HANDBOOK OF ABNORMAL PSYCHOLOGY

EDITED BY

Professor H. J. Eysenck Ph D, D Sc

Professor of Psychology, University of London

PITMAN MEDICAL

First published 1960
Second edition 1973

SIR ISAAC PITMAN AND SONS LTD
Pitman House, Parker Street, Kingsway, London, WC2B 5PB
P.O. Box 46038, Portal Street, Nairobi, Kenya
SIR ISAAC PITMAN (AUST) PTY LTD
Pitman House, 158 Bouverie Street, Carlton, Victoria 3053, Australia
PITMAN PUBLISHING COMPANY S.A. LTD
P.O. Box 11231, Johannesburg, S. Africa
PITMAN PUBLISHING CORPORATION
6 East 43rd Street, New York, NY 10017, USA
SIR ISAAC PITMAN (CANADA) LTD
495 Wellington Street West, Toronto 135, Canada
THE COPP CLARK PUBLISHING COMPANY
517 Wellington Street West, Toronto 135, Canada

Printed in Northern Ireland at the Universities Press, Belfast.
01 0840 81

This book is dedicated to the memory of
EMIL KRAEPELIN
*who first applied the methods and theories
of experimental psychology to the problems
of abnormal behaviour*

Contributors

M. BERGER, BA, Dip Psychol: Lecturer, Department of Psychology, Institute of Psychiatry, London

ANNE BROADHURST, BSc, Dip Psychol, PhD, ABPsS: Lecturer in Psychology, Department of Psychology, University of Birmingham

P. L. BROADHURST, MA, PhD, DSc, FBPsS, FIBiol: Professor of Psychology, University of Birmingham

G. CLARIDGE, BA, PhD, DSc: Senior Lecturer in Clinical Psychology, Department of Psychological Medicine, University of Glasgow

A. D. B. CLARKE, BA, PhD: Professor of Psychology, University of Hull

ANN M. CLARKE, BA, PhD: Research Fellow in Psychology, University of Hull

B. COOPER, MD, MRCPsych, DPM: Senior Lecturer, Department of Psychiatry, Institute of Psychiatry, London

W. B. ESSMAN, PhD: Professor of Psychology, Queens College of the City, University of New York

H. J. EYSENCK, PhD, DSc: Professor of Psychology, University of London

M. P. FELDMAN, BA, Dip Psychol, PhD: Senior Lecturer, Department of Psychology, University of Birmingham

C. D. FRITH, BA, Dip Psychol, PhD: Lecturer, Department of Psychology, Institute of Psychiatry, London

R. J. McGUIRE, BSc, MA, MEd: Senior Lecturer in Clinical Psychology, Departments of Psychiatry and Psychology, University of Edinburgh

IRENE MARTIN, PhD: Reader in Physiological Psychology, Institute of Psychiatry, London

R. E. PASSINGHAM, BA, MSc, PhD: Research Worker, Department of Experimental Psychology, University of Oxford

R. W. PAYNE, PhD: Professor of Psychology and Chairman, Department of Behavioural Science, Temple University School of Medicine and Senior Research Scientist, Eastern Pennsylvania Psychiatric Institute, U.S.A.

S. J. RACHMAN, MA, PhD: Senior Lecturer, Department of Psychology, Institute of Psychiatry, London

L. REES, MD, BSc, FRCP, FRCPsych, DPM: Professor of Psychiatry, St. Bartholomew's Hospital, London

R. D. SAVAGE, BA, PhD, FBPsS: Senior Lecturer in Applied Psychology, University of Newcastle upon Tyne

M. SHEPHERD, DM, FRCP, FRCPsych, DPM: Professor of Epidemiological Psychiatry, Institute of Psychiatry, London

J. SHIELDS, BA: Senior Lecturer, Department of Psychiatry, Institute of Psychiatry, London

J. D. TEASDALE, MA, Dip Psychol, PhD: Principal Psychologist, Whitchurch Hospital, Cardiff

G. B. TRASLER, MA, BSc, PhD: Professor of Psychology, University of Southampton

G. D. WILSON, BA, MA, PhD: Lecturer, Department of Psychology, Institute of Psychiatry, London

A. J. YATES, BA, PhD, Dip Psychol: Professor of Psychology, University of Western Australia

Preface

Textbooks on psychology usually preface the text with an apology for the difficulty of defining psychology. A *Handbook of Abnormal Psychology* ought to begin with a triple apology, because in addition to the obvious difficulties of defining the major subject it is not at all easy to define the concept of 'abnormality', and even the connotations of the word 'Handbook' are far from obvious. We shall not attempt to give any new meaning to the term 'psychology', but shall take it to denote the scientific study of the behaviour of organisms. Nor shall we worry overmuch about the general designation of this book; handbook is as handbook does. But we shall devote a little time to a discussion of the meaning of 'abnormal', if only because our use of the term will be found to differ somewhat from that often accepted in psychiatry and clinical psychology.

As has been frequently pointed out, the word 'abnormal' is used in at least two quite distinct senses. It may be equated with the *statistically unusual*, or it may be equated with *deviations from the ideal norm*. Often the two are combined, so that deviations from the norm which are decidedly unusual are called 'abnormal' only when they are in an undesirable direction. Thus, an IQ of 50 is considered abnormal, but not one of 150; cowardice, but not bravery; neurosis, but not superior adjustment.

As used in psychology, the term has come to refer to certain *unusual* and *maladaptive* states, such as schizophrenia, hysteria, anxiety state, and the like; this usage appears to have been taken over from psychiatry, where these behaviour patterns are regarded as medical diseases. As will be shown later (Chapter 1), this usage is not really justified by the facts; mental abnormalities do not represent qualitative disease entities having specific 'causes'. They resemble rather such continuously varying features as height, intelligence, hair colour, and the like, and demand quite a different type of analysis from that appropriate to 'diseases'.

It is for this reason that we have rejected the traditional arrangement of books on abnormal psychology, which closely follows the psychiatric mould. Hunt (1951) has put the situation very well—

'Clinical psychology in (the) methodological sense is a more mature science than psychiatry. It is definitely experimental, if at times somewhat shakily so. As an experimental science it has much to offer psychiatry, as I think many psychiatrists realise. For once, however, I am not advocating the 'team' concept, although it is one of my firmest beliefs. I would rather suggest that psychiatry attempt to stand upon its scientific feet, if only because of the good example it would set us in clinical psychology; far too many of us clinicians, instead of bringing our experimental tradition to the assistance of psychiatry, flee to the empirical ambiguities of psychiatry in an attempt to escape the rigorous scientific demands of our own discipline.'

This is precisely what we have attempted to do here—bring the experimental tradition of psychology to bear upon the 'abnormal' behaviour of the organism. For reasons that will become apparent, we have rejected the psychiatric framework outright, preferring not to be bound and constrained by diagnostic schemes of dubious validity and known unreliability. Where the experimental findings summarised by us were couched in terms of such a system, we have, of course, had to make such use of them as we could, but we have, whenever possible, translated these classificatory schemes into a more empirical framework along the lines of dimensional analysis, outlined in Chapter 1.

In thus attempting to break away from the traditional frame, we have encountered two main difficulties. In the first place, much discussion had to be devoted to methodological problems. As long as clinical and experimental psychologists are content to take psychiatric diagnosis as their criterion, so long will their experimental designs be of exemplary simplicity and elegance—and their results equivocal and unrepeatable! But once we begin to question the validity of psychiatric diagnosis, and demonstrate its obvious lack of reliability, we are cast adrift on rather more turbulent waters, and have to consider seriously the problem of experimental design and methodological adequacy.

In the second place, much of the published evidence was found to be useless for our purpose, and had to be discarded. Less than one-fifth of the papers and books examined have been included, and even so the reader will find that what remains often gives rise to critical discussion rather than enlightenment. We have preferred the positive to the negative approach, leaving out whole areas that traditionally would have been included (the vast literature of the Rorschach technique is one example) because detailed investigation revealed all dross and no gold (Zubin *et al.*, 1965), and including instead much less well-cultivated areas because these seemed to hold out a more definite promise of future usefulness. We have little doubt that our critical judgements, leading to *exclusion*, can be justified by factual reference; we have less confidence that the same would at present be possible with respect to those judgements leading to the *inclusion* of material about which there is as yet not very much evidence. The book as a whole presents a point of view; it is in recognition of the fact that this point of view may easily be mistaken that we have prefaced the book with a quotation from Terence which William Harvey included for a similar purpose in his *Exercitatio Anatomica de Motu Cordis et Sanguinis in Animalibus* (1628).

Our conception of abnormality, then, is not in terms of people suffering from mental diseases produced by definite 'causes'; it is rather in terms of the defective functioning of certain psychological systems. The delineation of these systems, and the mapping out of the laws according to which they work, is the task of experimental psychology. There is no pretence that all is known about these systems, or about the laws governing their working. We are only too well aware of the low level of knowledge, and the high degree of speculation, which are so characteristic of even the most developed parts of psychology. But poor as this may be as a base, it is all there is; good intentions cannot conjure up scientific knowledge, and it is better to rely on a small secure base than float on insubstantial clouds of putative and suppositious generalisations without reference in reality.

Whenever possible, we have supplanted the usual paradigm of psychiatric research—x members of class y showed behaviour z—by what to our way of thinking is a superior paradigm: change in the independent variable x effects a change y in function z. In this paradigm, change y might be in the direction of making function z more 'abnormal', or it might be in the opposite direction; provided the experiment included abnormality of functioning as a referent, it was considered to be relevant to our endeavour. Indeed, while nearly all of the material traditionally included in books on abnormal psychology would have been gathered from experiments on abnormal groups, such as neurotics and psychotics, much of our material comes from normal groups. Readers who do not feel in sympathy with this approach may like to consider that there are many textbooks written along the lines we have criticised; with one or two partial exceptions there is none that treats the subject in the manner here advocated.

A word may need to be added about the phrase 'change in the independent variable x'. These words have their usual meaning when we deal with the effects of administering a drug, carrying out an operation on the brain, or giving a series of cerebral electroshocks. It carries a slightly different meaning when this change in variable x is effected by choosing different groups of subjects (human or animal) whose positions on a continuum presumed to be highly correlated with x differ significantly. Thus, Spence and his colleagues carried out a series of investigations into the effects of anxiety, x, on conditioning and learning by comparing the performance of different groups of students scoring respectively high and low on a questionnaire presumed to be a measure of anxiety. While we cannot afford to reject any method of testing our hypotheses, attention should be drawn to the dangers inherent in this procedure. The continuum in question may not in fact be isomorphic with the hypothetical variable x; the method used for allocating people to positions on the continuum may have low reliability and low validity; position on the continuum may be indicative of a chronic state that produces different effects from those consequent upon acute and sudden stimulation-produced increases in x. Fortunately, all these points are open to empirical study, and much interesting material should emerge from a detailed investigation of the advantages and disadvantages of this paradigm.

Another point arises in connexion with the use of factors or continua in this type of research. As will be seen in Chapter 1, it is often possible to show that certain psychiatric groups have clearly assignable positions in the dimensional framework produced by the combination of factors or continua. The question is sometimes put whether the dimensional framework is not merely a restatement of the original psychiatric type of classification. The answer, of course, is simply that the degree of correspondence observed is of some interest in making possible the translation of experimental findings from one field to the other. It is not, however, used or intended in any sense as proof of the correctness of the dimensional system, which is derived independently from the empirical relationships between experimental and behavioural measures of an objective kind applied to groups of normal and abnormal subjects. Even if there were no correspondence at all with psychiatric diagnostic classifications, this would not in any way invalidate the empirical findings.

Accumulation of facts, while indispensable, is not enough in science: 'those who refuse to go beyond fact rarely get as far as fact'. Hence, we have been particularly concerned to do two things. We have tried to use the laws and hypotheses of general, experimental psychology to account for the facts presented; it will be noted, for instance, how the Yerkes-Dodson Law appears to integrate the superficially heterogeneous content of many different chapters. (A quick look through a score of textbooks of abnormal and clinical psychology shows that none of them even deigned to mention this law!) We have also tried, where this deductive process could not be used because of the absence of well-substantiated laws in a particular field, to form generalisations from the available data, and thus suggest certain general rules or hypotheses that are sufficiently precise to admit of experimental tests. Thus, there is throughout this book a stress on *integration through theory*, an attempt to see abnormal psychology as a part of general, experimental psychology. The laws of learning theory, to take but one example, apply no less to neurotics than to rats and college students; should it not be the task of the psychologist to deduce the details of abnormal behaviour from such general laws? This attitude has governed our view on the problem of treatment also, and on the relationship between abnormal psychology, or psychopathology and psychiatry. Jaspers has put the case very clearly in his classical *Psychopathologie*—

'Psychiatry always deals with individual people in their totality . . . But while the work of the psychiatrist is entirely with individual cases, he nevertheless also requires to be a psychopathologist, to look for general concepts and rules, in order to solve the problems presented by the single case. If the psychiatrist in the course of his practical work . . . makes use of science as only one of his aids, to the psychopathologist this science is an end in itself. He wishes to know and understand, characterise and analyse, not the individual person, but the general case. He is not concerned with the therapeutic use of his science . . . but only with truth, with facts, with connexions, and with proof. Not for him are empathy and understanding as such; they only furnish him with material. He requires ideas which can be conceptualised, which can be communicated, which can be fitted into an orderly scheme and which can be systematised . . . Science requires conceptual thinking which is systematic and can be communicated. Only in so far as such thinking has been developed can psychopathology claim to be scientific. The part of psychiatry which is art and expertise, which cannot be communicated but at best handed over in personal contact to susceptible disciples, cannot be the subject of printed explanation. Psychiatric instruction is more than the communication of conceptualised knowledge and more than the teaching of scientific facts. A book which is concerned with psychopathology can only offer scientific knowledge, and is valuable only in so far a sit does precisely that. With a full realisation of the importance of experience for practical treatment, and for the analysis of individual cases, we will nevertheless restrict ourselves consciously to those matters which are properly the subject matter of scientific knowledge.'

While we have thus concentrated on *facts*, and *laws* relating facts together into an organised whole, we have not tried to erect any kind of grand metaphysical system, all-embracing and all useless. As Robert Boyle said: 'It has long seemed to me to be none of the least impediments of the real advancement of true natural philosophy that men have been so forward to write systems of it.' And as Bacon said of such system builders, they had; 'with infinite agitation of wit, spun out of a small quantity of matter those laborious webs of learning which are extant in their books . . . To what purpose are these brain-creations and idle plays of power? . . . Everyone philosophises out of the cells of his own imagination, as out of Plato's cave.' In its present humble state, psychology can at best support on a factual basis certain low-order generalisations; to go beyond these is to court disaster. Such generalisations are the building stones for all future advance; hence the importance of deriving them from the facts in a proper quantified manner. 'Just as the ears are made for sound and the eyes for colour, so the mind of man is meant to consider quantity, and it wanders in darkness when it leaves the realm of quantitative thought.' Thus Kepler, and we may perhaps add Roger Bacon's dictum of seven hundred years ago: 'Physicians must know their science is impotent if they do not apply to it the power of mathematics.'

A point of overriding importance has always seemed to us to be the *choice of variables* to be measured in our attempts to describe abnormal behaviour. This choice has in the past been made too often in a haphazard manner, determined by fashion (Rorschach), ease of obtaining data (questionnaire), or whim. Measurement in science grows out of a theoretical system; alter the system and you alter the meaning and process of measurement. Only measurements so anchored have scientific meaning, and are capable of interpretation that is not arbitrary, subjective, and indeterminate. I have tried to make this point in detail elsewhere (Eysenck, 1967), and will not reiterate the arguments in its favour. It is necessary, though, to insist on it because several chapters are devoted to detailed discussions of the correct choice of variables in the investigation of mental abnormality. The discussion by I. Martin presents an obvious case in point.

This second edition will probably be considered to serve its purpose more adequately than did the first edition; at least the editor hopes so. There are several reasons for this. In the first place, much has happened in the last ten years to make the whole field more scientific; research design has improved, the general level of theorising is not so much overawed by psychoanalytic doctrines; novel practices, themselves deriving from experimental psychology, have become widely used and accepted, more people with a good background in experimental psychology have gone into the abnormal field and have used their knowledge to good advantage; psychiatrists have begun to accept the contribution which only psychologists can make, and have begun to co-operate in a more wholehearted manner than ever before—in short, there has been a veritable renaissance the fruits of which are apparent in the pages of the Handbook. Another ten years of this, and we might have the beginnings of a truly scientific account of abnormal behaviour; what we have now is, of course, little more than the promise of better things to come. In the second place, many fields are now included which in the first edition could not be accommodated. Disorders of old age, mental subnormality, psychosomatic disorders—these are only three examples of chapters that were lacking in the first edition, and that were definitely missed. Thus, the second edition is much more comprehensive, and will fill its niche much more adequately, than was possible previously.

Certain chapters previously included are not now retained. The reasons are varied, but mostly these omissions are simply due to the fact that since the first edition appeared little has happened to change the field to any noticeable extent. Lobotomy is one obvious example; there has been little research in the past ten years, and the method itself is falling into disuse. It would have been pointless to reproduce the chapter in the first edition, virtually unchanged; readers interested in this topic can still with advantage consult the first edition, without fear of missing anything important. The same is true of the chapter on expressive movements, for instance; little research interest has been manifested in this area, hence it has been omitted. In an ideal world, perhaps, these and other chapters might have been retained and brought up-to-date, and others, planned but finally rejected, been included; unfortunately, books have a finite capacity, and it seemed more important to concentrate on the most valuable contributions than pursue the impossible ideal of complete comprehensiveness.

The book is now divided into four parts, dealing respectively with: (1) the description and measurement of abnormal behaviour, (2) the experimental study of abnormal behaviour, (3) the causes and determinants of abnormal behaviour, and (4) the modification of abnormal behaviour. These divisions are, of course, in part artificial, and overlapping is inevitable; nevertheless, they do seem to mirror four rather separate aspects of research interest, and this subdivision helps in the organisation of the material. All classification must be part subjective, part heuristic, and nothing fundamental is claimed for the one here adopted; on the whole, it seems slightly superior to the threefold division adopted in the first edition. Many chapters contain material pertaining to more than one division; thus, the chapter on abnormalities of sexual behaviour deals not only with the description and measurement of such behaviour, but also with its causes, and with treatment. Similarly, the chapter on drug addiction deals not only with description and measurement, but also with experimental studies and with treatment. It would have been artificial to split chapters up to fit in more precisely with the fourfold division, and we believe that the present way of presenting the material is more acceptable to readers. There is no perfect arrangement, and the one here chosen seemed to us to have fewer contra-indications than others that suggested themselves—apart from the fact that expertise in the various fields dictated some such arrangement as that here offered.

We have tried, in selecting our material, to avoid overlapping with handbooks devoted to other fields of psychology. Stevens's *Handbook of Experimental Psychology*, Lindzey's *Handbook of Social Psychology*, Carmichael's *Manual of Child Psychology*, and Stone's *Comparative Psychology* mark out fields of study that are relatively separate from our own, and it will be seen that only a very small percentage of the references in this Handbook will be found in these other volumes. This may serve as evidence that the field of 'Abnormal Psychology' has indeed a separate and independent existence, even though its definition, as mentioned before, may be difficult and heuristic; indeed the contents of this Handbook may have to serve as a kind of operational definition of the field covered.

The selection of authors is clearly more widely based than it was before; yet even now the majority either are members of the Institute of Psychiatry (Maudsley Hospital) in the University of London, or else have left the Institute to carry on elsewhere the experimental tradition associated with it. No apology is made for their choice; this was not determined by considerations other than their competence and ability to do the job. Whether the editor's confidence was justified, only the reader can judge. Nor should it be assumed that because of this common parentage, therefore all authors must necessarily agree on major points; this is by no means so. Each author is completely responsible for his chapter, and although I have tried to fulfil my editorial function by avoiding unnecessary overlap, and suggesting the filling of lacunae, I have not considered it my duty to interfere in any way with the expression of views, or the drawing of conclusions, that I might not totally agree with in the form stated. In any active field of scientific advance, disagreements are not only unavoidable, but essential; without them a handbook would be a dead and useless piece of compromise. On one point, however, there is no disagreement whatever; the absolute necessity, namely, of applying the highest standards of experimental design and statistical treatment to the complex and perplexing problems offered by this fascinating but difficult field. It is for this reason that the dedication is to E. Kraepelin, the first person to be trained in the psychological laboratory and to apply experimental methods to abnormal psychology. It is sobering to consider, if only his outlook had prevailed in psychiatry, how much farther advanced our knowledge would now be! And how much less occasion there would be for what Huxley has called 'the great tragedy of Science—the slaying of a beautiful hypothesis by an ugly fact.'

H. J. Eysenck
Maudsley Hospital

REFERENCES

Carmichael, L. (1946) *Manual of Child Psychology*. New York: Wiley.

Eysenck, H. J. (1967) *The Biological Basis of Personality*. Springfield: C. C. Thomas.

Hunt, W. A. (1951) Clinical psychology—science or superstition? *Amer. Psychologist*, 6, 683–687.

Jaspers, K. (1948) *Allgemeine Psychopathologie*. Berlin: J. Springer.

Lindzey, G. (1957) *Handbook of Social Psychology* (2 vols). Cambridge, Mass.: Addison-Wesley.

Spence, K. W. (1956), *Behaviour Theory and Conditioning*. London: Oxford University Press.

Stevens, S. S. (1951) *Handbook of Experimental Psychology*. New York: Wiley.

Stone, C. P. (1951) *Comparative Psychology*. New York: Prentice-Hall.

Zubin, J., Eron, L. D., and Schumer, F. (1965) *An Experimental Approach to Projective Techniques*. London: Wiley.

Contents

ACKNOWLEDGEMENTS

Sources are indicated by parenthetical references on the page where cited material appears and are related to the References sections at the ends of chapters where the relevant citations are given in extended form.

PART ONE
Description and Measurement of Abnormal Behaviour

1

Classification and the Problem of Diagnosis

RALPH J. McGUIRE

Psychiatrists and clinical psychologists who turn to this chapter hoping to find the results of the latest research in the psychiatric field will be disappointed. It does not contain an account of recent advances in specific diagnoses. That would have been to turn the chapter into one on psychiatry. Nor, so that a new objective approach to diagnosis might be produced, is there an attempt to put together all the abnormalities considered in other chapters, useful though this would have been. Instead, an effort has been made to concentrate on the methods relevant to the solution of the problems of diagnosis, the 'how' and 'why' of diagnosis rather than the 'what'. This, it is hoped, explains some of the apparent lack of judgement in this chapter. Some excellent papers in the field have been ignored completely because, although their findings may have been important, their methods are not so novel as to need explanation or are so complex as not to be the best examples available. In other cases a very wide field of research may be covered rather succinctly because the general principle of the research can be explained very simply. In many such cases the direct results of the work are dealt with in detail in other chapters of this volume. Finally, some decidedly poor papers will be mentioned because they contain the germ of an idea in methodology that might be profitably applied elsewhere.

GENERAL INTRODUCTION TO THE PROBLEM OF CLASSIFICATION

When people refer to the classification problem in psychiatry they tend to include the mixture problem and the discrimination problem as well as the assignment problem. The mixture problem lies in detecting if a group is homogeneous or heterogeneous. The discrimination problem is in deciding if two or more apparently different groups, e.g. those diagnosed clinically as paranoid, hebephrenic, simple, and catatonic schizophrenics, do differ significantly from each other in the variable or variables under consideration. Finally, there is the assignment or identification problem in which one has to decide to which of the possible groups that have emerged a particular patient should be assigned on the basis of his scores on the relevant variables. All three of these problems will be considered in this chapter.

When only one variable is used, for example height, the mixture problem may boil down to deciding if the distribution is normal, bimodal, or multimodal. The discrimination approach may involve separating the group into such groups as are already accepted by the experts, or according to some other criterion, e.g. sex, race, or age, and, finally, when the groups have been established one may assign an individual to one or another according to his height, either by minimising his deviation from the mean of the group to which he is assigned or by using Bayes' theorem to assign him to the group to which he has the greatest likelihood of belonging. These two methods of assignment need not yield the same answer. For example, in a given population of children a small group may have mentally subnormal parents and have a mean IQ of 70, whereas the larger group consists of the children of normal parents and have a mean IQ of 100. Using

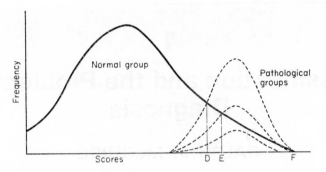

Fig. 1.1. The base rate problem

Fewest errors occur in assigning individuals to normal or pathological groups when the cut-off point used corresponds to the intersection point of the two distribution curves. However, this depends on the relative sizes of the two groups. Optimum cut-off point for the largest pathological group is *D*, for the middle group *E* and for the smallest group *F*, i.e. all cases classed as normal. A more efficient test would be one in which the within-groups variance was less, i.e. each group was taller and thinner but with the same mean.

the least deviation method, a child with an IQ of 75 would be assigned to the first group, whereas, because of the greater number in the second group, he should be assigned to it as being a more likely member of it. This is the difficulty that arises in psychological testing where the optimum cut off point between two groups is very dependent on the base rates, i.e. the relative proportions of the two groups in the population from which the individual to be assigned has come. The optimum cut-off point to minimise both types of error, i.e. 'false positives' and 'false negatives', is where the distributions of the two groups have the same frequency, but this obviously varies with the relative sizes of the distribution. (*See* Fig. 1.1).

There are many (Gleser, Eysenck) who argue that discrimination as outlined above is completely irrelevant in psychiatry. They would argue that the formation of subgroups and the assignment of individuals to them is essentially wasteful, necessitating as it does the discarding of continuous measures from an individual for the purpose of assigning him to a cluster of types whose very existence may hardly be tenable. Thus, progress may be impeded by erroneous assignment and by the sacrifice of a fine measure for a much coarser one.

It is certainly true that typologies that at first sight appear dichotomous usually reduce to continuous distributions when more accurate measurements and larger samples are used. A defence of the continued use of typologies in psychiatry, even among those who would not accept the disease concept in psychiatry, is that in an illness one is

dealing with those at the extremes of normal distributions, and we might therefore more readily accept that there will be discontinuities between the groups. Eysenck is able to avoid this difficulty and preserve his dimensional approach by evaluating his work on normal populations, so that even his Psychoticism factor (P) is verified as a dimension of personality in a normal population (Eysenck and Eysenck, 1968a,b; 1969b).

Where, as in most psychological and psychiatric situations, there are innumerable measures that can be made on an individual, one is usually forced at quite an early stage to try to reduce the number of variables to more manageable proportions. Before the advent of computers this would have meant reducing the data to five or ten measures at the most, but nowadays computers allow many more variables to be dealt with, although even with the largest today this is probably less than 200, which may sound enormous but which cannot allow all the items of the MMPI to be dealt with at one time.

The History of Psychiatric Classification

Mentally ill patients were regarded as a problem of religion, as much as of medicine, for a long time. Then, in the seventeenth century, Thomas Sydenham explained how in psychiatry, as in physical medicine, symptoms could be grouped into syndromes, with characteristic onset, cause, and outcome. Some physicians (Georget, in the early nineteenth century) argued there was only one psychosis that was organic in cause but that it had many different forms.

Kraepelin published his first textbook in 1883 but it was his 1899 publication that laid the basis of his classification system. There was nothing new in it, but it systematised the ideas of clinical psychiatrists that had been put forward in the previous twenty to thirty years. Multiple diagnostic criteria, including past and present symptoms and prognosis, were considered necessary, but aetiology was played down as being largely guesswork. The course of the illness was thus the predominant basis of his classification system. The manic-depressive psychoses formed one major group, and dementia praecox the other but with several forms. Poor prognosis was the essential feature for the diagnosis of dementia praecox. If the patient with such a diagnosis recovered, the diagnosis was regarded as having been erroneous.

Eugen Bleuler not only changed the name of dementia praecox to schizophrenia but revised the notion that poor prognosis was inevitable. He believed schizophrenia to be a group of organic diseases that were linked by a similar symptomatology, the basis of which was loosening of associations. Adolf Meyer rejected the disease concept although still attending to heredity and physical factors, and spoke of reaction types. He emphasised the individual's life history and reactions to various stresses that might occur in the course of his life. He had his own nomenclature, e.g. parergasia was equivalent to schizophrenia, but it was his reaction types that made the main impact on American psychiatric classification and it is only in the most recent revision of the US standard classification system that the term reaction types has been dropped.

Reliability of Present Psychiatric Classification

The practical problem of classification shows itself most clearly in the disagreement among psychiatrists in assigning a patient to a particular diagnostic group. At the individual level it is demonstrated in the wrangling that takes place at staff conferences throughout the world. At the group level it can be seen in the results of various attempts to measure the percentage agreement between different observers examining the same subjects and, also, in comparing the percentage incidence of different diagnoses found by different observers among populations that might be expected to be similar. Kreitman et al. (1961) have shown that percentage agreement between observers, even when assignment is into fairly broad categories such as organic, functional psychosis, psycho-neurosis, rarely rises above 80 per cent, and when it does it is often possible to detect contamination in that the observers' decisions were not completely independent (Table 1.1). When the

categories are finer, i.e. diagnosis within the broad groups, agreement fell to around 50 per cent on the average. These figures are confirmed by Zubin (1967) who includes not only the studies used by Kreitman but also some later ones.

Table 1.1. Reliability of Diagnosis
in Clinical Psychiatry

Summary of percentage agreement on diagnostic categories between psychiatrists found in several investigations

| Authors | No. Pts | Average percentage agreement | | Notes |
		Broad categories	Specific categories	
Ash (1949)	52	64	38	Joint interview
Hunt et al. (1953)	794	54	32	Between hospitals
Schmidt & Fonda (1956)	426	84	55	Jun. v. Sen. clinician
Krietman (1961)	90	78	63	
Beck et al. (1962)	153	70	54	
Sandifer et al. (1964)	91	73	57	

Kreitman (1961) examines the reasons for disagreement and suggests several sources of error. Some are not true error, in the sense that researchers have not always ensured that the two observers had equal experience or even equal opportunity of examining the patients. One suspects, nevertheless, that while the objections mean that the figures do not represent the best possible for clinical diagnosis they do fairly represent clinical practice. There are also to be taken into account the factors that tend to inflate the reliability measures, e.g. sometimes the second psychiatrist had the first one's diagnosis available, and sometimes, although the psychiatrists rated separately from each other, they had both been present at the same interview so that the trend of thinking of one of them might have been fairly obvious to the other.

Other sources of error mentioned by Kreitman are disagreement regarding nomenclature, which might be rectified by the use of standard terms such as the International Classification of Diseases, although most researchers on this subject (Schmidt and Fonda, 1956) did try to standardise. Ward et al. (1962) blamed 62 per cent of the disagreement among diagnosticians on the inadequacy of the nosological system, 33 per cent on inconsistent behaviour of the diagnosticians, and only 5 per cent on the inconsistent behaviour of the patient. They had also found, in a well-designed experiment, that agreement was 70 per cent on general categories and 56 per cent for subcategories, though this rose to 82 per cent if a second choice was allowed to count as close agreement.

It may be small consolation to the psychiatrists and psychologists operating within the present classification system to realise that the position is not significantly different in general medicine. Wilson and Deming (1927), horrified to find only 66 per cent agreement on their psychiatric diagnoses, found that this figure was very similar to the agreement between cause of death on the death certificate and the diagnosis arrived at by autopsy. The medical figure was, of course, a validation figure, whereas the psychiatric one was only reliability, in which case the validity is likely to be much less.

WHO International Classification of Diseases (ICD8)

To remove many of the difficulties in communication due to the separate classification systems used by psychiatrists in different parts of the world there has been a move to press for the adoption of the WHO International Classification of Diseases (ICD8), Table 1.2. WHO, naturally, has a psychiatric section. The American system DSM II, which is based on the WHO system, became official in July 1968. The previous American Psychiatric Association system (DSM I) had been based mainly on a Meyerian approach to psychiatric illness, but this is largely abandoned in the new one. One difference between the American and the international systems is in the different importance given to organic factors. In the American system, the organic always precedes the functional and the syndromes precede the symptoms even when one syndrome might be regarded as being merely a symptom of some other syndrome. The diagnostician is encouraged to make multiple diagnoses where relevant. Qualifying phrases such as mild, moderate, and severe can be added by means of symbols ($\times$ 6, $\times$ 7, or $\times$ 8) and so enable the clinical picture to be more easily reproduced from the coded diagnosis.

The use of a standard system should have the effect of improving international communication between psychiatrists, but whether by itself it represents an advance in knowledge is hotly debated. Some (Spitzer and Wilson, 1968) regard it as a nomenclature only, i.e. definitions of terms used, which is descriptive but not explanatory. Others (Jackson, 1969; Baldwin, 1969) criticise it as a classification system that is a hotch-potch of different classification systems with different bases of classification.

There is also a British version of the ICD8 and a cross-national study of diagnoses of the mental

Table 1.2
Main divisions of the Mental Disorders section of the *Manual of the International Statistical Classifications of Diseases, Injuries and Causes of Death*, W.H.O., Geneva (1967)

ICD 8 (1965), Mental Disorders

Psychoses
290 Senile and pre-senile dementia
291 Alcoholic Psychoses
292 Psychoses associated with intercranial infection
293 Psychoses associated with cerebral conditions
294 Psychoses associated with physical conditions
295 Schizophrenia
296 Affective Psychoses
297 Paranoid states
298 Other psychoses
299 Unspecified psychoses

Neuroses, personality disorders and other non-psychotic mental disorders
300 Neuroses
301 Personality disorders
302 Sexual deviation
303 Alcoholism
304 Drug dependence
305 Physical disorder of presumably psychogenic origin
306 Special symptoms not elsewhere classified
307 Transient situational disturbances
308 Behaviour disorders of childhood
309 Mental disorders not specified as psychotic associated with physical conditions

Mental retardation
310 Borderline mental retardation
311 Mild mental retardation
312 Moderate mental retardation
313 Severe mental retardation
314 Profound mental retardation
315 Unspecified mental retardation

Each of the 3 digit classifications is further subdivided .1, .2, etc., to cover more specific conditions.

disorders between the USA and the UK (APA, 1969) makes use of the ICD8 so that communication can be standard between the two countries. Some results arising from work in this field are given in Cooper *et al.* (1969) and show the advantages of an international classification system, poor though it may be in other respects, particularly when it is combined with a statistical method of assignment.

The next revision of the ICD, the 9th, is due in 1975, and working parties are already preparing for it by means of case histories and video-tape recordings. The paper by Shepherd *et al.* (1968) which used DIAGNO came from one of these. Psychotic disorders in childhood produced the topic for yet another (Rutter *et al.*, 1969) which produced a tri-axial classification system. The first axis deals with the clinical psychiatric disorders (developmental, conduct, neurotic, etc.). The second covers intellectual level (normal and three levels of sub-normality) and the third axis lists possible associated or aetiological factors (e.g. infective disease, allergies, disorders of various systems, and environmental factors). Multiple coding is possible in the third category only. This approach should help to remove some of the difficulties where features on each of the axes might lead to disagreement if the consultant for his main diagnosis had to choose from one only.

MODELS OF PSYCHIATRIC ILLNESS

Many models for disturbed behaviour are possible. Eysenck (1960a) considered some of these in his chapter in the previous edition of this handbook and the reader is referred there for his detailed comparison between the medical model and a learning model. Siegler and Osmond (1966) and Siegler *et al.* (1969) have produced no less than seven popular models for schizophrenia and the models probably have significance in the general psychiatric system. The authors point out that practitioners do not consistently apply a specific model, and many move from one model to another between diagnosis and treatment without realising they have done so. The authors attempt to clarify the issue by making such models explicit, and in the first paper six models emerge—medical, moral, psychoanalytic, family interaction, conspiratorial, and social (Table 1.3). Each is examined as far as

Table 1.3. Some models of schizophrenia derived by Siegler and Osmond (1966) and Siegler, Osmond, and Mann (1969). The table covers only part of their analyses and has been simplified for illusntratio here.

Model	Supporters	Definition of schiz.	Interpretation of behaviour	Treatment
1. Medical	Organically-orientated psychiatrists	Specific disease or group of diseases: a named syndrome	Manifestation of a pathological condition: may reflect severity of illness	Medicine, surgery, nursing care
2. Moral	Skinnerians, Mowrer	'Bad' habits that have been learned and that bring patient into conflict with himself or society	The behaviour is the illness: in the past reinforced by the environment	Conditioning therapy: a training programme to prevent reinforcement of 'bad' habits and to encourage 'good' habits
3. Psychoanalytic	Psycho-dynamically orientated psychiatrists	State of severe emotional disturbance, specific to that patient	The behaviour is symbolic of the patient's emotional problems	Psychotherapy: to decode the symbolism of the behaviour and thus give the patient insight into the true source of his problem
4. Family interaction	Bateson, Lidz	The family is 'sick' because its internal communication is grossly distorted or ambiguous	The patient is reacting with his own evasions and manipulations to those of his family	Group therapy for the whole family so that they might gain insight into their behaviour and thus alter it
5. Conspiratorial	Szasz, Laing, Goffman	A label attached to a deviant member of society to justify his being ignored	Frustration or resignation resulting from being treated as non-rational	Do not label the patient. Treat him a an individual with rights and duties
6. Social	Epidemiologists	An illness that is more frequent among deprived members of society	Reflects inability to cope with the stresses of situation	Social remedies: change society to make life simpler for its less well equipped members
7. Psychedelic	Laing	A legitimate and often worthwhile exploration of an inner world	Mode of experiencing, distorted by psychiatric intervention	Helping the subject to gain maximum benefit from the enlightening experience

possible for its implications on twelve specific points (called dimensions by the authors), namely: definition, aetiology, interpretation of behaviour, treatment, prognosis, suicide, function of hospital, termination of hospitalisation, personnel, rights, and duties of the patient, of his family, and of society.

The medical and psychoanalytic models do not need explanation here. The moral model includes the learning model and Mowrer's later theories. Family interaction models include Bateson and Lidz approaches and have as their basic premise that the whole family is 'sick' and needs treatment by group therapy so that they can experience healthier ways of interacting. The conspiratorial model includes Goffman (1961) as well as Szasz (1963), both of whom assert that the institution whether it is a building or society uses the schizophrenic for its own ends. Finally, the social model, supported, it is said, by epidemiologists, regards the schizophrenic as a member of a deprived group who has to be sheltered and supported because he has been too battered by life to live outside.

In the later paper (1969), Siegler *et al.* look at the three models implicit in Laing's book *The Politics of Experience* (1967) and find that, of the three, two of them have already been covered, namely the psychoanalytic and the conspiratorial, but a third is the psychedelic model in which schizophrenia is seen as 'a breakthrough' or 'liberation', an exploration of a legitimate 'inner world'. Laing himself has not realised, apparently, that there are three different models in his view of schizophrenia since he is inconsistent in their use. The authors also point out that he implicitly uses the medical model to gain status by his profession as a doctor, although this is irrelevant to the model of schizophrenia he advocates.

Medical Model

The modern medical model (or more specifically the disease model) works on the assumption that the individual's functioning (either physical or mental) is abnormal because of some underlying cause. In physical medicine, bacteria, viruses, infections, etc., are the causes of the signs and symptoms. Similar causes are sought in the psychiatric illnesses. This modern medical model has been in vogue only since the nineteenth century but it led to such major advances in treatment and understanding of disease that it is perhaps natural that in all disturbed behaviour a similar explanation should be assumed and its specific disease or organic cause of malfunctioning sought.

It is interesting that Freud, who was reared in the field of physiology and practised as a neurologist, should have produced a psychodynamic theory that

resembles the basic disease model very closely. The cause in psychoanalytic theory is not a virus that manifests its action through abnormal physiological functioning but a morbid idea or fixation that manifests itself through psychological malfunctioning in an equally subtle and multiformed way. Further, as physical medicine is not content with symptomatic treatment, so in psychoanalysis the aim is to isolate and render harmless the pathological 'mental' germ that is the cause of the symptoms. Once this has been done the individual will begin to recover and return to normal functioning.

It has been suggested by Bockoven (1963) that the introduction of the disease model into psychiatry in the 1850s had a disastrous effect in reversing what had been the beginning of a breakthrough in the form of moral treatment started by Pinel, Tuke, and their followers. Moral treatment had, according to Bockoven, already produced a higher remission rate in the years before 1850 than has been achieved since.

Various arguments are put forward in support of the disease model in psychiatry. The first is that not all physical changes can be regarded as continuous. Tissue destruction is not merely a further stage in some malfunctioning, but introduces a qualitative change in the function of the organism. It is further pointed out that some advances in medical knowledge, and to a certain extent in psychiatric knowledge, have come from discovering qualitatively different groups within previously apparently homogeneous groups with a normal distribution. For example, our knowledge of feeblemindedness has been advanced by the discovery of an organic basis to the condition in certain groups of patients, e.g. cretinism due to thyroid deficiency, mongolism due to chromosome abnormality and various metabolic and toxic effects such as phenylketonuria. Advance has thus been made, not by accepting the normal distribution of intelligence as evidence of a multigenetic distribution, but by slicing off from this apparently continuous group, those subgroups whose condition has an organic basis and whose differences have been discovered by the use of medical science rather than psychology.

Eisenberg (1966) also points out that even where there may be continuity in physiological measures between health and illness, e.g. blood lead and serum bilirubin, there may be a discontinuity of response because there is some threshold which, once it has been passed, leads either to a catastrophic response or even a reversed response. The latter effect is known also in psychology in the relationship between stress and performance in the Yerkes-Dodson law.

The medical model supporters would take it as

unquestionable that where there is a clear organic basis to the disturbed behaviour the patient must be regarded as a medical case. General paresis of the insane, which was described as early as the fourteenth century and which at the beginning of this century was a common diagnosis of the chronic psychiatric in-patient, is most often quoted as the paradigm of all such conditions. This illness had at various times been attributed to different types of psychological stress such as terrors of war, excessive sexuality, extremes of heat and cold, and intellectual effort. Statistical evidence was available to support each 'cause', but when the viral basis was unquestionably demonstrated by Naguchi in 1911, everything fell neatly into place: the spirochaetes of syphilis were the necessary and sufficient cause of the illness, and nowadays penicillin is the treatment of choice. When such advances are attributable to the medical approach it is natural that many believe that psychiatry will continue to break down in this way before scientific advances of geneticists, virologists, and biochemists, leaving the psychologist with the task of explaining only the manifest behaviour resulting from the latent organic 'causes', and even this may be only an academic exercise when genetic engineering, chemotherapy, and neurosurgery have produced techniques to remedy the organic defects that have been revealed.

Eysenck (1960a) has reminded us that in such an outcome the profession of clinical psychiatry will have been rendered redundant even before that of clinical psychology.

While many, justifiably perhaps, approach the problem of classification by discarding the whole of the present system and attempting to produce a nosology that is more reliable, more valid and, generally, more useful, there are others who attempt to improve the present system rather than jettison it completely. Some may feel that there is enough good in it to make a purification process worth while so that the gold may not be thrown out with the dross. There may also be some who take the view that the present system is too strongly entrenched and that there is more hope of acceptance if one changes the diagnostic system gradually. Both these latter groups will see some benefit, both immediate and long term, in making the clinical decision process more explicit and thus more objective, so that errors can be traced to their source and the decision process further improved.

STATISTICAL PREDICTION

Meehl (1954, 1965) has been the principal proponent of this view. He argues that increased reliability is almost always obtained if formal statistical techniques (regression equations, probability coefficients, and cut-off points) replace the clinical judgement of psychiatrists or psychologists no matter how well qualified. Several such attempts along these lines will now be discussed. There is no doubt that, mathematically, the most direct route between objective data and accepted groups is by multiple discriminant analysis (Rao, 1952). Consideration will, however, be given here only to the objective approaches that are based on the clinical decision process and, thus, might throw some light on that.

MMPI Data

The Mayo clinic program (Rome et al., 1965) uses configural analyses that take MMPI scores and print out statements based on the kinds of conclusions that trained psychologists draw from the data; hence, according to which scales are high and low the description of that score is printed out, e.g. if Pa is very high, 'resentful or suspicious of others, perhaps to the point of fixed false beliefs'. Modifying statements may also appear, so that a high Ma score may appear only as 'tense and restless' if some other psychotic scale is high and seems more diagnostically relevant. Kleinmuntz and his colleagues at the Carnegie Institute of Technology (1963a,b,c) used the MMPI profiles to predict maladjustment among college students (Table 1.4). Groups of students were supplied with a definition of 'maladjusted' persons; namely, 'one who is suspicious, difficult to get along with, chronically complains of aches and pains, gets into frequent trouble with people in authority, and is generally unpleasant'. Each was then asked to nominate the three most adjusted and the three least adjusted students in his group. Nominated criterion groups were thus obtained for each end of the adjustment scale and the MMPI profiles of these subjects were then supplied to trained psychologists to sort according to their views of adjustment versus maladjustment. Sorting was into fourteen classes using forced normal distribution.

The most accurate assessor, i.e. the one whose grouping corresponded most closely to the nominated groups, was then instructed to reason aloud regarding the reasons for them. His verbal comments might refer to only one scale or the balance of two or more scales or simply to a large number of highly abnormal scores. These decisions were then examined, using a computer, so that a logical flow diagram that would sort all MMPI profiles into either adjusted,

Table 1.4. MMPI Decision Rules

The first 8 decision rules derived from a clinician's reasoning aloud as he sorted MMPI profiles of college students into adjusted or maladjusted. Es = Ego strength and Mt = maladjustment are non-standard scales. The scores on these are raw scores marked with *r*. All other scores are in T-score form (Kleinmuntz, 1963).

---

1. If four or more clinical scales have T-scores $\geq$ 70, call maladjusted.
2. If scales Hs, D, Hy, Pd, Mf, Pa, Pt, Sc and Si are $\leq$ 60, and if Ma $\leq$ 80 and Mt $\leq$ 10_r, then call adjusted.
3. If the first two scales in the Hathaway code includes Pd, Pa or Sc, and at least one of these is $\geq$ 70, then call maladjusted.
4. If Pa or Sc $\geq$ 70 and Pa, Pt or Sc $\geq$ Hs, D, or Hy, call maladjusted.
5. Call maladjusted if Pa $\geq$ 70 unless Mt $\leq$ 6_r and K $\geq$ 65.
6. If Mt $\leq$ 6_r call adjusted.
7. Call maladjusted if (Pa + Sc $-$ 2Pt) $\geq$ 20 and Pa or Sc $\geq$ 65.
8. If D or Pt are the highest scores and Es $\geq$ 45_r, call adjusted.

---

maladjusted, or unclassified could be produced. The first use of the information was as follows. At each decision point a question was asked, e.g. 'Are 5 or more clinical scales >65 and is either Pa or Sc >65?'. If the answer was 'yes' the subject was put into the maladjusted group and no further decisions regarding him were made. If, on the other hand, the answer was 'no' he was passed on to the next decision point, and only those, who at the end of the 16 decision points were still in neither of the groups labelled 'adjusted' or 'maladjusted', were now labelled 'unclassified'. Even at this relatively simple level the computer program compared favourably with the expert. Some increase in prediction was obtained by submitting each profile to all 16 decision points and noting the ratio of the numbers of 'adjusted' to 'maladjusted' decisions. Finally, an examination was made by the computer of the validity of each decision rule, and patterns of decision rules were also included. Here, new decision rules, not originally supplied by the expert but suggested by examination of the false positives and negatives, were included. At this final stage the program's valid positives and negatives were 91 per cent and 84 per cent respectively, compared with 63 per cent and 88 per cent from the first computer program, and 80 per cent and 67 per cent for the original expert. Unfortunately, since the decision rules were based on the known results, the whole process had to be cross validated, and later, students supplied four new samples. As might be expected a lower validity was

now found. However, for even these poorer results the computerised decision process still detected 68 per cent of the maladjusted students. It would have been interesting to have compared the results of such a clinically based decision process with that obtained by a multiple discriminate approach based either on the 15 subscale scores or even by direct examination of the 550 answers to the total inventory. Computer facilities make this possible today, though it would have been a very time-consuming job even for most computers in 1963 when the original research was done. Other relevant papers are by Sarbin (1941, 1943) and Sines (1964, 1966).

DIAGNO

Another approach to psychiatric diagnosis based on the clinical method was published by Spitzer and Endicott (1968). The computer program DIAGNO that they produced was a logical decision tree model based on the differential diagnosis procedure common in medicine (Fig. 1.2). In programmed learning language, while Kleinmuntz's approach was a linear one, their approach allowed branching and returning to the main stream. The input to the program consisted of 39 scores obtained from the Mental Status Schedule devised by Spitzer *et al.* (1964). This consists of 492 items rated in a way similar to those of the IMPS (Lorr *et al.*, 1962) in that they emphasise behaviour during the past week, i.e. present status. The scores are grouped together to yield 39 subscales such as Grandiosity, Drug Abuse, Guilt, Delusions, and Hallucinations. The final classification inferred is one of twenty-five from the standard APA system (DSM, 1952) consisting of six brain syndromes, mania, involutional psychotic reaction, psychotic depression, six schizophrenic reactions, six psychoneurotic, four sociopath, two other neuroses, and 'not psychiatrically ill'. These were found to cover 88 per cent of psychiatric patients admitted to Belle Vue Hospital New York in 1964. The decisions were based on best clinical psychiatric practice and the more basic decisions were made earlier in the process; for example, the patient's level of orientation sent him down either the organic diagnosis branch or led on to the next fundamental disturbance, i.e. psychotic or not. This decision was based on the sum of the various psychotic scores. The patient who had normal scores at each major decision point was passed on to the next until, if he had no abnormal scores, he would be classified 'not psychiatrically ill'. Otherwise he would have been sent down one of the major branches where he would be passed on till a definite diagnosis had been arrived at. He could be moved from one major branch to another if his later scores

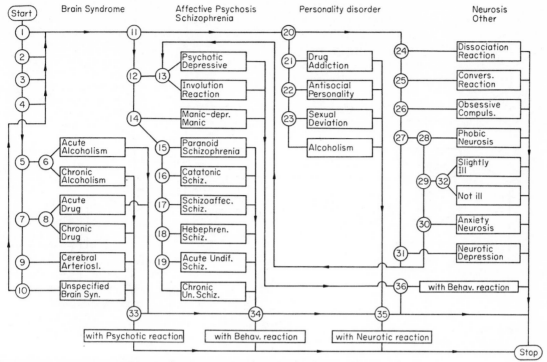

Fig. 1.2. Schematic flow chart for DIAGNO computer program

Numbered circles refer to decision rules based on the patient's scores or combination of scores on the 39 scales of the Psychiatric Status Schedule. Rectangles give diagnosis. (Spitzer & Endicott, 1968)

suggested that he had been mistakenly assigned to that branch.

The system was tested on 140 individuals, and the authors' own clinical decisions were compared with the computer diagnoses. Falsely diagnosed cases were traced back, and the decision points altered to eliminate those errors until all the decisions of the computer were in complete agreement with those of the authors. Cross validation was carried out for 55 patients, and the accuracy was considered promising by its authors. They quote its interrater reliability as 0·66, using a special statistic Kappa devised by them. The value of this statistic when two psychiatrists were compared with each other was only 0·50 and 0·59 for 31 and 36 patients respectively. A statistic such as Kappa is necessary for dealing with such data as this because the simple percentage concordance depends on the number of categories possible and the base rates for them.

A modified version of DIAGNO was also used in the cross-cultural study of diagnoses of the mental disorders (Cooper *et al.*, 1969) where it provided an objective test of the consistency of two groups of project psychiatrists in applying the diagnostic criteria of the ICD8. The reasoning was that, even if the computer and the psychiatrist used different criteria for arriving at the diagnosis, the ratio of cases diagnosed as, say, schizophrenic, by the computer and by the psychiatrist should be equal for the two cultures, assuming the base rates in the two cultures are the same.

Systems Analysis

Finally, Nathan (1967) has issued a book which, although offering no experimental validation, has a full discussion of a systems analytic approach utilising diagnostic cues culled from several standard textbooks of psychiatry, such as the *American Handbook of Psychiatry* (Arieti, 1959), Mayer-Gross *et al.* (1960), Noyes (1953), the works of Freud, the Psychiatric Dictionary by English, H. B. and English, A. C. (1958), and any other writings that seemed to be relevant to a particular problem. After consideration of the main psychotic versus psychoneurotic decision problem, each of the five chapters discusses some aspect of abnormal behaviour

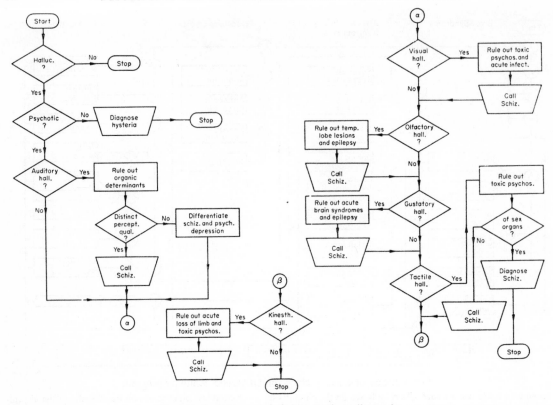

Fig. 1.3. A systems-analytic approach to diagnosis

The section illustrated deals with perception without an object (hallucinations). Diamonds represent decision points with choices; rectangles deal with organic conditions which must be ruled out before continuing; trapezoids represent tentative (call) or firm diagnoses. Other decision trees link up with this and cover other aspects of disturbed behaviour. (Nathan, 1967)

(Psychomotor, Affective, etc.) in order of reliability. For each disturbance of function flow diagrams based on computer programming convention, and using its set of statistical symbols, are produced. The symbols are: decision points are represented by diamonds; rectangles are used where further information is needed (in this book, specifically to rule out organic disease before continuing with the diagnosis of a functional condition); trapezoids contain functional diagnoses that must be noted either as a final diagnosis, e.g. 'diagnose schizophrenia', or as a tentative diagnosis 'call schizophrenia' which leads to further decision or processing points; Greek letters in circles show points of connection with other parts of the flow diagram; ellipses are starting and stopping points; direction of flow along the decision pathways is indicated by arrows (*see* Fig. 1.3). The book is rather a hotchpotch of discussion of psychopathology, textbook extracts, and quotations from a wide selection of

psychotic autobiographies, and, as I have already stated, there is no experimental evaluation of the program produced. The book is, nevertheless, a reasonably interesting introduction to the decision-tree procedure, and since all decision rules are freely discussed and references quoted it can be easily adapted to suit the emphasis of other researchers. The book may inspire some validation studies since nothing elaborate in the way of computer facilities is required to test the program as it stands.

Such approaches as have just been discussed may improve on present clinical diagnosis, but relying as they do on traditional diagnostic procedures it is unlikely that they will improve on the more direct statistical approach to diagnostic categories. They may, nevertheless, have value as intermediate steps to the acceptance of the statistical approach or even for the light they throw on the traditional clinical diagnostic process.

MATHEMATICAL MODELS IN CLASSIFICATION

The theory of how the individuals in a group differ from each other determines the mathematical model, which, in turn, determines the method used for classification (Torgerson, 1965; Greenhouse, 1965). Where there are no *a priori* grounds for knowing the type of distribution that exists, some hypothesis must be used to ensure that an appropriate mathematical technique is used. The hypothesis can then be confirmed by the information that emerges from the statistical treatment. One major decision about the distribution is whether the individuals represent a homogeneous group in which all the variables are continuous and unimodal, or whether the total group can itself be split into several subgroups. These hypotheses will be considered in turn.

Homogeneous Groups

Eysenck represents the best example of a researcher who bases his research on the continuous model; he initially assumes and proceeds to demonstrate that personality and symptom variables each use a continuum on which normal and abnormal are only quantitatively different. When all humans, at least from the same culture, are plotted in multidimensional space on his model the density cloud should yield a homogeneous normal multivariate distribution.

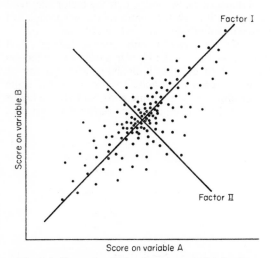

Fig. 1.4. Example of bivariate normal distribution

The distribution corresponds to correlation about +0·6, showing the directions of the principal component axes. Factor I explains about 80 per cent of the variance of the two variables and Factor II the remaining 20 per cent.

An example of such a distribution is given for a two dimensional model in Fig. 1.4. The axes represent variables and the points represent the distribution of individuals according to their measures on the two variables. The distribution corresponds to a correlation of approximately +0·6 and it can be seen that as a score increases on one variable the score on the other variable is likely also to be increasing. It should be fairly clear from the diagram that if an individual's position is reckoned from the two axes marked Factor I and Factor II, the relative positions of all the individuals remain the same. However, because Factor I is drawn through the major axis of the distribution, the differences between individuals is much greater for Factor I scores than for Factor II scores, or for either variable score. This effect increases as the correlation between the original variables increases because this has the effect of making the ellipse that envelopes the distribution longer and thinner. Figure 1.5 demonstrates the basis of principal component factor analysis, namely to choose new axes so that, in turn, each measures as much as it can of the remaining differences between individuals. If one has started with a large number of variables, say 20, it is not unusual to find that only 4 or 5 factors are needed to sum up most of the information about the relative positions of individuals.

When the distribution is of the homogeneous sort, factor analysis has the advantages both of reducing redundancy and of increasing the reliability by adding together with optimal weights those variables that correlate highly with each other. The principal component analysis produces factors that are not correlated with each other so that in the geometrical model the axes are still at right angles.

It is worth remembering that, although rotation can make the reduced number of factors more psychologically meaningful, the principal component analysis factors are mathematically more basic and, therefore, in some cases may be physiologically more meaningful. This is not to dispute that principal component analysis factors are less stable than rotated factors when the variables or subjects included in the analysis are changed.

When oblique axes are allowed, the factors are now correlated with each other. The British factor analysts have, on the whole, tended to prefer orthogonal factors because they are less subjective, while the Americans have, on the whole, favoured oblique factors since it is easier to get psychologically meaningful factors. Like orthogonal factors they are

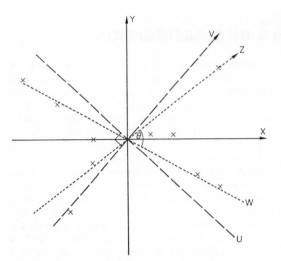

Fig. 1.5. Principal component analysis

The crosses represent 10 variables in 2-dimensional space. Principal component analysis yields orthogonal axes X, Y and most variables have moderate loadings on both. Orthogonal rotation to axes U, V gives most variables higher loadings on one factor and lower on the other. With oblique axes W, Z this trend goes still further so that 4 variables are almost completely aligned with one axis and 2 with the other. The meanings of the factors may then seem much clearer, but are likely to be measuring the same combinations of skills, etc. as the original variables, although more reliably.

also fewer in number and more reliable than the original variables used. Since oblique factors are correlated they can themselves be factor analysed to yield a smaller number of second order factors that can now be orthogonal if so decided. This is becoming a much more common practice and should reduce the differences between the American and the British factor analysts. For example, it has again and again been shown (Cattell, 1957; Eysenck and Eysenck, 1969a; Borgatta, 1962) that Eysenck's orthogonally derived factors of Extraversion, and Neuroticism emerge as second order factors in data originally analysed by oblique factor methods. To summarise, factor analysis has in the past been used for two purposes: firstly, to reduce the number of variables, where oblique rotation is probably best; and secondly, to reveal underlying traits of psychological importance, where orthogonal factors may be best.

In the past, both these purposes have tended to be tackled by one analysis because of the work involved, but the advent of modern computer techniques means that the data can now be subjected to several different techniques at the cost of only a few minutes, or even a few seconds, of computer time. The factor analyst can therefore now look at his data from

several directions and, accordingly, test several different hypotheses before deciding on what approach is most appropriate in his own particular study.

Eysenck and Cattell have both insisted on working with predominantly normal groups to decide their factors. This is very important in the dimensional approach since it postulates that the behaviour found among patients is only at the extreme end of that found in the general population. It is often necessary to look at patient groups in an attempt to identify the factors that have been found from the normal population, and this Eysenck has usually done. Nevertheless, there are many who find difficulty in accepting the labelling of dimensions such as Neuroticism and Psychoticism when these dimensions have been derived from a non-psychiatric population. Despite this, the technique is basic to the whole dimensional approach and although Eysenck and Eysenck (1969b) defer to such critics to the extent of suggesting the use of the term P factor rather than 'psychoticism', they are obviously confident from their other work that what is being measured by this factor is an aspect of behaviour that places normals at one end and the psychotic patient at the other.

While factor analysis can be used when the distributions of the variables are not continuous, i.e. when subgroups exist, the results can be misleading unless further analysis is carried out. Lorr (1966) points out several objections illustrated in Fig. 1.6. His first is that there may in fact be more subgroups than dimensions. Secondly, that the factor axes tend not to go through the centre of the subgroups but between subgroups so that individuals tend to correlate significantly with several factors. And thirdly, because of the bipolar nature of the factors that tend to emerge, individuals who are mirror images of each other tend to appear on the same factor although at opposite ends, so that the factor tends to define two subgroups rather than just one.

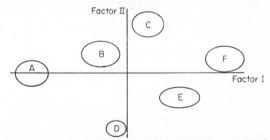

Fig. 1.6. Illustrating some objections to factor analysis Lorr (1966) has pointed out that when subjects in a factor analysis are in discrete groups; (a) there may be more clusters than factors, (b) axes tend to go between nearby groups, and (c) clusters may be found at each end of the factor.

The first objection is the converse of the problem that often arises of deciding how many dimensions are necessary to define a given set of subgroups, and of deciding if all the subgroups are independent. Rao's method of multivariate discriminate function is used in such cases (1952, 1965) and this will be considered later.

When the factor analysis has been done in the more common way of analysing correlations between variables (R technique) the way to detect subgroups is to calculate factor scores for each individual and then to plot each individual using two of his factors at a time as coordinates. The alternative is to start with the correlations between individuals (Q technique) and to factor analyse that matrix. In this case the individuals are plotted using two factor saturations at a time. Ryder (1964) has shown that, if appropriate standardisation procedures have been carried out and principal component analyses have been used, the results will be the same in both cases.

Factor Analytic Approaches to Classification

In a paper read at the International Congress of Psychiatry in 1929, Father T. V. Moore reported the first attempt to use a factor analytic approach to psychiatric classification. His introductory remarks (Moore, 1929) are unfortunately still as true now as they were over forty years ago.

'We have as yet only the vaguest notions about the pathology of the mind, and as a result the diagnostic entities of psychiatry are so poorly defined that the attempts to associate physical symptoms with definite mental conditions have been most disappointing. Likewise, psychological measurements of memory, associations, reaction time, etc., have been difficult of interpretation, when they had to be attached to the vague, overlapping, indeterminate entities of clinical psychiatry.'

Moore's 367 patients were rated on the presence or absence of certain psychiatric symptoms and, for nearly half of them, there were also available test results for reasoning, perception, and memory. Forty-one variables were selected for analysis. By the use of punched cards he was able to calculate tetrachoric correlations between all the variables and perform a rather crude form of cluster analysis, based on Spearman's technique of testing for the presence of a common factor in each selected group of four tests. The factors or groups that emerged were cognitive defect, catatonia, uninhibited, and manic (later split into two groups euphoric and non-euphoric), deluded-hallucinated, endogenous, and retarded depression. The factors were, as would be expected from the techniques used, not orthogonal, and had correlations as high as 0·69.

Both Thurstone (1947) and Degan (1952) have reanalysed Moore's original correlations using modern techniques. Degan found four second-order factors which he interpreted as mania, hebephrenic schizophrenia, paranoid-depression, catatonic schizophrenia. Lorr *et al.* (1963) accept six first-order factors: hyperexcitability, catatonia, hyperprojection, depression, schizophrenic dissociation, and traumatic hysteria, but reject hyperirritablity, deterioration, and neurasthenia as 'ward factors'.

The Trouton-Maxwell Study

Despite recent criticism (Grosz, 1968) concerning the reliability of the data used in the Trouton-Maxwell (1956) study, this is probably one of the most convincing pieces of evidence for the existence of the psychotic and neurotic dimensions in mental illness and their comparative orthogonality. In this study, use was made of the 11-page item-sheet used in the Maudsley and Royal Bethlem Hospitals, London, which records, mainly in terms of absence or presence, certain information of 500 aspects of the patient. These cover not only the symptoms exhibited at any time by the patient during his hospitalisation but also information concerning his own previous mental health and that of his family. These sheets are filled in by the junior psychiatrist on the patient's discharge from hospital and are also checked by the senior psychiatrist.

For the purpose of this study 45 items were selected, partly on the basis of their incidence, as those occurring in less than 10 per cent of the patients were excluded, and partly on *a priori* grounds as being of likely relevance to the psychotic-neurotic dimensions. This latter limitation is fraught with danger since it is well known that the differences in the selection of variables or subjects in a factor analysis can lead to differences in the factors that emerge. For example Guertin (1952a,b) in his attempt to discover if there is such a thing as schizophrenia included only schizophrenics in his analysis and thus precluded the chance of ever answering his question.

Trouton and Maxwell attempted also to avoid the stereotypy which so easily occurs in symptom rating, by grouping together as one variable any items that were likely to be the same piece of behaviour under different names according to the diagnosis given to the patient. Thus, overactivity, excitement, mania or hypomania, and non-manic euphoria, were all combined into one item since any two might tend to be given to the same piece of behaviour according

Table 1.5. Trouton-Maxwell Factor Analysis

Personal	*Symptoms*
1. Age under 40	21. other functional
2. Psychotic	disturbances
	22. retarded
Family History	23. overactive
3. of psychosis	24. agitated
4. of neurosis	25. impulsive
5. of abnormal	26. socially withdrawn
personality	27. compulsive/obsessional
	28. motor disturbances
Adjustment	29. depressed
6. unsatisfactory early	30. anxious
life	31. mood disturbances
7. unsatisfactory	32. suspicious
adolescence	33. irritable
8. poor/falling work	34. suicidal feelings
record	35. thought disorder
9. lacks confidence	36. psychogenic impairment
10. unsatisfactory home	of thought/memory
life	37. delusions of guilt
11. neurotic traits in	38. ideas of reference
childhood	39. other delusions
12. hysterical symptoms	40. hallucinations
13. obsessional symptoms	41. severe insomnia
14. anxiety symptoms	42. gross disturbance
15. previous mood swings	weight/food intake
16. energy output low	43. hypochondriacal
17. symptoms for over	44. unawareness of
1 year	symptoms
Onset	*Outcome*
18. gradual	45. recovered or much
19. constitutional causes	improved
20. environmental causes	

(From *Trouton and Maxwell*, 1956)

to the diagnosis already present in the psychiatrist's mind. Table 1.5 lists the items actually included.

The subjects used were male in-patients, selected at random from the files, whose ages were between 16 and 59 and whose diagnosis did not include organic disorder. Originally, those labelled personality disorder had also been excluded but they were included in the final factor analysis. This leads to a certain irregularity in the data recorded in the original paper since it sometimes refers to 700 patients and at other times to 819.

Tetrachoric correlations were calculated between each pair of the 45 items, and a Thurstone (1947) centroid method of factor analysis carried out. Six factors which accounted for 45 per cent of the variance were extracted and these were then orthogonally rotated. These six rotated factors were as follws—

Factor I which was fairly confidently labelled Psychoticism by the authors because it had high positive loadings on variables 26, 38, 39, 40, and 2.

Factor II was equally confidently labelled Neuroticism since it had high positive loadings on variables 11, 12, 9, etc.

There is no doubt that factors I and II do also tend to separate items into acute symptoms and long-standing symptoms in that factor II tends to have items from the section of the item sheet dealing with history and previous personality, but the authors defend their particular interpretation by reference to other research giving similar descriptions of the factors and, also, to the genetic evidence given by the loadings of items 3 and 4 in the two factors namely—

	Factor I	Factor II
Family history of psychosis		
(3)	0·28	−0·02
Family history of neurosis		
(4)	−0·03	0·32

Factor III has positive loadings on what would be generally regarded as schizophrenic symptoms 35, 28, and negative loadings on depressive symptoms 24, 41, 37, 30, 29, and might therefore be labelled the schizophrenic-psychotic depression dimension.

Factor IV is labelled inactivity-withdrawal by the authors since it includes at the positive end 26, 22, and at the negative end 23, 25.

Factors V and VI are dismissed as unimportant and unreliable by the authors, although they seem to relate to hypochondriasis and obsessionality respectively.

Eysenck (1960a) has a table relating the position of 26 patients with various psychiatric diagnoses in the first 4 factors and this tends to confirm the interpretation placed on the factors by Trouton and Maxwell.

Lorr and O'Connor (1957) are critical of this study, believing that it is impossible to make such sense out of data that was so heterogeneous in composition, i.e. combining symptoms, history of illness, family history, etc. Nevertheless, when they reanalysed the data, using oblique factors to obtain simple structure, their first factor corresponded to grossly disturbed behaviour that might reasonably be labelled psychotic; their second factor was based mainly on neurotic symptoms and a history of maladjustment that would not be considered by many to be radically different from Trouton and Maxwell's neuroticism factor. Their third factor was reactive depression, and the fourth paranoid symptoms.

CHILDREN'S CLASSIFICATION

In 1962, Collins and co-workers attempted a project similar to the Trouton and Maxwell study on information from children's files at the Institute of Psychiatry, London. Epileptic, psychotic, and mentally subnormal children were excluded, leaving

268 boys and 98 girls aged 8 or 9. From the 150 item sheet those items occurring in less than 10 per cent of the cases were excluded, leaving 59 items for the boys and 64 for the girls with 56 items in common. These items covered disturbances of behaviour or relationship as well as personal and family history, parental attitudes, etc. Principal component analyses were carried out separately on the item correlation matrices for the two sexes.

The first factor in each case accounted for only 8 per cent of the variance. For the boys this was labelled 'rebelliousness' and the second factor was labelled 'rootlessness'. It is surprising, as the authors point out, to find that these two factors are orthogonal, i.e. independent of each other. The third factor was labelled 'anxiety'. For the girls, the first factor combined the main variables of the boys' first two factors, e.g. disobediance, destructiveness, as well as restlessness. The girls' second factor had high positive loadings on unsatisfactory social adjustment, with negative loadings on delinquency variables. The low correlations between the items probably account for the small amount of variance extracted by the factors, and for the difficulty in labelling them with any confidence.

Earlier work on the factor analysis both of children's and adults' data is more than adequately covered by Eysenck's (1960a) chapter in the first edition of this volume and the reader is referred to that for further details.

Cluster Analysis

When the underlying theory is that there is a fixed (but unknown) number of discrete, qualitatively different classes of individuals within the population being studied, the methods of cluster analysis are frequently used. Some of the more popular techniques are described by Lyerly (1965). While factor analyses are usually carried out on the resemblances between variables, cluster analyses are usually done on the resemblances between persons, although these are by no means necessary limitations.

Starting with the scores of N subjects on k variables a matrix of $N \times N$ measures of similarity or dissimilarity are calculated and then analysed in such a way as to produce m subgroups so that subjects within each subgroup closely resemble each other on the original variables and at the same time differ from all other subjects in these same variables or, in the geometrical model, subjects who are close together in the multidimensional space form one group, and the other subjects farther away belong to other groups (Fig. 1.7).

The $N \times N$ matrix of (dis-) similarities can be formed in several ways. The most obvious might

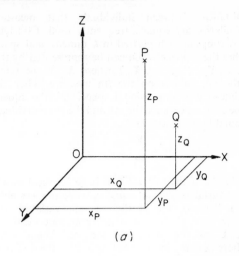

(a)

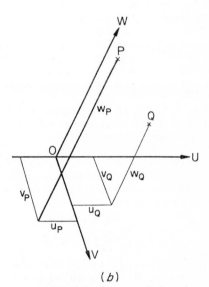

(b)

Fig. 1.7. Cluster analysis

O, P, and Q are points fixed relative to each other. In (a) orthogonal and in (b) oblique reference axes are used. Only in (a) can the distances between P and Q be calculated from their coordinates using Pythagoras's Theorem. In (b) the cosines of the angles between the axes enter into the calculation.

appear to be to calculate the correlations between persons, as Stephenson (1952) does, but there is more than one way of doing this and these will be considered later when profile analysis, which is also a person-to-person comparison and for which the mathematical problem is the same, is discussed.

Distances between individuals that measure dissimilarity are equally frequently used. Consider the N subjects each plotted in k dimensional space so that the scores of each can be represented by the vector $(X_{p1}, X_{p2}, \ldots, X_{pk})$, where X_{pj} is the score of the pth subject on the jth measure. Then, in Euclidean multidimensional space, D^2, the square of the distance between the pth and the qth individual, is found by the formula

$$D^2 = \sum_{i=1}^{k} (x_{pi} - x_{qi})^2$$

Obviously, if the two subjects have identical scores on all variables D^2 will equal 0, while the less alike the individuals are in the relevant variables the farther apart the points which represent them are placed, and the greater D^2 becomes. While some authors (Sawrey *et al.*, 1960) use D^2, others (Cronbach and Gleser, 1953) prefer to use D, which places less emphasis on large differences in one variable, compared to moderate differences in several variables. D also has the logical advantage of being more strictly a distance measure (Heerman, 1965). If raw scores are used, then the weight of each variable in the D^2 measure is proportional to its variance in the group. For this reason the variables are usually transformed into standard scores before calculating D^2 or, alternatively, the variables are deliberately weighted, either to take account of the experimenter's own views on their relative importance or according to some objective criterion such as using principal component analysis factors derived from the variables (Overall, 1964).

Cattell (1949) proposed a measure derived from D^2 as a measure of similarity between profiles and he advocates this for comparing 16 PF profiles. It is calculated by the formula

$$r_p = \frac{2_k \chi_{50}^2 \sum S_j^2 - kD^2}{2_k \chi_{50}^2 \sum S_j^2 + kD^2}$$

where $_k\chi_{50}^2$ represents the median χ^2 corresponding to the k variables. It varies from -1 to $+1$ as D^2 decreases from infinity to zero. It has the property of discriminating well between similar profiles but for very dissimilar profiles r_p has a value of nearly -1, which changes insignificantly as D^2 becomes very large.

Having used one system or another to obtain the $N \times N$ matrix of similarities or dissimilarities between subjects the next task is to start grouping together those subjects who are similar to each other. The important question here is how to decide when to stop adding to one group and start on the next group. The job is not made easier by the fact that there is seldom any *a priori* suggestion as to

how many subgroups exist. Several solutions have been offered to the clustering problem. Most of them are laborious; all are subjective at some stage or another. 'No formal rules can be laid down for finding clusters because a cluster is not a well-defined term' (Rao, 1952).

The general basis for clustering is to arrange it so that each individual in a cluster is more like the other individuals in the cluster than any other group of individuals. The earliest attempt was by Holzinger and Harman (1941) who chose as the starting nucleus of a group those two members who correlated most highly with each other, then other members were added one at a time. At each stage the average correlation of the members with each other was compared with the average correlation with all the non-members of the group. The ratio of these two averages multiplied by 100 was termed B (standing for belonging) coefficient. If B fell below 130, or if it showed a sharp fall at any stage, then that group was regarded as complete and all its members withdrawn from the population; the procedure then started again with the remaining measures. Holzinger and Harman introduced this approach in order to group variables but it can obviously also be applied to grouping individuals. Another early attempt at clustering by Thorndike (1953) started from the opposite point of view. The two individuals who least resembled each other were taken as the nucleus of separate groups, then a third individual who was furthest from the other two was found, and he formed the nucleus of a third cluster, and so on. Then each nucleus had allocated to it, in turn, the individual nearest to it, so that at the end each cluster had an equal number of members. Next, fringe members were reallocated where they clearly belonged to a nearby cluster. Each subgroup could also be split up by establishing new nuclei within it. No criteria are laid down and the whole procedure seems even more arbitrary (e.g. in making clusters initially at least equal in size) than can be accepted even for clustering techniques. Zubin *et al.* (1963) in an unpublished paper have apparently suggested an adaption of Thorndike's technique that has more adequately defined criteria, but even that is rejected by Lorr (1966) as having many drawbacks.

McQuitty has in successive papers (1954, 1960a,b,c, 1963) developed approaches to cluster analysis that have attracted much attention and have been used in several studies. His methods have the advantage of being relatively simple procedures which, once the $N \times N$ association matrix has been calculated, proceeds by simple comparison so that computers need not be used, although several computer programs have been written. Its simplest form is Elementary Linkage Analysis which classifies people into categories so that each member in a category resembles some member of that group more closely than he resembles any non-member of the category. This is done by including as a new member of an existing category any individual whose highest similarity score is with an existing member of that category. Typal Analysis tightens the criterion so that in a category each member resembles *every* member of that category more than he resembles any non-member. Finally, in his Hierarchial Syndrome Analysis, McQuitty starts with a large number of small groups and then shows how these small groups may, in turn, be amalgamated into large groups which can, in turn, be further amalgamated. McQuitty suggests that biologically this offers a basis of classification into species, genera, and families, etc. By allowing different levels of similarity, this approach may be favoured by clinicians who traditionally take the viewpoint that there are broad groups within which more specific groups can be observed.

Sawrey *et al.* (1960) used the D^2 measure. They start off with a nuclear pair who resemble each other most (i.e. lowest D^2) then add to this all the other individuals whose D^2 from the first pair is less than an assigned limit. The remaining cases are then dealt with in a similar way until all cases have been assigned. A limit of dissimilarity is also laid down to determine 'unassignable' cases.

Discriminant Function Analysis

The previous methods discussed have started by making no assumptions regarding the number of groups that may exist, or their composition. Sometimes, however, one may believe on other evidence that n groups exist and individuals can be placed uniquely in the groups. These assumptions must, however, be tested. In the univariate case this is done by analysis of variance. Each individual has some measure x and the question is whether the different groups differ significantly in their mean value of x. It is also possible to test which of the groups is significantly different from others (Snedecor, 1956). In the problem we have been considering so far there are many variables and these variables are usually not just additional information about the group but the basic information (history, symptoms, and signs) on which the groups have been formed. Rao (1952, 1962) has offered in multiple discriminate analysis a technique for solving this problem. Its aim is similar to multiple regression in that weights that will maximise the differences between groups are sought. It also determines how many dimensions are needed to explain these differences and may suggest that certain groups are

not significantly different from each other. Rao and Slater (1949) and Slater (1960) give examples of the technique. Nowadays, with the aid of computers the process is relatively straightforward. The reason it is not used more commonly is because many researchers in the classification field today prefer to start off with no assumptions regarding groups that may exist.

Lubin (1950) has proposed an alternative technique for the solution of the problem and this was used by Eysenck (1955) to separate normals, neurotics, and psychotics from each other. He showed that two dimensions were necessary to discriminate among the three groups so that psychotics could not be placed on the normal-neurotic continuum but required a second dimension. This is further discussed in Eysenck (1960a).

Numerical Taxonomy

Taxonomy is the process of biological classification used to arrange flora and fauna into species and genera. Numerical taxonomy is the application to this task of the statistical techniques of multivariate analysis, borrowed from the psychologists but now being borrowed back for new applications. Sokal and Sneath (1963) and Sokal (1966) outline the technique with zoological and botanical examples but Hope (1969) discusses its application to psychological problems while Pilowsky *et al.* (1969) have used it in the diagnosis of depression.

The methods used are those of clustering, but it is interesting to observe the kinds of results that are obtained in the zoological examples and are hoped for in the psychological application. Figure 1.8 shows how, if certain levels of similarity between individuals are differently shaded or coloured to show increasing similarity, the clusters show up as small triangles of dark shading, representing species, within larger triangles of lighter shading, representing genera. Figure 1.9 shows a two-dimensional representation, called a phenogram, of the stages of clustering as they occur. As in all two-dimensional representations of higher dimensional processes in psychology, the practical results may be much less clear than the artificial example shown, although examples from zoology can be very convincing with cut-off points for species and for genera standing out quite clearly.

Profile Analysis

It has long been a practice in psychological assessment, when several measures are available on patients, to display the scores of any patient as a profile. It is done for the WAIS, the MMPI and the Rorschach, to name but a few popular tests. How

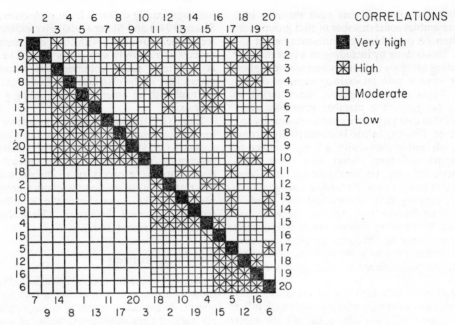

Fig. 1.8. Artificial example of numerical taxonomy

The upper right triangle represents half of the original symmetrical correlation matrix. The lower left triangle represents half of the symmetrical matrix obtained by transposing rows (and corresponding columns) so that those elements that correlate highly with each other are grouped together. This reveals small highly correlated clusters that represent subgroups and larger moderately correlated clusters that represent broader groups. (*After* Sokal, 1966)

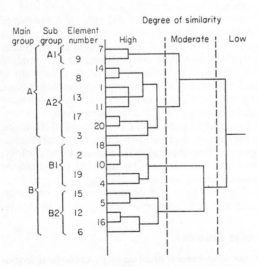

Fig. 1.9. A phenogram of stages of clustering

As the acceptable level of similarity is progressively lowered, the elements cluster in increasingly large groups. The data for this figure is the same as for Fig. 1.8. (*After* Sokal, 1966)

should one interpret such data? Usually, the psychologist is comparing this patient's profile with some 'typical' profiles. These typical profiles may be based on his own experience, supplied norms, or theoretical considerations. Mathematically, profile analysis on k variables is an almost identical problem to comparing points in the k dimensional space, as is done in the clustering analysis just considered, but problems do arise (Nunnally, 1962). Profiles can be displayed graphically in two dimensions and this undoubtedly gives them the advantages and disadvantages of the concrete compared to the abstract. Because of this, comparison between an individual and some typical case is easier for the profiles, but, unless the variables have been chosen to be independent of each other, there is a redundancy of information and a loss of reliability that is not present if factor scores are used. Profiles, however, indicate some features of the data that might be missed in the more abstract realm of multivariate analysis (Fig. 1.10).

It is assumed, as is usually the case, that before plotting the profile the subtest scores have been scaled so that they have the same mean and standard deviation on each variable for the population being

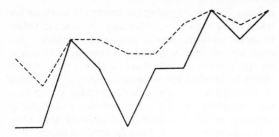

(*a*) Profiles differ both in elevation and scatter

(*b*) Profiles now differ only in scatter

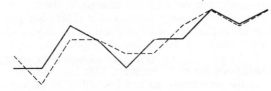

(*c*) Profiles now have same elevation (mean) and same scatter (s.d.)

Fig. 1.10. Profile analysis

Two profiles of 10 variables which correlate with $r = 0.8$ are successively equated for mean and standard deviation to bring out the similarity in their shape.

considered. This is certainly the case for the WAIS and the MMPI. If this is not done, those subscales with mean and/or standard deviations much greater than the others are liable to be given undue prominence in the interpretation. When comparing two profiles (Cronbach and Gleser, 1953) the first thing noticed is that they can differ in mean elevation. On the WAIS, for example, the mean elevation varies approximately with IQ. If the subtests have a mean score of 10 the IQ is about 100, whereas if the mean scaled score is 14 the IQ is likely to be about 120. In the MMPI the mean profile level may measure something like 'intensity of disturbance'. A factor analysis of crude cross products rather than correlations would be needed if elevation were to be allowed to play its part in an ordinary factor analysis. Of course, in some situations a rise in mean variable score has no implication since there is no common meaning that can be attributed to it. Some

variables may be measured in opposite directions to each other (Stephenson, 1952) and other variables may have no direct relevance to each other. Such would be the case for the Rorschach elevations even if the scoring categories were scaled in some way that removed the differences due to the different total number of responses. If, as in the WAIS, the mean elevation has a clear meaning it might seem most appropriate to remove it from the profile and to record it separately.

The next distinction between profiles that would then emerge would be that some are more variable than others. What is the meaning of this? It obviously depends on the variables listed. Using the WAIS the implication is that a level profile represents consistency of intellectual function while a jagged one represents discrepancies usually due to a pathological state either functional or organic. Again, differences in scatter, where the shape was the same, might represent that the individuals are of the same type (same diagnosis for example) but the one with the greater scatter is a more extreme example of that type. Lorr (1966) shows that, in acute psychosis, as the patient responds to treatment his profile retains roughly the same shape but shows less scatter (Fig. 1.11). In the multidimensional model he lies on the same line from the main position but moves nearer to the mean as he recovers. In that same paper, however, Lorr shows that there can be differences between acute and chronic patient types but these might be due to other factors, e.g. Institutional Neurosis.

It might seem reasonable, therefore, to remove this scatter. It can be recorded if relevant by the standard deviation of the individual's subtest scores, and since now every profile has a mean of zero and a standard deviation of 1 all that is left is the shape of the profile. If types exist, we might expect the

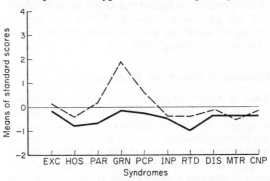

Fig. 1.11. IMPS profiles for acute Grandiose-Paranoid male types

The upper profile is that on admission and the lower that six months later or on discharge from hospital. Lorr points out that the profile shapes are similar. (Lorr, 1966)

profile of members to have shapes that are very similar to each other. The similarity of profile shapes is measured by the correlation between them. Note that the correlation coefficient automatically removes the elevation and scatter dimension from the profile. For this reason Cattell, who believes that elevation should not be discarded in comparing profiles, advocates (1949) the coefficient r_p, already quoted for use in comparing 16 PF profiles.

The danger of eliminating scatter is that those cases with very little scatter have this scatter amplified to the standard value so that the shape that results may represent little more than exaggerated error, and those individuals who are close together near the centre of the group may be scattered widely apart, as Cronbach and Gleser (1953) have pointed out.

It has been suggested (Overall, 1964; Osgood and Suci, 1962) that there are advantages in standardising deviation from the origin but to some extent retaining elevation, as in the normalised vector procedure, where the sum of squares of the corrected scores is made equal to unity in each individual case. This is done by dividing the original scores by the square root of the sum of their squares. This should be used only if a score of zero has the same meaning for each variable, usually symptom not present. The appropriate index of similarity according to Gleser (1965) is the normalised vector product.

$$\cos \theta_{pq} = \frac{\sum (x_{pi} \cdot x_{qi})}{\sqrt{(\sum x_{pi}{}^2 \cdot \sum x_{qi}{}^2)}}$$

where θpq will represent the angle subtended at the origin by the points p and q. The ordinary Pearson product moment correlation is equal to the cosine of the angle subtended at the mean by the two points in the multidimensional space. The normalised vector product, as indeed the crude cross products and the covariances, can be factor analysed in exactly the same way as correlations but the results have to be interpreted with care.

Criterion of Therapeutic Response

Since a major application of any classification system is to indicate treatment and to predict prognosis, an obvious approach is to use multiple regression techniques to select patients who, on the basis of past experience, are likely to benefit from a specific form of treatment, and then cross-validate these findings on another group. If such a regression equation can be found that is reliable and valid it needs no further justification: it is of immediate practical benefit in helping those patients who are predicted as likely to respond and in saving time and expense by not supplying the treatment to those for whom it is unlikely to have any therapeutic value. In so far as differences in therapeutic response give evidence of real differences between individuals, on the theoretical side there is also a gain, which might be further investigated. Anything that helps to separate an otherwise homogeneous group into separate groups usually helps to reduce within-group variance, which is a measure of residual ignorance. It is sometimes argued, from the medical model, that symptomatic response is a poor ground for equating groups, and this has to be admitted. The danger lies mainly in assuming that those who respond similarly are similar (Lubin, 1965), but one can avoid this trap and concentrate on its negative aspect; namely, that those who differ in response are likely to be different, and there is very much less danger in this. One of the troubles in psychiatry is that there are too few diagnostic groups. It is generally accepted that schizophrenia must contain several different categories of patients, yet work continues to be done with groups having just that label, so that within-group variance tends to be large compared to any between-group variance that emerges in the experiment. In an amusing paper, Lubin (1965) has put forward in the form of a dialogue the advantages and disadvantages of the therapeutic-response typology.

To be generally useful it is not enough to produce predictions for each treatment. One must also test that the treatments do not just differ in efficacy. There is little gain in predicting drug A responders and drug B responders if in fact the rank order of response for the two drugs is the same, in which case one is likely to be better than the other for nearly all patients, and the poorer drug can then be discarded. What one hopes to find is that different kinds of patients respond to each of the two drugs. Statistically this means that it is better if the drug by patient interaction is significant.

This is an important point that is often neglected in analysing results of controlled drug trials. If, in a drug trial, drugs A and B are not significantly different from each other in that each cures 50 per cent of the patients, it would obviously not be insignificant if it emerged that the 50 per cent of the patients cured by A were all the females and the 50 per cent cured by B were all the males. One should, therefore, examine, as far as possible, the characteristics of the responders in each group. Papers on controlled trials usually produce evidence that both groups were equated for age, sex, and duration of illness before treatment began, but few bother to test whether responders in each group were still equated on those same variables compared to non-responders, and whether responders on one drug differed from the responders to the other drug. It is not sufficient to test only whether A is on the whole better than B.

Clyde (1965) has had some mixed success in his research to produce typologies based on therapeutic response. The major part of his research and the most difficult to date was in deciding what constituted 'good response'. He had both doctors and nurses assess changes in patients by means of the Minnesota-Hartford Personality Assay which used 127 items for the doctors and 142 for the nurses. Each group's data were factor analysed separately, producing eleven factor scores for the doctors and seven for the nurses. Six of these factors were similar for both groups (e.g. thinking disorder, hostility, etc.), but tranquility appeared only in the nurses' scale, and five other factors, including anxiety, appeared only in the doctors' scale. A total of 278 schizophrenic patients were assessed before treatment and, five weeks later, after treatment. Raters also assessed global improvement on a seven point scale. The mean improvement score was the same for each group. What, however, was meant by 'improvement' by the two sets of raters? It emerged that this was more complex than at first seemed likely. For example, sometimes the raters agreed on the changes that had taken place, but while one group rated this as improvement the other group did not. This is not perhaps surprising when one considers the different relationships of the two raters with the patients. More surprising, however, was the second finding that, when prediction of improvement was attempted from the pre-test scores, the only predictors that were better than chance were those on which the raters disagreed. (Rice and Mattsson, 1966, found similar difficulty over 'improvement'.)

Three drugs had been used in the trial, and one of them was shown to be significantly better than the other two in producing improvement. The method of approach did not allow for different predictors for each drug, which would have been more useful. Drug by type interaction could then have been investigated. The research is, however, most important in exploring a difficulty in the therapeutic-response approach; namely, what is meant by 'good response', and who decides it.

McGuire and Wright (1971) have used therapeutic changes in symptoms to produce an index of disease activity. The method finds weights to maximise the significance of the difference from zero of the mean of the weighted sums of the drug-induced beneficial changes in the symptoms. Treatments similar in action should produce similar weights, and the method should also aid in finding subgroups within a larger group.

Therapeutic response by type interaction also serves as a criterion for the validation of any

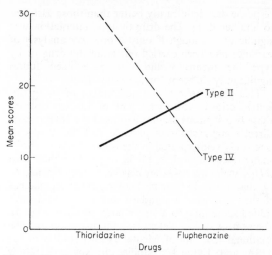

Fig. 1.12. Results that demonstrate drug by type interaction

Type II are withdrawn, periodically agitated schizophrenics and Type IV are withdrawn, helpless, suspicious schizophrenics (Lorr, 1966). In the 2-way analysis of variance only interaction was significant ($p < 0.01$). For the drugs separately, Type II differed from Type IV on thioridazine ($p < 0.05$). For the types separately, the drugs produced different responses only for Type IV ($p < 0.01$). (Katz, 1965)

classification system. Katz (1965) and Overall and Hollister (1964) have given predictive validation to their classification system by showing the interaction to be significant (Fig. 1.12). Klett and Moseley (1965), using data from two other studies—the first by Lasky and associates (1962) in a Veterans Administration Cooperative study, and the second an NIMH collaborative study (1964)—in both of which IMPS had been used, investigated the possibility of a therapeutic-responders classification. In the trial, three phenothiazine drugs had been used to treat acute schizophrenia, and for each pre-treatment scores were available on the IMPS for use as predictors, and three post-treatment scores were also available, so that the differences yielded improvement scores. Thus, for each drug, three multiple regression equations were calculated, each based on over 70 patients. This data all came from the Veterans Administration Project and the equations were then cross validated on 320 patients of the second study. From the pretreatment scores, three responses were predicted for each of the three drugs. Since this analysis was post-hoc some of the patients had actually been assigned to the drug predicted as being most suitable to them, others had not. Initial differences were adjusted by covariance. In every case, i.e. three criteria and three drugs, those patients assigned to their predicted best response did significantly better than those assigned to another drug. The drug by type interaction was significant, although if only a one-way analysis of variance had been carried out either by drug or by type the means would not have been found significantly different for the main effects.

This paper reflects the advantages of using objective criteria for assessment of illness. Because these two separate studies had used the IMPS scale, direct comparison was possible and the results of one study reinterpreted in the other. Unfortunately, many research workers prefer to produce their own *ad hoc* scales because they believe, usually erroneously, that it will do their particular job better, whereas if they had used a standard test they would have added something to a larger body of knowledge. In the same way, the Veterans Administration and the National Institute of Mental Health studies in the USA and Eysenck's studies in the UK show the tremendously magnified pay-off when one pursues a continuous and interlocking series of attacks on a common theme.

The Assignment Problem

In most methods so far discussed the techniques have produced defined groups to which some if not all of the original defining subjects have been assigned. What of the new individual who now appears with a vector of scores? To which group should he be assigned? To a complete dimensionalist the problem does not arise in this form. He does not assign the individual to a group but to a point in a reduced multidimensional space defined by his factor scores which can be accurately calculated according to the appropriate formula for the technique used. The dimensionalist would point out that clustering discards information about differences between individuals in the group, and this can be justified only if these differences are irrelevant or due to error.

In those cases where some clustering model has been adopted, the method used in forming the clusters may be adaptable to the new scores, or some other technique such as cut-off points, regression equations, multiple discrimination function, or probability function may be suitable.

Bayes' Theorem

This theorem, which was first put forward more than 200 years ago, states that the probability of disease D existing, given that a symptom complex S is present, is equal to the probability of the symptom complex S existing within the population with the disease D, multiplied by the probability of that disease in the total population, divided by the probability of symptom S in the same total population. It can be expressed mathematically as

$$P(D \mid S) = \frac{P(S \mid D) \cdot P(D)}{P(S)}$$

Before discussing the application of this formula to the classification problem it is worth noting that it demonstrates clearly the base rate problem; namely, discrimination must be very good if the probability of a diagnosis is rare. As in the base rate problem, the probabilities specific to the situation, i.e. the probability of disease D and the probability of symptom S, may vary from hospital to hospital and even from consultant to consultant. It can, however, usually be worked out from the frequencies that actually occur. If a moving average is kept, they can even be continually altering with the changing situation, thus coping with the situation where, once a consultant is expert in a field, the number of patients with conditions relevant to that field referred to him may increase compared to other patients. The probability of a given symptom within a disease is probably relatively constant, though even that can alter with the changing culture pattern. The social desirability value of an item in a self-rating questionnaire might alter in the course of time and thus alter the frequency of that response in all or in some types of patients. Many applications of Bayes' theorem use a computer to make the diagnosis so that it could easily be arranged that the computer program routinely updates both the probability of the disease and the probability of the symptom in the cases being presented to it (Fitzgerald *et al.*, 1966; Lusted, 1968).

The likelihood ratio is a deduction from Bayes' theorem in that if one is only interested in the differential diagnosis, $D1$ or $D2$, then the relative likelihood of the two diagnoses is

$$P(D_1 \mid S)/P(D_2 \mid S) = \frac{P(S \mid D1)}{P(S \mid D2)} \cdot \frac{P(D1)}{P(D2)}$$

In this form it may appeal to many clinicians because it is more straightforward.

In both Bayes' theorem and the likelihood ratio the number of errors can be reduced by using different values for different groups of the population, i.e. different probabilities for each sex and various age groups. The symptoms can also be any combination of signs, symptoms, scores, etc., one wishes to include, so long as one knows the relevant probabilities. Lusted (1968) provides an example of this approach to the diagnosis of bronchial asthma. Overall and Hollister (1964) used Bayesian techniques in testing their computer diagnostic system, mentioned elsewhere. Other research of a psychiatric nature using the model has been done by Birnbaum and Maxwell (1961), Overall and Gorham (1963), and Smith (1966). This last paper had 14 clinicians assess the probability of 41 symptoms in 38 mental disorders, and found good agreement for 80 per cent of them. Smith then applied Bayes' formula to predict the diagnosis of 30 new patients from the presence of the symptoms and found agreement with a clinical diagnosis for 26 out of the 30 patients, that is 87 per cent, which was better than had been found on the average between psychiatrists for similar data.

Eysenck's Inventories

Even before the Trouton and Maxwell study in 1956, Eysenck (1947, 1950, 1952, 1955) had been pressing the view that a few major orthogonal factors could summarise most of the variance in individual personality differences. The three dimensions he proposed were Neuroticism (N), Extraversion-Introversion (E), and Psychoticism (P). Much of the experimental work from the Institute of Psychiatry, London, and elsewhere, produced to support the existence of these dimensions, is discussed in other chapters of this volume.

The Maudsley Personality Inventory (Eysenck, 1959) and later the Eysenck Personality Inventory (Eysenck and Eysenck, 1964), and the Junior EPI (S.B.G. Eysenck, 1965), which provided self-rating scales to measure the first two dimensions N and E, did much to popularise these measures of personality. Many studies (Sainsbury, 1960; McGuire et al., 1963) showed the value of the scales in the psychiatric setting. More recently Eysenck and Eysenck (1968a,b; 1969b) have put forward new inventories which also measure the Psychoticism factor in adults and children.

It is characteristic of his scientific approach that Eysenck (1967, 1970) had made explicit his theories as to the physiological basis of his three factors. The E factor is believed to measure the excitation-inhibition balance which, in turn, is related to the arousal of the cortex and the threshold of the individual's reticular activating system. The N factor is related to individual differences in thresholds of emotional activation, which is determined by the threshold of the individual's visceral brain, which also determines autonomic reactivity. The P factor has been less well defined to date, but, in the normal population, it seems to be related to odd, cruel, antisocial behaviour and suspicion and a lack of feeling towards even those close to one. No clear physiological or psychological theory has yet been offered to explain the P factor.

The N and E type questions are probably too

Table 1.6. Some Questions Measuring Psychoticism (P) Factor (From the Junior and Adult PEN Inventories of Eysenck and Eysenck)

Junior PEN. Inventory (Eysenck and Eysenck, 1969b)		
6. Do you enjoy hurting people you like?	YES	NO
31. Would it upset you a lot to see a dog that has just been run over?	YES	NO
95. Do you like doing things that are a bit frightening?	YES	NO
PEN. Inventory (Eysenck and Eysenck, 1968a)		
19. Have you had an awful lot of bad luck?	YES	NO
27. Are there several people who keep trying to avoid you?	YES	NO
40. Do you have enemies that wish to harm you?	YES	NO

well known to need illustration, but typical P questions from the PEN Inventories are given in Table 1.6. Both the inventories measuring the P factor are still at the development stage. An up-to-date summary of his dimensional system is given in Eysenck (1970) *A Dimensional System of Psychodiagnostics.*

16 PF Test

This self-rating scale, like those of Eysenck, hardly needs introduction. It comes in six forms, labelled A to F. Three choices are given for each item, usually corresponding to 'True', 'False', 'In-between'. As the name implies, sixteen personality factors are measured. They were obtained from a normal population by oblique factor solutions, but since the intercorrelations tend to be low, most being below 0·3, Cattell claims they can be regarded as independent. Four higher order factors, Anxiety, Extraversion, Alert-poise and Independence, can be obtained by appropriate weighting, but the author believes this to be a less satisfactory procedure for most interpretations, as some information is inevitably lost. Personality descriptions are given in the manual for high and low scores on each factor. Score profiles are also given for certain broad psychiatric groups, but the emphasis is mainly on applications to the normal population.

Symptom Sign Inventory

Since the MMPI scales were collected by empirically selecting questions that differentiated specific groups from normals, positive intercorrelations between scales occur, e.g. a high score on Depression is almost always associated with a high score on Schizophrenia so that, while the test is useful for screening purposes in distinguishing psychiatric from non-psychiatric individuals, in its basic form it has many limitations for differential diagnosis. In particular, diagnoses that are similar in the clinical picture also tend to be similar in the scale score pattern. Foulds (1962) has attempted to improve on this by the use of his Sign-Symptom Inventory (SSI). From a questionnaire assumed to measure aspects of each of eight common psychiatric diagnoses (10 questions for each), those questions were selected that significantly differentiated between two specific clinical diagnoses of Anxiety state (50), Neurotic Depression (50), Psychotic Depression (50), Hysteria (40) and Paranoid Schizophrenia (30). These five diagnoses gave ten possible comparisons. The number of questions in each comparison ranged from 8 to 26 with an average of 18. For the 220 patients from whom the questions had been derived, 63 per cent were found with the same diagnoses as had been given to them clinically, with 12 per cent uncertain. With a cross-validation group of 40 patients the agreement rate had fallen to 55 per cent with 13 per cent uncertain. Most of the errors occurred in the Neurotic groups. Since there were five categories to which the 40 patients had to be assigned, an agreement of 55 per cent is obviously highly significant but is still a long way from satisfactory. However, Foulds discusses some of the misclassifications and suggests that in the diagnosis of Hysteria, for example, his objective assignment might be more correct than the clinical one because of the tendency of psychiatrists to assign patients to this category on the basis of their personality rather than on clinical signs and symptoms. This point is followed up more fully in other work by Foulds (1965, 1967).

IMPS

The In-patient Multidimensional Psychiatric Scale devised by Lorr and co-workers, and published in 1962, is a rating scale of 75 questions to be answered preferably by both an interviewer and an observer. The scoring takes about ten minutes and covers those aspects of the patient's behaviour, speech content, attitudes, etc., actually observed or reported by the patient during an unstructured interview lasting from thirty to sixty minutes. Some typical questions are shown in Table 1.7. The answers to the questions on intensity of symptoms have to be selected from a nine-point scale: Not at all (0), very slightly (1), a little (2), mildly (3), moderately (4), quite a bit (5), distinctly (6), markedly (7), extremely (8). It has been shown (Cliff, 1959) that such adverbs can provide an approximately equal interval scale of intensity. There is a similar five-point scale dealing with frequency of symptoms. Some questions on delusions and orientation are answered on a

Table 1.7.   In-patient Multidimensional Psychiatric Scale (IMPS). Some Questions from the Scale by Lorr *et al.* (1962)

Compared to the normal person to what degree does he—
5. Verbally express feelings of hostility, ill will, or dislike of others?
    Cues: Makes hostile comments regarding others such as attendants, other patients, his family, or persons in authority. Reports conflicts on the ward.
35. Exhibit an excess of speech?
    Cues: Difficult to stop flow of speech once started or to get a word in edgewise. Judge the amount of speech and not its rate or relevance.

How often did he—
53. Hear voices that accused, blamed, or said "bad" things about him (e.g. he is a spy, homosexual, murderer)?

Does he believe that—
62. Certain people are trying to or now do control his actions or thinking?

---

two-point scale. In arriving at subtest totals the latter two scales are multiplied by 2 and 8 respectively to produce a maximum of 8 for all items.

On the basis of earlier factor analyses, ten syndromes were believed by the authors to be necessary to explain psychotic behaviour. A multiple group factoring process (Guttman, 1952) was used to produce ten oblique factors and the fit tested by rejecting variables that did not show sufficient correlation with their assigned factors (< 0.30) or too high a correlation with some other factor (> 0.25). Most items correlated with their appropriate syndrome at about the ± 0.6 level. Because of the method, no factor loadings are given to the variables and the only scaling used is to give each variable the same range 0 to 8 before adding the actual scores together to give a factor or syndrome score.

Reliability both by interrater correlations and KR formulae are high, averaging about 0·88 and 0·85 respectively. Lorr *et al.* (1963) offer validation by showing the presence of the syndromes in the re-analysis of other factorial studies. Unfortunately, these are mainly the studies that were used to hypothesise the factors, so there must inevitably be some contamination.

It is an important feature of the scale to restrict scoring to that behaviour observed or revealed during the interview. This, although ignoring much valuable evidence from the reports of others or from the patient's earlier behaviour, means that the scores should have less inertia and make them more sensitive to change. The test is therefore particularly useful in drug trials.

In the earlier book *Syndromes of Psychosis* (Lorr

et al., 1963) a clustering procedure is applied to the IMPS scores of 566 psychotic patients split into five groups using the procedure of Sawrey *et al.* (1960). Six types were identified at this time, but in his later book, *Explorations in Typing Psychotics*, Lorr (1966) found 7 psychotic types common to both sexes, 2 for males only, and 2 for females only. Multiple cutting scores for assigning individuals to clusters were produced. One of the types common to both sexes required separate cutting scores for each sex. These allowed approximately 60 per cent of the patients to be assigned unequivocally to one psychotic type. An alternative assigning system was to correlate each case with the mean profile of each type and thus to assign the case to that type with which it correlated highest. Any case that failed to correlate at least 0·55, i.e. $p < 0.05$, was left unassigned and 20 per cent of the patients were in this group. Lorr's description of the types (1966, pp. 74–75) is given below.

'Seven of the patient types are essentially the same for men and women. These are the Excited, the Excited-Hostile, the Hostile Paranoid, the Hallucinated Paranoid, the Intropunitive, the Grandiose Paranoid and the Anxious-Disorganised types. The Retarded-Disorganized group among women appears to be differentiated into a Disoriented and a Retarded-Motor Disturbed class among men. The Excited-Disorganised group appeared only among women.

'Comparison of the types with standard psychiatric diagnostic classes suggests that there may be four types of paranoids: Excited-Hostile, Hostile, Hallucinated and Grandiose. Three of the acute psychotic types can be characterised as 'disorganised'. The bases for this designation are high scores on Disorientation, Motor Disturbances, and Conceptual Disorganisation. Among women there are Excited-, Anxious-, and Retarded-Disorganised types. Corresponding male types are labelled Disoriented, Retarded-Motor Disturbed and Anxious-Disorganised. The Excited patient class probably corresponds to the conventional Manic type while the Intropunitives appear to encompass the depressed psychotics. Further research is needed to ascertain whether the Intropunitives can be further differentiated.' (*See* Figs. 1.13 and 1.14.)

Other uses of the IMPS in Lorr (1966) are to establish differences between acute and chronic psychotics and the investigation of temporal changes in the patients (Rice and Mattsson, 1966).

The Brief Psychiatric Rating Scale (BPRS)

This scale was devised by Overall and Gorham (1962) from 16 symptom constructs of the MSRPP

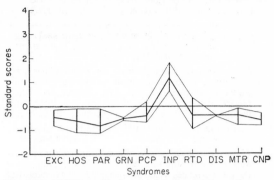

Fig. 1.13. IMPS profile for acute intropunitive male type

The means and range of ± 1 s.d. are shown. Roughly half of the group is diagnosed as Depressed, and the remainder as Schizo-affective, Acute undifferentiated or Paranoid. This is the most frequent of the types identified. (Lorr, 1966)

(Lorr *et al.*, 1953) and the IMPS (Lorr *et al.*, 1962). Each symptom is rated on a seven-point scale, preferably by two raters, either separately so that a measure of reliability is then available, or jointly to increase reliability. The interview is expected to last only eighteen minutes. It is non-structured, though the last five minutes is allowed for direct questions to clear up doubtful points. The actual rating takes two minutes, thus the test takes only twenty minutes in all.

The reliability of any one symptom has been shown to vary from 0·56 (anxiety) to 0·87 (guilt and hallucinatory behaviour). The last two items are illustrated in Table 1.8. Twenty experienced psychiatrists have supplied weights (0 to 4) for each of 13 diagnostic types, i.e. 'typal' patients, and the

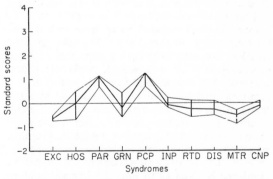

Fig. 1.14. IMPS profile for acute Hallucinated-Paranoid male type

The means and range of ± 1 s.d. are shown. In this and the Intropunitive type shown above the male and female profiles are almost identical. Clinically, this group is nearly always diagnosed as paranoid. (Lorr, 1966)

Table 1.8. Some Items from 'Brief Psychiatric Rating Scale' (BPRS) (Overall & Gorham, 1962)

DIRECTIONS: *Draw a circle around the term under each symptom which best describes the patient's present condition.*

5. *Guilt Feelings*—Over-concern or remorse for past behaviour. Rate on the basis of the patient's subjective experiences of guilt as evidenced by verbal report with appropriate affect; do not infer guilt feelings from depression, anxiety or neurotic defences.

Not present	Very mild	Mild	Moderate
Mod. Severe	Severe	Extremely severe	

12. *Hallucinatory Behaviour*—Perceptions without normal external stimulus correspondence. Rate only those experiences which are reported to have occurred within the last week and which are described as distinctly different from the thought and imagery processes of normal people.

Not present	Very mild	Mild	Moderate
Mod. Severe	Severe	Extremely severe	

average weights for each type provide a total pathology score which allows change within a type to be represented by a single score. Applications of the scale are mentioned elsewhere in this chapter.

Hamilton Depressive Rating Scale

Although several scales measure Depression as one of the several subscales, the most commonly used measure of Depression in patients is the Hamilton Rating Scale for Depression. This was first published in 1960 with an analysis and norms supplied by only 49 male depressive patients. The scale was intended to measure the syndrome of depression, and the seventeen items contributing to the total score were based on the traditional clinical description of Psychotic Depression. A factor analysis was carried out on this data at the time. A later publication by Hamilton (1967) included many more patients and now covered both sexes, with 152 males and 120 females. The data from both groups was analysed separately. The scale is scored, preferably simultaneously but independently by two raters, after a semistructured interview taking about 30 minutes. Some of the variables, e.g. depressed mood, guilt, retardation, agitation, are scored on a five-point scale (0–4) but other symptoms, e.g. general somatic symptoms, loss of libido, are scored on a three-point scale (0–2). In every case 0 was absence of symptoms. Guidance is given as to how the items should be rated and what should be rated.

In clinical psychiatry the scale has a use in measuring intensity of illness, and since its first publication it has been used in many drug trials to assess response to treatment. Here, only its factor analysis will be discussed, since it is the factor structure of the scale that has more relevance to this chapter. Hamilton, in his 1967 paper, describes how the correlation matrices of the 17 variables for the two groups were processed first by a principal component analysis from which 6 factors in each case emerged as probably significant, explaining between them 62 per cent and 61 per cent of the variance for the male and female patients respectively. These were then rotated orthogonally, using the Varimax method.

The first factor that emerged for each sex was labelled as the general factor of depressive illness since it correlates 0·93 with total score. The second factor (about 12 per cent of the variance for each) appeared to distinguish between agitation plus anxiety and retardation plus suicide. The third factor from the males corresponded with the fourth from the females, and was unlabelled. The fourth for the males, corresponding approximately to the third for the females, distinguishes patients with unstable and asocial personality from those with hypochondriacal complaints and loss of weight. It is worth noting that Hamilton named his factors not only from the factor saturations of the variables but also from the factor scores of individual patients. He supplies constants and weights so that factor scores can be found for any patient to whom the scale has been given. In his 1967 paper Hamilton found no factor contrasting endogeneous and neurotic depression, which has been found elsewhere.

Two Raters or One

It has become almost standard practice (Hamilton, 1960; Lorr, 1962; Overall and Gorham, 1962) to have an interviewer and observer independently rate each patient and then to combine their scores. Although this doubles the psychiatric time per patient, it has been believed that the increase in reliability makes the practice worth while. Overall *et al.* (1967) have investigated this assumption and have shown that for the BPRS at least, interobserver error is not a major source of unreliability. They calculate that when group differences are being examined, as in drug trials, using two raters only increased the sensitivity of the test enough to allow a 15 to 20 per cent reduction in sample size. It is therefore more economical to use only one rater and include more patients. The only situation where this is not best is where the number of available patients is limited and, therefore, maximum reliable information must be extracted from each patient, or where the treatment for ethical reasons should only be given to, or withheld from, as few patients as possible.

The NIMH Studies

To conclude and to illustrate how all the foregoing problems come together in a piece of research, there could be no better example than the NIMH research. Since about 1960, there has been a stream of publications from the Psychopharmacology branch of the US National Institute of Mental Health on the problems of producing meaningful classifications in psychiatry. By a team approach, using psychologists, psychiatrists, pharmacologists, statisticians, and by using patients in several hospitals, they have tackled every aspect of this from assessment through typologies, and assignment to therapeutic validation. It is an incomparable attack on a fairly broad front on the psychiatric battle field, and many papers quoted elsewhere in this chapter have a footnote 'supported in part by a grant from NIMH'. Six years of this research are reviewed by Overall and Hollister (1965).

The first stage of their work was the production of the Brief Psychiatric Rating Scale (BPRS) (Overall and Gorham, 1962) already described. The consensual validity of this rating instrument was assessed (Overall and Gorham, 1963; Overall, 1963; Overall and Hollister, 1964) by assessing its use within standard diagnostic nomenclature. Thirty-eight experts, psychologists, and psychiatrists rated theoretical 'typal' cases of 13 functional psychoses. The ratings thus provided 13 groups of 38 patients

whose mean scores provided a diagnostic profile and whose within group differences could be analysed. The first analysis was to compare different methods of assigning the individual patients to clusters using Bayesian and three other profile similarity methods. All gave very similar results. Unfortunately, in cross validation, when 314 'real' patients were used instead of 'ideal' patients, agreement was much poorer. In fact only 13 per cent of the patients were placed in mutually agreed categories. This is, however, better than chance, and it should be remembered that discrimination was being made within a fairly homogeneous group. Better results were obtained on two drug trials, using 98 and 40 patients respectively, which showed that the computer diagnoses were better than the clinicians at separating drug reactors from non-reactors. There would have been a 50 per cent improvement in response had the computer diagnoses been used rather than the clinicians in deciding treatment, i.e. if all the computer 'depressives' had been given anti-depressant drugs rather than the clinically assessed 'depressives'. The drug by computer diagnosis interaction was highly significant (Overall and Hollister, 1964).

The next approach was to devise types empirically from the BPRS data. Instead of analysing a broad spectrum of patients the researchers relied on clinical diagnoses to produce samples of 40 patients, 6 samples of schizophrenics and 4 of depressives.

Table 1.9.   Profiles of Modal Patients

Profiles of modal patients obtained by cluster analyses of BPRS scores of 240 schizophrenic and 160 clinically depressive patients (Overall and Hollister, 1965). If in drug research patients were labelled according to their similarity to modal types such as this, more specific information as to drug response might be forthcoming.

BPRS scales	Schizophrenic types					Depressive types		
	S1	S2	S3	S4	S5	D1	D2	D3
1. Somatic concern	0·8	1·6	1·7	1·4	1·8	2·5	3·6	1·4
2. Anxiety	0·8	3·9	3·0	2·6	3·9	4·3	3·4	1·9
3. Emotional withdrawal	3·0	2·2	2·7	3·0	1·3	0·4	1·9	4·2
4. Conceptual disorganisation	4·5	2·5	2·8	2·5	2·2	0·1	0·4	2·4
5. Guilt feeling	0·3	1·9	1·0	1·2	2·7	1·5	0·8	2·8
6. Tension	1·2	3·0	3·1	3·1	3·5	3·0	2·0	1·9
7. Mannerism posturing	1·8	1·3	1·4	1·6	1·0	0·2	1·1	0
8. Grandiosity	1·7	0·3	0·5	1·3	1·8	0	0	0
9. Depressive mood	0·4	2·4	2·0	1·3	2·0	4·5	3·7	4·1
10. Hostility	0·4	1·8	1·2	2·8	2·1	0·4	3·4	0·4
11. Suspicious	1·6	4·5	1·6	3·2	2·7	0·3	1·8	0·3
12. Hallucinatory behaviour	2·2	4·3	0·6	1·1	0·7	0	0·3	0·2
13. Motor retarded	1·0	1·2	1·6	0·9	0·6	1·8	1·3	3·5
14. Uncooperative	0·7	1·1	1·4	2·3	0·7	0·2	1·1	0·9
15. Unusual thought continued	3·6	3·9	2·2	1·7	3·7	0·1	0·6	0·4
16. Blunted affect	3·8	2·3	3·1	2·0	1·5	1·4	1·9	3·7

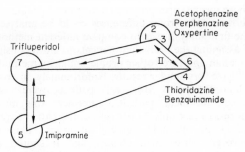

Fig. 1.15. Multiple discriminant analysis

The diagram shows that 3 orthogonal dimensions are sufficient to differentiate the pre-treatment BPRS profiles of 7 groups who responded well to one of seven drugs, and showed four different drug response types. (Overall and Hollister, 1965)

Each sample was factor analysed on the basis of between-person correlations to produce clusters. Each schizophrenic sample yielded 4 or 5 clusters from which, by further clustering, higher order model profiles were obtained defining 5 subtypes of schizophrenia. The four samples of depressives similarly yielded 3 depressive subtypes.

These original diagnostic groups were, in turn, cross validated by means of therapeutic response. It was shown that patients with the clinical diagnosis of depression showed no difference in therapeutic outcome between Imipramine and Thioridazine. However, when the general group of depressives was split into the three explicitly defined subgroups: D1, Anxious-tense depression, D2, Anxious-Hostile depression, and D3, withdrawn-retarded depression, the responses of the D2 group to the two drugs were the same, but the anxious group responded much

better to Thioridazine and the retarded group responded much better to Imipramine.

The third approach (Overall, 1963) was to use multiple discriminant analyses (Rao, 1952) to examine the between group variance compared to within group variance in multivariate space (Fig. 1.15). The patients used were those who had improved in response to one of seven drugs. Improvement meant a reduction of at least 15 points in BPRS total pathology score. 145 patients were thus obtained. The pretreatment BPRS profiles of the seven groups were different from each other at a level of high statistical significance, but only three dimensions were required to separate the groups, i.e. there are four different groups according to good response to: 1. Acetophenazine or Perphenazine or Oxypertine; 2. Thioridazine or Benzquinamide; 3. Imipramine; 4. Trifluperidol. Dimension I effectively separated 1 and 2 from 3 and 4, dimension II separated 1 from 2, and dimension III separated 3 from 4. This is a very interesting result but must be cross validated since the results were used to produce the predictors, i.e. separation was on a post-hoc basis.

A final debt must be acknowledged by this author to the NIMH who, together with the American Psychiatric Association, organised a conference in Washington in 1965, and whose proceedings, edited by Katz, Cole, and Barton under the title *The Role and Methodology of Classification in Psychiatry and Psychopathology* (1965), brought together the works of most of the experts in this field. Reference to this fund of wisdom and expertise prevented many errors and omissions, but for those that have persisted the author takes full responsibility and tenders his apologies to authors and readers alike.

REFERENCES

APA, (1969) Cross national study of diagnosis of the mental disorders Suppl. to *Amer. J. Psychiat.*, **125**, No. 10.

ARIETI, S. (Ed.) (1959) *American Handbook of Psychiatry*. New York: Basic Books.

ASH, P. (1949) The reliability of psychiatric diagnosis. *J. abn. soc. Psychol.*, **44**, 272–276.

BALDWIN, J. A. (1969) Statistical classification in psychiatry: a new international diagnostic code. *Int. J. Psychiat.*, **7**, 378–381.

BECK, A. T. (1962) Reliability of psychiatric diagnoses: 1. A critique of systematic studies. *Amer. J. Psychiat.*, **119**, 210–216.

BIRNBAUM, A. and MAXWELL, A. E. (1961) Classification procedures based on Bayes' formula. *Appl. Statistics*, **9**, 152–169.

BOCKOVEN, J. S. (1963) *Moral Treatment in American Psychiatry*. New York: Springer.

BORGATTA, E. F. (1962) The coincidence of sub-tests in four personality inventories. *J. soc. Psychol.*, **56**, 227–244.

CATTELL, R. B. (1949) rp and other coefficients of pattern similarity. *Psychometrika*, **14**, 279–298.

CATTELL, R. B. (1957) *Personality and Motivation Structure and Measurement*. London: Harrap.

CLIFF, N. (1959) Adverbs as multipliers. *Psychol. Rev.*, **66**, 27–44.

CLYDE, D. J. (1965) Pattern of reaction to drug treatments derived through multivariate procedures. In *The Role and Methodology of Classification in Psychiatry and Psychopathology* (Ed. Katz, M. M., Cole, J. O., Barton, W. E.). Chevy Chase, Md.: US Dept. of Hlth, Educ. and Welfare.

COLLINS, L. F., MAXWELL, A. E., and CAMERON, K. (1962) A factor analysis of some child psychiatric clinic data. *J. ment. Sci.*, **108**, 274–285.

COLLINS, L. F., MAXWELL, A. E., and CAMERON, K. (1963) An analysis of the case material of the younger maladjusted child. *Brit. J. Psychiat.*, **109**, 758–765.

COOPER, J. E., KENDELL, R. E., GURLAND, B. J., SARTORIUS, N., and FARKAS, T. (1969) Cross national study of diagnosis of the mental disorders: some results from the first comparative investigation. *Amer. J. Psychiat.*, **125**, April Supp., 21–29.

CRONBACH, L. J. and GLESER, G. C. (1953) Assessing similarity between profiles. *Psychol. Bull.*, **50**, 456–473.

DEGAN, J. W. (1952) *Dimensions of functional psychosis.* Psychometry Monogr. 6.

EISENBERG, L. (1966) Classification of the psychotic disorders in childhood. In *The Classification of Behaviour Disorders* (Ed. Eron, L. D.). Chicago: Aldine.

ENGLISH, H. B. and ENGLISH, A. C. (1958) *A Comprehensive Dictionary of Psychological and Psychoanalytic terms.* New York: Longmans Green.

EYSENCK, H. J. (1947) *Dimensions of Personality.* London: Routledge and Kegan Paul.

EYSENCK, H. J. (1950) Criterion analysis: an application of the hypothetico-deductive method to factor analysis. *Psychol. Rev.*, **57**, 38–53.

EYSENCK, H. J. (1952) *Scientific Study of Personality.* London: Routledge and Kegan Paul.

EYSENCK, H. J. (1955) Psychiatric diagnosis as a psychological and statistical problem. *Psychol. Rep.*, **1**, 3–17.

EYSENCK, H. J. (1959) *The Maudsley Personality Inventory.* London: Univ. of London Press.

EYSENCK, H. J. (1960a) Classification and the problem of diagnosis. In *The Handbook of Abnormal Psychology* (Ed. Eysenck, H. J.). London: Pitman Medical.

EYSENCK, H. J. (1960b) *Experiments in Personality.* London: Routledge and Kegan Paul.

EYSENCK, H. J. (1967) *The Biological Basis of Personality.* Springfield, Ill.: C. C. Thomas.

EYSENCK, H. J. (1970) A dimensional system of psycho-diagnostics. In *New Approaches to Psychodiagnostic Systems* (Ed. Mahrer). New York: Aldine.

EYSENCK, H. J. and EYSENCK, S. B. G. (1964) *The Eysenck Personality Inventory.* London: Univ. of London Press.

EYSENCK, H. J. and EYSENCK, S. B. G. (1969a) *Personality Structure and Measurement.* London: Routledge and Kegan Paul.

EYSENCK, H. J. and EYSENCK, S. B. G. (1968a) A factorial study of psychoticism as a dimension of personality. *Multivariate behav. Res.*, all-clinical special issue, **2**, 15–31.

EYSENCK, S. B. G. (1965) *The Junior Eysenck Personality Inventory.* London: Univ. of London Press.

EYSENCK, S. B. G. and EYSENCK, H. J. (1968b) The measurement of psychoticism: a study of factor stability and reliability. *Brit. J. soc. clin. Psychol.*, **7**, 286–294.

EYSENCK, S. B. G. and EYSENCK, H. J. (1969b) Psychoticism in children: a new personality variable. *Res. in Ed.*, **1**, 21–37.

FITZGERALD, L. T., OVERALL, J. E., and WILLIAMS, C. M. (1966) A computer program for the diagnosis of thyroid disease. *Amer. J. Roentgen.*, **97**, 901–905.

FOULDS, G. A. (1962) A quantification of diagnostic differentiae. *J. ment. Sci.*, **108**, 389–405.

FOULDS, G. A. (1965) *Personality and Personal Illness.* London: Tavistock Publications.

FOULDS, G. A. (1967) Some differences between neurotics and character disorders. *Brit. J. soc. clin. Psychol.*, **6**,

GLESER, G. C. (1965) Quantifying similarity between people. In *The Role and Methodology of Classification in Psychiatry and Psychopathology* (Ed. Katz, M. M., Cole, J. O., Barton, W.E.). Chevy Chase, Md.: US Dept. of Hlth, Educ. and Welfare.

GOFFMAN, E. (1961) On the characteristics of total institutions. In *Asylums.* (Ed. Goffman, E.) London: Pelican Books.

GREENHOUSE, S. W. (1965) On the meaning of discrimination, classification, mixture and clustering in statistics. In *The Role and Methodology of Classification in Psychiatry and Psychopathology.* (Ed. Katz, M. M., Cole, J. O., Barton, W. E.). Chevy Chase, Md.: US Dept. of Hlth, Educ. and Welfare.

GROSZ, H. J. (1968) The relation between neurosis and psychosis: observations on the reliability of the data defining the Trouton-Maxwell factors of neuroticism and psychoticism. *Brit. J. Psychiat.*, **114**, 189–192.

GUERTIN, W. H. (1952a) A factor-analytic study of schizophrenic symptoms. *J. consult. Psychol.*, **16**, 308–312.

GUERTIN, W. H. (1952b) An inverted factor-analytic of schizophrenics. *J. consult. Psychol.*, **16**, 371–375.

GUTTMAN, L. (1952) Multiple group methods for common factor analysis: their bases, computation and interpretation. *Psychometrika*, **17**, 209–222.

HAMILTON, M. (1960) A rating scale for depression. *J. Neurol. Neurosurg. Psychiat.*, **23**, 56–62.

HAMILTON, M. (1967) Development of a rating scale for primary depressive illness. *Brit. J. soc. clin. Psychol.*, **6**, 278–296.

HEERMAN, E. F. (1965) Comments on Overall's multivariate methods for profile analysis. *Psychol. Bull.*, **63**, 128.

HOLZINGER, K. J. and HARMAN, H. H. (1941) *Factor Analysis.* Chicago: Univ. of Chicago Press.

HOPE, K. (1969) The complete analysis of a data matrix. *Brit. J. Psychiat.*, **115**, 1069–1079.

HUNT, W. A., WITTSON, C. L., and HUNT, E. B. A. (1953) Theoretical and practical analysis of the diagnostic process. In *Current Problems in Psychiatric Diagnosis* (Ed. Hoch and Zubin). New York: Grune and Stratton.

JACKSON, B. (1969) Reflections on DSM II. *Int. J. Psychiat.*, **7**, 385–392.

KATZ, M. M. (1965) A phenomenological typology of schizophrenia. In *The Role and Methodology of Classification in Psychiatry and Psychopathology* (Ed. Katz, M. M., Cole, J. O., Barton, W.E.). Chevy Chase, Md.: US Dept. of Hlth, Educ. and Welfare.

KATZ, M. M., COLE, J. O., and BARTON, W. E. (Ed.) (1965) *The Role and methodology of Classification in Psychiatry and Psychopathology.* Chevy Chase, Md.: US Dept. of Hlth, Educ. and Welfare.

KLEINMUNTZ, B. (1963a) A portrait of the computer as a young clinician. *Behav. Sci.*, **8**, 154–156.

KLEINMUNTZ, B. (1963b) MMPI decision rules for the identification of college maladjustment: a digital computer approach. *Psychol. Monogr.*, **77**, No. 14 (577).

KLEINMUNTZ, B. (1963c) Personality test interpretation by digital computer. *Science*, **139**, 416–418.

KLETT, C. J. and MOSELEY, E. C. (1965) The right drug for the right patient. *J. Consult. Psychol.*, **29**, 546–551.

KREITMAN, N. (1961) The reliability of psychiatric diagnosis. *J. ment. Sci.*, **107**, 876–886.

KREITMAN, N., SAINSBURY, P., MORRISSEY, J. TOWERS, J., and SCRIVENER, J. (1961) The reliability of psychiatric assessment: an analysis. *J. ment. Sci.*, **107**, 887–908.

LAING, R. D. (1967) *The Politics of Experience*. London: Pelican Books.

LASKY, J. J., KLETT, C. J., CAFFEY, E. M., BENNETT, J. L., ROSENBLUM, M. P., and HOLLISTER, L. E. (1962) Drug treatment of schizophrenic patients. *Dis. nerv. System*, **23**, 698–706.

LORR, M., JENKINS, R. L., and HOLSOPPLE, J. Q. (1953) Multidimensional scale for rating psychotic patients. *V. A. Tech. Bull.*, No. 10, 507.

LORR, M. (Ed.) (1966) *Explorations in Typing Psychotics*. London: Pergamon.

LORR, M. and O'CONNOR, J. P. (1957) The relation between neurosis and psychosis: a reanalysis. *J. ment. Sci.*, **103**, 375–380.

LORR, M., KLETT, C. J., McNAIR, D. M., and LASKY, J. J. (1962) *Inpatient Multidimensional Psychiatric Scale: Manual*. Palo Alto: Consulting Psychologists Press.

LORR, M., KLETT, C. J., and McNAIR, D. M. (1963) *Syndromes of Psychosis*. New York: Macmillan.

LORR, M., KLETT, C. J., and McNAIR, D. M. (1966) Acute psychotic types. In *Explorations in Typing Psychotics* (Ed. Lorr, M.). London: Pergamon.

LUBIN, A. (1950) Some contributions to the testing of psychological hypotheses by means of statistical multivariate analysis. Unpubl. Ph.D. thesis, Univ. of London.

LUBIN, A. (1965) On typologies which maximize therapeutic validity. In *The Role and Methodology of Classification in Psychiatry and Psychopathology* (Ed. Kalz, M. M., Cole, J. O., Barton, W. E.). Chevy Chase, Md.: US Dept. of Hlth, Educ. and Welfare.

LUSTED, L. B. (1968) *Introduction to Medical Decision Making*. Springfield, Ill.: C. C. Thomas.

LYERLY, S. B. (1965) A survey of some empirical clustering procedures. In *The Role and Methodology of Classification in Psychiatry and Psychopathology* (Ed. Katz, M. M., Cole, J. O., Barton, W. E.). Chevy Chase, Md.: US Dept. of Hlth, Educ. and Welfare.

McGUIRE, R. J., MOWBRAY, R. M., and VALLANCE, R. C. (1963) The M.P.I. used with psychiatric in-patients. *Brit. J. Psychol.*, **54**, 157–166.

McGUIRE, R. J. and WRIGHT, V. (1971) A statistical approach to indices of disease activity in rheumatoid arthritis. *Ann. rheum. Dis.*, **30**, 574–580.

McQUITTY, L. L. (1954) Pattern analysis illustrated in classifying patients and normals. *Educ. psychol. Measmt.*, **14**, 598–604.

McQUITTY, L. L. (1960a) Comprehensive Hierarchical Analysis. *Educ. psychol. Measmt.*, **20**, 805–816.

McQUITTY, L. L. (1960b) Hierarchical linkage analysis for the isolation of types. *Educ. psychol. Measmt.*, **20**, 55–67.

McQUITTY, L. L. (1960c) Hierarchical syndrome analysis. *Educ. psychol. Measmt.*, **20**, 293–304.

McQUITTY, L. L. (1963) Rank order typal analysis. *Educ. psychol. Measmt.*, **23**, 55–61.

MAYER-GROSS, W., SLATER, E., and ROTH, M. (1960) *Clinical Psychiatry*. London: Cassell.

MEEHL, P. E. (1954) *Clinical versus Statistical Prediction*. Minneapolis: Univ. Press.

MEEHL, P. E. (1965) Seer over sign: the first good example. *J. exp. Res. in Pers.*, **1**, 27–32.

MOORE, T. V. (1929) The empirical determination of certain syndromes underlying praecox and manic depressive psychoses. *Amer. J. Psychiat.*, **9**, 719–738.

NATHAN, P. E. (1967) *Cues, Decisions and Diagnosis*. New York: Academic Press.

NATIONAL INSTITUTE OF MENTAL HEALTH (1964) Psychopharmacology service centre collaborative study group: phenothiazine treatment in acute schizophrenia. *Arch. gen. Psychiat.*, **10**, 246–261.

NORRIS, V. (1959) *Mental Illness in London*. Maudsley Monogr. No. 6. London: Chapman and Hall.

NOYES, A. P. (1953) *Modern Clinical Psychiatry*. Philadelphia: Saunders.

NUNNALLY, J. (1962) The analysis of profile data. *Psychol. Bull.*, **59**, 311–319.

OSGOOD, C. E. and SUCI, G. (1962) A measure of relation determined by both mean difference and profile information. *Psychol. Bull.*, **49**, 251–262.

OVERALL, J. E. (1963) A configural analysis of psychiatric diagnosis. *Behav. Sci.*, **8**, 211–219.

OVERALL, J. E. (1964) Notes on multivariate methods for profile analysis. *Psychol. Bull.*, **61**, 195–198.

OVERALL, J. E. and GORHAM, D. R. (1962) The Brief Psychiatric Rating Scale. *Psychol. Rpts.*, **10**, 799–812.

OVERALL, J. E. and GORHAM, D. R. (1963) A pattern probability model for the classification of psychiatric patients. *Behav. Sci.*, **8**, 108–116.

OVERALL, J. E. and HOLLISTER, L. E. (1964) Computer procedure for psychiatric classification. *J. Amer. med. Ass.*, **187**, 583–588.

OVERALL, J. E. and HOLLISTER, L. E. (1965) Studies of quantitative approaches to psychiatric classification. In *The Role and Methodology of Classification in Psychiatry and Psychopathology* (Ed. Katz, M. M., Cole, J. O., Barton, W. E.). Chevy Chase, Md.: US Dept. of Hlth, Educ. and Welfare.

OVERALL, J. E., HOLLISTER, L. E., and DALAL, S. N. (1967) Psychiatric drug research: sample size requirements for one v. two raters. *Arch. gen. Psychiat.* **16**, 152–161.

PILOWSKY, I., LEVINE, S., and BOULTON, D. M. (1969) The classification of depression by numerical taxonomy. *Brit. J. Psychiat.*, **115**, 937–945.

RAO, C. R. (1952) *Advanced Statistical Methods in Biometric Research*. New York: John Wiley & Sons.

RAO, C. R. (1965) Discrimination among groups and assigning new individuals. In *The Role and Methodology of Classification in Psychiatry and Psychopathology* (Ed. Katz, M. M., Cole, J. O., Barton, W. E.). Chevy Chase, Md.: US Dept. of Hlth, Educ. and Welfare.

RAO, C. R. (1962) Use of discriminant and allied functions in multivariate analysis, *Sankhya*, **22**, 317–338.

RAO, C. R. and SLATER, P. (1949) Multivariate analysis applied to differences between neurotic groups. *Brit. J. stat. Psychol.*, **2**, 17–29.

RICE, C. E. and MATTSSON, N. B. (1966) Types based on repeated measurement. In *Explorations in Typing Psychotics* (Ed. Lorr, M.). London: Pergamon.

ROME, H. P., MATAYA, P., PEARSON, J. S., SWENSON, W. M., and BRANNICK, T. L. (1965) Automatic personality assessment. In *Computers in Biomedical Research* (Ed. Stacy and Waxman). New York: Academic Press.

RUTTER, M., LEBOVICI, S., EISENBERG, L., SNEZNEVSKIJ, A. V., SADOUN, R., BROOKE, E., and LIN, T-Y. (1969) A triaxial classification of mental disorders in childhood. *J. child. Psychol. Psychiat.*, **10**, 41–61.

RYDER, R. G. (1964) Profile factor analysis and variable factor analysis. *Psychol. Rpts.*, **15**, 119–127.

SAINSBURY, P. (1960) Psychosomatic disorders and neurosis in outpatients attending a general hospital. *J. Psychosom. Res.*, **4**, 261–273.

SANDIFER, M. G., PETTUS, C., and QUADE, D. (1964) A study of psychiatric diagnosis. *J. nerv. ment. Dis.*, **139**, 350–356.

SARBIN, T. R. (1941) The relative accuracy of clinical and statistical predictions of academic achievement. *Psychol. Bull.*, **38**, 714.

SARBIN, T. R. (1943) A contribution to the study of actuarial and individual methods of prediction. *Amer. J. Sociol.*, **48**, 593–602.

SAWREY, W. L., KELLER, L., and CONGER, J. J. (1960) An objective method of grouping profiles by distance function and its relation to factor analysis. *Educ. Psychol. Measmt.*, **20**, 651–673.

SCHMIDT, H. O. and FONDA, C. P. (1956) The reliability of psychiatric diagnosis: a new look. *J. abn. soc. Psychol.*, **52**, 262–267.

SHEPHERD, M., BROOKE, E. M., COOPER, J. E., and LIN, T-Y. (1968) An experimental approach to psychiatric diagnosis. *Acta Psychiat. Scand.*, Suppl. 201.

SIEGLER, M. and OSMOND, H. (1966) Models of madness. *Brit. J. Psychiat.*, **112**, 1193–1203.

SIEGLER, M., OSMOND, H., and MANN, H. (1969) Laing's models of madness. *Brit. J. Psychiat.*, **115**, 947–958.

SINES, J. O. (1964) Actuarial method as the appropriate strategy for the validation of diagnostic tests. *Psychol. Rev.*, **71**, 517–523.

SINES, J. O. (1966) Actuarial methods in personality assessment. In *Progress in Experimental Personality Research* (Ed. Maher). New York: Academic Press.

SLATER, P. (1960) Canonical analysis of discriminance. In *Experiments in Personality* (Ed. Eysenck). London: Routledge and Kegan Paul.

SMITH, W. G. (1966) A model for psychiatric diagnosis. *Arch. gen. Psychiat.*, **14**, 521–529.

SNEDECOR, G. W. (1956) *Statistical Methods.* Iowa: State College Press.

SOKAL, R. R. (1966) Numerical Taxonomy. *Scientific American*, **215**, 106–116.

SOKAL, R. R. and SNEATH, P. H. A. (1963) *Principles of Numerical Taxonomy.* San Francisco: Freeman.

SPITZER, R. L., FLEISS, J. L., BURDOCK, E. I., and HARDESTY, A. S. (1964) The mental status schedule: rationale, reliability and validity. *Comprehens. Psychiat.*, **5**, 384–395.

SPITZER, R. L. and WILSON, P. T. (1968) A guide to the American Psychiatric Association's new diagnostic nomenclature. *Amer. J. Psychiat.*, **124**, 1619–1629.

SPITZER, R. L. and ENDICOTT, J. (1968) DIAGNO: a computer program for psychiatric diagnosis utilising the differential diagnostic procedure. *Arch. gen. Psychiat.*, **18**, 746–756.

STEPHENSON, W. (1952) Some observations on Q technique. *Psychol. Bull.*, **49**, 483–498.

SZASZ, T. S. (1963) *Law, Liberty and Psychiatry.* New York: Macmillan.

THORNDIKE, R. L. (1953) Who belongs to the family? *Psychometrika*, **18**, 267–276.

THURSTONE, L. L. (1947) *Multiple Factor Analysis.* Chicago: Univ. of Chicago.

TORGERSON, W. S. (1965) Multidimensional representation of similarity structures. In *The Role and Methodology of Classification in Psychiatry and Psychopathology* (Ed. Katz, M. M., Cole, J. O., Barton, W. E.). Chevy Chase, Md.: US Dept. of Hlth, Educ. and Welfare.

TROUTON, D. S. and MAXWELL, A. E. (1956) The relation between neurosis and psychosis. *J. ment. Sci.*, **102**, 1–21.

WARD, C. H., BECK, A. T., MENDELSON, M., MOCK, J. E., and ERBAUGH, J. K. (1962) The psychiatric nomenclature: reasons for diagnostic disagreement. *Arch. gen. Psychiat.*, **7**, 198–205.

WILSON, E. B. and DEMING, J. (1927) Statistical comparison of psychiatric diagnosis of some Massachussets state hospitals during 1925. *Q. Bull. Mass. Dept. ment. Dis.*, **11**, 1–15.

WRIGHT, W. S., MANWELL, M. K. C., and MERRETT, J. B. (1969) Anorexia nervosa: a discriminant function analysis. *Brit. J. Psychiat.*, **115**, 827–831.

ZUBIN, J. (1967) Classification of the behaviour disorders. In *Ann. Rev. Psychol.*, **18**.

2

Epidemiology and Abnormal Psychology

BRIAN COOPER and MICHAEL SHEPHERD

INTRODUCTION AND BACKGROUND

Definition of Terms

The field of enquiry reviewed in this chapter is concerned with the incidence and distribution of various abnormal psychological states in defined populations. While there exists, as yet, no general descriptive label for this branch of study, in a medical context it is placed by modern usage under the rubric of *epidemiology* (Shepherd and Cooper, 1964). Any study of this nature, whether or not it is undertaken in a medical setting, may fairly be described as 'epidemiological', provided it deals with forms of 'psychological abnormality' that are regarded as maladaptive and of clinical significance; it is in this restricted sense that both terms will be employed here. Population studies of non-clinical psychological variables are outside the compass of the present chapter, although there are good grounds for supposing that they make use of essentially similar techniques.

General Background

Research techniques for the investigation of psychologically determined variables in human populations are already common coinage throughout the behavioural sciences. To the social psychologist they are familiar in connection with the measurement of popular attitudes, most notably in market research surveys and studies of electoral behaviour (Edwards, 1956; Eysenck, 1954). In educational psychology, fundamentally the same approach has been utilised to chart the variation of intelligence among school-children, both by geographical area and over

intervals of time (Burt, 1950; Scottish Council for Research in Education, 1949). Indeed, the whole theory of standardisation of psychometric tests is based on the principle of representative population sampling, although here the practical difficulties have proved so great that even such widely employed instruments as the Stanford Binet and Wechsler Adult Intelligence Scales have fallen well short of the requirements of modern survey methodology (Terman and Merrill, 1937; Wechsler, 1958).

In essence, a morbidity survey is simply a type of social survey which focuses on illness as the dependent variable. Hence, as one social scientist has remarked—

'It is not uncommon for sociologists, ecologists, and social psychologists to discover, on being introduced to the field of epidemiology, that this is what they have been doing all their professional lives.' (Mechanic, 1970).

Basically similar problems of measurement are encountered in clinical psychology. In the words of Shapiro (1966)—

'Once a measure has been validated then it has to be calibrated. The only form available to psychologists is the method of so-called standardisation. This consists of giving the test to a representative sample of the population one is interested in, and then comparing the scores obtained by the subject with the distribution of scores of the standardisation sample.'

Against this background, the indifference of most modern clinical psychologists to field studies of mental disorders is all the more striking. Fortunately, this neglect has not been universal: one leading authority in the United States has repeatedly emphasised the importance of field surveys as a branch of biometrics (Zubin, 1961; Zubin and Burdock, 1965) while in this country the MRC Social Psychiatry Unit under the directorship of Sir Aubrey Lewis successfully integrated clinical psychologists into a research programme with epidemiological, clinical, and experimental facets (Shepherd and Davies, 1968). In general, none the less, points of contact between these different disciplines have been disappointingly few, while the concepts and preoccupations of each set of workers remain largely alien to the others.

There is a number of reasons why this should be so. To begin with, the professional structure and practice of clinical psychology in most countries has not tended to foster much concern with public health problems. Secondly, since for obvious reasons an experimental approach is either very difficult or downright impossible to apply to whole communities, or even to representative population samples, research in this field has been largely confined to observational studies. In consequence, the findings as a rule have corresponded to the formula, rightly deprecated by the editor of this volume, 'x members of class y showed behaviour z', rather than to the more stringent experimental paradigm. Thirdly, and perhaps most important, the great majority of relevant studies have employed medical conventions and terms of reference that do not always command the allegiance of clinical psychologists. While the lack of a common vocabulary hampers interdisciplinary communication in all branches of psychiatric research, this is especially true in the field of population studies because here the established models are derived not only from clinical medicine but also, and more immediately, from the public health field. For the non-medical worker to acquire an understanding of this subject, he must know something of its derivation from the mainstream of medical epidemiology.

Epidemiology as a Medical Discipline

Epidemiology was for long regarded as the science of epidemics, or major outbreaks of infectious disease, but there is no etymological justification for this restricted meaning. In modern usage, the term has acquired a much wider connotation, as is evident from definitions such as 'the study of health and disease of populations and groups' (Morris, 1957) and 'the study of factors that influence the occurrence and distribution of disease, defect, disability, and death in aggregations of individuals' (Leavell and Clark. 1953). The latter definition makes clearly explicit the relevance of epidemiology to preventive medicine and, indeed, epidemiological research may be considered the logical first step in any programme of public health action.

In this sense, epidemiology is today universally recognised as a major branch of medicine, while the epidemiological approach to disease problems is widely accepted as complementary to the clinical. Whereas the clinician is primarily concerned with the individual patient, the epidemiologist takes as his basic unit of observation the group or community, which at any given time comprises both sick and healthy persons. Hence, a *statistical* approach is essential to the epidemiologist's work. As a corollary, while clinicians are chiefly engaged in the treatment and management of established cases of illness, epidemiologists are concerned rather with problems of prevention and control of the spread of disease. In consequence, epidemiology as a science is largely bound up with the study of environmental influences on health and disease, a subject commonly referred to as *medical ecology* (Hare, 1952).

With the decline in Western society of mortality due to acute infectious diseases, the focus of epidemiological research has shifted to the ever-increasing public health problems of chronic, non-infectious diseases which, in the words of Ryle (1948): '. . . also have their epidemiologies and their correlations with social and occupational conditions, and must eventually be considered to be in greater or less degree preventable.' The extent of this shift over the past few decades may be gauged from the papers presented at an international study group which met in 1957 (Pemberton and Willard, 1958). Among the topics dealt with were the statistics of coronary artery disease and of motor vehicle accidents, the relationship of malignant disease in childhood to foetal irradiation, the effect of chronic bronchitis on industrial sickness-absence and the factors influencing the use of medical services on a new housing estate. Only one quarter of the contributions dealt with aspects of acute infectious disease. In so far as the range of subject matter reflected the interests of contemporary epidemiology and social medicine, it is noteworthy that two papers were devoted to the topic, 'Epidemiology applied to mental illness'.

Epidemiology and Psychiatry

The need to pay regard to the mass phenomena of mental illness has been a frequently recurring theme in the psychiatric literature for generations. Physicians such as Sydenham (1682) and Cheyne (1733) stressed the high prevalence of neurotic disorders in the general population, while at the beginning of the nineteenth century Pinel (1806) observed that: '. . . too generally has the philosophy of this disease, by which I mean the history of its symptoms, of its progress, of its varieties and of its treatment in and out of hospitals been most strangely neglected.'

The importance of the statistical approach to problems of aetiology was clearly perceived by Pinel and Esquirol, two of the founding fathers of modern psychiatry, and has never since been wholly lost from sight. Griesinger, whose textbook first propounded the modern approach, put the matter clearly—

'An influence of causation can naturally be attributed with most certainty to those circumstances whose mode of action can be clearly traced, and whose effects therefore may be considered as physiological necessities; or, where this is not the case, to those whose influence is established by reliable statistics.'

Again,

'The conclusion *post hoc ergo propter hoc* depends, therefore, on a single empirical (statistical) knowledge of the fact that these particular circumstances . . . very frequently coincide with, or precede, the commencement of the insanity.' (Griesinger, 1867)

During the latter half of the nineteenth century, the attention of psychiatrists with an actuarial bent was chiefly focused on institutional statistics. Nevertheless, the need for community surveys was not entirely forgotten. Kraepelin, besides himself carrying out a survey in Java (Kraepelin, 1909a) encouraged some of his collaborators to investigate the families of mental hospital patients and of samples of healthy individuals. Later members of the Munich school such as Rüdin, Luxenburger, and Brugger conducted genetically-orientated community studies in which population sampling and other modern techniques were utilised (Strömgren, 1950). For a number of reasons, such studies formed only a scattered handful until after the Second World War a rapid expansion of the subject began (Milbank Mem. Fund, 1950).

The assumptions underlying this new approach were clearly summarised in the report of a World Health Organisation Expert Committee. It had, they wrote, become increasingly apparent that

'the problems of studying personal susceptibility and the modifying effects of the environment or habit on the risks of attack were essentially similar in the communicable diseases and in other kinds of human illness. Consequently, the methods which had been used so successfully in uncovering

the origin and mode of spread of diseases associated with microbial infection came to be increasingly applied to the study of mental disorders and the use of the term 'epidemiology' to imply the study of their distribution and behaviour in differing conditions of life in human communities became widely accepted,' (W.H.O., 1960).

The application of epidemiological concepts to the field of psychiatry can thus be viewed as part of a more general change in medical attitudes towards the problems of chronic, non-infectious disease. For the behavioural scientist, as for the psychiatrist, the principal advantage resides in a unification of research strategies, a drawing together of such previously disparate threads as the analysis of institutional statistics (Malzberg, 1940; Norris, 1959), the use of psychometric tests in the screening of child populations (Lewis, 1929; Rutter *et al.*, 1970), the demographic and sociological studies of suicide from Durkheim onwards (Durkheim, 1897; Gibbs and Martin, 1964), the area population surveys of the German and Scandinavian geneticists (Strömgren, 1950; Astrup, 1957) the ecological research of the Chicago school (Faris and Dunham, 1939; Clark, 1949) and the many descriptive accounts of collective psychopathology (Brown, 1954; Gruenberg, 1957).

The Disease Model in Epidemiology

The use of epidemiological methods in psychiatry has been subjected to criticism, chiefly on the grounds that the terminology and techniques of classical infectious epidemiology are not appropriate to this field of enquiry. It is true that the pursuit of facile analogies between mental disorder and physical illness has handicapped psychiatric research for over a century. There are, however, no grounds for supposing epidemiologists to be more at fault in this respect than their fellow research workers in biochemistry, neurophysiology, or other related branches. On the contrary, advocates of the epidemiological approach have shown themselves well aware of the pitfalls (W.H.O., 1960; Shepherd and Cooper, 1964) and there is now an encouraging output of research that combines a sophisticated theoretical standpoint with a careful attention to survey methodology.

The crux of the difficulty lies in the disease concept of mental disorder (Kraupl Taylor, 1966). In general medicine, the disease model is more or less firmly based on an established structural pathology. In psychiatry, where for the most part such an established pathology is lacking, the presence of underlying disease may represent at best a convenient working hypothesis. The extent to which, in practice, this hypothesis serves to explain the observable phenomena differs widely among the various syndromes.

Two related aspects of the traditional disease model, as applied in psychiatry, are alien to the thinking of clinical psychologists: the concept of disease as *process* and the view of *deviation* as essentially a pathological rather than a statistical phenomenon. Of these the former, though less widely recognised, is probably the more potent cause of interdisciplinary misunderstanding.

The notion of disease as the expression of a process—or, to be precise, of a number of distinct processes of differing course and outcome—derived originally from the painstaking observation and recording of clinical phenomena. This, the 'natural history' approach to disease (Ryle, 1936), long antedated modern pathological science but remains basic to much contemporary thinking in epidemiology and preventive medicine, as is indicated by the following passage from an authoritative text—

'Any disease or morbid condition in man is the result of a process following a more or less characteristic series of events in the environment and in man from its earliest beginning until the affected individual returns to normal, reaches a state of equilibrium with the disease, defect or disability, or dies. Disease is not a static condition but a process following a more or less natural history.' (Leavell and Clark, 1953).

While this concept has found useful application in psychiatry, from the time of Kraepelin onwards, it has received very little attention from behavioural scientists. If psychiatrists have proved too ready uncritically to adopt notions derived from the general medical frame of reference, many psychologists appear to have gone to the opposite extreme. In rejecting what they take to be the medical model of the disease entity, they have also thrown out the related concept of the morbid process. Paradoxically, in seeking to construct a more flexible and dynamic model of their own, they have largely ignored the question of change over time. Only occasionally does one glimpse an uneasy awareness that the baby may have been lost with the bathwater. Thus, Bannister, in discussing the problems of research into schizophrenia, has commented that

'the tendency is for research workers in the field to be preoccupied with the question of defining the 'condition' rather than hypothesising a process .... This is clearly a further inheritance from the general medical framework carried over into psychiatry, but it illustrates the deficiencies of the transported form of the framework as opposed to its potential in its original habitat.' (Bannister, 1968).

Not unnaturally, an excessive preoccupation with the present condition has been associated with a lack of interest in prognostic factors. In this respect, the clinical psychiatrist has been less at fault than his non-medical colleagues: his professional role dictates the need for prediction in the individual patient, while his basic training has served to impress upon him the importance of the Richtungsprognose, the broad pattern of course and outcome which holds good for any given morbid condition. The clinical psychologist as a rule is less subject to these influences, being concerned mainly with the state of individual patients at a given point in time or over relatively brief periods. In the field of research, however, a too static view of abnormal mental states has long prevailed among workers drawn from both disciplines; to this extent one must accept the rough justice of Zubin's criticism—

'Much of the difficulty in abnormal psychology and psychiatry stems from the fact that these fields are focused on diagnosis and description of the present and past and pay insufficient attention to the future.' (Zubin *et al.*, 1961).

The second source of interdisciplinary confusion is the discrepancy between the pathological and statistical concepts of deviation. In this issue, the gap between modern medical and psychological teaching is actually much narrower than has been generally recognised. Cohen (1955), in reviewing the evolution of medical concepts of disease, has epitomised the modern position thus—

'... (a) disease indicates deviations from the norm—these are its symptoms and signs;
(b) symptoms and signs are commonly found to recur in constant patterns; these are the 'syndromes' or 'symptom-complexes';
(c) these syndromes always indicate one or more of three aspects of disease:
1. its site;
2. associated functional disturbances;
3. causative factors in terms of (i) morbid anatomy, physiology, and psychology, and (ii) aetiology.'

There is little in this statement with which clinical psychologists need seek to quarrel. Indeed, as Sir Cyril Burt has pointed out, in the field of abnormal psychology common experience leads the different professional groups to essentially the same conclusions—

'It was perhaps the First World War that most effectively brought home to the medical world the artificiality of the distinction between the normal mind on the one hand and its abnormal conditions on the other. The application of intelligence tests to nearly two million Americans led to the startling conclusion that nearly 40 per cent of the population had a mental age below the level then currently accepted as marking off the mentally defective . . . .

'The medical investigator was quicker to recognise this than the psychologist; for if the medical man based his notions of the abnormal on his experience of advanced disease, the psychologist had derived his picture of the normal from samples high above the average. Indeed, he tended to identify the normal with the perfect.' (Burt, 1955).

If, therefore, the epidemiological psychiatrist continues to make what sometimes seems to the observer a naive distinction between 'cases' and 'normals', he does so not out of any belief in mental disorder as a discrete entity, but because of an eminently practical need to establish priorities in terms of investigation, treatment, and social programmes.

The foregoing considerations suggest that, both for psychiatrists and for clinical psychologists, the chief obstacles to a common understanding and purpose in this field of research arise from traditional stereotypes and habits of thought, rather than from any major differences of substance. The aim of the present chapter is to provide an introduction to the subject which will help to overcome these obstacles.

Since in ordinary usage the term epidemiology embraces both a method of investigation and the body of knowledge amassed by its application, it would be artificial in a general review to consider the one in isolation from the other. At the present stage of development of the subject, serious research is still largely concerned with problems of definition and method; a broad understanding of these problems is thus an essential prerequisite for assessment of either the achievements or the potential value of the epidemiological approach.

PROBLEMS OF RESEARCH METHOD

The principal tasks of survey design that confront the epidemiologist are fourfold: he must define the population to be surveyed; he must define and classify the condition under investigation; he must locate and identify all cases existing in this population; finally, he must express his findings in terms of standard indices of morbidity so that they may be compared with those of other investigators.

1. Population Definition and Sampling Procedures

The epidemiologist's problems in defining the population at risk and selecting an appropriate sampling method are essentially similar to those encountered in any type of social survey (see, for example, Kish, 1965; Moser and Kalton, 1971). In practice, however, the problems of national coverage that tend to preoccupy survey statisticians have not greatly exercised epidemiologists, for the simple reason that field surveys of disease on a national scale have seldom been feasible: the inherent difficulties have been too great and the cost prohibitive. The nearest approach so far has been the sort of enquiry, typified by the British Survey of Sickness (Logan and Brooke, 1956), in which a national sample of persons living at private addresses was visited by lay interviewers using a check-list of medical complaints. In a survey of this kind carried out some years ago in the United States, a representative national sample of some 2,500 adults was selected for interview by a team from the University of Michigan Survey Research Center and asked for their own views of their mental health (Gurin et al., 1960). Investigations of this kind can provide a useful supplement to clinically-orientated surveys but the evaluation of interview responses presents obvious difficulties. For the most part, therefore, epidemiological psychiatrists have tended to prefer the techniques of the area survey in which the mental state of all members of the population at risk, or of a large probability sample, can be directly examined.

The choice of the area to be surveyed is influenced by a number of factors (Fletcher and Oldham, 1959b). It may be determined by the subject of enquiry; for example, the prevalence of Huntington's Chorea has been estimated for certain areas of Great Britain in which this condition is believed to be endemic (Bickford and Ellison, 1953; Pleydell, 1954). It may depend upon local administrative requirements, as in the setting up of new services (Roth and Luton, 1942; Kushlick, 1966). It may replicate a previous survey of the same area (Hagnell, 1966) or take advantage of a pre-existing sampling frame (Rawnsley, 1968a). Most commonly, it simply corresponds to the area on which the investigator happens to be based.

A question not always resolved—or even explicitly stated—in relation to area surveys may be posed thus: do the people residing within the defined boundaries constitute the population under enquiry, or are they to be regarded as part of some larger group such as the national population? To the statistician, no single area can be taken as representative of the country as a whole; hence, area morbidity rates cannot be extrapolated to the parent population. Even the use of a number of carefully selected areas with widely contrasting socio-economic and ecological features, as for example by Lewis (1929) in his survey of mental deficiency, has been subjected to heavy criticism on these grounds (Gruenberg, 1964). On the other hand, there is little doubt that intensive area surveys can provide results of an accuracy impossible to achieve on a national scale. One may take the surveys conducted on the Danish island of Bornholm (Fremming, 1951) and in a remote, isolated corner of Northern Norway during the Second World War (Bremer, 1951) as instances where the advantages of studying a captive population clearly outweighed the unrepresentativeness of the material.

This conflict can never be entirely resolved. In practical terms, the epidemiologist can justifiably draw some general conclusions if he is able to carry out a series of replicated area surveys whose results all point in the same direction (Durkheim, 1897); or, less satisfactorily, if his own survey reveals findings similar to those of a number of other workers in the same field. Thus, the ecological patterns for mental illness in Chicago reported by Faris and Dunham (1939) were subsequently confirmed both for other American cities (Gerard and Houston, 1953; Lapouse et al., 1956) and in other parts of the world (Lin, 1953; Hare, 1956a,b; Stein, 1957). Although some discrepant findings were also reported (Clausen and Kohn, 1959; Murphy, 1959), the association of schizophrenic illness with social isolation and low socio-economic status reported by the Chicago workers appeared to have validity in many large cities.

The population at risk should be defined in terms of residence within clearly stated geographical or administrative boundaries, so that it can be readily enumerated from local Census or other official data. In surveys aimed at a particular diagnostic category or public health problem, the population may be delimited by other than geographical factors. Surveys of childhood disorders, post-partum psychoses or senile psychoses will automatically determine the age-sex groups to be reviewed. In the interests of economy, the technique of stratification may be further refined, as in the Isle of Wight survey of schoolchildren (Rutter and Graham, 1966) which was deliberately restricted to 10- and 11-year-olds. In Great Britain, surveys of psychological abnormality have been undertaken on a variety of subgroups, including old people (Kay et al., 1964),

adolescents (Henderson et al., 1967), factory workers (Fraser, 1947), university students (Kidd, 1965) and West Indian immigrants (Hemsi, 1967). In some enquiries, the samples have been weighted to ensure adequate representation of each subcategory; the National Survey of Child Health, for example, is based on a sample stratified by social class (Douglas and Blomfield, 1958).

Whether the whole population or a probability sample is to be surveyed, care must be taken to account for all individuals at risk, including patients in institutions, members of the Armed Forces, temporary residents in hostels and boarding houses; indeed, all persons who enter or leave the area during the survey period. Problems of this kind may be aggravated by the presence of large airports or railway termini. The importance of checking on transient groups was strikingly illustrated by a recent census of a London Reception Centre which found 25 per cent of the residents to be chemically dependent on alcohol (Edwards et al., 1968).

2. Case-definition and Classification

Any satisfactory case-definition must meet two essential requirements: first, it must provide an acceptable formulation of the category under review; secondly, it must permit a clear differentiation between 'cases' and 'normals' (or rather, since the latter term is ambiguous, between 'cases' and 'not-cases'). In relation to psychological abnormality each of these requirements may give rise to serious difficulty: so much so that, to one worker, '. . . the recent history of epidemiological work in psychiatry is the history of attempts to define a case' (Hare, 1962).

The more comprehensive the survey, the greater the problem of formulating a definition. The epidemiologist is on reasonably firm ground in dealing with well-delineated syndromes of a kind whose clinical diagnosis is seldom in doubt. The ground is more treacherous, however, where large, miscellaneous categories such as 'depression' or 'schizophrenia' are under consideration; in surveys of 'total psychiatric prevalence' it becomes a quagmire.

The first of these situations obtains when the psychiatric state has well-marked physical concomitants, as in mongolism or Huntington's Chorea, or is accompanied by characteristic patterns of behaviour, as in infantile autism or drug dependency. For any such condition, the task of setting up an operational definition is apt to be relatively simple and, by the same token, a high standard of diagnostic reliability can be expected.

Unfortunately, in relation to the major categories

of psychiatric disorder, these problems are a good deal more complex. In the past, the reliability of psychiatric diagnosis has proved disappointingly poor (Eysenck, 1952; Kreitman, 1961) and, although with the introduction of more sophisticated techniques the picture is improving (Foulds, 1965), it is still very far from satisfactory. The results are apparent not only in routinely-collected morbidity statistics, but in the findings of intensive area surveys: Table 2.1, for example, compares the expectancy rates for affective disorders derived from a number of the more careful studies of this kind.

Table 2.1.   Expectation through Life of Affective Disorder

| | Per 1,000 births | |
	Male	Female
Bornholm (Fremming)	10·2	22·4
Sweden (Larsson and Sjögren)	9·0	12·0
Iceland (Helgason)	18·0	24·6
Norway (Ödegaard)	4·2	6·2
London (Norris)	8·0	14·4
Sweden (Essen-Möller)	17·0	28·0

Source: Rawnsley (1968b)

There is some evidence that differences of this order are attributable, at least in part, to a lack of agreement on the application of diagnostic terms. It has been shown, for example, that psychiatrists in the United States habitually class as schizophrenic many patients who in Great Britain would be regarded as cases of depression; a finding that helps to account for the major discrepancies between the two countries' psychiatric statistics (Cooper et al., 1969b).

The reliability of psychiatric diagnosis may be improved, and the findings of different surveys made more directly comparable, by the adoption of a standard taxonomy. The business of classifying and categorising disease is not primarily the duty of the epidemiologist, who in this regard must lean heavily upon his clinical colleagues. In psychiatry, where problems of case-definition and classification are so closely interlinked, survey findings have always been subject to influence by the diagnostic habits of individual clinicians.

From the epidemiological standpoint, the primary function of any classification is to serve as a means of communication (Stengel, 1960). No matter what 'private' classification the clinician favours, for the purpose of collaborative research he must be prepared to submit to a common 'public' system (Lewis, 1961). In Great Britain, a recent step in this direction has been the publication of an official glossary based on the Eighth Revision of the International Statistical Classification of Diseases (W.H.O., 1967; Registrar General, 1968).

On a wider scale, the selection of a research strategy is likely to be determined in part by the prevailing theoretical assumptions. Mechanic (1970), for example, has pointed out that while in recent years European workers have striven to sharpen their diagnostic tools, their American counterparts have shown a tendency to regard all psychiatric disorder as part of a unitary phenomenon, ranged on a continuum from psychosis, through neurosis and character disorder, to an ideal state of 'positive mental health'. Whatever the merits of this viewpoint, the resulting preoccupation with 'total prevalence' in field survey work has multiplied the problems of definition.

It is a commonplace that the clinical material of modern psychiatric practice comprises a heterogeneous mixture of cerebral pathology, idiopathic illness and abnormal behavioural patterns acquired through the ordinary processes of learning (Eysenck, 1957). It is also widely recognised that concepts of mental illness and mental health are in large measure culturally determined and vary among different societies (Opler, 1956; Wittkower and Fried, 1959). In such circumstances, no general definition of the term 'psychiatric disorder' seems feasible. Any figure given for total psychiatric prevalence in a defined population can represent no more than the summation of rates for a miscellaneous collection of morbid states that in large measure require different strategies of investigation.

Both in generic and specific terms, the concept of a 'case' has been greatly bedevilled by the fallacy of the excluded middle. Most forms of psychological abnormality show a steady gradation through the mildest pathological variants into the normal range; the threshold beyond which a person's experiences and behaviour are perceived as morbid depends largely on his own social background and on the attitudes of his family, his local community and his doctors (Mechanic, 1962; Cooper, 1964; Rawnsley, 1965).

In an attempt to solve this dilemma, some workers have introduced criteria based on disability or impairment of social function: so far with limited success. An Expert Committee of the World Health Organisation, for example, proposed an operational definition which runs as follows—

'A manifest disturbance of mental functioning, specific enough in clinical character to be consistently recognisable as conforming to a clearly defined standard pattern, and severe enough to cause loss of working or social capacity or both, of a degree which can be specified in terms of absence from work or of a taking of legal or other special action.' (W.H.O., 1960).

Quite apart from the weight placed upon such question-begging terms as 'manifest', 'consistently', and 'clearly', the criteria here listed would automatically exclude any housewife or retired person not actually under institutional care.

In the face of these difficulties, research workers have tended to fall back on operational definitions based on the need for treatment services, actual or hypothetical. Redlich (1957), for instance, proposed that the guide-line should be 'who should be treated by psychiatrists'—financial considerations apart, presumably. Similarly, Clausen (1959), a sociologist, commented that: 'all these administrative indices imply an operational definition of mental illness as diagnosis by a qualified psychiatrist. The indices differ in respect to the circumstances that influence the probability that a clinician will have an opportunity to make a diagnosis . . .' Though the wording is obscure, the point is obvious enough if one bears in mind the shortage of trained psychiatrists in many developing countries; or, for that matter, the wide range of minor psychiatric disorders that even in modern industrial society remain largely outside the purview of the psychiatrist (Shepherd *et al.*, 1966).

The threshold of clinically significant abnormality can be more precisely defined with the aid of symptom-rating scales, used in conjunction with standardised interview techniques. This approach, little used hitherto, is rapidly becoming practicable with the introduction of properly calibrated instruments (Wing *et al.*, 1967a; Goldberg *et al.*, 1970). In addition, clinical severity ratings will be increasingly supplemented by indices of social dysfunction as more reliable measures become available (Katz and Lyerly, 1963; Brown and Rutter, 1966).

3. Case-finding and case-identification

Once the nature of a 'case' has been defined, the epidemiologist must select a strategy for the enumeration of all such cases in his survey population. Broadly speaking, the choice of an appropriate strategy for any survey will be determined by the type and severity of morbidity that is to be ascertained. It is clear, for instance, that in Great Britain a fair approximation to the true incidence of acute major psychotic illnesses could be derived from the records of psychiatric agencies; or to that of severe subnormality from the records of local institutions and public health authorities. Equally clearly, such procedures would not reveal the extent

in the community of, say, chronic alcoholism or of phobic anxiety states.

To some degree, therefore, the choice of case-finding methods is a function of the *level* of morbidity at which the enquiry is aimed. This point can best be illustrated by a frequency distribution, as in Fig. 2.1.

The diagram is obviously an over-simplification, since it assumes that all forms of morbidity can be placed on a linear axis of severity, while at the same time ignoring the many personal and cultural differences in sickness-tolerance that determine the point at which individuals seek medical care. Nevertheless, it provides a useful model for planning

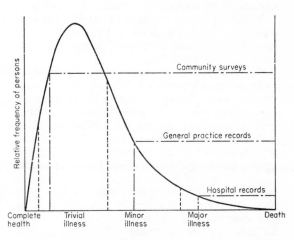

Fig. 2.1. Coverage of sickness continuum achieved by the major sources of morbidity statistics. (*Source:* Kalton, 1968, by permission of the Editor of the *Journal of the Royal College of Practitioners*)

area health surveys. The study of mental health in a New Town by Taylor and Chave (1964) provides a neat example. Considering no single index of health to be adequate for their purpose, these investigators set out to chart mental illness in their survey population in terms of mental hospital admissions, referrals to the local psychiatric out-patient clinic, general practice consultations for psychiatric symptoms and, finally, self-reported nervous complaints recorded in the course of door-to-door interviewing of a random sample of the population. The four reported complaints taken as *prima facie* evidence of psychiatric disturbance were 'nerves', depression, sleeplessness, and undue irritability. Persons with one or more of these complaints who were not under medical care were regarded as at increased risk for neurotic illness and were classed as a 'subclinical neurosis' group. On this basis, the findings of the enquiry were summarised as follows—

'Of the adult population of Newton in 1959—
330 per 1,000 reported sub-clinical neurotic symptoms,
81 per 1,000 were treated by general practitioners for definite psychiatric illness,
4·4 per 1,000 were referred to an out-patient psychiatric clinic,
1·9 per 1,000 were admitted as in-patients for psychiatric treatment.'

This type of approach goes some way to reducing the confusion in prevalence statistics and has great advantages for comparative studies. It is, however, quite inadequate as a means of establishing total prevalence, since too little is known about the general practice and 'subclinical' groups to permit of firm case-identification.

Whatever the respective importance to be accorded to these various sources, it is clear that the basic division in case-finding procedures lies between: (a) the enumeration of all cases known to existing medical agencies, and (b) the estimation of all undeclared cases in the community. For the first of these operations, the epidemiologist can in effect rely upon 'second-hand' information; that is to say, he can make use of the clinical and administrative records of the medical agencies that serve his chosen area. For the second operation, no such data are available; hence, special procedures must be set up for collecting the information at first hand. It is chiefly at this second stage that the major problems of method arise.

(A) ENUMERATION OF DECLARED CASES

In the past, mental hospital returns have constituted the principal source of statistics on the incidence and prevalence of psychiatric disorders. Their employment for this purpose has always been open to criticism on the grounds that various selective factors, other than clinical, may influence the probability of hospital admission (Terris, 1965). Of recent years, the growing emphasis on out-patient treatment and community care for the mentally sick has reinforced the need for extra-mural statistics. While the collation of out-patient records represents a step in this direction, the information so far available from this source is scanty. In this country, only the Bethlem Royal and Maudsley Hospitals publish detailed out-patient statistics (Hare, 1968) and even here the attendance figures cannot be related to a base-population. Moreover, hospital

out-patients are far from representative of morbidity in the community (Cooper, 1966; Shepherd et al., 1966).

A notable advance in the routine collection of morbidity statistics has been the establishment in some areas of Psychiatric Case Registers, so far chiefly in the United States (Miles et al., 1964; Bahn et al., 1966) and in Great Britain (Baldwin et al., 1965; Wing et al., 1967b). Essentially, the Case Register has three characteristics: it is a linked record system that collates information from all in-patient, out-patient, and domiciliary psychiatric agencies; it is based on a defined population and it is cumulative over time. Such an instrument can be helpful for the evaluation of services not only by the provision of routine descriptive statistics but also as a sampling frame for special intensive studies. By dint of its on-going nature it can facilitate prospective follow-up and cohort studies and it serves to bring into the net all those cases that run a remittent or episodic course.

The limitations of the case register as an epidemiological tool are readily apparent. For economic reasons, such registers are likely to remain confined to relatively few areas. Even within these areas, they cannot provide a true index of the prevalence of morbidity. Admittedly, the findings of psychiatric registers in different areas have proved remarkably similar, with reported annual prevalence rates of the order of $1\frac{1}{2}$ to 2 per cent of the population at risk. In all probability, however, this concordance merely 'says something about the proportion of the gross national product which industrial societies are prepared to devote to specialised services for the mentally ill' (Wing et al., 1969).

It need not be emphasised that the diagnostic findings of case registers are subject to the same vagaries as any other data on mental illness and the orientation of the individual psychiatrist remains an important determinant (Babigian et al., 1965; Kidd and Mackie, 1967).

(B) DETECTION OF UNDECLARED CASES

The chief difficulties of enumeration arise out of the need to detect cases that have not come into contact with any psychiatric agency. Relatively few common diseases of our society can be diagnosed on simple inspection. More frequently, a detailed medical examination is required, and often laboratory or other test procedures are needed for confirmation. In consequence, two related but distinct forms of activity are called for: in the words of Blum (1962), 'Case-finding . . . has two components. One component consists of the means which are employed to locate potential cases: the other component is concerned with the identification of actual cases'. If for the terms 'potential' and 'actual' we substitute suspected and confirmed, this statement accords well with orthodox epidemiological teaching. In psychiatric surveys, however, much confusion has been occasioned by failure to distinguish between these two forms of activity and to pay regard to the need for both.

A further point emphasised by Blum is that clinical examination constitutes the nearest approach to a yardstick in this field of enquiry: '. . . the ultimate criterion against which other means of identifying psychiatric disorders are validated'. It is a sobering reflection that, over almost the entire range of psychiatric disorder today, this point remains true. From it, two corollaries can be drawn. In the first place, no procedure other than clinical examination can be accepted as a valid method of psychiatric case-identification unless, when subjected to rigorous experimental testing, its results can be shown to correlate very highly with those of examination by trained psychiatrists. So far, it may be added, no method satisfies this criterion. Secondly, all other case-finding techniques have to be viewed simply as ways of nominating suspected or 'potential' cases which then require to be confirmed by detailed psychiatric examination. The most common shortcoming of field surveys of mental disorder has been their reliance on indirect methods of case-identification as a substitute for clinical assessment.

The examination by trained psychiatrists of all members of an area population, or even of a probability sample, presents formidable problems of logistics and, in practice, has been attempted in very few studies. The difficulties are apparent from the description by Essen-Möller (1956) of how he and three colleagues in their survey of the Swedish parish of 'Lundby' each interviewed daily up to fourteen persons '. . . in their homes, in the fields, or else in their places of work'. Such conditions are hardly conducive to high reliability and it is not altogether surprising that when the same population was reviewed a decade later the frequency of case-finding was double that of the original survey (Essen-Möller, 1961; Hagnell, 1966).

A variety of techniques has been employed to locate suspected cases. Each has its merits and its limitations: the choice will as a rule be decided by local conditions and resources. In rural areas, or wherever a close-knit, static community is under enquiry, the help of key informants such as priests, doctors, school-teachers, and welfare workers—or, in other cultures, village headmen and witch doctors—can be invaluable. In urban areas and modern industrial societies, sources of this kind are less rewarding, and the research worker may have to rely mainly on systematic sampling procedures and the use of standardised screening techniques.

The principal case-finding methods listed by Blum (1962) are structured and semistructured ('guided') interviews conducted by lay research assistants; psychological symptom and personality inventories; rating scales, including self-rating techniques such as the Q sort (Stephenson, 1953). In this type of enquiry, the potential contribution of the clinical psychologist cannot be over-emphasised. In addition, Blum discusses the use of indirect pointers such as the presence of physical illness or social dysfunction in selecting people with a high risk of psychiatric disorder.

All these methods have serious imperfections. The reports of lay interviewers are generally of low reliability, although a good deal can be achieved by means of intensive training (New York Department of Mental Hygiene, 1959). The evaluation of interview protocols can face the clinician with many uncertainties: to such an extent, indeed, that 'the attempt to make a diagnosis in the usual clinical sense must be abandoned' (Leighton et al., 1963).

Standardised symptom inventories have the advantage of being more reliable than interview techniques, but their validity as judged by their congruence with clinical findings appears to be of a low order (Little and Schneidman, 1959; Goldberg, 1969), while the distribution of scores on such instruments is heavily affected by demographic and socio-cultural factors (Dohrenwend and Dohrenwend, 1969). A variety of rating scales have been constructed, usually for the purpose of measuring clinical change in relation to treatment (Knowles, 1963; Marks, 1968). Most of these measures have been standardised on psychiatric populations and are unsuitable for use in field surveys. Ratings by parents and teachers have proved useful in screening child populations (Glidewell et al., 1959; Shepherd et al., 1971) but there exists no comparable body of work on adults. Social adjustment ratings (Katz and Lyerly, 1963) can serve as an adjunct to clinical assessment but cannot be regarded as an acceptable substitute.

Two recent developments in this field are of interest for the epidemiologist. One is the adaptation of Shapiro's Personal Questionnaire (Shapiro, 1961) for use in community surveys; the other is a refinement by Goldberg (1969) of the psychiatric complaint inventory. Ingham (1965) employed a number of symptom scales, derived by Shapiro's technique, in a preliminary investigation of a rural parish in South Wales. He found that they evoked consistent response patterns and discriminated effectively between clinically defined groups. On the other hand, one-quarter of the subjects either refused to take part or were unable to complete the test. Hence, it seems that this approach will be subject to at least the same degree of sampling bias as earlier case-finding methods.

From this point of view, Goldberg's General Health Questionnaire appears more promising. Essentially, this is a psychiatric symptom inventory that has been calibrated against three criterion groups: mental hospital in-patients, out-patients, and a healthy sample of the metropolitan population. It is designed to focus on symptoms rather than on personality traits (Foulds, 1965) and, by permitting a graduated response, to avoid the errors of bimodal response scales. The results of a series of tests of validity, reliability, and sensitivity indicate that this questionnaire compares favourably with any corresponding instrument.

In distinguishing between 'declared' and 'undeclared' cases, some ambiguity may arise over the position of those persons who are in contact with various kinds of medical agency. Many such individuals do literally 'declare' their psychological symptoms; yet the true nature of their complaints often goes unrecognised. In a sense, such patients may be thought of as comprising a special inter-mediate group of 'declared but unrecorded' cases.

In Great Britain under the National Health Service, general practitioners occupy a position of great potential importance as key informants in psychiatric surveys. It has been shown, for example, that only a small fraction of the psychiatric problems recognised by general practitioners are reported to psychiatric agencies (Shepherd et al., 1966). At the same time, the psychiatric case-reporting of medical practitioners without special training is apt to be of low reliability, quite apart from the problems of bias inherent in any survey confined to persons in contact with the medical services. Hence, the screening of medical contacts must be regarded as a supplement to, rather than a substitute for, other case-finding methods.

A MODEL SURVEY DESIGN

We are now in a position to set out the desiderata for case-identification in a community survey. The process should consist of two phases, in the first of which an economical screening method is employed to nominate suspected cases, while in the second the latter are subjected to detailed clinical examination. The prime requirement of the first phase screening procedure is that it should be highly sensitive: that is, the number of 'false negatives' should be small (Meehl and Rosen, 1955; Fletcher and Oldham, 1959a). Its specificity is of less importance, since 'false positives' can be discarded at the second phase.

At the present stage of knowledge, the most efficient method of primary screening is probably a combination of systematic recording by trained key informants (of whom, in the United Kingdom, the general practitioner is the outstanding example), together with the application to a probability sample of a complaint inventory such as the General Health Questionnaire (Goldberg, 1969). In the second stage, all possible suspected cases should undergo psychiatric examination; at this point the procedure can be made more valid and reliable by the use of a standardised clinical interview (Goldberg et al., 1970).

To date, very few investigations have conformed to this model, although in their very different ways the surveys of Lewis (1929) and of Lin (1953) can be cited as examples of the basic approach.

4. Indices of Morbidity

The same need to communicate by means of a generally accepted 'public' system, already discussed in relation to diagnosis, applies a fortiori to the measurement of morbidity in populations. Rates of morbidity are more difficult to compute than those for mortality, since they do not refer to an unequivocal point-event; in consequence, they have come to be regarded by many clinicians as something of an esoteric mystery. In truth, however, the number of relevant variables is small and the basic principles are simple.

To begin with, the basic unit of measurement can refer either to the person who is deemed sick, or to the 'illness' he experiences. Illnesses may be mild or severe in intensity; brief or of prolonged duration; continuous or episodic in course. The person who is ill may be more or less handicapped as a result, and may be under medical care for longer or shorter periods of time. These constructs provide the raw material from which virtually all morbidity data are derived.

The indices appropriate to any given survey depend upon the primary aims and objectives of the enquiry. If the main purpose is to assess the need for medical and ancillary services, the most useful measure will be concerned with prevalence—the total number of cases existing in the population at a given time—severity and handicap. If, on the other hand, the investigator is seeking to establish clues to the aetiology of a particular diagnostic entity, he will try to discover its rate of inception (incidence);

that is, the total number of new cases arising in the population during a defined time-period. In either event, the population at risk serves as the denominator in estimating rates.

Both these concepts can be related either to persons or to illnesses, so that the following operational definitions may be formulated (Reg. Gen., 1954; Kalton, 1968)—

1. Inception rate (spells):

$$\frac{\text{Number of spells of illness starting in a defined period}}{\text{Average number of persons exposed to risk in that period}}$$

2. Inception rate (persons):

$$\frac{\text{Number of persons starting at least one spell in a defined period}}{\text{Average number of persons exposed to risk in that period}}$$

3. Period prevalence rate (spells):

$$\frac{\text{Number of spells current at some time during a defined period}}{\text{Average number of persons exposed to risk during that period}}$$

4. Period prevalence rate (persons):

$$\frac{\text{Number of persons who are ill at some time during a defined period}}{\text{Average number of persons exposed to risk during that period}}$$

5. Point prevalence rate:

$$\frac{\text{Number of persons who are ill at some point in time}}{\text{Number of persons exposed to risk at that point in time}}$$

In this context, a 'spell' of illness (sickness) has been defined as a 'period during which a person is sick on one day (or shift) or on each of a consecutive series of days (or shifts)' (Reg. Gen., 1954). The industrial frame of reference is obvious enough, and limits the application of this concept. An alternative commonly employed in psychiatric surveys is to take as the 'spell' or 'episode' the total length of time during which a patient is continuously under a specified form of medical care.

In comparing period prevalence rates for different populations, or for the same population over different periods of time, it is essential to make use of a standard period of observation, since the rate of case-finding is unlikely to be uniform. Chronic cases, for example, and those in continuous contact with medical agencies, are normally identified in the early weeks of a survey, after which the process of enumeration slows down very markedly. Hence, the findings of, say, a six-month survey cannot be directly compared with those of a one-year survey simply by doubling up the numbers for the former. In practice, the one-year prevalence rate is the commonest form of cross-sectional survey index.

In some types of investigation, neither inception nor prevalence rates are regarded as satisfactory, because they take no account of differential mortality rates in the general population. This is especially true of population genetics, where the investigator wishes to examine the statistical association between psychiatric disorder and the genotype (see Chapter 16). In such enquiries, the morbidity-experience of any particular subgroup is usually expressed in terms of the 'morbid risk' or 'disease expectancy' of any individual member of that group; that is to say, the statistical probability that any individual who survives long enough to be 'at risk' for the disorder in question will in fact develop that disorder. Clearly, the only satisfactory means of ascertaining this value is by study of a representative cohort of the population throughout the risk period. In a small number of investigations, this aim has been achieved; notably by Fremming (1951) in his Bornholm survey. More commonly, indirect methods of computing morbid risk, such as that described by Weinberg, have been employed (Reid, 1960). These have the advantage that the relevant index can be calculated from the findings of a cross-sectional morbidity survey, provided the age and sex distribution of the population at risk is known. The notion of a period 'at risk' is, however, somewhat artificial with regard to psychiatric disorders. The definition of the risk period for schizophrenia, for example, as the range from 15 to 45 years, fails to accord with the findings of modern clinical investigation (Kay and Roth, 1961).

From this brief review, it is clear that many problems of research remain unsolved, and that the main interest of the epidemiological approach in this field lies in the possibility of future developments, rather than its achievements to date. Nevertheless, the volume and range of work published in this field during the past three or four decades is already sufficient to give a fair indication of the scope of epidemiological research on psychological abnormality.

THE SCOPE OF EPIDEMIOLOGICAL RESEARCH

Morris (1957) has enumerated the 'uses' of epidemiology under seven headings; namely, community diagnosis, completion of the clinical picture of disease, delineation of new syndromes, computation of individual morbid risk, charting of historical trends, evaluation of health services in action and, lastly but most important, the search for causative factors. This frame-work has been adopted by Shepherd and Cooper (1964) in reviewing the broad field of mental disorders and by Gruenberg (1964) in relation to mental subnormality. While such a classification can serve to bring order to a confused and obscure topic, its value is perhaps more obvious to the epidemiologist than to workers in other fields, who may fail to see what relevance population surveys have to their own professional needs. From their point of view, epidemiological research can be more usefully considered according to whether its primary interest is for (1) the public health administrator, (2) the clinician or (3) the professional research worker.

1. Administrative Studies: Prevalence and Trends

Public health administrators, both at national and local level, require estimates of the prevalence and distribution of mental disorders in the general population, in order to assess the need for medical and related services. In Great Britain, this need has been well recognised for over a century: by 1845, for example, John Thurnam could write that the public good called 'for the regular publication, on an uniform plan, of the statistics of institutions, so liable to neglect and abuse as are those for the insane' (Thurnam, 1845). Yet progress in the collation and publication of national statistics was slower in this country than in Scandinavia (Ödegaard, 1945; Astrup and Ödegaard, 1960) and in parts of the United States (Pollock, 1925; Malzberg, 1940). The first substantive British contribution to hospital morbidity statistics did not appear until after the Second World War (Mackay, 1951) and the first national census of patients in psychiatric beds until nearly twenty years later (Brooke, 1967).

The most rewarding application of mental hospital statistics so far has been the cohort study, which can provide useful pointers to future trends in the course and outcome of treated morbidity. Thus, Shepherd (1957), by comparing the subsequent fate of patients admitted to a County Mental Hospital during two triennia (1931–3 and 1945–7)

was able to demonstrate a trend towards more favourable outcome in terms both of a shorter mean duration of stay and of an increased discharge rate. That this trend accelerated in the ensuing decade was revealed by a cohort study of admissions and re-admissions to three London mental hospitals (Brown et al., 1961). Investigations of this kind can be of help in the assessment of new measures such as the introduction of tranquillising drugs, or of changes in official discharge policy (Lewis, 1959; Shepherd et al., 1961).

It is less easy to point to instances of the successful application of hospital statistics to the planning of future psychiatric services. Indeed, the best-known example serves to illustrate the hazards as well as the potential value of statistical prediction in this field.

In the mid-1950s, the resident mental hospital population of Great Britain, which up to that time had been rising steadily, unexpectedly began to fall. The change was due, not to any decrease in the admission numbers, but to a reduced average period of stay in hospital: fewer patients were now becoming chronic inmates. This trend, variously attributed to the impact of new drugs and to more active rehabilitation, soon began to relieve the pressure on mental hospital beds and to reduce the waiting lists for admission. Clearly, if continued, it could herald a permanent reduction in the bed requirements, and so wield an influence on the hospital building programme.

To examine this possibility, Tooth and Brooke (1961) undertook a survey of mental hospital beds in England and Wales, designed to predict future developments. Their technique consisted essentially of the analysis of two opposing trends. On the one hand, they tried to estimate the rate of attrition of the long-stay population resident at the end of 1954; on the other hand, they studied the progress of two patient cohorts, admitted in 1954 and 1956 respectively, in order to gauge the rate of accumulation of a new generation of chronic patients.

With regard to the former problem, Tooth and Brooke found that over the quinquennium 1954–9 there had been a reduction in the long-stay cohort amounting to 18 per cent of the men and 22 per cent of the women. By a process of simple extrapolation they calculated that, 'On this basis none of the long-stay patients resident on 31 December 1954 would be in hospital after about sixteen years'.

Turning to the admission cohorts, they reached the conclusion that the existing need for short-stay and medium-stay beds totalled about 870 per million of the general population. Furthermore, on the basis of current admission and discharge rates the bed requirement of the new generation of chronic patients was thought likely to rise over the next fifteen years to a maximum of about 890 per million of the population, and then stabilise. Hence, given the complete disappearance in the meantime of the existing chronic population, a total requirement of about 1,760 beds per million could be predicted for 1975.

As an academic contribution to the demography of mental illness, Tooth and Brooke's paper might have excited little comment. It gained, however, the unusual distinction of being taken seriously by government. A ten-year Hospital Plan, published in the following year, declared that—

'Because of the success of new methods of treatment combined with changed social attitudes, it may be expected that the recent decline in the number of hospital beds required for mental illness will continue. A recent statistical enquiry indicated that, by about 1975, only 1·8 beds per 1,000 population will be required (compared with the present figure of 3·3) on the assumption that the average length of stay of patients admitted in the years 1954–6 continues to apply. . . . A ratio of 1·8 per 1,000 population has therefore been taken as the probable limit of requirements by 1975' (Min. of Health, 1962).

At this pronouncement, which in effect heralded a reduction of some 60,000 psychiatric beds, many hospital physicians and administrators became alarmed, and the controversy that ensued was at times heated. The assumptions of the Hospital Plan were challenged: it was pointed out that the admission rate was still rising, and the effects of the nation's changing age-structure were emphasised. Rehin and Martin (1963) stressed the wide regional variation in bed rates and argued strongly against the imposition of any uniform national figure. Other critics seized on the statistical calculations in Tooth and Brooke's paper, showing that the known rate of decline of the chronic population corresponded to a geometric rather than an arithmetic progression. On grounds of clinical experience it was urged that once all the less severely impaired chronic patients had been 'creamed off' a large residue of intractable, severely handicapped patients would be left and that most of these would still be resident by 1975. Norton (1961) calculated that, according to which year was taken as the starting-point, the official estimate could be out by either 10,000 or 25,000 beds. Implicit in all these arguments was the fear that the observed decline in the demand for mental hospital beds might well prove to be only a temporary phenomenon, and that within a few years the earlier up-going trend might be resumed.

At the time of writing (1970), it is still unclear if Tooth and Brooke's prediction was seriously wide of the mark; up-to-date figures for their long-stay cohort are not available. To some extent, the Hospital Plan itself has served to obscure the picture, since a statistical prediction given the stamp of official approval is liable to become a self-fulfilling prophecy. On this score, one group of critics has commented that, 'Patients can be discharged, and beds can be emptied, by administrative decision: but, in the absence of some substantial and favourable change in the situation, this can be achieved only at the cost of much hardship to patients and their families' (Gore *et al.*, 1964).

That the overall trend towards fewer mental hospital beds has continued can be seen from Table 2.2, in which the fall in numbers over the past fourteen years is set out. Wide disparities occur between the different regions, emphasising the need for more detailed and intensive regional surveys as a basis for planning future requirements.

Table 2.2. Resident Hospital Patients per 1,000 Population in the Regions of England and Wales, 1954 and 1968

Regional hospital board	1954	1968	Per cent fall 1954–68
England and Wales	3·44	2·48	28
Newcastle	2·76	2·26	18
Leeds	3·74	2·73	27
Sheffield	2·55	1·80	29
East Anglia	3·30	2·46	25
Combined Metropolitan[1]		2·80	
Oxford	2·85	1·65	42
South Western	3·98	2·80	30
Welsh	3·32	2·51	24
Birmingham	3·05	2·22	27
Manchester	2·97	1·98	33
Liverpool	3·71	3·23	13
Wessex[1]		2·81	

[1] In 1954 Wessex was part of the South West Metropolitan region.
Source: Bransby (1969)

Hospital statistics alone, however interpreted, may be of limited value as aids to the rational planning of services. Indeed, the need for estimates of psychiatric prevalence is apt to be most urgent in precisely those situations where the existing services are too inadequate to furnish any guidance. In the developing countries, for example, it is obvious that the number of mental hospital beds bears little or no relation to the true needs (Lin, 1953; Hoenig and Srinivasan, 1959). Even in modern industrial societies, new kinds of needs arise that cannot be gauged from the existing provisions:

witness the current epidemic of narcotic addiction in Great Britain (de Alarcon and Rathod, 1968; Kosviner et al., 1968).

Case registers can serve a useful local function by spotlighting trends in the use of services and by revealing serious imbalance. By means of the Rochester Register, for example, Gardner (1970) was able to show up disparities between the facilities for middle-class and for lower-class areas, and to suggest appropriate modifications. Similarly, Wing and his colleagues have made good use of data from the Camberwell Register to argue the case for rationalising the local services (Wing et al., 1970). In most areas, however, the necessary information can be obtained only by means of ad hoc surveys.

It is no coincidence that survey techniques have found their most successful applications in that branch of psychiatry where case-finding is most reliable. Cases of 'severe subnormality', which for practical purposes can be equated with an IQ below 55 (Larsson and Sjögren, 1954), are readily identifiable in childhood. In England and Wales, about 3·7 per 1,000 of those who survive into their 'teens are likely to fall into this category. Table 2.3 summarises the findings of three recent surveys which yielded very similar results.

Table 2.3.　Prevalence of Severe Subnormality in Three Areas of England

Area of survey	Age-group	Severe Subnormality rate/1,000	Mongolism, rate/1,000
County of Middlesex, 1960	7–14	3·45	1·14
	10–14	3·61	N.K.
Salford, 1961	15–19	3·62	0·90
Wessex, 1964:			
Urban (County Boroughs)	15–19	3·54	1·15
Rural (Counties)	15–19	3·84	1·18

Source: Kushlick (1966)

In Great Britain, as in most industrial nations, severely subnormal children of school age are readily identifiable because they have been deemed unsuitable for the ordinary educational streams and as such have been notified to Local Authority Health Departments. By a process of extrapolation, the numbers of pre-school age children with primary amentia can be calculated for any standard population. It is thus possible to assess the need for services for children of all age-groups and to compare it with the existing state of affairs. The result may be disquieting, as Kushlick's figures for Wessex reveal (Table 2.4)

Table 2.4.　Estimated and Declared Prevalence of Severely Subnormal Children per 100,000 Population in Wessex

| | Age-group: | | |
	0–4	5–15	Total
Estimated total	30	66	96
Number known to Mental Health Department:	4	47	51
Home care only	2	7	9
Home care plus training centre	1	22	23
Hospital or hostel	1	16	17
Other	–	2	2
Estimated number not known to Mental Health Dept.	26	19	45

Source: Kushlick (1966)

As a result of Kushlick's survey, the Wessex Hospital Regional Board has accepted a scheme for an evaluative experiment in which locally based hostel accommodation will be provided for the estimated total number of severely subnormal children who are judged to be in need of residential care. It is planned to compare this experimental service with the traditional type of institutional care in terms of the children's progress, the problems experienced by their families, the administrative difficulties encountered and the relative costs (Wessex R.H.B., 1966). The advantages of such evaluative schemes are obvious.

2. Clinical Studies: Diagnosis and Prognosis

The importance of epidemiological research has been much more widely recognised by public health workers, who are professionally concerned with the mass aspects of disease, than by clinicians, who are inevitably preoccupied with the problems presented by individual patients. Nevertheless, modern clinical thinking in psychiatry draws heavily on statistical concepts, and every clinician, whether consciously or otherwise, is relying on actuarial data whenever he makes an individual diagnosis or prognosis. Emil Kraepelin, to whom this book is dedicated, based his system of classification on observation of the clinical symptoms of large numbers of mental hospital patients, together with an evaluation of their outcome (Kraepelin, 1909b; Ödegaard, 1967). So long as the aetiology and pathogenesis of most psychiatric disorders remain obscure, this approach provides the only practical basis for classification (Holmboe and Astrup, 1957) and as such has continued to be applied to a variety of conditions, ranging from senile psychoses (Roth and Morrissey, 1952; Roth, 1955) to the disorders of childhood (Hewitt and Jenkins, 1946; Robins, 1966). The development of modern statistical techniques such as factor analysis and canonical variate analysis (*see* Chapter 1 by H. J. Eysenck in the 1st edition of this book) has served to refine the Kraepelinian method without fundamentally changing it.

Kraepelin and his successors derived their views on taxonomy from the study of institutional populations, or of patients under specialist care. Field surveys and cross-cultural comparisons have been useful in revealing the kinds of bias that may ensue. Thus, many forms of behaviour regarded as morbid when they present to Child Guidance Clinics have been shown to occur frequently in the general child population (Lapouse and Monk, 1959; Shepherd *et al.*, 1971). Neurotic disorders do not reach their peak in early adult life, as hospital statistics suggest, but are equally represented in middle life (Kessel and Shepherd, 1962; Shepherd *et al.*, 1966). In non-European cultures, schizophrenic reactions are not necessarily associated with a prolonged illness and an unfavourable outcome (Rin and Lin, 1962). In these and other contexts, it seems clear that our notions have been unduly influenced by local conditions of clinical practice.

In a positive sense, the epidemiological contribution to taxonomy has been meagre, for the simple reason that the necessary investigations have still to be undertaken. As a rule, survey workers have preferred to utilise the ready-to-hand Kraepelinian categories, rather than to attempt any fresh delineation of syndromes; indeed, the sharp differences that have been found between the patterns of incidence and distribution of the main symptom-groupings have been adduced as evidence of their specificity (Lemkau, 1955). From time to time, nevertheless, survey reports have served to modify the prevailing views on nosology. Thus, the survey of mental deficiency in England and Wales (Lewis, 1929) indicated that a relatively mild, culturally-determined form of retardation could be differentiated from the more severe biological forms: this finding has since been repeatedly substantiated (Penrose, 1938; Stein and Susser, 1960). More recently, a survey of childhood autism in Middlesex (Lotter, 1967) has provided confirmation of the clinical impression that in its family and social distribution this disorder is entirely distinct from schizophrenia.

While the findings of socio-medical surveys have thus at times helped to mould diagnostic concepts, their major influence on clinical thinking has been in the area of prognosis. Longitudinal studies of psychological abnormality in the community have provided the clinician with valuable knowledge in a number of fields, of which we may take as instances

the natural history of minor psychiatric disorder, the effect of social factors on the outcome of schizophrenia, and the concept of 'high-risk' groups and individuals, particularly in relation to suicide.

Remarkably little is known about the normal course and outcome of the neuroses and related non-psychotic disorders. Greer and Cawley (1966), from an extensive review of the literature, concluded regretfully that, '. . . it is not possible to make legitimate generalisations about the prognosis of neurotic disorders from the published data'. Although their own very careful follow-up of a sample of Maudsley Hospital patients went some way to remedying the deficiency, they were at pains to emphasise the need for prospective enquiries and for investigation of the milder degrees of disability which do not as a rule necessitate in-patient treatment.

In Great Britain under the National Health Service, the registered lists of general practitioners constitute an ideal sampling frame for this kind of enquiry. Longitudinal studies of psychiatric illness in general practice populations (Cooper *et al.*, 1969a; Harvey-Smith and Cooper, 1970) suggest that the previous duration of illness is the most important prognostic factor for the neuroses, and that a rough dichotomy can be established between chronic disorders of poor prognosis, on the one hand, and short-term situational reactions, on the other. Figure 2.2 illustrates a simple model for the balance of neurotic disorders in a general practice population.

These findings place chronic neurotic syndromes in the forefront of psychiatric disorder in the community and in so doing point to the need for further research on the subject. In the past few years, a number of investigations have begun to define chronic neurosis in relation to personality and physical constitution (Hare and Shaw, 1965; Little

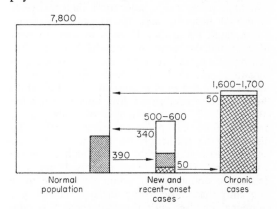

Fig. 2.2. A simple model of the changing distribution of psychiatric morbidity during one year in a standard population of 10,000 (By permission of the Editor of the *Journal of the Royal College of Practitioners*)

and Kerr, 1968), physical ill-health (Brown, 1965; Eastwood, 1969) and factors in the social environment (Cooper *et al.*, 1970).

The role of social factors in determining the outcome of schizophrenic illness has only recently begun to receive serious attention: even a decade ago it was possible for a leading authority on the subject to opine that 'nothing of much significance has been stated as to the influence of psychological and social factors on the course of schizophrenia' (Langfeldt, 1959). That such a comment would be unthinkable today is due in part to the pioneer work of men like Belknap (1956), Caudill (1958), and Goffman (1961), who have brought home to psychiatrists the full extent of the adverse influence of the 'total' institution; in part to a series of careful, detailed studies mounted by the MRC Social Psychiatry Unit (O'Connor, 1968).

The findings of these studies may be outlined as:

1. Schizophrenic patients who were visited during their first two months in hospital were less likely to become chronic inmates than those who received no visits during this period (Brown, 1959). Polish schizophrenic patients in this country, who received very few visits, were found to have a particularly marked tendency to become chronic (Brown, 1960).

2. Severely handicapped chronic schizophrenic patients showed a rapid response to social stimulation in a workshop environment, but relapsed as soon as the stimulation was withdrawn (Wing and Freudenberg, 1961).

3. Moderately disabled patients were found to improve in their attitudes to work when given the opportunity of industrial rehabilitation courses and as a result a proportion were successfully resettled in employment (Wing *et al.*, 1964a).

4. Male patients who, after more than two years in mental hospital, were discharged to parental homes fared worse than those who went to their wives; while the latter, in turn, did less well than patients discharged to other kin, or to lodgings (Brown *et al.*, 1958). This result appeared to be related to the degree of emotional arousal to which the patients were subjected. In a later investigation (Brown *et al.*, 1962) a sample of schizophrenic men was followed up for one year after hospital discharge, the prediction being made that those returning to relatives who showed 'high emotional involvement' (in terms of expressed emotion, dominance and hostility) would deteriorate more frequently than those whose relatives showed 'low emotional involvement': this hypothesis was confirmed.

5. Among female long-stay schizophrenic patients the severity of clinical symptoms was found to vary as between three mental hospitals with widely differing regimes. The clinical ratings correlated with a number of indices of the quality of hospital care, notably the degree of restriction of personal freedom, the extent of personal possessions granted the patients and the level of ward activities as judged from a time budget. Nurses' attitudes towards the patients likewise differed significantly between the three hospitals (Wing and Brown, 1961). Subsequent changes in these institutional regimes were associated with corresponding changes in the patients' clinical state, an increase in active pursuits having the most marked beneficial result (Wing, 1967).

6. In the high proportion of schizophrenic patients who relapsed within a year of hospital discharge, a characteristic pattern could be discerned of mounting family tension leading to serious distress in the relatives and culminating in a social crisis (Wing *et al.*, 1964b). In so far as such crises were commonly bound up with the recurrence of psychotic delusions, and with lapse from after-care supervision, they might be taken as manifestations of the underlying pathological process. An intensive controlled study of the events preceding acute schizophrenic breakdown, however, showed a significant excess even of those types of stressful experience which could not be in any way ascribed to the patients' mental state (Brown and Birley, 1968).

By the standards of social psychiatry, this series of investigations constitutes a substantial body of work. The research method has been largely of a standard to withstand criticism, so that it is now difficult for anybody to maintain that social determinants do not play a part in the course and outcome of schizophrenia. For the clinician, these studies have prognostic significance not merely in the deterministic sense that they render prediction more accurate in the individual case, but because they point to relatively specific ways of taking social action and modifying the long-term outcome.

Predictive factors, once identified, can be evaluated by means of anterospective enquiry: a technique that has been exploited to some purpose by criminologists (Mannheim and Wilkins, 1956; Glueck and Glueck, 1959). In the same way, the clinical psychiatrist can be helped by longitudinal surveys to assess the risk of future morbidity in persons whose current mental state is normal or only mildly disturbed. This principle has been applied to the calculation of illness-expectancy among the relatives of patients with established mental disorder: the method of the 'empirische Erbprognose' (*see* Chapter 16). It is equally relevant to the assessment of morbid risk for the patient himself in conditions where the occurrence of one or more previous attacks is held to influence the probability of future episodes. Affective psychosis is an obvious case in point, since the periodicity of attack forms an integral part of the Kraepelinian concept of manic-depressive illness and, indeed, long-term follow-up studies have substantially confirmed this view (Rennie, 1942). Unfortunately, as we have seen, the diagnostic reliability for this category has proved too poor for the findings of area surveys to show any consistency; while only recently have more homogeneous subcategories begun, possibly, to emerge (Leonhard, 1959; Perris, 1966).

Greater rewards have accrued from the study of suicidal risk in populations. Here, statistical surveys have amply demonstrated the importance of a variety of biological and social determinants including sex, age, physical health, occupation, marital state, fertility, religious faith, ethnic origin, and socio-economic status (Dublin, 1963). Local surveys have rounded out the picture and provided some indications of the possibilities for preventive action (Robins et al., 1959; Kessel and McCulloch, 1966).

One subgroup of the population with a greatly increased suicide risk comprises those persons who have already made one or more unsuccessful attempts on their own lives. By following up representative samples of such individuals, it becomes possible to evaluate predictive factors in terms of subsequent suicidal attempts and final self-destruction. Thus, of 1,112 adults whose suicidal attempts had come to the attention of the Philadelphia Police Department over a two-year period, 16 were found to have committed suicide over the ensuing twelve months (Tuckman and Youngman, 1963a,b). The one-year suicide rate for this sample, adjusted for age, sex, and racial distribution, was calculated to be 1,950 per 100,000, compared with a corresponding rate of 14 per 100,000 for the adult population of Philadelphia as a whole: a ratio of 140 to one. The data revealed that the suicide risk was greatest for those subgroups that most closely approximated in sex, age, and racial distribution to the statistics for suicide in the general population.

From the police records, it was possible to extend this investigation beyond the simple demographic characteristics of the sample. Altogether, 27 factors derived from the police reports were reviewed, and of these eleven were selected as being of predictive value: the findings are set out in Table 2.5.

From these eleven factors, together with those of

Table 2.5. Suicide Rates per 1,000 Population among 1,112 Attempted Suicides, by High- and Low-risk Categories of Risk-related Factors

Factor	High-risk category	Suicide rate	Low-risk category	Suicide rate
Marital status	Separated, divorced, widowed	41·9	Single, married	12·4
Employment status[1]	Unemployed, retired	24·8	Employed[2]	16·3
Living arrangements	Alone	71·4	With others	11·1
Health	Poor (acute or chronic condition in the 6-month period preceding the attempt)	18·0	Good[2]	13·8
Mental condition	Nervous or mental disorder, mood or behavioural symptoms including alcoholism	17·6	Presumably normal, including brief situational reactions[2]	11·7
Method	Hanging, firearms, jumping, drowning	45·5	Cutting or piercing, gas or carbon monoxide, poison, combination of methods, other	13·1
Potential consequences of method	Likely to be fatal[3]	31·5	Harmless, illness-producing	6·0
Police description of attempted suicide's condition	Unconscious, semiconscious	16·3	Presumably normal, disturbed, drinking, physically ill, other	13·0
Suicide note	Yes	22·5	No[2]	13·7
Previous attempt or threat	Yes	22·6	No[2]	13·3
Disposition	Admitted to psychiatric evaluation center	21·0	Discharged to self or relative; referred to family doctor, clergyman, or social agency; or other disposition	11·6

[1] Does not include housewives and students.
[2] Includes cases for which information on this factor was not given in the police report.
[3] Several criteria used in estimating whether the method used was likely to be fatal.
Source: Tuckman and Youngman, 1963b.

age, sex, and ethnic status, a simple 14-point scale of suicidal risk was constructed. Using a score of 4 as the cut-off point, the suicide rate was found to be 0·0 per 1,000 for the low-score group and 35·2 per 1,000 for the high-score group: a highly significant difference. While in this enquiry the number of suicide deaths was too small to warrant any more detailed analysis, it is evident that with larger survey samples the differential contribution of individual risk factors could be computed; hence, weighted scales of greater predictive accuracy might be derived.

The potential value of any such scale lies in its application to individual patients not only by clinical psychiatrists but by general hospital physicians, casualty officers, general practitioners, and others whose need to make decisions about the immediate disposal of attempted suicides constitutes a heavy responsibility.

From investigations of this nature it is only a stone's throw to the identification of high-risk groups as a means of picking out possible causal factors. By examining the differences in frequency of a given disorder between different populations, or different sections of the same population, it becomes possible to test for associations between its rate of inception and various biological or environmental indices. This, the 'search for causes', is held by many authorities to be the principal function of the epidemiologist.

3. Heuristic Studies: Aetiology and Pathogenesis

In order to view the epidemiologist's contribution in perspective, it is necessary to understand an important feature that limits his method of enquiry: being concerned solely with *associations* between morbidity and environmental factors he cannot, except by inference, draw any conclusions about the nature of causal connections. For elucidation of the pathophysiological mechanisms underlying the manifestations of disease, he has to rely upon the findings of experimental workers. This is not to deny the crucial part epidemiology can play in establishing a causal chain: the point requiring emphasis is the need for co-operation between different research disciplines if the chain is to be completed. The relationship between bronchial carcinoma and smoking habits provides a topical case in point (Doll and Hill, 1956; Wynder, 1959; Eysenck *et al.*, 1960), while the extensive table of complementary studies in clinical medicine, laboratory science, and epidemiology compiled by Morris (1957) amply illustrates the same theme. The extent and relative importance of the different contributions must vary with the nature of the disease under scrutiny and the

available resources; the principle of scientific interdependence remains.

In the field of abnormal psychology, exactly the same considerations apply. The epidemiologist seeks to establish associations between any given behavioural abnormality and the strength of certain environmental factors; the psychophysiological mechanisms that mediate the particular form of behaviour can be uncovered only by means of experimental investigation.

It need hardly be emphasised that, in the long run, experimental workers are just as dependent on survey techniques as are epidemiologists on laboratory findings. The history of psychiatric research is littered with the debris of exploded theories and abandoned projects; not a little of this wastage can be attributed to the neglect of simple epidemiological principles by workers who in their own fields of competence have maintained high standards.

In this context, the commonest weaknesses have stemmed from reliance on unrepresentative samples and the failure to use appropriate controls. Recent research on schizophrenia provides a number of telling examples. Thus, Lidz and his colleagues (Lidz *et al.*, 1965) developed their hypothesis of the 'double bind' in parent-child interaction from intensive study of the families of a small group of schizophrenic patients undergoing long-term private treatment. Of this research, Brown (1967) has justly remarked that:

'the generally confident tone of published work may distract the reader from recognising the lack of any evidence for the association of schizophrenia with this kind of communication, let alone any role in aetiology. The group have not published information on the frequency of double-binds in different kinds of family. The risk of overlooking such deficiencies seems greatest when, as in this case, the basic ideas are original and have obvious relevance outside the study of schizophrenia.'

Some investigators have been understandably reluctant to submit their hypotheses to the test because of the practical problems of method that would be entailed. Bowlby (1962), in discussing the aetiological significance of early maternal deprivation, has stated the dilemma with his customary frankness:

'As regards research strategies, the investigator has a choice .... An obvious possibility is to examine a sample of older children and adults who had the experience in their early years with a view to discovering whether or not they differ from a comparable sample who did not have the experience ... this strategy has many practical difficulties. The principal ones are locating a suitable sample, selecting and examining appropriate controls, and finding reliable instruments to measure the features of personality that are expected to show differences. An alternative approach is to study the child's responses at the time of and in the period immediately subsequent to the experience. After spending several not very productive years following the first strategy, my research group has concentrated during most of the past decade on the second. This has been much more rewarding.'

Although one can readily sympathise with this statement, it has to be said that the two strategies here outlined are complementary, not alternative, and that no findings based solely on the second can be accepted as proof of the hypothesis in question. If psycho-analytically-orientated research has, on the whole, been notoriously deficient in methodology, the same criticism can hardly be levelled at biochemical investigations. Yet the early, enthusiastic reports on the 'pink spot' in schizophrenia were also based on highly unrepresentative case-material, and have proved misleading in consequence. Thus, one series of experiments (Bourdillon et al., 1965) purported to show that the pink spot on urinary chromatography was characteristic of patients with first-rank symptoms of schizophrenia and seldom found either in conjunction with other forms of mental disorder or among mentally normal persons. In these studies, however, the index patients had been drawn from the patient population of three mental hospitals, many being chronic inmates. The principal control groups, in contrast, comprised: (a) 265 healthy individuals, mainly university staff and undergraduates; (b) 126 mentally normal hospital in-patients with a variety of physical disorders. Subsequent reports by a number of other workers indicated that the pink spot was found in only a minority of schizophrenics and was, in fact, commoner in patients with Parkinson's disease (Lancet, 1966). More recent work suggests that this phenomenon is related more to dietary factors than to the biochemistry of schizophrenia (Perry et al., 1967). In a field where laboratory investigation is so highly skilled and expensive, attention to survey techniques could have effected a considerable saving of resources.

The positive achievements of epidemiological research have been most impressive where a single, readily defined causal agent is operative. Thus, the spread of drug abuse, and hence of addiction, in a community can be treated, for practical purposes, exactly like that of a contagious disease. By means of this approach, de Alarcon (1969) was able to trace the growth of heroin dependence among the population of a New Town from the point at which four individuals were initiated into its use while living outside the area. The spread by 'contagion' is strikingly illustrated in Fig. 2.3.

Where the causal agent is not communicable, the pattern of incidence will be entirely different, a fact that can provide valuable clues to the epidemiologist. When Moss and McEvedy (1966) investigated an acute epidemic in a Blackburn girls' school, they found that all the evidence pointed to a psychological rather than an infectious causation. No infectious agent was identified, and all laboratory investigations were negative. The condition had developed first among the older girls and spread to those in the younger age-groups, who appeared to be less severely affected. The outbreak followed soon after an epidemic of poliomyelitis, which had received a great deal of publicity, and immediately after a school church-parade during which some children had fainted. In its mode of onset and of spread, this condition was readily distinguishable from an acute bacterial or viral infection (McEvedy et al., 1966).

More recently, a retrospective investigation of the epidemic of 'benign myalgic encephalomyelitis' which closed the Royal Free Hospital some years ago has raised the suspicion that this perplexing episode may also have been attributable to 'epidemic hysteria' (McEvedy and Beard, 1970). Here, although the evidence was far from conclusive, the investigators were impressed by the fact that the outbreak had been confined to the nursing staff, and almost entirely to females.

Half a century earlier, Joseph Goldberger had been led by similar reasoning to the conclusion that pellagra was not an infectious disease. In 1914, when Goldberger was assigned to take charge of the US Public Health Services studies of pellagra, the Surgeon General described it as '... one of the knottiest and most urgent problems facing the service at the present time' (Parsons, 1943). At that time, the aetiology of pellagra was obscure, although it was widely supposed to be '... in all probability a specific infectious disease communicable from person to person by means at present unknown' (Siler et al., 1917). A widespread cause of disability with a mortality of up to 40 per cent, pellagra included among its manifestations an organic psychosis in a small proportion of cases and a chronic neurasthenic syndrome in a high proportion.

At the very outset of his enquiries, Goldberger decided that the pattern of incidence of pellagra in hospitals and institutions ruled out the possibility of a contagious infection since, although many inmates developed the disease years after their admission, the nursing staff appeared to be exempt. Believing the explanation to reside in the different diets of the

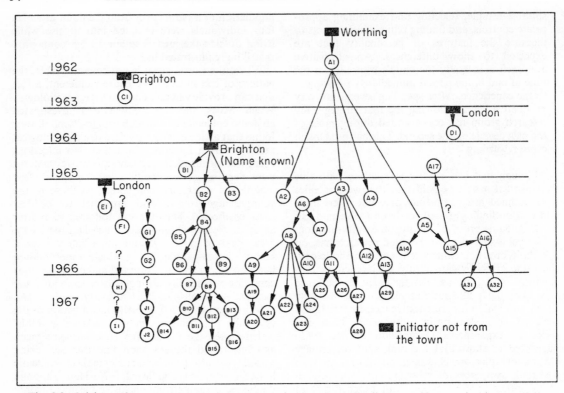

Fig. 2.3. Origins and pattern of transmission of heroin abuse in an English town (*Source:* de Alarcon, 1969 by permission of the Editor of the *Bulletin of Narcotics.*)

two groups, Goldberger at this stage already felt confident in urging '. . . the reduction in cereals, vegetables, and canned foods that enter to so large an extent into the dietary of many of the people in the South and an increase in the fresh animal food component, such as fresh meats, eggs, and milk' (Goldberger, 1914).

The story of how, over the ensuing years, Goldberger confirmed his hypothesis by means of a remarkably thorough series of field surveys and experiments has become one of the classics of epidemiology. Having established that the cause lay in a dietary deficiency. Goldberger and his co-workers set out to explore the whole causal chain, including not only the nature of the specific deficiency but also the social and economic nexus of the faulty diet. By the time of his death in 1929, he had reached the conclusion that the pellagra-preventive factor was to be found in the heat-resistant fraction of the 'water-soluble B' vitamin. Eight years later, this substance was identified as nicotinic acid; subsequent laboratory work demonstrated how the amino-acid tryptophan, derived from fresh animal protein foods, is converted into nicotinic acid in man. Thus, the causal chain was completed and the way open to eradication of a major scourge (Terris, 1964).

Of recent years, epidemiologists in common with other medical research workers have become increasingly preoccupied with problems of multi-factorial causation. This trend has not been in any way peculiar to psychiatry; it has been shown, for example, that the incidence of coronary heart disease is related to diet, exercise, body weight, smoking habits, blood pressure, and serum cholesterol level (Morris, 1957; Dawber *et al.*, 1962), while psychological stress and personality factors have also been implicated (Mai, 1968). No single necessary and sufficient cause has been identified, but the co-existence of two or more of the established risk factors undoubtedly increases the probability of coronary disease in the individual patient. Under these circumstances, it seems realistic to speak of 'multiple causation' or of '. . . a pattern or complex of causes . . . very likely of differing importance and directness, adding together, possibly compounding each other' (Morris, 1957).

In so far as the incidence of any given disorder may be related to biological, socio-economic, cultural or individual psychological factors, each with its own problems of measurement, their total evaluation can present formidable difficulties for the research worker. It is hardly remarkable, therefore, that since Goldberger's day individual studies have made only piecemeal contributions to aetiology. Most of the published work falls readily enough into one or other of three principal categories: (1) studies of social concomitants, (2) studies of precipitating factors and (3) studies of predisposing factors.

1. SOCIAL CONCOMITANTS

The search for demographic and social correlates constitutes, in one sense, the lowest level of aetiological research; it is, indeed, simply an extension of the use of official statistics for public health planning. This comment in no way detracts from the achievement of such pioneers as Lewis (1929), Ödegaard (1932), and Faris and Dunham (1939), whose work has done so much to extend the range of psychiatric research. In the long run, nevertheless, surveys focused on variables as crude as 'social class', 'social isolation', and 'mobility' have added disappointingly little to our knowledge of the genesis of psychological abnormality and it has become increasingly apparent that more refined concepts and techniques will be required. Aside from the obvious need for more accurate and sensitive measuring instruments, the search for ecological correlates must give way to direct study of the association between clinical and social variables. Furthermore, the nature of *temporal* relationships will have to be more carefully defined. This latter point has been taken most seriously in research into the 'proximal precipitants' of mental disorder (Reid, 1961).

2. PRECIPITATING FACTORS

Remarkably little scientific research has been undertaken in this field, in part because of the conflicting preconceptions on 'reactivity' held by different schools of clinical psychiatrists. Many British and American workers, largely as a result of the influence of Adolf Meyer, have preferred to speak of 'reaction-types' rather than diseases in psychiatry. Continental writers, on the other hand, have tended to reserve the term 'reactive' for certain circumscribed groups of disorder which in their view can be distinguished on clinical grounds; thus, 'schizophreniform reactions' can be differentiated from true, or 'process', schizophrenia (Langfeldt, 1937). In their definitions of reactivity, the advocates of this school of thought exact high standards: Jaspers (1923), for example, proposed that there should be a clearly adequate

precipitating factor closely proximate in time to the onset of illness; that the content of the illness should be manifestly related to this factor, and that recovery should follow on its removal. The range of psychiatric disorders that would satisfy all three requirements is very small indeed.

From the epidemiological standpoint, only one criterion need be established: a significant association between the onset of illness in a population and the occurrence of clearly defined environmental change (Cooper and Shepherd, 1970). In these terms, there is precious little evidence to justify limitation of the term 'reactive' to any specific diagnostic labels.

Broadly speaking, the epidemiological evidence on reactivity has been derived from two main types of investigation: (a) studies of populations or large groups exposed to acute stress-situations; (b) controlled studies of events antecedent to the onset of psychiatric disorder. A third source, that of experimental studies, has yielded some indirect evidence but is of minor importance.

(a) Studies of Acute Stress-situations

In modern times, the most dramatic illustrations have come from military sources. The experience of the First World War led to official recognition of the importance of psychiatric casualties in the armed forces; as a result, British psychiatrists played a much more prominent part in the second conflict (Ahrenfeldt, 1958). They were not slow to grasp the effect of battle conditions on the psychiatric rates—

'The numbers correlate indirectly with the surgical casualties—following about three days behind the curve of daily incidence. But it is not a parallel curve; as the surgical casualties rise, the psychiatric casualties rise out of all proportion. Depending on the type of battle, 2% to 30% of all casualties may be psychiatric.' (Main, 1946)

In the US Army, careful and systematic recording likewise revealed a close correlation between the psychiatric and the surgical casualty rates (Glass and Bernucci, 1966).

Under peace-time conditions, the effects on exposed populations have been documented for a variety of forms of social change, including migration, displacement, social mobility, economic cycles and, most notably, rapid processes of acculturation (Murphy, 1961). The methodological difficulties in this field are considerable, and none of these studies can be regarded as in any sense definitive. More compelling evidence has come from research on those types of life-change which include a major biological component: of these the paradigm is childbearing (Thomas and Gordon, 1959).

Table 2.6. Observed and Expected Numbers* of First Admissions to Mental Hospitals among the Married Child-bearing Population (Massachusetts, 1950) according to Stage of Childbearing and Category of Psychiatric Diagnosis

Stage of child-bearing	Month	Number observed	Number expected	Chi-square value†	p Value
Psychoses:					
Pregnancy	0–2	1	6·3	2·89	0·10–0·05
	3–5	1	6·3	2·89	0·10–0·05
	6–8	—	6·3	4·42	0·05–0·02
After delivery	0–2	30	6·4	85·99	0·001
	3–5	10	6·4	1·55	0·30–0·20
	6–8	10	6·4	1·55	0·30–0·20
Other Diagnoses:					
Pregnancy	0–2	2	4·1	0·49	0·50–0·30
	3–5	—	4·1	2·90	0·10–0·05
	6–8	1	4·1	1·44	0·30–0·20
After delivery	0–2	9	4·2	4·43	0·05–0·02
	3–5	6	4·2	0·41	0·70–0·50
	6–8	6	4·2	0·41	0·70–0·50

* Observed and expected in 40 per cent sample of admissions.
† All values for chi-square based on Yates correction for small expected numbers.
Source: Pugh *et al.* (1963).

In a survey of Massachusetts (Pugh *et al.*, 1963), data on mental hospital first admissions during 1950 were related to estimates of the general population of women of 15 to 45 years, according to defined childbearing status during that year. Comparison of the observed and expected numbers of first admissions revealed a large excess for psychosis, and a smaller excess for non-psychotic disorders, during the three months post partum. Admission rates for both these categories remained high over the ensuing six months, although only significantly so for the psychotic group. The findings are summarised in Table 2.6.

Comparable findings have been reported from a more recent survey of Hamilton County, Ohio (Paffenbarger, 1964); here also investigation revealed a diminished frequency of mental disorder during pregnancy, followed by a dramatic increase in the post-partum months. The epidemiological evidence thus leaves little doubt that childbearing can serve to precipitate mental illness, at any rate among predisposed women (Seager, 1960).

(b) Studies of Antecedent Events

In clinical psychiatry, the traditional approach to problems of reactivity has been through the individual biography, or 'life-chart' (Meyer, 1951), in which major events in the patient's life are plotted against the occurrence of illness-episodes. The extension of this method to representative samples can provide a useful epidemiological tool where adequate records are available. Such conditions may obtain in industry (Hinkle and Wolff, 1957), in the armed services (Rahe *et al.*, 1967) and—potentially,

at least—in general medical practice under the National Health Service (Kellner, 1963; Marinker, 1969). The consensus of findings from such sources has been that illnesses are not randomly distributed over the life-span but occurs in clusters, often of two or three years' duration. Such clusters can be related to periods of environmental change and individual difficulties of adaptation. Rahe and his co-workers have attempted to quantify life-change according to prevailing cultural standards, and have reported a positive correlation between annual morbidity experience and the corresponding total of 'Life Change Units' (Rahe *et al.*, 1967).

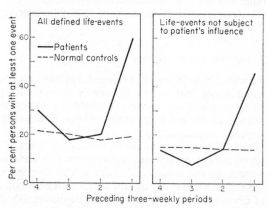

Fig. 2.4. Experience of life-events during four consecutive three-weekly periods

(*a*) Fifty patients immediately prior to onset of schizophrenic illness;
(*b*) 325 normal controls immediately prior to interview
(*Source:* derived from Brown and Birley, 1968)

A more precise technique for studying the relationship between environmental change and the acute onset of mental illness has been developed by two British workers (Brown and Birley, 1968). By means of a careful check of all events and changes that had occurred over a three-month period, they were able to compare the recent life-experience of a sample of patients admitted to hospital for acute schizophrenia with that of a large group of normal controls. The findings, which are illustrated by Fig. 2.4, showed that the index group had experienced a sharp increase in the number of life-events, including those of a fortuitous nature, in the three-week period prior to the onset of acute symptoms.

Although research of this kind deliberately focuses on the immediate precursors of illness, it may incidentally point to the equal importance of predisposition. Indeed, no aetiological model in psychiatry can be regarded as complete unless it pays attention both to proximal and to distal causative factors.

3. PREDISPOSING FACTORS

The primary influences that bear on the individual's expectancy of psychiatric disorder are to be found in his genetic endowment, the nature of his biological environment *in utero* and during infancy, and the socio-cultural factors that determine his early learning experiences. Epidemiological surveys have supplied vital evidence in all these fields, of which the genetic is undoubtedly the most fully charted. Population genetic studies are reviewed in Chapter 16.

The role of prenatal and paranatal factors has been less well substantiated, despite the growth of an extensive literature on the subject (MacMahon and Sawa, 1961). Where neurological deficits are in evidence, the importance of such influences as metabolic disorders, maternal infections and immunological reactions has been firmly established. The grounds for incriminating such factors in functional psychiatric disorder are much weaker. Nevertheless, the theory advanced by Pasamanick and his co-workers of a 'continuum of reproductive casualty' has provided a stimulating challenge for the epidemiologist. Paranatal complications such as prematurity, birth injury, and hypoxia of the newborn are known to be associated with neonatal mortality, most commonly as a result of brain damage. It is a plausible hypothesis that, in Pasamanick's own words—

'there must remain a fraction so injured who do not die; depending upon the degree and location of trauma they go on to develop a series of disorders extending from cerebral palsy, epilepsy, and mental deficiency through all types of

behavioural and learning disabilities which are a result of lesser degrees of damage sufficient to disorganize behavioural development and lower thresholds to stress; and, further, these abnormalities of pregnancy are associated with certain life-experiences, usually socio-economically determined, with the consequence that they themselves and their resulting neuro-psychiatric disorders find greater aggregation in the lower strata of our society' (Pasamanick, 1961).

In a series of studies based on the records of Baltimore maternity hospitals, Pasamanick and his co-workers have established connections between, on the one hand, such complications of childbirth as toxaemia of pregnancy, delayed labour, haemorrhage in pregnancy or labour and foetal malpresentation; and, on the other hand, a range of conditions including cerebral palsy, epilepsy, mental retardation, and reading disability. A tentative connection has also been established between obstetric complications and subsequent behaviour disorders of childhood, although here the findings are more open to question.

Further investigations are urgently needed in this field; in particular prospective surveys in which factors such as socio-economic status can be adequately controlled. Meanwhile, the findings of cross-sectional surveys have yielded strong indirect evidence in support of Pasamanick's views. Thus, a survey undertaken on the Isle of Wight (Rutter and Graham, 1966) estimated independently the prevalence both of psychiatric and of neurological disorders among the child population, and revealed a strong positive association between them (Table 2.7).

Children too mentally handicapped for the school system were excluded from this sample. Even so, it can be seen that those children with some evidence of brain damage contributed disproportionately to the overall psychiatric prevalence. In particular, the rate for psychiatric disorder in this group was three times that for the children with other kinds of physical handicap: statistically a highly significant difference.

This latter finding indicates that some at least of the psychiatric disturbance found in the neuro-epileptic group of children was a direct consequence of cerebral dysfunction, rather than a secondary effect of the psycho-social stress of ill-health and disability. Although a cross-sectional survey of this type cannot point to causal relationships, the results in this instance conform well to Pasamanick's views on the role of reproductive damage in childhood behaviour disorders.

Evidence for the importance of early psycho-social factors in predisposing to psychiatric disorder remains disappointingly fragmentary and conflicting.

Table 2.7.   Prevalence of Psychiatric Disorder in Neuro-epileptic Children aged 5–14 years attending School

	With psychiatric disorder		Total
	No.	%	
General population (10- and 11-year-old children)	144	6·6	2,189
Physical disorders not involving brain	16	11·5	139
Blind only	1	16·6	6
Deaf only	2	15·4	13
Lesion at or below brain stem	2	13·3	15
Miscellaneous other physical disorders*	11	10·3	107
Brain disorder	34	34·3	99
Uncomplicated epilepsy	18	28·6	63
Lesion above brain stem (but no fits)	9	37·5	24
Lesion above brain stem (with fits)	7	58·3	12

* This group includes 2 children who also have lesions below the brain stem.
Source: Graham and Rutter (1968).

The original, excessive claims for the maternal deprivation hypothesis were subjected to a heavy barrage of criticism (Wootton, 1959; O'Connor and Franks, 1961) and its theoretical basis has never been entirely restored. Nevertheless, cohort studies have repeatedly shown that the incidence of juvenile delinquency is related to the quality of maternal care and of the home environment in childhood (Glueck and Glueck, 1950; McCord and McCord, 1959) and these findings have been related to the psychology of character development (Peck and Havighurst, 1960). Findings of this kind have encouraged research workers to construct predictive indices that can be applied in the early years of childhood (Glueck and Glueck, 1959), but their value remains in some doubt.

More recently, a number of surveys have reported positive associations between the loss of one or both parents during childhood and the risk of adult mental illness, especially depressive states (Dennehy, 1966; Hill and Price, 1967). Furthermore, there is good evidence that psychiatric patients who have suffered parental loss during childhood carry a higher risk for suicidal attempts than others without such a history (Bruhn, 1962; Greer, 1964).

In view of the formidable problems of method in this field, none of the findings so far published can be regarded as conclusive. Apart from the usual difficulties of demographic matching, the investigator has to take into account such related variables as birth order and parental age at the time of birth (Granville-Grossman, 1968). Reliance on the official vital statistics may be misleading, since the expectancy of orphanhood has changed over the years and differs from place to place (Gregory, 1965; Dennehy, 1966). Almost all the reported findings have been derived from retrospectively collected data, with all the attendant faults of this technique. In very few can the index samples be taken as representative of their parent populations. Finally, patients who commit suicide differ in certain important respects from those who unsuccessfully attempt suicide (Stengel and Cook, 1958).

Against this background, the survey of male American university students by Paffenbarger and Asnes (1966) has unusual advantages, in that the investigators acquired access to medical and psychological data, previously collected, on a group of individuals who had since committed suicide. By selecting an appropriate control group, they were thus able to evaluate a number of possible predisposing factors. At the University of Pennsylvania, the college case-records over a ten-year period (1931–40) consistently provided responses to a questionnaire enquiry on nervous symptoms and personality traits. The responses to this enquiry of the 50 students who had later committed suicide were compared with those of 100 controls, 2 students from the same intake year being randomly selected to match each index case. The results are shown in Table 2.8.

Information of this kind clearly comes into the predictive category already discussed in relation to clinical prognosis. In addition, however, there are implications for aetiology. When the numbers were increased by combining the University of Pennsylvania sample with a comparable Harvard sample, the index and control students were found to resemble each other in area of origin, size of community of residence, family wealth, number of siblings, and marital status, but to differ in some important family characteristics. Significantly more often, the index group had reported separation of the parents, death of the father or ill-health of the father at the time of their entrance to university. In contrast, death or ill-health of the mother did not distinguish between these two male groups. In short, this exceptionally well-matched, reliable study pointed to the importance of parental loss and a broken home in early life, largely independent of socio-economic status, in determining subsequent psychiatric illness and suicide.

Table 2.8. Comparison of Questionnaire Responses of Students who later Committed Suicide with those of a Random Control Group (University of Pennsylvania, 1931–04)

Item	Percentage of affirmative responses Suicides ($N = 50$)	Controls ($N = 100$)	P-value
Instruction: Place a tick mark after those conditions to which you are subject and a 0 after those which you never have.			
Sensation of heart beating	20	14	0·34
Nervousness	28	17	0·12
Insomnia (sleeplessness)	16	6	<0·05
Sense of exhaustion	16	12	0·49
Instruction: Put tick after affirmative replies, 0 for negative.			
Are you subject to worries	50	29	0·01
Are you particularly self-conscious	42	20	<0·01
Are you bothered by a feeling that people are watching or talking about you	20	8	0·03
Are you subject to moods	40	30	0·21
Are you subject to periods of alternating gloom and cheerfulness	46	31	0·07
Are you inclined to be secretive and seclusive	22	10	<0·05
'Anxiety-depression index'*	30	10	<0·01

* Affirmative responses to five or more of the above items.
Source: Paffenbarger and Asnes (1966)

CONCLUSION

This review gives some indication of the wide range of enquiry into the mass aspects of psychological abnormality which may be subsumed by the term 'epidemiology'. While this approach has already made a substantial contribution to our knowledge of the major mental disorders, its achievements so far have been limited both by deficiencies of method and by its relative isolation from other branches of psychiatric and psychological research. Future progress in this field will depend, therefore, in part upon the development and application of scientific survey techniques, but also upon the growth of co-ordinated research programmes in which epidemiological methods take their place alongside clinical and laboratory investigation,

These considerations provide a clear challenge to the behavioural sciences. In order to improve survey techniques, the measurement of psychological variables in the general population must be tackled with the same attention to problems of validity, reliability and discrimination as has hitherto characterised hospital and laboratory research: for such a task, the clinical psychologist is uniquely equipped by his training and experience. By the same token, collaboration in epidemiological research offers him the prospect of rich rewards in his own field, since it is only by the study of representative population samples that his test procedures can be adequately standardised and his clinical and experimental data properly evaluated. For these reasons it can be safely predicted that participation in community and survey research will become increasingly accepted as an essential part of the clinical psychologist's function.

REFERENCES

AHRENFELDT, R. H. (1958) *Psychiatry in the British Army in the Second World War*. London: Routledge and Kegan Paul.

ALARCON, R. de (1969) The spread of heroin abuse in a community. *W.H.O. Bulletin on Narcotics*, **29**, 17–22.

ALARCON, R. de and RATHOD, N. H. (1968) Prevalence and early detection of heroin abuse. *Brit. med. J.*, **2**, 549–553.

ASTRUP, C. (1957) Scandinavian literature on psychiatric genetics and epidemiology. *Acta psychiat. neurol. Scand.*, **32**, 399–424.

ASTRUP, C. and Ödegaard, Ö. (1960) The influence of hospital facilities and other local factors upon admission to psychiatric hospitals. *Acta psychiat. Scand.*, **35**, 289–301.

BABIGIAN, H. M., GARDNER, E. A., MILES, H. C., and

ROMANO, J. (1965) Diagnostic consistency and change in a follow-up study of 1,215 patients. *Amer. J. Psychiat.*, **121**, 895–901.

BAHN, A. K., GARDNER, E. A., ALLTOP, L., KNALTERUD, G. K., and SOLOMON, M. (1966) Admission and prevalence rates for psychiatric facilities in four Register areas. *Amer. J. pub. Hlth.*, **56**, 2,033–2,051.

BALDWIN, J. A., INNES, G., MILLAR, W. M., SHARP, G. A., and DORICOTT, N. (1965) A psychiatric case-register in N.E. Scotland. *Brit. J. prev. soc. Med.*, **19**, 38–42.

BANNISTER, D. (1968) The logical requirements of research into schizophrenia. *Brit. J. Psychiat.*, **114**, 181–188.

BELKNAP, I. (1956) *Human Problems of a State Mental Hospital.* New York: McGraw-Hill.

BICKFORD, J. A. R. and ELLISON, R. M. (1953) The high incidence of Huntington's chorea in the Duchy of Cornwall. *J. ment. Sci.*, **99**, 291–294.

BLUM, R. H. (1962) Case identification in psychiatric epidemiology: methods and problems. *Milbank Mem. Fund Quart.*, **40**, 253–288.

BOURDILLON, R. E., CLARKE, C. A., RIDGES, A. P., SHEPPARD, P. M., HARPER, P., and LESLIE, S. A. (1965) 'Pink spot' in the urine of schizophrenics. *Nature* (Lond.), **208**, 453–455.

BOWLBY, J. (1962) Childhood bereavement and psychiatric illness. In *Aspects of Psychiatric Research* (Ed. Richter, D., Tanner, J. M., Taylor, Lord, and Zangwill, O.L.) London: Oxford Univ. Press, p. 264.

BRANSBY, E. R. (1969) Personal communication. London: Statistics Division, Dept. of Health and Social Security.

BREMER, J. (1951) Social psychiatric investigation of a small community in Northern Norway. *Acta psychiat. neurol. Scand.*, Suppl. 62.

BROOKE, E. M. (1967) A census of patients in psychiatric beds, 1963. *Min. of Health Reports on Public Health and Medical Subjects*, No. 116. London: H.M.S.O.

BROWN, A. C. (1965) *The general morbidity of neurotic patients.* Cambridge University M.D. thesis. Unpublished.

BROWN, G. W. (1959) Experience of discharged chronic schizophrenic patients in various types of living group. *Milbank Mem. Fund Quart.*, **37**, 105–131.

BROWN, G. W. (1960) Length of hospital stay and schizophrenia: a review of statistical studies. *Acta psychiat. neurol. Scand.*, **35**, 414–430.

BROWN, G. W. (1967) The Family of the Schizophrenic Patient. In *Recent Developments in Schizophrenia: a symposium* (Ed. Coppen, A. & Walk, A.). Ashford, Kent: Headley Bros. for RMPA.

BROWN, G. W. and BIRLEY, J. L. T. (1968) Crises and life changes and the onset of schizophrenia. *J. Hlth. soc. Behav.*, **9**, 203–214.

BROWN, G. W., CARSTAIRS, G. M., and TOPPING, G. (1958) Post-hospital adjustment of chronic mental patients. *Lancet*, **ii**, 685–689.

BROWN, G. W., MONCK, E. M., CARSTAIRS, G. M., and WING, J. K. (1962) Influence of family life on the course of schizophrenic illness. *Brit. J. prev. soc. Med.*, **16**, 55–68.

BROWN, G. W., PARKES, C. M., and WING, J. K. (1961) Admissions and re-admissions to three London mental hospitals. *J. ment. Sci.*, **107**, 1,070–1,077.

BROWN, G. W. and RUTTER, M. (1966) The measurement of family activities and relationships: a methodological study. *Human Relations*, **19**, 241–263.

BROWN, R. W. (1954) Mass Phenomena (Ch. 23). In *Handbook of Social Psychology* (Ed. Lindzey, G.) vol. II. Reading, Mass.: Addison-Wesley.

BRUHN, J. G. (1962) Broken homes among attempted suicides and psychiatric out-patients: a comparative study. *J. ment. Sci.*, **108**, 772–779.

BURT, C. (1950) *The Backward Child* (3rd ed.). The Sub-normal Child, vol. II. London: University of London Press.

BURT, C. (1955) *The Subnormal Mind* (3rd ed.). London: O.U.P. Quotation taken from p. 5.

CAUDILL, W. (1958) *The Psychiatric Hospital as a Small Society.* Boston: Harvard University Press.

CHEYNE, G. (1733) *The English Malady: or, a treatise of nervous diseases of all kinds, as spleen, vapours, lowness of spirits, hypochondriacal and hysterical distempers, etc.* London: G. Strahan.

CLARK, R. E. (1949) Psychosis, income and occupational prestige. *Amer. J. Sociol.*, **54**, 433–440.

CLAUSEN, J. A. (1959) The Sociology of Mental Illness. In *Sociology Today: problems and prospects* (Ed. Merton, R. K., Broom, L. and Cottrell, L. S.). New York: Basic Books.

CLAUSEN, J. A. and KOHN, M. L. (1959) Relation of schizophrenia to the social structure of a small city. In *Epidemiology of Mental Disorder* (Ed. Pasamanick, B.). Washington D.C.: American Association for the Advancement of Science, Publication No. 60.

COHEN, H. (1955) The evolution of the concept of disease. *Proc. Roy. Soc. Med.*, **48**, 155–160.

COOPER, B. (1964) General practitioners' attitudes to psychiatry. *De Medicina Tuenda* **1**, 43–48.

COOPER, B. (1966). Psychiatric disorder in hospital and general practice. *Soc. Psychiat.*, **1**, 7–10.

COOPER, B., EASTWOOD, M. R., and SYLPH, J. (1970) Psychiatric morbidity and social adjustment in a general practice population. In *Psychiatric Epidemiology* (Ed. Hare, E. H. and Wing, J. K.). London: Oxford University Press for Nuffield Provincial Hospitals Trust.

COOPER, B., FRY, J., and KALTON, G. (1969a) A longitudinal study of psychiatric morbidity in a general practice population. *Brit. J. prev. soc. Med.*, **23**, 210–217.

COOPER, B. and SHEPHERD, M. (1970) Life change, stress and mental disorder: the ecological approach. In *Modern Trends in Psychological Medicine* (Ed. Price, J. H.). London: Butterworth.

COOPER, J. E., KENDELL, R. E., GURLAND, B. J., SARTORIUS, N., and FARKAS, T. (1969b) Cross-national study of diagnosis of the mental disorders: some results from the first comparative investigation. *Amer. J. Psychiat.*, **125**: April 1969 supplement.

DAWBER, T. R., KANNEL, W. B., REVOTSKIE, M., and KAGAN, A. (1962) The epidemiology of coronary heart disease—the Framingham enquiry. *Proc. Roy. Soc. Med.*, **55**, 265–270.

DENNEHY, C. M. (1966) Childhood bereavement and psychiatric illness. *Brit. J. Psychiat.*, **112**, 1,049–1,069.

DOHRENWEND, B. P. and DOHRENWEND, B. S. (1969) *Social Status and Psychological Disorder: A Causal Inquiry.* New York: Wiley.

DOLL, R. and HILL, A. B. (1956) Lung cancer and other causes of death in relation to smoking. *Brit. med. J.*, **2**, 1,071–1,081.

DOUGLAS, J. W. B. and BLOMFIELD, J. M. (1958) *Children under Five: the results of a national survey.* London: Allen and Unwin.

DUBLIN, L. I. (1963) *Suicide.* New York: Ronald Press.

DURKHEIM, E. (1897) *Suicide: a study in sociology.* Transl. Spaulding, J. A. and Simpson, G. Glencoe, Illinois: Free Press (1951).

EASTWOOD, M. R. (1969) *The physical status of psychiatric patients in general practice.* University of Edinburgh M.D. thesis. Unpublished.

EDWARDS, F. (Ed.) (1956) *Readings in Market Research.* London: British Market Research Bureau.

EDWARDS, G., WILLIAMSON, V., HAWKER, A., HENSMAN, C., and POSTOYAN, S. (1968) Census of a reception centre. *Brit. J. Psychiat.*, **114**, 1,031–1,039.

ESSEN-MÖLLER, E. (1956) Individual traits and morbidity in a Swedish rural population. *Acta psychiat. Scand.*, Suppl. 100.

ESSEN-MÖLLER, E. (1961) Discussion to Technical aspects of procedures in field observation. In *Field Studies in the Mental Disorders* (Ed. Zubin, J.). New York: Grune and Stratton.

EYSENCK, H. J. (1952) *The Scientific Study of Personality.* London: Routledge and Kegan Paul.

EYSENCK, H. J. (1954) *The Psychology of Politics.* London: Routledge and Kegan Paul.

EYSENCK, H. J. (1957) *The Dynamics of Anxiety and Hysteria.* London: Routledge and Kegan Paul.

EYSENCK, H. J., TARRANT, M., WOOLF, M. and ENGLAND, L. (1960) Smoking and personality. *Brit. med. J.*, **1**, 1,456–1,460.

FARIS, R. E. L. and DUNHAM, H. W. (1939) *Mental Disorders in Urban Areas: an ecological study of schizophrenia and other psychoses.* Chicago: University of Chicago Press.

FLETCHER, C. M. and OLDHAM, P. D. (1959a) Diagnosis in group research, in *Medical Surveys and Clinical Trials* (Ed. Witts, L. J.). London: Oxford University Press.

FLETCHER, C. M. and OLDHAM, P. D. (1959b) Prevalence surveys. In *Medical Surveys and Clinical Trials* (Ed. Witts, L. J.). London: Oxford University Press.

FOULDS, G. A. (1965) Personality and Personal Illness. London: Tavistock Press.

FRASER, T. R. C. (1947) The incidence of neurosis among factory workers. *M.R.C. Industrial Health Research Board*, Report No. 90. London: H.M.S.O.

FREMMING, K. H. (1951) *The Expectation of Mental Infirmity in a Sample of the Danish Population.* Occasional Papers on Eugenics, No. 7. London: Cassell.

GARDNER, E. (1967) Psychological care for the poor: the need for new service patterns with a proposal for meeting this need. In *Emergent Approaches to Mental Health Problems* (Ed. Cowen, E., Gardner, E. & Zax, M.). New York: Appleton-Century-Crofts.

GERARD, D. L. and HOUSTON, L. G. (1953) Family setting and the social ecology of schizophrenia. *Psychiat. Quart.*, **27**, 90–101.

GIBBS, J. and MARTIN, W. (1964) *Status Integration and Suicide.* Seattle: University of Oregan Press.

GLASS, A. J. and BERNUCCI, R. J. (Ed.) (1966) *Neuropsychiatry in World War II.* Office of the Surgeon General, Dept. of the Army, Washington D.C., p. 402.

GLIDEWELL, J. C., GILDEA, M. C. L., DOMKE, H. R., and KANTOR, M. B. (1959) Behavior symptoms in children and adjustment in public school. *Human Organization*, **17**, 123–130.

GLUECK, S. and GLUECK, E. T. (1950) *Unravelling Juvenile Delinquency.* New York: Commonwealth Fund.

GLUECK, S. and GLUECK, E. T. (1959) *Predicting Delinquency and Crime.* Cambridge, Mass.: Harvard University Press.

GOFFMAN, E. (1961) *Asylums.* New York: Anchor Books, Doubleday.

GOLDBERG, D. P. (1969) *The identification and assessment of non-psychotic psychiatric illness by means of a questionnaire.* University of Oxford D.M. thesis. Unpublished.

GOLDBERG, D. P., COOPER, B., EASTWOOD, M. R., KEDWARD, H. B., and SHEPHERD, M. (1970) A standardized psychiatric interview for use in community surveys. *Brit. J. prev. soc. Med.*, **24**, 18–23.

GOLDBERGER, J. (1914) The etiology of pellagra. The significance of certain epidemiological observations with respect thereto. *Publ. Hlth. Rep.* (Wash.) **29**, 1,683–1,686. Reprinted in *Goldberger on Pellagra* (Ed. Terris, M.). Baton Rouge: Louisiana State University Press (1964).

GORE, C. P., JONES, K., TAYLOR, W., and WARD, B. (1964) Needs and Beds: a regional census of psychiatric hospital patients. *Lancet*, **ii**, 457–60.

GRAHAM, P. and RUTTER, M. (1968) Organic brain dysfunction and child psychiatric disorder. *Brit. med. J.*, **3**, 695–700.

GRANVILLE-GROSSMAN, K. L. (1968) The early environment in affective disorder. In *Recent Developments in Affective Disorders: a symposium* (Ed. Coppen, A. and Walk, A.) Ashford, Kent: Headley Bros. for RMPA.

GREER, H. S. and CAWLEY, R. H. (1966) *Some observations on the natural history of neurotic illness.* Australian Medical Association. Mervyn Archdall Medical Monograph No. 3. Glebe, New South Wales: Australasian Medical Publishing Co.

GREER, S. (1964) The relationship between parental loss and attempted suicide: a control study. *Brit. J. Psychiat.*, **110**, 698–705.

GREGORY, I. (1965) Retrospective estimates of orphanhood from generation life tables. *Milbank Mem. Fund Quart.*, **43**, 323–348.

GRIESINGER, W. (1867) *Mental Pathology and Therapeutics.* Transl. Robertson, C. L. and Rutherford, J. London: The New Sydenham Society, p. 127–130.

GRUENBERG, E. M. (1957) Socially shared psychopathology. In *Explorations in Social Psychiatry* (Ed. Leighton, A. H., Clausen, J. A., and Wilson, R. N.). London: Tavistock Press.

GRUENBERG, E. M. (1964) Epidemiology. In *Mental Retardation: a review of research* (Ed. Stevens, H. A. and Heber, R.). Chicago and London: University of Chicago Press.

GURIN, G., VERHOFF, J., and FELD, S. (1960) *Americans view their Mental Health*. Joint Commission on Mental Illness and Health, Monograph No. 4. New York: Basic Books.

HAGNELL, O. (1966) *A Prospective Study of the Incidence of Mental Disorder*. Stockholm: Svenska Bokförlaget, Norstedts-Bonniers.

HARE, E. H. (1952) The ecology of mental disease. *J. ment. Sci.*, **98**, 579–594.

HARE, E. H. (1956a) Mental illness and social conditions in Bristol. *J. ment. Sci.*, **102**, 349–357.

HARE, E. H. (1956b) Family setting and the urban distribution of schizophrenia. *J. ment. Sci.*, **102**, 753–760.

HARE, E. H. (1962) The distribution of mental illness in the community. In *Aspects of Psychiatric Research* (Ed. Richter, D., Tanner, J. M., Taylor, Lord and Zangwill, O. L.). London: Oxford University Press.

HARE, E. H. (1968) *Triennial Statistical Report, 1964–66*. London: The Bethlem Royal Hospital and the Maudsley Hospital.

HARE, E. H. and SHAW, G. (1965) *Mental Health in a New Housing Estate*. Maudsley Monograph No. 12. London: Oxford University Press.

HARVEY-SMITH, E. A. and COOPER, B. (1970) Patterns of neurotic illness in the community. *J. Roy. Coll. gen. Practit.*, **19**, 132–139.

HEMSI, L. K. (1967) Psychiatric morbidity of West Indian immigrants. *Soc. Psychiat.*, **2**, 95–100.

HENDERSON, A. S., McCULLOCH, J. W., and PHILIP, A. E. (1967) Survey of mental illness in adolescence. *Brit. med. J.*, **1**, 83–84.

HEWITT, L. E. and JENKINS, R. L. (1946) *The Fundamental Patterns of Maladjustment*. Springfield, Ill.: Michigan Child Guidance Institute.

HILL, O. and PRICE, J. (1967) Childhood bereavement and adult depression. *Brit. J. Psychiat.*, **113**, 743–751.

HINKLE, L. E. Jr. and WOLFF, H. G. (1957) Health and the social environment: experimental investigations. In *Explorations in Social Psychiatry* (Ed. Leighton, A. H., Clausen, J. A., and Wilson, R. N.). London: Tavistock Press.

HOENIG, J. and SRINIVASAN, U. (1959). Aspects of the mental health service—past and present. *J. All-India Inst. ment. Hlth.*, **2**, 13–25.

HOLMBOE, R. and ASTRUP, C. (1957) A follow-up study of 255 patients with acute schizophrenia and schizophreniform psychoses. *Acta psychiat. neurol. Scand.*, Suppl., **115**.

INGHAM, J. G. (1965) A method for observing symptoms and attitudes. *Brit. J. clin. Psychol.*, **4**, 131–140.

JASPERS, K. (1923) *General Psychopathology* (7th ed.) transl. Hoenig, J. and Hamilton, M. W. Manchester: Manchester Univ. Press, pp. 383–393.

KALTON, G. (1968) The contribution of research in general practice to the study of morbidity. *J. Roy. Coll. gen. Practit.*, **15**, 81–95.

KATZ, M. M. and LYERLY, S. B. (1963) Methods for measuring adjustment and behaviour in the community. *Psychol. Rep.*, **13**, 503–535.

KAY, D. W. K., BEAMISH, P., and ROTH, M. (1964) Old age mental disorders in Newcastle-upon-Tyne (I). *Brit. J. Psychiat.*, **110**, 146–158.

KAY, D. W. K. and ROTH, M. (1961) Environmental and hereditary factors in the schizophrenias of old age ('late paraphrenia') and their bearing on the general problem of causation in schizophrenia. *J. Ment. Sci.*, **107**, 649–686.

KELLNER, R. (1963) *Family Ill-health: an investigation in general practice*. London: Tavistock Press.

KESSEL, N. and McCULLOCH, J. W. (1966) Repeated acts of self-poisoning and self-injury. *Proc. Roy. Soc. Med.*, **59**, 89–92.

KESSEL, W. I. N. and SHEPHERD, M. (1962) Neurosis in hospital and general practice. *J. ment. Sci.*, **108**, 159–166.

KIDD, C. B. (1965) Psychiatric morbidity among students. *Brit. J. prev. soc. Med.*, **19**, 143–150.

KIDD, C. B. and MACKIE, R. E. (1967) The psychiatrist factor in case register data interpretation. *Soc. Psychiat.*, **2**, 168–173.

KISH, L. (1965) *Survey Sampling*. New York: J. Wiley.

KNOWLES, J. B. (1963) Rating methods and measurement of behaviour. In *Methods of Psychiatric Research: an introduction for clinical psychiatrists* (Ed. Sainsbury, P. and Kreitman, N.). London: Oxford University Press.

KOSVINER, A., MITCHESON, M. C., MYERS, K., OGBORNE, A., STIMSON, G. V., ZACUNE, J., and EDWARDS, G. (1968) Heroin use in a provincial town. *Lancet*, **i**, 189–1,192.

KRAEPELIN, E. (1909) *Psychiatrie: ein Lehrbuch für Studierende und Ärtze* 8th ed. Leipzig: Barth, Band I, pp. 152–159.

KRAEPELIN, E. (1913) *Psychiatrie: ein Lehrbuch für Studierende und Ärtze* 8th ed. Leipzig: Barth, Band III.

KRAUPL TAYLOR, F. (1966) *Psychopathology: its causes and symptoms*. London: Butterworth.

KREITMAN, N. (1961) The reliability of psychiatric diagnosis. *J. Ment. Sci.*, **107**, 876–886.

KUSHLICK, A. (1966) A community service for the mentally subnormal. *Soc. Psychiat.*, **1**, 73–82.

Lancet (1966) *The Pink Spot: a red herring?* Annotation in vol. ii, 848–849.

LANGFELDT, G. (1937) The prognosis in schizophrenia and the factors influencing the course of the disease. *Acta psychiat. neurol. Scand.*, Suppl. **13**.

LANGFELDT, G. (1959) The prognosis in schizophrenia, in *Report of the Second International Congress of Psychiatry* (Ed. Stoll, W. A.) Vol. I. p. 220. Zürich: Orell Füssli Arts.

LAPOUSE, R., MONK, M. A., and TERRIS, M. (1956) The drift hypothesis and socio-economic differentials in schizophrenia. *Amer. J. pub. Hlth.* **46**, 978–986.

LAPOUSE, R. and MONK, M. A. (1959) Fears and worries in a representative sample of children. *Amer. J. Orthopsychiat.*, **29**, 803–818.

LARSSON, T. and SJÖGREN, T. (1954) A methodological, psychiatric and statistical study of a large Swedish rural population. *Acta psychiat. neurol. Scand.* Suppl., **89**.

LEAVELL, H. R. and CLARK, E. G. (1953) *Textbook of Preventive Medicine*. New York: McGraw-Hill.

LEIGHTON, D. C., HARDING, J. S., MACKLIN, D. B., MacMILLAN, A. M., and LEIGHTON, A. H. (1963) *The Character of Danger*. New York: Basic Books.

LEMKAU, P. V. (1935) The epidemiological study of mental illnesses and mental health. *Amer. J. Psychiat.*, 111, 801–809.

LEONHARD, K. (1959) *Aufteilung der endogenen Psychosen*. Berlin: Akademie-Verlag.

LEWIS, A. J. (1959) The impact of psychotropic drugs on the structure, function and future of psychiatric services in hospitals. In *Neuro-psychopharmacology. Proc. First International Congress of Neuro-psychopharmacology*, Rome, 1958. (Ed. Bradley, P. B., Deniker, P. and Radouco-Thomas, C.) Amsterdam: Elsevier.

LEWIS, A. J. (1961) Discussion: problems of taxonomy and their application to nosology and nomenclature in the mental disorders. In *Field Studies in the Mental Disorders* (Ed. Zubin, J.), p. 34. New York and London: Grune and Stratton.

LEWIS, E. O. (1929) *Report on an investigation into the incidence of mental deficiency in six areas, 1925–7*. Report of the Mental Deficiency Committee of the Board of Education and Board of Control (the Wood Report), Part IV. London: H.M.S.O.

LIDZ, T., FLECK, S., and CORNELISON, A. R. (1965) *Schizophrenia and the Family*. Monograph series on Schizophrenia, No. 7. New York: International Universities Press.

LIN, T. (1953) A study of the incidence of mental disorder in Chinese and other cultures. *Psychiatry*, 16, 313–336.

LITTLE, J. C. and KERR, T. A. (1968) Some differences between published norms and data from matched controls as a basis for comparison with psychologically-disturbed groups. *Brit. J. Psychiat.*, 114, 883–890.

LITTLE, K. B. and SCHNEIDMAN, E. S. (1959) *Congruencies among interpretations of psychological test and anamnestic data*. Psychological Monographs, vol. LXXIII.

LOGAN, W. P. D. and BROOKE, E. M. (1956) *The Survey of Sickness, 1943 to 1952*. Studies on Medical and Population Subjects, No. 12. London: H.M.S.O.

LOTTER, V. (1967) Epidemiology of autistic conditions in young children. Pt. II, some characteristics of the parents and children. *Soc. Psychiat.*, 1, 163–173.

McCORD, W. and McCORD, J. (1959) *Origins of Crime*. New York: Columbia University Press.

McEVEDY, C. P. and BEARD, A. W. (1970) Royal Free epidemic of 1955: a reconsideration. *Brit. med. J.*, 1, 7–11.

McEVEDY, C. P., GRIFFITH, A., and HALL, T. (1966). Two school epidemics. *Brit. med. J.*, 2, 1,300–1,302.

MACKAY, D. (1951) *Hospital Morbidity Statistics*. General Register Office Studies on Medical and Population Subjects, No. 4. London: H.M.S.O.

MacMAHON, B. and SAWA, J. M. (1961) Physical damage to the fetus. (Conference on causes of mental disorders: a review of epidemiological knowledge, 1959). *Milbank Mem. Fund Quart.*, 39, 14–73.

MAI, F. M. M. (1968) Personality and stress in coronary disease. *J. psychosom. Res.*, 12, 275–287.

MAIN, T. F. (1946) Discussion: forward psychiatry in the Army. *Proc. Roy. soc. Med.*, 39, 137–142.

MALZBERG, B. (1940) *Social and Biological Aspects of Mental Disease*. Utica, New York: State Hospital Press.

MANNHEIM, H. and WILKINS, L. T. (1956) *Prediction Methods in Relation to Borstal Training*. London: H.M.S.O.

MARINKER, M. L. (1969) The general practitioner as family doctor. *J. Roy. Coll. gen. Practit.*, 17, 227–236.

MARKS, I. (1968) Measurement of personality and attitude: applications to clinical research. *Postgrad. med. J.*, 44, 277–285.

MECHANIC, D. (1962) Some factors in identifying and defining mental illness. *Ment. Hyg.*, 44, 66–74.

MECHANIC, D. (1970) *Problems and Prospects in Psychiatric Epidemiology*. In *Psychiatric Epidemiology* (Ed. Hare, E. H. and Wing, J. K.). London: Oxford Univ. Press for Nuffield Provincial Hospitals Trust.

MEEHL, P. E. and ROSEN, A. (1955) Antecedent probability and the efficiency of psychometric signs, patterns or cutting scores. *Psychol. Bull.*, 52, 194–216.

MEYER, A. (1951) *Collected Papers* (Ed. Winters, E. E.), Vol. III, pp. 52–56. Baltimore: Johns Hopkins Press.

Milbank Memorial Fund (1950) *Epidemiology of Mental Disorder*. New York.

MILES, H. C., GARDNER, E. A., BODIAN, C., and ROMANO, J. (1964) A cumulative survey of all psychiatric experience in Monroe County, New York: summary data for the first year (1960). *Psychiat. Quart.*, 38, 458–487.

Ministry of Health (1962) *A Hospital Plan for England and Wales*. Cmnd. 1604. London: H.M.S.O.

MORRIS, J. N. (1957) *Uses of Epidemiology*. Edinburgh: Livingstone.

MOSER, C. A. and KALTON, G. (1971) *Survey Methods in Social Investigation* (2nd edition). London: Heinemann.

MOSS, P. D. and McEVEDY, C. P. (1966) An epidemic of over-breathing among schoolgirls. *Brit. med. J.*, 2, 1,295–1,300.

MURPHY, H. B. M. (1959) *Culture, society and mental disorder in South East Asia*. Thesis, Edinburgh University, Scotland. Unpublished.

MURPHY, H. B. M. (1961) Social change and mental health. *Milbank Mem. Fund Quart.*, 39, 385–434.

New York State Dept. of Mental Hygiene (1959) A mental health survey of older people. *Psychiat. Quart. Supplement*, 45–99 and 252–300.

NORRIS, V. (1959) *Mental Illness in London*. Maudsley Monograph No. 6. London: Chapman and Hall.

NORTON, A. (1961) Correspondence. *Lancet* i, 608.

O'CONNOR, N. (1968) The origins of the Medical Research Council Social Psychiatry Unit. In *Studies in Psychiatry* (Ed. Shepherd, M. and Davies, D. L.). London: Oxford University Press.

O'CONNOR, N. and FRANKS, C. M. (1961) Childhood upbringing and other environmental factors. In *Handbook of Abnormal Psychology* 1st ed. (Ed. Eysenck, H. J.) London: Pitman Medical.

ÖDEGAARD, Ö. (1932) Emigration and insanity. *Acta psychiat. Scand.*, Suppl. 4.

ÖDEGAARD, Ö. (1945) The distribution of mental disease in Norway: a contribution to the ecology of mental disorder. *Acta psychiat. Scand.*, **20**, 247–284.

ÖDEGAARD, Ö. (1967) Changes in the prognosis of functional psychoses since the days of Kraepelin. *Brit. J. Psychiat.*, **113**, 813–822.

OPLER, M. K. (1956) *Culture, Psychiatry and Human Values.* Springfield, Ill.: Chas. C. Thomas.

PAFFENBARGER, R. (1964) Epidemiological aspects of post-partum mental illness. *Brit. J. prev. soc. Med.*, **18**, 189–195.

PAFFENBARGER, R. S. and ASNES, D. P. (1966) Chronic disease in former college students. III. Precursors of suicide in early and middle life. *Amer. J. pub. Hlth.*, **56**, 1,026–1,036.

PARSONS, R. P. (1943) *Trail of Light.* Indianapolis: Bobbs-Merrill.

PASAMANICK, B. (1961) Epidemiological investigations of some prenatal factors in the production of neuro-psychiatric disorder. In *Comparative Epidemiology of the Mental Disorders*, p. 260. (Ed. Hoch, P. H. and Zubin, J.). New York and London: Grune and Stratton.

PECK, P. F. and HAVIGHURST, R. J. (1960) *The Psychology of Character Development.* New York: Wiley.

PEMBERTON, J. and WILLARD, H. (Ed.) (1958) *Recent Studies in Epidemiology.* Oxford: Blackwell.

PENROSE, L. S. (1938) A clinical and genetic study of 1,280 cases of mental defect (Colchester Survey). *Sp. Rep. Med. Res. Coun.* No. 229. London: H.M.S.O.

PERRIS, C. (1966) A study of bipolar (manic-depressive) and unipolar recurrent depressive psychoses. *Acta psychiat. Scand.*, **42**, Suppl. 194.

PERRY, T. L., HANSEN, S., MacDOUGALL, L., and SCHWARZ, C. J. (1967) Studies of amines in normal and schizophrenic subjects. In *Amines and Schizophrenia* (Ed. Himwich, H. E., Kety, S. S., and Smythies, J. R.). London: Pergamon Press.

PINEL, P. (1806) *A Treatise on Insanity.* (Transl. Davis, D. D., 1962), p. 5. New York: Hafner

PLEYDELL, M. J. (1954) Huntington's chorea in Northamptonshire. *Brit. med. J.*, **2**, 121–1,128.

POLLOCK, H. M. (1925) *What happens to patients with mental disease during the first year of hospital life?* Albany: State Hospital Commission.

PUGH, T. F., JERATH, B. K., SCHMIDT, W. M., and REED, R. B. (1963) Rates of mental disease related to childbearing. *New England J. Med.*, **268**, 1,224–1,228.

RAHE, R. H., McKEAN, J. D. Jr., and RANSOM, J. A. (1967) A longitudinal study of life-change and illness patterns. *J. psychosom. Res.*, **10**, 355–366.

RAWNSLEY, K. (1965) Studies of social attitudes and values in relation to psychiatric epidemiology. *Postgrad. med. J.*, **41.**, 401–407.

RAWNSLEY, K. (1968a) Social Attitudes and Psychiatric Epidemiology. In *Studies in Psychiatry* (Ed. Shepherd, M. and Davies, D. L.). London: Oxford University Press.

RAWNSLEY, K. (1968b) Epidemiology of Affective Disorders. In *Recent Developments in Affective Disorders: a symposium* (Ed. Coppen, A. and Walk, A.). Ashford, Kent: Headley Bros. for RMPA.

REDLICH, F. C. (1957) The Concept of Health in Psychiatry. In *Explorations in Social Psychiatry* (Ed. Leighton, A. H., Clausen, J. A., and Wilson, R. N.), Chapter 5. London: Tavistock Press.

Registrar General (1954) *Measurement of Morbidity.* Report of the Statistics Sub-committee on Medical Nomenclature and Statistics. General Register Office Studies of Medical and Population Subjects, No. 8. London: H.M.S.O.

Registrar General (1968) *A Glossary of Mental Disorders.* General Register Office Studies on Medical and Population Subjects No. 22. London: H.M.S.O.

REHIN, G. F. and MARTIN, F. M. (1963) Psychiatric Services in 1975. *Planning Broadsheets* Vol. **29**, No. 468. London: P.E.P.

REID, D. D. (1960) *Epidemiological Methods in the Study of Mental Disorders.* Public Health Papers No. 2. Geneva: W.H.O.

REID, D. D. (1961) Precipitating proximal factors in the occurrence of mental disorders: epidemiological evidence. *Milbank Mem. Fund Quart.*, **39**, 229–248.

RENNIE, T. A. C. (1942) Prognosis in manic-depressive psychoses. *Amer. J. Psychiat.*, **98**, 801–814.

RIN, H. and LIN, T-Y. (1962) Mental illness among Formosan aborigines as compared with the Chinese in Taiwan. *J. ment. Sci.*, **108**, 134–146.

ROBINS, E., MURPHY, G. E., WILKINSON, R. H., GASSNER, S., and KAYES, J. (1959) Some clinical considerations in the prevention of suicide based on a study of 134 successful suicides. *Amer. J. pub. Hlth.* **49**, 888–898.

ROBINS, L. N. (1966) *Deviant children grown up: a sociological and psychiatric study of sociopathic personality.* Baltimore: Williams and Wilkins.

ROTH, M. (1955) The natural history of mental disorder in old age. *J. ment. Sci.*, **101**, 281–301.

ROTH, M. and MORRISSEY, J. D. (1952) Problems in the diagnosis and classification of mental disorder in old age. *J. ment. Sci.*, **98**, 66–80.

ROTH, W. F. and LUTON, F. H. (1942) The mental health program in Tennessee. *Amer. J. Psychiat.*, **99**, 662–675.

RUTTER, M. and GRAHAM, P. (1966) Psychiatric disorder in 10- and 11-year-old children. *Proc. Roy. Soc. Med.*, **59**, 382–387.

RUTTER, M., TIZARD, J., and WHITMORE, K. (1970) *Education, Health and Behaviour.* London: Longmans, Green.

RYLE, J. A. (1936) *The Natural History of Disease.* London: Oxford University Press.

RYLE, J. A. (1948) *Changing Disciplines.* London: Oxford University Press.

Scottish Council for Research in Education (1949) *The Trend of Scottish Intelligence.* London: University of London Press.

SEAGER, C. P. (1960) A controlled study of post-partum mental illness. *J. ment. Sci.*, **106**, 214–230.

SHAPIRO, M. B. (1961) A method of measuring psychological changes specific to the individual psychiatric patient. *Brit. J. med. Psychol.*, **34**, 151–155.

SHAPIRO, M. B. (1966) *Function of the clinical psychologist* (Mimeograph). London: the author. Institute of Psychiatry.

SHEPHERD, M. (1957) *A Study of the Major Psychoses in an English Country.* Maudsley Monographs No. 3. London: Chapman and Hall.

SHEPHERD, M. and COOPER, B. (1964) Epidemiology and mental disorder: a review. *J. Neurol. Neurosurg. Psychiat.*, **27**, 277–290.

SHEPHERD, M., COOPER, B., BROWN, A. C., and KALTON, G. W. (1966) *Psychiatric Illness in General Practice.* London: Oxford University Press.

SHEPHERD, M. and DAVIES, D. L. (Ed.) (1968) *Studies in Psychiatry.* London: Oxford University Press.

SHEPHERD, M., GOODMAN, N., and WATT, D. C. (1961) The application of hospital statistics in the evaluation of pharmacotherapy in a psychiatric population. *Comprehens. Psychiat.*, **2**, 11–19.

SHEPHERD, M., OPPENHEIM, B., and MITCHELL, S. (1971) *Childhood Behaviour and Mental Health.* London: University of London Press.

SILER, J. F., GARRISON, P. E., and MacNEAL, W. J. (1917) *Third Report of the Robt. M. Thompson Pellagra Commission of the New York Postgraduate Medical School and Hospital, New York.*

STEIN, L. (1957) Social class gradient in schizophrenia. *Brit. J. prev. soc. Med.*, **11**, 181–195.

STEIN, Z. and SUSSER, M. (1960) Families of dull children. III. Social selection by family type. *J. ment. Sci.*, **106**, 1,304–1,310.

STENGEL, E. (1960) Classification of mental disorders. *Bull. Wld. Hlth Org.*, **21**, 601–663.

STENGEL, E. and COOK, N. E. (1958) *Attempted Suicide.* Maudsley Monographs No. 4. London: Chapman and Hall.

STEPHENSON, W. (1953) *The Study of Behaviour: Q technique and its methodology.* Chicago: University of Chicago Press.

STRÖMGREN, E. (1950) *Statistical and genetical population studies within psychiatry: methods and principal results.* Paris: Congrès International de Psychiatrie.

SYDENHAM, T. (1682) Dissertatio epistolaris ad ... Gulielmum Cole ... de affectione hysterica. In *The Entire Works of Dr. Thomas Sydenham, newly made English from the Originals ... by John Swan, M.D. (1742)* London: Cave.

TAYLOR, Lord and CHAVE, S. (1964) *Mental Health and Environment.* London: Longmans, Green.

TERMAN, L. M. and MERRILL, M. A. (1937) *Measuring Intelligence.* London: Harrap.

TERRIS, M. (Ed.) (1964) *Goldberger on Pellagra.* Baton Rouge: Louisiana State University Press.

TERRIS, M. (1965) Use of hospital admissions in epidemiological studies of mental disease. *Arch. gen. Psychiat.*, **12**, 420–426.

THOMAS, C. L. and GORDON, J. E. (1959) Psychosis after childbirth: ecological aspects of a single impact stress. *Amer. J. med. Sci.*, **238**, 363–388.

THURNAM, J. (1845) *Observations and essays on the statistics of insanity.* London: Simpkin, Marshall.

TOOTH, G. C. and BROOKE, E. (1961) Trends in the mental hospital population and their effect on future planning. *Lancet*, **i**, 710–713.

TUCKMAN, J. and YOUNGMAN, W. F. (1963a) Suicide risk among persons attempting suicide. *U.S. Public Health Reports* **78**, 585–587.

TUCKMAN, J. and YOUNGMAN, W. F. (1963b) Identifying suicide risk groups among attempted suicides. *U.S. Public Health Reports* **78**, 763–766.

WECHSLER, D. (1958) *The Measurement of Adult Intelligence.* 4th ed. Baltimore: Williams and Wilkins.

Wessex Regional Hospital Board (1966) *Provision of further accommodation for the mentally subnormal.* Working Party Report.

WING, J. K. (1967) Social treatment, rehabilitation and management. In *Recent Developments in Schizophrenia: a symposium* (Ed. Coppen, A. and Walk, A.) Ashford, Kent: Headley Bros. for RMPA.

WING, J. K., BENNETT, D. H. and DENHAM, J. (1964a) The industrial rehabilitation of long-stay schizophrenic patients. *Medical Research Council Memorandum* No. 42. London: H.M.S.O.

WING, J. K., BIRLEY, J. L., COOPER, J. E., GRAHAM, P., and ISAACS, A. D. (1967a) Reliability of a procedure for measuring and classifying present psychiatric state. *Brit. J. Psychiat.*, **113**, 499–515.

WING, J. K. and BROWN, G. W. (1961) Social treatment of chronic schizophrenia: a comparative survey of three mental hospitals. *J. ment. Sci.*, **107**, 847–861.

WING, J. K. and FREUDENBERG, R. K. (1961) The response of severely ill chronic schizophrenic patients to social stimulation. *Amer. J. Psychiat.*, **118**, 311–322.

WING, J. K., MONCK, E. M., BROWN, G. W., and CARSTAIRS, G. M. (1964b) Morbidity in the community of schizophrenic patients discharged from London mental hospitals in 1959. *Brit. J. Psychiat.*, **110**, 10–21.

WING, J. K., WING, L., and HAILEY, A. (1970) The use of case registers for evaluating and planning psychiatric services. In *Psychiatric Case Registers* (Ed. Wing, J. K. and Bransby, R.). Dept of Health Statistical Report Series.

WING, L., WING, J. K., HAILEY, A., BAHN, A. K., SMITH, H. E., and BALDWIN, J. A. (1967b). The use of psychiatric services in three urban areas: an international Case Register study. *Soc. Psychiat.*, **2**, 158–167.

WITTKOWER, E. D. and FRIED, J. (1959). A cross-cultural approach to mental health problems. *Amer. J. Psychiat.*, **116**, 423–428.

WOOTTON, B. (1959) *Social Science and Social Pathology.* London: Allen and Unwin.

World Health Organization (1960) *Epidemiology of mental disorders.* 8th Report of the Expert Committee on Mental Health. Techn. Rep. Ser. No. 185, p. 4. Geneva: W.H.O.

World Health Organization (1967) *International Classification of Diseases: manual of the international statistical classification of diseases, injuries and causes of death, based on the recommendations of the 8th Revision Conference.* Geneva: W.H.O.

WYNDER, E. L. (1959) Laboratory contributions to the tobacco-cancer problem. *Brit. med. J.*, **1**, 318–322.

ZUBIN, J. (1961) Summary: from the point of view of biometrics, in *Field Studies in the Mental Disorders* (Ed. Zubin, J.) New York and London: Grune and Stratton.

ZUBIN, J., SUTTON, S., SALZINGER, K., SALZINGER, S., BURDOCK, E. I., and PERETZ, D. (1961) A biometric approach to prognosis in schizophrenia. In *Comparative Epidemiology of the Mental Disorders* (Ed. Hoch, P. H. and Zubin, J.) p. 144. New York and London: Grune and Stratton.

ZUBIN, J. and BURDOCK, E. I. (1965) The revolution in psychopathology and its implications for public health. *Acta Psychiat. Scand.*, **41**, 348–359.

3

Criminal Behaviour

GORDON TRASLER

INTRODUCTION

It is not immediately obvious that criminal behaviour constitutes a viable field of scientific discourse. For one thing, both crimes and criminals are immensely diverse in their characteristics. As we shall see, repeated attempts to show that offenders as a class can be sharply distinguished from the law-abiding in respect to intelligence, emotionality, extraversion, physique, and social origin have generally met with little success. The range of behaviours currently treated as crimes is enormous, extending from gross physical violence to minor infractions of laws relating to currency and to the sale of liquor. Furthermore, what is and what is not criminal is defined by laws of the state presently in force; consequently the meaning of the categories 'criminal' and 'crime' varies substantially between one society and another, and indeed from one generation to the next—an effect greatly amplified by local and temporal variations in police practice (Walker, 1965; Wootton, 1959).

It has been argued, on the one hand, that behavioural scientists ought to focus their attention on particular kinds of crime and offenders, thus abandoning the attempt to construct general hypotheses about the nature of criminality (Wootton, 1959), and on the other, that a more appropriate designation of the field of investigation would be deviant social behaviour, irrespective of whether it happens to attract conviction in the criminal courts. But the common belief that those who repeatedly break the law always commit the same kind of offence is not substantiated by studies of the records of habitual offenders, many of whom have convictions for a variety of acquisitive, aggressive and sexual crimes (West, 1963; Hammond and Chayen, 1963); the notion of criminality as an attribute seems, therefore,

to have some meaning. It appears unlikely that the illegality of an action is ever wholly without significance to the actor; an adequate explanation of a crime must account for the fact that the offender acted despite the knowledge that he might incur a judicial penalty.

MULTIPLE CAUSATION

A rather different objection is raised by those writers who wish to distinguish between 'psychological' and 'social' offenders, arguing that in some instances criminality is genuinely an attribute of the individual, perhaps arising from some inherent defect or condition of maladjustment, while in other cases criminal activity is to be seen as a rational adaptation to prevailing social circumstances, such as poverty or participation in a criminal subculture. This argument is essentially a version of the principle of 'multiple causation' which implies that criminality cannot be amenable to a single explanatory model: 'There are no causes of crime which are both sufficient and necessary. There are only factors which may be "necessary" to produce crime in conjunction with other factors' (Mannheim, 1965). This position is somewhat ambiguous; its validity depends upon whether it is taken to mean that different explanatory hypotheses may be set up to account for clearly-distinguished categories of criminals or of offences, applying unequivocally to all cases included within the categories to which they relate, and thus falsifiable by the discovery of a single contrary instance. Such an interpretation of 'multiple causation' is consistent with the ordinary procedures of science. However, some writers have invested the expression with a different meaning, asserting that criminality may be the consequence of any combination of a number of antecedent conditions, the nature and interrelations of which can only be inferred by retrospective study of the particular case. As Wilkins (1964) points out, this view of 'multiple causation' '. . . could be considered an anti-theory which proposes that no theory can be formed regarding crime', for it implies that genuinely falsifiable hypotheses are impossible in this field.

It must be admitted that the present state of research into criminal behaviour offers some encouragement to those who oppose any attempt to construct a formal theory of criminality. Most of our information is in the form of low-level correlations between criminality and an apparently random assortment of sociological, psychiatric, psychological, and physiological variables, often derived from studies of highly-selected groups of offenders in penal institutions or psychiatric clinics, posing considerable problems of interpretation and comparison. A further difficulty arises from the wide variation in theoretical orientation and scientific sophistication of those who have conducted research in this field. Some investigations were designed to explore elaborate psychodynamic conceptions of the origins of criminality, others to test quite specific hypotheses, and others again to search in an apparently non-theoretical, commonsense fashion for social conditions that give rise to delinquency.

For these reasons it is by no means easy adequately to review the present state of knowledge of criminal behaviour. Some basic theoretical framework is needed if the task is to be attempted at all—not as a formal model to be tested against the evidence, for this, unfortunately, is not yet feasible, but as a means of organising the material.

THE PARALLEL WITH AVOIDANCE PHENOMENA

Most crimes take the form of acquisitive, violent or sexually-aggressive behaviour (Walker, 1965) which may reasonably be attributed to basic and universal human motives. They are distinguished from non-criminal actions by the fact that they are forbidden by the criminal law (and usually, though not invariably, by the *mores* of the society in which they occur) and attract judicial penalties. Although some crimes demand special techniques or skills (for example, the forgery of documents) most do not. It follows that the fundamental problem in explaining criminality is not to discover the manner in which criminal habits are acquired, but to explain why some individuals fail to inhibit those kinds of actions that are socially-proscribed, which the rest of the population has learned to avoid. This may come about if the techniques of training applied to

the individual in the course of socialisation are inadequate, or if his capacity to respond to training is limited by some defect. It will also occur if the effects of such training are eroded by some kind of extinction, or temporarily or permanently impaired by the action of some kind of stress or trauma.

There is a close and interesting parallel between the manner in which individuals learn to inhibit certain forms of proscribed social behaviour and the phenomenon of avoidance, which has been extensively investigated in the laboratory (Eysenck, 1955, 1970; Hare, 1965a,b; Trasler, 1962). The appropriate paradigm is what Mowrer (1960a) terms *passive avoidance*—that is to say, a set of conditions in which the individual can avoid punishment by refraining from a particular kind of activity, in contradistinction to the active avoidance situation,

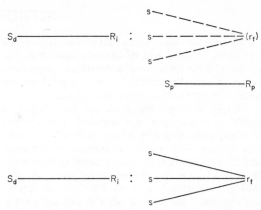

Fig. 3.1. Schematic representation of avoidance (*after* Mowrer, 1969a, by permission). For explanation *see* text.

which requires him to perform some action in order to evade punishment. Mowrer argues that passive avoidance is mediated by an acquired fear reaction which, when elicited by appropriate signal stimuli, effectively blocks that form of behaviour which attracts punishment. His model hypothesises that such fear reactions are acquired through a process of classical conditioning: the CS consists of a pattern of stimuli produced by the individual himself in the preparatory stages of the prohibited behaviour, which (after a number of 'trials') become associated with the fear or distress caused by the punishment which immediately follows the proscribed action. Thus, in the course of time these initial or preparatory stages come to elicit a conditioned fear reaction that is sufficiently powerful to block the consummatory component of the behavioural chain—the individual sees something that he might steal, feels anxious or afraid, and turns away. This sequence of events is depicted in Fig. 3.1.

'. . . a problem situation or drive, S_d, produces an overt, instrumental response, R_i. R_i is followed by punishment, which is here represented as S_p. The punishment elicits a response R_p of which r_f, or fear, is a component. But when R_i occurs, it not only elicits the extrinsic stimulus, S_p; it also produces a number of other stimuli, s, s, s, which are inherently associated with the occurrence of R_i. The result: a part of the reaction produced by S_p, namely fear, gets conditioned to these response-produced stimuli, s, s, s. Consequently, when S_d recurs and the organism starts to perform R_i, the resulting stimuli "remind" the organism of the antecedent punishment, i.e. cue off r_f, which tends to inhibit R_i.' (Mowrer, 1960a, p. 255).

Mowrer's model is based on theoretical arguments of some complexity which cannot be adequately treated here. But it has considerable heuristic value in the attempt to explain criminality, and we shall use it as a basis for organising the rather unmanageable body of research which it is the business of this chapter to review. It is possible to deduce from the model a specification of the conditions necessary for the establishment of effective and enduring avoidance behaviour. First, the mechanism depends upon an unpleasant state of arousal, r_f, which is sufficiently intense, and well enough differentiated from the normal state of the individual, to block the executive phase of the proscribed action, R_i—that is to say, to reinforce avoidance behaviour. This state of arousal is elicited by a complex of conditioned stimuli (s, s, s) which Mowrer describes as 'response-produced', but which presumably also include perceptions of the situation in which the individual finds himself in the preparatory stages of R_i—that is to say, the recognition of characteristics of the situation which define R_i as criminal rather than permissible. It is assumed that the conditioned stimuli derive their significance through a Pavlovian relation of contiguity with a punishing state of affairs, R_p, induced by a sanction (as we shall term it here), with which it is reliably associated. The model demands that the subject should accurately recognise the conditioned stimulus-complex (s, s, s); and, in practice, that he should generalise this to other, comparable, situations.

With these reflections in mind, we shall direct our attention to two groups of parameters: those which may determine individual differences in responsiveness to that part of the socialisation process which normally mediates 'ethical learning'—that is to say,

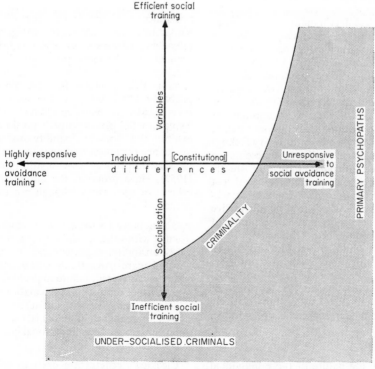

Fig. 3.2. Relations between individual (constitutional) and social variables

training in the avoidance of delinquent behaviour—and the characteristics of the socialisation process itself, in so far as these may be relevant to the efficiency of training or to the value-system which is thus transmitted to the individual. There is no reason to suspect the existence of any connexion or correlation between these two sets of variables, and indeed it seems much more likely that they are quite independent.

RELATIONS BETWEEN SOCIAL AND INDIVIDUAL VARIABLES

This state of affairs is depicted in Fig. 3.2, which contains an important implication about the relation between these two sets of parameters and criminality. It suggests that there may be extreme cases in which the individual is so unresponsive to social training that not even the most efficient techniques of socialisation could prevent him from becoming criminal, and also that there may be some individuals who are normally susceptible to avoidance training, but have encountered such inefficient socialisation that they have never had an opportunity to acquire

effective avoidance responses. But we may expect to find some (perhaps many) criminals in the lower right-hand quadrant—people who are not wholly insusceptible to avoidance training, who might have responded to particularly efficient socialisation, but did not receive it.

This model contains several working assumptions, which may have to be revised in due course. For example, it treats susceptibility to avoidance training as a continuous variable, and implies that the techniques of socialisation employed by parents and others also vary from highly efficient to very inefficient. It also suggests that the system as a whole exhibits a certain degree of surplus efficiency—that is to say, that most individuals in the population are subjected to a régime of social avoidance training that is more than adequate to secure conforming behaviour. These assumptions are consistent with our present knowledge of the incidence of criminality; delinquents and criminals constitute a minority of the population, and the modest frequency of reconviction exhibited by first offenders (Walker, 1965) suggests that the failure of socialisation among some delinquents may be marginal.

INDIVIDUAL DIFFERENCES OF CONSTITUTIONAL ORIGIN

The belief that persistent criminality is sometimes the result of a constitutional defect which renders the individual incapable of acquiring normal ethical values has a long history (Maughs, 1941; Gurvitz, 1951). The terms 'moral idiocy', 'moral insanity', and (more recently) 'constitutional psychopathy' were used to indicate that this disability was to be found in people who did not show symptoms of psychotic or neurotic disturbance, or subnormality, but were distinguished by a lack of ordinary feelings of guilt or remorse. Clinical studies of representative samples of convicted offenders have consistently identified a small group of particularly persistent criminals drawn, for the most part, from unremarkable social backgrounds, who show the distinctive qualities of 'consciencelessness' and lack of guilt that earlier writers had described (Karpman, 1961; Lindner, 1942, 1943; McCord and McCord, 1964). More extensive investigations using psychological tests (Finney, 1966; Peterson et al., 1961) and case-history data (Quay, 1964) indicate the existence of a dimension or continuum, of which this relatively small percentage of offenders represents one extreme.

Primary Psychopathy

Attempts to identify the nature of those individual differences that impede the acquisition of social

avoidance responses have, for obvious reasons, tended to concentrate on this category of persistent offenders. However, as Hare (1963, 1968a) has pointed out, the term 'psychopath' is insufficiently precise in connotation for scientific purposes; certain discrepancies in research findings are probably attributable to the inclusion, by some investigators, of neurotic offenders ('secondary' or 'symptomatic' psychopaths) who do not necessarily exhibit the specific inability to acquire social avoidance responses that appears to characterise the classical or 'primary' psychopath. Following Lykken (1957), Hare proposes the adoption of Cleckley's criteria of sociopathy (though not the term itself); namely—

'an inability to form lasting emotional relationships with others, failure to grasp the meaning of responsibility, repeated and inadequately motivated aggressive acts, absence of neurotic guilt and anxiety, apparent failure to profit from experience, absence of delusions, hallucinations or intellectual defect, inability to distinguish truth from lies, lack of real insight into his own behavior, and promiscuous but impersonal sexual behavior' (Hare, 1965).

Cleckley's criteria are open to criticism on two grounds; they involve reliance upon qualitative clinical judgements, and they define a type rather than a continuum. But in practice they have proved valuable; applied conservatively (i.e. excluding individuals who do not meet all the stipulated criteria) they apparently identify a reasonably homogeneous group of people who differ in important respects from other persistent offenders, and their use by several investigators has at least ensured some comparability of experimental populations. We shall have occasion to refer to a number of studies of this particular type of psychopath in the course of our review of individual differences in relation to criminality, upon which we shall now embark.

Conditionability and Extraversion

The Mowrer model proposes (as we have seen) that passive avoidance behaviour is mediated by a conditioned fear response, originally derived from the experience of punishment. It is reasonable to suspect that the psychopath's characteristic failure to inhibit socially-unacceptable behaviour may be the consequence of some kind of constitutional inability to form such conditioned responses. Several hypotheses of this nature have been proposed during the last fifteen years. One of these, based on Eysenck's (1955) theory of personality, postulates the existence of stable individual differences in 'conditionability' (i.e. in rapidity of acquisition and resistance to extinction of conditioned responses of all kinds), which is a function of introversion (Eysenck, 1962). Thus, Franks (1956a) suggested that, 'there are two kinds of recidivists; the introverted ones, who condition well and who readily learn the rules of their (undesirable) environment, and the extraverted—possibly psychopathic—ones, who condition poorly and who find great difficulty in learning the rules of their environment (desirable or otherwise)'. This line of argument was later developed by Eysenck (1970). However, several investigators have failed to demonstrate differences between psychopaths and others in rate of conditioning, using eyelid responses (Miller, 1966; Warren and Grant, 1955; see also Hare, 1965a). The notion of 'conditionability' as a personality variable has given rise to much dispute (Willett, 1960; Franks, 1963; Storms and Sigal, 1958; Eysenck, 1959). There is evidence that such differences as may exist in responsiveness to conditioning are less general than was originally supposed; it seems likely that the conditioning schedule adopted (Eysenck, 1965, 1967; Eysenck and Levey, 1967), the nature and intensity of the unconditioned stimulus (Johns and Quay, 1962; Gray, 1970), and possibly the type of response to be conditioned (Willett, 1960), govern the cir-

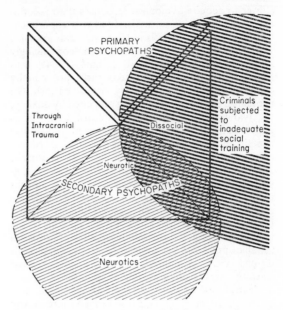

Fig. 3.3. Types of categories of psychopathy

cumstances in which such differences can be expected (Fig. 3.3).

It is important to remember that Eysenck's hypothesis concerned the relations between rates of conditioning and extraversion—not specifically psychopathy. The Maudsley school uses the term 'psychopath' to denote individuals whose social behaviour is markedly deviant and antisocial; in practice, the population thus defined tends to have high scores on measures of both extraversion and neuroticism (Eysenck, 1967, 1970). The Cleckley/Lykken criteria of primary psychopathy used by such investigators as Hare and Miller (op. cit.) effectively exclude neurotic individuals, whom Hare would classify as 'secondary' psychopaths (Hare, 1965a); indeed, Schoenherr (1964) reports that his group of primary psychopaths, selected upon Cleckley criteria, were not significantly neurotic or extraverted on the psychometric tests which he employed.

Avoidance Learning

A more direct approach to the problem of why psychopaths fail to establish normal social-conforming responses is to look for specific defects in avoidance learning, rather than in responsiveness to conditioning in general. Using a complex experimental arrangement resembling a maze, in which incorrect responses were punished by an electric shock, Lykken (1957) was able to show that primary psychopaths were slower to acquire avoidance responses than secondary psychopaths or normals. Lykken's experiment has not escaped criticism (Persons and Persons, 1965); however, his results were convincingly replicated by Schachter and Latané (1964), who found that: 'normals and sociopaths are equally capable of learning a positively reinforced task. On avoidance learning, presumably mediated by anxiety, the two groups differ—normals learn well, sociopaths not at all.' Schoenherr (1964) employed similar experimental arrangements, and obtained results consonant with Lykken's, though less dramatic. Another study (Hetherington and Klinger, 1964) suggests that the relation between response to punishment and psychopathy is not confined to extreme groups. They used women undergraduates selected because of high or low scores on the *Pd* scale of the MMPI, and required them to learn a list of nonsense syllables presented on a memory drum. Three conditions were compared; verbal encouragement (reward), verbal discouragement (punishment), and a neutral condition in which no comment was offered. Low *Pd* subjects learned much more slowly in the 'punishment' condition; high *Pd* subjects, on the other hand, showed no significant variation in rates of learning between the three conditions. The authors conclude that punishment-induced fear interfered with the learning of non-psychopathic (low *Pd*) subjects, but high *Pd* subjects were unaffected. On the other hand, Blaylock (1960) found no differences between psychopaths and non-psychopaths in a verbal-conditioning experiment employing similar reinforcers. However, the manner in which his experimental groups were selected (from prison and hospital populations) makes it difficult to compare his study with that of Hetherington and Klinger, and he indicates that his psychopathic subjects differed from his controls in other ways (e.g. being more introverted), which may have influenced his results.

The suggestion that the psychopath's poor performance in avoidance training is due to an inability to form anticipatory fear responses is supported by three studies of 'shock stress threat'—i.e. the knowledge that punishment is imminent. Hare (1965d) used three groups of subjects: primary psychopaths from a penitentiary, non-psychopathic criminals from the same institution, and student control subjects. He informed them that they would receive an electric shock when the number 8 appeared in a memory drum. Digits from 1 to 12 were then presented consecutively, changes in skin conductance being continuously recorded. His data show that the psychopaths, unlike the other two groups, exhibited virtually no anticipatory increase in conductance, although they reacted strongly to the shock itself.

Hare concluded: 'This is consistent with the hypothesis that psychopaths can be characterised by a steeper than normal gradient of fear arousal and response inhibition. Presumably, cues associated with future punishment are incapable of generating sufficient fear in the psychopath for immediate behaviour to be inhibited.' A similar experiment using student subjects selected for high and low scores on the *Pd* scale of the MMPI yielded comparable results, suggesting that the effect is not peculiar to extremely psychopathic individuals (Hare, 1965c).

Lippert and Senter (1966) used an ingenious technique to test the same hypothesis. Their subjects (apparently 'mixed' psychopaths, and non-psychopathic delinquent controls) were told—falsely, as it turned out—that they would receive a shock after ten minutes had elapsed, and were allowed to watch a clock. Towards the end of this period more than half the non-psychopathic subjects showed an abrupt increase in skin conductance; none of the psychopaths exhibited an anticipatory GSR.

Hare (1965a) suggests that the absence of anticipatory fear responses in the psychopath is merely one manifestation of 'a steeper than normal avoidance gradient' which is also reflected in other kinds of generalisation. He conducted another experiment with primary psychopaths and non-psychopathic controls in a penitentiary, the results of which lend some support to this view. GSR was conditioned to an auditory stimulus (a 1,000 c/s tone), and electric shock served as the UCS. Generalisation was measured by the amplitude of GSRs elicited by two novel auditory stimuli of 468 and 153 c/s respectively. The psychopathic subjects produced weaker responses to both of these stimuli than did the controls, indicating that 'conditioned fear responses . . . once acquired, are generalised less by psychopaths than by non-psychopaths' (Hare, 1965b). This is an interesting result, but it should be interpreted with caution. Lykken (1957) was unable to demonstrate differences between psychopaths and others in the strength of GSR to an auditory stimulus resembling the CS, although (as Hare points out) his experiment complicated the issue by presenting the generalisation stimulus from the beginning of acquisition trials. It would be rash to regard Hare's findings as proof of differences in the slope of generalisation gradients for psychopaths and others, but the matter is certainly worth further investigation. Hare himself offers an original theoretical interpretation which relates his notion of avoidance gradients to Miller's (1959) approach-avoidance conflict theory of behaviour (Hare, 1965a).

It is conceivable that punishing stimuli may be less unpleasant to psychopaths than to normal subjects, and consequently less threatening. Two investigators (Schoenherr, 1964; Hare, 1968b) found that the detection threshold for electric shock in psychopaths was slightly higher than in non-psychopathic subjects; on the other hand, they seem unwilling to tolerate more intense shocks than normals (cf. Hare, 1965d, 1966; Latané and Schachter, 1964). Indeed, Hare (1968b) found that those primary psychopaths with the highest detection threshold had the lowest tolerance level; as he remarks, 'whether this means that these Ss experienced an extremely rapid increase in subjective intensity or that they were the most psychopathic and hence least ready to tolerate pain is unknown'—and presumably unknowable.

It is the usual practice, in experiments that make use of an unpleasant electric shock as the UCS, to carry out preliminary tests in which each subject is asked to identify the highest intensity of stimulation he can bear. This is clearly, on Hare's argument, an unsatisfactory way of compensating for individual differences in the tolerance threshold, and may have the effect of introducing a serious source of error into comparative studies of response to avoidance training. Fortunately, the Lippert and Senter (1966) design eliminates the necessity for this precaution, as no shock is actually administered; it is reassuring to find that their results were concordant with those of investigators who did use it. But although this suggests that threshold differences can hardly be the sole explanation for the psychopath's failure to acquire anticipatory fear responses, it may still be the case, as Eysenck (1970) maintains, that sanctions sufficient to deter normal individuals from deviant behaviour may be insufficiently unpleasant to effect avoidance training in highly extraverted people.

Autonomic Reactivity

Much attention has been devoted to the question whether psychopaths differ from non-psychopaths in respect of any of several parameters of autonomic functioning. Hare (1968a) conducted a careful review of a number of relevant studies, and found a considerable conflict of evidence (*see* Table 3.1) which seems to be due, at least in part, to the fact that investigators have used a variety of indices of arousal and reactivity, and have done so in differently defined populations—some adhering to Cleckley's category of primary psychopaths, and others using mixed groups of primary and secondary psychopaths. An experiment, reported in the same paper, attempts to resolve some of the ambiguities in the literature. Hare concludes that differences in autonomic functioning between primary psycho-

paths and non-psychopaths, though genuine, are probably much more complex than previous writers have assumed. His psychopathic subjects showed less marked response to novel stimuli ('orienting reflex') than the controls, which, he argues, is consistent with the psychopath's lack of attentiveness to his environment, and his poor performance in discriminative conditioning situations (Warren and Grant, 1955). He offers some support for the hypothesis that the psychopath is autonomically hyporeactive.

Schachter and Latané (1964) emphasise the key rôle of internal (autonomic) cues in mediating avoidance behaviour, in the Mowrer model, and offer an hypothesis that partially conflicts with Hare's conception of the psychopath as an under-reactive individual who does not attend to subtle changes in his environment which, for the normal person, signal impending punishment. They suggest that the basic defect is an inability to recognise and to discriminate autonomic changes that ought to give rise to aversive emotion. Their argument depends on the premise that, 'sympathetic arousal is not necessarily associated with an emotional state; cognitive and situational factors determine whether or not a state of physiological arousal will be labeled as an emotion'—a proposition which they support with evidence from experiments in drug-induced arousal.

They insist that, far from being underresponsive: 'sociopaths appear to be more responsive to virtually every titillating event ... the sociopath reacts sympathetically to events that are labeled frightening by others, but he also reacts to events labeled as relatively harmless by others. Such generalised, relatively indiscriminate reactivity is, we would suggest, almost the equivalent of no reactivity at all. If almost every event provokes strong autonomic discharge, then, in terms of internal autonomic cues, the subject feels no differently during times of danger than during relatively tranquil times.' The authors offer a striking experimental finding to support their argument. Using the Lykken maze task, they first replicated his finding (Lykken, 1957) that sociopaths do not differ from normals in the 'manifest' (reward) task, but show markedly inferior avoidance learning in the punished, 'latent' task. A small intramuscular injection of adrenalin was then administered, with dramatic effect: the sociopaths showed a rate of avoidance learning which equalled that which had been achieved by the normal controls in the no-drug trials. This is interpreted as the consequence of exaggerating autonomic changes so that they 'stand out' or become discriminable from the 'noise' or random activity that normally characterises the autonomic system of the psychopath—a state of

Table 3.1. Summary of Studies of Autonomic Functioning in the Psychopath
(*from* Hare, 1968a)

Investigator	Subjects[a]	Variables[b]	Stimuli	Findings Resting level	Findings Responsivity
Lindner (1942)	M, NPC	SR, HR, RR	Tones and shock	No significant difference.	No significant difference.
Ruilmann & Gulo (1950)	M, NC	SR, HR, RR, BP	'Sensory stimuli', questions, arithmetic problems	No significant difference.	Group M showed less GSR activity; no significant difference in other variables.
Lykken (1955)	P, S, NC	GSR	Tones and shock	Group P had lowest SR.	Groups P and S less reactive to shock and to tones signalling shock.
Tong (1959)	M, NC	GSR	Heat, tones, tactile, frustration	Not reported	Some Group M hyperreactive, others hyporeactive.
Fox & Lippert (1963)	N, NPC	SC, NSP	None	Group M gave fewer NSP.	
Schachter & Latané (1964)	P, NPC	HR	Injection of adrenalin	No significant difference.	Group P more reactive.
Goldstein (1965)	M, NC	SC, HR, RR, BP, MAPs	White noise	No significant difference	No significant difference.
Hare (1965b)	P, NPC, NC	SC	Shock and threat of shock	Group P had lowest SC.	No significant difference. However, Group P less reactive to threat of shock.
Hare (1965c)	P, NPC	SC	Tones and shock	Group P had lower SC.	No significant difference. However, Group P less reactive to tones signalling shock.
Lippert & Senter (1966)	M, NPC	SC, NSP	Lights, tones, threatened shock	No significant difference.	No significant difference. However, Group M less reactive to threat of shock.

[a] M = mixed group of psychopaths; P = primary psychopaths; S = secondary psychopaths; NPC = nonpsychopathic criminals or patients; NC = noninstitutionalised controls.
[b] SR = skin resistance; SC = skin conductance; NSP = spontaneous or nonspecific GSRs; HR = heart rate; RR = respiration rate; BP = blood pressure; MAP = muscle action potentials.

affairs the authors regard as a pharmacological equivalent of 'labeling'.

The Schachter and Latané study presents formidable theoretical and technical difficulties, and has been extensively criticised (Hare, 1968a). However, it represents an original and promising line of research, and there are interesting similarities between their conception of the characteristics of the psychopath and the theory of psychopathic behaviour proposed by the Maudsley school (Eysenck, 1967, 1970).

SUMMARY

It is clear, even in this brief and incomplete review, that experimental investigations of the characteristics of psychopaths have yielded findings which are consistent in certain respects and in sharp disagreement in others. It is tempting to concentrate on the points of agreement and to attribute conflicting findings to defects in research designs; however, as Hare (1968a, 1970) points out, at least some of the discrepancies in experimental results that appear in the literature may prove, on further scrutiny, to be theoretically significant.

While several investigators have failed to find any evidence that psychopaths learn more slowly than non-psychopathic subjects under reward conditions, there is substantial evidence that they respond poorly to fear conditioning, particularly in an avoidance-training situation (for example, the several studies of Hare, Lykken, Schachter, and others, to which reference has been made). This finding is consistent with several alternative theoretical accounts of psychopathic functioning, including those of Eysenck (1967, 1970b), Hare (1970) and Schachter and Latané (1964) and with Gray's (1970) modified account of the relations between passive avoidance conditioning, neuroticism, and introversion. On the other hand, the evidence does not offer much support for Eysenck's (1955) and Franks's (1956a) contention that this deficit in fear conditioning is a manifestation of poor conditionability in general. The question is by no means resolved, however. Eysenck's model is intended to apply to a differently defined and probably more heterogeneous group of individuals ('secondary psychopaths' in Hare's terminology) than those studied by American investigators. It may be that failure to learn avoidance responses has a different origin in neurotic, extraverted individuals, who seem to predominate in the Maudsley samples; it is possible, also—as Eysenck (1965) argues—that in the case of neurotic psychopaths, but not of 'primary' psychopaths, resistance to conditioning will be evident only in conditions of partial reinforcement. These are questions that can only be resolved by further experiment, using more carefully selected groups of subjects. However, the basic point of agreement—that failure to respond to avoidance training is characteristic of some persistent criminals—is a discovery of considerable heuristic value.

The second point of general agreement is that failure to acquire inhibitory (avoidance) responses has something to do with the psychopath's inability to recognise stimuli (both external and internal) that signal impending punishment. The nature of this defect is still a matter of dispute: it has been variously explained in terms of autonomic hypo-reactivity (e.g. Claridge and Herrington, 1963), deficiency in orienting response (Hare, 1968a), high threshold to stimulation (Eysenck, 1970; Quay, 1965) and autonomic lability, generating so much 'noise' that the individual is unable to discriminate between significant and irrelevant increases in activation (Schachter and Latané, 1964). In this case, also, the consensus of empirical findings is striking, and (as we shall see later) prompts interesting and important questions about the mechanisms of social training processes. Much further experiment will be required to resolve the theoretical issues that have been raised, and it may well turn out, as Hare suggests (1970), that failure to respond to appropriate stimuli can occur in more than one way.

These rather general reflections are relevant to the question: Is the study of psychopathic individuals an appropriate starting point in the attempt to identify constitutional characteristics which predispose people to become criminals? It is clear that 'primary psychopaths' are unusual individuals in two senses: they constitute a small minority of the criminal population, and they are in certain respects markedly different from other criminals and from the remainder of the population. But the research to which we have referred suggests that these differences are quantitative rather than qualitative; the psychopath appears to be peculiarly unresponsive to the kind of training that mediates conforming social behaviour, but it is reasonable to suppose that his defects are shared, in a smaller degree, by others. There is some indication, also, that 'primary' psychopathy represents the conjunction of several adverse factors—autonomic, cortical, sensory. These considerations point to the possibility of constructing a general theoretical scheme which will account for individual differences in responsiveness to avoidance training, explaining both the extremely psychopathic and the mildly resistant. Such a model will have (on present evidence) to be based on precise and sophisticated information about the physiological mechanisms of arousal and the relations between cortical and autonomic processes, and it is clear that its construction will not be an easy matter.

Inheritance

The notion that criminality may have an hereditary basis is an old one. Lombroso (1876) attempted to identify a category of persistent offenders whose physical characteristics appeared to reflect some kind of degeneracy—a kind of evolutionary 'throwback' in which criminality was the consequence of unbridled primitive instincts. His work was developed by Goring (1913) in a careful statistical study of more than three thousand English convicts. In recent years there has been a renewed interest in the relations between physical constitution and personality (Sheldon, 1940, 1942; Eysenck, 1947), which has prompted several studies of the body-build of delinquents and criminals. Sheldon (1949) compared 200 young offenders with a large control sample of college students, and found a preponderance of endomorphic-mesomorphs (i.e. of muscular, thickset individuals) among the delinquents. Gibbens (1963) found a similarly high incidence of mesomorphs in a group of 58 Borstal inmates, and showed that they were physically very different from other samples of undergraduates and officer cadets. These apparently clear-cut results should be treated with some caution. Young offenders are not randomly drawn from the general population, but are most frequently recruited from urban working-class families. The differences in physique these investigators have observed may be at least in part a function of socio-economic level rather than specifically of delinquency (Walker,

1965). The validity of Gibbens's results may also be affected by a very high rate (42 per cent) of refusal in his original sample; it seems possible that those who consented to somatotyping may have done so because they were not ashamed of their muscular physique.

However, a study by Glueck and Glueck (1956), which obtained fairly similar results, is exempt from these criticisms. They matched 495 persistent juvenile delinquents with 484 non-delinquents in respect of age, intelligence, racial origin, and socio-economic status, so that both groups were recruited from poor neighbourhoods, and investigated temperamental characteristics and social attitudes as well as body build. Sixty per cent of the delinquents were of mesomorphic physique (compared with 31 per cent of the non-delinquents) and they appeared to be more vigorous, destructive, and uninhibited than boys of different physical type.

Although the existence of a correlation between delinquency and physical type is fairly well established, this is not in itself evidence of the inheritance of a predisposition to criminality. The connexion may depend on the interplay between the temperamental correlates of physical types and the social environment (Eysenck, 1970b; Mannheim, 1965), and in any case the extent to which physique is itself influenced by the socio-economic status of the family within which the individual grows up (for example, through nutritional differences) is extremely difficult to determine. More direct investigations of the relations between heredity and criminal behaviour have relied on the twin-study method and (more recently) the identification of chromosomal abnormalities.

TWIN STUDIES

The rationale of twin studies as a means of identifying genetic determinants of behavioural differences is explained at length elsewhere in this volume by Shields (Chapter 16). One of the earliest essays in the twin-study method was concerned with criminality. Lange (1929) investigated the histories of thirty male criminals who were known to have twins of the same sex. Thirteen of the resulting pairs were judged to be uniovular ('identical'); in ten of these the other twin also proved to have a criminal record. Among the seventeen pairs of binovular twins, on the other hand, there were only two cases in which both twins had criminal records. Lange's work has been heavily criticised; he used fairly crude criteria to determine monozygocity, and did not report some of his measurements (Wheelan, 1951), and his sample was collected in a way that may

have exaggerated the degree of concordance present (Slater, 1953).

A more extensive study by Rosanoff *et al.* (1934) included both adult criminals and juvenile delinquents. They were 33 pairs of male adult uniovular twins, of which 22 were concordant for criminal conviction; in the juvenile group 25 of 27 pairs of male monozygotes showed delinquency in both twins, and a similarly high rate of concordance (21 of 25) was recorded in a sample of children, the *propositi* being selected for behaviour disorders that had not attracted legal proceedings. The corresponding concordance figures for dizygotic pairs (both male in all cases) were 3:23 and 24:39 for adults and juveniles respectively. Stumpfl (1936) reported concordance rates for criminality of 61 per cent for uniovular twins, and 37 per cent for binovular pairs of the same sex. Kranz (1936), in a similar study, found 66 per cent of monozygotic pairs, and 54 per cent of same-sexed dizygotic twins, concordant for criminality. Yoshimasu (1961) reports figures of 61 per cent and 11 per cent respectively, but also quotes evidence that concordance rates are influenced by prevailing social conditions, having increased since the Second World War (Mannheim, 1965).

These figures are not easy to interpret. 'It is sometimes assumed that any similarities shown by uniovular twins can be attributed to heredity, any differences to the environment, but only the latter half of this assumption can be safely held' (Slater, 1953). Most studies of monozygotic criminal twins inevitably reflect the consequences of similar childhood environment as well as identical genetic inheritance. It is arguable that their principal heuristic value consists in the opportunity to explore the environmental factors that result in differences in social behaviour (Wheelan, 1951). Penrose (1955) argues that criminality *per se* is too diffuse a territory for genetic science, and suggests that twin studies are only likely to be useful if they are directed at the investigation of criminality 'when it is associated with a clearly defined pathological condition'. His thesis is supported by two studies of psychopathy in uniovular twins (Slater, 1953; Wheelan, 1951) already mentioned, which—by concentrating on a form of criminality that seems to have an important constitutional basis—throw an interesting light on the complex and cumulative interaction between inherited characteristics and social environment.

CHROMOSOME ANOMALIES

In recent years much interest has been aroused by the suggestion that certain chromosomal abnormalities may be associated with a tendency to antisocial behaviour and criminality. The matter is a complex one; an admirably clear outline of the nature and origin of chromosomal anomalies, and a description of the techniques used in identifying them, is given by Forssman and Hambert (1967). Most of the published studies have dealt with the possession of extra X chromosomes or with individuals who have additional Y chromosomes; mosaicism (mixed chromosome complement) has not as yet been given much attention as a possible source of delinquent tendencies. Although some research has been directed at chromosomal abnormalities in the female, this facet of the problem presents peculiar difficulties because of the small and highly-selected nature of institutional populations of female offenders. This brief review will therefore be limited to studies carried out on male subjects; it will be convenient to deal separately with the evidence relating to extra X and Y chromosomes respectively.

The X Chromosome

The possession of more than one X chromosome can be readily discerned by the Barr method of staining for sex-chromatin, which can be applied to large populations. It is known that the incidence of sex-chromatin positive males in the general population is of the order of two per thousand; the corresponding figure for males in institutions for the subnormal is about ten per thousand (MacLean et al., 1962, 1964). Casey et al. (1966b) found that 2·2 per cent of male patients in two state hospitals for subnormal patients with violent, aggressive or criminal tendencies (Rampton and Moss Side) were sex-chromatin positive: of the total count of 21, 12 had an XXY complement, 7 showed the XXYY configuration, and 2 'were presumed to have XXY/XY mosaicism.' This survey supports an earlier note by Court Brown (1962), who reported that an apparently high proportion of sex-chromatin positive males in institutions for the mentally defective had histories of 'such anti-social acts as larceny, fire-raising, and indecent exposure', but gave no details of the manner in which his sample was drawn; nor did he indicate the frequency of these offences among patients with normal chromosome pattern. Nielsen (1964) found four delinquents in a group of ten men with an extra complement of X chromosomes in a mental hospital; Hunter (1966), in an extensive survey of subnormal patients in the Sheffield area, reported that sex-chromatin positive patients included an abnormally high proportion of men with 'anti-social behaviour abnormalities' (64·7 per cent, compared with the figure of 19·5 per cent for all male patients) and especially of aggressive

offences (45·5 per cent against 17 per cent). Several other studies of subnormal populations have yielded similar findings (Forssman and Hambert, 1967). But while the association between behaviour disorders and the possession of one or more supernumerary X chromosomes seems to have been convincingly established in subnormal populations, it is not clear whether the association holds for those of normal intelligence. It is significant that Wegmann and Smith (1963) found only two sex-chromatin positive individuals among 1,232 boys and young men in three state institutions for delinquents—a lower incidence than in the general population, according to MacLean's estimate.

The Y Chromosome

Identification of individuals with an abnormal complement of Y chromosomes is technically much more difficult, as it is necessary to prepare cultures. Consequently, reliable parametric information about normal populations is lacking. It is believed that XYY males must be less common than XXY males; Slater (1967) suggests that the frequency may be of the order of one per 2,000—that is to say, one for every four males of the XXY karyotype. The identification of nine men with the XYY complement (together with an XXYY individual and an XY/XYY mosaic) in a group of 315 patients in a secure hospital for dangerous (mainly criminal) subnormals was therefore particularly striking (Jacobs et al., 1965). Careful studies of these men (Price et al., 1966; Price and Whatmore, 1967a,b; Jacobs et al., 1968), comparing them against the rest of the population from which they were drawn, reveals differences of considerable criminological interest. Their criminal records were no worse than those of the controls, and included relatively few crimes of violence against the person. But their criminal careers had started earlier; the average age at which they were first convicted was 13 years, against a mean of 18 years for patients with normal chromosome patterns. They exhibited no sign of psychotic illness, and did not differ from the rest of the hospital population in respect of intelligence-level; two were of average intelligence, and the other seven had 'only a mild degree' of subnormality. It is reported that, as a group, 'they demonstrated an absence of genuine remorse or guilt, a limited capacity for affection and an inability to establish normal interpersonal relationships'—a description that suggests psychopathy. It is significant that the authors also remark that these nine individuals did not appear to be socially underprivileged or handicapped by a familial record of crime or mental illness (Jacobs et al., 1968).

Males of the XYY karyotype seldom exhibit physical abnormalities, except that they tend to be unusually tall. Casey *et al.* (1966a) made use of this fact to search several populations for men with this chromosomal pattern. They found 18 individuals with the XYY complement among 124 men, six feet or more in height, detained in hospitals or prison because of antisocial behaviour. On the other hand, they could find no instance of this karyotype among 30 equally tall, non-criminal patients in a psychiatric hospital, or in a similar group of 'normal' men. Welch *et al.* (1969) were unable to replicate this finding in a large American institution for 'defective delinquents', but—as they point out—their data were rather equivocal.

It has been suggested that the presence of an extra Y chromosome, rather than some consequence of the XYY karyotype itself, might be related to criminality—a possibility that stimulates interest in the XXYY pattern, apparently unusually prevalent in institutions for criminal subnormals (Casey *et al.*, 1966b). It has been argued that the high incidence of XXYY individuals in such populations is sufficient, in strictly numerical terms, to account for the observed excess of sex-chromatin positive males to which we have already referred. An interesting speculation on the reasons for this state of affairs has been advanced by Slater (1967). He points out that criminality and delinquency are much more frequent in males than in females; moreover, comparisons between offenders of the two sexes

suggest that obvious psychiatric causes or marked environmental stress are present much more often in female delinquency—in this sense crime is 'normal' in the male, but an aberration in the female. It is possible, he argues, that the possession of an extra Y chromosome exaggerates masculine attributes—'it is the masculinity as such that increases the tendencies to delinquency'. It is interesting to note that Price *et al.* (1966) remarked that their sample of XYY subnormals were 'often aggressive and violent' in their behaviour while in hospital—though, paradoxically, their criminal records included rather fewer violent offences.

Forssman and Hambert (1967) offer an alternative explanation, that chromosome abnormalities may be associated with 'minimum brain damage'—that is to say, 'microscopic or submicroscopic cerebral injury . . . of a diffuse nature' leading to restlessness, lack of concentration and aggressiveness, thus interfering with the individual's social adjustment, particularly during childhood. However, there is as yet no evidence of a connexion between this syndrome and the possession of an extra Y chromosome.

In summary, it may be said that the evidence of some association between certain chromosomal anomalies and antisocial behaviour in subnormals is fairly convincing. The nature of the relationship is at present obscure; nor is it known whether unusual chromosome patterns occurring in individuals who are not subnormal carry an increased risk of delinquency.

SOCIAL VARIABLES

Socio-Economic Status and Risk of Criminal Behaviour

The results of a number of investigations of the social backgrounds of delinquents and young criminals indicate that the sons of unskilled workers and of the unemployed are substantially overrepresented; the children of skilled working-class, white-collar and professional parents are much less likely to be convicted of criminal offences. Thus, Mannheim *et al.* (1947), in a study of 400 juvenile delinquents from London courts, found that 53 per cent came from households that would be included in Class V of the Registrar-General's scheme, which is certainly more than double the proportion to be expected if there were no differences between occupational groups in the frequency of delinquency. Morris (1957) discovered a similarly high incidence of sons of unskilled workers in a smaller sample of delinquents in Croydon. Ferguson (1952), Little and Ntsekhe

(1959), and Glueck and Glueck (1950) all report a preponderance of lower working-class children among their groups of delinquents, although the differences were not so pronounced as those in the studies cited above. Little and Ntsekhe suggest that the social-class differential may be diminishing, but this is not borne out by the most recent British figures (Douglas *et al.*, 1966), derived from a large developmental study, which indicate that 'children of non-manual workers are only half as likely to be cautioned or [to] come before the courts as the children of manual workers'.

A similar picture emerges from studies of young men (normally in the age-range 17–20 +) committed to borstal institutions (e.g., Rose, 1954; Gibbens, 1963). Unfortunately it is impossible to obtain reliable information about the social backgrounds of the whole population of adult offenders in British prisons (Mannheim, 1965), though something is known of the socio-economic status of those who commit certain kinds of crimes, such as sexual offences (Radzinowicz, 1957; Fitch, 1962), shoplifting (Gibbens and Prince, 1962), motoring offences (Willett, 1964), homicides (Wolfgang, 1958; see also Wolfgang and Ferracuti, 1967), and offences relating to drunkenness (Parr, 1962). These data, and less systematic observations of those who commit larcenies, indicate an overall preponderance of individuals from the lower working class which cannot be explained by the proportion of such families in the population (Walker, 1965). More reliable parametric information is available in Denmark; Wolf (1962) investigated the incidence of criminal convictions in more than three thousand adult males, and found that 15 per cent of those in unskilled manual occupations had been convicted of offences, compared with 4 or 5 per cent of middle-class men.

These figures describe the frequency of criminal convictions, not the incidence of illegal acts. Investigators who have asked children and adolescents, in strict confidence, about their delinquencies have not found marked differences between the social classes (Nye et al., 1958; Nye, 1958; Dentler and Monroe, 1961), and have concluded that the higher frequency of convictions in children from working-class families is an artefact of police practice. However, there is another explanation of the discrepant findings of these two kinds of investigation. Clark and Wenninger (1962), who also found no real relationship between the socio-economic status of the child's family and the number of delinquencies which he admitted, when this question was investigated in neighbourhoods in which most families belonged to the same status-group, were able to demonstrate genuine variations in both the frequency and the nature of reported delinquencies *between* communities dominated by different socio-economic classes. They report that, 'the lower class areas have higher illegal behavior rates, particularly in the more serious types of offences'; they were also able to show that when social-class groups are compared *across* communities, so that the population sampled is heterogeneous in respect of 'status areas', a significant relationship between socio-economic status and admitted delinquency does emerge. Other studies have yielded similar findings (Reiss and Rhodes, 1961; *see also* Downes, 1966, for a review of this material). It is reasonable to conclude that the crucial variable is the general style of life of the family rather than its immediate economic circumstances and status—a proposition that gains some support from the investigations of Douglas et al. (1966) and of Sprott et al. (1954).

There is good reason to suppose that studies of the inmate populations of prisons and correctional institutions are likely to present an exaggerated picture of social-class differentials in the incidence of delinquency because of the tendency of sentencers to prescribe institutional penalties for offenders from 'bad' homes (Clinard, 1958; Short and Nye, 1957), although it is not easy to demonstrate this effect (*see* Hood, 1962). It is even more difficult to assess the extent to which the figures are influenced by the fact that delinquencies of middle-class children may be dealt with by the parents or the school rather than by the police (Wootton, 1959). Even if the police do decide to take action themselves, they may still deal differently with the delinquent from a middle-class home, administering a formal 'caution' instead of preferring charges in the courts (Douglas et al., 1966). Estimates of the *size* of the social-class differential in the incidence of delinquency based on surveys of groups of 'official' offenders must therefore be treated with great reserve. On the other hand, the evidence we have reviewed here supports the contention that the sons of unskilled workers *brought up in neighbourhoods in which families of this socio-economic class predominate* are more likely to commit criminal offences, and to commit more numerous and more serious offences, than the sons of middle-class or skilled working-class parents, at least during adolescence and early manhood. It remains to be seen whether this tendency is a permanent feature of criminal statistics, and whether it also holds true for female offenders and for mature male offenders.

Although the association between socio-economic status and criminality may have been overestimated, it has furnished impetus for some interesting studies of social-class differences in styles of child training; for it is reasonable to assume that if the families of unskilled workers provide a disproportionate number of offences, they must (*ceteris paribus*) be less efficient, as agents of socialisation, than middle-class or upper working-class families. This argument relies, of course, on the assumption that 'primary psychopathy', as we have defined it, is equally infrequent in all social strata. There is no reason to suppose that this assumption is incorrect, but the evidence that supports it is both slight and indirect. It entails two testable, related assumptions: (1) that 'undersocialised' individuals will make up a greater proportion of lower working class delinquents than of those recruited from middle-class or skilled working-class families (Trasler, 1962), and (2) that the socio-economic status of the families from which offenders are derived will be found, in any randomly chosen group of delinquents or criminals, to be statistically independent of those attributes that define primary psychopathy or neurotic delinquency. The second of these propositions receives some support from the dimensional studies of Marcus (1960), Quay (1964) and Jenkins and Glickman (1947). Conger and Miller (1966), while contesting the theoretical basis of a similar prediction advanced by Kvaraceus and Miller (1959), present data that are not inconsistent with our argument. On the other hand, proposition (1) has yet to be tested.

The Parameters of Social Training

That part of the socialisation process which furnishes the conditions in which the developing individual is trained to inhibit socially-proscribed behaviour is extremely difficult to investigate—because of its complexity and the interdependence of its several aspects, and also because it is hard to discover how parents and other agents of socialisation actually behave. As Robbins (1963) demonstrates, people's descriptions of their methods of dealing with children are seldom accurate, and it is rarely possible actually to observe this kind of interaction without greatly distorting it. In the discussion that follows we shall attempt only to identify a few of those aspects of child-training processes which seem, on present evidence, to be especially important in determining their effectiveness in promoting social avoidance learning.

We shall use two avenues of approach to this problem. Firstly, if it is the case that some socio-economic groups are less efficient than others in the task of social training, such differences as may emerge from a comparison of their characteristic patterns of child rearing may point to the reasons for this. There is, however, a particular reason for caution in interpreting such comparisons. Styles of child rearing are subject to continuous change; they are strongly influenced by tradition, it is true, but they also reflect, and are modified by, the physical surroundings, the economic circumstances and the prevailing religious beliefs and social values of each generation. Some of the investigations to which we shall refer relate, fortunately, to the period in which the greater number of contemporary delinquents were passing through the formative years of child-hood; some do not, and in any event it would be unwise to assume that even those differences in parental practice that were quite clear-cut ten or fifteen years ago have persisted to the present time.

Clues of a rather different order may be derived from Mowrer's analysis of passive avoidance learning, which implies that certain conditions must be met if training is to be effective. The model was initially devised to account for the behaviour of animals in the laboratory but—by analogy, if not in precise equivalence—its essential parameters can be identified in the child training situation. First, the process relies on the unprompted occurrence of the behaviour that is to be inhibited. Second, this behaviour must be systematically (and quickly) followed by the application of a punishing stimulus capable of eliciting an unpleasant state of arousal. Third, it is necessary for the subject to recognise those features of the total situation that indicate that punishment is imminent. It is implied that some of these cues are response-produced (i.e. are 'within the organism') and that others are perceived features of the external environment; a rat which has learned to inhibit the action of walking towards the manipulandum in the experimental chamber will have no hesitation in approaching other attractive objects, with similar gait, in a free situation. Thus what has to be discriminated is a complex of cues—a consideration which we shall see to be important in the application of this model to the child-training situation. Fourth, some degree of generalisation is necessary if avoidance is to be maintained. The animal in the laboratory learns to inhibit a category of behaviours rather than an exactly specified sequence of motor movements; for example, both frontal and oblique approaches to the manipulandum incur punishment.

In transferring these notions to the socialisation process a further assumption of some importance is necessary. It is that childish misdemeanours are in a special sense analogues of adult crimes, so that avoidance responses acquired during the early years of life will extend, in due course, to whole categories of behaviour of which a child is incapable. It seems reasonable to assume that pilfering, aggressiveness and 'immodesty' for which children are rebuked can be treated as paradigms for the larcenies and thefts, violent offences, and sexual crimes which make up the great majority of 'ordinary' delinquency, and indeed parents generally assume that in eradicating the former they have some hope of preventing the latter. It is significant, also, that these are the kinds of crime about which most people feel aversion and guilt; by contrast, the 'technical' and 'white-collar' crimes which have no parallel in childhood, such as evasion of tax and customs laws, motoring offences and financial swindles, are much less likely to provoke strong feelings, although in some cases they result in a great deal more harm to individuals and to the community (Wootton, 1959).

SANCTIONS

Investigations of social-class differences in styles of child-rearing have devoted much attention to the kinds of sanctions parents employ in training their children. In particular, a distinction is drawn between physical punishments (such as spanking) and those that involve the interruption of social relations by isolating the child, or temporarily withholding expressions of parental affection and approval. A number of studies in the United States (Bronfenbrenner, 1958; Allinsmith, 1960—but see also Eron *et al.*, 1963) and in Britain (cf. Sprott *et al.*, 1954) showed that middle-class parents usually relied upon 'love-oriented' techniques, while parents of lower socio-economic status made fairly extensive use of physical punishments. Sears *et al.* (1957) furnish evidence that the withholding of parental approval is much more effective in securing socially-conforming behaviour than the infliction of pain. Argyle (1964) has suggested that this finding is damaging to theories which regard socialisation as an analogue of avoidance training, but his argument appears to be based on a misconception of the rôle of the sanction in avoidance training. Although in the animal laboratory the punishing stimulus S_p (*see* Fig. 3.1) is generally a painful one (such as an electric shock) its essential function is not to create pain, but to generate 'an unpleasant state of arousal', r_t, which will mediate avoidance behaviour in subsequent trials. The distinction is important; avoidance training can be effected in human subjects by the use of stimuli that are unpleasant but not painful, such as loud noises (Watson and Rayner, 1920), and indeed this fact has proved useful in the modification of abnormal behaviour (*see* chapter 22, 'The Effects of Psychological Treatment').

In practice, few parents are prepared to inflict pain of sufficient intensity to induce a strong autonomic response; it seems likely, therefore, that physical punishment administered within the family derives most or all of its effect from its symbolic significance. But if this is the case it is not immediately clear why techniques of socialisation which employ physical punishments should be less effective than 'love-oriented' methods in which the temporary withholding of parental approval is signalled verbally or by facial expression, for both presumably rely on the exploitation of the child's emotional dependence on his parents. Some clues to the reason for this can be found in the differing social circumstances in which the two kinds of sanctions are employed. Middle-class traditions of family life emphasise the internal cohesiveness of the family; the young child is encouraged to find almost all of his social contacts within the family group, and the phase of his life in which he is wholly dependent upon his parents and siblings for affection and reassurance is relatively long. He does not begin to establish warm interpersonal relations with people outside the family group (who might constitute alternative sources of comfort and reassurance) until

he is old enough to go to school; until that time, being out of favour with his parents implies a high degree of isolation, and gives rise to considerable anxiety. In these circumstances temporary withholding of parental affection is an extremely powerful sanction. By contrast, those families that rely on physical punishments generally live in high-density neighbourhoods in which a much higher incidence of casual contacts is inevitable, even if these were not encouraged by traditions of sociability and neighbourliness. The child begins to establish relations with children and with adults in other families; the first phase of his social development during which he is wholly dependent on his parents is comparatively short, and soon gives way to a state of affairs in which he has alternative sources of reassurance if he is in trouble at home (Trasler, 1965a).

ATTITUDES TO PARENTHOOD

The kind of sanction which parents employ seems also to be related to their conception of the task of bringing up children. As we have already noted, avoidance training can only be applied to behaviour that occurs spontaneously; the parents must wait until the child does something he ought not to do, and then apply an appropriate punishment, in order to establish the response that will inhibit such behaviour in the future. It is also necessary that they should do so with reasonable consistency; they may occasionally overlook examples of misbehaviour, but it is important that they should never reward it.

In practice, parents punish childish misbehaviour for two reasons: to abate an immediate nuisance to others or danger to the child, and (secondly) in the belief that they are shaping his character. Much depends on the relative importance they assign to these two aspects of their rôle. It is a simple matter to distract a child from annoying others by administering a slap or a sharp rebuke; on the other hand, consistent training demands a great deal of time and attention. It also means correcting the child if he unknowingly contravenes the rules of social conduct (as, for example, when he helps himself to candy, not realising that he needs permission), and this sometimes interrupts pleasant family interaction. Parents will not do this, and neither will they feel and show genuine concern at the child's action, unless they believe that childish misdemeanours have more than ephemeral significance. There is evidence that concern for long-term character formation is more marked among middle-class parents than in lower-class families (Sears *et al.*, 1957; Sprott *et al.*, 1954). It involves paying attention to the principles implicit in the child's behaviour, and sometimes to his motives, rather than to the practical details of his misdemeanour, which may be quite trivial (Kohn, 1957, 1959), Thus, while some parents may simply be amused at their infant's ineffectual attempts to inflict physical harm, others may treat such behaviour seriously, believing that unless it is curbed this aggressive impulse will in due course become a dangerous propensity for violence. In an interesting analysis of social-class variations in parental behaviour, Kohn argues that these are partly a function of the differing conditions of life encountered by individuals of different socio-economic status; middle-class parents, who follow occupations which require a degree of self-direction, tend to respond to the child's intentions, while working-class parents, accustomed to accepting the instructions of others, emphasise the need for conformity to external rules (Kohn, 1963; *see also* Stolz, 1967).

VALUES

It is frequently suggested that the high incidence of criminality in certain sections of the population is to be explained by differences in the values and rules of behaviour that prevail in those groups, rather than ineffective methods of child training. Although this argument has been used to explain social-class differences in the prevalence of crime, it is difficult to reconcile with the fact that (at least if recorded contacts with the police are used as the index) non-criminals greatly outnumber offenders even in those socio-economic groups and neighbourhoods that exhibit the highest incidence of delinquency (Trasler, 1962). It is conceivable that, as Franks (1956) and Eysenck (1970b) argue, there are some families which positively encourage stealing and other antisocial activities so that the children are efficiently conditioned to the wrong stimuli. But there is no evidence that there exists any sizeable number of criminals, in other respects normal in their social functioning, who possess a genuinely inverted value-system. What seems more likely is that certain specific kinds of delinquency are condoned in some social groups (for instance, the theft of public property, or violence towards members of other races), so that while the general proscription of stealing and physical aggression is maintained, the kinds of behaviour to which these terms apply are rather differently defined.

The question, as Kohn points out, is a complicated one. Surveys designed to discover the qualities parents regard as important in their children have not demonstrated any marked differences between social class groups; honesty, consideration for others, self-control and unwillingness to resort to violence are apparently valued by most, if not all,

parents (Kohn, 1959, 1963). But data of this kind are of little help in resolving the problem, for two reasons. First, it is by no means certain that the expressed values of parents are a reliable guide to the behavioural rules they actually apply in training their children, or to the emphasis they give to them in practice. A mother who says that one of her main aims is to bring up her child to be honest may nevertheless overlook some kinds of behaviour that other parents would regard as grossly dishonest. In the second place, it is important to recognise the extent to which the individual's behaviour is shaped and modified by his membership of social groups other than the family. It is quite clear that peer-groups and other adolescent and adult groups, with behavioural norms and values at variance with those expressed in the criminal law, do exist; that they are more common in certain socio-economic strata and in certain kinds of neighbourhoods than in others; and that they exert considerable (and possibly enduring) influence on their members (Downes, 1966; Mannheim, 1965). But this is a question—or rather, a universe of questions—of great complexity which cannot, unfortunately, be dealt with here.

LANGUAGE

It is evident that if the individual is to be trained to inhibit socially-proscribed behaviour he must first learn to distinguish it from similar, but permissible, actions. The distinction is often a nice one, depending on cues that are not easy to recognise. A small child will pick up any coins which he sees lying on a shop counter; a few years later he will discriminate without hesitation between the change from his own transaction and someone else's money, and his behavioural response will be quite different. The parents' task, in training their child, is not simply to visit misbehaviour with a sanction, but to help him to identify those characteristics of the situation that have evoked their disapproval. This is mainly accomplished by some kind of verbal explanation, which has three related functions: (1) to draw attention to the action that is being punished (as distinct from other actions the child may perform at almost the same time); (2) to indicate what distinguishes it from other actions that are permissible; and (3) to identify it as an example of a class of behaviours, all of which are wrong. Thus the verbal component of training mediates both discrimination and generalisation to future situations.

The extent to which parents make use of reasoned explanations in disciplining their children varies, as one would expect, according to their social status and the kind of sanction on which they normally rely

(Sears *et al.*, 1957). Techniques of child training based on the temporary withholding of approval necessarily involve some verbal labelling of the child's action as 'naughty', and, in practice, usually entail more elaborate explanations in which other general terms are used to indicate the relations between specific misdemeanours and general rules— 'mother doesn't like dirty little boys'; 'you mustn't take things that don't belong to you'; 'nobody wants to play with rough children'—but are not essential to it. It seems probable, however, that the willingness of middle class and upper working class parents to expend time and trouble in explaining to the child why what he has done is wrong reflects the emphasis on the long-term moulding of character which distinguishes these groups from the lower working class—a view that necessarily focuses attention on the principles implicit in acts of misbehaviour rather than their immediate consequences.

There is reason to believe that the disposition to refer to general rules of conduct in order to distinguish between right and wrong actions is promoted by formal education; the less-educated tend to think in terms of specific prohibitions without recognising underlying ethical principles. Certainly the task of explaining such matters precisely (and clearly enough for a child to understand) demands some skill in the use of language. In this connexion Bernstein's (1960, 1961, 1962, 1965) distinction between two kinds or styles of speech is of particular interest. One of these (which Bernstein terms *restricted code*) is relatively simple and crude in structure, and is universally used for everyday purposes. It relies on the existence of a background of common experiences, shared by speaker and hearer; it can convey simple exhortations, demands, statements of fact, and expressions of attitude, but it is limited to the rôle of invoking or alluding to matters which are so familiar to both parties to the conversation that they do not have to be spelled out. On the other hand, when it is necessary to communicate information more exactly—to specify logical relations, enunciate general principles, and identify their implications in particular instances—a more sophisticated and precise mode of speech (*elaborated code*) is required. Bernstein suggests that practice and skill in the use of elaborated codes of speech is largely a function of formal education, and for that reason is more characteristic of middle-class people than of unskilled workers and their families, who seldom need (or have the opportunity to become familiar with) this kind of linguistic code. Bernstein's typology is supported by some empirical studies which indicate that children from lower working class homes have much less facility in the use of elaborated codes of speech than those from upper working-class or middle-class families (Lawton 1968; Robinson and Rackstraw, 1971), presumably because they rarely encounter this kind of language.

Most work in this field has been concerned to establish the existence of differences between the social classes in language behaviour. The crucial question for the study of criminality, which apparently has yet to be systematically explored, is whether persistent delinquents who do not exhibit symptoms of primary psychopathy have particular difficulty in understanding speech in the style of elaborated code; if this is the case, the line of argument set out in this section may be considered tenable. But there are other reasons for investigating the language characteristics of criminals. As Mowrer (1960b) implies, verbal cues probably play an important part in the 'once-always generalisation' which mediates avoidance learning in human social situations, where the temporal relations between stimuli are seldom optimal and there is a great deal of 'noise' in the form of irrelevant concurrent events. Several writers have suggested that some disturbance of language—or at least of logical processes or conceptual systems normally derived from verbal interaction with others—may play some part in the psychopath's characteristic inability to respond to signals of social disapproval or impending punishment (e.g. Cleckley, 1964).

SUMMARY

It is clear that those aspects of social training within the family which, on theoretical grounds, seem likely to influence the efficiency of such training are by no means independent. There is a close relation between parents' conceptions of their rôle, the kinds of sanctions they employ, and the extent to which they furnish verbal explanations that facilitate accurate and reliable discrimination of the crucial from the irrelevant, and consequently promote effective generalisation to future situations. It seems to be the case, at least in contemporary Western societies, that the most effective style of child training depends on the systematic exploitation of the child's dependence upon his parents for emotional support and security, and that in order to implement this technique of training, parents must exercise certain linguistic skills. However, two reservations must be made. First, although we have made use of observed differences between socio-economic classes in trying to identify some of those aspects of parental practice that influence the efficiency with which they train their children, it must be recognised that such differences may be transitory (Bronfenbrenner, 1958); it is unsafe to assume that lower working class parents of today are less efficient than their

Table 3.2. Wechsler-Bellevue Intelligence Scale Scores of Delinquent Samples[a] (*from* Prentice and Kelly, 1963)

Study	Year	N	Sample[b]	Age			Form		P.S.	V.S.	F.S.
Altus & Clark	1949	53	Training camp (includes 31 Mexicans)	R 14–18	$\bar{X}$ SD		I	$\bar{X}$ SD	98·0[c,d]	82·0[c]	89·0[c]
Bernstein & Corsini	1953	100	Females in institutions	R	$\bar{X}$ SD		I[e]	$\bar{X}$ SD	100·8 15·3	90·1 14·9	94·8 15·2
		100	(As above)	R	$\bar{X}$ SD		I[e]	$\bar{X}$ SD	99·9 15·5	90·2 14·8	93·9 15·1
Blank	1958	67	Training school	R 14–16	$\bar{X}$ SD		I	$\bar{X}$ SD	99·7[d]	87·4	92·5
		49	High school students	R 12–16	$\bar{X}$ SD		I	$\bar{X}$ SD	103·2	101·3	102·9
DeStephens	1953	200	Reformatory	R 16–30[f]	$\bar{X}$ SD	22·0 3·2	I, II	$\bar{X}$ SD	98·3[d] 17·6	90·1 14·5	93·6 15·9
		100	Reformatory (Negroes)	R 16–30[f]	$\bar{X}$ SD	22·7 3·1	I, II	$\bar{X}$ SD	91·2 15·3	86·7 12·7	87·9 14·1
Diller	1952	80	Female clinic outpatients (court referrals)	R 14–17	$\bar{X}$ SD	15·5	I	$\bar{X}$ SD	86·2 14·7	80·8 12·8	83·6 15·4
Doppelt & Seashore	1959	98	Federal training school	R 16–17	$\bar{X}$ SD		WAIS	$\bar{X}$ SD			100·5[g] 13·1
		61	Federal & state institutions	R 18–19	$\bar{X}$ SD		WAIS	$\bar{X}$ SD			99·7[g] 11·9
		95	Federal reformatory	R 20–24	$\bar{X}$ SD		WAIS	$\bar{X}$ SD			100·6[g] 10·5
		194	Federal penitentiary	R 25–35	$\bar{X}$ SD		WAIS	$\bar{X}$ SD			97·2[g] 14·4
Durea & Taylor	1948	109	Industrial school	R 11–18	$\bar{X}$ SD		I	$\bar{X}$ SD	94·5[c,d]	83·8[d]	87·6
Foster	1959	44	Adolescent delinquents	R 11/5–16/11	$\bar{X}$ SD	15·0	I	$\bar{X}$ SD	98·3	96·3	
Franklin	1945	276	Training school (Negroes)	R 9/7–20/1	$\bar{X}$ SD	14·6 1·6	I	$\bar{X}$ SD	80·4 18·2	76·2 14·5	76·5 15·4
Glueck & Glueck	1950	500	Training schools	R	$\bar{X}$ SD	14·7 1·6	I	$\bar{X}$ SD	97·2 13·4	88·6 14·6	92·3 13·3
		500	Matched non-delinquents	R	$\bar{X}$ SD	14·5 1·4	I	$\bar{X}$ SD	98·1 12·9	92·0 12·2	92·2 12·0
Graham & Kamona	1958	33	Federal institution (unsuccessful readers)	R 16–17/11	$\bar{X}$ SD	17·0	WAIS	$\bar{X}$ SD	99·8	90·3	93·9
		35	Federal institution (successful readers)	R 16–17/11	$\bar{X}$ SD	17·2	WAIS	$\bar{X}$ SD	104·3	105·2	105·1
Harris	1957	25	Training school (Nova Scotia)	R 13–16	$\bar{X}$ SD		WISC	$\bar{X}$ SD	98·8	84·3	
		25	Matched non-delinquents (Nova Scotia)	R 13–16	$\bar{X}$ SD		WISC	$\bar{X}$ SD	93·4	90·0	
Jastak & Allen	1944	50	Clinic outpatients referred by court primarily	R 10–17	$\bar{X}$ SD		I	$\bar{X}$ SD			85·0[h]
		50	Females as above	R 10–17	$\bar{X}$ SD		I	$\bar{X}$ SD			81·0[h]
Kingsley	1960	20	Psychopathic prisoners (military disciplinary barracks)	R 19/10–33/1	$\bar{X}$ SD	22·2		$\bar{X}$ SD			99·9[i] 10·9
	1960	20	Matched prisoners (non-psychopathic)	R 21/10–27/6	$\bar{X}$ SD	26·3 4·2		$\bar{X}$ SD			
		40	Military personnel		$\bar{X}$ SD			$\bar{X}$ SD			98·2 10·6

Table 3.2. (Continued)

Study	Year	N	Sample[b]	Age		Form		P.S.	V.S.	F.S.
Prentice & Kelly	1960	100	Diagnostic reception center	R 8/1–17/11	$\bar{X}$ 15.5	WAIS,I WISC,II	$\bar{X}$	98.0[d]	90.9	94.1
					SD 1.8		SD	11.8	12.4	11.9
		100	Females as above	R 13/0–17/11	$\bar{X}$ 15.4	WISC I, II	$\bar{X}$	95.4[d]	89.4	91.8
					SD 0.9		SD	12.2	11.8	11.8
Richardson & Surko	1956	105	Inpatients referred by court for study (includes 15 girls)	R 8/4–16/0	$\bar{X}$ 12.3[e]	WISC	$\bar{X}$	92.4[d]	87.0	88.4
					SD		SD	18.2	15.0	16.6
Strother	1944	14	Psychopathic outpatients & inpatients of hospital	R 16–21	$\bar{X}$	I	$\bar{X}$	101.7	99.4	
					SD		SD	13.4	11.0	
Vane & Eisen	1954	100	Females in reformatory	R 16–25	$\bar{X}$ 18.5	I	$\bar{X}$	98.5[d]	93.6	95.2
					SD 1.5		SD	10.1	9.7	8.4
		100	Matched non-delinquents in high school	R 16–25	$\bar{X}$ 17.3	I	$\bar{X}$	100.9[d]	93.1	96.8
					SD 0.9		SD	8.9	7.7	6.9
Walters	1953	50	New Zealanders (European descent) in main security prison	R 20–45	$\bar{X}$	I	$\bar{X}$	101.9	101.1	101.8
					SD		SD	12.2	13.7	13.3
	1953	50	New Zealanders (Maori descent) as above	R 20–45	$\bar{X}$	I	$\bar{X}$	89.1	82.1	84.4
					SD		SD	12.1	13.2	13.0
Wechsler	1955	52	Reformatory	R 16–26	$\bar{X}$ 27.8	WAIS	$\bar{X}$	98.3	93.8	95.4
					SD		SD	12.6	10.9	11.7
Wiens *et al.*	1959	112	Convicted sex offenders in state diagnostic hospital	R 14–64	$\bar{X}$ 32.4	WAIS WISC, I	$\bar{X}$	104.0	97.6	100.1
					SD		SD	15.0	17.3	15.3
Weider *et al.*	1943	61	Delinquent & behaviour problem clinic patients on observation ward (includes 13 girls)	R 8/0–16/1	$\bar{X}$ 12.3	I	$\bar{X}$	94.0	82.0	87.0
					SD		SD	17.5	16.1	16.6

[a] For clarity of presentation, all Wechsler scale entries are rounded to tenths, all age ranges expressed in months, all age $\bar{X}$s and SDs converted to decimals.

[b] All samples are white delinquent males in state correctional institutions except where stated otherwise.

[c] Median scores only reported.

[d] P > V at 0·05 level or greater where reported in study.

[e] While not stated, Form I was apparently administered to adolescent delinquents.

[f] Reported for entire group of 300 only.

[g] While no Performance or Verbal means are reported, 'In all age groups, the Performance IQ was higher than the Verbal IQ. The difference was only 1·7 IQ points for the oldest group, although it was 4 to 5 IQ points for the younger groups' (Doppelt and Seashore, 1959, pp. 86–87).

[h] While no Verbal or Performance means are reported, 'only eleven children out of the 100 have a balanced pattern of perceptual orientation. There is only one true verbalist in the group. Eighty-nine have a strong non-verbal orientation. Both boys and girls show the same degree of deviation' (Harris, 1944, p. 102).

[i] Presented for combined prisoner groups only. 'P IQ was greater than V IQ, at 1 per cent level of confidence, in all three groups. This difference was not significantly greater in the psychopaths as compared to the other prisoners not in the general prisoner group as compared with the controls' (Jastak and Allen, 1960, p. 373). Form of Wechsler administered not reported.

middle-class contemporaries as agents of socialisation. Second, the apparently quite distinct patterns of child training which emerge from the literature should be treated with some caution. Most of the data on which we have relied consist of correlations between a few parameters of parental techniques in sizeable samples of families; although they are illuminating, they almost certainly obscure the existence of some households in which different, and possibly equally effective, styles of training are employed.

Intelligence and Educational Performance

The belief that there is a connexion between subnormality of intelligence and criminality has a long history (Woodward, 1963) and probably originated in the observation that many convicted offenders were illiterate, or almost so, and that (to judge by their responses to punishment) they were incapable of learning by experience. Early studies of prison populations, in which simple interrogation formed the basis of assessment, seemed to confirm the hypothesis. But when intelligence tests were introduced they showed a much lower incidence of subnormality than had been suspected. An extensive study of inmates in Illinois penitentiaries undertaken by Tulchin (1939), using the Army Alpha and Beta tests, yielded a distribution of scores which was not significantly different from that found in men drafted into the armed forces. Similar results were reported in a number of investigations of young delinquents (e.g. Shulman, 1950; Harris, 1957). Caplan and Siebert (1964) examined the intelligence-test scores of more than fifty-one thousand delinquents, collected over a period of 34 years. They noted that the mean score had steadily risen from 80 to 92 during that time, but concluded that most (if not all) of this apparent gain was attributable to improvements in the tests employed. Wheway (1958) reviewing a number of British studies of adult and young offenders, predicted that '. . . as tests become less culturally loaded the IQ of delinquents will approach the same level as that of the normal population'. The effects of cultural handicaps are most readily distinguished when a battery of verbal and non-verbal tests is used. Prentice and Kelly's (1963) searching analysis of 24 investigations of delinquent groups in which one of the Wechsler tests was employed showed that most of these had yielded a mean Performance score within the normal range, although mean scores in the Verbal division of the test were usually substantially lower (*see* Table 3.2). They also concluded that 'the "true" incidence of intelligence in delinquency may not be significantly different from the general population.'

The tendency for delinquents to achieve higher scores on performance tests than in verbal tests had been noted by a number of investigators. Wechsler himself suggested that the 'P > V discrepancy' might be used in the diagnosis of psychopathy, though he also drew attention to other features in the pattern of subtest scores which ought to be taken into account in drawing this inference (Wechsler, 1944), a precaution that has not always been observed. Several investigations have found the P > V discrepancy to be common among institutionalised delinquents (Manne *et al.*, 1962; Fisher, 1961; Blank, 1958; Harris, 1957; Frost and Frost, 1962); on the other hand, Foster (1959) and Field (1960) failed to demonstrate significant differentials in adolescent psychopaths and adult recidivists respectively, and there are indications that the pattern is not usually discernible in subnormals or in Negro delinquents.

Prentice and Kelly (1963) list several studies of delinquent groups in which the P > V discrepancy did not appear, and point out that, on the other hand, it has been observed among individuals who are obviously not psychopathic. They conclude that 'there is little evidence to justify Wechsler's contention that the P > V pattern is a useful one in differentiating psychopathy *per se* although it may be diagnostic of some kinds of learning disabilities.' It certainly seems to be correlated with educational failure. Graham and Kamano (1958) divided a group of persistent young offenders into successful and unsuccessful readers, and found that those who could read well obtained equally high scores on both verbal and performance divisions of the WAIS; the group of unsuccessful readers, on the other hand, yielded a mean performance score more than nine points above the verbal quotient. This is supported by an extensive investigation of young delinquents by Henning and Levy (1967). Where the P > V pattern does occur it is usually the result of particularly low scores on the Information, Arithmetic, and Vocabulary subtests, and sometimes in Comprehension also (Wechsler 1944; Panton, 1960; Harris, 1957; Richardson and Surko, 1956).

There is much evidence that youthful delinquency is associated with educational underachievement—that is to say, delinquents' attainments in school subjects tend to be meagre by comparison with those of non-delinquents of similar intelligence (e.g. Glueck and Glueck, 1950; Ferguson, 1952). Richardson and Surko (1956) report that 'the lowest scores are in tests which are most dependent on school learning or which require concentration and persistency of effort in a task involving symbols. By far the lowest ratings for the group are those in the school achievement tests in reading and arithmetic.'

This is not, as one might suspect, simply a reflection of the socio-economic classes from which delinquents are recruited. Manne *et al.* (1962) showed that the P > V discrepancy was, if anything, more pronounced in sociopaths from superior homes than in those from lower working class families; and West (1969) found that within a relatively homogeneous urban working-class group, low educational attainment was highly predictive of both 'official' and 'unofficial' delinquency. This study is of interest for another reason. It was found, not unexpectedly, that most of the delinquents obtained very poor results in a test of verbal comprehension; more surprisingly, they also achieved low scores on the Raven Progressive Matrices test, a non-verbal measure of intelligence. This proved, in fact, to be a better predictor of delinquency than the Mill Hill vocabulary scale—a finding which apparently conflicts with those of most other investigations of the characteristics of young offenders. The authors are inclined to attribute this to lack of motivation in the test situation (Gibson and West, 1968), but it is not clear why this effect should occur in their study when it has not been evident in others. It may be significant, on the other hand, that the Raven test differs from most non-verbal measures in requiring the subject to discover the principles underlying arrangements of symbols and, by logical inference, to deduce the characteristics of the remaining item in the pattern. Thus, although it is a non-verbal test, it samples reasoning processes of the kind normally mediated by language. Indeed, Barratt (1956) found (in a population of similar age to Gibson and West's sample) that its correlations with the verbal and performance scales of the WISC were virtually identical.

All of this indicates that the relations between intelligence-test performance, school achievement and delinquency are complex. It is reasonable to suggest that the backwardness which many young delinquents exhibit during the early years of formal education is partly attributable to the fact that their experiences within the family have not equipped them with basic intellectual skills (such as the use of precise styles of language, the manipulation of symbols, and logical reasoning) which form the foundation for later progress in learning to read and in grasping the principles of arithmetic. The P > V discrepancy is an indication that such basic skills are lacking. We may argue, further, that the rudiments, at least, of these skills are usually acquired through verbal interaction with parents—and this (as we noted earlier) plays an important rôle in avoidance training. On these grounds some statistical relationship between delinquency, specific deficiencies in verbal tests, and poor school performance is to be expected, as each of these things depends to some extent on the characteristics of the child's linguistic environment during the first few years of his life.

Yet this explanation is not sufficient. The acquisition of social inhibitions is normally mediated, as we have seen, by the manipulation of the child's emotional dependence on his parents. 'Withholding of approval' is only effective if the child has learned to value, and to rely on, the security of his parents' affection. The development of speech and linguistic skills is stimulated and reinforced by their encouragement: thus both aspects of the child's early development depend, to some degree, on the motivating quality of affectionate interaction between child and parents. The disruption of this relationship during crucial phases of childhood tends to result in a characteristic syndrome of retarded speech development, delinquent behaviour, and discrepant scores on verbal tests of intelligence in comparison with those attained in performance tests (Kellmer Pringle, 1965) which closely resembles the pattern that emerges, in less striking form, from many of the studies of young sociopaths we have reviewed. The parallel is suggestive; and although these speculations are presently based on very little firm evidence, there is reason to hope that more intensive controlled investigations of the intellectual characteristics of young offenders (and also of mature criminals) will throw more light on the social conditions that impede the inhibition of socially-proscribed behaviour.

Discontinuities in Parent-Child Relations

If social avoidance training normally relies on the manipulation of the child's dependence on his parents it presumably follows that temporary or permanent interruption of this relationship during the early years of childhood is likely to prejudice the effectiveness of such training. Much will depend, obviously, on the age of the child at the time of separation, the circumstances in which loss of the parents occurs, and the quality of substitute care that is provided (*see* Chapter 16 and discussions in Ainsworth *et al.*, 1962; Monahan, 1960; Trasler, 1960; Yarrow, 1961). But one would expect to find, in the histories of any large, randomly chosen sample of delinquents, a greater frequency of family disruption than obtains in the population at large. The problem is complicated by the absence of 'baseline' information about the likelihood of losing one's parents during childhood, and the possibility that the risk is higher in some socio-economic groups than in others. However, three studies employing control samples matched for the social status of the family (Glueck and Glueck, 1950; Carr-Saunders *et al.*, 1942;

Hooke, 1966) have shown a higher incidence of broken homes among delinquents.

There is some indication in the Carr-Saunders study that the death of one or both parents is less likely to precipitate delinquency than divorce or separation. This is supported by the developmental investigation that is being conducted by Douglas and his colleagues, who report that, 'it is the families broken by divorce or separation that produce the high incidence of delinquence—23 per cent of children in these families were delinquent as compared with 12 per cent of those in families broken by death, and this difference cannot be explained in terms of the social classes from which these families came' (Douglas et al., 1966). Ferguson (1952) found a similar state of affairs in his Glasgow sample. Studies of the populations of correctional institutions usually show a higher incidence of family breakdown among inmates than in the general population of corresponding age (Mannheim and Wilkins, 1955; Little, 1965; Cline and Wangrow, 1959), though this may be partly a consequence of sentencing policy; it is interesting to note, however, that Banks (1965), in an analysis of boys in detention centres, found that family breakdown through divorce or separation was over-represented (compared with the corresponding age-group in the normal population) by a factor of five, while the number of boys who had lost parents through death was three times the expected incidence.

Much interest in the relations between deprivation of parental care and delinquent behaviour was aroused by Bowlby's contention that prolonged separation from the mother during the early years of a child's life was likely to result in a gross disturbance of social behaviour ('affectionless character') which closely resembles Cleckley's (1959) description of sociopathy, and which (in Bowlby's view) often leads to persistent delinquency and adult criminality (Bowlby, 1946, 1951). Bowlby's original sample was a highly selected one, derived from youthful patients in a child guidance clinic; although other workers have also found a high incidence of separation from the mother during early childhood among child-guidance populations (e.g. Wardle, 1961), attempts to test the 'maternal deprivation hypothesis' in its original form in more representative delinquent populations have not been very successful (Naess, 1959, 1962; Andry, 1960). It is admittedly difficult to secure accurate information about temporary interruptions in the mother-child relationship that have occurred many years ago; it should also be remembered that Bowlby's argument is concerned not simply with breaks in the continuity of maternal care, but also with its quality and with the kind of substitute care provided in its

place, which makes the hypothesis peculiarly difficult to test (Ainsworth et al., 1962; Yarrow, 1961). Grygier et al. (1959), presenting an analysis of the family relations of delinquent boys in training schools in Ontario, found that in this sample separation from the mother usually entailed general disruption of the family. Their study is open to the objection that sentencers may be more inclined to send homeless delinquents to training schools (cf. Nye, 1958), but it may well be the case, as they contend, that concentration on mother-child separation has caused some earlier investigators to overlook the relations between dissolution of the family and subsequent delinquency. It is of interest, in this connexion, that in a follow-up study of two hundred parentless children in New York, Theis (1924) found that those who had not received adequate substitute care were three times as likely to become persistent criminals in adult life as those who had been placed in good foster homes.

On theoretical grounds one would expect that the break-up of the family during the early years of childhood would be associated not simply with a higher risk of delinquency, but with a greater chance of becoming a persistent or recidivist offender. The evidence on this point is rather equivocal. Neither Little (1965) nor Field (1962) could demonstrate any reliable relation between maternal separation and frequency of offending in institutional groups of persistent criminals; however, both relied on prison records for their information, and they were dealing with populations which were already highly selected for recidivism. Craft et al. (1964), comparing the histories of large groups of patients in special hospitals (including subnormals and psychopaths), approved school boys, and non-delinquents from similar neighbourhoods, concluded that there was some evidence of a connexion between severity of delinquency and other disturbances of behaviour, on the one hand, and separation from the parents during childhood, on the other. But this (as the authors point out) was simply a pilot study; one may suspect that their data, like those of Field and Little, were unreliable, and the rather odd design of the research makes it impossible to determine how strong the correlation was. Robins, who conducted a long-term follow-up study of 524 children referred to a child guidance clinic for delinquency or similar behaviour problems, found that a slightly higher proportion (27 per cent as against 19 per cent) of those whose families were broken by divorce or separation were subsequently diagnosed as suffering from sociopathic personality, but children who lost their parents through death were no more likely to become sociopaths in later life than those whose families remained intact (Robins, 1966).

It appears that there is no simple relationship between separation from the parents in childhood and delinquency. There is no reason to doubt the findings of Goldfarb (1943, 1945) and others, that permanent *privation* (i.e. total absence) of a dependent relationship with a mother figure from an early age (Ainsworth and Bowlby, 1954) is likely to result in failure to inhibit antisocial behaviour; but modern techniques of child care are designed to prevent this state of affairs through the provision of substitute parents. On the other hand, certain kinds of family breakdown—particularly those caused by divorce or separation of the parents—usually represent the outcome of a prolonged period of stress, which can seriously interfere with the training of children. Several writers have proposed complex theories of the connexions between intrafamilial stress and delinquency (e.g. Stott, 1950; Bennett, 1960). But it can be argued that such statistical evidence as presently exists can also be adequately explained by the simpler assumptions of the avoidance-training model; namely, that socialisation demands consistent manipulation of a stable, reliable dependent relationship between the child and his parents, and also—by implication—the capacity to recognise and respond to the approval of others, which is presumably acquired through experience of normal family relationships (Sarbin *et al.*, 1965).

Time Orientation

The observation that delinquents seem to prefer immediate satisfactions to the achievement of longer-term, more worthwhile ends occurs frequently in criminological literature, and has some experimental support (e.g. Mischel, 1961). Various techniques have been devised for investigating 'temporal experience' (Wallace and Rabin, 1960), and some of these have recently been employed in attempts to demonstrate systematic differences between offenders and non-offenders in respect of 'time perspective' and accuracy in estimating brief periods of time.

TIME PERSPECTIVE

Barndt and Johnson (1955) asked delinquent boys to complete an unfinished story, and were able to show that, in comparison with carefully matched non-delinquent controls, the events they described took place in a relatively short period of time; this finding was confirmed by Davids *et al.* (1962) in a similar study. Siegman (1961), borrowing a technique from Wallace (1956) in which the subject is asked to furnish a list of ten future events involving himself, also reported that delinquents had a shorter time

perspective than non-delinquents. Siegman's study was particularly well-designed; he took care to control for the effects of institutionalisation by selecting, as his non-delinquent group, young men inducted into the Israeli Army. On the other hand, Schneiderman, using non-institutionalised groups (from a public school) could find no difference in time perspective. He made a further comparison between inmates of a secure state institution and non-delinquents in a boy's club; not surprisingly, he found that the fantasies of boys confined in prison were more future-oriented than those of boys living at home. But this is hardly a fair test of the hypothesis. Ricks (1964) reported that psychotherapy designed to combat delinquent tendencies in adolescents also had the effect of increasing their time perspective, but gave few details of his data.

On the whole, the available evidence seems to suggest that there are probably genuine differences in time perspective between delinquents and non-delinquents, but the origin and consequences of these differences are a matter of conjecture. Some writers have suggested that they simply reflect the social background from which offenders are recruited. As we have already noted, there is evidence that middle-class parents tend to pay more attention to the long-term implications of their children's behaviour, and probably encourage them to think in terms of goals and achievements that are relatively distant in time, in comparison with parents of low socio-economic status. One might expect these differences in parental behaviour to affect the time-perspective of their children, and indeed LeShan (1952) was able to demonstrate this in a comparative study of 'lower-lower class' children and those from families of higher social status. However, this cannot be the whole explanation as Barndt and Johnson (1955), for example, used samples which were carefully matched for social-class origin, but still found reliable differences between delinquents and non-delinquents.

TIME ESTIMATION

Siegman, in the study to which we have referred, predicted that delinquents would tend to give lower estimates of short periods of elapsed time than non-offenders. He based his hypothesis on the notion of the 'internal clock': '. . . the range of one's future time perspective is a significant source of variance in the experience of duration . . . the more the subject desires that an interval of time pass rapidly, the longer it will appear to be . . . subjects with a long range future time perspective are relatively more motivated that time pass rapidly' (Siegman, 1961).

This proved to be the case; his sample of institution-alised delinquents showed shorter time perspective and lower estimates of elapsed time than his control group of non-delinquents performing military service. Schneiderman made the opposite prediction, arguing that delinquents would have 'a feeling that time passes slowly', and would consequently tend to overestimate elapsed time. He found no significant differences in his younger samples of non-institution-alised delinquents; on the other hand, his older group of inmates in a maximum-security state institution did make higher estimates of the duration of short periods of time than non-offenders living in their own homes. Because of the way in which he selected his experimental samples, these results are difficult to interpret. It seems probable that any differences in 'internal clock' that might have obtained between delinquents and non-delinquents have been obscured by the effect of incarceration, which presumably makes time appear to pass slowly.

Mischel (1961) found that delinquents preferred 'immediate, smaller reinforcement as opposed to delayed, larger reinforcement', and reported that this tendency was associated with marked inaccuracy in long-term 'time recall'—estimating how long ago important events took place. Rutkin (1966), working with brief time intervals marked by either auditory or visual signals in the laboratory, found that delin-quents showed much greater variability in their judgements of the duration of elapsed time than a matched group of non-delinquent controls.

The evidence tends to support the contention that delinquency is associated with disturbance of time-sense so far as that is reflected in estimates of brief periods of elapsed time. But the theoretical signifi-cance of this effect is far from clear; in particular, the notion of the 'internal clock' does not appear to be very illuminating. The discrepancy between Schnei-derman's findings and those of other investigators suggests that the effects of detention in a penal institution may be considerable, and underlines the importance of ensuring that experimental and con-trol groups are tested in comparable conditions.

CONCLUDING NOTE

The principal object of this chapter was to trace connexions and relationships between some of the established facts about delinquents and criminals. An exhaustive review of existing materials would need ten times the space available here. We excluded studies that seemed to us to be defective in design and those that are not susceptible of replication because details of the manner in which samples were selected or of the measures employed are lacking in the published reports. A considerable number of well designed investigations remained; in choosing among them we concentrated, for the most part, on those that seemed to throw light on the patterns of inter-action between the individual and his social envi-ronment that give rise to criminality. We were concerned, *inter alia*, to explore the extent to which a simple model of avoidance learning of the kind proposed by Mowrer and Eysenck was capable of articulating these data into a reasonably coherent scheme. It is clear that such integration is feasible; whether it is heuristically advantageous remains to be seen. However, even this brief and preliminary survey has drawn attention to several questions that seem to be important and amenable to investigation.

One of these concerns the relations between pri-mary psychopathy and other kinds of behaviour disorder which entail the disposition to commit crimes. We have seen that there are striking differ-ences in results between experimental studies of groups selected by Cleckley's criteria (for instance, the work of Hare) and those investigations, such as the research of Eysenck and his colleagues, that have employed mixed groups of psychopaths. In par-ticular, the distinction between 'primary' and 'neurotic' psychopathy may prove to be of major importance. The more general question of the relations between psychopathy (however it is de-fined) and variations in responsiveness to social training among 'normal' people merits further investigation; here the experimental techniques devised by Lykken and Lippert have obvious application.

Although it has long been recognised that certain types of intracranial damage, resulting from trau-matic injury or cortical disease, may give rise to persistent criminality and other grossly deviant social behaviour, the way in which this occurs has not been established. Similar ignorance surrounds the mechanism through which normal social inhibitions are rendered temporarily ineffective by drugs (including alcohol) and by episodes of acute anxiety or environmental stress. The work of Eysenck, Hare, and Schachter and Latané generates rather different hypotheses about these matters. Crucial tests on carefully-defined experimental groups, designed to identify anomalies and changes in autonomic lability and reactivity, in discrimination, and perhaps in temporal gradients of generalisation, would certainly promote a better understanding of the precipitation of criminal behaviour in these special circumstances, and might also contribute to the general theory of social avoidance learning.

In the past, the study of criminality has been greatly hampered by the length and complexity of the chain of events that connects supposed antecedent variables, such as those relating to socialisation within the family, with adult criminal behaviour (a difficulty that is further compounded by the uncertainty of detection and inequalities in opportunity for crime). Attempts to establish measures of aspects of present functioning which will discriminate between individuals in respect of the likelihood that they will commit crimes have so far met with little success; those tests that have some predictive validity seem to derive this from indirect sampling of the social circumstances which tend to give rise to delinquency, and not from the psychological characteristics of the individual himself (Waldo and Dinitz, 1967; Mannheim and Wilkins, 1955). Yet the identification of relevant personality differences is an urgent need, not simply in the development of the theory of criminality, but as a basic condition for the construction of rational systems of classification of offenders for correctional purposes and for the validation of penal treatments, neither of which can make much progress without some means of assessing the degree of criminality of the individual, as distinct from the 'risk category' from which he is drawn (Trasler, 1964).

Our review yields some hints as to the way in which this problem may be tackled. It seems fairly clear that although differences in such primary characteristics as autonomic reactivity, behavioural extraversion, and rate of habituation to novel stimuli may be of fundamental importance in the genesis of criminality, they operate through interaction with a complex of environmental variables, and consequently are unlikely to furnish an accurate index of present criminality. A more direct measure of the subject's established avoidance responses is required. One aspect of the problem worth pursuing is the exploration of 'input' characteristics, such as the readiness with which the individual can detect and recognise relevant stimuli, presented aurally or visually (or in combination of these modalities) against a background of irrelevant noise, the extent of semantic generalisation, and the amplitude and rate of habituation that characterise his autonomic responses to such stimuli. Major and unavoidable problems arise in the selection of response measures (Hare, 1968a; *see also* Chapter 10). It should theoretically be possible to devise an experimental task in which established avoidance responses constrain or modify performance in some way, but no satisfactory method of doing this has yet been reported.

As we have seen, most existing studies of the mechanisms of social learning have concentrated on that part of the socialisation process which takes place within the family. But it is apparent that later social experiences, in the peer groups of childhood and adolescence, in the school and in working groups, exert a considerable effect on the individual's behaviour, including his response to social rules and proscriptions. There is substantial sociological evidence that such groups may, in some circumstances, demand conformity to values which are markedly different from, and perhaps antagonistic to, those transmitted by parents. Perhaps the most interesting of the psychological problems this raises concerns individual differences in responsiveness to group pressures. The variations in styles of child rearing to which we referred earlier have implications for this question. It is reasonable to suppose that in those social groups in which the period of exclusive dependence on the parents is relatively short, the child will look to the peer-group for social support and reassurance, and in doing so will develop a habit of depending on his peers, and a sensitiveness to group norms and group approval, to a greater extent than, say, a middle-class child, whose dependency needs are met by his parents until he has reached a phase in his development at which he has less need to rely on the immediate support of others. On these grounds one might expect individuals brought up in lower working class families to be more sensitive to peer-group norms, and less inclined to respond to parent-like figures of authority, than people brought up in the middle-class style. This argument is no more than speculative, although it does correspond with the impressions of workers in correctional institutions. It would, of course, have consequences for the treatment of delinquents. One might guess that two-person relationships (for example, between probation officers and their clients) would be less effective in modifying the behaviour of delinquents from those social groups in which peer-relations are established early; on the other hand, they might be expected to respond to such techniques as group therapy. The implications of this notion for the institutional treatment of offenders are disturbing; it can be argued that those offenders who are most likely to be committed to prisons and training institutions are also, by reason of their social backgrounds, the most receptive to the deviant values of the inmate culture, and the most resistant to the attempts of custodial staff to modify their behaviour (Trasler, 1965b).

Criminality is not the only form of deviant social

behaviour, nor the most common, but there are certain advantages in concentrating attention on this kind of deviancy. Convicted offenders are reasonably accessible, and published statistics furnish some information about the incidence of certain kinds of crimes, if not of criminals. Some of the hypotheses reviewed here have more general relevance; it is legitimate to hope that the development and consolidation of knowledge of criminality will also shed light on the origins of other kinds of deviant social behaviour, and perhaps contribute to the understanding of the socialisation process itself.

REFERENCES

AINSWORTH, M. D., ANDRY, R. G., HARLOW, R. G., LEBOVICI, S., MEAD, M., PRUGH, D. G., and WOOTTON B. (1962) *Deprivation of Maternal Care*. Geneva: WHO.

AINSWORTH, M. D. and BOWLBY, J. (1954) Research strategy in the study of mother-child separation, *Courrier du Centre International de l'Enfance*, **4**, 105–31.

ALLINSMITH, B. B. (1960) Expressive styles: II. Directness with which anger is expressed. In *Inner Conflict and Defense* (Ed. Miller D. R. and Swanson G. E.). New York: Holt.

ANDRY, R. G. (1964) *Delinquency and Parental Pathology*. London: Methuen.

ARGYLE, J. M. (1964) Introjection: a form of social learning. *Brit. J. Psychol.*, **55**, 391–402.

BANKS, C. (1965) Boys in detention centres. In *Studies in Psychology* (Ed. Banks, C. L. and Broadhurst, P. L.). London: London Univ. Press.

BARNDT, R. J. and JOHNSON, D. M. (1955) Time orientation in delinquents, *J. abnorm. soc. Psychol.*, **51**, 343–5.

BARRATT, E. S. (1956) The relationship of the Progressive Matrices (1938) and the Columbia Maturity Scale to the WISC. *J. consult. Psychol.*, **20**, 294–6.

BENNETT, I. (1960) *Delinquent and Neurotic Children*. London: Tavistock Press.

BERNSTEIN, B. B. (1960) Language and social class. *Brit. J. Sociol.*, **11**, 271.

BERNSTEIN, B. B. (1961) Social structure, language and learning. *Educ. Research*, **3**, 163–76.

BERNSTEIN, B. B. (1962) Social class, linguistic codes and grammatical elements. *Lang. and Speech*, **5**, 221–40.

BERNSTEIN, B. B. (1965) A socio-linguistic approach to social learning. In *Penguin Survey of the Social Sciences* (Ed. Gould, J.) London: Penguin.

BLANK, L. (1958) The intellectual functioning of delinquents. *J. soc. Psychol.*, **47**, 9–14.

BLAYLOCK, J. J. (1960) Verbal conditioning performance of psychopaths and non-psychopaths under verbal reward and punishment. *Diss. Abstr.*, **21**, 1628–9.

BOWLBY, J. (1946) *Forty-Four Juvenile Thieves: Their Characters and Home-Life*. London: Baillière, Tindall & Cox.

BOWLBY, J. (1951) *Maternal Care and Mental Health*. Geneva: W.H.O.

BOWLBY, J., AINSWORTH, M. D., BOSTON, M., and ROSENBLUTH, D. (1956) The effects of mother-child separation; a follow-up study. *Brit. J. med. Psychol.*, **29**, 211–44.

BRONFENBRENNER, U. (1958) Socialization and social class through time and space. In *Readings in Social Psychology*, 3rd edn. (Ed. E. E. Maccoby, T. M. Newcomb, and E. L. Hartley) New York: Holt.

CAPLAN, N. S. and SIEBERT, L. A. (1964) Distribution of juvenile delinquent intelligence test scores over a thirty-four year period ($N = 51,808$). *J. clin. Psychol.*, **20**, 2, 242–7.

CARR-SAUNDERS, A. M., MANNHEIM, H., and RHODES, E. C. (1942) *Young Offenders*. Cambridge: Cambridge Univ. Press.

CASEY, M. D., BLANK, C. E., STREET, D. R. K., SEGALL, L. J., McDOUGALL, J. H., McGRATH, P. J., and SKINNER, J. L. (1966a) YY chromosomes and antisocial behaviour, *Lancet*, **ii**, 859–60.

CASEY, M. D., SEGALL, L. J., STREET, D. R. K., and BLANK, C. E. (1966b) Sex chromosome abnormalities in two state hospitals for patients requiring special security. *Nature*, **209**, 641.

CASEY, M. D., STREET, D. R. K., SEGALL, L. J., and BLANK, C. E. (1968) Patients with sex chromatin abnormality in two state hospitals. *Ann. hum. Genet.*, **32**, 53–63.

CLARIDGE, G. S. and HERRINGTON, R. N. (1963) Excitation-inhibition and the theory of neurosis: a study of the sedation threshold. In *Experiments with Drugs* (Ed. Eysenck, H. J.) London: Pergamon.

CLARK, J. P. and WENNINGER, E. P. (1962) Socioeconomic class and area as correlates of illegal behavior among juveniles. *Amer. Sociol. Rev.*, **27**, 826–34.

CLINARD, M. B. (1958) *Sociology of Deviant Behavior*. New York: Rinehart.

CLINE, V. B. and WANGROW, A. S. (1959) Life history correlates of delinquent and psychopathic behavior. *J. clin. Psychol.*, **15**, 266–70.

CLECKLEY, H. M. (1959) Psychopathic states. In *American Handbook of Psychiatry* (Ed. S. Arieti) New York: Basic Books.

CLECKLEY, H. (1964) *The Mask of Sanity*, 4th edn. St. Louis: Mosby.

CONGER, J. J. and MILLER, W. C. (1966) *Personality, Social Class, and Delinquency*. New York: John Wiley.

COURT BROWN, W. M. (1962) Sex chromosomes and the law. *Lancet*, **ii**, 508.

CRAFT, M., STEPHENSON, G., and GRANGER, C. (1964) The relationship between severity of personality disorder and certain adverse childhood influences. *Brit. J. Psychiat.*, **110**, 392–6.

DAVIDS, A., KIDDER, K., and REICH, M. (1962) Time orientation in male and female juvenile delinquents. *J. abnorm. soc. Psychol.*, **64**, 3, 239–40.

DENTLER, R. A. and MONROE, L. J. (1961) Early adolescent theft. *Amer. Sociol. Rev.*, **26**, 733–43.

DOPPELT, J. E. and SEASHORE, H. G. (1959) Psychological testing in correctional institutions. *J. Counsel. Psychol.*, **6**, 81–92.

DOUGLAS, J. W. B., ROSS, J. M., HAMMOND, W. A., and MULLIGAN, D. G. (1966) Delinquency and social class. *Brit. J. Criminol.*, **6**, 294–302.

DOWNES, D. M. (1966) *The Delinquent Solution*. London: Routledge & Kegan Paul.

ERON, L. D., WALDER, L. O., TOIGO, R., and LEFKOWITZ, M. M. (1963) Social class, parental punishment for aggression, and child aggression. *Child Develpm.*, **34**, 4, 849–67.

EYSENCK, H. J. (1947) *Dimensions of Personality*. London: Routledge & Kegan Paul.

EYSENCK, H. J. (1955) A dynamic theory of anxiety and hysteria. *J. Ment. Sci.*, **101**, 28–51.

EYSENCK, H. J. (1959) Scientific methodology and the dynamics of anxiety and hysteria. *Brit. J. Med. Psychol.*, **32**, 56–63.

EYSENCK, H. J. (1962) Conditioning and personality. *Brit. J. Psychol.*, **53**, 3, 299–305.

EYSENCK, H. J. (1965) Extraversion and the acquisition of eyeblink and GSR conditioned responses. *Psychol. Bull.*, **63**, 258–70.

EYSENCK, H. J. (1967) *The Biological Basis of Personality*. Springfield: Thomas.

EYSENCK, H. J. (1970) *Crime and personality* (2nd edn). London: Granada Press.

EYSENCK, H. J. and LEVEY, A. (1967) Konditionerung, Introversion-Extraversion und die Stärke des Nervensystems. *Zeitschrift für Psychologie*, **174**, 96–106.

EYSENCK, S. B. G. and EYSENCK, H. J. (1970) Crime and personality: an empirical study of the three-factor theory. *Brit. J. Criminol.*, **10**, 3, 225–39.

FERGUSON, T. (1952) *The Young Delinquent in his Social Setting*. London: Oxford Univ. Press.

FIELD, J. G. (1960) The performance-verbal I.Q. discrepancy in a group of sociopaths. *J. clin. Psychol.*, **16**, 321–2.

FIELD, J. G. (1962) Two types of recidivist and maternal deprivation. *Brit. J. Criminol.*, **2**, 377–81.

FINNEY, J. C. (1966) Relations and meaning of the new MMPI scales. *Psychol. Rep.*, **18**, 459–70.

FISHER, G. M. (1961) Discrepancy in verbal and performance I.Q. in adolescent sociopaths. *J. clin. Psychol.*, **17**, 60.

FITCH, J. H. (1962) Men convicted of sexual offences against children. *Brit. J. Criminol.*, **3**, 18–37.

FORSSMAN, H. and HAMBERT, G. (1967) Chromosomes and antisocial behavior. *Excerpta Criminologica*. **7**, 113–7.

FOSTER, A. L. (1959) A note concerning the intelligence of delinquents. *J. clin. Psychol.*, **15**, 78–9.

FOX, R. and LIPPERT, W. W. (1963) Spontaneous g.s.r. and anxiety level in sociopathic delinquents. *J. consult. Psychol.*, **27**, 368.

FRANKS, C. M. (1956a) Recidivism, psychopathy and personality. *Brit. J. Delinq.*, **6**, 192–201.

FRANKS, C. M. (1956b) Conditioning and personality: a study of normal and neurotic subjects. *J. abnorm. soc. Psychol.*, **52**, 143–50.

FRANKS, C. M. (1957) Personality factors and the rate of conditioning. *Brit. J. Psychol.*, **48**, 119–26.

FRANKS, C. M. (1963) Personality and eyeblink conditioning seven years later. *Acta Psychologica*. **21**, 295–312.

FROST, B. P., and FROST, R. (1962) The pattern of WISC scores in a group of juvenile sociopaths. *J. clin. Psychol.*, **18**, 354–5.

GIBBENS, T. C. N. (1963) *Psychiatric Studies of Borstal Lads*. London: Oxford Univ. Press.

GIBBENS, T. C. N. and PRINCE, J. E. (1962) *Shoplifting*. London: I.S.T.D.

GIBSON, H. B. and WEST, D. J. (1968) Some concomitants of early delinquency. *Proc. Third Nat. Conf. on Res. & Teaching in Criminol.* Cambridge: Institute of Criminol.

GLUECK, S., and GLUECK, E. T. (1950) *Unraveling Juvenile Delinquency*. New York: Commonwealth Fund.

GLUECK, S., and GLUECK, E. T. (1956) *Physique and Delinquency*. New York: Harper.

GOLDFARB, W. (1943) Infant rearing and problem behavior. *Amer. J. Orthopsychiat.*, **13**, 249–65.

GOLDFARB, W. (1945) The effects of psychological deprivation in infancy and subsequent stimulation. *Amer. J. Psychiat.*, **102**, 18–33.

GORING, C. (1913) *The English Convict*. London: H.M.S.O.

GRAHAM, E. E. and KAMANO, D. (1958) Reading failure as a factor in the WAIS subtest patterns of youthful offenders. *J. clin. Psychol.*, **14**, 302–5.

GRAY, J. A. (1970) The psychophysiological basis of introversion-extraversion. *Behav. Res. and Therapy*, **8**, 249–66.

GRYGIER, T., CHESLEY, J., and TUTERS, E. W. (1969) Parental deprivation: a study of delinquent children. *Brit. J. Criminol.*, **9**, 3, 209–53.

GURVITZ, M. (1951) Developments in the concept of psychopathic personality (1900–1950). *Brit. J. Delinq.*, **2**, 88–143.

HAMBERT, G. (1966) Males with positive sex chromatin. Quoted in Forssman, H. and Hambert, G. (1967).

HAMMOND, W. H. and CHAYEN, E. (1963) *Persistent Criminals*. London: H.M.S.O.

HARE, R. D. (1965a) A conflict and learning theory analysis of psychopathic behavior. *J. Res. Crime & Delinq.*, **2**, 12–19.

HARE, R. D. (1965b) Acquisition and generalization of a conditioned-fear response in psychopathic and non-psychopathic criminals. *J. Psychol.*, **59**, 367–70.

HARE, R. D. (1965c) Psychopathy, fear arousal and anticipated pain. *Psychol. Rep.*, **16**, 499–502.

HARE, R. D. (1965a) Temporal gradient of fear arousal in psychopaths. *J. abnorm. Psychol.*, **70**, 6, 442–5.

HARE, R. D. (1968a) Psychopathy, autonomic functioning, and the orienting response. *J. abnorm. Psychol. Monogr. Suppl.*, **73**, 3, 2, 1–24.

HARE, R. D. (1968b) Detection threshold for electric shock in psychopaths. *J. abnorm. Psychol.*, **73**, 3, 268–72.

HARE, R. D. (1970) *Psychopathy: Theory and Research*. New York: Wiley.

HARRIS, R. (1957) A comparative study of two groups of boys, delinquent and non-delinquent, on the basis of their Wechsler and Rorschach test performances. *Bull. Maritime Psychol. Assoc.*, **6**, 21–8.

HENNING, J. J. and LEVY, R. H. (1967) Verbal-performance I.Q. differences of white and negro delinquents on the WISC and WAIS. *J. clin. Psychol.*, **23**, 164–8.

HETHERINGTON, E. M. and KLINGER, E. (1964) Psychopathy and punishment. *J. abnorm. soc. Psychol.*, **69**, 1, 113–5.

HOOD, R. G. (1962) *Sentencing in Magistrates' Courts*. London: Stevens.

HOOKE, J. F. (1966) Correlates of adolescent delinquent behavior: a multivariate approach. *Diss. Abstr.* 2136-B.

HUNTER, H. (1966) YY chromosomes and Klinefelter's syndrome. *Lancet*, **i**, 984.

JACOBS, P. A., BRUNTON, M., MELVILLE, M., BRITTAIN, R. P., and McCLEMONT, W. F. (1965) Aggressive behaviour, mental sub-normality and the XYY male. *Nature*, **208**, 1351–2.

JASTAK, J. and ALLEN, A. (1944) Psychological traits of juvenile delinquents. *Delaware State Med. J.*, **16**, 100–104.

KARPMAN, B. (1961) The structure of neurosis: with special differentials between neurosis, psychosis, homosexuality, alcoholism, psychopathy and criminality. *Arch. crim. Psychodyn.*, **4**, 599–646.

KELLMER PRINGLE, M. L. (1965) *Deprivation and Education*. London: Longmans Green.

KOHN, M. L. (1957) Social class and the exercise of parental authority. *Amer. Sociol. Rev.*, **24**, 352–66.

KOHN, M. L. (1959) Social class and parental values. *Amer. J. Sociol.*, **64**, 4, 337–51.

KOHN, M. L. (1963) Social class and parent-child relationships: an interpretation. *Amer. J. Sociol.*, **68**, 471–80.

KRANZ, H. (1936) *Lebensschicksale krimineller Zwillinge*. Berlin: Springer.

KVALE, J. N. and FISHMAN, J. R. (1965) The psychosocial aspects of Klinefelter's syndrome. *J. Amer. med. Ass.*, **193**, 567.

KVARACEUS, W. C. (1954) *The Community and the Delinquent*. New York: World Books.

KVARACEUS, W. C. and MILLER, W. B. (Ed.) (1959) *Delinquent Behavior: Culture and the Individual*. Washington: Nat. Educ. Assoc.

LANGE, J. (1929) *Verbrechen als Shicksal: Studien an Kriminellen Zwillingen*. Leipzig: Thieme. (English translation by C. Haldane, as *Crime as Destiny*. New York: Boni, 1930).

LAWTON, D. (1968) *Social Class, Language and Education*. London: Routledge & Kegan Paul.

LESHAN, L. L. (1952) Time orientation and social class. *J. abnorm. soc. Psychol.*, **47**, 589–76.

LINDNER, R. (1942) Experimental studies in constitutional psychopathic inferiority—I. *J. crim. Psychopath.*, 252–76.

LINDNER, R. (1943) Experimental studies in constitutional psychopathic inferiority—II. *J. crim. Psychopath.*, 484–500.

LIPPERT, W. W. and SENTER, R. J. (1966) Electrodermal responses in the sociopath. *Psychon. Sci.*, **4**, 25–6.

LITTLE, A. (1965) Parental deprivation, separation and crime: a test on adolescent recidivists. *Brit. J. Criminol.*, **4**, 419–30.

LITTLE, W. R. and NTSEKHE, V. R. (1959) Social class background of young offenders from London. *Brit. J. Delinq.*, **10**, 130–5.

LOMBROSO, C. (1876) *L'uomo delinquente*. Torino: Bocca.

LYKKEN, D. T. (1957) A study of anxiety in the sociopathic personality. *J. abnorm. soc. Psychol.*, **55**, 6–10.

MacLEAN, N., MITCHELL, J. M., HARNDEN, D. G., WILLIAMS, J., JACOBS, P. A., BUCKTON, K. E., BAIKIE, A. G., COURT BROWN, W. M., McBRIDE, J. A., STRONG, J. A., CLOSE, H. G., and JONES, D. C. (1962) A survey of sex chromosome abnormalities among 4,514 mental defectives. *Lancet*, **i**, 293.

MacLEAN, N., HARNDEN, D. G., COURT BROWN, W. M., BOND, J., and MANTLE, D. J. (1964) Sex chromosome abnormalities in newborn babies. *Lancet*, **i**, 286.

McCORD, W., and McCORD, J. (1964) *The Psychopath: An Essay on the Criminal Mind*. Princeton: Van Nostrand.

MANNE, S. H., KANDEL, A., and ROSENTHAL, D. (1962) Differences between performance I.Q. and verbal I.Q. in a severely sociopathic population. *J. clin. Psychol.*, **18**, 1, 73–7.

MANNHEIM, H. (1965) *Comparative Criminology*. London: Routledge & Kegan Paul.

MANNHEIM, H., SPENCER, J., and LYNCH, G. (1947) Magisterial policy in the London juvenile courts. *Brit. J. Delinq.*, **8**, 13–33.

MANNHEIM, H. and WILKINS, L. T. (1955) *Prediction Methods in Relation to Borstal Training*. London: H.M.S.O.

MARCUS, B. (1955) Intelligence, criminality, and the expectation of recidivism. *Brit. J. Delinq.*, **6**, 147–51.

MARCUS, B. (1960) A dimensional study of a prison population. *Brit. J. Criminol.*, **1**, 130–53.

MATHER, K. (1964) *Human Diversity*. London: Oliver & Boyd.

MAUGHS, S. (1941) A conception of the psychopathic personality. *J. crim. Psychopath.*, **2**, 329–56.

MILLER, J. G (1966) Eyeblink conditioning of primary and neurotic psychopaths. *Diss. Abstr.*, 27B, III.

MILLER, N. E. (1959) Liberalization of basic S-R concepts: extensions to conflict behavior, motivation and social learning. In *Psychology: A Study of a Science* (Ed. S. Koch) New York: McGraw-Hill.

MISCHEL, W. (1961) Preference for delayed reinforcement and social responsibility. *J. abnorm. soc. Psychol.*, **62**, 1, 1–7.

MONAHAN, T. P. (1960) Broken homes by age of delinquent children. *J. soc. Psychol.*, **51**, 387–97.

MORRIS, T. P. (1957) *The Criminal Area*. London: Routledge & Kegan Paul.

MOWRER, O. H. (1960a) *Learning Theory and Behavior*. New York: Wiley.

MOWRER, O. H. (1960b) *Learning Theory and the Symbolic Processes*. New York: Wiley.

NAESS, S. (1959) Mother-child separation and delinquency. *Brit. J. Delinq.*, **10**, 22–35.

NAESS, S. (1962) Mother-separation and delinquency. Further evidence. *Brit. J. Criminol.*, **2**, 4, 361–74.

NIELSEN, J. (1964) Klinefelter's syndrome and behaviour. *Lancet*, **ii**, 587–8.

NYE, F. I. (1958) *Family Relationships and Delinquent Behavior*. New York: Wiley.

NYE, F. I., SHORT, J. F., and OLSON, V. J. (1958) Socioeconomic status and delinquent behavior. *Amer. J. Sociol.*, **63**, 381–8.

PANTON, J. H. (1960) Beta-WAIS comparisons and WAIS sub-test configurations within a state prison population, *J. clin. Psychol.*, **16**, 312–7.

PENROSE, L. S. (1955) Genetics and the criminal. *Brit. J. Delinq.*, **6**, 15–25.

PERSONS, R. W. and PERSONS, C. E. (1965) Some experimental support of psychopathic theory: a critique. *Psychol. Rep.*, **16**, 745–9.

PETERSON, D. R., QUAY, H. C., and TIFFANY, T. L. (1961) Personality factors related to juvenile delinquency. *Child Develpm.*, **32**, 355–72.

PRENTICE, N. M. and KELLY, F. J. (1963) Intelligence and delinquency: a reconsideration. *J. soc. Psychol.*, **60**, 327–37.

PRICE, W. H., STRONG, J. A., WHATMORE, P. B., and McCLEMONT, W. F. (1966) Criminal patients with XYY sex-chromosome complement. *Lancet*, **i**, 565–6.

PRICE, W. H. and WHATMORE, P. B. (1967a) Criminal behaviour and the XYY male. *Nature*, **213**, 815.

PRICE, W. H. and WHATMORE, P. B. (1967b) Behaviour disorders and the pattern of crime among XYY males identified at a maximum security hospital. *Brit. med. J.*, **i**, 533.

QUAY, H. C. (1964) Dimensions of personality in delinquent boys as inferred from the factor analysis of case history data. *Child Develpm.*, **35**, 479–84.

QUAY, H. C. (1965) Psychopathic personality as pathological stimulation-seeking. *Amer. J. Psychiat.*, **122**, 180–3.

RADZINOWICZ, L. (Ed.) (1957) *Sexual Offences*. London: Macmillan.

REISS, A. J. and RHODES, A. L. (1961) The distribution of juvenile delinquency in the social class structure. *Amer. Sociol. Rev.*, **26**, 720–32.

RICHARDSON, H. M. and SURKO, E. F. (1956) WISC scores and status in reading and arithmetic of delinquent children. *J. genet. Psychol.*, **89**, 251–62.

RICKS, D., UMBARGER, C., and MACK, R. (1964) A measure of increased temporal perspective in successfully treated adolescent delinquent boys. *J. abnorm. soc. Psychol.*, **69**, 6, 685–9.

ROBBINS, L. C. (1963) The accuracy of parental recall of aspects of child development and of child rearing practices. *J. abnorm. soc. Psychol.*, **66**, 3, 261–70.

ROBINS, L. N. (1966) *Deviant Children Grown Up*. Baltimore: Williams & Wilkins.

ROBINSON, W. P. and RACKSTRAW, S. J. (1971) *A Question of Answers*. London: Routledge & Kegan Paul.

ROSANOFF, A. J., HANDY, L. M., and ROSANOFF, J. A. (1934) Criminality and delinquency in twins. *J. crim. Law & Criminol.*, **24**, 923–34.

ROSANOFF, A. J., HANDY, L. M., and PLESSET, I. R. (1941) Etiology of child behavior. *Psychiat. Monogr.*, 1.

ROSE, A. G. (1954) *Five Hundred Borstal Boys*. Oxford: Blackwell.

RUTKIN, R. (1966) The time judgment of delinquent and neglected children. *Diss. Abstr.*, **27**, 802–3A.

SARBIN, T. R., ALLEN, V. L., and RUTHERFORD, E. E. (1965) Social reinforcement, socialization, and chronic delinquency. *Brit. J. soc. clin. Psychol.*, **4**, 179–84.

SCHACHTER, S. and LATANÉ, B. (1964) Crime, cognition, and the autonomic nervous system. In *Nebraska Symposium on Motivation, 1964* (Ed. M. R. Jones) Lincoln: Univ. of Nebraska Press.

SCHNEIDERMAN, D. F. (1964) The time sense of delinquents. *Diss. Abstr.*, **25**, 3118–9.

SCHOENHERR, J. C. (1964) Avoidance of noxious stimulation in psychopathic personality. *Diss. Abstr.*, **25**, 2055–6.

SEARS, R. R., MACCOBY, E. E., and LEVIN, H. (1957) *Patterns of Child Rearing*. Evanston: Row Peterson.

SHELDON, W. H. (1940) *Varieties of Human Physique*. New York: Harper.

SHELDON, W. H. (1942) *Varieties of Temperament*. New York: Harper.

SHELDON, W. H. (1949) *Varieties of Delinquent Youth*. New York: Harper.

SHORT, J. F. and NYE, F. I. (1957) Reported behavior as a criterion of deviant behavior. *Soc. Probl.*, **5**, '207–13.

SHULMAN, H. M. (1950) Intelligence and juvenile delinquency. *J. crim. Law and Criminol.*, **41**, 763–81.

SIEGMAN, A. W. (1961) The relationship between future time perspective, time estimation, and impulse control in a group of young offenders and in a control group. *J. consult. Psychol.*, **25**, 6, 470–5.

SLATER, E. (1953) *Psychotic and Neurotic Illness in Twins*. London: H.M.S.O.

SLATER, E. (1967) Genetics of criminals. *World Med.*, March 21, 44–5.

SPROTT, W. J. H., JEPHCOTT, A. P., and CARTER, M. P. (1954) *The Social Background of Delinquency*. Cyclostyled publn.: Univ. of Nottingham.

STOLZ, L. M. (1967) *Influences on Parent Behaviour*. London: Tavistock.

STORMS, L. H. and SIGAL, J. J. (1958) Eysenck's personality theory with special references to 'The Dynamics of Anxiety and Hysteria'. *Brit. J. Med. Psychol.*, 3 & 4, 228–46.

STOTT, D. H. (1950) *Delinquency and Human Nature*. Dunfermline: Carnegie UK Trust.

STUMPFL, F. (1936) *Die Ursprünge des Verbrechens*. Leipzig: Thieme.

THEIS, S. van S. (1924) *How Foster Children Turn Out*. New York: State Charities Aid Assocn.

TONG, J. E. and MURPHY, I. C. (1960) A review of stress reactivity research in relation to psychopathology and psychopathic behaviour disorders. *J. ment. Sci.*, **106**, 1273–95.

TRASLER, G. B. (1960) *In Place of Parents*. London: Routledge & Kegan Paul.

TRASLER, G. B. (1962) *The Explanation of Criminality*. London: Routledge & Kegan Paul.

TRASLER, G. B. (1964) Strategic problems in the study of criminal behaviour. *Brit. J. Criminol.*, **4**, 422–42.

TRASLER, G. B. (1965a) Criminality and the socialization process. *Advmt. Sci.*, **21**, 94, 545–50.

TRASLER, G. B. (1965b) The social relations of persistent offenders. In *Sociological Studies in the British Penal Services* (Ed. P. Halmos) Keele: Univ. Press.

TRASLER, G. B. (1968) Socialization. In *The Formative Years*. London: B.B.C.

TULCHIN, S. H. (1939) *Intelligence and Crime*. Chicago: Univ. Press.

WALDO, G. P. and DINITZ, S. (1967) Personality attributes of the criminal: an analysis of research studies, 1950–65. *J. Res. Crime & Delinq.*, **4**, 2, 185–202.

WALKER, N. D. (1965) *Crime and Punishment in Britain.* Edinburgh: Univ. Press.

WALLACE, M. (1956) Future time perspective in schizophrenia. *J. abnorm. soc. Psychol.*, **52**, 240–5.

WALLACE, M. and RABIN, A. (1960) Temporal experience. *Psychol. Bull.*, **57**, 213–6.

WARDLE, C. J. (1961) Two generations of broken homes in the genesis of conduct and behaviour disorders in children. *Brit. med. J.*, **2**, 349–54.

WARREN, A. B. and GRANT, D. A. (1955) The relation of conditioned discrimination to the M.M.P.I. *Pd* personality variable. *J. exp. Psychol.*, **49**, 1, 23–7.

WATSON, J. B. and RAYNER, R. (1920) Conditioned emotional reactions. *J. exp. Psychol.*, **3**, 1–14.

WECHSLER, D. (1944) *The Measurement of Adult Intelligence*, 3rd edn., Baltimore: Williams & Wilkins.

WEGMANN, T. G. and SMITH, D. W. (1963) Incidence of Klinefelter's Syndrome among juvenile delinquents and felons. *Lancet*, **i**, 274.

WELCH, J. P., BORGAONKAR, D. S., and HERR, H. M. (1967) Psychopathy, mental deficiency, aggressiveness and the XYY syndrome. *Nature*, **214**, 500–1.

WEST, D. J. (1963) *The Habitual Prisoner*. London: Macmillan.

WEST, D. J. (1967) *The Young Offender*. London: Duckworth.

WEST, D. J. (1969) *Present Conduct and Future Delinquency*. London: Heinemann.

WHEELAN, L. (1951) Aggressive psychopathy in one of a pair of uniovular twins. *Brit. J. Delinq.*, **2**, 2, 130–43.

WHEWAY, J. P. (1958) Intelligence and delinquency. *Durham Res. Rev.*, **2**, 208–14.

WILKINS, L. T. (1964) *Social Deviance*. London: Tavistock.

WILLETT, R. A. (1960) Measures of learning and conditioning. In *Experiments in Personality*. Vol. II (Ed. H. J. Eysenck) London: Routledge & Kegan Paul.

WILLETT, T. C. (1964) *Criminal on the Road*. London: Tavistock.

WOLF, P. (1962) Crime and social class in Denmark. *Brit. J. Criminol.*, **3**, 5–17.

WOLFGANG, M. E. (1958) *Patterns in Criminal Homicide*. Philadelphia: Univ. of Pennsylvania Press.

WOLFGANG, M. E. and FERRACUTI, F. (1967) *The Subculture of Violence*. London: Tavistock.

WOODWARD, M. (1963) *Low Intelligence and Delinquency* (revised edn) London: I.S.T.D.

WOOTTON, B. (1959) *Social Science and Social Pathology*. London: Allen & Unwin.

YARROW, L. J. (1961) Maternal deprivation: toward an empirical and conceptual re-evaluation. *Psychol. Bull.*, **58**, 6, 459–90.

YOSHIMASU, S. (1961) The criminological significance of the family in the light of the study of criminal twins. *Acta Criminologiae et Medicinae Legalis Japonica*, **27**, 4, 117–41.

4

Drug Dependence

JOHN D. TEASDALE

As defined by the World Health Organisation Expert Committee on Drug Dependence (1969), drug dependence is: 'A state, psychic and sometimes also physical, resulting from the interaction between a living organism and a drug, characterised by behavioural and other responses that always include a compulsion to take the drug on a continuous or periodic basis in order to experience its psychic effects, and sometimes to avoid the discomfort of its absence. Tolerance may or may not be present. A person may be dependent on more than one drug.'

Such a definition is quite wide, and obviously could include dependence on alcohol, tobacco, or even coffee. These drugs will be largely excluded from this review, which will be concerned mainly with the drugs typically abused by patients labelled 'drug addicts', i.e. the opiates, amphetamines and other stimulants, barbiturates and other sedatives, and the psychedelic drugs such as cannabis and LSD.

This review is restricted largely to the findings of psychological investigations of drug dependence, both in animals and man. This is done in full recognition that the findings of other disciplines, such as pharmacology and sociology, must be included in any total approach to a problem as complex as drug dependence.

ANIMAL STUDIES

The considerable literature on studies of drug dependence in experimental animals has been recently reviewed by Schuster and Thompson (1969), Thompson (1968), and Steinberg et al. (1968). The importance of these animal studies is that they permit more rigorous experimental control than is usually feasible in studies of dependence in man. Further, they offer the hope of revealing the learning mechanisms basic to the processes of dependence in both animals and man, without the confounding influence of factors such as personality disorder, social influence, expectation and the like, which complicate the interpretation of studies in human subjects.

Experimental studies of drug dependence in animals take as their starting point the potential addict as he takes his first dose of drugs. They do not attempt to answer the question of how the addict came to his first experience of drugs;

experimental conditions are arranged so that all animals have this opportunity.

As the framework of the review, the learning processes involved in becoming addicted will be followed chronologically. That is, starting with the animal as he takes his first dose of drugs, the factors determining the acquisition, maintenance, cessation, and relapse back to drug-taking will be discussed, in turn. At each stage, questions will be formulated which it would seem the experiments were designed to answer. The first of these is below.

Are the consequences of self-administration of addictive drugs positively reinforcing?

We can tell whether animals find their first experiences of addictive drugs 'pleasant' only by observing whether they repeat the responses that have led up to their first consumption of drugs. The question posed above is thus, essentially, asking whether we can establish instrumental responses based on drug reinforcement.

It is necessary to distinguish at this stage between two possible ways in which a drug might be reinforcing. The first would be that, for a naïve animal, with no previous experience of drugs, the first experience of drugs is positively 'pleasurable'. To demonstrate the existence of such 'psychogenically' based reinforcement, it is necessary to show that animals voluntarily take, or attempt to take, repeated doses of the drug for no other purpose than to experience the effects of the drug. Consumption of a drug solution to relieve thirst or suppress abstinence symptoms would not be evidence for the existence of psychogenic dependence.

The other way in which a drug could be reinforcing would be by relieving abstinence symptoms in animals that are already physically dependent on the drug, i.e. animals which, by repeated administration of the drug, have reached the state where the drug is essential to their 'normal' physiological functioning.

Experiments investigating these effects have been of two main types. In the first, the animal consumes the drug orally in aqueous solution, so that the habit established is drinking the drug solution in preference to water. In the second, an intravenous catheter is introduced surgically into the experimental animal and connected to an infusion pump, which, on depression of a lever by the animal, injects a solution of the drug into the animal. The habit established in this case is depression of the lever.

Claghorn *et al.* (1965) and Deneau and Seevers (1964) report that naïve, unpremedicated monkeys will voluntarily initiate the habit of drinking morphine solution in preference to water. Other workers (e.g. Nichols, 1963, 1965) have failed to confirm this finding for rats. This probably results from the fact that morphine solutions have a bitter taste, a factor complicating the interpretation of the studies using the oral route of administration, which does not arise in studies using the intravenous route. Another advantage of this latter route is that it is a much closer approximation to the human addict 'mainlining' his drug; the effects of orally administered drugs are likely to be less powerful than the same drugs administered intravenously as, in the latter, the drug has its immediate effect concentrated in a short space of time, whereas in the former the effects of the drug will be drawn out over a longer period of time.

Rats that have been made physically dependent on morphine by injections given by the experimenter

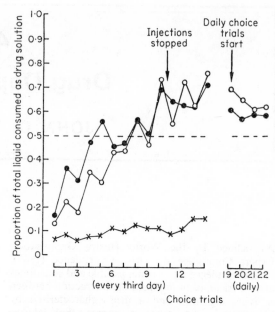

Fig. 4.1. Development of preference for morphine in rats given a choice between morphine solution and water every third day

On the intervening days morphine solution only was available. Premedicated rats (Group 1: ●–●) had had morphine injections for 15 days before drinking trials began and up to the tenth choice trial. Unpremedicated rats (group 2: ○–○) received saline injections only. A clear preference for morphine developed in both groups and they continued to drink more morphine solution than water even when water was available as an alternative to morphine every day. No preference developed in a control group given quinine solution (Group 3: ×–×) (*from* Kumar, Steinberg, and Stolerman, 1969a)

will readily learn the habit of drinking morphine solution to relieve their withdrawal distress (Nichols, 1963, 1965; Kumar *et al.*, 1969a) (Fig. 4.1).

Turning to the intravenous route of drug self-administration, it has been shown that unpremedicated rats will learn to make a bar-press response to obtain injections of a variety of drugs including cocaine, dextro-amphetamine, and meth-amphetamine (Pickens, 1968). Seevers (1967) has reported that these drugs can also serve as the reinforcers for the establishment of bar-pressing habits in unpremedicated monkeys. As none of these drugs produces a recognised abstinence syndrome on withdrawal, the dependence induced in these experiments is of the psychogenic type. Seevers also showed that even for morphine, and pentobarbital, drugs that on repeated administration lead to physical dependence, bar-pressing habits can be established by using them as reinforcers in monkeys that had not reached the state of physical dependence.

Weeks and Collins (1968) and Thompson and Schuster (1964) have demonstrated the learning of a bar-pressing habit for intravenous morphine reinforcement in experimental animals physically dependent on morphine.

It thus seems clear that, at least in the rat and monkey, drugs that are addictive in man can serve as reinforcers for the establishment and maintenance of motor responses. Some of these responses may be extremely persistent, e.g. Seevers (1967) reports that monkeys will continue to self-administer cocaine until they die. Having established that addictive drugs can act as reinforcers in experimental animals, the question obviously arises:

What is the nature of the reinforcement provided by the drugs?

It was mentioned above that drugs could be reinforcing either 'in their own right' or by relieving some unpleasant withdrawal state resulting from their absence in a physically dependent animal. Only two classes of addictive drugs, opiates and barbiturates, produce an obviously observable abstinence syndrome when they are withdrawn from animals that have been receiving them regularly. In the case of opiates this takes the form of increased activity, hypothermia, loss of body weight, decreased water intake, and increased defaecation, urination, and hostility (Wikler and Pescor, 1967). In the case of the barbiturates, the withdrawal symptoms include delirium and grand mal seizures (Seevers, 1967).

It has thus been assumed that the reinforcement attending self-administration of other classes of drugs, e.g. the amphetamines, cocaine, nicotine, is psychogenic, by which it is often implied that the drugs produce a positive 'euphoria'. However, there is evidence that the distinction between psychogenic and physical dependence may not be so clear. Thus, although withdrawal of amphetamines from an animal dependent on them does not produce the marked autonomic symptoms characteristic of opiate withdrawal, there is evidence in humans (*see* page 120) that it does produce a marked change in brain function, as shown by the sleep EEG. It may be that no sharp distinction is possible between 'psychogenic' and 'physical' dependence; the apparent distinction that is now recognised may simply reflect the lack of sensitivity of existing methods for detecting 'withdrawal phenomena'.

The initiation and maintenance of 'psychogenic' dependence on, for example, amphetamines might thus occur as follows; in exploring its experimental environment, the animal will accidentally operate the lever that causes the delivery of an amphetamine injection; the first few injections, accidentally delivered, are sufficient to cause some change in the animal's physiology such that it 'needs' amphetamines for its normal functioning. Learning the operant of bar-pressing then occurs, based on the reinforcement of reduction of this need. This account differs from that normally implied by the term 'psychogenic' dependence, which assumes that the amphetamine injection is an inherently 'pleasurable' event, and directly reinforces the behaviour preceding it. The evidence from human studies (page 117), where subjective accounts of drug experiences are available, tends to support the latter account. However, the possible role of the former mechanism should not be neglected. Wikler and Carter (1953) have demonstrated that if administration of morphine to previously unmedicated animals is followed by the administration of nalorphine (a morphine antagonist) one hour later, in some animals the nalorphine precipitates a morphine abstinence syndrome. Nalorphine does not have this effect if administered alone or simultaneously with morphine. Wikler and Carter concluded that, even in single doses, morphine may produce some degree of physical dependence, although this is not normally observed unless nalorphine is administered some time after the morphine. Thus, there is evidence that single doses of drugs can produce changes in an animal's physiology such that it may 'need' the presence of the drug for its normal function, although no obvious withdrawal symptoms appear if no more drug is administered.

Any discussion of the relative importance of reinforcement based on 'euphoria' and that based on relief of hypothetical unobserved 'withdrawal phenomena' in psychogenic dependence would obviously be highly speculative. However, in the case of morphine dependence, where withdrawal symptoms are easily recognisable, there is some relevant experimental evidence.

Nichols and his co-workers were among the first to investigate the hypothesis that relief of withdrawal symptoms was an important component of the reinforcement for sustained opiate-directed behaviour in animals physically dependent on morphine (Nichols, 1965; Davis and Nichols, 1962). In one of their experiments, three groups of rats were used, varying in the extent to which they manifested withdrawal distress at the start of the procedure by which they were trained to drink morphine solution. It was found that the amount of opiate-directed behaviour (quantity of morphine solution drunk) increased with the level of withdrawal distress at the start of training. This supports the hypothesis that relief of withdrawal distress provides reinforcement for opiate-directed behaviour; the more severe was the withdrawal distress, the greater was the relief obtained by drinking morphine solution, the greater was the reinforcement for the opiate-directed behaviour, and so, the greater was the extent of that behaviour.

Nichols tested the withdrawal-relief hypothesis in a further experiment utilising three groups of animals. Group I were dependent on morphine, but trained on quinine solution, a substance tasting like morphine solution but without narcotic properties, i.e. this group experienced withdrawal but no withdrawal-relief. Group II were not dependent on morphine, but were trained on morphine solution, i.e. this group experienced minimal withdrawal, so they had the possibility of only minimal reinforcement from withdrawal-relief. They also experienced any other reinforcing effects consumption of morphine solution might provide. Group III were dependent on morphine, and trained on morphine solution, i.e. this group experienced both withdrawal and withdrawal-relief.

At the choice tests conducted after the training period, only Group III showed any degree of opiate-directed behaviour, as measured by consumption of morphine solution, in accord with the withdrawal-relief hypothesis.

Further support for the withdrawal-relief hypothesis is provided by another experiment reported by Nichols, which compared the amount of morphine drunk by dependent animals trained while receiving morphine injections under two different regimes. One group received a single daily injection of 400 mg/kg, the other received six-hourly injections of 150 mg/kg. It was found, both during training and at the choice tests after withdrawal, that the latter group showed less maintained opiate-directed behaviour than the former. Nichols offers two possible explanations for this. One is that the larger amount of morphine received by the second group depressed performance. The other is that, as the second group never experienced such severe withdrawal as the first group during training, the withdrawal-relief, and, therefore, the reinforcement contingent on drinking the morphine solution, was greater in the first group than in the second.

Nichols rejects the first explanation on the grounds that, while the rats in the second group drank less morphine solution than those in the first group, they drank more water. He thus accepts the second explanation, which gives further support to the withdrawal-relief hypothesis.

Nichols's experiments, taken together, give strong support to the hypothesis that the relief of withdrawal symptoms is an important component of the reinforcement provided by morphine in physically

dependent animals. His experiments studied the oral consumption of drug solutions. Experiments utilising the intravenous route of drug administration have given added support to the hypothesis. These experiments have generally taken the form of demonstrating that, when a physically dependent experimental animal is prevented from experiencing withdrawal distress by the experimenter supplying it with opiate drugs in addition to those it gains by its own efforts at lever-pressing, the rate of lever pressing falls. Thus, Thompson and Schuster (1964) pretreated physically dependent monkeys with 1, 2, or 3 mg/kg of morphine 45 minutes before periods when the animals were scheduled to self-administer 1 mg/kg of morphine. The length of time required to complete the morphine-reinforced fixed ratio 25 varied directly with the pretreatment dose. Thompson (1968) reported that hourly injections of the opioid methadone suppressed morphine-reinforced responding by monkeys. This finding is particularly interesting in view of the use of this drug in the treatment of human heroin addicts by Dole and Nyswander (*see* page 125). Etonitazene, a synthetic opioid, suppresses morphine-reinforced lever-pressing, whether introduced into the rats' drinking water (Weeks, 1964) (Fig. 4.2) or continuously infused intravenously (Weeks and Collins, 1964). Weeks and Collins (1964) reported that continuous morphine infusions at rates of 0·5 to 1·0

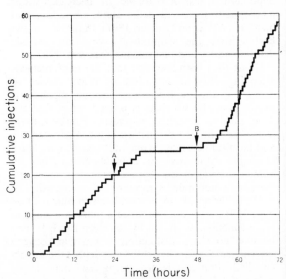

Fig. 4.2. The effect of adding the morphine-like drug etonitazene to the drinking water of a morphine-dependent rat, self-administering morphine injections

The etonitazene was added at *A*, and removed at *B* (*from* Weeks, 1964, copyright © 1964 by Scientific American, Inc., all rights reserved)

mg/kg per hour suppressed morphine self-administration in most rats.

The converse of these procedures has been to study the effects of precipitating withdrawal symptoms by the administration of the morphine antagonist, nalorphine, to physically dependent monkeys. Weeks (1962) and Thompson and Schuster (1964) have both reported that this procedure results in an increased rate of responding for self-administration of morphine.

The importance of the withdrawal-relief component of morphine reinforcement seems well established. However, there is some evidence that other components exist. Thus, as was pointed out earlier, animals will voluntarily initiate morphine self-administration without being obviously physically dependent on the drug. Further, Woods and Schuster (1968) have demonstrated that monkeys will initiate and maintain lever-pressing for intravenously administered morphine at dosages as low as 10 µg/kg; at this low dosage the monkeys failed to show any signs of physical dependence when saline was substituted for morphine.

Most authors (e.g. Schuster and Thompson, 1969) have taken such findings as evidence suggesting that morphine possesses positive reinforcing properties independent of its ability to ameliorate the withdrawal syndrome. However, the possibility, raised earlier in this section, that such findings may be interpreted in terms of relief of 'covert withdrawal symptomatology' should also be borne in mind.

A series of experiments by Beach (1957a,b) attempted to demonstrate that morphine reinforcement could have a 'euphoria' component as well as its withdrawal-relief component.

In his first experiment, Beach demonstrated that rats physically dependent on morphine preferred the arm of a Y-maze, into which they had been run following an injection of morphine, to the other arm, into which they had been run following an injection of saline. This result was obtained whether the rats were in 'need' of morphine (i.e. in withdrawal) or whether they were sated for morphine (2 to 4 hours after injection). Beach interpreted this result as demonstrating the reinforcing properties of the combined withdrawal-relief and euphoria experienced following the morphine injection. However, his results could be interpreted equally well in terms of the rats avoiding the arm of the maze into which they had been run following the saline injection, as this arm would have been associated with the unpleasant state of withdrawal distress.

In his second experiment, Beach attempted to separate the euphoria and withdrawal-relief aspects of morphine reinforcement. He had observed that there was a latency of 10 to 15 minutes between the subcutaneous injection of morphine and its having any observable effects in rats. Beach thus assumed that if the rats were not run into the arm of the Y-maze until 20 minutes after the injection of morphine, the correction of the state of withdrawal would have occurred before the rats were run into the maze, and any reinforcement occurring in the maze could be attributed to a longer-lasting euphoric effect of morphine. When this modification was made to the first experiment, the rats still showed a preference for the arm of the maze associated with the effects of morphine injection. Again, this was shown whether the rats were in need of or sated with morphine. Beach concluded that this result demonstrated the existence of morphine-induced euphoria, independent of the withdrawal-relief effect of morphine. However, the same objection that was raised to the interpretation of the first experiment could be raised to this conclusion.

The third experiment in Beach's first series was designed to see whether the motor habits trained by morphine reinforcement would persist after administration of the drug had ceased and withdrawal symptoms had disappeared. It was intended to compare habits established by the combined reinforcement of withdrawal-relief and euphoria with those established using only the reinforcement of drug-induced euphoria. Groups of rats were trained under both these conditions, by the methods described above, and then withdrawn from all contact with the drug and the training apparatus for a period of three weeks. The rats were then given the preference test to see which arm they would enter when placed in the maze. It was found that rats that had received the combined reinforcement still showed a significant preference for the arm associated with the drug effects, while the rats that had been trained on only euphoria reinforcement did not. Beach concluded that, in rats, the euphoric effects of morphine do not constitute reinforcement that leads to the learning of a durable habit, while the withdrawal-relief (drive reduction) effects do.

In his second series of experiments (Beach 1957b), Beach compared the habits established by morphine reinforcement with those established by food reinforcement. He was particularly interested to see how the two types of habit responded to variations in drive; would the habits be manifest in the absence of the drive (withdrawal distress or hunger) whose reduction constituted their reinforcement during training?

The morphine habit was established by a procedure essentially similar to that employed in the first series of experiments, using the combined reinforcement of withdrawal-relief and euphoria. At the post-training preference test, it was found, as in the first series of experiments, that the rats showed a significant preference for the arm that had been associated with the drug effects. This preference was shown whether the rats were tested while they were in 'need' of morphine (24 hours abstinent) or while they were sated with morphine (2 hours after their injection with morphine). That is, the habit established on the basis of morphine reinforcement did not seem to require the presence of the drive of withdrawal distress for its manifestation.

The rats trained for food reward went through a procedure analogous to that experienced by the animals receiving drug reward.

The post-training preference tests were conducted under conditions of 2 and 12 hours food deprivation. Under the latter condition, rats showed a significant preference for the arm where they had been fed. However, in contrast to the animals trained for morphine reinforcement, these showed no significant preference for the food goal-box, when tested under conditions in which the relevant drive, hunger, was at a low level (2 hours food deprivation).

Beach interpreted his results as showing that, while a habit established using food reinforcement needs the drive of hunger for it to be manifested, habits established by morphine reinforcement are displayed whether the animal is in need of morphine or whether it is sated with morphine. Beach suggests that morphine habits are qualitatively different from food habits in that the nature of the reinforcement provided by morphine is not dependent on the correction of a state of physiological need. Evidence pointing to similar conclusions has been mentioned earlier. However, Beach's results could be explained by the alternative hypothesis we have already mentioned, i.e. the rats prefer the arm associated with morphine reinforcement because they are avoiding the other arm, which has been associated with an unpleasant withdrawal state. The reason why a similar situation does not arise in the case of the food habit (i.e. that the originally preferred arm is avoided because it has the unpleasant properties associated with 12 hours food deprivation conditioned to it) would seem to be that the distress after 12 hours food deprivation is less than that after 24 hours morphine deprivation in physically dependent animals, especially as the rats in the food experiment were adapted to the food deprivation schedule before the experiment began.

In summary of this section, it can be said that addictive drugs can be reinforcing to experimental animals either by relief of withdrawal distress in animals showing obvious signs of physical dependence, or by other means in animals receiving drugs that do not produce obvious physical dependence, or in animals receiving drugs that can produce

physical dependence but that have not yet reached that state. The second mode of reinforcement is probably based on the drugs being unconditioned positive reinforcers, but could, possibly, be based on the drugs relieving 'covert' withdrawal symptoms. In connection with this second mode of reinforcement, various writers (e.g. Collier, 1968) have suggested that the drugs may be stimulating the 'pleasure centres' suggested in the light of the work on brain self-stimulation (Olds and Milner, 1954). This is an interesting idea, but at the moment there is insufficient evidence to assess it thoroughly.

As has been pointed out, most animals, given the opportunity, will become dependent on most of the traditional drugs of addiction. However, a number of workers (e.g. Yanagita et al., 1965) have pointed out that animals vary in their susceptibility to becoming addicted. The question arises:

Are there individual differences in susceptibility to becoming dependent on addictive drugs?

AGE

Nichols (1965) has reported that young rats acquire conditioned morphine-seeking behaviour more readily than adult rats (Fig. 4.3). He suggested that this finding might parallel the observation made by Winick (1962) that human addicts tend to stop using opiates as they grow older, the 'maturing out' process.

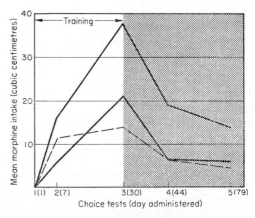

Fig. 4.3. Reduced opiate-directed behaviour is exhibited as an organism ages

Young rats (upper black curve) drank more morphine than middle-aged rats (lower black curve) and old rats (broken curve). All three groups were trained to drink the drug and were tested on five occasions (*from* Nichols, 1965, copyright © 1965 by Scientific American, Inc., all rights reserved)

Steinberg *et al.* (1968) report a number of studies which have shown that younger rats are more susceptible to the behavioural effects of a number of addictive drugs (e.g. amphetamines, amphetamine-barbiturate mixtures) than older animals.

GENETIC DIFFERENCES

Nichols and Hsiao (1967) have reported that rats can be selectively bred for their tendency to 'relapse' back to morphine drinking. The rats were trained to make this response while physically dependent and then withdrawn from the drug so that, at the time of testing for 'relapse', only minimal withdrawal symptoms were present. Inbreeding of the 'suscep-tible' rats from an unselected population produced 'susceptible' offspring. Similarly, inbreeding 'resist-ant' rats produced 'resistant' offspring. Further inbreeding increased the strain differences in suc-cessive generations. Cross-fostering studies showed that these differences could not be accounted for in terms of differences in maternal care. Further, the fact that there were no differences between the strains in the consumption of morphine solution before the start of training suggests that the differ-ences between the strains are not explicable simply in terms of differences in taste threshold, preference for novel stimuli, or naïve preference for morphine (Fig. 4.4).

The strain differences were not related to differ-ences in emotionality, as measured by the Hall open-field test (Nichols, 1967). It was found that the susceptible and resistant rats in the F-3 generation differed in their alcohol intake in preference tests conducted 14 days after being conditioned to drink alcohol. However, Nichols (1968) also found that the susceptible strain learned to solve maze problems

more rapidly than the resistant strain. It is possible that Nichols was not actually breeding for sus-ceptibility to morphine or alcohol addiction but for learning ability; the measures of susceptibility to addiction involve the learning of the drug con-sumption habit, and thus, presumably, would also reflect differences in learning ability between the strains of rats.

EFFECTS OF PREVIOUS EXPERIENCE WITH DRUGS

As has been pointed out already, previous experience with drugs producing physical dependence, such that the experimental animal is physically dependent on the drug, can have an effect on the animal's drug self-administration behaviour. A somewhat different phenomenon is that of drug 'escalation'. This term is used to describe the progression that may occur from the initial use of so called 'soft' drugs, such as cannabis, amphetamines, etc. to the use of 'harder' drugs such as heroin. One study (Kumar *et al.* 1969b) has investigated whether this phenomenon can be demonstrated in experimental animals. Rats were allowed the opportunity to drink solutions of amylobarbitone, dexamphetamine, or chlordiaze-poxide for a period of days. Access to these drugs was then discontinued, and the rats were subjected to a morphine-drinking procedure which had previously been shown to produce behavioural dependence on morphine. No differences in the rates at which the rats developed behavioural dependence on morphine were found between any of the groups pretreated with another drug and a control group that had received no drug pretreat-ment. This may have been related to the fact that the rats did not seem to develop any marked degree of dependence on the amylobarbitone, dexamphet-amine, or chlordiazepoxide. A more likely expla-nation is that drug escalation in human addicts is a sociological rather than pharmacological phenom-enon.

Having discussed factors that may determine initial susceptibilities to becoming dependent on drugs, the discussion will turn to the question:

What factors affect drug self-administration in an animal which is already dependent?

THE OPIATES

Weeks and Collins (1968) have usefully summarised their own investigations into patterns of intravenous self-injection by morphine-dependent rats. The rats were initially made dependent over 5 to 8 days by hourly injections of drugs through an indwelling

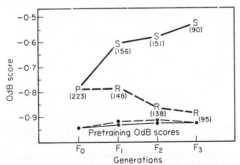

Fig. 4.4. Curves showing the effect of selective breeding on morphine drinking by rats

From an unselected population (*P*) an addiction-susceptible strain (*S*, solid line) and an addiction-resistant strain (*R*, broken line) were bred. The number of subjects in each group is given in parenthesis. The *ODB* score is a measure of opiate-directed behaviour (*from* Nichols and Hsiao, 1967)

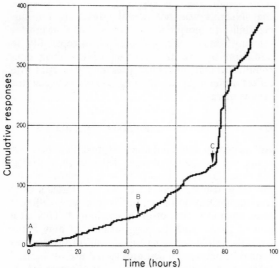

Fig. 4.5. Variation of response rate with size of dose

After addiction, the rat began to respond (*A*), at first receiving 10 mg of morphine per kg body weight. When the dose was cut to 3·2 mg/kg (*B*), the rate increased. When the drug was then cut off completely (*C*), the response rate rose sharply again, then slowed (*from* Weeks, 1964, copyright © 1964 by Scientific American, Inc., all rights reserved)

cannula. They were then put on a fixed ratio schedule (FR10) in which they obtained injections of morphine (10 mg/kg) by lever pressing. On this schedule, rats characteristically responded rapidly to obtain morphine and then did not touch the lever for about two hours. In this way, an average of 12 to 14 injections were received each day. More than one injection at a time seldom occurred. However, if the dose was decreased to 3·2 mg/kg double and triple injections occurred, and the total number of doses increased. When morphine injections were discontinued, there was an immediate increase in responding which then gradually diminished (extinction). A severe abstinence syndrome developed and the rats lost 15 to 25 per cent of their body weight overnight (Weeks, 1962) (Fig. 4.5).

From the observation that dose frequency increased as dose size decreased, the hypothesis arose that the rats titrated their morphine requirements so that they maintained a constant total daily morphine intake despite variations in the size of the dose they received per injection. Weeks and Collins (1964) tested this hypothesis by arranging a daily reduction of dose from 10 mg/kg in decrements of about one third (−0·5 log intervals) on a continuous reinforcement schedule. They found that each daily reduction in dose led to only approximately a doubling of the total number of doses taken each day, and therefore

to a decrease in the total morphine intake. Below 0·32 mg/kg to 0·1 mg/kg there was no further increase in the daily number of injections and only an insignificant amount of morphine was obtained. Weeks and Collins suggested that one reason for the lower total morphine intake at lower doses might be a reduction in tolerance at these doses, i.e. the rats might require less morphine to achieve the same effect.

Woods and Schuster (1968) examined the effects of variation of morphine dosage in monkeys using a 2·5 minute variable interval (VI) schedule of reinforcement. They found a ∩-shaped relation between response rate and dose size; rates increased for doses from 10 mcg/kg to 100 mcg/kg, and then decreased at the higher doses of 250 to 1000 mcg/kg, in some cases falling within the range of the saline control rate (Fig. 4.6). Woods and Schuster attributed the

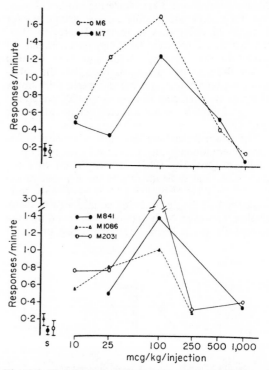

Fig. 4.6. Variable-interval response rate as a function of morphine dose delivered as reinforcement

The morphine data points are the average rates obtained in the last 5 of 15 days at each dose. The saline control data points (*S*) are the averages and ranges of averages of all of the last 5 of 10 days of saline administration interpolated between morphine doses. The monkeys shown in the upper portion of the figure received different doses of morphine in a descending order, the monkeys in the lower portion received doses in an ascending order (*from* Woods and Schuster, 1968, *by courtesy of* Marcel Dekker, Inc.)

decrease in response rate to the dose-related depressant effects of morphine. In their experiment, the generally low response rates did not produce the maximum possible number of reinforcements that could be obtained. In fact, approximately thirty reinforcements were received daily at each dosage. Like Weeks and Collins, Woods and Schuster found that total daily intake was an increasing function of dosage.

Weeks and Collins also report the results of progressively increasing the value of a fixed ratio (FR) schedule of morphine reinforcement. The FR was increased by about 50 per cent each day, until the rats were obtaining less than four injections. Up to FR 75, it was found that, once the rats started responding, they did not stop until they had obtained an injection. There was relatively little responding between injections. At higher ratios, the rats, having started responding, would stop for a few minutes and then resume responding. There was a consequent increase in the time between doses and a decrease in the total morphine intake. Above

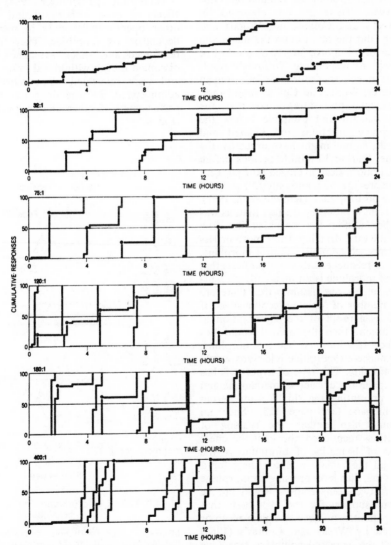

Fig. 4.7. The effect of variation of the value of the fixed-ratio schedule from 10 : 1 to 400 : 1 on total morphine intake

The dose remained constant at 10 mg/kg per injection, dots marking the injections
(*from* Weeks, 1964, copyright © 1964 by Scientific American, Inc., all rights reserved)

FR 180, little morphine was obtained. At the higher ratios the interval between one injection and starting to work for the next increased. This may have been related to prolonged working times enforcing decreased morphine intake with consequent loss of tolerance to morphine (Fig. 4.7).

What implications do the results of these studies have for an understanding of the nature of morphine reinforcement? If the effects of the morphine injection were intensely pleasurable one would expect high steady rates of responding for the drug, as are seen in studies of brain self-stimulation (Olds and Milner, 1954). These are not observed; in neither the Weeks and Collins, nor Woods and Schuster, studies did the rats obtain the maximum possible number of injections, largely as a result of long intervals with no responding. This might result from the depressant effects of morphine following an injection. However, Weeks and Collins found that, in their experimental procedure, rather than the animals being wakeful and excitable before the voluntary morphine injection, and sedated and sleepy afterwards, as one might have expected, the reverse was true. During 30 minute periods before and after the injection, sleep averaged 60·7 per cent of the total time pre-injection, and only 13·7 per cent of the total time post-injection (Khazan et al., 1967).

Another problem is raised by the fact that, as was mentioned earlier, adding the morphine-like drug etonitazene to the rats' drinking water more or less eliminated the rats self-administration of morphine. This is difficult to reconcile with the hypothesis that each injection of morphine is an inherently pleasurable experience, unless one assumes that there are only a limited number of 'opiate receptor sites'. If these are filled as a result of the consumption of etonitazene solution, then the animal could not register the effects of additional injected morphine, and so self-administered morphine injections would cease to be reinforcing. This type of hypothesis has been used to explain the efficacy of methadone and cyclazocine in preventing the 'high' from heroin injections in humans (see page 125). Such an hypothesis would also explain the spacing of morphine injections mentioned above; if the effect of an injection of 10 mg/kg of morphine is the occupation of all the 'opiate receptor sites' for a period of two hours, then lever pressing for morphine injections before two hours elapsed would not be reinforced. Some support for the hypothesis that there are only a limited number of opiate receptor sites is provided by Weeks and Collins's (1964) observation that the increased voluntary morphine intake resulting from the infusion of nalorphine is proportional to the nalorphine infusion rate only up to a point above which no additional increase in

morphine intake occurs. Once the nalorphine occupies all the receptor sites, further increments in morphine dosage would be ineffective.

The fact that the rats did not maintain a constant morphine intake as the size of the dose per injection was changed is still a problem. Weeks (1964) has suggested that the size of the individual injection may be a factor in maintaining a high drug intake as a result of a 'jolt' at the moment of injection or some effect of a momentarily high drug level in the blood.

Thompson and Schuster (1964) have studied the effects of drug withdrawal and reinstatement in other operant behaviours in monkeys physically dependent on morphine. They found that food-reinforced and shock avoidance behaviour were disrupted during withdrawal (after about 18 hours) and were reinstated when morphine was again administered, i.e. the drug was essential for the performance of other non-drug related behaviours (Fig. 4.8).

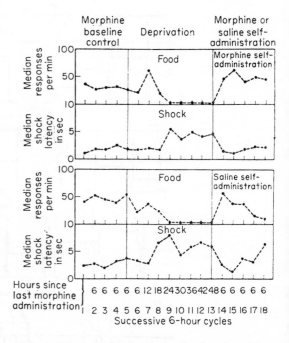

Fig. 4.8. Effects of deprivation on food and avoidance behaviour

Monkeys under conditions of morphine baseline control, 48 hours without the opportunity to self-administer morphine, followed by (upper graph) return to morphine baseline control procedure, or (lower graph) return to baseline condition with saline substituted for morphine self-administration (*from* Thompson and Schuster, 1964)

STIMULANTS

Pickens (1968) has summarised the results of experiments he has conducted with a number of other workers on self-administration of d-amphetamine (Pickens and Harris, 1968), methamphetamine (Pickens *et al.*, 1967) and cocaine (Pickens and Thompson, 1968) in rats with indwelling cannulae.

For the first day or two, responding for all three drugs was low and variable. Thereafter, responding increased and had usually stabilised by the fourth day with a fairly constant interval separating infusions. A pattern of drug intake developed in which periods of drug self-administration alternated with periods of drug abstinence. The mean lengths of drug self-administration periods were 48, 36, and 23 hours, while those of the abstinence periods were 30, 33, and 14 hours respectively for d-amphetamine, methamphetamine, and cocaine. During abstinence periods the animals typically slept and ate. Following an abstinence period of several hours, a self-administration period could be initiated by the experimenter 'priming' the animal by administering a single drug injection. Weight loss and drug tolerance were observed with animals receiving the amphetamines, but not with those receiving cocaine.

To check that the self-administration of stimulants represented a genuine reinforcement effect and not simply the result of drug-produced increases in general activity, a number of experimental manipulations were performed. Some of the manipulations were carried out using only one or two of the drugs, others involved all three.

The results were essentially similar for all three drugs. When drug infusions were discontinued or saline substituted for drug solution, an extinction-like initial increase in response rate followed by cessation of responding was observed. When drug infusions were delivered automatically at a rate equal to that observed during self-administration, an abrupt cessation of responding resembling satiation resulted. In a two-lever cage, when responses on one lever produced drug infusion and responses on the other had no effect, the animal responded on the drug lever only. When the lever contingencies were reversed, the animal's lever preference also reversed. Finally, in a situation where rats were yoked so that responding by one animal produced drug infusion for both, while responding by the other animal had no consequence, it was found that the response rate of the first animal was significantly higher than that of the other.

Overall, these results strongly suggest that self-administration of the drugs represents a real reinforcement effect.

When the size of the dose per infusion of the stimulant drug was varied, an inverse relation between size of dose and frequency of response was observed, with the result that about the same amount of drug per hour was taken at all doses. Woods and Schuster (1968) obtained essentially similar results for cocaine and SPA (1,2-diphenyl-1-dimethylamine-ethane hydrochloride, a stimulant drug abused in Japan) in monkeys (Fig 4.9). Pickens and Thompson (1968) compared the effects they had noted in varying the size of the cocaine reinforcement with the effects of varying the size of the food reinforcement on a food reinforcement schedule. They found, as with cocaine, that increasing the number of food pellets per reinforcement led to a decrease in response rate, and

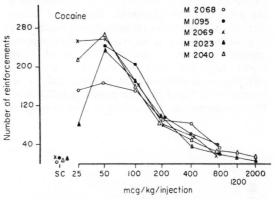

Fig. 4.9. Number of cocaine reinforcements as a function of cocaine dose delivered as reinforcement

The cocaine data points are the averages of all days spent at each dose. The saline control data points (*SC*) are the 5-day average number of injections taken before the monkeys were conditioned to respond for cocaine (*from* Woods and Schuster, 1968, *by courtesy of* Marcel Dekker, Inc.)

about the same daily amount of food was consumed at each reinforcement value. However, no regularly spaced pauses after reinforcement were evident with food, as had been found with cocaine. The effect of intravenous cocaine on an animal responding on an FR 10 schedule of food reinforcement was to produce a complete cessation of responding for an interval after the injection. The fact that the length of the pauses produced in this way was similar to that following cocaine administration in a cocaine reinforcement schedule suggests that the 'pausing' in the latter case may reflect some effect of the drug in inhibiting response other than through drug satiation.

The relatively constant stimulant drug intake over varying dose sizes stands in contrast to the situation occurring with the opiate drugs, already described.

Another difference between the two is the fact that opiate self-administration continues uninterrupted over a relatively long period of time, whereas the self-administration of stimulants by rats is normally interspersed with periods of drug abstinence.

Pickens also reports the effect of varying the value of the fixed-ratio (FR) schedule on total intake of stimulant drugs. It was found that as the value of the FR was increased, response frequency increased accordingly, so that, again, the total intake of drug remained more or less constant.

BARBITURATES

Seevers (1967) has reported that naïve monkeys will self-administer pentobarbital by the intravenous route. The pattern involves self-administration to the point of unconsciousness. The animal wakens after 15 to 20 minutes to continue bar-pressing until unconsciousness again occurs. The cycle is repeated around the clock. However, Davis *et al.* (1968) report very low rates of self-administration of intravenous amobarbital or hexobarbital in unstressed rats. These rates increased considerably if the rats were stressed by receiving unavoidable shocks

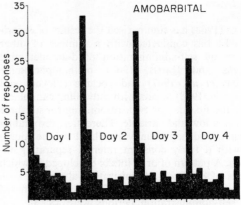

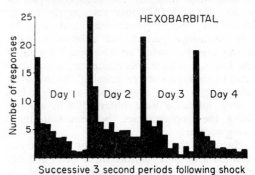

Fig. 4.11. The temporal distribution of responses made by experimental animals

The total number of responses made in ten, 3-second intervals following each shock is plotted for the first four experimental days. The tenth interval contains all responses made in the last 30 seconds of each one minute inter-shock interval (*from* Davis, Lulenski, and Miller, 1968, *by courtesy of* Marcel Dekker, Inc.)

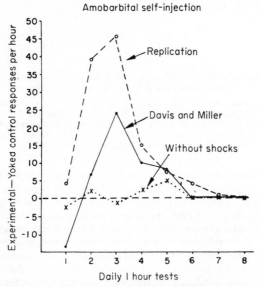

Fig. 4.10. The mean difference between the number of responses made by experimental animals and the yoked control animals in eight daily 1-hour sessions of amobarbital self-administration

Results of the experiment of Davis and Miller (1963) are compared with the replication by Davis, Lulenski, and Miller (1968). The dotted line indicates the difference in response rate of six pairs of experimental and yoked control animals run without shock (*from* Davis, Lulenski, and Miller, 1968, *by courtesy of* Marcel Dekker, Inc.)

every minute. This increase was only temporary, however, and, for the majority of animals, the response rate had returned to a very low level by the sixth or seventh daily session. This result had been obtained previously with amobarbital by Davis and Miller (1963) (Fig. 4.10).

One very interesting observation noted by Davis and co-workers, was that the modal frequency of response for self-administration of amobarbital or hexobarbital occurred within the first three-second period following shock (Fig. 4.11), and could not be attributed to the shock-induced startle reaction. This lends some support to the hypothesis that anxiety or pain-relief provided some of the reinforcement for barbiturate consumption. The decline in barbiturate self-adminstration may have been related to the rats becoming habituated to the painful effects of the shock.

All the studies discussed so far in this review have investigated the reinforcing effects of the addictive drugs themselves, i.e. primary reinforcement effects. A number of studies have attempted to answer the question:

Can drug reinforcement serve as the basis for the establishment of secondary reinforcement?

All the studies that have investigated this question have used morphine as the addictive drug. In an experiment reported by Schuster and Woods (1968) a red light accompanied the infusion of morphine in monkeys self-administering morphine on a variable interval schedule. After the animals had been on the drug for 60 days, morphine reinforcement was discontinued. In extinction, pressing the lever under the discriminative stimulus that morphine was available (in fact, of course, it was not) led to either no programmed consequence, or to the infusion of saline and presentation of the

reconditioned on a smaller dose of morphine as reinforcement for 12 days. They were then withdrawn from the drug and left for 15 days away from the experimental cage, after which time there was no evidence of withdrawal symptoms. The monkeys were then replaced in the experimental cages and the extinction procedure repeated as before, saline and the red light following pressing of the lever on alternate days. Again, higher rates of responding were observed when the red light and saline infusion followed the red light than when there was no programmed consequence. The conditioned reinforcing effect showed a similar decline over extinction to that observed in the first extinction phase.

It should be noted that the results from the second extinction phase showed that the conditioned reinforcer maintained its reinforcing effect, *even when no signs of withdrawal distress were apparent*. This result is similar to that obtained by Beach (page 102), and seems extremely important. Schuster and Woods point this out: 'That conditioned rein-

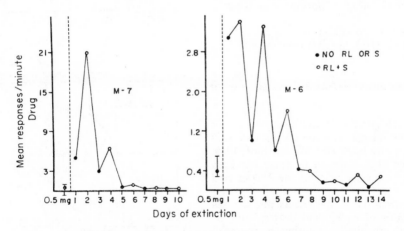

Fig. 4.12. Average response rates for two monkeys

The far-left point is the final 5-day average of response rate for morphine reinforcement. Brackets indicate the range of daily response rate over the 5 days. Points to show right of the dashed line show extinction data, with solid points indicating the absence of response consequence, and with open circles indicating the response consequences of infusion of saline and the presentation of the red light. Note the difference in scale for the two animals (*from* Schuster and Woods, 1968, *by courtesy of* Marcel Dekker, Inc.)

red light previously paired with morphine infusion, on alternate days. It was found that the rate of lever-pressing was higher on the days when it produced saline infusions and the red light than on the other days, demonstrating the conditioned reinforcing properties of the red light.

The secondary reinforcing effects of the red light diminished as extinction proceeded (Fig. 4.12).

After this first extinction phase, the monkeys were

forcement effects can be obtained subsequent to the primary period of morphine withdrawal should be surprising to those who assume that avoidance or escape from withdrawal is the motive for responding for morphine and its associated stimuli, If, on the other hand, the avoidance or escape motive assumption is not made, conditioned reinforcement effects would be expected since morphine responding has not been extinguished.'

As has been already mentioned, Thompson and Schuster (1964) found that when the opportunity to self-administer morphine was withdrawn from morphine-dependent monkeys, their food-reinforced and shock-avoidance behaviours progressively deteriorated. A single morphine self-administration reinstated these behaviours. It was found that, when the animals were allowed to self-administer saline accompanied by a light that had previously been paired with morphine infusion, there was a similar recovery of food-reinforced and shock-avoidance behaviours. The ameliorative effects of morphine had become conditioned to the light paired with morphine infusion. However, this conditioned effect progressively declined with repeated administrations of saline and light (*see* Fig. 4.8).

There seems strong evidence that stimuli associated with drug administration can acquire secondary reinforcing properties. This is particularly interesting in view of the clinical observation that the whole 'ritual' of injection becomes reinforcing in heroin addicts, to the extent that they will inject water if they cannot obtain drugs (Thomson and Rathod, 1968).

Having seen that the effects of drug administration can be conditioned, the next question is:

Can the withdrawal symptoms resulting from the absence of an opiate be conditioned to external stimuli?

The answer to this question is particularly important to a theory of relapse to drug-taking following withdrawal proposed by Wikler (Wikler, 1961, 1965, 1968) (*see* page 112). Relevant evidence has been obtained in experiments reported by Wikler and Pescor (1967).

The procedure in these experiments was to associate the periods of withdrawal distress and its absence, which normally occur during the course of a day in rats maintained on single daily doses of morphine, with different environmental situations. It was found that the frequency of withdrawal signs was significantly higher when the rats were placed in situations previously associated with the morphine abstinence syndrome than when placed in situations which had previously not been associated with the abstinence syndrome. These conditioned abstinence symptoms could be demonstrated up to five months after withdrawal of morphine from the rats, by which time the frequency of withdrawal symptoms in their home environment was very low.

Further evidence for the possibility of conditioning withdrawal symptoms to external stimuli is provided by Goldberg and Schuster (1967). As already mentioned, the drug nalorphine is a morphine

antagonist, and precipitates withdrawal symptoms when administered to morphine-dependent animals. Goldberg and Schuster demonstrated that a stimulus paired with nalorphine infusion in physically dependent monkeys elicits withdrawal symptoms. Monkeys working for food on a fixed ratio schedule were presented with a 5-minute tone followed by an infusion of nalorphine. After several sessions of pairings, the onset of the tone was followed by complete suppression of the operant responding. In addition, signs of acute withdrawal distress, including salivation and vomiting occurred during the tone. After 40 to 45 sessions in which the tone was paired with a saline injection, the conditioned suppression of the food lever response rate and the conditioned autonomic changes were extinguished (Fig. 4.13).

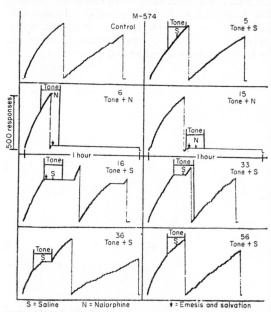

Fig. 4.13. Cumulative response curves from one monkey
Each segment shown is a complete FR10 food component record extracted from a 2-hr session. A control session before tone-injection pairings is shown first; 5 was a session, establishing tone and saline injection as neutral stimuli; 6 was the first conditioning session, 15 was the tenth conditioning session; 16 was the first extinction session, 33 the eighteenth, 36 the twenty-first, and 56 the forty-first extinction session. Arrows indicate observations of emesis and excessive salivation (*from* Goldberg and Schuster, 1967)

Irwin and Seevers (1956) have provided further experimental evidence that nalorphine-induced withdrawal can be classically conditioned. Morphine-dependent monkeys that had undergone repeated nalorphine-induced withdrawal continued to show a 'withdrawal-like response' to both nalorphine and saline injections several months after they had been withdrawn from morphine. After repeated injections of saline, the withdrawal-like response was no longer elicited.

The final question to be discussed in this section is, perhaps, the most important in relation to attempts to treat human addicts. It is:

What are the factors affecting the return to drug-taking behaviour after a period in which the animals have been removed from the drug-taking situation?

Most of the experiments on drug self-administration have shown that, if the drug reinforcement contingent on the drug-seeking behaviour is discontinued, extinction of the drug-seeking behaviour occurs. Animals show an initial increase in the frequency of drug-seeking behaviour, which then declines to a low level.

Investigation of what occurs if the animal is then replaced in the situation where it can obtain drugs after an interval of absence seems to have occurred only for the opiate drugs.

Nichols (1965) and Wikler and Pescor (1967) have reported relapse back to opioid-drinking up to seven weeks following total withdrawal of opioids. Weeks and Collins (1968) report that rats withdrawn from intravenously administered morphine for one to three months all promptly resumed self-administration when returned to the experimental cages and offered morphine.

The interpretation of such studies is complicated by the fact that the short-lived (3 to 5 days) primary abstinence syndrome, which includes the characteristic withdrawal symptoms already mentioned, is succeeded by a milder and qualitatively different secondary abstinence syndrome, characterised by increased water intake, colonic temperatures, metabolic rate, activity, and frequency of 'wet dog shakes' lasting up to six months (Martin *et al.*, 1963). Cochin and Kornetsky (1964) demonstrated residual tolerance to the analgesic action of morphine in post-addict rats one year after withdrawal. It seems that morphine dependence is followed by an altered physiology long after the more obvious withdrawal symptoms have abated, and this factor could affect the tendency to resume drug intake.

It is not in the least surprising that animals, having once been dependent, should later return to drug use, given the chance. The same factors that led to voluntary initiation of drug self-administration in the first place could still be operating, and the fact that the animal now has the motor responses required to produce drug reinforcement in its behavioural repertoire should increase the tendency to self-administer drugs at relapse tests.

An experiment reported by Weeks and Collins (1968) was designed to assess the relative contributions of prior exposure to morphine, and the learning of the appropriate operant response to the tendency to relapse. Five groups of rats were used. One group self-administered morphine during the first three weeks of the experiment. A second group received prior morphine exposure alone, i.e. the rats were given all their morphine injections automatically at the same average rate as the group of self-maintained addict rats for three weeks. A third group, the operant conditioning alone group, wore the same saddle as the addict rats but received no injections. Instead, they were required to press a lever to obtain their drinking water for three weeks, the rate of pressing being approximately similar to that shown by Group I pressing for morphine. A fourth group received essentially the same treatment as the third group, receiving, in addition, injections of morphine programmed automatically. The fifth group consisted of naïve untreated rats and was used to control for the effects of spontaneous primary addiction at the relapse tests.

All groups were subjected to their particular special treatment for three weeks. They were then removed from the experimental cage for four weeks (withdrawal without extinction of the learned response). After this period, they were replaced in the experimental cage for a week of relapse tests, during which they were offered either 10 mg/kg of morphine or an equal volume of water on the FR 10 schedule used in training.

It was found that Group 1 rats promptly resumed morphine intake at the relapse tests and increased their intake throughout the week, all 10 rats showing increased morphine intake between the first and seventh day. Normal untreated rats (Group 5) also took morphine but at a much lower level, and only 3 of the 10 rats in this group showed an increased morphine intake over the week. Rats that had received automatic injections of morphine (Group 2) did not differ significantly from the normal untreated (Group 5) rats in their morphine intake.

It was concluded that neither primary addiction as a result of spontaneous exploratory behaviour nor morphine pretreatment alone could account for the relapse of the 'post-addict' (Group I) rats.

To study the effects of prior operant conditioning in determining tendency to relapse, the post-addict rats were compared with the water-conditioned rats (Group 3) and with the rats receiving combined water-conditioning and morphine pre-treatment (Group 4). It was found that at no time was there a significant difference between the behaviour of post-addict rats and the combined water-conditioned and morphine pretreatment rats at the relapse tests.

The rats that had received water-conditioning alone, but no morphine pretreatment, took less morphine than the post-addicts. While, on a day-to-day basis, the difference between these two groups reached borderline significance only on two days, on all days the post-addicts consistently took about 50 per cent more morphine than the water-conditioned rats.

These results suggest that neither morphine pretreatment nor the existence of the required operant in the animal's behavioural repertoire can alone account for the relapse of post-addict rats. The presence of both seems essential. However, the fact that the morphine-pretreated water-conditioned rats behaved very similarly to the post-addicts suggests that it is only necessary for the rats to have the appropriate operant in their behavioural repertoire, rather than for it necessarily to have been the operant previously associated with the injection of morphine.

A final part of their experiment was designed to cast light on a theory of relapse proposed by Wikler (1961, 1965, 1968). Based on clinical observation, Wikler hypothesised that a factor leading to relapse in addicts who had been kept off drugs for very long periods (e.g. in prison) was the relief of classically conditioned withdrawal symptoms. In the course of

addict has 'hustled' for drugs. It is hypothesised that, by virtue of this association, withdrawal symptoms become classically conditioned to these stimuli, so that, on the addict's return to his old haunts, even after a number of years, the addict experiences conditioned withdrawal symptoms and resumes drug use in order to relieve them. Evidence that withdrawal symptoms can be classically conditioned was presented in the previous section, and an experiment by Wikler himself testing his hypothesis will be discussed below.

Weeks and Collins note that the abstinence syndrome in addicted rats is associated with a marked increase in lever-pressing activity. If, during the three weeks training period, the experimental cage becomes a conditioned stimulus for withdrawal symptoms, then return to the experimental cage at the relapse tests should produce a conditioned abstinence syndrome which should, in turn, produce marked lever-pressing activity. To test this prediction, post-addict rats relapsing to saline and morphine injections were compared with water-conditioned rats relapsing to saline. It was found that, while the water-conditioned rats did not show excessive or sustained regular lever pressing, the post-addict rats showed a high rate of lever-pressing when

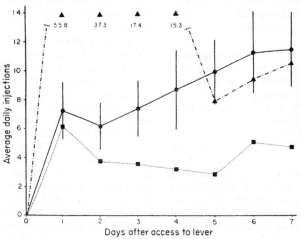

Fig. 4.14. Relapse of 10 post-addict rats to morphine (●———●), 10 to saline (▲–·–▲), and 11 water-conditioned rats to saline (■ – – – ■)

Confidence limits for the saline rats are not shown because they were extremely large. However, post-addict rats on relapse to saline took significantly more injections ($p = 0.05$) than the other groups on days 1, 2, and 3 (*from* Weeks and Collins, 1968)

his addictive career, the addict will have experienced withdrawal symptoms many times, and these will have been associated with the stimuli associated with drug-taking, drug-friends, and the areas where the

relapsing to saline, and an intermediate rate when pressing for morphine (Fig. 4.14). At this time the rats showed no signs of withdrawal (weight loss and hyperirritability). Weeks and Collins state that their evidence is consistent with the development of a conditioned abstinence syndrome. However, as they have no measure of this other than the rate of lever pressing, which is also the measure of extent of relapse, it is difficult to see that they have actually obtained evidence in support of the hypothesis that this motivates relapse.

Wikler (Wikler and Pescor, 1967) tested his theory of the importance of conditioned abstinence symptoms, in precipitating relapse in an experiment already mentioned (page 110). He found that rats showed an increased frequency of withdrawal symptoms when placed in situations previously associated with withdrawal distress, thus demonstrating the existence of conditioned abstinence symptoms. However, no differences in the tendency to relapse to drinking a solution of the opioid etonitazene were found between rats that relapsed in situations previously associated with abstinence symptoms, and those that relapsed in situations with no such associations. This result is contrary to the prediction from Wikler's theory. Further, no differences in the tendency to relapse were found between rats that had previously been trained to reduce withdrawal symptoms by drinking etonitazene solution and those that had had no experience of such relief, but had simply been made physically dependent. This finding differs from that of Weeks and Collins, just described, where it was found that previous morphine dependence alone was not sufficient to account for relapse. This may be related to the fact that the response used by Wikler in the relapse test, drinking, would already be in the behavioural repertoire of the rat, whereas the response used by Weeks and Collins, lever pressing, would not be, without special training. However, Wikler's results also differ from those reported by Nichols (1965) where, using a drinking response, he found that only those animals that had previous experience of relieving abstinence symptoms by drinking morphine solution showed appreciable morphine drinking at relapse tests; those that had been made dependent but not trained to relieve abstinence symptoms by drinking showed little morphine drinking at relapse. Wikler (1968) suggests that this difference might be accounted for by the fact that morphine solution has a bitter taste which rats might find aversive, while etonitazene apparently has not. Thus, rats not previously trained would be more likely to consume enough etonitazene solution at relapse to discover its ability to relieve their residual withdrawal symptoms than rats drinking the more aversive morphine solution. That procedural variables can have such profound effects in altering the results of experiments which, in principle, are studying the same phenomenon should urge caution in the interpretation of such studies.

Wikler and Pescor (1967) summarised the results of their experiments as follows: 'It is concluded that although classical conditioning of morphine abstinence phenomena (and by inference, "craving" for the drug) is demonstrable, the pre-potent factor in disposing to relapse, at least in the rat under the experimental conditions described, is the long-term persistence of unconditioned disturbances in homeostasis following withdrawal of morphine which can provide a source of reinforcement for operant-conditioning of opioid-seeking behaviour during "relapse-testing" sessions even without benefit of previous "training".'

Results apparently contrary to Wikler's hypothesis were obtained in an experiment reported by Thompson and Ostlund (1965). In this experiment, rats were orally addicted to morphine solution, experienced 30 days of withdrawal, and were then re-addicted. Half the rats experienced withdrawal in the same environment as that in which addiction occurred, and half in a different environment. Each of the withdrawal groups was then subdivided and re-addicted in either the same or different environments. Rats re-addicted in the same environment in which original addiction occurred, re-addicted more rapidly then those re-addicted in a new environment. Initial preference for morphine during re-addiction was greater for rats that had experienced withdrawal in a different environment from that in which re-addiction occurred.

The first finding is consistent with Wikler's hypothesis. However, the second is the opposite of what his hypothesis would predict, suggesting that the first finding might have resulted from a simple discriminative function of the stimuli of the original environment, rather than from any abstinence symptoms conditioned to them. However, the results cannot be interpreted unambiguously in relation to Wikler's hypothesis; during the withdrawal period water was placed in the bottle that had previously contained morphine, and thus the response of drinking from this bottle to obtain withdrawal-relief would extinguish. If the animal is placed for re-addiction in an environment different from that in which extinction has occurred, generalisation decrement of the extinction will occur. This factor will operate in the opposite direction to the effects of any conditioned withdrawal effects, and the results obtained might simply demonstrate that the effects of generalisation decrement of extinction outweigh those of conditioned withdrawal symptoms, rather than that the latter do not exist. The relevance of Thompson and Ostlund's findings to the management of human addicts is discussed on page 124.

Findings similar to Thompson and Ostlund's were informally observed by Nichols (1968). This worker noted that, in a long experiment with many replications, in one of the replications the rats had not relapsed nearly as much as in other replications. It was found that the experimental cages had been scrubbed and sterilised between the end of training and the return of the rats for their relapse test, apparently removing a number of stimuli that had been associated with previous addiction, so reducing the relapse rate.

It seems that, in order to explain the evidence available from animal experiments, Wikler's theory may be unnecessarily complicated; relapse to drug-taking at the intervals after withdrawal studied could be explained in terms of relief of residual withdrawal symptoms, as Wikler himself has suggested. Indeed, if drugs do have some inherently pleasurable properties, as some of the experimental evidence suggests, it would not even be necessary to postulate any physiological imbalance in the animal, either conditioned or unconditioned, to explain the return to drug taking. All that would be necessary would be for the animal to have had 'pleasant' experiences from drugs and to have the responses that led to these experiences in its behavioural repertoire. No physiologically-based drive would then be necessary to explain relapse, much in the same way as it is not easy to account for the tendency of food-sated rats to work to obtain condensed milk (which seems 'inherently pleasant' to them) in terms of a physiologically-based hunger drive.

Alternatively, as Nichols (1965) has suggested, as morphine reduces drives other than withdrawal distress such as pain, hunger, anxiety, and sex (although there seems to be little experimental evidence for such effects in animals), these drives could motivate relapse to drug-taking even when there is no longer any withdrawal-based need for the drugs.

Summarising the evidence from animal experiments, it can be said that the initiation and maintenance of drug-taking have been demonstrated for a considerable number of the drugs abused by man, and that relapse after a drug-free period has been demonstrated for the opiates. These findings make Lindesmith's (1947) contention that such behaviour depends on the use of symbolic stimuli and language, and, therefore, is restricted to man, strangely archaic. The animal studies strongly point to the conclusion that, whatever the disorders of personality or factors of social influence leading to drug use in the first place, once the addict has used drugs there are powerful behavioural factors maintaining his further use of drugs.

The fact that the majority of experimental animals will, given the chance, become dependent on drugs abused by human addicts, while only a small minority of humans do, suggests that an interesting way to investigate why addicts take drugs would be to look at why the majority of people do not.

HUMAN STUDIES

The literature on human studies presents a generally less clear-cut picture than that emerging from the animal studies. This reflects the greater difficulties, both practical and ethical, in doing research in this field with humans and also the fact that the situation seems in reality more complex as a result of factors that operate in the human situation but not in the experimental situation with animals. These factors often make it difficult to extrapolate from the animal studies to man, e.g. Nichols (1965) has suggested that the reason most hospital patients receiving morphine injections for the relief of pain do not become morphine addicts is that they do not actually give themselves the injection; it is given by a nurse. This suggestion is based on his finding that morphine-drinking behaviour is only shown to any degree by rats that have learned this as a way of relieving withdrawal symptoms; if rats have been given the same amount of morphine by injection from the experimenter, they show little morphine-drinking behaviour. An alternative, equally plausible explanation for medical patients not normally becoming morphine addicts is that they differ in personality and ease of access to the drug from those people who do become morphine addicts.

The review of studies on animals was fairly comprehensive; the literature on human studies is much

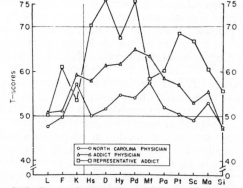

Fig. 4.15. Composite MMPI profiles for addict and non-addict physicians and general white hospitalised Caucasian addicts (*from* Hill, Haertzen, and Yamahiro, 1968)

larger, and it would be impossible to attempt an overall review of it in the space of this chapter. A sample of studies will be discussed, selected on their relevance to the questions posed in the section on animal studies.

The framework used in the first section will be used here, though some of the questions will be altered or omitted due to lack of relevant experimental evidence.

The first question to be asked is:

How does the potential addict become exposed to his first experience of drugs?

This question is obviously irrelevant to the animal studies because, there, experimental conditions are arranged so that all animals have this experience. In

humans, however, this question is highly relevant; abuse of drugs can begin only where there is access to a supply of drugs. The importance of ease of access to drugs in increasing the likelihood of becoming dependent on them is demonstrated by the fact that, in the United States, the addiction rate among physicians is estimated at 1 in 40 to 1 in 100, whereas that in the general population is 1 in 3,000 to 1 in 10,000. (Hill *et al.*, 1968). Further, the availability of the drug might interact with personality, so that the more freely available the drug, the less disturbed need the personality of the person be to become a user. Hill and his colleagues present evidence that addict physicians have personalities more abnormal than non-addict physicians but less abnormal than non-physician addicts (Fig. 4.15).

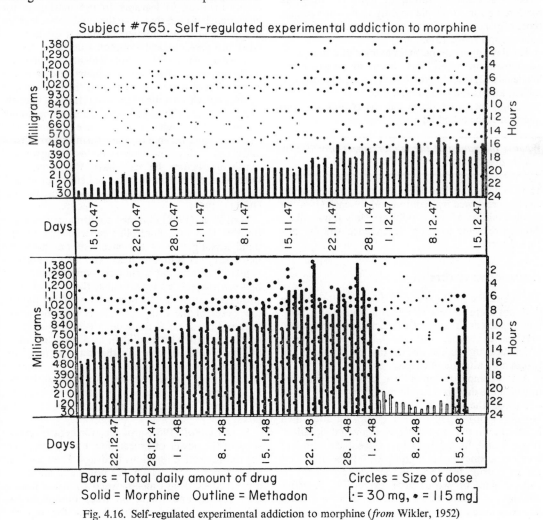

Fig. 4.16. Self-regulated experimental addiction to morphine (*from* Wikler, 1952)

Introduction to drugs seems to occur through friendship networks (Chein *et al.*, 1964; de Alarcon *et al.*, 1969; Zacune *et al.*, 1969). However, as this is the field of sociology and epidemiology, it will not be discussed further. The next question is:

Are the consequences of self-administration of addictive drugs positively reinforcing?

Using the criterion that was used to determine whether drug self-administration was positively reinforcing in animals, i.e. whether the subject would 'voluntarily' initiate and maintain drug self-administration, the very existence of drug addicts is sufficient evidence that drug self-administration can be positively reinforcing in man. A controversial issue is whether self-administration of addictive drugs is reinforcing for all people or only those with certain types of personality. This issue will be discussed in a later section (page 121).

The development and maintenance of a drug self-administration habit has been investigated by Wikler (1962) in an intensive study of an ex-morphine addict, and is shown in Fig. 4.16.

Having seen that drugs can be reinforcing, the question to be asked is:

What is the nature of the reinforcement provided by addictive drugs?

The effects of a variety of drugs on human behaviour has been reviewed by Trouton and Eysenck (1960) in the first edition of this handbook. Only those effects directly relevant to drug dependence will be discussed here.

1. SUBJECTIVE EFFECTS

The subjective effect experienced as a result of a drug does not seem to be a simple function of the drug; factors such as the subject's expectation, personality, previous experience with the drug, the setting in which the drug is taken, and the task requirements can profoundly alter these effects.

A neat demonstration of the effects of the situation in which the drug is taken in modifying the reported effects of the drug is described by Nowlis and Nowlis (1956). They studied groups of four men interacting in the same basic experimental situation. It was found, for example, that if a subject who had received seconal was in a group with three others on the same drug, there was an increased frequency of endorsement of words like expansive, forceful, courageous, daring, elated, and impulsive on a mood adjective check-list. However, if he was, 'cooped up

with, say, the egotistical benzedrine partner, the withdrawn, indifferent dramamine partner, and the slightly bored lactose man, the second subject reports that he is distractible, dizzy, drifting, glum, defiant, languid, sluggish, discouraged, dull, gloomy, lazy, and slow'.

The effect of the environment in determining the nature of drug-induced subjective experience has also been demonstrated by the work of Schacter (1966). This worker has shown, for example, that the subject's cognitive appraisal of what is happening to him can powerfully influence the subjective effects of injected epinephrine. Schacter suggests that such cognitive appraisal is important in determining the subjective consequences of drugs taken for pleasure, and cites the work of Becker (1953) in support of this suggestion. Becker studied the sequence of events involved in learning to use marijuana for pleasure. He found that once the smoker has learned the techniques of smoking, he must then learn to label the physiological symptoms as being 'high'; '. . . being high consists of two elements: the presence of symptoms caused by marijuana use and the recognition of these symptoms and their connection by the user with his use of the drug. It is not enough, that is, that the effects are present; they alone do not automatically provide the experience of being high. The user must be able to point them out to himself and consciously connect them with his having smoked marijuana before he can have this experience. Otherwise, regardless of the actual effects produced, he considers that the drug has no effect on him' (Becker, 1953).

Weil *et al.* (1968) obtained confirmatory evidence for this idea in a controlled experimental double-blind investigation of the effects of marijuana on naïve subjects and on those who had smoked it regularly. While naïve subjects could differentiate between placebo and marijuana, they reported no strong subjective experiences after smoking high or low doses of the drug; the effects they did report were not the same as those described by the regular users. The latter became high, as a result of taking the same doses of drugs in the same setting. That the marijuana was actually having a physiological effect on the naïve subjects was shown by the impairment it produced in the performance of simple intellectual tests and psychomotor tasks.

Bozzetti *et al.* (1967) produced further evidence to support the power of expectation, etc., in determining the subjective reactions to drugs. They analysed dried banana peel, which was popularly smoked as a psychedelic drug ('mellow yellow') at the time of their report, and found no trace of any known hallucinogen. They concluded that the reported psychedelic effects of the 'drug' could be accounted for entirely in terms of expectation, suggestion, etc.

Reed and Witt (1965) report the occurrence of an LSD type response to a placebo, and effectively no response to LSD, in an experiment they undertook. They interpreted these results in terms of the subject's expectations, etc.

It should be pointed out that, while cognitive factors are obviously important in determining the reinforcing effects of drugs, the work with animals suggests that they cannot account for them entirely, i.e. it is not all 'in the mind'.

In addition to modifying the reinforcing effects of drugs, cognitive factors also seem important in determining the relation between reinforcement and behaviour. Chein *et al.* (1964) state that while approximately half the heroin users they interviewed reported that their first reactions to heroin were definitely pleasant, about one third reported that they had had negative reactions. Willis (1969) reports somewhat similar findings. On a simple reinforcement view, one would have predicted that those experiencing initial adverse reactions would not go on to take further injections of heroin. In fact, they do, although not so immediately as those who experienced initial positive reactions. Chein *et al.* report that while two-thirds of those whose initial reactions were favourable continued heroin use immediately, only one-fifth of those whose reactions has been unfavourable did so.

Workers at the Addiction Research Center, Lexington, Kentucky, have conducted experimental investigations into the subjective effects of a number of drugs, using ex-heroin addicts as their experimental subjects. Hill and co-workers (1963a) describe the empirical construction of scales of questionnaire items which significantly differentiated the subjective effects of these drugs from a placebo condition. These scales are given in Hill *et al.* (1963b). Examples of items from the morphine and amphetamine scales are given in Table 4.1.

It can be seen that there are several items common to both scales. Hill *et al.* (1963a) conclude: 'It is quite apparent that considered *individually* very few of the subjective changes measured are unique for any of the drugs studied. On the other hand, it is quite clear that viewed as a spectrum of concurrent changes, subjective effects of drugs do exhibit a high degree of pattern specificity.'

In order to examine this 'pattern specificity' further, Haertzen (1965) factor analysed the items of the Addiction Research Center Inventory (from which the drug scales had been derived) using the responses of 100 post-addict male subjects given LSD 25. Ten factors were extracted but only two of these were substantially related to the effects of the

Table 4.1. Examples of Items from the Morphine and Amphetamine Scales Derived from the Addiction Research Center Inventory
(Hill, Haertzen, Wolbach, and Miner, 1963a, 1963b)

Item No.	Item	Scoring
Morphine		
2	I have a pleasant feeling in my stomach	T
3	I feel as if I would be more popular with people to-day	T
345	I feel so good that I know other people can tell it	T
457	My nose itches	T
541	My speech is not as loud as usual	T
Amphetamine		
2	I have a pleasant feeling in my stomach	T
3	I feel as if I would be more popular with people to-day	T
59	My thoughts come more easily than usual	T
152	My memory seems sharper than usual	T
279	I feel a very pleasant emptiness	T

eight drugs that were investigated: LSD, morphine, amphetamine, pentobarbital, chlorpromazine, pyrahexyl, alcohol, and scopolamine.

Figure 4.17 shows the distribution of the items in the factor space obtained when plotting only the first two factors. The names of the drugs are adjacent to those items that show the greatest effect following administration of that drug.

The first factor was labelled 'reactivity', and it was found that all eight drugs produced a significant change on this factor. The second factor, 'efficiency', was polar in the sense that some drugs produced on it effects that were opposite to those under placebo. Thus, amphetamine increased the feeling of energy and memory capacity, but other drugs such as scopolamine decreased the feeling.

By using the two factors, the general spectrum of similarities and differences between drugs can be demonstrated. The factor space serves as an organising principle for relating subjective drug effects. The similarities in some areas of their subjective effects might explain why, for example, drug users will quite happily switch from a drug like heroin to one with quite different pharmacological properties, such as methylamphetamine (Hawks *et al.*, 1969).

The role of differences in personality in determining subjective reactions to drugs will be discussed later (page 121).

2. EXPERIMENTAL INVESTIGATIONS OF THE EFFECTS OF MORPHINE

A number of experimental investigations have been aimed at elucidating the effects of morphine in man, in particular, its analgesic effects.

Hill and colleagues (1952a) studied the effects of

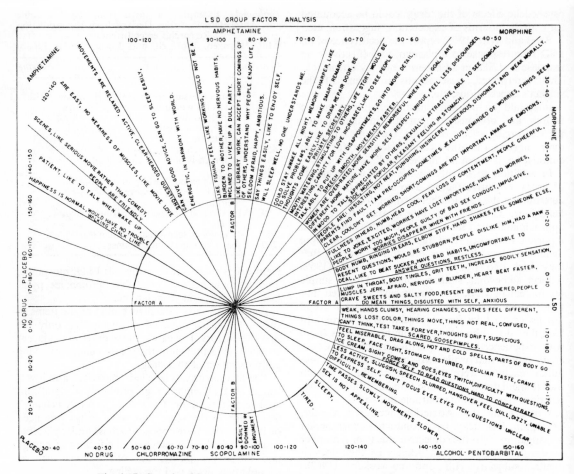

Fig. 4.17. Sample of item content for the reactivity (*A*) and efficiency (*B*) factors

The axes for factors *A* and *B* were rotated starting from the *A* axis as indicated by degrees around the periphery. Content was sampled along each rotated axis among items that had factor loadings of 0·4 or greater on the axis in question. Drug names are indicated on the axis where a drug has its principal effect as compared with no-drug and placebo. However, on any one axis drugs can be ordered in terms of the magnitude of difference from the no-drug and placebo conditions. To illustrate, LSD produces the highest effect using questions on the *A*-axis. LSD is followed by morphine, alcohol, pentobarbital, scopolamine, pyrahexyl, chloropromazine, and amphetamine. The ordering of the drugs is a function of the dose. Although the average *S* under placebo is located in the centre of the circle, *S*s with extremely high scores are not. The performance of such *S*s is related somewhat to drug-effect profiles (*from* Haertzen, 1965)

morphine on the ability of former opiate addicts to judge the intensity of painful electric shocks under two experimental conditions. Under the formal condition, the subjects were not familiarised with the potentially fear-inspiring experimental situation. Under the informal condition, the experiment was preceded with reassurance and a demonstration and explanation designed to allay the subject's anxiety. It was found that under the formal condition, subjects tended to overestimate the intensities of powerful shocks, but that if the subject had received

morphine before the experiment this effect did not occur. Placebos had no effect in reducing anxiety in this condition. In the informal condition, however, little, if any, overestimation of the intensities of painful stimuli occurred. Morphine had no effect on the accuracy of judgement in this situation, where experimental conditions were arranged to minimise the subject's anxiety. It was concluded that the analgesic action of morphine was attributable to its effect on pain-produced anxiety rather than to its effect on the sensory threshold for pain. In fact,

Wolff *et al.* (1940) reported that morphine improves the ability to estimate pain.

Findings essentially similar to those obtained by Hill *et al.* (1952a) were obtained in an experiment by Kornetsky (1954) investigating the effects of morphine on the anticipation and perception of painful radiant thermal stimuli. It was found that morphine was effective in reducing anticipatory responses to pain only in the anxiety-provoking 'formal' condition, and not in the more reassuring 'informal' condition.

In another experiment, Hill and co-workers (1952b) studied the effects of morphine on the disruptive effects of anxiety anticipatory to pain on psychomotor performance. The hand reaction times to visual stimuli of former opiate addicts were compared on days when they had received a pre-injection of morphine with their performance on days when they had received no morphine, under two conditions. In the first condition, subjects were motivated only by the general knowledge of their performance. In the second condition, the subjects were penalised by the self-administration of brief, strong, electric shocks to one hand immediately after each response that was slower than the previous median value.

The shortest reaction times were obtained in non-morphinised subjects under the first condition. In this condition, morphine significantly increased reaction times. Under the second condition, non-morphinised subjects gave significantly longer reaction times than in the first condition, presumably reflecting the disruptive effects of the anxiety produced by anticipation of pain. However, morphinised subjects showed no such increase in reaction times from condition 1 to condition 2. The authors interpreted their result as demonstrating that morphine reduces the disruptive effects on performance that are associated with the anxiety produced by the anticipation of pain. They suggested an interesting parallel between the effects of morphine and those of frontal lobectomy; Malmo and Shagass (1950) reported that lobotomy markedly reduced the motor responses anticipatory of painful stimuli, in contrast to its effect on the direct responses to painful stimuli, which might actually be enhanced (Chapman *et al.* 1948).

A later study (Hill *et al.* 1955) confirmed the effects of morphine in reducing the disruption of performance due to anticipatory anxiety in the experimental situation described above. Pentobarbital failed to show the same effect, however. That the effect of morphine in reducing the effect of anxiety on performance might be one example of a more general action of morphine in reducing the effects of a variety of motivational effects on behaviour was suggested by the authors in an

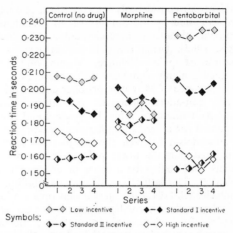

Symbols:
◇—◇ Low incentive   ◆—◆ Standard I incentive
◆—◆ Standard II incentive   ◇—◇ High incentive

Fig. 4.18. Effect of incentives on mean reaction time under various drug conditions (*from* Hill, Belleville, and Wikler, 1957)

experiment reported by Hill *et al.* (1957). In this experiment on former opiate addicts, motivation was manipulated by variations in the contingency between performance on the reaction time task and a reward of morphine for good performance, to give a low, standard, and high level of motivation to perform well. It was found that the differences in performance on the reaction time task under different motivation conditions were less after the subject had a pre-injection of morphine than in the no-drug condition. Pretreatment with pentobarbital enhanced the differences between the performance under different conditions of motivation (Fig. 4.18). The authors suggested that the effect of morphine in this experimental situation, which was to make the subjects less sensitive to variations in motivation, paralleled clinical reports of morphine and its derivatives, making addicts less sensitive to pain and discomfort, to sexual objects, and to other social influences, effectively shielding them from the unpleasant pressures these factors might exert on them.

Unfortunately, an alternative explanation is possible; the high motivation condition relied on producing good performance by rewarding with morphine for such performance; pre-injection with morphine could have a direct effect on weakening this source of motivation, as the subjects would be under the influence of morphine already and the prospect of more morphine might be less attractive than for subjects not already morphinised. This, rather than any general 'shielding' from motivational influences, could explain the results of the above experiment.

That people who become opiate addicts may actually be more than usually sensitive to pain, and so might gain considerably from the effects of opiates, was suggested by the authors of an investigation into pain tolerance in narcotic addicts (Martin and Inglis, 1965). Using the cold-pressor test as the measure of pain tolerance, Martin and Inglis obtained a highly significant difference between the pain tolerance of 24 female prisoner addicts and 24 female non-addict prisoners, the addicts having lower pain tolerance. This difference could not be accounted for in terms of differences in extraversion or neuroticism between the groups. The authors recognised that the lower pain tolerance of their addicts could either be a cause or effect of opiate addiction. The latter is a distinct possibility, for Himmelsbach (1941) has shown that opiate addicts show lower than normal pain thresholds up to six months after withdrawal from drugs, although these had returned to normal by 17 to 18 months after withdrawal. Unfortunately, Martin and Inglis do not state the period after withdrawal at which their subjects were tested.

3. WHAT ARE THE RELATIVE ROLES OF 'EUPHORIA' AND WITHDRAWAL-RELIEF REINFORCEMENT IN MAINTAINING OPIATE SELF-ADMINISTRATION?

No adequate experimental evidence is available on this question. Wikler, on the basis of clinical observations and the results of his intensive study of a single case of experimental re-addiction to morphine, (Wikler, 1965, 1961, 1952) states that patients consistently report that with successive doses of opiates repeated several times daily, the 'euphoric' effects decline progressively. Such 'tolerance' can be overcome to a considerable extent by progressively increasing the dose, but the intensity of the initial euphoria is not regained as long as the uninterrupted schedule of drug administration is maintained. The reason given by most addicts for continuing to take opiates in the face of this declining euphoria, Wikler states, is that they fear the distress of acute abstinence, having reached the stage of physical dependence. The picture presented by the addicts is that they take drugs simply to avoid abstinence symptoms and stay 'normal' without achieving very much pleasure out of their whole addiction system. Wikler doubts this picture; he suggests that if the whole addiction system in the physically dependent addict gives so little pleasure, then the addicts should gradually withdraw themselves from drugs, knowing from experience that this could be done without great discomfort. They could then start taking opiates again and recapture the initially powerful euphoric effects, or simply lead a life not plagued by the regular misery of withdrawal symptoms.

Wikler's alternative explanation was derived from his intensive single-case investigation of experimental morphine re-addiction (Wikler, 1953). The subject of this study, having acquired a high degree tolerance to morphine by repeated self-injections, commented that, although he could not regain the initial euphoric effects, the drug produced another sort of pleasure, that arising from the relief of such abstinence discomfort as developed towards the end of the intervals between injections. The subject drew the analogy that while a steak always tastes good, it tastes even better when one is hungry. The impression given is that drug-taking is not simply on an avoidance conditioning paradigm, to avoid the distress of abstinence, but that the consumption of drugs in a state of abstinence leads to withdrawal-relief which is actually experienced as pleasurable. Wikler *et al.* (1953) have shown that the morphine antagonist nalorphine can precipitate an abstinence syndrome in post-addicts after they have been receiving opiates four times daily for as short a period as two or three days. This result suggests that, in man as in animals, some degree of physical dependence may develop very rapidly after the onset of drug use, so that withdrawal relief may be an important aspect of drug reinforcement even in the early stages of drug use.

4. CORRECTION OF SLEEP ABNORMALITIES

From a number of studies they review, Oswald and co-workers (1969) conclude: 'The present evidence suggests that all the common *drugs of addiction at first suppress paradoxical sleep and that after their withdrawal a rebound excess occurs*, and that this second disturbance of brain physiology may take weeks to disappear' (their italics).

Amphetamines, barbiturates, amphetamine-barbiturate mixtures, and morphine have been shown to have this effect; after consumption of the drug for some time, the amount of paradoxical sleep (REM sleep) is normal, but stays normal only so long as the drugs continue to be taken. If drugs are discontinued, excess paradoxical sleep occurs (Fig. 4.19), often accompanied by nightmares, and the authors suggest that one reason for continued consumption of addictive drugs may be to avoid such 'psychophysiological withdrawal symptoms' occurring when the drug is stopped. Some support for this hypothesis is provided by the observation reported by the same workers that, while a number of drugs can lead to the suppression of REM sleep, only those that also produce a rebound excess on withdrawal are actually addictive. Further, they suggest that these effects on sleep, which are common to a variety of addictive drugs, may explain the use by the same individual of

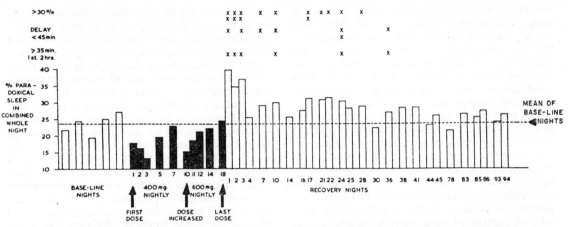

Fig. 4.19. Effect of sodium amylobarbitone on the sleep of two men who serve as their own controls

The hypnotic at first causes suppression of paradoxical sleep and withdrawal or rebound increase. The time scale is not linear. Where either or both volunteers spent over 30 per cent of the whole night in paradoxical sleep, had a delay of less than 45 min between first falling asleep and first rapid eye movements of paradoxical sleep, or spent more than 35 minutes of the first two hours of sleep in paradoxical sleep, a cross has been placed over the night concerned. The crosses, which indicate extreme or frankly abnormal values, are seen only after drug withdrawal and peter out in the sixth recovery week (*from* Oswald and Priest, 1965)

drugs of otherwise widely differing pharmacological action, e.g. opiates and amphetamines.

This hypothesis, like other withdrawal-relief hypotheses, applies only to the maintenance of drug-taking, once established, rather than to its initiation.

Having reviewed the reinforcing effects drugs can have, the next question concerns how widespread such effects are in the human population:

Are there individual differences in susceptibility to becoming dependent on addictive drugs?

AGE

Dependence on drugs such as the opiates or amphetamines seems commonest among the younger age groups, e.g. Zacune *et al.* (1969), who report a mean age of 21·1 years for the males and of 18 for the females, in a group of British heroin users they studied; such results seem fairly typical. Further, Winick (1962) presents evidence to support the idea that opiate addicts 'mature out' of their addiction as they get older, and Vaillant (1966a) has shown a progressive decline in the numbers addicted over a twelve-year follow up of a group of 100 narcotic addicts (Fig. 4.20).

These results are obviously very similar to the findings reported for animals, where 'addiction susceptibility' seemed to decline with age. Whether this reflects a pharmacological/physiological phenomenon common to animals and man, or whether

the results in man are better explained in terms of sociological or psychological processes it is impossible to say.

PERSONALITY

Personality could operate in a number of ways in determining susceptibility to addiction. For example, it could determine whether a person mixed with groups where drugs were available; whether, given the availability of drugs, the person experimented

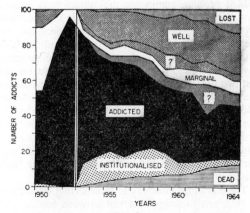

Fig. 4.20. Drug use of 100 addicts over a 15-year period (admitted to hospital between 1st August 1952 and 31st January 1953) (*from* Vaillant, 1966a)

with them; whether, having had some experience of drugs, the person continued to use them, how strongly the person would want to stop taking them, and how successful his attempts would be. The discussion in this section will be restricted to one of the most important influences of personality, from a behavioural point of view, namely, its influence on the reinforcing properties of the drug.

This problem has been looked at in two ways. The first is to look at the relation between drug effects and personality within the population of drug addicts. The second has been to look at differences in drug reactions in drug addicts and normal subjects. As early as 1925, Kolb (1925), on the basis of clinical observation, suggested the existence of two reaction patterns to narcotic drugs in addicts. The first, labelled 'negative pleasure', was the use of opiates by neurotic individuals to allay their anxiety, i.e. a form of self-medication to make them more 'normal'. The experimental evidence suggesting the anxiety-reducing properties of morphine has already been discussed (page 118).

The second pattern, labelled 'positive pleasure', was shown by sociopaths who used drugs, not to allay anxiety, but to take them to a supernormal state of 'euphoria'.

A number of studies have used the MMPI to demonstrate the existence of different 'types' of narcotic addicts (e.g. Hill et al., 1960; Hill et al., 1962; Astin, 1959) and 'psychopathic' and 'neurotic' types have in fact emerged. Haertzen and Hill (1959) studied the response to morphine and pentobarbital in 55 post-addicts, giving them the MMPI in balanced order under control, morphine, and pentobarbital conditions. No significant overall effect of the drugs was found. However, when the subjects were split into different 'types' of addicts, on the basis of their MMPI profiles, significant differences were found. It was found, for example, that, while the 'neurotic psychopaths' showed a significant decrease on Depression, Welsh's Anxiety Index, and Welsh's Internalisation Ratio under morphine, the 'primary psychopaths' showed a significant *increase* on the last two measures, and a non-significant increase on the first. These results support the idea that different addicts obtain different effects from the same drug in the same setting, suggesting that the reasons for drug-taking may be different for different groups of addicts. The results also support the hypothesis that part of the reasons for taking drugs may be 'self-medication'.

There is more difficulty in interpreting differences in reactions to drugs observed between addicts and non-addicts in terms of differences in personality. One difficulty is that the addicts used in the studies are generally institutionalised, and, further, may have only recently been withdrawn from their drugs, e.g. in the study by Lasagna et al. (1955) none of the post-addicts had been more than a week without a narcotic drug before the experiment began. Himmelsbach (1942) has shown that it can take up to six months after the withdrawal of opiates for physiological functions to return to normal; the relief of such residual physiological imbalance, rather than any differences in personality, might account for differences observed in the effects of opiates on normal and post-addict subjects. A further difficulty is that, as pointed out above (page 117), it may be necessary to learn to interpret the physiological effects of drugs as pleasant before one experiences pleasure from them; post-addicts would have had this learning experience, whereas drug-naïve normal subjects would not. Route of administration is also likely to effect the subjective effects obtained; the 'thrill' or 'buzz' reported by heroin addicts seems to depend on intravenous injection, whereas experiments on normal subjects are more likely to use the subcutaneous route.

Lasagna et al. (1955) review a number of reports of incidental observations on the effects of morphine on non-addict subjects, all of which suggested that drug-induced euphoria was a relatively rare occurrence, e.g. the authors note that, in their own experience, of 356 doses of morphine administered to 150 patients after surgical operations, in only three patients were the responses really euphoric. Lindesmith (1947) cites observational evidence suggesting the opposite conclusion. Lasagna et al. (1955) conducted an experimental investigation of this problem. Placebo, amphetamine, pentobarbital, heroin, and morphine were given subcutaneously (except pentobarbital) to normal subjects and to ex-opiate addicts (all of whom had had contact with narcotics in the previous week). It was found that for the normal subjects, amphetamine was a more potent euphoriant than morphine, or heroin, neither of which, in the doses and situation used, were pleasant to the majority of the subjects. In contrast, the ex-addicts picked morphine as the most pleasant drug, and amphetamine as the most unpleasant drug, for which they expressed an actual dislike. However, in this group there was a marked absence of euphoria after injection of heroin. This may have been related to the small doses used (2 or 4 mg) or to the subcutaneous route of administration. The results for morphine are similar to those reported in an experiment by Fraser and Isbell (1952): 'The former morphine addict finds the sensation caused by an injection of morphine agreeable, even though he may experience nausea, gagging, and repeated vomiting, whereas the non-addict is mainly indifferent, experiences no pleasure or even dislikes the sensation evoked by the injection.'

In another paper, von Felsinger *et al.* (1955) examined the relation between personality and reaction to drugs in the group of normal subjects reported in Lasagna *et al.* (1955) in more detail. Estimates of personality were obtained by interview and the Rorschach, and were related to the response to the drugs in terms of whether these were typical of most of the subjects or atypical. The typical reactions to amphetamines were euphoria and alertness, to heroin and morphine dysphoria and sedation, and to pentobarbital euphoria and sedation. It was found that those subjects showing atypical dysphoria or sedation under amphetamines were judged to have, generally, less adequate personalities than those showing the typical reaction. Similarly, those seven of the twenty subjects who had responded with unequivocal euphoria to heroin or morphine or both, were characterised by immaturity, impulsiveness, and self-centred and emotional tendencies. Pentobarbital typically produced sedation; only two subjects felt stimulated by the drug, and both of these had reacted with euphoria to the opiates. Further, five of the seven people with an atypical reaction to opiates had also atypical reactions to pentobarbital in that they showed only slight sedation. In terms of the effect of pentobarbital on mood, those showing a dysphoric reaction were described as showing less self-confidence than those showing the more typical euphoric effect. Six patients showed definite changes to the placebo, five reporting pleasant effects, one unpleasant. Of these six, four had atypical reactions to opiates, and one had experience of a slightly pleasant reaction to opiates.

The results suggested that the subjects exhibiting atypical reactions to one drug tended to show atypical reactions to other drugs. If the seven subjects who fell into at least two of the four major atypical groups (dysphoria with amphetamine, sedation with amphetamine, euphoria with opiates, and dysphoria with pentobarbital) were considered as a group, the following composite picture emerged:

1. immature personalities, dominated by impulsive and egocentric tendencies, and inadequately controlled emotion, of which the subjects were frequently consciously aware;
2. strong, diffuse, unrealistic striving;
3. moodiness and depression;
4. these were the most anxious and hostile group.

Both in terms of their reaction to drugs, and description of their personality, these patients seem to resemble the post-addicts also studied. The fact that seven out of twenty of the 'normal' subjects

were considered atypical in these respects suggests that, in terms of personality and reaction to drugs, the post-addicts were not particularly unusual.

It would be tempting to interpret the results of this investigation in terms of an 'arousal' hypothesis: atypical reactors and opiate addicts are generally 'over-aroused' (over the optimal point on a Yerkes-Dodson curve) so that 'sedative' drugs, such as the opiates, will bring the arousal level down closer to the optimum, and be experienced as pleasant; whereas 'stimulant' drugs, such as amphetamine, would take the arousal level even further away from the optimum, and so be experienced as unpleasant. Conversely, 'normal' subjects could be viewed as being generally at a sub-optimal point of arousal; opiates would be experienced as unpleasant as they would take them even further away from the optimal arousal level, whereas amphetamine would be experienced as pleasant, as it would bring them up closer to the optimal arousal level.

Unfortunately, there are several difficulties with this simple hypothesis. Firstly, pentobarbital, a 'sedative' drug, produced euphoria in the 'normal' subjects and dysphoria in the atypical subjects. Secondly, amphetamine, while sedating the atypical subjects, had a dysphoric effect on them. Thirdly, the empirical amphetamine scale developed by Hill *et al.* (1963a, 1963b) (*see* page 117) which was developed on ex-opiate addicts, contains items suggesting amphetamine had a pleasant effect on them. Fourthly, drug users will not necessarily restrict themselves to the use of either stimulant or sedative drugs, e.g. Hawks *et al.* (1969) found that methylamphetamine users would switch to opiates when these were available, not necessarily to 'sedate' them from the stimulant effects of the amphetamine.

If, as a number of authors have suggested, opiates are reinforcing to only a minority of humans with inadequate personalities, the situation in man seems different from that in animals where, apparently, the majority of animals find such drugs reinforcing. This difference may seem less marked if one considers the situations in which the experimental animals are studied; confined in small cages, carrying harnesses on their backs, having undergone major surgery for the implementation of the indwelling cannulas, the animals are in a situation that might be expected to produce 'unhappiness' that could be relieved by the drugs.

The next question to be discussed is:

What factors affect drug self-administration in a person already dependent on drugs?

Owing to the practical and ethical problems in conducting, in man, the type of experiments that have been conducted with animals, there is virtually no experimental evidence on this point.

The single-case study by Wikler (1952) has already been mentioned. As consumption of morphine was self-regulated by this patient (i.e. frequency of injection was not determined by the amount of drug available) the fact that he took relatively few (approximately 7 to 10) injections each day, and that these were spaced at fairly regular intervals (*see* Fig. 4.16) provides an interesting parallel with the results from animal investigations.

Consumption of stimulants by animals seems to occur in a pattern of alternating periods of administration and abstinence, the periods lasting 20 to 40 hours. A similar phenomenon has been reported in human users of methylamphetamine by Kramer and co-workers (1967); typically, the drug is injected approximately every two hours around the clock for three to six days, during which time the users are continually awake. Following such a 'run' the user 'falls out', that is, stops injecting and falls into a sleep, from which he cannot be wakened, which lasts 12 to 18 hours following a run of three to four days. The period of sleep is longer following longer runs. On waking, the user feels lethargic, and terminates this lethargy with the first injection of the next run.

In contrast to Kramer *et al.*'s findings, Hawks *et al.* (1969) found such a cyclic pattern of drug use in only 8 per cent of their sample of methylamphetamine users; the majority used the drug continuously.

Can drug reinforcement serve as the basis for the establishment of secondary reinforcement?

Here, only clinical evidence is available. Thomson and Rathod (1968) report that heroin addicts will inject themselves with water if drugs are not available; it seems that, by association with the unconditioned reinforcement of the drug, the whole 'ritual' of drug administration will acquire reinforcing properties, and may be prolonged to maximise the reinforcement from this source.

Can the withdrawal symptoms resulting from the absence of an opiate be conditioned to external stimuli?

Again, no experimental evidence is available in humans. Clinical observations, such as post-addicts experiencing withdrawal symptoms long after withdrawal from drugs had been completed, in situations previously associated with drug-taking, e.g. meeting an old addict friend in the street, were the original basis of Wikler's theory of relapse precipitated by conditioned abstinence symptoms (Wikler, 1965, 1961, 1953) (*see* page 112).

Vaillant (1969) cites several types of anecdotal illustration to support the thesis that withdrawal symptoms can be conditioned to external stimuli. First, when nutmeg, which Vaillant describes as a non-narcotic stimulant, was smuggled into the addiction treatment centre, the patients went through certain rituals, previously associated with heroin distribution, while dividing it among themselves. At such times, patients might experience signs and symptoms characteristic of withdrawal. Another observation cited was that, on the research ward, patients who had been abstinent for months could experience acute craving and withdrawal symptoms while watching another patient receive an injection of narcotics.

Such observations would suggest the utility of testing Wikler's theory more rigorously in human subjects, despite the lack of support it has received from animal experiments.

What are the factors affecting the return to drug-taking behaviour after a period in which the patients have been removed from the drug-taking situation?

Discussion of this question will be restricted to dependence on opiates, on which more data is available than on other drugs.

It is extremely difficult to get clear evidence in support of hypotheses derived from animal experiments from follow-up studies of human addicts; there seem to be many interacting factors determining whether a drug user ceases to use drugs, and *post-hoc* examination of the facts with a view to obtaining support for experimentally derived hypotheses holds the danger of selecting only the more 'desirable' facts.

A good example of the problem is the question whether drug users are more likely to remain abstinent if, after withdrawal from drugs, they are returned to the same environment in which they originally became addicted, or to a different environment. The experiment by Thompson and Ostlund (1965) (*see* page 113) clearly predicts that readdiction will be less likely if addicts are returned to an environment different from that in which addiction originally developed. However, if this result were in fact observed it could occur for reasons quite different from those accounting for the results in this experiment, e.g. it is probable that for addicts placed in a totally new environment (probably one where drug-taking is less endemic than in the area they originally came from) access to drugs would be more difficult than if replaced in their original environment, either because there were fewer drugs in the area, or because the ex-addict would no longer have such easy access to the distribution network. Further, from the experimental evidence, one could equally explain the opposite result (i.e. that readdiction would be less likely if the addict is returned to his old environment), e.g. Vaillant (1969) suggests that the reason why abstinence maintained under parole in the community is more enduring than that achieved during voluntary hospitalisation is that the former occurs in the presence of many stimuli with conditioned reinforcing properties (or with conditioned abstinence properties). Continued abstinence while surrounded by such stimuli would lead to extinction of their conditioned effects, and thus reduce the chance of relapse. In support of this hypothesis, Vaillant cites the fact that less than a third of the long abstinences observed in his study were associated with the addict moving out of areas of high endemic drug use.

For such reasons, the data from follow-up studies, while of great clinical and practical importance, is not a very fruitful source for obtaining evidence relevant to the type of behavioural model suggested by the animal studies. For a discussion of such studies the reader is referred to Vaillant (1966a, 1966b, 1966c, 1966d, 1969) and O'Donnell (1965).

In contrast to this section, the evidence obtained from studies of treatment methods is highly relevant to the behavioural model of drug dependence.

TREATMENT

Again, the discussion will be largely concerned with opiate addiction.

Most attempts at treatment of opiate addicts have consisted of withdrawing them from their drugs, and attempting,, by psychotherapy, milieu therapy, rehabilitative procedures, etc., to change their 'personality disorders' which, it is assumed, contributed to the development and maintenance of their drug use. Such attempts have, in general, had very little immediate success, e.g. Vaillant (1969) reports that virtually all the 100 patients he studied relapsed after leaving hospital in Lexington, Kentucky.

Recently, a number of techniques employing a more 'behavioural' approach (i.e. an approach that would be as applicable to animal 'addicts' as to humans) have been employed, apparently with considerable success.

The animal experiments suggested that the reinforcement provided by withdrawal-relief and/or drug-induced 'euphoria' was responsible for the maintenance of drug self-administration. It follows that, if one could prevent the occurrence of these events following an injection of opiates, the reinforcement for the injection should be removed and drug-taking should extinguish. In fact, one can achieve this effect pharmacologically by the use of either of the drugs methadone or cyclazocine.

The use of methadone in the treatment of heroin dependence has been developed by Dole and Nyswander (Dole and Nyswander, 1965, 1967; Dole et al., 1966). Methadone, an opiate, like heroin, when given in relatively high doses prevents injections of heroin having any subjective effect, a phenomenon that Dole and Nyswander label 'methadone blockade' (Dole et al., 1966). Further, as methadone is an opiate whose absence does not lead to the appearance of withdrawal symptoms as rapidly as the absence of heroin in physically dependent patients, those receiving it regularly will not experience abstinence distress. This will eliminate this factor as an element of motivation for drug-taking and also eliminate the possibility of reinforcement of heroin injection by withdrawal-relief. As we noted on page 100, animals receiving infusions of methadone at high doses will reduce almost to zero their rate of responding for morphine injections.

The treatment procedure consists of progressively increasing the quantity of methadone the patient receives until he is stabilised on his blockading dose of methadone. He is then released into the community, where he attends an out-patient clinic for his daily dose of methadone, which is drunk, not injected. The treatment is continued as a 'maintenance' therapy, i.e. the patient continues to receive daily methadone on a more or less permanent basis.

The results of this treatment are impressive. Dole and Nyswander (1967) report that of the 304 patients admitted to their programme, 91 per cent had continued in the programme, and approximately 70 per cent of the patients who had been in the programme for six months or longer were employed or in school; the rest had ended heroin usage and related antisocial behaviour.

Another striking finding is that the signs of 'disordered personality', which reputedly characterise heroin addicts, apparently disappear when the addicts are placed on the methadone maintenance programme. Dole states: 'The patients on the methadone program are normal people by every test we have been able to devise. The psychiatrists report them as normal, the medical people see only a normal variety of minor illnesses, the counsellors and social workers discuss normal reality problems with them, the employers have not found any reason to separate them from other normal employees and the experimental psychologists, with detailed psychometric tests, have not been able to distinguish them from normal controls by any test' (Dole, in Wikler, 1968, p. 376 discussion).

In the light of this finding, Dole and Nyswander

(1967) have questioned the psychogenic theory of addiction, i.e. the theory that addiction is caused by an antecedent character defect. They discuss the main arguments they have found used to support the psychogenic theory. The most important of these is the fact that addicts characteristically exhibit sociopathic traits. Dole and Nyswander maintain that such behaviour is a result rather than a cause of addiction. They maintain that the results of those studies which show that addicts exhibited problems of adjustment in areas such as delinquency, educational attainment, and employment record before addiction began (e.g. Vaillant 1966c, 1969) fail to show that there is an identifiable 'addictive personality' different from the 'delinquent' personality. It seems that, on the one hand, Dole and Nyswander accept that addicts may have shown delinquent, sociopathic traits before addiction, but maintain, on the other hand, that the need to obtain drugs once they are addicted leads to such sociopathic traits. To maintain that any psychogenic theory of addiction must posit a characteristic 'addictive personality' seems unwarranted; so many factors may operate to determine whether a person starts using drugs that a psychogenic theory that suggested that addicts might display a similar range of personality disorders as delinquents is tenable, and the presence of such personality traits could be an

important element in the aetiology of addiction. Because all delinquents do not become drug addicts does not necessarily refute the possibility that delinquent-type personality traits could lead to drug use where other circumstances are conducive; Chein et al. (1964) report that only 4 of the 50 non-heroin-using delinquents they interviewed had ever tried taking heroin, and so it is not surprising that these delinquents did not become addicts.

Another possible objection to Dole and Nyswander's hypothesis is that if addicts use heroin as self-medication for what problems of personality they have, methadone, also an opiate, may serve the same function and explain the apparent normality of patients on methadone maintenance.

Dole and Nyswander suggest that the fact that some people become addicts whereas others do not is not the result of personality differences that make heroin more reinforcing for the more disordered group, but the result of some physiological difference between these two groups which accounts for the difference in reaction to heroin. The 'metabolic' and 'psychological' theories are diagrammed in Fig. 4.21.

Despite these objections, Dole and Nyswander's technique certainly appears effective in eliminating drug-taking and the social deterioration directly attributable to it. The fact that such good results were obtained with a technique aimed entirely at

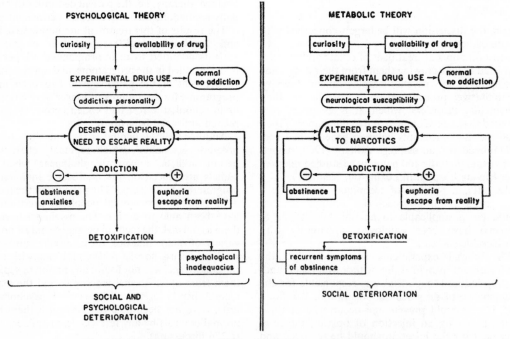

Fig. 4.21. Theories of drug addiction (*from* Dole and Nyswander, 1967)

the 'behavioural' aspects maintaining drug administration, which would be equally applicable to man or animals, does stress the importance of those aspects in maintaining drug use, whatever the problems of personality, etc., that may have led to drug-taking in the first place.

The use of cyclazocine in the treatment of heroin addiction has been described by a number of authors (e.g. Jaffe, 1967; Martin and Gorodetzky, 1967; Freedman *et al.*, 1967). Cyclazocine, unlike methadone, is not an opiate; it is an opiate antagonist, like nalorphine, and apparently acts by occupying the morphine 'receptor sites' (Jaffe, 1967). Heroin, if administered to subjects on antagonistic doses of cyclazocine, leads to little, if any, subjective effect or physical dependence (Martin *et al.*, 1966) nor to any effect on the EEG (Freedman *et al.*, 1967). While cyclazocine can prevent the development of physical dependence as a result of heroin injection, it cannot, unlike methadone, correct a residual state of physical dependence resulting from chronic heroin administration before it was itself administered. The rationale in its therapeutic use is that, by blocking the effects of heroin injections, it removes the reinforcement attendant on them, thereby producing extinction of the injection habit, and also extinction of any drug effects conditioned to external stimuli. It also prevents the initiation of another cycle of physical dependence resulting from injections of heroin.

Preliminary reports suggest that this method of treatment, again aimed purely at the 'behavioural' aspects of drug taking, is promising (Jaffe, 1967; Freedman *et al.*, 1967).

Another method of treatment aimed at the behavioural aspects of heroin addiction, but employing psychological rather than pharmacological procedures, is reported by Thomson and Rathod (1968). The intention in this treatment was to strip the act of heroin injection, and the preceding ritual, of positively reinforcing properties by pairing them with an intensely noxious stimulus. The noxious stimulus used was respiratory paralysis, induced by the injection of scoline. The treatment procedure was arranged so that within one second of the heroin addict injecting himself with heroin, he collapsed and was unable to breathe, as a result of a previous injection of scoline. This procedure occurred daily on five consecutive days. The results of this brief, traumatic, treatment are impressive: of the ten patients completing the treatment, eight had not used heroin since treatment, one relapsed once, was retreated and remained abstinent thereafter, and one patient injected chloral hydrate, but not heroin, after treatment. The average drug-free period for the first nine patients was 33 weeks at the time of the report. Of a group of nine patients not receiving the treatment (but not strictly forming an adequate control group), all relapsed to regular heroin use.

The success of scoline aversion in treating heroin dependence is surprising compared with the poor results obtained from its application to alcoholism (Rachman and Teasdale, 1969).

A number of other studies have reported the use of aversion procedures in treating drug addicts (Liberman, 1968; Raymond, 1964; Lesser, 1967; and Wolpe, 1965) but, as each report concerns only one or two cases, it is difficult to assess the efficacy of these procedures.

Although in human drug users there is a number of factors making the situation more complex than it is in animals, relatively 'simple-minded' treatments directed mainly at the actual behavioural mechanisms of drug use have been very successful. This suggests that such mechanisms, rather than disordered personalities, may account for the maintenance of drug use and the difficulties in terminating drug use.

Conclusion

The studies on human subjects reviewed here are in many ways inadequate in giving a convincing picture of the importance in humans of the mechanisms demonstrated in the animal studies. That attempts at treatment largely aimed at these behavioural mechanisms have been so successful would suggest that experimental investigations of these mechanisms in human subjects, while difficult, could be extremely worthwhile, and would help to reduce the extrapolation gap that must always exist in applying the results of animal studies to man.

REFERENCES

ASTIN, A. (1959) A factor study of the MMPI psychopathic deviate scale. *J. Consult. Psychol.*, **23**, 550–554.

BEACH, H. D. (1957a) Morphine addiction in rats. *Canad. J. Psychol.*, **11**, 104–112.

BEACH, H. D. (1957b) Some effects of morphine on habit function. *Canad. J. Psychol.*, **11**, 193–198.

BECKER, H. S. (1953) Becoming a marihuana user. *Amer. J. Sociol.*, **59**, 235–242.

BOZZETTI, LOUIS JR., GOLDSMITH, S., and UNGERLEIDER, J. T. (1967) The Great Banana Hoax. *Amer. J. Psychiat.*, **124**, 678–679.

CHAPMAN, W. P., ROSE, A. S., and SOLOMON, H. C. (1948)

Measurements of heat stimulus producing motor withdrawal reaction in patients following frontal lobotomy. *The Frontal Lobes. Res. Publ. Ass. Nerv. Ment. Dis.*, **27**, 754.

CHEIN, I., GERARD, D. L., LEE, R. S., and ROSENFELD, E. (1964) *Narcotics, Delinquency and Social Policy: The The Road to H.* London: Tavistock.

CLAGHORN, J. L., ORDY, J. M., and NAGY, A. (1965) Spontaneous opiate addiction in rhesus monkeys. *Science*, **149**, 440–441.

COCHIN, J. and KORNETSKY, C. (1964) Development and loss of tolerance to morphine in the rat after single and multiple injections. *J. Pharmacol. and Exper. Therap.*, **145**, 1–10.

COLLIER, H. O. J. (1968) Supersensitivity and dependence. *Nature*, **220**, 228–231.

DAVIS, J. D., LULENSKI, G. C., and MILLER, N. E. (1968) Comparative studies of barbiturate self-administration. *Int. J. Addict.*, **3**, 207–214.

DAVIS, J. D. and MILLER, N. E. (1963) Fear and pain: their effects on self-injection of amobarbital sodium by rats. *Science*, **141**, 1286–1287.

DAVIS, W. M. and NICHOLS, J. R. (1962) Physical dependence and sustained opiate-directed behaviour in the rat. *Psychopharmacologia* (Berl.), **3**, 139–145.

de ALARCON, R., RATHOD, N. H., and THOMSON, I. G. (1969) Observations on heroin abuse by young people in Crawley New Town. In *Scientific Basis of Drug Dependence* (Ed. H. Steinberg). London: Churchill.

DENEAU, G. A. and SEEVERS, M. M. (1964) Drug Dependence. In *Evaluation of Drug Activities: Pharmacometrics* (Ed. D. R. Lawrence and A. L. Bacharach). London: Academic Press.

DOLE, V. P. and NYSWANDER, M. E. (1965) A medical treatment for diacetyl-morphine (heroin) addiction. *J. Amer. med. Assn.*, **193**, 646–650.

DOLE, V. P. and NYSWANDER, M. E. (1967) Heroin addiction—a metabolic disease. *Arch. Intern. Med.*, **120**, 19–24.

DOLE, V. P., NYSWANDER, M. E., and KREEK, M. J. (1966) Narcotic blockade. *Arch. Intern. Med.*, **118**, 304–309.

FRASER, H. F. and ISBELL, H. (1952) Comparative effects of 20 mg. of morphine sulfate on non-addicts and former morphine addicts. *J. Pharmacol. Exper. Ther.*, **105**, 498–502.

FREEDMAN, A. M., FINK, M., SHAROFF, R., and ZAKS, A. (1967) Cyclazocine and methadone in narcotic addiction. *J. Amer. med. Assn.*, **202**, 191–194.

GOLDBERG, S. and SCHUSTER, C. R. (1967) Conditioned suppression by a stimulus associated with nalorphine in morphine-dependent monkeys. *J. exp. Anal. Behav.*, **10**, 235–242.

HAERTZEN, C. A. (1965) Subjective drug effects: a factorial representation of subjective drug effects on the Addiction Research Center Inventory. *J. Nerv. Ment. Dis.*, **140**, 280–289.

HAERTZEN, C. A. and HILL, H. E. (1959) Effects of morphine and pentobarbital on differential MMPI profiles. *J. Clin. Psychol.*, **15**, 434–437.

HAWKS, D., MITCHESON, M., OGBORNE, A., and EDWARDS, G. (1969) Abuse of methylamphetamine. *Brit. med. J.*, **2**, 715–721.

HILL, H. E., BELLEVILLE, R., and WIKLER, A. (1955) Studies on anxiety associated with anticipation of pain: II Comparative effects of pentobarbital and morphine. *AMA Arch. Neurol. Psychiat.*, **73**, 602–608.

HILL, H. E., BELLEVILLE, R. E., and WIKLER, A. (1957) Motivational determinants in modification of behaviour by morphine and pentobarbital. *AMA Arch. Neurol. Psychiat.*, **77**, 28–35.

HILL, H. E., HAERTZEN, C. A., and DAVIS, H. (1962) An MMPI Factor Analytic Study of Alcoholics, Narcotic Addicts, and Criminals. *Quart. J. Stud. Alcohol.*, **23**, 411–431.

HILL, H. E., HAERTZEN, C. A., and GLASER, R. (1960) Personality characteristics of narcotic addicts as indicated by the MMPI. *J. gen. Psychol.*, **62**, 127–139.

HILL, H. E., HAERTZEN, C. A., WOLBACH, A. B., and MINER, E. J. (1963a) The Addiction Research Center Inventory: Standardisation of scales which evaluate subjective effects of morphine, amphetamine, pentobarbital, alcohol, LSD-25, pyrahexyl and chlorpromazine. *Psychopharmacologia*, **4**, 167–183.

HILL, H. E., HAERTZEN, C. A., WOLBACH, A. B., and MINER, E. J. (1963b) The Addiction Research Center Inventory: Appendix 1. Items comprising empirical scales for seven drugs. 2. Items which do not differentiate placebo from any drug condition. *Psychopharmacologia*, **4**, 184–205.

HILL, H. E., HAERTZEN, C. A. and YAMAHIRO, R. (1968) The addict physician: a Minnesota Multiphasic Personality Inventory study of the interaction of personality characteristics and the availability of drugs. In *The Addictive States* (Ed. A. Wikler) Association for Research in Nervous and Mental Disease, Vol. 46. Baltimore: The Williams and Wilkin Company.

HILL, H. E., KORNETSKY, C., FLANARY, H., and WIKLER, A. (1952a) Effects of anxiety and morphine on discrimination of intensities of painful stimuli. *J. Clin. Invest.*, **31**, 473–480.

HILL, H. E., KORNETSKY, C., FLANARY, H., and WIKLER, A. (1952b) Studies on anxiety associated with anticipation of pain: I Effects of morphine. *AMA Arch. Neurol. Psychiat.*, **67**, 612–619.

HIMMELSBACH, C. K. (1941) Studies on the relation of drug addiction to the autonomic nervous system: Results of Cold Pressor Tests. *J. Pharmacol. Exp. Therap.*, **73**, 91.

HIMMELSBACH, C. K. (1942) Clinical studies on drug addiction. Physical dependence, withdrawal and recovery. *Arch. intern. Med.*, **69**, 766–772.

IRWIN, S. and SEEVERS, M. H. (1956) Altered response to drugs in the post-addict Macaca Mulatta. *J. Pharmacol. and Exper. Therap.*, **116**, 31–32.

JAFFE, J. H. (1967) Cyclazocine in the treatment of narcotic addiction. In *Current Psychiatric Therapies*, Vol. 7. New York: Grune and Stratton.

KHAZAN, N., WEEKS, J. R., and SCHROEDER, L. A. (1967) Electroencephalographic, electromyographic, and behavioural correlates during a cycle of self-maintained morphine addiction in the rat. *J. Pharmacol. and Exper. Therap.*, **155**, 521–531.

KOLB, L. (1925) Types and characteristics of drug addicts. *Mental Hygiene*, **9**, 300–313.

KORNETSKY, C. H. (1954) Effects of anxiety and morphine on the anticipation and perception of painful radiant thermal stimuli. *J. Comp. Physiol. Psychol.*, **47**, 130–132.

KRAMER, J. C., FISCHMANN, V. C., and LITTLEFIELD, D. C. (1967) Amphetamine abuse. *J. Amer. med. Assn.*, **201**, 305–309.

KUMAR, R., STEINBERG, H., and STOLERMAN, I. P. (1969a) How rats can become dependent on morphine in the course of relieving another need. In *Scientific Basis of Drug Dependence* (Ed. H. Steinberg) London: Churchill.

KUMAR, R., STEINBERG, H., and STOLERMAN, I. P. (1969b) Analysis of drug dependence in rats. Paper presented at the XIX International Congress of Psychology, London.

LASAGNA, L., von FELSINGER, J. M., and BEECHER, H. K. (1955) Drug-induced changes in man; observations on healthy subjects, chronically ill patients, and post-addicts. *J. Amer. med. Assn.*, **157**, 1006–1020.

LESSER, E. (1967) Behaviour therapy with a narcotics user: a case report. *Behav. Res. Ther.*, **5**, 251–252.

LIBERMAN, R. Aversive conditioning of drug addicts: a pilot study. *Behav. Res. Ther.*, **6**, 229–32.

LINDESMITH, A. R. (1947) *Opiate addiction*. Evanston: Principia Press of Illinois, Inc.

MALMO, R. B. and SHAGASS, C. (1950) Behavioural and physiologic changes under stress after operations on the frontal lobes. *AMA Arch. Neurol. Psychiat.*, **63**, 113–124.

MARTIN, J. E. and INGLIS, J. (1965) Pain tolerance and narcotic addiction. *Brit. J. Soc. and Clin. Psychol.*, **4**, 224–229.

MARTIN, W. R. and GORODETZKY, C. W. (1967) Cyclazocine, an adjunct in the treatment of narcotic addiction. *Int. J. Addict.*, **2**, 85–93.

MARTIN, W. R., GORODETZKY, C. W., and McCLANE, T. K. (1966) An experimental study in the treatment of narcotic addicts with cyclazocine. *Clin. Pharmacol. Therap.*, **7**, 455–465.

MARTIN, W. R., WIKLER, A., EADES, C. G., and PESCOR, F. T. (1968) Tolerance to and physical dependence on morphine in rats. *Psychopharmacologia*, **4**, 247–260.

NICHOLS, J. R. (1963) A procedure which produces sustained opiate-directed behavior (morphine addiction) in the rat. *Psychological Reports*, **13**, 895–904.

NICHOLS, J. R. (1965) How opiates change behavior. *Scientific American* **21**, 2 80–88.

NICHOLS, J. R. (1969) Opiates as reinforcing agents: some variables which influence drug seeking in animals. Symposium presented at *Amer. Psychol. Assoc. Washington, D.C.* 1967, cited by Schuster and Thompson (1969).

NICHOLS, J. R. (1968) Discussion following Chapters 21, 22, and 23. In *The Addictive States*. (Ed. Wikler, A.) Association for Research in Nervous and Mental Disease, Vol. 46. Baltimore: Williams and Wilkins.

NICHOLS, J. R. and HSIAO, S. (1967) Addiction liability of albino rats: breeding for quantitative differences in morphine drinking. *Science*, **157**, 561–563.

NOWLIS, V. and NOWLIS, H. H. (1956) The description and analysis of mood. *Ann. N.Y. Acad. Sci.*, **65**, 345–355.

O'DONNELL, J. A. (1965) The relapse rate in narcotic addition: A critique of follow-up studies. In *Narcotics* (Ed. Wilner, D. M. and Kasselbaum, G. G.) New York: McGraw-Hill.

OLDS, J. and MILNER, P. (1954) Positive reinforcement produced by electrical stimulation of septal area and other regions of rat brain. *J. comp. Physiol. Psychol.*, **47**, 419–427.

OSWALD, I., EVANS, J. I., and LEWIS, S. A. (1969) Addictive drugs cause suppression of paradoxical sleep and withdrawal rebound. In *Scientific Basis of Drug Dependence* (Ed. Steinberg, H.) London: Churchill.

OSWALD, I. and PRIEST, R. G. (1965) Five weeks to escape the sleeping pill habit. *Brit. med. J.*, **2**, 1093–1095.

PICKENS, R. (1968) Self-administration of stimulants by rats. *Int. J. Addict.*, **3**, 215–221.

PICKENS, R. and HARRIS, W. (1968) Self-administration of d-amphetamine by rats. *Psychopharmacologia* (Berl.), **12**, 158–163.

PICKENS, R., MEISCH, R., and McGUIRE, L. E. (1967) Methamphetamine reinforcement in rats. *Psychon. Sci.*, **8**, 371–372.

PICKENS, R. and THOMPSON, T. (1968) Cocaine-reinforced behaviour in rats: effects of reinforcement magnitude and fixed ratio size. *J. Pharm. exp. Ther.*, **161**, 122–129.

RACHMAN, S. and TEASDALE, J. (1969) *Aversion therapy and behaviour disorders: an analysis*. London: Routledge and Kegan Paul.

RAYMOND, M. (1964) The treatment of addiction by aversion conditioning with apomorphine. *Behav. Res. Ther.*, **1**, 287–291.

REED, C. F. and WITT, P. N. (1965) Factors contributing to unexpected reactions in two human drug-placebo experiments. *Confin. Psychiat.*, **8**, 57–68.

SCHACTER, S. (1966) The interaction of cognitive and physiological determinants of emotional state. In *Anxiety and Behaviour* (Ed. Spielberger, C. D.). New York and London: Academic Press.

SCHUSTER, C. R. and THOMPSON, T. (1969) Self administration of an behavioural dependence on drugs. *Ann. Rev. Pharmacol.*, **9**, 483–502.

SCHUSTER, C. R. and WOODS, J. H. (1968) The conditioned reinforcing effects of stimuli associated with morphine reinforcement. *Int. J. Addict.*, **3**, 223–230.

SEEVERS, M. H. (1967) Laboratory evaluation for drug dependence. In *New Concepts in Pain and Its Clinical Management*. Philadelphia: F. A. Davis Company.

STEINBERG, H., KUMAR, R., KEMP, I., and BARTLEY, H. (1968) Animal behaviour studies and some possible implications for man. *Proc. Symp. the Pharmacological and Epidemiological Aspects of Adolescent Drug Dependence*. Oxford: Pergamon Press, pp. 29–40.

THOMPSON, T. (1968) Drugs as reinforcers: experimental addiction. *Int. J. Addict.*, **3**, 199–206.

THOMPSON, T. and OSTLUND, W. (1965) Susceptibility to readdiction as a function of the addiction and withdrawal environments. *J. comp. Physiol. Pyschol.*, **60**, 388–392.

THOMPSON, T. and SCHUSTER, C. R. (1964) Morphine self-administration, food-reinforced and avoidance behaviors in rhesus monkeys. *Psychopharmacologia*, 5, 87–94.

THOMSON, I. G. and RATHOD, N. H. (1968) Aversion therapy for heroin dependence. *Lancet*, ii, 382–384.

TROUTON, D. and EYSENCK, H. J. (1960) The effects of drugs on behaviour. In *Handbook of abnormal psychology* (Ed. H. J. Eysenck). London: Pitman Medical.

VAILLANT, G. E. (1966a) A twelve-year follow-up of New York narcotic addicts: I. The relation of treatment to outcome. *Amer. J. Psychiat.*, 122, 727–737.

VAILLANT, G. E. (1966b) A twelve-year follow-up of New York narcotic addicts: II. The natural history of a chronic disease. *New Engl. J. Med.*, 275, 1282–1288.

VAILLANT, G. E. (1966c) A twelve-year follow-up of New York narcotic addicts. III. Some social and psychiatric characteristics. *Arch. Gen. Psychiat.*, 15, 599–609.

VAILLANT, G. E. (1966d) A twelve-year follow-up of New York narcotic addicts. IV. Some characteristics and determinants of abstinence. *Amer. J. Psychiat.*, 123, 573–584.

VAILLANT, G. E. (1969) The natural history of urban narcotic drug addiction—some determinants. In *Scientific Basis of Drug Dependence* (Ed. H. Steinberg). London: Churchill.

VON FELSINGER, J. M., LASAGNA, L., and BEECHER, H. K. (1955) Drug-induced mood changes in man: 2. Personality and reaction to drugs. *J. Amer. med. Assn.*, 157, 1113–1119.

WEEKS, J. R. (1962) Experimental morphine addiction: method for automatic intravenous injections in unrestrained rats. *Science*, 138, 143.

WEEKS, J. R. (1964) Experimental narcotic addiction. *Scientific American*, 210 (3), 46–52.

WEEKS, J. R. and COLLINS, R. J. (1964) Factors affecting voluntary morphine intake in self-maintained addicted rats. *Psychopharmacologia*, 6, 267–279.

WEEKS, J. R. and COLLINS, R. J. (1968) Patterns of intravenous self-injection by morphine-addicted rats. In *The Addictive States* (Ed. A. Wikler). Association for Research in Nervous and Mental Disease, Vol. 46. Baltimore: Williams and Wilkins.

WEIL, T. W., ZINBERG, N. E., and NELSEN, J. M. (1968) Clinical and psychological effects of marihuana. *Science*, 162, 1234–1242.

WIKLER, A. (1952) A psychodynamic study of a patient during self-regulated readdiction to morphine. *Psychiat. Quart.*, 26, 270–293.

WIKLER, A. (1953) *Opiate Addiction*. Springfield, Ill.: Charles C. Thomas.

WIKLER, A. (1961) On the nature of addiction and habituation. *Brit. J. Addict.*, 57, 73.

WIKLER, A. (1965) Conditioning factors in opiate addiction and relapse. In *Narcotics* (Ed. Wilner D. M. and Kassebaum, G. G.). New York: McGraw-Hill.

WIKLER, A. (1968) Interaction of physical dependence and classical and operant conditioning in the genesis of relapse. In *The Addictive States* (Ed. A. Wikler) Association for Research in Nervous and Mental Disease, Vol. 46. Baltimore: Williams and Wilkins.

WIKLER, A. and CARTER, R. L. (1953) Effects of single doses of *n*-allylnormorphine on hindlimb reflexes of chronic spinal dogs during cycles of morphine addiction. *J. Pharmacol. Exper. Therap.*, 109, 92–101.

WIKLER, A., FRASER, H. F., and ISBELL, H. (1953) *N*-allylnormorphine: effect of single doses and precipitation of acute "abstinence syndromes" during addiction to morphine, methadone, or heroin in man (postaddicts). *J. Pharmacol. Exper. Therap.*, 109, 8–20.

WIKLER, A. and PESCOR, F. T. (1967) Classical conditioning of a morphine abstinence phenomenon, reinforcement of opioid drinking behaviour and relapse in morphine-addicted rats. *Psychopharmacologia* (Berl.), 10 (3), 255–284.

WILLIS, J. H. (1969) The natural history of drug dependence: some comparative observations on UK and US subjects. In *Scientific Basis of Drug Dependence* (Ed. H. Steinberg). London: Churchill.

WINICK, C. (1962) Maturing out of narcotic addiction. *Bull. Narcotics U.N. Dept. Social Affairs*, 14, (1).

WOLFF, H. G., HARDY, J. D., and GOODELL, H. (1940) Studies on pain: measurement of the effect of morphine, codeine and other opiates on the pain threshold and an analysis of their relation to the pain experience. *J. Clin. Invest.*, 19, 659–680.

WOLPE, J. (1965) Conditioned inhibition of craving in drug addiction. *Behav. Res. Ther.*, 2, 285–287.

WOODS, J. H. and SCHUSTER, C. H. (1968) Reinforcement properties of morphine, cocaine, and SPA as a function of unit dose. *Int. J. Addict.*, 3, 231–238.

World Health Organisation (1969) Expert Committee on Drug Dependence Sixteenth Report. World Health Org. Techn. Rep. Serv. No. 407.

YANAGITA, T., DENEAU, G. A., and SEEVERS, M. H. (1965) Evaluation of pharmacologic agents in the monkey by long-term intravenous self or programmed administration. *Proceedings of the XXIIIrd International Congress of Physiological Sciences.* Excerpat Medica International Congress Series No. 87, 453–457.

ZACUNE, J., STIMSON, G., OGBORNE, A., MITCHESON, M., and KOSVINER, A. (1969) The assessment of heroin usage in a provincial community. In *Scientific Basis of Drug Dependence* (Ed. H. Steinberg). London: Churchill.

5

Abnormal Sexual Behaviour—
Males

P. FELDMAN

A. Types of Sexual Deviation

1. HOMOSEXUALITY

Despite occurring in all cultures in which its presence has been sought (Ford and Beach, 1952) homosexual behaviour represents a form of activity that in most cultures is socially unacceptable to one degree or another. The result is that there is no certainty concerning the precise incidence of the behaviour, and no one has yet attempted a systematic survey over the population in general, even of heterosexual behaviour, based on a statistically acceptable random sample. The nearest attempt to this in the United Kingdom was made by Schofield (1965a). He carried out a detailed survey of the self-reported hetero-sexual behaviour of a satisfactorily random sample of adolescents between the ages of fifteen and nineteen. He has commented (personal communication, Schofield, 1967) on the great difficulty of obtaining information even on sexual behaviour considered normal, and felt that the difficulties of obtaining reliable information on abnormal sexual behaviour (e.g. homosexuality) were so great as to be almost insuperable.

DEFINITION

A widely acceptable definition of homosexuality has been very difficult to attain, partly because of the confusion between description (homosexual *behaviour*) and explanation (*homosexuality*—an explanation abstracted from observed or self-reported overt behaviour). Ideally, any definition should stem from observable, publicly communicable, behaviour.

In the case of sexual behaviour in general, it frequently happens that a desire for an overt response cannot be put into practice, so that instead the individual substitutes the expression of the behaviour in his fantasy life. Hence, definition and, in turn, assessment and classification require not only ascertaining what people do, but also what they would like to do given the opportunity, i.e. an available and consenting sexual partner. Homo-sexual behaviour may be usefully defined as homo-sexual activity or fantasy directed towards orgasm with a partner of the same sex, which is persistently recurrent, and not merely a substitute for a preferred behaviour, that is heterosexual behaviour, made difficult of attainment by the immediate environment. (This is an adaptation of a definition of sexual perversions in general, given by Scott, 1964.)

The homosexual behaviour may be overtly sexual; equally overt but the sexual nature of the behaviour (e.g. eye contact or standing in close proximity to another individual) may need to be inferred—procedure of as yet uncertain validity; or entirely covert, so that self-report has to be relied upon for evidence of the homosexual interest. (However, at a later stage of this section, some recent developments in the assessment of homosexual interest by physio-logical techniques are described.) Because homo-sexual behaviour may be preferred only at one stage in the individual's life, it is more useful to think of homosexual *behaviour*, where behaviour also in-cludes fantasy, rather than *homosexuality*, which implies some internal, underlying, always present influence which *causes* the individual to behave in a homosexual manner. The mere *fact* of homosexual behaviour alone is not enough to bring the individual within the boundaries of the research interests of this chapter. Individuals who engage in homosexual behaviour only when deprived of access to females, as when in prison, but return immediately to heterosexual behaviour on leaving their confinement, are not appropriate as subjects for research which attempts to account for homosexual behaviour when heterosexual outlets are available.

INCIDENCE

Much the largest scale survey of homosexual behaviour was carried out by Kinsey (Kinsey *et al.*, 1947) as part of a detailed survey of the sexual behaviour of several thousand US males. Kinsey recognised the near impossibility of a totally random sample, and in several instances attempted to obtain one hundred per cent samples of particular social groups. The following data from the Kinsey report are relevant to the present purpose. Thirty-seven per cent of the total male population surveyed (4,480 in all) reported at least incidental overt homosexual experience to the point of orgasm between adolescence and old age; 25 per cent reported more than incidental homosexual experience or reactions for at least three years between the ages of 16 and 55; eighteen per cent reported at least as much homosexual as heterosexual behaviour in their histories for at least three years between the ages of 16 and 55; 10 per cent were more or less exclusively homosexual for a period of three years between the ages of 16 and 55; finally, 4 per cent of white males were exclusively homosexual throughout their lives after the onset of adolescence, and a further 4 per cent of white males were exclusively homosexual for at least three years between the ages of 16 and 55. Whatever the argument about the detailed size of the proportions who reported homosexual behaviour for various periods of their lives, several facts emerge clearly from the Kinsey data. A small but noticeable minority of males are exclusively homosexual throughout their lives. A rather larger, but still small minority, of males are exclusively homosexual for a period of their lives. A further group display homosexual behaviour at some time in their lives, varying in amount from a considerable proportion of their total sexual outlet to a very tiny proportion. Finally, the majority of the male population are likely never to have responded either in fantasy or in practice to homosexual stimuli.

The above statements make clear the shifting nature of the sexual behaviour of a substantial proportion of the population. However, with increasing age a gradual polarisation occurs so that the proportion of individuals in the Kinsey survey who were 'bisexual', i.e. displayed both homosexual and heterosexual behaviour to a significant degree, tended to decline with increasing age. Kinsey proposed a scale from 0 to 6, where 0 was totally heterosexual in the three years before interview, and 6 totally homosexual in the three years before interview, the points in between showing a changing weight of homosexual to heterosexual interest and behaviour. This is a useful working scheme, which is widely used.

Classification

There is no general agreement on the classification of homosexuality, partly, at least, because of the confusion between homosexuality and homosexual behaviour. Attempts to classify in terms if a dichotomy between 'latent' and 'overt' homosexuality have foundered on the difficulty of defining, let alone measuring, 'latent' behaviour. A distinction between 'active' and 'passive' types, according to the role adopted in homosexual intercourse, has been attempted, but has found little acceptance (West, 1968). Scott (1964) has proposed a scheme based on the 'quality of the personality'. He classified his patients into five groups, the basis of the classification being rather wide ranging, so that some of his group of 63 are described in terms of effeminacy, others in terms of social integration, and still others in terms of anti-social tendencies.

Feldman and MacCulloch (1971) while utilising personality descriptions to predict the outcome of treatment by aversion therapy used *heterosexual* behaviour as the classificatory criterion, homosexually behaving individuals (termed homosexuals from this point on for convenience) not differing in any systematic way according to the nature or extent of their homosexual behaviour. Feldman and MacCulloch termed as 'primary' homosexuals those homosexuals without heterosexual interest or practice at any stage in their lives, and 'secondary' homosexuals those who have such a history. The reasons for this approach will be elaborated in the section on Causation.

A reasonable degree of similarity in the proportions of these two types is found in the relatively few British surveys that provide data on heterosexual, as well as homosexual, behaviour. In a sample of 117 non-patient male homosexuals interviewed by Westwood (1960) some 64 per cent were of the primary type. Schofield (1965) interviewed six groups of individuals; patient and non-patient homosexuals, heterosexuals in psychiatric treatment, homosexuals and paedophiles in prison, and heterosexual non-patient controls. The proportion of the primary type among the non-patient homosexuals was 60 per cent. A similar two-thirds to one-third ratio was found by Kolaszynska (1969) in a non-patient series of male and female homosexuals. Saghir *et al.* (1969) report the same proportions in a US series of non-patient male and female homosexuals. The criterion of 'heterosexual cognitional rehearsals' was found by these authors to be 'the most reliable index for heterosexual responses', and is the basis for their figures reported above. In all the series of homosexuals given above the pattern is one of decreasing heterosexual interest and arousal after the early twenties; that is, an increasing polarisation towards a solely homosexual outlet. Unfortunately, many series of homosexual individuals have not paid much attention to the heterosexual aspect of behaviour, so that information on this point is often lacking.

Measurement

There are at least four reasons for measuring homosexual behaviour. First, for the purpose of establishing the incidence of homosexual behaviour in a random sample of the general population. Secondly, as a dependent variable in studies concerned to seek explanations for homosexual behaviour. Thirdly, as a diagnostic tool to ascertain whether overt or covert homosexual behaviour or interests are the 'real' problem of a psychiatric patient, who presents with a problem apparently quite different, and, lastly, in order to establish a base line from which to assess the effects of the therapy of homosexual patients.

It is important that the purpose for which the measuring instrument is intended be specified; otherwise it is difficult to evaluate the usefulness of the instrument. For instance, a measurement procedure ultimately designed to ascertain the incidence of homosexual behaviour in a survey population of non-self reporting individuals and which has been standardised on a population of self-reporting homosexuals, has not yet demonstrated its efficacy for its intended purpose. This highlights the fact that, unlike many other behaviours of interest in abnormal psychology, sexual deviations frequently do not result in the deviant individual asking for help, and raises the possibility that those sexually deviant individuals who do ask for help may differ in some major way from those who do not, so that it becomes difficult to generalise from samples of patients to the general population of non-patient homosexuals.

Unfortunately, the majority of research on homosexual behaviour has used samples of patients in the same way as research on anti-social behaviour has used samples of convicted offenders, who may be unrepresentative of the larger population of non-apprehended offenders. When a research sample is both sexually deviant *and* in prison, the strictures concerning doubtful generalisations apply with added force, and particularly so when the individuals comprising the research sample have been in the institution, whether prison or hospital, for more than a very minimal length of time, so that the effects of the deprivation, total or partial, of heterosexual stimuli, may have further heightened or distorted the pre-existing behavioural or test responses of the subject. There is a strong case for research on sexual behaviour, both normal and deviant, to be carried out on samples of non-prison non-patient individuals. The evidence described below shows in large part that homosexuals who seek psychiatric treatment are more similar to non-homosexual psychiatric patients than to non-patient samples, of either sexual orientation, in many aspects of their personalities.

(a) PERSONALITY MEASURES

Since the first study by Terman and Miles (1936) several attempts have been made to develop personality tests for 'masculine' and 'feminine' personality traits. These have been reviewed by Maccoby (1967). Much of the variance in these measures is accounted for by factors other than either male or female sexuality or sexual object preference. For instance, highly educated males tend to obtain 'feminine' scores because the less-educated majority of males score rather low on cultural interests, whereas even the less well-educated females score more highly.

A male/female vocabulary test devised by Slater (1948) was based on the assumption that certain words would be more familiar to men than to women, and that homosexuals would be more familiar with the female words than would non-homosexual males. This seems related to the man in the street's notion of the typical homosexual as effeminate in voice, gait, and interests. Slater and Slater (1947) reported that the test distinguished between homosexuals and normals but with a considerable degree of overlap. Clarke (1965) showed that scores on the Slater test were highly related to age, IQ, and social class. When these factors were controlled the non-homosexual group correctly defined more masculine words than did a homosexual group, but at a rather low level of significance ($p = 0.05$). There was no difference in the number of female words correctly defined. The degree of overlap between the groups, even on the masculine set of words, was so great as to render the test useless for practical purposes.

The MMPI has been used as an item pool to derive scales that might discriminate between homosexuals and non-homosexuals. One of the first such attempts was made by Marsh et al. (1955). They described a scale of 100 items which picked up among undergraduate students 88 per cent of two samples of 'sexual psychopaths' with only 11 per cent false positives. They suggested, however, that it might be psychiatric disorder that was being discriminated.

A validation of the Marsh et al. scale was carried out by Peek and Storms (1956) who compared a group of 13 mixed sex offenders, 30 non-sex offenders (male psychiatric patients), and 30 male nurses. The scale failed to discriminate between the patients and the sex offenders and the correlations of the scale with other MMPI scales showed that it measured gross maladjustment.

A further attempt was made by Panton (1960) who restricted his abnormal sample to self-reporting homosexuals. Panton assembled two sets of MMPI items, one being termed the masculinity-femininity (MF) scale and the other the homosexuality scale. He claimed that the combination of the scales successfully picked out three out of four homosexuals. His study was cross validated by Friberg (1967), who tested the two scales on four groups. The first of these were in-patients whose primary complaint was homosexuality, the second a mixed group of sexual deviants, the third a mixed group of abnormals (55 per cent neurotics, 33 per cent psychotics), and the fourth the normative sample from the original standardisation group for the MMPI. On the masculinity-femininity scale the homosexuals were significantly different at the 0·01 level both from the mixed abnormals and the normal controls. The scores of the sexual deviants and the abnormals were the same, and both were different from the normals at the 0·01 level. On the homosexual scale the homosexual group was different from all other groups (0·01), but the general abnormals had a significantly lower homosexual score than the normals (0·01). The two scales did not correlate significantly. The best cutting score for the MF correctly classified 59 per cent of the homosexuals, but 19 per cent of the sexual deviants, 25 per cent of the general abnormals, and 2 per cent of the normals were misclassified. The best homosexual cutting score gave false positive rates for the general abnormals and normals of 10 per cent and 18 per cent respectively, and correctly classified only 44 per cent of the homosexuals. There was a small improvement if the two scales were combined, but

Friberg's final conclusion was, 'a positive assertion made on the basis of a positive test is still more likely to be incorrect than correct' (page 90).

Dean and Richardson (1964) compared 40 homosexuals, only 2 of whom were in psychotherapy and 9 in legal difficulties, with 40 control undergraduates. The two groups differed at the 0·01 level on the psychopathic deviate and MF scales, and beyond 0·05 on the schizophrenia and manic-depressive scales, with the homosexuals higher than the controls in each case. However, the overall profile of the homosexual group showed T scores of below 70, except for the masculinity/femininity scale; that is, they were within the normal range for the MMPI scales. They concluded that the homosexual group was not seriously neurotic or psychotic.

Zucker and Manosevitz (1966), re-interpreting Dean and Richardson's study, criticised it for lack of attention to stylistic differences between homosexuals and normals. They carried out a profile analysis on the Dean and Richardson data which indicated that three major profile codes occurred. Zucker and Manosevitz suggested that it is inappropriate to use a unit dimensional adjustment-maladjustment model for conceptualising the homosexual population.

That not only discrimination of the patterns of scores may be needed, but also discrimination of the type of homosexual is indicated by a study by Oliver and Mosher (1968) who compared 'insertors' and 'insertees' (defined in 75 per cent of the sample—reformatory inmates—by having been seen in a sexual act with another inmate). They reported 'considerably more confusion re personal and sexual identity' in the insertees than in a heterosexual control group drawn from the same reformatory. This was based on the findings for the masculinity-femininity scale of the MMPI, on which there was no difference between the control group and the insertors. However, the insertees were significantly different from the heterosexual controls at beyond the 0·01 level. The insertors were distinguished from the insertees at only the 0·10 level.

No studies have been reported seeking masculinity-femininity differences between groups of primary and secondary homosexuals as defined by Feldman and MacCulloch (1971).

Only two studies have compared homosexuals with controls on the 16PF test. The first was a report by Cattell and Morony (1962) who compared 100 male prisoners convicted of one or more homosexual acts with 33 uncharged male homosexuals. Cattell and Morony found the personality profile of the two samples of homosexuals more similar to each other than to normals, and both resembled that profile characteristic of anxiety neurotics. In discussing the differences between this finding—that is of similarity in personality scores for convicted and unconvicted homosexuals—and their own, Dean and Richardson (1964) comment that it is possible that the non-convicted homosexuals either had been in jail in the past, or may not have been functioning well anyway, or that the 16PF measures different traits from the MMPI, or, finally, that there is less social pressure against homosexuality in the United States than in Australia. This last point is made in connection with their own finding of relatively little increased incidence of psychiatric symptoms in non-patient homosexuals as compared to heterosexuals.

Orford (1971) administered the 16PF to a sample of thirty British homosexual patients prior to treatment by aversion therapy. The results showed that the British homosexuals differed significantly from both the 100 Scottish normals with whose scores they were compared and the sample of convicted Australian homosexuals reported by Cattell and Morony. The highest degree of association was found with the latter group, apparently supporting the conclusion of Cattell and Morony that it is possible to talk of homosexual profiles. However, there is a substantially lower correlation between the British homosexual patient profile and that of the Australian uncharged homosexuals.

Orford comments that it is those homosexuals who are not sufficiently well adjusted either to keep clear of the law or to avoid seeking psychiatric help who may have certain features of personality in common, features that may not necessarily be shared by better adjusted homosexuals. As compared with the Scottish normals, the British homosexuals are seen as more emotional, apprehensive, tense, imaginative, tender-minded, shy (translating the 16PF factor descriptions into everyday language). Three of the scales load on the 16PF second order factor of anxiety, and these results are therefore very much in line with the further finding of Orford that neuroticism (as measured by the EPI) was significantly higher than the standardisation group (Eysenck and Eysenck, 1964) for this sample ($P > 0.001$). They were also significantly less extraverted ($P > 0.01$)

Kenyon (1968) has also found EPI N scores to be significantly higher than normals in a group of 123 non-patient female homosexuals. It is of interest that Kolaszynska's (1969) findings indicate that three-quarters of the self-reported psychiatric symptoms in her male and female non-patient homosexual groups were secondary to their homosexual behaviour. It seems, therefore, that the psychoanalytic notion of homosexuality as inevitably psychopathological (arising out of an incompletely worked through oedipal situation) is unlikely to be correct. When the homosexual is functioning in a tolerant environment—such as that of a college campus—(see the findings of Dean and Richardson, 1964), the probability of his sexual deviance leading to psychiatric symptoms is rather small. When the culture is unsympathetic, there will be an increased likelihood of psychiatric symptomatology, presumably more so in those who are predisposed to respond to stress in this way.

It is clear from all the foregoing that both patient and convicted groups of homosexuals are at least partially unrepresentative of the population of homosexuals in general, and particularly so on measures of personality.

The Rorschach test has been used widely in the assessment of homosexuality, as it has for many other problems. Davids et al. (1956) compared 20 overt homosexual students who were concerned about their homosexuality, 20 neurotic students, and 20 non-neurotic students. The Rorschach data were scored blind and the signs suggested by Wheeler (1949) were used. The homosexual group produced significantly more Wheeler signs than did neurotic and normal groups and this remained when the total response frequency was controlled. However, only four of the twenty signs discriminated significantly between homosexual and non-homosexual groups and the authors doubted the usefulness of the signs for individual work. They also compared the groups for a number of signs on the Thematic Apperception Test, and several of these also discriminated significantly. However, they provided no data on the proportion of false positives and false negatives.

Gelfried (1956) has carried out a very detailed review on the use of the Rorschach for diagnosing homosexuality, particularly of the Wheeler signs. He concluded that only six held up reasonably well on empirical test—although there was as yet no separate study on the six 'good' signs. Gelfried concluded, 'the only real justification for a Rorschach measure of homosexuality is in those instances where the individual is unable or unwilling to reveal this information to the clinician directly'. He goes on, 'the value of the Rorschach for the homosexual is its ability to detect those individuals for whom homosexual thought or behaviour presents a problem'. However, Goldfried also concludes that no data are available relative to these questions!

It is clear that at the present time personality measures, whether questionnaire or projective, do not provide a means of detecting the presence of homosexual interests in otherwise undiagnosed individuals.

(b) ATTITUDINAL MEASURES

A number of reports have appeared of techniques in which the number of times a subject operates a shutter or other form of viewer to reveal pictures of males and females is used to index the relative levels of homo- and heterosexual interest.

A single case report by Brown (1964) was followed by a thorough critique of such methods by Koenig (1965). Zamansky (1956) described a study on 20 overt practising homosexuals, none of whom had had psychotherapy, compared to 20 undergraduate controls. It was found that the homosexuals looked significantly more at male pictures (0·001) than did the controls, in each case as compared with the proportion of time they looked at female pictures. He also found that there was a tendency, significant at the 0·05 level, for the homosexuals to show a greater avoidance of female than control pictures, as compared with the heterosexuals—a particularly severe test. Zamansky concluded 'anxiety aroused by the idea of heterosexual relations, as well as being a compensation for aggressive urges, plays a large role in the development of homosexuality.' Martin, (1964) has shown the importance of the setting of the experiment, and has reported that a greater degree of time is spent looking at nude photographs when the atmosphere is 'permissive' rather than 'inhibitory'.

A less direct approach was used by Keuthe and Weingartner (1964) who studied 100 inmates, 50 identified as homosexual by the administrative and psychological staff of the penitentiary. The task of the subjects was to place felt male and female figures on a felt field. It was found that of 20 subjects who failed to pair male and female figures together at least once in four opportunities, sixteen were homosexuals and four were heterosexuals; that is, the measure identified 32 per cent of the homosexuals, and misidentified 8 per cent of the expected heterosexuals. A further section of the study in which the subjects had to replace two male figures after they had been handed them by the experimenter showed that 36 of the homosexuals and 14 of the heterosexuals ($P < 0.001$) replaced them closer together than when the two figures were of a male and a female. However, what seems a promising technique is vitiated by the admission of the authors that 'none of the homosexual group was committed for homosexuality but had made a homosexual adjustment in prison'. That is, an unknown proportion may have been what Scott (1964) has called 'facultative' homosexuals—adopting homosexuality only when deprived of heterosexual outlets.

Feldman and co-workers (1966) have described a questionnaire technique of assessing the relative levels of homo- and heteroerotic orientation as part of a research project on the treatment of homosexuality by anticipatory avoidance learning. The design of this technique borrowed both from the semantic differential (Osgood et al., 1957) and personal questionnaire (Shapiro, 1961) techniques. The technique of Feldman et al. is termed the Sexual Orientation Method (SOM). The authors presented data on internal consistency, unidimensionality, reliability, and validity (the test discriminated without overlap a group of homosexuals prior to treatment, from two groups of heterosexual controls). Following treatment, successful patients were discriminated without overlap from unsuccessful patients but overlapped with the normal controls. The test was designed specifically for assessing the degree of change following treatment, and not as a method of detecting homosexuality in those not otherwise presenting with it. It has not yet been applied to the latter problem.

(c) PHYSICAL MEASURES

A method that seemed at first to be promising, namely, an increase in eye pupil response to sexually arousing homosexual and heterosexual pictures (Hess et al., 1965) has been replicated by Scott et al. (1967) who found that pupillary response was an index of general arousal rather than of sexual arousal in particular. Moreover, Chapman et al. (1969) reported that male undergraduates showed more pupil dilation to female than male slides when tested by an experimenter who was 'casual and outgoing' than when tested by one who was 'aloof and businesslike'.

A penile plethysmograph for recording erectile responses to sexual stimuli was first described by Freund (1963), and in a more developed form by Bancroft et al. (1966) who reported that at a penile volume level above the threshold for detection of the instrument subjects were usually aware of no more than an incipient reaction. That is, they claim that the plethysmographic response is a more subtle index of sexual arousal even than the subject's self awareness. A further report by Freund (1965) extended his earlier work on homosexuality to heterosexual paedophilia and he concluded that the technique might serve, but was as yet a crude instrument.

The only clinical application of this method to date has been in work by Bancroft (1969) and by McConaghy (1969) the former of whom used the penile volume change to homosexual slides as the response to be punished by shock. Both Bancroft and McConaghy used penile volume change as a dependent measure of the effect of treatment. It is desirable, as Koenig (1965) has pointed out, that the dependent measure of the effect of treatment should be different from the response to be punished, or acquired, in treatment. A further disadvantage of the plethysmographic method is that erection may not occur as a direct involuntary response to visual stimulation but that it may be possible to fake responses, in either direction, by using the appropriate imagery. Laws and Rubin (1969) showed that subjects, when instructed to do so, were able to inhibit previously maximal erection by 50 per cent in the presence of erotically stimulating motion pictures. When instructed to develop an erection in the absence of a film, subjects were able to reach a peak of 30 per cent of their maximum.

The need to overcome subject faking, or dissimulation, is central to all techniques that attempt to assess either the presence of homosexual behaviour or interest in otherwise undiagnosed or non-self reporting individuals, or changes in homosexual interest following treatment. At the present time there seems to be no technique available that is definitely proof against such problems. Feldman *et al.* (1966) described a method of assessing the internal consistency of the SOM (the less consistent the response the more the patient was considered likely to be faking). Further work on this very simple measure is now under way.

It would be useful if measures that were totally insusceptible to voluntary control could be devised. A. T. Carr has suggested (personal communication, 1970) that the rate of habituation of the orientation reaction to a sexual stimulus would be both a precise measure of sexual interest, and totally outside voluntary control. One such possibility lies in the measurement of hormonal levels of homosexual and heterosexual subjects. West (1968) has surveyed the data on adult hormonal differences between homosexuals and controls and has concluded that they do not exist, at least in the present state of knowledge of assay techniques. As will be seen later in this chapter there is some reason to believe that hormonal influences on the developing foetus may be responsible, at least in part, for a predisposition to adult homosexual behaviour.

The Causation of Homosexuality

The major theories of homosexuality can be considered in terms of the age at which the effect on later behaviour is deemed to occur, beginning with the view that homosexuality is genetically determined, and proceeding through perinatal influences, to early infantile experiences (such as the 'oedipal' situation), specific learning events in pre- and early adolescence, and finally, to heterosexual deprivation, or fears, during adolescence.

(a) TWIN STUDIES

Much the largest sample of twin studies with respect to homosexual behaviour was reported by Kalmann (1952a,b), who described the results of a study of 85 twins. Information on sexual behaviour was available for 37 of the 40 monozygotic homosexual pairs and for 26 of the 45 dizygotic pairs. Whereas all the monozygotic pairs were concordant for homosexuality, this was true for less than half the dizygotic group. The effect of these two papers was to support the view that homosexuality was very largely genetically determined. However, Kalmann's own formulation was rather more cautious: 'on the whole, adaptational equilibrium between the potentialities of organic sex differentiation and consequent patterns of psychosexual behaviour, seems to be so labile that the attainment of maturational balance may be disarranged at different developmental stages by a variety of disturbing mechanisms'. Kalmann seems to be hinting strongly at the possibility of genetic-environmental interaction in the causation of homosexual behaviour. A year later, Kalmann (1953) considered the 100 per cent concordance obtained between monozygotic twins in his earlier study to be 'a statistical artifact'. In the same book he reported, in the form of a footnote (page 116), a monozygotic pair, one of whom was both schizophrenic and homosexual, the other of whom was neither.

Several authors (Rainer *et al.*, 1960; Klintworth, 1962; Parker, 1964) have reported pairs of monozygotic twins discordant for homosexuality. The report by Rainer *et al.* was concerned with two pairs of monozygotic twins, one female and one male, and in both cases the authors claim an early discrepancy in handling by the mother of each of the two pairs of twins. They emphasise the extent to which twins that cannot be easily distinguished induce maternal anxiety, and consequently a need, felt by the mother, to differentiate the twins, a need she expresses by the accentuation, deliberately or otherwise, of relatively small initial differences. A similar emphasis on differences in the way the twins were handled was made by Parker in his report on three discordant homosexual pairs, two male and one female.

Heston and Shields (1968) report two sets of data, the first being concerned with a family with a sibship of fourteen, which contained three pairs of male monozygotic twins. The second set of data consisted of all the twin pairs in the Maudsley Twin Register, which has been kept since 1948, in which at least one member of the pair had a primary or a secondary (to psychiatric disorder) diagnosis of homosexuality. In the first set of data two of the three monozygotic twin pairs were concordant for homosexuality, and one for heterosexuality. All six individuals grew up in 'a severely disruptive environment'. Heston and Shields considered that both genetic and environmental factors were required to explain the aetiology of sexual behaviour in this family. Of the twelve male twins with a primary or secondary diagnosis of homosexuality five were monozygotic, and of these, three were concordant and two discordant (one of the latter two formed part of the series reported by Parker). Of the seven dizygotic twins only one was concordant and six were not. In seeking alternative explanations for the apparently strong association between genetic determinants and homosexuality they conclude that there is no evidence to support an increased likelihood of homosexuality due to monozygocity *per se*, nor of an increased likelihood of all kinds of psychiatric disturbance in twins.

Emery *et al.* (1970) have described the case of a monozygotic twin pair discordant for homosexuality, in which the homosexual twin was of the primary type described by Feldman and McCulloch (1971). Despite being highly motivated for treatment the homosexual twin failed to respond to 24 sessions of anticipatory avoidance learning, followed by 24 sessions of classical conditioning. This appears to be the only report in which there is sufficiently full data to assign the homosexual twin in a discordant pair confidently to either the primary or the secondary type. It might be that the ability to make this assignation would be a powerful research weapon in considering the question of the aetiology of homosexuality.

At the present stage it can be said that where twins are monozygotic but discordant and the homosexual twin is of either homosexual type it suggests that a genetic explanation cannot be the only one operating, and environmental influences are strongly suggested. In view of a possible association between homosexual behaviour and inappropriate sex-typed behaviour it is of interest that the homosexual twin patient of MacCulloch *et al.* was effeminate, unaggressive and dependent as a child, in contrast to his heterosexual co-twin. The effects of the postnatal psychological environment would have had to have been particularly powerful to produce such major and generalised differences in behaviour between the members of the twin pair, and the possibility is therefore raised that the source of the environmental influence determining primary homosexuality, as exemplified in the MacCulloch *et al.* patient, is likely to be perinatal, and specifically intrauterine, as described below.

(b) FOETAL PRE-NATAL CIRCULATING STEROIDS

While there is no evidence of hormonal differences between homosexual adults and other adults (Appel, 1937; Glass *et al.* 1940; Kupperman, 1967) there is a considerable animal literature on the effects on adult behaviour of variations in the level and type of gonadal hormones present in the new born mammal.

Early work was concerned with the transplantation of gonads (Young *et al.*, 1965). More recent work has involved prenatal or postnatal injection of hormones. Harris and Levine (1965) and Whalen (1964) showed that injection of oestrogen to intact newborn rats disturbed male reproductive function. Harris and Levine (1965) also showed that the postnatal administration of androgen during critical periods markedly and irreversibly affected subsequent reproductive behavioural functions. Injections when the rat was more than a week old were ineffective. Male rats given oestrogen in infancy showed excessive aberrant mounting, rarely achieved intromission, and failed to ejaculate. Sexual behaviour in the male rat was also markedly affected by early infantile castration. Such rats exhibited complete female sexual behaviour if they were given injections of oestrogen and progesterone. By contrast, males castrated in adulthood showed no such behaviour after these procedures.

It has been suggested (Young *et al.*, 1965) that gonadal hormones exert a dual influence on the central nervous system, organisational during development, and excitatory or activational in the adult. Their studies show that the presence of either androgen or oestrogen in the newborn rat causes the sexually differentiating brain to be organised so that the acyclic common male pattern of hormone activity occurs in the adult. In the absence of gonadal hormones, the basic female hormone release pattern becomes established, and these patterns of hormone release form part of a 'hormonostat' whereby the concentration of sex steroids circulating acts as a 'feedback' to influence the central nervous system which, in turn, controls the rate of steroid production, or release, or both.

These effects have been shown to be true for higher mammals also. Young and co-workers (1965) produced female pseudohermaphroditic monkeys by injecting testosterone into the mother during pregnancy. They showed that the behaviour of the pseudohermaphrodite offspring became similar in type to that of a normal male monkey and different from that of female controls. Further evidence for a specifically susceptible area in the developing brain in relation to circulating sex hormones is provided by the work of Pfaff (1964) and Altmann and Das (1964). In addition, work by Fisher (1956) showed that, using an implantation technique, it was possible to produce an exaggerated male mating response in rats by introducing testosterone into the lateral preoptic areas in the brain.

Detailed evidence for the control of sexual

behaviour by specific *loci* in the brain is provided by McLean and Ploog (1962) who have carried out extensive studies on the cerebral representation of penile erection in the squirrel monkey. These authors mapped out areas in the limbic system and its projection pathways, which, when stimulated, produced penile erection. It seems clear that adult sexual behaviour and sex associated behaviour in mammals depends on a neurophysiological substrate, and it may be that some neuronal circuits are composed of cells that are specifically sensitive to sex hormones. These *loci* may well turn out to be the centres that govern sexual behaviour, possibly under the influence of feedback hormones or stimulation from higher centres.

Neumann and Elgar (1966) summarised evidence to support their view that the target organ in relation to circulating sex steroids is not the pituitary but the hypothalamus. They have shown that antiadrenogenically active steroid effectively inhibits the differentiation of the pituitary diencephalic system only during the critical phase of receptivity in the rat. Furthermore, they have also shown that feminised, but genotypically male rats, will show female phenotypic sexual behaviour. It can be concluded that in the human foetal brain there are possible male and female areas that are critically susceptible to circulating levels of male and female hormones. It may well be that the level of circulating sex steroids in the unborn foetus is influenced by placental activity and it is even possible that the circulations of two monozygotic twins are affected differentially in this respect, thus enabling postnatal discordance for sexual orientation.

If the human foetal brain is preconditioned by circulating sex steroids, then one possible mechanism for the development of the primary type of homosexuality is thus available. In setting out this argument Feldman and MacCulloch (1971) hypothesise that primary homosexuals differ from secondary homosexuals in that their developing brains have been preconditioned, prior to birth, by an imbalance of sex steroids, derived either from maternal or placental sources. It is unlikely that the sex steroids affecting the brain of the developing foetus are either in perfect balance, leading to a sexually normal person, or in total imbalance, inevitably leading to primary homosexuality. A continuous variation in the degree of balance of prenatal sex steroids seems more likely, so that the probability of the infant developing, postnatally, a total pattern of behaviours inappropriate to the morphological sex increases the greater the degree of steroid imbalance. By the total behaviour pattern is meant a constellation (e.g. in the morphologically male child) of low aggression, interpersonal deference, preference for female children as friends and for 'feminine' toys;

the converse pattern being regarded as inappropriate for morphologically female children.

It is considered that such behaviour patterns are not all-or-none, but lie on a continuum, from what may be termed for convenience, 'highly masculine', to 'highly feminine'. The extent to which prenatal hormonal influences are reflected in the behaviour pattern of the developing infant will be a function of the type of reinforcement, positive or negative, and the intensity and frequency of such reinforcement, provided by the parents for the display of sex—appropriate or inappropriate behaviours. A male child, behaving in the manner of the monozygotic twin patient described by Emery *et al.* (1970), who is consistently and positively reinforced for such behaviours would be more likely to develop and strengthen them, than one who is punished. Feldman and MacCulloch (1971) consider that a child displaying a behaviour pattern inappropriate to his morphological sex would have an increased probability of developing another form of inappropriate behaviour, namely emotional and sexual attachments to a person of the same sex. Once such homosexual behaviour has occurred, and has been enjoyed, there is a raised probability that it will continue.

Two specific predictions from the above argument are as follows. First, interviews of adult primary homosexuals will reveal childhood behaviour patterns inappropriate to the morphological sex, as compared both to adult secondary homosexuals and adult heterosexuals. Secondly, there will be a positive correlation between the prenatal circulating maternal sex steroids to which the developing foetus is exposed and postnatal behaviour patterns. (It seems likely that modern hormone assay techniques will make it possible to measure circulating maternal androgen and oestrogen during all stages of pregnancy—personal communication, Rudd, 1969.)

The next stage would be to study a cohort of children produced by such pregnancies and investigate the rate and direction of acquisition of sex-typed behaviour patterns postnatally. However, it is still not possible to measure the levels of circulating foetal steroids, and the success of such a study would therefore depend on the assumption that levels of sex steroids in the foetal circulation are a relatively precise reflection of circulating maternal sex steroids; or, if the placenta is the relevant site of sex steroid source, that its output is also reflected in the maternal circulation. It is also possible that there may be a relative insensitivity, or lack of responsiveness, of neural target organs. In order to test the above theory completely careful observations would also have to be taken of the reinforcing behaviour of the parents for the appropriate or inappropriate sex behaviours of the children of these pregnancies.

A biological theory of homosexuality might also seem to implicate differences in body build between homosexuals and controls. In practice, the conventional notion of the homosexual as having a mincing gait, a lisping voice, and an epicene build is rarely found to operate (West, 1968).

Coppen (1959) studied the body build of three groups of individuals. Thirty-one were homosexual patients at the Maudsley Hospital (the majority referrals by the Courts), 53 were non-patient heterosexual controls, and 22 neurotic patients at the Maudsley. When matched for social class the androgny scores [1 × the bone diameter (mm) −0·4 × fat diameter (mm) at the maximum diameter of the calf] of the homosexual group was significantly lower than those of the heterosexual controls (0·01 level of significance). However, there was much overlap between the two groups and a poor degree of overall discrimination. Moreover, the heterosexual neurotics also differed significantly from the non-patient controls and were not different from the homosexual group. Hence, body build in homosexual psychiatric patients is not different from that of non-homosexual psychiatric patients, although, as Coppen did not differentiate his homosexual group into primary and secondary types, a final test of the body-build hypothesis is still to be made.

(c) PARENTAL CHILD-REARING PRACTICES

West (1968) has reviewed the theoretical and research evidence for the view that the nature of the relationships between parents and their children plays a major part in the determination of homosexual behaviour in later years. As he points out, most of the published evidence is unsatisfactory, as control groups are lacking, so that the psychoanalytic theory relating, for instance, an 'intense' or an 'over possessive' mother to the development of homosexuality cannot properly be evaluated.

Even the studies that have employed a control group have usually been carried out retrospectively, the source of evidence being the adult homosexual's recollection of the nature of his childhood relationship with his parents and his perceptions of these. Bene (1965) compared 83 non-patient homosexuals with the same number of married (and therefore presumed heterosexual) males of roughly equivalent age and social class. Both groups were administered the Family Relations Test (Bene and Anthony, 1962) in order to ascertain the nature of the child-parent relationships. Her results showed that homosexual men recalled unsatisfactory relationships with their fathers more frequently than with their mothers.

O'Connor (1964) compared 50 non-homosexual neurotic patients serving in the Royal Air Force with 50 homosexual referrals. The homosexuals had a significantly higher frequency of close attachment to the mother, and poor relations with the father, as well as a history of long absence from father during adolescence. The extent of interviewer bias in determining the differences between the groups is unknown, as the same person interviewed both groups, and the answers may therefore have been affected by a theoretical preconception on the part of O'Connor.

A similar stricture applies to a study by West (1959) which compared descriptions contained in Maudsley case notes of 50 overt male homosexual patients and 50 non-homosexual neurotic controls. The descriptions were independently rated for the nature of the relationship with the parents, and it was found that a combination of a very intense maternal relationship and an unsatisfactory paternal relationship occurred more commonly among homosexuals than among the controls. Although, once the descriptions had found their way into the case histories, they were independently rated, no such constraint was present on the original interviewer, whose questions, and impressions of the answers to them, may have been influenced to an unknown degree by the theory that West later tested. In addition, the answers to such retrospective questions given by adult homosexuals may be influenced, again to an unknown degree, by their own acceptance of the theory in question.

One of the very rare studies of a prospective kind was carried out by McCord et al. (1962). They abstracted information from the participants in the well-known Cambridge Somerville Project. Observation began at the age of eleven (an earlier age would have been preferable) and continued for five years. Three types of sexually disturbed adolescents were identified: the 'anxious-inhibited' type who feared any form of sexual contact; the 'perverted' type who indulged in a variety of deviant activities in addition to ordinary heterosexual outlets; and the 'feminine-attitude' type who were clearly unhappy in the male role, preferring feminine company and pursuits and being liable to overt homosexual activity. All three types seemed to come from parental homes characterised by sexual anxiety and prudishness, maternal authoritarianism, quarrels between parents, and maternal punitiveness. In addition, it was noted that the feminine type of deviant had been exposed to a particularly unsatisfactory father. Finally, half the fathers were absent from home most of the time and most of them 'openly despised or neglected' their sons.

A study of the absence of the father from home

was carried out by Tiller (1968) in which he compared the families of Danish sailors with a control group of families of a similar social level. The mothers whose husbands were persistently absent appeared to over-protect their children and the boys displayed a distinct excess of feminine traits. However, some boys appeared to fight against their own feminine characteristics by compensatory assertiveness of masculine status and attitude in particular situations. The degree to which this study was carried out blind is unclear, as is the extent to which the descriptions of behaviour were objective.

Barclay and Cusmano (1967) investigated the effects of father absence on cross-sex identity and field-dependency in male adolescence. Masculinity scores on the MF scale of the MMPI (*see* earlier) did not distinguish the two groups (father present and father absent). Nor were there differences in indices of cross-sex identity 'at least at an overt level'.

It is possible that a particular kind of mother and/ or a particular kind of father, or an absent father, interacting with a particular kind of child, may increase an existing predisposition to develop homo-sexual behaviour, but the research techniques concerned with child-rearing practices require considerable improvement before the extent of the influence of parental environment on sexual develop-ment can properly be evaluated.

(d) SOCIAL ISOLATION

There is evidence to link the isolation of animals from access to the opposite sex with disturbed hetero-sexual behaviour and occasional homosexual be-haviour. Although in natural surroundings mam-malian homosexual behaviour takes place when animals are strongly sexually aroused, it usually does so only in addition to normal heterosexual behaviour. A preference for males in adult male rats can be induced by prolonged segregation from females (Jenkins, 1928). A proportion of the sample who were isolated continued for an indefinite period to prefer homosexual behaviour, even when allowed access to females. Similarly, Rasmussen (1955) showed that male rats given an electric shock when they attempted to copulate with females were discouraged from further attempts at heterosexual behaviour.

The concept of imprinting at a critical period of development (Sluckin, 1965) has been used to account for such effects. The degree of reversibility of imprinted responses appears to be partly a function of the level of maturation of the organism. Harlow (1965) showed that baby monkeys, separated from their mothers during the first six months of life, were relatively incapable either of sexual behaviour with

the opposite sex or of appropriate maternal behaviour to their own first born offspring. However, there seemed to be some degree of recovery, because mating behaviour improved at a later age and their response to the second born offspring was also nor-mal. Moreover, the deleterious effects of early deprivation of mothering appeared to be at least partially overcome by being allowed access early in life to peers of the same sex.

The psychoanalytic emphasis on the importance of the emotional experiences of infancy for later social development finds support in such studies, as it does in one by Miller *et al.* (1967) who found striking differences in co-operative avoidance conditioning between normally reared monkeys and those reared in isolation, the latter being particularly poor at responding to facial signals of distress emitted by another monkey.

Human infants and adolescents are rarely isolated completely; hence it is difficult to separate out the effects of isolation *per se* from the opportunities to imitate, or be modelled by, other youngsters who are behaving in a homosexual manner, which they, in turn, have acquired from a particular subculture. There is ample evidence for the importance of model-ling, and vicarious (i.e. self-provided) reinforcement in the acquisition of behaviour in social situations (Bandura and Walters, 1963). The extent to which the model is imitated depends on many factors, such as observed similarity between model and imitator, the receipt of reinforcement for imitation, and the occurrence of vicarious reinforcement and the appropriateness of such reinforcement to the needs of the imitator. (In the field of juvenile delinquency, the acquisition of antisocial attitudes through physical contiguity with the members of the criminal subculture forms the basis of the influential Associ-ation theory of crime [Sutherland, 1955].) Member-ship of a single sex subculture such as a boarding school, the norm in which was homosexual behaviour, might provide a similarly powerful environment for the acquisition of homosexual behaviour.

Unfortunately, there is very little evidence for or against such a hypothesised increase in homosexual behaviour in single sex environments, other than of an anecdotal or autobiographical kind (Lewis, 1955). Schofield (1965a), as a minor aspect of his excellent survey of the heterosexual behaviour of adolescents, asked his subjects questions concerning their homosexual experiences. A very much higher pro-portion of those educated in single sex boarding schools reported such experiences than did those educated in day schools, whether co-educational or single sex. However, Schofield did not question his subjects concerning their present preferred orienta-tion, and, as his sample went up to the age of nineteen years only, the persistence of the effects of school experiences is not known.

West (1968) cited anecdotal evidence of the acquisition of homosexual behaviour by previously heterosexual males incarcerated in prisons or prisoner of war camps. He suggests that the post-confinement persistence of such homosexual behaviour is dependent on whether it afforded a sexual outlet only, or was associated also with emotional gratification.

(e) SPECIFIC LEARNING EXPERIENCES: POSITIVE AND NEGATIVE

It has been strongly argued by McGuire et al. (1965) that the nature of the first sexual experience, followed by orgasm, is crucial for the establishment of the direction of sexual orientation, and they cite several case studies in support of this theory. Some supporting evidence, although not of a directly relevant kind is provided in an account by Evans (1968) who reported that of two groups of exhibitionists deconditioned with emotive imagery and aversive conditioning, the group that used heterosexual masturbatory fantasy deconditioned significantly faster than the group with deviant masturbatory fantasy. There is also a striking piece of anecdotal evidence by Gebhard (1965); and Bandura (1969, p. 512–513) cites several similar reports of deviant sexual behaviour reinforced by social learning processes.

McGuire et al. (1965) emphasised the importance of the fantasy of the deviant behaviour maintaining the behaviour, by becoming the cue for sexual response (such as masturbation). This raises the importance of the incubation of behavioural experiences through cognitive rehearsal. Eysenck (1968) has proposed a theory of incubation concerning the stage in learning in which repeated presentations of the CS alone (i.e. without the UCS) results not in extinction, as might be expected, but an increase in the intensity of the CR.

Feldman and MacCulloch (1971, Appendix B) report a striking example of such a phenomenon in two normal volunteer subjects exposed to three sessions of avoidance learning. In both cases there was an increase in intensity of response, both behavioural and physiological, after the removal of the shock electrodes and the continued presentation of a stimulus which was originally attractive but which had become aversive in the course of avoidance learning. Feldman and MacCulloch (1971) have extended Eysenck's views on incubation to include the time *between* learning sessions, in which the subject may be cognitively rehearsing the behavioural experiences that occurred in training.

They propose that there are individual differences in the frequency and intensity of such rehearsal, which affect the nature of the response the next time a subject is re-exposed to the original CS. That is, positive approach learning to homosexual stimuli may be either extinguished or incubated by cognitive rehearsal following the learning experience, depending on the intensity of the original learning experience, the habitual intensity of cognitive rehearsal, and whether the individual has a tendency to incubate positive or negative experiences.

It might be that positively reinforced learning experiences with sexual stimuli would be particularly crucial in determining the direction of sexual orientation if they occurred at a particular, and possibly critical, stage of development. The stage at which secondary sexual characteristics are developed (i.e. adolescence) would be an obvious candidate for such a critical period. Those educated at single sex boarding schools, from before adolescence until well past adolescence, would be very much at risk as compared with day school attenders, who are exposed, in addition, to heterosexual stimuli.

Thus far we have been concerned with positive reward conditioning to homosexual stimuli as a major explanation of homosexual orientation. Another possibility is the occurrence of unpleasant heterosexual experiences which might lead to the development of heterosexual avoidance, and by implication, to homosexual approach behaviour becoming more acceptable. There is a considerable psychoanalytic emphasis on this point, e.g. Ovesey et al. (1963) and Bieber et al. (1963). The latter conclude that heterosexual fear is one of the main elements of homosexuality, and some form of attempt to reduce such heterosexual avoidance seems to be involved in several of the reports of the treatment of homosexuality by psychotherapy. Similarly, Stevenson and Wolpe (1960) stress the desensitisation of heterosexual avoidance in their patients treated by reciprocal inhibition, and Feldman and MacCulloch (1965, 1971) have attempted to build into their aversion therapy technique the reduction of heterosexual avoidance as well as a decrease in homosexual approach.

A questionnaire study of non-patient homosexual and heterosexual males was reported by Ramsay and Van Velzen (1968). They found highly significant differences between the groups, with homosexuals reporting more dislike of intimate heterosexual situations. No data were reported by Ramsey and Van Velzen on the occurrence of unpleasant heterosexual experiences during adolescence which might provide the basis for adult heterosexual avoidance behaviours. Kolaszynska (1969) found a similarly strong emphasis on hetero-sexual avoidance in both male and female groups of non-patient homosexuals.

Feldman and MacCulloch (1971) have proposed a theory for the secondary type of homosexual behaviour. They suggest that many adolescents may have encountered pleasant homosexual experiences (these probably occur to a considerable proportion of adolescents—*see* Schofield, 1965) and unpleasant heterosexual experiences. They suggest that if such a combination of experiences occur to individuals who have a tendency to incubate unpleasant experiences, the outcome is likely to be a gradual shifting, through the process of cognitive dissonance reduction, from a heterosexual orientation to a homosexual orientation. A detailed account of this theory is given in Feldman and MacCulloch (1971).

West (1968) has reviewed the psychoanalytic theory relating homosexuality and paranoia. The theory was proposed by Freud following the case of Dr Schreber, who wrote a detailed description of his delusion. Freud argued that Schreber's account showed the unmistakable homosexual significance of much of the content of the delusion. Briefly, the supposed enemy of the paranoiac is someone towards whom the person really experiences a sexual feeling, but a violent reaction against the guilty attraction causes him to fly to the opposite extreme and assert that the individual is an object of hate and not of love. That is, the insanity consists of an extreme instance of overcompensation for repressed homosexual feelings. Planansky and Johnston (1962) surveyed the incidence of 'heterosexual problems and homosexual concerns' in 150 schizophrenic in-patients. At the end of a detailed and careful study they concluded that there was no significant relationship between the degree of paranoidness and either of the above types of problem: 'Paranoia and the development of homosexuality, as found in schizophrenia, are not specially related to each other'. A less direct study by Kendrick and Clarke (1967) was carried out on 20 homosexual and 20 heterosexual males, in the form of an attitudinal measure of various aspects of familial social relationships, to test the notion that homosexuals are in a state of cognitive dissonance. While the homosexual group had less favourable attitudes to certain aspects of the family and society than had the controls, in no way could they be considered to hold paranoid attitudes.

No single theory of the acquisition of homosexual behaviour has yet emerged as dominating its competitors. The most useful research strategy would be to carry out a prospective and long-term behavioural study as soon after conception as possible. One aspect of such a study would be to relate maternal prenatal circulating hormonal levels to the development of postnatal sexual and sex-linked behaviours. A second aspect would look at the socio-sexual experiences with both sexes of developing infants and attempt to relate the development and direction of sexual interests over several years to the form and outcome of such behavioural experiences. The first section of the study would be concerned with the development of the primary type of homosexual, the second with the secondary type (Feldman and MacCulloch, 1971). Studies that would be useful, in addition, would relate both of the above areas of research to the social setting of the developing child and adolescent, and particularly the nature of the reinforcements provided by parents and other significant persons for the display of sexual and sex-typed behaviours—that is, behaviours considered appropriate or inappropriate by society in general for the morphological sex.

2. FETISHISM AND TRANSVESTISM

Fetishism refers to sexual behaviour in which a human partner is not required, that is, an object is substituted as the stimulus for sexual arousal, which may or may not lead to orgasm. The nature of the object varies enormously, but frequently involves shoes (or boots) or the whole or part of female clothing (fetishistic behaviour appears to be confined almost entirely to males). In the latter case the sexual deviation is known as transvestism. It is to be distinguished very clearly from trans-sexualism, which is discussed in the next section and involves a desire to be thought of as a female. The transvestite has no desire to be regarded as a female, or to 'change' his sex. Hence, there is a very much closer relationship between fetishism and transvestism, which may be regarded simply as a form of fetishism, than between transvestism and trans-sexualism.

Two papers, by Rachman (1966) and Rachman and Hodgson (1968) provide one of the few examples of experimental research on transvestism. Rachman studied the possibility that sexual fetishism was a learned response, a suggestion originally made by Binet in 1888. (The bizarre nature of many of the sexual fetishisms does suggest *a priori* that a chance conditioning of neutral stimuli to arousal might have occurred.) In his first experiment Rachman conditioned sexual responses (monitored by the phallo-plethysmograph) to slides of boots of various types, which were displayed on a screen immediately prior to the presentation of slides of sexually arousing nude females. All three volunteer subjects acquired the criterion of five successive plethysmograph reactions to the CS within a maximum of 65 paired trials. Rachman was also able to demonstrate extinction and spontaneous recovery. It is of interest that the subject who took twice as long to condition as the other two showed the greatest resistance to extinction, and that all the subjects displayed stimulus generalisation to at least one other stimulus (low-heeled black shoes) which had not been originally paired with the UCS (the slides of nude females).

In a further study, Rachman and Hodgson (1968) conditioned five volunteer subjects to give a sexual response to a slide of a pair of knee-length boots which was paired with a UCS of a slide of a nude female. In order to control for pseudo-conditioning a control condition was used in which the UCS was presented prior to the CS. While all five subjects reached the criterion of five successive responses to the CS with forward conditioning, none did so with backward conditioning. Three of the five subjects showed evidence of stimulus generalisation, and the subject who showed the most generalisation was the one who took the longest to condition.

The fact that a conditioning model can be used to explain fetishism does not mean that the chance association of a neutral CS with a sexual UCS is sufficient to account for the development of fetishism. It seems a reasonable assumption that the number of individuals exposed to such chance contiguities vastly exceeds the number who develop a full-blown fetishism. It may be, therefore, that either the intensity of the UCS, of the CS, or of the 'drive' state of the organism may be of major importance. The last possibility underlies the view of several authors that the development of fetishism is associated with some form of cerebral dysfunction.

For example, Epstein (1960) divided the development of fetishistic phenomena into two general stages: (a) a state of increased 'organismic excitability' which he considers the primary disturbance in fetishism, the state being the product of cerebral pathophysiology such as seizures and other episodic phenomena found in temporal lobe dysfunction; (b) the development of fetishisms is potentiated by the attempts of the individual to maintain 'organismic control'. That is, increased cerebral activity provides the basis for increased responsiveness to sexual stimulation, and increased libido provides the basis for orgasm to occur more frequently and, hence, with an increased probability of being conditioned to neutral non-sexual stimuli. The fetishist then tries to achieve control over his hyperresponsivity and this ritualises the fetishistic act. Epstein supports his theory by citing ten cases reported elsewhere in the literature.

A similar view has been put forward by Wålinder (1965) who provides a review of reports relating cerebral dysfunction (particularly temporal lobe disorder) and sexual deviations. He includes several cases of concurrent sexual deviation and temporal lobe epilepsy in which both the convulsion and the deviation disappeared following surgical intervention. Wålinder also presents EEG data on 26 cases of transvestism. Of these, eight records were normal, six probably normal, two were borderline, and ten abnormal. Six of the EEG records considered abnormal showed the site of the abnormality to be in one or both temporal lobes. No controls were used, and it is not known to what extent the analysis of the records was carried out blind.

Further reports of an apparent association between temporal lobe leisons and sexual deviations have been provided by Davies and Morgenstern (1960), Ball (1968), and Kolarsky et al. (1967). The last-named study presented data on 86 male epileptic outpatients in an attempt to relate sexual deviations to the inferred localisation of the lesion and the age of onset of the lesion. Nineteen of these 86 were psychosexually deviant, and eleven of the 19 had their lesion localised in the temporal lobe. Irrespective of the site of lesion, the lesions of the sexually deviant subjects had an earlier age of onset than did those of non-deviant subjects. The authors hypothesise that 'an early brain lesion destroys primordial programmes controlling the selection of stimuli and activities, the learning of which is necessary for further specification and elaboration of these primordial programmes. Deviant sexual programmes may develop as a compensation, provided that the brain lesion is present during the critical period of life'. They consider that this period in man is unlikely to extend beyond the end of the second year in life.

While Kolarsky et al. do not hypothesise that all cases of sexual deviation have their origin in brain lesions, there is a strong presumption that at least a significant proportion of cases of transvestism and fetishism are associated with brain lesions. That is, brain lesions, particularly of the temporal lobe, predispose to the development of fetishisms, although they do not make them inevitable. The bizarre nature of fetishisms makes a combination of abnormal brain functioning and classical conditioning a useful and heuristic theory, and further studies on these lines would be valuable.

The psychoanalytic theory of fetishism, as set out

by Gillespie, (1964) emphasises fetishism as a means adopted by the individual of overcoming castration anxiety. The fetish remains as the sign of triumph over the castration threat and spares the fetishist any need to become homosexual by making the female into a tolerable sexual object. Gillespie also emphasises the importance of identification in fetishism. Identification serves as a further defence mechanism, the identification being with a female figure. That is, there is the same sort of defence, according to the psychoanalysts, as is used by the homosexual. The criticisms frequently made of psychoanalytic theory in general apply equally to particular instances.

However, the psychoanalytic theory of transvestism and fetishism does highlight one of the most important facts in this area, namely that fetishism is very rare in females—at any rate in the absence of published reports it can be said that females rarely *complain* of fetishistic problems. Returning to the earlier discussion on brain dysfunction and fetishism, it seems likely that early differences in cerebral development between males and females might be well worth looking at.

3. TRANSSEXUALISM

DEFINITION

The syndrome of transsexualism was discussed for the first time by Benjamin (1953), according to whom the major characteristics of the syndrome are a complete identification with the opposite sex and the urge to have an operation in order to change the sex. Although the direction of sexual orientation is a homosexual one, transsexuals do not consider themselves homosexual, because they strongly believe they 'really' belong to the opposite sex. The identification with the opposite sex extends to all aspects of their lives. Benjamin (1953) considers that the urge for the change of sex operation is the best pathognomonic sign for transsexualism.

This raises the question of how to classify patients who request operations short of a total reforming of the external sexual organs, such as a mastectomy. However, the criterion of the sex change operation does enable workers to classify transsexuals into two groups, as follows. Firstly, those patients who hate their external genitalia and wish these to be altered. This group are the 'true' transsexuals. Secondly, those individuals who want to keep their genitalia but dress in clothes of the opposite sex. These are feminine homosexuals (the 'drag queens') or in the case of physical females, masculine lesbians (the 'butch' type). Both are separate from the transvestites, whose sexual orientation is usually heterosexual, but who, in addition, are aroused by clothes of the opposite sex as sexual ends in themselves. This can be considered, as mentioned earlier, as an example of fetishistic behaviour. Kockott (1970) states that the heterosexual transvestite very rarely becomes a transsexual.

Benjamin (1953) discusses the problem of distinguishing between transvestism and transsexualism. He considers that there may be only one form of gender role disorientation—transsexualism—found in varying degrees. If the intensity is low enough there is the clinical picture of transvestism. If it is high, surgery would be demanded. That is, transsexuals differ in the degree of emotional distress they feel concerning their desire to change their sex. Some are satisfied merely to dress in the clothes of the opposite sex, by day, and to be regarded as a female in terms of superficial appearance. Others want more than the mere outward appearance, and want to possess some of the physical characteristics too. Similarly, some physical females who wish to be regarded as males are satisfied to wear male clothes, while others require operations aimed at transforming their external physical appearance. Similar distinctions between the milder and the more extreme forms of transsexualism are made by Lukianowicz (1959) who has provided a useful survey of the literature concerning transvestism and transsexualism up to that date.

Benjamin has missed the major point concerning the difference between transvestism and transsexualism. The former term describes the individual who does not wish to be seen by *others* in his female clothing, whether by day or night. The latter term refers to the person who *does* wish to be seen, not for sexually arousing reasons, but to give him at least the partial illusion of being regarded by others as a female, or at least as possibly not a male.

Kockott (1970) discusses the psychopathology of transsexualism and makes the following major points. Firstly, there is a complete identification with the opposite sex; the identification is a fixed idea, and in the extreme form the wish to achieve a sex change operation becomes the only goal in life. Next, patients often show bodily illusions—they believe they have noticed changes of their body towards that of the opposite sex—hence a female may believe her shoulders have become bigger and broader and her hips narrower. There is a remarkable similarity in the histories presented by many patients, and Kockott raises the question that these may be changed by the patients in relation to their fixed idea. Many transsexuals show an exaggerated behaviour they think is typical for the opposite sex, but which is more of a travesty than an accurate representation.

Lukianowicz (1959) considers that all transsexuals are homosexual; however, because the (male) patients feel they are really women, he accepts that they are not homosexuals! Benjamin (1967) has a similar view, stating that transsexuals are largely heterosexual, but occasionally bisexual. He agrees that they are attracted only to members of their own morphological sex; however, they cannot be called homosexual because they feel they 'belong' to the sex opposite to that of the chosen partner. He further states, 'the trans-sexual man loves another man as a woman does, in spite of his phenotype and in spite of his genital apparatus which he feels he must change'. All this would imply that persons of the opposite morphological sex who marry or have a sexual association with a transsexual individual should themselves be heterosexual.

Money (1969) described a series of 20 morphologically male transsexuals who had undergone a 'sex change' operation, and reported that nearly half of these had married physically normal males who were not transsexuals or homosexuals. He adduced this as evidence for the view that the male to female transsexual is not homosexual. However, he also reported that in all cases the 9 post-operative transsexuals had met their partners in homosexual bars! On *a priori* grounds it seems rather unlikely that a heterosexual male would seek as a sexual partner a facsimile of a female. A similar doubt must be raised about the likelihood of a female-to-male transsexual attracting a heterosexual female as a partner.

INCIDENCE

No reliable figures for the incidence of transsexualism are available, as there has not yet been a survey of a random sample of the population to assess the frequency of the syndrome. As more Gender Identity Clinics are set up, more transsexuals come to light. Benjamin (1967) stated that he had seen and examined 300 transsexuals during the fourteen years prior to 1967. Hamburger (1953) reported that, following an article by him, he received personal letters from 465 men and women, all of whom desired a change of sex. It seems likely that the problem occurs with sufficient frequency to confirm its practical importance; perhaps more pertinent to research purposes is the theoretical interest for the problems of the acquisition of gender identity, and

sex-typed behaviour, of the existence of individuals whose gender identity is at total variance with their morphological structure.

MEASUREMENT

Money and Epstein (1967) report intelligence test scores for male and female transsexuals and for nineteen prepubertal 'effeminate' boys. All three groups showed significantly higher mean verbal than non-verbal score. No information is provided by the authors on the social class background of the subjects, and as it is well known that middle-class subjects have on average superior verbal than performance score it is not possible to assign the reason for the obtained disparity to the transsexual or 'effeminate' nature of the sample. Dorbar (1967) reported a group of 34 male transsexual patients to whom were administered a number of cognitive, personality, and perceptual tests. The distribution of Wechsler IQ test scores showed a preponderance towards the upper end of the scale. This supports the possibility that both Dorbar's sample and Money and Epstein's sample were drawn from a socially advantaged (i.e. middle class) section of the population. As Dorbar points out, transsexual patients are persons who have taken the initiative in seeking a solution to their problem by contacting agencies whom they hope will help them. This suggests a degree of sophistication more likely to be found in middle-class than working-class individuals.

The personality data reported by Dorbar (1967) are potentially of more interest. Unfortunately, most of the data are concerned with the House-Tree-Person Test and only qualitative and anecdotal accounts of the results of this test are given. However, the finding that in not a single case was a body drawn naked might be of some interest. Dorbar also states, 'it is quite clear that these patients have intense disgust for their own male bodies'. She reports that they took great care never to view themselves in the mirror and also employed a variety of means to make their morphological sex as inconspicuous as possible.

Dorbar is engaged on the psychological re-testing of operated patients, within six months to a year after their operation, and further reports would be of interest. At present very little evidence is available concerning changes on personality measure following sexual re-assignment. Berg (1963) described the history of a boy with hypospadias (a relatively superficial genitial deformity) who was mistakenly regarded as a girl until puberty. He had accepted his sex assignation, and only came to medical attention because his voice broke. The genital deformity was successfully repaired, and the boy showed a strong willingness to discard things female and to take up life as a boy. There was also a change towards imaginative fantasy of a masculine type on a projective test. However, this case is not really comparable to that of someone who clings to a strong belief in his 'true' gender role despite anatomical evidence to the contrary.

In general, it seems that the detailed psychological assessment of transsexualism has barely begun. Prospective developmental studies are indicated, particularly of 'effeminate' boys or 'masculine' girls. A study of a long-term nature, which is now under way, has been described by Stoller (1967). He is following up over the years all children who are brought to a Gender Identity Research Clinic because their parents consider them to be effeminate, usually because of the boys' cross-dressing. It is to be hoped that both Stoller—and Green (1969), who is carrying out a similar long-term study—will make detailed observations of the sex appropriate and inappropriate behaviour of the children and also of the reinforcement behaviour towards these responses of the parents.

Causation

Much the most influential early theory on the causation of transsexualism arose from studies on individuals who were physically intersexual. That is, those who have internal organs or chromosomal constitutions that have characteristics both of the male and the female.

The first survey of intersexuals was carried out by Ellis (1945), who abstracted from the medical literature all the cases in which both the glandular constitution and sexual preferences of intersexuals were known. Of 39 intersexuals who were reared as males, 34 showed sexual desires of a definite type; in all 34 cases their desires were heterosexual. This was despite the fact that 23 of them had either mixed or female sex glands. It seemed that the sexual inclination of intersexuals correlated more closely with their upbringing than with their hormonal constitution.

In a study of a consecutive series of 100 patients with different types of intersexuality, Money and Hampson (1957) confirmed that, with an occasional exception, the behaviour of these patients followed the sex of rearing, even in cases in which their chromosomes and the predominant characteristics of their external genitalia and their internal reproductive organs were those of the opposite sex. It seemed that the sex of assignment and the sense of gender identity were firmly established in the child's behaviour by the age of two or three and that

attempts to change either became increasingly difficult after that age.

One criticism of this approach concerns the great difficulty of generalising from individuals who are intersexes to those who anatomically and physiologically quite clearly belong to one sex or the other. Certainly the major distinguishing feature of the transsexual, the fixed belief in the fact that he should have been born as a member of the opposite sex, is quite lacking in the intersexuals. Hence, the theory described above, in connection with the aetiology of homosexuality concerning neuro-endrocrine influences on the development of sexual behaviour and sex-typed behaviours, would appear more relevant.

Summarising this, it can be said that there is a hypothalamic brain centre controlling sexual behaviour which is fundamentally female in all foetuses, whether they are genetically male or female. It has also been discovered, at any rate in animals, that a critical period exists when, in a genetically male foetus, masculinisation of this female centre occurs, due to androgen production in the newly formed testicles. Something interferes, such as a lack of internal androgen, or lack of response of the neutral target organ, and the centre remains female, determining the later sexual behaviour and possibly causing gender role disorientation. That is, the sexual centre in the brain is female in persons otherwise physically male in all respects. Vice versa, through an increase in the level of male sex hormones affecting the female foetus, a 'masculinisation' occurs. No evidence of endocrine differences would be expected in the adult patient, and indeed none has been found (Kupperman 1967). This does not invalidate the thesis described above.

Several workers (e.g. Stoller, 1967; Baker and Stoller, 1968) are beginning to change their earlier views concerning aetiology and to agree that there could be 'a biological force' which operates irrespective of parental attitudes. Feldman and MacCulloch (1971) have suggested that adult primary homosexuality would be associated with sex-inappropriate childhood behaviour, and that there is a relatively close association between primary homosexuality, transsexualism and homosexual transvestism. The view of Feldman and MacCulloch is that transsexuals are primary homosexuals who in addition have a delusion concerning their 'real' sex. The problem remains why a relative minority of primary homosexuals (who are then termed transsexuals) not only display sex inappropriate behaviour, but, in addition, wish to change their bodily appearance so that morphology and behaviour will be consistent.

4. EXHIBITIONISM

As far as criminal statistics are concerned, exhibitionism is one of the commonest sexual deviations in the United Kingdom. The offence 'indecent exposure' formed one quarter (490) of Radzinowicz's total of 1,985 sexual offenders in his 1957 study, and represented approximately one third of the sexual offenders found guilty in 1959. However, as pointed out by Schofield (1965b), the likelihood of the very much more common homosexual behaviour resulting in a conviction is so minimal as to be almost non-existent Hence, one cannot argue from the incidence of a behaviour in the criminal statistics to the incidence of the behaviour in the population at large. It is impossible to know exactly the frequency of exhibitionist behaviour solely from the complaints of the victims—and this is the only means by which an exhibiting individual becomes known. The frequency of complaint will depend on the threshold of complaint of those against whom the behaviour is carried out.

The literature on exhibitionism is rather sparse; that up to 1950 has been reviewed by Rickles (1950). Rosen (1964) defines an exhibitionist as a man who exposes his genitals to someone of the opposite sex outside the context of the sexual act. When this serves as the major source of sexual pleasure, or is compulsive or repetitious, exhibitionism is regarded as a perversion. Mohr et al. (1964) define exhibitionism rather similarly, except to add as an important feature of the definition 'not leading to an aggressive act'. The behaviour appears to be confined to males, even in non-western cultures (Ford and Beach, 1952). In those few societies where women deliberately expose their genitals, exhibitionism appears to be a stage of courting behaviour.

Mohr et al. categorise exhibitionism as, (a) secondary to a recognised illness, and (b) as arising out of an 'obsessional drive'. Rosen also divides exhibitionists into two types. In the first, simple or regressive type, the exhibitionist act follows as the result of some rather obvious social or sexual trauma, disappointment or loss, or as an accompaniment to a severe mental or physical illness. The second type he calls phobic impulsive, and states that personality disturbances are much more intense in this type. A detailed analysis of exhibitionism from the point of view of psychoanalytic theory is given by Rosen. This cannot be considered apart from a general appraisal of psychoanalytic theory as an adequate explanation for sexual deviation, and in view of the usual difficulties of testing psychoanalytic hypotheses, such a survey will not be attempted here, as it has not been elsewhere in this chapter. Rosen recognises the importance of a precipitating event, and states that this may be of one or two types. In the first type there is an internal sexual excitement arising spontaneously, as in the adolescent, or aroused in the adult exhibitionist by sexually stimulating sights. In the second type, exposures occur as a result of a non-sexual tension situation which nevertheless has 'the symbolic meaning of loss of security or castration'.

Rosen relates exhibitionism to voyeurism, in that both involve a sexual pleasure from looking at a sexual stimulus. However, in the case of exhibitionism the pleasure is intended to be felt by the other person; in voyeurism it is felt by the one who looks at the stimulus. No data are provided by either Rosen or Mohr et al., who describe a series of 54 exhibitionists seen at the Toronto Psychiatric Clinic, which would enable anything more than a descriptive approach to be made at the present time. Even this is handicapped by the lack of data on control subjects.

Mohr et al., surveying the nature of the act, state that in their series there was no particular age of victim, the victim was always a stranger and no further relationship between the offender and the victim was sought. The specific stimuli were part of the person, rather than the whole of the person, the act was as often as not carried out in a public place, and varied from partial exposure to open masturbation. It was intended to arouse a strong emotional response in the victim. The responses of the victim are likely to vary widely, hence whether there is a complaint and a subsequent arrest are largely matters of chance. It is important to point out that some exhibitionists may not be true exhibitionists but, more likely, compulsive masturbators—who did not intend a visual display to the 'victim'. Such a case has been described by MacCulloch et al. (1968).

In the series of Mohr et al. the peak incidence was in the age group twenty to thirty, thereafter decreasing. They state that when exhibitionism occurs for the first time, it is usually secondary to some other psychiatric problem. The IQs of the Mohr et al. sample were normally distributed, but there was a tendency to educational under-achievement. However, as there are no data on social class the specific importance of this factor cannot be estimated. While the majority of the series had good work records, Mohr et al. state that, 'they seem to have difficulty with the supervisors'; again, no evidence for this statement of a quantitative kind is supplied. One third of the Mohr et al. series had fathers absent for prolonged periods of time and also claimed to have more distant feelings for their fathers than for their mothers—in the absence of control data the importance of this cannot be assessed.

Mohr *et al.* cite several series of exhibitionists reported in the literature, in which the proportion of the series who were married varied between 40 per cent and 63 per cent. Some anecdotal description is given of the nature of the relationship with the wife and of the personality characteristics of the wife; the former is said to involve considerable difficulty in the sexual area but no clear data are supplied. The characteristics of the wife are said to involve dependence and ambivalence—again, the evidence is merely anecdotal. Mohr *et al.* cite personality assessments by Rickles (1950) to the effect that exhibitionists tend to be 'tense, compulsive, with a rigid control over emotions'. No quantitative data, or data on controls are supplied, but there does seem to be general agreement in the literature that the exhibitionist act has the phenomenological quality of a compulsion.

Rosen, surveying a series of 24 exhibitionists who were treated at the Portman Clinic over a two-year period, considers that there is a functional equivalence between exhibitionism and the expression of aggression. This conclusion is drawn from the fact that it was 'possible to deal indirectly with the sexuality of the patients a great deal of the time by discussing their aggressions'. These last two points—the possible equation between sexuality and aggression (the near absence of exhibitionism in females may be related to male-female differences in aggression), and the obsessional nature of the act—appear worthy of systematic research, as does the sexual satisfaction derived from either looking at another person or being looked at. The latter question should be studied in the context of a wider research into the role of visual factors in sexual behaviour in general.

5. IMPOTENCE

This section is based largely on the work of Johnson (1970). Johnson begins by pointing out the pervasive and widely observed occurrence of impotence—for instance every psychiatric patient is at some time impotent. Johnson distinguishes between disorders of sexual potency due to disorders of ejaculation and those which are due to disorders of erection, with associated loss of sexual drive. The disorders of ejaculation are further distinguished into impotence of ejaculation and premature ejaculation. The author of the other major survey on impotence (Cooper, 1968) organises the field in a similar way. Both surveys were based entirely on individuals who had sought psychiatric help for impotence.

Much the largest survey on the population at large forms part of the data presented by Kinsey *et al.* (1947). Kinsey's sample was by no means a random one of the male population of the United States, but it is possible to base tentative conclusions on it, True ejaculatory impotence was found to be a very rare phenomenon (only six out of 4,108 cases). Erectile impotence was less uncommon (66 cases of more or less permanent erectile impotence in subjects aged between 10 and 80.) Of those under the age of 30 the incidence of impotence was less than 1 per cent, and was under 2·5 per cent between the ages of 30 and 45. By the age of 60 it had reached 18 per cent, and 75 per cent by the age of 80, although the very small number of cases available at the upper age ranges impels caution.

Johnson (1970) cites work by Klüver and Bucy (1939) who showed that a bilateral temporal lobec-tomy produced a syndrome in monkeys which included hypersexual behaviour. Hence, there seems to be some localisation of sexual function in the temporal lobe. This relates to the work described earlier concerning the possible connection between fetishism and temporal lobe damage. It is possible that hyposexual behaviour (impotence) also may be related to temporal lobe dysfunction. The psychoanalytic theory of impotence is that it is due to the fear of symbolically incestuous relationships (Fenichel, 1943). Freud related impotence to homosexuality, and from a rather different point of view, Kinsey saw the conflict between homosexual and heterosexual behaviour as important for the development of impotence. Feldman and MacCulloch (1971) have discussed the concept of heterophobia—that is, the avoidance of potential sexual contact with females—which, in addition to the attraction to males, is a major feature of the secondary type of homosexuality. They state that heterophobia is unlikely to be shown only by homosexuals, and that milder forms are probably to be found in many otherwise heterosexual individuals. Some cases of erectile impotence might be an extreme variation of the fear of heterosexual stimuli. Johnson found homosexuality 'to be surprisingly rare' in his series, with no consistent type of disorder of potency associated with a history of homosexual behaviour.

However, Johnson made no specific attempt to assess the direction of sexual orientation in his subjects, and in addition, heterosexually impotent homosexuals would be less likely to seek help for their impotence if, in addition, a satisfactory sexual outlet—homosexuality—still remained open to them. The possibility of conceptualising at least a proportion of cases of impotence within an approach-avoidance conflict model, enables learning theory analyses to be applied to the problem, and suggests the usefulness of treatment techniques such as desensitisation and graded practice.

Johnson's series consisted of 76 patients in all, in whom the primary complaint was impotence. He described 44 per cent of them as displaying the neurotic constitution, defined by Slater (1943) as a combination of clinically assessed abnormal personality, a history of neurotic behaviour in childhood, a previous neurotic breakdown, and a positive family history of neurotic breakdowns. The suggestion that the sample of impotent individuals seen by Johnson was rather similar to other groups of neurotics is supported by an anthropometric study of the sample which used the androgyny score of Tanner (1951). The androgyny measurements in the 44 per cent of the sample with a 'neurotic constitution' were significantly different from those of a group of normal controls, whereas those of the patients with a non-neurotic constitution were not significantly different from the controls. Johnson concludes that the anthropomorphic variation he demonstrated in some patients with disorders of sexual potency is probably related to the same factor as determines the neurotic constitution. It is therefore not specifically related to the sexual disorder. This is reminiscent of the finding of Coppen (1959), described earlier, concerning the relationship between homosexuality, neurosis, and anthropometric scores.

As mentioned above, Johnson divided his sample into disorders of impotence (72·4 per cent) and disorders of ejaculation (27·6 per cent). The latter were further divided into premature ejaculation and the very rare inability to ejaculate. A further way of dividing the group was by time of onset—46 per cent were impotent from the first attempt at coitus, the

remaining 54 per cent were of late onset. It is worth asking why the early onset type of individual marries, what is the personality and sexual nature of his marital partner, and why he seeks help—perhaps after being content for many years? Johnson considers the impotence of the early onset group to be more likely to be caused by constitutional factors. This is borne out by the androgyny scores for the early onset group being significantly different from those of the controls ($P = 0·02$), whereas those of the late onset group were not significantly different from the controls. An extension of the analysis to compare the early and late onset groups in terms of neurotic constitution would have been useful.

Johnson suggests that individuals differ in the rate at which they come to ejaculation, with the disorders of ejaculation being at two extremes of the normal distribution. Hence, the male who can learn to delay his ejaculation in order to reduce disparity with the speed of the female response will ultimately achieve a mutually satisfactory sexual relationship. Failure to delay orgasm and ejaculation will, in some cases, especially where the marital partner is sexually inhibited, be labelled as a disorder of ejaculation. Considered from this viewpoint, premature ejaculation is not so much a pathological state as a failure to learn an adaptive response. A high proportion of the ejaculatory difficulties were in the group of early onset. Johnson's view of the patient's inability to learn to delay ejaculation, and so relate it to his wife's speed of orgasm, is supported by Cooper (1968) who reported a series of 54 cases of impotence, and supports, in general, the findings of Johnson concerning typology and onset. Cooper reports that in nine cases out of ten of premature ejaculation the female had instigated the referral of her spouse.

The relationship between the time of onset of disorder, the type of disorder, and the outcome of treatment are discussed in the section on the treatment of abnormal sexual behaviour.

6. PAEDOPHILIA

In view of the fact that homosexuals, like heterosexuals, usually choose as their partner either an adult or prepubertal individuals (Curran and Parr, 1957) and rarely both, paedophilia will be discussed separately from homosexual behaviour in general. Two surveys of paedophiliacs will be considered in this section.

The first was carried out by Mohr *et al.* (1964) at the Toronto Psychiatric Clinic, and includes all paedophiliac referrals (55 in number) between the years of 1956 and 1959. The second survey was

carried out in Britain by Schofield (1965b). He studied six groups of subjects in all, four homosexual and two nonhomosexual, as mentioned earlier in this chapter. The paedophile group consisted of the first 50 individuals in sequence of the total paedophile group in three London prisons at the time of the study. Two-thirds of the group were in Wormwood Scrubs, which deals mainly with first offenders. The group of 50 homosexual prisoners with whom Schofield compared his group of paedophiliacs (i.e. homosexuals whose preferred partner was over 21) were drawn from the same three prisons, but half were from Wandsworth, which deals mainly with recidivists. Whereas Mohr *et al.* defined paedophilia as 'the expressed desire for immature sexual gratification with a pre-pubertal child,' where pre-pubertal means before the development of secondary sexual characteristics, Schofield defined paedophilia as those whose preferred sexual object is under the age of sixteen. Hence, some of Schofield's sample would not be regarded by Mohr *et al.* as paedophiliacs, because the average age of onset of puberty is well before sixteen.

This basic difference in defining the samples makes it difficult to compare the two groups; the same problem of definition applies, of course, throughout the field of abnormal sexual behaviour.

The relationship between the differences in definition, and the differing composition of the groups of Mohr *et al.* and Schofield is shown by the emphasis in the former on 'immature sexual gratification'. By 'immature' Mohr *et al.* mean sex acts appropriate to the age of the victim, such as mutual genital display, fondling, etc. However, when one looks in more detail at the precise nature of the act which took place with the victim it can be seen that of the twenty-six of Mohr's subjects who were homosexual paedophiliacs, in only six instances was the major act fondling the victim, and in only one did it consist of looking; by contrast, fourteen of the major acts consisted of undoubted overt adult behaviour, including fellatio, anal or intercrural intercourse, and masturbation. In addition, Mohr *et al.* cite other studies, particularly that carried out at the Institute of Criminology in Cambridge (Radzinowicz, 1957) in which only nine per cent of the homosexual offences consisted of fondling, and the California study (Department of Mental Hygiene, California Sexual Deviation Research, 1954) in which the vast majority of homosexual paedophiliac acts consisted of overt sexual behaviour. Even in the case of heterosexual paedophiliac acts, only a minority of the acts with the victim involved 'immature' behaviour such as fondling or display.

However, no generalisation to the total population of paedophiliacs can be made from these samples of offenders seen in prison, or in psychiatric centres, as it may be that complaints are not made either by the victims or their parents unless sexual behaviour of a more active kind than fondling or display is involved.

In the Mohr *et al.* sample the majority of the heterosexual paedophiliacs were married; less than a half of the homosexual paedophiliacs were married. A similar figure is reported for Schofield's paedophiliac homosexuals. Mohr *et al.* reports that the marriages of the heterosexual paedophiliacs lasted longer than those of the homosexual paedophiliacs. Comparing Schofield's paedophiliacs (PC) with his homosexual offenders group, there were significantly more married men in the PC group ($P < 0.005$). The same tendency for marriages to break down was reported by Schofield in his PC group as noted by Mohr *et al.*

Both Mohr *et al.* and Schofield emphasise the tendency for homosexual paedophilia to begin relatively late in life. Mohr *et al.* describe three peaks, one in puberty, one in the mid to late thirties, and one in the mid to late fifties, and state 'a small minority are paedophiliac from childhood on'. By way of contrast, Feldman and MacCulloch (1971) found that all seven of the paedophiliac patients whom they treated by aversion therapy had an unbroken history of paedophiliac behaviour from adolescence onward. The difference between the findings of Feldman and MacCulloch, and those of Mohr *et al.* and Schofield (22 of Schofield's series claimed they had no sexual experience with boys before the age of twenty-one, 15 of whom claimed none until the age of thirty, and 6 until over the age of fifty, while another 11 had shown paedophiliac behaviour in their teens but had then stopped until middle age) may reflect the different degrees of thoroughness of interview used by the various workers. Feldman and MacCulloch interviewed their patients in hospital for up to several hours in each case. By way of contrast, Schofield's interviews were carried out in prison, and lasted no more than fifty minutes.

Schofield links the occurrence of homosexual paedophiliac behaviour, in his sample, rather closely to lack of opportunities for heterosexual outlets in middle life. Of the 50 in the PC sample, 33 had heterosexual experience of an extensive nature, but only 14 had had heterosexual experience in the year prior to their arrest. Of the 33 just mentioned, 19 began their paedophiliac behaviour after the age of twenty-one, and 15 of the 19 after the age of thirty. Schofield provides further data on the heterosexual interests of his PC sample: 22 of the 50 PC men maintained that they had felt a strong sexual attraction to at least one girl at some period of their lives, as compared with an average of 8·3 out of 50 for the other three homosexual groups (convicted homosexuals, non-convicted non-patients, and patients). Only 34 per cent PC men said that they did not find women sexually attractive, as compared with an average of 56 per cent in the other three homosexual groups. Moreover, 83 per cent of the PC men with heterosexual experience preferred this to homosexual experience, as compared to only 16·4 per cent of the men with heterosexual experience in the other three homosexual groups.

The extent to which the impression of paedophilia as substitute behaviour for a heterosexual outlet, given by these reports, can be relied upon is unclear; as mentioned above, Schofield's interviews were not only rather brief, but were carried out in a prison setting, and, although the prisoners were assured that the information would be confidential, Schofield himself doubts whether the prisoners behaved as if they believed this. 'There is little doubt that the two groups seen in the prisons produced the least satisfactory interviews'.

The extent to which the victims of paedophiles are affected by their experiences has been looked at by several authors. Mohr *et al.* review evidence to show that there is little tendency for the victims to show sexual pathology as adults of a gross kind, but that there is a tendency for some individuals to show problems in their social and emotional adjustment. In none of the surveys cited by Mohr *et al.* were control groups used. In any future study it should be mandatory for control children to be used and they should be matched with the attacked group for variables such as degree of psychological disturbance at an age equivalent to that at which the victim group were attacked. Gibbens (1957) reports that there was no difference in the percentage of Borstal boys of known homosexual trends who reported 'being made a pass at' by a stranger, as compared with those without homosexual tendencies. Doshay (1943)

followed up 108 boy sex offenders aged from seven to sixteen. None had been convicted for other kinds of crime (in itself rather surprising) but over half had been involved in homosexual offences either with older males or with other boys. In the whole group there was not a single instance of a sex violation in adult life. Similarly, Tolsma (1957) followed up 133 boys who had had homosexual experience with adults. All but eight were married and had not continued homosexual practices. Finally, Schofield (1965b) reports that three-quarters of his non-patient homosexual group had started homosexual practices before the age of seventeen and most often with boys of the same age. Only a relatively small proportion (16 per cent) had a homosexual initiation by an adult.

The evidence concerning the personality of the paedophile offender is so limited as to be unworthy of review. Perhaps the most interesting and important question is to ask why an adult person is attracted to sexually immature persons, whether of the same sex or his own sex. There may be a considerable degree of overlap in personality between hetero- and homopaedophiles. The empirical work to date has hardly begun to answer this problem; perhaps the most revealing account is that of Humbert Humbert in *Lolita* (Nabokov, 1959).

B. The Treatment of Sexual Deviations

1. HOMOSEXUALITY

From the end of the nineteenth century to the early 1960s the treatment of homosexuality usually meant one form or other of psychotherapy. Eysenck (1952) argued forcibly that there was little evidence for the efficacy of psychotherapy in the treatment of neuroses in general. Since then, several controlled attempts have been made to compare the efficacy of psychotherapy and desensitisation in the treatment of phobias (reviewed by Marks, 1969). Until very recently (Feldman and MacCulloch, 1971; Bancroft, personal communication, 1969; McConaghy, 1969) no such comparisons have been made in the treatment of sexual deviations. Only indirect comparisons were reported and inevitably these were between widely differing samples of patients, treated by different therapies, often using unstated variations of the various possible techniques. A brief listing follows of the information that should be provided in research reports on the treatment of sexual deviations.

Perhaps most important there should be a clear and unequivocal statement of the proportion of referred patients who actually received treatment. If any selection was involved the criteria should be stated. Information should be provided on the full history of the sexual behaviour of the patients in the sample and the nature of their sexual activities at the time of referral for treatment. There should also be data on the patients' motivation for treatment and their future aspirations, both sexual and marital, as well as the source of referral for treatment. The psychiatric status of the patient and the presence or absence of other sexual deviations should also be stated, as should the extent to which the sample of patients were involved in the homosexual subculture. Appearances in Court for homosexual and other offences, and the number of such offences, are also relevant, as is the manner in which the information provided in the research report was obtained—by hearsay, surmise, or by direct statement from the patient. In the last case it should be stated whether this was obtained by interview, or by letter. The degree to which the patient's claim of a successful response to treatment was accepted unquestioningly, or was probed in detail, may also make a considerable difference to the level of success reported.

Information is needed concerning the form of the treatment, the length of time during which it was received and the number of sessions involved, together with the length of each session. Finally, the mode of assessment of changes both in sexual behaviour and interest, and of non-sexual behaviour, if elicited, should be stated. The assessment may be based on the verbal testimony of the patient, on direct observation, on attitude measurement techniques, or on some form of supposedly objective measurement such as the penile plethysmograph. The assessment of change as reported may have been made immediately after treatment or after follow up, or both, and the time of assessment should always be clearly stated.

It is likely (Goldstein, 1962) that the expectations of neurotic patients concerning psychotherapy play an important part in determining the outcome of treatment by that method. It is also likely that such criteria apply to homosexual patients. For example, the vast majority of a non-patient sample of 127 homosexuals who gave interviews to Westwood (1960) were pessimistic as to the likelihood of treatment altering their sexual orientation. About 20 per cent of the sample had received some form of treatment for their homosexual behaviour, mainly by psychiatrists, and of these one half left their treatment within three months and before it had been completed. Nearly one half of those who received treatment had been followed up from six to eighteen months and none reported any change in the direction of their sexual orientation. A further 20 per cent reported a previous desire to change, usually in their late 'teens or early twenties, but had not sought treatment actively.

It seems possible that a considerable proportion of those who do seek treatment are pessimistic about the likelihood of a successful outcome. The majority of the reports of treatment outcome reported in this section (with the exception of some forms of aversion therapy) provide ample support for such pessimism. Whereas the majority of patients seeking psychiatric help for their problems do not gain from the nature of the problem behaviour, and are relieved when these problems ease, such a statement would not be entirely true in the case of homosexuality. In addition to causing distress and unhappiness to the individual displaying the behaviour, homosexual behaviour has at the same time pleasurable consequences, leading as it does to

sexual and in some cases social gratification. Hence, the prospect of a successful outcome of treatment is not an unmixed blessing. It implies both giving up something which, however distressing, has also produced satisfaction and that the individual will have to learn new social skills, or at any rate re-learn skills that have been long dormant.

The extent to which the therapist is able to change the expectation of success of the patient may have an important effect in raising the potential number of those who will respond to treatment. It follows that for any treatment to have the best possible chance of success it should be carried out in an atmosphere of therapeutic optimism. Of course, to guard against the biasing of the results of treatment by such optimism, when evaluating a technique it is necessary to provide a control group, having an alternative form of treatment in a therapeutic atmosphere that is equally optimistic.

In reviewing the results of the treatment of homosexuality, more attention will be paid to the rare examples of controlled trials, than to reports of uncontrolled series of patients, and the very much more frequent instances of single cases or small groups. The last-named type of report will be referred to in any detail only when some aspect of the treatment exemplifies an important theoretical point, or is a clear-cut example of a direct transition from the experimental laboratory to the treatment context.

Psychotherapy and Psychoanalysis

Curran and Parr (1957) reported 100 male homosexual patients treated in the first author's private practice. Only 25 of the sample sought help because of direct personal anxiety concerning homosexuality; seventeen did so because of pressure from friends or relatives, and nearly one third had been referred following a charge, or on an order of the Court. Slightly over half the sample were considered free from gross personality disorder, neurosis, or psychosis during their adult lives. Kinsey ratings for 42 per cent were five and six, 29 per cent as Kinsey four, 16 per cent as Kinsey one to three, and the remainder were unclassified. For 66 patients treatment was limited to discussion at the initial interview, simple counselling, etc. The remainder received psychotherapy, either as in-patients or out-patients. Follow-up information was available on 59, 9 of whom reported either less intense homosexual feelings, or an increased capacity for heterosexual arousal. Of the total series of 100, 25 who had received psychotherapy were compared with a matched group of another 25 out of the 100 who had not received psychotherapy of any kind. The mean follow-up was four and a half years. At that time no difference could be found between the two groups in sexual orientation.

Two papers reporting homosexuals treated by psychotherapy at the Portman Clinic are only slightly more optimistic. The Portman specialises in the study and treatment of delinquency, so that a large proportion of the homosexuals treated there are referrals from the Courts. The first series was reported by Woodward (1958) and consists of 113 cases discharged from the Portman Clinic in 1952 and 1953. The breakdown of the sample, in terms of Kinsey ratings, was similar to that of Curran and Parr. Unfortunately, in very few of the reported series of treated homosexuals is there direct information on pretreatment heterosexual history.

Of the series, 97 were recommended for treatment, of whom 81 actually started it, and 64 patients either completed their treatment or interrupted it for some good reason, of whom 48 were regarded as having satisfactorily completed the treatment. Of the 48, 33 received 29 sessions of psychotherapy or less. While many psychotherapists would regard this as a rather small number of sessions, 29 hours (sessions) is rather longer than is received by the majority of patients in aversion therapy. Woodward states that 21 of the 48 had 'no homosexual impulse' on completion of treatment. Neither, however, did they have any heterosexual impulses. It is a frequent finding (Feldman and MacCulloch, 1971) that patients relapse unless it has been possible to replace homosexual by heterosexual interests. Only 7 out of the 48 showed such a re-orientation of sexual interest. All 7 had a Kinsey rating of five or less at the outset of treatment, and 6 of the 7 were aged under 30. Follow-up data on this series are so scanty that the only tentative conclusion that could be drawn is that in a series of patients largely referred by the Courts and treated by psychotherapy only about 15 per cent responded to treatment with both reducd homosexual interest and increased heterosexual interest.

A further series of 45 homosexuals treated at the Portman Clinic was reported by Coates (1962). Data on length of treatment are provided for 33 of the sample, 14 of whom received 300 sessions or more and 19 less than 300 sessions. No distinction is made in presenting the follow-up data between those who had completed, and those who were still undergoing, treatment. In these follow-up reports, 5 of those receiving more than 300 sessions were considered definitely improved as compared with none of those who received less than 300.

Much the largest scale psychoanalytic study is that reported by Beiber et al. (1963). They report a series of 106 homosexual males and a comparison group of 100 heterosexual males all of whom had been treated by 77 American psychoanalysts. Of the 106 homosexual patients 78 had a heterosexual genital experience, and 55 of these had experienced successful heterosexual intercourse at some stage prior to treatment. At the time the data on the results of treatment were collected, 74 of the total series had terminated psychoanalysis, while 32 had not yet done so. Only 2 of the 28 patients who had received fewer than 150 sessions were exclusively heterosexual at the time of report. The success rate of those with pretreatment heterosexual experience was just under 40 per cent; none of the primary type was successful. The total failure with those who had never had any prior heterosexual experience is found throughout all the reported series, both those treated by psychotherapy and aversion therapy.

The relatively high degree of success reported by Bieber et al. as compared with the three previous psychotherapy series, may reflect both the highly selective nature of a fee-paying sample, and a great deal of effort represented by several hundred hours of treatment. Moreover, there is no knowledge of the degree of selection in reporting exercised by the 77 psychoanalysts represented in the Bieber series.

There are two other reports of series of patients treated by psychotherapy, both of which claim a considerable degree of success. The first is by Ellis (1956) who reported on 28 males and 12 females treated for 'homosexual problems'. Ellis states that his emphasis was not on inducing his patients to forgo homosexual activities; it was rather to free the homosexual from fear or antagonism towards heterosexual relations. Hence, Ellis puts his emphasis on desensitising heterosexual avoidance rather than averting the patient from his interest in his own sex. He claims 64 per cent of his male patients, and 100 per cent of his female patients were either 'improved' or 'considerably improved'. The meaning of these terms is not stated, nor are data provided on the length of follow up or on the selection of patients. It is possible to interpret the post-treatment behaviour of Ellis's patients as indicating an increase in heterosexual activity, accompanied by the continuance of homosexual activity.

Allen (1958) is similarly optimistic, but in view of the paucity of data presented by him and the strong possibility of bias in selection, very little weight can be attached to his results.

A series of three cases has been reported by Ovesey et al. (1963). Despite the small number of cases, this series is of interest because of the explicit emphasis of the therapists on the reduction of heterosexual avoidance, even though this tends to be phrased in psychoanalytic language.

Many psychoanalysts would seem to accept the

1938 dictum of Freund, cited by Jones (1964): 'In a certain number of cases we succeed . . . in the majority of cases it is no longer possible . . . the results of our treatment cannot be predicted' (page 624).

To conclude: despite a very large number of sessions, which in the psychoanalytic form of psychotherapy can exceed 350 hours, the best reported outcome of treatment by this method is no more than 40 per cent in the secondary type of homosexuality, in a possibly selected sample of fee-paying patients. Also of interest is the very explicit emphasis, by some psychotherapists, on the need for the reduction of heterosexual avoidance in homosexual patients.

Behaviour Therapy

Although *aversion therapy* has been used for many years in the treatment of alcoholism (Franks, 1960) prior to the 1950s, there appears to be only one reference (Max, 1935) to the treatment of sexual deviations by aversion therapy. Max used a classical conditioning approach in which the patient fantasised the attractive sexual stimulus in conjunction with electric shocks. Four months after treatment the patient reported a '95 per cent degree of success', but no further details are given. Max foreshadowed the emphasis on electrical aversion which marks the current literature on the treatment of homosexuality.

The first series of homosexual patients treated by aversion therapy was reported by Freund (1960). He administered to his patients a mixture of caffeine and apomorphine, and the number of sessions of treatment never exceeded 24. When the emetic mixture became effective, slides of dressed and undressed men were shown to the patients. During a second phase of treatment, the patient was shown films of nude, or semi-nude women, seven hours after he had been administered testosterone propionate. Sixty-seven patients are reported in this paper; treatment was refused to none. Out of 20 Court referrals, only 3 achieved any kind of heterosexual adaptation, and in no case did this last more than a few weeks. The first follow up was carried out after three years. Out of the 47 patients who presented other than due to Court referral, 12 had shown some long-term adaptation. A second follow-up two years later traced the histories of these 12. At that time none of them could claim complete absence of homosexual desire, and only 6 a complete absence of homosexual behaviour. Of the group of 12, 3 were practising homosexual behaviour fairly frequently. Although 10 had heterosexual intercourse at least once every two weeks, only 3 found females other than their wives sexually desirable. (On a commonsense basis this would seem likely to be encountered relatively rarely in heterosexual individuals.) The results of Freund did not engender optimism about the use of chemical aversion. However, his is one of the few series in the field that includes a satisfactorily long follow-up.

Freund used a classical conditioning procedure, as did McGuire and Vallance (1964), in the first reported series that used electrical, rather than chemical, aversion. In their technique the patient was required to signal to the therapist when the image of his usual fantasy was clear. When he did so a shock was administered, and the procedure was repeated throughout a twenty to thirty minute session, which was held up to six times a day. A major interest in this report is the fact that the patient was provided with a completely portable electrical apparatus so that he was able to treat himself in his own home. He was told to use this apparatus whenever he was tempted to indulge in the fantasy concerned.

One doubt (Feldman, 1966) concerning this technique lies in the interpretation of the term 'clear'. If this meant that the patient had achieved a completed representation of his usual fantasy, it might be that the authors were carrying out a variety of punishment learning (Estes, 1944). In this paradigm, the noxious stimulus occurs following the completion of the undesired response. Estes reported that the extinction of a newly acquired avoidance response (in animal subjects) was particularly rapid with this technique.

Perhaps a more important doubt is that the patient himself was free to set the level of the shock. Sandler (1964) has discussed the concept of masochism, defining this as the situation in which a noxious stimulus does not result in the subject receiving it displaying avoidance behaviour, but conversely it appears not only to be tolerated but even sought after. In one variety of masochistic behaviour, aversive stimuli might be paired with the reinforcer that followed a given activity. The end result might be that 'the aversive stimulus becomes positively reinforcing in the same process' (Skinner, 1953, p. 367). Writing from a psychoanalytic point of view, Fenichel (1945) states: 'Certain experiences may have so firmly established the conviction that sexual pleasure must be associated with pain, that suffering has become the prerequisite for homosexual pleasure' (page 357). In the context of the McGuire and Vallance technique it might be that self-treating patients would use a fairly low level of shock. This level might then become associated with a very well-reinforced event, namely sexual gratification, so that it might serve as a positive reinforcer. Thus, far from the electric shock being aversive, it might simply become part of the normal fantasy situation.

McGuire and Vallance (1964) present the result of treatment for six homosexual patients of whom three discontinued treatment and three showed an improvement. They also state that the follow-up time in most cases was one month; a much longer one is clearly required. In a later paper (McGuire et al., 1965) these workers claimed 'at least as good results as the more elaborate mimes and cues provided by other aversion therapists' (p. 187). Unfortunately, they provided no data to support their claim.

A further series of homosexual patients treated by electrical aversion, was reported by Schmidt et al. (1965). A detailed critique of three earlier papers by this group (Thorpe et al., 1963; Thorpe and Schmidt, 1964; and Thorpe et al., 1964) in each of which one case was described, is provided by Feldman (1966). In their 1965 paper they report 42 cases displaying a wide variety of problems including homosexuality. Of the 42, 16 were diagnosed as homosexual, and of these 13 were treated by 'aversion relief therapy'. A disc containing up to 24 appropriate words, e.g. homosexual and its synonyms, was prepared for each patient. In each instance the last word on the disc was associated with heterosexual behaviour. The patient was told to read the word aloud, as it appeared in an illuminated aperture for about two and a half seconds, about ten seconds being allowed between each word. As he did so he received a shock; if he failed to do so he received a more intense shock. In each session there were five such trials, each having a different number and order of words, but all were terminated by relief words. Each trial was separated by five minutes, and about one session a day was administered. The rationale behind shocking the patient as he read a homosexual word clearly involved classical conditioning. The rationale behind shocking him when he failed to do so is somewhat less clear. It could be argued in fact that he was shocked for *avoiding* the previously attractive stimulus, the avoidance response having been set up by the classical conditioning procedure. This is analogous to the finding of Solomon et al. (1953) in which they found that in order to extinguish the instrumental anticipatory avoidance response in dogs, they had to shock the dog for avoiding.

Ten of the 16 homosexual patients were described by the authors as practising homosexuals and 6 as latent homosexuals, the latter term seeming to mean those whose homosexual behaviour was confined to their fantasy lives. Seven of the 10 practising homosexuals refused to continue with treatment before it was judged to have been completed. However effective a technique, if some aspect of it is so distasteful to the patient that he leaves treatment prematurely, the practical value of the technique

must be doubtful. The remaining 3 patients were described as being markedly improved on discharge from treatment. Five of the 6 latent homosexuals were described on discharge as being markedly improved and one as moderately improved. The follow-up data on the homosexual patients were provided as an undifferentiated part of the data on all the patients in the series. Hence, no conclusions can be drawn on the long-term effectiveness of this form of aversion therapy.

McConaghy (1969) reported a series of 20 homosexual patients who were randomly assigned either to apomorphine aversion therapy, or aversion relief therapy (a modified version of the Thorpe et al. technique). The objective index of changes in sexual orientation was provided by penile pleythsmography (discussed earlier in this chapter in the section on the assessment of homosexual behaviour, when serious doubts about the usefulness of the technique were raised). The penile plethysmograph response was assessed two weeks after therapy, and was compared to the changes in such responses in a control group of 20 subjects who had not received any treatment over the same period. McConaghy reports a trend for more patients to improve following apomorphine aversion, than after aversion relief therapy. However, the difference was not statistically significant.

McConaghy states that a greater number of patients with previous heterosexual experience received the apormorphine therapy. In addition, in view of the doubts raised above concerning the Thorpe et al. technique, the possible inadequacy of the plethysmograph response as an indicant of change, and particularly the very short period of follow-up, further reports from McConaghy must be awaited before his results can be fully evaluated. It can be said at the present stage, that his conclusion concerning the greater adequacy of apomorphine aversion as compared to electrical aversion is quite unacceptable.

A report by Meyer (1966) seems at first sight to describe a controlled trial of psychoanalysis and behaviour therapy in the treatment of homosexuality. In fact, it is a comparison between the series separately reported by Freund (1960) and by Bieber et al. (1963). Meyer's conclusion that the Bieber series showed a higher degree of success is obviously inadmissible. The comparison was between a sample of possibly selected fee-paying American patients treated by highly trained analysts, and a sample of patients from Eastern Europe, probably unselected, receiving less than one sixth of the hours of treatment of the Bieber series and treated by a technically unsound form of aversion therapy (*see* Rachman and Teasdale, 1969, and Feldman and

MacCulloch, 1971, for detailed arguments supporting electrical as against apomorphine aversion, the more important of which are given later in this chapter).

Bancroft has recently contributed two reports on the behavioural treatment of homosexual patients. The first of these (Bancroft, 1969) consists of a series of 10 cases treated by a method that combined features from techniques reported by several other workers. The patient was asked to produce his homosexual fantasies while looking at photographs of males, and whenever an erection developed beyond a predetermined threshold, as measured by the penile plethysmograph, he received an electric shock. Each session also included two further types of trial; one homosexual trial with no threat of shock, and three heterosexual trials in which photographs of females were used and the patient was encouraged to produce heterosexual fantasy. This last variant was hoped to have an 'anxiety relief' effect. In addition, the McGuire and Vallance (1964) technique was used with 3 of the 10 patients. Each patient received between 30 and 40 sessions, each lasting from one to one and a half hours. All patients who asked for treatment were offered it, and all were followed up for a period of two years. Although 7 of the 10 patients showed 'significant changes in sexual activities following treatment' in only 3 were such changes sustained, and 'in only one can the result be called completely successful'.

Several criticisms may be made of this report. First, no details were provided as to whether the same male photographs were used for all patients or whether they were tailored to each patient's particular interests. Nor did Bancroft state whether they were presented in a hierarchical order of attractiveness or in random order. The doubts concerning the validity of the plethysmograph technique have been outlined earlier in this chapter. Bancroft (1969) agrees that the penile response criterion provides a poor discriminative stimulus for the patient, and concludes 'a clear and equivocal type of response is perhaps more likely to be effective. MacCulloch and Feldman's method may be superior in this respect' (p. 1429). (An account of the Feldman and MacCulloch technique follows shortly.) The Bancroft technique took a minimum of 30, and a possible maximum, of 60 hours of skilled time. In evaluating any treatment, both its *efficiency* as well as its *efficacy* have to be taken into account. Bancroft does, however, provide a considerable amount of interesting data, and his paper is one of the more praiseworthy efforts in a difficult field.

In his second report, Bancroft (personal communication, 1969) describes the treatment of two groups

each containing 15 homosexual patients, the first being treated by desensitisation, and the second by the aversive technique described in his 1969 paper. Both methods involved 30 sessions of treatment, on an out-patient basis, usually twice a week. The dependent variables were sexual behaviour ratings based on interview, penile erections to homo- and heterosexual stimuli as measured by the penile plethysmograph, and sexual attitudes before, during, and after treatment as measured by a semantic differential technique. Bancroft concludes; 'there was very little difference to choose between them with a slight edge to desensitisation. Because of the unpleasantness of aversion it would seem that desensitisation was the treatment of choice. But it is quite possible that some cases would do better with aversion and these are likely to be with the younger male with low general anxiety but with some anxiety in relation to homosexuality before treatment.' He notes that one effect of the aversive method was to increase heterosexual erections. Bancroft (1969) has also noted that there was a re-emergence in the later stages of treatment of initially suppressed homosexual erections. This 'paradoxical' effect throws further doubt both on the particular technique of aversion therapy used, and on the penile plethysmograph as the dependent measure of the effect of treatment.

In a series of papers published between 1964 and 1971, Feldman and MacCulloch have carried out a sustained investigation into the treatment of homosexuality by anticipatory avoidance learning. The attraction of this technique to its authors was that it produced an avoidance response with a reasonably good rate of acquisition and a very high resistance to extinction (Solomon and Brush, 1956). Turner and Solomon (1962) extended the anticipatory avoidance technique to humans, and found the same results as were obtained earlier with dogs. Solomon et al. (1968) carried out further research on avoidance learning in dogs, but instead of a neutral stimulus (buzzer) they used an attractive and very strongly learned stimulus (meat) as the CS. Finally, the same technique was used with child subjects by Aronfreed and Reber (1965); in this case the attractive stimulus was a toy, and the aversive stimulus verbal disapproval. A common factor throughout the above research was the finding of a greater resistance to extinction when the aversive stimulus was applied at an early point, as opposed to later, in the behaviour sequence.

A detailed account of the Feldman and MacCulloch technique is provided in Feldman and MacCulloch, 1965 and 1971. Briefly, the situation is as follows. The homosexual patient views a male slide which is back-projected on to a screen. He is instructed to leave the picture on for as long as he finds it attractive. After the slide has been on the screen for eight seconds, the patient receives a shock if he has not by then removed it by means of a switch with which he is provided. If he does switch it off within the eight-second period, he avoids the shock.

Once the patient is avoiding regularly, he is placed on a standardised reinforcement schedule, which consists of three types of trial, randomly interspersed. The first type consists of reinforced trials (the patient's attempt to switch off succeeds immediately). The second consists of delay trials (the patient's attempt to switch off is held up for varying intervals of time within the eight-second period. He does, however, eventually succeed in avoiding). Finally, one-third of all trials are non-reinforced (the patient receives a shock irrespective of his attempts to switch off), the eventual termination of shock and slide removal being contiguous and associated with an avoidance response. In addition, on two-fifths of the trials, selected at random, a female slide is projected onto the screen at the request of the patient, contiguous with the removal of the male slide, and is left on for about ten seconds. It is then removed by the therapist and the patient can, if he wishes, request that it be returned. However, his request is met in an entirely random manner.

A further feature is the use of hierarchies of male and female slides. The patient places the slides in the order of attractiveness for him, so that treatment starts with the least attractive male slide being paired with the most attractive female slide; the two hierarchies then being moved along simultaneously. The interstimulus interval varies between 15 and 45 seconds randomly, and about 24 stimulus presentations (trials) are given per session, which lasts about 20 minutes.

MacCulloch and Feldman (1967a) reported the results of treatment of an unselected series of 43 homosexual patients treated by anticipatory avoidance learning, all of whom had been followed up for at least one year. Nearly 60 per cent of the cases were considered successfully treated at the end of the follow-up period. Success was defined as a cessation of homosexual behaviour, the use of no more than occasional and mild homosexual fantasy and/or mild homosexual interest in directly observed males together with at least strong heterosexual fantasy and, in the majority of cases, overt heterosexual behaviour. The post-treatment measures used to ascertain change, if any, were a structured clinical interview, and the Sexual Orientation Method questionnaire (Feldman et al., 1966). In addition, within-treatment measures were taken of avoidance response latencies, and changes in pulse rate to the male slides used as conditional stimuli. Illustrative examples of the last two measures were provided by MacCulloch et al. (1965).

There was a marked tendency for all the measures to cohere in indicating change, or lack of change. The most clearcut favourable prognostic sign was a pre-treatment history of pleasurable heterosexual behaviour, at some time in the patient's life history. The next most favourable sign was the absence of a disorder of personality of the weak-willed or attention-seeking types (using the classification of Schneider, 1959). Detailed data on the relationship between clinically assessed personality and the outcome of treatment were provided by MacCulloch and Feldman (1967b). In the latter report it was shown that there was a relationship between personality and outcome even with age controlled.

The satisfactory degree of success obtained in their series of 43 prompted the same authors to carry out a controlled trial of anticipatory avoidance learning, classical conditioning, and psychotherapy in the treatment of homosexuality. This is described in detail in Feldman and MacCulloch (1971). The use of classical conditioning was intended to control for the possibility that a classical (Pavlovian) explanation could partially account for the comparative degree of success obtained in the series of 43 (a possibility strongly argued by Rachman and Teasdale, 1969). Psychotherapy was intended to control for the possible contribution to success of a positive relationship between therapist and patient. In contrast to the policy which obtained with the series of 43, 5 potential patients were excluded from the controlled trial on various grounds; patients with no prior pleasurable heterosexual history were not excluded as the major importance of this variable was not then appreciated. The follow-up was at least three months, and averaged 44 weeks.

Both avoidance learning techniques were successful with the majority of patients who had a prior heterosexual history (secondary homosexuals); psychotherapy was initially successful with two such patients, but both quickly relapsed. All three treatments were almost totally unsuccessful with patients with no prior pleasurable heterosexual history (primary homosexuals). Patients who failed with psychotherapy were randomly assigned to one of the two learning techniques. A severe personality disorder of the attention-seeking or weak-willed types (Schneider, 1959) was once more associated with failure to respond to treatment in the secondary homosexuals.

Combining the series of 43 and the controlled trial (Table 5.1) 70 per cent of secondary homosexuals were successfully treated by aversion

Table 5.1.   Response to Avoidance Learning
The association between homosexual type (primary or secondary) and success at latest follow-up in response to avoidance learning. Series and trial patients are combined.

	Primary	*Secondary*	*Total*
Sucess	5	36	41
Failure	12	10	22
Total	17	46	63

$\chi^2 = 12{\cdot}21, P = 0{\cdot}001$

therapy (AA or CC, see later for a discussion of the two techniques of aversion). This figure is considerably superior to the 40 per cent rate of success in the Bieber *et al.* (1963) series (*see* above). Even if it were no better, the treatment of choice, psychoanalysis or aversion therapy, would be the latter, in view of its vastly more efficient use of therapist time (the average number of sessions per patient in the Feldman and MacCulloch series was between 20 and 24), as well as the relative rarity of trained psychoanalysts.

J. F. Orford (in Feldman and MacCulloch, 1971) carried out a psychometric study on the 30 patients in the trial and showed that the combination of a pretreatment history of heterosexual practice—which correlated very highly with the pretreatment SOM heterosexual scores—and a combined personality scale (contributed to by the personality of the patient as clinically assessed and the C scale of the 16PF) predicted the outcome of treatment almost perfectly (*see* Table 5.2). If these results are confirmed by other workers (Mellor, personal communication, 1970, has reported this to have occurred) then the following procedures should be systematically applied in the selection for treatment of homosexual patients by anticipatory avoidance learning (AA). Only patients who have pretreatment SOM heterosexual scores of 20 or more (the scale goes from 6 to 48), and in addition score beyond a cut-off point of 2 on the combined measure of personality, would be regarded as suitable for treatment by avoidance learning (AA or CC). Patients who are either of 'poor' personality, irrespective of heterosexual interest, or are of the

primary heterosexual type, irrespective of personality, are very likely to fail with either AA or CC.

At least two major problems remain from the work carried out by Feldman and MacCulloch. First, there is as yet no treatment available that is successful with the primary type of homosexual; in view of the fact that a proportion of such individuals have a very strong desire to change their sexual orientation, it is highly desirable that research should be carried out towards the development of a technique that will be effective. Secondly, there is a need to quantify the findings on personality predictors obtained by Feldman and MacCulloch. The clinical interview has been useful in showing the desirable direction of research on the relationship between personality and outcome; ultimately, a method of assessment that is completely communicable and generalisable is required.

Several reports have appeared to date of other therapists using the anticipatory avoidance technique. Among these are Hawks (personal communication, 1970) who reports the treatment of 3 homosexuals and 1 fetishist, in all instances successfully, although follow-up data are incomplete; Stern (1969) who very briefly reports the treatment of 20 homosexual patients 'the degree of success being the same as that obtained by Feldman and MacCulloch', and Levin *et al.* (1968) who supplemented by desensitisation the AA technique, which they used without the incorporation of heterosexual relief stimuli. Hawks's report is of particular interest, in that he combined both auditory and visual homosexual stimuli.

Because of the ethical qualms felt by many therapists at inflicting electric shocks on patients, attempts have been made to develop the techniques of *covert desensitisation* (Gold and Neufeld, 1965; Barlow *et al.*, 1969). This technique involves the patient visualising a succession of homosexual images in association with unpleasant suggestions such as physical nausea. Later sessions include imagining both attractive females associated with pleasant suggestions, and homosexual stimuli associated with unpleasant suggestions. A detailed account of the covert sensitisation technique, though mainly as applied to alcholism, is provided by Rachman and Teasdale (1969). A major argument against the use of the technique is that which applies to the use of fantasy stimuli in general. The reduced degree of control by the therapist over the stimuli may not be sufficient compensation for the improvement in the ethical aspects of treatment allowed by the use of covert techniques. As yet, the only reports available of the treatment of homosexual behaviour by covert sensitisation are single cases or very small series of cases.

Other than the trial of desensitisation and aversion

Table 5.2.   The Success Rates of the Four 'Types' of Homosexual Patient generated by combining Personality and Pre-Treatment Heterosexual Scores

Personality	*Pre-treatment SOM heterosexual score*	
	Less than 20	*20 or more*
'Good'	3/6 successes	13/14 successes
'Poor'	0/4 successes	0/3 successes

described by Bancroft (*see* above) there are few reports of the use of systematic desensitisation in the treatment of homosexuality. Stevenson and Wolpe (1960) reported 3 patients, 2 of whom were homosexuals, treated by desensitisation which was intended to increase assertive behaviour towards other people in general, and to females in particular. Both cases were described as being completely successful after a follow up of at least three years. Kraft (1967) also reports the successful use of systematic desensitisation with a single homosexual patient. It should not be thought that there is necessarily a complete opposition in technique between aversion therapy and desensitisation. Indeed, Feldman and Mac-Culloch (1971) have conceptualised their anticipatory avoidance method as combining both aversion and desensitisation within the same technique. (It will be recalled that the attempt is made to associate the relief of anxiety the patient feels when the homosexual slide leaves the screen with the appearance of the female slide.)

The desensitisation of heterosexual anxiety is inevitably an indirect approach to the problem of increasing heterosexual approach behaviour.

Feldman (1968) has strongly urged the desirability of research on the acquisition of such behaviour. The first direct attempt to solve this problem was reported by Quinn *et al.* (1970) who carried out a pilot study of the acquisition by heterosexual stimulus of discriminative control over phallic responses in a secondary homosexual patient who had partially relapsed from an earlier reduction in homosexual interest following AA treatment. Prior to each session of treatment he was placed on 18 hours fluid deprivation, as an antecedent for behaviour control with fluid reinforcement. He also received three doses of sodium chloride and one dose of an oral diuretic to increase the effect of fluid deprivation. The receipt, at the end of each of the ten sessions of treatment, of the reward (a drink of iced lime) was consequent on either 30 phallic responses to female slides (monitored by the plethysmograph, and signalled to the patient by a cue light) or the passing of 45 minutes. There was a marked change in the amplitude of the heterosexual phallic response from the beginning to the end of the experiment, together with concomitant changes in SOM scores (Feldman *et al.*, 1966).

2. TRANSVESTISM AND FETISHISM

The behaviour therapy literature on the treatment of transvestism and fetishism is largely restricted to single case studies. Examples are reports by Raymond (1956), Oswald (1962), Cooper (1963), and Clark (1963) all of whom paired fetishistic stimuli with apomorphine-induced nausea. Barker (1965) reported the treatment of two transvestite patients, one by apomorphine aversion, the other by electrical aversion. A detailed critique of the above reports is provided by Feldman (1966). Further single case reports, which appeared after the completion of Feldman's review (mid-1965), include Raymond and O'Keefe (1965), and Davison (1967). This last report is of some technical interest in that the patient, whose problem concerned sadism, was treated without the use of an aversive stimulus. Instead, socially acceptable heterosexual stimuli were paired with the sexual feelings aroused by the patient's sadistic fantasy.

There are only four reports in this field, which consist of more than one or two patients. The first of these is a series of 19 transvestite patients reported by Morgenstern *et al.* (1965). Of these patients, 6 relapsed after completing treatment but practised much less frequently than prior to treatment, and seven ceased to cross-dress altogether. The 13 patients who completed treatment received 39 sessions given three times a day. Apomorphine was used

as the aversive stimulus, and injections were graded so that the peak effect of nausea and vomiting coincided with the completion of the cross-dressing ritual. The authors report on the relationship of a battery of tests to the treatment outcome, the most significant relationship being that between outcome and a verbal conditioning (instrumental) procedure whereas eyeblink (classical) conditioning showed no relationship with outcome. Only the cured patients showed evidence of verbal conditioning. Morgenstern *et al.* conclude that an instrumental form of conditioning is involved in aversion therapy, a conclusion that is vigorously attacked by Rachman and Teasdale (1969).

McGuire and Vallence (1964) reported eight varied cases of sexual deviation treated by associating fantasy with self-administered electric shocks. All eight were stated to have improved. In no case did the follow-up exceed one month.

Feldman and colleagues (1967) described the treatment by anticipatory avoidance learning of a heterogeneous group of 5 cases of sexual deviation, 2 of whom complained of transvestite behaviour; for one the fetish object was females many years older than himself. The technique of treatment was very similar to that used for the homosexual patients treated by this group of workers. In each instance a photograph of the deviant sexual stimulus was used

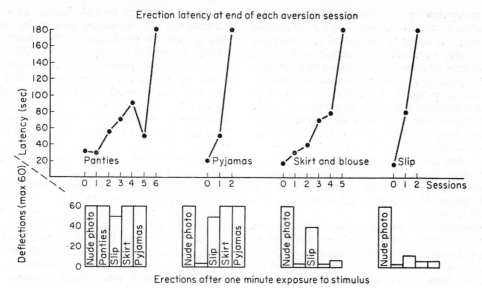

Fig. 5.1. The selective effect of electrical aversion

Reductions in sexual reaction are restricted to treated items. (*Courtesy* Marks and Gelder (1967) and the Editor of the *British Journal of Psychiatry*)

as the CS. In the case of the 2 transvestite patients this consisted of a series of photographs of the patient wearing his transvestite clothing in a hierarchical order of attractiveness. Relief stimuli consisted of photographs of the wife or girl friend of the patient. Two of the above 3 patients improved completely in response to treatment; the partial improvement of the third was attributed by the authors to his wife being a most unwilling sexual partner, so that there was no alternative sexual outlet for the suppressed transvestite behaviour.

Much the most detailed report of the treatment of fetishist patients was provided by Marks and Gelder (1967), who described a group of 5 patients all of whom were treated as in-patients by electrical aversion. In the early stages of treatment the shock was delivered when the patient imagined himself in a sexually provocative and arousing situation which incorporated some features of his deviant behaviour. In the second stage of treatment the patients were shocked when they carried out the deviant behaviour in reality, such as putting on female clothing. The shock was delivered on an intermittent schedule—

approximately one quarter of all trials were non-shocked and the penile plethysmograph was used to monitor the progress of treatment throughout; further monitoring was made possible by the use of a version of the Osgood Semantic Differential technique.

Many interesting findings came out of this work. For example, with repeated exposure to the aversive stimulus, the patients' reported increasing difficulty in fantasising the fetish image. Moreover, the time taken to obtain the image increased, and in several instances the patients reached a point when they were unable to obtain the images at all (*see* Fig. 5.1). It was also shown that the change in ability to obtain the abnormal sexual image was probably attributable to the effects of the aversive stimulation and not to simple habituation effects. With increasing time in treatment there was an increasing difficulty in obtaining an erectile response to the fetishistic stimulus. Finally, there was a remarkable specificity of the erectile changes in treatment to the particular stimuli that had been associated with the aversive stimulus.

3. THEORETICAL PROBLEMS IN AVERSION THERAPY

(a) Electrical vs. Chemical Aversion

Despite a revival of apomorphine aversion (McConaghy, 1969) there is wide agreement on the superiority of electrical aversion (Rachman and

Teasdale, 1969; Feldman and MacCulloch, 1971) for the following reasons; electrical stimulation can be precisely controlled; the shock can be given for a precise period of time, at a measured intensity and at exactly the desired moment. These variables can all be manipulated as the therapist desires, so that the treatment situation becomes much more flexible. Moreover, it is easier to use partial reinforcement, and this may be particularly important from the point of view of increasing resistance to extinction. It is also possible to make more accurate measurements of the progress of treatment—the data on avoidance response latencies, and autonomic events, reported by Feldman and MacCulloch (1971) would not have been possible with the use of chemical aversive stimuli. The use of an electrical aversive stimulus does not require more than one therapist to be present; hence it is less arduous to administer. The likelihood of physical side effects, particularly of of a dangerous kind, is also rather less than with chemical aversion.

In contrast to these advantages of electrical aversion, the arduous and complicated nature of the chemical aversive conditioning situation makes it impracticable to provide frequent repetitions of the association between the conditioned and unconditioned stimuli. The number of trials within any one session is therefore considerably limited. A further restriction is the heavy demands made on the nursing staff. These demands are not only in terms of time but also of the unpleasantness of the situation, which has frequently led to complaints from nursing staff (Rachman and Teasdale, 1969).

However, Rachman and Teasdale (1969) have drawn attention to the disadvantages of electrical aversion. For instance, the administration of electrical aversive stimuli in laboratory experiments has been known to give rise to aggressive behaviour. Similar reports have been given of aggressiveness, negativism, and hostility in clinical practice. People sometimes have an initial fear of electric shocks even before experiencing them in the clinical situation. This emphasises the importance of using a level of shock no higher than that just necessary to lead to avoidance behaviour. Bombarding the patient with very high levels of shock may only result in his leaving the treatment situation prematurely.

(b) Classical vs. Instrumental Conditioning

One aspect of this controversy centres around whether the effects of aversion therapy, irrespective of the stated nature of the technique, are explicable by a classical or an instrumental model. Rachman and Teasdale (1969) argue strongly for the former. The results of the controlled trial of anticipatory avoidance learning and classical conditioning carried out by Feldman and MacCulloch (1971) might seem to support the classical conditioning point of view. However, in discussing the results of their trial, Feldman and MacCulloch (1971) point

out that there are several factors in common between the two techniques as used by them, so that a clear-cut conclusion of the source of the effects of aversion therapy is not possible. Firstly, both techniques provided an alternative sexual outlet by the use of heterosexual relief slides. Secondly, the classical conditioning technique as used in the trial involved the onset of the male slide some two seconds before the onset of the shock. That is, it served as a warning signal in an unavoidable shock situation. Thirdly, a proportion of trials in the AA technique were non-reinforced (were associated with shock). Despite these important points in which the two techniques overlapped, it is quite clear that the provision for patients of response manipulanda is not a necessary element for the success of treatment by aversion therapy.

It has been argued, by Feldman and MacCulloch (1971), that despite the lack of difference in efficacy of outcome, the anticipatory avoidance technique is potentially very much more efficient. Firstly, avoidance response latencies provide a constant flow of quantitative information positively correlated with the rate of response to treatment. Examples of such avoidance latency data from a successfully treated, and an unsuccessfully treated, patient are given in Fig. 5.2.

It should be possible systematically to modify the course of treatment as a function of the response latencies of the patient, in order to maximise the speed, and hence the efficiency, of treatment. This is partially achieved by an automated aversion therapy apparatus described by MacCulloch et al. (1971). An even more satisfactory development would be to control the aversion therapy procedure by computer, on-line to the patient, so that there was an immediate matching of the form of the next trial to the outcome of the immediately previous one. Such a development is now under way (MacCulloch, personal communication, 1970). The increased potential efficiency of treatment by the anticipatory avoidance technique, because of the constant feed-back of information, enables the saving both of patient time (and hence of time away from employment) and of therapist time (and hence, an increased number of patients treatable in any given unit of time).

The second argument for preferring the AA technique is that a higher level of heart rate during treatment tends to be associated with a successful response (Feldman and MacCulloch, 1971). It should be possible, again because of the flexibility of the AA technique, deliberately to produce the optimal level of autonomic activity for rapid avoidance learning. It is less easy to do so in the CC situation—the fact that the shock is used on every trial makes the monitoring of autonomic measures very

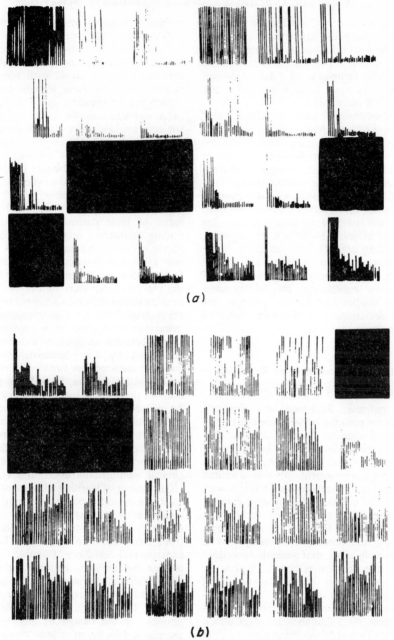

Fig. 5.2. Automatically recorded avoidance latencies

(a) Sessions 1–13, 16–17, 20–24. The conditioned stimulus (male slide) was changed every three sessions. There was a tendency for a greater proportion of longer latencies in sessions 1, 4, 7, 10 compared with sessions 3, 6, 9, 12

(b) Sessions 1–5, 9–24. Compare with (a) the relative lack of contrast between sessions 1 and 3, 10 and 12, 13 and 15, etc.

difficult. Nor does the CC technique provide information concerning the latency of avoidance responses. The flow of information during the AA technique also makes it possible, at any rate in theory, to use the technique of false feed-back (Valins, 1966). This may further maximise the efficiency of the AA technique.

On a more fundamental level, the elegant and crucial experiments of Neale Miller and his colleagues (e.g. Miller, 1969) have provided powerful evidence that instrumental learning can produce changes in many autonomic variables once thought modifiable solely by classical conditioning techniques, and then only to a limited and uncertain degree. Such changes cannot be accounted for in classical terms, and have been found to be relatively long lasting in rats—up to at least three months. Miller's work suggests, first (as he has long argued) the artificiality of the traditional distinction between classical and instrumental learning, and secondly, the great range of visceral responses modifiable by instrumental techniques. The implications for the therapy, not only of sexual deviations, but of a wide range of problems, are enormous.

(c) Generalisation from Treatment to Real Life

In discussing the results of Marks and Gelder (1967) with fetishist patients, Rachman and Teasdale (1969) point out the paradox between the apparently selective effects of aversion therapy, and the fact that these effects generalised to the behaviour of the patients in the external world. They state, 'it is evident that during the treatment only a very limited number of deviant stimuli can be dealt with. Nevertheless the effects of aversion therapy appear to be widespread. These effects spread from the clinic to the external world from a few selective sexual items to a wide range of stimulated conditions' (page 49). That is, they agree, in effect, that generalisation does occur, and that the problem is how to explain its occurrence. Later in their book, Rachman and Teasdale also comment on their difficulty in understanding how the equally specific behaviour manipulated in treatment by Feldman and MacCulloch (1971) generalised to real life situations works ('the surprising thing about aversion therapy is not that its effects are uncertain but that it works at all').

In attempting to account for the occurrence of generalisation, Feldman and MacCulloch (1971) begin by referring to a review of the concept of incubation (Eysenck, 1968). He cites reports of an increment in response when the CS is presented alone, in the absence of the UCS. Feldman and MacCulloch (1971) report an experiment on two normal volunteers who received three sessions of anticipatory avoidance learning. At the end of the third session the electrodes were removed, and the CS was presented alone for ten trials. Both subjects continued both to avoid with very short response latencies and to show physiological indicants of anxiety on the presentation of the CS alone (a slide of a squirrel, initially rated as attractive). Both subjects avoided after they knew that they could not be shocked. No attempt was made to study the possible occurrence of incubation following an interval of time after the end of the last session, a possibility that is central to the extended concept of incubation discussed below.

Feldman and MacCulloch (1970) reported that many of their patients spontaneously mentioned finding themselves in real life looking away from previously attractive males and looking at previously less attractive females, as well as rehearsing in fantasy both the sequence of events in treatment and the real life behaviours that represented the reproduction of the responses acquired in treatment. They argue that both laboratory research workers and behaviour therapists have grossly neglected the events between sessions of treatment that are uncontrolled by the therapist. Hence, additional concepts are necessary for a complete account of the generalisation process. In order to provide such an account they extend Eysenck's concept of incubation by introducing cognitive and personality variables.

Generalisation is assisted by a number of *within* treatment features, which are under the control of the therapist. One of the major differences between laboratory studies of avoidance learning and clinical administered aversion therapy is the very large number of learning trials involved in the latter, so that a considerable overlearning is likely, with a consequently greater resistance to extinction of responses learned in treatment following the transfer from treatment into real life. There is extensive experimental evidence (Kimble, 1961) that the greater the similarity between training stimuli and real-life stimuli, the smaller is the amount of extinction, and the greater the amount of transfer of training that occurs. This provides an important pointer for the design of any behaviour-therapy technique. Finally, in at least some of the aversion-therapy techniques, the patient is provided with an alternative sexual outlet to the one that is being suppressed in treatment. Unless this is done, the likelihood of a failure of generalisation is very great indeed.

In addition to the references mentioned above, useful discussions on theoretical aspects of aversion therapy have been provided by Kushner and Sandler (1966) and Wilson and Davison (1969).

4. OTHER DEVIATIONS

Because the vast majority of reports on the behaviour therapy of sexual deviations have been concerned with homosexuality (potentially this includes paedophilia), transvestism, and fetishism, only brief mention will be made of the behavioural treatment of two other types of sexual deviation, discussed earlier in this chapter, namely impotence and exhibitionism. The treatment of transsexualism will not be discussed, as the transsexual patient may desire surgical intervention to provide tangible support for his beliefs, and not behavioural modification in the other direction. Behaviour therapy appears to be contra-indicated, a conclusion supported by the total absence of published reports. Psychotherapy has been confined to superficial support.

Impotence

Cooper (1969) has provided a brief review of previous reports of treatment. The level of success obtained seemed to be low, irrespective of the technique used. Cooper carried out a treatment regime consisting of what he describes as an optimal combination of: deep muscular relaxation; the provision of optimal sexual stimulation for the male; sexual education, and psychotherapy. This regime was designed according to the individual case and is described in detail in Cooper (1968). He reports the response to therapy to be comparatively poor; 39 per cent of his series were rated as recovered or improved, while the remainder were unchanged or worse. Cooper (1969) lists a number of factors that were associated, at a level of significance of at least $p = 0.05$, with a poor outcome of treatment. The most significant prognostic factors were: premature ejaculation; insidious onset of impotence; long duration of impotence; personality disorder in the male; absence of motivation for therapy; and unwillingness or inability of the female to co-operate in treatment. The opposite of each of the above factors was significantly associated with a favourable outcome.

Cooper's is a useful preliminary study in that it begins to organise the field for more incisive research, particularly for the application of such behavioural techniques as systematic desensitisation and the sophisticated operant approach of Quinn et al. (1969).

Exhibitionism

Rosen (1964) has described the psychoanalytic treatment of a series of 24 exhibitionists who were treated by him over a two year period, but it is difficult to draw firm conclusions from his report.

Evans (1968) has reported the results of the treatment of 10 exhibitionist patients using a variant of the anticipatory avoidance technique of Feldman and MacCulloch (described in detail in Evans, 1967). All 10 patients reached the criterion of a period of six months during which they reported no further display of exhibitionist behaviour, nor any urge to do so. Evans also reports that the deviant behaviour was deconditioned more rapidly in those patients who used normal fantasy than in those who used deviant fantasy; that is, fantasies of exhibiting. This report by Evans is rather brief and more detail would be valuable. The successful treatment of an adolescent exhibitionist by AA learning has been carried out by MacCulloch (personal communication, 1970) using a specially designed apparatus.

In conclusion, a review of the literature on the treatment of sexual deviations indicates that behavioural techniques have considerable promise. The more closely the techniques are related to the findings of general experimental psychology, and the greater the emphasis on objectivity of recording and reporting, the more effective and efficient they are. The widespread occurrence of sexual deviations, and the distress felt by many of those displaying them, indicates a continuing demand for treatment, which may even increase as the possibility of a successful outcome in response to behavioural techniques becomes more widely known.

REFERENCES

ALLEN, C. (1958) *Homosexuality: Its Nature, Causation, and Treatment.* London: Staples Press.

ALTMAN, J. A. and DASS, G. (1964) Auto-radiographic and histological evidence of postnatal hippocompal neurogenis in rats. Unpublished manuscript (1964). Cited by J. Money in Hormones and Sexual Behaviour in Sex Research. In *Sexual Research: New Developments* (Ed. J. Money) New York: Rinehart & Winston.

APPEL, K. E. (1937) Endocrine studies in cases of homosexuality. *Arch. Neurol. Psychiat.*, **37**, 1206–7.

ARONFREED, J. and REBER, A. (1965) Internalised behavioural suppression and the timing of social punishment. *J. Person. Soc. Psychol.*, **1**, 3–16.

BAKER, H. J. and STOLLER, R. J. (1968) Sexual psychopathology in the hypogonadal male. *Arch. Gen. Psychiat.* **18**, 631–634.

BALL, J. R. B. (1968) A case of hair fetishism, transvestism, and organic cerebral disorder. *Acta Psychiat. Scand.*, **44**, 249–254.

BANCROFT, J. H. J. (1969) Aversion therapy of homosexuality. *Brit. J. Psychiat.*, **115**, 1417–1433.

BANCROFT, J. H. J., JONES, GWYNNE H., and PULLAN, B. (1966) A simple transducer for measuring penile erections, with comments on its use in the treatment of sexual disorders. *Behav. Res. Ther.*, **4**, 239–241.

BANDURA, A. (1969) *Behaviour Modification.* New York: Wiley.

BANDURA, A. and WALTERS, R. (1963) *Social Learning and Personality Development.* New York: Holt, Rhinehart and Winston.

BARCLAY, A. and CUSMANO, D. R. (1967) Father, absence, cross-sex identity, and field dependent behaviour in male adolescents. *Child Dev.*, **38**, 243–250.

BARKER, J. C. (1965) Behaviour therapy for transvestism. a comparison of pharmacological and electrical aversion techniques. *Brit. J. Psychiat.*, **111**, 268–276.

BARLOW, D. H., LEITENBERG, H., and AGRAS, W. S. (1969) Experimental control of sexual deviation through manipulation of the noxious scene in covert sensitization. *J. Abnorm. Psychol.*, **74**, 596–601.

BENE, EVA (1965) On the genesis of male homosexuality: an attempt at clarifying the role of the parents. *Brit. J. Psychiat.*, **3**, 803–13.

BENE, E. and ANTHONY, J. (1962) *Bene-Anthony Family Relations Test.* London: N.F.E.R.

BENJAMIN, H. (1953) Transvestism and trans-sexualism. *Int. J. Sexol.*, **7**, 12–14.

BENJAMIN, H. (1967) Transexualism. *Trans. N. Y. Acad. Sci.*, **29**, 428–433.

BERG, I. (1963) Change of assigned sex at puberty. *Lancet*, **ii**, 1216–17.

BIEBER, B., BIEBER, I., DAIN, H. J., DINCE, P. R., DRELLICH, M. G., GRAND, H. G., GRUNDLACH, R. H., KREMER, MALVINA W., WILBER, CORNELIA B., and BIEBER, T. D. (1963) *Homosexuality.* New York: Basic Books.

BINET, A. (1888) *Etudes de Psychologie Experimentale.* Paris.

BROWN, P. T. (1964) On the differentiation of homo- or hetero-erotic interest in the male: an operant technique illustrated in the case of a motor-cycle fetishist. *Behav. Res. Ther.*, **2**, 31–37.

CALIFORNIA, STATE OF (1954) Department of Mental Hygiene, California Sexual Deviations Research.

CATTELL, R. B. and MORONY, J. H. (1962) The use of the 16PF in distinguishing homosexuals, normals and general criminals. *J. Consult. Psychol.*, **26**, 531–540.

CHAPMAN, L. J., CHAPMAN, JEAN P., and BRELJE, T. (1969) Influence of the experimenter on pupillary dilation to sexually provocative pictures. *J. Abnorm. Psychol.*, **74**, 396–400.

CLARK, D. F. (1963) Fetishism treated by negative conditioning. *Brit. J. Psychol.*, **109**, 404–408.

CLARKE, R. G. V. (1965) The Slater Selective Vocabulary Test and male homosexuality. *Brit. J. Med. Psychol.*, **38**, 339–341.

COATES, S. (1962) Homosexuality and the Rorschach Test. *Brit. J. Med. Psychol.*, **35**, 177–90.

COOPER, A. J. (1963) A case of fetishism and impotence treated by behaviour therapy. *Brit. J. Psychiat.*, **109**, 649–652.

COOPER, A. J. (1968) A factual study of male potency disorders. *Brit. J. Psychiat.*, **114**, 719–730.

COOPER, A. J. (1969) Disorders of sexual potency in the male: a clinical and statistical study of some factors related to short-term prognosis. *Brit. J. Psychiat.*, **115**, 709–719.

COPPEN, A. J. (1959) Body-build of male homosexuals, *Brit. med. J.*, **2**, 1443–1445.

CURRAN, D. and PARR, D. (1957) Homosexuality: an analysis of 100 male cases seen in private practice. *Brit. med. J.*, **1**, 797–801.

DAVIDS, A., JOELSON, N., and McARTHUR, C. (1956) Rorschach and TAT indices of homosexuality in overt homosexuals, neurotics and normal males. *J. Abnorm. (Soc.) Psychol.*, **53**, 161–172.

DAVIES, B. M. and MORGENSTERN, F. S. (1960) A case of cysticercosis, temporal lobe epilepsy and transvestism. *J. Neurol. Neurosurg. Psychiat.*, **23**, 247.

DAVIDSON, G. C. (1967) The elimination of a sadistic fantasy by a client-controlled counter conditioning technique: a case study. *J. Abnorm. Psychol.*, **73**, 84–90.

DEAN, R. B. and RICHARDSON, H. (1964) Analysis of MMPI profiles of forty college-educated overt male homosexuals. *J. Consult. Psychol.*, **28**, 483–486.

DORBAR, RUTH R. (1967) Psychological testing of transsexuals: a brief report of results from the Wechsler Intelligence Scale, the Thematic Apperception Test, and the House-Tree Person Test. *Trans. N. Y. Acad. Sci.*, **29**, 455–462.

DOSHAY, L. J. (1943) *The Boy Sex Offender and His Later Career.* New York: Grune & Stratton.

ELLIS, A. (1956) The effectiveness of psycho-therapy with individuals who have severe homosexual problems. *J. Consult. Psychol.*, **20**, 58–60.

ELLIS, A. (1945) The sexual psychology of human hermaphrodites. *Psychosom. Med.*, **7**, 108–125.

EMERY, A. E., MacCULLOCH, M. J., and FELDMAN, M. P. (1970) The treatment by aversion therapy of an identical twin discordant for homosexuality. Unpublished manuscript, Univ. of Edinburgh.

EPSTEIN, A. W. (1960) Fetishism: a study of its psychopathology with particular reference to a proposed disorder in brain mechanisms as an etiological factor. *J. Nerv. Ment. Dis.*, **130**, 107–120.

ESTES, W. K. (1944) An experimental study of punishment. *Psychol. Monog.*, **57**, No. 263.

EVANS, D. R. (1967) An exploratory study into the treatment of exhibitionism by means of emotive imagery and aversive conditioning. *Canad. J. Psychol.*, **8**, 161.

EVANS, D. R. (1968) Masturbatory fantasy and sexual deviation. *Behav. Res. Ther.*, **6**, 17–19.

EYSENCK, H. J. (1952) The effects of psychotherapy: an evaluation. *J. Cons. Psychol.*, **16**, 319–324.

EYSENCK, H. J. (1968) A theory of the incubation of anxiety/fear responses. *Behav. Res. Ther.*, **6**, 309–322.

EYSENCK, H. J. and EYSENCK, SYBIL B. G. (1964) *Manual of the Eysenck Personality Inventory.* London: Univ. of London Press.

FELDMAN, M. P. (1966) Aversion therapy for sexual deviation: A critical review. *Psychol. Bull.*, **65**, 65–79.

FELDMAN, M. P. and MacCULLOCH, M. J. (1965) The application of anticipatory avoidance learning to the treatment of homosexuality. I. Theory, technique and preliminary results. *Behav. Res. Ther.*, **3**, 165–183.

FELDMAN, M. P. and MacCULLOCH, M. J. (1971) *Homosexual Behaviour: Therapy and Assessment.* Oxford: Pergamon Press.

FELDMAN, M. P., MacCULLOCH, M. J., MELLOR, VALERIE and PINSCHOF, J. M. (1966) The application of anticipatory avoidance learning to the treatment of homosexuality–III. The Sexual Orientation Method. *Behav. Res. Ther.*, **4**, 289–299.

FELDMAN, M. P., MacCULLOCH, M. J., and MacCULLOCH, MARY C. (1968) The aversion therapy treatment of a heterogeneous group of five cases of sexual deviation. *Acta Psychiat. Scand.*, **44**, 113–124.

FENICHEL, O. (1945) *The Psychoanalytic Theory of the Neuroses.* New York: Norton.

FISHER, A. E. (1956) Maternal and sexual behavior induced by intra-cranial chemical stimulation. *Science*, **124**, 228–229.

FORD, C. S. and BEACH, F. A. (1952) *Patterns of Sexual Behavior.* New York: Harper.

FRANKS, C. M. (1960) Conditioning and abnormal behaviour. In *Behaviour Therapy and the Neuroses* (Ed. H. J. Eysenck). Oxford: Pergamon Press, 457–487.

FREUND, K. (1960) Some problems in the treatment of homosexuality. In *Behaviour Therapy and the Neuroses* (Ed. H. J. Eysenck) Oxford: Pergamon Press, 312–326.

FREUND, K. (1963) A laboratory method for diagnosing predominance of homo- or heteroerotic interest in the male. *Behav. Res. Therp.*, **1**, 85–93.

FREUND, K. (1965) Diagnosing heterosexual paedophilia by means of a test for sexual interest. *Behav. Res. Ther.*, **3**, 229–235.

FRIBERG, R. R. (1967) Measures of homosexuality: cross-validation of two MMPI scales and implications for usage. *J. Consult. Psychol.*, **31**, 88–92.

GEBHARD, P. H. (1965) Situational factors affecting human sexual behaviour. In *Sexual Behaviour* (Ed. F. A. Beach) New York: Wiley, 483–492.

GIBBENS, T. C. N. (1957) The sexual behaviour of young criminals. *J. Ment. Sci.*, **103**, 527–540.

GILLESPIE, W. H. (1964) Fetishism. In *The Pathology and Treatment of Sexual Deviations* (Ed. I. Rosen) London: Oxford Univ. Press.

GLASS, S. J., DEVEL, H. J., and WRIGHT, C.A. (1940) Sex hormone studies in male homosexuality. *J. Clin. Endocrinol.*, **26**, 590–594.

GOLD, S. and NEUFELD, INGE L. (1965) A learning approach to the treatment of homosexuality. *Behav. Res. Ther.*, **3**, 201–204.

GOLDFRIED, M. R. (1966) The diagnosis of homosexuality from the Rorschach. *J. Consult. Psychol.*, **30**, 338–349.

GOLDSTEIN, A. P. (1962) *Therapist-Patient Expectancies in Psychotherapy.* New York: Pergamon Press.

GREEN, R. (1967) Physician emotionalism in the treatment of the transexual. *Trans. N.Y. Acad. Sci.*, **29**, 440–443.

HAMBURGER, C. (1953) The desire for change of sex. *Acta Endocrin.*, **14**, 361–375.

HARLOW, H. F. (1965) Sexual behaviour in the rhesus monkey. In *Sex and Behavior* (Ed. F. A. Beach) New York: Wiley, 243–265.

HARRIS, G. W. and LEVINE, S. (1965) Sexual differentiations of the brain and its experimental control. *J. Physiol.*, **181**, 379–390.

HESS, H., SELTZER, L., and SHLIEN, M. (1965) Pupil response of hetero- and homosexual males to Pictures of men and women: a pilot study. *J. Abnorm. psychol.*, **70**, 165–168.

HESTON, L. and SHIELDS, J. (1968) Homosexuality in twins: a family study and a registry study. *Arch. Gen. Psychiat.*, **18**, 149–160.

JENKINS, M. (1928) The effect of segregation on the sex behaviour of the white rat. *Genet. Psyohcl. Monog.*, **3**, 461–471.

JOHNSON, J. (1970) *Disorders of Sexual Potency in the Male.* Oxford: Pergamon Press.

JONES, E. (1964) *The Life and Work of Sigmund Freud.* London: Pelican Books.

KALLMANN, F. J. (1952a) Comparative twin study of the genetic aspects of male homosexuality. *J. Nerv. Ment. Dis.*, **115**, 283–298.

KALLMANN, F. J. (1952b) Twin sibships and the study of male homosexuality. *Amer. J. Human Genet.*, **4**, 136–146.

KALLMANN, F. J. (1953) *Heredity in Health and Mental Disorder.* New York: Norton.

KENDRICK, D. C. and CLARKE, R. V. G. (1967) Attitudinal differences between heterosexually and homosexually oriented males. *Brit. J. Psychiat*, **113**, 95–99.

KENYON, F. E. (1968) Studies in female homosexuality, *J. consult. clin. Psychol.*, **32**, 510–513.

KIMBLE, G. (1961) *Conditioning and Learning.* London: Methuen.

KINSEY, A. C., POMEROY, W. B., and MARTIN, C. I. (1947) *Sexual Behaviour in the Human Male.* Philadelphia: Saunders.

KLINTWORTH, G. K. (1962) A pair of male monozygotic twins discordant for homosexuality. *J. Nerv. Ment. Dis.*, **135**, 113–125.

KLÜVER, H. and BUCY, P. C. (1939) Preliminary analysis of the functions of the temporal lobes in monkeys *Amer. Med. Assoc. Arch. Neurol. Psychiat.*, **42**, 979–1000.

KOCKOTT, G. (1970) Psychiatrische und lerntheoretische Aspekte der Transsexualität. In *Sexualforschung: Kritik und Tendenzen.* In Press.

KOENIG, K. P. (1965) The differentiation of hetero- or homo-erotic interests in the male: Some comments on articles by Brown and Freund. *Behav. Res. Ther.*, **3**, 305–307.

KOLARSKY, A., FREUND, J., MACHEK, J., and POLAK, O. (1967) Male sexual deviation, *Arch. Gen. Psychiat.*, **17**, 735–743.

KOLASZYNSKA, ANNE (1969) Unpublished M.Sc. Thesis, University of Birmingham.

KRAFT, T. (1967) A case of homosexuality treated by systematic desensitization, *Amer. J. Psychother.*, **21** 815–821.

KUETHE, J. L. and WEINGARTNER, H. (1964) Male-female schemata of homosexual and non-homosexual penitentiary inmates. *J. Person.*, **32**, 23–31.

KUPPERMAN, H. S. (1967) The endocrine status of the transexual patient. *Trans. N. Y. Acad. Sci.*, **29**, 434–439.

KUSHNER, M. and SANDLER, J. (1966) Aversion therapy and the concept of punishment, *Behav. Res. Ther.*, **4**, 179–186.

LAWS, D. R. and RUBIN, H. B. (1969) Instructional control of a behavioural response. *J. App. Behav. Analys.*, **2**, 93–99.

LEVIN, S. M. (1968) Treatment of a homosexual problem with avoidance conditioning and reciprocal inhibition. (*Symp. on the use of aversive techniques in behaviour therapy, 76th Ann. Conven. A.P.A., San Francisco*).

LEWIS, C. S. (1955) *Surprised by Joy: the Shape of My Early Life.* London: Bles.

LUKIANOWICZ, N. (1959) Survey of various aspects of transvestism in the light of our present knowledge. *J. Nerv. Ment. Dis.*, **128**, 36–64.

MACCOBY, ELEANOR K. (1967) *The Development of Sex Differences.* London: Tavistock.

McCONAGHY, N. (1969) Subjective and penile plethysmograph responses following aversion-relief and apormorphine aversion therapy for homosexual impulses. *Brit. J. Psychiat.*, **115**, 723–730.

McCORD, W., McCORD, JOAN, and VERDEN, P. (1962) Family relationships and sexual deviance in lower class adolescents. *Int. J. Soc. Psychiat.*, **8**, 165–179.

MacCULLOCH, M. J. and FELDMAN, M. P. (1967a) Aversion therapy in the management of 43 homosexuals. *Brit. med. J.*, **2**, 594–597.

MacCULLOCH, M. J. and FELDMAN, M. P. (1967b) Personality and the treatment of homosexuality. *Acta Psychiat. Scand.*, **43**, 300–317.

MacCULLOCH, M. J., BIRTLES, C. J., and FELDMAN, M. P. (1971) Anticipatory avoidance learning for the treatment of homosexuality: recent developments and an automatic aversion therapy system. *Behav. Ther.*, **2**, 151–169.

MacCULLOCH, M. J., FELDMAN, M. P., and PINSCHOF, J. S. (1965) The application of anticipatory avoidance learning to the treatment of homosexuality. II. Avoidance response latencies and pulse rate changes. *Behav. Res. Ther.*, **3**, 21–43.

McGUIRE, R. J. and VALLANCE, M. (1964) Aversion therapy vs. electric shock: a simple technique. *Brit. med. J.*, **1**, 151–153.

McGUIRE, R. J., CARLISE, J. M., and YOUNG, B. G. (1965) Sexual deviations as conditioned behaviour: A hypothesis. *Behav. Res. Ther.*, **3**, 185–190.

MacLEAN, P. D. and PLOOG, D. W. (1962) Cerebral representation of penile erection. *J. Neurophysiol.*, **25**, 29–41.

MARKS, I. M. (1969) *Fears and Phobias.* London: Heinemann Medical.

MARKS, I. M. and GELDER, M. G. (1967) Transvestism and fetishism: clinical and psychological changes during faradic aversion. *Brit. J. Psychiat.*, **113**, 711–729.

MARSH, J. T., HILLIARD, J., and LEICHTI, E. (1955) A sexual deviation scale for the MMPI. *J. Consult. Psychol.*, **19**, 55–59.

MARTIN, B. (1964) Expression and inhibition of sex motive arousal in college males. *J. Abnorm. (Soc.) Psychol.*, **68**, 307–312.

MAX, L. W. (1935) Breaking up a homosexual fixation by the conditioned reaction technique: a case study. *Psychol. Bull.*, **32**, 734.

MEYER, A. E. (1966) Psycho-analytic versus behaviour therapy of male homosexuals: A statistical evaluation of clinical outcome. *Comp. Psychiat.*, **7**, 110–117.

MILLER, N. E. (1969) Learning of visceral and glandular responses. *Science*, **163**, 434–445.

MILLER, R. E., CAUL, W. F., and MIRSKY, I. A. (1967) Communication of affects between feral and socially isolated monkeys. *J. Person. Soc. Psychol.*, **7**, 231–239.

MOHR, J. W., TURNER, R. E., and JERRY, M. B. (1965) *Paedophilia and Exhibitionism.* London: Oxford Univ. Press.

MONEY, J. (1969) Heterosexual vs. homosexual attitudes: Male partners' perception of the feminine image of male trans-sexuals. *First. Inter. Symp. Gender Identity,* London.

MONEY, J. and EPSTEIN, R. (1967) Verbal aptitude in eonism and prepubertal effeminancy. *Trans. N.Y. Acad. Sci.*, **29**, 448–454.

MONEY, J. and HAMPSON, R. (1957) Imprinting and the establishment of gender role, *Arch. Neurol. Psychiat.*, **77**, 333–336.

MORGENSTERN, F. S., PEARCE, J. F., and REES, L. W. (1965) Predicting the outcome of behaviour therapy by psychological tests. *Behav. Res. Ther.*, **3**, 191–200.

NABOKOV, V. (1959) *Lolita.* London: Weidenfeld & Nicholson.

NEUMANN, F. and ELGAR, W. (1966) Permanent changes in gonadal function and sexual behaviour as a result of early feminisation of male rats by treatment with an anti-adrenogenic steroid. *Endokrinologie*, **50**, 209–224.

O'CONNOR, P. J. (1964) Aetiological factors in homosexuality as seen in R.A.F. psychiatric practice. *Brit. J. Psychiat.*, **110**, 381–391.

OLIVER, W. A. and MOSHER, D. L. (1968) Psychopathology and guilt in heterosexual and subgroups of homosexual reformatory inmates. *J. Abnorm. (Soc.) Psychol.*, **73**, 323–329.

ORFORD, J. F. (1971) The assessment of personality and its influence on the outcome of treatment. In *Homosexual Behaviour: Therapy and Assessment* (Ed. M. P. Feldman and M. J. MacCulloch) Oxford: Pergamon.

OSGOOD, C. E., SUCCI, G. J., and TANNENBAUM, P. (1957) *The Measurement of Meaning.* Urbana, Ill.: Univ. of Illinois Press.

OSWALD, I. (1962) Induction of illusory and hallucinatory voices with consideration of behaviour therapy. *J. Ment. Sci.*, **108**, 196–212.

OVESEY, L., GAYLIN, W., and HENDIN, H. (1963) Psychotherapy of male homosexuality. *Arch. Gen. Psychiat.*, **9**, 19–31.

PANTON, J. H. (1960) A new MMPI scale for the identification of homosexuality. *J. Clin. Psychol.*, **16**, 17–21.

PARKER, N. (1964) Twins: A psychiatric study of a neurotic group. *Med. J. Austral.*, **2**, 735.

PEEK, R. M. and STORMS, C. H. (1956) Validity of the Marsh-Hilliard-Liechti MMPI Sexual Deviation Scale in a state hospital population. *J. Consult. Psychol.*, **20**, 132–136.

PFAFF, D. W. (1965) Cerebral implantation and auto-radiographic studies of sex hormones. In *Sexual Research; New Developments* (Ed. Money, J.). New York: Holt, Rhinehart, and Winston, 219–231.

PLANANSKY, K. and JOHNSTON, R. (1962) The incidence and relationship of homosexual and paranoid features in schizophrenia. *J. ment. Sci.*, **108**, 604–615.

QUINN, J. T., HARBISON, J. J. M., and McALLISTER, H. (1970) An attempt to shape penile response. *Behav. Res. Ther.*, **8**, 8–10.

RACHMAN, S. J. (1966) Sexual fetishism: an experimental analogue. *Psychol. Rec.*, **16**, 294–296.

RACHMAN, S. J. and HODGSON, R. J. (1968) Experimentally-induced sexual fetishism: replication and development. *Psychol. Rec.*, **18**, 25–27.

RACHMAN, S. J. and TEASDALE, J. (1969) *Aversion Therapy and Behaviour Disorders: An Analysis*. London: Routledge & Kegan Paul.

RADZINOWICZ, L. (1957) *Sexual Offences*. London: Macmillan.

RAINER, J. D., MESNIKOFF, A., KOLB, L. C., and CARR, A. (1960) Homosexuality and heterosexuality in identical twins. *Psychosom. Med.*, **22**, 251–259.

RAMSAY, R. W. and VANVELZEN, V. (1968) Behaviour therapy for sexual perversions. *Behav. Res. Ther.*, **6**, 233.

RASMUSSEN, E. W. (1955) Experimental homosexual behaviour in male albino rats. *Acta Psychol.*, **11**, 303–334.

RAYMOND, M. J. (1956) Case of fetishism treated by behaviour therapy. *Brit. med. J.*, **2**, 854–857.

RAYMOND, M. J. and O'KEEFE, K. (1965) A case of pin-up fetishism treated by aversion conditioning. *Brit. J. Psychiat.*, **111**, 570–581.

RICKLES, N. K. (1950) *Exhibitionism*. Philadelphia: Lippencott.

ROSEN, I. (1964) Exhibitionism. In *The Pathology and Treatment of Sexual Deviation* (Ed. I. Rosen) London: Oxford Univ. Press.

SAGHIR, M. T., ROBINS, E., and WALBRAM, B. (1969) Homosexuality II. Sexual behaviour of the male homosexual. *Arch. Gen. Psychiat.*, **21**, 219–229.

SANDLER, J. (1964) Masochism: an empirical analysis. *Psychol. Bull.*, **62**, 197–205.

SCHMIDT, ELSA, CASTELL, D., and BROWN, P. (1965) A retrospective study of 42 cases of behaviour therapy. *Behav. Res. Ther.*, **3**, 9–20.

SCHNEIDER, K. (1959) *Psychopathic Personalities*, 9th ed. London: Cassell.

SCHOFIELD, M. (1965a) *The Sexual Behaviour of Young People*. London: Longmans.

SCHOFIELD, M. (1965b) *Sociological Aspects of Homosexuality*. London: Longmans.

SCOTT, P. D. (1964) Definition, classification, prognosis and treatment. In *The Pathology and Treatment of Sexual Deviations* (Ed. I. Rosen) London: Oxford Univ. Press.

SCOTT, T. R. WELLS, W. H. WOOD, DOROTHY Z., and MORGAN, D. I. (1967) Pupillary response and sexual interest reexamined. *J. Clin. Psychol.*, **31**, 433–438.

SHAPIRO, M. B. (1961) *Manual of the Personal Questionnaire*. London: Institute of Psychiatry.

SKINNER, B. F. (1953) *Science and Human Behaviour*, New York: Macmillan.

SLATER, E. (1943) The neurotic constitution. *J. Neurol.*, **6**, 1–16.

SLATER, E. and SLATER, P. (1947) A study in the assessment of homosexual traits. *Brit. J. Med. Psychol.*, **21**: 61–74.

SLATER, P. (1948) *The Selective Vocabulary Test*. London. Harrap.

SLUCKIN, W. (1965) *Imprinting and Early Learning*. Chicago: Aldine.

SOLOMON, R. L. and BRUSH, E. S. (1956) Experimentally derived conceptions of anxiety and aversion. In *Nebraska Symposium on Motivation* (Ed. M. R. Jones) Lincoln, Neb.: Univ. of Neb. Press, 212–305.

SOLOMON, R. L., KAMIN, L. T., and WYNNE, L. C. (1953) Traumatic avoidance learning: the outcomes of sexual extinction procedures with dogs. *J. Abnorm. (Soc.) Psychol.*, **48**, 291–302.

STERN, R. S. (1969) Aversion therapy for homosexual impulses (correspondence). *Brit. J. Psychiat.*, **115**, 1101.

STEVENSON, I. and WOLPE, J. (1960) Recovery from sexual deviations through overcoming non-sexual neurotic response. *Amer. J. Psychiat.*, **116**, 737–742.

STOLLER, R. J. (1967) Etiological factors in male transsexualism. *Trans. N.Y. Acad. Sci.*, **29**, 431–433.

SUTHERLAND, H. (1955) *Principles of Criminology*, 5th Ed. (revised by R. Cressey) Chicago: Lippincott.

TANNER, J. M. (1951) Current advances in the study of physique. Photogramometric anthropametry and an androgymy scale. *Lancet*, **i**, 574.

TERMAN, L. M. and MILES, C. C. (1936) *Sex and Personality*. New York: McGraw-Hill.

THORPE, J. G. and SCHMIDT, ELSA (1964) Therapeutic failure in a case of aversion therapy. *Behav. Res. Ther.*, **2**, 293–296.

THORPE, J. G., SCHMIDT, ELSA, and CASTELL, D. (1963) A comparison of positive and negative (aversive) conditioning in the treatment of homosexuality. *Behav. Res. Ther.*, **1**, 357–362.

THORPE, J. G., SCHMIDT, ELSA, BROWN, P. T., and CASTELL, D. (1964) Aversion-relief therapy: a new method for general application. *Behav. Res. Ther.*, **2**, 71–82.

TILLER, P. O. (1968) Parental role division and the child's personality development. In *The Changing Roles of Men and Women* (Ed. E. Dahlstrom) London: Duckworth, 79–105.

TOLSMA, F. J. (1957) De Betekenis van der Verleiding. In *Homofiele Ontirikkelingen*. Amsterdam: Psychiatri-juridical Society.

TURNER, LUCILLE H. and SOLOMON, C. (1962) Human traumatic avoidance learning: theory and experiments on the operant-respondent distinction and failures to learn. *Psychol. Monog.*, **76**, No. 559.

VALINS, S. (1966) Cognitive effects of false heart-rate feedback. *J. Person. Soc. Psychol.*, **4**, 400–408.

WÅLINDER, J. (1965) Transvestism, definition and evidence in favour of occasional deviation from cerebral dysfunction. *Int. J. Neuropsychiat.*, **1**, 567–572.

WEST, D. J. (1959) Parental figures in the genesis of male homosexuality. *Int. J. Soc. Psychiat.*, **5**, 85–97.

WEST, D. J. (1968) *Homosexuality*, 3rd ed. London: Penguin Books.

WESTWOOD, G. (1960) *A Minority: Homosexuality in Great Britain*. London: Longmans.

WHALEN, R. E. (1964) Hormone induced changes in the organization of sexual behaviour in the male rat. *J. Comp. Physiol. Psychol.*, **57**, 175–182.

WHEELER, W. M. (1949) An analysis of Rorschach indices of male homosexuality. *J. Proj. Tech.*, **13**, 97–126.

WILSON, G. T. and DAVISON, G. C. (1969) Aversion techniques in behaviour therapy: some theoretical and metatheoretical considerations. *J. Consult. Clin. Psychol.*, **33**, 327–329.

WOODWARD, MARY (1958) The diagnosis and treatment of homosexual offenders, *Brit. J. Delinq.*, **9**, 44–59.

YOUNG, W. C., GOY, R. W., and PHOENIX, C. H. (1965) Hormones and sexual behaviour. In *Sexual Research: New Developments* (Ed. J. Money) New York: Holt, Rinehart & Winston, 176–196.

ZAMANSKY, H. S. (1956) A technique for assessing homosexual tendencies. *J. Person.*, **24**, 436–448.

ZUCKER, R. A. and MANOSEVITZ, M. (1966) MMPI patterns of overt male homosexuals: reinterpretation and comment on Dean and Richardson's study. *J. Consult. Psychol.*, **30**, 555–557.

6

Abnormal Sexual Behaviour—Females

ANNE BROADHURST

Sexual behaviour of the human female appears particularly unamenable to systematic or unified classification. It comprises not only the female's biological ability to reproduce and her actual reproductive behaviour, but also her social behaviour in relation both to the group from which a mate is selected and to the spouse or long-term mate, as well as her success in bringing offspring to maturity and independence. We are thus concerned with the abnormality (for example, in the normative statistical sense) of sex-associated behaviour, as well as with sexual behaviour that causes abnormalities either in the participant or offspring, and with the relationship between psychiatric disorders and sexual behaviour.

Lacking the possibility of achieving complete coverage of all these various facets of female abnormal sexuality, we have chosen to consider, first, the major periods of reproductive functioning in chronological order from menstruation and on to coitus and childbirth, followed by consideration of postnatal disturbances and then the menopause Abnormal behaviour of the woman in relation to her sexual partner forms another major section, and consideration of abnormal female sexuality ends with a survey of the sexual disturbances occurring in various abnormal circumstances. Emphasis has been placed on the literature 1950–1969, but exhaustive coverage has not been attempted. Earlier work is referred to for its classical or historical interest or when later work on the same topic is scanty. Comparative work is, similarly, not emphasised unless it provides information not available from human studies.

A. SEXUALITY IN RELATION TO CAPACITY TO REPRODUCE

1. Menstrual Functioning and Pre-coital Aspects of Abnormal Sexuality

AGE OF MENARCHE AND PERSONALITY

Although it is at the menarche—the age when menstruation first occurs—that the woman first becomes reproductively viable, and the preparation for, and the onset of, menses might be thought to be of major importance in the development of adult sexuality and personality generally (Shainess, 1961), little study has been given to examining this point in a woman's life, or to the variations or abnormalities to which the menarche is subject.

Age at menarche is lower with increasing maternal age (Newton and Issekutz-Wolsky, 1969). It is to some extent genetically determined (polygenically) and also environmentally manipulable, for example, by stress in infancy, which, as in comparative studies, advances the menarcheal date (Whiting, 1965). In Britain, as in Norway, the average age at menarche has fallen from 15·5 years, in 1855, to around 13 years in the 1950s (Tanner, 1962). If we take the average age at menarche as 12·8 years $\pm$ s.d. 1·1 (Nicolson and Hanley, 1953) then there is evidence that mental defectives show both a retardation (at 13·2 years; Domino, 1966) of this sign of sexual development and considerably greater variation in age of onset (Mosier *et al.*, 1962; Domino, 1966). This is of interest since several workers report psychological, as well as physical, differences between early and late maturing adolescents. The major interest in this area was in possible intellectual differences between pre- and post-menarcheal girls of the same age (Stone and Barker, 1934, 1937) but little evidence of cognitive discrepancy appeared, and Domino (1966) found no significant differences between early and late maturing mental defectives.

On the other hand, personality rather consistently shows differences between early and late maturers. Some writers claim to be able to predict the onset of menses from the earlier instability of the girl (Davidson and Gottlieb, 1955). Eichorn (1963) summarises studies showing that psychological differences can distinguish the sexually mature girl or boy from the immature. Physical maturity, accompanied by accelerated growth, is said to have less favourable social implications for girls than for boys, but there is some conflict of opinion over this (Eichorn, 1963) and no firm evidence. Shipman (1964) administered Cattell's 16 Personality Factor (16 PF) test to adult women, and related the results to their age at menarche. Those with menarche before 12 were conservative and dependent; those at age 12 to 13 were most feminine, while menarche at age 14 years or older went with a personality that was dominant, critical, and self-controlled. Kroth (1968) gave the IPAT Anxiety scale to two groups of 12 girls (pre-menarche and post-menarche) matched for age (14·2 years), religion, parentage, and race. He showed a higher anxiety score for the pre-menarcheal girls in this small but carefully selected older group of girls. While this appears to confirm commonsense expectation, there is also contrary evidence (e.g. Domino, 1966) showing better adjustment for the pre-menarcheal group. Clearly, the influence of menarche on anxiety levels and personality adjustment must be further explored with due attention to the clue from Kroth that early and late maturing personality differences may vary with age.

Age at menarche has been found to be associated positively with age at marriage (Buck and Stavraky, 1967) and to psychiatric disorder (Wertheimer, 1962). Wertheimer took the records of 1,094 hospitalised female schizophrenics for whom information on menarche was available and investigated the diagnostic distributions of early (8 to 12 years), modal (13 years) and late (14 to 18 years) developers. Among the late menarche group there were significantly more chronic schizophrenics than acute or paranoid forms.

AMENORRHOEA

Menstruation, however, may not appear at all within the normal range of menarcheal ages, in which case we may speak of primary amenorrhoea—defined as failure of onset of monthly bleeding in phenotypic women by the age of 18 years. Philip *et al.* (1965) found abnormalities of chromosome complement in 41 out of 101 patients with primary amenorrhoea, and, in those patients with normal female chromosome complement (46/XX), abnormalities of the gonads were found or suspected. There is thus no serious implication of psychological causation in primary amenorrhoea and we turn therefore to the problem of secondary amenorrhoea, or amenorrhoea developing after a number of normal menstrual periods.

Secondary amenorrhoea is so frequent a phenomenon and can be attributable to such a variety of normal or near normal causes, from pregnancy to emotional shock, that for many decades there was little attempt to establish its incidence or to distinguish normal from abnormal amenorrhoea. Many reports also suggest wide variability of normal menstrual cycle length, so that criteria for absence of a menstruation would differ according to the occasion and the individual. Arey (1939) gives normative data on cycle length from a study of over 20,000 cycles and confirms the variability between and within subjects but sets the average cycle length at 29·3 days; there has been general agreement with this finding. On this basis, and since menstruation may on occasion be so light as to pass unnoticed, secondary amenorrhoea is frequently judged present only when there has been no menstural flow for sixty days or more.

Apart from the normal secondary amenorrhoea of pregnancy, this condition occurs in various normal and abnormal groups, e.g. those with ovarian or adrenal neoplasm (Kalstone and Jaffe, 1969), but there is very wide disagreement about its incidence. Loeser (1943) and Drew (1961), reviewing work on the incidence of secondary amenorrhoea, find it is reported to vary from 1·9 to 100 per cent in different groups studied. Between 2 and 7 per cent of healthy young women will have an episode of amenorrhoea but it often goes unreported because it is considered of no importance or because of the fear of pregnancy. Notably, however, the incidence is increased when women leave home, either for work or other reasons, or when undergoing acute stress.

The association between amenorrhoea and mental illness, particularly catatonic schizophrenia, affective disorders (Gregory, 1957b) and anorexia nervosa, led many workers to support the hypothesis of amenorrhoea caused by denial of the feminine role and lack of healthy maternal identification (Loftus, 1962; Shanan, 1965). However, Peskin (1968) could find no confirmation of this in a comparison of women with short and long menses: extrapolating from the denial-of-femininity hypothesis, he had predicted greater femininity among the latter. Furthermore, the denial-of-femininity hypothesis cannot adequately account for the suddenness of amenorrhoea. Loeser (1943) for example, reporting on amenorrhoea following such incidents as a bomb explosion that could be precisely dated, found that atrophic changes in the uterus wall were such as to indicate cessation of normal physiological activity on the exact day of the trauma.

In this connection the observations of women in conditions of war are of considerable interest. Amenorrhoea increases under these stressful conditions and early workers thought that 'war amenorrhoea' could be attributed to the absence of men rather than to faulty nutrition (Engels et al., 1964). Sher (1946) adequately disposed of dietary deficiency as a major cause of amenorrhoea when he showed that it occurred markedly in a large group of Women's Auxiliary Air Force personnel who ate a more balanced diet than they had known before joining the Service. It is concluded that a change of environment was the major causative factor.

Remarkable uniformity appears in the reports of amenorrhoea among women in the truly harsh conditions of prison and concentration camps (Whitacre and Barrera, 1944; Sydenham, 1946; Bass, 1947). Amenorrhoea occurred in 15 to 54 per cent of internees, the more severe conditions producing decidedly higher incidence. It was frequently accompanied by a gain in weight, while non-amenorrhoeic women did not gain and the men of the camp lost weight. Since amenorrhoea was also more common among the younger women, it may be due to non-maturation of the ovum and, hence, a preservative mechanism for the ovaries (Bass, 1947). Writers on this subject agree that amenorrhoea appeared immediately on arrival at a concentration camp (Kral, 1951). Of Bass's cases, 60 per cent appeared in the first month and 25 per cent in the second month. Nutritional factors could not be expected to have affected these women with such speed and Sydenham (1946) makes the point that very prolonged malnutrition does not give rise to amenorrhoea. Starvation could contribute to the incidence of amenorrhoea, but its occurrence in prison camps is attributed primarily to the emotional shock of war and, particularly, of sudden adverse changes in living conditions.

Neither is sexual deprivation a causative factor in amenorrhoea, since Bass (1947) found amenorrhoea as common among virgins as among other women in the Theresienstadt concentration camp. Two other findings in these deplorable conditions are worthy of note: Whitacre and Barrera (1944) found that interned Army nurses were more susceptible to amenorrhoea (incidence of 23 per cent as against the camp total in this case of 15 per cent) and Drew (1961) reports that nuns were the only group not to become amenorrhoeic. Possibly missionary nuns are already pre-selected to withstand stress or they may suffer less from the factors of separation and hopelessness which Drew considers of importance in explaining the camp amenorrhoea.

There is little doubt therefore of emotional factors in the production of secondary amenorrhoea and there are reports of therapeutic success by psychotherapy (Loftus, 1962). Interest has also been shown in the personality or type of woman who is susceptible to psychogenic amenorrhoea (Piotrowski, 1962) and hence supposedly suitable for treatment by psychotherapy. However, psychotherapy is often supplemented with hormone treatments the effectiveness of which emphasises the obvious endocrine imbalance associated with amenorrhoea. Igarashi et al. (1965) investigated 16 women with amenorrhoea following trauma and found urinary follicular stimulating hormone (FSH) was below normal, and urinary oestrogen was low. From this they conclude that stress leads to oversecretion of corticotrophin releasing factor and a corresponding undersecretion of FSH and luteal hormone (LH) releasers at the hypothalamus, with resulting undersecretion of FSH and LH at the pituitary. Reduced secretion of FSH and LH will cause amenorrhoea or anovulation. While this explanation is to some extent speculative it is amenable to rigorous test and, hence, preferable to the vague hypotheses of disordered mother-daughter relationships and inadequate feminity.

UTERINE BLEEDING

The converse of amenorrhoea, continuous uterine bleeding, is a known but rare disorder of the uterine endometrium. It is thought to be stress-related and has been likened to a mourning or weeping reaction due to sudden loss of or separation from a love object (Heiman, 1962). Objective studies (rather than historico-religious anecdotes such as the miraculous cure by Jesus of the woman who 'had an issue of blood twelve years') are unlikely, owing to paucity of sufferers.

DYSMENORRHOEA

Dysmenorrhoea is pain occurring in the back or lower abdomen at or about the time of the menstrual period. Reports of incidence place the figure between 1 and 34 per cent (Gregory, 1957a) and the incidence is said to be particularly low in Russia (Hopkins, 1965) where the status of women is high. Dysmenorrhoea can, like amenorrhoea, be due to pelvic abnormalities. However, a large proportion of these complaints are not due to known physical abnormality and these have for some time been associated clinically with the neurotic personality or with development of neurosis. Again, like amenorrhoea, dysmenorrhoea has been attributed to unpleasant, unloving experiences in relation to the mother (Shainess, 1961) and to rejection of the feminine role (Lucas, 1963) even to the point of using improvement of the condition as an index of acceptance of femininity (Lucas, 963). 1Coppen and Kessel (1963) ably review the literature prior to their study, and refer to the lack of uniform views, particularly between psychiatrists and gynaecologists, on aetiology, gynaecologists being less likely to attribute neuroticism to their dysmenorrhoeic patients. Paulson and Wood (1966) to some extent confirm this remark on the two medical specialities. Psychiatrists and gynaecologists were asked to judge how a dysmenorrhoeic patient would respond to questionnaire items and were found to have diverse attitudes concerning the aetiology: psychiatrists, as a group, recognised a strong psychosomatic component, while many of the gynaecologists considered psychogenic aspects relatively unimportant.

Aetiological discussion is further complicated by the high incidence of dysmenorrhoea in the general population (Drillien, 1946; Rose, 1949; Golub, Lang and Menduke, 1958) and by the reported lowering of pain threshold in dysmenorrhoeics (Haman, 1944). Careful work relating the incidence of dysmenorrhoea to personality characteristics was provided by the Coppen and Kessel study of 1963. They employ also the concept of premenstrual tension which is said to have been described by Hippocrates (Kramp, 1968) but was first popularised by Frank (1931). In addition to pain at menstruation, many women report tension, irritability, depression, headaches, and swelling of the breast and abdomen, particularly prior to the onset of blood flow. Rees (1953) compared the incidence of premenstrual tension in normals and neurotics and found neurotics more susceptible, but there was no simple relationship.

Coppen and Kessel (1963) aimed to find the relationship between the premenstrual syndrome, including dysmenorrhoea, and personality in a group of normal women. Five hundred menstruating women were chosen from the lists of ten general practitioners and circulated with the Maudsley Personality Inventory (MPI) and a questionnaire on menstrual symptoms. A series of reminders brought the response

rate to 93 per cent. The authors found severe dysmenorrhoea in 12 per cent of their sample and moderate dysmenorrhoea in 45 per cent. The frequency was significantly reduced by parity and by age. Thus, Coppen and Kessel show that the incidence is great enough to raise doubts about the propriety of considering dysmenorrhoea as abnormal. Furthermore, they failed to find any significant correlation between dysmenorrhoea and neuroticism. However, dysmenorrhoea was significantly related to the other symptoms of the premenstrual syndrome (irritability, depression, headache, and sensations of swelling) which were themselves strongly correlated with neuroticism. Dysmenorrhoea was the sole symptom that increased from premenstrual to menstrual phases, but 40 per cent of those with other premenstrual symptoms also complained of pain premenstrually. The authors conclude that, 'one sort of period pain occurs premenstrually and can be regarded as an uncommon feature of the premenstrual syndrome, whilst the more usual sort is maximal during the period and is not part of the syndrome . . . . This survey provides no evidence to justify dysmenorrhoea being regarded as a psychosomatic condition or one that calls for psychological treatment' (Coppen and Kessel, 1963, p. 720).

This careful study, replicated in Spain with similar findings (Théano, 1968), can be criticised on grounds of non-randomness of the samples chosen and finally co-operating. Nor was there any check on the veracity and memory of the subjects. Since these are points considered carefully by the authors they might concur that their conclusion cannot be the final word on the topic. Coppen's (1965) later work, using a very similar approach with 49 neurotic patients, 41 depressives, and 61 schizophrenic women showed a significant increase in menstrual pain in neurosis, in line with the poorer adjustment found in groups with increased premenstrual and menstrual pain (Rose, 1949). Despite Coppen and Kessel's conclusion, there is, moreover, evidence of the successful treatment of dysmenorrhoea by the psychological technique of desensitisation (Mullen, 1968, 1969) as well as by pharmacological agents such as chlordiazepoxide (Moore, 1962).

The development of a Menstrual Distress Questionnaire (Moos, 1968, 1969), which assesses one complete cycle, can be used repeatedly and has scales for the measurement both of the respondent's accuracy and her tendency to report an overabundance of symptoms, will further improve research in this area. Using this questionnaire on 839 wives of graduate students, Moos (1968) found that older women complain more of premenstrual symptoms while the younger show relatively greater symptoms in the menstrual phase. In so far as the menstrual complaint is more often of pain (Coppen and Kessel, 1963), this is a confirmation of the finding of negative correlations between pain and age and pain and parity. Only Kramp (1968) is at variance on this point. Moos found menstrual cycle length had no correlation with symptom intensity, but variability of cycle length and length of menstrual flow correlated significantly with pain and other symptoms.

Mention has already been made of Coppen's (1965) investigation of menstrual disorders in psychiatric patients. Menstrual pain was found to be significantly increased in neurosis, normal in prevalence in the depressives, and below normal in the schizophrenics. Similar findings emerged concerning irritability at the menses and depression, anxiety, and tension. Schizophrenics show a definite reduction of menstrual symptoms in comparison with the normal.

'MITTELSCHMERZ'

A further pain of menstruation, termed 'mittelschmerz', is known to occur occasionally and is associated with the mid period (14th day of the cycle) and, specifically, with ovulation. The incidence of this pain is not well documented and there has been little suggestion that its incidence is increased in psycho-pathological groups.

MENSTRUATION AND PERSONALITY; THE PREMENSTRUAL SYNDROME

That there might be personality changes with the endocrinological variations of the menstrual phases has long been suspected on clinical grounds. The concept of the premenstrual tension syndrome (Frank, 1931) has developed from these clinical suspicions. Direct assessment, however, has as yet proved difficult. Rees (1969) gave the Eysenck Personality Inventory (EPI) and the Multiple Affect Adjective Checklist (MAACL) (Zuckerman and Lubin, 1965) to young women and ascertained menstrual stage accurately. No significant differences in personality between menstrual phases emerged. Similar work is reported elsewhere with results that are more positive (Moos et al., 1969). However, it may well be that personality questionnaires are not yet sensitive enough for these undoubtedly small effects. Even measures of arousal have not uniformly shown menstrual phase variation (Koppell et al., 1969). A more successful approach has been used by Bardwick and her colleagues (Bardwick, 1967; Bardwick and Behrman, 1967; Ivey and Bardwick, 1968) who combined physiological measures of uterine activity, derived from

intrauterine balloon pressure, and emotional indices such as the Verbal Anxiety Scale (VAS) (Gottschalk et al., 1962). They have been able to show that reactions to experimentally induced stresses and sexual stimuli vary with menstrual phase, women in the premenstrual phase showing more anxiety than in the ovulatory mid-phase period. Thus, with the neatest experimentation encountered in this field, they have provided a factual basis for the claim of Benedek (1963) that she could identify ovulatory (calm) and non-ovulatory (anxious) phases from the verbal productions of women in psychoanalytic treatment.

That there should be psychophysiological correlates of menstrual state is not surprising. Rapid Eye Movement (REM) sleep varies with menstrual phase (Hartmann, 1966), and reaction time studies show an increase of speed premenstrually (Akita, 1965). The electroencephalograph also shows variations with menstrual stage (Barenne and Gibbs, 1942; Lamb et al., 1953; Margerison et al., 1964) and this, in turn, has been shown to have a complex relationship with personality measures (Savage, 1964; Broadhurst and Glass, 1969; Gale et al., 1969).

We have seen that environmental factors can cause amenorrhoea (Loeser, 1943; Sher, 1946; Sydenham, 1946; Drew, 1961; Engels et al., 1964). Menstruation can also be altered, though perhaps less drastically, by hypnotic techniques (Dunbar, 1954; Hartland, 1966) and by electric shock applied therapeutically. This last is of particular interest to the study of the abnormal manifestations. Comparative psychological research (e.g. Jenson and Stainbrook, 1949) suggests that electroconvulsive shock can produce disturbances of the oestrus cycle (though Nolan (1952) failed to confirm this) and foetal resorption (Myers and Poole, 1962) in rats. The human relevance of these findings on the disturbance of reproductive function is emphasised by Kalinowski (1948), Michael (1954) and Gregory (1957b) who all report reduced menstrual flow after electroconvulsive therapy (ECT). Michael (1954) reports that amenorrhoea 'was the conspicuous finding' of his investigations on 687 patients in a New York Psychiatric Institute. It was especially likely to occur when ECT was combined with deep insulin therapy, when the number of treatments was increased (Michael, 1954), and when ECT occurred in the first ten days of the cycle (Gregory, 1957b). However, ECT is prescribed chiefly for schizophrenia and for depression, both of which conditions can themselves be related to reduced or irregular menses (Coppen, 1965; Gregory, 1957b).

Another way of looking at menstruation and personality is to consider the individual differences in menstrual pattern and their relationships with

7

personality types. Peskin's (1968) work on the personalities of women with short or long menstrual flow marks a beginning in these investigations but, having proved negative, may not be followed up. Other studies on the relationship between personality and menstruation have been decidedly influenced by the premenstrual tension concept to which we now return.

The numerous reports of behavioural disorders occurring in close relationship to menstrual phase, and particularly in the premenstrual phase, certainly cannot be disregarded. Suicides (Mackinnon and Mackinnon, 1956; Mackinnon et al., 1959; Tonks et al., 1968), accidents (Dalton, 1960), deterioration of work (Dalton, 1964) and crime (Cooke, 1945; Pollak, 1950; Dalton, 1961) are all found more frequently than could be expected by chance in women in the premenstrual phase. Epilepsy has been found to vary in some patients concomitant with menstruation (Healey, 1928; Almquist, 1955), as also does migraine in a proportion of sufferers, though simple headaches are more equitably spread through all phases of the cycle (Ostfeld, 1962). The observation that admissions to psychiatric hospitals is increased in the premenstrual phase (Dalton, 1959; Petersen and Kramp, 1965) coupled with sporadic reports of psychiatric patients whose disorder fluctuates with the menstrual cycle (e.g. Janowsky et al., 1967) also led to the postulation of a 'menstrual psychosis' but this must now be abandoned as a specific entity (Gregory, 1957a) in place of the concept of exacerbation of existing disorder at this time.

The evidence is conclusive that extensive physiological changes occur premenstrually which lead in many instances to no more than food cravings (Smith and Sauder, 1969) or lethargy, but can also constitute the premenstrual tension syndrome, earlier described, including 'a desire to find relief by foolish and ill considered actions' (Frank, 1931) with even fatal consequences. Sutherland and Stewart (1965) confirmed the picture of cyclical disorder in a careful study of 100 female students and 50 nurses and cast doubt only on the terminology. Since the symptoms can appear premenarcheally and continue postmenopausally they prefer the term 'cyclic syndrome' which, however, has not yet received much acceptance.

2. Disturbances Manifested between Coitus and Childbirth

ILLEGITIMACIES

The number of illegitimacies can be variously assessed. Gebhard et al. (1958) found approximately 10 per cent of their large sample of women had a premarital pregnancy. While other estimates vary (3 to 30 per cent), this is in any case very different from the figures on illegitimate births. These authors show that the majority of the unmarried pregnant marry subsequently, and before the birth. A large proportion also arrange abortion (see later). Another measure of illegitimacy is by percentage of all births. Prior to 1950 the figures for the United States were 1·6 to 2·4, European figures being higher (e.g. 4·8 England; 16·5 Austria).

The social problems associated with these illegitimate pregnancies and, particularly, the proportional increase reported recently in these births has turned the attention of psychiatrists and psychologists to the personalities of the women concerned. At one time it seemed that unmarried mothers had, on average, lower than normal intelligence (McClure, 1931). However, a large-scale survey (Pearson and Amacher, 1956) of 3,394 women, covering 40 per cent of all illegitimate births in the State of Minnesota in the period 1946–1951, and whose intelligence was assessed in connection with the adoption of the child, showed a mean intelligence (IQ) of 100·19 ± s.d. 18·36. The observed distribution of intelligence was, however, significantly different from normal, having an excess of both the intellectually defective and the bright normal—hence the large standard deviation—and an underrepresentation of the dull normals (IQ 83 to 91). This over- and underrepresentation of bright and dull normals respectively is difficult to explain, but mental deficiency does still appear as a small, contributory factor in illegitimacy, particularly as the 'repeaters' (i.e. with more than one illegitimate pregnancy) were found to be duller than normal.

Concern over the fertility of defectives and the consequent negative correlation of IQ with family size (Cattell, 1937) produced the investigations of national intelligence (Scottish Council for Research in Education, 1949) which provided some evidence against the decline attributable to the 'submerged fifth'. (For further arguments on 'Cattell's paradox' see Higgins et al., 1962.) Nevertheless, interest in the fertility of defectives remains as a humane consideration, both for the mother and her offspring. Wignall and Meredith (1968) surveyed reports from institutions for mental defectives in the United States and found the incidence of illegitimate pregnancies to be one-fifth that for the total population, due both to supervision of the patients and, in some States, to the administration to them of contraceptive pills.

Attempts have frequently been made to ascertain non-cognitive personality characteristics of the unmarried mother. Objective testing by S. Eysenck (1961) found unmarried mothers more neurotic and extraverted than the general population and there is evidence also of prepregnancy instability among unmarried student mothers (Giel and Kidd, 1965). Little evidence of psychosis as a major determinant appears (Pearson and Amacher, 1956) and writers, instead, refer to 'characterological disturbances' (Malmquist *et al.*, 1966), 'hysterical dissociation' or 'deviant personality development' (Hoffmeyer, 1964), but these descriptions are frankly based on clinical impressions. The perpetual search for personality profiles characteristic of various malfunctioning groups in society has not been successful often enough to be considered a valuable exercise. Thoughtful workers have admitted that they 'found it impossible to apply psychiatric diagnoses to our patients' difficulties, and could not even say consistently that they were "emotionally disturbed" ' (Barglow *et al.*, 1968, p. 682). 'Symbolic explanations of unwed motherhood . . . have included: a wish to restore the symbolic tie to the mother; a conscious wish for pregnancy; a wish for revenge on the mother, or a wish to have a child for her; the masochistic replacement of the missing penis; and the regressive use of the vagina as a rectum' (*op. cit.* p. 683). But these authors could not verify any of these psychoanalytic notions and emphasise the contrary finding of a complete absence of prepregnancy wishes for a child.

An incidental finding of this last study (Barglow *et al.*, 1968) of 78 unmarried schoolgirls was that learning ability and concentration improved during pregnancy for 60 per cent of the group. This observation, supported by teachers' reports, deserves further exploration. It can hardly be relevant only to the young and the unmarried.

Closely linked with the problem of illegitimacy are the sexual disorders of sexual psychopathy, promiscuity, and nymphomania. Anant (1968) reports successful aversion therapy in a case of promiscuity in a defective girl, lending support to theories of deficient training or socialisation in such cases. While sexual psychopathy in the male has been subjected to considerable, albeit inadequate, investigation, even sound survey work is lacking for the human female.

Much has been written on the prostitute and her personality (Gagnon and Simon, 1967; Glover, 1969). Though it appears unlikely from the mass of anecdotal evidence (e.g. Bennett, 1954) that she is nymphomaniac, and, in fact, frigidity is more often stated to be characteristic (Glover, 1969), she may well be psychopathic and most certainly is promiscuous. But objective data both on sexual responsiveness and on other personality traits are lacking. Gibbens (1957) provides a rare study with psychometry on adolescent prostitutes which suggests that

intellectual retardation in this group of women may be another of the myths of abnormal sexuality.

INFERTILITY

While not concerned with the excellent research on the psychopharmacology of infertility, mainly of non-humans, (reviewed by Fridhandler and Pincus, 1964), we may note that a monoamine oxidase inhibitor decreased fertility in rats (Spector, 1961). This strictly subhuman report may, nevertheless, give additional reason to welcome the decreasing use of these antidepressants. The relief of infertility by administration of the muscle relaxant chlordiazepoxide has been reported (Schwartz and Smith, 1963). In contrast, there is a vast literature suggesting that much reported infertility is psychogenic, and there is certain evidence that stress can block pregnancy in mice (Weir and DeFries, 1963).

The quality of the work on man, however, is poor, as indicated by Noyes and Chapnick (1964) who surveyed the literature 1935–1963. They rarely found material well presented or with clear-cut conclusions, probably a consequence of the lack of clearly stated hypotheses. Fifty psychological factors were mentioned in this period as having an influence on human female fertility and of these the following ten were most frequent: masculine aggressive personality, feminine immature personality, functional disturbances, rejection of pregnancy, adoption, frigidity, hostile dependence on the mother, conflict over feminine role, mothering of dependent husband, superficial psychotherapy. Less frequently reported but still influential in the literature surveyed is the notion that desire for a child precipitates the discharge of unripe ova from the ovaries (Dunbar, 1935). It can be seen that many of these factors show the influence of psychoanalytic writers (e.g. Deutsch, 1944) and are too ill-defined to be suitable for investigation. For example, Bos and Cleghorn (1958) claim that factors associated with infertility in one patient may be associated with hyperfertility in another, no clue being offered to predict the response of the individual.

Criteria can be set up for research on psychogenic factors in infertility that would avoid these pitfalls. Before a psychogenic factor can be proved operative it must be identified in unmarried or virginal women who, when married, prove to be infertile. Treatment directed solely at the factor in question would have to be shown to be effective in reducing infertility. Logically, the further proof of the causative agency requires the production of infertility in otherwise normal women. These criteria rule out all the research effort to date, but some few of the recent studies deserve mention.

Seward and her colleagues (1965, 1967), starting from the assumption 'that underlying the overt wish for a child indicated by the couple's seeking medical help was a covert wish to avoid conception', set up clear hypotheses concerning the infertile woman's role conflict and dependence on the husband. They tested the hypotheses in matched groups of fertile and infertile women using sentence completion, Thematic Apperception Test (TAT) and human figure drawing administered by one person and scored blind by another. No confirmation for the psychogenic hypotheses was found. The authors draw attention to the possible effects of test administration by a person who knows the group assignment of the women. If this factor were indeed relevant here, it would be evidence against the operation of an experimenter bias (Rosenthal, 1964), or perhaps could be adduced as evidence of the experimenter's unconscious wish to prove herself wrong! However, an extension of the study to other groups, in which the tester was kept ignorant of the group assignment, produced essentially the same negative findings. Added to the dissatisfaction with the framing of many psychoanalytically influenced hypotheses, this negative from sympathetic researchers should shake the firm beliefs of some.

More mundane perhaps is the report of an association between smoking and infertility (Tokuhata, 1968) obtained from records of the dead. Despite its necessarily retrospective nature, this careful study adds further evidence of the harms linked with smoking to the well-established association between maternal smoking and lower infant birth weight. It is suggested that concomitant disorders such as spontaneous abortions and deformities may also be associated with smoking. Since the husband's smoking history is unrelated to the infertility, a prezygotic impairment of reproduction is implicated.

Whitelaw (1968) presents evidence on the vexed topic of the use of oral contraception as a means of reducing infertility. Particularly the *withdrawal* of the oestrogenic-progestational norethynodrel has been reported to enhance pregnancy. This claim, however, has never been adequately substantiated, and Whitelaw reports that 30 per cent of his patients have failed on this treatment when prescribed by others and, in his own uncontrolled trial, only three of 38 patients conceived within two months of cessation. There were also various undesirable side reactions, including ovarian degeneration. Hence, norethynodrel is judged to be not only ineffective but positively contra-indicated for infertility.

There is still a widespread belief that adoption of a baby increases the infertile woman's likelihood of conception (Benedek *et al.*, 1953). Thus, Kroger (1962) states that 'psychosomatic infertility ... may be alleviated by adoption through a dissolution of the psychological defences against motherhood' (p. 635). Certainly, conception can *occur* after adoption, but is its occurrence *enhanced* by the adoption? Sandler (1965), criticising the sampling techniques and the methods used by previous workers, reports 32 fully-investigated infertile couples who were advised to adopt when no further treatment could be offered. Fifty-six per cent of these conceived later and this finding agrees closely with the finding of 55 per cent later conceptions in women primarily diagnosed as infertility of emotional origin and exceeds the 45·5 per cent success for treatment of organic infertilities in this clinic. After referring briefly to the impossibility of establishing controls in such work, Sandler concludes that the hypothesis is supported. However, appropriate control groups can be used as was shown by the much more extensive study of Rock *et al.* (1965) who found a significantly higher proportion of non-adopters to conceive (35·4 per cent) than adopters (22·9 per cent) with organic conditions excluded.

Essentially this finding was confirmed by Weir and Weir (1966) who, however, criticised the previous workers for comparing groups with varying durations of infertility (Rock *et al.*, 1965). They studied 438 couples all of whom were potentially fertile, but had had infertile unions for at least 18 months. Full investigation and treatment had been completed and all had been discharged non-pregnant from the clinic and followed up for at least five years. A group of 197 adopted and 241 did not. Weir and Weir point out that their groups were comparable in respect of length of infertility or showed only minor differences favouring conception among the adopters. The actual conception rate of the two groups was essentially the same, 18·2 per cent and 16·2 per cent for the non-adopting and adopting groups respectively, the difference being non-significant. Credibility is strengthened by the modesty of the claims from recent work as well as by the larger samples. Adoption clearly cannot be recommended as a cure for psychogenic infertility.

Another possible approach to the problem of infertility is to consider artificial insemination (AI) either by husband's semen (AIH) or a donor's (AID). AIH was first reported by Home (1797) to have been carried out successfully by John Hunter several years before his death in 1793. The procedure is thus of considerable antiquity, but has recently come to the fore with improved techniques for semen storage. Various legal problems are apparent, particularly for AID but these are now in process of clarification. Suspected psychological problems have not yet materialised. Rubin (1965) reviews the medical, legal, and theological concerns over AI and found in a questionnaire approach to 85 recipients of AI (of whom 43 responded) that there was notable lack of concern for anonymity, which contrasts with the medical fears and concerns on this point. The group showed few differentiating characteristics from a comparable group of mothers conceiving naturally. Only a pervading concern over the possibility of an incestuous conception appeared. Similarly Benedek *et al.* (1953) present dreams of women impregnated by AI as evidence of incest anxiety. However, since the thesis of these authors is of the presence of deep unconscious fears of incest, it may be that the findings are contaminated.

A neglected aspect of AI is the attitude and response of the husband, men being said to prefer AI to adoption as a solution to the problems of infertility (Benedek *et al.*, 1953). Another neglected aspect is of interest, namely, the low success rate of AI in humans. In cattle, artificial insemination is known to be 99 per cent successful on single application. Yet in women, the reports of ultimate success are as low as 4 to 30 per cent and the average number of inseminations before conception is eight (Benedek *et al.*, 1953). One factor reducing the success rate is the variable ovulation date of the human female. But, even allowing for the inaccuracies of estimation of ovulation time, the low conception rate for AI makes plausible the existence of a psychogenic pregnancy block meriting the attention of psychosomatically interested gynaecologists.

For the couple who choose neither to adopt nor to attempt artificial insemination, problems of adjustment to their infertility remain. Social case work reports anecdotally on the outcomes: thus it is suspected that instances of child stealing may occur in such circumstances, but hard facts are lacking.

PHEROMONE INFLUENCE ON HUMAN SEXUALITY

Although there is increasing evidence that olfactory acuity shows sex differences (LeMagnen, 1953) and changes with menstrual phase (LeMagnen, 1952; Kloek, 1961) and with androgen injection (Beidler, 1961) in women, there is nothing to suggest the existence of the Bruce effect—pregnancy blocked by presence or mere scent of other males (Parkes and Bruce, 1961; Bruce, 1962, 1966)—in human sexual behaviour (Gleason and Reynierse, 1969). Furthermore, although there have been attempts to show influence of external chemical messengers (pheromones) on human behaviour (Wiener, 1966, 1967a, 1967b), man is clearly not dominated by olfactory sensitivity, and the evidence is decidedly thin. For reviews of comparative findings on such

pregnancy blocking, as well as pseudocyesis, etc., the reader is referred to Michael and Keverne (1968) and to Parkes and Bruce (1961).

ABORTION

If a child that is conceived is not carried to full term we have, as far as reproductive success is concerned, a disorder of sexuality. This survey is concerned primarily with factors that can cause this abnormality in those wishing for children and, with the possible abnormal consequences of abortion when artificially produced, in those not wishing for the child in question.

A single spontaneous abortion—variously defined as occurring before 22 or 28 weeks of gestation, that is, before the foetus is viable (Vanden Bergh *et al.*, 1966)—may well be the result of chance factors and occurs in about 10 per cent of pregnancies in Western societies. It is known, however, that a very high proportion of foetal malformations is found in these cases of spontaneous abortion (Hertig, 1967), which may therefore be a normal protective mechanism of adaptive significance.

Nevertheless, there are abortifacient factors whose study is of importance if we recognise that they probably contribute not only to the abortion, but also to the earlier teratogenic development of the foetus. Such a one is the ubiquitous cigarette which Tokuhata (1968) has shown increases infertility and foetal loss, including the rarer disorder of stillbirth. Psychopharmacology points to various abortifacient drugs but also emphasises the species variability in this respect. Cortisone, for example, is an abortifacient when given in large doses to mice and rabbits but has no such effect on rats and humans (Meier, 1963), which makes the rat the experimental animal of choice for studying this resistance to cortisone effect in humans. From comparative studies, also, we find that overcrowding is associated with abortions, stillbirths and foetal resorptions (Myers and Poole, 1962). This may well be another hormonal effect since increase in adrenal size and adrenocortical hormones (including cortisone) are associated also with overcrowding. The effect of overcrowding on human births cannot readily be judged since cramped living conditions go with so many other adverse environmental factors that the associated raised infant mortality clearly has a multifactorial aetiology.

The possible dangers of ECT therapy are suggested by further comparative studies (Bacon and Rosvold, 1948; Rosvold, 1949b; Stone and Walker, 1949) which have shown foetal resorption and abortion caused by electric shock in the early phases of pregnancy in the rat, the earlier the greater the disruption of reproduction. Alternatively, the possibility has been raised that shocks cause pseudopregnancy in rats (Jensen and Stainbrook, 1949) but Nolan (1952) failed to replicate this finding and in the treatment of human psychiatric conditions ECT is not generally thought to be contra-indicated, at least until late pregnancy.

However, greatest psychological interest centres round the personality factors associated with women who have a series of spontaneous abortions. Habitual abortion is generally accepted as a complaint when there have been three or more successive abortions. No abortifacient pathology can usually be found (Grimm, 1962) but various nutritional and hormone replacement therapies are applied empirically. Dunbar (1962), writing of the emotional concomitants of this condition, sought to dispose of the prevalent idea that it is only the neurotic and the ill who break down during pregnancy. She emphasised that bodily homeostasis is strained in pregnancy, which, though normal, creates its own stresses. Successful weathering of these stresses, we are told, depends upon 'ego strength' and personality 'integration'. But these ill-defined terms may represent aspects of the neuroticism dimension, so that Dunbar scarcely makes her point.

In fact, neurotic women are more likely to have miscarriages (Mandelbrote and Monro, 1964); and Tupper (1962), in an uncritical and subjective report finds neurotic characteristics in a group of habitual aborters. Only slightly more sophisticated is the approach of Grimm (1962), who compared 70 habitual aborters with 35 non-aborters of similar intelligence on Rorschach and TAT scores. Analysis showed some projective test score differences which are interpreted to show increased proneness to guilt in aborters.

Such a study, however, even if modified to include objective tests, can tell us little of the causes of habitual abortion since the personality of the woman aware of her problem may undergo further change as a consequence. More significant, therefore, is the note that projective test scores changed for the better in a small group of women who finally brought a child to term, and that 80 per cent success, that is, a successful pregnancy, can be achieved for habitual aborters with psychotherapy (Grimm, 1962). If substantiated, this would suggest a psychogenic causative factor more than usually amenable to this form of therapy.

The psychoanalytic explanation of habitual abortion is that the woman is unconsciously reluctant to accept the roles of woman and mother. Following this theory to its psychoanalytic conclusion, Vanden Bergh et al. (1966) predicted that women operated upon (having a suture of the

incompetent cervical os) to improve their pregnancy success would suffer psychic disturbance if they did in fact have a child. A study of the medical history in nine such cases suggested that these women had postpartum psychoses and, later, a need for psychotherapy more often than did an equally small control group. However, the bias of the interviewers and the small size of the sample reduce the significance of this conclusion.

Artificially induced abortions have been much more fully, though not exhaustively, investigated. Recent alterations in legislature both here and abroad (Heller and Whittington, 1968) have brought the topic before the public and the medical profession in a new light and the result has been a flood of literature (see review by Simon and Senturia, 1966). Public attitude in the United States has been tested by opinion polls and found not to support abortions carried out for the major reasons for which they are sought (Gebhard et al., 1958), namely economic reasons, illegitimacy and simply not wanting the child. Medical opinion on abortion varies greatly, and the overt anxieties of the profession on this point (Rodger, 1968) have caused comment (Peck, 1968). Psychiatrists are generally in favour of liberalising procedures (Crowley and Laidlaw, 1967) but fear that the legal need for psychiatric opinion in 77 per cent (Ingram et al., 1967) or 91 per cent (Heller and Whittington, 1968) of cases reduces their role to that of an accomplice (Bolter, 1962) in what has until recently been considered a crime.

Argument, after consideration of the ethical 'gift of life' problem (Rodger, 1968), usually hinges on the benefits of reducing dangerous illegal abortion if abortion is legalised, and on the psychiatric consequences of abortion for the woman, depressions (Deutscher, 1965) and psychoses being particularly predicted. On neither point are facts readily obtained. Goodhart (1966) argues that the estimate of illegal abortions in Britain, generally set at 100,000 per year, is much too high. The true figure could be considerably below 30,000. With such indeterminables a rise or fall would be difficult to detect.

The psychiatric consequences of abortion are reviewed by Simon and Senturia (1966) who conclude that on this topic 'deeply held personal convictions frequently seem to outweigh the importance of data'. There is some consensus of agreement that previously disturbed patients continue to have difficulty following abortion, but a properly controlled study on the lines these authors suggest has yet to be carried out. Large-scale follow-up in Sweden suggests that few psychoses follow abortion (Ekblad, 1955) and those who are refused abortions can also have psychiatric sequelae (Hook, 1963; Pare and Raven, 1970). Peck and Marcus (1966) found improvement or no change and Patt et al. (1969) found mainly favourable effects after therapeutic abortion, but the psychiatric interview technique without controls in these reports resembles much of previous work. Kenyon (1969) provides psychiatric controls for descriptive comparison but no follow-up data. For a socio-cultural examination of abortion problems in many countries, the reader is referred to Gebhard et al. (1958).

PREMATURITY

Two studies report on women who unaccountably give birth prematurely (Gunter, 1963; Blau et al., 1963). Both compare mothers of the premature with matched controls on a series of intelligence and projective tests and clinical rating scales and show more immaturity and inadequacy in the former, leading to the conclusion that these personality factors and related life situations may in part cause the prematurity. The conclusion hardly follows from the semi-subjective measures used, and if there is a psychogenic factor here it remains to be proved. On the other hand, it is adequately established that maternal smoking is related to premature delivery (Joffe, 1969).

PREGNANCY DISORDERS

Little attention has been paid to the possible effect of pregnancy on the personality (McDonald and Gynther, 1965) or of the personality in relation to likelihood of desiring a pregnancy (Flapan, 1969). As an introduction to the former, McDonald and Parham (1964) found lower scores on Minnesota Multiphasic Personality Inventory (MMPI) neurotic and psychotic scales after delivery. In a large survey of a random sample of Oxfordshire women, the neurotic were found to be more likely to become pregnant, as well as more likely to miscarry, than the normals (Mandelbrote and Monro, 1964). If higher frequency of conception is a pointer to desire for children, this is as far as the investigations to date will take us in attempting to link personality and maternal wishes.

Psychiatric health is normal (Osterman, 1965) or unaccountably high during pregnancy (Pugh et al., 1963) and suicides rare (Shainess, 1966). Sexual desire may, however, be reduced (Kane et al., 1968). No evidence for a predicted regression of personality was found in psychological testing in pregnancy (Wenner et al., 1969).

More attention has been given to the problem of the relationship between factors operating during pregnancy, both innate personality and environmental factors, and the course of pregnancy, of delivery, and the health of offspring. Disorders of the course of pregnancy, especially pre-eclampsia, have been found to be related to the expectant mother's youth, primiparity and unwed status (Salerno, 1962). Nausea, occurring in 60 per cent of pregnancies, may be increased by the physician's and society's expectations of its presence as an early sign of pregnancy (Taylor, 1962)—possibly a case of the patient living up to role expectations. Interpersonal, economic and occupational problems have been found to be greater among those with complications of pregnancy (Hetzel et al., 1961) but this was in a group of unmarried women who would, in any case, be expected to have problems beyond the average.

A considerable literature has built up on the relationship between anxiety in pregnancy and complications of delivery. Stott and Marston (1969) find a small but significant relationship between maternal ill health during pregnancy and the birth of a child with the minimal brain-damage syndrome. In a series of prospective blind studies Davids and DeVault (Davids et al., 1961a,b; Davids and DeVault, 1962) have shown that psychological assessment, using Manifest Anxiety Scale, and careful ratings of anxiety by patient and clinician, as well as by sentence completion and objectively coded TAT, made during pregnancy can differentiate those who will later suffer difficulties in delivery. They have not yet demonstrated the power of their measures by predicting from their scores, but clearly this would be both possible and useful. Similarly McDonald and co-workers (McDonald and Christakos, 1963; McDonald, et al., 1963) have shown increased anxiety and neuroticism in those mothers who will later have obstetric complications. Non-confirmatory reports are rarer (Brown, 1964; McDonald and Gynther, 1965; Grimm and Venet, 1966) and, within the limitations of clinical research, the relationship shown bears out the known effect of severe stress on the pregnancies of experimental animals (Caldwell, 1962). James's evidence (1969) is based on public records of infant mortality, marriage and deformities, and also leads to the conclusion that there is a relationship between anxiety or pregnancy stress, defined in various ways, and delivery complications, especially stillbirths, though whether this is a cause and effect relationship or two effects of a single cause cannot be determined at present. Possibly the development of objective continuous daily ratings of symptoms during pregnancy (Erickson, 1967) will improve research and Joffe's (1969) discussion of methodological problems is exemplary for workers in this field.

There is growing evidence (*see* reviews by Montagu, 1962, and Ferreira, 1965) that maternal pregnancy stress is also associated with 'a continuum of reproductive casualty' from the minor to the most severe and fatal deformities (Pasamanick *et al.*, 1956). This is a scientifically respectable revival of many superstitious beliefs concerning pregnancy (McLaren, 1964). Evidence can be brought for a relationship between maternal ill health in pregnancy and the child's later behaviour disorders (Rogers *et al.*, 1955), reading defects, epilepsy, mental deficiency and also stillbirths and neonatal deaths (Kawi and Pasamanick, 1959). Furthermore, a strange group of problem children has been brought to psychiatric and guidance clinics with parental complaints of distractibility and restlessness not confirmable by the clinicians. These too have been found more frequently among mothers whose pregnancies and deliveries were difficult (Cohen, 1966). Possibly the stress of pregnancy influences the mother's anticipation and perception of her child's behaviour and development. If so, this is an area of interpersonal influence as yet insufficiently explored.

The mechanisms of these as yet rather tenuous connections between mother's pregnancy and child's behaviour also remain unexplored. Stott and Marston (1969) mention the importance of inheritance in this connection. But we must not overlook the now extensive comparative work on prenatal determination of behaviour, reviewed by Joffe (1969), the more sophisticated of which has specified the genetic/environmental interaction very precisely. Nor must we forget that animal study shows us clearly that early experiences of the mother can affect the course of pregnancy (Yaron *et al.*, 1963). Also relevant here is the work on human foetal conditioning (Spelt, 1948). Sontag (1962) relates foetal adaptation to external stimuli directly to some rather anecdotal observations on mothers undergoing real life stresses such as fear of a psychotic husband, or news that the child's father was already married, both of which increased foetal activity and heart rate.

PSEUDOCYESIS

Signs and symptoms of pregnancy may be false, an abnormal condition reported by Hippocrates (Fischer, 1962) and known in animals and man as pseudocyesis. The clinical picture is almost exactly that of advancing pregnancy and has confused many. While clearly a disorder primarily of women (Abram, 1969), it has been recorded in a girl of seven years and in a man (Knight, 1960). The cause is said to be wish for or fear of pregnancy (Fischer, 1962),

though these wishes can hardly be of importance in the comparative studies. Subhuman pseudopregnancy (*see* Everett, 1961) can throw some light on the physiology of pregnancy. Shelesnyak (1938) draws a conclusion of a naso-genital relationship from the feasibility of inducing pseudopregnancy in the rat by nasal stimulation. It is also a known consequence of suckling in the rat (Selye and McKeown, 1934). More usual direct antecedents in the human situation have been sterilisation, menopausal changes and isolated intercourse in the unmarried, so that the pregnancy fear and pregnancy wish hypotheses appear superficially plausible.

STERILISATION

Barglow (1964) found pregnancy fantasies persisting years after an operation for sterilisation in 90 per cent of a large sample of women. Twenty-five per cent of these women were said to be psychiatrically disturbed and showed bizarre manifestations of pseudocyesis. However, this investigator was seeking disorders and so some caution must be exercised in following him.

As with abortion, the fears of psychiatric sequelae are great in this, often medically necessary, operation. The major investigations (Ekblad, 1963; Kaij and Malmquist, 1965) on this point have been in Scandinavia, where legal difficulties over female sterilisation have until recently been less than elsewhere. Peel and Potts (1969) review the field and find general agreement that the majority of patients are well and satisfied after sterilisation. The dissatisfied, who also report depression and nervousness postoperatively, are among those who had not had children previously or who are under thirty years of age at the time of marriage. Prior psychiatric disturbance increases the likelihood of dissatisfaction. But the number of children (above one) and length of marriage were not found to be important predictors of satisfaction with sterilisation.

3. Disturbances at Childbirth

DELIVERY COMPLICATIONS AND NEONATE
ABNORMALITIES

Difficulties in the delivery and neonate abnormalities have usually been considered together in studies of the disturbances of childbirth. Joffe (1969) has critically reviewed the work in this area and points out the methodological difficulties inherent in human clinical research where the groups are always to some extent self-selecting. As with pregnancy disturbances, on the topic of delivery room abnormalities excellent work comes from the team of

Pasamanick and his co-workers. Typically they identify from the records of the city of Baltimore all children with a particular disability and compare them with appropriate controls (e.g. from the same class-room or next birth). Hospital birth records yield data on abnormalities of the children's birth. To date they have shown that retarded children, behaviour disorders, reading disorders, cerebral palsy, epilepsy, mental deficiency, etc., all show a significantly higher proportion of premature births and pre- and perinatal abnormalities than their controls (Rogers et al., 1955; Kawi and Pasamanick, 1959; Knobloch and Pasamanick, 1966; Pasamanick and Knobloch, 1966), but as regards lowered intelligence, other investigators are not in accord. Barker (1966) found little evidence of increased prematurity or delivery abnormality among children of low intelligence in Birmingham. The investigators' methods and data presentation differ, so that it is impossible to recommend one over the other—only the volume of confirmatory studies on related disorders of offspring lends some weight to the Baltimore reports. Approaching the problem in the reverse direction, Friedman et al. (1969) retested 1933 infants eight months or a year after a fully documented birth. Comparison of those from dysfunctional and from normal labours revealed no major differences though there were greater tendencies for the former to show motor disorders. Thus, it seems plausible that perinatal factors can be related to the child's development and behaviour though the degree and explanation of the relationship, if established, remains obscure.

DELIVERY COMPLICATIONS AND PERSONALITY OF MOTHER

Investigating the factors associated with the delivery itself, Jansson and Selldén (1966) found no EEG change in records taken from mothers before and after delivery, but differences have appeared in the personalities of women suffering prolonged rather than short labour (Kapp et al., 1963), or painful rather than a painfree one (Chertok, 1969). Illegitimate pregnancies have been noted to present fewer, rather than more, than the normal number of difficulties at time of delivery (Malmquist et al., 1966). If this finding holds up when same age controls are investigated it will require explanation by those who view the reproductive disorders of women as due to rejection of the child. One might expect the unmarried to show a high proportion of child rejections. Delivery room behaviour is said to be improved, and complications reduced, by training in relaxation (Chertok, 1959). Delivery is also said to be rapid and easy in some primitive tribes (Kanner, 1956)

but too few cross-cultural surveys have been carried out for generalisation on this point.

MULTIPLE BIRTHS

Twinning and multiple births are rare statistically, and some gynaecologists incline to the view that, the human uterus being designed for a singleton, a twin or multiple pregnancy is ipso facto abnormal. Such pregnancies also produce a high proportion of prematures and birth complications. The recent cases of quintuplets and sextuplets due to the administration of gonadotropins to subfertile women (Fridhandler and Pincus, 1964) have not yet been the subject of psychological investigation, although there are undoubtedly sociological and psychological difficulties to be faced by the parents and children.

COUVADE

There has recently been a series of papers showing that Western fathers show physical abnormalities at or around the time of their wives' deliveries (Jarvis, 1962; Trethowan, 1965; Trethowan and Conlon, 1965; Wainwright, 1966; Retterstöl, 1968). Everything from toothache to full-blown psychosis is apparently possible in association with the birth of a child. A related study, comparing expectant fathers examined in a court psychiatric clinic with a matched group of men whose wives were not pregnant (Hartman and Nicolay, 1965) found increased sexual deviance among the fathers-to-be. This makes some sense during a wife's pregnancy while the physical disorders of the so-called couvade (Dawson, 1929) syndrome are less meaningful.

4. Postnatal Disturbances

CHILD REJECTION AND INADEQUATE MOTHERING

While there are numerous purely clinical records of inadequate mothering, little systematic work has been carried out on the factors that increase or decrease the likelihood of its occurrence in humans. Infant rejection occurs temporarily in some puerperal psychoses (see later) and in other psychotic states. Infanticide, which differs legally from murder in that the child is under one year old, can occur in psychosis but the incidence is minute.

Later inadequacies of mothering, including such extremes as the battering of babies (Helfer and Kempe, 1968), become social problems and are treated possibly by environmental manipulation. Despite the seriousness of the problem there has been no systematic attempt at behaviour modification. Equally prone to tragic consequences is the rare disorder of child-stealing. No group of child stealers or 'baby snatchers' (almost invariably young women) has been investigated, but psychiatrists believe that the culprits have frustrated 'maternal instinct' (*see* under 'Infertility', page 177).

Some suggestive leads on mothering can be gathered from comparative studies (Rheingold, 1963). Rats with median cortex lesions are found to be inadequate mothers (Stamm, 1955). Rosvold (1949a) found that maternal behaviour (nest-building and retrieval of pups) was disrupted by electroconvulsive shock given to the mother rat in the latter days of pregnancy. Some protection from this deleterious effect is found when the shocks are given under ether anaesthesia (Stone and Walker, 1949) which abolishes the convulsion. It is possible, therefore, that the usual practice of giving electric shock therapy with a muscle relaxant may be beneficial to the patient post-treatment as well as reducing the risk of physical damage during treatment.

Eisner (1960) reviewing parental behaviour in birds (nest-building, egg-laying, incubation, etc.) found the hormonal controls difficult to establish. Increases in prolactin and suppression of gonadal activity facilitate the elicitation of parental behaviour, but care of the young can be induced in birds and many mammals without hormone treatment. The ensuing decade has seen the work explaining many such discrepancies by further knowledge of the brain-pituitary link (Lehrman, 1964; Levine and Trieman, 1969). It is now increasingly clear that pituitary control is established after priming with minute amounts of gonadal hormones secreted at a critical phase in the organism's life.

The quality of maternal behaviour is definitely related to early experience in both monkeys (Harlow, 1962) and chimpanzees (Tinklepaugh, 1932) and may be mediated by a general responsiveness to young animals. Mason and Green (1962), for example, found wild monkeys more responsive to and prone to mother small white rats than were socially deprived laboratory monkeys. There is also evidence that adequacy of maternal care increases with parity in chimpanzees (Nissen and Yerkes, 1943) suggesting that learning occurs despite the fact that maternal care of the young is traditionally considered to be instinctive in sub-humans. It is generally considered also that improvement by learning occurs in human mothers' child care, but documentation is wanting.

LACTATION

Although oxytocin is responsible to a major degree for both the uterine contractions during labour and for the ejection of milk (MacLeod, 1964), and though the former may be inhibited by the toco-phobic patient, there has been neglect of the relationship between personality, especially anxiety, and the secretion and ejection of milk. Kaij and Nilsson (1964) found no correlation between psychiatric symptoms, if any, and length of breastfeeding or feeding troubles in 404 Swedish women interrogated postpartum.

Once again it is mainly from comparative experiments that our meagre psychological information comes. It is known that pseudo-pregnancy can follow from suckling of the nipples of the laboratory rat (Selye and McKeown, 1934) and suckling has also been found to prolong rats' lactation up to 12 months (Bruce, 1961) when strongly suckling foster pups were continually replaced. Oestrus, mating, and further pregnancies could be initiated during the prolonged lactation. Adult rats could be induced to lactate by suckling alone if they had previously given birth and yielded milk, but immature or virgin rats could not be so stimulated. Weak suckling, as by very young pups, tended to allow the milk flow to dry up. It has also been neatly and convincingly demonstrated that the immature rat's mammary gland growth is stimulated during pregnancy by the mechanical self-licking of the glands and genitalia in which the female rat indulges. Roth and Rosenblatt (1965, 1966) showed relative atrophy of the glands in rats prevented from self-licking by a neck collar. Control groups wearing less restrictive collars indicated that the burden and stress of the collar could not be implicated in this finding, which has been used as the justification of a self-stimulation massaging technique designed to increase women's mammary size and milk production for breast-feeding.

The advantages and disadvantages of breast feeding (*see* Newton and Newton, 1951) cannot be covered in this review, particularly as many of the factors adduced in this argument are strictly physical. However, where breast- and bottle-feeding produce behavioural differences in the infant this appears relevant. Bell (1966) compared breast-fed and bottle-fed infants at three and four days old on measures of pre-feeding arousal, based on observations of bodily movement, eye movement, and vocalisation, and found that the breast-fed infants, both male and female, more frequently showed high levels of arousal and vocalisation than the bottle-fed. He suggests that breast-feeding provides a slightly slower and smaller milk yield than bottle-feeding and that the infants are therefore aroused by hunger. Whatever the explanation, and, though behavioural arousal of this sort may be the inverse of cortical arousal (Eysenck, 1967), this finding if confirmed could have important implications for the understanding of developmental personality differences.

PUERPERAL DISORDERS

Much evidence has now accumulated to suggest that during the puerperium, or immediate post-partum period and in contrast with the period of pregnancy, the woman is particularly vulnerable to mental illness, more so than at any time in her life (Pugh et al., 1963). Illnesses reported range from affective disorders and schizophrenia to neurotic conditions (Kaij et al., 1967) and transient 'blues' (Yalom et al., 1968). Rutherford and co-workers (1962) refer to frigidity developing at this specific time, but do not report the frequency of occurrence. Melges (1968) finds a syndrome of shame, helplessness, and confusion. A full review is provided by Hamilton (1962).

Interest has attached to the factors that might contribute to this phenomenon of vulnerability and to the mechanism that produces it. Long ago, Anderson (1933) rejected the view that puerperal psychosis was a product of abnormal sexual conduct or constitution. Smalldon (1940) found a higher proportion of Jews showing puerperal disorders, but this has not been confirmed in better controlled surveys (Foundeur et al., 1957). Writers are agreed that primiparae are most at risk and that post-partum disturbance is preceded by insomnia in pregnancy (Karacon et al., 1969). Women with a family history of psychosis are more likely to succumb (Jansson, 1963) and personality factors are of major importance in this presumed reaction to stress. However, it is still not possible to predict accurately those primiparae who will develop post-delivery symptoms.

Protheroe (1969) has recently published a long-term study of puerperal psychosis among admissions to a Newcastle mental hospital. He examined the records 1927–1961 and included all admissions of whom it was known that the onset of illness occurred within six weeks following labour. In fact, the majority fell ill in the first fortnight and this six-week criterion is arbitrary. Psychiatrists may call psychoses that develop many months after delivery peurperal—a factor making for terminological confusion. From further careful search of hospital records of the 134 patients meeting his criterion, Protheroe analysed the clinical features, treatment, and outcome as well as attempting to follow up the patients and to collect familial data. The diagnoses of his patients included 91 affective reactions, 37 schizophrenics, and 6 organic psychoses, thus confirming the impression that affective disturbance is most common postpartum. In all cases the symptoms followed closely those found in non-puerperal conditions, so that it is now usual to consider puerperal disorder not as a unique clinical entity but as a manifestation at this time of psychosis in

a woman who is constitutionally prone. Early work (discussed by Protheroe) had indicated an association between illegitimacy and puerperal psychosis, while more recently this has been doubted. Protheroe's long-term study provided confirmation of both these views by showing that over the years in question there has been a change from positive correlation between illness and illegitimacy in the 1920s to none at present.

The question then arises as to whether another pregnancy is advisable. Protheroe emphasises that the likelihood of recurrence is great and, of course, recurrence may be unassociated with pregnancy (Hegarty, 1955). However, puerperal psychoses were recorded, in his study, in first to twelfth pregnancies, and recurrence or rehospitalisation was examined. In general, the chance of having further puerperal psychosis is to be placed, on the basis of Protheroe's findings, at 20 per cent, which is high enough to raise the question of therapeutic abortion, particularly in cases where the woman has already had two puerperal breakdowns.

It is noteworthy that over the period studied there has been considerable improvement in the treatments offered. A high proportion of patients prior to 1943 were sedated but otherwise untreated, with the consequence that chronic psychoses developed and deaths in hospital are recorded. Nowadays there is excellent prognosis with electroconvulsive therapy and medication. It is also increasingly possible for mothers to be admitted with their babies (Albretsen, 1968) so that, even when the disorder takes the form of rejection of or delusions concerning the child, the patient can be gradually trained in child care during her recovery.

The puzzle of puerperal psychosis remains. Why should psychosis appear only at this time for some women? The similarity between the peurperal psychoses and the postoperative psychoses (Stengel et al., 1958) has been noted. Both disorders occur after surgical or quasi-surgical procedures, but frequently show a latent period of two or three days before making their appearance. Some women with postoperative psychosis are reported to have suffered puerperal disorder also, though the reverse has not been recorded in the studies on puerperal psychosis.

The value of objective measures in women with normal pregnancies has been recognised in a number of studies bearing on the problem of why the puerperium should be a time of disorder. Kear-Colwell (1965) using the Cattell Neuroticism Scale Questionnaire (NSQ) on 100 women in the first week after delivery found increased neuroticism as compared with 50 control women who were neither pregnant nor within one year of delivery. Kane and co-workers (1968) administered the Clyde Mood

Scale and ratings on lability of mood to 137 mothers at a clinic on the third day post-partum. This pilot study showed some anxiety in the sample post-delivery and suggested also some deficit in cognitive functioning as assessed by clinical methods such as serial subtraction. This tentative finding was essentially confirmed in a larger sample (86) of white mothers compared with controls on the Trail Making Test, Porteus Mazes, MMPI and the NSQ again (Jarrahi-Zadeh et al., 1969). Choice of objective tests and methods of analysis might well have been improved upon so that the findings on cognitive deficit await replication. Karacon and co-workers (1969) suggest an intriguing relationship between rhythms during pregnancy and puerperal breakdown.

5. Menopausal Disturbances

The well-known changes in reproductive physiology of women at the menopause are noteworthy for several reasons. Firstly, because only the human and primate female loses reproductive capacity at an age much younger than the expected chronological life span (Engle, 1952); many species (rat, cat, goat, mare) continue to reproduce at relatively advanced ages. Secondly, while the menopause is essentially normal, the symptoms experienced can be decidedly uncomfortable, inconvenient or entirely traumatic for the woman. An early survey of 1,187 menopausal English women (Council of the Medical Women's Federation, 1933) showed 15·8 per cent symptom free; 20·6 per cent had only minor and transitory disturbances; 62 per cent experienced hot flushes; 45 per cent headaches; 40 per cent giddiness; 34 per cent increase in weight; 31 per cent moodiness; and 24 per cent rheumatic pains. The time of the menopause varied in this study from age 23 to

age 60 years (average 50·1 years in another report, Benjamin, 1960). It is a time of endocrinological adjustment, which usually takes about 18 months. Some physical disorders are said to delay the menopause (Benjamin, 1960) while others may advance it. Contrary to popular belief there has been found no relationship between age at menarche and age at menopause (Benjamin, 1960), and reports conflict on whether the current decrease in menarcheal age (see earlier) gives a corresponding change in menopausal age (Burch and Rowell, 1963; Frommer, 1964). Childbearing does not influence age at menopause (Malleson, 1963) though it does appear to increase the symptomatic discomforts of the menopause (Allen, 1942). There is also evidence that a history of dysmenorrhoea is associated with more severe symptoms at the time of the menopause (Council of the Medical Women's Federation, 1933). Evidence on the effect of oral contraception on menopausal date is awaited.

Menopausal changes can follow artificial reduction of ovarian activity, for example, by disease, surgical removal, or by X-irradiation (Allen, 1942) and some of the symptoms, particularly the hot flushing, can occur also in middle-aged men (Reynolds, 1962). Hormone replacement therapy, particularly the use of oestrogen, can be beneficial if prescribed with caution, and is widely used when the discomfort is excessive. The symptom of hot flushes, the physiological basis of which is not known, nevertheless appears to implicate a malfunction of the basic heat-regulating mechanism at this time (Reynolds, 1962). This is also the period of false accusations of sexual molestation, and possibly also of poison-pen letter writing—disorders that may be stimulated by the psychological distress of terminated fertility. Systematic study yet remains to be done.

B. FEMALE SEXUALITY IN RELATION TO THE PARTNER

1. Choice of Heterosexual Partner

For a survey of marriage counselling the reader is referred to Sanctuary (1968), who gives a full account of such services throughout the world. This section will be concerned with mate selection in normal individuals, since this does not always lead to successful marriage, and the concern of researchers has been to establish the reasons for marriage breakdown. It is also concerned with mate selection among psychiatrically abnormal groups with all its implications for genetic predisposition of the offspring to further psychiatric disorder.

MATE SELECTION IN NORMAL GROUPS

Psychologists and sociologists have done much over the past eighty years or so to elucidate the problems surrounding mate selection and marital satisfaction (Adams, 1966). Recent work involving both test and interview procedures is claimed to show areas of stress and weakness in new marriage relationships (Hooper and Sheldon, 1969). A fundamental question, however, has always been, 'Does like marry like? Is there generally homogamy or heterogamy?' Similarity has been found not to increase mutual attraction in problem-solving groups (Hoffman and Maier, 1966), but, for married partners, the evidence has accumulated in favour of homogamy or assortative mating which occurs specifically with regard to race, age, religion, ethnic origin, social class, and residential propinquity (Katz and Hill, 1958; Luckey, 1963). However, Winch and his associates (Winch, 1958) have proposed the theory that, while homogamy of social characteristics is operative and establishes a 'field of eligibles', mate selection is determined by a specific kind of motivational heterogamy—namely, need-complementarity—by which partners differ in degree or kind of the felt needs. Tharp (1963), who reviews this area incisively, concludes that the need-complementarity hypothesis has not been established although it has stimulated research. Levinger (1964) is less certain that this concept has no value and clarifies some of the interpretations of need-complementarity.

Our concern remains with the research findings around such controversies that have contributed to understanding of the will-o-the-wisp of marital success or lack of it. The classic work in this area was by Terman (1938). Since then, a large number of studies, in which married couples, average well-adjusted couples, and those seeking marriage guidance, answer for themselves and for their spouses—giving their prediction of their spouse's view of themselves on adjectival Q-sorts, MMPI responses, or on personality ratings of the traditional kind—have combined to show that congruence between self-perception and perception by the spouse is associated with marital success. This is particularly true for the male for whom it appears that it is important that he conforms to the socio-cultural norm or widely held pattern of qualities of the ideal husband. 'The maximally happy marital situation can be described as follows: husband and wife agree that he is as *he* wishes to be, namely, like his father; and as *she* wishes him to be, namely, like hers' (Tharp, 1963, p. 101–102). In view of this conclusion, it might seem desirable to study the similarity between fathers and fathers-in-law and the relationship between this and marriage success. But the findings suggest that it is required of the man in his marriage, as in society at large, that he conforms to the male sex-role, and that in so far as he can do this his marriage is more likely to be stable and satisfactory.

Evidence concerning the process of training in sex-role introduces the concept of identification, which leads one to suppose that men marry women who resemble their mothers. Investigation of this point has been generally negative or inconclusive (Sears, 1942; Strauss, 1946). Nevertheless, roles are learned, and Tharp (1963, 1964) argues for role theory as offering to psychologists the best available

approach to the socio-psychological phenomena of marriage.

Husbands and wives have also been found similar in certain important attitudes (Byrne and Blaylock, 1963; Luckey, 1963), but their perceptions of one another's attitudes agree even more closely. It may be that misperception of the spouse is easier than changing the actual attitude towards some aspect of the other's behaviour or personality. Testing hypotheses derived from these ideas, namely that spouses' assumed agreement exceeds their actual agreement about topics important for the marriage, and that assumed agreement varies directly with marital satisfaction, Levinger and Breedlove (1966) measured actual and assumed agreement for 60 married couples of whom 24 were clients at a marriage counselling service. They used a lengthy interview technique in the course of which individuals ranked the relative importance of nine different marriage goals and of 11 marital communication topics. They also filled in a Traditional Family Ideology Scale and described the couple's real and ideal behaviour in several areas of marriage such as decision making, frequency of communication, and frequency of sexual relations. Marital satisfaction was measured by a composite derived from 15 separate indices, and was found to confirm the second hypothesis, particularly for the husbands. The authors have thus shown convincingly that assumed interpersonal agreement and mutual attraction are correlated, but they point out that the parameters of this association have yet to be worked out. Their findings lend some support to their suggestion that an important parameter is that of to-be-agreed-upon objects central to the marriage as opposed to those peripheral to it.

Quite central to marriage is sexual behaviour (Adams, 1966). In a large-scale study of 1,000 couples married from one to nine years, Wallin and Clark (1958) found marital satisfaction correlated with equivalence of preferred frequency of intercourse. Sexual satisfaction was very significantly associated with equivalence of preferred frequency. In another study (Mudd et al., 1961), 100 husbands and wives at a Philadelphia marriage counselling service filled in a Marriage Adjustment Schedule which gave information on preferred frequency of coitus, and satisfaction after coitus, as well as estimates of the spouses' answers in these areas. Consistent with Kinsey's finding (Kinsey et al., 1953) that there is a low correlation between spouses on reported frequency of marital coitus, these workers found that 35 per cent of the couples disagreed in their reports—the male reporting greater frequency. However, the partners agreed more often about frequency than about satisfaction, an aspect of sexuality not emphasised by Kinsey. Wives overestimated their husbands' desires, and altogether the male is seen by both as the partner wanting more sexual intercourse. While this is plausible, in relation to Tharp's (1963) theory of role playing, in that it is perhaps accepted as part of the socio-cultural male role to be sexually demanding, it must be remembered that these were already problem couples.

In later work, Tharp and Otis (1966) have suggested, as an alternative to the mental illness concept, that 'identifiable psychopathology occurs only when the absence of satisfying role-reciprocations produces conflict' (p. 426). A basic hypothesis then is that psychiatric patients experience marital role disturbances more than the average person. This hypothesis was confirmed (Crago and Tharp, 1968), when a group of 35 married psychiatric patients and their spouses were compared with 67 students and their spouses on a Marriage Role Questionnaire giving information on role expectation and role enactment in five classes of family behaviour (solidarity, sexuality, external relations, internal instrumentality, and division of responsibility). Interestingly, only the area of sexuality produced no significant difference between the clinical and normal groups. As Tharp and Otis (1966) suggest, sexual difficulties may have been overemphasised by the dynamic theorists. It may be that family discord can be beneficially approached with greater emphasis on the disturbances in other areas of marital life, to which the sexual difficulties are secondary.

Aside from the interpersonal interactions of marriage, some light is thrown on problem marriages by work in social case history and in therapy. Hurvitz (1967) points to the dangers for a marriage of giving psychotherapy to one partner: often the woman partner receives therapy from a male of whom the husband may become jealous. This is a particular aspect of 'transference'—a situation that many non-psychoanalytic therapists seek in any case to avoid (Johnson and Masters, 1964). That marriage following birth of an illegitimate child presents problems (Dame et al., 1966) should not cause surprise. Unsatisfactory marital adjustment follows emotional disturbances in childhood (Pond et al., 1963) and is to some extent correlated with neuroticism (Ryle, 1966).

DIVORCE

The previous section has in the main reviewed investigations on normal couples or couples seeking guidance where the aim was to avoid divorce or separation. Studies of divorcees suggest that sexual maladjustment between the former partners looms large as an aetiological factor (Kephart, 1954). Kinsey (Kinsey et al., 1953, Table 93) suggests that divorced women prefer a below-average coital frequency. However, achievement of orgasm, Kinsey's criterial measure, is not found to be strongly related to enjoyment of sexual intercourse (Wallin and Clark, 1963). But personality factors other than sexual inclination must also have a bearing on divorce (Tharp and Otis, 1966). Psychiatric disorder was noted in 65 per cent of cases in one large survey as a reason for divorce (Blumenthal, 1967). Few workers, however, have assessed personality before marriage and then obtained data on marriage and divorce for group comparisons. This was the approach of Loeb (1966), who obtained records of students' personality as assessed by MMPI while at college and followed them up more than ten years later, finding that those who later were divorced were on average more disturbed than those who maintained stable marriages. The divorced group had higher psychopathic deviate score (Pd) on the MMPI.

The problem of pathological jealousy should be mentioned as a condition that comes to the attention of psychiatry usually in the marital context. However, only clinical reports exist.

MATE SELECTION IN ABNORMAL GROUPS

A beginning has been made in determining personality characteristics of those who choose to marry schizophrenics (Planansky and Johnston, 1967). Were it to be shown that homogamy or assortative mating is a potent force in determining mate selection among psychiatric patients (Slater and Woodside, 1951), then, with neuroticism shown to have a high heritability (Eysenck and Prell, 1952) and psychosis also demonstrably subject to complex inheritance (Kringlen, 1967), the progeny of such homogamous unions would have an increased chance of becoming the psychiatric patients of tomorrow. There is evidence of a higher than expected frequency of mental illness in the spouses of mental patients (Nielsen, 1964; Kreitman, 1968). Recent work, reviewed by Kreitman (1964) and Neilsen (1964), suggests, however, that the assortative mating hypothesis does not account for all the available facts. In particular, the correlations between spouses for neuroticism (derived from the Cornell Medical Index (CMI) and the Maudsley Personality Inventory), which are high for both patient (0·45) and non-patient (0·36) groups, show changes with duration of marriage inconsistent as between the two groups (Kreitman, 1964). Assortative mating would ensure that husband-wife correlations which are high at marriage should remain so over the years. While this is found to be true of the controls investigated, psychiatric patients show a low correlation at the time of marriage (0·27) which increases during the marriage to 0·47 after 12 years. Such a result suggests interaction between the spouses rather than assortative mating and, although this is still unlikely to be the whole story (Nielsen, 1964), there is considerable confirmatory evidence (Pond *et al.*, 1963; Buck and Ladd, 1965). The development of an objective measure of marital behaviour, the Marital Patterns Test (Ryle, 1966), is a welcome addition to research in this field.

Kreitman (1968) has subsequently confirmed this increase in concordance over the years of marriage for pairs both developing neurotic disorder, but found no increase in concordance postmaritally for pairs containing a psychotic partner. The assortative mating hypothesis is therefore consistent with the data from functional psychotics and from control groups, but is not supported by the findings for neurosis and the personality disorders.

Although alcoholics' daughters are said to marry alcoholic husbands (Kreitman, 1968), investigations of mate selection among alcoholics has not progressed so far as among psychiatric patients. The Interpersonal Perception Technique developed by Drewery and Rae (1969) (an extension of the interpersonal perception research among normals, using, instead of personality ratings, the Edwards Personal Preference Schedule for self, spouse and self-as-seen-by-spouse) suggests that alcoholics have as much insight into their marriages as have comparable controls. Most remarkable, however, is the difference between the females. Wives of controls described their husbands much as they (the controls) described themselves, whereas male patients' self descriptions and descriptions of them as given by their wives are markedly at variance. This finding is attributable to a shared concept of the male personality among the control couples. The alcoholics and their wives either did not have this socio-cultural sex-role stereotype or found it inapplicable to themselves. The interpersonal relationship of patients and their wives showed socio-sexual role confusion and ambivalent dependence-independence needs. This brief consideration of another abnormal group re-emphasises the fruitfulness of considering marital success as well as psychopathology in terms of role playing.

2. Disturbances at Coitus

FREQUENCY OF COITUS

Frequency (Udry and Morris, 1968) and season (Takahashi, 1964) of coitus have been further documented since the Kinsey (Kinsey *et al.*, 1953)

report, despite the clear difficulties of accurate investigations in these intimate areas of behaviour. Aside from their normative value, such investigations have relevance for a study of abnormal sexuality since German (1968) proposed that Down's syndrome may be the result of delayed fertilisation following sporadic or infrequent coitus. While this effect is not yet confirmed, Welch (1968) adduces evidence to show the value of continuing to establish the relationship and suggests testing the hypothesis by comparisons of incidence of Down's syndrome in married and unmarried mothers, in Catholics, who use the 'safe period' as a contraceptive, and non-Catholics, and in divorcees, because Kinsey *et al.* (1953) suggested that divorcees have below average interest in coitus. He further suggests that infrequent coitus may be associated with other chromosomal and teratous aberrations in the offspring and with spontaneous abortions which, as previously noted, are frequently malformed (Hertig, 1967). Since this effect of infrequent coitus may be small, the investigation of cumulative abnormalities rather than of Down's syndrome exclusively could lead to more definitive results.

ORGASM IN COITUS

Using the orgasm as their major index of sexual behaviour, Kinsey *et al.*, (1953) have extensively documented its frequency in American women. The work of Coppen (1965) provides some further evidence on groups of psychiatric patients in Britain. Neurotic patients show very marked differences from the normals, 50 per cent falling in their grades 4–5 of sexual satisfaction, indicating frigidity. Schizophrenics and those suffering from affective disorders show lesser but still significant differences from normal. Even allowing for inaccuracies due to self report, especially by psychotically disturbed patients, these disturbances of sexuality in the psychiatrically ill are striking. However, investigators disagree on the significance of orgasm in the totality of sexuality, a major criticism of the Kinsey approach (Geddes, 1954), and its significance for sexual satisfaction and marriage success is even more dubious (Terman, 1951; Wallin and Clark, 1963).

Since some workers place significance on the first orgasm, particularly in connection with the development of sexual deviations (McGuire *et al.*, 1965) it is of value to have the Brackbills' (Brackbill and Brackbill, 1966) preliminary report on reactions to first-remembered sexual climax.

FANTASIES DURING COITUS

Although rape and prostitution fantasies are described as frequent (Maslow *et al.*, 1966) experimental work in the area of women's sexual fantasies connected with coitus is entirely lacking. Clark (1955) presents incompletely controlled data on males. Hollander (1963) deduces that coital fantasies are associated with masturbation, but her involved analytic reasoning fails to convince and her data are not clearly supportive of her thesis. Moreover, the connection between coital and masturbatory fantasy is apparent from the major part that both coitus and masturbation play in total sexuality. DeMartino (1966) lists fantasies reported by women subjects of another type of investigation.

DYSPAREUNIA, FRIGIDITY, AND NON-CONSUMMATION OF MARRIAGE

Three major disorders of sexual behaviour are recognised in relation to the woman's ability to enjoy or to tolerate sexual intercourse. Dyspareunia or pain on attempted penile penetration is often associated with vaginismus or painful contraction of the vaginal musculature. Frigidity refers to indifference to intercourse or, in some cases, to positive dislike of genital contacts. Less severe may be the absence of orgasm despite sexual enjoyment. This may still be termed frigidity though this is relatively common (Wallin and Clark, 1963, found it occurring in 17 per cent of 417 women) and is less likely to come for any form of therapy or behaviour change. Non-consummation of marriage refers to the complete failure of penile penetration after attempts at sexual intercourse. Occasionally, shallow penetration may have been achieved, and not infrequently conception has occurred so that the hymen may or may not be intact. These then are disorders of sexual relationships which, although separate problems, distinctly overlap and may therefore be considered together.

Incidence of these conditions has never been adequately determined and as there are all degrees of the disorders there is unlikely to be an easily accepted figure. Moulton (1966) notes that frequency of frigidity varies from 15 to 90 per cent according to the observer. For non-consummation specifically, the situation is reviewed by Friedman (1962) but we learn only that selected general practitioners see 8 to 60 'virgin wives' a year in their practices and that all three disorders make up 1·5 to 5 per cent of gynaecological cases. The incidence in the total population is not known.

Leaving aside those patients who can be helped to overcome physical abnormalities, aetiological theory varies with the background of the writer. Blair and Pasmore (1965) attempt a psychoanalytic classification of their 58 cases of frigidity. Problem areas are said to centre round the patient's relationships with her own body, feelings of inadequacy as a woman, anger over being a woman, and a need to deny all feeling, but they admit that 'no patient corresponds completely to one of these' (p. 6), so that we are little further advanced.

Clinical experience indicates an over-representation of sexual traumata (molestation and rape) in the past histories. This is consistent with explanations of frigidity as a learned phenomenon. Malleson (1954) suggests that conditioning is the cause of sex problems in marriage and implicates chiefly rectal examination which may be traumatic for the child and later elaborated in fantasy. The similarity of innervation of the anal and vaginal areas would be sufficient to account for the generalisation of such an experience from one body area to another. Such generalisations are commonplace in the learning theory explanations of phobic conditions. Medical writers usually recommend reassurance, relaxation, and the insertion of graduated dilators (Malleson, 1954; Dawkins and Taylor, 1961) thus, in effect, operating a simple desensitisation schedule. Fear of some aspect of the penile insertion is the almost universally encountered phenomenon here, and has proved amenable to systematic desensitisation (Wolpe, 1958, 1969). Hierarchies of approach to the vagina and vaginal contact are usually employed (Lazarus, 1963; Haslam, 1965) and hierarchies of increasing ease in social situations have also proved of value (Kraft and Al-Issa, 1967). Cooper (1964) mentions a case of frigidity that cleared with the alleviation of asthma treated by desensitisation. The usual methods of relaxation, including hypnosis and the use of methohexitone sodium (Brady, 1966) have been found effective. More recently, there has been increasing emphasis on the participation of the husband in the presentation of the hierarchy (Madsen and Ullman, 1967; Cooper, 1969). Leventhal (1968) reports the therapy of an atypical case of sexual phobia by desensitisation techniques within the more traditional psychotherapy. While the psychoanalytic approach claims 71 per cent improvement for non-consummation (Friedman, 1962), these reports of application of general psychological principles to the treatment of coital disorders within marriage reveal 66 per cent improvement on a conservative estimate, with considerable reduction of therapists' time with each patient. Thus, they confirm Malleson's (1954) view that learning has contributed to the development of these disorders and offer hope for the further refinement of rational techniques for alleviating these uncommon but maritally disastrous difficulties.

3. Homosexuality

Much less has been written on the subject of homosexuality in women or lesbianism than on male homosexuality. Some attempt has been made to relate female homosexuality to masculine body build (Henry and Galbraith, 1934) but many women exhibiting the found characteristics, low voice, under-developed breasts etc., are definitely heterosexual. In the special case of women in prison, Ward and Kassebaum (1967) find homosexual behaviour is no more than a continuation of the woman's role 'outside' where her life is based on an intense relationship with husband, child, or parent. Berecz, (1968) reviews the evidence for an association between childhood schoolphobia and later developing homosexuality. This is a link with psychoanalytic thought which emphasises the aetiological role of the dominant mother and the detached, 'maternal' or passive father (*see* Wilbur, 1965, for a summary of various analytic aetiologies). For those who accept these aetiological hypotheses it follows that psychotherapy offers considerable promise of change (Socarides, 1963; Romm, 1965; Mayerson and Lief, 1965) but the groups reported on are selected, uncontrolled, and too small for generalisation (Mayerson and Lief, 1965). The fact remains that homosexual women rarely seek change (Kaye *et al.*, 1967; Kenyon, 1968b, 1968c).

In the last few years a definite attempt has been made to establish normative data on the present characteristics and developmental factors in the lives of women homosexuals. Bene (1965), using the far from objective Bene-Anthony Family Relations Test and a questionnaire, investigated 37 non-psychiatric lesbians from a lesbian society and 80 married women controls. She confirmed the even more subjective work of Kaye *et al.* (1967) finding that homosexuals retrospectively report a very different picture of their fathers from controls. Memory of the mother is essentially the same for the two groups. The homosexuals' father image, however, is of a weak, incompetent person towards whom they felt fear or hostility as children. (Similarly, Kremer *et al.* (1969) found no 'close-binding' fathers in their group of adolescent lesbians.) Significantly, more of the homosexuals than controls believed their parents would have preferred a son.

Kenyon (1968a, 1968b, 1968c) and Hopkins (1969) in Britain, and Saghir and co-workers (Saghir and Robins, 1969; Saghir *et al.*, 1969) in the United States bring the study of homosexuality up to date. In both countries, the co-operation of lesbian societies was gained. Kenyon contacted 123 homosexual women and an equal number of married women as controls. Subjects took psychological tests (MPI and CMI), provided anthropometric data and answered an extensive questionnaire. While much depends on the subjects' willingness to co-operate and report truthfully and to recall past

events, this study remains a most comprehensive and detailed collection of data on female homosexuality. It emerged that the homosexuals, as a group, are significantly higher on neuroticism than the heterosexuals. No significant differences on extraversion were found (Kenyon, 1968a). Compared with controls, homosexual women had poorer work records, were more inclined to reject organised religion, and had much more evidence of disturbed childhoods and home lives—poor relationship with parents, death of mothers, parental discord, homosexuality in the families, and greater incidence of having been adopted. Homosexuals had more frequently received psychiatric help, but only 5 per cent had required in-patient treatment and the commonest reason for treatment was depression rather than homosexuality. The homosexual group rated themselves on the Kinsey Scale from 1 to 6, only 37 per cent using the rating of 6 (exclusively homosexual) and this group was more stable than the mixed or bisexual group.

Hopkins (1969) has been more concerned with personality assessment than the social history data emphasised by Kenyon. She gave Cattell's 16PF test to 24 lesbians and 24 matched controls and could not confirm Kenyon's finding of higher neuroticism in the homosexuals. She does report more reserve and more dominance as well as more compromise, resilience, and self-sufficiency among the homosexuals.

The American study (Saghir and Robins, 1969) incorporates interview data from 57 lesbians who had never been hospitalised for psychiatric reasons. Unfortunately, no control group of heterosexual women was seen, the authors being more interested in comparisons with homosexual men similarly contacted and investigated (Saghir *et al.*, 1969). They found twice as much self-stimulation (masturbation) among male homosexuals as among females. Development of homosexuality was similar in these male and female groups, with heterosexual arousal occurring more in early—70 per cent in women and 49 per cent in men—than in later life. Women, however, started their homosexual practices significantly later than men. Women had fewer homosexual partners than men and had more long-term attachments with strong emotional basis than had men, both comparisons reaching a very high level of significance. Similarly, heterosexual intercourse was also commoner among homosexual women (79 per cent) than men (48 per cent). The lack of population controls is almost compensated for in this American study by the availability of Kinsey's data (Kinsey *et al.*, 1953) and much valuable normative data on lesbian practices is tabulated here. Unpublished work (Kolaszynska, 1969) gathered similarly from co-operating non-patient members of British homosexual organisations suggests that heterosexual fantasy is frequent among lesbians but that heterosexual attraction is weak and heterosexual experiences generally induce negative attitudes of dislike rather than fear. Kenyon (1970) ably reviews and summarises the previously published literature including animal and cross-cultural studies and clinical associations of lesbianism. There is a uniform finding of lesser incidence of homosexual behaviour in females than in males.

Feldman and MacCulloch (1970) put forward a theory of strengthening of homosexuality in women by their aggressive response to male approaches. This initially anxiety-reducing behaviour may be ultimately maladaptive as it limits the opportunities for desensitisation to heterosexual experiences.

4. Fetishism and other Sexual Disorders

The various disorders of sexuality that occur among men and, on occasions, bring them to the attention of psychiatrists or the courts are little discussed in writings on female sexuality. It has been wrongly stated that fetishism, for example, is totally confined to men, but cases of fetishism in women are known. However, the much reduced incidence of female fetishism (Socarides, 1963) still requires explanation. Occasional cases of female transvestism are also reported (Barahal, 1953), but Stoller (1968) maintains this is a symptom of transsexualism and does not occur with true sexual arousal in women.

Similarly, frotteurism, voyeurism, exhibitionism, sadism, masochism are known to be operative in female sexuality, though the incidence is apparently greatly reduced relative to males and the significance of the behaviour when it occurs may well vary between the sexes. But in women these behaviours do not create the social problem that they create when performed by men and, hence, both counter-legislation and objective enquiry are rare.

C. FEMALE SEXUALITY IN ABNORMAL CONDITIONS

1. Extremes of Intelligence

Little information is available on sexuality among the intellectually gifted. Terman (1951) found that gifted women's orgasmic adequacy was by no means the most important factor in their marital happiness. Meade and Parkes (1966) show that the gifted are now increasing their family size, but studies of family size and intelligence (Scottish Council for Research in Education, 1953) are confounded with many other factors.

Though basically directed towards problems arising from the now out-of-date nature-nurture controversy, studies relating illegitimacy with intelligence (McClure, 1931; Nottingham, 1937; Schmideberg, 1952) may perhaps give some indication of a relationship between sexuality and intelligence. Many workers (e.g. McNemar, 1940) have criticised the studies for having a biased sample of unmarried mothers since the higher social groups are less likely to come to the attention of the welfare agencies, or may otherwise escape assessment. But the careful study, referred to earlier, by Pearson and Amacher (1956), who tested approximately 40 per cent of all unmarried mothers in the state of Minnesota over the 5-year period 1946–1951, showed an average very close to IQ 100 and standard deviation also close to the population standard deviation.

Tizard (1954), reporting on a 5 per cent sample of the 12,000 mental defectives in institutions in (then) Greater London found under 4 per cent of the women had venereal disease or were pregnant and approximately 5 per cent of male patients had histories of indecent assault or exposure. There is therefore little in these reports to suggest hypersexuality in those of low intelligence, though no doubt, with lack of training and appropriate opportunity, expressions of sexuality in this group may be socially undesirable.

2. Brain Damage and Epilepsy

The early discovery (Klüver and Bucy, 1939) that bilateral temporal lobectomy led to hypersexuality in monkeys suggested that a cerebral centre governing sexual control might eventually be found. Klüver (1965) has more recently expounded the view that bilaterally lobectomised animals suffer a more general deficit of olfactory, sexual, and emotional functioning, these activities being subsumed under the rubric of 'poikilofunctioning'. Ball (1968) describes a case of (male) sexual disorder possibly caused by organic (temporal lobe) deficit, but, in a postoperative study of 100 temporal lobe epileptics, Taylor (1969) found hyposexuality more common than hypersexuality.

As already noted, Healey (1928) and Almquist (1955) have observed an association between menstrual phases and increase of epileptic attacks in some individuals. Occasional reports of linkage between sexual behaviour or subjective experience and epilepsy appear from time to time. A tumour on the medial surface of the right cerebral hemisphere caused hypersexuality in a woman of menopausal age. Her condition was only diagnosed when it deteriorated sufficiently to include motor seizures with aurae of 'passionate feelings' on the left side of the body, and confirmed when recovery followed removal of the tumour (Erikson, 1945). Epilepsy is reported to be precipitated by orgasm (Hoenig and Hamilton, 1960; Taylor, 1969). A case of epilepsy with impotence due to frontal oligodendroglioma is on record (Johnson, 1965) and there is thought to be an association between impotence and temporal lobe epilepsy. Temporal lobe sexual seizures with vaginal aurae are reported by Scott (1964) and Freemon and Nevis (1969): epilepsy was proposed as an aetiological factor in the development of one patient's homosexuality, while the second included such vulgar verbal and non-verbal sexual automatisms that the patient was vilified and threatened with institutionalisation by her family.

3. Genetically Determined Abnormalities

Almost all behaviour may be considered to have genetic and environmental determinants which interact, and the strength if not the exact size of the genetic component has been shown for such conditions as homosexuality and psychosis (Kallman, 1953) both of which have direct and indirect effects upon sexuality. However, we confine attention here to abnormalities of the human chromosome complement which produce the various forms of intersexuality (Overzier, 1963).

It is now well known that the normal human chromosome complement comprises 23 pairs of chromosomes among which the sex chromosome takes the form XX in women and XY in men. The additional X chromosome in women is apparently inactivated during embryogenesis and forms the sex chromatin body regularly found in the cell nuclei of normal females but not found in the cell nuclei of normal males (Brown, 1968). This chromatin is readily stained and identified microscopically to give positive (chromatin present; nuclear sex female) or negative (chromatin absent; nuclear sex male) findings. Full information, particularly on the presence or otherwise of the Y chromosome requires the much more time-consuming chromosome studies that determine chromosomal sex (karyotyping). While normal women are XX and normal men XY chromosome carriers, a large number of genetic abnormalities are logically possible and quite a few of these are viable though producing physical and behavioural abnormalities now coming to be more widely studied and understood.

True hermaphrodites have both male and female gonadal tissue and may be of nuclear sex male or

female. Overzier (1963) advises that, if the patient's inclination and nuclear sex are not in agreement, plastic surgery or endocrine replacement therapy should be in the direction that the patient wishes, rather than be consistent with the nuclear sex. But he notes that in cases of doubt it is often easier for these hormone-deficient individuals to live as females. This observation is supported by the more frequent reports of criminality and personality deviation in the phenotypic males with chromosome disorders (Nielsen and Tsuboi, 1969).

Pseudohermaphrodites have unisexual gonads compatible with their nuclear sex but show deformities of the external genitalia and genital ducts. Female pseudohermaphrodites are rare, but males relatively more frequent. It can be appreciated that these individuals face psychological difficulties both from the derision of their school-mates and their difficulties in sexual adjustment. Corrective surgery may be enormously beneficial.

Testicular feminisation appears as a female phenotype of male genotype and nuclear sex. Without ovaries or uterus and with the vagina short or absent, no menarche is possible and it is this which brings these otherwise normal 'women' to medical attention. It may be that the normality of the feminine somatotype contributes to the personality stability noted as characterising these people (Negulici et al., 1968). Despite the presence of testes, sexual feelings and inclinations are predominantly feminine and it is possible for these patients to lead a normal woman's sex life including marriage, intercourse, and orgasm, though, of course, remaining sterile. Their interest in sexual intercourse is said to be normal or even heightened, with a lower than average incidence of frigidity. They are also said to be of high intelligence and stable personality so that they are found among professional women and, if married, may very successfully adopt children. Removal of the (non-functional) testes has, however, been known to lead to depression and psychosis (Overzier, 1963).

The chromatin positive (XXY) phenotypic male is the true Klinefelter's syndrome patient. The extra female chromosome causes reduction of testicular development and spermatogenesis, impotence and mental retardation (Hoaken et al., 1964) so that many of these patients are found in mental deficiency hospitals or show various forms of anti-social behaviour (Nielsen, 1964). They also suffer from epilepsy above the population incidence level.

Absence of female gonads (gonadal aplasia) in people with female external genitalia was first described by Turner and, hence, takes the name of Turner's syndrome. There are varieties of this disorder from the chromosomally XO type to various mosaics. Shaffer (1963) reviews the literature on intellectual and personality assessment of these patients and himself provides a study of 13 cases. He finds intelligence not significantly lower than the general population mean, and personality to be characteristically feminine. Low levels of activity and inhibition of emotions were noted but serious emotional disturbance did not occur. Mellbin (1966), however, in a smaller sample, found a high proportion of psychiatric disorder and abnormality of the EEG.

A condition of complete agonadism has also been reported in individuals who are phenotypic 'women' but lack menstruation and breast development in adolescence. Overzier (1963) provides personality descriptions of a number of these abnormal types. Despite his immense knowledge of these physical disturbances, the numbers seen of any one type are, however, too small to warrant group personality description. As a whole, it appears that individuals with either more or less than the usual number of sex chromosomes or sex organs will be crippled in sexual and social activities if not also obviously deformed or intellectually retarded or both. It is of interest that schizophrenics were over-represented among the hospitalised female subnormals found to have sex chromatin abnormalities (Ridler et al., 1963) although male patients with Klinefelter's syndrome are rarely reported with schizophrenic symptoms.

4. Endocrine Disorder

While studies of mental deficiency, pituitary disorder, and hormonal imbalance frequently refer to precocious development of the primary and secondary sexual characteristics, it is unlikely that precocious genital development is associated with abnormal hypersexuality. The reverse is more likely, and the boy with precocious physical sexual development, as for example in a case of Von Recklinghausen's disease with hyperpituitarism (Jordan, 1956), may be described as quiet and affable with no evidence of sexual drive. Thus, we find the sexual 'cripples' (Overzier, 1963) among those with severely disordered sexual hormone production.

Variations in endocrine levels in otherwise normal groups have thrown further light on the role of the hormones in the establishment and maintenance of normal sexuality. Reviews of comparative work show the association of the hypothalamus with sexuality (Michael and Harris, 1958), and the feasibility of pseudohermaphrodite production by injection of testosterone propionate (masculinising) or oestrogen (feminising) in pregnant rats and guinea-pigs (Young, 1961; Young and Goy, 1964). A similar virilising

effect on offspring when testosterone is taken in pregnancy has been noted in humans (Overzier, 1963). Michael (1964) reviews the evidence from hormone injection studies that 'the potential for both male and female patterns is present in the nervous system of many adult vertebrates' (p. 48). Anthropological evidence (Mead, 1961) suggests that bisexual expression is common in humans also and, hence, a characteristic shared with other mammals. Although the genetic sex of mammals may not be alterable by hormone injection (Barraclough, 1967) sexual behaviour is more susceptible to endocrine change (Levine and Mullins, 1966; Young, 1967). For further reviews of comparative work on sexual response see Martini and Ganong (1967).

Studies of hormone control of human female sexuality have centred round the question of the relative importance of the ovarian and other sexual hormones. Maslow (1965) argues that the ovarian hormones play little part in female sexuality since women report a peak of sexual desire premenstrually when the hormonal level is low, and since ovariectomy causes little change in sexuality (Waxenberg et al., 1960), a finding that Waxenberg (1963) cites as evidence for the dependence of female sexuality on androgens rather than oestrogens. Administration of the androgen testoterone is also reported to increase female libido (Kupperman, 1963).

However, the importance of oestrogens in female sexual behaviour may have been underestimated. The method of daily data collection throughout the menstrual cycle shows, not a premenstrual peak in sexual activity, but, a mid-cycle peak (Udry and Morris, 1967). In any case, there are several studies which show that very small amounts of oestrogen are all that is required to prime subhuman experimental animals to respond sexually (Michael, 1964) and since the adrenal glands produce oestrogen in small amounts the hypothesis that minimal oestrogen is essential is consistent with Waxenberg's findings of the change after adrenalectomy. Sexual behaviour change during pregnancy and in the postmenopausal period when hormone levels are known to be altering would be informative, and work is beginning (Kane et al., 1969). Generally, the work in this area is inconclusive, being retrospective, uncontrolled, and on small selected samples of the population. (For an introduction to behavioural consequences of ingestion of oral contraceptives see Section 6, below.)

5. Psychiatric Disorder

While many of the interactions between sexuality and psychiatric disorder have been referred to in earlier sections, this section is concerned with some remaining aspects of sexuality in psychiatric patients.

SCHIZOPHRENIA

Epidemiological studies suggest that, despite retaining an interest in the opposite sex and showing considerable sexual content in the hallucinations and delusions of disorder, schizophrenic women (Gittleson and Dawson-Butterworth, 1967) and men (Gittleson and Levine, 1966) are more friendless and therefore more likely to remain single (Stevens, 1969). Conversely, it is found that single patients are over-represented among schizophrenics (Gittelman-Klein and Klein, 1968). Married or unmarried, they are more likely to be passive sexually (Kringlen, 1967) and the number of pregnancies is reduced in comparison with co-twin controls (Slater, 1953; Stevens, 1969). It is not surprising to find, with low marriage rate, a raised illegitimate fertility in schizophrenia (Stevens, 1970). In general, these findings in Western populations have been confirmed also in an Arab community (El-Islam and El-Deeb, 1968) where in addition it was noted that 'forced marriage', i.e. marriage under family pressure, was found among the schizophrenics although very rare for men in general. Forced marriage did not appear to have any effect either for good or ill on the prognosis of the schizophrenic, an observation supported by the careful work of Gittelman-Klein and Klein (1968) in the United States. They conclude that, 'the process of the illness is not reversible by marriage'.

Some interest has thus been shown in the, possibly, causative or supportive or protective role played by the schizophrenic's spouse or sexual partner. But childbirth has seemed to be the aspect of sexuality with greatest aetiological significance in schizophrenia since, as we have seen earlier, schizophrenia may occur puerperally. Yet only one investigation of the effect of childbirth on known schizophrenic women has come to hand. Yarden and his colleagues (1966) compared 67 schizophrenic women who become pregnant soon after the onset of symptoms, with an equal number of carefully matched control schizophrenic women who did not become pregnant. Although there were trends towards worsened prognosis for the pregnant (and delivered) group in the first year of follow-up, there was no significant difference between the two groups in the longer, five-year follow-up. This confirms the general clinical view that pregnancy should not be discouraged and does not necessarily lead to a worsening of schizophrenia.

Yet another aspect of schizophrenic disorder and sexuality concerns Freud's (1934) hypothesis that paranoid schizophrenia results from homosexuality—specifically, that paranoid symptoms represent a failure of defences which would normally result in repression of the homosexuality. Klaf and Davis (Klaf and Davis, 1960; Klaf, 1961) have deduced consequences of Freud's hypothesis and tested these on large numbers of male and female paranoids and non-psychotic controls. Some of the consequences were confirmed for males and some for females, but over the whole group of paranoid patients the results do not strongly support Freud, particularly as the paranoid patients were not significantly different from Kinsey's normals (Kinsey et al., 1948) on, for example, incidence of early homosexual episodes.

DEPRESSION

While depression is frequently found to cause a reduction of sexual desire (Palmer and Sheridan, 1938; Kraines, 1957), the opposite or over-compensatory reaction of hypereroticism is also reported particularly in the manic phase of manic-depressive psychosis (Trethowan, 1968). Guilt and fear concerning certain sexual behaviours are more characteristic of depression than are sexual hallucinations or delusions.

Understandably, evidence on sexual performance is hard to obtain but is inferred from marriage rates and numbers of offspring. Late marriage seems to characterise psychiatric patients. Kreitman (1968) and Kallman (1953) found a high rate of celibacy among manic-depressives. Stenstedt (1952) confirmed this for manic-depressives but was less certain about the group of involutional melancholics and it seemed likely that marriage and fertility are related to age of onset of depressive disorder, involutional melancholia occurring later in life than manic-depressive psychosis. However, Hopkinson (1963) and Stevens (1969) in Britain were not able to confirm the lower marriage rate (higher celibacy) of depressives. The former investigator found no relationship between celibacy and age of onset of depressive disorder, although the fertility of depressive women was tentatively related to age of onset.

NEUROSIS

Interest in the relationship between sexuality and neurosis has in some quarters been confined to the relatively simple question of the extent to which neurosis modifies sexuality. (Slater, 1943, 1945, showed that sexual inadequacy correlates with neurotic constitution.) But the major controversy centres around Freud's clearly stated conviction that disturbed sexuality, including masturbation, is aetiological for all cases of neurosis. 'Phobias do not occur when the *vita sexualis* is normal', Freud wrote (1934) and, without the major fact-finding attempts represented by the Kinsey volumes, such a statement is difficult to refute. Certainly Freud has been used as justification by numerous psychiatrists who confidently assume that sexual behaviour is disturbed on the sole evidence of current mild depression, over-anxiety concerning the children, or incidents of stealing and so on.

But what emerges from a study of sexuality and neurosis? Surprisingly long after the early Freudian pronouncements came the careful investigations of Winokur and Holemon (1963) on 31 anxiety neurotics male and female. Following Kinsey, they used an interview technique and assessed total sexual outlet (intercourse, masturbation and nocturnal orgasm). In many respects their group corresponded well to Kinsey's (1948, 1953) norms for the same age group and social class. Relatively few patients found that illness had decreased their sexual activities and some reported that sexual activity served to decrease their anxieties. Only in one respect did these anxiety neurotics differ sexually from controls. Of the 18 women investigated, eight (44 per cent) reported that they had experienced nocturnal orgasm—a higher percentage than reported by Kinsey (below 40 per cent). However, this finding is not specific to anxiety neurosis. Winokur (1963) has found high frequency of nocturnal orgasm to be characteristic of all psychiatric patients. The phenomenon of spontaneous diurnal orgasm has also been observed in psychiatric patients, but its frequency in normal groups remains conjectural.

However, of even greater relevance to the testing of Freudian pronouncements is the investigation of sexuality in hysteria. Classically, of course, this was a condition said to be due to movements of or absence of the womb in women. If these were indeed the aetiological factors then the disorder would necessarily be confined to women and there is a strong tendency to limit the discussion of hysteria to women patients. Perley and Guze (1962) state that hysteria, properly defined, occurs only in women. In fact, the term hysteria is not popular now in psychiatry. In any case, few would go as far as Perley and Guze, and their system of diagnosis by symptom checklist is not in accord with the promising classification of disorder by personality dimensions such as neuroticism and extraversion (Eysenck, 1960). A man can have high scores on both neuroticism and extraversion which, in Eysenckian terminology, defines an 'hysteric'. Such a clearly defined term is to be preferred to the usual diagnosis of 'hysteria', although the terms may have common features.

Among other findings, Winokur and Holemon (1963) noted that dysmenorrhoea and dyspareunia were commoner in hysteria than in their group of anxiety neurotics. Perley and Guze (1962) consider frigidity to be almost diagnostic of hysteria though not all agree (Prosen, 1967). Hence, although malign influence is no longer attributed directly to the womb, evidence relating sexuality to hysteria is forthcoming and must be checked. With this in mind, Bragg (1965) studied 1,601 hysterectomy cases and found a slight but non-significant relationship between hysterectomy and later admission to mental hospital. The possibility that neurosis may predispose to hysterectomy (Lund, 1964; Munro, 1969) is, however, duly noted. Bragg, however, relies heavily on the notion of hysterectomy as being more disturbing than other operations by virtue of the symbolic significance of the sex organs. Whatever the findings, and they are not impressive, there are plenty of reasons, endocrinological and sociological, for disturbance following hysterectomy other than its sexual symbolism.

A contrasting experimental study by O'Neill and Kempler (1969) shows that 'hysterics'—normals selected on the basis of personality questionnaire responses—were inconsistent in responses with sexual connotation. The authors predicted approach-avoidance conflict behaviour to be characteristic of hysterics and confirmed their prediction in learning and visual recognition tasks. This is but one of the growing number of sound researches into sexuality and personality relationships (De-Martino, 1966; Eysenck, 1970) too often ignored by clinicians. Even in clinical studies, despite the numerous dogmatic statements to the contrary, there is little positive evidence of sexual abnormality among neurotics, either dysthymics (introverted neurotics) or hysterics (extraverted neurotics), and, hence, little to support Freud's theory of a sexual basis of disorder.

However, in this connection the disorder known as anorexia nervosa is of particular importance. Although it is often questioned whether this is a syndrome in its own right or a symptom variously caused, the diagnosis is generally applied to those patients who cease to eat, and maintain their obstinate abstention even when body weight has been reduced to dangerous levels. It occurs only very rarely in married, parous women, being characteristically limited to single women between the ages of 14 and 20 years, though occasionally young men are reported as anorexic and Warren (1968) reports on a group of girls whose onset was in the main prepubertal. This markedly uneven sex distribution alone would suggest the importance of this disorder for a survey of abnormal sexuality. In addition, anorexia nervosa is commonly accompanied by amenorrhoea and is reputed to be related to sexual difficulties. Crisp (1966) refers to poor premorbid sexual adjustment, but his patients were adolescents who might not yet have experienced any opportunity for sexual adjustment. He also found novel and distressing sexual experiences in the past history of 16 of his 21 cases. Such observations seem to support the 'dynamic' explanations of anorexia nervosa in terms of denial of sexuality and fear of pregnancy. Experimental test of these hypotheses by assessing the strength of relationship between food and sex in subliminal perception gave some confirmatory findings in a single case study (Beech, 1959). On the other hand, the continuing reports of therapeutic successes by symptomatic treatments from chlorpromazine (Crisp, 1966) to operant control (Bachrach et al., 1965; Leitenberg et al., 1968) and desensitisation (Hallsten, 1965) suggest again that too much has already been made of the disturbed sexuality hypothesis. Poor sexual adjustment did not distinguish anorexics from psychiatric controls (Wright et al., 1969) in a careful discriminant function analyses. It must again be concluded that this hypothesis has not proved to be tenable.

6. Effects of Drugs

Practically nothing is known of the effects on sexual behaviour in normal women of pharmacological agents other than those with endocrine effects. Our main interest is in the effects of antipsychotic drugs, the effects of oral contraceptives, and the effects of addictive drugs including alcohol.

ANTIPSYCHOTIC DRUGS

Many psychoactive drugs have anticholinergic side effects which adversely affect male sexuality—particularly penile erection and ejaculation (Blair and Simpson, 1966). No report has come to hand of the effect of these drugs on sexuality in women, but it can be assumed that the action would similarly resemble the hyperactivity of parasympathetic functioning and, hence, both desire and orgasmic adequacy would be reduced.

ORAL CONTRACEPTIVES

Since the recent rapid rise in the use of oral contraceptives there has been a growing number of reports of undesirable side-effects. Harris (1969) reports a case of malignant hypertension which abated after cessation of oral contraceptive (Lyndiol) and there is fear of oral contraceptives as possibly causing cancer (see Strong, 1936) or sterility of later generations. These fears, however, are as yet unproven. Fears of thrombosis are more firmly founded, but the risk of fatality is no greater than, for example, caused

by pregnancy. The undoubted changes in menstruation are generally for the better (Moos, 1968) and electroencephalographic changes are also known (Matsumoto et al., 1966). But it is with the more directly behavioural side effects that we are concerned. Glick (1967), reviewing mood and behavioural changes following oral contraception, concluded that lack of control data and variation in dosage made it impossible to state anything definitively. Many patients report that they 'feel better' and have more frequent sexual intercourse with greater pleasure. But this is not specific to oral contraceptives since it is reported also with other contraceptive devices and is attributed to removal of the fear of pregnancy. A small number of patients report mood changes for the worse, but the majority are unchanged (Glick, 1967).

Since 1967, however, there has been increasing concern over the likelihood of inducing depression. Many writers affirm that depressions of varying degrees, but reaching psychotic and suicidal levels, can be related to ingestion of oral contraceptives (Nilsson et al., 1967; Nilsson and Almgren, 1968; Grant and Pryse-Davies, 1968) especially with longer periods of medication and increased progestin content of the 'pill' (Lewis and Hoghughi, 1969). Although the perfect control study has probably not yet been achieved, informed medical practice avoids prescription of contraceptives containing mainly progestin and avoids any oral contraceptives when there is already a history of depression or mood swings.

While those reporting depression with oral contraceptives may refer to concomitant loss of libido (Grant and Pryse-Davies, 1968), and freedom from inhibitions concerning pregnancy may increase sexuality, changes in sexual activity following oral contraception were not marked in the only study that specifically sought information on this point (Rodgers and Ziegler, 1968). If, then, a desire to avoid pregnancy, which can be presumed to be strong in those starting a contraceptive regime, does not in itself inhibit sexuality it becomes important to assess not only the effectiveness of the contraceptives used but also the efficiency of the user. Bakker and Dightman (1964) used MMPI and 16PF scales to assess the personalities of those women who consistently took their oral contraceptive and those who had lapses of memory in this connection. They found that 'forgetters' were also immature women who avoided responsibility and tended towards impulsive action rather than contemplation. Since their forgetting was enhanced by discord and conflict with husbands and since their irresponsible attitude would extend also to mechanical forms of contraception, these authors suggest that surgical contraception is the method of choice for this group if pregnancy must be avoided.

ADDICTIVE DRUGS

Until recently it was assumed that alcohol reduces inhibition and so releases sexual drive, but at the same time diminishes potency. The experimental work of Gantt (Gantt, 1952; Teitelbaum and Gantt, 1958) on dogs has put these assumptions on a firmer than anecdotal basis. However, such findings remain to be replicated on humans, and in any case, since the emphasis is on erectile and ejaculatory reflexes in males, they add nothing to our understanding of the sexuality of women. A clinical survey of alcoholics (Levine, 1955) in hospital records, and including 16 women, suggests that, while promiscuity may occur, orgasm is almost entirely absent and disinterest in men is typical. Frigidity is common in those who do have sexual partners—a finding confirmed by Gebhard (1965).

Despite their growing use in the community, even less is written on the effect of other addictive drugs on sexual behaviour. 'Marihuana has been said to improve sexual potency, probably because of the distortion of the passage of time . . . that makes a period of sexual contact . . . seem much longer' (Winick, 1965, p. 22). Such an observation with all its implications awaits verification. Drug addicts frequently engage in little or no sexual activity (Gebhard, 1965) but this may, in part, be attributed to the malnutrition from which they may suffer.

7. Privation

The effects on man's sexuality of privations and extreme conditions should throw some light both on the strength of sexual drives and habits as well as on future requirements for enabling groups to withstand stresses. For convenience we will consider the privations of social isolation, of starvation and, specifically, sexual privation, although recognising that in many real situations these are not suffered singly. In fact, much of our information comes from observations—often meticulous although admittedly biased, particularly by the experimenter as participant—of real life situations since experimental deprivation of basic needs in man can rarely be carried out under ethically sound conditions. We are also, for present purposes, too often limited to observations on the human male.

ISOLATION

Comparative psychological workers have provided convincing evidence of the harmful effects on both male and female sexuality of social isolation during infancy (Harlow, 1962; Harlow et al., 1965; Gerall, 1965). Dogs perceptually deprived in infancy fail to discriminate sexually relevant cues and avoid the approaches of the female in heat (Melzack, 1965). Harlow's extensive work has shown that female as well as male rhesus monkeys display disturbed or infantile sexual behaviour if reared without opportunity for mother or peer contact. Observation on more normally reared monkeys shows the continual development of sexual play and the early sex differentiation of sex play and sex posturing (Harlow, 1962). Males brought up in isolation hardly recovered even after months of sexual training with a docile female. Females reared in isolation were unwilling to mate and breed but could be induced to do so, again by months of social training in the adult stage and by being paired with gentle and persistent males. However, they emerged as poor mothers, neglecting their offspring and treating the infants with dangerous cruelty. Thus, early social isolation can be seen to cause disruption of the development of adequate sexuality in the widest sense. Harlow believes these findings have generality for man and much anecdotal evidence can be adduced to support this belief. The enormous difficulty of testing it experimentally is likely to preclude more reliable evidence bearing on generality for some time.

Isolation in later life does, however, occur with some frequency though here we are almost entirely limited to group isolation and to male groups. Prisons are usually single sex communities in addition to being isolated from the rest of the world. This factor alone can produce much of the reported homosexuality of prisons. Indeed Scott (1964) has classified as 'facultative homosexuals' those individuals who adopt this form of sexual behaviour only when deprived of heterosexual outlets. Data collected in the specialised circumstances of exploration in Antarctica (Rohrer, 1960; Palmai, 1963) do not suggest an increase in homosexuality, however, but indicate that sexual deprivation is better tolerated by the sexually satisfied and mature than by the single and separated.

STARVATION

In natural famine, human sexual activity is much reduced or ceases altogether (Keys et al., 1950). Women may increasingly offer themselves for prostitution but even this is merely a means to the food goal in this context. In experimental semi-starvation 36 male conscientious objectors lost one quarter of their pre-experimental weight and reported loss of sex drive, reduced masturbation and nocturnal emissions. Sex drive improved only very slowly after rehabilitation (Brožek *et al.*, 1950). Biskind (1947) relates the waning of sexuality with age (*see* Section 8) to the reduced sexuality of avitaminosis. Such findings then are consistent with those of Gantt (1950) who showed that food deprivation reduced conditioned sexual reflexes in dogs. McClure (1966) has also demonstrated reduced fertility in fasting mice—particularly fasting females.

A considerable literature is available on the effects, some of them already mentioned (*see* Section A.1 in this chapter), of extreme conditions on human behaviour in concentration camps. Few writers are concerned with sexual behaviour primarily, but sporadic references occur. While these organised horrors included much more than mere starvation, the following observations are relevant to the study of abnormal female sexuality. Sexual desire was generally reduced (Leyton, 1946; Kral, 1951) but rarely disappeared. Pregnancies did occur (Kral, 1951) and there were some observations of greatly exaggerated sexual appetite (Leyton, 1946; Niremberski, 1946). For many inmates, however, with loss of self-respect and even of identity there was reduced 'consciousness of sex' (Lipscomb, 1945) with instances of women undressing publicly (Niremberski, 1946) and many more who were careless of appearances and looked sexless even beyond the imposed limitations of dress.

When followed up after liberation it was found that concentration camp inmates had frequently contracted hasty marriages (Eitinger, 1965) no doubt in an attempt to rebuild the families they had lost. Under these circumstances marital disharmony was frequent, but the divorce rate was low (Klein *et al.*, 1963). Otherwise, it is suggested that sexual disorders were rare and when present had antedated the concentration camp experience (Eitinger, 1965). Maternal instinct is said to have been reduced in camp and remained low on liberation (Niremberski, 1946). Klebanow (1949) shows that a high proportion of mentally defective children were born to concentration camp survivors and links this to the reports of ill-health prior to conception and to the impoverished conditions which have been associated with giving birth to defectives and other malformed infants (Edwards, 1952).

SEXUAL PRIVATION AND CELIBACY

The sexual privation of prisoners and isolated research teams has already been mentioned. Newman (1944) mentions the fear of prisoners-of-war that sexual privation would later cause impotence. There is, however, no evidence of such an effect nor of such an effect following masturbation, which may well

have been the fear underlying such a notion. Although the strain of celibacy on the man or woman at the height of sexual powers is likely to be intense, no survey of the effects is known. Walker (1954) believes that voluntary celibacy is easier to bear, while anxiety-provoked abstention is dangerous. De Berker (1960) finds a high proportion of offenders remanded for psychiatric examination are celibate (*see also* Kallman, 1953). This last, however, may be cause or effect, or unrelated to the social offence, although there was a larger number of minor sexual offences noted in the series.

All this information relates chiefly to deprived or celibate males. Although women take religious vows of chastity, the consequences of their decision have been little studied. Only the evidence of males determining coital frequency (Mudd *et al.*, 1961) suggests that celibacy presents fewer problems for women.

8. Age

Age is a vital factor in the development and continuation of sexual functioning. Kinsey (Kinsey *et al.*, 1948; Kinsey *et al.*, 1953) has documented this fact for both men and women and no attempt will be made here to reiterate his findings. We are concerned with old age as an extreme or near-extreme condition and with sexuality in this period. The physiology of the ageing reproductive system in women has been adequately described (Masters, 1952; Masters and Johnson, 1966). Since age brings irreversible changes in the reproductive organs of even the healthy woman it follows that sexuality will change with age, even beyond the changes that might be associated with infertility after the menopause.

It is generally accepted that sexual behaviour to orgasm will decrease in frequency with advancing years (Hamilton, 1942; Rubin, 1966), though testosterone (Stafford-Clark, 1954) and vitamin-rich diets (Biskind, 1947) have been used *inter alia* in attempts to reverse the decline. Zubin and Katz (1964) attribute the waning of sexual arousal with age at least in part to a system of conceptual expectations. Post (1968) observes that, consistent with the role expectations of reduced sexuality, the elderly present few sexual problems. Nevertheless, their continuing interest in sexual matters can be seen in the sexual content of delusions of the involutional melancholic, for example. Surveys, at first based on the data collected by Kinsey (Kinsey *et al.*, 1953) show that sexual behaviour is certainly not absent even in women in their ninth decade (Christenson, 1964; Christenson and Gagnon, 1965). Cross-sectional surveys confirm the expected gradual decline of interest and activity with increasing age.

However, in a longitudinal study (Pfeiffer *et al.*, 1968) it is shown that some individuals increase in both sexual activity and interest in sexual matters with age. Workers agree, however, in finding that the aged husband is the regulator of frequency of intercourse rather than the aged wife. Thus, even after decades of experience the man remains the instigator in much of marital sexuality.

CONCLUSIONS

This survey of findings on abnormal sexual behaviour of the human female was prompted by dissatisfaction with the availability of data in this area reputedly of major relevance for many a psychiatric problem. But we end with continuing dissatisfaction. The search for facts reveals much work of such glaring scientific incompetence that it should never have been done let alone published, and large areas of importance that have never been subjected to scientific scrutiny. Isolated instances of carefully planned fact-finding surveys are welcome. Even more welcome, however, are the early signs of true experimentation (e.g. Bardwick, 1967; Bardwick and Behrman, 1967; O'Neill and Kempler, 1969; Levi, 1969) and of sexual behaviour modification (e.g. Lazarus, 1963; Mullen, 1968) by methods based on general psychological principles. While the scientific study of human female sexuality has lagged seriously behind that of the male, it can be confidently predicted for both fields of study that a sexual behaviour survey conducted in 1980 will show advances of knowledge and of techniques for the accumulation of further knowledge which will shame our present ignorance.

REFERENCES

ABRAM, H. S. (1969) Pseudocyesis followed by true pregnancy in the termination phase of an analysis. *Brit. J. med. Psychol.*, **42**, 255–262

ADAMS, C. R. (1966) An informal preliminary report on some factors relating to sexual responsiveness of certain college wives. In *Sexual Behavior and Personality Characteristics* (Ed. M. F. DeMartino) 208–226. New York: Grove Press.

AKITA, K. (1965) The influence of monthly periodicity in women students on the physical and mental phases. *J. Sci. Labour* (Tokyo), **41**, 469–473.

ALBRETSEN, C. S. (1968) Hospitalization of post partum psychotic patients together with babies and husbands. *Acta Psychiat. Scand.*, Suppl., **203**, 179–182.

ALLEN, E. (1942) Female reproductive system. In *Problems of Ageing*, 2nd ed. (Ed. E. V. Cowdry) 446–474. Baltimore: Williams & Wilkins.

ALMQUIST, R. (1955) The rhythm of epileptic attacks and its relationship to the menstrual cycle. *Acta Psychiat. Neurol. Scand.*, Suppl., **105**, 1–116.

ANANT, S. S. (1968) Verbal aversion therapy with a promiscuous girl. Case report. *Psychol. Rep.*, **22**, 795–796.

ANDERSON, E. W. (1933) A study of the sexual life in psychoses associated with childbirth. *J. ment. Sci.*, **79**, 137–149.

AREY, L. B. (1939) The degree of normal menstrual irregularity. *Amer. J. Obstet. Gynec.*, **37**, 12–29.

BACHRACH, A. J., ERWIN, W. J., and MOHR, J. P. (1965) The control of eating behavior in an anorexic by operant conditioning techniques. In *Case Studies in Behavior Modification* (Ed. L. P. Ullman and L. Krasner) 153–163. New York: Holt, Rinehart & Winston.

BACON, R. L. and ROSVOLD, H. E. (1948) Effects of electroconvulsive shock on pregnancy in the rat. *Proc. Soc. Exp. Biol.*, N.Y., **69**, 287–288.

BAKKER, C. B. and DIGHTMAN, C. R. (1964) Psychological factors in fertility control. *Fertil. Steril.*, **15**, 559–567.

BALL, J. R. B. (1968) A case of hair fetishism, transvestitism, and organic cerebral disorder. *Acta Psychiat. Scand.*, **44**, 249–254.

BARAHAL, H. S. (1953) Female transvestitism and homosexuality. *Psychiat. Quart.*, **27**, 390–438.

BARDWICK, JUDITH, M. (1967) Need for individual assessment of *S*s in psychosomatic research. *Psychol. Rep.*, **21**, 81–86.

BARDWICK, JUDITH M., and BEHRMAN, S. J. (1967) Investigation into the effects of anxiety, sexual arousal, and menstrual cycle phase on uterine contractions. *Psychosom. Med.*, **29**, 468–482.

BARENNE, DOROTHEA D. de, and GIBBS, F. A. (1942) Variations in the electroencephalogram during the menstrual cycle. *Amer. J. Obstet. Gynec.*, **4**, 687–690.

BARGLOW, P. (1964) Pseudocyesis and psychiatric sequelae of sterilization. *Arch. Gen. Psychiat.*, **11**, 571–580.

BARGLOW, P., BORNSTEIN, M., EXUM, DOLORES B., WRIGHT, MATTIE K., and VISOTSKY, H. M. (1968) Some psychiatric aspects of illegitimate pregnancy in early adolescence. *Amer. J. Orthopsychiat.*, **38**, 672–687.

BARKER, D. J. P. (1966) Low intelligence and obstetric complications. *Brit. J. Prevent. Soc. Med.*, **20**, 15–21.

BARRACLOUGH, C. A. (1967) Modifications in reproductive function after exposure to hormones during the prenatal and early postnatal period. In *Neuroendocrinology* Vol. II (Ed. L. Martini and W. F. Ganong) 61–99. New York: Academic Press.

BASS, F. (1947) L'amenorrhée au camp de concentration de Terezin (Theresienstadt). *Gynaecologia*, **123**, 211–219.

BEECH, H. R. (1959) An experimental investigation of sexual symbolism in anorexia nervosa employing a subliminal stimulation technique. *Psychosom. Med.*, **21**, 277–280.

BEIDLER, L. M. (1961) The chemical senses. *Ann. Rev. Psychol.*, **12**, 363–388

BELL, R. Q. (1966) Level of arousal in breast-fed and bottle-fed human newborns. *Psychosom. Med.*, **28**, 177–180.

BENE, EVA (1965) On the genesis of female homosexuality. *Brit. J. Psychiat.*, **111**, 815–821.

BENEDEK, THERESE (1963) An investigation of the sexual cycle in women: methodologic considerations. *Arch. Gen. Psychiat.*, **8**, 311–322.

BENEDEK, THERESE, HAM, G. C., ROBBINS, F. P., and RUBENSTEIN, B. B. (1953) Some emotional factors in infertility. *Psychosom. Med.*, **15**, 485–498.

BENJAMIN, F. (1960) The age of the menarche and of the menopause in white South African women and certan factors influencing these times. *S. Afr. med. J.*, **34**, 316–320.

BENNETT, R. (1954) The problem of prostitution. *Practitioner*, **172**, 381–388.

BERECZ, J. M. (1968) Phobias of childhood. *Psychol. Bull.*, **70**, 694–720.

BISKIND, M. S. (1947) The relation of nutritional deficiency to impaired libido and potency in the male. *J. Gerontol.*, **2**, 303–314.

BLAIR, J. H. and SIMPSON, G. M. (1966) Effect of anti-psychotic drugs on reproductive functions. *Dis. Nerv. Syst.*, **27**, 645–647.

BLAIR, MARGARET, and PASMORE, JEAN (1965) Frigid wives. A clinical classification. In *Proc. 6th Int. Congr. of Psychotherapy, London 1964, Selected Lectures*, (Ed. M. Pines and T. Spoerri) 1–7. New York: S. Karger.

BLAU, A., SLAFF, B., EASTON, K., WELKOWITZ, JOAN, SPRINGARN, J., and COHEN, J. (1963) The psychogenic etiology of premature births. *Psychosom. Med.*, **25**, 201–211.

BLUMENTHAL, M. D. (1967) Mental health among the divorced. A field study of divorced and never divorced persons. *Arch. Gen. Psychiat.*, **16**, 603–608.

BOLTER, S. (1962) The psychiatrist's role in therapeutic abortion: the unwitting accomplice. *Amer. J. Psychiat.*, **119**, 312–318.

BOS, C. and CLEGHORN, R. A. (1958) Psychogenic sterility. *Fertil. Steril.*, **9**, 84–98.

BRACKBILL, G. A. and BRACKBILL, YVONNE (1966) Some reactions to first remembered sexual climax. In *Sexual Behavior and Personality Characteristics* (Ed. M. F. DeMartino) 227–233. New York: Grove Press.

BRADY, J. P. (1966) Brevital relaxation treatment of frigidity. *Behav. Res. Ther.*, **4**, 71–78.

BRAGG, R. L. (1965) Risk of admission to mental hospital following hysterectomy or cholecystectomy. *Amer. J. Pub. Health*, **55**, 1403–1410.

BROADHURST, ANNE and GLASS, A. (1969) Relationship of personality measures to the alpha rhythm of the electroencephalogram. *Brit. J. Psychiat.*, **115**, 199–204.

BROWN, L. B. (1964) Anxiety in pregnancy. *Brit. J. med. Psychol.*, **37**, 47–58.

BROWN, W. M. C. (1968) The study of human sex chromosome abnormalities with particular reference to intelligence and behaviour. *Advance. Sci.*, **24**, 390–397.

BROŽEK, J., GUETZKOW, H., and BALDWIN, MARCELLA V. (1950) A quantitative study of perception and association in experimental semistarvation. *J. Personal.*, **19**, 245–264.

BRUCE, HILDA M. (1961) Observations on the suckling stimulus and lactation in the rat. *J. Reprod. Fertil.*, **2**, 17–34.

BRUCE, HILDA M. (1962) Continued suppression of pituitary luteotrophic activity and fertility in the female mouse. *J. Reprod. Fertil.*, **4**, 313–318.

BRUCE, HILDA M. (1966) Smell as an exteroceptive factor. *J. Anim. Sci. Suppl.*, **25**, 83–87.

BUCK, CAROL W. and LADD, KATHERINE L. (1965) Psychoneurosis in marital partners. *Brit. J. Psychiat.*, **111**, 587–590.

BUCK, CAROL W. and STAVRAKY, KATHLEEN (1967) The relationship between age at menarche and age at marriage among childbearing women. *Hum. Biol.*, **39**, 93–102.

BURCH, P. R. J. and ROWELL, N. R. (1963) Menarche and menopause. *Lancet*, **ii**, 784–785.

BYRNE, D. and BLAYLOCK, BARBARA (1963) Similarity and assumed similarity of attitudes between husbands and wives. *J. Abnorm. Soc. Psychol.*, **67**, 636–640.

CALDWELL, D. F. (1962) Stillbirths from adrenal deme-dullated mice subjected to chronic stress throughout gestation. *J. Embryol. Exper. Morphol.*, **10**, 471–475.

CATTELL, R. B. (1937) *The Fight for Our National Intelligence*. London: King.

CHERTOK, L. (1959) *Psychosomatic Methods in Painless Childbirth*. London: Pergamon.

CHERTOK, L. (1969) *Motherhood and Personality. Psychosomatic Aspects of Childbirth*. London: Tavistock.

CHRISTENSON, CORNELIA V. (1964) Sexual behavior in a sample of older women. *Amer. Psychol.*, **19**, 546, abstract.

CHRISTENSON, CORNELIA V. and GAGNON, J. H. (1965) Sexual behavior in a group of older women. *J. Geront.*, **20**, 351–356.

CLARK, R. A. (1955) The effects of sexual motivation on phantasy. In *Studies in Motivation* (Ed. D. C. McClelland) 44–57. New York: Appleton-Century-Crofts.

COHEN, R. L. (1966) Pregnancy stress and maternal perceptions of infant endowment. *J. ment. Subnorm.*, **12**, 18–23.

COOKE, W. R. (1945) Presidential address; the differential psychology of the American woman. *Amer. J. Obstet. Gynec.*, **49**, 457–472.

COOPER, A. J. (1964) A case of bronchial asthma treated by behaviour therapy. *Behav. Res. Ther.*, **1**, 351–356.

COOPER, A. J. (1969) An innovation in the 'behavioural' treatment of a case of non-consummation due to vaginismus. *Brit. J. Psychiat.*, **115**, 721–722.

COPPEN, A. J. (1965) The prevalence of menstrual disorders in psychiatric patients. *Brit. J. Psychiat.*, **111**, 155–167.

COPPEN, A. J. and KESSEL, N. (1963) Menstruation and personality. *Brit. J. Psychiat.*, **109**, 711–721.

COUNCIL OF THE MEDICAL WOMEN'S FEDERATION (1933) An investigation of the menopause in one thousand women. *Lancet*, **i**, 106–108.

CRAGO, MARJORIE and THARP, R. G. (1968) Psychopathology and marital role disturbance: A test of the Tharp-Otis descriptive hypothesis. *J. Consult. Clin. Psychol.*, **32**, 338–341.

CRISP, A. H. (1966) A treatment regime for anorexia nervosa. *Brit. J. Psychiat.*, **112**, 505–512.

CROWLEY, R. M. and LAIDLOW, R. W. (1967) Psychiatric opinion regarding abortion: preliminary report of a survey. *Amer. J. Psychiat.*, **124**, 559–562.

DALTON, KATHERINA (1959) Menstruation and acute psychiatric illness. *Brit. med. J.*, **1**, 148–151.

DALTON, KATHERINA (1960) Menstruation and accidents. *Brit. med. J.*, **2**, 1425–1426.

DALTON, KATHERINA (1961) Menstruation and crime. *Brit. med. J.*, **2**, 1752–1753.

DALTON, KATHERINA (1964) *The Premenstrual Syndrome*. London: Heinemann.

DAME, NENABELLE G., FINCK, G. H., MAYOS, RUTH G., REINER, BEATRICE S., and SMITH, B. O. (1966) Conflict in marriage following premarital pregnancy. *Amer. J. Orthopsychiat.*, **36**, 468–475.

DAVIDS, A. and DEVAULT, S. (1962) Maternal anxiety during pregnancy and childbirth abnormalities. *Psychosom. Med.*, **24**, 464–470.

DAVIDS, A., DEVAULT, S., and TALMADGE, M. (1961a) Psychological study of emotional factors in pregnancy: a preliminary report. *Psychosom. Med.*, **23**, 93–103.

DAVIDS, A., DEVAULT, S., and TALMADGE, M. (1961b) Anxiety, pregnancy, and childbirth abnormalities. *J. Consult. Psychol.*, **25**, 74–77.

DAVIDSON, HELEN H. and GOTTLIEB, LUCILLE S. (1955) The emotional maturity of pre and post menarcheal girls. *J. Genet. Psychol.*, **86**, 261–266.

DAWKINS, SYLVIA and TAYLOR, ROSALIE (1961) Non-consummation of marriage. *Lancet*, **ii**, 1029–1033.

DAWSON, W. R. (1929) *The Custom of Couvade*. Manchester: Manchester University Press.

DE BERKER, P. U. (1960) 'State of mind' reports. *Brit. J. Criminol.*, **1**, 6–20.

DEMARTINO, M. F. (1966) *Sexual Behavior and Personality Characteristics*. New York: Grove Press.

DEUTSCH, HELENE (1944) *The Psychology of Women*. New York: Grune & Stratton.

DEUTSCHER, M. (1965) Some observations on the psychological consequence of induced abortion. *Amer. J. Orthopsychiat.*, **35**, 212–213.

DOMINO, G. (1966) Relation of early and late menarche to personality characteristics in mentally deficient women. *Amer. J. ment. Def.*, **71**, 381–386.

DREW, FRANCES L. (1961) The epidemiology of secondary amenorrhoea. *J. chron. Dis.*, **14**, 396–407.

DREWERY, J. and RAE, J. B. (1969) A group comparison of alcoholic and non-alcoholic marriages using the interpersonal perception technique. *Brit. J. Psychiat.*, **115**, 287–300.

DRILLIEN, C. M. (1946) A study of normal and abnormal menstrual function in the Auxiliary Territorial Service.

J. Obstet. Gynaec. Brit. Emp., **53**, 228–241.

DUNBAR, HELEN F. (1954) *Emotions and Bodily Changes* 4th ed. New York: Columbia University Press.

DUNBAR, HELEN F. (1962) Emotional factors in spontaneous abortion. In *Psychosomatic Obstetrics, Gynecology and Endocrinology* (Ed. W. S. Kroger) 135–143. Springfield, Ill.: C. C. Thomas.

EDWARDS, J. H. (1958) Congenital malformations of the central nervous system in Scotland. *Brit. J. Prev. Soc. Med.*, **12**, 115–130.

EICHORN, DOROTHY H. (1963) Biological correlates of behavior. In *Child Psychology* (Ed. H. W. Stevenson) 4–61. Chicago: Nat. Soc. Stud. Educ. Yearbk.

EISNER, ERICA (1960) The relationship of hormones to the reproductive behaviour of birds, referring especially to parental behaviour: a review. *Anim. Behav.*, **8**, 155–179.

EITINGER, L. (1965) *Concentration Camp Survivors in Norway and Israel*. New York: Humanities Press.

EKBLAD, M. (1955) Induced abortion on psychiatric grounds. *Acta Psychiat. Scand. Suppl.*, **99**, 1–238.

EKBLAD, M. (1963) Social-psychiatric prognosis after sterilization of women without children. *Acta Psychiat. Scand.*, **39**, 481–514.

EL-ISLAM, M. F. and EL-DEEB, H. A. (1968) Marriage and fertility of psychotics. A study at an Arab psychiatric clinic. *Soc. Psychiat.*, **3**, 24–27.

ENGELS, W. D., PATTEE, C. J., and WITTKOWER, E. D. (1964) Emotional settings of functional amenorrhea. *Psychosom. Med.*, **26**, 682–700.

ENGLE, E. T. (1952) The male reproductive system. In *Cowdry's Problems of Ageing*, 3rd ed. (Ed. A. I. Lansing) 708–729. Baltimore: Williams & Wilkins.

ERICKSON, MARILYN T. (1967) Method for frequent assessment of symptomatology during pregnancy. *Psychol. Rep.*, **20**, 447–450.

ERIKSON, T. C. (1945) Erotomania (nymphomania) as an expression of cortical epileptiform discharge. *Arch. Neurol. Psychiat.*, **53**, 226–231.

EVERETT, J. W. (1961) The mammalian female reproductive cycle and its controlling mechanism. In *Sex and Internal Secretions*, 3rd ed., Vol. I. (Ed. W. C. Young) 497–555. Baltimore: Williams & Wilkins.

EYSENCK, H. J. (1960) Classification and the problem of diagnosis. In *Handbook of Abnormal Psychology* (Ed. H. J. Eysenck) 1–31. London: Pitman Medical.

EYSENCK, H. J. (1967) *The Biological Basis of Personality*. Springfield, Ill.: C. C. Thomas.

EYSENCK, H. J. (1970) Personality, sexual behaviour and attitudes to sex. *Bull. Brit. Psychol. Soc.*, **23**, 151.

EYSENCK, H. J. and PRELL, D. B. (1952) A note on the differentiation of normal and neurotic children by means of objective tests. *J. clin. Psychol.*, **8**, 202–204.

EYSENCK, SYBIL B. G. (1961) Personality, and pain assessment in childbirth of married and unmarried mothers. *J. ment. Sci.*, **107**, 417–430.

FELDMAN, M. P. and MACCULLOCH, M. J. (1970) *Homosexual Behaviour: Therapy and Assessment*. Oxford: Pergamon Press.

FERREIRA, A. J. (1965) Emotional factors in prenatal environment: a review. *J. nerv. ment. Dis.*, **141**, 108–118.

FISCHER, I. C. (1962) Hypothalamic amenorrhea: Pseudo-cyesis. In *Psychosomatic Obstetrics, Gynecology and Endocrinology* (Ed. W. S. Kroger) 291–297. Springfield, Ill.: C. C. Thomas.

FLAPAN, M. (1969) A paradigm for the analysis of child-bearing motivations of married women prior to birth of the first child. *Amer. J. Orthopsychiat.*, **39**, 402–417.

FOUNDEUR, M., FIXSEN, C., TRIEBEL, W. A., and WHITE, MARY A. (1957) Postpartum mental illness: A controlled study. *Arch. Neurol. Psychiat.*, **77**, 503–512.

FRANK, R. T. (1931) The hormonal causes of premenstrual tension. *Arch. Neurol. Psychiat.*, **26**, 1053–1057.

FREEMON, F. R. and NEVIS, A. H. (1969) Temporal lobe sexual seizures. *Neurology*, **19**, 81–86.

FREUD, S. (1934) *Collected Papers*. London: Hogarth.

FRIDHANDLER, L. and PINCUS, G. (1964) Pharmacology of reproduction and fertility. *Ann. Rev. Pharmacol.*, **4**, 177–188.

FRIEDMAN, E. A., NISWANDER, K. R., and SACHTLEBEN, MARLENE R. (1969) Dysfunctional labour. XI. Neurologic and developmental effects on surviving infants. *Obstet. Gynec.*, **33**, 785–791.

FRIEDMAN, L. J. (1962) *Virgin Wives*. London: Tavistock.

FROMMER, D. J. (1964) Changing age of the menopause. *Brit. med. J.*, **2**, 349–351.

GAGNON, J. H. and SIMON, W. (Ed.) (1967) *Sexual Deviance*. New York: Harper & Row.

GALE, A., COLES, M., and BLAYDON, J. (1969) Extraversion-introversion and the EEG. *Brit. J. Psychiat.*, **60**, 209–224.

GANTT, W. H. (1950) Food deprivation and sexual reflexes. *Fed. Proc.*, **9**, 46–47, abstract.

GANTT, W. H. (1952) Effect of alcohol on the sexual reflexes of normal and neurotic male dogs. *Psychosom. Med.*, **14**, 174–181.

GEBHARD, P. H. (1965) Situational factors affecting human sexual behavior. In *Sex and Behavior* (Ed. F. A. Beach) 483–495. New York: Wiley.

GEBHARD, P. H., POMEROY, W. B., MARTIN, C. E., and CHRISTENSON, CORNELIA V. (1958) *Pregnancy, Birth and Abortion*. New York: Harper.

GEDDES, D. P. (Ed.) (1954) *An Analysis of the Kinsey Reports on Sexual Behavior in the Human Male and Female*. New York: New American Library.

GERALL, HELENE D. (1965) Effect of social isolation and physical confinement on motor and sexual behavior of guinea pigs. *J. Personal. Soc. Psychol.*, **2**, 460–464.

GERMAN, J. (1968) Mongolism, delayed fertilization and human sexual behaviour. *Nature*, **217**, 516–518.

GIBBENS, T. C. N. (1957) Juvenile prostitution. *Brit. J. Delinquency*, **8**, 3–12.

GIEL, R. and KIDD, C. (1965) Some psychiatric observations on pregnancy in the unmarried student. *Brit. J. Psychiat.*, **111**, 591–594.

GITTELMAN-KLEIN, RACHEL and KLEIN, D. F. (1968) Marital status as a prognostic indicator in schizophrenia. *J. nerv. ment. Dis.*, **147**, 289–296.

GITTLESON, N. L. and DAWSON-BUTTERWORTH, K. (1967) Subjective ideas of sexual change in female schizophrenics. *Brit. J. Psychiat.*, **113**, 491–494.

GITTLESON, N. L. and LEVINE, S. (1966) Subjective ideas of sexual change in male schizophrenics. *Brit. J. Psychiat.*, **112**, 779–782.

GLEASON, KATHRYN K. and REYNIERSE, J. H. (1969) The behavioral significance of pheromones in vertebrates. *Psychol. Bull.*, **71**, 58–73.

GLICK, IRA D. (1967) Mood and behavioral changes associated with the use of the oral contraceptive agents. A review of the literature. *Psychopharmacologia*, **10**, 363–374.

GLOVER, E. (1969) *The Psychopathology of Prostitution*, 3rd ed. Dorking, Surrey: Institute for the Study and Treatment of Delinquency.

GOLUB, L. J., LANG, W. R., and MENDUKE, H. (1958) Dysmenorrhea in high school and college girls; relationships to sports participation. *West. J. Surg. Obstet. Gynecol.*, **66**, 163–165.

GOODHART, C. B. (1966) How many illegal abortions? *New Society*, **8**, 720.

GOTTSCHALK, L. A., KAPLAN, S., GLESER, G. C., and WINGET, C. M. (1962) Variations in magnitude of emotion: a method applied to anxiety and hostility during phases of the menstrual cycle. *Psychosom. Med.*, **23**, 300–311.

GRANT, ELLEN C. G. and PRYSE-DAVIES, J. (1968) Effect of oral contraceptives on depressive mood changes and on endometrial monoamine oxidase and phosphates. *Brit. med. J.*, **3**, 777–780.

GREGORY, B. A. J. C. (1957a) The menstrual cycle and its disorders in psychiatric patients—I. Review of the literature. *J. Psychosom. Res.*, **2**, 61–79.

GREGORY, B. A. J. C. (1957b) The menstrual cycle and its disorders in psychiatric patients—II. Clinical studies. *J. Psychosom. Res.*, **2**, 199–224.

GRIMM, ELAINE R. (1962) Psychological investigation of habitual abortion. *Psychosom. Med.*, **24**, 369–378.

GRIMM, ELAINE R. and VENET, WANDA R. (1966) The relationship of emotional adjustment and attitudes to the course and outcome of pregnancy. *Psychosom. Med.*, **28**, 34–49.

GUNTER, LAURIE M. (1963) Psychopathology and stress in the life experience of mothers of premature infants. A comparative study. *Amer. J. Obstet. Gynec.*, **86**, 333–340.

HALLSTEN, E. A., Jr. (1965) Adolescent anorexia nervosa treated by desensitization. *Behav. Res. Ther.*, **3**, 87–91.

HAMAN, J. O. (1944) Pain threshold in dysmenorrhea. *Amer. J. Obstet. Gynec.*, **47**, 686–691.

HAMILTON, G. V. (1942) Changes in personality and psychosexual phenomena with age. In *Problems of Aging*, 2nd ed. (Ed. E. V. Cowdry) 810–831. Baltimore: Williams & Wilkins.

HAMILTON, J. A. (1962) *Postpartum Psychiatric Problems*. St. Louis: Mosby.

HARLOW, H. F. (1962) The heterosexual affectional system in monkeys. *Amer. Psychol.*, **17**, 1–9.

HARLOW, H. F., DODSWORTH, R. O., and HARLOW, MARGARET K. (1965) Total isolation in monkeys. *Proc. Nat. Acad. Sci., USA*, **54**, 90–97.

HARRIS, G. W. and LEVINE, S. (1965) Sexual differentiation and its experimental control. *J. Physiol.*, **181**, 379–400.

HARRIS, P. W. R. (1969) Malignant hypertension associated with oral contraceptives. *Lancet*, **ii**, 466–467.

HARTLAND, J. (1966) *Medical and Dental Hypnosis and its Clinical Applications.* London: Baillière, Tindall & Cassell.

HARTMAN, A. A. and NICOLAY, R. C. (1966) Sexually deviant behavior in expectant fathers. *J. Abnorm. Psychol.*, **71**, 232–234.

HARTMANN, E. (1966) Dreaming sleep (the D-state) and the menstrual cycle. *J. nerv. ment. Dis.*, **143**, 406–416.

HASLAM, M. T. (1965) The treatment of psychogenic dyspareunia by reciprocal inhibition. *Brit. J. Psychiat.*, **111**, 280–282.

HEALEY, F. H. (1928) Menstruation in relation to mental disorders. *J. ment. Sci.*, **74**, 488–492.

HEGARTY, A. B. (1955) Post-puerperal recurrent depression. *Brit. med. J.*, **1**, 637–640.

HEIMAN, M. (1962) Functional uterine bleeding as psychosomatic disorder: separation bleeding. In *Psychosomatic Obstetrics, Gynecology and Endocrinology* (Ed. W. S. Kroger) 262–271. Springfield, Ill.: C. C. Thomas.

HELFER, R. E. and KEMPE, C. H. (1968) *The Battered Child.* Chicago: Univ. Chicago Press.

HELLER, A. and WHITTINGTON, H. G. (1968) The Colorado story: Denver General Hospital experience with the change in the law on therapeutic abortion. *Amer. J. Psychiat.*, **125**, 809–816.

HENRY, G. W. and GALBRAITH, H. M. (1934) Constitutional factors in homosexuality. *Amer. J. Psychiat.*, **91**, 1249–1270.

HERTIG, A. T. (1967) The overall problem in man. In *Comparative Aspects of Reproductive Failure* (Ed. K. Beurschke) New York: Springer-Verlag.

HETZEL, B. S., BRUER, BRIGID, and POIDEVIN, L. O. S. (1961) A survey of the relation between certain common antenatal complications in primiparae and stressful situations during pregnancy. *J. Psychosom. Res.*, **5**, 175–182.

HIGGINS, J. V., REED, ELIZABETH W., and REED, S. C. (1962) Intelligence and family size: a paradox resolved. *Eugen. Quart.*, **9**, 84–90.

HOAKEN, P. C. S., CLARKE, MARY, and BRESLIN, MARIANNE (1964) Psychopathology in Klinefelter's syndrome. *Psychosom. Med.*, **26**, 207–223.

HOENIG, J. and HAMILTON, CHRISTINA M. (1960) Epilepsy and sexual orgasm. *Acta Psychiat. Neurol. Scand.*, **35**, 448–456.

HOFFMAN, L. R. and MAIER, N. R. F. (1966) An experimental reexamination of the similarity-attraction hypothesis. *J. Personal. Soc. Psychol.*, **3**, 145–152.

HOFFMEYER, H. (1964) The psychological background of pregnancies in puberty and adolescence. *Acta Psychiat. Scand.*, **40**, 245–246.

HOLLENDER, M. H. (1963) Women's fantasies during sexual intercourse. *Arch. Gen. Psychiat.*, **8**, 86–90.

HOME, E. (1799) Account of dissection of hermaphrodite dog. *Philosoph. Trans. Roy. Soc.*, **89**, 157–178.

HOOK, K. (1963) Refused abortion. *Acta Psychiat. Scand.* Suppl., **168**, 1–156.

HOOPER, D. and SHELDON, A. (1969) Evaluating newly-married couples. *Brit. J. Soc. Clin. Psychol.*, **8**, 169–182.

HOPKINS, JUNE H. (1969) The lesbian personality. *Brit. J. Psychiat.*, **115**, 1433–1436.

HOPKINS, P. (1965) Menstrual disorders. In *Psychosomatic Disorders in Adolescents and Young Adults* (Ed. J. Hambling and P. Hopkins) 55–60. Oxford: Pergamon.

HOPKINSON, G. (1963) Celibacy and marital fertility in manic-depressive patients. *Acta Psychiat. Scand.*, **39**, 473–476.

HURVITZ, N. (1967) Marital problems following psychotherapy with one spouse. *J. Consult. Psychol.*, **31**, 38–47.

IGARASHI, M., TOHMA, K., OZAWA, M., HOSAKA, H., and MATSUMOTO, S. (1965) Pathogenesis of psychogenic amenorrhea and anovulation. *Int. J. Fertil.*, **10**, 311–319.

INGRAM, J. M., TRELOAR, H. S. B., THOMAS, G. P., and ROOD, E. B. (1967) Interruption of pregnancy for psychiatric indication—a suggested method of control. *Obstet. Gynec.*, **29**, 251–255.

IVEY, M. E. and BARDWICK, JUDITH M. (1968) Patterns of affective fluctuations in the menstrual cycle. *Psychosom. Med.*, **30**, 336–345.

JAMES, W. H. (1969) The effect of maternal psychological stress on the foetus. *Brit. J. Psychiat.*, **115**, 811–825.

JANOWSKY, D. S., GORNEY, R., and MANDELL, A. J. (1967) The menstrual cycle. Psychiatric and ovarian-adrenocortical hormone correlates: Case study and literature review. *Arch. Gen. Psychiat.*, **17**, 459–469.

JANSSON, B. (1963) Psychic insufficiencies associated with childbearing. *Acta Psychiat. Scand.* Suppl., **39**, no. 172.

JANSSON, B. and SELLDÉN, ULLA (1966) Electroencephalographic investigation of women with psychic insufficiencies associated with childbearing. *Acta Psychiat. Scand.*, **42**, 89–96.

JARRAHI-ZADEH, A., KANE, F. J., Jr., CASTLE, R. L. VAN DE, LACHENBRUCH, P. A., and EWING, J. A. (1969) Emotional and cognitive changes in pregnancy and early puerperium. *Brit. J. Psychiat.*, **115**, 797–805.

JARVIS, W. (1962) Some effects of pregnancy and childbirth on men. *J. Amer. Psychoanal. Ass.*, **10**, 689–700.

JENSEN, G. D. and STAINBROOK, E. (1949) The effect of electrogenic convulsions on the estrus cycle and the weight of rats. *J. Comp. Physiol. Psychol.*, **42**, 502–505.

JOFFE, J. M. (1969) *Prenatal Determinants of Behaviour.* Oxford: Pergamon.

JOHNSON, J. (1965) Sexual impotence and the limbic system. *Brit. J. Psychiat.*, **111**, 300–303.

JOHNSON, VIRGINIA E. and MASTERS, W. H. (1964) A team approach to the rapid diagnosis and treatment of sexual incompatibility. *Pacific Med. Surg.*, **72**, 371–375.

JORDAN, T. E. (1956) Psychological findings in a case of Von Recklinghausen's disease and hyperpituitarism. *J. clin. Psychol.*, **12**, 389–391.

KAIJ, L., JACOBSON, L., and NILSSON, Å. (1967) Postpartum mental disorder in an unselected sample. *J. psychosom. Res.*, **10**, 317–347.

KAIJ, L. and MALMQUIST, ANN (1965) Prognosis after sterilization in connection with parturition. *Acta Psychiat. Scand.*, **41**, 204–217.

KAIJ, L. and NILSSON, Å. (1964) Mental disorders following parturition. *Acta Psychiat. Scand.*, **40**, 189–190.

KALINOWSKI, L. B. (1948) Variation in body weight and

menstruation in mental illness. *J. nerv. ment. Dis.*, **108**, 423–427.

KALLMAN, F. J. (1953) *Heredity in Health and Mental Disorder.* New York: Chapman.

KALSTONE, C. E. and JAFFE, R. B. (1969) Secondary amenorrhea, infertility and hirsutism. *Postgrad. Med.*, **45**, 181–189.

KANE, F. J., Jr., HARMAN, W. J., Jr., KELLER, M. H., and EWING, J. A. (1968) Emotional and cognitive disturbance in the early puerperium. *Brit. J. Psychiat.*, **114**, 99–102.

KANE, F. J., Jr., LIPTON, M. A., and EWING, J. A. (1969) Hormonal influences in female sexual response. *Arch. Gen. Psychiat.*, **20**, 202–209.

KANNER, L. (1956) Psychiatric aspects of pregnancy and childbirth. In *Williams's Obstetrics* (Ed. N. J. Eastman) 346–364. New York: Appleton-Century-Crofts.

KAPP, F. T., HORNSTEIN, S., and GRAHAM, V. T. (1963) Some psychologic factors in prolonged labor due to inefficient uterine action. *Comp. Psychiat.*, **4**, 9–18.

KARACON, I., WILLIAMS, R. L., HURSCH, C. J., McCAULLEY, M., and HEINE, M. W. (1969) Some implications of the sleep patterns of pregnancy for postpartum emotional disturbances. *Brit. J. Psychiat.*, **115**, 929–935.

KATZ, A. M. and HILL, R. (1958) Residential propinquity and marital selection: A review of theory, method, and fact. *Marriage and Family Living*, **20**, 27–35.

KAWI, A. A. and PASAMANICK, B. (1959) Prenatal and paranatal factors in the development of childhood reading disorders. *Child Developm. Monogr.*, **24**, 1–80.

KAYE, H. E., BERL, S., CLARE, J., ELESTON, MARY R., GERSHWIN, B. S., GERSHWIN, PATRICIA, KOGAN, L. S., TORDA, CLARE, and WILBUR, CORNELIA B. (1967) Homosexuality in women. *Arch. Gen. Psychiat.*, **17**, 626–634.

KEAR-COLWELL, J. J. (1965) Neuroticism in the early puerperium. *Brit. J. Psychiat.*, **111**, 1189–1192.

KENYON, F. E. (1968a) Studies in female homosexuality—psychological test results. *J. consult. clin. Psychol.*, **32**, 510–513.

KENYON, F. E. (1968b) Studies in female homosexuality. IV. Social and psychiatric aspects. V. Sexual development, attitudes and experience. *Brit. J. Psychiat.*, **114**, 1343–1350.

KENYON, F. E. (1968c) Studies in female homosexuality. VI—The exclusively homosexual group. *Acta Psychiat. Scand.*, **44**, 224–237.

KENYON, F. E. (1969) Termination of pregnancy on psychiatric grounds: a comparative study of 61 cases. *Brit. J. med. Psychol.*, **42**, 243–254.

KENYON, F. E. (1970) Homosexuality in the female. *Brit. J. Hosp. Med.*, **3**, 183–206.

KEPHART, W. M. (1954) Some variables in cases of reported sexual maladjustment. *Marriage and Family Living*, **16**, 241–243.

KEYS, A., BROŽEK, J., HENSCHEL, A., MICKELSON, O., and TAYLOR, H. L. (1950) *The Biology of Human Starvation*, Vol. 2. Minneapolis: University of Minnesota Press.

KING, J. A. (1967) Behavioral modification of the gene pool. In *Behavior-genetic Analysis* (Ed. J. Hirsch) 22–43. New York: McGraw-Hill.

KINSEY, A. C., POMEROY, W. B., and MARTIN, C. E. (1948) *Sexual Behavior in the Human Male.* Philadelphia: W. B. Saunders.

KINSEY, A. C., POMEROY, W. B., MARTIN, C. E., and GEBHARD, P. H. (1953) *Sexual Behavior in the Human Female.* Philadelphia: W. B. Saunders.

KLAF, F. (1961) Female homosexuality and paranoid schizophrenia. *Arch. Gen. Psychiat.*, **4**, 84–86.

KLAF, F. and DAVIS, C. (1960) Homosexuality and paranoid schizophrenia: A survey of 150 cases and controls. *Amer. J. Psychiat.*, **116**, 1070–1075.

KLEBANOW, D. (1949) Die Gefahr der Keimschädigung bei Ruckbildungsvorgängen in den weiblichen Gonaden. *Dtsch. Med. Wschr.*, **74**, 606–610.

KLEIN, H., ZELLERMEYER, J., and SHANAN, J. (1963) Former concentration camp inmates on a psychiatric ward. *Arch. Gen. Psychiat.*, **8**, 334–342.

KLOEK, J. (1962) The smell of some steroid sex-hormones and their metabolites. Reflections and experiments concerning the significance of smell for the mutual relation of the sexes. *Psychiat. Neurol. Neurochir.*, **64**, 309–344.

KLÜVER, H. (1965) Neurobiology of normal and abnormal perception. In *Psychopathology of Perception* (Ed. P. H. Hoch and J. Zubin) 1–40. New York: Grune & Stratton.

KLÜVER, H. and BUCY, P. C. (1939) Preliminary analysis of functions of the temporal lobes in monkeys. *Arch. Neurol. Psychiat.* (Chicago), **42**, 979–1000.

KNIGHT, J. A. (1960) False pregnancy in a male. *Psychosom. Med.*, **22**, 260–266.

KNOBLOCH, HILDA and PASAMANICK, B. (1966) Prospective studies on the epidemiology of reproductive casualty: methods, findings, and some implications. *Merrill-Palmer Quart.*, **12**, 27–43.

KOLASZYNSKA, ANNE B. (1969) *A questionnaire study of the attitudes to heterosexuality of homosexual men and women.* Unpubl. M.Sc. thesis, Univer. Birmingham.

KOPELL, B. S., LUNDE, D. T., CLAYTON, R. B., and MOOS, R. H. (1969) Variations in some measures of arousal during the menstrual cycle. *J. nerv. ment. Dis.*, **148**, 180–187.

KRAFT, T. and AL-ISSA, I. (1967) Behavior therapy and the treatment of frigidity. *Amer. J. Psychother.*, **21**, 116–120.

KRAINES, S. H. (1957) *Mental Depressions and Their Treatment.* New York: Macmillan.

KRAL, V. A. (1951) Psychiatric observations under severe chronic stress. *Amer. J. Psychiat.*, **108**, 185–192.

KRAMP, J. L. (1968) Studies on the premenstrual syndrome in relation to psychiatry. *Acta Psychiat. Scand.* Suppl., **203**, 261–267.

KREITMAN, N. (1964) The patient's spouse. *Brit. J. Psychiat.*, **110**, 159–173.

KREITMAN, N. (1968) Married couples admitted to mental hospital. Part I: Diagnostic similarity and the relation of illness to marriage. Part II: Family history, age and duration of marriage. *Brit. J. Psychiat.*, **114**, 699–718.

KREMER, MALVINA W. and RIFKIN, A. H. (1969) The early development of homosexuality: A study of adolescent lesbians. *Amer. J. Psychiat.*, **126**, 91–96.

KRINGLEN, E. (1967) *Heredity and Environment in the Functional Psychoses: an epidemiological-clinical Twin study*. London: Heinemann.

KROGER, W. S. (1962) Fertility after adoption. In *Psychosomatic Obstetrics, Gynecology and Endocrinology* (Ed. W. S. Kroger) 632–637. Springfield, Ill.: C. C. Thomas.

KROTH, J. A. (1968) Relationship between anxiety and menarcheal onset. *Psychol. Rep.*, **23**, 801–802.

KUPPERMAN, H. S. (1963) *Human Endocrinology*, Vol. 2. Oxford: Blackwell.

LAMB, WANDA M., ULETT, G. A., MASTERS, W. H., and ROBINSON, D. W. (1953) Premenstrual tension: EEG, hormonal and psychiatric evaluation. *Amer. J. Psychiat.*, **109**, 840–848.

LAZARUS, A. A. (1963) The treatment of chronic frigidity by systematic desensitization. *J. nerv. ment. Dis.*, **136**, 272–278.

LEHRMAN, D. S. (1964) The reproductive behavior of ring doves. *Sci. Amer.*, **211**, 48–54.

LEHRMAN, D. S. (1967) Reproductive behavior. In *Encyclopedia of Science and Technology*, Vol. 11, 454–462. New York: McGraw-Hill.

LEITENBERG, H., AGRAS, W. S., and THOMSON, L. E (1968) A sequential analysis of the effect of selective positive reinforcement in modifying anorexia nervosa. *Behav. Res. Ther.*, **6**, 211–218.

LEMAGNEN, J. (1952) Les phénomènes olfacto-sexuals chez l'homme. *Arch. Sci. Physiol.*, **6**, 125–160.

LEMAGNEN, J. (1953) L'olfaction. Le fonctionnement olfactif et son intervention dans les régulations psychophysiologiques. *J. Physiol. Path. Gen.*, **45**, 285–326.

LEVENTHAL, A. M. (1968) Use of a behavioral approach within a traditional psychotherapeutic context: a case study. *J. abnorm. Psychol.*, **73**, 178–182.

LEVI, L. (1969) Sympatho-adrenomedullary activity, diuresis, and emotional reactions during visual sexual stimulation in human females and males. *Psychosom. Med.*, **31**, 251–268.

LEVINE, J. (1955) The sexual adjustment of alcholics. A clinical study of a selected sample. *Quart. J. Stud. Alcohol*, **16**, 675–680.

LEVINE, S. and MULLINS, R. F., Jr. (1966) Hormonal influences on brain organization in infant rats. *Science*, **152**, 1585–1592.

LEVINE, S. and TREIMAN, L. J. (1969) Role of hormones in programming the central nervous system. In *Foetal Autonomy* (Ed. G. E. Wolstenholme and M. O'Connor) 271–281. London: Churchill.

LEVINGER, G. (1964) Note on need complementarity in marriage. *Psychol. Bull.*, **61**, 153–157.

LEVINGER, G. and BREEDLOVE, J. (1966) Interpersonal attraction and agreement: a study of marriage partners. *J. Personal. Soc. Psychol.*, **3**, 367–372.

LEWIS, ANNE and HOGHUGI, M. (1969) An evaluation of depression as a side effect of oral contraceptives. *Brit. J. Psychiat.*, **115**, 697–701.

LEYTON, G. B. (1946) *A survey of the effects of slow starvation on man*. Unpubl. M.D. thesis, Univer. Cambridge.

LIPSCOMB, F. M. (1945) Medical aspects of Belsen concentration camp. *Lancet*, ii, 313–315.

LOEB, JANICE (1966) The personality factor in divorce. *J. Consult. Psychol.*, **30**, 562.

LOESER, A. A. (1943) Effect of emotional shock on hormone release and endometrial development. *Lancet*, ii, 518–519.

LOFTUS, T. A. (1962) Symposium: Psychogenic factors in anovulatory women: III. Behavioral and psychoanalytic aspects of anovulatory amenorrhea. *Fertil. Steril.*, **13**, 20–28.

LUCAS, ANN F. (1963) The relationship between attitude of student nurses toward childbearing and certain selected individual and background characteristics. *Amer. Psychol.*, **18**, 403, abstract.

LUCKEY, ELEANOR B. (1963) Self- and spouse perceptions concomitant with marital satisfaction. *Amer. Psychol.*, **18**, 367, abstract.

LUND, M. A. (1964) Gynaecological psycho-syndromes. *Acta Psychiat. Scand.*, **40**, 191–197.

MCCLURE, T. J. (1966) Infertility in mice caused by fasting at about the time of mating. I. Mating behaviour and littering rates. *J. Reprod. Fertil.*, **12**, 243–248.

MCCLURE, W. E. (1931) Intelligence of unmarried mothers, II. *Psychol. Clin.*, **20**, 154–157.

MCDONALD, R. L. and CHRISTAKOS, A. C. (1963) Relationship of emotional adjustment during pregnancy to obstetric complications. *Amer. J. Obstet. Gynec.*, **86**, 341–348.

MCDONALD, R. L. and GYNTHER, M. D. (1965) Relations between self and parental perceptions of unwed mothers and obstetric complications. *Psychosom. Med.*, **27**, 31–38.

MCDONALD, R. L., GYNTHER, M. D., and CHRISTAKOS, A. C. (1963) Relations between maternal anxiety and obstetric complications. *Psychosom. Med.*, **25**, 357–363.

MCDONALD, R. L. and PARHAM, K. J. (1964) Relation of emotional changes during pregnancy to obstetric complications in unmarried primigravidas. *Amer. J. Obstet. Gynec.*, **90**, 195–201.

MCGUIRE, R. J., CARLISLE, J. M., and YOUNG, B. G. (1965) Sexual deviations as conditioned behaviour: a hypothesis. *Behav. Res. Ther.*, **2**, 185–190.

MACKINNON, I. L., MACKINNON, P. C. B., and THOMSON, A. D. (1959) Lethal hazards of the luteal phase of the menstrual cycle. *Brit. med. J.*, **1**, 1015–1017.

MACKINNON, P. C. B. and MACKINNON, I. L. (1956) Hazards of the menstrual cycle. *Brit. med. J.*, **1**, 555.

MCLAREN, ANNE (1964) 'Maternal impressions': an old wives' tale reconsidered. *New Scientist*, **22**, No. 386, 97–100.

MACLEOD, A. W. (1964) Some psychogenic aspects of infertility. *Fertil. Steril.*, **15**, 124–133.

MCNEMAR, Q. (1940) Critical examination of the University of Iowa studies of environmental influences upon the IQ. *Psychol. Bull.*, **37**, 63–92.

MADSEN, C. H., Jr. and ULLMAN, L. P. (1967) Innovations in the desensitization of frigidity. *Behav. Res. Ther.*, **5**, 67–68.

MALLESON, JOAN (1954) Sex problems in marriage. *Practitioner*, **172**, 389–396.

MALLESON, JOAN (1963) *Change of Life: Facts and Fallacies of Middle Age*. Harmondsworth, Middlesex: Penguin.

MALMQUIST, C. P., KIRESUK, T. J., and SPANO, R. M. (1966) Personality characteristics of women with repeated illegitimacies: descriptive aspects. *Amer. J. Orthopsychiat.*, **36**, 476–484.

MANDELBROTE, B. M. and MONRO, M. (1964) Neurotic illness as a factor in reproduction. *Acta Psychiat. Scand.*, **40**, 419–426.

MARGERISON, J. H., ANDERSON, W. McC., and DAWSON, J. (1964) Plasma sodium and the EEG during the menstrual cycle of normal human females. *Electroenceph. Clin. Neurophysiol.*, **17**, 540–544.

MARTINI, L. and GANONG, W. F. (1967) *Neuroendocrinology*, Vol. II. New York: Academic Press.

MASLOW, A. (1965) Critique and discussion. In *Sex Research: New Developments* (Ed. J. Money), 3–23. New York: Holt, Rinehart & Winston.

MASLOW, A. H., RAND, H., and NEWMAN, S. (1966) Some parallels between sexual and dominance behavior of infra-human primates and the fantasies of patients in psychotherapy. In *Sexual Behavior and Personality Characteristics* (Ed. M. F. DeMartino) 154–174. New York: Grove Press.

MASON, W. A. and GREEN, P. H. (1962) The effects of social restriction on the behavior of rhesus monkeys: IV. Responses to a novel environment and to an alien species. *J. Comp. Physiol. Psychol.*, **55**, 363–368.

MASTERS, W. H. (1952) The female reproductive system. In *Cowdry's Problems of Ageing*, 3rd ed. (Ed. A. I. Lansing) 651–685. Baltimore: Williams & Wilkins.

MASTERS, W. H. and JOHNSON, VIRGINIA E. (1966) *Human Sexual Response*. London: Churchill.

MATSUMOTO, S., SATO, I., ITO, T., and MATSUOKA, A. (1966) Electroencephalographic changes during long term treatment with oral contraceptives. *Int. J. Fertil.*, **11**, 195–204.

MAYERSON, P. and LIEF, H. I. (1965) Psychotherapy of homosexuals: a follow-up study of nineteen cases. In *Sexual Inversion. The Multiple Roots of Homosexuality* (Ed. J. Marmor) 302–344. New York: Basic Books.

MEAD, MARGARET (1961) Cultural determinants of sexual behavior. In *Sex and Internal Secretions* (Ed. W. C. Young) 1433–1479. Baltimore: Williams & Wilkins.

MEADE, J. E. and PARKES, A. S. (1966) *Genetic and Environmental Factors in Human Ability*. Edinburgh: Oliver & Boyd.

MEIER, H. (1963) *Experimental Pharmacogenetics*. New York: Academic Press.

MELGES, F. T. (1968) Postpartum psychiatric syndromes. *Psychosom. Med.*, **30**, 95–107.

MELLBIN, G. (1966) Neuropsychiatric disorders in sex chromatin negative women. *Brit. J. Psychiat.*, **112**, 145–148.

MELZACK, R. (1965) Effects of early experience on behavior: experimental and conceptual considerations. In *Psychopathology of Perception* (Ed. P. H. Hoch and J. Zubin) 271–290. New York: Grune & Stratton.

MICHAEL, R. P. (1964) Biological factors in the organization and expression of sexual behaviour. In *The Pathology and Treatment of Sexual Deviation* (Ed. I. P. Rosen) 24–54. London: Oxford University Press.

MICHAEL, R. P., HARRIS, G. W., and SCOTT, P. R. (1958) *Neurological Basis of Behaviour*. London: CIBA Foundation.

MICHAEL, R. P. and KEVERNE, E. B. (1968) Pheromones in the communication of sexual status in primates. *Nature*, **218**, 746–749.

MICHAEL, S. T. (1954) Electric shock treatment and the menstrual cycle. *Arch. Neurol. Psychiat.*, **71**, 198–207.

MONTAGU, M. F. A. (1962) *Prenatal Influences*. Springfield, Ill.: C. C. Thomas.

MOORE, S. F. (1962) Therapy of psychosomatic symptoms in gynecology. An evaluation of chlordiazepoxide. *Curr. Ther. Res.*, **4**, 249–257.

MOOS, R. H. (1968) Psychological aspects of oral contraceptives. *Arch. Gen. Psychiat.*, **19**, 87–94.

MOOS, R. H. (1968) The development of a menstrual distress questionnaire. *Psychosom. Med.*, **30**, 853–867.

MOOS, R. H. (1969) *Menstrual Distress Questionnaire*. Preliminary manual. California: Dept. Psychiat., Stanford University.

MOOS, R. H., KOPELL, B. S., MELGES, F., YALOM, I., LUNDE, D. T., CLAYTON, R. B. and HAMBURG, D. (1969) Fluctuations in symptoms and mood during the menstrual cycle. *J. Psychosom. Res.*, **13**, 37–44.

MOSIER, P. H., GROSSMAN, H. J., and DINGMAN, H. F. (1962) Secondary sex development in mentally deficient individuals. *Child Development*, **33**, 273–286.

MOULTON, RUTH (1966) Multiple factors in frigidity. In *Sexuality of Women* (Ed. J. H. Masserman) 75–93. New York: Grune & Stratton.

MUDD, EMILY H., STEIN, M., and MITCHELL, H. E. (1961) Paired reports of sexual behavior of husbands and wives in conflicted marriages. *Compr. Psychiat.*, **2**, 149–156.

MULLEN, F. G., Jr. (1968) The treatment of a case of dysmenorrhea by behavior therapy techniques. *J. nerv. ment. Dis.*, **147**, 371–376.

MULLEN, F. G., Jr. (1969) Personal communication.

MUNRO, A. (1969) Psychiatric illness in gynaecological outpatients: a preliminary study. *Brit. J. Psychiat.*, **115**, 807–809.

MYERS, K. and POOLE, W. E. (1962) A study of the biology of the wild rabbit, *oryctolagus cuniculus* (L.) in confined populations. III. Reproduction. *Austral. J. Zool.*, **10**, 225–267.

NEGULICI, EUGENIA, CHRISTODORESCU, D., and ALEXANDRU, S. (1968) Psychological aspects of the testicular feminization syndrome. *Psychosom. Med.*, **30**, 45–50.

NEWMAN, P. H. (1944) The prisoner-of-war mentality: Its effect after repatriation. *Brit. med. J.*, **1**, 8–10.

NEWTON, MARY B. and ISSEKUTZ-WOLSKY, MARIA DE (1969) The effect of parental age on the rate of female maturation. *Gerontologia*, **15**, 328–331.

NEWTON, N. R. and NEWTON, M. (1951) Recent trends in breast feeding: a review. *Amer. J. Med. Sci.*, **221**, 691–698.

NICOLSON, A. B. and HANLEY, C. (1953) Indices of physiological maturity: derivations and interrelationships. *Child Development*, **24**, 3–28.

NIELSEN, J. (1964) Klinefelter's syndrome and behaviour. *Lancet*, **ii**, 587–588.

NIELSEN, J. (1964) Mental disorder in married couples (assortative mating). *Brit. J. Psychiat.*, **110**, 683–697.

NIELSEN, J. and TSUBOI, T. (1969) Intelligence, EEG, personality deviation, and criminality in patients with the XYY syndrome. *Brit. J. Psychiat.*, **115**, 965.

NILSSON, Å. and ALMGREN, P.-E. (1968) Psychiatric symptoms during the postpartum period as related to use of oral contraceptive. *Brit. med. J.*, **2**, 453–455.

NILSSON, Å., JACOBSON, L., and INGEMANSON, C.-A. (1967) Side-effects of an oral contraceptive with particular attention to mental symptoms and sexual adaptation. *Acta Obst. Gynec. Scand.*, **46**, 537–556.

NIREMBERSKI, M. (1946) Psychological investigations of a group of internees at Belsen camp. *J. ment. Sci.*, **92**, 60–74.

NISSEN, H. W. and YERKES, R. M. (1943) Reproduction in the chimpanzee: report on forty-nine births. *Anat. Rec.*, **86**, 567–578.

NOLAN, C. Y. (1952) Stimulational seizures without pseudopregnancy in white rats. *J. Comp. Physiol. Psychol.*, **45**, 183–187.

NOTTINGHAM, R. (1937) A psychological study of forty unmarried mothers. *Genet. Psychol. Monogr.*, **19**, 155–228.

NOYES, R. W. and CHAPNICK, ELEANOR M. (1964) Literature on psychology and infertility: a critical analysis. *Fertil. Steril.*, **15**, 543–558.

O'NEILL, MARION and KEMPLER, B. (1969) Approach and avoidance responses of the hysterical personality to sexual stimuli. *J. abnorm. Psychol.*, **74**, 300–305.

OSTERMAN, E. (1965) Les troubles mentaux au cours de la grossesse. *Encephale*, **1**, 36–54.

OSTFELD, A. M. (1962) Studies in headache: migraine and the menstrual cycle. In *Psychosomatic Obstetrics, Gynecology and Endocrinology* (Ed. W. S. Kroger) 327–333. Springfield, Ill.: C. C. Thomas.

OVERZIER, C. (1963) *Intersexuality: A comprehensive treatise*. Basle: Karger Libri.

PALMAI, G. (1963) Psychological observations on an isolated group in Antarctica. *Brit. J. Psychiat.*, **109**, 364–370.

PALMER, H. D. and SHERIDAN, S. H. (1938) The involutional melancholia process. *Arch. Neurol. Psychiat.* (Chicago), **40**, 762–788.

PARE, C. H. B. and RAVEN, HERMIONE (1970) Follow-up of patients referred for termination of pregnancy. *Lancet*, **i**, 635–638.

PARKES, A. S. and BRUCE, HILDA M. (1961) Olfactory stimuli in mammalian reproduction. *Science*, **134**, 1049–1054.

PASAMANICK, B. and KNOBLOCH, HILDA (1966) Retrospective studies on the epidemiology of reproductive casualty: old and new. *Merrill-Palmer Quart.*, **12**, 7–26.

PASAMANICK, B., KNOBLOCH, HILDA, and LILIENFELD, A. M. (1956) Socioeconomic status and some precursors of neuropsychiatric disorders. *Amer. J. Orthopsychiat.*, **26**, 594–601.

PATT, S. L., RAPPAPORT, R. G., and BARGLOW, P. (1969) Follow-up of therapeutic abortion. *Arch. Gen. Psychiat.*, **20**, 408–414.

PAULSON, M. J. and WOOD, K. R. (1966) Perceptions of the emotional correlates of dysmenorrhea. *Amer. J. Obstet. Gynec.*, **95**, 991–996.

PEARSON, J. S. and AMACHER, PHYLLIS L. (1956) Intelligence test results and observations of personality disorder among 3594 unwed mothers in Minnesota. *J. clin. Psychol.*, **12**, 16–21.

PECK, A. (1968) Therapeutic abortion: Patients, doctors, and society. *Amer. J. Psychiat.*, **125**, 797–804.

PECK, A. and MARCUS, H. (1966) Psychiatric sequelae of therapeutic interruption of pregnancy. *J. nerv. ment. Dis.*, **143**, 417–425.

PEEL, J. and POTTS, M. (1969) *Textbook of Contraceptive Practice*. Cambridge: Cambridge Univ. Press.

PERLEY, M. J. and GUZE, S. B. (1962) Hysteria—the stability and usefulness of clinical criteria. *New Engl. J. Med.*, **266**, 421–426.

PESKIN, H. (1968) The duration of normal menses as a psychosomatic phenomenon. *Psychosom. Med.*, **30**, 378–389.

PETERSEN, W. G. and KRAMP, J. L. (1965) The premenstrual syndrome: Its significance for admission to a psychiatric department. *Ugeskr. Laeg.*, **127**, 1536–1540.

PFEIFFER, E., VERWOERDT, A., and WANG, H.-S. (1968) Sexual behavior in aged men and women. I. Observations on 254 community volunteers. *Arch. Gen. Psychiat.*, **19**, 753–758.

PHILIP, J., SELE, V., and TROLLE, D. (1965) Primary amenorrhea: a study of 101 cases. *Fertil. Steril.*, **16**, 795–804.

PIOTROWSKI, Z. A. (1962) Psychogenic factors in anovulatory women: II. Psychological evaluation. *Fertil. Steril.*, **13**, 11–19.

PLANANSKY, K. and JOHNSTON, R. (1967) Mate selection in schizophrenia. *Acta Psychiat. Scand.*, **43**, 397–409.

POLLAK, O. (1950) *The Criminology of Women*. Philadelphia: Univer. Penn. Press.

POND, D. A., RYLE, A., and HAMILTON, MADGE (1963) Marriage and neurosis in a working-class population. *Brit. J. Psychiat.*, **109**, 592–598.

POST, F. (1968) Disorders of sex in the elderly. In *Sex and Its Problems* (Ed. W. A. R. Thomson) 67–72. Edinburgh: Livingstone.

PROSEN, H. (1967) Sexuality in females with 'hysteria'. *Amer. J. Psychiat.*, **124**, 687–692.

PROTHEROE, C. (1969) Puerperal psychoses: A long term study 1927–1961. *Brit. J. Psychiat.*, **115**, 9–30.

PUGH, T. F., JERATH, B. K., SCHMIDT, W. M., and REED, R. B. (1963) Rates of mental disease related to childbearing. *New Engl. J. Med.*, **268**, 1224–1228.

REES, CAROLYN E. Y. (1969) Personal communication.

REES, L. (1953) Psychosomatic aspects of the premenstrual tension syndrome. *J. ment. Sci.*, **99**, 62–73.

RETTERSTÖL, N. (1968) Paranoid psychosis associated with impending or newly established fatherhood. *Acta Psychiat. Scand.*, **44**, 51–61.

REYNOLDS, S. R. M. (1962) Physiological and psychogenic factors in the menopausal flush syndrome. In *Psychosomatic Obstetrics, Gynecology and Endocrinology* (Ed. W. S. Kroger) 618–624. Springfield, Ill.: C. C. Thomas.

RHEINGOLD, HARRIET L. (Ed.) (1963) *Maternal Behavior in Mammals*. New York: Wiley.

RIDLER, M. A. C., SHAPIRO, A., and McKIBBEN, W. R. (1963) Sex chromatin abnormalities in female subnormal patients. *Brit. J. Psychiat.*, **109**, 390–394.

ROCK, J., TIETZE, C., and McLAUGHLIN, HELEN B. (1965) Effect of adoption on infertility. *Fertil. Steril.*, **16**, 305–312.

RODGER, T. F. (1968) Attitudes toward abortion. *Amer. J. Psychiat.*, **125**, 804–808.

RODGERS, D. A. and ZIEGLER, F. J. (1968) Changes in sexual behavior consequent to use of noncoital procedures of contraception. *Psychosom. Med.*, **30**, 495–505.

ROGERS, M. E., PASAMANICK, B., and LILIENFELD, A. M. (1955) Prenatal and paranatal factors in the development of childhood behavior disorders. *Acta Psychiat. Neurol. Scand.*, Suppl., **102**, 1–157.

ROHRER, J. H. (1960) *Human adjustment to Antarctic isolation*. Armed Services Technical Information Agency, Publication AD 246610, 1–25. Arlington Hall Station, Arlington, Va.

ROMM, MAY E. (1965) Sexuality and homosexuality in women. In *Sexual Inversion* (Ed. J. Marmor) 282–301. New York: Basic Books.

ROSE, ANNELIES A. (1949) Menstrual pain and personal adjustment. *J. Pers.*, **17**, 287–302.

ROSENTHAL, R. (1964) The effect of the experimenter on the results of psychological research. In *Progress in Experimental Personality Research*, Vol. I (Ed. B. A. Maher). New York: Academic Press.

ROSVOLD, H. E. (1949a) The effects of electroconvulsive shocks on gestation and maternal behavior. I. *J. Comp. Physiol. Psychol.*, **42**, 118–136.

ROSVOLD, H. E. (1949b) The effects of electroconvulsive shocks on gestation and maternal behavior. II. *J. Comp. Physiol. Psychol.*, **42**, 207–219.

ROTH, LORRAINE L. and ROSENBLATT, J. S. (1965) Self-licking as a stimulus for mammary development in the pregnant rat. *Amer. Zool.*, **5**, 234, abstract.

ROTH, LORRAINE L. and ROSENBLATT, J. S. (1966) Mammary glands of pregnant rats: development stimulated by licking. *Science*, **151**, 1403–1404.

RUBIN, B. (1965) Psychological aspects of human artificial insemination. *Arch. Gen. Psychiat.*, **13**, 121–132.

RUBIN, I. (1966) *Sexual Life After Sixty*. London: Allen & Unwin.

RUTHERFORD, R. N., BANKS, A. L., and COBURN, W. A. (1962) Frigidity in the female partner with special reference to postpartum frigidity: some clinical observations and study programs. In *Psychosomatic Obstetrics, Gynecology and Endocrinology* (Ed. W. S. Kroger) 400–414. Springfield, Ill.: C. C. Thomas.

RYLE, A. (1966) A marital patterns test for use in psychiatric research. *Brit. J. Psychiat.*, **112**, 285–293.

SAGHIR, M. T. and ROBINS, E. (1969) Homosexuality I. Sexual behavior of the female homosexual. *Arch. Gen. Psychiat.*, **20**, 192–201.

SAGHIR, M. T., ROBINS, E., and WALBRAN, B. (1969) Homosexuality II. Sexual behavior of the male homosexual. *Arch. Gen. Psychiat.*, **21**, 219–229.

SALERNO, L. J. (1962) Psychophysiologic aspects of the toxemias of pregnancy. In *Psychosomatic Obstetrics,*

Gynecology and Endocrinology (Ed. W. S. Kroger) 104–112. Springfield, Ill.: C. C. Thomas.

SANCTUARY, G. (1968) *Marriage Under Stress*. London: Allen & Unwin.

SANDLER, B. (1965) Conception after adoption: A comparison of conception rates. *Fertil. Steril.*, **16**, 313–322.

SAVAGE, R. D. (1964) Electro-cerebral activity, extraversion and neuroticism. *Brit. J. Psychiat.*, **110**, 98–100.

SCHMIDEBERG, M. (1952) Psychiatric social factors in young unmarried mothers. *Bull. National. Comm. on Service to Unmarried Parents*, Cleveland, Ohio.

SCHWARTZ, E. D. and SMITH, J. J. (1963) The effect of chlordiazepoxide on the female reproductive cycle as tested in infertility patients. *West. J. Surg.*, **71**, 74–76.

SCOTT, P. D. (1964) Definition, classification, prognosis and treatment. In *The Pathology and Treatment of Sexual Deviation* (Ed. I. P. Rosen.) London: Oxford Univ. Press.

SCOTTISH COUNCIL FOR RESEARCH IN EDUCATION (1949) *The Trend of Scottish Intelligence*. London: Univ. London Press.

SCOTTISH COUNCIL FOR RESEARCH IN EDUCATION (1953) *Social Implications of the 1947 Scottish Mental Survey*. London: Univ. London Press.

SEARS, R. (1942) *Survey of Objective Studies of Psychoanalytic Concepts*. New York: Social Science Research Council.

SELYE, H. and McKEOWN, T. (1934) Production of pseudo-pregnancy by mechanical stimulation of the nipples. *Proc. Soc. Exp. Biol.*, **31**, 683–687.

SEWARD, GEORGENE H., BLOCH, S. K., and HEINRICH, J. F. (1967) The question of psychophysiologic infertility: some negative answers: A postscript. *Psychosom. Med.*, **29**, 151–152.

SEWARD, GEORGENE H., WAGNER, P. S., HEINRICH, J. F., BLOCH, S. K., and MYERHOFF, H. L. (1965) The question of psychophysiologic infertility: some negative answers. *Psychosom. Med.*, **27**, 533–545.

SHAFFER, J. W. (1963) Masculinity-femininity and other personality traits in gonadal aplasia (Turner's syndrome). In *Advances in Sex Research* (Ed. H. G. Beigel) 219–232. New York: Hoeber.

SHAINESS, NATALIE (1961) A re-evaluation of some aspects of femininity through a study of menstruation: A preliminary report. *Comp. Psychiat.*, **2**, 20–26.

SHAINESS, NATALIE (1966) Psychological problems associated with motherhood. In *American Handbook of Psychiatry*, Vol. III (Ed. S. Arieti) 47–65. New York: Basic Books.

SHANAN, J. (1965) Family structure as predictor of transient amenorrhea. *2nd Int. Congr. Psychosom. Med. Obstet. Gynaecol.*, 377–380.

SHELESNYAK, M. C. and ROSEN, S. (1938) Naso-genital relationship: Induction of pseudo-pregnancy in rat by nasal treatment. *Endocrin.*, **23**, 58–63.

SHER, N. (1946) Causes of delayed menstruation and its treatment. An investigation in the Women's Auxiliary Air Force. *Brit. med. J.*, **1**, 347–349.

SHIPMAN, W. G. (1964) Age at menarche and adult personality. *Arch. Gen. Psychiat.*, **10**, 155–159.

SIMON, N. M. and SENTURIA, AUDREY G. (1966)

Psychiatric sequelae of abortion. *Arch. Gen. Psychiat.*, **15**, 378–389.

SLATER, E. (1943) Neurotic constitution; statistical study of 2,000 neurotic soldiers. *J. Neurol. Psychiat.*, **6**, 1–16.

SLATER, E. (1945) Neurosis and sexuality. *J. Neurol. Neurosurg. Psychiat.*, **8**, 12–14.

SLATER, E. (1953) *Psychiatry, in Clinical Genetics* (Ed. A. Sorsby) London: Butterworths.

SLATER, E. and WOODSIDE, M. (1951) *Patterns of Marriage*. London: Cassell.

SMALLDON, J. L. (1940) A survey of mental illness associated with pregnancy and childbirth. *Amer. J. Psychiat.*, **97**, 80–101.

SMITH, S. L. and SAUDER, CYNTHIA (1969) Food cravings, depression, and premenstrual problems. *Psychosomat. Med.*, **31**, 281–287.

SOCARIDES, C. W. (1963) The historical development of theoretical and clinical concepts of overt female homosexuality. *J. Amer. Psychoanal. Ass.*, **11**, 386–412.

SONTAG, L. W. (1962) Effect of maternal emotions on fetal development. In *Psychosomatic Obstetrics, Gynecology and Endocrinology* (Ed. W. S. Kroger) 8–13. Springfield, Ill.: C. C. Thomas.

SPECTOR, W. G. (1961) Suppression of fertility in rats by an inhibitor of monoamine oxidase. *J. Reprod. Fertility*, **2**, 362–368.

SPELT, D. K. (1948) The conditioning of the human fetus in utero. *J. Exp. Psychol.*, **38**, 338–346.

STAFFORD-CLARK, D. (1954) The etiology and treatment of impotence. *Practitioner*, **172**, 397–404.

STAMM, J. S. (1955) The function of the median cerebral cortex in maternal behavior of rats. *J. Comp. Physiol. Psychol.*, **4**, 324–326.

STENGEL, E., ZEITLYN, B. B., and RAYNER, E. H. (1958) Post-operative psychoses. *J. ment. Sci.*, **104**, 389–402.

STENSTEDT, Å. (1952) A study in manic-depressive psychosis. *Acta Psychiat. Scand.* Suppl., **79**.

STEVENS, BARBARA C. (1969) Probability of marriage and fertility of women suffering from schizophrenia or affective disorders. *Population Studies*, **23**, 435–454.

STEVENS, BARBARA C. (1970) Illegitimate fertility of psychotic women. *J. Biosoc. Sci.*, **2**, 17–30.

STOLLER, R. J. (1968) *Sex and Gender*. London: Hogarth Press.

STONE, C. P. and BARKER, R. G. (1934) On the relationships between menarcheal age and certain aspects of personality, intelligence and physique in college women. *J. Genet. Psychol.*, **65**, 121–135.

STONE, C. P. and BARKER, R. G. (1937) Aspects of personality and intelligence in postmenarcheal and premenarcheal girls of the same chronological age. *J. Comp. Psychol.*, **23**, 439–445.

STONE, C. P. and WALKER, A. H. (1949) Note on modification of effects of electroconvulsive shocks on maternal behavior by ether anesthesia. *J. Comp. Physiol. Psychol.*, **42**, 429–432.

STOTT, D. H. and MARSTON, N. (1969) A primary form of behavior disturbance (inconsequence) related to physical and mental stress during pregnancy. Personal communication.

STRAUSS, A. (1946) The influence of parent-images upon marital choice. *Amer. Sociol. Rev.*, **11**, 554–559.

STRONG, L. C. (1936) Establishment of "A" strain of inbred mice. *J. Hered.*, **27**, 21–34.

SUTHERLAND, H. and STEWART, I. (1965) A critical analysis of the premenstrual syndrome. *Lancet*, **i**, 1180–1183.

SYDENHAM, ANNIE (1946) Amenorrhea at Stanley Camp, Hong Kong, during internment. *Brit. med. J.*, **2**, 159.

TAKAHASHI, E. (1964) Seasonal variation of conception and suicide. *Tohuko. J. exp. Med.*, **84**, 215–227.

TANNER, J. M. (1962) *Growth at Adolescence*, 2nd ed. Oxford: Blackwell.

TAYLOR, D. C. (1969) Sexual behavior and temporal lobe epilepsy. *Arch. Neurol.*, **21**, 510–516.

TAYLOR, H. P. (1962) Nausea and vomiting of pregnancy: hyperemesis gravidarum. In *Psychosomatic Obstetrics, Gynecology and Endocrinology* (Ed. W. S. Kroger) 117–126. Springfield, Ill.: C. C. Thomas.

TAYLOR, M. A. (1969) Sex ratios of newborns: associated with prepartum and postpartum schizophrenia. *Science*, **164**, 723–724.

TEITELBAUM, H. A. and GANTT, W. H. (1958) The effect of alcohol on sexual reflexes and sperm count. *Quart. J. Stud. Alc.*, **19**, 394–398.

TERMAN, L. M. (1938) *Psychological Factors in Marital Happiness*. New York: McGraw-Hill.

TERMAN, L. M. (1951) Correlates of orgasm adequacy in a group of 556 wives. *J. Psychol.*, **32**, 115–172.

THARP, R. G. (1963) Psychological patterning in marriage. *Psychol. Bull.*, **60**, 97–117.

THARP, R. G. (1964) Reply to Levinger's note. *Psychol. Bull.*, **61**, 158–160.

THARP, R. G. and OTIS, G. D. (1966) Toward a theory for therapeutic intervention in families. *J. Consult. Psychol.*, **30**, 426–434.

THÉANO, GINETTE (1968) The prevalence of menstrual symptoms in Spanish students. *Brit. J. Psychiat.*, **114**, 771–773.

TINKLEPAUGH, O. L. (1932) Parturition and puerperal sepsis in a chimpanzee. *Anat. Rec.*, **53**, 193–205.

TIZARD, J. (1954) Institutional defectives. *Amer. J. Ment. Defic.*, **59**, 158–165.

TOKUHATA, G. K. (1968) Smoking in relation to infertility and fetal loss. *Arch. Environ. Health*, **17**, 353–359.

TONKS, C. M., RACK, P. H., and ROSE, M. J. (1968) Attempted suicide and the menstrual cycle. *J. Psychosom. Res.*, **11**, 319–323.

TRETHOWAN, W. H. (1965) Sympathy pains. *Discovery*, **26**, 30–33.

TRETHOWAN, W. H. (1968) Psychiatric emergencies in general practice. *Brit. med. J.*, **4**, 164–166.

TRETHOWAN, W. H. and CONLON, M. F. (1965) The couvade syndrome. *Brit. J. Psychiat.*, **111**, 57–66.

TUPPER, W. R. C. (1962) The psychosomatic aspects of spontaneous and habitual abortion. In *Psychosomatic Obstetrics, Gynecology and Endocrinology* (Ed. W. S. Kroger) 144–152. Springfield, Ill.: C. C. Thomas.

UDRY, J. R. and MORRIS, N. M. (1967) A method for validation of reported sexual data. *J. Marriage Family*, **29**, 442–446.

VANDEN BERG, R. L., TAYLOR, E. S., and DROSE, VERA (1966) Emotional illness in habitual aborters following suturing of the incompetent cervical os. *Psychosom. Med.*, **28**, 257–263.

WAINWRIGHT, W. H. (1966) Fatherhood as a precipitant of mental illness. *Amer. J. Psychiat.*, **123**, 40–44.

WALKER, J. (1954) The celibate male. *Practitioner*, **172**, 411–414.

WALLIN, P. and CLARK, A. L. (1958) Marital satisfaction and husbands' and wives' perception of similarity in their preferred frequency of coitus. *J. Abnorm. Soc. Psychol.*, **57**, 370–373.

WALLIN, P. and CLARK, A. L. (1963) A study of orgasm as a condition of women's enjoyment of coitus in the middle years of marriage. *Hum. Biol.*, **35**, 131–139.

WARD, D. A. and KASSEBAUM, G. G. (1965) *Women's Prison: Sex and Social Culture*. Chicago: Aldine.

WARREN, W. (1968) A study of anorexia nervosa in young girls. *J. Child Psychol. Psychiat.*, **9**, 27–40.

WAXENBERG, S. E. (1963) Some biological correlatives of sexual behavior. In *Determinants of Human Sexual Behavior* (Ed. G. Winokur) 52–73. Springfield, Ill.: C. C. Thomas.

WAXENBERG, S. E., FINKBEINER, J. A., DRELLICH, M. G., and SUTHERLAND, A. M. (1960) The role of hormones in human behavior: II. Changes in sexual behavior in relation to vaginal smears of breast-cancer patients after oophorectomy and adrenalectomy. *Psychosom. Med.*, **22**, 435–442.

WEIR, M. W. and DEFRIES, C. (1963) Blocking of pregnancy in mice as a function of stress. *Psychol. Rep.*, **13**, 365–366.

WEIR, W. C. and WEIR, D. R. (1966) Adoption and subsequent conceptions. *Fertil. Steril.*, **17**, 283–288.

WELCH, J. P. (1968) Down's syndrome and human behaviour. *Nature*, **219**, 506.

WENNER, NAOMI K., COHEN, MABEL B., WEIGERT, EDITH V., KVARNES, R. G., OHANESON, E. M., and FEARING, J. M. (1969) Emotional problems in pregnancy. *Psychiatry*, **32**, 389–410.

WERTHEIMER, NANCY M. (1962) Schizophrenic subdiagnosis and age at menarche. *J. Ment. Sci.*, **108**, 786–789.

WHITACRE, R. E. and BARRERA, B. (1944) War amenorrhea. *J. Amer. Med. Assn.*, **124**, 399–403.

WHITELAW, M. J. (1968) The myth of oral contraceptives in the treatment of infertility. *Fertil. Steril.*, **19**, 372–375.

WHITING, J. W. M. (1965) Menarcheal age and infant stress in humans. In *Sex and Behavior* (Ed. F. A. Beach) 221–233. New York: Wiley.

WIENER, H. (1966) External chemical messengers. I. Emission and reception in man. *New York State J. Med.*, **66**, 3153–3170.

WIENER, H. (1967a) External chemical messengers. II. Natural history of schizophrenia. *New York State J. Med.*, **67**, 1144–1165.

WIENER, H. (1967b) External chemical messengers. III.

Mind and body in schizophrenia. *New York State J. Med.*, **67**, 1287–1310.

WIGNALL, C. M. and MEREDITH, C. E. (1968) Illegitimate pregnancies in state institutes. *Arch. Gen. Psychiat.*, **18**, 580–583.

WILBUR, CORNELIA B. (1965) Clinical aspects of female homosexuality. In *Sexual Inversion: The Multiple Roots of Homosexuality* (Ed. J. Marmor) 268–281. New York: Basic Books.

WINCH, R. F. (1958) *Mate-selection: A Study of Complementary Needs*. New York: Harper.

WINICK, C. (1965) Marihuana use by young people. In *Drug Addiction in Youth* (Ed. E. Harms) 19–35. Oxford: Pergamon.

WINOKUR, G. (1963) Sexual behavior: its relationship to certain affects and psychiatric diseases. In *Determinants of Human Sexual Behavior* (Ed. G. Winokur) 76–100. Springfield, Ill.: C. C. Thomas.

WINOKUR, G. and HOLEMON, E. (1963) Chronic anxiety neurosis: clinical and sexual aspects. *Acta Psychiat. Scand.*, **39**, 384–412.

WOLPE, J. (1958) *Psychotherapy by reciprocal inhibition*. Stanford, Calif.: Stanford Univ. Press.

WOLPE, J. (1969) *The Practice of Behavior Therapy*. New York: Pergamon.

WRIGHT, W. S., MANWELL, M. K. C., and MERRETT, J. D. (1969) Anorexia nervosa: a discriminant function analysis. *Brit. J. Psychiat.*, **115**, 827–831.

YALOM, I. D., LUNDE, D. T., MOOS, R. H., and HAMBURG, D. A. (1968) 'Postpartum blues' syndrome: A description and related variables. *Arch. Gen. Psychiat.*, **18**, 16–27.

YARDEN, P. E., MAX, D. M., and EISENBACH, Z. (1966) The effect of childbirth on the prognosis of married schizophrenic women. *Brit. J. Psychiat.*, **112**, 491–499.

YARON, E., CHOVES, I., LOCKER, A., and GROEN, J. J. (1963) Influence of handling on the reproductive behaviour of the Syrian hamster in captivity. *J. Psychosom. Res.*, **7**, 69–82.

YOUNG, W. C. (1961) The hormones and mating behavior. In *Sex and Internal Secretions*, Vol. II (Ed. W. C. Young) 1173–1839. Baltimore: Williams & Wilkins.

YOUNG, W. C. (1967) Prenatal gonadal hormones and behavior in the adult. In *Comparative Psychopathology: Animal and Human* (Ed. J. Zubin and H. F. Hunt) 173–183. New York: Grune & Stratton.

YOUNG, W. C., GOY, R. W., and PHOENIX, C. H. (1964) Hormones and sexual behavior. *Science*, **143**, 212–218.

ZUBIN, J. and KATZ, M. M. (1964) Psychopharmacology and personality. In *Personality Change* (Ed. P. Worchel and D. Byrne) 367–395. New York: Wiley.

ZUCKERMAN, M. and LUBIN, B. (1965) Normative data for the Multiple Affect Adjective Check List. *Psychol. Rep.*, **16**, 438.

7

Mental Subnormality*

ANN M. CLARKE and A. D. B. CLARKE

INTRODUCTION

Definition

In the past, different countries have employed widely different practices for, and concepts of, mental subnormality. It is scarcely surprising, therefore, that there are many different definitions of these conditions. It is probable that at all times and within all cultures, the severely handicapped have been identified as such because of their difficulty, without help, in adapting themselves to social demands. Hence, one finds a greater agreement in defining the more severe than the milder forms of subnormality. Indeed, these latter will only tend to come to notice when the complexity of society advances above the limits of their spontaneous competence.

The World Health Organisation (1954) referred to mental subnormality as 'incomplete or insufficient general development of the mental capacities . . . it is intended to cover only cases in which general mental development is insufficient'. The American Association on Mental Deficiency (Heber, 1959) defined mental retardation as, 'sub-average general intellectual functioning which originates during the development period and is associated with impairment in one or more of the following: (1) maturation, (2) learning, and (3) social adjustment'. Here 'sub-average' refers to performance more than one standard deviation below the population mean; 'general intellectual functioning' may be assessed by one or more of the objective tests developed for the purpose; and the upper age limit of the 'development period' is regarded as about sixteen years. Maturation and learning are also carefully discussed and 'social adjustment' at the adult level is regarded as the degree to which the individual is able to maintain himself independently in the community and in gainful employment, as well as his ability to meet and conform to other personal and social standards as set by the community. In its *Manual of the International Statistical Classification of Diseases, Injuries, and Causes of Death*, the World Health Organisation (1967) follows the American suggestion in defining 'border-line mental retardation' (and, hence, all lower levels of subnormality) as lying between IQ 85 and 68. The WHO Expert Committee (1968), however, deplored this widening of the concept, believing both that the quality of available services, geared to lower ability, would be damaged and that the category would become a repository for other conditions. Our own Mental Health Act (1959) defined subnormality as 'a state of arrested or incomplete development of mind (not amounting to severe subnormality) which includes subnormality of intelligence and is of a nature or degree which requires or is susceptible to medical treatment or other special care or training of the patient'. Severe subnormality is referred to in the same general terms but with the qualification that 'the patient is incapable of living an independent life or of guarding himself against serious exploitation, or will be so incapable when of an age to do so'.

These definitions use rather similar phrases, such as 'incomplete or insufficient general mental development', 'sub-average general intellectual functioning', and 'arrested or incomplete development of mind . . . which includes subnormality of intelligence', and focus on lack of intelligence as an essential criterion. Indeed, with such a wide group

* This Chapter was written as part of a research project generously financed by the Association for the Aid of Crippled Children, New York.

212

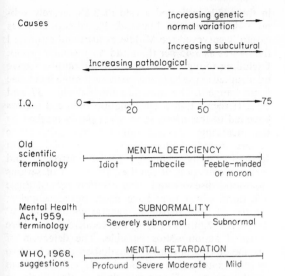

Fig. 7.1. The relation between main causes of mental subnormality, IQ, British terminology, and recent WHO suggestions

The WHO committee considered that, taken in conjunction with social factors, the subclassifications should be associated with IQ as follows—

mild	—2·0 to	—3·3
moderate	—3·3 to	—4·3
severe	—4·3 to	—5·3
profound	more than	—5.3

Standard deviations from a mean of 100.

as the subnormal, heterogeneous in aetiology, level of functioning and prognosis, low or very low intelligence is perhaps the only quality its members have in common. Nevertheless, such criteria as social adjustment are never precisely identified so that in practice all such definitions, particularly of the higher levels of subnormality, permit wide differences in interpretation and in practice. These problems are discussed in detail by A. M. Clarke (Clarke and Clarke, 1965).

Attempts have been made, with some over-simplification, to identify three headlines in the aetiology of the many conditions subsumed under the heading of subnormality, and to relate them to the levels of ability within the whole group (see Fig. 7.1).

First, ordinary polygenic variation is certainly responsible for a fair proportion of those in the higher grades. With parent-child IQ correlations of about 0·5, it is obvious that children may show different levels of ability from their parents, even though there is a clear tendency for parent-child resemblance. Thus, for parents who are themselves

below average there is some chance of their producing children of average levels or above, as well as the milder grades of subnormality. No unusual mechanism need therefore necessarily be invoked for those subnormals (a) whose conditions of childhood have been reasonable, (b) whose parents are of average or below average ability themselves, and (c) who have no history, or signs suggestive of, an organic pathology.

The second aetiological group usually identified is termed 'subcultural'. With perhaps dull parents, together with adversity of social and child-rearing conditions, their level is considered to result from a complex interaction of poor genetic endowment and poor environment. It is this group that is thought most likely to benefit from social and special educational programmes.

Thirdly, there are those whose condition is largely pathological in origin. Obviously, pathological changes in the central nervous system may operate at almost any grade of ability, reducing its functional level by various amounts. Within the range of subnormality, however, we are dealing with grosser changes and grosser effects. And as one descends the IQ scale, the more likely it is that a given condition is pathological in origin.

An interesting change, as Penrose (1962) has pointed out, has occurred in our understanding of aetiological mechanisms. Whereas, in the past, most cases of pathological, mainly low-grade, subnormality were thought to result from trauma, infection or toxicity, it is now increasingly recognised that rare (often recessive) genetic mechanisms are frequently responsible for the damage (e.g. phenylketonuria). And whereas the subnormals of IQ 50 upward were at one time thought to owe their condition largely to unfavourable genetic mechanisms, evidence now suggests that early and prolonged social adversity may be an important (though not the sole) feature. The dichotomy between pathological/subcultural, recognised in the early nineteen-thirties, remains valid, although its interpretation has been to some extent reversed. Obviously, too, some cases of subnormality may result from mixed aetiology.

Mental subnormality poses two main problems; first, the task of primary prevention of these conditions, whether they be of medico-biological or socio-cultural origin, or, more commonly, resulting from the interaction of both. The second problem is the amelioration of existing mental subnormality wherever possible, again whether by medical, social or educational means. Of course, these aspects overlap to some extent; if amelioration is highly effective it becomes prevention, so that division of research into two categories is to some extent artificial. There have been recent important theoretical advances in the first sphere, leading to some practical results, though it is very unlikely that, in the immediately foreseeable future, mental subnormality will be substantially reduced in incidence. In the second, however, the increased awareness of mental subnormality as a special problem in learning has already borne practical fruit. Although not wishing to minimise our continuing ignorance, it is now obvious from a variety of broad educational and training programmes that much can be done to use, develop, and indeed sometimes to create, limited assets in a way thought impossible a mere fifteen years ago. The ground has thereby been cleared and the way is now open for behavioural scientists to explore in depth the details of learning and other processes. Perhaps the most important recent development in the field of amelioration is the increasing concern by experimental scientists with perception, attention, memory, language, and concept attainment. Work of this nature takes time to yield applicable knowledge; it seems to us, however, that the foundations of adequate educational programmes for the future will be laid on the basis of research carried out under conditions sufficiently controlled to indicate causes of behavioural deficits and precise methods of overcoming them.

Most of this chapter will be concerned with experimental studies of subnormal behaviour. These must, however, be set in a broader context if their significance is to be appreciated. Hence, in concluding this Introduction, it is proposed first to indicate very briefly the scope and limitations of work relating to prevention of subnormality, and second, to its amelioration. These problems are outlined in greater detail by Clarke (1969).

Prevention

Estimates of the effectiveness of preventive methods must in the last resort depend on accurate studies of incidence and prevalence. The complex issues involved in such studies have been outlined in detail by Tizard (1964) and more briefly by O'Connor (1965). Overall prevalence is usually taken as about 2 per cent of the population with an upper limit of IQ 70 or thereabouts. Three-quarters of the subnormal have IQs between 50 and 70, about 20 per cent between 20 and 50 and the remaining 5 per cent below IQ 20.

True prevalence can best be estimated for those grades where the condition is easily recognisable and where diagnosis (of retardation, though not necessarily the specific aetiology) is thus not in dispute. In practice, the severely subnormal in later childhood are most easily identified. A careful study in the 1920s indicated a rate of 3·88 severely subnormal children per thousand. Tizard (op. cit.) has carefully surveyed the Middlesex area and estimated the figures as 3·45 per thousand for a similar group. Excluding mongols, whose surviving numbers have quadrupled in the last forty years (although incidence is unchanged), the rates are respectively 3·37 and 2·31. It seems that a constellation of social factors have led to this decrease which is partly masked by the increasing survival rate for mongols. These factors include better maternal and child health services, family planning, earlier marriage, and earlier completion of families, reduction of serious childhood diseases and immunisation against those infections which may have neurological sequelae, the use of 'risk registers', genetic counselling and the early diagnosis of some metabolic defects where remedial action seems possible. The detection of enzyme defects or chromosomal aberrations *in utero* by the examination of foetal cells cultured from small amounts of amniotic fluid is also likely to prove a practical method that would aid decisions to terminate pregnancy in families at risk (Steele and Breg, 1966).

It has long been known that some rare types of subnormality (e.g. cretinism) can be successfully treated by means of replacement therapy. Or again, an understanding of haemolytic disease of the newborn due to Rhesus incompatibility has enabled successful exchange transfusions to be made, consequently affecting the incidence of subnormality from this cause. More importantly, Clarke (1967) has shown that it is possible to immunise rhesus-negative mothers and prevent Rh sensitisation by rhesus-positive foetuses. Controlled studies in Liverpool indicated a high degree of protection. Much publicity has also been given to the treatment of phenylketonuric children with a diet low in phenylalanine. A number of authorities, such as Birch and Tizard (1967) and Bessman, Due Logue and Wapnir (1968), however, have cast doubt on the rationale of PKU treatment. It has been shown that some children exhibiting PKU do not suffer mental subnormality, while others do. It is possible, therefore, that some of the successes claimed for treatment occur in those who would have anyway developed normally. Thus, currently the PKU model is being re-evaluated.

The prevention of higher grades of mental defect turns on many complex and interacting factors. Those who owe their condition to pathological agents may be reduced in number for such reasons as those advanced above, but mild subnormality is much more often caused by normal genetic variation and subcultural factors. It is in the latter category that the hopes for prevention are greatest. Although the evidence is not always unequivocal, it seems that extremely adverse social conditions play a part in retarding development. These studies have been critically reviewed by McCandless (1964), Clarke and Clarke (1965), Clarke (1968), and Sarason and Doris (1969); they indicate that if the period of deprivation is not too long there is a certain degree of reversibility in such effects. Intervention programmes such as the American 'Headstart' educational schemes have attempted to prevent the development of mild subnormality, but their duration is all too short and the children remain in conditions that militate against any permanent change in their developmental path. Moreover, Bereiter and Engelmann (1966) argue that the educational methods used are often inappropriate for this sort of child. Nevertheless, a few studies indicate a successful outcome, and currently Heber (1968) is undertaking an ambitious, controlled experimental study in Milwaukee, the outcome of which will do much to establish precisely how far mild defect can be prevented where its origins are thought to include powerful social factors. This study, in an area of high prevalence for mental retardation, shows a statistical risk factor for 14 year-olds of 0·90 when the mother's IQ is less than 80, and only 0·13 when maternal IQ is 80 or above. Hence, low intelligence mothers in this area have been randomly assigned either to experimental or control conditions. The newly born children of the former group are being stimulated intensively from birth onwards to see whether or not it is possible to reduce the occurrence of mental retardation. From four months of age the babies attend a special Infant Education Centre and follow an intensive programme of sensory and language stimulation. At the same time, the retarded mothers are relieved of the day care of other pre-school children and offered training in home-making and child care techniques. This Project may well indicate that shorter-term attempts at prevention of mild subnormality need to be greatly extended and supplemented by changes in the home if 'Headstart' effects are to be anything more than transitory. If successful, they would provide a very important rationale for up-grading a section of the dull and mildly subnormal members of the population. Early results look promising (Heber, 1971).

Amelioration

This sub-section overlaps to some extent with the previous one, for really successful amelioration becomes prevention. Amelioration may take place through social improvements, educational or training methods, through administrative changes and above all through the careful step-by-step investigation of what may be broadly termed the learning processes—simple words used to describe the highly complex modes of modification of behaviour that occur throughout life. There can be little doubt that the amelioration of subnormality, sometimes profound, sometimes barely measurable, can and does occur. The gap, however, between research findings and administrative practice remains wide. These problems have been discussed in detail by Clarke and Clarke (1965) and Baumeister (1967a) among other writers. A few examples of recent work are given below, and, of course, some of the experimental studies to be reviewed later are relevant.

(a) THE SEVERELY SUBNORMAL

The problems of the severely subnormal in the community have been carefully described by Saenger (1957) and by Tizard and Grad (1961).

The effects on development in the severely subnormal of different forms of residential care have been described by Lyle (1959; 1960a,b) and by Tizard (1960). Institutionalisation clearly retards verbal development, but the effect may be reduced in small units generously staffed (e.g. the Brooklands Experiment, Tizard, op. cit.). It was the view of the experimenter that considerably better social and emotional adjustment resulted from the greater attention given to the children in the residential unit. Tizard et al. (1968) have studied differences in child management techniques, and believe that the social organisation of our present residential institutions is the main factor responsible for the poor quality of care that many of them provide.

Most studies on the effects of special class training of imbecile children have been poorly controlled and of short duration. Charney (1963) gives a useful over-view of this field. It is significant that, in a lengthy and more recent review on educational research, Guskin and Spicker (1968) are able to devote less than three pages to the educational and training problems of the severely subnormal. They cite, among others, a carefully controlled study by Cain and Levine (1963) which showed that home-based children, attending or not attending school, increased significantly in social competence over a two-year period, although they failed to differ significantly from each other. Institutionalised groups decreased substantially in social competence over this period. The lack of significant differences between school and non-school children substantiates some earlier findings. Careful surveys of curriculum content forced the authors to conclude that two of the major reasons why educational programmes have not been shown to facilitate social competence are: (*a*) inadequacy of curriculum content, and (*b*) poor teaching. They conclude also, 'that special classes for the trainable as presently constituted cannot be defended on the basis of benefit to parents'.

Such findings are in sharp contrast with those of the early experimental laboratory and workshop studies on imbecile adults in this country. Gordon, O'Connor, and Tizard (1954 and 1955), Tizard and Loos (1954) and Clarke and Hermelin (1955) gave evidence for substantial modifications of perceptual-motor behaviour. Much of this, together with corroborative independent findings in sheltered workshops in Holland, laid the basis for the better training and sheltered employment now available.

There appear to be several reasons for greater ignorance of appropriate training methods for children than for adults. First and foremost, until recently, educational research on severely subnormal children was, on the whole, poorly controlled and scanty. Second, both in the United States and in the United Kingdom, that section of the teaching profession concerned with these children has been accorded short and inadequate training and low professional status. Third, the commendable provision of beautiful buildings as training centres seems to have diverted educational authorities from precise evaluation of what goes on inside them.

This sub-section can be concluded by a re-affirmation of the earlier statement that to varying extents (sometimes large, sometimes negligible) the behaviour processes of the severely subnormal are subject to modification. More is known about the appropriate methods for adults than for children, but there is a dearth of properly controlled long-term evaluative studies. As some of the later reviews of experimental research will indicate, the starting level for learning is usually poor on most tasks, and yet subsequent learning and retention can often occur. This suggests, as a main deficit, a relative inability to learn from ordinary life experience, a disability that individual training under special conditions can do something to overcome. (*See*, in particular, the Section on Operant Learning.) Although our ignorance cannot be minimised, it is already clear from experimental studies that novel curricula could be devised for the education and training of the severely subnormal, which would allow controlled evaluation and identification of critical aspects of such methods.

(*b*) THE MILDLY SUBNORMAL

It is generally estimated that about 2 per cent of the population may be regarded as intellectually subnormal and severely subnormal, in the propor-

Table 7.1.   Total Identified Subnormal Population (Subnormal and Severely Subnormal) in England and Wales, 1966

Population of England and Wales	approx. 48 million
2% of total population	960,000
In schools for the ESN	approx. 45,000
On ESN waiting lists	approx. 10,000
In mental subnormality hospitals	approx. 65,000
On mental subnormality hospital waiting lists	approx. 5,000
* Under care of local health authorities	approx. 93,000
* In Junior Training Centres	approx. 17,000
* In Adult Training Centres	approx. 18,000
	approx. 253,000

* The total of 253,000 is considerably inflated because the Training Centre numbers are almost certainly also included in those under care of local health authorities. Moreover, in mental subnormality hospitals and training centres, the majority will be of severely subnormal grade.

It should be added that in 1966 there were a little over four million children under five; 2 per cent of this figure is 80,000. Of these, perhaps 60,000 are potentially ESN but these will not have been identified until the school years. The balance, about 20,000, is severely subnormal and some of these pre-school children will be under the care of local health authorities or in special care units or in subnormality hospitals. All these considerations justify the conclusion that a relatively small percentage of the *mildly* subnormal (unlike the severely subnormal) are in receipt of special facilities at any one time. (Part of this information is taken from Table 7 in Worters, 1968.)

tion of three to one, respectively. With a population in England and Wales of about 48 million, therefore, one would expect something like 960,000 subnormal persons of all grades. What do we know of the status of this large group? It is possible, in a rough-and-ready way, to account for a proportion by examining statistics for a given year, in this case 1966 (Table 7.1).

The Table accounts for all those specifically designated subnormal (whether of mild or severe grade) and dealt with as such by various social agencies. It is certain that it includes the vast majority of those who are severely subnormal. There remains the possibility, however, that other types of community provision include significant numbers of the mildly subnormal, of which the criminal population is the only one worth serious consideration. In an as yet unpublished recent study, Dr C Banks (personal communication) gave individual Stanford-Binet tests to 900 randomly sampled men aged 17 to 20, in detention, prison, or Borstal. She found that 2 per cent (i.e. roughly the expected representation from the total population) had IQ of 70 and below. Unfortunately, there is no study available of the intelligence of a randomly selected prison population, but according to Dr R. V. G Clarke (personal communication) studies of selected samples of the prison population, while showing a over-representation of the dull normal, do not suggest any marked over-representation of the subnormal.

If one were to add, say, a further 25,000 (probably a considerable over-estimate) to cover the mildly subnormal receiving care in prisons, Borstals, approved schools, or charitable hostels, one would only account for less than a third of the estimated total subnormal and severely subnormal population. The conclusion seems inescapable that at any one point in time, the majority of the *mildly subnormal* (who comprise three-quarters of the total) function within the limits of community tolerance in a welfare state, receiving no special official provision. For these very reasons, little is known of the 'ordinary' mildly subnormal in the community, and precise data relate in the main to the most disadvantaged members of the group.

The rather crude analysis offered above is supported by the results of long-term social follow-up of mildly retarded persons (Charles, 1953; Miller, 1965). A large group identified as retarded and attending 'opportunity classes' was originally studied in the 1930s. Detailed analysis of the ways in which its members differed from the general population has been provided and the successively improving outcome carefully documented. A final monograph by Baller *et al.* (1967) indicated that the majority were functioning adequately as low-average members of the population, working in unskilled or semi-skilled employment. Of average age 53 years, this group has 'continued to fare much better than could have been predicted or even hoped for'.

A detailed summary of American work on social and occupational adjustment of mental retardates is provided by Goldstein (1964), who concluded that: (1) the results of follow-up studies of former inmates of institutions for the mentally retarded indicated that the pervading pessimism of professional and lay people is unwarranted; (2) comparative studies of the social adjustment of adult retardates and normal peers indicated that the former were generally inferior on most criteria, including employment, but it was difficult to be sure whether these differences might be accounted for by intellectual differences or by social factors; (3)

occupationally the retarded cluster in the unskilled category or service occupations—they did not appear to change jobs more frequently than normal workers, but tended to be the first to be discharged during slack periods; and (4) there was encouraging evidence that training programmes and counselling services were effective. Guskin and Spicker (1968) have reviewed educational research undertaken in America with both educable and trainable mental defectives of school age; although the results of special educational intervention have not always shown gains, on the whole there are grounds for cautious optimism in this area.

Another source of supportive evidence for their thesis emerges from prevalence studies. Analysis of age rates (Penrose, 1949) indicates a marked reduction in numbers from adolescence onwards, a fact confirmed, in general, by more recent surveys in Baltimore and Onondaga County in the United States. According to Clarke (1969) this is accounted for by three factors:

1. 'camouflage' which implies no change in the individual but a lowering of intellectual demands following school age and hence reasonable adjustment,
2. prolonged but ultimately successful social learning, and
3. delayed maturation, characterised by IQ increments which tend to occur in some subcultural members of the mildly subnormal population. These factors, singly or in combination, may account for the diminution in identifiable numbers as age increases.

In summary, it seems that among the mildly subnormal there are those whose condition, to varying extents, spontaneously improves. Other studies (e.g. Skeels and Dye, 1939; Skeels, 1966; Skodak, 1968) suggest that planned intervention, initiated early and reinforced throughout life, can result in more profound changes. Many such studies can be criticised on methodological grounds but, even so, the data have been carefully collected and have led to methodologically purer research (Gray and Klaus, 1965, 1970; Heber, 1968). It is likely that in the next few years the detailed results of these more recent studies will give a fuller understanding of the problems of amelioration of mild subnormality.

THEORIES OF SUBNORMAL BEHAVIOUR

In any new scientific field, after a period of large-scale data collection, some general hypotheses or general attitudes arise to which research workers, wittingly or unwittingly, adhere. Currently, three positions with respect to mental subnormality may

be outlined. These are as yet embryonic and are perhaps less important in their own right as psychological theories than for the rôle they play in determining research projects and type of experimental design.

1. The Defect Theory

Adherents to this view consider that the mentally subnormal differ from the normal not only quantitatively but qualitatively. The argument rests on the many studies comparing subnormal and normal subjects *matched for MA* which show inferior performance in the former group, and the special difficulties of most subnormals in the area of language development and verbal mediation. Most defect theorists (Ellis, 1963; Spitz, 1963; Luria, 1961) have elaborated their own physiological models which serve as guidelines in formulating hypotheses for behavioural research. Although their views are sometimes ambiguous, a strong impression is gained that they see the mentally subnormal, regardless of aetiology or level of intellect, as neurologically different from the normal population. As Ellis (1969), one of the chief exponents of this theory, puts it, MA, IQ, or 'developmental level', however defined, are rejected as an *explanation* of behaviour. Given that there are behavioural differences between normals and retardates of equal CA, the primary task for a behavioural science is to describe these differences. In view of Ellis's position it is logical that he believes the term 'defectives' more accurately describes this population than 'retardates', the latter term holding connotations of a developmental lag, which might in time be made good.

2. The Retardation or Developmental Lag Theory

This states that the cognitive development of the mentally retarded is characterised by a slower progression through the same sequence of cognitive stages as the normal, and by lower limits to full development. Thus, the difference between normal and subnormal is analogous with the difference between the very superior and normal. The developmental position generates the hypothesis that there are no differences in formal cognitive functioning between *familial* (biogenic) retardates and normals matched on general level of cognition (typically measured by MA). Zigler (1969) has contributed an excellent statement of this position and critique of the defect theory. He (1967) believes that many of the reported differences in performance between normal and mentally retarded individuals of the same MA may be traced to such variables as motivation and experience, rather than to basic cognitive deficiencies.

Although the differences in theoretical position between adherents of these views of subnormality sometimes appear wide, in fact there is considerable overlap, and the most important point of contention probably resides in the question as to whether the broad aetiological classification (biogenic versus pathological) is so basic to a consideration of any problem in mental retardation that research workers are in error to include in one group subjects selected on intellectual level as the sole criterion. Zigler (1969) would have it that a developmental lag theory applies best to the familial/cultural subnormals, reserving the defect theory for the pathological. By contrast, Leland (1969) and others argue that it is not to the scientist's advantage to dichotomise mentally retarded groups on the basis of presumed aetiologies. Most of them are so labelled because of maladaptation and behavioural difficulties. The only serviceable classification system is one that groups individuals by their ability to cope with specific critical demands, and that provides a guide to the modification and reversal of these behaviours.

3. The Skinnerian Position

The latter position has something in common with Skinnerian theory, elaborated for retardation by Bijou (1963 and 1966), which is important not so much for its effectiveness in describing the nature of subnormality, as in focusing the research of its adherents on to the antecedent conditions, and future methods of shaping the behaviours of sometimes profoundly subnormal individuals who might not otherwise be seen as promising material for psychological research. (*See* Operant Learning.)

Bijou eschews the use of hypothetical mental constructs such as defective intelligence and hypothetical biological abnormalities such as 'clinically inferred brain injury' in the classification of mental retardation. He maintains that, since it is the behaviour that is retarded, correlates must be sought for this retarded behaviour. These must be observable events that clearly limit or control behaviour; antecedent events are grouped in classes such as abnormal anatomical structure and physiological functioning, the consequences of severe punishment, or inadequate reinforcement history. Once the relationship is established the basis for behaviour control is reached.

In summary, the main point of contention in the recent experimental literature on mental subnormality has related to the first two hypotheses outlined above, and frequent references to this issue will be found in the following pages. The recent polemic between Milgram (1969), Zigler (1969), and Ellis (1969) suggests a considerable overlap between the 'defect' and 'retardation' theories, and some misunderstanding by the main protagonists of the others' position. But Ellis now considers that a sharp distinction between developmental and defect approaches lacks substance. However, much research stems from one or other of these positions.

PROBLEMS OF RESEARCH DESIGN

A majority of the experimental studies reviewed in this chapter contrast a group or groups of mentally retarded subjects' performance on a task or tasks with that of normal subjects matched for MA or CA. In both cases, IQ differences between groups will be inevitable and sometimes considerable. With MA matches, up to 50-point IQ differences may be found and with CA matches, 30 points is usual and up to about 70 points has been reported, when retarded children are compared with groups of intellectually superior subjects. Although in many cases of MA-matched groups, psychologists have clearly stated that they were looking for qualitative differences between groups, who on intelligence tests had performed similarly, the suspicion arises that, on occasion, inclusion of normal controls in a research design was due to a blind adherence to a fashionable trend. Only recently have scientists looked critically at research designs in common use and at the questions that may legitimately be answered in any particular case.

Zeaman (1965) points out that the psychologist may attack the problems of subnormality in at least two ways, either by finding the laws, principles, or regularities that govern the behaviour of retardates, or by finding the *unique* laws of their behaviour. If the latter is to be attempted, comparisons with normal children are essential, but control in such comparisons is fraught with difficulty. 'If you match for CA, then MA is out of control. If you match for MA, then CA is necessarily out of control. If you assume CA is not a relevant variable and match for MA, then other differences appear to be out of control. Length of institutionalisation, home environments, previous schooling, tender-loving-care, and socio-economic status are factors likely to be different for retardates and normals.' To tackle such problems realistically would require heroic investigators matched by heroic budgets; hence, Zeaman and some others confine their interest to laws about subnormal behaviour rather than unique laws.

Baumeister (1967b) discusses in detail the difficulties encountered in comparing subnormals and normals. Obviously, the fundamental problem is one of ensuring that the task is an equivalent measure of the same psychological processes for both groups. If one is investigating some cognitive process, and differences emerge, it is necessary to be able to exclude sensory, motor, motivational, and other differences, but this can seldom be achieved. Obvious violations of this principle occur in studies of institutionalised subnormals and non-institutionalised normals. Zigler (1969) quotes the following example. Rohwer and Lynch (1968) compared the paired-associate learning efficiency of institutionalised retardates (having a mean CA of about 25) with groups of normal children of varying economic strata (having CAs ranging from about 5 to 12). The finding that the institutionalised retarded group did worse than MA-matched normals (and even normals having lower MAs than the retarded) was interpreted as convincing evidence of the erroneousness of the retardation theory. However, in another article in the same journal, Baumeister (1968a) reported a study of paired-associate learning of MA-matched groups of institutionalised retardates, non-institutionalised retardates, and children of normal intellect. There was no difference between the latter two groups, but the institutionalised retardates were inferior to both. Furthermore, there was a significant correlation between length of institutionalisation and trials to criterion: the longer the child was institutionalised, the worse was his performance.

Another example of a questionable comparison of groups is provided by some early work on short-term memory in which innumerate severely subnormal children were contrasted with normal schoolchildren on digit repetition.

Transcending the developmental *vs.* defect controversy, there is agreement that the essential problem of mentally retarded individuals is their intellectual or cognitive inadequacy. Zigler (op. cit.) reasons that since cognitive functioning lies at the core of retardation phenomena, it is easy to see why, in this particular area, workers have concentrated on cognitive functioning, often totally ignoring the possibility that other factors such as temperament, educational opportunities, motivation, social class, and environmental background might contribute at all to the current status, and consequent task performance of the retardate. Indeed, this chapter is itself testimony to the imbalance of experimental research in mental deficiency since the interactions of these factors with cognitive development have not been systematically explored. A notable exception is the work of Zigler and his colleagues (*see* Section on Personality and Motivation).

A few investigators have argued against attempts to match experimentally on either an MA or CA basis, on the grounds that it is not always a valid assumption that either of these is the most relevant variable that could be used, and may lead to the introduction of systematic differences between groups on variables other than these. Furthermore, experimental matching normally results in biased selection of subjects due to the necessity for discarding those who cannot be paired with others, or who alter means or variances on the matching variable. Stanley and Beeman (quoted by Prehm, 1966b) advocated statistical matching: subjects should be drawn at random from a specified population, and assigned at random to the various treatment conditions, a procedure that should result in subjects varying at random on any antecedent variable. Matching of subjects could then be accomplished through analysis of covariance. Prehm (op. cit.) discussed this suggestion, and adopted it in a study of paired-associate learning (Prehm, 1966a); however, experimental matching remains the preferred method by a majority of investigators.

Baumeister argues that comparison of subnormals and normals is most appropriate where their behaviour is observed as a function of systematic variations in task or environmental variables; this calls for a multiple factor design in which subject characteristics are co-manipulated with experimental factors. The question then posed is not whether the subnormal is inferior but whether experimental manipulation will produce the same behavioural adjustment in both groups. One is thus no longer concerned with showing that there are deficits in the subnormal (this is taken for granted) but with determining the conditions that produce variability in group differences. This procedure does not assume that the task is exactly the same for the two groups, but that task and subject characteristics are constant for all values of the experimental variables. This latter is normally a far safer assumption.

Where, after an MA match, performance differences emerge, the researcher has identified a difference not residing in the MA scores themselves. 'That this difference is any more fundamental and theoretically meaningful than one which happens to correlate with test performance is dubious. One might say that such a result shows that intelligence tests do not measure all adaptive behaviours . . . we may have done nothing more than to discover another way of diagnosing mental retardation' (Baumeister, op. cit.). Moreover, the MA is itself compounded of many factors, equal MAs may be reached by several routes, and are a reflection of an interaction between the content of the test, the experience of the subject and his 'true' ability. As such, the MA has little explanatory value. Baumeister notes that far more attention has been devoted to MA than to other variables such as reinforcement history, comprehension of instructions, and so on. In effect, like Zeaman, he concludes

that to understand the behaviour of subnormals one must study the behaviour of subnormals, and the study of normal behaviour 'is quite irrelevant to this purpose'. He does not entirely dismiss the usefulness of comparative studies, but considers that observations of normals will not, of themselves, tell us about the behaviour of subnormals. At best it may raise hypotheses.

'Floor' and 'ceiling' effects are a further source of difficulty in group comparisons, particularly in learning studies. Clarke and Blakemore (1961), for example, compared adults, adolescent and child imbeciles from the same institution on their learning and transfer on various pairs of perceptual-motor tasks. They found that there was greater transfer in the children than in the adolescents and adults. This resulted from a 'ceiling effect' which prevented the adolescents and adults from improving their performance on tasks not especially difficult for them. When Clarke and Cooper (1966) repeated some of this work but adjusted task difficulty to achieve equal starting points for older and younger subnormals, no transfer differences were found.

Ellis (op. cit.) makes a masterly contribution to this whole problem. The apparent rationale of an equal MA match is that this equalises 'development'. Rarely, however, is the meaning of 'development' scrutinised. There is the additional and already noted problem of whether equal MA scores are based on equal sub-test performance, and there is also the possibility that MA may reflect past and present motivational status as well as cognitive factors.

Ellis believes that the equal CA matching procedure is directed to the primary characteristic of subnormality. There are, however, serious problems with this design. Behavioural differences (except for the mildly retarded) are often so great that measurement on the same scale is impossible. 'Floor' and 'ceiling' effects (noted above) are inevitable hazards (Ellis and Anders, 1968). Nevertheless, Ellis argues that for certain purposes CA matches appear to carry more theoretical significance than a comparison of adult mental retardates with normal children on the basis of an MA match.

Finally, Baumeister (1968b), who makes a habit of tackling difficult methodological problems, which are easily swept under the carpet, has pointed to the problem of greater performance variability of defective than normal subjects, a matter that must surely have been observed by all research workers who have studied both groups. He reviews the literature, which is not extensive, and concludes that it is almost certain that the two intelligence groups do differ on this characteristic to a significat extent; he suggests, tentatively, that variables related to arousal, attentional, or motivational processes may be implicated in normal-retardate efficiency differences.

These problems have been outlined at some length because, although they permit no easy solution, it seems essential that research workers should be aware of them, since the conclusions derived from much of the early experimental work on mental retardation must be regarded as equivocal, due to a failure on the part of investigators fully to understand the many pitfalls. Furthermore, the fact that in most areas included in this review, both results and interpretations by different authors conflict, is acknowledged to be largely due to differing methodological preferences.

Bortner and Birch (1970) review a large number of studies of subnormal and normal children and experimental animals which demonstrate that performance levels under particular conditions are but fragmentary indicators of capacity (or potential). Glaring differences occur in the estimates of potential when significant alterations are made in the conditions for performance. This distinction between capacity and performance, more often implicit in the literature than explicit, has led some workers to start investigating systematically the appropriate conditions, both cognitive and motivational, for maximising performance.

In considering the following text, which reviews a selection of studies published up to 1970, readers should bear firmly in mind the problems discussed above and, also, that the subjects used in the various experiments range from helpless idiots (*see* Operant Learning) through imbeciles (often malformed, malcoordinated with severe speech defects) to the mildly subnormal many of whom in later life are barely distinguishable from members of the normal working population, but who, while young, by virtue of learning difficulties, find their way into special classes, schools, or institutions, for the retarded.

PERCEPTUAL PROCESSES

Although sensory perception may be considered basic to cognitive functioning, psychologists have concerned themselves much less with the operation of sensory and perceptual processes in the mentally subnormal than with problems of learning and memory. Spivack (1963) reviewing this field concluded that the paucity of research data on perceptual processes is striking, and the results are too fragmentary to permit of meaningful integration. 'Too often the "single-shot" study raises more questions than are answered and is rarely followed up by others.' The situation has not changed substantially to date and, with certain important exceptions, there is as yet little theoretical debate of the sort likely to give rise to hypothetico-deductive studies. Moreover, the problem is complicated by the fact that some influential clinical theorists, notably Goldstein and Scheerer (1941), Werner (*see* Diller and Birch, 1964), Strauss and Lehtinen (1947), and Strauss and Kephart (1955) suggested that cortical lesions interfere with perception, and in consequence special training and educational methods have been devised to take account of the effects of brain injury (either demonstrable or assumed). A vast literature exists on the psychological diagnosis of brain damage, and the differentiation of exogenous from endogeneous mental defectives. This will not be reviewed here, but the reader is referred to a summary by Diller and Birch (op. cit.) who raise a number of methodological problems that affect interpretation of the data. Haywood (1966), in a discussion of training programmes for the perceptually handicapped, concludes that no definite criteria reliably differentiate the perceptually handicapped (or minimally brain damaged) child from the emotionally disturbed or generally mentally retarded. No systematic research has been conducted to demonstrate the validity of these programmes, and it is suggested that 'perceptual handicap' may be 'an artifact of our ignorance and lack of solid descriptive research' (*see also* Sternlicht *et al.*, 1968).

The difficulty some brain-damaged children experience with visuo-motor tasks, such as copying a diamond or reproducing a block design, by comparison with controls matched for mental and chronological age, has given rise to a debate as to whether the basic problem is visuoperceptual or visuomotor. Bortner and Birch (1960), working with adult hemiplegics and cerebral-palsied children, found that these subjects made many more errors than did control subjects in copying block designs. However, in the vast majority of cases the brain-damaged subjects were able to select the correct design (over their own reproductions and a standard incorrect copy) when the task was presented in multiple-choice version. The investigators concluded that the difficulty of the brain-damaged lies not in the perceptual system but in the perceptual-action system.

Support for this view is provided by Ball and Wilsoncroft (1967) who used the phi-phenomenon to investigate perceptual-motor deficits. The technique used was based on Orlansky's (1940) demonstration that type of form used as stimuli influences phi thresholds. If two squares are used, a certain threshold is obtained; if a square is paired with a diamond, the threshold changes significantly. It is assumed that if a subject obtains thresholds that differ for homogeneous (two squares) and heterogeneous (square and diamond) forms, it is due to his perceptual ability to discriminate these forms. Three groups, normals, institutionalised retardates, and cerebral-palsied were studied; the latter two groups were tested on the Stanford-Binet task of copying a diamond (MA 7) as well as reproduction of a straight line and a diamond on a peg-board. Since all subjects had MAs over eight, the inability by some to copy or construct a diamond represented a specific perceptual-motor deficit. There were no differences in ability to discriminate form as measured by phi-thresholds among the groups and sub-groups studied, although there was a significant difference in overall reactivity to phi motion in favour of the normals. The authors conclude that the results substantiate the position advocated by Bortner and Birch (op. cit.) and are at variance with Kephart's theory which emphasises the rôle of perception in accounting for perceptual-motor deficits.

On the other hand, Deich (1968) challenged this conclusion by demonstrating that retardates at two MA levels, matched on this variable with normal children, aged 6 and 8·9 years, were significantly inferior in both reproduction *and* recognition of block designs, although all groups performed better on the latter than the former. Deich believes her results support the view that retardates are perceptually impaired, at least for complex visual stimuli. In this connection, Gaudreau (1968) points to the great difficulty of discriminating between the rôles played by perception and those by intelligence when complex problems are used. Krop and Smith (1969) showed that performance by retardates on the Bender-Gestalt test improves with participation in an educational programme, and further improvement resulted from specific instruction in drawing geometric patterns.

A marked contrast to the single-shot studies of perception, deplored by Spivack, is provided by the systematic work on illusions conducted recently over several years by Herman Spitz and his colleagues. Spitz (1963) offers a cogent defence of Gestalt theories in the study of mental retardation; more specifically, the application of Köhler and Wallach's (1944) theory of cortical satiation to the results of experiments on figural after effects (Spitz and Blackman, 1959), kinesthetic after effects (Spitz and

Lipman, 1961), and perspective reversal (Necker cube) led him to postulate (1964) that cortical changes take place more slowly in retardates than in normals. Therefore retardates should be *less* susceptible to 'physiological' illusions than normal subjects, but *equally* susceptible to 'experiential' illusions, a classification applied to those illusions induced primarily by distorting the stimulus and/or reducing the viewer's observing power, apparently causing the viewer to resort to faulty assumptions and inferences based on past experience (Spitz, 1967).

Mental retardates were found to be less capable than equal CA controls of perceiving visual after effects, and had a lower reversal rate on the Necker cube. Winters (1965) and Winters and Gerjuoy (1965; 1967) compared college students with high-grade retardates on sensitivity to gamma movement (the apparent expansion and contraction of a briefly exposed figure) and concluded that, unlike normals, retardates do not perceive gamma at 0·2 sec, but that it was possible to induce gamma in retardates by lengthening the exposure time. The authors believe that slower electro-chemical processes in the cortex rather than an attention deficit account for the differences observed between their groups (*see* Section on EEG Studies).

Of the experimental illusions, Spitz (1964) found retardates equally susceptible as normals on the rotating trapezoidal window illusion, and on the distorted room illusion (Spitz, 1967). In the latter study, adolescent retardates were compared with college students on a table model of the Ames distorted room—a trapezoidal room which simulated rectangularity—and a control room that was truly rectangular. Loss of size constancy in judging two unequal circles was the illusion indicator. No significant differences between groups was found on either room. Even under visual restraint retardates maintained as much size constancy as equal CA normals.

Spitz (1965) has also reported *greater* susceptibility on the part of retardates than of normals to a physiological illusion that can be countered by an awareness of the depth cue of interposition (the rotating cube illusion). The results of all these experiments lend support to Spitz's contention that retardates differ from normals in their sensitivity to 'physiological' and 'experiential' illusions.

Winters (1969) took the argument further by postulating that if the only prerequisite for demonstrating physiological visual illusions is that a subject possesses a healthy central nervous system, then young normals (of equal MA to retardates) should demonstrate physiological illusions to the same degree as older normals (matched for CA to retardates), but should differ from older retardates;

furthermore, that on a presumably experiential illusion different age groups will be differentially affected. Winters contrasted perception of gamma-movement (physiological illusion) with two-dimensional size constancy (experiential illusion) using institutionalised male retardates (CA 16·4; IQ 63·7), normal adolescent males (CA 16·7; IQ 103·8) and normal male children (CA 10·8, no IQs available). The retardates did not demonstrate the physiological illusion, whereas both normal groups did, though not differing from each other. All three groups exhibited size constancy, with greater constancy of retardates over equal MA normals reaching only marginal significance. Winters interprets the results as confirming the defect theory of mental deficiency and offering evidence against the retardation theory.

The important question of the interdependence of perceptual and intellectual development was considered by Doyle (1967). Starting with the observation of an adult retardate whose perceptual skills appeared so well developed that by capitalising on them she was able to perform tasks beyond her intellectual capacity, Doyle advanced the hypothesis that perceptual skill development might proceed independently of intellectual development. One hundred and eight children from special classes for the mentally retarded were allocated to CA groups (at 7, 9, and 11) and MA groups (at 7, 9, and 11) so that each MA level was represented at each CA level, and vice versa. The children's susceptibility to the horizontal-vertical illusion for hearing, sight, and touch was determined by the method of constant stimuli. Susceptibility to the illusion was associated with independently varied MA and CA; (e.g. retarded children in the highest CA group were less susceptible to the illusion than their younger MA counterparts) and the findings were interpreted as supporting the hypothesis. Although this conclusion should probably be accepted with caution until more studies have been conducted, the experimental design might be used to good effect to investigate other aspects of perception.

EEG STUDIES

There is some, but by no means conclusive, evidence that EEG tracings are related to IQ (Ellingson, 1966; Vogel and Broverman, 1964; 1966).

The literature up to and including 1961 has been well reviewed by Berkson (1963), and Clevenger (1966) has provided an annotated bibliography of over 100 references. The former author distinguishes five main parameters of the alpha rhythm that have been studied. These are: (1) the frequency of alpha rhythm; average frequencies for normals and subnormals are closely similar, although there is a suggestion that the range for subnormals is greater; (2) the average amplitude of alpha rhythm; and (3) the proportion of time during a resting period for the subjects, when the rhythm is exhibited. Some studies show a relationship with MA while others do not; (4) and (5) are measures of response to short duration stimuli. If the subject is resting quietly in a darkened room, the alpha rhythm is most pronounced. With the presentation of a short-duration stimulus (e.g. light flash) the alpha rhythm is blocked, and the length of time of the block has been termed perseveration time. Berkson offers no information on speed of alpha blocking except from an unpublished study where no differences were found between normals and subnormals. The perseveration time of normals was, however, rather longer. Later work by Wolfensberger and O'Connor (1965) failed to confirm this finding. This later study also yielded information that subnormals were slower to block than normals.

Baumeister and Hawkins (1967) note the above discrepancies in the published findings and believe that difficulties may arise when widely disparate intelligence groups are compared. They aimed, therefore, to study the relationship between alpha phenomena and intelligence within subnormal groups, using 21 male adult cultural-familial subnormals. One second duration light stimuli were used during the presence of alpha rhythm for twenty trials. IQ and alpha block duration were not correlated within this group, but the correlation between IQ and number of blocks was significant (0·05 level), the more intelligent blocking more frequently. Brighter subjects were also slower to block, and a significant habituation effect was noted, the block duration decreasing over trials. This appeared to be unrelated to other measures. These findings are interpreted as indicating that decreasing intelligence seems to be associated with a reduction in responsiveness to external stimulation, a view that corresponds closely to clinical impressions, which should be considered in conjunction with the conclusions of Butler and Conrad (1964). These authors interpret the EEG findings as indicating an impaired speed of integration of complex sensory information.

Vogel and co-workers (1969) noted the lack of studies of behavioural correlates of abnormal EEG phenomena among the mentally subnormal, and attributed this to a consensual assumption that a group of people with abnormal EEGs will, on average, evidence more cortical pathology and therefore more maladaptive behaviour than those with normal EEGs. They investigated 45 retardates with abnormal EEGs and an equal number with normal EEGs, matched for age and diagnosis. The groups were compared for test intelligence, school, and occupational performance, personal skills, social behaviours, and psychiatric status for three separate periods: year of admission, year of EEG examination, and current year. EEG abnormality was associated with deficits on intelligence test performance, but not with deficits in broader categories of adjustment. However, mean alpha frequency of EEG was associated with behavioural adjustment as reflected in personal skills (e.g. dressing) and social behaviours (e.g. co-operation with ward staff), as well as test intelligence and classroom performance. The authors suggest that quantitatively derived EEG indices, such as alpha frequency, which are thought to reflect particular underlying neurological processes, relate more effectively to retardates' behaviour than do clinically derived categories such as EEG 'normality' or 'abnormality'.

REACTION TIME

Studies of reaction time (RT) using mentally subnormal subjects have been carried out by several investigators, particularly Baumeister and Berkson and their associates.

Baumeister and Kellas (1968c), reviewing the literature, concluded that:

1. Intelligence is functionally related to RT, not only when normal and subnormal subjects are compared (Scott, 1940), but also within the retarded population (Pascal, 1953; Ellis and Sloan, 1957; Berkson, 1960b). Although there has been some dispute on the nature of the function, it is suggested that it can best be described as linear.

2. Intensity of the stimulus influences retardates' response speed more than that of normals (Baumeister et al., 1964; Baumeister et al., 1965a,b). As the intensity of the signal to respond increases, RT correspondingly decreases. However, at stimulus values near threshold, normals and retardates are similarly affected.

3. Compound reaction stimuli appear to decrease RT in a manner similar to intensity. Holden (1965) showed that trimodal stimulation (auditory, visual, cutaneous) yielded faster reactions than any of these stimuli presented singly, possibly implying increased arousal. However, compound warning stimuli did not influence RT (Baumeister et al., 1965).

4. In conditions of stimulus complexity requiring choice, response speed of normals and defectives are equally affected (Berkson, 1960a,b). Berkson also found that when both stimulus and response complexity were varied, IQ interacted with the latter but not the former. Berkson concluded that IQ is not relevant to making a choice or planning a movement, but is related to the performance of that movement. Hawkins et al. (1965) compared college students and retardates on simple and choice RT tasks, using a verbal rather than motor response. Normals were faster than defectives and both groups showed slower choice RTs, but there was no interaction between type of task and intelligence level.

5. Temporal factors are related to the performance of mental defectives; these include the uncertainty, length of warning interval, psychological refractory period, and warning signal duration.

6. Attempts have been made to relate parameters of the alpha rhythm to RT of retardates. Since it has been shown that alpha blocks are shorter in defectives than normals (Baumeister et al., 1963; Berkson et al., 1961), it seems possible that EEG responsivity is related to slow RT. Furthermore, reaction signals presented during the period of alpha block are associated in normal subjects with faster RT than stimuli presented during a no block period (Fedio et al., 1961; Lansing et al., 1959). Thus, Baumeister and Hawkins (1967) suggested that retarded subjects whose alpha waves are particularly responsive to visual stimulation might be rapid responders. Their findings failed to support the hypothesis. Hermelin and Venables (1964) used visual warning stimuli of different duration and a wide range of warning interval. Reaction times to a sound stimulus were equally fast during periods of alpha and during alpha blocks.

7. Incentive conditions have been found to influence speed of RT (Baumeister and Ward, 1967).

8. Within-subject variability of RT is greater in defectives than normal subjects. Berkson and Baumeister (1967) examining variability in RTs of bright and dull subjects, found substantial correlations between medians and standard deviations (see also Baumeister and Kellas, 1968a,b, and Baumeister, 1968b). Baumeister believes that greater variability of response generally characterises the defective individual, and suggests that to determine the source of this variability offers an important subject for future research.

Baumeister, Wilcox, and Greeson (1969) used a reaction-time experiment to test the hypothesis that mental retardates are at a particular disadvantage in situations that require rapid adjustment to a complex and uncertain environment. Two experiments were conducted to compare the reaction times of normals and retardates as a function of the relative frequency of reaction signal occurrence, using a buzzer and a light as signals. The results indicated that both groups displayed increased reaction times as the probability of a particular stimulus decreased. Only when the frequencies of stimulus occurrence were markedly different did the interaction between intelligence group and event probability reach significance.

HYPERACTIVITY AND DISTRACTIBILITY

Clinicians have noted that among the retarded, and particularly severely retarded brain-injured children, many are hyperkinetic and distractible to a point where these characteristics actively interfere with attempts to educate or train them. Strauss and Lehtinen (1947) vividly describe the difficulties presented by such children; recently, research workers have attempted to explore factors affecting activity level and distractibility in the mentally retarded. Cromwell and co-workers (1963) summarise findings and theories concerning activity level, and rightly question whether it can be considered a unitary topic of review. The same point can justifiably be made concerning distractibility, and in consequence only a few very recent studies from these areas are included here.

Tizard (1968a) notes that, although hyperkinesis is a very real phenomenon to parents and teachers, it has proved strangely elusive to laboratory investigation. Neither McConnel et al. (1964) nor Schulman et al. (1965) were able to establish a relation between observers' ratings of overactivity and objective measures (by ballistograph or actometers). On the other hand, Hutt and Hutt (1964), who measured locomotion, found higher movement scores in hyperkinetic than normal children, and suggested that their activity was comparatively unmodifiable by any environmental influence, whether social or otherwise. In a preliminary study, Tizard observed two groups of severely subnormal children, rated very overactive and not overactive, during free play. The overactive children moved about significantly more often than the control children but were not rebuked more often nor did they receive more attention from their teachers. They were not more aggressive than the non-overactive group, but they made significantly fewer friendly contacts. The classical hyperkinetic syndrome was not seen; instead, the overactive children showed a wide range of personality characteristics. There was some evidence that they had suffered brain damage of a different kind from that found in the control group.

Since theories to account for overactivity postulate an inhibitory defect, as a result of which the child is unable to stop attending to, or responding to, irrelevant stimuli, or is slow to habituate, Tizard (1968b) conducted an experiment to determine (a) the effect of stimulus variation on the amount of locomotion, and (b) the effect of increasing familiarity with the environment on the amount of locomotion. Overactive and non-overactive severely subnormal children were tested four times, with and without toys, in an experimental room. There was no significant difference in the movement scores of the two groups and no significant habituation in the amount of movement recorded over four sessions for either group. Stimulus variation did not affect overall movement score, although it did affect the nature of the children's activity. Tizard concludes from the two studies that overactivity is a real characteristic of children designated overactive and one that is difficult to modify, and that delayed maturation or general retardation are inadequate concepts to account for the behaviour studied.

In an attempt to investigate the 'inhibitory defect' theory, Tizard (1968c) tested: the responsiveness of overactive imbeciles to auditory stimuli using EEG and skin potential changes as measures of response; and the habituation of these responses while awake and while asleep. Control groups of non-overactive imbeciles and normal children were used. Only the normal children showed habituation of skin potential while awake; while asleep no habituation occurred in any group. There was no difference in the frequency of EEG and skin potential changes in response to sound in the three groups; a difference in alertness while awake was a confounding variable. Tizard (1968d) analysed the all-night EEGs, electro-oculograms, and movement records for the three groups. Apart from clinical EEG abnormalities, few group differences were found. The overactive group tended to have more but briefer periods of deep sleep, while the normal children tended to have longer waking periods. Over half the imbeciles, and a quarter of the normal children had periods resembling Stage I Rapid Eye Movement sleep without REMs. All groups spent longer in deep sleep, and less time in Stage I REM sleep than adults. Tizard notes with interest that children whose daytime behaviour is very abnormal and severely retarded, and in whom electro-physiological habituation is disturbed, have sleep patterns barely distinguishable from those of normal children.

Turning now to studies of distractibility, the experimental literature suggests that comparisons of the intellectually normal with the mentally retarded (and particularly brain-injured) do not always support the view that the latter are more distractible. Schulman and co-workers (1965) suggest that in view of the wide range of types of brain-damage, the failure to differentiate between heterogeneous groups of brain-injured and non-brain-injured is not surprising. It is also clear that 'distractibility' cannot be viewed as a unitary characteristic, but one that must be seen both in terms of individual differences and situational variables. Ellis and colleagues (1963) compared 'familial', 'subcultural', 'brain-injured', and defectives of unknown aetiology and normal children of equivalent MA on an oddity problem under two kinds of distraction: attention value of stimulus objects and the presence of a large mirror. The main hypothesis, that defective subjects would be more distractible than normal, was not confirmed, and the mirror actually facilitated the normal group's performance. Similarly, Baumeister and Ellis (1963) found that a potential distractor resulted in improved performance in a group of retardates. Girardeau and Ellis (1964) found no effect of various background noises (train-noise, buzzer, playground noise, music, conversation, automobile horn, dog barking) on serial and paired-associate learning by normal and mentally retarded children. Sen and Clarke (1968) conducted a series of experiments, using subnormal subjects of two IQ levels, which showed that: (1) subjects' susceptibility to extraneous stimuli designed to act as distractors is clearly related to the level of task difficulty, and (2) not all external stimuli operate as distractors for a given task. In addition it was suggested that the following variables are important: (*a*) nature of the task; (*b*) its duration; (*c*) intensity of the distracting stimuli; (*d*) relevance of the distractors to the task; and (*e*) in case of conversation or stories, their attention value. The findings of these studies are consistent with the view that retardates, as a group, are more likely to show distractible behaviour than normal subjects (since more tasks will be at a level of difficulty producing distractible behaviour), but also suggest that a blanket description of retardates as distractible serves only to cloud the issue of why and in what circumstances they manifest this behaviour, and how it may be overcome.

Rather similar conclusions were reached by Belmont and Ellis (1968), who studied the effects of extraneous stimulation on discrimination learning in normals and retardates. Bright lights produced a decrement in two-choice discrimination learning of normal subjects, but *facilitated* retardate learning. In two further experiments, retardates learned a series of six two-choice problems, on which postresponse extraneous stimulation (meaningful pictures) was at first found to facilitate learning. The same stimuli distracted the subjects later in the series. It was concluded that current notions regarding distractibility in retardation require serious qualification.

OPERANT LEARNING

The application of operant conditioning techniques to the mentally subnormal has aroused considerable interest within the last few years, and it is clear that further developments are to be expected.

This area is, however, different from the others reviewed in that no comparative studies have been undertaken, and there has, until recently, been little controversy over method and interpretation of findings. The question raised by the Skinnerians is rarely 'Can a subnormal person learn by operant methods task X as well as a normal person matched on MA or CA?' The orientation is much more that since operant methods have been shown to be useful in shaping behaviour in animals and normal human beings, the same principles should result in efficient shaping in the subnormal at all levels. The evidence suggests that this faith has been justified.

As Dent (1968) indicates in an admirably succinct review, man's interaction with his environment results in the development of both simple and complex forms of behaviour. According to behaviour theory, these behaviours are acquired, altered, or maintained by the reinforcement received from the environment; the frequency of a response is subject to the consequences of that response. Broadly speaking, reinforcement may be positive (pleasant, rewarding) or negative (noxious, punishing). The former is assumed to increase, and the latter to decrease, the frequency of a particular response. There are four simple schedules of reinforcement: fixed ratio; variable ratio; fixed interval; and variable interval. Dent stresses that since society skilfully dispenses its reinforcement on a variable interval schedule, the ultimate goal in training the subnormal is to achieve control of the particular behaviour in such a way that it will eventually be maintained by society. This, in turn, suggests that the desired response should be established by means of a fixed ratio reinforcement schedule (i.e. rewards given in a fixed ratio to the subject's response rate) which is then gradually shifted to variable interval reinforcement; at the same time there should be a shift from primary reinforcers (e.g. edibles) to secondary (e.g. social approval).

Operant techniques are important, since they have often been applied to subnormals with IQs below 35, and in particular to those of idiot grade who are normally regarded as unresponsive to the more usual modes of training. Positive reinforcement is used to create desirable forms of behaviour and negative (e.g. aversive) reinforcement to eliminate undesirable traits such as aggressive, destructive, or self-destructive behaviour. Various studies have concerned the development, by means of operant conditioning, of personal self-care skills and social and verbal skills. Useful and comprehensive reviews have been produced by Watson and Lawson (1966); Spradlin and Girardeau (1966); Watson (1967); and Baumeister (1967a). An Orwellian twist has been provided by Henker, according to Dent (1968). She contends that the mentally subnormal can be trained to apply operant procedures in the training of other subnormals. This will create 'therapeutic pyramids' whereby a small number of professionals train a larger number of subnormals who, in turn, train a still larger number of their peers.

Of the general reviews, the most detailed appears to be that of Watson (1967) to whose work the writers are indebted. He discusses four types of positive reinforcement: edible, manipulatable, social, and token or generalised. In considering a number of studies in which comparisons between different reinforcers were made, he concludes that token reinforcement possesses two major advantages: first, it is possible that a summation effect may occur because of numerous associations with each of the edible, manipulatable, or social reinforcement with which it has been related; and second, it is relatively independent of specific deprivation states. An annotated bibliography with many references has been provided by Gardner and Watson (1969).

Positive reinforcement is not always a sufficient condition for developing certain behaviours while eliminating others, and the use of negative reinforcement at the same time has been found appropriate (Giles and Wolf, 1966; Watson, 1967). Time-out procedures have been used effectively to eliminate head banging, window-breaking, and other aggressive behaviour (Watson, 1967).

Studies have been mainly carried out in the following areas and some examples are given below:

1. *Toilet training*. (Baumeister and Klosowski, 1965; Bensberg *et al.*, 1965; Hundziak *et al.*, 1965; Giles and Wolf, 1966; Watson, 1967)
2. *Self-feeding*. (Gorton and Hollis, 1965; Henriksen and Doughty, 1967)
3. *Self-dressing*. (Bensberg *et al.*, 1965; Gorton and Hollis, 1965; Roos, 1965; Watson, 1967)
4. *Self-grooming*. (Girardeau and Spradlin, 1964; Bensberg *et al.*, 1965; Gorton and Hollis, 1965)
5. *Social play behaviour*. (Girardeau and Spradlin, 1964; Bensberg *et al.*, 1965; Watson, 1967)
6. *Undesirable behaviour*. (Girardeau and Spradlin, 1964; Giles and Wolf, 1966; Hamilton *et al.*, 1967; Watson, 1967; Wiesen and Watson, 1967)
7. *Speech*. (Kerr *et al.*, 1965; Doubros, 1966; Hamilton and Stephens, 1967; Sloane and Mac Aulay, 1968) *See also* Section on Language.
8. *Work skills*. (Girardeau and Spradlin, 1964; Bensberg *et al.*, 1965)

In controlling undesirable behaviour, Gorton and Hollis (1965) and Bensberg *et al.* (op. cit.) found that with few exceptions, operant procedures were effective in maintaining desirable behaviour without the aid of tranquillisers, energisers, or sleeping medication. As Watson and Lawson (1966) put it, 'instrumental learning research is providing the basis for a new, effective technology of educating and training mental retardates, with both academic and social implications . . . . Of significance is the fact that . . . (these conditioning techniques) . . . have succeeded with the severely and profoundly retarded, where other training methods have failed.'

Despite the large number of studies reported, Watson (1967) concluded that, although they indicate that severely and profoundly retarded children can develop skills when systematic training procedures are used, it is not clear what variables are responsible for the success of these programmes and which are either irrelevant or possibly even interfering. Gardner (1969) examined the methodology and results of operant conditioning techniques, and concluded that, to some extent, all the studies have violated one or more of the following requirements of good experimental design: (1) exact specification of *all* relevant independent variables; (2) proper sampling techniques; (3) use of adequate controls; (4) proper assessment of the dependent variable; and (5) evaluation of long-term gains. Gardner recommends: (1) direct and indirect measures of both specific and general changes in behaviour; (2) individual as well as group presentation of results; (3) pre- and post-treatment evaluations, including periodic assessment to measure long-term gain; and (4) multivariate manipulation of the independent variables, particularly specific techniques. Progress in elucidating these problems can confidently be expected.

LEARNING SETS AND TRANSFER OF LEARNING

As Deese (1958) puts it, 'There is no more important topic in the whole of the psychology of learning than transfer of training. Nearly everyone knows that transfer of training is basic to educational theory. Practically all educational and training programs are built upon the fundamental premise that human beings have the ability to transfer what they have learned from one situation to another.' The question at once arises whether the subnormal in addition to his deficiencies in acquisition is also defective in the extent to which previously learned responses may be generalised to new situations.

The first part of this section is concerned with learning set formation in the mentally subnormal; studies of transfer of training among problems of disparate classes, and the effects of special programmes of instruction upon test performance are reviewed later.

Learning Set Acquisition

A learning set (Harlow, 1949) is acquired through practice on problems that have a common basis for solution. Once the solution is apparent, performance on subsequent problems of the same type changes from a trial-and-error response pattern to one approximating single-trial learning. Learning set acquisition is based on a history of discrimination experience and represents a particular kind of transfer of training, transfer among many problems of a single class. The main variable of interest is, thus, interproblem learning as opposed to intraproblem learning.

Watson and Lawson (1966) provide a detailed review of the vast number of experiments using mentally retarded subjects on the Wisconsin General Test Apparatus, most of which have been concerned with object-quality discriminations, reversal learning and oddity learning. Only a highly compressed summary of some of the findings will be included here.

The relation between mental age and speed of acquisition of an object-quality learning set was one of the first problems to be investigated. Ellis (1958) investigated object-quality discrimination at 'low' (5·05) and high (8·02) MA levels. Ten successive problems were given and on each the subject had to reach a criterion of 20 successive correct responses ('finding the marble'). While both MA groups developed discrimination learning sets, the higher made fewer errors per problem and acquired learning sets more rapidly. Efficiency in learning set formation thus appeared to be a function of MA but,

as Watson and Lawson point out, the possible effect of IQ was not partialled out. Stevenson and Swartz (1958) carried out a somewhat similar study but comparing two not greatly different MA groups. The lower of these (MA 4·1) failed to develop a set. Ellis and colleagues (1962), however, were able to show that even those with lower MAs were in some circumstances able to form object-quality discrimination sets. It seems probable that discrepancies between the findings of different studies can be accounted for by such factors as the nature of the discriminanda, number of problems, length of training, learning criterion, background experience, and type of reinforcement offered, as well as to such factors as MA (*see also* Wischner *et al.*, 1962). Kaufman (1963) and Girardeau (1959) also point to the influence on discrimination of factors other than MA. Hayes and co-workers (1953) believed that learning set acquisition is a joint function of trials-per-problem and level of performance.

Studies of reversal discrimination learning, show that, in general, the subnormal learn a position discrimination reversal most easily, followed in order of difficulty by intradimensional reversal shift and extradimensional reversal shift (Watson and Lawson, op. cit.). Subnormals with MAs as low as two years were able to master reversal position problems (House and Zeaman, 1959). Some studies have found no difference between the reversal performance of retardates and equal MA normals (Plenderleith, 1956; Stevenson and Zigler, 1957). There appears to be little relationship between MA and position reversal performance, but there may be a relationship between MA and stimulus reversal, particularly where an extradimensional shift is required.

Oddity discrimination learning has been shown to be related to MA. The general finding is that subnormals with MAs below five years do not form oddity learning sets, but above this level, speed of learning set acquisition is related to MA (Ellis and Sloan, 1959; Ellis *et al.*, 1963; House, 1964).

Watson and Lawson point out that all conclusions concerning the relationship between MA and discrimination learning are open to the alternative interpretation of an IQ relationship, since both MA and IQ control procedures were not used. Furthermore, it is possible that institutionalised retardates, who were the subjects of these studies, may by virtue of the restricted environment, be specifically deficient with respect to learning visual discriminations. These authors also conclude that the learning set acquisition is a function of the particular method employed. For maximising the possibility of a low MA subnormal acquiring, for example, an object-quality set it is necessary to: (1) use many trials per problem or a high learning criterion; (2) employ a non-correction stimulus presentation technique; and (3) present the negative stimulus only on the first trial of each new problem.

Zeaman and House (1963) have provided an important theory of retardate discrimination learning that distinguishes two responses: (1) attending to the relevant stimulus dimension, and (2) approaching the correct cue of that dimension. From a large amount of data on visual discrimination learning in severely retarded subjects, they plotted the forward learning curves of subgroups of subject homogeneous with respect to the number of trials taken to reach criterion of learning. From this it emerged that slow learners stayed close to chance performance for varying numbers of trials, but once performance started to improve, it moved relatively fast. Plotting the same data as backward learning curves (Hayes, 1953) showed that the final rates of all groups, fast or slow, were similar. It was concluded that the difference between fast and slow learning was not so much the rate at which improvement takes place *once it starts*, but rather the number of trials taken for learning to start. It was concluded that the difficulty retardates have in discrimination learning is related to the attention phase of the dual process, rather than to approaching the correct cue of the relevant stimulus dimension. Those who are familiar with studies of animal discrimination learning will note the similarity of this theoretical formulation with that of Sutherland (1964) and Mackintosh (1965). Zeaman and House present a number of stochastic models organised by the dual process theory and demonstrate the application of these to discrimination experiments with lower-level retardates, including original learning, reversals, effects of intelligence, stimulus factors, schedules of reinforcement, and transfer operations.

The discrimination reversal problem has been used to test verbal mediation deficiency hypotheses in mental retardates; these studies are reviewed in the section on Verbal Mediation.

Shepp and Turrisi (1966) have provided an important review (46 references) of work on learning and transfer of mediating responses in discrimination learning. In addition to discussing individual papers, as well as methodological problems, these authors offer some general process laws. As already noted, intradimensional shifts are learned faster than extradimensional and this is held to support the proposition that the mediating process is dimensional in nature. Subjects learn to respond to a discriminative cue common to a class of stimuli, and they can transfer these responses to subsequent discriminations. Secondly, intradimensional shift performance improves with increasing amounts of overtraining, this being directly implied in the theories of Sutherland and Zeaman and House. These state that the strength of a relevant mediator approaches its asymptote slower than does the strength of an instrumental response. 'Consequently, with a weak criterion or just a few overtraining trials, the relevant mediator may be weak, and any intra-dimensional and extra-dimensional shift difference may be attenuated. With increasing amounts of overtraining, the strength of the relevant mediator increases, and the probability of this response approaches unity. There is also some evidence that extra-dimensional shifts become progressively more difficult with increases in amount of overtraining. This finding also supports the notion that the relevant mediator becomes stronger as a function of overtraining.' (Shepp and Turrisi, op. cit.)

A third and much less certain 'law' is related to the type of irrelevant dimension presented during original learning (Shepp and Turrisi, op. cit.). In most experiments that have shown dimensional mediating-response transfer, the irrelevant dimension during training was presented with a variable—within arrangement. In one study, however, the irrelevant dimension was constant and there was subsequently no intra- or extradimensional shift difference and no evidence for mediating response transfer. Now mediating-response theories have not specified the variable—within irrelevant condition as a prerequisite for the acquisition of a mediating response. This poses an important theoretical question, and the authors suggest that the two types of shift should be compared with constant irrelevant and variable irrelevant dimensions to settle the question of whether the acquisition of a mediating response requires a variable irrelevant dimension during training.

Retention of Learning Sets

Wischner and colleagues (1962) used a large number of problems (twelve a day for ten days) with mildly subnormal subjects, to study the formation of object-quality learning sets. The authors studied retention six months later, using an additional two days of practice on twelve three-trial problems a day. For those who had reached criterion in the earlier learning, the additional practice was sufficient to restore performance to its final level. For those who had earlier learned less well, however, per-formance was only a little above chance at the end of the two days of practice.

Clarke (1962) reported that a group of adult imbeciles, re-tested on the learning of the four Minnesota formboards seven years after initial learning (32 trials), showed greatly enhanced performance, particularly on the first board. This could not be attributed to maturation but may, however, have resulted from the reinforcement provided by perceptual-motor experience in industrial workshops. However, Clarke and Cookson (1962) showed impressive retention of perceptual-motor learning by child and adult imbeciles over six months and one year, respectively, of non-reinforcement. In both these studies learning had been taken to asymptote, and motivation was apparently very high indeed.

Kaufman (Kaufman and Prehm, 1966), however, carried out a study on retention by mongols of three-trial object-quality problems. This experiment was marred by an institutional epidemic but limited findings failed to indicate retention by this group.

Much more information is needed on the degree to which learning sets may be retained. Apart from the nature of the tasks, at least two powerful factors seem to be involved. Firstly, the amount of learning and overlearning undertaken is clearly relevant, and secondly, the degree to which the ordinary life experience of these subjects possesses relevant reinforcers or makes direct use of the induced sets. (*See also* the Section on Memory.)

Transfer of Training

Despite the acknowledged importance of transfer effects on all human activities, surprisingly little systematic research has been conducted in this area using mentally retarded subjects. In their comprehensive review, Kaufman and Prehm (1966) point to the diversity of work in this area and to the difficulty of coming to any precise conclusion concerning the conditions under which retardates will show positive (or negative) transfer.

An illustration of the importance of method to experimental outcome and, thus, to conclusions is given in a later section on the Role of Input Organisation in Memory. Gerjuoy and Alvarez (1969) failed to find any effect on amount recalled or amount of clustering one week after a single training session of five trials in which material to be recalled was presented clustered. By contrast, the present authors, using a different design, a long-term training procedure, and only one day between the end of training and initial transfer tests, did find significant effects. Both types of experiment are clearly necessary if the precise conditions in which transfer will occur are ever to be specified.

In the absence of data on which to base an analysis of transfer effects in the subnormal, this section will be confined to a summary of the only two long-term programmes of research on transfer reported in the literature, apart from the already discussed and monumental work by Zeaman and House on learning sets. This will be followed by discussion of three attempts to alter test behaviour on the basis of widely based programmes of instruction.

Using pairs of perceptual-motor learning tasks of equal difficulty, each of which made similar demands but had a different content from the other, Clarke and Blakemore (1961) showed that transfer, using a time score for 20 trials, was easily demonstrated, particularly among the younger imbeciles. Subsequent work suggested that this latter result was due to a ceiling effect for the adults. Clarke and Cookson (1962) using similar tasks, and the same subjects showed that earlier easier learning transferred six months later to more difficult learning, without intervening practice. Clarke and Cooper (1966) evolved a method for directly comparing adult and child imbeciles on the same tasks. Either the difficulty of the task pairs could be increased for the adults so that the time taken for initial performance was equal to that of the children, or difficulty could be decreased for the children so that their starting point was the same as for adults. Both methods gave similar results, showing that adults and children in these tasks exhibited similar learning and transfer curves. More importantly, it seemed that task complexity might, within limits, facilitate transfer. This notion was now tested by Clarke et al. (1966) who evolved a new experimental design, and, holding age constant, gave matched groups of imbeciles training on conceptual sorting tasks of different complexity. It was found that: (1) transfer was related to training task complexity; (2) it occurred across tasks that possessed no identical elements other than that they were conceptual problems; (3) differential effects of differing degrees of complex training were subsequently persistent over ten trials of the transfer task; and (4) the amount of overlearning of the complex training task was also relevant. This work was replicated, with rather more striking results on normal pre-school children (for review of these studies see Clarke et al., 1967).

The question of the nature of transfer between different conceptual tasks using normal pre-school children was then studied by Clarke et al. (1967). Among other findings, it seemed that improved performance did not result from an increased arousal arising from exposure to a difficult problem, but rather from the practice of relatively unpractised processes—in this case the reduction of stimulus variability by categorisation. The authors interpreted these and some later findings in terms of the subject's increased sensitivity to the categorical properties of the stimuli (Clarke *et al.*, 1970) a process not normally high in the hierarchy of preferred responses for these populations.

Bryant (1964) used apparently simple discrimination tasks and tested the ability of his severely subnormal subjects to abstract. Half were given verbal instruction on the first task, while the others were not. Against Bryant's expectancies, it emerged that verbal instruction heavily impeded transfer. A later experiment (Bryant, 1965a) showed that verbalisation had interfered with the component on which imbeciles tend to base their transfer in discrimination learning, namely, learning to avoid the irrelevant dimension. Nevertheless, verbal instruction improved learning at the time when the instruction was given.

Subsequent work by Bryant (1967a) was aimed at elucidating the effect of verbal instruction: first, on the response about which instruction was being given, and second, on the response about which no instruction was given. Subjects were required to sort cards of two different colours into different boxes. Without verbal instructions, errors were equal for both. With instruction, errors were reduced but equal; and with instruction about one colour, errors were reduced for that colour, but for the other, errors remained equal to the earlier situation where no instruction was given. A transfer post-test showed many more errors with unfamiliar than with familiar colours. It seems, writes Bryant (1968) that learning strategies adopted by subnormals might be maladaptive to the introduction of language.

The author raises the question whether verbal instruction improves learning by directing attention or by affecting memory processes. His preliminary investigations (1965b and 1967b) suggested that memory is improved only when verbal labelling relates to a verbal problem, and that attentional processes are affected only when the stimulus array is a complex one.

The effects of specific, fairly long-term programmes of instruction, as measured by standard tests, have been explored in three recent studies.

Rouse (1965) found significant changes in educable retarded children after exposure to a special curriculum aimed at enhancing productive thinking. The training programme for the 47 experimental subjects comprised 30 half-hour lessons over a period of six weeks, and included a wide range of carefully specified activities; members of a control group meanwhile attended their regular classes. Budoff and colleagues (1968) repeated the experiment, but their subjects failed to show gains on the Minnesota Tests of Creative Thinking commensurate

with those previously reported; the authors were unable to offer precise reasons why the outcome of the two experiments differed.

Corter and McKinney (1968) conducted an experiment on flexibility training with educable retarded and bright normal children. Although much work on the alleged rigidity of the subnormal can be found in the literature, the authors were unable to identify any previous attempts to improve flexibility.

The major purpose of the study was to develop a process-oriented programme of training designed to provide subjects with reinforced practice in making cognitive shifts. The effectiveness of this training was then evaluated on 'flexibility tasks', the Binet scale, and five tests developed by the authors selected from a larger number by factor analytic techniques.

Training employed a large number of different exercises involving a variety of materials. Three general areas, perceptual, conceptual, and spontaneous flexibility, were sub-divided into two kinds of exercises for each. The perceptual area, for example, involved figure-ground reversal and embedded figures. The conceptual exercises used similarities-differences and concept shifting. For spontaneous flexibility, exercises included tasks in both structured and constructed fluency such as class naming, rhymes, and cancellation. Efforts were also made to teach appropriate verbal concepts such as 'figure', 'ground', 'part', 'whole', 'alike', and 'different'.

The subjects were 32 mildly subnormal children attending special education classes and 32 normal children in kindergarten, matched for MA and sex, and allocated randomly to teaching or control conditions. The experimental groups received cognitive flexibility training for 20 days in sessions that lasted between 30 and 45 minutes. Control groups participated in their usual classroom activities. At the conclusion, experimental and control groups were retested on the Stanford-Binet and with the Cognitive Flexibility test battery. The Stanford-Binet re-tests were carried out by three experienced examiners, who had not pretested the same children and had not taken part in the training programme.

Results indicated that for the experimental groups the mean change in flexibility score between pre- and post-test was highly significant ($p < 0.001$). The mean change for the retarded controls was not significantly different from zero, although the normal controls had achieved significantly higher scores ($p < 0.001$). Mean IQ increases for experimental groups were as follows: for retarded, 6·25 and for normals 10·19, these both being significant. For the controls, however, non-significant gains were reported.

The authors consider that their results support earlier findings of greater difficulty in concept shifting in retardates as compared with normals, but, as they indicate, their normals were 'bright' and the two groups were not matched for social class so that such results are somewhat equivocal. However, the training programme was effective in producing significant increases in flexibility, and it is of interest that a hypothesis that retardates and normals would respond differentially was unsupported. The IQ increases were significantly greater for the trained than the controls, and this appeared to indicate generalisation from training to other areas of cognitive functioning. However, the authors properly list the limitations of their study and are cautious in their interpretations. An important point emerging from this study is that, although retardates may gain significantly from a training programme, it is likely that normal children, subjected to the same programme, will gain more, particularly if, as in this case, they are above average in intelligence.

The present authors conclude with Kaufman and Prehm (op. cit.) that there is a need for greatly increased research activity on transfer of training. It is difficult to see how efficient programmes for use in schools and rehabilitation centres can be evolved without a great deal more knowledge of factors underlying the generalisation of learning in the subnormal.

MEMORY

Studies of memory in the mentally retarded have focused attention on the problem of identifying deficits in short-term memory, long-term memory, and the rôle of input organisation, usually by contrast with normal control groups, matched for MA or CA. Most of the studies on short- and long-term memory have used rote memory or rote learning techniques and either digits, letters of the alphabet, or conceptually unrelated words or pictures. Those interested in input organisation have used word lists or picture displays in which the stimulus material can be grouped into common conceptual categories.

Short-term Memory (STM)

The importance of short-term memory is emphasised in a number of psychological theories (e.g. Broadbent, 1958; Miller *et al.*, 1960) which assume that if information cannot pass from STM into permanent storage, learning will not occur. It should follow that where the major distinguishing feature of a group is their inability to learn as efficiently as others of similar age, the key to their deficiency might well be found in the processes underlying STM.

Ellis (1963) elaborated a theory embodying two constructs, stimulus trace and central nervous system integrity, to account for the behavioural inadequacies of the mentally retarded. The stimulus trace is a hypothetical neural event or response which varies with the intensity, duration, and meaning of the stimulus situation. CNS integrity is defined by indices of adaptability such as intelligence test score, and serves as a limiting function for the stimulus trace. The central hypothesis is that the duration and amplitude of a trace are diminished in the subnormal organism. Ellis further hypothesised that the apparent learning deficit in the subnormal organism is due to noncontinuity of events as a result of an impoverished stimulus trace. He presents an account of his physiological model and cites evidence in support of it from a wide range of behavioural research with mental defectives. These included the areas of serial verbal learning, paired associate learning, reaction time, EEG studies, and factor analytic studies of intelligence test profiles.

Further support for this theory is provided by Hermelin and O'Connor, 1964; O'Connor and Hermelin, 1965), whose evidence suggested that recall deficits in STM might be due to both memory decay and input restriction, and Madsen (1966) who reported a series of five experiments involving the assessment of the recall performance of normal and retarded subjects for a single paired associate, under different conditions. Performance of the retarded subjects was consistently inferior to that of the normal controls. On the other hand, Butterfield (1968a) investigated several predictions from the stimulus trace theory concerning serial learning in normal and retarded subjects, and concluded from a review of the research literature that these predictions had not been supported. In order to determine whether the central organismic variable of stimulus trace theory (i.e. neural integrity) was more closely related to MA or IQ, Butterfield (1968b) compared digit span performance of groups who were matched on either MA or CA but who differed in IQ. Differences were found between normal, borderline, and retarded IQ groups matched on CA, but not between those matched on MA. It was concluded that stimulus trace theory may best be regarded as a developmental rather than a defect approach to mental retardation. Further experimental studies on STM are reported by Ellis and Munger (1966), Ellis and Anders (1968), and Baumeister *et al.* (1967).

Neufeldt (1966) conducted a series of experiments to investigate STM in mental retardates using the dichotic listening technique initiated by Broadbent (1954). The experiments were devised to discover whether STM *capacity* and/or *strategy of encoding information* would account for some of the differences between retardates and normals. Four groups of subjects were compared: two groups of retardates (IQ range 53 to 79), one Organic and one Cultural-Familial in aetiology; a normal group matched for MA, and a second normal control group matched for CA. The evidence indicated that STM capacity was indeed an important difference between retardates and CA controls, but not between retardates and MA controls. The most important differences lay in the superior strategies manifested by both normal control groups, who, by comparison with the retardates, demonstrated a marked degree of flexibility in their adaptation of different recall strategies to various rates of informational input, and an ability to use more ambiguous strategies; familial defectives were somewhat better in this respect than organic retardates. The differences between the two normal control groups (of different ages) were indicative of the degree to which both memoric capacity and ability to apply useful strategies develops in normal individuals over time. The discussion and interpretation of these findings is consistent with the 'developmental lag' theory of familial retardation.

Kouw (1968) investigated the stimulus trace construct as an explanatory mechanism in retardate STM. He argued that (*a*) the capacity of retarded subjects to perform a delayed response task will vary as a function of CNS integrity; and (*b*) their delayed response capacity will vary as a function of both the intensity and duration of the pre-delay stimulus as well as the interaction of these variables. Using the Knox Cubes Test to classify 181 retardates as high or low on STM adequacy, he found that stimulus intensity affected delayed response as predicted, but that stimulus duration had no effect on performance. The author does not accept the latter results as necessarily conclusive, suggesting refinements in the technique for further investigation. He concludes that the limitations imposed on behavioural adequacy in STM functioning in organisms with subnormal CNS integrity were shown to change in the direction of greater adequacy, and this change was greatest for those with the lowest degree of CNS integrity. He concurs with Ellis's (1963) suggestion that the investigation of learning difference between

retardates and normals must focus attention on the acquisition aspects, rather than long-term retention.

Gordon (1968) showed how stimulus presentation rate may both enhance and hinder recall of stimuli, depending on the interacting effects of stimulus complexity and the level of intellectual competency of the subjects. Using mildly subnormal and normal adults, three levels of stimulus complexity and three rates of presentation (40, 60, or 120 units per minute) he showed that: (*a*) subnormal subjects were inferior to normals in all conditions; (*b*) while normal subjects recalled simple concepts at a high level under all rate conditions, subnormal performance was adversely affected by high-speed presentation; (*c*) the normal group curve of performance was positively decelerated with increasing stimulus complexity, while the retarded group curve was negatively decelerated; (*d*) the variance in normal performance decreased with increase in presentation rate, while the opposite occurred for the retarded; and (*e*) that the error pattern for the two groups differed, suggesting differences in both accuracy of perception and in the ability to organise, encode, or associate what has been perceived.

Scott and Scott (1968) in reviewing a vast literature on STM, comment on the importance of Ellis's theory in providing a focal point for investigation in this area, and suggest, further, that two relatively new experimental techniques show promise of major theoretical importance. These are Broadbent's dichotic listening technique used by Neufeldt (op. cit.) and the miniature experiment technique elaborated by House and Zeaman (1963), which are seen as providing an essential bridge between research on attention and memory and the relations between these two processes.

Serial Anticipation and the McCrary-Hunter Hypothesis

If a list of items is learned to perfection and the number of errors made in the course of learning is plotted for each item in the series, according to its position, a bow-shaped curve is obtained. The degree of bowing may be influenced by several conditions such as distribution of practice, rate of presentation, familiarity of material, and individual differences in learning ability. McCrary and Hunter (1953) showed that, if the curve is plotted in terms of *percentage* of total errors occurring at each position, the effect of differing conditions and subject differences disappears and the distribution of errors remains invariant.

Lipman (1963) reviews many of the studies of this hypothesis using contrasted groups of subnormals and normals. Subsequent work by Girardeau and

Ellis (1964), McManis (1965), and Sen and Sen (1968) has confirmed the invariance hypothesis, using subjects of different intellectual levels under various conditions of learning. Butterfield (1968a), reviewing studies of serial learning in mental retardates, points out that the McCrary-Hunter procedure does not take account of learning efficiency, and suggests that a correction be made to subject's percentage error scores prior to evaluating the relation between learning rate and the shape of the serial curve. He re-analysed data and found a significant interaction between rate of learning and serial position, reflecting the fact that slow learners made relatively more errors in the middle positions of the list. Butterfield points to the growing body of evidence showing the inadequacy of trace-interference explanations of the serial position curve, and suggests that strategy analysis might provide a testable framework within which to study individual differences in rate of learning and relative position errors.

The von-Restorff effect has been investigated in mental retardates by McManis (1966), Sternlicht and Deutsch (1966), and Sen et al. (1968), with results that are consistent with the view that while serial learning performance in the subnormal is inferior to the normal, the effects of varying experimental conditions operate in a similar way in both groups. McManis (1969a), however, obtained results that supported a stimulus and response generalisation explanation of the isolation effect for normals but not for retardates.

In summary, the findings in the area of short-term memory and serial learning generally support the thesis that comparisons of mental retardates with normally intelligent subjects, whether matched for CA or, in some cases, MA is likely to result in a demonstration of inferior performance on the part of the mentally subnormal, but that the effects of varying conditions operate in a similar way for both groups. Any precise theoretical interpretation of these findings must await the resolution of some of the methodological problems that bedevil this area, and that were discussed earlier in this chapter.

Long-term Retention

Although learning ability in subnormals is typically impaired, their retention of learned material is usually found to be as good as that of normal subjects. Haywood and Heal (1968) provide the following succinct review of the literature:

'Experimenters have typically failed to find differences in long term retention between retardates and non-retardates of comparable mental age (M.A.) (Cantor and Ryan, 1962, relearning of picture paired associates; Johnson, 1958, recognition, recall, and relearning with nonsense syllables learned serially; O'Connor and Hermelin, 1963a, recall of word paired associates; Plenderleith, 1956, reversal learning with picture paired associates). Furthermore, experimenters have failed to find differences in retention between retardates and non-retardates of comparable chronological age (C.A.), provided adjustments were made for differences in learning level (Klausmeier, Feldhusen, and Check, 1959, savings in reworking simple arithmetic problems; Lance, 1965, savings scores with nonsense syllable paired associates; Pryer, 1960, savings scores with words in a serial anticipation task; Vergason, 1964, 30-day savings scores with picture paired associates). Only Heber, Prehm, Nardi and Simpson (1962, relearning with nonsense syllable paired associates adjusted for original learning by co-variance) and Vergason (1964, 1-day savings scores with picture paired associates) have reported poorer retention by retardates than by non-retardates of comparable C.A. when adjustments were made for original learning level.'

Nevertheless, interpretation of these data must take account of a number of methodological problems, discussed in detail by Belmont (1966), who considers the literature in the light of critical analyses made by Underwood (1954, 1964) and Keppel (1965). Belmont abstracts certain principles considered essential to the construction of a viable experiment:

(a) level of learning, defined as probability of performance, must be equalised for all subjects, especially where subject variables are studied independently;

(b) the optimum level of learning must be less than maximal at the beginning of the retention interval; and

(c) there must be a criterion against which retention test performance will be judged. This criterion should take the form of a reliable evaluation of what subjects would have done had there been no retention interval, thus permitting an evaluation of the retention interval per se.

Implicit in this analysis are two further principles: the original learning phase must be regulated to yield sufficient acquisition data for all subjects, while avoiding asymptotic performance, and the retention test conditions must be identical to the conditions prevailing at the time of immediate memory assessment. Belmont reviewed twelve studies of retention in the mentally retarded and found that most suffered in varying degree from one or more methodological weakness, principally failure to demonstrate equal original learning and problems of floor versus ceiling effects. The single study (by Klausmeier *et al.*, op. cit.) which seemed to overcome these problems found that normals and retardates were equal in long-term memory.

Haywood and Heal (1968) conducted a retention experiment in the light of the foregoing analysis, taking account of the important methodological principles arising from it.

'Experimentally naïve institutionalised retardates at four IQ levels were trained in a group procedure by the study-test technique over 15 presentations of a visual code task. Each IQ level was divided into the top, middle, and bottom thirds according to the number of codes correctly recalled during the 15 acquisition trials. Retention tests were given all Ss at post-training intervals of one hour, 24 hours, one week, two weeks, and four weeks. There were no differences among IQ levels in either training or retention performance. Those in any IQ group who made more correct responses during acquisition retained the learned associations best and appeared to forget them at a slower rate.'

The Role of Input Organisation

Miller's (1956) paper on memory and the storage of information is too familiar to need summarising. Suffice it to say that considerable research investment in the general area of input and storage organisation has subsequently been made.

A further stimulus had been provided by Bousfield (1953) who studied associative clustering in free recall. Words from the same category tend to be recalled consecutively even though they may have been presented randomly. Recall of word lists is improved where categorisable words are included. Tulving (1962, 1964, 1966) took matters further by demonstrating the presence of organising activities even with apparently unrelated words. It seems clear that this organisational process takes place at or during memory storage.

Turning to the field of subnormality, Osborn (1960) carefully selected two groups of 'organic' and 'familial' mildly subnormal institutionalised patients, together with normal MA-matched school controls. Using pictures, rather than words, as experimental material, no significant differences were found between 'organics' and 'familials', both groups recalling and organising them in recall as efficiently as the controls. Osborn draws attention, however, to some qualitative differences that might be the result of inappropriate learning habits.

Rossi (1963) compared the clustering of normal and subnormal children using a list of 20 stimulus words, five from each of four categories, randomised in five different ways. Each subject was given five trials with the same words arranged in different order to minimise serial learning order effects. The words were almost identical with these employed by Osborn (op. cit.). Using three PPVT MA levels for normal children (4–6; 7–3; and 10–0), he matched three subnormal groups, finding that there was no significant difference between normals and subnormals in amount of recall. The normals showed a superior clustering performance only when a special clustering measure which eliminated categorical intrusions was employed. Practice effects as well as MA were associated with clustering within each diagnostic group.

Evans (1964) used Rossi's methods with adult subnormals, which he divided into two intelligence groups with mean WAIS IQs of 69 and 47, respectively. Each was subdivided into subgroups with or without material incentives. This latter had a negligible effect, but the brighter subjects tended to recall more words than the duller. Neither main group differed on clustering. Evans also discusses the problem of intrusions in relation to indices of clustering.

Gerjuoy and Spitz (1966) review the literature and in the findings point to inconsistencies that may result from the use of two different measures of clustering. Moreover, neither measure takes into account the number of words recalled by the subject. The investigation summarised here had as its aims the study of the growth of clustering and free recall as a function of age, intelligence, and practice, as well as an elucidation of the relationship between clustering and free recall. Five populations were used: 20 middle-grade subnormals (mean IQ 53), 20 high-grades (mean IQ 72), 19 matched normal MA subjects (mean IQ 107), 14 matched CA subjects (mean IQ 117) and finally, a group of 20 college students.

The experimental material consisted of 20 nouns, five from each of four categories (animals, body parts, clothing, and food). Using an identical procedure to that of Rossi (op. cit.), five separate randomisations of this test were used.

Two measures of clustering were used; the first was the amount of clustering above chance. Chance clustering, or expected repetitions was defined as follows—

$$E(R) = \frac{m_1^2 + m_2^2 + m_3^2 + m_4^2 - 1}{n}$$

where m_1, m_2, m_3, and m_4 are the number of items recalled from the categories, and n the total number of items recalled. Observed repetitions, $O(R)$, were defined as the number of times a stimulus word was followed by one or more stimulus words from the same category. Categorical or irrelevant intrusions, and perseverations were not counted. The amount of clustering of each subject was defined as the difference between expected and observed repetitions.

The authors developed a second measure of clustering: the observed/maximum ratio, which again takes into account the number of stimulus words recalled. Maximum possible clustering, Max (R), was defined as $(m_1 - 1) + (m_2 - 1) + (m_3 - 1) + (m_4 - 1)$. The observed/maximum ratio formula is—

$$\frac{O(R) - E(R)}{\text{Max }(R) - E(R)}$$

which indicates the amount of above chance clustering achieved in relation to the maximum possible clustering based on the number of stimulus words recalled.

Data for middle and high-grade subnormals were pooled since there were no significant differences between them on recall or amount of clustering. Comparison of the subnormals with the other populations was made by means of a Lindquist Type I analysis of variance. Significant Population and Trial effects (both with $p < 0.001$) with non-significant interactions were demonstrated. There were no significant differences between the two lower MA groups, nor between the two higher MA groups. The latter, however, both recalled more words than the former.

Subnormals and their MA matched controls clustered very little, and only on Trial 5 for the subnormals were the scores significantly above chance. Equal CA normals clustered significantly on Trials 4 and 5 ($p < 0.02$), and college students on Trials 3, 4, and 5 ($p < 0.001$). Significant correlations between clustering and recall were found only for equal CA normals on Trial 5 ($r = 0.55$, $p < 0.05$) and for college students on Trials 4 ($r = 0.81$, $p < 0.01$) and 5 ($r = 0.85$, $p < 0.01$).

A second experiment was planned to determine whether conditions designed to increase clustering would aid the recall of the retarded. Two different methods were used: the Presented Clustered (PC) method where the stimulus words were presented in categories, and the Requested Clustered (RC) method where the experimenter requested the words by category name. Fifteen institutionalised subnormals were randomly assigned to each condition, and the same stimulus material was used as earlier. For the first group (PC), however, 5 new orders of the 20 stimulus words were produced with the 5 words of each category placed consecutively but with the order of categories, and the order of words within categories, randomised.

The recall data were compared with those from the subnormals in the first experiment. There were significant effects of Treatment ($p < 0.005$), Trials ($p < 0.001$), and Treatment × Trials ($p < 0.005$). Results from the two induced clustering groups did not differ significantly but induced clustering significantly increased the recall of both of these groups and produced steeper learning curves.

The clustering data were equally interesting. The PC group on Trial 1 clustered almost twice as much as the subnormals in the first experiment, and significantly above chance. On Trial 4 the correlation between clustering and recall ($r = 0.63$, $p < 0.05$) was significant, decreasing to a non-significant 0.39 on Trial 5. The observed/maximum clustering scores on the PC group were 0.72, 0.35, 0.19, 0.24, and 0.26 for the five trials, respectively.

Irrelevant intrusions were few in all three conditions, but categorical intrusions were somewhat higher. The RC group gave significantly more categorical intrusions than the first experiment or PC subjects.

Spitz (1966) offers an important review of the literature and concludes that subnormals are primarily deficient in the categorisation and chunking of incoming information rather than in simple memory. In a sense this notion is supported by much work on long-term memory which indicates that this process may be specifically less defective than some others.

Madsen and Connor (1968) investigated the extent to which high-grade subnormals categorise verbal material during the storage process in comparison with college students. Small groups were selected and given pre-training in the coding of 18 categories of 4 words each. They were then tested for the free recall of lists of 12 words which differed in the amount and type of categorisation. With increased degrees of categorisation in the lists, an increased recall score by both groups was apparent. When an uncorrected categorisation score was used, the students showed a significantly higher rate than the subnormals. When, however, the score was based on the number of words recalled, there were no significant differences. These results are in marked contrast with those of Gerjuoy and Spitz (op. cit.) and may result from the pre-training procedure used by Madsen and Connor, which ensured that the categories and words were available to the subjects. It is clear that the mildly subnormal can use clustering processes and information reduction under the above-stated conditions.

Gerjuoy and Alvarez (1969) failed to produce a set to cluster in educable retarded adolescents (CA 15·2 years, IQ 59·4) and normal children matched for MA, using one training session of five trials and a transfer session one week later. Two lists of 20 familiar words were used, five words from each of four categories. Half the subjects in each population received List 1 during training and List 2 for transfer, and the other half had the converse. Half the subjects were trained with randomised word lists, while the other half were given clustered presentation; all subjects had randomised lists in the second (transfer session). Both populations exhibited increased clustering and recall when the list was presented in a clustered, rather than a randomised order, thus confirming previous findings. Neither practice and familiarity with the task, nor experience with a clustered list aided performance at the second session.

By contrast, Clarke and co-workers (1970) found significant effects of a learned set on the free recall of retarded adults (mean PPVT IQ 60). Two groups of subjects matched for score on a pictorial similarities test and ability to recall unrelated words, were trained as follows: the Blocks Group was required to recall a list of 16 words, four in each of four categories, presented in clusters (i.e. 'blocks'), twice every day until a criterion of four consecutive scores of 15 or 16/16 words was reached, *or* they had completed 24 trials. The orders of words within clusters, and position of clusters within the list were systematically changed from trial to trial. The Random Group was required to recall a list of 16 unrelated high-frequency words (Thorndike-Lorge) to the same criterion, the order of presentation of words varying from trial to trial. Both groups were subsequently presented with the same new list of 16 words, four words in each of four categories in which no two conceptually related words were ever juxta-posed, and neither words nor categories were common to either of the two training lists. There was a significant difference in *amount* recalled ($p < 0.025$) on the first two trials of transfer, favouring the Blocks Group, but neither group showed much tendency to cluster; on trials 3 and 4 the differences between the groups in terms of amount recalled was reduced to non-significance, but there was a significant difference ($p < 0.05$) in cluster index (taking account of score) in favour of the Blocks Group. A further study by the authors, using memory for pictures as the transfer task, and groups of subjects, including an equal number of educable and trainable (imbecile) adolescents, showed a significant difference in score only between Blocks and Random Groups on trials 1 and 2 of transfer, and no difference whatever in clustering, educable subjects in both groups clustering above chance, and the imbeciles showing little tendency to cluster. It was concluded that if categorical relations among words are repeatedly demonstrated by clustered presentation, a set to perceive inter-item associations develops. This is available for use with new categorisable material so that the categorical relations are perceived at the input-coding stage with consequent augmentation of total output (recall score). Clustering at any significant level is a reflection of organisation of input material in store, and is an activity that occurs after at least two repetitions of a list, predominantly among subjects of higher intelligence. The results point to the importance of total recall score as a measure of categorisation, in addition to clustering, which latter may well depend on different psychological processes.

LANGUAGE, VERBAL MEDIATION, AND CONCEPTUAL BEHAVIOUR

Language

The proposition that language development in the mentally subnormal tends to fall below the general level of their other abilities has commanded almost universal support for many years. Recently, Alper (1967), analysing the WISC test results of 713 institutionalised children aged five to sixteen, found performance IQs were significantly higher than verbal IQs; within the verbal scale the Comprehension and Similarities subtests were consistently higher than Arithmetic and Vocabulary, while within the performance scale Picture Completion and Object Assembly tended to be high and Picture Arrangement and Coding lower. Belmont and colleagues (1967) compared WISC performance of a total population sample of home-based educable mental retardates aged 8 to 10, in Aberdeen, with the performance of normal children. The subtest profile for the subnormal group differed from that of the normal, the outstanding feature being their lack of verbal facility, with Vocabulary the lowest subtest score. The factorial organisation of intellectual patterning also differentiated the groups and led to the suggestion that the limited level of functioning in the retarded children may be directly related to their less-developed verbal skills and to the non-availability of such skills in the service of perceptual-motor performance.

As in other areas of research, however, two divergent positions, the 'developmental lag' and the 'defect' theories, have been used to account for such findings; Luria (1961) and Luria and Vinogradova (1959) have been the chief exponents, along with other Pavlovian 'defectologists', of the latter view. Thus, Luria has contended not only that speech and thinking are intimately related, and that speech plays a vital part in the regulation and integration of normal behaviour, but that in the retarded there is a pathological inertia of the nervous processes. Unlike the normal child, the subnormal also suffers a dissociation between speech and motor signalling systems. These facts are said to account for 'the extreme difficulties with which their training is connected'.

Luria's approach has involved ingenious experimentation but there remains some doubt about his methodology. In the famous Luria and Vinogradova (op. cit.) experiment, for example, it was shown that imbeciles generalised to homonyms, while normal children generalised to synonyms. It is, however, unclear whether the words used were equally familiar to the subnormals as to the normals. If the words were not understood very well by the former, the results are entirely to be expected.

Work on language has been well reviewed by O'Connor and Hermelin (1963b) who also outline their own experiments. While these authors find some merit in the approach of Luria they believe that the prediction that the dissociation between speech and motor behaviour cannot be overcome to be too pessimistic. Part of the subnormal's incapacity to handle symbols comes from a reluctance to use them. Thus, 'a verbal disinclination as well as a verbal disability seems to be present' (op. cit.).

Lenneberg (1967), unlike Luria, espouses a developmental view of language. Recognising that each disease giving rise to retardation has its typical manifestations, he nevertheless states that: 'the development of language, insofar as it occurs at all in these patients, follows some general laws of evolvement which may be traced among all of these conditions, and which, indeed, are not different in nature from the unfolding of language in healthy children. Among the retarded the entire developmental process is merely slowed down or stretched out during childhood and is regularly arrested during the early teens.' Support for this view is provided by Lenneberg et al. (1964) who studied over a three-year period, sixty-one mongoloid children reared in their own homes. The children were visited periodically, and data consisted of psychological test results, tape recordings of spontaneous utterances during play, performance on an articulation test and a sentence-repetition test, assessments of vocabulary, understanding of commands, and nature of vocalisation. Lenneberg points out that the IQ threshold for language development is quite low, and that above it, chronological age is the better predictor for language development. In this sample, the sequence of learning phases and the synchrony of emergence of different aspects of language was normal; progress in one field of language learning was well correlated with progress in all fields other than articulation. Poor articulation seemed to be to some extent a motivational factor and not primarily due to structural abnormalities.

Two important review papers on language functions in mental retardation have been published by Spreen (1965a,b). In the first, evidence is presented on the relationship between intellectual and language development and consideration is given to specific types of retardation and to factors identified as contributing to the severity of language handicaps. The second concentrates on the role of language in higher intellectual functions such as abstraction, concept formation, learning, and verbal mediation.

Spreen indicates that language dysfunction occurs in 100 per cent of those below IQ 20, in 90 per cent of those between IQ 21 and 50, and in around 45 per cent for the mildly subnormal. It is also argued that the abstract-concrete dimension in vocabulary definitions is of some value in differentiating subnormals matched for mental age with younger normals, and there is some indication that the brain-damaged are more handicapped in abstraction ability than familial subnormals.

In Spreen's second paper, attention is again directed to the work of Luria, and to the broad question of verbal mediation. He reviews the Dissociation Hypothesis as put forward by Luria, where, in the final stage (about the age of 6 in the normal child) spoken language becomes more and more replaced with inner language which 'constitutes the essential component of thought and volitional action'. If this is so, the fact that subnormals are on the average markedly deficient in language in comparison with their other deficiencies, may be particularly significant. That this view is at least over-simple has been shown in the work of Furth and Youniss (1964) and Furth and Milgram (1965). All that can be repeated with certainty is that there tends to a particular language deficit in the subnormal, and this may have a bearing on the rest of their cognitive development. Spreen concludes his review of this complicated problem by suggesting that although some of the evidence points to a specific innate verbal deficit in the retarded, the effects of environment and interpersonal communication, and the effects of general anxiety and motivation are probably important additional factors in determining the retardate's poor performance in this area.

Blount (1969) has reviewed studies of language in the more severely retarded, below IQ 50. He points to the dearth of research in this area and draws attention to the important work of Lyle (1959, 1960a). Lyle (1960b) in collaboration with Tizard, studied the experimental manipulation of environment and its effect on verbal development in a sample of imbecile children. In this, the Brooklands experiment, a control group was left in impoverished institutional surroundings while the experimental group was moved to a small 'child centred' family unit. Over a two-year period very significant verbal gains (e.g. on the Minnesota Pre-School Scale) were demonstrated in the experimental group. Later work (Lyle, 1961) also supported the findings of Karlin and Strazzulla (1952). The more severely retarded are delayed in language development but follow the same sequence as normals. Poor home environments as well as the restricting effects of institutionalisation are among the relevant factors. Other important descriptive studies have been provided by Mein and O'Connor (1960), Mein (1961) and Wolfensberger *et al.* (1963).

Beier and co-workers (1969) studied vocabulary usage in thirty institutionalised mentally retarded male subjects aged 11 to 24, IQ range 23 to 75, who were known to talk and whose articulation was good. Data on normal children, aged 12 and 16, IQ range 90 to 110, were available from a previous study. The subnormal group spoke more slowly than normals; used more positive words such as 'yes' and 'okay', and used more self-reference words. There was very little difference between the samples in extent of vocabulary: both had a vocabulary of about forty words which comprised 50 per cent of their language; the same high agreement was true for the ten most frequently used words. The authors conclude that the deficit in mental retardation is not so much in vocabulary as in conceptualisation, organisation, language structure, grammar, and syntax usage.

It would be surprising if some degree of language remediation were not possible with the mentally retarded. Indeed, Lyle's (1960b) experiment showed that considerable gains could be induced in a deprived imbecile group. A much shorter five months' programme by Kolstoe (1958) with a mongol group was, however, largely unsuccessful. On the other hand, a two-year study by Harvey *et al.* (1966) showed highly significant improvements. In the present writers' view, a major research attack on the question of remediation of verbal deficiencies is now overdue; these need to be explored in much the same way as did earlier experimental work on manual skills. In particular, the question of length of training as well as the most appropriate methods need to be evaluated. It seems probable that if significant effects are to be obtained, training programmes will have to be carried out over long periods of time.

Verbal Mediation

Since there is general agreement that the mentally subnormal tend to be particularly handicapped in the area of language development, a number of experimental studies has been undertaken to determine whether they can use verbal mediators to facilitate learning, and whether, as suggested by Jensen and Rohwer (1963) and Jensen (1965), retardates have a specific deficit in this ability. The methods used have commonly been reversal and non-reversal shift learning and paired-associate learning.

O'Connor and Hermelin (1959) found that eleven-year-old imbeciles were greatly superior to five-year-old normal subjects (matched for MA) on a reversal shift, although the groups had not differed on the original discrimination. However, the normal children would verbalise the principle, while the imbeciles would not. A second group of imbeciles, required to verbalise their choices on the initial discrimination, showed no facilitation on reversal, resembling the normal controls in that discrimination and reversal scores were equal. A possible interpretation is that the original learning was not under verbal control in the retarded subjects and, consequently, they did not have to inhibit a strong pre-experimental verbal set in the reversal situation, as did the normal children.

Balla and Zigler (1964) replicated this experiment, and found no difference in discrimination or reversal learning between retardates and normals at MA levels five and six. They challenged the view that the cognitive functioning of retarded subjects is inherently different from normal children of equivalent MA.

Milgram and Furth (1964) compared normal and educable retarded children at two MA levels on a variety of reversal, non-reversal, and control shift conditions. They found evidence for the mediational deficiency hypothesis in significant age and IQ differences on dimension reversal, the greater difficulty of non-reversal over reversal shift, and in the relation of retrospective verbalisation about relevant cues with age and task variables.

The finding reported by Kendler and Kendler (1959, 1960) and others that reversal shifts are easier than non-reversal shifts for normal elementary school children was confirmed by Sanders *et al.* (1965). Retarded children of similar MA, however, performed equally well on each problem, thus presenting ambiguous data for a theory that proposes presence or absence of verbal mediation as the basis for the difference in ease of learning the two types of problem.

Heal and colleagues (1966) compared retarded children (MA 6·4, CA 14–8) with normal children (MA 6·5, CA 5–4) on three reversal problems. While the groups did not differ on original learning, the retardates were inferior to the normals in overall reversal, results discrepant with those of O'Connor and Hermelin (op. cit.). The authors suggested two deficits in retardates: inability to inhibit a previously acquired habit, and susceptibility to disruption by novel stimuli, and speculated that increasing mental age may be associated with increasing retardate inferiority on a discrimination reversal.

The data on reversal shifts are thus to some extent inconsistent, and it seems unlikely that this method will yield crucial evidence on possible mediational deficiencies in retardates. (*See also* Section on Learning Sets.)

Evidence on mediation in retardates from studies of paired-associate learning is more extensive, and excellent summaries are provided by Prehm (1966a,b), Goulet (1968), and Mordock (1968).

Of those early workers who matched subjects for CA, Eisman (1958), Akutagawa and Benoit (1959), and Vergason (1964) failed to find significant differences between their retardates and normals. Berkson and Cantor (1960) compared normal and retarded children matched for CA in a three-stage mediation paradigm, where the mediator was based on laboratory acquired associations. They found no difference between the groups for mediated facilitation, but the normal subjects learned the test stage faster than the retardates. Blue (1963), Carrier *et al.* (1961), Madsen (1963), and Ring and Palermo (1961) also found differences between groups on rate of initial learning. Of those workers who matched on MA, Cantor and Ryan (1962), Girardeau and Ellis (1964), and Vergason (op. cit.) found no differences between normal and subnormal groups, while Blake (1960) and Heber *et al.* (1962) did find retardates significantly inferior.

Lipman (1963) suggested that the meaningfulness of the stimulus material was a major variable in determining outcome of experiments such as these, the less meaningful the material, the greater would be the performance deficit in retardates. Evidence in support of this notion comes from Noble and McKeely (1957), Cieutat *et al.* (1958), Lance (1965), and Prehm (1966a). Mordock (op. cit.), commenting on these findings points out that although there is empirical support for Lipman's contention, the relationship between decreasing meaningfulness and deficit in retardates is not linear, since both Lance and Prehm imply that at certain levels decreases in meaningfulness do not further handicap the subnormal.

The effect of different exposure times and anticipation intervals is considered to be another possible source of variation among reported results (*see* Section on Reaction Time). Recently, Penney and colleagues (1968) used a similar experimental design to that of Berkson and Cantor (op. cit.), but matched their subjects on MA. They found that the retardates were mediationally deficient relative to normal children when a relatively short anticipation interval was used during the mediation test. Lengthening the interval facilitated mediation in the former group but was detrimental to the latter.

The nature of the stimulus and response items and their relative similarity or dissimilarity is also relevant to the outcome of comparative studies of paired-associate learning. It is suggested by Mordock that since subnormal subjects have weaker associative strengths to the same words than have average subjects (Evans, 1964; Silverstein and McLain, 1966), it is possible that stimulus differentiation will be more difficult for them. Furthermore, if subnormal and average subjects are differentially affected by stimulus similarity, then they should differ in R–S recall. Rieber (1964) found that subnormal subjects do not differ from average in learning simple verbal responses to stimuli but they do differ considerably in their ability to use these responses; this suggests a relative inability in the retardate to acquire mediating responses, and a greater rigidity once these have been established.

Milgram has investigated the mediational deficiency hypothesis in a series of studies. A comparison of educable and trainable retardates of comparable MA with young normal children at two age levels on paired associate learning with response competition, showed a relationship between susceptibility to interference and a combination of MA and IQ variables (Milgram and Furth, 1966). Retardates were found to be inferior in long-term retention of a mediational set (Milgram, 1967), although they had benefited significantly from verbal mediation instructions. Milgram draws attention to Macoby's (1964) distinction between *production deficiency* (failure to employ verbal statements that are potentially available and useful) and a genuine *mediation deficiency* (actually producing these verbalisations without using them to elicit effective covert mediating responses) and suggests that his data support a production deficiency in retardates (*see also* Section on Concept Learning). This line of argument is further elaborated by Milgram (1968) in a study of verbal mediation in paired-associate learning in severely retarded subjects compared with four-year-old children.

Mediational facilitation was of borderline significance for the retardates, but was effective in the young normals. However, Milgram, drawing on a great deal of evidence, suggests that as yet the question of production versus mediational deficiency has not been resolved.

Prehm (1968) gives the following summary of a series of experiments by Martin and his associates (Martin *et al.*, 1968; Berch, 1967; Bulgarella, 1967; Hohn, 1967; Van der Veen, 1967).

'Martin, Boersma, and Bulgarella studied the use of associative strategies (mediators) by retarded and normal adolescents. Using a seven-level schema for classifying subjects' verbal reports about how they learned pairs of dissyllables developed in a previous study (Martin, Boersma, and Cox, 1965), they found that significantly more normal than retarded subjects used high-level, and fewer normal than retarded subjects used low-level, strategies. Both groups used intermediate-level strategies to a comparable degree. Hohn provided groups of retarded and normal subjects with associative strategy aids and found that, although the provision of aids facilitated the performance of the retarded subjects, their acquisition performance was still below that of unaided normal subjects. Berch found that the performance of retarded subjects who were made familiar with stimulus elements was superior to the performance of subjects who were familiar with the entire stimulus. Bulgarella found that retarded subjects could be conditioned to use high-level strategies and that acquisition performance of subjects so conditioned was superior to control subjects.'

Evidence that mental retardates can be persuaded to use mediators, granted the appropriate learning opportunities, is provided by two recent papers. Borkowski and Johnson (1968) replicated the Berkson and Cantor (1960) experiment, but used an MA control group as well as a CA control. Furthermore, the control paradigm in the three-stage chaining experimental model differed from the mediational paradigm in stage II rather than in stage I to prevent the occurrence of differential stimulus familiarity in stage III learning. The paired-associate learning of retardates was inferior to that of MA and CA controls when mediators were not available. However, when mediating links were provided, retardates used these associations in learning as well as the MA control group though not as efficiently as the CA controls. Furthermore, comparison of higher IQ levels with lower, within the retarded group, showed that the beneficial effects of mediation were not restricted to the former.

In a further carefully controlled study, again using a three-list paired-associate task, Penney *et al.* (1968) explored the possibility of creating a set to mediate, by giving half their mentally retarded subjects a learning set task, while the other half were given an operant task. Both groups were then again given the three-list paired-associate task as a post-test of their mediational ability. The results showed that learning-set training enhanced mediation, while operant conditioning retarded mediation; the former result is consistent with the emerging notion that mentally retarded subjects can learn to organise behaviour verbally and to use mediators. The latter result, which was unexpected, is, however, difficult to explain.

The important question of the retention of mediational sets in retardates has not as yet been adequately explored; thus, this remains a crucial area for investigation, with the probability of major theoretical and practical implications.

Gallagher (1969) used a variant of the three-stage chaining paradigm to investigate with normal and retarded subjects (MA 8·76, CA 15–6) the influence of free association strength (FAS) as an *inferred* mediator between word pairs that are non-associated according to normative data (e.g. table–chair: A–B stage; chair–sit: B–C stage; both normal associations, should lead to table–sit: A–C faster than a control condition, A–D, where no associative links are available). Each subject received a list of six pairs. Two pairs had high FAS between both the A–B and B–C links; two pairs had low FAS between these links, and two pairs were non-associated. As predicted on the basis of previous work with normal subjects, paired-associate learning was a function on the multiplicative value of the FAS values from stages A–B and B–C for both normal and retarded subjects. Normals learned faster than retardates for both types of A–C pairs (high and low multiplicative FAS values), and for the A–D control pairs. The findings are further evidence that retardates use verbal associations to facilitate learning, although dependence on their natural repertoire may result in less efficient learning than laboratory controlled associations (Berkson and Cantor, op. cit.; Borkowski and Johnson, op. cit.).

Studies of Conceptual Behaviour

The material to be reviewed in this section overlaps to a considerable extent with much of the foregoing research data on verbal mediation, and organisation of input for memory storage. The chief difference lies in the type of problem studied, being less dependent on rote learning or memory components (as in paired-associate learning) and more dependent on spontaneous processes of abstraction. Useful summaries of some of the evidence are provided by Rosenberg (1963) and Blount (1968).

An important study by Miller and associates (1968) sought to determine a hierarchy of problems that might differentiate the mentally retarded from normal controls. The investigation is unique in that it employed a repeated measures design and used films in presenting nine different tasks to 96 retarded adolescents, 100 normal adolescents of similar CA, and 109 normal children of similar MA to the retarded. The tasks included: paired-associate learning, discrimination learning, probability learning, incidental learning, concept of probability, conservation of volume, age estimation, verbal memory, and ability to construct anagrams. All subjects were non-institutionalised and testing took place in school classrooms.

The results offer clear evidence of less effective performance in learning and problem solving tasks by retarded subjects than by normal people of either similar CA or MA. The only task in which retarded subjects performed at a higher level than normals was probability learning (confirming previous findings by Stevenson and Zigler, 1958); on paired-associate and discrimination learning the differences failed to reach the 0·05 level of significance; on all other tasks, significant inferiority of performance by the retarded, as compared with CA or MA matched peers, was demonstrated. The authors conclude that the ability of the retarded to organise verbal material, and to apply conceptual schemes to its analysis, is more drastically impaired than is their ability to modify their responses in a learning task as a consequence of the information they receive. A very important subsidiary finding lay in the difference between normals and retardates in their pattern of relations between IQ and performance on the nine tasks. The correlations for the two groups of normal subjects were consistently positive and significant for the majority of tasks. By contrast, few significant correlations between IQ and performance were found for the retarded subjects. The authors suggest that variables other than intelligence, possibly motivation and attention (*see* Zigler, 1967), play a greater part in retardate than normal performance.

The results of Miller *et al.* (op. cit.) lead to the proposition, which many assume tacitly, that if out of a number of tasks (given in the same circumstances to groups of normal and retarded subjects) some differentiate between the groups better than others, those that differentiate will be: (*a*) more difficult, and (*b*) have a larger verbal/conceptual component than those that do not. A study by Milgram and Furth (1963) is important in showing that these two factors are not always correlated. They compared retarded school children in the IQ range 50–75 with normal children matched by CA to sub-groups of MA 6, 7, 8, and 10 (approximately) on three tasks previously used by Furth (1961) in a study of deaf children. The Sameness task involved discrimination between two identical geometrical figures and two different shapes; the Symmetry task required discrimination between symmetrical and asymmetrical figures (both these tasks were assumed to be predominantly perceptual); the Opposition task, which was assumed to involve language-mediation, required choosing the opposite to one examplar among a series of objects varying (on any one occasion) in size, volume, length, member brightness, position, and texture. Size opposition was used as the standard, subjects being required to reach a criterion of six consecutive correct choices; the others (one trial each) were used as transfer tasks. Trials to a given criterion was used as the measure to compare groups, which did not differ on the Sameness discrimination task, differed in favour of the retarded on Symmetry ($p < 0.05$), and differed very significantly in favour of normal subjects ($p < 0.001$) on Opposition. Further analysis of the data, however, revealed that this latter task was much the *easiest* of the three for both retarded and normal subjects. The authors interpret their findings as showing that the retarded are not adept at the discovery and application of a language-relevant concept within their realm of comprehension, but do as well as normals in (more difficult) problems where perceptual rather than verbal modes of solution might be more appropriate.

An important theoretical point arises from the work of Furth on concept learning in the deaf, elaborated by Furth and Milgram in studies using mentally retarded subjects of different levels of ability. Furth and Milgram (1965) challenge the commonly held assumption that thought and language are so inextricably related as to be to all intents and purposes identical. While not disregarding the presumed interaction of language and cognitive behaviour, they believe that many views about the relationship of the two are oversimplified and potentially confusing, and point out the dangers inherent in procedures adopted by Piaget, Vigotsky, and Kendler which rely on verbal operations as mechanisms for advanced stages of conceptual ability. It might be added that the hazards involved in demanding a verbal response as evidence even of verbal comprehension (let alone potential non-verbal concepts) are underlined by Lenneberg (1962) who described a case which he claims is typical of a larger category of patients, where an organic defect prevented the acquisition of the motor skill necessary for *speaking* a language but who showed evidence of a complete *understanding* of language.

In an attempt to explore non-verbal and verbal classificatory behaviour, Furth and Milgram (op. cit.) constructed a pictorial similarities task. Eighteen sets of seven pictures were presented, and from each set the subject was required to select three (out of seven) which belonged together (*picture sorting*). The subjects were presented with the 18 sets of three conceptually related pictures and asked to explain why they belonged together (*picture verbalisation*); the material was presented verbally, i.e. 18 sets of seven words (*word sorting*); and subjects were given three related words and asked to verbalise the basis for the relation (*word verbalisation*). In the first of a series of experiments 38 non-institutionalised retardates (CA 12 years, IQ 70, MA 9 years) were compared with 38 normal school children (CA 9·1). Half the children in each group were used for the first two tasks, and half for the latter. For both groups the two word tasks were more difficult than the picture tasks; there was no difference between the groups on picture sorting; retardates were, however, significantly inferior to the normals on the remaining three verbal tasks.

In a further experiment the authors used lower CA–MA groups: 16 retardates (CA 9·2; IQ 66·9; MA 6) and 16 normal children (CA 6·1). As before, the groups were equal on picture sorting; they were also similar on picture verbalisation, a fact interpreted as showing with normal children that, developmentally, verbal formulation lags behind cognitive behaviour at the 6-year level. A statistical analysis of the data from both experiments showed a significant IQ × CA × Modality (pictures/words) interaction, suggesting that retardates improve (from MA 6 to 9) significantly less than do normals on the verbalisation task by contrast to the sorting task.

Milgram (1966) using the same procedure, compared severely retarded (trainable, institutionalised), mildly retarded (educable, non-institutionalised) and normal groups of similar MA (6) but with an IQ difference of 30 points between adjacent groups. No difference was found among the three groups on Picture sorting, but the severely retarded were significantly inferior to the other two groups with respect to verbalisation. As before, at this MA level, the mild retardates and normals did not differ on verbalisation. Milgram concludes that the greater the severity of mental defect, the greater the deficiency in verbal formulation of adequate conceptual performance.

Somewhat different results are reported by Stephens who conducted a series of investigations into the presence and use of categories by mentally retarded school children. He (1964) compared 30 mildly subnormal (mean IQ 60) boys with 30 normals (mean IQ 101) using a CA match. Cards, each containing seven pictures, four of which represented a particular category, were presented to the subjects. The experimenter named the category and the boy was required to point out the four exemplars. The normals gave significantly more correct responses than the subnormals and could identify all exemplars of more categories.

Stephens (1966a) repeated the earlier study, using CA matched groups. The subnormals were selected in three CA ranges: 90 to 101 months; 102 to 113 months; and 114 to 126 months. On this occasion, the cards were demonstrated twice. First, the subject was asked to point out which four pictures went together and why; and second, with the same instructions as in the earlier experiment. The normals were able to indicate more of the exemplars of categories, and could also label more of the correctly identified categories under both experimental conditions. It appeared that the concepts were present but were poorly delineated in the subnormals, with, for example, not all exemplars being correctly identified.

In a further study (Stephens, 1966b) subnormals did not differ from MA controls, both these groups being significantly less efficient than CA controls. All subjects were more effective when the category was named by the experimenter than when they had to discover the category for themselves.

Stephens (1968) studied the linguistic deficiencies of mentally subnormal children by investigating the types of errors they exhibited when required to provide verbal labels for concepts they had used successfully. Seven types of error were discovered, ranging from over- or undergeneralisation to inability to state a category by name. Further support is thus provided for the view that it is possible successfully to use categories for problem solving without being able to provide an appropriate verbal label (*see* Furth and Milgram, op. cit.). The author suggests two possible conclusions. 'On the one hand, there may exist a developmental sequence in concept learning and utilisation which begins with no knowledge of a concept, proceeds to a functional ability to use the concept, and is concluded by the higher level development of the ability to label the concept appropriately, as well as to employ it correctly.' The second possibility is that it may be 'easier, and less threatening, to respond to a labelling task by citing a series of low level descriptive features of the stimuli than by risking failure'. This reference to a possible problem of motivation is reminiscent of O'Connor and Hermelin's (1963b) conclusion that there is a disinclination on the part of the subnormal to use speech. Allen and Wallach (1969) found that educable retardates (IQ range, 41 to 77) were considerably less efficient at word definition than recognition on the PPVT (with the recognition score corrected for guessing) and conclude that the major functional weakness of this population is verbal encoding.

The relative importance of the alternative explanations will be determined only after a great deal more experimental work has been undertaken contrasting retarded groups with normal (IQ 90 to 110) and normal with superior (IQ 130 and above), at all ages, including adults.

A series of experiments on conceptual behaviour has been reported by Griffith and his colleagues. Griffith and Spitz (1958) presented eight groups of three nouns each, requiring institutionalised retarded subjects (IQ 66, CA 17 years) to state the relationship of the words in the triad, i.e. to abstract. An additional vocabulary test included eighteen of the twenty-four words already used, and the subject was asked to define these. The definitions of each word in the triad were checked for the presence of identical characteristics having been stated which might serve as a common abstraction. The data were then compared with results from the other test (order of presentation having been controlled). Subjects who defined at least two of the triad words by mentioning a common characteristic were ten times more likely to offer the abstraction common to the triad. Conversely, if they defined less than two words with a mention of common characteristics, they were unlikely to offer the abstraction common to the words in the triad. Had the subnormals been 'testing hypotheses', only one abstraction suitable to relate the constituents of the triad would need to appear in the definitions; hence, the authors concluded that they were not testing hypotheses. Moreover, the subnormals, while offering adequate definitions, found it difficult to produce adequate abstractions.

Griffith and colleagues (1959) used a similar procedure with institutionalised retardates but added normal MA matched controls. Their purpose was to cast light on the relationship between concept formation and the availability of mediators. Retardates and normal seven-year-old children were not very successful in concept attainment unless they defined at least two words in terms of an acceptable abstraction. Normal nine-year-olds, however, were relatively successful even when they defined only one word in terms of an abstraction. The authors consider that conceptual tasks are sensitive indicators of retardation.

Further work by Griffith (1960) aimed to establish whether retarded subjects' performance in reporting similarities depended on their defining a threshold number or some constant proportion of the presented stimulus words in terms of an appropriate similarity for the entire set of presented words. Subjects were required to respond to three- and six-word sets of stimulus words. Those with IQs below 65 showed little success unless they could define, in terms of a possible abstraction, approximately two-thirds of the words. The results for those of IQ 65 and above did not clearly support either hypothesis.

Miller and Griffith (1961) studied the effect of a brief period of training (three sessions) upon abstraction. Social reinforcement appeared to exercise little influence on abstraction performance, but training produced significant conceptual effects on materials used in training. This did not transfer to new material. The conclusion that any improvement in the conceptual behaviour of retardates, effected through training, may be limited to the materials used, must, however, be viewed in the context of the short duration of these experiments.

Concept attainment by induction and deduction was investigated by Blake and Williams (1968) using retarded, normal, and superior subjects, all from state schools. Two sets of subjects were used, one equated for MA (approximately 11), and the other for CA (approximately 14), with the same group of retardates in each set. The task was concept-identification with object-level words from four categories used as specific instances to be associated with two-digit numerals, which served as category labels. Subjects were allocated to the following conditions: induction-discovery, induction-demonstration, or deduction. No significant groups effect was shown in the equal MA comparison; it was, however, significant in the equal CA comparison (where analysis of covariance was used to adjust for a superior group younger than the retarded group). In this comparison the superior group exceeded the normal and the retarded, while the normal exceeded the retarded. Furthermore, the difference between the superior and the normal was larger and more significant than that between the normal and retarded. Although the authors do not comment on it (perhaps because the groups were statistically rather than experimentally matched for age), this finding raises the question of whether differences between superior and average 'normal' children may be as great as differences between mildly retarded and normal (see Osler and Fivel, 1961; Osler and Trautman, 1961), an important point in considering the 'defect' versus 'retardation' view of mental subnormality. The methods of concept attainment did not differentially affect the relationships among the groups. Deduction was the most effective method for all three types of subject; induction was less effective, and no difference was found between the discovery and demonstration methods. The authors rightly suggest, in view of findings with normal populations, that the lack of qualitative difference should be interpreted with caution, and may not hold with different tasks and different material.

Gozali (1969) investigated cognitive style in mental retardates, using a method devised by Kagan (1966) for normal children. A circular version of Kagan's Matching Familiar Figures test was administered to eighty educable retardates and measures of response latency, number of errors and order of errors were obtained. The findings were similar to those reported for normal children: subjects with long time response latencies and few errors (reflective children) made consistent efforts to solve test items; subjects with short latencies and high error scores (impulsive) tended to employ a position response set. The findings are important in showing the lack of homogeneity in behaviour among a retarded group which was representative of a limited age range (8 to 10·5 years), IQ range (55 to 78) and drawn from special classes within one city.

The question of some variables affecting the development of relative thinking by retardates has been explored by McManis (1968), using a technique designed by Piaget (1928) and investigated with normal children by Elkind (1961 and 1962). The 'right-left' test and 'mother-sister' test both assess a subject's ability to handle certain abstract relations without a necessary reference to himself. Thus, questions in the former test range from concrete, 'Show me your left hand, show me your right hand' to the abstract connotation of spatial relations between three objects *opposite* to the subject; in the latter test, questions range between 'How many brothers have you, how many sisters.' to 'Ernest has three brothers: Paul, Henry, and Charles. How many brothers has Paul? Henry? Charles?'

The subjects were 140 institutionalised subnormals with an IQ range of 30 to 60, CA 7 to 8 to 21 to 11, and MA from 5–0 to 8–11. The normal controls were provided from Elkind's data. A succinct description of the results has been provided by McManis. 'Retardate MA and normal CA correspondence was good for concrete understanding of both concepts. Abstract right-left understanding was CA related (low IQ retardates > high IQ retardates > normals). Abstract understanding of kinship, however, was not a simple function of either MA or CA (high IQ retardates > normals > low IQ retardates). Understanding of the class concept of brother–sister was a function of IQ (normals > high IQ retardates > low IQ retardates).'

Commenting on these results, McManis points out that his data support the view that relative thinking development is hierarchically ordered. Success at the abstract-relative level was invariably associated with success with the concrete problems but the reverse relationship was not found.

In a study of mass, weight, and volume conservation, McManis (1969b) found conservation to be MA rather than CA related, and more or less in the expected order of difficulty, although there were several reversals. Conservation of volume was poor for both groups, and both failed to show MA related improvement on this task. In a further study, McManis (1969c) showed that retardates attained transitivity of weight and length considerably later than normals. Conservation developed prior to transitivity, with more retardates between MA 7 and 10 being in a transitional stage of the sequence.

In view of the recent plethora of Piagetian studies on normal children, one must expect this fashionable trend to extend to the field of subnormality. It is to be hoped that experimenters will not be content with describing Piagetian stages in relation to MA, CA, and IQ, but will also conduct rigorous, long-term learning experiments to establish the conditions in which conservation, transitivity, and other processes may be acquired.

Evidence already exists to suggest that neither the hierarchical sequence nor the developmental ages at which these types of thinking occur can be regarded as anything like as clear and predictable as has been claimed by Piagetian enthusiasts.

PERSONALITY AND MOTIVATION

The emphasis of this chapter is on research connected with aspects of cognitive functioning, and important problems such as the general motivation, need achievement, or anxiety level of subjects taking part in the many experiments have largely been ignored. Writing on personality disorders and characteristics of the mentally retarded, Heber (1964) stated:

'Despite the generally acknowledged importance of personality factors in problem solving there has been relatively little experimental work relative to personality development and characteristics of the retarded. Not one of such commonly purported attributes of the retarded as passivity, anxiety, impulsivity, rigidity, suggestibility, a lack of persistence, immaturity, withdrawal, low frustration tolerance, unrealistic self-concept or level of aspiration can be either substantiated or refuted on the basis of available research data.'

It is beyond the scope of this chapter to summarise research findings in the area of personality assessment; we will confine ourselves to a brief outline of two related theories of personality and motivation which in each case have served as a focus for systematic investigation. Both Cromwell and Zigler have been concerned to analyse the motivational effects of failure experiences and failure expectancies; Zigler has concentrated on the outcome of general deprivation suffered by most retardates in institutions.

Cromwell (1963) summarises his social learning theory, emphasising the critical rôle of failure experience and generalised expectancies for failure which typically characterise the retardate. Based on careful studies over many years he concluded that: retardates (1) enter a novel situation with a performance level which is depressed below their level of constitutional ability, (2) have fewer tendencies to be 'moved' by failure experience than normals, and (3) have fewer tendencies than normals to increase effort following a mild failure experience. Evidence was also obtained which gave partial support to the notion of separate approach and avoidance motivational systems. Stronger avoidance tendency was sometimes, but not always, shown by retardates. From this research there gradually developed a theoretical formulation that posited a success-approach and failure-avoidance motivational system which was separate from the hedonistic system typically described in terms of primary and secondary drives.

Zigler and his colleagues believe that many of the reported differences between the retarded and their normal MA matched controls may arise from a variety of differences in their motivational systems, associated with their impoverished experience and social deprivation. Zigler's interest arose in connection with a careful testing of the 'rigidity' hypothesis first advanced by Lewin and Kounin, a typical 'defect' theory of subnormality. This hypothesis was rejected, and in its place a social deprivation motivational hypothesis proposed (Zigler, 1966). Differences in 'rigidity' between the subnormal and their MA matched controls may be related to motivational differences for obtaining adult contact and approval. Those in institutions are likely to suffer a degree of deprivation and be more highly motivated to seek contact and approval. This view was supported by experimental evidence and led to an extension of the hypothesis that 'the greater the amount of pre-institutional social deprivation experienced by the feeble-minded child, the greater will be his motivation to interact with an adult, making such interaction and any adult approval or support that accompany it more reinforcing for his responses than for the responses of a feebleminded child who

has experienced a less amount of social deprivation' (op. cit., p. 85). For example, sixty retarded children were divided into two groups, high and low socially deprived, but matched on all other relevant variables. The study employed a two-part satiation game and three out of four predictions were confirmed. The more socially deprived children: (1) spent a greater amount of time on the game; (2) more frequently made the maximum number of responses allowed; and (3) showed a greater increase in time spent on part two over that on part one of the game. The predictions that the more socially deprived would make fewer errors, however, reached only borderline significance.

Zigler pursued the point by demonstrating significant differences in performance of institutionalised retardates by comparison with home-based retardates and normal children matched for MA, the latter two groups showing no difference in performance; further, he found similar differences between institutionalised children of normal intelligence, by comparison with non-institutionalised controls (summarised in Zigler, 1966).

Butterfield and Zigler (1965) studied two institutions in the same state, having identical admission policies, but very different social climates in terms of staff attitudes to rehabilitation of their charges. In one institution, all except the most severely retarded were regarded as potentially capable of returning to the community, granted adequate preparation; in the other, a custodial attitude predominated. Butterfield and Zigler found that retardates in the latter institution had a greater need for social reinforcement than had those in the former (see also, Butterfield, 1967).

Additional research yielded data supporting the following hypotheses—

'(1) Institutionalised retarded children tend to have been relatively deprived of adult contact and approval, and hence have a higher motivation to secure such contact and approval than do normal children.

(2) While retarded children have a higher positive-reaction tendency than normal children, due to a higher motivation to interact with an approving adult, they also have a higher negative-reaction tendency. This higher negative-reaction tendency is the result of a wariness which stems from retarded children's more frequent negative encounters with adults.

(3) The motive structure of the institutionalised retardate is influenced by an interaction between pre-institutional social history and the effects of institutionalisation. This effect is complicated by the fact that institutionalisation does not constitute

a homogeneous psychological variable. Instead, institutions differ, and underlying psychological features of the particular institutions must be considered before predictions can be made concerning the effects of institutionalisation on any particular child.

(4) The positions of various reinforcers in a reinforcer hierarchy differ as a function of environmental events. Due to the environmental differences experienced by institutionalised retarded children, the positions of reinforcers in their reinforcer hierarchy will differ from the positions of the same reinforcers in the reinforcer hierarchy of normal children.

(5) Institutionalised retarded children have learned to expect and settle for lower degrees of success than have normal children.

(6) An inner- versus outer-directed cognitive dimension may be employed to describe differences in the characteristic mode of attacking environmentally presented problems. The inner-directed person is one who employs his own thought processes and the solutions they provide in dealing with problems. The outer-directed person is one who focuses on external cues provided either by the stimuli of the problem or other persons in the belief that such attention will provide him with a guide to action. The style which characterises the individual's approach may be viewed as a result of his past history. Individuals whose internal solutions meet with a high proportion of failures will become distrustful of their own efforts and adopt an outer-directed style in their problem-solving. Since retardates unquestionably experience a disproportionate amount of failure, they are characterised by this outer-directedness. Many behaviours that are thought to inhere in mental retardation, e.g. distractibility, may be a product of this cognitive style.' (Zigler, 1966).

Zigler's position must not be misconstrued as denying cognitive deficiencies of varying degree and quality in the mentally subnormal. He is, however, persistent in his assertion that factors other than 'pure' cognition determine performance in most behavioural situations, and that research workers should attempt some control of these factors in selecting groups for comparison (Zigler, 1969). He has shown that the institutionalised retarded, when confronted with an experimental task, tend to look for cues and solutions provided by others, rather than relying on their own judgement, as the intellectually normal tend to do (Turnure and Zigler, 1964; Sanders et al., 1968).

The emphasis by both Cromwell and Zigler on failure experiences as an important motivational factor find support in Zeaman's (1965) summary of his research on discrimination learning sets. 'We have, on the other hand, observed *failure sets*. Prolonged failure on difficult problems leads to an inability to solve even the easiest problems, ordinarily solved in a trial or two' (op. cit., p. 112).

Gardner (1968), in a careful review of research on personality characteristics, notes the paucity of systematic studies (other than those by Cromwell and Zigler), and that the results reported in the areas of self-concept and anxiety level are conflicting and inconclusive. He can see no reason why personality characteristics in the subnormal should not be studied in an objective and meaningful fashion provided that the special problems of measurements in a population characterised by language deficits can be overcome.

OVERVIEW

If the reader of this chapter expected to gain clear knowledge from experimental studies of the precise nature and extent of the retardate's deficiencies and the methods by which these can be ameliorated, he will have been disappointed. In almost every area in which the methods of experimental psychology have been applied, apparently conflicting results have been reported. The wide range of subject and situational characteristics, (including age, intellectual ability, and social background), experimental techniques, stimulus material, and criterion measures that have been employed, makes a critical evaluation of the literature exceedingly difficult, and it would at present be unwise to attempt to draw many firm conclusions. There is, however, an increasing awareness of methodological problems, and an increasing sophistication in the planning of experiments, which, combined with the differing attitudes of experimenters towards the problem of subnormality should, it is to be hoped, bring about a deeper understanding of this branch of psychology during the next decade.

The evidence summarised leads the authors to the following selective evaluation:

1. The question of whether the mentally subnormal is qualitatively deficient, due to general CNS impairment, or a retarded normal, remains to be resolved, if indeed it is susceptible of resolution. The fact that a large section of institutionalised populations are

known to be the victims of chromosomal or metabolic defects, or conditions involving brain injury, makes the defect position tempting. There are, however, two problems: first, the fact that there is by no means clear evidence that the behaviour of diagnosed organically impaired retardates differs from matched groups in whom no impairment can be demonstrated (Haywood, 1966; Sternlicht *et al.*, 1968; Zeaman, 1965); second, that the few comparisons made of normal with super-normal children tend to show similar differences to those between normals and the mildly subnormal (Osler and Fivel, 1961; Blake and Williams, 1968; discussed on p. 244). If the hundreds of studies comparing retarded with normal subjects were repeated, but comparing normal children (preferably from orphanages or other institutions) with superior children, it might be concluded that on the whole people with IQs above 130 are qualitatively superior to those with IQs of 100, and that the latter were inferior in CNS functioning to the former. Such a (hypothetical) conclusion might be entirely valid, but would invalidate suggestions that the majority of the mentally subnormal are to be regarded as a race apart.

Despite the persuasive evidence presented by Spitz (1967) and Winters (1969) suggesting that normal and subnormal subjects differ with respect to their perception of 'physiological' but not to 'experiential' illusions (p. 221–22), the present authors conclude with Zeaman (1965) that the emphasis of psychological research is best directed to an examination of the laws governing the retardate's behaviour, rather than a search for unique laws (p. 222–23). In this connection, there is no systematic evidence suggesting that the laws governing learning, including language acquisition, or retention, are essentially different from those underlying these processes in normal human beings, or, in some cases, other animals. Zeaman and House's analysis of discrimination learning in the subnormal bears a striking similarity to that of Sutherland (1964) and Mackintosh (1965) in the field of animal behaviour. The principles of operant learning, successfully applied in many cases to the subnormal, all originated in the animal laboratory.

Baumeister and others found that, although RT is functionally related to intelligence, alteration of experimental conditions similarly affected reaction times of normals and subnormals (pp. 224–25); Sen and Clarke showed within a defective population that susceptibility to external distractors was related to task difficulty, as previously demonstrated with normal subjects (p. 226); factors affecting verbal mediation, such as meaningfulness, exposure time and free-association strength (pp. 240–41) appear on

balance to apply to retardate behaviour in a similar manner to the normal population. Blake and Williams (p. 244) showed that methods of concept attainment did not differentiate superior, normal, and mildly retarded subjects, although there was a clear difference in levels of performance. Other examples could be cited from the text.

2. Altogether too much of the evidence concerning different aspects of behaviour in the subnormal is based on institutionalised samples. Since a majority of the subnormal never go to an institution, and those who do must be regarded as an unrepresentative sample (*see* Introduction) there is a danger that inaccurate generalisations may be made.

There is sufficient evidence suggesting that institutionalised retardates differ from non-institutionalised retardates of similar level (Kaufman, 1963, learning sets; Baumeister, 1968a, paired-associate learning; Lyle, 1959, 1960a, language; Zigler, 1966, personality and motivation) to render suspect any conclusions relating to cognitive difference based on differences between institutionalised retardates and normal subjects. Fortunately, this point seems at last to have been taken, and recent studies have tended to compare normal and subnormal children in the same schools, or retardates of different levels in the same institution or workshop.

3. Zeaman and House's (1963; Zeaman, 1965) careful analysis of retardate discrimination learning have led them to conclude that this process is mediated, not by verbal behaviour, but by attention. Discrimination learning involves a chain of at least two responses, the first being that of attending to the relevant dimension, the second being to approach the positive cue of that dimension; it is in the former aspect that retardates are deficient (this behaviour being MA-related) rather than in the latter. Learning and extinction, only the process starts, do not appear to be related to intelligence (p. 229).

4. Although studies of short-term memory greatly outnumber those on long-term retention, and there is no consensus as to whether retardates generally are inferior to MA-matched controls, as they clearly are to CA-matched on short-term memory (pp. 232–34), there do seem to be reasonable grounds for tentatively concluding that the acquisition of new material is the chief area of deficit in the subnormal, while retention of well-learned material is good (pp. 234-35).

5. The fact that subnormals often show variability of performance (Baumeister, 1968b), low degree of intercorrelation among tasks, and low correlation with intelligence test performance (Miller *et al.*, 1968) suggests either a lack of a firmly based, well-ordered repertoire of response tendencies enabling

the subject to select an appropriate strategy when first confronted with a task, or fluctuating motivation to succeed, or both in combination.

Work on verbal mediation (Borkowski and Johnson, 1968; Penney *et al.*, 1968; Gallagher, 1969) suggests that mental retardates can be shaped in the laboratory to use mediators, but the strong possibility exists that without long-term over-learning they would quickly lapse back into their lower-order response habits. Milgram (1967) found that retardates, although benefiting significantly from verbal mediation instructions, were inferior to normal controls in their long-term retention of a mediational set.

6. There is impressive evidence that retardates are particularly handicapped with respect to verbal and higher-order conceptual abilities (Alper, 1967; Belmont *et al.*, 1967; Miller *et al.*, 1968). This is to be expected, almost by definition, and may reasonably be accepted as evidence of constitutional deficits. It should, however, be immediately apparent that differences between the subnormal and normal in these respects find a direct parallel in differences between the average and intellectually gifted, and the entire nature-nurture controversy (which will not be elaborated here) can be applied to the findings (*see* Introduction). It has been suggested that, even among the severely retarded, environmental influences significantly influence the level attained (Lyle, 1959, 1960a,b).

It is equally clear from the work of many investigators, and particularly Furth and Milgram (p. 243) that even fairly low-grade subnormals are not wholly devoid of conceptual categories, but that the greater the severity of defect, the greater the deficiency in *verbal formulation* of conceptual activity.

Bortner and Birch (1970) make the important point that the performance of a subnormal or normal child in a particular experimental situation does not necessarily give an accurate indication of his capacity, or of his potential for learning. These authors assert that 'it is clear that we have but begun to explore the universe conditions for learning and performance which will facilitate most effectively the expression of the potentialities for adaptation which exist in mentally subnormal children'.

Granted that the subnormal are impaired in their ability to learn, verbalise, and abstract, the question remains open concerning the extent to which they can be made more competent in these respects. Such evidence as is available suggests that they might. On the other hand, the criticisms voiced by Watson (1967) and Gardner (1969) of studies of operant learning (p. 227) would with profit be borne in mind by any potential researcher in this area. Neither short-term periods of specific instruction nor blunderbuss educational programmes are likely to lead to the detailed understanding of how verbal and conceptual training of the retarded should most effectively proceed. Obvious, but frequently overlooked problems, are 'Hawthorne' effects and the personal qualities of the instructor. Both of these should be controlled in the experimental design, in addition to other variables. Research on higher cognitive processes, to be of any value, will probably need considerable financial support, and the services of a team of scientists; it seems to the present writers that it offers a most challenging and potentially interesting area for endeavour—whatever the outcome.

REFERENCES

AKUTAGAWA, D. and BENOIT, E. P. (1959) The effect of age and relative brightness on associative learning in children. *Child Developm.*, **30**, 229–238.

ALLEN, M. R. and WALLACH, E. S. (1969) Word recognition and definition by educable retardates. *Amer. J. Ment. Defic.*, **73**, 883–885.

ALPER, A. E. (1967) An analysis of the Wechsler Intelligence Scale for Children with institutionalized mental retardates. *Amer. J. Ment. Defic.*, **71**, 624–630.

BALL, T. S. and WILSONCROFT, W. E. (1967) Perceptual-motor deficits and the phi-phenomenon. *Amer. J. Ment. Defic.*, **71**, 797–800.

BALLA, D. and ZIGLER, E. (1964) Discrimination and switching learning in normal, familial retarded, and organic retarded children. *J. Abnorm. (Soc.) Psychol.*, **69**, 664–669.

BALLER, W. R., CHARLES, D. C., and MILLER, E. L. (1967) Mid-life attainment of the mentally retarded: a longitudinal study. *Genet. Psychol. Monogr.*, **75**, 235–329.

BAUMEISTER, A. A. (1967a) Learning abilities of the mentally retarded. In *Mental Retardation: Appraisal, Education and Rehabilitation* (Ed. A. A. Baumeister) London: Univ. of London Press.

BAUMEISTER, A. A. (1967b) Problems in comparative studies of mental retardates and normals. *Amer. J. Ment. Defic.*, **71**, 869–875.

BAUMEISTER, A. A. (1968a) Paired-associate learning by institutionalized and non-institutionalized retardates and normal children. *Amer. J. Ment. Defic.*, **73**, 102–104.

BAUMEISTER, A. A. (1968b) Behavioral inadequacy and variability of performance. *Amer. J. Ment. Defic.*, **73**, 477–483.

BAUMEISTER, A. A. and ELLIS, N. R. (1963) Delayed response performance of retardates. *Amer. J. Ment. Defic.*, **67**, 714–722.

BAUMEISTER, A. A. and HAWKINS, W. F. (1967) Alpha responsiveness to photic stimulation in mental defectives. *Amer. J. Ment. Defic.*, **71**, 783–786.

BAUMEISTER, A. A., HAWKINS, W. F., and HOLLAND, J. M. (1967) Retroactive inhibition in short-term recall in normals and retardates. *Amer. J. Ment. Defic.*, **72**, 253–256.

BAUMEISTER, A. A., HAWKINS, W. F., and KELLAS, G. (1965a) The inter-active effects of stimulus intensity and intelligence upon reaction time. *Amer. J. Ment. Defic.*, **69**, 526–530.

BAUMEISTER, A. A., HAWKINS, W. F., and KELLAS, G. (1965b) Reaction speed as a function of stimulus intensity in normals and retardates. *Percept. Mot. Skills*, **20**, 649–652.

BAUMEISTER, A. A., HAWKINS, W. F., and KOENINGS-KNECHT, R. (1965) Effects of variation in complexity of the warning signal upon reaction time. *Amer. J. Ment. Defic.*, **69**, 860–864.

BAUMEISTER, A. A. and KELLAS, G. (1968a) Distributions of reaction times of retardates and normals. *Amer. J. Ment. Defic.*, **72**, 715–718.

BAUMEISTER, A. A. and KELLAS G. (1968b) Intrasubject response variability in relation to intelligence. *J. Abnorm. Psychol.*, **73**, 421–423.

BAUMEISTER, A. A. and KELLAS, G. (1968c) Reaction time and mental retardation. In *International Review of Research in Mental Retardation*, Vol. 3 (Ed. N. R. Ellis) New York: Academic Press.

BAUMEISTER, A. A. and KLOSOWSKI, R. (1965) An attempt to group toilet train severely retarded patients. *Ment. Retard.*, **3**, 24–26.

BAUMEISTER, A. A., SPAIN, C. J., and ELLIS, N. R. (1963) A note on alpha block duration in normals and retardates. *Amer. J. Ment. Defic.*, **67**, 723–725.

BAUMEISTER, A. A., URQUHART, D., BEEDLE, R., and SMITH, T. E. (1964) Reaction time of normals and retardates under different stimulus intensity changes. *Amer. J. Ment. Defic.*, **69**, 126–130.

BAUMEISTER, A. A. and WARD, L. C. (1967) Effects of rewards upon the reaction time of mental defectives. *Amer. J. Ment. Defic.*, **71**, 801–805.

BAUMEISTER, A. A., WILCOX, S., and GREESON, J. (1969) Reaction times of retardates and normals as a function of relative stimulus frequency. *Amer. J. Ment. Defic.*, **73**, 935–941.

BEIER, E. G., STARKWEATHER, J. A., and LAMBERT, M. J. (1969) Vocabulary usage of mentally retarded children. *Amer. J. Ment. Defic.*, **73**, 927–934.

BELMONT, I., BIRCH, H. G., and BELMONT, L. (1967) The organization of intelligence test performance in educable mentally subnormal children. *Amer. J. Ment. Defic.*, **71**, 969–976.

BELMONT, J. M. (1966) Long term memory in mental retardation. In *International Review of Research in Mental Retardation*, Vol. 1 (Ed. N. R. Ellis) New York: Academic Press.

BELMONT, J. M. and ELLIS, N. R. (1968) Effects of extraneous stimulation upon discrimination learning in normals and retardates. *Amer. J. Ment. Defic.*, **72**, 525–532.

BENSBERG, G. J., COLWELL, C. N., and CASSEL, R. H. (1965) Teaching the profoundly retarded self-help activities by behavior shaping techniques. *Amer. J. Ment. Defic.*, **69**, 674–679.

BERCH, D. (1967) Comparison of training methods in effective utilization of high level associative strategies. *Unpublished paper presented at the 91st Ann. Conven. Amer. Assoc. on Ment. Defic.*, Denver, Colo.

BEREITER, C. and ENGELMANN, S. (1966) *Teaching Disadvantaged Children in the Preschool.* New Jersey: Prentice Hall.

BERKSON, G. (1960a) An analysis of reaction time in normal and mentally deficient young men. II. Variation of complexity in reaction time tasks. *J. Ment. Defic. Res.*, **4**, 59–67.

BERKSON, G. (1960b) An analysis of reaction time in normal and mentally deficient young men. III. Variation of stimulus and of response complexity. *J. Ment. Defic. Res.*, **4**, 69–77.

BERKSON, G. (1963) Psychophysiological studies in mental deficiency. In *Handbook of Mental Deficiency* (Ed. N. R. Ellis) New York: McGraw-Hill.

BERKSON, G. and BAUMEISTER, A. A. (1967) Reaction time variability of mental defectives and normals. *Amer. J. Ment. Defic.*, **72**, 262–266.

BERKSON, G. and CANTOR, G. N. (1960) A study of mediation in mentally retarded and normal school children. *J. Educ. Psychol.*, **51**, 82–86.

BERKSON, G., HERMELIN, B., and O'CONNOR, N. (1961) Physiological responses of normals and institutionalized mental defectives to repeated stimuli. *J. Ment. Defic. Res.*, **5**, 30–39.

BESSMAN, S. P., DUE LOGUE, D., and WAPNIR, R. A. (1968) Phenylketonuria—certainty versus uncertainty. *Proc. First Congr. Internat. Assoc. Scient. Stud. Ment. Defic.*, 182–193. Reigate: Michael Jackson.

BIJOU, S. W. (1963) Theory and research in mental (developmental) retardation. *Psychol. Rec.*, **13**, 95–110.

BIJOU, S. W. (1966) A functional analysis of retarded development. In *International Review of Research in Mental Retardation*, Vol. 1 (Ed. N. R. Ellis) New York: Academic Press.

BIRCH, H. G. and TIZARD, J. (1967) The dietary treatment of phenylketonuria: not proven? *Developm. Med. Child Neurol.*, **9**, 9–12.

BLAKE, K. A. (1960) Direct learning and transfer. In *Learning Performance of Retarded and Normal Children* (Ed. G. O. Johnson and K. A. Blake) New York: Syracuse Univ. Press.

BLAKE, K. A. and WILLIAMS, C. L. (1968) Induction and deduction and retarded, normal and superior subjects' concept attainment. *Amer. J. Ment. Defic.*, **73**, 226–231.

BLOUNT, W. R. (1968) Concept usage research with the mentally retarded. *Psychol. Bull.*, **69**, 281–294.

BLOUNT, W. R. (1969) Language and the more severely retarded: a review. *Amer. J. Ment. Defic.*, **73**, 21–29.

BLUE, C. M. (1963) Performance of normal and retarded subjects on a modified paired-associate task. *Amer. J. Ment. Defic.*, **68**, 228–234.

BORKOWSKI, J. G. and JOHNSON, L. O. (1968) Mediation and the paired-associate learning of normals and retardates. *Amer. J. Ment. Defic.*, **72**, 610–613.

BORTNER, M. and BIRCH, H. G. (1960) Perception and perceptual-motor dissociation in cerebral palsied children. *J. Nerv. Ment. Dis.*, **130**, 49–53.

BORTNER, M. and BIRCH, H. G. (1970) Cognitive capacity and cognitive competence. *Amer. J. Ment. Defic.*, **74**, 735–744.

BOUSFIELD, W. A. (1953) The occurrence of clustering in the recall of randomly arranged associates. *J. Gen. Psychol.*, **49**, 229–240.

BROADBENT, D. E. (1954) The role of auditory localization in attention and memory span. *J. Exp. Psychol.*, **47**, 191–196.

BROADBENT, D. E. (1958) *Perception and Communication*. Oxford: Pergamon.

BRYANT, P. E. (1964) The effect of a verbal instruction on transfer in normal and severely subnormal children. *J. Ment. Defic. Res.*, **8**, 35–43.

BRYANT, P. E. (1965a) The transfer of positive and negative learning by normal and severely subnormal children. *Brit. J. Psychol.*, **56**, 81–86.

BRYANT, P. E. (1965b) The effects of verbal labelling on recall and recognition in severely subnormal and normal children. *J. Ment. Defic. Res.*, **9**, 229–236.

BRYANT, P. E. (1967a) Verbal labelling and learning strategies in normal and severely subnormal children. *Quart. J. Exp. Psychol.*, **19**, 155–161.

BRYANT, P. E. (1967b) Verbalisation and immediate memory of complex stimuli in normal and severely subnormal children. *Brit. J. (Soc.) Clin. Psychol.*, **6**, 212–219.

BRYANT, P. E. (1968) Practical implications of studies of transfer. *Proc. First Congr. Internat. Assoc. Scient. Stud. Ment. Defic.*, 865–868. Reigate: Michael Jackson.

BUDOFF, M., MESKIN, J. D., and KEMLER, D. J. (1968) Training productive thinking of E.M.R.'s: a failure to replicate. *Amer. J. Ment. Defic.*, **73**, 195–199.

BULGARELLA, R. (1967) Conditionability of associative strategies among educable retardates. *Unpublished paper presented at the 91st Ann. Conven. Amer. Assoc. on Ment. Defic.*, Denver, Colo.

BUTLER, A. J. and CONRAD, W. G. (1964) Psychological correlates of abnormal electroencephalographic patterns in familial retardates. *J. Clin. Psychol.*, **20**, 338–343.

BUTTERFIELD, E. C. (1967) The rôle of environmental factors in the treatment of institutionalized mental retardates. In *Mental Retardation: Appraisal, Education and Rehabilitation* (Ed. A. A. Baumeister) London: Univ. of London Press.

BUTTERFIELD, E. C. (1968a) Serial learning and the stimulus trace theory of mental retardation. *Amer. J. Ment. Defic.*, **72**, 778–787.

BUTTERFIELD, E. C. (1968b) Stimulus trace in the mentally retarded: defect or developmental lag? *J. Abnorm. Psychol.*, **73**, 358–362.

BUTTERFIELD, E. C. and ZIGLER, E. (1965) The influence of differing institutional social climates on the effectiveness of social reinforcement in the mentally retarded. *Amer. J. Ment. Defic.*, **70**, 48–56.

CAIN, L. F. and LEVINE, S. (1963) Effects of community and institutional school programs on trainable mentally retarded children. *CEC Research Monogr.*, Series B, No. B-1.

CANTOR, G. N. and RYAN, T. J. (1962) Retention of verbal paired-associates in normals and retardates. *Amer. J. Ment. Defic.*, **66**, 861–865.

CARRIER, N. A., MALPASS, L. F., and ORTON, K. D. (1961) *Responses of Bright, Normal, and Retarded Children to Learning Tasks*, Office of Education co-operative project No. 578. Carbondale: Southern Illinois Univ.

CHARLES, D. C. (1953) Ability and accomplishment of persons earlier judged mentally deficient. *Genet. Psychol. Monogr.*, **47**, 3–71.

CHARNEY, L. (1963) The trainable mentally retarded. In *Behavioral Research on Exceptional Children* (Ed. S. A. Kirk and B. B. Weiner) Washington, D.C.: Council for Exceptional Children.

CIEUTAT, V., STOCKWELL, F., and NOBLE, C. (1958) The interaction of ability and amount of practice with stimulus and response meaningfulness (m, m′) in paired-associate learning. *J. Exp. Psychol.*, **56**, 193–202.

CLARKE, A. D. B. (1962) Laboratory and workshop studies of imbecile learning processes. *Proc. Lond. Conf. Scient. Stud. Ment. Defic.*, **1**, 89–96.

CLARKE, A. D. B. (1968) Learning and human development. *Brit. J. Psychiat.*, **114**, 1061–1077.

CLARKE, A. D. B. (1969) *Recent Advances in the Study of Subnormality*. London: National Association for Mental Health.

CLARKE, A. D. B. and BLAKEMORE, C. B. (1961) Age and perceptual-motor transfer in imbeciles. *Brit. J. Psychol.*, **52**, 125–131.

CLARKE, A. D. B. and COOKSON, M. (1962) Perceptual-motor transfer in imbeciles: a second series of experiments. *Brit. J. Psychol.*, **53**, 321–330.

CLARKE, A. D. B. and COOPER, G. M. (1966) Age and perceptual-motor transfer in imbeciles: task complexity as a variable. *Brit. J. Psychol.*, **57**, 113–119.

CLARKE, A. D. B. and HERMELIN, B. F. (1955) Adult imbeciles: their abilities and trainability. *Lancet*, **ii**, 337–339.

CLARKE, A. M. and CLARKE, A. D. B. (1965) *Mental Deficiency: the Changing Outlook*. London: Methuen.

CLARKE, A. M., CLARKE, A. D. B., and COOPER, G. M. (1967) Learning transfer and cognitive development. In *Psychopathology of Mental Development* (Ed. J. Zubin and G. Jervis) New York: Grune and Stratton.

CLARKE, A. M., CLARKE, A. D. B., and COOPER, G. M. (1970) The development of a set to perceive categorical relations. In *Social-Cultural Aspects of Mental Retardation* (Ed. H. C. Haywood) New York: Appleton Century Crofts.

CLARKE, A. M., COOPER, G. M., and CLARKE, A. D. B. (1967) Task complexity and transfer in the development of cognitive structures. *J. Exp. Child Psychol.*, **5**, 562–576.

CLARKE, A. M., COOPER, G. M., and HENNEY, A. S. (1966) Width of transfer and task complexity in the conceptual learning of imbeciles. *Brit. J. Psychol.*, **57**, 121–128.

CLARKE, C. A. (1967) Prevention of Rh-haemolytic disease. *Brit. med. J.*, **4**, 484–485.

CLEVENGER, L. J. (1966) Electroencephalographic studies relating to mental retardation. *Ment. Retard. Abstrs.*, **3**, 170–178.

CORTER, H. M. and McKINNEY, J. D. (1968) Flexibility training with educable retarded and bright normal children. *Amer. J. Ment. Defic.*, **72**, 603–609.

CROMWELL, R. L. (1963) A social learning approach to mental retardation. In *Handbook of Mental Deficiency* (Ed. N. R. Ellis) New York: McGraw-Hill.

CROMWELL, R. L., BAUMEISTER, A. A., and HAWKINS, W. F. (1963) Research in activity level. In *Handbook of Mental Deficiency* (Ed. N. R. Ellis) New York: McGraw-Hill.

DEESE, J. (1958) *The Psychology of Learning*. New York: McGraw-Hill.

DEICH, R. (1968) Reproduction and recognition as indices of perceptual impairment. *Amer. J. Ment. Defic.*, **73**, 9–12.

DENT, H. E. (1968) Operant conditioning as a tool in the habilitation of the mentally retarded. *Proc. First Congr. Internat. Assoc. Scient. Stud. Ment. Defic.*, 873–876. (Reigate: Michael Jackson).

DILLER, L. and BIRCH, H. G. (1964) Psychological evaluation of children with cerebral damage. In *Brain Damage in Children* (Ed. H. G. Birch) New York: Williams and Wilkins.

DOUBROS, S. G. (1966) Behavior therapy with high level, institutionalized retarded adolescents. *Except. Children*, **33**, 229–233.

DOYLE, M. (1967) Perceptual skill development—a possible resource for the intellectually handicapped. *Amer. J. Ment. Defic.*, **71**, 776–782.

EISMAN, B. (1958) Paired associate learning, generalization, and retention as a function of intelligence. *Amer. J. Ment. Defic.*, **63**, 481–489.

ELKIND, D. (1961) Children's conception of right and left: Piaget replication study IV. *J. Genet. Psychol.*, **99**, 269–276.

ELKIND, D. (1962) Children's conception of brother and sister: Piaget replication study V. *J. Genet. Psychol.*, **100**, 129–136.

ELLINGSON, R. J. (1966) Relationship between E.E.G. and test intelligence: a commentary. *Psychol. Bull.*, **65**, 91–98.

ELLIS, N. R. (1958) Object-quality discrimination learning sets in mental defectives. *J. Comp. Physiol. Psychol.*, **51**, 79–81.

ELLIS, N. R. (1963) The stimulus trace and behavioral inadequacy. In *Handbook of Mental Deficiency* (Ed. N. R. Ellis) New York: McGraw-Hill.

ELLIS, N. R. (1969) A behavioral research strategy in mental retardation: defense and critique. *Amer. J. Ment. Defic.*, **73**, 557–566.

ELLIS, N. R. and ANDERS, T. R. (1968) Short-term memory in the mental retardate. *Amer. J. Ment. Defic.*, **72**, 931–936.

ELLIS, N. R., GIRARDEAU, F. L., and PRYER, M. W. (1962) Analysis of learning sets in normal and severely defective humans. *J. Comp. Physiol. Psychol.*, **55**, 860–865.

ELLIS, N. R., HAWKINS, W. F., PRYER, M. W., and JONES, R. W. (1963) Distraction effects in oddity learning by normal and mentally defective humans. *Amer. J. Ment. Defic.*, **67**, 576–583.

ELLIS, N. R. and MUNGER, M. (1966) Short-term memory in normal children and mental retardates. *Psychon. Sci.*, **6**, 381–382.

ELLIS, N. R. and SLOAN, W. (1957) Relationship between intelligence and simple reaction time in mental defectives. *Percept. Mot. Skills*, **7**, 65–67.

ELLIS, N. R. and SLOAN, W. (1959) Oddity learning as a function of mental age. *J. Comp. Physiol. Psychol.*, **52**, 228–230.

EVANS, R. A. (1964) Word recall and associative clustering in mental retardates. *Amer. J. Ment. Defic.*, **69**, 413–418.

FEDIO, P. M., MIRSKY, A. F., SMITH, W. J., and PARRY, D. (1961) Reaction time and E.E.G. activation in normal and schizophrenic subjects. *Electroencephalog. Clin. Neurophysiol.*, **13**, 923–926.

FURTH, H. G. (1961) The influence of language on the development of concept formation in deaf children. *J. Abnorm. (Soc.) Psychol.*, **63**, 386–389.

FURTH, H. G. and MILGRAM, N. A. (1965) The influence of language on classification: a theoretical model applied to normal, retarded and deaf children. *Genet. Psychol. Monogr.*, **72**, 317–351.

FURTH, H. G. and YOUNISS, J. (1964) Colour-object paired-associates in deaf and hearing children with and without response competition. *J. Consult. Psychol.*, **28**, 224–227.

GALLAGHER, J. W. (1969) Mediation as a function of associative chains in normal and retarded children. *Amer. J. Ment. Defic.*, **73**, 886–889.

GARDNER, J. M. (1969) Behavior modification research in mental retardation: search for an adequate paradigm. *Amer. J. Ment. Defic.*, **73**, 844–851.

GARDNER, J. M. and WATSON, L. S. (1969) Behavior modification of the mentally retarded: an annotated bibliography. *Ment. Retard. Abstrs.*, **6**, 181–193.

GARDNER, W. I. (1968) Personality characteristics of the mentally retarded: review and critique. In *Behavioral Research in Mental Retardation* (Ed. H. J. Prehm, L. A. Hamerlynck, J. E. Crosson) Oregon: Univ. of Oregon.

GAUDREAU, J. (1968) Interrelations among perception, learning ability and intelligence in mentally deficient school children. *J. Learning Disabilities*, **1**, 301–306.

GERJUOY, I. R. and ALVAREZ, J. M. (1969) Transfer of learning in associative clustering of retardates and normals. *Amer. J. Ment. Defic.*, **73**, 733–738.

GERJUOY, I. R. and SPITZ, H. H. (1966) Associative clustering in free recall: intellectual and developmental variables. *Amer. J. Ment. Defic.*, **70**, 918–927.

GILES, I. K. and WOLF, M. M. (1966) Toilet training institutionalized, severe retardates: an application of operant behavior modification techniques. *Amer. J. Ment. Defic.*, **70**, 766–780.

GIRARDEAU, F. L. (1959) The formation of discrimination learning sets in mongoloid and normal children. *J. Comp. Physiol. Psychol.*, **52**, 566–570.

GIRARDEAU, F. L. and ELLIS, N. R. (1964) Rote verbal learning by normal and mentally retarded children. *Amer. J. Ment. Defic.*, **68**, 525–532.

GIRARDEAU, F. L. and SPRADLIN, J. E. (1964) Token rewards in a cottage program. *Ment. Retard.*, **2**, 345–351.

GOLDSTEIN, H. (1964) Social and occupational adjustment. In *Mental Retardation* (Ed. H. A. Stevens and R. Heber) Chicago: Univ. of Chicago Press.

GOLDSTEIN, K. and SCHEERER, M. (1941) Abstract and concrete behavior: an experimental study with special tests. *Psychol. Monogr.*, **53**, 25–42.

GORDON, M. C. (1968) Some effects of stimulus presentation rate and complexity on perception and retention. *Amer. J. Ment. Defic.*, **73**, 437–445.

GORDON, S., O'CONNOR, N., and TIZARD, J. (1954) Some effects of incentives on the performance of imbeciles. *Brit. J. Psychol.*, **45**, 277–287.

GORDON, S., O'CONNOR, N., and TIZARD, J. (1955) Some effects of incentives on the performance of imbeciles on a repetitive task. *Amer. J. Ment. Defic.*, **60**, 371–377.

GORTON, C. E. and HOLLIS, J. H. (1965) Redesigning a cottage unit for better programming and research for the severely retarded. *Ment. Retard.*, **3**, 16–21.

GOULET, L. R. (1968) Verbal learning and memory research with retardates: an attempt to assess developmental trends. In *International Review of Research in Mental Retardation* Vol. 3 (Ed. N. R. Ellis) New York: Academic Press.

GOZALI, J. (1969) Impulsivity-reflectivity as problem solving styles among educable mentally retarded children. *Amer. J. Ment. Defic.*, **73**, 864–867.

GRAY, S. and KLAUS, R. A. (1965) An experimental preschool program for culturally deprived children. *Child Developm.*, **36**, 887–898.

GRAY, S. and KLAUS, R. A. (1970) The early training project: a seventh year report. *Child Developm.*, **41**, 909–924.

GRIFFITH, B. C. (1960) The use of verbal mediators in concept formation by retarded subjects at different intelligence levels. *Child Developm.*, **31**, 633–641.

GRIFFITH, B. C. and SPITZ, H. H. (1958) Some relationships between abstraction and word meaning in retarded adolescents. *Amer. J. Ment. Defic.*, **63**, 247–251.

GRIFFITH, B. C., SPITZ, H. H., and LIPMAN, R. S. (1959) Verbal mediation and concept formation in retarded and normal subjects. *J. Exp. Psychol.*, **58**, 247–251.

GUSKIN, S. L. and SPICKER, H. H. (1968) Educational research in mental retardation. In *International Review of Research in Mental Retardation*, Vol. 3 (Ed. N. R. Ellis) New York: Academic Press.

HAMILTON, J. W. and STEPHENS, L. Y. (1967) Reinstating speech in an emotionally disturbed, mentally retarded young woman. *J. Speech Hear. Disord.*, **32**, 383–389.

HAMILTON, J., STEPHENS, L., and ALLEN, P. (1967) Controlling aggressive and destructive behavior in severely retarded institutionalized residents. *Amer. J. Ment. Defic.*, **71**, 852–856.

HARLOW, H. F. (1949) The formation of learning sets. *Psychol. Rev.*, **56**, 51–65.

HARVEY, A., YEP, B., and SELLIN, D. (1966) Developmental achievement of trainable mentally retarded children. *Trng. Sch. Bull.*, **63**, 100–108.

HAWKINS, W. F., BAUMEISTER, A. A., KOENINGSKNECHT, R. A., and KELLAS, G. (1965) Simple and disjunctive reaction times of normals and retardates. *Amer. J. Ment. Defic.*, **69**, 536–540.

HAYES, K. J. (1953) The backward curve: a method for the study of learning. *Psychol. Rev.*, **60**, 269–275.

HAYES, K. J., THOMPSON, R., and HAYES, C. (1953) Discrimination learning sets in chimpanzees. *J. Comp. Physiol. Psychol.*, **46**, 99–104.

HAYWOOD, H. C. (1966) Perceptual handicap: fact or artifact? *Ment. Retard.* (Canada) **16**, 9–16.

HAYWOOD, H. C. and HEAL, L. W. (1968) Retention of learned visual associations as a function of I.Q. and learning levels. *Amer. J. Ment. Defic.*, **72**, 828–838.

HEAL, L. W., ROSS, L. E., and SANDERS, B. (1966) Reversal and partial reversal in mental defectives and normal children of a comparable mental age. *Amer. J. Ment. Defic.*, **71**, 411–416.

HEBER, R. (1959) A manual on terminology and classification in mental retardation. *Amer. J. Ment. Defic. Monogr. Suppl.*, **64**.

HEBER, R. (1964) Personality. In *Mental Retardation* (Ed. H. A. Stevens and R. Heber) Chicago: Univ. of Chicago Press.

HEBER, R. (1968) The rôle of environmental variables in the etiology of cultural-familial mental retardation. *Proc. First Congr. Internat. Assoc. Scient. Stud. Ment. Defic.*, 456–465. (Reigate: Michael Jackson).

HEBER, R. (1971) An experiment in prevention of 'cultural-familial' mental retardation. *Proc. Second Congr. Internat. Assoc. Scient. Stud. Ment. Defic.* (Holland: Swets and Zeitlinger, and Warsaw: Ars Polonia. In press.)

HEBER, R., PREHM, H., NARDI, G., and SIMPSON, N. (1962) Learning and retention of retarded and normal children on a paired-associate task. *Paper read at the annual meeting, Amer. Assoc. Ment. Defic.*, New York.

HENRIKSEN, K. and DOUGHTY, R. (1967) Decelerating undesired meal time behavior in a group of profoundly retarded boys. *Amer. J. Ment. Defic.*, **72**, 40–44.

HERMELIN, B. F. and O'CONNOR, N. (1964) Short-term memory in normal and subnormal children. *Amer. J. Ment. Defic.*, **69**, 121–125.

HERMELIN, B. F. and VENABLES, P. H. (1964) Reaction time and alpha blocking in normal and severely subnormal subjects. *J. Exp. Psychol.*, **67**, 365–372.

HOHN, R. (1967) Facilitation in associative learning ability among educable retardates. *Unpublished paper presented at the 91st Ann. Conven. Amer. Assoc. on Ment. Defic.*, Denver, Colo.

HOLDEN, E. A. Jr. (1965) Reaction time during unimodal and trimodal stimulation in educable retardates. *J. Ment. Defic. Res.*, **9**, 183–190.

HOUSE, B. J. (1964) The effect of distinctive responses on discrimination reversals in retardates. *Amer. J. Ment. Defic.*, **69**, 79–85.

HOUSE, B. J. and ZEAMAN, D. (1959) Position discrimination and reversals in low-grade retardates. *J. Comp. Physiol. Psychol.*, **52**, 564–565.

HOUSE, B. J. and ZEAMAN, D. (1962) Reversal and non-reversal shifts in discrimination learning in retardates. *J. Exp. Psychol.*, **63**, 444–451.

HOUSE, B. J. and ZEAMAN, D. (1963) Miniature experiments in the discrimination learning of retardates. In *Advances in Child Development and Behavior* (Ed. L. P. Lipsitt and C. C. Spiker) New York: Academic Press.

HUNDZIAK, M., MAURER, R. A., and WATSON, L. S. (1965) Operant conditioning in toilet training of severely mentally retarded boys. *Amer. J. Ment. Defic.*, **70**, 120–124.

HUTT, S. J. and HUTT, C. (1964) Hyperactivity in a group of epileptic (and some non-epileptic) brain damaged children. *Epilepsia Journal*, **5**, 334–351.

JENSEN, A. R. (1965) Rote learning in retarded adults and normal children. *Amer. J. Ment. Defic.*, **69**, 828–834.

JENSEN, A. R. and ROHWER, W. D. (1963) The effect of verbal mediation on the learning and retention of paired-associates by retarded adults. *Amer. J. Ment. Defic.*, **68**, 80–84.

JOHNSON, G. O. (1958) *Comparative Studies of Some Learning Characteristics in Mentally Retarded and Normal Children of the Same Mental Age.* New York: Syracuse Univ. Press.

KAGAN, J. (1966) A developmental approach to conceptual growth. In *Analysis of Concept Learning* (Ed. H. J. Klausmeier and C. W. Harris) New York: Academic Press.

KARLIN, I. W. and STRAZZULLA, M. (1952) Speech and language problems of mentally deficient children. *J. Speech Hear. Dis.*, **17**, 286–294.

KAUFMAN, M. E. (1963) The formation of a learning set in institutionalized and non-institutionalized mental defectives. *Amer. J. Ment. Defic.*, **67**, 601–605.

KAUFMAN, M. E. and PREHM, H. J. (1966) A review of research on learning sets and transfer of training in mental defectives. In *International Review of Research in Mental Retardation*, Vol. 2 (Ed. N. R. Ellis) New York: Academic Press.

KENDLER, T. S. and KENDLER, H. H. (1959) Reversal and non-reversal shifts in kindergarten children. *J. Exp. Psychol.*, **58**, 56–60.

KENDLER, T. S., KENDLER, H. H., and WELLS, D. (1960) Reversal and non-reversal shifts in nursery school children. *J. Comp. Physiol Psychol.*, **53**, 83–88.

KEPPEL, G. (1965) Problems of method in the study of short-term memory. *Psychol. Bull.*, **63**, 1–13.

KERR, N., MEYERSON, L., and MICHAEL, J. (1965) A procedure for shaping vocalizations in a mute child. In *Case Studies in Behavior Modification* (Ed. L. P. Ullman and L. Krasner) New York: Holt, Rinehart, and Winston.

KLAUSMEIER, H. J., FELDHUSEN, J., and CHECK, J. (1959) *An Analysis of Learning Efficiency in Arithmetic of Mentally Retarded Children in Comparison with Children of Average and High Intelligence.* Madison: Univ. of Wisconsin Press.

KÖHLER, W. and WALLACH, H. (1944) Figural aftereffects: an investigation of visual processes. *Proc. Amer. Phil. Soc.*, **88**, 269–357.

KOLSTOE, O. P. (1958) Language training of low grade mongoloid children. *Amer. J. Ment. Defic.*, **63**, 17–30.

KOUW, W. A. (1968) Effects of stimulus intensity and duration upon retardates' short-term memory. *Amer. J. Ment. Defic.*, **72**, 734–739.

KROP, H. D. and SMITH, C. R. (1969) Effects of special education on Bender-Gestalt performance of the mentally retarded. *Amer. J. Ment. Defic.*, **73**, 693–699.

LANCE, W. D. (1965) Effects of meaningfulness and overlearning on retention in normal and retarded adolescents. *Amer. J. Ment. Defic.*, **70**, 270–275.

LANSING, R. W., SCHWARTZ, E., and LINDSLEY, D. B. (1959) Reaction time and E.E.G. activation under alerted and non-alerted conditions. *J. Exp. Psychol.*, **58**, 1–7.

LELAND, H. (1969) The relationship between 'intelligence' and mental retardation. *Amer. J. Ment. Defic.*, **73**, 533–535.

LENNEBERG, E. H. (1962) Understanding language without ability to speak. *J. Abnorm. (Soc.) Psychol.*, **65**, 419–425.

LENNEBERG, E. H. (1967) *Biological Foundation of Language.* New York: Wiley.

LENNEBERG, E. H., NICHOLS, I. A., and ROSENBERGER, E. F. (1964) Primitive stages of language development in mongolism. In *Disorders of Communication*, Vol. XLII. Res. Pub., A.R.N.M.D., 119–137.

LIPMAN, R. S. (1963) Learning: verbal, perceptual-motor, and classical conditioning. In *Handbook of Mental Deficiency* (Ed. N. R. Ellis) New York: McGraw-Hill.

LURIA, A. R. (1961) *The Role of Speech in the Regulation of Normal and Abnormal Behaviour.* London: Pergamon.

LURIA, A. R. and VINOGRADOVA, O. S. (1959) An objective investigation of the dynamics of semantic systems. *Brit. J. Psychol.*, **50**, 89–105.

LYLE, J. G. (1959) The effect of an institution environment upon the verbal development of imbecile children: I. Verbal intelligence. *J. Ment. Defic. Res.*, **3**, 122–128.

LYLE, J. G. (1960a) The effect of an institution environment upon the verbal development of imbecile children: II. Speech and language. *J. Ment. Defic. Res.*, **4**, 1–13.

LYLE, J. G. (1960b) The effect of an institution environment upon the verbal development of imbecile children: III. The Brooklands residential family unit. *J. Ment. Defic. Res.*, **4**, 14–23.

LYLE, J. G. (1961) A comparison of the verbal intelligence of normal and imbecile children. *J. Genet. Psychol.*, **99**, 227–234.

MCCANDLESS, B. R. (1964) Relation of environmental factors to intellectual functioning. In *Mental Retardation* (Ed. H. A. Stevens and R. Heber) Chicago: Univ. of Chicago Press.

MCCONNEL, T. R., CROMWELL, R. L., BIALER, I., and SON, C. D. (1964) Studies in activity level VII. *Amer. J. Ment. Defic.*, **68**, 647–651.

MCCRARY, J. W. and HUNTER, W. S. (1953) Serial position curves in verbal learning. *Science*, **117**, 131–134.

MACKINTOSH, N. J. (1965) Selective attention in animal discrimination learning. *Psychol. Bull.*, **64**, 124–150.

MCMANIS, D. L. (1965) Relative errors with serial lists of different lengths. *Amer. J. Ment. Defic.*, **70**, 125–128.

MCMANIS, D. L. (1966) The von Restorff effect in serial learning by normal and retarded subjects. *Amer. J. Ment. Defic.*, **70**, 569–575.

MCMANIS, D. L. (1968) Relative thinking by retardates. *Amer. J. Ment. Defic.*, **73**, 484–492.

MCMANIS, D. L. (1969a) Intralist differentiation and the isolation effect in serial learning by normals and retardates. *Amer. J. Ment. Defic.*, **73**, 819–825.

McManis, D. L. (1969b) Conservation of mass, weight, and volume by normal and retarded children. *Amer. J. Ment. Defic.*, **73**, 762–767.

McManis, D. L. (1969c) Conservation and transitivity of weight and length by normals and retardates. *Developm. Psychol.*, **1**, 373–382.

Macoby, E. E. (1964) Developmental psychology. *Annu. Rev. Psychol.*, **15**, 203–250.

Madsen, M. C. (1963) Distribution of practice and level of intelligence. *Psychol. Rep.*, **13**, 39–42.

Madsen, M. C. (1966) Individual differences and temporal factors in memory consolidation. *Amer. J. Ment. Defic.*, **71**, 501–507.

Madsen, M. C. and Connor K. J. (1968) Categorization and information reduction in short-term memory at two levels of intelligence. *Amer. J. Ment. Defic,*. **73**, 232–238.

Martin, C. J., Boersma, F. J., and Cox, D. L. (1965) A classification of associative strategies in paired associate learning. *Psychol. Sci.*, **3**, 455–456.

Martin, C. J., Boersma, F. J., and Bulgarella, R. (1968) Verbalization of associative strategies by normal and retarded children. *J. Gen. Psychol.*, **78**, 209–218.

Mein, R. (1961) A study of the oral vocabularies of severely subnormal patients: II. Grammatical analysis of speech samples. *J. Ment. Defic. Res.*, **5**, 52–59.

Mein, R. and O'Connor, N. (1960) A study of the oral vocabularies of severely subnormal patients. *J. Ment. Defic. Res.*, **4**, 130–143.

Milgram, N. A. (1966) Verbalization and conceptual classification in trainable mentally retarded children. *Amer. J. Ment. Defic.*, **70**, 763–765.

Milgram, N. A. (1967) Retention of mediation set in paired-associate learning of normal children and retardates. *J. Exp. Child Psychol.*, **5**, 341–349.

Milgram, N. A. (1968) The effect of verbal mediation in paired-associate learning in trainable retardates. *Amer. J. Ment. Defic.*, **72**, 518–524.

Milgram, N. A. (1969) The rational and irrational in Zigler's motivational approach to mental retardation. *Amer. J. Ment. Defic.*, **73**, 527–531.

Milgram, N. A. and Furth, H. G. (1963) The influence of language on concept attainment in educable retarded children. *Amer. J. Ment. Defic.*, **67**, 733–739.

Milgram, N. A. and Furth, H. G. (1964) Position reversal versus dimension reversal in normal and retarded children. *Child Developm.*, **35**, 701–708.

Milgram, N. A. and Furth, H. G. (1966) Response competition in paired associate learning by educable and trainable retarded children. *Amer. J. Ment. Defic.*, **70**, 849–854.

Miller, E. L. (1965) Ability and social adjustment at midlife of persons earlier judged mentally deficient. *Genet. Psychol. Monogr.*, **72**, 139–198.

Miller, G. A. (1956) The magical number seven, plus or minus two: some limits on our capacity for processing information. *Psychol. Rev.*, **63**, 81–97.

Miller, G. A., Galanter, E., and Pribram, K. (1960) *Plans and the Structure of Behavior.* New York: Holt, Rinehart, and Winston.

Miller, L. K., Hale, G. A., and Stevenson, H. W (1968) Learning and problem solving by retarded and normal Ss. *Amer. J. Ment. Defic.*, **72**, 681–690.

Miller, M. B. and Griffith, B. C. (1961) The effects of training verbal associates on the performance of a conceptual task, *Amer. J. Ment. Defic*, **66**, 270–276.

Mordock, J. B. (1968) Paired associate learning in mental retardation: a review. *Amer. J. Ment. Defic.*, **72**, 857–865.

Neufeldt, A. H. (1966) Short-term memory in the mentally retarded: an application of the dichotic listening technique. *Psychol. Monogr.*, **80**, No. 620, 1–31.

Noble, C. E. and McKeely, D. A. (1957) The rôle of meaningfulness (m′) in paired-associate verbal learning. *J. Exp. Psychol.*, **53**, 16–22.

O'Connor, N. (1965) The prevalence of mental defect. In *Mental Deficiency: the Changing Outlook* (Ed. A. M. Clarke and A. D. B. Clarke) London: Methuen.

O'Connor, N. and Hermelin, B. F. (1959) Discrimination and reversal learning in imbeciles. *J. Abnorm. (Soc.) Psychol.*, **59**, 409–413.

O'Connor, N. and Hermelin, B. F. (1963a) Recall in normals and subnormals of like mental age. *J. Abnorm. (Soc.) Psychol.*, **66**, 81–84.

O'Connor, N. and Hermelin, B. F. (1963b) *Speech and Thought in Severe Subnormality.* London: Pergamon.

O'Connor, N. and Hermelin, B. F. (1965) Input restriction and immediate memory decay in normal and subnormal children. *Quart. J. Exp. Psychol.*, **17**, 323–328.

Orlansky, J. (1940) The effect of similarity and difference in form on apparent visual movement. *Arch. Psychol.*, **40**, No. 246. p. 85.

Osborn, W. J. (1960) Associative clustering in organic and familial retardates. *Amer. J. Ment. Defic.*, **65**, 351–357.

Osler, S. F. and Fivel, M. W. (1961) Concept attainment: I. The rôle of age and intelligence in concept attainment by induction. *J. Exp. Psychol.*, **62**, 1–8.

Osler, S. F. and Trautman, G. E. (1961) Concept attainment: II. Effect of stimulus complexity upon concept attainment at two levels of intelligence. *J. Exp. Psychol.*, **62**, 9–13.

Pascal, G. R. (1953) The effect of a disturbing noise on the reaction time of mental defectives. *Amer. J. Ment. Defic.*, **57**, 691–699.

Penney, R. K., Seim, R., and Peters, R. DeV. (1968) The mediational deficiency of mentally retarded children: I. The establishment of retardates' mediational deficiency. *Amer. J. Ment. Defic.*, **72**, 626–630.

Penney, R. K., Peters, R. DeV., and Willows, D. M. (1968) The mediational deficiency of mentally retarded children: II. Learning set's effect on mediational deficiency. *Amer. J. Ment. Defic.*, **73**, 262–266.

Penrose, L. S. (1949) *The Biology of Mental Defect.* London: Sidgwick and Jackson.

Penrose, L. S. (1962) Biological aspects. *Proc. Lond. Conf. Scient. Stud. Ment. Defic.*, **1**, 11–18.

Piaget, J. (1928) *Judgement and Reasoning in the Child.* London: Routledge and Kegan Paul.

PLENDERLEITH, M. (1956) Discrimination learning and discrimination reversal learning in normal and feeble minded children. *J. Genet. Psychol.*, **88**, 107–112.

PREHM, H. J. (1966a) Associative learning in retarded and normal children as a function of task difficulty and meaningfulness. *Amer. J. Ment. Defic.*, **70**, 860–865.

PREHM, H. J. (1966b) Verbal learning research in mental retardation. *Amer. J. Ment. Defic.*, **71**, 42–47.

PREHM, H. J. (1968) Rote verbal learning and memory in the retarded. In *Behavioral Research in Mental Retardation* (Ed. H. J. Prehm, L. A. Hamerlynck, and J. E. Crosson) Oregon: Univ. of Oregon.

PRYER, R. S. (1960) Retroactive inhibition in normals and defectives as a function of temporal position of the interpolated task. *Amer. J. Ment. Defic.*, **64**, 1004–1011.

RIEBER, M. (1964) Verbal mediation in normal and retarded children. *Amer. J. Ment. Defic.*, **68**, 634–641.

RING, E. M. and PALERMO, D. S. (1961) Paired associate learning of retarded and normal children. *Amer. J. Ment. Defic.*, **66**, 100–107.

ROHWER, W. D. and LYNCH, S. (1968) Retardation, school strata, and learning proficiency. *Amer. J. Ment. Defic.*, **73**, 91–96.

ROOS, P. (1965) Development of an intensive habit training unit at Austin State School. *Ment. Retard.*, **3**, 12–15.

ROSENBERG, S. (1963) Problem-solving and conceptual behavior. In *Handbook of Mental Deficiency* (Ed. N. R. Ellis) New York: McGraw-Hill.

ROSSI, E. L. (1963) Associative clustering in normal and retarded children. *Amer. J. Ment. Defic.*, **67**, 691–699.

ROUSE, S. T. (1965) Effects of a training program on the productive thinking of educable mental retardates. *Amer. J. Ment. Defic.*, **69**, 666–673.

SAENGER, G. (1957) The adjustment of severely retarded adults to the community. *Report to the New York Inter-Departmental Health Resources Board.*

SANDERS, B., ROSS, L. E., and HEAL, L. W. (1965) Reversal and non-reversal shift learning in normal children and retardates of comparable mental age. *J. Exp. Psychol.*, **69**, 84–88.

SANDERS, B., ZIGLER, E., and BUTTERFIELD, E. C. (1968) Outer-directedness in the discrimination learning of normal and mentally retarded children. *J. Abnorm. Psychol.*, **73**, 368–375.

SARASON, S. B. and DORIS, J. (1969) *Psychological Problems in Mental Deficiency.* New York: Harper and Row.

SCHULMAN, J. L., KASPAR, J. C., and THRONE, F. M. (1965) *Brain Damage and Behavior. A Clinical-Experimental Study.* Springfield, Ill.: C. C. Thomas.

SCOTT, K. G. and SCOTT, M. S. (1968) Research and theory in short-term memory. In *International Review of Research in Mental Retardation*, Vol. 3 (Ed. N. R. Ellis) New York: Academic Press.

SCOTT, W. S. (1940) Reaction time in young intellectual deviates. *Arch. Psychol.*, **36**, 1–64.

SEN, A. and CLARKE, A. M. (1968) Some factors affecting distractibility in the mental retardate. *Amer. J. Ment. Defic.*, **73**, 50–60.

SEN, A. K., CLARKE, A. M., and COOPER, G. M. (1968) The effect of isolating items in serial learning in severely retarded subjects. *Amer. J. Ment. Defic.*, **72**, 851–856.

SEN, A. K. and SEN, A. (1968) A test of the McCrary-Hunter hypothesis in mentally retarded subjects. *J. Ment. Defic. Res.*, **12**, 36–46.

SHEPP, B. E. and TURRISI, F. D. (1966) Learning and transfer of mediating responses in discriminative learning. In *International Review of Research in Mental Retardation*, Vol. 2 (Ed. N. R. Ellis) New York: Academic Press.

SILVERSTEIN, A. B. and McLAIN, R. E. (1966) Associative processes of the mentally retarded: III. A developmental study. *Amer. J. Ment. Defic.*, **70**, 722–725.

SKEELS, H. M. (1966) Adult status of children with contrasting early life experiences. *Monogr. Soc. Res. Child Developm.*, **31**, No. 3.

SKEELS, H. M. and DYE, H. B. (1939) A study of the effects of differential stimulation on mentally retarded children. *Proc. Amer. Assoc. Ment. Defic.*, **44**, 114–136.

SKODAK, M. (1968) Adult status of individuals who experienced early intervention. *Proc. First Congr. Internat. Assoc. Scient. Stud. Ment. Defic.*, 11–18. Reigate: Michael Jackson.

SLOANE, H. and MACAULAY, B. (1968) (Eds) *Operant Procedures in Remedial Speech and Language Training.* Boston: Houghton-Mifflin.

SPITZ, H. H. (1963) Field theory in mental deficiency. In *Handbook of Mental Deficiency* (Ed. N. R. Ellis) New York: McGraw-Hill.

SPITZ, H. H. (1964) A comparison of mental retardates and normals on the rotating trapezoidal window illusion. *J. Abnorm. (Soc.) Psychol.*, **68**, 574–578.

SPITZ, H. H. (1965) The effect of a single monocular depth cue deficit on retardates' perception of the rotating cube illusion. *Amer. J. Ment. Defic.*, **69**, 703–711.

SPITZ, H. H. (1966) The rôle of input organization in the learning and memory of mental retardates. In *International Review of Research in Mental Retardation*, Vol. 2 (Ed. N. R. Ellis) New York: Academic Press.

SPITZ, H. H. (1967) A comparison of mental retardates and normals on the distorted room illusion. *Amer. J. Ment. Defic.*, **72**, 34–49.

SPITZ, H. H. and BLACKMAN, L. S. (1959) A comparison of mental retardates and normals on visual figural aftereffects and reversible figures. *J. Abnorm. (Soc.) Psychol.*, **58**, 105–110.

SPITZ, H. H. and LIPMAN, R. S. (1961) A comparison of mental retardates and normals on kinesthetic figural aftereffects. *J. Abnorm. (Soc.) Psychol.*, **62**, 686–687.

SPIVACK, G. (1963) Perceptual processes. In *Handbook of Mental Deficiency* (Ed. N. R. Ellis) New York: McGraw-Hill.

SPRADLIN, J. E. and GIRARDEAU, F. L. (1966) The behavior of moderately and severely retarded persons. In *International Review of Research in Mental Retardation*, Vol. 1 (Ed. N. R. Ellis) New York: Academic Press.

SPREEN, O. (1965a) Language functions in mental retardation: a review I. Language development, types of retardation, and intelligence level. *Amer. J. Ment. Defic.*, **69**, 482–494.

SPREEN, O. (1965b) Language functions in mental retardation: a review II. Language in higher level performance. *Amer. J. Ment. Defic.*, **70**, 351–362.

STEELE, M. W. and BREG, W. R. (1966) Chromosome analysis of human amniotic-fluid cells. *Lancet.*, **i**, 383–385.

STEPHENS, W. E. (1964) A comparison of the performance of normal and subnormal boys on structured categorization tasks. *Except. Children*, **30**, 311–315.

STEPHENS, W. E. (1966a) Category usage by normal and mentally retarded boys. *Child Developm*, **37**, 355–361.

STEPHENS, W. E. (1966b) Category usage of normal and subnormal children on three types of categories. *Amer. J. Ment. Defic.*, **71**, 266–273.

STEPHENS, W. E. (1968) Labelling errors of mentally subnormal children in a concept attainment task. *Amer. J. Ment. Defic.*, **73**, 273–278.

STERNLICHT, M. and DEUTSCH, M. R. (1966) Cognition in the mentally retarded: the von Restorff effect. *J. Ment. Defic. Res.*, **10**, 63–68.

STERNLICHT, M., PUSTEL, G., and SIEGEL, L. (1968) Comparison of organic and cultural-familial retardates on two visual-motor tasks. *Amer. J. Ment. Defic.*, **72**, 887–889.

STEVENSON, H. W. and SWARTZ, J. D. (1958) Learning set in children as a function of intellectual level. *J. Comp. Physiol. Psychol.*, **51**, 755–757.

STEVENSON, H. W. and ZIGLER, E. F. (1957) Discrimination learning and rigidity in normal and feeble minded individuals. *J. Personal.*, **25**, 699–711.

STEVENSON, H. W. and ZIGLER, E. F. (1958) Probability learning in children. *J. Exp. Psychol.*, **56**, 185–192.

STRAUSS, A. A. and KEPHART, N. C. (1955) *Psychopathology and Education of the Brain Injured Child*, Vol. II, *Progress in Theory and Clinic*. New York: Grune and Stratton.

STRAUSS, A. A. and LEHTINEN, L. E. (1947) *Psychopathology and Education of the Brain Injured Child*. New York: Grune and Stratton.

SUTHERLAND, N. S. (1964) The learning of discriminations by animals. *Endeavour*, **23**, 148–152.

TIZARD, B. (1968a) Observations of over-active imbecile children in controlled and uncontrolled environments: I. Classroom studies. *Amer. J. Ment. Defic.*, **72**, 540–547.

TIZARD, B. (1968b) Observations of over-active imbecile children in controlled and uncontrolled environments: II. Experimental studies. *Amer. J. Ment. Defic.*, **72**, 548–553.

TIZARD, B. (1968c) Habituation of E.E.G. and skin potential changes in normal and severely subnormal children. *Amer. J. Ment. Defic.*, **73**, 34–40.

TIZARD, B. (1968d) A controlled study of all-night sleep in over-active imbecile children. *Amer. J. Ment. Defic.*, **73**, 209–213.

TIZARD, J. (1960) Residential care of mentally handicapped children. *Brit. med. J.*, **i**, 1041–1046.

TIZARD, J. (1964) *Community Services for the Mentally Handicapped*. London: Oxford Univ. Press.

TIZARD, J. and GRAD, J. G. (1961) *The Mentally Handicapped and their Families*. London: Oxford Univ. Press.

TIZARD, J. and LOOS, F. M. (1954) The learning of a spatial relations test by adult imbeciles. *Amer. J. Ment. Defic.*, **59**, 85–90.

TIZARD, J., RAYNES, N. V., KING, R. D., and KUSHLICK, A. (1968) Symposium: residential care for the mentally retarded. *Proc. First Congr. Internat. Assoc. Scient. Stud. Ment. Defic.*, 632–653. Reigate: Michael Jackson.

TULVING, E. (1962) Subjective organization in free recall of 'unrelated' words. *Psychol. Rev.*, **69**, 344–354.

TULVING, E. (1964) Intratrial and intertrial retention: notes towards a theory of free-recall verbal learning. *Psychol. Rev.*, **71**, 219–237.

TULVING, E. (1966) Subjective organization and effects of repetition in multi-trial free-recall learning. *J. Verb. Learn. Verb. Behav.*, **5**, 193–197.

TURNURE, J. and ZIGLER, E. (1964) Outer-directedness in the problem solving of normal and retarded children. *J. Abnorm. (Soc.) Psychol.*, **69**, 427–436.

UNDERWOOD, B. J. (1954) Speed of learning and amount retained: a consideration of methodology. *Psychol. Bull.*, **51**, 276–282.

UNDERWOOD, B. J. (1964) Degree of learning and the measurement of forgetting. *J. Verb. Learn. Verb. Behav.*, **3**, 112–129.

VAN DER VEEN, C. (1967) Verbalization of associative learning strategies among educable retardates and normal children. *Unpublished paper presented at the 91st Ann. Conven. Amer. Assoc. on Ment. Defic.*, Denver, Colo.

VERGASON, G. A. (1964) Retention in retarded and normal subjects as a function of amount of original learning. *Amer. J. Ment. Defic.*, **68**, 623–629.

VOGEL, W. and BROVERMAN, D. M. (1964) Relationship between E.E.G. and test intelligence: a critical review. *Psychol. Bull.*, **62**, 132–144.

VOGEL, W. and BROVERMAN, D. M. (1966) A reply to 'Relationship between E.E.G. and test intelligence: a commentary'. *Psychol. Bull.*, **65**, 99–109.

VOGEL, W., KUN, K. J., MESHORER, E., BROVERMAN, D. M., and KLAIBER, E. L. (1969) The behavioral significance of E.E.G. abnormality in mental defectives. *Amer. J. Ment. Defic.*, **74**, 62–68.

WATSON, L. S. (1967) Application of operant conditioning techniques to institutionalized severely and profoundly retarded children. *Ment. Retard. Abstrs.*, **4**, 1–18.

WATSON, L. S. and LAWSON, R. (1966) Instrumental learning in mental retardates. *Ment. Retard. Abstrs.*, **3**, 1–20.

WIESEN, A. E. and WATSON, E. (1967) Elimination of attention seeking behavior in a retarded child. *Amer. J. Ment. Defic.*, **72**, 50–52.

WINTERS, J. J. (1965) Gamma movement: a comparison of normals and retardates. *Amer. J. Ment. Defic.*, **69**, 697–702.

WINTERS, J. J. (1969) A comparison of normals and retardates on physiological and experiential visual illusions. *Amer. J. Ment. Defic.*, **73**, 956–962.

WINTERS, J. J. and GERJUOY, I. R. (1965) Gamma movement: field brightness, series, and side of the standard. *Psychon. Sci.*, **2**, 273–274.

WINTERS, J. J. and GERJUOY, I. R. (1967) Gamma movement: a comparison of normals and retardates under several temporal conditions. *Amer. J. Ment. Defic.*, **71**, 542–545.

WISCHNER, G. J., BRAUN, H. W., and PATTON, R. A. (1962) Acquisition and long-term retention of an object quality learning set by retarded children. *J. Comp. Physiol. Psychol.*, **55**, 518–523.

WOLFENSBERGER, W. and O'CONNOR, N. (1965) Stimulus intensity and duration effects on E.E.G. and G.S.R. responses of normals and retardates. *Amer. J. Ment. Defic.*, **70**, 21–37.

WOLFENSBERGER, W., MEIN, R., and O'CONNOR, N. (1963) A study of the oral vocabularies of severely subnormal patients. *J. Ment. Defic. Res.*, **7**, 38–45.

WORLD HEALTH ORGANIZATION (1954) *The Mentally Subnormal Child, Wld. Hlth. Org. Techn. Rep. Ser. No. 75.* Geneva: W.H.O.

WORLD HEALTH ORGANIZATION (1967) *Manual of the International Statistical Classification of Diseases, Injuries, and Causes of Death, 1965. Revision.* Geneva.

WORLD HEALTH ORGANIZATION (1968) *Organization of Services for the Mentally Retarded,* 15th Report of the W.H.O. Expert Committee on Mental Health. *Wld. Hlth. Org. Techn. Rep. Ser.,* No. 392. Geneva: W.H.O.

WORLD HEALTH ORGANIZATION (1969) *Genetic Counselling,* 3rd Report of the W.H.O. Expert Committee on Human Genetics. *Wld. Hlth. Org. Techn. Rep. Ser. No. 416.* Geneva: W.H.O.

WORTERS, A. R. (1968) Subnormality—terminology and prevalence. In *Modern Trends in Mental Health and Subnormality* (Ed. G. O'Gorman) London: Butterworths.

ZEAMAN, D. (1965) Learning processes of the mentally retarded. In *The Biosocial Basis of Mental Retardation* (Ed. S. F. Osler and R. E. Cooke) Baltimore: Johns Hopkins Press.

ZEAMAN, D. and HOUSE, B. J. (1963) The rôle of attention in retardate discrimination learning. In *Handbook of Mental Deficiency* (Ed. N. R. Ellis) New York: McGraw-Hill.

ZIGLER, E. (1966) Research on personality structure in the retardate. In *International Review of Research in Mental Retardation,* Vol. 1 (Ed. N. R. Ellis) New York: Academic Press.

ZIGLER, E. (1967) Familial mental retardation: a continuing dilemma. *Science,* **155**, 292–298.

ZIGLER, E. (1969) Developmental versus difference theories of mental retardation and the problem of motivation. *Amer. J. Ment. Defic.,* **73**, 536–556.

PART TWO
Experimental Studies of Abnormal Behaviour

PART TWO

8

Abnormalities of Psychomotor Functions

AUBREY J. YATES

I. INTRODUCTION

Interest in the psychomotor functioning of abnormal subjects should not be confused with interest in psychomotor abilities (Guilford, 1958). In examining reaction time in schizophrenics, for example, the experimenter is not concerned with the subject's *skill* in lifting his finger off the key (any more than in an eyeblink conditioning experiment the interest lies in the subject's ability to blink). It is, in fact, implicitly assumed in many psychomotor studies that all subjects are equal in their ability as far as the motor act itself is concerned. Psychomotor tests are used rather as a means of measuring the *speed* and *accuracy* of central functioning. Interest lies in what goes on *between* the objective onset of the stimulus (e.g. the light in an RT experiment) and the objectively observed motor response (e.g. lifting the finger). Even where records of complex psychomotor responses have been analysed (e.g. Luria, 1932; Davis, 1948), it has been assumed that disorganised responses do not indicate impairment of the motor system itself (such as might follow on injury to the motor cortex) but rather some kind of central disorganisation which is *reflected* in the motor response.

A large variety of psychomotor tasks have been used in attempts to elucidate the nature of the supposed deficit in various categories of abnormality. In this section, examples of the range of tasks used will be given, without any attempt at an exhaustive classification. Then dimensional problems of psychomotor performance will be considered, followed by a brief discussion of the problem of learning in psychomotor performance.

A. Types of Psychomotor Tests

Four broad types of psychomotor tests may be distinguished: (*a*) those involving the measurement of general speed of responding in a given situation involving a motor response; (*b*) those involving a specific response to a discrete stimulus; (*c*) those involving a complex motor response; (*d*) those involving a continuous motor response where speed is not a factor. The categories are purely arbitrary and some tests included in one category could equally well have been included in another.

1. GENERAL SPEED OF RESPONDING

In this category may be included such tests as the Trail-Making test (Alvarez, 1962) in which S is required to connect randomly distributed numbers or letters in their correct sequential order; the Digit Symbol test (Beck *et al.*, 1964); dotting tests (Rafi, 1960), and so on. Payne and Hewlett (1960) have derived a number of motor speed scores from tests not usually considered as psychomotor tests. These measures may be considered as measuring the general speed of functioning of abnormal subjects and, as pointed out above, are primarily intended as measures of rate of central processing, rather than of motor speed as such. Thus, if a patient is excessively slow in writing the phrase 'United States of America', it is assumed that his slow motor performance is not due to motor impairment as such but rather to central events (not related to impairment of the motor cortex area) which result in slow motor performance. Under this category may also be

261

included the classical cancellation test and the tapping test.

Of special interest are the fluency tests which involve the rate of production of verbal responses, either in free form or in response to a specific instruction (e.g. all birds beginning with a particular letter). Several fluency factors have been identified. Rogers (1953) found a general factor of fluency which he identified as 'g' plus Vernon's 'v-ed' factor, as well as two additional orthogonal factors (*oral* fluency and *written* fluency). Rim (1955) suggested the existence of two further factors. One of these defined three tests of oral verbal fluency where relatively less constriction is given in the instructions (this factor appears to be equivalent to Rogers's oral fluency factor). The other defined three tests of oral verbal fluency, where more constriction is given in the instructions, and appears also to be similar to one found by Rogers which he defined as 'dealing with words in which one or more formal restrictions were placed on the responses'. This factor, however, cuts across the factors of oral and written fluency, since Rogers's study showed that it was defined by both oral and written tests.

2. SPECIFIC RESPONSE TO A DISCRETE STIMULUS

Under this category may be listed the study of simple and complex reaction time; cancellation; and the kind of tests used by Davis (1946a, 1946b, 1947, 1948, 1949a, 1949b).

(a) Reaction Time (RT)

The RT test has perhaps been more frequently used in the study of psychomotor function in abnormal subjects than any other test. The methodology of RT studies has, however, varied so widely as to make direct comparison between different studies often very difficult.

Thus, the investigator may require a specific response to a specific stimulus (simple RT) or a choice among several possible responses depending on which of several stimuli occurs (choice RT). The interval between successive stimuli may be short or long, regular or irregular. The stimulus may or may not be preceded by a 'ready' signal; and the stimulus or 'ready' signal may be visual, auditory, or in some other modality. The type of response required may vary from pressing a key to releasing it, to moving it from one point to another. The musculature involved may be the hand (left or right) or the foot (left or right) or even some other part of the body.

Research with abnormal groups has, however, in recent years, tended to make increasing use of the methodology developed by Shakow and his colleagues. The stimulus (usually a sound, but sometimes a light) to which a response is required is presented at regular or irregular intervals after a warning signal. When the regular interval is used, there will be a number of succesive trials for each interval (the intervals being of the order of 1, 2, 4, 7·5, 15, and 25 seconds), each set of trials for a given interval being completed before the next interval is started. The inter-trial interval is usually of the order of 5 seconds and the interseries interval usually of the order of one minute. Thus, within each group of trials the subject knows, after the first trial, how much time will elapse before the next stimulus appears. In the irregular system, however, the interval between the warning signal and the appearance of the stimulus is varied randomly within each block of trials in such a way that each interval is presented an equal number of times. Thus, the subject does not know, for any given trial, how much time will elapse between the occurrence of the warning signal and the appearance of the stimulus. The Shakow technique has been used both with and without drugs, and with sound or light as the stimulus. Simple RT is usually measured in preference to choice RT, presumably because choice RT is considered too difficult a situation for many patients.

Other investigators (e.g. Hall and Stride, 1954; King, 1954) have used simple RT with a standard interval (5 seconds) with no warning signal, or delayed RT with a long interval (10 seconds) but with a warning signal.

(b) Cancellation

The cancellation test is a classic example of a psycho-motor task. It is clearly analogous to a choice RT test in that the subject is required to respond only to certain stimuli with specified characteristics and ignore all other stimuli. The task also involves the use of irregular intervals between relevant stimuli.

(c) Control Movements

Davis (1946a, 1946b, 1947, 1948, 1949a, 1949b) used a simulated cockpit in which instruments on a panel respond realistically to movements of the controls; and an apparatus in which a pointer can be moved to a given position to the right or left of a start point. The techniques permit the observation of two types of error: those involving over-reaction; and those involving inertia. Overactive errors involve large scores on control movements, excessive responses to instrument deviations, and frequent overcorrection. Errors of inertia, on the other hand, involve errors that are large and of long duration, whereas activity, as represented by control movement scores, is relatively small.

3. COMPLEX MOTOR RESPONSES

Here may be considered the use of the Luria technique; mirror-drawing; and manual and finger dexterity.

(a) The Luria Technique

This method was developed by Luria (1932) based on the original work of Nunberg (1918) who had combined Jung's Word Association test with measurements of hand movement at the time of, and between, verbal movements. The underlying rationale is that the internal conflict believed to occur when S is required to respond to an emotionally disturbing stimulus will be reflected in motor movements. Four types of dependent variables have been measured. Reaction-time measures include time of verbal response; time of manual response; and variability of time of response. Measurement of the right-hand response (usually a voluntarily produced response requested of S at the time of responding verbally) involves assessment of its regularity, duration, and height. In addition, the number of disturbances, and double depressions, and the omission of depressions may be recorded. A composite measure based on the three largest, minus the three shortest responses may be computed. Rather similar measures may be applied to the left-hand response (usually made involuntarily, both at the time of, and between, the voluntary right-hand responses). Finally, Eysenck (S. B. G., 1955) has measured the length of the base line, i.e. the actual length of the record.

Little attention has been paid to the degree of relationship between these dependent variables. Malmo *et al.* (1951), and others, have produced evidence indicating low positive correlations between left- and right-hand disturbance, but no correlation between amount of motor disturbance and speed of response.

(b) Mirror Drawing

This test is so well known as scarcely to require description. It involves essentially the production of a discrepancy between kinaesthetic feedback from the motor movements involved in drawing and visual feedback from the same movements, the latter being distorted by being perceived in a mirror rather than by direct vision.

(c) Manual and Finger Dexterity

Manual dexterity tests involve more gross motor movements than finger dexterity tests. In the former case, S may be required to handle relatively large objects; in the latter case, very small objects must be manipulated.

4. CONTINUOUS MOTOR RESPONSE TESTS

Under this heading may be considered static ataxia, body sway, rail-walking, finger tremor, perseveration, persistence, and work decrement.

(a) Static Ataxia

In this test, S is told to stand still and relax, with the eyes closed and the hands hanging down the side, feet together. A trial usually lasts for 30 seconds and the score is the maximum sway, either forward or backward.

(b) Rail-Walking

This test, as devised by Heath (1942), employs two nine-foot long rails (one four inches, and one two inches, wide), and one six-foot long rail (one inch wide). The test is given in an untimed form, S being required to walk along the rail in his stockinged feet. It was extensively standardised by Heath (1942, 1944, 1949) who found it to have a high reliability.

Static ataxia, rail-walking, and body sway (*see* below) tests may be regarded as measures of equilibrium and may be given with or without suggestions that Ss balance will be disturbed (in which case they are used as measures of suggestibility, though rail-walking does not actually appear to have been used in this way). Recently, Graybiel and Fregly (1966) have developed a new battery of ataxia tests which include both rail-walking, with eyes open, on each of six rails of varying length; and standing still, with eyes open or closed, on a rail. Standardised data for large numbers of Ss have been provided. The importance of adequate standardisation data against which to assess the performance of abnormal Ss is shown in a second study by Fregly and Graybiel (1968) who also developed a new set of ataxia tests not requiring the use of rails. The four tests for which data are provided consist of the Sharpened Romberg (SR) test in which S stands with eyes closed for 60 seconds; the Stand On One Leg Eyes Closed (SOLEC) test, with a time period of 30 seconds; the Walk A Line, Eyes Closed (WALEC) test, the distance walked being 12 feet; and the Walk on Floor, Eyes Closed (WOFEC) test. The standardisation data indicated a severe decline in performance as a function of age; and a significant sex difference at all age levels, with females inferior in performance to males.

(c) Body Sway (Suggestibility)

In this test, S stands with his eyes closed and is subjected to verbal suggestions that he is falling forward. The resulting sway may be forwards or backwards (or both) and a few Ss may actually fall over. The interesting methodological problems involved in the use of this test have been fully discussed by Eysenck and Furneaux (1945). The question whether a factor of motor suggestibility exists was investigated by Eysenck (1943) who used eight tests of suggestibility and factor-analysed the resulting correlations, with results shown in Table 8.1.

Table 8.1.   Factor Analysis of Eight Tests of Suggestibility

Test	Loadings Factor I	Factor II
1. Weights (personal)	+0·509	−0·371
2. Lines (personal)	+0·772	−0·002
3. Weights (impersonal)	+0·558	+0·048
4. Lines (impersonal)	+0·386	+0·016
5. Pendulum	+0·094	+0·386
6. Body Sway	−0·041	+0·623
7. Levitation up	−0·194	+0·370
8. Levitation down	−0·100	+0·546
(*Source:* Eysenck, 1943)		

The analysis identified a clear-cut factor defined by tests of the ideomotor type, that is, by psychomotor tests in which a motor movement is executed by S following the repeated suggestion of E that such a movement will take place, without conscious participation in the movement by S. The body sway test most clearly defines this factor. According to Eysenck (1943) the main characteristics of primary suggestibility (as he named this factor) are as follows:

(i) It is distributed in the experimental population as a U-curve, this, however, being an artefact of the method of measurement (Eysenck and Furneaux, 1945).

(ii) It correlates in a significantly nonlinear way with intelligence (Ss of average intelligence being most suggestible).

(iii) It may manifest itself as a positive or negative response to suggestion.

(iv) It is a highly reliable phenomenon.

A recent review of the literature on suggestibility in the normal waking state (Evans, 1967) concluded that more recent research has not cast serious doubt on the validity of Eysenck's demonstration of a factor of primary suggestibility (which Evans prefers to call 'passive motor suggestibility').

(d) Finger Tremor

In this type of test, the intention is to measure the amount of involuntary movement that appears when the finger, hand, arm, or body as a whole is held as motionless as possible. The difference between this type of test and static ataxia tests lies in the conscious effort on the part of S to hold the body part still. Its correlation with static ataxia and body sway tests is not known.

(e) Perseveration*

Perseveration has been defined in various ways. Thus, Cameron and Caunt (1933) define it in behavioural terms as 'the tendency for an activity to persist after the subject has decided to change that activity, this persistence in the primary activity being shown by a transitory interference with the new activity which follows it' and a similar definition was given by Kleemeier and Dudek (1950) and by Scheier and Ferguson (1952). On the other hand, Jasper (1931) invoked central processes, defining it as 'the tendency of a set of neurones, once excited, to persist in the state of excitation autonomously, showing resistance to any change in this state'.

The concept of perseveration derives originally from the work of Gross (1902) who distinguished between primary and secondary function. The intensity of the primary function would determine how long it would perseverate after the stimulus had been removed, whereas secondary function referred to the duration of the response. An intense primary response would be followed by a long secondary function, a weak primary response by a short secondary response.

Secondary function may manifest itself in four ways: by the perseveration of a response after the stimulus has ceased; by the spontaneous reappearance of a response after the original stimulus and response have ceased; by the interference of a first response with a subsequent response; and by the interference of an habitual response to a new response required to the same stimulus.

Stephenson (1934) had defined three different kinds of perseveration tests (alternation; creative

---

* The previous version of this chapter included a very detailed review of the literature relating to the dimensional analysis of perseveration. Since in the intervening period of ten years interest has shifted from the study of perseveration to the study of rigidity (Leach, 1967), the present account has been considerably curtailed. For the earlier studies, *see* Yates (1960, p. 44–48).

effort; and direct). Cattell (1946a) intercorrelated scores on a large number of such tests and distinguished two perseveration factors. The first of these he named 'inertia of mental processes', shown in alternation tests, perseveration manifesting itself by the interference of one activity on the other, and vice versa. The second he named 'disposition rigidity' shown in creative effort tasks in which S has to substitute a new activity for a more customary one. Subsequent studies have tended to confirm Cattell's argument that disposition rigidity is a motor perseveration factor (e.g. Jasper, 1931; Notcutt, 1943; Rethlingshafer, 1942; Rim, 1955; Scheier and Ferguson, 1952) and that the factor he called 'inertia of mental processes' may be an artefact of scoring technique. In any event, it seems clear that perseveration factors play a relatively small part in those tests commonly called tests of perseveration (Rim, 1955), a claim that has been empirically substantiated by Scheier and Ferguson (1952).

(f) Persistence

Like perseveration, persistence tests have been subjected to a great deal of analysis in an effort to discover whether a general factor of persistence can be demonstrated or not. Much of the work has been inconclusive and unsatisfactory* but on the whole appears to point to the existence of a general factor. The existence of a trait of motor persistence seems to be well documented, however. Thornton (1939) described a factor of 'ability and/or willingness to withstand discomfort in order to achieve a goal' with high loadings on 'time holding breath', 'time standing shock', 'time standing pressure' and 'maintained hand grip'. MacArthur (1951) described a factor of persistence defined by a group of physical tests—leg persistence (time foot is held over and just clear of a chair), maintained hand grip (dynamometer test), time of holding breath, and arm extension.

(g) Work Decrement

The 'curve of work' (Thorndike, 1912) (i.e. the changes occurring in performance under conditions of prolonged performance of mental or physical work) has mediated a large amount of research on normal subjects. The work studied may be either physical in nature (e.g. ergographic) or 'mental' (e.g. continual addition, naming colours, etc.). Among the major trends noted in the objective work curve are: (a) warm-up effect; (b) practice effect; (c) spurts and rhythms; (d) general (work) decrement;

* For an excellent review of persistence see Eysenck (1960) or Feather (1962).

(e) blocking. The two latter phenomena are of particular importance. Work decrement refers to the decline in amount of work done per unit time during a period of continuous practice. Blocking refers to temporary complete stoppages of work under the same conditions of practice. Such blockages and work decrements have been observed in both physical and mental work, but are more easily observed in the former since the phenomena appear to be directly related to the lack of rest pauses. Such rest pauses are naturally more common in 'continuous' physical work than in 'continuous' mental work. However, under appropriate conditions of forced continuous mental work (such as naming colours) the involuntary blockages can be readily observed.

Both phenomena have been considered to be functions of fatigue induced by continuous work. Blockings could be obviated by enforcing rest pauses at about the same rate; while they could be increased by making the material more homogeneous. Thus, where conditions of work were most homogeneous, the average blocks per minute were 2·1; where they were least homogeneous, only 1·4 per minute (Robinson and Bills, 1926).

B The Dimensional Problem

The question of the existence of a general factor of 'psychomotility' (King, 1961) has received a good deal of attention. The earlier studies suggested that specificity of psychomotor function existed and this has been largely confirmed by subsequent factor analytic work. For example, the analysis of 38 psychomotor tests by Fleishman (1954) produced ten independent group factors which are listed in Table 8.2. It is apparent that each factor defines a very narrow range of abilities. The wrist-finger factor, for example, is defined primarily by two simple tapping tests, while the reaction-time factor is defined by visual and auditory RT only. The intercorrelation of these four tests shows clearly that

Table 8.2. Some Psychomotor Factors Identified by Factor Analysis

I. Wrist-finger speed
II. Finger dexterity
III. Rate of arm movement
IV. Aiming
V. Arm-hand steadiness
VI. Reaction-time
VII. Manual dexterity
VIII. Psychomotor speed
IX. Psychomotor coordination
X. Spatial relations

(*Source:* Fleishman, 1954)

proficiency in RT bears little relationship to proficiency in tapping—a surprising finding in view of
the apparent simplicity of the two tasks, which
appear to be measures of simple motor speed.

However, the factors isolated by Fleishman should
not be regarded as definitive. The first factor in an
unrotated solution usually accounts for about 25 per
cent of the total variance, indicating a general factor
is present in psychomotor performance and it is
apparent that the factors obtained in such analyses
depend on the nature of the tests included in the
analysis. Thus, Seashore and colleagues (1940)
factor-analysed a rather different group of 21 tests
and isolated five factors which they designated:
speed of single reaction; finger, hand, and forearm
speed in restricted oscillatory movement; forearm
and hand speed in oscillatory movements of moderate
extent; steadiness or precision; and skill in manipulating spatial relations. The first factor was
defined by four RT tests, horizontal tapping, and
rotation of speed drill, in contrast with Fleishman,
who found tapping and RT to define independent
factors. King (1961) identified three distinct factors
in psychomotor tasks involving fine movements:
time to initiate response (e.g. reaction time); speed
of maintaining ongoing responses (e.g. tapping); and
speed of carefully controlled movements (e.g. finger
dexterity). The existence of a general psychomotor
speed factor was confirmed by Birren et al. (1962)
who factor analysed (by the principal components
method) 22 tasks ranging from simple movement
and reaction time to numbers, letters, colours,
symbols, and word relationships. In a young group
of subjects, the first factor accounted for 29 per cent
of the total variance; whereas, in elderly subjects it
accounted for 44 per cent of the total variance.

A second major problem arises from the fact that
correlations between scores on psychomotor tasks
tend to be significantly higher in abnormal groups.
This difference was clearly shown in a study by
Shapiro and Nelson (1955) who correlated scores on
a number of simple motor speed tests of the Babcock
series on which no errors were made. The results are

Table 8.3.   Number of Significant Correlations Between
Error-Free Speed Tests
(Total number of correlations in each sample = 45)

Sample	5 per cent level $r = 0.44$ to 0.55	1 per cent level $r > 0.56$
Normals	3	1
Schizophrenics	8	19
Manic-depressives	3	22
Organics	8	12
Neurotics	9	13

(*Source:* Shapiro and Nelson, 1955)

shown in Table 8.3. That the explanation of the
difference is not an artefact due to a restriction of
range of scores in normal subjects is shown quite
clearly by data available from Fleishman's (1954)
study in which the spread of scores of normal
subjects is quite satisfactory for correlation purposes.
Furthermore, Birren et al. (1962), in the study
already referred to, found that the correlations
between psychomotor speed tests were generally
higher in their elderly subjects as compared with
their younger subjects. The difference would appear
to reflect the general tendency of abnormality to
produce more uniform performance relative to other
subjects.

C Learning, Motivation, and Psychomotor Performance

The role of learning in psychomotor performance is a
somewhat neglected problem. Factor analytic
studies of psychomotor tests (e.g. Fleishman, 1954;
Guilford, 1958) have included both simple measures
in which learning, if it occurs at all, is minimal, and
much more complex tasks in which a good deal of
learning is clearly involved. Thus, the factorial
structure of psychomotor *performance* may be
confounded by the uncontrolled effects of *learning*,
where several trials are given; and, indeed, Fleishman
and Hempel (1954) showed that the factorial
composition of psychomotor tests was significantly
altered as function of practice. In general, however,
it has been assumed that learning is unimportant in
psychomotor performance, since the tasks involved
are so simple that the subject performs at his
optimal level right from the start. King (1954) has
shown that this assumption is false, even for such
tasks as simple tapping and dexterity tests. The
importance of this demonstration, of course, lies in
the possibility that abnormal *S*s may perform
initially at a very low level compared with normal
control groups but may show a higher rate of
learning so that their final level of performance is
much closer to that of the controls. Alternatively, of
course, the improvement with practice in abnormal
groups may be a function rather of change of
motivation. Shakow, in particular, has concerned
himself with this problem, and has repeatedly
pointed out that differences between normal and
abnormal groups in performance may result from
motivational deficiencies (whether these result from
the abnormality *per se* or from ancillary factors such
as length of hospitalisation resulting in apathy)
rather than cognitive or other factors often put
forward in explanation of the differences. Failure to
take account of such factors may well account for

some of the contradictory results found in studies of normal and abnormal groups on psychomotor tests, particularly where the comparisons involve the use of psychotic patients.

II. PSYCHOMOTOR PERFORMANCE OF PSYCHOTICS

The empirical results obtained will be considered first. Theoretical models to account for these results will be confined to those relating to schizophrenia since nearly all theoretical accounts have been directed towards this aim.

A Empirical Results

1. REACTION TIME (RT)

The results obtained with the methods described in Section I present a somewhat confused picture but the following results would seem to be relatively clear-cut.

(a) Undifferentiated schizophrenic groups are significantly slower than depressives and neurotics (Hall and Stride, 1954); normals (Huston et al., 1937; Huston and Singer, 1945; Rodnick and Shakow, 1940; Tizard and Venables, 1956); and defectives (Tizard and Venables, 1956).

(b) Chronic schizophrenics are significantly slower than acute schizophrenics, depressives, and neurotics (Huston and Senf, 1952) and normals (King, 1954) on both simple and complex RT (Benton et al., 1959). Chronic psychotics are poorer than acute psychotics on a complex RT test (Windle and Hamwi, 1953; King, 1954).

(c) Acute schizophrenics are not significantly slower than depressives, but are significantly slower than neurotics (Huston and Senf, 1952).

(d) The difference between chronic schizophrenics and hospitalised normal controls is greater for simple RT than for complex RT (Benton et al., 1959).

(e) Neurotics are significantly faster than depressives (Hall and Stride, 1954; Huston and Senf, 1952), chronic and acute schizophrenics (Huston and Senf, 1952).

(f) Depressives are not significantly different from normals if the groups are matched for age (Hall and Stride, 1954).

The one consistently clear-cut result seems to be that chronic schizophrenics have consistently been found to be significantly slower than all other psychiatric groups, and than normals, except where a simple reflex reaction with minimal central processing involved (such as the patellar tendon reflex) is concerned (Huston, 1935).

Certain other characteristics of RT have been investigated also. Thus, schizophrenics show more inter- and intraindividual variability in their RT responses than do normals (Benton et al., 1959; Huston et al., 1937; Huston and Senf, 1952; Huston and Singer, 1945; King, 1954; Knehr, 1954; Rodnick and Shakow, 1940; Tizard and Venables, 1956), this increased variability being shown both under normal testing conditions and under the influence of drugs.

These early results led to a series of important studies by Shakow and his colleagues in which RT was evaluated as a function of preparatory interval (PI), preceding preparatory interval (PPI) and whether a regular or irregular procedure in presentation of the stimulus was used. Thus, Rodnick and Shakow (1940) showed that, with a short PI, the irregular procedure leads to a longer RT than does the regular procedure (for the same intervals). With longer intervals, the pattern is reversed, the change in behaviour apparently occurring somewhere between a PI of 4 seconds and 7·5 seconds. The results of one study with chronic schizophrenics and normals are shown in Table 8.4.

Table 8.4. Change in RT under Varying Preparatory Intervals for Regular and Irregular Procedures in Normals and Schizophrenics

Intervals (seconds)	Regular procedure mean Milliseconds	Irregular procedure mean Milliseconds
A. 25 Schizophrenics		
1	668·7	722·5
2	544·4	665·6
4	531·0	619·5
7·5	648·5	583·0
15	639·3	587·9
25	653·5	560·8
B. 10 Normal controls		
1	262·7	315·2
2	239·2	290·7
4	261·1	296·6
7·5	275·5	303·6
15	278·1	296·0
25	312·3	305·3

(Source: Rodnick and Shakow, 1940)

These findings were confirmed by Tizard and Venables (1956) and in subsequent studies by Shakow and his colleagues.* An interesting feature of the data in Table 8.4 relates to the consistently

* Similar findings with schizophrenic children have been reported by Czudner and Marshall (1967).

faster RT found for longer PIs under the irregular procedure in the schizophrenic, but not in the normal group. This finding has also been replicated and led to a study by Zahn *et al.* (1963) in which two experiments were performed. In both, the irregular procedure was used with PIs of 1, 2, 4, 7·5, 15, and 25 seconds (in the first experiment) and 1, 2, 4, 7, and 15 seconds (in the second experiment). The main difference between the two experiments was the omission of the ready signal in the second, the PI being initiated by *S*s pressing the reaction key (the response required was lift RT). The data were analysed to assess the effect of the PPI on RT and it was found that a PPI equal to or shorter than the PI to the stimulus evoking the response produced a faster RT whereas the reverse was the case when the PPI was longer than the PI. This effect was significantly greater in the schizophrenic than in the control group. In a second study, Zahn and his colleagues (1961), using the regular procedure, showed that a single series of long PIs produce effects on RT that carry over into short PIs. Zahn and co-workers (1961) showed that the slowing down effects on RT of long PIs with the regular procedure are not a function of the slower rate of stimulation produced by long PIs. They varied both PI and intertrial interval (ITI) and found that the PI effect remained constant as ITI varied.

All the above studies were carried out on chronic schizophrenics. Zahn and Rosenthal (1965) used the regular and irregular PI procedures to compare RT performance in chronic and acute schizophrenics. The results, shown in Fig. 8.1 for the acute schizophrenics and controls only, indicate that the same features are apparent for the acute schizophrenics as had previously been demonstrated for chronic schizophrenics, though to a less marked degree. The acute schizophrenics performed overall at a superior level to the chronic schizophrenics.

2. SIMPLE SPEED TESTS

Babcock (1930, 1933) demonstrated that performance on a number of simple speed tests was significantly impaired in schizophrenics, and this finding has been repeatedly confirmed, most notably in a large-scale study by Payne and Hewlett (1960). They compared the performance of carefully selected groups of normal controls, neurotics (hysterics and dysthymics), endogeneous depressives, and acute schizophrenics on a number of such tests. The principal results for the motor speed tests they used are shown in Table 8.5. In general, the acute schizophrenics were significantly slower than the other groups with the exception of the depressives who tended to be slower still. A group of chronic

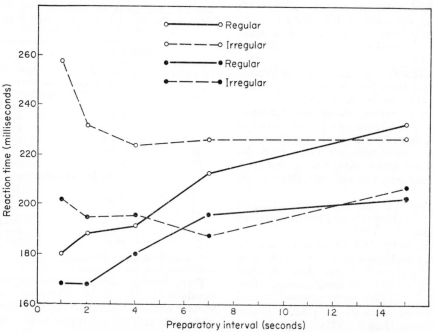

Fig. 8.1. Median RT at each PI under regular and irregular procedures for acute schizophrenic and nonschizophrenic Ss (*Source:* Zahn and Rosenthal, 1965)

Table 8.5. Comparative Performance of Four Groups on Motor Speed Tests

Test	Normals	Dysthymics	Mean Scores Hysterics	Depressives	Schizophrenics	Significance
Writing USA	1·35	3·00	2·14	3·00	2·95	<0·05
Writing Sentence	2·25	3·42	3·14	3·65	3·30	<0·05
Writing Name	2·45	4·25	4·00	4·35	4·95	<0·01
Substitution Test	2·25	2·75	2·38	4·55	3·90	<0·01
3-Squares Test	1·10	2·25	2·43	2·84	3·25	<0·01

(*Source:* Payne and Hewlett, 1960)

schizophrenics would be expected to be at least as slow as the depressives, if not slower.

3. TAPPING

Shakow and Huston (1936) found that psychotics were significantly slower in tapping rate than normals (with schizophrenics slower than manic-depressives within the psychotic group). This finding was confirmed by King (1954) for chronic schizophrenics as compared with both normals and neurotics. S. B. G. Eysenck (1955) found that while individual left- or right-hand scores did not differentiate between normals, neurotics, and psychotics, the latter were slower than either of the other two groups on a combined score. Wulfeck (1941), however, found no differences in tapping speed between normals, schizophrenics, depressives, and neurotics, whereas Rafi (1960) did.

4. OTHER MEASURES OF PSYCHOMOTOR PERFORMANCE

Psychotics are significantly less *fluent* than either normals or neurotics (Eysenck, 1952a; Eysenck, S. B. G., 1955). With respect to *perseveration*, although early studies suggested that low 'p' scores were characteristic of manics (e.g. Jones, 1928; Pinard, 1932b; Stephenson, 1932a) while high 'p' scores were characteristic of depressives (Stephenson, 1932a) and schizophrenics (Pinard, 1932b; Stephenson, 1932b), this trait has subsequently been related primarily to differences in neuroticism and introversion-extraversion. More recently, however, Crumpton (1963) found that schizophrenics had more difficulty than normals in shifting from a learned psychomotor response to a new response. There was some evidence that the persistence of the maladaptive response was related to the severity of the disorder. There is relatively weak evidence that psychotics are significantly less *persistent* on dynamometer performance than normals but not neurotics (Eysenck, S. B. G., 1955); but no differences in leg persistence were found between normals and psychotics by Eysenck (1952a).

The study of *work-decrement* in psychotics has received a good deal of attention. Kraepelin (1902) found that the performance of schizophrenics on a simple 10-minute addition test was characterised by rapid deterioration; if a rest was introduced after five minutes, performance increased markedly in the sixth minute, but then deteriorated rapidly again in the remaining four minutes. Hoch (1901), on the other hand, reported that manic-depressives increased in strength of performance on the ergograph in the early stages of performance before showing the usual fatigue effects. Mailloux and Newburger (1941) presented patients with a task involving four coloured lights with corresponding keys. Depression of the appropriate key extinguished a light and activated another. Thus, continuous work was carried on for 10 minutes.* Patients were classified into six groups according to speed and type of response activity. Compared with the normal rate of 72 responses a minute, psychotics averaged a rate of only 52·5, only one psychotic exceeding the normal group's mean score. Psychotics averaged five blocks a minute, compared with three for the normal group. The deficit appeared related to psychosis *per se*, rather than type of psychosis. This study was repeated in its essentials by Venables and Tizard (1956) and O'Connor *et al.* (1956). Venables and Tizard found an initial rise in performance (probably due to practice effects) followed by a fall, a further rise after rest, and subsequent deterioration, in schizophrenics. Long-stay schizophrenics performed consistently below short-stay schizophrenics at all stages of performance. Endogenous depressives were intermediate between the two schizophrenic groups but showed no deterioration in performance, either before or after the rest pauses (however, it should be pointed out that Venables and Tizard did not divide the endogenous depressives into long-stay and short-stay groups and, hence, it is not known whether similar effects would have been found). The rapid work decrement and blockings shown by schizophrenics were also found in a study by Baruk *et al.* (1953).

Since psychotics tend to show impairment on very

* This task is now known as the serial reaction time test.

Table 8.6. Differences Between Normals, Neurotics, and Psychotics on the Luria Test

Variables	Controls (n = 123)	Neurotics (n = 55)	Psychotics (n = 55)	F	p
	M	M	M		
1. *Motor RT*					
No. of delays	22·7	27·0	29·1	16·61	0·001
$\sum$ total delays	112·2	233·3	294·5	20·13	0·001
2. *R-hand Disturbances*					
No. double depressions	2·0	4·7	5·9	11·71	0·001
No. omitted depressions	0·1	0·3	1·8	9·79	0·001
$\sum$ 3 longest—$\sum$ 3 shortest RT	14·2	16·7	18·6	5·21	0·01
3. *L-hand Disturbances*					
No. reversals	8·2	8·4	13·5	4·18	0·01
Max. distance from base line	1·5	1·9	2·2	3·69	0·05
4. Length of baseline	297·9	406·9	503·2	21·74	0·001

(*Source:* S. B. G. Eysenck, 1955)

simple psychomotor tasks, it would be expected that they would show impairment on more complex types of task; and this, indeed, has proved to be the case. On the Luria test, psychotics show at least as much disorganisation as neurotics (Malmo *et al.*, 1951), if not more. A well-controlled study by S. B. G. Eysenck (1955) confirmed this. Using 123 controls, 55 psychotics and 55 neurotics, she obtained the results shown in Table 8.6. From these data she concluded that R-hand disturbance differentiates better than L-hand disturbance and that psychotics show even greater disorganisation than do neurotics. S. B. G. Eysenck (1956) also found that *manual and finger dexterity tests* of the USES battery discriminated psychotics from normals, a finding that has since been replicated by Payne and Hewlett (1960). S. B. G. Eysenck (1955) further demonstrated that psychotics were significantly poorer than either neurotics or normals on five speed measures derived from performance on the *mirror-drawing test*, thus replicating an earlier finding of Eysenck (1952a).

With respect to *static ataxia* and *body sway suggestibility* early studies suggested that catatonic schizophrenics may be negatively suggestible; paranoid schizophrenics positively suggestible; and manics non-suggestible. A careful study by Das and O'Connor (1959) measured amount of both forward and backward sway with static ataxia and body sway instruction conditions in paranoid and non-paranoid patients. They found that the paranoids swayed significantly more under both static ataxia and body sway conditions, but that there was no evidence of a greater tendency in the non-paranoids to sway backwards rather than forwards. Payne and Hewlett (1960), on the other hand, found that maximum

backward sway was greater in acute schizophrenics than in endogenous depressives, neurotics, or normals. With regard to *finger tremor*, it has been found that schizophrenics have significantly greater finger tremor than normals (Edwards and Harris, 1953).

B Theoretical Analysis

The past ten years have witnessed significant advances in theory construction in relation to the psychoses, with most attention being paid to schizophrenia. It is interesting, in this connection, to note that the more recent theories represent a complete about-face by comparison with the most influential theory of ten years ago, that of Kretschmer.

(*a*) The dissociative-integrative hypothesis of Kretschmer mediated a large amount of experimental work over a period of more than twenty years. By dissociation, Kretschmer meant the ability to form separate and partial groupings within a single act of consciousness; from this resulted the ability to dissect complex material into its constituent parts. Normal schizothymes (and schizophrenics) were said to be characterised by dissociative capacity; normal cyclothymes (and manic depressives) by integrative capacity. On the basis of this theory it was predicted that leptosomes* would be superior to pyknics in simultaneous performance

* As Eysenck (1950) points out, Kretschmer tried to show the general validity of the concept of schizothymia-cyclothymia beyond the psychotic realm by using body build as a *tertium quid;* his method of proof was to show that normal people of leptosomatic or pyknic body build react to certain psychological experiences in a manner similar to that of schizophrenes and manic-depressives, who are known to be also leptosomatic or pyknic.

on two tasks such as adding while performing a manual task; motor activities such as manual dexterity, quality of handwriting, bimanual co-ordination, and fine steadiness tests; speed of motor activities such as tapping; and speed of reaction time under distraction.* However, Payne (1955) showed conclusively that the tests used by Kretschmer as measures of the hypothesised trait of dissociation (spaltungsfähigkeit) do not define such a factor. Hence, even if the tests did discriminate between schizophrenics and manic-depressives, it could not be because of the operation of the hypothesised factor. Furthermore, Eysenck (1952a, 1952b) was unable to find evidence of a dimension of cyclo-thymia-schizothymia as demanded by the theory. Not surprisingly, therefore, Kretschmer's theory has received much less attention in the past ten years.

(b) Interest has shifted in recent years to the construction of theoretical models which lay stress on the rate of information processing in psychotics as compared with other patients and normal subjects. These models have taken two main forms, broadly speaking. On the one hand, there are the models that suggest (contrary to Kretschmer's theorising) that schizophrenics are unable to deal adequately with the mass of incoming data, largely because they are unable to screen out irrelevant stimuli and thus find their 'channel capacity' (Broadbent, 1958) overloaded. Studies by Chapman and his colleagues have provided most of the experimental evidence on which such models are based (Chapman and McGhie, 1962, 1963, 1964; Lawson et al., 1964; McGhie and Chapman, 1961; McGhie et al., 1964, 1965a, 1965b). They showed that on some tasks not involving distraction, schizophrenics performed as well as normals, but when attention had to be selective, especially when competing channels were involved, the performance of schizophrenics tended to deteriorate. The capacity for temporal integration, particularly of the reception of speech, tends to break down in schizophrenia.

The inability to screen out irrelevant from relevant incoming data is especially stressed by Chapman and his colleagues. A rather different formulation has recently been advanced by Yates (1966a) who has argued that the fundamental deficit in schizophrenia may be an inability to handle incoming *relevant* data. Yates's model is essentially based on the empirical evidence, reviewed above, that schizophrenics are abnormally slow in their handling of incoming relevant data, a finding first reported many years ago by Babcock (1930, 1933). Yates pointed out that the basic deficit in schizophrenia may lie, not at the highest cortical level, as argued by those who

laid most stress on thought disorder in schizophrenia, nor at the peripheral sensory/perceptual level, but rather at what he called the data-processing level, at which the incoming data is organised (or coded) for presentation to the highest cortical (mediational or cognitive) centres where the coded data is assimilated to the apperceptive mass (to use a term coined by Herbart over a century ago). If breakdown occurs at the data-processing level, then all subsequent operations will be adversely affected (just as an intact motor car engine will function inefficiently if it receives an inadequate supply of fuel).

Yates argued that, if the basic deficit in schizophrenia is the extreme slowness with which incoming relevant data are processed, then it follows that, in terms of Broadbent's (1958) theory of the human operator as having a limited channel capacity, it will be necessary for the schizophrenic to place more material per unit of time into the short-term memory (STM) system. This, in turn, will mean (since the STM has itself a limited capacity and, by definition, can hold material placed in it only for a limited time) that much of the material placed temporarily in the STM will be irretrievably lost, either through its capacity being exceeded, or through loss by decay over time. Hence, in a very real sense, schizophrenics will demonstrate 'a reduced rate of integration in basic conceptual assimilation which thereby deprives higher mental processes of an adequate supply of material to manipulate' (Harwood and Naylor, 1963, p. 35). Thus, in principle, it may be argued that the schizophrenic literally is trying to perform adequately on the basis of incoming information that is randomly interrupted. If this is so, it is not surprising that the highest cortical processes operate inefficiently ('thought disorder') and that eventually disorganised motor responses occur. There is evidence that, where schizophrenics are allowed to control the rate of incoming information, their responses may be greatly improved (Donahoe et al., 1961); and that schizophrenic-like responses may be evoked in normal subjects under increased rates of stimulus presentation (Usdansky and Chapman, 1960).

Similar formulations to those outlined above have been put forward frequently in the past few years. Thus, Moran and colleagues (1964) refer to temporary inaccessibility of essentially normal structures; Payne and co-workers (1963) to a defect in the screening mechanism; and Pishkin and his associates (1962) to a deterioration in channel capacity. Venables (1964) has used the term 'input dysfunction' to summarise the empirical studies he reviewed. Studies by McReynolds (1963) and Sidle et al. (1963) have provided empirical evidence that schizophrenics inhibit the input of novel stimulation,

* For the German literature relating to these predictions, see Eysenck (1950).

a finding in line with Russian work on the role of protective inhibition in schizophrenia (Lynn, 1963). And although Shakow's theory of 'segmental set', advanced to account for his findings on reaction time in schizophrenia, may appear superficially somewhat different, he, too, refers to a failure in the scanning process (Shakow, 1962, 1963).

It is, of course, not yet clear whether the notion of input dysfunction should be applied to the psychoses as a whole; to schizophrenia; or only to chronic schizophrenia. It seems likely that different theoretical models may be required to account for the two basic dimensions of schizophrenia recently delineated—acute/chronic (process/reactive; good/

poor premorbid), on the one hand; paranoid/non-paranoid, on the other (Johannsen et al., 1963). This distinction has thus far received little attention in model building. However, Silverman (1964) has utilised the concepts of scanning control and field-articulation within this framework. He has related extensive scanning and field-articulation responsiveness to the paranoid subtype, while minimal scanning and undifferentiated field-articulation characterise the other dimension. It may be predicted that differential models for the two basic dimensions will receive much more attention in the near future.

III. PSYCHOMOTOR PERFORMANCE OF NEUROTICS

If the existence of a dimension of neuroticism is accepted, then the general empirical results of investigations with psychomotor tests suggest that neurotics show disorganisation of behaviour on such tests, the degree of disorganisation being roughly proportional to the degree of complexity inherent in a particular psychomotor task. The evidence is more striking for some psychomotor tasks than others. These will be dealt with in some detail, with brief mention of other measures.

A. Empirical Results

1. CONTROL MOVEMENTS

Davis (1948) showed that, if responses on his task are classified into three categories (normal, overactive, and inert), only 33 per cent of neurotic pilots showed a normal reaction, compared with 75 per cent of non-neurotic controls; and he confirmed this result in a second study (Davis, 1946b), the percentage of normal responses decreasing with increasing predisposition to neurosis. He concluded from his studies that neurotics tend to make more errors of judgement in this kind of task compared with normals.

2. LURIA TECHNIQUE

It has been shown that R-hand voluntary response is significantly more disturbed in neurotics than in normals (Malmo et al., 1951; Eysenck, S. B. G., 1955), as is L-hand involuntary response (Albino, 1948; Malmo et al., 1951; Eysenck, S. B. G., 1955). Both local and general motor disturbance is greater in neurotics than in normals (Barnacle et al., 1935; Ebaugh, 1936). The principal findings on this test in

S. B. G. Eysenck's study with normals, psychotics, and neurotics, are shown in Table 8.6.

3. MANUAL AND FINGER DEXTERITY

S. B. G. Eysenck (1955) found that parts M, N, O, and P of the USES battery all discriminated significantly between neurotics and normals, confirming the earlier results of Eysenck (1952a). A comparison of the two studies is shown in Table 8.7.

Table 8.7. A Comparison of Two Studies on Manual and Finger Dexterity Tests

| | S. B. G. Eysenck, 1955 | | Eysenck, 1952 | |
| | Controls | Neurotics | Controls | Neurotics |
	M	M	M	M
Part M	75·45	72·62	77·29	71·87
Part N	88·60	86·75	83·06	75·58
Part O	27·76	25·29	26·22	23·60
Part P	25·65	23·95	25·56	22·90
Total	217·36	208·61	212·13	193·95

(Sources: Eysenck, 1952a; S. B. G. Eysenck, 1956)

Tizard and O'Connor (1951) also found that manual and finger dexterity tests had significant loadings on a factor of neuroticism.

4. STATIC ATAXIA AND BODY SWAY

Early studies (reviewed by Eysenck, 1947) suggested that suggestibility is related to neuroticism, and this has been confirmed by empirical results. Using data on 120 normal controls and 1,230 neurotics, Eysenck (1952a) found that 81 per cent of normals swayed less than one inch, compared with only 32 per cent of neurotics on a static ataxia measure. No normals swayed more than two inches, whereas

31 per cent of neurotics did so. In another study on static ataxia, Eysenck (1944) found that four times as many neurotics swayed more than one inch when compared with normals.

Turning to body sway suggestibility, Eysenck (1944) in a study of 110 normals and 110 neurotics, found that 63 per cent of male, and 42 per cent of female neurotics were suggestible compared with only 7 per cent of male, and 8 per cent of female, normal subjects. Sixteen neurotics fell outright, whereas no normal did. The correlation between primary suggestibility and neuroticism was 0·66. Later researches demonstrated a strong correlation between amount of sway and amount of neuroticism. Figure 8.2 shows the average amount of suggestibility on the Body Sway test for six groups of neurotic patients, totalling 960 males and 390 females. It is clear that sway increases with increase in neuroticism.

The large number of subjects used by Eysenck in these studies and the clear-cut nature of the results obtained with respect to the correlation between suggestibility and neuroticism have led to general acceptance of the validity of the relationship formed, though conflicting results (usually based on quite inadequate results) have since been reported (Rickels et al., 1964; Webb and Nesmith, 1964). As will be seen, however, results reported by Furneaux (1961) suggest that the matter may be more complex than it appears. Consideration of Furneaux's results will be deferred to the theoretical section.

5. PERSEVERATION

Pinard (1932a) appeared to relate extreme 'p' scores to neurosis. Thus, in a study on children, he found that 75 per cent of the most difficult and unreliable children were perseverators, while self-controlled children showed only moderate perseveration. These results were confirmed for adult neurotics. Cattell (1946b) found a negative correlation between 'w' and 'p' in neurotics, supporting the earlier finding by Brogden (1940) whose first factor was identified as one of perseveration and was said by Brogden to resemble closely Webb's 'w' factor. This would suggest a relationship between perseveration and neuroticism, since Eysenck (1960) showed that Webb's 'w' factor is the normal pole of a normal/ neuroticism dimension. However, no relationship of this kind was apparent in studies by Rim (1955) and Petrie (1948). It would appear that factors of perseveration are of little importance in defining differences between neurotics and normals.

6. PERSISTENCE

Neurotics are not differentiable from normals on leg persistence tests (Eysenck, 1952a; S. B. G. Eysenck,

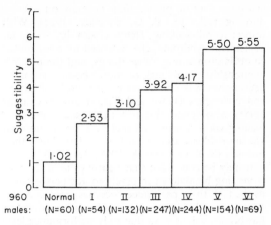

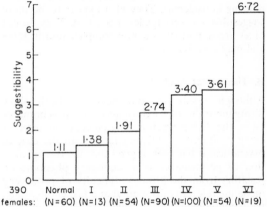

Fig. 8.2. Average suggestibility of normals and neurotics, showing increase in suggestibility correlated with increase in neuroticism (*Source:* Eysenck, 1947)

1955; Himmelweit and Petrie, 1951). A difference in dynamometer persistence was reported by S. B. G. Eysenck (1955). As, however, the neurotics showed a much weaker initial maximum grip, it is possible that this affected their subsequent persistence. Similar results for children were reported by Himmelweit and Petrie (1951). Like perseveration, persistence would appear to be a trait of relatively small significance in delineating differences between neurotics and normals.

7. OTHER PSYCHOMOTOR MEASURES

Reaction-time measures do not appear to discriminate between normals and neurotics though it seems likely that complex RT would do so. Rate of tapping does not discriminate though there is a suggestion that scatter of tapping may do so (Eysenck, 1952a). There is slight evidence that neurotics may be poorer than normals on mirror-drawing tasks (S. B. G. Eysenck, 1955). With respect to rail-walking, Heath (1946) discovered an adjustment syndrome, characterised by poor motor co-ordination among other things, and the possible relationship of this lack of motor co-ordination to neuroticism was confirmed by the work of Tizard and colleagues (1950) and Tizard and O'Connor (1951) who found this test to have a significant loading on a neuroticism factor. There is no convincing evidence that neurotics are less fluent than normals (S. B. G. Eysenck, 1955; Rim, 1955).

It may be concluded that neurotics tend to show increasing breakdown in psychomotor performance as the task to be performed becomes more complex (it is assumed that learning is either not involved or has been maximised so that only performance level is being considered). They also appear to be more suggestible and perhaps less persistent. They do not differ from normals on non-complex motor tasks and may even be superior.

B. Theoretical Analysis

Although psychotics and neurotics both show disorganisation of performance on psychomotor tasks, the disorganisation may be conceptualised as being produced by different factors. In the case of psychotics, it has been argued that the disorganisation of performance is a secondary phenomenon resulting from the primary difficulty of processing incoming relevant information at a fast enough rate, with consequent irretrievable loss of information from the short-term memory system. The theoretical model developed to account for the performance of neurotics on psychomotor tasks may best be put forward as a number of relatively well-supported empirical statements:

1. Efficiency of performance on a psychomotor task is a function of drive interacting with task complexity. High drive facilitates performance when the task is of low complexity, but interferes with performance when the task is of high complexity. Drive is here defined as lability of the autonomic nervous system; complexity is defined in terms of the number of competing responses available, with the correct response being low in the response hierarchy.

2. Neurotics* are characterised by high drive (autonomic lability) such that a stimulus that would be neutral for a non-neurotic person will trigger off a strong autonomic response in the neurotic person.

---

* Actually, the reference here is to *neuroticism*, considered as an inherited predisposition; whereas *neurosis* refers to the actual state of breakdown, resulting from the interaction of neuroticism with stress.

3. Persons high in neuroticism will perform better than persons low in neuroticism where the task does not involve competing responses; the contrary will be true where competing responses are involved.

These postulates would mediate the following predictions:

(a) Neurotics will show psychomotor disorganisation compared with normal subjects on complex but not simple tasks. The evidence in favour of this has been reviewed at length above.

(b) An increase in the strength of the stimulus will lead to an increased amplitude and speed of response in normal subjects. This prediction has been abundantly verified, particularly in the field of reaction-time studies. Thus, Johnson (1922) in an early study showed that increasing the strength of the stimulus led to a faster RT, as did Chocholle (1945); Steinman and Veniar (1944) found that faster reactions to a constant stimulus ratio were obtained at the stronger of two levels of visual intensity. Higher muscular tension levels (Travis and Kennedy, 1947), increased motivation (Hipple, 1954) and mild electric shock (Henry, 1951) all facilitate speed of simple reaction-time. Above a certain intensity, however, a stimulus ceases to facilitate response and begins to inhibit it. This was shown by Johnson (1922) and by Pascal (1953) who found that when a loud disturbing noise was given with the ready signal for reaction-time, some subjects showed complete disruption of performance. This result would be expected from the Yerkes-Dodson law since it specifies *optimal* levels of intensity for most adequate performance.

(c) An increase in induced anxiety in normals (usually by means of some stressful situation) will facilitate amplitude and speed of simple responses. An important study relevant here is that by Castaneda (1956) which links anxiety as drive and stimulus intensity as drive. His subjects were high- and low-anxiety high-school boys and girls; the stimulus a buzzer with two intensities; the response, squeezing a dynamometer; and the scores recorded, amplitude and speed of reaction. On the theory that differences in intensity produce differences in relevant drive he predicted that (1) speed of reaction of anxious subjects should be faster than that of non-anxious subjects; and (2) the increase in speed of reaction attributed to increased stimulus intensity should be relatively greater for non-anxious subjects, thus reducing the difference between anxious and non-anxious subjects. With regard to amplitude Castaneda found that anxious subjects did indeed show significantly higher amplitude at weak intensities and that there was a greater increase with the more intense stimulus in non-anxious as compared with anxious (though the latter finding held only for boys). With regard to speed of reaction, Castaneda found no difference at the weaker intensity between anxious and non-anxious subjects and, contrary to prediction, found a greater increase in speed at the higher intensity for the anxious subjects.

(d) Whereas increasing stimulus strength, inducing anxiety or stress in normals appears on the whole to facilitate response amplitude and speed in normals where the response required is simple in nature, it is predicted from the theory that the same factors would disrupt performance where the response required had to be selected from a range of possible choices or where the response itself is of a complex nature. There is a reasonable amount of evidence indicating the correctness of this prediction. Thus, a study by Grice (1955) indicates a significant increase in discrimination response time under conditions of induced anxiety or stress.

Several studies on induced conflict (stress) indicate that 'the probability of blockage as a reaction to conflict increases with the approach of the strengths of the conflicting responses to equality' (Sears and Hovland, 1941) and this conclusion is supported by several other studies (Hovland and Sears, 1938; Cartwright, 1941).

Similarly, it has been shown that complex motor reactions deteriorate markedly under stress in normal subjects. This holds for steadiness (Parsons *et al.*, 1954; Ross *et al.*, 1954); the work curve (Burghmann, 1939) and more complex tasks (Lofchie, 1955; Starer, 1942; Hill, 1954).

Thus, we may reasonably conclude with Davis (1947) that in normal subjects: 'under conditions . . . in which . . . anticipatory tension was increased, skilled responses were more extensive, more precipitate, more disturbed by restless movements and less accurate than single conditions (simple stimuli) in which anticipatory tension was normal.' The above results and those reported in the body of the chapter do seem to support the hypothesis that neurotics are characterised by a high state of drive which facilitates the correct response in a simple situation but impedes the correct response in a complex situation.

IV. PSYCHOMOTOR PERFORMANCE OF INTROVERTS AND EXTRAVERTS

Eysenck has argued that, in the event of neurotic breakdown, the patient's position on the introversion/extraversion dimension will determine whether the neurosis takes the form of dysthymia or hysteria. In terms of performance on psychomotor tasks, this may be translated into an argument that, whereas neurotics as an undifferentiated group will show disorganisation of psychomotor behaviour, position on the introversion/extraversion dimension will determine the nature of the disorganisation. That is, introverted and extraverted neurotics will manifest different kinds of disorganisation of motor behaviour. It has already been shown that neurotics do show motor disorganisation; and it will now be shown that introverted and extraverted neurotics do indeed manifest this disorganisation in different forms.

A. Empirical Results

1. CONTROL MOVEMENTS

The most cogent evidence remains that provided by the classical studies of Davis. As already pointed out, he observed two types of errors: those involving *overaction;* and those involving inertia. Subjects who were overactive 'obtained large scores on control movements . . . responses to instrument deviations were excessive, the extent and gradient of the movements being greatly increased and over-correcting frequent. Numerous restless movements were observed . . . subjects felt excited and under strain, tense and irritable and sometimes frankly anxious.' Subjects who were inert, on the other hand, made 'errors which were large and of long duration, whereas activity, represented by scores of control movements, was relatively little . . . . The individual responses were less hurried and less disturbed by restless movements than were those of the pilots showing the overactivity reaction, but they were often more extensive than at the beginning of the test . . . . Subjects reported that their interest had flagged and that their concentration had failed. A feeling of strain had now given way to one of mild boredom, tedium, or tiredness.'

Davis (1948) went on to show that pilots suffering from anxiety states showed a strong tendency to make overactive responses; whereas pilots suffering from hysteria tended to display inert responses. In another experiment, Davis (1949a), using a simple pointer apparatus, found similar results, as shown in Table 8.8. Davis also reported that errors of inertia tended to increase in all subjects as a function of length of testing.

Table 8.8.   Degree of Error of Normal, Anxious, and Hysteric Pilots

| | *Distribution of cases* *(Extent scores in arbitrary unit)* | | | | | | |
	3	4	5	6	7	8	Total
Healthy pilots	1	3	21	29	14	1	69
Acutely anxious	1	1	2	3	6	2	15
Hysterics	4	5	2	1	0	0	12

(*Source:* Davis, 1949a)

2. LURIA TECHNIQUE

There is some evidence that the motor disorganisation shown by dysthymics is different from that shown by hysterics (Barnacle *et al.*, 1935; Malmo *et al.*, 1951). Speer (1937) related introversion/extraversion to the amount of L-hand disturbance, and concluded that introverts tended to respond more than extraverts with the L-hand (that is, showed more involuntary disturbance.) A study by Ebaugh (1936) indicated that anxiety cases showed more general disturbance than hysterics; and possibly more local disturbance. These results, of course, need to be treated cautiously since the criterion groups were not identified in terms of Eysenck's dimensional system.

3. BODY-SWAY SUGGESTIBILITY

It has been shown that body-sway suggestibility is primarily a function of neuroticism rather than introversion/extraversion and, hence, that it is not related to hysteria as had long been supposed. On the contrary, there is some suggestion that dysthymics are more suggestible than hysterics. Eysenck (1947) reported correlations between anxiety as a symptom and suggestibility of +0·26 for men and +0·33 for women, while for conversion hysteria correlations of +0·12 for men and −0·08 for women were found. In an earlier study, however, Eysenck (1943) using very carefully matched groups of conversion hysterics and dysthymics found no significant differences on tests of primary suggestibility; similarly, Roach (1947) found no differences between introverted and extraverted normals.

Eysenck (1943) provided some evidence that suggestible patients are of two kinds in relation to tests of primary suggestibility. On the one hand, there are suggestible subjects who constitute an active, alert group; on the other, there are suggestible subjects who constitute a passive, lethargic group. The similarity of these two groups to the overactive/inert dichotomy found by Davis will be readily apparent.

4. PERSEVERATION

Numerous attempts have been made to relate perseveration to introversion/extraversion but with singularly little success. Pinard (1932b), for example, found the extreme perseverator to be effeminate, 'nervous', sensitive, sentimental, serious, shy, and solitary, whereas the extreme non-perseverator was suspicious, inconsiderate, critical, impatient of criticism, tactless, silent and anxious, and in a state of general tension with ups and downs in mood. Cattell (1946b) found that *p*-scores were negatively correlated with his Dominance-Submission factor and that the relationship was curvilinear. These suggestions of a relationship between perseveration and introversion/extraversion have not, in general, been confirmed by more recent studies. Thus, Rim (1955) failed to find any significant differences in perseveration between hysterics and psychopaths, on the one hand, and anxiety states and obsessives, on the other; and found an insignificant correlation between perseveration and introversion/extraversion. Similarly, Petrie (1948) found no differences between hysterics and dysthymics on four tests of perseveration. Thus, it must be concluded that perseveration is of little importance in defining differences between introverts and extraverts.

5. FLUENCY

Early suggestions that fluency may be related to differences in extraversion/introversion have not been confirmed. Himmelweit (1946) and Rim (1955) found no differences between hysterics and dysthymics. Rogers (1956) found a significant relationship between fluency in dealing with words and introversion/extraversion.

6. PERSISTENCE

Several studies suggest that there are no significant differences between hysterics and dysthymics on leg persistence (Eysenck, 1952a; S. B. G. Eysenck, 1955). Petrie (1948), on the other hand, found that dysthymics persisted over twice as long as hysterics.*

B. Theoretical Analysis

The most clear-cut result obtained in the study of the psychomotor performance of introverts and extraverts appears to be the demonstration that the *type* of motor response on a given task will differ for

---

* Test instructions (e.g. whether the subject is allowed to flex the extended leg) appear to play an important role in leg persistence tests.

extraverts as compared with introverts, provided the experimental conditions are appropriate. Within the neurotic disorganisation apparent on complex tasks, hysterics will tend to react with inertia, dysthymics with overaction. This distinction may well be very similar to the finding (Eysenck, 1947; Himmelweit, 1946) that hysterics prefer speed to accuracy, the reverse being the case with dysthymics.

Eysenck (1957) postulated that differences between introverts and extraverts are due to differences in the rate of growth, magnitude, and persistence of reactive inhibition (I_R), hysterics being characterised by rapid growth, high level, and slow dissipation of reactive inhibition, the reverse being true of dysthymics. It is possible to derive predictions from this theory relating to psychomotor task performance. Thus, for example, in a simple repetitive tapping task, it would be predicted that extraverts would build up I_R more rapidly than introverts and that this difference would manifest itself in two ways: the interval between taps would increase more rapidly for extraverts than for introverts over an extended period of practice; and, over a sufficiently long period of tapping, extraverts would produce fewer taps than introverts. This apparently straightforward prediction is unfortunately vitiated by a number of other considerations. Boder (1935), for example, has shown that even such a simple activity as tapping has at least four components (movement up, upper reversal, movement down, and bottom reversal). Oscillograph recordings showed that between both progressions there is a definite stop which, in finger tapping, lasts from twice to four times as long as the progressions. He found that concomitant activities led to reduced speed, alterations in pattern of tapping, *differences in duration of arrested movement*, and reduction in tapping excursion. Now it is possible that taking an overall tapping rate as score on this test obscures significant differences in duration of arrested movement since extraverts (who tend to trade accuracy for speed) may well 'catch up' on other aspects of performance. In other words, the prediction is relevant only to one aspect of performance, and failure to isolate that aspect may lead to negative results in relation to the theory without truly invalidating the theory. Secondly, if *neuroticism* also affects performance on a tapping task in the direction of producing greater scatter of tapping, the effects of inhibitory processes may be partially obscured if neurotic introverts and extraverts are used as criterion groups.* Thirdly, the prediction in terms of differences in rate of growth of I_R between extraverts and introverts is significantly complicated by the subsequent inclusion within Eysenck's theoretical system of differences in 'excitation' (Eysenck, 1957, 1968). Finally, the prediction is complicated by the selection of criterion groups of extraverts and introverts based on questionnaire responses, since such groups will consist of 'extraverts' and 'introverts' who are the confounded end-result of the interaction between constitutional predisposition and subsequent environmental exposure to differential socialisation (some of the 'extraverts' thus being constitutional introverts whose socialisation has been neglected, while some of the 'introverts' will be constitutional extraverts whose socialisation has been exceptionally severe).

It is unnecessary to labour further this point, except to indicate that similar complications have arisen in relation to other findings reported earlier in this chapter. Thus, Furneaux (1961) has cast serious doubt on the validity of the linear relationship between degree of neuroticism and body-sway suggestibility. He has demonstrated that large body-sway scores are obtained by stable extraverts and neurotic introverts, whereas much smaller scores are obtained by stable introverts and neurotic extraverts. From these results, he has hypothesised that neuroticism and introversion/extraversion *interact* to produce a particular degree of body sway.

It is unfortunately true that the detailed theoretical analysis and empirical investigations in relation to psychomotor performance have not yet been carried out so that a more comprehensive model of individual differences in psychomotor performance as related to personality factors may be constructed.

* Frith (1968) has recently discussed these problems, while Smith and Smith (1962) have similarly analysed the components involved in manual transport tasks (e.g. pegboard performance).

V. PSYCHOMOTOR PERFORMANCE MOTIVATION AND PSYCHOLOGICAL DEFICIT REDUCTION

A great deal of work (mostly with schizophrenic patients) has been carried out in recent years on the effects of various kinds of motivation and reinforcement in reducing the deficits in behaviour described in earlier sections of this review. It is impossible to describe this work in detail here and extensive reviews already exist (e.g. Johannsen, 1964; Silverman, 1963; Yates, 1966b), to which the reader is referred. Several studies in this area have, however, made use of psychomotor tasks and are worthy of special mention here.

Noxious stimulation (e.g. verbal censure, noise, or

electric shock) appears to lead to significant improvement in the performance of schizophrenics, provided the stimulation is specific to a particular task (that is, provided it is response contingent). Such contingent stimulation may lead to escape behaviour (if the stimulation can be turned off, but not avoided) or to avoidance behaviour (if the stimulation can be avoided provided the response is made fast enough). An early study utilising noxious physical stimulation was that by Pascal and Swensen (1952). A stimulus requiring a disjunctive RT was accompanied by unpleasant white noise which could be turned off only by making the response. Under these conditions, the performance of schizophrenics tended to be normalised. Similar results were found by Rosenbaum and associates (1957), Lang (1959), and Karras (1962), using shock or white noise as the noxious stimuli. Using an avoidance training paradigm, Cavanaugh and co-workers (1960) investigated the effects of verbal censure on disjunctive RT, the noxious stimulus being presented if the subject responded too slowly (the subject could thus avoid the noxious stimulus by responding more rapidly). Verbal censure led to a significant improvement in RT, whereas in a subsequent experiment verbal praise did not produce a similar improvement.

The effects of motivating instructions in general have also been extensively investigated and it has been shown that, with schizophrenics at least, verbal censure has produced greater improvement in psychomotor performance than verbal praise or neutral instructions (Goodstein *et al.*, 1961; Johannsen, 1962; Long, 1961; Olsen, 1958). Silverman (1963), after reviewing much of this work, concluded that it is possible to modify the avoidance and escape habits of schizophrenics by means of these techniques, and that the crucial factor involved is the contingency of the stimulation following upon a particular response. The more general extrapolation of these findings to the modification of the behaviour of psychotic patients is dealt with elsewhere in this book (*see also* Yates, 1969, Chapters 13 and 14).

VI. PREDICTIVE VALIDITY OF PSYCHOMOTOR TESTS

The possibility of utilising psychomotor tests as prognostic indicators has received increasing attention in recent years. Of particular importance in this respect are the monumental studies of Weaver and Brooks. In their first study, Weaver and Brooks (1964) divided 407 schizophrenics into four groups according to whether, at the time of completion of the study, they had been discharged from hospital and not returned ($n = 136$); been discharged, returned, and discharged again ($n = 57$); been discharged but returned and not discharged again ($n = 62$); or had not been discharged at all ($n = 148$). All subjects received intensive treatment and, at the beginning of the study, were given four tests prior to treatment (visual and auditory simple lift RT); rate of tapping; serial RT; and a transport-assembly pegboard task). Table 8.9 shows, for the first three groups (those subjects who had been discharged at least once) and for the fourth group (not discharged at any time), the percentage falling above the median on each test. It is clear that the tests indicate prognosis under an intensive treatment regime to a highly significant degree. Weaver and Brooks additionally showed that the differences were not a function of age. Correlation of each test with the criterion measure (in *vs.* out) were all significant (tapping, 0·374; serial RT, 0·434; transport, 0·409; assembly, 0·446, RT, 0·459), while for all five measures combined, the multiple correlation was 0·516.

In a subsequent study, Weaver and Brooks (1967a) replicated these results with 637 schizophrenics, and additionally showed that the tests served as prognostic indicators with other disorders as well (manic-depressives, chronic brain syndrome, personality disorder, and mental deficiency) though the criteria used with schizophrenic groups were found to be not directly applicable to the other groups.

In a third study, Weaver and Brooks (1967b) differentiated between acute (hospitalised less than 90 days on first admission at time of test, $n = 336$)

Table 8.9. Percentage Falling Above the Median on Five Measures

Group	Test				
	Tapping	Reaction Time	Serial Reaction Time	Transport	Assembly
I, II, III	62·4	62·7	62·4	62·3	64·3
IV	29·1	28·2	29·0	29·0	25·4

(*Source:* Weaver and Brooks, 1964)

and chronic (hospitalised more than two years at time of test, $n = 347$) groups of patients (schizophrenic; manic-depressive; brain damaged; personality disorder; mental defectives). These patients were twice given the same four tests described earlier, with a test-retest interval of one year. The hypothesis under investigation in this study was that a good initial score indicates a favourable prognosis in acute patients, whereas the reverse was hypothesised to be the case for chronic patients. The hypothesis was not supported: good initial performance was positively correlated with discharge, irrespective of acute/chronic status.

Thus, the potential usefulness of psychomotor tests for prognostic purposes appears to have been clearly demonstrated and could have important consequences for decisions as to where treatment is likely to be most useful when demand is greater than resources. The Brooks/Weaver results have been confirmed in a smaller but important study by Burstein and associates (1967), who added one more test (pinboard) to those used by Brooks and Weaver. Their results were obtained with chronic schizophrenics allocated one of three conditions of treatment (workshop training; recreational and occupational therapy; or a no treatment control group). A significant correlation with discharge was found for all the tests used, except simple RT, with the pinboard test being the best predictor. Similar confirmatory findings with similar tests have been reported by Court (1964), Haywood and Moelis (1963), and Payne (1966).

REFERENCES

ALBINO, R. C. (1948) The stable and labile personality types of Luria in clinically normal individuals. *Brit. J. Psychol.*, **39**, 54–60.

ALVAREZ, R. R. (1962) Comparison of depressive and brain-injured subjects on the trail-making test. *Percept. Motor Skills*, **14**, 91–96.

BABCOCK, H. (1930) An experiment in the measurement of mental deterioration. *Arch. Psychol.*, **18**, (No. 117).

BABCOCK, H. (1933) *Dementia Praecox: A Psychological Study*. New York: Science Press.

BARNACLE, C. H. (1935) EBAUGH, F. G. and LEMERE, F. Association-motor investigations of the psychoneuroses. *Amer. J. Psychiat.*, **91**, 925–937.

BARUK, H., LIFSCHITZ, A. G. Y., and MELZER, R. (1953) Etude de l'initiative psychomotrice et de la mise en train volontaire chez le sujet normal et en psychopathologie. *Encéphale*, **42**, 193–218.

BECK, A. T., FESHBACH, S., and LEGG, D. (1962) The clinical validity of the digit symbol test. *J. consult. Psychol.*, **26**, 263–268.

BENTON, A. L., JENTSCH, R. C., and WAHLER, H. J. (1959) Simple and choice reaction times in schizophrenia. *Arch. Neurol. Psychiat.*, **81**, 373–376.

BIRREN, J. E., RIEGEL, K. F., and MORRISON, D. F. (1962) Age differences in response speed as a function of controlled variations of stimulus conditions: evidence of a general speed factor. *Gerontologia*, **6**, 1–18.

BODER, D. P. (1935) The influence of concomitant activity and fatigue upon certain forms of reciprocal hand movement and its fundamental components. *Comp. psychol. Monogr.*, **11**, 4.

BROADBENT, D. E. (1958) *Perception and Communication*. London: Pergamon.

BROGDEN, H. E. (1940) A factor analysis of forty character tests. *Psychol. Monogr.*, **52**, No. 3.

BURGHMANN, J. (1939) The effect of distraction, both manual and mental, on the ergograph curve. *Austr. J. Psychol. Phil.*, **17**, 273–276.

BURSTEIN, A. G., SOLOFF, A., GILLESPIE, H., and HAASE, M. (1967) Prediction of hospital discharge of mental patients by psychomotor performance: partial replication of Brooks and Weaver. *Percept. Motor Skills*, **24**, 127–134.

CAMERON, D. E. and CAUNT, T. G. B. (1953) Studies in perseveration. *J. ment. Sci.*, **79**, 735–745.

CARTWRIGHT, D. (1941) Relation of decision time to the categories of response. *Amer. J. Psychol.*, **54**, 174–196.

CASTANEDA, A. (1956) Reaction time and response amplitude as a function of anxiety and stimulus intensity. *J. abnorm. soc. Psychol.*, **53**, 225–228.

CATTELL, R. B. (1946a) The riddle of perseveration: I. 'Creative effort' and disposition rigidity. *J. Personality*, **14**, 229–238.

CATTELL, R. B. (1946b) The riddle of perseveration: II. Solution in terms of personality structure. *J. Personality*, **14**, 239–267.

CAVANAUGH, D. K., COHEN, W., and LANG, P. (1960) The effect of 'social censure' and 'social approval' on the psychomotor performance of schizophrenics. *J. abnorm. soc. Psychol.*, **60**, 213–218.

CHAPMAN, J. and MCGHIE, A. (1962) A comparative study of disordered attention in schizophrenia. *J. ment. Sci.*, **108**, 487–500.

CHAPMAN, J. and MCGHIE, A. (1963) An approach to the psychotherapy of cognitive dysfunction. *Brit. J. med. Psychol.*, **36**, 253–260.

CHAPMAN, J. and MCGHIE, A. (1964) Echopraxia in schizophrenia. *Brit. J. Psychiat.*, **110**, 365–374.

CHOCHOLLE, R. (1945) Variations des temps de la réaction auditive en fonction de l'intensité à diverses fréquences. *Année Psychol.*, **41–42**, 65–124.

COURT, J. H. (1964) A longitudinal study of psychomotor functioning in acute psychiatric patients. *Brit. J. med. Psychol.*, **37**, 167–173.

CRUMPTON, E. (1963) Persistence of maladaptive responses in schizophrenia. *J. abnorm. soc. Psychol.*, **66**, 615–618.

CZUDNER, G. and MARSHALL, M. (1967) Simple reaction

time in schizophrenic, retarded, and normal children under regular and irregular preparatory interval conditions. *Canad. J. Psychol.*, **21**, 369–380.

DAS, J. P. and O'CONNOR, N. (1959) Body-sway suggestibility in paranoid and non-paranoid schizophrenics. *Internat. J. clin. exp. Hyp.*, **7**, 121–128.

DAVIS, D. R. (1946a) The disorganization of behaviour in fatigue. *J. Neurol. Psychiat.*, **9**, 23–29.

DAVIS, D. R. (1946b) Neurotic predisposition and the disorganization observed in experiments with the Cambridge cockpit. *J. Neurol. Psychiat.*, **9**, 119–124.

DAVIS, D. R. (1947) Disorders of skill: an experimental approach to some problems of neurosis. *Proc. Roy. soc. Med.*, **40**, 583–584.

DAVIS, D. R. (1948) *Pilot Error: Some Laboratory Experiments.* London: H.M.S.O.

DAVIS, D. R. (1949a) Increase in strength of a secondary drive as a cause of disorganization. *Quart. J. exp. Psychol.*, **1**, 22–28.

DAVIS, D. R. (1949b) The disorder of skill responsible for accidents. *Quart. J. exp. Psychol.*, **1**, 136–142.

DONAHOE, J. W., CURTIN, M. E., and LIPTON, L. (1961) Interference effects with schizophrenic subjects in the acquisition and retention of verbal material. *J. abnorm. soc. Psychol.*, **62**, 553–558.

EBAUGH, F. G. (1936) Association motor investigation in clinical psychiatry. *J. ment. Sci.*, **82**, 731–743.

EDWARDS, A. S. and HARRIS, A. C. (1953) Laboratory measurements of deterioration and improvement among schizophrenics. *J. gen. Psychol.*, **49**, 153–156.

EVANS, F. J. (1967) Suggestibility in the normal waking state. *Psychol. Bull.*, **67**, 114–129.

EYSENCK, H. J. (1943) Suggestibility and hysteria. *J. Neurol. Psychiat.*, **6**, 22–31.

EYSENCK, H. J. (1944) States of high suggestibility and the neuroses. *Amer. J. Psychol.*, **57**, 406–411.

EYSENCK, H. J. (1947) *Dimensions of Personality.* London: Routledge and Kegan Paul.

EYSENCK, H. J. (1950) Cyclothymia—schizothymia as a dimension of personality: I. Historical review. *J. Personality*, **19**, 123–152.

EYSENCK, H. J. (1952a) *The Scientific Study of Personality.* London: Routledge and Kegan Paul.

EYSENCK, H. J. (1952b) Schizothymia—cyclothymia as a dimension of personality: II. Experimental. *J. Personality*, **20**, 345–384.

EYSENCK, H. J. (1955) A dynamic theory of anxiety and hysteria. *J. ment. Sci.*, **101**, 28–51.

EYSENCK, H. J. (1957) *Dynamics of Anxiety and Hysteria.* London: Routledge and Kegan Paul.

EYSENCK, H. J. (1960) *The Structure of Human Personality*, 2nd ed. London: Methuen.

EYSENCK, H. J. (1968) *The Biological Basis of Personality.* Springfield: C. C. Thomas.

EYSENCK, H. J. and FURNEAUX, W. D. (1945) Primary and secondary suggestibility: an experimental and statistical study. *J. exp. Psychol.*, **35**, 485–503.

EYSENCK, S. B. G. (1955) A dimensional analysis of mental abnormality. *Unpubl. Ph.D Thesis*, U. of London Library.

EYSENCK, S. B. G. (1956) Neurosis and psychosis: an experimental analysis. *J. ment. Sci.*, **102**, 517–529.

FEATHER, N. T. (1962) The study of persistence. *Psychol. Bull.*, **59**, 94–115.

FLEISHMAN, E. A. (1954) Dimensional analysis of psychomotor abilities. *J. exp. Psychol.*, **48**, 437–454.

FLEISHMAN, E. A. and HEMPEL, W. E. (1954) Changes in factor structure of a complex psychomotor test as a function of practice. *Psychometrika*, **19**, 239–252.

FREGLY, A. R. and GRAYBIEL, A. (1968) An ataxia test battery not requiring rails. *Aerospace Med.*, **39**, 277–282.

FRITH, C. D. (1968) Strategies in rotary pursuit-tracking and their relation to inhibition and personality. *Life Sciences*, **7**, 65–76.

FURNEAUX, W. D. (1961) Neuroticism, extraversion, drive, and suggestibility. *Internat. J. clin. exp. Hyp.*, **9**, 195–214.

GOODSTEIN, L., GUERTIN, W., and BLACKBURN, H. (1961) Effects of social motivational variables on choice reaction time of schizophrenics. *J. abnorm. soc. Psychol.*, **62**, 24–27.

GRAYBIEL, A. and FREGLY, A. R. (1966) A new quantitative ataxia test battery. *Acta Otolaryng.*, **61**, 292–312.

GRICE, G. R. (1955) Discrimination reaction time as a function of anxiety and intelligence. *J. abnorm. soc. Psychol.*, **50**, 71–74.

GROSS, O. (1902) Die cerebrale Sekundärfunktion. Leipzig.

GUILFORD, J. P. (1958) A system of the psychomotor abilities. *Amer. J. Psychol.*, **71**, 164–174.

HALL, K. R. L. and STRIDE, E. (1954) Some factors affecting reaction times to auditory stimuli in mental patients. *J. ment. Sci.*, **100**, 462–477.

HARWOOD, E. and NAYLOR, G. F. K. (1963) Nature and extent of basic cognitive deterioration in a sample of institutionalized mental patients. *Austr. J. Psychol.*, **15**, 29–36.

HAYWOOD, H. C. and MOELIS, I. (1963) Effect of symptom change on intellectual function in schizophrenia. *J. abnorm. soc. Psychol.*, **67**, 76–78.

HEATH, S. R. (1942) Rail-walking performance as related to mental age and etiological type among the mentally retarded. *Amer. J. Psychol.*, **55**, 240–247.

HEATH, S. R. (1944) Clinical significance of motor defect with military implications. *Amer. J. Psychol.*, **57**, 482–499.

HEATH, S. R. (1946) A mental pattern found in motor deviates. *J. abnorm. soc. Psychol.*, **41**, 223–225.

HEATH, S. R. (1949) The rail-walking test: preliminary maturational norms for boys and girls. *Mot. Skills Res. Exch.*, **1**, 34–36.

HENRY, F. M. (1951) Increase in speed of movement by motivation and by transfer of motivated improvements. *Res. Quart. Amer. Assoc. Hlth. Phys. Educ.*, **22**, 219–228.

HILL, H. E. (1954) An experimental study of disorganization of speech and manual responses in normal subjects. *J. Speech Dis.*, **19**, 295–305.

HIMMELWEIT, H. T. (1946) Speed and accuracy of work as related to temperament. *Brit. J. Psychol.*, **36**, 132–144.

HIMMELWEIT, H. T. and PETRIE, A. (1951) The measurement of personality in children: an experimental investigation of neuroticism. *Brit. J. educ. Psychol.*, **21**, 9–29.

HIPPLE, J. E. (1954) Racial differences in the influence of motivation on muscular tensions, reaction time, and speed of movement. *Res. Quart. Amer. Assoc. Hlth. Phys. Educ.*, **25**, 297–306.

HOCH, A. (1901) On certain studies with the ergograph. *J. nerv. ment. Dis.*, **28**, 620–628.

HOVLAND, C. I. and SEARS, R. R. (1938) Experiments on motor conflict: I. Types of conflict and their modes of resolution. *J. exp. Psychol.*, **23**, 477–493.

HUSTON, P. E. (1935) The reflex time of the patellar tendon reflex in normal and schizophrenic subjects. *J. gen. Psychol.*, **13**, 3–41.

HUSTON, P. E. and SENF, R. (1952) Psychopathology of schizophrenia and depression: I. Effect of amytal and amphetamine sulphate on level and maintenance of attention. *Amer. J. Psychiat.*, **109**, 131–138.

HUSTON, P. E., SHAKOW, D., and RIGGS, L. A. (1937) Studies of motor function in schizophrenia: II. Reaction time. *J. gen. Psychol.*, **16**, 39–82.

HUSTON, P. E. and SINGER, M. M. (1945) Effect of sodium amytal and amphetamine sulphate on mental set in schizophrenia. *Arch. Neurol. Psychiat., Chicago*, **53**, 365–369.

JASPER, H. N. (1931) Is perseveration a functional unity participating in all behaviour processes? *J. soc. Psychol.*, **2**, 28–52.

JOHANNSEN, W. J. (1962) Effect of reward and punishment on motor learning by chronic schizophrenics and normals. *J. clin. Psychol.*, **18**, 204–207.

JOHANNSEN, W. J. (1964) Motivation in schizophrenic performance: a review. *Psychol. Rep.*, **15**, 839–870.

JOHANNSEN, W. J., FRIEDMAN, S. H., LEITSCHUH, T. H., and AMMONS, H. (1963) A study of certain schizophrenic dimensions and their relationship to double alternation. *J. consult. Psychol.*, **27**, 375–382.

JOHNSON, A. M. (1922) Influence of incentive and punishment upon reaction time. *Arch. Psychol.*, **8**, 54–93.

JONES, L. W. (1928) An investigation into the significance of perseveration. *J. ment. Sci.*, **74**, 653–659.

KARRAS, A. (1962) The effects of reinforcement and arousal on the psychomotor performance of chronic schizophrenics. *J. abnorm. soc. Psychol.*, **65**, 104–111.

KING, H. E. (1954) *Psychomotor Aspects of Mental Disease*. Commonwealth Fund: Harvard Univer. Press.

KING, H. E. (1961) Some explorations in psychomotility. *Psychiat. Res. Rep.*, **14**, 62–86.

KLEEMEIER, R. W. and DUDEK, F. J. (1950) A factorial investigation of flexibility. *Educ. Psychol. Measmt.*, **10**, 107–118.

KNEHR, C. A. (1954) Schizophrenic reaction time responses to variable preparatory intervals. *Amer. J. Psychiat.*, **110**, 585–588.

KRAEPELIN, E. (1902) Die arbeitskurve. *Philos. Stud.*, **19**, 459–507.

LANG, P. J. (1959) The effect of aversive stimuli on reaction time in schizophrenia. *J. abnorm. soc. Psychol.*, **59**, 263–268.

LAWSON, J. S., McGHIE, A., and CHAPMAN, J. (1964) Perception of speech in schizophrenia. *Brit. J. Psychiat.*, **110**, 375–380.

LEACH, P. J. (1967) A critical study of the literature concerning rigidity. *Brit. J. soc. clin. Psychol.*, **6**, 11–22.

LOFCHIE, S. H. (1955) The performance of adults under distraction stress: a developmental approach. *J. Psychol.*, **39**, 109–116.

LONG, R. C. (1961) Praise and censure as motivating variables in the motor behaviour and learning of schizophrenia. *J. abnorm. soc. Psychol.*, **63**, 283–288.

LURIA, A. R. (1932) *The Nature of Human Conflicts*. New York: Liveright.

LYNN, R. (1963) Russian theory and research on schizophrenia. *Psychol. Bull.*, **60**, 486–498.

MACARTHUR, R. S. (1951) An experimental investigation of persistence and its measurement at the secondary school level. *Unpubl. Ph.D Thesis*, Univer. London Library.

McGHIE, A. and CHAPMAN, J. (1961) Disorders of attention and perception in early schizophrenia. *Brit. J. med. Psychol.*, **34**, 103–116.

McGHIE, A., CHAPMAN, J., and LAWSON, J. S. (1964) Disturbances in selective attention in schizophrenia. *Proc. Roy. Soc. Med.*, **57**, 419–422.

McGHIE, A., CHAPMAN, J., and LAWSON, J. S. (1965a) The effect of distraction on schizophrenic performance: I. Perception and immediate memory. *Brit. J. Psychiat.*, **111**, 383–390.

McGHIE, A., CHAPMAN, J., and LAWSON, J. S. (1965b) The effect of distraction on schizophrenic performance: II. Psychomotor ability. *Brit. J. Psychiat.*, **111**, 391–398.

McREYNOLDS, P. (1963) Reactions to novel and familiar stimuli as a function of schizophrenic withdrawal. *Percept. Motor Skills*, **16**, 847–850.

MAILLOUX, N. M. and NEWBURGER, M. (1941) The work curves of psychotic individuals. *J. abnorm. soc. Psychol.*, **36**, 110–114.

MALMO, R. B., SHAGASS, C., BELANGER, D. J., and SMITH, A. A. (1951) Motor control in psychiatric patients under experimental stress. *J. abnorm. soc. Psychol.*, **46**, 539–547.

MORAN, L. J., MEFFERD, R. B., and KIMBLE, J. P. (1964) Idiodynamic sets in word association. *Psychol. Monogr.*, **78**, No. 2 (Whole No. 579).

NOTCUTT, B. (1943) Perseveration and fluency. *Brit. J. Psychol.*, **33**, 200–208.

NUNBERG, H. (1918) On the physical accompaniments of association processes. In *Studies in Word Association*. (Ed. Jung, G. C.) London: Heinemann.

O'CONNOR, N., HERON, A., and CARSTAIRS, G. M. (1956) Work performance of chronic schizophrenics. *Occupat. Psychol.*, **30**, 153–164.

OLSON, G. W. (1958) Failure and the subsequent performance of schizophrenics. *J. abnorm. soc. Psychol.*, **57**, 310–314.

PARSONS, O. A., PHILLIPS, L., and LANE, J. E. (1954) Performance on the same psychomotor task under different stressful conditions. *J. Psychol.*, **38**, 457–466.

PASCAL, G. R. (1953) The effect of a disturbing noise on the reaction time of mental defectives. *Amer. J. ment. Def.*, **57**, 691–699.

PASCAL, G. R. and SWENSEN, C. (1952) Learning in

mentally ill patients under conditions of unusual motivation. *J. Personality*, **21**, 240–249.

PAYNE, R. W. (1955) Experimentelle Untersuchungen zum Spaltungsbegriff von Kretschmer. *Zeit. für exp. und angew. Psychol.*, **3**, 65–97.

PAYNE, R. W. (1966) The long-term prognostic implications of overinclusive thinking in mental patients: a follow-up study using objective tests. *Proc. IV World Congress Psychiat.*, pp. 2657–2660.

PAYNE, R. W., ANCEVICH, S. S., and LAVERTY, S. G. (1963) Overinclusive thinking in symptom-free schizophrenics. *Canad. psychiat. Assoc. J.*, **8**, 225–234.

PAYNE, R. W., CAIRD, W. K., and LAVERTY, S. G. (1964) Overinclusive thinking and delusions in schizophrenic patients. *J. abnorm. soc. Psychol.*, **68**, 562–566.

PAYNE, R. W. and HEWLETT, J. G. (1960) Thought disorder in psychotic patients: In *Experiments in Personality*, Vol. II (Ed. Eysenck, H. J.) 3–104. London: Routledge and Kegan Paul.

PETRIE, A. (1948) Repression and suggestibility as related to temperament. *J. Personality*, **16**, 445–458.

PINARD, J. W. (1932a) Tests of perseveration: I. Their relation to character. *Brit. J. Psychol.*, **23**, 5–19.

PINARD, J. W. (1932b) Tests of perseveration: II. Their relation to certain psychopathic conditions and to introversion. *Brit. J. Psychol.*, **23**, 114–128.

PISHKIN, V., SMITH, T. E., and LEIBOWITZ, H. W. (1962) The influence of symbolic stimulus value on perceived size in chronic schizophrenia. *J. consult. Psychol.*, **26**, 323–330.

RAFI, A. A. (1960) Motor performance of certain categories of mental patients. *Percept. Motor Skills*, **10**, 39–42.

RETHLINGSHAFER, D. (1942) Relationship of tests of persistence to other measures of continuance of activities. *J. abnorm. soc. Psychol.*, **37**, 71–82.

RICKELS, K., DOWNING, R., and APPEL, H. (1964) Some personality correlates of suggestibility in normals and neurotics. *Psychol. Rep.*, **14**, 715–719.

RIM, Y. (1955) Perseveration and fluency as measures of introversion-extraversion in abnormal subjects. *J. Personality*, **23**, 324–334.

ROACH, J. H. L. (1947) Autosuggestion in extraverts and introverts. *J. Personality*, **15**, 215–221.

ROBINSON, E. S. and BILLS, A. C. (1926) Two factors in the work decrement. *J. exp. Psychol.*, **9**, 413–433.

RODNICK, E. H. and SHAKOW, D. (1940) Set in the schizophrenic as measured by a composite reaction time index. *Amer. J. Psychiat.*, **97**, 214–225.

ROGERS, C. A. (1956) The orectic relations of verbal fluency. *Austr. J. Psychol.*, **8**, 27–46.

ROGERS, C. A. (1953) The structure of verbal fluency. *Brit. J. Psychol.*, **44**, 368–380.

ROSENBAUM, G., GRISELL, J. L., and MACKEVEY, W. R. (1957) The relationship of age and privilege status to reaction time indices of schizophrenic motivation. *J. abnorm. soc. Psychol.*, **55**, 202–207.

ROSS, S., HUSSMAN, T. A., and ANDREWS, T. G. (1954) Effects of fatigue and anxiety on certain psychomotor and visual functions. *J. appl. Psychol.*, **38**, 119–125.

SCHEIER, I. H. and FERGUSON, G. A. (1952) Further factorial studies of tests of rigidity. *Canad. J. Psychol.*, **6**, 18–30.

SEARS, R. R. and HOVLAND, C. I. (1941) Experiments on motor conflict: II. Determination of mode of resolution by comparative strengths of conflicting responses. *J. exp. Psychol.*, **28**, 280–286.

SEASHORE, R. H., BUXTON, C. E., and McCOLLOM, I. N. (1940) Multiple factorial analysis of fine motor skills. *Amer. J. Psychol.*, **53**, 251–259.

SHAKOW, D. (1962) Segmental set: a theory of the formal psychological deficit in schizophrenia. *Arch. gen. Psychiat.*, **6**, 1–17.

SHAKOW, D. (1963) Psychological deficit in schizophrenia. *Behav. Sci.*, **8**, 275–305.

SHAKOW, D. and HUSTON, P. E. (1936) Studies of motor function in schizophrenia: I. Speed of tapping. *J. gen. Psychol.*, **15**, 63–103.

SHAPIRO, M. B. and NELSON, E. H. (1955) An investigation of the nature of cognitive impairment in co-operative psychiatric patients. *Brit. J. med. Psychol.*, **28**, 239–256.

SIDLE, A., ACKER, M., and McREYNOLDS, P. (1963) 'Stimulus-seeking' behavior in schizophrenics and non-schizophrenics. *Percept. Motor Skills*, **17**, 811–816.

SILVERMAN, J. (1963) Psychological deficit reduction in schizophrenia through response-contingent noxious reinforcement. *Psychol. Rep.*, **13**, 187–210.

SILVERMAN, J. (1964) The problem of attention in research and theory in schizophrenia. *Psychol. Rev.*, **71**, 352–379.

SMITH, K. U. and SMITH, W. M. (1962) *Perception and Motion*. Philadelphia: Saunders.

SPEER, G. S. (1937) The measurement of emotions aroused in response to personality test items. *J. Psychol.*, **3**, 445–461.

STARER, E. (1952) The effects of two simultaneous cognitive and affective stimuli. *J. clin. Psychol.*, **8**, 402–405.

STEINMAN, A. and VENIAR, S. (1944) Simple RT to change as a substitute for the disjunctive reaction. *J. exp. Psychol.*, **34**, 152–158.

STEPHENSON, W. (1932a) Studies in experimental psychiatry: II. Some contact of p-factor with psychiatry. *J. ment. Sci.*, **78**, 318–330.

STEPHENSON, W. (1932b) Studies in experimental psychiatry: III. p-score and inhibition for high-p praecox cases. *J. ment. Sci.*, **78**, 908–928.

STEPHENSON, W. (1934) An introduction to so-called motor perseveration tests. *Brit. J. educ. Psychol.*, **4**, 186–208.

THORNDIKE, E. L. (1912) The curve of work. *Psychol. Rev.*, **19**, 105–194.

THORNTON, G. R. (1939) A factor analysis of tests designed to measure persistence. *Psychol. Monogr.*, **51**, 1–42.

TIZARD, J. and O'CONNOR, N. (1951) Predicting the occupational adequacy of certified mental defectives: an empirical investigation using a battery of psychological tests and ratings. *Occup. Psychol.*, **25**, 205–211.

TIZARD, J., O'CONNOR, N., and CRAWFORD, J. M. (1950) The abilities of adolescent and adult high-grade male defectives. *J. ment. Sci.*, **96**, 888–907.

TIZARD, J. and VENABLES, P. H. (1956) Reaction time responses by schizophrenics, mental defectives, and normal adults. *Amer. J. Psychiat.*, **112**, 803–807.

TRAVIS, R. C. and KENNEDY, J. L. (1947) Prediction and automatic control of alertness: I. Control of lookout alertness. *J. comp. physiol. Psychol.*, **40**, 457–461.

USDANSKY, G. and CHAPMAN, L. J. (1960) Schizophrenic-like responses in normal subjects under time pressure. *J. abnorm. soc. Psychol.*, **60**, 143–146.

VENABLES, P. H. (1964) Input dysfunction in schizophrenia. In *Progress in Experimental Personality Research*, Vol. 1 (Ed. Maher, B. A.) New York: Academic Press, pp. 1–47.

VENABLES, P. H. and TIZARD, J. (1956) Performance of functional psychotics on a repetitive task. *J. abnorm. soc. Psychol.*, **53**, 23–26.

WEAVER, L. A. and BROOKS, G. W. (1964) The use of psychomotor tests in predicting the potential of chronic schizophrenics. *J. Neuropsychiat.*, **5**, 170–180.

WEAVER, L. A. and BROOKS, G. W. (1967a) The prediction of release from a mental hospital from psychomotor test performance. *J. gen. Psychol.*, **76**, 207–229.

WEAVER, L. A. and BROOKS, G. W. (1967b) Differential performance on psychomotor tests by hospitalized acute and chronic mental patients. *Psychiat. Quart.*, **41**, 286–295.

WEBB, R. A. and NESMITH, C. C. (1964) A normative study of suggestibility in a mental patient population. *Internat. J. clin. exp. Hyp.*, **12**, 181–183.

WINDLE, C. and HAMWI, V. (1953) An exploratory study of the prognostic value of the complex reaction time test in early and chronic psychotics. *J. clin. Psychol.*, **9**, 156–161.

WULFECK, W. H. (1941) Motor dysfunction in the mentally disordered: I. A comparative investigation of motor function in psychotics, psychoneurotics, and normals. *Psychol. Rec.*, **4**, 271–323.

YATES, A. J. (1960) Abnormalities of psychomotor functions. In *Handbook of Abnormal Psychology* (Ed. Eysenck, H. J.) London: Pitman.

YATES, A. J. (1966a) Data-processing levels and thought disorder in schizophrenia. *Austr. J. Psychol.*, **18**, 103–117.

YATES, A. J. (1966b) Psychological deficit. *Ann. Rev. Psychol.*, **17**, 111–144.

YATES, A. J. (1969) *Behaviour Therapy*. New York: Wiley.

ZAHN, T. P. and ROSENTHAL, D. (1966) Simple reaction time as a function of the relative frequency of the preparatory interval. *J. exp. Psychol.*, **72**, 15–19.

ZAHN, T. P., ROSENTHAL, D., and SHAKOW, D. (1961) Reaction time in schizophrenic and normal subjects in relation to the sequence of series of regular preparatory intervals. *J. abnorm. soc. Psychol.*, **63**, 161–168.

ZAHN, T. P., ROSENTHAL, D., and SHAKOW, D. (1963) Effects of irregular preparatory intervals on reaction time in schizophrenia. *J. abnorm. Psychol.*, **67**, 44–52.

ZAHN, T. P., SHAKOW, D., and ROSENTHAL, D. (1961) Reaction time in schizophrenic and normal subjects as a function of preparatory and intertrial intervals. *J. nerv. ment. Dis.*, **33**, 283–287.

9

Abnormalities of Perception

C. D. FRITH

INTRODUCTION

In the following discussion of abnormalities of perception a very wide definition of perception, extending from sensory thresholds to the more cognitive processes involved in the perception of complex patterns such as speech has been adopted. It would be impossible to cover this field adequately in the small space available without reducing the material to a list of references linked by redundant phrases in the manner of the *Annual Review of Psychology*, hence the chapter has been limited to a discussion in more detail of a few particularly important topics, and, as far as possible only the most recent experiments and reviews are considered. The interested reader can obtain references to earlier work from these sources.

The number of abnormal groups considered has also been limited to psychiatric groups and patients suffering from cerebral damage. Straightforward physical abnormalities of perception such as blindness and deafness have not been considered. Furthermore, most of the studies mentioned concern schizophrenia rather than any other group. This, however, I believe to be a fair reflection of the literature over the last ten years. With the coming of behaviour therapy many psychologists involved with abnormal groups have turned from 'pure' experimentation to experimental treatment. Thus, the study of perception, as yet unrelated to treatment, has been restricted to schizophrenic patients, as yet untreatable. There is still much argument about whether schizophrenia is a real or useful clinical entity and much work has been done on various subsystems of classification within this group. This means that when a study is reported on a group of schizophrenics it is not at all clear how similar these are to schizophrenics of other groups reported in

other studies. These difficulties are not discussed in this chapter, which is concerned only with the types of abnormalities of perception that have been discovered and investigated. However, there does seem to emerge from the various studies of schizophrenia a consistent pattern of perceptual dysfunctioning. Experimental work with normal people, in which the techniques used could be usefully applied to the study of abnormal groups even if there are, as yet, few reports of such applications, has also been given consideration.

The Cognitive Approach to Perception

The remarkable ability of people to perceive and comprehend complex patterns such as speech and writing has resulted in a recent movement in psychology to consider perception as a cognitive process. This approach is exemplified by Neisser (1967). The basis of this approach is revealed in the title of a paper by Garner (1966): 'To perceive is to know.' Garner considers that perception is an active process in which a person defines and organises sets of stimuli. Pribram (1963) has also said that only stimuli for which cognitive models are available can be perceived, and Simon (1967) has proposed an information processing model of perception derived from his earlier model of problem-solving behaviour. A cognitive theory of perception assumes that a person will perceive any stimulus array as being, in some sense, organised, and that he will continue to perceive this organisation until there is a sufficient change in the stimulation to produce a new organisation. The kind of organisation perceived will depend very much on the person perceiving. Organisations can be defined mathematically, and this aspect of

284

their study has been greatly advanced by the use of computers as pattern-recognising machines (Uhr, 1966). The use of machines as pattern recognisers has also made it clear that the human brain is capable of perceiving only a small subset of all theoretically possible organisations. This results in certain perceptual biases which probably make the human brain especially suited for dealing with certain special kinds of material such as speech. It is perhaps for this reason that computers, starting out with no biases and with all theoretically possible organising principles available to them, have, as yet, been notably unsuccessful in processing language or even typewritten alphabetic characters (Proceedings of the conference on pattern recognition, 1968).

Some Organising Mechanisms Involved in Perception

If a complex set of stimuli is perceived as organised, then this implies that various predictable and systematic relationships are seen to exist between various parts of the stimulus set. However, if systematic and predictable relations exist between parts of the set then the whole set can be reconstructed from a subset of stimuli. Thus, by organising the stimulus set, a person can reduce the amount of information required to describe that stimulus set.

Von Békésy (1967) has pointed out that the suppression of excess information is a basic necessity for dealing with the complex mass of information with which a person is constantly bombarded. He has demonstrated that inhibition and, particularly lateral inhibition, is one of the basic physiological means by which this suppression is achieved. Although von Békésy has shown that it is operating in all modalities, lateral inhibition has been studied principally in vision. The neural basis of lateral inhibition which was first demonstrated by Hartline *et al.* (1956) is the receptive field. When the centre of such a field is stimulated, the resultant output is a central area of positive excitation surrounded by a ring of negative excitation. A large array of such overlapping fields will suppress information by a process of contour sharpening. An approximate indication of the effect of this mechanism is that the excitation produced at any point is proportional to the change in illumination at that point. Thus, if there is no change in illumination there is no excitation, while a sharp change in illumination produces a large amount of excitation. By a lucky coincidence the same effect is produced by a Xerox copier, and so can be easily demonstrated (Fig. 9.1). Von Békésy has shown that lateral inhibition will account for various phenomena such as Mach bands and the Müller-Lyer illusion.

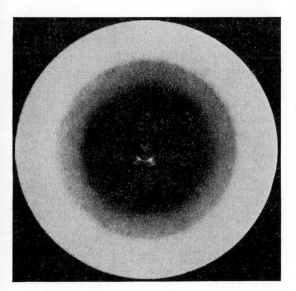

(a)

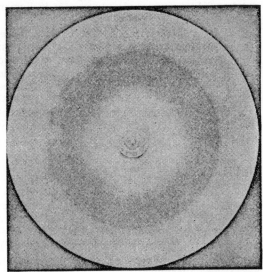

(b)

Fig. 9.1. Contour extraction by lateral inhibition

(*a*) A photograph of Mach's rotating disk from Sitzungsberichte der Akademie der Wissenschaften in Wien, Math.-nat. Cl. (1865, **52**, 303–322). The central black area has a constant intensity. The surrounding grey area has a gradient of intensity. (*b*) A Xerox copy of (*a*). Areas of constant illumination intensity, whether black or white, are reproduced lighter than areas of intensity gradients, demonstrating contour extraction by lateral inhibition.

Attneave (1954) has tried to quantify different parts of complex visual stimuli in terms of information theory. Using Shannon's (1951) guessing technique applied to a matrix of black and white squares he demonstrated that the maximum information was located at the contours, and particularly where the contours changed direction. This simply means that contours and changes in direction of contours are the least predictable part of a stimulus. Thus, it appears that at a very early stage in the perceptual process there is a built-in mechanism for organising stimulus sets in terms of contours. If the role of this organisation in selecting and rejecting information were to be emphasised then it might be referred to as a 'feature extracting' system, the feature in this case being the contour. In terms of Attneave's measure this system is also selecting those parts of the stimulus set with the highest information content.

There is evidence that there are other innate organising and feature-extracting systems occurring at relatively early stages in the perceptual process. Milner and Teuber (1968) conclude that the primary stages of the perceptual system are undoubtedly innate, quoting work of Hubel and Wiesel on the line and direction extracting cells found in the cortex of the cat (Hubel and Wiesel, 1963; 1965). Bower (1967) has found that many of the Gestalt principles of phenomenal identity such as object permanence and form constancy are already present in human infants 36 days old.

It is not yet known at what level the various organising principles of perception cease to rely on innate, built-in mechanisms and have to involve systems using learning and past experience. The elegant experiments of Held and his colleagues (Held and Freeman, 1963; Held and Hein, 1963) have demonstrated that some major aspects of perceptual organisation depend on experience of visuo-motor interaction.

Methods for Studying the Principles of Organisation Involved in Perception

The development of more sophisticated techniques of experimentation and analysis has resulted in a new lease of life for the study of the Gestalt principles of perceptual organisation (Wertheimer, 1922; 1923). In particular, the principle of 'grouping by similarity' has received attention.

Figure 9.2 (Beck, 1966) shows that orientation is the most powerful feature of the stimulus elements for organisation into groups, although this would not be expected from the judged differentness of the stimulus elements. In Fig. 9.3 (Goldstein, 1967), although the embedded figure is made up of circles

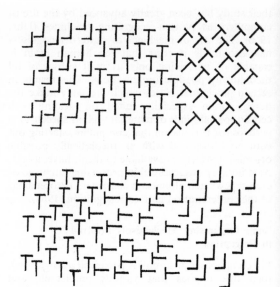

Fig. 9.2. Perceptual organisation by similarity
It can be seen that 45° rotation differences permit grouping more readily than shape differences (*after* Beck, 1966).

Fig. 9.3. The embedded figure cannot easily be seen although the circles of which it is composed are clearly smaller than the circles surrounding it (*after* Goldstein, 1967)

readily perceived as smaller than the surrounding ones, this principle of organisation cannot be used to perceive the embedded figure. Another powerful feature for producing grouping is movement of the stimulus elements. Since single-cell detectors for movement and orientation have been found in the cat cortex, one is tempted to speculate that features that readily produce grouping are detected by some such simple mechanism, while features that do not so readily produce grouping, such as size and shape, involve more complex mechanisms. Grouping has also been studied in the auditory modality using the technique of dichotic listening. When unstructured material (a string of digits) is presented, grouping tends to be based on physical characteristics; e.g. ear by ear or in terms of the spatial locations of the two sources (Broadbent, 1958). However, with structured material (sentences switching from ear to ear) the grouping tends to be determined by the structure (Yntema and Trask, 1963). Thus, dichotic listening provides another technique for investigating which stimulus features favour grouping.

Perception as a Hierarchical Processing System

Egeth (1967) has suggested that recognition, both in vision and audition, is the result of a hierarchy of tests performed on the sensory input. A similar model for the processing of sensory input in general is being proposed here. Sensory input is processed through a hierarchy of mechanisms that extract progressively more complex organisational principles or features. The lower level mechanisms are built-in and innate. The higher level mechanisms may also involve learning and past experience. Such a processing system retains only some parts of the sensory input, the rejected parts being predictable on the basis of those parts retained. Other systems of information reduction that do not have this effect will also be involved. Parts of the sensory input can be discarded with no possibility of prediction. This would occur, for example, if one modality were attended to at the expense of another. Also, parts of the sensory input might be rejected on the basis of organisations that were not actually present in the sensory input. In this case, predictions from the extracted features of the sensory input would be false. This 'imposition' of organisation would presumably occur at a relatively high level of the hierarchical system. The system is illustrated schematically in Fig. 9.4.

When very short-term storage is considered, memory and perception are intimately linked, and it is from studies of very short-term memory that there is good evidence of a hierarchical processing system. For both the auditory and the visual

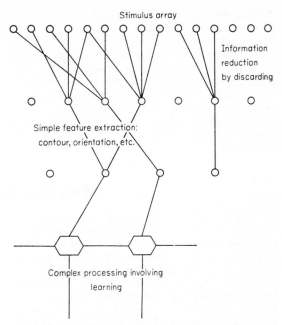

Fig. 9.4. Schematic illustration of some hypothetical perceptual processes

modalities there is evidence for the existence of very short-term stores from which stimulus material is rapidly lost (in less than two seconds). At this point the material is still stored in terms of its physical characteristics (Broadbent, 1958; Sperling, 1960; Craik, 1966). When the material is transferred to longer-term stores it is said to be 'recoded' into some more abstract form. This re-coding is identical to processing by the higher level organising systems referred to above, and the two memory stores clearly correspond to different levels in the perceptual hierarchy. It is clear that lower levels of the hierarchy will be more modality specific than higher levels. Sperling (1963) and Conrad (1963) have shown that once visually presented patterns have left the very short-term visual store they are placed in a longer-term auditory store, resulting in errors determined by acoustic confusability. Also, Garner and Gottwald (1968) have shown that recall of binary patterns is modality specific at high rates of presentation, but not at low rates of presentation. These results are explained by assuming that at low rates of presentation more processing of the input is possible so that higher levels of the perceptual hierarchy are involved.

It must be borne in mind that performance of mechanisms in the lower levels of the perceptual hierarchy can probably be modified by signals from the cortex and the reticular formation. Such modification would apply, for example, to the responsivity of the sense organs.

A Framework for the Discussion of Abnormalities of Perception

The framework for the discussion of abnormalities of perception will be based on the hypothetical hierarchy of perceptual processing. First, the preperceptual processes determining sensory thresholds will be considered with some discussion of the modification of these processes by the person's level of 'arousal'. Secondly, the 'simple' organising processes at low levels of the hierarchy will be considered. Since these are innate, built-in mechanisms, their abnormalities will be found most probably in people with unequivocal brain damage. Unfortunately, there is little work in this area. Methods for studying this kind of abnormality will be discussed. Thirdly, the 'complex' organising processes at high levels of the perceptual hierarchy will be considered in conjunction with the perception of complex patterns. Fourthly, perceptions that are not based on sensory input will be considered. In this section hallucinations and impositions of perceptual organisations will be discussed.

SENSORY THRESHOLDS

It is not just in the perception of complex stimuli that internal factors of the person perceiving play an important part. Signal detection theory and other methods have shown that subject variables play an important role in the determination of sensory thresholds. These subject variables principally concern various types of response bias and are, clearly, particularly important in the study of individual differences whether these differences have a normal or an abnormal source.

The Importance of Distinguishing Effects of Perception and Effects of Response Bias

1. THE THEORETICAL BACKGROUND

Several methods have been proposed to distinguish the effects of perception and response bias in studies of detection and recognition. An early example was the 'correction for guessing' procedure which Luce has shown to be unsatisfactory. Several methods for achieving this separation have now been developed (Luce, 1963) of which perhaps the most well known and easiest to apply is that derived from signal detection theory. Accounts of the principles and methods of signal detection theory are available from many sources (Swets, 1964; Swets *et al.*, 1961; Weintraub and Hake, 1962). However, a brief account of it is given here in an attempt to dispel the idea many seem to hold that it is accessible only to trained mathematicians. The theory assumes that any stimulus will, by the time it comes to be processed by the nervous system, have added to it random fluctuations known as noise. At least some of this noise is unavoidably present in the nervous system resulting, perhaps, from random firing of neurones. The situation is shown schematically in Fig. 9.5, where a person has to distinguish between noise and signal + noise.

It is assumed that the perceived intensities of the signal and the noise vary normally about some mean level. It can be seen from the diagram that whether a subject reports signal or noise will depend not only on the distance in perceptual intensity, d', between the signal and noise distributions, but also on the point at which the subject decides to place an arbitrary cut-off point to determine whether he will give the response 'signal' or 'no signal'. There are many different measures available for this criterion point. One of those used is β, which is the ratio of signal to noise probabilities at the criterion point. In some circumstances β may not be a useful measure of bias since its variability depends on the detectability of the signal. An alternative measure of bias might be the distance of the criterion from the mean of the noise distribution, c. If it is assumed that distributions of noise and signal are normal and have equal standard deviations, then it is a simple matter to calculate d' and β from the probability of a correct detection (number of correct detections over number of signals presented) and the probability of a false positive (number of false detections over number of non-signals presented). This can be done either with tables of the normal distribution or directly from tables of d' and β provided by Freeman (1964).

This, of course, is only the simplest example of a signal detection model. The theory will deal also

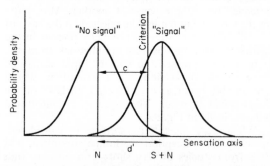

Fig. 9.5. The assumptions underlying the simplest version of signal detection theory

with situations where the distribution of noise is neither constant nor normal. For example, if a person qualifies his decisions by giving a confidence rating, the values for correct detection probabilities and false positive probabilities can be plotted against each other for different confidence levels. The resulting curve (known as the Receiver-Operating-Characteristic or ROC) can be used to describe the person's performance without making any assumptions about the underlying distributions of signal and noise.

The drawback of the psychophysical methods of measuring thresholds such as the method of limits, etc., is that the threshold measures they produce confuse effects due to the perceived difference between stimuli and those of the person's criterion for responding. A difference in response criteria between two groups, or a change in response criteria produced by a drug clearly demands a very different interpretation from a change in the detectability of a signal. Not only will traditional psychophysical methods confuse response criteria and detectability, but also they will give different results depending on which particular method is used. Pollack (1968), using a computer simulation, found that large differences in threshold were obtained using different procedures available for the method of limits, despite the fact that the underlying threshold distribution remained fixed.

2. EXPERIMENTAL COMPARISONS OF PSYCHOPHYSICAL AND SIGNAL DETECTION METHODS

The relation between signal detection theory and psychophysical threshold procedures has been discussed in detail by Treisman and Watts (1966). They showed that one traditional method, the method of constant stimuli, does give the parameters of signal detection theory unambiguously. They also suggest that signal detection methods may be fruitfully applied to tests of personality. They found a significant relationship between a person's criterion in a signal detection experiment and a measure of 'rigidity'. People using a cautious criterion were also unwilling to use a strategy previously associated with failure in a problem-solving task. Price (1966) has discussed the advantage of the signal detection methods over the traditional psychophysical procedures and has reviewed many studies that directly compare the two methods. Clark (1966; Clark et al., 1967) has compared traditional and signal detection theory methods in measuring flicker thresholds in psychiatric patients. In one experiment, facilitating instructions produced a change in threshold in terms of the traditional method which the signal detection method revealed to be due to a change in response

criteria rather than in sensitivity. In another experiment, psychiatric patients were found to have higher thresholds than normals, when this was measured with the method of limits, but with a forced choice method the difference disappeared. Since the forced choice method gives an unambiguous measure of sensitivity alone, the difference between the groups found with the method of limits must have resulted from a difference in response criteria, the patients being more cautious.

Clark (1969) has also studied the effect of a placebo on the pain response. After administration of what was described as a powerful analgesic, normal subjects sharply reduced the proportion of pain responses to a radiant heat stimulus. Analysis in terms of signal detection theory demonstrated that pain sensitivity remained unchanged. The effect of the placebo was to alter the subjects' response criteria.

Erikson (1960) has used signal detection theory to demonstrate the meaninglessness of the concept of 'subliminal' perception. The demonstration that a stimulus is below a threshold indicates the position of the subject's response criterion. In the laboratory, people tend to adopt, and are often trained to adopt, particularly cautious response criteria so as to minimise the number of false positives. Thus, it is likely that a large amount of information is available to the subject from stimuli that are apparently below 'threshold'. Similar criticisms can probably be made of studies of intersensory facilitation. Gregson and Wilson (1966) found that changes in taste threshold associated with changes in ambient light were related to changes in response strategy rather than taste sensitivity. Of particular interest was their finding (Wilson and Gregson, 1967) that the apparent facilitation effects were most marked when the taste stimuli were most difficult to discriminate. It would thus appear that when relevant cues are not available a person is prepared to use irrelevant ones to organise incoming stimuli.

Abnormalities of Sensory Thresholds

Unfortunately, although there is much evidence in the early literature, which has been extensively reviewed by Granger (1953, 1957, 1960), of abnormalities in the sensory thresholds of various psychiatric groups, few attempts have been made to elucidate these differences further by the application of signal detection methods. A similar state of affairs exists in the study of the effects of drugs on sensory thresholds (e.g. Misiak et al., 1966). The study by Clark et al. (1967) already mentioned and another by Kuechler and Dodwell (1968) found that differences between normal and psychiatric groups resided in the response criterion rather than the sensitivity. A study by Waggoner (1960) on response latency in a flicker fusion task showed that highly anxious subjects had high response latencies near threshold, suggesting that decision-making processes also play an important part in any threshold abnormalities shown by such subjects. Milner (1966) has pointed out the probable importance of decision-making processes in determining the thresholds of obsessional neurotics. Milner also found that at least some of the rise in sensory threshold that occurs with age is due to an increasingly cautious response criterion.

However, studies of thresholds probably have rather limited usefulness in relation to abnormal groups. The sensitivity to most sensory stimuli seems largely to be determined by mechanisms that are innate and peripheral. Levinson (1968) has proposed a model of flicker fusion in which the temporal behaviour of the human visual system is likened to that of a linear low-pass filter. This model is very similar to that described by Fuortes and Hodgkin (1964) for the time behaviour of the receptors in Limulus, and thus Levinson concludes that the location of this mechanism in man is most probably retinal. Application of this model has led to the discovery of hitherto unobserved pseudoflash and real flash phenomena. In accord with this theory Granger and Ikeda (1968) found that the site of action of alcohol, which decreases sensitivity to flicker, was in the retina, lying between the pigment cell layer and the bipolar layer. Similar mechanisms for the sense of flutter vibration have been studied by Talbot *et al.* (1968). It is also clear that some more complex perceptual functions such as contour sharpening and various coding operations are carried out by peripheral and/or innate neurological mechanisms (von Bekesy, 1967; Hubel and Wiesel, 1967; Whitfield, 1967). Thus, any abnormalities in the sensitivity of these mechanisms must be due either to neurological damage or to temporary centrally induced modification. Work on selective attention (Hernandez-Peon *et al.*, 1956; Treisman, 1964) suggests that such modification is possible of specific sensory mechanisms, but in relation to abnormal groups a general modification resulting from some change in state of, for example, 'arousal', has been most commonly studied.

Sensory Thresholds as Indices of 'Arousal'

Arousal is an elusive concept derived from the continuum of a person's activity from sleep to wakefulness and is discussed in greater detail in Irene Martin's chapters on Somatic Reactivity (Chapters 10 and 11). The concept of arousal is usually related to some underlying brain mechanism for which the reticular activating system is a favoured candidate (Eysenck, 1968). Since it is assumed to be a general state of the organism there are many ways of measuring arousal. However, the situation is complicated by the observation that high as well as low levels of arousal are detrimental to performance, there being an optimal level of arousal for any particular task (Yerkes and Dodson, 1908; Broadhurst, 1959).

Frith (1967) found that when arousal was increased by the presentation of auditory noise, sensitivity to flicker measured with a forced choice technique increased in extraverted but not in introverted people. This would be consistent with the theory (Eysenck, 1968) that introverts are consistently more highly aroused than extraverts, increased arousal taking the introverts beyond the optimum level for CFF performance. Kuechler and Dodwell (1968) studied auditory signal detection as a function of pre-stimulus shock. Sensitivity, d', increased for normals, but decreased for neurotics and schizophrenics. This also would be consistent with the abnormal groups being initially more highly aroused than the normals. The arousing effect of the pre-stimulus shock did not affect the response criterion β.

Two-flash- and Two-click Thresholds as Measures of Arousal in Schizophrenic Patients

A theory of schizophrenia largely due to Venables (1966a; 1969) suggests that most of the disorder can be accounted for in terms of a breakdown in the mechanisms regulating arousal, resulting in chronic over-arousal. In support of this theory Venables (1963) has shown that while there is a positive relationship between skin potential and two-flash threshold in normal subjects and paranoid schizophrenic patients, for non-paranoid schizophrenic patients the relationship is negative. A similar distinction was found between paranoid and non-paranoid schizophrenic patients when two-click thresholds were related to a measure of withdrawal (Venables, 1967). While the most withdrawn paranoid patients were less highly aroused (i.e. a longer interstimulus interval was required for the perception of two flashes), the non-paranoid schizophrenic patients were more aroused (i.e. a shorter interstimulus interval was required in the perception of two flashes) when most withdrawn. Hieatt and Tong (1969) studied the effects of increasing arousal on two-flash thresholds in normal people and schizophrenic patients. Arousal was increased with a non-distracting pedalling task. The sensitivity of the normal people increased with increased arousal, while the sensitivity of the schizophrenic patients decreased. This finding, too, would be consistent with over-arousal in the schizophrenic group.

However, another finding of Venables (1966b) does not seem to support the concept of arousal as a general state since the schizophrenic disorders seem to be partially modality specific. In a comparison of two-flash and two-click thresholds schizophrenic subjects showed relatively higher two-click thresholds than normals, indicating that it is auditory temporal discrimination that is particularly impaired in the schizophrenic group. A similar modality specific effect was found by Hermelin and O'Connor (1968) who studied the effects of light and sound stimuli on the arousal of normal and autistic children in terms of percentage of EEG alpha rhythm. Light stimuli did not differentiate the groups, but the autistic children were relatively more aroused by continuous sound than either the normal or subnormal controls. Ornitz (1969) has proposed that there is a disorder of perception common to both early infantile autism and schizophrenia. This disorder results from the breakdown of the homeostatic mechanisms of sensory input resulting in sometimes too much and sometimes too little stimulation. In view of the proposed role of the reticular formation as a mechanism controlling cortical arousal by determining the effect of sensory input on the cortex, it is clear that Ornitz's theory is very similar to that of Venables. Crucial to the testing of such theories is the discovery of a relatively 'pure' measure of cortical arousal. It is unfortunately the case that studies that have compared the various measures proposed (usually various sensory thresholds and physiological measures) have tended to find rather small relationships between them (Duffy, 1962; Hume, 1968).

Assuming there is indeed some underlying dimension that partially determines these various measures, then the lack of relationship between them could result from the various peripheral and un-related effects that are involved. (*See* Bartenwerfer, 1969, for discussion of this problem with physiological measures.) The extent to which Critical Flicker Fusion (CFF) thresholds may be determined by peripheral mechanisms have already been mentioned. Venables states that he measures two-flash threshold rather than CFF threshold since the former is a more direct measure of cortical arousal being unaffected by the brightness of the flashes over a wide range. Experiments by Hirsh and Sherrick (1961) suggest that the threshold for the correctly perceived order of two events might be even more closely related to some cortical mechanism since the same threshold is found both with different modali-

ties and crossmodally. However, they do not report correlations between these different measures. In the work of Venables described here, two-flash threshold has been measured with a modified version of the method of limits and, hence, sensitivity and response criteria have been confused. Venables is currently replicating this work using signal detection theory methods. So far only work with normal people has been reported, but this has suggested that a much more complex model must be invoked to account for two-flash and two-click thresholds. Venables and Warwick-Evans (1968) found that two-flash threshold was affected by the relative brightness of the two flashes. This is explained by supposing that the signal from the second flash cannot be detected until the 'noise' produced by the first flash is dissipated. On the basis of this, Venables (1968) proposes a two-factor theory of two-flash threshold. First, there is an arousal component determining the minimum detectable interflash interval, and secondly, there is the speed of dissipation of noise generated by the first stimulus. Murphy (1969) applied signal detection theory to the study of two-click thresholds. She found that, in certain circumstances, there was a difference in sensitivity, d', between the left and right ears, the left ear being more sensitive than the right. She suggests therefore that the two cerebral hemispheres may normally differ in their state of arousal.

Spitz and his colleagues (Spitz *et al.*, 1968; Spitz and Thor, 1968) have studied the perception of repeated visual stimuli in subnormal people. In a recent report of this work (Thor and Holden, 1970) in which people were required to count repeated light flashes, differences were found between normals and subnormals of the same mental age. Thor and Holden suggest that these results were due to a slower rate of processing of repeated visual stimuli in the subnormal group.

Time Estimation as a Measure of Arousal

The perception of time is often neglected, perhaps because there is no obvious sense organ involved. This might in fact be an advantage, since time perception might thus be more directly related to central, cortical processes. Many studies of the estimation of time provide some evidence that this measure might be a useful index of arousal. Treisman (1963) has studied temporal discrimination and proposed a model of the 'internal clock'. He found that, during a session of estimations, produced intervals lengthened and estimates of fixed intervals decreased. Both these effects would be consistent with a slowing down of the internal clock. Treisman suggests that these changes have similar origin to the decrements found in vigilance experiments (and so has von Sturmer, 1968). Emley and associates (1968) found similar trends during time-estimation sessions. They also found that there was more overestimation of fixed intervals in the morning than in the afternoon. This effect of time of day on time estimation was confirmed by Pfaff (1968). He also measured body temperature and found a close relationship between the changes in temperature and the changes in the estimated length of fixed intervals that occurred during the day. He suggested that the internal clock accelerates when temperature is raised. Cahoun (1969) studied time estimation explicitly in relation to physiological arousal. He found a relation between EEG alpha rhythm, heart rate, and time estimation in chronically aroused subjects. Goldstone (1967) found that barbiturates slowed down the clock, producing underestimations, while amphetamines produced the reverse effect. All these results are consistent with the idea that the speed of the internal clock, which determines how time will be estimated, is closely related to the level of arousal or activation of the person estimating.

Abnormalities of Time Perception

Two studies of time estimation in schizophrenic patients (Normington, 1967; Goldstone, 1967) revealed no systematic errors, but a greater inaccuracy. Goldstone also states that his schizophrenic subjects showed excessive over- and underestimation. This situation might be clarified by dividing the schizophrenic patients into some of the subgroups that have been proposed. Disorders of time perception are a common clinical feature of schizophrenia, and similar effects are also obtained with psychomimetic drugs. These disorders have been described by Cohen (1967). They include disorientation as to the time of day or the year and also abnormalities in the perception of the flow of time. There is no reason why such disorders should have any relation to abnormalities in the estimation of time, particularly as the time estimated in the experiments listed are all in the region of minutes or seconds rather than of hours. However, Banks et al. (1966) have confirmed this point, showing that feelings of disorientation of time in psychiatric patients were not necessarily associated with abnormal estimations.

Neurological Damage and the Perception of Simple Stimuli

1. CEREBRAL DAMAGE AND SENSORY THRESHOLDS

Milner and Teuber (1968) have extensively reviewed studies of the alterations in perception and memory

in vision, touch, and audition produced by brain lesions. Cerebral damage tends to cause reductions in the responsivity of the sense organs, resulting in raised sensory thresholds. Wilson and Wilson (1967) have studied abnormalities of touch sensitivity in cerebral palsied patients and have obtained with various measures evidence of a lowered touch sensitivity. Reduction of sensory thresholds in all modalities have been found associated with cerebral lesions to the primary and secondary receiving areas. In particular, more subtle and local changes such as the local reduction in sensitivity to flicker, in acuity, etc., and warping of subjective visual coordinates, have been found at the boundaries of central scotoma (areas of acquired blindness produced by penetrating missile wounds) (Milner and Teuber, 1968). If such lesions can be assumed to be entirely central then the question remains as to how they can alter sensory thresholds while the sensitivity of the sense organs has remained unchanged.

One suggestion that has been offered for the auditory modality is that there has been an increase in 'neural noise' (Gregory and Wallace, 1958) so that a low intensity signal remains buried in the noise. This noise might appear at a high level in the perceptual system. This account could be extended to all modalities, and receives support from results reported by Milner and Teuber (1968) for patients with hemisensory syndromes (i.e. with elevated touch thresholds on one side of the body opposite an injured cerebral hemisphere). For detection, these patients require a stimulus of greater physical intensity on their defective than on their normal side. However, as intensity of stimulation is increased, the subjective magnitude of the resulting pressure sensation increases more rapidly on the impaired side than on the normal side. Thus, at a sufficiently high level of physical intensity, sensations on the two sides will be subjectively as well as physically matched although the threshold on the defective side is greatly elevated. This finding is clearly consistent with the theory of increased noise on the defective side. This hypothesis could be tested using some of the methods described by Luce (1963). One of these would be the method derived from signal detection theory. However, it would be possible, if it were desired to retain the concept of threshold, to use methods based on the more sophisticated forms of threshold theory, e.g. the neural quantum theory (von Békésy, 1930; Stevens et al., 1941).

2. EFFECTS ASSOCIATED WITH SCOTOMA

A patient with a central scotoma will not complain of a large blind spot in the centre of his visual field

Fig. 9.6. This highly redundant figure tends to produce illustrations of movement at right angles to the lines, particularly if a field of randomly moving dots is projected on to it (*from* Mackay, 1957 by permission of the author, and the Editor of *Nature*)

but will report only that his acuity is diminished (Teuber, 1966). That the patient is making an active completion can be shown by his failure to perceive a gap in a line when this gap falls in the blind area. Such completion is most readily elicited by very redundant line patterns such as those used by MacKay (1957) (Fig. 9.6).

However, completion also occurs with fields completely filled with randomly moving dots (visual noise) (Milner and Teuber, 1968). The use of the word 'completion' in this context presupposes the hypothesis that the patients are reconstructing the sensory input on the basis of extracted features or organisations. For the blind area, where there is no input, they can be tricked into making false predictions.

3. ANALYSIS OF THE PERCEPTUAL DEFICITS PRODUCED BY CEREBRAL LESIONS

From the results discussed so far it seems likely that cerebral lesions will tend to affect processing at an early stage of the perceptual hierarchy, with the sense organs and the lowest level processing mechanisms remaining intact. If this is so, then the study of cerebral lesion effects should be of particular interest in that it should reveal something about the mechanisms in the early stages of the perceptual hierarchy. For example, if the early stages are concerned with simple feature extraction (orientation, movement, etc.) then the different lesions might differentially affect these various extractors. The resulting perceptual deficits would then give some

indication as to what features are normally extracted.

Warrington and her colleagues (personal communication, Warrington and Rabin, 1969a,b), are currently engaged in a series of experiments designed to define in more detail the various types of perceptual deficit produced by lesions in various parts of the cerebral cortex. In general, there is a tendency for patients with right hemisphere lesions to be more impaired on visuo-perceptual tasks than those with left hemisphere lesions (Milner and Teuber, 1968). Warrington has attempted to analyse visual perception into various stages distinguishing components of memory, space perception, form perception, etc. Of particular interest is her finding that in a successive perceptual matching, task division of errors into false positives and false negatives discriminated between groups that had been indistinguishable in terms of total errors. This finding suggests that signal detection methods could be usefully applied in this area.

4. NEW METHODS FOR STUDYING SIMPLE PERCEPTUAL DEFICITS

In addition to the necessity of a distinction between errors due to perceptual deficits and those due to response biases, it has also been considered necessary to distinguish between errors due to perceptual deficits and those due to memory deficits. Hermelin and O'Connor (1970), Warrington and Rabin (1969a) and others (reviewed by Milner and Teuber, 1968) have attempted this by comparing simultaneous with successive matching tasks. Probably this distinction between perception and memory will gradually disappear as the underlying mechanisms are elucidated. For example, if the transfer from an immediate to a short-term memory store requires a recoding of the sensory input, then it is valueless to distinguish between perception and memory in this process since coding is indistinguishable from perceptual organising. The futility of this distinction is demonstrated by the work of Kinchla and his colleagues (Kinchla and Smyzer, 1967; Allan, 1968) which also provides a useful methodology for studying perceptual processing at these low levels of the perceptual hierarchy.

Kinchla has studied the perception of the displacement of dots. A dot is presented, and after a variable interval a second dot is presented at the same or at a different point. This task can be considered either as perception of movement or as memory for position. This distinction is purely semantic. Kinchla assumes that this task involves the comparison of the second stimulus with the stored image of the first. In terms of this model, signal detection theory methods allow the measurement of the disintegration of the stored image with time (i.e. the extent to which change in

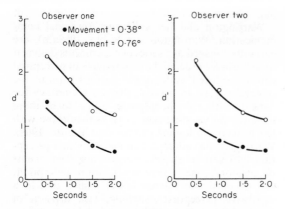

Fig. 9.7. Data demonstrating the disintegration of memory for the position of a dot with the passage of time (*from* Kinchla and Smyzer, 1967 by permission of the authors and Psychonomic Journals Inc.)

position becomes more difficult to detect as the time interval is increased (Fig. 9.7).

This method has been used to study other stimulus features such as the intensity of tones. Using this method it should be possible to study the various hypothetical feature-extracting mechanisms, and perhaps even to obtain evidence that certain stimulus features are extracted independently of each other. The method could throw considerable light on the hypothetical deficits of perception and storage produced by various cerebral lesions. Also,

by extending the time intervals used, it might be possible to demonstrate and elucidate the transfer and recoding of material from short-term to long-term stores. Since these stores are supposed to have different properties, such a transfer should appear as a discontinuity in the function relating detectability and time.

Another method for studying perception and storage at this early stage of the perceptual hierarchy has been developed by Eriksen and Collins (1968). Essentially this technique involves the successive, tachistoscopic presentation of two stimulus arrays. Viewed alone, each array contains only random dots. However, if the two arrays are fused a word is seen. The maximum interpresentation interval at which the word can still be seen gives an accurate estimation of the length of time that the physical characteristics of the first array could be stored. This method, too, could be extended for the study of the extraction and storage of various stimulus features.

Exactly this kind of analysis has been carried out using a slightly different methodology in some experiments by Julesz (1966). These experiments were concerned with the depth perception that results when stimuli containing areas of binocular disparity are fused. This impression of depth will occur even from monocularly shapeless and contourless random dot textures. Of particular interest is the finding that octal symmetry present monocularly will be suppressed in the binocular percept (Fig. 9.8).

Fig. 9.8. When the two figures are viewed stereoscopically a figure in depth is perceived and the octal symmetry of the right-hand figure disappears (*from* Suppression of Monocalarly Perceivable Symmetry during Binocular Fusion, *BSTJ*, Vol. 49, 1967, B. Julesz. Copyright, 1967, The American Telephone and Telegraph Co., reprinted by permission.)

Julesz suggests that a hierarchy of pre-processors exists (these correspond to simple feature extractors) from which the binocular fusion process selects only those that give some consistent global organisation. Thus, for instance, if edge detectors cannot provide a consistent organisation, the binocular fusion process may interrogate a lower level where there are dot detectors. It would be predicted that a patient with damage to any of these feature extractors would be unable to base binocular fusion upon them.

Sekuler and his colleagues (Houlihan and Sekuler, 1968; Pantle and Sekuler, 1968) have attempted to study the properties of the feature-extracting mechanisms in human vision, using a masking technique. They have found evidence for extractors of contour orientation and contour movement. The technique can be illustrated by considering the study of contour orientation. A test stimulus was presented tachistoscopically followed at a brief interval by a masking stimulus. If the angle between the test bar and the lines in the masking grating was 45 degrees or greater, then the masking grating was no more effective than a homogeneous masking field of equal luminance. However, as the angle between test bar and masking grating was decreased below 45 degrees, the masking became progressively more effective. The study of contour movement was essentially the same, but involved adapting stimuli rather than masking stimuli. Clearly, this technique could be used to study many different kinds of stimulus features, and could reveal any abnormalities of feature extraction at this low level of the perceptual processing hierarchy.

THE PERCEPTION OF COMPLEX STIMULI

1. THE ROLE OF EYE MOVEMENTS IN PERCEPTION

It appears that the rejection of the parts of a stimulus containing little information and suppressions of information by not looking are closely linked. Mackworth and Morandi (1967) found that the areas of a picture that received most fixations contained unpredictable contours or unusual details. Predictable outlines and regular textures received few fixations and were probably processed by the peripheral (anterior) retina. Mackworth and Morandi suggest that these predictable areas were processed and discarded in less than two seconds. An extensive study of the role of eye movements in visual perception has been carried out by Yarbus (1967). He also found that fixations tended to concentrate on areas of a picture that contained particularly important or unusual features. However, whether a feature is important or not will not depend entirely on the picture. Yarbus could show that when a person was asked to make some inference from what he saw in the picture, the pattern of eye movements made would depend on the information the person was trying to extract. Thus, as Gould (1967) has pointed out, eye movements provide a basis for inferences about higher order processing of visual stimuli. It is for this reason that a discussion of eye movements has a place in a chapter on abnormalities of perception.

Movement of the eye is basically a motor system controlled by muscles and therefore will not be discussed at any length here. Bartz (1967) studied fixation errors in eye movements to peripheral stimuli. Investigation of over- and undershoot errors showed them to be similar to those produced by body limbs pursuit tracking. In relation to the purely motor aspects of eye movements there has also been much discussion as to how movement of objects across the retina due to movements of the eye can be ignored. Starr (1967) has discussed some of these theories and has shown that a patient with disordered saccadic efferents had deficiency in localisation. He concluded that knowledge of the position of the eye depends in part on efferent information. Gibson (1968), however, has suggested that displacement of the retinal image is irrelevant. He proposes that various types of motion (i.e. of the observer, object or eye) are distinguished by various possible changes in the relationships of the components of the retinal image.

2. INDIVIDUAL DIFFERENCES IN EYE MOVEMENTS

Of more interest are studies in which eye movements provide information about the processing of visual stimuli. Dizney et al. (1969) studied fixations in reading in relation to anxiety. They found that anxious people made more eye movements when reading. Possible interpretations of this result would be that either the anxious people were gaining less information from each fixation or that they were cautious about accepting the information they did gain as being correct. These hypotheses might be tested by studying the detectability of words presented tachistoscopically, using a signal-detection paradigm. Conklin et al. (1968) studied the relationship between field dependency–independency and eye movement patterns. They found significant differences for track length and informative search, but none for the duration of fixations, and conclude that field independent people used a more effective search pattern. However, since field independence was defined by success with an embedded figures test, it might be argued that the concept of field dependency–independency was irrelevant to the experiment, which had simply revealed that an effective search pattern of eye movements is associated with success in finding embedded figures. Some of the perceptual deficits of schizophrenic patients, particularly those relating to size and distance judgements, have been accounted for in terms of scanning disorders (Silverman, 1964). These theories will be discussed in more detail later since eye movements have not usually been studied directly. However, Silverman and Gardner (1967) have studied the rates of saccadic eye movements and size judgements in normals and schizophrenic patients. For those people who underestimated size, there was no difference between the groups, but, for those who overestimated size there was a difference in that non-schizophrenics had unusually low rates of saccadic eye movements whereas schizophrenics had unusually high rates. McKinnon and Singer (1969) have criticised the scanning theory of size estimation. They found that medication was associated with a lower eye movement rate, but that a diagnosis of schizophrenia was not. Medication was also found to affect size judgement scores. However, eye movement rate did not relate to size judgement scores. Clarification of these conflicting results could probably be achieved by studying the exact relationship between fixation points and the parts of the object of which the size is being judged. Study simply of the rate of eye movements cannot give a proper indication of the underlying scanning process.

The pioneering work of Yarbus in studying these relationships has already been mentioned. He and his colleagues (Luria *et al.*, 1961) also studied the eye movements of brain-damaged and schizophrenic patients. These patients did not show the highly structured pattern of fixations of normal people. Their fixations appeared to be scattered randomly about the display, suggesting that they were unable to pick out the important features of the picture. Thomas and Stasiak (1964) found similar results with an undifferentiated group of psychiatric patients. These and a control group of non-patients looked at full-length pictures of people. The patients tended to have much longer or shorter fixation times than the normal group, but also the amount of fixations on the various body areas distinguished the groups. The non-patients looked at all body levels, but spent much more time looking at the head. This is also a characteristic feature of Yarbus's results. The patients, however, paid much more attention to other parts of the body. Thomas and Stasiak interpret this as a deliberate avoiding of faces on the part of the patients. Another interpretation might be that the patients were unable to select for fixation the most important aspects of the display, for it seems likely that the face carries the most information in a full-length picture of someone. This deficit of patients would then apply to any complex stimulus and not just those with social connotations.

It is clear that the detailed study of eye movements can throw much light on the underlying mechanism for processing visual stimuli. Unfortunately, the techniques for doing this are expensive and complex. It would be extremely useful if simple methods could be developed for studying fixation points. O'Connor and Hermelin (1967) report a very simple method they used to study the selective visual attention of autistic children. In this experiment the children could look at one of two displays or at a matt black background. The experimenter could easily see which the child was looking at at any time. It was found that the autistic children spent more time looking at the background than either the normal or subnormal controls. This group difference was independent of the nature of the display, and all children spent more time looking at a display of a face than at a random picture. Thus, in autistic children, also, there seems to be a breakdown of the principle that the important aspects of a complex stimulus display will receive the most fixations. This hypothesis can account for the clinical observation of 'gaze avoidance' of autistic children, suggesting that this does not necessarily have any emotional or social causes.

Size and Distance Judgements in Schizophrenia

Many studies have been carried out concerning how accurately schizophrenics can judge size and distance. In order to make such judgements it is necessary to observe and integrate many different aspects of a complex stimulus array, including the object and its background. Thus, study of size and distance judgements can give information about the processing of complex visual stimuli.

The literature on size constancy and schizophrenia has been reviewed by Price and Erikson (1966). They suggest that much of the confusion and lack of consistency is due to methodological faults. Particularly inconsistent are those studies that have compared unspecified schizophrenics with a normal control group. More consistent results have been obtained when the schizophrenic patients have been subclassified into paranoid, non-paranoid and into acute-chronic. A second methodological fault of most of these studies is that perceptual capabilities have been confused with the subjective criteria used by the subjects in making the judgements. This is the same criticism that has been applied to studies of sensory thresholds. Once again, one possible solution is the application of signal detection theory methods. Price and Erikson (1966) carried out a study of size constancy in which these methodological errors did not apply. Paranoid and non-paranoid schizophrenic patients and normal people were compared using a signal detection method involving confidence ratings for each judgement. There was no difference in the point of subjective equality for the three groups, although all groups showed a slight amount of under-constancy. However, a signal detection analysis showed that the perceptual sensitivity of the non-paranoid schizophrenic patients was significantly lower than that of the other two groups. Another significant difference was revealed by a study of the response categories used. The paranoid schizophrenics made excessive use of the extreme confidence rating 'positive'. A similar type of response bias was found in certain schizophrenic patients by Miller and Chapman (1968). Thus, in Price and Erikson's study the signal detection method revealed perceptual differences and response biases, all of which would have been concealed or confused using traditional psychophysical methods. The finding of low perceptual sensitivity in the non-paranoid schizophrenic patients might shed some light on the confusion as to whether over- or under-constancy is characteristic of this group. Low sensitivity alone should not give rise to systematic error in either direction, but it might well exaggerate any tendency produced by the properties of the stimulus presented.

The effect of purely perceptual (as opposed to content) aspects of the stimulus configuration on these types of judgements was found in a slightly different area by Wells and Caldwell (1967). They studied perception of the vertical and found that normal people were more accurate than schizophrenic patients in adjusting objects to the vertical. Several different objects were used as stimuli and while the content did not affect the performance of the two groups differently, one particular object, a cat, was consistently tilted by all subjects. This effect was almost certainly due to the cat being poorly drawn and distorted. The effect of such aspects of the stimulus on such judgements is of particular concern in interpreting the studies that have claimed an effect of the thematic content on the size or distance judgements of schizophrenics (e.g. Webb et al., 1966). It is almost impossible for stimuli to differ in thematic content without also differing in purely perceptual, geometric properties also. For example, it would be likely that in an experiment comparing the judgement of objects and people the stimuli would also differ in complexity. In view of these various methodological flaws there is probably no good evidence that the size and distance judgements of schizophrenic patients is affected by the thematic content of the stimuli. Blumenthal and Meltzoff (1967) found that schizophrenic patients were less accurate in judging the distance apart of two objects than normal people, and that social aspects of the stimuli had no effect.

Some possible artefacts that have been studied in this type of experiment are those relating to the definition of the schizophrenic group. For example, Silverman et al. (1966) suggest that the perceptual deficits found in schizophrenia may be partially, at least, due to effects of institutionalisation rather than the disease itself. They found that differences between acute and chronic schizophrenic patients were similar to those between short- and long-term prisoners. However, duration of illness and length of institutionalisation will tend to be confounded. Johannsen and O'Connell (1965) found that, when duration of illness was held constant, differences in length of institutionalisation did not affect performance on various perceptual tasks.

Studies of this perceptual deficit in schizophrenia will not be very fruitful unless some attempt is made at delineating the underlying mechanisms. There seems to be reasonably good evidence that non-paranoid schizophrenics are less accurate than normal people in their judgement of the size and distance of objects. The next step required is a detailed analysis of their performance in an attempt to reveal how their bad performance arises. Stannard et al. (1966) studied the effects of information feedback on the size judgement of schizophrenic patients. They found that feedback produced a reduction of errors in the schizophrenic group and concluded that the differences in size judgement were due to instructional control (i.e. pay-off, response bias) rather than perception. With regard to the perceptual differences of the type that Price and Eriksen (1966) found, a useful methodology for further investigation is suggested by some work of Humphrey and Weiskrantz (1969) on size constancy in monkeys. They found that breakdown in constancy after infro-temporal lesions was due to oscillations between one 'correct' and two 'incorrect' strategies. 'Incorrect' strategies involved using retinal size or distance information alone in judging size. That is, the animals with lesions were less able to integrate information coming from different aspects of the stimulus. Weckowicz and Blewett (1959) have suggested that size constancy judgements and abstract thinking in schizophrenics should be related on the grounds that the ability to select and integrate relevant stimuli is necessary for both activities.

Theories of the Deficit in Processing Complex Stimuli by Schizophrenic Patients

Any search for the underlying mechanisms of schizophrenic perceptual dysfunction must be guided by prior speculation. The theory of scanning in relation to experiments on eye movements has been mentioned, and has been discussed in detail by Silverman (1964, 1968). The theory considers the perceptual deficits of schizophrenia in terms of cognitive strategies for dealing with complex stimulus arrays, and derives from Piaget's (1950) theories about the development of intelligence in children. Silverman proposes two stages for perceptual processing. The first involves stimulus sampling in a sensory or perceptual field that may be more or less extensive ('scanning control'). The second involves attention to some aspects and inhibition of attention to other aspects of the field ('field articulation'). These proposed mechanisms clearly show a close relationship to the idea of feature extraction outlined in the introduction to this chapter. Silverman suggests that paranoid schizophrenic patients show extensive scanning and field articulation, whereas non-paranoid schizophrenic patients show the opposite. Cromwell (1968) has suggested that an explanation in terms of unnecessary attention to redundant stimuli rather than in terms of eye movements might be preferable. However, as already pointed out, eye movements almost certainly play a vital role in the selection of key stimulus elements for attention, and in the rejection of redundant ones.

Broen (1966, 1969) suggests that response disorganisation characterises both chronic and acute schizophrenic patients. However, he also considers that breadth of observation is an important variable and suggests that chronic schizophrenic patients attempt to cope with their deficits by observing fewer stimuli.

Summarising these theories in slightly different words might be useful both in organising the various studies of the perception of complex stimuli that remain to be discussed and also in suggesting further experiments. Schizophrenic perception, it is suggested, might be deficient in the mechanism for selecting the important and relevant information from a complex stimulus array and rejecting the rest. This is closely similar to the field articulation theory of Silverman. However, I would think that this selection process begins even before the scanning process (in terms of eye movements). It is because he is unable to reject the irrelevant aspects of the perceptual environment that the acute schizophrenic patient is bombarded with excess stimulation (Ornitz, 1969) and may indulge in excessive scanning since he has no information available to organise and direct it. Chronic schizophrenic patients may learn to deal with this deficit by rejecting information on the basis of some simpler organisation of the perceptual environment than that used by normal people. Broen has suggested (personal communication) that chronic schizophrenic patients might organise incoming stimuli on the basis of modality, so that if visual information was of primary importance, auditory information would be completely ignored. He has confirmed this in an as yet unpublished study in which he found that the detectability of tones was significantly lower for chronic than acute schizophrenics when they were performing a visual task, than when the tones were of primary concern. This effect on detectability suggests that an actual attenuation of the signal was involved rather than an effect on response bias. A similar finding has been reported by Al-Far (1968) who studied dichotic listening in schizophrenic patients. He found that the most severely ill nonparanoid schizophrenic patients were able to report only the numbers presented to one of their ears, although there was no difference between the ears in acuity. This suggests that they were completely rejecting information from one ear.

Methods for Analysing the Perception of Complex Stimuli

In order to investigate this proposed theory and to gain more information about the perceptual strategies of schizophrenic patients and other abnormal groups it is necessary to control the various aspects of the total perceptual field and to be aware of various ways in which they might be organised to allow the selection of the important and relevant parts.

Pishkin and Bourne (1969) studied concept identification in normal and schizophrenic subjects paying particular attention to the use made of the various cues provided. Normal people made more use of the relevant stimulus information than the schizophrenic patients; however, the normal people were also more sensitive to the irrelevant background cues. The groups were particularly differentiated in terms of the use they made of 'social' cues, that is, information coming from a stooge. Schizophrenic patients almost entirely failed to make use of such information. Pishkin (1966) has reported a similar study of size judgement in normals and schizophrenics. In this study also the schizophrenics showed particular difficulty in making use of cues provided by people.

Bemporad (1967) found that schizophrenics had difficulty in ordering parts of stimuli into a whole. When asked to describe the Ishihara colour blindness cards, they mentioned the coloured dots before the numerals. Wescott and Tolchin (1968) studied individual and age differences in the ability to recognise fragmented pictures. They found stable differences relating to the degree of completeness needed for the first attempt at identification and for the degree of completeness needed for correct identification. Ebner and Ritzler (1969) studied this ability in chronic and acute schizophrenic patients. Chronic schizophrenic patients needed more completeness for correct recognition than either acute schizophrenic patients or normal people, although they did not differ in terms of completeness needed for first response or in the number of pre-recognition hypotheses.

Johannsen and Testin (1966) studied the assimilation of visual information in schizophrenic patients by requiring the reproduction of the position of a dot in a matrix presented tachistoscopically. The performance of chronic schizophrenic patients deteriorated considerably in comparison to acute schizophrenic patients when the grid lines defining the matrix were removed.

The perceptual processing of a complex stimulus array can be conveniently studied using tasks requiring a person to search for certain elements in the array. Search of some kind is required, for example, when it is necessary to decide whether two complex arrays are the same or different. Sekuler and Abrams (1968) have studied this process in normal people. They found that search for similarity took longer than search for identity, and suggest that this reflects the difference between serial search and Gestalt processing. Talland and Quarton (1966) have studied the effects of drugs on continuous search, but their results suggest that it was the vigilance aspect of this task, rather than the perceptual processing, that was affected by the drugs. Cowan (1968) has proposed a model of visual search behaviour in terms of a series of discrete observing responses that can be described in terms of an absorbing Markov process. Clearly all these methods would be very useful for studying perceptual processing in schizophrenic and other abnormal groups. However, as far as I know, they have yet to be applied.

Multivariate analysis provides a convenient framework for studying the organisation of stimuli in an array. Schiffman and Falkenberg (1968) have proposed a method (very similar to factor analysis) for finding such underlying organisations from a matrix relating stimulation and the output of single neurones. They have validated the method by studying colour vision for which the underlying neural organisation is known, and also applied it to the sense of taste for which the underlying organisation is less clear. The same technique can be applied to the perception of more complex stimuli. Grodin and Brown (1967) presented schematised faces for which certain dimensions were varied, and required people to give a judgement of their degree of friendliness (Fig. 9.9). Grodin and Brown tested the hypothesis that this judgement could be reliably predicted on the basis of some linear function of the characteristics in the schematised faces that was stable for any one person. They found that normal people performed more often in a consistently linear fashion than paranoid schizophrenic patients.

In more detail, this hypothesis, originally put forward by Rodwan and Hake (1964), states that a person's judgement of some characteristics of the schematised face is determined by two sets of parameters, one set provided by the stimulus and the other by the person judging. Thus, judged degree of friendliness is assessed as $F = aX_1 + bX_2 + cX_3$, where X_1, X_2, X_3 are dimensions of the face (length of chin, distance between the eyes, length of forehead) and a, b, c are constants determined for an individual judge. This technique could be extended to study any complex stimulus array and also could be used to investigate to what extent the different features of the array were processed independently.

It can be seen that there is a striking similarity between this experimental method and the test of

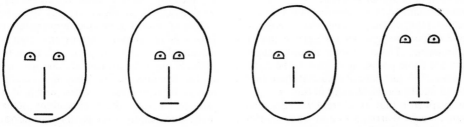

Fig. 9.9. Schematic faces variable along four dimensions (*after* Brunswik and Reiter, 1937)

thought disorder in schizophrenia developed by Bannister and Fransella (1966). In this test, people are required to judge photographs of faces along various scales such as 'kind', 'honest', etc. A major difference is that, since photographs are used rather than schematised faces, the underlying characteristics on the basis of which the judgements are arrived at cannot be specified. Bannister and Fransella believe that it is the understanding of the 'constructs' ('kind', 'honest', etc.) rather than the perceptual processing of the faces that is disordered in certain schizophrenic patients, but there is still the need for experimentation on this point. For example, Miller and Chapman (1968) report an experiment using a procedure very similar to this test. Normal people and schizophrenic patients had to judge photographs of people along two logically related scales. The schizophrenics made more random errors than the normals (i.e. they had a lower test-retest correlation). When the groups were matched on the basis of test-retest reliability it was found that the schizophrenics showed an accentuation of normal response biases in terms of an extreme similarity of ordering on the two related scales. In the Bannister and Fransella test no direct measure of test-retest reliability is inferred, although almost certainly it will influence both the scores ('Intensity' and 'Consistency') that are derived. Calculations of test-retest reliabilities as well as these scores might shed more light on the processes underlying performance on this test (Frith and Lillie, 1971; Williams, 1971).

In concluding this section on the perception of complex stimulus arrays mention will be made of studies of some peculiar asymmetries of human visual perception that cannot easily be accounted for in terms of the various processing models that have been proposed. Sekuler and Houlihan (1968) studied the discrimination of mirror images in adults. Using a choice time analysis they found that left-right reversals were more difficult to discriminate than up-down reversals. It has often been observed that people tend to process visual stimuli from left to right and this has been attributed to Western reading habits. However, Braine (1968) found that young Israelis also processed from left to right although they had read nothing but Hebrew.

Another asymmetry was observed by Hochberg and Galper (1967). They found that recognition accuracy for faces was greater for upright than for inverted viewing. These various findings suggest that there are some perceptual biases in the human visual system. It is just conceivable that these biases might be related to the asymmetry of function of the brain hemispheres that is currently being much investigated (e.g. Warrington and James, 1967; Milner and Teuber, 1968).

The Perception of Speech and Other Sequential Patterns

In the study of auditory sequential patterns, like speech, there is no direct indicator analogous to eye fixations to show which aspects are receiving particular attention. However, in speech there are powerful methods available for controlling the amount of redundancy (i.e. unnecessary information) in any message. Shannon (1951) devised a method of guessing to generate passages of text with varying degrees of contextual constraint or redundancy. Miller and Selfridge (1950) used such passages to demonstrate that in normal people immediate memory was facilitated by increasing redundancy. Lawson et al. (1964) studied the effect of this contextual constraint on the perception of speech in schizophrenic patients. They found that the schizophrenic patients did not differ from normal people in their recall of random word strings, but became progressively more impaired as the degree of contextual constraint increased. Raeburn and Tong (1968) have suggested that such results might be an artefact due to low vocabulary levels and slower written responses in the schizophrenic group. However, the results have been replicated in a carefully controlled study by Levy and Maxwell (1968). They showed that the finding could not be a result of drugs, hospitalisation or vocabulary level. However, they found that depressed patients showed the same inability to use contextual constraint as the schizophrenic ones.

The deficit underlying this inability to make use of contextual constraint might lie either in the area of syntactics or of semantics. If the deficit lay in the area of semantics it would be expected that schizophrenics would show less appreciation of the meaning of words and, thus, a weakening of the associations between words. Studies of word associations in schizophrenia (Pavy, 1968) have suggested that schizophrenics do indeed show abnormal word associations. Deckner and Blanton (1969) found that schizophrenics performed as well as normal people when rewarded for choosing the strong associations of stimulus words, but were significantly inferior when rewarded for choosing weak associations. However, this might be due to a failure of reward to produce appropriate behaviour. Moon et al. (1968) demonstrated that apparently abnormal associations produced by schizophrenic patients might be an artefact due to misperception of the stimulus words. They first required people merely to repeat the stimulus words as quickly as possible. Under these conditions schizophrenics made significantly more errors than normals. Then, a normal word-association test was given. Accepting stimuli and responses at face value in this test it appeared that the schizophrenics gave more unusual and poor associations. However, when the data were re-analysed for mis-hearings this effect disappeared. A mishearing was considered to have occurred if a response was a 'good' association for a word phonetically similar to the stimulus word. Application of this procedure removed all the apparently abnormal associations, so that the associations given by the schizophrenic group were no different from those given by normal people. This greater mishearing of words in the schizophrenic group could not be accounted for by any simple auditory abnormalities.

If the inability of schizophrenics to make use of contextual constraint does not lie in the area of semantics, then it might be a result of a failure to recognise or use syntactic structure. In this case, schizophrenics might have difficulties with any kind of sequential patterning and not just with that produced in speech by the underlying grammatical rules. I am unaware of any attempt to study the appreciation of such sequential patterns by adult schizophrenic patients, but such studies have been made with autistic children. Hermelin and O'Connor (1967) have shown that autistic children also show an inability to make use of contextual constraint. Whereas a normal and a subnormal control group showed much better recall of sentences than of random word strings, the recall of autistic children was less affected by the increased structuring provided by the sentences.

This finding was followed up by Frith (1970a; 1970b), who investigated the ability of children to make use of simple sequential structures not associated with language. The children had to recall binary sequences with varying degrees of structure. The structure was provided by simple repetitions, e.g. 'spoon spoon spoon spoon horse horse'; or by repeating sub-units, e.g. 'spoon horse spoon spoon horse spoon'. It was confirmed that, while the children did not differ in their ability to recall quasi-random sequences, the autistic children did not benefit as much from structure as the normal and subnormal control groups. All the lists presented were approximately double the digit span of the children who had to recall them. However, with the structured lists, normal children were able to remember more words than would have been predicted on the basis of their digit span. Frith proposed a two-stage mechanism to account for this. First the child reduces a list to its important features and remembers only these. Then, during recall an attempt is made to reconstruct the list by applying rules based on these features. She found evidence for this mechanism in the errors made by the children. In these simple binary sequences only two basic features or rules are possible; repetitions and alternations. It was found that the errors made by normal children tended to result from exaggerations of these features. Thus, if a sequence containing predominantly alternations was presented, the child would recall a list with an even greater predominance of alternations and, similarly, with perseverations. However, with the autistic children, the errors did not reflect the predominant features of the presented list, but tended to consist of repetitions whatever had been presented. Frith concluded that the autistic children were unable to perceive the important features in the structured lists. She found similar results with visually presented sequences. If random sequences were presented, then the differences between the children disappeared. All children imposed structure on the perceived sequences, the type of structure imposed not differentiating the autistic from the normal children. Thus, it seems that autistic children treat all sequences as if they were random with no important features to be extracted, and thus impose their own structure.

This imposition of structure on to stimulus arrays seems to be a necessary activity in people of all ages (especially psychologists). Adults asked to guess the next event in a random sequence will produce responses that are far from random. This was particularly noted in the famous Zenith Radio experiments on ESP (Goodfellow, 1938). Wundt (1896) also observed that people listening to a metronome where every beat was of equal intensity could not prevent themselves from actually hearing rhythmic patterns of stronger and weaker beats.

Perception Uncontrolled by Stimuli: Perceptual Biases and Preferences

The tendency to impose structure, if this is not already present in the stimulus array, provides a means of studying the perceptual biases present in a person. This is, of course, the basis of projective tests like the Rorschach. Unfortunately, in such tests there has been too little control of the minimal stimuli on which the perceiver pins his structure, and the interpretations of his perceptions have been carried out at some very deep level without a proper understanding of the primary perceptual biases. There are very few studies that have attempted to look at perceptual biases at this very simple and basic level. Yacorzynski (1941) looked for the perceptual principles involved in the prediction of the occurrence of binary patterns selected by chance. Normal people tended to select non-symmetrical patterns producing fewer strings of alternations and perseverations than would be expected by chance.

This probably reflects their concept of what a random sequence should be like. Schizophrenic and manic-depressive patients, on the other hand, showed different preferences, particularly for strings of alternations. However, this difference between the groups may not reflect different perceptual biases, but differences in the effects of task instructions. In situations where they are not explicitly told to produce random sequences, normal people will also produce patterned sequences although random ones have been presented. Hodge and Reige (1966) looked at response patterns in binary choice tasks with non-discriminable stimuli. They found that normal people produced a moderate degree of patterning, particularly favouring repetitions.

The preference of people for different kinds of stimulus arrays might reveal something of their perceptual biases. Boesch et al. (1968) and Baltes et al. (1968) have carried out detailed surveys of the preferences of many age groups for very simple visual and auditory sequences. There was great similarity across modalities, showing that older people prefer increasingly slower stimulus sequences.

Berlyne (Berlyne et al., 1963) has done much work on preference for complexity. He has shown that higher arousal tends to be associated with preference for a lesser degree of complexity. It is thus consistent with the theory that schizophrenic patients are chronically over-aroused; Neale and Cromwell (1969) found that schizophrenic patients showed the greatest preference for the least complex shapes. These authors also suggest that there is a match between preference for environmental information and input processing capacities. Consistent with this notion is the clinical observation that autistic children, who also have poor information processing capabilities, show an 'insistence on sameness' in the environment, and perform ritualistic acts. Also consistent with theories relating arousal and preference for complexity is an experiment by Skrzypek (1969). He compared psychopathic and neurotic delinquents and found a significant negative correlation between complexity preference and anxiety. He also found that after perceptual isolation, psychopaths increased their complexity preference, whereas after an arousing task neurotics increased in anxiety and showed decreased complexity preferences.

Hallucinations as Impositions of Organisation

I have discussed very briefly some perceptual biases that appear in preference for stimuli and in perception of unstructured stimuli. It seems plausible, though somewhat of an oversimplification, to suggest that it is the attempt to impose some kind of 'meaning' on random input that underlies hallucinations. Katz et al. (1968), discussing the effects of LSD, suggest that Bartlett's (1932) 'effort after meaning' will apply when a person is confronted with experiences not comprehensible in terms of his previous experience. There is clearly no difference between incomprehensible experience and unstructured experience since comprehension means structuring. Forgus and Dewolfe (1969) showed that the perceptual biases revealed in hallucinations also occurred in more normal situations. When hallucinating patients were given stories containing many themes to recall, the dominant recall theme could be predicted from the dominant theme present in their hallucinations in 18 out of 23 subjects.

The stimulation that a person is continually experiencing will be a mixture of signals and random noise. Thus, the amount of random stimulation a person is receiving can be increased either by increasing the noise or by decreasing the signal. This decrease of the signal is the essential feature of many experiments on sensory and perceptual deprivation. These studies and the theories based on them have been extensively reviewed by Zuckerman and Cohen (1964) and Zubek (1964). There is a tendency for fewer hallucinations to be reported in the more recent studies than were reported in the early studies. However, this is almost certainly an effect of the criteria adopted to define hallucinations. Thus, with the very strict criterion that a hallucination is 'an uncontrolled change in sensation that the subject believes to be true', only about 2 per cent of people undergoing deprivation have hallucinations. If visual or auditory experiences of varying degrees of complexity are considered, then these commonly occur even after relatively short periods of deprivation (Schulman et al., 1967). Thus, there is some evidence that exposing normal people to unstructured stimulation can induce experiences that have similarities to those described by psychiatric patients and labelled hallucinations.

Other methods that induce hallucinations in normal people have also been found. It is claimed that positive and negative hallucinations can be induced by hypnosis. However, an experiment by Stewart (1968) suggests that these have little similarity to hallucinations induced by other methods. Stewart found that the loudness of a person's voice varied directly as a function of actual sound level, but not at all as a function of hallucinated sound level. This would be consistent with the view that under hypnosis people feel compelled to 'fake' an hallucination; however, their inadequate knowledge ensures that there will be flaws in their performance.

There has been much interest in the hallucinations

induced by drugs like LSD. Although these are certainly true perceptions, there are nevertheless striking differences between them and the hallucinations found in psychoses. Malitz *et al.* (1962) found that the predominant hallucinatory response to LSD and similar drugs was visual, whereas among a random selection of chronic schizophrenic patients there was a 50 per cent incidence of auditory hallucinations and only a 9 per cent incidence of visual hallucinations. Feinberg (1962) also found differences in the type of visual hallucinations found in schizophrenic patients. For example, the geometric patterns and distortions of colour that are an essential feature of LSD and Mescaline induced hallucinations are rarely reported by schizophrenic patients. All the topics mentioned above are discussed in the book on hallucinations edited by West (1962).

The Experimental Study of Hallucinations

Apart from these different attempts to induce them, the experimental study of hallucinations has largely been neglected, probably because the experimenter must depend on the subjective reports of his subjects. An ingenious technique applied by Haber and Haber (1964) to the study of eidetic imagary in children might also be applicable to the study of visual hallucinations. Haber and Haber systematically relied on eye movements in this study, and using this criterion could clearly distinguish children with eidetic imagery. These children all clearly scanned their images while other children virtually never did. In addition, the eidetikers were far more accurate in recall of the pictures from which the image derived, their images lasted much longer, and tended to be positively coloured.

Eye movements have also been used in an attempt to study visual imagery in dreams. Roffwarg *et al.* (1962) were relatively successful in an attempt to relate the recorded eye movement of a sleeper with those inferred from his subsequent report of his dream. Using eye movements in this way it might be possible to have an objective indication of when a person was having a visual hallucination and also of what might be the content of the hallucination.

The difficulties that result from the dependence on subjective reports are pointed out by Miller *et al.* (1965). They found that hallucinating schizophrenics had an overall impoverishment in descriptive language skills. Because their patients were soldiers, intelligence test data was available to show that a longstanding cognitive deficit had been noted on testing prior to illness. Miller *et al.* suggest that, when a patient has to describe incomprehensible and stressful internal experiences, a low level of descriptive language skills will result in a more deviant description.

Hoehn-Saric and Gross (1968) attempted to describe the changes in auditory hallucinations that occur with drug treatment and drug withdrawal. They found that frequency, loudness, and emotional reaction were the characteristics that changed significantly rather than perceptual and cognitive characteristics. This probably reflects the greater objectivity of the former measures. McGuigan (1966) studied the relation between covert oral behaviour and auditory hallucinations. He found that just before auditory hallucinations were reported there was a significant increase in whispering and tongue muscle action potentials. Chin muscle action potentials and breathing amplitude also increased. These changes were specific to speech mechanisms and not related to general bodily arousal. Reimer and Hauss (1966) attempted to do an experiment that required presenting pictures tachistoscopically to a group of recovered schizophrenics. However, this procedure reactivated the patients, producing anxiety, illusory misperception, and hallucinations. Saravay and Parde (1967) studied the so-called 'elementary' auditory hallucinations found in alcohol withdrawal psychosis. They concluded that the sounds reported were not hallucinations but actual sounds produced by pathological contraction states of the muscles governing the middle ear. This result suggests a possible source for random stimulation on which a person might, in some circumstances, try to impose meaning.

Hallucinations and Reality

The imposition of meaning on random stimulation is clearly not sufficient to account for the genesis of hallucinations. In addition, the person must accept this perception as representing reality. This may be the crucial component of schizophrenic hallucinations. The images produced by LSD are generally perceived as unreal although very vivid, whereas dreamers and schizophrenics believe in the reality of their images although they may be very indistinct (Neisser, 1967). Neurophysiological theories of hallucinations have been proposed (Hernandez-Peon, 1966; Evarts, 1962) which attempt to account for this acceptance of internally generated perceptions as reality. Hernandez-Peon and Evarts both assume that dreams and hallucinations are essentially similar in origin. It is suggested that the dream system involves structures concerned with recent memory and is inhibited by the vigilance system during wakefulness. Similar inhibition is applied to structures involving remote memories and emotions

11

and motivations. Hallucinations thus result when there is a failure of this inhibition during wakefulness. Control and inhibition of these various systems is thought to depend on the arousal system, mediated by the ubiquitous ascending reticular formation. West (1962), for example, suggests that there is a curvilinear relationship between arousal and the 'integration of consciousness'. The disintegration resulting in dreams or hallucinations would then occur both at very high and at very low levels of arousal. These neurophysiological theories are clearly more concerned with explaining how

hallucinations come to be accepted as reality rather than with the mechanisms of the percepts themselves.

Viscott (1968) has reported some interesting results that seem consistent with the common origin of dreams and hallucinations. He found seven cases of patients who had hallucinations when taking Clordiazepoxide (Librium). These hallucinations occurred just before sleep or after waking. It was as if the patient continued to dream for a short while even after waking up, suggesting an impairment of the inhibition of dream material.

CONCLUSIONS

By discussing perception in terms of information processing, the boundaries between concepts such as memory, cognition, and perception have tended to become blurred, and thus have not been used as a framework. Probably these distinctions are no longer very useful, and certainly very interesting techniques and hypotheses have been developed which cut across these categories. Although this approach has suggested new hypotheses that could

be applied to the study of abnormalities of perception in various groups, there are still no definite statements that can be made about any existing perceptual dysfunctions. However, a survey of the literature shows that, in the field of general experimental psychology, this approach is producing a wealth of new techniques. The possibilities that may result from the application of these new techniques to the study of abnormalities of perception are very exciting.

REFERENCES

AL-FAR, B. (1968) Short term memory, alternation of attention, and perceptual confusion in schizophrenia. Unpubl. Ph.D. thesis, Univ. of London lib.

ALLAN, L. G. (1968) Visual position discrimination: A model relating temporal and spatial factors. *Percept. and Psychophys.*, **4**, 267–278.

ATTNEAVE, F. (1954) Some informational aspects of visual perception. *Psychol. Rev.*, **61**, 183–193.

BALTES, P. B., SCHMIDT, L. R., and BOESCH, E. E. (1968) Preference for different visual stimulus sequences in children, adolescents, and young adults. *Psychonom. Sci.*, **11**, 271–272.

BANKS, C., CAPPON, C., and HAGEN, R. (1966) Time estimation by psychiatric patients. *Percept. and motor skills*, **23**, 1294.

BANNISTER, D. and FRANSELLA, F. (1966) A grid test of schizophrenic thought disorder. *Brit. J. Soc. and Clin. Psychol.*, **5**, 95–102.

BARTENWERFER, H. (1969) Einige praktische Konsequenzen aus der Aktivierungs-Theorie. *Zeitschrift für experimentelle und angewandte Psychologie*, **16**, 195–222.

BARTLETT, F. (1932) *Remembering*. London: Cambridge University Press.

BARTZ, A. E. (1967) Fixation errors in eye movements to peripheral stimuli. *J. Exp. Psychol.*, **75**, 444–446.

BECK, J. (1966) Effect of orientation and of slope similarity on perceptual grouping. *Percept. and Psychophys.*, **1**, 300–302.

BEMPORAD, J. R. (1967) Perceptual disorders in schizophrenia. *Amer. J. Psychiat.*, **123**, 971–976.

BERLYNE, D. E., CRAW, M. A., SALAPATEK, P. H., and LEWIS, J. L. (1963) Novelty, complexity, incongruity, extrinsic motivation and the G.S.R. *J. Exp. Psychol.*, **66**, 560–567.

BLUMENTHAL, R. and MELTZOFF, J. (1967) Social schemas and perceptual accuracy in schizophrenia. *Brit. J. Soc. and Clin. Psychol.*, **6**, 119–128.

BOESCH, E. E., BALTES, P. B., and SCHMIDT, L. R. (1968) Preferences for different auditory stimulus sequences in various age groups. *Psychon. Sci.*, **10**, 205–206.

BOWER, T. G. R. (1967) Phenomenal identity and form perception in infants. *Percept. and Psychophys.*, **2**, 74–76.

BRAINE, L. G. (1968) Asymmetries of pattern perception observed in Israelis. *Neuropsychologia*, **6**, 73–88.

BROADBENT, D. E. (1958) *Perception and Communication*. London: Pergamon.

BROADHURST, P. L. (1959) The interaction of task difficulty and motivation: The Yerkes-Dodson law revived. *Acta Psychol.*, **16**, 32–38.

BROEN, W. E. (1966) Response disorganisation and breadth of observation in schizophrenia. *Psychol. Rev.*, **73**, 579–585.

BROEN, W. E. (1969) *Schizophrenia: Research and Theory*. New York: Academic Press.

BRUNSWIK, E. and REITER, L. (1937) Eindruckscharaktere schematisierter Gesichter. *Z. Psychol.*, **142**, 67–134.

CAHOON, R. L. (1969) Physiological arousal and time estimation. *Percept. and motor Skills*, **28**, 259–268.

CLARK, W. C. (1966) The psyche in psychophysics. *Psychol. Bul.*, **65**, 358–366.

CLARK, W. C. (1969) Sensory decision theory analysis of the placebo effect on the criterion for pain and thermal sensitivity (*d'*). *J. Abn. Psychol.*, **74**, 363–371.

CLARK, W. C., BROWN, J. C., and RUTSCHMANN, J. (1967) Flicker sensitivity and response bias in psychiatric patients and normal subjects. *J. Abn. Psychol.*, **72**, 35–42.

COHEN, J. (1967) *Psychological Time in Health and Disease.* Springfield: Thomas.

CONKLIN, R. C., MUIR, W., and BOERSMA, F. J. (1968) Field dependency-independency and eyemovement patterns. *Percept. and motor Skills*, **26**, 59–65.

CONRAD, R. (1963) Acoustic confusions and memory span for words. *Nature*, **197**, 1029–1030.

COWAN, T. M. (1968) An observing response analysis of visual search. *Psychol. Rev.*, **75**, 265–270.

CRAIK, F. I. M. (1966) Short-term memory: Echo box plus search process? *Bul. Brit. Psychol. Soc.*, **66**, 3A.

CROMWELL, R. L. (1968) Stimulus redundancy and schizophrenia. *J. Nerv. Ment. Dis.*, **146**, 360–375.

DECKNER, C. W. and BLANTON, R. L. (1969) Effect of context and strength of association on schizophrenic verbal behaviour. *J. Abn. Psychol.*, **74**, 348–351.

DIZNEY, H., RANKIN, R., and JOHNSTON, J. (1969) Eye movement fixations in reading as related to anxiety in college females. *Percept. and motor Skills*, **28**, 851–854.

DUFFY, E. (1962) *Activation and Behaviour.* New York: Wiley.

EBNER, E. and RITZLER, B. (1969) Perceptual recognition in chronic and acute schizophrenics. *J. Consul. and Clin. Psychol.*, **33**, 200–206.

EGETH, H. (1967) Selective attention. *Psychol. Bul.*, **67**, 41–57.

EMLEY, G. S., SCHUSTER, C. R., and LUCCHESI, B. R. (1968) Trends observed in the time estimation of three stimulus intervals within and across sessions. *Percept. and motor Skills*, **26**, 391–398.

ERIKSEN, C. W. (1960) Discrimination and learning without awareness: A methodological survey and evaluation. *Psychol. Rev.*, **67**, 279–300.

ERIKSEN, C. W. and COLLINS, J. F. (1968) Sensory traces versus the psychological moment in temporal organisation of form. *J. Exp. Psychol.*, **77**, 376–382.

EVARTS, E. V. (1962) A neurophysiological theory of hallucinations. In *Hallucinations* (Ed. L. J. West) New York: Grune and Stratton.

EYSENCK, H. J. (1967) *The Biological Basis of Personality.* Springfield: Thomas.

FEINBERG, I. (1962) A comparison of the visual hallucinations in schizophrenia with those induced by Mescaline and LSD-25. In *Hallucinations* (Ed. L. J. West) New York: Grune and Stratton.

FORGUS, R. H. and DEWOLFE, A. S. (1962) Perceptual selectivity in hallucinatory schizophrenics. *J. Abn. Psychol.*, **74**, 288–292.

FREEMAN, P. R. (1964) *Table of d' and β, Document 529/64.* Cambridge Medical Research Council Applied Psychology Research Unit.

FRITH, C. D. (1967) The interaction of noise and personality with critical flicker fusion performance. *Brit. J. Psychol.*, **58**, 127–131.

FRITH, C. D. and LILLIE, F. J. (1971) A loose construct system does not explain thought disorder. *Bul. Brit. Psychol. Soc.*, **24**, 55.

FRITH, U. (1970) Studies in pattern detection in normal and autistic children: I. Immediate recall of auditory sequences. *J. Abnorm. Psychol.*, **76**, 412–420.

FRITH, U. (1970) Studies in pattern detection in normal and autistic children: II. Reproduction and production of colour sequences. *J. Exp. Child Psychol.*, **19**, 120–135.

FUORTES, M. G. F. and HODGKIN, A. L. (1964) Changes in time scale and sensitivity in the ommatidia of Limulus. *J. Physiol.*, **172**, 239–263.

GARNER, W. R. (1966) To perceive is to know. *Amer. Psychol.*, **21**, 11–19.

GARNER, W. R. and GOTTWALD, R. L. (1968) The perception and learning of temporal patterns. *Q. J. Exp. Psychol.*, **20**, 97–109.

GIBSON, J. J. (1968) What gives rise to the perception of motion? *Psychol. Rev.*, **75**, 335–346.

GOLDSTEIN, A. G. (1967) Gestalt similarity principle, difference thresholds and pattern discriminability. *Percept. and Psychophys.*, **2**, 377–382.

GOLDSTONE, S. (1967) The human clock: A framework for the study of healthy and deviant time perception. *Ann. New York Acad. Sci.*, **138**, 767–783.

GOODFELLOW, L. D. (1938) A psychological interpretation of the results of the Zenith Radio experiments in telepathy. *J. Exp. Psychol.*, **23**, 601–632.

GOULD, J. D. (1967) Pattern perception and eyemovement parameters. *Percept. and Psychophys.*, **2**, 399–407.

GRANGER, G. W. (1953) Personality and visual perception; a review. *J. Ment. Sci.*, **99**, 8–43.

GRANGER, G. W. (1957) Effect of psychiatric disorders on visual threshold. *Science*, **125**, 500–501.

GRANGER, G. W. (1960) Abnormalities of sensory perception. In *Handbook of Abnormal Psychology* (Ed. H. J. Eysenck) London: Pitman Medical.

GRANGER, G. W. and IKEDA, H. (1968) Drugs and visual perception. In *Drugs and Sensory Functions* (Ed. A. Herxheimer) London: Churchill.

GREGORY, R. L. and WALLACE, J. G. (1958) A theory of nerve deafness. *Lancet*, **i**, 83–84.

GREGSON, R. A. M. and WILSON, G. D. (1966) *Effects of illumination on the detection and perceived relative intensity of acid tastes.* Univ. Canterbury, (N.Z.), Dept. Psychol. and Sociol., Res. Rep. 10.

GRODIN, M. and BROWN, D. R. (1967) Multivariate stimulus processing by normal and paranoid schizophrenic subjects. *Psychonomic Sci.*, **8**, 525–526.

HABER, R. N. and HABER, R. B. (1964) Eidetic imaginery: 1. Frequency. *Percept. and motor skills*, **19**, 131–138.

HARTLINE, H. K., WAGNER, H. G., and RATLIFF, F. (1956) Inhibition in the eye of Limulus. *J. Gen. Physiol.*, **39**, 651–673.

HELD, R. and FREEDMAN, S. J. (1963) Plasticity in human sensori-motor control. *Science*, **142**, 455–462.

HELD, R. and HEIN, A. (1963) Movement produced stimulation in the development of visually guided behaviour. *J. Comp. Physiol. Psychol.*, **56**, 872–876.

HERMELIN, B. and O'CONNOR, N. (1967) Remembering of words by psychotic and subnormal children. *Brit. J. Psychol.*, **58**, 213–218.

HERMELIN, B. and O'CONNOR, N. (1968) Measures of occipital alpha rythm in normal, subnormal, and autistic children. *Brit. J. Psychiat.*, **114**, 603–610.

HERMELIN, B. and O'CONNOR, N. (1971) Children's judgement of duration. *Brit. J. Psychol.*, **62**, 13–20.

HERNANDEZ-PEON, R. (1966) A neurophysiological model of dreams and hallucinations. *J. Nerv. Ment. Dis.*, **141**, 623–650.

HERNANDEZ-PEON, R., SCHERRER, H., and JOUVET, M. (1956) Modification of electrical activity in the cochlear nucleus during 'attention' in unanesthetised cats. *Science*, **123**, 331–332.

HIEATT, D. J. and TONG, J. E. (1969) Differences between normals and schizophrenics on activation-induced change in two-flash fusion threshold. *Brit. J. Psychiat.*, **115**, 477–478.

HIRSH, I. J. and SHERRICK, C. E. (1961) Perceived order in different sense modalities. *J. Exp. Psychol.*, **62**, 423–432.

HOCHBERG, J. and GALPER, R. E. (1967) Recognition of faces: 1. An exploratory study. *Psychon. Sci.*, **9**, 619–620.

HODGE, M. H. and RIELE, W. H. (1966) Individual response patterns in binary choice tasks with non-discriminable stimuli. *Percept. and Psychophys.*, **1**, 421–425.

HOEHN-SARIC, R. and GROSS, M. (1968) Auditory hallucinations in schizophrenia: Early changes under drug treatment and drug withdrawal. *Amer. J. Psychiat.*, **124**, 1132–1135.

HOULIHAN, K. and SEKULER, R. W. (1968) Contour interactions in visual masking. *J. Exp. Psychol.*, **77**, 281–285.

HUBEL, D. H. and WIESEL, T. M. (1963) Receptive fields of cells in striate cortex of very young, visually inexperienced kittens. *J. Neurophysiol.*, **26**, 994–1002.

HUBEL, D. H. and WIESEL, T. M. (1965) Receptive fields and functional architecture in two non-striate visual areas (18 and 19) of the cat. *J. Neurophysiol.*, **28**, 229–289.

HUME, W. I. (1968) The dimensions of central nervous arousal. *Bul. Brit. Psychol. Soc.*, **21**, 111.

HUMPHREY, N. K. and WEISKRANTZ, L. (1969) Size constancy in monkeys with inferotemporal lesions. *Q. J. Exp. Psychol.*, **21**, 225–258.

Institute of Electrical Engineers (1968) *Proc. Conf. Pattern Recognition.* London: Nat. Phys. Lab.

JOHANNSEN, W. J. and O'CONNELL, M. J. (1965) Institutionalisation and perceptual deficit in schizophrenia *Percept, and motor Skills*, **21**, 244–246.

JOHANSSEN, W. J. and TESTIN, R. F. (1966) Assimilation of visual information as a function of chronicity in schizophrenia. *Arch. Gen. Psychiat.*, **15**, 492–498.

JONES, R. T., BLACKER, K. H., and CALLAWAY, E. (1966) Perceptual dysfunction in schizophrenia: clinical and auditory evoked response findings. *Amer. J. Psychiat.*, **123**, 639–645.

JULESZ, B. (1966) Binocular disappearance of monocular symmetry. *Science*, **153**, 657–658.

KATZ, M. M., WASKOW, I. E., and OLSSON, J. (1968) Characterising the psychological state produced by L.S.D. *J. Abn. Psychol.*, **73**, 1–14.

KINCHLA, R. A. and SMYZER, F. (1967) A diffusion model of perceptual memory. *Percept. and Psychophys.*, **2**, 219–229.

KUECHLER, H. A. and DODWELL, P. C. (1968) Auditory signal detection as a function of prestimulus shock. *Q. J. Exp. Psychol.*, **20**, 305–308.

LAWSON, J. S., McGHIE, A., and CHAPMAN, J. (1964) Perception of speech in schizophrenia. *Brit. J. Psychiat.*, **110**, 375–380.

LEVINSON, J. Z. (1968) Flicker fusion phenomena. *Science*, **160**, 21–28.

LEVY, R. and MAXWELL, A. E. (1968) The effect of verbal context on the recall of schizophrenics and other psychiatric patients. *Brit. J. Psychiat.*, **114**, 311–316.

LUCE, R. D. (1963) Detection and recognition. In *Handbook of Mathematical Psychology*, Vol. 1 (Ed. R. D. Luce, R. R. Bush, and E. Galanter). New York: Wiley.

LURIYA, A. R., PRAVDINA-VINARSKAYA, E. N., and YARBUS, A. L. (1961) Mechanisms of eye movements in the process of visual perception and their pathology. *Voprosy Psikhologii*, No. 5, 160.

MACKAY, D. (1957) Moving visual images produced by regular stationary patterns. *Nature*, **180**, 849–850.

MACKWORTH, N. H. and MORANDI, A. J. (1967) The gage selects informative details within pictures. *Percept. and Psychophys.*, **2**, 547–552.

MALITZ, S., WILKENS, B., and ESECOVER, H. (1962) A comparison of drug-induced hallucinations with those seen in spontaneously occurring psychoses. In *Hallucinations* (Ed. L. J. West). New York: Grune and Stratton.

McGUIGAN, F. J. (1966) Covert oral behaviour and auditory hallucinations. *Psychophysiology*, **3**, 73–80.

McKINNON, T. and SINGER, G. (1969) Schizophrenia and the scanning cognitive control: A reevaluation. *J. Abn. Psychol.*, **74**, 242–248.

MILLER, G. A. and CHAPMAN, L. J. (1968) Response bias and schizophrenic beliefs. *J. Abn. Psychol.*, **73**, 252–255.

MILLER, G. A. and SELFRIDGE, J. A. (1950) Verbal context and the recall of meaningful material. *Amer. J. Psychol.*, **63**, 176–185.

MILLER, M. D., JOHNSONN, R. L., and RICHMOND, L. H. (1965) Auditory hallucinations and descriptive language skills. *J. Psychiat. Res.*, **3**, 43–56.

MILNER, A. D. (1966) A decision theory approach to obsessional behaviour. *Unpubl. Dipl. Psychol. Diss.*, Univ. of London Lib.

MILNER, B. and TEUBER, H-L. (1968) Alteration of perception and memory in man. In *Behavioural Change* (Ed. L. Weiskrantz) London: Harper and Row.

MISIAK, H., ZEUHAUSERN, R., and SALAFIA, W. R. (1966) Continuous temporal evaluation of the effect of Meprobamate on critical flicker frequency in normal subjects. *Psychopharmacologia*, **9**, 457–461.

MOON, A. F., MEFFERD, R. B., WIELAND, B. A., POKORNY, A. D., and FALCONER, G. A. (1968) Perceptual dysfunction as a determinant of schizophrenic word associations. *J. Nerv. Ment. Dis.*, **146**, 80–84.

MURPHY, E. H. (1969) Differentiation of function in the right and left cerebral hemispheres in man. *Unpubl. Ph.D. Thesis*, Univ. London Lib.

NEALE, J. M. and CROMWELL, R. L. (1968) Size estimation in schizophrenics as a function of stimulus presentation time. *J. Abn. Psychol.*, **73**, 44–48.

NEALE, J. M. and CROMWELL, R. L. (1969) Preference for complexity in acute schizophrenics. *J. Consul. and Clin. Psychol.*, **33**, 245–246.

NEISSER, U. (1967) *Cognitive Psychology*. New York: Appleton-Century-Crofts.

NORMINGTON, C. J. (1967) Time estimation in process-reactive schizophrenics. *J. Consul. Psychol.*, **31**, 222.

O'CONNOR, N. and HERMELIN, B. (1967) The selective visual attention of psychotic children. *J. Child Psychol. Psychiat.*, **8**, 167–179.

ORNITZ, E. M. (1969) Disorders of perception common to early infantile autism and schizophrenia. *Comprehensive Psychiat.*, **10**, 259–274.

PANTLE, A. J. and SEKULER, R. W. (1968) Velocity-sensitive elements in human vision: Initial psychophysical evidence. *Vision Res.*, **8**, 445–450.

PAVY, D. (1968) Verbal behaviour in schizophrenia: A review of recent studies. *Psychol. Bul.*, **70**, 164–178.

PFAFF, D. (1968) Effects of temperature and time of day on time judgements. *J. Exp. Psychol.*, **76**, 419–422.

PIAGET, J. (1950) *The Psychology of Intelligence*. London: Routledge and Kegan Paul.

PISHKIN, V. (1966) Perceptual judgement of schizophrenics and normals as a function of social cues and symbolic stimuli. *J. Clin. Psychol.*, **22**, 3–10.

PISHKIN, V. and BOURNE, L. E. (1969) Concept identification by schizophrenic and normal subjects as a function of problem complexity and relevance of social cues. *J. Abn. Psychol.*, **74**, 314–320.

POLLACK, I. (1968) Computer simulation of threshold observations by the method of limits. *Percept. and motor Skills*, **26**, 583–586.

PRIBRAM, K. H. (1963) Reinforcement revisited: A structural view. In *Nebraska Symposium on Motivation* (Ed. M. R. Jones) **11**, 113–159.

PRICE, R. H. (1966) Signal detection methods in personality and perception. *Psychol. Bul.*, **1**, 55–62.

PRICE, R. H. and ERIKSEN, C. W. (1966) Size constancy in schizophrenia: A reanalysis. *J. Ab. Psychol.*, **71**, 155–160.

RAEBURN, J. M. and TONG, J. E. (1968) Experiments on contextural constraint in schizophrenia. *Brit. J. Psychol.*, **114**, 43–52.

REIMER, F. and HAUSS, K. (1966) Provizierte Trugwahrnehmungen im psychologischen Experiment. *Z. Exp. u. Ang. Psychol.*, **13**, 596–601.

RODWAN, A. S. and HAKE, H. W. (1964) The discriminant-function as a model for perception. *Amer. J. Psychol.*, **77**, 380–392.

ROFFWANG, H. P., DEMENT, W. C., MUZIO, J. N., and FISHER, C. (1962) Dream imagery: Relation to rapid eyemovements of sleep. *Arch. Gen. Psychiat.*, **7**, 235–258.

SARAVAY, S. M. and PARDES, H. (1967) Auditory elementary hallucinations in alcohol withdrawal psychosis. *Arch. Gen. Psychiat.*, **16**, 652–658.

SCHIFFMAN, H. and FALKENBERG, P. (1968) The organisation of stimuli and sensory neurones. *Physiology and Behaviour*, **3**, 197–201.

SCHULMAN, C. A., MILTON, R., and WEINSTEIN, S. (1967) Hallucinations and disturbances of affect, cognition, and physical state as a function of sensory deprivation. *Percept. and motor Skills*, **25**, 1001–1024.

SEKULER, R. W. and ABRAMS, M. (1968) Visual sameness; a choice time analysis of pattern recognition processes. *J. Exp. Psychol.*, **77**, 232–238.

SEKULER, R. W. and HOULIHAN, K. (1968) Discrimination of mirror images: Choice time analysis of human adult performance. *Q. J. Exp. Psychol.*, **20**, 204–207.

SHANNON, C. E. (1951) Prediction and entropy of printed English. *Bell Syst. Tech. J.*, **30**, 50–64.

SILVERMAN, J. (1964) The problem of attention in research and theory in schizophrenia. *Psychol. Rev.*, **71**, 352–379.

SILVERMAN, J. (1968) A paradigm for the study of altered states of consciousness. *Brit. J. Psychiat.*, **114**, 1201–1218.

SILVERMAN, J., BERG, P. S. D., and KANTOR, R. (1966) Some perceptual correlates of institutionalisation. *J. Nerv. Ment. Dis.*, **141**, 651–657.

SILVERMAN, J. and GAARDER, K. (1967) Rates of saccadic eye movement and size judgements of normals and schizophrenics. *Percept. and motor skills*, **25**, 661–667.

SIMON, H. A. (1967) An information-processing explanation of some perceptual phenomena. *Brit. J. Psychol.*, **58**, 1–12.

SKRZYPEK, G. J. (1969) Effect of perceptual isolation and arousal on anxiety, complexity preference, and novelty preference in psychopathic and neurotic delinquents. *J. Abn. Psychol.*, **74**, 321–329.

SPERLING, G. (1960) The information available in brief visual presentations. *Psychol. Monogr.*, **74**, No. 11 (whole No. 498).

SPERLING, G. (1963) A model for visual memory tasks. *Human Factors*, **5**, 19–31.

SPITZ, H. H., HOATS, D. L., and HOLDEN, E. A. (1968) Numerosity discrimination of tachistoscopically presented dots by mental retardates and normals. *Amer. J. Mental. Def.*, **73**, 127–138.

SPITZ, H. H. and THOR, D. H. (1968) Visual backward masking in retardates and normals. *Percept. and Psychophys.*, **4**, 245–246.

STANNARD, R., SINGER, G., and OVER, R. (1966) The effect of information feedback on size judgements of schizophrenic patients. *Brit. J. Psychol.*, **57**, 329–333.

STARR, A. (1967) Localisation of objects in visual space with abnormal saccadic eye movements. *Brain*, **90**, 541–544.

STEVENS, S. S., MORGAN, C. T., and VOLKMANN, J. (1941) Theory of the neural quantum in the discrimination of loudness and pitch. *Amer. J. Psychol.*, **54**, 315–335.

STEWART, C. G. (1968) The effect of auditory hallucinations on loudness of verbal report. *Psychon. Sci.*, **13**, 197–198.

SWETS, J. A. (1964) *Signal Detection and Recognition by Human Observers*. New York: Wiley.

SWETS, J. A., TANNER, W. P., and BIRDSALL, T. G. (1961) Decision processes in perception. *Psychol. Rev.*, **68**, 301–340.

TALBOT, W. H., DARIAN-SMITH, I., KORNHUBER, H. H., and MOUNTCASTLE, B. (1968) The sense of flutter-vibration: Comparison of the human capacity with response patterns of mechanoreceptive afferents from the monkey hand. *J. Neurophys*, **31**, 301–324.

TALLAND, G. A. and QUARTON, G. C. (1966) The effects of drugs and familiarity on performance in continuous visual search. *J. Nerv. Ment. Dis.*, **143**, 266–274.

TEUBER, H-L. (1966) Effects of occipital lobe lesion on pattern vision. *Neurol.*, **3**, 79–102.

THOMAS, L. E. and STASIAK, E. (1964) Eye movements and body images. *Canad. Psychiat. Ass. J.*, **9**, 336–344.

THOR, D. H. and HOLDEN, E. A. (1970) Visual perception of sequential numerosity by normals and retardates. *J. Abn. Psychol.*, **74**, 676–681.

TREISMAN, A. M. (1964) Selective attention in man. *Brit. med. Bul.*, **20**, 12–16.

TREISMAN, M. (1963) Temporal discrimination and the indifference interval: Implications for a model of the 'internal clock'. *Psychol. Mon.*, **77**, 13.

TREISMAN, M. and WATTS, T. R. (1966) Signal detectability theory and sensory thresholds. *Psychol. Bul.*, **66**, 438–454.

UHR, L. (1966) *Pattern Recognition: Theory, Experiment, Computer Simulations, and Dynamic Models of Form Perception and Discovery*. New York: Wiley.

VENABLES, P. H. (1963) The relationship between level of skin potential and fusion of paired light flashes in schizophrenic and normal subjects. *J. Psychiat. Res.*, **1**, 279–287.

VENABLES, P. H. (1966a) Psychophysiological aspects of schizophrenia. *Brit. J. Med. Psychol.*, **39**, 289–297.

VENABLES, P. H. (1966b) A comparison of two flash and two click thresholds in schizophrenic and normal subjects. *Q. J. Exp. Psychol.*, **18**, 371–373.

VENABLES, P. H. (1967) The relation of two flash and two click thresholds to withdrawal in paranoid and non-paranoid schizophrenics. *Brit. J. Soc. and Clin. Psychol.*, **6**, 60–62.

VENABLES, P. H. (1968) *Signals, noise, refractoriness and storage: Some concepts of value to psychopathology?* *Biometrics Research Workshop*, Session 3.

VENABLES, P. H. (1969) Sensory aspects of psychopathology. In *Neurobiological Aspects of Psychopathology* (Ed. J. Zubin and C. Shagass) New York: Grune and Stratton.

VENABLES, P. H. and WARWICK-EVANS, L. A. (1968) The effect of stimulus amplitude on the threshold of fusion of two flashes. *Q. J. Exp. Psychol.*, **20**, 30–37.

VISCOTT, D. S. (1968) Chlordiazepoxide and hallucinations. *Arch. Gen. Psychiat.*, **19**, 370–376.

VON BEKESY, G. (1930) Über das Fechner'sche Gesetz und seine Bedentung für die Theorie der akustischen Beobachtungsfehler und die Theorie des Hörens. *Ann. Phys.*, **7**, 329–359.

VON BEKESY, G. (1967) *Sensory Inhibition*. Princeton: Princeton Univ. Press.

VON STURMER, G. (1968) Time perception, vigilance, and decision theory. *Percept. and Psychophys.*, **3**, 197–201.

WAGGONER, R. A. (1960) Differences in response latency and response variability between high and low anxiety subjects in a flicker-fusion task. *J. Abn. and Soc. Psychol.*, **61**, 355–359.

WARRINGTON, E. K. and JAMES, M. (1967) Disorders of visual perception in patients with localised cerebral lesions. *Neuropsychologia*, **5**, 253–260.

WARRINGTON, E. K. and RABIN, P. (1970) Perceptual matching in patients with cerebral lesions. *Neuropsychologia*, **8**, 475–487.

WARRINGTON, E. K. and RABIN, P. (1970) A preliminary investigation of the relationship between visual perception and visual memory. *Cortex*, **6**, 87–96.

WEBB, W. W., DAVIS, D., and CROMWELL, R. L. (1966) Size estimation in schizophrenics as a function of thematic content of the stimuli. *J. Nerv. Ment. Dis.*, **143**, 252–255.

WECKOWICZ, T. E. and BLEWETT, D. B. (1959) Size constancy and abstract thinking in schizophrenic patients. *J. Ment. Sci.*, **105**, 909–934.

WEINTRAUB, D. and HAKE, H. (1962) Visual discrimination, an interpretation in terms of detectability theory. *J. Opt. Soc. Amer.*, **52**, 1179–1184.

WELLS, J. D. and CALDWELL, W. E. (1967) Perception of the vertical as a function of effective stimuli and extraneous stimulation in schizophrenic and normal subjects. *Genetic Psychol. Mon.*, **75**, 209–234.

WERTHEIMER, M. (1922) Untersuchungen zur Lehre von der Gestalt. I. Prinzipielle Bemerkungen. *Psychol. Forsch.*, **1**, 47–58.

WERTHEIMER, M. (1923) Untersuchungen zur Lehre von der Gestalt. II. *Psychol. Forsch.*, **4**, 301–350.

WESCOTT, M. R. and TOLCHIN, M. (1968) Individual and age differences in perceptual inference behaviour. *Percept. and motor Skills*, **26**, 683–697.

WEST, L. J. (1962) *Hallucinations*. New York: Grune and Stratton.

WHITFIELD, I. C. (1967) Coding in the auditory nervous system. *Nature*, **213**, 756–760.

WILLIAMS, E. (1971) The effect of varying the elements in the Bannister-Fransella Grid Test of thought disorder. *Brit. J. Psychiat.* (in press).

WILSON, B. C. and WILSON, J. H. (1967) Sensory and perceptual functions in the cerebral palsied: I. Pressure thresholds and two point discrimination. *J. Nerv. Ment. Dis.*, **145**, 53–68.

WILSON, G. D. and GREGSON, R. A. M. (1967) Effects of illumination on perceived intensity of acid tastes. *Austral. J. Psychol.*, **19**, 69–73.

WUNDT, W. (1896) *Grundriss der Psychologie*. Leipzig: Engelmann.

YACORZYNSKI, G. K. (1941) Perceptual principles involved in the disintegration of a configuration formed in predicting the occurrence of patterns selected by chance. *J. Exp. Psychol.*, **29**, 401–406.

YARBUS, A. L. (1967) *Eye Movements and Vision*. New York: Plenum Press.

YERKES, R. M. and DODSON, J. D. (1908) The relation of strength of stimulus to rapidity of habit formation. *J. Comp. Neurol. Psychol.*, **18**, 458–482.

YNTEMA, D. B. and TRASK, F. P. (1963) Recall as a search process. *J. Verb. Learn. verb. Behav.*, **2**, 65–74.

ZUBEK, J. P. (1964) Effects of prolonged sensory and perceptual deprivation. *Brit. med. Bul.*, **20**, 38–42.

ZUCKERMAN, M. and COHEN, N. (1964) Sources of reports of visual and auditory sensations in perceptual isolation experiments. *Psychol. Bul.*, **62**, 1–20.

10

Somatic Reactivity: Methodology

IRENE MARTIN

Introduction

The physiology of the organism is sometimes compared to tidal ebb and flow, upon which layer after layer, pattern upon pattern of shifting activity takes place. The problem is to detect the patterns and to establish their functional significance for living organisms. The substantive area deemed significant at any time will depend on the current fabric of ideas; empirical testing will increasingly be dependent on technical skills.

Darrow, in 1961, anticipated that within a very short time the technology of recording and analysing data would reach ideals of efficiency and reliability; that automation and computers would help us 'pursue the psyche to its fastnesses within the brain and gut . . .'. His anticipations on methodological advances are realities today. Electronic equipment is available that fulfils our specifications. Recording techniques are greatly improved. Computer analysis is daily routine. A far greater proportion of the recorded physiological data can be processed and utilised than ever before, and as a result of all these developments contemporary methodological problems are different from those of ten years ago.

Those of relevance today are the question of response definition, units of measurement, pre- and post-stimulus relationships, change over time, and these will be discussed in this chapter. Methodological analysis is necessarily bound up with interpretative problems, and these, too, have shifted during the past decade. One would hesitate to claim that physiology alone can define 'so-called mental mechanisms' or 'reveal' the 'phenomena of the mind' (to use Darrow's terms). Physiological responses are appraised now rather as *an aspect* of a total, complicated, behavioural response pattern. Our area of interest may lead us to emphasise physiological aspects, but at least as far as understanding human behaviour is concerned, they are best considered *in conjunction with* (and not separate from) perceptions, cognitions, verbal analyses, and other facets of responding. It follows from this that to distinguish a subject matter of 'somatic reactivity' from areas such as learning, emotion, and perception is of little value. It is reasonable, nevertheless, to view such topics from a psychophysiological point of view, and this is the one adopted in this chapter, and Chapter 11.

The placement of somatic reactivity in better perspective is characteristic of much current work. Lang's (1968) attempt to measure fear, for example, starts with the assumption that it is a response expressed in three main behavioural systems: verbal (cognitive), overt motor, and somatic. Lazarus (1968) takes a similar view. What would an emotion be, he asks, without its motoric impulses, its causal appraisal as well as its physiological changes? When one component is missing, as it is in sham rage or in the physiological arousal produced by an epinephrine injection, the reaction does not seem like a 'real' emotion. Current experimental work focuses on the ways of measuring the many components accurately and comprehensively. This must be done in the context of determining the relationship among them and the nature of their interactions (i.e. the functional significance of the response pattern). One current area for example, concerns the connection between cognitive processes and emotional disturbance; Lazarus (1968) and Pribram (1967) are examining such cognitive concepts as reappraisal and re-evaluation, treating them as mechanisms of coping with disturbance and of leading to re-equilibration. This research involves measurement both of subjective report and physiological responsiveness.

This recognition of a multidimensional response pattern is evident not only in the difficult context of

309

human emotional responses but in other areas such as conditioning (Dykman *et al.*, 1965; Germana, 1969) and perception (Sokolov, 1963). Current research is much concerned with the interaction of physiological arousal and overt behaviour. Is successful avoidance of a noxious stimulus, for example, followed by a reduction of physiological activity; put in other words, is successful direct action upon the environment yet another way of establishing re-equilibration. The point again is that somatic reactivity is seen in the context of a wide range of reactions, as interacting with other ways of responding.

The basic analysis must therefore centre on response function. It would be an inadequate representation of behaviour to describe the pattern of response as if it were a still-life. The pattern clearly shifts in time. From the interpretative point of view, it has complex relations with the environment: with the perception of objects and their significance. Its analysis forms part of the general movement towards psychological models involving cognition and information processing, feedback and control theory. The methodological-statistical requirement is that we examine change of the response pattern in time; the interpretative problem is that of viewing a biological/adaptive organism whose responses serve a purpose, have endpoints, achieve goals appraised as desirable or not desirable.

The contents of this chapter and Chapter 11 will try to reflect some of these current trends. Methodology will be considered in this chapter. The emphasis will be not so much on recording techniques as on problems of measurement: distinguishing types of responses, examining relationships among them and between responses and levels, discussing transformations of data and methods of analysing changes over time. The second section, titled interpretation, will discuss some of the contemporary work on arousal, emotion, and stress. As in the previous version of this chapter, the material covered will be largely restricted to psychophysiological research involving human subjects.

METHODOLOGY

The aim of psychophysiological methods is to increase the reliability and quality of observation and measurement and to decrease unwanted sources of interference. Several handbooks are available on this topic (Brown, 1967; Lykken, 1969; Venables and Martin, 1967). These deal with recording techniques and give details of transducers, electrodes, and apparatus. They cover the usual range of variables: skin resistance, skin potential, cardiovascular activity (heart rate, blood pressure, and plethysmography), respiration, salivation, gastric motility, electromyography, pupillography, and electroencephalography. In addition, they include sections on electronic storage and computer analysis and telemetry of psychophysiological variables. Their aims are to provide the necessary background for the employment of each technique and to supply principles and specifications on which the experimenter may rationally equip his laboratory.

In addition to these books there have been innumerable notes and articles in various journals concerning techniques for improved recordings. Many journals that cover topics in psychophysiology and medical engineering include sections on instrumentation. Indeed, so great has been the expansion and publication of information in this area that levels of efficiency and reliability are extremely high today. There is little point in further reviewing this work. Instead, attention can be turned to a number of problems that remain with us if we are to make best use of the data.

The past decade has seen the introduction of analogue to digital conversion systems, often in conjunction with laboratory computers. Most workers in the field are all too familiar with the drudgery of hand-scoring miles of record charts and with the arbitrary constraints that hand scoring can place on data analysis. Not the least significant of these are decisions about what to include as a response measurement. The advent of A–D conversion on a scale of general availability substantially increases the range of data available to routine analysis and has interesting implications.

Response Definition

In most areas of measurement in the field it would be possible to define a classical period of investigation during which response limits were defined: latency and amplitude criteria for single waveform responses, frequency rates for continuous responses, and so on. It would also be fair to say that these limits were heavily influenced by the crude scoring methods available at the time. A–D conversion facilities, tape storage, and digital computer capabilities now offer the possibility of analysing the whole record or a substantial part of it. Further, they offer a formidable range of analytic methods: serial and autocorrelation, power-spectrum analysis, etc., formerly restricted to highly specialised studies. Transient averages, running estimates of power and/or variance, and a variety of summary measures also become available to routine data analysis. One result of this new activity is certain to be a renewed interest in response definition. Older concepts of the response are likely to be questioned.

This technical trend has, in fact, coincided with, and will give impetus to, a recent swing of interest away from preoccupation with stimulus characteristics and towards the analysis of response characteristics. Many workers, for example, have been concerned with the complicated nature of the heart rate response to simple stimuli (Graham and Clifton, 1966; Lacey and Lacey, 1958; Obrist *et al.*, 1965; Zeaman and Smith, 1965). Others have analysed different conditioned responses in skin resistance records (Grings *et al.*, 1962; Kimmel, 1965). Response characteristics of the conditioned eyelid response have been examined in some detail (Martin and Levey, 1969; Pennypacker, 1964; Prokasy, 1965).

Isolated studies have appeared over the years, examining such topographic elements of the single waveform as latency, rise time, area, duration, or amplitude. Through routine digitisation and appropriate programming, it is now possible to include these response characteristics systematically in our investigations. Most important of all, however, it is now necessary to specify the rationale for selecting some measurements rather than others. In analysing the conditioned eyelid response, for example, questions such as: Does the response stabilise towards an equilibrium? Does it optimise its energy output over time? can be meaningfully examined (Martin and Levey, 1969). These questions concern the nature of response *development* and have been largely ignored in the past because of the formidable scoring difficulties involved. There is clearly evidence that analysis of the response as a developing whole can shed light on adaptive behaviour (Levey and Martin, 1968), and we may find ourselves able to ask the more fundamental question: how does the response benefit the organism?

Levels and Responses

It has always seemed necessary to make a clear distinction between *levels* of physiological activity and *responses* with characteristic waveforms superimposed on these levels. Various attempts have been made to propose a standard nomenclature that distinguishes between measurement of levels and responses.

Such a distinction seems appropriate for most current laboratory experimentation, where there is some degree of control over the external stimuli given to the subject. Typically there are periods of 'rest' and periods of 'stimulation'. Where stimuli are of the simple, discrete variety, there may indeed be a characteristic response, usually a transient increase in activity with reasonably well-defined parameters of latency, amplitude, duration, etc. Indeed, stimuli are typically selected because of the clear-cut responses they produce. How representative such simple stimuli and simple responses are of much real-life responsiveness must remain an open question. However, even within the laboratory the nature of the stimulus employed may vary greatly; it may be simple or complex, short or long; it may or may not be a signal to overt activity.

Up to some years ago it was customary to take 'basal' readings, hopefully as representing the characteristic resting level of the individual. It would now be recognised that individuals have a wide spectrum of levels, ranging from sleep, relaxation, resting, through to alert, active, excited, and so on. There is an interesting area of study examining the range of psychophysiological variables over this sleep-waking continuum, especially in the various stages of sleep. It would seem that some variables are better able to distinguish levels at one end of the spectrum, say different stages of sleep, while others may be more sensitive to changes at the alert end of the spectrum.

In addition, there is the empirical question of ascertaining for the individual his range of values for a particular psychophysiological variable. We cannot expect the effector organ to exhibit the same absolute level of activity in all individuals for the same level of central activity. In their study of cardiac activity in infants, Bridger and Reiser (1959) observed 'that babies in the same activity state—from profound sleep to violent crying—may have different heart rate levels, and that babies with the same heart rate levels may be in different states of excitability'. Individual differences in the range of skin conductance values are probably still greater. One subject's range of skin conductance may be from one micromho during sleep to five micromhos in high excitement; another may show values of five and ten micromhos respectively under the same conditions.

Lykken (1969) points out that even with no sudomotor innervation, the skin displays a certain minimum conductance which will vary among individuals in relation to local anatomical and physiological peculiarities. Similarly, the maximum conductance produced under conditions of maximal central activation will also vary from person to person. Because of the number of specific peripheral factors involved, many of which will be irrelevant so far as assessing central processes is concerned, there will be only a relatively poor correlation between the obtained measurements of skin conductance and properties of central processes such as arousal. The extent of the correlation between peripheral and central events remains an empirical (and extremely difficult) problem. One way round the problem is to try to determine minima and maxima for individuals, i.e. their *range* on any particular psychophysiological variable. Lykken *et al.* (1966) have suggested how this might be done and how it can be used to obtain a more rational measuring unit for assessing change to a stimulus.

If levels of peripheral activity do reflect underlying changes of some central sleep-waking dimension it seems inevitable that any experimental situation must contend with shifts in physiological activity as the subject becomes interested, anxious, annoyed, tired, and bored. Indeed, the problem is often met in studies trying to relate levels of performance to levels of arousal, where it is desirable to keep one factor, usually arousal, constant throughout the course of the experiment. Subjects show a distressing tendency to shift upwards or downwards in physiological levels, and in no regular pattern. The implication is that levels of activity are far from constant, and that a single measure, say the average for a 30-minute session in which thirty one-minute readings are made, is likely to be very inadequate. Some measure of trend is required to reflect change from beginning to end of the period.

Changes in physiological activity during performance of various tasks have been observed and investigated by several workers. Progressively rising gradients were reported in skeletal muscle activity (often in muscles not engaged in activity) and in cardiovascular and respiratory systems (Malmo, 1965). They have also been found to accompany periods of sustained attention, and Malmo has suggested that the steepness of the gradients is a function of motivational level.

Whether the gradient shows a general increase or decrease in activity depends on the nature of the stimulus conditions as well as on the individual concerned. Nevertheless, a reduction of levels in time is a commonly reported phenomenon, especially when the subject becomes relaxed or sleepy. The finding that reduction of basal level activity lasts across sessions lends support to the view that some situational habituation is taking place (Duffy, 1962; Frankenhaeuser *et al.*, 1967; Martin, 1960). The relationship of the gradient to its initial level must also be examined, since the initial level may determine the steepness of the gradient.

We therefore have to accept the idea that so-called 'levels' of activity themselves show marked changes (responses?) depending on a large number of internal as well as situational factors. The distinction between levels and responses along a time base—level shifts being 'longer', more gradual, etc., whereas responses are brief and discrete—may to some extent be a function of employing experimental conditions which emphasise such differences (e.g. a long period of relaxation followed by a brief, discrete electric shock). When more complicated longer-duration stimuli, perhaps involving task performance, are used, the distinction becomes more difficult to sustain. As Sharpless and Jasper (1956) found in a much-quoted experiment, tonic and phasic changes to brief sensory stimuli could be discerned and described, but it was exceedingly difficult to differentiate the two except under very special conditions. The phasic reaction is described as rarely outlasting the stimulus by more than 10 or 15 seconds, having a short latency, being very resistant to habituation, and once habituated, as recovering within a few minutes. The other, the tonic reaction, varies in duration from a few seconds to many minutes, may have a long latent period (up to 30 seconds), is labile, subject to rapid habituation, and tends to recover slowly, over periods of hours or days. The two occur together in normal animals but can be dissociated by brain stem lesions.

This distinction seems close to Sokolov's (1963) differentiation of localised and generalised orientation reactions. The generalised orientation is widespread, can be long lasting and habituate quickly; the localised reaction is more confined to the cortical area of the particular sensory modality, subsides quickly, and is more resistant to habituation. It is unclear at present what the precise relationship is between the two schemes; or to what extent they relate to the common use of phasic to describe brief responses, and tonic to refer to changes in background level.

It would therefore seem appropriate at this stage to take a flexible view of level/response differentiation and keep open the possibility that they may be far from distinct categories of physiological activity. It is well known, of course, that there are complicated functional relationships between pre- and post-stimulus activity, and these will be discussed in a later section.

Before considering the specific characteristics of stimulus-evoked responses, some mention must be made of the apparently spontaneous fluctuations that occur in many physiological systems.

Spontaneous Activity

This is described by Lacey and Lacey (1958) as periodic oscillatory changes that are uncorrelated in time with specifically imposed stimuli or with detectable specific episodes of affective response. The older view of spontaneous activity as biological 'noise' with little functional significance has been replaced more recently by one that regards it as important in maintaining the level of CNS activity necessary for the organism to be able to respond to changes in stimulation. This concept of spontaneous responses refers to waveforms that have a shorter period than circadian rhythms (Stern, 1966).

The Laceys have offered several hypotheses to account for the occurrence of these variations. In view of the likelihood that oscillatory variations will be analysed with much greater interest in the near future, their hypotheses will be reviewed.

First, they suggest, response to specific stimulation may consist not simply in one massive displacement of autonomic function, but in the evocation of an oscillatory disturbance, with the oscillations dying out in a short time. This set of circumstances undoubtedly occurs and has been amply documented.

'The second explanation accepts the first notion of stimulus-produced chained responses and adds to it the tempting idea that the stimuli are either covert or undetected and thus escape the knowledge of the experimenter . . . . This possibility cannot be logically or experimentally discounted.' It cannot, however, adequately explain the high correlations found between resting autonomic activity and autonomic activity during various experimental tasks, nor the relatively constant rate of resting autonomic 'bursts'. Further, the variation in clear records can be seen as a low frequency, almost periodic oscillation.

The Laceys' third explanation has the scientific and theoretical advantage of placing their results in a framework of general biological significance.

'If we search for a known biological process which accounts for a periodic variation, which is relatively constant for fixed environmental circumstances, but which varies with changing environmental input (to account for the significant increase in frequency of discharge during demanding activity), we immediately arrive at what has come to be known as "spontaneous activity". Roeder (1955) has recently given an excellent review of this inherent "restlessness of living matter", and Granit (1955) has set forth in detail the evidence for spontaneous activity in sense organs and has elaborated on its biological significance. Investigators have been slow to accept the notion, but it now seems clear that no matter how carefully the ambient stimulus-level is controlled and maintained at as close to zero level as one can approximate, living tissue will discharge spontaneously at characteristic rates. The rate is subject to control by chemical variation

and environmental stimulation, but is non-specific. It responds only in a generalised way to specific input; it is an expression of inherent instability; it is "biological noise". This explanation, unlike the first two, renders the resting autonomic variation psychologically "silent". The source of the autonomic oscillation is to be sought, not in adventitious stimuli, nor in fleeting disturbing ideation, but in physicochemical processes at the level of localised cell aggregates. Autonomic effectors are thus put on a biologically equal footing with sense organs, receptor tracts, isolated slabs of cat cortex, and motor cells.'

They develop this hypothesis further, and suggest that episodes of autonomic discharge (whether spontaneous or stimulus-evoked) may be paralleled by episodes of changes in cortical arousal. They postulate close functional links between autonomic-cortical coupling and autonomic-somatic coupling. The latter leads to facilitated and augmented, or inhibited, motor activity. Hence, the subject of their study: the relationship of spontaneous autonomic activity with motor performance.

Since then, a number of workers have investigated aspects of spontaneous activity. Johnson (1963) examined spontaneous activity in a number of systems—skin resistance, heart rate, temperature, and respiration—under rest and during stimulation. He found it possible to divide subjects on the basis of spontaneous skin resistance and heart-rate activity into two groups, one showing a smooth, regular, stable record and the other a highly irregular labile record. Degree of lability has been found to relate to speed of habituation (Mundy-Castle and McKiever, 1953) and to speed of conditioning (Stern et al., 1961). Stern (1966) has suggested that what is true of the laboratory is equally true of real-life situations, lability in a system being indicative of easier conditionability of that system by life stresses.

Amount of spontaneous activity in one variable, however, is apparently unrelated to spontaneous activity in other variables. Further, the course of change over time is different in different variables. Spontaneous skin resistance activity was found to show an initial increase as a result of stimulation and also adaptation to repetitive presentations of a stimulus; this kind of responsiveness did not characterise spontaneous heart-rate activity (Johnson, 1963).

The relationship between levels and spontaneous activity within a single system is discussed by Lader and Wing (1966). Most authors have worked with skin conductance measures and have reported definite relationships (Mundy-Castle and McKiever, 1953; Silverman et al., 1959; Sternbach, 1960).

Others have expressed doubts as to whether the observed slight relationship was real (Johnson, 1963; Lacey and Lacey, 1958); yet others have denied a relationship (Wilson and Dykman, 1960). Lader and Wing obtained a correlation of +0·49 and accept that a relationship does exist.

Several workers have expressed concern about the variety of different criteria employed in the measurement of spontaneous fluctuations. Lacey and Lacey (1958) counted the number of 30-second periods in which a spontaneous fluctuation occurred, and Dykman et al. (1959) used a 15-second interval. It is more usual, however, to count the number of fluctuations that are larger than a certain criterion, usually a change of resistance such as one kilohm, or, if extremely sensitive amplifiers are employed, about 20 ohms (Silverman et al., 1959). Lader and Wing argue that if a log conductance unit is used for the stimulus-evoked response, it is consistent to use a criterion of change in log conductance for the spontaneous fluctuation. Boyle et al. (1965) further discuss the scoring of spontaneous activity for skin resistance, heart rate, respiratory rate, muscle action potentials, and EEG records.

In summary, it seems that spontaneous physiological activity, in particular skin resistance activity, is a measure that shows meaningful relationships with arousal, performance, stimulation, and stress (Lader and Wing, 1966; McDonald et al., 1966; Silverman et al., 1959). In early experiments the number of spontaneous fluctuations in skin conductance was believed to reflect, in a roughly linear way, the level of activation of the central nervous system. Lacey and Lacey (1958) have pointed out that much physiological activity shows spontaneous activity, and discuss possible links with cortical and with somatic functioning.

Stimulus Evoked Responses

The concern of this section is with detection of meaningful patterns in the surging, restless, unceasing waves of electrical activity that characterise living organisms. Within the range of organismic-environmental interaction we typically select a very few, simple aspects for experimental analysis. It is in this very narrow context that we ask the question: what is the characteristic response of a particular system (skin resistance, heart rate, respiration, etc.) to a discrete stimulus?

In the usual psychophysiological experiment simple sensory stimuli are used. We must be mindful of the characteristics of these stimuli, of what they are and what they are not. They are not usually stimuli carrying much information; they are not commonly of long duration. They usually have specifiable physical properties (frequency, voltage, etc.) and they have such properties as fast rise times. Thus, they represent a sudden, sharp energy change on the receptors. It is useful in this context to remember Schneirla's (1959) distinction between stimuli that elicit withdrawal behaviour and those eliciting approach behaviour. It is likely that the short, sharp stimuli most commonly used can be classified in the former category, as 'negative' and productive of defensive reactions rather than 'positive'; as unpleasant rather than pleasant.

Following a discrete stimulus, say a brief tone, events happen with almost inconceivable speed. The 'Bickford twitch', a celebrated electromyographic artefact occurring in the recording of evoked responses, occurs within the first 50 msec; reflex eyelid closure can occur with latencies in the region of 50 msec, as well as muscular components of the startle reflex. Various components of the vertex potential occur within the 50–300 msec range. The pupil will begin to dilate with onset latencies between 300 to 400 msec. Many of these responses will be completed or in the process of recovery by the time that EEG changes and, especially, the slower autonomic responses get under way.

Latencies of peripheral responses can be understood in terms of transmission rates along effector fibres and innervation of peripheral end organs. The amplitude of a response and its recovery function are far less clearly understood. They will relate to properties of end organs and undoubtedly to homeostatic factors that act to reduce the disturbance. They also seem to relate more significantly to a variety of psychological factors.

The change in electrical activity to a short, discrete and virtually meaningless stimulus is, therefore, like a richly orchestrated score; to study one fragment of it represents an achievement, but a small one. We may focus on skin resistance, or the heart or pupil, and find in these measures an abundant source of information; yet they represent one small instrumental sequence in an incredibly complex symphonic movement. This is not to undervalue the great amount that has been achieved; indeed, it is the purpose of the following brief review to illustrate the fruitfulness of precise examination of response characteristics.

SKIN RESISTANCE AND SKIN POTENTIAL
RESPONSES (SRRs AND SPRs)

The SRR is typically a decrease in resistance; the SPR is often biphasic in nature, a negative followed by a positive change (Fig. 10.1). However, the waveform of the latter is extremely variable, the character

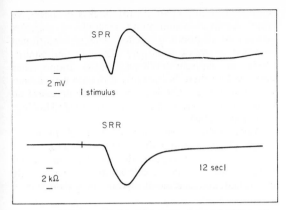

Fig. 10.1. Characteristic skin potential and skin resistance responses (*from* Venables and Martin, 1967)

of the negative component depending on the amplitude and time delay of the positive component if present (Holmquest and Edelberg, 1964).

The latency of the SRR and of the negative component of the SPR appears to be of the order of 1 to 4 sec. The best latency criteria to adopt would seem to be those derived from distributions obtained within the study itself. On such a basis Kleinman and Stern (1968) applied a latency criterion of 0·8 to 3·5 sec, a range very close to the figure of 1·0 to 3·6 sec obtained by Slubicka (1971) from data digitised at a sampling rate of 5 per sec. Amplitude criteria are often determined by the sensitivity of the amplifiers in use. One kilohm is a common unit, but some workers measure considerably smaller responses (of one to two hundred ohms).

Freeman (1948) proposed a measure of recovery, the recovery quotient (RQ), arguing that it provides an estimate of homeostatic behaviour; he obtained data to show that RQ was independent of base-level. It was measured from a reasonably stable level, A, a peak level, B, and recovery at some defined point, C, following the stimulus. Thus, the formula for RQ was $B - C/B - A$ giving a value of 1·00 for perfect recovery. Freeman believed that individuals differed in their ability to re-equilibrate basic disturbances, and that defective homeostatic adjustment could be assessed in terms of speed of recovery to stress. Surprisingly few studies since have employed this measure in the comparison of individuals. An exception is in Mednick and Schulsinger (1968) who found that a measure of SRR recovery differentiated behaviour of children suffering a psychiatric breakdown from that of controls.

Evaluation of the SPR presents certain difficulties because of the possibility that it may be produced by two opposing components that exhibit different waveform characteristics and a variable phase

relationship. Theories and research concerned with the mechanisms underlying palmar SP have been reviewed by Fowles and Venables, 1970; Holmquest and Edelberg, 1964; Martin and Venables, 1966. It is suggested that two components are involved: (1) a fast negative-going component probably arising in the sweat gland, and (2), a slower positive-going component, probably arising in the epidermal layer of the skin. The problem faced in attempting to analyse this two-component response is basically that of trying to separate a single complex waveform into two opposing components that are interacting in any number of combinations to produce cancellations and alterations in amplitude and wave shape (Holmquest and Edelberg, 1964).

A great deal of work with the SPR waveform has been concerned with the possible physiological mechanisms underlying the two components. Some excellent analytical work has been done by Edelberg (1963) and readers are referred to his articles for discussion of the problem. In addition, many workers have been concerned with the differential relationship of the two components to different types of stimuli.

CARDIAC ACTIVITY

Of the many measurable aspects of cardiac activity, the analysis of successive interbeat intervals is one of the most common measures of heart rate in the psychological literature. There are many current debates on the precise form of the change (whether decelerative or accelerative) and on appropriate scoring methods. There are several bases for the current enthusiasm for heart-rate analysis. First, heart rate has been implicated in the mediation of organism-environmental interactions (Graham and Clifton, 1966; Lacey et al., 1963), where, among other things, it would seem to be involved in attention processes. Second, the cardiac deceleration that has been observed to anticipate both aversive and non-aversive stimuli is puzzling in view of traditional expectations of a 'sympathetic-like effect' with heightened motivation or emotionality (Wood and Obrist, 1964, 1968). Third, heart-rate changes form a readily detectable component of the fear response and can be monitored with relative ease in the therapy situation.

The pattern of cardiac activity has always been viewed in the context of the physiological mechanisms underlying and controlling the response. Sympathetic-parasympathetic innervation and its role in determining the shape of the cardiac response has been discussed by Lacey (1956); the influence of respiration has been extensively investigated (Wood and Obrist, 1964; Zeaman and Smith, 1965) especially in conditioning studies. Mutual inter-actions with somatic-motor activity have long been recognised (Obrist and Webb, 1967; Obrist *et al.*, 1969).

Methods of scoring the cardiac response are varied; their advantages and disadvantages are discussed by Hallam (1971). Lang and Hnatiow (1962) used a purely post-stimulus score, suited to an acceleration/deceleration pattern of response. Dykman and colleagues (1959) took pre-stimulus level into account in their measure which reflects only the accelerative component. A problem that must be examined before any particular scoring method is selected is that the form of the cardiac response may change over trials.

An alternative method to that of deriving single scores is to average the heart rate during successive time intervals following stimulus onset. This method can be applied to the data of an individual subject or to single responses across a group of subjects.

It would be somewhat arbitrary to describe the nature of the heart-rate response even to simple stimuli: its course would depend on the kind of stimulus used, the nature of respiratory controls, and the nature of motor activity, if any, required of the subject. In addition, there are wide variations in the methods of data scoring and analysis.

These qualifications having been stated, the 'typical' cardiac response to an auditory stimulus seems to be biphasic, an accelerative followed by a decelerative component (Fig. 10.2). As to the relative prominence of each phase, factors such as loudness, pitch, rise time, and prior instructions are doubtless important (Wilson, 1969). When an

auditory stimulus is paired with shock over successive trials, as in a conditioning schedule, a complex pattern of responding occurs. The unconditioned response to shock is largely (Zeaman and Smith, 1965) or entirely (Wilson, 1969) monophasic accelerative; there is currently a debate on whether the 'true' cardiac CR is a monophasic acceleration or deceleration (Zeaman and Smith, 1965; Hastings and Obrist, 1964).

Other workers have observed a triphasic response, which Graham and Clifton (1966) describe as a short latency acceleration due to decreased vagal tone, a longer latency acceleration, sympathetically controlled, and a deceleration due to vagal discharge.

CHANGES IN BLOOD VOLUME

Recording this type of response has several inter-esting applications. It is commonly used in studies of orientating reactions, especially since Sokolov's distinction between orientating and defensive reactions, in conditioning studies, and, more recently, in the measurement of anxiety (Gelder and Mathews, 1968; Kelly, 1966) and male sexual reactions (Freund, 1967; McConaghy, 1967).

The type of measure obtained is related to the technique employed. Photo-electric and digital pulse volume techniques provide continuous re-cordings, and latency measures can be derived. Gale and Stern (1968) observed a latency range of 2·0 to 5·5 sec. With venous occlusion methods only intermittent readings can be obtained; charac-teristically, a saw-tooth waveform is obtained at minute or half-minute intervals and the slope is measured, rate of blood flow being proportional to slope. McConaghy (1967) has discussed the quantifi-cation of the penile volume change. This is usually a relatively simple measure of maximum amplitude during a 10-second period (in his case the duration of a visual stimulus). He observed both increases and decreases in volume to stimuli.

Most findings are of vasoconstriction to discrete stimuli. There is still some argument concerning the occurrence of vasodilation. Sokolov distinguished the OR from the defensive reflex (DR) by means of the cephalic vasomotor response: the OR is ac-companied by vasodilatation in the skin of the forehead and the DR by vasoconstriction in forehead skin. Only few investigators have actually measured the cephalic vasomotor response, and they seemed to have reached very different conclusions.

Some have, others have not, obtained a vasodila-tion of forehead blood vessels. Some have argued that there is little evidence of vasodilator fibres directly affecting cutaneous blood vessels and that vasomotor control of cutaneous blood flow is solely

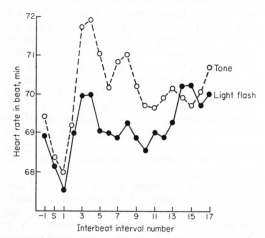

Fig. 10.2. **Mean HR** response for a tone and light flash averaged over all Ss on trials 1 and 2, and trial blocks (TB) 1–5 (*from* Smith and Strawbridge, 1969, by permis-sion of the authors, and the Editor of *Psychophysiology*)

constrictive. Others have asserted that in some areas (digits, ears, lips, nose) vascular changes are regulated by constrictive tone whereas in the skin of the forehead, scalp, chin, and neck, regulation is achieved mainly by dilatative tone (Royer, 1965). The problem of relating cephalic vasomotor responses to ORs and DRs is further complicated by a total absence of quantification of responses in many studies.

PUPILLARY RESPONSES

The value of the pupillary reaction as a diagnostic indicator has long been recognised in neurology and ophthalmology. This has tempted investigators to search for similar relations between pupillary reactions and psychiatric illness, and from early this century abnormal reactions of the pupil to light and other sensory stimuli have been reported in the context of psychopathology.

The work of Lowenstein is outstanding in pupillography and must be acknowledged. He advocated the view that, above all, central sympathetic tonus exerts a decisive influence on the phenomenology of the pupillary light reflex, and was much concerned with sympathetic/parasympathetic balance. This same theme, rephrased in terms of adrenergic/cholinergic balance, has recently been discussed by Rubin (1962) who examines pupillary reactivity as a method for investigating patterns of disordered adrenergic/cholinergic steady states in psychotic disorders.

There are several reasons, then, for measuring pupillary reactions. There is a substantial early literature in which pupillary motility was found to relate to physiological and psychiatric abnormalities. More recent interest centres on the effect of biogenic amines and enzyme disorders on pupillary reactions. Second, the pupil is easily accessible and can be measured with a high degree of accuracy and no discomfort to the subject. More recently there has been a number of studies showing that mental activity is accompanied by an increase in pupil size and that this increase is related to the difficulty of the cognitive task (Simpson, 1969).

Techniques of recording have much improved in recent years. They have moved from direct observation to photography of different kinds and to mechanical and electronic infra-red scanning devices. A description of these techniques has been given in Hakerem (1967).

The response of the pupil to light is constriction, and to a variety of other, including painful, stimuli is dilation. Hakerem and Lidsky (1968) report a latency of about 420 msec to a light stimulus and longer latencies (in the region of 480 msec) with near threshold stimuli. Scholander (1961) obtained onset latencies of between 300 and 400 msec to an auditory stimulus, maximal dilation occurring between 1·5 and 3·0 seconds.

Initial pupillary diameter is reported at about 6·9 mm for normal subjects, and the extent of contraction to a light stimulus about 1·79 mm (Hakerem and Lidsky, 1968). Schaefer et al. (1968) report a mean of about 5·0 mm during rest and 6·3 mm during mental performance. These latter authors measured pupil size to the nearest 0·1 mm. Hakerem has reported that signals of the order of 0·01 mm can be discerned in an average response curve of 50 trials. A common measure is rate of change in time, usually over a 5-second period. Various ratio measures have been used to index change: percent change (Schaefer et al., 1968); final minus initial level, divided by final level (Rubin, 1962). Considerable attention has been given to rates of constriction, dilation and of recovery.

The duration of phasic changes in the pupil following a stimulus is still somewhat controversial. Lowenstein and Loewenfeld (1952) observed that the habituation of the response to light progresses in a peculiar rhythmical way. During the first 5 to 10 reactions in a series there is a general decline of practically all characteristics, initial pupillary diameter, extent, and duration of contraction, etc. Starting with about the sixth reaction, the steady decline starts to vary rhythmically up and down. Cüppers (1951) has criticised Lowenstein and Loewenfeld's results on the grounds of methodological artefact; Dureman and Scholander (1959), however, also reported a rhythmical course in the habituation curve.

Hakerem and Lidsky have more recently described a phenomenon of substantially delayed, yet orderly, continuation of dilation and contraction in a flickering light series. They point out that a pupillary reaction to a given light stimulus (say No. 1) will occur while the next stimulus (No. 2) is being presented. Contraction to stimulus No. 2 begins while stimulus No. 3 is still on, and so forth. It was consistently observed that all the input information from the retina was precisely executed by the pupil but with a delay of over 400 msec. In other words, input and output were out of phase by 420 msec with no apparent degradation of information. The authors suggest that this and other observations are hardly explicable by a simple input-output reflex arc, and that it seems necessary to evoke the existence of some delay or storage mechanism in the response system.

The pupil is another response that has an interesting and controversial role so far as conditioning is concerned. This area has recently been discussed by

Young (1965) who contrasts attempts to condition the pupillary constriction reflex (using light stimuli as UCSs) with those attempting to condition pupillary dilation using shock stimuli. He points out that light stimuli elicit reflex constriction of the pupil itself, whereas noxious stimuli elicit pupillary dilation as part of the fear or startle pattern. It is the latter that seems to be conditionable, and Young concludes that it is the generalised fear pattern, including pupillary dilation, that is conditioned to shock. This distinction between the local and more general systemic responsivity to stimuli is an interesting one, applicable to many kinds of autonomic responses that have a local role, as it were, as well as participating in the general emergency reaction.

SALIVATION

As Ost and Lauer (1965) observe on salivary conditioning, for a method with such a long history there is still a surprising number of technical details to be cleared up. Their efforts are directed towards systematic parametric analysis using salivary conditioning techniques, in order to reappraise the generality of some of the phenomena studied by Pavlovian psychophysiologists, and their experimental subjects are dogs. Work carried out with human subjects has met an almost overwhelming array of difficulties, and very little has been firmly established concerning response characteristics.

Brown and Katz (1967) recently investigated stimulus intensity and salivary output. Although the relationship varied with the measure employed, it was in no case linear. Several measures of the characteristic salivary response curve were taken: maximum amplitude, time to reach maximum amplitude, duration of decline and duration of response. (The authors express doubts about the latter two, suggesting that they may contain errors due to instrumental limitations.)

The difficulties of trying to define a salivary CR by its latency and form have been illustrated in a study by Wells and Feather (1968). Although a definite peak of responding is obtained during CSs at different CS–UCS intervals, the level of salivation following CS offset remains high and may even ascend to a second peak.

Feather showed that much of the undulating or oscillating characteristic of the salivary UCR was associated with concomitant mouth and tongue movements. Feather and Wells (1966) measured salivary response in terms of number of drops in each of two 30-sec intervals following the presentation of acid. They point out that since a salivary response is a change in ongoing rate, any criterion

of the latency of the response to a discrete stimulus is to some extent arbitrary; however, given the digital form of the data (drops) their criterion was in terms of intervals between drops. Response onset was defined as the midpoint of the first of at least two decreasing interdrop intervals. The mean latency obtained from subjects who could swallow immediately after the stimulus was 5·0 sec; from subjects whose swallowing was delayed for 30 sec the latency was 16·9 sec. The authors attributed this long latency to delay of effective stimulation, arguing that when there are no mouth movements to cause redistribution of the acid across the tongue, only few receptors are stimulated, and these so rapidly undergo adaptation that they do not provide sufficient stimulation for a significant increase in salivation. During periods of mouth activity, however, the acid is constantly redistributed across the tongue, reaching previously unstimulated receptor cells and cells that have had time to recover.

The above studies have employed relatively refined techniques of recording and measuring salivation, and, as the authors ruefully realise, their data are meagre in psychological significance compared with the overwhelming impact salivary conditioning has had on the course of psychology. Mention should also be made of work that has been carried out in a psychiatric context; in particular, to test the hypothesis that a reduction of salivary output is characteristic of patients with endogenous depressions.

In these studies salivation has usually been measured by means of the dental-roll technique, in which dental swabs are used in the mouth to absorb total salivary flow. Measuring units are therefore based on the weights of each roll per period of testing; obviously no very precise response pattern can be discerned, although several studies include samples obtained at two minute intervals.

EEG DATA

Continuous Recording

In the majority of studies carried out prior to computer analysis, records were scored by visual inspection. The most visually obvious change that occurs is the blocking response (desynchrony), and it is hardly surprising that there has been almost exclusive interest in this type of response.

Attempts to specify criteria (reviewed by Philips, 1971) have therefore centred on the detection of decrease in ongoing alpha wave activity, even though there is considerable evidence for an enhancement (paradoxical response) effect, especially in drowsy states (McDonald et al., 1964). Desynchrony is typically measured by comparing alpha following a stimulus with that immediately preceding, often only three or so alpha waves. This amounts to about $\frac{3}{8}$ to $\frac{3}{10}$ sec of prestimulus activity and represents a weak attempt at assessing change. Duration of reduced voltage or fast frequency is another response characteristic that has been employed.

In order to simplify response detection it is quite usual to use only highly selected groups of subjects who show high alpha activity when resting. This makes the definition of a phasic response in terms of desynchrony dependent on a specific prestimulus EEG state, namely high alpha wave activity, and this is usually associated with a relaxed awake state. Philips (1971) points out that desynchrony is therefore a state dependent definition.

As with many, if not all, psychophysiological variables, the detection of a response is the problem of detecting a specific time-linked change in a changing system. A number of spontaneous EEG changes occur, and enveloping of the alpha and its disintegration will produce patches of reduced alpha indistinguishable from blocking.

The Evoked Response

This is a measure of neural activity immediately following a discrete stimulus; it is distributed over a large area of the scalp, but since its amplitude is usually largest when recorded from the vertex, it is commonly referred to as the vertex potential.

The record of a single occurrence is riddled with random activity, and it is necessary to employ an averaging technique that allows noise to cancel and signal to accumulate. This technique is discussed by Cooper et al. (1969). In the typical procedure, a stimulus is repeated many times and regular samples of the continuous voltage are obtained and averaged, hence the label averaged evoked response (AER). Averaging may be done on as many as 100 responses, but there may be little gain above an average of 32 or so.

The waveform obtained is complex, with many peaks (Fig. 10.3). The problem of measurement is one of identifying the major components. A component is a pronounced peak or trough in the waveform. Measures of interest are latencies and amplitudes of the major components; amplitude is usually measured from some base point to the peak of a component, or from peak to trough. Three major components of the waveform have been distinguished: a 'primary response' occurring during the first 80 msec after stimulus onset; a 'secondary response' lasting from 80–300 msec; and an oscillatory after-discharge starting at around 300 msec which marks the end of the specific response to the sensory input (Davis et al., 1966).

It is useful to label the components for ease of

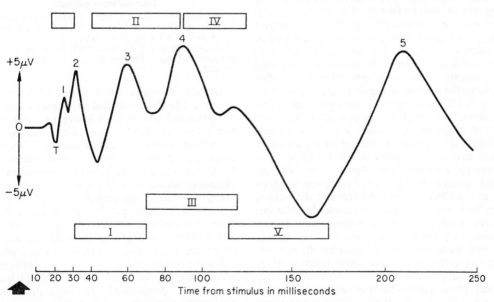

Fig. 10.3. Idealised averaged evoked response

The Arabic numerals on the positive peaks represent a numbering system that has been suggested for somatosensory AERs. The bars labelled with Roman numerals indicate the distribution of positive and negative peaks in visual evoked responses found by Kooi and Bagchi (1964) (*from* Callaway, 1966, by permission of the author, and of the publishers of *J. nerv. ment. Dis.*)

reference, since they appear to be differentially related to psychological factors. It has been suggested that specific characteristics of the waveform may reflect different stages in the brain's processing of sensory input (Kooi and Bagchi, 1964). In general, the primary response seems to relate to simple transmission and reception of the physical stimulus and the secondary response to cortical processing and appraisal of stimulus significance. Latencies of peaks 3 and 4, for example, have been shown to correlate with intelligence (Chalke and Ertl, 1965; Horn, 1969); long duration waves (up to 1 second following stimulus onset) have been shown to relate to complexity of visual material (Lifshitz, 1966).

In addition to the waves shown in Fig. 10.3 three other relatively persistent changes have been observed. These are: (1) ringing, (2) contingent negative variation, and (3) drive related d.c. shifts. The latter two will be examined in the following section. Ringing is described as a prolonged regular oscillation, reminiscent of 'ringing' in a resonant circuit and lasting for several seconds. Although it suggests a return of alpha following the response it has been shown to be statistically distinct from it (Callaway, 1966).

Contingent Negative Variation (CNV)

Walter *et al.* (1964) have described a sustained potential change involving mainly the frontal cortex, during which the surface of the brain becomes electronegative by about 20 microvolts with respect to deeper structures or remote reference electrodes. The effect can be recorded accurately only with equipotential non-polarisable electrodes and long time-constants or d.c. amplifiers. They have called this change the contingent negative variation (CNV), arguing that it is contingent on the significance of an association, and that its amplitude reflects the degree of subjective probability felt by the subject.

It is typically investigated during the time interval between two stimuli, either a CS or UCS, or a preparatory and reaction signal. The shortest interval between the signals for complete development of the CNV is about 0·5 sec and the longest 20 sec. With normal subjects in standard conditions and with moderate intervals between stimuli, the appearance of the CNV is remarkably constant, reaching a mean potential of 20 microvolts between vertex and common mastoid after 1-second (Fig. 10.4). Although records are most commonly obtained from vertico-mastoid electrodes, some use transcephalic recordings of d.c. potential (TCDC) obtained from the midline surface of the head over frontal and occipital emissary veins (Friedman and Taub, 1969).

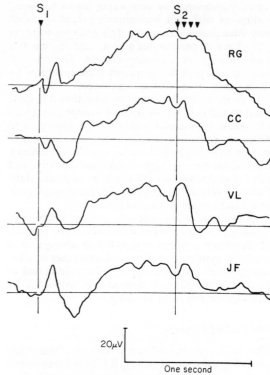

Fig. 10.4. Specimen of fully-developed CNV waves from four different subjects

S_1 was a single flash and S_2 was a train of clicks, terminated by the subject's manual response. Each tracing is the computer sum of 6 consecutive CNVs. Negativity is upwards (*from* Hillyard and Galambos, 1967, by permission of the authors, and the publishers of *Electroenceph. clin. Neurophysiol.*)

Usually, averages are obtained of 6 or 12 responses. The data obtained in Walter's laboratory are processed first as a set of averages and then as histograms of CNV amplitude. The averaging procedure permits measurement of amplitude, latency, duration, and general development of the CNV over trials. The response has been found to be extremely sensitive to changes in the mental and emotional state of the subject.

Walter (1968) has put forward a theory that the brain distinguishes between trivial and important events on the basis of the statistical significance of their association—their contingency. The implication is that the pattern of responses to a particular type of stimulus should vary according to whether it is novel, predictable, conditional, or imperative. Recent work with telemetric recordings has shown that the CNV is present in freely moving subjects performing everyday tasks (Walter *et al.*, 1967).

Although the response described above is negative

in sign, it has been found that interoceptive afferents produce a positive going d.c. frontal deflection, while exteroceptive afferents produce a negative frontal d.c. shift (Cowen, 1967).

In summary, it has been suggested that one of the important methodological concerns in the study of somatic reactivity is the appropriate identification and description of responses. The brief preceding review of some of the commonly employed variables and their measurement is not meant to be comprehensive. Other variables in use include blood pressure, respiration, eye movements, blink rate, the electromyogram and gastrogram. It is hoped, however, that sufficient has been said to indicate the variety of response characteristics that can be measured, and to illustrate the psychological usefulness of such measurement.

It has also been emphasised that more information is usually available than is ever analysed. Computer analysis will undoubtedly remedy this—may indeed produce too much data for intelligible analysis. However, such data must contribute to an improved detection of patterns of responding and to a better understanding of their functional significance.

So far the multidimensional nature of the pattern has been emphasised, in cross section as it were. We must now consider the response in its temporal sequence and consider such questions as: How do preceding events affect the response? How does the response affect successive events? In other words, we must take into account the time-dependent nature of the patterns of activity. One of the earliest factors to be recognised was that subsumed under the title 'law of initial values'.

Pre- and Poststimulus Relationships

The 'Law of Initial Values'

The relationship between pre-stimulation level and the response to stimulation has come to be known as the law of initial values (LIV). The 'law' states that the magnitude of a psychophysiological reaction to a stimulus is dependent on the prestimulus level; when the stimulus is excitatory, subjects with low prestimulus levels tend to show a greater reactivity than subjects with high initial levels, who in some instances may even show 'paradoxical reactions'. Unfortunately, the 'law' has been treated as such very often, instead of being what it is—the statement of a very general kind of relationship requiring empirical examination. The first question one might ask, therefore, concerns the nature of the evidence.

Hord and his colleagues (1964) have asked an important set of questions. Does the 'law of initial value' operate in the same direction for all autonomic variables, that is, is it always the case that the higher

the prestimulus level the smaller the response will be? Second, where the 'law' does apply, how reliable is the relationship of stress to prestimulus level? They attempted to answer these questions by carrying out a regression analysis of stress levels on prestimulus levels of skin conductance, heart rate, respiration rate, and finger temperature responses. Their results are shown in Fig. 10.5. Of the four variables measured, only heart rate and respiration rate have regression line slopes that are less than unity. For these two variables, the higher the prestimulus level, the smaller the response; but this holds only up to a point. A look at the plotted raw data and their regression lines shows that the stress level is essentially a linear function of the prestimulus level, as indicated in Fig. 10.5. The change model in each case can be summarised by relating the regression line to the line of equality, which is the solid line in each of the four sets of co-ordinates. The line of equality is simply the line $Y = X$. The regression line is the dashed line. The point at which the slopes intersect (the cross-over point described by Bridger and Reiser, 1959) is that point above which activation leads to decreased output (paradoxical reactions) and below which the output increases with stimulation.

A similar approach has been adopted for EEG data (Griesel, 1968). He found that the slopes of the regression lines for different types of stimulation for two EEG measures, alpha frequency and abundance scores, were less than 45°, suggesting that the measures are likely to follow the LIV in their response to stress. Further, the slopes appeared to differentiate between different types of stress, some slopes being steeper than others. This steepness of slope was earlier discussed by Bridger and Reiser who suggested that the tighter the homeostatic control of a system the steeper the slope.

The above studies have used *group* data. They and others (e.g. Block and Bridger, 1962) are well aware of the need to examine pre- and post-stimulus relationships for *individuals*. Block and Bridger point out that the LIV may operate for group data among subjects whose individual responses demonstrate an opposite relation. It is often the case that the relative response magnitude of the individual is inferred with respect to the group; Block and Bridger present data showing that the slopes of individual curves are rarely the same as that of the group. Many individual curves intersect the group curve. In these cases, the portion of the individual curve lying above the group curve is composed of responses that are above the average of the group, and the portion below the group curve is composed of responses that are below the average of the group. Whether a particular response is scored as being

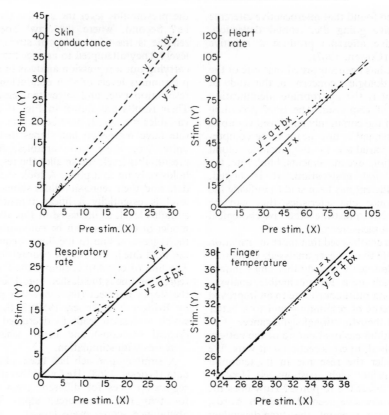

Fig. 10.5. Regression lines for autonomic responses (*from* Hord, Johnson and Lubin, 1964, by permission of the authors and the Editor of *Psychophysiology*)

above or below the group is largely dependent on the prestimulus value at which the stimulus was applied.

Unfortunately, intra-individual regressions are themselves subject to many difficulties. While it would undoubtedly be preferable to describe the prestimulus/poststimulus regression in terms of data for a single individual, such data would be confounded with habituation effects. In adult subjects (the question may be open for very young children), repetition of a stimulus very frequently produces adaptation of the response to it. When there is no effect of repeated stimulation (in particular, no habituation), such parameters can be calculated for each subject and used as measures of the stimulus effect. Lubin and co-workers (1964) have attempted to derive an equation for each subject that can be used even when habituation is present. The position of these latter authors is that the blanket use of any fixed procedure is to be avoided. For each purpose the score that will best suit that purpose should be

calculated, and there is no score that will suit all situations.

One of the most important purposes, and one stated explicitly in Lacey's 1956 paper, was the comparison of responses between individuals. The method he proposed was a landmark in the discussion of this particular problem. In the use of his technique, a single response is obtained from a number of subjects, and essentially a group regression (response magnitude as a function of initial level) is determined. The response magnitude for a given subject is then compared to that expected on the basis of the group regression, and an autonomic lability score (ALS) computed. This ALS is linearly uncorrelated with the prestimulus level. That individual is most responsive who demonstrates the largest ALS.

The method has been criticised by Block and Bridger (1962) and Steinschneider and Lipton (1965), essentially on the basis that Lacey's technique assumes there is a single score that could describe the relative standing of the subject within the group.

Stated in another way, it assumes that an individual's ALS would remain the same regardless of the initial level at which he was tested. These critics maintain that such an assumption can be satisfied only if the intra-individual slope of the regression of response magnitude as a function of initial level is the same for all individuals. But the difficulty of the intra-individual slope, as indicated above, is that in most instances it is likely to be confounded with habituation effects.

There have been other suggestions concerning ways of looking at pre-post stimulus relationships. The notion of the cross-over point suggested by Bridger and Reiser (1959) has already been discussed. Steinschneider and Lipton (1965) have pointed out that measuring the magnitude relationship is not the only means for evaluating the importance of initial level as a determiner of the subsequent response. The LIV can be expressed as the extent to which the estimate of the response is improved by knowledge of the initial value. Another way of viewing this is to consider the extent to which the variability around the regression line (S^2yx) is decreased relative to the variance obtained *without* consideration of the initial value (S^2y). The ratio, S^2yx/S^2y, expresses the proportion of variance still remaining after the initial value is taken into account.

Benjamin (1967) has reviewed the many miscellaneous artefacts said to be associated with analysis of covariance, which is the most appropriate method of 'getting rid of' the influence of prestimulus levels, if this is the aim. Some of these are: that it can cause a loss of valuable information (Heath and Oken, 1965); that it introduces an artefactual association with final level (Heath and Oken, 1965); that LIV can be an artefact of whether resistance or conductance happens to be chosen (Hord *et al.*, 1964), and that in certain instances where groups are defined by a fixed variable its assumptions will be violated (Lubin, 1965).

In fact, the scores obtained from each subject and the subsequent statistical analysis depend in a direct way on the question being asked, the relation between pre-post stimulus values, and nature of the treatment (or effect), etc. (Lubin *et al.*, 1964). These latter authors come to the conclusion that the ALS is inherently no 'fairer' than the difference score, percent change score, difference between standardised scores, etc. Various scoring procedures may be appropriate and effective in situations where other scoring procedures would be inappropriate or less effective.

It is interesting that many workers in allied areas face very similar problems of pre-post stimulus relationships, without ascribing to these relationships the status of a 'law'. An extended empirical examination of the data is required, and also some attempt to interpret the physiological basis for the relationship. The 'mutually antagonistic action' of the sympathetic and parasympathetic systems was early suggested as contributing to the magnitude of peripheral autonomic response (Darrow, 1943), a theme taken up by Lacey (1956), who considers the evidence on the homeostatic restraint of cardiovascular responses, and further emphasised by Lubin *et al.* (1964) who suggest that LIV can hold only if there are two or more antagonistic neural mechanisms involved. Hord *et al.* (1964) have speculated on the physiological mechanisms affecting the four variables (skin conductance, heart rate, respiration rate, and skin temperature) which they observed to show different pre-post stimulus relationships. They point out that the two variables to which the LIV applies (heart rate and respiration) have direct negative feedback mechanisms: chemoreceptors and baroceptors in the carotid sinus and aortic arch as well as afferent fibres originating in the pulmonary apparatus provide direct information on breathing rate and blood pressure (and indirectly on heart rate) to central nervous system centres. On the other hand, there is little if any neurophysiological evidence to suggest a direct negative feedback mechanism for skin conductance and skin temperature.

They deduce the existence of at least two kinds of autonomic variables: quick equilibrium variables and slow equilibrium variables. Heart rate and respiration rate would be quick equilibrium types, with direct neurochemical negative feedback guaranteeing a quick recovery. Other autonomic variables may show a different kind of relationship (pre- and poststimulus) or none at all. In accordance with these observations, Hord *et al.* propose a more general set of linear models of change, the precise nature of which could be made explicit for a given autonomic variable by knowledge of the regression equation and the value of the cross-over point.

From this very brief review it can be seen that solutions are being sought to a wide variety of questions. These include the comparison of individual responsiveness, examination of group differences, the testing of a conditions effect on responses. The empirical evidence available is very slight; what there is is almost entirely plotted in terms of group curves, difficult to plot for the individual subject because of the change in pattern of pre-post stimulus interactions over time, and apparently different for different types of responses. In addition, these empirical data are plotted with a variety of measures, although the basic data are two: a pre- and a post-stimulus value, from which a third, the difference, is commonly derived. This is, of course, a gross understatement of the true complexity, for any response will have many values, some of magnitude, some of time.

Finally, it must be remembered that the LIV problem has in the past been discussed in the context of discrete responses occurring against a background level which 'unfortunately' seemed to vary. The present view is more inclined towards recognising an ongoing stream or sequence of activity, most of it meaningful and essentially time dependent.

Consideration of the LIV leads directly to two further problems in the assessment of patterns of somatic reactivity: the problem of choosing appropriate units of measurement, and the problem of identifying and measuring change. Having decided what aspects of the response are to be measured, we must choose units of measurement that reflect them accurately. The original units of psychophysiological recordings are usually physical units: resistance, voltage, frequency, and time. These units, however, often give rise to skewed distribution; means and variances obtained at different levels of activity tend to be highly correlated; and pre- and poststimulus levels are often highly related. The two former factors are undesirable for statistical, and the third problematical for interpretative reasons.

Units of Measurement

Raw or Transformed?

The problem, then, is whether to use the original units of measurement, or whether to apply transformations. The debate on this issue has lasted several decades, and seems as lively and as far from solution as ever. There is a wide spectrum of opinions and practices.

Most investigators are strongly against 'the use of arbitrary mathematical transformations, which have not been rooted in physiological fact or theory but have emerged entirely as a result of statistical manipulations' (Lacey, 1956; *see also* Lykken, 1968, and Oken and Heath, 1963, for a similar point of view). Nevertheless, most workers are clearly uneasy with raw physiological data and fall into a pattern of applying some conventional transformation, often without checking that it achieves its purpose. All that a monotonic transformation does is to rescale the units of measurement, the main reasons for requiring adjustment being either statistical or theoretical.

The *statistical* reason is usually that of meeting assumptional requirements of the statistical method used regarding the distribution of significance tests.

Any statistic can be used to get an interpretable estimate, but if its assumptions are violated the significance tests do not apply. Analysis of variance, for example, requires a normally distributed variate, independent means and variances, and homogenous variances. Correlation requires bivariate normal distributions. The specific problem of transformations consists simply in determining which one should be used for a particular set of data in order to fulfil these requirements. It should be noted that many 'short-cut' statistics used as approximations to more powerful methods, e.g. X^2, tetrachoric R, and rank correlation, still assume an underlying normality. Distribution free statistics do not assume normality, but suffer a loss of power.

The *theoretical* reason for applying a transformation is usually to make the data conform to some model or expectation based either on theory or assumptions about the variates involved. An example has just been considered—the law of initial values—in which the assumption is made that pre- and poststimulus levels should be treated as if they were independent. It must be realised that the justification for removing the base line is not rooted in physiological fact or any 'law' of initial values. The justification lies, instead, in the statistical control of the experiment. If the question asked is: What would phasic responses be if all subjects had the same pre-stimulus level?, then the appropriate method is to partial out by means of covariance techniques. This assumes linearity throughout the range of measurements; an interesting and relevant point is that the range must include all the experimental conditions. To partial out the base line for purposes of statistical control is to assume that the relationship between pre- and poststimulus levels is the same under all conditions, i.e. the within cell regressions are assumed to be equal. A better approach would be multiple discriminant function analysis or multivariate analysis of variance, to assess the contribution of base levels under each experimental condition. This is a different aim from statistical control, however.

It is unfortunate that statistical control of the experiment and assumptions of independence have been confused in the literature. Modern statistical methods allow for the identification of components and estimates of their functional contribution, hence we can identify the *contribution* of the baseline without *discarding* it (see the later section on measurement of change).

It would seem that transformation of raw data is a necessary step in many physiological measurements. The problem of the investigator is to choose the appropriate transformation wisely. Transformation methods currently in use can be grouped under three headings: (1) mathematical, (2) empirical (*ad hoc*), and (3) theoretical.

1. *Mathematical.* The choice of a transformation will depend on certain characteristics of the distribution: its shape, relation between means and variances, etc. These are purely mathematical requirements and most statistical texts include their discussion. Maxwell (1958), for example, gives convenient rules of thumb for selecting square-root, reciprocal and logarithmic transformations on these grounds.

2. *Empirical.* The mathematical requirements can be produced by arbitrary manipulation of the units of measurement, though this method has never been popular. It is not necessary to know anything about the data or the underlying physiology. Tabled values of the normal equivalents of ranked data may be used, for example, in this way (Fisher and Yates, 1943). Recently, Dolby (1963) has suggested a general formula the constants of which can be fitted to provide an arbitrary transformation. These methods assume, however, that the underlying distributions satisfy the statistical requirements; they should not be used to force observed variates into the model without good reason for the assumption.

3. *Theoretical.* This term is used to distinguish the substantive area from the mathematical. Where something is known of the nature of the underlying process, transformations can take advantage of this knowledge to achieve greater simplicity or parsimony of description. Simple examples of this are judgements of pitch on a logarithmic scale, ceiling effects on an antilog scale, proportionality of responding on an arc sine scale, i.e. transformations that achieve linearity.

In the case of somatic responses, transformations should ideally be based on known physiology, where available. It is not enough to assert that 'most biological variates are normally distributed', that 'many biological functions are logarithmic', etc. Regrettably, for most variates the underlying physiology is not sufficiently explicit. Possible mechanisms have been discussed by Lacey (1956) in connection with heart rate, and by Lader and Wing (1966) and Lykken (1968) in connection with sweat gland activity. The argument applied to skin resistance measures is as follows: the main effect of sudomotor innervation is to increase the density of active sweat glands, which would amount to adding more conduction paths in parallel to those already present; hence, conductance is the logical unit to employ since it is linearly related to the density of active glands.

There is a danger of tautology in this type of argument. If sweat glands are in parallel, conductance is additive and resistance is not; but if sweat glands are in series, resistance is additive and conductance is not. We cannot apply a transformation to prove the case. In fact, current models of sweat gland activity as they relate to obtained skin resistance measures are exceedingly complex, and it is still not certain how increases and decreases relate to underlying activity.

To conclude, the tendency to apply transformations in an arbitrary manner to the obtained units of measurement must be deplored. Two examples of the effect of several different transformations of SRR are given in Figs. 10.6 and 10.7. It is clear from Fig. 10.7 that, although some transformations achieve a better distribution than others, they all have a prolonged spread at the upper end, and a good case might be made for excluding some of the subjects on the grounds that they do not belong within the sample. Objective criteria for excluding deviant observations have long been used in the physical sciences (e.g. Chauvenet's criterion, *see* Parrat, 1961) though they have been discouraged in the biological sciences. Further, the transformation that comes closest to normality also alters the correlation with base-line level. This is 0·35 for raw

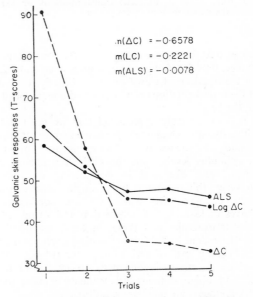

Fig. 10.6. Habituation functions to two intensities of auditory stimulation (50 and 90 db)

Comparison is made between two response measures: change in conductance and autonomic lability score (ALS). Hyperbolic slope (*m*) values are associated with each function (*from* Germana, 1968, by permission of the authors, and the Editor of *Psychophysiology*)

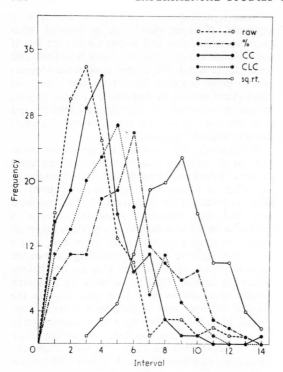

Fig. 10.7. Effect of different transformations on skin resistance response data (*from* Levey, 1970)

scores, 0·02 for percent change, 0·06 for conductance change, 0·04 for change in log conductance and 0·25 for the square root transformation. Clearly, no one of the transformations can be selected unequivocally as 'the best'.

It is increasingly appreciated that we must deal with a dynamic changing organism when we attempt to study somatic reactivity. The change from pre- to poststimulus levels, and the difficult problems it raises, were discussed in considering the LIV. However, this represents but a single aspect of the many changes with which we are confronted. Curves of learning, of habituation and so on, are familiar examples and these, in turn, are usually interdependent on initial and resting levels, and on the ongoing level of activation of the subject. The problem of measuring change, however, and the related problem of the interdependence of successive measurements are far from solution.

Estimates of Change

Perhaps the simplest, and not necessarily the least informative measure of change is a difference score, computed by subtracting initial from final values of

any measure. It yields a single value to express the degree of change, and if the rate of change is constant or a constant function this score subsumes it. Thus, average amplitude or latency of responding during a first block of trials forms the baseline for the average level of a final block. Similarly, the baseline may be expressed in a ratio, but in this case the assumption is made that growth or change can be represented by a constant of proportionality. The limitations and advantages of ratio and difference scores were early described in the standard texts (Snedecor, 1938). These and other scores comparing initial with final values have the serious disadvantage that by omitting the intervening trial values they miss information on the course of change, which is assumed to be constant.

The regression methods discussed earlier may also be used in the analysis of change. If we define change as that part of an individual's score that cannot be predicted from his initial or preceding level, we can use the discrepancy between the observed level and the level predicted by the regression formula as a measure of change. This approach has been discussed by Lord (1963) at some length. It is important to note that the method implies a model of change, and the assumptions of the model must be scrutinised before it is applied indiscriminately to a particular set of data.

In recent years, the use of trend analysis has increased in response to the limitations of the methods just discussed. This is a method that takes account of all the observations in a series, and reduces them to a set of independent components of trend, based on the polynomial expression that best reproduces the series. It consists, essentially, in estimating, by analysis of variance, the successive contribution of each of these orthogonal components, representing linear, quadratic, cubic, and ascending orders to the serial form of any ordered set of observations. The computations, using tabled coefficients, have been summarised by Grant (1956) and computational methods are available for the case in which unequal number of subjects respond at unequally spaced intervals (Gaito, 1965).

It is essential to keep clear the distinction between group trends, based on the averaged values for successive trials, and individual trends. The group trend is not necessarily representative of any individual trend, as has been mentioned earlier. Where there has been interest both in individual differences and in overall differences in performance, it has seemed appropriate to analyse the data for each individual separately over successive trials. Individual estimates of change, using the method of orthogonal polynomials, have been applied to eyelid conditioning data (Levey, 1966), autonomic conditioning data (Morgenson, 1967), and to EEG habituation data (Philips, 1971). Plotting of individual curves from these estimates is both a rewarding and frustrating task. All the data examined so far in this way reveal a great variety of curves. In general, however, linear and quadratic components are dominant in conditioning and habituation experiments, higher order polynomials contributing little.

Trend analysis should not be taken as providing a solution that is true to nature, in the sense of identifying the parameters of an underlying process. Rather it provides a summary of the available information in the form of a linear equation that simply identifies the significant inflections in the curve. A final advantage of this approach, however, is that individual coefficients can be used as scores in further analyses, for example of group or treatment effects. Here they function as summary scores describing the course of change, and bring the results of complex analyses within an interpretable range.

None of these estimates of change so far discussed takes account of the mutual interdependence of observations taken from living organisms over a period of time. Two aspects of the measurement of change must be sharply distinguished.

We can regard the course of change—increment, decrement or fluctuation—as a fixed function of successive observations and write an equation that describes it, as in the case of the polynomial regression equation of trend analysis. In this case we assume that time is the determinant, and such methods require that the successive observations be independent of one another. We know, however, that for living organisms this is seldom the case; the immediate and distant past history is an important determinant of responses in the present. The second aspect of change, therefore, regards the behaviour of a single occasion of measurement as a function of previous occasions. Both of these aspects are essential, and they are closely interwoven. No satisfactory method exists, however, for their simultaneous analysis.

The linear covariance matrix among successive measures represents a summary of the data that takes account both of the ordering of measures and their interdependence. Methods of analysing the information in such matrices are now readily available for routine use through high-speed computing facilities. Three such methods will be briefly described. None offers a complete or final answer to the problems of measuring change, but they make it possible to take account of the mutual dependency of responses that probably characterises most living response systems.

Tucker (1966) has offered one solution to the problem in a factor analytic method of measuring the components of change. This method identifies orthogonal contributions from successive measures, and essentially describes the relationship among them in terms of their individual contributions to one or more response curves. The performance of individuals or groups can be described by the relative strength of these change components in their recordings. While originally devised to account for learning data, the method would seem to hold promise for the data of somatic reactivity. It has the advantage of summarising the information contained in successive interrelated measures while retaining their serial positions as dependent variables.

While the analysis of variance has become an indispensible tool in the treatment of univariate data, its extension to multivariate observations has been undeservedly neglected. Multivariate analysis of variance offers a method of comparing treatments among mutually dependent measures such that their components are weighted to achieve the best separation between treatments. This method yields a profile of weights across measures which identifies the degree to which each of them contributes to the separation. Since it takes account of covariance among measures it can readily be extended to the treatment of successive interdependent observations, to provide a description of the course of change. A full discussion of the method would lie beyond the scope of this chapter, but excellent introductory accounts are available (Morrison, 1967) and the method is fully discussed in advanced texts (Kendall and Stuart, 1968).

Finally, brief mention must be made of methods derived from the physical laboratory, whose application to the data of somatic reactivity is relatively recent. Of these, the use of the autoregressive series to analyse the course of change appears to hold particular promise. The autoregressive series describes the level of responding observed on a single occasion in terms of the contribution from previous or adjacent occasions. The equation defines coefficients for weighting the previous occasions in terms of their contribution to any current measurement. Again, the reader must be referred to introductory accounts (Goldberg, 1958; Hannon, 1967) or to the advanced texts (Kendall and Stuart, 1968; Rao, 1952) for a fuller description.

The interest of this approach is twofold. The method gives rise to an extensive family of curves based on exponential and sinusoidal components. These include increasing and decreasing monotonic functions, oscillating functions with and without damping, and so on, which bear a close resemblance to the kind of curves generated in psychophysiological recordings. These may be regarded as statistical descriptions, and tests of goodness of fit and significance are available (Quenouille, 1949). In these terms, one advantage of the method is that where no real or complex solution can be found we have evidence that the method is inappropriate, and this contrasts with other methods of 'curve fitting' in which, by appropriate manipulation some 'solution' is forced, however misleading.

Apart from description of a wide variety of change patterns the method is of interest in that it can serve as a model of the underlying process. It can be used to define the impulse function of the system that generates the response output measured. In this sense it offers hypotheses about the nature of the generators; for example in EEG recordings. It can also be used to identify feedback components in the system, since the contribution of previous measures may represent components still active. In application to psychological data the number of components required may be surprisingly low (Jones *et al.*, 1969).

The method suffers the practical disadvantage that the covariance elements are not allowed to change through time, i.e. every segment of the record must bear the same interrelation among measures. This may impose severe limits on the length of recording epoch, depending on the response system being recorded. Conversely, the method can be used to identify state changes in the system, for example after a change in stimulation, by determining whether the defined function continues to hold.

In summary, it is suggested that the choice of an appropriate model to represent change in living systems must be made on the basis of all available information. As with the data transformations, it is not enough to apply a routine method. Although the problem of measuring change remains largely unsolved, there is a number of guiding principles. In the first instance the assumptions of the model can be examined. The methods discussed earlier, difference and ratio scores, regression scores and trend analysis, all imply that the occasions of measurement are independent. The three methods discussed above take advantage of the mutual dependence among measures but, in general, require that the sampling interval of responses be rigidly controlled, since time dependency is limited to the ordering of the measures. In particular, the method of autoregressive analysis implies that the ongoing process is in a constant state. If applied to habituation data, for example, it would imply that habituation is itself a constant process. If the investigator regards habituation as a change in the state of the organism, and wishes to measure the changes occurring during habituation the method would be inappropriate.

Apart from the assumption of the models, practical criteria may determine the method of analysis. In general, the method that yields the best statistical criteria of goodness of fit is to be preferred. Similarly, the model that effects a description of change by using only a few elements or terms is preferable on grounds of parsimony to one that requires a large number. Finally, the exigencies of recording in a particular system may determine the number of observations it is feasible to collect, and thus exclude methods that require a large number of observations.

SUMMARY

Some major shifts of emphasis in the study of somatic reactivity have occurred during the past decade. In this chapter an attempt has been made to trace out and underline these changes: the shift from technical problems of recording to methodological problems of analysis; the swing away from stimulus-orientated studies and toward response characteristics; the renewal of interest in adaptive and problem solving aspects of responding.

It has been suggested that four problems have emerged in response to these changes. They are: the problem of response definition; the problem of relating responses and levels; the problem of units of measurement; and the problem of estimating change.

The theme is the unity of the organism as a living system, adaptive and self-regulatory, whose responses are embedded in a context and mutually dependent through time.

REFERENCES

BENJAMIN, LORNA S. (1967) Facts and artifacts in using analysis of covariance to 'undo' the law of initial values. *Psychophysiology*, **4**, 187–206.

BLOCK, J. D. and BRIDGER, W. H. (1962) The law of initial value in psychophysiology: a reformulation in terms of experimental and theoretical considerations. *Ann. New York Acad. Sci.*, **98**, 1229–1241.

BOYLE, R. H., DYKMAN, R. A., and ACKERMAN, PEGGY T.

(1965) Relationships of resting autonomic activity, motor impulsivity, and EEG tracings in children. *Arch. Genl. Psychiatry*, **12**, 314–323.

BRIDGER, W. H. and REISER, M. F. (1959) Psychophysiologic studies of the neonate; an approach toward the methodological problems involved. *Psychosom. Med.*, **21**, 265–276.

BROWN, C. C. (Ed.) (1967) *Methods in Psychophysiology*. Baltimore: Williams and Wilkins.

BROWN, C. C. and KATZ, RUTH A. (1967) Psychophysiological aspects of parotid salivation in man: 1. Stimulus intensity and salivary output. *Psychophysiology*, **3**, 273–279.

CALLAWAY, E. (1966) Averaged evoked responses in psychiatry. *J. nerv. ment. Dis.*, **143**, 80–94.

CHALKE, F. C. R. and ERTL, J. P. (1965) Evoked potentials and intelligence. *Life Sciences*, **4**, 1319–1322.

COOPER, R., OSSELTON, J. W., and SHAW, J. C. (1969) *EEG technology*. London: Butterworths.

COWEN, M. A. (1967) Elementary functional correlates of the transcephalic DC circuit. *Psychophysiology*, **3**, 262–272.

CÜPPERS, C. (1951) Eine neue Methode zur stetigen Registrierung der direkten und der konsensuellen Pupillenreaktion. *Klinische Monatsblätter für Augenheilkunde*, Stuttgart, **119**, 411.

DARROW, C. W. (1943) Physiological and clinical tests of autonomic function and autonomic balance. *Physiological Rev.*, **23**, 1–36.

DARROW, C. W. (1964) Psychophysiology, yesterday, today, and tomorrow. *Psychophysiology*, **1**, 4–7.

DAVIS, H., MAST, T., YOSHIE, N., and ZERLIN, S. (1966) The slow response of the human cortex to auditory stimuli: recovery process. *Electroencephal. Clin. Neurophysiol.*, **21**, 105–113.

DOLBY, J. L. (1963) A quick method for choosing a transformation. *Technometrics*, **5**, 317–325.

DUFFY, ELIZABETH (1962) *Activation and Behaviour*. New York: Wiley.

DUREMAN, I. and SCHOLANDER, T. (1959) *Studies in the psychosensory reflex*. 1. Habituation to auditory stimuli. Reports from the Psychological Laboratories, Univ. of Uppsala, 2.

DYKMAN, R. A., REESE, W. G., GALBRECHT, C. R., and THOMASSON, P. J. (1959) Psychophysiological reactions to novel stimuli: measurement, adaptation, and relationship of psychological and physiological variables in the normal human. *Ann. New York Acad. Sci.*, **79**, 43–107.

DYKMAN, R. A., MACK, R. L., and ACKERMAN, PEGGY T. (1965) The evaluation of autonomic and motor components of the non-avoidance conditioned response in the dog. *Psychophysiology*, **1**, 209–230.

EDELBERG, R. (1963) *Electrophysiologic characteristics and interpretation of skin potentials*. Technical Documentary Report No. SAM-tdr-63-95, USAF School of Aerospace Medicine.

FEATHER, B. W. and WELLS, D. T. (1966) Effects of concurrent motor activity on the unconditioned salivary reflex. *Psychophysiology*, **2**, 338–343.

FISHER, R. A. and YATES, F. (1943) *Statistical Tables for Biological, Agricultural, and Medical Research*. London: Oliver and Boyd.

FOWLES, D. C. and VENABLES, P. H. (1970) The effects of epidermal hydration and sodium reabsorption on palmar skin potential. *Psycholog. Bull.* **73**, 363–378.

FRANKENHAEUSER, MARIANNE, FROBERG, J., HAGDAHL, R., RISSLER, ANITA, BJORKVALL, C., and WOLFF, B. (1967) Physiological, behavioral, and subjective indices of habituation to psychological stress. *Physiology and Behav.*, **2**, 229–237.

FREEMAN, G. L. (1948) *The Energetics of Human Behaviour*. Ithaca: Cornell Univ. Press.

FREUND, K. (1967) Diagnosing homo or heterosexuality and erotic age-preference by means of a psychophysiological test. *Behav. Res. Therapy*, **5**, 43–48.

FRIEDMAN, H. and TAUB, H. A. (1969) The transcephalic DC potential and reaction time performance. *Psychophysiology*, **5**, 504–509.

GAITO, J. (1965) Unequal intervals and unequal *n* in trend analyses. *Psycholog. Bull.*, **63**, 125–127.

GALE, E. N. and STERN, J. A. (1968) Classical conditioning of the peripheral vasomotor orienting response. *Psychophysiology*, **4**, 342–348.

GELDER, M. G. and MATHEWS, A. M. (1968) Forearm blood flow and phobic anxiety. *Brit. J. Psychiat.*, **114**, 1371–1376.

GERMANA, J. (1968) Rate of habituation and the law of initial values. *Psychophysiology*, **5**, 31–36.

GERMANA, J. (1969) Patterns of autonomic and somatic activity during classical conditioning of a motor response. *J. comparat. physiolog. Psychol.*, **69**, 173–178.

GOLDBERG, S. (1958) *Introduction to Difference Equations: with illustrated examples from economics, psychology, and sociology*. London: Chapman and Hall.

GRAHAM, F. K. and CLIFTON, R. K. (1966) Heart-rate change as a component of the orienting response. *Psycholog. Bull.*, **65**, 305–320.

GRANIT, R. (1955) *Receptors and Sensory Perception*. New Haven: Yale Univ. Press.

GRANT, D. A. (1956) Analysis of variance tests in the analysis and comparison of curves. *Psycholog. Bull.*, **53**, 141–154.

GRIESEL, R. D. (1968) The applicability of Wilder's law of initial value to changes in the alpha rhythm of the EEG. *Psychologia Africana*, **12**, 122–132.

GRINGS, W. W., LOCKART, R. A., and DAMERON, L. E. (1962) Conditioning autonomic responses of mentally abnormal individuals. *Psychological Monographs*, **76**, 39, whole No: 558.

HAKEREM, G. (1967) Pupillography. In *Manual of Psychophysiological Methods* (Ed. Venables, P. and Martin, Irene). Amsterdam: North Holland Pubg. Co., pp. 335–349.

HAKEREM, G. and LIDSKY, A. (1968) *Characteristics of pupillary reactions in psychiatric patients and normals*. Paper presented at the Biometrics Research Workshop on objective indicators of psychopathology, New York.

HALLAM, R. (1971) The role of cognitive factors and conditioning in aversion therapy. Unpublished doctoral dissertation, University of London.

HANNAN, E. J. (1967) *Time Series Analysis*. London: Methuen.

HASTINGS, SHIRLY E. and OBRIST, P. A. (1967) Heart rate

during conditioning in humans: Effect of varying the interstimulus (CS-UCS) interval. *J. exp. Psychol.*, **74**, 431–442.

HEATH, H. A. and OKEN, D. (1965) The quantification of 'response' to experimental stimuli. *Psychosomat. Med.*, **27**, 457–471.

HILLYARD, S. A. and GALAMBOS, R. (1967) Effects of stimulus and response contingencies on a surface negative slow potential shift in man. *Electroencephalography and Clin. neurophysiol.*, **22**, 297–304.

HOLMQUEST, D. and EDELBERG, R. (1964) Problems in the analysis of the endosomatic galvanic skin response. *Psychophysiology*, **1**, 48–54.

HORD, D. J., JOHNSON, L. C., and LUBIN, A. (1964) Differential effect of the law of initial value (LIV) on autonomic variables. *Psychophysiology*, **1**, 79–87.

HORN, J. L. (1969) *The relationship between evoked potential recordings and intelligence test measures.* Paper given at the International conference of the Society of Multivariate Psychology, Oxford.

JOHNSON, L. C. (1963) Some attributes of spontaneous autonomic activity. *J. comp. physiol. Psychol.*, **56**, 415–422.

JONES, R. H., CROMWELL, D. H., and KAPUNAI, LINDA E. (1969) Change detection model for serially correlated data. *Psycholog. Bull.*, **71**, 352–358.

KELLY, D. H. W. (1966) Measurement of anxiety by forearm blood flow. *Brit. J. Psychiat.*, **112**, 789–798.

KENDALL, M. G. and STUART, A. (1968) *The Advanced Theory of Statistics.* (Rev. Ed.) Boston: Houghton.

KIMMEL, H. D. (1965) Instrumental inhibitory factors in classical conditioning. In *Classical Conditioning* (Ed. Prokasy, W. F.) New York: Appleton-Century-Crofts.

KLEINMAN, K. M. and STERN, J. A. (1968) Task complexity, electrodermal activity and reaction time. *Psychophysiology*, **5**, 51–60.

KOOI, K. A. and BAGCHI, B. K. (1964) Visual evoked responses in man: Normative data. *Ann. New York Acad. Sci.*, **112**, 254–269.

LACEY, J. (1956) The evaluation of autonomic responses: toward a general solution. *Ann. New York Acad. Sci.*, **67**, 125–163.

LACEY, J. I. and LACEY, B. C. (1958) The relationship of resting autonomic activity to motor impulsivity. *Proc. Assoc. Res. in Nerv. and Ment. Dis.*, **36**, 144–209.

LACEY, J. I., KEGAN, J., LACEY, B. C., and MOSS, H. A. (1963) Situational determinants and behavioural correlates of autonomic response patterns. In *Expression of the Emotions in Man* (Ed. Knapp, P. J.) New York: International Universities Press, pp. 191–196.

LADER, M. H. and WING, LORNA (1966) *Physiological Measures, Sedative Drugs, and Morbid Anxiety.* Institute of Psychiatry, Maudsley Monographs, No. 14. London: Oxford Univ. Press.

LANG, P. J. (1968) Fear reduction and fear behaviour: Problems in treating a construct. In *Research in Psychotherapy*, Vol. 3 (Ed. Shlien, J. M.). Washington: American Psychological Association.

LANG, P. J. and HNATIOW, M. (1962) Stimulus repetition and the heart rate responses. *J. comp. physiol. Psychol.*, **55**, 781–785.

LAZARUS, R. S. (1968) Emotions and adaptation: conceptual and empirical relations. In *Nebraska Symposium of Motivation* (Ed. Arnold, W. J.). Lincoln, Nebr.: University of Nebraska Press.

LEVEY, A. B. (1966) *Some measures of response efficiency for the conditioned eyelid response.* Paper read at the Fourth World Cong. Psychiat. Symposium on higher nervous activity. Madrid.

LEVEY, A. B. (1970) The use of transformations on psychophysiological data. Unpublished.

LEVEY, A. B. and MARTIN, IRENE (1968) Shape of the conditioned eyelid response. *Psychol. Rev.*, **75**, 398–408.

LIFSHITZ, K. (1966) The averaged evoked cortical response to complex visual stimuli. *Psychophysiology*, **3**, 55–68.

LORD, F. M. (1963) Elementary models for measuring change. In *Problems in Measuring change* (Ed. Harris, C. W.). Madison: Univ. of Wisconsin Press.

LOWENSTEIN, O. and LOEWENFELD, I. (1950) Role of sympathetic and parasympathetic systems in reflex dilation of the pupil: pupillographic studies. *Arch. Neurol. Psychiat.*, **64**, 313–340.

LUBIN, A. (1965) Book Review of 'Problems of Measuring Change' (Ed. Harris G.) *Amer. J. Psychol.*, **78**, 324–327.

LUBIN, A., HORD, D. J., and JOHNSON, L. C. (1964) *On the Validity and Reliability of the Autonomic Lability Score.* U.S. Navy Med. Neuropsychiatric Res. Unit, San Diego, Report No. 64-20.

LYKKEN, D. T. (1969) Psychophysiological techniques and personality theory. In *Handbook of Personality Theory and Research* (Ed. Borgatta, E. F. and Lambert, W. W.) Chicago: Rand McNally.

LYKKEN, D. T., ROSE, R., LUTHER, B., and MALEY, M. (1966) Correcting psychophysiological measures for individual differences in range. *Psychol. Bull.*, **66**, 481–484.

MALMO, R. B. (1965) Physiological gradients and behaviour. *Psychol. Bull.*, **64**, 225–234.

MARTIN, IRENE (1960) The effects of depressant drugs on palmar skin resistance and adaptation. In *Experiments in Personality*, Vol. 1 (Ed. Eysenck, H. J.) London: Routledge and Kegan Paul.

MARTIN, IRENE and LEVEY, A. B. (1969) *The Genesis of the Classical Conditioned Response.* International Series of Monographs in Experimental Psychology, Vol. 8. Oxford: Pergamon Press.

MARTIN, IRENE and VENABLES, P. (1966) Mechanisms of palmar skin resistance and skin potential. *Psychol. Bull.*, **65**, 347–357.

MAXWELL, A. E. (1958) *Experimental Design in Psychology and the Medical Sciences.* London: Methuen.

McCONAGHY, N. (1967) Penile volume change to moving pictures of male and female nudes in heterosexual and homosexual males. *Behav. Res. Therapy*, **5**, 43–48.

McDONALD, D. G., JOHNSON, L. C., and HORD, D. J. (1964) Habituation of the orienting response in alert and drowsy subjects. *Psychophysiology*, **1**, 163–173.

MEDNICK, S. A. and SCHULSINGER, F. (1968) Some premorbid characteristics related to breakdown in children with schizophrenic mothers. *J. Psychiat. Res.*, **6**, (Supplement 1) 267–291.

MORGENSON, D. (1967) Cognitive factors in autonomic

conditioning. Unpublished doctoral dissertation. University of London.

MORRISON, D. F. (1967) *Multivariate Statistical Methods*. New York: McGraw Hill.

MUNDY-CASTLE, A. C. and McKIEVER, B. L. (1953) The psychophysiological significance of the galvanic skin response. *J. exp. Psychol.*, **46**, 15–24.

OBRIST, P. A. and WEBB, R. A. (1967) Heart rate during conditioning in dogs: Relationship to somatic-motor activity. *Psychophysiology*, **4**, 7–34.

OBRIST, P. A., WEBB, R. A., and SUTTERER, J. R. (1969) Heart rate and somatic changes during aversive conditioning and a simple reaction time task. *Psychophysiology*, **5**, 696–723.

OBRIST, P. A., WOOD, D. M., and PEREZ-REYES, M. (1965) Heart rate during conditioning in humans: Effects of UCS intensity, vagal blockage, and adrenergic block of vasomotor activity. *J. exp. Psychol.*, **70**, 32–42.

OKEN, D. and HEATH, HELEN A. (1963) The law of initial values: some further considerations. *Psychosomat. Med.*, **25**, 3–12.

OST, J. W. P. and LAUER, D. W. (1965) Some investigations of classical salivary conditioning in the dog. In *Classical Conditioning: a symposium* (Ed. Prokasy, W. F.) New York: Appleton-Century-Crofts, pp. 192–207.

PARRAT, L. G. (1961) Probability and Experimental Errors in Science. New York: Wiley.

PENNYPACKER, H. S. (1964) Measurement of the conditioned eyelid reflex. *Science*, **144**, 1248–1249.

PHILIPS, CLARE. (1971) An experimental investigation of EEG habituation. Unpublished doctoral dissertation. University of London.

PRIBRAM, K. H. (1967) The new neurology and the biology of emotion: A structural approach. *Amer. Psychol.*, **22**, 830–838.

PROKASY, W. F. (1965) Classical eyelid conditioning: Experimenter operations, task demands, and response shaping. In *Classical Conditioning* (Ed. Prokasy, W. F.) New York: Appleton-Century-Crofts, pp. 208–225.

QUENOUILLE, M. N. (1949) Approximate tests of correlation in time-series. *J. roy. statistical Society*, Series B, **11**, 68–84.

RAO, C. R. (1952) *Advanced Statistical Methods in Biometric Research*. New York: Wiley.

ROEDER, K. D. (1955) Spontaneous activity and behaviour. *Scientific Monthly*, **80**, 362–370.

ROYER, F. L. (1965) Cutaneous vasomotor components of the orienting reflex. *Behav. Res. Therapy*, **3**, 161–170.

RUBIN, L. S. (1962) Patterns of adrenergic-cholinergic imbalance in the functional psychoses. *Psychol. Rev.*, **69**, 501–519.

SCHAEFER, T., BRINTON FERGUSON, J., KLEIN, J. A., and RAWSON, E. B. (1968) Pupillary responses during mental activities. *Psychonomic Sci.*, **12**, 137–138.

SCHNEIRLA, T. C. (1959) An evolutionary and developmental theory of a biphasic process underlying approach and withdrawal. In *Nebraska Symposium on Motivation* (Ed. M. R. Jones) Lincoln, Nebr.: University of Nebraska Press.

SCHOLANDER, T. (1961) *Habituation Processes*. Annales Academiae Regiae Scientiarum Upsaliensis.

SHARPLESS, S. and JASPER, H. (1956) Habituation of the arousal reaction. *Brain*, **79**, 655–680.

SILVERMAN, A. J., COHEN, S. I., and SHMAVONIAN, B. H. (1959) Investigation of psychophysiologic relationships with skin resistance measures. *J. Psychosomat. Res.*, **4**, 65–87.

SIMPSON, H. M. (1969) Effects of a task-relevant response on pupil size. *Psychophysiology*, **6**, 115–121.

SLUBICKA, BARBARA (1971) Changes in electrodermal responses during classical conditioning and their relationship to personality and awareness. Unpublished.

SMITH, D. B. D. and STRAWBRIDGE, PHYLLIS, J. (1969) The heart rate response to a brief auditory and visual stimulus. *Psychophysiology*, **6**, 317–329.

SNEDECOR, G. W. (1938) *Statistical Methods*. Ames: Iowa State College Press.

SOKOLOV, E. N. (1963) *Perception and the Conditioned Reflex*. New York: Pergamon Press.

STEINSCHNEIDER, A. and LIPTON, E. L. (1965) Individual difference in autonomic responsivity. Problems of Measurement. *Psychosomat. Med.*, **27**, 446–456.

STERN, J. A. (1966) Stability-lability of physiological response systems. *Ann. New York Acad. Sci.*, **134**, 1018–1027.

STERN, J. A., STEWART, M. A., and WINOKUR, G. (1961) An investigation of some relationships between various measures of the galvanic skin response. *J. Psychosomat. Res.*, **5**, 215–223.

STERNBACH, R. A. (1960) Some relationships among various 'dimensions' of autonomic activity. *Psychomat. Med.*, **22**, 430–434.

TUCKER, L. R. (1966) Some mathematical notes on three mode factor analysis. *Psychometrika*, **31**, 279–311.

TUKEY, J. W. (1957) On the comparative anatomy of transformations. *Ann. of Mathemat. Statist.*, **28**, 602–632.

VENABLES, P. H. and MARTIN, IRENE (1967) Skin resistance and skin potential. In *Manual of Psychophysiological Methods*. Amsterdam: North-Holland Publishing Co.

VENABLES, P. H. and MARTIN, IRENE (Eds) (1967) In *Manual of Psychophysiological Methods*. Amsterdam: North-Holland Publishing Co.

WALTER, W. C. (1968) *The contingent negative variation as an aid to psychiatric diagnosis*. Paper presented at the Biometrics Research Workshop on objective indicators of psychopathology, New York.

WALTER, W. G., COOPER, R., ALDRIDGE, V. J., McCALLUM, W. C., and WINTER, A. (1964) Contingent negative variation: an electric sign of sensorimotor association and expectancy in the human brain. *Nature* (London) **203**, 380–384.

WALTER, W. G., COOPER, R., CROW, H. J., McCALLUM, W. C., WARREN, W. J., and ALDRIDGE, V. J., and STORM VAN LEEUWEN, W., and KAMP, A. (1967) Contingent negative variation and evoked responses recorded by radio-telemetry in free-ranging subjects. *Electroencephalography clin. Neurophysiol.*, **23**, 197–206.

WELLS, D. T. and FEATHER, B. W. (1968) Effects of changing the CS-UCS interval on human salivary responses. *Psychophysiology*, **4**, 278–283.

WILSON, J. W. D. and DYKMAN, R. A. (1960) Background autonomic activity in medical students. *J. comp. physiol. Psychol.*, **53**, 405–411.

WILSON, R. S. (1969) Cardiac response: determinants of conditioning. *J. comp. physiol. Psychol.*, **68**, No. 1. Part 2.

WOOD, D. M. and OBRIST, P. A. (1964) The effects of controlled and uncontrolled respiration on the conditioned heart rate response in human beings. *J. exp. Psychol.*, **68**, 221–229.

WOOD, D. M. and OBRIST, P. A. (1968) Heart rate during conditioning in humans: Effect of unconditioned stimuli with minimal and maximal sensory input. *J. exp. Psychol.*, **76**, 254–262.

YOUNG, F. A. (1965) Classical conditioning of autonomic functions. In *Classical Conditioning* (Ed. Prokasy, W. F.) New York: Appleton-Century-Crofts, pp. 358–377.

ZEAMAN, D. and SMITH, R. W. (1965) Review of some recent findings in human cardiac conditioning. In *Classical Conditioning* (Ed. Prokasy, W. F.) New York: Appleton-Century-Crofts.

11

Somatic Reactivity: Interpretation

IRENE MARTIN

Biologists have long been absorbed with the excitability of living matter, its capacity for growth (we would include learning as a form of growth) and self-organisation. Evidence on excitability compels us to accept that no matter how slight, brief, and even trivial, the sensory data that bombard our receptors, widespread electrophysiological changes occur. This electric field is Sherrington's 'enchanted loom where millions of flashing shuttles weave a dissolving pattern, always a meaningful pattern though never an abiding one'. We have examined the autonomic, cortical and muscular components of this pattern, and the methodological requirements of considering it as a matrix of interdependencies among components over time. We must now examine the organisation of the response matrix in terms of biologically significant themes: of arousal, emotion, stress, and learning, all of which are relevant to abnormal behaviour.

Of the millions of electrical changes that occur to a stimulus we can only measure a fractionally small subset. Of this possible subset we shall be interested in relatively few, and it is important that we judge which few are relevant to abnormal behaviour. We must therefore face the question: is our relevant pattern best composed solely of traditional psychophysiological measures, or ought we to include other components such as cognitive, perceptual and motor behavioural? As we have seen in Chapter 10, there is already an increasing tendency towards including these other components, both in the practical clinical context (Lang, 1968) and in the experimental-theoretical (Lazarus, 1968; Pribram, 1967).

Three major types of response pattern have been distinguished in the study of abnormal behaviour: they are conveniently labelled arousal, emotion, and stress reactions. These patterns are subject to

continuous flux and change, hence a fourth feature must be included: change that is attributable to learning. This chapter will follow these four major divisions.

When we speak of an individual's *arousal* level we refer to some allegedly stable, characteristic level of organismic activity; characteristic, that is, of a waking, relatively non-active, non-stimulated state. Several theories relate arousal level to personality, suggesting that one or other personality type is more or less aroused than others. In addition to this concept of characteristic levels is the notion of arousability (Claridge, 1967). Arousability refers to the limits arousal levels can reach when stimulated; it also refers to the way in which a person responds to stimuli.

When we measure an orientating reaction, we are measuring relatively transient psychophysiological events in response to simple stimuli, superimposed on an ongoing level of arousal. This kind of work examines the way in which information is perceived, attended to, and processed, and, in general it is not much concerned with overt skeletal muscle or behavioural activity. This is not the case with the multiresponse pattern to which we give the label *emotion*. This is not only a more complicated pattern, in that its elements show complex and subtle relationships with one another, but it takes place over a much longer time span, includes extensive hormonal changes, and often involves strong impulses toward overt activity. An emotional response to a stimulus is unlikely to occur and disappear within a few seconds: it may last for minutes or hours and lead to complex patterns of overt behaviour. *Stress* reactions of the type described by Selye (1956), as well as psychosomatic disorders, frequently have a particularly extended time course in which semi-permanent physiological response changes ultimately occur. The composition and structure of all response patterns is undoubtedly modified in time, although we do not have very adequate models to describe the course of change. In some sense modification occurs in accordance with *learning* principles, and it is in part the problem of learning theory to account for the genesis, maintenance, and change over time in the overall pattern of responding.

Individual Differences

The purpose of much of the work to be discussed is the differentiation of levels and patterns of psychophysiological reactivity as they occur in different individuals. Typically, individuals are grouped according to certain diagnostic criteria, the groups being labelled schizophrenic, depressive, psychopathic, and so on. The underlying assumption very often is that there are diagnostic categories in psychiatry comparable to the disease entities of physical medicine. While this view may be held in question by contemporary workers, who stress the almost insoluble problems of diagnosis, there is a dearth of practical alternatives. Subdivision of categories is sometimes employed, e.g. process/reactive in schizophrenia; endogenous/reactive in depression. Another approach is to examine somatic reactivity in relation to the current emotional state of the person: whether he is depressed, anxious or aggressive, irrespective of the psychiatric label that may be attached to him. The problem of ratings, however, is no less difficult than that of diagnosis.

Perhaps one of the most potentially attractive ideas is that of describing personality and behaviour (normal and abnormal) in terms of a number of underlying dimensions. Eysenck (1957) has argued convincingly in favour of this approach. What these dimensions or continua are and how they can be established is an important problem that has been fully examined elsewhere (Eysenck and Eysenck, 1969).

Arousal

The idea that there is some alteration in the characteristic arousal levels of psychiatric patients has inevitably been discussed at length in the past decade (Duffy, 1962; Claridge, 1967; Lader and Wing, 1966). Unfortunately, the arousal theory is often examined purely from a neurophysiological rather than from a behavioural/subjective point of view. The structural/anatomical evidence of the ascending reticular activating system (ARAS) and the diffuse thalamic projection system (DTPS) as well as their functional properties (Brodal, 1969; Grossman,

1967; Thompson, 1967) testify to the intricacy of these systems. Several recent papers have been highly critical of the unitary concept of arousal, and have elaborated it in various ways. A two-arousal hypothesis centred on the reticular formation and the limbic system has been proposed (Eysenck, 1967; Gellhorn and Loofbourrow, 1963; Routtenberg, 1968). It has also been pointed out that a number of inhibitory and facilitatory interrelationships remain unexplained, for example between the reticular formation and the cortex, between the reticular formation and peripheral autonomic and skeletal muscle effectors (Magoun, 1963).

This is a rapidly expanding conceptual and empirical area, and we must examine with care the contribution of human psychophysiology to its development (and vice versa). There was, of course, a considerable amount of early evidence concerning the shift in tonic autonomic and skeletal muscle activity along a continuum of behavioural sleep/wakefulness (Kleitman, 1939; Duffy, 1951). Neurophysiological evidence on the ARAS and DTPS provided a neural basis for the earlier psychological concepts, and psychologists have been quick to see the implications of contemporary neurophysiology for their own discipline. Most arousal theorists have suggested links between the continuum of behavioural arousal, patterns of autonomic/skeletal muscle activity, and specific CNS centres.

As is now realised, there is no one-to-one relationship between these different systems. Johnson (1970) reviews the problems and disappointments of using EEG and autonomic data as measures of sleep and wakefulness. Lacey (1967) has questioned the validity of a unified concept of arousal, particularly in view of the low correlations obtained between central and peripheral indices of arousal. His criticisms centre around four empirical findings:

(a) the dissociation of somatic and behavioural arousal,
(b) the dissociation of the physiological functions that indicate activation,
(c) somatic response patterning, and
(d) visceral afferent feedback from the cardiovascular system to the brain, which has inhibitory rather than excitatory effects.

It can be deduced from this that much of the current neurophysiological evidence and controversies concern us somewhat indirectly, although we must certainly be alert to their implications. As Lacey has suggested, we probably need, at present, a greater emphasis on our more immediate problems: the relationships between stimulus conditions, physiological response patterns, and overt performance.

As yet, the range of psychological functions encompassed by the notion of arousal remains unexplored. However, they broadly seem to relate to two major areas; one is the range and characteristic tonic level of arousal in different individuals along a behavioural dimension of sleep/wakefulness; the second is that of responding to sensory input, of information processing, attention and filtering, classification, coding, and storing. Within these areas it is meaningful to ask how characteristic positions along the sleep/wakefulness dimension might be inferred from different measures and shown to be altered in different affective states such as anxiety and depression. This would relate to shifts in tonic levels. So far as responding to stimulus input is concerned, it would be meaningful to analyse the person's mode of responding, the amplitude, duration, and recovery pattern of the physiological response. Such information could then be related to attention, coding, and storage processes, as they occur in different individuals or in different abnormal states.

From this point of view, then, it is of more importance to relate physiological response patterns to patterns of psychological functioning, than it is to consider them in relation to brain centres. Indeed, instead of beginning with primary neurophysiological data in the examination of behavioural arousal it is possible to accept another starting point: introspective evidence. Bartenwerfer (1969), for example, has tried to measure the experience of *activation* and suggests that there is a general dimension of activation which can be described verbally by means of concepts such as inner tension, concentration and attention. Although long rejected as a useful source of information, verbal report is being increasingly employed—especially in clinical studies—and if activation can be meaningfully described and measured in this way, it would have much to commend it. It would be of additional value to relate such a dimension to physiological response patterns, and Bartenwerfer has attempted to do this with a measure of heart rate.

AROUSAL AND PERSONALITY

Eysenck (1967) argues that there are two major independent dimensions of personality relating to arousal and emotion: Extraversion (*E*) and Neuroticism (*N*). He identifies differences in behaviour of *E* with differential thresholds in the various parts of the ARAS. It is postulated that introverts and extraverts differ both in their level of arousal and in their reaction to stimulus input, introverts tending to amplify, and extraverts tending to damp down stimulation. Differences in behaviour of *N* are identified with differential thresholds of arousal in the visceral brain, i.e. the hippocampus, amygdala, cingulum, septum, and hypothalamus. *N*, therefore, is primarily concerned with emotional responsiveness or excitation.

It follows from the general scheme presented by Eysenck and other authors (e.g. Gellhorn and Loofbourrow, 1963) that cortical arousal can be produced along two quite distinct and separate pathways. It can be produced by sensory stimulation or by problem-solving activity of the brain, without necessarily involving the visceral brain at all. The extent to which peripheral autonomic/muscular components are involved is somewhat less certain; they indubitably occur, but whether in a specific pattern or with specific intensity cannot be stated with any certainty. Cortical arousal can also be produced by emotion, in which case the reticular formation is involved through the ascending and descending pathways connecting it with the hypothalamus. The fact that cortical and autonomic arousal are involved in both types of loops does not mean that these loops are identical and it is therefore dangerous to assume that indices of cortical or autonomic arousal can be used as measures of emotional involvement.

'It might be true to say that emotional arousal can be indexed in terms of cortical arousal, but this proposition cannot be inverted: cortical arousal can take place without any marked degree of autonomic/emotional arousal. Thus, it is not sufficient to prove that a given change in EEG, GSR, or EMG follows upon the presentation of an emotion-producing stimulus in order to argue that these manifestations are pure measures of emotional activation. They may be measures of cortical arousal accompanying many other types of stimuli which are not emotional in nature and which do not in any way involve the hypothalamus, the visceral brain, or the autonomic system as a whole.'

Thus, Eysenck sees some degree of partial independence between autonomic activation and cortical arousal; activation always leads to arousal, but arousal very frequently arises from types of stimulation that do not involve activation. (Note the terms activation and arousal are used in a specialised sense, as referring to autonomic and reticular activity respectively.)

From the viewpoint of peripheral responses it is uncertain at present what the precise patterns of activity would be. One implication is that the arousal pattern involves minimal autonomic activity that is not particularly widespread, is of low intensity and quick recovery, possibly without much in the way of skeletal-muscle involvement, and that its function is primarily to do with perception of stimuli and cognitive activities such as problem-solving. The activation pattern, on the other hand, would represent the generalised sympathetic emergency reaction, with strong skeletal-motor involvement. Thus, the cortical and autonomic patterns of activity in arousal and emotion may be composed largely of common elements but with different overall organisation.

By incorporating the essential features of Pavlov, Hull, and Jung, Eysenck has brought within the framework of modern personality theory the concept that introverts and extraverts differ in the nature of their nervous activity, specifically along a dimension of arousal. The original description had been in terms of a dimension of excitation/inhibition, again a single dimension such that strong inhibition implied weak excitation. This view is at variance with Pavlov's opinion, as well as contemporary Russian views, that both excitatory and inhibitory processes of the nervous system can vary independently in strength (Gray, 1967).

The empirical data that bear on these views of inhibition/excitation are extremely numerous, and range over a wide variety of perceptual functions, motor-performance tests, measures of conditioning and learning, and a large number of psycho-physiological measures. The techniques, methods, and results of all these extensive measures require careful evaluation. Gray (1967) has reviewed in detail the evidence obtained in Nebylitsyn's laboratory, much of it concerning measures of EEG activity during conditioning experiments. The point at issue in Gray's paper is the degree of correspondence between Eysenck's E and N factors, and the Russian concepts of strength of the nervous system and equilibrium in dynamism (the latter referring to the predominance of excitation or inhibition). Extraversion is defined by questionnaire measures largely relating to impulsivity and sociability (these form two first-order factors); N by items relating to anxiety and to physiological over-activity (Eysenck and Eysenck, 1969). The strength of the nervous system factor is defined in terms of objective performance measures: individuals with a weak nervous system have low absolute sensory thresholds in both visual and auditory modalities, amplify stimuli, and have a poor capacity to endure stimulation that is extreme in duration and intensity.

The relationship of much of this evidence to arousal theory is quite apparent. Eysenck's general statement relating introversion-extraversion and the reticular formation postulates a higher level of arousal in introverts and a higher level of inhibition in extraverts. He has also suggested an identification of the Russian factor of weak/strong nervous systems with arousal, the weak nervous system being more easily or more highly aroused. Gray sums up his survey by saying

'The weak nervous system is more *sensitive* than the strong: it begins to respond at stimulus intensities which are ineffective for the strong nervous system; throughout the stimulus-intensity continuum its responses are closer to its maximum level of responding than the responses of the strong nervous system; and it displays its maximum response, or the response decrement which follows this maximum, at lower stimulus intensities than the strong system .... Further, we may say that, where some function of responding to stimulation is bounded by a lower threshold, beyond which the organism does not respond, and an upper threshold beyond which the organism's response ceases to grow greater, or starts to grow smaller, both thresholds being measured in units of stimulus intensity, the weaker the nervous system the earlier both thresholds are reached.'

As will be seen later, the idea that introverted (or weak nervous system individuals) begin to respond to low levels of stimuli earlier than the extraverts has been fruitfully applied to predictions concerning the conditionability of these groups.

Another interpretation of arousal theory, this time in the immediate context of psychiatric disorder, has been proposed by Claridge (1967). He is careful to distinguish arousal from arousability, i.e. the maximum degree to which the individual can be aroused by stimulation. Arousal level refers to his prevailing state at a particular time; this may or may not reflect his maximum potential for arousal. Claridge develops his views largely on the basis of two specific tests, the sedation threshold (Shagass, 1954) and the spiral after-effect (Holland, 1965). Analysis of the results of these tests, and their relationship with other psychological, autonomic, and EEG measures, led him to conclude that sedation threshold reflects the activity of a tonic arousal system that is responsible for maintaining the individual's characteristic level of arousal. Measures of spiral after-effect are related to an arousal modulating system that serves the joint function of controlling, through inhibitory effects, the level of activity in the tonic arousal system and integrating the stimulus input into both systems by appropriate facilitation and inhibition of incoming information. Claridge therefore introduces the notion of feedback into the system; his model assumes that under normal circumstances a balance is maintained between the tonic arousal and the arousal modulating systems, the arrangement forming an efficient negative feedback loop.

Two main sources of individual variation are proposed.

'The first is the overall level of excitability at which the total system operates. The second is the degree of equilibrium or homeostasis that is maintained between the two arousal mechanisms. It is assumed that the behavioural continuum from dysthymia to hysteria represents a state of affairs in which the tonic arousal and arousal modulating systems operate in equilibrium, but at varying levels of excitability. In the dysthymic, high tonic arousal is matched by an efficient modulating inhibitory system. In the hysteric the reverse is true, both tonic arousal and arousal modulation being at a low level.'

This model is illustrated in Fig. 11.1 which shows the two behavioural continua of neuroticism and psychoticism running, respectively, from dysthymia to hysteria and from active psychosis to retarded psychosis.

'Weak arousal modulation and high tonic arousal are assumed to be characteristic of the active, emotionally responsive, or paranoid patient shown to have a high sedation threshold, low spiral after-effect, and a greater tendency to over-inclusive thinking. The more withdrawn, emotionally retarded psychotic, having a low sedation threshold and long spiral after-effect would be characterised by a low level of tonic arousal and a highly excitable arousal modulating system with its consequently greater inhibitory and facilitatory control over the stimulus input. The assumption in psychosis, therefore, is that the active patient, because of his poor modulation of arousal, will tend to make weak orienting responses to a greater range of stimuli than normal. The retarded psychotic, on the other hand, will respond with considerable intensity to an excessively narrow range of stimuli.'

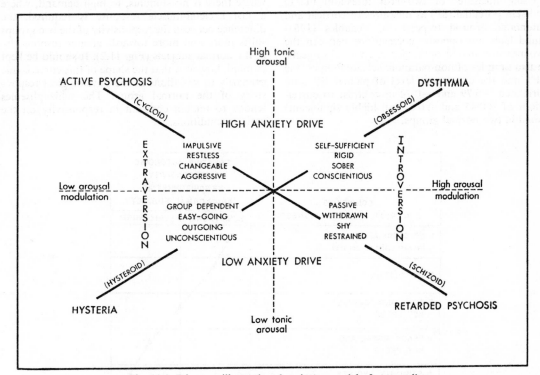

Fig. 11.1. Diagram illustrating descriptive model of personality

Broken lines refer to two underlying causal mechanisms determining two behavioural continua of neuroticism and psychoticism, represented by solid lines. Existing typologies from which the model was derived are also shown, together with some of the descriptive features of normal individuals falling in various positions along the two continua (*from* Claridge, 1967 by permission)

AROUSAL, ORIENTATING RESPONSES (ORs)
AND SCHIZOPHRENIA

So far as Western work is concerned, the impression of earlier studies that autonomic activity was lowered in chronic schizophrenics has tended to be reversed in more recent research. Although there are inconsistencies in the evidence, much of it suggests that some kinds of schizophrenics are under chronic high arousal, showing high levels of autonomic activity and hyper-responsive skin resistance responses (SRRs) to a variety of stimuli.

Authors who have reported lower skin resistance levels in schizophrenic groups include Ax (1972), Lykken and Maley (1968), Wenger (1966), and Zahn *et al.* (1968). Data from other measures such as heart rate and pulse volume levels are slight and of low statistical significance. Hakerem and his colleagues (1964) have found pupillary diameter to be smaller in acute schizophrenics than in either chronic or normals; both they and Rubin (1962) suggest that this indicates a greater parasympathetic dominance in schizophrenics.

Using measures of two-flash threshold (TFT) and skin potential (SP) as measures of cortical and autonomic arousal respectively, Venables (1963) found high but opposite correlations between the two measures in schizophrenics and normal subjects. In two samples of non-paranoid schizophrenics, the TFT and the concurrent level of palmar SP were correlated −0·79 and −0·72 in contrast to correlations of +0·45 and +0·61 (all highly significant) found in two normal groups.

Venables proposed an interpretation of his results in terms of a cortical regulatory system which is present in normals but relatively non-functional in non-paranoid schizophrenics. Lykken and Maley (1968) failed to confirm the findings of Venables in obtaining positive correlations in both groups. These authors have recently collaborated in an attempt to ascertain the reason for their different results; they suggest that it relates to the level of arousal or habituation of subjects when tested (Gruzelier *et al.*, 1972).

Venables and Wing (1962) observed a close and consistent relationship between degree of social withdrawal and level of physiological arousal: the more withdrawn the patient the higher his arousal. The only exception to this general rule is found among patients who exhibit marked coherent delusions. They suggest that withdrawal from the environment, both social and material, may be a protective mechanism.

Along similar lines, Zahn (1964) has shown that as the demandingness of the situation increases from zero demand in the case of non-specific responses, where there is no stimulus, to high demand, where a fast skeletal-muscle response is required, the difference between the responsivity of the two groups shifts more and more towards greater responsivity in the normal subjects (Fig. 11.2). It should be kept in mind, however, that the shape of this curve is due primarily to variations in the physiological responsivity of the normal group. The schizophrenics tended to remain constant in responsivity on the various conditions.

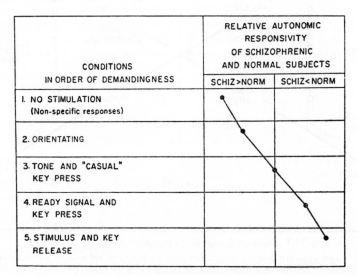

CONDITIONS IN ORDER OF DEMANDINGNESS	RELATIVE AUTONOMIC RESPONSIVITY OF SCHIZOPHRENIC AND NORMAL SUBJECTS	
	SCHIZ > NORM	SCHIZ < NORM
1. NO STIMULATION (Non-specific responses)		
2. ORIENTATING		
3. TONE AND "CASUAL" KEY PRESS		
4. READY SIGNAL AND KEY PRESS		
5. STIMULUS AND KEY RELEASE		

Fig. 11.2. Schematic representation of the relative autonomic responsivity of schizophrenic and normal groups (*from* Zahn, 1964)

Zahn discusses the proposals of Deutsch and Deutsch (1963) that while increases in the general level of arousal may lower the threshold for responding to all stimuli, whether relevant or irrelevant, there exists a specific alerting system which increases responsivity only to relevant stimuli. Thus, the relative hyperreactivity of his patients to irrelevant and meaningless stimuli would be due to their persistent high arousal level, while the relative hyporeactivity, both autonomically and behaviourally, to more demanding stimuli would reflect a defective specific alerting system. It may be inferred that a person whose specific alerting system is relatively weak, and whose non-specific arousal system is relatively strong, would be subject to marked fluctuations of attention between relevant stimuli and irrelevant external and internal stimuli.

The idea of impaired attention as a prominent feature of schizophrenia, particularly the inability to attend selectively, has been discussed by a number of workers (e.g. Venables, 1972). The justification for viewing the average evoked response (AER) as a complex indicator of attention and central processing has been examined by Callaway (1966) and Jones et al. (1966). Shagass and Schwartz (1965) observed significantly less after-rhythm or 'ringing' (see p. 320) in schizophrenics, although it is uncertain whether 'ringing' is augmented or abolished by heightened attention and alertness. Grey Walter (1972) reported differences in CNV amplitude between schizophrenics and controls, being lower in the patient groups; he suggests that this may correspond with fluctuations in cortical involvement due to internal distraction.

Mednick and Schulsinger (1968) have found that SRR measures discriminate between sick, well, and control groups of children, in their study of the children of schizophrenic mothers. Comparison of the sick with the other groups showed the former to have a shorter latency, a decreasing latency over a habituation series, and a *faster* recovery. These authors, too, conclude that hyperarousal is characteristic of the schizophrenic, and discuss the role of hippocampal damage and failure to inhibit ACTH as a contributing factor to the development of schizophrenia. This theme is further developed by Venables (1972).

The work on autonomic responses, particularly SRRs, is therefore reasonably extensive and provides some convincing evidence of hyper-responsivity in schizophrenics. Zahn (1972) and Venables (1972) both review and discuss habituation of the orienting response in these subjects. Venables's tentative conclusion is that acute and/or paranoid patients tend to be responsive to their environment and show less habituation than normals, while the chronic or regressed patient tends to be slow in response and to show fewer and smaller responses. Lynn's (1963) review of Russian work, however, suggests a general tendency towards unreactivity. He distinguishes two major types of schizophrenics: a majority group characterised by low sympathetic tone and reactivity; and a minority group in whom sympathetic tone and reactivity are unusually high. The majority group would appear to consist mainly of acute and agitated patients, especially paranoics. Much of the Russian work is based on Pavlov's theory that schizophrenia results from the generation of protective inhibition in the cerebral cortex. Protective inhibition can be generated as a result of various kinds of shocks, drugs, or physical illnesses.

There is also an important constitutional factor in liability to schizophrenia, namely the strength of the nervous system. A weak nervous system that is sensitive to stimulation is more likely to become overstimulated, generate protective inhibition and, hence, succumb to schizophrenia. The presence of protective inhibition in the cortex accounts for the slowness and poor conditionability of schizophrenics.

It is virtually impossible to make any coherent assessment of these findings; those who have recently reviewed the area (e.g. Stern and McDonald, 1965) point to the many possible sources of discrepancy in methods of diagnosis and problems of adequate controls. In addition, the kind of variables employed tends to be different, Western workers concentrating rather more on skin resistance and Russian workers on the EEG and blood volume. If we can judge research in this area in terms of either theoretical or therapeutic advancement, it is questionable whether psychophysiology has contributed very much. The currently popular models of perceptual and attentional dysfunction have obvious connections with arousal theory, but they have arisen more from work on cognitive performance than from autonomic measurement.

AROUSAL, ORs, AND PSYCHOPATHY

When we turn to research on psychopathic states the same uncertainty prevails. Some studies report lowered autonomic levels, some no differences. Similarly, the psychopath has been found to be 'autonomically hyper-responsive, hypo-responsive and normally responsive to a variety of neutral stimuli' (Hare, 1968). Hare gives a survey of studies of autonomic functioning in the psychopath that are depressingly inconsistent. These provide little support for the various attractive hypotheses that have been put forward concerning a hypothetical deficiency in the autonomic correlates of anxiety necessary for the development and maintenance of certain required patterns of behaviour. The trouble is, as most investigators themselves freely admit even of their own studies, that problems of diagnosis, drugs, hospitalisation, controls and measurement (to name but a few) are so impossibly difficult to cope with that one can never be sure that the hypothesis has, in fact, been adequately tested.

And, to return to our theme, if the response configuration is at all complex we must remember that when we sample heart rate or skin resistance we are doing little more than catching a few ripples on the ocean. It is rarely possible to take measures from all three cortical, autonomic, and muscular systems, let alone hormonal and metabolic changes. Even the measures we take, say of skin resistance, may be of latency, amplitude, duration, or recovery: the choice is just as great for cardiac, pupillary, EEG, adrenalin, and other variables, and there is often little rationale to guide the selection of measures.

AROUSAL AND DEPRESSION

This is another area where hopes of rapid progress remain unfulfilled. Indeed, there has been little, if any, significant advance during the past decade in relating depression to psychophysiological (autonomic) measurement. As in the previous section, one of the major problems has appeared to be that of diagnosis, especially the differentiation of neurotic and endogenous depression; even with the increasing use of sophisticated statistical techniques this problem remains unsolved (Kiloh and Garside, 1963; Cropley and Weckowicz, 1966; Kendell, 1968; *see also* Eysenck, 1970, for a discussion of the problem).

Shagass's use of the sedation threshold to measure excitability of the CNS in neurotic and endogenous depression (Shagass and Mihalik, 1956) has met with difficulties in that many workers are unable to replicate the earlier findings. (Claridge (1967) reviews these studies, and Herrington (1967) discusses the pharmacological factors involved in this use of amylobarbitone sodium.) The significant changes in blood pressure responses to epinephrine and mecholyl reported by Funkenstein and his colleagues, (Funkenstein and Greenblatt, 1949; Funkenstein *et al.*, 1951) have not been confirmed by other reports (Davies, 1960).

Studies on autonomic reactivity have continued in a somewhat desultory fashion, mainly on measures of salivation and skin resistance. Several more positive reports of diminished salivary secretion in depression have appeared in the past few years (Busfield and Wechsler, 1961; Davies and Gurland,

1961; Loew, 1965). Palmai and Blackwell (1965) demonstrated a diurnal rhythm in salivary flow which was significantly diminished in depressed patients. Greenfield *et al.* (1963) suggest that depressed mood may be a more important determinant of skin resistance hyporesponsivity than psychiatric classification as such, and show the Depression scale score of the MMPI to be significantly different in high and low SR responders.

In spite of the rather slight evidence available, it is frequently concluded (e.g. Greenfield *et al.*) that depressed patients show decreased responsivity. No new hypotheses have been put forward, however, to account for any lowered responsivity that might occur, and again one is forced to the conclusion that studies of autonomic reactivity have contributed little to the problem as it has been traditionally studied. There has been a somewhat greater impetus, however, in the study of biochemical factors of physiological responsiveness such as 17-hydroxycorticosteriods (Bunney *et al.*, 1965) and mineral metabolism (Coppen, 1965) which appears to hold considerable promise.

AROUSAL AND ANXIETY

Malmo, in 1957, suggested that anxiety may be produced by keeping level of arousal very high over long periods of time. He cites neuro-physiological findings that continuous over-arousal may result in impairment of central inhibitory mechanisms. In his use of the concept, arousal has no steering function. It refers to physiological *levels* only, i.e. to tonic not phasic measures, whereas Duffy (1962) discusses both level and response measure as indices of arousal.

The arousal theme has more recently been continued by Lader and Wing (1966) who also suggest that morbid anxiety is the experience of abnormally prolonged and excessive CNS activity. Using a measure of skin resistance, they found that patients with anxiety states adapted less, habituated less, and had more fluctuations than normal control subjects. These differences were lessened but not abolished by treating the patients with sedative drugs. Subsequently, Lader (1967) divided anxious patients into several groups:

  (i) anxiety with depression,
  (ii) anxiety states,
  (iii) agoraphobics,
  (iv) social phobics and
  (v) specific phobics (usually of small animals such as spiders, dogs, and cats).

Specific phobics were found to differ significantly from the other groups in that they showed more rapid habituation and fewer spontaneous fluctuations. In these respects they did not differ significantly from normals, whereas the remaining patients differed in the direction of increased arousal.

Kelly (1966) found that patients with chronic anxiety-states had a mean basal forearm blood flow more than twice as great as that of mixed neurotics and normal controls. It was postulated that this is evidence of 'persistent arousal' of the defence reaction, which is the fundamental pathological feature of these patients. A stressful mental arithmetic task produced a much larger reaction in controls. Gelder and Mathews (1968) followed up Kelly's work and used the measure of forearm blood flow in the assessment and treatment of phobic states using desensitisation therapy.

The mechanisms underlying desensitisation treatment, although not completely understood, are generally thought to involve small increases of anxiety in patients imagining phobic scenes, which are then inhibited by the use of muscular relaxation. One method of investigating this hypothetical process is the use of physiological measures during both imagination of phobic scenes and subsequent relaxation. Gelder and Mathews attempted to relate forearm blood flow to the subjective assessment of anxiety during the imagination of phobic scenes. Comparison of the mean blood flow scores showed a progressive increase from the neutral to the most stressful phobic scene, and subjective ratings of anxiety also increased with increasing stressfulness of the imagined scenes. Forearm blood flow increases were greatest, however, in response to a stressful mental arithmetic task; yet reported changes in anxiety on this task, while varying considerably among subjects, were sometimes quite small.

The psychophysiological studies reviewed in this section have been concerned with shifts in level of autonomic activity in different psychiatric categories, usually under some hypothesis of under- or over-arousal. They have also examined the way in which individuals respond over, say, the stimulus intensity dimension, as in the Russian work on the weak/strong nervous system, changes over time as in habituation of the orientating response, and the relationship of stimulus-induced changes to arousal level (which can readily be rephrased in terms of pre- and poststimulus relationships). In general, the arousal hypotheses are loosely phrased and apparently equally applicable to quite different kinds of psychiatric disorder. More specific hypotheses have been developed in the area of attention and perceptual dysfunction in schizophrenics, and it may be possible to relate this to autonomic responsiveness in a meaningful way. Certainly, autonomic changes

seem to be involved in the perception and registration of significant stimulus characteristics, possibly ensuring storage and consolidation.

They are also involved in the responses that we call emotion. One popular theory has been that of a single dimension of activation, on which emotion can be placed at the upper end. It seems more likely, however, that it is response patterning as well as intensity that differentiates arousal from emotion. We have suggested that impulses to overt activity contribute to the emotional pattern, as does subjective experience. And, as Eysenck (1967) has suggested, all emotional states are probably states of high arousal, although the converse is not necessarily true. The problem of distinguishing between them is evident in the case of anxiety, which can be considered as a high arousal state or, when subjective report and overt behaviour are included, as an emotional state.

Emotion

The last few examples of the preceding section have illustrated the transition from anxiety considered within the framework of arousal theory, mainly in terms of excessive physiological activity, to that of anxiety as an emotion. There are many aspects of anxiety theory. Anxiety can be considered from an experiential viewpoint, as a clinical syndrome, as an energiser to action, as conflict, and as a conditioned emotional response. Psychologists have most commonly examined anxiety in this latter role, suggesting that anxiety acts as a drive and that the diminution of anxiety has the properties of reinforcement and, hence, can serve to cause learning. Because the concept of anxiety (and emotions in general) is not explicitly defined it is difficult to place the subject matter within any of the usual categories of psychological analysis such as perception, arousal, learning, and so on. It can equally well be considered from any one of these viewpoints since they are all contributory factors. Comprehensive reviews of this variety of viewpoints and theories have been made by Arnold (1960) and Hillman (1960).

The problem of explicit definition of the emotions has always generated controversy, and in the experimental literature, emotion all but vanished for a while as a substantive topic. In 1951, in one of the most influential and forceful arguments on this topic, Brown and Farber examined the difficulties in treating emotions as intervening variables, and they rejected the concept of emotion as a substantive, scientifically discoverable state or reaction. Part of the difficulty has been that of reconciling emotion as experience with emotion as behaviour. When verbal self-reports and introspection were in disrepute, the view of emotion as behaviour was ascendent. This view carried with it an emphasis on animal experimentation and generated a search for brain centres that controlled the autonomic-motoric pattern of reaction. Goldstein (1968) reviews physiological theories of emotion. More recently, subjective experience has become recognised not only as an essential but as a measurable component; hence, human studies and cognitive/perceptual modes of responding have come to dominate research in the emotions. Combining both these approaches leads to the current view that emotion differs from arousal in comprising—

(i) strong experiential/perceptual components which assume a great significance for the individual and
(ii) some felt impulse to overt behaviour.

These may be viewed in relation to adaptive behaviour or coping processes.

Lazarus (1968) sets forth a forceful argument for treating emotion as response, thereby emphasising its substantive qualities and its determinants, rather than its motivational function. He analyses many of the disadvantages that have arisen from conceptualising emotions as motivators, discussing how this viewpoint has shaped research, over-emphasing some problems and overlooking other, equally important, areas such as the complex relational aspects of emotion and the specification of antecedents of emotional states. He recognises the difficulties in defining emotions as intervening variables, but does not think that difficulty is any good reason for abandoning the attempt.

'I think it is likely that one day specific physiological patterns, specific cognitive patterns, and specific behavioural patterns, in association with given eliciting conditions, will be identified and shown to be organised in such a way as to clearly distinguish one emotional state from another . . . No single response component is capable of producing adequate inferences about any internal state, be it an emotion or some other conceptual entity. Motoric-expressive cues are unreliable because people wear masks. Self-report fails for similar reasons, and is also confounded with response sets, self-justifications, etc. Physiological changes can also be produced by conditions of non-emotional relevance. Thus, there is substantial lack of agreement between single indexes of emotions.'

Lazarus is arguing for emotion as a response configuration, and suggests some of its components. Contrary to those early views, which assumed a one-to-one correspondence between self report,

physiological change and overt behaviour in emotions, Lazarus discusses the reasons why divergence could well occur among major components without necessarily invalidating the inferences about a given emotion.

'The key point is that each response system from which inferences about emotional reactions are generally made has its own adaptive functions and, taken individually, communicates some special *transaction* taking place between the person and his environment. Thus, what the person reports to the observer and, to an extent, his instrumental actions reflect intentions concerning the social being with whom he is interacting. At the same time, the physiological state should also reflect the direct action tendencies which are mobilised for dealing in some fashion with the appraised threat.'

Obviously, the total response configuration changes in time. His own emphasis, as can be seen in Fig. 11.3, is on the contribution cognitive processes of appraisal make to change (i.e. coping behaviour) occurring in the response sequence.

The problem of response patterning is particularly relevant to the assessment and treatment of anxiety. Lang and his colleagues (Lang, 1969, 1967; Lang and Lazovik, 1963; Lang et al., 1965) have been concerned with the study of fear and anxiety in the laboratory and have tried both to measure fear in its various manifestations and to treat it by means of systematic desensitisation therapy. These and other workers in this area assume that fear is a response that is expressed in three main behavioural systems: verbal (cognitive), physiological (autonomic), and overt motor behaviour. The assessment of emotionality has been to a very large extent based on one or more of these categories.

The group of verbal responses includes questionnaires that measure anxiety, depression, neuroticism, etc. There are also various kinds of mood scales in which the subject is asked to endorse a large list of adjectives if they apply to him. Another technique is for the subject to rate himself along a hypothetical continuum; for example, a mood scale of depression might include a scale ranging from 'feeling cheerful, on top of the world' at one end, to 'feeling unhappy and miserable all the time' at the other end. The *a priori* construction of questionnaires and the naive notion that because a questionnaire is given a particular label it therefore measures that particular trait must, however, be deplored. Very careful statistical analysis is required to sort out this kind of problem (Eysenck and Eysenck, 1969).

Eysenck's use of factor analysis in this field suggests that items that characterise neuroticism (or

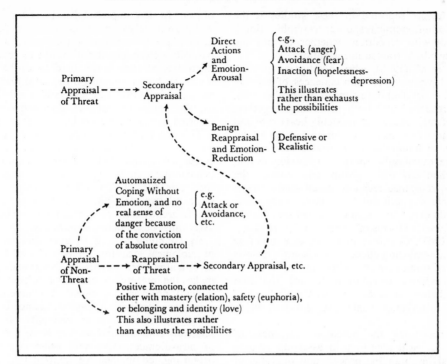

Fig. 11.3. Outline of a theoretical analysis of emotions (*from* Lazarus, 1968, the *Nebraska Symposium on Motivation*, by permission of the author, and the University of Nebraska Press)

emotional instability) include nervousness, hypersensitivity, depression, and inferiority feelings. The neurotic is emotionally unstable, hypochondriacal, worried, excitable, impatient, etc. Eysenck postulates that differences between people in emotionality or neuroticism are mediated by inherited differences in the lability and excitability of the autonomic nervous system. Some people are constitutionally predisposed to show a strong reaction of the sympathetic nervous system towards stimuli of various kinds, whereas other people are predisposed to react much less strongly. Eysenck (1967, 1969) has extensively reviewed the evidence on autonomic responsiveness in this connection. Differentiated emotional states are seen within this dimensional framework: the introverted neurotic, for example, is predisposed to suffer anxiety and depression.

The significance of somatic reactivity in emotion is rarely disputed. Its manifestations are diffuse and have been repeatedly described. Cannon systematised earlier descriptions by demonstrating that emotional excitement results in sympathetic (neural) discharges both to peripheral structures and to the adrenal medulla. Adrenaline (epinephrine) secretion stimulates the same activities that are stimulated neurally by the sympathetic, but on a longer time base; thus sympathetic effects are automatically augmented and prolonged through direct chemical action on the organs themselves. The utility of bodily changes was discussed by Cannon in terms of mobilising the animal for prompt and efficient struggle. This point of view has remained influential throughout subsequent decades, when many forms of emotions were discussed within the context of the 'emergency reaction'.

Many of the bodily effects of sympathetic arousal can be readily recorded from the surface of the body; there are, however, many problems of measurement, as is evident from Chapter 10. In addition, there is ample evidence of patterning of reaction even within the autonomic nervous system.

Mathews (1971) reviews attempts to study the physiological concomitants of fear and fear change in phobic patients, and concludes that measures of skin resistance, forearm blood flow and heart rate reliably differentiate between phobic and neutral stimuli, and also between items in the desensitisation hierarchy. Heart rate may be a particularly responsive measure during phobic imagery, as opposed to real life stimuli, because of the tendency described by Lacey (1967) for heart rate to decelerate during orientation reactions to external stimuli, and to accelerate during mental tasks when stimuli from the external environment are ignored. One almost universal feature reported in these studies is the tendency for autonomic responses to phobic stimuli to diminish with repetition, whether or not the subjects have been trained in relaxation.

Folkins *et al.* (1968), who investigated physiological and psychological consequences of viewing stressful films, studied the effects of prior relaxation, cognitive rehearsal and both procedures together, in terms of their efficacy in reducing heart rate and skin resistance responses to a film portraying a fatal accident. They found that subjects who had received cognitive rehearsal only reported less anxiety during the film than any other group, and showed the lowest skin resistance response. Such studies highlight 'the role of experimentally imposed or suggested forms of adaptive thinking in the reduction of stress when direct-action forms of coping are not possible' (Lazarus, 1968). Cognitive processes can therefore have emotion-reducing effects, and Lazarus reviews a number of studies where the attempt to influence subjects' cognitive orientation toward the film events predictably lowered or raised their level of emotional disturbance while the film was being watched.

While recognising the potential usefulness of psychophysiological measures in assessing anxiety and in studying both the process and outcome of desensitisation, Mathews points to some of the problems of interpretation that arise. It often remains unclear to what extent autonomic responses can be entirely attributable to anxiety and to what extent factors such as expectation, attention, or cues given by the therapist may be involved. From the practical point of view, one interesting use that has been made of autonomic responses (usually skin resistance responses) is that of predicting the outcome of phobic patients to desensitisation treatment (Lader *et al.*, 1967) and the prognosis of schizophrenic patients (Stern *et al.*, 1965).

The group of overt motor responses, like the other two categories, is fraught with measurement problems. Various techniques have been used to investigate the communication of emotional meaning by facial and vocal expression in experimental studies, with no very great success (Davitz, 1964). Ratings of emotional change based on observations of patients' behaviour are subject to many criticisms (Eysenck, 1969). Measurement of gesture and motor attitudes have again contributed little on an experimental basis, in spite of their significance in everyday human interaction.

One simple measure that has been found of use in the treatment of phobias is that of behavioural approach and withdrawal in connection with the feared object. Treatment often involves manipulation of the distance between the patient and this object. In a comprehensive review of approach withdrawal behaviour in comparative psychology, Schneirla (1959) suggests that stimulus intensity basically determines the direction of reaction: low intensities of stimulation tend to evoke approach reactions, high intensities withdrawal reactions. The relationship between arousal and a variety of performance measures has been described in terms of an inverted U-shape function by a number of workers.

This very brief outline suggests some of the possible ways in which fear can be assessed. Lang and his colleagues found that different measures of fear behaviour, even though taken concurrently from the same subject, do not yield responses of the same relative strength. High relationships among the different measures cannot therefore be assumed. They must be examined empirically.

By confining himself to questionnaires only, or physiological measures, or behavioural ratings, the investigator narrows his informational input and makes the interpretation of his results unnecessarily difficult or even impossible. The investigation of emotional reactivity, therefore, cannot be confined to measures of somatic reactivity. It must be relatively complex and involve more than one type of measurement. This way offers a much more promising, comprehensive approach to the treatment of fears than that based on the assumption that 'fear' is a unitary whole.

RESPONSE PATTERNING AND DIFFERENT EMOTIONS

One of the first attempts to specify and list different kinds of emotions was based on the then current instinct theories (McDougall, 1910). McDougall cited a long list of instincts each with its own associated emotion that was believed to be innate; ready made to serve the instinct by providing the appropriate driving force. A second and more influential view was that different emotional states relate to a differential pattern of physiological activation. Relatively few of the studies carried out have provided positive results. Among those that have, Wolf and Wolff (1943) found that fear regularly reduced gastric activity and blood flow; Ax (1953) showed that anxiety and anger produced different cardiovascular patterns. These and other findings cited by Arnold (1960) offer the best evidence available that fear and anger may be differentiated in terms of the pattern of autonomic arousal.

In most of the emotional states experimentally produced with human subjects, results have shown a rather general pattern of excitation of the sympathetic nervous system. Whether or not there are physiological distinctions in different emotions remains an open question. Averill (1969) has recently discussed evidence relating to sadness and mirth which shows that sympathetic activation is common to both. Current work might be taken to indicate that such differences are at best rather subtle and that the variety of emotion, mood and feeling states experienced are by no means matched by an equal variety of visceral patterns.

This rather ambiguous situation has led many to suggest that cognitive factors may be major determinants of emotional states. Granted a general pattern of sympathetic excitation as characteristic of the emotional state, it may be that one labels, interprets, and identifies this stirred-up state in terms of the characteristics of the precipitating situation and the general perceptual state. This suggests that an emotional state may be considered a function of a state of physiological arousal and of a cognition appropriate to this state. The cognition, in a sense, exerts a steering function (Schachter, 1966). While agreeing with Schachter on the importance of cognitive processes in emotion, Lazarus questions the implication of Schachter's argument that emotions are mainly a single state of physiological arousal. He feels that, probably, there are different physiological patterns in anger, fear, depression, grief, sexual excitement, guilt, shame, etc., even though admitting that they may have some common core of excitement or mobilisation which we call arousal. In any case, Lazarus argues, it seems shortsighted to focus exclusively on the excitement these emotions have in common and to ignore the particular kinds of organised behavioural activity that are different in different emotions. This tendency to include introspective report in the assessment of emotion has obvious implications for theories of emotional behaviour. Theories of human emotion, i.e. those that include emotional experience in their major postulates, cannot be tested by animal experimentation. Moreover, the concept of neural centres, so relevant to understanding the organisation of patterns of autonomic-somatic behaviour (as in attack or flight), hardly helps us with the organisational principles of human behaviour.

Perhaps the most serious criticism of experimental work on the emotions has been the almost universal concentration on noxious stimuli of sharp onset and high intensity. Many writers (e.g. Schneirla) have distinguished between stimuli that elicit approach behaviour and lead to pleasure, and those that elicit avoidance and are associated with pain or negative feelings. This distinction has in recent years been given experimental support. Olds and others have demonstrated the existence of 'positive' and 'negative' emotive systems by electrical stimulation of the brain (Olds, 1962), and have suggested

that they are activated respectively by parasympathetic and sympathetic centres in the hypothalamus. The emotional implications of low intensity stimuli and their gradual onset have been virtually ignored. The application of Cannon's work, with its emphasis on the biological-adaptive nature of behaviour, to the area of human emotion has led to an emphasis on emotions such as pain, rage, fear, anxiety, i.e. the energy-mobilising adreno-toxic 'hit-run-mate-devour' category. Positive emotional experience such as love, awe, wonder, religious, and aesthetic feelings have been relatively ignored. From the experiential viewpoint, these positive emotions are seen to lead to growth, expansion and self-development.

Stress

The concept of stress has proved useful both in examining the problems of somatic reactivity, and in accounting for some forms of psychiatric illness. When we consider stress in relation to emotion and arousal we encounter a further extension of the time continuum from the momentary fluctuations of phasic arousal and emotional response, through the slower oscillations of tonic arousal levels, to the prolonged reaction of the stress syndrome. We also encounter another underlying dimension, that of the role of biochemical agents in influencing behaviour. In the stress reaction we see clearly the involvement of hormonal activity, particularly in the mediating role of the adrenocortical hormones, and it seems likely that it is this molecular level of chemical activity that underlies the reactions of emotionality and arousal. There is every reason, then, to implicate biochemical factors in the response configuration of arousal, emotion, and stress. The difficulties are those of determining the components of the response, their interdependencies, and their time courses.

It is important to define the concept of stress, and to point to some of its characteristics. Selye (1950) has suggested the term be reserved for a specific physiological reaction pattern (described below) while the term 'stressor' is applied to the variety of agents that produce the pattern. One of the useful aspects of this distinction is to limit the use of a term that may otherwise become too generalised, because of its explanatory plausibility. More important, it reserves to the category of stressors the function of antecedents of the stress reaction. It is peculiarly the case that, unlike emotion and orientating responses for which we can usually identify the antecedent stimuli, the stress response is identified by its characteristics from which the action of antecendent stressors must usually be inferred.

Nevertheless, useful inferences may be drawn, as for example in the finding that chronic hypertension may be preceded by some years of exposure to environmental stressors (Heine *et al.*, 1969).

Largely as a result of the work of Cannon (1932) and Selye (1950) the hormones of the sympathetic nervous system and the adrenal cortex have been recognised as crucial mediators of the mammalian stress response. Technological advances in the determination of the catecholamine levels have stimulated interest in their role both in normal and abnormal psychological states. A further stimulus has been the finding that many of the drugs used in the psychiatric treatment of patients with affective disorders also cause significant changes in the metabolism and function of various biogenic amines, peripherally and centrally. This area has been well reviewed by a number of authors (*see* Schildkraut and Kety, 1967).

THE STRESS SYNDROME

The stress reaction described originally by Selye (1950) is organised around the pituitary-adrenal cortical axis and mediated by adrenocorticotrophic hormone (ACTH). When the stress is prolonged the syndrome typically includes three stages:

(i) an alarm reaction, including an initial shock phase of lowered resistance and a countershock phase, in which defensive mechanisms begin to operate;

(ii) a stage of resistance in which adaptation is optimal, and

(iii) a stage of exhaustion, marked by the collapse of the adaptive response.

Selye's emphasis was on the physiological patterning of the stress response and on its elaborate course of change over time (Fig. 11.4). He also emphasised the problem as one of adaptation, rephrasing the old question 'what do the hormones do' in terms of 'what adaptive reactions do they influence'. A recurring theme was that of a finite amount of 'adaptation energy' which gets 'used up' (Selye, 1956), of physiological and psychological integrative capacities that are taxed to the limit (Basowitz *et al.*, 1955). The overall reaction was construed as a disruption of the normal equilibrium between anabolic processes, represented by the actions of the

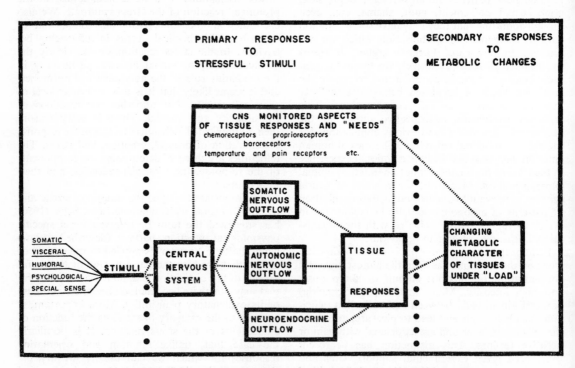

Figure 11.4. Schematic representation of two phases in the adaptation to stress

The first phase is considered to be an immediate complex of CNS responses; the second phase derives from the metabolic consequences of sustained activity of tissues (*from* Goldstein and Ramey, 1957).

glucocorticoids, and catabolic reactions involving the mineralocorticoids.

The nature of the pituitary-adrenal involvement in the stress response has since been much debated, and the physiological mechanisms involved extensively investigated (Levine, 1968; Ramey and Goldstein, 1957; Selye, 1959). Much of this work has a history of animal experimentation, although relationships with psychiatric disorder were early discussed by Selye and others.

Attempts to translate Selye's idea of general systemic stress to include psychological aspects have met many problems. In the first place the nature of stressors is very different. Selye discussed systemic stressor agents like heat, cold, infections, intoxicants, injury, shock, and surgical trauma. The range of possible psychological stressors is so wide as to be virtually endless. Cofer and Appley (1964) argue that such stressors are effective only when they threaten the life or integrity of the individual exposed to them. They offer a definition of stress as, 'the state of the organism when he perceives that his well-being (or integrity) is endangered and that he must elevate all of his energies to its protection'.

Central issues in psychological stress are the conditions and processes—

(i) that lead the individual to differentiate between benign and damaging conditions, and
(ii) that determine the kind of coping behaviour which ensues.

Once a stimulus has been appraised as threatening, various methods of coping are adopted. Pribram, (1967) has suggested that cognitive re-evaluation may obviate the necessity for overt behavioural adjustment, i.e. an individual's appraisal of the situation can reduce the stress reaction. The stress reaction when examined in a psychological context must therefore take account of complex cognitive processes as well as physiological reactions and feedback from the effects of these reactions.

Second, the nature of the physiological reaction is not now seen as a general, well-defined pattern. The result of two decades of research suggests that individual differences, styles, patterns of response and pre-potent tendencies lead to idiosyncratic response patterns. These may relate to inherited responsivity, e.g. of the sympathetic nervous system (Eysenck, 1967) and possibly to various personality characteristics that determine stress thresholds and stress tolerance.

We should undoubtedly discriminate between the immediate physiological disturbance produced by a discrete stimulus and a chronic, long-term stress reaction in which basic physiological changes that result in a detrimental shift in equilibratory processes are produced. Psychological stresses of an inescapable kind may lead to a sustained stress reaction eventuating in tissue damage, disruption of adreno-cortical functioning and psychosomatic disorder. This type of reaction may well differ from a neurotic 'coping' reaction in which sustained tissue damage is avoided by some behavioural solution, for example the use of escape mechanisms and conditioned avoidance responses.

BEHAVIOURAL AND CLINICAL SIGNIFICANCE OF CATECHOLAMINES

The work on stress and the implication of the adrenocortical hormones as important mediators of somatic reactivity has inevitably drawn attention to the role of other endogenous chemical agents, particularly the catecholamines. Here the emphasis is on more transitory states, such as anxiety and aggression. The role of biochemical agents in mediating short term changes is less clear in this context than in the context of prolonged reactions of the type just discussed.

Exogenous administration has produced no clear-cut answer to the question: Does adrenaline produce anxiety? Kety (1966) has suggested that peripherally released catecholamines acting directly on the brain or by visceral proprioceptors represent limited and rudimentary components of a variety of emotional states. Similarly, Schachter's (1966) view is that epinephrine infusion may produce a non-specific state of arousal and that it is cognitive evaluation of the situation that leads to labelling of the emotion (see p. 342). Arousal may be a component in both 'negative' and 'positive' emotions: Levi (1965) has reported that the excretion of amines is similar in pleasant and unpleasant emotional states, suggesting that the important factor is intensity rather than quality of affect.

Several authors have pointed to an association between nor-epinephrine excretion and aggressive states (Frankenhaueser, 1967, reviews of many these studies). Work with infra-human animals has shown that nor-adrenaline predominates in the suprarenals of aggressive, attacking animals while adrenaline predominates in non-aggressive, escaping animals. In his early work on the differentiation of emotions, Ax (1953) concluded that the physiological response during experimentally induced anger resembles the reaction to nor-epinephrine, whereas the response during experimentally induced anxiety resembles the reaction to an injection of both nor-epinephrine and epinephrine. Along similar lines, Funkenstein (1956) postulated an endocrine basis for anxiety and aggression. Much of this work remains unreplicated and is extremely difficult to evaluate.

Urinary catecholamine excretion in schizophrenia has shown no consistent pattern. Ax (1970) is following up his early work on autonomic epinephrine and nor-epinephrine-like patterns of response in relation to aggressive and hostile *vs.* passive and anxious reactions in schizophrenics.

Mention must also be made of the continuing work on adrenaline and anxiety by Pitts and McClure (1967). This suggests that it is excess lactate production resulting from an increased flow of adrenaline that stimulates anxiety symptoms. The anxiety state was shown to be particularly sensitive to infusions of sodium lactate, which produced anxiety attacks in the patients but in very few of the controls. It is hypothesised that this reaction of the anxiety neurotic may be attributed to the effect of adrenaline on lactate production.

Frankenhaeuser has examined relationships between catecholamine secretion and subjective reactions to experimental stressors (Frankenhaeuser, 1965) and has been concerned with efficiency of performance as related to adrenaline release (Frankenhaeuser, 1968).

Although momentary blood-levels of the catecholamines may reflect with greater sensitivity their release in response to transient situations, the concentrations involved are low and the methods of determination are fraught with difficulty. Most investigators have relied on urinary excretion as the basis for their measurements. Fine and Sweeney (1968) discuss the possible relation of hormone levels to personality traits (as relatively enduring conditions) rather than to momentary emotional states. They review the literature and, in conjunction with their own results, come to the conclusion that subjects characterised as having highly aggressive personality traits excrete more norepinephrine and have higher nor-epinephrine/ epinephrine ratios than subjects characterised as low on the aggression dimension (*see also* Silverman *et al.*, 1961). Frankenhaeuser and Patkai (1965) have approached the problem by a factor analytic study in which personality traits and catecholamine excretion were measured; results obtained, however, failed to support the view that predominantly anxious *vs* aggressive individuals vary in their catecholamine response. Instead, they found that individuals with depressive tendencies had a relatively weaker adrenaline reaction during stress.

Schildkraut and Kety (1967) have reviewed a number of studies showing a fairly consistent relationship between the effects of drugs on biogenic amines, particularly nor-epinephrine, and affective or behavioural states. Drugs that cause central depletion and inactivation of nor-epinephine produce sedation or depression, while drugs that increase or potentiate brain nor-epinephrine are associated with behavioural stimulation or excitement and generally have an antidepressant effect in man. 'From these findings, a number of investigators have formulated the concept, designated the catecholamine hypothesis of affective disorders, that some, if not all, depressions may be associated with a relative deficiency of nor-epinephrine at functionally important adrenergic receptor sites in the brain, whereas elations may be associated with an excess of such amines' (Schildkraut and Kety, 1967).

In 1954, Hoffer and co-workers proposed the hypothesis that oxidised derivations of epinephrine are aetiologic factors in the genesis of schizophrenia; more explicitly, that epinephrine released by increased sympathetic activity is degraded by a phenolase which predominates in schizophrenia with the production of the psychotomimetic quinone indoles, adrenochrome and adrenolutin. The evidence that has since been collected is reviewed by Kety (1966) and Stern and McDonald (1965); much of it is inconsistent, and the conclusions of these reviewers are phrased in cautious terms.

In summary, these and other biochemical agents have links with arousal, emotion, and with psychiatric illness, as well as with the stress response. There are probably metabolic and biochemical accompaniments or determinants of the characteristic tonic level of the individual. It also seems likely that there are oscillations in this level that accompany or produce mood changes and other day-to-day changes in arousal level. These oscillations also may well be biochemical in origin. Superimposed on these slower changes are the more rapid shifts in autonomic functioning with which we are more familiar: orientating responses and transitory emotional states. When the stress is very prolonged, as it seems to be, for example, in unresolved conflict situations, a long series of changes occur—those described by Selye—which seem to result in extensive and possibly irreversible metabolic shifts such that the individual's characteristic tonic level of functioning may be profoundly disturbed.

The immense amount of detailed work triggered by the hypotheses of Cannon and Selye has provided us with a greatly enlarged (albeit incomplete) understanding of the intricate network of autonomic, hormonal, electrolytic, and metabolic functioning during stress. Kety (1966) has recently concluded, however, that biochemical mechanisms will always be essential but rarely sufficient to the understanding of this aspect of somatic reactivity.

'Although it is possible that there may be affective disorders in which inherent biochemical dysfunction may be of primary etiologic significance, human affect in general represents an interplay between the biochemical substrate and psychologic factors derived from individual experience. A valid understanding of its nature will depend upon information from both of these spheres.'

In this, as in so much of human psychophysiology, the recognised pattern of responding is being expanded to include psychological components, especially subjective reactions, and also to include behavioural-adaptive factors. The way in which such a vast response configuration—not only the autonomic, cognitive, and behavioural/motor components discussed earlier, but, in addition, the infinitely subtle but effective chemical agents operating in living organisms—is organized within the central nervous system remains largely unknown. Yet it is reasonably certain that such organisation occurs and that individual experience plays a large part in determining the overall response pattern. In the following and last section of this chapter we will examine response development and change in the context of conditioning and learning.

Conditioning

In the preceding sections we have discussed the patterns of responses that occur in states of arousal, emotion, and prolonged stress. It is the purpose of the present section to examine some of the changes in response pattern that occur over time and as a function of learning. The extensive literature on animal studies in this area will not be included. (Animal studies of conditioning are reviewed by Broadhurst, Chapter 20.) Instead, the subject matter will be confined very largely to human studies, from which we have chosen a sample to illustrate some of the newer trends. Some of these are not directly concerned with somatic reactivity as such, but serve to underline points of method or interpretation that may well be applied to this field. It is one of the themes of this section that studies of human reactivity have suffered from the limiting influence of older methods and viewpoints derived from classical learning theory. In particular, the treatment of anxiety has been forced into models that are in need of revision.

The history of research into conditioned anxiety is so well known, and its theoretical problems so frequently examined that further review here is unnecessary (Miller, 1951; Mowrer, 1939, 1960; Solomon, 1964; Solomon and Wynne, 1954). During the past few years there has been a greater emphasis on the application of learning principles to the treatment of various psychiatric disorders (Eysenck, 1960), including severe anxiety (Wolpe, 1958), phobias (Rachman, 1968) and psychopathy (Eysenck, 1964). The effects of this emphasis have been to promote interest in *human* conditioning, and to emphasise the specifically human components of anxiety. They have also brought into focus the inadequacies of academic learning theory. It is not so much that learning principles are invalid but rather that they are only very generally related to the practical usages of the clinician.

In addition, there has been a recent period of development in which much of conventional learning theory has been questioned. It has been questioned at the conceptual level, especially with some of the old-established concepts like drive, habit, and reinforcement. It has been questioned at the measurement level, where earlier oversimplified methods of measurement are being replaced by detailed analysis of response characteristics. Both Hull and Skinner have overemphasised frequency and rate of responding as dependent variables, Skinner once suggesting that the investigation of response rate would change psychology in the way that the analysis of weight changed alchemy into modern chemistry. In retrospect it now appears merely ridiculous that conditioned anxiety should have been equated with a single measure—of skin resistance response amplitude, perhaps, or a verbal report, or worse, a bar-pressing response. Anxiety is a response complex comprising many parts: it cannot be indexed by any single measure. Undoubtedly, Hull's influence can be detected here, since he assumed that all response elements—frequency, amplitude, latency, etc.—index a single, unitary concept of learning, i.e. habit strength.

Once these constraints of theory and measurement are loosened we can empirically examine the interdependencies among measures of conditioning. These do not all correlate very highly with one another; what is of importance is the way the response components are organised into an overall response pattern, and how this organisation shifts in time. In measurement terms this amounts to specifying the covariance matrices at different points of the learning process. The nature of the interdependencies is of great importance for the application of deconditioning techniques, since there is ample experimental evidence that interaction among response components occurs: one response system may have profound effects on another. Instructional set may reduce not only verbal report of stress intensity but also autonomic responses associated with fear arousal; this factor has been shown to affect the course of conditioning in experimental studies. In like fashion, the reduction of autonomic activity by various means (drugs and relaxation) may have marked effects on subjects' self reports of anxiety, and on the appearance or non-appearance of CRs. It is in this sense that there is interaction between response characteristics and the organisation of the response pattern; modification of some of the elements can produce a marked change in the structure of the whole.

Because the focus of the present section is on conditioning and human anxiety reactions, it is appropriate to begin an analysis of the concepts of learning theory by referring to the assumptions held by behaviour therapists in seeking to modify anxiety. It is generally accepted that anxiety is a learned response; it has been widely postulated that classical conditioning is involved in the genesis of neurotic illnesses characterised by anxiety and phobias, and that, in addition, some form of operant conditioning may be involved in the maintenance of conditioned fears over time. Wolpe (1958) who has so imaginatively applied learning theory to behaviour therapy, bases his approach largely on the work of Pavlov and Hull. Neurotic behaviour is defined as any persistent habit of unadaptive behaviour acquired by learning in a physiologically normal organism. Anxiety is accorded a central role in this behaviour.

It is useful in the present context to examine this summary statement and to consider its separate clauses with the question in mind: How valid and how acceptable are the theoretical concepts to which it refers? What is their potential usefulness as foundations of the kind of learning theory of relevance to the problems of treatment?

HABIT

Central to most contemporary learning theories is the concept of Habit. The attributes of this concept can be briefly summarised as follows—

  (i) Habit is identified as the learning component in behaviour.
 (ii) It is energised by a separate drive factor.
(iii) It increments gradually in strength as a function of trial frequency.
 (iv) Its strength increases to a limit beyond which there is no further gain.
  (v) It is measured by a number of response elements (frequency, latency, amplitude) which are all assumed to index habit strength.

These six attributes are shared by a number of behaviour theories, and have gained wide general acceptance. The habit construct they define, and that has come to assume the status of a 'real' variable

in the learning process, is the major definition of learning on which many theories of abnormal behaviour are based. Yet on close examination, only two of them (iii) and (iv) refer even remotely to empirical observation of behaviour. *The remainder are assumptions, with no observable reference.* These assumptions are largely derived from a tradition of associationism which has little current status today.

It would be much more in line with modern conceptions of learning to replace the bond-forging, path-wearing, connectionist approach with one closer to Sokolov's (1963) conception of the neuronal model. This suggests that incoming stimuli leave traces of all their analysed characteristics within the nervous system and that subsequent stimuli are compared with already existing neuronal models by means of a comparator system. This general concept of stimulus registration, used by Sokolov in the context of habituation, can readily be extended to a complex stimulus like the combined CS and UCS. Such a stimulus model, it has been suggested, determines the shape of the learned complex, which usually takes the form of a CR/UCR blend (Martin and Levey, 1969). In this view, it is the stimulus model and its characteristics that shape and modify the response as it develops over trials. This is a radically different conception from the Associationist view since it involves neither S—R/S—S bonds (or bonds of any sort) nor the concept of habit strength. Bridger (1967) has used a similar line of thought in connection with learning of emotional responses.

The empirical data of learning experiments all rest solely on a single class of evidence: response change. Initially, in a learning experiment the response-to-be-learned is not present: at some point it appears. This is the first empirical datum: *the change from no-responding to responding.* Once the response is occurring in overt behaviour, its changing properties can be measured as latency, amplitude, duration, frequency, etc. This is the second empirical datum: *the course of change in the response over trials.* Any learning theory must be expected to account for these empirical data, i.e. the change from no-responding to responding, and the change in the response once responding occurs. It can be argued that the point at which the first CR appears is largely determined by performance factors; the second, response change, may be much better understood in terms of an engram or neuronal model which gradually incorporates features of the environment as well as the subject's own responses.

The S—R theorists from Thorndike through Guthrie, Hull, and Spence have proposed that only stimulus-response associations are learned. The cognitive (S—S) theorists such as Tolman and Lashley have preferred to believe that it is stimulus connections that are learned. The issue is still alive today in the form of cognitive *vs* response theories, as a paper by Breger and McGaugh (1965) testifies. Their essential position is that only a cognitive, mediational type of theory can explain the complex behaviour that behaviour therapists face, and they suggest that response learning is a later stage, coming from the learning of strategies, programs, plans, and hypotheses. The S—R *vs* S—S issue remains insoluble, however, because the decision to favour an S—R or S—S model is not based on evidence but on the *a priori* assumption that an association must exist.

CR AND UCR ANALYSIS

Responses in the typical conditioning experiment, then, can be classified as—

1. presence or absence of a response, and
2. change in response form.

More attention has traditionally been paid to class (1), i.e. the frequency measure, either a count of CRs, number of correct *vs* incorrect responses, or number of trials to a criterion of correct responding.

Changes in response *form*, however, have been examined in several recent studies of human conditioning. The UCR changes in amplitude, latency and rise-time through acquisition trials (Kimmel, 1965; Martin and Levey, 1969; Prokasy, 1965). Changes in similar features of the CR have also been reported. Further, CR and UCR interact; CS/UCS pairing produces a decrement in UCR amplitude, which Lykken (1962) has labelled the preception phenomenon. CR and UCR characteristically blend in eyelid conditioning experiments. Changes in response characteristics have, therefore, been amply documented though their significance has remained somewhat doubtful. Sokolov's suggestion of the stimulus model and the array of earlier notions relating to schemata, engrams, programs, cognitive maps, etc. are but variants of the theme that information is stored in such a way that it can (*a*) be readily accessed, and (*b*) trigger action when required. It seems perfectly possible to conceive of these 'stores' as containing not only environmental stimulus characteristics but programs of appropriate responses. This implies that both registration of stimulus characteristics and response development are taking place during learning.

This kind of analysis of CS, UCS, CR, and UCR characteristics would probably be appreciated by the clinician who has genuine difficulties in deciding in relation to his patient which stimulus is 'the'

CS or 'the' UCS; which response 'the' CR or UCR. We probably need no longer worry whether the CS is learned and the UCS unlearned, whether the UCR is a reflex or not. The current tendency is to speak of CS and UCS as two stimuli in rapid succession, the second of which has greater arousal or activation properties than the first and is perceived as being more important or significant or more intense. The basic differentiating feature of CSs and UCSs is their capacity to produce weak and strong responses respectively. The arousal generated by the second stimulus seems, in ways as yet imperfectly understood, to ensure storage of the contents of immediate memory. In addition, it may ensure a greater permanence and accessibility of the memory trace through consolidation (*see* Eysenck, Chapter 13). The application of this type of approach to the problem of anxiety, emotion, and arousal in conditioning almost certainly holds more promise than the traditional point of view.

CONDITIONING AND EMOTION

Bridger (1967) has discussed the possibility of failure to distinguish between CS and UCS in strong emotional arousal. He comments as follows—

'When the data from behavioural, neuropharmacological, and electrophysiological levels are integrated, it would seem that there is evidence at the neocortical level of differentiated responses to the CS and UCS. At the level of the more primitive limbic system the evidence does not indicate such a differentiation. In an emotional learning situation which produces hippocampal activity, mescaline will increase this activity while simultaneously inhibiting the neocortex. I therefore suggest that any condition which would inhibit the neocortex and simultaneously activate the limbic system will produce a confusion between the CS and the UCS; between the signal and what is being signalised. This lack of differentiation between signifier and what is being signified occurs primarily in strong emotional situations when hippocampal activity is present . . . I therefore propose that the distinction between the symbol and the object symbolised will be determined by the balance between neocortical and limbic system activity. The more effectively charged an experience is the greater will be the limbic system activity and the closer will be the bond between the symbol and the object symbolised. Neo-cortical inhibition will also decrease the distinction between the symbol and the object symbolised.'

He relates his discussion to the Solomon and Wynne (1954) experiment involving traumatic avoidance conditioning in dogs. After the dog had been conditioned to avoid a very painful electric shock by jumping a hurdle, this response was found to be remarkably resistant to extinction. A further attempt to extinguish the response was made by presenting the CS when the hurdle was absent and the animal could not avoid the anxiety-producing situation. However, when the hurdle was replaced, the CS again elicited the hurdle-jumping response. Solomon concluded that conventional learning theory could not explain this so-called fixated pathological phenomenon and hypothesised partial irreversibility of the traumatic classical emotional response. Bridger suggests that if the limbic system is markedly activated in a conditioning situation, the organism would have great difficulty in distinguishing the CS from the UCS. 'In Solomon's experiment perhaps the dog was not able to distinguish the CS from the electric shock, which was also true in my mescaline experiment. This suggests a mechanism for the so-called partial irreversibility of the pathological conditioned response.' Bridger goes on to discuss certain neuro-physiological experiments that shed further light on the role of the neocortex in reality testing.

Stampfl (1967) and Levis (1967) have interesting data that extend these general ideas concerning the differentiation of CSs and UCSs and their relationship to the role of anxiety. They stress that conditioning occurs to a stimulus complex, not just to (say) the tone that precedes shock; and that this complex may often take the form of a stimulus *sequence* (say a tone followed by a light followed by a buzzer followed by a shock). Such a serial procedure preserves the anxiety to the first CS in the series in the following manner: as extinction occurs to the first CS component within the series, the next component upon re-exposure will reinforce secondarily the first component because of the second CS component's higher arousal (anxiety) properties. This point is perhaps best illustrated by an experiment of Levis (1967) using rats in a shuttlebox situation. An 18-sec CS-UCS interval was used, consisting of three distinct stimulus segments each of 6-sec duration ordered serially. The first 6-sec segment consisted of a gate being raised (permitting a response) followed by a period of silence. From the 6th to 12th-sec, flashing lights were presented, and from the 12th–18th sec a buzzer was presented. The offset of the buzzer on the 18th sec was followed by shock.

Levis reports as follows:

'Only one to three shock trials were required for Ss to reach the acquisition criterion of ten consecutive avoidance responses. The shock was turned off initiating the extinction phase of the experiment. The first three or four avoidance responses occurred to the buzzer and/or to the lights. However, by the fifth trial Ss were responding to the first 6-sec CS segment. Apparently some of the aversiveness associated with the shock transferred back to the onset of the CS-UCS intervals. In fact, for approximately the first 100 trials most Ss responded within one or two seconds after the onset of the CS-UCS interval. These short latency responses helped conserve the anxiety associated with the remaining segments of the chain since short latency responses prevent exposure to the remaining segments. As the number of avoidance responses increased, overt signs of fear (e.g. defecation, urination) diminished. It appeared that as the skeletal avoidance response became overlearned, only a minimal amount of anxiety was needed to produce the response. After a number of short CS exposures longer latency responses started to occur, although most Ss responded to the first 6-sec segment for two to three hundred trials. Finally, after sufficient extinction occurred to the first 6-sec segment, S would remain in the situation long enough to be exposed to the second segment of flashing lights. Since in the Ss conditioning history there was little exposure to the lights without subsequent shock, this segment still generated a high level of anxiety. Upon its exposure most Ss displayed overt signs of fear with quick avoidance of the stimulus. On the next few trials, a short latency response usually would be made to the first 6-sec segment. Apparently the second segment in the series 'recharged' or secondarily reinforced anxiety to the first segment for another 50 or 100 trials. Exposure to the second segment again recharged the first segment. However, with more and more exposure to the lights, extinction to the lights increased. The S now responded mainly to the second segment. After approximately 500 or 600 trials enough extinction occurred to the lights for Ss to remain in the situation long enough to be exposed to the buzzer, the third stimulus segment in the series. The buzzer, which probably had the highest anxiety attachment since it was the closest segment to shock onset, recharged the lights which in turn reinforced the silent period, again resulting in short latency responses. Thus, by this process of intermittent secondary reinforcement, a sort of "seesaw" effect occurred which resulted in extreme resistance to extinction.'

This experiment among other things illustrates the difficulty if not impossibility of specifying which is 'the' UCS. Indeed, it becomes partially irrelevant to do so. What seems to happen is that a sequence of stimuli (CSs in conventional terminology) terminate in a situation or stimulus that is more fear-provoking than any of the preceding ones. These CSs gain in arousal value as they approach this high fear-provoking situation. It also illustrates (as does Eysenck's discussion below) the importance of the *effect* of the stimulus on the individual.

The work of Stampfl and Levis thus emphasises the extended sequential elements of stimulus/response interactions in behaviour. The hierarchy in desensitisation methods also recognises that order is important: the order of proceeding from the least traumatic CS or stimulus, up to the feared object itself, in carefully graduated steps. Stampfl's analysis is interesting in that he suggests that the sequence of stimuli and responses leads to a 'core of fear' that incorporates certain dynamic notions underlying the neurotic's fear and anticipation of abandonment, injury and annihilation, condemnation and disapproval, humiliation, loss of love, and rejection. Put in conditioning terms, it refers to sequences in which CSs are more and more able to elicit strong anxiety reactions, up to the very 'core' (the UCS or UCR) which involves not only fear of a particular object or situation, but fear of failure to cope, fear of ego destruction, fear of loss of status, and so on. Thus, it is necessary, Stampfl maintains, to pursue the series until it reaches the UCR-core, which can then be defused, as it were, and, hence, reduce anxiety to all the preceding CS series that led up to the core. Unless one gets to the UCS-core and reduces the reaction to it, the CSs that lead up to it will get reinforced and will fail to extinguish, as Levis's experiment demonstrates.

This experiment of Levis's on failure to extinguish is interestingly connected with Eysenck's description of the incubation phenomenon. It also shows how the rigid CS/UCS: CR/UCR distinction needs to be made more flexible to allow for the complicated chaining of responses and stimuli that occur in complex situations, a fact conventional S—R analyses have tended to ignore. What is being suggested is that conditioning sets in motion a positive feedback cycle in which the CR provides the reinforcement for the CS. Eysenck's description of the incubation of anxiety/fear responses well illustrates this newer approach to the conditioning process.

Eysenck (1968) uses the term incubation to refer to an *increment* in CR over a period of time when the CS is applied once or a number of times but without reinforcement. Normally, this procedure would give rise to extinction; instead, however, it may give rise to an increment in the size of the CR that is substantially larger than that which in control experiments follows paired CS/UCS exposures. Eysenck's description of the process also illustrates the loosening of rigid CS, UCS, CR, and UCR distinctions referred to earlier. He argues as follows:

'Consider the usual account of aversive conditioning. A CS is followed by a UCS, say shock, which produces a great variety of UCRs; some of these, or even one of these, may then be singled out for study. After a single pairing, or after repeated pairings of CS and UCS, $\overline{CS}$ (i.e. a CS unaccompanied by a UCS) produces some, or at least segments of some, of the responses originally produced by the UCS. Fear/anxiety responses are of particular interest in this connection; they are frequently produced by nocive UCSs and are readily conditioned .... CS and $\overline{CS}$ acquire the function of signalling danger and coming pain, discomfort, fear, and annoyance; let us denote these nocive consequences as NRs (nocive responses). Through the intermediacy of the UCS, CS has become associated with the NRs and signals their arrival to the organism. (For reasons which will become obvious later, we prefer the term NR in this connection to the use of the terms UCR and CR. It will be argued that the classical account, which is implicitly accepted when we use the classical terms, is somewhat deficient, and that a novel nomenclature will be useful in putting over a theory which departs in some ways from the usual one.) Each reinforcement (which may be defined as a NR following CS) increments the habit strength associating CS and NR; consequently each CS/UCS pairing serves to increment the CR. When we administer a CS, however, so classical theory assures us, this reinforcement is missing, and consequently extinction weakens the habit strength associating CR and NR.

'It is here suggested that this account is partly erroneous. $\overline{CS}$, although unaccompanied by UCS or UCR, is in fact accompanied by CR, which is a partial, possibly weak but real NR. Hence, some reinforcement is provided, although perhaps this is so much weaker than that accompanying the UCS that its presence may not be very important under certain circumstances. Yet in principle it is always present, and its presence would theoretically lead to a strengthening of the CS/NR bond, and hence to some form of incubation. What is being suggested, in other words, is that conditioning sets in motion a positive feed-back cycle in which the CR provides reinforcement for the $\overline{CS}$. Usually the extinction process will be stronger than this form of reinforcement, leading to overall extinction and making the action of CS/NR reinforcement unobservable, but under certain circumstances (e.g. when the UCS is exceptionally strong) the extinction process may be weaker than the CS/NR reinforcement process and observable incubation will result.'

In a footnote, Eysenck explains the apparent implausibility of making a response (CR) act as its own reinforcer by pointing out that it is not the CR itself that acts as reinforcer, but rather the response-produced stimuli; not the autonomic, hormonal and muscular reactions themselves but rather the experience of fear/anxiety based upon them. In so far as these CR-produced are identical with the UCR-produced stimuli, it seems likely that they will be reinforcing in exactly the same manner; in so far as they are different they will act as reinforcers to the extent that they are nocive and aversive.

This proposal, in summary, adds to the conventional picture of classical conditioning the notion that fear is a painful event, and the stimuli associated with it (i.e. $\overline{CS}$) come to evoke more fear, thus producing a positive feedback. This mechanism is well known descriptively in psychiatric disorders; it brings to mind the famous saying about 'having nothing to fear but fear itself'.

These various points of view just discussed, all amply backed up by experimental evidence, illustrate very well the shift away from the traditional emphasis placed on the role of the *stimulus* and towards a greater emphasis on the *response*. Where the classical account links CS with UCS, these writers concentrate far more on the CR and UCR. The differentiation between UCS and UCR reflects the experimenter's preoccupation with control. From the Ss point of view (and after all it is in the subject that the process of conditioning takes place) the differentiation is of doubtful relevance and value. Bridger's point that CS and UCS may be poorly differentiated under high emotional arousal is part of a general trend toward understanding the conditioning process not so much in terms of externally defined events but more in terms of the effect of such events on the individual, and, further, the effect of the individual's response on the environment. In this context it becomes meaningful to ask what the developing CR/UCR achieves for the individual in his interaction with the environment. Thus, we are led to an examination of the endpoints of conditioning.

ADAPTIVE BEHAVIOUR AND THE CONCEPT
OF ENDPOINTS

There have been many discussions concerning the nature of both adaptive and unadaptive behaviour.

Making maladaptiveness the defining characteristic of the behaviour disorders raises many problems: how it can be defined; how it can be judged sufficiently maladaptive that some attempt should be made to alter it. In the clinical context it becomes the problem of how a maladaptive pattern of behaviour can be changed into an adaptive one.

The concept of adaptation is biological in origin, relating to factors that promote survival of the individual or of the species. It now has a wider usage, and has been applied to personality, to psychopathology, and to the behaviour of social groups. Cofer and Appley (1964) offer a useful discussion of the term in these contexts. In so far as somatic reactivity is concerned it has long been put forward as a persistent theme in the notion of energy conservation. Selye (1956) refers to adaptation energy, Duffy (1962) to inappropriate energy release, Freeman (1948) to basic energy level, and Thorpe (1956) to learning that is 'economical' in that it saves the animal's energies. For these writers (and for many others) adaptive behaviour is that which guards energy expenditure; it is the minimum output necessary for efficient performance. In terms of more recent models, optimum responding is achieved by a trade off between energy expenditure and defensive activity.

Such a criterion is considerably wider than its purely biological implications. In accounting for psychiatric disorders, adaptiveness can be further defined in social terms. Ullman and Krasner (1965) characterise maladaptive behaviour as that considered inappropriate by those key people in a person's life who control reinforcers, and as leading to a reduction in the amount of positive reinforcement given to the individual. However, this kind of definition ignores the facts of diversity of goals in a complex society and also conceals important distinctions within the realm of the maladjusted (Buchwald and Young, 1969). There are those who seek the typical rewards of society but are unable to achieve them; there are others who seek rewards that are sufficiently atypical for them to be considered 'disordered' even though they achieve them. Both could well show maladaptive behaviour in the sense of failing to maximise the extent to which they receive forms of reinforcement.

It is interesting that some of the most recent discussions of what once would have been called maladaptive behaviour do not now use this term. Perhaps indicative of this trend is a brief discussion by Paul (1969) concerning behaviour modification, in which he refers to 'distressing behaviour', i.e. 'clients will come to treatment in order to obtain "help" in changing some aspect of their behaviour which they, or someone else, find distressing. This distressing behaviour may be motoric, autonomic and emotional, or it may be cognitive and ideational. Both the number and nature of distressing behaviours may vary within an individual client and across clients, and may change over a period of time'.

Such views seem to be shifting towards a criterion of adaptation with reference to some standard of what a satisfactory human life can be in society. They imply a balance between the person and his environment, and begin to incorporate notions such as happiness and self-actualisation. Cofer and Appley examine these and allied concepts with care, concluding that as yet they are difficult to test empirically. In such a complicated social environment as our own, we are clearly dealing with an overall complex set of social responses that must comprise innumerable response components, innumerable interactions, and perhaps—if growth, maturation, conditioning, and learning processes go well—an optimum *balance* among the elements that represent some degree of personal self-optimisation. These kinds of subtle adaptations are indeed beyond empirical test. But simple analogues can be readily discerned within the conditioning/experimental framework. Two factors of relevance in ideas of self-optimisation are that (*a*) they implicate endpoints of behaviour, and (*b*) they suggest that only one or a few of the response components need be modified in order to achieve a better balance (or acceptance) of the overall response. That this represents a perfectly feasible experimental approach can be illustrated in work on eyelid conditioning which examines how shaping of the response is achieved through the interaction of single response components (latency, amplitude, duration, etc.) and how their appropriate co-ordination places the CR in relation to specified endpoints such as successful avoidance (Levey and Martin, 1968).

This approach was discussed by Logan in 1956 as a form of equilibrium analysis. He instanced economic theory based on the mutual interdependence of price and quantity. Or, viewed within classical learning experiments: 'when reinforcement varies with speed, the organism will be viewed as running at just that speed which provides just that amount of reward which produces just that degree of incentive which will motivate just that speed'. The similarity between this kind of behavioural solution and notions of self-optimisation are remarkably close, even though the latter is obviously more difficult to measure. It also bears an analogy to the treatment situation where response components are manipulated in order to modify the overall topography of the response, as it were, to a point where the patient no longer exhibits or feels distressed by his particular disability.

Modification of an undesirable fear response can be achieved by a variety of techniques, which can be split into two main groups. One is aimed at the modification of response probability or response maintenance. The other aims to modify *components* of the total fear response. From the viewpoint of traditional conditioning theory these two main groups seem directed at the drive (i.e. arousal) and the habit (i.e. learning) concepts respectively. The first group employs methods to reduce level of arousal, usually by means of relaxation, such that the conditioned fear response is less easily evoked; this would represent reduction of drive to a point below the threshold of CR responding in overt performance. The second employs methods of re-learning, for example by operant re-training of autonomic responses, or by counter-conditioning, such that the elements of the old CR are replaced by new, antagonistic responses. This is Guthrie's notion of extrinsic interference, Wolpe's of reciprocal inhibition.

These two aims—to reduce emotional CRs either by lowering level of arousal or by reshaping the learned response—are very similar to the distinction between performance and learning made in learning theory. It should be recognised that most of the acquisition curves reported in the traditional literature simply depict whether or not Ss give CRs. Presumably, a subject who gives CRs has been successfully conditioned; however, it seems almost certain from the available evidence that some Ss condition but do not give overt CRs. From this it can be concluded that the conditioning curves that employ frequency measures of conditioning are completely confounded with performance. They do not reflect the course of development of the conditioned response.

Granted that a response has been well learned, there are many conditions that will then determine whether or not it will appear in overt performance. One of the most widely accepted is a change in drive level or level of arousal. In applying this to a phobic patient suffering from anxiety, it can be hypothesised that if the ongoing, tonic *level* of arousal is reduced the phobic response will be less likely to occur. This, in part, is the argument put forward by Lader and Mathews (1968). The second part of their argument is that systematic desensitisation may be regarded as habituation occurring when the rate of habituation is maximal, that is, when level of arousal is low. The question that must be raised is that although habituation may *appear* to be quicker at low arousal levels, only subsequent testing would show whether *learning* not to respond has actually occurred. In other words, responding will be lower at relaxed levels, but this may be a performance and not a learning factor.

Their argument is of interest since it is one of the few that examine anxiety as possibly comprising two factors: an abnormally elevated tonic level of arousal, and an abnormally high rate of responding to stimuli. Tonic arousal levels are normally equated with an unlearned drive factor. If arousal levels can be modified on a long-term basis by means of relaxation training, it suggests that the hard-and-fast conceptual distinction between drive and habit (learning) becomes impossible to maintain. At the empirical level, the fact of complex relationships between responding and tonic levels is amply documented. This is discussed in the previous chapter under the law of initial values.

When we consider the multiple and complex nature of the response components in conditioned human anxiety, and when we consider the complex course of development of these components it becomes apparent that a preferable way of examining CR development is in terms of the nature or topography of the response: what it comprises, what its shape and characteristics are, what it achieves in terms of effective subject/environment interaction, and so on. This aspect of learning is relatively independent of response frequency, i.e. the probability that a response will be given.

COGNITIVE-PERCEPTUAL FACTORS

It is worth recalling Bridger's comment that while the CS and UCS can be discriminated at a cortical level, there is a failure to discriminate when emotional arousal is very great; hence, if the subject can be trained by means of cognitive/instructional factors towards discrimination of the cues this may be transferable to a level of emotional discrimination of CS and UCS.

A careful discussion of the role of verbal-perceptual factors in the conditioning of autonomic responses has been made by Grings (1965) which documents the contention that cortical effects can have an influence on autonomic nervous system responding. He considers whether or not cognitive learning should be considered within the confines of conditioning.

'It is well known that during conditioning experiments with human Ss, S is usually trying to figure out what is going on .... He may "catch on" to the relations among stimuli and many perceptual features of the task may influence his learning behaviour. When he "catches on" should the resulting behaviour change be called "classical conditioning"? If not, what form of learning is it? To what degree, if any, can classical conditioning be studied with human Ss without this "other" kind of learning complicating or confusing the picture.

'The central issue becomes this. Classical conditioning is defined in terms of certain operations of stimulus pairing. Some theorists, e.g. Spence (1956, 1960) appear to assume that these operations are sufficient for conditioning to occur as long as various limiting requirements are met (e.g. stimulus intensity, time relations, etc.). It is not clear whether these theorists would treat cognitive-perceptual variables as a special class of independent variables determining classical conditioning, or whether the use of the term "classical conditioning" should be restricted to those operations where perception of relations can be excluded. Spence seems to favour the former when he states that "extinction of the conditioned eyelid response in humans is to a considerable degree a function of cognitive factors relating to observation on the part of the subject of procedural changes with the shift to extinction. Attempts to infer the quantitative properties of an intervening theoretical variable, for example inhibition, that results from the operation of nonreinforcement will need to take account of these potent cognitive factors" (1963, p. 1225).

'Razran (1955), on the other hand, holds the second view. He would divide learning into two major classes, perceptual and nonperceptual, and asserts that "the chief determinant of the division is the presence or absence of perceived—or reacted—relations between stimuli and reactions involved in learning rather than the mere nature and history of the stimulus and reaction *per se* ... conditioning with perceived relationships is neither "mere conditioning" nor "conditioning plus" but something else; it is relational or perceptual learning.' (1955, p. 91–92)

Grings has observed in a series of studies that some Ss behaved with sudden shifts of behaviour as if they were responding to notions about stimulus relations, whereas some Ss gave gradual acquisition curves. Complete control of various forms of verbal-perceptual trial and error behaviour on the part of the Ss was never achieved. He subscribes to the view that what is required is a direct study of verbal-perceptual determiners of human performance in the classical conditioning situation rather than a perseveration of the negative view that such variables are sources of confounding. He discusses four or five major areas of overlap between classical conditioning and perceptual learning as they apply to human autonomic behaviour observed in the classical conditioning paradigm. The areas can be described as (*a*) conditioning-like behaviour arising from verbal instruction or association, (*b*) conditioning-like behaviour changes resulting from changes in perception of the total environment, (c) verbalisation of stimulus relations (awareness) as a factor in autonomic conditioning, (d) verbal association as a conditioning transfer dimension, and (e) efforts to demonstrate preparatory (perceptual) phenomena in conditioning situations.

INDIVIDUAL DIFFERENCES

No summary of conditioning would be complete without some attempt to examine the role of individual differences. That they exist and are meaningful few would dispute. How precisely they can be measured and integrated with learning theory is controversial.

The difficulties of psychiatric diagnosis, ratings, subcategories, etc., were mentioned in an earlier section of this chapter, together with Eysenck's proposal to use dimensions of personality in the description of psychiatric disorders. Many applied workers would claim that the personality dimensions are still only of potential rather than immediate value in applied work. Nevertheless, the relation between personality and conditioning has been very extensively investigated during the past few decades. Recent experimental work has furthered the theory of differential conditioning between introverts and extraverts in terms of the experimental schedule employed. This work has been reported by Eysenck (1967) and Martin and Levey (1972). Subjects received either continuous or partial (66%) reinforcement; a strong or weak airpuff (6 lb in.² vs 3 lb in.²) and a short or long CS-UCS interval (400 vs 800 msec) in a balanced factorial design. Stimulus conditions favourable for high CR responding in extraverts are those that tend to be highly arousing, i.e. strong UCS intensity, continuous reinforcement and long CS-UCS interval. Under low arousal stimulus conditions, i.e. weak UCS intensity, partial reinforcement and short CS-UCS interval, the introverts give many CRs and extraverts very few. These results support Eysenck's theory of introversion-extraversion (outlined in the arousal section) and his contention that when stimulus conditions are selected on the basis of this theory, meaningful and significant results are found.

The whole area of personality and conditioning is so extensive that it cannot adequately be reviewed here; controversial features have been well discussed by Spence (1964) and by Eysenck (1965). Gray (1967) discusses Russian work on conditioning and individual differences. Ax (1972) and Mednick (1972) consider conditioning in relation to schizophrenic withdrawal reactions.

Conditioning studies are among the more solid and consistent of the data reported in this chapter. There can be no doubt that learning and conditioning are of fundamental significance to the understanding of behaviour. Clinicians have treated it unsystematically (if they have treated it at all) and experimental psychologists, while thoroughly systematic, may have been unduly limited in their experimental subjects, their conditions, and their conclusions. But the fact remains that, even if we reformulate all of existing learning theory there is a richness and abundance of well-collected evidence that will serve well any rebuilding operations. If conditioning studies have appeared trivial, mechanical and artificial this is due more to the limited measurements and interpretations that have been imposed than to any inherent triviality. It is hoped the sample of studies that have been described above illustrates a variety of ways in which the old mechanics of reflexology can be extended to more contemporary models of self-organising, self-optimising human behaviour.

REFERENCES

ARNOLD, MAGDA B. (1960) *Emotion and Personality.* New York: Columbia University Press, 2 vols.

AVERILL, J. R. (1969) Autonomic response patterns during sadness and mirth. *Psychophysiology*, **4**, 399–414.

AX, A. F. (1953) The physiological differentiation between fear and anger in humans. *Psychosom. Med.*, **15**, 433–442.

AX, A. F. (1972) The psychophysiology of schizophrenia. In *Objective Indicators of Psychopathology* (Ed. Zubin, J., Sutton, S., and Kietzman, M. L.) New York: Academic Press.

BARTERNWERFER, H. (1969) Some practical consequences of activation theory, *Zeitschrift für experimentelle und angewardte Psychologie*, Band XVI, Heft **2**, 195–222.

BASOWITZ, H., PERSKY, H., KORCHIN, S. J., and GRINKER, R. R. (1955) *Anxiety and Stress.* New York: McGraw-Hill.

BREGER, L. and McGAUGH, J. L. (1965) Critique and reformulation of 'learning-theory' approaches to psychotherapy and neurosis. *Psychologic. Bull.*, **63**, 5, 338–358.

BRIDGER, W. H. (1967) Contributions of conditioning principles to psychiatry. In *Foundations of Conditioning and Learning* (Ed. Kimble, G. A.). New York: Appleton-Century, pp. 587–599.

BRODAL, A. (1969) *Neurological Anatomy in Relation to Clinical Medicine* (2nd. edition). London: Oxford University Press.

BROWN, J. S. and FARBER, I. E. (1951) Emotions conceptualized as intervening variables: with suggestions toward a theory of frustration. *Psychologic. Bull.*, **48**, 465–495.

BUCHWALD, A. M. and YOUNG, R. D. (1969) Some comments on the foundations of behavior therapy. In *Behavior Therapy: Appraisal and status* (Ed. Franks, C. M.) New York: McGraw-Hill.

BUNNEY, W. E., MASON, J. W., and HAMBURG, D. A. (1965) Correlations between behavioral variables and urinary 17-hydroxycorticosteriods in depressed patients. *Psychosomat. Med.*, **27**, 299–308.

BUSFIELD, B. L. and WECHSLER, M. (1961) Studies of salivation in depression. *Arch. gen. Psychiat.*, **4**, 10–15.

CALLAWAY, E. (1966) Averaged evoked responses in psychiatry. *J. nerv. ment. Dis.*, **143**, 80–94.

CANNON, W. B. (1932) *The Wisdom of the Body.* New York: Norton.

CLARIDGE, G. S. (1967) *Personality and Arousal. A psychophysiological study of psychiatric disorder.* Internat. Series Monogr. Experimental Psychology. Oxford: Pergamon.

COFER, C. N. and APPLEY, N. H. (1964) Frustration, conflict and stress. In *Motivation: Theory and Research.* New York: Wiley, 412–465.

COPPEN, A. (1965) Mineral metabolism in affective disorders. *Brit. J. Psychiat.*, **111**, 1133–1142.

CROPLEY, A. J. and WECKOWICZ, T. E. (1966) The dimensionality of clinical depression. *Austral. J. Psychol.*, **18**, 18–25.

DAVIES, B. M. (1960) The methacholine test in depressive states. *A.M.A. Archives of general psychiatry*, **3**, 14–16.

DAVIES, B. M. and GURLAND, J. B. (1968) Salivary secretion in depressive illness. *J. Psychosomat. Res.*, **5**, 269–271.

DAVITZ, J. R. (1964) *The Communication of Emotional Meaning.* New York: McGraw-Hill.

DEUTSCH, J. A. and DEUTSCH, D. (1963) Attention: some theoretical considerations. *Psychologic. Rev.*, **70**, 80–90.

DUFFY, ELIZABETH (1951) The concept of energy mobilization. *Psychologic. Rev.*, **58**, 30–40.

DUFFY, ELIZABETH (1962) *Activation and Behaviour.* New York: Wiley.

EYSENCK, H. J. (1957) *The Dynamics of Anxiety and Hysteria.* London: Routledge and Kegan Paul.

EYSENCK, H. J. (1960) *Behaviour Therapy and the Neuroses.* New York: Pergamon.

EYSENCK, H. J. (1964) *Crime and Personality.* London: Routledge and Kegan Paul.

EYSENCK, H. J. (1965) Extraversion and the acquisition of eyeblink and GSR conditioned responses. *Psychologic. Bull.*, **63**, 258–270.

EYSENCK, H. J. (1967) *The Biological Basis of Personality.* Springfield: Thomas.

EYSENCK, H. J. (1968) A theory of the incubation of anxiety/fear responses. *Behav. Res. Therapy*, **6**, 309–321.

EYSENCK, H. J. (1969) *The Structure of Human Personality.* 3rd. edn. London: Methuen.

EYSENCK, H. J. (1970) The classification of depressive illnesses. *Brit. J. Psychiat.*, **117**, 241–250.

EYSENCK, H. J. and EYSENCK, S. B. G. (1969) *Personality Structure and Measurement.* London: Routledge and Kegan Paul.

FINE, B. J. and SWEENEY, D. R. (1968) Personality traits, and situational factors, and catecholamine excretion. *J. exp. res. Personality*, **3**, 15–27.

FOLKINS, C. H., LAWSON, KAREN D., OPTON, E. M. Jr., and LAZARUS, R. S. (1968) Desensitization and the experimental reduction of threat. *J. abn. Psychol.*, **73**, Part 2, 100–113.

FRANKENHAEUSER, MARIANNE (1965) *Physiological, behavioral and subjective reactions to stress.* In Second Internat. Symp. on man in space, Paris.

FRANKENHAEUSER, MARIANNE, and PATKAI, PAULA (1965) Interindividual differences in catecholamine excretion during stress. *Scand. J. Psychol.*, **6**, 117–123.

FRANKENHAEUSER, MARIANNE (1967) *Catecholamine Excretion and Behavior. A survey of experimental studies.* Rep. Psychological Laboratories, University of Stockholm, No. 227.

FRANKENHAEUSER, MARIANNE (1968) *Behavioral Efficiency as related to Adrenaline Release.* Rep. Psychological Laboratories, University of Stockholm, No. 268.

FREEMAN, G. L. (1948) *The Energetics of Human Behavior.* Ithaca: Cornell University Press.

FUNKENSTEIN, D. H. (1956) Nor-epinephrine-like and epinephrine-like substances in relation to human behavior. *J. nerv. ment. Dis.*, **124**, 58–68.

FUNKENSTEIN, D. H. and GREENBLATT, M. (1949) Changes in the autonomic nervous system following electric shock therapy in psycho-neurotic patients. *J. nerv. ment. Dis.*, **109**, 272–277.

FUNKENSTEIN, D. H., GREENBLATT, M., and SOLOMON, H. (1951) Autonomic changes paralleling physiologic changes in mentally ill patients. *J. nerv. ment. Dis.*, **114**, 1–18.

GELDER, M. G. and MATHEWS, A. M. (1968) Forearm blood flow and phobic anxiety. *Brit. J. Psychiat.*, **114**, 1371–1376.

GELLHORN, E. and LOOFBOURROW, G. N. (1963) *Emotions and Emotional Disorders.* New York: Harper.

GOLDSTEIN, M. L. (1968) Physiological theories of emotion: a critical historical review from the standpoint of behaviour theory. *Psychologic. Bull.*, **69**, 23–40.

GOLDSTEIN, M. S. and RAMEY, E. R. (1957) Non-endocrine aspects of stress. *Perspectives Biol. Med.*, **1**, 33–47.

GRAY, J. A. (1967) Strength of the nervous system, introversion-extraversion, conditionability and arousal. *Behav. Res. Therapy*, **5**, 151–170.

GREENFIELD, N. S., KATZ, DEBORAH, ALEXANDER, A. A., and ROESSLER, R. (1963) The relationship between physiological and psychological responsivity: depression and galvanic skin response. *J. nerv. ment. Dis.*, **136**, 535–539.

GRINGS, W. W. (1965) Verbal-perceptual factors in the conditioning of autonomic responses. In *Classical Conditioning* (Ed. Prokasy, W. F.) New York: Appleton Century, pp. 71–89.

GROSSMAN, S. P. (1967) *A Textbook of Physiological Psychology.* New York: Wiley.

GRUZELIER, J. H., LYKKEN, D. T., and VENABLES, P. H. (1972) Schizophrenia and arousal revisited. Two flash thresholds and electrodermal activity in activated and non-activated conditions. *Arch. gen. Psychiat.* (in press).

HAKEREM, G., SUTTON, S., and ZUBIN, J. (1964) Pupillary reactions to light in schizophrenic patients and normals. *Amer. New York Acad. Sci.*, **105**, 820–831.

HARE, R. D. (1968) Psychopathy, autonomic functioning, and the orienting response. *J. abnr. Psychol. Monogr. Supplement*, **73**, 1–24.

HEINE, B. E., SAINSBURY, P., and CHYNOWETH, R. C. (1969) Hypertension and emotional disturbance. *J. Psychiat. Res.*, **7**, 119–130.

HERRINGTON, R. N. (1967) The sedation threshold: pharmacological considerations. Appendix to CLARIDGE, G. S. (1967).

HILLMAN, J. (1960) *Emotion: A comprehensive phenomenology of theories and their meanings for therapy*. London: Routledge and Kegan Paul.

HOFFER, A., OSMOND, H., and SMYTHIES, J. (1954) Schizophrenia: A new approach. 11. Result of a year's research. *J. ment. Sci.*, **100**, 29–45.

HOLLAND, H. C. (1965) *The Spiral After-effect*. Internat. Series of Monographs in Experimental Psychology. Oxford: Pergamon.

JOHNSON, L. C. (1970) A psychophysiology for all states. *Psychophysiology*, **6**, 501–516.

JONES, R. T., BLACKER, K. H., and CALLAWAY, E. (1966) Perceptual dysfunction in schizophrenia: clinical and auditory evoked response findings. *Amer. J. Psychiat.*, **123**, 639–645.

KELLY, D. H. W. (1966) Measurement of anxiety by forearm blood flow. *Brit. J. Psychiat.*, **112**, 789–798.

KENDELL, R. E. (1968) *The Classification of Depressive Illnesses*. London: Oxford University Press.

KETY, S. S. (1966) H. Catecholamines in Neuropsychiatric States. *Pharmacological Rev.*, **18**, 787–798.

KILOH, L. G. and GARSIDE, R. F. (1963) The independence of neurotic depression and endogenous depression. *Brit. J. Psychiat.*, **109**, 451–463.

KIMMEL, H. D. (1965) Instrumental inhibitory factors in classical conditioning. In *Classical Conditioning* (Ed. Prokasy, W. F.). New York: Appleton Century.

KLEITMAN, N. (1939) *Sleep and Wakefulness*. Chicago: University of Chicago Press.

LACEY, J. I. (1967) Somatic response patterning and stress: some revisions of activation theory. In *Psychological Stress* (Ed. Appley, M. H. and Trumbull, R.). New York: Appleton-Century-Crofts.

LADER, M. H. (1967) Palmar skin conductance measures in anxiety and phobic states. *J. psychosomat. Res.*, **11**, 271–281.

LADER, M. H. and MATHEWS, A. M. (1968) A physiological model of phobic anxiety and desensitization. *Behav. res. Therapy*, **6**, 411–421.

LADER, M. H. and WING, LORNA (1966) *Physiological Measures, Sedative Drugs and Morbid Anxiety*. London: Oxford University Press.

LADER, M. H., GELDER, M. G., and MARKS, I. M. (1967) Palmar skin conductance measures as predictors of response to desensitization. *J. psychosomat. Res.*, **11**, 283–290.

LANG, P. J. (1968) Fear reduction and fear behavior: Problems in treating a construct. In *Research in Psychotherapy* (Ed. Shlien, J. M.). Vol. 3. Washington: American Psychological Association.

LANG, P. J. (1969) The mechanics of desensitization and the laboratory study of human fears. In *Behavior Therapy: Appraisal and Status*. (Ed. Franks, C. M.). New York: McGraw-Hill.

LANG, P. J. and LAZOVIK, A. D. (1963) Experimental desensitization of a phobia. *J. abn. soc. Psychol.*, **66**, 519–525.

LANG, P. J., LAZOVIK, A. D., and REYNOLDS, D. J. (1965) Desensitization, suggestibility and pseudo therapy. *J. abn. Psychol.*, **70**, 395–402.

LAZARUS, R. (1968) Emotions and adaptation: conceptual and empirical relations. In *Nebraska Symposium on Motivation*. (Ed. Arnold, W. J.) Lincoln, Nebr.: University of Nebraska Press, pp. 175–266.

LEVEY, A. B. and MARTIN, IRENE (1968) Shape of the conditioned eyelid response. *Psychologic. Rev.*, **75**, 398–408.

LEVI, L. (1965) The urinary output of adrenaline and nor-adrenaline during pleasant and unpleasant emotional states. *Psychosomat. Med.*, **27**, 80–85.

LEVINE, S. (1968) Hormones and Conditioning. In *Nebraska Symposium on Motivation*. (Ed. Arnold, W. J.). Lincoln, Nebr.: University of Nebraska Press, pp. 85–101.

LEVIS, D. J. (1967) Implosive Therapy: Part 2. The subhuman analogue, the strategy, and the technique. In *Behavior Modification Techniques in the Treatment of Emotional Disorders*. (Ed. Armitage, S. C.) Battle Creek, Michigan: V. A. Publications, pp. 22–37.

LOEW, D. (1965) Syndrom, Diagnose und Speichelsekretion bei depresseven Patienton. *Psychopharmacologia*, **7**, 339–348.

LOGAN, F. A. (1956) A micromolar approach to behavior theory. *Psychologic. Rev.*, **63**, 63–73.

LYKKEN, D. T. (1962) Preception in the rat: autonomic response to shock as a function of length of warning signal. *Science*, **137**, 665–666.

LYKKEN, D. T. and MALEY, M. (1968) Autonomic versus cortical arousal in schizophrenics and non-psychotics. *J. Psychiat. Res.*, **6**, 21–32.

LYNN, R. (1963) Russian theory and research on schizophrenia. *Psychologic. Bull.*, **60**, 486–498.

MAGOUN, H. W. (1963) *The Waking Brain*. Springfield: Thomas.

MALMO, R. B. (1957) Anxiety and behavioral arousal. *Psychologic. Rev.*, **64**, 276–287.

MARTIN, IRENE and LEVEY, A. B. (1969) *Genesis of the classical conditioned response*. Internat. Monog. Experimental Psychology. Vol. 8. Oxford: Pergamon Press.

MARTIN, IRENE and LEVEY, A. B. (1972) Learning and performance in human conditioning. In *Objective Indicators of Psychopathology* (Ed. Zubin, J., Sutton, S., and Kietzman, M. L.). New York: Academic Press.

MATHEWS, A. (1971) Psycho-physiological approaches to the investigation of desensitization and related procedures. *Psychologic. Bull.* **76**, 73–91.

MCDOUGALL, W. (1912) *Introduction to Social Psychology.* Boston: Luce.

MEDNICK, S. A. (1972) Breakdown in individuals at high risk for schizophrenia: behavioral and autonomic characteristics and possible role of perinatal complications. In *Objective Indicators of Psychopathology* (Ed. Zubin, J., Sutton, S., and Kietzman, M. L.) New York: Academic Press.

MEDNICK, S. A. and SCHULSINGER, F. (1968) Some premorbid characteristics related to breakdown in children with schizophrenic mothers. *J. Psychiat. Res.,* 6, 267–291.

MILLER, N. E. (1951) Learnable drives and rewards. In *Handbook of Experimental Psychology* (Ed. Stevens, S. S.) New York: Wiley.

MOWRER, O. H. (1939) A stimulus-response analysis of anxiety and its role as a reinforcing agent. *Psychologic. Rev.,* 46, 553–566.

MOWRER, O. H. (1960) *Learning Theory and Behavior.* New York: Wiley.

OLDS, J. (1962) Hypothalamic substrates of reward. *Physiologic. Rev.,* 42, 554–604.

PALMAI, G. and BLACKWELL, B. (1965) The diurnal pattern of salivary flow in normal and depressed patients. *Brit. J. Psychiat.,* 111, 334–338.

PAUL, G. L. (1969) Behavior modification research: Design and tactics. In *Behavior Therapy: Appraisal and Status* (Ed. Franks, C. M.) New York: McGraw-Hill.

PITTS, F. N. and MCCLURE, J. N. (1967) Lactate metabolism in anxiety neurosis. *New Engl. J. Med.,* 277, 1329–1336.

PRIBRAM, K. H. (1967) The new neurology and the biology of emotion: a structural approach. *Amer. Psychol.,* 22, 830–838.

PROKASY, W. F. (1965) Classical eyelid conditioning: experimenter operations, task demands and response shaping. In *Classical Conditioning* (Ed. Prokasy, W. F.) New York: Appleton Century.

RACHMAN, S. (1968) *Phobias. Their Nature and Control.* Springfield: Thomas.

RAMEY, E. R. and GOLDSTEIN, M. S. (1957) The adrenal cortex and the sympathetic nervous system. *Physiologic. Rev.,* 37, 155–195.

RAZRAN, G. (1955) Conditioning and perception. *Psychologic. Rev.,* 62, 83–95.

ROUTTENBERG, A. (1968) The two-arousal hypothesis: reticular formation and limbic system. *Psychologic. Rev.,* 75, 51–80.

RUBIN, L. S. (1962) Patterns of adrenergic-cholinergic imbalance in the functional psychoses. *Psychologic. Rev.,* 69, 501–519.

SCHACHTER, S. (1966) The interaction of cognitive and physiological determinants of emotional state. In *Anxiety and Behavior.* (Ed. Spielberger, C. D.) New York: Academic Press, 193–224.

SCHILDKRAUT, J. J. and KETY, S. S. (1967) Biogenic amines and emotion. *Science,* 156, 21–30.

SCHNEIRLA, T. C. (1959) An evolutionary and developmental theory of the biphasic process underlying approach and withdrawal. In *Nebraska Symposium on Motivation* (Ed. Jones, M. R.) Lincoln, Nebr.: University of Nebraska Press.

SELYE, H. (1950) *Stress.* Montreal: Acta Inc.

SELYE, H. (1956) *The Stress of Life.* New York: McGraw-Hill.

SELYE, H. (1959) Perspectives in stress research. *Perspectives biologic. Med.,* 2, 403–416.

SHAGASS, C. (1954) The sedation threshold. A method for estimating tension in psychiatric patients. *Electroenceph. clin. Neurophysiol.,* 6, 221–233.

SHAGASS, C. and MIHALIK, J. (1956) An objective test which differentiates between neurotic and psychotic depression. *Amer. med. assoc. arch. neurol. Psychiat.,* 75, 461–471.

SHAGASS, C. and SCHWARTZ, M. (1965) Visual cerebral evoked response characteristics in a psychiatric population. *Amer. J. Psychiat.,* 121, 979–987.

SILVERMAN, A. J., COHEN, S. I., SHMAVONIAN, B. M., and KIRSHNER, N. (1961) Catecholamines in psychophysiological studies. *Rec. Adv. biologic. Psychiat.,* 3, 104–118.

SOKOLOV, E. N. (1963) Higher nervous functions: the orienting reflex. *Ann. rev. Physiol.,* 25, 545–580.

SOLOMON, R. L. (1964) Punishment. *Amer. Psychologist,* 19, 239–254.

SOLOMON, R. L. and WYNNE, L. C. (1954) Traumatic avoidance learning: the principles of anxiety conservation and partial irreversibility. *Psychologic. Rev.,* 61, 353–385.

SPENCE, K. W. (1956) *Behaviour Theory and Conditioning.* New Haven: Yale University Press.

SPENCE, K. W. (1960) *Behaviour Theory and Learning.* Englewood Cliffs, N.J.: Prentice-Hall.

SPENCE, K. W. (1963) Cognitive factors in the extinction of the conditioned eyelid response in humans. *Science,* 140, 1224–1225.

SPENCE, K. W. (1964) Anxiety (drive) level and performance in eyelid conditioning. *Psychologic. Bull.,* 16, 129–139.

STAMPFL, T. G. (1967) Implosive therapy: Part 1. The theory, the subhuman analogue, the strategy, and the technique. In *Behaviour Modification Techniques in the Treatment of Emotional Disorders* (Ed. Armitage, S. C.) Battle Creek, Michigan: V. A. Publication, pp. 12–21.

STERN, J. A. and MCDONALD, D. G. (1965) Physiological correlates of mental disease. *Ann. Rev. Psychol.,* 16, 225–264.

STERN, J. A., SURPHLIS, W., and KOFF, E. (1965) Electrodermal responsiveness as related to psychiatric diagnosis and prognosis. *Psychophysiology,* 2, 51–61.

THOMPSON, R. F. (1967) *Foundations of Physiological Psychology.* London: Harper.

THORPE, W. H. (1956) *Learning and Instinct in Animals.* London: Methuen.

ULLMAN, B. P. and KRASNER, L. (1965) *Case Studies in Behaviour Modification.* New York: Holt, Rinehart and Winston.

VENABLES, P. H. (1963) The relationship between level of skin potential and fusion of paired light flashes in schizophrenics and normal subjects. *J. Psychiat. Res.,* 1, 279–287.

VENABLES, P. H. (1972) Input regulation and psycho-pathology. In *Towards a Science of Psychopathology* (Ed. Hanner, M., Salzinger, K., and Sutton, S.) New York: Wiley.

VENABLES, P. H. and WING, J. K. (1962) Level of arousal and the subclassification of schizophrenia. *Arch. gen. Psychiat.*, **7**, 114–119.

WALTER, W. GREY (1972) The contingent negative variation as an aid to psychiatric diagnosis. In *Objective Indicators of Psychopathology* (Ed. Zubin, J., Sutton, S., and Kietzman, M. L.) New York: Academic Press.

WENGER, M. A. (1966) Studies of autonomic balance: a summary. *Psychophysiology*, **2**, 173–186.

WOLF, S. and WOLFF, H. G. (1943) *Human Gastric Function.* New York: Oxford University Press.

WOLPE, J. (1958) *Psychotherapy by Reciprocal Inhibition.* Stanford: Stanford University Press.

ZAHN, T. P. (1964) *Autonomic Reactivity and Behaviour in Schizophrenia.* Psychiatric Research Report 19, American Psychiatric Association pp. 156–173.

ZAHN, T. P. (1972) Psychophysiological concomitants of task performance in schizophrenia. In *Objective Indicators of Psychopathology* (Ed. Zubin, J., Sutton, S., and Kietzman, M. L.) New York: Academic Press.

ZAHN, T. P., ROSENTHAL, D., and LAWLOR, W. G. (1968) Electrodermal and heart rate orienting reactions in chronic schizophrenia. *J. Psychiat. Res.*, **6**, 117–134.

12

Abnormalities of Motivation

GLENN D. WILSON

INTRODUCTION

The concept of 'motivation' has various meanings in psychology, and overlaps to a considerable extent with most other broad areas such as perception, learning, personality, and psychophysiology. It is therefore necessary at the outset to state the limits on the scope of this chapter. This review is restricted to consideration of those experiments dealing with motivation that is *generalised* and *work-related*, rather than that which is goal-specific or closely associated with a particular physiological need such as hunger or sex. This usage of the term motivation is similar to that adopted by many behavioural psychologists, notably Hull, Spence, and Eysenck, and corresponds closely to the *energising* function of drive, as distinguished from its various cue functions (Hebb, 1955).

In accordance with the general plan of this handbook, emphasis is given to studies that involve either *abnormal subjects*, or normal subjects under *extreme or unusual environmental conditions*. In addition, this chapter is limited to consideration of studies employing human subjects; space does not allow for a review of the many animal studies relevant to this field. (The interested reader is referred to chapter 20, by Broadhurst.) Even so, the task remains enormous and no claim to comprehensive coverage can be made. Other things being equal, greater attention has been paid to recent research that has not been reviewed elsewhere, but some amount of selectivity must still be put down to the idiosyncratic preferences of the writer.

Although the concepts to be dealt with in this chapter overlap considerably, and in many situations have been used interchangeably, each of them has a slightly specialised referent. The elusive differences among these concepts may be clarified to some extent by reference to two systems of classification—

1. according to whether the orientation is primarily *biological or social*, and
2. according to the *source of the variability* in drive or motivation.

Biological versus Social Drive Concepts

This classification of motivational concepts is fairly straightforward, and will be adopted as the major basis for division of the chapter. Concepts such as anxiety, arousal, and reminiscence are psychological concepts, but are thought of as being closely related to fundamental biological processes (e.g. reticular activity, neuroendocrine factors, etc.). On the other hand, concepts such as achievement motivation, level of aspiration, and the Zeigarnik Effect are regarded as being more closely associated with social learning phenomena. Although it might be more accurate to think in terms of a continuum rather than a dichotomy, such an arbitrary division provides a convenient way of organising the chapter.

Sources of Drive Variability

Much of the confusion surrounding the use of the various drive-related concepts undoubtedly results from the fact that they have been used to describe variations resulting from several different sources—

1. Relatively stable or 'chronic' intersubject drive differences (e.g. need achievement).
2. Environmental factors that contribute to temporary drive state differences (e.g. motivating instructions).

3. Personality traits that determine differential susceptibility to arousal of drive by environmental factors (e.g. neuroticism).

4. Environmental factors that effect lasting changes in one or other of the drive trait groups (e.g. history of childhood failure).

5. Differences in transient drive states *per se*, that are the resultant of the particular combination of personal and situational factors operative at a given moment of time (e.g. arousal as measured by skin conductance).

6. It will shortly be suggested that in studies of task performance it may often be useful to treat certain characteristics of the task itself as a separate source of drive (e.g. complexity and pacing).

Since different operational definitions of drive reflect different combinations of these kinds of drive variation, they are not always directly comparable one with another. For example, the Manifest Anxiety Scale is specifically designed to measure individual differences in susceptibility to external drive, while, on the other hand, physiological indices such as skin conductance have been employed to assess variations in drive originating from all sources, separately and simultaneously.

The Yerkes-Dodson Law: A Three-Dimensional Model

From the literature concerned with the relationship between drive and task performance, two generalisations consistently emerge:

1. An inverted-U function relates efficiency of task performance and learning to strength of drive, whether the origin of drive be internal (subject-based) or external (environment-based), or some combination of these two major groups of drive source. This relationship has been discussed by many writers, including Malmo (1959), Cofer (1959), Duffy (1957), and Fiske and Maddi (1961).

2. Increased drive tends to be facilitatory on the efficiency of performance on tasks that are simple or well learned, but interferes with performance on tasks that are more difficult or in the early stages of being learned. The work of Spence (1958) and his associates is perhaps best known in connection with this generalisation.

Together, these two generalisations have come to be known as the *Yerkes-Dodson Law* relating motivation and performance (Broadhurst, 1959), support for which has come from experiments employing physiological measures of drive (Vogel *et al.*, 1959; Burgess and Hokanson, 1968), and situationally-induced drive (Eysenck, 1964), as well as the studies of Spence and Eysenck using questionnaire-defined drive (Eysenck, 1967).

It is the opinion of the present author that the various relationships subsumed under the Yerkes-Dodson Law can best be summarised by reference to three major groups of variables which have most frequently been investigated in relation to task performance, and which may be viewed as different sources of drive. They are: (1) *subject-based*, (2) *environmental*, and (3) *task-based* variations in drive level (Table 12.1). The first two of these are arrived at by broadly grouping the more detailed list of drive sources given above, and are fairly self-explanatory, but the concept of 'task drive' is perhaps less obvious. The idea of treating certain characteristics of the task itself as a source of drive is not new, however (*see* Jones, 1960; Haywood and Weaver, 1967), and in fact, the task is really only a specialised aspect of the environment. It is ascribed an importance equal to intersubject variability and the remaining environmental influences in the present context simply because it has, in the experimental literature, regularly been considered as a third major variable determining performance.

In the present analysis it is hypothesised that, other things being equal, the relationship between task

Table 12.1. Three Major Sources of Drive Influencing Task Performance

Subject drive		Environmental drive		Task drive	
low	*high*	*low*	*high*	*low*	*high*
Non-anxious	Anxious	Low ego-involvement	High ego-involvement	Easy	Difficult
Stable-extravert	Neurotic-introvert	'Research' context	'Selection' context	Simple	Complex
Low *n* Ach	High *n* Ach	Neutral instructions	Exhortive instructions	Unpaced	Paced
Low aspiration level	High aspiration level	No monetary incentive	Monetary incentive	Familiar	Novel
External control	Internal control	No audience	Audience	Chance situation	Skill situation
Low dissonance	High dissonance				

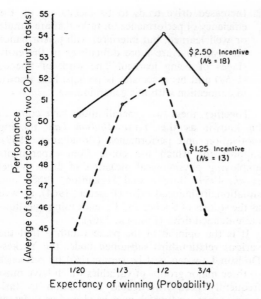

Fig. 12.1. Relationship between performance on arithmetic and clerical tasks and probability of success (*from* Atkinson, 1958)

performance and each of these three types of drive, taken separately, will tend to take the form of an inverted-U function. As already stated, there is substantial evidence to support this hypothesis in the cases of subject drive and environmental drive, and it also seems reasonable to assume that there will be an optimum level of difficulty, pacing, etc., at which a task is neither boring nor impossible, but of a moderately challenging nature. Indeed, such a result has been found in several studies (e.g. Atkinson, 1958, Fig. 12.1).

Now since these three sources of drive are conceptually independent of one another, they can be represented as orthogonal dimensions in a three-dimensional Euclidean 'drive space'. The major generalisations that constitute the Yerkes-Dodson Law can then be summarised by reference to this model (Fig 12.2). Triangle *ETS* is the plane of optimal performance, while all planes parallel to *ETS* are isometric with respect to performance. At point *L*, drive from all sources is at zero value and no work will occur. At the diagonally opposite corner (point *H*), all forms of drive are at maximum and the resultant performance is again poor. Optimal performance may be expected to occur either when drive from all three sources is within the low-moderate range, or when the almost complete lack of drive from any two of these sources is compensated by very high levels of drive from the third.

The limitation of this model as it stands, of course, is that the units of measurement along the three axes cannot be specified in advance, but must be adjusted with each new set of circumstances so as to yield the simple isometric performance planes illustrated in Fig. 12.2. Thus, in this very general form, the model is descriptive rather than quantitative. A further practical difficulty with the model relates to the fact intimated earlier, that the instruments used to measure the motivational effects derived from the subject, the environment, and the task itself, are often sensitive to more than one of these influences simultaneously. When the effects of the three variables are not easily separated, the task of evaluating experimental results in terms of the three-dimensional Yerkes-Dodson Law is complicated.

Nevertheless, the present model does appear to permit the evaluation of a vast number of experimental observations within a unified framework. Few experimenters have been ambitious enough to consider variations in all three dimensions within a single investigation. In most cases, performance has been studied as a function of one drive dimension only, while the other two are held, or assumed to be, constant. Others have manipulated two of these drive variables and undertaken to analyse the interaction between them in determining performance. In both cases, the three-dimensional model may be useful because it draws attention to the importance of other major sources of variation that

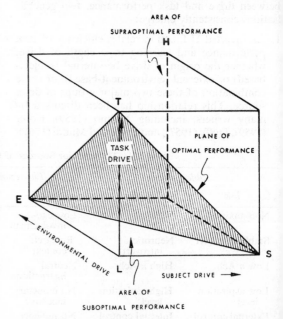

Fig. 12.2. A three-dimensional model of the Yerkes-Dodson law

may have to be taken into account in order to interpret the results.

An example may clarify this point. In a recent experiment, Hays and Worell (1967) investigated the effects of drive as measured by three different motivation questionnaires upon performance of a digit-symbol task at two levels of complexity. In accordance with the optimal drive hypothesis, low-drive subjects were at a significantly greater advantage over high-drive subjects on the more difficult task as compared to the easier task. An unexpected finding, however, was that superior performance was shown by low-drive subjects even on the easier task. In the interpretation of these results, the authors had taken account of the subject and task variables, i.e. those which had been experimentally manipulated. Reference to our three-dimensional Yerkes-Dodson model, however, would lead one to suppose that the environment had probably been contributing a considerable amount of additional drive to the total situation, thereby causing the performance of the low-drive subjects to fall closer to the optimal performance plane than high-drive subjects, even when the task was comparatively easy (task-drive low). This, in fact, seems to have been the case. The subjects used in this study were students from introductory psychology classes. They were tested in small groups 'in an attempt to create a competitive atmosphere', and the task was represented to them as a 'very sensitive' test which 'gives a good indication of a person's intelligence and the likelihood of career success'. Clearly, this was a highly competitive and ego-threatening situation, which, in terms of the present model, is necessary to explain why low-drive subjects performed better than high-drive subjects even on the relatively easy task.

This experiment has been considered in some detail simply to illustrate how a Yerkes-Dodson model which emphasises three major sources of drive might prove useful in explaining certain seemingly paradoxical results. This model will be found to have relevance throughout the chapter.

Eysenck's Personality Dimensions

Another major framework within which the experiments described in this chapter will be evaluated is that of Eysenck's dimensional analysis of personality. From a long and painstaking series of factor-analytic studies of behaviour on a wide variety of verbal, perceptual, and motor tests, using both patient and non-patient samples, Eysenck (1968) has established the usefulness of summarising the structure of personality in terms of three higher-order factors called *extraversion-introversion* (E), *neuroticism* (N), and *psychoticism* (P). Since the weight of the empirical evidence indicated a continuity between normal and abnormal behaviour along these dimensions, Eysenck's analysis of personality also provides a relatively objective system of psychodiagnostics, which has long been recognised as one of the most fundamental needs of clinical psychology.

A questionnaire for measuring the E and N dimensions has been available for some time; this is the Maudsley Personality Inventory (MPI), now up-dated and renamed the Eysenck Personality Inventory (EPI; Eysenck and Eysenck, 1964). Although these dimensions have been shown to be independent, the interactions between them are very important, and they will usually be considered together when their relevance to the various motivational concepts is discussed in the chapter. Also, because the locations of most of the clinically diagnosed neurotic groups in relation to these two dimensions are fairly well established, experiments using patient samples may be evaluated within the same framework.

The situation with respect to the psychoticism dimension is rather different. Satisfactory questionnaire measures of this variable have only recently become available, and its interactions with the other two dimensions have been little researched. Therefore, the relevance of this factor must be considered separately, and it will be necessary to employ the traditional psychiatric diagnostic labels, whatever the extent of their unreliability.

BIOLOGICALLY-BASED MOTIVATIONAL CONCEPTS

1. Arousal

(a) DESCRIPTION AND MEASUREMENT

Most researchers in the field of psychophysiology have found it necessary to postulate some kind of generalised, work-related, motivational continuum, which has been variously called 'energy mobilization' (Duffy, 1951), 'emotion' (Lindsley, 1951), 'activation' (Malmo, 1957), 'alertness' and 'arousal' (Lindsley, 1957). Probably the terms 'arousal' or 'general arousal' are most widely used today in reference to this continuum.

Changes in the behavioural continuum of arousal are known to be paralleled by changes occurring at other levels of description, e.g. physiological states and awareness (Table 12.2). Note that behavioural efficiency is regarded as having a curvilinear relationship to arousal, as described in our Yerkes-Dodson model.

Although some experimenters have employed

Table 12.2. Psychological States and their EEG, Conscious and Behavioural Correlates
(*from* Lindsley, 1952)

Behavioural continuum	Electro-encephalogram	State of awareness	Behavioural efficiency
Strong, excited emotion (fear) (rage) (anxiety)	Desynchronised: low to moderate amplitude; fast, mixed frequencies	Restricted awareness; divided attention; diffuse, hazy; 'Confusion'	Poor: (lack of control, freezing-up. disorganised)
Alert attentiveness	Partially synchronised: mainly fast, low amplitude waves	Selective attention, but may vary or shift. 'Concentration' anticipation, 'set'	Good: (efficient, selective, quick, reactions); organised for serial responses
Relaxed wakefulness	Synchronised: optimal alpha rhythm	Attention wanders-not forced. Favours free association	Good: (routine reactions and creative thought)
Light sleep	Spindle bursts and slow waves (larger); loss of alphas	Markedly reduced consciousness (loss of consciousness), dream state	Absent
Deep sleep	Large and very slow waves (synchrony but slow time base); random, irregular pattern	Complete loss of awareness (no memory for stimulation or for dreams)	Absent
Coma	Isoelectric to irregular large slow waves	Complete loss of consciousness, little or no response to stimulation; amnesia	Absent
Death	Isoelectric: gradual and permanent disappearance of all electrical activity	Complete loss of awareness as death ensues	Absent

self-ratings of arousal, or behavioural indices such as two-flash threshold, operational definition of the concept has, for the most part, been in terms of physiological measures, both central and autonomic (e.g. skin conductance, heart rate, EEG). Since variations in arousal can be environment-based as well as subject-based, definition may also be in terms of experimental manipulation (e.g. white noise intensity, stimulant *vs* depressant drugs), but in such cases most researchers also monitor arousal by one of the other means in order to check that the manipulation of arousal has been successful.

Chapter 10, by I. Martin, deals with the relationship of the arousal concept (particularly as defined physiologically) to abnormal behaviour, so that only a brief discussion of some of the experiments most relevant to this chapter are given here.

(*b*) RELATIONSHIP TO NEUROTICISM
    AND EXTRAVERSION

Eysenck (1967) hypothesises that the *N* dimension of personality is related at the genotypic level to the lability of the autonomic nervous system, while *E* is a function of the excitation-inhibition balance of the cerebral cortex. Therefore, he distinguishes the concepts of *activation*, which he says should be used to refer to autonomic activity only, and cortical *arousal*, which is a function of reticular activity. For normal persons under normal environmental conditions these two variables are independent, but because of the interconnections between the two underlying neural systems, sustained high levels of activation inevitably lead to high levels of arousal as well. Thus, *N* and *E* are normally independent, but are found to be negatively correlated under abnormal conditions and with highly neurotic subjects (Eysenck, 1959).

In case it has not been made clear, the concept of general arousal, as commonly used in the psychophysiological literature, falls diagonally between Eysenck's dimensions of neuroticism (activation) and introversion (cortical arousal), the exact tilt in relation to these two varying according to the method used for measuring the continuum. When arousal is defined in terms of EEG patterns or two-flash threshold it will probably be more closely related to introversion or cortical arousal. On the other hand, when the index of arousal is heart rate or GSR, it will be relatively more highly correlated with neuroticism or activation.

Evidence relating to the hypothesis that unstable-introverts and patient groups falling into that (dysthymic) quadrant show relatively high arousal patterns on physiological measures is reviewed by Martin (Chapter 10).

(c) SCHIZOPHRENIA

Venables and O'Connor (1959) identified two independent factors in schizophrenic symptomatology, designated *paranoid* and *withdrawal* behaviour respectively (Table 12.3). Since then, a great deal of evidence has accrued which points to the conclusion that withdrawal, but not paranoid, symptoms are positively related to degree of arousal.

Venables and Wing (1962) discovered that two-flash thresholds were lower in those schizophrenic patients who were independently rated as most withdrawn. The correlation held only for patients classified as non-paranoid, or for patients having some paranoid ideas but which were incoherently expressed. This important finding has been closely replicated on several occasions (e.g. Venables, 1967a; Clark, 1967), and essentially similar results have been found using skin potential as a measure of arousal (Venables and Wing, 1962; Spain, 1966) and with reaction time (Goldberg et al., 1968).

A series of prognostic studies using this classification of schizophrenic symptoms have shown results that might also be interpreted as consistent with the hypothesis that withdrawal is related to high arousal. Whereas paranoid symptoms were found to be responsive to variations in ward atmosphere (Kellam et al., 1967), and to placebo treatment (Goldberg et al., 1965), withdrawal symptoms did not respond to these social stimuli. On the other hand, withdrawal symptoms were found to improve more dramatically than paranoid symptoms with

Table 12.3.   Symptom Components of Paranoid
and Withdrawal Syndromes
(From Venables and O'Connor, 1959)

Paranoid	Withdrawal
Hostility	Indifference
Ideas of persecution	Slowed speech
Delusions of grandeur	Disorientation
	Self care
	Confusion
	Hebephrenic symptoms

phenothiazine (tranquillising) drugs (Goldberg et al., 1967). Experiments that have shown disruptive effects of forced social interaction on the behavioural efficiency of withdrawn schizophrenics (Hunter, 1961; Schooler and Spohn, 1960; Spohn and Wolk, 1963; Schooler and Zahn, 1968) are also consistent with this hypothesis if the Yerkes-Dodson Law is invoked. Thus, Goldberg and his colleagues (1968) note that therapeutic efforts directed towards increasing stimulation in withdrawn schizophrenics, either environmentally or pharmacologically, are bound to be self-defeating.

Other evidence comes from the finding that chronic, severely ill schizophrenics show a narrower span of attention than acute, less-disturbed patients, and normals (Clark, 1967). Since reduced perception is a well-recognised effect of increased arousal in normal subjects (e.g. Easterbrook, 1959), this finding also accords with the arousal-withdrawal hypothesis in chronic schizophrenia. Similarly, Silverman (1964, 1968) characterised paranoid schizophrenics as 'hyperscanners' of the environment, while non-paranoids (presumably those patients in whom withdrawal symptoms predominate) were described as 'hyposcanners'.

Venables (1967b) theorises that chronic (particularly non-paranoid) schizophrenia is associated with the partial failure of a homeostatic cortical-subcortical mechanism for the regulation of arousal, which forces the schizophrenic to fall back on various less fundamental means of dealing with arousing stimuli (e.g. narrowing the span of attention, avoidance of novel situations, withdrawal from social interaction). 'These tactics for maintaining a degree of homeostatic control when a more central mechanism is ineffective are to some extent competent to prevent what would otherwise be an intolerable degree of input to the organism. In them, however, may be seen the element of the disease process as it is manifest to the outside observer'.

This view of the symptoms of chronic schizophrenia as representing some kind of defensive reaction to abnormally high levels of arousal is reminiscent of Pavlov's concept of *protective inhibition*, which has remained very central to Russian theory and research on schizophrenia (Lynn, 1963). It will also be seen to be closely related to some accounts of chronic schizophrenia based on Hullian learning theory, which are discussed in the next section.

Finally, an interesting series of experiments by Zahn (1964) seems relevant to this formulation. Zahn was concerned with the question of why some studies of physiological responses in schizophrenics have found higher arousal patterns in this group as compared to normals, while other studies have

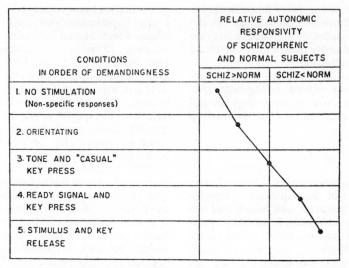

CONDITIONS IN ORDER OF DEMANDINGNESS	RELATIVE AUTONOMIC RESPONSIVITY OF SCHIZOPHRENIC AND NORMAL SUBJECTS	
	SCHIZ > NORM	SCHIZ < NORM
1. NO STIMULATION (Non-specific responses)		
2. ORIENTATING		
3. TONE AND "CASUAL" KEY PRESS		
4. READY SIGNAL AND KEY PRESS		
5. STIMULUS AND KEY RELEASE		

Fig. 12.3. Relative autonomic responsivity of schizophrenic and normal subjects as a function of situation 'demandingness' (*from* Zahn, 1964)

indicated lower arousal in schizophrenics than in normals, He found that an answer suggested itself when the various situations under which physiological responsiveness was measured were arranged along a continuum according to the extent to which demands for organised behaviour were placed on the subject. Situations that were low in 'demandingness' (e.g. resting levels of autonomic activity) indicated higher arousal in the schizophrenic group, compared to normals, while more demanding situations (e.g. a complex reaction time task) showed lower levels of arousal in the schizophrenics (Fig. 12.3). Although interpreted by Zahn as indicating a defective specific alerting system in the chronic schizophrenic, this finding might also be taken as evidence that some kind of secondary defence mechanism, similar to Pavlov's protective inhibition, operates to protect the schizophrenic against environmental stresses which threaten to elevate his already high level of arousal beyond the peak of endurance.

2. Anxiety (Drive)

(*a*) DESCRIPTION AND MEASUREMENT

The Hullian concept of generalised 'drive' (D) is very similar to the behavioural aspect of the 'arousal' continuum. This concept, also, is used to refer to changes that result from environmental conditions (e.g. dynamometer pressure) or to stable differences between subjects.

The use of the term 'anxiety' as a work-related motivational concept is probably best known in relation to the work of Spence (1956, 1958) and his associates at Iowa. In extending Hullian learning theory to experiments with human subjects, they have operationally defined between-subject variation in D in terms of scores on the Manifest Anxiety Scale (MAS; Taylor, 1953).

(*b*) RELATIONSHIP TO LEARNING AND PERFORMANCE

Numerous experiments have been conducted to examine the effects of drive, defined by anxiety questionnaires, on task learning and performance. Although this literature is not without contradictions (Feldman, 1964; Spielberger, 1966), high anxiety has generally been found to facilitate performance on tasks that are simple or well learned, but to cause decrements in performance on tasks that are complex or in the early stages of learning (Spence, 1958; Weiner, 1959; Sarason, 1961).

A second, frequently reported finding relates to the interaction between anxiety scores and the level of external drive (stress) operative in the experimental situation, in determining the efficiency of task performance. Typical stressors that have been employed include dynamometer pressure, monetary incentive, induced success or failure, exhortive instructions and threat of punishment. The concensus is that high-anxiety subjects perform better under low levels of stress, while low-anxiety subjects perform better under higher levels of stress (Walker, 1961; Ryan and Lakie, 1965; Cox, 1966; Carron and Morford, 1968; Ganzer, 1968; Martens and Lander, 1969).

Taken together, these findings indicate that there is an optimum level of drive for the performance of any task, which is dependent on certain characteristics of the task itself. Although normally interpreted as supporting certain predictions from Hullian learning theory, these results are also clearly consistent with the Yerkes-Dodson model outlined above.

(c) FACILITATING AND DEBILITATING ANXIETY

Some writers have argued that the concept of anxiety may itself be divided into components that are respectively facilitating and debilitating in their effects upon learning and performance. The Achievement Anxiety Test (AAT; Alpert and Haber, 1960) was designed to separate these two different kinds of anxiety as they relate to test-taking situations (normally situations high in external drive). Since these two kinds of anxiety are conceived as independent, it is possible to separate four basic achievement-anxiety personality types: (1) facilitators, (2) debilitators, (3) high-affecteds (individuals high on both types of anxiety), and (4) non-affecteds (individuals low on both).

That this formulation is not necessarily a substitute for the Yerkes-Dodson Law, however, is shown in an experiment by Munz and Smouse (1968), who found that the relative performance of a group of students in an examination could be best accounted for by arranging the mean scores of the four anxiety-achievement types according to an inverted-U curve (Fig. 12.4). Such an assumption was necessary to explain why the facilitators and high-affecteds had higher scores than both the debilitators and non-affecteds. This inverted-U hypothesis was specially tested, and confirmed in a subsequent experiment (Sweeney *et al.*, 1970).

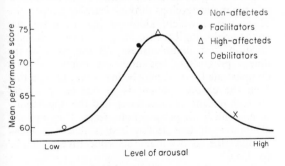

Fig. 12.4. Achievement test performance as a function of theoretical level of arousal (*from* Munz and Smouse, 1968)

Table 2.4. Higher-order Factor Loadings of Several Drive and Anxiety Measures (*from* Farley, 1968)

Variable	Second-order Factors	
	I	II
Nervousness self-rating	0·04	−0·41
Anxiety self-rating	0·12	−0·20
Drive self-rating	−0·31	−0·12
MAS	0·08	−0·45
Heron Maladjustment	0·64	0·13
Bendig Emotionality	0·52	−0·24
Heron Sociability	−0·11	−0·58
Bendig Social E-I	0·28	0·57
Brengelmann Drive	0·16	−0·06
Edwards n Achievement	0·20	−0·34
MPI-Lie	−0·08	−0·31
Marlowe-Crowne SD	−0·40	−0·28
Edwards SD	−0·62	0·23

(d) RELATIONSHIP TO NEUROTICISM AND EXTRAVERSION

The MAS and other 'anxiety' scales of this kind have been criticised by Eysenck (1967) for confounding what he sees as the two major orthogonal dimensions of personality. Anxiety scores are generally found to correlate highly with neuroticism, but also to load significantly on the extraversion-introversion dimension, high anxiety being associated with the introversion end of the continuum.

Recent support for this two-dimensional analysis of anxiety comes from a study by Farley (1968) who factor analysed a number of questionnaires and rating scales purporting to measure anxiety and drive, along with certain other 'marker' personality variables. Rotation by the Hendrickson-White procedure yielded two higher-order factors which corresponded closely to the familiar dimensions of neuroticism and extraversion (Table 12.4).

Studies of the relationships between E, N, and task performance are also consistent with the hypothesis that anxiety and drive are located on an axis between neuroticism and introversion. For example, performance on ability test items tends to show an inverted-U relationship with N scores, and optimal level of N depending on the perceived importance of the test, and the motivational value of the instructions (Eysenck, 1967). Similarly, studies involving the E dimension indicate that there is an optimum level of cortical arousal for learning and task performance which is a joint function of subject-arousal (introversion) and levels of environmental arousal-value, e.g. white noise, time of day (Corcoran, 1965; Eysenck, 1967).

Although there are often advantages in keeping these variables separate, they can also be considered simultaneously in their effect upon performance.

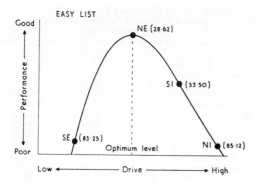

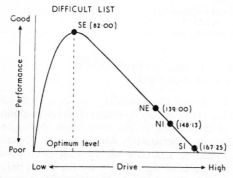

Fig. 12.5. Paired-associate learning performance as a function of drive and least difficulty (*from* McLaughlin and Eysenck, 1967)

For example, McLaughlin and Eysenck (1967) divided subjects into groups of neurotic-extraverts, neurotic-introverts, stable-extraverts, and stable-introverts, and tested them on either an easy or difficult list of paired associates. It was hypothesised that the optimum drive for the easy list would be higher than that for the difficult list, drive being defined by ordering the four groups of subjects on a theoretical continuum from *SE*, through *SI* and *NE*, to *NI*. As predicted, and in accordance with the Yerkes-Dodson model, results showed that in going from the easy to the difficult task the optimum performance level was shifted towards the low drive end of the continuum (Fig. 12.5).

Thus, the evidence suggests that the Hull-Spence concepts of drive and anxiety fall on an axis between Eysenck's dimensions of neuroticism (activation) and introversion (cortical arousal), although possibly closer to the former. The term 'anxiety' is a concept of the same order as *N* and *E* in that it is normally used to refer to between-subject differences. On the other hand, drive, activation, and arousal can all be used to refer either to between-subject differences or within-subject differences, or the resultant of variations arising from both these

sources. Apart from high-anxiety subjects as measured by the MAS, clinically diagnosed 'anxiety states' have also been found to fall within the neurotic-introvert (dysthymic) quadrant of this two-dimensional system (Eysenck, 1960a).

(*e*) SCHIZOPHRENIA

Several accounts of schizophrenia formulated within the framework of Hull-Spence learning theory have appeared. They have, in common, a view of the disorder as resulting from the incapacitating effects of abnormally high drive, but they differ in certain theoretical details.

Mednick (1958) reviews evidence that the behaviour of acute schizophrenics (in common with that of severe anxiety neuroses) can be reliably distinguished from that of normals in three ways—They

1. acquire conditioned responses more readily;
2. show greater stimulus generalisation; and
3. have difficulty in performing efficiently in complex situations, although doing at least as well as normals on tasks of low complexity.

All these characteristics, he says, would be predicted of a group working under very high drive. Mednick goes on to propose a theory of the acute schizophrenic 'break' in terms of the reciprocal augmentation of anxiety and generalisation following a precipitating event in the life of an individual highly susceptible to anxiety. This 'vicious spiralling' of drive pushes previously remote responses beyond the threshold of evocation, resulting in a loss of the ability to discriminate stimuli and the disruption of organised behaviour.

In Mednick's theory, the transition from the acute to the chronic phases of the schizophrenic illness is viewed as a secondary process involving the reinforcement, through anxiety reduction, of remote responses (e.g. irrelevant thoughts). Thus, the chronic schizophrenic develops through learning a repertoire of responses which, although inappropriate, are anxiety-reducing because they remove disturbing ideation from consciousness. As the term of the illness progresses, less and less emotionality is demonstrated, but 'it may be important to note that even the chronic patient is in one sense a very anxious patient. He has never had the opportunity to extinguish his pre-psychotic fears. They are still elicitable; all that is required is that one break through the schizophrenic's "associative curtain".' (p. 324).

Broen and Storms (1961, 1966) have produced a similar account of schizophrenic disorganisation, utilising the concept of drive as an energiser of

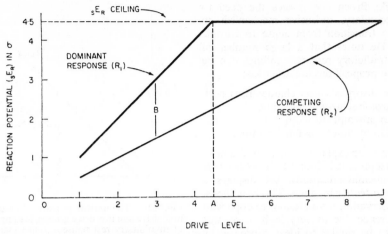

Fig. 12.6. Theoretical effects of drive level on reaction potentials of dominant
and competing responses (*from* Broen and Storms, 1961)

response hierarchies within a Hullian framework, but proposing the additional concept of *response-strength ceiling*. This implies that when the dominant response in a given situation has reached ceiling as a result of increased drive, then further increases of drive will have the effect of raising the relative strength of *competing responses* (Fig. 12.6). As a variety of different responses approach ceiling, their probabilities of evocation become nearly equal and a partial randomisation of the response hierarchy occurs. Schizophrenics are postulated to have lower average response-strength ceilings than normals (Fig. 12.7) and are therefore more susceptible to this ceiling effect.

Broen and Storms give reasons for preferring the response *ceiling* interpretation of drive decrements in both normal and abnormal subjects over the threshold theories of Spence and Mednick. In particular, they argue that, while the threshold theory accounts adequately for the performance decrements known to occur under very high drive, it takes the ceiling

theory to explain experimentally observed decrements occurring with less extreme drive levels but very high habit strength.

Some experiments involving schizophrenic patients have been conducted within the framework of this theory. Broen and colleagues (1963) showed that increased drive defined by dynanometer grip led to decrements in perceptual discrimination in two groups of psychiatric patients, and Broen and Storms (1964) showed this decrement to be greater in chronic schizophrenics than in normals. Storms and co-workers (1967) obtained associations to neutral and anxiety words under relaxed and time pressure conditions from each of 40 schizophrenics, 32 neurotics, and 27 normals, on two successive days. Schizophrenics and neurotics were less stable than normals in their associations, and schizophrenics were less stable than neurotics in their response to anxiety words. Time pressure made schizophrenics even less stable in their associations, but neurotics became more stable.

The results of all these experiments were interpreted as supporting the response-ceiling hypothesis concerning the mechanism involved in the schizophrenic deficit, although it seems that they are also consistent with other similar formulations, not least the Yerkes-Dodson model. Assuming that schizophrenics start off with a higher level of subject-based drive than either normals or neurotics, it is in accord with our three-dimensional model that increases in environmental and task-based drive, such as occurred in these experiments, should push the performance of this group further into the supraoptimal area than either of the other two groups.

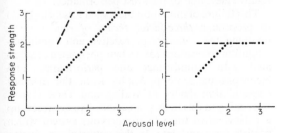

Fig. 12.7. Relative strengths of dominant and competing responses in (left) normal and (right) schizophrenic subjects (*from* Broen and Storms, 1966)

Like Mednick, Broen (1966) sees the need to postulate a secondary, defensive mechanism to account for the transition from acute to chronic schizophrenia. He notes that a large number of apparently contradictory research findings can be reconciled if two propositions are accepted:

1. that response disorganisation characterises both acute and chronic schizophrenics, and
2. that chronics attempt to cope with response disorganisation by observing fewer stimuli.

Only thus can it be explained why, for example, the chronic schizophrenic is found to be *distractible* in some experimental situations, yet displays a *narrower focus of attention* in others. This hypothesis, that reduced observation is an attempt to cope with response interference due to very high drive, was acknowledged to be similar to ideas expressed by other writers including Freeman (1960) and Zahn *et al.* (1963), and supported by them experimentally.

3. Reminiscence

(*a*) DESCRIPTION AND MEASUREMENT

When massed practice on a task is resumed after a period of rest, a considerable improvement in performance is frequently observed compared with the level of performance immediately preceding the rest period. This phenomenon is called reminiscence, and is normally measured by taking the difference between performance at the end of one practice session and performance at the beginning of the next practice session.

(*b*) KIMBLE'S INHIBITION THEORY

Kimble (1949, 1950) outlined certain deductions from Hullian theory according to which reminiscence should constitute a measure of drive. According to this theory, massed practice generates reactive inhibition, I_R, a fatigue-like product which progressively cancels out the positive drive, D, operative in the situation. After a certain duration of pactice, the critical point is reached where $I_R = D$, and an involuntary rest pause (IRP) ensues. During this rest pause I_R dissipates, and when it has fallen sufficiently below the level of D performance is restarted. This stop-start cycle continues until a longer, 'programmed' rest pause is introduced, which allows I_R to dissipate more completely. Since I_R is equivalent to D once the critical level has been passed, reminiscence ought to be a direct measure of drive, provided the rest period was long enough to allow most of the I_R to dissipate. Fig. 12.8 illustrates the theoretical growth of I_R in high and low drive

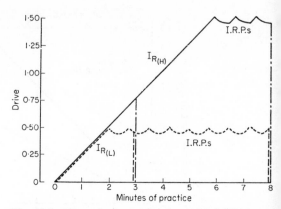

Fig. 12.8. Theoretical growth of reactive inhibition in high drive and low drive groups, leading to the occurrence of involuntary rest pauses (*from* Eysenck and Maxwell, 1961)

groups (or situations), leading to the occurrence of IRPs.

(*c*) EYSENCK'S THREE-FACTOR THEORY

This general hypothesis linking reminiscence and motivation was apparently well supported in a series of experiments in which reminiscence on the pursuit rotor task was compared for groups of subjects working under different levels of situation-induced drive (Eysenck and Maxwell, 1961; Eysenck and Willett, 1961; Willett and Eysenck, 1962; Eysenck, 1964; Farley, 1966). In addition to confirming the prediction that high-drive subjects would show higher reminiscence, these experiments also went a considerable way towards specifying the conditions under which the effects of drive could be optimally observed (Fig. 12.9). Contrary to prediction from the Hull-Kimble inhibition theory, however, these experiments consistently showed that the higher reminiscence scores of the high-drive subjects resulted not from the depression of pre-rest performance but from a relative elevation of post-rest performance.

This failure of inhibition theory led Eysenck (1965) to propose a *three-factor theory of reminiscence*, retaining the concepts of reactive and condition-inhibition to account for certain phenomena associated with reminiscence and performance, and incorporating some principles from the memory consolidation theory of Walker and Tarte (1963). According to this theory, an associative event sets up a perseverative trace in the nervous system which persists for some time. In this active phase, during which permanent memory is laid down, there is a degree of temporary inhibition of recall that serves

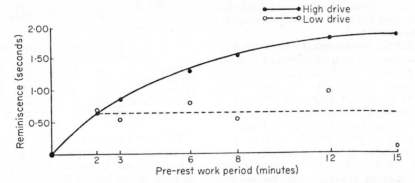

Fig. 12.9. Reminiscence in high-drive and low-drive groups as a function of length of pre-rest work period (*from* Willett and Eysenck, 1962)

to protect the consolidating trace against disruption. High arousal at the time of the associative event is postulated to result in a more intensely active trace process, which leads to superior ultimate memory, but also to a greater temporary inhibition against immediate recall. Support for this theory as it applies to verbal learning has been provided in numerous experiments demonstrating the predicted interaction between level of arousal and time of recall in determining paired-associate learning performance (McLean. 1969).

In the new theory, Eysenck suggests that whether reminiscence is due primarily to consolidation or to inhibition depends on certain characteristics of the task in question. Reminiscence on tasks that involve a great deal of new learning, those that are self-paced, and subject to drive-level manipulation, is hypothesised to reflect primarily the process of consolidation. On the other hand, with tasks that are not heavily dependent on new learning, those which are experimenter paced, and in which drive level is less implicated, reminiscence is hypothesised to result largely from the dissipation of I_R. Verbal learning and pursuit rotor are tasks of the former variety, whereas reaction time and vigilance fall into the latter group.

To summarise, there is good evidence that reminiscence can be used as a measure of motivation, but two separate mechanisms are apparently involved: (1) a negative motivational process (inhibition), which may depress performance at the end of a practice session, and (2) a positive motivational effect (arousal) which leads to greater consolidation of learning, and therefore a relative elevation of performance following a period of rest. Which of these processes will account for the major part of the variation in overall reminiscence scores is hypothesised to depend upon the nature of the task concerned.

(*d*) NEUROTICISM AND EXTRAVERSION

The consolidation explanation of reminiscence draws attention to the importance of the length of the rest period in mediating the size, and even the direction, of the relationship between personality and motivational variables, and reminiscence scores. With relatively short periods of rest, reminiscence scores would be expected to be lower for high drive subjects and situations than for subjects working under low drive, because of the interfering effect of arousal on immediate performance. On the other hand, with longer periods of rest the high-drive subjects should show superior learning, and therefore higher reminiscence scores. This hypothesis is illustrated in Fig. 12.10. The situation is, however, complicated a lot further by the Yerkes-Dodson

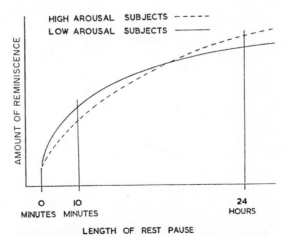

Fig. 12.10. Theoretical relationships between reminiscence, arousal and length of rest pause (*from* Clark, 1967)

Law, in that if drive levels are supraoptimal, learning and performance on tasks that are complex may also be expected to deteriorate.

The reminiscence phenomenon would seem to provide a good example of a situation in which it is particularly profitable to divide the concepts of drive or general arousal into the independent components of autonomic activation and cortical arousal preferred by Eysenck. The tasks with which reminiscence effects have been most frequently studied (verbal learning and pursuit rotor), are those in which consolidation of learning is attributed the primary role, therefore it might be expected that variations in cortical arousal (extraversion-introversion) would be most relevant to this consolidation process.

Since introverts are hypothesised to show higher cortical arousal than extraverts, the prediction based on consolidation theory would be that extraverts should show higher reminiscence scores than introverts when relatively short rest periods are involved, but that this relationship would be reversed with longer periods of rest. This interaction has been demonstrated most strikingly with a paired-associate learning task (Howarth and Eysenck, 1968, Fig. 12.11). A slight but significant interaction between extraversion and length of rest in determining the amount of reminiscence, in the predicted direction, has also been reported for the pursuit rotor task (Eysenck, 1960b). Claridge (1960) failed to find consistent differences in pursuit-rotor reminiscence scores between groups of dysthymic and hysteric patients, but since he used rest periods of ten minutes it is difficult to predict which way the difference should have gone.

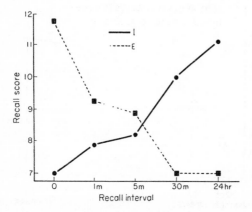

Fig. 12.11. Paired associate recall as a function of extraversion-intraversion and recall interval (*from* Howarth and Eysenck, 1968)

Table 12.5. Pursuit Rotor Reminiscence Scores (*From* Claridge, 1960)

	N	Score I Mean	S.D.	Score II Mean	S.D.
Normals	16	13·7	8·51	14·8	11·53
Dysthymics	16	8·3	7·91	6·2	14·07
Hysterics	16	8·0	9·76	12·3	9·67
Schizophrenics	16	1·9	7·62	3·9	13·53

The situation with respect to neuroticism is apparently more complicated. Eysenck (1967) has suggested that, 'it may be possible to regard N as a motivational variable exerting a positive or negative effect on learning or memory in accordance with the Yerkes-Dodson Law but not affecting the consolidation process in the manner characteristic of the cortical excitation associated with introversion'. Thus, with groups of normal subjects N has been found to correlate positively with pursuit rotor reminiscence (Eysenck, 1956) or to show no significant correlation (Eysenck, 1962), yet clinically neurotic subjects (both dysthymics and hysterics) have been found to yield lower reminiscence scores than normals (Claridge, 1960, Table 12.5; Grassi, 1968).

(e) SCHIZOPHRENIA

If schizophrenics are characterised by abnormally high drive or arousal, as the evidence reviewed in the previous sections suggests, then they may be expected to show abnormally low reminiscence with relatively short periods of rest but higher than normal reminiscence scores following longer rest periods. In general, the experimental evidence supports this hypothesis. Studies by Broadhurst and Broadhurst (1969) and Claridge (1960; Fig. 12.12, Table 12.5) have demonstrated a virtual absence of pursuit rotor reminiscence effects with short periods of rest which do produce significant reminiscence scores in normal subjects. Experiments by Ley (1961), Huston and Shakow (1948) and Rachman (1963; Fig. 12.13) have shown that with longer periods of rest (24 hours or more) schizophrenics do show a strong reminiscence effect, often higher than that obtained with normal subjects. In the field of verbal learning, as early as 1917 Hull reported that psychotics showed greater retention than normals when tested a week after learning.

Clark (1967) studied pursuit rotor reminiscence as a function of arousal and duration of rest *within* a group of 127 chronic schizophrenics. His main hypothesis was that those schizophrenics who were high in arousal would show greater reminiscence after a 24-hour rest period than after 10 minutes

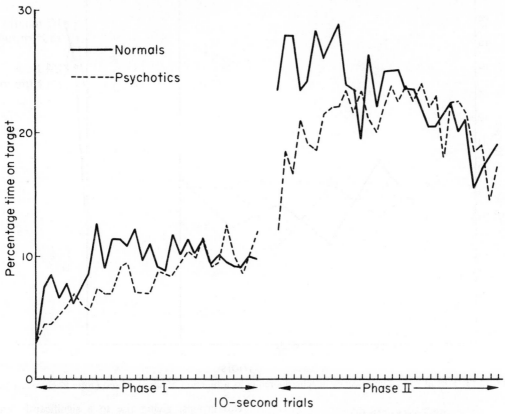

Fig. 12.12. Pursuit rotor reminiscence in normals and psychotics (*from* Claridge, 1960)

rest, while the reverse would hold true for those schizophrenics classified as low in arousal (*see* Fig. 12.10). Subjects were divided into low and high arousal groups on the basis of two-flash threshold scores, low TFTs being taken as indicating high arousal, and vice versa. All subjects were then given three five-minute blocks of massed practice on the pursuit rotor, the first and second blocks being separated by 10 minutes rest, while the second and third blocks were separated by 24 hours. Results showed clearly the predicted crossover of reminiscence scores for the two groups of schizophrenics as a function of length of rest (Fig. 12.14). In addition, it was found that arousal as measured by TFT was significantly correlated with ratings of degree of social withdrawal, and breadth of attention as measured by a card-sorting task.

An experiment by Bleke (1955) throws some light on the nature of processes that interfere with immediate performance in schizophrenic subjects. Groups of schizophrenics, subdivided according to whether their premorbid adjustment was good or poor, were compared with normals on a verbal-motor learning task. For half the subjects in each group learning took place under a *punishment* condition in which the word 'wrong' appeared whenever an error was made, while the others were tested under a *reward* condition with the word 'right' following each correct response. The poor premorbid schizophrenic group, tested under conditions of censure, showed significantly greater delayed reminiscence effects relative to all other groups. This result was taken as supporting the hypothesis that poor premorbid schizophrenics are unusually sensitive to censure, to which they react with 'more interfering and fewer adaptive responses'.

Venables and Tizard (1956) and Venables (1959) compared reminiscence scores of schizophrenics, normals, and depressives on a continuous, examiner-paced reaction time task. Their procedure involved two practice periods of ten minutes separated by a rest period of one minute. It was found that during the first practice session, performance of the schizophrenic group fell off faster than either of the other

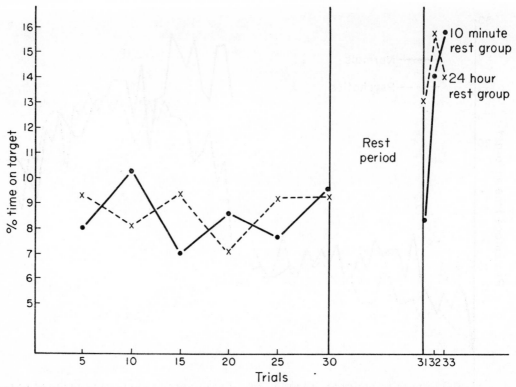

Fig. 12.13. Pursuit rotor reminiscence in schizophrenics as a function of length of rest (*from* Rachman, 1963)

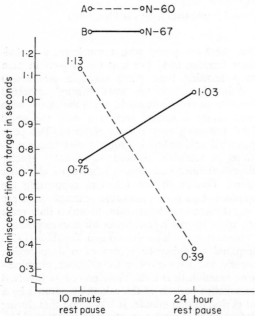

Fig. 12.14. Pursuit rotor reminiscence in low arousal (*A*) and high arousal (*B*) groups of schizophrenics as a function of length of rest (*from* Clark, 1967)

two groups, giving rise to a significantly greater reminiscence effect. With faster pacing of the task, however, the depressives and normals showed the same rate of decline in pre-rest performance as the schizophrenic group. These results seem better accounted for in terms of differential rates of the development of I_R, and are consistent with the Yerkes-Dodson model if is assumed that the schizophrenic group is one of comparatively high subject-drive, such that the resultant overall drive is supraoptimal for this group even with the slower task pacing condition.

(*f*) MENTAL RETARDATES

Differences in reminiscence scores on the pursuit rotor have also been reported between normals and mental retardates (Ellis *et al.*, 1960; Jones and Ellis, 1962; Wright and Hearn, 1964). In all of these studies reminiscence was found to be lower in retardates than normals, and the interpretation was that retardates accumulate less I_R because they are disinhibited to a greater extent by environmental distractions. In view of the findings of Eysenck and his associates concerning the importance of the consolidation factor in pursuit rotor learning, this inhibition account is unlikely to be adequate, and experiments designed to choose between these theories are indicated.

Matheny (1968) reasoned that if the inhibition hypothesis was valid, there should be differences in degrees of distractibility *within* the retardate population which would be associated with differences in the amount of I_R accumulated. Forty retarded children were divided into distractible and non-distractible groups on the basis of discrepancies between their general IQ and digit-span performance (the subtest assumed to load highest on an 'attention' factor). Results showed both a lower rate of acquisition of the pursuit rotor skill and less reminiscence with the distractible group compared to the non-distractibles. This was taken as supporting the disinhibition theory of the low reminiscence scores frequently found with retardates, although Matheny concedes that the results might equally well be interpreted in terms of differential arousal between the groups.

SOCIALLY-BASED MOTIVATIONAL CONCEPTS

1. Achievement Motivation

(a) DESCRIPTION AND MEASUREMENT

The concept of 'achievement motivation' came into widespread popularity with the work of McClelland and colleagues (1953). A descriptive definition is provided by Heckhausen (1967): 'the striving to increase, or keep as high as possible, one's own capability in all activities in which a standard of excellence is thought to apply, and where the execution of such activities can, therefore, either succeed or fail'.

Although a number of questionnaires for measuring achievement motivation have been produced, operational definition of the concept has, for the most part, been based on the analysis of fantasy elicited by TAT-like stimuli. The three most widely used projective measures of achievement motivation have been the McClelland-Atkinson test based on the TAT (McClelland *et al.* 1953), the Iowa Picture Interpretation Test (Hurley, 1955), and the French Test of Insight (French, 1958). They have all been criticised on the grounds of their frequently reported failure to show adequate reliability. Although interscorer and score-rescore correlations are reported to be quite high, test-retest and split-half reliability coefficients are generally low or even insignificant, and the various projective measures are largely uncorrelated (Klinger, 1966, Weinstein, 1969).

(b) NEED ACHIEVEMENT AND PERFORMANCE

The extent to which these measures predict performance on various tasks (often regarded as a form of validation) is examined by Klinger (1966). He found that only about half the published relationships between need achievement and performance reached an acceptable level of significance. Furthermore, the pattern of positive evidence did not support the assumption that the appearance of achievement imagery directly reflects the arousal of a motivational state. The addition of perceptual, cognitive, and developmental variables (e.g. modelling processes, sophistication about achievement situations) was shown to render the empirical evidence more theoretically tractable.

In view of the lack of stability and consistency displayed by these projective measures, it is perhaps not surprising that relationships with performance criteria do not reliably occur. There is, however, another possible reason why achievement motivation has often been reported to show no relationship with task performance, and this concerns the regular failure to consider non-linear relationships such as those implied by the Yerkes-Dodson Law. As Atkinson and Feather (1966) state, 'if efficiency of performance is decreased after a certain intensity of motivation has been reached, then much of the earlier work in which performance at particular tasks is the dependent variable must be thoughtfully re-examined. For all this work, at least within the programme of *n* achievement, has been interpreted on the premise of a positive monotonic relationship between strength of goal-directed tendency and level of performance' (p. 351).

(c) APPROACH-SUCCESS AND AVOID-FAILURE MOTIVES

Atkinson and Feather (1966) have produced a rather more sophisticated theory of the relationship of achievement motivation to task performance, in which prediction is based on the interaction of three major classes of variables:

1. personality dispositions;
2. expectations regarding the probabilities of success and failure; and
3. the incentive values of success and failure.

It will be seen that these three groups of variables correspond roughly to the subject, task, and environmental dimensions discussed earlier in the chapter. Atkinson and Feather separate the variability due to personality into two components: *achievement orientation*, which is measured by the TAT and *fear of failure*, measured by test-anxiety scales such as the Text Anxiety Questionnaire (Mandler and Cowen, 1958). The achievement-orientated personality is said to be attracted to competitive activities and is most challenged by tasks of intermediate difficulty. The failure-threatened individual avoids competition and defends himself against anxiety by undertaking tasks that are either so easy that success is assured, or so difficult that he cannot be blamed for failure. These two variables are treated as partly independent, and it is suggested that the best predictor of performance is the difference between scores on need achievement and fear-of-failure. The Success-Failure Inventory (SFI) was designed by Guevara (1965) as a questionnaire measure of both of these variables.

Unfortunately for the Atkinson theory, various measures of risk-taking preference are poorly correlated one with another, and are generally found to be unrelated to achievement motivation (Weinstein, 1969). In addition, the correlation between approach-success and avoid-failure motives is as high as can be expected considering the unreliability of the measures involved, so the evidence suggests these are merely converse ways of conceptualising the same underlying motive (McReynolds and Guevara, 1967).

(d) THE ROLE OF SOCIAL LEARNING

A number of studies, employing both projective and questionnaire measures, point to the importance of social factors as antecedents of high achievement motivation. Evidence that need achievement is related to parental attitudes regarding independence and achievement is reviewed by Heckhausen (1967), who also notes that religious affiliation is a relevant factor (Jews and Protestants tend to be more achievement-orientated than Catholics). First-born children have been found to be higher in achievement motivation than later-borns (Rhine, 1968; Munz et al., 1968), although this relationship may hold only for middle-class families.

(e) NEUROTICISM AND EXTRAVERSION

Little direct evidence is available concerning the relationship between Atkinson's personality dimensions and those of Eysenck. Atkinson's description of the fear-of-failure tendency does suggest high neuroticism, however, as does the finding of Feather (1961) that persons high in failure-anxiety show 'atypical' changes in aspiration following success and failure, as well as 'other non-adaptive behavioural trends, including dogged persistence when there is little obvious chance to succeed'. An experiment by Bartmann (1963) showing that under stress such as time pressure, performance of achievement orientated subjects tended to improve, while failure-threatened individuals tended to show deterioration of complex thought processes, also supports the identification of failure-threat with neuroticism.

On the other hand, Eysenck (1967) gives theoretical reasons for expecting that achievement-orientation would be an introverted characteristic. Introverts would be expected to introject the achievement values of our society more than extraverts, and their higher levels of cortical excitation make them better equipped for prolonged periods of work. He cites some experimental work that generally supports this hypothesis.

Against this must be set the finding mentioned above, that achievement-orientation and fear-of-failure are apparently polar opposites rather than independent dimensions. The only way to accommodate all these propositions simultaneously would be to suggest that the Atkinson dimension runs from *NE* (failure-threat) to *SI* (achievement-orientation) in the Eysenck system, but much more evidence would be needed before this hypothesis could be regarded as anywhere near established.

Rudin (1968) reports a study in which death rates attributed to psychological factors were predicted by international motive differentials. National motive strengths had been assessed earlier by McClelland on the basis of a content analysis of books and stories prescribed for children's reading about the year 1925 in a sample of 22 temperate, Westernised nations. On the basis of correlations

Table 12.6.   Correlations (rho) Between 1925 Motives and 1950 Death Rate Clusters, Death Rates, and Other Behaviour
N (number of countries) = 16
(*from* Rudin, 1968)

Behaviour	Motive	
	Need for achievement	Need for power
Aggressiveness cluster	−0·11	0·42
Murder	−0·03	0·22
Suicide	−0·09	0·52
Cirrhosis of liver	−0·31	0·13
Inhibition cluster	0·66	−0·02
Ulcers	0·57	0·20
Hypertension	0·52	−0·18
Film attendance	0·55	−0·05
Books published	−0·48	−0·02

Table 12.7. Comparison of Manic-depressives and Controls on Six Experimental Measures
(*from* Becker, 1960)

Measures	Manic Depressives (N = 24)			Controls (N = 30)			p
	Median	x	SD	Median	x	SD	
v Achievement	4·83	4·86	1·00	4·23	4·16	0·67	<0·02
F scale	4·62	4·57	0·87	4·17	4·09	0·83	<0·05
TFI scale	4·29	4·19	0·73	3·76	3·67	0·67	<0·01
n Achievement	4·25	5·38	3·98	5·00	5·77	4·68	0·88
Xs-in-Circles	562·00	571·17	122·28	560·00	573·83	114·92	0·83
Additions	505·00	534·58	230·17	388·50	497·13	220·00	0·37

Table 12.8. Items in Success-Failure Inventory (SFI), Showing Keys for Success Attainment (S)
and Failure Avoidance (FA) Scales, and Differences in Percentages of 'True'
Answers Given by Normals and Schizophrenics
(*from* McReynolds and Guevara, 1967)

Item	Keying		Percentage of 'True' responses		χ^2
	True	False	Normals (N = 103)	Schizophrenics (N = 136)	
I have a tendency to give up easily when I meet difficult problems.	FA	S	14	46	28·75***
I like to fool around with new ideas even if they turn out later to have been a total waste of time.	S	FA	75	54	10·43**
I am ambitious.	S	FA	88	58	26·12***
It's better to stick by what you have than to try new things you don't really know about.	FA	S	20	57	31·80***
Failure is not a disgrace when one has tried his best.		FA	96	86	5·82*
It is better to be an observer than a participant because one learns more and gets into less trouble.	FA	S	5	47	48·85***
Success is too transient an experience for a person to sacrifice much to obtain it.		S	16	32	8·12**
One of my primary or major aims in life is to accomplish something that would make people proud of me.	S		72	68	0·38
Any man who is able and willing to work hard has a good chance of succeeding.		FA	92	82	4·20*
I would rather remain free from commitments to others than risk serious disappointment or failure later.	FA		34	66	24·25***
When I am in a group or organization, I like to be appointed or selected for office.	S	FA	70	31	35·23***
I have a very strong desire to be a success in the world.	S		73	70	0·25
I like to follow routines and avoid risks.	FA	S	30	65	29·29***
Great ambitiousness usually brings great accomplishments.	S		67	60	1·13
I don't like to work on a problem unless there is the possibility of coming out with a clear cut and unambiguous answer.		S	34	68	26·68***
I dislike failure so much that I abstain from participating in competitive situations.	FA	S	8	38	27·80***
I sometimes keep on at a thing until others lose patience with me.	S		50	43	1·18
I used to like it very much when one of my papers was read to the class in school.	S	FA	64	60	0·47
I keep out of trouble at all costs.	FA		38	62	13·88***
I enjoy competitive sports.	S	FA	93	64	26·31***
It is better never to expect much; in that way you are rarely disappointed.	FA	S	35	59	13·43***
I like to avoid responsibilities and obligations.	FA	S	11	48	38·45***

*$p < 0.05$ **$p < 0.01$ ***$p < 0.001$

among 'psychogenic death rates', Rudin identified two clusters which he described as 'deaths due to aggressiveness and acting out' (murder, suicide, alcoholism), and 'deaths due to inhibition' (ulcers and hypertension). International death rates in the aggressiveness cluster in the year 1950 were apparently predicted by the 1925 need-for-power scores, while death rates in the inhibition cluster were predicted by need-achievement scores (Table 12.6). Since psychosomatic disorders are associated with introverted neurotics (Eysenck, 1960) these results are consistent with the hypothesis that need achievement is related to introversion. They would be far more convincing, however, if it could be demonstrated that within-nation variation in the strength of these motives also predicts the incidence of 'psychogenic death'.

(b) MANIC-DEPRESSIVES

McClelland *et al.* (1953) distinguished *value* achievement, which is a conscious valuing of achievement in response to parental demands, from *need* achievement, which is concerned with living up to an internalised standard of excellence. A series of studies by Becker (1960), Spielberger *et al.* (1963), and Becker and Nichols (1964) has indicated that, in general, male manic-depressives show the characteristics supposed to be associated with high value achievement (self-reported achievement values, conformity and authoritarianism), but do not differ from non-psychiatric controls on either need achievement or task performance itself (e.g. Table 12.7). More recent studies, however, have shown that this finding does not generalise to ordinary depressives (Katkin *et al.*, 1966), or to female manic-depressives (Becker and Altrocchi, 1968).

(g) SCHIZOPHRENICS

Following the suggestion of Rodnick and Garmezy (1957) that schizophrenics are characterised by extreme sensitivity to social censure, McReynolds and Guevara (1967) tested the hypothesis that they would be relatively more highly motivated to avoid failure than to achieve success as compared with normals. A sample of 136 hospitalised schizophrenics, 103 normals. and 52 neurotics, were administered the Success-Failure-Inventory. Table 12.8 shows the percentages of normals and schizophrenics responding 'Yes' to each item, chi-square values reflecting the differences between these two samples, and indicates the way in which the items were keyed for approach-success and avoid-failure scores. The interest of the authors was in the difference between these two scores, and means of these differences are

Table 12.9. D* Scores of Samples of Normals, Neurotics and Schizophrenics (*from* McReynolds and Guevara, 1967)

Sample	N	D	
		M	σ
Normals			
Firemen	50	10·16	4·07
Aides	18	10·22	5·47
Students	35	11·63	4·64
Total	103	10·67	4·28
Neurotics	52	4·50	6·86
Schizophrenics			
Chronic	72	0·83	5·36
Less chronic, active	32	1·94	6·97
Less chronic, remitted	32	4·44	6·66
Total	136	1·94	6·26

D* = Difference between approach-success and avoid-failure total scores.

shown for the various groups in Table 12.9. As predicted, the schizophrenic samples all manifested greater relative failure-avoidance than the normals. Furthermore, active schizophrenics evidenced greater failure-avoidance than did remitted schizophrenics, who showed scores similar to the group of neurotics (classified mostly as anxiety and depressive neuroses). Thus, the authors suggest that these difference, *D*, scores can be used as an inverse measure of the degree of psychiatric illness.

2. Level of Aspiration

(a) DESCRIPTION AND MEASUREMENT

In the classical level-of-aspiration experiment, the subject works for a number of trials at a task that permits different levels of performance, is informed of his score after each trial, and is required to set a goal for the succeeding trial. The possible scores that can be obtained from data gathered in this way are discussed by Lewin and co-workers (1944), and the most important of these are shown diagrammatically in Fig. 12.15.

The score most frequently studied is the *goal discrepancy* (GD), which is the difference between the level of aspiration on a given trial and performance on the previous trial. The difference between the level of aspiration on a given trial and the subsequent performance on that same trial is called the *attainment discrepancy* (AD), and amounts to a measure of success/failure. If, in addition, the subject is required to estimate his level of performance on the previous trial, then it is possible to calculate a *judgement discrepancy* (JD), the difference between actual and judged performance

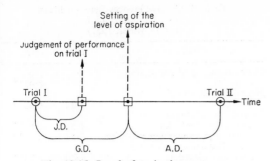

Fig. 12.15. Level-of-aspiration measures

J.D. = judgement discrepancy
    = difference between what you did get and what you
       think you got
G.D. = goal discrepancy
    = difference between what you did get and what you
       think you are going to get
A.D. = attainment discrepancy
    = difference between what you think you are going to
       get and what you do, in fact, get
(*from* Lewin *et al.*, 1944)

on a given trial. Secondary measures that have occasionally been considered include the *affective discrepancy* (the difference between GD and JD), the index of *flexibility* (the sum of all shifts in aspiration level), and the index of *typicality of response* (the number of times aspiration is raised after success and lowered after failure).

As Inglis (1960) points out, these measures of aspiration level phenomena will have usefulness only in so far as they can be demonstrated to show stability and generality. Reviewing a number of studies in the literature of the previous two decades, he found that split-half and test-retest reliability coefficients were generally quite high (about 0·5 to 0·9), while intercorrelations between aspiration measures based on different tasks were somewhat lower but still quite substantial (0·3 to 0·6). Although the exact nature of the task is apparently not critical in level-of-aspiration studies, the precise wording of the instructions does seem to be very important. Instructions worded in such a way that the subject believes he is being asked about his *expectations* regarding future performance tend to yield more realistic scores (lower GDs and ADs) than instructions which stress *aspirations and goals*.

(b) SOCIAL FACTORS

Level-of-aspiration scores are known to be very sensitive to social effects. For example, providing subjects with information (true or fictional) concerning the relative performance of other individuals or groups varying in prestige can result in a significant elevation of GDs, particularly when these

'anchors' are threatening to self-esteem (Chapman and Volkmann, 1939; Hansche and Gilchrist 1956). Sex and class differences in goal-setting behaviour have been explained in terms of differential social pressure toward achievement (Inglis, 1960). The influence of parents was demonstrated by Little and Cohen (1950) who found that a group of thirty asthmatic children who set abnormally high goals had mothers who also set high goals for them compared with the mothers of control children. Gibson (1958) studied the families of 39 manic-depressives and 17 controls, and interpreted his results as suggesting that the manic-depressives tended to have families who had trained the patient for upward mobility as a means of compensating for their low status.

(c) NEUROTICISM AND EXTRAVERSION

There is a considerable body of evidence indicating that individuals who characteristically show low positive GDs tend to be more stable and efficient in their work than subjects who show either high positive or negative GDs. Subjects adopting either of the latter two strategies have been variously reported to be socially maladjusted, tense and insecure (Sears, 1941; Gruen, 1945), less integrated (Ax, 1947), unstable, (Klugman, 1947, 1948), self-rejecting (Cohen, 1954, Steiner, 1956), poor at work (Jucknat, 1937; Sears, 1941) and disturbed (Subotnik, 1967). All these characteristics, taken together, suggest a picture of the neurotic personality in Eysenck's system.

The results of several experiments have indicated that classifying neurotics along the extraversion-introversion dimension of personality makes for increased precision in the prediction of level-of-aspiration behaviour in neurotic subjects. Eysenck and Himmelweit (1947) compared fifty dysthymic patients (neurotic introverts) with fifty hysterics (neurotic extraverts), using an adaptation of the pursuit rotor called the 'triple tester'. Although the two groups were comparable in age, intelligence, and actual performance on the test, significant differences appeared in several aspiration-level phenomena, particularly the GD and JD measures (Fig. 12.16). These results imply that the aspirations of dysthymics are significantly higher, and their evaluation of previous performance significantly lower, than those of hysterics. Similar results were found by Himmelweit (1947) using a symbol-substitution task and samples of 58 hysterics and 69 dysthymics. The goal-setting behaviour of the hysterics was described as more 'objective' and 'flexible' than either the normals or dysthymics. The dysthymics showed wide deviations from actual performance in their

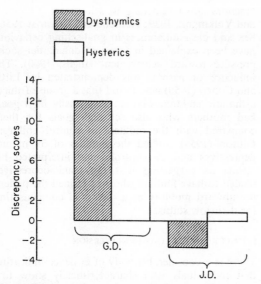

Fig. 12.16. Goal discrepancy and judgement discrepancy scores of dysthymic and hysteric patients (*from* Eysenck, 1947)

Table 12.11.   Differences Between Mean Goal Discrepancies (*from* Miller, 1951)

Groups	Diff.	t
Neurasthenics and conversion hysterics	2·57	8·43**
Neurasthenics and character disorders	1·92	6·62**
Paranoid schizophrenics and conversion hysterics	1·85	4·83**
Normals and conversion hysterics	1·59	5·13**
Paranoid schizophrenics and character disorders	1·20	3·23**
Normals and neurasthenics	0·98	6·33**
Normals and character disorders	0·94	3·24**
Paranoid schizophrenics and neurasthenics	0·72	2·61**
Character disorders and conversion hysterics	0·65	1·65
Normals and paranoid schizophrenics	0·26	0·93

** $p < 0.01$

estimates of both past and future performance, and their indices of flexibility were low. This behaviour was described as 'subjective' and 'rigid'. When motivation was increased by offering incentives, this differentiation of hysterics and dysthymics was accentuated.

Miller (1951) compared four clinical groups and a group of normal controls on a form-board task under conditions designed to be very competitive and ego-involving. Neurasthenics (neurotic-introverts in the Eysenck nomenclature) again produced high, positive GDs, while the character disorder and hysterical groups (Eysenck's neurotic-extraverts) gave negative mean GDs (Tables 12.10 and 12.11).

The conclusion that can be made on the basis of these three studies is that neurotics who are introverted tend to set abnormally high goals for themselves, and evaluate their performance as poor, while neurotics who are extraverted tend to set abnormally low goals, often below the level of previous performance, and thus evaluate their performance as satisfactory.

Table 12.10.   Mean Goal Discrepancies (*from* Miller, 1951)

Group	Mean goal discrepancy	σ_M
Neurasthenics	1·56	0·11
Paranoid schizophrenics	0·84	0·25
Normals	0·58	0·11
Character disorders	−0·36	0·27
Conversion hysterics	−1·01	0·29

Confirmatory data concerned with differences along the extraversion-introversion continuum in normal (non-patient) subjects is provided in studies by Himmelweit (1947), Gately (1954) and Broadbent (1958). Here again, the introverts were found to show higher CDs than extraverts. In a more applied study, Sevransky (1965) found that introverted schoolboys tended to aspire to occupations that were above their ability level, while extraverted schoolboys aspired to occupations that were below their ability level.

Other relevant studies suggest that individuals who might be classified as 'highly driven' (presumably those falling in the neurotic-introvert quadrant) tend to show abnormally high GDs. Raifman (1957) reported that peptic ulcer patients show high GDs, and Berkeley (1952) found that high GDs were associated with an increase in adrenal cortex activity as measured by steroid excretion.

Some experiments, which involve a partial contradiction of the Eysenck and Himmelweit experiments have, however, also been reported. Ausubel and colleagues (1953) did find that high-anxious subjects drawn from the normal population set high initial aspiration levels, but that, following the experience of failure, they eventually lowered their goals to approximate equivalence with the control group. Similarly, Hartogs (1949) found high GDs in anxious subjects drawn from the clinical population, but these subjects reacted to failure by lowering their aspirations below their actual performance level.

Also exceptional are the results of Loeb *et al.* (1964), and Loeb *et al.* (1967) which showed that depressed patients (who fall into Eysenck's dysthymic quadrant) set their goals 'more pessimistically' than non-depressed patients. Their finding that the depressed patients also evaluated their performance as poorer, when in reality it was just as good, is, however, consistent with previous findings. One thing that makes the experiments of Loeb *et al.* difficult to evaluate within this framework is their failure to describe the symptoms displayed by their 'non-depressed patients', so that they can be assigned some position along the extraversion-introversion dimension.

(d) SCHIZOPHRENIA

Attempts to differentiate schizophrenic groups from each other and from normals on level-of-aspiration measures have not proved very successful. Miller (1951) found that his group of paranoid schizophrenics did not differ significantly from normal controls in terms of GD scores (Table 10.11). Jost (1955), using a reaction time task, also failed to find differences in mean GD scores between schizophrenics and normals. He did report greater variance in the GD scores of the schizophrenic group compared to the normals, but this may have been attributable to the fact that the schizophrenics also showed greater variance in their actual performance on the task.

Winder (1952) subdivided a schizophrenic sample into groups of 35 paranoids and 35 non-paranoids, and found a slight tendency for the non-paranoids to show negative ('defeatist') GD scores, while the paranoids showed slightly positive GDs. Although this difference was not statistically significant, the low positive (normal) CGs shown by the paranoid group are congruent with the findings of Miller, while the slightly negative GDs of the non-paranoids seem consistent with the general pattern of withdrawal typically manifested by this group.

(e) INTERNAL VS. EXTERNAL CONTROL OF REINFORCEMENT

The dimension of internal-external control (Rotter, 1966) refers to individual differences in generalised expectancies as to whether outcomes are determined by one's own actions (skill) or are beyond personal control (luck). This 'locus of control' variable has been shown to be highly relevant to achievement-related behaviour, risk-taking and level of aspiration (Lefcourt, 1966). Cautious failure-avoidant strategies have been found to be characteristic of 'externals', while more aggressive achievement striving patterns appear to be more common to 'internals'.

The evidence reviewed by Lefcourt also suggests that perceived locus of control variable may also be useful in explaining the withdrawal and apathy characteristic of certain oppressed and pathological

groups. Several studies are described which indicate that oppressed groups such as the US Negroes are characterised by low expectancies that effort on their own behalf can affect the outcomes regarding goals they value. Cromwell and co-workers (1961) found schizophrenics to be higher in externality than normals, and demonstrated that the performance of schizophrenics deteriorates more markedly, compared to normals, in situations of autonomy (internal control).

(f) SOCIAL MOBILITY

On a more sociological level, the concept of 'mobility striving' is clearly related to achievement motivation and level of aspiration behaviour. Thus, Stacey (1968) reviews evidence of a positive relationship between strength of achievement motivation and intergeneration social mobility, and (1969) reviews the literature concerning the relationship between integration social mobility and mental disorder. Some of the conclusions that he was able to reach on the basis of the empirical evidence were as follows:

1. The downwardly mobile are characterised by a higher incidence of mental disorder than either the stationary or upward mobile, and have the poorest prognosis.

2. Neurosis and psychosomatic disorder are associated with upward mobility, while psychosis, character disorder, alcoholism, suicide, and mental deficiency are associated with downward mobility.

3. There are complex reciprocal relationships between mobility and mental disorder. For example, upward mobility can contribute to the aetiology of anxiety by bringing the individual into contact with unfamiliar life-stresses, but anxiety may also be a cause of ambitious striving and therefore upward mobility. Mental deficiency tends to be a cause of downward mobility, whereas character disorders and alcoholism are more often consequences.

3. The Zeigarnik Effect

(a) DESCRIPTION AND MEASUREMENT

In 1927, Zeigarnik reported that tasks interrupted before completion are better recalled by the subject than those that have been successfully completed. This differential recall of interrupted and completed tasks is called the Zeigarnik Effect, and has normally been measured as the ratio of I/C.

(b) EFFECTS OF EXTERNAL DRIVE

The Zeigarnik phenomenon was quickly adopted as support for Lewin's (1935) notion of enduring tension systems, which is now seen to be related to the theory of memory consolidation. It was subsequently discovered, however, that while this positive Zeigarnik Effect may be expected to occur under conditions of low external motivation, a *reversed* Zeigarnik Effect is likely to appear under conditions of high external drive, ego-involvement, etc. (Heckhausen, 1967). This reversed effect, a superior recall of completed over interrupted tasks, has been variously attributed to 'repression' (Rosenzweig, 1943), 'ego-enhancement' (Lewis and Franklin, 1944), and 'avoidance of anxiety mediators' (Inglis, 1960).

These findings may be regarded as consistent with the Yerkes-Dodson model if is assumed that failure to complete a task has positively motivating effects upon memory, but that the addition of further drive from external sources raises the total motivation level beyond the optimum, thus resulting in a relative impairment of memory for interrupted tasks. Our earlier discussion of the effects of arousal upon memory consolidation would also point to the importance of considering the recall interval in studies of the Ziegarnik Effect.

(c) NEUROTICISM AND EXTRAVERSION

Claeys (1969) was concerned with the interactions between different conditions of external motivation and the Eysenck personality dimensions in determining the direction and magnitude of the Zeigarnik Effect. He proposed that the variations in differential recall of interrupted and completed tasks could best be explained by postulating two processes:

1. a *completion tendency* which appears whenever a task is begun under either formal or informal conditions (high or low external drive), and which favours the recall of interrupted tasks: and

2. a *success factor* which favours the recall of tasks that lead to a good result (completed tasks). The success factor depends on the evaluation of completed and interrupted tasks as good and bad respectively, and is therefore more marked under 'formal' conditions.

Claeys goes on to consider the relevance of the EPI dimensions. Identifying N with general drive level, he hypothesised that high N subjects will have a stronger completion tendency, and will therefore show a more positive Zeigarnik Effect than stable subjects under either formal or informal conditions. Since introverts are 'oversocialized', he argued, they will be preoccupied about whether they are doing well, or not, even under conditions of low external motivation. Thus, they will tend to have a less positive Zeigarnik Effect than extraverts under informal conditions, but will not differ from them under formal conditions.

Using a sample of forty Congolese students, Claeys was able to confirm cross-culturally the positive Zeigarnik Effect under neutral conditions, and the reversed effect under ego-threat (intelligence test) conditions, as well as both the hypotheses concerning the relationships with personality (Fig. 12.17).

(d) SCHIZOPHRENIA

Tamkin (1957) compared 24 hospitalised schizophrenics and 24 normals who were matched on a number of variables, and found that a greater proportion of the schizophrenic group showed the

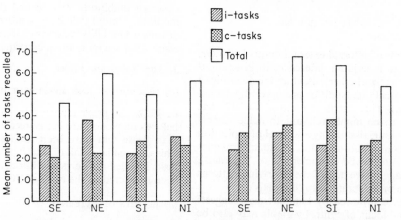

Fig. 12.17. Recall of completed and interrupted tasks for stable-extraverts, neurotic-extraverts, stable-introverts, and neurotic-introverts, under informal (neutral) and formal (intelligence test) conditions (*from* Claeys, 1969)

positive Zeigarnik Effect. This was taken as supporting a hypothesis that schizophrenics have a selective recall for experiences of failure in general.

Winder (1952) compared 35 paranoid schizophrenics with 35 non-paranoid schizophrenics, and observed a slight but significant tendency for the paranoids to show a positive Zeigarnik Effect while the non-paranoids showed a reversed effect. Assuming that the non-paranoids were characterised by withdrawal symptoms, this finding of a reversed Zeigarnik Effect is consistent with their general pattern of defence against arousal.

CONCLUSIONS

This review has been concerned with a number of areas that might at first seem quite unrelated. For example, the connection between 'arousal' as a biologically-based concept, and the sociological concept of 'intergeneration social mobility' is very tenuous indeed. Yet they may be regarded as representing fairly extreme points on a continuum of work-related motivational concepts that shade into each other almost imperceptibly.

Throughout this continuum the Yerkes-Dodson Law concerning the relationship between motivational level and performance was found to have relevance. This law implies that moderate levels of drive are optimal, and that differences between individuals, between environments, and between tasks, must all be taken into account in calculating the overall level of drive that is operative in a given situation.

With respect to the differences between individuals the following generalisations can be tentatively offered:

1. Individuals who are high on neuroticism and introversion as measured by the EPI, and patient groups that fall within this *NI* quadrant (dysthymics) may be characterised as manifesting a state of high drive or general arousal relative to other groups. Where the measure concerned is more closely associated with autonomic responsivity or emotion (e.g. heart rate, test anxiety) the *N* dimension is generally found to be a more powerful predictor. Similarly, where the measure concerned would be expected to reflect primarily cortical arousal (e.g. consolidation, two-flash thres-

hold) then the *E* dimension is found to be more relevant.

2. There is a very complex relationship between motivational variables and the schizophrenias. Acute and paranoid schizophrenics tend to manifest high drive states which are often similar, in their effects upon behaviour, to those observed in severe anxiety neuroses. On the other hand, chronic and non-paranoid schizophrenics tend to manifest symptoms often interpreted as reflecting low drive (withdrawal, apathy, etc), but on closer examination appear to indicate that they are defensive reactions to a state of abnormally *high* drive.

In conclusion, it should be pointed out that many of the motivational concepts discussed in this chapter present particular problems to the experimental psychologist in that non-linear, even non-monotonic, relationships are frequently hypothesised (and found) to be involved. This means that the same behavioural effects may be expected to occur at different levels of drive widely separated on the motivational continuum. In some cases this has given rise to unnecessary puzzlement over apparent discrepancies between experimental findings, but there is also the danger that principles such as the Yerkes-Dodson Law or 'protective inhibition' can be used to explain almost any outcome. Such a criticism has often been brought to bear, with and without justification, against various 'psychodynamic' concepts such as 'reaction formation'. Theories not susceptible to disproof are not scientific theories, and many motivational concepts require extremely careful handling if they are to be acceptable within the science of behaviour.

REFERENCES

ALPERT, R. and HABER, R. N. (1960) Anxiety in academic achievement situations. *J. Abnorm. (soc.) Psychol.*, **61**, 207–215.

ATKINSON, J. W. (Ed.) (1958) *Motives in Fantasy, Action, and Society*. Princeton: Van Nostrand.

ATKINSON, J. W. and FEATHER, N. T. (Ed.) (1966) *A Theory of Achievement Motivation*. New York: Wiley.

AUSUBEL, D. P., SCHIFF, H. M., and GOLDMAN, M. (1953) Qualitative characteristics in the learning process associated with anxiety. *J. Abnorm. (Soc.) Psychol.*, **48**, 537–547.

AX, A. F. (1947) A validation study of the Rotter-Jensen level of aspiration test. *J. Person.*, **15**, 166–172.

BARTMANN, T. (1963) Der Einfluss von Zeitdruck auf die Leistung und das Denkverhalten bei Volksschülern. *Psychol. Forsh.*, **27**, 1–61.

BECKER, J. (1960) Achievement related characteristics of manic-depressives. *J. Abnorm. (Soc.) Psychol.*, **60**, 334–339.

BECKER, J. and ALTROCCHI, J. (1968) Peer conformity and achievement in female manic-depressives. *J. Abnorm. Psychol.*, **73**, 585–589.

BECKER, J. and NICHOLS, C. H. (1964) Communality of manic-depressive and "mild" cyclothymic characteristics. *J. Abnorm. (Soc.) Psychol.*, **69**, 531–537.

BERKELEY, A. W. (1952) Level of aspiration in relation to adrenal cortical activity and the concept of stress. *J. Comp. Physiol. Psychol.*, **45**, 443–449.

BLEKE, R. C. (1955) Reward and punishment as determiners of reminiscence effects in schizophrenic and normal subjects. *J. Pers.*, **23**, 479–498.

BROADBENT, D. E. (1958) *Perception and Communication.* London: Pergamon.

BROADHURST, P. L. (1959) The interaction of task difficulty and motivation: The Yerkes-Dodson Law revived. *Acta. Psychol.*, **16**, 321–338.

BROADHURST, A. and BROADHURST, P. L. (1959) An analysis of the pursuit rotor learning of psychotics under massed and spaced practice. *Bull. Brit. Psychol. (Soc.)* **37**, 29.

BROEN, W. E. (1966) Response disorganization and breadth of observation in schizophrenia. *Psychol. Rev.*, **73**, 579–585.

BROEN, W. E. and STORMS, L. H. (1961) A reaction potential ceiling and response decrements in complex situations. *Psychol. Rev.*, 405–415.

BROEN, W. E. and STORMS, L. H. (1964) The differential effect of induced muscular tension (drive) on discrimination in schizophrenics and normals. *J. Abnorm. (Soc.) Psychol.*, **68**, 349–353.

BROEN, W. E. and STORMS, L. H. (1966) Lawful disorganization: The process underlying the schizophrenic syndrome. *Psychol. Rev.*, **73**, 265–279.

BROEN, W. E. STORMS, L. H., and GOLDBERG, D. H. (1963) Decreased discrimination as a function of increased drive. *J. Abnorm. (Soc.) Psychol.*, **67**, 266–273.

BURGESS, M. M. and HOKANSON, J. E. (1968) Effects of autonomic arousal level, sex, and frustration, on performance. *Percept. Mot. Skills.*, **26**, 919–930.

CARRON, A. V. and MORFORD, W. R. (1968) Anxiety stress and motor learning. *Mot. Percept. Skills.*, **27**, 507–511.

CHAPMAN, D. W. and VOLKMANN, J. A. (1939) A social determinant of the level of aspiration. *J. Abnorm. (Soc.) Psychol.*, **34**, 225–238.

CLAEYS, W. (1969) Zeigarnik Effect, 'Reversed Zeigarnik Effect', and personality. *J. Pers. Soc. Psychol.*, 320–327.

CLARIDGE, G. (1960) The excitation-inhibition balance in neurotics. In *Experiments in Personality* (Ed. Eysenck H. J.) London: Routledge and Kegan Paul.

CLARKE, A. M. (1967) The relationship of arousal to reminiscence, withdrawal, and the Hunter prognostic index in chronic schizophrenia. Unpublished Ph.D. thesis, Univ. London.

COFER, C. N. (1959) Motivation. *Annu. Rev. Psychol.*, **10**, 173–202.

COHEN, L. D. (1954) Level of aspiration and feelings of adequacy and self-acceptance. *J. Abnorm. (Soc.) Psychol.*, **49**, 84–86.

CORCORAN, D. W. J. (1965) Personality and the inverted-U relation. *Brit. J. Psychol.*, **56**, 267–274.

COX, F. N. (1966) Some effects of test anxiety and presence or absence of other persons on boys' performance on a repetitive motor task. *J. Exp. Child. Psychol.*, **3**, 100–112.

CROMWELL, R., ROSENTHAL, D. SHAKOW, and ZAHN, T. P. (1961) Reaction time, locus of control, choice behaviour and descriptions of parental behaviour in schizophrenic and normal subjects. *J. Person.*, **29**, 363–380.

DUFFY, E. (1951) The concept of energy mobilization. *Psychol. Rev.*, **58**, 30–40.

DUFFY, E. (1957) The psychological significance of the concept of 'arousal' or 'activation'. *Psychol. Rev.*, **64**, 265–275.

EASTERBROOK, J. A. (1959) The effect of emotion on cue utilization and the organization of behaviour. *Psychol. Rev.*, **66**, 183–201.

ELLIS, N. R., PRYER, M. W., and BARNETT, C. D. (1960) Motor learning and retention in normals and defectives. *Percept. Mot. Skills.* **10**, 83–91.

EYSENCK, H. J. (1947) *Dimensions of Personality.* New York: Praeger.

EYSENCK, H. J. (1956) Reminiscence, drive, and personality theory. *J. Abnorm. (Soc.) Psychol.*, **55**, 328–333.

EYSENCK, H. J. (1957) *Dynamics of Anxiety and Hysteria.* London: Routledge and Kegan Paul.

EYSENCK, H. J. (1960) Classification and the problem of diagnosis. In *Handbook of Abnormal Psychol.* (1st Edition), (Ed. Eysenck, H. J.) London: Pitman Med.

EYSENCK, H. J. (1960) Reminiscence as a function of rest, practice and personality. *Percept. Mot. Skills.*, **11**, 91–94.

EYSENCK, H. J. (1961) Psychosis, drive, and inhibition: A theoretical and experimental account. *Amer. J. Psychiat.* **118**, 198–204.

EYSENCK, H. J. (1962) Reminiscence, drive and personality—a revision and extension of a theory. *Brit. J. Soc. Clin. Psychol.*, **1**, 127–140.

EYSENCK, H. J. (Ed.) (1964) *Experiments in Motivation.* London: Pergamon.

EYSENCK, H. J. (1965) A three-factor theory of reminiscence. *Brit. J. Psychol.*, **56**, 163–182.

EYSENCK, H. J. (1967) *The Biological Basis of Personality.* New York: C. C. Thomas.

EYSENCK, H. J. (1968) A dimensional system of psychodiagnostics. In *New approaches to Psychodiagnostic Systems.* (Ed. Mahrer, A. R.) New York: Aldine.

EYSENCK, H. J. and EYSENCK, S. B. G. (1964) *Manual of the Eysenck Personality Inventory.* London: Univ. London Press.

EYSENCK, H. J. and HIMMELWEIT, H. T. (1946) An experimental study of the reactions of neurotics to experiences of success and failure. *J. Gen. Psychol.*, **35**, 59–75.

EYSENCK, H. J. and MAXWELL, A. E. (1961) Reminiscence as a function of drive. *Brit. J. Psychol.*, **52**, 43–52.

EYSENCK, H. J. and WILLETT, R. G. (1961) The measurement of motivation through the use of objective indices. *J. Ment. Sci.*, **107**, 961–968.

FARLEY, F. H. (1966) Reminiscence and post-rest performance as a function of length of rest, drive and personality. Unpublished Ph.D. thesis, University of London.

FARLEY, F. H. (1968) Global self-ratings, the independence of questionnaire drive and anxiety, and social desirability variance. *Acta. Psychol.*, **28**, 387–397.

FEATHER, N. T. (1961) The relationship of persistence at a task to expectation of success and achievement-related motives. *J. Abnorm. (Soc.) Psychol.*, **63**, 552–561.

FELDMAN, M. P. (1964a) Motivation and task performance: A review of the literature. In *Experiments in Motivation* (Ed. Eysenck, H. J.) London: Pergamon.

FELDMAN, M. P. (1964b) Pursuit rotor performance and reminiscence as a function of drive level. In *Experiments in Motivation* (Ed. Eysenck, H. J.) London: Pergamon.

FISKE, D.W. and MADDI, S. R. (Eds) (1961) *Functions of Varied Experience*. Homewood, Ill.: Dorsey Press.

FREEMAN, T. (1960) On the psychopathology of schizophrenia. *J. ment. Sci.*, **106**, 925–937.

FRENCH, E. G. (1958) Development of a measure of complex motivation. In *Motives in Fantasy Action and Society* (Ed. J. W. Atkinson) Princeton: Van Nostrand-242–248.

GANZER, V. J. (1968) Effects of audience presence and test anxiety on learning and retention in a serial learning situation. *J. Pers. Soc. Psychol.*, **8**, 194–199.

GATELY, G. M. (1954) The use of projection technique in an experimental study of level of aspiration. Unpublished Ph.D. thesis, University of London.

GIBSON, R. W. (1958) The family background and early life experiences of the manic-depressive patient. *Psychiatry*, **21**, 71–90.

GOLDBERG, S. C., KLERMAN, G. L., and COLE, J. O. (1965) Changes in schizophrenic psychopathology and ward behaviour as a function of phenothiazine treatment. *Brit. J. Psychiat.*, **111**, 120–133.

GOLDBERG, S. C., SCHOOLER, N. R., and MATTSSON, N. (1967) Paranoid and withdrawal symptoms in schizophrenia: Differential symptom reduction over time. *J. Nerv. Ment. Dis.*, **145**, 158–162.

GOLDBERG, S. C., SCHOOLER, N. R., and MATTSSON, N. (1968) Paranoid and withdrawal symptoms in schizophrenia: relationship to reaction time. *Brit. J. Psychiat.*, **114**, 1161–1165.

GRASSI, J. R. (1968) Performance and reminiscence of brain-damaged, behaviour-disordered and normal children on four psychomotor and perceptual tests. *J. Abnorm. Psychol.*, **73**, 492–499.

GRUEN, E. W. (1945) Level of aspiration in relation to personality factors in adolescents. *Child Developm.*, **16**, 181–185.

GUEVARA, C. I. (1965) The effects of success and failure experiences on schizophrenics' rate of learning under conditions of low and high expectancy of success. Unpubl. Doct. Diss., Stanford Univ.

HANSCHE, J. and GILCHRIST, J. C. (1956) Three determinants of the level of aspiration. *J. Abnorm. (Soc.) Psychol.*, **53**, 136–137 (1956).

HARTOGS, R. (1949) The clinical investigation and differential measurement of anxiety. *Amer. J. Psychiat.*, **53**, 136–137.

HAYS, L. W. and WORELL, L. (1967) Anxiety drive, anxiety habit, and achievement: A theoretical reformulation in terms of optimal motivation. *J. Person.*, **35**, 145–163.

HAYWOOD, H. C. and WEAVER, S. J. (1967) Differential effects of motivational orientations and incentive conditions on motor performance in institutionalized retardates. *Amer. J. Ment. Defic.*, **72**, 459–467.

HEBB, D. O. (1955) Drives and the C.N.S. *Psychol. Rev.*, **62**, 209–225.

HECKHAUSEN, H. (1967) *The Anatomy of Achievement Motivation*. New York: Academic.

HIMMELWEIT, H. T. (1947) A comparative study of the level of aspiration of normal and neurotic persons. *Brit. J. Psychol.*, **37**, 41–59.

HOWARTH, E. and EYSENCK, H. T. (1969) Extraversion, arousal and paired associate learning. *J. Exp. Res. Pers.*, **3**, 14–116.

HULL, C. L. (1917) The formation and retention of associations among the insane. *Amer. J. Psychol.*, **28**, 419–435.

HUNTER, M. (1961) The effects of interpersonal interaction upon task performance of chronic schizophrenics. *Diss. Abstracts.*, **21**, 2004.

HURLEY, J. R. (1955) The Iowa Picture Interpretation Test: A multiple choice variation of the TAT. *J. Consult. Psychol.*, **19**, 372–376.

HUSTON, P. and SHAKOW, D. (1948) Learning in schizophrenia. I: Pursuit learning. *J. Person.* **17**, 52–74.

INGLIS, J. (1960) Abnormalities of motivation and 'ego-functions'. In *Handbook of Abnormal Psychology*, 1st Edn. (Ed. Eysenck, H. J.) London: Pitman Med.

JONES, H. G. (1960) Learning and abnormal behaviour. In *Handbook of Abnormal Psychology*, 1st Edn. (Ed. Eysenck, H. J.) London: Pitman Med.

JONES, R. W. and ELLIS, N. R. (1962) Inhibitory potential in rotary pursuit acquisition by normal and defective subjects. *J. Exp. Psychol.*, **63**, 534–537.

JOST, K. (1955) The level of aspiration of schizophrenic and normal subjects. *J. Abnorm. (Soc.) Psychol.*, **50**, 315–320.

JUCKNAT, M. (1937) Leistung, anspruchsnivean und selbrbewusstsein. *Psychol Forsch.*, **22**, 89–179.

KATKIN, E. S., SASMOR, D. B., and TAN, R. (1966) Conformity and achievement—related characteristics of depressed patients. *J. Abnorm. Psychol.*, **71**, 407–412.

KELLAM, S. G., GOLDBERG, S. C., SCHOOLER, N. R., BERMAN, A., and SHMELZER, J. L. (1966) Ward atmosphere and outcome of treatment of acute schizophrenia. *Psychopharmacology. Res. Br. Pub. Rep. N.I.M.H.*

KIMBLE, G. A. (1949) An experimental test of a two-factor theory of inhibition. *J. Exp. Psychol.*, **39**, 15–23.

KIMBLE, G. A. (1950) Evidence for the role of motivation in determining the amount of reminiscence in pursuit rotor learning. *J. Exp. Psychol.*, **40**, 248–253.

KLINGER, E. (1966) Fantasy need achievement as a motivational construct. *Psychol Bull.*, **66**, 291–308.

KLUGMAN, S. F. (1948) Emotional stability and level of aspiration. *J. Gen. Psychol.*, **38**, 101–118.

KLUGMAN, S. F. (1947) Relationship between performance on the Rotter Aspiration Board and various types of test. *J. Psychol.*, **23**, 51–54.

LEFCOURT, H. M. (1966) Internal versus external control of reinforcement: A review. *Psychol. Bull.*, **65**, 206–220.

LEWIN, K. (1935) *A Dynamic Theory of Personality*. New York: McGraw-Hill.

LEWIN, K., DEMBO, T., FESTINGER, L., and SEARS, P. S. (1944) Level of aspiration. In *Personality and the Behaviour Disorders* (Ed. Hunt, J. McV.) New York: Ronald Press.

LEWIS, H. B. and FRANKLIN, M. (1944) An experimental study of the role of the ego in work II: The significance of task-orientation in work. *J. Exp. Psychol.*, **34**, 195–215.

LEY, P. (1961) Unpublished report cited by H. J. Eysenck. (1961) *r.s.*

LINDSLEY, D. B. (1951) Emotion. In *Handbook of Experimental Psychology* (Ed. Stevens, S. S.) New York: Wiley.

LINDSLEY, D. B. (1952) Psychological phenomena and the electroencephalogram. *EEG Clin. Neurophysiol.*, **4**, 443–456.

LINDSLEY, D. B. (1957) Psychophysiology and Motivation. *Nebraska Symposium on Motivation*. Lincoln, Nebr.: Univ. Nebraska Press, 44–105.

LITTLE, S. W. and COHEN, L. D. (1950) Goal setting behaviour of asthmatic children and of their mothers for them. *J. Person.*, **19**, 376–389.

LOEB, A. BECK, A. T., DIGGORY, J. C., and TUTHILL, R. (1967) Expectancy level of aspiration, performance, and self-evaluation in depression. *Proc. A.P.A.* **75**, 193–194.

LOEB, A. FESHBACH, S., BECK, A. T., and WOLF, A. (1964) Some effects of reward upon the social perception and motivation of psychiatric patients varying in depression. *J. Abnorm. (Soc.) Psychol.*, **68**, 609–616.

LYNN, R. (1963) Russian theory and research on schizophrenia. *Psychol. Bull.*, **60**, 486–498.

MCCLELLAND, D. C., ATKINSON, J. W., CLARKE, R. A., and LOWELL, E. L. (1953) *The Achievement Motive*. New York: Appleton-Century-Crofts.

MCLAUGHLIN, R. J. and EYSENCK, H. J. (1967) Extraversion, neuroticism and paired-associates learning. *J. Exp. Res. Pers.*, **2**, 128–132.

MCLEAN, P. D. (1969) Induced arousal and time of recall as determinants of paired associate learning. *Brit. J. Psychol.*, **60**, 55–62.

MCREYNOLDS, P. and GUEVARA, C. (1967) Attitudes of schizophrenics and normals towards success and failure. *J. Abnorm. Psychol.*, **72**, 303–310.

MALMO, R. B. (1959) Activation: A neurophysiological dimension. *Psychol. Rev.*, **66**, 367–386.

MANDLER, G. and COWEN, J. E. (1958) Test anxiety questionnaires. *J. Consult. Psychol.*, **22**, 228–229.

MARTENS, R. and LANDERS, D. M. (1969) Effect of anxiety, competition and failure on performance of a complex motor task. *J. Motor. Behav.*, **1**, 1–10.

MATHENY, A. P. (1968) Reactive inhibition as related to the mental retardate's distractibility. *Amer. J. Ment. Defic.*, **73**, 257–261.

MEDNICK, S. A. (1958) A learning theory approach to research in schizophrenia. *Psychol. Bull.*, **55**, 316–327.

MILLER, D. R. (1951) Responses of psychiatric patients to threat of failure. *J. Abnorm. (Soc.) Psychol.*, **46**-378–387.

MUNZ, D. C. and SMOUSE, A. D. (1968) Interaction effects of item-difficulty sequence and achievement-anxiety

reaction on academic performance. *J. Educ. Psychol.*, **59**, 370–374.

MUNZ, D. C., SMOUSE, A. D., and LETCHWORTH, G. (1968) Achievement motivation and ordinal position of birth. *Psychol. Rep.*, **23**, 175–180.

RACHMAN, S. (1963) Inhibition and disinhibition in schizophrenics. *Arch. Gen. Psychiat.*, **8**, 91–98.

RAIFMAN, I. (1957) Level of aspiration in a group of peptic ulcer patients. *J. Consult. Psychol.*, **21**, 229–231.

RHINE, W. R. (1962) Birth-order differences in conformity and level of achievement arousal. *Child Dev.*, **39**, 987–996.

RODNICK, E. H. and GARMEZY, N. (1957) An experimental approach to the study of motivation in schizophrenia. *Nebraska Symposium on Motivation*, Lincoln, Nebr.: Univ. Nebraska Press, 109–183.

ROSENWEIG, S. (1943) Experimental study of repression with specific reference to need-persistive and ego-defensive reactions to frustration. *J. Exp. Psychol.*, **32**, 64–74.

ROTTER, J. B. (1966) Generalized expectancies for internal versus external control of reinforcement. *Psychol. Monogr.*, **80**, (1, whole No. 609).

RUDIN, S. A. (1968) National motives predict psychogenic death rates 25 years later. *Science*, **160**, 901–903.

RYAN, E. D. and LAKIE, W. L. (1965) Competitive and non-competitive performance in relation to achievement motive and manifest anxiety. *J. Pers. Soc. Psychol.*, **51**, 253–260.

SARASON, I. G. (1961) The effects of anxiety and threat on the solution of a difficult task. *J. Abnorm. (Soc.) Psychol.*, **62**, 165–168.

SCHOOLER, C. and SPOHN, H. E. (1966) The susceptibility of chronic schizophrenics to social influence in the formation of perceptual judgements. *J. Abnorm. (Soc.) Psychol.*, **61**, 348–354.

SCHOOLER, C. and ZAHN, T. P. (1968) The effect of closeness of social interaction on task performance and arousal in chronic schizophrenia. *J. Nerv. Ment. Dis.*, **147**, 394–401.

SEARS, P. S. (1941) Levels of aspiration in relation to some variables of personality: Clinical studies. *J. Soc. Psychol.*, **14**, 311–336.

SEVRANSKY, C. (1965) Unpublished thesis, Colombia Univ. (Cited in Eysenck, 1967).

SILVERMAN, J. (1964) The scanning control mechanism and "cognitive" filtering in paranoid and non-paranoid schizophrenia. *J. Consult. Psychol.*, **28**, 385–393.

SILVERMAN, J. (1967) Variations in cognitive control and psycho-physiological defense in the schizophrenias. *Psychosom. Med.*, **29**, 225–251.

SPAIN, B. (1966) Eyelid conditioning and arousal in schizophrenic and normal subjects. *J. Abnorm. Psychol.*, **71**, 260–265.

SPENCE, K. W. (1956) *Behaviour Theory and Conditioning*. New Haven: Yale. Press.

SPENCE, K. W. (1958) A theory of emotionally based drive (D) and its relation to performance in simple learning situations. *Amer. Psychologist*, **13**, 131–141.

SPIELBERGER, C. D. (Ed.) (1966) *Anxiety and Behaviour*. New York: Academic Press.

SPIELBERGER, C. D., PARKER, J. B., and BECKER, J. (1963)

Conformity and achievement in remitted manic-depressive patients. *J. Nerv. Ment. Dis.*, **137**, 162–172.

SPOHN, H. and WOLK, W. (1963) Effect of group problem solving experience upon social withdrawal in chronic schizophrenics. *J. Abnorm. (Soc.) Psychol.*, **66**, 187–189.

STACEY, B. G. (1968) Achievement motivation, occupational choice and inter-generation occupational mobility. *Human Relations*, **22**, 275–281.

STEINER, I. D. (1956) Self-perception and goal-setting behaviour. *J. Person.*, **25**, 344–355.

STORMS, L. H., BROEN, W. E., and LEVIN, I. P. (1967) Verbal associative stability and commonality as a function of stress in schizophrenics, neurotics and normals. *J. Consult. Psychol.*, **31**, 181–187.

SUBOTNIK, L. (1967) Level of aspiration, emotional disturbance, and learning in institutionalized educable mentally retarded boys. *Amer. J. ment. Defic.*, **71**, 767–771.

SWEENY, C. J., SMOUSE, A. D., and RUPIPER, O. (1970). A test of the inverted-U hypothesis relating achievement anxiety and academic test performance. *J. Psychol.*, **74**, 267–273.

TAMKIN, A. S. (1957) Selective recall in schizophrenia and its relation to ego strength. *J. Abnorm. (Soc.) Psychol.*, **55**, 345–349.

TAYLOR, J. A. (1953) A personality scale of manifest anxiety. *J. Abnorm (Soc.) Psychol.*, **48**, 285–290.

VENABLES, P. H. (1959) Factors in the motor behaviour of functional psychotics. *J. Aborm. (Soc.) Psychol.*, **58**, 153–156.

VENABLES, P. H. (1967a) The relation of two-flash and two-click thresholds to withdrawal in paranoid and non-paranoid schizophrenics. *Brit. J. Soc. Clin Psychol.*, **6**, 60–62.

VENABLES, P. H. (1967b) Partial failure of cortical-subcortical integration as a factor underlying schizophrenic behaviour. *Exerpta Medica. Int. Cong. Series. No. 151.*

VENABLES, P. H. and O'CONNOR, N. (1959) A short scale for rating paranoid schizophrenia. *J. Ment. Sci.*, **105**, 815–818.

VENABLES, P. H. and WING, J. K. (1959) Level of arousal and the subclassification of schizophrenia. *Arch. Gen. Psychiat.*, **105**, 815–118.

VENABLES, P. and TIZARD, J. (1956) Performance of functional psychotics on a repetitive task. *J. Abnorm. (Soc.) Psychol.*, **53**, 23–26.

VOGEL, W. RAYMOND, S. and LAZARUS, R. S. (1959) Intrinsic motivation and psychological stress. *J. Abnorm. (Soc.) Psychol.*, 225–233.

WALKER, E. L. and TARTE, R. D. (1963) Memory storage as a function of time with homogeneous and heterogeneous lists. *J. Verb. Learn. Verb. Behav.*, **2**, 113–119.

WALKER, R. E. (1961) The interaction between failure, manifest-anxiety, and task-irrelevant responses in paired-associate learning. Unpubl. Doct. Diss. Northwestern Univ.

WEINER, G. (1960) The interaction among anxiety, stress instructions, and difficulty. *J. Consult. Psychol.*, **60**, 147–150.

WEINSTEIN, M. S. (1969) Achievement motivation and risk preference. *J. Pers. soc. Psychol.*, **13**, 153–172.

WILLETT, R. A. and EYSENCK, H. J. (1962) An experimental study of human motivation. *Life Sci.*, **1**, 119–127.

WINDER, C. L. (1952) On the personality structures of schizophrenics. *J. Abnorm (Soc.) Psychol.*, **47**, 86–100.

WRIGHT, L. and HEARN, C. B. (1964) Reactive inhibition in normals and defectives as measured from a common performance criterion. *J. Gen. Psychol.*, **71**, 57–64.

ZAHN, T. P. (1964) Autonomic reactivity and behaviour in schizophrenia. *Psychiat. Res. Rep., A.P.A.*

ZAHN, T. P., ROSENTHAL, D., and SHAKOW, D. (1963) Effects of irregular preparatory intervals on reaction time in schizophrenia. *J. Abnorm. (Soc.) Psychol.*, **67**, 44–52.

ZEIGARNIK, B. (1927) Über das Behalten von erledigten und unerledigten Handlungen. *Psychol. Forsch.*, **9**, 1–85.

13

Personality, Learning, and 'Anxiety'

H. J. EYSENCK

Most clinicians assume that anxiety and emotion generally have a profound effect on a person's ability to learn new material and to remember and recall what he has learned previously; psycho-analysts have formulated several hypotheses in this field which, however, have either not been submitted to experimental test, or have failed to give congruent results when submitted to such tests. The present chapter deals largely with laboratory investigations of this relationship, using normal subjects differing in anxiety or neuroticism as assessed by questionnaire methods, or manipulating external stimuli in order to produce changes in the anxiety level of subjects, or both; this necessarily imposes limitations on the conclusions that can be drawn from the results, and makes dangerous any direct extrapolation to patients suffering from severe forms of neurotic disorder, or to psychotics characterised by severe anxiety. However, until some systematic under-standing has been gained of the phenomena in question, and until some systematic formulations can be made of the kinds of relations expected on the basis of more general laws, there is little hope of gaining a proper understanding of the behaviour of anxious and emotionally disturbed patients. Unless it is assumed that the emotions and behaviour patterns and reactions of neurotics are entirely *sui generis*, and are quite unlike those shown by normal persons, or that the laws governing the behaviour of normal persons are not in any way applicable to neurotics, it seems reasonable to hope that such extension, cautious though it must of course be, of knowledge gained in the one field to the other will ultimately prove useful, and give a new way of approaching a very old and difficult problem. This way of approaching the problem certainly seems

more promising than does the formulation of purely *ad hoc* theories and hypotheses to deal with specific behaviour disorders, unrelated to the laboratory study of learning phenomena or the systematic generalisation of findings in the form of laws.

The formulation of relevant theories owes much to K. Spence, who based himself very much on Hull's general theory (Spence and Spence, 1966); for this reason our discussion will make use of certain Hullian terms and symbols, even though the general applicability of this system is not nowadays favoured very widely. However, in spite of its imperfections it does contain many well-established generalisations and observations, and these can usually be translated without loss into other systematic formulations (e.g. MacCorquodale and Meehl, 1954). The use of these terms and symbols should therefore not be interpreted as implying outright acceptance of the Hullian system; indeed several fundamental criticisms of Spence's theory will be given later on. Nevertheless, his pioneering efforts in this field are of such importance, and have had such influence, that a detailed discussion of his work, in his own terms, must precede any efforts to criticise or extend it. His theoretical position has already been indicated in a previous chapter (Chapter 11) dealing with conditioning; his work on learning is based essentially on the same principles which, therefore, will be indicated only very briefly. It is left open whether, as he believes, the same laws are applicable to conditioning and verbal learning, or whether quite different laws are required; to try to answer such a profound theoretical question would take us well beyond our immediate task (Melton, 1964). The division in this book into two chapters, one on conditioning and one on learning, is based more on heuristic than on fundamental and theoretical considerations.

Hullian learning theory makes much use of the concepts of 'drive' and 'reinforcement'; primary drives like hunger and thirst motivate the organism to activity, and drive-reduction (as in eating and drinking) causes conditioning of the stimuli which are associated in point of time with this drive-reduction by providing reinforcement for the activities in question. In addition, secondary drives and secondary reinforcement are posited in this system; anxiety in psychological parlance is a term denotative of a secondary drive, and also a source of secondary reinforcement. 'The primary drive involved in this case is pain; neutral stimuli associated with pain give rise to "fear" responses, very similar to responses to pain, and the proprioceptive consequences of these learned responses produce the drive stimulus (S_D) that serves the secondary drive.' (Hilgard, 1956, p. 131.) This conditioned fear response is the psychologist's conception of 'anxiety'; the diminution of anxiety has the properties of reinforcement, and hence can serve to cause learning. Anxiety may be unique in having both these functions; few other examples come to mind of secondary *drives*, although there are many studies using secondary *reinforcers*. Tokens that may be exchanged for food will act as secondary reinforcers for hungry chimps, but they will only cause him to work when hungry (primary drive). Miller (1948, 1951), in his classical studies, showed that anxiety, i.e. conditioned pain reactions, acted as a drive as well as providing reinforcement. In these studies he demonstrated,

'first, that neutral stimuli become fear arousing after association with noxious stimuli, and can serve as the basis for motivating an animal in a learning situation so that it strives to escape from them, and secondly, that reduction of the fear through cessation of the conditioned fear stimulus constitutes a reinforcing event in that it leads to the learning of those responses which it follows.' (Spence, 1956).

If anxiety has the status of a drive, then it would seem to follow that the general laws relating to drives should apply to anxiety. Pavlov formulated two such laws. The *Law of Strength* asserts that the strength of the response is proportional to the strength of the stimulus, and the *Law of Transmarginal Inhibition* asserts that there is a point of maximum response beyond which further increase in the strength of the stimulus leads to a lessening of response rather than a further increase. In English-speaking countries this is usually known as the Yerkes-Dodson Law (Broadhurst, 1959), which

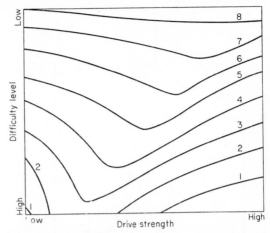

Fig. 13.1. Isometric levels of learning efficiency on an arbitrary scale from 1 (low) to 8 (high), plotted against difficulty level and drive strength (*from* Jones, 1960)

also comes in two parts, but goes somewhat further than does Pavlov. It asserts that the relation between drive and performance is curvilinear, in that low drive is sub-optimal and very high drive supra-optimal for performance, with intermediate drive levels optimal; it also asserts that the optimal drive level depends on the difficulty of the task, so that very simple tasks have high optimal drive levels, while very difficult tasks have low optimal drive levels. This law is also sometimes referred to as the inverted-U relation between drive and performance, although this notion does not contain the very important second part of the Yerkes-Dodson Law. Figure 13.1 shows the isometric levels of learning efficiency on an arbitrary scale from 1 (low) to 8 (high), plotted against difficulty level and drive strength (Jones, 1960).

Figure 13.2 shows the results of a typical experiment on the Yerkes-Dodson Law (Broadhurst, 1957). Underwater swimming provides the drive (air deprivation), different periods of delay before starting, the rat held in the starting box under water, providing different strengths of drive. The task of the rat was to choose that arm of a Y-maze which led to escape; the difference in brightness with which the two arms were illuminated provided the clue. The problem could be made easy, moderate, or difficult by making this difference in brightness large, medium, or small. It will be seen that for the easy task the optimal level of drive lay beyond the maximum used, while for the difficult task the optimal level lay towards the minimum used, with the inverted-U relation clearly marked. The moderately difficult task is intermediate. A thorough

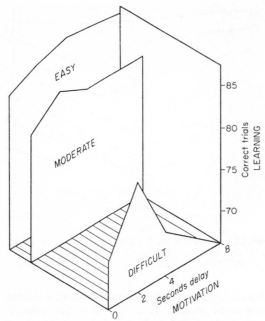

Fig. 13.2. Results of an experiment with rats demonstrating the Inverse-U relationship between drive and performance postulated by the Yerkes-Dodson law (*from* Broadhurst, 1957)

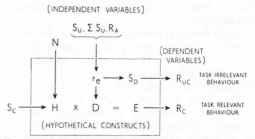

Fig. 13.3. Hypothetical constructs, independent and dependent variables contained in Spence's theory linking personality and learning (modified *from* Spence and Spence, 1966)

review of the whole field, with particular attention to cue utilisation, is given by Easterbrook (1959); his review is concerned especially with human subjects.

The Yerkes-Dodson Law has in recent years been revived under the title of the 'inverse-U' function of performance and drive; Malmo (1957, 1958, 1959) has been particularly active in pursuing this line of research, which was begun by Courts (1942) in his well-known study of the effects of different degrees of induced muscular tension. Under whatever title, this law is purely descriptive, like Bode's law in Astronomy (Hoyle, 1962); it is not derived from any more fundamental and more general set of laws and theories. (Pavlov might dispute this view, but his two laws are not, in fact, anything but generalised statements of empirical findings; they do not depend in any way on his general systematic view.) It is possible to derive the Yerkes-Dodson Law, or the Inverse-U Law, from Spence's (or rather Hull's) system of postulates, although this derivation does not enable us to make any quantitative predictions; however, quantification may come later, and the possibility of prediction implicit in this new formulation is of considerable interest and importance.

The Hull-Spence theory makes use of certain concepts which are presented diagrammatically in Fig. 13.3; this is modified from a less complete figure given in Spence and Spence (1966). On the left is the conditioned stimulus (S_C); at the top are certain independent variables which can be manipulated by the experimenter, such as N, the number of learning or paired conditioned trials; S_U, the unconditioned stimulus, and $\sum S_U$, the number of prior presentations of the unconditioned stimulus; and R_A, the score of the subject on an inventory or other measure of emotional responsiveness. In the body of the diagram are the H(abit) and D(rive) variables which multiply to give E(xcitatory potential). In addition to these three hypothetical constructs there is a further one, r_e, which is described by Spence and Spence as, 'a persistent emotional response aroused by aversive stimuli. This mechanism, it will be recognised, is similar to that proposed by Miller (1951) and Mowrer (1939) in connection with their work on the acquired drive of fear'. This r_e response not only determines the amount of D in the situation, but also that of the drive stimulus, S_D. Coming now again to observable variables, we have R_C, the conditioned response; this is an example of task-relevant behaviour. We also have task-irrelevant behaviour, instigated by S_D; this may be conditioned or unconditioned, hence is denoted in our diagram $R_{U.C}$. These are the main variables in the Hull-Spence system which have a bearing on our discussion; other variables must, of course, always be borne in mind, and will occasionally be mentioned.

Spence follows Hull in assuming that D always has a facilitative, energising effect on H, rather like Pavlov's Law of Strength; this relationship is therefore a monotonic one, rather than being shaped like an inverted U. Spence accounts for the inversion observable in the relation between drive and observed behaviour along two entirely different lines.*

* Our presentation of Spence's theory takes into account only its latest version; earlier ones are of purely historical interest. Quotations are from the Spence and Spence (1966) paper, unless otherwise indicated.

1. Contrasting complex, selective learning tasks with simple classical conditioning, he points out that the former typically employ a series of stimulus items each of which may evoke a number of competing responses with varying habit strengths. 'If, in the case of a single item, the initial habit strength of the correct response is stronger than the strength of the competing responses, the multiplicative relationship between H and D in determining excitatory potential, E, implies that the higher the level of D, the greater is the difference between the E values of the correct and the incorrect competing responses.' Assuming that we are concerned only with the magnitude of the difference in E values, it follows that when the correct responses are initially strong, performance should be positively related to the drive level. Conversely, if the correct to-be-learned response is weaker than wrong alternative responses, then the higher the drive level, the poorer will be performance during the early stages of learning. 'However, as learning of the correct responses increases over the trials, the habit strength of the responses would be expected to equal and then exceed those of competing responses.' Thus, the performance of high drive groups should become superior in later stages of learning. In so far as we are justified in calling tasks that have only one response (as in conditioning), or where the correct response is already predominant, *simple*, and those where a wrong response is predominant, *complex* or *difficult*, this derivation from Hullian theory would generate the type of fact on which the Yerkes-Dodson Law is based; it certainly demonstrates how the monotonic relation between D and E can lead to a curvilinear relationship between $(D \times H)$ and E, depending on the precise nature of H at the time.

2. The second line of argument employed by Spence relates to the existence of S_D variables, which, in turn, may generate task irrelevant behaviour that may interfere with the behaviour to be learned. 'The extensions of our notions concerning drive and anxiety involved what might be called the "response interference hypothesis", the hypothesis that states that task-irrelevant responses which in some situations may interfere with efficient performance are more easily elicited in high than in low anxiety Ss. (Spence, 1956; Taylor, 1956).' Animal studies have shown that whether an increase in D and S_D facilitates or interferes with performance depends in part on whether the response tendencies elicited by S_D are compatible with the response to be acquired or performed, or not (Amsel, 1950; Amsel and Maltzman, 1950). Strong anxiety may thus generate behaviour that interferes with learning even though the learning is of the *simple* kind, i.e. does not involve stimuli already possessing strong

but wrong responses; under these conditions, increasing drive might lead to worse performance. This mechanism is entirely different from the first mechanism discussed under (1), and resembles that put forward by Child (1954) in criticism of Spence's original theory. Both of the mechanisms postulated by Spence are qualitative rather than quantitative, and no precise predictions are possible; nevertheless, a general expectation can be found for different classes of learning situations, and experimentation has largely been concerned with confirming or disconfirming such broad expectations.

Spence's discussion applies equally to (*a*) conditions that produce heightened emotional drive, such as electric shock, or ego-involving instructions, and (*b*) personality features that make the individual more receptive to emotional stress, or keep him in a permanent state of high anxiety. The equivalence of these two sets of variables (S_U and R_A in our diagram) has been formally postulated by Savage and Eysenck (1964) in a paper that also furnishes experimental evidence which strongly supports it. In this paper, an analogy has been suggested with Hooke's law of elasticity; Stress = $k \times$ Strain, where k is a constant (the modulus of elasticity) which depends on the nature of the material and the type of stress used to produce the strain. This constant k, i.e. the ratio Stress/Strain, is called Young's modulus, and is illustrated (with certain simplifications) in Fig. 13.4a. A and B are two metals, differing in elasticity; they are stressed by increasing loads, the elongation corresponding to each load plotted on the abscissa. It will be seen that identical loads θ give rise to quite divergent elongations, α and β. Figure 13.4b illustrates a similar analysis of human behaviour in an experimental situation productive of emotion. Again the stress (independent variable) is plotted on the ordinate, and the strain (dependent variable) on the abscissa; A and B represent a non-anxious and an anxious group respectively. Identical stress θ_1, gives rise to quite different strains α and β. It would require stress θ_2 to make the strain in person A equal to that produced by θ_1, in person B. Differences between θ_1 and θ_2 are the kind of differences traditionally studied by experimental psychologists; differences between A and B are the kinds of differences traditionally studied by personality theorists. K in Young's formula is the equivalent of 'personality' in the psychologist's formulation.

Consider two experiments reported by Rosenbaum (1953, 1956) which illustrate the two sides of this comparison. In the first experiment he showed that threat of strong shock led to greater generalisation of a voluntary response than did threat of weak shock. This illustrates the difference between θ_1,

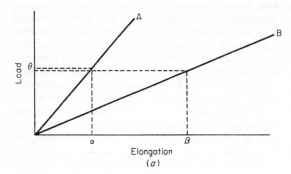

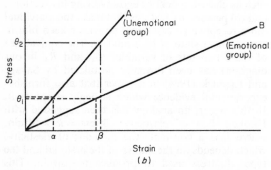

Fig. 13.4. The measurement of stress and strain in physics and psychology

(Upper) shows Young's modulus in diagrammatic form; (lower) shows, by analogy, the differential effect of stress on emotional and non-emotional subjects (*from* Savage and Eysenck, 1964).

and θ_2, i.e. the effects of stress differences on strain. In his second experiment he showed that anxious subjects exposed to identical stimuli as were non-anxious subjects, showed greater generalisation; this illustrates the differences between A and B, i.e. differences in k. Similarly, Savage and Eysenck, working with genetically pure strains of emotionally reactive and non-reactive rats (Eysenck and Broadhurst, 1964) showed that these strain differences paralleled in their effects those of anxiety-producing externally imposed stimuli, such as strong electric shocks. Personality (or strain) interacts with experimental conditions to produce R_C; it seems possible to exchange the one for the other, up to a point. Mild shock applied to anxious people (or emotional rats) gives results similar to strong shocks applied to non-anxious people (or non-emotional rats). Both variables obviously require to be taken into account; Eysenck (1967) has drawn attention to the curious and indefensible gap between experimentalists who refuse to look at individual differences in their work, and personality theorists who refuse to look at experimental work.

Apart from conditioning experiments, which of course depend for their interpretation on the same theoretical constructs, Spence has dealt with ten main types of investigation in the more complex human learning field.

1. Serial verbal or spatial mazes, where two response alternatives are presented at each point. Spence assumed that at many choice points anticipatory and perseverative tendencies would be present to such a degree that the incorrect choice would be stronger than the correct one. Using the Manifest Anxiety Scale (MAS) as in all his work, Spence therefore predicted that high scorers (high anxiety Ss) would exhibit a greater number of errors on the learning trials than a low drive group; he also expected to find a correlation between rank order of the 'difficulty' of the choice points (as indexed by the total number of errors made on each) and the magnitude of the difference between the errors made by the MAS+ and the MAS− groups. Several studies have confirmed one or other of these predictions (Faber and Spence, 1953; Taylor and Spence, 1952; Matarazzo et al., 1955; Axelrod et al., 1956); Hughes et al. (1954) failed to confirm either prediction. None of the experiments confirmed another prediction; the MAS+ group should have been superior to the MAS− group at the choice points where few errors were made, suggesting the absence of competing response tendencies. They were not. More fatal to the theory is an experiment by Buchwald and Yamaguchi (1955), who trained rats in a T-maze to a criterion of 10 correct responses out of twelve; they then reversed the maze and retrained rats under high and low drive conditions. Contrary to prediction, relearning was more rapid with high drive. In view of the much greater control over experimental conditions possible in rat experiments, this is a difficult result to explain for Spence.

2. Other early studies employed serial learning tasks in which Ss were presented with each successive item and required to anticipate the next item on the list. Lucas (1952) and Montague (1953) showed that the differences between the overall performance of MAS+ and MAS− groups increased in favour of the latter in conformity with intralist similarity and intralist competition. Similarly, on a serial rote learning task, Malmo and Amsel (1948) found anxious patients to make more errors than normals.

In spite of these promising results, Spence gave up the serial learning method because of certain deficiencies in the paradigm (Spence and Spence, 1966).

3. Instead, research was concentrated on paired-associate learning, using non-competitive lists 'in which the formation of each S-R association is isolated as much as possible from the others by

minimising the degree of formal and meaningful similarity among the stimulus and response terms as well as the degree of associative connection between each stimulus and the non-paired response terms. In several experiments the initial associative connection between the paired words was also at a minimum'. The prediction was made that after initial similarity the MAS+ group would progress more quickly than the MAS− group. Spence (1958), Taylor (1958), and Taylor and Chapman (1955) have confirmed the prediction; Kamin and Fedorchak (1957) and Lovaas (1960) have not. The evidence in favour of this prediction is thus not very impressive.

4. Another type of task used in the experimental testing of Spence's hypothesis 'employed a second type of non-competitive list in which there was an initial associative connection between each *S* and *R* term, acquired as a result of extra experimental experience. In this instance it was expected that performance would be well above zero on the first anticipation trial for both groups and that the performance curve for the high anxiety group would be consistently above that of the low anxiety group'. Results have, on the whole, been in favour of this prediction (Besch, 1959; Spence, Farber, and McFann, 1956; Spence, Taylor, and Ketchel, 1956; Standish and Champion, 1960).

5. Similar to this prediction is the complementary one 'that high anxiety (*D*) groups will be poorer in performance than low anxiety groups when the initial habit strength of the response term paired with a given stimulus is weaker than the strength of one or more competing response tendencies . . . . It was expected that *on the initial trials* the performance of high anxiety *Ss* would be inferior to that of low anxiety *Ss* on these competitive items.' Ramond (1953) and the two Spence *et al.* studies already cited provide evidence for this prediction. Standish and Champion (1960) also support it, and go further by showing that, as expected, on later learning trials the high anxiety *Ss* gradually became superior, in line with the greater response probability of newly learned response items. This study may be described in some detail, not only because it is perhaps the most impressive support of Spence's theories, but also because it has been repeated (Willett, 1964) with externally induced drive substituted for high anxiety scorers as the 'high drive' group. These experimenters used an 'easy' list of paired associates containing common associates from the Kent-Rosanoff list (e.g. foot-hand). A difficult list was also made up, containing the same stimulus words but unusual associates (e.g. foot–cheese). Since the aim of the experiment was to contrast performance where correct responses were dominant, with performance where incorrect responses were dominant, each subject learnt the 'easy' list first to a criterion of two correct repetitions plus eight further trials. (Trials 1 to 10.) Having completed the 'easy' list to this criterion, each subject learned the 'difficult' list, also to a criterion of two correct repetitions plus eight further trials. The first ten trials of the 'difficult' list are also labelled Trials 1 to 10 and the last 10 trials of this list, Trials A to J.

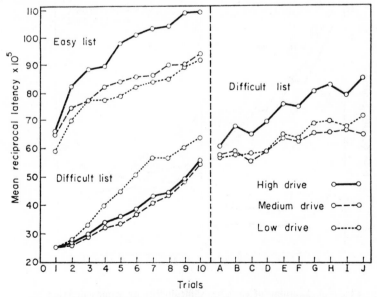

Fig. 13.5. Learning of easy and difficult lists by groups differing in manifest anxiety (*from* Standish and Champion, 1960)

The score taken was the latency of the subject's response to the stimulus word. Figure 13.5 shows the results of the Standish and Champion study; Trials 1 to 10 of the easy and the difficult lists constitute the crucial comparison; in the former case, the correct is clearly predominant, in the latter, the incorrect. In Trials A to J of the difficult list the correct response is dominant again, as these trials occur at the same stage of learning as Trials 1 to 10 of the easy list. High drive subjects are superior on the easy list, and on Trials A to J of the difficult list; low drive subjects are superior on Trials 1 to 10 of the difficult list.

Willett (1964) used exactly the same paradigm, but substituted for the MAS selected subjects, high and low drive groups made up by selection of industrial apprentices who were given the test as part of a selection procedure (high drive), or as part of a simple task-motivated experiment administered after they had already been accepted (low drive). There is considerable evidence that the principle of selection employed did, in fact, produce marked differences in drive (Eysenck, 1964). Results under these conditions were quite unlike those reported by Standish and Champion; at all stages the high drive group was superior to the low drive group! Figure 13.6 shows the main results; note that here latencies have been graphed, rather than their reciprocals, as in Fig. 13.5. We shall come across other evidence showing that MAS+ and MAS− subjects under

identical conditions of external motivation do not always differ in the same way as subjects not differing in personality, but working under externally imposed conditions of high and low drive. This demonstration is a powerful argument against Spence's form of the drive theory of anxiety.

A study demonstrating the importance of interaction between externally imposed drive (stress) and personality has been reported by Spielberger and Smith (1966) in which they employed serial-verbal learning of twelve nonsense syllables, using a neutral and a stress condition (in which the student subjects were told that speed of learning was strongly related to intelligence). Figure 13.7 shows that differences between anxious and non-anxious subjects emerge only under stress conditions, where high-anxious subjects do worse than low-anxious subjects in the first trials (when competing responses would be at a maximum), and better in the later trials.

The authors also compare the differences in learning speed for easy and hard words, defining these in terms of the position of words in the series to be learned. (It is well known that words in serial positions 1, 2, 3, and 12 are easiest to learn, while those in the middle, i.e. positions 6, 7, 8, and 9 are most difficult to learn.) The results are shown in Fig. 13.8; high-anxious subjects are superior for the easy words, but inferior for the difficult words, where competing responses are known to exist; they

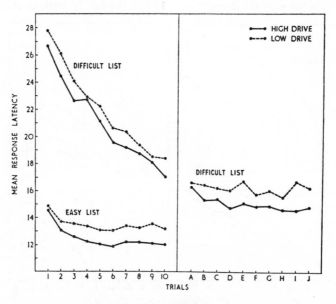

Fig. 13.6. Learning of easy and difficult lists by groups differing in externally imposed drive (*from* Willett, 1964)

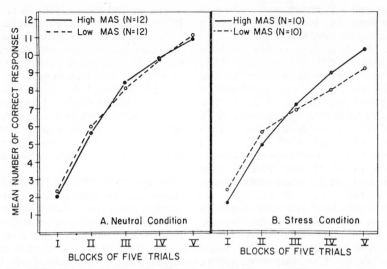

Fig. 13.7. Serial-verbal learning under neutral and stress conditions, of anxious and non-anxious subjects (*from* Spielberger and Smith, 1966)

finally achieve superiority towards the end, when competing responses may be supposed to have been eliminated.

This study supports the Spence theory. A similar point is made by Castaneda and Palermo (1955) in a study of psychomotor performance as a function of training and stress.

Katahn (1964) and Katahn and Lyda (1966) followed the Standish and Champion example by having subjects learn first a highly dominant response word to the stimulus word, then having

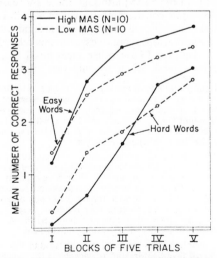

Fig. 13.8. Differences in learning speed for easy and hard words, for anxious and non-anxious subjects (*from* Spielberger and Smith, 1966)

the same subjects learn a non-dominant response word. MAS + subjects learned the dominant word more readily than MAS − subjects; for non-dominant responses the results were reversed. In these studies little attempt was made to control for ability differences; as Katahn (1966) has shown elsewhere, these may interact with anxiety as measured by the MAS. He failed to find poorer performance by MAS + subjects on verbal mazes, and in a highly-intelligent subgroup the MAS + subjects performed in fact better than the MAS − subjects. High ability may downgrade the anxiety-provoking properties of mental tests, even when these are presented under ego-involving instructions. It seems important in future work to control for this variable.

6. Work with children has also been concerned with the interaction between drive level and degree of intratask competition; using motor learning tasks, Castaneda and his co-workers used a children's version of the MAS, or manipulated the drive variable by means of time stress (Castaneda, 1956, 1961; Castaneda, Palermo, and McCandless, 1956; Castaneda and Lipsitt, 1959). Clark (1962) used a similar technique with adults; results have been favourable to the theory of the whole.

7. The next category of experimental researches is concerned with the interaction hypothesis, i.e. 'the hypothesis that states that task-irrelevant responses which in some situations may interfere with efficient performance are more easily elicited in high than in low anxiety Ss (Spence, 1956; Taylor, 1956).' Three main sets of stress stimuli have been involved in this

work; this paragraph will review work with ego-involving instructions, i.e. instructions suggesting that success in the experimental task has a bearing on the Ss IQ, his personality, or his scholastic standing. Nicholson (1958) and Sarason (1956, 1957a), using serial or paired-associate learning found that the introduction of ego-involving instructions impaired performance in the MAS+ group. Other tasks were used by Katchmar et al. (1958), Sarason (1961), and Sarason and Palola (1960) (coding and digit-symbol substitution.) Interactions were observed, but these are of necessity complex, involving as a third variable the difficulty level of the task itself; on the whole, results are in favour of the hypothesis.

8. Failure experiences have also been used in an attempt to induce psychological stress. Sarason (1956) failed to discover any interaction with MAS scores, but Gordon and Berlyne (1954), Lucas (1952), Sarason (1957b), Katchmar et al. (1958), and Taylor (1958) succeeded in supporting the interaction hypothesis, high MAS scorers being uniformly inferior under failure conditions.

9. Noxious stimulation (usually shock) has been studied by several investigators (Besch, 1959; Chiles, 1958; Lee, 1961), who used paired-associates learning; Deese et al. (1953) and Lazarus et al. (1954) who used serial learning, as did Silverman and Blitz (1956); and Davidson et al. (1956), who used colour-naming; (see also Westrope, 1953). Their results, as well as those of Bardach (1960), who used a single shock, are too contradictory to make any decision possible; possible reasons for this will be given later in connection with an alternative theoretical interpretation to Spence's.

10. Some of the earliest work of Spence and his collaborators related to predictions made for discrimination conditioning (Spence and Farber, 1954; Spence and Beecroft, 1954; Hilgard et al., 1951) and learning (Restle and Beecroft, 1955;

Stevenson and Iscoe, 1956; Bendig and Vaughan, 1957; Kamin, 1955). The results have been surveyed by Jones (1960); they are too inconsistent to allow of interpretation. Predictions depend critically on potential differences in stimulus generalisation, and in spite of the interesting work of Rosebaum, already mentioned, the relation of this variable to anxiety is still in doubt. There would appear to be an area of research here where clarification would be of considerable importance, both practically and theoretically, and it is disappointing that very little research appears, in fact, to have been done in this field in recent years.

As Spence and Spence recognise, 'whether these results can be generalised to other measures of manifest anxiety, e.g. clinical judgments, will require empirical demonstration'. Studies like those of Beam (1955), Diethelm and Jones (1947), Pascal and Swensen (1952) and Korchin and Levine (1957) suggest that the use of clinical criteria does not make impossible replication of MAS-type studies, and there are several papers that demonstrate that questionnaire investigations of anxiety or neuroticism correlate quite well with clinical ratings (e.g. Gleser and Ulett, 1952; Lauterbach, 1958; Eysenck, 1947; Eysenck and Eysenck, 1969). It is curious that so little work has in fact been done with clinical patients in this connection; it would seem that they would provide particularly apposite examples of high and low anxiety.* The generalisation Spence and Spence suggest seems likely to prove both possible and useful, but the evidence is not really available on which alone it could be based.

We have concentrated in this review on results achieved with the MAS; although there are reasons for criticising its construction (to which we will turn presently) it does provide a fixed point around which to group multifarious types of experiments related to Spence's theories. Many other measures have, of course, been used, often in only one study, and

---

* Experiments on learning in psychotics have been reviewed by Hunt and Cofer (1944) and by Jones (1960); no detailed review will be given here because they have not, on the whole, been carried out with any regard to theoretical problems of the kind considered in this chapter. Starting with the early work of Hull (1917) and the followers of Kraepelin, several workers have published data that are possibly relevant to the issues considered here; Simmins (1933), Babcock and Levy (1940), Hall and Crookes (1951), Peters (1953), Bleke (1954), and Brengelmann (1958) are examples. The results of this work have been summarised by Jones (1960), and more recent work has not made it necessary to alter his conclusions. He says:

'1. Psychotic patients of all types are capable of learning. 2. Despite this capacity, when compared with normal or psycho-neurotic subjects, psychotics display impaired learning efficiency but individual differences are considerable and overlap between groups is large. 3. This deficit may not, or not entirely, derive from a true impairment of learning capacity but may be a secondary effect of abnormal motivational or other processes. 4. In terms of learning processes, manic-depressives form a group distinct from schizophrenics. 5. Similarly, schizophrenics do not form a unitary group and paranoid schizophrenics, in particular, display specific tendencies. 6. Some types of schizophrenia may result in exaggerated inhibitory tendencies of a character yet undetermined. 7. Increased stimulus generalization may be characteristic of some types of schizophrenia. 8. Chronicity and severity of psychosis are related to the degree of learning impairment.'

Much light could be shed on these problems if experimenters were to phrase their hypotheses in terms more relevant to academic and 'fundamental' theories; there is little link at present between the clinical investigators and the academic theoreticians. Until a closer liaison is established it is unlikely that results of any great generality will be discovered through the use of psychotic subjects.

usually without information of how these measures might be related to the MAS, or to other more widely used tests. Such results are difficult to interpret, and hence no detailed discussion will be given. Waterhouse and Child (1953), for instance, used the Interference Tendency Questionnaire; Williams (1947) and Carlson and Lazarus (1953) used the Rorschach test; a group Rorschach was used by Ausubel *et al.* (1953); Crowne *et al.* (1968) used a 'need for approval' measure; Galbraith and Mosher (1970) a sex guilt test. It is one of the prevailing weaknesses of psychology that idiosyncratic devices for measuring personality dimensions (and many other variables as well!) are constantly being produced and used for no better reason than their novelty; this delight in 'one off' products makes evaluation quite impossible. It should be recognised that new devices are admissible only when it can be shown: 1. That they are in some demonstrable and measurable way 'better' than any existing device; and 2. When their relationship to existing and widely used measures has been clarified. These are minimum requirements, but neglect to pay attention to them has made this field into a stamping ground for untried and often meaningless scores. Where fad succeeds fad, science flies out of the window. It is also interesting to note that existing devices are almost completely immune to criticism; Kimble and Posnick's (1967) demonstration that the MAS could be completely rewritten, preserving the *formal* elements of each question but eliminating its anxiety-related content, while yet retaining a very high correlation with the original MAS has not diminished the popularity of this measure. Neither have the criticisms outlined in subsequent papers had any such effect. The continued use of the Rorschach in spite of continued devastating criticism is another case in point.

We must now turn to an evaluation and to possible criticisms of the Spence model. In order to carry out such a task satisfactorily, it is first necessary to clarify certain points that have been misunderstood in much of the criticism published to date. Thus, the use of the MAS has been criticised because it does not correlate at all well with physiological measures of emotional arousal or drive, which are believed to have greater validity and to be more fundamental, and it has been suggested that such physiological measures should be employed by preference instead of the MAS.

'Such suggestions seem to be based on a rather serious confusion between the drive concept as it is employed in the quantitative Hull-Spence behaviour theory and as it is employed in the physiological theories of such individuals as

Duffy (e.g. 1957) or Malmo (e.g. 1957; 1959). In these physiological theories, the term drive or such alternate expressions as motivation or arousal appear to be used to refer to an assumed physiological state of the organism, thus making it legitimate to seek methods of measuring this state and to compare proposed methods of measurement on the basis of directness, purity, etc. In the Hull-Spence system, on the other hand, the drive concept is purely mathematical in nature, being defined in terms of observable manipulations and related mathematically to other similarly defined concepts, deductions from the entire theoretical network permitting predictions to be made about behaviour. Since the concepts in this behavioural system are convenient mathematical fictions rather than speculations about physiological facts, it is totally inappropriate to refer, literally, to 'measuring' drive and thus to compare the directness, purity, or whatever of various methods of defining the concept.'

Thus, what Cronbach and Meehl call *concurrent* validity of the MAS is meaningless and impossible to achieve, and the same is true of all definitions of concepts within the Hullian network; *construct* validity is the only kind of test that may with advantage be applied to these concepts (Cronbach and Meehl, 1955).

Along similar lines, Spence follows the principle of *operational definition* of concepts and variables; he would argue that if anxiety (drive) is defined in terms of the operations involved in filling in and scoring the MAS, then no criticism is possible. In such a system, the medium is indeed the message; obviously, such a combination of mathematical concepts and operational definitions makes the task of the critic rather difficult as there are no obvious *points d'appui*. It is not even easy to see how such a system could be experimentally disconfirmed; its complexity is such that (as Hullian apologists well know) it is usually possible to adduce saving clauses for every prediction that goes awry. Formal criticism of the Spence theory is therefore probably not very useful; it is possible to argue, as many psychologists have done, that his type of mathematical logic is inappropriate to psychology, or to biology in general, but this, too, would not be a useful avenue to explore—if we knew with any degree of certainty just what are and what are not the most useful methods of approach, we would be much more advanced than we actually are. It may be more helpful to acknowledge the very real advances made by Spence, both in our thinking about these problems, and in our factual understanding of them, and to contrast his approach with possible alternatives. Such a comparison will not enable us to decide that one method of approach is superior, either in this particular instance or under all conceivable circumstances, but it may help us see more clearly the advantages and disadvantages of different approaches.

We have already mentioned the 'interference' theory (Child, 1954) as an alternative to Spence's original form of the simple anxiety/drive theory; Spence's inclusion of S_D within his system brings interference within his system, and indeed gives it a proper status, which it previously did not have. This, therefore, is not any longer an alternative to Spence's theory, as it was when Jones (1960) last reviewed this field. Another possibility, also mentioned by Jones, has already been alluded to. As he puts it, there is a possibility

'that there exists a stable curvilinear relationship between drive and efficiency with a stable optimum drive value (Hebb, 1955) but that increasing task difficulty, irrespective of the degree and nature of response competition, increases drive in a manner analogous to the drive increment postulated as following frustration (Brown and Farber, 1951; Child and Waterhouse, 1953; Marx, 1956). If so, the optimum pretask drive level would be lower the more difficult the task. This hypothesis is consistent with empirical studies of the relationship between task difficulty and such measures as muscle tension and palmar skin resistance (cf. Freeman and Giese, 1940) which tend to indicate that task difficulty is a stressor factor increasing drive.'

Willett and Eysenck (1962) have manipulated drive level experimentally, as well as difficulty level in serial rote learning; they found superior performance under high drive conditions, and, of course, with the easier task, but failed to find the interaction between the two that would be called for by this theory. They also found greater bowing of the error curve with low drive and with the easy list; again, no interaction was observed. This empirical finding, together with the powerful arguments produced by Spence and Spence (1966) against the use of 'difficulty' as a relevant dimension in this field, must speak against this hypothesis.

A further hypothesis is suggested by Jones (1960).

'This is concerned with the stimulus properties of drive, as such, and can best be illustrated by reference to discrimination learning. Discrimination is most difficult to achieve when the positive and negative stimuli are most nearly alike, i.e. when they have most elements in common. The incidental experimental stimuli contribute to what they have in common and one of these is the drive

stimulus. The stronger the drive, the more intense the drive stimulus, the greater its share of the stimulus complex, the greater the similarity between the positive and negative stimuli and, therefore, the greater the difficulty of discrimination. This effect would be opposed to any energising value of increased drive and the interaction of the two effects would determine the optimal level of drive, thus producing a pattern of results similar to those reported by Yerkes and Dodson. In simple conditioning, where a single stimulus is linked with a single response, no deleterious effect would result but in trial-and-error learning of all types, discriminations between stimuli are as important as in discrimination learning though the additional factor of response selection is also involved. This hypothesis is akin to that advanced by Hilgard, Jones, and Kaplan (1951) concerning the relationship between anxiety and discrimination learning. They suggest that anxious subjects perceive situations as more threatening than do non-anxious subjects and that "a person whose discriminations are dimmed by anxiety" is less likely to differentiate between the positive and negative stimuli.'

This hypothesis would account for much of the material reviewed by Easterbrook (1959) and could with advantage be made the subject of a determined experimental investigation. At present it has not been integrated experimentally with work on personality and anxiety in any direct fashion.

From the systematic side, the only attempt to elaborate a general theory that would link the phenomena of rote learning with personality has been that of the present writer (Eysenck, 1965, 1967); in this primary orientation it differs from that of Spence and Spence (1966) who point out that, 'the interests of those of us who developed and first used the scale can be described as being both broader and narrower than anxiety as a personality characteristic, the studies growing out of a series of investigations that have been concerned with the role of aversive motivational or drive factors in learning situations, primarily classical conditioning, within the framework of Hull-Spence behaviour theory'.

The starting point of the Eysenck series of studies, *per contra*, was the discovery that individual differences in behaviour, whether in social situations or in the laboratory, could be described with reasonable accuracy in terms of two major dimensions of personality, i.e. introversion-extraversion and neuroticism-stability, or emotionality *vs* non-emotionality (Eysenck and Eysenck, 1969.) These dimensions have emerged again and again from the most diverse types of studies, both of adults and children

(Eysenck, 1970), and although other writers frequently use quite different terms (Cattell, for instance, prefers exvia-invia for extraversion-introversion, and anxiety for neuroticism), yet the nature of their factors is demonstrably very similar. Given that some such two-dimensional system is indeed indicated by the facts, then it becomes important to enquire where the MAS fits in. Many investigations have shown that this scale correlates in the neighbourhood of 0·6 to 0·7 with neuroticism, and 0·3 to 0·4 with introversion; this makes good sense in terms of the Eysenck (1947, 1957) descriptive system as neurotic patients suffering from anxiety state, or having anxiety among their symptoms ('dysthymics' in Eysenck's nomenclature) are universally found to be high on both introversion and neuroticism. It also fits in with Eysenck's theory about the origin and nature of neurosis, which is conceived of as a set of conditioned autonomic responses (Eysenck and Rachman, 1965); *see also* Chapter 10. Thus, the MAS emerges as a factorially complex measure that picks out subjects for testing in the laboratory who are either introverted, or neurotic (in the non-clinical sense of that term), or both; clearly this makes interpretation of results reported by Spence extremely difficult, if not impossible. Findings could be mediated through the *N* construct, or the *I* construct, or both, to varying degree; it is impossible to tell by looking at the published results. It is even possible that the positive effects of MAS + might be due to the high degree of introversion of the sample tested, while the negative effects might be due to the high degree of neuroticism. Such criticisms do not touch Spence's purely operational definition of 'anxiety', but they may give others pause who are not committed to this particular definition. The only way to demonstrate the superiority of this two-factor approach to Spence's single factor approach is, of course, an experimental one; it remains to be shown that empirical data can be discovered through the use of the two-dimensional system which would not have been discovered through Spence's system, and could not be explained by his concepts.

Before turning to a consideration of this system, and the underlying hypothesis that it is introversion (characterised by high cortical arousal) that is responsible for the drive-properties of the MAS + subjects, rather than neuroticism (which when aroused through ego-involving instructions, or some other manipulation of the situation, produces the drive stimuli that interfere with performance), it may be useful to consider an important study in which an attempt has been made to test this hypothesis. Willoughby (1967) replicated the Spence *et al.* (1956) **study** on the relation of anxiety level to performance in competitional and non-competitional paired-associates learning, reviewed above, but with one important modification; instead of using the multi-dimensional, and, hence, equivocal MAS as his measure of 'anxiety', he employed a factorially purified measure of 'emotionality' or neuroticism, which had negligible correlation with a measure of introversion (0·14). He found high *N* subjects significantly inferior to low *N* subjects on the competitive paired-associated list, as expected on Spence's hypothesis; he also found high *N* subjects inferior on the non-competitive list, however, which is clearly contrary to Spence's hypothesis, and to the findings of the Spence *et al.* study. Willoughby comments:

'Since the procedures used in this study replicated those of Spence *et al.*, including the use of *S*s drawn from a collegiate population, the differences between the present findings and those of Spence can be attributed to a difference in the operational measures of "anxiety" employed in the two experiments. One possible basis for the discrepancy is that the "introversion" component is the main factor in the MAS producing a performance differential on the non-competitive pairs.'

He goes on to say that:

'the results of an unpublished study . . . support these notions. In that study *S*s scoring in the upper and lower quintiles of a unidimensional "anxiety" scale did not differ significantly in their rates of conditioning. These results were obtained despite the fact that the experimental procedures employed were similar to those used by Spence and associated in their conditioning studies. Such findings, taken in conjunction with those of the present study, indicate that Spence's results for non-competitive paired-associates may be obtained only when measures of anxiety include an "introversion" component (as for example in the MAS) but not when a more unidimensional emotionality scale is employed.'

This study illustrates very forcibly the weakness of 'operational definitions' when used in the absence of supporting evidence from independent studies of the univocal nature of the concepts employed, and the measures used. The continued and widespread use of the MAS in experimental studies of this kind finds little support in a consideration of the most appropriate methodology for the discovery of unequivocal relations between personality variables and learning, or even for the further investigation of the 'drive' concept; it inevitably produces confusion, contradictory results, and uninterpretable conclusions.

Eysenck has been mainly concerned with reminiscence, using in particular motor learning on the
pursuit rotor; his theories have undergone several
changes which will not be of interest here (1956,
1962, 1964, 1965).* According to the latest version
which has also been extended to verbal learning, the
process of consolidation of the memory trace is of
fundamental importance in all learning, and is, in
turn, influenced profoundly by the degree of cortical
arousal (itself probably mediated by the ascending
reticular activating system); the greater the degree
of arousal, the stronger and more prolonged the
consolidation process, and consequently, the greater
the permanence and accessibility of the memory
trace so laid down. (John, 1967, gives a good
discussion of the theoretical and experimental work
related to this theory.) To these postulates, which
essentially concern the transformation of short-
term memory, conceptualised as a set of reverberating
neural circuits, into long-term memory, conceptualised as a permanent chemical transformation of the
cell material through some form of protein synthesis,
must be added certain others (Walker, 1958;
Walker and Tarte, 1963) concerning what these
authors call the *action decrement*. In their own
words:

'(1) The occurrence of any psychological event . . .
sets up an active, perseverative trace process which
persists for a considerable period of time. (2) The
perseverative process has two important dynamic
characteristics: (*a*) permanent memory is laid
down during the active phase in a gradual fashion;
(*b*) during the active period, there is a degree of
temporary inhibition to recall, i.e. action decrement (this negative bias against repetition serves
to protect the consolidating trace against disruption.) (3) High arousal during the associative
process will result in a more intensely active trace
process. The more intense activity will result in
greater ultimate memory but greater temporary
inhibition against recall.'

Kleinsmith and Kaplan (1963, 1964) and Kleinsmith *et al.* (1963) have submitted the hypothesis of
'action decrement' to an experimental test, showing
that high arousal paired-associates were poorly
remembered after a short interval, well remembered
after a long interval (reminiscence), while low arousal
paired-associates were well remembered after a short
interval, poorly remembered after a long interval
(forgetting.) This cross-over effect with time is, of
course, precisely what is required by the theory.

* In so far as this is a theory of motivation as well as of
learning, a more detailed discussion will be found in Chapter
12, by G. Wilson, who also quotes some of the studies here
referred to.

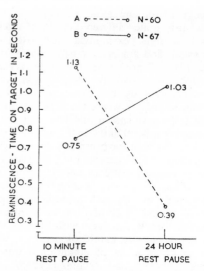

Fig. 13.9. Mean reminiscence scores on pursuit rotor of
high arousal group (*A*) and low arousal group (*A*) after
short and long rest pause (*from* Clark, 1967)

Similar results have been reported for the pursuit
rotor by Clark (1967), except that he did not
contrast, as had Kleinsmith and Kaplan, the fate
over time of high arousal and low arousal items, but
instead, graded his subjects as highly aroused or
poorly aroused on the basis of the two flash threshold
test (Lindsley, 1957; Venables, 1963a,b). Using
60 low-drive schizophrenics and 67 high-drive ones,
he gave both groups 5-minutes practice on the
pursuit rotor, followed by a 10-minute rest pause;
another 5 minutes of practice followed, then a 24-
hour rest pause, and finally another 5 minutes of
practice. Reminiscence was defined as the increase
in performance of the first post-rest 10 sec period
over the average of that on the last three pre-rest
10 sec periods; there were two such scores for each
subjects, following the short and the long rest period
respectively. Figure 13.9 shows the main results; it
will be seen that for the low-drive group reminiscence
is high after the 10-minute rest, but poor after the
24-hour rest, while for the high-drive group this
relationship is reversed. Analysis of variance shows
that neither for the 'between groups' nor for the
'between rest periods' variance is there any statistical
significance; for the interaction p < 0·001. This
study not only supports Walker's theory; it also
demonstrates the danger of averaging scores for
heterogeneous groups, a danger stressed very much
by Eysenck (1967). It is assumed by most writers
that maximum reminiscence has been reached after
rest periods of eight minutes or so because there is
on average no further increase in reminiscence;

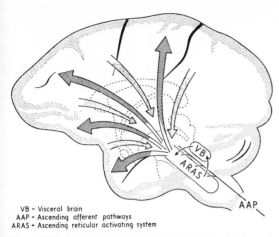

VB = Visceral brain
AAP = Ascending afferent pathways
ARAS = Ascending reticular activating system

Fig. 13.10. Cortical and pre-cortical representation of physiological bases of N and E in Eysenck's theory (*from* Eysenck, 1967)

clearly the possibility has been overlooked that some people (high arousal) might show an increase, others (low arousal) an actual decrement. The present experiment does not prove this point because the same subjects were exposed to both the long and the short rest period; nevertheless, even in this form the experiment does seem to establish the point that personality variables (in this case high or low arousal) may play a decisive part in determining the temporal fate of the memory trace. It may also be noted that the 'now you see it, now you don't' character of the verbal reminiscence phenomenon, which has led to the practical abandonment of research in that field, may be due to the failure to take arousal differences (whether experimentally produced, task material produced, or personality correlated) into account.

Eysenck's (1967) personality theory links the descriptive concepts of E (extraversion-introversion) and N (neuroticism-stability) with the arousal-activation mechanism along the lines suggested in Fig. 13.10. Unlike Duffy (1962) Eysenck postulates two such mechanisms, linked respectively with the reticular formation and the visceral brain; the former produces cortical arousal, and is, in turn, basic to individual differences in E, while the latter

produces autonomic activation, and is, in turn, basic to individual differences in N. (A hypothesis making a similar distinction between the reticular and the limbic forms of arousal/activation has been independently put forward by Routtenberg, 1968.)* According to this hypothesis, introverts are characterised by higher cortical arousal levels than extraverts, with ambiverts, of course, intermediate; high N scorers are characterised by high levels of limbic activation, low N scorers by low levels of activation. These two systems are postulated to be independent for most of the time, except on occasions when strong emotions are produced in the individual concerned; such strong emotions produce strong arousal in the cortex, either directly or through the reticular formation, so that a combination of strong emotion—low arousal is impossible, although the combination of high arousal—little emotion is possible. Evidence for some such system as that postulated has been reviewed in detail in Eysenck (1967), and no effort will be made to do so here; while, of course, not conclusive, the physiological evidence (largely relying on EEG recordings and other electro-physiological methods) and the psychological evidence (relying on laboratory experiments with conditioning, vigilance, sensory threshold, and other types of investigation) are on the whole in support of the hypothesis. If we accept the view that such a two-dimensional theory is at least along the right lines (although it would, of course, have to be supplemented by other dimensions and other physiological mechanisms to account for all of personality variance), then we would have to formulate a linking set of hypotheses to enable us to make predictions from personality to performance on learning tasks. Chapter 11 (I. Martin) has done so for simple conditioning; here we will be concerned with verbal and motor learning.

Mention has already been made of the writer's attempts to provide a satisfactory theory to encompass pursuit rotor learning, particularly reminiscence. The prediction was originally made that reminiscence would be more strongly marked in extraverted subjects; this hypothesis was mediated through an out-of-date reliance on Hullian mechanisms, particularly I_R. In terms of the consolidation hypothesis, however, a much more direct mediation

---

* Elliott (1966) and Elliott, Bankart and Light (1970) have made a similar distinction, linking arousal with what Berlyn (1960) has labelled the 'collative' properties of situations—novelty, complexity, uncertainty, surprisingness, and the like. They thus distinguish between 'arousal', a term applying to collative properties, and measurable by palmar conductance, and 'activation', which is linked with the instigation and initiation of responses, and measurable by increases in heart rate. Elliott and his colleagues report experimental studies in support of this distinction, and clearly a properly planned factorial study of physiological measures of arousal and activation would be of considerable interest in this connection. At the moment, the distinction made by these various writers cannot be said to be supported sufficiently to consider it acceptable without further experimental proof, but the evidence is strong enough to throw much doubt on the unidimensional hypothesis of Duffy and Spence. Elliott and his colleagues do not take into account in their work the possible interactions between arousal and activation; Eysenck (1967) has discussed this point in detail.

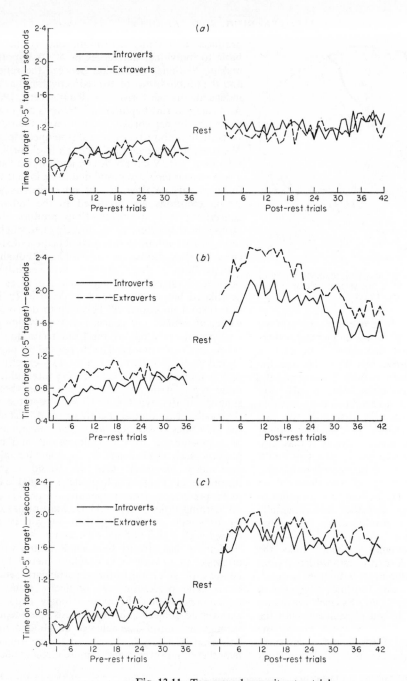

Fig. 13.11. Ten-second pursuit-rotor trials.

Pursuit rotor reminiscence data for groups of introverts and extraverts, after (*a*)
30 sec rest, (*b*) 10 min rest, and (*c*) 1 weeks rest, respectively (*from* Gray, 1968)

becomes possible. We have seen (in the Clark experiment cited above) that as predicted on the Walker hypothesis high arousal subjects show poor post-rest performance after a 10 minute rest pause, but good performance after a 24 hour rest pause, while low arousal subjects show the opposite pattern. If introverts are equated with high arousal subjects, and extraverts with low arousal subjects, then it would seem to follow that with the usual rest intervals of 5 to 10 minutes extraverts would show more reminiscence than introverts, while with longer rest intervals (24 hours or more) introverts would show more reminiscence than extraverts. There are some two dozen experiments using short rest intervals, mostly carried out to test Eysenck's original theory (Eysenck, 1962); almost all of these show the predicted superiority of extraverts in reminiscence. Studies using longer intervals of rest are, of course, crucial to the hypothesis, but are unfortunately rare. Gray (1968) used three groups of male university students, totalling 209 Ss; these were given 6 minutes of massed practice on the pursuit rotor, a rest of 30 seconds, 10 minutes or 1 week, and a further practice period of 7 minutes. Each group was divided into extraverts and introverts; Fig. 13.11 shows the results. As usual, extraverts show greater reminiscence after the ten-minute rest period, but they are not superior after 30 seconds, nor are they inferior after one week. The interaction term was quite insignificant. More successful was a series of studies carried out by Farley (1969). Using several different measures of extraversion-introversion on different groups (in addition to personality questionnaires; he also used the salivary increment test as described by Eysenck and Eysenck (1967) as a measure of introversion) he found the predicted cross-over effect in every case, although the interaction term was not always statistically significant. Clearly, the type of subject used, and the level of arousal produced in them by the testing operation must be crucial factors in the verification or disconfirmation of hypotheses of this kind; only further work can tell us whether the confirmatory nature of Farley's results or the disconfirmatory nature of Gray's results is more relevant to the theory under discussion. As far as motor learning and reminiscence are concerned, no definitive conclusion can be drawn at present. It should be noted, however, that the theory does account for the very numerous data on short-rest reminiscence; these would present considerable difficulty to alternative theories because it is the low arousal group (i.e. the extraverts) who perform better after the rest pause.

Work on verbal learning has usually concentrated on short rest pauses, possibly because it is more

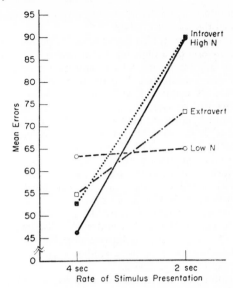

Fig. 13.12. Serial rote leaning as a function of rate of presentation and personality (*from* Jensen, 1962)

difficult to programme 24 hour intervals, and partly because the importance of the length of the rest intervals was not always recognised due to the absence of any clearly formulated theory. The first study to be mentioned was published by Jensen (1962). He presented his subjects with a serial rote learning task, varying rate of presentation by giving 2 sec intervals to one group, 4 sec intervals to the other group. His results, comparing introvert with extravert subjects, and high N with low N scorers, are shown in Fig. 13.12. It would seem that extraverts do better, as expected, with the short interval, while introverts do worse. (We are comparing the two groups with each other; absolutely, both groups do worse with the short rate of presentation, but the introverts suffer disproportionately.) Low N subjects are not affected by the difference in length of interval, but high N subjects clearly are penalised by the short interval. If our hypothesis regarding the longer consolidation periods of the introverts making them perform comparatively less well on the 2 sec rate of presentation is correct, then we may perhaps explain the poor performance of the high N group either in terms of interfering drive stimuli produced by the stress imposed by the short interval, or by the secondary cortical arousal produced by this stress, directly or indirectly through the ARAS. Jensen's main finding, as far as our theory is concerned, was that 'the overall correlation within the high and low N groups between extraversion and errors in learning was -0.31'. Thus, extraverts do better with these short intervals, on the whole, but disproportionately so with the shorter interval.

Howarth (1963) also found superior performance of extraverts on a digit repetition task in which the length of time during which information could be held was investigated. Extraverts gave a score of 14·0 sec as compared with introverts who scored 11·8 sec on the average. This agrees with prediction from our hypothesis; Howarth, working on another type of hypothesis altogether, had predicted the opposite. Siegman (1957) predicted superiority of introverts on simple serial learning tasks, and inferiority on complex ones, on the basis that arousal would mediate more intralist interference. Using Guilford's R scale as a measure of E, he found significant correlations (with MA held constant) of 0·35 between introversion and simple list learning, and of −0·34 between introversion and complex list learning. Both of these studies were somewhat tangential to our purpose.

Shanmugan and Santhanam (1964) tested personality differences in serial learning under conditions of no interference, and also when competing stimuli were presented at the marginal visual level. Ten learning trials were allowed for the twenty-word list, and the criterion test given after a period of 30 sec; this short term would lead us to predict superiority for the extraverted subjects. Regardless of interference, extraversion correlated positively and significantly with the number of words correctly anticipated. The concern of these investigators with the effects of interference on learning was shared by Jensen (1964) whose study has not been reported in the usual journals, but which constitutes the most concerted attack on the problem of personality as related to verbal learning.

Jensen carried out a large-scale experimental study involving many different types of learning and learning tasks, as well as measures of personality and intelligence; results were intercorrelated, factor analysed and the resulting factors submitted to oblique rotation. Two higher-order factors were obtained, of which the second is of particular interest here; its nature is to be inferred from the loadings given in Table 13.1. These figures show convincingly that extraversion correlates with *quick* performance on the Matrices intelligence test and with good performance on various learning/memory tasks; the size of the loadings is surprising, as a much less close relation between temperament and learning would perhaps have been expected, particularly in a group of students, where ability is relatively homogeneous. Even so, several types of learning task and several scores from those which figure in Table 13.1 do not correlate with extraversion, and form an independent factor of 'general learning ability'.

Table 13.1.

Variable	Loading
MPI Extraversion	0·78
EPI Extraversion, Form A	0·68
Serial retroactive interference, oscillation	−0·66
Serial Trigram learning, errors	−0·65
EPI Extraversion, Form B	0·61
Time for Progressive Matrices	−0·56
Serial retroactive interference, errors. (Relearning)	−0·54
Serial retroactive interference, errors. (Interpolated learning)	−0·46
Delayed digit span	0·41
Immediate digit span	0·40

(Actually the two factors are not quite independent, but are correlated to the extent of 0·34; a fourth-order factor was extracted by Jensen which included the majority of learning tasks and scores, as well as extraversion. Neuroticism did not have loadings here or elsewhere in Jensen's data.)

Gebhardt (1966) applied nine intelligence tests to 400 high-school children chosen from a much larger number because of their extreme N and E scores; 100 were chosen from each of the four quadrants. On overall performance, extraverts and introverts were well matched, but on an associative rote learning test of memory, the extraverts were significantly superior. Scores for the four groups were as follows:

	$N+$	$N-$	Mean
$E+$	107	110	109
$E-$	104	106	105

This difference, in addition to being fully significant statistically, is equal to over one-third of one SD and is, of course, in the same direction as the differences noted above; apparently group tests are capable of verifying the general theory linking rote learning and personality. Other studies relevant to this point are those of Meredith (1966) and Crawford and Snyder (1966); neither used the MPI or the EPI, but both found better learning with subjects who would be expected to score high on E, for reasons outlined in Eysenck (1967).

Howarth (1969a) took up the notion introduced by Siegman (1957) that extraverts are less subject to response-interference, due to their lower level of cortical arousal. He tested 11 introverts, 11 ambiverts, and 11 extraverts on three trials of paired associated learning, in which a colour name was paired with an animal name; pairings were changed from first to second, and from second to third test, with 2 minute intervals between series. No differences were found on the first two series, but on the third series extraverts showed improvement in performance rather than interference; introverts showed most interference. Howarth (1969b) returned to the fray with another experiment, using external distraction, rather like Shanmugan and Santhanam had done; he found extraverts learning faster under the most interfering conditions. However, the nature of the interfering task (numbers printed in front and/or behind sets of numbers to be learned) makes it difficult to interpret the results.

A rather complex experiment is reported by Purohit (1966). A paired associates learning task had as stimulus two digits with a sign of multiplication between them, and the response consisted of a two-digit number which was either a correct or an incorrect product of the stimulus. To maximise interpair competition, the stimuli of the four incorrect pairs were the reverse of the stimuli of the four correct pairs, and the same responses to the four correct pairs were used as responses to the incorrect pairs as well. Two groups of subjects were formed; in the stress group, subjects were asked to anticipate the response within 2 seconds of the presentation of the stimulus, while in the non-stress group subjects were allowed as much time as they required. MPI scores on E did not significantly correlate with scores, but measures of E derived from experimental tests (e.g. spiral after effect) found extraverts significantly superior on the difficult task under stress conditions. This experiment is difficult to evaluate because of its complexity, and the unusual nature of the stimuli used.

More clearly relevant from the theoretical point of view is a thesis by Grant (1969), in which he tested 16 extraverts and 16 introverts. A series of 48 items was presented singly to each S, consisting of 24 3-letter words and 24 trigrams. Eight items were tested after each of six retention intervals (3, 6, 9, 12, 15, and 18 sec). The retention interval was filled with counting backwards by threes or by fours from a 3-digit number. It is well known that under these conditions most forgetting takes place within the first 3 sec (Talland, 1967; Dillon and Reid, 1969); this suggests that consolidation of the memory trace (which is, of course, a very simple one in this case, being only made up of one single word or trigram) is by then almost complete. If this were so, then no competition of the consolidation process would take place, and the amount of remembering would be a direct function of the amount of arousal; hence one might expect, on our hypothesis, that introverts would be superior to extraverts, in spite of the short time interval involved. Meaningful material was found too easy to give much discrimination (although even here introverts did better on the whole); for the trigrams, results significantly favoured the introverts at the 0·001 level, with introverts scoring

14 per cent more than extraverts. Introverts were better at all 6 intervals, but significantly so only for intervals of 3, 6, 9, and 15 sec. This study is of particular interest because of its close relation with experimental work using this technique; no such relation exists for the type of study done by Purohit. Proper tests of the theory in question, particularly along quantitative lines, cannot be undertaken with any hope of success if investigators continue to make up new, untried tests, regarding which no general information is available.

Also relevant in this connection may be some experiments usually listed under the heading of 'immediate memory'; clearly, the distinction between learning and memory, unless specially worked out according to a sophisticated paradigm, does not have such meaning in this type of work. Moldawsky and Moldawsky (1952) demonstrated impairment in immediate memory (digit span) as a function of failure-criticism, and similar effects of stress-induced anxiety have been observed by Basowitz et al. (1955), comparing paratroop trainees with controls, and by Wright (1954), using patients confronted with threat of surgery. In the Moldawsky experiment, a useful control was introduced, in that a vocabulary-type intelligence test was not found to be affected by the experimental variable. Although these studies use the term 'anxiety' to characterise the experimentally-manipulated stress variable, interpretation comes most naturally in terms of the arousal concept, high arousal, contingent upon experimental manipulation of the situation, leading to strong consolidation, and hence poor immediate performance. These studies would have been of much greater interest if half the experimental population had been tested for recall after 24 hours or some other period that would permit consolidation to be completed, even in the high arousal group.

All these studies used a short interval between learning and reproduction, and in nearly every case extraverts, as predicted, performed better; the Grant study is the only exception, and there, of course, the known brevity of the consolidation period leads to the prediction of introvert superiority. Few studies have used variations in length of interval as an experimental variable; these, of course, furnish us with a crucial test of the hypothesis, while the superiority of the extraverts on short-interval tests could be accounted for along many different lines, the crossover between extraverts and introverts with lengthening of the interval would be difficult to explain along any other lines. One such experiment has been reported by Skanthakumari (1965), who used a task in which five geometrical figures are exposed inside a large circle; subjects have to remember their positions and indicate them after the stimulus has been withdrawn. Four periods of learning-reproduction interval were used: no rest, 24 hours, 7 days, and 21 days. Scoring errors in terms of degrees of rotation from true, Skantha-kumari found that for the shorter periods the extraverts did better, while for the longer periods there were no differences between groups; these results were of doubtful statistical significance. High N scorers were better throughout than low N scorers. It should be noted that in this study the same group of subjects was tested on all four occasions; it would, of course, have been better if four different groups had been used. The results, showing a relative improvement of introverts with increasing length of rest period, might have been more pro-nounced if the interpolated testing had not interfered with the process of consolidation. Also, the task itself is unusual and little understood; again, it is not entirely easy to apply knowledge gained from more orthodox tasks to explain the detailed findings with a novel and relatively untried test.

More relevant and indeed crucial to our argument is a study reported by Howarth and Eysenck (1968) who designed their experiment specially to test the theory under discussion. From over 600 students, 110 were selected on the basis of their EPI scores as being extraverted or introverted (+ or −1 SD or more from the mean) and having a relatively low score on N. Seven pairs of CVCs of medium association value were used in four orders of presentation; learning of the list was to a criterion of

once through correct. The subsequent retention interval (up to 30 min) was occupied with S making words out of a longer word. There were no differ-ences in learning rates, but there was a significant interaction effect between recall intervals (0, 1 min, 5 min, 30 min or 24 hours) and extraversion, with extraverts having superior recall at the short-term retention intervals, but inferior at the long-term intervals. The predicted cross-over occurred at about 5 min. Results are shown in detail in Fig. 13.13; it should be noted that each point represents a different group of subjects. There is a striking similarity between the results shown in this figure, and those reported by Kleinsmith and Kaplan; the curve showing the fate of the memory trace for extraverts resembles closely that of low-arousal words in their study, and the curve showing the fate of the memory trace for introverts resembles closely that of high-arousal words in their study. This resemblance is unlikely to be due to chance factors, and suggests that similar theories may be applicable to both conditions, i.e. high arousal may be inherent in the person (introvert) or may be produced by the stimulus. It remains to study the interaction between these two scores of arousal; no relevant study appears to have been reported.

McLaughlin has also reported a study (1968) varying the reproduction interval, using immediate reproduction and intervals of 1, 2, or 7 days; 75 students were tested after having been selected on the basis of the EPI from a larger group of 141 and assigned to one of four groups: $E + N+, E + N−,$ $E − N+,$ and $E − N−.$ The list to be learned consisted of 12 pairs with 3-letter words as stimuli and 40 per cent association value nonsense syllables as responses. The list was presented on a memory drum at a 2·2 sec rate with a 6 sec intertrial interval to a criterion of 10/12 correct responses for a maximum of 36 trials. The recall task consisted of 3 parts: (a) free stimulus and/or response recall, (b) filling in a sheet which listed the stimulus items with blanks for the responses, and (c) a multiple-choice recognition test. Extraverts were found to be superior in learning the task at the 0·05 level, but more detailed analysis of the stages of learning revealed interesting differences. Three such stages were recognised: Response learning was defined as the mean number of correct responses until each response was given correctly; no differences were found with respect to this stage. The association stage was defined as the mean number of trials between the trial on which responses were first given until it was first given to the appropriate stimulus; here extraverts performed worse than introverts, possibly because of greater 'risk-taking behaviour' leading them to give responses as soon as learned,

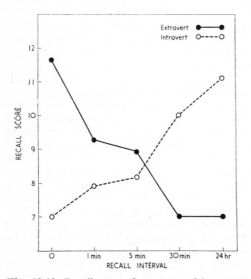

Fig. 13.13. Recall scores for groups of introverts and extraverts after different recall intervals (*from* Howarth and Eysenck, 1968)

but in response to the wrong stimulus word. Lastly, the integration stage, which was defined as the mean number of trials between the trial on which the response was first given to the appropriate stimulus until the response was last given incorrectly; on this extraverts were significantly better. (These stages are, of course, not independent, nevertheless analysis along these lines constitutes a welcome beginning for a proper analysis of the precise differences in performance between extraverts and introverts.) No differences were found in recall or recognition between the personality groups; possibly the periods chosen for the intervals were not very appropriate for such a test. N did not at any stage correlate with performance, either in learning or in reproduction.

A somewhat different approach to that exemplified in the studies listed so far was attempted by McLaughlin and Eysenck (1967). This study is based on the hypothesis that the four personality groups $(E + N+, E + N-, E - N+,$ and $E - N-)$ can be arranged along a continuum of arousal, from the lowest $(E + N-)$ to the highest $(E - N+)$, with the other two intermediate. On the basis of the Yerkes-Dodson Law, performance on a paired-associates nonsense syllable learning task should show the usual inverted-U shape when plotted against this continuum; for a difficult task, the optimum point of this interval-U shape should be shifted towards the low arousal side. Two lists were constructed to meet the requirements of having stimulus members of high meaningfulness, low similarity and response members of intermediate meaningfulness and either high similarity or low similarity. Stimulus and response members of low similarity had a minimal number of letters in common, while the responses of high similarity all had the same vowel and one consonant in common. In all pairs similarity between stimuli and responses was minimised as much as possible. Sixty-four subjects were assigned to one of the four personality groups; 8 members of each group were given the easy list, the other 8 the difficult list. Results are shown in Fig. 13.14; extraverts perform significantly better throughout, which is in line with expectation as testing immediately followed learning. Of greater interest is the fact that the second order interaction $(E \times N \times \text{Difficulty})$ is also significant beyond the 0·01 level; neurotic extraverts are superior to stable extraverts on the easy list, while the reverse is true on the difficult list. Similarly, neurotic introverts learn faster on the difficult task and slower on the easy task than stable introverts. While the overall results are in line with prediction, it should be noted that the inverted-U curves drawn in Fig. 13.14 to connect the results (number of errors) of the four personality groups give an exaggerated air of

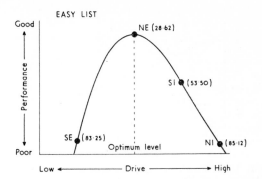

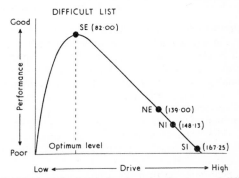

Fig. 13.14. Paired-associate learning for easy and difficult lists of four personality type groups (*from* McLaughlin and Eysenck, 1967)

numerical exactitude as no intermediate levels of arousal were, of course, available on the abscissa. Nevertheless, the results compare well with others already reported on response interference, and the theory suggested (high arousal producing greater interference) would seem to explain the occurrence of the Yerkes-Dodson (inverted-U) type of relation in this connection.

A very carefully controlled experiment by McLean (1968) must be mentioned to round off this brief survey of relevant work; it is too extensive to be described in detail, but essentially McLean controlled, in addition to the personality variable (through selection on the basis of EPI scores), by measuring within-subject arousal (through the use of psychophysiological measures), and by imposing low arousal or high arousal conditions (through the use of white noise in order to induce high arousal). He also compared incidental and intentional learning, using paired-associates learning of single digits paired with nonsense syllables. Figure 13.15 shows recall of paired-associates after incidental learning for low arousal and induced high arousal groups as a function of recall interval (2 mins *vs* 24 hours); Figure 13.16 shows recall as a function

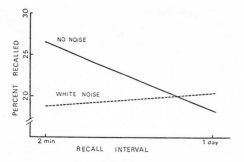

Fig. 13.15. Recall of paired-associates after incidental learning for low-arousal and induced high-arousal groups as a function of recall interval (*from* McLean, 1968)

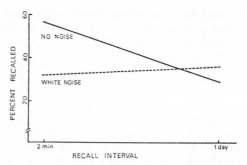

Fig. 13.17. Recall of paired-associates after intentional learning for low-arousal and induced high-arousal groups as a function of recall interval (*from* McLean, 1968)

of within-subject arousal. Figures 13.17 and 13.18 show the same relations for intentional learning; it will be clear in all these results that the expected cross-over effect does in fact occur. As far as personality was concerned, 'extraverts performed better than introverts on immediate (2 minute) paired-associate recall tests, but introverts performed better than extraverts on delayed (24 hours) recall tests. The interaction between extraversion and recall interval was ... statistically significant (p < 0·01)'.

McLean goes on to make a comparison between within-subject arousal, as measured psychophysiologically, and extraversion-introversion, in terms of the inverse-U curve relating 'arousal' to performance.

'That there is a strong curvilinear relationship between arousal and P–A performance becomes apparent when recall performance is plotted against within-subject arousal categories for both noise conditions and both recall intervals in incidental learning in terms of an inverted-U relationship.... As arousal increases, recall performance decreases when the P–A interval is 2 minutes. This relationship is almost completely

reversed in the delayed recall subjects, 24 hours later. In the case of 24 hour recall the optimal arousal category was the high arousal associates of the control group, while the same associates for the experimental group remained postoptimal for that recall period. On the other side of the inverted-U, low arousal associates for both noise conditions were suboptimal in recall performance for the 24 hour recall interval.'

Relationships with personality mirroring this were established

'when extreme introvert and extravert groups are selected separately from each noise category and arranged according to the inverted-U hypothesis as is done in [Fig. 13.19]. This pattern is remarkably similar to the arousal-recall relationship found as a function of time when the descriptor of arousal was percentage change in skin resistance. The indication is that differences along the E scale are equivalent to differences in the magnitude of skin resistance decrement in their effect on P–A recall performance. Introverts recalled fewer correct associates than extraverts when tested 2 minutes after P–A presentation but recalled more a day

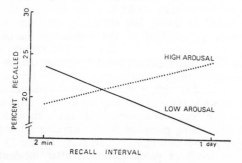

Fig. 13.16. Recall of paired-associates after incidental learning as a function of within-subject arousal and time of recall for both noise conditions (*from* McLean, 1968)

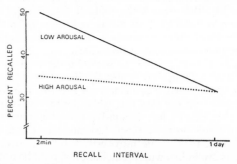

Fig. 13.18. Recall of paired-associates after intentional learning as a function of within-subject and time of recall for both noise conditions (*from* McLean, 1968)

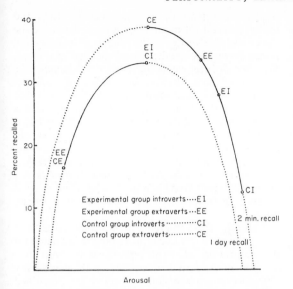

Fig. 13.19. Paired-associate recall and hypothetical inverted-U relationship with arousal as a function of time when personality-derived and experimentally-induced arousal are considered to be similar in effect (*from* McLean, 1968)

later. A point which adds credibility to the equation of personality derived arousal and experimentally induced arousal in terms of their effect on P–A recall performance is the sequential arrangement of P–A recall as a function of the combination of noise treatment and personality. For example, in the case of the 2 minute recall interval in [Fig. 13.19], the control group introverts appear to have been more highly aroused than were control group extraverts, but less aroused than experimental group extraverts, and so on.'

The figure mentioned by McLean refers to extraverts and introverts selected as being + or −1 SD above or below the mean; as he points out, the results should be even more clear cut when more extreme samples are chosen (1·5 SD above or below the mean). The figure here given, while essentially similar to that referred to in the above quotation, is in fact derived from this more extreme sample.

In connection with this figure, McLean comments: 'It is apparent that the personality derived arousal was stronger in effect than the experimentally induced arousal effects produced by white noise . . . . As can be seen, the sequential order of P–A recall performance decrement in [Fig. 13.19] for immediate recall, moved from the extraverts of both noise conditions to introverts in both noise conditions, while in delayed recall conditions there was no

difference in recall between personality categories.' McLean also comments on the relative absence of effect of the N variable; this was almost completely orthogonal to E in this population ($r = -0.13$). He concludes that 'the consistency and similarity with which personality derived arousal influences the magnitude of P–A recall as a function of time, compared to physiologically recorded arousal changes, adds considerable weight to the notion that introverts function at a higher state of cortical arousal than do extraverts'.

Of particular interest to our discussion is an experiment carried out by Michaelis (1969) with the explicit intention of testing the combination of Spence's and Eysenck's theories here outlined. He used as his test material a carefully chosen task which made possible the detailed analysis of information acquisition. A white or black disc was shown on grey background, either in the right or left position, and either in the up or down position. Thus, there are three variables to be considered, of which only two were relevant to the task, which consisted in identifying the correct combination of the other two variables by writing down one of the four letters. The different factors (brightness of the disc, vertical position, horizontal position) had different $_sH_R$ values, and the changes in these through learning could be quantified with considerable accuracy. A $2 \times 2 \times 2$ design was used, in which N and E scores were used to identify high and low scorers on these two personality dimensions respectively, and externally imposed high and low drive was manipulated by using male adolescent apprentices who were either being tested as part of an admission procedure (high drive) or had already been accepted and were merely task-motivated (low drive); Eysenck (1964) has described the setting for these experiments in some detail. Forty presentations of the stimuli were made in all, and detailed analyses carried out of the total number of false reactions made, as well as the information gained for each of the three factors separately. Of 645 Ss tested by means of the personality inventory, 192 were finally induced in the experimental groups. The very complex results of the experiment indicated considerable support for the theory of drive action on learning, with externally manipulated drive being used as the independent variable: 'Bei situationsinduziertem Angst-Drive wurden die schweren Teile des Konzeptionslerntests weniger gut und die leichten Teile besser erlernt als in einer angstfreien, entspannten Atmosphäre mit relative niedrigerem Drive'. (Under conditions of high drive, the difficult parts of a conceptual learning task were learned less well, and the easy parts better, than under conditions of low drive.)

The influence of the S_D could also be verified, but Michaelis concluded that it 'kann nur mit Einschränkungen für richtig gehalten werden'. S_D was indeed found to lower the effectiveness of conceptual learning, but a more complex explanation than that of Spence seemed to be required. The results showed that externally manipulated drive in this situation produced greater effects than did habitual anxiety level; this is not perhaps surprising when it is considered that the drive-inducing conditions in these experiments are such as to produce very considerable anxiety, while under low-drive conditions there is little effective motivation (Eysenck, 1964.) Even so, significant interactions between N and E, on the one hand, and drive condition, on the other, were observed. It was found, 'dass ängstliche Personen bei der Erlernung von schwierigem Material weniger ängstlichen Personen nur in einer entspannten Atmosphäre unterlegen sind, während in einer Stress-Situation kein Unterschied mehr zu verzeichnen ist'. This finding suggested the following hypothesis to Michaelis: The increase in drive and S_D produced in an examination situation only play their full part in persons who show relatively weak anxiety and S_D in normal situations. Michaelis appeals to certain task specific factors to explain the differences between his results in this respect and those obtained by other writers. As regards E, Michaelis found in his analysis of total errors that in the high drive situation extraverts made fewer mistakes, introverts more mistakes, than in the low drive situation; in other words, increase in externally manipulated drive improves the performance of extraverts and impairs the performance of introverts. For further details of this study the original report should be consulted; it seems that future work would benefit from adopting the design and method of analysis pioneered by Michaelis.

This completes our account of the experimental findings; we must now turn to a theoretical discussion of the implications of this work. It would probably not be useful to consider the Spence and Eysenck theories as rivals between which a choice had to be made. In the first place, much of the Spence work fits in perfectly well with the Eysenck set of postulates, both theoretically and empirically, and in the second place it is obvious that Eysenck's work owes much to Spence's prior experiments and theories. It would seem more useful to regard Eysenck's hypothesis as arising from those of Spence, and taking them farther along the same road—even though Spence himself would probably not have agreed with the direction taken. His reliance on what he called 'mathematical' theories and on operational definitions finds no counterpart in post-Hullian work which has abjured the notion of

the 'empty organism'; it seems an unnecessary and indeed suicidal act of filial devotion to renounce the use of such knowledge of the process of learning and remembering as modern biology has given us. Whether Spence would have tried to include the process of consolidation in his set of concepts cannot now be ascertained; what seems likely is that workers in the future will not wish to abandon a concept so relevant theoretically, and so firmly based experimentally. Granted, then, that Spence would almost certainly not have approved of this revamping of his set of postulates and theories, it nevertheless remains true that in spirit the new theory is not entirely different from his, and must be acknowledged to bear distinct marks of resemblance in many places.

That said, there still remain many differences. The most important of these is probably the insistence on the separation of MAS-type 'anxiety' into two components, arousal (identified with personality differences in extraversion) and activation (identified with personality differences in neuroticism). In this, our theory goes back to Hebb's (1955) notion of arousal as the physiological basis and correlate of Hull's drive, D, concept. It is very noticeable that in the group of studies inspired by the Maudsley group, it is in nearly every case introversion-extraversion that correlates with differences in remembering and learning; neuroticism is only very rarely implicated. This suggests that, in terms of our Fig. 13.4, task-relevant behaviour (D instigated behaviour) is related to arousal, and, hence, to differences in extraversion-introversion, while task-irrelevant behaviour (S_D instigated behaviour) is related to activation, and, hence, to differences in neuroticism. The data do not, of course, suffice to prove this theory, but they certainly do not contradict it, particularly when it is remembered that high degrees of activation have the power to produce increases in level of arousal (Eysenck, 1969).

Such a theory, while more in line with modern work on learning theory and in psychophysiology, still cannot really claim to be 'mathematical' or even quantitative in the Hull-Spence sense; indeed, it seems unlikely that this presents at the moment a viable ideal. Before our theory can be claimed to be quantitative, it will be necessary to measure, along some meaningful continuum, the concepts of 'arousal' and 'activation'; as Martin has shown in a previous chapter, we are still very far from achieving this goal. We can manipulate these concepts experimentally with some show of success, and produce a very rough-and-ready physiological correlate in terms of GSR and other responses; this hardly suffices for more refined purposes of measurement. Nor is it likely that our concepts of reticular activating system functions have taken us as far out of the realm of Hebb's 'conceptual nervous system' as might have been desired; recent work has thrown much doubt on the fundamental tenets of the orthodox view in this field (Thompson, 1967; Brodal, 1969). However, this is not a fatal weakness; from the psychological point of view it is not crucial whether cortical arousal is mediated by the ARAS, some minute portion or portions within it, or by some other structure. What is important is that the cortex should differentially respond with greater or lesser arousal to different types of stimuli, and that it should do so in differing degree in extraverted and introverted persons. It is, of course, desirable that our physiology should be as correct as possible, but we can hardly aspire to go beyond the results of the most modern research in that field. There can be no doubt that many changes in conceptualisation will take place before a definitive theory can be established in this context.

Given these general weaknesses, it is hardly surprising that Eysenck should prefer to deal with the experimental evidence in terms of a 'weak' rather than a 'strong' theory (Eysenck, 1960); such a theory, in J. J. Thomson's words, is 'a policy rather than a creed'—it is designed to guide research into fruitful channels, not to establish once-and-for-all eternal truths. The preference of Hull and Spence for the elaboration of 'strong' theories has had the rather unfortunate results of making many psychologists distrustful of theories altogether; such a distrust, generalised to all theories, is clearly misplaced. Much of the work described in this chapter was undertaken in direct response to Spence's theoretical formulations, and although we have criticised these from various points of view, it nevertheless remains true that imperfect though they may have been, these theories have led to the accumulation of much interesting and important empirical material. No theory in science can lay claim to more than that.

What is surprising in our review of the literature is not so much that isolated studies fail to fall into place, or that replication of previous findings has not always been possible; surprise is rather occasioned by the very large number of instances where prediction has been verified, or where replication has been successful. The reason for this surprise is, of course, the extreme complexity of the whole situation, and the large number of variables that enter into the final score of even the simplest learning task. A simple enumeration of just these variables that have been taken into account in one or other of these studies will reveal their multiplicity.

1. Personality factors, particularly introversion-extraversion; here we are dealing with a (probably) largely innate resting level of arousal which is characteristically high in introverts and low in extraverts.

2. Intrasubject measures of momentary state of arousal (EEG, GSR, etc.); this may or may not be correlated with personality, i.e. with a more enduring state of arousal.

3. Stimulus-produced arousal (as in the Kleinsmith and Kaplan studies); this may be indexed by the measures mentioned under (2), and interact with personality states mentioned under (1).

4. Experimentally induced arousal, e.g. by white noise or other sensory stimulation.

5. Arousal produced by differential task instructions, e.g. ego-orientated *vs* task orientated.

6. Temporal rhythms of arousal; Eysenck (1967) has reviewed some of the evidence indicating that introverts show higher arousal in the morning, comparatively speaking, extraverts in the afternoon. Time of day has not usually been controlled (except by McLean) and may in some cases act as an interfering variable.

7. Complexity of the task; this may be indexed either in terms of previously established habits (Spence) or in terms of interference factors (Eysenck) or both. Either way, complexity clearly interacts with the other factors mentioned.

Given this multiplicity of interacting variables, many of which are difficult to measure, one might be forgiven if one concluded that prediction would be rather hopeless; in practice this has not proved so, particularly when conscious choices have been made in the setting up of the experiment between different variables, and when control has been attempted over other variables. It is here that theory has been so important; random choice of variables has been rightly condemned by Spence as leading to uninterpretable results. The fact that proper control over, and choice of, experimental variables leads to predictable results suggests that there is sufficient truth in the theories we have been dealing with to make further work along these lines exciting and potentially fruitful. Greater rigour is, of course, desirable, but must inevitably be a function of further work, both theoretical and experimental; in particular, the practice of throwing together the E and N dimensions into one single non-univocal 'anxiety' variable will have to be given up and the MAS replaced by some such measure as the EPI. But with such improvement in methodology, there is every reason to hope that the next revision of this chapter will be able to give a much tighter and more consistent account of the phenomena of learning and personality.

Such an account would by preference also contain

references to improved ways of integrating question-naire measures of anxiety and physiological meas-ures; the position at the moment is very unsatisfactory (although Spence with his operational definition, claims to be unconcerned about the widespread failure of research workers to find significant correlations between these two types of measures). As Martin (1970) points out, 'the relationship of these self-report measures to physiological measures is . . . weak at best'. Various heart-rate measures (e.g. Hodges and Spielberger, 1966) and skin conductance and palmar sweating measures have resulted in low and non-significant relations (Beam, 1955; Burdick, 1966; Calvin et al., 1956; Endler et al., 1962; Katkin, 1965, 1966; Lotsof and Downing, 1956; Martin, 1959; and Silverman, 1957); admittedly there are a few positive and significant reports (Becker and Matteson, 1961; Rossi, 1959; Fiorca and Muehl, 1962; these workers used, respectively, initial skin conductance, muscle action potentials, and plasma 17—OH—CS level). Much of this dearth of positive evidence may be due to a neglect of Lacey's and Malmo's principle of autonomic response specificity (cf. Chapter 10, by I. Martin). Mandler and colleagues (1961) report non-significant correlations between the MAS and 11 individual autonomic measures, but when each subject's highest autonomic response was used as a score for him, this correlated with the MAS to the extent of 0·60. Opton and Lazarus (1967) using a positive comparison between autonomic effects of horror film or threat of shock, found that this difference correlated significantly with various self-reported personality measures, whereas the raw reactions did not. Martin and Sroufe (1970), who give a good review of this whole field, conclude: 'The implica-tions of the multiple response studies for anxiety assessment are (1) that the individual's characteristic pattern of autonomic response must be taken into account before degree of anxiety relative to other individuals can be inferred, and (2) that relative changes in different autonomic responses within the same individual tend to be correlated, and each response may have some validity for reflecting anxiety level.' To which it might be added that resting-level determinations of autonomic functioning are by definition unlikely to differentiate MAS+ and MAS− groups, as anxiety is not produced by the stimuli present in the situation (Eysenck, 1970).

More relevant to our theme, and also more in accord with the paradigm of personality differences as interchangeable with arousal-producing stimuli (Savage and Eysenck, 1964), is a rather different approach in which general theorems are tested by using self-ratings of anxiety level, and independently by using physiological measures. Because of the

greater ease of using inventories, and because of the possibility of selecting small groups of extreme scorers from much larger samples tested, most workers have used questionnaire measures of anxiety, or N and E; nevertheless, the possibility remains of using physiological variables for the same purpose, and the work of, inter alia, Burgess and Hokanson (1964), Hokanson and Burgess (1964), and particularly Doerr and Hokanson (1965) may be quoted as an example. In the former two studies, it was found that 'adult, human subjects with characteristically low resting heart rates achieved scores on simple performance tasks which were lower than those obtained by high heart-rate subjects; and after an imposed stress, which typically increased heart rate approximately 16 beats per minute, the low heart-rate subjects significantly improved in performance relative to a non-stressing control group, while high heart-rate subjects manifest a relative decrement'. In the most recent study, Doerr and Hokanson used three groups of children (ages 7, 9, and 11), subdivided, in turn, into low, medium, and high heart-rate categories on the basis of resting heart-rate measures. The experi-mental variable was arousal by a frustrating experience vs non-arousal; the number of items completed on a simple coding task prior to the arousal manipulations and the number of items completed on an alternate form after arousal served as a measure of performance. Heart-rate recordings made at each phase of the investigation served as an indicator of physiological stress. Main results are shown in Fig. 13.20; it will be seen that they duplicate those we have encountered so often in relation to inventory-indexed anxiety, or arousal, with the frustration variable interacting with heart rate in such a way that high-rate subjects show a worsening in performance, low-rate subjects an improvement; for the non-frustration subjects there is no difference in performance according to heart-rate. (The authors prefer an explanation in terms of the Yerkes-Dodson Law, but apparently without realising that this is a purely descriptive rule which itself is in need of explanation.)

No simple summary could do justice to the richly diversified literature in this field; instead we may with advantage conclude this chapter by stating a number of general conclusions that are suggested by the data. The first is that there can be no doubt that personality factors interact with experimental variables in complex ways to determine the rate of learning, of consolidation, and of performance. This simple fact has very important consequences; if taken seriously it means that no experiment in this field should be undertaken without taking into account the relevant personality scores of the

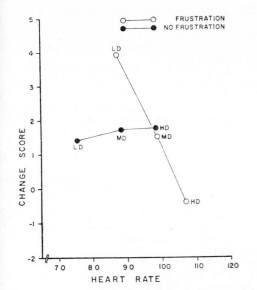

Fig. 13.20. Change in performance as a function of task-induced drive (frustration *vs* non-frustration) and within-subject drive (low, medium, and high heart rate) (*from* Doerr and Hokanson, 1965)

certain is that these individual-difference factors in experimental design should not be consigned to the rubbish-heap of error term; their influence is too profound to encourage the belief that disregarding them will make them go away. The second general conclusion is that work with patients would benefit considerably if it made greater use of the theoretical sophistication embodied in such approaches as Spence's; simple-minded inductive wool-gathering is not likely to result in meaningful, interpretable data. The design of experiments in the abnormal field has shown little improvement since Hull's 1917 paper; if anything, the standard has dropped. This is an interesting if profoundly discouraging discovery; to discuss its causes would take us too far into the pathology of social psychology. And the third and final general conclusion is that when all its limitations are taken into account, and all adverse empirical studies are listed, nevertheless the theoretical system erected by Spence on Hull's original foundation emerges with many important achievements and successes to its credit. We have argued that it can be improved in many ways, but it should not be forgotten that improvements can only be made on an existing system that has demonstrated its value in explaining existing data and predicting others; the Hull-Spence system has at the moment no rival in this connection. It is customary to smile at the naïveté of some of Hull's pronouncements; we might do well to remember, rather, their originality and fruitfulness.

subjects participating in the study. We have argued in favour of a two-factor personality theory, but, of course, it is quite likely that additional factors will need to be taken into account; intelligence is an obvious one, and there may be others. What seems

REFERENCES

AMSEL, A. (1950) The effect upon level of consummatory response of the addition of anxiety to a motivational complex. *J. exp. Psychol.*, **40**, 109–115.

AMSEL, A. and MALTZMAN, I. (1950) The effect upon generalized drive strength of emotionality as inferred from the level of consummatory response. *J. exp. Psychol.*, **40**, 563–569.

AUSUBEL, D. P., SCHIFF, H. M., and GOLDMAN, M. (1953) Qualitative characteristics in the learning process associated with anxiety. *J. abnorm. soc. Psychol.*, **48**, 537–547.

AXELROD, H. S., GOVEN, E. L., and HEILITZER, F. (1956) The correlates of manifest anxiety in style and image learning. *J. exp. Psychol.*, **51**, 131–138.

BABCOCK, H. and LEVY, L. (1940) *The Measurement of Efficiency of Mental Functioning*. Chicago: Stoelting.

BARDACH, J. L. (1960) Affects of situational anxiety at different stages of practice. *J. exp. Psychol.*, **59**, 420–424.

BASOWITZ, H., PERSKY, H., KORCHIN, S. J., and GRINKER, R. R. (1955) *Anxiety and Stress*. New York: McGraw-Hill.

BEAM, J. F. (1955) Serial learning and conditioning under real life stress. *J. abnorm soc. Psychol.*, **51**, 543–551.

BECKER, W. C. and MATTESON, H. H. (1961) GSR conditioning, anxiety and extraversion. *J. abnorm. soc. Psychol.*, **62**, 427–430.

BENDIG, A. W. and VAUGHAN, C. J. (1957) Manifest anxiety, discrimination, and trans position. *Amer. J. Psychol.*, **70**, 286–288.

BERLYN, D. E. (1960) *Conflict, arousal and curiosity*. New York: McGraw-Hill.

BESCH, N. F. (1959) Paired associate learning as a function of anxiety level and shock. *J. Person.*, **27**, 116–124.

BLEKE, R. (1954) Reward and punishment as determiners of reminiscence effects in schizophrenic and normal subjects. *J. Person.*, **23**, 479–498.

BRENGELMANN, J. C. (1958) Learning in neurotics and psychotics. *Acta Psychol.*, **13**, 371–388.

BROADHURST, P. L. (1957) Emotionality and the Yerkes-Dodson Law. *J. exp. Psychol.*, **54**, 345–352.

BROADHURST, P. L. (1959) The interaction of task difficulty and motivation: the Yerkes-Dodson Law reviewed. *Acta Psychol.*, **16**, 321–338.

BRODAL, A. (1969) *Neurological Anatomy in Relation to Clinical Medicine*. Oxford: University Press.

BROWN, J. S. and FARBER, I. E. (1951) Emotion conceptualised as interviewing variables with suggestions towards a theory of frustration. *Psychol. Bull.*, **48**, 465–480.

BUCHWALD, A. M. and YAMAGUCHI, H. G. (1955) The effect of change in drive level on habit reversal. *J. exp. Psychol.*, **50**, 265–268.

BURDICK, J. A. (1966) Autonomic lability and neuroticism. *J. psychosom. Res.*, **9**, 339–342.

BURGESS, M. and HOKANSON, J. E. (1964) Effects of increased heart rate in intelligence performance. *J. abnorm. soc. Psychol.*, **68**, 85–91.

CALVIN, A. P., McGRINGAN, F. J., TYRRELL, A., and SAYERS, M. (1956) Manifest anxiety and the palmar perspiration index. *J. consult. Psychol.*, **20**, 356.

CARLSON, V. R. and LAZARUS, R. S. (1953) A repetition of Meyer-William's study of intellectual control under stress and associated Rorschach factors. *J. consult. Psychol.*, **17**, 247–253.

CASTANEDA, A. (1956) Effects of stress on complex learning and performance. *J. exp. Psychol.*, **52**, 9–12.

CASTANEDA, A. (1961) Supplementary report: Differential position habits and anxiety in children as determinants of performance in learning. *J. exp. Psychol.*, **61**, 257–258.

CASTANEDA, A. and LIPSIT, L. P. (1959) Relation of stress and differential position habits to performance in motor learning. *J. exp. Psychol.*, **57**, 25–30.

CASTANEDA, A. and PALERMO, D. S. (1955) Psychomotor performance as a function of amount of training and stress. *J. exp. Psychol.*, **50**, 175–179.

CASTANEDA, A., PALERMO, D. S., and McCANDLESS, B. R. (1956) Complex learning and performance as a function of anxiety in children and task difficulty. *Child Developm.*, **27**, 327–332.

CHILD, I. L. (1954) Personality. *Ann. Rev. Psychol.*, **5**, 149–170.

CHILD, I. L. and WATERHOUSE, I. K. (1953) Frustration and the quality of performance: II. A theoretical statement. *Psychol. Rev.*, **60**, 127–139.

CHILES, W. D. (1958) Effects of shock-induced stress on verbal performance. *J. exp. Psychol.*, **56**, 159–165.

CLARK, A. M. (1967) The relationship of arousal to reminiscence, attention, withdrawal, and the Hunter Prognostic Index in chronic schizophrenia. London: Unpublished Ph.D. thesis.

CLARK, R. E. (1962) The role of drive (time stress) in complex learning: an emphasis on prelearning phenomena. *J. exp. Psychol.*, **63**, 57–61.

COURTS, F. A. (1942) The influence of practice on the dynamurgenic effect of muscular tension. *J. exp. Psychol.*, **30**, 504–511.

CRAWFORD, P. L. and SNYDER, W. U. (1966) Differentiating the psychopath and psychoneurotic with the LAIS. *J. consult. Psychol.*, **30**, 178.

CRONBACH, L. J. and MEEHL, P. E. (1955) Construct validity in psychological tests. *Psychol. Bull.*, **52**, 281–302.

CROWNE, D. P., HOLLAND, C. H., and CONN, L. K. (1968) Personality factors in discrimination learning in children. *J. Person. soc. Psychol.*, **10**, 420–430.

DAVIDSON, W. Z., ANDREWS, T. G., and ROSS, S. (1956) Effects of stress and anxiety on continuous high-speed colour naming. *J. exp. Psychol.*, **52**, 13–17.

DEESE, J., LAZARUS, R. S., and KEENAN, J. (1953) Anxiety, anxiety reduction, and stress in learning. *J. exp. Psychol.*, **46**, 55–60.

DIETHELM, O. and JONES, M. R. (1947) Influence of anxiety on attention, learning, retention and thinking. *Arch. Neurol. Psychiat.*, **58**, 325–336.

DILLON, R. F. and REID, L. S. (1969) Short-term memory as a function of information processing during the retention interval. *J. exp. Psychol.*, **81**, 261–269.

DOERR, H. O. and HOKANSON, J. E. (1965) A relation between heart rate and performance in children. *J. Person. soc. Psychol.*, **2**, 70–76.

DUFFY, E. (1957) The psychological significance of the concept of 'arousal' or 'activation'. *Psychol. Rev.*, **64**, 265–275.

DUFFY, E. (1962) *Activation and Behaviour*. London: Wiley

EASTERBROOK, J. A. (1959) The effect of emotion on cue utilization and the organization of behaviour. *Psychol. Rev.*, **66**, 183–201.

ELLIOTT, R. (1966) Effects of uncertainty about the nature and advent of a curious stimulus (shock) upon distress. *J. Person. soc. Psychol.*, **3**, 353–356.

ELLIOTT, R., BANKART, B., and LIGHT, T. (1970) Differences in the motivational significance of heart rate and palmar conductance: two tests of a hypothesis. *J. Person. soc. Psychol.*, **14**, 166–172.

ENDLER, N. S., HUNT, J. McV., and ROSENSTEIN, A. J. (1962) An S–R inventory of anxiousness. *Psychol. Monogr.*, **76**, 17 (Whole No. 336).

EYSENCK, H. J. (1947) *Dimensions of Personality*. London: Routledge & Kegan Paul.

EYSENCK, H. J. (1956) Reminiscence, drive and personality theory. *J. abnorm. soc. Psychol.*, **53**, 328–333.

EYSENCK, H. J. (1957) *The Dynamics of Anxiety and Hysteria*. London: Routledge & Kegan Paul.

EYSENCK, H. J. (1960) The place of theory in psychology. In *Experiments in Personality*, Vol. 2. (Ed. Eysenck H. J.) London: Routledge & Kegan Paul, pp. 303–315.

EYSENCK, H. J. (1962) Reminiscence, drive and personality—revision and extension of a theory. *Brit. J. soc. clin. Psychol.*, **1**, 127–140.

EYSENCK, H. J. (Ed.) (1964) *Experiments in Motivation*. Oxford: Pergamon Press.

EYSENCK, H. J. (1964) Personality and reminiscence—an experimental study of the 'reactive inhibition' and the 'conditioned inhibition' theories. *Life Science*, **3**, 189–198.

EYSENCK, H. J. (1965) A three-factor theory of reminiscence. *Brit. J. Psychol.*, **56**, 163–181.

EYSENCK, H. J. (1967) *The Biological Basis of Personality*. Springfield: C. C. Thomas.

EYSENCK, H. J. (1969) Psychological Aspects of Anxiety. *Brit. J. Psychiat*, Special Publication No. 3.

EYSENCK, H. J. (1970) *The Structure of Human Personality*, 3rd ed. London: Methuen.

EYSENCK, H. J. and BROADHURST, P. L. (1964) Experiments with Animals. Introduction. In *Experiments in Motivation* (Ed. Eysenck, H. J.). Oxford: Pergamon Press.

EYSENCK, H. J. and EYSENCK, S. B. G. (1967) Salivary response to lemon juice as a measure of introversion. *Percept. motor Skills*, **24**, 1047–1053.

EYSENCK, H. J. and EYSENCK, S. B. G. (Eds.) (1969) *Personality Structure and Measurement*. London: Routledge & Kegan Paul.

EYSENCK, H. J. and RACHMAN, S. (1965) *The Causes and Cures of Neurosis*. London: Routledge & Kegan Paul.

FARBER, I. E. and SPENCE, K. W. (1953) Complex learning and conditioning as a function of anxiety. *J. exp. Psychol.*, **45**, 120–125.

FARLEY, F. (1969) Personality and Reminiscence. Paper read at the International Congress of Psychology, London.

FIORCA, V. and MUEHL, S. (1962) Relationship between plasma levels of 17-hydroxy-corticosteroids (17-OH-CS) and a psychological measure of manifest anxiety. *Psychosom. Med.*, **24**, 596–599.

FREEMAN, G. L. and GIESE, W. J. (1970) The relationship between task difficulty and palmar skin resistance. *J. gen. Psychol.*, **23**, 217–220.

GALBRAITH, G. G. and MOSHER, D. L. (1970) Effects of sex guilt and sexual stimulation on the recall of word association. *J. consult. clin. Psychol.*, **34**, 67–71.

GEBHARDT, R. (1966) Unpublished work. Düsseldorf: Psychol. Inst.

GLESER, G. and ULETT, G. (1952) The Saslow Screening Test as a measure of anxiety-proneness. *J. clin. Psychol.*, **8**, 279–283.

GORDON, W. M. and BERLYNE, D. E. (1954) Drive-level and flexibility in paired-associate nonsense syllable learning. *Quart. J. exp. Psychol.*, **6**, 181–185.

GRANT, D. K. (1969) The relationship between personality and short-term memory. Durban Natal: Unpublished, thesis.

GRAY, J. E. (1968) Level of arousal and length of rest as determinants of pursuit rotor performance. London: Unpublished Ph.D. thesis.

HALL, K. R. L. and CROOKES, T. G. (1951) Studies in learning impairment: I. Schizophrenic and organic patients. *J. ment. Sci.*, **97**, 725–737.

HEBB, D. (1955) Drives of the CNS (Conceptual Nervous System). *Psychol. Rev.*, **62**, 243–254.

HILGARD, E. R. (1956) *Theories of Learning*, 2nd ed. New York: Appleton-Century-Crofts.

HILGARD, E. R., JONES, L. V., and KAPLAN, S. J. (1951) Conditioned discrimination as related to anxiety. *J. exp. Psychol.*, **42**, 94–99.

HODGES, W. F. and SPIELBERGER, C. D. (1966) The effects of threat of shock on heart rate for subjects who differ in manifest anxiety and fear of shock. *Psychophysiol.*, **2**, 287–294.

HOKANSON, J. E. and BURGESS, M. (1964) Effects of physiological arousal level, frustration, and task complexity on performance. *J. abnorm. soc. Psychol.*, **68**, 698–702.

HOYLE, F. (1962) *Astronomy*. London: Macdonald.

HOWARTH, E. (1963) Some laboratory measures of extraversion–introversion. *Percept. Mot. Skills.*, **17**, 55–60.

HOWARTH, E. (1969a) Extraversion and increased interference in paired-associate learning. *Percept. mot. Skills*, **29**, 403–406.

HOWARTH, E. (1969b) Personality differences in serial learning under distraction. *Percept. mot. Skills*, **28**, 379–382.

HOWARTH, E. and EYSENCK, H. J. (1968) Extraversion, arousal, and paired-associate recall. *J. exp. Res. in Person.*, **3**, 114–116.

HUGHES, J. B., SPRAGUE, J. L., and BENDIG, A. W. (1954) Anxiety level, response alteration, and performance in serial learning. *J. Psychol.*, **38**, 421–426.

HULL, C. L. (1917) The formation and retention of associations among the insane. *Amer. J. Psychol.*, **28**, 419–435.

HUNT, J. McV. and COFER, C. N. (1944) Psychological deficit. In *Personality and the Behaviour Disorders*, Vol. 2. (Ed. Hunt, J. McV.) New York: Ronald Press.

JENSEN, A. (1964) *Individual differences in learning: interference factor*. Washington: U.S. Dept. Health, Educ. & Welfare, Project Report No. 1867.

JENSEN, A. (1962) Extraversion, neuroticism and serial learning. *Acta Psychol.*, **20**, 69–77.

JOHN, E. R. (1967) *Mechanism of Memory*. New York: Academic Press.

JONES, GWYNNE H. (1960) Learning and abnormal behaviour. In *Handbook of Abnormal Psychology* (Ed. Eysenck H. J.) London: Pitman Med.

KAMIN, L. J. (1955) Relation between discrimination, apparatus stress, and the Taplow Scale. *J. abnorm. soc. Psychol.*, **51**, 595–599.

KAMIN, L. J. and FEDORCHAK, O. (1957) The Taylor scale, hunger, and verbal learning. *Canad. J. Psychol.*, **11**, 212–218.

KATAHN, M. (1964) Effects of anxiety (drive) on the acquisition and avoidance of a dominant intratask response. *J. Person.*, **32**, 642–650.

KATAHN, M. (1966) Interaction of anxiety and ability in complex learning situations. *J. Person. soc. Psychol.*, **3**, 475–479.

KATAHN, M. and LYDA, L. L. (1966) Anxiety and the learning of responses varying in initial rank in the response hierarchy. *J. Pers.*, **34**, 287–299.

KATCHMAR, L. T., ROSS, S., and ANDREWS, T. G. (1958) Effects of stress and anxiety on performance of a complex verbal-coding task. *J. exp. Psychol.*, **55**, 559–564.

KATKIN, E. S. (1965) Relationship between manifest anxiety and two indices of autonomic stress. *J. Person. soc. Psychol.*, **2**, 324–333.

KATKIN, E. S. (1966) The relationship between a measure of transitory anxiety and spontaneous autonomic activity. *J. abnorm. Psychol.*, **71**, 142–146.

KAYE, D., KIRSCHNER, P., and MANDLER, G. (1953) The effect of test anxiety on memory span in a group test situation. *J. consult. Psychol.*, **17**, 265–266.

KIMBLE, G. A. and POSNICK, G. M. (1967) Anxiety? *J. Person. soc. Psychol.*, **7**, 108–110.

KLEINSMITH, L. J. and KAPLAN, S. (1963) Paired-associate learning as a function of arousal and interpolated interval. *J. exp. Psychol.*, **65**, 190–193.

KLEINSMITH, L. J. and KAPLAN, S. (1964) Interaction of arousal and recall interval in nonsense and syllable paired-associate learning. *J. exp. Psychol.*, **67**, 124–126.

KLEINSMITH, L. J., KAPLAN, S., and TARTO, R. D. (1963) The relationship of arousal to short and long-term recall. *Canad. J. Psychol.*, **17**, 393–397.

KORCHIN, S. J. and LEVINE, S. (1957) Anxiety and verbal learning. *J. abnorm. soc. Psychol.*, **54**, 234–240.

LAUTERBACH, C. G. (1958) The Taylor A scale and clinical measures of anxiety. *J. consult. Psychol.*, **22**, 314.

LAZARUS, R. S., DEESE, J., and HAMILTON, R. (1954) Anxiety and stress in learning: the role of intraserial duplication. *J. exp. Psychol.*, **47**, 111–114.

LEE, C. (1961) The effects of anxiety level and shock as a paired-associate verbal task. *J. exp. Psychol.*, **61**, 213–217.

LINDSLEY, D. B. (1957) The reticular system and perceptual discrimination. In *Reticular Formation of the Brain* (Ed. Jasper H. H. *et al.*) London: Churchill.

LOTSOF, E. J. and DOWNING, W. L. (1956) Two measures of anxiety. *J. consult. Psychol.*, **20**, 170.

LOVAAS, O. I. (1960) The relationship of induced muscular tension, tension level, and manifest anxiety in learning. *J. exp. Psychol.*, **59**, 145–152.

LUCAS, J. P. (1952) The interactive effects of anxiety, failure, and intraserial duplication. *Amer. J. Psychol.*, **65**, 59–66.

MacCORQUODALE, K., and MEEHL, P. E., (1954) EDWARD C. TOLMAN. In *Modern Learning Theory* (Ed. Esher W. K. *et al.*) New York: Appleton-Century-Crofts.

McLAUGHLIN, R. J. (1968) Retention in paired-associate learning related to extraversion and neuroticism. Paper presented at Midwestern Psychol. Ass. Convention, Chicago.

McLAUGHLIN, R. J. and EYSENCK, H. J. (1967) Extraversion, neuroticism and paired-associate learning. *J. exp. Res. in Person.*, **2**, 128–132.

McLEAN, P. D. (1968) Paired-associate learning as a function of recall interval, personality and arousal. London: Unpublished Ph.D. thesis.

MALMO, R. B. (1957) Anxiety and behavioural arousal. *Psychol. Rev.*, **64**, 276–287.

MALMO, R. B. (1958) Measurement of drive: an unsolved problem in psychology. In *Nebraska Symposium on Motivation* (Ed. Jones M. R.) Lincoln, Nebraska: University of Nebraska Press, 1958.

MALMO, R. B. (1959) Activation: a neuropsychological dimension. *Psychol. Rev..* **66**, 367–386.

MALMO, R. B. and AMSEL, A. (1948) Anxiety-produced interference in serial rote learning with observations on rote learning after partial frontal lobectomy. *J. exp. Psychol.*, **38**, 440–454.

MANDLER, G., MANDLER, J. E., KREMEN, I., and SHOLITAN, R. D. (1961) The response to threat: relations among verbal and physiological indices. *Psychol. Monographs.*, 75 (Whole No. 513).

MARTIN, B. (1959) The validity of a self report measure of anxiety as a function of the time interval covered by the instructions. *J. consult. Psychol.*, **23**, 468.

MARTIN, B. and SROUFE, L. A. (1970) Anxiety. In *Symptoms of Psychopathology* (Ed. Costello, C. G.) London: Wiley.

MARX, M. H. (1956) Some relations between frustration and drive. In *Nebraska Symposium on Motivation* (Ed. Jones, M. R.) Lincoln, Nebraska: University of Nebraska Press.

MATARAZZO, J. P., ULETT, A. A., and SERLOV, G. (1955) Human maze performance on a function of increasing levels of anxiety. *J. gen. Psychol.*, **43**, 79–95.

MELTON, A. W. (Ed.) (1964) *Categories of Human Learning*. New York: Academic Press.

MEREDITH, G. M. (1966) Contending hypothesis of autogenesis for the exuberance-restraint personality factor, U.I.21. *J. genet. Psychol.*, **108**, 89–104.

MICHAELIS, W. (1969) Individuelle Differenzen Konzept Kiel: Unpublished Ph.D. thesis.

MILLER, N. E. (1948) Studies of fear as an acquirable drive: 5. Fear as motivation and fear-reduction as reinforcement in the learning of new responses. *J. exp. Psychol.*, **38**, 89–101.

MILLER, N. E. (1951) Learnable Drives and Rewards. In *Handbook of Experimental Psychology* (Ed. Shevens, S. S.) New York: Wiley.

MOLDAWSKY, S. and MOLDAWSKY, P. C. (1952) Digit span as an anxiety indicator. *J. consult. Psychol.*, **16**, 115–118.

MONTAGUE, E. K. (1953) The role of anxiety in serial rote learning. *J. exp. Psychol.*, **45**, 91–96.

NICHOLSON, W. M. (1958) The influence of anxiety upon learning: Interference or drive increment? *J. Person.*, **26**, 303–319.

OPTON, E. M. and LAZARUS, R. S. (1967) Personality determinants of psychophysiological response to stress: a theoretical analysis and experiment. *J. Person. soc. Psychol.*, **6**, 291–303.

PASCAL, G. R. and SVENSON, G. (1952) Learning in mentally ill patients under conditions of unusual motivation. *J. Person.*, **21**, 240–249.

PETERS, H. N. (1953) Multiple choice learning in the chronic schizophrenic. *J. clin. Psychol.*, **9**, 328–333.

PUROHIT, A. J. (1966) Levels of introversion and competitional paired-associate learning. *J. Person.*, **34**, 129–143.

RAMOND, C. K. (1953) Anxiety and task as determinants of verbal performance. *J. exp. Psychol.*, **46**, 120–124.

RESTLE, F. and BEECROFT, R. S. (1955) Anxiety, stimulus generalization and differential conditioning: a comparison of two theories. *Psychol. Rev.*, **62**, 433–437.

ROSENBAUM, R. (1953) Stimulus generalization as a function of level of experimentally induced anxiety. *J. exp. Psychol.*, **45**, 35–43.

ROSENBAUM, R. (1956) Stimulus generalization as a function of clinical anxiety. *J. abnorm. soc. Psychol.*, **53**, 281–285.

ROSSI, A. M. (1959) An evaluation of the Manifest Anxiety Scale by the use of electromyography. *J. exp. Psychol.*, **58**, 64–69.

ROUTHENBERG, A. (1968) The two-arousal hypothesis: reticular formation and limbic system. *Psychol. Rev.*, **75**, 51–80.

SARASON, I. G. (1956) Effect of anxiety, motivational instructions, and failure on serial learning. *J. exp. Psychol.*, **51**, 253–260.

SARASON, I. G. (1957a) Effect of anxiety and two kinds of

motivating instructions on verbal learning. *J. abnorm. soc. Psychol.*, **57**, 166–171.

SARASON, I. G. (1957b) The effect of anxiety and two kinds of failure on serial learning. *J. Person.*, **25**, 383–391.

SARASON, I. G. (1961) The effect of anxiety and threat on the solution of a difficult task. *J. abnorm. soc. Psychol.*, **62**, 165–168.

SARASON, I. G. and PALOLA, E. G. (1960) The relationship of test and general anxiety, difficulty of task, and experimental instructions to performance. *J. exp. Psychol.*, **59**, 185–191.

SAVAGE, R. D. and EYSENCK, H. J. (1964) Definition and measurement of emotionality. In *Experiments in Motivation* (Ed. Eysenck, H. J.). Oxford: Pergamon.

SILVERMAN, R. E. (1957) The manifest anxiety scale as a measure of drive. *J. abnorm. soc. Psychol.*, **55**, 94–97.

SILVERMAN, R. E. and BLITZ, B. (1956) Learning and two kinds of anxiety. *J. abnorm. soc. Psychol.*, **52**, 301–303.

SHANMUGAN, T. E. and SANTHANAM, M. C. (1964) Personality differences in serial learning when interference is presented at the marginal visual level. *J. Ind. Acad. App*. *Psychol.*, **1**, 25–28.

SIEGMAN, A. W. (1957) Some relationships of anxiety and introversion-extraversion to serial learning. Ann Arbor, Michigan: Unpublished Ph.D. thesis.

SIMMINS, C. (1933) Studies in experimental psychiatry; IV. Deterioration of "g" in psychotic patients. *J. ment. Sci.*, **79**, 704–734.

SKANTHAKUMARI, S. R. (1965) Personality differences in the rate of forgetting. *J. Ind. Acad, Appl. Psychol.*, **2**, 39–47.

SPENCE, J. T. and SPENCE, K. W. (1966) The motivational components of manifest anxiety: drive and drive stimuli. In *Anxiety and Behaviour* (Spielberger, C. D.) London: Academic Press.

SPENCE, K. W. (1956) *Behaviour Therapy and Conditioning*. New Haven: Yale Univ. Press.

SPENCE, K. W. (1958) A theory of emotionally based drive (D) and its relation to performance in simple learning situations. *Amer. Psychologist*, **13**, 131–141.

SPENCE, K. W. and BEECROFT, R. S. (1954) Differential conditioning and level of anxiety. *J. exp. Psychol.*, **48**, 399–403.

SPENCE, K. W. and PARKER, I. E. (1954) The relation of anxiety to differential eyelid conditioning. *J. exp. Psychol.*, **47**, 127–134.

SPENCE, K. W., PARKER, I. E., and McFANN, H. H. (1956) The relation of anxiety (drive) level to performance in occupational and non-occupational paired-associates learning. *J. exp. Psychol.*, **52**, 296–305.

SPENCE, K. W., TAYLOR, J., and KETCHEL, R. (1956) Anxiety (drive) level and degree of competition in paired-associates learning. *J. exp. Psychol.*, **52**, 306–310.

SPIELBERGER, C. D. and SMITH, L. H. (1966) Anxiety (drive), stress and serial-position effects in serial-verbal learning. *J. exp. Psychol.*, **72**, 585–595.

STANDISH, R. R. and CHAMPION, R. A. (1960) Task difficulty and drive in verbal learning. *J. exp. Psychol.*, **59**, 361–365.

STEVENSON, H. V. and ISCOE, I. (1956) Anxiety and discriminative learning. *Amer. J. Psychol.*, **69**, 113–114.

TALLAND, G. A. (1967) Short-term memory with interpolated activity. *J. verb. Learn., verb. Behav.*, **6**, 144–150.

TAYLOR, J. A. (1956) Drive theory and manifest anxiety. *Psychol. Bull.*, **53**, 303–320.

TAYLOR, J. A. (1958) The effects of anxiety level and psychological stress in verbal learning. *J. abnorm. soc. Psychol.*, **57**, 55–60.

TAYLOR, J. A. and HAYMAN, J. P. (1955) Anxiety and the learning of paired-associates. *Amer. J. Psychol.*, **68**, 671.

TAYLOR, J. A. and SPENCE, K. W. (1952) The relationship of anxiety level to performance in serial learning. *J. exp. Psychol.*, **44**, 61–64.

THOMPSON, R. F. (1967) *Foundations of Physiological Psychology*. London: Harper.

VENABLES, P. H. (1963a) The relationship between level and skin potential and fusion of paired flashes in schizophrenic and normal subjects. *J. Psychol. Res.*, **1**, 279–287.

VENABLES, P. H. (1963b) Changes due to noise in the threshold of fusion of paired light flashes in schizophrenics and normals. *Brit. J. soc. clin. Psychol.*, **2**, 94–99.

WALKER, E. L. (1968) Action decrement and its relation to learning. *Psychol. Rev.*, **65**, 129–142.

WALKER, E. L. and TARTE, R. D. (1963) Memory storage as a function of arousal and time with homogeneous and heterogeneous tests. *J. verb. Learn. verb. Behav.*, **2**, 113–119.

WATERHOUSE, I. K. and CHILD, I. L. (1953) Frustration and the quality of performance: III. An experimental study. *J. Person.*, **21**, 298–311.

WESTROPE, M. R. (1953) Relatives among Rorschach indices, manifest anxiety and performance under stress. *J. abnorm. soc. Psychol.*, **48**, 515–524.

WILLETT, R. A. (1964) Situation-induced drive and paired-associate learning. In: *Experiments in Motivation* (Ed. Eysenck, H. J.), Oxford: Pergamon Press.

WILLIAMS, J. E. (1955) Mode of failure, interference tendencies, and achievement imagery. *J. abnorm. soc. Psychol.*, **51**, 573–580.

WILLOUGHBY, R. H. (1967) Emotionality and performance in competitional and noncompetitional paired-associates. *Psychol. Rep.*, **20**, 659–662.

WRIGHT, M. W. (1954) A study of anxiety in a general hospital setting. *Canad. J. Psychol.*, **8**, 195–203.

14

Cognitive Abnormalities

R. W. PAYNE

INTRODUCTION

Thought disorder has always been regarded as one of the main criteria of mental illness. In fact, the ancients probably regarded all types of abnormal behaviour as stemming from a disordered intellect. Thus, for example, Plato (Zilboorg and Henry, 1941) thought that individuals who were too happy or too sad were devoid of reason. This view would make affective disorders secondary to intellectual disorders, being essentially due to a failure to understand and to interpret events correctly. Nevertheless, early in classical times, a clear distinction came to be made between disorders of the intellect and disorders of the affect, laying the basis for the main subdivision of the psychoses in the Kraepelinian system. The notion that cognitive and affective disorders are independent, was probably formulated most clearly by Aretaeus (30–90 AD) in Roman times, who thought that disorders of the intellect stemmed from the head, while disorders of the emotions stemmed from the stomach. He gave the first detailed account of manic depressive psychosis, which he believed carried with it a favourable prognosis, although it tended to recur. Manic depressive psychosis, Aretaeus believed, could produce a secondary impairment of intellectual functioning. Nevertheless, it was distinguished clearly from the primary disorders of the intellect, which were characterised by 'stupid, absent, and musing behaviour' (Zilboorg and Henry, 1941). The implication was that such disorders had a worse prognosis. All these views anticipated in some detail those of Kraepelin. Even in classical times, however, there were those who disagreed, and anticipated the views of some Freudian analysts that all psychotic symptoms are primarily the result of emotional disorders. An example is Asclepides, who wrote in the first century BC (Zilboorg and Henry, 1941). Asclepides was a careful observer of psychotic phenomena, evidently being the first to distinguish clearly between hallucinations and delusions. However, he regarded mental diseases as primarily due to emotional disturbances. It would seem that there have always been those who attributed emotional disorders to a failure of comprehension, those who attributed disordered thinking to emotional disturbances, and those who wished to regard the two as being quite independent disorders of different aspects of the human mind, 'cognition', and 'affect'.

In some respects, the three major psychiatric subdivisions follow the three ancient subdivisions of psychology. Thus, schizophrenia is usually regarded as primarily a cognitive disorder, manic depressive psychosis is regarded as primarily an affective disorder, and neurosis could be regarded as a disorder of conation. However, these classical psychological subdivisions have been abandoned by experimental psychology because they have not been found useful. It is very difficult to define 'cognition' in clear operational terms. This is probably why it was never possible for psychiatrists to decide for any particular condition, whether the basic disorder was cognitive or affective. Such a distinction may be impossible to draw, and the question may be a meaningless one in behavioural terms. For this reason it is difficult to decide what kind of disorders to include, and what to exclude in a chapter dealing with cognitive abnormalities.

1. General Intelligence

If psychologists have largely abandoned the term 'cognition', they have certainly not abandoned the term 'intelligence'. Nevertheless, this term is equally difficult to define operationally. Intelligence, broadly speaking, refers to the quality of one's cognition. The intelligent person has a higher level of cognitive ability. This, however, like most of the definitions that have been attempted, is too vague, and often intelligence is operationally defined as that which intelligence tests measure in common. Although this begs the question of what defines an intelligence test, it does underline the often repeated observation that people who are good at solving one type of problem tend also to be good at solving other types, even when the content, the mode of presentation, the type of response, and the type of reasoning involved seem to be different.

Although different kinds of intelligence tests, as scored conventionally intercorrelate fairly highly, and, therefore, yield a strong general factor when factor analysed, we cannot necessarily conclude from this that general intelligence is a unitary phenomenon. Furneaux (1961), investigated a typical test of g composed of Thurstone type letter series items (for example: 'complete the following series: ABBABB-'). He found that the IQ score obtained from an untimed version of the test is a function of three relatively independent characteristics of performance, speed (of solving correct, but not incorrect or abandoned items), accuracy, and persistence. He found that these three characteristics can each be measured very reliably, and he also gave reasons for regarding them as being of more fundamental importance than a single IQ score. For example, there appears to be a linear relation between log solution time and item difficulty level which has the same slope for all people. Furneaux pointed out that the same IQ score can be obtained in different ways (by a slow, accurate performance, or a fast inaccurate performance), so that measuring these characteristics separately is of more descriptive value, and is potentially of greater predictive value because of their relative independence.

Furneaux's work suggests that we should regard 'IQ' scores as being ambiguous. Thus, if we demonstrate that two different symptoms among the mentally ill both tend to be associated with a decline in general intelligence, we cannot necessarily conclude that the same 'general' ability is being affected in both conditions. The reduced IQ scores might be the result of two quite different abnormalities in the two cases (for example slowness in the first instance and inaccuracy in the second).

2. The Process of Problem Solving

The results of a great many studies in which intelligence tests have been employed have thrown remarkably little light on the process of problem solving itself. Problem solving is a purposeful activity that resolves some conflict, in that it suggests only one of a number of possible responses to the given situation. For any particular problem there is usually only one 'correct' answer which we must assume would satisfy everyone if he were aware of it, and if he could comprehend the way in which it related to the initial data of the problem. There has been a number of experimental attempts to investigate various stages of the problem solving process, but no attempt will be made to review this literature here, unless it is relevant to studies of abnormal behaviour. It is probably fair to say that the central process is still not understood. For example, after a number of possible solutions have been considered, how do we recognise the correct answer? Attempts have been made to reduce problem solving to internalised trial and error learning. Thus, for example, Maltzman (1955) has argued that, all the possible answers (internal representations of the 'response' to be made) are produced by trial and error. However, only one is 'reinforced' by evoking an 'anticipatory goal response'. This 'anticipatory goal response' is an internal representation of the rewarding state of affairs that will follow the emission of the correct response. Such accounts, however, do not explain why it is that only the correct response is internally reinforced in this way, unless the subject has already learned that this is the correct answer from past experience. But if this were the case, the problem wouldn't really be a problem.

For the purposes of the present chapter, the following, largely 'common sense' analysis of the stages of problem solving will be adopted. Abnormalities associated with each stage of this process will then be discussed.

(a) ATTENTION

In order to register all the data relevant to a problem, it is first necessary to attend to all the relevant stimuli. If one's attention wanders, important data may be missed, and a correct solution will be impossible.

(b) PERCEPTION

Perception is the process whereby incoming stimuli are grouped and interpreted in the light of past experience. This process often involves the suppression or enhancement of some aspects of the stimulus complex, in order to produce perceptual 'constancy'. The 'set' of the individual also influences the range and type of stimuli that will be perceived. If this perceptual set is too narrow or restrictive, essential data may be excluded, and problem solving will be affected. If it is too broad or 'over-inclusive', problem solving will be affected in a different way.

Perceptual distortions could also influence problem solving, as the data of the problem would not be correctly registered. It is also possible that some perceptions that do not arise from the sensory stimuli (hallucinations) might be registered, and this, too, could lead to erroneous conclusions.

(c) IMMEDIATE MEMORY SPAN

Those data that have been perceived, must be held in some kind of temporary store, which in some sense represents the focus of one's consciousness, while they are being manipulated. The capacity of this 'span of apprehension' varies from person to person, and individual differences are clearly associated with differences in problem solving ability. The evidence for this is that such tests as the Wechsler (1944) 'digit span' subtest correlate fairly highly with general intelligence. It is clearly an advantage to be able to hold more items of information in mind, and manipulate them simultaneously, and the capacity of this store may set a limit to the complexity of the problems an individual can solve. Any disorder that affects the capacity of one's immediate memory span could clearly affect thinking adversely.

(d) SHORT-TERM RETENTION

Relevant items of information that exceed the capacity of immediate memory span must presumably be stored temporarily somewhere else. There are individual differences in the capacity of this short-term store as well. Furthermore, information held in short-term store appears to decay as a function of time, and there are also, probably, individual differences in this decay rate, which could be independent of differences in storage capacity. The capacity of such a short-term store could limit the complexity of the problem that could be solved, but the decay rate could also influence thinking. For example, as Yates (1966) has pointed out, a very slow thinker may forget essential items of information he has stored temporarily before he has solved the problem, making the correct solution impossible.

(e) LEARNING ABILITY

Some problems may require more information than can be apprehended, or stored temporarily. Their solution depends on information that has been learned in the past. It goes without saying that the ability to memorise material may be a relevant variable in the solution of some types of problems.

(f) LONG-TERM RETENTION

Learning might be defined as the process whereby information is fed into some long-term storage system (perhaps chemical in nature). The subsequent retrieval of this information, however, may well be affected by a number of influences not well understood. It seems likely that, whatever the retrieval mechanism, there is some long-term decay of retained information through time. This, in conjunction with individual differences in initial experience, and learning ability, could account for the *amount* of information potentially available for recall. However, there must also exist some mechanism whereby the stored material can be retrieved. If long-term memory is chemical in nature, there must exist some neurological receptors that reconvert the chemically stored data into neural impulses. One source of individual differences is probably the speed with which this can occur. 'Fluent' individuals appear to be those who can rapidly scan stored data, and withdraw quickly from the memory pool, items of information that are needed. It is also possible that the efficiency of the hypothetical neurological receptor varies from person to person. Thus, some individuals may readily be able to recall a large proportion of the data stored. Others may need additional cues to aid this process, so that their 'recognition' may considerably exceed their recall. Defects in any of these processes could interfere with thinking in one way or another, although the processes themselves are as yet little understood.

(g) CONCEPTUALISATION

Conceptualisation refers to the process whereby discrete perceptions are in some way categorised by the central nervous system. A concept refers to a generalisation covering a wide range of perceptual data. In most problems, the elements that must be manipulated for the solution are concepts. Usually, these are represented by language symbols. There are undoubtedly individual differences in the way in which concepts are initially learned. Put another way, words do not mean the same things to all people. Since many problems are presented verbally, the problems themselves may convey different meanings to different people, depending on how they have been taught to use and define words (or other concepts). A life-long defect in the capacity to learn concepts could clearly be detrimental to problem solving.

Very often, however, in order to solve a particular problem, it is necessary to group the initial data in some novel way. That is to say, it is necessary to reorganise it by producing some new generalisation or conceptualisation. The term 'concreteness' has been used to refer to the inability to formulate any abstract generalisations about specific items of information. There is a good deal of evidence that some abnormal individuals are concrete. Some individuals are apparently even unable to employ previously learned concepts to organise new data. They seem to regard each individual item of information as unique, being unable to see common elements. This disorder can lead to a rather unusual use of words, because the concrete person acts as if he were unable to recognise the abstract connotations of the words he employs.

Another conceptual defect refers to the opposite extreme. There is evidence that some individuals define concepts (or words) so broadly that their thinking is affected for this reason. This defect, which has been labelled 'overinclusive' conceptualisation can also affect thinking by making it diffuse and imprecise.

(h) RIGIDITY

Another characteristic of problem solving performance has been called rigidity. The solution of a problem may require a number of different conceptual groupings of the data, and a number of different manipulations before a correct solution emerges. However, some people appear unable to perceive a different method of conceptualising data once they have produced an initial method. This restricts the range of possible solutions, and clearly affects thinking adversely.

(i) ACCURACY OF MANIPULATION

Once information has been perceived and classified, it is in some way manipulated until a correct solution emerges. This process, which is the core of problem solving, has still not been explained satisfactorily. The most obscure aspect of the process is the way in which the correct solution is recognised and checked against the initial data. All individuals occasionally produce an incorrect answer, and accuracy is an important source of individual differences, which Furneaux has found to be relatively independent of the speed of the problem solving process itself. As will be seen, the tendency to produce incorrect, or unusual responses appears to be an important characteristic of some mentally ill individuals.

(j) SPEED OF MANIPULATION

The speed of problem solving is a very important source of individual differences. Even in untimed IQ tests, Furneaux has demonstrated that slow thinkers frequently abandon a problem before they have solved it. The relationship between solution time and difficulty level is a logarithmic one, so that, for the slow thinker, a difficult problem may be insoluble, because for all practical purposes, he does not have time to solve it. The cause of individual differences in speed is an intriguing question. As Furneaux has demonstrated, although most people can speed up their thinking when required to do so, this can be done only within very narrow limits. It is possible that the speed of mental processes is related to some fundamental property of the central nervous system. A very interesting set of data were collected by Dispensa (1938) who administered Thurstone's Psychological Test for college entrance to a large number of college women. Measures of basal metabolism were also obtained. There was a significant tendency, even within this relatively homogeneous population, for those with an underactive thyroid to be duller, and those with an overactive thyroid to be brighter. It is tempting to explain these results in terms of individual differences in problem solving speed. As will be seen, extreme slowness in thinking is a very striking finding among many mentally ill individuals.

(k) PERSISTENCE

The final source of individual differences in problem solving ability, which Furneaux found to be relatively independent of speed and accuracy, is persistence. Individuals who are not prepared to persist for long enough in thinking about a problem are less likely to obtain a correct solution. Furneaux has demonstrated that for problems of a certain level of difficulty, for any individual, there is a relatively restricted span of time during which a correct solution can be obtained. A correct solution will never be given if the individual spends less than the minimum time needed. Persistence thus clearly interacts with problem solving speed, and very slow individuals who also happen not to be persistent will clearly abandon difficult items long before a correct solution could have emerged. Clearly, people who are abnormally lacking in persistence will be adversely affected in problem solving.

3. The Neurology of Problem Solving

No account of human problem solving would be complete without explaining what part or parts of the central nervous system mediate each different process. Unfortunately, it is not possible at present to give any such account. Once it is conceded that the notion that 'g' or general intelligence is housed in the 'silent areas' of the cortex is an entirely unsatisfactory account, some of the complexities required of any proposed neurological model are clear. It seems possible that the locus of information processing may be the synapse, since these structures appear to provide the means whereby generalisations can be made, and data reduced. They also appear to provide an active mechanism for the suppression of unwanted (incorrect?) responses. It is tempting to speculate that the speed of synaptic transmission

may be related to problem solving speed. Short-term memories may well be stored neurologically in some type of neural reverberating circuits. It seems more probable that long-term retention has a chemical basis, and also that whatever chemicals are responsible are relatively widespread, because extensive cortical lesions seem to have a surprisingly small effect on long-term memories. This suggests that some redundancy exists, both in the distribution of whatever chemical is concerned, and in the number of end organs that must exist to re-convert chemical information into neural impulses. Beyond these very vague speculations, however, it does not seem possible to go at present.

GENERAL INTELLIGENCE AND INTELLECTUAL DETERIORATION IN MENTAL ILLNESS

1. The Concept of Mental Syndromes

Most of the studies reviewed in the present chapter were designed to investigate the general or specific cognitive disabilities associated with specific psychiatric syndromes. The value of these studies rests largely on the validity of the Kraepelinian system of psychiatric classification. Nevertheless, attempts to provide some objective evidence of the validity of this scheme have met with inconclusive results.

A number of investigators have used rating scales applied to large groups of hospitalised mental patients in an attempt to demonstrate that those signs and symptoms that should correlate with one another in accordance with the traditional psychiatric syndromes do in fact do so. Usually, the technique of factor analysis has been used to demonstrate the existence of these anticipated symptom clusters. However, these studies have produced remarkably conflicting results, some supporting in general the Kraepelinian scheme, but some providing evidence for quite different symptom clusters.

Two shortcomings, unfortunately, render all these studies inconclusive. The first is a purely statistical one. In the factor analyses carried out, no explicit mathematical definition of what constitutes a syndrome ('cluster' or 'factor') has been agreed upon. That is to say, there has been no generally accepted mathematical criterion specifying those conditions under which the existence of a putative syndrome will be rejected. Different investigators have used somewhat different factor analytic techniques, and the same set of data can suggest different sets of clusters to different investigators.

A more important shortcoming, however, concerns the validity of the symptom ratings themselves. However objectively the symptoms may be described

in the rating scale, psychiatrists, or for that matter any raters with a knowledge of psychiatric classification, are likely to be influenced by their preconceptions. Thus, for instance, if the rater knows that symptoms A and B are supposed to occur together, when he elicits A, he is more likely to question the patient about B, more likely to encourage the patient to describe B, and, given an ambiguous response, more likely to rate B as being present. Thus, the statistical results may in part, or even largely reflect only the psychiatric training of the raters.

Another source of bias is the social context of the ratings made, and its interaction with the rater. In a study carried out on 24 psychiatric in-patients, 29 symptoms were rated independently both by the nurse who knew the patient best, and by the doctor in charge (Payne et al., 1970). The average intercorrelation between doctors' and nurses' ratings was only 0·32, and for only 8 of the 29 symptoms rated was there a statistically significant correlation. Either the doctors and nurses perceived the patient's behaviour differently, or else they elicited different sorts of behaviour from the patient, or both.

For all these reasons then, it must be concluded that these rating studies have thrown very little light on the nature of the different psychiatric syndromes that may exist.

In the present chapter, no attempt will be made to deal with mental deficiency, perhaps the most striking example of cognitive abnormality, since this is the subject of Chapter 6 (section A). Similarly, no attempt will be made to deal with cognitive abnormalities that result from brain damage, since this is the subject of Chapter 3 (section D). This chapter will be concerned with those cognitive defects regarded as 'functional' in nature, in that they are associated with neurosis or one of the psychoses. Of all the functional psychiatric disorders, it is generally agreed that schizophrenia is the psychosis that is characterised by the presence of thought disorder. Many authorities regard thought disorder as the primary diagnostic criterion of schizophrenia, and believe that when thought disorder occurs in other psychotic or neurotic conditions, it is secondary to the basic emotional disturbance.

The literature abounds with detailed clinical descriptions of the different types of thought disorder shown by schizophrenic patients, and many items of the rating scales referred to above refer to some kind of thinking disturbance. However, it is almost certainly the case that rating thought disorder from clinical interviews is not a very reliable procedure.

Ever since Kraepelin's major publications, experimentally orientated research workers have been developing objective techniques for measuring different kinds of schizophrenic thought disorder, either by laboratory experiments or by standardised formal psychological tests. There is now a considerable body of research findings. This evidence suggests unequivocally that, whatever else, schizophrenics are an extremely heterogeneous group of patients. Typically, on any single objective psychological measure, the range of schizophrenic performance extends from virtually the top of the normal range, to a score so low as to be not only completely outside the normal range, but to be two or even three standard deviations lower than the lowest normal score. In this respect, these studies are consistent with a large number of other chemical and biological investigations. Unfortunately, however, most of these studies are unhelpful in determining what specific types of thought disorder syndromes may exist among schizophrenic patients. This is because most investigators use only two or three measures of a particular kind of thought disorder, and demonstrate that schizophrenics, as a group, differ from normal people, or from other psychiatric control groups. Usually, no attempt is made to account for the extreme variability within the schizophrenic group, by trying to subdivide it on the basis of some behavioural or other characteristic. What is clearly needed is more large scale studies using a number of measures of quite different kinds of thought disorder, and also including other measurable behavioural or biological characteristics, in order to determine what empirical clusters do seem to occur within the schizophrenic population. This, of course, was the aim of the rating scale studies referred to above, but the use of objective tests and experimental data would eliminate some of the sources of observer bias that make the results of the rating scale studies ambiguous.

The other striking lack in the presently available data, is the almost complete absence of any long-, or even short-term follow-up studies of the same patients. Dementia praecox was originally regarded by Kraepelin as progressive. Even if many schizophrenics appear to recover, or at least to show remissions, many seem to get worse. There has been a considerable amount of interesting speculation about the possible intellectual changes that develop in those schizophrenics who seem to deteriorate, but objective data are almost completely unavailable.

2. Intellectual Level During Mental Illness

For many years, clinical psychologists have made a practice of administering tests of general intelligence to mental patients of all kinds shortly after their admission to mental hospital, as part of the routine assessment procedure. Since Wells and Kelley's (1920) study, articles have been appearing summarising the intelligence test results for different groups of patients. In the earlier studies, the Binet test was used, although since 1945 most published data have been obtained from the Wechsler Bellevue Scale (Wechsler, 1944), or Raven's (1950) Progressive Matrices Test. Extensive reviews of this literature have been published by Brody (1941), by Hunt and Cofer (1944) and more recently by Payne (1960). However, the popularity of this type of study seems to have declined markedly in recent years, and there appear to be no recent studies that necessitate any revisions of Payne's (1960) conclusions.

The mean IQ scores shown in Table 14.1 were obtained by adding together the results of a number of published studies (Payne, 1960), and refer to Wechsler Bellevue Full Scale IQ scores unless otherwise noted. It was not possible to calculate standard deviations for the entire group, although all IQs quoted are in terms of a mean of 100 and a standard deviation of 15. It is of interest that, on

Table 14.1. Intelligence Quotients in Abnormal Groups*
(Wechsler-Bellevue except where noted)

Category	Mean IQ	Number of cases
Civilian neurotics	105·01	987 (includes 145 on Matrices)
Neurotics (Army Service)	93	5,000 (all on Matrices)
Epileptics	107·51	425
Schizophrenics	96·08	1,284
Affective psychoses	94·87	65

* *From* Payne, 1960

Table 14.2. Intelligence Quotients in
Subgroups of Neurotics*
(civilians)

Category	Mean IQ	Number of cases
Neurotic (not specified)	103·63	676
Mixed neurosis	107·23	72 (includes 63 on Matrices)
Hysteric	106·11	43 (includes 25 on Matrices)
Psychopath	100·64	33 (includes 21 on Matrices)
Obsessive-compulsive	114·16	27 (includes 11 on Matrices)
Anxiety neurosis	109·65	120 (includes 25 on Matrices)
Neurotic depression	109·28	72 (includes 63 on Matrices)
Total introverted neurotics	110·36	163 (includes 36 on Matrices)
Total extraverted neurotics	103·74	76 (includes 46 on Matrices)

From Payne, 1960

Table 14.3. Intelligence Quotients in
Subgroups of Schizophrenia*
(Wechsler Bellevue—Full Scale IQ)

Category	Mean IQ	Number of cases
Schizophrenic (nor further specified)	97·53	928
Mixed schizophrenics	99·61	72
Paranoid schizophrenics	94·84	166
Simple schizophrenics	88·23	44
Catatonic schizophrenics	82·80	45
Hebephrenic schizophrenics	80·60	29

From Payne, 1960

average, the neurotics appear to be of slightly above average intelligence. A breakdown of the neurotic group by sub-classification (where available) is given in Table 14.2 which suggests that 'introverted' neurotic (i.e. those classified as obsessive compulsive, anxiety neurosis or neurotic depression) are brighter than extroverted neurotics. These results are in accord with earlier data reported by Eysenck (1947), who tested 904 'dysthymic' and 474 'hysteric' neurotic soldiers on the Matrices Test.

These data do not suggest that any degree of general intellectual impairment is associated with neuroses. The fact that neurotics are of above average intelligence might be due to their relatively high level of drive, which could be associated with their anxiety and general autonomic responsiveness. The exception to this rule is the sample of neurotics who broke down under service conditions during the Second World War, who were of below average intelligence. This rather striking discrepancy may merely reflect different labelling policies between wartime army psychiatrists, and peacetime psychiatrists. It is possible that many of these soldiers would not have been diagnosed 'neurotic' in peacetime by civilian psychiatrists, but given some different label. It is also possible that the population of soldiers from which this neurotic group was drawn was itself of below average intelligence.

Both psychotic groups shown in Table 14.1 are of below average intelligence, on average, but as can be seen from Table 14.3, there is considerable heterogeneity within the schizophrenic group when

it is broken down into sub-categories. Most noteworthy is the tendency for those labelled 'simple schizophrenic' to be dull, and those labelled 'catatonic' or 'hebephrenic' to be very dull. However, too much weight should not be given to these results in view of the way in which the data were assembled, as it is not certain how representative these combined samples may be. It is, for example, probable that the more seriously disturbed psychotics are not represented, as such patients are often too unco-operative to be tested. It is certainly possible to select groups of schizophrenics whose average tested IQ is very low. For instance, Mainord (1953) tested a group of 22 schizophrenics who were judged to have deteriorated, and they obtained a mean IQ of 84·5 on the Wechsler Bellevue. Similarly, Malamud and Palmer (1938) found that a group of 100 deteriorated schizophrenics had a mean mental age of only 126·3 months (SD, 14·4) on the Stanford-Binet Scale.

An interesting question in view of the generally lower IQs of psychotic patients tested when they are ill, is whether or not the dull are especially susceptible to develop psychosis. A large-scale study by Mason (1956) provides some interesting evidence. Mason obtained a sample of 510 inductees of the Second World War, all of whom, as veterans, later broke down with some functional psychiatric illness. All had been given the American Army General Classification Test on being accepted for service. The pre-illness IQ scores of this group were compared with those of a very large and carefully matched control group consisting of 290, 163 Fifth Service Command Inductees. Figure 14.1 compares the pre-illness IQs of the inductees who later broke down, with the normal controls. There is no statistically significant difference between these two distributions. In terms of IQ scores, there is no way in which the subsequent psychiatric breakdown of this group as a whole could have been predicted.

Mason also broke down the group that had developed psychiatric disorders according to the

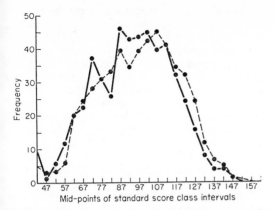

Fig. 14.1. Distribution of A.G.C.T. standard scores for 510 psychiatric in-patients (solid) and control distribution based on data for 290,163 fifth service command inductees (broken) (*from* Mason, 1956)

3. Direct Evidence for Intellectual Deterioration with Mental Illness

If intellectual impairment is an important feature of mental illness, one would expect that patients who are diagnosed as psychotic should have lower tested intelligence quotients on admission to hospital than they had before they became ill. Studies involving direct measurements of this sort are not easy because of the obvious difficulty of obtaining comparable pre-illness intelligence measures. Some investigators have been able to find schizophrenic patients who had been given IQ tests in high school prior to their illness, and retest them on the same measures (Rappaport and Webb, 1950). In most recent studies, newly admitted patients have been retested on selection tests which they had taken first when they were inducted into one of the armed services. Such data are available for relatively large groups of schizophrenics retested on the Army Classification Battery (Lubin *et al.*, 1962; Kingsley and Struening, 1966) and the Canadian Army M test (Schwartzman and Douglas, 1962). These three groups of investigators all report a decrease of approximately one-third of a standard deviation, or 6 IQ points from the pre-illness level. However, the normal controls were found to increase their scores over the same period by a similar amount, presumably due to practice. Thus, the deterioration shown by the schizophrenics may amount to as much as two thirds of a standard deviation on average.

However, other studies have produced no evidence for intellectual deterioration from the highest childhood level (Batman, Albee, and Lane, 1966; Albee *et al.*, 1963) or from Army induction level (Griffith *et al.*, 1962). These three negative studies have in common the fact that the subjects were retested on different tests from those they took first, so that differences would be harder to detect,

type of illness, as shown in Table 14.4. As can be seen, those who broke down with schizophrenia were significantly duller than the rest of the group. Those schizophrenics who were diagnosed as 'hebephrenic', 'simple', or 'other' were below average for the group in IQ, the 'paranoid' and 'catatonic' schizophrenics being average. Those who later became neurotic were average for the group, and, perhaps surprisingly, those who later became manic depressive were of above average in intelligence.

These data do suggest that people of below average intelligence are more likely to develop some types of schizophrenia than people of normal or high intelligence. Unfortunately, Mason did not attempt to retest any of these psychiatric patients, so that we do not know what effect the subsequent psychiatric breakdown might have had on the IQs of those who broke down.

Table 14.4. Differences in Pre-illness IQ Between Controls and Different Diagnostic Groups (*After* Mason, 1956)

Group	N	d.f.	Chi square	p	Trend
All Patients	510[1]	16	22·32	0·14	
All schizophrenics	368	16	32·60	0·02	low scores
Paranoid	66	3	3·10	0·39	
Catatonic	126	7	10·61	0·19	
Hebephrenic	122	7	17·55	0·02	low scores
Simple	33	2	12·46	0·002	low scores
Other	21	1	4·77	0·05	low scores
Non-schizophrenics	188	12	7·78	0·79	
Alcoholism	29	1	0·61	0·90	
Neurosis	79	5	1·93	0·20	
Manic-depressive	25	1	17·65	0·001	high scores
Character disorder	55	3	4·21	0·25	

[1] This total is reproduced from the original article. The author does not explain how it is related to the subtotals below.

due to the relative lack of correlation between the measures. Also, the patients in these studies were of nearly subnormal intelligence initially. For instance, Batman et al.'s chronic schizophrenics had a mean IQ of 81·2 in childhood. It is possible to speculate that the dull who had become psychotic deteriorate little intellectually. However, this may be, in part, an artefact of the kinds of tests used, which may not be sensitive enough to measure changes among the very dull, having too high a 'floor'.

Lane and Albee (1963) suggested that schizophrenic patients may, in fact, begin to deteriorate intellectually quite early in childhood. They produced evidence that seemed to suggest an intellectual deterioration between early and late childhood in individuals who became schizophrenic adults. However, a later statistical analysis (Lane and Albee, 1964) was unable to confirm the significance of this finding.

There is clear evidence that not all people deteriorate to the same extent when they become ill. Not surprisingly, the nature of the illness is a very important factor. Kingsley and Struening (1966) found that non-paranoid schizophrenics had dropped an average of 15 score units, while paranoid schizophrenics had dropped only 3·7 units on average. The findings of Lubin and his colleagues (1962) agree on this, but the difference is much less pronounced. It would appear that psychiatrists tend to attach the label 'paranoid schizophrenic' to those who are relatively undeteriorated intellectually.

Whether affective disorder or neurosis also produce any degree of general intellectual deterioration is not certain, as test-retest studies are lacking. However, the data on the level of functioning of such patients when ill, which is average, suggest that the general deterioration in these groups cannot be large.

A second question is whether or not deterioration is progressive if the illness continues. Kraepelin believed that most schizophrenic patients continue to deteriorate intellectually. Even if this were true, however, one need not necessarily indict the 'disease' process. Continued incarceration, with its relative sensory and social deprivation, could cause such a result. In fact, sensory deprivation could well mask the intellectual improvement normally associated with clinical improvement among those who remain in hospital.

Several direct test-retest studies have been reported which suggest that further intellectual deterioration does indeed take place among those who continue to be hospitalised as schizophrenic. Trapp and James (1937) retested 41 schizophrenics who had taken the Binet test within two weeks of admission. The retest interval varied from 4 months to 13 years. There was an average decline of 7·6 IQ points, and

the data also suggested that the longer the patients had been ill, the greater was the decline (Payne, 1961). Schwartzman and colleagues (1962) followed up 23 schizophrenics for ten years after they had first been tested in hospital, and found that the 10 who were still in hospital had continued to decline on the Canadian Army M test. However, those who had been released from hospital had improved significantly, almost to the level of their premorbid scores. Haywood and Moelis (1963) similarly found that 'improved' schizophrenics had increased their IQs five years after admission, while 'unimproved' schizophrenics had decreased their IQs although all were still hospitalised.

Three other studies (Batman et al., 1966; Hamlin and Ward, 1965; Smith, 1964) found no evidence for progressive deterioration after hospitalisation in groups of schizophrenics, although not all were well controlled.

These studies on the whole suggest that, apart from the initially very dull, intellectual deterioration can continue during hospitalisation among those regarded as schizophrenic, and at least a part of this decline may be due to some worsening disability and not just the effect of social and cultural isolation. However, it does not occur in all cases.

4. Indirect Evidence for Intellectual Deterioration with Mental Illness

Frequently, clinical psychologists are called upon to decide whether a particular patient has deteriorated, without having any pre-illness intelligence level to use as a baseline. In such circumstances it is common practice to use one of the standard indirect measures of deterioration. Three of the most common, the Babcock-Levy test for the measurement of efficiency of mental functioning (Babcock and Levy, 1940), the Shipley-Hartford test of deterioration (Shipley, 1940) and the Hunt-Minnesota test for organic brain damage (Hunt, 1943) utilise a vocabulary test to provide a measure of pre-illness intellectual level. The rationale for this is that in normal people, vocabulary is very highly correlated with most tests of general intelligence. Furthermore, there is a great deal of indirect evidence (Payne, 1960) that vocabulary is the ability least affected by mental illness, since conventionally scored vocabulary tests show the smallest difference between mentally ill groups of all types, and normal people.

The Babcock-Levy test measures current functioning ability by a battery of tests of mental and motor speed, and rote learning ability. These were chosen because the evidence suggested that these are the abilities most seriously affected by mental illness of all kinds. Thus, in theory, the Babcock deterioration index might be expected to underestimate current general level of functioning, and over-estimate the extent of general deterioration. The Shipley-Hartford test measures present intellectual level by means of a conventional verbal 'g' test of abstract reasoning. In principle, this would seem more reasonable. The Hunt-Minnesota test was not originally intended to be a test of deterioration, but a test of brain damage, so that the learning tests that are contrasted to vocabulary level were chosen because they are most affected by brain damage. A fourth common indirect measure is the Wechsler Bellevue Deterioration Index (Wechsler, 1944). This index measures present level by those subtests most affected by the normal ageing process, and measures past level by those subtests least affected by age. The somewhat dubious assumption is that the deterioration produced by age and mental illness is the same. A fifth test, not originally designed to measure deterioration at all, but very similar to the Shipley-Hartford Scale, is the combination of the Mill Hill Vocabulary Scale (Raven, 1958) and Raven's Progressive Matrices (Raven, 1938), a non-verbal test of general intelligence (Foulds and Dixon, 1962).

In all these tests, an estimate of previous IQ and an estimate of present IQ can be obtained, and the difference, expressed as an 'index' or a 'ratio' indicates the degree of deterioration.

Because normal people tend to keep adding to their vocabulary until about 30, and show no subsequent decline until about fifty, whereas they begin to decline in abstract ability before thirty, it is essential to standardise such scales very carefully over their entire age range. Unfortunately, the Babcock-Levy Scale utilised the Binet vocabulary test norms for very young adults, and the original standardisation of the Shipley-Hartford was based almost entirely on normal people under twenty. The result is that, when either test is given to middle-aged, normal people and the original norms are used, the score suggests a considerable degree of 'deterioration', no allowance being made for normal changes with age (Payne, 1960; Lewinsohn, 1963). Only two of these scales are adequately standardised for age, the Wechsler Deterioration Index and Mill Hill Vocabulary-Matrices combination (Foulds and Dixon, 1962). The latter is preferable because, since the correlation between the scales is available, it is possible to say for any given discrepancy how frequently it would have arisen in the standardisation population, and thus assess the statistical abnormality of the amount of indirectly assessed 'deterioration' shown by a particular patient (Payne and Jones, 1957).

Quite apart from the problem of standardisation, however, is the question of the validity of these measures. It has frequently been claimed that a conventional vocabulary test is not the best measure of premorbid intelligence, because some deterioration of vocabulary score does in fact occur in mental illness. There is a good deal of evidence, which has been reviewed by Payne (1960), that this is the case and more recent studies confirm this (Hamlin and Jones, 1963) although the rate of deterioration of vocabulary among the chronically ill may be very slow (Moran et al., 1960). It would probably be better to use the Ammons Full Range Picture Vocabulary Test in future attempts to develop indirect measures of deterioration, since the evidence (Payne, 1960; Blatt, 1959) suggests that this vocabulary test is minimally affected by mental disorder, as it involves recognition rather than recall, and requires the subject merely to point to the appropriate picture.

While indirect techniques of assessing deterioration may yet prove valuable, it is necessary first to demonstrate their validity by showing a substantial correlation between an indirect measure of deterioration, and a direct measure of deterioration based on a test-retest follow-up study. So far, no such studies seem to have been carried out. Studies in which the Wechsler and Shipley-Hartford indices of deterioration have been related to clinical ratings of the amount of deterioration have yielded insignificant results (Payne, 1960). However, one study (Dowis and Buchanan, 1961) using the Matrices as a measure of present intellectual level, and the Wide Range Vocabulary Test as a measure of former level, obtained very promising results. Seventy-five in-patients were tested when they were judged to be as well as possible, and again when their pathology was judged to be at maximal level. It was found that the vocabulary score remained the same, whereas the Matrices dropped significantly during the pathological state. One can conclude that, at least this combination of tests, which is logically the most satisfactory, may yet prove to be useful.

Because of all these defects, the results of studies using indirect tests of deterioration are inconclusive. These studies have been extensively reviewed by Payne (1960), who concluded that, when different clinical groups have been compared, neurotics usually show the least deterioration on the various indirect indices. There are very few studies of affective disorders, but depressed patients usually show more 'deterioration' than neurotics. Schizophrenics as a group are usually found to show most deterioration, the 'hebephrenics' and the 'chronics' being worse than the other subgroups. In this respect, the data from such studies are consistent with studies assessing the general intellectual level of mental patients while ill.

One interesting study which did not make use of any of the measures described above, was carried out by Binder (1956) using Thurstone's test of Primary Mental Abilities. Binder tested a group of young (mean age 29·2) and a group of old (mean age 53·6) schizophrenics, and compared them with matched groups of normals. Unlike the test discussed above, all the PMA tests are timed. The usual pattern of discrepancies was not found under these conditions in either the young or the old group of schizophrenics. That is to say, the young schizophrenics were uniformly worse than the normal controls on *all* the PMA subtests, including the verbal meaning (vocabulary) measure. In fact, the smallest discrepancy was on the abstract 'reasoning' test. This suggests that perhaps the usual discrepancy between vocabulary and 'g' test performance found among psychotics on indirect tests of deterioration can be attributed to slowness among psychotics (the vocabulary tests used are all untimed), and does not represent a 'general' intellectual deterioration. Granick (1963) also found that psychotic depressives were no worse than matched normal controls on speed-free intelligence tests. These results are consistent with the findings of Shapiro and Nelson (1955), which will be discussed below.

One other curious aspect of Binder's data, was the fact that the older schizophrenics differed much less from the normal controls than did the younger schizophrenics. It is hard to know how to interpret such a finding. One possibility is that normal adults slow down much more quickly with age than do schizophrenics. However, an alternative possibility is that the two groups of 'schizophrenics' may have been quite different. For instance, the older group may have had an illness that started much later in life, and that produced much less severe intellectual slowness than did the younger group.

5. The Reversibility of Intellectual Deterioration

A different question is whether the intellectual deterioration found in psychotic patients is reversible. Kraepelin originally thought that dementia praecox was, like organic dementia, progressive and irreversible. However, the experimental evidence on the whole suggests that when patients improve, their level of intelligence improves again. The findings of Schwartzman *et al.* (1962) and Haywood and Moelis (1963) which support this conclusion have already been described. Early studies by Davidson (1939) who used the Binet test, and Carp (1950) who used the Wechsler-Bellevue, found that

IQ level went up as the patients improved clinically, although they tested no control group to assess the effects of practice.

The evidence suggests, therefore, that intellectual deterioration in patients diagnosed as schizophrenic is not completely irreversible, but tends to recover if the patient's other symptoms improve.

6. Behavioural Abnormalities Associated with General Intellectual Deterioration

It has been found that when young (adolescent) schizophrenic patients are compared with older (middle-aged) patients, the young show a much lower level of tested intelligence (Pollack, 1960). This and other evidence suggests that, when schizophrenia is diagnosed in the young, an important diagnostic criterion is intellectual deterioration, whereas this is not the case in middle-aged individuals. In the young, schizophrenic deterioration may be mistaken for mental deficiency (Chapman and Pathman, 1959).

As was noted above, there is a tendency for schizophrenics with low levels of intellectual functioning while ill to be diagnosed as 'hebephrenic'. This suggests that there may be a tendency for these impaired patients to exhibit mood swings, and silly, bizarre, or grotesque forms of behaviour. Schizophrenic patients who are functioning at an average intellectual level or better, tend to be diagnosed as paranoid schizophrenic (Payne, 1960; Smith, 1964; Lubin *et al.*, 1962). More or less systematised delusions of persecution are for some reason common among intellectually well-preserved patients. This suggests that their cognitive defect may be relatively specific. Unfortunately, there seem to be very few objective studies of the specific symptomatology associated with different levels of intellectual functioning when ill.

Another common descriptive method of subdividing the very large and heterogeneous group diagnosed as 'schizophrenic', is by the form of onset of the condition, as defined in terms of some standard scale such as the Elgin Scale (Wittman, 1941) or the Phillips (1953) Scale. When the onset of the illness is very gradual and of long standing, associated with increasing social withdrawal but reactive to no discernible trauma, the condition is labelled 'process' schizophrenia. However, when the illness has a rapid onset, in persons who were formerly sociable and extraverted, and seems to be a response to some environmental trauma, the term 'reactive' schizophrenia is used. There is now a good deal of evidence that 'reactive' patients have a relatively good prognosis, whereas 'process' schizophrenics tend to become chronic patients (Chapman *et al.*, 1961;

Higgins, 1964). In spite of the popularity of this classification there seem to be no studies of the differences between these groups in general level of intellectual functioning when ill. It is, of course, quite possible that once the condition has developed, there are no marked differences in this respect.

7. Prognostic Significance of Poor Intellectual Performance

There is now a considerable body of evidence that individuals who have a low (dull normal to border-line defective) tested IQ in their childhood, are more likely to develop a breakdown that will be diagnosed as 'schizophrenic' when they are young adults, than will their peers of normal intelligence (Lane and Albee, 1964; Albee *et al.*, 1964; Pollack, 1960). Furthermore, in a group of adult schizophrenics, those who recover tend to have had a higher child-hood IQ than those who become chronic patients (Batman *et al.*, 1966). Similarly, chronic schizo-phrenics tend to have had a lower tested IQ on army induction than schizophrenics who recovered (Schwartzman and Douglas, 1962). It is also the case that schizophrenics who have a higher tested IQ on their hospital admission, more frequently tend to recover than patients with a lower tested admission IQ, who tend more often to become chronic (Payne, 1960).

It is possible that these findings are related to the process-reactive dimension. It may be the case that 'process schizophrenia' starts to develop very slowly even in childhood, so that some amount of de-terioration has occurred very early in life. It would seem to he this type of patient who has a poor prognosis (Phillips, *et al.*, 1965). A study by Heath and co-workers (1965) supports this view. Forty-six adult schizophrenics were given a standard Process-Reactive rating scale, and their childhood intelligence quotients on the Kuhlmann-Anderson Group Intelligence test were obtained. The process schizo-phrenics, as expected, were significantly duller as children. The process schizophrenics as children had also been significantly duller than their own siblings, but the reactive schizophrenics as children were not significantly different from their siblings.

8. The Possibility of Manipulating General Intelligence in Psychosis

The studies so far cited suggest that any procedure that improves the general clinical status of the patient is likely to improve his general intellectual level. However, there are very few carefully controlled studies about the specific effects of certain types of treatment on general intelligence.

Graham (1940) investigated the effect of insulin shock therapy on performance on the Stanford Binet in 33 schizophrenics, but found that the treatment produced no significant improvement. Carp (1950) studying 42 schizophrenics, found a 4·7 point rise on the Wechsler IQ following insulin treatment, but the lack of a control group made it impossible to rule out the effects of practice. Thorpe and Baker (1958) in a similarly uncontrolled study of the effects of insulin in 9 schizophrenics found a substantial improvement on the Matrices test score. However, the faulty design of these studies, which control neither for practice, nor for the well-known 'placebo' effect of suggestion, make it impossible to draw any conclusions about the possible specific effect of insulin therapy on general intellectual performance.

There is, similarly, no clear evidence that electro-convulsive therapy improves performance on in-telligence tests. Callagan (1952) found that ECT had no significant effect on improving the performance of 25 depressed patients on several Wechsler sub-tests. Thorpe and Baker (1958), on the other hand, found that 9 schizophrenics given ECT improved in their performance of Raven's Matrices. Again, the inadequate design failed to assess either the placebo effect or the effect of practice.

Another treatment that has been claimed to have temporary beneficial effects on the general in-tellectual performance of schizophrenics, is sodium amytal. Layman (1940), testing 20 schizophrenics with the Binet, before, during, and after amytal found a significant improvement with the drug, and a significant decline again when the drug was withdrawn. Mainord (1953) in an exactly similar study using the Wechsler Bellevue with 22 de-teriorated schizophrenics, found a pre-amytal mean IQ of 84·5, a highly significant mean improvement to 100·6 under amytal, and a decline to a mean of 86·4 when the effects of the amytal had worn off. However, Senf and colleagues (1955) using 24 chronic schizophrenics tested with three Wechsler verbal tests, could not obtain a significant effect. Similarly, Ogilvie (1954) and Broadhurst (1957) could not obtain this amytal effect with the Nufferno Level Test, although they report large practice effects over the three sessions among the acute undeteriorated schizophrenics they tested, which may partly have obscured the influence of amytal. It is likely that the drug, for some reason, works with some patients but not with others, and it is conceivable that it works only with very deteriorated patients. None of the studies allows the effect of suggestion *per se* to be evaluated.

A more recent form of treatment is phenothiazine medication. A very carefully controlled double blind study of the effects of nine weeks of Thorazine treatment as contrasted to a placebo on the intellectual performance of 40 chronic schizophrenics, is reported by Nickols (1958). He found that the drug produced a slight but statistically insignificant improvement on the performance of the Wechsler Bellevue test and the Arthur Point Stencil Design Test. The addition of a 'total push' regime for a further twelve weeks to the drug placebo treatment similarly had no statistically significant effect on test performance.

9. Intellectual Variability and Mental Illness

The data so far discussed are all intelligence quotient scores obtained from an entire test session. While it is clear that the tested IQ of some patients commonly declines, this fact tells us nothing about which particular intellectual process (or processes) is at fault. Clearly, different patients could get low IQ scores for different reasons.

Before turning to an assessment of specific intellectual processes, it is worth discussing briefly one descriptive hypothesis about the nature of intellectual deterioration in schizophrenia. It has frequently been maintained (Payne, 1960) that schizophrenics are characteristically very variable in their performance, and it is this that tends to bring down their average level of ability both individually and as a group. Thus, for some periods, a schizophrenic patient may perform normally, but he may then perform very badly, the fluctuations being unpredictable. Several measures of this supposed variability have been commonly used. The first, derived from the Binet test, is merely the difference between 'basal' mental age (at which all subtests are passed) and the 'ceiling' mental age (at which no subtests are passed) (Payne, 1960). A very variable performance, it was thought, would increase this difference. Several ways of assessing the subtest scatter on the Wechsler-Bellevue Scale have been used, although the best is probably that used by Monroe (1952) who calculated the standard deviation of the weighted subtest scores around their own mean, for each patient.

There is a considerable amount of evidence (Payne, 1960) that subtest scatter on the Binet and on the Wechsler, so measured, is increased in mental illness. However, this could be the result, either of an increased variability of performance *or* a reduction of the subtest intercorrelations within the mentally ill. Payne (1960) in reviewing the literature, concluded that the reliability studies on the Wechsler and the Binet do not in fact bear out the hypothesis that schizophrenics are more variable in their test performance over an entire testing

session. If anything, their scores are more consistent from one occasion to another, than are those of normal people both in subtest and full-scale performance. More recent studies reviewed by Guertin *et al.* (1962) similarly find high coefficients of reliability among mental patients on the Wechsler Bellevue. It therefore seems to be that the increased subtest discrepancies shown by schizophrenics are the result of a reduction in the average subtest intercorrelation. Indeed, such changes in subtest intercorrelations have been found in schizophrenic groups (Payne, 1960; Berger *et al.*, 1963). The clear implication of these results is that, among psychotics, certain subtests are probably affected by a relatively specific type of thought disorder, which does not affect the performance of normal people on these tests, and does not affect performance on other subtests. The intrusion of such an additional, specific source of subtest variance for psychotic patients would increase the size of subtest discrepancies, and reduce subtest intercorrelations in an abnormal population. In the following sections, several such specific types of impairment will be discussed, all of which could easily affect the performance of psychotics on specific Wechsler and Binet subtests.

These results do not, of course, rule out the possibility that the performance of some schizophrenics is very variable over much shorter periods of time than would be needed to complete the average intelligence subtest. Such moment-to-moment variability could produce an average decrement in performance over the entire test, and there is some evidence, which will be discussed below, that this type of variability does indeed occur in reaction time experiments.

10. Summary and Conclusions

1. Neurotic patients, tested when ill, appear to be of above average intelligence as a group, introverted neurotics being brighter than extraverted neurotics. The pre-illness intelligence of neurotic patients is also above average, and there is no evidence that this condition produces any general intellectual impairment.

2. On average, schizophrenic patients who are tested when they are ill are of low average intelligence, but they are unusually heterogeneous as a group. Those labelled 'hebephrenic', 'catatonic', or 'simple' seem to be duller than the other groups, often being of borderline defective general intelligence.

3. The pre-illness intelligence of schizophrenics as a group also tends to be low average, and those diagnosed as 'hebephrenic' or 'simple' are especially dull. It would appear that individuals of low general

intelligence are especially likely to develop an illness that is diagnosed as hebephrenic or simple schizophrenia.

4. Test-retest studies suggest that, on average, the IQ scores of schizophrenics who are tested when they are ill may have declined by as much as two-thirds of a standard deviation from their pre-illness level. This suggests that this disorder is associated with a significant decline in general intellectual level. However, paranoid schizophrenia appears to be the exception to this generalisation, as these patients show only a minimal decline.

5. There is some evidence that schizophrenic patients who do not recover continue to decline intellectually if they remain in hospital.

6. There is evidence that the intellectual level of those schizophrenics who recover may return nearly to their pre-illness level. This suggests that this process is by no means irreversible in all cases.

7. Among patients diagnosed as schizophrenic, those with a lower tested IQ appear to have a significantly poorer prognosis.

8. There is some evidence that children of dull intelligence are more likely to develop 'process' schizophrenia, whereas brighter children are more likely to develop 'reactive' schizophrenia.

9. There is no evidence to suggest that, prior to their illness, individuals who develop an affective disorder, can be distinguished from the general population on intelligence tests. While there is some indirect evidence that the affective psychoses may produce some deterioration in general intellectual performance, satisfactory test-retest studies are not available.

DIFFERENT TYPES OF PROBLEMS

1. Verbal vs. Performance Tasks

When the Wechsler Bellevue Intelligence Scale first became widely used, a number of investigators began to look for patterns of subtest discrepancies that were characteristic of specific groups of psychiatric patients. Indeed, for a period, many clinical psychologists attempted to use such patterns of discrepancies as a diagnostic tool.

Payne (1960) combined the results of a number of studies, in an attempt to determine to what extent the particular discrepancies found in specific studies cancelled out when all the available published data were combined. He concluded that there was no evidence for any particular psychiatric group to show a Wechsler Verbal-Performance IQ discrepancy. For example, combining the published data for schizophrenics as a group yielded a population of 663 cases, the mean Verbal IQ being 93·50, and the mean Performance IQ 92·67. A breakdown of these cases (where possible) by subtype similarly failed to suggest any striking differences, and it was noted that the larger the sample, the smaller the mean difference seemed to be. Similar results were obtained for the neurotic samples but too few cases of affective disorder were available to make such an analysis especially meaningful.

2. Wechsler Bellevue Subtest Scores

Payne (1960) carried out the same analysis for the Wechsler-Bellevue subtests. The largest combined group was one of 879 schizophrenics, whose highest mean weighted subtest score was 'Vocabulary' (9·73, SD 2·87) and whose lowest mean subtest score was 'Digit Symbol' (7·53, SD 2·97). Normals of the same mean age show an average discrepancy between the 'Information' and 'Digit Symbol' subtests of 0·6 points, in the same direction (data are not available for normals on vocabulary). Even if it were possible to demonstrate the probable statistical significance of this discrepancy, it is not a large one. None of the combined profiles for the different schizophrenic subgroups, showed any more clear cut profiles. These results suggested that the much more striking subtest profiles reported by specific workers may well have been partly the result of sampling errors. It must be concluded that Wechsler-Bellevue profile analysis could not be used diagnostically, especially in view of the relatively low reliabilities of the sub-tests. There appeared to be a slight general tendency for the schizophrenics to do best on tests of 'old learning' ('Vocabulary', 'Information') and worst on tests involving speed ('Digit Symbol', 'Arithmetic') or attention ('Digit Span'), a result very much like that observed earlier by Babcock (see below).

The combined sample of 127 introverted neurotics also did best on vocabulary, but unlike the schizophrenics they did worst on digit span, there being roughly a 2 point mean difference between these two extreme subtest scores. It has been argued that the digit span subtest is adversely affected by a high level of anxiety. Again, this discrepancy could not be used as a diagnostic measure with individuals because of the relatively low subtest reliability.

There were too few cases in the other diagnostic groups for any valid generalisations about Wechsler 'profiles' to be made.

It therefore seems likely that the apparent 'content' of the intelligence test may be of less relevance to mental abnormality than the type of thought processes involved in its solution. It should be noted that the scores on nearly all of the Wechsler-Bellevue subtests would seem to depend on the interaction of a number of different intellectual processes, so that a single subtest score would probably not reflect very clearly a defect in one specific process. Since the remainder of the chapter will deal in detail with specific stages of the problem solving process, the possible causes of differences in scores between different kinds of tests will not be discussed further here.

DISORDERS OF ATTENTION

Attention might be defined as the process whereby the organism remains orientated to a particular set of incoming stimuli. Clearly, people vary in their ability to do this, and there is evidence that an unusual degree of distractibility is associated with certain types of mental disorder. However, in any experiment, the incoming stimuli are 'perceived', or organised in some way, before any measurable response is made. Therefore 'attention' and 'perception' are inevitably confounded in most experiments. Accordingly, those experiments dealing with abnormal distractibility will be discussed below along with the other disorders of perception.

DISORDERS OF PERCEPTION

1. Perceptual Errors

Perceptual disorders are common among brain-damaged patients, and Kraepelin's original view that dementia praecox is an organic illness, has led some investigators to look for perceptual defects among schizophrenics. Some have even gone so far as to suggest that schizophrenia may be caused by a perceptual defect of some sort (e.g. Cooper, 1960). Groups of schizophrenics have been found to be significantly worse than normals at matching and reproducing patterns (Payne, 1960; Chapman and McGhie, 1962; Schwartz, 1967), estimating sizes (Cooper, 1960; Silverman, 1964), estimating distances (Blumenthal and Meltzoff, 1967) and perceiving apparent motion (Chambers and Wilson, 1968), although not all studies report significant differences (Rutschmann, 1961; Dean and Weckowicz, 1967).

Weight discrimination thresholds have been found to be raised in schizophrenics, and some studies suggest that the inability to judge weights may be a poor prognostic sign (Rosenbaum et al., 1965). Kelm and his colleagues (1968) also found that patients who show perceptual distortions on the Hoffer-Osmond Diagnostic test on admission, stay in hospital longer than other patients.

Some studies report more specific perceptual anomalies. Salzinger (1957) found in a weight judgement experiment, that acute schizophrenics have a much more pronounced 'anchor' effect than normals. They judge weights to be heavier after they have been given a very heavy weight to lift (but not to judge). Hoffer and Osmond (1963) in a very interesting study found that 25 schizophrenic patients were less accurate than normals in judging when an investigator was looking into their eyes. The authors speculate that such a disability might contribute to a common feeling among paranoid schizophrenic patients that people are watching them.

It is clear that such perceptual defects among schizophrenics could impair their ability to solve problems, because they may miss essential items of information. For example, Moon et. al. (1968) found evidence that schizophrenics mishear words when they are merely asked to repeat them.

Starr and co-workers (1968) found no differences between catatonic and non-catatonic schizophrenics in size-matching ability, but there appear to be no other recent studies into the differences in perceptual ability between the Kraepelinian subgroups of schizophrenia.

There is no evidence that perceptual defects are specific to schizophrenia, however. For example, Friedman (1964) found that psychotic depressives, by comparison with normal subjects, had poorer binocular acuity of vision on the Orthorater test. Unfortunately, there appear to be very few recent investigations of the perceptual accuracy of depressive patients.

These perceptual studies do not necessarily indicate that the sensory input is at fault. The apparent defective acuity found in some sensory threshold experiments can be shown to be due to a response bias (e.g. adopting a more conservative attitude) (Clark, 1966; Clark et al., 1967) and other apparent sensory defects may partly be defects of judgement and interpretation. Spiegel and Litrownik (1968) found that, like normals, the perceptual judgements of schizophrenics rated as 'dependent' or 'unassertive' could be influenced by group pressure.

The recent interest in psychotomimetic drugs has led to several attempts to produce the same type of perceptual disorders in normals as are found in schizophrenics. LSD 25 (Lysergic Acid Diethyl-amide) significantly impaired the size judgements of normal subjects in one study (Liebert *et al.*, 1958), and the ability to judge size, estimate eye level, and judge the upright in another study (Krus *et al.*, 1963). The theory that schizophrenics are resistant to the effect of this drug was also tested in both studies, and found not to be true. Schizophrenics were poorer than the normal subjects without LSD, but their perception deteriorated to the same extent as the normals under the influence of the drug.

Another reputedly psychotomimetic agent is Sernyl [1-(1-phenylcyclohexyl) piperidine mono-hydrochloride], a sensory blocking agent with anaesthetic and sedative properties which produces severe disturbances of the body image, affect, attention, and thinking. Depersonalisation and repetitive motor behaviour have also been observed clinically in normal people who have taken this drug. Rosenbaum and co-workers (1959) found that the ability to discriminate weights in normals is con-siderably impaired by this drug.

2. Perceptual Slowness

It is possible to measure the speed with which perception occurs as contrasted to its accuracy, and it is quite possible that this may prove to be an independent phenomenon. One of the earlier techniques for measuring perceptual speed, the 'Object Recognition Test', was developed by Brengelmann (Payne and Hewlett, 1960). This test consists of a group of three-dimensional objects viewed monocularly through a camera shutter. The purpose of the test is to discover at what shutter speed the subjects are able to recognise the objects. Eysenck and colleagues (Payne and Hewlett, 1960) found that psychotics as a group needed longer shutter speeds than neurotics or normals before they could identify the objects. Pinillos and Brengelmann (Payne, 1960) developed a different version of the test in which pictures instead of real objects were used, and found similar results, as did Payne and Hewlett (1960).

More recently, Friedman (1964) found that psychotic depressives were significantly slower than normal at recognising a chair viewed tachisto-scopically. Using a slightly different technique, Ford and Caldwell (1968) found that schizophrenics took longer than normals to recognise masked pictures presented stroboscopically.

These studies are consistent in suggesting that all psychotic groups are unusually slow in their percep-tions, and it is tempting to conclude that perceptual slowness is one aspect of the general psychomotor retardation that Payne and Hewlett (1960) found to characterise both schizophrenics and depressives. Indeed, Payne and Hewlett found that the Brengel-mann Picture Recognition test score had just as high a factor loading on a general retardation factor as other types of mental and motor speed tests.

None of the investigators so far mentioned attempted to explain perceptual slowness. Recently, however, Ebner and Ritzler (1969) have done so. Ebner and Ritzler used yet another technique to study perceptual speed. They presented their subjects with projected pictures that were completely out of focus, being only an unrecognisable blur of light. The pictures were then very slowly brought into perfect focus, 120 seconds elapsing between the initial projection of the picture and its resolution into perfect focus. The subjects were allowed to guess what the picture was at any time. Ebner and Ritzler tested 20 chronic schizophrenics, 20 acute schizophrenics, and 20 matched normal controls. As might be expected, they found that the chronic schizophrenics were significantly slower than the normals at recognising the pictures. Unexpectedly however, the acute schizophrenics were normal in this respect.

Ebner and Ritzler explained this phenomenon in terms of Silverman's theory of scanning. They argued that chronic schizophrenics (like process schizo-phrenics) tend to scan visually only a small portion of any given visual field. Accordingly, they miss data essential to the correct recognition of the picture, delaying correct identification. Acute schizophrenics (like reactive schizophrenics) on the other hand, indulge in an excessive range of visual scanning, which in this situation results in quick identification of the pictures.

3. Silverman's Theory of Perception

Julian Silverman (1964) has suggested that three independent processes underlie perception. This model is of interest because it has been applied extensively in the study both of abnormalities of perception and cognition. Recently, Schooler and Silverman (1969) have reported a factor analytic investigation that supports this three-dimensional analysis. Silverman's three variables are as follows:

Scanning Control. The first dimension Silverman postulates is concerned with the extensiveness with which individuals sample visual stimuli. This can be measured directly by recording eye movements. Some individuals characteristically scan a very wide visual field, while some restrict their scanning to a small area of any field presented to them. Individual differences along this dimension have been used to account for several perceptual anomalies which will be discussed below.

Field Articulation. In order to organise whatever visual field is being scanned, some data are attended to, but some are ignored or suppressed. The ability to abstract only certain features from a scanned field varies from individual to individual. Silverman has suggested that it is this perceptual dimension that underlies performance on the Witkin 'rod and frame' test. People who are 'field independent' on this test (ignoring the background frame) are said to have a high degree of field articulation.

Stimulus Intensity Control. This variable refers to the intensity with which sensations are registered by the central nervous system. Some individuals are hypersensitive, reacting strongly to any input. They react to this by attenuating their input, and Silverman labels these as 'reducers'. He associates the tendency to reduce with such features as a high pain tolerance, and a tendency to underestimate the size of a test bar following kinesthetic satiation, in the kinesthetic figural after effect test. At the opposite end of this dimension are the 'augmenters' who overreact to pain, and overestimate the test object in the kinesthetic after effects test following stimulation. Buchsbaum and Silverman (1968) found significant correlations between measures of the intensity of evoked cortical potentials and the kinesthetic figural after effect score which they held to support this aspect of the theory. Schooler and Silverman also (1969) found some evidence that acute schizophrenics who show strong affect are 'augmenters', although chronic schizophrenics who show strong affect are, paradoxically, 'reducers'.

4. Size Constancy and Scanning

One type of perceptual distortion that has often been studied is size constancy. As Silverman (1964) points out, judging the sizes of objects accurately at varying distances depends on observing distance cues carefully. Children tend to make their judgements in terms of the size of the retinal image. Therefore, distant objects are judged to be smaller than they really are, and objects that are near at hand are judged to be larger than they really are. Normal adults slightly over compensate for this, and tend to underestimate the size of objects close at hand, and overestimate the size of distant objects. A number of earlier studies (Weckowicz and Blewett, 1959; Silverman, 1964a, 1964b, 1968; Davis et al., 1967) suggested that paranoid schizophrenics show 'over-constancy' to an abnormal degree. That is to say,

they overestimate the size of distant objects even more than normal adults. Silverman has suggested that this is because paranoid schizophrenics scan their environment more carefully, and therefore observe distance cues more closely, which, like normal adults, they slightly overestimate. Scanning behaviour was measured by filming eye movements during size estimation experiments, and the early evidence supported this hypothesis (Silverman, 1964a). Paranoid schizophrenic patients were also found to indulge in an abnormal amount of scanning up to three years after they had been in hospital (Silverman, 1968).

Neale and co-workers (1969) in a review of the literature also concluded that several experiments carried out up to that time suggest that paranoid schizophrenic patients underestimate (overconstancy), while non-paranoid schizophrenics overestimate the sizes of near objects (underconstancy).

'Simple' or 'hebephrenic' schizophrenics, like children, show underconstancy, their size judgements being based largely on the size of the retinal image (Weckowicz and Blewett, 1959; Silverman, 1964a).

There is no *a priori* reason why paranoid delusions should be especially prevalent among reactive as contrasted to process schizophrenics. Nevertheless, there is also some evidence from earlier studies (Weckowicz and Blewett, 1959; Silverman, 1964a, 1964b, 1968; Davis et al., 1967) that reactive schizophrenics like paranoid schizophrenics, show overconstancy, while process schizophrenics and chronic schizophrenics show underconstancy.

One factor in perceptual disorders among chronic patients may well be the effect of continued institutionalisation. Silverman and colleagues (1966) found that the ability to judge the size of circles is significantly worse in long-term prison inmates than in short-term prison inmates. They attribute this to the decrease in scanning acquired over the years as a way of avoiding 'aversive inescapable surroundings'.

The studies in this area have also been reviewed by Neale *et al.* (1969) who conclude that '. . . acute good premorbid (reactive) schizophrenics show small but consistent size underestimation . . . (while) . . . acute poor premorbid (process) schizophrenics show a small but reliable tendency towards size overestimation'. However, they conclude that at present, differences between chronic and acute schizophrenics as a group have not been demonstrated.

Since Neale *et al.*'s review, two articles reporting conflicting results have appeared. In this area, as in so many others in a field in which the operational definition of such terms as 'schizophrenics' is not clear, completely consistent results can never be expected. Magaro (1969) tested 72 male schizophrenics, and found that the acutely ill reactive (good premorbid) schizophrenics overestimated the size of lines embedded in different backgrounds. On the other hand, acutely ill process (poor premorbid) schizophrenics underestimated the size of the lines. Chronically ill reactive (good premorbid) schizophrenics underestimated the size of lines, while chronically ill process (poor premorbid) schizophrenics overestimated the size of lines. He found no differences between paranoid and nonparanoid patients. These results are difficult to reconcile with the earlier findings, although they suggest that the differences between chronic and acute schizophrenics should be studied further, as perceptual styles may change as the illness develops.

Silverman (1964a), attributes perceptual underconstancy among process schizophrenics to an abnormal reduction in scanning. Following Berlyne, he suggests that the amount of scanning may be learned. 'The excessive scanner has learned that his most effective means of escaping or avoiding anxiety is to be hyperalert to the presence of cues which often precede or co-occur with noxious events' (Silverman, 1964a). The 'minimal-scanner', on the other hand, he postulates, avoids anxiety by directing his attention away from the environment and on to internal processes. This, Silverman believes, could lead to hallucinations. Silverman does not explain how reactive schizophrenics learn one technique of reducing anxiety, while process schizophrenics learn another.

McKinnon and Singer (1969) tested the hypothesis by measuring eye movements directly, and were unable to repeat Silverman's original observation that paranoid schizophrenics scan more widely than nonparanoid schizophrenics. They also found no correlation between the amount of scanning, as measured by eye movement, and size judgements. On retesting under medication, however, they found that tranquilising drugs reduced the level of scanning in their schizophrenics. Also, under conditions of medication they found that paranoid schizophrenics underestimated size more than nonparanoid schizophrenics. This study makes it clear that more attention should be paid in perceptual studies to drug effects, which may well become confounded with other variables unless it is certain that all subjects are drug free at the time of testing.

5. Perceptual Overinclusion—The 'Defective Filter' Hypothesis

Perhaps the most conclusive test of Silverman's hypothesis about the cause of size overconstancy was carried out by Neale and Cromwell (1968; Cromwell, 1968). Cromwell (1968) first quotes an experiment by Harris, which demonstrated that the

dimensions of 'process-reactive' (i.e. good–poor premorbid) and 'paranoid–nonparanoid' were independently related to size judgement in one experiment. Those who made the smallest size judgements were the reactive, paranoid schizophrenics. Next were the process paranoid schizophrenics, followed by the reactive, nonparanoid schizophrenics. The largest judgements were made by the process nonparanoid schizophrenics. In order to test Silverman's 'scanning' hypothesis, Neale and Cromwell (1968) gave a size judgement task to 15 reactive paranoid acute schizophrenics, 15 process nonparanoid acute schizophrenics and 15 normal controls. During one part of the experiment, the lines whose lengths were to be judged were presented for 10 seconds each. As expected, the process nonparanoid schizophrenics made significantly larger judgements than did the reactive paranoid group, the normals falling in between. However, in another part of the experiment, the lines to be judged were presented for only 100 milliseconds. Under these conditions, all the subjects judged the lines to be smaller, but the differences between the groups were just as large, and in precisely the same direction. As the authors point out, these results make Silverman's eye movement 'scanning' hypothesis completely untenable. In the first place, the 100 millisecond exposure time would give absolutely no time for any scanning or changes in fixation to take place. In the second place, if more scanning produces judgements of smaller sizes, the longer exposure times should have produced smaller rather than larger judgements.

The alternative explanation for these findings, offered by Cromwell (1968), is the 'filter' hypothesis. Cromwell's argument is that reactive, paranoid schizophrenics, when perceiving any visual field, do not 'filter out' any irrelevant stimuli ('perceptual overinclusion'). The fact that background details are not suppressed leads to a judgement of 'smaller'. The hypothesis is the same as that of Silverman, excepting that 'filtering' takes place immediately and is not the result of a limitation of the breadth of scanning over a period of time. According to the hypothesis, process nonparanoid schizophrenics, by comparison with normals, have a very restrictive filter that constricts their attention.

Cromwell (1968) also quotes a study by Griffith and colleagues, who found that amphetamine-users while taking the drug underestimate sizes (are unable to filter), but following withdrawal from the drug, overestimate sizes (filter excessively). Cromwell also argues that in the Müller-Lyer illusion, distracting background material should decrease the illusion, while the lack of such distracting background material should enhance it (lead to judgements of 'longer'). An experiment by Kar and

Cromwell supported this prediction. It was also found, as expected, that in the same Müller-Lyer illusion experiment, reactive paranoid schizophrenics were more affected by the distracting background material (being unable to filter it out) than were process, nonparanoid schizophrenics (who filter it out).

Perceptual overinclusion, or the 'defective filter' hypothesis, has been used for some time to account for some of the behaviour manifested by some schizophrenic patients. Payne and co-workers (1959), in explaining overinclusive thinking (which will be discussed below), suggested that:

'All purposeful behaviour depends for its success on the fact that some stimuli are "attended to" and some other stimuli are ignored. It is a well known fact that, when concentrating on one task, normal people are quite unaware of most stimuli irrelevant to the task. It is as if some "filter mechanism" cuts out or inhibits the stimuli, both internal and external, which are irrelevant to the task in hand, to allow the most efficient "processing" of incoming information. Over-inclusive thinking might be only one aspect of a general breakdown of this "filter mechanism".'

Payne and his associates (1964) suggested that such a 'defective filter' could be one cause (but not the only cause) of paranoid delusions. They suggest that, 'The overinclusive patient, in addition to perceiving the essential features of any problem or situation, is also apparently unable to screen out irrelevant perceptions . . . (which) . . . may also lead to an overgeneral conclusion which is unwarranted'. They go on to suggest that

'Many paranoid patients appear to perceive an unusually wide range of stimuli. Thus, for example, a patient may note that one of the two men across the street in shabby raincoats has a folded copy of *The Times* in his pocket, and that he periodically touches this in an unusual way. This the patient may interpret as a signal with some special significance. The delusion is of course abnormal, but what may also be abnormal is the amount of detailed perception on which the delusion is based. In normal people the range of perceptions around whatever engages the attention is very limited, such details go unnoticed, and could thus not form the basis of delusional ideas.'

6. Reaction Time, Scanning, and Distractibility

One of the earliest experimental observations made in psychiatry was that, as a group, schizophrenics have a slow and variable reaction time. This observation has been repeated many times, and the most generally accepted explanation of the phenomenon is that put forward by Rodnick and Shakow (1940) that schizophrenics are unable to preserve a 'set' to respond over a long period of time. Their performance instead, depends upon a series of minor 'sets'. The research in this area has recently been well reviewed by Broen (1968). Broen points out that the 'set' to respond has been related to scanning theory.

'Reaction-time (RT) tasks are of a kind in which information from previous events affects performance. A subject's readiness to respond to a "go" signal cannot be maintained at top efficiency for long periods of time and so subjects learn to use their prior experience with the task to estimate when the "go" signal will occur.'

'When the preparatory interval (PI—the interval between "ready" and "go" signals) varies, maximal readiness should be obtained by scanning past PI's held in memory . . . . We would expect that recent events would be dominant in memory and, if there are any restrictions on scanning, more remote events will be more likely to be ignored. This means that the pattern of readiness preparation should be determined by the length of the immediately preceding preparatory interval . . .'

(in those subjects with restricted scanning, such as process schizophrenics.) (Broen, 1968 pp. 141–142.)

Broen goes on to explain a number of the results of reaction time studies in terms of this scanning hypothesis.

Payne and Caird (1967), on the other hand, have put forward a different explanation of the slow and variable reaction times shown by many schizophrenics, using the 'defective filter' hypothesis. They argue that schizophrenics are unable to 'filter out' irrelevant stimuli during a reaction time experiment carried out under ordinary conditions. These randomly occurring irrelevant stimuli will periodically distract the overinclusive schizophrenic, producing on average a slow, but variable reaction time. They predicted that paranoid schizophrenics, having a 'defective filter', should be especially affected by distracting stimuli during a reaction time experiment.

Payne and Caird (1967) carried out a study to investigate the relations between distractibility in a reaction time experiment, overinclusive thinking and paranoid delusions. Fifteen paranoid schizophrenics, 15 non-paranoid schizophrenics and 15 non-schizophrenic psychiatric inpatients were given a simple and a multiple choice auditory reaction time test in which the presence and number of distracting stimuli were varied. The test stimuli were tones delivered through earphones, and the distracting stimuli, which the patients were told to ignore, were similar tones delivered from a loud speaker. Over-inclusive thinking was measured by the average number of words needed to explain the Benjamin Proverbs. As predicted, the reaction times of the paranoid patients were more affected by the distraction than those of the non-schizophrenics. The distractibility of the non-paranoid schizophrenics was intermediate. Also as expected, overinclusive subjects were more distractible than non-over-inclusive subjects, there being highly significant correlations between the proverbs test word count score and the reaction time under conditions of distraction.

7. Distractibility and the 'Defective Filter' Hypothesis

One clear prediction from the 'defective filter' hypothesis, is that individuals with this abnormality (and the above results suggest that these should be 'paranoid' and 'reactive' schizophrenics) should be unusually distractible in a variety of situations, being relatively unable to filter out irrelevant stimuli.

Rappaport (1968) carried out an experiment in which the subjects were asked to listen to a single (male) voice reading a list of random numbers through both of a pair of earphones. The task was to copy down the numbers. As a distraction, additional male voices were introduced reading different random lists of numbers simultaneously. These distracting voices were heard through only one of the two earphones, and the subject's task was to concentrate only on the original voice heard through both earphones. The number of distracting voices was systematically increased until, under the most difficult conditions, 13 different voices were being heard simultaneously. In a second, more difficult experiment, the voice to be concentrated on, like the distracting voices was heard through only one earphone, and could be identified only by its distinguishing characteristics. The subjects were 90 acute schizophrenics, 71 non acute schizophrenics, 12 chronic schizophrenics, and 37 normal controls. While performance dropped off as the number of distractions was increased for all the subjects, there were no differences in performance between the normals and the non acute schizophrenics. The chronic schizophrenics were affected slightly, but significantly. However, it was the group of acute schizophrenics in this study who proved to be extremely distractible, their performance falling off very dramatically. There was no tendency for paranoid patients to be especially distractible. The subjects were later retested under the influence of

different doses of phenothiazines, in the expectation that this drug would enable the acute patients to concentrate. The drug, however, had virtually no effect.

The results of this study are not exactly what would have been expected from the findings so far discussed, in that there was no evidence for 'defective filtering' among the paranoid patients. The process reactive variable was not assessed, so that this aspect of the prediction could not be tested.

Rappaport's (1968) finding that it is acute schizophrenics who are especially distractible is consistent with the results of Blum et al. (1969). They measured the extent to which digit span performance was affected by interpolated distracting letters in 10 schizophrenics who were periodically retested, and found that these patients became more distractible when they were disturbed. Similarly, Langer et al. (1969), using the Stroop Word-Color Interference test found that a group of 20 acute schizophrenics were significantly more distractible than a normal control group.

Unfortunately, it cannot be concluded that the evidence consistently suggests that distractibility is found primarily among acute rather than chronic schizophrenics. McGhie and associates (1965a, 1965b), carried out a large-scale study of distractibility in chronic schizophrenic patients, following an earlier clinical study by Chapman and McGhie (1962) of acute schizophrenics. McGhie, Chapman, and Lawson compared chronic paranoid schizophrenics, chronic non-paranoid schizophrenics, depressed patients, and normal control subjects on a large number of different measures. They found that simple (but not choice) visual and auditory reaction times were not significantly affected by distractions in the form of the sound of an irregular metronome rhythm, or a circle of randomly flashing white lights around the stimulus light, in any of the groups. However, they did find that distraction had a significant effect on more complex psychomotor performance containing some degree of uncertainty. In another test, the subjects were required to listen to digits read by a female voice, and to screen out those read by a male voice. The effect of auditory distraction on a visual task (reading letters, or digits) and visual distraction on an auditory task were also studied. The results were consistent in suggesting that as a group, the chronic schizophrenics were significantly more distractible than the non-schizophrenics or the normals. However, it was the chronic hebephrenic schizophrenics who were distractible in these situations. The chronic paranoid schizophrenic patients were not significantly different from normal. Although distractibility was related to symptomotology, it was not related to the degree of chronicity. Similar findings have been reported by Cohen *et al.* (1962).

A slightly different group of perceptual tasks are those which require the subject to recognise or to abstract some picture from a distracting irrelevant background. A good example of this is the Gottschaldt Figures Test (Weckowicz and Blewett, 1959). Studies in which such tests of selective visual perception have been used (Chapman and McGhie, 1962; Weckowicz and Blewett, 1959; Krus *et al.*, 1963; Bemporad, 1967; Schwarz, 1967; Weckowitz, 1960; Snyder *et al.*, 1961) consistently suggest that schizophrenics as a group are significantly worse than normal controls. Again, however, when symptomatology has been reported, paranoid patients have been found to be normal in this respect. This type of perceptual distractibility seems to characterise hebephrenic or chronic patients.

Very similar studies are those that present the patient auditorily with a word mixed with masking noise, or a picture masked by visual noise ('snow'), and systematically decrease the amount of noise until correct recognition occurs (Donovan and Webb, 1965; Stilson *et al.*, 1966). Schizophrenics as a group appear to be poor at these recognition tasks, and 'process' schizophrenics are worse than 'reactive' schizophrenics.

A quite different approach to the same problem has been taken by Callaway and his associates (Callaway *et al.*, 1965; Jones *et al.*, 1966; Jones *et al.*, 1965). They have measured, using an EEG, the cortical electrical response to both visual and auditory stimuli. These evoked cortical potentials vary in amplitude and in wave form. Normally, two identical stimuli produce identical cortical responses. However, the wave forms produced by two identical stimuli in schizophrenics tend to be quite dissimilar. This suggests that in some way, schizophrenics are paying attention to small differences in nearly identical stimuli, or are being distracted by extraneous events that do not register in normal people. It has been found that this lack of consistency in cortical response characterises schizophrenic patients while they are ill, and improves with clinical improvement. It is associated with disordered talk, disorganised delusions and thought disorder as rated clinically. It does not characterise paranoid schizophrenics who are nearly normal in this respect. It is more severe in process than in reactive schizophrenics, and is more severe in chronic than in acute schizophrenics.

8. Distractibility in Sorting Tests

A slightly different type of experiment makes use of sorting tests. Chapman (1956) produced a test in which the subjects were required to sort cards into three boxes. Each box was labelled with a stimulus card which contained four pictures. Only the picture in the lower right-hand corner was relevant to the task, the other three being distractors. The response cards, which were to be sorted into one of the three boxes, also had four pictures. Again, only the picture in the lower right-hand corner was relevant. The subjects were asked to sort each response card into the box labelled with the stimulus card which pictured 'something of the same kind'. The cards depicted such categories as numbers, letters, clothing, etc. The variable manipulated was the number of relevant distractor items. For some categories the cards to be sorted had distractor items identical to the picture defining one of the other (incorrect) categories. For some categories, the cards to be sorted had distractor items of the same kind as the card defining one of the other (incorrect) categories. Some categories had no relevant distractors, in order to estimate the baseline error rate. Chapman (1956a) found that chronic schizophrenics made significantly more errors due to the distractions, than did a matched group of normals.

Chapman (1956b) also found that chronic schizophrenics were more often distracted by the identical distractor items, whereas normals were more often distracted by different items in the same category. This result was confirmed with a slightly different test by Downing *et al.* (1963). Downing and associates (1966) in another study confirmed that the closer the associational link between distractor and stimulus word, the more effective the distractor, at least among schizophrenic patients.

In a somewhat different sorting experiment, Chapman (1958) asked subjects to sort cards with a single word on each into three boxes defined by a single stimulus word. Some of the words to be sorted had a connection with one stimulus word only, whereas some were of the same category as one of the stimulus words, but also had an association with one of the other stimulus words. This association, it was predicted, would lead to errors of distraction, and a group of chronic schizophrenics made more such errors than a matched normal group. In a different type of verbal distractor experiment, Blumberg and Giller (1965) tested chronic schizophrenics, acute schizophrenics, and non-schizophrenic patients with a test in which the subjects were asked to choose the synonym of a word from a group of words which also included an antonym, a homonym, and an irrelevant word. All subjects were distracted by the antonyms and homonyms, but the chronic schizophrenics were most seriously affected.

Feinberg and Mercer (1960) gave both types of

Chapman distraction tests to groups of schizophrenics and brain-damaged patients and found that the organic patients made more distraction errors than the schizophrenics.

Downing and co-workers (1963) developed a form of Chapman's distractor test in which the items to be sorted were cards containing one relevant word and two distractor words. They tested 37 acute schizophrenics and retested them after six weeks of treatment with Chorpromazine, Fluphenazine, Thioridazine, or placebo. Placebo and Chlorpromazine produced no significant improvement, but Fluphenazine and Thioridazine did. The authors note that neither of the drugs which were effective in cutting down distractibility are members of the 'Chlorpromazine model' group.

There appear to have been relatively few other attempts to manipulate distractibility experimentally. Rosenbaum and associates (1959), using the Rodnick and Shakow reaction time experiment as a measure of distractibility, found that neither LSD nor Sodium Amytal given to normal subjects could make them as slow as schizophrenics. However, the drug Sernyl did. On the other hand, if the subjects were given an electric shock until they reacted, normals drugged with Sernyl, and schizophrenics, produced normal reaction times. Undrugged normals were not affected by the shock. It is possible to speculate that the higher drive level induced by the shocks enhanced the ability of anaesthetised normals and schizophrenics to focus their attention.

9. Summary and Conclusions

The results of many of the perceptual experiments discussed above, especially those dealing with the estimation of sizes, can be explained in terms of a 'filter' hypothesis. It would seem that, usually, both paranoid and reactive schizophrenics tend to perceive an unusually wide range of stimuli, whereas process schizophrenics perceive an unusually narrow range of stimuli. However, it would appear that this hypothesis alone cannot explain the results of the fairly large group of distractibility experiments. Abnormal distractibility has been found among groups of acute schizophrenics, chronic schizophrenics in general, and chronic hebephrenics in

particular, process schizophrenics, and disturbed schizophrenics. The only consistent finding would seem to be that chronic paranoid schizophrenics are relatively normal with respect to distractibility. It is not certain, however, that in the acute stage of their illness, paranoid schizophrenics are not distractible. It would seem to be that while paranoid schizophrenics normally perceive a very wide range of stimuli, they are nevertheless able to focus their attention when required to do so. Because of the heterogeneity of the large group of distractible schizophrenics, it is not easy to suggest a very convincing single explanation of abnormal distractibility. It is also not certain that many psychotics with affective disorders are not equally distractible, because there are very few studies of this group of patients. Callaway and Dembo (1958) and Callaway and Stone (1960) found that a number of stimulant drugs that can be presumed to increase the general level of arousal tend to lower the response to peripheral stimuli and thus focus the attention more narrowly. Easterbrook (1959) also cites evidence that in states of high drive, the attention is more narrowly focused. Nevertheless, these results by no means prove that individuals who are under the influence of stimulant drugs, or in states of high drive, cannot very easily be *distracted*. It is also difficult to argue that the acutely disturbed schizophrenics who have been shown to be very distractible are not in a high state of arousal, without clear physiological evidence to the contrary. Venables (1963) measured the distractibility of a group of chronic schizophrenics by means of a special sorting test, and assessed their level of cortical activation by means of their 'two flash fusion' threshold level. He found that the schizophrenics with a higher level of cortical activation were less influenced by the distractions on the sorting test. Among the non-paranoid patients, those who were behaviourally withdrawn tended to be less distractible, but there was no such tendency within the paranoid group. It is possible to speculate that a relatively high level of cortical activation accounts for the relative lack of distractibility in paranoid patients. However, the data in this area are too few and too contradictory at the moment to have much confidence in this sort of explanatory hypothesis.

DISORDERS OF IMMEDIATE MEMORY SPAN

Perhaps the most satisfactory accounts of 'span of apprehension' or 'immediate memory span' has been given by Broadbent (1957). If this theory is correct, there is every reason to believe that immediate memory span is unrelated to learning and long-term

retention (Inglis, 1957). Broadbent believes that incoming information is held in temporary store until some action can be performed on it by some type of mechanism which 'circulates' it, feeding it back into the perceptual system at the end of each circuit. However, this mechanism can only hold (and circulate) a limited amount of information, and an excessive input 'crowds out' items already circulating, which are lost. Individuals differ in the capacity of this mechanism, and in the rate with which information circulating decays over time.

Memory span has been measured in a number of different ways. Unfortunately, whatever the technique used, it is never certain whether a low memory span is the result of the limited capacity of whatever holding mechanism is involved, or merely a failure to perceive the material in the first place. Distractible individuals will clearly do poorly for this reason alone.

The most frequently used technique for assessing memory span, is the typical 'digit span' test, in which random series of numbers of increasing length are read at one-second intervals to the subject, whose task is to repeat them at the end of the series. In the Wechsler-Bellevue digit span test, subjects are also asked to repeat the series backward in the second half of the test.

Payne (1960) reviewed those studies using the digit span test, which had appeared at that time. He concluded that immediate memory span appears to be an ability that is one of the most resistant to age in normal people. There is consistent evidence that in normal people, anxiety produces a reduction in memory span. However, this may merely reflect a decrease in the range of perception, which we have seen has been shown in some studies to occur at high levels of anxiety. On the whole, neurotic patients tend to have a slightly smaller digit span than normal people, presumably because they are more anxious as a group, but there appear to be no studies of the differences between specific neurotic groups.

Psychotics as a group have lower scores than neurotics on the digit span test, although there is no evidence of differences between schizophrenics and manic-depressive groups.

A somewhat different technique for assessing immediate memory span consists of presenting the subject with a set of stimuli (letters, shapes, words, numbers) visually, for very short periods of time using a tachistoscope, and then asking them to say what was presented. Payne (1960), in reviewing the experiments in which this technique was used, concluded that the results were the same as those reported for the digit span test.

Since that time, attention has been paid to individual differences in memory span within schizophrenic populations. Neale and associates (1969) presented their subjects with sets of eight letter arrays shown tachistoscopically. The task was merely to say whether or not one of two specified letters was present. They found that, as a group, schizophrenics receiving phenothiazine medication were significantly poorer than matched normal controls. The results suggested that the schizophrenics had a memory span about 50 per cent that of normal. However, there were no differences between process and reactive schizophrenics. Unfortunately, the possible effect of the drugs was not assessed.

Spohn and co-workers (1970) presented their subjects with sets of six nonsense syllables tachistoscopically, and asked them to write down what they had seen. Before and during the experiment, a number of physiological responses were monitored. They tested 32 schizophrenics, who were broken down into paranoid, nonparanoid, process-reactive and chronic-acute subgroups, as well as a normal control group. As usual, the schizophrenics, as a group, had very much smaller immediate memory spans than did the normal subjects. However, there were very small and mainly insignificant differences between the schizophrenic subgroups. The only significant difference was that the acute nonparanoid schizophrenics were significantly better than the acute paranoid schizophrenics (there were no differences among the chronic subjects). This result was unexpected, as it is inconsistent with the findings using measures of distractibility. Acute paranoid schizophrenics are usually better able to concentrate their attention than acute nonparanoid schizophrenics. This suggests that it is conceivable that genuine differences in memory were being measured in spite of the differences in ability to attend, which might have been expected to obscure them. However, no firm conclusions can be drawn until this experiment has been repeated.

Spohn et al. found that the schizophrenics had a lower base line level of skin conductance, but a higher basal heart rate than the normal controls. There was no correlation between memory span and base line heart rate or skin conductance levels, suggesting that the basal level of autonomic arousal is not relevant to the task. They did find, however, that in both the normal and the schizophrenic groups there was a significant correlation between memory span and the magnitude of change in both these autonomic measures during the course of the experiment. Curiously, the change, at least in skin conductance was in opposite directions in the two groups. Schizophrenics with the best memory span showed the largest *increase* in skin conductance during the experiment, while normals with the best memory span showed the largest *decrease* in skin conductance during the experiment. The authors speculate that there is some optimal level of arousal needed for the task, and that those who do best are those most able to adapt to this optimal level. In a subsidiary experiment it was found that although phenothiazine drugs affected the autonomic levels, they did not significantly effect immediate memory span.

A quite different technique for assessing immediate memory span was first used with abnormal subjects by Lawson et al. (1964). Lists of ten and twenty words each were read to the subjects in a monotone at one-second intervals over a tape recorder, a procedure exactly parallelling the usual digit span technique. At the end of the presentation, the subjects were asked to write down as many of the words as they could remember. There were eight lists of each length. The first word list in each set consisted of a set of randomly related words. However, the eighth list was in fact a complete English sentence. From the first to the eighth list in each series, the amount of 'contextual constraint' was increased. That is to say, the words became increasingly related, and should therefore be increasingly easy to remember, the complete sentence being easiest of all. As expected, the normal subjects did indeed find the lists increasingly easy to reproduce, their performance increasing sharply as the 'contextual constraint' increased. The schizophrenics, however, who were significantly poorer on the first list than the normal subjects, did not improve their performance at the same rate, so that they became increasingly worse than the normal subjects as each series progressed. It was as if they did not recognise that what they were hearing (in the last trial for instance) was a complete sentence, but continued to act as if it was a set of unrelated words. Levy and Maxwell (1968) repeated this experiment with 13 acute schizophrenics, 10 severe depressives, and 10 control cases of personality disorder, alcoholism, or homosexuality. While they found essentially the same differences between the schizo-phrenics and the control subjects, they found that the severe depressives behaved exactly like the acute schizophrenics, suggesting that this might be a phenomenon related to psychosis in general, perhaps resulting from disturbed attention.

Much more light has been thrown on this phenomenon recently, however, in a series of studies carried out by Raeburn and Tong (1968). These investigators studied schizophrenic and normal subjects, and demonstrated that two independent factors seem to explain the results. They found that schizophrenics with a high level of vocabulary benefited most by increased contextual constraint. That is to say, schizophrenics with a poor vocabulary are evidently less able to recognise the complete sentence for what it is, and recall it more nearly as they would a list of unrelated words. However, the second factor was merely one of writing speed. Raeburn and Tong were able to demonstrate that those schizophrenics who did worst, wrote most slowly. Thus, on the most meaningful lists, when they presumably had initially recalled most of the words, it took so long for them to write them down that they had forgotten many of them before they had completed the task.

These recent experiments suggest, therefore, that the poor performance of psychotic patients on tests of immediate memory span may be related to several factors, including their ability to concentrate on the stimulus material, their ability to organise this material, where this is possible, into larger units which are easier to recall (i.e. when the material is meaningful), and the speed with which they can reproduce the information before it decays with time. Only when all these factors are controlled is it possible to estimate individual differences in memory span *per se*. Therefore, no firm conclusions can be drawn at present.

DISORDERS OF SHORT-TERM RETENTION

Short-term retention can be operationally distinguished from immediate memory span in that in the case of short-term retention, the attention is directed away from the material presented before the subject is later asked to recall it. To ensure this, subjects are usually required to carry out some interpolated task before being asked to recall the initial material. Quite how 'short' the time interval between the initial perception of the material and its recall must be to qualify as 'short-term memory' is not certain. Theoretically, information held in this short-term store (reverberating neuronal circuits?) gradually decays with time, but at the same time it is being 'consolidated', so that, after a period of time, whatever remains has entered some long-term store (chemical in nature?), where its rate of decay is very much slower. It is not established how long this consolidation requires, but, as Inglis (1970) has suggested, the fact that retrograde amnesia following a trauma usually extends back for a period of about half an hour, suggests that this is the approximate consolidation time. Thus, recall measures must be taken within half an hour after the material has been perceived, before it is theoretically appropriate to regard them as measures of short-term memory. There are clearly individual differences in the rate of decay of information held in temporary store, and one variable known to influence this is the age of the individual (Inglis, 1970). Inglis has used the technique of 'dichotic stimulation' to provide an objective means of assessing short-term memory. In this procedure, subjects are given lists of numbers (or words) simultaneously to both ears, by giving one list through one earphone, and the other list through the other. The subjects are instructed to repeat the list heard through a specified ear first, and when this is done, they are asked to recall the list heard through the other ear. In this way, the attention is diverted to the first list, and the list recalled second must be stored temporarily. Inglis has demonstrated that the severe memory disorder found in some old people can be explained in terms of a gross defect in this short-term retention. These individuals cannot retain new information over a long period of time, presumably because it does not remain long enough in the short-term store to become consolidated.

A survey of the literature in this area will not be attempted here, as such a detailed account is outside the range of the present chapter, although its relevance to cognition is obvious. Individuals with a very fast rate of information decay will clearly be handicapped in solving any problem that takes a prolonged period of time, or that requires the switching of attention from one aspect of the information to another.

Only one set of data will be discussed here, because it is directly relevant to some results that will be discussed later.

Price (1968) carried out a concept identification experiment of the sort that will be discussed further in a later section, using a group of hospitalised schizophrenics and a non-schizophrenic psychiatric control group matched for degree of pathology. The test material consisted of a set of cards depicting items of various shapes and colours. For example, one card depicted two red triangles. The subjects were asked to say, of each card, whether it did or did not belong to a conceptual category. The conceptual category was defined in two ways in different parts of the experiment. In one part of the experiment, the concept was identified pictorially by a cue card. In another section, it was identified verbally, and the subjects had to read out its

definition from a card. Some of the dimensions along which the cards differed from one another were relevant to the concept (e.g. colour, number of objects) and some were not relevant, and were to be ignored (e.g. shape, size). The concepts according to which the cards were to be sorted, were periodically changed, some being difficult and some being easy. As is usual in experiments of this sort, the schizophrenics made significantly more errors in sorting than the non-schizophrenics. However, the errors they made tended to be of a certain kind. They tended incorrectly to identify a card as belonging to a concept when it did not. They were also much slower at carrying out the task. The authors explained their poor performance as being due to a defect in short-term memory. A schizophrenic subject would, for instance, correctly note for a particular card that in one of its characteristics, it belonged to the category in question. Because of their slowness in sorting, however, it was thought that schizophrenics tended to forget the second essential identifying dimension of the concept, and rate the card as 'belonging', on the basis of only the first of the two relevant dimensions. This hypothesis was tested in a second experiment, by presenting the cue card which identified the concept to the subject at the same time as he was asked to decide whether a particular card belonged or did not belong. In this way he could keep the cue card in front of him, could keep referring to it, and his performance need not depend on his memory of it. As predicted, under these circumstances the schizophrenics improved significantly, and, more important, improved in the direction of eliminating their 'false positive' errors.

This experiment is of considerable interest because in the past, the relative inability of schizophrenics to do tasks of this sort has been attributed to 'concreteness', which as an 'explanation', is not entirely satisfactory as it has few testable consequences. Price's experiment does not throw any light on which particular sort of schizophrenic patients (or non-schizophrenics for that matter) may have a short-term memory defect severe enough to impair performance on tests of reasoning, but it does suggest that further work in this area would be useful.

DISORDERS OF LONG-TERM RETENTION

The evidence discussed above suggests that those cognitive tests that appear to be least affected by any ability other than the capacity to recall information learned in the past (e.g. vocabulary tests, the Wechsler Information subtest) seem least affected by

mental illness. However, as Hull pointed out as early as 1917, in order to measure individual differences in long-term retention, it is essential to ensure that all subjects have learned the information to the same criterion. If this is not so, retention scores will be a function of both the ability to learn, and the ability to retain, and will thus be ambiguous. Routine memory tests such as the Wechsler Memory Scale combine measures of rote learning, span of apprehension, and long-term retention (inadequately controlled) as if they were identical functions, and thus produce completely inconclusive results.

There are still remarkably few well-controlled studies of long-term retention in abnormal subjects. Gladis (1967), in reviewing the literature up to that time, pointed out that in the two adequate studies that he discovered, there was no evidence of significant differences in long-term retention between students and schizophrenic subjects, although the methods used were often open to question (e.g. one study made use of the recall of narrative material). Gladis himself carried out a carefully controlled study using a paired associate learning test in which two-syllable adjectives had to be learned in response to nonsense syllables. All the subjects learned the material to a criterion. The subjects were 45 schizophrenic veterans and 36 matched normal controls. Retention was measured over 7, 14, and 28 day periods, (there being 15 schizophrenic subjects retested at each interval). There were no significant differences in initial learning rate between the schizophrenic and the control subjects. However, there were highly significant differences in the retention scores, the schizophrenics recalling only about half as much information as the control subjects. All the subjects recalled less with longer intervals. The subjects were also required to relearn the material to the same criterion, and although the schizophrenics were slightly worse at relearning, the differences were not significant. One difficulty in interpreting the results of this study is the fact that the schizophrenic subjects were taking tranquilising drugs at the time of testing.

The other study of long-term retention presently available was concerned with the differences between subgroups of schizophrenia. Bauman and Murray (1968) asked their subjects to learn word lists to a criterion, and assessed retention half an hour later. Twenty-four schizophrenics were divided into two groups on the basis of two of the tests of over-inclusive thinking developed by Payne and Hewlett (1960), the Goldstein Object Sorting test 'handing over' score and the Payne Object Classification test 'non-A' response score. A control group of normal subjects was given the same tests. Two different methods of measuring retention were compared, 'recall' and 'recognition'. It was found that there were no significant differences in retention between the overinclusive and the non-overinclusive subjects. As might be expected, all the subjects were better at

recognition than recall. The schizophrenics were no different from the normal controls at recognising the material, but they were significantly worse in unaided recall. This suggests a difficulty in retrieval from storage rather than a difference in retention as such. Unfortunately, these results are also obscured by the fact that the schizophrenics were taking drugs at the time of testing.

One factor makes the interpretation of the results of both studies difficult. Although the Gladis study suggests that schizophrenics may have a difficulty in long-term retention, it is equally possible that the basic difficulty is one of memory consolidation. If it is the case (and the evidence above suggests that it might be) that some schizophrenics have a defective short-term memory, this factor alone could prevent information from becoming consolidated in the 'long-term store'. Therefore, Gladis's results may not reflect the tendency for information in the long-term store to deteriorate quickly in time in some schizophrenics. It may merely reflect the fact that the information never reached this store in the first place. The fact still remains that other evidence suggests that, in psychosis, information learned *before* the psychosis developed seems minimally affected by the illness.

A quite different aspect of long-term memory is the process of information retrieval. Some individuals may be both quicker and/or more accurate at retrieving stored information than others. Measures most likely to reflect the speed of retrieval from memory are many of the so-called 'fluency' tests. Fluency tests typically require the subject to write down (for example) all the words he can think of beginning with the letter 'S' in a specified period of time. The number of words produced is clearly a function of the number of such words the subject knows (which are available in the stored memory pool) and the speed and efficiency of whatever scanning and retrieval mechanism is involved. The shorter the time limit given, the more likely the test score is to reflect the speed of retrieval as contrasted to the size of the total pool of information available.

Payne (1960) reviewed the literature up to that period, and since that time no new studies appear to have been carried out. Payne concluded that neurotic patients as a group are probably slightly below average in fluency, while both depressive patients and schizophrenics are considerably below average. As will be seen, these results are similar to the results obtained from a wide range of other tests of mental and motor speed, and it is possible that the speed of retrieving stored memories is a function of some more general factor that influences the speed of neural activity as a whole.

DISORDERS OF CONCEPTUALIZATION

1. Concreteness

Concreteness could be defined as the inability to formulate an abstract general principle from a group of particular items, or to recognise that a group of objects with some common characteristics can be grouped together under some general category. In effect, it is the inability to carry out inductive reasoning. Since inductive reasoning is required in a large number of intellectual tasks, it is hardly surprising to find that measures of concreteness have been found to be highly correlated with conventional measures of general intelligence (Payne and Hewlett, 1960; Payne, 1960; Shimkunas et al., 1966; Holtzman et al., 1964; Karson and Pool, 1957). It is, nevertheless, possible to conceive of someone whose deductive powers are intact, and who can perform satisfactorily on some tasks (e.g. mechanical arithmetic) but not on others that require inductive reasoning.

It has long been held that concreteness results from brain damage (Payne, 1960), and many authorities believe that schizophrenic patients resemble brain-damaged patients in this, as in several other respects. Nevertheless, in 1960, Payne after reviewing the literature, was forced to conclude that there was no unambiguous evidence for this proposition. This was mainly because most of the studies carried out prior to that time were ambiguous, either because they failed to control for crucial variables such as pre-illness intelligence, or age, or because they made use of tests whose evaluation was essentially subjective. Since that time, however, in addition to the proliferation of ill-controlled studies, a number of more adequate experiments make it possible to come to some more positive conclusions.

Since not all tests of 'concreteness' appear to involve the same process, it is best to review the literature in terms of the different sorts of experimental situations employed.

(a) THE INTERPRETATION OF PROVERBS

A proverb is a concrete illustration of a general principle, and the ability to interpret proverbs has been a popular method of assessing the ability to generalise for many years. Early proverbs tests, such as the Benjamin Proverbs (Payne, 1960) lacked a standardised scoring system. More recently, however, tests have been developed, such as Gorham's proverbs (Gorham, 1956a, 1956b, 1956c; Elmore and Gorham, 1957), with carefully standardised scoring criteria, which it has been demonstrated can

be applied reliably to the spontaneous interpretations of proverbs by patients. Proverb interpretation is obviously affected by educational background and word knowledge, so that a considerable amount of detailed normative data would be necessary if one were to use such a test clinically with an individual patient. Even the best standardised proverbs test so far available does not, for example, supply norms that specify the mean 'abstraction' scores (with standard deviations and ranges) that can be expected from normal people at different age levels, and of different levels of educational background, without which interpreting a score from an individual patient would be impossible. Proverbs tests can, nevertheless, be used in group studies, provided that care is taken to match the groups to be compared on these variables.

Two types of response are usually scored from proverb interpretations, an 'abstract' answer which correctly states the general principle illustrated by the proverb, and a 'concrete' answer which does not make any generalisation at all (e.g. Rome was not built in a day. Abstract answer, 'Great things come about slowly'. Concrete answer, 'It took years'.). One disadvantage with the 'clinical' form of the proverbs test is that a number of responses, sometimes called 'autistic' or 'idiosyncratic' are difficult to classify under either heading. This scoring problem is avoided by using a multiple choice version of the test.

Studies using the clinical versions of the proverbs test have employed either Benjamin's (1944) original proverbs and scoring, the Benjamin proverbs scored according to Becker's (1955) system, Gorham's (1956a) test, or the Friedes proverbs test (Friedes et al., 1963). Most studies have found that process schizophrenic patients give more concrete answers and fewer abstract answers than a matched group of normal people, or a matched group of reactive schizophrenics (Gregg and Frank, 1966; Johnson, 1966; Little, 1966), although the results have not always been statistically significant (Judson and Katahn, 1963). Reactive schizophrenics, on the other hand, appear relatively unimpaired. As might be expected, chronic schizophrenics are also concrete in their proverb interpretation (Gorham, 1956c; Lewinsohn and Riggs, 1962), as are brain-damaged patients (Gregg and Frank, 1966; Brattemo, 1962; Fogel, 1965).

The concreteness manifested by schizophrenic patients on the proverbs test while ill, improves significantly with clinical recovery (Schwartz, 1967a;

Shimkunas *et al.*, 1966). However, there is some evidence that the relatives (parents, siblings, children) of schizophrenics are significantly more concrete on proverbs than normal people (Phillips *et al.*, 1965). While this suggests a degree of pathology in the 'well' members of these families, this study throws no light on the aetiology of this particular disorder.

There has been at least one attempt to induce concrete thinking on the proverbs test in normals by the use of drugs (Cohen *et al.*, 1962). Two drugs, LSD 25 and sodium amytal had so significant effect, but Sernyl produced a significant increase in concrete responses.

There has been some suggestion that concreteness on proverbs is, at least in part, emotionally determined. The hypothesis is that an emotional response to the material can induce concrete behaviour. Lewinsohn and Riggs (1962), replicated a finding made by Lewis *et al.* (1959) that acute schizophrenics have more difficulty interpreting 'oral' proverbs than they do 'anal', 'phallic' or 'neutral' ones. Chronic schizophrenics, on the other hand, were significantly more concrete, and were uninfluenced by the content. Normals, similarly, were uninfluenced by the content. Using a different approach to the problem, Feffer (1961) found that a group of concrete schizophrenics, as selected by the Gorham test, showed an avoidance reaction to affect-laden words in that they did not recognise them when they were presented tachistoscopically as background material. Abstract schizophrenics did not behave in this way. However, this result is ambiguous, as concrete, (probably process) schizophrenics might be expected to make more errors in visual perception.

Two approaches have been made towards improving the concrete behaviour of schizophrenics in explaining proverbs. Hamlin and associates (1965), repeating a study by Blaufarb (1962), instead of using a single proverb to illustrate each principle, presented proverbs in groups of threes. Each set of three illustrated the same principle, and in this way the subjects had more instances from which to generalise. Under these circumstances, schizophrenics with a mild degree of concreteness improved to a normal level. However, the severely ill, closed-ward schizophrenics remained concrete.

Wagner (1968) tested 48 chronic schizophrenics on a proverbs test, and then gave them a period of training in abstracting. They were required to select one of three alternative pictures which were in the same category as a stimulus picture, and correct performance was rewarded with canteen coupons. Following this training there was a significant improvement on proverbs performance, as there

was in the ability to perform on a 'similarities' test.

Because of its apparent relation to the process-reactive continuum, one would expect that concreteness on the proverbs test would be a bad prognostic indication in early psychosis. However, no follow-up studies to test this hypothesis appear to have been conducted.

(b) THE USE OF WORDS

A second method of assessing concreteness is by studying how patients use words. Some words, in addition to having a concrete meaning, also symbolise an abstract principle, and can therefore be used in at least two different senses. It has been claimed that concrete individuals no longer use words in their abstract sense, and in this respect, words have reduced meaning for them.

One way of assessing this is by the use of a test designed by Flavell (1956) and modified by Milgram (1959). The subject is presented with a stimulus word and two response words. He is asked to underline the response word closest in meaning to the stimulus word. One association is always more abstract than the other, so that a measure of concreteness can be obtained. The results using this test are very similar to those obtained with the proverbs. Schizophrenics as a group appear to be concrete, but not so concrete as brain-damaged patients (Milgram, 1959), although schizophrenics in a state of remission are on average, no longer concrete (Schwartz, 1967a).

A rather different technique is a word meaning test designed by Chapman (1960), who was interested in measuring not only misinterpretations due to concreteness, but also figurative misinterpretations, or unusual abstract uses of words. This is a multiple choice test, and two typical items are as follows:

David turned yellow when he faced the enemy.
This means:
- A. David became cowardly (abstract correct)
- B. David became hungry (figurative incorrect)
- C. David's skin became discoloured (concrete incorrect)

Miss Bailey's illness turned her yellow.
This means:
- A. Miss Bailey became cowardly (abstract incorrect)
- B. Miss Bailey became hungry (figurative incorrect)
- C. Miss Bailey's skin became discoloured (concrete correct)

Chapman (1960; Chapman *et al.*, 1961) found that chronic schizophrenics made more errors of both types than normal adults. Brain-damaged patients made more figurative errors than chronic schizophrenics, while chronic schizophrenics made more literal errors than brain-damaged patients. Children were like chronic schizophrenics, and unlike brain-damaged patients, as they made concrete but not figurative errors.

One reason why chronic schizophrenics use words more concretely is suggested in another study by Chapman and Chapman (1965). They first ranked the strength of the different meanings of each of a group of words, as judged by the frequency with which the meaning was mentioned first by normals. They then asked normals and schizophrenics to rank the degree of similarity between pairs of words. They found that chronic schizophrenics in this task relied mainly on the strongest normal meaning response, ignoring subsidiary meanings. Thus, schizophrenics judged words to be identical in meaning if they had the same strongest meaning, but if not, they found them completely different in meaning, even though they shared a large number of subsidiary meanings. This reliance upon only the strongest meaning in a hierarchy of possible meanings may well be the essence of verbal 'concreteness'.

These findings have been confirmed in a study by Faibish (1961) who found that a group of schizophrenics defined words with multiple meanings more poorly than normal subjects, being able to give fewer of their meanings. Similarly, Benjamin and Watt (1969) found that schizophrenics tended to select only the primary meanings of words used in sentences, whatever the context.

Willner (1965) found that chronic schizophrenics could give fewer unfamiliar meanings of words than brain-damaged patients, and Klorman and Chapman (1969) found that the reliance on only the single strongest meaning of a word characterises younger children as contrasted to older children.

A slightly different test of Chapman's hypothesis was carried out by Deckner and Blanton (1969), who showed their subjects a stimulus word, and then asked them to select from a card one of two words to go with it. One was a 'nickel' word, the subjects receiving a nickel if they chose it. In one part of the experiment, the 'nickel' word had a strong association with the stimulus word, while in another part of the experiment, the word with a weak association was rewarded. A group of schizophrenics were no poorer than normal controls at learning to pick out the strong association, but were inferior at learning to select the word with the weak association. There were no significant differences between process and reactive schizophrenics.

Miller and Chapman (1968) have suggested that this oversimplified use of words by chronic schizophrenics might be one aspect of a more general tendency to oversimplify. That is to say, such individuals use fewer independent dimensions in their classification of verbal information, and make fewer fine discriminations. This theory was tested by asking a group of chronic schizophrenics to rank a list of items along two independent dimensions, and a third more general dimension. For instance, some of the items were the names of foods, which were rated on the two independent dimensions of 'most–least healthful' and 'weight—most per cupful–least per cupful', as well as the general dimension 'like best–like least'. As expected, there were higher overall correlations among these ratings in the chronic schizophrenic group than in the normal group. Miller and Chapman conclude that the beliefs of chronic schizophrenics might be more susceptible to this 'halo' effect which could lead them into logical errors. Some of the erroneous beliefs of chronic schizophrenics could in this way be due to an exaggeration of what is basically a normal response bias.

Chronic schizophrenics are not only restricted in their use of individual words, but they also appear to employ a reduced vocabulary. Hammer and Salzinger (1968) found their speech to be more stereotyped than normal, as judged by a lower 'type-token' ratio, indicating a greater amount of word repetition in a given speech sample.

It might be expected that these verbal disabilities would impair the ability of chronic schizophrenics to communicate with others, and there is evidence that this is the case. Cohen and Camhi (1967) and Smith (1970) found that chronic schizophrenics were less able than normal subjects to provide useful verbal clues, or even to select such clues when trying to convey information to normal people or to one another. However, they had no significant defect in understanding the speech of others. Two studies using the Flavell test (Payne, 1960) suggest that concrete subjects are less sociable, perhaps because they find communication with others more difficult.

Another line of research on the same problem has been carried out by Salzinger and his colleagues (Salzinger et al., 1966). Salzinger has used the 'Cloze' technique to assess the intelligibility of schizophrenic speech. Speech samples from chronic schizophrenics were typed out, and every fifth word was deleted. Normals were less able to guess the missing words in the schizophrenic speech samples than they were in normal speech samples. Similar results have been reported by Cheek and Amarel (1968) using the same technique. Cheek and Amarel investigated some possible causes of the relative unintelligibility of schizophrenic speech samples, and found that they used more content words, but fewer function words than normal people. These investigators concluded that it is the grammatical structure more than the content of schizophrenic speech that makes it unpredictable.

Deckner and Blanton (1969) applied the 'Cloze' technique in a different manner. Samples of *normal* speech with every tenth (and then with every fifth) word deleted were presented to schizophrenics. The schizophrenics were worse than the normal controls at guessing the deleted words. Perhaps surprisingly, the number of deleted words made no difference. There were also no differences between the process and the reactive schizophrenics.

At least two attempts have been made to induce abnormal verbal behaviour in normal subjects by the use of LSD. Krus and co-workers (1963) were able to increase the number of concrete verbal responses on the Flavell (1956) word definition test by giving LSD 25 to normal subjects. Cheek and Amarel (1968), gave the same drug to normal subjects, obtained 100-word speech samples from them under drugged and non-drugged conditions, and then analysed the speech samples using the Cloze technique. As expected, LSD made the speech of normal subjects less predictable. However, the drugged speech samples were different from those of schizophrenics. Unlike schizophrenics, who use more content and fewer function words than normal, LSD produced a change in the opposite direction. LSD led to an increase in the use of function words in the normal subjects.

In an attempt to see how far concrete verbal behaviour in schizophrenics is reversible, True (1966), following a period of base-line measurement positively reinforced abstract responses and negatively reinforced concrete responses in a word association task. He found that reactive schizophrenics could be made to respond normally, but the behaviour of the initially more concrete process schizophrenics could not be significantly altered in this way.

(c) THE USE OF SORTING TESTS

Requiring patients to sort objects into groups in order to determine whether they are able to formulate and employ abstract categories has been used for many years in assessing concreteness. One of the most commonly used tests of this sort, the Goldstein-Scheerer (1941) Object Sorting Test, consists of a set of everyday objects such as a pipe, cigar, cutlery, matches, and so on. Another of Goldstein and Scheerer's sorting tests, the Colour-Form test consists of a small set of plastic objects in three different shapes, squares, circles, and triangles, and four different colours, red, blue, green, and yellow.

Goldstein and Scheerer argued that concrete individuals would be unable to sort the objects into groups or, if they did, they would be unable to give an adequate account of the abstract principle that formed the basis of the grouping. However, they added a second criterion of what they regarded as a normal, abstract performance, namely the ability, having produced one type of abstract sorting, to 'shift' and re-sort the objects according to a quite different abstract principle. Clearly, people differ in respect to their 'rigidity' in this situation, but it has never been demonstrated that concreteness and rigidity on these tests are the same phenomenon.

There is, however, evidence that this type of rigidity can be reliably measured in different situations. Nolan (1968) obtained 72 schizophrenics who were unable to 'shift' on the Goldstein Colour-Form test, and 72 schizophrenics who were able to 'shift' successfully. All the subjects were given a different type of sorting task, using cards. The schizophrenics who could shift on the Goldstein test tended also to be able to do so on the second task. However, those who were rigid on the Goldstein test had much more difficulty, not only in learning to shift the basis of their sorting to some new dimension, but even in being able merely to reverse the direction of their sorting, a task it had been expected would be easier for them, as it still involved the same dimension. Altering the type of reinforcement used (verbal praise or candy) made no difference.

The difficulty with the Goldstein-Scheerer tests as they were originally used is that, while a more or less standard administration procedure was employed, no standard scoring system was laid down. Accordingly, earlier studies with these tests (Payne, 1960) are difficult to evaluate because of the subjective assessments involved. Rapaport (1946) has produced a standard technique for scoring concreteness on the Object Sorting Test, and Payne and associates (1959) have produced a standard scoring procedure for both the Object Sorting Test and the Colour Form Test.

Tutko and Spence (1962), using the Rapaport version of the Goldstein Object Sorting test found that acute 'process' schizophrenics were concrete like a group of brain-damaged patients, whereas a group of matched 'reactive' schizophrenics were not significantly different from normal. Payne and associates (1959) and Payne and Hewlett (1960), using both sorting tests, found no significant differences between a group of acute schizophrenics and a group of normal controls. However, the process-reactive variable was not considered in either study, and it is not known how many, if any, 'process' schizophrenics were included. Weckowicz and Blewett (1959) found that concreteness on these tests was associated with poor perceptual constancy among chronic schizophrenics. This suggests that concrete schizophrenics make use of a very restricted range of cues, both in perception and in concept formation.

Several sorting tests employ words or pictures rather than real objects, although the same principle is involved. Two-word 'similarities' tests, such as that in the Wechsler-Bellevue Scale, are sorting tests in this sense, and Tolor (1964) has developed a special multiple choice version of this test. Trunnell (1964, 1965) has developed a version in which subjects must say what three words have in common (e.g. car, bicycle, train), and Bernstein (1960) used a five-word test of the same sort. Schizophrenics as a group were inferior on these tests in some studies, but the process-reactive variable has not been investigated. An exception to this is a study by DeLuca (1968) who gave a set of similarities tests to groups of process and reactive schizophrenics, who performed similarly. He then gave some of the subjects instructions about how to improve their performance, and retested them. Curiously, the process schizophrenics receiving the instructions improved much more on retest than did the comparable group of reactive schizophrenics. However, the process schizophrenics who received no such instructions did much worse when retested, as compared with their reactive counterparts. Probably the instructions acted, in part, by motivating the subjects, but it is surprising that the process schizophrenics were more susceptible to motivation.

A slightly different sorting test has been employed by Feldman and Drasgow (1951; Drasgow and Feldman, 1957). It consists of a set of cards, each of which depicts four objects in a row. For example, the first card pictures four lines; three are horizontal, and one vertical, and one of the horizontal lines is coloured red. The subjects are asked to find three objects that can be grouped together for one reason (three horizontal lines), and then three objects that can be grouped together for a different reason (three black lines). Subjects must explain each grouping, and can score 0, 1, or 2 on each card, 2 indicating that both groupings were perceived. Payne and colleagues (1959) and Schwartz (1967a) used a similar test with different items, and Bernstein (1960) developed a version of the test using words instead of pictures. Nathan (1964) developed a multiple choice test along similar lines, except that no 'shift' was involved. Four pictures illustrate the concept and the subject must select the one of four sentences that best describes the concept. Studies using these tests are inconclusive, some (Feldman and Drasgow, 1951; Bernstein, 1960) finding schizophrenics to be concrete, and some (Payne *et al.*, 1959; Nathan, 1964) finding no evidence for this. Again, however, such variables as chronicity and the process-reactive dimension are not usually considered. Both studies that tested brain-damaged patients found them to be concrete (Bernstein, 1960; Feldman and Drasgow, 1951).

As with verbal tests, the introduction of emotionally disturbing material into sorting tests can make subjects more concrete in their performance. Brodsky (1963) tested groups of acute schizophrenics, chronic schizophrenics, and normal control subjects on a set of five sorting tests. The material consisted either of cards depicting abstract diagrams, or cards showing people in sexual, aggressive, or threatening situations. The schizophrenic patients were concrete in sorting the abstract cards but significantly more concrete when sorting the emotionally arousing cards. Similar results were obtained by Bernstein (1960).

(d) CONCEPT ATTAINMENT EXPERIMENTS

A somewhat more elaborate extension of the sorting test is the concept attainment technique developed by Heidbreder in experiments with normal subjects (Payne, 1960). This technique is exemplified by the Wisconsin Sorting Test (Payne, 1960), which consists of 64 cards. These have to be sorted one at a time with one of four meaningless stimulus cards. The subject is not told the basis of the sorting, but each time he sorts a card he is told 'right' or 'wrong'. When the subject has sorted ten cards correctly consecutively, the sorting principle is changed. The first principle is 'colour', the second 'form', and so on. When the same criterion is reached for the second principle, the principle is changed again. The test requires five shifts in all. The test is over when all five principles have been attained, or when all 64 cards have been sorted without the criterion of ten correct consecutive sortings being achieved.

Concept attainment tests differ in a number of ways. For example, the number of dimensions relevant to a particular method of sorting can be varied (e.g. sort all the square, red, large objects together—3 dimensions—or merely sort all the red objects together—1 dimension). The cards may also differ along irrelevant dimensions, which serve as distractors, although these extra dimensions may or may not be made relevant to later methods of sorting the cards. In most experiments, the subjects merely sort the cards into one of two piles, the sorting principle being changed periodically. However, in some experiments (e.g. Hall, 1962) sorting the cards into as many as six different categories has been required. Normally, the categories are originally identified in some meaningless way [e.g. the 'right' pile *vs* the 'wrong' pile (Fey, 1951) the 'A' *vs* the 'B' pile (Pishkin and Blanchard, 1963)]. Under these circumstances, the subject must learn by trial and error which properties define which particular concept, by observing which properties are reinforced. However, in some experiments (Furth and Youniss, 1968) the categories to be used are initially identified by a sample or 'cue' card, which illustrates without defining the category and still depends upon trial and error learning.

It is not certain whether the trial and error 'concept formation' being assessed in these experiments can be identified with the kind of conceptualisation required by the sorting tests that have been discussed above. One difference is that in concept attainment experiments there need be no single English word that defines the concept being developed (e.g. all red, striped diagrams with curved edges could define one concept). Sorting tests, on the other hand, usually require the subjects to employ simple concepts they have learned in the past (e.g. shape, colour, use).

In studies using concept attainment tests, it has generally been found that acute schizophrenics are significantly worse than normals (Fey, 1951; Hall, 1962). Remitted schizophrenics, however, are no worse than nonschizophrenic psychiatric patients (Schwartz, 1967a).

The two studies carried out with chronic schizophrenics have produced conflicting results. Snelbecker and associates (1966) found that chronic schizophrenics were not significantly different from a normal control group, while Phelan and coworkers (1967) found that they made more errors, and were slower than a normal control group.

Furth and Youniss (1968) tested a group of 15 litigious paranoid schizophrenics, and a group of 15 non-litigious non-paranoid schizophrenics (mainly catatonics), and, unexpectedly, found no significant differences between the groups.

Several studies have been carried out to investigate the extent to which schizophrenics can make use of social cues in concept attainment tasks (Pishkin and Blanchard, 1963; Wolfgang et al., 1968; Pishkin and Bourne, 1969). In these experiments, social cues were provided by another individual (normal or schizophrenic) who took the test at the same time, so that the subject could see how this person responded before responding himself. In some conditions the other person was always correct, while in some conditions he responded at a chance level. It was found that the schizophrenics were less able than normal subjects to benefit from these social cues. In one study (Wolfgang et al., 1968), male schizophrenics did no better under these social conditions than they did while working alone, and female schizophrenics did significantly better on their own.

Three studies (Price, 1968; Phelan et al., 1967; Furth and Youniss, 1968) have been carried out to test an hypothesis put forward by Yates (1966a) to explain concrete behaviour in sorting tasks. Yates suggested that because schizophrenics are so much slower than normal subjects, they tend to forget what they have learned from trial to trial. In all these studies, the schizophrenics not only made more errors than normal subjects, but were found to be slower at sorting the cards, and in this respect the results were consistent with this explanation.

(e) CONCLUSIONS

The evidence suggests that concreteness is a disability process schizophrenics share with brain-damaged patients. It seems likely that it is this disability that contributes largely to the low level of general intelligence of these patients, in view of the high correlation between IQ tests and tests of concreteness in psychiatric groups. Concreteness seems to be associated with the perceptual inaccuracies presumably caused by deficient 'scanning' and may be related to insufficient sensory input. It causes difficulties in verbal communication, and is associated with social withdrawal. It characterises at least some chronic schizophrenics and can be presumed to be a poor prognostic sign, although direct studies are not available. Emotionally disturbing material can increase the level of concreteness. At least in some concept attainment tasks, the poor scores of some schizophrenics may be the result of poor short-term retention, and slowness of performance.

2. Overinclusive Thinking

Norman Cameron thought that the essence of schizophrenic thought disorder was what he termed 'overinclusive thinking'. Cameron (1938a, 1938b, 1939a, 1939b, 1944, 1947; Cameron and Magaret, 1951) carried out several preliminary studies of the nature of conceptual thinking in schizophrenia, making use of an incomplete sentences task, and the Vigotsky sorting test. From an essentially subjective analysis of the results of these studies, Cameron concluded that overinclusive thinking is a conceptual disorder in which the boundaries of concepts become overextensive. Associated ideas, or even distantly related ideas become incorporated into the concepts of schizophrenics, making them broad, vague and imprecise. One result of this is that thinking itself becomes vague and imprecise. Indeed normally mutually exclusive concepts can come to share common elements, and hence overlap, and this can produce apparent logical contradictions.

A second aspect of overinclusive thinking,

according to Cameron, is the 'interpenetration' of irrelevant themes. Completely irrelevant, often personal ideas intrude themselves and become mixed up with the problem solving process.

Following Cameron's early work, a number of relatively objective measures of overinclusive thinking have been developed. For the sake of clarity, it is easiest to classify these roughly according to the type of test employed.

(a) VERBAL TESTS

Moran's (1953) Definitions Test

Moran developed a word-usage test with a number of sections, several of which were designed to assess overinclusive concept formation. In one section of the test, the subjects are asked to give as many synonyms as possible for each of 25 words. Moran found that 40 schizophrenics gave more, but less precise synonyms than did a matched group of 40 normals. In another section, each of the same 25 stimulus words is printed on a page and is followed by five to eight response words, including neologisms. The subjects are asked to underline every response word they believe is an essential part of the concept denoted by the stimulus word. Schizophrenics, because they are overinclusive in their definitions, were expected to underline more of the distantly related words (but not fewer of the correct responses). The results supported the prediction. When asked to free associate to the same words in another section, the schizophrenics produced more distant associations, and when asked to use the words in a sentence, their sentences were unclear, contradictory, and ungrammatical. When the same words were incorporated into a similarities and an analogies test, again the schizophrenics showed significantly inferior performance. Seth and Beloff (1959) succeeded in repeating Moran's findings in a later study.

The Epstein (1953) Test

Epstein developed a very similar test which consists of 50 stimulus words, each followed by 6 response words, including the word 'none'. Epstein's own results confirmed those of Moran. He found that schizophrenics underlined significantly more words than did a normal control group. Payne and co-workers (1959) also found that schizophrenics had a higher overinclusion score on this test than a matched control group of neurotics. However, the more recent results with this test, which have been reviewed by Sturm (1965), have been somewhat conflicting. Sturm points out that acute schizophrenics have usually been found to be more overinclusive than normals, although in one study neurotics were also overinclusive, and in another, psychotic depressives were found to be overinclusive (Payne and Hirst, 1957). No particular subgroup of schizophrenics appears to be especially overinclusive on this test, there being no consistently reported differences between deteriorated schizophrenics, acute schizophrenics, chronic schizophrenics, process schizophrenics, or reactive schizophrenics (Eliseo, 1963; Sturm, 1965). Schwartz (1967b) found no significant differences between remitted schizophrenics, nonschizophrenic psychiatric controls, and normal controls. Reed (1969), using a very similar test found that a group of neurotic patients with obsessional personalities were underinclusive, underlining significantly *fewer* words than a control group of mixed psychiatric patients.

There is, however, no evidence that the Epstein test is significantly related to any other measures of overinclusive concept formation. Payne and Hewlett (1960) found it to be the only overinclusion test that had no loading on their overinclusion factor. Watson (1967) found it to be unrelated to a proverbs overinclusion score or a measure of concept breadth derived from the Goldstein Object Sorting Test, and Phillips et al. (1965) found it unrelated to the Payne Object Classification Test 'Non-A' score.

One reason for these results is suggested by a study carried out by Desai (1960), who found that the overinclusion score on this test is a function of word knowledge. People with low vocabularies tend to get high overinclusion scores. In an effort to improve the test, Sturm (1965) revised it, but found no evidence that the revised overinclusion score differentiated significantly among groups of process schizophrenics, reactive schizophrenics, brain-damaged patients, and tubercular patients. It would appear that overinclusion is better measured by a test less influenced by vocabulary level.

Daston, King, and Armitage's (1953) Test

In this technique, two short stories were read aloud to 25 paranoid schizophrenics and 27 matched normal subjects. Afterwards the subjects were given a check list of 36 positive and 36 negative statements about the characters in the stories. The schizophrenic group checked off significantly more adjectives than did the normal controls.

The Shneidman (1948) Make-a-Picture-Story (MAPS) Test

In this test, the subjects are presented with a set of background cards depicting various outdoor and indoor settings. They are also given a large number of cardboard cut-out human figures in different positions and costumes. They are asked to select for each background card, as many figures as they like, place them on the background card, and then make up a story about the scene they have created. Shneidman gave the test to a group of 50 schizophrenics and 50 normal controls. Among other differences found, the schizophrenics tended to use an abnormally large number of figures on each background card. They seemed unable to restrict their attention to a few figures relevant to a simple theme, and tended to make up diffuse, overinclusive stories.

The Pettigrew (1958) Test

This is a pencil and paper test of 20 multiple choice items in which the subjects are asked to estimate the extremes of a number of different categories such as the length of whales, or the annual rainfall in Washington, D.C. Overinclusive subjects are expected to produce very broad ranges. There is no evidence that schizophrenics as a group produce wider categories than do normal college students (Silverman, 1964a; Silverman *et al.*, 1966) although college students were found to produce broader categories than convicts.

The Proverbs Test

Payne and associates (1959) suggested that, to an overinclusive individual, Benjamin's (1944) proverbs should illustrate a set of more extensive and elaborate generalisations than they do for normal people. Because of this, overinclusive subjects should use more words, and take longer to explain the proverbs. The overinclusion score used was the average number of words required to explain each proverb. Care must be taken, however, in specially instructing the subject to give a positive indication that he has completed his explanation before going on to the next proverb. It is also essential to tape record the answers, and to count the words from the tape. Whenever studies have relied on longhand recording, relatively few words per proverb have been reported, and the significant differences vanish (Payne *et al.*, 1959; Goldstein and Salzman, 1965) because it is almost impossible to record in longhand without condensation.

Payne and Hewlett (1960) found acute schizophrenics to be significantly more overinclusive than normals, neurotics, or depressives on this measure. Reed (1968) found similar results. Payne *et al.* (1964) found that among acute schizophrenics, paranoid schizophrenics were significantly more overinclusive

than nonparanoid schizophrenics, a finding confirmed by Lloyd (1967). However, Foulds and his associates (1968) found no significant correlation between the proverbs word count score and a rating of delusions in an acute schizophrenic group, although they did find a significant tendency within a chronic schizophrenic group for the deluded patients to use more words. Payne and co-workers (1963), on the other hand, found that chronic schizophrenics were not abnormally overinclusive on this measure.

These rather conflicting results may be due to the fact that this test could be especially susceptible to unconscious verbal reinforcement on the part of the examiner. It is probably relatively easy to encourage patients subtly to go on talking, and in future studies it would appear desirable to rule out the possible effect of examiner bias, perhaps by giving the test by means of a tape recorder.

(b) SORTING TESTS

The Zaslow (1950) Test

This test was designed to measure overinclusive concept formation. It consists of a set of 14 cards. Card one depicts an equilateral triangle, and card 14 a perfect circle. In the intervening cards the shape gradually changes from a triangle to a circle. In one part of the administration procedure the examiner places the cards in order and asks the subjects to indicate where the circles, and where the triangles end. Overinclusive subjects were expected to include more cards in each category. Zaslow (1950) found that 24 schizophrenics were significantly more overinclusive than 16 normal surgical patients. However, Kugelmass and Fondeur (1955) could not confirm these findings with 45 early schizophrenics, 23 acute schizophrenics and 23 normal controls. They also found that the test-retest reliabilities of the scores derived from this test were so low as to be insignificant in some cases.

The Payne (1962) Object Classification Test

The object classification test consists of 12 small objects, squares, circles, and triangles, which differ in their size, thickness, and weight, are made of different materials, and are painted in colours of different hues and saturations. Subjects are asked to sort the objects in as many ways as they can think of. There are intended to be 10 'correct' ways to sort the objects, and these are scored as 'A' responses. Any other sorting the subject is willing to explain is scored as a 'Non-A' response. The original rationale for regarding the number of 'Non-A' responses as a measure of overinclusion, was that normal people are able to 'screen out', or to disregard aspects of the material they regard as irrelevant, such as un-intentional scratches on the objects, the shadows cast by the objects on the table, their personal associations to the objects, and so on. Overinclusive schizophrenics, on the other hand, it was thought, are overinclusive because they are unable to screen out such irrelevant thoughts and perceptions. For this reason, these patients should have more data on which to base their sortings. Accordingly, they should produce more sortings than normal people, including both the usual 'A' sortings, but also a number of unusual or 'Non-A' sortings randomly interspersed. In the initial studies with this test (Payne *et al.*, 1959; Payne and Hewlett, 1960; Payne *et al.*, 1963) it was found that about 50 per cent of acute schizophrenics produce an abnormally large number of 'Non-A' responses, but that neither normals, neurotics, nor depressives behave in this way. Payne (1970) found that Non-A scores tend not to characterise chronic schizophrenic patients, who appear instead to be 'concrete', giving very few 'A' responses. However, Foulds *et al.* (1967) found no differences between chronic and acute schizo-phrenics. On the other hand, they did find that the paranoid schizophrenics in both groups gave significantly more Non-A responses than the non-paranoid schizophrenics.

Although Payne and his colleagues (1963) found that remitted schizophrenics did not produce an abnormal number of 'Non-A' responses, Phillips and co-workers (1965) have reported that an abnormal number of Non-A responses are produced by the relatives of schizophrenic patients. Claridge (1967) has reported that Non-A responses are given by reactive rather than by process schizophrenics, and are associated with a number of other charac-teristics such as a high drive level as assessed by sedation threshold, fast reactions, extraversion, mood swings, activity (in contrast to withdrawal) and a good prognosis. Other results with this test will be discussed below.

The Shaw Test (Howson, 1948)

The Shaw test of concept formation consists of a set of four wooden blocks varying in colour, height, shape, size, and weight. There are four shapes: hexagon, pentagon, square, and triangle. There are four shades of the colour grey. In addition, the blocks have other features by which they can be arranged in a number of sequences. On the bottom of each block is one of four names: rat, lamb, ox, and whale. The size of the printing varies. On the top surface, each block has one of four letters, A, B, C, or D. Each block has a hole in the centre varying in

depth and diameter, and on the side of each block there is a notch varying in width, depth, and position relative to the corner of the block. The task is to arrange the blocks in as many sequences as possible. There are 15 correct or 'abstract' sequences, but other less adequate, or unusual ways of arranging them are scored as 'B', 'C', or 'D' responses. The rationale for this test as a measure of overinclusion is identical to that of the Object Classification Test. Payne and Hewlett (1960) predicted that schizo-phrenics would produce more unusual ('C' or 'D') responses than neurotics, normals, or depressives, and the prediction was confirmed.

The Goldstein Object Sorting 'Handing Over' Score

Payne *et al.* (1959) developed a measure of over-inclusive thinking from the Goldstein-Scheerer (1941) Object Sorting Test. Goldstein and Scheerer's standard administration procedure is followed up to the end of the 'handing over' experiment. The 'male' set of everyday objects is placed in front of the subject, who is asked to select one ('point of departure') and hand it over to the examiner. He is then asked to hand over all the objects he thinks could be grouped together with this object for any reason at all, and then to explain his grouping. The experiment is repeated three more times. Payne and associates (1959) modified the procedure by using three standard 'points of departure', the red plate, the box of matches, and the bicycle bell. The overinclusion score is the average number of objects chosen in each group (excluding the 'point of departure'). The rationale is simply that over-inclusive subjects should build up a more over-inclusive concept around the 'point of departure', thus selecting more objects.

This score differentiated acute schizophrenics from normal, neurotic, and depressive control groups in two studies (Payne *et al.*, 1959; Payne and Hewlett, 1960). This test will be discussed further below.

Lovibond's (1954) Modification of the Goldstein Object Sorting Test

Lovibond used the standard Goldstein-Scheerer administration of the Object Sorting test, but developed a special system according to which the sorting categories employed by the subject can be scored according to their degree of overinclusiveness. He found that schizophrenics were more over-inclusive than normal controls. Other investigators (McConaghy, 1959; Lidz *et al.*, 1962; Rosman *et al.*, 1964) have shown that the parents of schizo-phrenic patients also tend to be significantly more overinclusive than normal on this test. Schopler and Loftin (1969) found that the parents of young psychotic children were significantly more over-inclusive than the parents of a control group of normal children on this measure. These results, by themselves, however, do not make it possible to say whether this sort of thought disorder is inherited or learned.

McGaughran's (1954) Modification of the Object Sorting Test

McGaughran (1954) suggested that the Goldstein-Scheerer Object Sorting Test could be scored on the basis of two independent dimensions. One of these he labelled 'open-closed'. This dimension refers to the number of objects contained in a category, an 'open' category containing a large number of objects. It has already been suggested that this could be taken as a measure of overinclusion. Studies using this measure suggest that paranoid schizophrenics use significantly more 'open' sortings than do normals (McGaughran and Moran, 1956) or neurotics (Silverman and Silverman, 1962), and that brain-damaged patients use significantly more 'closed' (concrete) sortings (McGaughran and Moran, 1957). Tutko and Spence (1962) found evidence that process schizophrenics and brain-damaged patients produced 'closed' (concrete) sortings, whereas reactive schizo-phrenics produced 'open' sortings, although Sturm (1964) was unable to repeat this finding by testing three groups.

Weckowicz and Blewett (1959) found that schizophrenics who produced 'closed' (concrete) sortings had a perceptual defect in the form of poor size constancy.

Chapman and Taylor's (1957) Sorting Test of Overinclusion

This sorting test makes use of a somewhat different principle. The test material consists of 30 words typed on index cards. The subjects are asked to sort all the cards illustrating a specific concept (e.g. 'alcoholic beverages') into one box, while sorting the remainder into a second box. While some cards contain items that are clearly irrelevant to the concept (e.g. names of insects), some contain items that are very similar to it (e.g. names of non-alcoholic beverages). Overinclusive subjects are expected to make errors of overinclusion by mis-sorting the similar but not the dissimilar cards. Chapman and Taylor found that chronic schizophrenics produced more errors of overinclusion than did a group of matched normals.

It is also possible to define errors of under-inclusion on this test (rejecting correct cards). Chapman (1961) found that the broader the categories used, the more errors of overinclusion were made by chronic schizophrenics. He also found that brain-damaged patients on this test made errors of underinclusion like children (Chapman et al., 1961), but unlike chronic schizophrenics and nor-mals. Chapman and Knowles (1964) found that phenothiazine treatment in chronic schizophrenics significantly reduced errors of overinclusion, did not change errors of underinclusion, but did increase random errors on this test. The implication is that phenothiazine therapy may specifically improve overinclusive conceptualisation, but at the expense of producing some generalised inefficiency.

The results using this test are consistent with those from other measures in so far as the performance of brain-damaged patients is concerned. However, on the other types of sorting tests, the acute (or reactive), but not the chronic schizophrenics tend to be over-inclusive. Studies of the relation between Chapman and Taylor's sorting test and other tests of over-inclusion are needed before this apparent contradic-tion can be resolved.

Hammer and Johnson's (1965) Sorting Test

A test very similar to that of Chapman and Taylor has been developed by Hammer and Johnson, who used cards with pictures. The category to be selected is illustrated by four different pictures (for example, four pictures of fruit), and the subject is also told what the category is. These four cards remain in front of the subject during the sorting, so that the correct category is constantly defined, and need not be held in mind. It was found that acute schizo-phrenics made significantly more errors of over-inclusion than normals, whereas organics made significantly more errors of underinclusion.

The Vigotsky Test

This test consists of a set of 22 blocks of various shapes painted in five different colours. Reed (1969b) asked a group of psychiatric patients to sort them into groups, and found that obsessional neurotics were the opposite of overinclusive. They overdefined their categories, and used more categories, with fewer objects in each.

Nickols's (1964) Sorting Test

In this test subjects are asked to select from a group of differently shaped figures of different sizes all those that 'seem to go with' a relatively amorphous multicoloured stimulus card. Nickols found that a group of chronic schizophrenics did not select significantly more objects per group than a normal control group. These results are consistent with the results from other tests of overinclusion in suggesting that chronic schizophrenics are not overinclusive. The exception is the finding with Chapman and Taylor's test discussed above.

Miscellaneous Sorting Tests

Other investigators have found that on word-sorting tests, schizophrenics as a group produce more unusual sortings than do normals (McReynolds and Collins, 1961; Rashkis, 1947; Rashkis *et al.*, 1946).

(c) INTERPRETATIONS OF AMBIGUOUS STIMULI: FAILURE TO DEVELOP A 'SET'

Payne and Hewlett (1960) argued that in normal people, focusing the attention is dependent on the ability to develop and maintain a 'set'. They suggested that overinclusive thinking may be associated with an inability to develop such a 'set'. The following tests of overinclusion can all he explained in terms of this rationale.

White's (1949) Test

White produced a set of cards on which were printed very blurred carbon copies of words that were almost undecipherable, and asked a group of normal subjects and a group of schizophrenics to say what they were. The normal subjects nearly always guessed a word, presumably because they rapidly developed a set to perceive only words. Schizophrenics, on the other hand, gave less evidence of such a set. They frequently gave responses that were not words at all, such as 'teeth' or 'spots'.

The Brengelmann Picture Recognition Test 'Incorrect Guesses' Score (Payne and Hewlett, 1960)

In this test, subjects are shown pictures in a tachistoscopic viewing box at exposures too brief to permit correct identification. The duration of the exposure is systematically increased until correct recognition occurs. When normal subjects make an incorrect guess at the very fast exposures, they tend to continue to make the same guess until the exposure times are long enough for them to identify the picture correctly. Presumably this is because their initial interpretation imposes a 'set' on them, and they continue to interpret what is essentially an ambiguous pattern of stimulation in the light of their initial expectation. Payne and Van Allen (1969)

argued that overinclusive subjects who should not develop such a set, would continue to notice aspects of the ambiguous stimulus that were inconsistent with their first guess, and would keep modifying their interpretation, producing a large number of different prerecognition guesses. In a sample of mainly schizophrenic psychiatric in-patients, the hypothesis was confirmed at a high level of significance, there being a correlation of 0·90 between the number of prerecognition guesses and the Non-A response score on the Payne Object Classification Test.

Ebner and Ritzler (1969) in an experiment described above, asked their subjects to recognise pictures that were slowly being brought into focus. They found no significant differences among groups of acute schizophrenics, chronic schizophrenics, and normal subjects in the number of prerecognition guesses, a result not entirely consistent with Payne and Hewlett's finding.

Payne and Hewlett's (1960) Modification of the Luchins 'Water-Jar' Test

Payne and Hewlett argued that 'Einstellung' rigidity is a special case of a learned set. The water-jar test presents the subjects with problems in measuring quantities of water using three jars of known capacity. During a series of 'set' problems, the subjects are presented items that can only be solved by following one specific sequence. Later, when this sequence no longer works, normal subjects find great difficulty in solving simple items they could easily solve before the set 'blinded' them to alternative methods of solving the problem. Payne and Hewlett modified the test by increasing the number of 'set' problems to such an extent that 15 out of 20 normals were completely unable to solve 5 subsequent problems requiring a different attack. They argued that, if overinclusion is associated with the inability to develop such a set, acute schizophrenics should be better able to solve the later problems. The prediction was verified, to the extent that half an acute schizophrenic group was able to solve three or more of the five problems given after the set had been established, a result that was statistically significant.

McCormack and colleagues (1967) modified the Luchins test in a different way, arranging a set of problems in such a way that in one part of the test, the set that was developed was useful, while in another part of the test it was a handicap. They tested 30 schizophrenics and 30 matched normal subjects, and, unlike Payne and Hewlett, found that the normal subjects were better than the schizophrenics at developing the useful set, and were also better than the schizophrenics at rejecting the inappropriate set. However, it is not possible to interpret this discrepancy without knowing more about the schizophrenic patients tested.

The Pathways Test

Payne and associates (1959) tested this same hypothesis in a somewhat different way, using the Leiter-Partington 'Pathways' test material. In the first part of the test, the subject is shown a piece of paper, on which is a set of circles drawn at random, and randomly numbered from 1 to 10. The examiner merely says 'watch me', and then connects the circles with a pencil in numerical order. The subject is then given a second sheet of paper containing many more randomly arranged numbered circles, which are in a different spatial arrangement. The subject is merely instructed 'do as I did'. It was predicted that normal people, while watching the examiner complete the demonstration item, would conclude that the only relevant variable was the numbers in the circles, and would ignore everything else. They should therefore make no errors in completing the test proper, even though the circles are arranged differently. Over-inclusive patients, on the other hand, it was predicted, would not immediately develop this 'numerical set', and would observe other aspects of the examiner's performance, such as the spatial pattern of the lines drawn. It was predicted that in the test proper, they would now be in a conflict, since, if they followed one aspect of the demonstration (the numerical order) they would not reproduce the same directional pattern of lines. This overcomplication of the task, it was expected, should lead both to a very slow performance, and errors among acute schizophrenics. A second section of the test is identical, except that both letters and numbers are used in an alternating alphabetical numerical sequence. Payne *et al.* (1959) found that all the differences were in the expected direction, although only the error score on the second section achieved statistical significance. Payne and Hewlett (1960), testing groups of schizophrenics, neurotics, depressives, and normals again found all the differences in the expected direction, but none attained statistical significance.

(d) FACTORIAL STUDIES OF OVERINCLUSIVE THINKING

Before it can be concluded that the various measures of overinclusive thinking that have been developed measure the same phenomenon, it is necessary to demonstrate that they do, in fact, measure something in common. However, relatively few correlational studies have been carried out. The largest

scale investigation appears to be that carried out by Payne and Hewlett (1960). They made use of a large battery of tests producing 60 different scores. Twenty-three were selected as being measures of overinclusion (13 of which were regarded *a priori* as being 'pure', probably being unaffected by contaminating variables). Fourteen were measures of speed, ranging from the speed of carrying out very simple psychomotor tasks, such as writing one's own name (from the Babcock Levy test battery) to tests of speed of carrying out letter series intelligence test items (Nufferno tests). Six were measures of general intelligence, 6 were measures of concreteness, and 11 were miscellaneous measures regarded by Eysenck as tests of 'psychoticism', such as the amount of body sway in a static ataxia experiment, and the size of drawing waves. The tests were given to carefully matched groups of 20 normal subjects, 20 neurotics, 20 depressives, and 20 acute schizophrenics. The matrix of test intercorrelations for all 80 subjects was factor analysed, and the first three centroid factors were identified. A discriminant function analysis was then carried out on the three factor scores. First, that function that maximised the separation between the psychotics as a group, and the other subjects was defined. A rotated factor defining this function was obtained. It was found that the tests that defined this factor were almost entirely tests of speed, and it was labelled a factor of 'retardation'. It did not differentiate between the two psychotic groups. Second, that function that maximised the separation between the depressives and the schizophrenics was defined. A rotated factor defining this function was obtained. This factor was defined almost exclusively by those tests that had been thought to be measures of overinclusive thinking. A third factor, orthogonal to the first two and which did not discriminate between any of the groups was obtained. It was largely defined by the tests of intelligence and concreteness.

This study suggested clearly that the tests of overinclusion did intercorrelate as anticipated, and further, that a factor score representing what they measured in common could differentiate the schizophrenics from all the other subjects, although when the distributions on this factor score were examined, it was clear that only about half the schizophrenic group had overinclusion factor scores outside the normal range. The remainder of the schizophrenics tended to be abnormally retarded.

The only other large-scale factorial study that appears to have been carried out was reported by Craig (1965), who gave a large battery of tests of overinclusive thinking to 66 newly admitted psychiatric patients, and factor analysed them. He was able to extract three factors, using a method of factor analysis different from that employed by Payne and Hewlett. Unfortunately, a direct comparison of the results obtained in the two studies is not possible, because Craig does not report the matrix of intercorrelations he obtained.

The other correlational studies that have been reported, used only a few tests. Hawks (1964) using three of Payne and Hewlett's overinclusion tests yielding four overinclusion scores with a group of 58 acutely ill patients who were suspected of having thought disorder, found that only two of the six intercorrelations were significantly greater than zero. Watson (1967), intercorrelating three tests used with 100 chronic schizophrenics found no significant correlations, and Phillips et al. (1965) found no significant correlation between two tests. It must be concluded that the evidence that overinclusive thinking can be regarded as a unitary phenomenon is still inconclusive.

(e) PAYNE AND FRIEDLANDER'S STANDARD OVERINCLUSION TEST BATTERY

Payne and Friedlander (1962) proposed that the three tests which were the best measure of Payne and Hewlett's overinclusion factor could provide the best operational definition of this concept. These measures, which have been described above, are the 'Non-A' response score from the Payne Object Classification Test, the average number of objects selected per group from the 'Handing over' experiment of the Goldstein-Scheerer object sorting test, and the average number of words used in explaining the Benjamin Proverbs. Payne and Friedlander suggested a single overinclusion score could be obtained, by summing the transformed scores used by Payne and Hewlett. Payne and Hewlett's transformations were designed to normalise the distributions, and equalise the variance on each test, so that the three scores are given equal weight.

The results of a number of studies using this standard test battery have recently been reviewed by Payne (1971) and will be summarised briefly here.

Test-Retest Reliability

Hawks (1967) found that this battery had a satisfactory test-retest reliability. The test-retest correlations obtained from a group of 54 psychiatric in-patients (36 of whom were schizophrenic) are as follows: Object Classification Test Non-A score, 0·773; Goldstein Object Sorting Test 'handing over' score, 0·799; Proverbs tests average number of words, 0·855; Combined Overinclusion Score, 0·869.

Intercorrelations Among the Tests

Payne (1971) summarising the results of several studies (Hawks, 1964, 1967; Hewlett, 1959; Hart, 1964; Foulds et al., 1967; Watson, 1967) concluded that moderately large and statistically significant intercorrelations have been found only when the sample tested included patients who had been carefully selected as showing typical signs of schizophrenic thought disorder (Hawks, 1967; Payne and Hewlett, 1960; Foulds et al., 1967). Studies using chronic schizophrenics (Foulds et al., 1967; Watson, 1967), doubtful cases (Hawks, 1964) or an unselected psychiatric group (Hart, 1964) did not find significant intercorrelations. This suggests that the variance of these tests in most populations is specific. Only when an extreme degree of thought disorder is present and is clinically obvious, are the test scores influenced by this, and share some common variance. Of the three measures, the Proverbs test score has least in common with the other two scores.

Relationship to General Intelligence

Payne (1971) summarising the results of several studies (Hart, 1964; Payne and Hewlett, 1960; Hawks, 1967; Phillips et al., 1965) concluded that in none of these studies has there been a significant correlation reported with any of a number of different tests of general intelligence. The only exception to this was a small correlation (0·26) found between the Nufferno Level Test (Furneaux, 1956) and the proverbs score. Brighter patients tend to use slightly more words.

Overinclusive Thinking and Paranoid Delusions

Two quite different attempts have been made to relate paranoid delusions to the breadth of conceptual categories. Silverman (1964b) following Bruner and Cameron, has suggested that paranoid individuals progressively decrease the breadth of any conceptual category that is painful. If it is a broad category, a wide range of perceptual input will be subsumed under this category, and in one sense it will be frequently reinforced. However, in order to reduce the extent to which painful categories are employed, Silverman argues that they become increasingly restricted, so that in the end, many incoming data remain unclassified. This serves the purpose of reducing the anxiety level of the patient.

On the face of it, this explanation seems to deny some of the main clinical features of paranoia. Paranoid delusions do *not* succeed in reducing anxiety. Rather than failing to classify relevant stimuli under their false beliefs (underinclusion), paranoid patients appear to interpret a wide range of irrelevant input in the light of their delusional system, thereby increasing and not decreasing their level of discomfort. Silverman (1964b) nevertheless has produced some evidence consistent with his position. Using the Pettigrew (1958) test, he found that a group of paranoid schizophrenics employed significantly more underinclusive categories than a group of non-paranoid schizophrenics.

Payne and associates (1964), on the other hand, formulated exactly the opposite explanation. They suggest that, in one sense, a delusion is by definition an unwarranted generalisation from the facts. Thus, a paranoid patient who hates one man, may incorporate all similar men into the hated category (e.g. all foreigners, all Jews). They therefore predicted that paranoid delusions would be associated with conceptual overinclusion.

The same workers (1964) tested their theory by using the Benjamin proverbs test. As predicted, they found that paranoid schizophrenics used more words per answer than did non-paranoid schizophrenics, a result they attributed to overinclusive thinking. This finding, again using the proverbs word count, was repeated by Lloyd (1967). It was not confirmed by Goldstein and Salzman (1965), but these investigators, who found no significant differences between their groups, relied on longhand recording rather than tape recording, and report an unusually small word count in all their groups. Other, rather inconsistent findings have been described above.

In order to rule out sample-to-sample variations, Payne (1971) combined the results obtained using the tests of Payne and Friedlander's standard battery of overinclusion tests from a number of different studies (Payne *et al.*, 1959; Payne, 1962; Payne and Hewlett, 1960; Hart, 1964; Payne *et al.*, 1963; Payne and Caird, 1967; Campbell, 1962; Payne *et al.*, 1963; Hawks, 1967; Kekes and Woods, unpublished; Payne and Van Allen, 1969). For the combined overinclusion score, data were available for a total of 38 paranoid schizophrenics, 55 non-paranoid schizophrenics, 20 acute undifferentiated schizophrenics, 17 chronic schizophrenics, 13 manics, 41 depressives, 7 organics, 12 alcoholics, 20 cases of character disorder, 55 neurotics, and 20 normals. Many more cases were available for some of the individual tests.

The pooled results are presented in Table 14.5. As can be seen, the difference between the groups for the combined score does not support the hypothesis, the very small difference between the means being in the direction opposite to prediction. The original findings (Payne *et al.*, 1964) were made on the proverbs test, and, as can be seen, when all the other

Table 14.5. Overinclusion Scores in Paranoid and Non-paranoid Schizophrenics

		Paranoid Schizophrenics	Non-paranoid Schizophrenics
Combined overinclusion score	Mean	8·70 (N = 38)	8·98 (N = 55)
	S.D.	3·74	4·07
Object classification test Non-A responses	Mean	6·31 (N = 48)	4·91 (N = 67)
	S.D.	7·20	4·31
Proverbs test Av. No. of words	Mean	27·30 (N = 55)	25·02 (N = 72)
	S.D.	18·79	25·54
Goldstein object sorting Av. No. objects per group	Mean	7·06 (N = 46)	9·80 (N = 65)
	S.D.	5·51	7·75

data are added to the initial groups, the difference almost entirely vanishes, suggesting that sample-to-sample variations were responsible for the conflicting results from this test described above.

These results are supported by a more detailed study carried out by Hawks and Payne (1971), who gave the standard battery of tests to a group of 54 psychiatric in-patients, 36 of whom were schizophrenic. A number of specific symptoms were independently rated by the doctor in charge of the case. Five specific delusional symptoms were rated, 'ideas of influence', 'ideas of reference', 'ideas of persecution', 'ideas of grandeur', and 'hypochondriacal delusions'. With the exception of 'hypochondriacal delusions', which correlated +0·26 with the combined overinclusion score (p < 0·05) the other four correlations were not significant.

Overinclusive Thinking among Different Psychiatric Groups

Table 14.6 shows the means and standard deviations found by pooling the available data for the combined overinclusion score for different psychiatric groups (Payne, 1971). A detailed inspection of the histograms for the combined overinclusion score suggested that almost no normal or neurotic subjects obtained a score greater than 12. There was, however, a distinct tendency for some neurotics to be more overinclusive than normals, although the size of the normal sample was small. The four groups that contained a sizeable proportion of patients obtaining a score greater than 12 were the paranoid schizophrenics, the nonparanoid schizophrenics, the acute undifferentiated schizophrenics, and the

Table 14.6. Combined Overinclusion Scores
For Different Psychiatric Groups

Group	Mean	S.D.	Number of cases
Paranoid schizophrenics	8·70	3·74	38
Nonparanoid schizophrenics	8·98	4·07	55
Acute undifferentiated schizophrenics	10·05	4·50	20
Chronic schizophrenics	5·33	2·43	17
Manics	10·92	4·62	13
Depressives	6·32	2·98	41
Organics	11·57	3·46	7
Alcoholics	8·00	2·86	12
Character disorders	7·10	2·95	20
Extraverted neurotics	8·58	3·46	12
Introverted neurotics	6·95	2·71	20
Combined neurotic group	7·29	2·93	55
Normals	4·90	1·58	20

manics. However, only about one quarter of the patients in these four groups obtained overinclusion scores over 12, clearly outside the neurotic range.

The distributions obtained from the individual tests were remarkably similar. A sizeable normal group ($N = 138$) was only available for the Object Classification test 'Non-A' score, but, again, the results for this test confirmed that a small proportion of neurotics is much more overinclusive than normal. Only one normal subject obtained more than 6 non-A responses, whereas 9 of the 76 neurotics obtained scores over 6, the highest neurotic score being 14. Again, about one third of each of the same three schizophrenic groups (paranoid, non-paranoid, acute undifferentiated) gave over 6 non-A responses. About one third of the manic group also gave over 6 non-A responses.

Prognostic Significance

There appears to be only one follow-up study of the prognostic significance of overinclusive thinking, using Payne and Friedlander's combined transformed overinclusion score. Payne (1968) reports a study in which 114 admissions to a mental hospital, the majority (88) of whom were later diagnosed as psychotic, and 67 of whom were finally diagnosed as schizophrenic, were given Payne and Friedlander's standard battery of overinclusion tests on admission, before medication had been started. The patients were followed up, on average, for a three-year period, at which time their level of adjustment was rated on a 9 point scale. This scale used relatively objective criteria. For example, score 1 (lowest level of adjustment) was defined as 'continuously in hospital since first seen', and score 9 (highest level of adjustment) was defined as 'no subsequent hospitalisation, at present at home, under no medication, working'.

There was a statistically significant tendency ($r = +0·329$) for patients who suffered from overinclusive thinking as measured on admission to have a better than average prognosis. The same patients also received tests of retardation on admission, and there was a significant tendency for those who were retarded to have a worse than average prognosis.

(*f*) EXPLANATIONS OF OVERINCLUSIVE THINKING

(*i*) The 'Defective Filter' Theory

Payne and colleagues (1959) suggested that over-inclusive thinking might be the result of a defect in some hypothetical 'filter' mechanism, which cuts out or inhibits those stimuli, both internal and external that are irrelevant to the task in hand to allow the most efficient processing of incoming information. If this explanation were correct, one would expect overinclusive thinking to be associated with an abnormal degree of distractibility under conditions in which irrelevant stimuli are present.

Payne and Caird (1967) carried out a study to investigate the relations between distractibility in a reaction time experiment, overinclusive thinking, and paranoid delusions. Fifteen paranoid schizophrenics, 15 non-paranoid schizophrenics and 15 non-schizophrenic in-patients were given a simple and a multiple choice auditory reaction time test in which the presence and the number of distracting stimuli were varied. The test stimuli were tones delivered through earphones, and the distracting stimuli, which the patients were told to ignore, were similar tones delivered from a loud-speaker. Over-inclusive thinking was measured by the proverbs test word count. As predicted, the reaction times of the paranoid patients were more affected by the distraction than were the reaction times of the non-schizophrenics. The distractibility of the non-paranoid schizophrenics was intermediate. As expected, there was a highly significant tendency for the paranoid schizophrenics to be more overinclusive than the non-paranoid schizophrenics or non-schizophrenics. Also as expected, there were highly significant correlations between the proverbs test word count score, and reaction time measured under conditions of distractibility.

These results appeared to be consistent with the 'defective filter' theory of overinclusive thinking. However, they are not consistent with the studies of distractibility reviewed above. In these studies, it was the chronic, hebephrenic, or process schizophrenics who were distractible. These results are, of course, not completely conclusive in so far as the relationship between distractibility and overinclusive thinking was not directly studied.

A direct test of the 'defective filter' hypothesis was carried out by Payne et al. (1970). They obtained a group of 12 schizophrenics who were unanimously judged by 3 independent raters to be suffering from overinclusive thinking in a clinical interview on the basis of carefully delineated criteria. These were matched in age, vocabulary, education, socio-economic level, and length of hospitalisation with 12 schizophrenics unanimously judged not to be suffering from overinclusive thinking by the same three raters, and a group of 12 normal controls. Payne et al. assessed the capacity of the subjects to 'filter' out irrelevant information by the same technique as that used by Broadbent, who originated the notion of a central 'filter', namely, dichotic listening. The subjects took part in two experiments in which they were required to 'shadow' (repeat simultaneously) verbal material presented through one of a pair of earphones, while being distracted by verbal material presented through the other earphone at exactly the same time. Word lists were used in the first experiment, and prose passages in the second. Measures of the increase in shadowing errors induced by the distraction, the 'interpenetration' of the distracting material, and the later recall or recognition of the distracting material were obtained. All these measures of the inability to 'filter' were shown to intercorrelate significantly. The subjects were also given Payne and Friedlander's standard set of overinclusion tests, which were also found to intercorrelate highly. However, there was no significant correlation between the combined over-inclusion score, and a combined score representing the inability to filter.

It must be concluded that, plausible though the 'defective filter' explanation of overinclusive thinking sounds, experiments have not supported it.

(ii) The 'Stimulus Generalisation' Hypothesis

Mednick (1955, 1958) was the first to advance the hypothesis that thought disorder in schizophrenia might be the result of an unusual amount of stimulus generalisation (i.e. a flat stimulus generalisation gradient). He argued that this might be the result of a very high level of anxiety, which characterises early acute schizophrenics.

Payne (1961) suggested that such a theory seemed especially relevant to overinclusive thinking in particular. The inability to exclude irrelevant thoughts or perceptions, could, in effect, be due to an inability to discriminate between somewhat similar stimuli. Payne predicted that an unusual amount of stimulus generalisation should be found among paranoid patients. Mednick has measured stimulus generalisation by means of a technique developed by Brown et al. (1951). The subject is seated in front of a row of lights, and is required to lift his finger from a key as quickly as possible whenever the centre light goes on (none of the other lights function during this training period). In a second period, the lights begin to go on at random. The measure of stimulus generalisation is the frequency with which the peripheral, irrelevant lights evoke a response, and the distance between the centre light and the most distant light reacted to.

Ralph (1968) tested this hypothesis with a group of chronic process schizophrenics, and found evidence in this particular group for an abnormal amount of stimulus generalisation. However, he found no differences between the paranoid and the non-paranoid patients, contrary to Payne's prediction.

There appear to have been only two studies directly investigating the relationships between overinclusive thinking stimulus generalisation and anxiety. May (1966) tested 50 schizophrenic patients with the Taylor Manifest Anxiety Scale, and Payne and Friedlander's standard battery of overinclusion tests. He found no significant correlation between any of the overinclusion tests and the Taylor scale, giving no support to the hypothesis. Watson (1967) gave Mednick's stimulus generalisation test to 100 male schizophrenics, who were also given the Epstein overinclusion test, the proverbs (word count) test, and the Goldstein Object Sorting 'Handing Over' Test. However, none of these measures correlated significantly with the two measures of stimulus generalisation obtained.

As Payne (1970) has pointed out, post hoc, it is perhaps not surprising that this hypothesis has not been supported. Presumably, subjects make errors in the Mednick experiment because they cannot discriminate between the lights. However, it is unlikely that subjects group together a large number of objects on the object sorting test (forming an overinclusive concept) simply because they cannot tell the objects apart. In any event, there is no evidence that overinclusive thinking can be explained in terms of stimulus generalisation.

(iii) The 'Defective Discrimination Learning' Hypothesis

Payne and colleagues (1959) also attempted to explain overinclusive concept formation as the result of defective discrimination learning. They argue:

'When a child first hears a word in a certain context, the word is associated with the entire situation (stimulus compound). As the word is heard again and again, only certain aspects of the stimulus compound are reinforced. Gradually the extraneous elements cease to evoke the response (the word), having become 'inhibited' through lack of "reinforcement". This 'inhibition' is in some sense an active process, as it suppresses a response which was formerly evoked by the stimulus. "Overinclusive thinking" may be the result of a disorder of the process whereby "inhibition" is built up to "circumscribe" and "define" the learned response (the word or "concept").'

This hypothesis led to the prediction that schizophrenics should tend not to build up a 'set', and the results obtained by Payne *et al.* and by Payne and Hewlett (1960), which have been described above, seemed to support the hypothesis. However, two more direct tests of the hypothesis have been carried out more recently.

Payne and Van Allen (1969) made use of two specially developed 'concept attainment' tests. The first consisted of a set of 30 cards which could be divided into three groups, 'A', 'AB', and 'B', of ten cards each. The cards in group 'A' depicted different types of fruit. The cards in group 'AB' depicted other types of food, while the cards in group 'B' depicted household items other than food. Groups A and AB shared the property of being edible. The second test also consisted of 30 cards, 10 in each group. In this test, group A depicted abstract figures with straight edges and hatched interiors. Group AB depicted figures with straight edges, but with no cross hatching, or figures with curved edges and cross hatching. Group B had figures with curved edges and no cross hatching. Thus, groups A and AB shared one of the two properties that defined group A.

In each part of the experiment, the subjects were given the deck of 30 cards randomly arranged, and were told merely to sort them into two piles. After each card was sorted, the subject was merely told 'right' or 'wrong'. The subjects continued until all 30 cards could be sorted consecutively correctly, or until the deck had been sorted 4 times. They were told 'right' whenever 'A' cards were sorted into pile 1, or 'AB' or 'B' cards were sorted into pile 2. It was predicted that, because of defective discrimination learning, overinclusive subjects would continue to mis-sort the AB cards into pile 1 because of their similarities, and would build up an overinclusive concept. These 'AB' errors represented the critical score derived from the experiments.

Payne and Van Allen tested 19 newly admitted psychiatric in-patients who showed overinclusive thinking on the Payne Object Classification Test

'Non-A' score, and 24 patients matched for age, IQ, and abstraction ability who were not overinclusive on this score. There were no significant differences between the groups in the number of AB errors in either experiment, nor were the mean differences even in the expected direction. The groups did not differ with respect to 'B' or 'A' errors. In short, overinclusive patients were just as quick at learning the concepts as were non-overinclusive patients, and did not learn overinclusive concepts.

A more elaborate experiment was carried out by Hawks and Payne (1972). Three types of concept identification problems were used, one presenting stimuli differing along one relevant and one irrelevant dimension, one presenting stimuli differing along one relevant and two irrelevant dimensions, and one presenting stimuli differing along two relevant and one irrelevant dimensions. Thirty-six schizophrenic, 18 non-schizophrenic psychiatric controls, and 18 normal controls, took part in the concept identification experiment, and were also given Payne and Friedlander's standard battery of overinclusion tests. It was anticipated that the overinclusive subjects would make more errors when more irrelevant dimensions were present, and take longer to learn the concept. However, there were no significant correlation coefficients between the number of trials needed to attain the concept, and the overinclusion score in any of the three types of problem. Two of the three error scores correlated with the overinclusion score at the 5 per cent level, but the values were so low (0·25 and 0·27 respectively) that the hypothesis can hardly be said to have received very strong support.

At present, therefore, there is no clear evidence that overinclusive thinking is the result of a specific defect in discrimination learning.

(g) SUMMARY AND CONCLUSIONS

It must he concluded that in spite of a very considerable amount of research, overinclusive thinking remains a somewhat elusive concept. While Payne and Friedlander's battery of three tests appear to be reliable, they seem to intercorrelate significantly only when given to groups that include patients who are clearly thought disordered by clinical criteria. It is by no means certain that all the other tests of overinclusive thinking measure the same dysfunction. The evidence, unsatisfactory though it is, suggests that overinclusive thinking, at least as measured by a score that averages the performance on three tests, and therefore is less likely to be affected by some specific factor, is a relatively uncommon disorder. It seems to occur in about one third of patients diagnosed as having acute schizophrenia. However, in spite of some promising earlier results that appeared plausible, there is no evidence that it is especially associated with delusional thinking. It appears to occur equally frequently among manic patients as it does among acute schizophrenics. Hawks and Payne (1971) found that it tended to be associated with talkativeness, overactivity, motor speed, overt hostility, and verbal responsiveness. Such patients also tend to be rated 'thought disordered' by their doctors.

Whether overinclusive thinking occurs among chronic schizophrenics is less certain. Overinclusion on Chapman's sorting test not only characterised chronic schizophrenics, but was found to respond to phenothiazine medication. Overinclusive thinking on Payne and Friedlander's tests, on the other hand, did not characterise chronic schizophrenics, and was not found to respond to phenothiazine medication (Payne et al., 1963). However, it is not certain that these tests measure the same thing.

There is no evidence that overinclusive thinking occurs among depressed patients. It does, however, seem to characterise some neurotic patients, and curiously enough, has been reported among the close relatives of schizophrenic patients. This suggests that this type of conceptual thinking could be partly learned at an early age. Bauman and Murray also found no difficulty in finding overinclusive individuals among the 'normal' staff members of a mental hospital.

The prognosis for patients suffering from overinclusive thinking is better than average. However, no satisfactory explanation of it has yet been advanced, and the several hypotheses that have been put forward to explain it have not been supported. One suggestive finding was reported by Payne (1966), who found that, in a small pilot study, a group of medical students were more overinclusive on a single standard test when tested under the effects of LSD, although many were too uncooperative under LSD to attend to the test. It is conceivable that, in view of some of the other associated symptoms (overactivity, talkativeness, manic behaviour) overinclusive thinking may ultimately be found to be the accompaniment of some relatively non-permanent toxic state.

3. Personal Construct Theory

A different approach to the problem of schizophrenic thought disorder has been made by Bannister (1960). Bannister has described schizophrenic thought disorder in terms of Kelly's Personal Construct theory. A construct can be regarded as a kind of hypothesis whereby individuals learn to predict the behaviour of others. It is a way of classifying one's experience. As Bannister (1960) writes, 'To construe a business as profitable or a woman as affectionate is to predict future events in relation to the elements construed and predictions are inevitably validated or invalidated... (by subsequent events)'.

Kelly has developed the Repertory Grid technique as a method of assessing the way in which constructs are employed. Subjects are asked to rate a number of people known to them (e.g. mother, father, close friend) on a number of different characteristics. '...if a subject nominates 40 people known personally to him, and categorises each in turn as Moral (emergent pole) or Not Moral (implicit pole) and Honest or Not Honest, and we find that the 20 designated as Honest are also designated as Moral, and the 20 designated as Not Honest are designated as Not Moral, then we can infer a high positive relationship (which can be measured in terms of its binomial probability) between the concepts Honest and Moral.' These constellations of concept ratings of groups of people are personal constructs. Constructs are formed when people behave consistently with respect to a number of characteristics. Constructs break down when the experience of an individual invalidates such interrelationships. Bannister's view is that in the early environment of the schizophrenic, people behave so inconsistently that normally related characteristics (e.g. 'friendly', 'good') are no longer found to cohere. Thus, schizophrenics on this test show a weakening of the relationship between normally associated ratings.

In a series of experiments Bannister (1960, 1962) found evidence for such a weakening of the relations between such ratings in schizophrenic subjects. As a further test of this hypothesis, Bannister (1960, 1965) attempted to produce this type of 'disassociative' thought disorder in normal subjects by asking them to rate ten photographs of people on a number of characteristics. This experiment was repeated on a number of days, but the subjects were told each day that their ratings were correct of some pictures, and of others that their ratings were incorrect. It was predicted that this consistent invalidation of the latter set of constructs (which hypothetically mimics the early experience of schizophrenics) would lead to a breakdown of the construct hierarchies (i.e. characteristics which formerly cohered would no longer cohere). These experiments supported this hypothesis.

There is some evidence that loosening of constructs is associated with thought disorder as clinically rated (Bannister and Fransella, 1966), and as assessed by a variety of cognitive tests (Al-Issa and Robertson, 1964). There is also evidence that the loosening of constructs in schizophrenics applies more to constructs about people than it does to constructs about inanimate objects, as one might expect if it were associated with a disturbed family background (Bannister and Salmon, 1966; Salmon et al., 1967).

There have been very few investigations into the relationship between Bannister and Fransella's measure of the loosening of constructs and other measures of thought disorder. Foulds and associates (1969), studying a group of 48 schizophrenics found that the Bannister-Fransella test was not significantly correlated with tests of psychomotor speed. This result was confirmed by Presley (1969) who tested a group of acute schizophrenics with a different battery of psychomotor speed tests. Foulds et al. also found the Bannister-Fransella test unrelated to Payne and Friedlander's overinclusion tests. They did, however, find that it was the non-paranoid rather than the paranoid schizophrenics who gave evidence of loosening of constructs, although there were no differences in this respect between chronic and acute schizophrenics.

RIGIDITY

There is some evidence (Payne, 1960) that two relatively independent kinds of mental rigidity are relevant to problem solving. One, 'adaptive' rigidity is the inability to change a set in order to meet the requirements imposed by changing problems. The other is the opposite of 'spontaneous flexibility', or the ability to produce a diversity of ideas in a problem-solving situation. Only 'adaptive rigidity' appears to have been studied in psychiatric subjects, although measures of the tendency to produce unusual responses, which will be discussed below, are similar to some tests of 'spontaneous flexibility'.

As has been seen, the results obtained using the Luchin's test of 'Einstellung' rigidity with acute schizophrenic patients have produced conflicting results.

All the other investigators of 'adaptive rigidity' in schizophrenics have used different techniques and have investigated chronic rather than acute schizophrenics.

Weiss and Nordtvedt (1964), using a perceptual task, found that schizophrenics were more rigid than normals, in the sense that they developed a set in conditions in which normals did not. Kristofferson (1967) used a reaction time task in which attention had to be switched from an auditory to a visual stimulus. She found that the reaction times of schizophrenics were more affected by the switch than the reaction times of normal subjects, suggesting an abnormal degree of rigidity in this situation. This finding is, in general, consistent with other similar studies reviewed by Kristofferson.

Payne (1960), reviewing the literature on perceptual tests of rigidity, concluded that normals tend to become more rigid when tested under stress, and suggested that 'adaptive rigidity' could be associated with high drive because it facilitates the learning of a 'set'. However, there appear to be no studies of the relation between 'adaptive rigidity' and neurotic behaviour in psychiatric groups.

Goldstein suggested that rigidity was one aspect of concrete behaviour. While there is still no clear evidence that this is so, it is a reasonable hypothesis in view of the characteristics of the concrete verbal behaviour of some schizophrenics which have been discussed above in detail. It is likely, therefore, that 'adaptive rigidity' will be found to be especially characteristic of the performance of process and chronic schizophrenic patients.

ERROR: THE TENDENCY TO PRODUCE UNUSUAL RESPONSES

Giving a wrong answer in a cognitive test in the mistaken belief that it is right is the most important single determinant of the score on untimed intelligence tests. Nevertheless, very little is known about the causes of errors in problem solving, and the nature of the checking process whereby a possible solution is verified.

Furneaux (1961) has found that there is a very low correlation between error and speed in normal people, although his standard measure of accuracy is obtained from test items that are at a relatively low level of difficulty. It would seem probable that errors can have many causes, including the inaccurate perception of the data of the problem, incorrect generalisations from the data due to conceptual difficulties and misunderstanding of the data because of an idiosyncratic use of words. One factor is clearly the complexity of the problem. Complex problems require more separate items of information to be held in mind and manipulated and it is not surprising that individuals with a larger immediate memory span make fewer errors. One would expect slow thinkers to be handicapped because they must hold information in temporary store for longer periods of time, and the probability becomes greater that relevant information will be forgotten before the problem is solved.

There is evidence that on such tests as the Porteus Mazes, 'delinquent' children make an abnormally large number of 'impulsive' errors which are due to disobeying the instructions not to cross lines or enter blind alleys in tracing the mazes (Payne, 1960). There is also evidence that on the Nufferno speed and level tests, extraverts make more errors than introverts, but whether this represents the 'careless-ness' of insufficient checking, or some 'cognitive' difference such as a smaller memory span, it is not possible to say.

There is, similarly, evidence that psychotic patients make more errors than normals on the Nufferno test at any given difficulty level (Payne, 1960).

In one sense, however, an error can be regarded as an unusual, or a statistically infrequent response to a given stimulus situation, and it has been pointed out frequently that schizophrenic responses in a variety of situations tend to be unusual. It has already been seen that several of the measures used to define 'overinclusive thinking' are in fact measures of unusual responses (the 'Non-A' response score on the Object Classification Test, the 'C' and 'D' responses on the Shaw Test, White's (1949 test).

Unusual Responses on the Goldstein Object Sorting Test

McGaughran (1954) suggested that a second, independent dimension of sorting performance on the Goldstein test is the 'public-private' classifica-tion, the term 'public' referring to usual, and the term 'private' referring to unusual responses. The results obtained suggest that chronic paranoid schizophrenics tend to produce more 'private' responses than either normals or brain-damaged patients (McGaughran and Moran, 1956, 1957; Leventhal et al., 1959). Undifferentiated schizo-phrenics have also been reported to produce more unusual sortings than neurotics (Silverman and Silverman, 1962; Payne and Hewlett, 1960). The only failure to find such differences on this test was reported by Sturm (1964) who was unable to differ-entiate significantly between groups of brain-damaged patients, tubercular patients, process schizophrenics, and reactive schizophrenics.

Unusual Responses to Proverbs

In addition to reporting 'abstract' or 'concrete' responses, several investigators have found responses to the proverbs test which could not be placed in either category. These responses are often labelled 'autistic'. While some workers have suggested that these responses might be related to overinclusive thinking (Shimkunas et al., 1967), correlations with other measures of overinclusive concept formation have not been reported. There is some evidence (Brattemo, 1965) that these kinds of responses diminish among schizophrenics following pheno-thiazine treatment, although properly controlled studies are lacking.

Unusual Responses to Other Stimuli

One technique that has often been used is to present subjects with some barely recognisable perceptual material and ask them to say what it is.

Adams and Berg (1961) made use of fifty tape-recorded sounds that were relatively meaningless, such as clicks, pure tones, chords, and so on, and asked subjects to rate how much they liked them. Schizophrenics produced more deviant ratings than normals. Another auditory technique that has been used is the 'tautophone' (Shakow et al., 1966) which was originally called the 'verbal summator' by Skinner. It consists of a recording of spoken vowel combinations that are in fact meaningless. The subjects are told that it is a record of a man who does not speak clearly, and are asked what he is saying. The evidence suggests that schizophrenics as a group tend to give more unusual interpretations than do normal subjects.

Unusual Responses on the Word Association Test

A somewhat similar technique that has been used for many years is the word association test. Pavy (1968) has recently reviewed the literature in this area, and concluded that as a group, schizophrenics produce unusual associations. There is some sugges-tion that process schizophrenics give more unusual responses than reactive schizophrenics (Dokecki et al., 1968), that chronic schizophrenics give more unusual responses than acute schizophrenics (Higgins, 1968) and that the tendency of chronic schizophrenics to give unusual responses cannot be altered by reinforcing more usual associations (Frankel and Buchwald, 1969).

Unusual Responses Assessed by the 'Cloze' Technique

Pavy (1968) gave a group of schizophrenics passages with words deleted, and asked them to fill in the missing words. He found that, perhaps surprisingly, reactive schizophrenics made more errors than process schizophrenics, who were normal in this respect. Non-paranoid schizophrenics made more errors than paranoid schizophrenics, but paranoid schizophrenics made more errors than a normal control group.

The Application of Silverman's Theory to Explain Errors

Livingston and Blum (1968) developed a verbal reasoning test, similar to the typical 'letter series' tests of general intelligence. Series of words were read to the subjects, who were asked to say what the next word should be. A typical item was: 'shovel dig chair sit pen write knife . . .'. Some series were long (7 words in length) and some were short (3 words long). In addition to the 'constrained' series, which could be completed logically, some series were in fact random and had no logical answer.

It was argued that two factors should be relevant to such a task. The first was breadth of scanning. Broad scanners should, in general, do better, since they should apprehend more data on which to base their answer. However, this should not be an advantage on the short series. The second factor was 'field articulation', which in this context was interpreted as the ability to abstract the principle underlying the series. It was found that, in general, reactive schizophrenics made more errors than normals or process schizophrenics, a finding explained in terms of their poor field articulation. Non-paranoid schizophrenics made more errors than paranoid schizophrenics, a finding that was also expected because of the hypothesised broader scanning in the paranoid group, although, unexpectedly, the paranoid patients were still less accurate than the normal controls. Also unexpectedly, the length of the series made no significant difference.

1. High Drive and Unusual Responses

It is probable that there is a group of schizophrenic patients who consistently produce unusual responses in a variety of different situations. This hypothesis nevertheless needs to be confirmed, for there appear to be no studies of the intercorrelations in psychiatric groups among the different measures of unusual response tendency that have been described. However, there is a wealth of clinical observation that suggests that some schizophrenic patients consistently have unusual thoughts and unusual responses in normal situations. One of the most widely investigated explanations of this type of schizophrenic thought disorder is that put forward by Mednick (1958).

Mednick argues that acutely disturbed schizophrenics are extremely anxious, and that this anxiety is evoked by a wide range of normal stimuli. This very high anxiety drive level has the effect of raising the response strengths of all the different competing responses to a particular stimulus (following Hull). A number of the less probable responses, whose response strengths are normally below the response threshold, become possible because their response strengths are now above the response threshold. By chance, occasionally, one of these very improbable responses occurs to a particular stimulus in the highly anxious person. When it does, Mednick argues, it receives an increment of reinforcement. This is because all the usual responses (thoughts or actions) have come to evoke anxiety. However, the unusual response does not. Accordingly, the acute schizophrenic gradually learns to produce unusual thoughts and behaviour as a means of reducing his anxiety. The end result is the 'affectless', 'flat' schizophrenic who is not anxious, but whose most probable responses are all bizarre.

Mednick tested this theory by measuring a somewhat different theoretical consequence of high drive, stimulus generalisation. A more direct test of the hypothesis, it might be argued, would have been to measure response generalisation, since it is this that causes unusual responses to appear in the early schizophrenic.

Mednick and his associates have measured stimulus generalisation in several ways. The reaction time test involving a row of peripheral distraction lights has already been described, and, although Mednick (1955) found that a group of schizophrenics showed more generalisation on this test than a group of normals or a group of brain-damaged patients, this study is open to criticism on the grounds that such variables as the tendency to produce random errors and age were uncontrolled. It is also curious that the schizophrenics in this sample were chronic, and presumably no longer highly anxious. In a subsequent study, Gaines et al. (1963) made use of a different procedure. Subjects were trained to respond to a tone of 2·25 seconds duration, and then tested on tones of a different duration (2·50 seconds and 3 seconds) to see how much generalisation occurred. As expected, acute schizophrenics showed more stimulus generalisation than normals, but chronics did not. In another study, Mednick (1966) investigated the generalisation of a GSR response which had been conditioned to a specific tone and found that the children of schizophrenics showed more generalisation than normal children. Buss and Daniell (1967) carried out a stimulus generalisation experiment in which the stimuli were lines of different lengths. They found no difference in stimulus generalisation gradient between chronic schizophrenics and normals, as might be predicted, but no acute patients were tested for comparison.

Ralph (1968) has recently reviewed the literature in this area. He pointed out that in an earlier 1965 review, Lang and Buss concluded that there was no evidence for increased stimulus generalisation in schizophrenia. However, Ralph drew attention to three more recent studies which had found significant differences, and concluded that it was still an open question as to whether any specific schizophrenic group has an unusual stimulus generalisation gradient. Ralph himself found evidence for an unusual amount of stimulus generalisation among a group of chronic, process schizophrenics.

Another relevant question is whether or not a high level of anxiety is in fact associated with an abnormally broad (or flat) stimulus generalisation gradient. Murray (1969) tested 90 normal male subjects and 90 normal female subjects, and found no evidence that chronic anxiety, as measured by the Taylor Manifest Anxiety Scale, or experimentally induced anxiety produced a significant amount of stimulus generalisation. Brilliant (1968) similarly found no evidence that stimulus generalisation was related to anxiety level in 80 psychiatric patients.

It can, however, be argued that all these stimulus generalisation experiments are irrelevant. The theory as formulated, suggests that the high level of (anxiety) drive energises more *responses*, producing more response competition. There is no real reason for supposing that it would necessarily have any effect on stimulus generalisation.

In a more relevant test of the theory, Higgins *et al.* (1966) found that process schizophrenics in a learning experiment retained remote associations better than reactive schizophrenics, a result thought to confirm the hypothesis.

Spence and Lair (1964) investigated another hypothetical effect of high drive on the rote learning of schizophrenics, associative interference, but found no support for Mednick's theory.

Streiner (1969) predicted on the basis of Mednick's theory that reactive schizophrenics should perform better than normals or process schizophrenics on an easy (but not on a difficult) paired associate learning task because of their high level of drive. The prediction was not confirmed. There were no differences between a group of process and a group of reactive schizophrenics, both of whom performed significantly poorer than the normal control group.

Kapche (1969) gave a chronic schizophrenic and a normal group three lists of paired associates to learn. On the first list there was a minimal association between the stimulus and the correct response. On the other two lists, some of the stimulus words had a weak association value with some of the incorrect stimulus words. It was predicted that this would make the schizophrenic group learn less easily

because of the response competition suggested by Mednick's theory. In fact, contrary to prediction, the normal subjects and the schizophrenics were equally affected by response competition, although the schizophrenic performance was generally poorer on all lists. Kapche concluded that the results were not consistent with Mednick's theory. However, it is not certain that Mednick's theory would predict response competition due to high drive in a chronic schizophrenic group (as contrasted to an acute group).

It would appear that the experimental evidence in support of Mednick's theory is still inconclusive.

Broen and Storms (1966; Broen, 1966, 1968) have suggested an elaboration of Mednick's theory that avoids most of the theoretical difficulties of his original formulation. They believe that there is a 'ceiling' to the possible strength of any response. When high drive increases the strength of a less probable competing response, if the dominant response is already at the ceiling, the difference between the strengths (probability of evocation) of the two responses will diminish, and the competing response will become *more likely* to occur. Thus, high drive not only makes more responses possible, because unlikely responses become suprathreshold, but it also alters the probability of evocation of all the responses in the response hierarchy, making the probabilities of all the alternatives more nearly the same. Schizophrenics, they postulate, have a lower response strength ceiling than normal people. Thus, their response hierarchies are more susceptible to disruption by high levels of anxiety. In this way, they explain the apparent frequency with which uncommon responses seem to occur in highly anxious early schizophrenics.

Broen (1968) has elaborated this hypothesis in considerable detail, and is able to account for a great many of the experimental findings in schizophrenia.

He suggests that early (acute) schizophrenics who are in a high state of arousal, have an abnormally large number of competing responses to the normal range of stimuli. He argues that in a number of the experimental situations that have been discussed above, the large number of unusual responses produced in some of the 'overinclusion tests' (e.g. the Payne Object Classification Test) are the result of this abnormal response competition, rather than some 'defective filter' which allows too many stimuli to impinge on consciousness. It is this abnormal response competition, he argues, that gives the impression that early schizophrenics suffer from 'information overload'. 'Response overload' would be a more accurate descriptive term. Because this response generalisation is so disruptive of their behaviour, he argues that schizophrenics learn to restrict the range of their attention. This accounts for the reduction of scanning among chronic schizophrenics, which does not necessarily reduce their basic level of anxiety; it merely allows them to adjust better to their surroundings. According to Broen's hypothesis, process schizophrenics, who are like chronic schizophrenics in these respects (they appear 'concrete' and seem to have reduced their scanning) might be regarded as reactive schizophrenics in a later stage of adjustment to their psychosis.

Broen and associates (1963) produced evidence supporting this hypothesis. The drive level of two samples of psychiatric patients was increased by having them grip a hand dynamometer during a discrimination task involving a response to different shades of grey. Under these conditions, the appropriate (strongest) responses occurred less frequently. Storms *et al.* (1967) also found that 40 acute schizophrenics gave more uncommon associations to words than normals or neurotics. All subjects gave more uncommon associations to anxiety words than to neutral words. This tendency was exacerbated in the schizophrenic group by the stress of time pressure, but time pressure had the opposite effect on the neurotics. This result is held to support the view that the schizophrenic has a lower response strength ceiling than the neurotic or the normal, so that his response strength hierarchy is more susceptible to disruption by stress. However, why stress should have the opposite effect on neurotics is not clear.

2. Unusual Responses, High Drive, and Paranoid Delusions

As has been seen, the formation of paranoid delusions cannot be explained as being the result of overinclusive thinking. Storms and Broen's hypothesis offers an alternative explanation. Occasionally, an improbable response to a situation might not only alleviate anxiety, but might also receive more specific reinforcement. Supposing, for instance, an anxious person draws the improbable (and incorrect) conclusion that he is hated by an associate, he might also act on this conclusion by returning the believed aggression. Once he is aggressive himself, however, he is likely to evoke hostility in return, thus reinforcing his initially unlikely hypothesis. Certainly, one characteristic of deluded patients is that they entertain possible interpretations of situations that do not occur to normal people. They are also usually willing to concede that their paranoid interpretation is only one of a number of possible alternative interpreta-

tions, which they can specify if required. It may not be the strength with which a delusional idea is held that characterises the early paranoid patient, so much as the fact that it is held at all under the circumstances. This hypothesis also suggests that the strength with which delusional beliefs are held only gradually increases, as the behaviour of the deluded person produces a consistent pattern of reinforcement from his environment. A similar account of the development of delusions has also been put forward by Storms and Broen (1969).

A study by Sheppard and colleagues (1969) provides some support for this theory, in so far as they found evidence among narcotic users, that individuals high on the MMPI paranoia scale made more unexpected errors than other narcotic users on the Matrices Test.

A much larger scale study consistent with this theoretical formulation was carried out by Claridge (1967). Claridge studied a group of reactive and a group of process schizophrenics on a number of different measures. He found that reactive schizophrenics tended to give a large number of unusual responses on the Payne Object Classification test, they tended to have more paranoid delusions, they tended to be extraverted rather than introverted, they tended to be active rather than withdrawn, they tended to have mood swings, and they tended to have a good prognosis. They also gave evidence of having an unusually high level of cortical arousal, which would be consistent with the hypothesis that it is a high anxiety level that disrupts the response hierarchies of reactive schizophrenic patients, producing unusual responses which can lead to the formation of delusions. Claridge assessed arousal level by means of the sedation threshold, and the duration of the afterimage produced by the Archimedes Spiral Test (a short afterimage suggests quick recovery from fatigue and high cortical arousal). Process schizophrenics were opposite on all these characteristics, and gave evidence of an unusually low level of cortical arousal.

These findings are consistent with several other studies. Ward and Carlson (1966) also found that reactive schizophrenics were characterised by a high level of GSR responsiveness, while process schizophrenics were characterised by a low level. Stern and co-workers (1965) found that a low level of autonomic responsiveness is a poor prognostic sign. Goldstein and associates (1968), evaluating 98 schizophrenics, found that reactive (good premorbid) schizophrenics are evenly distributed between paranoid and non-paranoid, whereas process schizophrenics are predominantly non-paranoid. As a group, they found that paranoid schizophrenics are predominantly reactive.

It is possible, then, to speculate that the tendency to produce unusual responses, which often leads to the formation of paranoid delusions, is the result of the high level of anxiety, and its resultant cortical arousal, which characterises reactive schizophrenics. These patients have a better than average prognosis.

There is also evidence, however, that many chronic schizophrenics also have a very high level of cortical arousal. Venables and his colleagues (Venables, 1960, 1963a, 1963b, 1963c, 1964, 1966a, 1966b, 1967; Venables and Wing, 1962) have produced a good deal of evidence that among chronic non-paranoid schizophrenic patients, it is those who are behaviourally withdrawn who show signs of a high level of arousal, as measured by the 'two flash' or 'two click' fusion threshold. Such chronic patients also have a high level of autonomic arousal as assessed by the GSR basal level, although Lykken and Maley (1968), unlike Venables, found no correlation between two flash threshold and skin potential in a chronic schizophrenic group. Venables (1963) also found that these patients were not distractible, a characteristic of reactive rather than process schizophrenics. In spite of the high basal level of autonomic arousal that characterises this group of chronic schizophrenics, as assessed by GSR baseline level, and GSR spontaneous fluctuations, the evidence suggests that such chronic patients actually show *less* specific GSR responsiveness to specific stimuli (Bernstein, 1970). This could possibly be some kind of 'protective inhibition' phenomenon, as the opposite is true in normal people, that is to say, among normal people, those who have a higher basal arousal level, are also more reactive to specific stimuli (Katkin and McCubbin, 1969).

3. Summary and Conclusions

It is rather difficult to integrate all these somewhat conflicting results into a single hypothesis. However, they could suggest that reactive schizophrenics are characterised by a high level of anxiety, which leads to the production of unusual responses. Among some reactive schizophrenics, this leads to the formation of paranoid delusions, but those patients who develop delusions tend not to become chronic, and, presumably have a better prognosis. Those reactive schizophrenics who do not develop delusions tend to become chronic, but when they do so, they typically become withdrawn. They nevertheless remain in a high state of cortical arousal. It is almost as if none of the plethora of competing responses has proven of adaptive value and has not become reinforced, so that they are left in a high state of arousal, with no adaptive behaviour, but a number of competing response tendencies. Nevertheless, they still show characteristics of reactive schizophrenia; for example they can concentrate their attention when the need arises (Venables, 1963). This suggests that in some way, the development of delusions by reactive schizophrenics has some adaptive value, a view put forward by Storms and Broen (1969). It is almost as if the development of some very strong (if incorrect) response tendency prevents the complete disruption of behaviour by the large number of competing responses. Storms and Broen argue that this suggests the presence of a higher response strength ceiling among paranoid patients.

SPEED: ABNORMAL RETARDATION

Individual differences in the speed of motor and cognitive processes have been investigated for as long as psychology has been a science, and many have considered that the speed of carrying out even the simplest decision may reflect some fundamental property of the central nervous system.

One of the most interesting studies in this area is still that carried out by Furneaux (1956a, 1956b). Furneaux demonstrated that on the Thurstone letter-series test of general intelligence, problem-solving speed is one of the major determinants of final score, whether a timed or untimed (as far as the subjects are aware) version of the test is used. In Furneaux's experiments, each test item was timed individually, and incorrect or abandoned items were not scored. Furneaux found that in normal people there is a linear relation between the logarithm of the solution time and the difficulty level of an item. Furthermore, the slope of this linear function is the same from one person to another, people differing only with respect to the origin. This suggests that speed may be a basic characteristic of an individual's problem solving, and that it represents the time taken to carry out a single operation of some 'mental search' process. Difficulty refers to the number of such 'searches' a problem requires, and increases exponentially with problem complexity.

There is some evidence (Payne, 1960) that in normal people, speed may depend largely on the kind of task involved. However, there is a large body of evidence suggesting that nearly every form of mental illness is accompanied by a degree of general psychomotor retardation. Some psychotic patients are so slow that the range of speed scores in any mixed psychiatric group is very broad. A wide range of speed tests, varying all the way from the speed of such simple tasks as counting or writing ones own name, to the speed of solving Nufferno intelligence test items has been found to intercorrelate highly in such abnormal populations (Shapiro and Nelson, 1955; Payne and Hewlett, 1960). This suggests the presence of at least one pathological factor of such importance that its presence overshadows the comparatively small differences in speed due to the specific nature of the individual task.

One of the earlier investigators to draw attention to the importance of extreme slowness in mental illness was Harriet Babcock. Indeed, Babcock and Levy's (1940) test battery for assessing intellectual efficiency (deterioration) in psychosis is largely made up of a variety of tests of mental and motor speed. The work using the Babcock speed tests, which has been reviewed by Payne (1960), suggests that psychomotor speed is a relatively sensitive barometer of the severity of the mental illness. Thus, a number of studies suggest that neurotic patients, on average, are slightly retarded, both depressive *and* manic patients are very retarded, and, on average, schizophrenics are as retarded as depressives. Although depressed patients and schizophrenics can be distinguished by some tests of thought disorder, both groups share the characteristic of retardation (Payne and Hewlett, 1960).

As a group, schizophrenics are, however, extremely heterogeneous on tests of retardation, as in most things, some being nearly as fast as normals, but some being much slower than the slowest depressed patient. The evidence suggests that, on the whole, it is those who are diagnosed as hebephrenic or catatonic who tend to be among the slowest.

Most studies suggest that while acute schizophrenics are very variable in their speed of performance, chronic schizophrenics tend to be more consistently severely retarded (Payne, 1960; King, 1967, 1969; Pugh, 1968). The evidence also tends to suggest that process schizophrenics may be slower than reactive schizophrenics (Ward and Carlson, 1966; Claridge, 1967) although not all studies report significant differences (Foulds et al., 1969).

The evidence suggests that retardation, as an abnormality, is probably independent of at least one of the other types of thought disorder discussed above. In normal people, speed and error are relatively independent (Furneaux, 1960), but there appear to be no studies of abnormal groups. There is fairly consistent evidence from several studies reviewed by Payne (1970) and in a study by Foulds et al. (1969) that retardation and overinclusive thinking are independent.

RETARDATION AND SPECIFIC SYMPTOMOTOLOGY

There seems to be little doubt that a moderate degree of slowness is associated with a depressed affect, as suggested by the fact that depressed patients are usually slow.

There is conflicting evidence about the relationship between paranoid delusions and slowness. Foulds and co-workers (1968) found no differences between paranoid and non-paranoid schizophrenics on a group of simple psychomotor speed tests. Goldberg et al. (1968) also found no differences in reaction times, but Court and Garwoli (1968) found that paranoid schizophrenics were significantly faster than non-paranoid schizophrenics.

Generally speaking, retardation appears to be associated with the more severe type of schizophrenic symptoms. Harris and Metcalfe (1956, 1959) found that extreme slowness was associated with 'flattening of affect' and 'incongruous affect'. Goldberg and associates (1968) found that a very slow reaction time was associated with the presence of auditory hallucinations. Raskin (1967) also found that a recent history of hallucinations was associated with a slow reaction time. Goldberg et al. found a slow reaction time to be associated with a number of symptoms of withdrawal. On the other hand, Raskin (1967) found that, in a schizophrenic population, anxiety was associated with a relatively fast reaction time. The remission of symptoms in schizophrenics seems to be associated with an improvement in retardation (Schwartz, 1967a, 1967b).

All these results are consistent with the findings that process schizophrenics tend to be slow, while reactive schizophrenics tend to be fast.

THE RESPONSE TO DRUGS

Some earlier experiments (Layman, 1940; Mainord, 1953; Senf et al., 1955) suggested that sodium amytal might increase the speed of performance of schizophrenics. However, these studies did not take into account the well-known 'placebo' effect. More adequately controlled 'double blind' studies, using a placebo group, were carried out by Ogilvie (1954) and Broadhurst (1958a, 1958b). Both studies made use of the Nufferno speed tests, and while considerable practice effects were reported, there was no significant drug effect. Broadhurst (1958a, 1958b) also found that a stimulant drug (dexamphetamine sulphate) had no significant effect.

More recently, Pugh (1968) investigated the effect of chlorpromazine on reaction times. He tested 57 chronic schizophrenics whose reaction times, on average, were twice as slow as normal. Chlorpromazine had no significant effect on reaction time, although it did significantly reduce the level of arousal in the subjects, as measured by spontaneous GSR fluctuations, and GSR reactions to emotional words.

RETARDATION AND PROGNOSIS

The fact that slowness seems to characterise process and chronic schizophrenic patients suggests that it is probably a poor prognostic sign. Harris and Metcalfe (1956, 1959) produced other indirect evidence supporting this suggestion.

The only direct study of the prognostic implications of extreme retardation has been carried out by Payne (1968). As described above, Payne gave a battery of tests to a large group of newly admitted mental patients before treatment started. The tests included three measures of overinclusiveness as defined by Payne and Friedlander (1962) and three measures of retardation, as defined by Payne and Hewlett (1960). It was found in a three-year follow-up study that the patients who were retarded on admission had a significantly worse than average prognosis, as judged by a small but significant correlation of −0·228 between the retardation score and follow-up status.

CAUSES OF RETARDATION

Shapiro and Nelson (1955) gave a large number of speed tests to a group of 20 normal subjects, 20 neurotics, 20 schizophrenics, 20 manic depressives, and 20 brain-damaged patients, and factor analysed the matrix of test intercorrelations for the entire group. They found that two independent factors were needed to account for the matrix of correlations. This suggests that there may be two independent causes of slowness among abnormal subjects. It seems highly probable that some patients are slow largely because they are distracted in some way. There is some evidence (Payne, 1960) that introverted neurotic patients are slower than extraverted neurotic patients, which suggests the possibility that the performance of such patients may be slowed by task-interfering anxiety responses. It is possible that some of the slowness manifested by depressed patients might also be the result of the distraction produced by their anxieties, worries, and depressive thoughts.

Payne and Caird (1967) hypothesised that a slow reaction time could be a function of either over-inclusion, which produces a variable slowness as a function of the number of external distractions, or retardation which produces a consistent slowness that is not a function of the amount of distraction. As expected, they found that some of the patients (those who were paranoid, and overinclusive) were indeed significantly affected by the presence and numbers of distracting stimuli. However, they found that the group of 'retarded' schizophrenic patients, as defined by a group of psychomotor speed tests, also had slow reaction times, although these were relatively unaffected by the distracting stimuli.

Ashem (1969) also showed that the tapping speed of acute schizophrenics could be influenced by distractions in the form of words repeated (e.g. 'slower' or 'faster') by either the experimenter or the subject himself while working. Curiously, the schizophrenics, unlike the normals, were more distracted by their own speech than by that of the examiner.

If distractions are one cause of slowness, there is some evidence to suggest that the other cause may well be some physiological abnormality. Payne (1960) suggested that speed might be a function of the level of cortical arousal, and cited some evidence, that, even in a relatively homogeneous student group, it is highly correlated with thyroid function. Payne also suggested that a higher level of 'neuroticism' in normal subjects might be associated with an increased level of arousal, and an increase in speed. Some evidence derived from the Nufferno speed tests given to university students supports this idea, although the suggestion was that, in the special case of introverted subjects, this advantage might partly be offset by the task-interfering anxiety responses of introverted neurotics. The evidence seemed to support this view. Claridge's (1967) results, which suggest that reactive schizophrenics, who have a higher level of arousal, also tend to be faster, while process schizophrenics, who have an unusually low level of arousal, tend to be slower, also supports this hypothesis. Venables (1966b) and his associates (Tizard and Venables, 1955, 1957; Venables and O'Connor, 1959) have also found evidence for an association between reaction time speed and cortical arousal, as measured by the 'two-click' and 'two-flash threshold' among chronic schizophrenic patients. Schooler and Zahn (1968) also found some evidence that, among chronic schizophrenics, those who performed best on the Koh's block test were those whose general GSR level increased most during the testing period.

PERSISTENCE

Furneaux has demonstrated that persistence is another important determinant of the score on cognitive tests, and that it becomes increasingly important when the tests are given with no time limit. It is obvious that individuals abnormally lacking in persistence would obtain reduced scores on most cognitive tests.

Factorial studies in normals (Payne, 1960)

suggest that there may be two fairly well-defined and relatively independent types of persistence, 'ideational' and 'physical'. The former refers to the amount of time spent on very difficult or unsolvable intellectual problems, and the latter to the length of time people are prepared to submit to boring, fatiguing, or uncomfortable physical tasks.

Most of the work with abnormal subjects appears to refer to tests of physical persistence (Payne, 1960). These studies suggest that neurotics as a group may be less persistent than normals, and that extraverted neurotics are less persistent than introverted neurotics. The data on psychotics are inconsistent, but it appears that they are less persistent than neurotics on most physical tests.

Although there are only a few investigations of persistence on cognitive tests, Lynn and Gordon (1961) and Payne (1960) have demonstrated that introverts are more persistent than extraverts on the Raven's Matrices test. In both these investigations, extraverted neurotics tended to do as well as, or better than, the introverted neurotics at the beginning of the test, but then became much worse at the end of the test. The reason for this is unclear but it is possible that extraverts become more fatigued and tend to give up on the later problems.

There is some evidence that ambulatory schizophrenics are significantly more persistent than hospitalised schizophrenics on cognitive tests (Blumenthal *et al.*, 1965).

SUMMARY AND CONCLUSIONS

Any general conclusions are bound to be tentative in view of the various shortcomings and inconsistencies of the present research literature. Nevertheless, some overall generalisations, if they are regarded as hypotheses are probably useful.

It seems to be the case that thought disorder, *per se* is not an important aspect of neurotic behaviour. The thinking of neurotic patients may be somewhat faster in some situations because they have a higher general level of arousal. However, they are often slightly handicapped by anxiety responses, which may interfere with their performance, and by lack of persistence, in the case of extraverted neurotics.

Depressed patients, especially those who are regarded as 'psychotic', appear to be slow and distractible in most mental and motor tasks. This slowness may be only the result of their distractibility and preoccupations, but it may also result from some physiological dysfunction. Very little work has been done in this area.

However, there do appear to be three relatively distinct 'syndromes' in which thought disorder is an important feature. Indeed tests of thought disorder might be used to provide a tentative operational definition of each syndrome.

The first is probably best labelled 'Process Schizophrenia' as this term is now very widely used. This term refers to a relatively distinct group of psychotic patients whose abnormality may begin in childhood. As children, these patients tend to be of low average to borderline defective intelligence, and to do poorly in school, without any indications of gross brain damage, or any very clear-cut neurological signs. The development of further symptoms takes place gradually, but by the time they reach adolescence or early adulthood, they typically require hospitalisation, and have deteriorated even

further intellectually on standard tests of intelligence. They are often unsociable, and withdrawn, appear to lack drive and to have a flattened or incongruous affect, and are frequently hallucinated. They are most usually diagnosed as 'process schizophrenics' or 'simple schizophrenics', but those who are very dull and who exhibit very 'silly' or especially inappropriate behaviour may sometimes be labelled as 'hebephrenic' schizophrenics. When tested during their illness, they tend to have a low level of general intelligence, and a severe degree of general psychomotor retardation, including a slow and variable reaction time. They tend to display perceptual 'underconstancy' and are concrete in their thought and in their use of language. They are also very distractible in a wide range of situations. They may develop paranoid delusions as a result of their concrete thinking, but these are usually not systematised. These patients tend to have a poor prognosis, and frequently become chronically ill. One possible hypothesis is that all these characteristics may be the result of an abnormally low level of cortical arousal. The drug Sernyl appears capable of producing many of these features in normal subjects, but neither sodium amytal nor LSD have been found consistently to produce any of these effects in normal people. These patients tend not to respond satisfactorily to treatment with drugs such as the phenothiazines.

The second syndrome is probably best labelled 'Psychotic Anxiety Reaction' to avoid implying that it necessarily has anything to do with the first condition described. In this group of patients, the illness appears to start much more dramatically, often in response to some environmental trauma or stress in early adulthood, or, not infrequently in early middle age. These patients frequently develop relatively well-organised paranoid delusions. They show little general intellectual deterioration, and, even if they remain ill for many years, they remain well preserved intellectually. They show no perceptual disabilities, are better than average at concentrating and at focusing their attention, and are not distractible. They show no evidence of such features as concreteness or psychomotor retardation. They are often labelled as 'reactive schizophrenics' or 'paranoid schizophrenics'. When tested during their illness, they have a normal or even an above average IQ. They characteristically exhibit a large number of unusual responses in a variety of situations, which causes them to have a relatively high error rate in standard cognitive tests. They tend to give unusual associations to words, and to ambiguous stimuli. They also show unusual responses on sorting tests. Characteristically, they show perceptual overconstancy, which may be the result of an unusual amount of scanning. This condition may result from a very high level of anxiety, interacting with some constitutional peculiarity that in some way lowers their response strength ceiling, in such a way that their normal response hierarchies are disorganised. Their tendency gradually to develop organised paranoid delusions may result from their tendency to produce unusual responses in social situations. If these unusual reactions are hostile, they may become systematically reinforced by the environment, and thus are maintained and strengthened. On the whole, the prognosis for this condition is relatively good. It is possible that the prognosis for those who develop delusions is better than for those who do not. Those who become chronic patients may remain in a very high state of arousal, but may become withdrawn because their responses are too often inappropriate and maladaptive.

The third syndrome might be labelled 'Overinclusive Psychosis'. This is probably a less common disorder, and little can be said at present about the typical age or form of onset. These patients characteristically exhibit excited, overactive hostile talkative behaviour with mood swings. The condition is best recognised by a typical sort of thought disorder that has been labelled overinclusive thinking. Basically, this is a conceptual disorder in which words and ideas come to be defined broadly and vaguely. Non-essential ideas come to be incorporated into their concepts, and their thinking itself becomes vague, imprecise and often contradictory. This can be demonstrated on a number of sorting tests, in which they tend to subsume an abnormally large number of different objects under the same conceptual label. This overly general definition of categories produces characteristic errors in sorting tests. Their explanations of such things as proverbs are often overly discussive, and vague. These patients are most frequently diagnosed as 'manic', but may be labelled 'acute schizophrenic', or 'schizo-affective'. However, only a minority of patients diagnosed as schizophrenic suffer from this syndrome. The prognosis for this condition is relatively good, although it is not known what drug may hasten remission. It is tempting to speculate that this may be basically a toxic condition of some sort. There is some evidence that some of these abnormalities might be produced in normal subjects by LSD. If this is so, and if it is also the case that the habitual use of LSD can lead to a relatively permanent disorder of this sort, it is possible that it may become a more widespread condition in the future.

REFERENCES

ABSE, D. W., DAHLSTROM, W. G., and TOLLEY, A. G. (1960) Evaluation of tranquilizing drugs in the management of acute mental disturbance. *Amer. J. Psychiat.*, 116, 973–980.

ADAMS, H. E. and BERG, I. A. (1961) Schizophrenia and deviant response sets produced by auditory and visual test content. *J. Psychol.*, 51, 393–398.

ALBEE, G. W., LANE, ELLEN A., CORCORAN, CLARE, and WERNEKE, ANN. (1963) Childhood and intercurrent intellectual performance of adult schizophrenics. *J. consult. Psychol.*, 27, 364–366.

ALBEE, G. W., LANE, ELLEN A., and REUTER, JEANETTE M. (1964) Childhood intelligence of the future schizophrenics and neighborhood peers. *J. Psychol.*, 58, 141–144.

AL-ISSA, I. and ROBERTSON, J. P. S. (1964) Divergent thinking abilities in chronic schizophrenia. *J. clin. Psychol.*, 20, 433–435.

ARIETI, S. (1959) Schizophrenia: the manifest symptomatology, the psychodynamic and formal mechanisms. In *American Handbook of Psychiatry, Volume I.* (Ed. S. Arieti). New York: Basic Books, pp. 455–484.

ARMSTRONG, H. E., Jr., JOHNSON, M., RIES, H. A., and Holmes, D. S. (1967) Extraversion-introversion and process-reactive schizophrenia. *Brit. J. soc. clin. Psychol.*, 6, 69.

ASHEM, BEATRICE A. (1969) Use of speech in the inhibitory control of motoric behavior of schizophrenic patients. *J. consult. and clin. Psychol*, 33, 226–234.

BABCOCK, HARRIET and LEVY, LYDIA. (1940) *Manual of Directions for the Revised Examination of the Measurement of Efficiency of Mental Functioning.* Chicago: Stoelting.

BANNISTER, D. (1960) Conceptual structure in thought-disordered schizophrenics. *J. ment. Sci.*, 106, 1230–1249.

BANNISTER, D. (1962) The nature and measurement of schizophrenic thought disorder. *J. ment. Sci.*, **108**, 825–842.

BANNISTER, D. (1963) The genesis of schizophrenic thought disorder: A serial invalidation hypothesis. *Brit. J. Psychiat.*, **109**, 680–686.

BANNISTER, D. (1965) The genesis of schizophrenic thought disorder: Retest of the serial invalidation hypothesis. *Brit. J. Psychiat.*, **111**, 377–382.

BANNISTER, D. and FRANSELLA, FAY. (1966) A grid test of schizophrenic thought disorder. *Brit. J. soc. clin. Psychol.*, **5**, 95–102.

BANNISTER, D. and SALMON, PHILLIDA. (1966) Schizophrenic thought disorder: Specific or diffuse? *Brit. J. med. Psychol.*, **39**, 215–219.

BATMAN, R., ALBEE, G. W., and LANE, ELLEN A. (1966) Intelligence test performance of chronic and recovered schizophrenics. *Proc. 74th Ann. Convent. Amer. Psychological Assn.* Washington: American Psychological Association, 173–174.

BAUMAN, E. and MURRAY, D. J. (1968) Recognition versus recall in schizophrenia. *Canad. J. Psychol.*, **22**, 18–25.

BECKER, W. C. (1955) The relation of severity of thinking disorder to the process-reactive concept of schizophrenia. Unpublished doctoral dissertation, Stanford University.

BEMPORAD, J. R. (1967) Perceptual disorders in schizophrenia. *Amer. J. Psychiat.*, **123**, 971–976.

BENJAMIN, J. D. (1944) A method for distinguishing and evaluating formal thinking disorders in schizophrenia. In *Language and Thought in Schizophrenia* (Ed. J. S. Kasanin). Berkeley and Los Angeles: University of California Press, 65–90.

BENJAMIN, T. B. and WATT, N. F. (1969) Psychopathology and semantic interpretation of ambiguous words. *J. abnorm. Psychol.*, **74**, 706–714.

BERGER, L., BERNSTEIN, A., KLEIN, E., COHEN, J., and LUCAS, G. (1963) Effects of aging and pathology on the factoral structure of intelligence. *Newsletter for Res. in Psychol.*, **5**, 35–36.

BERNSTEIN, A. S. (1970) Phasic eletrodermal orienting response in chronic schizophrenics: II Response to auditory signals of varying intensity. *J. abnorm. Psychol.*, **72**, 146–156.

BERNSTEIN, L. (1960) The interaction of process and content on thought disorders of schizophrenic and brain-damaged patients. *J. gen. Psychol.*, **62**, 53–68.

BINDER, A. (1956) Schizophrenic intellectual impairment: Uniform or differential? *J. abnorm. and soc. Psychol.*, **52**, 11–18.

BLATT, S. J. (1959) Recall and recognition vocabulary: Implications for intellectual deterioration. *Amer. med. assoc. Arch. gen. Psychiat.*, **1**, 473–476.

BLAUFARB, H. (1962) A demonstration of verbal abstracting ability in chronic schizophrenics under enriched stimulus and instructional conditions. *J. consult. Psychol.*, **26**, 471–475.

BLUM, R. A., LIVINGSTON, P. B., and SHADER, R. I. (1969) Changes in cognition, attention, and language in acute schizophrenia. *Dis. nerv. System*, **30**, 31–36.

BLUMBERG, S. and GILLER, D. W. (1965) Some verbal aspects of primary-process thought: A partial replication. *J. person. soc. Psychol.*, **1**, 517–520.

BLUMENTHAL, R. and MELTZOFF, J. (1967) Social schemes and perceptual accuracy in schizophrenia. *Brit. J. soc. clin. Psychol.*, **6**, 119–128.

BLUMENTHAL, R., MELTZOFF, J., and ROSENBERG, S. (1965) Some determinants of persistence in chronic schizophrenic subjects. *J. abnorm. Psychol.*, **70**, 246.

BRATTEMO, C. E. (1962) Interpretations of proverbs in schizophrenic patients: Further studies. *Acta Psychologica*, **20**, 254–263.

BRATTEMO, C. E. (1965) The effectiveness of a non-standardized categorization in differentiating schizophrenic patients of various levels of abstracting functioning. *Acta Psychologica*, **24**, 314–328.

BRILLIANT, P. J. (1968) Differences in stimulus generalization among psychiatric patients as a function of anxiety level, ego strength, sex and time of testing. *J. abnorm. Psychol.*, **73**, 581–584.

BROADBENT, D. E. (1957) A mechanical model for human attention and immediate memory. *Psychologic. Rev.*, **64**, 205–215.

BROADBENT, D. E. (1958) *Perception and Communication.* London: Pergamon Press.

BROADHURST, ANNE H. (1957) Some variables affecting speed of mental functioning in schizophrenics. Unpublished doctoral dissertation, University of London Library.

BROADHURST, ANNE H. (1958a) Experimental studies of the mental speed of schizophrenics: I. Effects of a stimulant and a depressant drug. *J. ment. Sci.*, **104**, 1123–1129.

BROADHURST, ANNE H. (1958b) Experimental studies of the mental speed of schizophrenics: II. Effects of practice. *J. ment. Sci.*, **104**, 1130–1135.

BRODSKY, M. (1963) Interpersonal stimuli as interference in a sorting task. *J. Pers.*, **31**, 517–533.

BRODY, M. B. (1941–43) A survey of the results of intelligence tests in psychosis. *Brit. J. med. Psychol.*, **19**, 215–261.

BROEN, W. E. (1966) Response disorganization and breadth of observation in schizophrenia. *Psychologic. Rev.*, **73**, 579–585.

BROEN, W. E., Jr. (1968) *Schizophrenia: Research and Theory.* New York: Academic Press.

BROEN, W. E. and STORMS, L. H. (1966) Lawful disorganization: The process underlying a schizophrenic syndrome. *Psychologic. Rev.*, **73**, 265–279.

BROEN, W. E., STORMS, L. H., and GOLDBERG, D. H. (1963) Decreased discrimination as a function of increased drive. *J. abnorm. Soc. Psychol.*, **67**, 266–273.

BROWN, J. E., BILODEAU, E. A., and BARON, M. R. (1951) Bidirectional gradients in the strength of a generalized voluntary response to stimuli on a visual-spatial dimension. *J. exp. Psychol.*, **41**, 52–61.

BUCHSBAUM, M. and SILVERMAN, J. (1968) Stimulus intensity control and the cortical evoked response. *Psychosom. Med.*, **30**, 12–22.

BUSS, A. and DANIELL, EDNA F. (1967) Stimulus generalization and schizophrenia. *J. abnorm. Psychol.*, **72**, 50.

CALLAWAY, E. III, and DEMBO, D. (1958) Narrowed attention. *Arch. Neurol. Psychiat.*, **79**, 74–90.

Callaway, E. III, Jones, R. T., and Layne, R. S. (1965) Evoked responses and segmental set of schizophrenia. *Arch. gen. Psychiat.*, **12**, 83–89.

Callaway, E. III, and Stone, G. (1960) Re-evaluating focus of attention. In *Drugs and Behavior* (Ed. Uhr, L. and Miller, J. G.). New York: Wiley.

Cameron, N. (1938a) Reasoning, regression and communication in schizophrenics. *Psychologic. Monogr.*, **50**, 1–33.

Cameron, N. (1938b) A study of thinking in senile deterioration and schizophrenic disorganization. *Amer. J. Psychol.*, **51**, 650–664.

Cameron, N. (1939a) Deterioration and regression in schizophrenic thinking. *J. abnorm. soc. Psychol.*, **34**, 265–270.

Cameron, N. (1939b) Schizophrenic thinking in a problem-solving situation. *J. ment. Sci.*, **85**, 1012–1035.

Cameron, N. (1944) The functional psychoses. In *Personality and the Behavior Disorders, Volume II* (Ed. Hunt, J. McV.). New York: Ronald Press.

Cameron, N. (1947) *The Psychology of Behavior Disorders.* Boston: Houghton Mifflin.

Cameron, N. and Magaret, Ann. (1951) *Behavior Pathology.* Boston: Houghton Mifflin.

Campbell, Dawn A. (1962) Attentional variables and the reaction time of overinclusive schizophrenics and depressives. Unpublished M.A. thesis, Queen's University, Ontario.

Carp, A. (1950) Performance on the Wechsler-Bellevue scale and insulin shock therapy. *J. abnorm. soc. Psychol.*, **45**, 127–136.

Chapman, J. and McGhie, A. (1962) A comparative study of disordered attention in schizophrenia. *J. ment. Sci.*, **108**, 487–500.

Chapman, L. J. (1956a) Distractibility in the conceptual performance of schizophrenics. *J. abnorm. soc. Psychol.*, **53**, 286–291.

Chapman, L. J. (1956b) The role of type of distractor in the "concrete" conceptual performance of schizophrenics. *J. Person.*, **25**, 130–141.

Chapman, L. J. (1958) Intrusion of associative responses into schizophrenic conceptual performance. *J. abnorm. Soc. Psychol.*, **56**, 374–379.

Chapman, L. J. (1960) Confusion of figurative and literal usages of words by schizophrenics and brain damaged patients. *J. abnorm. Soc. Psychol.*, **60**, 412–416.

Chapman, L. J. (1961) A reinterpretation of some pathological disturbances in conceptual breadth. *J. abnorm. soc. Psychol.*, **62**, 514–519.

Chapman, L. J., Burstein, A. G., Day, Dorothy, and Verdone, P. (1961) Regression and disorders of thought. *J. abnorm. Soc. Psychol.*, **63**, 540–545.

Chapman, L. J. and Chapman, Jean P. (1959) Atmosphere effect re-examined. *J. exp. Psychol.*, **58**, 220–226.

Chapman, L. J. and Chapman, Jean P. (1965) Interpretation of words in schizophrenia. *J. person. soc. Psychol.*, **1**, 135–146.

Chapman, L. J., Day, Dorothy, and Burstein, A. G. (1961) The process-reactive distinction and prognosis in schizophrenia. *J. nerv. Ment. Dis.*, **133**, 383–391.

Chapman, L. J. and Knowles, R. R. (1964) The effects

of phenothiazine on disordered thought in schizophrenia. *J. consult. Psychol.*, **28**, 165–169.

Chapman, L. J. and Pathman, J. H. (1959) Errors in the diagnosis of mental deficiency in schizophrenics. *J. consult. Psychol.*, **23**, 432–434.

Chapman, L. J. and Taylor, J. A. (1957) Breadth of deviate concepts used by schizophrenics. *J. abnorm. soc. Psychol.*, **54**, 118–123.

Cheek, Frances E. and Amarel, M. (1968) Studies in the sources of variation in close scores: II Verbal passages. *J. abnorm. Psychol.*, **73**, 424–430.

Claridge, G. S. (1967) *Personality and Arousal. A psychophysiological study of psychiatric disorder.* London: Pergamon.

Clark, W. C. (1966) The psyche in psychophysics: A sensory-decision theory analysis of the effect of instructions on flicker sensitivity and response bias. *Psychologic. Bull.*, **65**, 358–366.

Cohen, B. D. and Camhi, J. (1967) Schizophrenic performance in a word-communication task. *J. abnorm. Psychol.*, **72**, 240–246.

Cohen, B. D., Rosenbaum, G., Luby, E. D., and Gottlieb, J. S. (1962) Comparison of phencyclidine hydrochloride (Sernyl) with other drugs: Simulation of schizophrenic performance with phencyclidine hydrochloride (Sernyl), lysergic acid diethylamide (LSD-25) and amobarbital (Amytal) sodium, II. Symbolic and sequential thinking. *Arch. gen. Psychiat.*, **6**, 395–401.

Cooper, Ruth (1960) Objective measures of perception in schizophrenics and normals. *J. consult. Psychol.*, **24**, 209–214.

Court, J. H. and Garwoli, E. (1968) Schizophrenic performance on a reaction time task with increasing levels of complexity. *Brit. J. soc. clin. Psychol.*, **7**, 216–223.

Craig, W. J. (1965) Objective measures of thinking integrated with psychiatric symptoms. *Psychologic. Reps.*, **16**, 539–546.

Cromwell, R. L. (1968) Stimulus redundancy and schizophrenia. *J. nerv. ment. Dis.*, **146**, 360–375.

Czudner, G. and Marshall, Marilyn (1967) Simple reaction time in schizophrenic, retarded, and normal children under regular and irregular preparatory interval conditions. *Canad. J. Psychol.*, **21**, 369–380.

Daston, P. G. (1959) Effects of two phenothiazine drugs on concentrative attention span of chronic schizophrenics. *J. clin. Psychol.*, **15**, 106–109.

Daston, P. G., King, G. F., and Armitage, S. G. (1953) Distortion in paranoid schizophrenia. *J. consult. Psychol.*, **17**, 50–53.

Davidson, M. (1939) Studies in the application of mental tests to psychotic patients. *Brit. J. med. Psychol.*, **18**, 44–52.

Davis, D., Cromwell, R. L., and Held, Joan (1967) Size estimation in emotionally disturbed children and schizophrenic adults. *J. abnorm. Psychol.*, **72**, 395–401.

Dean, G. W. and Weckowicz, T. E. (1967) Brightness constancy in schizophrenic patients. *J. Schizo.*, **1**, 225–238.

Deckner, C. W. and Blanton, R. L. (1969) Effect of context and strength of association on schizophrenic verbal behavior. *J. Abnorm. Psychol.*, **74**, 348–351.

DeLUCA, J. N. (1968) Motivation and performance in chronic schizophrenia. *Psychologic. Reps.*, **22**, 1261–1269.

DESAI, M. M. (1960) Intelligence and verbal knowledge in relation to Epstein's overinclusion test. *J. clin. Psychol.*, **16**, 417–419.

DISPENSA, JOHNETTE (1938) Relationship of the thyroid with intelligence and personality. *J. Psychol.*, **6**, 181–186.

DOKECKI, P. R., CROMWELL, R. L., and POLIDORO, L. G. (1968) The premorbid adjustment and chronicity dimensions as they relate to commonality and stability of word associations in schizophrenics. *J. nerv. ment. Dis.*, **146**, 310–311.

DONOVAN, M. J. and WEBB, W. W. (1965) Meaning dimensions and male–female voice perception in schizophrenics with good and poor premorbid adjustment. *J. abnorm. Psychol.*, **70**, 426.

DOWIS, J. L. and BUCHANAN, C. E. (1961) Some relationships between intellectual efficiency and the severity of psychiatric illness. *J. Psychol.*, **51**, 371–381.

DOWNING, R. W., EBERT, J. N., and SHUBROOKS, S. J. (1963a) Effect of phenothiazines on the thinking of acute schizophrenics. *Percept. motor Skills*, **17**, 511–520.

DOWNING, R. W., EBERT, J. N., and SHUBROOKS, S. J. (1963b) Effects of three types of verbal distractors on thinking in acute schizophrenia. *Percept. motor Skills*, **17**, 881–882.

DOWNING, R. W., SHUBROOKS, S. J., and EBERT, J. N. (1966) Intrusion of associative distractors into conceptual performance by acute schizophrenics: Role of associative strength. *Percept. motor Skills*, **22**, 460–462.

DRASGOW, J. and FELDMAN, M. J. (1957) Conceptual processes in schizophrenia revealed by the visual-verbal test. *Percept. motor Skills*, **7**, 251–264.

EASTERBROOK, J. A. (1959) The effect of emotion on cue utilization and the organization of behavior. *Psychologic. Rev.*, **66**, 183–200.

EBNER, E. and RITZLER, B. (1969) Perceptual recognition in chronic and acute schizophrenics. *J. consult. clin. Psychol.*, **33**, 200–206.

ELISEO, T. S. (1963) Overinclusive thinking in process and reactive schizophrenics. *J. consult. Psychol.*, **27**, 447–449.

ELMORE, C. M. and GORHAM, D. R. (1957) Measuring the impairment of the abstracting function with the proverbs test. *J. clin. Psychol.*, **13**, 263–266.

EPSTEIN, S. (1953) Overinclusive thinking in a schizophrenic and a control group. *J. Consult. Psychol.*, **17**, 384–388.

EYSENCK, H. J. (1947) *The Dimensions of Personality.* London: Kegan Paul.

FAIBISH, G. M. (1961) Schizophrenic response to words of multiple meaning. *J. Person.*, **29**, 414–427.

FEFFER, M. H. (1961) The influence of affective factors on conceptualization in schizophrenia. *J. abnorm. soc. Psychol.*, **63**, 588–596.

FEINBERG, I. and MERCER, MARGARET (1960) Studies of thought disorder in schizophrenia. *Amer. med. Assoc. Arch. gen. Psychiat.*, **2**, 504–511.

FELDMAN, M. J. and DRASGOW, J. (1951) A visual-verbal test for schizophrenics. *Psychiat. Quart. Suppl.*, **25**, 55–64.

FEY, ELIZABETH T. (1951) The performance of young schizophrenics and young normals on the Wisconsin card sorting test. *J. consult. Psychol.*, **15**, 311–319.

FLAVELL J. H., (1956) Abstract thinking and social behavior in schizophrenia. *J. abnorm. soc. Psychol.*, **52**, 208–211.

FORD, J. R. and CALDWELL W. E. (1968) The (ASF) phenomena: An exploratory investigation of apparent stationary form perception of neutral and affective stimuli. *J. gen. Psychol.*, **79**, 34–46.

FOULDS, G. A. and DIXON, PENELOPE (1962) The nature of intellectual deficit in schizophrenia and neurotics: I A comparison of schizophrenics and neurotics. *Brit. J. soc. clin. Psychol.*, **1**, 7–19.

FOULDS, G. A., HOPE, K., McPHERSON, F. M., and MAYO, P. R. (1967a) Cognitive disorder among the schizophrenias: I The validity of some tests of thought process disorder. *Brit. J. Psychiat.*, **113**, 1361–1368.

FOULDS, G. A., HOPE, K., McPHERSON, F. M., and MAYO, P. R. (1967b) Cognitive disorder among the schizophrenias: II Differences between the sub-categories. *Brit. J. Psychiat.*, **113**, 1369–1374.

FOULDS, G. A., HOPE, K., McPHERSON, F. M., and MAYO, P. R. (1968) Paranoid delusions, retardation, and overinclusive thinking. *J. clin. Psychol.*, **24**, 177–178.

FOULDS, G. A., HOPE, K., McPHERSON, F. M., and MAYO, P. R. (1969) Cognitive disorder among the schizophrenias: III Retardation. *Brit. J. Psychiat.*, **115**, 177–180.

FRANKEL, A. S. and BUCHWALD, A. M. (1969) Verbal conditioning of common associations in long-term schizophrenics: A failure. *J. Abnorm. Psychol.*, **74**, 372–374.

FREIDES, D., FREDENTHAL, B., GRISELL, J. L., and COHEN, B. D. (1963) Changes in two dimensions of cognition during adolescence. *Child Development*, **34**, 1047–1055.

FRIEDHOFF, A. J. and ALPERT, M. (1960) The effect of chlorpromazine on the variability of motor task performance in schizophrenics. *J. nerv. ment. Dis.*, **131**, 110–116.

FRIEDMAN, A. S. (1964) Minimal effects of severe depression on cognitive functioning. *J. abnorm. soc. Psychol.*, **69**, 237–243.

FURNEAUX, W. D. (1956a) *Manual of Nufferno Speed Tests.* London: National Foundation of Educational Research.

FURNEAUX, W. D. (1956b) *Manual of Nufferno Level Tests.* London: National Foundation of Educational Research.

FURNEAUX, W. D. (1960) Intellectual abilities and problem solving behaviour. *Handbook of Abnormal Psychology* (Ed. Eysenck, H. J.) London: Pitman Medical; New York: Basic Books, 167–193.

FURTH, H. G. and YOUNISS, J. (1968) Schizophrenic thinking on nonverbal conceptual, discovery, and transfer tests. *J. nerv. ment. Dis.*, **146**, 376–383.

GAINES, JULIE A., MEDNICK, S. A., and HIGGINS, J. (1963) Stimulus generalization in acute and chronic schizophrenia. *Acta Psychiat. Scand.*, **39**, 601–605.

GARDNER, G. E. (1940) Childhood physical and mental measurements of psychotic patients. *Amer. J. Orthopsychiat.*, **10**, 327–342.

GLADIS, M. (1967) Retention of verbal paired associates by schizophrenic subjects. *Psychologic. Reps*, **21**, 241–246.

GOLDBERG, S. C., SCHOOLER, NINA R., and MATTSSON, N. (1968) Paranoid and withdrawal symptoms in schizophrenia: Relationship to reaction time. *Brit. J. Psychiat.*, **114**, 1161–1165.

GOLDSTEIN, K. and SCHEERER, M. (1941) Abstract and concrete behavior, an experimental study with special tests. *Psychologic. Monogr.*, 53.

GOLDSTEIN, M. J., HELD, JOAN M., and CROMWELL, R. L. (1968) Premorbid adjustment and paranoid-nonparanoid status in schizophrenia. *Psychologic. Bull.*, **70**, 382–386.

GOLDSTEIN, R. H. and SALZMAN, L. F. (1965) Proverb word counts as a measure of overinclusiveness in delusional schizophrenics. *J. abnorm. Psychol.*, **70**, 244–245.

GORHAM, D. R. (1956a) A proverbs test for clinical and experimental use. *Psychologic. Reps*, **2** 1–12.

GORHAM, D. R. (1956b) *Clinical Manual for the Proverbs Test.* Missoula, Mont.: Psychological Test Specialists.

GORHAM, D. R. (1956c) Use of the proverbs test for differentiating schizophrenics from normals. *J. consult. Psychol.*, **20**, 435–440.

GOTTESMAN, L. and CHAPMAN, L. J. (1960) Syllogistic reasoning errors in schizophrenia. *J. consult. Psychol.*, **24** 250–255

GRAHAM, VIRGINIA T. (1940) Psychological studies of hypoglycemia theory. *J. Psychol.*, **10**, 327–358.

GRANICK, S. (1963) Comparative analysis of psychotic depressives with matched normals on some untimed verbal intelligence tests. *J. consult. Psychol.*, **27**, 439–443.

GREGG, A. H. and FRANK, G. H. (1966) An analysis of conceptual thinking in process and reactive schizophrenics. *Proc. 74th Ann. Convent. Amer. Psychologic. Assoc.* Washington: American Psychological Association, 183–184.

GRIFFITH, R. M., ESTES, BETSY W., and ZEROF, S. A. (1962) Intellectual impairment in schizophrenia. *J. consult. Psychol.*, **26**, 336–339.

GUERTIN, W. H., RABIN, A. I., FRANK, G. H., and LADD, C. E. (1962) Research with the Wechsler Intelligence Scales for adults: 1955–60. *Psychologic. Bull.*, **59**, 1–26.

HALL, G. C. (1962) Conceptual attainment in schizophrenics and nonpsychotics as a function of task structure. *J. Psychol.*, **53**, 3–13.

HAMLIN, R. M., HAYWOOD, H. C., and FOLSOM, ANGELA T. (1965) Effect of enriched input on schizophrenic abstraction. *J. abnorm. Psychol.*, **70**, 390–394.

HAMLIN, R. M. and JONES, R. E. (1963) Vocabulary deficit in improved and unimproved schizophrenic subjects. *J. nerv. ment. Dis.*, **136**, 360–364.

HAMLIN, R. M. and WARD, W. D. (1965) Aging, hospitalization, and schizophrenic intelligence. *Proc. 73rd Ann. Convent. Amer. Psychologic. Assoc.*, Washington: American Psychological Association, 221–222.

HAMMER, A. G. and JOHNSON, LAUREL (1965) Overinclusiveness in schizophrenia and organic psychosis. *Brit. J. soc. clin. Psychol.*, **4**, 47–51.

HAMMER, MURIEL and SALZINGER, K. (1964) Some formal characteristics of schizophrenic speech as a measure of social deviance. *Ann. New York Acad. Sci.*, **105**, 861–889.

HARRIS, A. and METCALFE, MARYSE (1956) Inappropriate affect. *J. Neurol. Neurosur. Psychiat.*, **19**, 308–313.

HARRIS, A. and METCALFE, MARYSE (1959) Slowness in schizophrenia. *J. Neurol., Neurosur. and Psychiat.*, **22**, 239–242.

HART, D. S. (1964) Language and overinclusive thought disorder. Unpublished doctoral dissertation, Queen's University, Ontario.

HAWKS, D. V. (1964) The clinical usefulness of some tests of over-inclusive thinking in psychiatric patients. *Brit. J. soc. clin. Psychol.*, **3**, 186–195.

HAWKS, D. V. (1967) Overinclusive thought disorder in psychiatric patients. Unpublished doctoral dissertation, Queen's University, Ontario.

HAWKS, D. V. and PAYNE, R. W. (1971) Overinclusive thought disorder and symptomatology. *Brit. J. Psychiat.*, **118**, 663–670.

HAWKS, D. V. and PAYNE, R. W. (1972) Overinclusive thinking and concept identification in psychotic patients. *Brit. J. med. Psychol.* (to appear).

HAYWOOD, H. C. and MOELIS, I. (1963) Effect of symptom change on intellectual function in schizophrenia. *J. abnorm. Soc. Psychol.*, **67**, 76–78.

HEATH, ELAINE B., ALBEE, G. W., and LANE, ELLEN A. (1965) Predisorder intelligence of process and reactive schizophrenics and their siblings. *Proc. 73rd Ann. Convent. Amer. Psychologic. Assoc.* Washington: American Psychological Association, 223–224.

HERMELIN, BEATE M. and VENEABLES, P. H. (1964) Reaction time and alpha blocking in normal and severely subnormal subjects. *J. exp. Psychol.*, **67**, 365–372.

HEWLETT, J. H. G. (1959) An investigation into some aspects of thought disorder in abnormal groups. Unpublished doctoral dissertation, University of London.

HIGGINS, J. (1964) The concept of process-reactive schizophrenia: Criteria and related research. *J. nerv. ment. Dis.*, **138**, 9–25.

HIGGINS, J. (1968) Commonality of word association responses in schizophrenia as a function of chronicity and adjustment: A response to Dokecki, Cromwell and Polidoro. *J. nerv. ment. Dis.*, **146**, 312–313.

HIGGINS, J., MEDNICK, S. A., and THOMPSON, R. E. (1966) Acquisition and retention of remote associates in process-reactive schizophrenia. *J. nerv. ment. Dis.*, **142**, 418–423.

HOFFER, A. and OSMOND, H. (1963) People are watching me. *Psychiat. Quart.*, **37**, 7–18.

HOLTZMAN, W. H., GORHAM, D. R., and MORAN, L. J. (1964) A factor-analytic study of schizophrenic thought processes. *J. abnorm. soc. Psychol.*, **69**, 355–364.

HOWSON, J. D. (1948) Intellectual impairment associated with brain injured patients as revealed in the Shaw test of abstract thought. *Canad. J. Psychol.*, **2**, 125–133.

HUNT, H. F. (1943) A practical clinical test for organic brain damage. *J. appl. Psychol.*, **27**, 375–386.

HUNT, J. McV. and COFER, C. N. (1944) Psychological deficit. In *Personality and the Behavior Disorders, Volume II*. (Ed. Hunt, J. McV.). New York: Ronald.

HUSTON, P., COHEN, B., and SENF, RITA (1955) Shifting of set and goals orientation in schizophrenia. *J. ment. Sci.*, **101**, 344–350.

INGLIS, J. (1957) An experimental study of learning and 'memory functions' in elderly psychiatric patients. *J. ment. Sci.*, **103**, 796–803.

INGLIS, J. (1970) Memory disorder. In *Symptoms of Psychopathology: a handbook* (Ed. Costello, C. G.) New York: Wiley, 96–133.

JOHNSON, M. H. (1966) Verbal abstracting ability and schizophrenia. *J. consult. Psychol.*, **30**, 275–277.

JONES, R. T., BLACKER, K. H., and CALLAWAY, E. (1966) Perceptual dysfunction in schizophrenia: Clinical and auditory evoked response findings. *Amer. J. Psychol.*, **123**, 639–645.

JONES, R. T., BLACKER, K. H., CALLAWAY, E., and LAYNE, R. S. (1965) The auditory evoked response as a diagnostic and prognostic measure in schizophrenia. *Amer. J. Psychol.*, **122**, 33–41.

JUDSON, A. J. and KATAHN, M. (1963) The relationship of autonomic responsiveness to process-reactive schizophrenia and abstract thinking. *Psychiat. Quart.*, **37**, 19–24.

KAPCHE, R. (1969) Association response competition in schizophrenia. *J. abnorm. Psychol.*, **74**, 75–78.

KARSON, S. and POOL, K. B. (1957) The abstract thinking abilities in mental patients. *J. clin. Psychol.*, **13**, 126–132.

KATKIN, E. S. and MCCUBBIN, R. J. (1969) Habituation of the orienting response as a function of individual differences in anxiety and autonomic lability. *J. abnorm. Psychol.*, **74**, 54–60.

KELM, H., HALL, R. W., and HOFFER, A. (1968) A biochemical and perceptual measure related to length of hospitalization. *Dis. nerv. System*, **29**, 844–845.

KING, H. E. (1967) Trail making performance as related to psychotic stage, age, intelligence, education, and fine psychomotor ability. *Percept. motor Skills*, **25**, 649–658.

KING, H. E. (1969) Limited foreview tracing: Normal and schizophrenic. *Percept. motor Skills*, **28**, 13–14.

KINGSLEY, L. and STRUENING, E. L. (1966) Changes in intellectual performance of acute and chronic schizophrenics. *Psychologic. Reps*, **18**, 791–800.

KIRSCHNER, D. (1964) Differences in gradients of stimulus generalization as a function of 'abstract' and 'concrete' attitude. *J. consult. Psychol.*, **28**, 160–164.

KLEIN, E. B., CICCHETTI, D., and SPOHN, H. (1967) A test of the censure-deficit model and its relation to premorbidity in the performance of schizophrenics. *J. abnorm. Psychol.*, **72**, 174–181.

KLORMAN, R. and CHAPMAN, L. J. (1969) Regression in schizophrenic thought disorder. *J. abnorm. Psychol.*, **74**, 199–204.

KNEHR, C. A. and BROWN, NATALIE L. (1957) Perseveration in schizophrenic and brain damaged patients. *J. Psychol.*, **43**, 269–275.

KRISTOFFERSON, MARIANNE (1967) Shifting attention between modalities: A comparison of schizophrenics and normals. *J. abnorm. Psychol.*, **72**, 388–394.

KRUS, D. M., WAPNER, S., FREEMAN, H., and CASEY, T. M. (1963) Differential behavior responsivity to LSD-25: Study in normal and schizophrenic adults. *Arch. gen. Psychiat.*, **8**, 557–563.

KUGELMASS, S. and FONDEUR, M. R. (1955) Zaslow's test of concept formation reliability and validity. *J. consult. Psychol.*, **19**, 227–229.

LANE, ELLEN and ALBEE, G. W. (1963) Childhood intellectual development of adult schizophrenics. *J. abnorm. soc. Psychol.*, **67**, 186–189.

LANE, ELLEN A. and ALBEE, G. W. (1964) Early childhood intellectual differences between schizophrenic adults and their siblings. *J. abnorm. soc. Psychol.*, **68**, 193–195.

LANE, ELLEN A. and ALBEE, G. W. (1968) On childhood intellectual decline of adult schizophrenics: A reassessment of an earlier study. *J. abnorm. Psychol.*, **73**, 174–177.

LANGER, J., STEIN, K. B., and ROSENBERG, B. G. (1969) Cognitive interference by nonverbal symbols in schizophrenics. *J. abnorm. Psychol.*, **74**, 474–476.

LAWSON, J. S., MCGHIE, A., and CHAPMAN, J. (1964) Perception of speech in schizophrenia. *Brit. J. Psychiat.*, **110**, 375–380.

LAYMAN, J. W. (1940) A quantitative study of certain changes in schizophrenic patients under the influence of sodium amytal. *J. gen. Psychol.*, **22**, 67–86.

LESTER, J. (1960) Production of associative sequences in schizophrenia and chronic brain syndrome. *J. abnorm. soc. Psychol.*, **60**, 225–233.

LEVENTHAL, D. B., MCGAUGHRAN, L. S., and MORAN, L. J. (1959) Multivariable analysis of the conceptual behavior of schizophrenic and brain-damaged patients. *J. abnorm. soc. Psychol.*, **58**, 84–90.

LEVY, R. and MAXWELL, A. E. (1968) The effect of verbal context on the recall of schizophrenics and other psychiatric patients. *Brit. J. Psychiat.*, **114**, 311–316.

LEWINSOHN, P. M. (1963) Use of the Shipley-Hartford Conceptual Quotient as a measure of intellectual impairment. *J. consult. Psychol.*, **27**, 444–447.

LEWINSOHN, P. M. and RIGGS, ANN (1962) The effect of content upon the thinking of acute and chronic schizophrenics. *J. abnorm. soc. Psychol.*, **65**, 206–207.

LEWIS, J. M., GRIFFITH, E. C., RIEDEL, A. F., and SIMMONS, B. A. (1959) Studies in abstraction: Schizophrenia and orality: Preliminary results. *J. nerv. ment. Dis.*, **129**, 564–567.

LIDZ, T., WILD, CYNTHIA, SCHAFER, SARAH, ROSMAN, BERNICE, and FLECK, S. (1962) Thought disorders in the parents of schizophrenic patients: A study utilizing the object sorting test. *J. psychiat. Res.*, **1**, 193–200.

LIEBERT, R. S., WERNER, H., and WAPNER, S. (1958) Studies in the effect of LSD-25: Self- and object-size perception in schizophrenics and normal adults. *Amer. med. assoc. Arch. Neurol. Psychiat.*, **79**, 580–584.

LITTLE, L. K. (1966) Effects of the interpersonal interaction on abstract thinking performance in schizophrenics. *J. consult. Psychol.*, **30**, 158–164.

LIVINGSTON, P. B. and BLUM, R. A. (1968) Attention and speech in actue schizophrenia: An experimental study. *Arch. gen. Psychiat*, **18**, 373–381.

LLOYD, D. N. (1967) Overinclusive thinking and delusions in schizophrenic patients: a critique. *J. abnorm. Psychol.*, **72**, 451–453.

LOVIBOND, S. H. (1954) The object sorting test and conceptual thinking in schizophrenia. *Austral. J. Psychol.*, **6**, 52–70.

LUBIN, A., GIESEKING, C. F., and WILLIAMS, H. L. (1962) Direct measurement of cognitive deficit in schizophrenia. *J. consult. Psychol.*, **26**, 130–143.

LYDECKER, W. A. (1966) Effects of different reinforcement conditions on the learning of schizophrenics and normals. *Proc. 74th ann. convent. Amer. Psychologic. Assoc.* Washington: American Psychological Association, 179–180.

LYKKEN, D. T. and MALEY, M. (1968) Automic versus cortical arousal in schizophrenics and non-psychotics. *J. Psychiat. Res.*, **6**, 21–32.

LYNN, R. and GORDON, I. E. (1961) The relation of neuroticism and extraversion to intelligence and educational attainment. *Brit. J. Educ. Psychol.*, **31**, 194–203.

McCONAGHY, N. (1959) The use of an object sorting test in elucidating the hereditary factor in schizophrenia. *J. Neurol. Psychiat.*, **22**, 243–246.

McCORMACK, J. H., PHELAN, J. G., and TANG, T. (1967) Experimental studies of cognitive and motor sets: An aspect of psychological deficit in schizophrenia. *J. clin. Psychol.*, **23**, 443–446.

McGAUGHRAN, L. S. (1954) Predicting language behavior from object sorting. *J. abnorm. soc. Psychol.*, **49**, 183–195.

McGAUGHRAN, L. S. and MORAN, L. J. (1956) 'Conceptual level' *v.* 'Conceptual area' analysis of object-sorting behavior of schizophrenic and nonpsychiatric groups. *J. abnorm. soc. Psychol.*, **52**, 43–50.

McGAUGHRAN, L. S. and MORAN, L. J. (1957) Differences between schizophrenic and brain-damaged groups in conceptual aspects of object sorting. *J. abnorm. soc. Psychol.*, **54**, 44–49.

McGHIE, A. (1966) Psychological studies of schizophrenia. *Brit. J. med. Psychol.*, **39**, 281–288.

McGHIE, A., CHAPMAN, J., and LAWSON, J. S. (1965a) The effect of distraction on schizophrenic performance: I Perception and immediate memory. *Brit. J. Psychiat.*, **111**, 383–390.

McGHIE, A., CHAPMAN, J., and LAWSON, J. S. (1965b) The effect of distraction on schizophrenic performance: II Psychomotor ability. *Brit. J. Psychiat.*, **111**, 391–398.

McKINNON, T. and SINGER, G. (1969) Schizophrenia and the scanning cognitive control: A reevaluation. *J. abnorm. Psychol.*, **74**, 242–248.

McREYNOLDS, P. and COLLINS, BEVERLY (1961) Concept-forming behavior in schizophrenic and non-schizophrenic subjects. *J. Psychol.*, **52**, 369–378.

MAGARO, P. A. (1969) Size estimation in schizophrenia as a function of censure diagnosis, premorbid adjustment and chronicity. *J. abnorm. Psychol.*, **74**, 306–313.

MAINORD, W. A. (1953) Some effects of Sodium Amytal on deteriorated schizophrenics. *J. consult. Psychol.*, **17**, 54–57.

MALAMUD, W. and PALMER, E. M. (1938) Intellectual deterioration in the psychoses. *Archs. Neurol. Psychiat.*, **39**, 68–81.

MALTZMAN, I. (1955) Thinking: From a behavioristic point of view. *Psychologic. Rev.*, **62**, 275–286.

MASON, C. F. (1956) Pre-illness intelligence of mental hospital patients. *J. consult. Psychol.*, **20**, 297–300.

MAY, A. E. (1966) Anxiety and overinclusion. *Brit. J. Psychiat.*, **112**, 41–42.

MEDNICK, S. A. (1955) Distortions in the gradient of stimulus generalization related to cortical brain damage and schizophrenia. *J. abnorm. soc. Psychol.*, **51**, 536–542.

MEDNICK, S. A. (1958) A learning theory approach to research in schizophrenia. *Psychologic. Bull.*, **55**, 316–327.

MEDNICK, S. A. (1966) A longitudinal study of children with a high risk for schizophrenia. *Ment. Hygiene*, **50**, 522–535.

MILGRAM, N. A. (1959) Preference for abstract versus concrete word meanings in schizophrenic and brain-damaged patients. *J. clin. Psychol.*, **15**, 207–212.

MILLER, G. A. and CHAPMAN, L. J. (1968) Response bias and schizophrenic beliefs. *J. abnorm. Psychol.*, **73**, 252–255.

MONROE, J. J. (1952) The effects of emotional adjustment and intelligence upon Bellevue scatter. *J. consult. Psychol.*, **16**, 110–114.

MOON, A. F., MEFFERD, R. B., Jr., WIELAND, B. A., POKORNY, A. D., and FALCONER, G. A. (1968) Perceptual dysfunction as a determinant of schizophrenic word associations. *J. nerv. ment. Dis.*, **146**, 80–84.

MORAN, L. J. (1953) Vocabulary knowledge and usage among normal and schizophrenic subjects. *Psychological Monogr.*, 1953, **67**, (20, whole no. 370).

MORAN, L. J., GORHAM, D. R., and HOLTZMAN, W. H. (1960) Vocabulary knowledge and usage of schizophrenic subjects: A six year follow-up. *J. abnorm. soc. Psychol.*, **61**, 246–254.

MURRAY, E. N. (1969) Anxiety and overgeneralization: Negative results. *J. abnorm. Psychol.*, **74**, 602–605.

NATHAN, P. E. (1964) A comparative investigation of schizophrenic and normal conceptual performance. *J. nerv. ment. Dis.*, **138**, 443–451.

NEALE, J. M and CROMWELL, R. L. (1968) Size estimation in schizophrenics as a function of stimulus-presentation time. *J. abnorm. Psychol.*, **73**, 44–48.

NEALE, J. M., McINTYRE, C. W., FOX, R., and CROMWELL, R. L. (1969) Span of apprehension in acute schizophrenics. *J. abnorm. Psychol.*, **74**, 593–595.

NICKOLS, J. E., Jr. (1958) A controlled exploratory investigation into the effects of thorazine upon mental test scores of chronic hospitalized schizophrenics. *Psychologic. Rec.*, **8**, 67–76.

NICKOLS, J. E., Jr. (1964) Overinclusion under unstructured conditions. *J. clin. Psychol.*, **20**, 422–429.

NOLAN, J. D. (1968) Reversal and extradimensional shifts in abstract and concrete schizophrenics. *J. abnorm. Psychol.*, **73**, 330–335.

OGILVIE, B. C. (1954) A study of intellectual slowness in schizophrenia. Unpublished doctoral dissertation. University of London.

PAVY, D. (1968) Verbal behavior in schizophrenia:

Review of recent studies. *Psychological Bulletin*, **70**, 164–178.

PAYNE, R. W. (1960) Cognitive abnormalities. In *Handbook of Abnormal Psychology* (Ed. Eysenck, H. J.) London: Pitman Medical, 193–261.

PAYNE, R. W. (1962) An object classification test as a measure of overinclusive thinking in schizophrenic patients. *Brit. J. soc. clin. Psychol.*, **1**, 213–221.

PAYNE, R. W. (1966) The measurement and significance of overinclusive thinking and retardation in schizophrenic patients. In *Psychopathology of Schizophrenia* (Ed. Hoch, P. H. and Zubin, J.) New York: Grune and Stratton, 77–97.

PAYNE, R. W. (1968) The long-term prognostic implications of overinclusive thinking in mental patients: A follow-up study using objective tests. *Proc. IV World Cong. Psychiat., Madrid, 1966.* New York: Excerpta Medica Foundation, 2657–2666.

PAYNE, R. W. (1970) Disorders of thinking. In *Symptoms of Psychopathology: A handbook* (Ed. Costello, C. G.) New York: Wiley, 49–94.

PAYNE, R. W. (1971) Cognitive defects in schizophrenia: Overinclusive thinking. In *Cognitive Studies, Volume II. Deficits in Cognition* (Ed. Hellmuth. J.). New York: Brunner Mazel; London: Butterworths, 53–89.

PAYNE, R. W., ANCEVICH, SINGRIDA S., and LAVERTY, S. G. (1963) Overinclusive thinking in symptom-free schizophrenics. *Canad. psychiat. Assoc. J.*, **8**, 225–234.

PAYNE, R. W. and CAIRD, W. K. (1967) Reaction time, distractibility and overinclusive thinking in psychotics. *J. abnorm. Psychol.*, **72**, 112–121.

PAYNE, R. W., CAIRD, W. K., and LAVERTY, S. G. (1964) Overinclusive thinking and delusions in schizophrenic patients. *J. abnorm. soc. Psychol.*, **68**, 562–566.

PAYNE, R. W. and FRIEDLANDER, D. (1962) A short battery of simple tests for measuring overinclusive thinking. *J. ment. Sci.*, **108**, 362–367.

PAYNE, R. W., FRIEDLANDER, D., LAVERTY, S. G., and HADEN, P. (1963) Overinclusive thought disorder in chronic schizophrenics and its response to 'Proketazine'. *Brit. J. Psychiat.*, **109**, 523–530.

PAYNE, R. W., HOCHBERG, A. C., and HAWKS, D. V. (1970) Dichotic stimulation as a method of assessing the disorder of attention in overinclusive schizophrenic patients. *J. abnorm. Psychol.*, **76**, 185–193.

PAYNE, R. W. and HEWLETT, J. H. G. (1960) Thought disorder in psychotic patients. In *Experiments in Personality volume II, Psychodiagnostics and psychodynamics* (Ed. Eysenck, H. J.). London: Routledge and Kegan Paul, 3–104.

PAYNE, R. W. and JONES, H. G. (1957) Statistics for the investigation of individual cases. *J. clin. Psychol.*, **13**, 115–121.

PAYNE, R. W., MATUSSEK, P., and GEORGE, E. I. (1959) An experimental study of schizophrenic thought disorder. *J. ment. Sci.*, **105**, 627–652.

PAYNE, R. W. and SLOANE, R. B. (1968) Can schizophrenia be defined? *Dis. nerv. System*, **29**, 113–117.

PAYNE, R. W. and VAN ALLEN, R. K. (1969) The relationship between overinclusive thinking, perceptual rigidity, and the discrimination learning of new concepts. *Canad. J. behav. Sci.*, **1**, 193–203.

PETTIGREW, T. F. (1958) The measurement and correlates of category width as a cognitive variable. *J. Person.*, **26**, 532–544.

PHELAN, J. G., LEVY, HARRIET C., and THORPE, J. W. (1967) Concept learning in schizophrenics and normals: Selection and addition of cues: Effect of amount and type of memory information. *J. Psychol.*, **67**, 303–311.

PHILLIPS, J. E., JACOBSON, NAOMI, and TURNER, WM. J. (1965) Conceptual thinking in schizophrenics and their relatives. *Brit. J. Psychiat.*, **478**, 823–839.

PHILLIPS, L. (1953) Case history data and prognosis in schizophrenia. *J. nerv. ment. Dis.*, **117**, 515–525.

PISHKIN, V. and BLANCHARD, R. J. (1963) Stimulus and social cues in concept identification of schizophrenics and normals. *J. abnorm. soc. Psychol.*, **67**, 454–463.

PISHKIN, V. and BOURNE, L. E., Jr. (1969) Concept identification by schizophrenic and normal subjects as a function of problem complexity and relevance of social cues. *J. abnorm. Psychol.*, **74**, 314–320.

POLLACK, M. (1960) Comparison of childhood adolescent and adult schizophrenics. *Amer. med. assoc. Arch. gen. Psychiat.*, **2**, 652–660.

PRESLY, A. S. (1969) 'Slowness' and performance on the Grid Test for thought disorder. *Brit. J. soc. clin. Psychol.*, **8**, 79–80.

PRICE, R. H. (1968) Analysis of task requirements in schizophrenic concept-identification performance. *J. abnorm. Psychol.*, **73**, 285–293.

PUGH, L. A. (1968) Response time and electrodermal measures in chronic schizophrenia: The effects of chlorpromazine. *J. nerv. ment. Dis.*, **146**, 62–70.

RAEBURN, J. H. and TONG, J. E. (1968) Experiments on contextual constraint in schizophrenia. *Brit. J. Psychiat.*, **114**, 43–52.

RALPH, D. E. (1968) Stimulus generalization among schizophrenics and normal subjects. *J. abnorm. Psychol.*, **73**, 605–609.

RAPAPORT, D. (1946) *Diagnostic Psychological Testing.* Chicago: The Year Book Publishers.

RAPPAPORT, M. (1968) Attention to competing voice messages by nonacute schizophrenic patients: Effects of message load, drugs, dosage levels, and patient background. *J. nerv. ment. Dis.*, **146**, 404–411.

RAPPAPORT, S. R. and WEBB, W. (1950) An attempt to study intellectual deterioration by premorbid and psychotic testing. *J. consult. Psychol.*, **14**, 95–98.

RASHKIS, H. A. (1947) Three types of thinking disorder. *J. nerv. ment. Dis.*, **106**, 650–670.

RASHKIS, H. A., CUSHMAN, T. F., and LANDIS, C. (1946) A new method for studying disorders of conceptual thinking. *J. abnorm. soc. Psychol.*, **41**, 70–74.

RASKIN, A. (1967) Effect of background conversation and darkness on reaction time in anxious, hallucinating and severely ill schizophrenics. *Percept. motor Skills*, **25**, 353–358.

RAVEN, J. C. (1958) *Guide to using the Mill Hill Vocabulary Scale with the Progressive Matrices Scales.* London: H. K. Lewis.

REED, G. F. (1969a) 'Under-inclusion'—A characteristic of obsessional personality disorder: I. *Brit. J. Psychiat.*, **115**, 781–785.

REED, G. F. (1969b) 'Under-inclusion'—A characteristic of obsessional personality disorder: II. *Brit. J. Psychiat.*, 115, 787–790.

REED, J. L. (1968) The Proverbs Test in schizophrenia. *Brit. J. Psychiat.*, 114, 317–321.

RODNICK, E. H. and SHAKOW, D. (1940–41) Set in the schizophrenic as measured by a composite reaction time index. *Amer. J. Psychiat.*, 97, 214–225.

ROSENBAUM, G., COHEN, B. D., LUBY, E. D., GOTTLIEB, J. S., and YELEN, D. (1959) Comparison of Sernyl with other drugs: Simulation of schizophrenic performance with Sernyl, LSD-25, and Amobarbital (Amytal) Sodium: I. Attention, motor function and proprioception. *Amer. med. assoc. Archs. gen. Psychiat.*, 1, 651–656.

ROSENBAUM, G., FLENNING, F., and ROSEN, H. (1965) Effects of weight intensity on discrimination thresholds of normals and schizophrenics. *J. abnorm. Psychol.*, 70, 446–450.

ROSMAN, BERNICE, WILD, CYNTHIA, RICCI, JUDITH, FLECK, S., and LIDZ, T. (1964) Thought disorders in the parents of schizophrenic patients: A further study utilizing the object sorting test. *J. psychiat. Res.*, 2, 211–221.

RUTSCHMANN, J. (1961) Oppel-Kundt illusion in normals and schizophrenic patients: An examination of the perceptual primitivization hypothesis. *Percept. motor Skills*, 13, 399–415.

SALMON, PHILLIDA, BRAMLEY, JUDITH, and PRESLY, A. S. (1967) The word-in-context test as a measure of conceptualization in schizophrenics with and without thought disorder. *Brit. J. med. Psychol.*, 40, 253–259.

SALZINGER, K. (1957) Shift in judgment of weights as a function of anchoring stimuli and instructions in early schizophrenics and normals. *J. abnorm. soc. Psychol.*, 55, 43–49.

SALZINGER, K., PORTNOY, STEPHANIE, and FELDMAN, R. S. (1966) Verbal behavior in schizophrenics and some comments toward a theory of schizophrenia. In *Psychopathology of Schizophrenia* (Ed. Hoch, P. H. and Zubin, J.) New York: Grune and Stratton, 98–128.

SCHOOLER, CARMI and SILVERMAN, J. (1969) Perceptual styles and their correlates among schizophrenic patients. *J. abnorm. Psychol.*, 74, 459–470.

SCHOOLER, CARMI and ZAHN, T. P. (1968) The effect of closeness of social interaction on task performance and arousal in chronic schizophrenia. *J. nerv. ment. Dis.*, 147, 394–401.

SCHOPLER, E. and LOFTIN, JULIE (1969) Thinking disorders in parents of young psychotic children. *J. abnorm. Psychol.*, 74, 281–287.

SCHWARTZ, S. (1967a) Cognitive deficit among remitted schizophrenics: The role of a life-history variable. *J. abnorm. Psychol.*, 72, 54–58.

SCHWARTZ, S. (1967b) Diagnosis, level of social adjustment, and cognitive deficits. *J. abnorm. Psychol.*, 72, 446–453.

SCHWARTZMAN, A. E. and DOUGLAS, VIRGINIA I. (1962) Intellectual loss in schizophrenia: Part I. *Canad. J. Psychol.*, 16, 1–10.

SCHWARTZMAN, A. E., DOUGLAS, VIRGINIA I., and MUIR, W. R. (1962) Intellectual loss in schizophrenia: Part II. *Canad. J. Psychol.*, 16, 161–168.

SENF, RITA, HUSTON, P. E., and COHEN, B. D. (1955) Thinking deficit in schizophrenia and changes with amytal. *J. abnorm. soc. Psychol.*, 50, 383–387.

SETH, G. and BELOFF, H. (1959) Language impairment in a group of schizophrenics. *Brit. J. med. Psychol.*, 32, 288–293.

SHAKOW, D. (1946) The nature of deterioration in schizophrenic conditions. *Nerv. ment. dis. Monogr.*, 70, 1–88.

SHAKOW, D. (1962) Segmental Set. *Arch. gen. Psychiat.*, 6, 1–17.

SHAKOW, D. (1963) Psychological deficit in schizophrenia. *Behav. Sci.*, 8, 275–305.

SHAKOW, D. and MCCORMICK, M. Y. (1965) Mental set in schizophrenia studied in a discrimination reaction setting. *J. Person. Soc. Psychol.*, 1, 88–95.

SHAKOW, D., ROSENZWEIG, S., and HOLLANDER, L. (1966) Auditory apperceptive reactions to the tautophone by schizophrenic and normal subjects. *J. nerv. ment. Dis.*, 143, 1–15.

SHAPIRO, M. B. and NELSON, ELIZABETH H. (1955) An investigation of the nature of cognitive impairment in co-operative psychiatric patients. *Brit. J. med. Psychol.*, 28, 239–256.

SHAPIRO, M. B., SLATER, P., and CAMPBELL, D. (1962) The effects of distraction on psycho-motor slowness in co-operative, depressed, and schizophrenic subjects. *Brit. J. soc. clin. Psychol.*, 1, 121–126.

SHEPPARD, C., FIORENTINO, DIANE, COLLINS, LOIS, and MERLIS, S. (1969) Further study of performance errors on Raven's Progressive Matrices (1938). *J. Psychol.*, 71, 127–132.

SHIMKUNAS, A. M., GYNTHER, M. D., and SMITH, KATHLEEN (1966) Abstracting ability of schizophrenics before and during phenothiazine therapy. *Arch. of gen. Psychiat.*, 14, 79–83.

SHIMKUNAS, A. M., GYNTHER, M. D., and SMITH, KATHLEEN (1967) Schizophrenic responses to the Proverbs Test: Abstract, concrete, or autistic? *J. abnorm. Psychol.*, 72, 128–133.

SHIPLEY, W. C. (1940) A self-administering scale for measuring intellectual impairment and deterioration. *J. Psychol.*, 9, 371–377.

SHNEIDMAN, E. S. (1948) Schizophrenia and the MAPS test: A study of certain formal psycho-social aspects of fantasy production in schizophrenia as revealed by performance on the Make-A-Picture-Story (MAPS) test. *Genet. Psychol. Monogr.*, 38, 145–223.

SIBILIO, J. P., ANDREW, O., DART, DOROTHY, MOORE, K., and STEHMAN, V. (1959) Effects of Promazine Hydrochloride on attention in chronic schizophrenia. *Amer. med. assoc. Arch. Neurol. Psychiat.*, 81, 114–120.

SILVERMAN, J. (1964a) Perceptual control of stimulus intensity in paranoid and nonparanoid schizophrenia. *J. nerv. ment. Dis.*, 139, 545–549.

SILVERMAN, J. (1964b) The problem of attention in research and theory in schizophrenia. *Psychologic. Rev.*, 71, 352–379.

SILVERMAN, J. (1964c) Scanning-control mechanism and "cognitive filtering" in paranoid and nonparanoid schizophrenia. *J. consult. Psychol.*, 28, 385–393.

SILVERMAN, J. (1967) Variations in cognitive control and psychophysiological defense in the schizophrenias. *Psychosom. Med.*, **29**, 225–245.

SILVERMAN, J. (1968) Towards a more complex formulation of rod-and-frame performance in the schizophrenias. *Percept. motor Skills*, **27**, 1111–1114.

SILVERMAN, J., BERB, P. S. D., and KANTOR, R. (1966) Some perceptual correlates of institutionalization. *J. nerv. ment. Dis.*, **141**, 651–657.

SILVERMAN, L. H. and SILVERMAN, DORIS K. (1962) Ego impairment in schizophrenia as reflected in the object sorting test. *J. abnorm. soc. Psychol.*, **64**, 381–385.

SMITH, A. (1964) Mental deterioration in chronic schizophrenia. *J. nerv. ment. Dis.*, **139**, 479–487.

SMITH, E. E. (1970) Associative and editing processes in schizophrenic communication. *J. abnorm. Psychol.*, **75**, 182–186.

SNELBECKER, G. E., SHERMAN, L. J., ROTHSTEIN, E., and DOWNES, R. C. (1966) Schizophrenic and normal behavior on programmed inductive reasoning problems. *J. clin. Psychol.*, **22**, 415–417.

SNYDER, S., ROSENTHAL, D., and TAYLOR, I. A. (1961) Perceptual closure in schizophrenia. *J. abnorm. soc. Psychol.*, **63**, 131–136.

SPENCE, JANET T. and LAIR, C. V. (1964) Associative interference in the verbal learning performance of schizophrenics and normals. *J. abnorm. soc. Psychol.*, **68**, 204–209.

SPIEGEL, D. E. and LITROWNIK, A. J. (1968) The effects of dependency and self-assertiveness of schizophrenic patients on susceptibility to group influence in perceptual tasks. *J. clin. Psychol.*, **24**, 12–16.

SPOHN, H. E., THETFORD, P. E., and WOODHAM, F. L. (1970) Span of apprehension and arousal in schizophrenia. *J. abnorm. Psychol.*, **75**, 113–123.

STARR, B. J., LEIBOWITZ, H. W., and LUNDY, R. M. (1968) Size constancy in catatonia. *Percept. motor Skills*, **26**, 747–752.

STERN, J. A., SURPHLIS, W., and KOFF, E. (1965) Electrodermal responsiveness as related to psychiatric diagnosis and prognosis. *Psychophysiology*, **2**, 51–61.

STILSON, D. W. and KOPELL, B. S. (1964) The recognition of visual signals in the presence of visual noise by psychiatric patients. *J. nerv. ment. Dis.*, **139**, 209–221.

STILSON, D. W., KOPELL, B. S., VANDENBERGH, R., and DOWNS, MARION P. (1966) Perceptual recognition in the presence of noise by psychiatric patients. *J. nerv. ment. Dis.*, **142**, 235–247.

STORMS, L. H. and BROEN, W. E., Jr. (1969) A theory of schizophrenic behavioral disorganization. *Arch. gen. Psychiat.*, **20**, 129–144.

STORMS, L. H., BROEN, W. E., and LEVIN, I. P. (1967) Verbal associative stability and commonality as a function of stress in schizophrenics, neurotics, and normals. *J. consult. Psychol.*, **31**, 181–187.

STREINER, D. L. (1969) Effects of task complexity and verbal evaluation on the learning of normals and schizophrenics. *J. abnorm. Psychol.*, **74**, 606–611.

STURM, E. I. (1964) 'Conceptual area' among pathological groups: A failure to replicate. *J. abnorm. soc. Psychol.*, **69**, 216–223.

STURM, E. I. (1965) Overinclusion and concreteness among pathological groups. *J. Consult. Psychol.*, **29**, 9–18.

SUGERMAN, A. A. and CANCRO, R. (1968) Field independence and outcome in schizophrenia: A U-shaped relationship. *Percept. motor Skills*, **27**, 1007–1013.

THORPE, J. G. and BAKER, A. A. (1958) The effects of physical treatment on some psychological functions. *J. ment. Sci.*, **104**, 865–869.

TIZARD, J. and VENABLES, P. H. (1955–56) Reaction time responses by schizophrenics, mental defectives, and normal adults. *Amer. J. Psychiat.*, **112**, 803–807.

TIZARD, J. and VENABLES, P. H. (1957) The influence of extraneous stimulation on the reaction time of schizophrenics. *Brit. J. Psychol.*, **48**, 299–305.

TOLOR, A. (1964) Abstract ability in organics and schizophrenics. *J. Project. Techniques Person. Assess.*, **28**, 357–362.

TRUE, J. E. (1966) Learning of abstract responses by process and reactive schizophrenic patients. *Psychologic. Reps*, **18**, 51–55.

TRUNNELL, T. L. (1964) Thought disturbance in schizophrenia. *Arch. gen. Psychiat.*, **11**, 126–136.

TRUNNELL, T. L. (1965) Thought disturbance in schizophrenia: Replication study utilizing Piaget's theories. *Arch. gen. Psychiat.*, **13**, 9–18.

TUTKO, T. A. and SPENCE, JANET T. (1962) The performance of process and reactive schizophrenics and brain injured subjects on a conceptual task. *J. abnorm. soc. Psychol.*, **65**, 387–394.

VENABLES, P. H. (1960) The effect of auditory and visual stimulation on the skin potential response of schizophrenics. *Brain*, **83**, 77–92.

VENABLES, P. H. (1963a) Selectivity of attention, withdrawal, and cortical activation. *Arch. gen. Psychiat.*, **9**, 92–96.

VENABLES, P. H. (1963b) The relationship between level of skin potential and fusion of paired light flashes in schizophrenic and normal subjects. *J. Psychiat. Res.*, **1**, 279–287.

VENABLES, P. H. (1963c) Changes due to noise in the threshold of fusion of paired light flashes in schizophrenics and normals. *Brit. J. soc. clin. Psychol.*, **2**, 94–99.

VENABLES, P. H. (1964) Performance and level of activation in schizophrenics and normals. *Brit. J. Psychol.*, **55**, 207–218.

VENABLES, P. H. (1966a) Psychophysiological aspects of schizophrenia. *Brit. J. med. Psychol.*, **39**, 289–297.

VENABLES, P. H. (1966b) A comparison of two-flash and two-click thresholds in schizophrenic and normal subjects. *Quart. J. exp. Psychol.*, **18**, 371–373.

VENABLES, P. H. (1967) The relation of two-flash and two-click thresholds to withdrawal in paranoid and non-paranoid schizophrenics. *Brit. J. soc. clin. Psychol.*, **6**, 60–62.

VENABLES, P. H. and O'CONNOR, N. (1959) Reaction times to auditory and visual stimulation in schizophrenic and normal subjects. *Quart. J. exp. Psychol.*, **11**, 175–179.

VENABLES, P. H. and WING, J. K. (1962) Level of arousal and the subclassification of schizophrenia. *Arch. gen. Psychiat.*, **7**, 114–119.

WADSWORTH, W. V., WELLS, B. W. P., and SCOTT, R. F. (1962) A comparative study of chronic schizophrenic and normal subjects on a work task involving sequential operations. *J. ment. Sci.*, **108**, 309–316.

WARD, W. D. and CARLSON, W. A. (1966) Autonomic responsivity to variable input rates among schizophrenics classified on the process-reactive dimension. *J. abnorm. Psychol.*, **71**, 10–16.

WATSON, C. G. (1967) Interrelationships of six over-inclusive measures. *J. consult. Psychol.*, **31**, 517–520.

WECHSLER, D. (1944) *The Measurement of Adult Intelligence.* Baltimore: Williams and Wilkins.

WECKOWICZ, T. E. (1960) Perception of hidden pictures by schizophrenic patients. *Amer. med. assoc. Arch. gen. Psychiat.*, **2**, 521–527.

WECKOWICZ, T. E. and BLEWETT, D. B. (1959) Size constancy and abstract thinking in schizophrenic patients. *J. ment. Sci.*, **105**, 909–934.

WEISS, R. L. and NORDTVEDT, EMILIA I. (1964) Programmed stimulus input and the development of a perceptual set in schizophrenic and normal subjects. *Psychonomic Sci.*, **1**, 195–196.

WELLS, F. L. and KELLEY, C. M. (1920) Intelligence and psychosis. *Amer. J. Insanity*, **77**, 17–45.

WHITE, MARY A. (1949) A study of schizophrenic language. *J. abnorm. soc. Psychol.*, **44**, 61–74.

WILLIAMS, E. B. (1964) Deductive reasoning in schizophrenia. *J. abnorm. Psychol.*, **69**, 47–61.

WILLNER, A. (1965) Impairment of knowledge of unusual meanings of familiar words in brain damage and schizophrenia. *J. abnorm. Psychol.*, **70**, 405.

WITTMAN, M. P. (1941) A scale for measuring prognosis in schizophrenic patients. *Elgin State Hospital Papers*, **4**, 20–33.

WOLFGANG, A., PISHKIN, V., and ROSENBLUH, E. S. (1968) Concept identification of schizophrenics as a function of social interaction, sex, and task complexity. *J. abnorm. Psychol.*, **73**, 336–342.

YATES, A. J. (1966a) Data-processing levels and thought disorder in schizophrenia. *Austral. J. Psychol.*, **18**, 103–117.

YATES, A. J. (1966b) Psychological deficit. In *Annual Review of Psychology* (Ed. Farnsworth, P. R.). New York: Annual Reviews Inc., 111–144.

ZAHN, T. P., ROSENTHAL, D., and SHAKOW, D. (1963) Effects of irregular preparatory intervals on reaction time in schizophrenia. *J. abnorm. soc. Psychol.*, **67**, 44–52.

ZASLOW, R. W. (1950) A new approach to the problem of conceptual thinking in schizophrenia. *J. consult. Psychol.*, **14**, 335–339.

ZILBOORG, G. and HENRY, G. W. (1941) *A History of Medical Psychology.* New York: Norton.

PART THREE
Causes and Determinants of Abnormal Behaviour

15

Constitutional Factors and Abnormal Behaviour

LINFORD REES

During the nine years following the period covered by the last review (Rees, 1960) advances in the field of human constitution have been concerned with the refinement, evaluation, and extension of existing methods of investigating human constitution rather than the development of radically new methods. The application of sophisticated methods of statistical analysis dealing with complex data in this field has been greatly facilitated by the use of computers.

Improved methods of assessing psychological attributes, biochemical, physiological, and endocrinological characteristics have also contributed to advances in our knowledge in this field.

The study of human constitution has for one of its major objectives the discovery of stable organic correlations (integrated biological relations between the morphological, psychological, and pathological characteristics of the individual) and, eventually, the precise numerical measurement of such correlations (Pearl and Ciocco, 1934).

The term constitution is variously used and most frequently in the limited sense of susceptibility to disease. In this work the term is used in its wider connotation and refers to the sum total of the morphological, psychological, and physiological characters of an individual, all being mainly determined by heredity but influenced, in varying degrees, by environmental factors.

Physique lends itself more readily to exact measurement than other constitutional attributes, and provides a convenient starting point for the study of correlations between the various aspects of human constitution.

There is an infinite choice of morphological and other constitutional attributes for the study of human constitution. Attributes that show marked variability between individuals and relative constancy within the individual are more likely to be the most useful and relevant for human constitutional research. The choice of variable will ultimately be determined by practical results, namely its usefulness, fruitfulness and validity in studying constitutional correlates. The concept of human constitution connotes predominant genetic determination and the relative constancy of constitutional attributes within the individual. Observable and measurable morphological characteristics are conveniently referred to as the morphophenotype. The morphophenotype is the resultant of the interaction of the morphogenotype (i.e. the sum total of the genetically determined morphological characteristics) and environmental influences.

The various aspects of human constitution that may be investigated can be classified into—

1. *Morphological.* Among various morphological characteristics studied in human constitutional research are general bodily configuration (physical type, bodily *habitus*, somatotype); body size; the distribution and relative development of tissue components, e.g. muscle, fat, skeletal and connective tissue; relative development of various physical attributes, e.g. disharmonious growth (dysplasia), the relative development of masculine and feminine characteristics (androgyny, gynandromorphy), etc.

2. *Physiological.* Particularly relevant in constitutional studies are the functional characteristics of the autonomic, central, and peripheral nervous systems; cardiovascular and other visceral functions; anabolic-catabolic processes; biochemical characteristics; endocrine balance, etc.

3. *Psychological.* Aspects of human constitution include personality in its manifold aspects, temperament, character, intelligence, perceptive characteristics, psychomotor functions, etc.

487

4. *Immunological.* This classification includes relationships between various constitutional attributes and disease susceptibility, including physical illnesses, psychiatric, and psychosomatic disorders.

The origin of concepts regarding possible relationships between physical and psychological characteristics and predisposition to diseases is rooted in antiquity, and the present status of constitutional research can best be considered against the background of its historical development.

Historical Development of Concepts Relating Physical and Psychological Characteristics

The tendency to classify one's fellow beings into types according to physical characteristics is deep-rooted in human nature and has been carried out from ancient times. Classification into types serves to bring the chaos of manifold individual differences into some degree of order.

The ancient Hindus classified men, according to physical and behavioural characteristics, into types designated the hare, the bull, and the horse, and women, into types referred to as the mare, the elephant, and the deer.

Physicians of ancient Graeco-Roman medicine described a number of different physical types with alleged specific susceptibility to certain diseases. Other writers attempted to correlate external lineaments of the body with mental and moral qualities.

The tendency to correlate physical and mental attributes can be described historically, in three main fields—

(*a*) Social-cultural notions of stereotypes, as exemplified by quotations from the literature.
(*b*) Medical. The attempt to discover correlations between various types of somatic *habitus*, temperament, and susceptibility to diseases.
(*c*) Physiognomy, or the study of man's external lineaments, as a clue to his mental and moral qualities.

POPULAR NOTIONS OF PHYSICAL TYPE CORRELATES

In literature we find popular notions, dating from antiquity, that persons of certain physical types are associated with characteristic personality, character, or degree of intelligence. In Plutarch's *Lives* (Chap. 62, Sect. 5) Julius Caesar exclaims: 'I am not much in fear of those fat, sleek fellows but rather of those pale, thin ones'. He refers to Anthony and Dolabella as the fat ones and to Brutus and Cassius as the thin ones. Shakespeare refers to relationships between physique and personality in a number of plays, the best example probably being in Caesar's remarks to Anthony (*Julius Caesar*, I, ii, 192)—

Let me have men about me that are fat;
Sleek-headed men and such as sleep o' nights.
Yond' Cassius has a lean and hungry look;
He thinks too much: such men are dangerous ...
Would he be fatter! but I fear him not:
Yet if my name were liable to fear,
I do not know the man I should avoid
So soon as that spare Cassius.

The idea of a relationship between physique and intelligence is expressed in the old Italian proverb *Capo grasso, cervello magro* (Fat heads, lean brains); in an old Greek proverb which states: 'A gross belly does not produce a refined mind' and in Shakespeare's *Love's Labour's Lost* (I, i, 26)—

Fat paunches have lean pates, and dainty bits
Make rich the ribs, but bankrupt quite the wits.

The good humoured jollity and physical proportions of Falstaff are well known. Finally, the old English apothegm, 'Fat and merry, lean and sad,' may be quoted as it describes succinctly the popular notion of association between personality and physique.

Similarly, we can trace the concepts of the relationship between physical and temperamental characteristics right back to the time of the ancient Greek scholars and physicians. It is possible, as described by Ciocco (1936), to trace two parallel lines of development in the study of relationship between physical and mental attributes. The first is concerned with the humoral theories of the early Graeco-Roman writers, and the second is the science of physiognomy, founded by Aristotle.

HUMORAL CONCEPTS OF CONSTITUTION

Physical characteristics played a prominent part in the humoral theories of ancient Graeco-Roman medicine. Hippocrates (460–377 B.C.) thought sound health to be due to an optimum mixture of humours and disease to a disturbance of this relationship.

The humours were four in number, because, according to Empedocles and Pythagoras, there were four primary elements from which all substances were constituted, namely fire, water, earth, and air, to which corresponded the four humours, blood, lymph, and black and yellow bile. Galen (*c.* A.D. 129–199) gave detailed descriptions of nine temperamental types, which were considered to be determined by various mixtures of the humours. The various temperamental types were characterised by variations in the character of skin, hair, fat, skeleton, muscle, shape of chest, etc. The perfect temperament was characterised by physical symmetry. The Galenic doctrine of temperaments was, in fact, a general theory of disease causation as well as an attempt to explain individual differences in behaviour. Galen's teaching dominated medical thought and practice for many centuries. It was reproduced by Sir Thomas Elyot in 1534 in his book *Castell of Helth*. Stahl (1660–1734), being influenced by the then recent discovery of the circulation of the blood by Harvey, modified Galen's doctrine and attributed temperamental differences to the passage of various humours through channels of varying size. The fourfold classification of temperaments into sanguine, phlegmatic, choleric, and melancholic types was reproduced in the eighteenth century, by Thomas Laycock, Professor at Edinburgh.

Parallel to the study of constitution in relation to disease was the study of physiognomy.

DEVELOPMENT OF THE STUDY OF PHYSIOGNOMY

Aristotle (384–322 B.C.) is regarded as the founder of the subject physiognomy, which attempted to justify popular and traditional concepts relating man's external lineaments with his mental and moral qualities. He published his beliefs in a book entitled *Physiognomonica*, in which he stated that the mental character is conditioned by the state of the body.

The study of physiognomy was carried on, as described by Ciocco (1936), in a similar fashion by Polemonis, a Greek writer of the third century A.D., and Adamantius, a Jewish physician of the fourth century A.D.

Della Porta (1536–1615) published a book *De humana physiognomonica*, in which he reported many facial characteristics that were alleged to accompany different moral and intellectual traits. This work is mostly speculation and based on a minimum of observation, as is Lavater's book on physiognomy (1841).

In the late eighteenth and early nineteenth centuries, the study of physiognomy was deflected by the work of Combe, Gall, and Spurzheim (1809) into the now discredited science of phrenology, and later in the nineteenth century by the work of Lombroso (1889, 1911), who founded the doctrine of criminal anthropology, which postulated that the criminal as found in prison was an atavistic anomaly presenting morbid physical stigmata.

MODERN DEVELOPMENT OF KNOWLEDGE OF HUMAN CONSTITUTION

No significant progress was made in the study of the relationship between physical constitution, character

and susceptibility to disease from the time of Hippocrates and Galen until the late nineteenth century, when Beneke (1878), a pathologist of Marburg, published data on the measurements of various internal organs, and the variations in size associated with age, disease, and physical type. He described two main physical types: (1) the scrofulous-phthisical, and (2) the rachito-carcinomatous, which roughly correspond to the modern distinction of the narrow and the broad types of body build.

Working round about the same time, was an Italian physician, Di Giovanni (1919) who made an extensive study of the relationship between physical constitution and susceptibility to diseases and who may be regarded as the founder of clinical anthropometry. He, however, went to the extreme to trying to prove that the cause of the special morbidity of an organ resided in its disproportionate development relative to that of other organs. He classified individuals by means of combinations of certain physical characteristics. His first and third combinations corresponded to the modern narrow and broad types. The Italian school of clinical anthropology, founded by Di Giovanni, was continued by Viola (1925 and 1932), who made extensive investigations into physical characteristics of the population of Northern Italy. He concluded that different physical types were due to differences in the relative development of the trunk and limbs. Viola's index has trunk volume (eight measurements) as the denominator and the length of the arm and leg as the numerator. He recognised three morphological types—

1. the megalosplanchnic, characterised by a preponderance of the vegetative or digestive system, having a large trunk and short limbs;
2. the microsplanchnic, characterised by preponderance of the limbs over the vegetative or digestive system, having a small trunk and long limbs;
3. the normosplanchnic, which is midway between (1) and (2), having the harmonious relationship of trunk and limb.

Other workers of the Italian school included M. Boldrini (1929, 1931), who corroborated Viola's thesis of the fundamental relationship between trunk volume and limb length for discriminating physical types. He demonstrated statistically that chest circumference and stature could be substituted for the trunk volume and limb value of Viola's unwieldy index. Using an index consisting of circumference/stature he found that brevitypes, corresponding to the megalosplanchnic type, tended to have numerous progeny, whereas longitypes, corresponding to the microsplanchnic type, tended to have a higher age of death and a smaller number of progeny.

Boldrini's system was statistically strong, but anatomically weak, whereas Viola's system was strong anatomically, but weak statistically.

The Work of Kretschmer

The modern revival of interest in the relationship between physical constitution, temperament, personality, and psychiatric disorders was greatly stimulated by the work of Ernst Kretschmer, who, in 1921, published his book entitled *Körperbau und Charakter.*

Starting with the study of psychotic and potentially psychotic patients, he described, using a limited number of physical measurements, four main types of physique—

1. the asthenic or leptosomatic type, characterised by deficiency in thickness in all parts of the body. Length tends to preponderate in comparison with breadth and circumferential measurements;
2. the athletic type with a strong development of skeletal and muscular systems. The shoulders are wide, the chest is well developed and the trunk tapers in its lower part;
3. pyknic or pyknosomatic type is characterised by pronounced development of the body cavities and a tendency to increased fat deposition on the trunk. The extremities are short relative to circumferential measurements. The feet and hands tend to be broad and well upholstered with fat;
4. dysplastic group, which includes certain marked dysglandular syndromes.

He studied the distribution of these types in eighty-five manic depressive patients and one hundred and seventy-five schizophrenics and concluded—

1. that there was a clear biological affinity between the psychic disposition of manic-depressives and the pyknic type of body build;
2. that schizophrenes exhibit, with many varieties of crossing and blending, the characteristic features of a diversity of physical types, the most common of which are the leptosomatic, asthenic, and certain types of dysplasia (namely, certain varieties of eunuchoid, polyglandular obesity, infantilistic and hypoplastic physiques);
3. that there was a weak affinity between schizophrenia and pyknic body build and likewise between manic-depressive psychosis and leptomsomatic, athletic, and dysplastic types of body build.

Kretschmer extended his theory from the realm of psychotic types to normal personality types. He traced a graduation of temperamental characteristics from the pathological schizophrenic patient through schizoid psychopathy to the well-adjusted schizothymic personality. Likewise, he traced a gradation of characteristics from manic-depressives through cycloid psychopathy, to normal well-adjusted cyclothymic personality. He contended that schizoid psychopaths and schizothymes tend to have leptosomatic, athletic and certain types of dysplastic physique, and that cycloid psychopaths and cyclothymes tended to have a pyknic type of physique.

The work of Kretschmer must be accorded due importance, not only because he elucidated relationships between physical types and certain psychotic illnesses, but because of the tremendous amount of research stimulated by his theory. The value of his work was limited because of certain methodological difficulties; for example, his description of types was to a large extent based on clinical impression and only to a very limited degree defined by anthropometric measurements and indices. His classification tended to emphasise the existence of physical types as discrete and independent entities, although he does stress that the types described by him should be regarded as focal points around which a number of variations are distributed.

A large number of workers subjected Kretschmer's hypothesis to experimental investigation. Some investigators were unable to support Kretschmer's hypothesis from their findings, others only in part, and some were able to give strong support to the theory; these will be discussed more fully later.

Much of the work that followed the publication of Kretschmer's (1921) theory was handicapped because the variations in body build in the normal population had not been ascertained by satisfactory objective inductive methods. Knowledge regarding factors underlying such variations was lacking, and indices of body build that were available were not based on an inductive approach designed to determine which measurements in fact were likely to discriminate physical types.

Survey of Classifications of Physical Types

A large variety of typological classifications of physique have appeared since Hippocrates delineated the *habitus phthisicus* and the *habitus apoplecticus*. A list of such classifications is given in Table 15.1.

The basis used for various classifications is diverse, varying from general body shape and other morphological characteristics to theories based on alleged physiological, immunological, dietetic, and developmental features.

Table 15.1. Comparison of Classsification of Physical Types

	1	2	3
Hippocrates (460–400 B.C.)	*H. apoplecticus*	—	*H. phthisicus*
Rostan (1828)	Digestive	Muscular	Respiratory-cerebral
Beneke (1876)	Rachitic	Carcinomatous	Scrofulous-phthisical
di Giovanni (1880)	3rd Comb.	2nd Comb.	1st Comb.
Manouvrier (1902)	Brachyskeletal	Mesoskeletal	Macroskeletal
Virenius (1904)	Connective	Muscular	Epithelial
Stiller (1907)	—	Hypertonic	Atonic
Sigaud (1908)	Digestive	Muscular	Respiratory-cerebral
Bean (1912)	Hypo-entomorph	Meso-entomorph	Hyper-entomorph
Bryant (1915)	Herbivorous	Normal	Carnivorous
Mills (1917)	Hypersthenic	Sthenic	Asthenic
Viola (1919)	Macrosplanchnic	Normosplanchnic	Microsplanchnic
Kretschmer (1921)	Pyknic	Athletic	Leptosomatic
Bauer (1924)	Hypersthenic	Sthenic	Asthenic
Aschner (1924)	Broad	Normal	Slender
Bounak (1924)	Euryplastic	—	Stenoplastic
McAuliffe (1925)	Round	—	Flat
Stockard (1925)	Lateral	Intermediate	Linear
Draper (1925)	Gall bladder	—	Ulcer
Weidendreich (1926)	Eurysome	—	Leptosome
Pearl (1926)	Pyknic	Intermediate	Asthenic
Pende (1927)	Macrosplanchnic	Normosplanchnic	Microsplanchnic
Von Rohden (1928)	Endodermic	Mesodermic	Ectodermic
Boldrini	Brachytype	—	Longitype
Wiersma (1933)	Eurysomic	—	Leptosomic
Sheldon (1940)	Endomorph	Mesomorph	Ectomorph
Conrad (1941)	Pyknomorphy	Metromorphy	Leptomorphy
Burt (1947)	Pachysome	—	Leptosome
Martigny (1948)	Entoblastique	Mesoblastique	Ectoblastique
Hammond (1953)	Pachymorph	—	Leptomorph
Hammond (1957)	Eurysome	Mesosome	Leptosome
Rees and Eysenck (1945) and Rees (1950) .	Eurymorph	Mesomorph	Leptomorph
Lindegard (1953)	Fat factor high	Muscle and sturdiness factors high	Length factor high
Parnell (1957)	Fat factor (F) dominant	Muscle factor (M) dominant	Linear factor (L) dominant

It is noteworthy that the majority of authors, many unknown to each other, have described more or less corresponding physical types as shown in the respective columns of Table 15.1. Generally, a dichotomy of physique is described with contrasting antithetical types in columns 1 and 3, with a third type in some classifications.

The theory of physical types as disparate and mutually exclusive categories of body build has had to be abandoned in the light of more recent research and is now replaced by the concept of a continuous variation in body build (Rees, 1943).

During recent years several new techniques have been applied to the study of body build. These include—

1. factorial analysis and other statistical procedures for investigating variations in body build;
2. Sheldon's system of somatotypes;
3. Lindegard's method;
4. miscellaneous techniques such as analysis of tissue components, body disproportions, androgyny, etc.

Factorial Analysis of Human Physique

Until comparatively recently, constitutional research has been severely handicapped by the lack of reliable data concerning the variations in physique in the normal population and a lack of effective and economical description.

The problem was to develop a method that could deal inductively with the observed variations in physical dimensions, and that did not depend on preconceived ideas regarding the nature of the variations of body build and their determinants.

The technique of factorial analysis, which had proved fruitful in the study of intelligence, provided a relatively objective and inductive method of elucidating the variations in body build and their description in the most economical way.

Factorial analysis is concerned with the resolution of a set of variables in terms of a smaller number of categories or factors. Essentially, it is a method that reduces a large number of correlations or covariations between variables to a small number of factors accounting for the correlations or covariations.

Factorial analysis is of particular advantage in the study of human physique as it provides a holistic representation of the human body far more comprehensive than that given by anthropometric measurements alone. Factorial analysis may be applied to the study of physique in two distinct ways, i.e. either applied to traits (anthropometric measurements) or to persons.

The majority of factorial studies on physique deal with traits as these studies provide an inductive method of ascertaining the nature of variations in physique. Factorial analysis of persons instead of traits provides, as indicated by Burt (1943), a method of determining how true an individual is to a particular type. It involves the specification of the type in question by a set of representative measurements expressed in standard measure. The correlation of a given individual with the standard pattern indicates how nearly he approximates to a perfect representative of the type.

The steps undertaken in the factorial analysis of anthropometric measurements are—

1. The calculation of correlations or covariations between all measurements for the entire group giving a matrix of correlations or covariations.
2. Determining the factors underlying the observed correlations or covariations and removing the effect of each factor from the matrix before extracting the next factor; this process is repeated until the residual correlations are not significant statistically.

There are a number of different techniques of factorial analysis but, basically, each is concerned with analysing correlations or covariations in terms of factors which may refer—

1. to all the correlations or covariations in the matrix, i.e. general factors;
2. some of the correlations or covariations only, i.e. group factors;
3. specific or error factors that relate to separate measurements.

Table 15.2

Investigator	Group studied			Factor	
	Age in years	Sex	Composition	I per cent	II per cent
Cohen (1938)	Adults	M	British students	44	24
Cohen (1940)	Adults	M	British psychotics	46	19
Cohen (1941)	Adults	M	Jewish psychotics	35	25
Dearborn and Rothney (1941) . .	Children	—	American	59	8
Hammond (1942)	Adults	M	Irish	31	9
Burt (1944)	21	M	British students	50–60	—
	16	M	American		
Rees and Eysenck (1945) . . .	Adults	M	British soldiers	35	25
Burt (1947)				55	14
Burt (1949)	12–13	M	British schoolboys	45	13
Burt and Banks (1947)					
Mullen (1940) (1)	7	F	American	43	5
(2)	9	F	American	41	5
(3)	11	F	American	48	4
(4)	13	F	American	39	9
(5)	15	F	American	32	11
(6)	17	F	American	29	12
Rees (1950)	Adults	F	British	—	—
Hammond (1957)	1	M	British schoolchildren	35	7
	1	F	British schoolchildren	35	5
	2	M	British schoolchildren	40	8
	2	F	British schoolchildren	50	8
	2	M	British schoolchildren	41	7
	3	F	British schoolchildren	50	8
	4	M	British schoolchildren	47	8
	4	F	British schoolchildren	43	8
	5	M	British schoolchildren	41	12
	5	F	British schoolchildren	47	8
	7–11	M	British schoolchildren	57	7
	7–11	F	British schoolchildren	53	9
	0–5	M	Aberdeen children	29	6
	0–5	F	Aberdeen children	43	4

In the factorial methods usually employed in Great Britain, the factors extracted are independent or uncorrelated and are designated orthogonal factors.

Some factorial techniques involve rotation of factors in an attempt to get the best descriptions of groups of correlations, thus providing oblique or correlated factors.

The most frequently used factorial procedure is to extract a general factor first and then group factors relating to the shape of the body as a whole or of its constituent parts. Factorial analysis, whichever technique is used, provides a means of classifying body build with the fewest differentia covering the largest number of anthropometric data. The results of factorial analysis of physique also tell us which measurements help to discriminate and measure physical types. These may be combined in the form of a regression equation of weighted measurements, or in the form of suitably constructed ratios as indices of body build.

Factorial analysis was first applied to the study of physique by Spearman (1927); it was later employed by Cyril Burt (1938) and subsequently by Cohen (1938, 1940, 1941) and Hammond (1942); there are more recent papers by Burt (1947, 1947, 1950, 1950), and by Burt and Banks (1947).

A description will be given of factorial studies of physique in adult men carried out by Rees and Eysenck (1945), and in adult women by Rees (1950) and the findings will be discussed in relation to those of a number of other workers who have employed factorial methods.

Some of the results are shown in Table 15.2 and will be referred to later.

FACTORIAL STUDIES OF PHYSIQUE IN ADULTS

Rees and Eysenck (1945) calculated the intercorrelations of eighteen variables (age and seventeen body measurements) for a group of 200 soldiers successively admitted to Mill Hill Emergency Hospital. The measurements utilised in the study were taken according to the standardised procedures described by Hrdlicka (1939), Martin (1914) and Wilder (1920), and included stature, suprasternal height, symphysis height, breadth, and length of skull, biacromial diameter, transverse chest diameter, sagittal chest diameter, bicristal diameter, trunk length, sternal length, arm length to radial styloid, arm length to tip of medius, chest circumference at inspiration, chest circumference at expiration, hip circumference and weight.

It was found that all the correlation coefficients between physical measurements were positive, indicating the existence of a general factor. A factorial

analysis was carried out by Burt's (1940) summation method. Two main factors were extracted. The first factor, which had positive saturations throughout, contributed 34 per cent of the variance. The second factor was bipolar, having positive saturations with length measurements and negative saturations with breadth and circumferential measurements. This was clearly a factor of physical type, differentiating the *linear type* of physique at one extreme preponderating in length measurements in comparison with breadth and circumferential measurements, and a *broad type* at the other extreme, preponderating in breadth, width, and circumferential measurements relative to length.

The factor saturations of body measurements are shown diagrammatically in Fig. 15.1.

A similar study was carried out by Rees (1950) on a group of 200 female members of the Armed Forces suffering from neurosis, successively admitted to Mill Hill Emergency Hospital. The measurements taken in this group included stature, suprasternal height, symphysis height, breadth and length of skull, biacromial diameter, transverse chest diameter, sagittal chest diameter, bicristal diameter, length of sternum, length of arm, chest circumference at full inspiration and full expiration, hip circumference, and weight.

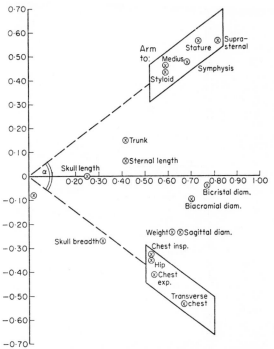

Fig. 15.1. Saturation of anthropometric measurements with general and type factors, men

Each of the fifteen variables was correlated with the others and the matrix of intercorrelation was analysed by Burt's (1940) summation method. Again it was found that all the measurements were positively correlated, indicating the existence of a general factor. When the effect of the general factor was removed, it was found that the residual co-efficients were significant and varied from −0·33 to +0·59. The second factor extracted was bipolar, having positive saturations for length measurements and negative saturations for breadth, width, and circumferential measurements. This factor, as in the male group, accounts for the existence of two antithetical types of bodily architecture, namely, the narrow, linear or leptomorphic type at one extreme and its antithesis, the broad, lateral, or eurymorphic type at the other.

The saturations of anthropometric measurements with the general and type factor in women are shown in Fig. 15.2.

These findings derived from factorial analysis of physique in British adult men and women are supported by a large number of other workers using factorial methods in groups of different ages, racial composition and socio-economic status.

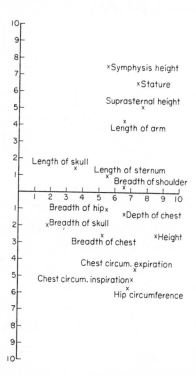

Fig. 15.2. Saturation of anthropometric measurements with general and type factors in two hundred women

It was strikingly shown by Burt (1947), from an anthropometric study of 30,000 men of the Royal Air Force, that in almost every age group and nationality the same two main factors emerged. Burt (1938) in his pioneering paper, describing factorial analysis of physical measurements in groups of British children and adults, also elicited a well-marked general factor and factors making for disproportionate growth in length, on the one extreme, and breadth, thickness, girth, and weight on the other extreme.

Similar factors have been found from factorial studies on groups of different racial composition, e.g. Cohen (1941), in a group of 100 Jewish patients in a mental hospital, Hammond (1942) in a group of 100 adult Irishmen, and Burt (1944) in groups of young British and American men.

Thurstone (1946) re-analysed data provided by Hammond (1942) consisting of twelve body measurements in a group of adult Irish males. He considered that there were four primary factors, two of these concerned with size and the other two concerned with length and breadth measurements, namely (1) head size, (2) bone length, (3) transverse girth dimensions, and (4) a factor considered to be related to the size of the extremities.

The factors elicited from factorial analysis of body measurements will, of course, depend on the number and selection of the original measurements used. For example, Howells (1951) carried out a factorial analysis of physical measurements in 153 university students. The data included a large number of head and face dimensions. There were three limb measurements and three facial length measurements. Howells elicited factors for limb and facial length and concluded that the factors extracted probably depended more on the measurements chosen than on growth patterns. He elicited, in all, seven factors, which he interpreted as relating to general body size, long bone length, cranial size, brain size, lateral facial cranial development, face length, and ear size. These can be grouped into four size factors, two length factors and a breadth factor.

Heath (1952) carried out a second order factorial analysis on twenty-nine measurements obtained on 4,128 women, taken in a study for women's clothing size standards. She extracted five first order factors, which were interpreted as length of bones, cancellous bone size, lower body girth, girth of extremities and upper body girth. Second-order factors were closely related to the usual length and breadth factors and the similarity between this solution and that obtained by the results of Rees and Eysenck (1945) and Rees (1950) was pointed out by Eysenck (1953).

Moore and Hsu (1946) carried out a factorial analysis of thirty-one measurements of head and body in a group of psychotic patients and found a general size factor; a factor of leptosomia, shown particularly in the length of hands, face, nose, long bones of the limbs, and stature; a factor of girth, or lateral type of body build, shown in chest, waist measurements, and breadth of face; a factor of robustness, shown in forearm circumference, calf circumference, and thickness of the neck. These can be grouped into a general size factor and a bipolar factor for leptosomia *vs.* lateral and circumferential measurements.

FACTORIAL STUDIES OF PHYSIQUE IN CHILDREN AND ADOLESCENTS

The question arises whether the factors of physique elicited in adults are also found during the growth period of childhood and adolescence.

Carter and Krause (1936) analysed data provided by Bakwin and Bakwin (1929) on neonates. A factorial analysis was carried out on groups of newborn babies, 608 male and 609 female. In both groups the results gave strong evidence of a general factor of size, the other factors elicited being difficult to characterise. Marshall (1936) factor-analysed eighteen measurements taken on children ranging in age from birth to 6 years. He considered that there was evidence for four group factors, one of which was identified with subcutaneous fatty tissue roughly corresponding to our general factor, but the other three group factors were difficult to characterise. Hammond (1957) reported factorial studies of physique in children ranging in age from birth to 18 years. In addition to his own data he used, for comparison, data obtained from Carter and Krause's (1936) analysis of the Bakwen's data and that provided from Low's (1952) Aberdeen study. In all age groups both in boys and girls, he found evidence of a general factor and a type factor that differentiated between the growth of long bones, on the one hand, and breadth of trunk and limbs, on the other. He found, in addition, evidence of two subgroups corresponding to limb-breadth development and trunk-breadth development, which were related to some extent. McCloy (1940) carried out a factorial analysis on nineteen measurements on groups of boys and girls ranging in age from infancy to adult life. The first factor extracted was interpreted as being concerned with the development of fat and subcutaneous tissue. The second factor was one of linearity and the third was described as a cross-section type factor having saturations with girth, width, and depth measurements. The second and third factors could be regarded as the opposite manifestations of a bipolar factor. The fourth factor extracted could not be clearly identified, but was most prominently related to chest measurements and shoulder width. Mullen (1940) studied groups of girls between 7 and 17 years of age and carried out a factorial analysis of anthropometric measurements in each age group. She found a general factor of size and two group factors, one being concerned with length and the other related to weight, bi-iliac width, bitrochanteric diameter, chest girth, chest width, and chest depth.

Rees (1950) found that the results obtained by Mullen (1940) in American girls corresponded closely with the results of his investigation of 200 adult British women. For example, there was a correlation of +0·64 between the first factor saturation of the traits in Mullen's groups and Rees's group (Rees, 1950).

Burt (1949) gave further results derived from factorial analysis of 457 boys aged 12 to 13 years. The correlations between physical measurements were first analysed by the method of simple summation and subsequently by the method of subdivided factors. The results of analysis involving subdivided factors indicated that the leptomorphic factor had two subfactors, one for limb length and the other for trunk length, and the pyknic factor had two

Classification of Physique in Terms of Orthogonal Subdivided Group Factors

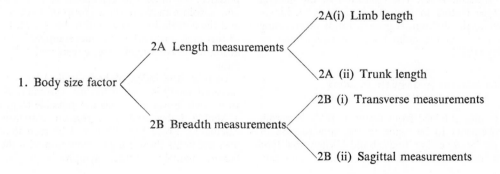

subfactors, one for transverse measurements and the other for sagittal measurements.

When it is considered that the various factorial studies of physique have differed not only in factorial method but in selection of measurements, and have dealt with groups differing in age, sex, and racial status, there is a noteworthy consistency in the results. When marked differences occur in results they may be accounted for by: (1) particular choice of anthropometric measurements (e.g. Howells, 1951), (2) the factorial technique used, or (3) the interpretations of the factors extracted.

It is agreed with Hammond (1957) that the most direct method of analysis is that of extracting a general factor and then bipolar contrasting factors. Group factors need be invoked only if this method proves to be inadequate to express the relations satisfactorily, as for example, when there is evidence of an odd number of groups, or when relationships appear to apply to a small part of the correlation matrix.

Accurate comparison of the results of different workers is possible only if the body measurements are the same. Alternatively, the analysis must be confined to those measurements common to the respective groups. This requirement would involve re-analysis from the correlation stage and has the twofold disadvantage of being laborious and limiting the data eligible for comparison.

It should be remembered that the factors elicited by factorial analysis are primarily statistical abstractions and further research will be needed to ascertain their relationship to genetic factors and growth processes and to endocrine, metabolic, or other biochemical processes.

The importance and possible biological significance of the general and type factors are attested by their discovery at all ages during the growth period and in adult life, in each sex, and also in different racial and social-cultural groups. Similar factors have been found in the animal kingdom, e.g. factorial analysis of physique of cows (Tanner and Burt, 1954), rabbits (Tanner and Sawin, 1953), and rats (Watson, 1956). The operation of the general and type factors in human physique is strikingly similar to the differential growth ratios determining body forms in the animal kingdom described by Huxley (1932).

INDICES FOR THE ASSESSMENT OF BODY
BUILD DERIVED FROM FACTORIAL STUDIES

The results obtained from factorial analysis permit improvements to be made in the construction of indices for assessing body build. When the type factor has been isolated, it is possible to ascertain which measurements are correlated most highly with it, and, therefore, the ones most likely to be useful in the discrimination of physical types. There is a number of possible ways in which such information might be used to construct indices of body build. Undoubtedly, the best measure of body type would be given by a regression equation using body measurements as terms, weighted according to their correlation with the type factor. Such indices are, however, complicated, cumbersome, and involve tedious calculations, thus limiting their practical usefulness.

Rees and Eysenck (1945) found that two measurements were highly correlated with the type factor, namely stature and transverse chest diameter. These measurements had similar saturations with the size factor and had similar saturations, but of opposite sign, with the type factor. The combination of these measurements in a ratio such as

$$\frac{\text{stature}}{\text{transverse chest diameter}}$$

would be free of the size factor and would tell us the individual's position the body-type continuum. In order to have a convenient figure without decimals, and a mean near 100, stature was multiplied by 100 and transverse chest diameter by 6. The Rees-Eysenck body-build index for males is therefore

$$\frac{\text{stature} \times 100}{\text{transverse chest diameter} \times 6.}$$

Tables for the ready calculation of the index are provided by Rees and Eysenck (1945) and a nomogram has been devised by Hamilton (1950) to permit ready calculation of the index.

As stature and transverse chest diameter differ with regard to variability, it might be suggested, on statistical grounds, that standard measure (i.e. the measurement expressed in terms of standard deviation units from the mean) rather than absolute measurements should be used in the index. To determine whether this was, in fact, necessary in practice, the index was calculated both in standard and absolute measure on a group of 1,100 soldiers and the correlation was found to be +0·94. In view of this high correlation, the more convenient use of absolute measurements was considered fully justifiable.

In men, the index of body build, derived from factorial analysis was, therefore, extremely simple. In women, however, it was not possible to produce a simple index and a regression equation was calculated. From Fig. 9.2 it will be seen that four measurements show a high correlation with the type factor, namely stature, symphysis height, hip

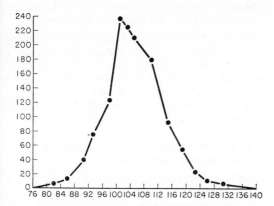

Fig. 15.3. Frequency distribution curve of

$$\frac{\text{Stature} \times 100}{\text{Transverse chest diameter} \times 6}$$

index in a group of 1,000 soldiers suffering from neurosis

circumference and chest circumference. These four measurements were utilised to form a regression equation as follows—

Index of female body build
   = +0·59 stature +0·47 symphysis height
     −0·31 chest circumference
     −0·164 hip circumference.

The measurements in the regression equation are expressed in standard measure. The pros and cons for ratios and partial regression equations for

assessing body build will be considered in greater detail later.

DISTRIBUTION OF THE REES-EYSENCK BODY-BUILD INDEX FOR MALES AND FEMALES

The Rees-Eysenck index of body build for men was calculated for normal groups, neurotic groups and psychotic groups, and it was always found that body build was distributed along a unimodal frequency distribution curve, approximating the normal frequency curve with evidence of some degree of skewness in some of the groups studied. In 100 normal soldiers, with a mean age of 30 ± 6 years, the Rees-Eysenck index had a mean of 100·1 ± 7·6. Figure 15.3 shows the distribution in 1,000 neurotic men, the mean being 104·4 ± 7·9. The Rees-Eysenck index has also been calculated on 2,423 normal miners and ex-miners in the Rhondda Fach area of South Wales by members of the Medical Research Council Pneumoconiosis Unit (Fig. 15.4). It was found that the distribution in this group was slightly skewed to the right, showing that very high values of the index were relatively more frequent than very low values. It was found that the deviations from normality, though significant, were not marked.

The index of female body build consisting of the regression equation, which is a function of stature, symphysis height, chest circumference, and hip circumference was calculated for 400 female Service neurosis patients successively admitted to Mill Hill Emergency Hospital. The mean was found to be

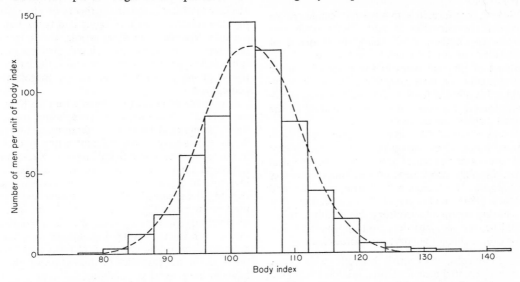

Fig. 15.4. The distribution of Rees's and Eysenck's body index among 2,423 normal miners and ex-miners in the Rhondda Fach

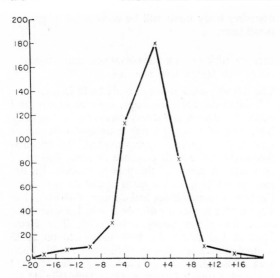

Fig. 15.5. Frequency distribution curve of a new index of body build in a group of four hundred women

+0·385 and standard deviation ±3·68. The frequency distribution curve of the index in this group is shown in Fig. 15.5. It will be seen that the distribution of the index of female body build approximates the normal frequency curve with some tendency to positive skewness. We find, as in the male group, a continuous variation in physique from the broad type, with high index values at one extreme, and a narrow type as its antithesis with low index values at the other.

We find, therefore, in both male and female groups a continuous variation in body build from one extreme to another, there being no evidence of bimodality or multimodality indicative of the existence of physical types in the sense of discrete and mutually exclusive categories. The male body-build index and the female body-build index, therefore, measure the position of the individual in the normal distribution curve of body build.

The extremes of the curve only, impress as well-marked types. There are no natural dividing points and any demarcation of the curve into physical types, although convenient and at times necessary for purposes of research, will be arbitrary. Rees and Eysenck (1945) and Rees (1950), considered that statistically acceptable arbitrary demarcation points would be one standard deviation above and below the mean, dividing the curve into three classes—

1. Leptomorphs, with small breadth, width, and circumferential measurements, relative to length.
2. Eurymorphs, with large circumferential measurements relative to length.

3. Mesomorphs with an intermediate relationship between lateral and linear measurements.

This division of the normal frequency distribution of body build is not intended in any way to convey the impression that these classes are disparate types. These categories of physique are ranges of body build objectively measured by new indices of body build and demarcated by statistical criteria for purposes of description and research.

An Evaluation of Anthropometric Indices in the Assessment of Body Build

Bodily measurements may be taken directly on the body or on standardised photographs or X-rays. From such measurements various indices of body build have been devised with the aim of providing objective methods of assessing physical type. A comprehensive list of such indices is given by Tucker and Lessa (1940).

It seems that, in the past, the construction of many of these indices has been based on an arbitrary selection of measurements that were combined in various ways in the hope that they would differentiate physical types.

Such arbitrary methods have hitherto been unavoidable, since inductively derived criteria for discovering which measurements were likely to be most discriminating in delineating and assessing physical types have, in the past, been lacking. Some indices were based on theories regarding the nature and origin of physical types; for example, the index of Viola, and its modification by Wertheimer and Hesketh (1926) is based on the theory of Viola (1925) that the relative growth of limbs and trunk volume are interdependent, in other words, the longer the limb the smaller the trunk volume, giving a microsplanchnic type; the shorter the limbs, the larger the trunk, giving a macrosplanchnic (or megalosplanchnic) type.

A number of indices has been based on Kretschmer's (1921) description of types, using measurements thought to be useful in differentiating his types. Some studies have segregated contrasting types, such as the leptosomatic and pyknic types of Kretschmer, by visual impression. The two groups were then investigated anthropometrically, and measurements showing the greatest differences between the groups used to form indices. This method has inherent disadvantages in that it merely provides an objective method of discriminating individuals, subjectively segregated into different physical types and cannot prove either the existence of the nature of physical types in the general population.

This method has been used to the best advantage by Strömgren (1937), who, by the method of least

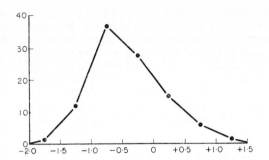

Fig. 15.6. Frequency distribution curve of Strömgren's index

squares, was able to ascertain which measurements in combination most efficiently discriminated the leptosomatic types of physique from the pyknic types of physique. Strömgren's index is a function of stature, transverse chest diameter, and sagittal chest diameter according to the following equation: Strömgren's index = -0.04 stature $+0.12$ transverse chest diameter $+0.156$ sagittal chest diameter. Strömgren called the range $+0.15$ to -0.15 the frontier zone, and index value outside these were said to denote pyknic and leptosomatic types respectively. He said that the average values for pyknics is $+1$ and the average value for leptosomes is -1. These index values imply that the *habitus* of the majority of individuals can be classified into leptosomatic or pyknic types with a narrow frontier range separating the two antithetical types. If we plot the frequency distribution curve of Strömgren's index for random samples of the normal population, neurotic groups and psychotic groups, as shown by Rees (1943), we find a continuous gradation from one extreme to the other. If physique were naturally divisible into leptosomatic and pyknic types, we would expect the frequency distribution curve to be bimodal, but, in fact, we find it is invariably unimodal and approximating normal frequency distribution curve (Fig. 15.6).

Rees (1943) compared pyknic, intermediate and leptosomatic physical types assessed by impression with the types delineated by the index values given by Strömgren. The distribution of types assessed by visual impression, in a group of 100 normal soldiers was pyknic 24 per cent, intermediate 53 per cent, leptosomatic 23 per cent. It is interesting to note that this corresponds closely to the distribution of macrosplanchnic, normosplanchnic and microsplanchnic types found in Northern Italy by Viola (1932). Out of the 24 pyknics determined somatoscopically, only 9 would be pyknic according to Strömgren's criteria, 9 were in the frontier zone and 6 had leptosomatic values. Of the 53 individuals somatoscopically

assessed as being of intermediate physique 45 were leptosomatic according to Strömgren's criteria, only 5 were in the frontier zone and 3 would be called pyknics. There was, however, complete agreement regarding the leptosomatic type. Taking the group as a whole 74 per cent would be assessed as leptosomatic according to Strömgren's criteria, only 14 per cent intermediate, and only 12 per cent pyknic. These findings do not necessarily mean that the index is thereby invalidated, but suggest that Strömgren's range of values for different physical types needs revision. Rees (1943) found that if one took the values of the 24th and 77th percentile as the upper and lower limits for the pyknic range and leptosomatic range respectively, giving values of -0.13 and higher as indicating a pyknic physique, values between -0.133 and -0.79 indicating intermediate range of physique and values -0.79 and lower as leptosomatic physique, this gave a close agreement between the index value and somatoscopic diagnosis of type.

Strömgren's index has been criticised in recent years by Hjortsjo (1951, 1952), who stated that Strömgren's index did not take into account any variation in the relationship between sagittal and transverse chest diameters. He was able to demonstrate that persons of the same stature having either broad flat chests or narrow deep chests, can give identical values for Strömgren's indices.

CORRELATION BETWEEN VARIOUS INDICES

Ciocco (1936) pointed out that not only were we ignorant of the principles that should underlie the construction of various indices of body build or of the principles that had been utilised in the construction of indices in the past, but that we did not even know the degree to which they correlated with each other.

Rees (1949) pointed out that the correlation between various body-build indices was not only of intrinsic interest, but, under certain conditions, could provide a method of evaluating these indices. For example, if it were possible to take a number of body-build indices made up from different physical measurements on a random sample of the population and each index correlated with the others, this would provide a matrix of correlations that could be factor-analysed. If a general factor were found it would presumably relate to body type as this is what the indices are supposed to measure. It would then be possible to determine the saturations of the various indices with this general factor, and those indices having the highest saturation with it should be the most valid ones for discriminating physical types.

This was done by Rees (1949) using thirteen body-build indices in a group of 100 normal soldiers. Most of the indices were selected from the list given by Tucker and Lessa (1940) and were chosen because they contained the measurements available in the group (*see* appendix to this chapter). The list, therefore, does not necessarily comprise a representative sample and it will be seen that many of the indices are made up of similar measurements that would tend to result in high intercorrelations. The fact that stature and chest measurements are common to so many indices undoubtedly influences the size of the correlations found and will result in these body indices being highly correlated with the general factor. This method, in this instance, could not be used as a means of validation but only as a means of determining the degree of correlation between various indices.

It was found that the Rees-Eysenck body-build index correlated highly with other indices and had a correlation of 0·76 with the general factor. The following indices also correlated highly with other indices: Brugsch's index, Pignet's index, Wertheimer and Hesketh's index, B. Marburg's index and the ratio stature/sagittal chest diameter. Other indices had a very low correlation and clearly did not measure the same thing.

COMPARISON OF INDICES WITH SOMATOSCOPIC GRADING

Rees (1949) anthroposcopically classified 100 soldiers into seven grades according to descriptions given by Kretschmer and others. The seven-point scale ranged from the extreme pyknic to extreme leptosomatic type. Various body-build indices were subsequently calculated independently and correlated with the anthroposcopic grading. The Rees-Eysenck index was found to have the highest correlation and had an index of forecasting efficiency of 73 (Rees and Eysenck, 1945).

It was concluded that the Rees-Eysenck index reproduces the subjective rating of the anthropometric worker more faithfully than other indices and, therefore, provides an objective method that effectively replaces anthroposcopic grading.

THE RELATIVE MERITS OF BODY-BUILD INDICES CONSTRUCTED IN THE FORM OF RATIOS AND REGRESSION EQUATIONS

As we have seen, the data obtained from factorial analysis of anthropometric measurements provide us with relevant information for the selection of measurements likely to be effective in discriminating physical types. The saturations of various anthropometric measurements with the leptomorphic-eurymorphic factor indicate which measurements are likely to be most effective in assessing physical types. The ideal method, undoubtedly, is one that uses all those measurements having a reasonably high saturation with the type factor in the form of a regression equation. To establish a regression equation utilising a large number of measurements would, as already noted, be of limited practical usefulness in view of the fact that it would be extremely cumbersome and would involve tedious calculations.

Rees (1950) in his factorial analysis of physical constitution in women found that it was not feasible to devise a simple ratio as a body-build index as in the male group studied by Rees and Eysenck (1945), and utilised a regression equation consisting of four measurements having a high saturation with the type factor, namely stature, symphysis height, hip circumference, and chest circumference. Burt and Banks (1947), found that a good multiple correlation with physical type could be obtained from stature, leg length, abdominal and shoulder girth and weight, which had a correlation of +0·95 with physical type as determined by nine or more measurements.

Hammond (1953) calculated a series of regression equations for the type factors found in children. He points out that even with four or five measurements regression equations are rather cumbersome, since they require different weights for each age and sex group and, possibly also social group, to allow for the different means of standard deviations. He suggests, as an alternative simplification, the use of the ratio of measurements indicating opposite type tendencies. Hammond (1953) found that the ratio

$$\frac{\text{height}}{2 \times \text{chest circumference}}$$

had a correlation of 0·66 with the type factor in six-year-old boys and 0·73 in ten-year-old girls, and that it showed considerable constancy during the growth period. Another ratio he found useful was $\frac{\text{height}}{\text{hip girth}}$ which had a correlation with type of 0·83 for girls and, also, a high degree of constancy when calculated three years later.

The available evidence indicates that suitably constructed indices based on the results of factor analysis satisfactorily serve the purpose of providing a simple type assessment and have the great practical advantage of being more easily computed than indices consisting of regression equations.

Sheldon's Method of Classifying Varieties of Physique

Sheldon (1940) took standardised photographs of 4,000 college students. He sorted out these photographs and concluded that there were three main components in physique, which he termed endomorphy, mesomorphy, and ectomorphy. These terms were applied because it was considered that the three components of body build were derived from the three primary germinal layers, namely the endoderm, mesoderm, and the ectoderm. Each individual was rated, by inspection, regarding each component on a 7-point scale, and the individual classified according to his rating in the three components.

Thus, a 711 rating would be an extreme endomorph; this type would perponderate in breadth and circumferential dimensions. He has a round head, large, fat abdomen, weak arms, with a great deal of fat in the upper arm and thigh but with slender wrists and ankles. He has, relative to his general size, a large liver, spleen, alimentary canal and lungs, and a great deal of subcutaneous fat.

A 171 rating would indicate the extreme in mesomorphy. his somatotype shows bone and muscle development, predominantly, he has a cuboid massive head, broad shoulders and chest, muscular arms and legs, with the distal segments strong in relation to the proximal, having a minimum amount of subcutaneous fat.

A person rated as 117 would be an extreme ectomorph. This somatotype is characterised by linearity having a preponderance of length measurements and a relatively poor development in breadth, width, and circumferential measurements. He has a thin face with receding chin, thin narrow chest and abdomen, spindly arms and legs; the development of muscle and fat is small in relation to his size, with a relatively large skin area and nervous system. Sheldon (1940) described 88 somatotypes of which about 50 are common.

Sheldon's method may be regarded as an advance on previous typologies which tended to emphasise physical types as disparate and mutually exclusive categories. The method, essentially, describes human physique as a continuous variation in three components of body build with the somatotype representing an arbitrary demarcation of the person's position in the continuous scale.

Sheldon's (1940) method of classifying physique aroused great interest and has been used in all parts of the world. The method has incurred criticism on the following grounds—

1. *Subjectivity of method.* It is essentially a subjective method based on anthroposcopy of standardised photographs.

Sheldon (1940) tried to provide a more objective assessment of somatotype for the age range 16 to 21 by a series of seventeen diameters taken from the photograph in relation to the ponderal index $\left(\dfrac{\text{stature}}{\sqrt[3]{\text{weight}}}\right)$. This, however, has not been found satisfactory and nowadays somatotype ratings are made from inspection of standardised photographs aided by reference to ponderal index values, which are now available for ages 16 to 35 years.

As the rating of components is a subjective procedure there is no certainty of agreement between different observers. It has, however, been demonstrated that the retest reliability of ratings is high with experienced workers. Brouwer (1956) found that ratings did not differ by more than half a unit by the same observer within an interval of some months. He also showed that two experienced observers did not differ on more than half a point in 81 per cent of cases. Tanner (1954) also provided evidence that the correlation between highly trained experienced somatotypers is high but that some differences do occur between observers, and should be taken into account when comparing results from different laboratories.

2. *Somatotype not necessarily constant.* Sheldon's somatotype, by definition, should not change with age, nutritional state, physical activity or training. However, Lasker (1947) found that the somatotype ratings of photographs taken before and after partial starvation are usually unalike. Furthermore, Newman (1952) found significant somatotype changes with increase in age in adult men.

3. Sheldon's hypothesis that the three components of physique are derived from the three primary germinal layers has not been established scientifically and, in fact, is not generally accepted.

4. The validity of the number of primary components is also contested. Humphreys (1957), for example, found that the correlations between endomorphy, mesomorphy, and ectomorphy on 4,000 individuals calculated from Sheldon's data provided evidence for the existence of only two independent (but not necessarily valid) types of physique.

Similarly, Howells (1952) found from a factorial analysis of persons (instead of traits) in a group of individuals who were markedly dominant in one of the three components, endomorphy, mesomorphy, or ectomorphy, that the three factors or scale arrangements of the persons extracted did not correspond to Sheldon's three components. His results suggest that ectomorphy and endomorphy are not independent factors, but are opposite manifestations of one underlying factor and basically one continuum. These results are confirmed by a similar investigation carried out by Ekman (1951) which also strongly indicates that two rather than three components are appropriate to account for Sheldon's data; Sills (1950), who correlated somatotype ratings with a number of measurement ratios, also found that ectomorphy was the opposite of endomorphy, rather than a separate factor.

MODIFICATIONS OF SHELDON'S METHOD

Parnell (1954) pointed out that Sheldon's system had inherent practical disadvantages. Standards of somatotype dominance are subjectively determined; many people object to being photographed in the nude and there are technical difficulties, also, in finding the necessary accommodation for the photographic and other equipment required. He accordingly modified Sheldon's method and proposed in its place a deviation chart profile of physique. The chart gives a standardised scale for height, weight, and the ponderal index, for (1) bicondylar measurements of the humerus and femur, (2) for maximal girth of the arm and calf, and (3) for the total of three skinfold measurements of subcutaneous fat. Parnell (1954) claims that the appropriate measurements for a given person recorded on the deviation chart give, at a glance, the main physical characteristics of the person and, with the aid of Sheldon's somatotype-ponderal index tables, a fairly accurate estimate of somatotype. Parnell (1957) further modified his technique and proposed ratings of the following: fat, F, muscularity, M, linearity, L, in place of Sheldon's endomorphy, mesomorphy, and ectomorphy. He does not assert that the method is as suitable for somatotyping as photoscopy, but claims, in its favour, consistency and objectivity. Parnell's (1954) modifications are criticised by Tanner (1954) on methodological and statistical grounds.

Hunt (1952) reports that Professor Hooton and his colleagues have attempted to devise a relatively fixed rating system, applicable to all adult ages and having an advantage of greater objectivity and simplicity than Sheldon's somatotyping technique. The system has three component 7-point scales. The first component is called fat and the second muscularity, both being rated from the inspection of nude photographs in much the same way as endomorphy and mesomorphy are by Sheldon's method. The third component is called attenuation and is derived from a 7-point scale based on the ponderal index

$$\left(\frac{\text{stature}}{\sqrt[3]{\text{weight}}} \right)$$

Hunt (1952) reviewing Hooton's approach, concluded that it expressed an unwillingness to dogmatise on the respective roles of heredity and environment, and is rather more operational than Sheldon's.

The existence of a high negative correlation between the first and third components (corresponding to endomorphy and ectomorphy respectively) in Hooton's system again raises the question whether they are opposite aspects of one continuum rather than a separate factor.

It will be noted that there is a marked similarity between Parnell's and Hooton's systems and both appear to acknowledge that one of the fundamental variations in body build appears to be linearity-laterality, corresponding to the leptomorphic-eurymorphic continuum, described by Rees and Eysenck (1945), with muscle and fat as additional factors determining variations in human physique.

Lindegard's Method of Assessing Body Build

Lindegard (1953) studied the variations in human body build, by means of anthropometric measurements, X-ray cephalometry, and dynamometry and concluded that there were four factors mainly responsible. These factors were designated length, sturdiness, muscle, and fat factors. The method operates with continuous variables and involves rating the position of a person in scales for each factor. The factors are assessed as follows—

1. Length factor, from length of radius and length of tibia.
2. Sturdiness factor, from the breadth of the femoral condyle, bimaleolar and bistyloid breadths, distance between the nasion and centre of *sella turcica*, as determined by X-ray cephalometry.
3. Muscle factor, from dynamometric recordings of handgrip and foot press.
4. Fat factor, from body weight and extremital girths.

Lindegard (1953) showed that the length and sturdiness factors were correlated with the morphology of the skeleton in different parts of the body. For example, an individual with a large length factor and an average sturdiness factor, is characterised by long extremities, a broad deep and long trunk, a flattened cranial base form, a high upper face and a long mandible.

An individual with a large sturdiness factor, but average length factor, would have long hands and long feet, a broad chest, large biacromial diameter and bi-iliac breadth, large cranium and large face length.

An individual with a large muscle factor tends to have large extremital girths and high urinary creatinine excretion. A large fat factor is associated with softness and roundness of the body. Lindegard (1953) claimed that these variables express not only the outer configuration of the body, but also its inner structure.

The length, sturdiness, and muscle factors are determined directly on the individual. The fat factor is deduced by comparing the weight and extremital girths with the skeletal build and the muscle factor.

Lindegard (1953) plots the four factors on a graph in terms of standard deviation units and he claims that this gives a clear impression of the entire body build of an individual.

He finds that length, sturdiness, and muscle factors are interdependent, and he attempts to deal with this by regression techniques giving a relative sturdiness factor and a relative muscle factor. The relative sturdiness factor expresses the skeletal sturdiness in relation to the length factor. The relative muscle factor is expressed by the dynamometric recording in relation to skeletal build as represented by stature.

Lindegard's (1953) method has been criticised because of the possibility that dynamometric recordings may be considerably altered within a short space of time by training and exercise, and may also be influenced by age, disease, etc. The method however, has the great advantage of being objective.

Comparison of Factorial Types with Sheldon's Somatotype

The results obtained from factorial analysis of groups different not only in age, sex, and racial status, but also in selection of anthropometric measurements and technique of analysis used, exhibit a high degree of agreement in the factors elicited, but provide no factors comparable to Sheldon's somatotypes. Even when factorial analysis has been specifically carried out to validate Sheldon's somatotypes, e.g. the analysis of persons by Howells (1952) and Lorr and Field (1954), the results do not support Sheldon's threefold primary components of physique.

The available evidence suggests that endomorphy-ectomorphy is one continuum rather than two separate components.

Tanner (1952) demonstrated that ectomorphy is practically the same as Burt's leptosome factor, and Hammond (1957) considers that the pachysome pole of the type factor approximates to the endomorph. Parnell (1957) compared the Rees-Eysenck index with somatotype in a group of students. He found the highest index values were found in Sheldon's

extreme ectomorphs and that Sheldon's ectomorphs and Rees and Eysenck's leptomorphs had much in common. He found that the lowest values of the Rees-Eysenck index were found in ectopenic mesomorphs, i.e. subjects who are low in ecto-morphy, but who exhibit mesomorphy rather than endomorphy. Comparison is not really feasible as Parnell's types include assessments of muscle and fat whereas the Rees-Eysenck index is based on skeletal measurements. Thus, the results of factorial analysis do not provide support for Sheldon's threefold component somatotype system.

RECENT APPRAISALS OF DIFFERENT METHODS OF ASSESSING PHYSIQUE

Somatotyping

Parnell's (1954) method is open to the same criticism as Sheldon's method, with the exception that the techniques Parnell uses for classifying physique are objective.

Zerssen (1964) showed that the ratings derived from Parnell's method were intercorrelated and, furthermore, that certain of the measurements are included for dubious reasons, e.g. bicondylar width was included because of Parnell's impression that football players have larger knees and elbows than those less mesomorphic (Parnell 1968).

Fowlie (1962) in a study of the reliability of the Parnell rating system found that 7 out of 16 people were placed in different somatotype sections upon re-examination.

Zerssen (1968) investigated the interrelationships of 14 photometric and 13 somatometric measurements including Parnell's variables; four body build indices, including the Rees-Eysenck Index and Tanner's androgyny scale, together with three photoscopic ratings. Zerssen (1968) carried out two separate factorial analyses of the data, each analysis yielding comparable results. Firstly, intercorrelations were factor-analysed by the centroid method and rotated to simple structure by Varimax. The first three factors elicited accounted for 80 per cent of the variance and were factors of body width, body size, and androgyny. The second method of graphical rotation reproduced the same factors even more clearly.

Zerssen (1968) concluded that it was possible to differentiate between three dimensions of physique: (1) general growth (body size); (2) proportional growth relating to relative stoutness; and (3) relative development of masculinity and femininity in body build.

Barnard and Cepeda (1968) carried out a detailed and comprehensive study of interrelationships of

Table 15.3. Comparison between Sheldon's (Hooton's) Components and Lindegard's Factors

Sheldon's system (*Hooton's modifications*)	*Length*	Lindegard's (1953) *factors* *Sturdiness*	*Fat*	*Muscle*
Endomorphy (Hooton's 1st component)	Low positive insignificant correlation (+ 0·05)	Not related	+ + + + (r = 0·96)	+ (+ 0·20)
Mesomorphy (Hooton's 2nd component)	Small negative correlation (− 0·19)	Not related	+ + (+ 0·32)	+ + (r + 0·29)
Ectomorphy (Hooton's factor of attenuation)	+ + + (r = 0·21)	Not related	− − − High negative correlation (− 0·8)	− Small negative correlation (− 0·14)

various methods of assessing body build. Their study was on 88 male students aged about 21 years in whom 106 anthropometric measurements were taken. Each subject was also assessed for somatotype score by Sheldon's system, and the Rees Eysenck Body Index was calculated.

A factorial analysis with Varimax rotation was carried out on the 106 anthropometric variables, and 17 factor groupings were extracted. Thirty-one variables having the highest correlation with these 17 factors were selected and correlational analysis was then carried out between them and Sheldon somatotype scores and the Rees-Eysenck Body Index. It was found that high values of the Rees-Eysenck Index corresponded in a high degree with ectomorphy and that low values of the body index represented a preponderance of endomorphy.

These comprehensive appraisal studies of different methods of physique strongly support the validity of the results obtained by factorial methods of assessing physique.

COMPARISON OF SHELDON'S AND LINDEGARD'S SYSTEMS

Lindegard (1956) compared his classification of physique with that of Hooton's modification of Sheldon's method and the results are given in Table 15.3.

It is noteworthy that here again we find evidence suggesting that ectomorphy-endomorphy is probably a continuum as it has high negative and high positive correlations respectively with the fat factor of Lindegard (1953). The validity of mesomorphy is sometimes questioned, and Lindegard found that mesomorphy correlated with muscle but not with the sturdiness factor. This suggests that Sheldon's method is based on the outer configuration of the body rather than on its composition as implied by Sheldon (1940).

Tissue Component Analysis

The assessment of the relative development of tissues such as bone, connective tissue, fat and muscle is a newly developing and promising field of somatology. It is by no means a substitute for other systems or methods of studying body build and could be complementary to factorial studies of physique, Sheldon's (1940) and Lindegard's (1953) systems.

The relative thickness of bone, fat, and muscle can be measured by standardised X-rays of the calf (Stuart and Sobel, 1946; Reynolds, 1949; Reynolds and Askawa, 1950). It has been shown that the relative amounts of fat, muscle, and bone in the calf are more or less independent of each other. Ectomorphs have the smallest amount of bone, muscle, and fat, mesomorphs the largest amount of muscle and bone, and endomorphs the largest amount of fat (Reynolds, 1949; Reynolds and Askawa, 1950).

ASSESSMENT OF FAT

The development of adipose tissue can be assessed by a number of methods, in addition to the above X-ray method.

1. *Measurement of thickness of skinfolds.* This is described by Cureton (1947), Edwards (1950a,b), Brozek and Keys (1951), Brozek (1953), Tanner and Whitehouse (1955), Parnell (1954a, 1957).

Special calipers are used for this purpose and optimal requirements for such instruments are described by Edwards *et al.* (1955). A caliper designed to meet these requirements has been produced by Tanner and Whitehouse (1955).

Edwards (1950) took repeated skinfold measurements in some fifty different sites and was able to demonstrate that variation in body weight is accompanied by variation in the subcutaneous thickness of skinfolds.

2. *Physico-chemical methods.* McCance and Widdowson (1951) utilised physico-chemical methods

for estimating body fat. The total body water was assessed by measuring the dilution of an introduced chemical substance, which is freely diffusible in all the body fluids (e.g. antipyrine) and from this the lean body mass is calculated. This subtracted from the total body weight leaves the weight of fat and bones. The weight of bones can be estimated from the weight of a comparable dry skeleton. This method is complicated and is of doubtful reliability.

3. *Specific gravity method.* Another method involves the calculation of the total amount of fat and water in the body. The amount of fat is directly related to the specific gravity which can be calculated by measuring the body volume by stereoscopic photographs, or by underwater weighing. The total body water content can be estimated by chemical means and it has been found that total body water and total body fat content are inversely proportional to each other.

4. Lindegard (1953) assesses the fat factor by eliminating the influence of bone and muscle tissues on body weight and from the girths of the extremities by partial regression calculations. He finds that the fat factor measured in this way correlated to the extent of +0·55 with subcutaneous fat as measured by the technique of Reynolds (1950).

Brozek and Keys (1951) using the specific gravity method, found that age and sex factors influenced fat content in the body. Between ages 19 to 25 years 10 per cent of body weight was fat, and between 45 and 55 years fat accounts for 21 per cent of body weight. The mean fat content was found to be about 10 per cent higher in normal females than in normal males of the same age.

THE MUSCLE FACTOR

An assessment of the development of muscular tissue in relationship to other morphological characteristics is included in the typological systems of Sheldon (1940), Parnell (1954, 1957) and Lindegard (1953). If muscular development is to be used for assessing body build and physical type, it is important to know its degree of constancy during a person's life. Muscularity is a factor which, theoretically, is capable of being modified by a number of conditions. Apart from disease, a number of conditions during normal active life may influence muscularity, e.g. the habitual level of physical activity a person engages in during his occupational or recreational pursuits. Muscularity may also be altered by intensive physical activity over a comparatively short period of time. An attempt was made to assess the effect of habitual physical activity on the muscle factor by Lindegard (1956) in a group of 208 Swedish men who had left different occupations to enter military service. They were examined soon after entry to military service and subsequently after a period of six months during which time the men had been subjected to ordinary military training. The muscle factor was assessed by dynamometric recordings of the gross muscular strength of certain groups of muscles, namely, handgrip, shoulder thrust, and shoulder pull. It was found that the dynamometric values initially recorded on entry for military service were highest in individuals belonging to the heavy or manual worker group, and were lowest in clerical workers. It was found that dynamometric measurements increased on the average by about 3 kg during the observation period of six months. Shoulder thrust and shoulder pull exhibited more variability than handgrip. These findings indicate that dynamometric measurements as an index of the muscular factor show considerable variability during a short space of time, and accordingly are less valid and reliable as measures of constitution. The effect of intense physical activity on a group of healthy men was studied by Tanner (1952). The group consisted of ten healthy men predominantly of mesomorphic physique who underwent a course of physical training by weight lifting over a period. The effect of the weight training on the physique was studied by means of anthropometric measurements and by standardised photographs from which further measurements were taken. These were taken twice before the onset of training, at intervals of three weeks during training and at four months after training had ceased. The largest increase was found in upper-arm circumference in which every subject showed a significant increase. All measurements tended to revert to their pre-training values at four months after cessation of training. Tanner (1952) found that there were no significant changes in somatotype rating, but that the effect on regional somatotypes and dysplasia (as defined by Sheldon) was more marked. There were significant increases in strength in various tests ranging from 10 to 80 per cent.

Lindegard (1956) found that the muscle factor was positively correlated with the sturdiness factor to the extent +0·26. This indicates that when the muscle factor is compared with other variables, it should be analysed independently of the sturdiness factor by means of partial correlation calculations. A positive correlation of 0·22 was found between muscle and length factors.

In conclusion, we may state that the muscle component of body build is difficult to measure satisfactorily. In addition to this disadvantage, it has been demonstrated that significant changes can occur with intensive exercise and as a result of habitual level of physical activity.

The available evidence indicates that muscle and fat are capable of showing marked variations in the individual during a comparatively short period of time and are far less constant than skeletal measurements for the study of the physical aspects of human constitution.

Tanner (1964, 1965) provides further validation of the method of tissue component analysis. He took soft tissue X-rays of the upper arm, thigh, and calf which were used to measure the width of subcutaneous fat, muscle, and bone. Measurements from all three sites are added to give an estimate of the magnitude of each tissue component.

In a study of some 300 subjects the inter-tissue correlations were found to be low, ranging from −0·07 to 0·13 and the intra-tissue correlations were fairly high, ranging from 0·37 to 0·75. It was therefore concluded that it is possible to measure three orthogonal dimensions of body composition. In the factor analysis of the nine X-ray measurements, together with measurements of sitting height, leg length, biacromial and bi-iliac diameters, humerus and femur bicondylar width, five orthogonal factors were extracted: (1) skeletal frame size, (2) limb bone width, (3) limb bone length, (4) muscle width, (5) fat width.

Segraves (1969) points out that taking into account the rather unbalanced representation of bodily measurements entering this factor analysis the results are roughly comparable to those of Rees and Eysenck (1945).

The Role of Genetic Factors in Determining Body Build

Body size, body shape, as well as many other morphological attributes such as the relative development of different organs and tissues, are a function of growth rates which, in turn, are largely determined by genes. Environmental factors, particularly nutrition and disease, can modify, to some extent, these genetically determined characteristics, particularly if they occur during the growth period.

An assessment of the relative importance of genetic and environmental factors in determining various bodily dimensions can be made from the results of twin studies. Dahlberg (1926) compared the variability of anthropometric measurements in identical and non-identical twins. The results showed that heredity accounted for 90 per cent of the variability of body length measurements and slightly less for the variability of body breadth, head, and face dimensions. This finding is also supported by the results of Newman et al. (1937), derived from a study of nineteen identical twins brought up apart from infancy. Newman et al. (1937), also found

that there were no significant differences in height, weight, head length, and head breadth in identical twins from a group of fifty pairs brought up together in the same environment.

The majority of bodily dimensions and the variations in body size and body shape have normal frequency distributions. This is in keeping with the hypothesis of multifactorial inheritance of these attributes. Davenport (1923) who classified individuals according to degree of linearity of body build for comparing physical type in parents and offsprings, produced results that also supported the view that multiple genetic factors are responsible for the inheritance of physical type. Palmer (1934) put forward evidence that the genes controlling the rate of physical growth are, to a large extent, independent in action from those controlling the final size achieved. It has also been shown that in animals, general body size is largely determined by genetic factors. That this is true of mammals was shown by Castle (1922, 1941) and of birds by Walters (1931). It is interesting to note in this connexion that Gregory and Castle (1931) demonstrated that large and small races of rabbits exist which, as early as thirty hours after fertilisation, show a difference in the number of blastomeres.

There is a great deal to be learnt about the genetics of the factors underlying body size, body shape, and the relative development of different parts and tissues of the body, and this is a field that urgently merits the serious attention of genetic research workers.

The Relationship between Physical Type and Growth Processes

D'Arcy Thompson (1916) pointed out that the form of an organism is a function of growth, whose rate varies in different directions and must be regarded as an event in space-time and not merely a configuration in space.

Studies of growth in the human being and in animals have considerably elucidated the nature of the factors underlying the variations in human physique and promise to be a fruitful field for future research. Studies of growth in the human are of two main kinds—

1. Longitudinal studies which deal with the changes in an individual over a period of time. A number of longitudinal studies on growth and development during childhood, adolescence and later, are now in progress in various parts of the world, and the results should provide invaluable information for the science of somatology. A review of these projects is given by Garn (1957).

2. Cross-sectional studies which deal with individual differences at different ages. Most of the published work on growth utilises this method.

In so far as the form of the human being is determined by the rate of growth in various directions, it is of fundamental importance to know how and when the types of physique found in the adult are determined. There is evidence that there are not only changes in growth resulting in increase in size of the body but also changes in differential growth, giving rise to changes in bodily configuration; D'Arcy Thompson (1916), from study of growth curves of weight and stature, found differences corresponding to changes in the shape of the child as he grows. He states that the infant stores fat, and the active child runs it off again. Between 4 and 5 years the increase of weight is at a minimum, but a fresh start is then made and the small schoolboy grows stout and strong. There is evidence, according to Tanner (1947a), of an increase in the rate of growth between $5\frac{1}{2}$ to $7\frac{1}{2}$ years, which has been referred to as the midgrowth spurt, and the changes that appear to be mainly concerned with the midgrowth spurt are lateral dimensions. A person who exhibits a large midgrowth spurt and a small adolescent spurt will end up different in bodily form from a previously similar individual who had had a large adolescent but a small midgrowth spurt. The nature and significance of the midgrowth spurt is still *sub judice*, and it will probably be necessary to await the results of longitudinal studies of individuals from birth to adult life before its significance can be determined. The available evidence, however, indicates that all leptomorphic-eurymorphic differences found in adults cannot be attributed to differences between midgrowth and adolescent spurts.

Tanner and co-workers (1956) carried out an interesting study on a group of individuals who had been measured anthropometrically between 1925 and 1932 by the late Professor Alexander Low. Low (1952) measured a series of sixty-five boys and fifty-nine girls at birth and at subsequent birthdays up to and including age 5. Tanner *et al.* (1956) remeasured and somatotyped as adults aged 25 to 30 years, about two-thirds of the group. They found that the correlation of birth measurements with later measurements was much lower than the intercorrelation of later measurements between themselves. It was evident that the size of the new-born babe was only very slightly related to the size of the adult or even to the size of the two-year-old. They found evidence that the inherent growth characteristics of the child asserted themselves after birth, and the correlation between the childhood measurements and

adult measurements rose sharply. They concluded that it was possible to predict adult size as reliably at the age of 3 as it was at the age of 4 or 5 years.

Carter and Krause (1936) analysing the data of Bakwin and Bakwin (1929) on neonates, found evidence of a general factor and of a well-marked bipolar leptomorphic-eurymorphic factor, which accounted for 10 per cent or more of the variance. Bailey and Davis (1935) in a study of growth during the first three years of life also found evidence of a general growth factor which retarded rapidly at first then more slowly throughout the thirty-six months. They found that disproportionate growth rates occurred at certain periods, and corresponded to changes in body build. They found that lateral growth, giving rise to chubbiness, increased rapidly during the first eleven months, with a more gradual increase of longitudinal growth up to this age.

Mullen (1940) carried out a factorial analysis of anthropometric measurements in groups of girls, ranging in age from 7 to 17 years, and found in all age groups a general factor and two group factors corresponding to the bipolar leptomorphic-eurymorphic factor of Rees and Eysenck (1945). Similarly, McCloy (1940) in a study of groups of boys and girls at various ages from birth to puberty, found evidence of a general factor as well as a type factor. Hammond (1957) carried out a factorial analysis of anthropometric data for individuals covering the period from birth to the age of 5. He included a group of infants from Leeds, data from Aberdeen, the infants collected by Professor Low, referred to above, and also Carter and Krause's (1936) analysis of infants' measurements. He found that the evidence indicated length, girth and breadth types similar to those found in later life, and was uniform throughout the age range. He found that the type consistency was low in infancy and increased throughout the school ages. Hammond (1953) reported results of studies of groups of English children ranging in age from 5 to 18 years and consisting of groups differing in socio-economic status, comprising 1,430 private school children and 1,537 free school children. Measurements were repeated after three years in the children still attending the schools. He found in all groups a body size and a type factor indicating a pachysome-leptosome dichotomy corresponding to the leptomorphic-eurymorphic dichotomy of Rees and Eysenck (1945). He also found that the constancy of individual type values over periods of two or three years, as shown by the correlation between the first and second measurements, ranged from 0·65 to 0·92 for the different age, sex, and racial groups, but the correlation tended to be lower about the time of puberty. He found that 11 per cent of the boys up to the age of 13 had changed their type, and up to the age of 14 this figure was 18 per cent. Among the girls, 8 per cent of those who had reached the age of 9, and 22 per cent of those who had reached age 10 to 13 years were found to have changed their physical type, and after 14 years the figure fell to 12 per cent. He found the ratios $\frac{\text{height}}{\text{chest circumference}}$ and $\frac{\text{height}}{\text{hip girth}}$ were useful in the assessment of physical type and changed very little with age.

The available evidence suggests that the two main factors isolated by Rees and Eysenck (1945), and by Burt (1937) and his followers, occur in all age groups in both sexes.

The evidence also strongly indicates that physical type in a large proportion of individuals tends to remain relatively constant, as shown by the work of Hammond (1953, 1957).

Sex Differences in Body Build

A number of investigations have recently been devoted to the study of the differences in various morphological characteristics between males and females. These studies have utilised different methods including—

1. anthropometric measurements treated by statistical techniques, such as factorial analysis and discriminant functions;
2. comparison of the distribution of physical types;
3. comparison of the distribution of the relative amounts of various tissue components such as fat muscle, bone, etc;
4. anthroposcopy, including general appearance, contours of the body and ratings of specific features.

ANTHROPOMETRIC DIFFERENCES AND DIFFERENTIAL GROWTH RATES BETWEEN SEXES

Rees (1950) carried out a factorial analysis of anthropometric measurements on 200 adult females and compared this anthropometric data with that of 200 neurotic soldiers and 100 normal soldiers of similar age distribution. It was found that the male groups exceeded the female groups in all measurements except hip circumference. Females, however, were found to have a longer trunk relative to stature. There was considerable overlapping in all measurements. The variations in body build were found to be determined, as already indicated, by a general factor of body size and a type factor. In the female group, the anthropometric measurements having the highest correlation with the type factor were symphysis height, stature, chest circumference, and hip circumference, whereas in the male group stature and transverse chest diameter had the highest saturations with the type factor.

Tanner (1951) used the statistical method of discriminant functions to ascertain the best possible discrimination between males and females with regard to biacromial diameter and bi-iliac diameter. He found that the best index for discriminating the sexes was 3 × biacromial diameter − bi-iliac diameter − 82. He found that this only misclassified 6 per cent of males and 20 per cent of females.

Lindegard (1953) compared a group of adult men and women anthropometrically. He found that the males were significantly greater in the mean value of the majority of measurements than the female group. Differences between the sexes were smallest regarding two measures of pelvic breadth, namely the bi-iliac and interspinous breadth. Tanner (1955) reports that the chief differences in body shape between men and women are that men have, on the average, broader shoulders, narrower hips, and longer upper and lower extremities than women, which is in contradistinction to the findings of Lindegard (1953).

The differences found in physique between adult men and women can be explained by sex differentials in growth and growth rates. Thomson (1946) reviewing the relevant literature, concluded that boys exceed girls in mean weight until 11 years, and that from 11 to 14 years girls exceed boys, and by 15 to 16 years superiority is regained by boys. By 20 years the mean weight of males exceeds that of females by 20 per cent. Girls, although smaller physically, tend to be more mature than boys in development, as shown by the earlier puberty and by the earlier pre-adolescent growth spurt. In males from puberty to maturity the growth in trunk and limbs is at first equal, then there follows a period of rapid trunk growth, circumferential growth continuing longer than growth in length. In females from puberty to maturity, the trunk elongates in the lumbar region and the pelvis enlarges, while the lower extremities cease to grow in proportion to the trunk. Tanner (1955) confirms that girls gain a temporary lead when their adolescent growth spurt starts and, for a time, are larger in all dimensions than boys. This lasts for the period 11 to 13 years, and then the boys' adolescent growth spurt starts and continues with greater intensity. Tanner (1947a) pointed out that the major relative growth velocity during the adolescent spurt is, of the hips in girls, and of the shoulders in boys.

Differences in physique have been observed between those who mature early and those who mature late. Baldwin (1921) found that boys and girls who were tall before puberty begin adolescence earlier than those who are short. Tanner (1955) demonstrated that somatotypes are related to the age of maturity. He found, for example, that ectomorphy increases steadily from a rating of 3·4 in the earliest maturers, to a rating of 4 in the latest maturers. Mesomorphy had the highest rating in the earliest maturers, whereas endomorphy showed no consistent trend at all. Barker and Stone (1936) and Worrell (1939) found that pyknic girls have the menarche eight months earlier than leptosomatic girls. Tanner (1955) states that early maturers, especially boys, are likely to be high in mesomorphy and low in ectomorphy. In girls, early maturers may be somewhat high in endomorphy, but he states that these conclusions are tentative and that further data are required before definite conclusions can be reached.

SEX DIFFERENCES IN DISTRIBUTION OF PHYSICAL TYPES AND IN TISSUE COMPONENT ANALYSIS

The study of body types has, in the past, received far less attention in women than in men. Kretschmer (1921) pointed out that the types of physique described by him were less easily diagnosed in women, and Sheldon (1940) pays comparatively little attention to somatotypes in women. Sheldon and co-workers (1954) discuss the sex factor in somatotypes and state that women are much more endomorphic than men and that all ages are heavier in proportion to stature. The mean $\dfrac{\text{height}}{\text{weight}}$ index for 4,000 college men was 13·19 and for 4,000 college women was 12·84, and the distribution of somatotypes in women was markedly different from that in men.

A comparison of the distribution in tissue components in males and females was carried out by Reynolds (1949) who utilised X-ray photographs of the calf and confirmed that females have on the average greater thickness of subcutaneous fat than men. Reynolds and Askawa (1950) claimed that the sex of a person X-rayed can be told with 90 per cent success from the relative amounts of fat and bone in the calf. Edwards (1950b) using skinfold calipers, found that skinfolds were one and a half times as thick in women as in men, and that this was due to subcutaneous fat.

Anthroposcopic Differences

Draper and colleagues (1944) give descriptions of impressionistically determined morphological differences between males and females. They emphasise such features as the carrying angle of the upper extremity, the relative dimensions of pelvic and shoulder breadth, the characteristic outline of the space between the lower extremities when the heels are approximated, the silhouette of the outer part of the calf, the slope of the shoulders, and the outward curve of the hip and thigh, all of which tend to show characteristic differences between males and females.

Androgyny (Gynandromorphy)

The terms androgyny and gynandromorphy refer to the degree of feminity of body build in the male and the degree of masculinity in body build of the female.

The study of androgyny and various other constitutional attributes has been the subject of a number of investigations recently. Androgyny has been assessed by two distinct methods—

1. Subjective procedures consisting of assessment of general appearance and ratings of special features. This method was used by Sheldon (1940), Seltzer (1945), Bailey and Bayer (1946), Draper *et al.* (1944) and Parnell (1954).

2. Objective, anthropometric methods, as used by Tanner (1951).

Tanner (1955) considers that androgyny, in contrast to somatotype, is determined by events taking place at adolescence. Relationships between androgyny and various other attributes have recently been studied. Parnell (1954) studied the relationship between the relative incidence of masculine and feminine physical traits and academic and athletic performance. He found that academic distinction was associated with a significant trend towards a greater degree of feminine traits and that athletes, as would be expected, showed a higher incidence of strong masculine traits.

Lindegard and co-workers (1956) correlated various traits of masculinity with Sjobring's personality variables and with various endocrine functions, but found no significant relationships. Seltzer and Brouha (1943) found that a superior degree of physical fitness could only be achieved by persons with a strong masculine component in their body build, and that individuals having physiques weak in masculinity, tended to have poor effort tolerance. In a recent study by Coppen (1957), using Tanner's index in a study of toxaemia in pregnancy, it was found that patients who developed toxaemia had a higher incidence of masculine features in body build than those who did not develop toxaemia.

Dysplasia in Physique

Dysplasia is the term applied to the disharmonious development of one or more parts of the body and is assessed by the extent to which one part of the body fails to harmonise with another. The term is used differently by various workers who use different methods and criteria when they are making assessment.

Kretschmer (1921) described a number of dysplastic types of physique that he considered were due to glandular disturbances. He assessed these types anthroposcopically and considered that they had a biological affinity to schizophrenia.

Viola (1932) attempted to make a statistical assessment of dysplasia by finding the total of the percentage deviation of various bodily measurements from the average.

Sheldon (1940) uses the term dysplasia to denote the degree with which somatotype ratings for different parts of the body fail to agree with each other. Sheldon (1940) assesses dysplasia anthroposcopically and there are no objective methods available. The assessment of Sheldon's dysplasia is a complex task and probably can be done with accuracy only when the dysplasia is gross.

Howells (1952) from his factorial study of Sheldon's somatotypes, found that the results only supported the existence of two main components (or factors) underlying physique, and that therefore the whole concept of dysplasia, as expressed by Sheldon (1940), needed revision.

The causes of dysplasia are not known. The questions, whether genetic factors are the main determinants of the disharmonious growth of different parts of the body or whether disturbances interfering with the growth of certain parts of the body during the developmental period are predominantly responsible, cannot be answered at present and must await further research.

Constancy of Body Type in Adult Life

The question of the degree of constancy of body type during adult life is of fundamental importance in studies on human constitution. Little research work has been carried out on the changes in physical dimensions and proportions during adult life, and published results differ widely. Brugsch (1918) found that narrow-chested types developed into normal-chested types in one-third of all cases, between the age of 25 and 35 years, and that some normal-chested individuals can change with increasing age, to the wide-chested type.

Mills (1917), however, found in a study of 1,000 persons that no individual changed from one major class to another with increasing age, and that the only changes were in subtypes. Similarly, Viola (1932) maintained that the types of *habitus* described by him, namely the longitype and the brachytype, were not altered by age.

Bauer (1926), using Sigaud's (1914) classification of types, found that the broad type (the digestive type) occurred more frequently among subjects of advancing age.

The ideal method of investigating the effect of age on body type would be to carry out anthropometric investigations in a random sample of the normal population at regular intervals throughout infancy, childhood, adolescence, maturity, and senescence. Results from such studies are not yet available. Another method available, but which must be regarded as second best, is to make a cross-sectional study of a random sample of adults of different ages.

Rees and Eysenck (1945) carried out a factorial analysis of seventeen anthropometric measurements in a series of 200 soldiers. The age ranged from 19 to 55 years, with a mean of 34 years and standard deviation of 5·89. The Pearson product moment correlation coefficients between age and seventeen absolute physical measurements are shown in a table from which it will be seen that most of the traits show a negative correlation with age, indicating a slight tendency for individuals of the old-age groups to be smaller in these measurements. Chest and hip circumference, trunk, and sternal length, show low positive correlations indicating a slight tendency for the older individuals to be larger in these measurements. The only statistically significant correlations are trunk, sternal length, and sagittal chest diameter. The statistical significance is of a low order, the odds against the correlation being due to chance, being about 20:1.

Four body-build indices (*see* appendix to this chapter for formulae) were calculated for the group and correlated with age—

1. The Morphological index.
2. The Pignet index.
3. Strömgren index.
4. Brugsch's index.

The Morphological index showed the highest correlation, namely, −0·245. Brugsch's index was next with a correlation coefficient of +0·141. The correlation for Pignet index was −0·098, and the Strömgren index +0·097. All the correlations suggest a slight tendency for older individuals to be broader in build. The correlation coefficient of the Morphological index is statistically significant at the 1 per cent level and Brugsch's index at the 5 per cent level.

Age was found to have a saturation of −0·236 with the type factor, indicating a tendency for older members of the group to have relatively greater breadth, width, and circumferential dimensions in contrast to length. The results obtained by Newman

(1952), who studied the problem of stability in body-build by examining a series of 40,000 individuals photographed by the US Army and typed at Harvard University according to Hooton's modification of Sheldon's method, are in conformity with these findings. The age range varied from 18 to 35 years. It was found that definite, although limited, changes associated with age occur in this group. The first and second components, corresponding with endomorphy and mesomorphy increased with age, while the third component corresponding to ectomorphy, decreased. The correlation between the first and second components, and the first and third components, increased with age, but the second and third components retained the same magnitude of association.

Lasker (1953) in a study of adult Mexican males, and Hooton and Dupertuis (1951) in a series of 10,000 Irish males, found that stature and sitting height reach a maximum in the thirties, and decline thereafter. Hooton and Dupertuis (1951) found a tendency for chest measurements to increase throughout adult life. These findings conform with our results.

Increase in head measurements has also been reported by these workers and also by Buchi (1950) in a study of 196 Swiss adults who were re-examined after an interval of nine years.

Lasker (1953) discussing the possible reasons for variation of anthropometric measurements with age, suggests that the change may occur mainly in the soft tissues, particularly cartilaginous and adipose tissues. The effect of adipose tissue on anthropometric measurements was clearly demonstrated by the work of Keys *et al.* (1950), who found a significant decrease in various bodily measurements during starvation.

Lasker (1953) believes there is strong evidence that the increased size of the face may, to some extent, be caused by oppositional growth of bone, although there may possibly be some changes in overlying soft tissue. He considers that it is probable that incremental growth changes continue for much longer than most anthropologists previously thought possible.

Environmental modifications of physique may occur as late as the third decade and subsequently. Lasker (1951) demonstrated the extent to which this was possible. Mexicans, who had resided in the United States, even temporarily, differed in size and proportions from their less perambulatory neighbours. He found that the differences were a function both of length of residence and age at emigration.

The available evidence, therefore, indicates that limited, but significant changes can occur in bodily dimensions and proportions with increasing age during adult life, and this emphasises the extreme importance of controlling the age factor in constitutional studies in adults as well as in children.

Physiological Functions in Relation to Body Build

The physiological attributes of human constitution and their possible relationships to morphological, psychological, and immunological features, have received comparatively little attention from research workers. The field of physiology, including endocrine and metabolic studies, is clearly an important one, as it might serve to bridge the gap between morphology, temperament, and susceptibility to disease.

Tanner (1944) studied the relationship between Sheldon's components of physique and body temperature, cardiovascular functions, and respiratory rate. He found that oral temperature and respiratory rate at rest were correlated positively with ectomorphy and negatively with endomorphy. When he used an estimated leptosomatic factor score instead of ectomorphy, the correlations were higher, $+0.32$ with respiratory rate, and -0.39 with oral temperature. Both ectomorphy and mesomorphy were found independently to have a tendency for higher oral temperature.

Gertler and co-workers (1950) and Tanner (1951a) have shown that the level of blood cholesterol is positively correlated with endomorphy. Kretschmer (1948) reported that serum albumin and serum antitrypsin are higher in leptosomes than pyknics.

The relationship between body build and the excretion rate of adrenal corticoids has been studied by a number of workers recently. Gertler *et al.* (1954), in a study of fifty individuals suffering from coronary disease, found that those with predominantly mesomorphic body build tended to excrete the highest amounts of 17-ketosteroids. The ectomorph, on the average, excreted the lowest amount of 17-ketosteroids, and endomorphic individuals were intermediate in this respect. Tanner (1955) found a correlation between increased excretion of androgens and the accelerated development of muscular strength in a longitudinal study of growth in adolescent boys. Genell *et al.* (1956) studied the urinary excretion of a number of different adrenal cortical hormones in 197 Swedish twenty-year-old healthy army men and found that the muscle factor was positively correlated with secretion of 17-ketosteroids and 17-hydroxycorticoids.

Seltzer (1940) compared oxygen uptake and utilisation in different types of physique and found that leptomorphic individuals has a lower level of mechanical deficiency as measured by oxygen-uptake experiments than those of broader body build. Seltzer and Brouha (1943) also found that the higher the androgyny the worse the exercise tolerance in normal men.

The study of relationships between physical type and physiological and biochemical functions is in its infancy and it remains to be seen whether the advent of improved techniques in physiology, biochemistry, and body-build assessment will reveal greater correlations.

Physique, Personality, and Neurosis

The tendency to relate physical with psychological characteristics has its roots in antiquity and indeed formed a prominent part of the humoral theories of Graeco-Roman physicians. During recent times studies designed to investigate such relationships can conveniently be classified according to the physical characteristics or the particular physical typology used as the basis for investigating correlations with personality, temperament, character, behaviour, neurotic illness, etc.

STUDIES BASED ON VIOLA'S TYPOLOGY

Viola (1925) described three main types of physique; the macrosplanchnic type, possessing a large trunk, in comparison with the development of the limbs, having large development of horizontal and circumferential dimensions and relatively small development of vertical dimensions. The microsplanchnic type, its antithesis, has a small trunk and long limbs with vertical dimensions preponderating over horizontal dimensions. Intermediate between these types in the normosplanchnic type having a harmonious development of trunk and limbs. Viola considered that the macrosplanchnic type had an overdevelopment of the vegetative system, whereas the microsplanchnic type had an overdevelopment of the animal or locomotive system (namely, the body musculature, nervous system and skeleton). The macrosplanchnic and microsplanchnic types were believed to differ in intellectual capacity and temperamental characteristics attributable to differences in the relative development and activity of the vegetative and animal systems.

Pende (1928), a pupil of Viola, extended Viola's classification by introducing a number of endocrine variations. He considered that there were two main physiological biotypes—

1. The anabolic biotype, which he equated with megalosplanchnic body build, having specific temperamental and hormonal characteristics;

2. The catabolic biotype which was equated with microsplanchnic physique, having specific endocrine and neuro-vegetative characteristics.

However, these relationships are mainly speculative and lack scientific and experimental validation.

Naccarati (1934), using an index based on that of Viola, investigated the body build of 100 male neurotic subjects. By means of the index he classified individuals into microsplanchnic, normosplanchnic, and macrosplanchnic types. He found that the neurotic group has a higher proportion of extreme physical types than a normal group of similar sex and age distribution. He found that emotional neuroses (under which category he included both hysteria and anxiety states), were associated with a more macrosplanchnic type of physique than the normal group, whereas neurasthenic patients were more microsplanchnic than both the normal and the emotional neurosis groups. Naccarati's work is difficult to assess because of his terminology and classification of neurosis. There would appear to be no valid reason for including such contrasting conditions as hysteria and anxiety state in the same diagnostic class. Similarly, the term neurasthenia is extremely unsatisfactory, having for many years been ill-used and over-used. His findings are also unacceptable because of lack of statistical treatment of the data.

Greenwood and Smith (1941), following the work of Boldrini (1925), who demonstrated that chest circumference and stature could be substituted for trunk volume and limb length in Viola's indices, used the ratio $\dfrac{\text{chest circumference}}{\text{stature}}$ as an anthropometric index. They correlated the index with intelligence, efficiency, neurotic manifestations such as anxiety and obsessional symptoms, and found all the correlations were in the realm of chance, the highest being $+0.23$.

INVESTIGATIONS BASED ON KRETSCHMER'S TYPOLOGY

A great deal of research was stimulated by Kretschmer's theory of an association between body types and temperamental types. A number of these studies selected well-defined types as described by Kretschmer and compared them with respect to a variety of psychological attributes by various methods. Thus, van der Horst (1916) and Kibler (1925) utilised questionnaires, and their results confirmed the association between leptosomatic body build and schizothymic temperament, on the one hand, and pyknic body build and cyclothymic temperament, on the other.

A series of investigations carried out by van der

Horst (1916), Kibler (1925) and Enke (1928), indicated that persons of pyknic physique, compared with those of leptosomatic physique, were more easily distracted in reaction-time experiments, were able to remember a smaller number of differently coloured squares on a card given at a certain speed, were poorer in the tachistoscopic perception of nonsense syllables. In further experiments on the tachistoscopic perception of longer unfamiliar words, leptosomatic individuals were found to use an abstractive, analytic, dissociative method in which the total work was built up by reading successive letters and syllables and constructing the whole from the parts. Pyknic individuals, on the other hand, tended to use a synthetic integrative method. Persons with athletic physique occupied an intermediate position in the results of these tests. There is also evidence that pyknics tended to respond predominantly to colour in tachistoscopic experiments, and also tended to react to colours on the Rorschach test.

Lindberg (1938) reviewing the relevant literature concluded that the evidence indicated that persons of pyknic physique had a distinct tendency towards colour reactivity, whereas schizothymes and leptosomatics showed a distinct tendency for form reactivity. Lindberg (1938), using his own special tests, was able to demonstrate that manic-depressives had a greater tendency to colour reactivity, and schizophrenics a greater form reactivity. Using Strömgren's index, he was able to demonstrate significant relationships between pyknic body build, manic-depressive illness with a greater tendency to colour reaction, on the one hand, and between leptosomatic body build and schizophrenic illness and form reactivity, on the other. His evidence suggests, but not conclusively, that pyknics differ

significantly from leptosomatics in colour-form reactivity. The work of Keehn (1953) has thrown doubt on the interpretation of the tests used as being measures of 'colour-form reactivity'.

Misiak and Pickford (1944) found that leptosomes react more to mental and physical stimuli on the psychogalvanic reflex and are more persevering and have a lower tendency to perseveration than pyknics. Smith and Boyarsky (1943) found that leptosomatic individuals have a higher tempo (as measured by tapping rate) and also a quicker reaction-time. Kretschmer (1941) showed that leptosomes had a more sudden onset of fatigue on the ergograph, and also showed more sudden and variable pressure in writing. Klineberg et al. (1934) compared a number of psychological tests on groups of leptosome and groups of pyknic subjects. Tests included cancellation of letters, intelligence tests, and tests of emotional adjustment and six tests specially designed to measure alleged characteristics of the two opposed constitutional types. They found no statistically significant differences between leptosomes and pyknics in these tests.

Similarly, Pillsbury (1939) and Kraines (1938) found no evidence to support Kretschmer's theory in a study of introversion-extraversion measured by personality inventories and physique measured by body-build indices.

More recently, Brattgard (1950) studied the relationship between personality attitude and physical make-up in a series of 1,000 patients attending a psychiatric clinic. This study is of special interest because the ratings of personality attitude had been made some time before the assessment of body build, and were not initially carried out with the intention of determining psychophysical correlates. He used Strömgren's index to assess body

Table 15.4. Classification of Personality and Physical Correlates by Orthogonal Subdivided Group Factors (Burt, 1949)

Factor	Designation	Attribute of disposition	Body size, physical types and subtypes
I	General factor of all round emotionality	Less emotionality	1. Small body size or 2. Pyknic—obese subtype
		More emotionality	Thin and slender physique (Leptomorph)
II	Extraversion versus introversion	Extraversion	1. Large body size 2. Pyknic—eurymorphic subtype
		Introversion	Leptomorphic physique
III	Euthymic versus dysthymic	Euthymic	Broader eurymorphic physique
		Dysthymic	Leptomorphic physique

build, which was used for comparison with ratings previously made regarding patients' syntonic, psychasthenic and hysterical attitudes. He found that syntonic attitudes were associated with a pyknic physique, whereas psychasthenic attitudes were associated with leptosomatic physique.

Thus, the results of investigations carried out to test Kretschmer's hypothesis of an affinity between personality and physical type are not all in agreement; some provide confirmation and others none.

FACTORIAL STUDIES OF THE RELATIONSHIP BETWEEN PHYSIQUE AND TEMPERAMENT

1. Children

Burt (1938), in a study of physique and temperament in schoolchildren, found that there were comparatively low correlations between stoutness and cheerful emotions, on the one hand, and between thinness with inhibitive and repressive tendencies, on the other. In adults he found that leptomorphic body build tended to be associated with repressive and introvertive temperament, and eurymorphic body build with depression. Burt (1949), in a study of 457 boys aged 11 to 13 years utilised the method of subdivided factors and found that the leptomorphic factor included two subfactors, one for limb length and the other for trunk length. The pyknic factor also had two subfactors, one for transverse and the other for sagittal measurements. He carried out a similar analysis of temperament, and his results, together with physical type correlates, are shown in Table 15.4.

2. Adults

Body-build indices derived from factorial analysis of physique were used for studying relationships between physical type and personality and neurosis in adult men by Rees and Eysenck, first in a group of 400 soldiers (Rees and Eysenck, 1945) and subsequently in a further group giving a total of 1,000 soldiers (Eysenck, 1947). Physique was assessed by the Rees-Eysenck body-build index for men as already described.

Rees (1950) carried out a similar study in a group of 400 women service patients suffering from neurosis, utilising a new regression equation for classifying body build in women derived from factorial analysis. Table 15.5 gives a summary of the findings, given as percentages, in the male group, and Table 15.6 the results for the female group. It should be emphasised that the clinical ratings and assessments were made quite independently of the assessment of physique, and were part

Table 15.5.

	Lepto-morphs (150) per cent	Meso-morphs (730) per cent	Eury-morphs (120) per cent
Age 16–20	9	7	1
21–25	25	27	18
26–30	23	28	34
31–40	36	34	42
40 +	7	4	4
Hysterical personality	23	23	30
Hysterical attitude	29	32	37
Hysterical conversion symptoms	29	33	40
Diagnosis conversion hysteria	11	20	24
Intelligence average or below	66	69	75
Vocabulary above average	38	28	22
Anxious	67	60	56
Obsessional	35	23	15
Depressed	73	65	56
Diagnosis anxiety state	47	42	43
Reactive depression	20	18	13
Endogeneous depression	1	2	4
Headaches	65	60	56
Dyspepsia	21	15	12
Tremor	31	36	25
Irritability	43	30	32

of the routine investigation and assessment by the medical staff of all patients admitted to Mill Hill Emergency Hospital. The results obtained in both male and female adult groups are very similar. Eysenck (1944) had previously found from a factorial study of neurotic symptoms and manifestations, that there was a dichotomy of clinical types into hysteria and dysthymia. Inspection of Tables 15.5 and 15.6 shows that in men and women, leptosomes tend towards dysthymic symptoms and traits, whereas eurymorphs tend towards hysterical traits and symptoms. Comparison of items relating to the introversion-extraversion dichotomy of Jung, and the schizothymic-cyclothymic dichotomy of Kretschmer (1934), shows that leptomorphs have a greater tendency to introversion or schizothyme tendencies, whereas eurymorphs tend to be more extraverted and cyclothymic. There is also evidence that leptomorphs tend to have a higher incidence of somatic manifestations of emotional tension and autonomic dysfunction than eurymorphs.

The results are similar to those found by Sanford *et al.* (1943) in normal children. Their tall-narrow type was found to be associated with autonomic dysfunction, good intelligence test results, satisfactory school progress, and also with guilt feelings, remorse and other features indicative of dysthymia. Their wide-heavy type, on the other hand, correlated negatively with autonomic dysfunction and positively with secure feelings and lively self expression.

Table 15.6.

	Lepto-morphs (60) per cent	Meso-morphs (263) per cent	Eury-morphs (77) per cent
1. Age			
16–20	12·2	17·5	20·2
21–25	61·1	51·2	45·9
26–30	10·7	19·6	24·3
31–40	7·7	9·8	8·1
41 +	2·2	1·7	1·3
2. Hysteria versus dysthymia			
Hysterical personality	14·4	23·9	20·2
Very marked hysterical traits	2	5	8
Hysterical, motor and sensory conversion symptoms	12	14	23
Headache	61	69	69
Anxiety, moderate and severe	71	55	49
Depression, moderate and severe	52	41	33
Irritability	54	44	37
Diagnosis—anxiety state, acute, severe	14	10	8
Diagnosis—anxiety state (all types)	60	59	51·3
3. Personality			
Marked schizoid personality	6·7	7	2·7
Very touchy and suspicious	7	6	1·5
Weak, dependent	89	55	46
Narrow interests	63	52	54
Inert, apathetic	15	6	9
Markedly cyclothymic	2·2	7	8·1
Hypochondriasis	37	27	25
4. Autonomic dysfunction			
Autonomic symptoms (palpitations, sweating, etc.)	49	44	40
Effort intolerance	65	62	55
5. Miscellaneous			
Duration of illness more than 1 year	40	45	27
Positive family history of marked neurosis	30	33	21
Childhood neurotic symptoms	48	43	42
Backward in elementary school	5	6	13
Good past physical health	57·7	71·7	22·9
Vocabulary test above average	22	22	14
Matrices test above average	13	10	12

Our findings of an association between eurymorphs and extraverted and cyclothymic tendencies and between leptomorphs and introverted and schizothymic tendencies, lends support to Kretschmer's theory of an affinity between body build and personality type. The higher incidence of symptoms of autonomic dysfunction in leptomorphs corresponds to the resuts of a study 'Physique and effort syndrome' by Rees (1945) in which it was found that, as a group, effort syndrome patients were more leptomorphic than normal controls, and the lepto-

morphic patients tended to have a lifelong history of symptoms of autonomic dysfunction in contrast to the eurymorphic effort syndrome patients in whom exogenous rather than constitutional factors were important.

STUDIES UTILISING SHELDON'S SOMATOTYPES

Sheldon (1942) calculated correlations between a large number of psychological traits and found that they tended to form three clusters in which traits showed positive intracorrelations but had negative correlations with traits of the other groups. He considered these three groupings to be indicative of three primary components of personality which he termed viscerotonia, somatotonia, and cerebrotonia. Viscerotonia is characterised by relative love of comfort, pleasure in digestion, greed for affection and approval and the need of people's company when in trouble. Sheldon states that the personality of viscerotonics seems to centre around the viscera. Somatotonia is characterised by an assertive posture, energy, a need of exercise, directness of manner, unrestrained voice, and a need for action when in trouble. Cerebrotonia is characterised by restraint in posture, quick reaction, socio-phobia, inhibited social address, vocal restraint, youthful intentness and a need of solitude when troubled.

In a group of 200 university men between the ages of 17 and 31 years, Sheldon (1942) found correlations between components of physique and temperament as follows: endomorphy and viscerotonia +0·79, mesomorphy and somatotonia +0·82, ectomorphy and cerebrotonia +0·83. These correlations are much higher than those reported by other workers in the field of physical temperamental relationships.

Sheldon's (1942) findings have been criticised because of the possibility that a 'halo' effect might have influenced the reported correlations as both physique and temperament were rated by the same observer.

Davidson and co-workers (1957) investigated body build in a group of 100 seven-year-old children with the object of determining what relationships existed between somatotype and psychiatric symptoms and psychological attributes. They found that symptoms of anxiety and emotional unrest were associated with ectomorphy. Among girls significant positive correlations were found between ectomorphy and meticulous, fussy, and conscientious traits of personality. The results on the Rorschach test showed that ectomorphs tended to be associated with movement responses and endomorphs with colour responses, but the correlations were not statistically significant. In general, the correlations between somatotype and psychological attributes were of a low order and none approached the high correlations reported by Sheldon (1942) between somatotypes and temperamental characteristics.

Parnell (1957) compared somatotype distribution in 405 healthy students with that in a group of 208 students who were advised by their general practitioners to seek psychiatric care. It was found that the linear person with poor muscular development, and below average in fat, was six times more common in the patient group. The averagely fat, rather muscular short man was found to be five times more common in the healthy group than in the patient group.

Wittman and colleagues (1948) studied the relationships between somatotype and psychiatric attributes based on Wittman's check-list. The first psychiatric component (designated manic-depressive) correlated 0·54 with endomorphy, 0·41 with mesomorphy, and −0·59 with ectomorphy. The second psychiatric component (paranoid) correlated −0·04 with endomorphy, 0·57 with mesomorphy, and −0·34 with ectomorphy. The third psychiatric component (hebephrenic) had a correlation of −0·25 with endomorphy, −0·68 with mesomorphy, and +0·64 with ectomorphy. Sheldon et al. (1949) also attempted to correlate neurotic behaviour reactions with somatotype. Hysteria was found to be associated with ectopenia, neurasthenia with lack of development of mesomorphy, and psychasthenia with lack of development of endomorphy.

Humphreys (1957) severely criticised Sheldon's methods and states that the evidence provided by Sheldon supported not more than two independent (but not necessarily valid) types of temperament.

Child and Sheldon (1941) studied the correlation between somatotype and tests of verbal and numerical aptitude, ascendance-submission, and masculinity-femininity. The correlations were uniformly low, the highest being 0·21. Fiske (1944) found no significant correlation between somatotype and intelligence test score in a group of 133 boys ranging in age from 13 to 17. Tanner (1957) refers to an investigation in which a group of boys aged 17 from an English boarding school were somatotyped by different observers from those assessing temperament by means of Sheldon's shortened scale. The results provided little to support Sheldon's claims for high correlations between somatotype and temperament. In so far as they go, the results of these studies are in good accord with those of Rees-Eysenck and of Burt, quoted above.

RECENT STUDIES OF PHYSIQUE AND PERSONALITY USING SHELDON'S SYSTEM AND ITS MODIFICATIONS

Cortes and Gatti (1965), using Parnell's method of somatotyping and a specially constructed questionnaire to measure cerebrotonia, somatotonia, and viscerotonia in 100 high school boys and 100 college girls and 20 prisoners, found very high correlations between physique and temperament. For example, among the college girls he found a correlation of +0·36 between viscerotonia and endomorphy, a correlation of +0·47 between somatotonia and mesomorphy, and a correlation of +0·49 between cerebrotonia and ectomorphy. Among prisoners they found a correlation of 0·47 between mesomorphy and somatotonia. Cortes and Gatti (1965) report much higher correlations between Sheldonian dimensions of personality and physique than other researchers, e.g. Zerssen (1965), Tanner (1956). Walker (1962, 1963) reported studies on children aged from two to four years, comprising 120 subjects at the Gessell Institute nursery school. The children were somatotyped photoscopically by three independent judges and rated independently by their teachers and parents regarding over 60 items. The results revealed an association between personality and somatotype, somewhat similar in form to that reported by Sheldon for cerebrotonia and somatotonia but with a much lower correlation. In boys, mesomorphy was significantly positively related to sociability and cheerfulness; in girls, endomorphy was related significantly to co-operativeness; mesomorphy to energy; ectomorphy was negatively correlated with cheerfulness.

Hood (1963) using the ponderal index on the series of 10,000 male students found that ectomorphs were significantly higher on depression and lower on mania as measured by the MMPI. Ectomorphs also had a significantly larger number of high psychasthenia items. The correlations between the ponderal index and the MMPI scales were around +0·2. The author stresses that these correlations were probably the highest obtainable as they were calculated on extreme groups. Zerssen (1965) carried out a study of the relationship between physical type and personality in 132 young male soldiers, using Parnell's system and a German translation of Child's questionnaire. The only significant findings were two negative correlations between cerebrotonia and mesomorphy and between somatotonia and ectomorphy, and a positive correlation between mesomorphy and somatotonia.

Bridges and Jones (1967, 1968) in a study on 18 male medical students using the Eysenck Personality Inventory and Parnell's method found that extroversion was correlated with linearity, to the extent 0·18, with muscle 0·06, with fat 0·06, neuroticism with linearity −0·21, with muscle 0·16, with fat 0·16. With a one-tailed test of significance only the correlation of neuroticism with linearity is significant beyond the 0·05 level; the correlation of extroversion with linearity is just short of this level of significance. This study supports the conclusions of Eysenck and Rees (1945).

Studies on obese subjects, by Levitt and Fellnar (1965), Werkman and Greenberg (1967), Leckie (1967), all support the view of an association between fatness and neuroticism, in contrast to the findings of Sheldon, who described endomorphs as cheerful and easy-going.

The work of Zerssen (1964) and Walker (1962, 1963) provide little support for Sheldon's claim of the physical correlates of viscerotonia.

STUDIES BASED ON LINDEGARD'S METHOD OF ASSESSING PHYSIQUE

Lindegard and Nyman (1956) attempted to correlate personality attributes and physique in a group of 320 men. Personality was assessed and rated according to the system of Sjobring and physique by Lindegard's (1953) method.

The results showed that the muscle factor correlated positively with 'validity' (i.e. expansivity and self confidence *vs.* unobtrusiveness). Both muscle and fat factors were negatively correlated with 'stability' (i.e. emotional warmth versus emotional coolness and sophistication and proficiency of motor pattern).

Lindegard and Nyman (1956) considered that the findings of Rees and Eysenck (1945), that subjects of tall, narrow body build have a high vocabulary score, was compatible with their own findings of a significant negative correlation between vocabulary score and muscularity in their series. It is interesting that Wretmark (1953), in a study of personality in peptic ulcer patients and normal controls, using Sjobring's system for assessing personality and anthropometric indices for assessing body build, found that stability was the only factor to be correlated with body build. He found that substable individuals were relatively wide-heavy and that superstable individuals tended to be tall-narrow in body build.

Lindegard and Nyman's (1956) results were not wholly in conformity with either those of Kretschmer (1921) or those obtained by Sheldon (1942) regarding the physical make-up of the cyclothymic and viscerotonic individuals, but the criteria and methods used differ so widely that it is impossible to make a satisfactory comparison of results.

BODY SIZE IN RELATION TO PERSONALITY AND NEUROSIS

The significance of body size as opposed to bodily proportion, has received little attention by investigators of physical-psychological correlates.

1. *Index of Body Size*

Rees and Eysenck (1945) found that the following measurements had the highest saturation with the general factor of body size and were therefore likely to be the most useful measurements for the construction of size indices—

(i) Suprasternal height
(ii) Bicristal diameter
(iii) Stature
(iv) Transverse chest diameter

Stature and transverse chest diameter were the measurements chosen as these measurements had already been taken on a group of 1,100 soldiers, successively admitted to Mill Hill Emergency Hospital, and on whom detailed psychological data recorded independently were also available. The product of these two measurements gives a convenient index of body size. The mean stature for the group of 1,100 soldiers was 172·067 cm with a standard deviation of 6·69, and a coefficient of variation of 3·38. The mean transverse chest diameter was 27·63 cm with a standard deviation of 1·902 and a coefficient of variation of 6·98. It will be seen that the coefficients of variation of these two measurements differ considerably and, therefore, absolute measurements could not be used for inclusion in an index of body size. Each measurement was, therefore, converted into standard measure, that is expressed in terms of standard deviation, and the product of stature and transverse chest diameter expressed in standard measure × 100 was calculated on each patient. From Fig. 15.7 it will be

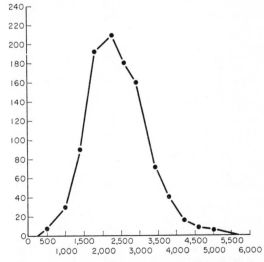

Fig. 15.7. Frequency distribution curve of the body size index in a group of 1,000 soldiers

seen that the index values are distributed along a normal frequency (Gaussian) curve with some positive skewness. The frequency curve shows no evidence of bimodality or multimodality, which would suggest the existence of disparate types of body size, but a continuous variation from one extreme to the other.

For the purposes of investigation it will be necessary to choose arbitrary points for classification of

Table 15.7.   Social Data and History

	Micro-somatics (156) per cent	Meso-somatics (688) per cent	Macro-somatics (156) per cent
Age			
16–20	7·7	7·3	3
21–25	25·6	25·4	26·9
26–30	25	28·3	30·1
31–40	37·2	34·7	36·5
41 +	4·48	4·2	3
Civilian occupation			
Unskilled	50·6	38·3	39·1
Semi-skilled	30·1	37·6	30·1
Skilled	12·1	20·5	23·7
Administrative or professional	5·8	4·5	4·5
Unduly frequent changes of employment	10·25	6·7	7·1
Civil state			
Married	55·8	65·8	62·8
Engaged	1·3	2·5	1·3
Single	37·1	26·2	30·1
Sexual activity			
Normal	73·7	80·7	76·3
Inhibited	17·3	11·2	8·9
Subject to worry	10·3	8·4	12·8
Education			
Elementary-poor	26·3	21·7	16·7
Elementary-good	58·9	63·1	59·6
Secondary or central	12·2	13·8	21·2
Higher	2·5	1·5	2·6
Past physical health			
Good	44·2	51·7	17·2
Medium	48·1	45·2	57·7
Poor	7·7	3·1	5·1
Alcohol consumption			
Teetotal	53·8	51·7	37·1
Moderate	44·2	45·2	57·7
Excessive	1·9	3	5·1
Family history			
Negative	12·8	11·4	12·2
Psychosis	5·1	4·9	6·4
Epilepsy	1·3	2·3	0·6
Mental deficiency	26·9	31·4	32·7
Pronounced neurosis	26·9	15	14·7
Slight neurosis	44·9	48·7	48·7

the group. The demarcation points chosen were one standard deviation above and below the mean, dividing the group into three classes—

(i) Small size or microsomatics, individuals of index values of 1,683 and less.

(ii) Medium size or mesomatics, comprising individuals with index values between 1,684 and 3,110.

(iii) Large size or macrosomatics, individuals with index values 3,110 and over.

An item sheet on each patient in the hospital had already been completed quite independently of physical assessment and contained over two hundred items relating to social data, personal and family history, personality, symptomatology, etc. The distribution of various items for the microsomatic, mesomatic and macrosomatic groups is given in Table 15.7. The significance of the differences in percentage incidence between the groups was tested by the critical ratio method and only ratios of 2 and over were taken as significant.

2. *Body Size, Intelligence and Personality Traits*

The results indicate that the microsomatic group tends to be lower in level of intellectual capacity that the macrosomatic group, as shown by the significantly higher proportion of individuals below average in intelligence in both progressive matrices and the vocabulary tests. Further evidence of a lower intellectual level in the microsomatic group is the higher proportion of individuals who failed to proceed beyond the second class from the top at primary school and the higher proportion of individuals who had unskilled civil employment. The microsomatic group tends to be of inadequate personality make-up, as shown by the higher incidence of weak dependent, anxious, and hypochondriacal traits of personality with narrow interests and hobbies. The macrosomatic group showed, in addition to greater body size, better musculature, tone and posture.

3. *Body Size and Neurosis*

Both microsomatics and macrosomatics show evidence of predisposition to a neurotic breakdown, as shown by the high incidence of childhood symptoms, by previous general behaviour indicative of a clear predisposition of mental illness and by the high proportion of individuals rated as being of unstable personality. The predisposition to neurosis in macrosomatics expressed itself differently from that in microsomatics in that they tended to be more active, rebellious and aggressive.

Table 15.8. Present Illness

Aetiology	Micro-somatics (156) per cent	Meso-somatics (688) per cent	Macro-somatics (156) per cent
Physical causes			
Unimportant	66·0	68·6	64·1
Precipitating	21·1	20·1	25·6
Important	12·2	10·2	10·9
Dominant	4·5	2·6	6·4
Psychological causes			
Unimportant	5·8	5·0	7·7
Precipitating	17·9	16·9	17·9
Important	39·1	40·0	44·2
Dominant	54·5	51·6	48·7
Stress of bombardment of exposure	20·5	26·5	25·0
War-time separation, regimentation	50·6	58·1	53·2
Unsuitable work	17·9	15·4	16·7
Domestic problems	26·9	33·4	30·1
Duration of illness before admission			
0–3 months	6·4	4·7	4·5
3–6 months	11·5	10·6	13·5
6–12 months	16·0	19·5	18·6
1 year +	66·0	65·1	63·5

In symptomatology and psychiatric diagnosis, there was a general similarity between the three groups; a notable difference was the higher incidence of depression as a symptom in the macrosomatic group. The mesosomatic group usually occupies an intermediate position in the percentage incidence of those traits that show statistically significant differences.

Rees (1950), discussing these findings, concludes that the general picture emerging from the study is that neurotics of large body size tend to be more active, having more stable personalities, better musculature, a higher intellectual level, and a better prognosis for return to military duties.

These findings are what one might expect on general considerations. The small person, apart from his constitutional make-up (i.e. his physical, psychological and physical attributes, determined in main, genetically), might react in many ways to his smallness, as Adler has indicated. A person may over-compensate for his smallness by assuming aggressive and dominating traits, or he may accept a more normal degree of compensation, or he may react by developing inferiority feelings. In our study we find little evidence that neurotics of small body size tend to over-compensate by aggressive or dominating behaviour. It might be contended that a socially acceptable degree of compensation in this direction might have had a salutary affect in

Table 15.9. Symptomatology and Diagnosis

	Micro-somatics (156) per cent	Meso-somatics (688) per cent	Macro-somatics (156) per cent
Somatic anxiety	53·8	48·8	53·8
Headache—			
Mild	46·8	47·5	42·9
Severe	12·8	13·8	10·9
Lassitude, fatigue	53·2	51·3	50·1
Dyspepsia, vomiting	18·6	14·8	13·5
Fainting	14·7	11·5	14·1
Pain not demonstrably organic in origin	18·0	23·7	22·4
Tremor	30·1	25·0	26·9
Stammer	0·6	9·4	7·7
Enuresis	3·2	2·9	2·6
Sexual anomalies	12·8	13·5	15·4
Anxiety	85·9	83·0	94·4
Depression	71·8	90·0	58·3
Paranoid	0	0·6	1·3
Elation	0	0·6	1·3
Irritability	30·1	31·7	38·5
Apathy	21·2	31·7	19·9
Hypochondriasis—			
Mild	19·2	25·6	23·1
Moderate	12·2	10·6	8·3
Severe	1·3	1·7	1·3
Hysterical attitude	28·8	33·4	28·8
Depersonalization	2·6	1·5	4·5
Hysterical conversion Symptoms	23·1	29·4	22·4
	10·3	5·7	3·8
Obsessive compulsive	2·6	6·4	7·1
Muscular tone—			
Good	18·6	28·2	48·7
Poor	28·8	12·1	5·8
Average	52·6	59·7	45·5
Anxiety state	57·7	66·0	63·5
Hysteria	25·0	23·5	19·2
Psychopathic personality	9·6	9·3	14·1
Depressive state	20·5	19·2	23·1
Paranoid state	2·6	1·7	1·3
Obsessional state	1·3	1·0	1·3
Mental deficiency	0·7	0	0·7
Epilepsy	1·3	0·6	1·3
Other mental disorders	0·7	0·3	0
Physical disease	2·6	2·6	5·8
Intelligence—			
Progressive matrices—			
Above average	24·2	30·8	31
Below average	36·2	29·0	25
Vocabulary—			
Above average	20·0	27·0	37
Below average	20·0	27·0	11

preventing neurosis. In fact, however, we find evidence of the opposite tendency, if anything, that is acceptance with feelings of inferiority, as shown by the high incidence of weak, dependent and timorous personalities, anxious highly strung types of personality (61%), hypochondriacal tendencies (27%), and the lack of such possible signs of over-compensation such as rebellious and aggressive tendencies (13%) or conspicuous energy and activity (4·5%).

Table 15.10.

	Micro-somatics (156) per cent	Meso-somatics (688) per cent	Macro-somatics (156) per cent
Clinically abnormal personality—			
General instability	45·5	48·8	52·6
Weak and dependent	57·7	49·7	37·8
Anxious	60·1	62·9	50·6
Touchy and suspicious	29·5	31·1	33·9
Cyclothymic	29·5	31·1	33·9
Schizoid	26·3	33·3	31·4
Hysterical	21·2	24·3	21·2
Obsessional	22·4	24·7	22·4
Hypochondriacal	26·9	32·7	16·7
Childhood neurosis	44·2	39·7	37·2
Positive family history	87·2	88·6	87·8
Poor work record	10·25	6·7	7·1
Repeated nervous breakdown	5·8	6·4	5·1

While it is clear that there was little evidence of over-compensation for any feelings of physical inferiority in the microsomatic group, it would not be safe to assume that lack of such compensation, and the adoption of a defeatist attitude, and the surrender to feelings of inferiority, had played an important role in the development of neurosis in the microsomatic group, although the adherent school would no doubt assume this to be the dominant factor. An aetiological study of this group showed that multiple aetiological factors were responsible, and that there was evidence of a high degree of assumed predisposition to neurosis or neurotic constitution, as defined by Slater (1943), in all groups as shown by the high incidence of clinically abnormal personality, positive family history, and the incidence of childhood neurotic sysmptoms.

It is interesting to note that the psychological correlates of body sizes are different from those associated with body type. Whereas the extreme types of body size show significant differences in the incidence of certain personality traits, the extremes of body type, the eurymorph and ectomorph, tend to be associated with hysterical and anxiety reactions respectively, which show no significant differences in groups classified according to body size.

Bodily Disproportions in Relation to Dominant Personality Traits

Seltzer (1946) described an investigation on a group of two 258 Harvard undergraduates by means of anthropometric measurements and body-build indices. He paid particular attention to body disproportion, which he defines as values of an index that are extremely divergent from the mean, usually in one direction. Examples of such disproportions are a combination of wide shoulders

and thin legs, or very broad hips relative to shoulder width, a very flat chest relative to shoulder width, very broad hips relative to chest breadth, broad face relative to chest width, etc. The term disproportion must not be confused with the term dysplasia. The term 'disproportion' was not intended to carry a stigma of abnormality, and the ratios are simply normal deviates from the mean of the group as a whole. Seltzer (1946) found that disproportions were more frequent among individuals of unstable autonomic functioning than in the series as a whole. Individuals who were extremely linear were virtually twice as frequent in this trait grouping. In basic personality the less well-integrated group was distinguished by a significant excess of individuals with extremely linear body builds, with flat chests relative to their shoulder breadths, and with small calf circumference relative to their shoulder breadths. He found significant excesses of one or more disproportions over the total series frequencies in the following trait groupings: unstable autonomic functions; less well integrated; mood fluctuations; sensitive affect; bland affect; meticulous traits; inhibited; self-conscious and introspective. Significant deficiencies, on the other hand, of one or more disproportions over the total series frequencies occurred in the following traits: well integrated; vital affect; practical organising; humanistic and pragmatic.

The first list contains trait groupings indicating lesser stability and integration together with sensitivity; a complexity of the personality, with lower capacity for making easy social adjustment. The second list is diametrically opposite to the first. Here the traits are suggestive of stability, good integration and ease of making adjustments. Seltzer (1946) found that disproportions were most common in strong ectomorphs and least common in marked endomorphs and marked mesomorphs. He considered that the disproportions were constitutional and possibly indicated a genetic element in the determination of personality and behaviour.

INTELLIGENCE LEVEL AND PHYSICAL STATUS

Psychologists and educationalists have for many years tried to discover relationships between physical attributes and level of intelligence with the aim of obtaining objective aids for the assessment of the latter.

1. *Isolated Morphological Variables and Intelligence*

Investigations have been carried out to ascertain possible relationships between intelligence level and isolated anthropometric measurements of the skull and the body. Meade (1914) studied the relationship, in children, between height and weight and general intelligence and found that the lower the intelligence the more checked is physical growth, this being more evident with height than with weight. Doll (1916), from a study of 333 children, reported a correlation of +0·31 between stature and mental age and one of +0·41 between standing height and mental age. Wheeler (1929) studied anthropometric data of the Harvard growth study on 154 mentally dull boys and 119 mentally dull girls and found consistent, though slight, differences in stature, sitting height, sternal length, leg length, trunk length, and bicristal diameter, which were smaller in the mentally dull groups than in normal children.

Sommerville (1924), in a study of 100 college students, found a correlation between intelligence and stature of +0·1, sitting height +0·13, weight +0·1, chest girth +0·01. None of the correlations was statistically significant.

Brooks (1928) studying groups of school and college pupils, reported that correlations between weight and intelligence varied between −0·08 and +0·31, and concluded that the results pointed to a zero correlation between weight and intelligence in adolescence.

Pearson and Moul (1925) conducted an elaborate biometric study of 616 boys and 580 girls of Jewish origin, resident in London, and found a negligible correlation between estimated intelligence and height and weight.

Lee *et al.* (1903) studied honours and pass men at Cambridge using scholastic standing as a criterion of intelligence. They found a non-significant correlation between weight and intelligence of +0·0502.

The product moment correlations between anthropometric measurements and intelligence level as measured by the Raven's progressive matrices in a group of 200 soldiers is given below. All the correlations are low and none is statistically significant. The consensus of results there indicates a zero correlation between absolute anthropometric measurements and intelligence level.

2. *Physical Type and Intelligence Level*

Viola (1933) regarded the macrosplanchnic type as tending to be lower in intelligence level than the microsplanchnic and normosplanchnic types. In keeping with this, Naccarati (1921) found that bright children, during the growth period, tended to microsplanchny in contrast to less bright or dull children. In other investigations Naccarati (1924), Naccarati and Garrett (1924), found that correlations between $\frac{\text{height}}{\text{weight}}$ index and intelligence varied

Table 15.11.

Variate	Pearson product moment correlation coefficient
Stature	+0·111
Suprasternal height	+0·08
Symphysis height	+0·055
Breadth of skull	−0·056
Length of skull	−0·036
Biacromial diameter	+0·012
Transverse chest diameter	−0·055
Sagittal chest diameter	+0·055
Bicristal diameter	+0·11
Trunk length	+0·097
Sternal length	+0·125
Arm length to radial styloid	+0·055
Arm length to tip of medius	+0·073
Chest circumference at inspiration	+0·051
Chest circumference at expiration	+0·101
Hip circumference	+0·177
Weight	+0·172

between +0·1 and +0·44, the average of thirteen correlation coefficients being +0·256.

Stalnaker (1923) found that there were correlations of +0·8 and +0·3 between the $\frac{\text{height}}{\text{weight}}$ index and intelligence in groups of 150 school pupils, whereas Heidbreder (1926), who studied a group of 1,000 students, and adequately controlled the data for sex distribution and reliability of intelligence tests, found that evidence pointed to a zero correlation.

Sheldon (1927) investigated 434 college freshmen by means of Naccarati's index of body build and found that its correlation with intelligence rating was +0·14 ± 0·03. Garratt and Kellogg (1928) also used the morphological index of Naccarati, calculated from photographs, and intelligence measured by psychological examination for college freshmen in a group of 206 individuals and found a correlation of +0·07 ± 0·05. Sheldon (1942) found that the correlations between intelligence quotient and morphological types were low, but there were correlations of +0·48 between 'aesthetic intelligence' and mesomorphy and ectomorphy.

Parnell (1955) studied groups of 371 boys and 421 girls aged 11 and concluded that the less muscular children tended to pass the grammar school examination. He found that linear subjects with more than average fat for their weight were best at examinations.

He found that all-rounders in university students, namely, those who played games and got a first-class degree, were somewhat more muscular. Endomorphic ectomorphs obtained a significantly high proportion of first-class honours (35%).

Mesomorphs (65%) obtained second-class honours. Ectomorphs were found to enjoy the widest range of possibilities for better or for worse. Mesomorphs were most consistent in obtaining a good level of performance with first- or second-class honours. Endomorphic ectomorphs who did exceptionally well in finals, received only a near average proportion of awards on entry.

BODY-BUILD INDICES AND INTELLIGENCE LEVEL

The following indices (*see* appendix to this chapter) were correlated with Progressive Matrices score in a series of 200 successive soldiers admitted to Mill Hill Emergency Hospital: Morphological index $+0.118 \pm 0.069$, Pignet index $+0.161 \pm 0.07$, Brugsch index $+0.061 \pm 0.07$. All these correlations are small and none is statistically significant.

A series of 976 successive soldiers admitted to Mill Hill Emergency Hospital were classified into leptomorph, eurymorph, and mesomorphic physical types by means of the Rees-Eysenck index; 33 per cent of the leptomorphs were above average, that is Grades 1 and 2, compared with 25 per cent of the eurymorphs; 29 per cent were below average in the leptomorphs compared with 34 per cent in the eurymorphs. The mesomorphs were intermediate. On the vocabulary scale, 37·5 per cent of leptomorphs were above average, compared with 22 per cent of eurymorphs. The difference of 8 per cent in the above average intelligence grades in the Matrices tests is not statistically significant. The difference of 15·4 per cent in the above average intelligence grades in the vocabulary test is statistically significant at the 5 per cent level, and is in conformity with Lindegard's (1956) results.

In conclusion we may say that the correlation between physique and intelligence is so low that a knowledge of a person's physical status will be of no value in the prediction of intelligence in the individual case.

PHYSIQUE IN RELATIONSHIP TO DELINQUENCY AND CRIMINALITY

Investigators have for many years attempted to ascertain whether any significant relationships exist between physical type and various morphological characteristics and delinquency and criminality.

Lombroso (1911) studied morphological anomalies in criminals and founded the doctrine that the criminal, as found in prison, was an atavistic anomaly presenting morbid physical stigmata.

In more recent years, interest has turned away from the question of physical stigmata to other aspects of body build. Hooton (1939) studied

17,000 prison and reformatory inmates and reported significant differences in various body measurements between persons convicted of different types of crime. Among his findings were that both the shortest sixth and the heaviest sixth of the group headed the list of crimes for rape, sex offences, and assault, but were lowest in murder, whereas the contrasting group consisting of tall and slender criminals had the highest incidence of murder and robbery, but the lowest or next lowest in crimes such as burglary, assult, rape, and other sex offences.

Glueck and Glueck (1950) compared a group of delinquents, consisting of 500 boys aged 11 to 18 years, with 500 non-delinquent controls, matched for age, intelligence, racial origin, and residence in underprivileged neighbourhoods. They compared anthropometric measurements and somatotype distribution and found that there was little difference in general body size, but that the delinquent group was considerably more mesomorphic and less ectomorphic than the nondelinquent group.

Sheldon *et al.* (1949), described a study of 200 delinquent youths who were somatotyped according to Sheldon's system and were compared in respect of somatotype distribution with 4,000 college students. They found that the sample of delinquents differed sharply from the college somatotype distribution, having a distinct and heavier massing in the endomorphic-mesomorphic sector. They found that mesopenes were, on the whole, rare. Ectomorphs were rare and also ectomorphic-mesomorphs in comparison with endomorphic-mesomorphs. As a generalisation, they concluded that the 200 delinquent youths were decidedly mesomorphic and also decidedly ectopenic, but that there appeared to be no strongly defined tendency, either way, with regard to endomorphy.

Epps and Parnell (1952) studied a group of 177 young women, between the ages of 16 and 21, undergoing Borstal training. Anthropometric measurements were carried out on the delinquent group and compared with a group of 123 university women aged between 18 and 21. They found that delinquents were heavier in body build and were more muscular and fat. In temperament they showed a predominance of somatotonia and viscerotonia. All these results are in good agreement with the Rees-Eysenck finding of a correlation between extraversion and eurymorph body build, and Eysenck's theory linking extraversion with psychopathy and criminality. (Cf. also Chapter 12.)

PHYSIQUE AND TYPE OF OCCUPATION

A good review of this subject is given by Damon and McFarland (1955), who point out that the first systematic study of physique of workers was carried out by Quetelet (1935), a Belgian statistician, who introduced the term anthropometry. Cathcart *et al.* (1935) found differences in strength and physique among individuals in different occupations. For example, they found that transport workers were taller, stronger, and heavier than clerical workers. Coerper (1929) classified individuals in various occupations according to Rostan's constitutional types and found that locksmiths, transport workers, and shoemakers tended to be of muscular type, and that lithographers, telegraphists, cabinet makers, and weavers tended to have the respiratory type of body build.

Garn and Gertler (1950) found that a group of research workers was significantly less endomorphic, less mesomorphic and more ectomorphic than a group of factory workers in the same establishment.

McFarland (1946, 1953) and Damon (1935) found that civilian air pilots were smaller, heavier, and stockier and generally more mesomorphic than the general population. Damon (1945) found that the more successful war-time aviators were more mesomorphic and masculine, with large chest girth, both relative and absolute to stature. Damon (1955), in a further study, utilising techniques that included classical anthropometry, Seltzer's (1946) disproportions, and an approximation of Sheldon's somatotyping, found that the more successful flyers were, on the average, more mesomorphic and masculine.

Woods and co-workers (1943) found that there was a significant association between masculinity of body build and high ratings for excellence as an officer. Seltzer (1945), in a study of 258 students, found significant relationships between choice of faculty and the masculinity component of physique. He found that in those individuals with low ratings of masculinity, there was a predeliction towards arts and philosophy. Parnell (1953) found that students of engineering, dentistry and medicine were more mesomorphic and less ectomorphic than students of physics and chemistry. Tanner (1955) criticises this work on the ground that many of the somatotypes have been obtained in an unconventional and an unwarranted manner, and also for its sketchy statistical treatment. Tanner (1955) compared the physique of 287 officer cadets, 171 Oxford University students, and 162 medical students. He found that the officer cadets were much more mesomorphic and somewhat lower in endomorphy and ectomorphy than Oxford University students. The medical students were in between the other two groups in mesomorphy, but in endomorphy they were the lowest group. Both student groups exceeded the officer cadets in ectomorphy, but did not differ between

themselves. In considering the possible determinants of these associations, Tanner (1955) discussed the possible role of (1) social background and early environmental effects; (2) self-selection by the individuals of their type of career; (3) institution selection; (4) physical changes after entry to the institution. He concluded that the type of occupation, social origin or educational attainment could not explain the differences and that self- and institutional-selection were undoubtedly the main factors involved.

In conclusion, one might say that the evidence suggests that there are tendencies for different types of physique to be associated with certain psychological characteristics, including personality traits and various neurotic symptoms, but the majority of investigations do not report any correlations as high as those reported by Sheldon (1942).

The available evidence suggests that the correlations between physical characteristics and personality traits, intelligence, and neurotic symptomatology, although often statistically significant, are nearly always too small to be trusted for the needs of diagnosis.

Physique and Susceptibility to Disease

Physicians have, from time immemorial, attempted to establish correlations between constitutional attributes and tendency to develop various diseases. The dichotomy in physique described by Hippocrates (namely, the *habitus pthisicus* and the *habitus apoplecticus*) was followed by Galen's detailed differentiation of physical types associated with specific temperamental qualities and disease susceptibility.

John Hunter (1728–1793) was a strong proponent of the theory that susceptibility to disease varied with the type of constitution, but it was nearly a hundred years after his death before serious study of the relationships between morphological characteristics and disease was carried out by Beneke (1881) in Germany, and Di Giovanni (1919) in Italy.

Interest in the constitutional aspects of medicine was relegated to the background as knowledge of bacteriology and pathology increased. In recent years greater interest has again been taken in the constitutional factors in disease, and this has been greatly stimulated by the marked prevalence at the present time of the so-called stress diseases or psychosomatic disorders in which constitution appears to play an important role.

There is a paucity of scientifically satisfactory investigations into the relationship between physical constitution and various diseases. Failure to utilise random samples of the disorder under consideration, and lack of satisfactory control groups and inadequate statistical evaluation of data, are some of the reasons for slow advance in this field.

PHYSIQUE AND PSYCHOSIS

Although Esquirol (1876) noted that the strong robust type has a tendency to be associated with an acute course of psychosis, with crises, whereas the lymphatic type tended to have a more chronic deteriorating course, Kretschmer (1921) must receive the main credit for elucidating relationships between physical type and psychotic type. The publication of his theory of a biological affinity between pyknic physique and manic-depressive psychosis, on the one hand, and between schizophrenia and leptosomatic, athletic and certain dysplastic physiques, on the other, stimulated research in all parts of the world.

The results of some of the investigations provide strong support for Kretschmer's hypothesis, others support it only in part, whereas some do not support it at all. Among the authors whose results supported Kretschmer's hypothesis, are Sioli and Meyer (1922), Olivier (1922), Jacob and Moser (1923), Michel and Weber (1924), Nenckel (1924), Weissenfeld (1925), Wyrsch (1924).

The work of Wertheimer and Hesketh (1926) merits more detailed consideration. They studied body build in sixty-five male patients by means of an index, based on that of Viola, which had leg length as the numerator and transverse chest diameter, sagittal chest diameter, and trunk length as the denominator. They found that among patients with low index values (indicating a pyknic physique) there was a predominance of manic-depressives, whereas among patients with high index values (indicating more narrow type of body build) schizophrenic psychosis predominated. Schizophrenic patients were found to be scattered over a wider variety of body types, but the greater number fell into the leptosomatic and athletic groups.

Only partial support for Kretschmer's theory was given by the results of Raphael et al. (1928), who compared a number of anthropometric measurements and body-build indices on sixty schizophrenics and sixty manic-depressives, and Clegg (1935), who studied 100 manic-depressives, 100 normals and 100 schizophrenics. Burchard (1936), who studied 407 male patients, including a group of 125 schizophrenics and a group of 125 manic-depressives, found that when the group was classified by impression into pyknic, athletic, and leptosomatic types, there was an association between pyknic type and manic-depressive psychosis and between the leptosomatic type and schizophrenia.

Comparison of anthropometric indices showed that transverse and sagittal chest diameters, bicristal diameter and certain body-build indices, showed statistically significant differences pointing to a more leptosomatic physique in schizophrenic patients. He found, however, that age influenced physical type. A more detailed analysis of the age factor on Burchard's data, carried out by Anastasi and Foley (1949), showed that there was a definite tendency towards a more pyknic body build with advancing age in each psychotic group as well as in the entire group. They found a correlation of −0·256 between age and body-build index values for the entire group. The findings indicate that some of the difference observed between the two psychotic groups could be attributed to age, and suggest that the relationship between body build and types of psychosis, as indicated by the results of this study, is rather slight.

Farber (1938) studied the stature, weight and height/weight ratio in eighty-one schizophrenics and eighty manic-depressive patients and considered that the tendency for pyknic type of physique to increase with age, and the greater tendency for physical deterioration in schizophrenia, would weaken if not entirely invalidate Kretschmer's theory. Connolly (1939) carried out an anthropometric study of 100 male psychotic subjects and found that schizophrenic patients (excluding paranoid schizophrenics) were below the average for all mesurements, and paranoid schizophrenics and manic-depressives were above the average in body measurements. Using the Pignet index, he found that there was a preponderance of the leptosomatic type in the schizophrenic group and of the pyknic type in the paranoid schizophrenic and manic-depressives. This work therefore supports Kretschmer's theory, and in addition finds that paranoid schizophrenics are more akin to manic-depressives in bodily *habitus* than to other types of schizophrenia.

Cohen (1940), in a study of forty-seven English male patients, found a significant correlation of 0·413 between the combined weighted measure of arm length, leg length, waist circumference and manic-depressive psychosis and schizophrenia. In a group of fifty-one female Jewish patients, he found a significant correlation of 0·557 between a combined weighted measure of chest depth, pelvic breadth and manic-depressive psychosis and schizophrenia, thus supporting Kretschmer's theory. Betz (1942), in a careful study of the physical status of 193 schizophrenic women, found that schizophrenes were small in general size, and showed a greater proportion of persons of asthenic build and a smaller proportion of persons of pyknic build than normal and non-schizophrenic groups. These findings were obtained both when the impression-istic method of assessing physical types and when anthropometric measurements were used.

Moore and Hsu (1946) carried out a factorial analysis on physical measurements in groups of psychotic patients and found significant relation-ships between body build and psychotic types at the 1 per cent level for the following relationships—

(a) Non-paranoid schizophrenics were below both manic-depressives and paranoid schizophrenics in the girth factor and were higher in the lepto-somia factor and particularly high in the ratio of leptosomia, girth, and robustness.

(b) Paranoid schizophrenics differed from manic-depressives in a lower ratio between the robust-ness factor and the girth factor.

AN ANTHROPOMETRIC STUDY OF MANIC-DEPRESSIVE PATIENTS

Rees (1953) carried out detailed anthropometric investigation of forty-two patients suffering from manic-depressive psychosis and compared the group with a group of one hundred normal subjects and forty-nine schizophrenic patients. The manic-depressive group was found to be significantly smaller in stature, suprasternal height and biacromial diameter, and was significantly larger in sagittal chest diameter than the normal group.

The Strömgren index significantly differentiated the manic-depressive group from the normal group indicating that the manic-depressive group was significantly more eurymorphic in body build.

Comparison of the manic-depressive and schizo-phrenic groups showed that the anthropometric measurement showing the greatest difference was sagittal chest diameter. The manic-depressive group was also significantly larger in bicristal diameter, hip circumference, and transverse chest diameter. Various body-build indices showed significant differences indicating a greater tendency to eury-morphic build in the manic-depressive group, these included $\frac{\text{stature}}{\text{sagittal chest diameter}}$, the index showing the highest discrimination; the next was Strömgren index, followed by the following indices in order of degree of statistical significance of difference between the groups: $\frac{\text{trunk length}}{\text{sagittal chest diameter}}$, Pignet index, $\frac{\text{trunk length}}{\text{bicristal diameter}}$, the Boldrini index and the Morphological index. All these indices, however, showed considerable overlapping and that the main differences between manic-depressive, normal, and schizophrenic groups, were in the central tendency of

a number of anthropometric measurements and body-build indices.

THE SIGNIFICANCE OF THE AGE FACTOR IN THE RELATIONSHIP BETWEEN PHYSICAL TYPE AND MANIC-DEPRESSIVE PSYCHOSIS

As both manic-depressive psychosis and eurymorphic physique tend to occur more frequently in middle age, the question arises whether the alleged affinity between the two could be attributable to this temporal coincidence. In view of the increased incidence of manic-depressive psychosis in middle age, it is likely that a random sample will have a relatively high mean age. This was found to be the case in Rees's group which had a mean age of 50·47 years. It is of interest to compare the mean age of other manic-depressive groups investigated to test Kretschmer's theory. The following are some examples: Wertheimer and Hesketh (1926) 39·3 years; Raphael et al. (1928) 47·5 years; Farber (1938) 44·5 years; Connolly (1939) 47·9 years. Thus, all these groups have a considerably greater mean age than Rees's normal and schizophrenic groups. When only the younger members of the manic-depressive group were considered, they were found to be more pyknic in body build than the normal group, but the difference only just approached statistical significance. It was concluded that the age factor plays some part in the affinity between manic-depressive psychosis and eurymorphic body build, but that it did not account for the entire association and did not completely invalidate Kretschmer's theory.

In view of recent researches which indicate that in adult life increasing age determines changes of physique, it is of the greatest importance that in future researches on body build in manic-depressive psychosis, the age factor should be strictly controlled. The present investigation provides some support for Kretschmer's hypothesis between pyknic *habitus* and manic-depressive psychosis, but the correlation is not by any means as high as suggested by Kretschmer.

AN ANTHROPOMETRIC STUDY OF SCHIZOPHRENIC AND NORMAL CONTROL GROUPS

In order to test Kretschmer's hypothesis of an affinity between schizophrenic and certain types of physique, Rees (1943) carried out a detailed anthropometric investigation of a random sample of forty-nine patients suffering from schizophrenia, and a control group of one hundred normal men of similar age distribution. The average age of the schizophrenic group was 28·75 years and did not differ significantly from that of the normal group (29·27 years). The schizophrenic group was found to be significantly smaller than the normal group in the following measurements: stature, chest circumference, hip circumference, biacromial diameter, suprasternal height, and symphysis height.

The schizophrenic group was also significantly more leptosomatic than the normal group, as was shown by statistically significant differences in the morphological, Boldrini and Pignet indices. The biserial coefficient of correlation between lepto-somatic build, measured by the Boldrini index, and schizophrenia, was 0·64 ± 0·06.

Comparison of distribution of physical types objectively delineated by various body-build indices showed the schizophrenic group to have a lower percentage of persons of intermediate physique. The incidence of patients with eurymorphic body build did not differ significantly from the normal control group. The results correspond closely to those of Betz (1942) who carried out a careful study of the body build in a group of 193 schizophrenic women and found that schizophrenics were smaller in general size and had a higher proportion of persons of leptosomatic body build than normal group.

BODY BUILD IN RELATIONSHIP TO TYPE OF SCHIZOPHRENIA

There is some evidence to suggest that paranoid schizophrenics tend to differ in physical constitution from catatonic, hebephrenic, and simple types of schizophrenia. Connolly (1939) found that paranoid schizophrenics were above the average for all measurements, and were more pyknic in body build than the other types of schizophrenic patients. This was also borne out by the factorial studies carried out by Moore and Hsu (1946). The work of Mauz (1930), Kisselew (1931), Plattner-Heberlein (1932), Vanelli (1932), Langfeldt (1937), and Betz (1942), suggests that schizophrenics with a leptomorphic body build tend to have an early age of onset, show a greater degree of withdrawal, apathy and scattered thinking, whereas schizophrenics of eurymorphic body build tend to have a later age of onset, better preservation of personality, and better affective relations with the environment.

We have already seen that there is now consider-able evidence that there is a tendency for pyknic body build to increase with age. The question arises therefore, whether the alleged association between paranoid schizophrenia and pyknic physique, and between leptomorphic physique and schizophrenia with an earlier age of onset, could be attributable largely or entirely to the age factor. There is a clear need for further research in this field utilising

diagnostic groups accurately matched for age, sex, socio-economic status, and investigated by adequate anthropometric and statistical methods.

BODY BUILD AND PROGNOSIS IN SCHIZOPHRENIA

Kallman (1953) found that the tendency to extreme deterioration during the course of a schizophrenic illness, was correlated with the presence of high asthenic and low athletic components of physique. He found that schizophrenics with the high athletic (mesomorphic) and low asthenic (ectomorphic) component in physique showed the relatively strongest resistance and were usually of the paranoid type of schizophrenia. He found, in agreement with the observations of Kline and Oppenheim (1952), that the pyknic component, although unrelated to differences in deterioration, was associated with a relatively poor prognosis. Kalman (1953) also found that concordant, monozygotic twins, without significant somatotypic differences, tended to have similar types of schizophrenia, developing usually at the same age and having a similar outcome. When there were differences in physique and physical development in such twins, there were usually differ-ences in the age of onset as well as in the severity of clinical schizophrenic symptoms. In the smaller group of monozygotic twins, discordant for schizo-phrenia, it was found that, as a rule, if one twin remained completely free from schizophrenic sym-toms, a definite difference was found in physical strength and body weight from early childhood consistently in favour of the more resistant twin.

Bleuler (1948) produced evidence in support of his hypothesis that certain types of schizophrenia show certain physical attributes related to endocrine abnormalities. He found, for example, a certain type of schizophrenia associated particularly with the acromegaloid type of *habitus*. This type is distinguished by having large hands, feet, and body size and a tendency to irritability and periodic exaggeration of the sexual urge. This type was frequently found to be associated with familial incidence of schizophrenia, and appeared to exert a favourable pathoplastic effect on the sympto-matology of a co-existing schizophrenic illness. Schizophrenic illnesses associated with the acro-megaloid *habitus* were found by Bleuler (1948) to be characterised by a later onset and a particularly mild clinical course.

RELATIONSHIPS BETWEEN OTHER CONSTITUTIONAL ATTRIBUTES AND TYPE OF SCHIZOPHRENIA

The cardiovascular system studied both macro-scopically and microscopically, has been extensively investigated in schizophrenic patients. Lewis (1936) reported that a hypoplastic circulatory apparatus was found consistently at autopsy in catatonic and hebephrenic types of schizophrenia. He found that the heart was approximately one-third smaller in these types of schizophrenia than in normal people, and he also found that heart size differentiated catatonic and hebephrenic patients from paranoid schizophrenics. This is of special interest in view of reports that paranoid schizophrenics differ from other types of schizophrenics in physique in that they have a greater tendency to eurymorphic physique. Capillary structure in schizophrenics has also interested research workers. Olkon (1939) found that schizophrenic patients showed striking deviations from the normal in their cutaneous capillaries. The differences found included a reduction in size in the number of capillaries per unit area, lack of uniformity, bizarre shapes, and the appearances of haemorrhages. Olkon (1939) considered that the severity of the disease was correlated with the degree of derangement of capillary structure. Hauptman and Meyerson (1948) studied capillary structure in the nailfold and found characteristic differences between normal subjects, paranoid schizophrenics and non-paranoid schizophrenics. This work was extended by Wertheimer and Wertheimer (1955), who found that schizophrenic patients showed thicker capillary loops than the normal, and they regarded this as being due to stasis of the blood and engorgement of the capillaries. They found that schizophrenics were also characterized by a great length and a greater degree of visibility of the subpapillary plexus. This feature was considered to be due to an underdevelopment of the mesodermal layer of the skin in which the capillaries lie. Paranoid schizophrenics were found to have capillaries more similar to the normal than catatonic, hebephrenic and simple schizophrenics. They found a negative correlation with mesomorphy and the degree of plexus visibility supporting the view that low mesomorphy and high plexus visibility are both manifestations of poor mesodermal development.

Shattock (1950) also found differences in vascular functions in catatonic schizophrenics compared with paranoid patients, and he found that improvement in systemic circulation coincided with the onset of remission.

To conclude, the available evidence on the whole lends confirmation, at least in part, to Kretschmer's theory of an affinity between schizophrenia and leptosomatic, athletic, and certain dysplastic physiques. The incidence of pyknic or eurymorphic body build is, however, higher in schizophrenic patients than is suggested by Kretschmer's theory. There is evidence, which is suggestive but not conclusive, that body build in schizophrenia may be related to age of onset, clinical status, course and prognosis of illness, and that paranoid schizophrenics tend to exhibit constitutional differences compared with simple hebephrenic and catatonic schizophrenics. If further research establishes significant relationships between physique and onset of schizophrenia, its clinical forms and prognosis, the basis of such relationships may prove to be genetic, with the various genes of small effect, which determine body build, acting as modifiers to the schizophrenic gene or genes, as described by Rees (1957).

Physical Type in Relationship to Physical and Psychosomatic Disorders

PULMONARY TUBERCULOSIS

Although the description of the *habitus pthisicus* by Hippocrates clearly implied an affinity between narrow body build and tuberculosis, the association has usually been put down to the effect of the disease on body weight and physique generally rather than possibly indicating a predispostion to tuberculosis.

Recent work utilising the findings obtained from mass radiography has helped to elucidate this age-old problem. Berry and Nash (1955) were able to demonstrate that the thickness of the skin and subcutaneous tissues measured from mass miniature radiographs, correlated to the extent of 0·86 with independent measurements of skinfold thickness made with fat calipers in the same series of individuals. They were thus able to show that subcutaneous fat may be estimated reasonably well from mass miniature radiographs and, in so doing, introduced a useful new technique for medical research.

These authors made a special study of a group of forty-nine people who had normal radiographs when first X-rayed and who later were found to have developed pulmonary tuberculosis. The interval between the first radiograph and that showing evidence of tuberculosis, ranged from two and a half to fifty-four months. They compared this group with a control group of similar age and sex distribution and matched as far as possible for occupation. They found that persons who developed tuberculosis had 17 per cent less fat than the controls.

They subdivided the groups into four types: Group 1, having long narrow chests, and Group 4, with short wide chests, with Groups 2 and 3 being intermediate. They found that individuals who developed tuberculosis had longer and narrower chests than the control subjects who did not develop tuberculosis, thus providing strong evidence in support of the *habitus phthisicus* of Hippocrates.

18

BODY TYPE AND ASTHMA

A number of investigators have, from time to time, claimed that there were special affinities between certain types of physique and the tendency to develop asthma. Hanse (1935) considered that asthmatics were predominantly of leptosomatic physique, and more recently Parnell (1954), using a modification of Sheldon's method in a group of university students, also considered that asthmatic patients were predominantly of ectomorphic physique. Horneck (1940), on the other hand, put forward the view that pyknic and muscular types were associated with asthma.

Rees (1957) studied a random sample of forty-two asthmatic men by means of the Rees-Eysenck body-build index. It was found that asthmatic subjects exhibited all ranges in physique, from the marked leptomorph to the marked eurymorph. Using the criteria of Rees and Eysenck (1945), the following distribution was found: eurymorphs 9, mesomorphs 21, leptomorphs 12. The mean value was identical to that of a normal healthy group of similar age distribution. The investigation yielded no evidence to suggest any significant relationship between asthma and body build. These conclusions are in agreement with those of Young (1953), who carried out anthropometric measurements both on a group of asthmatic children and a comparable control group, finding no significant differences in bodily measurements. The results are also in keeping with the work of Brouwer (1957), who used Sheldon's somatotyping method in groups of male and female asthmatic subjects. He found that asthmatics had a variety of somatotypes and did not differ significantly in somatotype distribution from the general population.

PEPTIC ULCER

During the present century a number of investigators have been interested in investigating the relationship between body build and the development of gastric or duodenal ulcers. Westphal (1914), Bauer (1918), Tscherning (1923), and Ruhmann (1926), reported that narrow types of body build were more common among ulcer patients. Draper and co-workers, in a series of publications since 1924, have reported relationships between body build and duodenal ulcer and gastric ulcer. They claimed that ulcer individuals had a smaller depth and breadth of the chest in relationship to height. They compared the physique of ulcer patients with those suffering from gall-bladder disease and stated that the index $\frac{\text{sagittal chest diameter}}{\text{length of the chest}}$ is lower

in ulcer patients than those suffering from gall-bladder disease. This work is largely vitiated by the lack of satisfactory control groups and also because the age factor was not controlled. The average age for gall-bladder patients is 8·6 years higher than for the duodenal ulcer individuals, so that the difference in ages may have wholly or partly determined the differences in body measurements and bodily proportions. Feigenbaum and Howat (1934, 1935) compared 67 patients who had ulcers with 79 who had diabetes, and 46 patients suffering from gall-bladder disease. They studied these groups anthropometrically and found no significant differences between the diabetic and gall-bladder groups, on the one hand, and the peptic ulcer patients, on the other. This work has been criticised by Wretmark (1953) both on grounds of methodology and with regard to the conclusions made. The work of many investigators has been partly vitiated because they did not separate duodenal ulcer from gastric ulcer patients.

A very carefully planned and well-controlled study of the relationship between personality, physique, and peptic ulcer was carried out by Wretmark (1953). This study is notable for the care with which a comparable control group was obtained, investigated and assessed by the same standards and criteria as the ulcer group. Body build was assessed by Strömgren's index and by indices described by Fürst (1933). It was found that duodenal ulcer patients had a more linear type of physique than the control group. The evidence regarding an affinity between gastric ulcer patients and similar types of physique was, however, not conclusive. The investigation also showed that there was a significant relationship between body build and the course of duodenal ulcer. The more leptomorphic the body build, the worse was the course of the illness.

Draper et al. (1944) found that peptic ulcer individuals showed more linearity of build, and that male duodenal ulcer patients were predominantly mesomorphic. Sheldon (1940) characterised duodenal ulcer and gastric ulcer patients as lacking in endomorphy (i.e. endopenic), but Brouwer (1956) points out that Sheldon's group of ninety-two male and twenty-five female duodenal ulcer patients had a strong tendency towards endomorphic mesomorphy which would indicate a heavy, stocky build but not endopenia. Brouwer (1956) found that his ulcer patients did not show mesomorphic body-build as Draper et al. (1944) reported, nor endomorphic mesomorphy as Sheldon's figures suggest, He found, in conformity with Wretmark (1953), that duodenal ulcer patients were more inclined to leptosomatic body build, but did not differ significantly in ectomorphy from healthy male controls or from his total groups of male patients.

GALL-BLADDER DISEASE

Draper (1944) described a gall-bladder physical type characterised by thick, round, stocky body build. Sheldon (1940, 1949) confirmed Draper's findings, and that gall-bladder patients were usually meso-morphic-endomorphic.

Draper's gall-bladder group was found to be thicker, rounder, and more stocky than his peptic ulcer patients. However, his gall-bladder group is considerably older than his peptic ulcer group, and as the age factor is not adequately controlled, it is possible that some or all the physical differences may be a function of the age difference rather than indicating a biological affinity between gall-bladder disease and the broad, round, stocky body build.

Brouwer (1936), using Sheldon's method of somatotyping, also observed a preponderance of endomorphy in female gall-stone patients, but not significantly greater than that of a comparable healthy female control group.

CARDIOVASCULAR DISORDERS

The description of the *habitus apoplecticus* by Hippocrates suggested that the broad type of body build was associated with arterial disease and presumably high blood-pressure. Support for this is given by Robinson and Brucer (1940), who found that persons with arterial hypertension are usually of wide-heavy body build and often show a tendency to obesity.

Ciocco (1936) in a review of the literature, also states that there is evidence to indicate that the pyknic type has a tendency to hypertension and cerebral haemorrhage. During recent years attempts have been made to correlate cardiovascular functions in normal subjects with physical types and Sheldon's components of physique. Tanner (1947) investigated physiological functions in fifty healthy students and found no correlation between the components of physique, on the one hand, and heart rate, cardiac output and blood-pressure, on the other. Parnell (1955) found that the broadest hearts were found in pyknic types, and that in asthenic people the hearts were not only narrow but were also small in relation to their body size. He found that men of muscular build had the largest hearts and the slowest pulse rates. Recent investigations have brought forward evidence that coronary artery disease has a higher incidence in more meso-morphic men (Gertler *et al.*, 1951; Spain *et al.*, 1955).

PHYSIQUE IN RELATIONSHIP TO EFFORT SYNDROME

Effort syndrome (synonyms: neurocirculatory asthenia, Da Costa's syndrome) is characterised by marked effort intolerance, by symptoms which unduly limit the patient's capacity for effort and by a number of signs depending on functional disturbance of the autonomic nervous system when such signs are not due to any organic disease. The cardinal symptoms are breathlessness, palpitations, fatigue, left chest pain, dizziness, and the cardinal signs are those of functional disturbances of the respiratory, vasomotor, muscular, and sudomotor systems (Paul Wood, 1941).

It is convenient to divide the various possible causative factors into intrinsic (constitutional) and extrinsic. The role of physical constitution in patients suffering from effort syndrome was investigated by Rees (1944). Anthropometric measurements were carried out on groups of 200 soldiers successively admitted to the effort syndrome unit at Mill Hill Emergency Hospital and groups of 200 normal soldiers of comparable age and military status. A number of statistically significant mean differences in anthropometric measurements were found indicating that the effort syndrome group was significantly narrower in body build than the control groups. Various anthropometric indices were also calculated and computed statistically. Significant differences were found in the Strömgren index and the Rees-Eysenck index, indicating that the effort syndrome group on the average was significantly more leptomorphic in body build than the normal groups.

Tanner (1951) considered that the data also provided evidence of marked differences in androgyny between the effort syndrome control group and a group of 237 Oxford students. He used formula 3 × biacromial diameter-bi-iliac breadth as a measure of androgyny and based his observations only on the mean value of the group. He remarks that the most striking features in the anthropometric data appear to be large hips, narrow shoulders, and short legs (i.e. symphysis height). However, as Rees (1943) demonstrated, the leg length (as shown by symphysis height) was not significantly different between the effort syndrome patients and the normal control group, that hip width was, in fact, somewhat smaller in the effort syndrome group than in the control group, but that the difference was not statistically significant. In the second group of 100 effort syndrome patients investigated, symphysis height was in fact greater than in the control group, but the difference was not statistically significant, and in the second hundred effort syndrome patients there was a greater hip circumference than in the normal group but the difference was again not statistically significant. The first hundred effort syndrome patients were significantly smaller than the control group in biacromial diameter; the second group was smaller in this measurement but not significantly so. Measurements showing the most significant differences in both groups of effort syndrome patients compared with the control groups were transverse and sagittal chest diameters, chest circumference, and chest expansion. In the second hundred effort syndrome patients the most striking difference was found in sagittal chest diameter. Tanner's assumption that effort syndrome patients are more androgynic is not therefore substantiated by the data. Rees's (1944) findings are in keeping with the work of Seltzer (1940), who found that patients of leptomorphic physique showed a much lower mechanical efficiency when assessed by means of oxygen uptake experiments.

Patients classified under the category effort syndrome are heterogeneous both with regard to psychiatric symptomatology and in aetiological factors, showing varying proportions of intrinsic compared with extrinsic causative factors. The significance of leptomorphic physique in the genesis of effort syndrome becomes considerably elucidated when we compare effort syndrome patients with marked leptomorphic physique with effort syndrome patients with marked eurymorphic physique. This was done by Rees (1944), who found that 85 per cent of the leptomorphic effort syndrome patients

had suffered from effort intolerance and symptoms of autonomic disequilibrium from an early age compared with 7 per cent in the eurymorphic group; 66 per cent of the leptomorphic group had evidence of longstanding personality traits of timidity, anxiety, and evidence of general neuroticism compared with 36 per cent in eurymorphic effort syndrome patients. The leptomorphic patients had a higher incidence of unsatisfactory factors in the family history of individuals with longstanding hypochondriacal tendencies. The eurymorphic effort syndrome patients were characterised by a comparatively short duration of illness. In 85 per cent the onset was less than two years before admission compared with 9 per cent in the leptomorphic group. Among the eurymorphic patients there was a higher proportion in whom exogenous factors were important aetiologically; for example, marked environmental stress, such as severe enemy action or precipitation by a febrile illness. It was, therefore, striking that leptomorphic effort syndrome patients had exhibited a predominance of constitutional factors in the aetiology as shown by the family history, longstanding symptoms of effort intolerance, autonomic disequilibrium, hypochondriasis and neuroticism. The eurymorphic effort syndrome patients, on the other hand, tended to have effort intolerance of recent origin, which was often brought on by extrinsic factors such as traumatic experiences and febrile illness.

GENERAL OBSERVATIONS AND CONCLUSIONS

The study of physical constitution has the respectable virtue of antiquity, but it is a field of investigation that has suffered from a surfeit of unverified hypotheses and a paucity of scientifically established facts. The majority of typological classifications which have from time to time been put forward, have lacked scientific basis and the entire concept of physical types in the sense of discrete and mutually exclusive categories has had to be abandoned in favour of a continuous variation ('dimensions') in body build. In order to facilitate the objective delineation of physical types, various anthropometric indices were devised, but most of these were not based on scientifically established criteria. Knowledge of the variations in human physique have been greatly advanced by modern methods, particularly factorial analysis and techniques, introduced by Sheldon (1940), Lindegard (1954), and others. Factorial analysis and allied mathematical techniques have proved to be among the most fruitful scientific approaches to the study of variations in human body build. It should be noted that very few studies have utilised measure-

ments specifically chosen for the purpose of factorial analysis. There is clearly a need for further research by factorial methods on well-selected and representative variables relating to all manifestations of physical constitution, including configuration of the body generally and of different regions as well as the distribution of various tissues in the body.

Faulty methodology has in the past been responsible for failure to make more rapid progress in this field of research, e.g. failure to use random or representative samples of the disorder under investigation, failure to use satisfactory control groups, failure to control factors of age, sex, race, and socio-economic status, etc. In some investigations the assessment of both psychological and physical attributes by the same observer has prevented the acceptance of the reported correlations at their face value in view of the possibility that bias or 'halo' effect could be responsible for part or all of the alleged correlation. Improved objective techniques are also needed for the assessment, not only of physique, but of personality, mental, and clinical status.

We have seen from the survey of available evidence that the correlations between physical and psychological attributes, although often statistically significant, are usually of a low order, and it remains to be seen whether in the future higher correlations will be found where improved research techniques and methodology are used. The very high correlations reported by Sheldon (1942) between somatotype and temperament, have not been confirmed by other workers. It is, therefore, possible that the correlations between the physical, psychological, and physiological aspects of human constitution and their relationship with disease susceptibility, although statistically significant and biologically important, may not be great enough to serve the needs of diagnosis.

If further research confirms or provides further evidence of significant relationships between physical attributes, personality and susceptibility to psychiatric, psychosomatic and physical disorders, the question will still remain regarding the precise nature of the factors or processes responsible for the associations. There appear to be two main possible explanations for correlations between certain physical and psychological attributes. Firstly, the association could be due to life experiences, reactions and conditioning processes, linking different psychological attributes to different physical attributes. An alternative and more probable explanation is that they constitute integrated biological correlations between constitutional attributes. If this proves to be the case, the basis may be genetic, with the genes responsible for various aspects of body build exerting an influence on the manifestation of development of genetically determined aspects of personality and neurosis, psychosis or other illness. There is an urgent need for further genetic investigations in this field, especially in combination with longitudinal investigations of growth and development. Such investigations should, in due course, provide a body of scientifically established, valid data, regarding the interrelationships of physical, psychological, physiological disease susceptibility as integrated components of the total personality.

Appendix

Indices of Body Build

Pignet Index = Stature (cm) − (chest circumference (cm) + weight (kg)).

Morphological Index is a modification of that of Wertheimer and Hesketh (1926)—

$$\frac{\text{Symphysis height} \times 10^3}{\text{Transverse chest diameter} \times \text{sagittal chest diameter} \times \text{trunk length}}$$

Strömgren Index = −0·04 stature + 0·127 transverse chest diameter + 0·56 sagittal chest diameter.

The following indices are quoted by Tucker and Lessa (1940)—

Bornhardt, A.

$$= \frac{\text{stature} \times \text{chest circumference}}{\text{weight}}$$

Brugsch's Index

$$= \frac{\text{chest circumference} \times 100}{\text{stature}}$$

Rohrer

$$= \frac{\text{weight} \times 100}{\text{stature} \times \text{shoulder breadth} \times \text{sagittal chest}}$$

Von Rohden

$$= \frac{\text{symphysis height}}{\text{chest circumference} \times \text{anterior trunk height}}$$

Lucas and Pryor

$$= \frac{\text{bi-iliac diameter} \times 1,000}{\text{stature}}$$

Pignet Ver Vaeck

$$= \frac{\text{weight} + \text{chest circumference} \times 100}{\text{stature}}$$

Martin

$$= \frac{\text{bicristal diameter}}{\text{shoulder breadth}}$$

Marburg, B.

$$= \frac{\text{leg length}}{(\text{transverse} + \text{sagittal chest diameter}) \times \text{trunk length} \times \text{shoulder breadth}}$$

REFERENCES

ADLER, H. M. and MOHR, G. J. (1928) Some considerations of the significance of physical constitution in relation to mental disorder. *Amer. J. Psychiat.*, **7**, 701–707.

ANASTASI, A. and FOLEY, J. P. (1949) *Differential Psychology*. New York: Macmillan.

ARISTOTLE (1913) Physiognomonica. Trans. by T. Loveday and E. S. Forster. In *The Works of Aristotle*. Oxford: Clarendon Press.

ASCHNER, B. (1924) *Die Konstitution der Frau und ihre Beziehungen zur Geburtsshilfe und Gynäkolgie* Munich: Bergmann.

BAKWIN, H. and BAKWIN, R. M. (1929) Types of body build in infants. *Amer. J. Dis. Child.*, **37**, 461–472.

BAKWIN, H. and BAKWIN, R. M. (1943) Body build in infants: V. Anthropometry of the newborn. *Hum. Biol.*, **6**, 612–626.

BALDWIN, B. T. (1921) The physical growth of children from birth to maturity. *Univ. Ia Stud. Child Welf.*, **1**, No. 1.

BARNARD, G. W. and CEPEDA, M. L. (1968) Personal communication.

BAUER, J. (1917) *Die konstitutionelle Disposition zur inneren Krankheiten*. Berlin: J. Springer.

BAUER, J. (1923) *Vorlesungen über allegemeine Konstitutions-Vererbungslehre*. Berlin: J. Springer.

BAYLEY, N. (1940) Factors influencing the growth and intelligence of young children. *39th Yearbook, Nat. Soc. Stud. Educ.*, Part II, 49–79.

BAYLEY, N. (1943) Size and body build of adolescents in relation to rate of skeletal maturing. *Child Develpm.*, **14**, 47–89.

BAYLEY, N. and BAYER, L. M. (1946) The assessment of somatic androgyny. *Amer. J. Phys. Anthropol.*, **4**, 433–461.

BEAN, R. B. (1912) Morbidity and Morphology. *Johns Hopk. Hosp. Bull.*, **23**, 363–370.

BEAN, R. B. (1923) The two European types. *Amer. J. Anat.*, **31**, 359–371.

BEAN, R. B. (1926) Human types. *Quart. Rev. Biol.*, **1**, 360–392.

BENEKE, F. W. (1878) *Die anatomischen Grundlagen der Constitutionsanomalien des Menschen*. Marburg Elwert.

BENEKE, F. W. (1881) *Konstitution und Konstitutionelles kranksein des Menschen*. Marburg: Elwert.

BERNREUTER, R. G. (1934) The imbrication of tests of introversion-extraversion and neurotic tendency. *J. Soc. Psychol.*, **5**, 184–201.

BERRY, W. T. C. and NASH, F. A. (1955) Studies in the aetiology of pulmonary tuberculosis. *Tubercle*, **36**, 164–174.

BETZ, B. (1942) Somatology of the schizophrenic patient. *Hum. Biol.*, **14**, 21–47; 192–234.

BLEULER, M. (1948) Untersuchungen aus dem Grenzgebiet zwischen Psycho-pathologie und Endokrinologin. *Arch. Psychiat. Nervenkr.*, **118**, 271–528.

BOLDRINI, M. (1925) Sivluppo corporeo e predisposizioni morbose. *Vita e Pensiero*. Milan.

BOLDRINI, M. (1931) La fertilità dei biotipi, *Vita e Pensiero*. Milan.

BORCHARDT, L. (1931) Funktionelle und tropische Momente als Ursachen des gegensätzlichen Verhaltens von Pyknikern und Asthenikern. *Z. Konst-Lehre*, **16**, 1–7.

BRAAT, J. P. (1937) Die experimentelle Psychologie und Kretschmer's Konstitutionstypen. *Mschr. Psychiat. Neurol.*, **94**, 273–297.

BRATTGARD, S. O. (1950) Personality attitude and physical make-up. *Acta Psychiat. Neurol. scand.*, **354**, 339–354.

BRIDGES, P. K. and JONES, M. T. (1967) Personality, physique and the adrenocortical response to a psychological stress. *Brit. J. Psychiat.* **113**, 601–605.

BRIDGES, P. K. and JONES, M. T. (1968) Relationship of personality and physique to plasma cortisol levels in respose to anxiety. *J. Neurol. Neurosurg. Psychiat.*, **31**, 57–60.

BROOKS, F. D. (1928) The organization of mental and physical traits during adolescence. *J. appl. Psychol.*, **12**, 228.

BROUWER, D. (1957) Somatotypes and psychosomatic diseases. *J. psychosom. Res.*, **2**, 23–34.

BROZEK, J. (1953) Measuring nutrition. *Amer. J. Phys. Anthropol.*, **11**, 147–180.

BROZEK, J. and KEYS, A. (1951) Evaluation of leanness-fatness in man: a survey of methods. *Nutr. Abstr. Rev*, **20**, 247–256.

BROZEK, J. and KEYS, A. (1951) Evaluation of leaness-fatness in man. *Brit. J. Nutr.*, **5**, 194–206.

BRUGSCH, T. (1918) *Allgemeine Prognostik, oder die Lehre von der ärtzlichen Beurteilung des gesunden und kranken Menschen*. Berlin: Urban & Schwarzenberg.

BRUGSCH, T. (1931) Die Morphologie der Person. In *Die Biologie der Person*, **2** (Ed. Brugsch, T. and Lewy, F. H.) Berlin and Vienna: Urban & Schwarzenberg, 1–114.

BRYANT, J. (1914) Stasis and human efficiency. *Int. Abstr. Surg.*, 449 (May).

BRYANT, J. (1915) The carnivorous and herbivorous types of man. *Boston Med. Surg. J.*, **172**, 321–326; **173**, 384–387.

BUCHI, E. C. (1950) Änderung der Körperform beim erwachsenen Menschen, eine Untersuchung nach der Individual-method. Anthropologische Forschungen. Horn: Ferdinand Berger. Vol. 1.

BURCHARD, M. L. (1936) Physique and psychosis. *Comp. Psychol. Mon.*, **13**, 84.

BURT, C. (1937) The analysis of temperament. *Brit. J. med. Psychol.*, **17**, 158–188.

BURT, C. (1940) *Factors of the Mind*. London: Univ. of London Press.

BURT, C. (1943) Factorial analysis of physical growth. *Nature*, **152**, 75.

BURT, C. (1944) The factorial study of physical types. *Man*, **44**, 82–86.

BURT, C. (1947) A comparison of factor analysis and

analysis of variance. *Brit. J. Psychol.* (Stat. Sect.), **1**, 3–26.

BURT, C. (1947) Factor analysis and physical types. *Psychometrika*, **12**, 171–188.

BURT, C. (1949) Subdivided factors. *Brit. J. Psychol.* (Stat. Sect.), **2**, 41–63.

BURT, C. and BANKS, CHARLOTTE (1947) A factor analysis of body measurements for British adult males. *Ann. Eugen.*, **13**, 238–256.

CABOT, P. S. de Q. (1938) The relationship between characteristics of personality and physique in adolescents. *Genet. Psychol. Monogr.*, **20**, 3–120.

CAMPBELL, J. K. (1932) The relation of the types of physique to the types of mental disease. *J. abnorm. (Soc.) Psychol.*, **27**, 147–151.

CARTER, H. D. and KRAUS, R. H. (1936) The physical proportions of the human infant. *Child Developm.*, **7**, 60–68.

CARUS, C. G. (1853) *Symbolik der menschlichen Gestalt* ed. 1925, Celle.

CASTLE, W. E. (1922) Genetic studies of rabbits and rats. *Pub. Carnegie Inst.* No. 320.

CASTLE, W. E. (1941) Size inheritance. *Amer. Nat.*, **75**, 488–498.

CATHCART, E. P., HUGHES, E. R., and CHALMERS, J. G. (1935) The physique of man in industry. *M.R.C. Industrial Health Research Board*, *Rep.* No. 71. London: H.M.S.O.

CATTELL, R. B. (1946) *Description and Measurement of Personality*. Yonkers-on-Hudson: World Books.

CHAILLOU, A. and MACAULIFFE, L. (1912) *Morphologie Médicale*. Paris: Octave Doin et Fils.

CHILD, I. L. and SHELDON, W. H. (1941) The correlation between components of physique and scores on certain psychological tests. *Character & Pers.*, **10**, 23–34.

CIOCCO, A. (1936) The historical background of the modern study of constitution. *Bull. Inst. hist. Med.*, **4**, 23–38.

CLEGG, J. L. (1935) The association of physique and mental condition. *J. ment. Sci.*, **81**, 297–316.

COERPER, C. (1926) Personelle Beurteilung nach der practischen Lepenseignung (a) körperlich. In *Die Biologie der Person* (Ed. T. Brugsch and F. H. Lewy). Berlin: Urban & Schwarzenburg.

COHEN, J. I. (1938) Determinants of physique. *J. ment. Sci.*, **84**, 495–512.

COHEN, J. I. (1940) Physical types and their relation to psychotic types. *J. ment. Sci.*, **86**, 602.

COHEN, J. I. (1941) Physique, size and proportions, *Brit. J. med. Psychol.*, **18**, 323–337.

CONNOLLY, C. J. (1939) Physique in relation to psychosis. *Stud. Psychol. Psychiat., Cath. Univ. Amer.*, **4**, No. 5.

CONRAD, K. (1941) *Der Konstitutionstypus als genetisches Problem*. Berlin.

COPPEN, A. J. (1958) Psychosomatic aspects of pre-eclamptic toxaemia. *J. psychosom. Res.*, **2**, 241–265.

CORTES, J. B. and GATTI, F. M. (1965) Physique and self-description of temperament. *J. consult. Psychol.* **29**, 432–439.

CURETON, T. K. (1947) *Physical Fitness, Appraisal and Guidance*. London: Kimpton.

DAHLBERG, G. (1926) *Twin Births and Twins from an Hereditary Point of View*. Stockholm: Tidens.

DAMON, A. (1955) Physique and success in military flying. *Amer. J. phys. Anthropol.*, **13**, 217–252.

DAMON, A. and McFARLAND, R. A. (1955) The physique of bus and truck drivers. *Amer. J. phys. Anthropol.*, **13**, 711–742.

DAVENPORT, C. B. (1920) Height-weight index of build. *Amer. J. phys. Anthropol.*, **3**, 567.

DAVENPORT, C. B. (1923) Body-build and its inheritance. *Pub. Carnegie Inst.*, No. 329.

DAVIDSON, M. A., McINNES, R. G., and PARNELL, R. W. (1957) The distribution of personality traits in seven-year-old children. *Brit. J. educ. Psychol.*, **27**, 48–61.

DEARBORN, W. F. and ROTHNEY, J. (1941) *Predicting the Child's Development*. 360. Cambridge, Mass.: Sci.-Art. Publ.

DI GIOVANNI, A. (1919) *Clinical Commentaries Deduced from the Morphology of the Human Body*. London and New York: J. J. Eyre.

DOLL, E. A. (1916) *Anthropometry as an Aid to Mental Diagnosis*. New Jersey: Williams & Wilkins.

DRAPER, G. (1924) *Human Constitution*. Philadelphia: Saunders.

DRAPER, G. (1942) The emotional component of the ulcer susceptible constitution. *Ann. intern. Med.*, **16**, 633.

DRAPER, G., DUNN, H. L., and SEEGAL, D. (1924) Studies in human constitution. I. Clinical anthropometry. *J. Amer. med. Assoc.*, **82**, 431.

DRAPER, G., DUPERTUIS, C. W., and CAUGHEY, J. L. (1944) *Human Constitution in Clinical Medicine*. New York: Hoeber.

DRAPER, G. and McGRAW, R. B. (1927) Studies in human constitution: V. The psychological panel. *Amer. J. med. Sci.*, **174**, 299.

DRAPER, G. and TOURAINE, G. A. (1932) The man-environment unit and peptic ulcer. *Arch. intern. Med.*, **49**, 616.

DUPERTUIS, C. W. (1950) Anthropometry of extreme somatotypes. *Amer. J. physiol. Anthropol.*, **8**, 367–385.

DUPERTUIS, C. W. (1950) Body build and specific gravity, Proc. 19th Ann. Meeting of Amer. Assoc. of Physical Anthropologists. *Amer. J. phys. Anthropol.*, **8**, 260.

DUPERTUIS, C. W., PITTS, G. C., OSSERMAN, E. F., WELHAM, W. C., and BEHNKE, A. R. (1951a) Relation of specific gravity to body build on a group of healthy men. *J. appl. Psychol.*, **3**, 676–680.

DUPERTUIS, C. W., PITTS, G. C., OSSERMAN, E. F., WELHAM, W. C., and BEHNKE, A. R. (1951b) Relation of body water content to body build in a group of healthy men. *J. appl. Psychol.*, **4**, 364–367.

EDWARDS, D. A. W. (1950) Observations on the distribution of subcutaneous fat. *Clin. Sci.*, **9**, 259–270.

EDWARDS, D. A. W. (1950) Observations on the distribution of subcutaneous fat. *Clin. Sci.*, **9**, 305–315.

EDWARDS, D. A. W., HAMMOND, W. H., HEALY, M. J. R., TANNER, J. M., and WHITEHOUSE, R. H. (1955) Design and accuracy of calipers for measuring subcutaneous tissue thickness. *Brit. J. Nutr.*, **9**, 133–143.

EKMAN, G. (1951) On typological and dimensional systems of reference in describing personality. *Acta Psychol.*, **8**, 1–24.

EKMAN, G. (1951) On the number and definition of dimensions in Kretschmer's and Sheldon's constitutional systems. *Essays in Psychology*. Uppsala: Almquist.

ENKE, W. (1928) Experimentalpsychologische Studien zur Konstitutionsforschung. *Z. ges. Neurol. Psychiat.*, **114**, 770–794.

ENKE, W. (1933) The affectivity of Kretschmer's constitutional types as revealed in psycho-galvanic experiment. *Character & Pers.*, **1**, 225–233.

EPPS, P. and PARNELL, R. W. (1952) Physique and temperament of women delinquents compared with women undergraduates. *Brit. J. med. Psychol.*, **25**, 249–255.

ESQUIROL (1816) *Dictionnaire des Sciences Médicales*, Vol. XVI. Paris: Panckoucke.

EYSENCK, H. J. (1947) *Dimensions of Personality*. London: Routledge & Kegan Paul.

EYSENCK, H. J. (1952) *The Scientific Study of Personality*. London: Routledge & Kegan Paul.

EYSENCK, H. J. (1953) *The Structure of Human Personality*. London: Methuen.

FARR, C. B. (1928) Bodily structure, personality and reaction type. *Amer. J. Psychiat.*, **7**, 231–244.

FEIGENBAUM, J. and HOWAT, D. (1934) The relation between physical constitution and the incidence of disease. *J. clin. Invest.*, **13**, 121.

FEIGENBAUM, J. and HOWAT, D. (1935) Physical constitution and disease: II. Absence of correlation between the anatomic constitution and predisposition to *diabetes mellitus*, cholecystitis and peptic ulcer. *Arch. intern. Med.*, **55**, 445–456.

FISKE, D. W. (1944) A study of relationship to somatotype. *J. appl. Psychol.*, **28**, 504.

FOWLIE, H. C. (1962) The physique of female psychiatric patients. *J. ment. Sci.*, **108**, 594–603.

FREEMAN, W. (1930) Psychological panel in diagnosis and prognosis; correlation of personality type with susceptibility to disease, based on 1,400 necropsies. *Ann. intern. Med.*, **IV**, 29–38.

FÜRST, C. M. (1933) Eine Zahlenbezeichnung für die Kombinationen der Indices der drei Dimensionen des Schädels (Tr. 1). *Anthrop. Anzeig.*, **10**, 209–214.

FÜRST, C. M. (1933) Graphische Darstellung der möglichen Kombinationen der Indices der drei Dimensionen des Schädels (Tr. I). *Anthrop. Anzeig.*, **10**, 321–322.

GALL, F. J. and SPURZHEIM, J. G. (1809) *Recherches sur le Système nerveux*. Paris.

GARN, S. M. (1957) Research in human growth. *Hum. Biol.*, **29**, 1–11.

GARN, S. M. and GERTLER, M. M. (1950) An association between type of work and physique in an industrial group. *Amer. J. phys. Anthropol.*, **8**, 387–397.

GARRETT, H. E. and KELLOGG, W. N. (1928) The relation of physical constitution to general intelligence, social intelligence and emotional stability. *J. exp. Psychol.*, **11**, 113–129.

GARVEY, C. R. (1930) Comparative body-build of manic-depressive and schizophrenic patients. *Psychol. Bull.*, **30**, 567–568.

GENELL, S., JENSEN, C. C., and LINDEGARD, B. (1956) On the quantitative relationship between some steroid substances excreted in the urine by adult males. In *Body-build, Body-function and Personality* (Ed. Lindegard, B.) Lund: Gleerup.

GERTLER, M. M., GARN, S. M., and LEVINE, S. A. (1951) Serum uric acid in relation to age and physique in health and in coronary heart disease. *Ann. intern. Med.*, **34**, 1, 421–1,431.

GERTLER, M. M., GARN, S. M., and SPRAGUE, H. B. (1950) Cholesterol, cholesterol esters and phospholipides in health and coronary artery disease: II. Morphology and serum lipides in man. *Circulation*, **2**, 380–391.

GERTLER, M. M., GARN, S. M. and WHITE, P. D. (1951) Young candidates for coronary disease. *J. Amer. med. Assoc.*, **147**, 621–625.

GILDEA, E. F., KAHN, E., and MAN, E. B. (1936) The relationship between body build and serum lipides and a discussion of these qualities as pyknophilic and leptophilic factors in the structure of the personality. *Amer. J. Psychiat.*, **92**, 1247–1260.

GLUECK, S. and GLUECK, E. (1950) *Unravelling Juvenile Delinquency*. New York: Commonwealth Fund.

GREENWOOD, M. and SMITH, M. (1934) Some pioneers of medical psychology. *Brit. J. med. Psychol.*, **14**, 1–30, 158–9.

GREGORY, R. W. and CASTLE, W. E. (1931) Further studies in the embryological basis of size inheritance in the rabbit. *J. exp. Zool.*, **59**, 199–211.

GRUHLE, H. W. (1926) Der Körper der Normalen. *Arch. psychiat. Nervenkr.*, **77**, 1–31.

HALL, W. S. (1896) Changes in the form of the body during the period of growth. *J. R. Anthrop. Inst.*, **25**, 21‑45.

HAMILTON, M. (1950) Nomogram for the Rees-Eysenck body index. *J. ment. Sci.*, **96**, 540.

HAMMOND, J. (1940) *Farm Animals. Their Breeding, Growth and Inheritance*. London: Arnold.

HAMMOND, W. H. (1942) An application of Burt's multiple general factor analysis to the delineation of physical types. *Man*, **52**, 4–11.

HAMMOND, W. H. (1953a) Measurement of physical types in children. *Hum. Biol.*, **25**, 65–80.

HAMMOND, W. H. (1953b) Physique and development of boys and girls from different types of school. *Brit. J. prevent. soc. Med.*, **7**, 231–239.

HAMMOND, W. H. (1955a) Measurement and interpretation of subcutaneous fat. *Brit. J. prevent. soc. Med.*, **9**, 201–211.

HAMMOND, W. H. (1955b) Body measurements of pre-school children. *Brit. J. prevent. soc. Med.*, **9**, 152–158.

HAMMOND, W. H. (1957) The constancy of physical types as determined by factorial analysis. *Hum. Biol.*, **29**, 40–61.

HAMMOND, W. H. (1957) The status of physical types. *Hum. Biol.*, **29**, 223–241.

HAUPTMAN, A. and MYERSON, A. (1948) Studies of finger capillaries in schizophrenia and manic-depressive psychosis. *J. nerv. ment. Dis.*, **108**, 91–108.

HEATH, C. W. (1945) *What People Are (a Study of Normal Young Men)*. Cambridge, Mass.: Harvard Univ. Press.

HEATH, H. A. (1950) A factor analysis of women's measurement taken for garment and pattern construction. *Doctoral Dissertation, Dept. of Psychiat., Univ. of Chicago* (available on microfilm).

HEATH, H. A. (1952) A factor analysis of women's measurements taken for garment and pattern construction. *Psychometrika*, **17**, 87–95.

HEIDBREDER, E. (1926) Intelligence and the height-weight ratio. *J. appl. Psychol.*, **10**, 52–62.

HENCKEL, K. O. (1924) Körperbaustudien an Schizophrenen, *Z. ges. Neurol. Psychiat.*, **89**, 82–106.

HENCKEL, K. O. (1925) Konstitutionstypen und eruopäische Rassen. *Klin. Wschr.* **4**, 2145–2148.

HIPPOCRATES (1891) *The Genuine Works of*, trans. from Greek with preliminary discourse and annotations by Francis Adams. New York: W. Wood.

HJORTSJO, C. H. (1951) Eine neuer Index gemass dem "Tres-Indices"—Princip als Hilfsmittel bei der Beurteilung der Korperkonstitution "Tri corp". *Lunds Universitets Arsskrift N.F.*, Avd. **2**, Bd. 47, Nr. 4.

HJORTSJO, C. H. (1952) Strömgren's constitutional index and the Tri Corp. A comparison. *Acta. Psychiat. Neurol. Scand.*, **27**, 57.

HJORTSJO, C. H. and LINDEGARD, B. (1953) Critical aspects of the use of indices in physical anthropology. *K. Fysiogr. Sällsk. Lund. Förh.*, **23**, No. 8.

HOOD, A. B. (1963) A study of the relationship between physique and personality variables measured by the M.M.P.I. *J. Personal.*, **31**, 97–107.

HOOTON, E. A. (1937) *Apes, Men and Morons.* New York: Putnam.

HOOTON, E. A. (1939) *Crime and the Man.* Cambridge, Mass.: Harvard Univ. Press.

HOOTON, E. A. (1939) *The American Criminal* (Vol. I). Cambridge, Mass.: Harvard Univ. Press.

HOWELLS, W. W. (1943) Physical anthropology as a technique. *Amer. J. phys. Anthropol.*, **1**, 355–361.

HOWELLS, W. W. (1948) Birth order and body size. *Amer. J. phys. Anthropol.*, **6**, 449–460.

HOWELLS, W. W. (1949) Body measurements in the light of familial influences. *Amer. J. phys. Anthropol.*, **7**, 101–108.

HOWELLS, W. W. (1951) Factors of human physique. *Amer. J. phys. Anthropol.*, **9**, 159–191.

HOWELLS, W. W. (1952) A factorial study of constitutional type. *Amer. J. phys. Anthropol.*, **10**, 91–118.

HRDLIČKA, A. (1947) *Practical Anthropometry.* 3rd ed. Philadelphia: Wistar Inst. of Anatomy and Biology.

HUMPHREYS, L. G. (1957) Characteristics of type concepts with special reference to Sheldon's typology. *Psychol. Bull.*, **54**, 218–228.

HUNT, E. E., Jr. (1952) Human constitution: an appraisal. *Amer. J. phys. Anthropol.*, **10**, 55–74.

HUNTER, J. (1835) *The Works of John Hunter, with Notes*, Vol. 1 (Ed. Palmer, J. F.). London: Longman.

HUXLEY, J. S. (1932) *Problems of Relative Growth.* London: Methuen.

JACOB, C. and MOSER, K. (1923) Messungen zur Kretschmer's Körpersbaulehre. *Arch. psychiat. Nervenkr.*, **70**, 93–108.

JOST, J. and SONTAG, L. W. (1944) The genetic factor in autonomic nervous system function. *Psychosom. Med.* **6**, 308–310.

KALLMAN, F. (1938) *The Genetics of Schizophrenia.* New York: J. J. Augustin.

KALLMAN, F. (1946) The genetic theory of schizophrenia. *Amer. J. Psychiat.*, **103**, 309–322.

KALLMAN, F. (1953) *Heredity in Health and Mental Disorders.* New York: Norton.

KEEHN, J. D. (1953) An experimental investigation into the validity of the use of attitude to colour and form in the assessment of personality. *Ph.D. Thesis, Univ. of London.*

KEYS, A. and BROZEK, J. (1953) Body fat in adult man. *Physiol. Rev.*, **33**, 245–325.

KIBLER, M. (1925) Experimentalpsychologischer Beitrag zur Typenforschung. *Z. ges. Neurol. Psychiat.*, **98**, 524–544.

KISSELEW, M. W. (1931) Der Körperbau und die besonderen Arten des Schizophreieverlaufs. *Z. ges. Neurol. Psychiat.*, **132**, 18–56.

KLINE, N. S. and OPPENHEIM, A. N. (1952) Constitutional factors in prognosis of schizophrenia, further observations. *Amer. J. Psychiat.*, **108**, 909.

KOLLE, K. (1925) Der Körperbau der Schizophrenen. *Arch. Psychiat. Nervenkr.*, **72**, 40–88.

KRETSCHMER, E. (1921) *Körperbau und Charakter.* Berlin: J. Springer.

KRETSCHMER, E. (1926) *Physique and Character.* New York: Harcourt & Brace.

KRETSCHMER, E. (1936) *Physique and Character. An investigation of the nature of constitution and of the theory of temperament.* 2nd ed. (Ed. Paul, K.). London: Trench Trubner.

KRETSCHMER, E. (1941) Tonus as a constitutional problem. *Z. ges. neurol. Psychiat.*, **171**, 401–407.

KRETSCHMER, E. (1948) *Körperbau und Charakter* (19th ed.) Berlin: J. Springer.

KROGMAN, W. M. (1956) The physical growth of children: An appraisal of studies 1950–1955. *Monogr. Soc. for Res. in Child Developmt.*, Ser. No. 60, 1.

LANGFELDT, G. (1947) *The Prognosis in Schizophrenia and the Factors Influencing the Course of the Disease.* Copenhagen: Levin and Munksgaard.

LASKER, G. W. (1947) The effects of partial starvation on somatotype. *Amer. J. phys. Anthropol.*, **5**, 323–341.

LASKER, G. W. (1953) The age factor in bodily measurements of adult male and female Mexicans. *Hum. Biol.*, **25**, 50–63.

LAVATER, J. C. (1804) *Essays on Physiognomy: For the Promotion of the Knowledge and the Love of Mankind* (Trans. Thomas Holcroft) London: Whittingham.

LAVATER, J. C. (1835) *L'art de connaître les Hommes par la Physiognomie.* Paris.

LAVATER, J. C. (1841) *La Physiognomie* (Trans. H. Bacharach). Paris: Librairie Française et Étrangère.

LAYCOCK, T. (1862) Physiognomical diagnosis. *Med. Times and Gazette*, **1**, 1–3, 51–54, 101–103, 185, 205–208, 287–289, 341–344, 449–451, 499–502, 551–554, 635–637.

LECKIE, S. V. (1967) Obesity and depression. *J. psychosom. Res.*, **11**, 1, 107–115.

LEE, A., LORENZ, M. D., and PEARSON, L. (1903) On the correlation of mental and physical characteristics in man. *Proc. roy. Soc.*, **71**, 106–114.

LEVITT, H., and FELLNER, C. (1965) M.M.P.I. profiles of three obesity subgroups. *J. consult. Psychol.*, **29**, 1, 91.

LEWIS, N. D. C. (1924) The constitutional factors in *dementia praecox. Nerv. Ment. Dis. Monogr.*, 39.

LEWIS, N. D. C. (1936) *Research in Dementia Praecox.* New York: National Committee for Mental Hygiene.

LINDBERG, B. J. (1938) Experimental studies of colour and non-colour attitude in school children and adults. *Diss. Acta Psychiat. et Neurol.*, Suppl. 16.

LINDEGARD, B. (1953) *Variations in Human Body Build.* Copenhagen: Munksgaard.

LINDEGARD, B., (Ed.) (1956) *Body Build, Body Function and Personality.* Lund: Gleerup.

LINDEGARD, B., MORSING, C., and NYMAN, E. G. (1956) Male sex characters in relation to body build, endocrine activity and personality. In *Body Build, Body Function and Personality* (Ed. B. Lindegard), Lund: Gleerup *vs.*

LINDEGARD, B. and NYMAN, E. G. (1956) Interrelations between psychologic, somatologic and endocrine dimensions. In *Body Build, Body Function and Personality* (Ed. B. Lindegard), Lund: Gleerup. *v.s.*

LOMBROSO, C. (1889) *L'Uomo Delinquente.* Flli. Bocca: Torina.

LOMBROSO, C. (1911) *Crime, Its Causes and Remedies* (Trans. Horton) Boston: Little, Brown.

LORR, M. and FIELDS, V. (1952) A factorial study of body types. *J. clin. Psychol.*, **10**, 182–185.

LOW, A. (1952) *Growth of Children.* Aberdeen: Aberdeen Univ. Press.

LUCAS, W. P. and PRYOR, H. B. (1933) The body build factor in the basal metabolism of children. *Amer. J. Dis. Child.* (Pt. II), **46**, 941–948.

LUCAS, W. P. and PRYOR, H. B. (1931) Physical measurements and physiological processes in young children. *J. Amer. med. Assoc.*, **97**, 1, 127.

MACAULIFFE, L. (1925) Les origines de la morphologie humaine. *Bull. Soc. d'Étude des Formes Humaines*, Nos. 2 & 3, 155.

McCANCE, R. A. and WIDDOWSON, E. M. (1951) A method of breaking down the body weights of living persons into terms of extra-cellular fluid, cell mass and fat and some applications of it to physiology and medicine. *Proc. roy. Soc.*, **138**, 115–130.

McCLOY, C. H. (1936) Appraising physical status and the selection of measurements. *Univ. Ia Stud. Child Welf.*, **12**, No. 2.

McCLOY, C. H. (1940) An analysis for multiple factors of physical growth at different age levels. *Child Develpm.*, **11**, 249–277.

McFARLAND, R. A. (1946) *Human Factors in Air Transport Design.* New York: McGraw-Hill.

McFARLAND, R. A. (1953) *Human Factors in Air Transportation.* New York: McGraw-Hill.

MANOUVRIER, L. (1902) Étude sur les rapports anthropométriques en général et sur les principale sproportions du corps. *Mém. de la Soc. d'Anth. de Paris*, Ser. 3, T. 2.

MARSHALL, E. L. (1938) A multiple factor study of 18 anthropometric measurements of Iowa City boys. *J. exp. Educ.*, **5**, 212.

MARTIGNY, M. (1948) *Essai de Biotypologie Humaine.* Peyronnet: Paris.

MARTIN, R. (1914) *Lehrbuch der Anthropologie.* Jena: Fisher.

MAUZ, F. (1930) *Die Prognostik der ergogensen Psychosen.* Leipzig: Thieme.

MEADE, C. D. (1914) Height and weight of children in relation to general intelligence. *Ped. Sem.*, **21**, 394–406.

MICHEL, R. and WEEBER, R. (1924) Körperbau und Charakter. *Arch. Psychiat. Nervenkr.*, **71**, 265.

MILLS, R. W. (1917) The relation of body *habitus* to visceral form, position, tonus and motility. *Amer. J. Roentgenol.*, **4**, 155.

MISIAK, H. and PICKFORD, R. W. (1944) Physique and perseveration. *Nature*, **153**, 622.

MOHR, G. J. and GUNDLACH, R. H. (1927) The relation between physique and performance. *J. exp. Psychol.*, **10**, 117–157.

MÖLLENHOFF, F., (1924) Zur Frage der Beziehungen zwischen Körperbau und Psychose. *Arch. Psychiat. Nervenkr.*, **71**, 98.

MOORE, T. V. and HSU, E. H. (1946) Factorial analysis of anthropological measurements in psychotic patients. *Hum. Biol.*, **18**, 133–157.

MULLEN, F. A. (1940) Factors in the growth of girls. *Child Develpm.*, **11**, 27.

NACCARATI, S. (1921) The morphological aspect of intelligence. *Arch. Psychol.*, No. 45.

NACCARATI, S. (1924) The morphologic basis of the psycho-neuroses. *Amer. J. Psychiat.*, **3**, 527–545.

NACCARATI, S. and GARRETT, H. E. (1924) The relation of morphology to temperament. *J. abnorm. (Soc.) Psychol.*, **19**, 3.

NEWMAN, H. H., FREEMAN, F. N., and HOLZINGER, K. J. (1937) *Twins: A Study of Heredity and Environment.* Chicago: Univ. of Chicago Press.

NEWMAN, R. W. (1952) Age changes in body build. *Amer. J. Phys. Anthropol.*, **10**, 75–90.

O'BRIEN, R., GIRSHICK, M. A., and HUNT, E. P. (1941) Body measurements of American boys and girls for garment and pattern construction. *U.S. Dept. Agric. Misc. Pub.* No. 366, 29–34.

OLIVIER, H. G. (1922) Der Körperbau der Schizophrenen. *Z. ges. Neurol. Psychiat.*, **80**, 489–498.

OLKON, D. M. (1939) Capillary structure in patients with schizophrenia. *Arch. neurol. Psychiat. Chicago*, **48**, 652–663.

PALMER, C. E. (1934) Age changes in physical resemblance of siblings. *Child Develpm.*, **5**, 351.

PARNELL, R. W. (1951) Some notes on physique and athletic training with special reference to heart size. *Brit. med. J.*, **1**, 1, 292.

PARNELL, R. W. (1957) Physique and mental breakdown in young adults. *Brit. med. J.*, **1**, 1,485–1,490.

PARNELL, R. W. (1952) Recording human constitution. *Eug. Rev.*, **XLIV**, **1**, 20.

PARNELL, R. W. (1953) Physique and choice of faculty. *Brit. med. J.*, **2**, 472–475.

PARNELL, R. W. (1953) Physical body measurements. *Trans. Assoc. indust. med. Officers*, **3**, 1.

PARNELL, R. W. (1954) The physique of Oxford undergraduates. *J. Hygiene*, **52**, 369–378.

PARNELL, R. W. (1954) Physique and performance: Honours class at Oxford. *Brit. med. J.*, **2**, 491.

PARNELL, R. W. (1954) Somatotyping by physical anthropometry. *Amer. J. phys. Anthropol.*, **12**, 209–240.

PARNELL, R. W. (1954) The relationship of masculine and feminine physical traits to academic and athletic performance. *Brit. J. med. Psychol.*, **XXVII**, 4, 247.

PARNELL, R. W. (1954) Constitutional aspects of psychosomatic medicine. In *Modern Trends in Psychosomatic Medicine*. London: Butterworth.

PARNELL, R. W. (1955) Strength of body and strength of mind. *Brit. J. physiol. Med.*, **18**, 7, 150–159.

PARNELL, R. W. (1968) Personal communication.

PARNELL, R. W., DAVIDSON, M. D., LEE, D., and SPENCER, S. J. G. (1955) The detection of psychological vulnerability in students. *J. ment. Sci.*, **101**, 425, 810–825.

PARNELL, R. W. and EPPS, P. (1952) Physique and temperament of women delinquents compared with women undergraduates. *Brit. J. med. Psychol.*, **XXV**, 4, 249.

PARNELL, R. W., PEIERLS, G. E., STANDLEY, C. C., and WESTROPP, C. K. (1955) Physique and the grammar school entrance examination. *Brit. med. J.*, **1**, 1,506–1,510.

PATERSON, D. G. (1930) *Physique and Intellect*. New York: Appleton-Century.

PEARL, R. (1933) *Constitution and Health*. London: Kegan Paul.

PEARL, R. and CIOCCO, A. (1934) Studies on constitution: II. Somatological differences associated with disease of the heart in white males. *Hum. Biol.*, **6**, 650–713.

PEARSON, K. (1906) Relationship of intelligence to size and shape of the head and other mental and physical characters. *Biometrika*, **5**, 105–146.

PEARSON, K. and MOULL, M. (1925–26) The problem of alien immigration into Great Britain, illustrated by an examination of Russian and Polish Jewish children. *Ann. Eugen.*, **1**, Pt II, 56–127.

PENDE, N. (1922) *Le debolezze di Costituzione* Rome: Bardi.

PENDE, N. (1928) *Constitutional Inadequacies* (Trans. by S. Naccarati) Philadelphia: Lea & Febiger.

PIGNET, L. (1901) Du coefficient de robusticité. *Bull. médicale*, 15 ann., 373–376.

PILLSBURY, W. B. (1936) Body form and success in studies. *J. soc. Psychol.*, **7**, 129–139.

PILLSBURY, W. B. (1939) Body form and introversion-extraversion. *J. abnorm.* (*soc.*) *Psychol.*, **34**, 400–401.

PLATTNER, W. (1932) Körperbauuntersuchungen bei Schizophrenen. *Arch. Klaus-Stift, VererbForsch.*

PLATTNER, W. (1938) Das Körperbauspektrum. *Z. ges. Neurol. Psychiat.*, **160**, 703–712.

PLATTNER-HEBERLEIN, F. (1932) Personlichkeit und Psychose asthenischer und pyknicscher Schizophrenen. *Z. ges. Neurol. Psychiat.*, **141**, 277–320.

QUETELET, A. (1842) *Sur l'homme et le développement de ses facultés* (1935, Engl. trans: *A Treatise on Man*). Edinburgh: Chambers.

QUETELET, A. (1871) *Anthropométrie*. Brussels: C. Muquardt.

RAPHAEL, T., FERGUSON, W. G., and SEARLE, O. M. (1928) Constitutional factors in schizophrenia. *Arch. Res. Neurol. ment. Dis.*, **5**, 100–132.

REED, L. J. (1933) Biometric studies on U.S. Army officers, somatological norms in disease. *Hum. Biol.*, **5**, 61–93.

REES, L. (1943) Physical constitution in relation to effort syndrome, neurotic and psychotic types. *M.D. Thesis, Univ. of Wales.*

REES, L. (1944) Physical constitution, neurosis and psychosis. *Proc. roy. soc. Med.*, **37**, 635–638.

REES, L. (1945) Physical and psychological aspects of constitution. *Eugen. Rev.*, **37**, 23–27.

REES, L. (1945) Physique and effort syndrome. *J. ment. Sci.*, **91**, 89–92.

REES, L. (1949) The value of anthropometric indices in the assessment of body build. *J. ment. Sci.*, **95**, 171–179.

REES, L. (1950a) A factorial study of physical constitution in women. *J. ment. Sci.*, **96**, 620–632.

REES, L. (1950b) Body build, personality and neurosis in women. *J. ment. Sci.*, **96**, 426–434.

REES, L. (1950c) Body size, personality and neurosis. *J. ment. Sci.*, **96**, 168–180.

REES, L. (1957) Physical characteristics of the schizophrenic patient. In *Somatic Aspects of Schizophrenia* (Ed. Richter, D.). London: Pergamon Press.

REES, L. (1947) The physical constitution and mental illness. *Eugen. Rev.*, **39**, 50–55.

REES, L. and EYSENCK, H. J. (1945) A factorial study of some morphological and psychological aspects of human constitution. *J. ment. Sci.*, **91**, 8.

REYNOLDS, E. L. (1943) Degree of kinship and pattern of ossification. *Amer. J. phys. Anthropol.*, **1**, 405–416.

REYNOLDS, E. L. (1949) The fat/bone index as a sex differentiating character in man. *Hum. Biol.*, **21**, 199–204.

REYNOLDS, E. L. and ASKAWA, T. (1950) A comparison of certain aspects of body structure and body shape in 200 adults. *Amer. J. phys. Anthropol.*, **8**, 343–365.

ROSTAN, L. (1828) *Cours élémentaire d'hygiène*. Paris.

RUHMANN, W. (1926) *Der Ulcuskranke. Studien zur Konstitution und Symptomatik am gesamten Status bei chronischem Ulcus Pepticum mit besonderer Berücksichtigung des vegetativen Nervensystems*. Berlin: Harger.

SANFORD, R. N., ADKINS, M. M., MILLER, R. B., and COBB, E. A. (1943) Physique, personality and scholarship. *Monogr. Soc. Res. Child. Develpm.*, **7**, No. 34, 73–174.

SCAMMON, R. E. (1927) The first seriatim study of human growth. *Amer. J. phys. Anthropol.*, **10**, 329–336.

SCHWERIN, O. (1936) Rasse und Körperbau bei 100 Schizophrenen an Baden. *Allg. Z. Psychiat.*, **105**, 121–129.

SEGRAVES, R. T. (1969) Adrenocortical Activity, Personality and Body Build. *Ph.D. Thesis, University of London.*

SELTZER, C. C. (1940) Body build and oxygen metabolism at rest and during exercise. *Amer. J. Physiol.*, **129**, 1.

SELTZER, C. C. (1945) The relationship between the masculine component and personality. *Amer. J. phys. Anthropol.*, **3**, 33.

SELTZER, C. C. (1946) Body disproportions and dominant personality traits. *Psychosom. Med.*, **8**, 75–97.

SELTZER, C. C. and BROUHA, L. (1943) The 'masculine' component and physical fitness. *Amer. J. phys. Anthropol.*, **1**, 95.

SELTZER, C. C., WELLS, F. L., and MCTERNAN, E. G. (1948) A relationsip between Sheldonian somatotype and psychotype. *J. Personality*, **16**, 431–436.

SHATTOCK, F. M. (1950) Somatic aspects of schizophrenia. *J. ment. Sci.*, **96**, 32–142.

SHAW, F. (1925) A morphological study of the functional psychoses. *State Hosp. Quart.*, **10**, 413–421.

SHELDON, W. H. (1927) Morphological types and mental ability. *J. person. Res.*, **5**, 447–451.

SHELDON, W. H. (1927) Social traits and morphological types. *Personnel J.*, **6**, No. 1, 47–55.

SHELDON, W. H. (1927) Ability and facial measurements. *Personnel J.*, **6**, No. 2.

SHELDON, W. H., STEVENS, S. S., and TUCKER, W. B. (1940) *The Varieties of Human Physique.* New York: Harper & Bros.

SHELDON, W. H., HARTL, E. M., and MCDERMOTT, E. (1949) *Varieties of Delinquent Youth.* New York: Harper & Bros.

SHELDON, W. H. and STEVENS, S. S. (1942) *The Varieties of Temperament.* New York: Harper & Bros.

SIGAUD, C. (1914) *Ma Forme Humaine.* Paris: A. Maloine.

SILLS, F. D. (1950) A factor analysis of somatotypes and their relationship to achievements in motor skills. *Res. Quart.*, **21**, 424–437.

SIOLI, F. and MEYER, A. (1922) Bemerkungen zu Kretschmers Buch "Körperbau und Charakter". *Z. ges. Neurol Psychiat.*, **80**, 439–453.

SLATER, E. (1943) The neurotic constitution. *J. Neurol.*, **6**, 1–16.

SLATER, E. (1950) The genetical aspects of personality and neurosis. *Congrès Internat. de Psychiatrie*, Paris. *VI. Psychiatrie Sociale, Génétique et Eugénique*, p. 119.

SMITH, H. C. and BOYARSKY, S. (1943) Relationship between physique and simple reaction time. *Character & Pers.*, **12**, 46–53.

SOMMERVILLE, R. C. (1924) Physical, motor and sensory traits. *Arch. Psychol.*, No. 75, **108**.

SPEARMAN, C. (1927) *Abilities of Man.* London: Macmillan.

SPURZHEIM, J. G. (1933) *Phrenology in Connexion with the Study of Physiognomy.* Boston: Capen & Lyon.

STALNAKER, E. M. (1923) A comparison of certain mental and physical measurements of school children and college students. *J. comp. Psychol.*, **3**, 181.

STALNAKER, E. M. and ROLLER, R. D. (Jnr.) (1927) A study of one hundred non-promoted children. *J. educ. Res.*, **16**, 265–270.

STILLER, B. (1907) Die astenische Konstitutionskrankheit. Stuttgart: Enke.

STOCKARD, C. R. (1923) Human types and growth reactions. *Amer. J. Anat.*, **31**, 261–269.

STOCKARD, C. R. (1931) *The Physical Basis of Personality.* New York: Norton.

STONE, C. P. and BARKER, R. G. (1934) On the relationship between menarcheal age and certain aspects of personality, intelligence and physique in college women. *J. Genet. Psychol.*, **45**, 121–135.

STRÖMGREN, E. (1937) Über anthropometrische Indices zur Unterschiedung von Körperbautypen. *Z. ges. Neurol. Psychiat.*, **159**, 75–81.

STUART, H. C. and SOBEL, E. H. (1946) The thickness of the skin and subcutaneous tissue by age and sex in childhood. *J. Pediat.*, **26**, 637–647.

TANNER, J. M. (1944) Intercorrelations between cardiovascular variables in healthy men and the relation of physique to these and other variables. Proc. Physiol. Soc. Phila. *Amer. J. med. Sci.*, **207**, 684.

TANNER, J. M. (1947) The morphological level of personality. *Proc. roy. soc. Med.*, **50**, 301–308.

TANNER, J. M. (1948) A guide to American growth studies. In *Yearbook of Physical Anthropology* (Ed. Lasker, S. W.). New York: The Viking Fund.

TANNER, J. M. (1951a) The relation between serum cholesterol and physique in healthy young men. *J. Physiol.*, **125**, 371–396.

TANNER, J. M. (1951b) The relationship between the frequency of heart, oral temperature and rectal temperature in man at rest. *J. Physiol.*, **125**, 391–409.

TANNER, J. M. (1951) Some notes on the reporting of growth data. *Hum. Biol.*, **23**, 93–159.

TANNER, J. M. (1951) Current advances in the study of physique. Photogrammetric anthropometry and an androgyny scale. *Lancet*, **i**, 574.

TANNER, J. M. (1952a) The physique of students: an experiment at Oxford. *Lancet*, **i**, 405–409.

TANNER, J. M. (1952b) The effect of weight-training on physique. *Amer. J. phys., Anthropol.*, **10**, 427–462.

TANNER, J. M. (1952) The assessment of growth and development in children. *Arch. Dis. Child.*, **27**, 10–33.

TANNER, J. M. (1953) Growth and Constitution. In *Anthropology Today* (Ed. Kroeber). Chicago: Univ. of Chicago Press.

TANNER, J. M. (1953a) Growth of the Human at the time of adolescence. In *Lectures on the Scientific Basis of Medicine* (Ed. Frazer, F.). London: Athlone Press.

TANNER, J. M. (1953b) The inheritance of morphological and psychological traits. In *Clinical Genetics* (Ed. Sorsby, A.) London: Butterworth.

TANNER, J. M. (1955) *Growth at Adolescence.* Springfield: C. C. Thomas.

TANNER, J. M. (1956) Physique, character, and disease. *Lancet*, **ii**, 635–637.

TANNER, J. M. (1954) The reliability of anthroposcopic somatotyping. *Amer. J. phys. Anthropol.*, **12**, 257.

TANNER, J. M. (1964) *Analysis and Classification of Physique.* In *Human Biology: an introduction to human evolution, variation and growth* (Ed. Wiener, J. S. and Barnicot, N. A.). Oxford: Clarendon Press.

TANNER, J. M. (1965) Radiographic studies of body composition in children and adults. In *Human Body Composition.* (Ed. Brozek, J.). Oxford: Pergamon Press.

TANNER, J. M. and BURT, W. A. (1954) Physique in the infra-human mammalia. A factor analysis of body measurements in dairy cows. *J. Genet.*, **52**, 37–51.

TANNER, J. M., HEALY, M. J. R., LOCKHARD, R. D., MACKENZIE, J. D., WHITEHOUSE, R. H. (1956) Aberdeen growth study: I. *Arch. Dis. Child*, **31**, 372–381.

TANNER, J. M. and SAWIN, P. P. (1953) Morphogenetic studies in the rabbit. Vol. XI. Genetic differences in the growth of the vertebral columns and their relation to growth and development in man. *J. Anat. London*, **87**, 54–65.

TANNER, J. M. and WEINER, J. S. (1949) The reliability of the photogrammetric method of anthropometry, with a description of a miniature camera technique. *Amer. J. phys. Anthropol.*, **7**, 145–185.

TANNER, J. M. and WHITEHOUSE, R. H. (1955) The Harpenden skinfold caliper. *Amer. J. phys. Anthropol.*, **13**, 743–746.

THOMPSON, D'A. W. (1916) *On Growth and Form.* London: Cambridge Univ. Press (revised ed. 1952)

THOMSON, G. H. (1946) *The Factorial Analysis of Human Ability.* London: Univ. of London Press.

THURSTONE, L. L. (1946a) *Analysis of Body Measurements.* The Psychometric Laboratory, Univ. of Chicago, No. 29.

THURSTONE, L. L. (1946b) Factor analysis and body types. *Psychometrika*, **11**, 15–21.

THURSTONE, L. L. (1947) Factorial analysis of body measurements. *Amer. J. phys. Anthropol.*, **5**, 15–28.

TIEDEMAN, D. V. (1951) The utility of the discriminant function in psychological and guidance investigations. *Harvard educ. Rev.*, **25**, 2, 71–80.

TOURAINE, G. A. and DRAPER, G. (1934) The migrainous patient—a constitutional study. *J. nerv. ment. Dis.*, **80**, No. 1, 183.

TSCHERNING, R. (1923) Über die somatische und psychische Konstitution bei Ulcus ventriculi. *Arch. Verdaukr.*, **31**, 351.

TUCKER, W. B. and LESSA, W. A. (1940) Man: a constitutional investigation. *Quart. Rev. Biol.*, **15**, 256–289, 411–455.

VANELLI, A. (1932) La costituzione somatica degli schizofrenici. *Schizofrenie*, **1**, 3–14.

VIOLA, G. (1925) L'*habitus phthisicus* et l'*habitus apoplecticus* comme conséquence d'une loi qui déforme normalement le type moyen de la race en ces deux types antithétiques. *Comptes rendus de l'Assoc. des anatomistes. Vingtiéme réunion* (Turin 6–8 April, 1925) p. 33 (of reprint).

VIOLA, G. (1932) *La Costituzione Individuale.* Bologna: Cappelli.

VIOLA, G. (1937) Il mio metodo di valutazione della costitutione individuale. *Endrocrinologia patologia costituzionale*, **12**, 387–480.

VON ROHDEN, F. (1927) Konstitutionelle Körperbauuntersuchungen an Gesunden und Kranken. *Arch. Psychiat.*, **79**, 786–815.

WALDROP, R. S. (1940) A factorial study of the components of body build (abstract). *Psychol. Bull.*, **37**, 578.

WALKER, R. N. (1962) Body build and behaviour in young children: Body build and nursery school teacher's ratings. *Monograph Soc. Res. Child. Dev.*, **27**, 3, 84.

WALKER, R. N. (1963) Body build and behaviour in young children. Body build and parent's ratings. *Child. Dev.*, **34**, 1–23.

WATSON, R. (1956) Unpublished data: Library of Institute of Psychiatry, London.

WEIDENREICH, F. (1926) *Rasse und Körperbau.* Berlin: J. Springer.

WEISSENFELD, F. (1925) Körperbau und Charakter. *Z. ges. Neurol. Psychiat.*, **96**, 175.

WELLS, F. (1938) Relation between psychosis and physical type: a statistical study. *Amer. J. Psychol.*, **51**, 136–145.

WELLS, S. R. (1869) *How to Read Character.* New York: Fowler & Wells.

WENGER, M. A. (1943) An attempt to appraise individual differences in level of muscular tension. *J. exp. Psychol.*, **32**, 213.

WERKMAN, S. J. and GREENBERG, E. S. (1967) Personality and interest patterns in obese adolescent girls. *Psychosom. Med.*, **29**, 72–80.

WERTHEIMER, F. I. and HESKETH, F. E. A. (1925) A minimum scheme for the study of the morphologic constitution in psychiatry with remarks on anthropometric technique. *Arch. Neurol. Psychiat. Chicago*, **17**, 93–98.

WERTHEIMER, F. I. and HESKETH, F. E. A. (1926) *The Significance of the Physical Constitution in Mental Disease.* Baltimore: Williams & Wilkins.

WERTHEIMER, N. and WERTHEIMER, M. (1955) Capillary structure, its relation to psychiatric diagnosis and morphology. *J. nerv. ment. Dis.*, **122**, 14–27.

WESTPHAL, K. (1914) Untersuchungen zur Frage der nervösen Entstehung peptischer Ulcera. *Dtsch. Arch. f. klin. Med.*, **114**, 327.

WHEELER, L. R. (1929) A comparative study of physical growth in dull children. *J. educ. Rev.*, **20**, 273.

WIERSMA, E. D. (1933) Bodily Build, Physiological and Psychological Function. *Ver. Akad. Wet. Amst. (b)*, **30**, No. 2.

WIGANT, V. (1933) Attempts at anthropometric determination of the body types of Kretschmer. *Acta Psychiat. Neurol.*, **8**, 465–481.

WILDER, H. H. (1920) *Laboratory Manual of Anthropometry.* Philadelphia.

WOOD, P. (1941) Da Costa's syndrome. *Brit. med. J.*, **1**, 767–772, 805–811, 845–850.

WOODS, W. L., BROUHA, L., and SELTZER, C. C. (1943) *Selection of Officer Candidates.* Cambridge, Mass.: Harvard Univ. Press.

WRETMARK, G. (1953) The peptic ulcer individual. *Acta Psychiat. Neurol. Scand.*, Suppl. 84.

WYRSCH, J. (1924) Beitrag zur Kretschmers Lehre von Körperbau und Charakter. *Z. ges. Neurol. Psychiat.*, **92**, 526–530.

ZERSSEN, D. v. (1964) Dimensionen der morphologischen Habitus-Variationen und ihre biometrische Erfassung. *Z. menschl. Vererb. u. Konstitutionslehre*, **37**, 611–625.

ZERSSEN, D. v. (1965) Eine biometrische Überprufung der Theorien von Sheldon über Zusammenhange zwischen Korperbau und Temperament. *Z. exp. angew. Psychol.*, **12**, 521–548.

16

Heredity and Psychological Abnormality*

JAMES SHIELDS

INTRODUCTION

In this chapter we consider the genetical causes of psychological abnormality. In so far as differences between individuals are due to differences between genes, which are the basic units of heredity, they ultimately rest on differences of a physical kind.

From Gene to Behaviour

In recent decades there have been outstanding advances in molecular biology. (For a popular account *see* Clowes, 1967.) The chemical structure of DNA (deoxyribose nucleic acid), the macromolecules of which the hereditary material consists, is well understood; and it is known in principle how DNA replicates itself. The difference between one gene and another depends on differences in the sequence in which four nucleotides are strung along the chains of the famous Watson-Crick double helix model of the structure of DNA. Furthermore, the three-letter genetic code for amino acids, contained in the sequence of nucleotides, has now been largely cracked so that it is known, at least in simple organisms such as bacteria, how the genetic information contained in the DNA of the cell nucleus is first transformed into messenger-RNA and then 'translated' into the sequence in which the 21 amino acids occur along a polypeptide chain in the synthesis of enzymes and other proteins. Sickle-cell anaemia is an example of a molecular disease in man.

The difference between the haemoglobin protein synthesised by the great majority of individuals and that synthesised by the carriers of the rare gene that causes sickle-cell anaemia consists in the substitution of one DNA base for another. In the abnormal haemoglobin a molecule of the amino-acid valine occurs at a particular point in a polypeptide chain instead of a molecule of glutamic acid. Those who have inherited the abnormal gene from both parents (i.e. the abnormal homozygotes) die of anaemia before reaching adult life. Ultimately, such a difference is due to a genetic mutation in the past. Mutation is a rare, essentially random event, which results in an error in the replication of a gene. If, on balance, a mutant gene is harmful, in the sense that the overall fertility of its carriers is reduced, it will be eliminated from the population gene pool by natural selection. The sickle-cell gene has been maintained in areas where malaria was endemic because those who have inherited the normal gene from one parent and this particular alternative form (allele) of the gene from the other parent synthesise a mixture of the two haemoglobins. There is still some tendency to anaemia, but the blood cells have increased resistance to the malaria parasite. Persons of this genetic constitution (heterozygotes) therefore more often survive to produce offspring than the normal homozygote. The relative increase in fertility of the heterozygote

* The chapter was completed in 1969. Only parts of it have been updated. I am indebted to Eliot Slater and Irving Gottesman for criticising the manuscript. The stimulus of their ideas in the past will be obvious and is gratefully acknowledged, but I am sure neither would wish to share responsibility for all the opinions expressed here. Eliot Slater has allowed me to use material from our joint Chapter 8 in the first edition of this *Handbook*. He and Valerie Cowie kindly allowed me to read chapters they had prepared for their book *The Genetics of Mental Disorders*, now published by Oxford University Press. Vera G. Seal has been of immense assistance in preparing this review, bibliographically and in many other ways.

balances the loss of sickle-cell genes caused by the infertility of the abnormal homozygote. The frequency of the normal and sickle-cell alleles has been in equilibrium in parts of the Mediterranean area and Africa where malaria is still endemic.

The sickle-cell gene has indirect effects on characters other than anaemia and resistance to malaria. Heterozygotes are liable to various minor forms of ill-health and, if the matter were gone into, would doubtless be found, on average, to differ by a small amount in measurable psychological variables. In general, *a gene that has a major effect on one trait will have a minor effect on many others* (*pleiotropy*).

Besides structural genes that control the synthesis of enzymes on the lines indicated above, there are also, at least in bacteria, *regulator genes*, first discovered by Jacob and Monod (1961), which control the activity of blocks of structural genes, switching them on and off, as it were, in response to external stimuli. An attempt to apply the concept of regulator genes to behavioural traits in man has been made by Meissner (1965). While the complexities of gene regulation in man are not well understood, the genes must be regarded as exerting their effects through their control of biochemical reactions, speeding up some and retarding others, or by inhibiting some reaction until the chemical environment is such as to trigger it off. Antibodies, the production of which is under close genetic control, are not produced until the specific antigen is present. The variation due to some genetic differences is seen very early in development, e.g. into a male or female constitution, but others show their effects much later, e.g. baldness in males, and Huntington's chorea. Far from 'genetic' being the equivalent of 'congenital' or manifest at birth, there is no point in life at which one can say that all genetic potentialities have been manifested.

Man is a highly variable creature genetically. Various estimates have been made of the number of human genes. According to Neel and Schull (1954), there are between 40,000 and 80,000. Most exist in one form only and so do not contribute to variation within the human species, but the proportion of loci for which the English population is polymorphic has been estimated at one third (Lewontin, 1967). Many of the mutant alleles are extremely rare. The number of already identifiable polymorphic genes, i.e. those existing in more than one form sufficiently advantageous to be maintained in the population without fresh mutation, is so great that, apart from monozygotic twins, each individual may be presumed to have his *unique biochemical individuality* (Williams, 1956; Harris, 1968). The basic question we have to consider is how this genetic variability is related to abnormalities of behaviour.

We must think of genetic-biochemical relationships as being of great complexity. H. J. Muller (1956) put it:

'Whatever may be the nature of the primary chemical products of genes within the cell, these products must be of thousands of different kinds, corresponding with the thousands of different genes, and these products must interact with one another in innumerable ways to form secondary products, tertiary products and those ever further removed from the genes. It is usually only after a most intricate web of these inter-actions has been followed through that those end-products are at last found which we become aware of as the characteristics of the organism.... Because of the great indirectness of the route connecting the genes with these end results, it is evident that any given characteristic must be a resultant of the action of many genes, some playing a major role in its development but many more playing only a minor role.'

Therefore although the genes are independent units, we must also think of the genetic constitution largely as a whole. We shall find that the cumulative effects of the minor end results of many genes (polygenic inheritance) will be just as important in some fields as the major effects of single genes (monogenic inheritance) in other fields. Once a major gene has produced its distinctive difference, this is not the end of the matter, for the specific abnormality so caused will become involved in a tangled web of secondary and tertiary consequences. And just as the effects of one gene may be many, so the same end result in some particular respect can be brought about by different genes or combinations of genes. It has even been said that every gene affects all characters and every character is affected by all genes.

In the first edition of the *Handbook* (Shields and Slater, 1960) we illustrated the point that a simple genetically-determined cartilage anomaly in the rat can have effects that are of an extremely various kind. Death, apparently arising from distinct diseases such as suffocation, pulmonary haemorrhage or starvation can, in the experimental animal, be traced back to the one main cause. In diabetes mellitus in man, the insulin deficiency to which the disease is primarily due is itself the result of a chain of causes genetically more complex than the cartilage anomaly in the rat, and it has even more varied secondary consequences, some of them due to the impaired ability to burn sugar, others to the efforts of the organism to compensate for this. The course taken is influenced by secondary factors, some genetic, others the products of the environment, including medical treatment.

The application of genetics to abnormal psychology is no different in principle from its application in biology or medicine. We may, indeed, suppose that the route from gene to the end result—from genotype to phenotype—will be more complex and indirect than ever; but we may still be able to show by appropriate methods whether a significant proportion of the total variation occurring in a given population is due to genetic causes. Here and there we may also be able to demonstrate in a more precise manner the mode of interaction between the genes and the environmental framework in which they must develop.

Approaches to the Genetic Aspects of Behaviour

Even if very few psychological abnormalities can be traced to inborn errors of metabolism, attributable to single mutant genes, or well understood at all stages of the development from the molecular to the psycho-social, this introduction has illustrated several points that are relevant to our subject. It is encouraging to know that the units of heredity are not just hypothetical constructs. In one or another of its aspects genetics encompasses most of the sciences. A complete account of the genetics of psychological abnormality, if such were possible, would include explanations in terms of evolution, cell biology, embryology, biochemistry, the social sciences and learning theory.

Taking a broad view, some workers (Freedman, 1968; Gottesman, 1965; Price, 1968) ask why it is that man has evolved such universal characteristics as extraversion-introversion and depression. Occasionally, geneticists have been able to apply a developmental approach; for example in trying to elucidate the nature of the pathway from the metabolic error of a liver enzyme in children with phenylketonuria (PKU) to the disturbed brain physiology and the resultant disorders of intelligence and behaviour. Elsewhere, formal mode of inheritance is the point at issue. For example, the two main types of defective colour vision, protanomaly and deuteranomaly, can be allocated to two different loci on the X-chromosome, each anomaly inherited as a sex-linked recessive trait. In schizophrenia one may compare the fit of the observed data on morbidity in the relatives with what is predicted on hypotheses of monogenic and polygenic inheritance. Another approach is to look for grossly identifiable genetic anomalies, such as an extra chromosome, in populations of different kinds. Such abnormalities may on occasion be found to play a major part in some cases of behavioural abnormality of a general kind, such as criminality. However, more often the task in behaviour genetics is to try to refute the null hypothesis that genetic variation is irrelevant to individual differences in intelligence and personality;

and, if the relevance of genetic variation is established, to estimate its contribution compared with that of the environment.

It is this last approach that is most favoured by experimental psychologists. The approach applies the methods of biometrical genetics—an extension of Mendelian genetics—which have been used with advantage, both theoretical and economic, by animal and plant breeders interested in estimating the degree of heritability of characters such as corn size and egg yield.

Difficulties of a Psychometric Approach to the Relatives of the Abnormal

Quite apart from the fact that heritability estimates, interesting though they may be, are not the final aim of human genetics, there are sound reasons why the approach has so far been little applied to the genetics of psychiatric abnormality. The method of analysis usually requires continuously and normally distributed variables, such as suitably scaled test scores, and these, if they are to carry conviction, must be repeatedly validated reciprocally against such external criteria as psychiatric consultation rates, conventional diagnosis, and criminal record. It is true that the best psychological tests are based on or checked against the responses of schizophrenics, neurotics, or prisoners as appropriate. But what is insufficiently known is how an individual's score when ill compares with his score not only after treatment, but more important, with what he would have scored *before* he became ill. The psychometric approach to psychiatric genetics envisages testing the relatives of patients. Unless the stability of the tests as a measure of constitutional predisposition to a particular type of abnormality is known, the interpretation of negative findings will be in doubt. Follow-up studies are therefore required of normal groups, or of high-risk but hitherto unaffected groups, tested initially on measures such as the neuroticism scale of the MPI (Maudsley Personality Inventory), the clinical scales of the MMPI (Minnesota Multiphasic Personality Inventory) or physiological reactivity. Prospective investigations of this kind would find out how subjects scored when retested on the same measure at different ages and what was the incidence and prevalence of psychiatric morbidity in them and in their relatives. Hagnell (1966) followed up an entire population which had been assessed in detail ten years earlier by Essen-Möller (1956). There was only a very moderate tendency for previously assessed complaints or personality traits such as sleep disturbance, headaches, tenseness or an asthenic temperament to be associated with the development of mental illness, mostly neurotic, in the later period. The development of reliable scales for the assessment by informants of the premorbid or normal personality of patients and relatives would also be most useful here (Price, 1969).

In fact, except in the genetics of subnormality, few studies have relied primarily on objective psychometric tests to assess the relatives of patients, and, again with the exception of tests measuring IQ, those that have been carried out have either been negative or inconclusive as regards their genetic interpretation. Though good indirect evidence for the importance of genetic factors comes from psychometric studies of normal twins, the direct evidence comes from the incidence of abnormality in the relatives of abnormal subjects, based on criteria such as hospitalisation and psychiatric diagnosis. There are, therefore, good grounds why most of the work reviewed in this chapter is in terms of a medical model of abnormality and why it is based on what Hirsch (1967) would disparagingly call 'typological thinking'. Much of the chapter describes and discusses topics such as the genetics of schizophrenia rather than genes, populations, and experimental measures of behaviour.

However, before reviewing the genetic aspects of different kinds of psychiatric and psychological abnormalities, we shall first say something about the incidence and behavioural effects of known genetic abnormalities.

CHROMOSOME ABNORMALITIES

The genes are organised on chromosomes of which there are 23 pairs in man, 22 homologous pairs of autosomes, and the sex chromosomes, XX in females and XY in males. By convention, the 22 autosomes are classified by size and shape into 7 groups, A to G. An individual inherits one chromosome of each pair from his father and the other from his mother. Pairs of homologous chromosomes may exchange segments through 'crossing over'. Occasionally, errors such as non-disjunction occur in cell division, so that an individual has too much or too little chromosomal material. With advances in techniques for studying the structure of the chromosomes under the microscope, abnormalities of many kinds have been recognised.

Autosomal Abnormalities other than Mongolism

The subject has been reviewed by Polani (1969). Foetuses with an extra autosome other than the smallest usually abort. Those that are born alive are developmentally abnormal and very severely retarded mentally. Patau's syndrome arises from trisomy (i.e. a third chromosome) of one of the chromosomes of the D group (Nos 13 to 15). Incidence at birth is about 1/9,000 and only a fifth survive to one year. Edwards's syndrome is due to trisomy of an E group (16 to 18) chromosome. It is about twice as frequent as Patau's syndrome, but 90 per cent die within a year, and the survivors are grossly defective. The *cri-du-chat* syndrome, so-called on account of the plaintive cry like a distressed kitten, which disappears after infancy, is usually accounted for, not by extra chromosomal material, but by a deletion of the short arm of a B group (4 to 5) chromosome. Its incidence may be as low as 1/100,000, but chances of survival are better, at least for females.

Mongolism

Frequency. Viability is greater when a small rather than a relatively large autosome is duplicated, presumably because less chromosomal material is involved. Indeed, in the form of mongolism (Down's syndrome or trisomy-21) a small extra chromosome of the G group (21 to 22) is the most frequent single pathological factor in severe subnormality. Incidence in the new-born is 1/666, to cite the representative findings of Carter and MacCarthy (1951) for the UK. With advances in medical care the chances of survival have greatly improved and in some hospitals for the subnormal mongols account for as much as 23 per cent of all patients (Berg and Kirman, 1959). The subject of mongolism has been comprehensively reviewed by Penrose and Smith (1966).

Chromosome Picture. In the standard trisomic mongol, 47 chromosomes can be identified instead of the normal 46, the additional chromosome being one of the G group. Such cases account for about 94 per cent of mongols. The remainder are mostly, and in about equal proportions (Richards, 1969), either one of the two commonest types of translocation mongolism or mosaic mongolism. In translocation mongolism there are 46 chromosomes, but extra G-chromosome material has become attached to a chromosome of the D or G groups. In mosaic mongolism there are two cell lines, one normal, the other trisomic.

Familial Incidence. Mongolism is genetic without, as a rule, being familial. In the rare event of a mongol producing children—only 13 cases have been reported—the chances are that half the children will be affected. However, monozygotic (genetically identical) co-twins are nearly always similarly affected. De Wolff *et al.* (1962) have described a pair where, exceptionally, only one twin was affected,

Table 16.1. Partition of Causes of Mongolism
(*from* Penrose and Smith, 1966)

Class	Cause	Possible proportion in an unselected group (%)
(A) Independent of mother's age	(i) Inevitable non-disjunction (parent partly or wholly trisomic)	10
	(ii) Abnormality in chromosome pairing (inherited translocation, inversion or other anomaly of the critical *G*-chromosome)	10
	(iii) Abnormal meiosis or mitosis (specific genes which cause non-disjunction)	10
	(iv) Environmental disturbance of cell division (infection, poison, radiation)	10
(B) Dependent on mother's age	Non-disjunction during oogenesis (deterioration of meiotic cell-division mechanism)	60

(*By Courtesy of* Professor L. S. Penrose, Dr G. F. Smith, and J. & A. Churchill Ltd.)

which they attributed to an anomaly in the division of the chromosomes; Penrose and Smith prefer to interpret the finding as mosaicism expressed as two separate people. Again, with only one reported exception, dizygotic (genetically dissimilar) co-twins of mongols are unaffected. The risk of recurrence in sibs depends on the karyotype (chromosome picture) of mongol and parents. With the standard trisomic karyotype in patient and normal karyotype in parents, i.e. in the majority of cases, genetic prognosis is good. The likelihood of an increased risk on account of undetected mosaicism in a parent or a gene facilitating non-disjunction is remote. However, in some cases of translocation mongolism there is a substantially increased risk. It is as high as one in three if the mother is the carrier of a D/G translocation in balanced form. Such unaffected carriers, with 45 chromosomes, have a single, fused D/G chromosome but no extra G-chromosome material. They can produce ova which, when fertilised and viable, result in normals, balanced carriers and mongols in about equal proportions. Karyotyping of parents greatly aids genetic counselling.

Aetiology. Except for the rare cases where the extra chromosomal material is transmitted genetically, the aetiology of the condition is obscure. The causes of the pathological non-disjunction of the chromosomes are associated with late maternal age in the majority of cases. In the general population the risk of a mother giving birth to a mongol increases with age until at forty-five and over it is as high as 1 in 50. The increased risk applies only to trisomic mongolism. Besides deterioration of the

cell-division mechanism through age, many environmental explanations have been suggested. They include emotional stress in the mother, infrequency of coitus, fluoridisation of water supplies and air pollution. More favoured but equally unestablished theories are infection, poison, and radiation. Table 16.1 shows Penrose's attempt to classify the definitely known and theoretically probable causes of mongolism in relation to the maternal age factor.

Psychological Aspects. The mean IQ of institutional cases is about 23 with an SD of 7; in groups selected because they were attending special schools mean IQs of up to 49 have been reported. The highest IQs are found in mosaic mongols (Shipe *et al.*, 1968). It is surprising that more has not been done to compare mongols with other types of subnormality in respect of psychological parameters. Work by O'Connor and his group (*see* O'Connor and Hermelin, 1963) showed that mongols were inferior to other imbeciles in tactual recognition. Compared with normals mongols had a reduced skin conductance, while other imbeciles, matched for intelligence, had an increased skin conductance. Mongols showed more eye movements than either normals or non-mongol imbeciles under different conditions of illumination. They were worse than other imbeciles in copying designs and had a slower reaction time in visual-motor tasks. O'Connor and Hermelin interpreted their findings in terms of hypotonia, which is a basic defect in mongolism, and an associated lack of kinesthetic feedback. Alternatively, they suggested that the low skin conductance and poor stereognosis might have been a function of their thick, dry skin. Clausen (1968) found mongols to be more impaired than controls in respect of sensory acuity and perceptual speech, but was unable to confirm the findings in tactual discrimination. Dingman (1968) could discover no systematic differences between mongols and other retarded patients in respect of the structure of their intelligence.

The stereotyped physical characteristics of the mongol are well known. From the time of Langdon Down, who first described the condition in 1866, to the present day clinical observers have tended to note a somewhat stereotyped similarity in personality, too, describing the mongol as happy, contented, affectionate, fond of mimicry and music. Penrose and Smith suggest that their reputation of being 'good' babies might be due to reduced responsiveness and hypotonia. Rollin (1946) and Blacketer-Simmonds (1953), who were the first to examine the subject methodically, were unable to find any more desirable qualities in mongols than in other subnormals or to show them to be a more homogeneous group. Tizard and Grad (1961) found mongols living at home to present their full share of problems. On the other hand, Silverstein (1964), comparing mongols and matched controls on Petersen's Behaviour Rating Schedules, found mongols to be better adjusted, though not more extraverted. Domino et al. (1964), using an adjective check list, found mongols to be more affectionate, contented, cheerful, clownish, and relaxed than control patients. Lyle (1959, 1960) concluded that the restricted environment of some hospitals had a more deleterious effect on the verbal development of mongols than non-mongols; in the institutional group mongols were relatively retarded by 9 months, while in more favourable conditions there was no difference between the groups. Golding (1968), investigating the prevalence of subnormality in Bedfordshire, found that only 2 out of 38 mongols were in hospital, compared with 26 out of 65 non-mongols. This suggests that mongols are more tractable.

Sex Chromosome Abnormalities

Apart from mosaics, the main types and their conventional designations are: (1) 45,XO (Turner's syndrome, ovarian dysgenesis); (2) XXX (triple-X syndrome); (3) 47,XXY (sex chromatin positive Klinefelter's syndrome); and (4) 47,XYY (found to excess among tall, subnormal psychopaths in maximum security hospitals).

1. In *Turner's syndrome*, one sex-chromosome has been deleted. According to Polani (1966) the condition may occur in as many as 0·7 per cent of conceptions, but 98 per cent of them abort. Survivors are phenotypical females of short stature, amenorrhoeic and sterile, and liable to have one or more of a number of physical stigmata, such as webbed neck; but they are not as a rule seriously handicapped mentally. Verbal intelligence is not reduced. In a study of 16 cases where mean verbal IQ was 103, Money (1963) found a mean performance IQ of only 86. He and his co-workers in studies summarised in Money (1968) reported three types of deficit— space-form dysgnosia, directional sense dysgnosia, and mild discalculia—which they claim suggests a developmental right parietal lobe anomaly related to the basic chromosomal defect. According to Hampson et al. (1955) and Sabbath et al. (1961), Turner's syndrome patients tend to be vague, bland, and passive in personality, perhaps largely for secondary reasons. Though psychiatric disorders of various kinds and with various EEG abnormalities have been reported (Mellbin, 1966), it is not yet certain whether there is an increased risk of psychosis. Maclean et al. (1968) found no instance of XO among 6,241 female patients in Scottish psychiatric hospitals.

2. *Triple-X females* are usually of normal stature and appearance and are fertile. Their live-born children, among whom there appears to be a deficiency of females (10 females to 21 males), have been found to have a normal chromosome complement (Bartalos and Baramki, 1967). Intelligence level is generally reduced. While the incidence of the XXX constitution at birth is 1·20 per 1,000, pooled data from three surveys in mental subnormality hospitals give a prevalence there of 4·5 per 1,000. Kidd et al. (1963) studied all 11 cases on a register of abnormal karyotypes known to be located in such hospitals, and found that as many as 4 of them had a psychosis in addition to subnormality. Conversely, in the study of Maclean et al. (1968), based on psychiatric hospitals not catering specifically for the subnormal, 4 of the 15 XXX females found were in fact diagnosed as mentally defective.

3. An *extra X chromosome in males* is the commonest of the major chromosome abnormalities. (Occasionally, an extra two or more X chromosomes are found.) Table 16.2 shows an excess in psychiatric and, more particularly, in higher grade subnormal populations. Physically there is usually testicular atrophy at puberty and some degree of feminisation. Subjects are generally infertile, though sexual function is normal. In the earlier studies of the condition (e.g. Pasqualini et al., 1957) they were characterised as tending to be childish, querulous, apathetic, and seclusive, with a mean IQ of 81. Behaviour disorders were highlighted in subsequent studies. Court Brown (1962) found those admitted to subnormality hospitals to be high-grade defectives

Table 16.2. Frequency of Chromatin Positive Males (Extra X-Chromosomes) in Normal and Abnormal Populations (*after* Court Brown *et al.*, 1968)

Population	Rate per 1,000	Size of pooled samples
Live born	1·7	41,688
Various non-institutional groups (recruits, out-patients etc.)	2·3	9,808
Various criminal groups	2·8	2,308
Mental hospital patients	5·0	6,000
Subnormality hospital patients	9·4	13,349
Ditto IQ > 50	15·2	864
British maximum security hospitals	19·1	1,257
Swedish hospitals for hard-to-manage subnormal males, IQ > 50	19·8	958

brought there for larceny, arson, or indecent exposure. There is probably no excess of homosexuality or transvestitism. Those admitted to psychiatric hospitals (Forssman and Hambert, 1963) suffered from a variety of disorders, including confusional episodes, paranoid states and epilepsy, EEG abnormalities being common. A controlled study of the EEG in 40 XXY subjects from different sources, including a mass survey of army recruits, found abnormalities in 73 per cent compared with 11 per cent in matched controls; the most specific abnormality was a low alpha frequency (Hambert and Frey, 1964). Maclean *et al.* (1968) carried out a sex chromatin screening of 6,000 male patients in Scottish psychiatric hospitals and found 30 positives (0·50%). Prevalence was highest in mental defectives (2·09%) and epileptics (2·2%); it was 0·38 per cent in schizophrenics (half of the XXY schizophrenics were paranoid) and 0·24 per cent in other diagnoses. In a sex chromatin study of chronic psychotic patients in Bexley Hospital, Anders *et al.* (1968) found 6 XXY cases among 529 males; all were paranoid and four were also defective or ?defective. From the above studies and that of Nielsen (1964), it would seem that there may be little appreciable increase, if any, in the risk for typical progressive schizophrenia; the vulnerability is rather towards low intelligence, character disorder, 'schizophreniform psychosis' and features suggesting some kind of brain damage.

4. The technique of nuclear sexing by buccal smear identifies extra or, in females, missing X chromosomes. To detect *extra Y chromosomes* and other abnormalities (OY has never been identified) the more difficult and time-consuming cytological technique of karyotyping from tissue culture has been required, at least until very recently (Pearson *et al.*, 1970). When 21 males from maximum security hospitals, identified in nuclear sexing surveys

as chromatin positive, were karyotyped, seven were found to have an extra Y chromosome as well as an extra X, i.e. to be XXYY (Casey *et al.*, 1966b). The subsequent work on the XYY sex chromosome complement is excellently summarised by Court Brown (1968). Jacobs, Court Brown and their colleagues in Edinburgh were led to look for cases of the recently discovered XYY karyotype in patients in the Scottish State Hospital at Carstairs—an institution provided for the detention of persons of dangerous, violent or criminal propensities. In the subnormal wing of the hospital, 7 out of 196 patients tested (36 per 1,000), and in the mental disease wing 2 out of 119 (17 per 1,000), were found to be XYY. (Other chromosome abnormalities were also discovered, all of them in the subnormal wing: one XXY, one XY/XXY/XXXY mosaic, one XXYY, and four autosomal structural abnormalities.) Most of the XYY cases were over 6 ft tall, and a quarter of all patients over 6 ft in the hospital had an extra Y chromosome. These findings were confirmed by Casey *et al.* (1966a) in the English special security hospitals of Rampton and Moss Side (catering mainly for the subnormal), where 12 out of 50 patients over 6 ft were XYY. This was so in 4 out of 50 at Broadmoor (catering mainly for the psychiatrically ill criminal). These developments led to further studies in various criminal and other populations, some selected for height and others not (Table 16.3).

Incidence of XYY in the newborn male is not yet known accurately on account of the problems involved in karyotyping a large enough sample. Probably it is something of the order of 1 in 1,000. If there is an increased early mortality, prevalence in the normal adult population will be less than this and the increased prevalence in tall, subnormal delinquents even more remarkable. Table 16.3

Table 16.3. Extra Y Chromosome in Males (*after* Court Brown, 1968)

Populations not selected for height			
Male births	1	in	1,392
Subfertility clinic	0	in	328
Scottish Borstals and Prison allocation centre	1	in	909
London remand centres	1	in	300
English subnormality hospitals	0	in	605
Epilepsy colony	1	in	75
Psychiatric prison	2	in	204
Maximum security hospital, Scotland	9	in	315
Tall populations			
Normal	0	in	401
Mental hospitals	1	in	142
Subnormality hospitals	10	in	79
Delinquency institutions (14 studies)	44	in	673

summarises the information contained in the detailed tables of Court Brown (1968) and Court Brown and Smith (1969) with two more recent surveys included (Nielsen *et al.*, 1968; Kahn, personal communication, 1969). Not surprisingly, there are differences between the studies, some of which are based on very small numbers. Some differences, such as the inconsistency between the findings from subnormal hospitals quoted in the upper and lower parts of the table, are due to differences in admission policies. The hospitals in which only tall patients were karyotyped more readily accepted referrals from the courts than the hospital in which 605 adult males were tested irrespective of height.

What, apart from height, are the characteristics of the abnormal XYY male? In the Carstairs population (Price and Whatmore, 1967) seven of the nine XYY subjects were classified as subnormal (IQ 60 to 80). This is a similar proportion to that found in the institution as a whole. The two who were of normal intelligence displayed the same pattern of behavioural characteristics as the seven who were subnormal. The XYY subjects had fewer convictions for offences against persons (0·9 per man) than 18 controls (2·6) in this highly selected population. Their offences, which were mostly against property, began at an earlier age. More notable was the difference in family background. Of the 31 sibs of the XYY cases only one had been convicted of an offence, while of the 63 sibs of the controls 12 (from 7 families) had 139 convictions recorded against them. The XYYs appeared as the black sheep in the family, with behaviour disorders going back to an early age, while the controls tended to come from a delinquency-prone subculture. Casey (1969), however, did not confirm this finding at Rampton and Moss Side. Hope *et al.* (1967) tested 7 XYY and 11 control subjects from Carstairs Hospital on a variety of psychological measures, including the Mill Hill Vocabulary Scale, the Coloured Progressive Matrices, and a modification of the *K* scale of the MMPI. Their results were inconclusive. The XYYs did not differ in intelligence or tested hostility, but they were more defensive (high *K*) in their responses. On a questionnaire measuring the extraversion dimension they were more introverted than the controls, a finding that agrees with the clinical impression of Price and Whatmore that the control patients were the more openly hostile.

Other recent studies based on criminal populations suggest a significant excess of convictions for arson among the numerically very few XYY cases identified (Nielsen *et al.*, 1968, two cases), coupled with schizoid and homosexual traits (Bartlett *et al.*, 1968, two cases). Traits of the latter kinds were also observed by Daly (1969) in the twelve tall subjects (11 from institutions and a boy of 5) studied by him from a neurological point of view. While Price *et al.* (1966) had been unable to find notable physical differences between their XYY cases and tall controls, Daly found tremor and body asymmetries to be frequent in his cases. Little is yet known about the fertility of the XYY male. Six sons and a daughter of one case were found by Thompson *et al.* (1967) to have a normal sex chromosome complement.

In evaluating the undoubted excess of XYYs among severely psychopathic criminals, one has to bear in mind the fact that the majority of studies so far have concentrated on such populations. Court Brown urged circumspection in interpreting the results and believed (Court Brown *et al.*, 1968) that the XYY male is subject to a wide variation of psychiatric disturbance. He pointed out (Court Brown, 1968) that there could be as many as 1,800 XYYs in the adult male population of Scotland, and if this is so, only 2 per cent of them have been identified so far in the many prisons and psychiatric and subnormality hospitals that have been surveyed. Some XYYs are known to be behaviourally normal, and perhaps the majority are. A number of those 'fortuitously' ascertained were examined because of gonadal abnormalities and Court Brown speculated that defective gonadal function may offset some of the risk of developing behavioural aberrations. In the end, he stated, there can be no substitute for an extensive and prolonged study of newborn children and the surveillance of identified XYY males in order to assess the risks and, if possible, to prevent extreme behavioural abnormalities. If the frequency of XYYs among newborn males in Scotland is now about 1 in 700 (Ratcliffe *et al.*, 1970), the 9 XYY men found in the Carstairs State Hospital represent a twentyfold increase in risk; in the other less specialised penal institutions surveyed in Scotland so far, the frequency of XYYs was not significantly raised (Jacobs *et al.*, 1971).

Having outlined the main sex chromosome abnormalities separately, we now make some general points. There are certain features that deviations in sex chromosome complement have in common. Their effects are variable and tend to be non-specific. They could be thought of as interfering with normal balanced development, largely in consequence of the disturbed dominance and recessivity relationships of the genetic material on the sex chromosomes. If this were so they would be expected to show individual variation. In so far as the effects result in a reduction of performance IQ, in EEG abnormalities or in tremor and asymmetries, they could be likened to mild chronic brain syndromes. Except for the possible dysgnosia in Turner's syndrome, psychological testing has as yet not led to any firm conclusions as to how patients with chromosome anomalies differ from controls. This is hardly surprising, since subjects are few in number and sometimes difficult to test on account of subnormality or lack of co-operation. The dangers of generalising about the XYY constitution from samples biased in the direction of psychopathy also apply to the other conditions, for the majority of those affected are not grossly abnormal; the type of abnormality found to distinguish them will differ, depending on whether the cases studied come from fertility clinics, psychiatric practice, subnormality hospitals, or penal institutions.

Sex chromosome abnormalities are not hereditary in the usual sense of the word. There may, however, in a few families be a genetic tendency to non-disjunction. Indeed, the first case of XYY was discovered because he was the father of a mongol. As in mongolism, MZ co-twins are probably similarly affected (cf. Rainer *et al.*, 1969; Vague *et al.*, 1968). Exceptionally, a Y chromosome may be deleted in MZ twins, resulting in the extremely rare anomaly of monozygotic twins of opposite sex (Edwards *et al.*, 1966), the one a phenotypic male, the other a phenotypic female with Turner's syndrome; both were XO/XY mosaics, presumably with different proportions of XY cells.

Sex chromosome anomalies have not been found in homosexuals or transvestites. In intersexual conditions in which there are discrepancies between nuclear sex, hormonal state, gonadal development or external genitalia, Money *et al.* (1955) found that registered sex at birth combined with upbringing congruent with this was the decisive factor for later personal sexual orientation in 72 out of 76 such patients with an unbalanced sexual constitution. These interesting findings do not, of course, lead to the conclusion that in the normal XX female or XY male congruent sexual orientation is entirely dependent on rearing and has nothing to do with whether they have a Y chromosome. Furthermore, the majority of boys can withstand a good deal of mollycoddling without becoming confirmed homosexuals or submitting themselves for a sex-change operation. Though this is not the place to discuss intersexuality (*see* Overzier, 1963) it is worth noting that, out of 94 cases affected with some form of hermaphroditism, Money *et al.* (1956) found as many as 79 to be psychologically healthy or else only mildly disturbed by the abnormalities of their physical sexual constitution.

ABNORMALITIES DUE TO THE MAJOR EFFECTS OF SINGLE GENES

Having considered gross chromosome abnormalities, we now turn to the influence on behaviour of recognised single-gene mutations. The first edition of this Handbook explained the principles of dominant, recessive and sex-linked inheritance, principles well described in many textbooks of genetics. Here we shall merely state them in summary form, giving examples of psychiatric abnormalities that are established as dependent on the presence of a highly penetrant mutant gene. The examples illustrate applications of types of genetic analysis that are occasionally possible for human abnormalities. Severe abnormalities of the kind under discussion are usually rare. They are catalogued by McKusick (1966) and, as far as neurological disorders are concerned, by Pratt (1967).

Recessive Conditions

The characteristics of autosomal recessive inheritance in respect of a condition where those affected seldom reproduce are these: (1) both parents are phenotypically normal heterozygotes, (2) other cases in the family are rare, except in sibs where, on average, 1 in 4 are affected, (3) the rarer the condition the more likely are the parents to be related by blood. The tendency is for recessive disorders that reduce fertility to be clinically uniform, severe, and of early onset. They are likely to show an enzyme deficiency (McKusick, 1966).

Phenylketonuria (PKU) is a typical example (*see* Hsia, 1967, for a recent review). Its frequency has been estimated at between 4 and 6 per 100,000 in most Western populations. About 1 per cent of subnormals in institutions have PKU. Close to 25 per cent of sibs are similarly affected. In various studies between 5 and 10 per cent of parents have been found to be first cousins. The disorder is one of the inborn errors of metabolism, homozygotes for the abnormal gene being unable to metabolise phenylalanine along the usual pathways. In 1956 Hsia *et al.* discovered that heterozygotes could frequently be detected; after the ingestion of phenylalanine the parents of phenylketonurics had twice the phenylalanine levels of controls. Although the biochemical nature of the initial defect is well understood, the pathway of the metabolic error in a liver enzyme to the brain and that from the brain to behaviour is still far from clear. Hsia thinks it 'likely that the mental defect is the end result of a critical shortage in the brain of 5-hydroxytriptamine during early infancy, caused in part by the physiological lack of this metabolite at birth, and in part by the excessive phenylalanine levels in this disease'.

By appropriate tests the condition can be identified at birth or soon after. Otherwise it usually does not become obvious before the fourth to sixth month that something is wrong, except sometimes for the occurrence of epileptic seizures. Clinically, frequently there is posturing, the occurrence of purposeless, rhythmic movements, a tremor of the hand and an habitual fiddling of the fingers close before the eyes. The EEG is usually abnormal, even in the absence of seizures, and patients are prone to irritability and severe temper tantrums (Paine, 1957). IQ in untreated cases is usually below 25 and rarely above 50. Occasionally, the same or a similar biochemical end result can be produced by a different mutant gene.

The PKU gene has effects on other characteristics besides intelligence. Phenylketonurics tend to be fair-haired and blue-eyed on account of their decreased production of melanin. It has been asked whether the gene in heterozygous form has any influence on behavioural traits. Munro (1947) and others have suggested that heterozygotes are liable to endogenous depression or other psychiatric conditions arising later in life. However, Pratt *et al.* (1963) failed to detect raised phenylalanine levels in a group of endogenous depressives, and other workers have generally failed to confirm Munro's suggestion (Perry *et al.*, 1966; Blumenthal, 1967; Larson and Nyman, 1968).

It is a serious mistake to think that because aetiology is genetic treatment is impossible. The intelligence level can be raised by a diet low in phenylalanine. In many centres it has been found that the earlier the treatment is initiated, the higher the eventual IQ. However, there is considerable variability of response (*see* Table 16.4). Treated patients do not usually reach the level of their unaffected sibs, and Hackney *et al.* (1968) found that their progress in school was poorer than would have been predicted from their IQ. Of 44 treated cases, 22 had neuropsychological handicaps such as hyperactivity and poor co-ordination and 9 were described as autistic in the sense of showing repetitive bizarre movements and stylised posturing; autistic behaviour patterns, however, diminished with age. In this study from Toronto, treatment was terminated between the ages of 5 and 8 in 14 cases, and on follow-up between 18 and 48 months later progress was satisfactory. It was suggested that some children may have been overtreated and on account of low phenylalanine levels received insufficient nourishment. Anderson and Siegel (1968) described

Table 16.4. Mean IQ of Phenylketonuric Patients, by Age at Initiation of Diet, and of their Normal Siblings (*from* Dobson *et al.*, 1968)

Age at beginning of diet	Age at testing yr	Mean IQ	Standard deviation	N
Birth–1 mo	5·4	89	11·7	11
1–4 mo	6·3	77	17·7	9
5–10 mo	5·2	68	26·8	11
11–17 mo	6·4	67	23·6	19
18–24 mo	7·3	73	22·6	21
25–36 mo	8·3	65	22·0	13
37–47 mo	6·5	63	24·7	16
48–72 mo	7·3	57	22·0	14
Sibling's Stanford-Binet IQs		109	12·8	58

(*By Courtesy of* Dr J. Dobson and the *New England Journal of Medicine*)

experimental work in progress in Minnesota, using psychomotor and other tests and aimed at discovering distinctive behavioural characteristics in PKU and the effect on them of treatment.

Other inborn errors of metabolism, inherited as recessive traits and having an effect on intelligence, include the lipoidoses (or Tay-Sachs disease), Maple Syrup urine disease (which like PKU is also treatable), and Hartnup's disease. They are mostly extremely rare. The commonest after PKU may be homocystinuria (Cusworth and Dent, 1969), but its frequency, according to studies made in Northern Ireland, is only about one-seventh that of PKU.

If marriage to a cousin increases the risk of bringing harmful recessive genes together, *incestuous unions* between first-degree relatives do so even more. In two prospective studies, summarised in a *British Medical Journal* annotation (1968), one from the UK (Carter, 1967) and one from the USA (Adams and Neel, 1967), 31 offspring of father-daughter or brother-sister unions were studied. Of the 25 survivors, 12 were normal. The abnormal children included 3 who were intellectually severely subnormal and 4 who were more mildly subnormal. While some of the subnormalities may well be due to single recessive genes, others may be attributable to multiple homozygosity and the low intellectual and social level of the parents. Six died from conditions such as cystic fibrosis, glycogen-storage disease, and cerebral degeneration with blindness, which are known or suspected recessive diseases.

Major disorders of perception are not infrequently attributed to single genes. A recessively inherited disorder is one of the commonest causes of deaf mutism (Stevenson and Cheeseman, 1956), maternal rubella being one of the commonest environmental causes. With regard to congenital blindness, while some cases are due to perinatal difficulties, a large

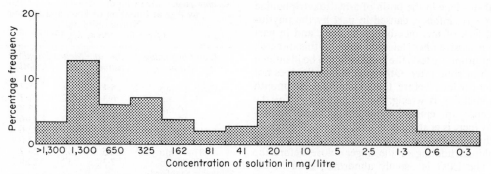

Fig. 16.1. Bimodal distribution of PTC taste thresholds in 150 English males (*after* Barnicot, 1950; *by courtesy of* Dr. N. A Barnicot and *Annals of Human Genetics*)

number are due to a variety of rare genetical causes. In a survey of 776 cases on the register of blind children in England and Wales, Fraser and Friedmann (1967) estimated that no less than 19 autosomal dominant, 30 autosomal recessive, and 10 sex-linked genetic entities can play the major part in the causation of childhood blindness. From the work of Blau and Mutton (1967) it would appear that some instances of the rare syndrome of congenital indifference to pain may be genetically caused: the eight cases reported included a pair of similarly affected twins and two who were the children of first cousins.

However, not all recessively inherited anomalies of perception are rare. By way of contrast the relative *inability to taste phenylthiocarbamide* (PTC) as a bitter substance is a common variant of taste perception, inherited as a recessive condition. This is a graded but bimodally distributed trait (Fig. 16.1) with about 33 per cent of most populations conventionally classified as non-tasters. Other factors besides the genetic polymorphism influence the threshold at which the individual recognises the bitter taste, among them smoking habits. Kaplan (1968) has shown that the slight decrease in sensitivity with increasing age—a decrease which has been found to be more marked in males than in females—is not observed when analysis is restricted to non-smokers. Kaplan's studies are based on 6-n-propylthiouracil (PROP), a substance closely related to PTC but completely odourless. He reports that sensitive tasters have more food dislikes and prefer milder foods than non-tasters. He believes that in some women there is a tendency for sensitivity to PROP to increase during menstruation. Persons insensitive both to PROP and to quinine (inherited independently) may be relatively low in general systemic reactivity. Based on very few cases (nine college students), there was also a tendency for sensitive

PROP tasters to have a more internalised pattern of scores on the WAIS than non-tasters, i.e. to be more introverted. Such a finding, if confirmed, would support the hypothesis that introverts are more highly reactive than extraverts. Again, based on fewer numbers than would be ideally desirable, Kaplan found a significant excess of tasters among subjects with duodenal ulcer compared with those with gastric ulcer and non-hospitalised controls. Other workers have established different proportions of PTC tasters and non-tasters in patients suffering from different forms of thyroid disease and from different kinds of glaucoma; but as Evans (1969) has recognised, the metabolic basis of associations between the PTC polymorphism and thyroid and glaucoma disorders remains obscure, and the same must be admitted for its possible associations with personality factors.

Dominant Conditions

The main characteristic of dominant inheritance is the transmission of the trait from generation to generation. Except for fresh mutations or incomplete penetrance, one parent of either sex and one sib out of two will carry the gene and manifest the trait. Dominant disorders when severe and of early onset will normally be eliminated from the population by natural selection. In the case of one such disorder, epiloia (*see* Penrose 1963), which is somewhat variable in manifestation, it has been estimated that one case in four is due to a fresh mutation. Dominant disorders that are not eliminated tend therefore to be milder than recessive disorders, more variable in their manifestation and, if severe, to have their onset postponed to an age during or later than the reproductive period. The degree and nature of manifestation will be influenced by other factors, genetic or environmental. According to McKusick

(1966), the genetic defect is more likely to be in a structural protein than an enzyme.

Huntington's chorea is a textbook example of dominant inheritance in mental disorder. (Myrianthopoulos (1966) has recently reviewed the literature.) Involuntary shaking movements of the limbs, mild at first, become increasingly severe and extensive and end in death. This distressing condition is fortunately rare. The prevalence of 6·5 per 100,000 estimated by Pleydell (1954, 1955) for Northamptonshire is representative of the rates calculated for several other Caucasian populations. Penetrance of the gene is virtually complete; in other words, when allowance is made for age at death it hardly ever skips a generation. In 962 affected individuals from New England early in this century the condition could be traced back through the family to immigrants, including three brothers, who left the east coast of England to settle in the area in the seventeenth century*. Investigating the genetic epidemiology of the condition in Michigan, Reed and Neel (1959) estimated the relative fertility of choreics to be slightly higher than that of their non-choreic sibs; but the fertility of the latter was lower than that of the general population, possibly because some of them may have limited their reproduction on account of their family history. They estimated the upper limit of the mutation rate for the Huntington's chorea gene to be 5×10^{-6}.

The pathology of Huntington's chorea is understood at the neuropathological level, where the essential features, according to Myrianthopoulos (1966) are 'a primary loss of cells in the caudate nucleus and the putamen, and similar involvement of the cerebral cortex, particularly that of the frontal lobes'. The biochemistry is not known, which might be regarded as in keeping with McKusick's generalisation concerning the difference between dominant and recessive disorders. Juvenile cases tend to show rigidity rather than hyperkinesis (Hansotia *et al.*, 1968).

Mean age at onset, according to Wendt (1959), is 44 years with a standard deviation of 10·9. Earlier estimates of 35 to 36 are probably underestimates, biased by the inclusion of too many individuals born in the later part of the period of investigation, which will include only cases of early onset. In Wendt's material, which consisted of 762 cases born in Western Germany between 1870 and 1899, the mean duration of the disease was 15 to 16 years. Table 16.5, derived by Slater and Cowie (1971) from Wendt's data, shows the distribution of age of onset, and the chance of being affected, if a gene

* However, the accuracy of this claim has been questioned (Hans and Gilmore, 1969).

Table 16.5. Distribution of Ages at Onset in Huntington's Chorea (Data of Wendt, 1959, as presented by Slater and Cowie, 1971)

Age period	Number	Per cent	Cumulative
1–5	—	—	—
6–10	1	0·1	0·1
11–15	5	0·7	0·8
16–20	11	1·4	2·2
21–25	24	3·2	5·4
26–30	58	7·6	13·0
31–35	68	8·9	21·9
36–40	102	13·4	35·3
41–45	125	16·4	51·7
46–50	151	19·8	71·5
51–55	107	14·0	85·5
56–60	73	9·6	95·1
61–65	27	3·5	98·6
66–70	8	1·1	99·7
71–75	2	0·3	100·0

(*By Courtesy of* Dr E. Slater, Dr V. A. Cowie and the Oxford University Press)

carrier, by a given age. Though it does not take into account correlation between relatives in age of onset, the table should be very useful in genetic counselling. The correlation between age at onset in sibs was 0·28 in Reed and Chandler's (1958) population-based material. Earlier calculations based on pooled data from the literature gave higher figures. According to Myrianthopoulos, age at onset is very close in those pairs of concordant MZ twins that have been reported: 22-22, 35-35, 41-41, 43-43, 45-45. A further pair with onset at 24 in both twins has been reported by Schiöttz-Christensen (1969). This would indicate that it is genetic rather than environmental modifying factors that influence age at onset.

Not only is age at onset extremely variable, but the psychiatric features of the disease, other than those entailed in the eventual organic deterioration, are very variable too. Sometimes behaviour disorders or delusions pre-date the first signs of choreic movements, sometimes they follow them, and sometimes they may never occur. Panse (1942) has described cases that with every seeming justification had been diagnosed as schizophrenic before the chorea became manifest. Increased irritability and the occurrence of paranoid ideas are often the first personality changes to be noted. Streletzki (1961), as described by Slater and Cowie, has made a detailed analysis from Wendt's large representative case material of the psychotic disorders, mostly of a paranoid kind, to which Huntington patients are liable. In Michigan, among those not hospitalised, suicide was the cause of death in 7·8 per cent of men and 6·4 per cent of women (Reed and Chandler, 1958).

Detailed psychometric studies aimed at differentiating Huntington patients from those with other forms of organic deterioration have not been considered necessary or appropriate. According to Hansotia *et al.* (1968) such tests may, however, be helpful in distinguishing early in the disease the siblings with mild impairment from those who are apparently unaffected. They found their proband and an elder brother, also affected early, to have shown changes in abstraction and problem-solving abilities and in motor sensory functions in advance of more obvious signs of deterioration. Goodman *et al.* (1966) studied 12 normal children of Huntington's chorea patients and found two, and possibly a further three, to show findings in psychological and language tests which were compatible with organic involvement. Up to now, however, attempts to identify the carriers of the Huntington gene at an early age have not met with success. The predictions of Patterson *et al.* (1948) based on somewhat non-specific EEG abnormalities were shown in an 18-year follow-up study by Chandler (1966) to be as often incorrect as correct. Attempts to identify changes pre-dating more obvious symptoms by a few years may be more promising. The low-voltage fast EEG activity typical of Huntington's chorea has been found in relatives (Leese *et al.*, 1952). In the family studied by Leese *et al.* it is now known that one of the normal sibs who showed the EEG abnormality developed the disease within a year of testing, and five years later at the age of 25 one of her daughters, previously with a normal record, developed the suspect EEG changes. The psychological test findings in the family of Hansotia *et al.* may be of similar significance and were also accompanied by low-voltage fast EEG activity.

Acute intermittent porphyria or AIP (Wetterberg, 1967), the 'Swedish' type of porphyria, is distinct from porphyria variegata, the 'South African' type which Macalpine and Hunter (1966, 1968) claimed was the cause of King George III's insanity, and present in some of his descendants. AIP is biochemically detectable in latent form and the *biochemical* abnormality is inherited as a highly penetrant dominant trait. The *disease* AIP is a good example of dominant inheritance with reduced penetrance.

The disease is characterised by abdominal, neurological, and psychiatric symptoms. Prevalence in Sweden is estimated at 1 in 13,000, except in the north of the country where it is higher. 1 in 600 patients in two mental hospitals was identified as having AIP. Wetterberg made a detailed genetic investigation of the families of 40 representative cases in Sweden. Among the siblings of probands only 73 per cent of females identified as carrying the gene manifested the disease, and only 49 per cent of male gene carriers. 20 probands had AIP and mental illness (*A*-group) while 20 had AIP without mental illness (*B*-group). *A*-group probands had 32 mentally ill siblings while *B*-group probands had 10. Some of the cases of mental illness in the *A*-group siblings were inherited independently of AIP, but there was a significant association between AIP gene carriers and mental illness. The psychiatric illnesses associated with AIP were of a varied kind but distinguished by a relative excess of confusion, visual hallucinations and neurological signs.

The condition illustrates one way in which a gene may contribute to the causes of psychological abnormality. Rare though porphyria is, models derived from it can be applied to the problem of the inheritance of a common psychosis such as schizophrenia. Under the theory of genetic heterogeneity most of the cases embraced by the wide term 'schizophrenia' would be thought of as representing the effects of one of a large number of rare genes, such as the AIP gene. Under monogenic inheritance, on the other hand, a gene much commoner than this is hypothesised and one which is necessary for the great majority of cases diagnosable as schizophrenic. Many gene carriers would be psychiatrically normal or show less specific conditions. According to polygenic theories of transmission of the type in which some genes are regarded as playing a more important part than others, genes analogous to the AIP gene, but commoner, would be seen as contributing to the specific genetic vulnerability. If the model of many equally common genes, each individually of minor effect, is preferred as being a simpler working hypothesis, a model derived from the example of porphyria might still help to explain the releasing of psychosis by specific kinds of stress in a multifactorially determined constitution or diathesis of a particular kind. In porphyria there are certain 'stresses' such as barbiturates which release an attack in the biochemically predisposed individual, but not in others. Diathesis and stress would be related as lock and key, rather than as independent, unspecific, additive forces.

Sex-linked Conditions

When a condition is dependent on a gene mutation on the X-chromosome and is inherited as a recessive trait, as most of them are, the typical pattern is for the condition to be passed on to sons by mothers who are unaffected carriers of the gene. Since father and son do not have an X-chromosome in common, affected fathers cannot pass the condition on to their sons.

Partial colour-blindness is a common anomaly of

perception inherited in such a manner. In this country it occurs in about 8 per cent of males and is rare in females. (For a detailed account, see Kalmus, 1965; recent views are summarised in Clarke, 1969.) It now appears that the deuteranoid anomalies, in which there is a relative lack of green sensations, are inherited at one locus on the X-chromosome, and the protanoid group, in which there is a relative lack of red sensations, at another. At the deutan locus there are three known alleles, for

1. normal vision, which is dominant over—
2. deuteranomaly (the commonest form of colour-blindness, affected persons being anomalous trichromats who cannot see green), which, in turn, is dominant over—
3. deuteranopia (dichromats who cannot see green).

Similarly, at the protan locus there are alleles, combinations of which determine the red vision defects of protanomaly and protanopia.

Colour-blindness is relatively common because it does not seriously affect survival. Post (1962), noting a higher frequency of colour-blindness in the more highly developed countries, suggested that natural selection against the trait may have become relaxed. There may also be compensating advantages for the colour-blind such as improved night-vision. Thoday (1965) noted that the colour-blind are in demand in the dyeing industry on account of their skill in matching tints of the same colour. He believes that society is the better for the existence of such genetic diversity.

Genetic analysis has shown that the deutan and protan loci lie close to one another on the X-chromosome, but are separated by the G6PD locus at which there are perhaps as many as 14 alleles determining various forms of glucose-6-phosphate dehydrogenase deficiency. A point of interest is that individuals suffering from these deficiencies are sometimes liable to drug sensitivity reactions. It is only on the X-chromosome that genetic linkage has been established, so far as genes that influence psychological abnormalities are concerned. Claims of genetic linkage between colour-blindness and alcoholism have not been substantiated.

It is important to distinguish genetic linkage, which refers to genes occurring at different loci on the same chromosome, from genetic association, which refers to the statistical excess of a condition (such as duodenal ulcer) in persons of a particular genotype (blood-group O). Linkage between colour-blindness and G6PD deficiency implies that in some families colour-blindness and the enzyme deficiency occur in the same individuals (except in the case of 'crossing-over'), while in other families the two conditions tend to be mutually exclusive.

It is also important to distinguish clearly between sex-linked inheritance (which in practice means X-linked inheritance, since it is doubtful whether there are any Y-linked traits) and sex-limitation. Sex-limitation or partial sex-limitation exists when a trait, whatever its genetics, is manifested exclusively or preponderantly in one sex. This distinction will have to be borne in mind when considering whether the excess of females affected by certain types of depression is to be accounted for, at least in part, by a dominant mutant gene on the X-chromosome, or whether it has other explanations.

THE PRINCIPLES OF POLYGENIC INHERITANCE

Having considered the abnormal psychological effects of the major chromosome abnormalities and single gene mutations, we now change our orientation and ask what contribution genetic variation makes towards the common abnormalities of intelligence and personality and to the established psychiatric illnesses as they are diagnosed in practice. Here we are not in the main concerned with the effects of single genes, but with the cumulative effects of individually indistinguishable genes at many different loci, each usually making only a small contribution to the abnormality, i.e. with polygenic rather than monogenic inheritance. The principles of polygenic inheritance can be understood most easily when applied to graded, normally distributed traits, though not all such traits are necessarily polygenic in the above sense. Furthermore, traits or diseases that, for whatever reason, are assessed as either present or absent may, in so far as they are genetically transmitted, represent the tail end of an underlying but at present unmeasurable normal distribution and be analysed according to the principles of polygenic inheritance.

To illustrate the principles, we present a simplified model. Let us suppose that a particular characteristic, say height, is determined by three gene pairs, A and a, B and b, C and c. We will suppose that the capital letters tend to cause tallness, the lower-case letters shortness, that there is neither dominance nor recessivity, that all genes are equally common, that no one gene has significantly more effect on the characteristic than any other, and that mating is taking place at random. Then the tallest individual we can find, with the constitution AABBCC, will be relatively uncommon; for every one of him there will be six individuals one degree less tall, consisting

Table 16.6.   Simplified Additive Polygenic Model for Quantitative Trait
Population distribution of genotypes and phenotypes with three gene pairs,
Aa, Bb, Cc, under assumptions stated in text

			AABbcc AAbBcc			
			AAbbCc AAbbcC			
			AaBBcc			
		aabbCC	aABBcc	AABBcc		
		aaBBcc	aaBBCc	AAbbCC		
		AAbbcc	aaBBcC	aaBBCC		
		aabBcC aabBCc	AabbCC aAbbCC	AABbCc AABbcC		
		aaBbcC aaBbCc	aaBbCC aabBCC	AAbBCc AAbBcC		
		aAbbcC aAbbCc	AaBbCc AaBbcC	AaBBCc AaBBcC		
	aabbcC aabbCc	AabbcC AabbCc	AabBCc AabBcC	aABBCc aABBcC	AABBCc AABBcC	
	aabBcc aaBbcc	aAbBcc aABbcc	aABbCc aABbcC	AaBbCC AabBCC	AABbCC AAbBCC	
	aAbbcc	AabBcc	aAbBCc	aABbCC	AaBBCC	
aabbcc	Aabbcc	AaBbcc	aAbBcC	aAbBCC	aABBCC	AABBCC

Low   ←   Phenotypic Score   →   High

Enhancing genes	0	1	2	3	4	5	6
Deviation from mean score (units per gene)	−3	−2	−1	0	+1	+2	+3
Percentage of population	1·6	9·4	23·4	31·2	23·4	9·4	1·6
Different genotypes	1	3	6	7	6	3	1

of three different genotypes: aABBCC or AaBBCC; AAbBCC or AABbCC; AABBcC or AABBCc. There will be fifteen combinations of four capitals with two lower-case letters, and in fact the population graded by height, will be distributed according to the terms of the expansion of $(\frac{1}{2} + \frac{1}{2})^6 = (1 + 6 + 15 + 20 + 15 + 6 + 1)/64$, as shown in Table 16.6. The commonest group (20 combinations) is the middle group of average height, comprising seven different genotypes, each with three genes enhancing tallness and three tallness-reducing genes. If we generalise and write the expansion of $(p + q)^n$, in which $p + q = 1$, as n gets bigger and bigger we get a closer and closer approximation to the normal curve. Like height, intelligence is for the greater part a graded, normally distributed characteristic. As Gottesman (1963a) has pointed out, a 5-pair model is sufficient to predict the IQ of the population (Table 16.7); but even with three gene pairs and small random effects caused by environmental factors and errors of measurement, there will already be a fairly close approximation to the normal curve. With contributions from many more gene pairs—perhaps of the order of one hundred—the genetic variability on such a model will be very considerable, even towards the extremes of the distribution; and where there is genotypic variability there will be phenotypic variability too, provided that the simplified assumption that every gene has identical effects is not taken too literally: all persons of the same height are not equally proportioned.

An important consequence of the hidden genetic variability in polygenic inheritance is that matings between phenotypically normal couples can give

Table 16.7. Theoretical Predictions of IQ
from a Five-pair Polygenic Model
(*from* Gottesman, 1963a)

Number of enhancing genes	Relative frequency of genotypes	Phenotypic IQ
0	1	50
1	10	60
2	45	70
3	120	80
4	210	90
5	252	100
6	210	110
7	120	120
8	45	130
9	10	140
10	1	150

(*By Courtesy of* Dr I. I. Gottesman and the McGraw-Hill Book Company)

rise to a wide variety of offspring. For example, a mating between persons who are both of the common genotype AaBbCc can produce children ranging between AABBCC to aabbcc. It can be shown that persons at the extremes of the distribution are more likely to have parents who are normal or mild deviants than parents who are themselves extreme deviants. If the characteristic in question is a threshold trait, manifest perhaps in the form of overt disease only in persons at the extreme of a hypothetical underlying distribution, it follows that affected subjects will frequently have no affected relatives. The expectations of disease in relatives are considerably lower here than under fully penetrant single gene inheritance, but in common disorders they may be very similar to those predicted by a hypothesis of dominant inheritance with low penetrance.*

In essence, the predictions from the simple additive model of polygenic inheritance outlined above derive from the expectation that correlations between measurements of relatives will correspond to the proportion of genes they have in common: 1·0 for MZ twins, 0·5 for first degree relatives (DZ twins, full sibs, parent-child), and 0·25 for second

* For an exposition of the principles of biometrical or quantitative genetics, based in large part on the assumptions of polygenic inheritance, the reader is referred to the textbook of Falconer (1960), and, with special reference to threshold traits or diseases in man, to the papers of Edwards (1960), Carter (1965) and Falconer (1965). R. A. Fisher's classical paper of 1918 has been reissued with a commentary by Moran and Smith (1966). Fuller and Thompson (1960), Parsons (1967) and Hirsch (1967) deal with the application of biometrical genetics to behaviour, mostly that of animals, while the volumes edited by Vandenberg (1965, 1968) deal with applications to man. The paper by Jinks and Fulker (1970) compares some of the most frequently recommended current approaches to the genetic analysis of quantitative traits, and sets out an example of an analysis of variance approach to family data on intelligence and personality.

degree relatives (half-sibs, uncle-niece, grandparent-grandchild, etc.) and 0·125 for third degree relatives (first cousins, etc.).

Different degrees of resemblance between relatives are obtained if the polygenes tend to produce their enhancing or reducing effects on the characteristic only in the homozygote, i.e. if there are *dominance-recessivity relationships* between the polygenes at most loci. Where there is dominance in this sense, the effects of the genes will no longer be additive, fixed and predictable, and resemblance between siblings will be less than when there is no dominance.

A similar or more marked effect on resemblance occurs if there is statistical *interaction* between genes at different loci. Let us suppose that the alleles A, B, and C enhance the characteristic only when all three are present in the same individual, while combinations such as AAB, ABB, and ACC do not. The likelihood that the sib of an ABC individual will have inherited the same three independent alleles necessary for him also to show the enhanced effect will be more remote than the likelihood that he will have this combination (ABC) or one of the other combinations of common alleles that would produce the same effect if there were not genetic interaction (epistasis).

While polygenic dominance and epistasis decrease resemblance between sibs, *assortative mating* increases it. When there is a tendency for like to marry like in respect of a measure that is to some extent genetically determined, there will be less variation in their children than if marriage were at random. In the population as a whole there will be relatively more individuals towards the extreme ends of the distribution. However, unless there are associations between high or low measurements and fertility, the mean of the population will remain the same from one generation to the next.

A character whose variability is determined by a large number of small independent *environmental factors* will have the same 'normal' distribution in the population as one that is determined by additive polygenes, but the familial distribution between generations and within sibships is unlikely to be the same as that predicted from the segregation of many genes. By making certain simplifying assumptions and by comparing appropriate groups of subjects (such as twins, adopted children etc., of which more later), biometrical genetics has developed elegant techniques for partitioning the total phenotypic variance of a characteristic according to how much is attributable to environmental variability, how much to additive genetic factors, how much to dominance, and how much to interaction effects of various kinds. We shall show the results of two such analyses later.

While such analytic methods have only relatively recently been applied to human behaviour, workers in agricultural genetics, where such methods have been pioneered and where they are easier to apply, are becoming increasingly aware of their present limitations even in an area where the interest is in the economic aspects of animal or plant breeding rather than in treating the abnormal individual; and many such workers look forward to further developments in biometrical or other genetic techniques (Robertson, 1967).

The above limitations may to a considerable extent be due to two further over-simplifications in the polygenic model, namely the assumptions that there are only two, equally frequent, alleles at each locus, and that no one polygene has more effect on the trait than any other. The situation in nature may well be different.

As regards the first assumption, work with human polymorphisms, such as blood groups and enzyme proteins, and with diseases such as those due to enzyme deficiencies shows that *multiple allelism* is far from infrequent (Harris, 1968); and when there are only two common alleles their relative frequencies

may well be 0·90 and 0·10 rather than 0·50 and 0·50. One consequence is that an alternative simple Mendelian model may account for some normal distributions—three alleles at a single locus, each genotypic combination of two alleles having its own reaction range, and the sum of the measures of each genotype combining to produce a bell-shaped distribution of the trait in the population. Red cell acid phosphatase activity is a case in point. Figure 16.2 shows the range of enzyme activity in persons of identifiably different genotype in proportion to the known frequency of these genotypes in the population. Penrose (1969) has developed a method of distinguishing between polygenic inheritance that is dependent on multiple loci and that which is dependent on multiple alleles. In the case of intelligence, polygenic inheritance can be shown to be of the former kind.

With regard to the second assumption, recent work in experimental genetics on lower organisms has shown that *a large proportion of the variance of a trait may be determined by relatively few genes*. In drosophila, 5 pairs of loci, partly additive and partly interactional, accounted for 87 per cent of the

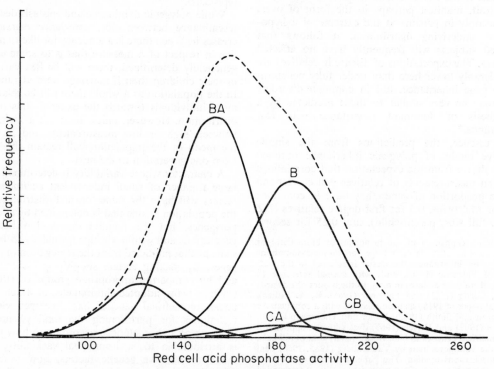

Fig. 16.2. Normal distribution determined by three alleles at one locus

Diagram showing distributions of red cell acid phosphatase activity in the general population (broken line) and in the separate enzyme types (*from* Harris, 1968; *by courtesy of* Professor Harris and *British Medical Journal*)

variance in bristle number between two selected lines, and the genes did not have identical effects on the trait (Thoday, 1967). There is hope that techniques may eventually be developed for identifying single polygenes or groups of polygenes influencing behavioural traits in man, allowing the study of their direct effects and interactions.

As long as this is not an immediate practical possibility, we may still hope to learn much from applying tests of the simple models of single-gene and multiple-gene inheritance and see how well or poorly they fit the best available data. However, the work alluded to above provides good theoretical reasons for supposing some genes to have a greater and more specific effect on a trait than others. The points at which we draw dividing lines between (a) major genes, (b) polygenes with a relatively large or specific effect on a trait, and (c) the modifying influences of the genetic background as a whole may to a considerable extent be arbitrary.

If genetic transmission is largely polygenic, the most hopeful hypotheses for tracing part of the pathway from genotype to phenotype are comparatively unspectacular. Gross biochemical differences are not to be expected. Hypotheses are more likely to concern the interaction between constitutional variables that are *indirectly* determined by genetic differences (e.g. introversion) and environmental influences of different kinds. Those who compare the effects of conditioning on introverts and extraverts may be doing developmental genetics in relation to polygenically determined behaviour as much as are those who study metabolic pathways in the single-gene character phenylketonuria. Eysenck (1967) is one of the few to appreciate the point.

Until recently, most sociologists and many psychologists, concerned with establishing the autonomy of their own disciplines, tended to ignore or deny the influence of genetics on behaviour. It is encouraging that there are now signs of a fruitful rapprochement from both sides. The Eugenics Society Symposia of 1964 (Meade and Parkes, 1965) and subsequent years, the report of the conference on genetics and behaviour organised by the Russell Sage Foundation, the Social Science Research Council and the Rockefeller University (Glass, 1968), and the transformation of the *Eugenics Review* and the *Eugenics Quarterly* into the *Journal of Biosocial Science* and the *Journal of Social Biology* respectively, are evidence of this trend. The report of the conference on *The Transmission of Schizophrenia* (Rosenthal and Kety, 1968), organised by the Foundations' Fund for Research in Psychiatry, will, it may be hoped, lead to a better mutual understanding between those who approach psychiatry from the genetic and the environmental or psycho-

dynamic ends, and to a consequent increase of useful knowledge in a difficult field.

Animal Studies

The application of polygenic models to human behaviour and the more widespread appreciation of genetic-environmental interaction coincide with advances in animal behaviour genetics ('psychogenetics') and with a growing interest in ethology. There is an increasing awareness of the artificiality of any sharp dichotomy between the innate and acquired when considering any complex adaptive behaviour. It would be an error to rely heavily on animal studies for evaluating genetic influences in human psychological abnormality. However, animal studies allow us to appreciate many important general points that cannot be llustrated so well in man.

1. Selective breeding for a variety of behaviour traits, including maze learning, emotionality, and wildness in the rat, shows that there is a wide range of genetic variability of a kind that influences behaviour within many outbred species in their natural environments (Fuller and Thompson, 1960).

2. Cross-fostering experiments, where the young of two inbred strains are interchanged, enable the effects of maternal training to be evaluated. While important for some traits, different types of maternal training have been found to have little effect on emotionality in the rat (Broadhurst, 1967) or on fighting behaviour in the mouse. In an experiment on the latter (Scott, 1958), when infant mice from the fierce strain attempted to take away food from their peaceful fosterparents, the adult mice began to compete: instead of cultural inheritance from parent to offspring, it was the biologically controlled behaviour of the offspring that influenced the parents (cf. Bell, 1968).

3. In any statement about the effects of genetic differences it is important to specify the environment, and in any statement about environmental differences to specify the strain. Inbred maze-bright and maze-dull rats do not show the same behaviour differences when they are reared either under radically restricted or radically enriched environments as they show when reared in their 'natural' laboratory environment (Cooper and Zubek, 1958). Strains of mice differ in their preference for alcohol (Rodgers and McClearn, 1962; McClearn, 1968).

4. Estimates of heritability are relative and not absolute. They need not be the same at different ages or after different lengths of exposure to an environment. Heritability may be defined as the proportion of the total variance of a trait, in a

specified population under specified environmental conditions, that can be attributed to genetic differences. As Broadhurst (1968) has pointed out, the heritability of maze running time in the laboratory mouse increases as a function of practice, while the heritability of defaecation in the rat in the open field test (a measure of emotionality) decreases on successive days of testing. Furthermore, the proportion of the variance due to additive and dominant genes changes in the rat on successive tests.

5. Estimates of heritability vary according to the tests used to measure a trait, the way in which the scores are scaled, and which of a number of different possible methods is used to make the estimate.

To mention these limitations is not to deny the usefulness of making heritability estimates. Indeed their great value lies in what can be learned from comparing estimates made from relatives varying in the nature of the environment they share, those made on different populations under varying conditions, and those made with different tests and by different analytic procedures. It is unrealistic to expect a global statement of how important heredity is for any general class of behaviour.

THE INHERITANCE OF INTELLIGENCE

The Distribution of IQ

As long ago as 1912 it became apparent that tested intelligence, like stature, was a continuous trait with a normal distribution. Jaederholm gave Binet-type tests to educationally subnormal children in Sweden (their scores shown shaded in Fig. 16.3) and to a representative sample of children attending the ordinary schools. There was a much better fit to the normal curve when those considered unsuited for ordinary schooling were included; and there was a good deal of overlap between the test-brighter subnormals and the test-duller schoolchildren. Similar findings were made in England (*see* Burt, 1962). Later, Roberts (1952) in a total sample of the children of Bath showed that there was an excess of severely subnormal children compared with the numbers expected on a Gaussian distribution. There are two broad classes of intellectual subnormality. On the whole, IQs below about 50 can be accounted for by single pathological causes of a gross kind, whether environmental or genetic, while the distribution of intelligence above that level can be accounted for by a combination of factors, polygenic and environmental. (An exception, as we have seen, is that sex-chromosome abnormalities tend to have only a small effect on IQ, being found to excess among the high-grade subnormal rather than the severely subnormal.) Except for those similarly affected with a disorder such as PKU, the distribution of IQ in the sibs of severely subnormal patients is close to that in the normal population, while the IQ of sibs of medium and high-grade cases lies about half-way between that of the patients and IQ 100, as predicted by a polygenic hypothesis. Even in the area where the IQs of the two classes overlap, IQ 35 to 60, Roberts in a further survey in Bath and Colchester succeeded in dividing the families of defectives into two groups, with results depicted in Fig. 16.4.

Single and Multiple Causes of Mental Subnormality

Only a very approximate notion can be given of the frequency of the different causes, as distinct from clinical types, of *severe* subnormality. Table 16.8 is based on a study of 800 such children admitted during the 1950s to the Fountain Hospital in London. The extra chromosome of mongolism is by far the most frequent single cause. Even in subnormality institutions where, as in many, approaching half the patients have an IQ above 50, some 10 per cent of patients are mongols (cf. Gruenberg, 1964). Subnormality resulting from incompatibility between the rhesus blood groups of Rh− mother and Rh+ father is now preventable (Clarke, 1967). Many of the 30 per cent of cases in the table where no aetiological factor was identified had physical abnormalities. Several may have relatively specific causes that remain to be discovered, while there may be

Table 16.8   Approximate Distribution of Aetiological Factors in Consecutive Admissions of Severely Subnormal Children to Subnormality Hospitals (Dr J. M. Berg, personal communication, 1969; estimated from data of Berg and Kirman, 1959, and Berg, 1963)

	%
Specific environmental factors (e.g. maternal rubella, probable or possible birth trauma, meningitis)	25
Specific genetic factors	
(*a*) Chromosomal aberrations (mainly mongolism)	25
(*b*) Gene defects (mainly recessive)	4
(*c*) Gene interaction (rhesus incompatibility)	1
Other possible genetic factors (e.g. family history of retardation, obscure syndromes)	15
No factors suggested	30
Total	100

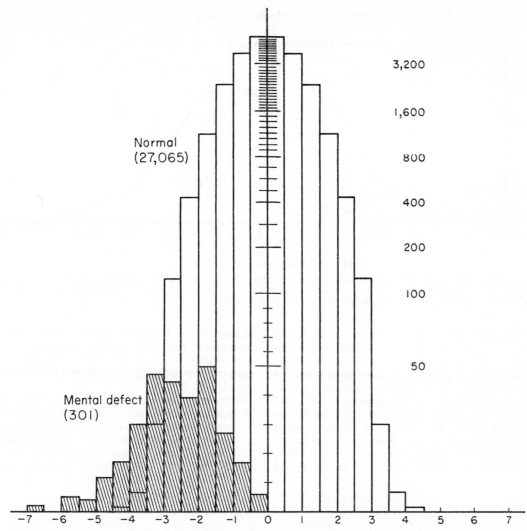

Fig. 16.3. Distribution of intelligence

Estimate based on Binet test scores of 301 defective children, and theoretical projection from the scores of 261 normal children. Jaederholm's data (Pearson and Jaederholm, 1914), *from* Pearson (1931). *By courtesy of Annals of Human Genetics*)

some where aetiology is multifactorial as in most high-grade subnormality. For the best estimate of the genetic contribution to the much larger group of the high-grade subnormal we shall turn shortly to studies on the normal range of intelligence. Mental subnormality is more frequent in the families of higher grade patients (Penrose, 1963).

Morbid Risk Figures for the Relatives of the Subnormal

Since this Handbook is concerned with abnormality, it will be of interest to give some further indication of the percentage of close relatives of mental defectives reported as similarly affected. A more detailed account is given by Reed and Reed (1965). Needless to say, findings vary, depending among other things on the thoroughness of the investigation, the criteria—social or psychometric—used, and the facilities for caring for and so knowing about the subnormal in the population. Nevertheless, agreement between some studies is impressive (Table 16.9). Fremming's (1951) estimate of 1·2 per cent is not unrepresentative of the expectation of mental subnormality in most general populations.

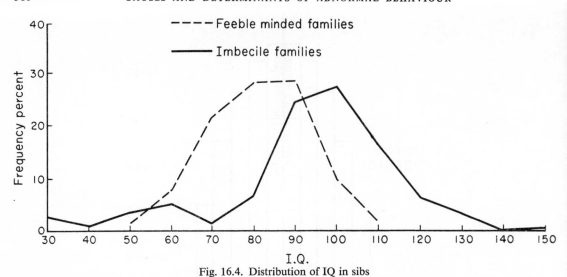

Fig. 16.4. Distribution of IQ in sibs

Terman-Merrill IQs of 562 sibs of 271 subnormal children of IQ 35–60, according to whether subnormality was classified as pathological (in 122 'imbecile families') or as part of the normal distribution (in 149 'feeble minded families') (*from* Roberts, 1952; *by courtesy of* Dr. J. A. Fraser Roberts and the *Eugenics Review*)

Taken in isolation, increased risks for relatives of around 30 per cent—which should be regarded as upper limits—do not enable one to distinguish the parts played by genetic and social inheritance. As regards the sibs, most studies show there is a greater risk of their being similarly assessed as abnormal if one or both parents are affected than if the parents are both of normal intelligence. However, when both parents are normal there is a considerably increased risk for the sib of a given case when there are uncles and aunts known to be subnormal (Table 16.10). If genetic factors were of little importance compared to environmental ones, subnormality in uncles and aunts would be irrelevant, but such a finding is predicted by a polygenic model.

If transmission were cultural and accounted for by factors associated with social class, there should be little variation between sibs and even less between genetically identical (monozygotic) and genetically dissimilar (dizygotic) twins. Both Rosanoff *et al.* (1937) and Juda (1939) found a much closer

Table 16.9.   Some Findings from Family Studies in Mental Subnormality

Author, Year, Country	Probands		Relatives
Ministry of Health, 1934, England (Brock Report)	3733 mental defectives known to local authorities	1848 children over age 13 and classified	32·4% (599) mentally defective (excluding dull and backward)
Penrose, 1938, England	1280 defectives in institution, Colchester	59 children whose ability was assessed	28·8% (17) mentally defective (various criteria)
Åkesson, 1962, Sweden	88 high-grade defectives of unknown aetiology, in 10 rural parishes	82 parents resident in area and tested	29·2% (24) IQ > 2 SD below mean, Swedish Binet test
Reed and Reed, 1965, USA	289 retardates in Minnesota institution, 1911–18	1897 parents, sibs and children	28·0% (532) IQ below 70
Scally, 1968, N. Ireland	All 342 defectives in country known to have had children and studied	454 children over age 6	30·2% (137) ineducable or educationally subnormal

Table 16.10. Frequency of Subnormality in Siblings of Affected Individuals, According to Type of Parental Mating (*from* Reed and Reed, 1965)

Parental mating	Number of Siblings	Percentage subnormal
Subnormal × subnormal	76	42·1
Subnormal × normal	317	19·9
Normal × normal with subnormal uncles or aunts	139	12·9
Normal × normal	104	5·7

(*By Courtesy of* Dr Elizabeth W. Reed, Dr S. C. Reed and Messrs. W. B. Saunders Co. Ltd.)

resemblance in monozygotic (MZ) pairs than in dizygotic (DZ) pairs. Twin studies based on the presence or absence of mental deficiency, however, are complicated by the fact that, largely on account of the hazards of twin pregnancy and birth, twins are more liable to subnormality of many kinds (Allen and Kallmann, 1962; Berg and Kirman, 1960) than are the singly born. What is more, in their New York study, Allen and Kallmann concluded that parents were inclined to institutionalise same-sex twins, especially boys, when both are subnormal, and to keep one member of opposite-sex pairs at home. Concordance was high in all same-sex (SS) pairs in respect of high-grade undifferentiated subnormality—nearly as high in SS DZ pairs (35/39) as in MZ pairs (41/41). They believed that factors such as parental rejection might contribute to the aetiology, in addition to the usual genetic and traumatic ones.

Correlations between Relatives in IQ

For further evidence we now turn to the normal range of tested intelligence. Erlenmeyer-Kimling and Jarvik (1963) summarised the evidence of 52 genetic studies from eight countries, spanning half a century of time and employing a wide variety of tests and subjects, including twins and adopted children. Table 16.11 shows the median correlation

Table 16.11. Intelligence Test Scores Median Correlation Coefficients in Family, Twin and Foster-child Studies (Number of studies in brackets) (*after* Erlenmeyer-Kimling and Jarvik, 1963)

	Reared apart		Reared together	
Unrelated	−0·01	(4)	0·23	(5)
Foster parent–child			0·20	(3)
Parent–child			0·50	(12)
Sibs	0·40	(2)	0·49	(35)
DZ twins				
Like-sex			0·53	(9)
Unlike-sex			0·53	(11)
MZ twins	0·75	(4)	0·87	(14)

for studies of each class indicated. Resemblances between first-degree relatives are all close to the 0·5 correlation predicted by the genetic hypotheses, although the kinds of environment shared by parent and child in their formative years, by sibs, by SS DZ twins and by twins of different sex, are not the same. The effect of the environment is seen in the lower correlations obtained when pairs are reared apart, or are not related (e.g. foster parent–child). The large effect of genetic differences is seen most clearly when one compares the correlation of 0·23 between unrelated persons reared together with that of 0·75 between MZ twins reared apart.

Adoption and Foster-home Studies. The earlier foster-home studies on intelligence were discussed in the first edition of this Handbook. Their results are included in the correlations of Table 16.11. Selective placement of a child in a home matching that of his biological parents makes interpretation of some findings difficult. In other studies, information about the intelligence of the biological parents may be inadequate. Too much weight may be given to predictions on IQ based on infant development tests. The early studies of Skodak and Skeels, recently followed up by Skeels (1966), are more remarkable for the tendency for the IQ to drop in the case of the 12 neglected children who were left in the unstimulating environment of the old-fashioned orphanage than for the rise in IQ in the case of the 13 who were adopted as 'guests' in a more encouraging environment, albeit that of a State School for the retarded. The latter subjects, of whom about half had an IQ below 80 at age 5, appear to have reached a level not very different from what might have been predicted on a genetic hypothesis. One is reminded of the study of rats in restricted and in enriched environments. One of the earlier studies (Freeman *et al.*, 1928), comparing children who, so far as could be judged, were of the same original potential, found a reaction range of IQ 96 to IQ 112, matching environments that had been globally assessed as ranging from poor to good.

Twins Reared Apart. The correlation coefficients reported for intelligence and educational achievement in the studies using MZ twins reared apart (MZ_A) and together (MZ_T) are shown in Table 16.12. In the Newman *et al.* (1937) study the within-pair difference in IQ shown by the 19 MZ_A pairs—most of them young adults when tested—was largely accounted for by the four pairs that had differed most in educational opportunity. As a group they were less alike than the children which Newman *et al.* used for their MZ_T and DZ_T groups. Burt's (1966) subjects were children and in both MZ groups he obtained high correlations with the tests

Table 16.12.   Studies Investigating MZ Twins
Reared Apart: Intra-pair Correlations for
Intelligence and for Educational Attainment

	MZ *Pairs*		DZ *Pairs*
	Reared apart	*Reared together*	*Reared together (mostly)*
	r	*r*	*r*
Newman *et al.* (1937)			
Binet IQ	0·767	0·881	0·631
Educational attainment	0·583	0·892	0·691
Shields (1962)			
Combined intelligence test score (Dominoes and Mill Hill Vocabulary)	0·77	0·76	0·51
Juel-Nielsen (1965)			
Raven Matrices	0·79	—	—
Wechsler-Bellevue IQ	0·62	—	—
Burt (1966)			
Intelligence (final assessment)	0·874	0·925	0·534
Educational attainment	0·623	0·983	0·831

he employed. MZ_A $r = 0.875$ (53 pairs) is remarkably high when it is noted that there was no tendency for the parents who reared the two members of the pair to be of the same social class.* In Shields's (1962) study, based on volunteers, most of them over the age of 30, the MZ_A and MZ_T groups, each consisting of 44 pairs in all, were matched for sex and age. Juel-Nielsen's (1965) 12 Danish MZ_A pairs were also adults and 8 elderly pairs came from a register of all twins born. The findings in the two latter studies are in quite good agreement. Newman *et al.* and Burt used tests of educational achievement as well as tests of intelligence, and, as expected, the former showed less evidence of genetic influence: DZ_T pairs were more alike than MZ_A pairs in their educational attainment.

In the present context the main reason for studying adopted children, and part of the reason for studying identical twins brought up apart, in addition to studying subjects reared with their biological families, is to assess the influence of between-family environment. If it is accepted that, so far as intelligence is concerned, the environments of MZ_T and DZ_T are sufficiently similar for one to conclude that within-family genetic differences account for most of the MZ:DZ difference, the same conclusions about the importance of heredity might not apply if between-family differences could be taken into account. It could be argued that differences such as

* Burt has stated (personal communication to P. Mittler) that the published DZ correlation of 0·453 was a misprint for 0·534.

those of social class might well overshadow the effect of genetic resemblance. The adoption and MZ_A studies suggest that between-family differences in early environment, so far as they have been tapped, contribute only a moderate amount. Of course, if one were to study only selected pairs of twins where the environment of one was grossly 'enriched' and that of the other grossly 'restricted' it would be surprising if they were still found to be so alike.

It is frequently objected that a finding of $rMZ_T >$ rDZ_T is for some traits a function, not of the genetic difference but of elements of the within-family environment which are more similar for MZ twins. To test the validity of this hypothesis is an equally important reason for studying MZ_A. Here it is no objection that the environments of a pair were not different enough, though it might be objected that the twins were not separated early enough. However, A. D. B. Clarke (1968) has argued that infancy is a bad time for learning, the important point being not whether an influence occurred early enough but whether it was sufficiently reinforced. So far as the influence of age at separation on IQ differences is concerned, this had no detectable influence in Shields's study, whereas, as noted by Vandenberg and Johnson (1968), the effect was paradoxical in the Newman and Juel-Nielsen studies. In the latter studies there was a significant tendency for the twins separated earlier to be more *alike* than those separated later. Further discussion of the validity of the twin method is reserved till later (pp. 569–70).

Biometrical Analysis

A biometrical analysis of investigations related to intelligence, listed in Table 16.13 and including some of those just mentioned, has been carried out by Jinks and Fulker (1970) with results (Table 16.14) that show some of the fascinating theoretical possibilities of such an analysis. Their analysis of extraversion and neuroticism follows later. 'Broad' heritability estimates the contribution of all the genetic variance, while 'narrow' heritability refers to the additive genetic component only.

Although they go further in their stated implications, Jinks and Fulker's conclusions based on IQ scores shown in Table 16.14 are not so very different from those of Sir Cyril Burt (1958), shown in Table 16.15. The latter were based on his own extensive data from a wide variety of relationships. In the older studies correlations of around 0·55 were reported between the IQs of husbands and wives (Jones, 1929). More recently, Garrison *et al.* (1968) report a correlation of 0·23, based on childhood IQ. Such degrees of resemblance would

Table 16.13. Description of Data on Intelligence and Educational Attainments
Subjected to Biometrical Reanalysis
(*After* Jinks and Fulker, 1970)

No.	Phenotype	Description of test used	Data available	Source
1	Intelligence	Synonyms section (set A) of Mill Hill Vocabulary test (Form B 1948)	MZ_T (24F and 12M pairs of Ss) MZ_A (25F and 15M pairs of Ss)	Shields (1962)
2	Intelligence	Dominoes intelligence test. Non-verbal 20 minutes test similar to Raven's progressive matrices	MZ_T (23F and 11M pairs of Ss) MZ_A (24F and 14M pairs of Ss)	Shields (1962)
3	Intelligence Quotient	Group test standardised by the London Revision of Terman-Binet Intelligence scale	Correlations only for MZ_T (95 pairs Ss) MZ_A (53 pairs Ss) DZ_T (127 pairs Ss) FS_T (264 pairs Ss) FS_A (151 pairs Ss) U_T (136 pairs Ss) parents and offspring (numbers unknown) husband and wife (numbers unknown)	Burt (1966) Burt and Howard (1956)
4	Educational Attainments	Group test devised for use with London school children including reading, spelling and arithmetic items (Burt 1921)	As above (excluding last two correlations)	Burt (1966)
5	Intelligence Quotient	IQ Scores deriving from a number of tests, preference given to individual tests administered at age 14	Sibs together (689 families size > 3)	Reed and Reed (1965)
6	Intelligence Quotient	Japanese version of the Wechsler Intelligence Scale for Children	1,511 inbred children ($f = 1/16$) 1,608 control children ($f = 0$)	Spuhler (1967)
7	Intelligence Quotient	Stanford-Binet Intelligence Scale and Otis Group Intelligence Scale	MZ_A (19 pairs Ss both sexes)	Newman Freeman and Holzinger (1937)

(*By courtesy of* Dr J. L. Jinks and Dr D. W. Fulker)

predict a sib correlation greater than 0·5 on the simple additive model, but this is offset by the element of dominance detected by Burt and others.

Heritability based on the raw scores of adult twins on the Dominoes and Mill Hill tests is a little lower than that based on IQ in children. Unfortunately, the range of scores on the Mill Hill Vocabulary Test was too restricted, in particular in the lower range of the MZ_T group, to permit as many conclusions to be drawn from the data as might otherwise have been the case. The conclusions from Jinks and Fulker's analysis are subject to the provisos already made about overgeneralising from heritabilities, though the consistency of findings in respect of intelligence is a ground for moderate confidence about the stability of the findings, which seem to make good sense.

Heritabilities calculated for a general factor of intelligence or for total test score are not as a rule any higher than those for individual subtests or separate abilities (Blewett, 1954, and later studies by others). Although the factor permits an economical summary of trait co-variation, no single element in the genotype or the environment accounts for the

Table 16.14.   Main Findings of Reanalysis of Data Shown in Table 16.13
(*after* Jinks and Fulker, 1970)

Example				Main findings		
No.	Phenotype	Correlated environments	Genotype-environment interaction	Heritability ± S.E. Broad	Narrow	Conclusions
1	Mill Hill Vocabulary	None, but poor sampling mimics correlation effect	Suggestion that unfavourable genotypes are more influenced by environment than favourable ones (p 0·1–0·05)	73 ± 12%	—	Poor sampling of genotypes vitiates attempt at more adequate analysis
2	Dominoes	None	None	71 ± 7%	—	Very simple genetical model adequate. Common family environment unimportant
4	Educational Attainments	Positive correlation of heredity and environment between families indicated (p < 0·001)	—	Uncertain but probably less than 30%	—	Simple model probably not adequate but sampling effects may be producing a false picture. No proper tests of assumptions possible without raw data. Assortative mating is indicated. Common family environment very important and accentuated by effect of correlated environments
3	IQ	None	—	86 ± 1%	71 ± 1%	Fairly simple model adequate to explain the inheritance of IQ. Assortative matings taking place. Additive and dominant gene action detected with level of dominance 0·74. Dominance for high IQ for many genes (about 100) and gene frequencies, on average, equal. Gene action strongly suggests that IQ has been subject to considerable directional natural selection during man's evolutionary history. Unlike educational attainments common family environment unimportant
5	IQ	—	—	—	—	
6	IQ	—	—	—	—	
7	IQ	—	None	—	—	

(*By courtesy of* Dr J. L. Jinks and Dr D. W. Fulker)

correlation (Gottesman, 1968), and intelligence is almost certainly not an entirely unitary trait genetically (Vandenberg, 1968). A twin who is more intelligent than his partner as judged by total score does not do better on all subtests, and this is more so in the case of DZ than MZ pairs. After applying a multivariate analysis to various data Vandenberg concluded that different tests probably measure independent as well as overlapping genetic components. Such a view is consistent with a polygenic model in which the genes may have somewhat different effects on the character.* The relative degree of heritability of the different abilities varies somewhat from study to study. In the setting of

* From the population data of Douglas *et al.* (1968), according to which myopia and IQ are positively related, one might be tempted to conclude that the polygenes determining myopia (Sorsby *et al.*, 1962) have at least an indirect effect on intelligence. Even if one does not regard them as overlapping with the polygenic system for intelligence, they might be construed as having a bearing on the general constitutional background that influences an individual's intellectual performance.

Table 16.15. Analysis of Variance for
Assessments of Intelligence
(*after* Burt, 1958)

Source	Unadjusted test scores	Adjusted assessments
Genetic component—		
additive	40·51	47·92
dominance	16·65	21·73
Assortative mating	19·90	17·91
Environment—		
systematic	10·60	1·43
random	5·91	5·77
Unreliability	6·43	5·24
Total	100·00	100·00

(*By courtesy of* Sir Cyril Burt and the American Psychological Association)

$MZ_T : DZ_T$ comparisons, Verbal intelligence generally has the highest heritability, as measured by the significance of the difference of the within-pair variances; in Memory and more surprisingly Reasoning heredity is less important. It may be of interest that children from different ethnic groups in New York—Jews, Chinese, Negroes and Puerto Ricans—of similar general ability and matched for social class, differed in their relative success with tests of Verbal, Reasoning, Number, and Spatial abilities (Lesser *et al.*, 1965). Subjects of the same cultural group from middle and lower class families had different levels of ability, but the profile of their scores on the tests tended to be similar.

Selection and Fertility

From the evidence presented it may be concluded that genetic variation contributes considerably to the causes of high-grade subnormality. This is not to deny the influence of social factors on the problems associated with low intelligence. What, then, is the prospect for future generations? At least until recently, the dull and backward tended to have larger families than the more prosperous and on the whole more intelligent; negative correlations of 0·2 or 0·3 were found between IQ and size of sibship. It was predicted that the mean IQ of the population would fall by 1·5 or 2 IQ points per generation (Burt, 1946). There was, however, no evidence of any such fall (Scottish Council for Research in Education, 1949). A solution to the paradox was proposed by Higgins *et al.* (1962). When sibships in the parental generation were studied, it was found that many of the very backward did not marry, and as a result those of low IQ were not contributing more than their share of genes to the next generation. With some reversal of differential fertility in recent years (Carter, 1962), some geneticists now cautiously suggest that there is positive selection for high intelligence and predict that the general level of inherent intellectual ability in the population should very slowly rise (Reed and Reed, 1965; Falconer, 1966; Jinks and Fulker, 1970).

GENETIC INFLUENCES ON PERSONALITY

Personality Questionnaires

The neuroses and personality disorders are usually assumed to be conditions to which individuals towards the extreme ends of normally distributed personality traits and dimensions are especially prone. It is therefore appropriate to outline the genetic work done, using assessments or measures of personality. This is based almost exclusively on twin studies. From the point of view of the experimental psychologist, it is very easy to criticise the earlier studies (summarised by Gedda, 1951; Eysenck and Prell, 1951; Shields, 1954) based on interviews and teachers' reports, which are liable to subjective bias, and on a variety of tests of uncertain reliability and validity. Nevertheless, later work has shown that the conclusions based on a clinical or uncontrolled approach, to the effect that MZ pairs are in many respects more similar than DZ pairs, may well have been correct. In an attempt to avoid subjectivity, Eysenck and Prell (1951) administered a number of performance tests of personality to a sample of normal twins and to a criterion group of children attending a child guidance clinic. A factor labelled neuroticism correlated 0·82 within MZ pairs and 0·22 within DZ pairs. Two years later, however, an attempt to replicate the findings resulted in the failure to identify a neuroticism factor from such tests (Blewett, 1953), and since then the paper-and-pencil type of personality questionnaire has been the method preferred by most investigators. The results of studies using such questionnaires have been comprehensively reviewed by Vandenberg (1967). Considering the differences between the tests used and the samples studied, it is not surprising that a trait or factor with the same name does not always reveal a MZ:DZ difference of the same significance. The Minnesota Multiphasic Personality Inventory

Table 16.16.   Summary of Findings from Twin Studies with Personality Questionnaires
(*from* Vandenberg, 1967)

Author, year N_{DZ} N_{MZ} Questionnaire	Significance level of the increased MZ concordance			
	0·01	0·05	Not significant	$r_{MZ} < r_{DZ}$
Carter, 1935 $\frac{44}{55}$ Bernreuter	Self-sufficiency Dominance Self-confidence	Neuroticism	Introversion Sociability	
Vandenberg, 1962 $\frac{35}{45}$ Thurstone	Active Vigorous	Impulsive Sociable	Dominant Stable Reflective	
Cattell *et al.*, 1955 Vandenberg, 1962 Gottesman, 1963*b* $\frac{102}{137}$ HSPQ	Surgency Neuroticism Energetic conformity	Adventurous cyclothymia *vs.* schizothymia Will control	Cyclothymia Dominance Tender—tough-minded Nervous tension Socialised morale	Impatient dominance
Gottesman, 1963b Gottesman, 1965 Reznikoff and Honeyman, 1967 $\frac{132}{120}$ MMPI	Social introversion Depression Psychasthenia	Psychopathic deviate Schizophrenia	Paranoia Hysteria Hypochondriasis Hypomania Masculinity-femininity	
Wilde, 1964 $\frac{42}{88}$ Amsterdam bio-graphical quest	Psychoneurotic complaints Psychosomatic complaints	Masculinity-femininity	Introversion Test-taking attitude	
Vandenberg *et al.*, 1966 $\frac{27}{40}$ Myers-Briggs		Introversion		Thinking-feeling Judgement-perception Sensing-intuition
Vandenberg *et al.*, 1966 $\frac{38}{50}$ Stern Activity-Index factors	Intellectual interests Closeness Sensuousness	Self-assertion Applied interests Orderliness Expressiveness-constraint Egoism-diffidence Educability	Audacity Motivation Submissiveness Friendliness	Dependency needs
Vandenberg *et al.*, 1966 $\frac{90}{111}$ Comrey	Achievement need Shyness	Compulsion Religious attitudes	Dependence Self-control Empathy Welfare-state attitude Punitive attitude Neuroticism	Hostility Ascendance
Scarr, 1966 $\frac{28}{24}$ Gough ACL Fels behavior list	Need for affiliation Friendliness Social apprehension Likeableness	Counseling readiness		

Table 16.16.   *(continued)*

Author, year N_{DZ} $\overline{N_{MZ}}$ Questionnaire	Significance level of the increased MZ concordance			
	0·01	0·05	*Not significant*	$r_{MZ} < r_{DZ}$
Gottesman, 1966 68 $\overline{79}$ CPI	Dominance Sociability Self-acceptance Originality	Social presence Good impression Socialisation Psychological mindedness	Status capacity Sense of well-being Self-control Tolerance Communality Responsibility Achievement via independence Intellectual efficiency Femininity Flexibility Psychoneurotic	Achievement via conformance
Partanen *et al.*, 1966 189 $\overline{159}$ Special questionnaire and interview	Sociability Frequency of drinking Average consumption		Need for achieve- ment Neuroticism Aggressiveness Lack of control	Not reported

(*By courtesy of* Dr S. G. Vandenberg and the Plenum Publishing Corporation)

(MMPI) and Cattell's High School Personality Questionnaire (HSPQ) are the only two tests that have been given in more than one study, though with somewhat different results. Within the same study there are frequently sex differences for which no consistent explanation has so far emerged. Nevertheless, Table 16.16 gives a good general picture of the present state of progress. A more recent review is provided by Mittler (1971).

The F test of significance used by Vandenberg in Table 16.16 is based on the ratio of the DZ and MZ within-pair variances. Although we are at present concerned simply with whether MZ pairs are more alike than DZ pairs, this may be the appropriate point at which to indicate how the various statistical measures sometimes used in the classical twin method are related to one another, as the method has been developed in the hands of recent American workers. Table 16.17 shows the basic principles of the method (1) (2) (3). V_H and V_E stand for variance due respectively to heredity and environment (including error). WPV is the observed within-pair variance. Holzinger's h^2, which is a measure of heritability in the 'broad' sense, is defined generally (4) and in terms of the within-pair variances (5) and of r, the intra-class correlation coefficient (6) (7). BPV is the between-pair variance. F is shown in terms of the variance ratio (8) and of h^2 (9). The significance level of F is found from statistical tables with degrees of freedom corresponding to the numbers of DZ and MZ pairs. The derivation of the formulas and some

of the limitations of h^2, as estimated from twins in the above manner, are discussed by Vandenberg (1966).

We now revert to Table 16.16. Clearly the most consistent finding is of a significant hereditary component in extraversion-introversion. Many studies also show the same with respect to a trait or factor that might be interpreted as neuroticism or as related to neuroticism, but the findings here are not

Table 16.17.   Principles of the Twin Method Relationship between Within-pair Variances, r, h^2 and F

$$\text{WPV}_{MZ} = V_E \tag{1}$$

$$\text{WPV}_{DZ} = V_H + V_E \tag{2}$$

$$\text{WPV}_{DZ} - \text{WPV}_{MZ} = V_H \tag{3}$$

$$h^2 = \frac{V_H}{V_H + V_E} \tag{4}$$

$$= \frac{\text{WPV}_{DZ} - \text{WPV}_{MZ}}{\text{WPV}_{DZ}} \tag{5}$$

$$\text{or} \quad \frac{r_{MZ} - r_{DZ}}{1 - r_{DZ}} \tag{6}$$

$$\text{where } r = \frac{\text{BPV} - \text{WPV}}{\text{BPV} + \text{WPV}} \tag{7}$$

$$F = \frac{\text{WPV}_{DZ}}{\text{WPV}_{MZ}} \tag{8}$$

$$= \frac{1}{1 - h^2} \tag{9}$$

Table 16.18. Studies Investigating Twins Reared
Apart Intra-pair Correlations for Personality
Questionnaire Scores

	MZ *Pairs*		DZ *Pairs*
	Reared apart	*Reared together*	*Reared together (mostly)*
	r	r	r
Newman *et al.* (1937)			
Neuroticism (Bernreuter)	0·583	0·562	0·371
Shields (1962)			
Self-rating questionnaire (Eysenck)			
Neuroticism	0·53	0·38	0·11
Extraversion	0·61	0·42	−0·17

so consistent. The latter dimension may be less stable and more difficult to measure than extraversion. In the large scale study of Partanen *et al.* (1966), the neuroticism scale used consisted of only nine items, so it is not surprising that correlations were low ($r_{MZ} = 0·28$, $r_{DZ} = 0·21$) and not significantly different from one another. Partanen *et al.* studied a population sample of adult Finnish male twins, Wilde (1964) studied volunteer twins from Amsterdam aged 13 to 69, and the small sample from Connecticut studied by Reznikoff and Honeyman (1967) also consisted of adults. Otherwise, the above reports were based on twins, mostly adolescents, from the US school system.

One of the few psychometric studies using information from twins and members of their families is that of Gottesman in his Harvard study (1965, 1966). Elston and Gottesman (1968) analysed the data on introversion, as measured by the Si scale of the MMPI, obtained from twins, their parents and their sibs. Provided the results of both sexes were pooled, a procedure the authors feel may not be justified, estimates of heritability of about 0·7 were

obtained by their method under two different sets of assumptions.

Another method of analysing twin and family data was first proposed by Cattell in 1953. Known as the MAVA method (multiple abstract variance analysis), it requires information on relatives reared apart in order to obtain estimates of between-family variance. Results so far obtained (Cattell *et al.*, 1955; Cattell *et al.*, 1957) are difficult to interpret.

Table 16.18 shows the present findings in studies of MZ twins reared apart which have employed personality questionnaires. MZ_A are slightly *more* alike than MZ_T as measured by the correlation coefficient, though in Shields's study the distribution of the differences and findings from the life histories and interviews revealed effects that were probably due to the environments of the MZ_A twins. As in other studies, r_{DZ} is sometimes low or insignificantly negative.

Jinks and Fulker (1970) re-analysed Shields's data. The self-rating questionnaire used, devised by Eysenck, was a forerunner of the MPI. Neuroticism and extraversion scores were examined for 29 female and 14 male MZ_T pairs, 26 female and 14 male MZ_A pairs and 16 female DZ_T pairs. There was no evidence of correlation between heredity and environment; but the introvert genotype was more modifiable than the extravert genotype by the within-family environment ($p < 0·02$). Table 16.19 shows the heritability estimates obtained by the biometrical method of analysis and Jinks and Fulker's conclusions about the genetics of personality. Since the data are less extensive than was the case with intelligence (*see* Tables 16.13 and 16.14) and since personality tests do not always produce consistent findings, some caution is required before assuming that the same results would be obtained on a different sample or with another test. Nevertheless, heritabilities of a similar order have been obtained in studies based on twins reared together.

Table 16.19. Main Findings of Biometrical Reanalysis of Shields's (1962) Data on
Personality Test Scores of Twins Reared Apart and Reared Together
(*after* Jinks and Fulker, 1970)

Phenotype	*Heritability* ± SE		Conclusions
	Broad	*Narrow*	
Neuroticism	54 ± 7%	54 ± 7%	Very simple genetical model adequate to explain data. Assortative mating indicated. Additive gene action only detected indicates intermediate expression of trait favoured by natural selection. Common family environment unimportant.
Extraversion	67 ± 8%	—	Simple model not adequate as DZ_T appear to react against each other producing negative correlation. Some evidence effect is built upon genetic differences. Common family environment unimportant.

(*By courtesy of* Dr J. L. Jinks and Dr D. W. Fulker)

Table 16.20. Intra-pair Correlations for Neuroticism
and Extraversion (EPI) in MZ Twins
(Dr J. S. Price, *personal communication*, 1969)

	Living apart	Living together	All pairs
	N = 57	N = 45	N = 102
Neuroticism	0·69	0·57	0·65
Extraversion	0·45	0·29	0·38

Jinks and Fulker have interpreted the negative DZ correlation in respect of extraversion as being due partly to the twins reacting against one another. From the time of Galton a similar tendency has been noted for MZ twins to adopt different roles, e.g. in one being the spokesman for the pair or in the development of dominance-submissiveness relationships, similar to the pecking order in chicks or the dominance hierarchy in primates. In Shields's MZ_T group the twin who as a child took the lead tended to have the higher extraversion score as an adult. The very closeness of the environment may act as a differentiating factor in twins reared together. Even when adult twins living apart are compared with those living together, there have been reports of the former being more alike (Wilde, 1964, with regard to DZ pairs in particular; Price, 1969, personal communication). Price gave the Eysenck Personality Inventory to 102 pairs of volunteer MZ twins aged 15 to 64, a sample in some ways comparable to Shields's (1962) MZ twins reared together. This time correlations were higher for neuroticism than for extraversion (Table 16.20).

Assessment of Bias in Twin Studies

The simplified assumptions of the twin method, especially when applied to psychological measures, have been questioned, notably the equating of environments shared by MZ and DZ pairs and the accuracy and validity of zygosity classification. Perhaps the main lesson to be drawn from the MZ_A studies about personality is that they have shown that any greater similarity of MZ_T than DZ_T is not mainly accounted for by intrafamilial environmental factors that are more similar for MZ_T. Further evidence to similar effect comes from the observation of Shields (1954) that those MZ twin schoolchildren who were assessed as being the most closely attached to one another were no more alike in personality or neurotic traits than the remainder. Parker (1964b) found psychiatric *discordance* in twins who stood out for their close degree of mutual identification; and in his series of neurotic twins (1964c) females were no more alike than males, although the former claimed a closer bond and so, in a sense, had a more similar environment.

A complementary approach to evaluating the possible bias in genetically orientated twin studies comes from observations, so far few in number, on pairs where parents are mistaken about the zygosity of their twins. Freedman (1965) found smiling response and fear reaction to be more similar in MZ than DZ infant twins, even though 6 out of 9 mothers of MZ twins thought their infants were fraternal, not identical. Scarr (1968) compared 11 misclassified pairs with 40 correctly classified pairs and concluded that 'differences in the parental treatment that twins receive are much more a function of the degree of their genetic relatedness than of parental beliefs about "identicalness" and "fraternalness".'

It is not denied that in certain respects the environment may be more similar for MZ than DZ twins. The points of interest are: in what ways is this so (cf. Husén, 1959; Jones, 1955; Smith, 1965; Zazzo, 1960), why is it so (e.g. to what extent is it the result of genotype-environment interaction such as MZ twins choosing more similar environments), and how relevant is it to resemblance in the trait under consideration?

Both kinds of twins differ from singletons in a number of respects (Mittler, 1971). For instance their mean verbal IQ is about 95 (Record *et al.*, 1970). These differences may be informative in their own right (*see* p. 561), but for most traits it is unlikely that they invalidate the comparison of MZ and DZ resemblance.

Faulty classification of zygosity, if it occurs at random with respect to psychological resemblance, will have the effect of obscuring any real differences between MZ and DZ pairs. While knowledge of zygosity might influence psychiatric diagnosis, or vice versa (Rosenthal, 1962a), this source of bias does not arise with objective psychological tests. Errors of zygosity determination may have been less frequent than some critics supposed. The introduction of extensive blood grouping as an aid in deciding whether twins are MZ or not has shown that criteria based on blood groups agree very closely with those based on a history or observation of resemblance in appearance (Cederlöf *et al.*, 1961; Jablon *et al.*, 1967).

Doubts on the validity of the twin method have been cast by claims that MZ twins are not always genetically identical (Storrs and Williams, 1968). We have already had occasion to refer to MZ twins of different sex and to a pair where only one had the extra chromosome that causes mongolism. The occurrence of such differences is almost certainly very rare and hardly relevant to abnormalities developing after early infancy. The role, if any, of cytoplasmic inheritance in the behaviour of man and whether MZ twins differ in cytoplasmic genes is not known (but cf. Nance, 1969). Probably of greater importance are the effects, peculiar to MZ twins, of asymmetries of development (e.g. through their developing from cells that might normally have been destined to become the right and left sides of a single individual) and of placental anastomosis (where one twin secures more of the placental blood supply than the other, Price, 1950). The result of such prenatal influences, some of them difficult to classify as genetic or environmental in the usual sense, will be to *underestimate* the importance of nuclear heredity.

From the work done with personality questionnaires and the discussion of some of the biases in twin studies we may conclude that genetic differences between individuals are relevant to variation in personality. In work on abnormal behaviour and in work using subjective ratings or diagnoses there are special biases which, unless precautions are taken to reduce or eliminate them, may influence findings in twin research. In particular there may be a selective or diagnostic bias in favour of concordant MZ pairs. Discussion will be concentrated on twin studies that have attempted to avoid these dangers. But before we come to such studies, we may first ask how it is that genes might influence personality.

How Genes May Influence Personality

There is a variety of ways in which genes may appear to exert an effect on personality. In general, one may think of their doing so through controlling the timing of the development of many different processes related directly or indirectly to personality. The genes may also set limits on these developments. Furthermore they can exert an influence by making one type of response to a stimulus more probable than another. Only a few examples can be briefly mentioned, based for the most part on careful studies.

Penrose (1961) has estimated that approximately 20 per cent of variation in birth weight is attributable to the maternal hereditary constitution and 18 per cent to the hereditary constitution of the foetus. It is generally accepted that differences in rates of early physical development are in part genetically determined (for references *see* first edition of this Handbook, Shields and Slater, 1960). From the previously mentioned work of Freedman and Keller (1963) and Freedman (1965) who studied infant twins, it appears that the same holds for the development of the early smiling response and fear reactions to strangers. Rutter *et al.* (1963) in a study of young twins and siblings concluded that primary reaction patterns such as withdrawal and activity were established early and were under some degree of genetic influence. Growth, in particular growth at adolescence, has been investigated by Tanner (1962) who has reviewed the subject in depth. As he demonstrates, sexual maturity indicated by age at menarche is influenced by genetic factors as well as by secular changes. Morphological variation in adult twins has been studied in detail by Osborne and De George (1959), while the subject of the relationship between body build (itself largely genetically determined) and personality is reviewed in this volume by Rees (Chapter 15). It presumably has a bearing on the greater similarity of MZ twins compared with DZ twins in their sporting abilities and interests (Grebe, 1955). The voices of MZ twins are similar and more alike than those of DZ twins, whether judged subjectively (Gedda *et al.*, 1955) or spectrographically (Flach *et al.*, 1968). From studies mentioned in the previous edition of this Handbook (Shields and Slater 1960) there is some evidence for genetical influence on involuntary expressive movements and motor and mechanical skills. There was a moderate genetic component in musicality as measured by the Wing test (Shuter, 1966), and Kalmus (1949, 1968) tentatively suggests the possibility of a major gene effect in tune deafness. From a content analysis of the verbal reports of their emotional experiences, Bloch (1969) infers that 'subjective experience' may be partially genetically determined.

Autonomic measures at rest or in response to mild stress have been studied in twins, among others by Eysenck (1956) and Vandenberg *et al.* (1965), and evidence found for genetic causes of variation. Lader and Wing (1966) showed MZ twins to be significantly more alike than DZ twins in the rate of habituation of the GSR, in the number of conductance fluctuations, and in pulse rate. Not only are the resting EEG records of MZ twins strikingly alike (Lennox *et al.*, 1939; Vogel, 1958), but marked similarity in evoked EEG potentials not found in DZ twins has been reported by Osborne (1970) and Young (1971), indicating genetic determinants in the response of the brain to the same simple visual or auditory stimulus.

Evidence of very specific effects of genetic differences comes from the study of response to drugs or pharmacogenetics (Porter, 1966; Evans, 1969). Such differences may well have an influence on the development and course of psychological abnormality. For instance, the severe side effects of phenelzine (Nardil), such as the reaction to eating cheese, occur only in slow inactivators of isoniazid (Evans *et al.*, 1965). It has also been claimed that the Parkinsonian side effects of chlorpromazine may depend on genetic factors (Myrianthopoulos *et al.*,

1962). Vesell and Page (1968a,b,c) have shown that the rate of elimination of certain drugs from the body is under significant genetic control. The half-life of doses of phenylbutazone and (independently) antipyrine was significantly more alike in MZ than DZ twins, as was the half-life of dicumarol. Alex-anderson et al. (1969) reached similar conclusions concerning genetic determination of concentrations of the anti-depressant nortriptyline in persons not exposed to other drugs.

Turning to abnormalities of development, there have been good family studies on stammering (Kay, 1964) and on dyslexia (Hallgren, 1950) and a family and a twin study on enuresis (Hallgren, 1957, 1960), which, together with evidence from other sources, strongly suggest that many forms of these disorders are considerably influenced by genetic factors. Once again, it must be stressed that such a claim does not deny the influence of other contributory aetiological factors. Far from denying the possibility of effective therapy, the conclusion points to the need for special methods for overcoming what may well be seen as genetically influenced learning disabilities. In so far as there is a polygenic basis for these disorders, the part played by the genes will be greater in some cases than in others.

In Japan, Abe and his colleagues in a series of papers (Abe and Shimakawa, 1966a,b,c; Abe et al., 1967; Naka et al., 1965) obtained information from grandparents about the behaviour of parents at the same age as these parents' children when the latter were examined in infant welfare clinics. Such information may, however, be particularly liable to retrospective falsification. They claim parent-child resemblance in a variety of childhood sleep disturbances, including insomnia, sleepwalking, and talking and teeth grinding, which they believe to be largely genetically determined traits, and also in other kinds of behaviour, including clinging to the mother, elective mutism, stubbornness and enuresis, which they consider may include a genetic component.

At the other end of life Kallmann and his colleagues in New York (Kallmann et al., 1951) studied twins over the age of 60 and found that even MZ twins who had led very different lives tended to be more alike than DZ twins of the same sex in longevity and in manner of ageing, as measured by adaptational assessments and psychometric tests.

We have ranged in our examples through a variety of fields, from birth weight to ageing, from the morphological to the psychological. How far some of the above medley of variables may be related to one another is a matter for investigation by multivariate analysis or other appropriate techniques. Eysenck (1967) hypothesises that, in so far as these parameters are related to personality and are dependent on the genotype, most of them are secondary to the theoretical construct of excitation-inhibition balance. On this view, virtually all the genes that influence personality do so primarily by determining the relative preponderance of excitatory or inhibitory potential in different people. On the other hand, if it is true that such diverse features of development as those referred to in this section are largely independent, a greater extent of genetic specificity for particular behaviour traits will be found than on the more general theory. It will not be unexpected that genetically identical twins—sharing genes which affect their behaviour in a variety of ways—will sometimes give the impression of being strikingly alike in total personality in a way seldom observed in genetically dissimilar twins, and for this to be so even when they have been reared apart (Shields, 1962). As regards deviations of personality the theory of multiple variegated genetic factors would predict that, given a deviation of a particular kind in one twin, the MZ co-twin will be at considerably greater risk of having the same kind of deviation than the DZ co-twin.

We now turn to look at work done on genetic aspects of the neuroses and personality disorders.

GENETIC ASPECTS OF NEUROSIS AND BEHAVIOUR ABNORMALITIES

Neurosis

If neurotic disorders represent the upper end of a dimension of neuroticism to which genetic factors make a significant contribution, one would expect the parents, sibs, and children of neurotic patients to score relatively highly in tests of neuroticism. Psychometric studies of the relatives of neurotics, such as those of Coppen et al. (1965) and Rosen-berg (1967) using the MPI, have not so far borne

this out. There are at least two possible reasons. First, much of the evidence for a genetic contribution to neuroticism comes from the contrast between moderate correlations in MZ twins and low correlations in DZ twins. Significantly high correlations between sibs or between parents and children are not therefore necessarily expected on the tests available. Secondly, intra-individual variability in test score may be especially high in neurotics. Ingham (1966) found recovered neurotics to have

Table 16.21. Extent of Neurotic Disorder in
Co-twins of Neurotics
(from Slater and Shields, 1969)

Investigator	MZ		DZ	
Slater (1953)	2/8	(25%)	8/43	(19%)
Ihda (1960)	10/20	(50%)	2/5	(40%)
Braconi (1961)	18/20	(90%)	13/30	(43%)
Tienari (1963)	12/21	(57%)	not studied	
Parker (1964c, 1965)	7/10	(70%)	4/11	(36%)
Shields and Slater (1966)	25/62	(40%)	13/84	(15%)

(By courtesy of Dr E. Slater and the British Journal of Psychiatry)

MPI scores virtually the same as a random normal sample, as did Coppen and Metcalfe (1965) in regard to recovered depressives.

There is, however, some direct evidence of an excess of neurotic relatives in the families of neurotic patients. McInnes (1937), Brown (1942), and Cohen et al. (1951) found a history of neurosis in about 15 per cent of parents and sibs of anxiety neurotics, a much higher rate than was found in the relatives of controls. There appears to be some degree of specificity as well as generality as to the type of neurosis found in relatives according to the findings of Brown (1942), Alanen (1966) and, with regard to obsessional neurosis, Lewis (1935) and Rüdin (1953). Studies of series of twins from various sources and countries support a genetic contribution to the reasons for the family resemblance in neurosis (Table 16.21). The genetic component was greatest in dysthymic neuroses such as obsessional neurosis (Ihda), anxiety states in childhood (Braconi) and neuroses with obsessional or phobic symptoms (Tienari).

In a family study of hysterics (Ljungberg, 1957) a significantly raised but absolutely low rate of hysteria was found in first-degree relatives. No other single diagnosis was found to excess among relatives, though there was an excess of other psychiatric disorders in the hysterics themselves. A twin study (Slater, 1961) based on patients with a hospital diagnosis of hysteria—usually in the sense of conversion symptoms—failed to find a single instance of the same disorder in either 12 MZ or 12 DZ co-twins, though some had other abnormalities. It was concluded that hysteria did not depend to any important extent on specific genetic factors, but was a symptom that could occur in conditions of different kinds, organic or functional, psychotic or neurotic. Arkonac and Guze (1963) defined hysteria more strictly, if less conventionally. For the Guze group a diagnosis of hysteria implies a personality disorder of early onset with recurrent symptoms in many different organ systems. The condition occurs almost exclusively in females. Hysteria was found

by Arkonac and Guze to be present in 15 per cent of the female relatives of hysterics, while the male relatives had an increased prevalence of alcoholism and perhaps sociopathy. Conversely, among the relatives of male criminals there was a raised prevalence of 'hysteria' in the females and of sociopathy and alcoholism, but not other psychiatric disorders, in the males (Guze et al., 1967).

Much of the evidence of twin and family studies in neurosis and personality disorder can be criticised as liable to bias through the investigator who assesses the history of the relative knowing the diagnosis of the patient and, in the case of twins, whether the pair is MZ or DZ. This criticism does not apply to the Maudsley twin study (Shields and Slater, 1966; Slater and Shields, 1969). It was based on consecutive admissions of all 192 adult twins diagnosed at the hospital as having a neurosis or personality disorder, 1948–58. Probands and co-twins were rediagnosed after a mean follow-up period of $7\frac{1}{2}$ years from individual summaries which did not mention diagnosis or zygosity of the twin partner. After exclusion of 46 pairs, where the proband was rediagnosed by Slater as organic or psychotic, the results shown in Table 16.22 were obtained. Anxiety neurosis and deviations of personality are in marked contrast to other neuroses, mostly mild reactive depressions in relatively normal personalities (see below, p. 575). As in the previous study of hospital diagnosed hysteria, the 'other' neuroses showed no MZ/DZ difference in overall psychiatric concordance, and where the twins were both rated as abnormal their diagnoses were

Table 16.22. Diagnostic Resemblance in
Maudsley Neurotic Twin Series
(from Slater and Shields, 1969)

	MZ	DZ
Anxiety state in proband	N = 17	N = 28
Any diagnosis in twin	47%	18%
Same diagnosis in twin	41%	4%
Other neurosis in proband	N = 12	N = 21
Any diagnosis in twin	25%	24%
Same diagnosis in twin	0%	0%
Personality disorder in proband	N = 33	N = 35
Any diagnosis in twin	55%	29%
Same diagnosis in twin	33%	6%
All probands	N = 62	N = 84
Any diagnosis in twin	47%	24%
Same diagnosis in twin	29%	4%

Probands accepted as neurotic or personality disordered on follow-up. Identity of diagnosis based on whole number of ICD classification.

(By courtesy of Dr E. Slater and the British Journal of Psychiatry)

different. Otherwise, what stands out in the study is the similarity in the form of the disorder in MZ as compared with DZ twins. The neuroses and personality disorders are not sufficiently similar in both MZ and DZ concordant pairs for them to be regarded as distinct genetic disease entities, and indeed this view has never been seriously entertained. Nevertheless, the qualitative resemblance in MZ pairs indicates some degree of genetic specificity: all the genes involved are not doing the same job. The findings support the view that the particular combination of many genetic factors in the neurotic individual influences the form of his neurosis to a greater extent than it influences whether or how severely he breaks down. Similar conclusions were reached in a study of twin schoolchildren unselected for neurosis or behaviour disorder (Shields, 1954), in which the presence of such conditions was found to be related to the nature of the home environment.

When MZ twins are alike in respect of an abnormality, it may be asked whether this could be on account of the hazards of monozygosity rather than shared genes. However, there is no excess of twins as such or of MZ twins in particular in the Maudsley Hospital clientele, and the great bulk of evidence shows that there is no excess of twins among the functional psychotics (Rosenthal, 1960; Kringlen, 1967).

The importance of genetic factors for psychopathic personality disorders is seen perhaps most clearly in the work on criminal twins reviewed below. Further support for the conclusion that genetic factors play a part in psychopathy comes from Schulsinger's (1972) recent comparison of the biological and adoptive relatives of psychopathic adoptees in Denmark.

Crime

Twin concordance rates for crime and delinquency and conclusions about the role of genetical factors that may be drawn from them vary depending upon the type of crime. The subject has been reviewed by Cowie et al. (1968); while the evidence in general must lead to stressing the importance of social and environmental factors, 'the type of crime into which [an individual] may drift, and the extent to which his life is governed by his criminal tendencies, would seem to be largely a reflection of his personality, with genetical factors lending much that is most characteristic.'

The earliest twin study on adult crime was that of Lange (1929). It was based on a sample that included a high proportion of psychopathic recidivists. Lange found that 10 out of 13 MZ co-twins had a criminal record, compared with only 2 out of 17 DZ co-twins of the same sex. The personalities and the criminal careers of the concordant MZ pairs were very similar, and Lange entitled his book *Crime as Destiny*. His conclusions proved one-sided. The studies of Stumpfl (1936) and Kranz (1936), based on more representative samples of criminals from south and north Germany respectively, showed 63 per cent concordance for crime in 49 MZ pairs and 48 per cent in 62 same-sex DZ pairs, a contrast that is not very striking. Nevertheless, Lange's findings were confirmed so far as the psychopathic criminal was concerned. Compared with DZ pairs, concordant MZ pairs were much more alike in personality and in criminal career. Both twins might have convictions for sexual offences, for fraud, or for crimes of violence. The latest study of adult criminal twins (Hauge et al., 1968) is based on all Danish twins born 1880 to 1910. Their names were matched against those on the Central Police Register. 48 out of 91 MZ twin individuals with an entry on the Register had co-twins who also had an entry, compared with 28 out of 128 DZ twin individuals. In terms of pairs, the concordance rates are 36 per cent and 12 per cent respectively, lower than in the German studies of Kranz and Stumpfl but showing a larger MZ/DZ difference. These figures include minor offences. Concordance with respect to more serious 'crime' was about twice as high as that for minor offences (Christiansen, 1968, 1970).

The situation is very different in juvenile delinquency. Rosanoff et al. (1941) found both MZ twins to be delinquent in 40 out of 41 pairs, but in same sex DZ pairs concordance was as high as 21 out of 26. The findings have been likened to those in measles and mumps. In twin boys referred to the Maudsley Children's Department on account of delinquency or aggressive behaviour disorders similar behaviour problems were found in 4 out of 5 MZ and in 7 out of 9 DZ co-twins (Shields, cited by Cowie et al. 1968). Home background and the mutual influence of the twins appear to be important in findings such as these. Concordant findings in single-born brothers (23%) were only about half those found in the DZ twin brothers (47%) of all male criminals studied by Rosanoff et al. (1941). Genetic studies often help to elucidate the importance of environmental factors.

Alcoholism

Åmark (1951) investigated the relatives of 645 alcoholic probands and found among them a considerable excess of both alcoholics and psychopaths, but not of psychotics. Bleuler (1955) confirmed these findings. Three twin studies report a closer resemblance in drinking habits in MZ than DZ twins. Kaij

(1960) made a clinical study of 214 pairs in which at least one twin appeared on the Swedish register of abusers of alcohol. There was an increasing concordance rate with increasing degrees of abuse in MZ as compared with DZ pairs. Kaij considered this observation to favour the existence of specific as well as general genetic factors in the aetiology of chronic alcoholism. Considering only those pairs where one twin was a chronic alcoholic, the other twin was also alcoholic in 71 per cent of 14 MZ pairs compared with 31 per cent of 31 DZ pairs. In an epidemiological study, also from Sweden, Jonsson and Nilsson (1968) investigated around 1,500 pairs born before 1925 by means of mailed questionnaires. They concluded that genetic factors were relevant for the consumption or non-consumption of large quantities of alcohol. In a population sample of 902 male pairs from Finland, Partanen et al. (1966) analysed the results of extensive questionnaires and interview schedules, using the methods of quantitative genetics. Their monograph contains a detailed account of the procedures and discussion of their limitations. There were significant MZ : DZ differences in whether the twins were abstainers or drinkers and, among the drinkers, in the frequency of drinking ($h^2 = 0.39$) and level of consumption ($h^2 = 0.36$) though not for lack of control. There were no significant differences in drinking habits between DZ twins and non-twin sibs.

The family and twin studies, together with the evidence of selection experiments for alcohol preference in rats and mice (Mardones et al., 1953; Rodgers and McClearn, 1962; McClearn, 1968), make it difficult to doubt that genetic differences between individuals have an influence on drinking behaviour, given the availability of alcohol. It has, of course, never been claimed that cultural milieu, occupation, and early learning experience have no influence. So far, MZ twins reared apart have not led to the identification of critical interactions between early family environment and a later history of heavy drinking. Of the five male pairs reported by Kaij (1960) and Shields (1962) four were essentially concordant for a history of above average consumption. It is clear that similar drinking histories do not depend on identical early environments. On the other hand, a foster study by Roe et al. (1945) reported that, at ages between 22 and 40, there were no alcoholics among 27 children of alcoholic parentage who had been brought up in foster homes.

Male Homosexuality

Slater (1962) found a tendency for male homosexuals, like mongols, to be born to elderly mothers, and argued that a proportion of cases might be caused by chromosome abnormalities. However, sex chromosome abnormalities have not so far been detected (Pare, 1956; Pritchard, 1962), and the late maternal age, which Abe and Moran (1969) have argued is secondary to late paternal age, is open to other, environmental, interpretations. The best evidence of a genetic contribution comes from twin studies, recently summarised by Heston and Shields (1968). The subject is difficult to investigate and most of the work has been done on psychiatric referrals or court cases that are not representative. Kallmann regarded his finding (1952) of 100 per cent concordance for overt homosexuality in 37 investigated MZ pairs and 12 per cent in 26 DZ pairs as a statistical artefact. His sample was restricted to confirmed homosexuals over the age of 30, and it may have been easier for him to make contact with those who had homosexual rather than heterosexual co-twins. Subsequently, discordance has been found even in pairs where the proband was a confirmed homosexual (Klintworth, 1962; Parker, 1964a) and in recent small series about half the MZ pairs have been discordant. Concordant pairs claim to develop their sexual inclinations independently of one another; there is no evidence that MZ twins per se are prone to homosexuality; and DZ pairs are much less frequently concordant. In the family studied in detail by Heston and Shields there were 14 sibs, including three sets of male MZ twins. In two pairs both twins were homosexual and in the third both were heterosexual. No environmental factors could be detected that differentiated the homosexual from the heterosexual sibs. All grew up in what must be regarded as a severely disruptive environment, yet most of the children were successful adults. From clinical differences between the two homosexual pairs and differences within each of them it was concluded that an aetiology based on the interaction of genetic and environmental factors was required to explain the findings.

THE DEPRESSIONS

Reactive and Endogenous

It is still a bone of contention among psychiatrists whether the neurotic (or reactive) and psychotic (or endogenous) depressions should be regarded clinically as poles of a unipolar continuum ranging from mild to severe (Kendell, 1968) or whether there is a dichotomy (Slater and Roth, 1969). Among those who favour a dichotomy there is uncertainty as to the best criteria for distinguishing between the

Table 16.23. Some Possible Relationships between Clinical Types of Depression and Genetic Factors

Clinical type:	A. Reactive	B. Endogenous (unipolar)	C. Bipolar (manic and depressive)
Frequency (relative to other types)	Common	Moderate	Rare
Inferred genetic factors			
Importance (relative to environment)	None or little	Fairly high, but some variability	High
Heterogeneity (genetic)	Some genetic overlap with B and other disorders	Some genetic overlap with C and other disorders, but with large homogeneous core	Homogeneous if mild upswings are excluded
Specificity of genes for disturbance of mood regulation	Non-specific	Specific, but manifestation influenced by personality, sex and age	Specific, less obviously influenced by background factors than B
Mode of transmission	—	Some authorities favour dominance or sex-linkage. Probably accumulation of polygenes, but possibility of some genes playing major part in predisposition	As for B, but gene or genes different from (or possibly additional to) those in B

types. McConaghy *et al.* (1967) in their Australian material were unable to replicate the results of a factor analysis by Kiloh and Garside (1963) of their Newcastle material. In a further study from Newcastle Kay *et al.* (1969a,b) extracted a bimodal factor which they identified as endogenous (retarded) *vs* neurotic (complaining) depression. On follow-up, significant differences in outcome were found between the two groups of patients.

Genetic studies support the existence of aetiological heterogeneity in the depressions but with some overlapping between inferred genotype and clinical classification. Table 16.23, which is inevitably speculative, presents one model of how the position may be construed at the present time. It may help to clarify the ensuing account.

We have already noted (p. 572) in the account given of the Maudsley twin study that there was no evidence for genetic factors in cases diagnosed there as reactive depression. Of 8 MZ probands 3 had co-twins who were classed as abnormal. All three had personality disorders. Of 16 DZ probands 4 had co-twins who suffered from a variety of psychotic and neurotic disorders, including one diagnosed as endogenous depression. There are few who would claim specific genetic factors for reactive depression. At most, genes may have some indirect influence in reactive depressions that occur in deviating personalities. Shapiro (1970) used the Danish Twin Register to study 'non-endogenous' depressions in 16 MZ and 14 DZ pairs. In so far as genetic factors operated, it was on personality structure.

Stenstedt (1966), in the latest of his three genetic studies of affective disorder in Sweden, investigated the families of 179 neurotic depressive patients, more severe cases than those diagnosed as reactive depression in the Maudsley study. The observed risk of affective disorder among their parents and sibs was 4·8 per cent, which was not appreciably higher than the risk of 3·0 per cent expected in the general population, using the same criteria. Some neurotic-depressive probands had affected relatives who were probands in Stenstedt's earlier (1952) study of manic-depressive psychosis. The former may be related genetically to endogenous depression, unlike the majority of patients diagnosed as neurotic depression in his 1966 study. Conversely, Kringlen (1967) diagnosed as neurotic depression two out of six MZ co-twins of unipolar manic-depressives.

In his investigation of 307 cases of so-called involutional melancholia, Stenstedt (1959) found higher risks for affective disorder in parents and sibs than he did in his study of neurotic depression (Table 16.24). He concluded that most cases of involutional melancholia had the same genetic

Table 16.24. Affective Disorders in Parents and Sibs (*after* Stenstedt, 1966)

Proband	Morbid risk (*per cent*)
Manic-depressive psychosis	10·2
Involutional melancholia	6·1
Neurotic depression	4·8

Table 16.25. Morbid Risks for First-degree
Relatives of Manic-Depressives:
Earlier work (to 1953)
(Derived from Zerbin-Rüdin, 1967)

	Risk (percent) for manic-depressive psychosis (including uncertain cases)		
	Investigations other than Kallmann or Luxenburger		*Investigations of Kallmann or Luxenburger*
	No. of studies	*Median risk*	*Risk*
Parents	9	10·3	23·4 (K)
Sibs	7	10·7	22·7 (K)
Children	5	10·9	24·1 (L)

aetiology as cases of typical manic-depressive psychosis, while others were attributable to a variety of different causes. As Price (1968), in his review of the genetics of depression has pointed out, the mean age of onset of illness in the relatives of the involutional cases (48·2 years) was half-way between that of the involutional probands themselves (57·7) and the endogenous depressive probands of Stenstedt's 1952 study (38·7). Further evidence that there is no major aetiological distinction between the involutional and earlier onset endogenous depressives comes from a study of Angst (1966), to which we shall refer in more detail later.

Stenstedt's (1952) study of manic-depressive psychosis was based on a representative sample of 216 probands. Findings were in good agreement with earlier work such as that of Slater (1938) on German material. As Table 16.25 shows, the median risks for parents, sibs and children reported in the earlier studies were very similar. In general they were around 10 per cent or 15 per cent if a different method of correcting for age was used. Kallmann and Luxenburger reported higher rates, but once again these were similar in the three kinds of first-degree relative. At that time, the similarity suggested dominant inheritance, with a reduced manifestation rate. According to recent trends in genetic theory it is equally compatible with polygenic inheritance. The latter hypothesis is probably the more plausible one for 'affective disorder' as it is broadly diagnosed

in this country today.* The condition is usually taken to cover a much wider spectrum of possibly related disorders, not all of them 'psychotic', than the older manic-depressive psychosis. It is unlikely that one gene underlies them all (Slater and Cowie, 1971).

A number of factors have been reported as decreasing or increasing the morbidity risk for the sib of an endogenous depressive. Late age at onset, as we have seen, is associated with a lower risk in some studies (Hopkinson, 1964; Hopkinson and Ley, 1969; Kay, 1959, among others), though not by Schulz (1951) or Stenstedt if one discounts his involutional probands. The observation, if accepted as true, is consistent with polygenic inheritance if one assumes that later onset implies carrying fewer of the predisposing genes. Other possibilities are (*a*) that many later onset cases have a different and less genetic kind of aetiology (heterogeneity), (*b*) that information about the relatives—in particular about the parents—of the late onset cases is incomplete, and (*c*) that insufficient allowance has been made for correlation of relatives in age of onset, so that many of the older but hitherto unaffected relatives of late onset cases would still be at risk. In Stenstedt's (1952) study factors in the probands associated with a *lower* risk for affective disorder in relatives included favourable childhood conditions, psychogenic precipitating factors, a deviant premorbid personality and atypical, schizophrenic-like features in the illness. In most studies, both earlier and later, there is a considerably *increased* risk for a sib if a parent is affected (Rüdin, 1923; Luxenburger, 1942; Winokur and Clayton, 1967). The data of Winokur and Clayton are shown in Table 16.26. Though the figure of 43 per cent when both parents are affected is based on very few cases, it is in agreement with the more extensive data of Elsässer (1952) on the children of 20 pairs of dual manic-depressive matings, in

* According to Slater and Roth (1969) the Registrar General's figures for 1960 show the expectation of admission to a mental hospital in the UK with a diagnosis of manic-depressive illness during a life-span of 75 years to be 2·4 per cent for males and 3·9 per cent for females. Earlier estimates of life-time expectancy had been of the order of 0·4 per cent (Slater, 1938, on German material) or 1·6 per cent (Fremming, 1951, on Danish material).

Table 16.26. Risks for Affective Disorder in Sibs, According to Affective Disorder in Parents
(*from* Winokur and Clayton, 1967)

	No. of probands	*Total No. of sibs (corrected)*	*No. of sibs affected*	*Morbid risk*
Neither parent affected	329	522	64	12 ± 1·4%
One parent affected	91	128	33	26 ± 3%
Both parents affected	6	7	3	43 ± 19%

(*By courtesy of* Dr G. Winokur, Dr Paula Clayton, and the Plenum Publishing Corporation) which the risk for the offspring was 44 per cent. A rise in the risk when one parent is affected supports polygenic rather than monogenic theory, at least when it is of such a degree as that reported by Winokur. It might be argued that the excess is due to environmental factors, but against this is the lack of any appreciable increase in neurosis and behaviour disorder.

Although attacks of 'endogenous' depression are frequently precipitated by physical or psychological stresses, the relevance of genetic factors has rarely been questioned. Twin studies consistently report higher concordance in MZ than DZ pairs. Kallmann (1950) reported much higher rates than other investigators: 22 out of 23 MZ pairs were concordant. Even when his findings are excluded, the pooled results of the seven remaining series* show there to be concordance for manic-depressive psychosis in 58 per cent of 80 MZ pairs and 23 per cent of 119 same-sexed DZ pairs. The DZ rate is reduced to 15 per cent if da Fonseca's (1959) series is omitted. His figure of 15 out of 39 is considerably higher than those of other investigators on account of the wider concept of affective disorder employed. The Danish and Norwegian studies (Harvald and Hauge, 1965; Kringlen, 1967), based on all twins born in a certain period, give results comparable with those of the other hospital-based studies. So far, 12 pairs of MZ twins reared apart have been reported in the literature where one or both has had some form of affective disorder. These have been summarized by Price (1968) who regards 8 as concordant. They are mostly rather mild illnesses.

Unipolar and Bipolar

Until recently, the majority view was that cases of endogenous affective psychosis with mania did not differ genetically from those with depression only. The school of Leonhard was an exception in holding that Kraepelinian manic-depressive insanity should be broken up into several separate entities. Leonhard (1934) considered that unipolar psychoses with only mania or only depression differed genetically from cycloid or bipolar psychoses with both manic and depressive phases. In 1966, independent studies by Angst in Switzerland and Perris in Sweden made the hypothesis of major heterogeneity an extremely likely one, at least so far as unipolar depression and bipolar psychosis is concerned. The position of recurrent mania without depression is unclear, since it is relatively rare.

Angst (1966) studied the families of all endogenous

* Luxenburger (1930), Rosanoff *et al.* (1935), Kallmann (1950), Slater (1953), da Fonseca (1959), Harvald and Hauge (1965), Kringlen (1967).

Table 16.27. Bipolar and Unipolar Affective Illness in Proband and Relative (*after* Perris, 1966)

Affective illness shown in relative as	Numbers of relatives of 138 bipolar and 139 unipolar probands	
	Bipolar	Unipolar
Bipolar psychosis	58	2
Unipolar psychosis	3	44
Not classifiable	14	16
Suicide	32	24

depressives admitted to a hospital over a 5-year period. 46 probands had mania as well as depression, 105 were unipolar depressions with onset before 50 in men or before the menopause in women, 103 were later onset 'involutional' depressives, and there were 73 mixed psychoses (schizo-affective). From the information on the families it was concluded that the last group did not belong with any of the others and was itself heterogeneous. For example, 7 per cent of the sibs were schizophrenic. The involutionals and unipolar depressives belonged together in that there was an excess of both types of depression in families of each. This group differed from the bipolar psychoses. Among 28 affected relatives of bipolar probands there were 7 who had manic phases, while among 44 affected relatives of unipolar probands there were only 3 with manic phases.

Perris (1966) compared the families of bipolar with those of unipolar depressives, the latter defined as having had at least three attacks without mania. As shown in Table 16.27 he found a remarkable tendency for the two types of disorder to breed true, though there were a number of relatives who could not be classified as unipolar or bipolar on his criteria. In a joint paper published in 1968 Angst and Perris compared their findings (Table 16.28). Both found the risk for affective disorder to be higher in the families of bipolar psychotics, and the difference is significant. They both found that male and female relatives were equally frequently affected in the bipolar families, while in the unipolar families female relatives were more often affected than male. Angst and Perris agreed that manic phases were rarely observed among the relatives of unipolar depressives but only Angst found many relatives of bipolars who had depression only.

Support for genetic heterogeneity comes from Zerbin-Rüdin's (1969) analysis of the twin data, from studies by Leonhard *et al.* (1962) and von Trostorff (1968), and in America from the work of Winokur and Clayton (1967). The latter compared cases with and without a family history of affective psychosis and found that the former group of cases

Table 16.28.   Risks for Affective Disorder in Parents and Sibs of Bipolar and Unipolar Cases
(*after* Angst and Perris, 1968)

Proband	No. of relatives (corrected)	Specific risks (%) for:			Total risk (%)
		Bipolar or mania	Recurrent depression	Other depressive psychoses or suicide*	
Bipolar (mania and depression)					
Angst	160	3·7	11·2	3·1	18·1
Perris	509	10·3	0·58	8·6	20·0
Unipolar (recurrent depression)					
Angst	341	0·29	9·1	2·3	11·7
Perris	571	0·35	7·4	6·8	14·6

* Or suicide only (Angst)

presented with mania significantly more often than the latter. Slater (1953) had already noted that pairs of relatives where both had affective disorder tended to resemble one another in whether they had manic phases or not. Stenstedt's (1952) data, however, offer no support.

If the hypothesis of two distinct genetic factors in endogenous depression is upheld, genetically bipolar depressives will exist who have only had depressive phases (which are commoner than manic phases) and so will be unidentifiable as genetically bipolar. Clinical unipolar cases will therefore to some extent be a heterogeneous group genetically. Clinical bipolar cases will be more homogeneous.

It may be asked whether depression with mania is transmitted differently from unipolar depressive psychosis. The former is comparatively rare. The upper limit of the lifetime risk in the general population is probably about 0·4 per cent, at one time the best estimate for the risk of developing typical manic-depressive psychosis (Slater, 1938). Since the risk for first degree relatives is around 20 per cent, a necessary dominant gene is a possibility. According to Edwards' (1960) principle a rate of 20 per cent would be too high for additive polygenic inheritance simulating Mendelism, since it is much higher than the square root of the population risk (6·25%). But if a major dominant gene is involved, one would expect other affected cases to occur predominantly on one side of the family (Slater, 1966), and the findings Perris (1971) and Slater *et al.* (1971) report are more consistent with polygenic inheritance according to this line of argument. If unipolar and bipolar depressions are each polygenic, the question arises to what extent the polygenic systems have genes in common. It could be that additional genes or alternative alleles are involved in the bipolar cases.

Since the time of Rosanoff *et al.* (1935) the possibility of a dominant sex-linked gene in manic-depressive illness has been put forward to account for the higher incidence of the condition in females, who have two X chromosomes, than in males who have only one. The theory was rejected for manic-depressive psychosis regarded as a unit (Slater, 1938). However, Perris (1968) has now raised the possibility of sex-linkage for unipolar but not bipolar depression, while Winokur and associates (Reich *et al.*, 1969) recently proposed it for bipolar psychosis but not unipolar. While the Winokur data are compatible with their hypothesis, data from other centres are not. There are too many reports of pairs of affected fathers and sons to be compatible with sex-linkage. A more likely possibility is the existence of a greater liability of the female to affective disturbance, without the implication of a specific genetic polymorphism on the X chromosome. Yet another source of heterogeneity may be the existence of a kind of depression to which only females are liable, possibly associated with their hormonal constitution, and this is a hypothesis that could be tested.

Experimental psychology has as yet been little used to elucidate the genetic problems of the depressions. For instance, can the premorbid personality of a sib predict his risk of falling ill? It will be interesting to know more accurately than at present how the previous personalities or psychophysiological status of depressive patients differ from the normal and from those of patients with other psychiatric disorders, and what differences there are between neurotic, unipolar and bipolar depressives in this respect. To assess premorbid personality Perris (1966) used a shorter version of the Marke-Nyman questionnaire (cf. Coppen, 1966) given to patients who were in a state of remission, while Angst relied on descriptions by patients and relatives. They agreed in finding bipolars to be relatively more often syntonic and cycloid and unipolars more asthenic (Angst and Perris, 1968). The general problem of the premorbid personality of depressives is discussed by Metcalfe (1968).

Suicide

Though there is an increased risk of suicide in depressive illness, the specific act of suicide is probably incidental. The risk for suicide is no higher for relatives of depressives who have taken their lives than for relatives of depressives who have not (d'Elia and Perris, 1969). At one time Kallmann and his colleagues (1947) thought that suicide in both members of a pair of twins, suicide pacts excluded, was so rare that the suicide of one might in some way protect the other from taking his life. They later (1949) considered that concordance occurred about as frequently as might be expected by chance. Recent figures based on death certificates of Danish twins (Hauge *et al.*, 1968) show concordance for suicide in 4 out of 19 MZ cases and in none out of 58 DZ cases, but it is not stated whether the concordant pairs were the result of suicide pacts.

SCHIZOPHRENIA

Twin and family studies on schizophrenia have been much more extensive than those on manic-depressive psychosis. With the exception of one twin study (Tienari, 1963), the results of which were difficult to account for on any theory, all of them are consistent with genetic theories. Yet the relevance of genetic factors in schizophrenia has been widely questioned, particularly in recent years. The usual alternative explanation is that it is a learned disorder of thought or behaviour to be accounted for in terms of the cultural or family environment.

There are five sources of evidence that lead to the conclusion that genetic factors cannot be disregarded.

1. No environmental causes have been found that will predictably produce schizophrenia in persons unrelated to a schizophrenic. In cases of so-called induced insanity or *folie à deux* there is, according to Scharfetter (1968), a high morbidity of schizophrenia among the relatives of the induced subjects, even when there is no consanguinity with the inducer.
2. Schizophrenia is present in all countries and populations that have been studied. It can occur with a similar frequency in countries of different culture.
3. In modern urban communities, the high prevalence of persons of Social Class V among schizophrenic admissions is best accounted for by the downward drift of the patient rather than by the environment in which he was reared (Goldberg and Morrison, 1963). On the other hand, there is an increasing risk of schizophrenia with an increasingly close blood relationship to a schizophrenic.
4. The familial incidence is not entirely due to environmental differences between families or to gross differences within families such as sex or place in sibship. There is a much higher incidence of schizophrenia in MZ co-twins of schizophrenics than in DZ co-twins of the same sex.
5. The findings in twins are not due merely to features of the within-family environment that are more similar for MZ than DZ twins. Studies of twins reared apart and adoption and fostering studies show a raised incidence of schizophrenia even when the relative of the schizophrenic is brought up in a different home.

That genetic factors are not sufficient is clear from the fact that concordance in MZ pairs is far from complete.

As recently as 1967 Lewis stated that 'the genetic study of schizophrenia has been virtually at a standstill'. Certainly there has been no major break-through, universally accepted as establishing the nature of the genetic factors involved. No simply inherited biochemical abnormality, directly observable in blood or urine, has been detected. It might even be considered that the genetic study of schizophrenia had taken several steps backwards in that genetic factors are minimised and their specificity denied by some recent workers. It could be claimed that we had retreated to the era of the general neuropathic taint. What cannot be denied is that there has been a spate of criticism, theoretical exposition, further twin studies, and new and valuable foster-home studies. Developments since the last edition of the Handbook have been so extensive that we can only summarise here points made more fully elsewhere.*

---

* Three volumes dealing with genetic aspects of schizophrenia may be specially mentioned. *The Genain Quadruplets* by Rosenthal and collaborators (1963) includes a useful discussion of what Rosenthal calls monogenic-biochemical, diathesis-stress and life-experience theories of schizophrenia, besides giving the detailed results of the many studies made on these MZ quadruplets. They included objective psychological tests. All four sisters had schizophrenic illnesses ranging from mild to severe. *The Transmission of Schizophrenia* (edited by Rosenthal and Kety, 1968) includes general papers on the genetic aspects by Slater and Shields, and accounts by the original investigators of the recent twin and adoption studies. There are also contributions on environmental aspects of transmission. Current genetic theories are discussed in the volume edited by Kaplan (in press) and by Gottesman and Shields (in press), Rosenthal (1970), and Slater and Cowie (1971).

Table 16.29.   Frequency of Schizophrenia in the General Population and in the
Relatives of Schizophrenics: Pooled Data*
(*after* Shields and Slater, 1967)

No. of investigations	No. of countries	Relationship to schizophrenic	No. of relatives investigated (corrected)	Morbid risk for schizophrenia (per cent)
19	6	Unrelated (gen. popn.)	330,752	0·86
14	8	Parents	6,622	5·07
12	7	Sibs	8,484·5	8·53
6	2	Children	1,226·5	12·31
4	4	Uncles and aunts	3,376	2·01
5	4	Nephews and nieces	2,315	2·24

* Based on Zerbin-Rüdin (1967); correction for age usually by shorter Weinberg method, risk period 15–39; only cases of definite schizophrenia counted.

Genetic Family Studies

Table 16.29 gives a picture of the findings of the earlier work on the familial incidence of the same disorder. Ideally data from different studies should not be pooled in this way. The schizophrenia empirical risks for sibs reported in Zerbin-Rüdin's (1967) review range from 3·3 per cent ± 0·07 in a study based on 200 families (Smith, 1936) to 14·3 per cent ± 0·09 in a study based on 691 families (Kallmann, 1946). Much of the variation can be accounted for by methodological or diagnostic procedures.

Probably of greater importance is the observation that the risk for the sib of a schizophrenic varies according to the presence of schizophrenia in a parent and the nature of schizophrenia in the proband. The pooled data on the risk for a sib when one parent is affected and the risk for the children of two schizophrenic parents is shown in Table 16.30. The rise to around 40 per cent when both parents are schizophrenic is not accounted for by the environment. When one parent is schizophrenic and the other is psychopathic—arguably a worse environment—the risk is only 15 per cent.

Table 16.30.   Schizophrenia Risks for Relatives
According to Schizophrenia in Parents
(*after* Slater and Cowie, 1971)

Relationship	Total relatives	Schizophrenic Number (a)	(b)	Per cent (a)	(b)
Sibs (neither parent schizophrenic)	7,535	621	731	8·2	9·7
Sibs (one parent schizophrenic)	675	93	116	13·8	17·2
Children (both parents schizophrenic)	134	49	62	36·6	46·3

(a) diagnostically certain cases only; (b) also including probable schizophrenics.

Both Kallmann (1938) and Hallgren and Sjögren (1959) found higher schizophrenia risks for the sibs of nuclear (hebephrenic and catatonic) than peripheral (paranoid, simple or atycpial) cases. Still lower schizophrenia risks are generally found if one starts with conditions such as late onset functional paranoid psychoses, whose relationship to schizophrenia is more problematic (*see* Shields, 1968).

It might be asked whether there is an excess of conditions other than schizophrenia among the close relatives of schizophrenics. One of the lessons of the earlier work was that the two major psychoses, schizophrenic and manic-depressive, were genetically independent. Except for a slight excess of schizophrenia in the children of what may have been somewhat atypical manic-depressives, it was claimed that there was no excess of one condition in the families of the other, at least when the investigator started with typical cases. When total samples of psychiatric patients were studied genetically, as by Slater (1953) and Ødegaard (1963), and not just 'pure' cases, considerable overlapping of the two types of clinical disorder was found. According to Tsuang (1967), the similarity of psychotic diagnosis within families is not close enough to give convincing support to a theory of two major genes, each associated with a distinct phenotype. On the other hand, the family resemblance is too close to support a theory of a single genetically undifferentiated *Einheitspsychose*.

It is agreed by all who have studied the families of schizophrenics that there is an excess of personality disorder as well as of psychosis among the relatives, who are frequently termed schizoid or 'borderline'. Understandably, there is considerable disagreement about the extent of these disorders, their precise nature, and their genetic relationship with schizophrenia. This is a perennial problem on which the methods of experimental psychology may one day shed some light. So far as concerns the premorbid

Table 16.31.   The Earlier Schizophrenic Twin Series
(after Gottesman and Shields, 1966b)

Investigator	Date	MZ pairs			SS DZ pairs		
		N	C	%	N	C	%
Luxenburger (Germany)	1928	19	11	58	13	0	0
Rosanoff et al. (USA)	1934	41	25	61	53	7	13
Essen-Möller (Sweden)	1941	11	7	64	27	4	15
Kallmann (USA)	1946	174	120	69	296	34	11
Slater (UK)	1953	37	24	65	58	8	14
Inouye (Japan)	1961	55	33	60	11	2	18

N = number of pairs;
C = number concordant for schizophrenia;
% = percentage concordant.

personality characteristics that distinguish schizophrenics from their healthy sibs or twins, all twin investigators from Slater (1953) onwards (e.g. Tienari, 1963, 1966), and Price (1969) who studied sibs, agree in finding these to be very similar to the characteristics that distinguish depressives and neurotics from their healthy twins or sibs. The future patient tends to be described in terms such as more anxious, sensitive, submissive, and setting himself higher standards; in fact, he is generally more dysthymic. The tendency may well be otherwise with psychopaths and (possibly) bipolar psychotics and their sibs.

Reverting to Table 16.29, it is worth mentioning that the risk of a member of the general population of the UK being admitted to a mental hospital for schizophrenia, provided he lives long enough, is about 1·2 per cent (Slater and Roth, 1969). This may be on account of a wider use of the diagnosis than in the older studies from which the figure of 0·86 per cent was obtained. (In the USA schizophrenia is very much more readily diagnosed. The risk of an individual being diagnosed schizophrenic, as out-patient or in-patient, has been calculated by Yolles and Kramer, 1969, as lying between 2 and 6 per cent.) The general population risk shown in the table is probably appropriate for the studies summarised there, which are mostly from Europe. The lower risk for parents than for sibs can be related to the fact that being sufficiently intact to marry and produce a family and falling ill with schizophrenia are to some extent antagonistic. It is questionable whether the difference between sibs and children is genuine. A higher proportion of the children studied than the sibs comes from studies by Kallmann, who generally reported higher rates than other investigators. The figures in the table cannot be accounted for by any Mendelian mode of inheritance without making additional assumptions. Current theories as to the likely mode of transmission are mentioned below.

Twin Studies

The results of the earlier twin studies are shown in Table 16.31. Pairs where the second twin's schizophrenia was doubtful or borderline have been counted as concordant. Only in Essen-Möller's series (see his 1970 follow-up) do such uncertain cases account for the majority of the concordant pairs. The findings in the recent twin studies are given in Table 16.32 with the range of concordance rates for schizophrenia or borderline conditions given by the investigators themselves. In Tables 16.31 and 16.32 no pair has been entered twice and no correction has been made for age.

The earlier concordance rates have been criticised as being spuriously high. The most trenchant criticisms were those of Rosenthal (1959, 1960, 1961, 1962a,b) who, nevertheless, concluded that at that time the twin evidence was the best we had for the existence of genetic factors in schizophrenia and should not be rejected because it contained errors. The later work has shown some of the criticisms to be justified. Very great efforts were made by the early investigators themselves to avoid the bias of preferential notification of concordant pairs. Luxenburger and Essen-Möller went to the lengths of

Table 16.32.   Recent Schizophrenic Twin Series[a]

Investigation	MZ pairs	Per cent concordant	DZ pairs	Per cent concordant
Tienari (Finland)[b]	16	6–36	20	5–14
Kringlen (Norway)	55	25–38	90	4–10
Fischer et al. (Denmark)	21	24–48	41	10–19
Gottesman and Shields (UK)	24	40–50	33	9–10
Pollin et al. (USA)[b]	80	14–35	146	4–10

[a] Range of uncorrected pairwise concordance rates reported by investigators (various criteria, including borderline features, when diagnosed).
[b] Males only.

checking the birth records of thousands of schizo-phrenics in order not to miss any that were twins. Such a procedure, however, was not open to Rosanoff, Kallmann, or Slater who, so it was argued, may therefore have missed discordant pairs. Perhaps more justified as an explanation of the higher rates found in the earlier studies is that they were to a large extent based on severe cases of schizophrenia from the resident population of long-stay mental hospitals. Most studies, early and late, show there to be an association between severity of schizophrenia in the proband and the likelihood of schizophrenia in the co-twin. The criticism that the earlier studies gave too high rates because they contained an excess of female pairs is perhaps less to the point. The later studies do not find the higher concordance rates in female pairs that were reported in the Rosanoff *et al.* and Slater samples. The criticism, reasonable at the time it was made, that Kallmann may have been more likely to diagnose a co-twin as schizophrenic if he knew the pair was MZ than if it was DZ, or to diagnose the pair as MZ if he knew both twins to be schizophrenic, now appears to be unjustified in the light of later information available about the hospitalization and hospital diagnoses of the co-twins (Shields *et al.*, 1967). Kallmann's reported concordance rate of 86 per cent for MZ pairs, however, was obtained by a method of correcting for age which, as Slater (1953) pointed out, was unrealistic for such pairs.

When factors such as the severity of the probands in the earlier series are taken into account, Gottes-man and Shields (1966b) argued that all the twin studies could be viewed as replications of the same experiment. Even among those who were previously most critical of the genetic twin studies this point of view is now more generally appreciated (Stabenau, 1968).

The recent population-based twin studies by Kringlen (1967) and Fischer *et al.* (1969) were carried out by matching names on a register of all twins born during specified years in Norway or Denmark respectively with the names on a national psychosis register. This was followed by personal investigation which was very detailed in Kringlen's study. Tienari made extensive personal investigations of all male twins born in Finland between 1909 and 1920. There is no psychosis register in Finland. It is difficult to be certain why he found such low rates of concordance for schizophrenia in MZ twins. In his first report (1963) none of the 16 MZ co-twins was schizophrenic though about 10 per cent of DZ pairs were. Various possibilities suggested by Shields (1965) included the loss of concordant pairs through mortality. By the time of Tienari's later report (1968) one pair had become concordant.

When two probands whose 'schizophrenia' may have been attributable to organic brain damage were omitted and four 'possible borderline' co-twins counted as concordant, a rate of 5 out of 14 (36%) was obtained. The co-twins counted as concordant in the higher of the rates reported by Gottesman and Shields (1966a, and in press) and Fischer *et al.* were all psychotic. Concordance for psychosis in Kringlen's series was 31 per cent.

The Gottesman and Shields study was based on consecutive admissions to the Maudsley Hospital out-patient department and short-stay in-patient facilities. The twinship of all patients was enquired about systematically at the time of admission. Diagnosis was based on the consensus of diagnostic opinions given blind by an international panel of six experts.

Unlike some of the earlier studies, the recent studies allow concordance to be reported as a casewise as opposed to a pairwise rate, corrected (downwards!) for mode of ascertainment by the proband method. Such proband-based casewise rates (Allen *et al.*, 1967) enable an estimate to be made of the risk for the co-twin of independently ascertained schizophrenics in such a way that it may be compared with the corresponding risk for other relatives or for a person from the general population. The writer estimates that the rate for functional schizophreniform psychosis for the co-twin of a proband in the four studies just men-tioned, taken together and using comparable diag-nostic criteria, is 47 per cent for MZ co-twins and 17 per cent for DZ co-twins. The corresponding rate for schizophrenia or schizophreniform psychosis in the general population is probably nearer 1 than 2 per cent.

The American study by Pollin *et al.* (1969) referred to in Table 16.32 should be treated separately. It was based on all twins known to the US Veterans Administration during the period spanning the Second World War and the Korean war where *both* twins had been passed as fit to serve in the armed forces. It was therefore a sample selected for health. There were nearly 16,000 such pairs. No personal investigation has been done and the diagnoses are those available on the VA files. It may be expected that they include as schizophrenic many cases that in Europe might be regarded as personality disorders or acute neurotic reactions. Prevalence of 'schizophrenia' in Veteran twins was as high as 1·14 per cent, though this is not higher than prevalence in US control populations (cf. Deming, 1968). Perhaps for this reason, lower concordance rates are to be expected. Nevertheless, there are many advantages in a total twin population of this kind. It can be shown, for example, that the

MZ co-twin of a VA-diagnosed schizophrenic is 25 times more likely to be so diagnosed than a Veteran twin taken at random, and the DZ co-twin 6·5 times as likely. The higher of the rates shown in Table 16.32 includes hospitalised psychiatric illness of any kind (Hoffer and Pollin, 1970). Despite the low concordance rate, schizophrenia was recognised by the authors as likely to be more genetically determined than any of the 11 other psychiatric or non-psychiatric diagnoses they investigated. In a climate of opinion that is sceptical of conclusions implicating genetics, such a view may seem surprising. Perhaps the recent foster-home studies are having the effect of justifying the earlier interpretations of twin studies.

Adoption and Fostering Studies

All genetic theories allow for interaction with the environment. A very plausible hypothesis is that the most important environmental factors for the development of schizophrenia in persons with the genetic predisposition are those provided by the family of a known schizophrenic. Such a theory would predict a significantly lower rate of schizophrenia in the relatives of schizophrenics when they are not reared in the same environment as the schizophrenics than when they are.

The present tally of MZ twins reared apart where one or both are schizophrenic is 17 pairs*; 11 were concordant. All but one were found in the course of other twin studies and were not reported in the literature simply because they were concordant. Half the pairs come from Japan (Mitsuda, 1967, p. 8, Table 4). These data seriously undermine the view that identification with a sick sib or subtle factors in the shared common environment are the cause of the higher concordance in MZ than DZ pairs.

Three good recent studies of genetic-environmental interaction in schizophrenia using adopted or fostered children may be specially mentioned. All three support the hypothesis that the raised incidence of schizophrenia in the families of schizophrenics is to be accounted for by shared genes and not by having been reared by a mentally ill parent. There was no support for the particular interaction effect suggested.

The essentials of Heston's (1966) study are shown in Table 16.33. He followed up children born in Oregon State Mental Hospitals to chronic schizophrenic mothers and separated from them and the

*These are the 16 pairs listed by Slater (1968) with the addition of a further pair of twins reported by Kringlen (1967) who were separated at 3 months and became concordant for schizophreniform psychosis.

Table 16.33. Psychiatric Disorders in Foster-home-reared Children (*after* Heston, 1966)

	Mother schizophrenic	Controls
Number studied	47	50
Mean age	35·8	36·3
Schizophrenia	5	—
Mental deficiency, IQ < 70	4	—
Sociopathic personality	9	2
Neurotic personality disorder	13	7

mothers' families at birth. They were brought up in a variety of adoptive homes and institutions and, as adults, were compared with a control group of non-psychotic parentage matched for type of upbringing. Schizophrenia was found only in the offspring of schizophrenics and to an extent similar to that reported for the children of schizophrenics in general. There was also an excess of psychiatric abnormalities of other kinds among the children of schizophrenics.

The other two studies made use of registers available in Denmark of adoptions, of mentally ill persons, and of the changes of address of the populace. The work was a joint Danish and US (National Institute of Mental Health) project. Extreme precautions were taken to avoid the hazards of contaminated diagnosis. The study reported by Rosenthal et al. (1968), like that of Heston, compared the children of psychotics placed for non-familial adoption with the children of non-psychotic parents so placed. At a mean age of 31, 8 (or 21%) of the 39 children of psychotics, compared with only 1 (or 2%) of 47 controls, were blindly diagnosed as schizophrenia or borderline schizophrenia. The provisional results are shown in more detail in Table 16.34.* It may be noted that diagnoses of schizophrenia without reservation were made only in children of chronic or '? chronic' schizophrenics. The addition of '? borderline' and schizoid and paranoid diagnoses did not help to discriminate between the groups. Though there are differences in the findings of the Copenhagen and Oregon studies, the crude rate of schizophrenia in the index adoptees, 11 per cent, is the same in both.

Kety et al. (1968) used the Danish adoption register in a different way. They identified adoptees who had become schizophrenic and then examined the psychiatric records of their adoptive and biological relatives. A matched control group of normal adoptees was also selected and their adoptive and biological relatives studied. The results are given in

*Later findings are reported in Rosenthal (1971).

Table 16.34.   Diagnosis of Adoptees by Diagnosis of Biological Parent
(Data of Rosenthal *et al.*, 1968)

| Diagnosis of offspring | 39 Index Cases | | | | 47 Controls | |
| | One parent chronic schizophrenia or ?chronic schizophrenia | | One parent other diagnosis* | | Both parents normal | |
	Number diagnosed	Cumulative total	Number diagnosed	Cumulative total	Number diagnosed	Cumulative total
Schizophrenia	3	3 (11%)	—	— (0%)	—	— (0%)
Borderline schizophrenia	3	6 (22%)	2	2 (17%)	1	1 (2%)
?Borderline schizophrenia	2	8 (29%)	—	2 (17%)	2	3 (6%)
Schizoid or paranoid tendencies	1	9 (33%)	2	4 (33%)	4	7 (15%)
None of above	18	27	8	12	40	47
Total offspring so far diagnosed	27	(100%)	12	(100%)	47	(100%)

* Acute schizophrenia (5), borderline schizophrenia (2) and manic-depressive or ?manic-depressive (5)

Table 16.35. The greatest amount of abnormality was found among the biological relatives of the schizophrenic adoptees. 13 out of 150 relatives (8·7%) had what were termed schizophrenia spectrum disorders as defined in the table. Of these, 7 were 'definite' schizophrenics. A surprisingly high proportion was accounted for by half-sibs with borderline schizophrenia. It can also be seen from the table that the biological parents of schizophrenics had an excess of personality disorders which the authors tentatively call 'extended spectrum'. When analysis was restricted to adoptees who had been separated from their biological parents in the first month of life, the difference between the groups

actually increased in significance. The authors concluded that their findings supported the importance of genetic factors in the transmission of schizophrenia. There was no evidence that the presence of schizophrenia or related disorder in the rearing family was a relevant stress influencing the future development of schizophrenia.

Studies by Karlsson (1966), Higgins (1966), Wender *et al.* (1968) and Fischer (1971) make similar points in different ways. Among other strategies currently employed by the NIH Group, one compares kibbutz and family reared children of schizophrenics in Israel. Another endeavours to complete the cross-fostering design used in animal genetics by

Table 16.35.   Psychiatric Abnormalities in Biological and Adoptive Relatives
(Data of Kety *et al.*, 1968)

| | Biological Relatives | | | | Adoptive Relatives | | | |
	Parents	Sibs	Half-sibs	Total	Parents	Sibs	Half-sibs	Total
Index Group: Relatives of 33 Schizophrenic Adoptees								
Schizophrenia spectrum disorders[a]	3	1	9	**13**	2	0	0	**2**
Extended spectrum disorders[b]	9	0	3	12	2	1	0	3
Other psychiatric diagnoses	3	0	2	5	6	1	0	7
No psychiatric diagnosis	48	1	71	120	53	6	3	62
Total relatives identified	63	2	85	**150**	63	8	3	**74**
Control Group: Relatives of 33 Non-schizophrenic Adoptees								
Schizophrenia spectrum disorders[a]	2	1	0	**3**	0	3	0	**3**
Extended spectrum disorders[b]	2	0	2	4	3	0	0	3
Other psychiatric diagnoses	6	1	3	10	2	0	0	2
No psychiatric diagnosis	53	3	83	139	58	14	0	75
Total relatives identified	63	5	88	**156**	63	17	0	**83**

[a] Schizophrenia (chronic, acute or borderline), certain or uncertain; inadequate personality.
[b] Character disorders, psychopathy (including imprisonment and delinquency); suicide; failure to reach consensus diagnosis, 2 out of 4 judges favouring certain schizophrenia.

studying children of normal parentage who have been adopted by schizophrenics.

Is the Concept of Schizophrenia Too Narrow?

The fostering studies revealed the widespread presence of disorders other than schizophrenia in the families of schizophrenics. This has focused attention on the possibility that a wider phenotype than schizophrenic psychosis would be a better starting point for genetic analysis. Heston (1970), for instance, has suggested the concept of 'schizoid disease'. This would include not only schizophrenia but also other conditions such as those that used to be called schizoid psychopathy, those that are currently called 'borderline' in contemporary US psychiatry, and perhaps others. He believes it is worth testing the hypothesis that all these conditions in the population can be accounted for by the theory of a highly penetrant dominant gene. The somewhat similar concept of schizophrenia spectrum disorder is open to the interpretation that what is inherited is an undifferentiated predisposition to 'spectrum disorder'. Whether this manifests itself as schizophrenia or in some less malignant way would depend on the environment. It is, of course, fully realised that it is currently difficult to decide what should be included in categories such as schizoid disease and spectrum disorder. While many interesting possibilities are open to investigation (see below for discussion of a psychometric approach), it seems likely that, as the concept of schizophrenia is widened, increasing aetiological heterogeneity is introduced (Shields, 1971). There may be an excess of suicides and 'inadequate personalities' among the relatives of schizophrenics, while not all suicides and 'inadequate personalities' have inherited the hard core 'spectrum' diathesis. Studies starting with psychopaths and neurotics have not usually found an excess of schizophrenia in their families.

Mode of Genetic Transmission

Four main types of theory are put forward by those who work on the subject, as models for explaining what we know or for generating fresh hypotheses.

1. Genetic factors, presumably polygenic in nature, are of minor importance. They relate to mental illness in general and not to schizophrenia in particular. Attention should therefore be paid to social factors, not to genetic ones. This opinion, which is close to Kringlen's (1967), is favoured by many psychodynamic psychiatrists (e.g. Alanen, 1966). It derives from the comparatively low concordance in MZ twins and the presence of other disorders such as neurosis in co-twins and other family members. In the writer's opinion it does not allow sufficient weight to the similarity in the nature of the psychosis in concordant twins across the whole field of psychiatric abnormality; nor does it give enough weight to the fact that schizophrenia is a relatively rare condition while neurosis is common.

Bleuler (1963) holds that there are no specific genetic factors in schizophrenia. He supposes that the genetic elements involved in the causation of the disorder consist of the disharmonious interaction of genes that are in themselves not morbid, rather than the consequence of too many genes of one kind. However, he believes genetic factors to be of considerable importance in schizophrenia, and his theory is probably nearer to those 'harder,' more specific polygenic theories discussed in para 4 below than they are to the type of theory we have just mentioned.

2. Genetical heterogeneity. Some human geneticists consider that schizophrenia may consist of a high risk group, comprising several different entities, each attributable to a different rare and possibly recessive gene, with a residue of sporadic low risk cases (cf. Erlenmeyer-Kimling and Paradowski, 1966; Morton, 1967a,b). Although some families have been reported (e.g. by Kaij, 1967) in which an atypical psychosis appears to be passed on genetically in a way suggestive of dominant inheritance, no picture has emerged of how many different conditions may be involved or of the size of the probably large residue. In particular, the Kraepelinian subtypes of schizophrenia do not show themselves on genetic analysis to be discrete genetic entities. There is some family resemblance in subtype but it is far from complete (e.g. Kallmann, 1938). The same is true for the Leonhardian classification according to van Epen (1969). Heterogeneity at present looks a less likely hypothesis for schizophrenia than for the depressions. Nevertheless, the possibility remains that some forms of schizophrenia that are due to rare genes may be identified, as with mental subnormality. Similarly, some cases may be environmental phenocopies. This may be so with the schizophrenic-like psychoses of epilepsy (Slater et al., 1963).

3. Monogenic theories. Of current theories which attribute at least the great bulk of cases diagnosed as schizophrenia to the effects of the same necessary gene, the most viable is Slater's monogenic theory (Slater, 1958; Slater and Roth, 1969; Slater and Cowie, 1971). According to this hypothesis all persons who are homozygous for the abnormal allele are affected; however, over 90 per cent of schizophrenics are heterozygotes, and only about 20 per cent of them develop schizophrenia. Whether heterozygotes become schizophrenic or not depends on

auxiliary polygenes and on the environment. The theory fits the data quite well, though it is not the only theory that can be made to do so. The hypothesis suggests that there is still promise in looking for a simple genetical biochemical defect in schizophrenia and for some advantage, such as resistance to infection in early life (*see* Erlenmeyer-Kimling, 1968; Carter and Watts, 1971), to balance the loss of genes caused by the fact that so many schizophrenics have no children.

4. Polygenic inheritance. To many who come to psychiatric genetics from psychology (e.g. Rosenthal) or from animal behaviour genetics, a polygenic model appears more plausible. In a sense this is a more parsimonious theory than a major gene plus polygenes. It is easier to account for the phenotypic variability found in the families of schizophrenics on some kind of polygenic theory than on a monogenic one. The association between severity and concordance in twins and the fall in the risk for second degree relatives from that for first degree relatives favours polygenic theory; and the lower fertility of schizophrenics is less of a problem than it is for monogenic theory. On the other hand, there are many possible versions of polygenic theory (Shields, 1968), and some of them are very vague. It seems best to start with a simple additive theory and see where it breaks down. However, even on simple polygenic theories the mathematics becomes too complex for predictions to be easily made for (say) the expected risk for the children of two schizophrenics: but Smith (1971) has now tackled this problem.

Polygenic theories for schizophrenia have been suggested by Ødegaard (1952, 1963 and in press) and by Kay (1963) among others. Gottesman and Shields (1967) were the first to apply the method of analysis suggested by Falconer (1965). This assumes that there is an underlying, normally distributed predisposition or 'liability' to schizophrenia which is partly genetically and partly environmentally determined, but which cannot at present be directly measured. Once a threshold of the liability is passed the individual is schizophrenic (Fig. 16.5). The method suggests a way of estimating, from the population incidence of schizophrenia and the risks for relatives of schizophrenics, how much of the liability can be accounted for by genetic variability in the population. A simple account of the theory is given by Carter (1969). Gottesman and Shields used what appeared to be the best data available from studies in different countries and from relatives sharing different kinds of environment with a schizophrenic. All the estimates showed substantial heritability. Some estimates were too high, notably those from twins. However the method may not be

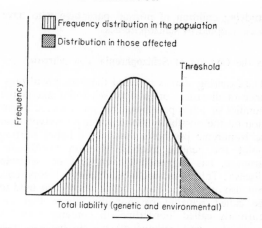

Fig. 16.5. Falconer's model of polygenic inheritance (*from* Carter, 1969; *by courtesy of* Dr. C. O. Carter and *The Lancet*)

appropriate for MZ twins (Falconer, 1967),* and the SEs of the DZ estimates were very large. Some of the data may be unreliable. Another explanation for the seemingly high heritabilities may be that some comparatively rare genes have a relatively large effect on the liability.

Polygenic theories are more open-ended if less specific than monogenic theories in the further hypotheses they suggest. Those favouring a polygenic approach might be expected to be interested in elucidating the part played by contributory factors, in attempts at measuring the underlying liability or parts of it, and in trying to disentangle the mode of genetic-environmental interaction. Are there specific environmental triggering stresses or only a greater vulnerability to ubiquitous stresses? Do the genes have their influence only through their effect on underlying personality traits, perhaps in evidence at an early age? Or does the essential genetic contribution come into play only later in the inability to deal adequately with certain psychosomatic states? Some models of genetic-environmental interaction have been suggested by Rosenthal (1963).

Psychological Measures of Relatives of Schizophrenics

Considerable effort has been devoted to attempts to differentiate the relatives of schizophrenics from controls by means of psychometry. From the point of view of the human psychogeneticist the hope is that such tests will provide a graded measure of schizophrenia, more objective than clinical diagnosis, and

* Smith (1970) suggests a way round this difficulty.

also a phenotype more closely related to the underlying genotype. To date neither of these hopes has been achieved.

In 1959, McConaghy tested the conceptual thinking of both parents of 10 schizophrenics with thought disorder. The test used was Lovibond's (1954) object-sorting test (OST), a modification of the Goldstein-Scheerer test, scores of 7 and over being taken as abnormal. Of the 20 parents—at least one parent of each case—12 showed looseness of thinking, compared with only 9 per cent of 65 controls. McConaghy's hypothesis was that an abnormal score would identify heterozygotic gene carriers. Lidz et al. (1962) did not confirm these promising findings. When they first scored their data only 5 out of 20 parents were abnormal on the test. A revised method of scoring was more successful but the difference remained non-significant and not all schizophrenics had an abnormal parent; a median cutting point, however, significantly discriminated the two classes of parent. A further study by the Lidz group (Rosman et al., 1964), based on larger numbers, found a numerically smaller but statistically significant difference in the proportion of parents with abnormal scores. The difference was accounted for by mothers rather than fathers and by parents of higher rather than lower intelligence. While 51 per cent of 68 parents of schizophrenics scored 7 or higher, so did 37 per cent of 125 control parents. The authors interpreted their findings in terms of the environmental transmission of irrational thinking. Phillips et al. (1965) reported that siblings as well as parents of schizophrenics had abnormal scores on other tests of thought disorder.

Later work has not been entirely confirmatory. Impressed by the frequency of high scorers in some control groups, McConaghy and Clancy (1968) found that many university students were high scorers on the OST. Since high scorers did not differ from low scorers in academic record or on the F-scale of the MMPI, the validity of the test as a specific measure of schizophrenic pathology was questioned. McConaghy and Clancy considered looseness of association to be a normal mode of allusive abstract thinking, found in a high proportion of schizophrenics but also in many normal individuals. Since the parents of 11 low scorers had significantly less allusive thinking according to the OST than the parents of 16 high scorers, they concluded that this *mode* of thinking was inherited.

There is also some doubt about the genetic basis of OST scores, at least in the families of schizophrenics. While Romney (1969) confirmed that 30 unequivocal schizophrenics in hospital were more thought disordered than 20 neurotics and 20 normals, he was unable to show that the parents or sibs of

these patients differed significantly, either on the OST or on Bannister's Grid test of thought disorder. In all, 119 relatives were tested, and the three groups of relatives were fairly comparable as regards age, education and occupational status, variables which may effect the scores. Muntz and Power (1970), however, found the parents of clinically thought-disordered schizophrenics to be significantly more abnormal on the Grid test than the parents of matched psychiatric patients who were not thought disordered.

Gottesman and Shields (in press) studied schizophrenics, their twins and their parents by means of the OST. The test did not discriminate efficiently between the schizophrenics, many of whom were in remission and on medication known to reduce thought disorder, and their non-schizophrenic relatives. MZ pairs were no more alike in test score then DZ pairs.

An interesting hypothesis has been put forward by Schopler and Loftin (1969) to account for the relatively high OST scores of parents of schizophrenics found in several studies, namely that anxiety increases looseness of association. When approached for testing in connection with their psychotic child, mothers were found to score more highly on the OST than when they were led to believe they had been selected as the parent of one of their normal children. If this work is confirmed, tested thought disorder in schizophrenic families would be seen in part as an effect of the psychosis rather than as a cause or as a predisposing genetic trait.

Singer and Wynne (1963, 1965) have predicted the diagnosis of the patient and his type of thought disorder from the styles of thought and communication of the parents. Thought disorder was assessed blindly from protocols of speech and test-taking behaviour. Their work is difficult to replicate and may depend on unusual clinical sensitivity. However, a careful attempt to replicate some of their work was made by Hirsch and Leff (1971), who compared the parents of 20 schizophrenics with the parents of 20 neurotics on the 41-category Rorschach scoring method devised by Wynne and Singer. While Wynne (in press) reported virtually no overlap between the deviance scores of parents of schizophrenics and neurotics, Hirsch and Leff found 97·5 per cent overlap.

In twin and family studies based on psychiatric cases psychological testing can be a useful adjunct to life history information, but it is not a substitute for it. Gottesman and Shields (1968, and in press) found the MZ co-twins of schizophrenics to be more abnormal than the DZ co-twins in mean MMPI profile, and in many concordant pairs a comparison of the twins highlighted points of resemblance if they were in the same clinical stage of illness. But MZ intrapair correlations on the MMPI scales were low, probably on account of the fluctuating course of the psychosis and consequently of test response in many subjects. The questionnaire as used in practice was not very helpful in identifying latent or borderline schizophrenics among parents and twins judged normal by psychiatric history.

Psychophysiological testing was a notable feature of Mednick and Schulsinger's (1968) prospective study of a high-risk group of 207 adolescent children of schizophrenics. Compared with matched controls they had a more labile autonomic response system. Their GSR responses had a shorter latency, a greater amplitude, a quicker recovery rate and a greater tendency to stimulus-generalisation. The children of schizophrenics also more often gave idiosyncratic and fragmented responses on a word-association test. Psychiatrically more of them were rated blind as poorly adjusted. Though performing relatively adequately at school, they were assessed by teachers as tending to get easily upset and to withdraw. The specific relationship of the GSR and other variables to the development of schizophrenia will eventually be assessed when it is finally known which of the children become schizophrenic, which have other deviations, and which are psychiatrically normal.

These findings suggest that there is an excess of neurotic traits in the children of psychotics. Cowie (1961), however, using the MPI, did not find the children of schizophrenics to have a higher neuroticism score than the children of controls. From his review of the literature and his own work, Rutter (1966) concluded that parental mental disorder, particularly when chronic, can for environmental reasons lead to behavioural disturbance in children. The effects of chronic neurosis may be more severe than those of psychosis, and the social consequences of chronic physical illness are often similar. In the earlier studies, schizophrenia in one parent was not a potent cause of disturbance in the children. However, with present trends towards community care, Rutter considered it could not be assumed that children would do so well when a psychotic parent remained at home. Block (1969), using Q-sort information, could not differentiate the parents of neurotic children from those of psychotic children, but the 'schizophrenic' children in question had a mean age of 8 years, and should not be equated with schizophrenic patients in this country.

EPILEPSY AND RELATED ABNORMALITIES

In 15 twin series based on epileptic probands Koch (1967), in the course of his comprehensive review of genetic factors, reported that 61 per cent of 233 MZ and 12 per cent of 470 DZ pairs were concordant. Rates vary according to source of proband material and nature of the epilepsy. Highest rates were found by Conrad (1935) in a study based on institutionalised epileptics; when restricted to what appeared to be 'idiopathic' epilepsy, 19 out of 22 MZ pairs were concordant and there was far-reaching similarity in onset, type of fit and sequelae. Concordance tends to be lower when the investigator starts from milder cases or cases of later onset. None of the 4 MZ pairs found in the studies of Alström (1950) and Slater (1953) based on admissions to neurological or psychiatric clinics were concordant. Lennox and Jolly (1954) found less MZ concordance in psychomotor epilepsy than in grand mal or petit mal.

In the parents, sibs, and children of epileptics rates of about 4 per cent have generally been found (e.g. by Harvald, 1954) but lower figures were reported by Alström (1950) in an equally careful investigation and higher rates by Ounsted (1955) dealing with epileptic children. The corresponding rate for the general population is usually taken to be about 0·5 per cent. Harvald (1954) found 10 to 18 per cent of the first degree relatives of non-focal (centrencephalic) epileptics to have marked non-focal EEG abnormalities, but the EEG was not a reliable indicator of carrier status. Of 29 presumed carriers of the genetic predisposition for epilepsy only 8 had an abnormal EEG.

The general opinion (Slater and Roth, 1969) is that the tendency to produce cerebral paroxysmal discharges and for such discharges to spread is polygenically inherited in man as in other mammals (Fuller et al., 1950), with environmental factors playing a greater role in some cases than in others. Disorders such as the type of myoclonic epilepsy Lundborg (1903) found to be attributable to a single recessive gene would be rare exceptions. In normal MZ twins (Lennox et al., 1939; Vogel, 1958), including those reared apart (Juel-Nielsen and Harvald, 1958), EEG records, taken under standard conditions, are frequently so similar that they can be confused. DZ twins do not show this striking overall similarity. But there is the possibility that some of the individual rhythms that contribute to the total picture may be inherited as simple dominant traits with manifestation depending on age. One such gene may be particularly implicated in centrencephalic epilepsy. When Metrakos and Metrakos (1961) examined the sibs of centrencephalic epileptics they found similar 3/sec spikes and waves in 45 per cent of those aged between $4\frac{1}{2}$ and $16\frac{1}{2}$ with a considerably lower prevalence in younger and older age groups. Such a high rate in sibs suggests the contribution of a major gene. Doose et al. (1967) investigated the EEGs of the sibs of children whose convulsive disorders were associated with an abnormal theta rhythm. Once again the prevalence of a theta rhythm in sibs was high and remarkably age dependent. Between ages 2 to 4 as many as 54 per cent of 46 sibs showed this abnormality, compared with 12 per cent of 60 controls, the records having been judged blind. In normal subjects certain beta rhythms were suspected by Vogel (1966) of being dominant genetic traits, while Petersén and Åkesson (1968), studying 14 and 6 per second spikes, reported an age-corrected prevalence in sibs of 53 per cent as against 9 per cent in controls. The sensitivity of the EEG to photic stimulation may be independently inherited (Hedenström, 1969).

Temporal lobe epilepsy is the type of seizure believed most frequently to be associated with psychological abnormality such as depersonalisation, twilight states, hyperkinesis, catastrophic rage and psychosis. Ounsted et al. (1966) studied the sibs of 100 children with temporal lobe epilepsy. The overall risk for any kind of convulsive disorder in the sibs was around 15 per cent. It was highest in the sibs of those children who, without gross organic insult to the brain, had developed status epilepticus. Seizures in sibs generally consisted of brief febrile convulsions. Ounsted et al. concluded that the genetic predisposition related merely to the development of febrile convulsions. Temporal lobe epileptics with gross organic brain insult had no excess of sibs with convulsive disorder, and it was predominantly this group of epileptics who later developed the hyperkinetic syndrome. There was thus no evidence that genetic factors played any important part in the predisposition to the hyperkinetic syndrome of epilepsy. Somewhat similar

findings were reported with regard to catastrophic rage. When Slater et al. (1963) studied the families of patients suffering from schizophrenia-like psychoses associated with epilepsy they found no excess of psychoses. Thus, while aspects of the EEG in the absence of trauma have a high heritability and the same may be true for non-focal seizures, many of the psychological complications of epilepsy are associated with traumatic epilepsy or with chance secondary effects of the seizures.

In 1908, Gowers introduced the concept of the 'borderlands of epilepsy' to include spasmodic disorders such as migraine, syncope, nocturnal enuresis and night terrors, which were said to occur in excess among the relatives of epileptics and were thought to represent epileptic equivalents. In the more recent past the term 'epileptoid psychopath' was used to describe the excessively explosive, moody or perseverative individual on account of his possessing characteristics said to be typical of epileptics. The present tendency is to avoid such terms. The personality characteristics of epileptics, in so far as there are any that are specific, are generally thought to be secondary to brain damage, as we have seen, or to social factors (Pond and Bidwell, 1960). The genetic investigations of Alström (1950) and Harvald (1954) failed to confirm the excess of psychopaths in the families of epileptics, while EEG or family studies of enuretics and others (summarised by Koch, 1967) have given contradictory or equivocal results. There is still scope, however, for detailed EEG and psychological investigation into the families of aggressive and other psychopaths with EEG abnormalities (cf. Hill and Watterson, 1942; Wissfeld and Kaindl, 1961).

The interesting concepts of the Japanese psychiatrist Mitsuda (1967) suppose there to be genetic factors in common between epilepsy and atypical schizophrenia and atypical manic-depressive psychosis, but this is a minority view for which there is not much independent evidence.

The recent work on the relationship between EEG measures and extraversion is discussed by Fenton and Scotton (1967) and Broadhurst and Glass (1969).

PRESENILE AND SENILE MENTAL DISORDER

The probability of developing mental illness increases steeply after middle age. In populations where the proportion of old people is rising, the importance of these conditions is bound to grow. Of course, many of the depressive, neurotic, and paranoid disorders of the elderly are no different in aetiology from those of younger persons.

The chapter on ageing and the mental diseases of the aged in Mayer-Gross, Slater and Roth's

Clinical Psychiatry (Slater and Roth, 1969) includes a summary of what is known of their genetic aspects. The normal process of ageing varies in the population for reasons that are partly genetic, presumably multifactorial. So, too, does hypertension, to the secondary effects of which some of the psychoses associated with cerebrovascular disease are due. But in conditions arising after the end of the reproductive period, natural selection can no longer operate to eliminate harmful genes. 'The post-reproductive period is therefore an evolutionary backwater in which mutations detracting from full health and vigour have probably been deposited over the generations' (Slater and Roth, *loc. cit.*, p. 535). It would not be surprising if some conditions due to major genes were found. Pick's disease, one of the pathologically distinct forms of presenile dementia, is probably one such example (Sjögren *et al.*, 1952). Some of the familial cases of Alzheimer's disease, such as those reported by Wheelan (1959) and Heston *et al.* (1966), have all the hallmarks of dominant inheritance, though Sjögren *et al.* and Constantinides *et al.* (1965), who carried out systematic studies on unselected series, favour polygenic inheritance.

There is some dispute over the genetics of rapidly advancing senile dementia, which occurs about 4·3 times as frequently in the close relatives of patients as in control subjects of the same age. Larsson *et al.* (1963) made out a strong case for a dominant gene and variable age of onset on the basis of their family study of 377 Swedish probands. Probands and secondary cases were equally severely affected, and there was an absence of conditions in unaffected relatives intermediate between senile dementia and normal ageing. However, the finding might also be explained in terms of pronounced threshold effects in the evolution of the underlying pathological process.

The twin concordance rates for senile psychosis reported by Kallmann (1950) may be mentioned here: 43 per cent in 33 MZ pairs and 8 per cent in 75 DZ pairs. This MZ rate is the lowest of those reported for the psychoses by Kallmann. For involutional psychosis he reported concordance rates of 61 per cent (MZ) and 6 per cent (DZ).

CONCLUSION

In view of the very considerable advances in genetics it was decided to refer to the psychological aspects of genetic abnormalities as well as to the genetic aspects of psychological abnormalities. Lengthy though this chapter is, it is inevitable that an emphasis on breadth required sacrificing depth. It has been impossible to discuss all the sophisticated designs used or suggested for the genetic analysis of human behaviour. There is nothing on evolution or the possible genetic and biological basis of much behaviour that is universal for our species. Within the field of psychiatric disorder it has not even been possible to go into the most likely reasons for conflicting observations or to discuss fully the pros and cons of different interpretations of the same data. But it is hoped that some indication has been given of the work going on at the present time and its rationale.

Though it needs to be made, the conclusion that genetic differences are important over a wide range of abnormal behaviour is too general a statement to be entirely satisfactory. It might even be argued that the most instructive findings are those that show no resemblance between parents and children and where similarity is no greater in twins who have all their genes in common than in those twins who are not genetically identical. Such findings may suggest where to look for environmental causes, or they may lead to alternative methods of classification or measurement more closely related to underlying genetic factors. The study of discordant and partially discordant MZ twins has been little mentioned, mainly because it is not directly concerned with genetic causes of abnormality. It must be admitted, however, that this potentially promising method has not so far come up with any agreed conclusions of major importance, despite the information gleaned from representative series of twins, from the unique case of the Genain quadruplets (Rosenthal, 1963), the specially selected sample of discordant schizophrenic twins studied in detail by Pollin and his colleagues (1966, 1968; Mosher *et al.*, 1971) or from Abe's (1969) analysis of the time intervals between onset of psychosis in concordant pairs of twins. Even prospective studies of twins differing in environmental factors (Dencker, 1958; Kaij, 1960; Shields, 1962) have been of greater interest for what they have told us about similarities which occurred despite the environmental differences than for what they have told us about the effects of head injury, alcoholic excess, or being reared in different homes.

A great deal of genetic analysis is devoted to estimating *how much* a trait is genetically determined, i.e. to the question of heritability or penetrance. The dependence of such estimates on the population studied and the method used has been repeatedly stressed. Correctly interpreted, such estimates can be useful, at least as a first step. But perhaps of greater interest is *what* is inherited. In the case of schizophrenia, is it merely a predisposition to mental disorder in general, psychoticism, schizophrenia as such, thought disorder, or some premorbid characterological or physiological trait? There have been some shifts of opinion over the years as to how much different conditions were inherited and how they might be related to one another genetically. Fifteen or twenty years ago it was sometimes maintained that the psychoses were inherited as specific entities, while personality—and hence even more so neurosis—was essentially determined by the environment. There is now better evidence than formerly of a genetic component in personality, while lower twin concordance rates tend to be reported for the psychoses. According to Essen-Möller (1965) among others, the genetic element in schizophrenia may relate to certain specific personality traits. MZ concordance rates of about 40 per cent have been reported for both anxiety neurosis and for schizophrenia, DZ rates being considerably lower. However, it would be misleading to assume that heredity was of comparable importance in the two conditions. Anxiety neurosis is common, schizophrenia much rarer. There are environmental factors that can make anyone anxious. No environmental causes that can make anyone schizophrenic are known.

Conclusions about *how* an abnormality is inherited depend on current ideas in genetics. Views may change, not because new facts have emerged about the families of the mentally ill but because hypotheses that were previously considered unlikely now appear more plausible. For example, monogenic inheritance used to be the preferred model for discontinuous or bimodally distributed variables, especially if rare, while polygenic inheritance was generally assumed to be operating in graded characters (cf. Figs 16.1 and 16.3). This no longer holds (cf. Figs 16.2 and 16.5). If it is assumed that most psychiatric abnormalities are polygenic, presumably there are some genes that increase the liability to more than one disorder. Do the hypothesised manic-depressive and schizophrenic polygenic systems have genes in common which predispose to psychoticism (Eysenck, 1967)? How far do neurotic traits influence the manifestation of psychotic illness, as the comparison of sick and healthy family members suggests they do? Is there a genetic continuum spreading from progressive schizophrenia at one extreme, through periodic schizophrenia, to recurrent manic-depressive psychosis at the other extreme, as Shakhmatova-Pavlova (1967) suggested from the evidence of family studies? Clearly, many possibilities could be examined.

Conclusions of many kinds also vary, depending how mental disorders are grouped together or subdivided. Genetic analysis can be an aid in validating proposed diagnostic classifications. At the present time there are, as we have seen, hypotheses that the depressions should be subdivided

and the concept of schizophrenia enlarged. For the experimental psychologist it would be an immense advance if major psychological abnormality could be studied genetically by means of quantitative tests or rating scales. Outside intelligence the approach is relatively new and, for the reasons given in the sections on neurosis and schizophrenia, progress so far has been uncertain. Even in centrencephalic epilepsy the EEG is of limited value for measuring genetic predisposition.

Dalén (1969) has criticised polygenic theories of psychiatric abnormality on the grounds that such complex hypotheses are essentially irrefutable and, hence, valueless. He urges instead the testing of the consequences of simple single factor theories. However, he admits (Dalén, in press) that simple additive polygenic theories do have consequences that can be tested. It is such theories that are usually put forward in the first place in behaviour genetic analysis. A danger of some polygenic and interactional theorising is that it may give a false impression that we know more than we really do. Such is not the wish of those who believe that the truth is probably complex. They hope to identify contributing factors, particularly those that can be controlled. By doing so they could be regarded as refuting the simple theory that no one factor is more important than any other. There is a healthy diversity of approach to the problem, so that if an investigator does not himself refute his own hypothesis someone else may do so. The discovery of the extra chromosome in mongolism made some of the previously held complex theories look ridiculous. Increasing numbers of psychologists are being trained in behavioural genetics and among professional geneticists there is a growing interest in behaviour. Hopefully many major and minor specific elements in the aetiology of psychological abnormality remain to be discovered. Directly or indirectly, it is important to increase our knowledge of what aspects of a complex trait are most under genetic control. It is equally important to discover what we can about the nature of the contribution to trait variability of environmental factors, whether these be different learning regimes or physical traumata. In this way we may eventually be able to make more detailed statements about the central problem of genetic-environmental interaction, instead of having to fall back on the truism that seed and soil are both essential for development.

REFERENCES

ABE, K. (1969) The morbidity rate and environmental influence in monozygotic co-twins of schizophrenics. *Brit. J. Psychiat.*, **115**, 519–531.

ABE, K. and MORAN, P. A. P. (1969) Parental age of homosexuals. *Brit. J. Psychiat.*, **115**, 313–317.

ABE, K. and SHIMAKAWA, M. (1966a) Genetic and developmental aspects of sleeptalking and teeth-grinding. *Acta Paedopsychiat.*, **33**, 339–344.

ABE, K. and SHIMAKAWA, M. (1966b) Predisposition to sleep-walking. *Psychiat. Neurol.* (*Basel*), **152**, 306–312.

ABE, K. and SHIMAKAWA, M. (1966c) Genetic-constitutional factor and childhood insomnia. *Psychiat. Neurol.* (*Basel*), **152**, 363–369.

ABE, K., SHIMAKAWA, M., and KAJIYAMA, S. (1967) Interaction between genetic and psychological factors in acquisition of bladder control in children. *Psychiat. Neurol.* (*Basel*), **154**, 144–149.

ADAMS, M. S. and NEEL, J. V. (1967) Children of incest. *Pediatrics*, **40**, 55–62.

ÅKESSON, H. O. (1962) Empiric risk figures in mental deficiency. *Acta Genet.* (*Basel*), **12**, 28–32.

ALANEN, Y. O. (1966) The family in the pathogenesis of schizophrenic and neurotic disorders. *Acta Psychiat. Scand.*, Suppl. 189.

ALEXANDERSON, B., EVANS, D. A. PRICE, and SJÖQVIST, F. (1969) Steady-state plasma levels of nortriptyline in twins: influence of genetic factors and drug therapy. *Brit. med. J.*, **4**, 764–768.

ALLEN, G., HARVALD, B., and SHIELDS, J. (1967) Measures of twin concordance. *Acta Genet.* (*Basel*), **17**, 475–481.

ALLEN, G. and KALLMANN, F. J. (1962) Etiology of mental subnormality in twins. In *Expanding Goals of Genetics in Psychiatry* (Ed. F. J. Kallmann). New York: Grune and Stratton, 174–191.

ALSTRÖM, C. H. (1950) A study of epilepsy in its clinical, social and genetic aspects. *Acta Psychiat. Neurol. Scand.*, Suppl. 63.

ÅMARK, C. (1951) A study in alcoholism. *Acta Psychiat. Neurol. Scand.*, Suppl. 70.

ANDERS, J. M., JAGIELLO, G., POLANI, P. E., GIANNELLI, F., HAMERTON, J. L., and LEIBERMAN, D. M. (1968) Chromosome findings in chronic psychotic patients. *Brit. J. Psychiat.*, **114**, 1167–1174.

ANDERSON, V. E. and SIEGEL, F. (1968) Studies of behavior in genetically defined syndromes in man. In *Progress in Human Behavior Genetics* (Ed. S. G. Vandenberg), 7–17. Baltimore: Johns Hopkins Press.

ANGST, J. (1966) *Zur Ätiologie und Nosologie endogener depressiver Psychosen.* Monogr. Gesamtgeb. Neurol. Psychiat., **112**. Berlin: Springer.

ANGST, J. and PERRIS, C. (1968) Zur Nosologie endogener Depressionen. Vergleich der Ergebnisse zweier Untersuchungen. *Arch. Psychiat. Nervenkr.*, **210**, 373–386.

ARKONAC, O. and GUZE, S. B. (1963) A family study of hysteria. *New Eng. J. Med.*, **268**, 239–242.

BARNICOT, N. A. (1950) Taste deficiency for phenylthiourea in African negroes and Chinese. *Ann. Eugen.*, **15**, 248–254.

BARTALOS, M. and BARAMKI, T. A. (1967) *Medical Cytogenetics.* Baltimore: Williams & Wilkins.

BARTLETT, D. J., HURLEY, W. P., BRAND, C. R., and POOLE, E. W. (1968) Chromosomes of male patients in a security prison. *Nature* (*Lond.*), **219**, 351–354.

BELL, R. Q. (1968) A reinterpretation of the direction of effects in studies of socialization. *Psychol. Rev.*, **75**, 81–95.

BERG, J. M. (1963) Causal factors in severe mental retardation. *Proc. 2nd. Internat. Congr. Ment. Retard., Vienna ; 1961*: Part I, 170–173.

BERG, J. M. (1969) Personal communication.

BERG, J. M. and KIRMAN, B. H. (1959) Some aetiological problems in mental deficiency. *Brit. med. J.*, **2**, 848–852.

BERG, J. M. and KIRMAN, B. H. (1960) The mentally defective twin. *Brit. med. J.*, **1**, 1911–1917.

BLACKETER-SIMMONDS, D. A. (1953) An investigation into the supposed differences existing between mongols and other mentally defective subjects with regard to certain psychological traits. *J. ment. Sci.*, **99**, 702–719.

BLAU, J. N. and MUTTON, D. E. (1967) Chromosome studies in the 'sensory syndrome'. *Acta Genet.* (*Basel*), **17**, 226–233.

BLEULER, M. (1955) Familial and personal background of chronic alcoholics. In *Etiology of Chronic Alcoholism* (Ed. O. Diethelm). Springfield, Ill.: Thomas, 110–166.

BLEULER, M. (1963) Conception of schizophrenia within the last fifty years and today. *Proc. roy. soc. Med.*, **56**, 945–952.

BLEWETT, D. B. (1953) An experimental study of the inheritance of neuroticism and intelligence. *Ph.D. Thesis, Univ. of London.*

BLEWETT, D. B. (1954) An experimental study of the inheritance of intelligence. *J. ment. Sci.*, **100**, 922–933.

BLOCH, A. A. (1969) Remembrance of feelings past: a study of phenomenological genetics. *J. abnorm. Psychol.*, **74**, 340–347.

BLOCK, J. (1969) Parents of schizophrenic, neurotic, asthmatic, and congenitally ill children. *Arch. gen. Psychiat.*, **20**, 659–674.

BLUMENTHAL, M. D. (1967) Mental illness in parents of phenylketonuric children. *J. psychiat. Res.*, **5**, 59–74.

BRACONI, L. (1961) Le psiconevrosi e le psicosi nei gemelli. *Acta Genet. Med. Gemell.*, **10**, 100–136.

BRITISH MEDICAL JOURNAL (1968) leading article, Inbreeding and adoption. *Brit. med. J.*, **2**, 257–258.

BROADHURST, A. and GLASS, A. (1969) Relationship of personality measures to the alpha rhythm of the electroencephalogram. *Brit. J. Psychiat.*, **115**, 199–204.

BROADHURST, P. L. (1967) The biometrical analysis of behavioural inheritance. *Sci. Prog. Oxf.*, **55**, 123–139.

BROADHURST, P. L. (1968) Experimental approaches to the evolution of behaviour. In *Genetic and Environmental Influences on Behaviour* (Ed. J. M. Thoday and A. S. Parkes). Edinburgh: Oliver & Boyd, 15–36.

BROCK, L. G. (Chairman) (1934) Ministry of Health, Report of the departmental committee on sterilization. Cmd. 4485. London: H.M.S.O.

BROWN, F. W. (1942) Heredity in the psychoneuroses. *Proc. roy. soc. Med.*, **35**, 785–790.

BURT, C. (1921) *Mental and Scholastic Tests*, 1st ed. London: P. S. King.

BURT, C. (1946) *Intelligence and Fertility.* Eugenics Society Occasional Papers on Eugenics, No. 2. London: Hamish Hamilton.

BURT, C. (1958) The inheritance of mental ability. *Amer. Psychol.*, **13**, 1–15.

BURT, C. (1962) *Mental and Scholastic Tests*, 4th Edn. London: Staples Press.

BURT, C. (1966) The genetic determination of differences in intelligence: a study of monozygotic twins reared together and apart. *Brit. J. Psychol.*, **57**, 137–153.

BURT, C. and HOWARD, M. (1956) The multifactorial

theory of inheritance and its application to intelligence. *Brit. J. statist. Psychol.*, **9**, 95–131.

CARTER, C. O. (1962) *Human Heredity*. London: Penguin.

CARTER, C. O. (1965) The inheritance of common congenital malformations. In *Progress in Medical Genetics*, Vol. IV. (Ed. A. G. Steinberg and A. G. Bearn). New York: Grune & Stratton, 59–84.

CARTER, C. O. (1967) Risk to offspring of incest. *Lancet*, **i**, 436.

CARTER, C. O. (1969) An ABC of medical genetics. VI—Polygenic inheritance and common diseases. *Lancet*, **i**, 1252–1256.

CARTER, C. O. and MACCARTHY, D. (1951) Incidence of mongolism and its diagnosis in the newborn. *Brit. J. prev. soc. Med.*, **5**, 83–90.

CARTER, H. D. (1935) Twin-similarities in emotional traits. *Character and Pers.*, **4**, 61–78.

CARTER, M. and WATTS, C. A. H. (1971) Possible biological advantages among schizophrenics' relatives. *Brit. J. Psychiat.*, **118**, 453–460.

CASEY, M. D. (1969) The family and behavioural history of patients with chromosome abnormality in the special hospitals of Rampton and Moss Side. In *Criminological Implications of Chromosome Abnormalities* (Ed. D. J. West). Cambridge: Institute of Criminology, 49–60.

CASEY, M. D., BLANK, C. E., STREET, D. R. K., SEGALL, L. J., MCDOUGALL, J. H., MCGRATH, P. J., and SKINNER, J. L. (1966a) YY chromosomes and antisocial behaviour. *Lancet*, **ii**, 859–860.

CASEY, M. D., SEGALL, L. J., STREET, D. R. K., and BLANK, C. E. (1966b) Sex chromosome abnormalities in two state hospitals for patients requiring special security. *Nature (Lond.)*, **209**, 641–642.

CATTELL, R. B. (1953) Research designs in psychological genetics with special reference to the multiple variance method. *Amer. J. hum. Genet.*, **5**, 76–93.

CATTELL, R. B., BLEWETT, D. B., and BELOFF, J. R. (1955) The inheritance of personality: a multiple variance analysis determination of approximate nature-nurture ratios for primary personality factors in Q-data. *Amer. J. hum. Genet.*, **7**, 122–146.

CATTELL, R. B., STICE, G. F., and KRISTY, N. F. (1957) A first approximation to nature-nurture ratios for eleven primary personality factors in objective tests. *J. abnorm. soc. Psychol.*, **54**, 143–159.

CEDERLÖF, R., FRIBERG, L., JONSSON, E., and KAIJ, L. (1961) Studies on similarity diagnosis in twins with the aid of mailed questionnaires. *Acta Genet. (Basel)*, **11**, 338–362.

CHANDLER, J. H. (1966) EEG in prediction of Huntington's chorea. An eighteen year follow-up. *Electroenceph. clin. Neurophysiol.*, **21**, 79–80.

CHRISTIANSEN, K. O. (1968) Threshold of tolerance in various population groups illustrated by results from Danish criminological twin study. In *The Mentally Abnormal Offender*, a Ciba Foundation Symposium (Ed. A. V. S. de Reuck and R. Porter). London: Churchill, 107–120.

CHRISTIANSEN, K. O. (1970) Crime in a Danish twin population. *Acta Genet. Med. Gemell.*, **19**, 323–326.

CLARKE, A. D. B. (1968) Learning and human development. *Brit. J. Psychiat.*, **114**, 1061–1077.

CLARKE, C. A. (1967) Prevention of Rh-haemolytic disease. *Brit. med. J.*, **4**, 7–12.

CLARKE, C. A. (1969) Polymorphism. In *Selected Topics in Medical Genetics* (Ed. C. A. Clarke). London: Oxford University Press, 22–44.

CLAUSEN, J. (1968) Behavioral characteristics of Down syndrome subjects. *Amer. J. ment. Def.*, **73**, 118–126.

CLOWES, R. (1967) *The Structure of Life*. London: Penguin.

COHEN, M. E., BADAL, D. W., KILPATRICK, A., REED, E. W., and WHITE, P. D. (1951) The high familial prevalence of neurocirculatory asthenia (anxiety neurosis, effort syndrome). *Amer. J. hum. Genet.*, **3**, 126–158.

CONRAD, K. (1935) Erbanlage und Epilepsie. *Z. ges. Neurol. Psychiat.*, **153**, 271–326.

CONSTANTINIDIS, J., GARRONE, G., TISSOT, R., and de AJURIAGUERRA, J. (1965) L'incidence familiale des altérations neurofibrillaires corticales d'Alzheimer. *Psychiat. Neurol. (Basel)*, **150**, 235–247.

COOPER, R. M. and ZUBEK, J. P. (1958) Effects of enriched and restricted early environments on the learning ability of bright and dull rats. *Canad. J. Psychol.*, **12**, 159–164.

COPPEN, A. (1966) The Marke-Nyman temperament scale: an English translation. *Brit. J. med. Psychol.*, **39**, 55–59.

COPPEN, A., COWIE, V., and SLATER, E. (1965) Familial aspects of 'neuroticism' and 'extraversion', *Brit. J. Psychiat.*, **111**, 70–83.

COPPEN, A. and METCALFE, M. (1965) Effect of a depressive illness on MPI scores, *Brit. J. Psychiat.*, **111**, 236–239.

COURT BROWN, W. M. (1962) Sex chromosomes and the law. *Lancet*, **ii**, 508–509.

COURT BROWN, W. M. (1968) Males with an XYY sex chromosome complement. *J. med. Genet.*, **5**, 341–359.

COURT BROWN, W. M., JACOBS, P. A., and PRICE, W. H. (1968) Sex chromosome aneuploidy and criminal behaviour. In *Genetic and Environmental Influences on Behaviour* (Ed. J. M. Thoday and A. S. Parkes). Edinburgh: Oliver & Boyd, 180–193.

COURT BROWN, W. M. and SMITH, P. G. (1969) Human population cytogenetics. *Brit. med. Bull.*, **25**, 74–80.

COWIE, J., COWIE, V., and SLATER, E. (1968) *Delinquency in Girls*. London: Heinemann.

COWIE, V. (1961) The incidence of neurosis in the children of psychotics. *Acta Psychiat. Scand.*, **37**, 37–87.

CUSWORTH, D. C. and DENT, C. E. (1969) Homocystinuria, *Brit. med. Bull.*, **25**, 42–47.

DALÉN, P. (1969) Causal explanations in psychiatry: a critique of some current concepts. *Brit. J. Psychiat.*, **115**, 129–137.

DALÉN, P. (in press) One, two, or many? In *Genetic Factors in Schizophrenia* (Ed. A. R. Kaplan). Springfield, Ill.: Thomas.

DALY, R. F. (1969) Neurological abnormalities in XYY males. *Nature (Lond.)*, **221**, 472–473.

DEMING, W. E. (1968) A recursion formula for the proportion of persons having a first admission as schizophrenic, *Behavl. Sci.*, **13**, 467–476.

DENCKER, S. J. (1958) *A Follow-up Study of 128 Closed Head Injuries in Twins using Co-twins as Controls.* Copenhagen: Munksgaard.

DINGMAN, H. F. (1968) Psychological test patterns in Down's syndrome. In *Progress in Human Behavior Genetics* (Ed. S. G. Vandenberg). Baltimore: Johns Hopkins Press, 19–25.

DOBSON, J., KOCH, R., WILLIAMSON, M., SPECTOR, R., FRANKENBURG, W., O'FLYNN, M., WARNER, R., and HUDSON, F. (1968) Cognitive development and dietary therapy in phenylketonuric children. *New Engl. J. Med.*, **278**, 1142–1144.

DOMINO, G., GOLDSCHMID, M., and KAPLAN, M. (1964) Personality traits of institutionalized mongoloid girls. *Amer. J. ment. Def.*, **68**, 498–502.

DOOSE, H., GERKEN, H., and VÖLZKE, E. (1967) Electren-cephalographische Untersuchungen über die Genetik zentrencephaler Epilepsien. *Z. Kinderheilk.*, **101**, 242–257.

DOUGLAS, J. W. B., ROSS, J. M., and SIMPSON, H. R. (1968) *All Our Future.* London: Davies.

EDWARDS, J. H. (1960) The simulation of Mendelism. *Acta Genet. (Basel)*, **10**, 63–70.

EDWARDS, J. H., DENT, T., and KAHN J. (1966) Monozygotic twins of different sex, *J. med. Genet.*, **3**, 117–123.

ELIA, G. d' and PERRIS, C. (1969) Selbstmordversuche im Laufe unipolarer und bipolarer Depressionen. *Arch. Psychiat. Nervenkr.*, **212**, 339–356.

ELSÄSSER, G. (1952) *Die Nachkommen geisteskranker Elternpaare.* Stuttgart: Thieme.

ELSTON, R. C. and GOTTESMAN, I. I. (1968) The analysis of quantitative inheritance simultaneously from twin and family data. *Amer. J. hum. Genet.*, **20**, 512–521.

EPEN, J. H. van. (1969) Defect schizophrenic states (residual schizophrenia), *Psychiat. Neurol. Neurochir.*, **72**, 371–394.

ERLENMEYER-KIMLING, L. (1968) Mortality rates in the offspring of schizophrenic parents and a physiological advantage hypothesis. *Nature (Lond.)*, **220**, 798–800.

ERLENMEYER-KIMLING, L. and JARVIK, L. F. (1963) Genetics and intelligence: a review. *Science*, **142**, 1477–1479.

ERLENMEYER-KIMLING, L. and PARADOWSKI, W. (1966) Selection and schizophrenia, *Amer. Nat.*, **100**, 651–665.

ESSEN-MÖLLER, E. (1941) Psychiatrische Untersuchungen an einer Serie von Zwillingen, *Acta Psychiat. Neurol. Scand.*, Suppl. 23.

ESSEN-MÖLLER, E. (1956) Individual traits and morbidity in a Swedish rural population. *Acta Psychiat. Neurol. Scand.*, Suppl. 100.

ESSEN-MÖLLER, E. (1965) Environmental freedom and genetic determination. *Acta Psychiat. Scand.*, **41**, 478–482.

ESSEN-MÖLLER, E. (1970) Twenty-one psychiatric cases and their MZ cotwins: a thirty years' follow-up. *Acta Genet. Med. Gemell.*, **19**, 315–317.

EVANS, D. A. PRICE (1969) Pharmacogenetics. In *Selected Topics in Medical Genetics* (Ed. C. A. Clarke). London: Oxford Univ. Press, 69–109.

EVANS, D. A. P., DAVISON, K., and PRATT, R. T. C. (1965) The influence of acetylator phenotype on the effects of treating depression with phenelzine. *Clin. pharmacol. Therap.*, **6**, 430–435.

EYSENCK, H. J. (1956) The inheritance of extraversion-introversion. *Acta Psychol.*, **12**, 95–110.

EYSENCK, H. J. (1967) *The Biological Basis of Personality.* Springfield, Ill.: Thomas.

EYSENCK, H. J. and PRELL, D. B. (1951) The inheritance of neuroticism: an experimental study. *J. ment. Sci.*, **97**, 441–465.

FALCONER, D. S. (1960) *Introduction to Quantitative Genetics.* Edinburgh: Oliver & Boyd.

FALCONER, D. S. (1965) The inheritance of liability to certain diseases, estimated from the incidence among relatives. *Ann. hum. Genet.*, **29**, 51–76.

FALCONER, D. S. (1966) Genetic consequences of selection pressure. In *Genetic and Environmental Factors in Human Ability* (Ed. J. E. Meade and A. S. Parkes). Edinburgh: Oliver & Boyd, 219–232.

FALCONER, D. S. (1967) The inheritance of liability to diseases with variable age of onset, with particular reference to diabetes mellitus. *Ann. hum. Genet.*, **31**, 1–20.

FENTON, G. W. and SCOTTON, L. (1967) Personality and the alpha rhythm. *Brit. J. Psychiat.*, **113**, 1283–1289.

FISCHER, M. (1971) Psychoses in the offspring of schizophrenic monozygotic twins and their normal co-twins. *Brit. J. Psychiat.*, **118**, 43–52.

FISCHER, M., HARVALD, B., and HAUGE, M. (1969) A Danish twin study of schizophrenia. *Brit. J. Psychiat.*, **115**, 981–990.

FLACH, M., SCHWICKARDI, H., and STEINERT, R. (1968) Zur Frage des Einflusses erblicher Faktoren auf den Stimmklang (Zwillingsuntersuchungen). *Folia Phoniat.*, **20**, 369–378.

FONSECA, A. F. da (1959) *Análise Heredo-Clínica das Perturbações Afectivas.* Oporto: Faculdade de Medicina.

FORSSMAN, H. and HAMBERT, G. (1963) Incidence of Klinefelter's syndrome among mental patients. *Lancet*, **i**, 1327.

FRASER, G. R. and FRIEDMANN, A. I. (1967) *The Causes of Blindness in Childhood.* Baltimore: Johns Hopkins Press.

FREEDMAN, D. G. (1965) An ethological approach to the genetical study of human behavior. In *Methods and Goals in Human Behavior Genetics* (Ed. S. G. Vandenberg). New York: Academic Press, 141–161.

FREEDMAN, D. G. (1968) The ethological study of man. In *Genetic and Environmental Influences on Behaviour* (Ed. J. M. Thoday and A. S. Parkes). Edinburgh: Oliver & Boyd, 37–62.

FREEDMAN, D. G. and KELLER, B. (1963) Inheritance of behavior in infants. *Science*, **140**, 196–198.

FREEMAN, F. N., HOLZINGER, K. J., and MITCHELL, B. C. (1928) The influence of environment on the intelligence, school achievement and conduct of foster children. *National Society for the Study of Education, 27th Yearbook*, Part I. Bloomington: Public School Publishing Co., 102–217.

FREMMING, K. H. (1951) *The Expectation of Mental Infirmity in a Sample of the Danish Population*, Eugenics Society Occasional Papers on Eugenics, No. 7. London: Cassell.

FULLER, J. L., EASLER, C., and SMITH, M. E. (1950) Inheritance of audiogenic seizure susceptibility in the mouse. *Genetics*, **35**, 622–632.

FULLER, J. L. and THOMPSON, W. R. (1960) *Behavior Genetics*. New York: Wiley.

GARRISON, R. J., ANDERSON, V. E., and REED, S. C. (1968) Assortative marriage. *Eugen. Quart.*, **15**, 113–127.

GEDDA, L. (1951) *Studio dei Gemelli*. Rome: Edizioni Orizzonte Medico.

GEDDA, L., BIANCHI, A., and BIANCHI-NERONI, L. (1955) La voce dei gemelli. I. Prova di identificazione intra-geminale della voce in 104 coppie (58 MZ e 46 DZ). *Acta Genet. Med. Gemell.*, **4**, 121–130.

GLASS, D. C. (Ed.) (1968) *Genetics*. New York: Rocke-feller University Press and Russell Sage Foundation.

GOLDBERG, E. M. and MORRISON, S. L. (1963) Schizo-phrenia and social class. *Brit. J. Psychiat.*, **109**, 785–802.

GOLDING, A. M. B. (1968) Ascertainment of subnormality in Bedfordshire. *J. ment. Def. Res.*, **12**, 81–83.

GOODMAN, R. M., HALL, C. L., TERANGO, L., PERRINE, G. A., and ROBERTS, P. L. (1966) Huntington's chorea. *Arch. Neurol. (Chic.)*, **15**, 345–355.

GOTTESMAN, I. I. (1963a) Genetic aspects of intelligent behavior. In *The Handbook of Mental Deficiency* (Ed. N. Ellis). New York: McGraw-Hill, 253–296.

GOTTESMAN, I. I. (1963b) Heritability of personality: a demonstration. *Psychol. Monogr.*, **77**, 9, whole number 572.

GOTTESMAN, I. I. (1965) Personality and natural selection. In *Methods and Goals in Human Behavior Genetics* (Ed. S. G. Vandenberg). New York: Academic Press, 63–80.

GOTTESMAN, I. I. (1966) Genetic variance in adaptive personality traits. *J. Child Psychol. Psychiat.*, **7**, 199–208.

GOTTESMAN, I. I. (1968) A sampler of human behavioral genetics. In *Evolutionary Biology*, Vol. 2. (Ed. Th. Dobzhansky, M. K. Hecht, and W. C. Steere). New York: Appleton-Century-Crofts, 276–320.

GOTTESMAN, I. I. and SHIELDS, J. (1966a) Schizophrenia in twins: 16 years' consecutive admissions to a psychi-atric clinic. *Brit. J. Psychiat.*, **112**, 809–818.

GOTTESMAN, I. I. and SHIELDS, J. (1966b) Contributions of twin studies to perspectives on schizophrenia. In *Progress in Experimental Personality Research, Vol. 3* (Ed. B. A. Maher). New York: Academic Press, 1–84.

GOTTESMAN, I. I. and SHIELDS, J. (1967) A polygenic theory of schizophrenia, *Proc. Nat. Acad. Sci. (USA)*, **58**, 199–205.

GOTTESMAN, I. I. and SHIELDS, J. (1968) In pursuit of the schizophrenic genotype. In *Progress in Human Behavior Genetics* (Ed. S. G. Vandenberg). Baltimore: Johns Hopkins Press, 67–103.

GOTTESMAN, I. I. and SHIELDS, J. (in press) *Schizophrenia and Genetics: a Twin Study Vantage Point*. New York: Academic Press.

GOWERS, W. (1908) Heredity in diseases of the nervous system. *Brit. med. J.*, **2**, 1541–1543.

GREBE, H. (1955) Sport bei Zwillingen. *Acta Genet. Med. Gemell.*, **4**, 275–295.

GRUENBERG, E. M. (1964) Epidemiology. In *Mental Retardation* (Ed. H. A. Stevens and R. Heber). Chicago: University of Chicago Press, 259–306.

GUZE, S. B., WOLFGRAM, E. D., McKINNEY, J. K., and CANTWELL, D. P. (1967) Psychiatric illness in the families of convicted criminals: a study of 519 first-degree relatives. *Dis. nerv. Syst.*, **28**, 651–659.

HACKNEY, I. M., HANLEY, W. B., DAVIDSON, W., and LINSAO, L. (1968) Phenylketonuria: mental develop-ment, behavior, and termination of low phenylalanine diet. *J. Pediat.*, **72**, 646–655.

HAGNELL, O. (1966) *A Prospective Study of the Incidence of Mental Disorder*. Stockholm, Scand. Univ. Books.

HALLGREN, B. (1950) Specific dyslexia ('congenital word-blindness'): a clinical and genetic study. *Acta Psychiat. Neurol. Scand.*, Suppl. 65.

HALLGREN, B. (1957) Enuresis, a clinical and genetic study. *Acta Psychiat. Neurol. Scand.*, Suppl. 114.

HALLGREN, B. (1960) Nocturnal enuresis in twins. I. Methods and material. *Acta Psychiat. Neurol. Scand.*, **35**, 73–90.

HALLGREN, B. and SJÖGREN, T. (1959) A clinical and genetico-statistical study of schizophrenia and low-grade mental deficiency in a large Swedish rural population. *Acta Psychiat. Neurol. Scand.*, Suppl. 140.

HAMBERT, G. and FREY, T. S. (1964) The electroence-phalogram in the Klinefelter syndrome. *Acta Psychiat. Scand.*, **40**, 28–36.

HAMPSON, J. L., HAMPSON, J. G., and MONEY, J. (1955) The syndrome of gonadal agenesis (ovarian agenesis) and male chromosomal pattern in girls and women: psychologic studies. *Bull. Johns Hopkins Hosp.*, **97**, 207–226.

HANS, M. B. and GILMORE, T. H. (1969) Huntington's chorea and genealogical credibility. *J. nerv. ment. Dis.*, **148**, 5–13.

HANSOTIA, P., CLEELAND, C. S., and CHUN, R. W. M. (1968) Juvenile Huntington's chorea. *Neurol.*, **18**, 217–224.

HARRIS, H. (1968) Molecular basis of hereditary disease, *Brit. med. J.*, **2**, 135–141.

HARVALD, B. (1954) *Heredity in Epilepsy. An Electro-encephalographic Study of Relatives of Epileptics*. Copenhagen: Munksgaard.

HARVALD, B. and HAUGE, M. (1965) Hereditary factors elucidated by twin studies. In *Genetics and the Epi-demiology of Chronic Diseases* (Eds. J. V. Neel, M. W. Shaw and W. J. Schull) US Department of Health, Education and Welfare, Washington, 61–76.

HAUGE, M., HARVALD, B., FISCHER, M., GOTLIEB-JENSEN, K., JUEL-NIELSEN, N., RAEBILD, I., SHAPIRO, R., and VIDEBECH, T. (1968) The Danish Twin Register. *Acta Genet. Med. Gemell.*, **17**, 315–332.

HEDENSTRÖM, I. v. (1969) Sensitivity to photic stimula-tion in the relatives of epileptics. *J. Amer. med. wom. Assoc.*, **24**, 227–229.

HESTON, L. L. (1966) Psychiatric disorders in foster home reared children of schizophrenic mothers. *Brit. J. Psychiat.*, **112**, 819–825.

HESTON, L. L. (1970) The genetics of schizophrenic and schizoid disease. *Science*, **167**, 249–256.

HESTON, L. L., LOWTHER, D. L. W., and LEVENTHAL,

C. M. (1966) Alzheimer's disease: a family study. *Arch. Neurol. (Chic.)*, **15**, 225–233.

HESTON, L. L. and SHIELDS, J. (1968) Homosexuality in twins: a family study and a registry study. *Arch. gen. Psychiat.*, **18**, 149–160.

HIGGINS, J. (1966) Effects of child rearing by schizophrenic mothers. *J. Psychiat. Res.*, **4**, 153–167.

HIGGINS, J. V., REED, E. W., and REED, S. C. (1962) Intelligence and family size: a paradox resolved. *Eugen. Quart.*, **9**, 84–90.

HILL, D. and WATTERSON, D. (1942) Electro-encephalographic studies of psychopathic personalities. *J. Neurol. Psychiat.*, **5**, 47–65.

HIRSCH, J. (Ed.) (1967) *Behavior-Genetic Analysis*. New York: McGraw-Hill.

HIRSCH, S. R. and LEFF, J. P. (1971) Parental abnormalities of verbal communication in the transmission of schizophrenia. *Psychol. Med.*, **1**, 118–127.

HOFFER, A. and POLLIN, W. (1970) Schizophrenia in the NAS-NRC panel of 15,909 twin pairs. *Arch. gen. Psychiat.*, **23**, 469–477.

HOPE, K., PHILIP, A. E., and LOUGHRAN, J. M. (1967) Psychological characteristics associated with XYY sex-chromosome complement in a state mental hospital. *Brit. J. Psychiat.*, **113**, 495–498.

HOPKINSON, G. (1964) A genetic study of affective illness in patients over 50. *Brit. J. Psychiat.*, **110**, 244–254.

HOPKINSON, G. and LEY, P. (1969) A genetic study of affective disorder. *Brit. J. Psychiat.*, **115**, 917–922.

HSIA, D. Y.-Y. (1967) The hereditary metabolic diseases. In *Behavior-Genetic Analysis* (Ed. J. Hirsch). New York: McGraw-Hill, 176–193.

HSIA, D. Y.-Y., DRISCOLL, K. W., TROLL, W., and KNOX, W. E. (1956) Detection by phenylalanine tolerance tests of heterozygous carriers of phenylketonuria. *Nature (Lond.)*, **178**, 1239–1240.

HUSÉN, T. (1959) *Psychological Twin Research; I. A Methodological Study*. Stockholm: Almqvist & Wicksell.

IHDA, S. (1960) A study of neurosis by twin method. *Psychiat. Neurol. Japon.*, **63**, 861–892 (Japanese, English summary).

INGHAM, J. G. (1966) Changes in MPI scores in neurotic patients: a three year follow-up. *Brit. J. Psychiat.*, **112**, 931–939.

INOUYE, E. (1963) Similarity and dissimilarity of schizophrenia in twins. *Proc. Third Internat. Congr. Psychiat., 1961*, **1**, Montreal: University of Toronto Press, 524–530.

JABLON, S., NEEL, J. V., GERSHOWITZ, H., and ATKINSON, G. F. (1967) The NAS-NRC twin panel: methods of construction of the panel, zygosity diagnosis, and proposed use. *Amer. J. hum. Genet.*, **19**, 133–161.

JACOB, F. and MONOD, J. (1961) On the regulation of gene activity. *Cold Spring Harbor Sympos. Quant. Biol.*, **26**, 193–211.

JACOBS, P. A., PRICE, W. H., RICHMOND, S., and RATCLIFF, R. A. W. (1971) Chromosome surveys in penal institutions and approved schools. *J. med. Genet.*, **8**, 49–53.

JINKS, J. L. and FULKER, D. W. (1970) A comparison of the biometrical genetical, MAVA and classical approaches to the analysis of human behavior, *Psychol. Bull.*, **73**, 311–349.

JONES, H. E. (1929) Homogamy in intellectual abilities. *Amer. J. Sociol.*, **35**, 369–382.

JONES, H. E. (1955) Perceived differences among twins. *Eugen. Quart.*, **2**, 98–102.

JONSSON, E. and NILSSON, T. (1968) Alkoholkonsumtion hos monozygota och dizygota tvillingpar. *Hyg. Tidskrift*, **49**, 21–25.

JUDA, A. (1939) Neue psychiatrisch-genealogische Untersuchungen an Hilfsschulzwillingen und ihren Familien: I. Die Zwillingsprobanden und ihre Partner. *Z. ges. Neurol. Psychiat.*, **166**, 365–452.

JUEL-NIELSEN, N. (1965) Individual and environment. A psychiatric-psychological investigation of monozygotic twins reared apart. *Acta Psychiat. Scand.*, Suppl. 183.

JUEL-NIELSEN, N. and HARVALD, B. (1958) The electro-encephalogram in uniovular twins brought up apart. *Acta Genet. (Basel)*, **8**, 57–64.

KAHN, J. (1969) Personal communication.

KAIJ, L. (1960) *Alcoholism in Twins*. Stockholm: Almqvist and Wiksell.

KAIJ, L. (1967) Atypical endogenous psychosis. Report on a family. *Brit. J. Psychiat.*, **113**, 415–422.

KALLMANN, F. J. (1938) *The Genetics of Schizophrenia*. New York: Augustin.

KALLMANN, F. J. (1946) The genetic theory of schizophrenia. An analysis of 691 schizophrenic twin index families. *Amer. J. Psychiat.*, **103**, 309–322.

KALLMANN, F. J. (1950) The genetics of psychoses: an analysis of 1,232 twin index families. *Internat. Congr. Psychiat., Rapports*, **6**, 1–27. Paris: Hermann.

KALLMANN, F. J. (1952) Comparative twin study on the genetic aspects of male homosexuality. *J. nerv. ment. Dis.*, **115**, 283–298.

KALLMANN, F. J. and ANASTASIO, M. M. (1947) Twin studies on the psychopathology of suicide. *J. nerv. ment. Dis.*, **105**, 40–55.

KALLMANN, F. J., FEINGOLD, L., and BONDY, E. (1951) Comparative adaptational, social, and psychometric data on the life histories of senescent twin pairs. *Amer. J. hum. Genet.*, **3**, 65–73.

KALLMANN, F. J., DE PORTE, J., DE PORTE, E., and FEINGOLD, L. (1949) Suicide in twins and only children. *Amer. J. hum. Genet.*, **1**, 113–126.

KALMUS, H. (1949) Tune deafness and its inheritance. *Proc. 8th Internat. Congr. Genet., Hereditas*, Lund, Suppl., 605.

KALMUS, H. (1965) *Diagnosis and Genetics of Defective Colour Vision*. Oxford: Pergamon.

KALMUS, H. (1968) The worlds of the colour blind and the tune deaf. In *Genetic and Environmental Influences on Behaviour* (Ed. J. M. Thoday and A. S. Parkes). Edinburgh: Oliver & Boyd, 206–208.

KAPLAN, A. R. (1968) Physiological and pathological correlates of differences in taste acuity. In *Progress in Human Behavior Genetics* (Ed. S. G. Vandenberg). Baltimore: Johns Hopkins Press, 31–66.

KAPLAN, A. R. (Ed.) (in press) *Genetic Factors in Schizophrenia*. Springfield, Ill.: Thomas.

KARLSSON, J. L. (1966) *The Biologic Basis of Schizophrenia*. Springfield, Ill.: Thomas.

KAY, D. W. K. (1959) Observations on the natural history and genetics of old age psychoses: a Stockholm material, 1931–7. *Proc. roy. soc. Med.*, **52**, 791–794.

KAY, D. W. K. (1963) Late paraphrenia and its bearing on the aetiology of schizophrenia. *Acta Psychiat. Scand.*, **39**, 159–169.

KAY, D. W. K. (1964) The genetics of stuttering. In *The Syndrome of Stuttering* (G. Andrews and M. Harris) Clinics in Developmental Medicine, No. 17. London: Heinemann, 132–143.

KAY, D. W. K., GARSIDE, R. F., BEAMISH, P., and ROY, J. R. (1969a) Endogenous and neurotic syndromes of depression: a factor analytic study of 104 cases. Clinical features. *Brit. J. Psychiat.*, **115**, 377–388.

KAY, D. W. K., GARSIDE, R. F., ROY, J. R., and BEAMISH, P. (1969b) 'Endogenous' and 'neurotic' syndromes of depression: a 5- to 7-year follow-up of 104 cases. *Brit. J. Psychiat.*, **115**, 389–399.

KENDELL, R. E. (1968) *The Classification of Depressive Illnesses*. Maudsley Monographs No. 18. London: Oxford Univ. Press.

KETY, S. S., ROSENTHAL, D., WENDER, P. H., and SCHULSINGER, F. (1968) The types and prevalence of mental illness in the biological and adoptive families of adopted schizophrenics. In *The Transmission of Schizophrenia* (Ed. D. Rosenthal and S. S. Kety). Oxford: Pergamon, 345–362.

KIDD, C. B., KNOX, R. S., and MANTLE, D. J. (1963) A psychiatric investigation of triple-X chromosome females. *Brit. J. Psychiat.*, **109**, 90–94.

KILOH, L. G. and GARSIDE, R. F. (1963) The independence of neurotic depression and endogenous depression. *Brit. J. Psychiat.*, **109**, 451–463.

KLINTWORTH, G. K. (1962) A pair of male monozygotic twins discordant for homosexuality. *J. nerv. ment. Dis.*, **135**, 113–125.

KOCH, G. (1967) Epilepsien. In *Humangenetik, ein kurzes Handbuch, V/2* (Ed. P. E. Becker). Stuttgart: Thieme, 1–83.

KRANZ, H. (1936) *Lebensschicksale krimineller Zwillinge*. Berlin: Springer.

KRINGLEN, E. (1967) *Heredity and Environment in the Functional Psychoses*. London: Heinemann.

LADER, M. H. and WING, L. (1966) *Physiological Measures, Sedative Drugs, and Morbid Anxiety*. Maudsley Monographs No. 14. London: Oxford Univ. Press.

LANGE, J. (1929) *Verbrechen als Schicksal, Studien an kriminellen Zwillingen*. Leipzig: Thieme.

LARSON, C. A. and NYMAN, G. E. (1968) Phenylketonuria: mental illness in heterozygotes. *Psychiat. Clin.*, **1**, 367–374.

LARSSON, T., SJÖGREN, T., and JACOBSON, G. (1963) Senile dementia: a clinical, sociomedical and genetic study. *Acta Psychiat. Scand.*, Suppl. 167.

LEESE, S. M., POND, D. A., and SHIELDS, J. (1952) A pedigree of Huntington's chorea. *Ann. Eugen.*, **17**, 92–112.

LENNOX, W. G., GIBBS, E. L., and GIBBS, F. A. (1939) The inheritance of epilepsy as revealed by the electro-encephalograph. *J. Amer. med. Ass.*, **113**, 1,002–1,003.

LENNOX, W. G. and JOLLY, D. H. (1954) Seizures, brain waves and intelligence tests of epileptic twins. *Res. Publ. Ass. nerv. Ment. Dis.*, **33**, 325–345.

LEONHARD, K. (1934) Atypische endogene Psychosen im Lichte der Familienforschung, *Z. ges. Neurol. Psychiat.*, **149**, 520–562.

LEONHARD, K., KORFF, I., and SCHULZ, H. (1962) Die Temperamente in den Familien der monopolaren und bipolaren phasischen Psychosen. *Psychiat. Neurol. (Basel)*, **143**, 416–434.

LESSER, G. S., FIFER, G., and CLARK, D. H. (1965) Mental abilities of children from different social-class and cultural groups. *Monogr. Soc. Res. Child Develop.*, **30**, Serial No. 102, 1–115.

LEWIS, A. (1935) Problems of obsessional illness. *Proc. roy. soc. Med.*, **29**, 325–336.

LEWIS, A. (1967) Empirical or rational? the nature and basis of psychiatry. *Lancet*, **ii**, 1–9.

LEWONTIN, R. C. (1967) An estimate of average heterozygosity in man. *Amer. J. hum. Genet.*, **19**, 681–685.

LIDZ, T., WILD, C., SCHAFER, S., ROSMAN, B., and FLECK, S. (1962) Thought disorders in the parents of schizophrenic patients: a study utilizing the object sorting test. *J. Psychiat. Res.*, **1**, 193–200.

LJUNGBERG, L. (1957) Hysteria: a clinical, prognostic and genetic study. *Acta Psychiat. Neurol. Scand.*, Suppl. 112.

LOVIBOND, S. H. (1954) The object sorting test and conceptual thinking in schizophrenia. *Austral. J. Psychol.*, **6**, 52–70.

LUNDBORG, H. (1903) *Die progressive Myoklonus-Epilepsie*. Uppsala: Almquist & Wiksell.

LUXENBURGER, H. (1928) Vorläufiger Bericht über psychiatrische Serienuntersuchungen an Zwillingen. *Z. ges. Neurol. Psychiat.*, **116**, 297–326.

LUXENBURGER, H. (1930) Psychiatrisch-neurologische Zwillingspathologie. *Zbl. ges. Neurol. Psychiat.*, **56**, 145–180.

LYLE, J. G. (1959) The effect of an institution environment upon the verbal development of imbecile children. I. Verbal intelligence. *J. ment. Def. Res.*, **3**, 122–128.

LYLE, J. G. (1960) The effect of an institution environment upon the verbal development of imbecile children. III. The Brooklands residential family unit. *J. ment. Def. Res.*, **4**, 14–23.

MACALPINE, I. and HUNTER, R. (1966) The 'insanity' of King George III: a classic case of porphyria. *Brit. med. J.*, **1**, 65–71.

MACALPINE, I., HUNTER, R., and RIMINGTON, C. (1968) Porphyria in the royal houses of Stuart, Hanover, and Prussia: a follow-up study of George III's illness. *Brit. med. J.*, **1**, 7–18.

McCLEARN, G. E. (1968) Genetics and motivation of the mouse. In *Nebraska Symposium on Motivation, 1968*. (Ed. Wm. J. Arnold). Lincoln, Nebraska: Univ. Nebraska Press, 47–83.

McCONAGHY, N. (1959) The use of an object sorting test in elucidating the hereditary factor in schizophrenia. *J. Neurol. Neurosurg. Psychiat.*, **22**, 243–246.

McCONAGHY, N. and CLANCY, M. (1968) Familial

relationships of allusive thinking in university students and their parents. *Brit. J. Psychiat.*, **114**, 1079–1087.

McCONAGHY, N., JOFFE, A. D., and MURPHY, B. (1967) The independence of neurotic and endogenous depression. *Brit. J. Psychiat.*, **113**, 479–484.

McINNES, R. G. (1937) Observations on heredity in neurosis. *Proc. roy. soc. Med.*, **30**, 895–904.

McKUSICK, V. A. (1966) *Mendelian Inheritance in Man.* London: Heinemann.

MACLEAN, N., COURT BROWN, W. M., JACOBS, P. A., MANTLE, D. J., and STRONG, J. A. (1968) A survey of sex chromatin abnormalities in mental hospitals. *J. med. Genet.*, **5**, 165–172.

MARDONES, R. J., SEGOVIA, M. N., and HEDERRA, D. A. (1953) Heredity of experimental alcohol preference in rats. II. Coefficient of heredity. *Quart. J. Stud. Alc.*, **14**, 1–2.

MEADE, J. E. and PARKES, A. S. (1965) *Biological Aspects of Social Problems.* Edinburgh: Oliver & Boyd.

MEDNICK, S. A. and SCHULSINGER, F. (1968) Some premorbid characteristics related to breakdown in children with schizophrenic mothers. In *The Transmission of Schizophrenia* (Ed. D. Rosenthal and S. S. Kety). Oxford: Pergamon, 267–291.

MEISSNER, W. W. (1965) Functional and adaptive aspects of cellular regulatory mechanisms. *Psychol. Bull.*, **64**, 206–216.

MELLBIN, G. (1966) Neuropsychiatric disorders in sex chromatin negative women. *Brit. J. Psychiat.*, **112**, 145–148.

METCALFE, M. (1968) The personality of depressive patients: 1. Assessment of change. 2. Assessment of the premorbid personality. In *Recent Developments in Affective Disorders* (Ed. A. Coppen and A. Walk) Brit. J. Psychiat. Spec. Publn. No. 2. Ashford, Kent: Headley, 97–104.

METRAKOS, K. and METRAKOS, J. D. (1961) Genetics of convulsive disorders. II. Genetic and electroencephalographic studies in centrencephalic epilepsy. *Neurology*, **11**, 474–483.

MITSUDA, H. (Ed.) (1967) *Clinical Genetics in Psychiatry.* Tokio: Igaku Shoin.

MITTLER, P. (1971) *The Study of Twins*, Penguin Science of Behaviour. London: Penguin.

MONEY, J. (1963) Cytogenetic and psychosexual incongruities with a note on space-form blindness. *Amer. J. Psychiat.*, **119**, 820–827.

MONEY, J. (1968) Cognitive deficits in Turner's syndrome. In *Progress in Human Behavior Genetics* (Ed. S. G. Vandenberg). Baltimore: Johns Hopkins Press, 27–30.

MONEY, J., HAMPSON, J. G., and HAMPSON, J. L. (1955) An examination of some basic sexual concepts: the evidence of human hermaphroditism. *Bull. Johns Hopkins Hosp.*, **97**, 301–319.

MONEY, J., HAMPSON, J. G., and HAMPSON, J. L. (1956) Sexual incongruities and psychopathology: the evidence of human hermaphroditism. *Bull. Johns Hopkins Hosp.*, **98**, 43–57.

MORAN, P. A. P. and SMITH, C. A. B. (1966) *Commentary on R. A. Fisher's Paper on The Correlation Between Relatives on the Supposition of Mendelian Inheritance.*

London: Cambridge Univ. Press for Galton Laboratory.

MORTON, N. E. (1967a) The detection of major genes under additive continuous variation. *Amer. J. hum. Genet.*, **19**, 23–34.

MORTON, N. E. (1967b) Population genetics of mental illness. *Eugen. Quart.*, **14**, 181–184.

MOSHER, L. R., POLLIN, W., and STABENAU, J. R. (1971) Families with identical twins discordant for schizophrenia: some relationships between identification, thinking styles, psychopathology and dominance-submissiveness. *Brit. J. Psychiat.*, **118**, 29–42.

MULLER, H. J. (1956) Genetic principles in human populations. *Amer. J. Psychiat.*, **113**, 481–491.

MUNRO, T. A. (1947) Phenylketonuria: data on forty-seven British families. *Ann. Eugen.*, **14**, 60–88.

MUNTZ, H. J. and POWER, R. P. (1970) Thought disorder in the parents of thought disordered schizophrenics. *Brit. J. Psychiat.*, **117**, 707–708.

MYRIANTHOPOULOS, N. C. (1966) Huntington's chorea. *J. med. Genet.*, **3**, 298–314.

MYRIANTHOPOULOS, N. C., KURLAND, A. A., and KURLAND, L. T. (1962) Hereditary predisposition in drug-induced Parkinsonism. *Arch. Neurol. (Chic.)*, **6**, 5–9.

NAKA, S., ABE, K., and SUZUKI, H. (1965) Childhood behavior characteristics of the parents in certain behavior problems of children, *Acta Paedopsychiat. (Basel)*, **32**, 11–16.

NANCE, W. E. (1969) Anencephaly and spina bifida: a possible example of cytoplasmic inheritance in man. *Nature (Lond.)*, **224**, 373–375.

NEEL, J. V. and SCHULL, W. J. (1954) *Human Heredity.* Chicago: Univ. Chicago Press.

NEWMAN, H. H., FREEMAN, F. N., and HOLZINGER, K. J. (1937) *Twins: a Study of Heredity and Environment.* Chicago: Univ. Chicago Press.

NIELSEN, J. (1964) Prevalence of Klinefelter's syndrome in patients with mental disorders. *Lancet*, **i**, 1109.

NIELSEN, J., TSUBOI, T., STÜRUP, G., and ROMANO, D. (1968) XYY chromosomal constitution in criminal psychopaths. *Lancet*, **ii**, 576.

O'CONNOR, N. and HERMELIN, B. (1963) *Speech and Thought in Severe Subnormality.* Oxford: Pergamon.

ØDEGAARD, Ø. (1952) Genetics and eugenics: discussion. In *Internat. Congr. Psychiat., Comptes Rendus 6.* Paris: Hermann, 84–90.

ØDEGAARD, Ø. (1963) The psychiatric disease entities in the light of a genetic investigation. *Acta Psychiat. Scand.*, Suppl. 169, 94–104.

ØDEGAARD, Ø. (in press) Polygenic theory of schizophrenia etiology. In *Genetic Factors in Schizophrenia* (Ed. A. R. Kaplan). Springfield, Ill.: Thomas.

OSBORNE, R. H. and DE GEORGE, F. V. (1959) *Genetic Basis of Morphological Variation.* Cambridge, Mass.: Harvard Univ. Press.

OSBORNE, R. T. (1970) Heritability estimates for the visual evoked response. *Life Sci.*, **9**, Pt. 2, 481–490.

OUNSTED, C. (1955) Genetic and social aspects of the epilepsies of childhood. *Eugen. Rev.*, **47**, 33–49.

OUNSTED, C., LINDSAY, J., and NORMAN, R. (1966) *Biological Factors in Temporal Lobe Epilepsy*, Clinics in Developmental Medicine No. 22. London: Heinemann.

OVERZIER, C. (Ed.) (1963) *Intersexuality*. London: Academic Press.

PAINE, R. S. (1957) The variability in manifestations of untreated patients with phenylketonuria (phenylpyruvic acidurea). *Pediatrics*, **20**, 290–302.

PANSE, F. (1942) *Die Erbchorea*. Leipzig: Thieme.

PARE, C. M. B. (1956) Homosexuality and chromosomal sex. *J. psychosomat. Res.*, **1**, 247–251.

PARKER, N. (1964a) Homosexuality in twins: a report on three discordant pairs. *Brit. J. Psychiat.*, **110**, 489–495.

PARKER, N. (1964b) Close identification in twins discordant for obsessional neurosis. *Brit. J. Psychiat.*, **110**, 496–504.

PARKER, N. (1964c) Twins: a psychiatric study of a neurotic group. *Med. J. Austral.*, **2**, 735–742.

PARKER, N. (1965) *Twins: a psychiatric study*, unpublished MD thesis, University of Queensland, Australia.

PARSONS, P. A. (1967) *The Genetic Analysis of Behaviour*. London: Methuen.

PARTANEN, J., BRUUN, K., and MARKKANEN, T. (1966) *Inheritance of Drinking Behavior*. Helsinki: The Finnish Foundation for Alcohol Studies.

PASQUALINI, R. Q., VIDAL, G., and BUR, G. E. (1957) Psychopathology of Klinefelter's Syndrome: review of thirty-one cases. *Lancet*, **ii**, 164–167.

PATTERSON, R. M., BAGCHI, B. K., and TEST, A. (1948) The prediction of Huntington's chorea, an electroencephalographic and genetic study. *Amer. J. Psychiat.*, **104**, 786–797.

PEARSON, K. (1931) On the inheritance of mental disease. *Ann. Eugen.*, **4**, 362–380.

PEARSON, K. and JAEDERHOLM, G. A. (1914) *Mendelism and the Problem of Mental Defect*. London: Dulau.

PEARSON, P. L., BOBROW, M., and VOSA, C. G. (1970) Technique for identifying Y chromosomes in human interphase nuclei. *Nature*, **226**, 78–80.

PENROSE, L. S. (1938) A clinical and genetic study of 1280 cases of mental defect. *Med. Res. Coun. Spec. Rep. Ser.*, No. 229. London: H.M.S.O.

PENROSE, L. S. (1961) Genetics of growth and development of the foetus. In *Recent Advances in Human Genetics* (Ed. L. S. Penrose). London: Churchill, 56–75.

PENROSE, L. S. (1963) *The Biology of Mental Defect*, 2nd Edn. London: Sidgwick & Jackson.

PENROSE, L. S. (1969) Effects of additive genes at many loci compared with those of a set of alleles at one locus in parent-child and sib correlations. *Ann. hum. Genet.*, **33**, 15–21.

PENROSE, L. S. and SMITH, G. F. (1966) *Down's Anomaly*. London: Churchill.

PERRIS, C. (1966) A study of bipolar (manic-depressive) and unipolar recurrent depressive psychoses. *Acta Psychiat. Scand.*, Suppl. 194.

PERRIS, C. (1968) Genetic transmission of depressive psychoses. *Acta Psychiat. Scand.*, Suppl. 203, 45–52.

PERRIS, C. (1971) Abnormality on paternal and maternal sides: observations in bipolar (manic-depressive) and unipolar depressive psychoses. *Brit. J. Psychiat.*, **118**, 207–210.

PERRY, T. L., TISCHLER, B., and CHAPPLE, J. A. (1966) The incidence of mental illness in the relatives of individuals suffering from phenylketonuria or mongolism. *J. Psychiat. Res.*, **4**, 51–57.

PETERSÉN, I. and ÅKESSON, H. O. (1968) EEG studies of siblings of children showing 14 and 6 per second positive spikes. *Acta Genet. (Basel)*, **18**, 163–169.

PHILLIPS, J. E., JACOBSON, N., and TURNER, W. J. (1965) Conceptual thinking in schizophrenics and their relatives. *Brit. J. Psychiat.*, **111**, 823–839.

PLEYDELL, M. J. (1954) Huntington's chorea in Northamptonshire. *Brit. med. J.*, **ii**, 1121–1128.

PLEYDELL, M. J. (1955) Huntington's chorea in Northamptonshire. *Brit. med. J.*, **ii**, 889.

POLANI, P. E. (1966) Chromosome anomalies and abortions. *Develop. Med. Child Neurol.*, **8**, 67–70.

POLANI, P. E. (1969) Autosomal imbalance and its syndromes, excluding Down's. *Brit. med. Bull.*, **25**, 81–93.

POLLIN, W., ALLEN, M. G., HOFFER, A., STABENAU, J. R., and HRUBEC, Z. (1969) Psychopathology in 15,909 pairs of veteran twins: evidence for a genetic factor in the pathogenesis of schizophrenia and its relative absence in psychoneurosis. *Amer. J. Psychiat.*, **126**, 597–609.

POLLIN, W. and STABENAU, J. R. (1968) Biological, psychological and historical differences in a series of monozygotic twins discordant for schizophrenia. In *The Transmission of Schizophrenia* (Ed. D. Rosenthal and S. S. Kety). Oxford: Pergamon, 317–332.

POLLIN, W., STABENAU, J. R., MOSHER, L., and TUPIN, J. (1966) Life history differences in identical twins discordant for schizophrenia. *Amer. J. Orthopsychiat.*, **36**, 492–509.

POND, D. A. and BIDWELL, B. H. (1960) A survey of epilepsy in fourteen general practices. II. Social and psychological aspects. *Epilepsia*, **1**, 285–299.

PORTER, I. H. (1966) The genetics of drug susceptibility. *Dis. nerv. Syst.*, Monogr. Suppl., **27**, No. 7, 25–36.

POST, R. H. (1962) Population differences in red and green color vision deficiency: a review, and a query on selection relaxation. *Eugen. Quart.*, **9**, 131–146.

PRATT, R. T. C. (1967) *The Genetics of Neurological Disorders*. London: Oxford Univ. Press.

PRATT, R. T. C., GARDINER, D., CURZON, G., PIERCY, M. F., and CUMINGS, J. N. (1963) Phenylalanine tolerance in endogenous depression. *Brit. J. Psychiat.*, **109**, 624–628.

PRICE, B. (1950) Primary biases in twin studies. *Amer. J. hum. Genet.*, **2**, 293–352.

PRICE, J. S. (1968) The genetics of depressive behaviour. In *Recent Developments in Affective Disorders* (Ed. A. Coppen and A. Walk) Brit. J. Psychiat. Spec. Publn, No. 2. Headley: Ashford, Kent, 37–54.

PRICE, J. S. (1969) Personality differences within families: comparison of adult brothers and sisters. *J. biosoc. Sci.*, **1**, 177–205.

PRICE, J. S. (1969) Personal communication.

PRICE, W. H., STRONG, J. A., WHATMORE, P. B., and McCLEMONT, W. F. (1966) Criminal patients with XYY sex-chromosome complement. *Lancet*, **i**, 565–566.

PRICE, W. H. and WHATMORE, P. B. (1967) Behaviour disorders and pattern of crime among XYY males identified at a maximum security hospital. *Brit. med. J.*, **1**, 533–536.

PRITCHARD, M. (1962) Homosexuality and genetic sex. *J. ment. Sci.*, **108**, 616–623.

RAINER, J. D., JARVIK, L. F., ABDULLAH, S., and KATO, T. (1969) XYY karyotype in monozygotic twins, *Lancet*, **ii**, 60.

RATCLIFFE, S. G., STEWART, A. L., MELVILLE, M. M., JACOBS, P. A., and KEAY, A. J. (1970) Chromosome studies on 3,500 newborn male infants, *Lancet*, **i**, 121–122.

RECORD, R. G., McKEOWN, T., and EDWARDS, J. H. (1970) An investigation of the difference in measured intelligence between twins and single births, *Ann. hum. Genet.*, **34**, 11–20.

REED, E. W. and REED, S. C. (1965) *Mental Retardation: a Family Study*. Philadelphia: Saunders.

REED, T. E. and CHANDLER, J. H. (1958) Huntington's chorea in Michigan. 1. Demography and genetics. *Amer. J. hum. Genet.*, **10**, 201–225.

REED, T. E. and NEEL, J. V. (1959) Huntington's chorea in Michigan. 2. Selection and mutation. *Amer. J. hum. Genet.*, **11**, 107–136.

REICH, T., CLAYTON, P. J., and WINOKUR, G. (1969) Family history studies: V. The genetics of mania. *Amer. J. Psychiat.*, **125**, 1358–1369.

REZNIKOFF, M. and HONEYMAN, M. S. (1967) MMPI profiles of monozygotic and dizygotic twin pairs, *J. consult. Psychol.*, **31**, 100.

RICHARDS, B. W. (1969) Mosaic mongolism. *J. ment. Def. Res.*, **13**, 66–83.

ROBERTS, J. A. F. (1952) The genetics of mental deficiency. *Eugen. Rev.*, **44**, 71–83.

ROBERTSON, A. (1967) Animal breeding. In *Annual Review of Genetics*, Vol. 1 (Ed. H. L. Roman, L. M. Sandler, and G. S. Stent). Palo Alto: Calif., Annual Reviews, 295–312.

RODGERS, D. A. and McCLEARN, G. E. (1962) Alcohol preference of mice. In *Roots of Behavior* (Ed. E. L. Bliss). New York: Harper, 68–95.

ROE, A., BURKS, B. S., and MITTELMANN, B. (1945) Adult adjustment of foster-children of alcoholic and psychotic parentage and the influence of the foster-home. Memoirs of the Section on Alcohol Studies, Yale Univ., No. 3. *Quart. J. Stud. Alc.*, New Haven.

ROLLIN, H. R. (1946) Personality in mongolism with special reference to the incidence of catatonic psychosis. *Amer. J. ment. Def.*, **51**, 219–237.

ROMNEY, D. (1969) Psychometrically assessed thought disorder in schizophrenic and control patients and in their parents and siblings. *Brit. J. Psychiat.*, **115**, 999–1002.

ROSANOFF, A. J., HANDY, L. M., and PLESSET, I. R. (1935) The etiology of manic-depressive syndromes with special reference to their occurrence in twins. *Amer. J. Psychiat.*, **91**, 725–762.

ROSANOFF, A. J., HANDY, L. M., and PLESSET, I. R. (1937) The etiology of mental deficiency with special reference to its occurrence in twins. *Psychol. Monogr.*, **216**, 1–137.

ROSANOFF, A. J., HANDY, L. M., and PLESSET, I. R. (1941) The etiology of child behavior difficulties, juvenile

delinquency and adult criminality with special reference to their occurrence in twins. *Psychiat. Monogr. (California)* No. 1. Sacramento: Dept. of Institutions.

ROSANOFF, A. J., HANDY, L. M., PLESSET, I. R., and BRUSH, S. (1934) The etiology of so-called schizophrenic psychoses with special reference to their occurrence in twins. *Amer. J. Psychiat.*, **91**, 247–286.

ROSENBERG, C. M. (1967) Familial aspects of obsessional neurosis. *Brit. J. Psychiat.*, **113**, 405–413.

ROSENTHAL, D. (1959) Some factors associated with concordance and discordance with respect to schizophrenia in monozygotic twins. *J. nerv. ment. Dis.*, **129**, 1–10.

ROSENTHAL, D. (1960) Confusion of identity and the frequency of schizophrenia in twins. *Arch. gen. Psychiat.*, **3**, 297–304.

ROSENTHAL, D. (1961) Sex distribution and the severity of illness among samples of schizophrenic twins. *J. Psychiat. Res.*, **1**, 26–36.

ROSENTHAL, D. (1962a) Problems of sampling and diagnosis in the major twin studies of schizophrenia. *J. Psychiat. Res.*, **1**, 116–134.

ROSENTHAL, D. (1962b) Familial concordance by sex with respect to schizophrenia, *Psychol. Bull.*, **59**, 401–421.

ROSENTHAL, D. (1970) *Genetic Theory and Abnormal Behavior*. New York: McGraw-Hill.

ROSENTHAL, D. (1971) Two adoption studies of heredity in the schizophrenic disorders. In *The Origin of Schizophrenia* (Ed. M. Bleuler and J. Angst). Berne: Huber, 21–34.

ROSENTHAL, D. and Colleagues (1963) *The Genain Quadruplets*. New York: Basic Books.

ROSENTHAL, D. and KETY, S. S. (Ed.) (1968) *The Transmission of Schizophrenia*. Oxford: Pergamon.

ROSENTHAL, D., WENDER, P. H., KETY, S. S., SCHULSINGER, F., WELNER, J., and ØSTERGAARD, L. (1968) Schizophrenics' offspring reared in adoptive homes. In *The Transmission of Schizophrenia* (Ed. D. Rosenthal and S. S. Kety). Oxford: Pergamon, 377–391.

ROSMAN, B., WILD, C., RICCI, J., FLECK, S., and LIDZ, T. (1964) Thought disorders in the parents of schizophrenic patients: a further study utilizing the object sorting test. *J. Psychiat. Res.*, **2**, 211–221.

RÜDIN, E. (1923) Über Vererbung geistiger Störungen. *Z. ges. Neurol. Psychiat.*, **81**, 459–496.

RÜDIN, EDITH (1953) Ein Beitrag zur Frage der Zwangskrankheit, insbesondere ihrer hereditären Beziehungen. *Arch. Psychiat. Z. Neurol.*, **191**, 14–54.

RUTTER, M. (1966) *Children of Sick Parents: an Environmental and Psychiatric Study*. Maudsley Monographs No. 16. London: Oxford Univ. Press.

RUTTER, M., KORN, S., and BIRCH, H. G. (1963) Genetic and environmental factors in the development of 'primary reaction patterns'. *Brit. J. soc. clin. Psychol.*, **2**, 161–173.

SABBATH, J. C., MORRIS, T. A., MENZER-BENARON, D., and STURGIS, S. H. (1961) Psychiatric observations in adolescent girls lacking ovarian function. *Psychosom. Med.*, **23**, 224–231.

SCALLY, B. G. (1968) The offspring of mental defectives. In *Advances in Teratology*, Vol. 3 (Ed. D. H. M. Woollam). London: Logos Press, 65–84.

SCARR, S. (1966) The origins of individual differences in adjective check list scores. *J. consult. Psychol.*, **30**, 354–357.

SCARR, S. (1968) Environmental bias in twin studies. In *Progress in Human Behavior Genetics* (Ed. S. G. Vandenberg). Baltimore: Johns Hopkins Press, 205–213.

SCHARFETTER, C. (1968) Zur Erbbiologie der symbiontischen Psychosen. *Arch. Psychiat. Nervenkr.*, **211**, 405–413.

SCHIÖTTZ-CHRISTENSEN, E. (1969) Chorea Huntington and epilepsy in monozygotic twins. *Europ. Neurol.*, **2**, 250–255.

SCHOPLER, E. and LOFTIN, J. (1969) Thought disorders in parents of psychotic children. *Arch. gen. Psychiat.*, **20**, 174–181.

SCHULSINGER, F. (1972) Psychopathy: heredity and environment. In *Genetics and Mental Disorders* (Ed. L. Erlenmeyer-Kimling). *Internat. J. ment. Health*, **1**, Nos 1–2, 190–206.

SCHULZ, B. (1951) Auszählungen in der Verwandtschaft von nach Erkrankungsalter und Geschlecht gruppierten Manisch-Depressiven. *Arch. Psychiat. Z. Neurol.*, **186**, 560–576.

SCOTT, J. P. (1958) *Animal Behavior.* Chicago: Univ. Chicago Press.

SCOTTISH COUNCIL FOR RESEARCH IN EDUCATION (1949) *The Trend of Scottish Intelligence.* London: Univ. London Press.

SHAKHMATOVA-PAVLOVA, I. (1967) Clinical genetics and the problem of the homogeneity in schizophrenia. In *Biological Research in Schizophrenia* (Ed. D. Lozovskii, Trans. of Symp. Instit. Psychiat., Moscow). Moscow: Acad. Med. Sci., U.S.S.R., 252–255.

SHAPIRO, R. W. (1970) A twin study of non-endogenous depression. *Acta Jutlandica*, **42**, No. 2.

SHIELDS, J. (1954) Personality differences and neurotic traits in normal twin schoolchildren. *Eugen. Rev.*, **45**, 213–246.

SHIELDS, J. (1962) *Monozygotic Twins Brought up Apart and Brought up Together.* London: Oxford Univ. Press.

SHIELDS, J. (1965) Review of *Psychiatric Illnesses in Identical Twins* by P. Tienari. *Brit. J. Psychiat.*, **111**, 777–781.

SHIELDS, J. (1968) Summary of the genetic evidence. In *The Transmission of Schizophrenia* (Ed. D. Rosenthal and S. S. Kety). Oxford: Pergamon Press, 95–126.

SHIELDS, J. (1971) Concepts of heredity for schizophrenia. In *The Origin of Schizophrenia* (Ed. M. Bleuler and J. Angst). Berne: Huber, 59–75.

SHIELDS, J., GOTTESMAN, I. I., and SLATER, E. (1967) Kallmann's 1946 schizophrenic twin study in the light of new information. *Acta Psychiat. Scand.*, **43**, 385–396.

SHIELDS, J. and SLATER, E. (1960) Heredity and psychological abnormality. In *Handbook of Abnormal Psychology*, 1st ed. (Ed. H. J. Eysenck). London: Pitman Medical, 298–343.

SHIELDS, J. and SLATER, E. (1966) La similarité du diagnostic chez les jumeaux et le problème de la spécificité biologique dans les névroses et les troubles de la personnalité. *L'Évolut. Psychiat.*, **31**, 441–451. English version in *Man, Mind, and Heredity* (1971)

(Ed. J. Shields and I. I. Gottesman). Baltimore: Johns Hopkins Press, 252–257.

SHIELDS, J. and SLATER, E. (1967) Genetic aspects of schizophrenia. *Hosp. Med. (Lond.)*, **1**, 579–584.

SHIPE, D., REISMAN, L. E., CHUNG, C-Y., DARNELL, A., and KELLY, S. (1968) The relationship between cytogenetic constitution, physical stigmata, and intelligence in Down's syndrome. *Amer. J. ment. Def.*, **72**, 789–797.

SHUTER, R. (1966) Hereditary and environmental factors in musical ability. *Eugen. Rev.*, **58**, 149–156.

SILVERSTEIN, A. B. (1964) An empirical test of the mongoloid stereotype. *Amer. J. ment. Def.*, **68**, 493–497.

SINGER, M. T. and WYNNE, L. C. (1963) Differentiating characteristics of parents of childhood schizophrenics, childhood neurotics, and young adult schizophrenics. *Amer. J. Psychiat.*, **120**, 234–243.

SINGER, M. T. and WYNNE, L. C. (1965) Thought disorder and family relations of schizophrenics: IV. Results and implications. *Arch. gen. Psychiat.*, **12**, 201–212.

SJÖGREN, T., SJÖGREN, H., and LINDGREN, Å. G. H. (1952) Morbus Alzheimer and morbus Pick: a genetic, clinical and patho-anatomical study. *Acta Psychiat. Neurol. Scand.*, Suppl. 82.

SKEELS, H. M. (1966) Adult status of children with contrasting early life experiences. *Monogr. Soc. Res. Child Develop.*, **31**, Serial No. 105, 1–65.

SLATER, E. (1938) Zur Erbpathologie des manisch-depressiven Irreseins. Die Eltern und Kinder von Manisch-Depressiven. *Z. ges. Neurol. Psychiat.*, **163**, 1–47. English version in *Man, Mind, and Heredity* (1971) (Ed. J. Shields and I. I. Gottesman). Baltimore: Johns Hopkins Press, 55–67.

SLATER, E. (1953) Psychotic and neurotic illnesses in twins. *Med. Res. Coun. Spec. Rep. Ser.* No. 278. London: H.M.S.O.

SLATER, E. (1958) The monogenic theory of schizophrenia. *Acta Genet. (Basel)*, **8**, 50–56.

SLATER, E. (1961) The thirty-fifth Maudsley Lecture: 'hysteria 311', *J. ment. Sci.*, **107**, 359–381.

SLATER, E. (1962) Birth order and maternal age of homosexuals. *Lancet*, **i**, 69–71.

SLATER, E. (1966) Expectation of abnormality on paternal and maternal sides: a computational model. *J. med. Genet.*, **3**, 159–161.

SLATER, E. (1968) A review of earlier evidence on genetic factors in schizophrenia. In *The Transmission of Schizophrenia* (Ed. D. Rosenthal and S. S. Kety). Oxford: Pergamon, 15–26.

SLATER, E., BEARD, A. W., and GLITHERO, E. (1963) The schizophrenia-like psychoses of epilepsy. *Brit. J. Psychiat.*, **109**, 95–150.

SLATER, E. and COWIE, V. A. (1971) *The Genetics of Mental Disorders.* London: Oxford Univ. Press.

SLATER, E., MAXWELL, J., and PRICE, J. S. (1971) Distribution of ancestral secondary cases in bipolar affective disorders. *Brit. J. Psychiat.*, **118**, 215–218.

SLATER, E. and ROTH, M. (1969) *Mayer-Gross, Slater and Roth Clinical Psychiatry*, 3rd edition. London: Baillière, Tindall & Cassell.

SLATER, E. and SHIELDS, J. (1969) Genetical aspects of anxiety. In *Studies of Anxiety* (Ed. M. H. Lader)

Brit. J. Psychiat. Spec. Publn. No. 3. Ashford, Kent: Headley, 62–71.

SMITH, C. (1970) Heritability of liability and concordance in monozygous twins. Ann. hum. Genet., 34, 85–91.

SMITH, C. (1971) Recurrence risks for multifactorial inheritance. Amer. J. hum. Genet., 23, 577–588.

SMITH, J. C. (1936) Dementia praecox-Probleme. Z. ges. Neurol. Psychiat., 156, 361–381.

SMITH, R. T. (1965) A comparison of socioenvironmental factors in monozygotic and dizygotic twins, testing an assumption. In Methods and Goals in Human Behavior Genetics (Ed. S. G. Vandenberg). New York: Academic Press, 45–61.

SORSBY, A., SHERIDAN, M., and LEARY, G. A. (1962) Refraction and its components in twins. Med. Res. Coun. Spec. Rep. Ser. No. 303. London: H.M.S.O.

SPUHLER, J. N. (1967) Behavior and mating patterns in human populations. In Genetic Diversity and Human Behavior (Ed. J. N. Spuhler). Chicago: Aldine, 241–268.

STABENAU, J. R. (1968) Heredity and environment in schizophrenia. Arch. gen. Psychiat., 18, 458–463.

STENSTEDT, Å. (1952) A study in manic-depressive psychosis: clinical, social and genetic investigations. Acta Psychiat. Neurol. Scand., Suppl. 79.

STENSTEDT, Å. (1959) Involutional melancholia. Acta Psychiat. Neurol. Scand., Suppl. 127.

STENSTEDT, Å. (1966) Genetics of neurotic depression. Acta Psychiat. Scand., 42, 392–409.

STEVENSON, A. C. and CHEESEMAN, E. A. (1956) Hereditary deaf mutism, with particular reference to Northern Ireland. Ann. hum. Genet., 20, 177–231.

STORRS, E. E. and WILLIAMS, R. J. (1968) A study of monozygous quadruplet armadillos in relation to mammalian inheritance. Proc. Nat. Acad. Sci. (U.S.A.), 60, 910–914.

STRELETZKI, F. (1961) Psychosen im Verlauf der Huntingtonschen Chorea unter besonderer Berücksichtigung der Wahnbildungen. Arch. Psychiat. Nervenkr., 202, 202–214.

STUMPFL, F. (1936) Die Ursprünge des Verbrechens dargestellt am Lebenslauf von Zwillingen. Leipzig: Thieme.

TANNER, J. M. (1962) Growth at Adolescence, 2nd ed. Oxford: Blackwell.

THODAY, J. M. (1965) Geneticism and environmentalism. In Biological Aspects of Social Problems (Ed. J. E. Meade and A. S. Parkes). Edinburgh: Oliver & Boyd, 92–106.

THODAY, J. M. (1967) New insights into continuous variation. In Proceedings of the Third Internat. Congr. Hum. Genetics (Ed. J. F. Crow and J. V. Neel). Baltimore: Johns Hopkins Press, 339–350.

THOMPSON, H., MELNYK, J., and HECHT, F. (1967) Reproduction and meiosis in XYY, Lancet, ii, 831.

TIENARI, P. (1963) Psychiatric illnesses in identical twins. Acta Psychiat. Scand., Suppl. 171.

TIENARI, P. (1966) On intrapair differences in male twins with special reference to dominance-submissiveness. Acta Psychiat. Scand., Suppl. 188.

TIENARI, P. (1968) Schizophrenia in monozygotic male twins. In The Transmission of Schizophrenia (Ed. D. Rosenthal and S. S. Kety). Oxford: Pergamon, 27–36.

TIZARD, J. and GRAD, J. C. (1961) The Mentally Handicapped and Their Families. Maudsley Monographs No. 7. London: Oxford Univ. Press.

TROSTORFF, S. VON. (1968) Über die hereditäre Belastung bei den bipolaren und monopolaren phasischen Psychosen. Schweiz. Arch. Neurol. Neurochir. Psychiat., 102, 235–243.

TSUANG, M-t. (1967) A study of pairs of sibs both hospitalized for mental disorder. Brit. J. Psychiat., 113, 283–300.

VAGUE, J., BOYER, J., NICOLINO, J., MATTEI, A., LUCIANI, J., ARNAUD, A., POUCH, J., and VALETTE, A. (1968) Maladie de Klinefelter chez deux jumeaux monozygotes, Annales d'Endocrinologie, Paris, 29, 709–729.

VANDENBERG, S. G. (1962) The hereditary abilities study: hereditary components in a psychological test battery. Amer. J. hum. Genet., 14, 220–237.

VANDENBERG, S. G. (1966) Contributions of twin research to psychology. Psychol. Bull., 66, 327–352.

VANDENBERG, S. G. (1967) Hereditary factors in normal personality traits (as measured by inventories). In Recent Advances in Biological Psychiatry, Vol. 9 (Ed. J. Wortis). New York: Plenum Press, 65–104.

VANDENBERG, S. G. (1968) Primary mental abilities or general intelligence? Evidence from twin studies. In Genetic and Environmental Influences on Behaviour (Ed. J. M. Thoday and A. S. Parkes). Edinburgh: Oliver & Boyd, 146–160.

VANDENBERG, S. G. (Ed.) (1965) Methods and Goals in Human Behavior Genetics. New York: Academic Press.

VANDENBERG, S. G. (Ed.) (1968) Progress in Human Behavior Genetics. Baltimore: Johns Hopkins Press.

VANDENBERG, S. G., CLARK, P. J., and SAMUELS, I. (1965) Psychophysiological reactions of twins: hereditary factors in galvanic skin resistance, heartbeat, and breathing rates. Eugen. Quart., 12, 7–10.

VANDENBERG, S. G. and JOHNSON, R. C. (1968) Further evidence on the relation between age of separation and similarity in IQ among pairs of separated identical twins. In Progress in Human Behavior Genetics (Ed. S. G. Vandenberg). Baltimore: Johns Hopkins Press, 215–219.

VANDENBERG, S. G., STAFFORD, R. E., BROWN, A., and GRESHAM, J. (1966) The Louisville Twin Study, University of Louisville School of Medicine, Louisville, Kentucky. Cited by Vandenberg (1967).

VESELL, E. S. and PAGE, J. G. (1968a) Genetic control of drug levels in man: phenylbutazone. Science, 159, 1479–1480.

VESELL, E. S. and PAGE, J. G. (1968b) Genetic control of drug levels in man: antipyrine. Science, 161, 72–3.

VESELL, E. S. and PAGE, J. G. (1968c) Genetic control of dicumarol levels in man, J. clin. Invest., 47, 2657–2663.

VOGEL, F. (1958) Über die Erblichkeit des normalen Elektroenzephalogramms. Stuttgart: Thieme.

VOGEL, F. (1966) Zur genetischen Grundlage frontopräzentraler β-Wellen-Gruppen im EEG des Menschen. Humangenetik, 2, 227–237.

WENDER, P. H., ROSENTHAL, D., and KETY, S. S. (1968) A psychiatric assessment of the adoptive parents of schizophrenics. In The Transmission of Schizophrenia

(Ed. D. Rosenthal and S. S. Kety). Oxford: Pergamon, 235–250.

WENDT, G. G. (1959) Das Erkrankungsalter bei der Huntingtonschen Chorea. *Acta Genet. (Basel)*, 9, 18–32.

WETTERBERG, L. (1967) *A Neuropsychiatric and Genetical Investigation of Acute Intermittent Porphyria*. Stockholm: Scand. Univ. Books.

WHEELAN, L. (1959) Familial Alzheimer's disease. *Ann. hum. Genet.*, 23, 300–310.

WILDE, G. J. S. (1964) Inheritance of personality traits. *Acta Psychol.*, 22, 37–51.

WILLIAMS, R. J. (1956) *Biochemical Individuality*. New York: Wiley.

WINOKUR, G. and CLAYTON, P. (1967) Family history studies. I. Two types of affective disorders separated according to genetic and clinical factors. In *Recent Advances in Biological Psychiatry*, Vol. 9 (Ed. J. Wortis). New York: Plenum Press, 35–50.

WISSFELD, E. and KAINDL, E. (1961) Über die Deutung und den Wert abnormer EEG-Befunde bei psychopathischen Persönlichkeiten. *Nervenarzt*, 32, 57–66.

WOLFF, E. DE, SCHÄRER, K., and LEJEUNE, J. (1962) Contribution à l'étude des jumeaux mongoliens. Un cas de monozygotisme hétérocaryote. *Helv. Paediat. Acta (Basel)*, 17, 301–328.

WYNNE, L. (in press) Family research on the pathogenesis of schizophrenia. Proc. Internat. Sympos. on Psychosis, Institut Albert-Prevost, Montreal, Nov., 1969. *Excerpta Medica*. Cited by Hirsch and Leff (1971).

YOLLES, S. F. and KRAMER, M. (1969) Vital statistics. In *The Schizophrenic Syndrome* (Ed. L. Bellak and L. Loeb). New York: Grune & Stratton, 66–113.

YOUNG, J. P. R. (1971) An investigation of auditory evoked potentials in male twins. Thesis submitted for the degree of Doctor in Medicine in the University of Cambridge.

ZAZZO, R. (1960) *Les Jumeaux, le Couple et la Personne*. Paris: Presses Universitaires de France, 2 vol.

ZERBIN-RÜDIN, E. (1967) Endogene Psychosen. In *Humangenetik, ein kurzes Handbuch*, V/2 (Ed. P. E. Becker) Stuttgart: Thieme, 446–577.

ZERBIN-RÜDIN, E. (1969) Zur Genetik der depressiven Erkrankungen. In *Das depressive Syndrom*, Internat. Sympos., Berlin, Feb. 1968 (Ed. H. Hippius and H. Selbach). Munich: Urban & Schwarzenberg, 37–56.

17

Early Experience and Other Environmental Factors: an Overview

I. Studies with Humans

M. BERGER

A. INTRODUCTION

'The substitution of the structural for the colloidal conception of "the physical basis of life" was one of the great revolutions of modern biology; but it was a quiet revolution, for no one opposed it, and for that reason, I suppose, no one thought to read a funeral oration over protoplasm itself.'

MEDEWAR, 1969

'Early experience'... by what?... of what?

In a discussion of genetics and behaviour development, McClearn (1964) has drawn attention to the general principle that 'the description of the phenotypic effect of different genes is incomplete without specification of the environmental circumstances. Equally, no description of the effect of an environmental manipulation can be regarded as complete without specification of the genotype of the organism to which such a manipulation was applied'.

With few notable exceptions, research in psychology, both normal and abnormal, is concerned primarily with the second part of the above principle. Research problems generally assume the form: 'What happens to R, the behaviour, if there is a change in S, the stimulus or environment?' Little attention is paid to the possibility that certain characteristics of the individual may determine the effects of the environmental (stimulus) manipulation. Do we need to, as it were, 'specify the genotype?' It is with this question in view that we present, in some detail, two recent research reports.

1. The Development of Regulated Behaviour in the Neonate

Consider the following observations, from an ongoing project reported by Sander (1969). Three groups of normal neonates, from the day of birth, are being reared under somewhat different caretaking conditions. Twenty-four-hour records of activity, quiescence and crying, as well as the occurrence, duration, and nature of caretaking, are obtained for each neonate, these being recorded simultaneously on a multichannel event recorder. From these records, the day-night organisation of motility 'appears to be sensitive to very subtle influences which come into play during the first 10 days of life': if the neonate is moved from care in the nursery to care by an individual caretaker, who lives in the room with him, 'between the fourth and sixth day the predominance of activity shifts to the day-time segment', the motility and crying having previously been predominant in the nocturnal segment. During the second day of life, the records show caretaker interventions scattered throughout the entire twenty-four-hour period. On subsequent days, however, there emerges evidence of increasing 'clustering', 'in which a coincidence becomes clear between the periods of infant activity and of caretaking activity'. Eventually, the 'activity epoch of the caretaker matches activity epoch of infant in duration, as well as in onset'.

Also, from the continuously monitored records of crying, it is apparent that not only is there a wide range of individual differences in crying, but also, there are 'as wide group differences between groups of infants reared in different caretaking environments'. With regard to the sleep patterns of the neonates, Sander (1969) reports that it appears that some babies are regular in the onset of sleep, 'as though largely governed by inner regulations of sleep-wake cycling, with little regard for environmental conditions': other babies, 'even by the eighth day of life, appear most sensitive to any substitution for the familiar caretaker in respect of their ability to fall asleep'.

A number of conclusions can be drawn from these observations. Firstly, Sander's (1969) data make it apparent that the neonate is responsive to conditions in its environment. Secondly, it is also evident that neonates as a group are not all similarly responsive to a standard environment. Thirdly, the term *interaction*, it would seem, cannot fully convey what happened in the course of these studies. *Mutual modification* of neonate and caretaker behaviour would perhaps be the most appropriate description of what took place: the behaviour of the neonate determined the behaviour of the caretaker and patterns of caretaking activity produced *some* behavioural changes in the neonate.

2. The Development of Behaviour Disorders

The New York longitudinal study (Thomas *et al.*, 1964, 1968), begun in 1956 and currently ongoing, represents an attempt to assess the role of temperamental factors in the development of normal and disordered behaviour. Data on 136 children in the study were gathered from infancy onwards by means of periodic parental interviews, undertaken by trained interviewers. Satisfactory reliabilities were obtained, and observational studies on a subsample provided some evidence for the validity of the interview data and the conclusions drawn from these. The children selected were from middle- or upper-middle-class families resident in New York City. The social-class restrictions, while they tend to limit the generality of the findings, were deliberately imposed to reduce the possible influence of social-class-related determinants of behavioural differences between the children.

Nine categories of behavioural style (temperamental characteristics) were developed from an inductive analysis of the initial interview protocols. These were activity level, rhythmicity, approach or withdrawal, intensity of reaction, threshold of responsiveness, quality of mood, distractibility, and attention span and persistence. (These categories are described more fully in a later section.)

Forty-two of the 136 children who developed 'a

significant degree of behavioral disturbance constituted the clinical sample. Judgement that the child was sufficiently disturbed for inclusion in the clinical sample did not depend simply on the complaints of parents and/or teachers, but was made only after a detailed clinical diagnostic assessment by a psychiatrist.'

Two types of comparison were undertaken. Firstly, children with diagnosed behaviour disorders were compared with those who did not have such disorders, thus enabling a comparison of temperamental differences between the groups. In the second analysis, temperamental patterns were isolated, and for each pattern those who developed a disorder were compared with those who did not, thus enabling an identification of the reasons for the differential outcome. Analysis of the data revealed firstly, that both before and after the onset of symptoms, the clinical and non-clinical groups differed in the organisation of their temperamental characteristics. Thus, it appears that temperamental factors played a role in the genesis of behaviour disorders. However, in both groups, children were also found who had 'highly similar' patterns of organisation of temperament. As the authors point out, it is therefore 'insufficient to refer to temperamental organisation alone' if the aetiology of behaviour disorders is to be understood.

Three groups of children with similar patterns of temperament were identified.

DIFFICULT CHILDREN

Before two years of age, and well before any behavioural disturbance was manifest, one subgroup of children was particularly noticeable. Analysis of the records revealed that this group differed from the remainder of the sample in that their 'biological functions' were irregular, their predominant reaction to new stimuli was to withdraw, they were slow to adapt to changes, reacted with intensity, and negative mood was frequently expressed. Approximately 70 per cent of these difficult children developed behaviour problems, and they represented 23 per cent of the eventual psychiatrically diagnosed clinical sample. Only 4 per cent (four cases) who showed the early difficult pattern were found in the non-clinical group.

Although no data are presented, Thomas *et al.* (1968) report that the parents of the difficult children did not seem to differ from the parent group as a whole in respect of their approach to child care. Nor did there seem to be any systematic difference in their early attitudes to the difficult child as compared with their other children. However, attitudes regarded as unfavourable to 'healthy development' did arise as the infant grew older. Thomas *et al.* (1968) suggest that the parents were reacting to the problems entailed 'in coping with and caring for the child'. Some of the parents appeared to cope with some of the difficulties presented by their children: no 'global categorisation' could be used to describe 'the wide range of feelings and handling' techniques that were recorded. When the difficult children presented with clinical behaviour problems, they showed a wide range of disorders which were manifest in a variety of situations. It appears, however, that if parents were able to adapt to the difficult child, disorders requiring psychiatric attention could be averted.

EASY CHILDREN

These children were 'preponderantly positive in mood', were regular, adapted readily, were positive in their approaches to new situations, and reacted with mild or low intensity. These characteristics were apparent from early in life and most of these children did not develop behaviour disorders. Those who did, tended to do so in response to traumatic episodes, or their positive behaviours in the home came into conflict with the expectations of their peers or teachers. Some behaviours the parents fostered in the infant and young child became unacceptable when the child was older.

CHILDREN WHO ARE SLOW TO WARM UP

This group of children presented clinically with 'passive' symptoms. Early in life they had appeared to be slow in adapting, showed low intensity reaction, would initially withdraw from situations, and they showed a low activity level. As compared with the non-clinical cases, negative mood responses were more frequent. If parents and school were able to wait for the 'slow' child to adjust in its own time, major problems seemed not to arise; if not, difficulties appeared in a variety of situations.

A number of limitations attending these conclusions from the New York longitudinal study have already been noted, and as yet insufficient data have been published that would enable a full evaluation of the research. Nevertheless, such limitations cannot detract from the importance of the findings of this unique approach to the study of the emergence of behaviour disorders in children. It appears that any attempt to comprehend the development of the range and type of disordered behaviour described cannot but be incomplete if it fails to recognise the contributions of the child; the child shapes, and is shaped by his environment, and the characteristics of both need to be taken into consideration.

3. Systematic Considerations

Genes, according to Dobzhansky (1967), 'determine the pattern of development of the organism, including the pattern of its behavioral development . . . in the sense that, given a certain sequence of environmental influences, the development follows a certain path. . . . But the development of the carrier of a given genotype might also follow different paths in different environments'. The 'developmental fixity or plasticity of a trait is genetically conditioned'. Certain traits or qualities whose 'presence and precise form' are indispensable for survival and reproduction have the property of 'fixity': 'environmental variations within the normal range do not influence the phenotype to any appreciable extent. With very few exceptions, babies are born with two eyes, a four-chambered heart, . . . physiological mechanisms maintaining constant body temperature, and so forth'. In addition to showing fixity in certain traits, the human genotype 'has been so formed in the process of evolution that educability [viewed in the 'broad sense' of an ability to adjust to circumstances as a consequence of experience], is a universal property of all nonpathological individuals' (Dobzhansky, 1967).

It is not denied that man is 'educable'. But is this 'educability' unbounded in the sense that Dobshansky (1967) proposes? We would argue, given the observations of Sander (1969) and Thomas *et al.* (1964, 1968), that at least early in life, there are limits to change which are probably not imposed simply by neurophysiological immaturity and the like. To clarify our view, we will draw upon certain ideas current among theoretical biologists.

In discussing the shortcomings of the Darwinian theory of evolution, Whyte (1965) has proposed that 'organisms are highly co-ordinated structures' and that only 'certain avenues of change are compatible with their conditions of co-ordination'. Natural selection by external factors has been the basis of the theory of evolution. Whyte (1965) suggests that there are 'internal factors' in the organism that act as a 'second directive agency'. This view, at the evolutionary level, as Thorpe (1969) points out, is shared by other biologists such as Haldane, Spurway, Weiss, and von Bertalanffy, among others.

In considering human plasticity, one can, on the one hand, draw attention to the limits imposed by the structure of the sensory systems and, on the other, to the human capacity for learning. In addition, however, the research reported by Sander (1969) and by Thomas *et al.* (1964, 1968) suggests that there are 'internal factors' relating to the 'conditions of co-ordination' of the neurophysiological subsystems that mediate behaviour, which direct the modification of behaviour. These factors operate at the level of the individual, appear to be present in the neonatal period, and seem to influence the direction of individual behaviour development differentially. An examination of the evidence for these hypotheses will be undertaken in the initial sections of this chapter, in addition to a review of some of the findings on the capabilities of the neonate and infant.

B. INDIVIDUAL DIFFERENCES, TEMPERAMENT AND PERSONALITY

1. The Capabilities of the Neonate and Infant

Flavell and Hill (1969), reviewing recent research on the neonate and infant note that it 'is becoming clear that the "black box" begins its postnatal developmental career with considerable internal organisation on both the efferent and the afferent side'. The degree of complexity and organisation is only beginning to be fully appreciated.

In a discussion of the role of biological rhythms in early development, Wolff (1967) has noted that the investigation of periodicities in human behaviour has generally been restricted to macro-rhythms, such as sexual activity and the sleep-waking cycles, which have basic frequencies of hours, days or months. Periodic behaviours with much higher basic frequencies, in terms of seconds or fractions of a second, have been recorded in the human neonate. The behaviours are predominantly reflex activities, such as sucking and crying, and they appear to be stable over short observation periods. Wolff (1967) reports that during restful sleep in the period shortly before a meal, many infants make what appears as spontaneous rapid movements of the lips, jaw, and tongue. These can be readily differentiated from the 'sucking and chomping' movements observed in light sleep. Such rapid movements are grouped in bursts of four to twelve distinct events and are separated by rest periods of two- to ten-seconds duration. Individual differences have been observed in both the mean duration of activity bursts and rest periods, but individual patterns are reported to be stable over time. Wolff (1967) suggests that his observations, while not necessarily constituting proof, nevertheless support the 'proposition that the human central nervous system instigates motor rhythms analogous to the endogenous automatisms described by von Holst and Weiss for lower species'. These rhythms can also, he argues, 'influence anatomically unrelated motor activities'.

The stability and macro-cyclical nature of neonatal behaviour have been described by S. J. Hutt et al. (1969). The behaviours shown by the neonate, 'a large and varied repertoire', are considered by Hutt et al. (1969) to be both self-generated and stimulus-elicited. These authors have noted, after reviewing a number of studies, that the 'spontaneous behaviour of neonates consists of a succession of patterns that are morphologically similar in all infants'. Such behaviour is reported to be stable over time.

Brain electrical activity (EEG) in the infant has been studied extensively. Patterns observed at term birth, during wakefulness, appear to be relatively stable until about three to four months of age. All activity tends to be of low voltage, and bilateral synchrony, at first comparatively circumscribed, generalises across the brain as the infant matures. The EEG during the waking state can be differentiated from patterns seen during drowsiness and sleep. Polygraphic records have also enabled a reliable discrimination to be made between 'active sleep' and 'quiet sleep'. In the active phase, the pattern observed consists of rapid body movements, irregular respiration, an irregular heart rate and clusters of rapid eye movements. During quiet sleep, body movements are rare or absent, as are rapid eye movements. Occasional sucking movements appear, respiration is slow and irregular, and the heart rate is slightly slower but regular (Ellingson, 1967).

In a study of a group of twenty neonates (aged thirteen- to thirty-eight-hours), Lodge et al. (1969) made simultaneous recordings of electroretinograms (ERG) and EEG evoked responses to flashes of orange and white light. They found that the neonatal ERG shows wave form characteristics similar to those observed in adults, although latencies were slightly longer and amplitudes considerably lower. Cortical visual evoked responses also showed longer latencies but amplitudes were comparable to those observed in adults. They regard their findings as providing 'further electrophysiological support for behavioural indications that the newborn human infant possesses well-developed perceptual capacities'.

Three studies, reviewed by Cantor (1963) have provided considerable support for the view that infants show reliable preferences for visual forms; further evidence that the young infant shows pattern selectivity, as well as having the capacity for pattern vision, has been presented by Fantz and Nevis (1967). These latter authors report that the preference for pattern over uniform surface is evident from birth. Fantz (1967) commenting on his own and other studies, contends that they '... prove that the newborn infant can resolve, discriminate, and differentially attend to visual patterns'. Lipsitt (1967), in a series of studies of habituation in the newborn, has also observed that the neonate 'is capable of discriminating components of odorant compounds'.

In a recent review of research of the learning capacities of the human infant, Lipsitt (1969) has commented that although it is undeniable that 'some behavioural differences are related to age, . . . the human newborn can no longer be regarded as a spinal creature who can have no capacity for learning or cognitive activity . . . The normal human infant shows an exceptional talent for differential responding, conditioning and discrimination learning'. Brackbill and Fitzgerald (1969) have emphasised that 'infant conditionability is not the same as adult conditionability, nor is the infant simply a less well-developed or less efficient version of the second'. A range of conditioned behaviours has been reported: conditioned head-turning, free-operant head-turning and temporal conditioning have been elicited in the neonate. Rovee and Rovee (1969) report that they have been able to demonstrate the conditioning of leg flexion by a conjugate reinforcement technique in eighteen infants aged nine- to twelve-weeks. A mobile, suspended within the infant's field of view, was attached to the baby's left ankle by means of a cord in such a way that leg movements initiated movement of the mobile. Leg activity increased while the cord was attached and diminished when it was detached. Both quantitative and qualitative changes were observed: gross body movements, present early in the sessions diminished and the infants began using smooth directed thrust actions of the leg connected to the mobile. In conjugate reinforcement phases, a period of leg movement would be followed by quiescence during which the infant's gaze was directed at the mobile.

Although 'infants and young children are strikingly inferior to adults in many dimensions of learning' (Clarke, 1968), the research data nevertheless demonstrate that they are eminently 'conditionable'. Further, as Rheingold (1967) has noted, 'conclusions about the non-modifiability of a response . . . can be stated only with reference to the procedure used; history teaches, and caution warns, that with some other procedure, modifiability may be subsequently demonstrated'. We would anticipate that if 'early learning is continually reinforced' long-term effects may appear (Clarke, 1968). As yet, however, no studies have examined the long-term stability of particular behaviours that have been conditioned in early life. The research problem is one of determining either the reinforcement history of behaviour patterns or, preferably, continual monitoring to see

whether behaviour learned early in life shows temporal stability: lack of evidence does not constitute proof that early conditioning does not persist.

2. Individual Differences

Two general propositions about the neonate and infant are supported by contemporary research. The first of these is that at birth, the human is a complex and organised being, with capacities that are only now being revealed. The second proposition is that differences on many quantifiable characteristics—behavioural and physiological—are manifest at or shortly after birth. Some of the evidence for the latter proposition has already been presented. Further illustrations from recent research provides a setting for a consideration of the determinants and significance of individual differences observed early in life.

In a series of studies of the responses of two- to five-day-old babies to various forms of stimulation, Bridger and Birns (1968) have found that there are stable individual differences in cardiac response to tactile stimulation. Further, when babies are rank-ordered in terms of their behavioural responses to a standard stimulus, consistent individual differences in response intensity were observed. Korner et al. (1968) filmed the spontaneous oral behaviour of thirty-two full-term neonates, ranging in age from forty-five- to eighty-eight-hours. An analysis of the filmed material indicated 'most graphically how much infants differ from each other in the frequency with which they mouthed, sucked their fingers, established hand-face and hand-mouth contact'. It has also been observed (Korner, 1969) that 'startle' behaviour during regular sleep was the only behaviour common to all the neonates. However, major individual differences in the pattern of startle were shown: some infants would startle several times in rapid succession whereas others showed long intervals between startles. The occurrence of other behaviours also varied markedly. Some of the infants showed no mouthing movements, others no reflex smiles. Papoušek (1967) in his neonate studies has found marked individual differences on all of the measures of conditioning that he employed.

3. Some Determinants of Individual Differences

Given the variety of individual behavioural and physiological differences observed in relation to the common baseline of chronological age, several determinants can be implicated as potential sources of such variation. For purposes of discussion, these can be viewed independently. In practice, we would anticipate the interaction of at least several factors.

(a) GENETIC SOURCES

There is little doubt that genetic differences underlie the physiological and behavioural differences between individuals. However, as King (1968) has pointed out, genetic effects are not direct but act through various structural and metabolic pathways that affect behaviour. The genetic factors that produce diversity within a species are not well known (Dobzhansky, 1967). In the human species, genetic diversity has been 'explored quite inadequately' (Dobzhansky, 1967). Some of the reasons for this have been summarised by Caspari (1967). Among the problems encountered in attempting to specify the behavioural consequences of genetic differences are those of the description and analysis of behaviour, the determination of the mode of inheritance (unigenic or polygenic), and the precise ways in which gene actions are mediated. Also, as King (1968) recognizes, 'with few notable exceptions', the contributing genetic factors have not been sought.

(b) DIFFERENCES IN BRAIN GROWTH

In humans, it was thought until recently, that the brain 'growth spurt' occurred in the weeks prior to birth (Dobbing, 1968, p. 183, Fig. 1), and continued at high rates in the months thereafter, particularly within the first three months. Recent evidence however, suggests that two major 'spurts' occur (Dobbing and Sands, 1970). The first takes place from the fifteenth to the twentieth week of pregnancy, and the second, which begins in the twenty-fifth week, appears to last until the second postnatal year. It is unlikely that the rate of brain growth is uniform across individuals, using chronological age as the baseline unit, as is indirectly indicated by differences in head circumference at and after birth. The 3rd and 97th percentiles for the head circumference of boys at birth are 32·1 cm and 37·4 cm, respectively (Silver et al., 1969). Comparable data for girls show similar variability, slightly reduced in range. Whether or not the extent of variability is a consequence of the baseline metric requires further investigation. It is possible that if gestational age were used (Neligan, 1970) the degree of variation might be reduced. It is probable that individual differences observed in the neonatal period and in infancy are a function, to some extent, of differences in the development of the various central nervous sub-systems, as indexed by these differences in head circumference.

(c) SEX-LINKED DETERMINANTS

The physical and physiological consequences of genotypic sex differences are evident at birth and through the life span of the individual. The ratio of male to female births is of the order of 1·25:1; using age as a common baseline, boys are generally larger and stronger than girls but girls tend to be physically more mature than boys—the differences may be several weeks at birth, one year by the time they enter school and there may be as much as a two-year difference in chronological age at the onset of puberty. Further, males die at an age which is, on average, less than that for females (Rutter, 1970a).

Sex differences in neonatal behaviour have been reported by Korner (1969), Korner et al. (1968); in the behaviour of infants aged 3 months (Moss, 1967; Kagan, 1969) and at later ages (Kagan, 1969; Goldberg and Lewis, 1969). Theories of child development pay little attention to sex differences as has been pointed out by Rutter (1970a), and some research workers studying infants, share this oversight (Kron et al., 1968; Dubignan et al., 1969; Wolff, 1967). Whether or not they are justified in doing so is an empirical question. Research data suggest that differences may be found if sought after, and that there may be major differential behavioural consequences of sex differences. Moss (1967) observed thirty first-born infants with their mothers over the first three-months of life. He found that males slept less and cried more than did females, and that these behaviours had different effects on the mother, depending on the sex of the infant. There also appear to be major sex differences in response to family stress, as well as to the stresses encountered prenatally and at birth (Rutter, 1970a). Cultural factors, as has been noted by McClearn (1967), have generally been accorded the primary status in discussions of sex differences. In some recent studies, however, interpretations have shown a shift to an interactional view (Goldberg and Lewis, 1969). It is suggested by these latter authors, that as a consequence of the already extensive body of information on sex differences, pooling of data should not be undertaken until it is established that sex effects are absent.

Present research data therefore appear to suggest that the extent of differences within groups of neonates or infants may be partially determined by sex-linked factors.

(d) PRENATAL AND PERINATAL FACTORS

Some of the factors, apart from post-natal 'experiences', which may determine individual differences in various characteristics, have been isolated in studies on animals, and others, through examination of humans who are deviant in some way. It is not certain in all cases that the determinants have acted singly. An example is to be found in research into the effects of malnutrition on human learning and behaviour (Scrimshaw and Gordon, 1968). If some behavioural or physiological abnormality is evident in a malnourished group, it is difficult to ascertain whether this is due simply to malnutrition, or to the other circumstances that are found in association with malnutrition, namely, infectious diseases, poor physical and educational environments, and so on. The various 'determinants' considered below are also presented singly for purposes of discussion.

Joffe (1969) points out that in the past decade there has been a considerable growth in the interest shown in the effects of prenatal influences on later physiological and behavioural characteristics. With the increase in systematically derived information on prenatal influences, 'it soon became evident that almost any treatment applied to a pregnant animal would result in differences of some kind between her offspring and those of untreated controls'. Prenatal treatments include a variety of forms of stimulation, ranging from exposure to X-irradiation, exposure to stress situations, to nutritional and pharmacological modifications. Major methodologic problems (discussed by Joffe, 1969) are encountered in research on the prenatal determinants of behaviour and, together with species differences, act as limiting factors on the validity of cross-species generalisations. Methodological limitations are particularly evident in the research on humans. While it 'appears reasonably certain that some agents acting on the mother during pregnancy cause abnormalities in her child' (e.g. infections, drugs, Joffe, 1969) it is more difficult to be precise about other factors such as the effects of maternal emotions on foetal and neonatal behaviour. Animal studies, demonstrating that maternal emotional stress affects offspring behaviour, tend to make it 'quite likely that a human mother's emotional state during pregnancy will affect her child's behaviour, although few of the studies of humans force one to this conclusion' (Joffe, 1969).

Many factors and circumstances present before conception and gestation, or arising during birth, appear to be associated with some of the more obvious abnormalities of structure and function.

The role of nutritional deficiencies, prenatally and postnatally are complex and not as yet clearly delineated. The probability that nutritional differences (in addition to nutritional deficiencies) are implicated in both anatomic-physiological and behavioural differences in the neonate infant must be given due weight. Support for such a contention can be found in the proceedings of a recent conference on the effects of malnutrition on learning and behaviour (Scrimshaw and Gordon, 1968), as well as in the research of Dobbing and Sands (1970). Nutritional factors have been considered to be of major import in a recent report (Naeye *et al.*, 1969) which found that infants from poor families had multiple anatomic signs of prenatal undernutrition.

Drillen (1967) notes that low birth weight is associated with an increased incidence of various handicaps. In one-half of a group of handicapped children, it appeared likely that the defect was of developmental origin (i.e. had arisen at an early stage of gestation), and that the low birth weight, associated or not with premature delivery, was the result rather than the cause of the defect. In one-quarter of the children, it appeared probable that intrauterine hypoxia leading to cerebral damage was responsible for the handicap; in the remainder of the group, the cause of the handicap was uncertain. Most of the latter group had weighed less than 1,500 g at birth and came from very poor homes.

There are a number of 'complications of pregnancy and the perinatal period which are generally considered capable of giving rise to late sequelae', such as disorders of physical and intellectual development (Neligan, 1970). Parity, age, socio-economic status, ethnic group membership, physique, and cigarette smoking, are among the various factors that place the foetus at risk (Russell and Thompson, 1970; Birch, 1968a).

It has been suggested by Eichenwald (1968) that certain effects of prenatal and postnatal infectious diseases of the central nervous system may be very difficult to detect. Certain congenital infections may run their full course during gestation so that their effects may not be clinically detectable at birth. Eichenwald (1968) implies that because of this, the effects of such diseases may be more prevalent than those of other diseases whose effects are more readily discernable. General behavioural and neurological examinations are, according to Birch (1968b) 'notoriously insensitive'. When detailed assessments of perinatal status were undertaken on a group of two- to three-day-old infants who did not show clinical signs of neurological or behavioural abnormality, 'neurointegrative disturbances on more refined and sensitive examination' (conditioned head-turning) were revealed (Birch, 1968b). Until recently, indicators of possible foetal asphyxia before or during birth were mainly clinical. More sophisticated methods—electrocardiography, blood gas measurements—'have not been in use long enough yet for follow-up studies to have been carried out' to determine fully the effects of foetal asphyxia (Neligan, 1970).

Given the range and degree of structural and behavioural complexity of the neonate, as well as the relative lack of sophistication of devices for assessing structural and functional integrity, it is difficult to specify, at this point in time, all the factors that promote individual differences already apparent in the neonatal period. It is obvious, however, that certain influences may be operating that have escaped detection, and that it would be inappropriate to view individual differences early in life as a reflection simply of genetic and 'maturational' differences, although these are no doubt implicated.

4. Individual Differences in Formal Characteristics: 'Internal Directional Influences'

In their prefatory comments in a recent paper, Bridger and Birns (1968) note that prior to the advent of Watsonian behaviourism and the Freudian era, it was 'common to ascribe various personality types to biological predispositions'. With the advent of behaviourism and psychoanalysis, prime responsibility for the behavioural characteristics of children became vested in the child-rearing practices of the parents. However, as Bridger and Birns (1968) point out, an interactionist approach, amalgamating biological predisposition with environmental factors, 'has been gaining theoretical acceptance'. Such views have, of course, been elaborated and their implications incorporated in adult personality research (Eysenck, 1967), and have been brought into prominence in research on infants and young children (Thomas et al., 1964, 1968; McGrade, 1968; Korner et al., 1968), as well as older children (Eysenck and Eysenck, 1969).

A convenient starting point in the search for 'biological predisposition' is the newly-born. The primary advantage is that the effects of the 'environmentalist's environment' are minimised: the human is seen 'before early experience could have a significant influence' (Bridger and Birns, 1968).

Behavioural phenomena manifest at birth and onwards can be conceptualised in terms of contents and formal characteristics (Thomas et al., 1964). The contents or classes of behaviour would include such features as crying, playing, clinging to mother, exploring a new situation, among many others. Formal characteristics are abstracted from the different contents: the child may persist in crying (despite attempts to pacify him), persist in trying to solve a difficult problem (despite lack of a solution). 'Persistence' is conceptualised as a formal characteristic of behaviour. Whereas 'content is continually changing', formal characteristics are 'present in a variety of behaviours, irrespective of content' (Thomas et al., 1964). The formal characteristics of a child's behaviour have been identified with the temperament or behavioural style of the individual

(Thomas et al., 1968). These characteristics refer to 'the how rather than the what (abilities and content) or why (motivations) of behaviour. Temperament is a phenomenologic term used to describe the characteristic tempo, rhythmicity, adaptability, energy expenditure, mood, and focus of attention of a child . . .' without reference to the content of any specific behaviour. Thomas et al. (1964) proposed the distinction between content and formal characteristics as a precursor to their project (the New-York longitudinal study): it was anticipated that formal characteristics, being independent of content could be expected to show some degree of temporal stability, without necessarily being immutable. Temperamental characteristics are regarded as aspects of personality, which includes the other aspects of abilities and motivations, and it is recognised that temperamental characteristics can undergo developmental changes in response to environmental influences. In their earlier monograph, Thomas et al. (1964) propose that temperamental differences may arise from any, a combination, or all the number of influences: genetic familial, prenatal influences, paranatal influences, and early life experiences, particularly within the first two-months of life. Evidence from a study of twins suggests that behavioural style may have a genetic basis (Rutter et al., 1963).

Bridger and Birns (1968) view temperamental factors in terms of excitatory and inhibitory processes in the central nervous system which 'influence the experiential effect of a given environmental variation'. In addition, they recognise the possible role of genetic predisposition interacting with pre- and postnatal events. By way of example, they cite the hypothetical effects of a given stimulus on individuals who may have high and low thresholds to such stimuli. The individual with high threshold may show only a moderate response to the given stimulus, whereas the low threshold individual responds as if he were being 'stressed'. It is plausible, they suggest, that 'while undergoing identical environmental variations' the infants may be 'having different infantile experiences' in the sense of physiological and hormonal changes, which, in turn, may modify 'sensory thresholds and general responsiveness'. Such changes are differentiated from those central nervous system effects that lead to the learning of specific behaviours. Korner et al. (1968) recognise that their observations of neonatal oral behaviour may be related to individual differences in behavioural style: 'individual differences at birth may contain rudiments of dispositional factors which may differentially affect later development', and that 'individual differences may influence the way in which universal childhood events are experienced by any given child'. The possibility that these characteristics may influence the caretaker is also commented on. The infant who shows a potentiality for 'self-comforting' behaviour—a greater frequency of hand-mouth contact and, hence, increased probability of thumb or finger sucking—may be less demanding of the mother than the infant who does not show such propensities. Differences in reactivity are thus recognised as being potentially influential in the interaction of mother and child. These implications were foreseen by Thomas *et al.* (1964), and appear as significant in the development of behaviour disorders in children (Thomas *et al.*, 1968), as already noted.

Can formal characteristics be abstracted from the extensive behavioural repertoire of the neonate and do these persist into infancy and beyond?

Bridger and Birns (1968) note that individual differences in response to a standard stimulus have been frequently observed by nurses, pediatricians, and especially mothers. However, a major problem in using such observations, particularly if they refer to the neonatal and early infancy period, is associated with what is called the 'state' or 'behavioural condition' of the neonate. Certain of the self generated (endogenous) behavioural and physiological activities of the neonate cluster together in cyclical patterns which are called 'states' and the probability that the neonate will respond to a stimulus, and the magnitude of any response to such a stimulus, is 'almost without exception a function of state' (Hutt *et al.*, 1969). Simultaneous polygraph records of several parameters reveal 'considerable independent fluctuations' among the various measures, and on this basis Hutt *et al.* (1969) reject the view that changes in state can be monitored by changes in a single variable. They do, however, recognise that 'there is a certain degree of relationship between many systemic functions under various conditions such as deep sleep or extreme alertness'. While state cycles have great stability, both duration and stability can be responsive to environmental conditions as is illustrated by Sander's (1969) observations described in the introductory paragraphs, and by the observations of the persisting effects on the neonate of drugs administered to the mother during labour (Hutt *et al.*, 1969). Studies of neonatal behaviour that do not control for state can lead to equivocal results (*see* for example Hutt and Hutt, 1970, p. 16–17).

Bridger and Birns (1968) have found that within the first five days of life, normal, healthy full-term infants could be reliably differentiated by the intensity of their behavioural responses to a set of standard stimuli. Thirty infants, two- to five-days-old, in a series of experiments, were presented with stimuli such as soft and loud tones, and a cold disc applied to the thigh. The reactions of the neonates were rated on a six-point scale by three observers. Two of the raters agreed in their ratings in 95 per cent of the trials, and in less than 1 per cent of the trials was there a disagreement of more than 1 point. Reliability studies were undertaken on ten babies. Each stimulus was applied three times in a session, and observations were spread over four sessions. In addition to observing major individual differences in reactivity, the babies tended to maintain their relative ranking in behavioural responsiveness to all of the stimuli used and those who responded at a certain intensity during the first session, responded at a similar intensity during subsequent sessions.

Korner *et al.* (1968) have observed inter-individual variation in the frequency of oral behaviours. The neonates, ranging in age from forty-five- to eighty-eight-hours were also found to be consistent in the type of oral behaviour shown over the four observation periods. In particular, finger sucking, hand-face and hand-mouth contacting were found to be significantly associated with high motility and with endurance of crying. In interpreting their observations, Korner *et al.* (1968) suggest that this association 'may point to temperamental differences in the neonate in the tendency to be active or passive under conditions of need.'

Bridger and Birns (1968) found marked individual differences, in another study of neonates, in responses to various attempts at pacification following a standard stress stimulus, placing the baby's foot in ice-water for ten seconds. For two of the twelve babies, neither head-rocking by the experimenter, nor sucking, diminished the behavioural or autonomic response to stress, whereas seven of the twelve responded to both types of stress-reducing technique on both the behavioural and autonomic measures. For three of the babies, the techniques reduced the behavioural responses but not the autonomic response. Marked individual differences were also observed in the relative effectiveness of these soothing techniques. Four babies responded equally well to both head rocking and sucking, four were more effectively soothed by head holding or rocking rather than sucking. In two babies, sucking was the most effective technique, and for two neonates, neither was effective.

In both the abovementioned studies (Korner *et al.*, 1968; Bridger and Birns, 1968) the short-term stability of the individual differences in reactivity was apparent. Two studies (McGrade, 1968; and the New York longitudinal study, Thomas *et al.*, 1964, 1968) suggest that there is stability in reactivity over varying periods of time.

McGrade (1968) has found significant correlations

between the reactions of newborn males and females to nipple withdrawal, and independent ratings of activity, tension and happiness eight months later. The behaviours of the neonates were measured from filmed samples of behaviour in response to a series of stimuli. The behavioural ratings at eight-months were made while the infants were being assessed on developmental tests. McGrade (1968) interprets her results as indicating that stress reactions to nipple removal at three- to four-days 'were associated with stress reactions during developmental testing'.

Thomas et al. (1964) began recording observations made in the 'first months of life' of the children. In all but 14 per cent of the eighty subjects, the initial parental interviews were conducted within the first four months, the average age of the infants at that time being 3·3-months. Half the infants, were less than 2·5-months of age. The temperamental characteristics isolated were—

1. Activity Level:
   level and frequency of motor components of behaviour.
2. Rhythmicity:
   regularity of repetitive biological functions.
3. Approach or Withdrawal:
   initial responses to new stimuli.
4. Adaptability:
   degree to which initial responses can be directed by circumstances.
5. Intensity of Reaction:
   energy content of the response.
6. Threshold of Responsiveness:
   level of stimulation required to elicit a response.
7. Quality of Mood:
   amount of pleasant, joyful, friendly contrasted with unpleasant crying, unfriendly behaviour.
8. Distractibility:
   effectiveness of extraneous stimuli in disrupting ongoing behaviour.
9. Attention Span and Persistence: (Two sub-categories).
   Attention span relates to 'the length of time a particular activity is pursued'. Persistence relates to continuation of behaviour despite obstacles.

After following these children to a median age of about two years, Thomas et al. (1964) report finding that 'initially identifiable characteristics of reactivity are persistent features of the child's behaviour throughout the first two years of life'. Information on the longitudinal stability of temperamental characteristics over the first five years of life of this sample is not yet published.

In the neonatal period individual differences are manifest in both the type of behaviours (contents) shown, and in formal behavioural characteristics. Evidence from at least one study (McGrade, 1968), that certain patterns of neonatal reactivity or temperament continue to be evident at eight-months of age, provides a basis for suggesting that at least some patterns of reactivity discernable at later ages (Thomas et al., 1964) are probably present at birth. This hypothesis, and the extent to which all nine patterns of reactivity are detectable within the first one- or two-weeks of life, require systematic investigation. The ingenuity of research workers demonstrates that a variety of systematic observation techniques can be introduced from the first hours after birth, and suggests that longitudinal research on formal behavioural characteristics could begin in maternity ward nurseries.

This section of the chapter was introduced with the question 'What was experiencing what?'. From the evidence considered to this point, it should be apparent that the first 'what' is not simply the neonate or infant. Rather, the postnatal human appears with many capacities as well as with certain biases in the ways it will interact with the extrauterine environment.

5. Personality and Temperament in Childhood: The Evidence for Continuity

In a recent review of research on personality organisation in children, Rachman (1969) records that 'it is possible to identify two dimensions which recur with extraordinary regularity', those of introversion-extraversion, E, and neuroticism-stability, N. Further, as Rachman (1969) notes, the evidence suggests that the E and N dimensions as observed in childhood are probably the same as the E and N dimensions isolated in studies of adult personality organisation (Eysenck, 1967).

The theoretical and experimental status of the current Eysenckian model of personality are presented in detail in two recent publications (Eysenck, 1967; Eysenck and Eysenck, 1969) and only certain features need be described here. The dimensions E and N consistently emerge in factor analytic studies as independent factors that 'find a ready explanation in theoretical psychology and experimental psysiology' (Eysenck and Eysenck, 1969). Neuroticism is linked to the sympathetic branch of the autonomic nervous system and is associated with the persistence, rather than the strength, of emotional arousal. The dimension E is identified with the concepts of excitation and inhibition. Eysenck (1969) has also proposed a four-level descriptive scheme for personality. At the lowest level are found the specific responses (SRs), which may or may not be typical for the individual. At the next level are the habitual responses (HRs). They are habitual in the sense that if the life situation recurs, the individual tends to react consistently. In effect, HRs are situation specific behaviours. At the trait level, T, habitual acts are organised into traits such as 'persistence': traits are conceptualised as 'theoretical constructs based on observed intercorrelations between a number of habitual responses'. Traits themselves are organised into a general type conception, for example, E, this organisation being derived empirically from the intercorrelations of traits. These four levels 'correspond closely to the four types of factor distinguished by analysts; error factors, specific factors, group factors, and general factors' (Eysenck, 1969).

English and American psychologists investigating personality organisation (and cognitive structure) have tended in the past to emphasise few type (higher order) as opposed to many trait (primary) factors, respectively. Currently both recognise the 'descriptive value of primary traits as well as the existence of type factors' such as E and N. The current dispute concerns the 'practical, theoretical and heuristic' utility of the higher order factors as opposed to the lower order primary traits (Eysenck and Eysenck, 1969). Several practical and theoretical problems are posed by the use of primary factors in personality research. The following summary (a detailed exposition can be found in Eysenck and Eysenck, 1969), will serve to highlight two main problems. The primary factors that have been isolated in personality research are not unitary in the sense that the items are used in their measurement intercorrelate. Further, such factors are not invariant across sample properties such as sex differences, age, education, and social class: factors derived from samples that differ in these characteristics will tend to vary as a function of such parameters. Higher order factors tend not to show such deficiencies and, hence, have greater value for purposes of prediction.

The primary categories of reactivity employed in the New York longitudinal study are, in Eysenck's (1969) terminology, trait-level descriptions. Data from the New York study indicated that there is a degree of overlap between the traits, albeit small, with statistically significant intercorrelations (Thomas *et al.*, 1968). (To some extent, the low level of correlation is a likely consequence of the homogeneity of the sample.) The presence of correlated traits suggests that higher order factors may be extracted from these data and there is some evidence, discussed in the next section, to suggest that these factors will be consistent with the E and N model. Whether or not such a conception is preferable to trait-level conceptions is an empirical question, although the advantages of higher-order factors would seem to favour such a model. It is also possible that the use of higher-order factors may enable developmental continuity to be measured from the neonatal period onwards. The theoretical and practical ramifications of this possibility cannot be explored here, although contemporary research in personality structure points to such developmental continuity.

While there is as yet no direct evidence of the continuity of E and N, from the neonatal period through infancy and childhood to adolescence and beyond, the observations derived from a number of independent longitudinal studies have been interpreted as being consistent with the E and N dimensions. Rachman (1969) suggests that E and N can probably be reliably assessed in children, perhaps even as young as four-to five-years. Evidence from the Berkeley Growth Study (Bronson, 1969) confirms this.

Bronson's (1969) research, reported for the ages five- to sixteen-years, has led to the identification of two dimensions of behaviour, 'Expressiveness-Reserve' and 'Placidity-Explosiveness'. Bronson regards these dimensions as manifestations of 'orientations' which she views as 'characteristic and relatively unmodifiable predispositions to certain modes of interaction'. These predispositions determine the nature of the individual's experience, including the 'kinds of beliefs about himself and others that he eventually comes to maintain'. These observations have been replicated, and Bronson has found that the 'definers of each dimension are among the most central and persistent of the behaviours assessed; the dimensions again represent tight groups of measures interrelated at all periods and for both sexes; as dimensions, they are both central and enduring'. An examination of the behavioural characteristics used in defining each dimension reveals a strong similarity to E and N: in fact, Bronson accepts the Eysenckian E and N dimensions as consistent with those she has proposed. Further, as she comments, 'it is reassuring that the main consensus of longitudinal studies lies in findings of persistence of behaviors quite similar to those I rely upon . . . and also that it is widely accepted that individual differences . . . can all be established at very early stages of development . . .'. She also recognises that the stability and developmental course 'is not yet well documented'.

Scarr (1969) has examined a number of longitudinal and twin studies, to determine if there is evidence of long-term stability of 'social introversion-extraversion' (SIE). She has concluded that SIE is a '. . . basic dimension of responsiveness to the environment. Individual differences are observable in the first years of life; it is relatively stable over the developing years; twin studies find significant genetic contributions to it; and it is constantly rediscovered as a source of individual differences in behavior.' Scarr's definition of SIE, in broad terms, includes 'sociability, social anxiety, friendliness to strangers and social spontaneity'. This definition confounds the Eysenckian dimensions of E and N. In examining the data she presents (Scarr, 1969, Table 2, p. 282–283) it is evident that the studies cited employ trait-level descriptions. Nevertheless, in view of current trends in the evidence, it is not unlikely that in future longitudinal research, employing type-level descriptions and appropriate observation techniques, evidence will be found for the early emergence of E and N.

Kagan (1966), in a series of papers (*see* Yando and Kagan, 1968) has isolated 'a stable psychological dimension called reflection-impulsivity'. The dimension describes a consistent tendency, stable over time, for the individual to display fast or slow decision times when confronted with problem situations with high response uncertainty. There is evidence to suggest that individual styles on this dimension pervade a number of performances, such as reading recognition, serial learning and inductive reasoning (Yando and Kagan, 1968). Further support for the generality and pervasiveness of reflection-impulsivity has been provided by Ward (1968) as a result of experiments on kindergarten children (41 males, 46 females, mean age 68·9-months). Ward (1968) does, however, caution that contextual cues can influence the performance, and Yando and Kagan (1968) report that 'teacher tempo', conceptualised as on the R-I dimension, can effect modifications in the behavioural style of the children.

There is a strong similiarity between the type of behaviour that defines *R-I* and the behaviours sampled by the impulsiveness items that define part of the E dimension. Empirical studies with children would be needed to confirm that this similarity is not simply nominal. It would also appear that 'impulsivity' in pre-school children may be associated with the presence of minor physical anomalies (Waldrop *et al.*, 1968) or could be related to low Apgar scores (ratings of various characteristics of the neonate—colour, pulse rate, muscle tone—made just after birth and used to index its physical status) (Shipe *et al.*, 1968), suggesting that the behavioural similarity may not necessarily reflect common 'underlying' determinants.

It is therefore important to differentiate the 'phenocopies' from the 'phenotypes' in research on personality structure. It is not unlikely that, as a result of certain experiential factors (such as those that arise from 'complications of pregnancy and delivery'), some children may present with behaviours that simulate those characteristic of children without such histories. Overactivity can be found in many childhood disorders and high levels of activity can be normal in young children (Rutter, 1965). The fact that some characteristics change (or remain stable) in some children could simply be a consequence of some individuals in the sample having minor physiological or neurological abnormalities.

The tendency towards congruence of personality schemata is accompanied by some degree of similarity in orientation among the various researchers: Eysenck (1967), Thomas *et al.* (1964) and Bridger and Birns (1968), among others, accept the likely biological/genetic basis of personality/temperament, even to the extent of involving the concepts of excitation-inhibition, and in recognising the implications of their work for the understanding of psychological disorder. Differences of detail do, however, exist, (for example, trait-level *vs* type-level description); no doubt such differences will be resolved as the theoretical and practical implications of alternatives are subjected to empirical testing.

6. Conclusions

In deference to current practice, we have used the term 'early experience' in the title of this chapter. Newton and Levine (1968) point out that this term focuses attention on the role of 'nurture' in shaping behaviour, in particular, the future behaviour of the infant. They do, however, emphasise that their point of view, which they term 'epigenetic', does take biological factors into consideration. Moltz (1968) characterises the epigenetic view as one that, in addition to focusing on maturational processes, also 'seeks to understand the manner in which these processes combine with extrinsic stimulative conditions to structure and organise temporally integrated behavior'.

The epigenetic view, while it represents an advance over the notion of the *tabula rasa* organism, is itself limited. It fails to take into account the evidence, albeit limited, that temperament/personality characteristics also appear to play a role in the development of 'temporally integrated behavior'. Recognition must be given to the ways in which these factors, which appear to be inherent and stable, can also determine the effects of early experiences.

In summary, the research considered in the preceding paragraphs suggests that the 'colloidal neonate is dead'; that humans show a marked degree of complexity and plasticity at birth and subsequently, and that they also show a degree of enduring 'bias', varying between individuals, in the ways in which they interact with the postnatal world. While experiences may appear to be standard, they meet with individuals who do not appear to be so.

C. BEHAVIOUR DISORDERS

1. An Overview of the Problem of Disordered Behaviour in Children

In a recent (Rutter *et al.*, 1970) epidemiologic study of the total population of 2,199 children, aged 10 and 11 years, on the Isle of Wight, 5·4 per cent 'were found to have a clinically significant psychiatric disorder'. (When corrected for children likely to have been missed in the initial screening, the prevalence rate was found to be 6·8 per cent.) Uncomplicated mental and educational retardation and monosymptomatic enuresis were not included in this estimate. Neurotic and conduct disorders (Rutter, 1965; Rutter *et al.*, 1969) were most commonly observed and the two diagnoses were made with about equal frequency. In addition, a large group of children showed mixed conduct and neurotic disorders and 'resembled the antisocial group in many characteristics, including sex ratio, family size and associated reading retardation'. Combining the mixed and conduct disorder groups, the corrected prevalence of antisocial or conduct disorders was found to be 4 per cent. For neurotic disorders, the comparable rate was 2·5 per cent. Neurotic conditions were more often observed in girls, whereas conduct disorders were more often found in boys, and in the antisocial group a third of the children were found to be seriously retarded in their reading attainment (Rutter *et al.*, 1970). (Reporting on the findings of a thirty-year follow-up study of children initially referred to a guidance clinic in St Louis, Robins (1966) notes that 'not having had serious school difficulties may be a rather efficient predictor of absence of gross maladjustment' in adult life. In the clinic sample it was found that 68 per cent of adult sociopaths and 55 per cent of other patients were retarded in their school work when referred to the clinic (Robins, 1966, p. 294, Table 13.1). These children were within the average range of intelligence.)

As part of the Isle of Wight study, the parents and teachers of ten-, eleven-, and twelve-year-old children completed a behaviour questionnaire on nearly all the children at these ages (3,064 and 3,426, out of approximately 3,500 questionnaires, were returned by parents and teachers, respectively). Both parents and teachers indicated the presence of 'difficult or distressing' characteristics in a 'high proportion of boys and girls' (Rutter *et al.*, 1970). Not all these characteristics constituted signs of psychiatric disorder: some behaviours were regarded as normal variations that arose in the process of development. In many cases, disorders of eating, sleeping, thumb sucking, and nail biting were not regarded as symptomatic of psychiatric disorder. On the other hand, neurotic symptoms, antisocial or delinquent behaviour, poor concentration and difficulties in peer relationships, reported by parents and teachers, 'were often part of a more widespread and handicapping psychiatric disorder'. Such behaviours could, however, appear in isolation. Neurotic items were found to be about equally recorded for boys and girls but other features were decidedly commoner in boys. No particular association with social class was detected and IQ was 'somewhat below average' in children with these behaviours (Rutter *et al.*, 1970).

Two general questions arise in relation to the observations. The first concerns the evidence for the persistence of disorders into adolescence and adult life, and the second, which is of major concern here, is the emergence of disordered behaviour. Partial answers to these questions can be found in follow-up and longitudinal studies.

The St Louis study (Robins, 1966) examined the adult psychiatric status of 524 individuals who were seen at a child guidance clinic thirty-years previously. Ninety per cent of the parents were located in the follow-up and 82 per cent of the total group were interviewed. Other records were available for 98 per cent of the sample. 'Reasonably specific' diagnoses were made for 71 per cent, and an assessment of the presence or absence of psychiatric disorder was possible in 88 per cent of the cases.

Whatever criteria of adult adjustment were used, the general conclusion was that 'clinic children were more maladjusted and sicker adults than were control subjects'. Included among the symptoms that did not predict adult psychiatric illness were withdrawn—reticent behaviour, nervousness, irritability, restlessness, tantrums, fears and thumb sucking. Also, symptoms that 'frequently bring children to psychiatric attention' but that do not appear to be significantly related later to psychiatric status include such characteristics as fearfulness, hypersensitivity, and shyness, among others. In contrast, almost all the common antisocial symptoms predict later difficulties: the major differences in adult outcome appear to be related to the presence of antisocial characteristics. Four per cent of 'control subjects had five or more antisocial symptoms as adults compared with 45 per cent of the patient group'. In their adult lives, 52 per cent of the controls as compared with 20 per cent of the patients were thought to be free of adult psychiatric disorder throughout the period of adulthood.

The general pattern, illustrated by the St Louis study, is that the long-term prognosis for neurotic disorders is more favourable than that for aggressive antisocial disorders which may persist, with delinquency, antisocial behaviour or 'schizophrenia' the eventual but not the invariable outcome. (Rutter, 1965, 1970b).

In the Isle of Wight ten- and eleven-year-old sample, in most of the children with neurotic and antisocial disorders, it appeared that the condition had been present for at least three years, when the children would have been aged seven- to eight-years (Rutter *et al.*, 1970), suggesting that for some children at least, the symptoms had been present before this time. In the St Louis study sample, Robins (1966) reports that 'the early years of school attendance ages 6 to 10 years, are the most common period of onset reported for all childhood behaviour problems'. Fifty-two per cent of the sociopathic group and 42 per cent of those with other diagnoses had begun to manifest their disorders between these ages. Robins (1966) also notes that problems can be reported as beginning at any point in childhood for sociopathic adults and for those with most other diagnoses.

In the 'anterospective' data (teachers reports, recorded and stored in school files, made before the child was classed as delinquent), in the study reported by Conger and Miller (1966), future delinquents could be differentiated from closely matched future non-delinquents in the period 'kindergarten to 3rd grade'. Aggressive behaviour, poor social relationships, distractability, were among the differentiating characteristics. While the data from the early part of this study are not satisfactory, the observations appear to be consistent with those described above.

In the New York longitudinal study, the age at onset of symptoms in children selected for the clinical sample (selection based on the judgement of only one psychiatrist) ranged from 24- to 104-months.

This sample of studies is intended to indicate (not prove) that disorders of behaviour in children, small in terms of percentages, but sizeable when translated into absolute numbers in the population, can appear early in life and persist, with major consequences, into adulthood. Many qualifications are, however, needed: abnormal characteristics may appear but not have long-term consequences; they may appear but not be recognised; they may appear beyond childhood; they may appear early in a tolerant or indifferent setting or in settings which can contain their expression. Criteria other than psychiatric can also be used in their definition with a consequent variation in what is considered to be deviant or abnormal.

In summary, antisocial and neurotic disorders appear to be the most prevalent of the childhood psychiatric disorders, with the former having the worse prognosis. Psychiatric disorders may appear throughout the early part of the individual life-span, and in some individuals their effects may persist at least into middle-age.

In general, studies appear to be directed in a search for broad classes of predisposing factors and individual differences in outcome are not emphasised. Apart from the New York project, which demonstrates a need to include a consideration of individual reaction patterns, the role of the individual in moulding his disorder is also not given due weight. In presenting some of the commonly implicated 'early experiences' therefore, evidence on individual differences is introduced in an attempt to obtain a more balanced perspective.

D. EARLY EXPERIENCE AND ABNORMAL BEHAVIOUR

1. Introduction
The main purpose of this section is to highlight certain major trends in research on the effects of early experiences, particularly those circumstances that appear to have some association with the phenomena of abnormal behaviour. The factors to be considered are intended to reflect some of the major preoccupations of writers who are concerned with early-occurring events that may predispose the child, or later, the adult, to develop psychological disorder.

2. Patterns of Infant Care and Child-rearing Practices
Research on the relationship between infant feeding practices and toilet-training procedures, and later

behaviour and personality development has been reviewed by Caldwell (1964). From her review, it appears that the hypothesised pathogenic potential of these variations in early experiences is as yet not clearly detected by empirical studies. The observations of Thomas *et al.* (1968) would suggest that if relationships are to be found, then the temperamental characteristics of both infant and mother would need to be assessed.

Perhaps the most sobering appraisal of the literature on the effects of parental child-rearing practices on the child's behaviour, is the recent account by Marian Yarrow and her colleagues (M. Yarrow *et al.*, 1968). Their conclusion, simply, was that the 'compelling legend of maternal influences on child behaviour that has evolved does not have its roots in solid data'. Specifically, they have examined, and attempted to replicate, the findings on dependency and aggression in children, and the factors associated with the development of conscience in the child, as a function of parental, particularly maternal, child-rearing practices. No strong support was found for the view that dependency in the child relates simply and directly to the 'affectional bond between parent and child', nor is there 'any sort of clear relation between children's dependency strivings' and the manner of parental response to these behaviours. The evidence on general child-control practices of the parent and dependency is also equivocal. A consistent finding has been the absence of significant associations between measures of frustration arising from parental demands and restrictions, and aggression in the child. Also, the findings on the relationship between punishment and aggression are such as to 'leave most questions unsettled'. This conclusion applies as well to the likely role of permissiveness as a contributor to aggression.

An observation of some import which has emerged from these analyses, is the possible sex-linked interaction between maternal acceptance and rejection, and the measures of conscience in the child: the associations between non-rejecting be-haviours and 'warmth', in the mother, and high 'conscience' scores, are closer for boys than for girls. Given this type of interaction, and the many methodological deficiencies in the research that has attempted to demonstrate a linkage between parent attributes and child characteristics, it is not surprising that commonly held hypotheses about the relation-ship between parent behaviour and the child's conscience 'are not with any certainty supported by the available evidence'. Correlational studies, as Yarrow et al. (1968) emphasise, do not indicate the direction of the effect. Theoretical supposition has been in the direction parent to child. That the process is interactional would be supported by the obser-vations of Thomas et al. (1968), and by Moss's (1967) observations of the mother-infant interaction. The exclusion from consideration of the role of temperamental factors, in his review of the conse-quences of parental discipline, must to a great extent limit the validity of the general conclusions drawn by Becker (1964).

The evidence on inconsistent discipline, as summarised by Becker (1964) is perhaps best interpreted in associational rather than in causal terms. There appears to be an association between inconsistent discipline and antisocial behaviour in children, as shown particularly in studies of delin-quents (McCord et al., 1959), the inconsistency being both intraparental and interparental (Becker, 1964). However, the precise meaning of incon-sistency is uncertain. Also, although not found to be statistically significant, an association was observed in the rates of antisocial behaviour in the children in the St Louis study who eventually became sociopathic, and the modes of discipline, particularly its absence, used by their parents. Robins (1966) suggests that strict discipline may in fact deter expression of antisocial behaviour later in life. With the number of childhood antisocial symptoms held constant, 21 per cent of the most severely antisocial children whose parents practised 'good or strict' discipline were diagnosed sociopathic later in life, as compared to 48 per cent whose parents were excessively lenient or disinterested.

The principles of operant conditioning (Ferster and Perrott, 1968) and current research on the use of behaviour modification techniques in the class-room (Becker et al., 1967; Hall et al., 1968; Berger, 1971) point to some of the difficulties encountered in using parental reports for assessing behaviour management practices, and to some of the problems encountered in using concepts such as permissiveness or inconsistency. The classroom data, based on direct observation studies, suggest that immediate praise for acceptable behaviour and ignoring the inappropriate behaviour of school children, can lead to an increment in the positively reinforced be-haviour. An important element in this procedure is that there be an immediate response by the teacher to 'good' behaviour; that is, contingent reinforce-ment. (Would parents who ignored bad behaviour be considered permissive or lax?) Teachers may report that they use praise for appropriate behaviour and ignore unacceptable behaviour as part of their classroom-behaviour control practices. Direct obser-vation of their behaviour in the classroom reveals that they may do so, but react inappropriately, that is, non-contingently. It is suggested that the problems inherent in the studies reviewed by Yarrow et al. (1968) and by Becker (1964), are unlikely to be resolved without recourse to direct observation of parent-child interaction, rather than accepting what the mother says she does, even if she says so consistently.

3. Social and Emotional Development and Separation

In a well-controlled study of the emergence of social behaviour in fraternal and identical twins, from one-to twelve-months of age, Freedman (1965) has concluded that hereditary factors are important in the development of a positive social orientation (including smiling), and in the emergence of the fear of strangers. He notes, for example, that in identical twins, the 'age of onset and the intensity of visual fixation of the adult's face was generally the same' despite even substantial differences in birth weight.

The general developmental sequence of social responsiveness of the infant has been described by Ricciuti (1968), and specific departures from the general pattern are noted by Freedman (1965). Reflex smiling in the neonate (Korner, 1969), is apparent during the first month during certain state-related periods, but tends to diminish in frequency towards the end of the first month. It does not appear to be linked to particular external stimuli. During the second month, smiling behaviour can be elicited by external stimulation (Freedman, 1965), and distinctly 'pleasureful social responses' do not emerge until near the end of the second month (Ricciuti, 1968). However, in some samples, socially elicited smiling appeared before the end of the first month (Wolff, 1963). Late in the second month, smiling and pleasureful responses are elicited by any human face, and indiscriminate responsiveness to humans persists until approximately the fifth or sixth month, when the smiling at strangers seems to diminish to a considerable extent. Towards the end of the first year, there emerges what may be described as a 'marked fear of strangers', with the tendency for infants to 'respond with considerable stress and anxiety' to the approach of a stranger. In the latter half of the first year, 'affectional attachments to specific adults such as the parents' is increasingly discernible, and this continues into the second year. In the latter part of the second year, increasing social and affectional interaction with other children becomes apparent. Although the trend is 'reasonably well established' (Ricciuti 1968), individual differences are very striking. Freedman (1965) reports that one pair of identical twins showed fear of strangers only over the age range five- to eight-months. Concordance in timing and intensity of reaction were noted in identical pairs, whereas the appearance, intensity, and duration of the reaction to strangers varied markedly in fraternal pairs.

The literature on the reactions of the infant and child to separation from it's parents, particularly the mother, has been analysed in a number of reviews: these reviews document the enduring interest in the effects of early separation (Yarrow, 1961, 1964; Casler, 1961, 1968; O'Conner, 1956, 1968; Clarke, 1968; Ambrose, 1968; Bronfenbrenner 1968). The past decade, too, as Ainsworth (1969) records, has been a 'period of ferment' in developmental psychology, the 'development of attachment' being one of the subjects of 'unprecedented research activity'. There is little doubt that Bowlby's (1951) monograph *Maternal Care and Mental Health* exerted a major directive influence, and that his more recent views (Bowlby, 1969a) will likely provoke a comparable expenditure of energy.

The event of separation, and the consequences that follow, appear to be a function of a multitude of interrelated factors. Yarrow (1964) points out that there are at 'least a dozen different types of separation experiences'. Further, the consequences of separation do not appear to be uniform: a variety of individual differences may interact with the variety of circumstances producing differential outcomes (Yarrow, 1964; Ucko, 1965; Clarke, 1968; O'Conner, 1968). A crucial factor, as Yarrow (1964) points out, is whether or not a 'focused relationship' with the mother has been established at the time of the separation event. The most severe disturbances appear to follow *after* the development of a 'focused relationship', a proposition supported by Bronfenbrenner (1968) and others.

4. Experimental Separations

Spontaneous separations from the mother have been observed by Rhinegold and Eckerman (1969). In a standard experimental setting, they found that ten-month-old infants left their mothers and with no distress entered a new environment whether it was empty or contained a toy. Their behaviour was controlled by the number and locality of the toys, and by whether the objects were there initially or were added later. This behaviour contrasted markedly with that shown by another group of infants who were placed in a new setting. The latter groups showed marked distress and an almost complete inhibition of locomotion (Rhinegold, 1969). The interpretation that the mother acts as a 'secure base' who affords the infant safety (Ainsworth, 1963) is queried by Rhinegold and Eckerman (1969). Firstly, on many occasions the infants did not touch their mothers in the course of their exits from the 'new' setting. Seeing their mothers appeared to be sufficient and 'often' the return was 'accompanied by facial and vocal expressions of pleasure and not by signs of fear or of relief from fear'. The presence or absence of the mother appears to have a significant effect on what the infant will do in a strange setting. Ainsworth and Bell (1970) have reported that, for fifty-six white, middle-class infants, forty-nine- to fifty-one-weeks of age, the presence of the mother encouraged exploratory behaviour whereas exploration was depressed in her absence. During the separation episodes, there was an increase in crying and search behaviour. When reunited with the mother, there was an increase in 'proximity-seeking' and 'contact maintaining' behaviour. A 'substantial proportion' of the infants also showed an increase in 'contact-resisting' behaviour, usually in conjunction with behaviour aimed at maintaining contact. Some of the subjects tended to avoid proximity to their mothers when reunited after a short separation.

During these nuclear separation events, individual differences in reaction were marked. Thirty-seven per cent cried minimally, if at all, but 'searched strongly'; 20 per cent cried 'desperately but searched weakly or not at all'; 32 per cent cried and searched, and 11 per cent did not appear to react when left alone (*see also*: Ainsworth and Wittig, 1969).

It is interesting to note the similarities in behaviour between these infants and young chimpanzees in laboratory play situations (Mason, 1967). In particular, it has been reported that the play or clinging behaviour of chimpanzees can be readily manipulated by the use of amphetamine and barbiturates (Mason, 1967; Mason *et al.*, 1968). Mason's interpretation introduces the 'arousal' properties of the 'novel' situation, a view that would be consonant with the observations on the effects of the stimulant and depressant drugs. It would be enlightening—but unethical?—to observe the reactions of separated infants given such drugs, to the Rhinegold- Ainsworth-type experimental situation!

5. Short-term Separations: Hospitalisation and Placement in Care

There are now very many studies (Bowlby, 1969a, p. 24–26) that document the reactions of infants and children to more enduring separations from 'the mother'. These subjects, as Bowlby (1969a) notes, come from a variety of settings, vary in age, and in both the institutional settings in which they are placed and in the duration of the separation, among other characteristics, there are marked differences. Despite such differences and irrespective of the 'backgrounds and expectations' of those who have reported their observations, 'there is a remarkable uniformity in the findings'. The prototypical separation situations described by Bowlby are those involving the placement of children in their second to third years of life in residential nurseries and hospital wards. They are placed for varying periods and are cared for 'in traditional ways'. The behaviour of these children on return to their homes is also observed directly, and further information is obtained from parents. Given a 'reasonably secure relationship with his mother' and no previous history of separation, the predictable sequence of behaviours that appears with separation are characterised by the merging phases of 'Protest, Despair and Detachment' (Bowlby, 1969a).

The initial phase of protest may begin immediately or may be delayed. It may last from a few hours to a week or more. In this phase, the young child appears greatly distressed, 'will often cry loudly, shake his cot, throw himself about, and look eagerly towards any sight or sound which might prove to be his missing mother'. At this time the child may reject other people, or some may cling to a nurse. During the second phase, the active physical behaviour may diminish or cease, and the child may cry monotonously or only intermittently. He tends to be withdrawn and inactive, making no demands of people in the environment, 'and appears to be in a state of deep mourning'. In the detachment phase, the child no longer appears to reject the caretakers, accepting their care and the food and toys they bring, and may even smile and be sociable. During this phase, should the mother visit, the child appears to be indifferent to her. On return to the home environment, certain characteristics are seen which do not appear in children not separated. On encountering the mother after a two- to three-week separation, the child appears 'distant and detached'. Proximity seeking behaviour, which tends to be a usual pattern at this age, is absent for varying periods of time ranging from minutes or hours to days. The degree of detachment is highly correlated with the length of separation (Heinicke and Westheimer, 1965). With the resumption of the attachment, the child tends to be more clinging than before the separation. How this is resolved appears to be a function of the management practices and the reactions of the mother. Heinicke and Westheimer (1965) report that six of the ten separated children showed strong and persistent hostile behaviour and negativism to the mother. Four of the ten children showed little or no evidence of this type of response to separation, as did the ten control group children.

(In view of the observations of Mason (1967) and Mason *et al.*, (1968), one may wonder how those children who showed strong reactions to hospitalisation and clinging behaviour at home on their return, would have reacted had they been given mild sedatives before their entry into the hospital and before their return home. And what if those who showed minimal disturbance in these situations were given amphetamine . . . ?)

Although the succession of phases may be predictable in general terms, it is obvious from even this brief account of reactions to longer separations, that individual differences exist (Heinicke and Westheimer, 1965). This would be anticipated to some extent from the observations of Ainsworth and Wittig (1969), and Ainsworth and Bell (1970). The factors that differentiate those individuals who react strongly from those who show minimal or no reaction, have not been fully examined. In young infants, at least, reactions to hospitalisation appear in part to be determined by organismic/constitutional characteristics (Schaffer, 1966). Twenty-two infants, ranging in age from 1 to 29 weeks were observed during a period of hospitalisation and were seen again in their homes ten to eighteeen days after being discharged. Developmental quotients were obtained three days prior to discharge (when they had recuperated) and again during the home observation. Shaffer (1966) found that the more active infants showed the least DQ change over the two periods and he suggests that reactions to deprivation appear to be a function of organismic characteristics, presumed to be constitutional in origin.

While the general pattern of response to what Clarke (1968) terms 'short periods of adversity' is well-recognised (Yarrow, 1964; Clarke, 1968; O'Connor, 1968), Yarrow (1964) notes that even these short-term reactions may be diluted by appropriate preparation of the child, and through such alterations in hospital policy as flexible arrangements for visitors and the provision of rooming-in facilities for parents. Both Clarke (1968) and O'Connor (1968) emphasise that while the short, intense experiences may have immediate effects they need not have any long-term consequences. That the child may become 'sensitised' to hospitals and the associated paraphanalia as a consequence, cannot be excluded, but such circumscribed 'phobias' can likely be overcome if they persist (Eysenck and Rachman, 1965; Rachman, 1968).

6. Long-term Separations: Institutionalisation

In a closely argued assessment of the effects of early separation experiences, Bronfenbrenner (1968), in agreement with Casler (1968), concludes that the event of maternal separation before a focused relationship has developed, does not give rise to serious emotional disorder or deficits, provided that the infant or child is not subjected to simultaneous perceptual or stimulus deprivation. If stimulus deprivation (or privation) occurs early in infancy and persists into late infancy and early childhood, there is a strong chance that serious disturbances and deficits would result, and that these would become permanently disabling (Bronfenbrenner, 1968). In middle infancy, at the period when attachment to the mother appears to be at its strongest, separation from the mother and placement in an adverse environment introduces the compound effects of separation and relative stimulus deprivation. Later on in infancy, the effects of deprivation are similar but not as extreme. The evidence for this general

pattern of reaction in humans is substantial (Bronfenbrenner, 1968). There is no evidence however, of irreversible debilitations consequent on 'deprivation of the type encountered in institutions'. This conclusion is consistent with those of Clarke (1968) and O'Connor (1968). As Clarke (1968) suggests, the apparent 'discrepancies between some of the classic studies of the effects of early institutional upbringing are largely resolved if (*a*) differences in institutions, (*b*) differences in later placement and (*c*) differences in length of follow-up are taken into account'. Clarke (1968) also emphasises, as does O'Connor (1968) that there seems to be large individual differences in vulnerability to adverse experiences encountered early in life. Bronfenbrenner (1968) does, however, stress that the evidence that deprived children reach normal levels of functioning is not very satisfactory. We cannot exclude the possibility that deficits or disabilities may remain. Several not necessarily mutually exclusive points need to be made. To some extent, whether or not disabilities are detected will be a function of the comprehensiveness and sensitivity of the assessments made at the time of follow-up. It strongly doubted that objective or other psychological tests could satisfy these requirements of sensitivity and comprehensiveness (*see* Suinn and Oskamp, 1969). Further, the extent to which less formal assessment procedures, such as the interview, will be able to exclude the possibility of more subtle aspects of disorder, is also likely to be restricted. For example, in a study of the reliability and validity of a short (half-hour) diagnostic interview, using children as subjects, Rutter and Graham (1968) have found that judgements about the presence or absence of psychiatric disorder could be made reliably (interrater agreement). However, they found that generally, 'individual ratings on specific aspects of behaviour proved to be less reliable'.

The presence of disabilities may, however, suggest little else than the possibility that 'the environments which these individuals have experienced' have been rather inefficient in capitalising on what the research evidence demonstrates, namely, that children brought up in institutions are educable! We have no proof that any residual difficulties would be incapable of modification, particularly by the application of systematic behaviour modification techniques such as those described by Bandura (1969), or the methods of social skills training suggested by Argyle (1969). Pessimism would be acceptable if adverse institutional experiences had effects similar to those that appear as a consequence of congenital or early-acquired cataracts. Humans deprived of patterned visual input early in life, 'show, often entirely unperturbed, the behaviour patterns of the blind when vision is introduced' (Ganz, 1968). This appears to be a consequence of the neural mechanisms responsible for patterned vision not being 'sustained or normally developed in the absence of patterned stimulus experience' (Ganz, 1968). Institutional environments do not, however, eliminate patterned inputs, nor do they totally deprive their inmates of contact with caretakers or with other children (Bronfenbrenner, 1968; King and Raynes, 1967).

In part, Bronfenbrenner's (1968) caution about the extent of recovery from 'isolation' arises from the major effects observed in research on mammals, particularly monkeys. It is possible however, that some of the observed effects are methodological artefacts. There is evidence, albeit limited, that primates need not be severely affected by gross deprivation. While further research is needed, Mason *et al.* (1968) suggest that the effects of perceptual deprivation and isolation may be a function of the *manner* in which the transition from rearing environment to the test situation is accomplished. Sudden exposure of visually deprived animals to complex visual surroundings produced striking and persisting emotional reactions which were not greatly reduced by prolonging the period of exposure. The effects are, however, 'much attenuated' if the transition is gradually introduced. Mason *et al.* (1968) also refer to evidence that suggests that by providing 'a graded series of experiences it may be possible to increase substantially the range of stimulation which is accepted by an isolation-reared subject'. Chimpanzees so 'prepared' responded, at the age of five- to six-years, to human and chimpanzee strangers, 'in much the same manner as African-born animals of comparable age'. While recognising that certain difficulties of the institutionalised child may be overcome by suitable modification techniques, it must also be appreciated that the child himself may impose limits on what can be done. Casler (1968) has emphasised that infants and children placed in institutions (or in special care) are undoubtedly a highly selected and atypical group. There is some evidence (Casler, 1968) that many 'institutionalised babies result from unwanted pregnancies' and these pregnancies are associated with possibly harmful circumstances for the foetus and neonate. Whether or not these 'experiences' limit the remedial efficiency of even good institutional environments and whether they may undermine the application of systematic modification techniques, needs to be fully examined.

7. Bond Disruption and Psychopathology

Bowlby's (1969a) current theorising is concerned firstly with the establishment of attachment (affectional bonds) in humans, and secondly, with the consequences of bond disruption, particularly as a determinant of psychiatric disorder (e.g. Bowlby, 1969b; Melges and Bowlby, 1969). Bowlby (1969b) has asserted that the broad classes of psychiatric disorder in adulthood, psychoneurotic, sociopathic and psychotic, 'always show impairment of the capacity for affectional bonding, an impairment that is often both severe and lasting'. The impairment may be secondary to the disorder but in 'many' instances it is thought to be primary and 'derives from faulty development having occurred during a childhood spent in an atypical family environment'. Childhood psychiatric disorders are also thought to have antecedent bond disturbances, although he accepts that, in the latter instances at least, the causal relationship is debatable (Bowlby, 1969b).

The psychiatric syndromes of psychopathic personality and depression, and the symptoms of persistent delinquency and suicide are, according to Bowlby (1969b) 'consistently found to be preceded by a high incidence of disrupted affectional bonds during childhood'. Differential antecedent conditions are associated with these syndromes and symptoms.

The studies Bowlby (1969b) cites in support of his arguments (Hill and Price, 1967; Dennehey, 1966; Greer et al., 1966; Greer and Gunn, 1966; Munro, 1966; among others), are said to show that 'the incidence of disruption of affectional bonds during childhood is significantly raised'. He does, however, concede that raised incidence and cause are not synonymous.

The evidence for 'raised incidence' in certain disorders has been questioned by Munro (1969a,b) in his review of the same studies, and by Munro and Griffiths (1968, 1969). As Munro (1969b) notes, methodological faults are abundant in the research on parental deprivation. Uncomplicated 'depressive illness seems to be the condition which has been shown most convincingly not to be associated with deprivation' and there is equivocal evidence of the role of parental loss as a major predisposing factor for particular psychoneurosis (Munro, 1969b). There is evidence (Munro and Griffiths, 1968) from studies on two geographically distinct groups of psychiatrically normal subjects, that parental deprivation 'is an extremely common experience in normal childhood; so common, in fact, that it is very difficult to see how it can be related directly to the aetiology of psychiatric illness'.

While there is some evidence for the raised incidence of parental loss/broken homes in attempted suicides (Munro, 1969b; Greer et al., 1966; Greer and Gunn, 1966), the pattern of determinants is by no means distinct. Greer et al. (1966) found that parental loss occurred in only 49 per cent of suicidal patients; Greer and Gunn (1966), analysing the data from this study, found that age, diagnosis and disruption of a close interpersonal relationship, were significant factors in distinguishing the attempted suicides brought up in intact homes, from those who had suffered parental loss. They recognise that further research needs to be undertaken to clarify these relationships. It should be noted that nearly all these studies have the disadvantage of being retrospective (Munro, 1969b).

It is not particularly clear what Bowlby (1969b) means by 'disrupted affectional bonds'. His emphasis appears to be directed mainly at parent-child bond *severance* through death, divorce, or separation of parents; the prototypical circumstances are those where the child is separated from both parents, through hospitalisation or placement in care. However, in the same paper, Bowlby (1969b) refers to the impaired capacity for affectional bonding arising as a consequence of 'a childhood spent in an atypical family environment'. There is no direct evidence, Bowlby's assertions apart, that all, or nearly all, psychiatric patients show an impaired capacity for forming affectional attachments. The evidence from the Munro and Griffiths (1968, 1969) studies suggests as well that parent-child separations *per se* do not necessarily lead to psychiatric sequelae. That 'atypical environments' may play an important role in the aetiology of various disorders is becoming more apparent in the research studies: if Bowlby includes 'disturbed families and parental discord' in the compass of 'atypical', then there would be some basis for his views as regards raised incidence, but not necessarily for those on the primacy of the disturbed capacity for 'bonding'.

8. Family Stress

Evidence is accumulating to suggest that family discord is a major factor in the development of delinquency (McCord *et al.*, 1959; Rutter, 1970b) and behaviour disorders in children (Rutter, 1969, 1970a,b), and that certain adult disorders may be a continuation of the earlier disturbances (Robins, 1966). Males in particular appear to be most vulnerable to the effects of family discord (Rutter, 1970a). In the St Louis follow-up study, Robins (1966, Table 13.1, pp. 294–295) has found that 67 per cent of sociopathic and 63 per cent of other patients were from broken homes. Robins has suggested that 'parental discord', rather than the experience of a broken home, is related to a later diagnosis of sociopathic personality. Twenty-seven per cent of the parents of sociopaths were divorced and 24 per cent were not, whereas 26 per cent came from discordant homes (parents separated or not) as compared with only 16 per cent who came from 'harmonious homes'. This latter difference was statistically significant. Eighty-five per cent of the sociopaths and other patients, respectively, were males.

An important predictor of antisocial characteristic in children, in the St Louis sample, was the presence of antisocial behaviour in the father. The risk was only slightly increased when both father and mother were antisocial. Thirty-two per cent of the fathers of the non-sociopathic patients, and 53 per cent of the fathers of the sociopathic patients, were sociopathic or alcoholic (Robins, 1966, Table 13.1, pp. 294–295). Robins (1966) has indicated that among the consequences of having an antisocial father are high rates of quarrelling, separation, and divorce between parents, as well as a lack of adequate discipline. While the St Louis sample is a selected one, carrying with it the disadvantages of clinic-derived groups, a number of features observed by Robins (1966) reappear, more clearly delineated in the Family Illness study (Rutter, 1970a), which is currently assessing the effects of psychiatric illness in one or both parents, on the behaviour of their children. Rutter (1970a), in a preliminary report of some of the findings, has stated that 'discord and disruption in the home were consistently and strongly associated with antisocial disorders in boys, but not in girls'. The characteristics of these families were not consistently associated with neurosis in either boys or girls.

Rutter's (1970a) observations suggest that where the clinical picture of a parent was one of an antisocial personality, a higher rate of disorder was found in boys. When the quality of family relationships was assessed, it was found that a combination of parental personality disorder and a poor marriage 'as indicated by such characteristics as frequency of quarrelling, quality of interaction in household activities and leisure pursuits', produced the highest rate of disorder in boys.

It should be noted that the measure of deviance of the child used in this particular study, was a questionnaire (Rutter, 1967) completed by the child's teacher, and similar to that used for general screening purposes in the Isle of Wight study (Rutter *et al.*, 1970). It has been reported (Tizard, 1968) that of 157 children (of a total group of 2,193 children for whom both parents and teachers had completed questionnaires), selected as maladjusted by teachers on this questionnaire, sixty-four were finally diagnosed as maladjusted by psychiatrists. Taking account of the likely misclassifications by questionnaires such as that used in this study, Tizard (1968) has concluded that teacher questionnaires alone cannot be regarded as valid indices of maladjustment. Rutter (1970a) is aware of this limitation and only compares rates of maladjustment operationally defined, within the samples.

To some extent, it is likely that the degree of association reported by Rutter (1970a) is a function of the relative homogeneity of social class in his sample. Robins (1966) found that no measure of social status operated independently of the child's antisocial behaviour and such behaviour in his father. The findings of Conger and Miller (1966) would also support this view and, in addition, suggest that other influences need to be taken into consideration, particularly, the interactions between personality factors, social class, and IQ in delinquency in boys. In referring to their initial findings in a parallel study of delinquency in girls, they note as well that 'even at this point it appears safe to state that sex differences exist in the number, extent, and nature of over-all delinquent-nondelinquent differences, as well as in the relation of social class and IQ status to personality and behavioral differences between delinquents and nondelinquents'.

A major implication of the aforementioned studies is that they point to the need to structure research in such a way that intrafamilial processes can be directly observed. Additionally, objective assessments of qualitative factors are needed. The trends in the research evidence point to these requirements. The studies reported by Moss (1969) and Rutter (1970a) show that such methods are feasible. Also, the recent research of Hess and Shipman (1967), in which mother-child interactions are observed in deliberately structured situations in the laboratory, suggest a model for future studies. It is probable that only under conditions that allow direct observation will psychologists also be able to observe the role of the phenomena of imitation (Aronfreed, 1969), for example, in the genesis of disorders. It is also presupposed that in such studies temperamental characteristics, sex differences and the like, would be taken into account.

E. CONCLUSIONS

In the first edition of this *Handbook*, Eysenck (1960) drew the distinction between the concepts of medical and behavioural disorders. It was emphasised at that time that the most important difference between these conceptions was the absence, in behavioural disorders, of a 'single cause'. With few exceptions, the research that appeared in the following decade continued to be directed in a unifactorial search. We have attempted to argue here, on the basis of individual differences in psychological characteristics and in response to various circumstances that arise early in life, that such a model does not account for the observed variation in outcome.

Studies that find evidence of 'raised incidence' serve the important function of directing attention to particular factors, but generally, do not clarify the pattern of relationships that has led to the raised incidence. Many papers conclude that X may be, or is, important, but that further research is needed. It would not grossly misrepresent the contemporary situation if it is asserted that perhaps the major contribution of much of the research on human psychological disorder has been to point out those variables that may be aetiologically significant. What are needed, are studies that combine the variety of factors in multivariate designs that allow interaction effects to manifest their significance. How much weight will be given to each factor is a problem for future research.

II. Studies with Non-human Primates

R. E. PASSINGHAM

A. INTRODUCTION

Beach (1950, 1960) has criticised psychologists for their 'anthropocentric' use of animals as substitutes for people, and argued that evidence is required that valid generalisations can be made from animals to man. He has pointed out that the choice of the rat as the animal most commonly studied was historically accidental and is scientifically questionable. Furthermore, he has demonstrated that psychologists tend to study only a very limited range of the natural behavioural repertoire of the rat, confining their attention mainly to learning, on the grounds that this is the field of study of most interest from the anthropocentric viewpoint. It should be stressed that the same problem arises with the anthropocentric use of carnivores and non-human primates. There is, even within the mammalian class, no *scala natura* such that clear phylogenetic trends can be discerned, on the basis of which conclusions can be drawn in relation to man (Hodos and Campbell, 1969). Different orders and families within the mammalian class are specialised for different ecological niches, both in their physical and behavioural make-up. Even where a behavioural trait is not clearly species-specific, it may be 'species typical' (Hinde and Tinbergen, 1958; Mason, 1968). Differences in behavioural repertoire would be predicted within the mammalian class on the basis of differences in brain structure and organisation alone, especially in relation to the extent of association cortex (Thompson, 1967). Furthermore, there are specialisations within the class for brain function, as for example in carnivores, for whom the cortex is specialised in relation to audition (Diamond and Hall, 1969). The choice of experimental animal for anthropocentric studies on the effects of early experience is, therefore, a difficult but crucial one.

For the purposes of this chapter evidence will be reviewed on the effects of early experience on non-human primates; that is on animals within the same order as man.* Detailed evidence is available for non-human primates on their behaviour both in the wild (DeVore, 1965) and in the laboratory (Schrier *et al.*, 1965), although the greater proportion of the evidence is available for the genus *Macaca*. However, even here there are dangers in generalising, since there are large differences in specialisation within non-human primates (Jay, 1968). Wherever possible, evidence is given for chimpanzees (*Pan troglodytes*) and gorillas (*Gorilla gorilla*) since both immunological and blood protein studies have shown that man is most closely related to these Pongidae, and that man is more closely related to

the Pongidae than are the Pongidae to Old World monkeys (Cercopithecoidea) (Sarich, 1968; Doolittle and Mross, 1970). Furthermore, as Mason *et al.* (1968, pp. 440) have pointed out, the higher 'primates are characterised by a long period of dependency on the mother, which brings with it many opportunities for social learning'. By the principle of neoteny (Mason *et al.*, 1968) the Pongidae have a very much longer period of infancy and dependency (3 to 5 years) than do Old World monkeys (about 1 year) and chimpanzees may be closely associated with their mothers for 13 or more years (Goodall, 1968). Finally, there are several major field studies on the social development and organisation of chimpanzees (Goodall, 1968; Reynolds and Reynolds, 1965) and gorillas (Schaller, 1963), although the evidence is much more extensive for the chimpanzee than the gorilla. Data are also available on the social development of chimpanzees in the laboratory (Mason, 1965a; Mason, 1965b).

Even when non-human primates are used as 'dummy humans' (Morris, 1967, pp. 1) there are considerable dangers in assuming that it will always be possible to generalise behavioural results to man (Drewe *et al.*, 1970). Experiments on non-human primates have the advantage that more severe and controlled environmental manipulations can be made than can be made on man, and it is thus more easy to isolate relevant causative variables. However, in view of the problem of the generalisability of the results both within non-human primates and between non-human primates and man, it is advisable to concentrate anthropocentric study on those areas in which it is likely that generalisations can most validly be made. Since the neural structures subserving emotional behaviour have undergone least change within the mammalian class and from non-human primates to man (Pribram and Kruger, 1954) it would seem likely *a priori* that generalisations would would be made with least risk from research on emotional behaviour. This review will concentrate, therefore, on the effects of early experience on emotional behaviour, although not totally neglecting other evidence where available. Since there are already in the literature several excellent and comprehensive reviews of the effects of early experience on the emotional behaviour of primates (Harlow and Harlow, 1965; Sackett, 1967; Sackett, 1969; Mason *et al.*, 1968) this review will concentrate mainly on questions of methodology and on the relevance of these studies for man.

---

* Evidence of the effects of early experience on mammals other than primates can be found in the following reviews: rodents (Broadhurst, 1971; Bronfenbrenner, 1968), carnivores (Fuller and Thompson, 1964; Bronfenbrenner, 1968; Melzack, 1968; Scott, 1968). Data on the maternal behaviour of mammals may be found in Rheingold (1963).

Evidence on the effects of the prenatal environment may be found in Joffé (1969).

B. METHODOLOGY

1. Biological Factors

As Mason *et al.* (1968, pp. 440) state, 'no one doubts that the social development of monkeys and

apes is dependent on experience'. Psychologists have for many years stressed environmental variables in the causation of both normal and abnormal behaviour, while tending to ignore innate factors, maturational factors, and individual differences. For example, Ullman and Krasner (1969) stress environmental schedules in the aetiology of mental disorder and give little discussion to the evidence on biological and neurological factors. As Hebb (1947, pp. 6) put it, 'in man, neurosis or psychosis again and again occurs without apparent cause in experience. It is common to assume that if we only know enough about the subject's past history we should find such a cause.... Only dogma, unsupported and even contradicted by fact, can assert that neurotic behaviour in man results always from psychological stress alone'. As Hebb goes on to say, the same assumption is often made in studies of 'neurosis' in non-human primates and may be as little justified as it is in the case of man. A more biological approach would stress the interaction between innate factors and environment in the explanation of behaviour in the phenotype (Eysenck, 1966; Eysenck, 1967). Such an approach has been gaining more support recently, due partly to the development of the study of behavioural genetics (for rodents, Eysenck and Broadhurst, 1960; for carnivores, Scott and Fuller, 1964; Fuller and Thompson, 1960). Another factor is the increase in interaction between the biologically trained zoologists and ethologists and the non-biologically trained psychologists, leading both to increasing stress on evolutionary questions (Roe and Simpson, 1958) and on studies of animals in their natural surroundings (Thorpe, 1957; Hinde, 1966). There is thus, now the possibility of a synthesis between ethology and comparative psychology (Hinde, 1966). This brings with it both stress on species-specific behaviour in invertebrates and lower vertebrates, and species-typical behaviour in higher mammals.

Eysenck (1966) has stressed the behavioural differences both between species and within species, these differences being phenotypic and thus affected by both genetic and environmental factors. It is worth stressing that within the primate order subdivisions can be made into suborder, superfamily, family, subfamily, genus, species and subspecies (Washburn and Hamburg, 1965; Schrier et al., 1965). It needs to be shown, therefore, that valid generalisations can be made about 'monkeys' or 'apes' as opposed to animals of a particular genus, species, and subspecies. There are other differences that need to be taken into account. For example, it is known that rhesus monkey (Macaca mulatta) mothers treat their male and female infants in differing ways (Mitchell, 1968) and that infant males both leave their mother earlier than females and engage in more rough and tumble play (Sackett, 1967). Chamove et al. (1967) have also reported

innate differences in the behaviour of preadolescent rhesus monkeys towards infants according to the sex of the preadolescent animals. There are also suggestions that males may be more disturbed than females by partial isolation during infancy (Sackett, 1967). Another relevant variable is that of age. Arling et al. (1969) reported that nulliparous female rhesus monkeys who had experienced isolation from birth were, at the age of 8 years, less aggressive toward infants than were others tested at the age of 4 years. Harlow and Harlow (1965) have also reported that 'motherless' mothers (i.e. reared apart from their mothers) were more rejecting of their first infant than they were of the second. This difference may reflect both the change in experience and in age. A further important variable is that of individual differences within a species or subspecies. Hinde (1969) has pointed out that there are individual differences in the patterns of interaction of mother, infant rhesus monkey pairs, and that, in particular the more demanding infants were more affected by maternal deprivation. These differences are, of course, phenotypic and there is no evidence yet on whether or not they reflect genotypic differences. However, Goodall (1969) comments on the large differences in aggressive behaviour between two of the chimpanzees studied by her who were of the same sex, age, and position in the social hierarchy. Unfortunately, the relevant breeding studies to isolate the causative variables would be prohibitive with primates, but it would seem unlikely that such differences can be accounted for by environmental factors alone.

2. Environmental Factors

Most of the studies on the effects of early experience reviewed in this chapter have used animals kept in laboratory cages. The animals have been studied, therefore, in an artificial environment. As pointed out by Gartlan and Brain (1968) the act of placing a non-human primate in a cage, after taking it from its natural environment, involves a change in many variables. For example, the animal has changes in type and variety of diet, short feeding times, lack of social contact (if isolated) and often overcrowding and abnormal sex ratios when kept in group cages. Furthermore, the caged animal is able to display only a small sample of its natural behavioural repertoire, especially since much of the naturalistic behaviour is social behaviour, which takes place naturally in large social groups. The behaviour of caged non-human primates may also be abnormal when compared with that of the free-living animal. Thus, Mason (in McKinney and Bunney, 1969) has observed that callicebus monkeys (Callicebus moloch) become depressed, at least initially, when placed in cages. As a result of the restricted and abnormal behaviour observed in caged animals it is not clear to what extent generalisations on the effects of environmental variables, such as early experience, can be made from the laboratory animal to the animal living in its natural environment.

Fortunately, there is now a certain amount of data on the behaviour of at least some species of non-human primates living in their natural environment (DeVore, 1965; Jay, 1968; Goodall, 1968). Where available, this evidence can be used to check on generalisations made from laboratory studies. However, Hall (1968a, 1968b), in particular, has stressed the importance of taking into account ecological variables when studying non-human primates in the wild. Different species are adapted both physically and behaviourally to different ecological niches. This means that it will not always be possible to make generalisations about 'non-human primates' on the basis of field studies of only a limited number of species and subspecies. For example, there are considerable differences between the social organisation of different species of baboons, the South African baboon (*Papio cynocephalus*) being adapted to relatively enclosed savannah, and the North African baboon (*Papio hamadryas*) being adapted to open desert (Kummer, 1968). There may also be considerable differences in the behaviour patterns of non-human primate groups within the same species. For example, the studies of Southwick *et al.* (1965) and Southwick (1969) have shown differences in behaviour patterns between forest, rural and urban-living rhesus monkeys in Northern India.

The behavioural adaptations of non-human primates to different ecological niches may be both genetically and socially transmitted. The extent to which 'cultural' behaviour patterns specific to particular troups may be learnt by social transmission has been well documented in the research on Japanese Macaques (*Macaca fuscata*) (Imanishi, 1957; Kawamura, 1959; Tsumori, 1967; Frisch, 1968). Furthermore, it has been shown that the social transmission of specific behaviour patterns in these animals may be affected by such variables as the sex and age of the animals transmitting or receiving the behaviour pattern. Goodall (1968) has also documented in detail 'cultural' transmission of specific skills in a group of chimpanzees.

3. Discussion

In view of the biological and environmental or ecological variables discussed above, it would be unwise to attempt any generalisations about the effect on non-human primates of early experience. In considering the results of any one study it is necessary to take into account the species, sex, age, and environment of the animals studied. The relevance of biological factors is well shown by the results of the study of Kaufman and Rosenblum (1969) on the effects of maternal deprivation on two species of macaque. They found that infant pig-tailed monkeys (*Macaca nemestrima*) showed grossly abnormal behaviour when their mothers were removed from the cage, even though the rest of the social group remained intact. On the other hand, these behavioural changes were not observed in bonnet macaques (*Macaca radiata*). (These results are discussed in detail later.) Similarly, there is suggestive evidence that the results of social deprivation may differ as between rhesus monkeys and chimpanzees. Mason (1968, pp. 475) has reviewed the relevant evidence, and comments that 'some of the effects of social deprivation are more persistent and severe in monkeys' than chimpanzees. The relevance of environmental variables is illustrated by the studies of Rowell *et al.* (1964, 1968). These studies have shown that there are differences in the maternal behaviour of rhesus monkeys as between those living only with their infants and those living in group cages with other adult females present (Rowell *et al.*, 1964; Hinde, 1965). Furthermore, there are differences in the maternal behaviour of baboons as between those living under natural conditions and those living in group cages (Rowell *et al.*, 1968). Another example of the relevance of environmental variables is provided by the observations of Itani (1963) who showed that there were considerable differences in the pattern of paternal care in Japanese macaques between different troups.

The above considerations suggest that considerable care should be exercised in generalising about the effects of early experience even within non-human primates, quite apart from generalising from non-human primates to man. Before such generalisations can be made considerably more information is necessary on the effect of the relevant biological and environmental variables. In particular, there is a need to integrate research carried out in the laboratory and research carried out in the field, so that the relevance of laboratory findings to the natural behaviour of the animals may be seen, and so that experiments may be carried out in the laboratory on factors that cannot be controlled and manipulated in the field. There is also a need for experiments in the field where these are feasible (Hall, 1968c; Mason, 1968). There is a particular need for more long-term observational studies of the kind that have been carried out by Goodall (1968) so that more information may be acquired on the effects of early experience on non-human primates in their natural surroundings.

4. Abnormal Behaviour

Non-human primates can be studied with a view to generalising the results both to the normal and abnormal behaviour of man. It is necessary in both areas of research to decide to what extent similarities in behaviour are merely analogous and to what extent they are homologous.

In the study of abnormal behaviour of non-human primates it is important to distinguish between arrested development and deviant behaviour, in particular in relation to studies of the short- or long-term effects of such experiences as maternal deprivation. It is also necessary to attempt to define what is meant by behavioural 'abnormality'. Wherever possible, behaviour patterns should be compared with normative data.* Finally, it is essential to attempt to isolate which behavioural abnormalities seen in non-human primates are, and which are not, relevant to behavioural abnormalities observed in man. As Hebb (1947, pp. 77) has said 'there is a great deal of chimpanzee behaviour which, from one point of view or another is aberrant; but where is a line to be drawn between aberrant behaviour which is relevant to the problem of neurosis and aberrant behaviour which is not?'

It is most useful to discuss the question of whether the abnormal behaviour of non-human primates is analogous or homologous to that of man in relation to each syndrome separately.

(a) FEAR-PHOBIAS

The review of animal fears in Marks (1969) makes it quite clear that many examples can be found of stimuli that elicit innate or learnt fears in animals and, in particular, non-human primates. For example, fears have been reported in animals of heights, novelty, snakes etc. However, to be analogous or homologous to human phobias it has to be shown that these fears are in some sense maladaptive, whereas the examples of fear quoted above are of possible adaptive and survival value. Hebb (1947) has reported a case of 2 'spontaneous' fear of solid food objects in one chimpanzee kept in captivity, this fear alternating with a fear of the human keeper. Hebb also comments that some of the other objects feared by this animal such as carrots could easily be given a Freudian interpretation, indicating how

* There are data on the normal development of some species of monkey (Kaufman and Rosenblum, 1965; Harlow and Harlow, 1965; Hansen, 1966) and of chimpanzees (Mason, 1965a).

easy it is to assume that a human fear is a fear of what is symbolised by the stimulus rather than of the stimulus itself (Wolpe and Rachman, 1960).

(b) ANXIETY-NEUROSIS

The similarities and differences between animal 'experimental neurosis' and human neurosis have already been extensively discussed by Hebb (1947) and Broadhurst (1971) so that no further general review is needed here. However, it should be pointed out that there are studies of experimental neurosis in non-human primates, although the interpretation of these is unclear. Fulton and Jacobsen (1935) reported temper tantrums in one chimpanzee performing on a delayed response task when the animal failed correctly to choose the stimulus associated with reward. On the basis of this observation they state (p. 119) that 'it was as complete an "experimental neurosis" as those obtained by Pavlovian conditioned reflex procedures'. But this conclusion is quite unwarranted by the evidence, since the same animal would perform without behavioural disturbance on other tasks; that is, the frustration response was task specific, and is therefore more akin to a human school or work phobia than to human neurosis. Masserman and Pechtel (1956a, 1956b) have described the setting up of what they call an 'experimental neurosis' in monkeys of differing species. However, all that was in fact demonstrated is that it is possible by associating a rewarded stimulus with negative and punishing stimuli to set up a feeding inhibition, which may be alleviated by drugs or brain lesions. Although they claimed more general behavioural disturbance, the data they provide are not adequate to evaluate the generality of the disturbance. In view of the methodological points made earlier, it is interesting to observe that Masserman and Pechtel (1956a, p. 110) comment that 'it is impossible to state the effects of any drug on any organism without considering the latter's genetic characteristics, past experiences, biologic status, and perceptions, motivations towards and evaluations of its current physical and social mileu'. Weiskrantz (1968, chapter 4) comments that it is not possible to set up an experimental neurosis in monkeys by titrating the difficulty of a discrimination, a method claimed by Pavlov to produce an experimental neurosis in dogs (Broadhurst, 1971). It would seem to be necessary to use punishment, in a situation in which either the animal is in conflict or in which the animal cannot avoid the punishment. Nonetheless, it would be wise to practise the caution shown by Hebb (1947, p. 6) who comments that 'despite a number of things about chimpanzee behaviour which *remind* one of the neurotic, I know of no other instances in which clear identification is possible'. More recent evidence does not essentially alter the correctness of this conclusion.

(c) OBSESSIONS AND COMPULSIONS

Stereotyped behaviour patterns are commonly reported in both rhesus monkeys and chimpanzee after partial or total isolation in infancy (Harlow and Harlow, 1965; Sackett, 1969; Mason et al., 1968). These patterns include rocking, thumb-sucking and hand movements in front of the eyes. However, as Berkson and Karrer (1968) have pointed out, these patterns appear also in infancy in normal monkeys, and what is abnormal is merely their continuation into later infancy. Furthermore, as Mason et al. (1968) argue, these behaviours can in each case be regarded as functional in the sense that they provide the stimulation for the animal which it would otherwise obtain from its mother, peers, and nonsocial environment. The patterns are, therefore, clearly not homologous to human adult obsessional and compulsive psychiatric disorder. They are, if anything, more akin to the rituals seen in autistic children (Wing, 1966) and mentally handicapped children in institutions (Clarke and Clarke, 1965).

(d) AGGRESSION

Clearly, it is possible to study aggressive behaviour in non-human primates. It is necessary, however, to decide at what point the aggression becomes abnormal. There are clear cases in which certain animals are more aggressive than others (Goodall, 1968) and in which individual dominant animals increase the aggression of a monkey troup (Carpenter, 1942, 1958), but it is not easy to judge whether or not these are examples of hyperaggression.

Examples of what seems to be hyperaggression when judged against control or normative data can be found. Sackett (1969) has reviewed the evidence showing that rhesus monkeys that have suffered partial or total isolation from birth are hyper-aggressive. However, Mason et al. (1968) have pointed out that increases in aggression in such animals may be due to the failure to learn to interpret and produce social cues; that is, to a failure in perceptual learning rather than a change in emotionality per se. Sackett (1969) and Mason et al. (1968) also report in rhesus monkeys and chimpanzees an increase in self-directed aggression in partially or totally isolated animals, particularly when they are faced with frustrating or punishing situations. This behaviour is strikingly reminiscent of the self-directed aggressive behaviour reported by McKerracher et al. (1966) for human female mentally subnormal patients.

One environmental factor of importance in determining the incidence of aggression in non-human primates is that of crowding. In a pioneering study Zuckerman (1932) observed a highly increased incidence of aggression in overcrowded baboons (Papio hamadryas). It is not clear, however, to what extent these results were not also due to the abnormal sex ratios, since Kummer (1968) has shown that in this species of baboon the natural social organisation is that of single adult males with an associated group of females and infants, the males not tolerating the presence of any other adult male. Carpenter (1942) also observed hyperaggression in adult females being transported with their infants under crowded conditions, 8 or 10 females actually killing their infants. Furthermore, adult males were observed to kill infants when 350 animals were released on an island of only 36 acres. Southwick et al. (1965) and Southwick (1969) have made important observations on the different incidence of intraspecific aggression in rhesus monkey bands living in rural and urban areas. They have reported, in particular, a highly raised incidence of aggression between groups in Temple-living monkeys. Southwick (1969) carried out an experimental study to isolate the relevant variables accounting for the hyperaggression in crowded groups. He found that limited space rather than food competition was the most important factor, although this contrasts with the observations of Goodall (1968) that in chimpanzees aggression was seen to occur mainly in a situation of food competition. Rosenblum et al. (1968) have reported, however, that squirrel monkeys (Saimiri sciurea), unlike the rhesus monkeys of Southwick (1968) tolerated the introduction of strangers into their cages without undue increase in aggression. It is not clear to what extent this represents a species difference and to what extent the different results are due to differing experimental procedures.

(e) SEXUAL BEHAVIOUR

The evidence on sexual abnormalities in non-human primates is incomplete. Disorders of sexual behaviour such that animals mate or attempt to mate in incorrect postures and with incorrect movements have been reported for both rhesus monkeys (Harlow and Harlow, 1965; Sackett, 1969) and chimpanzees (Mason et al., 1968) reared under conditions of isolation. Mason et al. (1968) also point out that there is a greater disturbance in the behaviour of the male than the female, but that this may be due to the more complex behaviour required of the male.

The evidence suggests that it is necessary for non-human primates to have social experience with peers prepubertally if they are to develop normal sexual behaviour as adults. Goodall (1968) points out that in their natural surroundings chimpanzees have many opportunities when young of watching adult sexual and maternal behaviour. The evidence showing disturbance of sexual behaviour in isolated monkeys and chimpanzees cannot, therefore, be used as evidence that they show sexual 'perversions'; rather it is true only that vicarious and personal experience is necessary for correct adult mating behaviour.

(f) MOOD-DEPRESSION

McKinney and Bunney (1969, pp. 24) have reviewed the evidence for the existence of model depression in non-human primates. They suggest that in humans 'the primary symptoms ... consist of a despairing emotional and depressive mood. The secondary symptoms vary and are less regularly found. They may include such things as social withdrawal, psychomotor retardation, anorexia, weight loss, and sleep disturbance. No experimental model exists at present for such depressive states in animals'. They argue, therefore, that an operational definition of depression be used when studying animals, including such features as response to external environment, changes in play activity, decreased appetite and weight, decreased motor activity, huddling posture and sleep disturbance. Hebb (1947) has reported a case of one chimpanzee which showed spontaneous mood swings, such that when it was 'depressed' it showed little spontaneous activity or reactivity, and when it was 'elated' it showed intolerance or frustration. He further points out that 'criticism of the conclusion that mental depression can be recognised in an ape is not sound, if it bases merely on an observer's failure to recognise anything of the sort in a week or two of observation' (Hebb, 1947, pp. 5). A very convincing description of a depressive syndrome has been described by Kaufman and Rosenblum (1967, 1969) in pig-tailed monkeys. Their observation was that taking the infant monkey's mother out of the social group led to a series of mood and emotional changes in the infant. At first it showed agitated behaviour and crying. It then, for a week or so, sat huddled alone without making social responses to other animals. Finally, it slowly remade social contact with the other animals in the group and increased in play activity. However, as shown by Rosenblum and Kaufman (1965, 1967) there are considerable

differences between the child-rearing practices of pig-tailed monkeys and bonnet macaques, the pig-tailed monkeys being more restrictive and the bonnet macaques more permissive and sociable. Furthermore, if the mothers of bonnet macaques were removed from the social group, the infants did not show the depression observed in pig-tailed monkeys, but rather they interacted with other members of the group and were 'adopted' by other females (Rosenblum and Kaufman, 1968). It is plausible to account for this difference in terms of the differing child-rearing practices of the two species. However, there are several important ways in which the results of these studies differ from those on adult man. Firstly, the study was on infant monkeys and not adults. Secondly, the monkeys did not show anorexia Thirdly, the monkeys recovered in a short space of time. The results are of more relevance to the childhood syndrome reported for hospitalised children (Bowlby, 1952, 1969b) than they are to the adult syndromes of endogenous or exogenous depression.

(g) SCHIZOPHRENIA-AUTISM-SOCIAL WITHDRAWAL

Unfortunately, the symptom of social withdrawal is common to both the main psychotic illnesses in man and it is not, therefore, possible to argue that social withdrawal is more closely related to schizophrenic states in man than to depressed states. It should further be pointed out that the diagnosis of autism and autistic symptoms of social withdrawal in children can be distinguished from schizophrenia (Rutter, 1966). The stereotyped movements and social withdrawal of partially and totally isolated rhesus monkeys and chimpanzees have been described earlier (Mason et al., 1968; Sackett, 1969). It is important to note, however, that the fear shown by these animals is not peculiar to social stimuli but extends to all complex and novel stimuli. As Sackett (1969, pp. 305) puts it, 'isolation-reared monkeys spend hours rocking and crouching in a manner reminiscent of withdrawal responses seen in schizophrenia and childhood autism. This physical similarity could indicate a causal and functional equivalence between abnormal man and abnormal monkey, yet this interpretation based solely on motor-response evidence is certainly unwarranted'.

In conclusion, there would seem to be a danger of generalising from abnormal and deviant behaviour in non-human primates to psychiatric disorders in man, without showing that the behaviour patterns are homologous or even closely analogous.

C. RESULTS

1. Sensory Deprivation—Isolation

The effects of sensory deprivation during infancy on non-human primates have been well reviewed by Riesen (1966). Total visual deprivation from birth leads to both retinal and lateral geniculate degeneration in both carnivores and non-human primates. This makes difficult the interpretation of poor discrimination performance after visual sensory deprivation (Riesen, 1966), and suggests, not that these studies show that perception is learnt but only that sensory input is essential after birth to maintain adequate neural functioning. In an important study, Berkson and Karrer (1968) reported that crab-eating monkeys (*Macaca fascicularis*) who were blinded after birth developed stereotyped self-directed behaviour patterns, and, in particular, showed the unusual behaviour of holding their hands still in front of their eyes for long periods of time. Berkson (1968) and Berkson and Karrer (1968) comment that most of the stereotyped behaviour patterns of sensorily deprived and/or isolated monkeys are also seen during the development of normal monkeys. What is unusual in sensorily deprived animals is the persistence of these patterns. The similarity of the hand movements to those reported for autistic children (Rutter, 1966) should not be overstressed, since these children move their hands in front of their face instead of simply holding them there motionless.

Harlow and Harlow (1965) have reported a series of experiments on the effects of total and partial isolation in infant rhesus monkeys on their behaviour both during infancy and adulthood. Such isolation produces both immediate and long-lasting behavioural changes in the direction of increased fear, in particular of novel stimuli, hyperaggression, and lack of social responses. One critical variable is the length of the isolation experience, the evidence suggesting that isolation for six months to a year produces effects in rhesus monkeys that are much more severe than those of three months' isolation. Sackett (1968) also reviews evidence showing that there is a relatively critical period between three and six months for the behavioural abnormality produced by early isolation. Mason *et al.* (1968) have argued that there is evidence that chimpanzees are less affected by partial cage isolation than are rhesus monkeys, and that they recover from the effects if given later adequate social and non-social stimulation. However, the methods used in the studies of Harlow and Harlow (1965) and Mason *et al.* (1968)

are not strictly comparable. It is particularly important to note that, since the chimpanzee has a longer infancy than the rhesus monkey, comparable behavioural effects may be found only if the chimpanzee is isolated for a length of time that is the same proportion of its infancy as is the proportion studied in rhesus monkeys. Finally, it should be pointed out that although the studies referred to above have been used by some authors to make generalisations to man, they cannot generally be so used, since the only strictly comparable human situation is that of a prisoner in solitary confinement.

2. Motivational Deprivation

There is only one major study on motivational deprivation in non-human primates, that of Benjamin (1961). In this study, bottle-fed and cup-fed monkeys were compared, and it was shown that the bottle-fed animals showed more non-nutritive sucking, whereas the cup-fed animals spent more time in other oral activities such as biting and licking. Furthermore, more non-nutritive sucking was found in those animals bottle-fed on a rocking than on a a non-rocking mother. These results suggest that some components of sucking are learnt to some extent and, also, that deprivation of nutritive sucking leads to an increase in both self-directed and externally directed sucking to make up for the motivational deprivation.

3. Paternal Deprivation

In the human literature (Bowlby, 1952, 1969b), it is the affectional bonds between mother and infant that have been particularly stressed. However, it should be noted that Andry (1960) has produced evidence suggesting that the father's role is particularly important in the development of adequate social behaviour and that separation from the father may be one of the factors that predisposes a child towards delinquency. Mitchell (1969) has reviewed the evidence for the role of the father in the socialisation of young monkeys and apes and in the protection of the social group. It will be seen from this review that there are very marked differences in the role played by the father in different species of non-human primate. In monogamous groups as with callicebus monkeys and gibbons (*Hylobates lar*), the role may be an important one. In some Old World monkeys such as baboons the males may play in protecting the group but have little part to play in the upbringing of the children. However, it may be noted that there is considerable evidence for an important male role in some Japanese macaques. The male's as well as the female's position in the dominance hierarchy may determine the position of the infant later in life. However, there are no experiments on the effects of deprivation of paternal as opposed to maternal care in non-human primates, and the role of the father, therefore, cannot further be discussed in relation to deprivation experience.

4. Maternal Deprivation

Hinde and his colleagues (1966) reported a study in which the mothers of infant rhesus monkeys were withdrawn from the social group for six days. At first, the infants became agitated and cried, but then they became 'depressed', showing much less activity. When the mothers were returned to the group the infants became more dependent on them than before and left them less than control animals. The effects differed in severity in different infants, two animals showing effects still one month later, and one animal up to a year later. Jensen and Tolman (1962) reported the stage of agitation and crying in pig-tailed monkeys whose mothers were withdrawn for less than one hour. The important studies of Kaufman and Rosenblum (1969) have already been described above, the period of separation being 28 days. Not only were the changes specific to pig-tailed monkeys, but there were also individual differences within pig-tailed monkeys. The infant of a dominant female suffered less change since it was already accustomed to interaction with adults other than its mother and was accepted by the adults when the mother was removed. Rosenblum and Kaufman (1968) comment that 'without question, it was the overwhelming increase in interaction with other adults which characterized the reaction of these bonnet infants to separation from their mothers and seemed to provide quite adequate substitution for her during, and to some degree even after, her absence'. Four out of the five bonnet macaques were adopted by other females, and even the unadopted bonnet engaged in social interaction with adults. The adult bonnet males were also solicitous towards the separated infants.

Mason *et al.* (1968) review the evidence on the effects of separation from the mother of chimpanzees. Unfortunately, in most of these studies conditions of isolation of the infants were used, so that it is not clear to what extent the results were due to isolation and to what extent to maternal deprivation. However, Mason (1965b) has reported a study in which the effect of separation from the mother for a minimal time, for one hour or for three hours, was studied. When the mother was returned it was found that the infants who had been separated for the longest time clung longer to the mother than those who had been separated for a lesser time. Goodall (1968) has reported some very important observations in the wild of the behaviour of two infant chimpanzees after the death of their mothers. Both animals became agitated at first and cried, this period being followed by one of depression. Finally, they were adopted by their female siblings, who had earlier during the mother's life had some practice at looking after the infants. The symptoms of depression that were observed were of emaciation, abnormal social behaviour, stereotyped movements, and an increase in aggression. Patterns of play activity slowly returned during the phase of recovery and adoption. Goodall (1968) points out that such factors as the lack of the mother's milk were not controlled for, and further experimental studies would be required to follow up Goodall's important observations from field data. However, as Goodall (1968, pp. 263) comments 'this rather inconclusive evidence suggests that the death of the mother, even during the fourth year of the infant's life, may cause profound psychological disturbance. It also suggests that, in some cases at least, constant opportunity to interact with other chimpanzees (including play with youngsters), and in particular with the sibling foster-mother, may eventually offset (completely or partially) the loss of the mother'.

5. Peer Deprivation

The results reviewed above on the effects of maternal deprivation suggest that the deleterious effects may be completely or partly suppressed if adequate social experience both with peers and adults is provided. Harlow and Harlow (1965) argue that peer deprivation is as bad in its effects on social behaviour as is maternal deprivation. Peer deprived animals are hyperaggressive towards their age mates, whereas infants reared apart from their mothers but with other cagemates show much less disturbance. Harlow and Harlow (1965, p. 322) comment that, 'animals denied the opportunity to form affectional feelings for their age-mates before aggression starts to mature are less capable of modulating and controlling these responses than normally raised monkeys'. Furthermore, they state (ibid p. 322) that 'our data make it quite clear that aggression is a complex response in monkeys, modulated, inhibited and exaggerated by various types of early experience. Furthermore, it is evident that aggression depends on an adequate aggression-provoking stimulus'.

Sackett (1963, p. 311) has also reviewed the relevant evidence and suggests that 'peer contact, rather than mothering, is crucial in developing important social behaviour'. Furthermore, Chamove (1966) has shown that the more peers with whom an infant is permitted to interact, whether in pairs or groups, the less disturbed is its behaviour. Peer contact allows the infant to learn the requisite skills of interaction during play behaviour, and peer deprivation may lead to a complete or partial inability to learn these skills in later life. Finally, it should be noted that socially deprived males fail to show normal sexual mounting behaviour in later life (Missakian, 1969) and the evidence suggests that later social experience does not correct the deficiency. Again, it seems likely that play and observational learning are necessary to develop complex behaviour patterns such as sexual behaviour in rhesus monkeys. The importance of play behaviour in chimpanzees has been particularly stressed by Mason (1965a) and Goodall (1968) both in relation to learning skills of interaction and to learning about the non-social environment.

6. Short and Long Term Effects

It is necessary to distinguish between the short- and the long-term effects of isolation and separation, both in the animal and in human literature. For example, Bowlby (1952, 1969b) has reviewed evidence that hospitalisation in young children produces an immediate grief reaction or depression and may retard the child's development. However, he has not yet shown convincingly that such child-hood experiences produce clinical depression in the adult. Most of the studies referred to in the previous sections have been concerned with the immediate effects in the short term of maternal separation. It is very important to know to what extent these effects are lasting and to what extent they can be alleviated by later therapeutic experiences.

Sackett (1967, 1968, 1969) has shown that the effects of prolonged total and partial isolation during infancy last up to at least four years. There is essentially an order effect such that the more severe and long the deprivation experience the more severe and long lasting the effects. Sackett (1967, p. 11) summarises the evidence as follows: 'After extensive experience in social and non-social situations as juveniles, pre-adults and adults, isolates still showed bizarre personal behaviour, low motor activity, little or no non-social exploration or preference for complex stimulation, abnormal social interaction including hyper-aggressiveness, and sexual and maternal inadequacies'. Harlow and Harlow (1965) and Sackett (1969) have stressed that the early reports of the punishing and

rejecting behaviour of motherless mothers towards their infants now require qualification in view of the later evidence that their behaviour towards their second infants is much more adequate and less punishing. Sackett (1969) also refers to an 'incubation' effect such that the results of certain early experiences may become more obvious later than immediately after them. For example, the children of motherless mothers were not abnormal at first but showed hyperaggression at the age of three to four years. As already noted above, Arling et al. (1969) also reported the waning of certain effects with age from the age of four years to eight years. However, it should be noted that isolation is rarely experienced by humans so that this evidence cannot be used to generalise the persistence of effects to man. More relevant are the results of Kaufman and Rosenblum (1969) who reported that maternal separation in infant pig-tailed monkeys produced 'a prolonged emotional impact'. Here, however, 'prolonged' refers to months rather than years. As has been noted above, Hinde (1969) reported individual differences in the length of the effects of separation, and reported, in one animal, effects lasting up to one year.

It should be noted that in none of the available studies has either immediate or long-term effects been found of early isolation or separation experience on cognitive functions. Harlow and Griffin (1965) failed to find a deficit on discrimination learning tasks and Sackett (1967) reports a study in which no effects were found on discrimination learning set. It would seem unlikely that these negative findings are due to inadequate sampling of cognitive behaviour as these tests are sensitive to the effects of other variables such as brain lesions.

Several methods have been tried of alleviating the deleterious effects of isolation. Harlow and Harlow (1965) have reported studies in which infants were raised on surrogate terry cloth mothers. The infants showed clinging behaviour towards the surrogate mother, especially when in a novel environment. When tested, the infants were not as impaired as total isolates. Mason et al. (1968) also comments that chimpanzees who are isolated derive comfort from clinging to soft things such as diapers or a rag mop. Harlow and Harlow (1965) also report studies in which the infant is given visual but not tactile access to its mother. Under these conditions immediate emotional effects are still found leading to a decrease in play. Sackett (1967; 1969) has shown that the immediate effects of isolation may be alleviated if the infant is given visual access to films and photos of other monkeys and objects. However, on testing later in life, these animals were found to be emotionally disturbed.

Methods have also been tried to countercondition the emotional disturbance. Thus, Sackett (1968) taught isolates to cling to other monkeys so as to avoid electric shocks. However, little generalisation was found of the effects outside the experimental avoidance situation, although it was reported that more generalisation was found with the younger than the older animals. Mason *et al.* (1968) have reviewed studies with both rhesus monkeys and chimpanzees in which they have tried the method of gradual reintroduction to and desensitisation to social and non-social situations. Unlike the negative report in Sackett (1968) they report some success in decreasing the emotional disturbance in this way. In the case of chimpanzees, which had been isolated for twenty months, it was shown that responses could be gradually increased towards a human companion. Mason *et al.* (1968) suggest, furthermore, that the effects of social deprivation are less persistent and severe than they are in monkeys, a factor that would have to be taken into account when attempting to generalise to man. However, as already pointed out above, all the studies on isolation and, therefore, on therapy for isolation, are largely irrelevant to man since conditions of infant isolation are rarely, if ever, found in man.

7. Imprinting

The phenomenon of imprinting or 'Prägung' was first well described and publicised by Lorenz (1933, 1937) in goslings and ducklings. Lorenz (1935) argued that 'imprinting has a number of features which distinguish it fundamentally from a learning process. It has not an equal in the psychology of any other animal, least of all in a mammal'. This latter comment has turned out to be overcautious, since imprinting has been described not only in precocial birds (Sluckin, 1964) but also in precocial mammals such as guinea-pigs (Sluckin, 1968). However, the use of the term has varied from author to author and it is important, therefore, to be clear as to what behaviour it should be taken to denote. Hinde (1961) pointed out that Lorenz put forward four criteria to distinguish imprinting from other forms of learning, that it took place only during a critical period, that it was irreversible, that it constituted supra-individual learning and that it influenced behaviour patterns that had not yet developed. Hinde (1961) has challenged the concept of imprinting as a type of learning separate from other known learning processes on the grounds that either some of the criteria given above are not fulfilled by imprinting in precocial birds (e.g. supra-individual learning) or they are also fulfilled by other types of learning (e.g. a critical period). He also criticises the suggestion that there is a very sharply delimited critical period during which imprinting takes place. He concludes that, 'it seems, then, that on the basis of Lorenz's four criteria, imprinting is not a special type of learning' (Hinde, 1961, pp. 229). The work of Bateson (1966), which is also reviewed in Hinde (1966) make it likely that the phenomenon observed by Lorenz (1935, 1937) can be explained as being due to a combination of two developmental and learning processes, the first being perceptual learning and habituation, and the second an increase in emotional responsiveness to novel and complex stimuli. Bowlby (1969a) has reviewed the literature on imprinting and concludes that the word can be used in a specific way or a general way, the first applying to following behaviour in precocial animals and, in particular, wild-fowl, and the second to mammals, including non-human and human primates. However, it is not clear why the word should be used at all in the general way since the phrase 'attachment behaviour' used both by Bowlby (1969a) and Ainsworth (1969) is a preferable substitute, since it carries none of the overtones of the specific process of 'imprinting'. As Bowlby (1969a) points out, there is considerable evidence both in humans and in non-human primates and other mammals for an important early process of attachment behaviour which may or may not be partly or wholly innate (*see*, for review, Harlow and Harlow, 1965; Bronfenbrenner, 1968). It is important to note that the attempt to show that the attachment 'drive' is learnt is difficult in view of the possibility that maturational and developmental factors which are innately programmed into the organism are almost certainly involved. It will not, therefore, be sufficient to point out that attachment behaviour develops during infancy to argue to the conclusion that it is a learnt 'drive' (Bronfenbrenner, 1968; Ainsworth, 1969). It has already been noted above that there is evidence for a relatively critical period for isolation but the evidence for such a period for maternal separation is not yet conclusive either as to its existence or to the time it covers in the life of either a chimpanzee or a rhesus monkey. Furthermore, it probably differs between the two species. However, Sackett *et al.* (1965) have shown that monkeys reared with humans may become attached to humans rather than to monkeys. It may finally be noted that the most relevant behaviour for attachment and positive affectional-systems in non-human and human primates is that of clinging by the infant rather than following, since the child is dependent for some time on its mother for locomotion. Rather than requiring only a mechanism by which the infant follows the mother it is necessary to programme into the organism the capacity both for the infant to cling to the mother and for the mother to hold, protect, and look after the infant. The complexity of the role played by the mother is well described for chimpanzees in Goodall (1968).

Much use has been made by Morris (1969) of the concept of 'malimprinting'. By this, Morris refers to the attachment of an animal or human to another animal, human or object that is inappropriate. Morris uses the word 'imprinting' in what Bowlby has described as the general way rather than the specific. Morris (1969) tries to explain, in man, several sexual disorders, such as fetishism, masochism, sadism, and homosexuality, as being due to 'malimprinting'. But evidence that these commonly or always develop during or after puberty is not evidence that they occur during a 'critical period'. Nor does evidence that they are due to 'traumatic' learning show that they are learnt by imprinting, since one-trial classical conditioning and instrumental avoidance conditioning are well described in both animals and men (Solomon and Wynne, 1953, 1954; Eysenck and Rachman, 1965). Nor, finally, can evidence that they are resistant to change be used as evidence that they are learnt by a process of imprinting, since behaviour learnt in other ways may also be resistant to extinction (Solomon and Wynne, 1954; Eysenck and Rachman, 1965). It can only be concluded that the usefulness of the term 'malimprinting' remains to be demonstrated.

8. Infant-rearing Methods

In a highly critical review of the hypotheses put forward by some ethologists to account for aggression in man, Montagu (1968, p. 16) comments that, 'it is not man's nature, but his nurture, in such a world, that requires our attention'. It has sometimes been assumed in the case of animals that it is towards their 'nature' that one might look for an explanation of behaviour, and of aggression in particular. It is perhaps significant that those who have written most about innate factors in relation to aggression have worked mainly on lower vertebrates such as fish and birds (Lorenz, 1966; Eibl-Eibelsfeldt, 1961) whereas those who have written most about learnt factors have worked with mammals (Scott, 1958), and non-human primates in particular (Hall, 1968d, 1968e; Washburn and Hamburg, 1968). Learnt factors are more likely to be of importance as one ascends the phylogenetic scale. However, there is, unfortunately, little evidence for non-human primates on the effects on aggression either of early experiences or of differing infant-rearing methods. It could even be argued that it is not possible to talk of methods of child-rearing in non-human primates in so far as this implied

consciously used and applied methods of rearing infants. However, it has already been persuasively argued by Barnett (1968) that the use of the word 'teaching' is not wholly inappropriate for a certain class of mammalian behaviour, and there is no need for the use of the word 'rearing methods' to carry the assumption that they are methods that are consciously and deliberately applied towards a certain end. Goodall (1968) has documented in detail for the chimpanzee the many examples of behaviour patterns learnt by infants from observing their mother, peers, and other adult animals. During the very long period of infancy the mother is essential for the protection, feeding, and transport of the infant. Furthermore, examples are reported by Goodall (1968) of the mother encouraging a certain type of behaviour in the infant and also of the infant imitating the mother, for example the infant's building a 'practice' nest. This latter behaviour is reported also by Schaller (1963) for the gorilla.

There is, unfortunately, little evidence on the effects of differing infant-rearing methods on the behaviour in the short and long term of the infant. No full treatment of the evidence on non-human primates as compared with that on humans can be attempted. However, what little evidence there is can be briefly reviewed. Harlow and Harlow (1965) have studied the behaviour of motherless mothers towards their own first infant and shown that they are very punitive and almost totally rejecting. Sackett (1967) has reviewed evidence showing that the infants of these mothers show few immediate signs of behavioural abnormality but become hyperaggressive when compared with control animals when tested at the age of three to four years. In relation to the use of punishment in general it is interesting to note that Goodall (1968) reports that chimpanzee mothers control the behaviour of their infants more by the withdrawal of desired things than by the administration of physical punishment. Studies have also been carried out by Harlow et al. (1963) on the effects of maternal overprotection of the infant. It was shown that in the short term this leads to an almost complete lack of social responses by the infant towards its peers, but there is no evidence reported so far of longer-term effects. Studies have also been carried out in the laboratory at Wisconsin on the effects of inconsistent mothering. By this is meant, not the effects on the infant of inconsistent behaviour by the mother, but rather the effects of giving the infant experience with several different mothers. Griffin (1967) has reported that there are no ill effects after such treatment. As already mentioned earlier, putting the infant with several different peers was beneficial rather than damaging to the child's behavioural normality (Chamove, 1966). Goodall (1968) has again provided important field observations on the methods of infant-rearing used by the chimpanzee. She found that the mothers were often inconsistent in the sense that, after punishing the infant, they responded to its distress by putting it to the nipple and comforting it. From the limited data available it does not seem that this practice is harmful in chimpanzees. Goodall (1968) has also noted that mothers differ in the competence with which they handle and rear their infants. Harlow *et al.* (1966) have also shown that early experiences affect the competence a female rhesus monkey will show towards its first infant; that is, whether it will be indifferent, abusive or adequate. No data are given, however, for the effect on the infants of incompetence in handling by the mother. In summary, the only finding of note is that hyperaggression may be produced in the infant later in life if it is heavily punished and rejected by its mother. As Seay *et al.* (1964) have shown at least the immediate effects of being reared by motherless mothers who had peer experience are negligible compared with the hyperaggression shown by the infants of motherless mothers who had not had peer experience.

There is also a limited amount of data on the practices of certain macaques and of chimpanzees in relation to other aspects of infant rearing. Rhesus monkeys (Harlow *et al.*, 1963) and pig-tailed monkeys (Kaufman and Rosenblum, 1965) are more punishing and less permissive in general than are either bonnet macaques or chimpanzees (Goodall, 1968). This difference is very marked in the suddenness and severity with which they wean their infants. However, there is no evidence on the effects on the infants in the long term of different methods of weaning. Goodall (1968) reported temper tantrums at the time of weaning by one chimpanzee, suggesting that weaning can be a negative experience even in the permissive chimpanzee. Goodall (1968) has also reported that there is no incest with the mother of a male child in the chimpanzee, although early sexual approaches towards the mother by the infant have been reported. These, however, die out and no further such advances are seen when the infant grows up. Furthermore, incest between siblings, though observed, is unusual and appears only to take place under protest by the female sibling. These observations suggest that the ideas of incest taboo as a cultural phenomenon as put forward by Freud (1919) are unfounded, and that an incest barrier has evolutionary advantages. Finally, an important observation has been made by Kaufman and Rosenblum (1969) that a mild and transient depres-

sion may be seen in pig-tailed monkeys after their mother has given birth to another infant. Such a finding would not be expected in the more permissive and social bonnet macaque, and there is no evidence of long-term effects even in pig-tailed monkeys.

Observations have also been made by Goodall (1968) on the fear response of chimpanzees to snakes and scorpions. The mother and other adults may have at least two effects on the fear shown by the infant in later life. The infant may learn fears by observing its mother and avoiding those dangers from which she protects it (Kawamura, 1959). The fact that the fear shown by adult animals of snakes was adaptive, in the sense that greater fear was shown of live than dead snakes, suggests that the fears of the infant, whether innate or learnt, may wane with age and that the animals may become better adapted to coping with real dangers and behaving in an adaptive way towards those animals and objects that are not of real danger (Hamburg, 1965). It would seem likely that the waning of fears may occur not only because of the experiences of the individual with the feared stimulus, but also because of observing the behaviour of the mother and other adults towards it. These two effects are not mutually incompatible since the one increases the fear of stimuli of real danger and the other decreases the fear of stimuli of no real danger. Hall and DeVore (1965) have also observed that baboons may merely step over snakes rather than show a panic fear, as was suggested by earlier reports (for which *see* Marks, 1969). The waning of fear suggested to occur, parallels the waning of fears seen in human children (Jershild and Holmes, 1936). In relation to aggression there are reports only that the infant Japanese macaques may take on the position in the dominance hierarchy held by their mothers (Imanishi, 1957). This may take place due to association in infancy with dominant males in infants with dominant mothers. It could also reflect and increase in either innate or learnt aggression.

As already noted above, some authors have tended to stress overmuch the innate components of emotional behaviour and the control of emotional behaviour in animals. Particularly in respect of the non-human primates it is important to take into account factors of social learning and socialisation. It is clear that social controls that are partly learnt are exercised in bands of baboons (Washburn and Hamburg, 1968) so as not to disrupt the social harmony. Furthermore, as Aronfreed (1969, p. 238) comments, 'a great deal of evidence points, not surprisingly, to a relatively powerful capacity for observational learning among primates'. It is necessary to distinguish, as Aronfreed (1969) does, between several types of behaviour that might be termed imitative or observational learning. Firstly, there is social facilitation in which the behaviour of one animal encourages the same behaviour in another. Secondly, there is choice matching in which one animal follows another in its locomotor and choice behaviour. Thirdly, there is observational learning in which one animal acquires information by observing the behaviour and the consequences of that behaviour in another animal. Finally, there is imitative learning in which a new skill or other motor pattern is acquired by copying the movements of another animal. Both the third (Hall, 1968e) and the fourth (Goodall, 1968) have been reported in non-human primates, and though they may not be specific to primates they are especially well developed in them. True observational and imitative learning may be regarded as a higher stage of learning than individual learning, that is as vicarious learning, having the advantage that the animal can learn about a situation by observational learning without itself being in the situation, and the advantage that the animal can learn by imitative learning culturally transmitted skills it would not necessarily acquire on its own. The transmission of food preferences and skills has been documented in Japanese monkeys and chimpanzees (Kawamura, 1959; Tsumori, 1967; Frisch, 1968; Goodall, 1968). Goodall (1968, pp. 109–110) states that, 'although the evidence is somewhat slender, it seems possible that much of the tool-using behaviour described on the preceding pages can be regarded as a series of primitive cultural traditions, passed down from one generation to another by processes of learning and imitation'. The Japanese workers also talk of 'subcultural propagation' (Kawamura, 1959).

Given the evidence that social learning takes place in non-human primates (Hall, 1968d, 1968e) it becomes important to consider to what extent controls of social behaviour are or are not learnt among monkeys and apes and to what extent the observations on non-human primates parallel those on the socialisation of human children. Hall (1968e) has talked of baboons as being 'so socially conditionable' and points out that they can learn very quickly to anticipate punishment from adult dominant males and avoid the behaviour that would incur such punishment. Some authors, for example Trasler (1962) and Eysenck (1970), have suggested that the process of socialisation in humans is one of avoidance conditioning. They therefore use evidence such as that of Solomon and Wynne (1953, 1954) on conditioned emotional and avoidance in rats when generalising to man. However, as Argyle (1964, 1965) points out, it is not clear that the human 'conscience' is learnt simply by avoidance conditioning with feared punishment as the UCS. The phenomenon of guilt is the phenomenon of a person's feeling bad about doing something even when he knows that there is no danger of external sanctions or punishment. It is best conceptualised, as by Bandura and Walters (1964) and Aronfreed (1969), as being a process of self-punishment and self-criticism acquired by observational and imitation learning. It is necessary to consider, therefore, if conscience when seen in this way could exist in non-human primates. There is no doubt that they can learn social controls of behaviour, but it is not clear whether these controls can be thought of as constituting a 'conscience'. It could be argued that they can not, since the ability to perform acts of self-criticism and self-punishment involves the use of language. Furthermore, it might very tentatively be suggested that the feeling of 'guilt' is due to cognitive dissonance in humans, there being dissonance between the person's attitude to himself or self-ideal and his actual or intended behaviour. Since non-human primates cannot be thought of as having attitudes, and in particular attitudes to themselves, they cannot either be thought of as suffering from cognitive dissonance and they therefore lack what may be an essential component of the human 'conscience'; none of which is to deny that they learn social controls by fear and avoidance conditioning. In summary, in so far as human self-control *is* learnt by conditioned emotional and avoidance conditioning and by imitation it is also learnt by non-human primates: but in so far as it depends on the ability to suffer cognitive dissonance it could not be learnt by non-human primates.

D. CONCLUSIONS

The process of arguing from the behaviour of present day non-human primates to either early or modern man is one that is fraught with dangers. Jay (1968b) has discussed very well the use to which data on non-human primates can be put when trying to reconstruct the behaviour of early man. In particular, it is difficult to decide whether to lay more stress on data on baboons and rhesus monkeys whose surroundings and social organisation are nearer than that of chimpanzee to early man, or on chimpanzees who are much more closely related, as mentioned at the beginning of this section of the chapter.

Montagu (1968) argues that 'there is, in fact, not

the slightest evidence or ground for assuming that the alleged "Phylogenetically adapted instinctive" behaviour of other animals is in any way relevant to the discussion of the motive-forces of human behaviour'. However, this position is difficult to maintain in view of the similarity of many of the expressions of emotional behaviour by chimpanzees to those of man (Goodall, 1968). Furthermore, even if homologies did not exist for instinctive behaviour it would be difficult to argue that no useful comparisons can be made for learnt behaviour. In particular, the evidence on the effects of early experience on non-human primates reviewed here suggests that hypotheses and evidence may be derived from this source and may be of relevance to man. However, the evidence reviewed here also suggests that, as recommended by Beach (1950, 1960), more caution should be exercised by psychologists in generalising from animals to man than has been exercised in the past.

REFERENCES

AINSWORTH, M. D. S. (1963) The development of infant-mother interaction among the Ganda. In *Determinants of Infant Behaviour II.* (Ed. Foss, B. M.). London: Methuen.

AINSWORTH, M. D. S. (1969) Object relations, dependency, an attachment: A theoretical review of the infant-mother relationship. *Child Dev.*, **40**, 969–1025.

AINSWORTH, M. D. S. and BELL, S. M. (1970) Attachment, exploration, and separation: illustrated by the behavior of one-year-olds in a strange situation. *Child Dev.*, **41**, 49–65.

AINSWORTH, M. D. S. and WITTIG, B. A. (1969) Attachment and exploratory behavior of one-year-olds in a strange situation. In *Determinants of Infant Behaviour IV* (Ed. Foss, B. M.). London: Methuen.

AMBROSE, A. (1968) The comparative approach to early child development: the data of ethology. In *Foundations of Child Psychiatry* (Ed. Miller, E.). London: Pergamon Press.

ANDRY, R. G. (1960) *Delinquency and Parental Pathology.* London: Methuen.

ARGYLE, M. (1964) Introjection: a form of social learning. *Brit. J. Psychol.*, **55**, 391–402.

ARGYLE, M. (1965) Eysenck's theory of conscience: a reply. *Brit. J. Psychol.*, 309–310.

ARGYLE, M. (1969) *Social Interaction.* London: Methuen.

ARLING, G. L., RUPPENTHAL, G. C., and MITCHELL, G. D. (1969) Aggressive behaviour of the eight-year old nulliparous isolate female monkey. *Anim. Behav.*, **17**, 109–113.

ARONFREED, J. (1969) The problem of imitation. In *Advances in Child Development and Behavior*, Vol. 4 (Ed. Lipsitt, L. P. and Reese, H. W.). New York: Academic Press.

BANDURA, A. (1969) *Principles of Behavior Modification.* New York: Holt, Rinehart and Winston.

BANDURA, A. and WALTERS, R. H. (1963) *Social Learning and Personality Development.* New York, Holt, Rinehart and Winston.

BARNETT, S. A. (1968) The 'instinct to teach'. *Nature*, **220**, 747–749.

BATESON, P. P. G. (1966) The characteristics and context of imprinting. *Biol. Rev.*, **41**, 177–220.

BEACH, F. A. (1950) The snark was a boojum. *Amer. Psychol.*, **5**, 115–124.

BEACH, F. A. (1960) Experimental investigations of species-specific behaviour. *Amer. Psychol.*, **15**, 1–18.

BECKER, W. C. (1964) Consequences of different kinds of parental discipline. In *Review of Child Development Research, Vol. 1* (Ed. Hoffman, M. L. and Hoffman, L. W.). New York: Russell Sage Foundation.

BECKER, W. C., MADSEN, C. H. Jnr., ARNOLD, R., and THOMAS, D. R. (1967) The contingent use of teacher attention and praise in reducing classroom behaviour problems. *J. spec. Educ.*, **1**, 287–307.

BENJAMIN, L. S. (1961) The effect of bottle and cup feeding on the non-nutritive sucking of the infant rhesus monkey. *J. comp. physiol. Psychol.*, **54**, 230–237.

BERGER, M. (1971) An introduction to behaviour modification in the classroom. *Proc. Conf. on Behavioural Modification, Dublin, 1969.* Belfast: Behavioural Engineering Assn.

BERKSON, G. (1968) Development of abnormal stereotyped behaviors. *Devel. Psychobiol.*, **1**, 118–132.

BERKSON, G. and KARRER, R. (1968) Travel vision in infant monkeys: maturation rate and abnormal stereotyped behaviors. *Devel. Psychobiol.*, **1**, 170–174.

BIRCH, H. G. (1968a) Health and education of socially disadvantaged children. *Dev. med. child Neurol.*, **10**, 580–599.

BIRCH, H. G. (1968b) Field measurement in nutrition, learning, and behavior. In *Malnutrition, Learning and Behavior.* (Ed. Scrimshaw, N. S. and Gordon, J. E.). Cambridge, Mass.: M.I.T. Press.

BOWLBY, J. (1951) *Maternal Care and Mental Health.* Monogr. No. 2., Geneva, World Health Organization. 2nd ed. 1952.

BOWLBY, J. (1969a) *Attachment and Loss, Vol. 1, Attachment.* London: Hogarth Press.

BOWLBY, J. (1969b) Disruption of affectional bonds and its effects on behavior. *Canada's Mental Health Supplement No. 59.*

BRACKBILL, Y. and FITZGERALD, H. E. (1969) Development of the sensory analyzers during infancy. In *Advances in Child Development and Behavior* (Ed. Lipsitt, L. P. and Reese, H. W.). New York: Academic Press, 173–208.

BRIDGER, W. H. and BIRNS, B. (1968) Experience and temperament in human neonates. In *Early Experience and Behavior* (Ed. Newton, R. and Levine, S.). Springfield, Illinois: Charles C. Thomas.

BROADHURST, P. L. (1971) Animal studies bearing on abnormal behaviour. In *Handbook of Abnormal Psychology*, 2nd Edn. (Ed. Eysenck, H. J.). London: Pitman Medical.

BRONFENBRENNER, U. (1968) Early deprivation in mammals: a cross-species analysis. In *Early Experience and Behavior* (Ed. Newton, R. and Levine, S.). Springfield, Illinois: Charles C. Thomas.

BRONSON, W. C. (1969) Stable patterns of behavior: The significance of enduring orientations for personality development. In *Minnesota Symposia on Child Psychology*, Vol. 2. (Ed. Hill, J. P.). Minneapolis: University of Minnesota Press.

CALDWELL, B. (1964) The effects of infant care. In *Review of Child Development Research, Vol. 1* (Ed. Hoffman, M. L. and Hoffman, L. W.). New York: Russell Sage Foundation.

CANTOR, G. N. (1963) Responses of infants and children to complex and novel stimulation. In *Advances in Child Development and Behavior, Vol. 1* (Ed. Lipsitt, L. P. and Spiker, C. C.). New York: Academic Press.

CARPENTER, C. R. (1942) Societies of monkeys and apes. *Biol. Symposia*, **18**, 172–204.

CARPENTER, C. R. (1958) Territoriality: A Review of concepts and problems. In *Behavior and Evolution* (Ed. Roe A. and Simpson, G. G.). New Haven: Yale University Press.

CASLER, L. (1961) Maternal deprivation: a critical review of the literature. *Monogr. Soc. Res. child Developm.* No. 26.

CASLER, L. (1968) Perceptual deprivation in institutional setting. In *Early Experience and Behavior* (Ed. Newton, R. and Levine, S.). Springfield, Illinois: Charles C. Thomas.

CASPARI, E. W. (1967) Behavioral consequences of genetic differences in man. In *Genetic Diversity and Human Behavior* (Ed. Spuhler, J. N.). Chicago: Aldine.

CHAMOVE, A. S. (1966) The effects of varying quantity of infant peer experience on subsequent social behavior in the rhesus monkey. Unpub. M.A. thesis, University of Wisconsin.

CHAMOVE, A., HARLOW, H. F., and MITCHELL, G. (1967) Sex Differences in the infant directed behaviour of preadolescent rhesus monkeys. *Child Dev.*, **38**, 329–335.

CLARKE, A. D. B. (1968) Problems in assessing the later effects of early experience. In *Foundations of Child Psychiatry* (Ed. Miller, E.). London: Pergamon Press.

CLARK, A. M. and CLARK, A. D. (1965) *Mental Deficiency: the Changing Outlook*, 2nd ed. London: Methuen.

CONGER, J. J. and MILLER, W. C. (1966) *Personality, Social Class and Delinquency*. New York: Wiley.

DENNEHEY, C. M. (1966) Childhood bereavement and psychiatric illness. *Brit. J. Psychiat.*, **112**, 1049–1069.

DEVORE, I. (Ed.) (1965) *Primate Behavior. Field Studies of Monkeys and Apes*. New York: Holt, Rinehart and Winston.

DIAMOND, I. T. and HALL, W. C. (1969) Evolution of neocortex. *Science*, **164**, 251–262.

DOBBING, J. (1968) Effects of experimental undernutrition on development of the nervous system. In *Malnutrition, Learning, and Behavior* (Ed. Scrimshaw, N. S. and Gordon, J. E.). Cambridge, Mass.: M.I.T. Press.

DOBBING, J. and SANDS, J. (1970) The timing of neuroblast multiplication in developing human brain. *Nature*, **226**, 639–640.

DOBZHANSKY, T. (1967) On types, genotypes, and the genetic diversity in populations. In *Genetic Diversity and Human Behavior* (Ed. Spuhler, J. N.). Chicago: Aldine.

DOOLITTLE, R. F. and MROSS, G. A. (1970) Identity of Chimpanzee with human fibrinopeptides. *Nature*, **225**, 643–644.

DREWE, E. A., ETTLINGER, G., MILNER, A. D., and PASSINGHAM, R. E. (1970) A comparative review of neuropsychological research on man and monkey. *Cortex* **6**, 129–163.

DRILLEN, C. M. (1967) The long-term prospects for babies of low birth weight. *Brit. J. hospital Medicine*, **1**, 937–944.

DUBIGNAN, J., CAMPBELL, D., CURTIS, M., and PARTINGTON, M. W. (1969) The relation between laboratory measures of sucking, food intake, and prenatal factors during the newborn period. *Child Dev.*, **40**, 1107–1120, 1969.

EIBL-EIBESFELDT, I. (1961) The fighting behavior of animals. *Sc. Amer.*, December.

EICHENWALD, H. F. (1968) Prenatal and postnatal infectious diseases affecting the central nervous system. In *Malnutrition, Learning, and Behavior* (Ed. Scrimshaw, N. S. and Gordon, J. E.). Cambridge, Mass.: M.I.T. Press.

ELLINGSON, R. J. (1967) The study of brain electrical activity in infants. In *Advances in Child Development and Behavior, Vol. 3* (Ed. Lipsitt, L. P. and Spiker, C. C.). New York: Academic Press.

EYSENCK, H. J. (1960) Classification and the problem of diagnosis. In *Handbook of Abnormal Psychology* (Ed. Eysenck, H. J.). London: Pitman Medical.

EYSENCK, H. J. (1966) Personality and Experimental Psychology. *Bull. of Brit. psychol. Soc.*, **19**, 1–28.

EYSENCK, H. J. (1967) *The Biological Basis of Personality*. Springfield, Illinois: Charles C. Thomas.

EYSENCK, H. J. (1970) *Crime and Personality*. 2nd ed. London: Granada Press.

EYSENCK, H. J. (1969) Part one: nature and history of human typology. In *Personality Structure and Measurement* (Ed. Eysenck, H. J. and Eysenck, S. B. G.) London: Routledge and Kegan Paul.

EYSENCK, H. J. and BROADHURST, P. L. (1960) Experiments with animals. In *Experiments in Personality*, Vol. 1 (Ed. Eysenck, H. J.). London: Routledge and Kegan Paul.

EYSENCK, H. J. and EYSENCK, S. B. G. (1969) *Personality Structure and Measurement*. London: Routledge and Kegan Paul.

EYSENCK, H. J. and RACHMAN, S. J. (1965) *The Causes and Cures of Neurosis*. London: Routledge and Kegan Paul.

FANTZ, R. L. (1967) Visual perception and experience in early infancy: A look at the hidden side of behavior development. In *Early Behavior* (Ed. Stevenson, R. W., Hess, E. H. and Rhinegold, H. L.) New York: Wiley.

FANTZ, R. L. and NEVIS, S. (1967) Pattern preferences and perceptual-cognitive development in early infancy. *Merrill-Palmer Quart.*, **13**, 77–108.

FERSTER, C. B. and PERROTT, M. C. (1968) *Behavior Principles*. New York: Appleton-Century-Crofts.

FLAVELL, J. H. and HILL, J. P. (1969) Developmental psychology. *Ann. Rev. Psychol.*, **20**, 1–56.

FREEDMAN, D. (1965) Hereditary control of early social behaviour. In *Determinants in Infant Behaviour III* (Ed. Foss, B. M.). London: Methuen.

FREUD, S. (1919) *Totem and Toboo.* London: Kegan Paul, French and Trubner.

FRISCH, J. E. (1968) Individual behavior and intertroop variability in Japanese macaques. In *Primates: Studies in Adaptation and Variability* (Ed. Jay, P. C.). New York: Holt, Rinehart and Winston.

FULLER, J. L. and THOMPSON, W. R. (1960) *Behavior Genetics.* New York: Wiley.

FULTON, J. F. and JACOBSEN, C. F. (1935) The functions of the frontal lobes, a comparative study in monkeys, chimpanzees and man. *Advances in Modern Biology,* 4, 113–123.

GANZ, L. (1968) An analysis of generalization behavior in the stimulus-deprived organism. In *Early Experience and Behavior* (Ed. Newton, R. and Levine, S.). Springfield, Illinois: Charles C. Thomas.

GARTLAN, J. S. and BRAIN, C. K. (1968) Ecology and social variability in *Cercopithecus aethiops* and *C. Mitis.* In *Primates: Studies in Adaptation and Variability* (Ed. Jay, P. C.). New York: Holt, Rinehart and Winston.

GOLDBERG, S. and LEWIS, M. (1969) Play behavior in the year-old infant: Early sex differences. *Child Dev.,* 40, 21–31.

GOODALL, J. VAN LAWICK (1968) The behaviour of free-living chimpanzees in the Gombe Stream Reserve. *Anim. Behav. Monographs,* 1, 161–311.

GREER, S., GUNN, J. C., and KOLLER, K. M. (1966) Aetiological factors in attempted suicide. *Brit. med. J.,* 2, 1352–1355.

GREER, S. and GUNN, J. C. (1966) Attempted suicides from intact and broken parental homes. *Brit. J. Psychiat.,* 2, 1355–1357.

GRIFFIN, G. A. (1967) The effects of multiple mothering in the infant-mother and infant-infant affectional systems. *Dissertation Absts.,* 28, 1226–1227.

HALL, K. R. L. (1968a) Social organization of the Old-World monkeys and apes. In *Primates: Studies in Adaptation and Variability* (Ed. Jay, P. C.). New York: Holt, Rinehart and Winston.

HALL, K. R. L. (1968b) Behavior and ecology of the wild patas monkeys. In *Primates: Studies in Adaptation and Variability* (Ed. Jay, P. C.). New York: Holt, Rinehart & Winston.

HALL, K. R. L. (1968c) Experiments and qualification in the study of baboon behaviour in its natural habitat. In *Primates: Studies in Adaptation and Variability* (Ed. Jay, P. C.). New York: Holt, Rinehart and Winston.

HALL, K. R. L. (1968d) Aggression in monkey and ape societies. In *Primates: Studies in Adaptation and Variability* (Ed. Jay, P. C.). New York: Holt, Rinehart and Winston.

HALL, K. R. L. (1968e) Social learning in monkeys. In *Primates: Studies in Adaptation and Variability* (Ed. Jay, P. C.). New York: Holt, Rinehart and Winston.

HALL, K. R. L. and DEVORE, I. (1965) Baboon social behavior. In *Primate Behavior: Field Studies of Monkeys and Apes* (Ed. DeVore, I.). New York: Holt, Rinehart and Winston.

HALL, R. V., LUND, D., and JACKSON, D. (1968) Effects of teacher attention on study behavior. *J. of app. behav. Anal.,* 1, 1–12.

HAMBURG, D. A. (1965) Observation of mother-infant interactions in primate field studies. In *Determinants of Infant Behaviour,* IV (Ed. Foss, B. M.). London: Methuen.

HANSEN, E. W. (1966) The development of maternal and infant behavior in the rhesus monkey. *Behav.,* 27, 107–149.

HARLOW, H. F. and GRIFFIN, G. A. (1965) Induced mental and social deficits in rhesus monkeys. In *The Bisocial Basis of Mental Retardation* (Ed. Osler, S. F. and Cooke, R. E.). Baltimore: Johns Hopkins Press.

HARLOW, H. F. and HARLOW, M. K. (1965) The affectional systems, In *Behavior of Nonhuman Primates.* Vol. 2 (Ed. Schrier, A. M., Harlow, H. F., and Stollnitz, F.). New York: Academic Press.

HARLOW, H. F., HARLOW, M. K., DODSWORTH, R. O., and ARLING, G. L. (1966) Maternal Behavior of rhesus monkeys deprived of mothering and peer associations in infancy. *Proc. Amer. Phil. Soc.,* 110, 58–66.

HARLOW, H. F., HARLOW, M. K., and HANSEN, E. W. (1963) The maternal affectional system of rhesus monkeys. In *Maternal Behavior in Mammals* (Ed. Rheingold, H. L.). New York: Wiley.

HEBB, D. O. (1947) Spontaneous neurosis in chimpanzees and experimental phenomena. *Psychosom. Med.,* 9, 3–19.

HEINICKE, C. M. and WESTHEIMER, I. J. (1965) *Brief Separations.* London: Longmans.

HESS, R. D. and SHIPMAN, V. C. (1967) Cognitive elements in maternal behavior. In *Minnesota Symposia on Child Psychology, Vol. 1* (Ed. Hill, J. P.). Minneapolis: University of Minnesota Press.

HILL, O. W. and PRICE, J. S. (1967) Childhood bereavement and adult depression. *Brit. J. Psychiat.,* 113, 743–751.

HINDE, R. A. (1961) The nature of imprinting. In *Determinants of Infant Behaviour,* II (Ed. Foss, B. M.). London: Methuen.

HINDE, R. A. (1965) Rhesus monkey aunts. In *Determinants of Infant Behaviour,* III (Ed. Foss, D. M.). London: Methuen.

HINDE, R. A. (1966) *Animal Behaviour: a synthesis of ethology and comparative psychology.* New York: McGraw-Hill.

HINDE, R. A. (1969) Analyzing the roles of the partners in a behavioral interaction—mother-infant relations in rhesus macaques. In *Experimental Approaches to the Study of Emotional Behavior* (Ed. Tobach, E.). Ann. New York Acad. Sci., Vol. 159.

HINDE, R. A., SPENCER-BOOTH, Y., and BRUCE, M. (1966) Effects of 6-day maternal deprivation on rhesus monkey infants. *Nature,* 210, 1021-1023.

HINDE, R. A. and TINBERGEN, N. (1958) The comparative study of species-specific behavior. In *Behavior and Evolution* (Ed. Roe, A. and Simpson, G.). New Haven: Yale University Press.

Hodos, W. and Campbell, C. B. G. (1969) Scala Naturae: why there is no theory in comparative psychology. *Psych. Rev.*, **76**, 337–350.

Hutt, S. J., Lenard, H. G., and Prechtl, M. F. R. (1969) Psychophysiological studies in newborn infants. In *Advances in Child Development and Behavior*, *Vol. 4* (Ed. Lipsitt, L. P. and Reese, H. W.). New York: Academic Press, 127–172.

Hutt, S. J. and Hutt, C. (1970) *Direct Observation and Measurement of Behavior*. Springfield, Illinois: Charles C. Thomas.

Imanishi, K. (1957) Social behavior in Japanese monkeys, *Macaca fuscata. Psychologia*, **1**, 47–54.

Itani, J. (1963) Paternal care in the wild Japanese monkey, *Macaca fuscata*. Reprinted in *Primate Social Behaviour* (Ed. Southwick, C. H.). Princeton: Van Nostrand.

Jay, P. C. (1968a) Primates; *Studies in Adaptation and Variability* (Ed. Jay, P. C.). New York: Holt, Rinehart and Winston.

Jay, P. C. (1968b) Primate field studies in human evolution. In *Primates: Studies in Adaptation and Variability* (Ed. Jay, P. C.). New York: Holt, Rinehart and Winston.

Jensen, G. D. and Tolman, C. W. (1962) Mother-infant relationship in the monkey, *Macaca Nemestrina*. The effect of brief separation and mother-infant specificity. *J. comp. physiol. Psychol.*, **55**, 131–136.

Jersild, A. T. and Holmes, F. B. (1936) Methods of overcoming children's fears. J. Psychol., **1**, 95-104.

Joffe, J. M. (1969) *Prenatal Determinants of Behaviour*. London: Pergamon Press.

Kagan, J. (1966) Reflection-impulsivity: the generality and dynamics of conceptual tempo. *J. ab. soc. Psychol.*, **71**, 17–24.

Kagan, J. (1969) On the meaning of behavior: Illustrations from the infant. *Child. Dev.*, **40**, 1121–1134.

Kaufman, I. C. and Rosenblum, L. A. (1965) The waning of the mother-infant bond in two species of macaque. In *Determinants of Infant Behaviour*, IV (Ed. Foss, B. M.). London: Methuen.

Kaufman, I. C. and Rosenblum, L. A. (1967) Depression in infant monkeys separated from their mothers. *Science*, **155**, 1030–1031.

Kaufman, I. C. and Rosenblum, L. A. (1969) Effects of separation from mother on the emotional behavior of infant monkeys. In Experimental approaches to the study of emotional behaviour (Ed. Tobach, E.). *Ann. New York Acad. Sci.*, **159**.

Kawamura, S. (1963) The process of sub-culture propagation among Japanese macaques. 1959. Reprinted in *Primate Social Behavior* (Ed. Southwick, C. H.). New Jersey: Van Nostrand.

King, J. A. (1968) Species specificity and early experience. In *Early Experience* (Ed. Newton, G. and Levine, S.). Springfield, Illinois: Charles C. Thomas, 42–64.

King, R. D. and Raynes, N. V. (1967) Patterns of institutional care for the severely subnormal. *Amer. J. ment. Defic.*, **72**, 700–709.

Korner, A. F. (1969) Neonatal startles, smiles, erections, and reflex sucks as related to state, sex and individuality. *Child Dev.*, **40**, 1039–1053.

Korner, A. F., Chuck, B., and Dontchos, S. (1968) Organismic determinants of spontaneous oral behavior in neonates. *Child Dev.*, **39**, 1145–1157.

Kron, R. E., Ipsen, J., and Goddard, K. E. (1968) Consistent individual differences in the nutritive sucking behavior of the human newborn. *Psychosom. Med.*, **30**, 151–161.

Kummer, H. (1968) Two variations in the social organization of baboons. In *Primates: Studies in Adaptation and Variability* (Ed. Jay, P. C.). New York: Holt, Rinehart and Winston.

Lipsitt, L. P., Learning in the human infant. In *Early Behavior* (Ed. Stevenson, M. W., Hess, E. M., and Rheingold, H. L.). New York: Wiley.

Lipsitt, L. P. (1969) Learning capacities of the human infant. In *Brain and Early Behaviour* (Ed. Robinson, R. J.). London: Academic Press.

Lodge, A., Armington, J. F., Barnet, A. B., Shanks, B. L., and Newcomb, C. N. (1969) Newborn infants' electroretinograms and evoked electroencephalographic responses to orange and white light. *Child Dev.*, **40**, 267–293.

Lorenz, K. (1957) Companionship in bird life; fellow members of the species as releasers of social behavior, 1935. Reprinted in *Instinctive Behavior* (Ed. Schiller, C. H.). New York: Intern. University Press.

Lorenz, K. (1957) The nature of instinct, 1937. Reprinted in *Instinctive Behavior* (Ed. Schiller, C. H.). New York: Intern. University Press.

Marks, I. M. (1969) *Fears and Phobias*. London: Heinemann.

Mason, W. A. (1965a) The social development of monkeys and apes. In *Primate Behavior: Field Studies of Monkeys and Apes* (Ed. DeVore, I.). New York: Holt, Rinehart and Winston.

Mason, W. A. (1965b) Determinants of social behavior in young chimpanzees. In *Behavior of Non-human Primates* (Ed. Schrier, A. M., Harlow, H. F. and Stollnitz, F.). New York: Academic Press.

Mason, W. A. (1967) Motivational aspects of social responsiveness in young chimpanzees. In *Early Behavior* (Ed. Stevenson, H. W., Hess, E. H. and Rhinegold, H. W.). New York: John Wiley.

Mason, W. A. (1968) Naturalistic and Experimental Investigations of the Social Behavior of Monkeys and Apes. In *Primates: Studies in Adaptation and Variability* (Ed. Jay, P. C.). New York: Holt, Rinehart and Winston.

Mason, W. A., Davenport, R. K. Jnr., and Menzel, E. W. Jnr. (1968) Early experience and the social development of monkeys and chimpanzees. In *Early Experience and Behavior* (Ed. Newton, R. and Levine, S.). Springfield, Illinois: Charles C. Thomas.

McClearn, G. E. (1964) Genetics and behavior development. In *Review of Child Development Research, Vol. 1* (Ed. Hoffman, M. L. and Hoffman, L. W.). New York: Russell Sage Foundation.

McClearn, G. E. (1967) Psychological research and behavioral phenotypes. In *Genetic Diversity and Human Behavior* (Ed. Spuhler, J. N.). Chicago: Aldine.

McCord, W., McCord, J., and Zola, I. K. (1959) *Origins of Crime*. New York: Columbia University Press.

McGRADE, B. J. (1968) Newborn activity and emotional response at eight months. *Child. Dev.*, **39**, 1247–1252.

McKERRACHER, D. W., STREET, D. R. K., and SEGAL, L. T. (1966) A comparison of the behaviour problems presented by male and female subnormal offenders. *Brit. J. Psychiat.*, **112**, 891–897.

McKINNEY, W. T. and BUNNEY, W. E. (1969) Animal model of depression. *Archiv. gen. Psychiat.*, **21**, 240–248.

MASSERMAN, J. H. and PECHTEL, C. (1956a) Neurophysiologic and pharmacologic influences on experimental neuroses. *Amer. J. Psychiat.*, **113**, 510–514.

MASSERMAN, J. H. and PECHTEL, C. (1956b) How brain lesions effect normal and neurotic behavior. *Amer. J. Psychiat.*, **112**, 865–871.

MEDEWAR, P. B. (1969) A biological retrospect. In *The Art of the Soluble*. London: Penguin Books, 111–124.

MELGES, F. T. and BOWLBY, J. (1969) Types of hopelessness in psychopathological process. *Arch. Gen. Psychiat.*, **20**, 690–699.

MELZACK, R. (1968) Early experience; a neurophysiological approach to heredity-environment interactions. In *Early Experience and Behavior* (Ed. Newton, G. and Levine, S.). Springfield: Thomas.

MISSAKIAN, E. A. (1969) Reproductive behavior of socially deprived male rhesus monkeys (*Macaca mulatta*). *J. comp. physiol. Psychol.*, **69**, 403–407.

MITCHELL, G. D. (1968) Attachment differences in male and female infant monkeys. *Child Dev.*, **39**, 611–620.

MITCHELL, G. D. (1969) Paternalistic behavior in primates. *Psychol. Bull.*, **71**, 399–417.

MOLTZ, H. (1968) An epigenetic interpretation of the imprinting phenomenon. In *Early Experience and Behavior* (Ed. Newton, G. and Levine, S.). Springfield, Illinois: Charles C. Thomas.

MONTAGU, M. F. A. (1968) *Man and Aggression*. London: Oxford Univ. Press.

MORRIS, D. (1967) *Primate Ethology*. London: Weidenfeld and Nicolson.

MORRIS, D. (1969) *The Human Zoo*. London: Cape.

MOSS, H. A. (1967) Sex, age and state as determinants of mother-infant interaction. *Merrill-Palmer Quart.*, **13**, 19–36.

MUNRO, A. (1966) Parental deprivation in depressive patients. *Brit. J. Psychiat.*, **112**, 443–457.

MUNRO, A. (1969a) The theoretical importance of parental deprivation in the aetiology of psychiatric illness. A critical review. *Appl. soc. Studies*, **1**, 81–92.

MUNRO, A. (1969b) Parent-child separation. *Arch. gen. Psychiat.*, **20**, 598–604.

MUNRO, A. and GRIFFITHS, A. B. (1968) Further data on childhood parent-loss in psychiatric normals. *Acta psychiat. Scand.*, **44**, 385–400.

MUNRO, A. and GRIFFITHS, A. B. (1969) Some psychiatric non-sequelae of childhood bereavement. *Brit. J. Psychiat.*, **115**, 305–311.

NAEYE, R. L., DIENER, M. M., and DELLINGER, W. S. (1969) Urban poverty: Effects on prenatal nutrition. *Science*, **166**, 1026.

NELIGAN, G. A. (1970) Late sequelae of perinatal complications. *Brit. J. hospital Med.*, **3**, 587–594.

NEWTON, G. and LEVINE, S. (Eds.) (1968) *Early Experience and Behavior*. Springfield, Illinois: Charles C. Thomas.

O'CONNOR, N. (1956) The evidence for the permanently disturbing effects of mother-child separation. *Acta Psychol.*, **12**, 174–191.

O'CONNOR, N. (1968) Children in restricted environments. In *Early Experience and Behavior* (Ed. Newton, R. and Levine S.). Springfield, Illinois: Charles C. Thomas.

PAPOUŠEK, H. (1967) Genetics and child development. In *Genetic Diversity and Human Behavior* (Ed. Spuhler, J. N.). Chicago: Aldine.

PRIBRAM, K. H. and KRUGER, L. (1954) Functions of the "olfactory brain". *Ann. New York Acad. Sci.*, **58**, 109–138.

RACHMAN, S. (1968) *Phobias*. Springfield, Illinois: Charles C. Thomas.

RACHMAN, S. J. (1969) Extraversion and neuroticism in childhood. In *Personality Structure and Measurement* (Ed. Eysenck, H. J. and Eysenck, S. B. G.). London: Routledge and Kegan Paul.

REYNOLDS, V. and REYNOLDS, F. (1965) Chimpanzees in the Budongo forest. In *Primate Behavior: Field Studies of Monkeys and Apes* (Ed. DeVore, I.). New York: Holt, Rinehart and Winston.

RHEINGOLD, H. L. (Ed.) (1963) *Maternal Behavior in Mammals*. New York: Wiley.

RHEINGOLD, H. L. (1967) A comparative psychology of development. In *Early Behavior* (Ed. Stevenson, H. W., Hess, E. H. and Rheingold, H. L.). New York: Wiley.

RHEINGOLD, H. L. (1969) The effects of a strange environment on the behaviour of infants. In *Determinants of Infant Behaviour IV* (Ed. Foss, B. M.). London: Methuen.

RHEINGOLD, H. L. and ECKERMAN, C. O. (1969) The infant's free entry into an environment. *J. exptl. child Psychol.*, **8**, 271–283.

RICCIUTI, H. N. (1968) Social and emotional behavior in infancy. Some developmental issues and problems. *Merrill-Palmer Quart.*, **14**, 82–100.

RIESEN, A. H. (1966) Sensory deprivation. In *Progress in Physiological Psychology* (Ed. Stellar, E. and Sprague, J. M.). New York: Academic Press.

ROBINS, L. N. (1966) *Deviant Children Grown Up*. Baltimore: Williams and Wilkins.

ROE, A. and SIMPSON (Ed.) (1958) *Behavior and Evolution*. New Haven: Yale Univ. Press.

ROSENBLUM, L. A. and KAUFMAN, I. C. (1968) Variations in infant development and response to maternal loss in monkeys. *Amer. J. Orthopsychiat.*, **38**, 418–426.

ROSENBLUM, L. A., LEVY, E. J., and KAUFMAN, I. C. (1968) Social behavior of Squirrel monkeys and the reaction to strangers. *Anim. Behav.*, **16**, 288–293.

ROVEE, C. K. and ROVEE, D. T. (1969) Conjugate reinforcement of infant exploratory behavior. *J. exptl. child Psychol.*, **8**, 33–39.

ROWELL, T. E., DIN, N. A., and OMAR, A. (1968) The social development of baboons in their first three months. *J. Zool. Lond.*, **155**, 461–483.

ROWELL, T. E., HINDE, R. A., and SPENCER-BOOTH, Y. (1964) Aunt-infant interaction in captive rhesus monkeys. *Anim. Behav.*, **12**, 219–226.

RUSSELL, J. K. and THOMPSON, A. M. (1970) Fetal complications and the selection of high-risk cases. *Brit. J. hospital Med.*, **3**, 594–555.

RUTTER, M. (1965) Classification and categorization in child psychiatry. *J. child Psychol. Psychiat.*, **6**, 71–83.

RUTTER, M. (1966) Behavioural and cognitive characteristics. In *Early Childhood Autism* (Ed. Wing, J. K.). Oxford: Pergamon.

RUTTER, M. (1967) A children's behaviour questionnaire for completion by teachers: preliminary findings. *J. child. Psychol. Psychiat.*, **8**, 1–11.

RUTTER, M. (1970a) Sex differences in children's responses to family stress. In *International Yearbook of Child Psychiatry, Vol. 1* (Ed. Anthony, E. J. and Koupernik, C.). New York: Wiley.

RUTTER, M. (1970b) Psycho-social disorders in childhood, and their outcome in adult life. *J. roy. coll. Phycns. Lond.*, **4**, 211–218.

RUTTER, M. and GRAHAM, P. (1968) The reliability and validity of the psychiatric assessment of the child: 1. Interview with the child. *Brit. J. Psychiat.*, **114**, 563–579.

RUTTER, M., KORN, S., and BIRCH, H. G. (1963) Genetic and environmental factors in the development of 'primary reaction patterns'. *Brit. J. soc. clin. Psychol.*, **2**, 161–173.

RUTTER, M., LEBOVICI, S., EISENBERG, L., SNEZNEVSKIJ, A. V., SADOUN, R., BROOKE, E., and TSUNG-YI LIN (1969) A tri-axial classification of mental disorders in childhood. *J. child. Psychol. Psychiat.*, **10**, 41–61.

RUTTER, M., TIZARD, J., and WHITMORE, K. (Eds.) (1970) *Education, Health and Behaviour*. London: Longmans.

SACKETT, G. P. (1967) Some effects of social and sensory deprivation during rearing on behavioral development of monkeys. *Revista Interameric. de Psicol.*, **1**, 55–79.

SACKETT, G. P. (1968) The persistence of abnormal behaviour in monkeys following isolation rearing. In *The Role of Learning in Psychotherapy* (Ed. Porter, R.). London: Churchill.

SACKETT, G. P. (1969) Abnormal behavior in laboratory-reared rhesus monkeys. In *Abnormal Behavior in Animals* (Ed. Fox, M. W.). New York: Saunders.

SACKETT, G. P., PORTER, M., and HOLMES, H. (1965) Choice behavior in rhesus monkeys: effect of stimulation during the first month of life. *Science*, **147**, 304–306.

SANDER, L. W. (1969) Regulation and organization in the early infant-caretaker system. In *Brain and Early Behaviour* (Ed. Robinson, R. J.). London: Academic Press.

SARICH, J. M. (1968) The origin of the hominids: an immunological approach. In *Perspectives in Human Evolution* (Ed. Washburn, S. L. and Jay, P. C.). New York: Holt, Rinehart and Winston.

SCARR, S. (1969) Social introversion-extraversion as a heritable response. *Child. Dev.*, **40**, 823–832.

SCHAFFER, H. R. (1966) Activity level as a determinant of infantile reaction to deprivation. *Child Dev.*, **37**, 595–602.

SCHALLER, G. (1963) *The Mountain Gorilla: Ecology and Behavior*. Chicago: Chicago Univ. Press.

SCHRIER, A. M., HARLOW, H. F., and STOLLNITZ, F.

(1965) *Behavior of Nonhuman Primates*. New York: Academic Press.

SCOTT, J. P. (1958) *Aggression*. Chicago: Chicago Univ. Press.

SCOTT, J. P. (1968) The process of primary socialization in the dog. In *Early Experience and Behavior* (Ed. Newton, G. and Levine, S.). Springfield: Thomas.

SCOTT, J. P. and FULLER, J. L. (1964) *Genetics and the Social Behavior of the Dog*. Chicago: Chicago Univ. Press.

SCRIMSHAW, N. S. and GORDON, J. E. (Eds.) (1968) *Malnutrition, Learning, and Behavior*. Cambridge, Mass.: M.I.T. Press.

SEAY, B., ALEXANDER, B. K., and HARLOW, H. F. (1964) Maternal Behaviour of socially deprived rhesus monkeys. *J. abnorm. soc. Psychol.*, **69**, 345–354.

SHIPE, D., VANDENBERG, S., and WILLIAMS, R. D. B. (1968) Neonatal apgar ratings as related to intelligence and behavior in preschool children. *Child Dev.*, **39**, 862–866.

SILVER, H. K., KEMPEE, C. H., and BRUYN, H. C. (1969) *Handbook of Pediatrics*. Los Altos, California: Lange Medical Publications.

SLUCKIN, W. (1964) *Imprinting and Early Learning*. London: Methuen.

SLUCKIN, W. (1968) Imprinting in guinea-pigs. *Nature*, **220**, 1148.

SOLOMON, R. L. and WYNNE, L. (1953) Traumatic avoidance learning. *Psychol. Mon.*, 67.

SOLOMON, R. L. and WYNNE, L. (1954) Traumatic avoidance learning: the principles of anxiety conversion and partial irreversibility. *Psychol. Rev.*, 353–385.

SOUTHWICK, C. H. (1969) Aggressive behavior of rhesus monkeys in natural and captive groups. In *Aggressive Behavior* (Ed. Garattini, S. and Sigg, E. B.). Amsterdam: Excerpta Medica.

SOUTHWICK, C. H., BEG, M. A., and SIDDIQUI, M. R. (1965) Rhesus monkeys in North India. In *Primate Behavior Field Studies in Monkeys and Apes* (Ed. DeVore, I.). New York: Holt, Rinehart and Winston.

SUINN, R. M. and OSKAMP, S. (1969) *The Predictive Validity of Projective Measures*. Springfield, Illinois: Charles C. Thomas.

THOMAS, A., CHESS, S., BIRCH, H. G., HERTZIG, M. E., and KORN, S. (1964) *Behavioral Individuality in Early Childhood*. London: University of London Press.

THOMAS, A., CHESS, S., and BIRCH, H. G. (1968) *Temperament and Behavior Disorders in Children*. London: University of London Press.

THOMPSON, R. F. (1967) *Foundations of Physiological Psychology*. New York: Harper.

THORPE, W. H. (1963) *Learning and Instinct in Animals*, 2nd ed. London: Methuen.

THORPE, W. H. (1969) Retrospect. In *Beyond Reductionism* (Ed. Koestler, A. and Smythies, J. R.). London: Hutchinson.

TIZARD, J. (1968) Questionnaire measures of maladjustment: a post-script to the symposium. *Brit. J. educ. Psychol.*, **38**, 9–13.

TRASLER, G. (1962) *The Explanation of Criminality*. London: Routledge and Kegan Paul.

TSUMORI, A. (1967) Newly acquired behavior and social interactions of Japanese monkeys. In *Social Communication among Primates* (Ed. Altmann, S. A.). Chicago: Chicago Univ. Press.

UCKO, L. E. (1965) A comparative study of asphyxiated and non-asphyxiated boys from birth to five years. *Develop. med. child. Neurol.*, **7**, 643–657.

ULLMANN, L. P. and KRASNER, L. (1969) *A Psychological Approach to Abnormal Behavior.* Englewood Cliffs: Prentice-Hall.

WALDROP, M. F., PEDERSEN, F. A., and BELL, R. Q. (1968) Minor physical anomalies and behavior problems in preschool children. *Child Dev.*, **39**, 391–400.

WARD, W. C. (1968) Reflection-impulsivity in kindergarten children. *Child Dev.*, **39**, 867–874.

WASHBURN, S. L. and HAMBURG, D. A. (1965) The study of primate behavior. In *Primate Behavior: Field Studies of Monkeys and Apes* (Ed. DeVore, I.). New York: Holt, Rinehart and Winston.

WASHBURN, S. L. and HAMBURG, D. A. (1968) Aggressive behavior in Old World monkeys and apes. In *Primates: Studies in Adaptation and Variability* (Ed. Jay, P. C.). New York: Holt, Rinehart and Winston.

WEISKRANTZ, L. (1968) Emotion. In *Analysis of Behavioral Change* (Ed. Weiskrantz, L.). New York: Harper.

WHYTE, L. L. (1965) *Internal Factors in Evolution.* London: Tavistock Publications.

WING, J. K. (Ed.) (1966) *Early Childhood Autism.* Oxford: Pergamon.

WOLFF, P. (1963) Observations on the early development of smiling. In *Determinants of Infant Behaviour II* (Ed. Foss, B. M.). London: Methuen.

WOLFF, P. H. (1967) The role of biological rhythms in early psychological development. *Bull. Menninger Clinic*, **31**, 197–218.

WOLPE, J. and RACHMAN, S. (1960) Psychoanalytic evidence: a critique based on Freud's Case of Little Hans. *J. nerv. ment. Dis.*, **130**, 135–148.

YANDO, R. M. and KAGAN, J. (1968) The effect of teacher tempo on the child. *Child Dev.*, **39**, 27–34.

YARROW, L. J. (1961) Maternal deprivation: Toward an empirical and conceptual re-evaluation. *Psychol. Bull.*, **58**, 459–490.

YARROW, L. J. (1964) Separation from parents during early childhood. In *Review of Child Development Research, Vol. 1* (Ed. Hoffman, M. L.). New York: Russell Sage Foundation.

YARROW, M. R., CAMPBELL, J. D., and BURTON, R. V. (1968) *Child Rearing.* San Francisco: Jossey-Bass.

ZUCKERMAN, S. (1932) *The Social Life of Monkeys and Apes.* London: Kegan Paul.

18

Old Age

R. D. SAVAGE*

The definition or measurement of normality and abnormality in old age presents numerous, complex problems. Any attempt to find answers requires certain assumptions to be made: Havighurst and his colleagues (1953–1963) have tried to define and measure successful ageing on the basis of a study of public opinion concerning the activities of older people. Roth and his associates (1955–1970) have stressed the natural history and classification of mental disorders in old age based on clinical practice and methodology. The identification of gross psychiatric abnormalities and organic diseases in the aged have been immensely improved (Birren, 1959; Roth, 1955; Slater and Roth, 1969). However, most attention has been given to the intellectual aspects of functioning in the aged by such investigators as Birren (1959; 1963), Riegel (1963; 1967; 1968), Savage (1966; 1967; 1968), and their colleagues. Our understanding of the processes and changes in behavioural skilled performance with age have also been vastly increased by the work of Welford (1958; 1964; 1968) and others. Nevertheless, as this review will show, we lack normative data on many psychological or behavioural aspects of old age and developmental studies of the aged are few. *Assumptions, or perhaps limits, had to be made even to begin writing this chapter; old age is therefore regarded chronologically to be at beyond 65 years of age (or perhaps 60), and the review will concentrate on psychometric studies of cognitive and personality characteristics in the elderly.*

Professor P. B. Medawar (1955), in his address to a Ciba Foundation Colloquia on Ageing, stated that 'nothing is clearer evidence of the immaturity of gerontological science than the tentative and probationary character of its systems of definitions and measurements'. We know of one master process, 'ageing', all that can be done is to measure the several manifestations of change with chronological age. The psychologist may concentrate on the 'functional' or 'behavioural' laws and processes associated with old age. The extent to which such behaviour and/or behavioural change are genetically and environmentally determined is also of considerable theoretical and practical importance. However, despite passages in Plato's Republic and from Cicero's *De Senectute*, gerontology in any real scientific sense dates from about 1950.

There have been a number of comprehensive reviews of various aspects of old age including those by Kubo (1938), Lorge (1941; 1944; 1947), Miles (1942), Kaplan (1945; 1956), Anderson (1949), Donahue (1949), Granick (1950), Shock (1950), Grewel (1953), and Watson (1954). *The Handbook of Aging and the Individual*, edited by Birren (1959), and Anderson's (1956) *Psychological Aspects of Aging* may be regarded as the initial attempts to organise the inaccessible and complex literature in this area, and research workers are considerably indebted to the *Annual Reviews of Psychology*, in particular chapters by Shock (1950), Lorge (1956), Birren (1960), and Chown and Heron (1965), and to books by Botwinick, *Cognitive Processes in Maturity and Old Age* (1967); by Post, *Clinical Psychiatry of Late Life* (1965); and by Slater and Roth, *Clinical Psychiatry* (1969). We look forward to a further report by Botwinick on investigations in gerontology which appears in the 1970 edition of the *Annual Review of Psychology*.

Over the past 15 to 20 years, increasing attention has been paid to ageing and old age in terms of psychological or behavioural development. There

* I am grateful to Mrs E. Hall for her assistance with this chapter.

has been a considerable output of research and further concern for the problems of old age, spurred perhaps more by actual or potential economic necessity than ethical or academic virtue. Nevertheless, this work on old age has vital contributions to make to the resolution of many theoretical and practical problems in psychology in general. As the United Nations Organisation for Economic Cooperation and Development stated in 1962, 'The capacity for the medical department to assist in promoting the health and working efficiency of people in all grades would be considerably enlarged were it possible to develop simple and practical measures for the assessment of functional age'.

COGNITIVE FUNCTIONING IN THE AGED

There have been numerous publications on the effects of age on cognitive functioning, Thorndike (1928), Jones and Conrad (1933), Wechsler (1944; 1958), Granick (1950), Shock (1951), Lorge (1941; 1944; 1950; 1956), Birren (1959; 1960), Chown and Heron (1965), Botwinick (1967), and Heron and Chown (1967), to mention but a few. The area, however, is beset with many difficulties and a radical rethinking of the situation has only recently emerged. Nevertheless, investigations of the elderly have an important part to play in our understanding of both normal and abnormal cognitive functioning and its change with age. The theoretical and practical problems here are only just being revealed and the measures available at present to assess cognitive functioning in the elderly are far from satisfactory. Intellectual functioning is vital to adaptability: normative data on intellectual level, its change and its structure in normal and abnormal elderly people are urgently required. Studies of intellectua lability over wide age ranges have suggested that intellectual functioning declines slowly from the third decade of life to the sixth, and more abruptly thereafter. Much of this work is noted in the *Annual Review of Psychology* articles by Shock (1950), Birren (1960), and Chown and Heron (1965).

The pioneer investigations of Thorndike and his associates published in *Adult Learning* (1928) reported that in learning on a large series of tasks by several ages and socio-economic levels, subjects reached a peak between 20 and 25 followed by a slow, uniform decline attributable to age of about $\frac{1}{2}$ per cent per annum to about 50 years of age. Furthermore, the decline from 22 to 42 was similar in proportion for both dull and gifted people. These conclusions were supported by the investigations of Robert Miles with the Otis Mental Ability Test (1932), Jones and Conrad using the Army Alpha Test (1933), the work of Sorenson (1933), Ruch (1934), and Birren (1955). Wechsler's (1944) extensive investigations of intellectual measurement also found a gradual decline in cognitive functioning with age. He summed up this position in 1955b:

'Intellectual ability, as we measure it, follows very closely the curve of growth and decline observed in other human traits of ability. It is a logistic curve which begins to level off in most instances at about age 15. From this age on, test scores show negligible increments with age until a maximum is reached in the age interval 20 to 25. Beyond this age all test scores begin to decline. The decline at first is relatively slow, but after 35 becomes increasingly apparent. The decline is continuous for most abilities and by age 60 amounts on the average to a drop of about 25 per cent in test score.'

This view was widely accepted, and developed to postulate that the more extensive decline in intellectual ability associated with cerebral damage or functional mental illness was similar in nature, differing only in quantity to those changes seen with age. Wechsler (1944; 1958), like Babcock (1930), Brody (1942a,b), Granick (1950), Yates (1956; 1966), Inglis (1958), Payne (1960), Savage (1970a,b) did, however, note differential rates of decline with age for different aspects of intellectual ability.

A number of serious criticisms, however, have been made of cross-sectional studies. In examining intellectual levels, various and different groups were used on the assumption that intellectual ability would be affected only by age. This is obviously not so, and even Thorndike in his original work was aware of the effects of education and the like on intelligence test scores. Longitudinal studies of the same subjects confirmed the suggestion that cross-sectional data comparisons were suspect even within the 20 to 50 age range. Two celebrated studies may be mentioned to illustrate this point. Owen's (1953) genetic psychology monograph indicated that college entrants showed significant gains in overall intellectual ability on the Army Alpha Test after a 31-year period from entrance to Iowa State College. In 1959, Terman and Ogden reported that the Concept Mastery Test given in 1939–40 and re-administered in 1950–52 to the same subjects showed the same picture. To quote:

'There were 768 gifted subjects (422 men and 346 women) and 335 spouses (144 husbands and 191 wives) who took both Form A and Form T. The elapsed time between the two testings was from 11 to 12 years. The average age of the subjects at the earlier testings was 29·5 years and at the later testing it was approximately 41·5 years .... The data shows that the scores of both the gifted and the spouse groups were consistently higher at the second testing when the subjects were approximately 12 years older. The increases in score for each of the subgroups were highly significant statistically .... The data from the retests of the gifted group and of their spouses (also intellectually superior on the average, though less highly selected than the gifted) give strong evidence that intelligence of the type tested by the Concept Mastery Test continues to increase at least through 50 years of age'.

The investigations of Bayley (1955) confirmed that intellectual ability gradually inclines upward between 20 and 50 years of age. These and similar studies have untold implications for the assessment of intellect in the aged. Not least is the fact that by far the most frequent measure used in assessing the aged is the Wechsler Adult Intelligence Scale which uses the age decline concept in calculating intelligence quotients. Recent studies of the aged relevant to this problem are discussed in detail later in this section.

A second major criticism of investigations relating age to cognitive ability is our understanding of the part played by 'speed' or 'performance' factors as against 'power'. Considerable argument has raged over the possible differential decline of various aspects of intellectual functioning with age or psychiatric abnormality (Payne, 1960; Yates, 1954; 1956; 1966; Savage, 1970b). Lorge *et al.* (1956) stressed the influence of changes in speed of functioning with age. He differentiates between 'speed' (or 'performance') and 'power' tests. The former showed decrement with age, while on the latter, 'power tests', subjects up to 60 did not demonstrate any decline in intellectual ability level. Lorge (1956) wrote:

'Whenever learning ability is measured in terms of power-ability, i.e. without stringent time limits, the evidence is clear that the learning ability does not change significantly from age 20 to 60 years. Bright people of 20 do not become dull by 60, nor do dull young people become moronic by 60. An individual at 60 can learn the same kinds of knowledge, skill, and appreciation at 60 that he could at 20 years of age .... The individual from 20 to 50 years probably does not decline in ability to learn or in power intelligence. His performance

may be reduced because of shifts in his motivations, speed, self-concept, or sensory acuities. Age as age probably does little to affect his power to learn or to think. Aging brings different values, goals, self-concepts, and responsibilities. Such changes in values together with the physiological changes may affect performance but not power.'

Even Wechsler (1958) has modified his views on the problems of ageing and intellectual functioning.

He asks and replies:

'Does intelligence, like the abilities by which it is now measured, also reach a peak in early maturity and then decline with increasing years?... The fact of the matter is that no unqualified answer can be given. What is definitely established is: (1) that our intelligence tests can and do measure intelligence in older as well as younger subjects to a substantial, although not necessarily to an equal, degree; (2) that the abilities by which intelligence is measured do in fact decline with age; and (3) that this decline is systematic and after age 30 more or less linear.

'In spite of the above findings, intelligence when appraised by other criteria does not always manifest the same decline with age as do the abilities (test scores) by which it is measured. Two principal reasons would seem to account for this discrepancy. The first is that while intellectual ability is the basic "factor" in intelligence behaviour, it does not constitute all of intelligence; the second, that intellectual ability whether expressed in terms of g or specific factors does not enter equally at all ages. To these must be added yet a third factor, namely, that with increasing age, experience plays an ever increasing role in the individual's capacity to deal effectively with his environment.

'The problem may be summed up as follows. General intelligence, as evaluated by pragmatic criteria, appears to maintain itself unimpaired over a much greater portion of adult life, and to decline at a much slower rate than do the mental abilities by which it is inevitably measured .... What we are proposing then is that general intelligence is a multivariate construct, the differentiae of which may and do alter with successive periods in the individual's life. There will be differences in how we define intelligence at different ages ....'

It is clear from recent research that the popular misconception that after a certain age one is too old to learn, has no basis in fact below 60, and much more needs to be known of the role of motivational and personality factors in the learning process.

Table 18.1. Intellectual Assessment in the Aged: Community and Normal Investigations

	Measure	N	Age	VIQ	PIQ	FSIQ	
Madonick and Solomon (1947)	W–B	50	60–85	117·1	115·1	—	
Fox and Birren (1950)	W–B	50	64·3	—	—	100·8	
Dorken and Greenbloom (1953)	W–B	20	72·2	—	—	104·0	
Berkowitz (1953)	W–B	278	60–64	—	—	100·3	
	W–B	64	65–69	—	—	99·81	
	W–B	33	70–74	—	—	101·73	
	W–B	24	75–79	—	—	104·71	
Busse *et al.* (1956)	W–B	180	71·53	—	—	103·47	
Howell (1955)	WAIS	100	60–89	127·4	105·2	110·7	
Norman and Daley (1959)	WAIS	25	60+	124	109	119	(special population: superior women)
Levinson (1960)	WAIS	33	68·9	87·15	80·30	—*	(special populations:
	WAIS	33	70·55	83·21	85·45	—**	* Jewish men
							** Italian men)
Eisdorfer and Cohen (1961)	WAIS	47	60–64	104·0	92·68	99·08	
	WAIS	67	65–69	100·01	91·26	96·04	
	WAIS	62	70–74	108·2	97·72	104·0	
	WAIS	63	75+	106·77	97·69	102·88	
Dibner and Cummins (1962)	WAIS	23	77·6	110·5	110·5	108·7	
	WAIS	27	82·8	109·2	113·7	109·9	
Obrist *et al.* (1962)	WAIS	245	70·7	—	—	100	
	WAIS	115	77·0	—	—	101	
White and Knox (1965)	WAIS	76	71·22	—	—	105·79	
Comalli (1965)	W–B	20	83·2	—	—	113·1	
Green and Berkowitz (1965)	W–B	61	53·34	100·08	100·25	99·67	
Bolton *et al.* (1966)	WAIS	29	60–74	107·2	98·9	104·1	
	WAIS	13	75+	103·8	101·1	102·2	
Bromley (1966)	WAIS	68	66·5	—	—	121	
Britton and Savage (1966)	WAIS	86	70+	100·1	95·5	98·1	
White and Patten (1968)	WAIS	76	71·22	—	—	105·79	
Savage and Britton (1968)	Short WAIS	86	70+	102·4	98·2	100·7	
Savage (1970b)	Short WAIS	176	70+	103·8	96·1	101·4	

				Score			
Foulds and Raven (1948)	Ravens Progressive Matrices (RPM)	77	50+	10·5			
Bromley (1953)	RPM	35	40–80	21·3			
Roth and Hopkins (1953)	RPM	12	77·5	13			
Orme (1957)	RPM	32	66·81	21·41			
	RPM	19	74·47	20·84			
Birren *et al.* (1963)	RPM	27	71	25·59			
	RPM	20	73	24·0			
Wetherick (1966)	RPM	45	60–69	34·8			
Heron and Chown (1967)	RPM (40-minute version)	90	60–69	36·95			
		90	70+	29·65			
Heron and Chown (1967)	RPM (20-minute version)	90	60–69	28·7			
		90	70+	20·0			

Foulds and Raven (1948)	Mill Hill Vocabulary Scale (MHVS)	77	50+	31			
Orme (1957)	MHVS	32	66·81	44·06			
	MHVS	19	77·47	46·63			

More crucial, however, is the fact that the so-called popular view has dominated supposedly scientifically respectable theories and investigations, particularly in the field of cognitive functioning and mental illness. What in fact does happen to intellectual functioning after 60? Does its level and/or its structure change? How is it affected by organic and functional psychiatric illness? How do the data from cross-sectional and longitudinal investigations of cognitive functioning in the elderly compare? What do such studies tell us about the measurement and nature of intellect? Are age and pathological changes in intellect in the aged similar or divergent?

Intellectual Levels

A number of problems exist in trying to present data on intellectual levels in the aged. Several different measures have been used by the investigators; age cut-off points have varied from one investigation to another, sampling, to say the least, has been haphazard, and various forms and amounts of data presented. Despite these and other limitations surrounding the studies of intellectual functioning in the aged, an attempt will be made to present the data and their implications.

The prime need in order to assess intellectual ability in the aged is to evaluate the adequacy of the normative data available. Tables 18.1 to 18.4 present a summary of the studies from which it was possible to extract Full Scale, Verbal, and Performance Intelligence Quotients on normal and mentally ill subjects beyond the age of 60. It is appreciated that the usual concept of Intelligence Quotient has severe limitations as far as the elderly are concerned. However, a detailed analysis of subtest scores and the various types of data presentation is not possible here for two major reasons. Firstly, space would not permit it, but more to the point is that the inconsistent way in which data on age, sex, subtests, etc. are presented in published work makes a complete coverage almost impossible. It must also be remembered that the assumption of a decline in intelligence with age after the third decade has pervaded work on the measurement of intelligence in the aged, particularly in its application to the clinical area. However, these widely used conventions must at least be adequately appreciated for both their value and limitations.

Problems of estimating the decline of intelligence with age and/or mental abnormality have dominated cognitive studies with the elderly for the past two decades. It is of interest first to look at the cross-sectional studies of normal or community aged samples in an effort to establish reliable normative data. By far the most widely used intellectual assessment procedures in both research investigations and clinical practice with the aged are the Wechsler-Bellevue and Wechsler Adult Intelligence Scales (Wechsler, 1944; 1955a). The Raven's Progressive Matrices (Raven, 1938; 1962) and Mill Hill Vocabulary Scale (Raven, 1943a) appear next in order of precedence. A summary of the data from the major studies of *normal elderly subjects* is presented in Table 18.1. It is somewhat unfortunate that investigators frequently publish incomplete data, some have given only VIQ, PIQ, FSIQ, others just subtest scaled scores, others subtest raw scores, some present combined, others separate male and female results, and few give adequate age group data. The position is even more confusing when comparisons between the various intellectual measures are attempted. Raven's Matrices data, for example, are variously reported in total score, qualitative differences, and IQ forms.

Madonick and Solomon (1947), using the Wechsler-Bellevue Scale on 50 normal subjects, reported mean verbal and performance IQs well above average for 60 to 85 year olds. This data no doubt partially results from the method of calculating IQ with this test, but it is hardly indicative of a severe decline in intelligence with age. Normal aged data described by Fox and Birren (1950) on a further 50 subjects with an average age of 64·3 showed an FSIQ of 100·8, and a larger sample of 342 normal elderly subjects 60 to 69 years of age had a mean FSIQ of 100·6 in the Berkowitz 1953 study. These studies raise the crucial problem of how to calculate and evaluate Intelligence Quotients in elderly subjects. The large sample data, however, appear more indicative of the 'true' position regarding intellect in the aged. Further studies using subjects over 70 by Berkowitz (1953) and Dorken and Greenbloom (1953) totalled eighty-four subjects and presented FSIQ scores ranging between 95·85 and 104·71 with age groupings between 70 and 84. The larger investigations of Busse *et al.* (1954) and Howell (1955) show an FSIQ of about 103·47 and 110·7 respectively. However, the mean VIQ of 127·4 of Howell (1955) can hardly be regarded as representative. A number of other studies in Table 18.1 refer to special populations such as those representing certain nationalities (Levinson, 1960) and intellectual superiority (Norman and Daley, 1959).

The first major attempt to provide standardisation data on an adequate aged sample was by Doppelt and Wallace (1955) on 495 subjects over 65 years old for inclusion in the WAIS (Wechsler, 1955a) This investigation was criticised by Eisdorfer and Cohen (1961) as being doubtful because of the influence of possible regional, cultural, and demographic factors on intellectual functioning. They presented data on 239 subjects over 60 which differed in a number of respects from that of Doppelt and Wallace. However, studies by Riegel and Riegel (1959) in Germany, by Beverfelt et al. (1964) in Norway, and by Britton and Savage (1966) and Savage and Britton (1968) on British community populations confirmed the original standardisation data of Doppelt and Wallace (1955) rather than those of Eisdorfer and Cohen.

The basic data from these and other studies are presented in Table 18.1. Obrist and his colleagues' (1962) data did not show that a decline in FSIQ is associated with old age, but most other studies do. Generally speaking, the VIQs are higher than the PIQs, but there are some exceptions, usually where the samples are small and probably not representative of the aged population at large. We can conclude from this that reasonable normative data is now available for aged subjects on the WAIS. From the most representative samples the mean FSIQ, VIQ, and PIQ for the over 60 are 106·8, 104·66, and 97·8 respectively, and mean PIQ significantly less than that for VIQ. It would be of value to readers to compare the subtest scores from the various national studies. However, overall comparisons are extremely difficult, as Doppelt and Wallace gave joint sex verbal scores, but separate sex scores for performance abilities and others vary in their age, sex, and score breakdown. Consequently, to illustrate the present position on assessment with the WAIS, Table 18.2 presents a summary of the Savage and Britton data on 86 British community subjects over 70 years of age on the full WAIS divided into two age groups, 70 to 74 and 75+, selected at random from the Newcastle upon Tyne Community Sample described by Kay et al. (1964a,b). There were 31 males, 22 aged 70 to 74 and 9 over 75, and 55 females, 27 aged 70 to 74 and 28 over 75. Age differences were seen in significantly lower scores for the over 75s, the older age group, for Comprehension, Similarities, Digit Span, Vocabulary, Digit Symbol, and Picture Completion subtests and the Verbal, Performance, and Full-scale scores, but sex differences occurred in only one subtest, Picture Completion, so the sex data are not presented separately (Savage and Britton, 1968). FSIQ, VIQ, and PIQ were not significantly different between the aged groups. Performance IQs were, however, significantly lower than verbal IQs for both age groups. It is interesting to speculate that in these aged groups of 70 to 90 years the limits of testable drop in performance IQ may almost have been reached, but that verbal IQs are continuing to decline, or at least that verbal intelligence is reducing at a faster rate than performance, even though both are being further

Table 18.2. Intellectual Assessment in the Aged: WAIS, FSIQ, VIQ, PIQ, and subtest scaled scores for two age groups from a community population: means and standard deviations (*from* Savage and Britton, 1968)

| | Age (Years) | | | |
| | 70–74 (N = 49) | | 75+ (N = 37) | |
	M	SD	M	SD
Information	8·12	2·58	7·40	2·51
Comprehension	7·67	3·15	6·46	2·42*
Arithmetic	7·73	2·51	6·94	1·97
Similarities	7·65	2·41	6·46	2·40*
Digit span	8·75	3·34	6·81	3·38†
Vocabulary	9·88	3·19	8·51	3·06*
Digit symbol	2·45	2·27	1·49	1·57*
Picture completion	6·90	1·98	5·38	2·14†
Block design	5·63	2·32	4·81	1·91
Picture arrangement	6·18	3·08	5·24	2·57
Object assembly	5·31	2·20	4·67	2·13
Verbal score	49·28	15·18	42·67	13·63*
Performance score	25·96	9·82	21·59	8·15*
Full scale score	75·24	23·81	64·27	21·03*
Verbal IQ	102·20	14·38	100·23	14·21
Performance IQ	95·85	13·30	96·16	13·27
Full scale IQ	99·58	14·03	98·14	13·98

* Significant at P < 0·05
† Significant at P < 0·01

impaired. Performance intelligence is well established as declining at a greater rate than verbal in the 50 to 70 year age group, but are there differential rates of drop for verbal and performance abilities in the 70+ age groups? Such a situation has vital implications for the use of the V/P discrepancy and the evaluation of intellectual status in the very old, particularly in the clinical setting. Indeed, the work of Bolton et al. (1966), Savage and Britton (1966), and Britton and Savage (1966) has cast considerable doubt on the assumption of PIQ = VIQ of Wechsler (1944; 1955a; 1958).

Britton and Savage (1966) have proposed a short form of the WAIS for elderly subjects which has certain advantages over the full WAIS. It consists of two verbal and two performance subtests, Comprehension and Vocabulary with Block Design and Object Assembly, and was developed by factorial and item analysis on 86 community subtests, then checked on a further sample of 90. Table 18.3 shows that the correlations between the full WAIS and the Britton and Savage short form are positive and highly significant and mean FSIQ, VIQ, and PIQ scores are not significantly different from each other. As this short form of the WAIS has been found to be an extremely useful measure of intelligence for the over-70-year-olds, the normative data are also presented in Table 18.3.

Cross-sectional studies using the Raven's

Table 18.3.   Intellectual Assessment in the Aged:
A Short WAIS for the Aged
(*from* Britton and Savage, 1966; Savage, 1970b)

	Community Aged: Validity Data (*N* = 86)				
	Aged Short WAIS scores		Standard WAIS scores		Correlation of Aged Short and Standard WAIS
	M	*SD*	*M*	*SD*	
Verbal IQ	102·4	15·6	100·1	14·2	0·960
Performance IQ	98·2	12·8	95·5	11·0	0·924
Full scale IQ	100·7	14·3	98·1	13·3	0·968
Verbal-performance IQ discrepancy	4·20	11·61	5·59	8·11	0·944

Community Aged Short WAIS: Normative Data (N = 176)

	M	*SD*
Age	75·0	4·9
Comprehension	7·83	3·69
Vocabulary	9·47	3·39
Block design	5·47	2·47
Object assembly	5·06	2·56
Verbal IQ	103·8	19·8
Performance IQ	96·1	15·4
Full Scale IQ	101·4	18·1
Verbal-performance IQ discrepancy	5·95	12·2

Progressive Matrices and the Mill Hill Vocabulary Scales have generally speaking confirmed the views derived from the Wechsler studies. Intelligence overall declines between 60 and 90 and performance ability is significantly lower than verbal ability throughout. Raven (1948) and Foulds and Raven (1948) found a mean score of 10·5 for over-50-year-olds and Bromley a mean score of 21·3 for 40 to 80-year-olds, while Roth and Hopkins quoted a mean of 13 for 12 people in the 70s. Normative data by Orme (1957) on 60 to 80-year-olds, Wetherick (1966) on 60 to 69-year-olds and in Heron and Chown (1967) on 60 to 69 and 70+ age groups with the Matrices show distinctly higher mean scores than the earlier work.

These Matrices investigations also suggested that old people required to break away from old habits to do the test and that older people give qualitatively different types of response, more personal associations, more simplified and concrete ideas, more global impressions, pattern reversals, and mechanical matching than younger subjects. The elderly were also unable to hold two aspects of the pattern simultaneously. This, incidentally, is consistent with the difficulties in short-term memory and dichotic stimulation in the work on the aged by Inglis and Caird (1963) and Welford (1964; 1968).

The Mill Hill Vocabulary scores on a number of studies are also presented in Table 18.4. Where comparison is possible, it would appear that verbal intelligence exceeds that of performance in the normal aged samples.

Moyra Williams (1961) also presented procedures and data from 239 subjects over 65 years of age for the measurement of mental performance in older people. Two parallel tests are available using material from the W-B, Wechsler Memory Scale, Raven's Matrices, and measures of delayed recall and manual dexterity. Scores are based on the amounts of assistance needed to reach certain criteria and cut-off points diagnose dementia.

The work of Horn and Cattell (1966; 1967) using various measures, and Cattell's theoretical views are of some interest. It would appear that fluid ability may decrease at a different rate from crystallised ability and could well account for many normal and clinical age-related intellectual phenomenon up to 60 years of age. The investigations of Margaret Eysenck (1945a,b; 1946), Pinkerton and Kelly (1952), Savage and Bolton (1968), and Savage and Britton (1968) suggest that the concepts of fluid and crystallised intelligence have considerable application to the measurement and understanding of intellect in the aged.

Table 18.4.   Intellectual Assessment in the Aged: Abnormal Sample Investigations

	Measure	N	Age	Diagnosis	VIQ	PIQ	FSIQ
Organic Samples							
Halstead (1943)	W-B	20	68–83	Dementia	—	—	106 (only 3 subtests)
Cleveland and Dysinger (1944)	W-B	20	75·1	Senile dementia	89·5 ($N = 18$)	52·82 ($N = 17$)	93·3 ($N = 6$)
Lovett Doust *et al.* (1953)	W-B	89	73·89	Senile dementia	—	—	84·45
Dorken and Greenbloom (1953)	W-B	67	77·2	Senile dementia	—	—	77·6
Busse *et al.* (1956)	W-B	80	76·6	Inability to function in community	—	—	85·7
Sanderson and Inglis (1961)	WAIS	15	68·83	Memory-disordered	89	—	—
Green and Berkowitz (1965)	W-B	164	56·51	Brain-damaged	92·63	93·92	94·43
Kendrick *et al.* (1965)	WAIS	20	70·9	Brain-damaged	93·05	79·2	—
Bolton *et al.* (1966)	WAIS	47	60+	Organic	83·6	77·1	79·7
Kendrick and Post (1967)	WAIS	10	70·48	Brain-damaged	96·0	79·5	—
Psychotic Samples							
Cleveland and Dysinger (1944)	W-B	5	75·0	Schizophrenic	94·4 ($N = 5$)	92·0 ($N = 5$)	94·0 ($N = 4$)
Sanderson and Inglis (1961)	WAIS	15	66–84	Miscellaneous Psychotic	95·4	—	—
Obrist *et al.* (1962)	WAIS	37	69·8	Miscellaneous Psychiatric (15 organic)	—	—	81
Green and Berkowitz (1965)	W-B	96	53·34	Psychotic	102·04	101·36	101·41
	W-B	61	53·34	Personality disorder	103·64	104·6	103·61
Kendrick *et al.* (1965)	WAIS	40	68·3	Depression	102·38	94·05	—
Bolton *et al.* (1966)	WAIS	40	60+	Psychotic	86·2	77·6	81·6
Kendrick and Post (1967)	WAIS	30		Normal and depressed	108·4	101·67	—
Neurotic Samples							
Green and Berkowitz (1965)	W-B	184	53·34	Neurotic	104·58	103·91	104·35
Bolton *et al.* (1966)	WAIS	39	60+	Community Neurotic	96·3	92·6	94·2

	Measure	N	Age	Diagnosis	*Score*		
Organic Samples							
Pinkerton and Kelly (1952)	Ravens Progressive Matrices (RPM)	40	65+	Senile and arteriosclerotic psychosis	21·05		
Roth and Hopkins (1953)	RPM	12	78 (median)	Senile psychosis	4·5		
Hopkins and Roth (1953b)	RPM	14	76·0	Arteriosclerotic psychosis	7·8		
	RPM	14	78·1	Senile psychosis	4·8		
Orme (1957)	RPM	25	73·84	Senile psychosis	15·0		
Newcombe and Steinberg (1964)	RPM	9	68·6	Organic cerebral disease	21·4		
Kendrick and Post (1967)	CPM	10	70·48	Brain-damaged	86·3 (converted to IQ)		
Psychotic Samples							
Roth and Hopkins (1953)	RPM	36	67 (median)	Affective psychosis	16·5		
	RPM	37	67 (median)	Affective psychosis	20·0		
Hopkins and Roth (1953)	RPM	20	73·4	Affective psychosis	17·2		
	RPM	12	75·6	Paraphrenia	14·9		
	RPM	7	71·0	Acute confusional state	17·6		

Table 18.4. Intellectual Assessment in the Aged: Abnormal Sample Investigations (contd.)

	Measure	N	Age	Diagnosis	VIQ
Orme (1957)	RPM	25	69·19	Depression	22·92
Riddell (1962a)	RPM	26	69·35	{Psychotic 21 \ Senile 5}	17·1
Newcombe and Steinberg (1964)	RPM	13	69·0	Functional	22·4
Kendrick and Post (1967)	CPM	30	70·48	Depressed + normal	105·17 (converted to IQ score
Organic Samples Pinkerton and Kelly (1952)	Mill Hill Vocabulary Scale (MHVS)	40	65+	Senile and arteriosclerotic psychosis	43·65
Orme (1957)	MHVS	25	73·84	Senile psychosis	41·64
Newcombe and Steinberg (1964)	MHVS	9	68·6	Organic cerebral disease	21·1
Kendrick *et al.* (1965)	MHVS	20	70·9	Brain-damaged	100·6 (converted to IQ)
Psychotic Samples Orme (1967)	MHVS	24	68·17	Depression	53·08
Riddell (1962a)	MHVS	26	69·35	{Psychotic 21 \ Senile 5}	48·7
Newcombe and Steinberg (1964)	MHVS	13	69·0	Functional	25·5
Kendrick (1965)	MHVS	60	60+	{Brain-damaged 20 \ Depression 40}	102·82 (converted to IQ)
Kendrick *et al.* (1965)	MHVS	40	68·3	Depression	101·5 (converted to IQ)
Kendrick (1967)	MHVS	40	68·96	{Brain-damaged 9 \ Psychotic 31}	99·2 (converted to IQ)
Kendrick and Post (1967)	MHVS	40	70·48	{Depression + normal 30 \ Brain-damaged 10}	105·73 (converted to IQ)

Developmental Studies

Our understanding of developmental changes in intellectual functioning with advancing age, and the associated clinical problems, has been complicated by the contrasting results obtained from 'cross-sectional' and 'longitudinal' studies. It is debatable to what extent latitudinal estimates of intellectual ability represent individual change in intellect with age.

Eisdorfer (1963), in a longitudinal re-examination of an earlier cross-sectional study concerning the WAIS performance of the aged, concluded that the pattern of decline has been exaggerated by the cross-sectional technique. Similar conclusions have been reached by Jarvik *et al.* (1962) and Berkowitz and Green (1963). These studies have led to caution in the interpretation of cross-sectional data and to attempts to increase the scope and quantity of longitudinal or developmental studies.

An attempt was made to clarify some of the issues surrounding the interpretation of cross-sectional and longitudinal studies by Schaie and Strother (1968). In general, cross-sectional data were found to overestimate age decrement on non-speeded cognitive tasks, while underestimating the corresponding decrement on speeded tasks. On the other hand, studies employing repeated measurement from

stable samples were thought to be more prone to errors in inference than independent random sampling from the available population on each occasion of testing.

It is quite possible that some of the difficulties surrounding interpretation of these data are due to the different age levels and samples used in the respective studies. The arguments advanced by Schaie and Strother (1968) for independent random sampling on each occasion of testing may not be as appropriate to 'the older' aged groups in which the primary explanation of loss from cohort sample will be the death of subjects. Many studies of the 'aged' have a rather low age limit for their definition of 'aged', often containing few, if any, subjects aged 65 or over. In addition, many apparently contradictory data in the literature may well be accounted for by attempts to generalise findings across excessive age ranges. This view is supported by the findings of Riegel *et al.* (1967b) who examined in detail the implications of 'drop-out' in longitudinal samples aged over 55.

A cross-sectional examination of intellectual functioning in community aged subjects by Savage and Britton (1968) shows a pattern of subtest scores similar to that found by Doppelt and Wallace (1955). In an attempt to clarify some of the issues involved, data were obtained from a longitudinal

Table 18.5. Intellectual Assessment in the Aged: Longitudinal Changes in Intellectual Functioning
(*from* Savage *et al.*, 1972)

	Single Tested Group (at initial assessment) N = 65		Re-tested Group (at initial assessment)		(at 2nd assessment) N = 111	
	M	SD	M	SD	M	SD
Age	77·2	5·6	73·7	4·1††	77·0	4·2
WAIS Comprehension	7·06	3·47	8·28	3·74†	7·76	3·53
Vocabulary	8·60	3·81	9·98	3·00†	7·82	3·4**
Block design	4·96	2·58	5·77	2·35†	6·56	2·81*
Object assembly	4·77	2·55	5·23	2·55	4·42	2·76*
Verbal IQ	96·8	19·8	107·9	18·6††	101·0	21·1*
Performance IQ	90·1	14·0	99·6	15·6††	101·9	16·0
Full scale IQ	96·3	18·8	104·4	17·0††	101·8	17·2
Verbal-performance IQ discrepancy	3·08	9·62	7·63	13·0	0·14	15·33**

** indicates re-tested group difference between initial and 2nd assessment significant at $p < 0.01$
* indicates re-tested group difference between initial and 2nd assessment significant at $p < 0.05$
†† indicates re-tested/single tested group difference significant at $p < 0.01$
† indicates re-tested/single tested group difference significant at $p < 0.05$

	Measure	N re-tested group	N single-tested group	Age range	Age differences at initial assessment	Differences at initial assessment		
						VIQ	PIQ	FSIQ
Riegel *et al.* (1967a)	WAIS	99	53	55–64	−0·6	2·2	0·9	2·8
	WAIS	103	125	65+	−2·3	6·4	5·7	6·3
Savage *et al.* (1972)	WAIS	111	65	70+	−4·5	11·1	9·5	8·1

− indicates that re-tested group are less than single-tested group

re-testing of the original Newcastle upon Tyne community subjects.

Table 18.5 shows the means and standard deviations for the WAIS subtest scores, Verbal, Performance, and Full Scale IQs, together with the Verbal-Performance IQ discrepancy for the Britton and Savage (1967) Short WAIS for the aged. These data are presented for the single-tested (65) and re-tested groups (111). Forty of the single-tested group had died. The initial Verbal, Performance, and Full Scale IQs are all significantly higher at the one per cent level for the re-tested than the single-tested group. The WAIS subtests also shows superior initial scores for the re-tested compared with the single-tested subtests, significant at $p < 0.05$, except in the case of Object Assembly where the difference does not quite reach statistical significance.

When the initial and follow-up data for the re-tested subjects are compared, a complex situation emerges. On three of the subtests, Vocabulary, Object Assembly, and Comprehension, a fall in subtest scaled score is evident, significant at $p < 0.01$ in the case of the Vocabulary subtest, and at $p < 0.05$ for the Object Assembly subtest. The drop in score in the Comprehension subtest does not reach

a satisfactory level of statistical significance. However, on one subtest, Block Design, a rise in subtest score, significant at $p < 0.05$ is obtained. Overall there is a significant drop in Verbal IQ ($p < 0.05$) on re-test, while the Performance and Full Scale IQs do not differ significantly, although the latter is lower. The significant $p < 0.01$ drop in the Verbal-Performance IQ discrepancy is of considerable interest and appears to reflect the complex changes in subtest score in old age. The results are not altogether unexpected as Performance IQ is known to fall earlier than Verbal IQ in the ageing (Chown and Heron, 1965). In these 'older' subjects there may well have been more room for verbal than performance drop.

However, discussion of changes with age should, perhaps, concentrate on the subtest scores, as the IQs are already contaminated by the age correction methods used in the WAIS assessment procedures. When the results outlined in Table 18.6 are compared with the cross-sectional data from the same investigation and with other studies, some interesting points emerge. Savage *et al.* (1972) showed that on three of the four subtests, comparable trends emerged for both the longitudinal and latitudinal

Table 18.6.   Developmental Studies of Normal Aged Samples:
Mean Differences Between Initial and Second Assessment

	Measure	N	Age at second assessment	VIQ	PIQ	FSIQ	Time between initial and second assessment
Eisdorfer (1963)	WAIS	85	64·8	3·19	4·94	4·14	41·1 months
	WAIS	80	74·6	−0·467	−0·09	0·527	38·67 months
Berkowitz and Green (1963)	W–B	184	64·97	−2·31	−1·07	−3·01	8·65 years
Berkowitz and Green (1965)	WAIS	64	61·2*	2·36	3·80	3·05	104 days
Riegel et al. (1967a)	HAWIE	51	60–64	1·4	4·8	2·7	60 months
	HAWIE	48	65–69	1·2	0·1	0·5	60 months
	HAWIE	44	70–74	3·5	0·5	1·9	60 months
	HAWIE	34	75+	−3·5	−3·2	−3·4	60 months
Savage et al. (1972)	WAIS	111	77·0	−6·9	2·3	−2·6	3 years

− indicates that performance at second assessment is lower than at initial assessment.
*at initial assessment

data for the age ranges 65 to 74·9 and 75 +, namely, a decline in subtest scores with advancing age on both Verbal and Performance subtests. However, other earlier studies using the Wechsler scales found that longitudinal results did not support the decline in subtest scores found in cross-sectional data (Eisdorfer, 1963; Jarvik et al., 1962). One possible explanation for these differences may lie in the composition of the samples used. Berkowitz and Green (1963) have drawn attention to the distortions in the rate of score decline that are introduced by lack of balance in the range of IQs included in a sample. The studies of both Eisdorfer (1963) and Jarvik et al. (1962) included large numbers of high IQ subjects. In the Berkowitz and Green (1963) sample, drawn from a Veterans Administration Hospital with high IQ groups poorly represented, there was a much greater decline in score on a longitudinal basis. The Savage data, from a representative community sample, show a pattern of decline somewhere between these previous results.

It can be seen from Table 18.6, which summarises difference scores for the main developmental studies, that re-testing of subjects below the age of approximately 74 results, generally, in an increase in Verbal, Performance, and Full Scale IQs (Eisdorfer, 1963; Berkowitz and Green, 1965; Riegel et al., 1967a). However, at the age of 75 and above, VIQ drops considerably in both the Riegel et al. (1967a) and the Savage et al. (1972) studies. PIQ, on the other hand, shows a decline in the Riegel study of 3·2 points and an increase in the Savage study of 2·3. The FSIQ drops in the older groups for both investigations.

The Verbal-Performance IQ discrepancy difference observed on re-test in the aged (Savage et al., 1972) reinforces earlier warnings on the unsuitability of this and similar indices for diagnostic use with the

aged in the absence of appropriate normative data (Berkowitz and Green, 1963; Bolton et al., 1966). An increase in Verbal-Performance IQ discrepancy has been suggested as an indication of cognitive abnormality. However, considerable care will be needed when interpreting this index if a decline in verbal intellectual functioning in later old age reduces the Verbal-Performance discrepancy. The apparent differential rate of decline of 'normal' verbal and performance impairment in advanced age must lead to many problems if they are not employed with extreme care when used as diagnostic aids.

The two developmental studies of community aged, analysing initial and re-tested intellectual levels (Riegel et al., 1967a; Savage et al., 1972), showed that the initial scores of those unable to be re-tested, due to death, illness, and refusal were generally lower than for those who were re-tested. A further study of developmental changes in intellect in mentally ill aged subjects, which has just been completed by Hall et al. (1972), confirms the above views (Table 18.5).

Assessment of Intellectual Impairment in the Aged

Much has been written on the concept and measurement of intellectual impairment, as can be seen in the reviews by Hunt and Cofer (1944), Yates (1954; 1966), Payne (1960), Guertin et al. (1962; 1966), Savage (1964; 1970a,b), and others. Several authors have proposed methods of assessing intellectual impairment and these can be broadly classified into three types:

1. Those by Babcock and Levy (1941), Hunt (1943), and Shipley (1940) which concentrate on the view that vocabulary remains less affected by age and/or mental illness than other aspects of intelligence.

2. Those derived from Wechsler's formulations that certain W-B and WAIS subscales 'hold', while others 'don't hold' with age or mental illness.

Both (1) and (2) assume that ageing, mental illness, or organic disorders result in intellectual loss of a similar kind or quality, differing only in quantity.

3. Finally, there are the techniques suggested by Walton and Black (1957), Inglis (1957; 1959a), and others,which differentiate between already 'acquired' intelligence and the ability to 'acquire new material'. The latter is thought more susceptible to generalised brain damage than to normal ageing.

Several reports suggested that some kind of V/P discrepancy existed in cases of senile dementia (Brody, 1942b; Halstead, 1943; Botwinick and Birren, 1951a; Dorken and Greenbloom, 1953; Cleveland and Dysinger, 1954). The recent work of Bolton and co-workers (1966), Britton and Savage (1968), and Savage (1970b) demonstrated that the Wechsler (1944; 1958) assumption of a zero V/P discrepancy in normal aged subjects cannot be accepted. They present useful normative data on V/P for normal, neurotic, psychotic, and organic groups of aged subjects. Only 66⅔ per cent of organics were correctly identified using this index and there was some misclassification into organic of some of the other groups. Considerable caution is needed in using V/P as a diagnostic index of organic brain damage, but it is recommended as an index of intellectual impairment when used with the appropriate normative data.

The Wechsler Deterioration Indices have also been used to measure intellectual impairment in the aged. Their success as diagnostic indicators of brain damage seems about as high as for younger subjects. Botwinick and Birren (1951a) examined the validity of the W-B Deterioration Quotient, Babcock's Efficiency Index, and the Senescent Decline Formula devised by Copple. Senile psychotic and cerebral arteriosclerotic patients were significantly lower than normal on EI and SDF, but not on the DQ. They suggested that future measures of intellectual deficit might exploit learning tests. Dorken and Greenbloom (1953) found similar results with Copple's SDF and Wechsler's DQ. The data provided by Bolton et al. (1966) on various Wechsler deterioration indices cast doubt on Wechsler's assumptions about the WB and WAIS DQ, Allen's and Reynell's Indices, and the Hewson Ratios as indices of organic disorder. Considerable overlap with functional disorder groups, especially affective depressed groups was seen (Bolton, 1967; Savage, 1970b). They do, however, present overall normative data on these deterioration indices by age and disorder groups for subjects over 60 years of age. Used correctly, the WAIS DQ and the V/P may be useful measures of intellectual impairment in the aged (Bolton et al., 1966; Savage and Britton, 1967; Savage, 1970b, Table 18.7). A detailed analysis of the structure of intellectual functioning in normal and abnormal aged is required before any definite conclusions regarding the usefulness of Wechsler type Deterioration Indices can be made. It would appear, however, from the work of Cattell (1943), Eysenck (1946), Cattell (1963), Horn and Cattell (1966; 1967), Savage and Britton (1968), and Savage and Bolton (1968) that the Wechsler DQ may measure decline in Cattell type crystallised ability. Savage (1970b) has put forward a theory of the structure of intellect in the aged consistent with this view. This and the evidence on learning and memory measures will be discussed later.

For the moment, learning measures as indices of intellectual impairment in the aged will be briefly evaluated. Babcock (1930) suggested that a significant discrepancy between past and present learning ability was an important factor in the diagnosis of dementia. Much work in the 1940s and the 1950s tried to evaluate this theory (Payne, 1960). Subjects had to learn and retain the meanings of previously unknown material. However, it was found that these measures failed to discriminate significantly between organic and non-organic patients.

Walton and Black (1957) increased the difficulty of the learning tests in the hope that this modification would lead to increased sensitivity to brain damage.

Table 18.7.   Intellectual Assessment in the Aged:
Normal and Mental Illness Data—WAIS, FSIQ, VIQ, PIQ,
V/P and DQ for the Aged (*from* Savage, 1970b)

| | Normals N = 29 | | Affectives N = 42 | | Schizophrenics N = 31 | | Organics N = 42 | |
	M	SD	M	SD	M	SD	M	SD
FSIQ	101·0	15·6	86·0	16·2	86·4	16·5	81·7	14·6
VIQ	103·9	15·4	90·3	15·8	90·8	17·7	86·7	14·6
PIQ	96·8	15·5	82·6	15·3	82·1	14·7	77·7	13·1
WAIS V/P	8·0	9·7	7·5	7·6	8·6	10·7	9·6	9·7
WAIS DQ	0·5	11·2	−2·5	29·9	2·3	28·3	17·3	25·8

They found that with aged subjects (Walton and Black, 1958) with the Modified Word Learning Test (MWLT), it was possible to identify correctly 85 per cent of the organics and 100 per cent of the functionals. IQ, vocabulary level, and age were found to exert some influence on the scores, but this influence was not sufficient to produce 'organic' scores independently of the presence of brain damage. The diagnostic efficiency of a modified form of the MWLT on the aged, the Synonym Learning Test, has been found to be improved by using a Bayesian statistical approach (Kendrick, 1965) to clinical classification. Kendrick (1967) and Bolton et al. (1967) suggested a possible explanation for the varying amounts of misclassification reported in earlier studies using the MWLT. They found a significant correlation between the scores obtained on the MWLT and WAIS full scale IQs. This suggested that misclassification resulted, in part, from the less intelligent non-organic subjects who obtained organic scores.

The Paired Associate Learning (PALT) or the Auditory Recall Test (ART) of Inglis (1957; 1959a) set out to measure the acquisition phase in memory. He successfully discriminated elderly psychiatric patients with memory disorder from others, and Caird et al. (1962) confirmed these results. Kendrick (1963) and Bolton et al. (1967) showed that the ART and the MWLT or Synonym Learning Test were significantly correlated, unlike Riddell (1966), who had suggested that they were measuring different things. His claim that the ART measures memory loss, while the MWLT is more significantly related to 'organic' involvement has not been substantiated. The specific relationships between these tests and brain damage are not easy to analyse; they are more often assumed than proven.

From recent investigations by Bolton and co-workers (1967) and Savage (1970b), it can be seen that on verbal learning and memory tests the aged organics did significantly worse than all other groups of elderly psychiatric patients. The only exception is the notably high scoring of the affective group which, in the case of the ART, was not significantly lower than that of the organics. Generally speaking, the performance of the aged affectives and the schizophrenics, though different from that of the normals, could not be distinguished from each other. The affective group results are consistent with the findings of Post (1962a; 1967) that aged depressives also have learning difficulties.

These tests may be extremely useful in diagnosing organically based intellectual impairment, as 'organic' performance is considerably worse than that of other aged groups. It should be remembered, however, that these aged organic patients were usually suffering from generalised cerebral disorders rather than specific lesions. At the same time, the normative data presented on the MWLT and ART on aged subjects by Inglis (1959a), Caird et al. (1962), Riddell (1962a,b), Kendrick (1965), Kendrick and Post (1967), Bolton et al. (1967), and Savage (1970b) should be extremely useful in assessing learning impairment in normal and the psychiatrically ill aged (Tables 18.7, p. 656, and 18.8, p. 664).

The Structure of Intellect in the Aged

Much of the confusion in the results of intellectual measurement on normal and abnormal aged individuals and groups will remain until a more satisfactory theory of the structure of intellect of the aged is available. A number of factorial and experimental studies have suggested pointers in the right direction.

Several investigators in the fields of ageing and senility have accounted for their findings by contrasting tests that measure the stored experiences of subjects with tests that measure learning or problem-solving ability. The former are said to be more resistant to the effects of ageing and brain damage than the latter. Thus, Wechsler (1944; 1958) distinguishes between 'hold' and 'don't hold' subtests of the Wechsler-Bellevue and Adult Intelligence Scales (W-B and WAIS) on this basis, claiming that a comparison of the two sets of scores yields a measure of intellectual deterioration. Eysenck (1946) and Inglis (1958), speculating upon their results with senile patients, invoked Cattell's theory of fluid and crystallised ability, in which fluid ability (GF) is said to show itself best in novel or culture-free material, while crystallised ability (GC) has its highest loadings in acquired, familiar, cultural activities (Cattell, 1963). Cattell (1957) has argued that his distinction parallels Wechsler's, suggesting that the 'hold' subtests reflect GC and the 'don't hold' subtests GF. In the same vein, Reed and Reitan (1963) have differentiated between tests that demand 'immediate adaptive ability' and tests that tap 'stored information'.

Factorial analyses of the Wechsler scales have produced equivocal conclusions with regard to possible changes in their factorial complexity with advancing age. Cohen (1957), Green and Berkowitz (1964) with the W-B, and Berger et al. (1964) with the WAIS have suggested that the factorial complexity of the scales is reduced in old age. On the other hand, Radcliffe (1966), although his sample was restricted to subjects under age 55, concluded that the factorial structure of the WAIS became more complex with advancing age. Riegel and Riegel (1962) considered that the factor structure of the WAIS and its German equivalent (HAWIE) remained constant across the age range examined, and Maxwell (1961) also found little change in factorial structure in the aged.

Theoretical preconceptions concerning the methodology of the analysis may well have had some bearing on the solutions that have been obtained. The studies quoted have involved a variety of factor-analytic methods. In the initial extraction of factors, both Centroid (Cohen, 1957; Berger *et al.*, 1964) and Principal Component (Maxwell, 1961) techniques have been employed. Rotation techniques, ranging from graphical rotation (Maxwell, 1961) to the mathematically more complex oblique analytic rotation techniques (Berger *et al.*, 1964), showed an even greater variety of results between studies. Much controversy has also surrounded the criteria for the significance of factors (Radcliffe, 1966).

With the diversity of approach, it is, perhaps, not surprising that rather different conclusions have been drawn from the data. However, the interpretations of the structures obtained have produced a number of consistent trends. It is thought that there is a tendency for the 'memory' factor to lose some, if not all, of its independence in the aged and to load the first two factors, which usually have a 'verbal' and 'performance' bias. Details of these changes in the factorial structure of the WAIS with aged can be found in Cohen (1957) and Berger *et al.* (1964).

Various explanations have been advanced to explain this phenomenon. Radcliffe (1966) considered that 'an increasing emphasis on the role of experience in the measurement of adult intelligence' was a possible explanation. The concepts of 'fluid' and 'crystalline' intelligence proposed by Cattell and his associates (Horn and Cattell, 1966; 1967) are of interest in this context. In the aged, 'crystalline', experiential factors may be expected to prove more stable, while the 'fluid', biologically influenced processes become susceptible to age changes. Such a change may be shown in factor analyses as a shift in the 'fluid' variance, as manifested in the separate 'memory' factor in younger groups distributing into the 'verbal' and 'space-performance' factors later. In the factor analysis of the WAIS, such a shift should be readily apparent in an increase in the factor loadings on the first two factors of those subtests having a 'fluid' bias, and of a decrease in the proportion of overall variance accounted for by the 'memory' factor.

Two studies by Savage and Britton (1968) and Savage and Bolton (1968) have cast some light on the problem of the structure of intellect in the aged. The WAIS was administered to an aged community sample. Factor analysis of the data from a normal community sample of aged was carried out using Principal Component procedures followed by 'Varimax' rotation. The Principal Component solution yielded three interpretable factors; a first general factor, a second Verbal-Performance factor, and a third factor appeared to be Picture Completion specific. Varimax rotation also produced three significant factors, the first having a 'verbal' bias and the second a 'performance' bias. However, in each case there was a tendency for those subtests that had an emphasis on immediate memory to have the highest loadings on the factors. The third factor was again specific to the Picture Completion subtest. These results provided confirmation for previous studies which have commented on the increasing involvement of spread of immediate memory in the structure of intellect in the aged (Savage and Britton, 1968).

A principal component analysis by Savage and Bolton (1968) of normal and abnormal aged group data from the WAIS, MWLT, ART, and MPI revealed a general intelligence factor, with all the WAIS subtests, except Digit Span, loading very highly; an intellectual deterioration factor, identified by loadings on WAIS DQ, Wechsler-Bellevue DQ, Reynell's Index, and Allen's Index; a verbal-performance factor; a learning factor, identified by the MWLT and ART; a neuroticism factor; and an extraversion factor. These findings were interpreted as indicating that, contrary to expectation, learning impairment in the elderly is distinct from intellectual deterioration, as defined by the patterning of WAIS subtest scores, so that the two types of deficit may have different diagnostic implications.

Savage (1970b) advanced theoretical and practical views on the structure and measurement of intellect in the aged. Analysis of the structure or organisation of intellect in normal and psychiatrically ill aged subjects suggested that several major factors were involved in the intellectual functioning of the aged and that this analysis may have implications for clinical diagnosis in the elderly. A four-factor theory is proposed to clarify the organisation of intellectual functioning and, possibly, improve its measurement in the aged. Two factors are represented by those measures that assess *intellectual level:* a factor of general intellectual level, and a factor representing verbal versus performance intellectual level. The WAIS appears to be an acceptable measure of these intellectual levels in terms of full scale, verbal, and performance IQs. A further two factors appear to represent *two types of intellectual impairment.* The first is general impairment of acquired level of intelligence and is best measured by the WAIS-based deterioration indices, in particular the WAIS DQ. The second, unrelated factor, concerns learning impairment and is best measured by the MWLT and, to a lesser degree, by the ART.

These results do not agree with the theoretical position of Wechsler (1958) and others, but tend to support Cattell's (1963) distinction between 'fluid' and 'crystallised' intellectual ability. They are also consistent with the previous findings in this area by Margaret Eysenck (1945a,b), Inglis (1957; 1958), and the others referred to earlier.

This four factor theory also has implications for clinical diagnosis in the aged. In the first place, any battery of intellectual measures used in diagnosis with the aged must cover these four basic areas:

1. General intellectual level
2. Verbal and performance intellectual levels
3. General intellectual deterioration
4. Learning impairment—verbal and perceptual-motor

In practice, this can be done by using (a) The Wechsler Adult Intelligence Scale (Wechsler, 1955) or the Newcastle Short Form of the WAIS (Britton and Savage, 1966), and (b) The Modified Word Learning Test (Walton and Black, 1957; 1959) in conjunction with the normative data presented here and by Bolton et al. (1966), Britton and Savage (1966), and Bolton et al. (1967). General ageing intellectual changes are probably associated chiefly with factors 1, 2, 3; clinical dementia additionally with factor 4. Many problems, however, remain unresolved in this area.

Intellect and Mental Illness

Many psychologists have concerned themselves with cognitive assessment of the mentally ill, and comprehensive reviews of this work have been published by Yates (1954; 1966), Meyer (1960), Payne (1960), Willett (1960), Piercy (1964), Zangwill (1964), and Savage (1964; 1970a). There is no doubt that intellectual functioning is severely affected by psychiatric illness of both functional and organic origin. However, there is relatively little of this research on aged populations, as the reviews by Granick (1950) and Inglis (1958) demonstrated. A brief synopsis of the major investigations over the past 30 years is presented in Table 18.4. The main problems of this area can perhaps be best illustrated by asking a series of questions—

1. *Can intellectual measures be used with confidence to diagnose intellectual level and/or impairment in psychiatric disorders in the aged?*

To which the answer is generally 'Yes', though many specific problems of the nature or structure of intellectual functioning and its change in the aged still remain unsolved.

2. *Can intellectual measures be used with confidence to diagnose psychiatric disorders in the elderly?*

To which the answer is almost certainly 'No'. The classification of abnormal disorders used in psychiatric practice is based on completely different assumptions from those employed to develop intellectual measures. Because *a* is slightly correlated with *b*, it does not mean that *a* is *b*: psychiatric and cognitive taxonomic systems are not interchangeable, even though the evidence suggests that psychiatric illness is in many cases accompanied by intellectual disability of one form or another.

3. *Can psychometric methodology be employed with any confidence to improve psychiatric clinical methods of diagnosing and classifying disorders?*

To which the answer is generally 'Yes'. The work of Kiloh and Garside (1963), Roth and co-workers (1969), and others on depressive and neurotic disorders illustrate this point.

Much work in this area has concentrated on the problems of differential diagnosis of functional and organic disorders in individuals or groups of aged following the lines of clinical investigations with younger groups. Attempts to diagnose the organic disorders in the aged—arteriosclerotic and senile dementia—have been particularly dominant. However, investigators, like those working with younger age groups, have found that intellectual functioning is adversely affected by functional as well as organic psychiatric disorders. Furthermore, the nature and extent of intellectual impairment appears extremely complex.

Pre-1955 studies of intellectual functioning in the elderly pointed to a significant decline in several of its aspects with age and mental illness. The importance of deteriorated language was demonstrated on elderly patients by Truebold (1935) and vocabulary was found to be more disturbed in aged arteriosclerotic and senile psychotics than could be accounted for by age in the study by Shakow et al. (1941). Furthermore, Roth and Hopkins (1953) reported that senile psychotics (age range, 67 to 85), whom they tested, were largely inferior on a vocabulary test to a group of affective psychotics (age range, 60 to 86). Orme (1955) showed a group of 25 senile dements, with mean age of 73·84, to be significantly worse on a vocabulary test than a group of 25 elderly depressive patients with a mean age of 68·17 years. There was, however, also a significant difference between the mean ages of the groups in the latter study. It has also been suggested by Pichot (1955) that verbal deterioration may take place to a more marked degree in cerebral arteriosclerosis than in senile dementia. He showed that when 27 aged arteriosclerotics were matched with

25 senile dements, in terms of general intellectual status on Raven's Progressive Matrices, the arteriosclerotic patients had a very significantly poorer Vocabulary score.

It may be concluded that while it is possible that verbal ability may decline more slowly than certain other abilities in the aged, there is little doubt that it, too, can be affected. These data and views are consistent with the findings and opinions on younger normal and abnormal persons, well reviewed by Yates (1954; 1956; 1966) and by Payne (1960) in the first edition of this book.

Brody (1942) adapted Babcock's Test of Mental Efficiency for use with elderly psychiatric patients aged 50 to 69 categorised into four degrees of severity of dementia. He demonstrated that the 'discrepancy scores' of the groups were significantly different and suggested that cut-off points of 0–24 for probably not or doubtfully demented, 25–40 for mildly or moderately demented and 40 plus for those seriously demented. Brody concluded that—

'The only positive conclusion suggested by study of the psychometric pattern in the present patients is that while, in dementia, vocabulary ability is comparatively well preserved, other abilities severely decline, levelling down in a fashion which obscures the common pattern in simple psychosis and normal senility. Otherwise there is no trace of a specific pattern of abilities in dementia.'

A somewhat similar approach was adopted by Halstead (1943), who gave a battery of 25 items to 20 senile patients aged 68 to 83. He was able to divide the tests into three groups in terms of the difficulty patients showed in coping with them. The least difficult involved old mental habits, visual recognition, and simple motor tasks. Vocabulary, simple arithmetic, rote memory, and fluency came next. The most difficult tests were those that required the subjects to break away from old mental habits. When, however, Halstead (1944) gave the same tests to a further 18 aged patients judged clinically to be more demented, they were shown to be worse than the first group on nearly every test. All the tests differentiated between the dementia and a standardisation group. Data on a further 20 psychological and motor measures were provided by Margaret Eysenck (1945a) who stressed that the organisation of mental functioning in 75 senile dementia patients was markedly different from that of normal adults. The senile group's lowest scores were on tests involving abstract reasoning, and their highest scores on measures requiring the reactivation of past experience and knowledge. Pinkerton and Kelly (1952) used the Raven's Progressive Matrices and

examined 40 patients (age range, 60 to 90) clinically graded into five groups from A to E, E being the most demented. Their data were consistent with that of previous investigators. Bromley's (1953) results on the Matrices test of 35 elderly psychiatric patients (mean age, 61, SD 11·3), including eight diagnosed as senile, 10 paranoid states, 12 depressives, and 5 organics, also agreed, in the main, with those obtained by Eysenck, in showing a diminished total quantitative score, but little qualitative difference from normals. Cleveland and Dysinger (1944), on the other hand, found that 20 senile psychotics, aged 64 to 84, were able to respond on an abstract level to the verbal materials of the Wechsler-Bellevue Intelligence Scale, though they had great difficulty with the non-verbal items and the abstract requirements of Goldstein-Scheerer Sorting Test. Total quantitative scores on the W-B scale were also found by Rabin (1945) to be lower in 60 to 83-year-old senile, psychotic, and arteriosclerotic patients than in two other groups described as miscellaneous and non-psychotic, but there were no subtest pattern differences between the groups. The V/P discrepancy varied in size; that for the senile, arteriosclerotic was highest, followed by those for the miscellaneous and non-psychotic groups. The mean age differences between the groups, however, were also significant.

Speed of writing digits and words was found by Birren and Botwinick (1951) to differentiate normal from patient groups of aged subjects 60 to 70 years. This data confirms Lorge's earlier notions on the differential role of intellectual speed and power factors with age, and is seen as important for differential diagnosis in more recent work by Kendrick et al. (1965; 1967). Silverman et al. (1953) found that elderly persons with mixed or 'diffuse' EEG abnormality did worse on the intelligence tests than those with 'normal' or 'focal' EEGs, is also of interest for clinical diagnosis. A relationship between physiological indices of oxygen saturation and intellectual functioning in senile dements, 62 to 88 years of age, was found by Lovett Doust et al. (1953). On the other hand, conceptual tasks such as the Goldstein-Scheerer Cubes and Colour Form Sorting Test, do not appear to show themselves as useful in differential diagnosis within psychiatric groups (Hall, 1952: Hopkins and Post, 1955; Thaler, 1956).

It would appear, in general, from the pre-1955 studies that, to paraphrase Inglis (1958), pp. 203–4—(1) Senile dements have poorer intellectual functioning than psychotic or normal elderly persons; (2) There is evidence of a verbal/performance discrepancy in cases of senile deterioration, though both verbal and performance ability drop off with age and mental illness, albeit at different rates. Recent evidence on this point has been presented by Savage (1970b) which is crucial to the clinical interpretation of such data; (3) Cattell's theory of 'fluid' and 'crystallised' intellectual ability in relation to the concept of intelligence in the elderly is of considerable importance.

Eysenck (1945a) also factor analysed the results of a battery of 20 tests given to 84 senile patients (mean age 73·4, SD, 6·5). She extracted one general and three group factors (speed, memory, and strength) accounting for 43 per cent of the variance in all. Her main conclusion from this analysis was that the factor structure extracted gave a different picture of the mental organisation for abnormal patients as compared with normal. The test with the highest saturation on the general factor was Vocabulary (0·71) whereas the Matrices showed a low saturation (0·34). Eysenck attempted to explain these results in terms of Cattell's (1943) notions regarding 'fluid' and 'crystallised' intelligence. She concluded that, on the basis of these conceptions:

'we should expect tests of fluid ability, such as the matrix, to have very high factor saturations in a study of adolescents and young people generally, but to give low factor saturations in extreme old age; while, conversely, crystallised abilities would give comparatively high factor saturations in old age. This is precisely what we do find in this analysis and we may, therefore, consider that this analysis gives a certain measure of support to the theory set forth by Cattell.'

Bolton et al. came to the same conclusion in 1967, yet, surprisingly, little notice was taken of this view in between.

More recent studies have generally supported the view that organic diagnosis in the aged is significantly associated with lower than normal verbal, performance, and full scale IQs on Wechsler's and Raven's measures (Busse et al., 1956; Green and Berkowitz, 1965; Sanderson and Inglis, 1961; Bolton et al., 1966; Kendrick and Post, 1967) (Table 18.4).

Aged psychotic patients have also received increased attention in respect of their intellectual functioning in the last decade. The early studies of Cleveland and Dysinger on schizophrenics (1944) and Rabin (1945) on miscellaneous psychotics have been supplemented by several reports on senile psychosis, affective disorders, paraphrenia, acute confusional states, depression, and personality disorders listed in Table 18.4. The major finding is that in aged psychotic patients intellectual functioning is often quite severely affected when measured by the W-B or WAIS. It is, generally speaking,

significantly lower than for normal groups of aged in terms of Full Scale, verbal, and performance intelligence (Cleveland and Dysinger, 1944; Obrist et al., 1962; Kendrick et al., 1965, 1967; Bolton et al., 1966; Savage, 1970b; and others). The Matrices data from Roth and Hopkins (1953) and Hopkins and Roth (1953) on affective psychoses, paraphrenia, and acute confusional states, and that of Orme (1957) on depressives support the view that intelligence is lowered by psychotic mental illness. Green and Berkowitz (1965), however, present data on psychotic and personality disordered patients that are not lower than in the standardised WAIS data for the aged. A further important point seems to be that for psychotic, like organic disorders, performance ability is usually significantly lower than verbal intelligence in all the groups, except for personality disorders (Green and Berkowitz, 1965).

There are, however, many problems in this area. Few studies use adequate, or even bother to fully describe their psychiatric classificatory procedures or frame of reference, so that direct comparison of the data is difficult and may even be misleading. Even less have sampled the possible range of old age psychiatric disorders in a single investigation. Furthermore, longitudinal data is virtually non-existent on psychiatric groups. Readers, therefore, may excuse the presentation of some recent information from the author's ongoing investigations which may help clarify the situation.

Since 1963, Savage and his colleagues have pursued the psychometric investigation of intellectual functioning in normal and abnormal groups of aged subjects diagnosed according to the criteria and classification system prescribed by Roth (1955). The data to be presented here are derived from 144 subjects aged over 65 divided into four groups of 29 community normals, 42 affective, 31 paraphrenic and recurrent schizophrenic and 42 organic—senile and arteriosclerotic—dements.

It will be seen from Table 18.7 that the psychiatric groups generally show significantly lower intellectual levels than the aged normals on full scale, verbal, and performance IQs. However, the intelligence scores do not significantly differentiate the affectives, paraphrenics, and organics from each other. Performance ability is significantly lower than verbal both for the sample as a whole and for each diagnostic group. It would appear, therefore, that functionally and organically ill, as well as normal aged, decline differentially in these two aspects of intelligence. Incidentally, data published by Bolton and co-workers (1966) confirms these results on normal and neurotic samples. V/P discrepancy and Deterioration Quotient normative data are also presented in Table 18.7. The organics all had significantly higher DQ indices than the rest, and a higher V/P score. Normals, affectives, and schizophrenics were not significantly different from each other on V/P nor on DQ.

These studies on the intellectual levels of normal and abnormal groups of aged have obvious implications for the assessment of intellectual impairment in the aged. When can a given level be regarded as impaired? The improved normative data should help here. What aspects decline and at what rate? Much more information is still needed in this area. Quite obviously PIQ goes before VIQ. However, in very old groups, VIQ begins to go down more rapidly than PIQ. Is decline the same for normal aged as for those with mental illness? On the WAIS this would appear to be the case, but what of other aspects of cognitive functioning when learning is required?

Memory and Learning

The importance of memory in terms of recognition and recall in the clinical diagnosis of elderly patients has long been recognised. However, neither the status of the memory function concept, nor its relation to other cognitive abilities has ever been clearly defined. It has commonly been considered distinct from general intelligence in young age groups. However, the WAIS factorial studies suggest that, in the elderly, memory spreads over several factors rather than being a distinct entity (Cohen, 1957; Green and Berkowitz, 1964; Berger et al., 1964; Savage and Britton, 1968; Savage and Bolton, 1968).

Furthermore, Inglis (1958) pointed out that Hull's (1917) concept of 'memory', as commonly used, is too restricted in meaning, since it has come to refer almost entirely to the process of reproduction of learned material. Instead, he suggests that 'learning ability' could be usefully substituted for 'memory', so that both acquisition and retention can be taken into account. Kral (1962) distinguished two types of senescent forgetfulness; the first type, which he calls 'benign', is characterised by the inability of the subject to recall relatively unimportant experiences; data not available for recall on one occasion may be recalled at another time. The second type is a 'malignant' memory impairment which is characterised by the inability of the subject to recall events of the recent past, when not only relatively unimportant data and parts of an experience, but the experience as such, cannot be recalled. This type of dysfunction, says Kral, bears the essential characteristics of the amnestic syndrome, namely, loss of recent memories, disorientation, and confabulation, and forms the amnestic syndrome in senile dementia.

This view is in accordance with the work of Walton and Black (1957; 1959), which demonstrated that the ability to learn is an important variable distinguishing brain-damaged from non-brain-damaged subjects. It is interesting to note that Kral's malignant memory dysfunction is characterised by loss of *recent* memories and may indicate that brain-damage affects principally the first stage of memory, namely, acquisition, and that the patient cannot remember recent events because they were never learned. On the other hand, earlier experiences have been acquired and are remembered.

Empirical studies of memory in the aged have been reported for over fifty years. Achilles (1917) examined a group of mainly elderly psychiatric patients suffering from Korsakoff's syndrome, arteriosclerotic dementia, and general paralysis of the insane. He concluded: 'No attempt will be made . . . to average the results of the insane but . . . all show a memory defect and the defect is present in both recall and recognition'. In 1919, Moore reported a study of 30 patients, ranging in age from 28 to 74, including cases suffering from GPI, senile dementia, and alcoholic deterioration. These subjects were presented once with eight stimuli in each of four series, real objects, pictures of objects, and printed and spoken words. These had to be recalled immediately and then again one minute later. The patients were also required to name 50 pictures. Moore found evidence suggesting that, while immediate memory, retention, and perception all tended to deteriorate together, they could still be regarded as 'two distinct mental functions'. Lilliencrants (1922), though he examined only four abnormal cases, also concluded that both comprehension and reproduction are affected in cases of memory disorder, when the patients are required to recall or recognise meaningful or non-meaningful visual stimuli.

Seven senile, three pre-senile, and six paretic 'deteriorated' cases (aged between 25 and 87) were investigated by Wylie (1930). Her results suggested that such patients could neither acquire, nor retain, in situations in which they had to remember pictures or to learn paired associates, of meaningful and non-meaningful material. They failed both in the recognition and recall of such material. Shakow and associates, in 1941, used a version of the Wells Memory Test (Wells and Martin, 1923), which involves both old recall (e.g. of personal information) and new recall (e.g. memory for a sentence). They examined 56 arteriosclerotic psychoses and 48 senile psychotics, aged between 65 and 85, and compared the performance of these groups with that of normal controls selected from the same age range. They found consistently, although not markedly, poorer results on these memory tests in the psychotic groups. All groups were better on old than on new recall and senile psychotics were poorer than patients with cerebral arteriosclerosis on both. The authors do not, however, present any statistical significance levels.

Several psychometric tests of memory and learning are available (Table 18.7). The Wechsler Memory Scale I and II (WMS) was published in 1945, though few studies have reported using it on elderly subjects. The original scale assumed a mean Memory Quotient of 100 with a standard deviation of 15. The WMS normative data on old people, presented by Kral and Durost (1953), was on ten senile dements (mean age 78) and ten Korsakoff's psychoses (mean age 51). Immediate recall was found to be impaired in all clinical groups. However, the control group was totally inadequate, consisting of ten hospital personnel with a mean age of 29. A high percentage of misclassification of patients has been reported, using a single testing with the Wechsler Memory Scales (Walton, 1958), but four repetitions of the test apparently produced different responses in the functional and organic patients. The functional patient improved his performance significantly more than the organic patient, and these differences were related to diagnostic change. It is important to note that this differentiation occurred only after four repetitions of the Wechsler Memory Scale.

Hulicka (1966) examined the age-related changes in WMS raw scores. She found that the age-related drop in raw score on the WMS was primarily a function of an age-related decline in performance on certain, rather than all of the WMS subtests, namely logical memory, visual reproduction, and associate learning. The WMS was not regarded as suitable for use with elderly individuals, and is seen as a test of general orientation and learning efficiency, rather than as a measure of memory functioning. No significant differences in WMS scores between age groups of subjects with an overall range of 80 to 92 years were found by Klonoff and Kennedy (1965). These data suggest that there is no significant decline in memory functioning once the age of 80 is reached. However, they did find that the WMS revealed greater loss in recent than in remote memory.

It appears, therefore, that the efficiency in the ability to learn new material and of short-term, rather than long-term, memory decreases in old age, particularly where organic brain damage is involved. This conclusion has been largely substantiated by experimental studies of learning and short-term memory (Welford 1958; 1968; Inglis 1960; 1962; Inglis and Caird, 1963; etc.) and a number of

psychometric learning measures have been developed which are useful in relation to diagnostic problems in the aged. Consequently, the normative data for the aged on some of these measures is presented in Table 18.8.

The notion that learning impairment is an important factor in the diagnosis of mental deterioration was first systematically developed by Babcock (1930) who hypothesised that in dementia old learning remains practically unimpaired, while ability to learn new information shows weakness in varying degrees according to the extent of deterioration. The validity of the Efficiency Index as a measure of deterioration has been seriously questioned (Yates, 1954, 1966; Payne, 1960 and others), but more recent attempts have been made to test Babcock's hypothesis that a significant discrepancy between past and present learning is consistent with dementia by Nelson (1953) and Shapiro and Nelson (1955). A modification of the New Word Learning and Retention Test (Shapiro and Nelson) was used in two studies of the memory function of psychiatric patients over the age of 65 (Inglis et al., 1956; Shapiro et al., 1956). In these studies the Wechsler Vocabulary subtest was used. Although initially highly significant differences were established between functionals, doubtful organics, and organics, these differences were not found when the psychiatric and psychological assessments used uncontaminated diagnostic criteria. The spuriously high validity obtained initially results from the fact that both psychological and psychiatric criteria were similar.

Walton and Black (1957) felt that the New Word Learning and Retention Test was too easy to be useful in the detection of brain damage. By extending the Learning Test to ten new words and by giving the subject greater opportunity to learn, it was hoped that the successful differentiation of the functional from the organic patient would result. They developed the Modified Word Learning Test and initial results with MWLT were very encouraging. By using a cut-off point of 30+, 93·5 per cent of organics and only 0·5 per cent of the functionals were identified as organic. IQ, vocabulary level, and age were found to exert some influence on the scores, but this influence was not sufficient to produce 'organic' scores independently of the presence of organicity. Orme et al. (1964) suggested that schizophrenic patients were misclassified 'organic' by the MWLT. However, further studies by Walton et al. (1959), Riddell (1962a), Kendrick (1963), Bolton et al. (1967), and others on young and aged samples have confirmed the success of the MWLT in identifying the impairment of verbal learning ability associated with generalised brain damage.

Table 18.8.   Learning in the Aged

	Measure	N	Age	Diagnosis	Mean score	% classified as organics
Walton (1958)	MWLT	31	73·17	Senile	30·32	76·5
		17	70·0	Functional	19·45	33·3
Sanderson and Inglis	MWLT	15	68–83	Memory disorder	52·0	—
		15	66–84	No memory disorder	11·33	—
Riddell (1962b)	MWLT (using Terman-Merrill vocabulary)	22	60+	Functional 16	5·95	—*
	MWLT (using WAIS vocabulary)	22	60+	Organic 6	5·68	*
White and Knox (1965)	MWLT	76	71·22	Normal	approximately 10·82	9·2
Bolton *et al.* (1967)	MWLT	29	73·7	Normal	9·34	0
		42	68·5	Affective	16·14	28·6
		31	69·5	Schizophrenic	12·70	22·6
		42	74·3	Organic	22·42	71·4
Kendrick *et al.* (1965)	SLT	20	70·9	Brain-damaged	13·7	—
		40	68·3	Depression	70·88	—
Inglis (1959)	ART	18	68·56	Memory disorder	59·0	—
	ART	18	69·61	Normal	13·0	—
Caird *et al.* (1962)	ART	30	79·90	Memory disorder	83·63	—
	ART	30	74·56	No memory disorder	17·80	—
Riddell (1962a)	ART (Form A)	26	69·35	Brain-damaged 5 / Psychotic 21	39·27	—
	ART (Form B)	26	69·35	Brain-damaged 5 / Psychotic 21	28·05	—
Riddell (1962b)	ART (Form A)	22	60+	6 organic / 16 functional	26·11	—
	ART (Form B)	22	60+	6 organic / 16 functional	23·75	—
Kendrick *et al.* (1965)	ART	20	70·9	Brain-damaged	26·45	—*
	ART	40	68·3	Depression	72·88	—*
Kendrick and Post (1967)	ART	30	70·48	Depression + normal	80·97	—*
	ART	10		Brain-damaged	29·7	—*
Bolton *et al.* (1967)	ART	29	73·7	Normal	14·93	
		42	68·5	Affective	24·95	
		31	69·7	Schizophrenic	17·77	
		42	74·3	Organic	30·14	
Krawiecki *et al.* (1957)	WMS	25	72·6	Senile with memory deficit	69·8	
		25	71·3	Senile with memory deficit	71·6	
Walton (1958)	WMS	27	70+	Organic	61·7 (Memory quotient)	
		21	70+	Functional	75·75 (Memory quotient)	
Klonoff and Kennedy (1965)	WMS	172	82·70	Normal	109·97 (Memory quotient)	
Hulicka (1966)	WMS	70	60–69	Normal	51·93	
	WMS	46	70–79	Normal	50·46 Raw scores	
	WMS	25	80–89	Normal	48·30	

* Adapted scoring system: low score is poor

It has also been found that the MWLT score of psychiatric patients over 65 predicted favourable or unfavourable (usually death) outcome better than did the provisional diagnosis (Inglis, 1959b; Sanderson and Inglis, 1961). The MWLT scores have also been shown to be capable of giving a high correct classification of organically based learning impairment in the aged (Bolton *et al.*, 1967). The normative data in this respect is presented in Table 18.8.

Kendrick *et al.* (1965) redesigned the MWLT so that it was more suitable for use with elderly subjects. They found that their Synonym Learning Test (SLT) correctly classified normal and psychiatric subjects nearly 90 per cent of the time. The major source of misclassification occurred with the depressed subjects, 16 per cent of whom were misclassified as organics. It was also found with the depressed group that over 63 per cent of those misclassified had IQs below 95. Bolton *et al.* (1967) have confirmed that misclassification results in part from affective, mostly depressive symptoms and low intelligence.

A second important learning test, the Paired Associate Learning Test, also called the Auditory Recall Test (ART), was devised by Inglis (1957; 1959a) in an attempt to measure the acquisition phase of memory. Acquisition is measured by the number of trials taken to learn word associations to a given criterion. It was found that the PALT or ART successfully discriminated between elderly psychiatric patients with clinically diagnosed 'memory disorder' and elderly patients without such a disorder. The validity of the test was later confirmed on a Canadian sample by Caird *et al.* (1962). More recently, it has been suggested (Zaretsky and Halberstam, 1968) that age, rather than brain-damaged status, appears to be the significant factor in impaired performance on the ART. In this study, pairs of words with different associative strength were used in addition to the standard ART words. Older subjects (age range 60 to 85), both with and without brain damage, performed best on material that utilised prior learning experiences (i.e. with the word pairs that were highly associated together), and less well on material requiring the learning of new associations. Savage (1970b) reported normative data on abnormal and psychiatric aged samples on the ART (Table 18.8). The effect of affective disorder on scores was noticeable, but, as an index of organic involvement in learning impairment, the ART was considered adequate, though slightly less valid than the MWLT.

In view of the fact that the measure of memory impairment derived from the ART is a measure of acquisition or learning, one would expect that 'memory impairment', as assessed by the ART, would correlate highly with 'learning impairment', as assessed by the MWLT. It is surprising, therefore, that Riddell (1962a), who administered the tests to groups of functional and organic, elderly, psychiatric patients, did not find a significant correlation between them. He interpreted this result as suggesting that the MWLT and the ART are not equivalent tests and that memory impairment as assessed by the ART differs from impairment of learning with organic involvement as assessed by the MWLT.

This conclusion, however, was not supported by Kendrick and his co-workers (1965), who found a correlation of 0·61 (significant at the one per cent

level) between the SLT and the ART. The discrepancy between these findings and Riddell's may, of course, be due to differences in procedure between the SLT and the MWLT. In the former, the subject learns a synonym of the word whose meaning he does not know; in the MWLT, on the other hand, the examiner can supply the subject with the meaning of the word in various ways. Thus, the SLT resembles the ART more than does the MWLT and should, on this reasoning, correlate more highly. It would be surprising, however, if this difference in form accounted completely for the discrepant findings, since all three tests are designed to reflect learning impairment. The work of Bolton and colleagues (1967) also fails to confirm the Riddell view. They suggested that the Inglis Paired Associate Learning Test and the Modified Word Learning Test measure essentially the same thing in elderly normal and abnormal subjects. This was further supported by Savage and Bolton (1968) who, in a factor analysis of cognitive functioning in normal subjects and mentally ill patients, found a distinct learning impairment factor on which the MWLT and ART loaded highly. This factor is quite distinct from WAIS general IQ, V/P intelligence and deterioration factors.

Perceptual Motor Ability

Perceptual motor functioning is by far the most neglected area of cognitive functioning measurement in the elderly. It is by no means clear how age changes in perceptual-motor functioning are to be distinguished from pathological changes. Generally, it appears that perceptual-motor efficiency declines with normal ageing (Wechsler, 1944, 1958; Kendall, 1962; Klonoff and Kennedy, 1965; Bromley, 1966; Davies, 1965, 1967). There is considerable evidence, as pointed out in the section on intelligence, from performance intelligence measures, that perceptual-motor functioning declines with age and is probably affected by psychiatric functional and organic illness. It is only recently, however, that attempts are being made to separate normal and pathological changes in perceptual-motor functioning *per se* in the elderly.

Early studies using the Bender-Gestalt Test (Bender, 1938; 1946) suggested that elderly organic subjects (mean age 71·0) were less accurate in copying the Bender designs than other elderly psychiatric groups whose mean age was 68·07 (Shapiro *et al.*, 1956; 1957) but no distinction is made in these studies between age related and pathological changes. Rosencrans and Schaffer (1969) found that a reduction in accuracy on the Bender-Gestalt is associated with brain damage but not with ageing. No difference was found between the accuracy of young brain-damaged subjects (mean age 36·55) and of elderly brain-damaged subjects (mean age 63·13). However, comparison of these two groups with a group of younger psychiatric patients (mean age 35·04) showed that the older group had a significantly slower time score. Thus, age related changes appear to take the form of a slowing of perceptual-motor responses rather than of a decrease in the accuracy with which these responses are carried out (Klonoff and Kennedy, 1965).

Normative data for subjects over 60 are only occasionally available for psychometric measures of perceptual-motor abilities and attempts to establish norms have met with limited success. Using the Memory for Designs Test, Graham and Kendall (1946–1960) and Kendall (1962) compared 36 brain-damaged subjects over the age of 60 with 36 control subjects, most of whom were psychotic, matched for age, education, and occupation. Two-thirds of the psychotic controls had organic scores, and significantly more perseveration and orientation errors were made by the elderly controls than by the younger samples (Graham and Kendall, 1960). Davies (1967; 1968) confirmed that the discrimination power of the Memory for Designs Test was poor with elderly subjects, while Newcombe and Steinberg (1964) found that the incidence of 'organic' responses increased after the age of 60 with 23 per cent of normal subjects over 70 obtaining organic scores. Alexander (1970), however, using aged normal and psychiatric patients, failed to distinguish between brain-damaged and non-brain-damaged subjects.

Another measure fairly widely used with elderly subjects is the Benton Visual Retention Test (Benton, 1955; 1963). Benton (1963) provided norms up to the age of 64 and suggested that 'while performance level declines merely as a function of age, when defined in terms of number correct score, it declines more precipitously when defined in terms of the total error score'. This hypothesis has been substantiated in a study by Klonoff and Kennedy (1965) using normal subjects over the age of 80. They found that a number of errors occurred with each incorrect response.

Probably the most successful attempt at providing normative data on perceptual-motor functioning in the aged has been with the Perceptual Maze Test (Elithorn, 1955). Davies (1965; 1968) used 90 normal subjects (50 men and 40 women) in each of the age decades from 20 to 29 and 70 to 79 in a study using the PMT. She found that the marked sex differences of younger groups in PMT performance were reduced to insignificance in the subjects over 60. There is a gradual decline in performance scores with increasing age, thus suggesting that the test is sensitive to normal ageing. However, performance on the test was also found to be positively related to non-verbal intelligence which is known to decline with age.

Finally, there are two other psychometric measures that have been used with limited success: the Porteous Mazes (Porteous, 1952, 1955) and the Trail Making Test (TMT) (Reitan, 1955). The Porteous Mazes are supposed to measure prudence and foresight or the more 'practical' aspects of general intelligence. Old people over the age of 70 have been found to perform as well as the average adolescent or young adult on the Porteous Mazes, although they found it difficult to cope with new ideas and methods of working (Loranger and Misiak, 1960).

On the other hand, Bromley (1966) found that elderly subjects (mean age 66·5) took considerably longer to complete each maze than younger subjects. The proportional increases in time for old subjects were not found to be directly related to difficulty. Bromley suggested that age changes in performance time on the Porteous Mazes are due to 'reduced "storage" and "control" capacities' and not to weaker motivation or poorer concentration. He concluded that the test needs considerable revision before it can be successfully used with the aged.

Performance of elderly subjects on the Trail Making Test led Reed and Reitan (1963) to suggest that there is a close resemblance of the effects of normal ageing and of brain damage. This suggestion has been supported by Davies (1968) who found that a very large number of elderly subjects were misclassified as organic, using the credit score norms in Reitan's manual. In the age range 70 to 79, 92 per cent of the male subjects were misclassified as organic. Thus, it appears that, on the basis of the TMT, little distinction can be made between the effects of normal age changes and of pathological changes. Nevertheless, Lindsey and Coppinger (1969) tentatively conclude that age does not contribute very much to Trail Making Performance.

Many problems exist in relation to the measurement of perceptual-motor functioning in the elderly. The influence of intelligence and age on these functions is crucial. The factorial analysis of intellect in the aged presented by Savage and Bolton (1968) and by Savage (1970b) suggests that a distinction between perceptual-motor level and perceptual-motor learning ability has important theoretical and practical implications for the assessment of functioning in normal and abnormal aged groups and individuals. Savage and his colleagues hope to modify the Digit Symbol subtest of the WAIS so that it is possible to assess the improvement of performance over a period of time and obtain a perceptual-motor learning score. This method has an advantage over Stein's (1961)

'Symbol-Gestalt Test' in that at least a partial control for intellectual level, as in the MWLT, can be built into the test, and age correction scores can be obtained for the basic WAIS performance. Similarly, the Block Design subtest of the WAIS has potential. The BD was considered by Wechsler to be one of the subtests that did not hold with age and later investigations confirmed this view (Fox and Birren, 1950; Berkowitz and Green, 1963; Savage and Britton, 1968). Howell (1955) found that older subjects 'very often decided on a possible method of constructing the design, and then proceeded without further reference to the design model'.

There have also been many attempts to modify the BD subtest of the WAIS to increase its sensitivity to organic brain disease (Grassi, 1947; Shapiro, 1951; 1952; 1953), and it has been suggested as potentially useful in assessing organic deterioration. For this reason, it seems suitable for modification into a learning test. The test in its standard form is also part of the short form of the WAIS devised by Britton and Savage (1966) for use with the aged.

PERSONALITY FUNCTIONING IN THE AGED

Mental Illness

The problem of mental illness in old age is increasingly important to modern society. A number of studies over the past three decades have illuminated the nature and size of this problem on an international basis in terms of diagnostic categories and treatment procedures. Recently, the World Health Organisation has been increasingly active in this field as well as several national bodies in supporting research and international conferences.

Early clinical diagnoses of old age psychiatric disorders were effectively dominated by the accounts of senile psychosis and dementia (Kraepelin, 1909–1913; and Bleuler, 1916). The scientific advances necessary to tackle the problems of mental illness in the aged more realistically are a product of the twentieth century, but readers will find remarkably full accounts of the ageing phenomenon in Burdach (1890–1926) and Burstein (1949) who summarise the early literature in this area. Historically the work of Rothschild (1937, 1942) is an important landmark in our understanding of the aged. He recognised that factors other than degenerative changes in the brain, such as the influence of personality and environment, played a role in mental disturbances in old age, even though these were still included under the general heading of senile and arteriosclerotic psychoses. Pathological studies by Grunthal (1927) and Gellerstedt (1933) established that the changes in the brains of senile dements could also be found in the brains of normal old people and pointed to the need to clarify the relationship between clinical and pathological phenomena.

In practice, however, the term 'senile psychosis' continued to be applied until quite recently to a wide range of syndromes with onset in old age. Many patients were considered to be suffering from illness or abnormality due to senility and to have a poor prognosis. They tended to be segregated in wards of mental hospitals set aside for the aged. The presence of hypertension, peripheral arteriosclerosis, or minor neurological changes, all of which are common in the aged, appeared to confirm the brain-damage aetiology of their illness. This was an era of pessimism and therapeutic nihilism as far as the elderly were concerned.

The increasing numerical importance of mental disorder among the aged, the burden on the community, and the threat to the hospital services, in modern civilised society stimulated an interest in the problems of the aged in the 1945 period (Pollock, 1945; Kaplan, 1945; Lewis, 1946). Studies by Semrad and McKeon (1941) and Williams et al. (1942) showed that in mental patients over the age of 70 committed to hospital for the first time, most had long histories of personality and financial difficulties with the breakdown of their home environments as a major precipitating cause. On investigating comparable groups of arteriosclerotic and senile dements, they concluded that personality factors were insignificant in the former. Clow (1940), however, reported contradictory results. He stressed that psychotics with cerebral arteriosclerosis had abnormal anxiety and tension in their adult lives, narrow interest ranges, and sexual maladjustment. At this time, several short-term follow-up studies of elderly patients showed that those with predominantly depressive symptomatology had a relatively good outcome compared with those with 'organic brain syndromes' (Post, 1951; Clow and Allen, 1951). Moreover, favourable responses were reported in depressed patients after ECT, even in the very old (Evans, 1943; Mayer-Gross, 1945; Feldman et al., 1946), and further served to demarcate the functional from the organic states. This acceptance of functional as well as organically based mental illness in the aged was of paramount importance. It allowed new perspectives for the diagnosis and treatment, especially as it was paralleled by an increased availability of pharmacological agents.

Table 18.9.   Mental Illness in the Aged:
Estimated incidence for the main psychiatric disorders per 1,000 population aged 65 years or over
(*modified from* Slater and Roth, 1969, p. 541)

	Institutional cases per 1,000	*Cases living at home per* 1,000	*Total incidence per* 1,000
Senile and arteriosclerotic dementia	6·8	38·8	45·6
Other severe brain syndromes	0·8	9·7	10·5
Organic syndromes, mild cases	5·3	51·8	57·1
Organics, all cases	12·9	100·3	113·2
Manic-depressive disorder	0·7	12·9	13·6
Schizophrenia, chronic	(0·2)*	9·7⎤	10·8
Paraphrenia, late onset	0·9	0·0⎦	
Character disorders, including paranoid states	0·5	35·6	36·1
Psychoses, all forms	2·3	58·2	50·5
Neuroses and allied disorders (Moderate/severe forms)	1·9	87·4	89·3
All disorders	17·1	245·9	263·0

* Long-stay mental hospital schizophrenics not included

Epidemiology

The prevalence of psychiatric disorders in the elderly has been investigated in a number of community surveys, general practice studies, and by means of hospital statistics. The World Health Organisation (1959) pointed out that first and second or more admissions of old people into mental hospitals is taking place at an increasing rate in many countries. In the USA between 1904 and 1950, the number of persons over 60 multiplied by four, yet the number of first admissions to mental hospitals increased nine times. Figures presented by the Registrar General (1964) for England and Wales show a similar progressive rise. The number of people over 65 increased by 1 per cent between 1951–60, but first admission rates rose by over 35 per cent. About 50 per cent of aged in mental hospitals had been there many years, the other 50 per cent were late onset admissions (Kidd and Smith, 1966). The relative incidence of various mental disorders in old age is indicated by these hospital admission rates, but the picture is incomplete as far as the total incidence and distribution is concerned. In this respect population surveys are extremely important and since the pioneer work of Sheldon (1948) several population surveys have appeared. (Bremer, 1951; Hobson and Pemberton, 1955; Essen-Möller, 1956; Gruenberg, 1961; Primrose, 1962; Kay *et al.*, 1962; 1964a,b; Watts *et al.*, 1962; Miller, 1963; Nielsen, 1963; Williamson *et al.*, 1964; Garside *et al.*, 1965; Parsons, 1965). These

writers' estimates of the prevalence of the main psychiatric disorders and less disabling mental illness of old age diverge to some extent owing to differences in diagnostic criteria. Table 18.9, modified from Slater and Roth (1969), represents a summary of the estimated prevalence rates for the main psychiatric disorders of the 65 plus age group per 1,000 of that population.

The investigations suggested that between 20 and 30 per cent of persons over 60 exhibit psychiatric symptoms or psychological deviations. Some 10 per cent showed conditions consistent with pathological brain damage, of which about half were seriously disabling. Psychotic disorders were diagnosed in 5 to 7 per cent of the population, severe depressive and paranoid illness to 2 per cent, and neurotic classification in about 10 per cent, but a further 10 to 15 per cent of minor neurotic symptomatology are noted (Gruenberg, 1961; Kay *et al.*, 1964a,b; 1966; Nielsen, 1963; Parsons, 1965). Functional, particularly affective disorders predominate up to the age of 70, thereafter psycho-organic states increasingly account for the rising psychiatric morbidity. However, even beyond 85, some 70 per cent of community residents are free from severe forms of mental deterioration (Gruenberg, 1961). Successful suicides in both sexes tend to increase with age, though the attempted suicide incidence decreases and probably half of them are associated with depression and/or physical illness (O'Neal *et al.*, 1956; Stengel and Cook, 1958; Capstick, 1960; Sainsbury, 1962). However, it is important to keep things in perspective and remember that the over-whelming majority of elderly people pass through a normal aged period without recognisable or diagnosed mental illness. Minor emotional and cognitive adjustment problems are common and increase between 60 and 90 years of age but for serious old age mental disorders the main risk found is between 60 and 80 (Kay, personal communication, 1969).

General practice studies have also made a vital contribution to the understanding of old age mental disorders. Kessel (1960) and Kessel and Shepherd (1962) suggested that minor psychiatric illness tends to remain unrecognised by general practitioners and this was confirmed in further investigations by Williamson et al. (1964). Shepherd et al. (1966) pointed out that family doctors were aware of about 50 per cent of the psychiatric disorders in their elderly patients and that very few of the milder cases were receiving any form of treatment or support. As Post has suggested, this shows that elderly psychiatric patients tend to be sent for specialist care only late in their illness, with requests for in-patient care rather than curative treatment. Nevertheless, it is now fair to say that a great deal can be done to successfully treat functional mental illness in the elderly and to alleviate the burden of those suffering from organic pathologically based senile disorders (Post, 1951, 1962a,b, 1965, 1966, 1968; Slater and Roth, 1969). Every effort must be made to identify and diagnose the potential recipient and thus improve the general quality of life in old age.

Modern Classification

The classification of mental illness in the aged has undergone fundamental changes over the years, but the taxonomy proposed by Roth and his colleagues has now been generally accepted (Roth and Morrissey, 1952; Roth, 1955; Slater and Roth, 1969; Kay et al., 1964a,b; Post, 1965, 1967). Roth's classification is based on symptomatological rather than aetiological considerations. However, the groups of patients so defined have been found to differ from each other not only in prognosis and cause of death (Kay, 1959; Post, 1962) but also on several psychological measurement techniques (Hopkins and Roth, 1953; Roth and Hopkins, 1953; Britton et al., 1966; Bolton et al., 1967), in association with somatic illness (Kay and Roth, 1955; Slater and Roth, 1969), in their EEGs, genetically (Kay, 1959; Larsson and Sjorgren, 1954), and in the postmortem findings (Corsellis, 1962). Within the 'organic' groups, the neuropathological studies of Corsellis confirmed the clinical differentiation into senile, arteriosclerotic, and acute confusional psychoses; and within the functional groups, the

course of illness (Kay, 1962) and the response to different forms of treatment (Post, 1962a) are in accord with the clinical separation into affective and paranoid psychoses. More recent work by Roth et al. (1967) and Blessed et al. (1968) has developed the analysis of the relationships between neuropathological and mental illness phenomena in the aged. The identification of mental illness proposed by Roth has been widely accepted on an international basis. One would like to see studies of normal and abnormal behavioural functioning in the aged relating their findings to this taxonomic system more frequently than at present.

The general classification for old age mental disorders from Roth (1955) and in Slater and Roth (1969) Clinical Psychiatry (Chapter 10) divided psychiatric features into 5 categories:

1. Affective disorder
2. Late paraphrenia
3. Acute or sub-acute delirious state
4. Senile dementia
5. Arteriosclerotic psychosis

The affective disorders have been subclassified into neurotic and endogenous depressions, and neurotic disorders as such have since been found to be prevalent among the aged. Late onset depression appears to have less genetic loading than early onset depression, and significantly more late onset manic depressives experience clear physical or social stress compared with that for early onset (Stendstedt, 1959; Kay, 1959; Post, 1962a; Chesser, 1965). Persons developing depression late in life also have more robust previous personalities than those with previous depressive episodes (Roth, 1955; Chesser, 1965). Several diagnostic subcategories of depression are presented by Slater and Roth (1969) which include atypical depression, pseudo-demented depression, depression with clouding of consciousness, physical illness and depression, 'reactive' depressions and organic depression. Attacks of mania or hypomania are also noted as constituting 5 to 10 per cent of the affective disorders in old age.

Early reports suggested that the success of treatment for depression in old age is limited, but there seems no doubt that some alleviation of the situation is possible (Post, 1962a). Indeed, recent studies discussed by Post (1968) support the view that depression in old age responds very well to modern methods of treatment and that depressives do not develop de novo senile dementia or arteriosclerotic dementia any more frequently than the elderly population as a whole.

Mild or moderate neurotic disorders are possibly much more frequent in the aged than they were thought to be, probably 10 to 15 per cent of the elderly population (Kay *et al.*, 1964a,b; Bergmann, 1966). The severe neurotic disorders in the elderly tend to be present in those with a longstanding predisposition to respond adversely to various kinds of stress, who tend to be less sociable, moody and have an anxious concern about their health (Vispo, 1962; Garside *et al.*, 1965; Bergmann, 1966). Both Post (1967) and Slater and Roth (1969) also stress that anxiety is usually associated with some degree of depression. Physical health emerges clearly as a causative factor in late onset neurotic disorders. In other recurrent old age neurotics, marriage is usually late or not at all: the divorce or separation incidence is high in this group, and a proportion had suffered breakdown in middle age. To quote Slater and Roth (1969) in *Mental Disease in the Aged*, p. 578: 'Viewed in retrospect, the lives of many of those who breakdown in old age, look rather like a protracted game of chess in the early stages of which some powerful figures have been eliminated from the game thus restricting the possibilities of effective action and survival for the remainder.'

When obsessions, phobias, or hypochondriasis occur for the first time in late life, they are usually much less permanently incapacitating and tend to be associated with introversion. Hysterical conversion symptoms rarely, if ever, present in old age and when they do are indicative of functional psychosis or organic disease rather than being of neurotic origin (Post, 1965; Slater and Roth, 1969). On the other hand, McDonald (1965) in a general practice survey concluded that neurotic symptoms were not the forerunners of dementia.

Treatment of neurosis tends to concentrate on the use of antidepressant and minor tranquillising drugs and advice or help to family. Psychotherapy is considered difficult for financial and theoretical reasons and as well as for other practical considerations (Post, 1965), though general supportive therapy is helpful. One must generally suggest that a great deal more work into functional disorders in the aged would be most profitable to the health and life satisfaction of that aged population.

Late Paraphrenia

The symptoms of schizophrenia in the aged have been known for some considerable time and were described by Bleuler in a review article in 1943. Early clinical practice tended to regard these disorders as of organic origin, but Roth (1955) drew attention to a group of patients whose first illness occurred in senescence, in whom the most prominent features of the illness were paranoid delusions and hallucinations often with unclear schizophrenic features, and who tended to be diagnosed as suffering from senile or arteriosclerotic psychoses. He called this condition *late paraphrenia*. Unlike early schizophrenia, it is mainly confined to women, about 8 to 9 per cent of female first admissions over the age of 65. According to Slater and Roth (1969) personality deterioration does not appear to accompany late paraphrenia, except after such long periods of observation that senile degenerative changes are a more likely explanation than a schizophrenic process and the disease does not run in families to the extent that schizophrenia appears to do (Kay, 1959; Kay and Roth, 1961). This view of the reduced significance of genetic factors in elderly schizoid type illness, was confirmed by Post (1966) in a review of the literature in this area and by Herbert and Nicholson (1967).

It has been suggested that there are many elderly ill of this type in the community tolerated as eccentrics (Macmillan and Shaw, 1966). This condition does, however, seem very responsive to treatment by the pharmacological agents used therapeutically on younger age group schizophrenics (Post, 1966a; Slater and Roth, 1969). Roth (1963) maintains that the circumstances surrounding breakdown and the features of the illness in paraphrenia are in some ways more reminiscent of the course of events in neurotic illness (except presumably its late onset) than of that associated with schizophrenia in early life.

Senile Dementia

Senile dementia is the most common mental disorder in the aged associated with degenerative diseases of the nervous system and the disorganisation of all aspects of personality (Larsson *et al.*, 1963; Kay *et al.*, 1964a,b). Simchowicz (1910) regarded senile dementia as an accentuation of the normal processes of ageing. This view was obviously implicit in Wechsler's (1944; 1958) concept of intelligence and its decline in normal and abnormal aged. However, the psychometric evidence, much of which was discussed earlier, suggests that there may be qualitative as well as quantitative differences between the cognitive functioning of senile dements and normal aged persons (Botwinick and Birren, 1951b; Savage, 1970b). Clinical evidence by Kral (1962) and Kay *et al.* (1966) supports this view.

It has long been suspected that hereditary factors are important in the development of senile dementia (Meggendorfer, 1926; Kallmann, 1948; 1951) and this appears to be supported by the work of Larsson *et al.* (1963) who found a higher incidence of senile dementia in families of dements than in the comparable general aged population. A link between senile organic psychoses and neuropathology has been establshed by the work of Corsellis (1962),

Roth *et al.* (1967), and Blessed *et al.* (1968) and it is also of interest to note that the survival period for 'uncomplicated senile dements' is shorter than for those whose dementia is coloured with loosely knit paranoid delusions or depressive symptoms (Kay, 1962). Presumably the pure senile dements have a more organic pathological basis to their disorder. It would certainly appear that the occurrence of senile plaques and associated neuropathological changes are correlated with changes in psychological performance. All the pathological changes described in senile dementia—argentophil plaques, neurofibrillary changes, and granulovacuolar degeneration—have been found in normal old subjects at death. Neurofibrillary change is often confined to the hippocampal region (Gellerstedt, 1933; Tomlinson *et al.*, 1968) and this has potential importance in view of the role of the limbic system in memory functioning.

The independence of arteriosclerotic and senile dementia has been discussed by both clinical and pathological investigators. Corsellis (1962) showed that the processes were distinct to a large extent neuropathologically; 45 per cent of his cases were due to cerebrovascular disease, 34 per cent showed changes associated with senile dementia, and 21 per cent of the patients had both disease processes. Clinically, arteriosclerotic psychosis is frequently associated with hypertension and follows a number of cerebrovascular accidents. Intellectual impairment and other symptoms show marked fluctuation in the course of the illness and total disintegration, as seen in senile dementia, does not show until very late in the illness. Prognosis in arteriosclerotic dementia is better than for senile dementia, but even so within two years of diagnosis, mortality is 70 per cent (Roth, 1955).

Psychodynamic factors operating in patients with chronic brain syndromes may result in difficulties in coping with the organically based difficulties (Katz *et al.*, 1961). Several investigators have also reported that additional brain damage results from circulatory inefficiency (Albert, 1964; Mueller, 1967). The early hope of Rothschild (1937; 1942) that ability to compensate for cerebral deterioration might be more important than actual anatomical changes in chronic brain syndromes cannot, unfortunately, now be accepted, nor can the implicit socio-medical therapeutic possibilities. Treatment of associated symptoms of depression, anxiety, paranoid episodes and the like, along with adequate social-environmental conditions will probably result in the main improvements in life for these patients.

Acute Confusional or Delirious States

These are probably the most frequent, yet least understood conditions in old age, occurring and seen by general practitioner and specialist alike during both physical and mental illnesses. The principal causes of delirium in old age are cardiac failure, chronic and acute respiratory disease, anaemias, malignant disease, alcoholism, overdosage of drugs, vitamin and nutritional deficiency, surgical operations, dehydration, and electrolyte disturbances. Patients are usually incoherent, hyperactive, and levels of awareness fluctuate. A considerable need for research into behaviour functioning associated with pre- and post-acute and chronic delirious states is evident as they appear to be the least understood of the five major categories of old age outlined by Roth and his colleagues.

In general, psychiatric classification of disorders in the aged has taken considerable strides over the past twenty years, even though more refinement in diagnostic techniques and treatment methods is necessary and will undoubtedly follow. I regret that the same cannot be said for psychometric and experimental psychological research in this area, where the dearth of investigations of real value is only too evident.

Adjustment in Old Age

'Adjustment' has been a major concept in the development of practical measurement devices and in elucidating theoretical problems related to ageing. Though much of the work covers the age range 40 to 65, some studies have investigated older samples. Conkey (1933) stressed three factors relating to good adjustment in old age. Most important was (1) strong and varied interests or activities, followed by (2) economic independence or security, and (3) freedom from physical handicaps. She also pointed out that good adjustment in old age is largely a product of good adjustment prior to old age. The better adjusted also wished more frequently to relive their lives. These conclusions were reinforced by the subsequent investigations of Morgan (1937), Lawton *et al.* (1940), and Landis (1941; 1942). In view of the stress laid on interests and activities in relation to adjustment, one might ask how stable or changing these are over age. Strong (1943) suggested that age and the experience that goes with age change an adult man's interests very little. Kuhlen (1945), on the other hand, notes that while the 25- and 65 year-old may be essentially alike in interests, the age differences that do exist in the correlational data are extremely important in the understanding of the older as compared with the younger man. One might have the same interests, but does one have the same ability or opportunity to enjoy them at 65 plus?

Since the 1940s, considerable emphasis has been

placed on the development of methods of extracting quantitative scores for 'adjustment' from subjects at various age levels. Cavan and colleagues (1949) reported the use of the Adult Activity Schedule. This inventory 'Your Attitudes and Activities' consists of some statements which are checked, others answered by 'yes' or 'no', while others have a four or five point intensity distribution. Categories covered in the inventory include health, family, friends, leisure, and recreation clubs and organisations, employment history, financial security, early life, and attitudes. The inventory was despatched to a total of 8,441 individuals geographically distributed over the entire United States. This sample was a fairly close representation of the population of the United States aged 60 years and over, with the exception that a much smaller representation of rural farm subjects was obtained. Subscores for the following categories were calculated: leisure activities (including organisations), religious activities, intimate contacts (friends and family), health, and security. The authors devoted considerable attention to the reliability and validity of the inventory and conclude that although improvements could be made, both reliability and validity are high enough to warrant the use of the scale. For instance, the correlation between ratings of adjustment made by two to five judges and scores on the schedule, range from 0·53 to 0·78. In the sample studies, increasing age was associated with a decrease in the amount of close companionship, in less participation in many activities as shown by attendance at meetings and in fewer number of hobbies and plans for the future. There was also an increase in physical handicaps, illness, and nervousness, and a decrease in feeling of satisfaction with health. Religious activities and dependence upon religion increased with age, whereas feelings of happiness, usefulness, zest, and interest in life decreased. In general, the older subjects responded with lower median attitude scores indicating *poorer adjustment*. An increased feeling of economic security, despite a lower amount of income, was reported by many of the respondents. Sex differences in adjustment were also apparent; for instance, women reported more physical handicaps, illness, nervous and neurotic symptoms, and accidents than men. Women had more religious activity and more favourable attitudes toward religion than did men, but were less happy than men.

A number of other studies have compared adjustment scores on the above questionnaire between specified groups of older people. Havighurst and Shanas (1950) obtained data on 28 members of the Fossils Club, a retired men's club in Washington D.C. composed of former professional or adminis-

trative people. Responses were obtained from 30 per cent of the total membership of the club with a mean age of 73 years. This group of subjects showed much better adjustment to old age than that observed in the general population. The important factors seem to be economic security, relatively late retirement, and congenial housing and living arrangements. Other studies on retired YMCA secretaries and public-school teachers have shown a wide range in adjustment patterns (Britton, 1949). Older people living in institutions were found by Pan (1950) to have lower adjustment scores on this inventory than those living in the community. All these studies suffer from methodological difficulties, such as lack of control for educational background, socioeconomic status, cultural pattern of the community, and home influences. *They have, however, served to focus attention on the many variables involved in the adequate social adjustment of older people* and in defining what one may consider abnormal.

Fried (1949) found that inactivity in elderly people was six times greater among the lower economic groups than in the higher. The elderly people interviewed complained of inactivity and indicated preference for doing something. A desire for continued activity has important social implications and indicates the need for re-education both in individuals and in the community with respect to attitudes toward older people. It also seems evident that our educational system has not succeeded in giving individuals inner resources for continued expansion of interests and activities throughout life, particularly in the latter decades.

The interrelationships between 'social' and 'personal' adjustment evident in the earlier work continue to provide a need for more detailed analysis in this area. Moberg (1953) reported that those old people who had formerly been leaders in the church were better adjusted than those who had never held leadership positions, but that there was no difference between church members and non-church members in personal adjustment to old age. Older people must adapt to many new life demands such as retirement, death of family and friends, changes in standards and styles of living, as well as to personal, psychological, and biological changes. These important changes are largely initiated by forces beyond the individual's control. It would also appear that individual differences in social roles determine many features of adjustment in old age (Phillips, 1957; Beckman et al., 1958; Pappas and Silver, 1958). Empirically there appears to be a significant correlation between the number of social roles and adjustment: activity and interpersonal contact may be prophylactic for many problems of later life (Shepard, 1955; Havighurst, 1957; 1959).

The onset of illness in late life does have marked effects on personal and social adjustment (Mack, 1953; Kahn *et al.*, 1954), but there is also considerable evidence that persons lacking successful adjustment in early or middle life continue to do so in old age (Shepard, 1955; Slater and Roth, 1969).

The measurement of *personal adjustment in terms of happiness* as well as social activity has also attracted considerable attention, though the reports offer conflicting results. Early studies by Morgan (1937) and Landis (1942), based on interview material, concluded that most people of advanced age considered the happiest period of their lives to have been that between 25 and 45 years. Kuhlen (1948), on the other hand, in a study of 300 adults between the ages of 20 and 80, reported that happiness ratings tended to increase up to the 20s and 30s and to decrease thereafter. The primary sources of unhappiness were bereavement and poor health. Though most of the foregoing subjects reported higher degrees of happiness at early ages, it is important to note that only 3 per cent of the aged people (two-thirds being 70 or over) interviewed by Gardner (1948), reported that they were unhappy. Furthermore, wide individual differences in happiness ratings were found by Lawton (1943). One should remember, however, that happiness is almost certainly a multi-dimensional quality that requires precise definition, and dependence on retrospective information about happiness in previous decades of life is hazardous. There is also considerable evidence that happiness and successful adjustment, both personal and social, in old age are intimately bound up with physical and mental health. Lebo (1953) and Mack (1953) found that happiness in old age depended on health and minimal financial support. Happy old people were more alert and flexible than those who were unhappy. Interestingly, the ill did not see themselves as different from normal, and the hopefully ill were better adjusted.

There are obviously many difficulties in assessing and defining 'adjustment' or 'successful ageing' as it is undoubtedly a multidimensional concept both in terms of definition and aetiology. However, the work of Havighurst (1949; 1950; 1953; 1963) and his colleagues gives many useful indications of the nature and for the measurement of old age adjustment. To quote Havighurst (1963)

'The practical purpose of gerontology is to help people live better in their later years. However, we do not have general agreement on what good living in later years is. We agree on some of the determining conditions of good living, such as health, economic security, presence of friends and family, but there is disagreement on the actual signs of good living in the feelings and behaviour of a person as he grows older. Some believe that good living in old age consists of maintaining activity and involvement as in middle age, others believe that good living for elderly people is just the opposite—a retirement to a rocking chair and decrease of activity as the years pass by. Thus, the definition of successful ageing may appear to require a value judgement on which people are bound to disagree.'

As he also points out, however, it should be possible to develop an instrument to measure the various aspects of success in ageing or in old age. Havighurst and Albrecht published a scale in 1953 based on a study of public opinion concerning the activities of older people.

Cavan *et al.* (1949) and Havighurst's own work mentioned earlier (1953; 1957) and later developments have concentrated on the definition of successful ageing in terms of social competence. Several measures recognise the inner and outer aspects of successful ageing, in particular the Chicago Attitude Inventory (Cavan *et al.*, 1949; Havighurst and Albrecht, 1953; Havighurst, 1957). Scores are a combination of attitudes about activities in several areas and inner feelings of happiness independent, to some extent, of outward behaviour. This area has been extended by the work of Bernice Neugarten in 50 to 80 year olds in the Kansas City study. The research group began by examining measures of adjustment morale used by other investigators. After extensive interview assessments, they produced an operational definition of life satisfaction in five components: (1) zest *vs* apathy (2) resolution and fortitude (3) goods of fit between desired and achieved goals (4) positive self-concept and mood tone. Each component can be rated on a five point scale (Neugarten *et al.*, 1961; Havighurst, 1963) and the ratings can be added to get a life satisfaction rating ranging from 5 to 25.

Two forms of self-report instruments are now available from the work of this research team (Havighurst, 1963): (1) *Life Satisfaction Index A*—an attitude inventory of 20 items which correlates 0·58 with the interview scale, $N = 90$, mean 12·4, SD 4·4 (2) *Life Satisfaction Index B*—consists of six open-ended and six check list items scored 0, 1, or 2 which correlates 0·71 with the rating scale, $N = 92$, mean 15·1, SD 4·7. A and B correlate 0·73, total mean 27·6, SD 6·7.

These procedures for measuring life satisfaction all depend on inner definitions of successful ageing. They can be used to study the effects of social and economic conditions on people, to assess their life satisfaction. The definition of successful ageing as satisfaction with present and past life does not favour either of the apparently rival, though one might add not mutually exclusive, activity and disengagement theories.

The activity theory is favoured by most of the practical workers in gerontology. They believe that people should maintain the activities and attitudes of middle age as long as possible and then find substitutes for the activities they must give up—for work when they are forced to retire, for clubs and associations, for friends and loved ones whom they lose by death. Disengagement theory is based on the observation that as people grow older they generally curtail the activities of middle age. As stated by Cumming and McCaffrey (1960):

'This theory starts from the commonsense observation that in America, the old person is less involved in the life around him than he was when he was younger and proceeds without making assumptions about the desirability of this fact. Ageing in the modal person is thought of in this theory as a mutual withdrawal or disengagement which takes place between the ageing person and others in the social systems to which he belongs. He may withdraw more markedly from some classes of people and remain relatively close to others. This withdrawal may be accompanied at the outset by increased preoccupation with himself. When the ageing process is complete, the equilibrium which existed in middle life between the individual and his society has given way to a new equilibrium characterised by a greater distance and an altered type of relationship. In a previous report, we have presented data which suggest that one of the early stages of disengagement occurs when the ageing individual withdraws emotional investment from the environment. We have thought of the inner process as being an ego change in which object cathexis is reduced; this results in an appearance of self-centredness, and an orientation to others which betrays less sense of mutual obligation. This is accompanied by a somewhat freer and more expressive manner. The fully disengaged person can be thought of as having transferred much of his cathexis to his own inner life; his memories, his fantasies, his image of himself as someone who was something, and did accomplish things.'

There is no doubt that disengagement does take place with ageing, but proponents of the activity theory regard this as a result of society's withdrawal from the ageing person against his will and desire. However, the disengagement theory stated by Cumming and co-workers (1960) regards disengagement as a natural process the ageing person accepts and desires. They speak of disengagement as being 'primary intrinsic, and secondarily responsive'.

Cumming *et al.* (1960) have stated and tested three hypotheses about the process of disengagement—

1. Rate of interaction and variety of interaction will lessen with age.
2. Changes in amount, and variety, of interaction will be accompanied by concomitant changes in perception of the size of the life space.
3. A change in the quality of interaction will accompany decrease in the social life space, from absorption with others to absorption with self, and from evaluative to carefree.

One might suggest, however, that unless the process of disengagement is so thoroughly intrinsic that there is no stopping or delaying it, there is a considerable margin of social and individual choice between activity and disengagement, and within this area it would be useful to test the two theories to find out how they are related to life satisfaction. Life satisfaction may be positively related to activity for some people and to disengagement for others. A person with an active, achieving, and outward-directed way of life style will be best satisfied to continue this into old age with only slight diminution. Other people with a passive, dependent, home-centred way of life will be best satisfied with disengagement. Cumming and McCaffrey (1960) suggested this when they said that there may be 'important non-modal groups of the die-with-your-boots-on school. We do not yet know who they are except that there is evidence that academics do not disengage, in the sense that we are using it here, to the same degree that, for example, skilled workmen or clerical workers do'. Reichard *et al.* (1962) in a study of working-class men found three types of successful agers, one active, one passive, and one mature, who almost certainly would be differentiated if their activity-disengagement processes were studied. Indeed, disengagement itself refers primarily to the weakening of the bonds that tie the individual to his social environment. It may result in rocking-chair inaction, but it may also result in a carefree attitude combined with assertiveness and activity.

These complex interrelationships between inner satisfaction with life and outer behaviour in society need careful investigation in the elderly. We can thank workers for their efforts, but wish for considerably more *evidence* on large representative samples of the aged and hope for longitudinal studies to help unravel the confusions in this area which are not only theoretically fascinating to psychologists, but of *vital* practical importance to a society with an increasing aged population. The effect of retirement, for example, shows interesting variations between classes, across cultures and within economic conditions. In Great Britain 70 per cent of men compulsorily retired at 65 would have continued working if it had been possible, though only 25 per cent actually tried to find work (Clark, 1959). On the other hand, in America, where pensions are less generally available, Gordon (1960) found men tended to retire only when ill health forced the issue. Furthermore, forced retirement will differentially affect those who have enjoyed rather than those who have tolerated or disliked their work. The evidence from Emerson (1959), Thompson *et al.* (1960) and Heron (1963) suggested that there is a 'retirement impact' that varies with occupational class. When and under what conditions one might ask does the 'retirement impact' become abnormal?

Some recent studies have cast doubt on the necessity of a polarised activity *vs* disengagement approach to understanding life satisfaction or abnormality in old age. What are successful or unsuccessful, normal or abnormal aged types? An interview project by Bühler (1961) named four groups of older people: (1) those who want to rest and relax, (2) those who wish to be active, (3) those dissatisfied with the past but resigned, (4) those who have led meaningless lives and are now frustrated, guilty, and regretful. On the other hand, Reichard *et al.* (1962) in their book *Personality and Ageing* suggested three types of 'successful' agers; one active, one passive, and one mature (ego-integrated). There were two unsuccessful types: extra-punitive and self-rejective. 'Life satisfaction', 'activity', and 'disengagement' would obviously mean different things for each of these groups. A review article by Jones (1961) pointed out that there are individual life styles (active, passive, social, asocial, etc.), environmental pressures (economic, social, familial, etc.) and, last but not least, biological deteriorations and disabilities, to be taken into account when defining normal and abnormal, successful or unsuccessful ageing. Because of the ways in which pressures and personality interact, it seems likely that we shall learn most about the aged by a thorough analysis of the components or the structure of aged personality and continuous longitudinal investigations.

Personality Measurement in Old Age

The identification, description, and presentation of adequate techniques for the measurement of personality in the aged has lagged behind that of cognitive assessment in the elderly. The development of more adequate personality assessment procedures by Cattell, Eysenck, and others gives hope for the future, but one cannot help but be disappointed by the small amount of research in this area on old people. It is an area of investigation, for example, where latitudinal studies, because of the problems of sampling and natural selection, could give extremely misleading results. The difficulties, particularly the considerable expense of longitudinal studies, must be accepted if we are to make any real progress.

Emotionality or neuroticism was one of the first most important personality characteristics of the elderly to receive the attention of investigators. Willoughby in 1938 concluded that neuroticism increased significantly between the sixth and eight decades of life. He suggested that old age was one of the periods of greatest stress for both sexes, married or single, and noted the important, but often forgotten point, that the diagnostic significance of a particular behaviour or scores on test items may vary significantly with age. However, even now, few methods of measuring personality have any, let alone satisfactory, normative data for the elderly. The personality theorists have given little or no attention to changes in old age or even to adequately describing old age personality until very recently. Watson, in a review of the situation in 1954, suggested that research of personality in the elderly was in a naturalistic, exploratory stage rather than at a theoretically or experimentally based level.

Investigations using *projective techniques of personality measurement have been reported*. The developmental changes accompanying increasing age were mentioned rather briefly by Rorschach (1942), who commented that 'the older individual loses the capacity for introversion and becomes more coartated or constricted'. He described further influences of age as an increase in stereotype and a decrease in the freedom of associations, and claimed that the protocols of normal subjects 70 to 80 years of age closely resembled those of cases of dementia simplex.

A study by Klopfer (1946) reported the results of individual examinations of fifty people over 60 years of age, thirty of whom were institutionalised and twenty of whom lived outside an institution. Personality characteristics describing the groups included a slowing down in the intellectual sphere both in terms of productivity and efficiency. The senescents had difficulty in thinking conventionally and at the same time showed stereotyped thought processes. For the most part the intellectual ties to reality were adequate, but somewhat loose. Their capacity for making use of inner resources seemed diminished, and emotional responsiveness tended either to be egocentric and labile or highly restricted. The ability to establish satisfactory relationships with others was considerably reduced. Klopfer also mentioned that, while there were some differences between his institutionalised and non-institutionalised samples, the patterns suggested more similarities than differences between the two groups.

Another Rorschach study was reported by Prados and Fried (1947) who examined 35 persons ranging in age from 50 to 80 years and reported results in terms of trends for the three decades. By this division, they hoped to learn something about the evolution of changes in personality structure. Their findings were similar to those of Klopfer, except for their observation of greater productivity and more frequent use of both movement and colour. They suggested that with increasing age, impoverishment of the creative intellectual faculties occurred, with the oldest subjects resigned to this deficit, but the younger groups still showing some anxiety about it. They also stated that the capacity for emotional responsiveness and control over instinctual demands diminished with age, resulting in a return to some of the primitive manifestations of early childhood.

Davidson and Kruglov (1952), who were concerned only with institutionalised subjects, administered the Rorschach to 46 men and women, ranging in age from 61 to 91. Means of the various scoring categories were reported for the total group and for the younger and older subgroups. In addition, the authors scored all the protocols on the seventeen Davidson adjustment signs which had been established on younger groups. The personality characteristics of this elderly group were listed as decreased productivity and drive, faulty perception of reality, bizarre thought processes, and decreased capacity for creative and original thinking. Emotional responsiveness was diminished, and general adjustment was less adequate than that found in younger subjects, with the women showing better adjustment than the men. The outstanding formal attributes of the records upon which these interpretations were based included low numbers of responses, overemphasis of form responses, high numbers of poor form responses, relatively few movement responses, extreme paucity of responses to colour, and a limited range of interests. However, their conclusion that the group showed less adequate adjustment than younger groups may be open to question, as in their sample the average number of adjustment signs was 8 out of 17, while in younger samples it has been found to be 9, a difference of only one point. Caldwell's (1954) paper presents similar results for 47 women aged 61 to 92 with a mean IQ of 85. She comments

'A comparison of the similarity in test protocols as reported by the various investigators provides one

method of evaluating the Rorschach for use in personality research with the aged. That is, the fact that different samples have yielded roughly comparable quantitative results indicates that whatever is being measured appears with a fairly respectable degree of consistency. One can say little, however, of the quantitative accuracy of the data in terms of evaluating personality in the aged. Furthermore, the titles of the three studies reviewed, namely, "Personality Patterns of Old Age", "Personality Structure of the Older Age Groups", and "Personality Characteristics of the Institutionalised Aged", respectively, clearly illustrate how Rorschach findings are assumed to be synonymous with personality characteristics. It is significant to note that none of the studies stated as its explicit purpose the establishment of norms for older groups, although it is highly probable that this was implicit in all of them. Logically, it would seem that this should come first.'

Light and Amick presented a paper on Rorschach responses in normal aged, and follow-up studies have been published by Ames (1960a,b) and Vinson (1961). Both suggested that personality changes with age in the aged. Sixty-one elderly subjects aged 70 to 102 were retested by Ames after a four- to five-year period. A restriction in the number responses, decreased variety of content, less use of colour, but increased F and M type responses were reported. Vinson's work showed that 20 geriatric patients without organic brain damage became more stimulus bound, but still had adequate emotional adjustment after one year.

The conclusions given in all the studies, as well as the meaning implied in the titles, have reflected this willing transposition of the assumed rationale of the Rorschach scoring categories for younger into the older age groups. Implicit in all the investigations is the fact that more credit has been given to the integrity of the test than to the integrity of the subjects. That is, the assumption is made that the rationale of the test variables does not change with age and, since different profiles are found at different age levels, these must represent change within the individual. This may well be true, but in view of the lack of conclusive evidence, it seems that one should more parsimoniously assume that either is equally plausible.

The Thematic Apperception Test (Murray, 1943) (TAT) has also been used on the aged in an effort to describe and understand their personality. A series of studies from the Kansas City project followed up the work of Peck (1956), Peck and Berkowitz (1959), and others who had not found statistically significant age differences in the analysis of ratings of flexibility, collection, mental flexibility, ego transcendence, body transcendences, body satisfaction or sexual integration from six TAT cards with 40 to 64 year olds. Neugarten argued that the same information from the TAT given by a 40- or a 70-year-old may have a very different meaning. She investigated 131 working and middleclass men and women 40 to 70 years of age. The older person felt that the world was more complex and dangerous, and that he or she was passively manipulated by it. The elderly felt that they were no longer in control of the situation; ego qualities were contracted and turned inward. Sex differences were also seen. A further study by Gutmann and co-workers (1959) using four standard TAT cards on over 60-year-olds suggested that these men had resolved many conflicts, stories were conforming, friendly, and mild. Aggression was ascribed only to the external world.

In their 1960 study, Rosen and Neugarten looked at the hypothesis that four dimensions of ego functioning diminish in effectiveness with age. The Thematic Apperception Test was used on 144 subjects aged 40 to 71 years divided by age, sex, and social class; the older subjects showed fewer extra characteristics in their stories, used less conflict, less strong emotion, and described less vigorous activities. Neugarten (1963) concluded that personality does change significantly with age to give way to passive mastery of the situation in 60 to 70 year olds and that important sex differences remain. Lakin and Eisdorfer (1960) showed a similar pattern of personality in the aged with the Reitman stick figures and Dean (1962), in her questionnaire investigation of 200 aged men, 50 to 95, also commented on the decrease in emotional responsiveness, anger, and imitation with age. However, the studies of aged on the MMPI, 16PF, and MPI to be discussed in detail later suggest that average or normative levels of emotionality, anxiety, and the like are increased in old age. It is possible that the average levels of emotionality are high, though they may not show themselves in the same type of emotional behaviour as seen at younger age levels.

Recent years have seen the introduction of psychometric personality questionnaires into research on old age personality measurement. This work is still in its infancy, for the practical and financial difficulties in this area of investigation are considerable. Indeed, the available data are far from adequate. The Minnesota Multiphasic Personality Inventory has been used in most of the investigations and has highlighted the need for caution when applying tests to the aged that have not been specifically standardised on the appropriate populations. Application of this large inventory to old people is in itself a somewhat difficult task and no

doubt accounts for the limited extent of publication in this area, though one has the impression that the MMPI enjoys extensive clinical use, particularly in the USA.

Hathaway and McKinley (1956) reported that on D and Pt scales the mean of their 56 to 65-year-old male sample of 13 deviated from the mean of the general population standardisation group. MMPI T scores were presented by Calden and Hokanson (1959) on 15 TB patients aged 60 to 69 along with these for younger age groups. They noted the significant elevation of Hs, D, and Si scaled scores in the old age sample and stressed the need for age-related normative data.

Several investigations have been interested in personality changes with age on the MMPI (Brozeck, 1955; Aaronson, 1958, 1960, 1964; Calden and Hokanson, 1959; Coppinger et al., 1963; Edwards and Wine, 1963; Hardyck, 1964), but have presented only limited normative data on samples beyond 65 years of age. The work of Aaronson (1958; 1960; 1964) on an MMPI ageing index also highlights the need for information about personality in old age. The first full-scale attempt to present normative data on the aged was by Swenson (1961) who reported on the validity and basic clinical scales of the MMPI from the records of 95 subjects of both sexes, aged 60+. Kornetsky (1963) administered the MMPI to 43 aged males and found significant elevations on the D and Mf scales. This tendency for a rise in D scale score with advancing age had also been reported by Canter et al. (1962).

British normative data on the MMPI were published from a community investigation carried out on a sample of the aged (70+) resident in Newcastle-upon-Tyne. The full card form of the MMPI was administered to 83 subjects representing both sexes who were selected at random from the aged community sample of Kay et al. (1964a,b) which was selected to represent socio-economic groupings in Newcastle-upon-Tyne. The questionnaire items were read to each subject during two sessions in his own home.

Table 18.10 presents the means and standard deviations in terms of the standard K corrected T scores for each of the validity and basic clinical scales for the investigations available.

The 1965 Britton and Savage data showed significant deviations ($p < 0.01$) on all except the Pd and Si scales from the standard MMPI normative data which had a mean of 50 and a standard deviation of 10 on each scale. The means of the K, D, and Sc scales are raised by more than one standard deviation and the means of Hs and Hy scales by more than two standard deviations.

A comparison between the Swenson (1961),

Table 18.10. Personality Assessment in the Aged:
Minnesota Multiphasic Personality Inventory

	McKinley and Hathaway 1956	Calden and Hokansen 1959	Swenson 1961		Kornetsky 1963	Britton and Savage 1965	Uecker 1969
N	13	15	66 (geriatric)	95 (normal)	43	83	3 0 (chronic brain syndrome)
Age	56–65	60–69		71·4	70+	70+	65+
L	—	51·73	7·50	6·137	5·44	41·3	—
F	—	57·67	9·86	4·432	5·65	54·8	—
K	—	48·27	15·91	14·389	14·16	61·5	—
Hs	—	67·53	62·23	57·95	14·49	73·2	62·97
D	21·46	67·20	65·18	59·21	22·23	67·4	66·70
Hy	—	57·93	61·26	55·91	19·91	72·5	56·80
Pd	—	57·40	62·71	51·02	20·47	49·6	64·47
Mf	—	53·73	57·39	55·62	25·63	56·8	59·53
Pa	—	53·40	65·85	52·43	8·98	54·5	67·20
Pt	12·38	52·27	59·00	53·17	24·65	58·1	67·77
Sc	—	53·67	65·70	52·45	24·81	62·3	76·73
Ma	—	56·53	57·24	47·22	18·41	42·3	67·83
Si	—	56·80	60·07	56·54	29·05	47·5	56·50

Kornetsky (1963), and Britton and Savage (1965) data shows the British sample as having higher scores than those obtained by the American subjects, but the profile patterns to be similar. Even allowing for any possible sampling bias, the results presented confirm the suggestion that the standard normative data for the MMPI should not be applied to aged subjects.

An interesting study has recently been reported by Uecker (1969) on the comparability of two methods of administering the MMPI to brain-damaged geriatric patients. The two methods of card form and oral presentation, given to 30 highly selected elderly male patients with a diagnosis of chronic brain syndrome, did not result in any significant scale differences. However, the test-retest reliability was very low, correlations ranging from 0·43 to 0·70 and the authors concluded that the use of the MMPI on elderly brain-damaged patients was not justified. It might be interesting to add here that an attempt by Britton and Savage to administer the Cattell 16PF scale to 20 elderly people living in the community, but diagnosed 'organic' was even less successful; only six were able to complete the inventory, even though it was read to them.

There are, however, other considerations to be taken into account when assessing the value of the MMPI as an instrument for assessing old age personality. What is the structure of personality it measures? Several recent studies have drawn attention to changes in personality as measured on the MMPI and attempts to interpret consistent trends in the personality characteristics of the elderly (Slater and Scarr, 1964; Gynther and Shimkunas, 1966; Postema and Schell, 1967).

The factorial studies of the MMPI by Kassebaum and associates (1959) have provided a basis for comparison of structure across a wide age range. With the use of factor-analytic procedures that facilitated comparison of results, a basic similarity of structure was found between young and old samples. The major factors of 'ego weakness *vs* ego strength' and 'introversion *vs* extraversion' appeared in both analyses. However, in the aged, a factor of 'dissociated personality', with a strong somatic emphasis was interpolated between the above factors. This finding is of interest in the context of personality change with age suggested by Birren (1964). Successful personality adaptation in old age is thought to depend on a relationship between stable, long-term components of personality rather than on those components that are more sensitive to the ageing processes. In old age a somatic emphasis might be expected in the latter, reflecting physiological change. This could be evident in MMPI factor-analyses as a factor similar to the 'dissociated personality' identified by Slater and Scarr (1964). However, the aged sample used by Slater and Scarr, although obtained from a non-hospitalised, normal population, was biased towards subjects of high socio-economic status and was thus not wholly representative.

Factor analysis of data from a community aged study by Britton and Savage (1969) yielded three major factors in 83 male and female subjects mean age 75·8, SD 3·7: (1) a general factor of psychopathology, (2) social withdrawal, and (3) aggressive-asocial reaction. These are not directly related to those described by Slater and Scarr (1964) and even less to those for the younger subjects of Kassebaum

Table 18.11. Personality Assessment in the Aged:
Maudsley Personality Inventory (*from* Bolton 1967)

	N	Age	Neuroticism (N)		Extraversion (E)		Correlation of E with N
			M	SD	M	SD	
Normals	29	73·7	20·0	11·2	25·8	8·2	−0·11 (ns)
Affectives	42	68·5	24·2	13·1	24·0	8·9	−0·22 (ns)
Schizophrenics	31	69·7	18·7	10·8	22·3	8·0	−0·01 (ns)
Organics	42	74·3	26·8	9·8	25·8	8·0	−0·18 (ns)
All Subjects	144	71·5	22·9	11·7	24·5	8·3	−0·12 (ns)

et al. (1959). There are, however, some underlying similarities. The first factor in the present analysis included certain features of their 'ego-weakness *vs* ego-strength' and 'dissociated personality' factors. In addition, the above second and third factors appear to resemble the 'fusion factor', *A*, 'acceptance of vulnerability *vs* defensiveness' proposed by Slater and Scarr (1964). 'Social withdrawal' may relate to passive acceptance of, and integration within, the changing environment, while 'aggressive, asocial reaction' reflects a defensive reaction to social change.

A study by Garside and co-workers (1965) outlined the factor structure of psychiatric material derived from the Newcastle-upon-Tyne aged sample. Four recognisable factors emerged from their Principal Component analysis: (*a*) general illness, (*b*) social isolation, (*c*) organic-functional, (*d*) income and social class. The first two factors show close general agreement with those of Britton and Savage from the MMPI (1969). Garside *et al.* rotated their third factor to emphasise organic-functional diagnostic differentiation; and the 'aggressive, asocial reaction', third factor in the present MMPI analysis, reflects a similarity of content.

The structure of personality in Britton and Savage's (1969) non-hospitalised aged sample would appear to emphasise their continued ability to adapt to physiological and environmental changes associated with advancing age. It is evident that administration of the Inventory and similar personality measures has much to offer in the quest for greater understanding of personality in old age. In particular, studies involving pathological groups might be expected to show a restriction in the flexibility of personality adaptation. Greater understanding of the underlying processes of personality and its change with age would be expected to add much to the diagnostic efficiency of the MMPI or new scales derived from it. For example, on the basis of their factor analysis of the MMPI, Britton and Savage (1967) have proposed a screening test for mental illness in the aged. It consists of a simple 'yes-no' answer, 15 item scale derived from a general factor

and item analysis of the MMPI. The scale measures general psychopathology and a cut-off point of 6+ suggests that mental illness is present. The scale was validated against psychiatric diagnosis, 95 per cent of those diagnosed mentally ill on clinical criteria were identified as such by the Britton and Savage aged mental health scale.

The paucity of studies on the aged with Cattell's and Eysenck's well-developed measures of personality assessment is of some considerable concern. Lynn in 1964 discussed the implications of Eysenck's theory of personality and age. He argues that the behaviour of older persons is like that of extraverts on a number of laboratory tests, but that their behaviour patterns are like those of introverts. Evidence on the responses of 144 normal and mentally ill aged to a questionnaire measure of neuroticism and extraversion is provided by Bolton (1967). The Maudsley Personality Inventory data can be seen in Table 18.11. Surprisingly, the *E* scale scores for normals, affectives, schizophrenics and organics were not significantly different from one another, nor were organics distinguishable even from normals on extraversion. On the other hand, organics did differ from both the normal and schizophrenic groups on the neuroticism scale. This high organic *N* score confirms the work of Choppy and Eysenck (1963). The high *N* score for the affectives is not surprising as the group was mainly aged depressives.

No normative data on Cattell's 16PF could be presented. Byrd (1959) suggested that anxiety increased with age on Cattell's measure and Sealy (1965) used the 16PF on several thousand Americans aged between 16 to 70, but separate data for the aged are not available. It was suggested, however, that men and women become more depressed and gloomy (F), more adventurous and outgoing (H), more unconventional (M) and more tough-minded (I) with age. Sex differences also emerged—the women became less dominant (E), the men more radical. Sealey also described interesting pre- and post-four-year-old patterns of change. We await, hopefully and with interest, more data on the aged.

REFERENCES

AARONSON, B. S. (1958) Age and sex influences on MMPI profile peak in an abnormal population. *J. consult. Psychol.*, **22**, 203–206.

AARONSON, B. S. (1960) A dimension of personality change with ageing. *J. clin. Psychol.*, **16**, 63–65.

AARONSON, B. S. (1964) Ageing, personality change and psychiatric diagnosis. *J. Gerontol.*, **19**, 144–148.

ACHILLES, EDITH M. (1917) Experimental studies in recall and recognition. *Arch. Psychol.*, **6**, No. 44.

ALBERT, E. (1964) Senile Demenz und Alzheimersche Krankheit als Ansdruck des gleichen Krankheits geschehens. *Fortschr. Neurol. Psychiat.*, **32**, 625.

ALEXANDER, D. A. (1970) The application of the Graham-Kendall Memory-for-Designs Test to elderly normal and psychiatric groups. *Brit. J. soc. clin. Psychol.*, **9**, 85–6.

AMES, L. B. (1960a) Age changes in the Rorschach responses of individual elderly subjects. *J. genet. Psychol.*, **97**, 257–85.

AMES, L. B. (1960b) Age changes in the Rorschach responses of a group of elderly individuals. *J. genet. Psychol.*, **97**, 287–315.

ANDERSON, J. E. (1949) *The Psychology of Development and Personal Adjustment*. New York: Henry Holt.

ANDERSON, J. E. (Ed.) (1956) *Psychological Aspects of Aging*. Washington, D.C.: Amer. Psychol. Assoc.

BABCOCK, HARRIET (1930) An experiment in measurement of mental deterioration. *Arch. Psychol. N.Y.*, No. 117.

BABCOCK, HARRIET and LEVY, LYDIA (1941) *Manual of Directions for the Revised Examination of the Measurement of Efficiency of Mental Functioning*. Chicago: Stoelting.

BAYLEY, NANCY (1956) The place of longitudinal studies in research on intellectual factors in ageing. In *Psychological Aspects of Aging* (Ed. Anderson, J. E.). Washington, D.C.: Amer. Psychol. Assoc.

BECKMAN, R. O., WILLIAMS, C. O., and FISHER, G. C. (1958) Adjustment to life in later maturity. *Geriatrics*, **13**, 662–67.

BENDER, LAURETTA (1938) A visual-motor test and its clinical use. *Amer. J. Orthopsychiat.*, Monogr. No. 3.

BENDER, LAURETTA (1946) *Instructions for the use of the Visual Motor Gestalt Test*. New York: Amer. Orthopsychiat. Assoc.

BENTON, A. L. (1946) *The Visual Retention Test*. New York: Psychological Corporation.

BENTON, A. L. (1963) *The Revised Visual Retention Test*, 3rd ed. Iowa City: Iowa State Univ., pp. 1–70.

BERGER, L., BERNSTEIN, A., KLEIN, E., COHEN, J., and LUCAS, A. (1964) Effects of ageing and pathology on the factorial structure of intelligence. *J. consult. Psychol.*, **28**, 199–207.

BERGMANN, K. (1966) Observations on the causation of neurotic disorder in old age with special reference to physical illness. *Proc. 7th Int. Congr. Geront.*, Vienna. pp. 623.

BERKOWITZ, B. (1953) The W-B performance of white males past age 50. *J. Gerontol.*, **8**, 76–80.

BERKOWITZ, B. and GREEN, R. I. (1963) Changes in intellect with age: Longitudinal study of Wechsler-Bellevue Scores. *J. genet. Psychol.*, **103**, 3–21.

BEVERFELT, E., NYGARD, M., and NORDVIK, R. (1964) Factor analysis of WAIS performance of elderly Norwegians. *J. Gerontol.*, **19**, 49–53.

BIRREN, J. E. (1955) Age changes in speed of simple responses and perception and their significance for complex behaviour. In *Old Age in the Modern World*. Report of the Third Congress of the International Association of Gerentology. London: Livingstone.

BIRREN, J. E. (Ed.) (1959) *Handbook of Aging and the Individual*. Chicago: Univ. of Chicago Press.

BIRREN, J. E. (1960) Psychological Aspects of Ageing. *Ann. Rev. Psychol.*, **2**, 161–198.

BIRREN, J. E. (1964) *The Psychology of Aging*. Englewood Cliffs: Prentice-Hall.

BIRREN, J. E. and BOTWINICK, J. (1951) The relation of writing speed to age and to the senile psychoses. *J. consult. Psychol.*, **15**, 243–249.

BIRREN, J. E., BUTLER, H. N., GREENHOUSE, S. W., BOROLOFF, L., and YARROW, M. R. (1963) *Human Aging: a Biological and Behavioural Study*. Bethesda, Md.: U.S. Dept. of Health, Education & Welfare.

BLESSED, G., TOMLINSON, B. E., and ROTH, M. (1968) The association between quantitative measures of dementia and of degenerative changes in the cerebral grey matter of elderly subjects. *Brit. J. Psychiat.*, **114**, 797–811.

BLEULER, E. (1916) *Textbook of Psychiatry*. Berlin: Springer.

BLEULER, E. (1943) The Clinical Features of the Late Schizophrenics. *Fortschr. neurol. psychiat.*, **15**, 259.

BOLTON, N. (1967) A psychometric investigation of the psychiatric syndromes of old age: measures of intelligence, learning, memory, extraversion and neuroticism. Unpub. Ph.D. thesis, Univ. of Newcastle upon Tyne.

BOLTON, N., BRITTON, P. G., and SAVAGE, R. D. (1966) Some normative data on the WAIS and its indices in an aged population. *J. clin. Psychol.*, **22**, 184–8.

BOLTON, N., SAVAGE, R. D., and ROTH, M. (1967) The MWLT on an aged psychiatric population. *Brit. J. Psychiat.*, **113**, 1139–1140.

BOTWINICK, J. (1967) *Cognitive Processes in Maturity and Old Age*. New York: Springer.

BOTWINICK, J. and BIRREN, J. E. (1951a) Differential decline in the W-B subtest in the senile psychoses. *J. Gerontol.*, **6**, 365–368.

BOTWINICK, J. and BIRREN, J. E. (1951b) The measurement of intellectual decline in senile psychoses. *J. consult. Psychol.*, **15**, 145–150.

BREMER, J. (1951) A social psychiatric investigation of a small community in Northern Norway. *Acta Psychiat. Neurol., Kbh.*, Suppl. 62.

BRITTON, J. H. (1949) A study of the adjustment of retired school teachers. *Amer. Psychologist*, **4**, 308.

BRITTON, P. G. (1967) An investigation of cognitive and personality functions in a sample of the aged in the community. Unpubl. Ph.D. thesis, Univ. of Newcastle upon Tyne.

BRITTON, P. G. and SAVAGE, R. D. (1965) The MMPI and the aged—some normative data from a community sample. *Brit. J. Psychiat.*, **112**, 941–943.

BRITTON, P. G. and SAVAGE, R. D. (1966) A short form of the WAIS for use with the aged. *Brit. J. Psychiat.*, **112**, 417–418.

BRITTON, P. G. and SAVAGE, R. D. (1967) A short scale for the assessment of mental health in the community aged. *Brit. J. Psychiat.*, **113**, 521–23.

BRITTON, P. G. and SAVAGE, R. D. (1969) The factorial structure of the Minnesota Multiphasic Personality Inventory from an aged sample. *J. genet. Psychol.*, **114**, 13–17.

BRODY, M. B. (1942a) The measurement of dementia. *J. ment. Sci.*, **88**, 317–27.

BRODY, M. B. (1942b) A psychometric study of dementia. *J. ment. Sci.*, **88**, 512–533.

BROMLEY, D. B. (1953) Primitive forms of responses to the Matrices test. *J. ment. Sci.*, **99**, 374–393.

BROMLEY, D. B. (1966) Age differences in the Porteous Maze Tests. *Proc. 7th Internat. Cong. Geront.*, Vol. 6, 225–228. Wien: Wien Med. Akad.

BROZECK, J. (1955) Personality changes with age: an item analysis of the MMPI. *J. Gerontol.*, **10**, 194–206.

BUHLER, C. (1961) Old age and fulfillment of life with considerations of the use of time in old age. *Acta Psychol.*, **19**, 126–48.

BURDACH, K. F. (1890–1926) *Vom Baue und Leben des Gehirns.* Leipzig.

BURSTEIN, S. R. (1949) Aspects of the psychopathology of old age. *Brit. med. Bull.*, **6**, 63.

BUSSE, E. W., BARNES, R. H., FRIEDMAN, E. L., and KELLY, E. J. (1956) Psychological functioning of aged individuals with normal and abnormal electroencephalograms. I a study of non-hospitalized community volunteers. *J. nerv. ment. Dis.*, **124**, 135–141.

BYRD, E. (1959) Measured anxiety in old age. *Psychol. Rep.*, **5**, 439–40.

CAIRD, W. T., SANDERSON, R. F., and INGLIS, J. (1962). Cross validation of a learning test for use with elderly psychiatric patients. *J. ment. Sci.*, **108**, 368–370.

CALDEN, G. and HOKANSON, J. E. (1959) The influence of age on MMPI responses. *J. clin. Psychol.*, **15**, 194–5.

CALDWELL, BETTYE McD. (1954) The use of the Rorschach in personality research with the aged. *J. Gerontol.*, **9**, 316–23.

CANTER, A., DAY, E. W., IMBODEN, J. B., and CLUFF, J. E. (1962) The influence of age and health status on the MMPI scores of a normal population. *J. clin. Psychol.*, **18**, 71–3.

CAPSTICK, A. (1960) Recognition of emotional disturbance and the prevention of suicide. *Brit. med. J.*, **1**, 1179–1182.

CATTELL, R. B. (1943) The measurement of adult intelligence. *Psychol. Bull.*, **40**, 153–192.

CATTELL, R. B. (1957) *Personality and Motivation Structure and Measurement.* New York: Word Book.

CATTELL, R. B. (1963) The theory of fluid and crystallized intelligence: a critical experiment. *J. educ. Psychol.*, **54**, 1–22.

CAVAN, RUTH S., BURGESS, E. W., HAVIGHURST, R. J., and GOLDHAMER, H. (1949) *Personal Adjustment in Old Age.* Chicago: Science Research Associates.

CHESSER, E. S. (1965) A study of some aetiological factors in the affective disorders of old age. Unpub. dissertation, Institute of Psychiatry, London.

CHOPPY, M. and EYSENCK, H. J. (1963) Brain damage and depressant drugs; an experimental study of interaction. In *Experiments with Drugs* (Ed. Eysenck, H. J.). London: Pergamon Press, Ch. 12, 313–324.

CHOWN, SHEILA M. and HERON, A. (1965) Psychological aspects of ageing in man. *Ann. Rev. Psychol.*, **16**, 417–450.

CLARK, F. LEGROS (1959) *Age and the Working Lives of Men.* London: Nuffield Foundation.

CLEVELAND, S. and DYSINGER, D. (1944) Mental deterioration in senile psychosis. *J. abnorm. soc. Psychol.*, **39**, 368–372.

CLOW, H. E. (1940) A study of one hundred patients suffering from psychosis with cerebral arteriosclerosis. *Amer. J. Psychiat.*, **97**, 16–26.

CLOW, H. E. and ALLEN, E. B. (1951) Manifestations of psychoneuroses occurring in later life. *Geriatrics*, **6**, 31–39.

COHEN, J. (1957) The factorial structure of the WAIS between early adulthood and old age. *J. consult. Psychol.*, **21**, 283–90.

COMALLI, P. E. Jr. (1965) Cognitive functioning in a group of 80–90 year old men. *J. Gerontol.*, **20**, 14–17.

CONKEY, FRANCES (1933) The adaptation of fifty men and women to old age. *J. Home Economics*, **25**, 387–389.

COPPINGER, N. W., BORTNER, R. W., and SANCER, R. T. (1963) A factor analysis of psychological deficit. *J. Genet. Psychol.*, **103**, 23–43.

CORSELLIS, J. A. N. (1962) *Mental Illness and the Ageing Brain.* London: Oxford Univ. Press.

CUMMING, ELAINE, DEAN, LOIS R., NEWELL, D. S., and McCAFFREY, ISOBEL (1960) Disengagement—a tentative theory of ageing. *Sociometry*, **23**, 23–35.

CUMMING, ELAINE and McCAFFREY, ISOBEL (1960) Some conditions associated with morale among the ageing. Paper presented at the Annual Meeting of the American Psychopathological Association, New York.

DAVIDSON, H. H. and KRUGLOV, L. (1952) Personality characteristics in the institutionalized aged. *J. consult. Psychol.*, **16**, 5–12.

DAVIES, ANN D. M. (1965) The perceptual maze test in a normal population. *Percept. Mot. Skills*, **20**, 287–93.

DAVIES, ANN D. M. (1967) Age and the Memory for Designs Test. *Brit. J. soc. clin. Psychol.*, **6**, 228–233.

DAVIES, ANN D. M. (1968) Measures of mental deterioration in ageing and brain damage. *Interdiscipl. Topics Geront.*, **1**, 78–90.

DEAN, LOIS R. (1962) Ageing and the decline of affect. *J. Gerontol.*, **17**, 440–6.

DIBNER, A. S. and CUMMINS, J. F. (1961) Intellectual functioning in a group of normal octogenarians. *J. consult. Psychol.*, **25**, 137–41.

DONAHUE, WILMA (1949) Living through the older years. In *Living Through the Older Years* (Ed. Tibbits, C.) Ann Arbor, Michigan: Univ. of Michigan Press, pp. 63–84.

DOPPELT, J. E. and WALLACE, W. L. (1955) Standardization

of the WAIS scale for older persons. *J. abnorm. soc. Psychol.*, **51**, 312–20.

DORKEN, H. and GREENBLOOM, GRACE C. (1953) Psychological investigations of senile dementia II the Wechsler-Bellevue Adult Intelligence Scale. *Geriatrics*, **8**, 324–333.

EDWARDS, A. E. and WINE, D. B. (1963) Personality changes with age; their dependence on concomitant intellectual decline. *J. Gerontol.*, **18**, 182–184.

EISDORFER, C. (1963) The WAIS performance of the aged; a retest evaluation. *J. Gerontol.*, **18**, 169–72.

EISDORFER, C. and COHEN, L. D. (1961) The generality of the WAIS standardisation for the aged; a regional comparison. *J. abnorm. soc. Psychol.*, **62**, 520–527.

ELITHORN, A. (1955) A preliminary report on a perceptual maze test sensitive to brain damage. *J. neurol. neurosurg. Psychiat.*, **18**, 287–292.

EMERSON, A. R. (1959) The first year of retirement. *Occup. Psychol.*, **33**, 197–208.

ESSEN-MOLLER, E. (1956) Individual traits and morbidity in a Swedish rural population. *Acta psychiat. neurol. Scand.*, Suppl. 100.

EVANS, V. L. (1943) Convulsive shock therapy in elderly patients—risks and results. *Amer. J. Psychiat.*, **99**, 531–3.

EYSENCK, MARGARET D. (1945a) An exploratory study of mental organization in senility. *J. neurol. Psychiat.*, **8**, 15–21.

EYSENCK, MARGARET D. (1945b) A study of certain qualitative aspects of problem solving behaviour in senile dementia patients. *J. ment. Sci.*, **91**, 337–345.

EYSENCK, MARGARET D. (1946) The psychological aspects of ageing and senility. *J. ment. Sci.*, **92**, 171–181.

FELDMAN, F., SUSSELMAN, S., LIPETZ, B., and BARRERA, S. E. (1946) Electric shock therapy of elderly patients. *Arch. Neurol. Psychiat.*, **56**, 158–170.

FOULDS, G. A. and RAVEN, J. C. (1948) Normal changes in the mental abilities of adults as age advances. *J. ment. Sci.*, **94**, 133–142.

FOX, CHARLOTTE and BIRREN, J. E. (1950) The differential decline of subtest scores of the W-B intelligence scale in 60–69 year old individuals. *J. genet. Psychol.*, **77**, 313–317.

FRIED, EDRITA G. (1949) Attitudes of the older population groups toward activity and inactivity. *J. Gerontol.*, **4**, 141–51.

GARDNER, L. PEARL (1948) Attitudes and activities of the middle-aged and aged. *Amer. Psychologist*, **3**, 307.

GARSIDE, R. F., KAY, D. W. K., and ROTH, M. (1965) Old age mental disorders in Newcastle upon Tyne. Part III a factorial study of medical, psychiatric and social characteristics. *Brit. J. Psychiat.*, **111**, 939–46.

GELLERSTEDT, N. (1932–1933) Our knowledge of cerebral changes in normal involution of old age. *Uppsala Lak Fören Förh.*, **38**, 193.

GORDON, M. S. (1960) Changing patterns of retirement. *J. Gerontol.*, **15**, 300–4.

GRAHAM, FRANCES K. and KENDALL, BARBARA S. (1946) Performance of brain damaged cases on a memory-for-designs test. *J. abnorm. soc. Psychol.*, **41**, 303–314.

GRAHAM, FRANCES K. and KENDALL, BARBARA S. (1960) *Memory for Designs Test.* New York: Psychological Test Specialists.

GRANICK, S. (1950) Studies of psychopathology in later maturity—a review. *J. Gerontol.*, **5**, 44–58.

GRASSI, J. R. (1947) The Fairfield Block Substitution Test for measuring intellectual impairment. *Psychiat. Quart.*, **21**, 474–85.

GREEN, R. F. and BERKOWITZ, B. (1964) Changes in intellect with age; II Factorial analysis of Wechsler-Bellevue scores. *J. genet. Psychol.*, **104**, 3–18.

GREEN, R. F. and BERKOWITZ, B. (1965) Changes in intellect with age; III The relationship of heterogeneous brain damage to achievement in older people. *J. genet. Psychol.*, **106**, 349–359.

GREWEL, F. (1953) Testing psychology of dementias. *Folia Psychiat. Neur.*, **56**, 305–339.

GRUENBERG, E. (1961) *A Mental Health Survey of Older People.* New York: Utica.

GRUNTHAL, E. (1927) Clinical and anatomical investigations on senile dementia. *Z. ges. Neurol. Psychiat.*, **111**, 763.

GUERTIN, W. H., LADD, C. E., FRANK, G., RABIN, A., and HIESTER, D. S. (1966) Research with the Wechsler Intelligence Scales for Adults, 1960–65. *Psychol. Bull.*, **5**, 385–409.

GUERTIN, W. H., RABIN, A., FRANK, G. H., and LADD, C. E. (1962) Research with the Wechsler Intelligence Scales for Adults, 1955–60. *Psychol. Bull.*, **59**, 1–26.

GUTMANN, D. L., HENRY, W. E., and NEUGARTEN, BERNICE L. (1959) Personality development in middle aged men. Unpub. paper read at American Psychological Association meeting, Cincinatti. Sept.

GYNTHER, M. D. and SHIMKUNAS, A. M. (1966) Age and MMPI performance. *J. consult. Psychol.*, **30**, 118–121.

HALL, ELIZABETH H., SAVAGE, R. D., BOLTON, N., PIDWELL, DIANA M., and BLESSED, G. (1972) Intellect, mental illness and survival in the aged: a longitudinal investigation. In press.

HALL, K. R. L. (1952) Conceptual impairment in depressive and organic patients of the pre-senile age group. *J. ment. Sci.*, **98**, 256–264.

HALSTEAD, H. (1943) A psychometric study of senility. *J. ment. Sci.*, **89**, 863–73.

HALSTEAD, H. (1944) Mental tests in senile dementia. *J. ment. Sci.*, **90**, 720–726.

HARDYCK, C. D. (1964) Sex differences in personality changes with age. *J. Gerontol.*, **19**, 78–82.

HATHAWAY, S. R. and McKINLEY, J. C. (1956) Scale 2 (Depression). In *Basic Readings on the MMPI in Psychology and Medicine* (Ed. Welsh, G. S. and Dahlstrom, W. G.) University of Minnesota Press, pp. 73–80.

HAVIGHURST, R. J. (1949) Old age—an American problem. *J. Gerontol.*, **4**, 298–304.

HAVIGHURST, R. J. (1950) Public attitudes towards various activities of older people. In *Planning the Older Years* (Ed. Donahue, Wilma and Tibbits, C.) Ann Arbor: Univ. of Michigan Press, pp. 141–148.

HAVIGHURST, R. J. (1953) *Human Development and Education.* New York: Longmans Green.

HAVIGHURST, R. J. (1957) The social competence of middle aged people. *Genet. Psychol. Monogr.*, **56**, 297–375.

HAVIGHURST, R. J. (1959) Life styles of middle aged people. *Vita Humana*, **2**, 25–34.

HAVIGHURST, R. J. (1963) Successful Ageing. In *Processes of Ageing*, (Vol. I) (Ed. Williams, R. H., Tibbits, C., and Donahue, Wilma) New York: Atherton Press.

HAVIGHURST, R. J. and ALBRECHT, R. (1953) *Older People*. New York: Longmans Green.

HAVIGHURST, R. J. and SHANAS, E. (1950) Adjustment to retirement. *Sociol. Soc. Res.*, **34**, 169–76.

HENRY, W. E. and CUMMING, ELAINE (1959) Personality development in adulthood and old age. *J. Proj. Tech.*, **23**, 383–90.

HERBERT, M. E. and JACOBSON, S. (1967) Late paraphrenia. *Brit. J. Psychiat.*, **113**, 461.

HERON, A. (1963) Retirement attitudes among industrial workers in the sixth decade of life. *Vita Humana*, **6**, 152–9.

HERON, A. and CHOWN, SHEILA (1967) *Age and Function*. London: Churchill.

HOBSON, W. and PEMBERTON, J. (1955) *The Health of the Elderly at Home*. London: Churchill.

HOPKINS, BARBARA and POST, F. (1955) The significance of abstract and concrete behaviour in elderly psychiatric patients and control subjects. *J. ment. Sci.*, **101**, 841–850.

HOPKINS, BARBARA and ROTH, M. (1953) Psychological test performance in patients over sixty: II paraphrenics, arteriosclerotic psychosis and acute confusion. *J. ment. Sci.*, **99**, 451–463.

HORN, J. L. and CATTELL, R. B. (1966) Age differences in primary mental ability factors. *J. Gerontol.*, **21**, 210–220.

HORN, J. L. and CATTELL, R. B. (1967) Age differences in fluid and crystallized intelligence. *Acta Psychol.*, **26**, 107–29.

HOWELL, R. J. (1955) Sex differences and educational influences on a mental deterioration scale. *J. Gerontol.*, **10**, 190–193.

HULICKA, IRENE M. (1966) Age differences in Wechsler Memory Scores. *J. Genet. Psychol.*, **109**, 135–145.

HULL, C. L. (1917) The formation and retention of associations among the insane. *Amer. J. Psychol.*, **28**, 419–35.

HUNT, H. F. (1943) A practical clinical test for organic brain damage. *J. appl. Psychol.*, **27**, 375–386.

HUNT, J. McV. and COPER, C. N. (1944) Psychological deficit. In *Personality and the Behaviour Disorders* (Vol. II) (Ed. Hunt, J. McV.). New York: Ronald Press.

INGLIS, J. (1957) An experimental study of learning and 'memory function' in elderly psychiatric patients. *J. ment. Sci.*, **103**, 796–803.

INGLIS, J. (1958) Psychological investigations of cognitive deficit in elderly psychiatric patients. *Psychol. Bull.*, **54**, 197–214.

INGLIS, J. (1959a) A paired-associate test for use with elderly psychiatric patients. *J. ment. Sci.*, **105**, 440–443.

INGLIS, J. (1959b) On the prognostic value of the modified word learning test in psychiatric patients over 65. *J. ment. Sci.*, **105**, 1100–1101.

INGLIS, J. (1960) Dichotic stimulation and memory disorder. *Nature*, **186**, 181–2.

INGLIS, J. (1962) Effect of age on responses to dichotic stimulation. *Nature*, **194**, 1101.

INGLIS, J. and CAIRD, W. J. (1963) Age differences in successive responses to simultaneous stimulation. *Canad. J. Psychol.*, **17**, 98–105.

INGLIS, J., SHAPIRO, M. B., and POST, F. (1956) Memory function in psychiatric patients over 60: the role of memory tests in discriminating between 'functional' and 'organic' groups. *J. ment. Sci.*, **102**, 589–98.

JARVIK, L. F., KALMANN, F. J., and FALEK, A. (1962) Intellectual changes in aged twins. *J. Gerontol.*, **17**, 289–294.

JONES, H. E. (1961) The age-relative study of personality. *Acta Psychol.*, **19**, 140–2.

JONES, H. E. and CONRAD, H. S. (1933) The growth and decline of intelligence: a study of a homogeneous population between the ages of ten and sixty. *Genet. Psychol. Monogr.*, **13**, 233–298.

KAHN, R. L., SEAMAN, F. D., and GOLDFARB, A. J. (1958) Attitudes towards illness in the aged. *Geriatrics*, **13**, 246–50.

KALLMANN, F. J. (1948) Preliminary data on life histories of senescent twins. *Amer. Psychologist*, **3**, 307–8.

KALLMANN, F. J. (1951) Comparative adaptational, social and psychometric data on life histories of senescent twin pairs. *Amer. J. hum. Genet.*, **3**, 65.

KAPLAN, O. J. (Ed.) (1945) *Mental Disorders in Later Life*. Stanford, Calif: Stanford Univ. Press.

KAPLAN, O. J. (1956) The aged subnormal. In *Mental Disorders in Later Life*, 2nd Edn. (Ed. Kaplan, O. J.). Stanford, Calif.: Stanford Univ. Press, pp. 383–97.

KASSEBAUM, G. G., COUCH, A. S., and SLATER, P. E. (1959) The factorial dimensions of the MMPI. *J. consult. Psychol.*, **23**, 226–236.

KATZ, L., NEAL, M. W., and SIMON, A. (1961) Observations on psychic mechanisms in organic psychoses of the aged. In *Psychopathology of Aging* (Ed. Hoch, P. H. and Zubin, J.). New York: Grune & Shatton.

KAY, D. W. K. (1959) Observations on the natural history and genetics of old age psychoses: a Stockholm material, 1931–1937 (abridged). *Proc. roy. soc. med.*, **52**, 791–794.

KAY, D. W. K. (1962) Outcome and cause of death in mental disorders of old age: a long-term follow-up of functional and organic psychoses. *Acta Psychiat. Scand.*, **38**, 249–276.

KAY, D. W. K., BEAMISH, PAMELA and ROTH, M. (1962) Some medical and social characteristics of elderly people under State care. A comparison of geriatric wards, mental hospitals and welfare homes. *The Sociolog. Review Monogr.*, No. 5, 173–193.

KAY, D. W. K., BEAMISH, PAMELA and ROTH, M. (1964a) Old age mental disorders in Newcastle upon Tyne. Part I: a study of prevalence. *Brit. J. Psychiat.*, **110**, 146–158.

KAY, D. W. K., BEAMISH, PAMELA, and ROTH, M. (1964b) Old age mental disorders in Newcastle upon Tyne. Part II: a study of possible social and medical causes. *Brit. J. Psychiat.*, **110**, 668–682.

KAY, D. W. K. and BERGMANN, K. (1966) Physical disability and mental health in old age: a follow-up of elderly people seen at home. *J. psychosomat. Res.*, 10, 3–10.

KAY, D. W. K., BERGMANN, K., FOSTER, ELEANOR, and GARSIDE, R. F. (1966) A four year follow-up of a random sample of old people originally seen in their own homes; a physical, social and psychiatric enquiry. *Excepta Medica Internat. Congress Series. No. 250.* 1668–70. *Proc. IVth World Congr. Psychiat.*

KAY, D. W. K. and ROTH, M. (1955) Physical accompaniments of mental disorder in old age. *Lancet*, ii, 740–745.

KENDALL, BARBARA S. (1962) Memory for designs performance in the seventh and eighth decades of life. *Percept. Mot. Skills*, 14, 399–405.

KENDRICK, D. C. (1963) The Walton-Black Modified New Word Learning Test: a tribute to Donald Walton. *Bull. Brit. psychol. Soc.*, 16, 51.

KENDRICK, D. C. (1965) Speed and learning in the diagnosis of diffuse brain damage in elderly subjects. A Bayesian statistical approach. *Brit. J. soc. clin. Psychol.*, 4, 141–148.

KENDRICK, D. C. (1967) A cross-validation study of the use of the SLT and DCT in screening for diffuse brain pathology in elderly subjects. *Brit. J. med. Psychol.*, 40, 173–178.

KENDRICK, D. C., PARBOOSINGH, ROSE CECILE, and POST, F. (1965) A synonym word learning test for use with elderly psychiatric patients. *Brit. J. soc. clin. Psychol.*, 4, 63–71.

KENDRICK, D. C. and POST, F. (1967) Differences in cognitive status between healthy psychiatrically ill and diffusely brain damaged elderly subjects. *Brit. J. Psychiat.*, 113, 75–81.

KESSEL, W. I. N. (1960) Psychiatric morbidity in a London general practice. *Brit. J. prev. soc. Med.*, 14, 16–22.

KESSEL, W. I. N. and SHEPHERD, M. (1962) Neurosis in hospital and general practice. *J. ment. Sci.*, 108, 159–166.

KIDD, C. B. and SMITH, V. E. M. (1966) A regional survey of old people in North-East Scottish mental hospitals. *Scot. med. J.*, 11, 132–136.

KILOH, L. G. and GARSIDE, R. F. (1963) The independence of neurotic depression and endogenous depression. *Brit. J. Psychiat.*, 109, 451–63.

KLONOFF, H. and KENNEDY, MARGARET (1965) Memory and perceptual functioning in octogenarians and nonagenarians in the community. *J. Gerontol.*, 20, 328–333.

KLOPFER, W. G. (1946) Personality patterns of old age. *Rorschach Res. Exch.*, 10, 145–166.

KORNETSKY, C. (1963) Minnesota Multiphasic Personality Inventory: Results obtained from a population of aged men. In *Human Aging: a biological and behavioural study* (Ed. Birren, J. E. *et al.*) Bethesda, Md.: U.S. Dept. of Health, Education and Welfare, Chapter 13.

KRAEPELIN, E. (1909–13) *Psychiatry*, 8th ed. Leipzig: Thieme.

KRAL, V. A. (1962) Senescent forgetfulness: benign and malignant. *Canad. med. Assoc. J.*, 86, 257–260.

KRAL, V. A. and DUROST, H. B. (1953) A comparative study of the amnestic syndrome in various organic conditions. *Amer. J. Psychiat.*, 110, 41–47.

KRAWIECKI, J. A., COUPER, L., and WALTON, D. (1957) The efficacy of Parentrovite in the treatment of a group of senile psychotics. *J. ment. Sci.*, 77, 126–133.

KUBO, Y. (1938) Mental and physical changes in old age. *J. Genet Psychol.*, 53, 101–8.

KUHLEN, R. G. (1945) Age differences in personality during adult years. *Psychol. Bull.*, 42, 333–358.

KUHLEN, R. G. (1948) Age trends in adjustment during the adult years as reflected in happiness ratings. Paper read at a meeting of the American Psychological Association, Boston.

LAKIN, M. and EISDORFER, C. (1960) Affective expression among the aged. *J. Proj. Tech.*, 24, 403–8.

LANDIS, J. T. (1941) Hobbies and happiness in old age. *Recreation*, 35, 607.

LANDIS, J. T. (1942) Social psychological factors of aging. *Social forces*, 20, 468–70.

LARSSON, T. and SJÖGREN, T. (1954) A methodological, psychiatric and statistical study of a large Swedish rural population. *Acta psychiat. neurol. scand.*, Suppl. 79.

LARSSON, T., SJÖGREN, T., and JACOBSON, G. (1963) Senile dementia. *Acta psychiat. scand.*, 39, Suppl., 167.

LAWTON, G. (1943) *New goals for old age*. New York: Columbia Press.

LAWTON, G. (Chairman) and others (1940) Old age and aging, the present status of scientific knowledge. *Amer. J. Orthopsychiat.*, 10, 27–87.

LEBO, D. (1953) Some factors said to make for happiness in old age. *J. clin. Psychol.*, 9, 385–87.

LEVINSON, B. M. (1960) A research note on subcultural differences in WAIS between aged Italians and Jews. *J. Gerontol.*, 15, 197–198.

LEWIS, A. (1946) Ageing and senility: a major problem of psychiatry, *J. ment. Sci.*, 92, 150–70.

LIGHT, B. H. and AMICK, J. H. (1956) Rorschach responses of normal aged. *J. Proj. Tech.*, 20, 185–95.

LILLIENCRANTS, J. (1923) Memory defects in organic psychoses, *Psychol. Monogr.*, 32, No. 143.

LINDSEY, B. A. and COPPINGER, N. W. (1969) Age related deficits in simple capabilities and their consequences for trail making performance. *J. clin. Psychol.*, 25, 156–9.

LORANGER, A. W. and MISIAK, H. (1960) The performance of aged females on five non-language tests of intelligence functions. *J. clin. Psychol.*, 16, 189–191.

LORGE, I. (1941) Intellectual changes during maturity and old age. *Rev. educ. Res.*, 11, 553–561.

LORGE, I. (1944) Intellectual changes during maturity and old age. *Rev. educ. Res.*, 14, 438–445.

LORGE, I. (1955) Capacities of older adults. In *Education for Later Maturity—a Handbook* (Ed. Donahue, Wilma). New York: Whiteside; and Morrow Chapter 3.

LORGE, I. (1956) Gerontology (Later maturity). *Ann. Rev. Psychol.*, 7, 349–364.

LOVETT DOUST, J. W., SCHNEIDER, R. A., TALLAND, G. A., WALSH, M. A. and BARKER, G. B. (1953) Studies on the physiology of awareness: the correlation between intelligence and anoxemia in senile dementia, *J. nerv. ment. Dis.*, 117, 383–398.

LYNN, R. (1964) Personality changes with aging. *Behav. Res. Therapy.*, **1**, 343–9.

MACK, M. J. (1953) Personal adjustment of chronically ill old people under home care. *Geriatrics*, **8**, 407–416.

MACMILLAN, D. and SHAW, P. (1966) Senile breakdown in standards of personal and environmental cleanliness. *Brit. med. J.*, ii, 1032.

MADONICK, M. J. and SOLOMON, M. (1947) The Wechsler-Bellevue Scale in individuals past sixty. *Geriatrics*, **2**, 34–40.

MAXWELL, A. E. (1961) Trends in cognitive ability in the older age ranges. *J. abnorm. soc. Psychol.*, **63**, 449–452.

MAYER-GROSS, W. (1945) Electric convulsive treatment in patients over sixty. *J. ment. Sci.*, **91**, 101–103.

MAYER-GROSS, W. (1969) *Clinical Psychiatry.* 3rd ed. (Ed. Slater, E. and Roth, M.). London: Bailliere, Tindall.

MCDONALD, C. (1965) Psychoneurosis in the elderly. *Postgrad. med. J.*, **38**, 432.

MEDAWAR, P. B. (1955) *Presidential address* to CIBA Foundation Colloquia on Ageing.

MEGGENDORFER, F. (1926) Über die hereditäre Disposition zur Dementia senilis. *Z. ges. Neurol. Psychiat.*, **101**, 604.

MEYER, V. (1960) Psychological effects of brain damage. In *Handbook of Abnormal Psychology* (Ed. Eysenck, H. J.). London: Pitman Medical.

MILES, W. R. (1942) Psychological aspects of aging. In *Problems of Aging*, 2nd. Edn. (Ed. Cowdry, E. V.). Baltimore: Williams and Wilkins, pp. 756–784.

MILLER, H. C. (1963) *The Ageing Countryman.* London: National Corporation for the Care of Old People.

MOBERG, D. O. (1953) Leadership in the church and personal adjustment in old age. *Sociol. Social Res.*, **37**, 499–509.

MOORE, T. V. (1919) The correlation between memory and perception in the presence of diffuse cortical degeneration. *Psychol. Monogr.*, **27**, 120.

MORGAN, M. (1937) The attitudes and adjustments of recipients of old age assistance in upstate and metropolitan New York. *Arch. Psychol.*, **30**, No. 214, 131.

MUELLER, C. (1967) *Alterspsychiatrie.* Stuttgart: Thieme.

MURRAY, H. A. (1943) *Thematic Apperception Test.* (3rd revision). Cambridge, Mass: Harvard Univ. Press.

NELSON, E. H. (1953) *An experimental investigation of intellectual speed and power in mental disorders.* Unpublished Ph.D. Thesis, University of London.

NEUGARTEN, BERNICE L. (1963) In *Processes of Aging*, Vol. I (Ed. Williams, R. H., Tibbits, C., and Donahue, Wilma). New York: Atherton Press.

NEUGARTEN, BERNICE L. and GUTMANN, D. L. (1958) Age-sex roles and personality in middle age: a Thematic Apperception study. *Psychol. Monogr.*, **72**, No. 17. Whole No. 470.

NEUGARTEN, BERNICE L., HAVIGHURST, R. J., and TOBIN, S. (1961) The measurement of life satisfaction. *Gerontology*, **16**, 134–143.

NEWCOMBE, FREDA and STEINBERG, B. (1964) Some aspects of learning and memory function in older psychiatric patients. *J. Gerontol.*, **19**, 490–493.

NIELSEN, J. (1963) Geronto-psychiatric period prevalence investigation in a geographically delimited population. *Acta psychiat. Scand.*, **38**, 307–328.

NORMAN, R. D. and DALEY, M. F. (1959) Senescent changes in intellectual ability among superior older women. *J. Gerontol.*, **14**, 457–464.

OBRIST, W. D., BUSSE, E. W., EISDORFER, C., and KLEEMEIER, R. W. (1962) Relation of the electro-encephalogram to intellectual function in senescence. *J. Gerontol.*, **17**, 197–206.

O'NEAL, P., ROBINS, E., and SCHMIDT, E. H. (1956) A psychiatric study of attempted suicide in persons over 60 years of age. *Arch. neurol. Psychiat.*, **75**, 275–284.

ORME, J. E. (1955) Intellectual and Rorschach test performances of a group of senile dementia patients and a group of elderly depressives. *J. ment. Sci.*, **101**, 863–870.

ORME, J. E. (1957) Non-verbal and verbal performance in normal old age senile dementia and elderly depressives. *J. Gerontol.*, **12**, 408–413.

ORME, J. E., LEE, D., and SMITH, M. P. (1964) Psychological assessment of brain damaged and intellectual impairment in elderly psychiatric patients. *Brit. J. soc. clin. Psychol.*, **3**, 161–167.

OWENS, W. A. (1953) Age and mental abilities. *Genet. Psychol. Monogr.*, **48**, 3–54.

PAN, J. S. (1950) Personal adjustment of old people in Church homes for the aged. *Geriatrics*, **5**, 166–170.

PAPPAS, W. and SILVER, R. J. (1958) Developmental differences between the successful and unsuccessful aged. *J. Amer. geriat. Soc.*, **6**, 360–367.

PARSONS, P. L. (1965) Mental health of Swansea's old folk. *Brit. J. prev. soc. Med.*, **19**, 43.

PAYNE, R. W. (1960) Cognitive abnormalities. In *Handbook of Abnormal Psychology* (Ed. Eysenck, H. J.) London: Pitman Medical.

PECK, R. F. (1956) Psychological developments in the second half of life. In *Psychological Aspects of Aging* (Ed. Anderson, J. E.) Washington, D.C.: Amer. Psychological Assoc., pp. 44–49.

PECK, R. F. and BERKOWITZ, H. (1959) *Personality and adjustments in middle age.* Unpublished manuscript on file with the Committee on Human Development. University of Chicago.

PHILLIPS, B. S. (1957) A role theory approach to adjustment to old age. *Amer. Soc. Rev.*, **22**, 212–217.

PICHOT, P. (1955) Language disturbances in cerebral disease. *Arch. Neurol. Psychiat.*, **74**, 92–95.

PIERCY, M. (1964) The effects of cerebral lesions on intellectual function: a review of current and research trends. *Brit. J. Psychiat.*, **110**, 310–352.

PINKERTON, P. and KELLY, J. (1952) An attempted correlation between clinical and psychometric findings in senile arteriosclerotic dementia. *J. ment. Sci.*, **98**, 244–255.

POLLOCK, H. M. (1945) A statistical review of mental disorders in later life. In *Mental Disorders in later life* (Ed. Kaplan, O. J.) Stanford, Calif.: Stanford Univ. Press, pp. 7–22.

PORTEOUS, S. D. (1952) *The Porteous Maze Test Manual.* London: Harrap.

PORTEOUS, S. D. (1955) *The Maze Test: Recent Advances.* Palo Alto: Pacific Books.

POST, F. (1951) The outcome of mental breakdown in old age. *Brit. med. J.*, **1**, 436–440.

POST, F. (1962a) *The significance of affective symptoms in old age*. Maudsley Monograph 10. London: Oxford Univ. Press.

POST, F. (1962b) The impact of modern drug treatment on old age schizophrenia. *Geront. Clin.*, **4**, 137–146.

POST, F. (1965) *The Clinical Psychiatry of Late Life*. Oxford: Pergamon Press.

POST, F. (1966a) Somatic and psychic factors in the treatment of elderly psychiatric patients. *J. Psychosomat. Res.*, **10**, 13.

POST, F. (1966b) *Persistent persecutory states of the elderly*. London: Pergamon Press.

POST, F. (1967) Aspects of psychiatry in the elderly. *Proc. roy. soc. Med.*, **60**, 249–260.

POST, F. (1968) The factors of ageing in affective disorders. In *Recent Developments in Affective Disorders* (Ed. Coppen, A. J.). London: Royal Medico-Psychological Assoc.

POSTEMA, L. J. and SCHELL, R. E. (1967) Ageing and psychopathology: some MMPI evidence for seemingly greater neurotic behaviour among older people. *J. clin. Psychol.*, **23**, 140–143.

PRADOS, M. and FRIED, EDRITA G. (1947) Personality structure in the older age groups. *J. clin. Psychol.*, **3**, 113–120.

PRIMROSE, E. J. R. (1962) *Psychological Illness: a community study*. London: Tavistock Publications.

RABIN, A. I. (1945) Psychometric trends in senility and psychoses of the senium. *J. gen. Psychol.*, **32**, 149–162.

RADCLIFFE, J. A. (1966) WAIS factorial structure and factor scores for ages 18–54. *Austral. J. Psychol.*, **18**, 228–38.

RAVEN, J. C. (1938) *Standard Progressive Matrices*. London: H. K. Lewis.

RAVEN, J. C. (1943) *Mill Hill Vocabulary Scales*. London: H. K. Lewis.

RAVEN, J. C. (1948) The comparative assessment of intellectual ability. *Brit. J. Psychol.*, **39**, 12–19.

RAVEN, J. C. (1962) *Revision of Advanced Progressive Matrices, Set 2*. London: H. K. Lewis.

REED, H. B. C. and REITAN, R. M. (1963a) A comparison of the effects of the normal ageing process with the effects of organic brain damage on adaptive abilities. *J. Gerontol.*, **18**, 177–79.

REED, H. B. C. and REITAN, R. M. (1963b) Changes in psychological test performance associated with the normal ageing process. *J. Gerontol.*, **18**, 271–274.

REGISTRAR-GENERAL (1964) *Statistical Review of England and Wales for the year 1960 (Suppl. on Ment. Hlth.)* London: H.M.S.O.

REICHARD, SUZANNE, LIVSON, FLORENCE, and PETERSON, P. G. (1962) *Ageing and Personality: a Study of Eighty-seven Older Men*. N.Y. and London: Wiley.

REITAN, R. M. (1955) The distribution according to age of a psychotic measure dependent upon organic brain functions. *J. Geront;* **10**, 338–340.

RIDDELL, S. A. (1962a) The performance of elderly psychiatric patients on equivalent forms of tests of memory and learning. *Brit.J.soc.clin.Psychol;* **1**, 70–71.

RIDDELL, S. A. (1962b) The relationship between tests of organic involvement, memory impairment and

diagnosis in elderly psychiatric patients. *Brit. J. soc. clin. Psychol.*, **1**, 228–31.

RIEGEL, K. F., RIEGEL, RUTH M., and MEYER, G. (1963) The prediction of intellectual development and death: a longitudinal analysis. Presented at 6th Internat. Congr. Gerontol., Copenhagen.

RIEGEL, K. F., RIEGEL, RUTH M., and MEYER, G. (1967a) Socio-psychological factors of aging; a cohort-sequential analysis. *Human Devel.*, **10**, 27–56.

RIEGEL, K. F., RIEGEL, RUTH M., and MEYER, G. (1967b) A study of the drop-out rates in longitudinal research on aging and the prediction of death. *J. pers. soc. Psychol.*, **5**, 342–8.

RIEGEL, K. F., RIEGEL, RUTH M., and MEYER, G. (1968) The prediction of retest resisters in research in aging. *J. Gerontol.*, **23**, 370–374.

RIEGEL, RUTH M. and RIEGEL, K. F. (1959) Standardisierung des Hamberg-Wechsler Intelligenz Tests für Erwachsenen (HAWIE) für die Altersstufen über 50 Jahre. *Diagnostica*, **5**, 97–128.

RIEGEL, RUTH M. and RIEGEL, K. F. (1962) A comparison and reinterpretation of factor structure of the W-B, the WAIS and the HAWIE on aged persons. *J. consult. Psychol.*, **26**, 31–37.

RORSCHACH, H. (1942) *Psychodiagnostics*. New York: Grune & Stratton.

ROSENCRANS, C. J. and SCHAFFER, HARRIET B. (1969) Bender-Gestalt time and score differences between matched groups of hospitalized psychiatric and brain damaged patients. *J. clin. Psychol.*, **25**, 409–410.

ROTH, M. (1955) The natural history of mental disorder in old age. *J. ment. Sci.*, **102**, 281–301.

ROTH, M. (1963) Neurosis, psychosis and the concept of disease in psychiatry. *Acta psychiat., Scand.*, **39**, 128–145.

ROTH, M., GURNEY, CLAIR, and GARSIDE, R. F. (1969) Quoted in MAYER-GROSS, W. (1969) *q.v.*

ROTH, M. and HOPKINS, B. (1953) Test performance of patients over 60. *J. ment. Sci.*, **99**, 439–450.

ROTH, M. and MORRISSEY, J. D. (1952) Problems in the diagnosis and classification of mental disorder in old age. *J. ment. Sci.*, **98**, 66–80.

ROTH, M., TOMLINSON, B. E., and BLESSED, G. (1967) The relationship between quantitative measures of dementia and of degenerative changes in the cerebral grey matter of elderly subjects. *Proc. roy. soc. Med.*, **60**, 254–260.

ROTHSCHILD, D. (1937) Pathologic changes in senile psychoses and their psychobiologic significance. *Amer. J. Psychiat.*, **93**, 757–88.

ROTHSCHILD, D. (1942) Neuropathological changes in arteriosclerotic psychosis and their psychiatric significance. *Arch. Neurol. Psychiat.*, **48**, 417–36.

RUCH, F. L. (1934) The differentiative effect of age upon learning. *J. gen. Psychol.*, **11**, 261–86.

SAINSBURY, P. (1962) Suicide in later age. *Geront. Clin.*, **4**, 161–170.

SANDERSON, R. E. and INGLIS, J. (1961). Learning and mortality in elderly psychiatric patients. *J. Gerontol.*, **16**, 375–6.

SAVAGE, R. D. (1964) Intellect and mental illness. *Univ. Durham Res. Rev.*, **15**, 145–15I.

SAVAGE, R. D. (1970a) Intellectual assessment. In *The Psychological Assessment of Mental and Physical Handicaps* (Ed. Mittler, P.). London: Methuen, pp. 29–81.

SAVAGE, R. D. (1970b) Psychometric Assessment and Clinical Diagnosis in the Aged. In *Recent Advances in Old Age* (Ed. Kay, D. W. K. and Walk, A.). London: Royal Medico-Psychological Association.

SAVAGE, R. D. and BOLTON, N. (1968) A factor analysis of learning impairment and intellectual deterioration in the elderly. *J. Genet. Psychol.*, **113**, 177–182.

SAVAGE, R. D. and BRITTON, P. G. (1968) The factor structure of the WAIS on an aged community sample. *J. Gerontol.*, **23**, 2, 183–186.

SAVAGE, R. D., BRITTON, P. G., GEORGE, SANDRA, O'CONNOR, D., and HALL, ELIZABETH H. (1972) A developmental investigation of intellectual functioning in the community aged. In press.

SCHAIE, K. W. and STROTHER, C. R. (1968) The effect of time and cohort differences on the interpretation of age changes in cognitive behaviour. *Multivariate Behav. Res.*, **3**, 259–294.

SEALY, A. P. E. L. (1965) Age trends in adult personality as measured by the 16PF test. *Bull. Brit. psychol. Soc.*, **18**, 59.

SEMRAD, E. V. and McKEON, C. C. (1941) Social factors in old age psychosis. *Dis. Nerv. System*, **2**, 58–62.

SHAKOW, D., DOLKART, M. B., and GOLDMAN, R. (1941) The memory function in psychoses of the aged. *Dis. Nerv. System*, **2**, 43–6.

SHAPIRO, M. B. (1951) Experimental studies of a perceptual anomaly. I: Initial experiments. *J. ment. Sci.*, **97**, 90–110.

SHAPIRO, M. B. (1952) Experimental studies of a perceptual anomaly; II: Confirmatory and explanatory experiments. *J. ment. Sci.*, **98**, 605–17.

SHAPIRO, M. B. (1953) Experimental studies of a perceptual anomaly. III: The testing of an exploratory theory. *J. ment. Sci.*, **99**, 394–409.

SHAPIRO, M. B., FIELD, J., and POST, F. (1957) An enquiry into the determinants of a differentiation between elderly 'organic' and 'non-organic' psychiatric patients on the Bender-Gestalt test. *J. ment. Sci.*, **103**, 364–74.

SHAPIRO, M. B. and NELSON, E. H. (1955) An investigation of the nature of cognitive impairment in co-operative psychiatric patients. *Brit. J. med. Psychol.*, **28**, 239–56.

SHAPIRO, M. B., POST, F., LOFVING, BARBRO, and INGLIS, J. (1956) 'Memory function' in psychiatric patients over sixty; some methodological and diagnostic implications. *J. ment. Sci.*, **102**, 233–246.

SHELDON, J. H. (1948) *The Social Medicine of Old Age*. London: Nuffield Foundation.

SHEPARD, W. P. (1955) Does the modern pace really kill? *J. Amer. geriat. Soc.*, **3**, 139–45.

SHEPHERD, M., COOPER, B., BROWN, A. C., and KALTON, G. W. (1966) *Psychiatric Illness in General Practice*. London: Oxford Univ. Press.

SHIPLEY, W. C. (1940) A self administering scale for measuring intellectual impairment and deterioration. *J. Psychol.*, **9**, 371–7.

SHOCK, N. W. (1951) Gerontology (Later maturity). *Ann. Rev. Psychol.*, **2**, 353–70.

SILVERMAN, A. J., BUSSE, E. W., BARNES, R. H., FROST, L. L., and THALER, MARGARET B. (1953) Studies on the processes of ageing. 4. Physiologic influences on psychic functioning in elderly people. *Geriatrics*, **8**, 370–76.

SIMCHOWICZ, I. (1910) Histologische Studien über die senile Demenz. *Histol. histopath. Arb.* **4**, 267–444.

SLATER, E. and ROTH, M. (1969). *See* MAYER-GROSS, W. (1969).

SLATER, P. E. and SCARR, M. A. (1964) Personality in old age. *Genet. Psychol. Monogr.*, **70**, 229–269.

SORENSON, H. (1933) Mental ability over a wide range of adult ages. *J. appl. Psychol.*, **17**, 729–41.

STEIN, K. B. (1961) The effect of brain damage upon speed, accuracy and improvement in visual motor functioning. *J. consult. Psychol.*, **25**, 171–7.

STENGEL, E. and COOK, NANCY G. (1961) Contrasting suicide rates in industrial communities. *J. ment. Sci.*, **107**, 1011–1019.

STENSTEDT, A. (1959) Involutional melancholia; an aetiological, clinical and social study of endogenous depression in later life with special reference to genetic factors. *Acta Psychiat. Neurol. Scand.*, **34**, Suppl. 127.

STRONG, E. K. J. (1943) *Vocational Interests of Men and Women*. Stanford University: Stanford Univ. Press.

SWENSON, W. M. (1961) Structured personality testing in the aged: an MMPI study of the geriatric population. *J. clin. Psychol.*, **17**, 302–304.

TERMAN, L. W. and OGDEN, MELITA H. (1959) The gifted group at mid-life: Thirty-five years' follow-up of the superior child. *Genetic Studies of Genius. Vol. V.* Stanford, California: Stanford Univ. Press.

THALER, MARGARET (1956) Relationships among Wechsler, Weigl, Rorschach, EEG findings, and abstract-concrete behaviour in a group of normal aged subjects. *J. Gerontol.*, **11**, 404–409.

THOMPSON, W. E., STREILS, G. F., and KOSA, J. (1960) The effect of retirement on personal adjustment: a panel analysis. *J. Gerontol.*, **15**, 165–169.

THORNDIKE, E. L. (1928) *Adult Learning*. New York: Macmillan.

TOMLINSON, B. E., BLESSED, G., and ROTH, M. (1968) Observations on the brain in non-demented old people. *J. neurol. Sci.*, **7**, 331–356.

TRUEBLOOD, C. K. (1935) The deterioration of language in senility. *Psychol. Bull.*, **2**, 735 (Abstract).

UECKER, A. E. (1969) Comparability of two methods of administering the MMPI to brain damaged geriatric patients. *J. clin. Psychol.*, **25**, 196–8.

VINSON, D. (1961) Objectivity in the assessment of psychobiologic decline. *Vita Humana*, **4**, 134–42.

VISPO, R. H. (1962) Pre-morbid personality in the functional psychoses of the senium. A comparison of ex-patients with healthy controls. *J. ment. Sci.*, **108**, 790–800.

WALTON, D. (1958) The diagnostic and predictive accuracy of the Wechsler Memory Scale in psychiatric patients over 65. *J. ment. Sci.*, **104**, 1111–1118.

WALTON, D. and BLACK, D. A. (1957) The validity of a

psychological test of brain damage. *Brit. J. med. Psychol.*, **30**, 270–279.

WALTON, D. and BLACK, D. A. (1959) The predictive validity of a psychological test of brain damage. *J. ment. Sci.*, **105**, 807–810.

WALTON, D., WHITE, J. G., BLACK, D. A., and YOUNG, A. S. (1959) The modified word-learning test: a cross-validation study. *Brit. J. med. Psychol.*, **33**, 213–220.

WATSON, R. I. (1954) The personality of the aged: a review. *J. Gerontol.*, **9**, 309–15.

WATTS, C. A. H. and WATTS, B. M. (1952) *Psychiatry in General Practice.* London: Churchill.

WECHSLER, D. (1944) *The Measurement of Adult Intelligence*, 3rd ed. Baltimore: Williams & Wilkins.

WECHSLER, D. (1945) A standardized memory scale for clinical use. *J. Psychol.*, **19**, 87–95.

WECHSLER, D. (1955a) *Manual for the Wechsler Adult Intelligence Scale.* New York: Psychological Corporation.

WECHSLER, D. (1955b) *In Old Age in the Modern World: Report of the Third Congress of the International Association of Gerontology, London, 1954.* London: Livingstone.

WECHSLER, D. (1958) *The Measurement and Appraisal of Adult Intelligence*, 4th ed. Baltimore : Williams & Wilkins.

WELFORD, A. T. (1958) *Ageing and Human Skill.* London: Oxford University Press (for Nuffield Foundation).

WELFORD, A. T. (1964) The study of ageing. In *Experimental Psychology* (Ed. Summerfield, A.). *Brit. med. Bull.*, **20**, 65–69.

WELFORD, A. T. (1968) *Fundamentals of Skill.* London: Methuen.

WELLS, F. L. and MARTIN, HELEN A. A. (1923) A method of memory examination suitable for psychotic cases. *Amer. J. Psychiat.*, **3**, 243–257.

WETHERICK, N. E. (1966) The responses of normal adult subjects to the Matrices Test. *Brit. J. Psychol.*, **57**, 297–300.

WHITE, J. G. and KNOX, S. J. (1965) Some psychological correlates of age and dementia. *Brit. J. soc. clin. Psychol.*, **4**, 259–265.

WHITE, J. G. and PATTEN, MARY P. (1968) Intellectual performance activity level and physical health in old age. *Geront. Clin.*, **10**, 157–170.

WILLETT, R. (1960) The effects of psychological procedures on behaviour. In *Handbook of Abnormal Psychology* (Ed. Eysenck, H. J.). London: Pitman Medical.

WILLIAMS, H. L., QUESNEL, E., FISH, V. W., and GOODMAN, L. (1942) Studies in senile and arteriosclerotic psychoses. *Amer. J. Psychiat.*, **98**, 712–715.

WILLIAMS, MOYRA (1961) *The Measurement of Mental Performance in Older People.* Booklet circulated privately.

WILLIAMSON, J., STOKOE, I. H., GRAY, S., FISHER, M., SMITH, A., McGHEE, A., and STEPHENSON, E. Old people at home; their unreported needs. *Lancet*, i, 1117–1120.

WILLOUGHBY, R. R. (1938) The relationship to emotionality of age, sex and conjugal condition. *Amer. J. Sociol.*, **43**, 920–31.

WORLD HEALTH ORGANISATION (1959) Mental health problems of ageing and the aged. *W.H.O. Techn. Rep. Ser.*, 171.

WYLIE, MARGARET (1930) An experimental study of recognition and recall in abnormal mental cases. *Psychol. Monogr.*, **39**, 180.

YATES, A. J. (1954) Validity of some psychological tests of brain damage. *Psychol. Bull.*, **51**, 359–379.

YATES, A. J. (1956) The use of vocabulary in the measurement of intellectual deterioration—a review. *J. ment. Sci.*, **102**, 409–440.

YATES, A. J. (1966) Psychological deficit. *Ann. Rev. Psychol.*, **17**, 111–114.

ZANGWILL, O. L. (1964) Neurological studies of human behaviour. In *Experimental Psychology.* (Ed. Summerfield, A.). *Brit. med. Bull.*, **20**, 43–48.

ZARETSKY, H. H. and HALBERSTAM, J. L. (1968) Effects of ageing, brain damage and associative strength on paired-associate learning and re-learning. *J. Genet. Psychol.*, **112**, 149–163.

19

Psychosomatic Relations in Physical Disease

GORDON CLARIDGE

INTRODUCTION

In planning this contribution on the causes and determinants of abnormal behaviour two difficulties were inherent in its subject matter. One was the obvious danger of overlapping too much with several other chapters, particularly those of Dr Martin on somatic reactivity. The other was the problem of remaining loyal to the expressed policy of this Handbook which, like its first edition, is organised not around diseases or syndromes but around psychological systems and their malfunctioning. Dr Martin has already considered in detail the psychophysiology of emotion, both from a methodological and a theoretical viewpoint. In calling on evidence from the field of abnormal psychology she has deliberately confined herself to the somatic dysfunction that accompanies functional mental disorders, the neuroses, and the functional psychoses. However, research on the basic mechanisms of emotion discussed by her has also been given impetus by, and indeed arose partly out of, concern with a problem of a slightly different kind; that is, the alleged role of psychological factors in the pathophysiology of physical disease. The term 'disease' is used here in its entirely acceptable sense to refer to a destructive or potentially destructive alteration in bodily functioning, the alteration being either a qualitative one, or a quantitative one of such degree that it takes on characteristics of a qualitative change. In a more conventional textbook this review might simply have been headed 'psychosomatic medicine' or 'psychosomatic disease'. Its presence here at all might be arguable, were it not for the fact that three reasons merit its inclusion.

The first has already been touched on, namely that the psychophysiological approach to behaviour owes some of its origins to research on the psychological factors in physical disease. An account of that work can therefore usefully complement the evidence reviewed by Martin. The second reason derives from the rather unsatisfactory nature of current theorising in psychosomatic medicine. Domination of the field by psychoanalytic thinking has meant that its theories have often had the quality of a conceptually uneasy mixture of the organic and the phenomenological. A new look at the problem within the context of this Handbook's more rigorous orientation will, it is hoped, prove valuable. The third justification for this chapter is that psychologists are slowly becoming more involved in research on physical disease and sometimes in the treatment of certain disorders that have been especially labelled 'psychosomatic'. Familiarity with some of the relevant literature should therefore be of benefit to the psychologist, both as a basic scientist and as a clinician.

A word, now, about the layout of this chapter. A deliberate attempt has been made to avoid sectioning it in terms of specific disorders. Instead, the chapter is divided up mainly on the basis of methodological approaches to psychosomatic medicine. The section that follows is in the nature of a brief orientation to the field, including its historical background and main theoretical issues. In the remaining sections the more important empirical studies will be reviewed, arranged under broad methodological headings.

ORIENTATION

Throughout the history of medicine the notion of a psychosomatic interaction in physical disease has appeared, disappeared, and reappeared. In recent times its scientific roots can be traced to the increasing interest, from the mid-nineteenth century onwards, in the psychophysiology of emotion. Because many of the early psychophysiologists were doctors, their studies of emotion were inextricably linked with a concern for the possible pathological effects of prolonged or intense emotional stress. Typical of this period in psychosomatic research are the writings of Charles Féré, a French physician whose remarkable, but little known, book, *The Pathology of Emotions* (1899), contains a wealth of experimental data on the physiological correlates of normal and 'morbid' emotions, as well as many astute clinical observations on the role of emotional factors in a variety of physical disorders, including cancer.

The real turning-point in the study of emotion, however, occurred earlier this century in the classical researches of Cannon and his colleagues. Although primarily concerned with the physiological mechanisms of the emotions seen from the viewpoint of their *utility* for the organism, Cannon also extended his observations to what he called the 'emotional derangement of bodily functions'. In his famous monograph *Bodily Changes in Pain Hunger Fear and Rage* he devoted a whole chapter to that topic which he introduced by saying:

'There are many systems in the body which, because of misuse or misfortune, may have their services to the organism as a whole so altered as to be actually harmful. Thus vicious circles of causation become established which may lead to death .... The development of pathological functions in a system is quite consistent with its usual performance of normal functions .... The problem is presented of attempting to learn under what circumstances the transformation occurs. And so, in an examination of the bodily changes which characterise the strong emotions, we may admit the common utility of the changes as preparations for action, we may admit also that such changes may become so persistent as to be a menace instead of a benefit, and we may also be stimulated by this contrast to attempt to understand how it may arise.'

Although Cannon and other early workers placed primary emphasis on the *physiological* aspects of the psychosomatic interaction, and in doing so, of course, stimulated a good deal of basic research on emotion, psychosomatic medicine as a clinical discipline developed in a rather different direction, at least in the West. In general, emphasis here has been placed less on the physiological and more on the psychical mechanisms through which emotion influences the disease process. This has meant that a good deal of clinically orientated research in psychosomatic medicine has been carried out within a psychoanalytic framework. The reasons for this are not hard to find. Inevitably, the growth of psychosomatic theories has been considerably influenced by theoretical developments in psychiatry, which until recently has not had the benefit of a mature scientific psychology. Furthermore, psychosomatic medicine had its formal origins in North America, where, of course, psychoanalytic notions have dominated both psychiatry and the psychology of personality. Thus, the bulk of the North American literature on psychosomatic disorder has traditionally been concerned with trying to correlate specific psychodynamic mechanisms with particular physical diseases, the aetiological link being sought through Freudian or neo-Freudian views on the psychobiology of emotional discharge. For example, Freud himself (1949) considered that damned-up psychic energy could find expression in physiological dysfunction, though he confined his own observations mainly to conditions in which the voluntary sensori-motor system was involved, namely conversion hysteria. However, later workers, notably Ferenczi (1926) and Klein (1948), extended this principle of 'organ neurosis' to dysfunction of an autonomic-vegetative kind. Using this general framework, various models of psychosomatic disease were formulated, that of Franz Alexander (1952) being typical of the psychoanalytic approach. Over many years he has tried to specify the psychodynamic factors present in various conditions by trying to match specific diseases to particular kinds of unconscious conflict; for example, peptic ulcer with a conflict involving oral dependency.

As might be expected from their psychoanalytic origins, the empirical data on which theories such as this are based have often left much to be desired, a fact that can be verified by glancing through the early (and not so early) issues of the journal *Psychosomatic Medicine*. Many of the studies published there show characteristic defects, poorly formulated hypotheses often being tested by equally poorly controlled observation or experimentation. Furthermore, many of the psychological variables focused on have often had only notional connections with the underlying biological mechanisms through which disease processes may be mediated.

The extent to which psychoanalytic thinking has influenced psychosomatic research can be judged from the fact that, as recently as 1954, it was possible to write in a major review of the field that 'we are still in the phase of Freud' (MacLeod *et al.*, 1954). Providing an interesting contrast is the situation in Soviet medicine. Writing about Russian psychosomatic research at roughly the same time as MacLeod and his colleagues were reviewing the American scene, Wortis (1950) commented that 'the general tendency to accord crucial emphasis to neural regulation in disease is a very important characteristic of Soviet medicine'. The growth of this 'corticovisceral medicine', as it is called, and the apparently readier acceptance of the psychosomatic principle by Russian workers are, of course, both largely due to the influence of Pavlovian principles in medicine generally and in psychiatry in particular. This more physiological flavour of Russian psychiatry and psychology has helped to avoid the awkward dualism inherent in many Western theories of psychosomatics and the distracting preoccupation with the mind-body problem as the 'nuclear question of psychosomatic medicine' (Margetts, 1954). It is chastening to note that Cannon (op. cit.) himself had deliberately avoided formulating the problem in such a way, for at the end of his chapter on 'emotional derangement' he concluded—

'In the foregoing discussion I have purposely emphasized the physiological mechanisms of emotional disturbance, and for two main reasons. First I wished to show that these remarkable perturbations could be described in terms of neurone processes. And again, I wished to show that these interesting phenomena need not be set aside as mystical events occurring in the realm of the "psyche".'

The very recent history of psychosomatic medicine indicates that there is now some tendency to return to a more objectively scientific approach to the problems it poses. At least, that is the conclusion reached in 1966 by Wittkower and Lipowski (1966) who reviewed current developments in the field during the previous five years. Recalling a survey made five years earlier and covering the preceding two decades (Wittkower, 1960), the authors concluded that during the period under review there had been a marked reduction in the number of psychoanalytically orientated studies and a shift from clinical observation to laboratory research. Methodology, they found, had tended to focus on the experimental study of psychological stresses,

particularly as reflected in various types of physiological response. On the theoretical side they commented that 'sweeping generalisations regarding the nature and influence of psychological variables in the causation of bodily disease which characterised the earlier phase of psychosomatic medicine have largely been replaced by sober research designs and low-level hypotheses.'

Despite the admitted failure of the earlier and more extravagant theories in psychosomatic medicine, continued interest and research in the area has thrown into relief a number of important questions about the role of psychological factors in the pathophysiology of disease. The most immediately obvious question concerns the generality of the psychosomatic principle or, put more concretely, the range of diseases in which psychological factors can be considered aetiologically important. Most doctors convinced of the value of a psychosomatic approach to disease would probably adopt a very catholic position on this issue, often to the dismay of their unconverted colleagues. Wittkower and Cleghorn (1954), for example, present a typical view. They comment that all medicine is psychosomatic medicine, which they suggest '. . . is perhaps the only field of research and study in medicine dedicated to its own dissolution'. Nevertheless, some boundaries to psychosomatic medicine as it stands at the present time can be defined, and a brief discussion of these will serve to delineate the kinds of study to be reviewed here.

Strictly speaking, psychosomatic medicine is concerned with the psychological factors involved in physical disease, in the sense in which that term was defined earlier. However, because the field has traditionally been the province of the medically trained psychiatrist, at least in the West, the term 'psychosomatic' has often been widened to include certain psychoneurotic reactions such as conversion hysterias. Most behaviourist psychologists, rejecting the medical model of psychiatric illness, would not agree to the psychoneuroses being classified as diseases at all. Of course, this is not meant to suggest that a study of the mechanisms mediating neurotic symptoms is irrelevant to an understanding of psychological factors in physical disease. On the contrary, the two fields of research are inextricably linked, as for example in the case of the psychophysiological relations involved in anxiety. However, that part of the evidence that relates specifically to the psychoneuroses has been adequately covered elsewhere in this book. For practical and theoretical reasons, therefore, such evidence will not be considered in detail here.

Among the physical diseases themselves it is possible to distinguish three, somewhat arbitrary, categories to which psychosomatic research has addressed itself. The first covers those diseases that have a known organic pathology and a known aetiology in the form of a virus or other micro-organism. In these conditions psychological factors are not considered to play a primary, or even essential, role in aetiology, but rather to provide a setting in which a disease may be more likely to manifest itself, presumably by lowering bodily resistance. Such has been claimed, for example, in pulmonary tuberculosis (Kissen, 1958). In the psychosomatic literature least attention has been paid to these diseases because psychological research on them has only limited implications for treatment. Thus, drug therapy or a programme of immunisation can be rightly regarded as the most effective way of dealing with a disease whose aetiology is well-established. In a second category are those diseases the exact causes of which are unknown but which, as part of the general search for the factors implicated in their aetiology, have been investigated from a psychosomatic point of view. Notable examples are the malignant diseases to which the psychosomatic approach has been applied, though often controversially. Finally there are the so-called 'stress diseases', the most commonly quoted examples of which are some forms of heart disease, essential hypertension, bronchial asthma, peptic ulcer, and a variety of other conditions in which there may also be visible organic pathology but in which psychosomatic interactions are thought to make a significant contribution to aetiology. These diseases have sometimes been named as the psychosomatic disorders proper and have formed the subject of

most research in the area. However, labelling only certain diseases as 'psychosomatic' is probably premature and unduly limits the range of legitimate psychosomatic enquiry. It has arisen partly because even many physicians are willing to admit the aetiological importance of psychological factors in this third category of disease and partly because the physiological links through which organic pathology may arise can, in principle at least, be readily identified; for example, in terms of autonomic nervous system dysfunction.

Given that psychological factors may play more than an incidental part in the aetiology of certain physical diseases, providing a very general theoretical model for how this occurs is not too difficult. It would view psychosomatic disease as the peripheral end-product of a state of central nervous arousal induced by stress. Two main issues arise when this model is used to try to give a more detailed account of psychosomatic interaction in disease. The first is concerned with the general principles of psychosomatic relations, particularly with the way in which cortical events influence the somatic response systems involved in disease. The second concerns the problem of individual differences, that is the variation observed between people, both in their susceptibility to disease in general and in their tendency to develop one disease rather than another. In a sense these two issues are interconnected because the study of individual differences, in this field as in any other, also throws light on basic mechanisms and vice versa. However, for the purposes of discussion they provide a convenient way of arranging studies in the area under review.

GENERAL PRINCIPLES OF PSYCHOSOMATIC DISORDER

Conceived in its broadest sense the literature on the general principles of psychosomatic disorder could be said to encompass any research that tries to link together psychological and somatic data. For reasons already given, however, it is necessary to restrict the kind of study reviewed here to those that are most immediately relevant. This can be done in a reasonably logical fashion by choosing only those studies that meet one or both of two criteria. The first is that causal connections or associations have been defined that actually involve a disease process rather than some normal physiological change which only by extrapolation can be considered of potential significance in the aetiology of disease. For example, investigations of disease produced by experimentally imposed stress would meet such a criterion, while general data on the role of the limbic system in emotion would not. The second criterion is that psychosomatic relations have been looked at

historically rather than cross-sectionally. Thus, a good deal of research on the bodily changes during emotional arousal has been concerned with the immediate and relatively transient effects of short-term acutely imposed stressors. However, if stress plays any part at all in the aetiology of psychosomatic disorder it presumably does so through its involvement in the life history of the organism. The most pertinent experimental data and theoretical models in stress research are, therefore, those that focus on the longitudinal aspects of stress. Studies of another kind also meet this second criterion, doing so almost by definition. These are experiments that explore psychosomatic, or more strictly corticovisceral, relations by means of conditioning procedures, thus trying to give an account of the dynamic mechanisms that may be involved in the aetiology of disease.

Stress and Disease

It is implicit in the naming of some diseases as stress disorders that psychological wear and tear makes a significant contribution to their aetiology. The scientific evidence on which this notion is based comes largely from extensive research on the physiological and endocrine changes that occur during emotional arousal and from work on the brain mechanisms that may mediate such changes. Most of that evidence has already been reviewed by Martin in Chapter 10, which can be regarded as a source of background literature for this section. The reader's attention is also drawn, however, to several other references. A good account of various ongoing lines of research on emotional stress is contained in Levi (1967). In addition, several authors have reviewed work on the brain and endocrine systems involved in emotion from the point of view of their relevance for psychosomatic disorder. Maclean (1949) has discussed the 'visceral brain' and Livingstone (1955) the brain-stem mechanisms relating to psychosomatic function; while very recently Mason (1968a,b) has reviewed psycho-endocrine research on the sympathetic-adrenal medullary and pituitary-adrenal cortical systems.

As noted above, a good deal of the experimentation on stress has been concerned with its acute effects in laboratory situations. As such, its main relevance to psychosomatic disorders is in defining the pathways through which pathophysiological changes may occur. While the existence of these pathways—both neurophysiological and neuroendocrine—is now well-established, the part they play in the causation of physical disease is by no means certain. Indeed, there have been surprisingly few attempts to provide a theoretical model that would link *chronic* stress effects to disease itself. A notable exception is that developed by Hans Selye.

SELYE'S ADAPTATION THEORY

Over many years, Selye and his co-workers at the University of Montreal have tried to give an account of the temporal sequence of events that occur during the body's response to stress (Selye, 1946, 1957). Selye views the stress reaction as essentially a normal adaptive response to threat which may nevertheless take on pathological features if the stress is unduly severe or prolonged. His adaptation theory focuses particularly on the effect of stress as it operates through the pituitary-adrenal cortical axis. The essence of the theory is that it views the response to stress as a triphasic reaction, known as the 'adaptation syndrome', which is said to follow a predictable course involving changes in the balance of adrenocorticotrophic hormone (ACTH), secreted by the anterior pituitary, and the corticoids, hormones of the adrenal cortex. It is known that these hormones are secreted as a stereotyped response to a variety of stressors, such as trauma, infections, nervous stimuli, and so on. The response is normally a biologically useful one because it helps the body survive emergencies, for example by suppressing excessive inflammatory reactions. Continued stimulation of this adaptive mechanism, however, may lead to its failure, to a lowered resistance to infection, and to pathological changes such as alterations in the size and constitution of the adrenal cortex. The disorders to which these changes give rise constitute, according to Selye, the diseases of adaptation.

As mentioned, Selye recognises three stages through which the adaptation syndrome may proceed. The first is the *alarm reaction* characterised by secretion of ACTH and, hence, increased activity of the adrenal cortex. During the second stage, that of *resistance*, this adaptive response reaches an optimum level. Finally, if the stress persists or becomes unduly severe a stage of *exhaustion* supervenes in which adrenal insufficiency occurs and the body's normal adaptive capacity is lost. Selye describes both a General Adaptation Syndrome (GAS) and a Local Adaptation Syndrome (LAS). Both are said to go through the same three phases, the difference lying in the degree to which the reaction is localised. Thus, the LAS refers to the response of one part of the organism to topically applied stress. The GAS, however, is not confined to one part of the body but is systemic, producing lesions not only peripherally but also in the central nervous system. It therefore presumably has wider implication than the LAS as a model for explaining human psychosomatic disease.

Evidence for Selye's theory has come chiefly from work by himself and his collaborators on the effects of non-specific stress in animals, mainly rats, in whom the physiological changes characteristic of the adaptation syndrome have been demonstrated. However, its application to human psychosomatic disorder has been limited despite what Cleghorn (1954) has called its 'beautiful coherence'. The latter author points out that one of the difficulties with the theory is that it leads to the prediction that hormonal activity in patients with psychosomatic diseases should be inadequate or disturbed; whereas in fact there is little evidence that such is the case, at least as anything other than a consequence of disease. In reply to this criticism Selye (1960) has argued that his theory does not postulate that there must necessarily be an absolute increase or decrease in hormone production in the diseases of adaptation, but rather a change in hormone activity which only becomes biologically significant in the presence of certain other, priming, stimuli. Thus, he points out, a nearly normal corticoid secretion that may be adequate to maintain homeostasis at rest, may be quite insufficient to maintain life in an adrenalecto-mised animal exposed to stress. As a concrete example of this interaction between the hormonal state of the organism and other factors, he cites work from his own laboratory on sudden cardiac death, an accident that is known clinically to follow exposure to acute stress, such as nervous excitement. If animals are pretreated with certain corticoids and sodium salts they do not develop a heart accident. They only do so if, following this sensitisation (or what Selye calls 'conditioning'), they are then exposed to stressors, such as hot or cold baths or physical restraint.

The significance of this sort of experiment for human psychosomatic reactions is clear. However, its results do imply a widening of the concept of adaptation syndrome to the point where some of its usefulness is lost, since it necessitates incorporating many additional features of the organism which in practice may be extremely difficult to specify. For Selye (1960) concludes:

'Dietary factors, interference with the normal function of an organ, hereditary predisposition and many other factors can selectively increase or decrease responsiveness of individual organs to the potentially pathogenic actions of stress or stress hormones. In the light of what we know about the widely different manifestations of infections with the same micro-organism (e.g. tuberculosis of the lungs, skin, bones, miliary tuberculosis), it is not unexpected that exposure to the same stressor may affect various individuals in essentially distinct ways.'

Unfortunately, it is these other variables that pose the main problem for psychosomatic research and in its present form Selye's theory is far too general (or too specific) to be immediately applicable to most physical disease. Nevertheless, there are two sets of data in psychosomatic medicine that can be considered relevant to Selye's general thesis concerning stress and disease. Neither is derived directly from his theory, but both are methodological approaches to psychosomatic disorder that it is appropriate to discuss at this point.

STRESS AND HUMAN DISEASE

In trying to relate stress to physical disease in man the usual research strategy adopted has been to take a group of individuals suffering from a particular illness and then to determine the frequency with which stress factors were present in their life histories. Thus, in one of the more carefully conducted studies of this type Rutter (1963) looked at a number of psychosocial variables, including immediate stress, in patients with peptic ulcer. He concluded that there was hardly any relationship between stress and the disease. Unfortunately, studies of this type suffer from the inherent weakness that it may be difficult, if not impossible, to specify which situations have been stressful for the individual. The range of stress covered is relatively narrow and, since the diseases in question are almost certainly multiply determined, the importance of stress *per se* as an aetiological factor is not easily isolated. An alternative approach is to define a set of life circumstances which are so threatening to the individual that all would agree upon their stressful nature. The incidence of physical disease in people subjected to such stress can then be determined. Fortunately, there are few such situations in modern society but, due to man's inhumanity to man, there is one whose evidence the scientist would happily have foregone; namely the prisoner-of-war camps. The later effects of internment in these camps has been of interest to some workers in psychiatry and psychosomatic medicine for the obvious reason that they provided conditions of sustained stress rarely encountered outside the animal laboratory. For as one such worker, Chodoff (1963), commented about the Nazi concentration camps:

'. . . if a diabolical intelligence were to plan an experimental situation which would be maximally productive of disordered behaviour in human beings, just as workers like Masserman and Liddell have done with animals, the German concentration camps could not be improved upon for this purpose.'

Studies of the survivors of military prisoner-of-war and civilian concentration camps have usually found a raised incidence of physical disease or of vegetative disturbances that may be incipient signs of disease. Thus, a six-year follow up of Americans held in Japanese camps showed that, compared with the general population of comparable age, such individuals had an increased mortality from cardio-vascular disease, gastro-intestinal disease, and carcinoma (Federal Security Agency, 1940–55). In his own small study of 23 Nazi concentration camp victims Chodoff (op. cit.) reported that common bodily manifestations of the earlier stress were dyspepsia, nausea, diarrhoea, neurodermatitis, and peptic ulcer. In a rather better controlled study Klein *et al.* (1963) examined 90 patients hospitalised in Jerusalem. Fifty of the patients had suffered oppression in concentration camps or ghettoes, while the remainder had spent the Second World War under cover underground. They found 'vegetative lability' to be over three times as common in the oppressed group, 38 per cent suffering from this syndrome as compared with 12·5 per cent in the control group. Rather surprisingly, actual physical disease proved to be somewhat less common in the previously interned patients, 12 per cent of the oppressed and 32·5 per cent of the non-oppressed group falling into what they termed a 'personality plus psychosomatic category'. However, as the authors themselves pointed out, it should be noted that even the so-called non-oppressed patients had been under constant stress, sometimes of considerable severity, during the war. The most detailed investigations of concentration camp stress have been those by Eitinger and his colleagues in Norway, and in a recent paper Eitinger (1969) himself reported on the frequency of psychosomatic symptoms in 227 Norwegian ex-prisoners. The most common psychosomatic disorders found were chronic diarrhoea (18·1 per cent) and peptic ulcer (16·3 per cent). In addition to those with manifest peptic ulcer a further 11·1 per cent complained of dyspepsia judged severe enough to be regarded as a significant prodroma of the disease.

In addition to symptoms of physical disease, all the above authors reported that severe psychological disturbance is extremely common in concentration camp survivors (*see also* Strassman *et al.*, 1956). The frequency with which certain kinds of psychological reaction recur has led to the description of a 'concentration camp syndrome', characterised by fatigue and apathy, difficulty in concentration, moodiness, sleep disturbance, and vegetative lability. Defining the syndrome according to eleven such symptoms Eitinger (op. cit.) found that five or more were present in 83 per cent of his sample. In an earlier paper Eitinger (1961) reported that the concentration camp syndrome—defined by the same eleven criteria—was more severe the more traumatic the original camp experience, as judged by the length and severity of internment and the amount of physical assault to which the victim had been subjected. In the same paper he also threw some light on the organic basis of the syndrome, demonstrating that its severity was positively related to the degree of brain pathology present, assessed by extensive neurological, EEG, and psychological examination. In fact, he claimed that of the 100 persons examined in that study 96 showed signs of meningo-encephalopathy.

Several interpretations can be put on the results of the last study quoted and, to some extent, of all investigations of concentration camp stress. On the one hand, they emphasise how physical hardship forms a significant part of the stress encountered under prisoner-of-war conditions. That fact might therefore be used as an argument against the pathology observed being due to emotional or psychological threat alone. On the other hand, such an interpretation begs the question about the nature of stress which, even under circumstances less extreme than those discussed here, is not clearly divisible into physical and psychological aspects. Perhaps the most reasonable conclusion one can reach is that there does seem to be some similarity between the central nervous and somatic changes said by Selye to characterise the adaptation syndrome in animals and the response of the human organism to severe and sustained threat.

PHYSICAL DISEASE AND PSYCHOLOGICAL DISORDER

Another research strategy that has been used to investigate the relationship between stress and human disease has been to examine the co-variation between physical and psychological illness. The rationale here is that, given a random degree of exposure to stress in the community, the more abnormal personalities should show a different incidence of physical disease from that observed in the general population. At a more physiological level Selye has also provided some rationale for this approach, even though the epidemiological studies that have been carried out to test its assumptions have rarely been undertaken with his theory in mind. In trying to apply his adaptation theory to human psychosomatic disease, Selye has relied almost entirely on what he views as the similarity between the endocrine changes produced by stress in animals and the abnormal endocrine response patterns reported in psychiatric patients (Selye and Fortier, 1950). Data of the latter kind are, of course, well-documented in the literature and while their significance may not be as well-understood, they do provide a second reason for carrying out the studies reviewed in this section.

The commonest, and perhaps the most obvious, hypothesis tested in this area is that certain individuals in the community will show a raised incidence of both physical and psychological disorder. The hypothesis has been stated most explicitly by Hinkle and Wolff (1957) who have argued that illnesses of all types can be viewed as part of man's total adaptation to his environment and, because of individual differences in stress tolerance, will not occur randomly. Instead, illness episodes will show a tendency to cluster, appearing more frequently in certain susceptible people and, in these people, during periods of experienced stress. Support for this thesis has come from a long-term investigation of a New York population where it was found that 25 per cent of the sample studied accounted for 50 per cent of the illness suffered (Hinkle, 1961). As part of that investigation, Hinkle and Wolff and their colleagues focused particular attention on two subgroups that were considered especially likely to have a history of difficult socio-cultural adjustment; namely a group of Hungarian refugees (Hinkle, op. cit.) and a group of immigrant Chinese (Hinkle *et al.*, 1958). In both cases it was found that episodes of illness tended to cluster around periods when the individual perceived his life situation as particularly stressful.

The patterning of disease incidence across the population—as distinct from within the individual—has usually been looked at by examining, in various ways, the concordance rates of physical and psychological disorders. A method used by Lovett Doust (1952) was to compare the physical disease histories of 354 healthy controls and 272 patients admitted to the Maudsley Hospital, excluding those with a current physical illness. Considering 38 bodily complaints and 72 somatic disease entities he found a significantly higher incidence of physical disease in the histories of psychiatric patients, while within the psychiatric group psychotics were more illness prone than neurotics or psychopaths. However, a criticism that can be levelled at Lovett Doust's study concerns his method of ascertaining his subjects' illness histories. This was done by questionnaire and it could be argued that psychiatric patients are more likely to report previous illnesses of all kinds than normal people.

In order to overcome this difficulty, Roessler and Greenfield (1961) carried out a similar investigation but using patients whose medical histories were documented in easily available form. Over a three-year period they compared 471 psychologically disturbed students referred to a university clinic with 480 psychiatrically healthy students. They reported that physical illnesses of various kinds were more common in the psychiatric group than in control subjects. Partly to counter the objection that mentally disturbed individuals might simply refer themselves more often to the clinic, they also demonstrated that the two groups did not differ in the frequency with which they attended during any particular illness episode. In a study similar to, though rather more limited than Roessler and Greenfield's, Lucas *et al.* (1965) also found that students with psychiatric symptoms were more likely to consult the London University health centre with physical complaints, though usually of a minor nature.

Both of the two studies just referred to were concerned with highly selected groups of individuals examined over a relatively short period of time. However, Kreitman *et al.* (1966) recently reported on the long-term concordance rates of different categories of illness found in a general practice, thus setting out to provide a more adequate test of Hinkle and Wolff's hypothesis that there is a parallelism in the occurrence of psychological and somatic disorders. Kreitman and his colleagues took an approximately 30 per cent random sample of patients who had continuously attended one general practitioner for a minimum period of 7 years (average 14 years). Entries in the patients' health records were classified according to six categories: major organic, minor organic, psychiatric, probably psychosomatic, possibly psychosomatic, and purely symptomatic. Analysing the results by a method that controlled for age and length of period of observation, few significant associations between different categories of illness were found. A relationship was observed between psychosomatic, minor organic, and symptomatic complaints but this was interpreted as probably due to a low threshold of consultation. The authors concluded that they could find no evidence for a general susceptibility theory of disease, at least using the methodology employed.

One interesting finding in the Kreitman study, and ascribed by the authors to chance, was a significant *negative* association observed, in men at least, between psychiatric and major organic illness. While the authors' interpretation may well be correct, the result does draw attention to an alternative hypothesis that has been considered in this field, namely that some physical diseases may actually be *less* common in patients with psychiatric disorder. Examination of this hypothesis has usually centred on the incidence of certain physical diseases, mainly peptic ulcer, in some forms of psychiatric disorder, principally schizophrenia. However, the discussion here may be usefully broadened somewhat to cover the general question of how, if at all, different types of physical and mental illness are related. Thus, if there are differential associations between psychological and somatic symptomatology, with occasional inversions of the expected relationships, then these may cancel each other out and fail to be revealed in studies where only very broad categories of illness are employed.

The notion that mental illness may confer immunity to some physical diseases derives partly from what West and Hecker (1952) termed the 'general and almost traditional impression' that peptic ulcers are uncommon in psychotic patients. Of the recent authors who have examined this question, Gosling (1958), after correcting for age, confirmed that the incidence of peptic ulcer was low in schizophrenics. He also reported that it was higher than normal in neurotics and, among neurotics, highest in those who were depressed. Swartz and Semrad (1951) studied a number of diseases, including hypertension, mucous colitis, and peptic ulcer, and found a generally low incidence of psychosomatic disease in psychotics, though no association between different types of physical and mental illness. In a similar study Ross *et al.* (1950b) surveyed 1,600 mental hospital patients and found that both ulcers and rheumatoid arthritis were uncommon in psychotics as a whole compared with a control group of non-psychotic patients; though in an accompanying paper the same authors reported that, among psychotics, manic patients showed a significantly higher incidence of peptic ulcer (Ross *et al.*, 1950a). The latter finding could be said to be partly confirmed by Ehrentheil (1957) who, in another large-scale survey, showed that ulcers were over eleven times more common in affective disorders than in non-psychotic controls. However, unlike Ross and his colleagues, Ehrentheil concluded that there was no evidence for a reduced incidence of ulcers in other psychotics, schizophrenics being twice as prone as control patients. West and Hecker (op. cit.), also challenged the notion of increased immunity to peptic ulcer in psychotics. Using case-history illustrations they suggested that the low incidences reported in the literature were probably due to the difficulty of eliciting symptoms of the condition in psychotic patients. They concluded that accurate estimates could be made only when diagnosis was based on laboratory tests or other objective evidence. Such evidence was used in the most recent study to be reported, that by Hussar (1968), who screened the autopsy protocols of over 1,200 institutionalised schizophrenics dying at the age of 40 or over. He found that the incidence of healed or active ulcers was about 6 per cent, a figure well within the range for unselected general hospital patients.

There is, then, no consistent evidence that schizophrenics, in particular, or psychotics, in general, are less likely to develop ulcers, or probably any other disease, than non-psychotic individuals. If anything, the tendency is the other way round, with some support for the notion that peptic ulcer, at least, may be more common in people suffering from or liable to suffer from affective disorders, a conclusion incidentally confirmed by Lovett Doust (op. cit.) in the study referred to earlier. He found that within his most illness prone group, namely psychotics, depressives had the highest loadings for gastro-intestinal disease.

A very recent study by Kerr *et al.* (1969) has also suggested that there may be a relationship between affective disorders and another common physical illness, namely carcinoma. They approached the problem by examining the causes of premature death in 135 patients with affective disorder, followed up for four years. The term 'affective disorder' was used to cover both anxiety and depression, the patients being evenly divided across these two categories. For males, though not for females, the observed mortality rate in both categories was significantly greater than expected. Patients who died during the follow-up period were considered under two headings: those who died of carcinoma and those who died from other causes. The latter group is of less interest because the patients concerned were evidently physically ill at the time of psychiatric admission and the authors quite rightly pointed out that a depressive reaction to the awareness of physical disease may have contributed to the apparent association between psychiatric and somatic illness. Nevertheless, their comments are important because they emphasise the need to take account of somato-psychic influences when evaluating studies of psychosomatic disorder. Such influences were not, however, present in those patients subsequently dying of carcinoma, since examination at the time of psychiatric admission failed to reveal any presence of the disease. The authors concluded that there may well be some aetiological link between carcinoma and depressive reaction in late middle age, though the mechanism remains obscure. They considered two possible explanations, which are not mutually exclusive. One was that there is a genetic association, mediated by some common biochemical abnormality, between carcinoma and depression; a view supported by the finding of Munro (1966) that the incidence of death from carcinoma is significantly raised in the mothers of depressed patients. The second explanation was based on the demonstration by Brain and Henson (1958) that non-metastatic neurological abnormalities can be found in cancer patients at least three years before the disease itself becomes manifest. Thus, it is possible that depressive mood is a significant central nervous prodroma of the somatic changes associated with carcinoma.

Although evidence of a statistical, epidemiological kind suggests that the association between psychiatric and physical disorder is, if anything, positive, there remains the possibility, and indeed it has been argued, that within the individual patient certain psychological and somatic syndromes may be mutually exclusive of each other. This is reflected in the clinically observed phenomenon of 'symptom alternation', namely the tendency for the symptoms of a somatic illness to disappear during episodes of psychiatric disorder, only to recur on recovery.

Although survey studies suggest that it is rare (O'Connor and Stern, 1967), the phenomenon does seem to be a genuine one. Kerman (1946), for example, described two cases in which bronchial asthma completely remitted during depressive episodes, but returned after successful treatment of the depression with ECT. Funkenstein (1950) also reported on six cases, again with asthma, in which the physical illness alternated with periods of psychosis. In order to throw light on the physiological basis of this reaction, Funkenstein carried out his Mecholyl test during phases of psychosis and normality. This test involves administering the drug Mecholyl in order to determine, from the blood pressure response, the degree of sympathetic/parasympathetic predominance. He found that when the patients were asthmatic but psychiatrically well they showed marked parasympathetic reactivity consistent with the physiological changes associated with asthma. On the other hand, parasympathetic reactivity was much reduced when the patients were free from asthma, but psychotic.

To conclude this section it may be said that the studies reviewed here illustrate both the methodological weaknesses and strengths of approaching psychosomatic relations through the association between psychiatric and physical illness. Certainly, general theories of illness such as that of Hinckle and Wolff appear to be too non-specific to provide useful explanatory concepts for disease. A not too-strained analogy is that they seem to be epidemiological equivalents of Selye's biochemical theory. Even attempts to relate together narrower categories of physical and mental illness are fraught with difficulties of sampling and diagnosis, particularly on the psychiatric side. On the other hand, epidemiological studies do provide the background data, such as the suggestive relation between affective disorder and gastro-intestinal disease, for more detailed investigations of the physiological mechanisms mediating the association. Perhaps the most useful studies are either those, like that of Funkenstein just described, which focus deliberately on relationships between specific somatic and psychiatric variables within the individual patient, or those that can at least offer plausible hypotheses to account for the aetiological link between physical and psychiatric illness. The study by Kerr et al. (op. cit.) of carcinoma in depressed patients is a good example of the latter approach. Unfortunately, investigations of either kind are rare in the psychosomatic literature.

Experimentally Induced Disease

Perhaps more than most areas of psychophysiology the study of the basic mechanisms of psychosomatic

disorder relies heavily, for obvious reasons, on the experimental induction of disease in lower animals. Selye's contribution in that area has already been touched on although, as we have seen, the theory to which his research has led is very non-specific. Consequently it has received more attention as a basis for speculation about human psychosomatic disease and less as a theoretical model for other animal investigators, who on the whole have tended to adopt a more empirical approach. They have followed two main research strategies in order to induce disease in animals. One has been through direct intervention in the brain, usually either by stimulation or by surgical lesions. The other has been through behaviourally induced stress of one kind or another. In both cases attention has been focused particularly on the pathogenesis of gastro-intestinal disease.

BRAIN INTERVENTION STUDIES

The use of brain intervention techniques to produce gastro-intestinal abnormalities in animals derives partly from early clinical observations on patients who, following operation for brain tumours, developed mucosal haemorrhage or peptic ulcer (Cushing, 1932). In one of the first experimental studies Watts and Fulton (1935) compared, in monkeys, the effects of lesions placed in the diencephalon with lesions placed elsewhere in the brainstem. They demonstrated that lesions in the hypothalamus were more likely than lesions elsewhere in the brain to cause mucosal bleeding and perforation, as well as cardiac irregularities. They did not, however, succeed in producing chronic peptic ulcers in their animals. In two other contemporaneous studies similar effects were demonstrated by Hoff and Sheehan (1935), also in monkeys, and by Keller in dogs (1936). At about the same time, however, Martin and Schnedorf (1938) reported that they were unable to produce any abnormalities of gastric activity, in either cats or monkeys, following small localised lesions in the hypothalamic area. They concluded that the changes described by other workers were due to the fact that the lesions produced previously had been more extensive than those in their own experiment.

However, more recent studies have confirmed that suitably placed lesions in the brain will induce gastro-intestinal defects of various kinds. Experimental evidence for this conclusion was provided in a classic study by French et al. (1952) who placed lesions in either the anterior or posterior hypothalamus in cats. Out of thirteen animals so treated twelve developed gastro-intestinal abnormalities, anterior lesions tending to produce mucosal haemorrhages and posterior lesions causing gastric ulcerations. French and his colleagues concluded that these findings were consistent with the clinical evidence on ulceration in brain-operated patients. After reviewing their own and other cases reported in the literature they found that in 50 per cent of such patients the hypothalamus was involved at operation; while in the remainder the lesions induced were in a position that would interfere with pathways connected with the hypothalamus.

In a further series of experiments the same group of workers used brain stimulation to produce gastric changes, this time in monkeys (French *et al.*, 1954, 1957). In the second of these studies 19 animals were electrically stimulated twice a day in the region of the hypothalamus, the total period of stimulation ranging from 30 to 86 days. Control animals consisted of 20 monkeys who, it was considered, had not received adequate stimulation due to various technical difficulties. None of these monkeys developed any symptoms, whereas among the test animals six developed focal lesions and two diffuse stomach changes. When the animals were subsequently sacrificed it was found that all eight who showed signs of disease had been stimulated in or near the central hypothalamic region. The eleven test animals free from disease, on the other hand, had been stimulated outside that area. Similar changes in the cat were demonstrated by Feldman *et al.* (1961), who produced acute erosion of the gastric and duodenal mucosa by stimulation of the anterior hypothalamus and preoptic region. In that study, 18 out of 31 stimulated animals developed signs of disease, while no control animals showed such symptoms.

Although the above studies were concerned with only one class of disease, of the gastro-intestinal tract, they could be said to have wider implications for the aetiology of other psychosomatic disorders. Central control of the autonomic nervous system as a whole is now well-established (*see* Grossman, 1967) and pathways certainly exist in the brain for the mediation of several diseases in which the autonomic nervous system is clearly involved, such as essential hypertension, cardiac disease, and asthma. In the case of other diseases the role of central nervous factors remains much more speculative though, as Selye's model suggests, the existence of hypothalamic influences on endocrine function, particularly those occurring through the pituitary-adrenal axis, leaves many possibilities open. Perhaps the most exciting, though certainly the most controversial, concerns malignant disease, the development of which may depend to some extent on the state of the central nervous system. Some support for this conclusion comes from a series of experiments carried out by Kavetsky and his colleagues in Kiev (Kavetsky *et al.*, 1966, 1969).

They have used a variety of brain intervention techniques to alter the resistance to tumour growth in a number of animal species. One method has been through the application of centrally acting drugs. It was found that excitation of the CNS with caffeine and strychnine hindered the growth of malignant tumours in mice and rabbits inoculated with two varieties of carcinoma. On the other hand, central nervous depression induced with amylo-barbitone sodium speeded up tumour growth. Other experiments involved decortication, which was shown to accelerate the development of inoculated tumours, in both pigeons and rabbits. Finally, the effect of more precise brain destruction was studied in a number of investigations in which electrolytic lesions were placed in the hypothalamus. It was found that hypothalamic damage, combined with prolonged illumination, favoured the growth of chemically induced mammary carcinoma in rats; while bilateral lesions to the anterior hypothalamus accelerated tumours of the thyroid gland in golden hamsters. Kavetsky and his colleagues concluded that it was possible to infer from their investigations that the hypothalamus, acting through the endocrine function of the organism, could alter the course of hormone-dependent carcinogenesis.

BEHAVIOURAL STRESS STUDIES

As an alternative to direct brain intervention a common way of inducing disease experimentally in animals has been through the use of some form of behaviourally induced stress. Historically, such research has been closely linked with studies of experimental neurosis in animals, as represented in the work of Gantt, Liddell, Masserman, and others. The reasons for this are fairly obvious. The production of experimental neurosis is often accompanied by widespread and persistent changes in autonomic activity which could provide the setting for the development of some forms of psycho-somatic disease. For example, an early study in Liddell's laboratory demonstrated the appearance of relatively permanent disorders of heart action in sheep following the conditioning of an experimental neurosis (Anderson *et al.*, 1939). Although observations such as these have often only been incidental to the main purpose of studying animal paradigms of neurotic behaviour, the techniques evolved have also been applied in research that focuses on the physiological changes themselves, particularly as they relate to the disease process. The present discussion will be confined to research of the latter kind, the background literature on experimental neurosis *per se* being reviewed elsewhere in this book (Chapter 20).

As with brain intervention studies, the production

of gastro-intestinal abnormalities has often been the aim of investigations using behavioural stress to induce disease in animals. Occasionally, in fact, both kinds of techniques have been combined. Hornbuckle and Isaac (1969) demonstrated that restriction of rats in dim illumination and/or removal of the frontal cortex led to an increase in gastric ulceration; while Luparello (1966) induced gastric erosions in the guinea-pig using a combination of behavioural restraint and lesions in the hypothalamus. Most studies, however, have been concerned with the use of behavioural stress alone. Porter *et al.* (1958) subjected monkeys to a wide variety of conditioning procedures given in different combinations. The procedures included lever pressing for food, followed by conditioned anxiety and conditioned avoidance sessions, and simple restraint. Eleven out of nineteen animals tested subsequently showed signs of gastrointestinal disease, the changes produced apparently correlating most highly with the severity of the total schedule to which particular animals had been exposed.

In other investigations attempts have been made to narrow down on specific features of the stress situation that may be critical for the production of ulcers. According to a recent study by Mikhail (1969) conditioned anxiety procedures as such do not lead to increases in stomach ulceration, at least in the rat; though Sawrey and Sawrey (1968), also working with rats, concluded that whether ulcers developed depended on the intensity (though not the duration) of the UCS employed. However, their animals were immobilised, which may have contributed to the fact that ulceration occurred at all. Thus, there is some evidence (Corrodi *et al.*, 1968) that immobilisation leads to quite specific central nervous changes in the form of increased activation of noradrenaline systems in the brain and spinal cord, a response that may play some part in the psychosomatic mediation of experimentally induced disease. This may also be true of milder forms of restriction. Certainly, restraint has been implicated in the pathogenesis of ulcers in laboratory animals (Brodie and Hanson, 1960), ulcers apparently being rare in animals living under more natural conditions (Chertok and Fontaine, 1963).

However, an equally important factor, and one that must contaminate many studies of stress-induced ulceration, is that of disturbed food scheduling. Thus, Frisone and Essman (1965) studied mice who were either immobilised or food-deprived for 48 hours. They found no difference in the number of gastric lesions produced, immunity to ulceration correlating most highly with degree of food retention and increased weight. The authors suggested that food deprivation was just as important as immobilisation in producing gastric ulcers. In a more elaborate experiment Weisz (1957) studied rats who were either exposed to an approach/avoidance conflict procedure, were placed in a fear-producing situation, or simply food and water deprived. Rats subjected to conflict developed significantly more ulcers than other animals. However, the other two conditions, including food and water deprivation by itself, also produced some ulceration.

In order to provide animal analogues of the human condition some workers have emphasised what may be variously described as the uncertainty, avoidability, or decision-making components in psychological stress. For example, Sawrey (1961) found that rats given electric shocks that unpredictably followed either a light or a buzzer stimulus developed more ulcers than a control group of animals who were shocked an equal number of times, but only following the light stimulus. However, the most widely quoted studies in this area are those of Brady and his colleagues. They showed that monkeys performing over a long period under shock avoidance conditions were more prone to stomach ulceration than animals exposed for a similar length of time to the same schedule of shocks (Brady *et al.*, 1958). The most famous of Brady's studies are his so-called 'executive monkey' experiments (Brady, 1958). Monkeys yoked together in pairs were given regular electric shocks which one member of the pair—the executive animal—could avoid, both for himself and his partner, by pressing a lever. It was found that several weeks on this schedule increased the incidence of ulcers in executive animals, but not in passive recipients of the shock. Whether ulcers developed, however, depended critically on the ratio of rest to lever-pressing performance employed. No ulcers were produced when what would appear to be very stressful schedules were used, namely 18 hours performance followed by six hours rest, or 30 minutes performance and 30 minutes rest. The optimum ratio was the superficially less stressful six hours performance and six hours rest, a schedule also shown by Rice (1963) to be the most effective one for producing ulcers in rats. As a possible explanation of this finding Brady (1958) suggested that whether emotional stress contributes to ulcerogenesis may depend on its being imposed on some natural biological rhythm of the organism. In partial support of his conclusion Brady quotes other work from his department in which measurements were made of gastric acid secretion in monkeys undergoing shock avoidance training. It was found that intermittent lever-pressing schedules produced increases in acid secretion *after performance had stopped* and that the greatest rises occurred following a six-hour performance session. Brady has considered that an important feature of the stress used in his experiments was the switching on and off of the nervous system coincident with a natural cycle of gastric secretion. Whether this explanation is correct or not, and quite apart from it, the fact that acid secretion rose regularly in between, rather than during, performance sessions is of interest in itself, since it indicates that the sustained nature of the arousal induced was probably critical for the production of ulcers. Thus, Mahl (1952) has shown that acute fear causes, if anything, a decrease in acid secretion, with a gradual changeover to increased secretion as the fear becomes more chronic.

The chronicity of the stress to which the organism is exposed is, in fact, probably a crucial element in the psychosomatic mediation of any disease. This, at least, is the conclusion reached by Corson (1966) whose own work has been concerned with stress-induced antidiuresis in dogs subjected to long-term conditioning procedures. Another important factor named by Corson is the unavoidability of the stress used and he has suggested that it is the *chronic* exposure to *unavoidable* stressful stimuli that is most likely to lead to somatic pathology. This point is illustrated by research on the effects of emotional stress in neoplastic disease. Some work, mainly Russian, has shown that tumours are more likely to develop in animals whose nervous systems have been 'weakened' by chronic stress. The classic studies are those of Petrova (1955) who reported that malignant tumours, both spontaneous and induced by application of coal tar to the skin, developed more frequently in dogs with experimental neurosis than in control animals. Results supporting these findings and supplementing their own work using brain intervention techniques have also been described by Kavetsky (op. cit.). In contrast, other workers have reported that stress either has no effect on tumour growth (Otis and Scholler, 1967) or actually retards the spread of malignant disease (Rashkis, 1952; Marsh *et al.*, 1959; Newton, 1964). However, as Corson (op. cit.) pointed out, these latter studies all employed stress involving muscular expression, like forced swimming, thus reducing the frustration element he considered to be important. The fact that such forms of stress actually lead to a *reduction* in tumour growth appears to be inexplicable, though superficially it may lend some support to hypotheses, like that of Kissen (1966), that human lung cancer is associated with a reduced outlet for emotional discharge.

If one accepts Corson's suggestion that chronicity and unavoidability are the crucial elements in psychosomatic stress, the problem still remains of defining situations that are maximally frustrating

for the organism. As Brady's experiments have shown, this may be more difficult than it appears at first sight, since intensive exposure to apparently unpleasant regimes may be less stressful (at least in terms of manifest disease) than intermittent exposure timed to coincide with physiological changes that contribute to the disease process. A second problem concerns the interaction between psychological stress and physical triggering factors which will vary and have different degrees of primacy in the aetiology of different diseases. Examples are the disturbance of food intake in the case of gastric ulceration and the exposure to carcinogens implicated in some forms of malignant disease. Finally, there is the problem of individual differences in the susceptibility to different diseases, a question that will be taken up later in the chapter.

Conditioning and Psychosomatic Relations

Apart from their use as a means of inducing stress, and sometimes disease, in the organism, conditioning procedures are of special relevance to the study of psychosomatic relations, for two reasons. First, they have been a basic research tool for investigating the way in which the central nervous system controls and integrates the bodily systems through which psychosomatic disease is mediated. Secondly, by their very nature they can give an account of the 'dynamics' of psychosomatic relations and, therefore, in principle at least, provide a scientific basis for understanding how the life-history of the organism can enter into the aetiology of physical disease. Here we shall concentrate on two sets of data from the field of conditioning that have special relevance to psychosomatic medicine. One comes from research using classical conditioning to explore the role of the central nervous system in the integration of activity in the internal organs. The other is concerned with recent work on the operant control of the autonomic nervous system.

CLASSICAL CONDITIONING STUDIES

The relatively slow acceptance of the psychosomatic principle in medicine derives partly from a somewhat dualistic view of the organism that has pervaded physiology, at least in the West. In classical physiology this is reflected in the relative importance that has been assigned to the central nervous system in the reception and integration of information coming from the external environment, on the one hand, and from the internal *milieu*, on the other. Information arriving at the exteroceptors clearly has direct access to the cortex, produces definable conscious sensations, and provides an obvious avenue for the analysis of higher mental activity. By comparison, the central influence of interoceptive stimuli is much less easily defined, both physiologically and psychologically.* Thus, Sherrington (1947) stated that interoceptive stimuli do not reach consciousness, and considered that the methods used in sensory physiology could not be applied to the analysis of visceral sensation. Consequently, study of the visceral afferent system has been concentrated on its peripheral mechanisms, often in isolated preparations, and has been slow to be incorporated into behavioural physiology.

As implied in the term 'corticovisceral', relegation of interoception to the periphery has been less evident in Russian physiology and among those influenced by it. Their somewhat different approach springs from a greater concern with the behaviour of the intact organism, with the nature of the central 'analysers' of afferent input into the nervous system, and with the use of the conditioned reflex as a method of investigation. Pavlov himself, of course, focused primarily on salivation, but his work was later extended to the study of the internal organs, principally by K. M. Bykov and his colleagues (Bykov, 1957). In the first stage of his research Bykov undertook to examine the range of interoceptive responses that could be conditioned by the usual methods developed by Pavlov. Thus, he argued that theoretically it should be possible to form a conditioned reflex to any unconditioned response. That this is essentially true was confirmed by a series of experiments carried out in Bykov's laboratory and elsewhere (Bykov, op. cit.). Conditioning was demonstrated for hormonally mediated diuresis, biliary and pancreatic secretion, splenic contraction, glycosuria and several other endocrine and physiological functions. These results laid the groundwork for a second group of experiments aimed at demonstrating what at that time was a more controversial fact, namely that stimuli arising from the internal organs were received in the higher nervous system and hence capable of influencing behaviour. Or, as Bykov himself put it (Bykov, op. cit., p. 246):

'Since the cerebral cortex is able to control, by means of temporary connections, the behaviour of the organism in its environment and, at the same time due to the very same mechanisms and in conformity with the developing outward reaction, to change the activity and state of the viscera, it is natural to expect the reverse phenomenon, i.e. that changes in the activity and state of

the viscera would effect, through the cerebral cortex, changes in the behaviour of the organism with respect to its environment.'

Methodologically, testing this possibility, of course, involved reversing the usual conditioning procedure and combining an indifferent (conditional) stimulus applied to an interoceptor with an unconditional exteroceptive stimulus. In one of the first experiments from Bykov's laboratory in which this procedure was used, a water injection into the stomach of a dog was combined with electrical stimulation to the animal's right-hand paw. It was found that irrigation of the gastric mucosa alone eventually caused the dog to lift its paw. Extensive subsequent research elaborated upon this finding and demonstrated that alimentary and defensive reflexes could be conditioned to several kinds of interoceptive stimulation. Furthermore, such responses were found to resemble exteroceptively conditioned reflexes in being subject to the same principles of differentiation, extinction, irradiation and so on. The results of these studies are detailed by Bykov himself (op. cit.) and are also discussed by the Hungarian physiologist G. Ádám (1967), whose recent monograph brings together the findings of his own research in the same area.

In his basic experiments Ádám was concerned with the elaboration of conditioned responses to distension of either the renal pelvis or the carotid sinus. He has reported that both forms of stimulation can be made to elicit a conditioned response. This was shown in two ways. One was by combining distension of the renal pelvis or carotid sinus with food, using salivation as the criterion of conditioning. The other was by conditioning renal pelvic stimulation to produce EEG desynchronisation. Once habituation to the first pelvic stimulus had taken place it was found to cause a conditioned desynchronisation of the EEG, after being combined with an auditory stimulus. In further investigations, in order to examine the brain mechanisms involved more closely, Ádám and his colleagues extended their experimental procedure to include intracerebral stimulation and ablation techniques. Thus, they have shown in the dog that desynchronisation of the EEG, produced by direct stimulation of the reticular formation, can be conditioned to intestinal stimuli. Furthermore, interoceptively conditioned reflexes were found to be disrupted by extirpation of various parts of the brain, particularly the cingulate gyrus.

Two other behavioural studies carried out in Ádám's laboratory are also of interest here in view of the experiments to be discussed in the next section. One was concerned with interoception as a

---

* The term 'interoception' is taken here to exclude 'proprioception' and is used synonymously with 'visceroception'.

source of discriminative stimuli for operant learning. Rhesus monkeys were trained on a fixed ratio schedule to press a lever for food. Once the response rate had been stabilised, intermittent visceral distension, via an intestinal balloon, was begun; first randomly to provide a baseline comparison and later as a discriminative stimulus for lever pressing. Random stimulation had the initial effect of desynchronising the EEG and producing a slight drop in lever pressing rate. However, these responses soon habituated and no sustained effect of interoceptive stimulation was observed. Further training using visceral distension as a reinforcer for lever pressing clearly demonstrated interoceptive control of the operant response. In one monkey, training was continued using a discrimination reversal procedure, and it was found that visceral stimulation could also act as a reinforcer for the termination of lever pressing. Ádám concluded that the source of background stimulation against which operant responses are elaborated must be taken to include both the internal and external environments, the visceral and somatic afferent systems being entirely interdependent in this respect.

The second group of studies referred to was concerned with the perception of interoceptive stimulation in man. Although conscious awareness of such stimulation is normally minimal a series of experiments reported by Ádám has suggested that visceral sensations, at least, can be shown to have measurable activating influences on the EEG and to be conditionable to verbal stimuli. In the first experiment subjects were stimulated by inflating a balloon inserted into the intestine. It was found that painless stretching of the duodenal wall in this way invariably caused blocking of resting alpha activity, EEG desynchronisation occurring in 70 per cent of the cases without any subjective feelings of abdominal discomfort being reported. In a second experiment a test was made of discrimination of stimuli from two balloons placed 15 to 20 cm apart in the intestine. After EEG habituation to duodenal stretching induced by one balloon, the second balloon was inflated. It was found that the alpha blocking response reappeared in 8 out of 14 subjects tested in this way. Finally, an attempt was made to condition subjects to become aware of previously unconscious duodenal stimuli. This was done in three stages. First, the objective threshold for duodenal pressure was determined, using the EEG desynchronisation method just described. Next, the balloon was inflated until the subject reported a definite sensation of distension (subjective threshold). Then balloon pressure was again reduced in steps, each step being accompanied by the verbal instruction that the intestinal stimulus was being applied.

This procedure resulted in a lowering of the subjective threshold, in some cases to a point very near to that of the original threshold at which EEG desynchronisation only had occurred.

OPERANT LEARNING STUDIES

The studies just described illustrate how interoception, via its afferent input to the brain, can influence higher nervous activity. Such evidence complements the results of another group of experiments, to be discussed now, which have been concerned with the effector control of interoceptive responses. These experiments have been aimed at challenging a commonly held view in psychology (e.g. Mowrer, 1950) that two kinds of learned response can be distinguished: those mediated by the autonomic nervous system and exclusively acquired according to classical conditioning principles, and those of a skeletal-muscular kind to which instrumental learning techniques can be applied. A vigorous critic of that standpoint has been Miller (1961) who, in a series of experiments, has demonstrated the applicability of operant training procedures to a wide range of autonomically mediated behaviour. For example, Miller and Carmona (1967) reported that thirsty dogs rewarded with water for bursts of spontaneous salivation showed a progressive increase in salivary output. Conversely, salivary output decreased in animals rewarded for periods without salivation.

A methodological difficulty with this kind of experiment is that the autonomic changes being studied are often themselves affected by skeletal activity and conditioning could conceivably be secondarily due to learned somatic responses. This problem has been overcome by working with curarised animals, thus eliminating the effects of muscular activity on the autonomic nervous system. Following this procedure, Miller and DiCara (1967), and also Trowill (1967), found that curarised rats showed the predicted cardiac changes when they were rewarded by direct stimulation of the brain for increasing or decreasing their heart rates. Similarly, using avoidance of a painful stimulus as the reward, it was demonstrated that rats could be trained to change their heart rates, and their blood pressure, in order to avoid an electric shock (DiCara and Miller, 1968a,b).

Further experiments have suggested that these conditioned responses are quite specific and not due to some general activating influence of the experimental situation. Thus, Miller and Banuazzi (1968) rewarded curarised rats for relaxation of the large intestine by electrically stimulating the medial forebrain bundle. Under these conditions spontaneous intestinal contractions decreased, but could be subsequently made to increase when contraction, rather than relaxation, of the intestine was rewarded. When reward was stopped altogether both responses extinguished. In this experiment the autonomic response was shown to be a specifically visceral one, heart rate for example showing no change. On the other hand, when heart rate itself was chosen for reinforcement, the appropriate change in this autonomic function was produced, with no alteration in intestinal activity. In another elegant example of the specificity of such changes DiCara and Miller (1968c) demonstrated that rats, rewarded by electrical stimulation of the brain, learned a vasomotor response in one ear which was independent of that occurring in the other ear or in either the forepaw or the tail. Furthermore, the conditioned response was unrelated to changes in heart rate or temperature.

The results of comparable experiments on man have been rather more equivocal, though a number of workers have reported operant conditioning of the heart rate in human subjects (Brener and Hothersall, 1967; Hnatiow and Lang, 1965; Brener et al., 1969). However, Harwood (1962) failed to condition slowing of the heart rate and, in general, conditioned deceleration of the heart has proved more difficult to achieve than its acceleration (Engel and Chism, 1967). Another feature of most experiments is that only a proportion of the subjects studied have been shown to gain control over their autonomic function. In this connection Engel and Hansen (1966) suggested that subjects learn better if they are unaware of the response they are trying to influence. The role of musculoskeletal feedback as a mechanism mediating the phenomenon in human subjects is clearly less easy to determine or control than it is in animals, but most authors who have considered the problem with respect to heart rate have concluded that respiration, at least, is not a significant variable affecting the results. Levene et al. (1968) confirmed this by carrying out a series of paced breathing experiments; though it is important to note that only two out of their five subjects were able to control their heart rates consistently.

Although most of the research has been concerned

with heart rate, attempts to condition operantly other autonomic responses in man have also been made. Brown and Katz (1967) claimed successful conditioning of salivary output, while Delse and Feather (1968) reported that three out of ten subjects were able to achieve significant differentiation between increases and decreases in salivation when given feedback in the form of being able to hear themselves salivate. In the case of electrodermal response Shapiro and Crider (1967) demonstrated that predictable shifts in palmar skin potential could be induced with a suitable operant reinforcement schedule. On the other hand, Mandler et al. (1962) found no evidence for operant conditioning of the galvanic skin response when drops in skin resistance were reinforced by a light stimulus. However, they did show that an increased emission of GSRs occurred during the reinforcement periods.

In a recent review of his own and other work in this area Miller (1969) has considered some of its implications for psychosomatic medicine. One important point he makes concerns the flexibility of instrumental learning and, therefore, the greater possibility for pathological autonomic responses to be acquired. Thus, in instrumental learning a given reward may reinforce any one of a number of different responses, while a given response may be reinforced by any one of a number of different rewards. By comparison, the conditioning of an autonomic response according to classical Pavlovian principles is much more restricted and requires reinforcement by an unconditioned stimulus that already elicits the specific behaviour pattern to be learned. The growing evidence that the acquisition of autonomic responses is not confined to one kind of learning is therefore of considerable importance for psychosomatic medicine because of the many kinds of reinforcement that may establish and maintain physiological reactions that are the vehicles for disease. An important corollary of this concerns the application of operant learning principles in the treatment of patients with existing disorders of the autonomic nervous system, and in this respect Miller (1969) quotes some evidence that instrumental training can be used successfully to treat cardiac arrhythmias of organic origin.

INDIVIDUAL DIFFERENCES IN SYMPTOM CHOICE

As noted earlier in this chapter, study of the basic mechanisms of psychosomatic disorder is inextricably linked with attempts to explain why individuals differ in their tendency to respond to stress by developing one disease rather than another. In fact, this latter problem has been the main focus of

attention for many Western workers in psychosomatic medicine. Preoccupied with psychoanalytic theory and methodology, they have often been exclusively concerned with the psychodynamic variables determining the individual patient's choice of symptoms. Unfortunately, extensive research from that point of view has resulted in more fanciful speculation than hard evidence and, at the risk of appearing overly didactic, such studies will not be considered here, despite the fact that they form a very large bulk of the psychosomatic literature. Instead, the discussion here will be confined to evidence and methodologies that seem to have more scientific validity than those derived from the psychoanalytic approach. These will be considered under three headings. The first is concerned with the measurement of definable and quantifiable personality characteristics in patients with physical disease. The second covers a variety of evidence on the patterning of physiological response, both within and between individuals. The third is concerned with the role of genetic factors.

Personality Factors in Disease

It was once the hope of some workers in psychosomatic medicine that the relationship between personality and disease was so specific that it would be possible to define personality types who were prone to develop particular diseases. The main proponent of that view was Flanders Dunbar (1948) who collected considerable clinical evidence which, she felt, supported the notion that disease and personality types could be matched together. Few authorities would now agree with that conclusion and in a recent critical review of work on the 'coronary personality', one of the major types to which attention has been directed, Mordkoff and Parsons (1967) decided that there was no evidence that such a personality type exists. Nevertheless, personality has remained as one of the obvious sources of variation to be examined in psychosomatic research, though the quest for global disease types has tended to be replaced, in the better validated studies, by investigation of more limited personality dimensions which it is thought may differentiate people prone to psychosomatic illness in general or to particular classes of disease. Here we shall look especially at work on the two personality dimensions of extraversion and neuroticism; doing so for three reasons. First, these are the two dimensions that have emerged most consistently from extensive psychometric research on personality. Secondly, the questionnaire measurement of extraversion and neuroticism has been developed to an acceptable level of reliability and validity. Thirdly, the existence of hypotheses anchoring these descriptive features of behaviour to their underlying causal substrate at least opens up the possibility of eventually linking personality variation to the physiological processes mediating psychosomatic disease.

In one of the most systematic studies that examined extraversion and neuroticism in relation to a range of physical diseases Sainsbury (1960) administered the Maudsley Personality Inventory to outpatients seen at a general hospital. The patients were divided into four groups: psychosomatic, possibly psychosomatic, control, and neurotic. He reported that both the psychosomatic and possibly psychosomatic groups had higher than normal neuroticism scores; while the psychosomatic, but not the possibly psychosomatic, patients were significantly more introverted than normal. Despite this average trend towards introversion, one group of patients, those suffering from warts, were significantly more extraverted (and neurotic) than normal. Sainsbury concluded that there was some evidence for distinguishing two types of psychosomatic reaction: those associated with dysthymic and those associated with hysterical personalities. Sainsbury's finding that, in general, psychosomatic patients have higher than average levels of neuroticism was confirmed by Barendregt (1961) and by Bendien (1963) both of whom used a Hebrew version of the Heron Scale.

Of other studies using the Maudsley scales Franks and Leigh (1959) found that asthmatics showed no tendency to abnormality in either extraversion or neuroticism. On the latter scale they fell between normals and neurotics. Nor did asthmatics differ from other groups when eye-blink conditioning was used as a genotypic personality measure. Heseltine (1963) reported equally negative findings on the MPI in patients with eczema, a disorder linked to asthma. Lucas and Ojha (1963) also found normal E and N scores in acne patients, although they showed that those whose symptoms worsened during stress were highest in neuroticism. In a study of different varieties of skin disorder Kenyon (1962), too, found that his sample as a whole did not differ from normal on either of the MPI scales. The most highly extraverted and neurotic of his patients, however, were those with warts, a finding confirming Sainsbury's.

Skin disorders are of particular interest because they bring out in a very obvious way a difficulty encountered in studies of questionnaire responses in physically ill patients: namely the permanent or transient influence of the disease itself on the personality. Thus, Kidd and Watt (1967), using Cattell's N-scale, demonstrated that skin patients with lesions producing visible disfigurement were more disturbed than those whose lesions were concealed. Such reactions to the presence of disease must also operate, if more subtly, in other conditions, a point made by most authors reporting in this area. Franks and Leigh (op. cit.), for example, concluded that the moderate degree of general neuroticism common to most asthmatics was probably reactive to the illness itself. Bendien (op. cit.) went further in interpreting his own finding that neuroticism is raised in psychosomatic patients and suggested that the N-scale he used simply measured the urge to complain. His grounds for saying so were that he also found raised N-scores in patients with internal disease of non-psychosomatic origin. Finally, Huggan (1968), reporting raised anxiety in women with cancer, argued strongly in favour of the result being due to a reaction to illness.

Although increases in anxiety/neuroticism in physically ill patients as a response to illness are understandable, it is less easy to explain in the same way the *lowered* levels of neuroticism that some authors have reported in certain physical diseases. Thus, Sainsbury (op. cit.) found that coronary patients had lower N-scores than controls, together with normal E-scores: a trend opposite, of course, to that shown by the remainder of his psychosomatic sample. Bendien and Groen (1963) reported a not too dissimilar finding in patients with myocardial infarction. Compared with other physically ill patients, the latter were significantly more extraverted and also less neurotic though not significantly so. In interpreting this result, Bendien and Groen reiterated the senior author's view of what their N-scale was measuring and suggested that infarct patients may have scored low on neuroticism because they were less likely to complain. However, they provide no evidence for such a conclusion.

Another group of patients in whom lowered neuroticism scores have been described are those with lung cancer. This result has been reported in a series of studies carried out by the late Dr Kissen and his collaborators who compared samples of male lung cancer patients with male patients suffering from other chest diseases. In the first account of this research Kissen and Eysenck (1962), using the short form of the MPI, found that lung cancer patients were significantly less neurotic than other chest patients. There was also a tendency towards increased extraversion in the lung cancer sample, but this was significant only in patients aged between 55 and 64 years. The latter result is consistent with that of Coppen and Metcalfe (1964) who described breast cancer patients as being extraverted, though the lowered N-score described by Kissen and Eysenck is somewhat at variance with Huggan's finding (op. cit.) that female cancer patients are more anxious.

Subsequent studies by Kissen and his colleagues have confirmed the unusually low N-scores of lung cancer patients, but the tendency to increased extraversion has not been maintained on the larger samples collected since the original study. In their latest paper Kissen et al. (1969) reported on the results for several hundred patients given either the short form of the MPI or the EPI. On both tests lung cancer patients proved to have significantly lower N-scores than other chest patients, but did not differ significantly from the latter on the E-scale.

Various interpretations have been put on the results just described. Eysenck himself has emphasized the slightly raised E-scores of lung cancer patients found in his original study with Kissen and has linked this to the finding that smokers tend to be more extraverted than average (Eysenck et al., 1960). He has suggested that both smoking and lung cancer may be the product of a common cause in the personality factor of extraversion (Eysenck, 1965). Kissen, however, placed greater emphasis on the findings for neuroticism in lung cancer which he interpreted as being in support of his clinical observation that lung cancer patients have a diminished outlet for emotional discharge (Kissen, 1966). Brown (1969), a colleague of Kissen, has also focused on neuroticism as the more important variable and has extended his research on it to a measure of autonomic awareness. He found that, compared with other chest cases, lung cancer patients reported being significantly less aware of their own autonomic activity; a result, of course, consistent with their low N-scores. Brown considered two possible interpretations of this finding. One, derived from that offered by Kissen, was that lung cancer patients have high physiological reactivity but do not admit to it. The other was that, in keeping with their self-description, they are autonomically poorly reactive. Brown has speculated that the second explanation would be nicely consistent with the demonstration (Bullough and Laurence, 1958) that low adrenaline levels are associated with a high rate of cell division. However, no evidence is as yet available to support either interpretation though research in progress is apparently examining the autonomic status of lung cancer patients in terms of their physiological response (Brown, personal communication) and catecholamine output (Rao, personal communication).

Returning to the general question of personality and disease, it would appear that of the two dimensions considered here neuroticism is most likely to show abnormality in psychosomatic patients; though this is not exclusively true. Even on neuroticism the degree of abnormality may vary over a considerable range, depending to some extent on the kind of illness being examined. Certainly, the most obvious hypothesis that psychosomatic patients will invariably show increased neuroticism or anxiety is by no means true, heart disease and lung cancer being notable exceptions.* The fact that the range of variation on this dimension is so great is encouraging since it suggests that the results described reflect genuine personality differences rather than some non-specific factor such as a transient reaction to illness. Nevertheless, the latter effect must inevitably complicate the interpretation of many studies of patients with an ongoing physical illness and it emphasises the importance of prospective research in this area.

Perhaps the main value of the studies reviewed is that they help to identify potentially important sources of individual variation at the descriptive level of personality which can then be examined more closely at the causal level. In this respect, the dimensions of extraversion and neuroticism are well-placed, both historically and theoretically. For one thing considerable research has already been undertaken to establish their psychophysiological determinants (Eysenck, 1967; Claridge, 1967). Furthermore, as Gray (1964) has pointed out, the models of personality to which such studies have given rise have important theoretical links with the Pavlovian notion of nervous typology, which has traditionally formed an essential part of Russian cortico-visceral research. The analysis of human nervous types has so far been confined to work on normal and psychiatric subjects but the general approach should be ideally suited to the study of psychosomatic relations in disease. Psychophysiological models of individual difference could therefore provide psychosomatic medicine with the viable theory of personality that it has so far lacked.

Physiological Response Patterning

Instead of emphasising broad personality differences some workers in psychosomatic research have focused on more narrowly defined sets of variables which determine the pattern of physiological response that the individual shows under stress. The assumption here is that physiological systems that are more frequently or more prone to be activated are potential vehicles for psychosomatic reactions. Several different kinds of study can be considered as falling under the heading of response patterning. Perhaps the most important theoretically are those concerned with the phenomenon of *response specificity*, which some authors (e.g. Sternbach, 1966) have considered provides a perfectly adequate model for explaining individual differences in

psychosomatic symptomatology. Response specificity refers to the observation that, under stress, the individual does not react with a uniform arousal in all physiological systems but shows an idiosyncratic patterning of response. The term was introduced by Lacey who, with his associates, demonstrated response specificity in both children and adults subjected to the stresses of hyperventilation, cold water, mental arithmetic, and a letter association test (Lacey and VanLehn, 1952; Lacey et al., 1953). Measuring skin conductance and various cardiovascular parameters they showed that, although the overall magnitude of response to different stressors varied, within the individual the hierarchical order of response in different systems tended to remain constant, whatever the stress. Thus, some subjects responded maximally in heart rate, others in blood pressure, others in skin conductance, and so on. This autonomic patterning was found to be reproducible on immediate retest and in some subjects to remain stable for longer periods. In a repetition of Lacey's work Wenger et al. (1961) also demonstrated the occurrence of response specificity but emphasised that not all subjects will show it, whether it appears depending partly on the method of scoring used. Lacey et al. (1953) had previously noted that the tendency to response specificity was itself a source of individual difference, some subjects showing more stable autonomic patterning than others.

A rather different approach to the problem of autonomic patterning was taken in two recent experiments by Fisher, who looked at the relationship between organ awareness and organ activation. In his first study (1966) Fisher demonstrated that subjects reporting heightened awareness of parts of their body surface consistently showed increased GSR responsiveness in the appropriate area. In his second study (1967) Fisher extended this procedure to other organ systems and found that scores of heart awareness correlated with heart rate. Similarly, reported awareness of stomach activity correlated with actual changes in the stomach.

The concept of response specificity was applied directly to psychosomatic symptomatology in two early studies by Malmo and Shagass, who formulated the allied principle of symptom specificity. In their first study (1949) they demonstrated that psychiatric patients with complaints of heart pain or headache did in fact tend to respond to stress with a change in the appropriate physiological system. Furthermore, cross-comparisons of physiological activity in the two groups showed that these responses were symptom specific. Thus, heart patients showed a significant change in heart activity, but not in muscle tension, and vice versa. In a second study (1950) Malmo and Shagass looked at the problem

---

* The possibility that low levels of neuroticism may also characterise people prone to hypertension is suggested by the recent finding of Davies (1970) who, in a survey of normal factory workers, demonstrated a significant *negative* relationship between blood pressure and the N-scale of the EPI.

longitudinally rather than cross-sectionally. There they sequentially examined muscle action potentials in three patients whose somatic symptoms were referable to muscle tension. Physiological recording during interview showed that periods of stress tended selectively to evoke increased muscle tension in the bodily areas appropriate to the somatic complaint; for example, in the forehead, but not in the arm, when the patient reported headache.

Symptom specificity was also demonstrated by Engel and Bickford (1961) and by Schacter (1957). Both showed that hypertensive patients reacted to stress with a greater change in blood pressure than normals, though Schacter also found that the variability of the blood pressure change was greater in hypertensives. In neither case, however, were there any differences between the groups in other kinds of autonomic change, such as galvanic skin response. Although these studies do seem to suggest that symptom specificity is a genuine phenomenon, Buck and Hobbs (1959), taking a different experimental approach, reached the opposite conclusion. They examined the extent to which individuals were liable to present with more than one psychosomatic illness. Five categories of illness were taken in pairs and it was found that the frequency with which patients had more than one psychosomatic disorder was greater than would be expected by chance. They decided on the basis of this evidence that there was no support for the specificity hypothesis.

The conclusions reached by Buck and Hobbs are perhaps somewhat sweeping since the concept of symptom specificity, as used by Malmo and Shagass, does not necessarily imply that the *possibility* for abnormal physiological response is confined to one bodily system, let alone to that of maximum reactivity. Nor, of course, does it follow that only one system in the response hierarchy will become pathologically activated during stress. Nevertheless, the fact that several organ systems may simultaneously become the targets of illness does raise the question of the general validity of the response and symptom specificity principles. Here a study by Broadhurst and Eysenck (1965) is relevant. They looked at the problem of emotionality in rats, comparing the Maudsley reactive and non-reactive strains, bidirectionally selected for emotional elimination on the open field test. They argued that, if extreme response specificity were operating, then selection for the defaecation response would not lead to any differentiation between the strains with respect to other physiological indices of emotionality. In fact, their results showed considerable generality of emotional responsiveness as a physiological characteristic. Both male and female animals in the two strains differed significantly in the weights of the gonads and the thyroid gland, while females also differed in pituitary and adrenal weights. Eysenck and Broadhurst concluded that response specificity was more in the nature of a limiting factor imposed upon a general factor of emotionality or emotional arousability.

Of course, it requires considerable extrapolation to relate these findings to work on human subjects, particularly as the latter has been mainly confined to autonomic activity. However, it seems probable that the same conclusions may be valid since, despite an established degree of patterning, the sympathetic division of the autonomic nervous system, at least, shows considerable uniformity in its activation under stress. Clearly more research needs to be done at the human level on the relative importance of response hierarchies compared with overall emotional reactivity as factors determining the individual's reaction to stress. Other problems that remain concern the reasons for individual differences in the stability of autonomic patterns and in the kind of patterning displayed. With regard to the latter, genetic influences might appear to be important. So far there is no direct evidence bearing on that question, though Richmond and Lustman (1955) and Lipton et al. (1963) did find that even in infants a few days old there were considerable individual differences in autonomic responsiveness. However, Miller (1969), in discussing his own work on operant conditioning of the ANS, has speculated that the response patterns may be learned through selective reinforcement. The probable answer is that both genetic factors and learning interact, organ systems high in the response hierarchy presumably being more readily activated under stress and, therefore, more subject to operant control.

Turning now to another potential source of individual variation, some attempts have been made to relate psychosomatic symptomatology to different affect states, on the assumption that these will manifest characteristic patterns of physiological arousal. Most of the basic research on emotion as such has been concerned with the differentiation between fear and anger in laboratory situations (e.g, Ax, 1953) and has already been dealt with by Martin in Chapter 10. However, it is appropriate to consider here some of the more clinically relevant evidence in that area as well as studies of more complex attitudes in relation to psychosomatic disorders. With regard to primitive emotional reactions there have been several studies of gastric function in different mood states. These have usually consisted of reports on single individuals whose gastric activity could, for one reason or another, be easily observed and recorded. The most well-documented example is the case of Tom who, due to an accident to the oesophagus, had his gastric mucosa partly open to view and who fed himself through a fistula. Wolf and Wolff (1943) who carried out intensive investigation of Tom reported that changes in his emotional state reliably produced marked alterations in gastric response. In situations involving anger or resentment it was found that the mucous membrane showed increased blood flow and took on a red, engorged appearance. At the same time, the secretion of acid increased. Conversely, when Tom was dejected, the membrane surface appeared pale and thin and acid secretion diminished. An important additional finding was that ulceration could be induced if, during periods of hypersecretion, the mucus which normally protects the stomach lining from acid was deficient or artificially removed.

In a later study of an infant with a gastric fistula Engel et al. (1956) also found changes in acid secretion in different emotional states. They reported that outgoing aggressive responses were associated with an increase in acid, which decreased during periods of withdrawal. Closely similar results were described by Coddington (1968) in a more recent study of a single pair of identical twins discordant for congenital abnormality of the oesophagus, though he noted that the correlation between mood and acid secretion was greatest during the early phase of development, and diminished later.

A somewhat different approach to mood-induced physiological reactions has been by the study of complex emotional attitudes and, procedurally, through the use of hypnosis. Thus, Ullman (1947) demonstrated that it was possible to produce second-degree burns under hypnosis, while Chapman et al. (1959) found that subjects given the hypnotic suggestion that their skin was 'vulnerable' showed extreme vasodilatation, inflammatory reaction and measurable tissue changes when a warm rod was applied to the skin. The most complete and relevant studies in this area, however, are those by Graham and his colleagues, who have used hypnotic suggestion to try to demonstrate that attitudes associated with different psychosomatic illnesses give rise to specific physiological responses that can be reproduced under hypnosis. In their first study, Grace and Graham (1952) described what, on the basis of clinical observation, they believed to be the emotional attitudes found in patients with several psychosomatic disorders. Thus, patients with eczema were seen as being frustrated, those with urticaria as feeling mistreated, those with duodenal ulcer as wanting to seek revenge and so on. Patients with Raynaud's disease were considered to be characterised by the feeling of wanting to hit others, and in a special study of individuals with this condition Graham

(1955) noted the effect of hostility in producing constriction of the minute blood vessels and the association between attacks of Raynaud spasm and the presence of a hostile attitude. Following these preliminary studies Graham and his collaborators hypnotically induced in normal subjects the attitudes thought to be characteristic of some of these conditions and measured the appropriate physiological parameters. Graham et al. (1958) contrasted the 'hives (urticaria) attitude' with the 'Raynaud's attitude' and found that, as predicted, the former produced a rise and the latter a fall in skin temperature when compared with a state of relaxation. In a later study, Graham et al. (1962) examined the 'hives attitude' against that for hypertension, which was considered to be one of feeling on guard against the world. Various autonomic responses were measured in normal subjects to whom these two attitudes were suggested under hypnosis. It was found that 'hives' produced a greater rise in skin temperature than 'hypertension', whereas the latter produced the greater rise in diastolic blood pressure. No differences were found in systolic blood pressure, heart rate, or respiration.

A slightly surprising feature of Graham's findings is the extreme specificity of physiological changes produced experimentally, despite considerable overlap in the attitudes elicited in the preliminary clinical enquiry. Thus, many psychosomatic disorders were found to have similar attitudes associated with them and in one case—asthma and vasomotor rhinitis—the attitudes elicited were exactly the same. Graham's results are the more surprising when it is considered that even very distinct emotions like anger and fear are not all that easily differentiated at a physiological level. In this connection it is pertinent to note that some authors, particularly Schacter (1966), have commented that it may be a fruitless quest to try to differentiate emotions purely in terms of their peripheral physiological concomitants. Schacter has emphasised, instead, the cognitive or 'labelling' aspects of emotion and it is possible that study of the subtler attitudinal components of emotional expression will throw more light on intra-individual differences in autonomic patterning than the investigation of crude affective states. The approach adopted by Graham may also be more relevant in the context of psychosomatic research because it is presumably getting at the autonomic patterns associated with chronically established attitudes rather than those found in acute emotion. This may be important since, as we saw in an earlier section with respect to gastric function, acute and chronic emotion may have different physiological concomitants. And it seems reasonably well-established that it is chronically sustained arousal that is most likely to enter into the aetiology of psychosomatic disorder.

Genetic Influences

Although use of the term 'stress disorder' as a synonym for psychosomatic disease emphasises the role of external factors in aetiology, there is usually an implicit assumption that genetic influences contribute to individual variations in symptom choice. As with most of the other research areas discussed here, the evidence bearing on that question could be said to come from many sources. Looking at the problem very broadly, the literature on the genetic basis of personality, particularly in relation to psychophysiological differences, should be considered relevant; but for a discussion of that evidence the reader is referred to Chapter 12. In a narrower sense, genetic studies in the field have been concerned with hereditary factors in disease itself, particularly vascular disease and peptic ulcer.

Several methodological approaches have been followed. Using the family pedigree method to study peptic ulcer, Doll and Buch (1950) demonstrated a significantly raised incidence of the condition in the relatives of affected patients. In a later paper, Doll and Kellock (1951) reported further that genetic factors may also partly determine the site at which ulcers occur. Thus, the affected relatives of patients with gastric ulcers themselves tended more frequently to have ulcers in the stomach. Similarly, the duodenum was more often the site of disease in the affected relatives of duodenal ulcer patients.

Some support for a specific heritability factor in ulcer susceptibility has also come from animal research. Sines (1959) found that in an unselected group of rats 58 per cent of males and 68 per cent of females developed ulcers after immobilisation stress combined with food and water deprivation. However, these figures rose to 79 per cent and 87 per cent, respectively, in the F1 generation of susceptible animals. In a later study, Sines and McDonald (1968) used 12-hour restraint as a stress in genetically bred strains of ulcer-susceptible rats. They concluded that over half the variability in ulcer susceptibility was genetically determined and that susceptibility was incompletely dominant over ulcer resistance. That the characteristic is inherited in a fairly specific manner would tend to be supported by the results of Mikhail and Broadhurst (1965) who compared the effects of immobilisation stress in the Maudsley strains of emotionally reactive and unreactive rats; that is, in animals not distinctly selected for ulcer susceptibility. They found no

difference between the two strains in the number and size of ulcers produced by stress.

Rather less positive evidence for the contribution of genetic factors in human peptic ulcer was reported by Harvald and Hauge (1958), using the conventional twin method. Taking as their criterion of concordance the hospitalisation of both twins on account of peptic ulcer they found that only 8 out of 44 monozygotic pairs were concordant for the disease. In dizygotic twins of the same sex the concordance rate was only slightly lower, there being 8 out of 54 pairs in which both members had ulcers. However, the authors pointed out that these differences might increase if thorough clinical examination, including X-ray, was used as the criterion of ulceration.

The results reported by Harvald and Hauge were part of a large-scale study of Danish twins in whom the concordance rates for various diseases were examined. Of the conditions more usually described as 'psychosomatic', bronchial asthma showed the greatest difference in concordance rates, both twins being asthmatic in 9 out of 16 monozygotic pairs, compared with 2 out of 33 in the dizygotic sample. Rather smaller differences between the two types of twin were found in the case of cerebral vascular disease, while no differences in concordance rates emerged for coronary occlusion. With respect to malignant disease the authors reported significantly higher concordance among monozygotic than among dizygotic twins, indicating a genetic component in aetiology. However, they suggested that there may be some differences with regard to site, higher concordance rates being found for breast cancer than other forms of the disease.

In summarising the results of their investigation Harvald and Hauge concluded that the findings throw light on the influence of heredity on what they described as the 'total load of life-shortening disabilities'. However, they also emphasised the important point that even in conditions in which significantly different concordance rates between monozygotic and dizygotic twins emerged, the number of *discordant* MZ pairs found was considerable. This, of course, is true of many characteristics studied by the twin survey method which tends to focus on the similarities rather than the differences between twins. However, a powerful refinement of the twin method is to examine the reasons for discordance between otherwise genetically identical individuals. In that way it should be possible to disentangle some of the interactions between genotypic and environmental influences. Few studies of disease have adopted this approach, though two exceptions are an investigation by Pilot et al. (1963) of a single pair of twins discordant for peptic ulcer and a study of three twin pairs discordant for leukaemia described by Greene and Swisher (1969). In the former study the differences between the twins were unfortunately presented as a clinical description of personality in psychoanalytic terms, the unaffected member being considered more over-controlled, repressed and having a conflict over oral-dependency needs. Greene and Swisher, however, presented a more complete chronological account of the life-history of their leukaemic and unaffected pairs. They concluded that in each of the three pairs the symptoms of leukaemia developed in the affected twin in the setting of major psychological stress.

Apart from peptic ulcer, genetic studies of psychosomatic disorder have concentrated particularly on vascular disease and on the associated problem of the heritability of blood pressure variations. As noted above, Harvald and Hauge, on the basis of their results in twins, concluded that heredity plays a minor role in coronary occlusion but a greater part in cerebral vascular disease, a finding they considered was due to the involvement of a genetically determined tendency to hypertension. A number of workers have examined blood pressure from a genetic point of view. Hamilton *et al.* (1954) and Miall and Oldham (1955) both reported that blood pressure was raised in the relatives of patients with essential hypertension. They also demonstrated a normal distribution of blood pressure, a finding consistent with a polygenic form of inheritance. According to that model, essential hypertension would be considered as blood pressure raised above an arbitrary cut-off point. However, as Roberts (1961) has discussed, it is also possible to postulate a limited gene hypothesis to explain hypertension, since bimodal distributions of blood pressure can be demonstrated if the data collected by Hamilton and others are analysed with respect to the older age groups only.

Studies using the twin method to investigate blood pressure variation have led to conflicting results, though they do agree in pointing to a complex relationship with age, sex and, in some cases, body type. Osborne *et al.* (1963) found no indication of a genetic component in blood pressure variability in twins aged 18 and over. However, Eisenberg *et al.* (1964) did find evidence for genetic determination of both systolic and diastolic pressures in females over 18, but none for individuals under that age. In a group of male twins aged between 30 and 40 years, Takkunen (1964) reported that variability of systolic blood pressure and pulse pressure depended on genetic factors, but this was not true of the diastolic pressure. He also concluded that there was significant genetic control over the covariation between blood pressure and body build, and between the latter and certain electrocardiographic parameters.

A possible familial association between raised blood pressure and vascular disease was suggested by Harlan *et al.* (1962), who undertook an 18-year follow-up of nearly 800 healthy young men. They found that individuals showing the greatest increase in blood pressure over the period of investigation more often had a positive family history of vascular disease. The authors also reported significant relationships between blood pressure change, weight, and initial somatotype. Although the existence of common genetic links between these various parameters and later disease seems fairly likely, equally certain is the interaction between hereditary factors and environmental influences. In an attempt to disentangle the relative significance of some of these factors in coronary heart disease Russek and Zohman (1958) studied a group of 100 patients with that condition. They concluded that the onset and progression of heart disease depended on three major factors: heredity, a high-fat diet, and emotional strain of occupational origin. At least two of these factors were present in 95 per cent of their sample compared with 12 per cent in a healthy control group. A family tendency to the disease was present in 93 per cent of patients, though in 17 per cent both parents were living and healthy. They concluded that the influences of heredity and diet may be age-dependent, in young adults the more important aetiological factor being emotional stress associated with job-responsibility.

In general, then, of the psychosomatic reactions that have been adequately studied none shows evidence of a simple genetic determination. This conclusion is not too unexpected since the very existence of psychosomatic medicine as a discipline rests on the assumption that the conditions with which it is mostly concerned are multiply determined. To specify the exact genetic mechanisms involved and the nature of their interaction with environmental influences will require research carried out on a very broad front. Of the methodological approaches considered here two seem to be particularly promising. One is the careful study of identical twins discordant for particular diseases. The other is the genetic analysis of animals in whom experimental disease is induced. In addition, if the results of studies of disease itself can be aligned with evidence about the genetic basis of behaviour as a whole, it might eventually be possible to give a coherent account of the contribution of heredity to individual variations in symptom choice.

CONCLUSIONS

In this chapter a number of very different kinds of study of psychosomatic disorder have been discussed. The studies concerned are so varied that no single conclusion can be reached about them as a whole. Rather they serve to illustrate several quite disparate methodological approaches to the problem under review. It can be said, therefore, that no adequate all-embracing theory of psychosomatic illness exists and that any attempt to provide such a theory based either on physiological, psychological, or sociological evidence is premature. Nevertheless, some important growing-points in the field can be discerned. One is certainly in the area of autonomic conditioning. The so-called involuntary nervous system has traditionally been assigned an inferior and somewhat separate role in behaviour, both with regard to its general participation in higher nervous activity, and specifically with respect to its modifiability. The increasing evidence that the internal *milieu* is as important in the regulation of behaviour as the external environment clearly has far-reaching implications for the study of psychological factors in physical disease. Among the most promising developments here are those pioneered by Miller and his colleagues on the operant control of autonomic response and it seems safe to predict that continued research on that problem will have important consequences for psychosomatic medicine.

The whole area of stress research also clearly has a central place in the sciences basic to psychosomatic medicine, though there is probably room here for greater concentration of effort on the effects of chronic, as distinct from acute, stress. This is admittedly difficult in humans though it should not be impossible to design experiments in which the physiological effects of relatively long-term stress were examined systematically. In animal research the situation is more favourable since it is possible to impose stress that will induce actual physical disease. Studies where that has been done certainly point to the chronicity of the stress as an important factor contributing to disease. However, more investigations of that kind might usefully incorporate within the experimental design the formal attempt to disentangle the influence of genetic factors; for example by using carefully selected animal strains whose physiological and behavioural characteristics are well-understood.

Any attempt in the future to give a comprehensive account of psychosomatic disorder must be able to explain individual differences in symptom choice. The search for a solution to that problem will certainly rely heavily on genetic studies of the predisposition to particular diseases. However, in a broader sense symptom choice is the same problem of individual variation in physiological make-up met in other behavioural research and at least two lines of enquiry promise to make an important contribution to psychosomatic medicine. One, that concerned with physiological patterning in the organism, offers considerable scope for research on its genetic and acquired determinants and on the extent to which it occurs in functions other than those conventionally studied by psychologists. Thus, it would be valuable to know whether consistent patterning of endocrine response could be demonstrated in human subjects. The second source of evidence about individual differences in symptom choice must surely be the general field of personality study. Admittedly, progress there has so far been limited and mainly confined to the use of relatively weak research instruments, namely personality questionnaires. Perhaps more important, however, are the conceptual advances that have occurred in personality theory. These must eventually begin to influence thinking in psychosomatic medicine, as psychoanalytic theories disappear and nervous typological models of personality begin to take their place.

REFERENCES

ÁDÁM, G. (1967) *Interoception and Behaviour.* Budapest: Hungarian Academy of Sciences.

ALEXANDER, F. (1952) *Psychosomatic Medicine. Its Principles and Applications.* London: Allen & Unwin.

ANDERSON, O. D., PARMENTER, R., and LIDDELL, H. S. (1939) Some cardiovascular manifestations of the experimental neurosis in sheep. *Psychosom. Med.,* **1,** 93–100.

AX, A. F. (1953) The physiological differentiation between fear and anger in humans. *Psychosom. Med.,* **15,** 433–42.

BARENDREGT, J. T. (1961) *Psychological Studies.* Vol. I. Research in Psychodiagnostics. The Hague: Mouton.

BENDIEN, J. (1963) The value of questionnaires testing the dimensions of neuroticism and extraversion in psychosomatic research. *J. psychosom. Res.,* **7,** 1–10.

BENDIEN, J. and GROEN, J. (1963) A psychological-statistical study of neuroticism and extraversion in patients with myocardial infarction. *J. psychosom. Res.*, **7**, 11–14.

BRADY, J. V. (1958) Ulcers in 'executive' monkeys. *Sci. Amer.* Oct.

BRADY, J. V., PORTER, R. W., CONRAD, D. G., and MASON, J. W. (1958) Avoidance behaviour and the development of gastro-duodenal ulcers. *J. exp. anim. Behav.*, **1**, 69–72.

BRAIN, W. R. and HENSON, R. A. (1958) Neurological syndromes associated with carcinoma. *Lancet*, **ii**, 971–4.

BRENER, J. and HOTHERSALL, D. (1967) Paced respiration and heart rate control. *Psychophysiology*, **4**, 1–6.

BRENER, J., KLEINMAN, R. A., and GOESLING, W. J. (1969) The effects of different exposures to augmented sensory feedback on the control of heart rate. *Psychophysiology*, **5**, 510–16.

BROADHURST, P. L. and EYSENCK, H. J. (1965) Emotionality in the rat: a problem of response specificity. In *Studies in Psychology* (Ed. Banks, C. and Broadhurst, P. L.). London: Univ. London Press.

BRODIE, D. A. and HANSON, H. M. (1960) A study of the factors involved in the production of gastric ulcers by the restraint technique. *Gastroenterology*, **38**, 353–60.

BROWN, C. C. and KATZ, R. A. (1967) Operant salivary conditioning in man. *Psychophysiology*, **4**, 156–160.

BROWN, R. I. F. (1969) Neuroticism, extraversion and awareness of autonomic activity in lung cancer patients. Paper presented to the British Psychological Society Annual Conference, Edinburgh.

BUCK, C. and HOBBS, G. E. (1959) The problem of specificity in illness. *J. psychosom. Res.*, **3**, 227–33.

BULLOUGH, W. S. and LAURENCE, E. P. V. (1958) Control of mytosis in mouse and hamster melanomeator by means of melocyte chalone. *Eur. J. Cancer.*, **4**, 672–6.

BYKOV, K. M. (1957) *The Cerebral Cortex and the Internal Organs.* (Trans. W. Horsley Gantt). New York: Chemical Publishing Co.

CANNON, W. B. (1953) *Bodily Changes in Pain, Hunger, Fear and Rage.* Boston: Charles T. Branford.

CHAPMAN, L. F., GOODELL, H., and WOLFF, H. G. (1959) Changes in tissue vulnerability induced during hypnotic suggestion. *J. psychosom. Res.*, **4**, 99–105.

CHERTOK, L. and FONTAINE, M. (1963) Psychosomatics in veterinary medicine. *J. psychosom. Res.*, **7**, 229–35.

CHODOFF, P. (1963) Late effects of the concentration camp syndrome. *Arch. gen. Psychiat.*, **8**, 323–33.

CLARIDGE, G. S. (1967) *Personality and Arousal.* Oxford: Pergamon.

CLEGHORN, R. A. (1954) The interplay between endocrine and psychological dysfunction. In *Recent Developments in Psychosomatic Medicine* (Ed. Wittkower, E. D. and Cleghorn, R. A.). London: Pitman Medical.

CODDINGTON, R. D. (1968) Study of an infant with a gastric fistula and her normal twin. *Psychosom. Med.*, **30**, 172–92.

COPPEN, A. J. and METCALFE, M. (1964) Cancer and extraversion. In *Psychosomatic Aspects of Neoplastic Disease* (Ed. Kissen, D.). London: Pitman Medical.

CORRODI, H., FUXE, K., and HÖKFELT, T. (1968) The effects of immobilization stress on the activity of

central monoamine neurons. *Life Sciences*, **7**, 107–12.

CORSON, S. A. (1966) Neuroendocrine and behavioural response patterns to psychologic stress and the problem of the target tissue in cerebrovisceral pathology. *Ann. N.Y. Acad. Sci.*, **125**, 890–918.

CUSHING, H. (1932) Peptic ulcers and interbrain. *Surg. Gynaec. and Obstet.*, **55**, 1–34.

DAVIES, M. H. (1970) Blood pressure and personality. *J. psychosom. Res.*, **14**, 89–104.

DELSE, F. C. and FEATHER, B. W. (1968) The effect of augmented sensory feedback on the control of salivation. *Psychophysiology*, **5**, 15–21.

DICARA, L. V. and MILLER, N. E. (1968a) Changes in heart rate instrumentally learned by curarized rats as avoidance responses. *J. comp. physiol. Psychol.*, **65**, 8–12.

DICARA, L. V. and MILLER, N. E. (1968b) Instrumental learning of systolic blood pressure responses by curarized rats: discussion of cardiac and vascular changes. *Psychosom. Med.*, **30**, 489–94.

DICARA, L. V. and MILLER, N. E. (1968c) Instrumental learning of vasomotor responses by rats: learning to respond differentially in the two ears. *Science*, **159**, 1485–86.

DOLL, R. and BUCH, J. (1950) Hereditary factors in peptic ulcer. *Ann. Eugen.* (London), **15**, 135–46.

DOLL, R. and KELLOCK, T. D. (1951) The separate inheritance of gastric and duodenal ulcers. *Ann. Eugen.* (London), **16**, 231–40.

DUNBAR, F. (1948) *Psychosomatic Diagnosis.* New York: Hoeber.

EISENBERG, H., HONEYMAN, M. S., and BARRETT, H. S. (1964) A twin family study of blood pressure. Paper presented at American Heart Association Annual Meeting.

EITINGER, L. (1961) Pathology of the concentration camp syndrome. *Arch. gen. Psychiat.*, **5**, 371–79.

EITINGER, L. (1969) Psychosomatic problems in concentration camp survivors. *J. psychosom. Res.*, **13**, 183–89.

EHRENTHEIL, O. F. (1957) Common medical disorders rarely found in psychotic patients. *Arch. Neurol. Psychiat.*, **77**, 178–86.

ENGEL, B. T. and BICKFORD, A. F. (1961) Response specificity. *Arch. gen. Psychiat.*, **5**, 478–89.

ENGEL, B. T. and CHISM, R. A. (1967) Operant conditioning of heart rate speeding. *Psychophysiology*, **3**, 18–26.

ENGEL, B. T. and HANSEN, S. P. (1966) Operant conditioning of heart rate slowing. *Psychophysiology*, **3**, 176–87.

ENGEL, G. L., REICHSMAN, F., and SEGAL, H. L. (1956) A study of an infant with a gastric fistula. I. Behaviour and the rate of total hydrochloric acid secretion. *Psychosom. Med.*, **18**, 374–98.

EYSENCK, H. J. (1965) *Smoking, Health and Personality.* London: Wiedenfeld and Nicholson.

EYSENCK, H. J. (1967) *The Biological Basis of Personality.* Springfield: Charles C. Thomas.

EYSENCK, H. J., TARRANT, M., WOOLF, M., and ENGLAND, L. (1960) Smoking and personality. *Brit. med. J.*, **1**, 1456–60.

FEDERAL SECURITY AGENCY (1940–55) *Vital statistics of the United States* (Annual Issues). Washington, D.C.: Government Printing Office.

FELDMAN, S., BEHAR, A. J., and BIRNBAUM, D. (1961) Gastric lesions following hypothalamic stimulation. *Arch. Neurol.*, **4**, 308–317.

FÉRÉ, C. (1899) *The Pathology of Emotions* (Trans. Park, R.). London: The University Press.

FERENCZI, S. (1926) *Further Contributions to the Theory and Technique of Psychoanalysis*. London: Hogarth.

FISHER, S. (1966) Body attention patterns and personality defenses. *Psychol. Monogr.*, **80**, 31 pp.

FISHER, S. (1967) Organ awareness and organ activation. *Psychosom. Med.*, **29**, 643–7.

FRANKS, C. M. and LEIGH, D. (1959) The theoretical and experimental application of a conditioning model to a consideration of bronchial asthma in man. *J. psychosom. Res.*, **4**, 88–98.

FRENCH, J. D., PORTER, R. W., CAVANAUGH, E. B., and LONGMIRE, R. L. (1954) Experimental observations on "psychosomatic" mechanisms. *Amer. med. assoc. Arch. Neurol. Psychiat.*, **72**, 267–81.

FRENCH, J. D., PORTER, R. W., CAVANAUGH, E. B., and LONGMIRE, R. L. (1957) Experimental gastro-duodenal lesions induced by stimulation of the brain. *Psychosom. Med.*, **19**, 209–20.

FRENCH, J. D., PORTER, R. W., VON AMERONGEN, F. K., and RANEY, R. B. (1952) Gastrointestinal haemorrhage and ulceration associated with intracranial lesions. *Surgery*, **32**, 395–407.

FREUD, S. (1949) *Inhibition, Symptoms and Anxiety* (Trans. A. Strachey). London: Hogarth.

FRISONE, J. D. and ESSMAN, W. B. (1965) Stress-induced gastric lesions in mice. *Psychol. Rep.*, **16**, 941–6.

FUNKENSTEIN, D. H. (1950) Psychophysiologic relationship of asthma and urticaria to mental illness. *Psychosom. Med.*, **12**, 377–85.

GOSLING, R. H. (1958) Peptic ulcer and mental disorder— II. *J. psychosom. Res.*, **2**, 285–301.

GRACE, W. J. and GRAHAM, D. T. (1952) Relationship of specific attitudes and emotions to certain bodily diseases. *Psychosom. Med.*, **14**, 241–51.

GRAHAM, D. T. (1955) Cutaneous vascular reactions in Raynaud's disease and in states of hostility, anxiety, and depression. *Psychosom. Med.*, **17**, 200–7.

GRAHAM, D. T., KABLER, J. D., and GRAHAM, F. K. (1962) Physiological response to the suggestion of attitudes specific for hives and hypertension. *Psychosom. Med.*, **24**, 159–69.

GRAHAM, D. T., STERN, J. A., and WINOKUR, G. (1958) Experimental investigation of the specificity of attitude hypothesis in psychosomatic disease. *Psychosom. Med.*, **20**, 446–57.

GRAY, J. A. (1964) *Pavlov's Typology*. Oxford: Pergamon.

GREENE, W. A. and SWISHER, S. N. (1969) Psychological and somatic variables associated with the development and course of monozygotic twins discordant for leukaemia. *Ann. N.Y. Acad. Sci.*, **164**, 394–408.

GROSSMAN, S. P. (1967) *A Textbook of Physiological Psychology*. New York: John Wiley.

HAMILTON, M., PICKERING, G. W., ROBERTS, J. A. F., and SOWRY, G. S. C. (1954) The aetiology of essential hypertension. 4. The role of inheritance. *Clin. Sci.*, **13**, 273–304.

HARLAN, W. R., OSBORNE, R. K., and GRAYBIEL, A. (1962) A longitudinal study of blood pressure. *USN Sch. Aviat. med. res. Rep.*, No. 4.

HARVALD, B. and HAUGE, M. (1958) A catamnestic investigation of Danish twins. *Acta genet.*, **8**, 287–94.

HARWOOD, C. W. (1962) Operant heart rate conditioning. *Psychol. Rec.*, **12**, 279–84.

HESELTINE, G. F. (1963) The site of onset of eczema and personality trait differences: an exploratory study. *J. psychosom. Res.*, **7**, 241–6.

HINKLE, L. E. (1961) Ecological observations of the relation of physical illness, mental illness, and the social environment. *Psychosom. Med.*, **23**, 289–96.

HINKLE, L. E., CHRISTENSON, W. N., KANE, F. D., OSTFELD, A., THETFORD, W. N., and WOLFF, H. G. (1958) An investigation of the relation between life experience, personality characteristics, and general susceptibility to illness. *Psychosom. Med.*, **20**, 278–95.

HINKLE, L. and WOLFF, H. G. (1957) The nature of man's adaptation to his total environment and the relation of this to illness. *Arch. intern. Med.*, **99**, 442–60.

HNATIOW, M. and LANG, P. J. (1965) Learned stabilization of cardiac rate. *Psychophysiology*, **1**, 330–36.

HOFF, E. C. and SHEEHAN, D. (1935) Experimental gastric erosions following hypothalamic lesions in monkeys. *Amer. J. Path.*, **11**, 789–802.

HORNBUCKLE, P. A. and ISAAC, W. (1969) Activation level and the production of gastric ulceration in the rat. *Psychosom. Med.*, **31**, 247–50.

HUGGAN, R. E. (1968) Neuroticism and anxiety among women with cancer. *J. psychosom. Res.*, **12**, 215–21.

HUSSAR, A. E. (1968) Peptic ulcer in long-term institutionalized schizophrenic patients. *Psychosom. Med.*, **30**, 374–77.

KAVETSKY, R. E., TURKEVICH, N. M., AKIMOVA, R. N., KHAYETSKY, I. K., and MATVEICHUK, Y. D. (1969) Induced carcinogenesis under various influences on the hypothalamus. *Ann. N.Y. Acad. Sci.*, **164**, 517–519.

KAVETSKY, R. E., TURKEVICH, N. M., and BALITKSY, K. P. (1966) On the psychophysiological mechanisms of the organism's resistance to tumour growth. *Ann. N.Y. Acad. Sci.*, **125**, 933–45.

KELLER, A. D. (1936) Ulceration in the digestive tract of the dog following intracranial procedures. *Arch. Path.*, **21**, 127–64.

KENYON, F. E. (1962) A psychiatric survey of a random sample of outpatients attending a dermatological hospital. *J. psychosom. Res.*, **6**, 129–35.

KERMAN, E. F. (1946) Bronchial asthma and affective psychoses. Report of two cases treated with electric shock. *Psychosom. Med.*, **8**, 53–57.

KERR, T. A., SCHAPIRA, K., and ROTH, M. (1969) The relationship between premature death and affective disorders. *Brit. J. Psychiat.*, **115**, 1277–82.

KIDD, C. B. and WATT, K. I. M. (1967) Neuroticism and distribution of lesions in patients with skin diseases. *J. psychosom. Res.*, **11**, 253–61.

KISSEN, D. M. (1958) *Emotional Factors in Pulmonary Tuberculosis*. London: Tavistock.

KISSEN, D. M. (1966) The significance of personality in lung cancer in men. *Ann. N.Y. Acad. Sci.*, **125**, 820–6.

KISSEN, D. M., BROWN, R. I. F., and KISSEN, M. (1969) A further report on personality and psychosocial factors in lung cancer. *Ann. N.Y. Acad. Sci.*, **164**, 535–544.

KISSEN, D. M. and EYSENCK, H. J. (1962) Personality in male lung cancer patients. *J. psychosom. Res.*, **6**, 123–27.

KLEIN, H., ZELLERMAYER, J., and SHANAN, J. (1963) Former concentration camp inmates in a psychiatric ward. *Arch. gen. Psychiat.*, **8**, 334–42.

KLEIN, M. (1948) *Contributions to Psychoanalysis 1921–45.* London: Hogarth.

KREITMAN, N., PEARCE, K. I., and RYLE, A. (1966) The relationship of psychiatric, psychosomatic and organic illness in a general practice. *Brit. J. Psychiat.*, **112**, 569–79.

LACEY, J. I., BATEMAN, D. E., and VANLEHN, R. (1953) Autonomic response specificity. An experimental study. *Psychosom. Med.*, **15**, 8–21.

LACEY, J. I. and VANLEHN, R. (1952) Differential emphasis in somatic response to stress. An experimental study. *Psychosom. Med.*, **14**, 71–81.

LEVENE, H. I., ENGEL, B. T., and PEARSON, J. A. (1968) Differential operant conditioning of heart rate. *Psychosom. Med.*, **30**, 837–45.

LEVI, L. (Ed.) (1967) *Emotional Stress.* Basel: S. Karger.

LIPTON, E. L., STEINSCHNEIDER, A., and RICHMOND, J. B. (1963) Auditory discrimination in the newborn infant (Abstract). *Psychosom. Med.*, **25**, 490.

LIVINGSTONE, R. B. (1955) Some brainstem mechanisms relating to psychosomatic functions. *Psychosom. Med.*, **17**, 347–54.

LOVETT DOUST, J. W. (1952) Psychiatric aspects of somatic immunity. *Brit. J. soc. Med.*, **6**, 49–67.

LUCAS, C., KELVIN, R., and OJHA, A. (1965) The psychological health of pre-clinical medical students. *Brit. J. Psychiat.*, **111**, 473–8.

LUCAS, C. J. and OJHA, A. B. (1963) Personality and acne. *J. psychosom. Res.*, **7**, 41–43.

LUPARELLO, T. J. (1966) Restraint and hypothalamic lesions in the production of gastroduodenal erosions in the guinea pig. *J. psychosom. Res.*, **10**, 251–54.

MACLEAN, P. D. (1949) Psychosomatic disease and the 'visceral brain'. *Psychosom. Med.*, **11**, 338–353.

MACLEOD, A. W., WITTKOWER, E. D., and MARGOLIN, S. G. (1954) Basic concepts of psychosomatic medicine. In *Recent Developments in Psychosomatic Medicine* (Ed. Wittkower, E. D. and Cleghorn, R. A.). London: Pitman Medical.

MAHL, G. F. (1952) Relationship between acute and chronic fear and the gastric acidity and blood sugar levels in macaca mulatta monkeys. *Psychosom. Med.*, **14**, 182–210.

MALMO, R. B. and SHAGASS, C. (1949) Physiologic study of symptom mechanisms in psychiatric patients under stress. *Psychosom. Med.*, **11**, 25–29.

MALMO, R. B., SHAGASS, C., and DAVIS, F. H. (1950) Symptom specificity and bodily mechanisms during psychiatric interview. *Psychosom. Med.*, **12**, 362–376.

MANDLER, G., PREVEN, D. W., and KUHLMAN, C. K.

(1962) Effects of operant reinforcement on the GSR. *J. exp. Anal. Behav.*, **5**, 317–321.

MARGETTS, E. L. (1954) Historical notes on psychosomatic medicine. In *Recent Developments in Psychosomatic Medicine* (Ed. Wittkower, E. D. and Cleghorn, R. A.). London: Pitman Medical.

MARSH, J. T., MILLER, B. E., and LAMSON, B. G. (1959) Effect of repeated brief stress on growth of Ehrlich carcinoma in the mouse. *U.S. Nat. Can. Inst., J.*, **22**, 961–77.

MARTIN, J. and SCHNEDORF, J. G. (1938) The absence of changes in gastric activity and of gastric intestinal ulceration following hypothalamic lesions in the monkey and cat. *Amer. J. Physiol.*, **122**, 81–85.

MASON, J. W. (1968a) A review of psychoendocrine research on the pituitary-adrenal cortical system. *Psychosom. Med.*, **30**, 576–607.

MASON, J. W. (1968b) A review of psychoendocrine research on the sympathetic-adrenal medullary system. *Psychosom. Med.*, **30**, 631–53.

MIALL, W. E. and OLDHAM, P. D. (1955) A study of arterial blood pressure and its inheritance in a sample of the general population. *Clin. Sci.*, **14**, 459–88.

MIKHAIL, A. A. (1969) Relationship of conditioned anxiety to stomach ulceration and acidity in rats. *J. comp. physiol. Psychol.*, **68**, 623–6.

MIKHAIL, A. A. and BROADHURST, P. L. (1965) Stomach ulceration and emotionality in selected strains of rats. *J. psychosom. Res.*, **8**, 477–9.

MILES, H. H. W., WALDFOGEL, S., BARRABEE, E. L., and COBB, S. (1954) Psychosomatic study of 46 young men with coronary artery disease. *Psychosom. Med.*, **16**, 455–77.

MILLER, N. E. (1961) Integration of neurophysiological and behavioural research. *Ann. N.Y. Acad. Sci.*, **92**, 830–9.

MILLER, N. E. (1969) Learning of visceral and glandular responses. *Science*, **163**, 434–445.

MILLER, N. E. and BANUAZZI, A. (1968) Instrumental learning by curarized rats of a specific visceral response, intestinal or cardiac. *J. comp. physiol. Psychol.*, **65**, 1–7.

MILLER, N. E. and CARMONA, A. (1967) Modification of a visceral response, salivation in thirsty dogs, by instrumental training with water reward. *J. comp. physiol. Psychol.*, **63**, 1–6.

MILLER, N. E. and DICARA, L. V. (1967) Instrumental learning of heart rate changes in curarized rats: shaping and specificity to discriminative stimuli. *J. comp. physiol. Psychol.*, **63**, 12–19.

MORDKOFF, A. M. and PARSONS, O. A. (1967) The coronary personality: a critique. *Psychosom. Med.*, **29**, 1–14.

MOWRER, O. H. (1950) Learning Theory and Personality Dynamics. New York: Ronald.

MUNRO, A. (1966) Parental deprivation in depressive patients. *Brit. J. Psychiat.*, **112**, 443–57.

NEWTON, G. (1964) Early experience and resistance to tumour growth. In *Psychosomatic Aspects of Neoplastic Disease* (Ed. Kissen, D.). London: Pitman Medical.

O'CONNOR, J. F. and STERN, L. O. (1967) Symptom

alternation. An evaluation of the theory. *Arch. gen. Psychiat.*, **16**, 432–36.

OSBORNE, R. H., DeGEORGE, F. V., and MATHERS, J. A. L. (1963) The variability of blood pressure; basal and casual measurements in adult twins. *Amer. Heart J.*, **66**, 176–83.

OTIS, L. S. and SCHOLLER, J. (1967) Effects of stress during infancy on tumour development and tumour growth. *Psychol. Rep.*, **20**, 167–73.

PETROVA, M. (1955) *The Role of a Functionally Weakened Cerebral Cortex in the Onset of Various Pathologic Processes in the Organism*. Moscow: Medgiz.

PILOT, M. L., RUBIN, J., SCHAFER, R., and SPIRO, H. M. (1963) Duodenal ulcer in one of identical twins. *Psychosom. Med.*, **25**, 285–91.

PORTER, R. W., BRADY, J. V., CONRAD, D., MASON, J. W., GALAMBOS, R., and RIOCH, D. McK. (1958) Some experimental observations on gastrointestinal lesions in behaviourally conditioned monkeys. *Psychosom. Med.*, **20**, 379–94.

RASHKIS, H. A. (1952) Systemic stress as an inhibitor of experimental tumours in Swiss mice. *Science*, **116**, 169–71.

RICE, H. K. (1963) The responding-rest ratio in the production of gastric ulcers in the rat. *Psychol. Rec.*, **13**, 11–14.

RICHMOND, J. B. and LUSTMAN, S. L. (1955) Autonomic function in the neonate. I. Implications for psychosomatic theory. *Psychosom. Med.*, **17**, 269–75.

ROBERTS, J. A. F. (1961) Multifactorial inheritance in relation to normal and abnormal human traits. *Brit. med. Bull.*, **17**, 241–6.

ROESSLER, R. and GREENFIELD, N. S. (1961) Incidence of somatic disease in psychiatric patients. *Psychosom. Med.*, **23**, 413–19.

ROSS, W. D., HAY, J., and McDOWALL, M. F. (1950a) The association of certain vegetative disturbances with various psychoses. *Psychosom. Med.*, **12**, 170–78.

ROSS, W. D., HAY, J., and McDOWALL, M. F. (1950b) The incidence of certain vegetative disturbances in relation to psychosis. *Psychosom. Med.*, **12**, 179–83.

RUSSEK, H. I. and ZOHMAN, B. L. (1958) Relative significance of heredity, diet and occupational stress in coronary heart disease in young adults. *Amer. J. med. Sci.*, **235**, 266–75.

RUTTER, M. (1963) Psychological factors in the short-term prognosis of physical disease. I. Peptic ulcer. *J. psychosom. Res.*, **7**, 45–60.

SAINSBURY, P. (1960) Psychosomatic disorders and neurosis in outpatients attending a general hospital. *J. psychosom. Res.*, **4**, 261–73.

SAWREY, W. L. (1961) Conditioned responses of fear in relationship to ulceration. *J. comp. physiol. Psychol.*, **54**, 347–8.

SAWREY, W. L. and SAWREY, J. M. (1968) UCS effects on ulceration following fear conditioning. *Psychonom. Sci.*, **10**, 85–6.

SCHACHTER, J. (1957) Pain, fear and anger in hypertensives and normotensives. *Psychosom. Med.*, **19**, 17–29.

SCHACTER, S. (1966) The interaction of cognitive and physiological determinants of emotional state. In *Anxiety and Behaviour* (Ed. Spielberger, C. D.). New York: Academic Press.

SELYE, H. (1946) The general adaptation syndrome and the diseases of adaptation. *J. clin. Endocrinol.*, **6**, 117–230.

SELYE, H. (1957) *The Stress of Life*. London: Longmans.

SELYE, H. (1960) The concept of stress in experimental physiology. In *Stress and Psychiatric Disorder* (Ed. Tanner, J. M.). Oxford: Blackwell.

SELYE, H. and FORTIER, C. (1950) Adaptive reactions to stress. In *Life Stress and Bodily Disease*. Baltimore: Williams and Wilkins.

SHAPIRO, D. and CRIDER, A. (1967) Operant electrodermal conditioning under multiple schedules of reinforcement. *Psychophysiology*, **4**, 168–75.

SHERRINGTON, C. S. (1947) *The Integrative Action of the Nervous System*. London: Cambridge Univ. Press.

SINES, J. O. (1959) Selective breeding for development of stomach lesions following stress in the rat. *J. comp. physiol. Psychol.*, **52**, 615–17.

SINES, J. O. and McDONALD, D. G. (1968) Heritability of stress-ulcer susceptibility in rats. *Psychosom. Med.*, **30**, 390–4.

STERN, J. A., WINOKUR, G., GRAHAM, D. T., and GRAHAM, F. K. (1961) Alterations in physiological measures during experimentally induced attitudes. *J. Psychosom. Res.*, **5**, 73–82.

STERNBACH, R. A. (1966) *Principles of Psychophysiology*. New York: Academic Press.

STRASSMAN, H. D., THALER, M. B., and SCHEIN, E. H. (1956) A prisoner-of-war syndrome: apathy as a reaction to severe stress. *Amer. J. Psychiat.*, **112**, 998–1003.

SWARTZ, J. and SEMRAD, E. V. (1951) Psychosomatic disorders in psychoses. *Psychosom. Med.*, **13**, 314–21.

TAKKUNEN, J. (1964) Anthropometric, electrocardiographic and blood pressure studies on adult male twins. *Ann. Acad. Sci. Fennicae, Series A. V. Medica*, **107**, pp. 82.

TROWILL, J. A. (1967) Instrumental conditioning of the heart rate in the curarized rat. *J. comp. physiol. Psychol.*, **63**, 7–11.

ULLMAN, M. (1947) Herpes simplex and second degree burn induced under hypnosis. *Amer. J. Psychiat.*, **103**, 828–30.

WARREN, I. A. and KOBERNICK, S. D. (1960) Studies with experimental neurosis and drug-induced ulceration of the colon in dogs. *Psychosom. Med.*, **22**, 443–47.

WATTS, J. W. and FULTON, J. F. (1935) The effect of the hypothalamus upon gastro-intestinal tract and heart in monkeys. *Ann. Surg.*, **101**, 363–72.

WEISZ, J. D. (1957) The aetiology of experimental gastric ulceration. *Psychosom. Med.*, **19**, 61–73.

WENGER, M. A., CLEMENS, T. L., COLEMAN, D. R., CULLEN, T. D., and ENGEL, B. T. (1961) Autonomic response specificity. *Psychosom. Med.*, **23**, 185–93.

WEST, B. M. and HECKER, A. O. (1952) Peptic ulcer. Incidence and diagnosis in psychotic patients. *Amer. J. Psychiat.*, **109**, 35–37.

WITTKOWER, E. D. (1960) Twenty years of North American psychosomatic medicine. *Psychosom. Med.*, **22**, 308–316.

WITTKOWER, E. D. and CLEGHORN, R. A. (Eds.) (1954) *Recent Developments in Psychosomatic Medicine.* London: Pitman.

WITTKOWER, E. D. and LIPOWSKI, Z. J. (1966) Recent developments in psychosomatic medicine. *Psychosom. Med.,* **28**, 722–37.

WOLF, S. and WOLFF, H. G. (1943) *Human Gastric Function. An Experimental Study of a Man and his Stomach.* London: Oxford Univ. Press.

WORTIS, J. (1950) *Soviet Psychiatry.* Baltimore: William and Wilkins.

PART FOUR

The Modification of Abnormal Behaviour

20

Animal Studies Bearing on Abnormal Behaviour

P. L. BROADHURST

INTRODUCTION

Comparative studies of non-human species continue to play an important role in the development of our understanding of abnormal behaviour. Indeed, recent theoretical developments and the more general acceptance of the view of neurosis as a disorder of learning have, if anything, increased their relevance and importance.

Paradoxically, the earlier studies purporting to demonstrate experimental neurosis thereby gain a stature which critical reviewers, including the present writer (Broadhurst, 1960), sought to minimise or deny, basing themselves, as we shall see, more strictly on an analogy drawn from the now discredited medical model. Hence, the first part of this chapter will be devoted to a review of this material, even though it is now largely of historical interest only, and consequently might have merited

much more cursory treatment were it not for the changing viewpoint.

The theoretical issues raised by this work will then be explored in some detail, to be followed by a discussion of the dimensional approach in so far as it has been applied using animals as subjects. The congruence of the factorial structure of personality at the human and infra-human level will be discussed. This will be followed by a treatment of modern contributions thought relevant to abnormal psychology and its applied field of clinical psychology. Here, distinction will be made among studies concerned with abnormal behaviour in animals in respect to their relevance to clinical psychology, the studies being judged as falling into three broad groupings of direct, less direct, and indirect relevance.

EXPERIMENTAL NEUROSIS

Early Russian Work

As is generally known, the idea of experimental neurosis originated with Pavlov. Most accounts give the name of Shenger-Krestovnikova (1921) as the first to observe an experimental neurosis. Her experiment is one of the classics of experimental psychology. A dog conditioned to salivate to the projected image of a circle, but not to an ellipse, was trained to make increasingly fine discriminations as the ellipse was made more and more circular, and disturbed behaviour occurred when the task was no longer possible for the animal. But such

behaviour had been observed previously in Pavlov's laboratory by Yerofeeva (1912, 1916), whose own account is therefore the pioneer report of behavioural disturbances due to conditioning techniques. She used electric shock as a conditioned stimulus for a salivary response to meat powder: the unconditioned defence reaction to this shock was abolished by training so that the shock became recognised as the signal for food, and gave rise to salivation, but when she attempted to show generalisation of the conditioned response, the defence reaction was restored whatever area of the dog's body was stimulated.

What appears to have impressed Pavlov is that

disordered behaviour similar to that found by Yero-feeva using electric shock was also found in Shenger-Krestovnikova's experiment employing more usual procedures. The programme of work initiated at that time absorbed Pavlov's last fifteen years of life (1927, 1941, 1961; Ivanov-Smolensky, 1954).

The work was next taken up by Pavlov's colleague Petrova (1924, 1926). She investigated two dogs chosen as extreme exemplars of nervous systems based on the dominance of excitation, or of inhibition. Five diverse sensory conditioned stimuli were used, and delays of up to five minutes between signal and reward were achieved with the inhibitable dog. But with only two minutes delay the excitable dog showed 'general excitation'. Practice with only one stimulus restored normal responses and the object of the experiment became the induction of abnormal behaviour. The technique of differentiation of positive and negative conditioned stimuli as used by Shenger-Krestovnikova, as well as others involving prolonged inhibition of the two dogs' responses, produced only transient general excitation in the excitable one. Accordingly, the painful stimulus used in Yerofeeva's original work was employed. Again, the dogs differed in their response to the shock. Initially, inhibition continued to weaken so that the excitable dog gave responses to the shock quite easily, but with practice it led to a decrease in the salivary response to this as well as to all other stimuli. Later, the 'ultra-paradoxical' phenomenon—Pavlov's descriptive term for the condition in which no response is made to positive stimuli, but only to previously negative ones—was observed, which he always regarded as evidence of abnormal cortical functioning. Pavlov's ideas about the types of nervous system of the experimental animals used in his laboratory and the extent to which they deter-mined the kind and course of the behavioural disorders observed originated in the early days of his studies of salivary conditioning, and certainly underwent considerable changes in the period after Petrova's work and before his death, but it is probably true to say that Petrova's work presented the problems especially clearly. The resolution of those problems, especially the classification of the 'type' to which one or other of her dogs belonged, reverberate in the subsequent writings of Pavlov himself, of his students and collaborators, and in the published transcripts of his famous 'Wednesday discussions'.

Pavlov's Types

These changes, and the subsequent developments, have been documented by several Russian writers whose work has been translated into English. In the previous Edition of this *Handbook* (Broadhurst, 1960), considerable reliance was placed on one of the few accounts then available (Ivanov-Smolensky, 1954), but the more recent treatment by Teplov in Gray's elegant translation (1964) is to be preferred. Teplov was not principally concerned with Pavlov's undoubted interest in abnormal behaviour—both in animals and man (Pavlov, 1961)—as such, but rather with the development of his possibly more enduring notions about the individual differences and the typology of central nervous system function-ing. Nevertheless Pavlov's final thoughts on these matters emerge with some clarity. It is, for example, plain that Pavlov came to appreciate and accept quite explicitly the fundamental distinction between phenotype and genotype, the latter signifying the hereditary endowment of the organism, which he called its 'type'. By this, however, he unfortunately understood all constitutional determinants, thus including prenatal factors operative before birth, which, for both conceptual and analytical purposes, are better treated as environmental determinants. Such determinants, largely operating postnatally, he recognised as contributing to the phenotype or 'character' which he regarded as the product or an amalgam of type and the environmental condi-tions under which the individual had been reared. Krushinskii (1962) has attempted to apply these ideas in a series of psychogenetic investigations, especially of defensive responses to stimulation in the dog.

Teplov traces Pavlov's thinking about types, as it evolved, in terms of his final classification of nervous function as comprising two processes having three properties. The processes are excitation and inhi-bition, and the properties are strength, mobility, and equilibrium. In respect of strength of nervous system, the strong is differentiated from the weak by a number of indices, particularly the speed with with conditioned responses are formed. He postu-lates the underlying basis of such differences as being due to variations in either the supply of a hypothetical excitatory substance, or the speed of its destruction. The property of mobility is concerned with the temporal characteristics of nervous function-ing, and differentiates the mobile from the inert types. Such differences are thought to be dependent on the speed of either the nervous processes them-selves, especially excitation, or the switching from one to the other, excitation to inhibition, or vice versa. The property of equilibrium or balance differentiates the equilibrated from the unstable types, and theoretically can operate in respect of either of the other two properties, thus giving a large number of possible unique types. In practice, how-ever, it has largely been confined, especially in recent years, to considerations of the effect of equilibrium on the dimension of strength of nervous system which may thus be balanced or not in respect of the relative strengths of the excitatory and inhibitory processes. For an account of Pavlov's later experimental work on experimental neurosis in dogs, the reader is referred to the sources cited (Ivanov-Smolensky, 1954; Broadhurst, 1960), as well as to Dinsmoor (1960). The last two attempt a critical evaluation. Other accounts may be found in the contributions by Russian workers to the book edited by Fox (1968), such as Kurtsin (1968) and Astrup (1968).

American Work

Three major American contributions to the literature appeared in the early 1940s (Anderson and Parmenter, 1941; Gantt, 1944; Masserman, reprinted 1964). This productivity originated in Liddell's pioneer work on conditioning in sheep (1926), and pride of place, because of its range, novelty, and volume, must go to the Cornell group associated with him.

Liddell

Liddell was studying thyroidectomy in sheep and goats and found no effects on maze learning. He therefore turned to conditioned reflex methods for a more precise measure. This led to the incidental production of experimental neurosis in a sheep, and the field of study changed. The techniques routinely used resemble the Russian but the motor response to an electric shock to the foreleg, which appears as a brisk muscular flexion, was used instead of the salivary reflex. Physiological measures, such as respiration, heart rate, and galvanic skin reflex, were recorded as well as movement of other parts of the body. From observations of the stressful aspects of the conditioned motor reflex procedure it is concluded that nervous strain develops when negative conditioned stimuli are introduced, and restraint is thus required of the animal.

This point is developed in a paper on four cases of experimental neurosis in sheep (Anderson and Liddell, 1935). The first animal showed persistent movement of the conditioned foreleg during intervals between the stimuli. Moreover, it now resisted entering the laboratory and had to be forced in, and onto the stand. Short periods of rest did not restore the former precision of the sheep's responses, but one-and-a-half years away from the laboratory did. Resuming work with delayed responses precipitated further 'interval activity' and resistance to experimentation. In a second sheep, the introduction of non-reinforced

conditioned signals caused similar symptoms, still apparent five years later. Rhythmical patterning caused similar restless and unmanageable behaviour in a fourth sheep. Thus, each neurosis was of an excitatory nature in Pavlov's sense.

An apparatus consisting of the chest-piece of a stethoscope attached to a long, flexible tube was used for measuring heart rate outside the conditioning chamber, and records of heart rate of six sheep were obtained. Two of those whose neurosis is described above are incuded in a group of four 'neurotics' and there were two normals. Evidence for rapidity of pulse comes from a systematic though unspecified number of observations which may or may not indicate a statistically significant elevation of rate. Thus, recognition of the methodological advance must be tempered by the absence of any satisfactory statistical treatment of the data. This criticism is also applicable to the major work of this group (Anderson and Parmenter, 1941). In this monograph the series is extended to ten (seven sheep and three dogs). All cases of experimental neurosis except one, a dog in whom salivary conditioning was developed, resulted from motor conditioned reflex procedures. Reproduction of polygraph recordings to illustrate the points discussed does not prevent the presentation from remaining anecdotal in flavour.

The signs of experimental neurosis are hyperirritability, restlessness, especially interval activity, and postural changes. One sheep regularly adopted an unusual posture with concavely flexed back; a dog showed 'pseudo-decerebrate rigidity' which allowed passive moulding of limbs. Records of respiration suggest that experimentally neurotic sheep have an increased breathing rate, persisting even in the animals' living quarters. Cardiac records reveal conditioning of cardiac responses. Elimination of urine and faeces in the laboratory was only observed among neurotic animals, and their social behaviour changed in the direction of greater solitariness. The conditioning procedures that gave rise to the signs of abnormal behaviour were, in order of importance, discrimination between positive and negative stimuli, experimental extinction of a positive conditioned response, and training according to a rigid time schedule.

Therapeutic procedures resemble Pavlov's with emphasis on rest from experimentation and the use of drugs. 'The degree of improvement did not seem to be a function of the duration of the period of rest' (Anderson and Parmenter, op. cit., p. 74). The effect of sedatives is unclear from the few data presented. Phenobarbital increased the magnitude of the conditioned motor responses, decreased the interval activity, and made the animal quieter in the barn. Thyroxin is said to be ineffective. Spontaneous remission of the neurosis in one old sheep may have resulted from senile changes.

The longitudinal approach is, unfortunately, marred by the absence of any standard experimental design. Procedures vary between subjects and with the same subject from time to time. The need for standardisation of experimentation on a sizeable number of subjects appears to have been recognised by provision for central polygraph recording (Liddell, 1950).

The Cornell group also did work on two additional species. The early work on the pig is diffusely reported with few experimental details. Later, Marcuse and Moore (1942) did work on several aspects of pig conditioning but in only one case was abnormal behaviour observed (1944). The work on goats is even more diffusely reported. A technique for conditioning in freely moving animals (Parmenter, 1940) was used later to investigate the protective effect of the mother goat. The results show that after relatively few trials a restriction of movement of isolated kids occurred. Liddell reported (1954) that two years later neurosis was precipitated in the now adult goats of the experimental group merely by restraining them in a conditioning harness, whereas adult controls were not affected.

Gantt

The work of the second major researcher, Gantt, is Pavlovian, yet, like Liddell, he was concerned with the generalisation of conditioned neuroses outside the laboratory. The accumulation of data on the abnormal behaviour of dogs led to his important monograph contribution (1944). Using salivary conditioning with food or acid as the unconditioned stimuli, Gantt reports on the effect of natural emotional shocks. Parturition in bitches, accidental disturbance, fighting, and restriction of freedom all caused altered behaviour. Experimental procedures that disturbed conditioned responses included conflict of drives, conflict of excitatory and inhibitory stimuli, and changes in conditioning routine. But the major part of the work is devoted to the case histories of three dogs who reacted to the experimental procedures with different degrees of disturbance.

Fritz, a male Alsatian, was a stable animal who developed conditioned differentiation. When the discrimination was made more difficult he showed some disturbance. A tactile differentiation was also achieved, and the responses to auditory stimuli well retained. The second dog, Peter, was a male beagle. He formed rather unstable salivary responses to the same tones and the same discrimination was

successfully accomplished; when made more difficult, he refused food, all conditioned responses disappeared, and he had to be forced into the room. After a rest he was quiet and gave responses.

The case history of the celebrated Nick—studied for 12 years—shows more severe disturbance. He was a male mongrel, active and playful, more restless than most dogs during adaptation, and slow in showing the conditioned salivary response. He refused food when auditory differentiation was introduced. A definite physical progression in the inhibitory effect of the experimental room was observed; Nick would eat the more readily the farther he was away. Rest caused only a slight improvement as judged by his eating and temporary recovery of responses. Nick was then fed his meat ration in the experimental room for seven months. But this attempt at therapy failed; and fresh abnormalities appeared including disturbed breathing and urination as much as twenty-five times in thirty minutes, despite punishment. Concurrently, abnormal sexual excitation— penile erection—was observed during stimulation occasioned by the experimental setting itself. Both the urinary and sexual abnormalities occurred after a bitch in oestrus had been used in the experimental situation to test the effect of normal sexual excitation on the other abnormal behaviour.

The rest of Nick's history was devoted to a study of his abnormalities, which did not proliferate further but fluctuated in intensity. Generalisation within the experimental situation was demonstrated and wide generalisation outside it was also observed, especially in the country, where Nick was kept for two periods. The food given as reinforcement in the experiment was consistently refused there, and penile erection, pollakiuria, disturbed respiration and heart rate were observed at the approach of people associated with the experiment, or members of their families.

The rests were therapeutic in that the anxiety and stereotyped responses in the experimental room were lessened though this may have been due to advancing age. The therapeutic effect of normal sexual activity was also investigated. Sexual activity inside the experimental situation showed that the experimental room decreased Nick's latent period for ejaculation and duration of erection. Alcohol appeared to abolish the anxiety responses temporarily (Gantt, 1940, 1952).

Gantt and his colleagues worked on another dog, V3, a male French poodle whose abnormalities of behaviour contrast markedly with those of Nick. His life history is described in detail by Newton and Gantt (1968). On occasion, he exhibited catatonic behaviour in which he would maintain bizarre postures and remain apparently insensitive to pain.

A visiting psychiatrist 'diagnosed' him as 'a schizophrenic dog'. Though he lived in the laboratory as long as Nick (14 years) he appears to have been quantitatively studied only intermittently. In addition to some observations on the effects of alcohol, which improved his otherwise very deficient sexual reflexes, and of the tranquiliser meprobamate, which normalised his behaviour towards people, the main findings relate to the quantification of what Gantt calls the 'effect of person' on V3's cardiac function. Petting the dog produced a pronounced bradycardia with the heart rate falling from his normally rather high 120 to 160 beats a minute to as low as 40 to 50 beats a minute. This is a considerable exaggeration of the normal effect of person on heart rate in the dog (Lynch and McCarthey, 1967, 1969; *see* also Anderson and Gantt, 1966). In addition, some behavioural observations of a somewhat anecdotal kind suggest possible homosexual interest in V3. All these symptoms were apparently spontaneous and not due to any conditioning procedure: they did not improve over the years and constitute an example of the self-sustaining and self-generating process which Gantt terms 'autokinesis', discussed below.

The third major American contribution to the literature on experimental neuroses during the pre- and early post-World War II period is that of Masserman. Like the contributions of Liddell and of Gantt, it is reviewed in detail up to 1958 by Broadhurst (1960): its subsequent development will be mentioned below in relation to psychoanalytic models of abnormal behaviour as they are exemplified in animal work.

Theoretical Issues

Our task now is to turn to the theoretical issues that emerge from this considerable body of experimental work.

Vigilance

Liddell's theoretical formulation of the disorders he and his colleagues studied stems from his view of conditioning as a stress situation based on the animal's self-imposed restraint. This conceals a tense expectancy, for which Liddell uses Head's term 'vigilance', so that when the capacity for maintaining vigilance is exceeded, pent-up nervous tension will disrupt conditioning and lead to chronic states of diffuse or congealed vigilance—experimental neurosis. Further stresses are loneliness, monotony, confusion, and overstimulation. Thus, a rise in tension or vigilance can be seen in indicators such as respiration rate during long conditioning

sessions, even in well-trained animals (Liddell, 1951, 1958, 1964). But the theory is not formulated in precise enough terms to have heuristic value; few testable deductions flow from it. Those that do, for example, the notion that waiting for shock is itself stressful and, indeed, may be even more stressful than the reinforcing shock itself, have received scant support in experimental work carried out on goats at Cornell (Campos, Moore, and Goldsmith, 1968) after Liddell's death in 1962. Block (1966) gives a bibliography of 64 publications by Liddell, the majority of those related to experimental neurosis being cited also in Broadhurst (1960).

Autokinesis and Schizokinesis

Gantt developed (1953) his theoretical views to employ two fundamental concepts: 'schizokinesis' and 'autokinesis'. The former implies a cleavage in response between the emotional and visceral systems (Gantt, 1964b) and the skeletal musculature, and has its origins in observations suggesting that cardiac conditioned responses are formed more quickly than motor ones, are of comparatively greater intensity, and are more resistant to extinction. Subsequent work (Dykman and Gantt, 1960b) extended this to, for example, hypertensive responses which parallel the heart rate changes. Consequently, emotional and endocrine responses may persist after the need for the appropriate accompanying motor response has passed. 'Autokinesis' refers to the internal development of responses on the basis of old excitations, as seen in the spontaneous restoration of extinguished conditioned responses and the appearance of signs of experimental neurosis long after the causal conflict has been removed. These might be seen as examples of the distinction made between positive, that is, beneficial and negative or harmful autokinesis, respectively (Gantt, Newton, and Royer, 1960). A particularly striking example of negative autokinesis is reported by Dykman and Gantt (1960a) in the behaviour of the dog Schnapps, a victim of one of those accidental experiments in which the literature on experimental neurosis abounds. He suffered three severe shocks in the conditioning chamber during a study on the orienting reflex which called for merely moderate electrical stimulation. After this single experience, which occasioned urination, defecation, vomiting, and penile erection, the dog's behaviour became progressively more disturbed. Fear of the experimenter, the animal technician, and the stairs to the experimental room all developed and intensified, and the autonomic responses in the conditioning laboratory were repeated. This behaviour persisted for over three weeks while every care was taken to restore normal behaviour. Ultimately, restoration was achieved by two sessions in which electrical stimuli were again given, but only of a mild kind, and thereafter Schnapps performed normally, though with slightly elevated heart rate.

Gantt's theoretical formulation shares with that of Liddell some characteristic imprecision, but it has merit in two respects. It does lead to testable deductions relating to the speed of development of visceral versus skeletal conditioning, and the dichotomy between the conditioning of the two kinds of body system has recently assumed importance with the development by Miller and his collaborators of methods of conditioning, by operant techniques rather than the classical methods, of various autonomic functions (see below). Moreover, the second of Gantt's two theoretical constructs, autokinesis (1962), has recently been revived in discussions of the so-called Napalkov phenomenon (1963) by, for example, Eysenck (1967a, 1968). Incubation has assumed importance as an explanatory concept, superior to the Yerkes-Dodson formulation (Broadhurst, 1960) in the attempts to improve upon Wolpe's (1952) explanation of the growth to disruptive proportions of the initially mildly anxious behaviour shown by many animals in the conditioning situation. In his careful review of theoretical explanations of experimental neuroses, Lovibond (1964) concludes: 'The attempts of Wolpe and Broadhurst to account for the phenomena of difficult differentiation neuroses in terms of emotional reactions, although ingenious, are scarcely convincing. Wolpe's assumption of an additive relationship between conditional and unconditional fear is somewhat implausible, especially in relation to the breakdown in the difficult differentiation experiment. Equally implausible is Broadhurst's hypothesis that increased drive level energises initial fear reactions to produce the "struggling, howling and agitated behavior' observed when breakdown occurs.' (p. 160). Eysenck, however, has proposed that the conditioned stimulus in itself, even when presented unreinforced by the unconditioned stimulus, nevertheless occasions an increase in the conditioned response by means of a positive feed-back mechanism because a small residual response to the conditioned stimulus is evoked on each of its presentations. 'Usually the extinction process will be stronger than this form of reinforcement, leading to overall extinction, ... but under certain circumstances (e.g. when the UCS is exceptionally strong) the extinction process may be weaker than the ... reinforcement process and observable incubation will result' (1968, p. 313). Eysenck reviews evidence from several animal

experiments which attests to the reality of the effects of incubation (see also Zammit-Montebello et al., 1969). Some subjects were observed over long time periods of weeks and even years which, he argues, would seem to rule out alternative explanations in terms of reminiscence or consolidation theories. Here, then, is a possible alternative explanation to those criticised by Lovibond and one that might plausibly be employed to account for the massive growth of autonomic responses in animal subjects displaying experimental neurosis. It is not, however, possible to argue this point at all persuasively, since the available data are insufficiently precise for retrospective appraisal in these terms, even if the experimental designs employed were sufficiently clear-cut to allow a separation of the effects of the conditioned stimuli when used with or without reinforcement.

Hebb's Views

As regards the assessment of these early experiments of both Russian and American workers in respect of their relevance to behavioural pathology, the tendency has been to move away from an effort to appraise them in terms of the extent to which they did or did not succeed in meeting a set of criteria, putatively related to human neurosis. Hebb (1947), in a characteristically penetrating analysis, provided such a set of criteria, defining human neurosis in behavioural terms that do not involve the use of the patient's report of his subjective state, thus allowing the use at the animal level of his definition: 'Neurosis is in practice an undesirable emotional condition which is generalised and persistent; it occurs in a minority of the population and has no origin in a gross neural lesion' (p. 11). It should be noted that this definition is to some extent idiosyncratic in that, while containing six elements considered to be essential, it excludes three that many psychiatrists and others diagnosing neurosis in terms of a disease model would consider essential. These are that neurosis produces a marked change from an earlier behavioural baseline, that it follows from some traumatic experience such as conflict or frustration (Seward, 1969), and that neurosis has no known physiological base. Hebb's approach, however, was a considerable advance on previous attempts to encompass the problem of animal neurosis. In the absence of direct ways of communicating anxiety and, usually, of societal structures which may be disturbed in important ways, maladaptive behaviours in animals are clearly difficult to define and there is a sense in which all conditioning possibly leading to maladaptive responses becomes relevant. But in the context of Hebb's analysis, this dilemma is avoided.

Following this approach to its logical conclusion involves us in examining the experimental neuroses reported in the literature to see whether they come within the terms of Hebb's definition. This was attempted in the previous edition of this *Handbook* to which the interested reader is referred (Broadhurst, 1960). The outcome was broadly negative in that though often inadequately reported—especially the Russian work—the literature showed no cases that met the criteria of Hebb's definition. This was especially true of Masserman's work using cats (1964) and primates (Masserman and Pechtel, 1956) and of the several attempts to precipitate experimental neuroses in rats. No animal analogue of neurosis as a disease entity had been demonstrated. It was concluded that what had been often shown was the unrecognised development of conditioned emotional responses similar to those demonstrated in humans (Watson and Rayner, 1924) and in animal subjects (Estes and Skinner, 1941).

Appraisal

Moreover, the value of the work on experimental neurosis for the more limited aim of furthering our understanding of either the mechanism of conditioned emotional responses as such, or the part that they play in the development of human neurosis, viewed as a phenomenon of maladaptive learning, has been minimal. The early Russian work, though very fruitful in stimulating research, in its later development led, as we have seen, to a concern with matters more related to general personality characteristics and typologies, the reconciliation of which with Western formulations is only now engaging attention (Gray, 1964, 1967). The rest of the work reviewed briefly here and in detail in the previous edition (Broadhurst, 1960) has been characterised by a poverty of experimental design, manifest in inadequate control, and the almost entire absence of quantitative data, appropriately analysed.

While some have not been so critical (Caïn, 1959; Wilson, 1963; Cosnier, 1966; Seward, 1969), others have arrived at similar conclusions: thus, Hunt (1964) notes '. . . unusual means were often required to produce unusual behavioral results. The paradigms for producing animal neuroses often have been so complex and confounded, viewed from the vantage

point of contemporary behavior theory, that much of the anticipated analytic power and experimental control was difficult to achieve and often lost altogether' (1964, p. 29). In similar vein, Sidman (1960) writes—

'With respect to pathologies of behavior . . . clinical practice and laboratory experimentation have yet to achieve a satisfactory working partnership. The origin of pathology in normal behavioral processes is beginning to be recognised . . . but in not a very large segment of current experimental or clinical practice. Experimental and clinical psychologists alike seem to equate the two terms abnormal and disorderly. Thus, when an experimenter isolates a lawful behavioral phenomenon, he is likely to consider that its very lawfulness removes it from the realm of clinical interest. Similarly, the clinician who does venture into the laboratory will, more often than not, try to demonstrate the absence of lawfulness in some behavioral phenomenon. Neither worker seems to give much thought to the possibility that maladaptive behavior can result from quantitative and qualitative combinations of processes which are themselves intrinsically orderly, strictly determined, and normal in origin' (1960, p. 61).

This coming together of the interests of the laboratory and the clinic has progressed considerably in the last decade with the use, on the one hand, of experimental techniques of the animal laboratory for the investigation, management, and sometimes therapy of human subjects, as in the use of operant methods with human subjects (Ayllon and Azrin, 1968), and the use of precisely controlled animal experimentation to investigate therapeutic and other clinical problems directly, a use pioneered by Wolpe (1952). This latter development has spread into a considerable body of work to be considered later, but first we must ask ourselves whether or not there remain ways in which animal experimentation can contribute to the study of abnormal behaviour without either pursuing the unlikely analogue of human neurosis or taking the circuitous, but probably in the long term more profitable, route of increasing our understanding of the normal lawful processes of learning and applying them to the apparently lawless behaviour observed by clinicians as advocated by Sidman.

CONTRIBUTIONS TO ABNORMAL PSYCHOLOGY

To the present writer it seems that there are two ways in which animal studies may still make a rather direct contribution to abnormal study generally.

The first relates to multivariate analyses designed to reveal the dimensions on which individual differences in animal behaviour may be ordered, for comparison with the similar factorial structure shown to be of importance in human behaviour, and upon which there is now a wide measure of agreement (Eysenck, 1967b; Eysenck and Eysenck, 1969). Since these dimensions encompass not only the average and normal in their range of variation, but also the extreme, abnormal, and often hospitalised, then it follows that if similar patterns could be identified in animal subjects with a degree of acceptance of the interspecies similarities underlying the various behavioural measures employed, we might accept that animal subjects showing the extremes of factor scores are in some measure equivalent to the human patients who also show them.

Factor Analytic Studies

With respect to factor-analytic studies of animal behaviour, Royce reviewed the literature in 1950 and again more recently (1966). He covered physiological and behavioural work on several species, including man, up to the early 1960s, the latest investigation included being that later published by McClearn and Meredith (1964). He discerns an encouraging measure of agreement between the various animal investigations, even though they are not very numerous. A factor that emerges with especial clarity from reports using all the animal species studied (rats, mice, and dogs) as well as from human subjects, is one related to autonomic balance. In the infrahuman subjects, the measures of emotional defecation and urination load heavily on this factor. Subsequent work by Wilcock and Broadhurst (1967) and especially by Whimbey and Denenberg (1967) has confirmed and clarified the factor structure for several measures from the open-field test in rats (Denenberg, 1969). While Becker (1969), as a result of the variations in factor structure

between the two sexes in rats, cast doubt on the unitary nature of emotionality as a construct, there nevertheless remains a considerable body of evidence. Hence, while the identification of this factor with the second order factor of neuroticism in humans (Eysenck and Eysenck, 1969) must remain tenuous at present, there seems little doubt that this is the best cross-species factor identification yet postulated. The other major personality factor in humans, introversion-extraversion, does not figure in the infrahuman analyses reviewed by Royce (1966). A docility factor emerges from many of the analyses of animal learning and factors apparently concerned with motor discharge and with activity level, the details of none of which encourage any cross-species identification of the kind possible with the autonomic factor. Attempts to seek this identification on a univariate basis would seem to be decidedly premature but will be discussed later.

Psychogenetics

The second way in which, it is suggested, animal studies can make a direct contribution to abnormal psychology is a psychogenetic one. If we can identify, perhaps by the factorial methods outlined above, particular behavioural syndromes in animals which mimic those associated with patients, or which may be argued to be indicative of disorder of physiological systems deranged in such patients, then it is possible literally to create in the animal laboratory populations extreme in this respect by genetic selection. Such selected strains may be extreme in either a positive or a negative direction in respect of the phenotypic scores of interest, or—perhaps most commonly—in both, bidirectional selection being practised. Examples will be cited in what follows.

CONTRIBUTIONS TO CLINICAL PSYCHOLOGY

Meanwhile, we must turn to the discussion of modern contributions from animal investigations to the problems of applied abnormal behaviour, that is, to clinical psychology. The decade after the first edition of this *Handbook* saw a considerable acceleration in the application of experimental psychology to treatment. The contribution of animal studies to the development of explanations of behaviour, of which the whole body of learning theory is perhaps the most conspicuous example, is widely appreciated and it is not intended to dwell on that theme. But with the increased use of behaviour therapeutic

techniques based on learning principles, there has been a comparably increasing traffic in the reverse direction—from the clinic to the laboratory—a path pioneered, albeit in a somewhat different theoretical climate, by Masserman, hotly pursued by Wolpe (1952) in an endeavour to prove him wrong. It is intended, therefore, to review recent work, using animals as subjects, of perceived importance to clinical psychology. Relevant contributions will be discussed in terms of three general categories: studies specifically concerned with or judged directly relevant to the application of learning theory in clinical practice; studies which the writer judges to be of less direct relevance to clinical psychology, but of importance, or perhaps potential importance, to it; and lastly, studies which seem to the writer to be of indirect relevance to clinical psychology. Obviously, much that is subjective must enter into this categorisation and the risk of errors of judgement is probably large. However, time will doubtless provide its amendments.

Direct Relevance

In the first area to be considered, in which we review studies having direct relevance to clinical psychology, pride of place must necessarily be given to work intended to provide animal analogues for behaviour therapy. The topic must necessarily be circumscribed since, if the view is accepted that much of the behaviour disorders with which the clinical psychologist is concerned and which are considered for behaviour therapeutic treatment are the product of maladaptive learning, all the large body of psychological literature on the topic of learning becomes relevant. Thus, for example, the proliferation of operant conditioning techniques in the clinical setting and directed towards the modification of behaviour, so conspicuous a feature of the approach to behaviour therapy in North America (Eysenck, 1964b; Krasner and Ullmann, 1965) is itself underpinned by numerous animal studies concerned with the kind, consequence, and scheduling of reinforcement. To review all this from the point of view of clinical psychology would be beyond the scope of this chapter and consequently is not attempted. Instead, attention will be focused on those animal studies that purport to be concerned with issues, problems, and techniques arising directly in the context of behaviour therapy.

According to Rachman and Teasdale (1969), the most commonly used methods of such therapy are desensitisation, aversion therapy, and operant conditioning, and of these we will concentrate first on desensitisation. Clearly, the key issue in learning theory in this connection is that of extinction, and consequently much of the animal work to be considered relates to this topic. In passing, we might add that, despite the apparently early use of aversion as a therapy (Rachman and Teasdale, 1969), methods based on extinction gained greater prominence sooner in the development of behaviour therapies in the 1950s and '60s and it is not surprising that more attention to animal work designed to underpin it should have appeared during the first of the two decades mentioned.

Desensitisation

The first area of interest to behaviour therapy concerns experimental work using animals and bearing on the extinction of anxiety—particularly desensitisation. No treatment will be attempted of the considerable body of work on the theory of extinction as such—an area of 'enormous complexity' (Kimble, 1961). A topic that might be expected to loom large in this connection is that of systematic desensitisation with relaxation—Wolpe's reciprocal inhibition therapy (1958)—which, according to Rachman's review (1967), 'usually features very prominently' in behaviour therapy. But the only animal experimentation Rachman cites, apart from that of Wolpe (1952) on the gradual deconditioning of conditioned emotional reactions in cats to electric shock, is a study by Gale, Sturmfels and Gale (1966). These authors' paper, albeit under another name, is also the only one that Lomont (1965) suggested showed positive results. In his not entirely comprehensive review of the relevant animal experimentation to that date, Lomont included work on both counter-conditioning and progressive procedures for extinction, analogous to the hierarchical approach. He notes he has—

'reviewed the available experimental research relevant to explaining the efficacy of reciprocal inhibition therapy. Only one of these experiments clearly indicated any feature of any reciprocal inhibition technique which could not be attributed to extinction, this characteristic being a superiority of a reciprocal inhibition procedure to extinction in eliminating fear in rats . . . . Thus, for explaining reciprocal inhibition therapy, it is still essentially an open question as to whether the concept of reciprocal inhibition, or counterconditioning, is more adequate than extinction' (p. 218).

Before proceeding to the paper in question it should perhaps be noted that Rachman (1967), on the basis of certain human studies, reaches diametrically opposite conclusions: 'At the very least, these three studies now justify the conclusion that reciprocal inhibition produced by relaxation is superior to extinction as a method for reducing fear' (Rachman, op. cit., pp. 98–99).

Basing themselves on earlier studies, such as those of Moltz (1954) and Sermat and Shephard (1959), reviewed by Lomont (1965), in which food or other stimuli had been used to assist the extinction of conditioned fear responses in animals, Gale *et al.*

(1966) sought to answer the question whether the reciprocal inhibition generated by such stimuli was the effective agent, or whether the mere fact of repeated exposure to the stimuli eliciting anxiety could have assisted the extinction process. Thus, Wolpe (1952) did not have an unfed control group of cats to explore this possibility. Gale and her colleagues' study avoids certain difficulties by having conditioned fear developed in hungry rats by associating a 1,500 Hz tone with shock to the feet and then dividing subjects into three groups—a reciprocal inhibition group given food during the extinction trials in which a tone, at first 300 Hz, was made progressively higher in frequency and thus more similar to the original conditioned stimulus; a desensitisation group merely exposed to the sequence of tones on successive trials without also being fed; and a control group not subjected to the extinction procedure at all. Two test extinction trials were then given to all groups before relearning began. The response measure employed was the amount of emotional elimination (number of fecal boluses) and it showed the superiority of the reciprocal inhibition procedure. The group treated by reciprocal inhibition ceased to defecate after the eleventh extinction trial whereas the desensitisation-only group continued over all 32 trials. No data are given for the two test extinction trials though it is stated that the control group defecated more and exhibited no diminution in conditioned emotional response as measured in this way. Neither are data presented for this group for the relearning of the original conditioned emotional response. The two experimental groups do not differ significantly, however, from which we may conclude, despite the deficiencies in the reporting of this study, that the reciprocal inhibition procedure did not have a prospectively protecting effect against the shock involved in the relearning. This study has also been criticised by Lader and Mathews (1968) in the context of their theory, put forward as an alternative to Wolpe's theory of reciprocal inhibition— a term they consider unfortunate—that desensitisation takes place as part of a process of maximising habituation to the anxiety-provoking stimuli. Relaxation is seen as part of the necessary process of de-arousal favouring habituation rather than as a reciprocally inhibiting activity, counter to anxiety. Thus, since all the rats in Gale and her colleagues' study were hungry (and therefore might be regarded as highly aroused) the group given food might be expected to have undergone a reduction in arousal with a consequent decrease in fear responding. Whether this interpretation supports the maximal habituation hypothesis is dubious, since it could plausibly be argued that finding of food might of itself have an arousing effect.

Lader and Mathews, it might be said in passing, seem to be on firmer ground in applying comparable criticism to the three studies with humans as subjects, referred to in the quotation from Rachman (1967) above as supporting the superiority of reciprocal inhibition over extinction procedures. In each case the control groups used could be said to have been subjected to procedures that might have maintained arousal, whereas the experimental, therapeutic groups were not.

Also relying, like Gale et al., on relatively simple indices of emotional reactivity, Willmuth and Peters (1964) sought to show that another possible artefact is inoperative in the extinction of anxiety by reciprocal inhibition. They argued that mere passage of time rather than any specific experience encountered during extinction could not account for their findings since rats exposed over several weeks to the box in which they had been shocked resumed activity therein more quickly, the oftener they were tested in it. Appropriate control groups equally often exposed but never shocked, allowed calculation of a difference score which supports this view. But the absence of adequate statistical analysis—itself somewhat startling nowadays—makes conclusions hazardous. In the shorter term, however, Melvin, Martin, and Parsons (1965) showed that increasing the delay immediately after training rats to escape shock and before extinction began caused an orderly decrease in the number of trials required for extinction. Korányi, Endroczi, and Lissak's findings (1965) are not presented in sufficient detail for evaluation.

Other work on the extinction of fear responses in animals, published since Lomont's review (1965), has been concerned with the topics of counter-conditioning versus exposure to the fear-arousing stimuli, the merits of the progressive approach to enhancing extinction and the assistance afforded by drugs. Nelson (1966) used feeding procedures, either placing hungry rats directly adjacent to food in a compartment in which they had previously been shocked, or by using a technique described by Page (1955) in an experiment not cited by Lomont. Page had shown that rats in whom a conditioned avoidance response had been developed would nevertheless approach food when hungry, even though it was exposed in the shock compartment. Using this method, Nelson found that the effect of feeding can be either to retard or to hasten the extinction of responses based on fear. In further work (1969), the same author took up the question of the nature of the exposure to the fear stimulation induced by feeding in the previous work. But forced exposure without feeding, equated in respect of the amount of free exposure a control group allowed itself, resulted in more rapid extinction, whereas, when combined with feeding in the extinction phase, previous free exposure was found to be more efficacious. Nelson seeks to resolve these apparently contradictory findings by noting that, in the second case, there was a greater similarity between the free exposure conditions and those of the fear acquisition than in the first. But it should also be noted that in neither of these experiments is Nelson concerned with the acquisition of an escape response in a situation in which the rat has previously been shocked. While he advances cogent arguments for preferring the clarity of this approach (1966), it might be thought to limit the applicability of his findings to clinical problems.

Page (1955; Coulter, Riccio, and Page, 1969), however, in his studies of counter-conditioning and exposure does provide evidence that, while performance of the avoidance response is affected, fear still persists. This was seen in the longer latencies to approaching the food in the group experiencing forced exposure as compared with a group undergoing normal extinction (Page, 1955), and Coulter et al., in a well-designed factorial experiment, were able to confirm the earlier finding and to extend it in several ways. They showed that blocking the avoidance response facilitated extinction of one-way avoidance, though not affecting residual fear as measured by latencies of entry to the shock chamber. The effect obtains irrespective of the strength of the original avoidance response. The duration of the blocking was also shown not to affect the extent of the residual fear.

In a series of studies more closely orientated to clinical psychology, Baum (1966, 1968, 1969a, 1969b, 1970; Baum and Oler, 1968; Lederhendler and Baum, 1970) has used the technique of forced exposure to fear stimuli which he has come to call 'flooding'—a term first used in this connection by Polin (1959)—and specifically relating this approach to the implosive therapy of Stampfl (Stampfl and Levis, 1967, 1968; see also Rachman's review, 1969). There is, of course, a sense in which all the work on the effects of blocking on subsequent avoidance responding could be subsumed under the term flooding, just as there is a sense in which it is perhaps better restricted to the discrete conditioning stimulus used in the primary fear conditioning. Polin's original meaning. However, Baum's usage of the term falls between the former, broad sense and the latter, narrower one because he employed a conditioned response involving jumping to a safe but retractable shelf from an intermittently charged grid floor, a procedure not using a discrete conditioned stimulus as a warning signal. In this situation, flooding is merely confinement in the shock box with the shelf unavailable

to the rat. Baum (1966) showed that this technique was highly effective in accelerating extinction of the jumping response. This finding is in accord with the results of a more extensive study using a conventional shuttle box, in which Weinberger (1965) exposed six groups of rats, matched for response acquisition, to the noise of a buzzer (a conditioning signal) for varying periods of time ranging from 0 to 20 sec. A reasonably lawful relationship for three different measures of extinction was found, but a difficulty was detected in that some subjects acquired a new response of crouching to the conditioned stimulus during detention. Crouching interfered with subsequent performance and hastened extinction. Baum (1969a) confirmed these general findings and also showed that more intense shock increased the likelihood of the development of the interfering response retarding extinction after a fixed period of detention.

Lederhendler and Baum (1970) further investigated the mechanism mediating the effect of the more severe shock in reducing the usual extinction facilitation of detention by the use of a mechanical paddle which prevented the development of crouching and freezing during the 5-min period of blocked response. The results suggested that sweeping rats around the box with the paddle did cause significantly fewer avoidance responses during extinction, but the authors do not comment on the finding that the experimental group had a much higher proportion of animals making no responses whatsoever during extinction than either of the control groups. Weinberger (1965) showed that the number of such unresponsive animals was a function of the length of the detention period during which response was prevented, and excluded them in some of his analyses on the grounds that such non-responding was evidence of the conditioning of responses competing with extinction. But the differences in technique may not allow this extension of the inference. Lederhendler and Baum suggest that the moving paddle may have functioned as did the presence of other animals in a previous experiment (Baum, 1969b) on the social facilitation of the beneficial effects of detention. The effects of more intense shock were markedly attenuated by the presence of two non-shocked rats during a 5-min detention period, but a 30-min period was sufficient to eliminate responding entirely, either with or without shock.

Continuing his admirable series of experiments, Baum (1968) explored the therapeutically important question of the effect on extinction of the degree of overlearning, as modified by response prevention of the usual duration of 5 min. He found a complex effect in which training involving 50 or 100 trials beyond the criterion of avoidance response acquisition in his standard apparatus either retarded or facilitated subsequent extinction, depending, respectively, on whether or not the rat had received any shocks during the overlearning. But the absence of a further control having no response detention means that these differences cannot also be evaluated in terms of the flooding procedure. The greater efficacy of the longer period of such treatment was further confirmed by Baum and Oler (1968) using massed extinction trials. Both for a single acquisition of an avoidance response and one that had been extinguished and then re-trained, the massing procedure was more effective than detention in facilitating extinction. In the only quasi-negative report that has come to hand, Benline and Simmel (1967) reported that blocking had no more than a transitory effect on fear responses in rats, the difference between such subjects and a control group diminishing as the number of trials increased. A similar phenomenon can be seen in data reported by others, (for example, Nelson, 1966), which suggests the operation of incubation in the manner discussed previously.

The progressive approach to extinction has received less attention from animal workers. In an early experiment not reviewed by Lomont (1965), Kimble and Kendall (1953) compared the effect on rats' conditioned avoidance response—wheel turning to a light signal—of exposure to the light at full intensity before extinction began (essentially a flooding procedure) or, alternatively, preceding this flooding experience with a series of graded exposures to the light at minimal intensities each increasing to the full value. They explain the marked superiority in speedy extinction of the group given this toleration method, which they attribute to Guthrie (1935), in the following terms, reminiscent of Wolpe's early formulations—

'In extinction by the toleration procedure, the stimulus for a fear reaction is presented first in a highly generalised form. This stimulus presumably tends to call out the conditioned fear, but to so small a degree that the instrumental response does not occur. Not because of the accumulation of inhibition, but simply because it is not reinforced, the fear reaction is partially extinguished and this extinction generalizes to adjacent stimulus intensities. Thus, when the intensity of the CS is raised slightly, the reaction will occur again, but still in a weak form, and the process described above is repeated. Successive application of the fear stimulus at intensities too weak to produce the avoidance reaction may then finally eliminate it by extinguishing its acquired motivational basis' (Kimble and Kendall, 1953, p. 89).

Reacting to his dissatisfaction with the lack of

clarity in the animal work in that it is rarely possible to disentangle the effects of extinction, counter-conditioning, and a progressive approach, Goldstein (1969) endeavoured to set up an experiment in which such effects could be isolated. Moreover, he sought a situation more nearly resembling a clinical one and used a species more nearly resembling those encountered in the clinic. Ten cebus monkeys had their fear of a teddy bear extinguished, using as a measure the distance they kept from the bear when it was placed together with sugar in an approach-avoidance runway. The effect on the runway response of various ways of exposing the subjects to the feared teddy bear with sugar in a separate smaller cage was investigated. A counter-conditioning group was fed half a sugar cube 10 sec after being exposed to the bear, while a second group had the same treatment but with a progressive approach of exposing bear to monkey, the distance being reduced on successive daily trials. A third group had this same progressive approach without counter-conditioning since the sugar was given before, rather than after, the fear stimulus, and the same occurred in a simple extinction group which, like the counterconditioning group, did not have the modified exposure of the progressive approach. Finally, a control group was given no treatments involving exposure to the bear other than in the runway tests. Despite the small numbers inevitable in a primate study, the results are remarkably clear cut. The combination of graduated exposure to the fear stimulus, combined with the counterconditioning procedure was most effective in extinguishing fear. There was little to choose between the other groups, depending upon which measures of extinction were employed, except that, of course, all were significantly superior to the untreated control group. Goldstein concludes that his results support Wolpe's theoretical position with its emphasis on reciprocal inhibition.

While the psychopharmacological literature on the effects of drugs on conditioned emotional responses and motivation generally is considerable, and no attempt will be made to review it here (see Miller, 1964), a few studies merit attention because of their explicit concern with the variables involved in experimentation just described. They include the work of Sherman (1967) who developed an approach avoidance conflict in rats by punishing with shock their bar-pressing for food. He then showed that injection of amylobarbital sodium restored responding as compared with a saline control group, but that abrupt withdrawal of the drug caused performance again to approximate the performance of the latter. On the other hand, a third group which had the drug withdrawn, but by progressive reductions in the dosage, showed no such relapse and extinction of the competing fear response proceeded. Implications for behaviour therapy are drawn in that transfer of the fear extinction from the drugged to the non-drugged state suggests that improvement (extinction) of phobic responses, for example, perhaps more pleasantly achieved by the sedated patient, will not thereby be lost later. Nelson (1967) explored the effect of chloropromazine on the variable of free versus forced exposure to the place in which rats had been shocked in so far as it determined subsequent learning of an escape response. He found that the effect of the drug was limited to the extent to which it increased free exposure, a result similar to his findings in relation to food as a counterconditioner.

Overall then, the burden of results from the comparative studies described seems broadly supportive of Wolpe's approach via reciprocal inhibition, as opposed to explanations primarily in terms of extinction or de-arousal. This up-dating of Lomont (1965) on the subject has produced little of decisive significance in this respect, but the general tenor of the results points in the direction indicated. If one study may be said especially to influence this conclusion, it is that of Goldstein (1969) whose findings, if replicable,* will be fundamental in this connection.

This review of work relating to the extinction of anxiety must be both interim and incomplete. Plainly, the last word has by no means been said on reciprocal inhibition and an active area of experimentation has been opened up. In particular, one might point to the work of Page and his collaborators which suggests that while performance may have extinguished under certain treatment, conditioned fear may yet remain.

Unfortunately, not all the work is of the quality that one has a right to demand nowadays, and clinicians who enter the animal laboratory cannot expect to adhere to the somewhat less rigorous standards of experimental control and design that often inevitably govern work in the clinic. It is perhaps salutary to note, in passing, a reverse trend in this connection; it is sometimes possible to apply to humans the demanding and rigorous techniques of experimentation deriving rather directly from the animal laboratory. Examples may be seen in the work of Orwin (1969) on escape-avoidance learning in neurotic subjects, and Quinn (Quinn and Patten,

1967; Quinn, Harbison and McAllister, 1970) in treating various sexual disorders.

Conditioned Inhibition

The next contribution to be considered concerning extinction is that of Kendrick (1958a, 1960) who mounted a series of experiments using rats to investigate theoretical issues related to the use of negative practice as a therapeutic technique. Kendrick himself, however, does not make this identification, except in the title of the second contribution cited. He does not, for example, discuss the importance the concepts of reactive and conditioned inhibition, whose effects on rats' alley running he is concerned to demonstrate, might have in the clinical treatment of undesirable habits, but the milieu in which his investigations were undertaken, and the placement of the second contribution alongside a reprinting (Eysenck, 1960) of Yates's pioneer 'Application of learning theory to the treatment of tics' (1958) make the point sufficiently well.

Kendrick's starting point arose from the criticism of the Hullian formulation of reactive and conditioned inhibition which suggested counter-intuitive outcomes in that the constant repetition of a habit must ultimately lead to the extinction of the response (*see* Mowrer, 1960a for review). He showed (1958a) that thirsty rats running in 10-ft-long runways for a very small (0·25 ml) water reward under conditions of massed trials (30 a day) did in fact extinguish their running response. In this well-controlled study all ten subjects met stringent extinction criteria within 40 days of the start of the experiment. He further demonstrated that there was no spontaneous recovery of the running habit after a long rest period of 36 days and concluded that some permanent decrement, which he identified as conditioned inhibition, had taken place. This interpretation was challenged by Keehn (1959; Keehn and Sabbagh, 1958), against whose criticisms Kendrick defended himself (1958b, 1959a). However, in a careful review of these studies together with the evidence from classical conditioning work, Prokasy (1960) reaches the conclusion that the demonstration of inhibition with reinforcement remains insecure. He instances the considerable evidence for persistance of responding over long periods, for example, in Skinner boxes, and feels that Kendrick's failure to provide a spaced trials control group which, presumably, should not have extinguished in the way the massed trials group did, precludes an identification of the motivational factors acting in his runway situation. In similar vein, Mowrer

---

* That this caveat was justified may be seen from a re-analysis of Goldstein's data which failed to support his conclusions, reported by Wilson and Davison (1971). This important review of somewhat wider coverage of the literature on desensitisation reaches conclusions opposite to mine.

(1960a) stresses the ambiguities in Kendrick's work but suspends judgement until the outcome of any replication of it, which, as we shall see, in the event turned out to be negative. Jensen (1961) reviews the efforts to reformulate the Hullian concepts of inhibition on which Kendrick's experiment depended, and comes to the conclusion that they are unsalvageable. It should perhaps be noted that Gray (1967) identifies the phenomenon of extinction with reinforcement, here, following Kendrick, attributed to conditioned inhibition, as being due to transmarginal inhibition in the Pavlovian system: that is to say, the inhibition postulated as being due to functional exhaustion of the cortical cells due to overstimulation, and having a protective function.

In further work, Kendrick (1959b, 1960) investigated the effect of drive and reinforcement variables in extinction developing during massed practice as before. He demonstrated (separately) that low drive and partial reinforcement were conducive to speedier extinction than high drive or 100 per cent reinforcement. Further work suggested that the amount of effort involved in making the response did not lead to faster inhibition of performance (though *see* Fischer *et al.*, 1968).

Others, however, have not been able to support Kendrick's main findings. Thus, Fuchs (1960) in an apparently careful attempt to repeat rather precisely the original conditions, found no extinction of the running response after 40 days at 30 massed trials a day, and Mountjoy, Edwin, and Rogers (1960), while varying some of the conditions parametrically (length of runway and intertrial block interval) and others arbitrarily (15 only massed trials), reported no change of running speed on retesting after periods shorter than Kendrick used. Wasserman and Jensen (1969) have drawn attention to possible artefacts in extinction experiments. On the other hand, Coons, Anderson, and Myers (1960) were unable to *prevent* extinction of avoidance responding in groups of rats given either two or six hours of testing a day for 15 or 10 days respectively, after having learned a wheel-turning response to avoid shock. However, these authors are inclined to rule out explanations in terms of inhibition concepts because of the absence of intrasessional performance decrement, and it may well be that the difficulties encountered parallel those often reported in training animals to make avoidance responses other than running (Beecroft, 1967). It would seem that the weight of evidence supports Prokasy's view of the matter. Hence perhaps, Kendrick's suggestive findings which stemmed rather directly from the problem of the treatment of multiples tics do not seem to have been followed up at all extensively in the clinical field (*see*, however, Clark, 1966).

Avoidance and Aversion

A third area of concern to behaviour therapy in which animal work has a part to play relates to avoidance and aversion. Here the problem is the opposite of that of the previous sections—rather than extinction with its implications for the elimination of undesired habits, the question of the positive conditioning, though of an aversive kind, of a new response arises. The formulations of Solomon and Wynne (1953, 1954) deriving from their work on traumatic avoidance learning in dogs have been influential in this connection (Feldman, 1966), but there has been little animal experimentation explicitly orientated towards clinical problems of the kind generated by the theory of reciprocal inhibition therapy and its critics. Instead, there has been a massive effort towards understanding the conditioned emotional response, especially in relation to conditioned suppression of ongoing behaviour in a Skinner box, together with a smaller but comparable effort to understand the nature of the processes involved in escape-avoidance conditioning. Once again it is beyond our present scope to review this whole area of animal work: Rachman and Teasdale (1969) and Feldman and MacCulloch (1971) provide useful summaries of some of the animal work relevant to the clinical treatments with which they are primarily concerned, and Campbell and Church (1969) bring together valuable discussions of many aspects of aversion and of punishment by various authors, some of whom are cited separately. In addition, Azrin and Holz (1966) review punishment from a more strictly operant point of view. In view of the considerable stress laid on the role of emotional conditioning in aversion therapy, particular importance attaches to work on this topic, a large segment of the behavioural aspects of which has been most competently reviewed by Beecroft (1967). He notes:

'The study of emotional conditioning in animals has a very short history. Although early investigators included such luminaries as Hunter and Warner, the real impetus to the analysis of emotional conditioning was associated with the work of Neal E. Miller and O. Hobart Mowrer at Yale University in the late 1930s. Nevertheless, two-thirds of the more than 200 papers cited in this monograph have been published in the 1960s. This bumper crop seems part of an effort of psychologists to bring their knowledge of the aversive side of learning up to the level which has been reached in the study of reward learning' (Beecroft, 1967, p. 45).

It is perhaps too much to expect, therefore, that what knowledge has been gained should have already been applied to clinical treatments involving aversion, in view of the recency of both the experimental work and of the upsurge of clinical interest in such techniques. Moreover this is an area that, it might be argued, is especially prone to misleading interpretations. Rachman and Teasdale express themselves on this point as follows:

'If, as seems to be the case, patients can acquire (conditioned?) aversive reactions . . . through the manipulations of purely imaginal events, then the implications of these clinical findings for general psychology are very considerable. A great deal of general psychology, and particularly the study of learning, is still peripheralist in conception. The findings on covert sensitisation underline the inadequacy of this type of approach and at the same time provide a striking example of the distance between learning in animals and in humans. Our traditional reliance on animal data in formulating theories of human learning is once again seen to be limiting' (1969, p. 105).

An example at the practical level they could have adduced lies in the demonstrations (*see* Campbell and Misanin, 1969) that acquisition of escape-avoidance responding is an *inverse* function of intensity of the shock used—an odd finding until it is noted that it relates to shuttle-box training only and seems to be best explicable in terms of a staying response or a freezing tendency (Miller and Weiss, 1969) on the part of rats made fearful of returning to the compartment in which they have been shocked. If such a staying response is itself a function of shock intensity then the result makes sense. But since humans are not made to shuttle backwards and forwards—even for therapeutic purposes—the finding is not directly relevant to clinical practice.

In view of the excellence of the review coverage indicated above little needs to be added except perhaps to emphasise the contribution that animal findings may have in the debate about the nature of the conditioning achieved with aversive methods. Rachman and Teasdale argue that the success of Feldman and MacCulloch's avoidance technique with homosexuals is due to classical conditioning rather than the two-factor, classical-instrumental paradigm they adapted from Solomon and Wynne's dog studies. Beecroft feels that the weight of animal evidence points towards emotional conditioning being of a classical kind, and it should be noted that Feldman and MacCulloch's (1971) clinical trial, admirably comparing the two methods, suggested little to choose between them in respect to therapeutic efficiency. However, these authors suggest that other clinical considerations argue in favour of avoidance techniques and here, of course, animal work can

have little by way of a direct contribution to make.

Once again, this survey must be incomplete, and in two ways; first, work on human subjects, often with direct bearing on therapeutic efficacy, is largely beyond the scope of this chapter and, hence, a one-sided view may have been presented, and, second, as was noted at the outset, it is not possible to devote attention to the body of experimental work on animals covering all the topics related to behaviour therapy. This work is especially well developed in the field of operant behaviour, and many convincing demonstrations of the applicability of animal-derived techniques as applied to human behaviour modification have been published, and much of consequence for further clinical application may ultimately lie therein. One example of what is meant must suffice. It comes from Hoffman (1969) who works with animals on conditioned suppression, motivated, as he says '. . . in the hope of acquiring information that might ultimately prove useful in the clinical management of anxiety and its related symptoms' (p. 232). This work is illustrated in Fig. 20.1. Pigeons trained to peck at a key were exposed to two signals, one a 1,000 Hz tone which was never followed by shock, and the other a noise

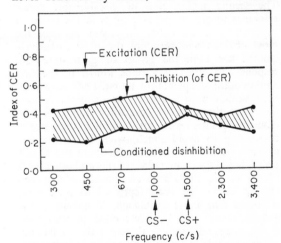

Fig. 20.1. Empirical gradients of inhibition and conditioned disinhibition of conditioned emotional response (CER) in pigeons

The pigeons are trained to press a key and then exposed to (*a*) noise associated with shock (CER), (*b*) a 1,000 Hz (=c/s) tone never associated with shock, CS−, yielding the inhibition of CER curve when combined with the noise and tested at the other frequencies shown, and (*c*) a 1,500 Hz tone also associated with shock, CS+, yielding the conditioned disinhibition curve when combined with the noise and tested at the other frequencies shown. (*Adapted with permission from* Hoffman, H. S. (1969) Stimulus factors in conditioned suppression, in *Punishment and Aversive Behavior* (Ed. B. A. Campbell and R. M. Church). New York: Appleton-Century-Crofts, 185–234.)

which was. Tests of the latter showed that it now evoked a conditioned emotional response as indicated by conditioned suppression of the primary pecking behaviour, whereas the tone did not. Sounding both together gave a frequency gradient of inhibition of the conditioned suppression which was minimal around 1,000 Hz, a process Hoffman notes as similar to Wolpe's reciprocal inhibition. Yet another step was to condition further suppression to a different tone, this time of 1,500 Hz by following it with shock. When this tone was itself combined with the aversive noise, it yielded another frequency gradient, this time of conditioned disinhibition (of the conditioned suppression) which, as might be expected, was maximal around the training frequency of 1,500 Hz. When this degree of precision of behavioural modification depending on stimulus discrimination is possible with human subjects, then many more clinical problems may yield to experimental manipulation.

PSYCHOSOMATICS

Stress Ulcers

The second major area of considerable direct relevance to clinical psychology is in the realm of psychosomatic disorders. Of these perhaps the most obvious and certainly the most intensively studied has been the group of gastro-intestinal responses to stress of various kinds. In the first edition of this chapter (Broadhurst, 1960) only a few such studies were available for mention. Among these was the work on 'executive' monkeys who developed gastric lesions attributable to the stress of responding to avoid shock, whereas their yoked controls did not (Porter *et al.*, 1958; *see also* Brady, 1966). Brady's account (1958) of this and other work (Brady *et al.*, 1958) aroused considerable interest (Brady, 1964), has been reprinted at least twice (Coopersmith, 1964; McGaugh, Weinberger, and Whalen, 1967) and is widely cited in textbooks. It is perhaps unfortunate therefore that it has not proved possible to repeat it, Foltz and Millett (1964) finding that only one of their yoked control subjects showed any ulceration. Further work, not using yoked controls, did show that a more severely stressful programme involving both conditioned avoidance and anxiety caused deaths from intussusception with acute intestinal obstruction (Foltz *et al.*, 1964). Nevertheless, in the decade since the pioneer studies appeared, the literature on gastric erosions has burgeoned so that there now exist numerous papers on this topic.

Most of this work has been done on rats, and some on mice, in both of which species gastric ulcers are relatively easily induced (Mikhail and Holland, 1966a). Considerable concern has been shown about the techniques of measurement best fitted to reflect the severity of ulceration (Mikhail and Holland, 1966b; Schmidt, 1966; Schmidt and Klopfer, 1965; Schmidt and Peckham, 1968). The susceptibility to gastric erosion has been shown to be influenced by many variables manipulable in the laboratory. Thus, the hereditary influence has been explored by the two standard psychogenetic techniques of selection (Sines, 1959, 1961, 1963, 1966; Sines and Eagleton, 1961; Eagleton and Sines, 1962; Sines, Cleeland, and Adkins, 1963; Martin *et al.*, 1968) and of strain comparison (Ader, Beels, and Tatum, 1960a; Sines, 1962; Ader, 1963; Mikhail and Broadhurst, 1965; Mikhail, 1969a; Sawrey and Long, 1962; Sines and McDonald, 1968). This programme of work on the inheritance of susceptibility is reviewed in detail up to 1963 by Robinson (1965): the later work confirmed that Sines's strain of rats genetically selected for susceptibility to immobilisation stress differed from non-selected stocks in having greater general and gastric motility. Mikhail (1969a) using improved techniques of assessment, succeeded in showing that the Maudsley emotionally reactive and nonreactive strains, bi-directionally selected for emotional elimination, differed in susceptibility, the reactives being more susceptible. Sines's most recent work suggests that about half the variation in ulcer susceptibility is attributable to genetic contributions. However, such an estimation should be applied with reservation in relation to human susceptibility: it should be noted that Sines and McDonald's heritability estimate, based on crossings between his susceptible strain and another is, like all such estimates, a property of a population and not of a trait and, hence, is subject to all manner of perturbations, not least among which are problems of cross-species comparisons.

Sex differences have been investigated by Schell and Elliot (1967) and other variables shown to affect susceptibility include group housing, which causes an increase in rats (Stern *et al.*, 1960) but a decrease in mice (Essman, 1966), infantile stimulation which causes a decrease in rats (Winokur, Stern, and Taylor, 1959) or interacts with other treatment variables such as group or individual housing (Ader, 1965) or has no effect on ulcer incidence (McMichael, 1966). In a well-controlled study Ader (1962) showed that early weaning (at 15 days) increased susceptibility, but among male rats only, confirming previous findings (Ader, Beels, and Tatum, 1960b; Ader, Tatum, and Beels, 1960).

Numerous other factors have been implicated in ulceration including diet (in swine—Perry *et al.*, 1963), gastric contents (in monkeys—Polish *et al.*,

1962), endocrines (Korányi and Endroczi, 1962) and various drugs have also been assayed in rats (Sines, 1960; Hartry, 1962; Simler, Schwartz, and Schmid, 1962; Sawrey, J. M. and Sawrey, W. L., 1964; Takagi, Kasuya, and Watanabe, 1964) among them banana, which protects (Sanyal, Banerji, and Das, 1963) and alcohol which apparently does not (Schmidt and Klopfer, 1968). Pregnancy protects mothers (Kahlson, Lilja, and Svensson, 1964), but female offspring of mothers manipulated during pregnancy show enhanced susceptibility (Ader and Plaut, 1968). Prior stress of various kinds increases susceptibility (Francois and Sines, 1961; Paré, 1962, 1964)—though not prior freezing of the stomach (McFee et al., 1963)—as does intercurrent cold stress (Rosenberg, 1967). Stressing rats in pairs or in threes, on the other hand, has a protective effect (Sawrey and Sawrey, 1966). While the effect of season has been shown to be present in rats (Lambert et al., 1966) and absent in swine (Muggenburg et al., 1964), Ader (1967a) has shown that rats immobilised at the peak as opposed to the trough of their activity cycle are significantly more susceptible to ulceration.

Of greater interest perhaps in the present context is the question of the relation of emotionality in the rat to susceptibility to gastric erosion. Ader (1967b) reviews the evidence, both from his own and others' work, to which that of Paré (1966) might be added, which fails to support the earlier identification (Sines, 1961, 1962) of rats judged emotionally reactive by such measures as emotional elimination in the open field as especially susceptible to ulcerogenic stress. The matter has been re-opened by Mikhail's study (1969a), referred to above, suggesting that rats of the Maudsley emotionally reactive strain can be shown to be more susceptible than the companion nonreactive strain. He attributes this to a hyperactivity of the parasympathetic system underlying both ulcerogenesis and emotional elimination. This contrasts with the absence of an increase in ulcer formation caused by conditioned anxiety of a kind likely to provoke hyperactivity of the sympathetic nervous system (Mikhail, 1969b), contrary to previous findings (Sawrey and Sawrey, 1964, 1968). Lovibond's findings (1969) that the application of a conditioned fear signal concurrent with immobilisation did not increase ulceration in Sines's susceptible strain of rats, supports this view.

Finally, the question of the determinants of ulcer production in stressed animals comes full circle in studies with rats and bearing on the role of anxiety in Brady's 'executive' monkeys. While early work had confirmed that the same overall time scheduling of rest pauses as used with monkeys was effective with rats (Rice, 1963), other work had shown the importance of irregularity in shock conditioning in giving rise to ulcers in rats (Sawrey, 1961; Sawrey and Sawrey, 1963). Groves and Diamond (1963) used the yoked-control method of Brady. In the hands of Weiss (1968) who used this method with rats, the outcome was just the opposite to that of the original work. Rats that could develop escape and avoidance responses showed less stress response than their yoked controls who could not avoid the shock, and who were more susceptible to gastric erosion. Seligman's (1968) work, in which rats having a warning signal for shock in a feeding situation were contrasted with others randomly stimulated which developed stomach lesions, probably pinpoints the reason: the possibility afforded of predicting the shock made it less stressful. As the author notes, the concept of 'learned helplessness' (see Maier, Seligman, and Solomon, 1969) may be important here. In commenting on these important differences between results from rather similar techniques in rat and monkey, Miller (1969b) notes the possible importance of the difficulty of the avoidance task, which was very simple for Weiss's rats as opposed to the more complex Sidman avoidance task which Brady's monkeys had to master. Miller and Weiss (1969) in a review of this experimentation are tempted to conclude 'It's easy to be an executive if you're a rat!' But they go on to point out that Brady may have unwittingly selected more susceptible monkeys for his control group in that less able learners were relegated to it. Also to be noted are the methodological problems associated with the yoked-control design, though Miller believes them not to have vitiated this work (Campbell and Church, 1969, pp. 522–523). All in all, therefore, it would seem that the question of the nature of the stress that may prove ulcerogenic is as yet unresolved but animal work has provided some important pointers.

Autonomic Conditioning

The next area of work with putative relevance to psychosomatic disorder brings us back to problems of conditioning—this time of autonomic responses. Increasing sophistication of technique has meant that recording of physiological parameters such as heart rate from animals as small as the rat is becoming commonplace, as compared with the relative paucity and tentative nature of those reviewed in the first edition of this *Handbook* (Broadhurst, 1960). Indeed, it has been said that the rat that does not have its electrocardiogram taken these days can justly feel deprived! A consequence of this increased expertise has been an upsurge of studies involving physiological variables, including those by Miller and his associates on the instrumental learning of visceral responses, which constitute a considerable break-through with possibly profound consequences.

Autonomic conditioning as such has long been demonstrated. Bykov's work (1957) is perhaps the best known in this connection. In his book he reports the details of numerous Pavlovian conditioning experiments dating back to the 1920s, using principally dogs, and dealing with the acquisition of conditioned responses of the kidney, liver, the cardiovascular system, the respiratory apparatus and the digestive tract and other metabolic functions. There is little doubt that control over numerous visceral functions can be achieved: Bykov has, as he puts it, shown 'that environmental agents (sound, light, smells) could influence an organ concealed in the depth of the body' (1957, p. 6). Moreover, these organs themselves are shown to be important sources of interoceptive stimuli which, in turn, can be used for conditioning. Gantt (1964a) provides a succinct review of further developments in this field, including some mention of confirmatory work from other laboratories on the visceral systems employed by Bykov, and notes the ubiquity of autonomic conditioning of the action of the heart, the classical conditioning of which may be seen in many striking ways. For example, Perez-Cruet and Gantt (1964) demonstrated that the centrally acting cataleptic drug, bulbocapnine, which produces a specific change in the electrocardiogram of dogs, can be used as an unconditioned stimulus to produce a conditioned electrocardiographic response to visual or auditory signals.

But the implications of the approach culminating in the investigations of Miller and his associates extend beyond the mere demonstration of the fact that autonomic functions can be conditioned, since the possibility that the responses of visceral organs can be brought under the control of instrumental techniques of the kind that enable such characteristics of Skinnerian techniques as delicate shaping and imperviousness to extinction to be utilised is an exciting one. The experimental work, largely using humans as subjects and designed to show that such instrumental conditioning of autonomic responses is possible is reviewed by Kimmel (1967) who takes a positive view of the evidence and by Katkin and Murray (1968) whose conclusions are broadly negative (see also Crider, Schwartz, and Schnidman, 1969; Katkin, Murray, and Lachman, 1969). They show that in most cases it is not possible to rule out artefacts arising either from the possible involvement in the conditioning process of skeletal musculature which might hence serve as a mediator under voluntary control, or from the influence of

cognitive processes which might themselves serve as mediators. Consider the difficulty encountered in this respect in attempting to condition instrumentally some aspect of sexual arousal in humans such as penile erection in males. While the reflex control over the response is almost exclusively mediated via the autonomic nervous system, volitional control might be completely dependent on a decision to think erotic thoughts—a proven possibility (Laws and Rubin, 1962). An experimenter could never be certain that artefacts of this kind were not contaminating his results. While neither of the comprehensive reviews mentioned deals with the precise example adduced, they relate comparable problems in studies of electrodermal, peripheral vascular, and cardiac conditioning. Katkin and Murray's review is saved from being entirely negative in tone and consequently having to endorse previous assertions that autonomic responses are susceptible only to classical but not to instrumental conditioning by the earlier reports of work of Miller's group using rats as subjects. The single major methodological advance here was the technique of completely paralysing the skeletal musculature by curare, thus obviating the possibility of skeletal conditioning (Trowill, 1967). Using this technique and either brain stimulation via implanted electrodes or shock to the tail as reinforcement, positive and negative respectively, Miller and his associates have been able to demonstrate instrumental conditioning of acceleration and deceleration of heart rate, increase and decrease of systolic blood pressure, intestinal contraction and relaxation, and increase and decrease of urine formation by the kidney. Moreover, they have shown that the changes are specific by monitoring two functions separately and demonstrating that only the conditioned one is altered whereas the other is not, and vice versa. Thus, Miller and Banuazizi (1968) conditioned heart rate and intestinal activity independently of each other. An even greater degree of specificity was shown in the demonstration of differential vasomotor conditioning of the two ears of the rat (DiCara and Miller, 1968). Katkin and Murray felt able to conclude 'Miller and his associates appear to have come as close as is possible to a truly definitive series of experiments establishing the phenomenon of instrumental conditioning of autonomically mediated responses' (1968, p. 65).

Further reviews of this work have already appeared (Miller, 1969a, 1969b; Miller and Weiss, 1969; DiCara, 1970) and accordingly it is intended neither to cite all the various studies individually nor to describe their details, but rather to concentrate attention on the few subsequent animal studies, especially confirmatory ones from other laboratories, and to assess the importance of this work from the psychosomatic point of view. Thus, Hothersall and Brener (1969) provided a replication of the work of Miller and his associates in an experiment with curarised rats rewarded with brain stimulation for increases or decreases in heart rate. Improvement over successive training sessions was shown, and extinction demonstrated. In further work from Miller's laboratory, DiCara and Weiss (1969) addressed themselves to the question of whether or not such autonomic responses, instrumentally learned under curare and already shown to be transferrable to the non-curarised state (DiCara and Miller, 1969), would affect the rat's subsequent adaptive reactions in a new situation. Curarised rats, maintained by artificial respiration, were trained in the now standard way to avoid electric shock to the tail by an increase or a decrease in heart rate. The response was shaped in the sense that the criterion was successively made more demanding in terms of the amount of change needed to avoid shock when the conditioned stimulus, a tone, sounded. The significant changes in heart rate to the tone thus achieved were shown, two weeks later, to have transferred to the normal, free-moving situation, and a further month later avoidance conditioning was developed. The results were quite definite: rats instrumentally trained to lower their heart rate to the tone learned the motor avoidance response to it by the second day of training, whereas the rats who had learned cardiac acceleration were much poorer, even failing to progress beyond the stage of learning the escape response to the shock heralded by the tone. Certain difficulties of interpretation arise in relation to these findings but the importance of the demonstration of the permanence and non-specificity of the learned cardiac changes transcends them.

Herein perhaps lies the potential importance for the clinical psychologist. At the therapeutic level the controversy over the relative involvement of classical and instrumental conditioning in relation to visceral and motor responses respectively, though important—witness the outcome of Miller's work to unravel this distinction by curarisation—is not vital, and the question whether avoidance develops as a two-factor process (Rescorla and Solomon, 1967) or not (Herrnstein, 1969) is again not of immediate consequence, however significant the theoretical implications may be in the long run. If patients can be brought relief for conditions—non-psychiatric as well as psychiatric—which distress them, then it may be immaterial that changes in autonomic functioning have been brought about by methods involving somatic or cognitive activities (Murray and Katkin, 1968). If, on the other hand,

it can be shown that it is important, perhaps in order to avoid extinction, that such mediators should be inoperative, then measures to reduce their influence will need to be evolved in behaviour therapy. One obvious approach to minimise somatic involvement (Miller, 1969a) might be to use the techniques of relaxation widely used in desensitisation. Another might be to develop hybrid techniques involving the conversion of, for example, classical conditioned responses into instrumental ones (Grant et al., 1969).

Here again, an incomplete assessment only is possible in a fast moving area of research and which, in the event of another edition of this *Handbook* a decade from now, will, it is almost certainly safe to predict, have changed out of recognition, and, with it, a considerable portion of applied abnormal psychology.

Less Direct Relevance

ANALOGUES OF PERSONALITY

We now turn to studies, using animals as subjects, that might be thought to have a bearing on applied abnormal psychology, though of a less direct kind than those discussed in the preceding sections. Of these, the first is concerned with the psychogenetic approach to the provision of animal analogues of personality dimensions in humans. Selective breeding can be used to create populations of animals that differ reliably in respect of the phenotype upon which the selection pressure has been exerted by means of assortative mating to create strains that are extreme in respect of the chosen characteristics. Such a procedure involving bidirectional selection for extremes of emotional elimination in the open-field test has led to the creation of the Maudsley reactive and nonreactive strains of rats. The programme was started in 1954 and the outcome was surveyed ten years later by Eysenck and Broadhurst (1964) in respect of the extent to which the phenotypic difference in emotional elimination, now a stable and reliable differentiating feature of the reactive and nonreactive strains, could be said to underlie the many other differences, physiological as well as behavioural, that characterise them. Reviewing some 50 different measures of all sorts taken from the two strains, we came to the conclusion that the manifold differences detected pointed to a very real effect on their general emotional responsiveness brought about by the selection for defecation in the open-field test. Since then the strains have been exported to other laboratories both in Britain and North America and nearly 50 further studies using them were reported prior to 1970. Reviewing this new body of evidence on their standing in respect of emotional reactivity, both in the original, open-field situation and in many other experiments, including psychopharmacological ones, compels the conclusion that the differentiation between the strains is well maintained. Further, the additional data fully support the generality of the autonomic responsiveness based on the genetical selection for a single aspect of it—emotional elimination. Thus, Broadhurst and Eysenck (1965) published the results of testing the two strains on a battery of tests including escape-avoidance conditioning, approach-avoidance conflict, measures of speed, startle and water intake, together with determinations of a range of endocrine function. A considerable degree of generality was demonstrated, even though there were some sex differences in the patterning of it.

Few studies explicitly concerned with the development of maladaptive behaviour as such and employing these strains for the purpose have been reported however. This may be because the emotionally reactive strain—the neurotic analogue—is less susceptible, rather than more, to conditioning of an escape avoidance kind (see for example, Broadhurst and Levine, 1963; Wilcock, 1968), while displaying greater susceptibility to the development of conditioned emotional responses which may, in fact, be causal in preventing the development of the more easily studied avoidance learning (see Joffe, 1964; Ferraro and York, 1968). Eysenck (1963) nevertheless developed an ingenious adaptation of an experiment of Mowrer and Ullman (1945) which involved subjecting rats of the two strains to a complex feeding procedure, the essence of which was that the subjects had to learn to delay taking the available food until the termination of a signal on pain of shock to the feet for transgression of the 'rule'. Two intensities of shock were used, and it was found that shock level did not interact with the strain differences observed. Emotionally reactive rats, as well as being slower at acquiring the initial feeding reactions also showed response to the imposition of the rule by a larger number of abnormal, non-waiting reactions, which Eysenck called 'psychopathic' if the food was taken before the buzzer signalling shock terminated or 'dysthymic' if food was refused altogether. The proportion of the two kinds of abnormal reaction developed did not separate the two strains however; both developed the psychopathic reaction more readily than the dysthymic. In discussing these results, Eysenck developed the argument that the one dimension of emotionality—the rodent analogue of neuroticism—is insufficient to account for them, suggesting that something akin to introversion-extraversion might be operative. He looked forward to the time when

selective breeding might give rise to populations as widely differentiated in this respect as are for example, the Maudsley rat strains in emotional elimination, the Roman strains in escape-avoidance conditioning (Broadhurst and Bignami, 1956), the Tryon strains in maze learning (Rosenzweig, 1964) or the strains selected for nonspecific excitability level (see Lát and Gollová-Hémon, 1969). But first a test satisfactorily convincing as an animal analogue of introversion-extraversion must be found and the efforts to provide this have not been especially encouraging as yet. Sinha, Franks, and Broadhurst (1958) showed the Maudsley strains were not differentiated in respect of alternation in a psychopharmacological study supporting Eysenck's drug postulate. The alternation measure, theoretically related to reactive inhibition, and hence, via the typological postulate, to introversion-extraversion in humans, was used also by Weldon (1967) who attacked the problem by running rats of the Maudsley strains in the Mowrer situation as well. But performances in the two tests were unrelated and, moreover, differences between the strains in alternation measures appeared which are attributable to inadequate extinction of fear of the apparatus. A further attempt to define an analogue in terms of stimulus satiation has been reported (Weldon, 1968) but so far the problem has remained intractable.

Meanwhile, the psychogenetics of emotional reactivity in the rat using the Maudsley and other strains has progressed. Broadhurst (1969) reviews the work to date of what has become the Birmingham group, presenting heritability estimates of emotional elimination and ambulation in the open field derived from a series of studies. In general, the former are higher than the latter. Analyses of genotype-environment interaction lead to speculations about the evolution of the behaviour measured which may serve to underpin similar ventures based on human data (Jinks and Fulker, 1970). Significant progress in the psychogenetics of the mouse has also been made, though there has been less concentration on emotional behaviour. Henderson's work (1968) on conditioned emotional response is an important exception.

ANALOGUES OF SOCIALISATION PROCESSES

Most studies of relevance to human socialisation are concerned with some aspect of deprivation and/or enrichment of the environment as the experimental variable. Berger and Passingham (see Chapter 17, this *Handbook*) review the work on non-human primates; other species are dealt with in addition by the various contributors to the book edited by Newton and Levine (1968). Morton (1968) provides a succinct review of the effects of infantile experiences on adult behaviour, and Joffe (1969) a thorough survey of prenatal determinants (including effects on humans). Woolpy discusses socialisation in wolves (1968) and Fuller (1967) surveys the after-effects of isolation in dogs. Of interest in this connection is some work by Solomon, Turner, and Lessac informally reported earlier by Mowrer (1960b—see also Eysenck, 1964a), on the development of conforming responses in hungry puppies who were punished for choosing a preferred food in the presence of the experimenter. Trials were run in which the experimenter was absent but observing the time taken for the puppy to react to the preferred food. This varied from six minutes to 16 daily sessions of 30 minutes, and allowed observations to be made on the original punishment and of breed differences in relation to the resistance to extinction of the fear conditioning. Other related examples are to be found in the book edited by Campbell and Church (1969) but few have the intuitive appeal of Solomon's work.

Studies of relevance to depressive behaviour have been reviewed by McKinney and Bunney (1969): Ferster (1966) also considers the problem from an operant conditioning viewpoint. That the disturbances of social relationships often held to be causal in such cases can have more serious outcomes is suggested by a report of coronary arteriosclerosis in pigs (Ratcliffe et al., 1969).

ANALOGUES OF CONFLICT, FRUSTRATION, AND
FIXATION

Maier's work (1949) on abnormal response fixations appears to be attracting increasing interest after a period of scepticism. Such fixations were often observed in rats forced by air blast to attempt insoluble two-choice problems in the Lashley jumping stand and revealed when the discrimination problem was later made soluble. They usually took the form of a stereotyped response to a position. Yates (1962) provides a comprehensive review of the work of Maier and his collaborators and analyses in detail both the experimentation itself and the criticisms of it. He concludes, perhaps reacting over-sympathetically to what he perceives to be the neglect shown it in American psychology, that the work is of considerable importance in endeavours to understand maladaptive habits resistant to extinction. He concedes that Maier's findings are more complex than Maier himself realised and that it is not possible to integrate them into conventional learning theory. More recent reviewers, Feldman and Green (1967), attempted to do this by proposing a model of the Maier situation as a double approach-avoidance

conflict. They confess that the model is unable to account for the persistence of stereotyped behaviour, but their review is valuable for the coverage of studies employing drugs and other procedures that show that fixations can be modified or prevented. Seward (1969), starting from the premise that conflict enhances drive, argues convincingly that the abnormal fixations described can be regarded as being due to powerful reinforcement arising from escape from the avoidance-avoidance conflict generated by the situation in which Maier's subjects were placed.

Liberson (1967) regards fixations as a rodent analogue of compulsions in humans and relates the outcome of pharmacological studies of fixation to brain biochemistry. Imada and Shikano (1968) inverted the procedure by which Ellen and Feldman (1958) showed that fixated rats could solve the subsequent discrimination problem if allowed to walk on runways to the stimulus windows rather than jumping to them. They devised an apparatus that required rats either to walk to, or, with a section removed, to jump to, one of five food cups. A group shocked at the starting point showed directional fixations when required to jump and not walk. Interesting as these findings are, the revised apparatus shares with Maier's the considerable situational complexity which several authors have commented on (Dinsmoor, 1960; Yates, 1962) and which make the analysis of abnormal fixations so difficult to encompass in conventional terms.

More profitable, perhaps, may be the study of what has come to be called 'vicious circle behaviour'. Brown (1969) prefers the term self-punitive behaviour for his review of work that shows that rats, trained to escape shock in a straight alley by running to a safe region, will fail to extinguish this behaviour when no longer shocked if required to pass through an intermediate electrified zone. Numerous factors appear to influence the appearance of such behaviour in which punishment appears facilitative rather than inhibitory. The explanation in terms of a generalisation of a conditioned fear, resulting from punishing the learned escape response, to the starting box, thus maintaining the escape motivation has been challenged by Delude (1969). He showed that the lower latencies that would be expected of rats on this view are not detectable.

ANALOGUES OF AGGRESSION AND SOCIAL
DENSITY PHENOMENA

Scott (1966) and Vernon (1969) review research on aggression and, between them, provide coverage of most areas. There is agreement that aggression is not a unitary concept. Moyer (1968) distinguishes the following classes: irritable, predatory, fear induced, territory defence, intermale, maternal, sexual, and instrumental (learned). Of particular interest in the present context are pain-induced (irritable) aggression—and interspecies or predatory aggression, both of which have been studied extensively in the laboratory.

Pain-induced aggression—the O'Kelly-Steckle reaction (1939)—against either animals or inanimate objects can be observed in many species. Azrin and his group have contributed extensively to the work on this topic. It is reviewed by Ulrich (1966), who notes the variety of independent variables that can affect the character and intensity of the aggressive reactions observed. Subsequent contributions include the methodological, such as Hutchinson, Azrin and Hake's (1966) bite sensor for automatically recording the rapidity and intensity of biting in the restrained monkey, and the substantive, such as Connor and co-workers' (1969) analysis of the role of sex hormones in pain-induced fighting in rats. It should be noted, in view of the obvious relevance of this work to the influential—though now much criticised (Kaufman, 1965)—frustration-aggression hypothesis of Dollard et al. (1939) that measured aggression may, for example, be increased in pigeons by extinction (Azrin, Hutchinson, and Hake, 1966) or in rats by non-reinforcement (Gallup, 1965) without the need for pain, induced by shock or otherwise.

Interspecies aggression is classified by Moyer as 'predatory' and is best so regarded. Extensive work on 'killer' rats has been done by Karli (1965; Karli and Vergnes, 1964) and by Myer (1964, 1968). Differences in brain biochemistry between rats that are regularly muricidal and those that are not have been detected (Goldberg and Salama, 1969). It can be shown that such responses to mice can be modified by aversive stimulation (Baenninger and Grossman, 1969; Baenninger and Ulm, 1969) as, indeed, can shock-induced aggression (Ulrich, Wolfe, and Dulaney, 1969).

Detailed consideration of the other aspects of animal aggression is beyond our present scope, but reference should be made to the use—or misuse—of the concept in extrapolations to human behaviour by Lorenz (1966) and, in more popular vein, Ardrey (1966) who is especially concerned with territorial defence. Crook's valuable survey (1968) of work in this latter field can serve as an antidote.

The influence of hereditary determinants of aggressive behaviour in mice has been demonstrated in a successful selection experiment by Lagerspetz (1961, 1964). Control for maternal effects by cross-fostering (Lagerspetz and Wuorinen,

1965) showed them to be minimal. Study of neurochemical and endocrinological differences between the selected strains suggests higher sympathetic nervous activity in the strain selected for aggressiveness (Lagerspetz, Tirri, and Lagerspetz, 1968).

Problems of social density are illustrated in animal work both with primates and non-primates. The former are discussed by Berger and Passingham (Chapter 17, this *Handbook*); the non-primates have been studied most intensively by Calhoun (*see* Thiessen's review, 1964). He has demonstrated experimentally the pathological consequences of excessive aggregations of rats termed, by analogy with geomorphic sinks, a 'behavioural sink' (Calhoun, 1962) and has developed theoretical expectations of the effects on social behaviour of various ecological factors that could be manipulated (Calhoun, 1963, 1968). Some of these have been shown to be operative (Calhoun, 1967). Endocrine responses to aggregation stress (Christian, 1964; Christian and Davies, 1964; Thiessen and Rodgers, 1969) are thought to be responsible for some of the pathology observed, such as excessive aggression and reproductive failures (Thiessen, 1966; Morrison and Thatcher, 1969).

ANALOGUES OF ADDICTION

Animals have frequently been used for studies of drug addiction or dependence: relevant work on the 'hard' drugs of abuse is considered elsewhere in this *Handbook* (*see* Chapter 4, by Teasdale). Among the socially accepted drugs the study of alcohol (ethanol, ethyl alcohol) has generated literature too ample to review here (*see* Franks, 1958, and the comprehensive survey by Wallgren and Barry, 1970). Concentration must therefore be focused on illustrative studies purporting or promising relevance to the development of human dependence, in which the property of alcohol of depressing many aspects of nervous function, including fear and anxiety, have been thought to be of importance. In addition, there will be some emphasis on constitutional, especially genetical, determinants, in view of the interest in physiological hypotheses, such as the genototrophic theory of Williams (1956).

The work of Masserman on the effects of ethanol on experimental neuroses in cats has been influential in connection with the first of these topics: it is critically reviewed by Broadhurst (1960) and a replication of it discussed below. Working with rats, Barry and Miller (1962) confirmed Conger's (1951) suggestion that approach-avoidance conflict was responsible for Masserman's findings in that it was possible to show that the administration of ethanol had a differential effect, depressing approach less than avoidance. More recent work has concentrated on self-administered alcohol, dilute solutions of which are preferred to water by many laboratory animals. Work of some saliency has included that by Mello and Mendelson, an example of whose admirable approach is seen in their careful study (1966) of the development of drinking in rhesus monkeys allowed access to ethanol before, during, and after exposure to a stress of the kind that led to ulcers in 'executive' monkeys. No addiction developed and no withdrawal symptoms were observed. In the work of Myers and his group methodological sophistication (Myers, 1966b) has been combined with manipulation of physiological parameters of possible importance (Myers and Cicero, 1969). Matters can be arranged so that quite large amounts of alcohol may be ingested by animals: Keehn (1969) made feeding contingent on intake of the drug and reports the blood alcohol level of one rat reached over 200 mg per cent, surpassing the previously reported record of 160 mg per cent (Lester, 1961) for ethanol polydipsia. Further experimentation involving an interaction with stress has been reported by Easterbrook (1963), Wallgren and Tirri (1963), and Ramsay and Dis (1967). Cicero, Myers, and Black (1968) appear to have succeeded in demonstrating a relationship in rats between the voluntary intake of ethanol and stress induced by shock (*see* also Casey, 1960). But no unequivocal evidence of addiction, involving the necessary elements of dependence, tolerance, and habituation (Mendelson and Mello, 1964), has so far been demonstrated in animal experiments using ethanol.

Despite this relatively discouraging outcome interest continues in the possibility of linking constitutional factors with differences in reaction to alcohol, often as measured by preference. Rodgers and McClearn (1962) and Rodgers (1967) ably review the work on alcohol preference in mice to which they have so largely contributed. They conclude that a strong genetic influence has been demonstrated, that it is related to metabolic capacity and does not result from stress. Brewster's reanalysis (1968) of preference data from cross-breeding mouse strains (McClearn and Rodgers, 1961; Fuller, 1964) confirms a high heritability and previous suggestions of polygenic determination. Among the numerous contributions to alcohol study from Wallgren's laboratory, Eriksson (1968) reports selection for alcohol preference in rats, resulting in the establishment of two strains that differ radically in this respect. Of the models of human addiction discussed or implied in this brief and selective review of animal work bearing on addiction to alcohol, the psychogenetic one seems especially promising.

Indirect Relevance

We now turn to studies of animal behaviour judged as being of indirect relevance to clinical psychology. Of these the work of ethologists is most uncertainly demoted into this category.

ETHOLOGICAL STUDIES

The last decade has seen considerable increase of interest in human behaviour by ethologists who vigorously attempted to apply their models of animal behaviour to a wider field. These models have been briefly reviewed by Grant (1965) and their application to child psychiatry outlined. The possibility of applying them to nonverbal behaviour in interviews with both schizophrenic and normal subjects has been demonstrated (Grant, 1968). Jones (1967), studying the behaviour of nursery-school children, draws a parallel with peer-group play in monkeys, and Mitchell (1969) seeks to relate masochism in humans to submissive behaviour in animals. These examples may give the flavour of this approach which has aroused interest among psychiatrists (Beer, 1968; Kramer, 1968) but which seems unnecessarily limited in its restriction to nonverbal behaviour when dealing with human subjects. Psychologists' theorising has not been conspicuously successful to date least of all, perhaps, in relation to abnormal behaviour, but it is probably safe to say that it would have been even less so if it had denied itself the possibility of studying communication psycholinguistically.

PSYCHOANALYTIC MODELS

Of the efforts to underpin a psychoanalytic approach by the use of animal studies, Masserman's has been the most sustained and the most influential. His 1943 monograph, *Behavior and Neurosis*, was reissued unamended in 1964, but with an appendix reviewing some of the later work of Masserman and his collaborators. The monograph includes, in addition to work on neurophysiology, a report of a series of experiments in which cats were subjected to traumata while feeding. Their subsequent behaviour and their responses to Masserman's therapeutic endeavours are interpreted in terms of his 'biodynamic principles'. This work, and many of the subsequent experiments, together with the controversy they aroused are reviewed in detail in the first edition of this *Handbook* (Broadhurst, 1960).

In further work with monkeys, Masserman, Aarons, and Wechkin (1963) exposed hungry normal pig-tail and rhesus monkeys to choices between two different but highly preferred foods. An experimental group which had been subjected to a conditioned emotional response formation during feeding, either by shock or fright (at a toy snake) a year previously, were similarly exposed to this approach-approach conflict. Agitated behaviour was noted for both groups, though the experimentally neurotic group are reported as showing significantly more of the various neurotic indices on which Masserman based his earlier work. In promising subsequent publication of the data and their analyses (which have not yet come to hand), the writers express Masserman's characteristic view that 'it is questionable whether this (publication) would provide evidence of any greater "objectivity", "reliability" or "validity" than the equally conscientious inferences summarized above' (p. 483). There is no question in the present writer's mind on this score, and the difficulty of assessing the significance of Masserman's work from a scientific point of view continues to be enhanced by such statements.

Moreover, the interpretation of Masserman's original work on experimental neurosis in cats as being a case of straightforward conditioned emotional response formation is strengthened by further work. Smart (1965a) notes that Wolpe (1952) failed to equate the number of shocks received by the essential control group he introduced with the number given in the group in which shock was associated with eating. This association provided the motivational conflict Masserman believed necessary to precipitate experimental neurosis. In Smart's well-controlled study, 30 cats learned to press a foot switch which activated a feeder and then to lift the lid of a box to obtain food. They were assigned to three treatments, given shock alone or before eating or after eating. Careful observation, primarily by means of rating scales, was undertaken, and the results showed no significant differential effect of the various treatments. Thus, all subjects showed disturbances of the learned behaviour and of other responses to the experimenter, to other cats, to caged mice, as well as showing autonomic responses. Neither was there any difference between the groups shocked before or after feeding. Smart concludes from his results that conflict is not necessary for the establishment of the kind of behaviour observed and that 'The results tend to support theories which attribute these types of behaviour to the creation of conditioned responses' (Smart, 1965a, p. 218).

In further work, Smart (1965b) extended his observations, just as Masserman had done (Masserman and Yum, 1946), to the effect of alcohol on the avoidance behaviour developed in his cats. Subjects were assigned to groups given, unknown to the experimenter, a single dose by stomach tube of either alcohol (1·5 cc per kg body weight of an 8 per cent solution by weight) or an equicaloric dose of dextrose of the same volume. The drugs were administered 30 min before testing in the feeding box. Analysis showed that the cats given alcohol showed significant reduction in certain of the ratings of disturbed behaviour, especially those relating to the apparatus, rather than those relating to social behaviours. Dextrose had no such effects, but there was no selective effect on treatments involving shock connected with feeding, as opposed to the control groups subjected to shock unassociated with feeding. To this limited extent, Masserman and Yum's findings are supported, though there are points of difference that remain unresolved, largely, as Smart notes, because of the inadequacy of the description of experimental details in the earlier report.

Masserman and his collaborators (Masserman, Wechkin and Terris, 1964; Wechkin, Masserman, and Terris, 1964) have also devoted some attention to so-called altruistic behaviour in rhesus monkeys in which one animal makes or inhibits an operant response apparently to secure the cessation of shock to another of the same species. Church (1959) showed a similar phenomenon in rats, confirmed by Rice and Gainer (1962), but it has also been interpreted in terms of fear (Rice, 1964) or arousal (Lavery and Foley, 1963).

NATURALISTIC STUDIES

Finally, we come to the category of naturalistic studies of animals which assert, sometimes vehemently, their relevance to human behaviour pathology. Usually, dependence on a medical model of such pathology is stated or implied. Examples continue to occur, and, indeed, two *collections*, largely devoted to such material, have appeared (Brion and Ey, 1964; Fox, 1968). Typically, such reports are anecdotal (Sanger and Hamdy, 1962; Fox, 1964; Chak and Sharma, 1965) and involve the egregious extrapolation Beach complained of long ago (1953). Other reports of abnormalities of behaviour are more restrained, though perhaps over-ready to label behaviour as experimentally neurotic (Richelle, 1965), and the sexual proclivities of cats in captivity continue to surprise investigators (Michael, 1961; Hagamen, Zitzmann, and Reeves, 1963).

CONCLUSIONS

It is clear that much has changed in the area of animal behaviour bearing on abnormal psychology in the decade between the two editions of this *Handbook*, and among these changes was the attitude of the author of the present chapter. This accounts for the different complexion discernible between the two treatments. In 1960 it seemed sufficient to explore the extent of the evidence for an experimental neurosis in the strict sense, that is to say, to decide if evidence for a clear-cut animal analogue of a clinical disease entity of some sort existed. The answer, not surprisingly it now seems, was 'No'. No animal preparation that convincingly mimicked such entity could be provided by experimental psychology for the study of aetiology, prognosis or therapy. The claims that such had been found failed to command general acceptance.

In the present account the search for the single solution has been abandoned, with the result that a more wide-ranging treatment of likely and perhaps less likely avenues of advance has been attempted. The answers arrived at to the questions more diffusely posed have, in consequence, been more diverse and less certain. Proving the negative, was, in this case, the easier course of action than proving the positive assertion of a connection transcending the difficult journey across species. In addition, the terms in which the question was put have altered: the demise of the disease model of neurosis has thrown a heavy burden of responsibility on psychology. This burden is not only the practical, clinical one, which the proponents of behaviour therapy and behaviour modification have manfully and even enthusiastically shouldered, but an explanatory one also. And the theoretical basis of behaviour therapy is, as we have seen, not always as clear as it might be, even in the relatively simple animal analogues with which we have been dealing. Moreover, it is a manifold burden of explanation, demanding explanations of numerous phenomena simultaneously. What will suffice for punishment may not be adequate for persuasion—desensitisation is different from dependence, and so on. Animal psychology will be hard put to supply more than a few of the answers to the problems thrown up in clinical psychology, but some of the material reviewed here gives grounds for cautious hope that the challenge can be met.

REFERENCES

ADER, R. (1962) Social factors affecting emotionality and resistance to disease in animals: III. Early weaning and susceptibility to gastric ulcers in the rat. A control for nutritional factors. *J. comp. physiol. Psychol.*, **55**, 600–602.

ADER, R. (1963) Plasma pepsinogen level in rat and man. *Psychosom. Med.*, **25**, 218–220.

ADER, R. (1964) Gastric erosions in the rat: Effects of immobilization at different points in the activity cycle. *Science*, **145**, 406–407.

ADER, R. (1965) Effects of early experience and differential housing on behavior and susceptibility to gastric erosions in the rat. *J. comp. physiol. Psychol.*, **60**, 233–238.

ADER, R. (1967a) Behavioral and physiological rhythms and the development of gastric erosions in the rat. *Psychosom. Med.*, **29**, 345–353.

ADER, R. (1967b) Emotional reactivity and susceptibility to gastric erosions. *Psychol. Rep.*, **20**, 1188–1190.

ADER, R., BEELS, C. C., and TATUM, R. (1960a) Blood pepsinogen and gastric erosions in the rat. *Psychosom. Med.*, **22**, 1–12.

ADER, R., BEELS, C., and TATUM, R. (1960b) Social factors affecting emotionality and resistance to disease in animals: II. Susceptibility to gastric ulceration as a function of interruptions in social interactions and the time at which they occur. *J. comp. physiol. Psychol.*, **53**, 455–458.

ADER, R. and PLAUT, S. M. (1968) Effects of prenatal maternal handling and differential housing on offspring emotionality, plasma corticosterone levels, and susceptibility to gastric erosions. *Psychosom. Med.*, **30**, 277–286.

ADER, R., TATUM, R., and BEELS, C. C. (1960) Social factors affecting emotionality and resistance to disease in animals: I. Age of separation from the mother and susceptibility to gastric ulcers in the rat. *J. comp. physiol. Psychol.*, **53**, 446–454.

ANDERSON, O. D. and LIDDELL, H. S. (1935) Observations on experimental neurosis in sheep. *Arch. Neurol. Psychiat.*, **34**, 330–354.

ANDERSON, O. D. and PARMENTER, R. (1941) A long-term study of the experimental neurosis in the sheep and dog. *Psychosom. Med. Monogr.*, **2**, 1–150.

ANDERSON, SANDRA L. and GANTT, W. H. (1966) The effect of person on cardiac and motor responsivity to shock in dogs. *Condit. Reflex.*, **1**, 181–189.

ARDREY, R. (1966) *The Territorial Imperative*. New York: Atheneum.

ASTRUP, C. (1968) Pavlovian concepts of abnormal behavior in man and animal. In *Abnormal Behavior in Animals* (Ed. M. W. Fox) 117–128. Philadelphia: Saunders.

AYLLON, T. and AZRIN, N. (1968) *The Token Economy: A Motivational System for Therapy and Rehabilitation*. New York: Appleton-Century-Crofts.

AZRIN, N. H. and HOLZ, W. C. (1969) Punishment. In *Operant Behavior: Areas of Research and Application* (Ed. W. K. Honig) 380–447. New York: Appleton-Century-Crofts.

AZRIN, N. H., HUTCHINSON, R. R., and HAKE, D. F. (1966) Extinction-induced aggression. *J. exp. Anal. Behav.*, **9**, 191–204.

BAENNINGER, R. and GROSSMAN, JAN C. (1969) Some effects of punishment on pain-elicited aggression. *J. exp. Anal. Behav.*, **12**, 1017–1022.

BAENNINGER, R. and ULM, R. R. (1969) Overcoming the effects of prior punishment on interspecies aggression in the rat. *J. comp. physiol. psychol.*, **69**, 628–635.

BARRY, H. III and MILLER, N. E. (1962) Effects of drugs on approach-avoidance conflict tested repeatedly by means of a 'telescope alley'. *J. comp. physiol. Psychol.*, **55**, 201–210.

BAUM, M. (1966) Rapid extinction of an avoidance response following a period of response prevention in the avoidance apparatus. *Psychol. Rep.*, **18**, 59–64.

BAUM, M. (1968) Efficacy of response prevention (flooding) in facilitating the extinction of an avoidance response in rats: The effect of overtraining the response. *Behav. Res. Ther.*, **6**, 197–203.

BAUM, M. (1969a) Extinction of an avoidance response following response prevention: Some parametric investigations. *Canad. J. Psychol.*, **23**, 1–10.

BAUM, M. (1969b) Extinction of an avoidance response motivated by intense fear: Social facilitation of the action of response prevention (flooding) in rats. *Behav. Res. Ther.*, **7**, 57–62.

BAUM, M. (1970) Extinction of avoidance responding through response prevention (flooding). *Psychol. Bull.*, **74**, 276–284.

BAUM, M. and OLER, I. D. (1968) Comparison of two techniques for hastening extinction of avoidance-responding in rats. *Psychol. Rep.*, **23**, 807–813.

BEACH, F. A. (1953) Animal research and psychiatric theory. *Psychosom. Med.*, **15**, 374–389.

BECKER, G. (1969) Initial and habituated autonomic reactivity in the male and female rat. *J. comp. physiol. Psychol.*, **69**, 459–464.

BEECROFT, R. S. (1967) Emotional conditioning. *Psychonom. Monogr. Suppl.*, **2**, 45–72.

BEER, C. (1968) Ethology on the couch. In *Science and Psychoanalysis Vol. XII. Animal and Human* (Ed. J. H. Masserman) 198–213. New York: Grune & Stratton.

BENLINE, T. A. and SIMMEL, E. C. (1967) Effects of blocking of the avoidance response on the elimination of the conditioned fear response. *Psychonom. Sci.*, **8**, 357–358.

BLOCK, J. D. (1966) Howard S. Liddell, Ph.D.: Scientist and humanitarian. *Condit. Reflex*, **1**, 171–180.

BRADY, J. V. (1958) Ulcers in 'executive' monkeys. *Scient. Amer.*, **199**, 95–104.

BRADY, J. V. (1964) Behavioral stress and physiological change: A comparative approach to the experimental analysis of some psychosomatic problems. *Trans. N.Y. Acad. Sci.*, **26**, 483–496.

BRADY, J. V. (1966) Operant methodology and the experimental production of altered physiological states. In *Operant Behavior: Areas of Research and Application* (Ed. W. K. Honig) 609–633. New York: Appleton-Century-Crofts.

BRADY, J. V., PORTER, R. W., CONRAD, D. G., and MASON, J. W. (1958) Avoidance behavior and the development of gastro-duodenal ulcers. *J. exp. Anal. Behav.*, **1**, 69–73.

BREWSTER, D. J. (1968) Genetic analysis of ethanol preference in rats selected for emotional reactivity. *J. Hered.*, **5**, 283–285.

BRION, A. and EY, H. (1964) *Psychiatrie Animale*. Paris: Desclée de Bouwer.

BROADHURST, P. L. (1960) Abnormal animal behaviour. In *Handbook of Abnormal Psychology* (Ed. H. J. Eysenck) 726–763. London: Pitman. (Reprinted in *Pavlovian Approaches to Psychiatry: History and Perspectives* (Ed. W. H. Gantt, L. Pickenhain and G. Zwingmann) 153–222. Oxford: Pergamon (1970).

BROADHURST, P. L. (1969) Psychogenetics of emotionality in the rat. *Ann. N.Y. Acad. Sci.*, **159**, 806–824.

BROADHURST, P. L. and BIGNAMI, G. (1965) Correlative effects of psychogenetic selection: A study of the Roman high and low avoidance strains of rats. *Behav. Res. Ther.*, **2**, 273–280.

BROADHURST, P. L. and EYSENCK, H. J. (1965) Emotionality in the rat: A problem of response specificity. In *Stephanos: Studies in Psychology Presented to Cyril Burt* (Ed. Charlotte Banks and P. L. Broadhurst) 205–222. London Univ. of London Press.

BROADHURST, P. L. and LEVINE, S. (1963) Behavioural consistency in strains of rats selectively bred for emotional elimination. *Brit. J. Psychol.*, **54**, 121–125.

BROWN, J. S. (1969) Factors affecting self-punitive locomotor behavior. In *Punishment and Aversive Behavior* (Ed. B. A. Campbell and R. M. Church) 467–514. New York: Appleton-Century-Crofts.

BYKOV, K. M. (1957) *The Cerebral Cortex and the Internal Organs*, 3rd ed. New York: Chemical Publishing Co.

CAÏN, J. (1959) *Le Problème des Névroses Expérimentales*. Paris: Desclée de Brouwer.

CALHOUN, J. B. (1962) A 'behavioral sink'. In *Roots of Behavior* (Ed. E. Bliss) 295–315. New York: Harper.

CALHOUN, J. B. (1963) The social use of space. In *Physiological Mammalogy Vol. 1. Mammalian Populations* (Ed. W. Mayer and R. Van Gelder) 1–187. New York: Academic Press.

CALHOUN, J. B. (1967) Ecological factors in the development of behavioral anomalies. In *Comparative Psychopathology: Animal and Human* (Ed. J. Zubin and H. F. Hunt) 1–51. New York: Grune & Stratton.

CALHOUN, J. B. (1968) Environmental control over four major paths of mammalian evolution. In *Genetic and Environmental Influences on Behaviour* (Ed. J. M. Thoday and A. S. Parkes) 65–93. Edinburgh: Oliver & Boyd.

CAMPBELL, B. A. and CHURCH, R. M. (1969) *Punishment and Aversive Behavior*. New York: Appleton-Century-Crofts.

CAMPBELL, B. A. and MISANIN, J. R. (1969) Basic drives. *Annu. Rev. Psychol.*, **20**, 57–84.

CAMPOS, J. J., MOORE, A. U., and GOLDSMITH, W. M. (1968) Vigilance and the reinforcing properties of shock. *Condit. Reflex*, **3**, 105–115.

CASEY, A. (1960) The effect of stress on the consumption of alcohol and reserpine. *Quart. J. Stud. Alcohol*, **21**, 208–216.

CHAK, I. M. and SHARMA, J. N. (1965) Effect of asarone on experimentally induced conflict neurosis in rats. *Ind. J. exp. Biol.*, **3**, 252–254.

CHRISTIAN, J. J. (1964) Physiological and pathological correlates of population density. *Proc. roy. soc. Med.*, **57**, 169–174.

CHRISTIAN, J. J. and DAVIES, D. E. (1964) Endocrines, behavior and population. *Science,* **146,** 1550–1560.

CHURCH, R. M. (1959) Emotional reactions of rats to the pain of others. *J. comp. physiol. Psychol.,* **52,** 132–134.

CICERO, T. J., MYERS, R. D., and BLACK, W. C. (1968) Increase in volitional ethanol consumption following interference with a learned avoidance response. *Physiol. Behav.,* **3,** 657–660.

CLARK, D. F. (1966) Behaviour therapy of Gilles de la Tourette's syndrome. *Brit. J. Psychiat.* **112,** 771–778.

CONGER, J. J. (1951) The effects of alcohol on conflict behavior in the albino rat. *Quart. J. Stud. Alcohol,* **12,** 1–29.

CONNOR, R. L., LEVINE, S., WERTHEIM, G. A., and CUMMER, J. F. (1969) Hormonal determinants of aggressive behavior. *Ann. N.Y. Acad. Sci.,* **159,** 760–776.

COONS, E. E., ANDERSON, N. H., and MYERS, A. K. (1960) Disappearance of avoidance responding during continued training. *J. comp. physiol. Psychol.,* **53,** 290–292.

COOPERSMITH, S. (1964) *Frontiers of Psychological Research: Readings from Scientific American.* London: W. H. Freeman.

COSNIER, J. (1966) *Les Névroses Expérimentales: De la Psychologie Animale à la Pathologie Humaine.* Paris: Editions du Seuil.

COULTER, XENIA, RICCIO, D. C., and PAGE, H. A. (1969) Effects of blocking an instrumental avoidance response: Facilitated extinction but persistence of 'fear', *J. comp. physiol. Psychol.,* **68,** 377–381.

CRIDER, A., SCHWARTZ, G., and SCHNIDMAN, SUSAN (1969) On the criteria for instrumental autonomic conditioning: A reply to Katkin and Murray. *Psychol. Bull.,* **71,** 455–461.

CROOK, J. H. (1968) The nature and function of territorial aggression. In *Man and Aggression* (Ed. M. F. A. Montagu) 141–178. Oxford: Univer. Press.

DELUDE, L. A. (1969) The vicious circle phenomenon: A result of measurement artifact. *J. comp. physiol. Psychol.,* **69,** 246–252.

DENENBERG, V. H. (1969) Open-field behavior in the rat: what does it mean? *Ann. N.Y. Acad. Sci.,* **159,** 852–859.

DiCARA, L. V. (1970) Learning in the autonomic nervous system. *Scient. Amer.,* **222,** 30–39.

DiCARA, L. V. and MILLER, N. E. (1968) Instrumental learning of vasomotor responses by rats: Learning to respond differentially in the two ears. *Science,* **159,** 1485–1486.

DiCARA, L. V. and MILLER, N. E. (1969) Transfer of instrumentally learned heart-rate changes from curarized to noncurarized state: Implications for a mediational hypothesis. *J. comp. physiol. Psychol.,* **68,** 159–162.

DiCARA, L. V. and WEISS, J. M. (1969) Effect of heart-rate learning under curare on subsequent noncurarized avoidance learning. *J. comp. physiol. Psychol.,* **69,** 368–374.

DINSMOOR, J. A. (1960) Abnormal behavior in animals. In *Principles of Comparative Psychology* (Ed. R. H. Waters, D. A. Rethlingshafer, and W. E. Caldwell) 289–324. London: McGraw-Hill.

DOLLARD, J., MILLER, N. E., DOOB, L. W., MOWRER, O. H., and SEARS, R. R. (1939) *Frustration and Aggression.* New Haven: Yale University Press.

DYKMAN, R. A. and GANTT, W. H. (1960a) A case of experimental neurosis and recovery in relation to the orienting response. *J. Psychol.,* **50,** 105–110.

DYKMAN, R. A. and GANTT, W. H. (1960b) Experimental psychogenic hypertension: Blood pressure changes conditioned to painful stimuli (schizokinesis). *Bull. Johns Hopkins Hosp.,* **107,** 72–89.

EAGLETON, G. and SINES, J. O. (1962) Free gastric acidity and intestinal motility in normal and stomach lesion susceptible rats. *J. psychosom. Res.,* **6,** 37–40.

EASTERBROOK, J. (1963) Ethyl alcohol and the effects of stress. In *Experiments with Drugs. Studies in the Relation Between Personality, Learning Theory and Drug Action* (Ed. H. J. Eysenck) 329–350. Oxford: Pergamon.

ELLEN, P. and FELDMAN, R. S. (1958) Generalization of fixated behavior in the rat. *J. comp. physiol. Psychol.,* **51,** 508–512.

ERIKSSON, K. (1968) Genetic selection for voluntary alcohol consumption in the albino rat. *Science,* **159,** 739–741.

ESSMAN, W. B. (1966) Gastric ulceration in differentially housed mice. *Psychol. Rep.,* **19,** 173–174.

ESTES, W. K. and SKINNER, B. F. (1941) Some quantitative properties of anxiety. *J. exp. Psychol.,* **29,** 390–400.

EYSENCK, H. J. (1960) *Behaviour Therapy and the Neuroses: Reading in Modern Methods of Treatment Derived from Learning Theory.* London: Pergamon.

EYSENCK, H. J. (1963) Emotion as a determinant in integrative learning: an experimental study. *Behav. Res. Ther.,* **1,** 197–211.

EYSENCK, H. J. (1964a) *Crime and Personality.* London: Routledge & Kegan Paul.

EYSENCK, H. J. (1964b) *Experiments in Behaviour Therapy: Readings in Modern Methods of Treatment of Mental Disorders Derived from Learning Theory.* Oxford: Pergamon .

EYSENCK, H. J. (1967a) Single-trial conditioning, neurosis, and the Napalkov phenomenon. *Behav. Res. Ther.,* **5,** 63–65.

EYSENCK, H. J. (1967b) *The Biological Basis of Personality.* Springfield, Ill.: C. C. Thomas.

EYSENCK, H. J. (1968) A theory of the incubation of anxiety/fear response. *Behav. Res. Ther.,* **6,** 309–321.

EYSENCK, H. J. and BROADHURST, P. L. (1964) Experiments with animals: Introduction. In *Experiments in Motivation* (Ed. H. J. Eysenck) 285–291. Oxford: Pergamon .

EYSENCK, H. J. and EYSENCK, SYBIL B. G. (1969) *Personality Structure and Measurement.* London: Routledge & Kegan Paul.

FELDMAN, M. P. (1966) Aversion therapy for sexual deviations: a critical review. *Psychol. Bull.,* **65,** 65–79. (Reprinted in *Review of Research in Behavior Pathology* (Ed. D. S. Homes) 50–93. New York: Wiley, 1968.)

FELDMAN, M. P. and MacCULLOCH, M. J. (1971) *Homosexual Behaviour: Therapy and Assessment.* Oxford: Pergamon.

FELDMAN, R. S. and GREEN, K. F. (1967) Antecedents to behavior fixations. *Psychol. Rev.*, **74**, 250–271.

FERRARO, D. P. and YORK, KATHLEEN M. (1968) Punishment effects in rats selectively bred for emotional elimination. *Psychosom. Sci.*, **10**, 177–178.

FERSTER, C. B. (1966) Animal behavior and mental illness. *Psychol. Rec.*, **16**, 345–356.

FISCHER, GLORIA, VINEY, W., KNIGHT, J., and JOHNSON, N. (1968) Response decrement as a function of effort. *Quart. J. exp. Psychol.*, **20**, 301–304.

FOLTZ, E. L. and MILLETT, FAY E. Jnr. (1964) Experimental psychosomatic disease states in monkeys: I. Peptic ulcer—'executive monkeys'. *J. surg. Res.*, **4**, 445–453.

FOLTZ, E. L., MILLETT, FAY E. Jnr., WEBER, D. E., and ALKSNE, J. F. (1964) Experimental psychosomatic disease states in monkeys. II. Gut hypermotility. *J. surg. Res.*, **4**, 454–464.

FOX, M. W. (1964) A sociosexual behavioral abnormality in the dog resembling Oedipus complex in man. *J. Amer. vet. med. Assoc.*, **144**, 868–869.

FOX, M. W. (1968) *Abnormal Behavior in Animals*. Philadelphia: W. B. Saunders.

FRANCOIS, G. R. and SINES, J. O. (1961) Stress induced stomach lesion as related to destruction of the sympathetic ganglia. *J. psychosom. Res.*, **5**, 191–193.

FRANKS, C. M. (1958) Alcohol, alcoholism and conditioning: A review of the literature and some theoretical considerations. *J. ment. Sci.*, **104**, 14–33.

FUCHS, STEPHANIE S. (1960) Replication report: An attempt to obtain inhibition with reinforcement. *J. exp. Psychol.*, **59**, 343–344.

FULLER, J. L. (1964) Measurement of alcohol preference in genetic experiments. *J. comp. physiol. Psychol.*, **57**, 85–88.

FULLER, J. L. (1967) Experiential deprivation and later behavior. *Science*, **158**, 1645–1652.

GALE, DIANE S., STURMFELS, GLORIA, and GALE, E. N. (1966) A comparison of reciprocal and experimental extinction in the psychotherapeutic process. *Behav. Res. Ther.*, **4**, 149–155.

GALLUP, G. G., Jnr. (1965) Aggression in rats as a function of frustrative nonreward in a straight alley. *Psychonom. Sci.*, **3**, 99–100.

GANTT, W. H. (1940) Effect of alcohol on sexual reflexes in dogs. *Amer. J. Physiol.*, **129**, 360, abstract.

GANTT, W. H. (1944) *Experimental Basis for Neurotic Behavior: Origin and Development of Artificially Produced Disturbances of Behavior in Dogs*. New York: Hoeber. (Also, *Psychosom. Med. Monogr.*, **3**, Nos. 3 and 4.)

GANTT, W. H. (1952) Effect of alcohol on the sexual reflexes of normal and neurotic male dogs. *Psychosom. Med.*, **14**, 174–181.

GANTT, W. H. (1962) Factors involved in the development of pathological Behavior: schizokinesis and autokinesis. *Perspect. Biol. Med.*, **5**, 473–482.

GANTT, W. H. (1964a) Autonomic conditioning. *Ann. N.Y. Acad. Sci.*, **117**, 132–137.

GANTT, W. H. (1964b) Autonomic conditioning. In *The Conditioning Therapies* (Ed. J. Wolpe, A. Salter, and

L. J. Reyna) 115–126. New York: Holt, Rinehart & Winston.

GANTT, W. H., NEWTON, J. E. O., and ROYER, F. L. (1960) Development of the experimental neurosis: Mechanism and factors. *Proc. 3rd. World Congr. Psychiat., Montreal*, 991–995.

GOLDBERG, M. E. and SALAMA, A. I. (1969) Norepinephrine turnover and brain monoamine levels in aggressive mouse-killing rats. *Biochem. Pharmacol.*, **18**, 532–534.

GOLDSTEIN, A. J. (1969) Separate effects of extinction, counter-conditioning and progressive approach in overcoming fear. *Behav. Res. Ther.*, **7**, 47–56.

GRANT, D. A., KROLL, N. E. A., KANTOWITZ, B., ZAJANO, M. J., and SOLBERG, K. B. (1969) Transfer of eyelid conditioning from instrumental to classical reinforcement and vice versa. *J. exp. Psychol.*, **82**, 503–510.

GRANT, E. C. (1965) The contribution of ethology to child psychiatry. In *Modern Perspectives in Child Psychiatry* (Ed. J. G. Howells) 20–37. Edinburgh: Oliver & Boyd.

GRANT, E. C. (1968) An ethological description of non-verbal behaviour during interviews. *Brit. J. med. Psychol.*, **41**, 177–183.

GRAY, J. A. (1964) *Pavlov's Typology: Recent Theoretical and Experimental Developments from the Laboratory of B. M. Teplov*. Oxford: Pergamon.

GRAY, J. A. (1967) Strength of the nervous system, introversion-extraversion, conditionability and arousal. *Behav. Res. Ther.*, **5**, 151–169.

GROVES, MARION H. and DIAMOND, P. T. (1963) Expectancy failure compared to food deprivation in its effect on ulcer development, self-aggression, and external aggression. *Amer. Psychol.*, **18**, 407, abstract.

GUTHRIE, E. R. (1935) *The Psychology of Learning*. New York: Harper.

HAGAMEN, W. D., ZITZMANN, E. K., and REEVES, A. G. (1963) Sexual mounting of diverse objects in a group of randomly selected, unoperated male cats. *J. comp. physiol. Psychol.*, **56**, 298–302.

HARTRY, ARLENE L. (1962) The effects of reserpine on the psychogenic production of gastric ulcers in rats. *J. comp. physiol. Psychol.*, **55**, 719–721.

HEBB, D. O. (1947) Spontaneous neurosis in chimpanzees: Theoretical relations with clinical and experimental phenomena. *Psychosom. Med.*, **9**, 3–16.

HENDERSON, N. D. (1968) Genetic analysis of acquisition and retention of conditioned fear in mice. *J. comp. physiol. Psychol.*, **65**, 325–329.

HERRNSTEIN, R. J. (1969) Method and theory in the study of avoidance. *Psychol. Rev.*, **76**, 49–69.

HOFFMAN, H. S. (1969) Stimulus factors in conditioned suppression. In *Punishment and Aversive Behavior* (Ed. B. A. Campbell and R. M. Church) 185–234. New York: Appleton-Century-Crofts.

HOTHERSALL, D. and BRENER, J. (1969) Operant conditioning of changes in heart rate in curarized rats. *J. comp. physiol. Psychol.*, **68**, 338–342.

HUNT, H. F. (1964) Problems in the interpretation of 'experimental neurosis'. *Psychol. Rep.*, **15**, 27–35.

HUTCHINSON, R. R., AZRIN, N. H., and HAKE, D. F.

(1966) An automatic method for the study of aggression in squirrel monkeys. *J. exp. Anal. Behav.*, **9**, 233–237.

IMADA, H. and SHIKANO, T. (1968) Studies on rigidity and crystallization of behavior: I. Preliminary report on the rigidity of fear-motivated behavior in the rat. *Jap. psychol. Res.*, **10**, 138–145.

IVANOV-SMOLENSKY, A. G. (1954) *Essays on the Patho-physiology of the Higher Nervous Activity: According to I. P. Pavlov and his School.* Moscow: Foreign Language Publishing House.

JENSEN, A. R. (1961) On the reformulation of inhibition in Hull's system. *Psychol. Bull.*, **58**, 274–298.

JINKS, J. L. and FULKER, D. W. (1970) A comparison of the biometrical genetical, MAVA and classical approaches to the analysis of human behavior. *Psychol. Bull.*, **73**, 311–349

JOFFE, J. M. (1964) Avoidance learning and failure to learn in two strains of rats selectively bred for emotion-ality. *Psychonom. Sci.*, **1**, 185–186.

JOFFE, J. M. (1969) *Prenatal Determinants of Behaviour.* Oxford: Pergamon.

JONES, N. G. B. (1967) An ethological study of some aspects of social behaviour of children in nursery school. In *Primate Ethology* (Ed. D. Morris) 347–368. London: Weidenfeld & Nicolson.

KAHLSON, G., LILJA, B., and SVENSSON, S. E. (1964) Physiological protection against gastric ulceration during pregnancy and lactation in the rat. *Lancet*, ii, 1269–1272.

KARLI, P. (1956) The Norway rat's killing response to the white mouse: An experimental analysis. *Behaviour*, **10**, 81–103

KARLI, P. and VERGNES, M. (1964) Dissociation expéri-mentale du comportement d'agression interspécifique rat-souris et du comportement alimentaire. *C.R. Soc. Biol.*, **158**, 650–653.

KATKIN, E. S. and MURRAY, E. N. (1968) Instrumental conditioning of autonomically mediated behavior: Theoretical and methodological issues. *Psychol. Bull.*, **70**, 52–68.

KATKIN, E. S., MURRAY, E. N., and LACHMAN, R. (1969) Concerning instrumental autonomic conditioning: A rejoinder. *Psychol. Bull.*, **71**, 462–466.

KAUFMANN, H. (1965) Definitions and methodology in the study of aggression. *Psychol. Bull.*, **64**, 351–364.

KEEHN, J. D. (1959) More about inhibition of reinforce-ment. *Psychol. Rep.*, **5**, 141–142.

KEEHN, J. D. (1969) 'Voluntary' consumption of alcohol by rats. *Quart. J. Stud. Alcohol*, **30**, 320–329.

KEEHN, J. D. and SABBAGH, U. (1958) Conditioned inhibition and avoidance learning. *Psychol. Rep.*, **4**, 547–552.

KENDRICK, D. C. (1958a) Inhibition with reinforcement (conditioned inhibition). *J. exp. Psychol.*, **56**, 313–318.

KENDRICK, D. C. (1958b) sI_R and drive level: A reply to Keehn and Sabbagh. *Psychol. Rep.*, **4**, 646.

KENDRICK, D. C. (1959a) Inhibition with reinforcement: II. Further reply to Keehn. *Psychol. Rep.*, **5**, 212.

KENDRICK, D. C. (1959b) Inhibition of, or with rein-forcement. *Psychol. Rep.*, **5**, 639–640.

KENDRICK, D. C. (1960) The theory of 'conditioned inhibition' as an explanation of negative practice

effects. In *Behaviour Therapy and the Neuroses: Readings in Modern Methods of Treatment Derived from Learning Theory* (Ed. H. J. Eysenck) 221–235. Oxford: Pergamon.

KIMBLE, G. A. (1961) *Hilgard and Marquis' Conditioning and Learning*, 2nd ed. New York: Appleton-Century-Crofts.

KIMBLE, G. A. and KENDALL, J. W. (1953) A comparison of two methods of producing experimental extinction. *J. exp. Psychol.*, **45**, 87–90.

KIMMEL, H. D. (1967) Instrumental conditioning of autonomically mediated behavior. *Psychol. Bull.*, **67**, 337–345.

KORÁNYI, L. and ENDROCZI, E. (1962) Role of endocrine factors in the development of gastric ulcer in the albino rat. *Acta Med.*, **18**, 357–362.

KORÁNYI, L., ENDROCZI, E., and LISSAK, K. (1965) Avoidance conditioned reflex elimination without somatomotor performance. *Acta Physiol.*, **27**, 149–153.

KRAMER, S. (1968) Fixed motor patterns in ethologic and psychoanalytic theory. In *Science and Psychoanalysis Vol. XII. Animal and Human* (Ed. J. H. Masserman) 124–155. New York: Grune & Stratton.

KRASNER, L. and ULLMANN, L. P. (1965) *Research in Behavior Modification: New Developments and Impli-cations.* New York: Holt, Rinehart & Winston.

KRUSHINSKII, L. V. (1962) *Animal Behavior—Its Normal and Abnormal Development.* New York: Consultants Bureau.

KURTSIN, I. T. (1968) Pavlov's concept of experimental neurosis and abnormal behavior in animals. In *Abnormal Behavior in Animals* (Ed. M. W. Fox) 77–106. Philadelphia: Saunders.

LADER, M. H. and MATHEWS, A. M. (1968) A physiologi-cal model of phobic anxiety and desensitization. *Behav. Res. Ther.*, **6**, 411–421.

LAGERSPETZ, KIRSTI (1961) Genetic and social causes of aggressive behavior in mice. *Scand. J. Psychol.*, **2**, 167–173.

LAGERSPETZ, KIRSTI (1964) Studies on the aggressive behaviour of mice. *Ann. Acad. Sci. Fenn.*, **131**, 1–131.

LAGERSPETZ, KIRSTI and WUORINEN, K. (1965) A cross fostering experiment with mice selectively bred for aggressiveness and non-aggressiveness. *Inst. Psychol., Univ. Turku*, No. 17, 1–6.

LAGERSPETZ, K. Y. H., TIRRI, R., and LAGERSPETZ, KIRSTI M. J. (1968) Neurochemical and endocrino-logical studies of mice selectively bred for aggressive-ness. *Scand. J. Psychol.*, **9**, 157–160.

LAMBERT, R., MARTIN, M. S., VOUILLON, G., and MARTIN, F. (1966) Facteurs constitutionnels et fréquence de l'ulcère de contrainte chez le rat. *C.R. Soc. Biol.*, **160**, 2127.

LÁT, J. and GOLLOVÁ-HÉMON, E. (1969) Permanent effects of nutritional and endocrinological intervention in early ontogeny on the level of nonspecific excit-ability and on lability (emotionality). *Ann. N.Y. Acad. Sci.*, **159**, 710–720.

LAVERY, J. J. and FOLEY, P. J. (1963) Altruism or arousal in the rat? *Science*, **140**, 172–173.

LAWS, D. R. and RUBIN, H. B. (1962) Instructional

control of an autonomic sexual response. *J. appl. Behav. Anal.*, **2**, 93–99.

LEDERHENDLER, I. and BAUM, M. (1970) Mechanical facilitation of the action of response prevention (flooding) in rats. *Behav. Res. Ther.*, **8**, 43–48.

LESTER, D. (1961) Self-maintenance of intoxication. *Quart. J. Stud. Alcohol*, **22**, 223–231.

LIBERSON, W. T. (1967) Withdrawal and fixation reactions in rodents. In *Comparative Psychopathology—Animal and Human* (Ed. J. Zubin and H. F. Hunt) 120–157. New York: Grune & Stratton.

LIDDELL, H. S. (1926) The effect of thyroidectomy in some unconditioned responses of the sheep and goat. *Amer. J. Physiol.*, **75**, 579–590.

LIDDELL, H. S. (1950) The role of vigilance in the development of animal neurosis. In *Anxiety* (Ed. P. Hoch and J. Zubin) 183–196. New York: Grune & Stratton.

LIDDELL, H. S. (1951) The influence of experimental neuroses on the respiratory function. In *Somatic and Psychiatric Treatment of Asthma* (Ed. H. A. Abramson) 126–147. Baltimore: Williams & Wilkins.

LIDDELL, H. S. (1954) Conditioning and emotions. *Scient. American*, **190**, 48–57.

LIDDELL, H. S. (1958) Presidential address: A biological basis for psychopathology. In *Problems of Addiction and Habituation* (Ed. P. H. Hoch and J. Zubin) 94–109. New York: Grune & Stratton.

LIDDELL, H. S. (1964) The challenge of Pavlovian conditioning and experimental neuroses in animals. In *The Conditioning Therapies* (Ed. J. Wolpe, A. Salter, and L. J. Reyna) 127–148. New York: Holt, Rinehart & Winston.

LOMONT, J. (1965) Reciprocal inhibition or extinction? *Behav. Res. Ther.*, **3**, 209–219.

LORENZ, K. (1966) *On Aggression*. London: Methuen.

LOVIBOND, S. H. (1964) Personality and conditioning. In *Progress in Experimental Personality Research* (Ed. B. A. Maher) 115–168. New York: Academic Press.

LOVIBOND, S. H. (1969) Effect of patterns of aversive and appetitive conditioned stimuli on the incidence of gastric lesions in the immobilized rat. *J. comp. physiol. Psychol.*, **69**, 636–639.

LYNCH, J. J. and MCCARTHY, J. F. (1967) The effect of petting on a classically conditioned emotional response. *Behav. Res. Ther.*, **5**, 55–62.

LYNCH, J. J. and MCCARTHY, J. F. (1969) Social responding in dogs: Heart rate changes to a person. *Psychophysiology*, **5**, 389–393.

MAIER, N. R. F. (1949) *Frustration: the Study of Behavior Without a Goal*. New York: McGraw-Hill.

MAIER, S. F., SELIGMAN, M. E. P., and SOLOMON, R. L. (1969) Pavlovian fear conditioning and learned helplessness: Effects on escape and avoidance behavior of (a) the CS-UCS contingency and (b) the independence of the US and voluntary responding. In *Punishment and Aversive Behavior* (Ed. B. A. Campbell and R. M. Church) 299–342. New York: Appleton-Century-Crofts.

MARCUSE, F. L. and MOORE, A. U. (1942) Conditioned reflexes in the pig. *Bull. Canad. psychol. Assoc.*, **2**, 13–14.

MARCUSE, F. L. and MOORE, A. U. (1944) Tantrum behavior in the pig. *J. comp. Psychol.*, **37**, 235–247.

MARTIN, M. S., MARTIN, F., ANDRÉ, C., and LAMBERT, R. (1968) Sélection du rat Wistar en fonction de sa sensibilité à l'ulcère de contrainte. *C.R. Soc. Biol.*, **162**, 2126–2128.

MASSERMAN, J. H. (1964) *Behavior and Neurosis: an Experimental Psychoanalytic Approach to Psychobiologic Principles*. New York: Hafner.

MASSERMAN, J. H., AARONS, L., and WECHKIN, S. (1963) The effect of positive-choice conflicts on normal and neurotic monkeys. *Amer. J. Psychiat.*, **120**, 481–484.

MASSERMAN, J. H. and PECHTEL, C. (1956) Normal and neurotic olfactory behavior in monkeys: a motion picture. *J. nerv. ment. Dis.*, **124**, 518–519.

MASSERMAN, J. H., WECHKIN, S. and TERRIS, W. (1964), 'Altruistic' behavior in rhesus monkeys. *Amer. J. Psychiat.*, **121**, 584–585.

MASSERMAN, J. H. and YUM, K. S. (1946) An analysis of the influence of alcohol on experimental neuroses in cats. *Psychosom. Med.*, **8**, 36–52.

MCCLEARN, G. E. and MEREDITH, W. (1964) Dimensional analysis of activity and elimination in a genetically heterogeneous group of mice (*Mus musculus*). *Anim. Behav.*, **12**, 1–9.

MCCLEARN, G. E. and RODGERS, D. A. (1961) Genetic factors in alcohol preference of laboratory mice. *J. comp. physiol. Psychol.*, **54**, 116–119.

MCFEE, A. S., STONE, N. H., GOODALE, R. L., BERNSTEIN, E. F., and WANGENSTEEN, O. H. (1963) Prevention of stress-induced ulcer in the rat by gastric freezing: A study showing protection afforded rats whose stomachs had been frozen. *J. Amer. med. Assoc.*, **186**, 917–919.

MCGAUGH, J. L., WEINBERGER, N. M., and WHALEN, R. E. (1967) *Psychobiology: The Biological Bases of Behavior. Readings from Scientific American*. London: W. H. Freeman.

MCKINNEY, W. T. Jnr. and BUNNEY, W. E. Jnr. (1969) Animal model of depression. I. Review of evidence: Implications for research. *Arch. gen. Psychiat.*, **21**, 240–248.

MCMICHAEL, R. E. (1966) Early-experience effects as a function of infant treatment and other experimental conditions. *J. comp. physiol. Psychol.*, **62**, 433–436.

MELLO, NANCY K. and MENDELSON, J. H. (1966) Factors affecting alcohol consumption in primates. *Psychosom. Med.*, **28**, 529–550.

MELVIN, K. B., MARTIN, R. C., and PARSONS, G. (1965) Delayed extinction of escape responses: A parametric study. *Psychonom. Sci.*, **2**, 247–248.

MENDELSON, J. H. and MELLO, N. K. (1964) Ethanol and whisky drinking patterns in rats under free-choice and forced-choice conditions. *Quart. J. Stud. Alcohol*, **25**, 1–25.

MICHAEL, R. P. (1961) Hypersexuality in male cats without brain damage. *Science*, **134**, 553–554.

MIKHAIL, A. A. (1969a) Genetic predisposition to stomach ulceration in emotionally reactive strains of rats. *Psychonom. Sci.*, **15**, 245–247.

MIKHAIL, A. A. (1969b) Relationship of conditioned anxiety to stomach ulceration and acidity in rats. *J. comp. physiol. Psychol.*, **68**, 623–626.

MIKHAIL, A. A. and BROADHURST, P. L. (1965) Stomach ulceration and emotionality in selected strains of rats. *J. psychosom. Res.*, **8**, 477–479.

MIKHAIL, A. A. and HOLLAND, H. C. (1966a) A simplified method of inducing stomach ulcers. *J. psychosom. Res.*, **9**, 343–347.

MIKHAIL, A. A. and HOLLAND, H. C. (1966b) Evaluating and photographing experimentally induced stomach ulcers. *J. psychosom. Res.*, **9**, 349–353.

MILLER, N. E. (1964) The analysis of motivational effects illustrated by experiments on amylobarbitone sodium. In *Animal Behaviour and Drug Action* (Ed. Hannah Steinberg, A. V. S. de Reuck, and Julie Knight) 1–18. Ciba Foundation Symposium jointly with Co-ordinating Committee for Symposia on Drug Action. London: Churchill.

MILLER, N. E. (1969a) Learning of visceral and glandular responses. *Science*, 163, 434–445.

MILLER, N. E. (1969b) Psychosomatic effects of specific types of training. *Ann. N.Y. Acad. Sci.*, **159**, 1025–1040.

MILLER, N. E. and BANUAZIZI, A. (1968) Instrumental learning by curarized rats of a specific visceral response, intestinal or cardiac. *J. comp. physiol. Psychol.*, **65**, 1–7.

MILLER, N. E. and WEISS, J. M. (1969) Effects of the somatic or visceral responses to punishment. In *Punishment and Aversive Behavior* (Ed. B. A. Campbell and R. M. Church) 343–372. New York: Appleton-Century-Crofts.

MITCHELL, W. M. (1969) Observations on animal behavior and its relationship to masochism. *Dis. nerv. Syst.*, 30, 124–128.

MOLTZ, H. (1954) Resistance to extinction as a function of variations in stimuli associated with shock. *J. exp. Psychol.*, **47**, 418–424.

MORRISON, B. J. and THATCHER, K. (1969) Overpopulation effects on social reduction of emotionality in the albino rat. *J. comp. physiol. Psychol.*, **69**, 658–662.

MORTON, J. R. C. (1968) Effects of early experience 'handling and gentling' in laboratory animals. In *Abnormal Behavior in Animals* (Ed. M. W. Fox) 261–292. Philadelphia: Saunders.

MOUNTJOY, P. T., EDWIN, A., and ROGERS, C. C. (1960) Response decrement under continuous reinforcement as a function of effort. *J. Sci. Lab. Denison U.*, 45, 124–128.

MOWRER, O. H. (1960a) *Learning Theory and Behavior.* New York: Wiley.

MOWRER, O. H. (1960b) *Learning Theory and the Symbolic Process.* New York: Wiley.

MOWRER, O. H. and ULLMAN, A. D. (1945) Time as a determinant in integrative learning. *Psychol. Rev.*, **52**, 61–90.

MOYER, K. E. (1968) Kinds of aggression and their physiological basis. *Commun. behav. Biol.*, Part A, 65–87. Abstract.

MUGGENBURG, B. A., REESE, N., KOWALCZYK, T., GRUMMER, R. H., and HOEKSTRA, W. G. (1964) Survey of the prevalence of gastric ulcers in swine. *Amer. J. vet. Res.*, **25**, 1673–1678.

MURRAY, E. N. and KATKIN, E. S. (1968) Comment on two recent reports of operant heart rate conditioning. *Psychophysiology*, **5**, 192–195.

MYER, J. S. (1964) Stimulus control of mouse-killing rats. *J. comp. physiol. Psychol.*, **58**, 112–117.

MYER, J. S. (1968) Associative and temporal determinants of facilitation and inhibition of attack by pain. *J. comp. physiol. Psychol.*, **66**, 17–21.

MYERS, R. D. (1966) Voluntary alcohol consumption in animals: Peripheral and intracerebral factors. *Psychosom. Med.*, **28**, 484–497.

MYERS, R. D. and CICERO, T. J. (1969) Effects of serotonin depletion on the volitional alcohol intake of rats during a condition of psychological stress. *Psychopharmacologia*, **15**, 373–381.

NAPALKOV, A. K. (1963) Information process of the brain. In *Progress in Brain Research. Vol. 2. Nerve, Brain and Memory Models* (Ed. N. Weiner and J. P. Schadé) 59–69. Amsterdam: Elsevier.

NELSON, F. (1966) Effects of two counterconditioning procedures on the extinction of fear. *J. comp. physiol. Psychol.*, **62**, 208–213.

NELSON, F. (1967) Effects of chlorpromazine on fear extinction. *J. comp. physiol. Psychol.*, **64**, 496–498.

NELSON, F. (1969) Free versus forced exposure with two procedures for conditioning and measuring fear in the rat. *J. comp. physiol. Psychol.*, **69**, 682–687.

NEWTON, G. and LEVINE, S. (1968) *Early Experience and Behavior: The Psychobiology of Development.* Springfield, Ill.: C. C. Thomas.

NEWTON, J. E. O. and GANTT, W. H. (1968) The history of a catatonic dog. *Condit. Reflex*, 3, 45–61.

O'KELLY, L. I. and STECKLE, L. C. (1939) A note on long enduring emotional responses in the rat. *J. Psychol.*, **8**, 125–131.

ORWIN, W. (1969) Escape and avoidance learning in extremely neurotic and extremely stable subjects. *Brit. J. soc. clin. Psychol.*, **8**, 362–374.

PAGE, H. A. (1955) The facilitation of experimental excitation by response prevention as a function of the acquisition of a new response. *J. comp. physiol. Psychol.*, **48**, 14–16.

PARÉ, W. (1962) The effect of conflict and shock stress on stomach ulceration in the rat. *J. psychosom. Res.*, **6**, 223–225.

PARÉ, W. P. (1964) The effect of chronic environmental stress on stomach ulceration, adrenal function, and consummatory behavior in the rat. *J. Psychol.*, **57**, 143–151.

PARÉ, W. P. (1966) Subject emotionality and susceptibility to environmental stress. *J. genet. Psychol.*, **108**, 303–310.

PARMENTER, R. (1940) Avoidance of nervous strain in experimental extinction of the conditioned motor reflex. *J. gen. Psychol.*, **23**, 55–63.

PAVLOV, I. P. (1927) *Conditioned Reflexes: an Investigation of the Physiological Activity of the Cerebral Cortex.* London: Oxford Univ. Press.

PAVLOV, I. P. (1941) *Lectures on Conditioned Reflexes: Vol. II. Conditioned Reflexes and Psychiatry.* London: Lawrence & Wishart.

PAVLOV, I. P. (1961) *Psychopathology and Psychiatry: Selected Works.* Moscow: Foreign Languages Publishing House.

PEREZ-CRUET, J. and GANTT, W. H. (1964) Conditioned

reflex electrocardiogram of bulbocapnine conditioning of the T wave. *Amer. Heart J.*, **67**, 61–72.

PERRY, T. W., JIMENEZ, A. A., SHIVELY, J. E., CURTIN, T. M., PICKETT, R. A., and BEESON, W. M. (1963) Incidence of gastric ulcers in swine. *Science*, **139**, 349–350.

PETROVA, M. K. (1924) Different kinds of internal inhibition under a particularly difficult situation. *Coll. Papers, Physiol. Lab. I. P. Pavlov*, **1**, 61–70.

PETROVA, M. K. (1926) Pathological deviations of the inhibitory and excitatory process in a case of their clashing. *Coll. Papers, Physiol. Lab. I. P. Pavlov*, **1**, 199–211.

PFEIFFER, C. J., GASS, G. H., and SCHWARTZ, C. S. (1963) Reduction by chlorpromazine of ulcers due to acute starvation in mice. *Nature, Lond.*, **197**, 1014–1015.

POLIN, A. T. (1959) The effects of flooding and physical suppression as extinction techniques on an anxiety motivated avoidance locomotor response. *J. Psychol.*, **47**, 235–245.

POLISH, E., BRADY, J. V., MASON, J. W., THACH, J. S., and NIEMECK, W. (1962) Gastric contents and the occurrence of duodenal lesions in the rhesus monkey during avoidance behavior. *Gastroenterology*, **43**, 193–201.

PORTER, R. W., BRADY, J. V., CONRAD, D., MASON, J. W., GALAMBOS, R., and RIOCH, D. McK. (1958) Some experimental observations on gastrointestinal lesions in behaviorally conditioned monkeys. *Psychosom. Med.*, **20**, 379–394.

PROKASY, W. F. (1960) Postasymptotic performance decrements during massed reinforcements. *Psychol. Bull.*, **57**, 237–247.

QUINN, J. T., HARBISON, J. J. M., and McALLISTER, H. (1970) An attempt to shape penile responses. *Behav. res. Ther.*, **8**, 213–216.

QUINN, J. T. and PATTEN, J. W. (1967) An attempt to use free operant techniques in the analysis and treatment of a case of transvestism complicated by masochism, *Bull. Brit. psychol. Soc.*, **20**, 25A. Abstract.

RACHMAN, S. (1967) Systematic desensitization. *Psychol. Bull.*, **67**, 93–103.

RACHMAN, S. (1969) Treatment by prolonged exposure to high intensity stimulation. *Behav. Res. Ther.*, **7**, 295–302.

RACHMAN, S. and TEASDALE, J. (1969) *Aversion Therapy and Behaviour Disorders: An Analysis*. London: Routledge & Kegan Paul.

RAMSAY, R. W. and DIS, H. VAN (1967) The role of punishment in the aetiology and continuance of alcohol drinking in rats. *Behav. Res. Ther.*, **5**, 229–235.

RATCLIFFE, H. L., LUGINBÜHL, H., SCHNARR, W. R., and CHACKO, K. (1969) Coronary arteriosclerosis in swine: Evidence of a relation to behavior. *J. comp. physiol. Psychol.*, **68**, 385–392.

RESCORLA, R. A. and SOLOMON, R. L. (1967) Two-process learning theory: Relationships between Pavlovian conditioning and instrumental learning. *Psychol. Rev.*, **74**, 151–182.

RICE, G. E. Jnr. (1964) Aiding behavior *vs.* fear in the albino rat. *Psychol. Rec.*, **14**, 165–170.

RICE, G. E. and GAINER, PRISCILLA (1962) 'Altruism' in the albino rat. *J. comp. physiol. Psychol.*, **55**, 123–125.

RICE, H. K. (1963) The responding-rest ratio in the production of gastric ulcers in the rat. *Psychol. Rec.*, **13**, 11–14.

RICHELLE, M. (1965) Névroses expérimentales dans des conditionnements à renforcement positif. *Psychol. Belg.*, **5**, 40–50.

ROBINSON, R. (1965) *Genetics of the Norway Rat*. Oxford: Pergamon.

RODGERS, D. A. (1967) Alcohol preference in mice. In *Comparative Psychopathology—Animal and Human* (Ed. J. Zubin and H. F. Hunt) 184–201. New York: Grune & Stratton.

RODGERS, D. A. and McCLEARN, G. E. (1962) Alcohol preference of mice. In *Roots of Behavior* (Ed. E. L. Bliss) 68–95. New York: Harper.

ROSENBERG, A. (1967) Production of gastric lesions in rats by combined cold and electrostress. *Amer. J. digest. Dis.*, **12**, 1140–1148.

ROSENZWEIG, M. R. (1964) Effects of heredity and environment on brain chemistry, brain anatomy, and learning ability in the rat. In *Physiological Determinants of Behavior: Implications for Mental Retardation*, 3–40, University of Kansas Symposium, 14.

ROYCE, J. R. (1950) The factorial analysis of animal behavior. *Psychol. Bull.*, **47**, 235–259.

ROYCE, J. R. (1966) Concepts generated in comparative and physiological psychological observations. In *Handbook of Multivariate Experimental Psychology* (Ed. R. B. Cattell) 642–683. Chicago: Rand McNally.

SANGER, V. L. and HAMDY, A. H. (1962) A strange fright-flight behavior pattern (hysteria) in hens. *J. Amer. vet. med. Assoc.*, **140**, 455–459.

SANYAL, A. K., BANERJI, C. R., and DAS, P. K. (1963) Banana and restraint ulcers in albino rats. *J. Pharm. Pharmac.*, **15**, 775–776.

SAWREY, J. M. and SAWREY, W. L. (1964) Ulcer production with reserpine and conflict. *J. comp. physiol. Psycnol.*, **57**, 307–309.

SAWREY, J. M. and SAWREY, W. L. (1966) Age, weight and social effects on ulceration rate in rats. *J. comp. physiol. Psychol.*, **61**, 464–466.

SAWREY, W. L. (1961) Conditioned responses of fear in relationship to ulceration. *J. comp. physiol. Psychol.*, **54**, 347-348.

SAWREY, W. L. and LONG, D. H. (1962) Strain and sex differences in ulceration in the rat. *J. comp. physiol. Psychol.*, **55**, 603-605.

SAWREY, W. L. and SAWREY, J. M. (1963) Fear conditioning and resistance to ulceration. *J. comp. physiol. Psychol.*, **56**, 821–823.

SAWREY, W. L. and SAWREY, J. M. (1964) Conditioned fear and restraint in ulceration. *J. comp. physiol. Psychol.*, **57**, 150–151.

SAWREY, W. L. and SAWREY, J. M. (1968) UCS effects on ulceration following fear conditioning. *Psychonom. Sci.*, **10**, 85–86.

SCHELL, R. E. and ELLIOT, R. (1967) Note on sex differences in response to stress in rats. *Psychol. Rep.*, **20**, 1201–1202.

SCHMIDT, K. M. (1966) The use of colored photographic

prints *vs.* the use of tissue specimens in evaluating severity of stomach ulceration. *J. psychosom. Res.*, **10**, 215–219.

SCHMIDT, K. M. and KLOPFER, F. D. (1965) The use of colored photographic slides in evaluating severity of stomach ulceration. *J. psychosom. Res.*, **8**, 379–384.

SCHMIDT, K. M. and KLOPFER, F. D. (1968) Ethanol and stomach ulcers: Absence of influence in the albino rat. *Quart. J. Stud. Alcohol*, **29**, 558–565.

SCHMIDT, K. M. and PECKHAM, J. C. (1968) The severity of stomach ulceration in the rat assessed by counting the number of ulcers. *J. psychosom. Res.*, **11**, 357–361.

SCOTT, J. P. (1966) Agonistic behavior of mice and rats: A review. *Amer. Zool.*, **6**, 683–701.

SELIGMAN, M. E. P. (1968) Chronic fear produced by unpredictable electric shock. *J. comp. physiol. Psychol.*, **66**, 402–411.

SERMAT, V. and SHEPHARD, A. H. (1959) The effect of a feeding procedure on persistent avoidance responses in rats. *J. comp. physiol. Psychol.*, **52**, 206–211.

SEWARD, J. P. (1969) The role of conflict in experimental neurosis. In *Punishment and Aversive Behavior* (Ed. B. A. Campbell and R. M. Church) 421–447. New York: Appleton-Century-Crofts.

SHENGER-KRESTOVNIKOVA, N. R. (1921) Contributions to the question of differentiation of visual stimuli and the limits of differentiation by the visual analyser of the dog. *Bull. Inst. sci. Leshaft*, **3**, 1–43.

SHERMAN, A. R. (1967) Therapy of a maladaptive fear-motivated behavior in the rat by the systematic gradual withdrawal of a fear-reducing drug. *Behav. Res. Ther.*, **5**, 121–129.

SIDMAN, M. (1960) Normal sources of pathological behavior. *Science*, **132**, 61–68.

SIMLER, M., SCHWARTZ, J., and SCHMID, F. (1962) Effets du chlorhydrate de morphine sur la prévention de l'ulcère de contrainte chez le rat. *C.R. Soc. Biol.*, **156**, 8–9.

SINES, J. O. (1959) Selective breeding for development of stomach lesions following stress in the rat. *J. comp. physiol. Psychol.*, **52**, 615–617.

SINES, J. O. (1960) Experimental production and control of stomach lesions in the rat. *J. psychosom. Res.*, **4**, 297–300.

SINES, J. O. (1961) Behavioral correlates of genetically enhanced stomach lesion development. *J. psychosom. Res.*, **5**, 120–126.

SINES, J. O. (1962) Strain differences in activity, emotionality, body weight and susceptibility to stress induced stomach lesions. *J. genet. Psychol.*, **101**, 209–216.

SINES, J. O. (1963) Physiological and behavioral characteristics of rats selectively bred for susceptibility to stomach lesion development. *J. Neuropsychiat.*, **4**, 396–398.

SINES, J. O. (1966) Elevated activation level as a primary characteristic of the restraint stress-ulcer-susceptible rat. *Psychosom. Med.*, **28**, 64–69.

SINES, J. O., CLEELAND, C., and ADKINS, J. (1963) The behavior of normal and stomach lesion susceptible rats in several learning situations. *J. genet. Psychol.*, **102**, 91–94.

SINES, J. O. and EAGLETON, G. (1961) Dominant behavior and weight loss following water deprivation in normal rats and rats susceptible to stomach lesions. *Psychol. Rep.*, **9**, 3–6.

SINES, J. O. and MCDONALD, D. G. (1968) Heritability of stress-ulcer susceptibility in rats. *Psychosom. Med.*, **30**, 390–394.

SINHA, S. N., FRANKS, C. M., and BROADHURST, P. L. (1958) The effect of a stimulant and a depressant drug on a measure of reactive inhibition. *J. exp. Psychol.*, **56**, 349–354.

SMART, R. G. (1965a) Conflict and conditioned aversive stimuli in the development of experimental neuroses. *Canad. J. Psychol.*, **19**, 208–223.

SMART, R. G. (1965b) Effects of alcohol on conflict and avoidance behavior. *Quart. J. Stud. Alcohol*, **26**, 187–205.

SOLOMON, R. L., TURNER, H., and LESSAC, M. S. (1968). Some effects of delay of punishment on resistance to temptation in dogs. *J. Pers. soc. Psychol.*, **8**, 233–238.

SOLOMON, R. L. and WYNNE, L. C. (1953) Traumatic avoidance learning acquisition in normal dogs. *Psychol. Monogr.*, **67**, No. 4.

SOLOMON, R. L. and WYNNE, L. C. (1954) Traumatic avoidance learning: The principles of anxiety conservation and partial irreversibility. *Psychol. Rev.*, **61**, 353–385.

STAMPFL, T. G. and LEVIS, D. J. (1967) Essentials of implosive therapy: A learning-theory-based psychodynamic behavioral therapy. *J. abnorm. Psychol.*, **72**, 496–503.

STAMPFL, T. G. and LEVIS, D. J. (1968) Implosive therapy—a behavioral therapy? *Behav. Res. Ther.*, **6**, 31–36.

STERN, J. A., WINOKUR, G., EISENSTEIN, A., TAYLOR, R., and SLY, M. (1960) The effect of group *vs.* individual housing on behavior and physiological responses to stress in the albino rat. *J. psychosom. Res.*, **4**, 185–190.

TAKAGI, K., KASUYA, Y., and WATANABE, K. (1964) Studies on the drugs for peptic ulcer: A reliable method for producing stress ulcer in rats. *Chem. pharmaceut. Bull.*, **12**, 465–472.

THIESSEN, D. D. (1964) Population density and behavior: A review of theoretical and physiological contributions. *Texas Rep. Biol. Med.*, **22**, 266–314.

THIESSEN, D. D. (1966) Role of physical injury in the physiological effects of population density in mice. *J. comp. physiol. Psychol.*, **62**, 322–324.

THIESSEN, D. D. and RODGERS, D. A. (1961) Population density and endocrine function. *Psychol. Bull.*, **58**, 441–451.

TROWILL, J. A. (1967) Instrumental conditioning of the heart rate in the curarized rat. *J. comp. physiol. Psychol.*, **63**, 7–11.

ULRICH, R. (1966) Pain as a cause of aggression. *Amer. Zool.*, **6**, 643–662.

ULRICH, R., WOLFE, M., and DULANEY, SYLVIA (1969) Punishment of shock-induced aggression. *J. exp. Anal. Behav.*, **12**, 1009–1015.

VERNON, W. M. (1969) Animal aggression: Review of research. *Genet. Psychol. Monogr.* **80**, 3–28.

WALLGREN, H. and BARRY, H. III. (1970) *Actions of Alcohol. Vol. I. Biochemical, Physiological and Psychological Aspects. Vol. II. Chronic and Clinical Aspects.* Amsterdam: Elsevier.

WALLGREN, H. and TIRRI, R. (1963) Studies on the mechanism of stress-induced reduction of alcohol intoxication in rats. *Acta pharmacol. Toxicol.*, **20**, 27–38.

WASSERMAN, E. A. and JENSEN, D. D. (1969) Olfactory stimuli and the 'pseudo-extinction' effect. *Science*, **166**, 1307–1308.

WATSON, J. B. and RAYNER, ROSALIE (1920) Conditioned emotional reactions. *J. exp. Psychol.*, **3**, 1–14. (Reprinted in *Behaviour Therapy and the Neuroses* (Ed. H. J. Eysenck) 28–37. Oxford: Pergamon, 1960.)

WECHKIN, S., MASSERMAN, J. H., and TERRIS, W. Jnr. (1964) Shock to a conspecific as an aversive stimulus. *Psychonom. Sci.*, **1**, 47–48.

WEINBERGER, N. M. (1965) Effect of detainment on extinction of avoidance responses. *J. comp. physiol. Psychol.*, **60**, 135–138.

WEISS, J. M. (1968) Effects of coping responses on stress. *J. comp. physiol. Psychol.*, **65**, 251–259.

WELDON, E. (1967) An analogue of extraversion as a determinant of individual differences in behaviour in the rat. *Brit. J. Psychol.*, **58**, 253–259.

WELDON, E. (1968) Stimulus or stimulation: Relevant cues in a learning situation involving differences in light reinforcement. *Psychonom. Sci.*, **10**, 239–240.

WHIMBEY, A. E. and DENENBERG, V. H. (1967) Two independent behavioral dimensions in open-field performance. *J. comp. physiol. Psychol.*, **63**, 500–504.

WILCOCK, J. (1968) Strain differences in response to shock in rats selectively bred for emotional elimination. *Anim. Behav.*, **16**, 294–297.

WILCOCK, J. and BROADHURST, P. L. (1967) Strain differences in emotionality: Open-field and conditioned avoidance behavior in the rat. *J. comp. physiol. Psychol.*, **63**, 335–338.

WILLIAMS, R. J. (1956) *Biochemical Individuality: The Basis for the Genetotrophic Concept.* New York: Wiley.

WILLMUTH, R. and PETERS, J. E. (1964) Recovery from traumatic experience in rats: Specific "treatment" *vs.* passage of time. *Behav. Res. Ther.*, **2**, 111–116.

WILSON, G. T. and DAVISON, G. C. (1971) Processes of fear-reduction in systematic desensitisation: Animal studies. *Psychol. Bull.*, **76**, 1–14.

WILSON, R. S. (1963) On behavior pathology. *Psychol. Bull.*, **60**, 130–146.

WINOKUR, G., STERN, J., and TAYLOR, R. (1959) Early handling and group housing: Effect on development and response to stress in the rat. *J. psychosom. Res.*, **4**, 1–4.

WOLPE, J. (1952) Experimental neuroses as learned behaviour. *Brit. J. Psychol.*, **43**, 243–268.

WOLPE, J. (1958) *Psychotherapy by Reciprocal Inhibition.* Stanford: Stanford Univ. Press.

WOOLPY, J. H. (1968) Socialization of wolves. In *Science and Psychoanalysis Vol. XII. Animal and Human* (Ed. J. H. Masserman) 82–94. New York: Grune & Stratton.

YATES, A. J. (1960) The application of learning theory to the treatment of tics. *J. abnorm. soc. Psychol.*, **56**, 175–182. (Reprinted in *Behaviour Therapy and the Neuroses* (Ed. H. J. Eysenck) 236–249. Oxford: Pergamon, 1960.)

YATES, A. J. (1962) *Frustration and Conflict.* London: Methuen.

YEROFEEVA, M. N. (1912) Electrical stimulation of the skin of the dog as a conditioned salivary stimulus, Thesis, St. Petersburg. (Reprinted Moscow: Akad. Med. Nauk., S.S.S.R., 1953.)

YEROFEEVA, M. N. (1916) Contribution à l'étude des réflexes conditionnels destructifs, *C.R. Soc. Biol.*, **79**, 239–240.

ZAMMIT-MONTEBELLO, A., BLACK, M., MARQUIS, H. A., and SUBOSKI, M. D. (1969) Incubation of passive avoidance in rats: shock intensity and pretraining. *J. comp. physiol. Psychol.*, **69**, 579–582.

21

Psychopharmacology*

WALTER B. ESSMAN

INTRODUCTION

In the years since publication of the first edition of the *Handbook of Abnormal Psychology* there has been a dramatic increase in the number of studies that have appeared dealing with the effects of drugs on behaviour. The field of psycho-pharmacology has emerged and grown within this period of time into an area that has seen the behavioural effects of drugs considered by psychologists, physiologists, pharmacologists, and biochemists from many differing theoretical and methodological approaches. It would be presumptuous to attempt a comprehensive summary of all of the pharmacological agents that have a behavioural effect in one form or another, or to deal with all those behavioural variables that are in some way altered by the effects of one or more pharmacological agents. What this chapter sets out to do is to provide a general overview of psycho-pharmacology in relation to the relevant classes of drugs that affect behaviour. These effects as dealt with here are not so much concerned with evaluating the therapeutic merits of any given drug or its clinical value in relation to other drugs, but are viewed within a context of the way drug effects on behaviour may be interrelated and involve complex systems within which they interact behaviourally as well as neurobiologically. The largest body of published research dealing with drugs and behaviour is in the animal literature rather than in the human literature; this is perhaps more a matter of convenience and accessibility, nevertheless it has created a gap between species that is often extremely difficult to bridge. The specific behavioural effect of an agent that may be considered psychoactive in some respects may not necessarily serve as a predicted index of its therapeutic potency in man, or

necessarily allow one to extrapolate dosage and time course data that would be applicable to man. A number of problems deserve attention in this chapter, most of which are, generally, concerned with the relevance and implications, or perhaps the generality, of the findings, and what specifically may be derived from experimental results that deal with drug effects on behaviour. One issue that will become immediately apparent is the obvious discrepancy between acute studies and those involving the chronic administration of drugs. In those rare instances where experiments have compared the behavioural effect of acute with those of chronic drug administration, the obvious conclusion emerges that the effects are vastly different and cannot be compared in terms of predicting the effect of one from the results of the other. This is perhaps a very relevant consideration in evaluating the meaningfulness of a vast majority of studies relating to acute drug administration that dominate the experimental literature.

Another consideration worthy of attention is the interaction between the behavioural effect of drugs and other systems affected over parallel time courses by that same agent. In this regard, studies of concurrent behavioural and physiological effects, behavioural and biochemical effects, behavioural and endocrine effects, etc., have not been clearly established in the literature. For example, in considering the behavioural effect of a presumed psychoactive agent, it would be extremely useful to have some information as to the amount of that compound, or, perhaps, its metabolites that are acting on the central nervous system, where they are, in fact, acting, and what the general nature of

* The literature surveyed in this chapter has covered material published up to September 1969.

their action is. To concern oneself with the behavioural effect of a drug that is still in the process of being metabolised in the liver before, in fact, it is capable of acting on the central nervous system, or prior to the point where concentrations approximating those required for central activity are reached, one would wonder just what relevance such consideration might actually have, both in terms of any emerging results or their generality. Unfortunately, considerations such as the aforementioned, do not occur too frequently but, nevertheless, do occur.

The separation of behavioural variables in psychopharmacology constitutes an extremely important aspect necessary to interpret the results that emerge. The ability, for example, to separate motivational effects from performance effects and from cognitive effects is sometimes, unfortunately, overlooked by a number of investigators. The use, for example, of a drug that affects appetite would seriously jeopardise the interpretation of results emerging from a learning task that was dependent on food reinforcement; similarly, agents that affect water balance could considerably alter the motivational properties of liquid reinforcement in an animal in which thirst was defined by the duration of water deprivation. Problems such as these, often created by information gaps regarding multisystem effects of psychoactive drugs, can raise serious questions as to the validity and meaning of behavioural findings.

Some attention has occasionally been given to the use of drugs in 'model' behavioural situations; i.e. where a given behavioural condition has been utilised as a 'model' for a behavioural situation or even a behaviour disorder. Common among such presumed 'models' are the animal prototypes of 'experimental neurosis', 'experimental anxiety', 'experimental depression', etc. The utility of such behavioural models for perhaps less well-defined behavioural studies is an issue of some controversy and it would perhaps be unwise to consider that specific effects of a pharmacological agent on an animal prototype can indeed serve as a model from which such results can be applied to the behavioural condition for which that model has been constructed.

The definition of the limits of psychopharmacology is at present difficult to set forth; concern with mechanisms underlying drug action that either parallel or are coincident with mechanisms underlying specific behaviours is drawing more and more on theory and methodology deriving from such areas as cell biology, immunochemistry, and electron microscopy. Significant advances in these areas have opened the door for the psychopharmacologist and have invited entry with the exciting promise of closing the gap between behavioural effects and specific mechanisms of actions of drugs. It is not our purpose in this chapter to explore what lies beyond all of these opened doors but, rather, to present an overview of some of the more relevant or representative psychoactive agents and the extent to which interdisciplinary approaches to their relationship with behaviour may lead us towards understanding their significance in a rapidly growing field of investigation.

The subject matter covered in this chapter has been dealt with in terms of a broad general classification of psychopharmacological agents, partly based on their general clinical or therapeutic application, and partly on their general mode of behavioural action. In the terminology used in describing these classes of psychoactive agents it will become apparent that there is a considerable degree of overlap and the choice of terms is more a matter of organisational convenience than of definition. The following is an outline of the geneol-sequence adopted, and the representative psychra active agent or agents which, perhaps, may be considered as best representing each of the classes outlined:

I. Anti-Psychotic and Anti-Anxiety Agents
    A. The Phenothiazine Derivatives
        Effects on Neurophysiological Activity
        1. Spinal Cord
        2. Brain Stem
        3. Hypothalamus
        4. Thalamus
        Behavioural Effects
        1. Behavioural Effects in Animals
            (a) Locomotor Activity
            (b) Learning
            (c) Emotionality, Aggression, and Fighting
        2. Behavioural Effects in Man
            (a) Experimental Studies
            (b) Clinical Studies
    B. Rauwolfia Alkaloids
        Effects on Neurological Activity
        Metabolic Effects
        1. Behavioural Effects in Animals

II. Mood Stabilising Agents
    A. Direct Stimulants
    B. Indirect Stimulants
    C. Miscellaneous Indirect Stimulants

III. Central Nervous System Stimulants

IV. Hypnotics, Sedatives, and Anaesthetics
    A. Barbiturates
    B. Sedatives
    C. General Anaesthetics

V. Psychomimetic Agents

I. ANTIPSYCHOTIC AND ANTI-ANXIETY AGENTS

A. The Phenothiazine Derivatives

The phenothiazines, as psychoactive agents, are probably best characterised by chlorpromazine, which was the first of this class of compounds to be applied in a psychiatric setting. Historically, the phenothiazines, as therapeutic agents, derive from methylene blue, which was utilised as an antimalarial agent by Ehrlich in 1891 and had received occasional, but only minor attention, in 1899 for its sedative effects. It would be unfair to attribute such casual clinical observation to any central effect of this compound, in as much as even small doses can lead to cardiovascular changes and thermolytic effects, while mental confusion in experimental animals and man can result from higher doses. Chlorpromazine was synthesised by Carpentier in 1950, as a result of searching for phenothiazine derivatives which had both anaesthetic potentiating activity as well as central effects. The 'tranquiliser-like' effect of this compound was observed when it was used by Laborit and co-workers; Laborit recognised the unique capacity of chlorpromazine to abolish anxiety and excitement in surgical patients. Through subsequently favourable reports of the clinical psychiatric efficacy of this compound (Delay *et al.*, 1952; Lehmann and Hanrahan, 1954) it gradually became accepted for treating a wide spectrum of behaviour pathologies, ranging from mild anxiety and psychomotor excitation to psychotic disorders of varied aetiology.

Chlorpromazine, in animals, results in decreased cardiac output and a fall in blood pressure, probably related to one of this compound's characteristic effects—adrenergic blocking action. By virtue of its autonomic action, chlorpromazine can lead to inhibition of gastro-intestinal motility. Several of these extrabehavioural effects may become relevant in evaluating the presumed, more direct, behavioural effects of this drug.

The phenothiazine derivatives, as a class of compounds with which central depressant action can be associated, has often found the referent 'tranquiliser' used descriptively; the 'tranquilisation' that attends initial doses of 50 to 100 mg in man, or the sedative effect characterised as the 'neuroleptic syndrome' by Delay (Delay and Deniker, 1952) hardly seems applicable to the nature of the improvement shown by psychiatric patients who benefit from chlorpromazine treatment, specifically, or phenothiazine therapy, more generally. When behavioural changes resulting from twelve weeks of phenothiazine treatment were assessed with the use of the Multi-dimensional Scale for Rating Psychiatric Patients (MSRPP), those variables sensitive to improvement were: (1) restlessness, (2) belligerance, (3) thinking disturbance, (4) perceptual disturbance, (5) mannerisms, and (6) paranoid projection (Casey *et al.*, 1960). It is apparent that the term 'tranquiliser' does not adequately describe the behavioural effect of these compounds when the therapeutic effect is considered.

Chlorpromazine was the earliest phenothiazine to be used experimentally and clinically, and has probably been studied more extensively than any of the other compounds in this class. It is probably one of the most extensively used clinical drugs, and for this reason it will be treated here as a model of the phenothiazines, to the extent that specific distinctions between chlorpromazine and other phenothiazines, where relevant, will be considered and, in addition, any directly relevant considerations for other derivatives.

EFFECTS ON NEUROPHYSIOLOGICAL ACTIVITY

The electroencephalogram in man shows a reduced amplitude and slowing of alpha activity, suggestive of normal drowsiness, following intravenous administration of small doses of chlorpromazine (Dobkin *et al.*, 1954; Szatmari, 1956; Terzian, 1952). In man, this effect has been observed subcortically as well (Monroe *et al.*, 1955). A basis for attributing a subcortical site of action to chlorpromazine derives from the slowing of alpha activity recorded from basal leads prior to its appearing in scalp-lead records (Voronin *et al.*, 1961). The effects of chlorpromazine on the EEG of man are very pronounced in the presence of brain damage (Swain and Litteral, 1960) and epilepsy (Bente and Itil, 1954); in the former there are abnormal EEG discharges, and in the latter there is an augmentation, by the drug, of spike and wave complexes and paroxysmal activity which has led to the suggestion that chlorpromazine may be of value in providing signs for diagnosing epilepsy (Turner *et al.*, 1956).

A vast amount of literature exists concerning the effects of chlorpromazine and its related derivatives on the electrical activity of the brain in animals. The mechanism of central action suggested by such studies is that the transmission of impulses that cause an arousing action on the cerebral cortex (sensory input to the posterior hypothalamus and reticular formation) is blocked by the suppressive action of chlorpromazine (Killam *et al.*, 1957), presumably via its antagonism to the activating properties of norepinephrine (Hiebel *et al.*, 1954). A summary of existing evidence suggests that the drug acts primarily on the bulbar reticular system, blocking the excitant effect of norepinephrine, and affecting, thereby, synaptic transmission in more diffuse areas and in more diverse ways in the brain. In other areas of the central nervous system the effects of chlorpromazine may be briefly summarised.

1. *Spinal Cord.* At this level there is some disagreement as to whether or not effects occur, and this seems to be dependent on whether or not the brain-stem reticular centres influence motor responses. In cats, monosynaptic spinal reflexes are selectively attenuated and polysynaptic reflexes are mildly affected (Dasgupta and Werner, 1955); these effects are not apparent in spinal cats (Preston, 1956).

2. *Brain Stem.* General effects of chlorpromazine at this level serve ultimately to depress function. A diminished frequency of response of reticular formation neurons during the recovery cycle from sciatic nerve stimulation, particularly for the slow component of this cycle, was produced by chlorpromazine (DeMaar *et al.*, 1958), which possibly suggests that the sedative effects of the drug may reside in the attenuated frequency response. Another view suggests that reticular input and conduction are increased by chlorpromazine, reticular filtering mechanisms thus being activated and information input reduced (Killam and Killam, 1959). There are several other views of the action of chlorpromazine on the reticular formation but they need not be detailed here; they range from dose-dependent depression-stimulation interpretations to a focus of action outside of the reticular system as bases for explaining the action of the drug.

3. *Hypothalamus.* The most suggestive effect implicating the hypothalamus in the sphere of phenothiazine effects is the thermolytic property possessed by these compounds. These thermoregulatory mechanisms, mediated by the hypothalamus when influenced by chlorpromazine, can lead to a partially poikilothermic state; thereby, body temperature can be profoundly influenced by ambient temperature which, unless isothermal with the organism, can lead to thermal change. Such changes can, under appropriate circumstances, alter the threshold response to the same drug, affect effective dosage of other compounds, alter electrical responses independent of drug effect, and directly influence behaviour.

4. *Thalamus.* The amplitude of the recruiting response (temporally-dependent amplitude increment recorded from cerebral cortex with low frequency stimulation of the diffuse thalamic projection system) is affected by chlorpromazine, depending on dosage and the waking status of the animal (Killam and Killam, 1956).

METABOLIC EFFECTS

The effects of chlorpromazine on brain biogenic amines are somewhat confused. Some investigators have reported no effect (Ehringer *et al.*, 1960; Pletscher and Gey, 1960), whereas, slight elevations in both serotonin and norepinephrine have been reported by others (Bartlet, 1960; Costa *et al.*, 1960). It is clear, though, that an elevation in brain serotonin produced by iproniazid (MAO inhibition) can be blocked by chlorpromazine (Ehringer *et al.*, 1960; Pletscher and Gey, 1960; Bartlet, 1960). In general, the effects of chlorpromazine on biogenic amines in brain are: (1) inhibition of serotonin and norepinephrine increments following treatment with either MAO inhibitors or amino acid precursors; (2) inhibition of the reserpine-induced monoamine decrease; and (3) an increase in the proportion of serotonin association with the 'free' brain tissue fraction. These effects may possibly support the view (Gey and Pletscher, 1961) that the passage of monoamines to and from their brain storage depots can be inhibited by chlorpromazine by either a decrease in the permeability of an intracellular membrane or of storage organelles.

Other metabolic effects observed experimentally with chlorpromazine include: (1) inhibition of both cerebral tissue respiration and the increase in such tissue respiration induced by electrical or electrolyte stimulation (Lindan *et al.*, 1957); (2) uncoupling of oxidative phosphorylation (Abood, 1955); (3) decreasing the synthesis of some brain phospholipids and stimulating synthesis of certain other phospholipids in brain (Strickland and Noble, 1961); and (4) possibly, affecting membrane permeability (Ernsting *et al.*, 1960).

BEHAVIOURAL EFFECTS

1. *Behavioural Effects in Animals*

In general, clinically effective doses of chlorpromazine lead to a reduced activity level associated with increased unresponsiveness, passivity, and motivational decrement.

(a) *Locomotor Activity*

A reduction in spontaneous locomotor activity was produced in mice given oral or subcutaneous chlorpromazine, ranging from 1 to 5 mg/kg; the activity reduction was dose-dependent. Complete suppression of locomotor activity occurred at 5 mg/kg, although ataxia was not apparent and co-ordinated responses could be elicited (Cook and Weidley, 1957). The proportionality of locomotor suppression and dose can be accounted for by brain concentration. Whereas quite small doses of chlorpromazine can lead to measurable changes in spontaneous locomotor activity in a variety of animal species, even doses as large as 365 mg/kg, i.p., did not induce sleep in mice (Brown, 1960). This type of behavioural finding draws a sharp contrast between the phenothiazines and the barbiturates.

A reduction, by chlorpromazine, in both nocturnal and diurnal activity has been observed; however, under these conditions no effect was exerted on the circadian rhythm (Sandberg, 1959; Schallek et al., 1956; Stone et al., 1960).

Exploratory behaviour of rodents has been modified by chlorpromazine in a number of varying experimental situations. The exploratory behaviour of mice was abolished at a dose lower than that required to inhibit motor activity (Buchel et al., 1962). Mice, exploring holes in a vertical panel, reduced the number of such explorations, as a function of dose, where the latter was varied from 0·25 to 2·00 mg/kg, i.p. In a multiple T-maze, the reduction in exploratory activity by chlorpromazine was similarly dose-dependent (Boissier and Simon, 1964; Boissier et al., 1964; Blogovski, 1959). Mice show a predictable tendency to climb inclined planes, when provided with a ladder, screening, mesh, or wire. Escape behaviour, by means of a wire-mesh ladder or screen to an exit from a jar or cage, was inhibited in mice by 1·9 to 4·2 mg/kg, s.c., or 5·6 mg/kg, i.p. (ED_{50}) (Boissier et al., 1961; Kneip, 1960; Sandberg, 1959).

When the motor activity of animals was elicited, using rotored performance, the effective dosage to interfere with performance closely paralleled the effective dose needed to disrupt spontaneous locomotor activity. Other tests in rodents, such as sloping planes to test for maintenance of position, activity wheel performance, pole climbing, backward tube climbing, rolling dowel traversal, wire clinging, and tube traversal have all been sensitive to the effects of chlorpromazine.

Another interesting chlorpromazine-induced alteration in motor activity of a specific type may be found in experiments in which chlorpromazine solutions given to spiders causes a marked cessation of web-spinning, lasting from one to three days after drug administration; any completed webs were still characteristic of normal webs (Witt, 1955). In contrast to these findings, oral doses of 50 µg/day for 10 successive days led to the construction of smaller webs with decreased radii in Aranea Sericata (Groh and Lemieux, 1964). These effects were irreversible, and persisted beyond the cessation of drug treatment. The spiders showed slowed reflexes, and the quality of the web silk decreased.

(b) Learning

The maze performance of rodents treated with chlorpromazine has been extensively investigated, with a variety of maze tasks. The general finding that has emerged from such studies is similar to what was observed for locomotor behaviour, the latency to complete a successful maze response and time spent in the maze were increased by drug treatment; this finding appears consistent with both positively as well as negatively reinforcing stimuli (Courvoisier et al., 1958; Herr et al., 1961; Latz, 1964). Utilising multiple T-maze performance, error frequency was not affected at low doses of the drug (1·0 to 6·0 mg kg) (Domer and Schueler, 1960), but at higher doses (10·0 to 20·0 mg/kg, s.c. and p.o.) error incidence was increased (Courvoisier et al., 1958). The use of a water maze to test the hypothesis that stereotyped behaviour caused by pre-trial water submersion could be eliminated by chlorpromazine-induced reduction in motivational strength yielded results suggesting impairment of acquisition and retention of stereotyped and non-stereotyped responses (Mitchell and King, 1960). In studies of this type it is difficult to separate the thermolytic effects of the phenothiazines from their direct behavioural effects. Whereas water temperature under normal circumstances serves as a basis for introducing differences in motivational level, drug-treated rodents, under these conditions, can become moderately hypothermic and show impaired maze performance as a result (Essman and Sudak, 1962). A possible exception to the behavioural effects of chlorpromazine-induced hypothermia in cold water derives from findings that indicate that the rate of core temperature reduction in cold (19 °C) water for chlorpromazine- and saline-treated rats forced to swim was the same, whereas at higher water temperature (32 °C), the drug-treated rats showed a more rapid rate of temperature loss (LeBlanc, 1958). At the low water temperature, 10 mg/kg, i.p. of chlorpromazine decreased endurance time by 50 per cent, whereas the same dose at the higher temperature had no apparent effect.

Conditioned responses, as affected by chlorpromazine, have been extensively studied; climbing by rats to avoid foot-shock onset signalled by an auditory stimulus was impaired (Courvoisier et al., 1953). At reduced drug dosage (1·0 mg/kg), although avoidance of shock was still impaired, escape from shock onset was not affected. The use of a pole-climbing technique in rats permitted study of the relationships between the unconditioned and conditioned responses (escape and avoidance). Selective impairment of avoidance was obtained at doses of 10·5 mg/kg, p.o., two to three hours following treatment, and the escape behaviour was impaired at higher doses (Cook and Weidley, 1957; Cook et al., 1953). The locomotor and avoidance-suppressant properties of eight phenothiazines were compared (Irwin, 1961) with results suggesting that there was a comparable degree of potency in suppressant effect. Avoidance behaviour in rats appears to be selectively affected by chlorpromazine within rather consistent dose ranges, regardless of the conditioned avoidance task specifically utilised to test such behaviour; these doses (ED_{50}) are approximately: 5 to 12 mg/kg, p.o.; 1·2 to 7·0 mg/kg, s.c.; and 2 to 5 mg/kg, i.p. These dose ranges derive from studies in which rats have been tested: rope climbing, pole climbing, lever-pressing avoidance, shuttle-box, hurdle-box, and hole-jumping.

Bar-pressing behaviour by rats has also been affected by chlorpromazine, where continuous reinforcement with food, water, or heat was given to maintain the behaviour. The dose required to initiate such decreased bar-pressing in motivated rats was somewhat lower than that previously indicated for abolition of conditioned avoidance (1 to 4 mg/kg, i.p.). In pigeons, a discriminative response, based on stimulus-specific fixed-ratio or fixed-interval acquisition, was not altered by 1·7 to 3·0 mg/kg, i.m., of chlorpromazine (Dews, 1956). The effect on response rate appears to be dose-dependent.

Dissociation of responses, as affected by chlorpromazine, has been demonstrated in rats trained after drug treatment and tested for following saline treatment, or a training-testing sequence in the reverse order (Otis, 1964). Rats that were trained under chlorpromazine (1·25 mg/kg) and tested under saline in an avoidance situation, or trained under saline and tested under chlorpromazine, showed less recovery of the avoidance response than rats trained and tested under both conditions with either chlorpromazine or saline. These results are interpreted as a drug-induced internal state that serves as a stimulus, where in a learning situation it may acquire associative connections with a response. In a similar study (Stewart, 1962) rats were given a somewhat higher drug dose (3 to 4 mg/kg, i.p.) and demonstrated dissociative learning in animals trained under the drug to choose one coloured goal box and, under saline, to choose another of a different colour. These observations have led to the speculation that the therapeutic gains of hospitalised patients maintained on drugs may be drug-dependent and may not survive discontinuance of drug therapy (Otis, 1964). These studies have a possible bearing on others that have investigated the effect of chlorpromazine on extinction. Rats trained to acquire a 'conditioned emotional response' (CER) in a grill box, either with or without chlorpromazine, and then tested under saline for extinction differed in that drug-treated rats showed a weaker CER, and extinguished more rapidly. Rats trained for a CER under saline conditions and given extinction trials under chlorpromazine showed CER behaviour for two days after the completion of the extinction series (Hunt, 1956). The effect of chlorpromazine on extinction appears dependent on the acquisition conditions, the complexity of the response, and the possible relationship between the drug-induced diminution of fear responses and/or pain. A relevant consideration in this latter regard is the possible analgesic property of the drug. In rats and mice, chlorpromazine-induced analgesia has been noted (Maxwell et al., 1961; Barkov, 1961a,b). Rats given 5 mg/kg, s.c. of chlorpromazine showed a significant increase in reaction time to thermal pain by 60 to 90 minutes after injection. An increase in reaction time to pain induced by infra-red rays was observed at even lower doses (Barkov, 1961a). These effects were attributed to the action of the drug on the spinal cord. The analgesic effect of 5 mg/kg of chlorpromazine in rats was determined as equivalent to the effect of a comparable dose of morphine (Barkov, 1961b), and combined treatment with 5 mg/kg of chlorpromazine and 5 mg/kg of morphine exceeded the analgesic potency of 10 mg/kg of morphine. Studies of this nature point toward an important consideration in evaluating the results of studies utilising aversive reinforcement, and offer a possible alternative to some of the rather broadly stated and usually generally accepted conclusions that derive from such investigations.

In a comparative study of several phenothiazines, it was shown that conditioned avoidance behaviour provided by auditory stimulation preceding pole-climbing was inhibited by chlorpromazine, but was blocked to a greater degree by prochlorperazine (2 to 3 times) and perphenazine (10 times). Thioridazine was less effective in its inhibitory effect on conditioned avoidance, but was highly effective in eliminating emotional defecation. While motor activity and emotional defecation were blocked by chlorpromazine and prochlorperazine, perphenazine appeared selective for only motor activity (Taeschler and Cerletti, 1959).

(c) Emotionality, Aggression, and Fighting

The open field behaviour of rats, with 'emotionality' measured as a function of the frequency of defecation has been used as one index of emotionality on which the effects of chlorpromazine (2 to 10 mg/kg, s.c.) appear to be inhibitory (Brimblecombe, 1963; Janssen et al., 1960). The stress-induced reduction in appetitive behaviour provided to rats by a novel environment was blocked by chlorpromazine (2 mg/kg) (Steinberg and Watson, 1959).

Aggressive behaviour can be induced in rodents by isolation, and such behaviour has been shown to be diminished by varying doses of chlorpromazine (Cook and Weidley, 1960; Janssen et al., 1960). Doses, generally within approximately 10 mg/kg for several administrative routes were shown effective in attenuating such isolation-induced aggression. It must be pointed out, however, that in addition to providing for enhanced aggressive behaviour in rodents, isolation also significantly alters the threshold for a number of psycho-active compounds (Garattini, 1969); in this respect, reduced ED threshold to the psychomotor effects of chlorpromazine in isolated rodents would be compatible with the results of such studies from which an aggression-reduction conclusion has been, perhaps prematurely, derived. Aggressive behaviour induced by foot shock has also been attenuated by chlorpromazine (Brunaud and Siou, 1959; Chen et al., 1963). An alternative explanation may again be present in the analgesic properties of this agent, so that reduced aggressive behaviour may be a simple concomitant of reduced pain.

In the cat, chlorpromazine was shown to increase sociability, and decrease hostility (Norton et al., 1957), but there appears to be a differential effect on 'hostile' behaviour, depending on whether such animals are aggressive or docile initially; aggressive behaviour, for example, has been augmented by chlorpromazine in docile cats (Bradley and Hance, 1957). The augmentation of aggressivity by chlorpromazine in presumably docile cats (Plas et al., 1962) is also accompanied by alterations in the dominance-submission hierarchy. In the monkey, chlorpromazine treatment (0·7 to 2·0 mg/kg, i.v.) usually results in marked attenuation of experimenter-directed hostility and aggression (Chen and Weston, 1960; Das et al., 1954).

2. Behavioural Effects in Man

(a) Experimental Studies

There are several problems associated with the initiation as well as the evaluation of experimental studies with the phenothiazines in man; these problems reside with the availability of an otherwise behaviourally and pharmacologically uncontaminated subject population, the heterogeneity of motivational and emotional variables inherent in any such population, and the subjective and semantic problems posed by the introduction of drugs.

Psychomotor functions, as evaluated on several tasks, including digit copying, digit-symbol substitution, addition speed, pursuit rotor performance, visual discrimination, and tactual perception, were shown to be differently affected by chlorpromazine (200 mg). Generally, there was a reduced score resulting in the drug-treated subjects (Kornetsky et al., 1957); however, such vigilance tasks as pursuit rotor performance, tapping speed, and continuously maintained performance were impaired by chlorpromazine to a greater degree than was a digit-symbol substitution test, which may generally be taken as an index of intellectual ability. The effects of chlorpromazine on these tasks was comparable to that produced by prolonged sleep deprivation. Those subjects that were minimally affected by chlorpromazine were greatly excited by dextroamphetamine following sleep deprivation (Kornetsky et al., 1959). Such individual variations in the depressant or stimulatory properties of psycho-active agents may well conform to the model of a dimensional framework in personality description within which the behavioural effects of drugs may be considered (Eysenck, 1960).

Subjects in whom a galvanic skin response was conditioned to a light flash did not show interference with the extinction of the unconditioned response as a result of chlorpromazine treatment, or any effect upon their response to an unconditioned stimulus, electric shock; there was, however, inhibition shown for the subsequent re-establishment of the response following extinction (Schneider and Costiloe, 1956).

In studies concerned with the comparative effects of four phenothiazines in 16 male students, a double-blind investigation, using single oral doses of chlorpromazine, promethazine (25, 50, 100, 200 mg/day), perphenazine, and trifluoperazine (2, 4, 8, 16 mg), revealed similar, but variable, differences in behaviour produced, as compared to the chlorpromazine effects. Psychomotor activity was inhibited, with concomitant confusion; changes in autonomic reactivity were accompanied by sedation; and mood anxiety was reduced (DiMascio et al., 1961). In a series of double-blind experiments (180) normal subjects, given a single dose of phenothiazines at four levels and tested 2, 4, or 7 hours after the drug, showed: psychomotor retardation, impairment on intellectual tasks, and drowsiness resulting from chlorpromazine and promethazine; perphenazine and trifluoperazine led to an elevation of mood and apposite behavioural effects. It is of interest to note here that rather contrasting behavioural differences emerged, depending on whether the phenothiazines were aliphatic or piperazine (Klerman and DiMascio, 1961).

The effects of chlorpromazine on eyelid conditioning in normal subjects (25 mg p.o.), given five hours or one hour prior to testing, was shown to lead to more conditioned eyelid responses than in a placebo-treated group. Chlorpromazine-treated subjects reported more of a subjective effect and performed at a higher level (Ludvigson, 1960).

Prolonged chlorpromazine administration (five weeks) to non-psychiatric patients (alcoholics) resulted in reduced critical flicker fusion values, initially, and then normalising with continued drug use (Hoehn-Saric et al., 1964). When visual after-images were measured, using two strong light flashes at $\frac{1}{4}$ second duration, separated by a $\frac{1}{2}$ second interval, the duration of the after-image and its colour were affected in children (average age, 13·6 yrs). Chlorpromazine, in a single dose (1 to 2 mg/kg), reduced the duration of the after-image and attenuated after-image colour; a reduction in the intensity of after-image reds and oranges occurred, and the intensity of greys and whites was increased (Agathon, 1964). In a double-blind crossover study the threshold for auditory flutter fusion was significantly depressed in male subjects (21 to 30 yrs) given oral doses of chlorpromazine (25, 50 mg). Perphenazine (2, 4 mg, p.o.), in contrast, had no effect on threshold (Besser et al., 1966). Again, as previously indicated, a distinction in behavioural effect may be made between the aliphatic and piperazine phenothiazine derivatives. In a task requiring a Euclidean-Pythagorean summation of pitch and loudness, doses of chlorpromazine of 150 mg and higher, given daily to students and psychiatric patients, diminished summation. Tiredness and fatigue accompanied the initial daily drug administration (Bergström et al., 1964). In a binaural hearing synthesis test 60 patients with normal hearing (average age, 29·5 yrs) were required to respond to questions with garbled speech, and repeat familiar words. Chlorpromazine (0·05 g, i.m.) reduced word synthesis, and this effect was attributed to its brain-stem action (Preibisch-Effenberger and Knothe, 1965). Oral administration of chlorpromazine (100 mg) to 21 subjects affected pause time per word (an index of cognition during speech) and breathing rate at rest (Goldman-Eisler, 1966). In a double-blind crossover study, students given chlorpromazine (50 mg), as compared with placebo (ascorbic acid, 50 mg) showed reduced verbal and numerical performance on the Morrisby Differential Test Battery, accompanied by drowsiness and other side-effects. Tests that involved judgements of conceptual relationships were also affected by the drug (Brimer et al., 1964).

(b) Clinical Studies

The clinical study of the phenothiazines covers a wide range of applications which has included treatment of psychoses, neuroses, and behaviour disorders in childhood. The efficacy of the phenothiazines as antipsychotic agents has several indicated differences; on a milligram basis, the piperazine derivatives (acetophenazine, fluphenazine, perphenazine, prochlorperazine, thiopropazate, and trifluoperazine) generally possess greater antipsychotic activity than compounds of the dimethylamine series (chlorpromazine, promazine, and triflupromazine) or the piperidyl series (mepazine and thioridazine). There are, of course, limiting factors that must apply to the above generality regarding the comparative efficacy of phenothiazines; one of these is the interaction between the drug and the type of patient. Among acutely schizophrenic patients thiopropazate was more effective therapeutically in paranoid than in non-paranoid patients (Hollister et al., 1962). Acetophenazine produced more variable results, with seemingly greater effectiveness in acute paranoid schizophrenics, than did perphenazine (Overall et al., 1963). In a schizophrenic population of older age, acetophenazine appeared to exert a selective effect on paranoid symptoms (Sheppard et al., 1964). Thioridazine was comparable in effect on depressed patients, to imipramine, but was more effective in alleviating schizophrenic symptoms (Overall et al., 1964). In a comprehensive evaluation of changes in schizophrenic psychopathology and ward behaviour with phenothiazine treatment, with data obtained in a collaborative multi-hospital study, it was found that: (1) more phenothiazine-treated patients improved than placebo-treated patients, (2) the greatest improvement among drug-treated patients occurred in Memory Deficit, (3) almost all relevant areas of psychopathology were improved in drug-treated patients, (4) drug-treatment clearly improved irritability, slowed speech and movements, hebephrenic symptoms, self-care, and indifference to environment, and (4) drug-treatment tended to prevent the development of symptoms that were not originally present (Goldberg et al., 1965). These data further indicate that the phenothiazines (at least chlorpromazine, fluphenazine, and thioridazine) have a wide range of clinically therapeutic effects over and above 'tranquilisation'. In a summary of double-blind controlled studies of the efficacy of phenothiazine-treatment in schizophrenia in hospitalised psychotic patients, this class of psychoactive drug was more effective than a placebo in 71 out of 92 separate studies (Davis, 1965). In none of the studies summarised were any of the phenothiazines considered therapeutically more effective than chlorpromazine; the latter was more effective in at least 13 out of 54 studies.

B. Rauwolfia Alkaloids

The rauwolfia alkaloids derive from the powdered root of *Rauwolfia serpentinea*, an ancient plant of India, the therapeutic value of which was described at least twenty years before the introduction of the Rauwolfia alkaloids for their tranquilising properties (Sen and Bose, 1931). The alkaloidal fraction of the *Rauwolfia serpentina* root (alseroxylon) and a semisynthetic derivative (syrosingopine) are primarily given in the treatment of hypertension. In addition to their antihypertensive properties, the Rauwolfia alkaloids, reserpine, deserpidine, and rescinnamine possess tranquilising activity. These agents are not indicated for as general a psychotherapeutic spectrum as are the phenothiazines, since (1) they do not appear as effective as the latter for treatment of more severe behavioural disturbances; (2) a stable level of control is difficult to maintain; and (3) the onset of action is considerably slower than that of the phenothiazines, and the effects are rather longer in duration. The Rauwolfia alkaloids appear more appropriately designated as 'tranquilisers', in as much as their effects on the central nervous system, and apparently centrally-mediated, secondary peripheral effects, such as depression of cardiovascular and respiratory reflexes, are behaviourally manifested to characterise 'tranquilisation' (sedation without sleep).

EFFECTS ON NEUROPHYSIOLOGICAL ACTIVITY

Since the administration of reserpine, as the representative of the Rauwolfia alkaloids, leads to primary effects that involve norepinephrine, serotonin, and acetylcholine changes in the brain, any effect of reserpine must also be considered in view of such metabolic alterations that it mediates.

The sequelae of reserpine administration—reduced alertness, anxiety, awareness, etc.—is some basis for suggesting that the drug may depress the reticular activating system. A 500 v/kg dose of reserpine given to cats, with brain-stem section rostral to the optic chiasm, in a state of sham-rage, rendered them completely tranquil within 30 minutes (Schneider, 1955). In the rhesus monkey,

aggressiveness became reduced and the animals became placid and handleable after injection of 0·5 to 1·0 mg/kg, i.v. of reserpine; there was an accompanying slight slowing of the EEG (Schneider and Earl, 1954). Although the behavioural effects emerged after drug treatment, the EEG changes were sometimes absent. Reticular or thalamic stimulation leading to evoked cortical spike and wave complexes in the rabbit were depressed by reserpine (Gangloff and Monnier, 1955). The threshold and duration of EEG arousal after peripheral or reticular stimulation were not altered by reserpine, nor were thalamocortical recruiting circuits (Killam and Killam, 1956). Facilitation of arousal by peripheral stimulation has been observed (Rinaldi and Himwich, 1955a,b) and for doses of reserpine causing behavioural sedation in the rabbit, arousal by such stimulation was prolonged. These discrepant findings between cat and rabbit preparations may reside in possible species differences in sensitivity to reserpine, or variations in the criteria used to assess arousal.

The EEG in man has not been subject to any marked alteration by reserpine, which comes as somewhat of a disappointment to those scientists whose working premise assumes electrophysiological changes attending gross behavioural changes. One could always assume that the EEG is too gross a measure to evaluate more complex time-locked or patterned alterations, or that the cortex is not involved in a direct mechanism of drug action, or that cessation of neural transmission in adrenergic fibres may not be reflected cortically, etc.

Schizophrenic patients given reserpine (5, 10 mg, i.v. or 3 mg, p.o.) did not show EEG changes as recorded for one week to one month, during drug treatment, measured from either scalp electrodes, cortical leads, or subcortical leads (Monroe *et al.*, 1955). A suggestion that rhinencephalic mechanisms are involved in the action of reserpine derives from data showing that delta and theta activity become produced or augmented, and seizures are activated in grand mal and petit mal epilepsy. This finding is consistent with other data that indicate reserpine as effective in reducing the threshold to a variety of experimentally-induced seizures (Arellano and Jeri, 1956).

Because of its sedative, autonomic, and thermolytic effects, reserpine action has also been linked with the hypothalamus; however, hypothalamic depressant features appear to be secondary to depression of medullary sympathetic centres (Bhargava and Borison, 1955).

It appears that the neurophysiological effects of reserpine in animals and man are difficult to assess without some consideration of its metabolic effects and how these may be related to neural functions.

METABOLIC EFFECTS

Reserpine has been shown to reduce brain serotonin levels (Pletscher *et al.*, 1955), to release stored norepinephrine (Paasonen and Vogt, 1956; Holzbauer and Vogt, 1956), exert a lowering effect on brain γ-amino-butyric acid (Balzer *et al.*, 1961a), increase brain glycogen (Balzer *et al.*, 1961b), affect the level of brain high-energy phosphate compounds (Kirpekar and Lewis, 1959), and increase hypothalamic acetylcholine levels (Malhotra and Pundlik, 1965).

The relationship between the behaviourally depressive effects of reserpine and its metabolic effects have been postulated in several respects: behavioural depression by reserpine depends on the selective depletion of serotonin; depletion of catecholamines (norepinephrine and dopamine) by reserpine results in the consequent sedation; sedation accounted for by a reduction in central sympathetic outflow; or sedation by reserpine caused by centrally mediated peripheral parasympathetic changes. While all these proposed mechanisms of action depend, in part, on the assumption that the molecule primarily involved with the mechanism of reserpine action is a mediator of central synaptic transmission, the assumptions are also limited by the extent to which the experimental evidence supports one or more such molecules in a transmitter role; it appears that considerably more work is necessary to define a mechanism of central metabolic action in this respect.

Behavioural Effects

1. *Behavioural Effects in Animals*

The behavioural effects of reserpine have been investigated in a variety of animal species with the same general result emerging—a calming, sedative effect which probably plays an important part in the behavioural situation in which its effects are considered. In such diverse species as the ant (*Formica rufa*) aggressive attack toward a beetle was markedly reduced, and calming and ataxia followed oral administration of reserpine (0·5 μg/mg); aggressive behaviour in mice and rats was also reduced by 1 to 6 hours after reserpine treatment (2 mg/kg, i.p.) and by 18 to 24 hours was completely suppressed (Kostowski, 1966). In the house fly (1 day old), fed 6 mg/ml of reserpine for 3 or 8 days, the life span was reduced from 14·6 days to 9·3 days. There was no egg laying and the 'tranquilising' effect persisted for at least 3 days after cessation of drug-treatment (Hays, 1965). The possible long-term behavioural effects of reserpine-treatment, beyond the period

within which one can account for the systemic elimination of the drug, has been observed in several respects; in mice trained with a buzzer-shock contingency, 1·3 and 1·5 mg/kg, i.p., of reserpine given pre-testing, abolished the CAR for 9 to 10 days; this was in considerable excess for a behavioural effect to persist beyond the two hours following injection, within which the reserpine was eliminated (Shugayev, 1965). Another example of such persistent reserpine effects may be found in a study in which rats were reserpinised during infancy (0·1 mg/kg/day, i.p. from 11 to 30 days of age) and as adults showed a reduced ability to learn to respond discriminatively during reinforcement (Kulkarni *et al.*, 1966). Studies such as these point to some methodological issues that bear on the assessment of behavioural effects of rauwolfia alkaloid; one such consideration is that the amine-depleting effects of reserpine may persist beyond its elimination; binding of the alkaloid to tissue may also account for effects that exceed accepted time periods for 'washout'. These issues appear contingent on such factors as dose and treatment-testing times, as well as on the nature of the motivational state of the animal and its sensory capacity.

In mice, reserpine (1·0 mg/kg, i.v.) led to a sedative effect by 40 minutes after treatment and produced inhibition of the orienting reflex; when the same dose of reserpine was given following inhibition of brain monoamine oxidase activity, the drug produced excitation and an increase in the orienting reflex (Wu, 1961). This study is again suggestive of the importance of the amine effect of reserpine and further indicates that its 'tranquilising' properties may be dependent on endogenous amine level. Exploratory behaviour of rats was impaired by reserpine (0·4 mg/kg) although in doses of 0·005 mg/100 g avoidance learning was facilitated when the injection-test interval was short. In doses of 0·025 mg/100 g there was a reduction in patterned discrimination learning (Walk *et al.*, 1961); this latter effect may have been attributable to the ability of the drug to initiate strabismus in the rat.

A differentiation between the escape and avoidance effects of reserpine in rats may be found with the use of a pole-climbing method; 25 mg/kg, p.o., in two doses, administered 17 hours apart, did not affect escape behaviour to shock onset, tested 3 hours after treatment; however, avoidance behaviour was blocked to an appreciable degree (Cook and Weidley, 1957; Cook *et al.*, 1953). Conditioning of a 'conditioned emotional response' in rats does not appear to be impaired by reserpine (0·5 mg/kg) (Stein, 1956), although an already established CER has been virtually eliminated by reserpine treatment (Brady, 1956). When hungry rats had bar-pressing for food suppressed by shock in the presence of a tone, the administration of reserpine (0·23 mg/kg, i.p. for 18 days) following each experimental session led to an increase in the number of shocks that were tolerated by the animals to obtain food (Geller *et al.*, 1963). There was a gradual decrease in a variable-interval response rate with continued drug treatment. With chronic reserpine treatment (0·2 mg/ kg) there was a decrease in 'conditioned emotional response' performance at low-shock intensity (0·8 mA), as measured by variable interval response rates and suppression ratios (Appel, 1963).

In evaluating the effects of reserpine on more complex behaviour, chains of alimentary reflexes were not affected by the drug (0·08 to 0·09 mg/kg); however, there was inhibition of chains of defensive reflexes and depression of efferent generalisation (Voronin and Napalkov, 1963). In doses of 0·1 mg/ kg there was an inhibitory effect on conditioned food reflexes, both in terms of positive reactions and for differentiation thereof; conditioned escape reflexes were not affected and differentiation inhibition was intensified (Hecht, 1963).

In the monkey, the effects of reserpine (0·7 mg/kg) on rated CER behaviour, established with a noise-shock contingency, was to increase the number of trials required to reach criterion; reserpine treatment during extinction (0·75 mg/kg) increased the number of criterion level extinction trials (Weiskrantz and Wilson, 1956). In rhesus monkeys receiving 0·2 to 0·5 mg/kg, i.m. of reserpine there was a deficit observed in auditory discrimination that could not be accounted for by an increased latency period; spatial delayed response performance was not changed (Gross and Weiskrantz, 1961). This effect has been viewed as a decreased use of information necessary for the animal to perform an auditory discrimination. It does become critical to consider that the specific sensory modality utilised in conditioning experiments may be important in evaluating the behavioural effect of reserpine and other Rauwolfia alkaloids.

Unlike chlorpromazine, where possible analgesic effects can account, in part, for changes in escape behaviour and, possibly, avoidance acquisition, reserpine does not appear to possess this property. At unusually high doses (2·5 mg/kg) mice became torpid and ataxic, yet escape from a 3·0 mA foot-shock in a grid box was not modified; the latency to escape by crossing to a 'safe' side was not elevated beyond that of saline-treated controls. Where mice, treated at the same dose, were given a single training trial for acquisition of a passive avoidance response, the incidence of acquisition and retention (tested 24 hours following injection) did not differ from that of controls. The unconditioned response (stepping from a light-exposed vestibule into a darkened chamber) and the conditioned response (passively avoiding the darkened chamber in which footshock was administered) were not modified by reserpine treatment (Essman, 1967). The administration of post-training electro-convulsive shock, which led to a retrograde amnesia for the passive avoidance behaviour in 78 per cent of saline-treated control mice, resulted in only 50 per cent of the reserpinised animals developing such a memory loss. Reserpine treatment given mice one hour prior to a one-trial active avoidance conditioning procedure (in which 35 per cent of control animals showed criterion acquisition) resulted in 30 per cent criterion acquisition (Essman, 1970); this finding suggests that the drug has little effect on active avoidance behaviour in mice, and that training during the reserpinised period is transferable to a subsequent non-drug testing period.

II. MOOD STABILISING AGENTS

A. Direct Stimulants

Amphetamines. Amphetamine action generally involves the major subdivisions of the central nervous system in that EEG activation has been observed in a number of species, both cortically and subcortically. A direct facilitatory effect on synaptic transmission has been indicated (Leico *et al.*, 1949), and it is possible that facilitation of monosynaptic and polysynaptic transmissions in the spinal cord may provide support for its generalised excitatory effects, including righting, postural activity, and the recovery period in animals with experimental lesions. There is also some indication that in addition to its stimulant properties, amphetamines may have depressant properties (Marazzi, 1953; Lond and Silvestrini, 1957). The suggestion has also been made that amphetamine acts on the reticular activating system by its ability to reverse the depressant effect of barbiturates on the reticular formation; it can lower the threshold for arousal by electrical stimulation of the reticular formation (Bradley and Key, 1958). The effect of amphetamines on the hypothalamic 'feeding centre' has been indicated, and inhibition of synaptic transmission of impulses in the mid-brain by this drug suggests that impulses to the lateral 'feeding centre' of the hippothalamus may be blocked (Marazzi and Hart, 1955).

There have been several suggestions made with regard to possible relationships between the central mechanism of action of the amphetamines and their effects on brain biogenic amines. Such hypotheses, unfortunately, do not take into account the total range of both stimulant and depressant effects of the amphetamines, nor do they clearly provide any basis on which the behavioural effects of these compounds may be explained.

The effect of amphetamines on operant behaviour in animals has been reviewed (Stein, 1964) and it is clear that this drug leads to decreases in the intake of both food and water; this, unfortunately, makes any assessment of behaviour maintained by either food or water reinforcement extremely difficult. In contrast, thirst-induced water intake in the rat was depressed by amphetamines. However, when these animals were forced to drink water in order to escape shock, there was increased drinking as a result of amphetamine treatment. The response pattern in the amphetamine-treated animals was also of interest in that escape of shock was modified to shock-avoidance by rapid licking (Teitelbaum and Derks, 1958). The i.p. administration of amphetamine, methamphetamine, and several other appetite depressants at several dose levels, led to increase in the current intensity required to elicit feeding in rats with chronically implanted electrodes in the lateral hypothalamus (Stark and Totty, 1967). For behaviour maintained with reinforcements other than food and water, the tendency to respond is generally enhanced by amphetamine. Under conditions of shock avoidance, performance is increased, and where electrical stimulation of the brain is utilised as a positive reinforcement, such behaviour is also increased. It has been suggested (Stein, 1964) that reward thresholds are lowered by amphetamines.

In rats which showed relatively poor performance in a discriminatory avoidance escape situation, 3 mg/kg of diamphetamine led to a significant improvement in avoidance performance without affecting lever responding during non-avoidance periods. The responding to exteroceptive stimuli, not previously associated with shock, was also affected by diamphetamines and this was interpreted as a disruption of central nervous system-induced freezing patterns (Hearst and Whalen, 1963). In rats maintaining environmental temperature in the cold by lever pressing for heat reinforcement, amphetamine increased the frequency of lever pressing for heat reinforcement beyond that required to maintain normal skin temperatures; this occurred in spite of the fact that the rat, in which body temperature fell in the cold, was not affected by amphetamine. It was concluded that behaviour thermoregulation is impaired by amphetamine through decreased optimal frequency of bursts of heat (Weiss and Laties, 1963). The effects of diamphetamine (2 mg/ kg, i.p.) did not lead to any difference in the number of conditioned avoidance responses made by rats in a shuttle box avoidance situation. Gross activity, measured by intertrial hurdle crossing, was increased; however, performance was not enhanced (Powell et al., 1965). There are several studies in which facilitation of avoidance conditioning has been reported with amphetamine treatment (Barry and Miller, 1965; Krieckhaus et al., 1965; Stein, 1965). The reduction in freezing by the animal may possibly be related to improved avoidance performance (Cole, 1966) and its effects on food consumption, with body activity able to vary with conditions under which food deprivation is maintained. Increased co-ordinated running and walking activity of mice has also been reported with amphetamine and metamphetamine (Dews, 1954).

The effects of amphetamine in man have been rather extensively studied, and it appears as if the behavioural effects rely on a number of rather complex factors. It has been indicated that oral doses of 10 to 30 mg can, in some individuals, result in wakefulness, alertness, decreased sense of fatigue, elevation of mood, increased initiative, difficulty in ability to concentrate, with associated elation with euphoria, and increases in motor and speech activity (Innes and Nickerson, 1965). The ability of amphetamine to accelerate physical endurance, and ability ability, and increase working time as well as ability form the results of several studies. An oral dose of 10 mg of amphetamine prevented a performance decrement in subjects operating muscle ergograph, and, at a higher dose (20 mg), an increase in work capability was observed (Alles and Feigen, 1943). In military field studies, subjective symptoms and motor testings seemed generally benefited by 10 mg of amphetamine sulphate (Seashore and Ivy, 1953). The effects of amphetamine on collegiate swimmers and track and field athletes was shown to be improved over that of placebo and, at higher doses of the drug, less variability was observed among the more proficient athletes (Smith and Beacher, 1959). In a review of the effects of amphetamine on human performance (Weiss and Laties, 1962), it was indicated that this drug appeared to lower reaction time, improve hold-steadiness and co-ordination, and counteract the motor-performance decrement produced by alcohol. Some further evidence was presented to indicate that amphetamine prevented the decrement in performance level and was capable of restoring deteriorated performance in a simulated light-control task. Performance on arithmetic tasks and complex verbal tasks can be improved by amphetamine treatment, especially in long task sessions. However, there has been no indication of improved intelligence test performance with this drug. Some indication of a facilitative effect of amphetamine on conditioning has been given; however, it is difficult to separate the effects of the drug on learning from those on performance. It has been shown that diamphetamine accelerates the rate of conditioning more than a placebo (Franks and Trouton, 1958).

Amphetamines have been shown to result in improved intellectual functioning in a variety of tasks, including abstract reasoning, addition, concealed figures, paired associations, etc., and to assert positive effects on tasks requiring subjects to operate to full capacity (Nash, 1962). A single dose of 10 mg of diamphetamine led to statistically significant increases in the number of arithmetic problems correctly solved. Proportionately fewer errors were made by amphetamine-treated subjects as compared to placebo-treated controls, and fatigued subjects did not show a characteristic performance decrement.

The behavioural effects of amphetamines in man seem to be most apparent for those tasks involving sustained performance, or in which fatigue may possibly operate to affect performance. It is difficult in separating, for specific tasks, the effects of amphetamine on performance, fatigue, cognitive ability, and judgement. There has been some indication that judgement may be distorted by this drug in that it has been observed that subjects given de-amphetamine overestimated auditory signal length (Goldstein et al., 1958).

The therapeutic uses of amphetamines as mood-altering agents has sometimes been indicated. Amphetamine-treated subjects, as compared with controls, reported euphoria, feelings of exhilaration, enhancing in energy and capacity to work, and reduced fatigue. There were some instances of mild or moderate insomnia and subjective feelings of increased tiredness by the end of the day (Nathanson, 1937). The use of the amphetamines in instances of depression have been limited by the resulting depression produced by the drug following its mood-elevating effects, the development of tolerance requiring increasing doses, its anorexogenic properties, and its cardiovascular effects (Biel, 1968).

B. Indirect Stimulants

Among the pharmacological agents that may be considered as indirect stimulants, one may broadly include the tricyclic compounds that are basically thymoleptic agents used primarily in the clinical situation for the treatment of depression, and also the monoamine oxidase inhibitors, the action of which in the central nervous system probably is of primary concern in so far as the modification of physiologically active brain amines are concerned. Since this treatment of psychoactive agents is to concern itself primarily with principal representatives of various classes of compounds, the behavioural effects of which parallel one another or bear a number of similarities to one another when dosage, onset, and duration of action are taken into consideration, only one representative of the compounds usually designated as indirect stimulants will be dealt with. Since the classification of any given psychoactive compound as 'antidepressive' is extremely difficult to adhere to, in view of the fact that the behaviour disorder characterising 'depression' is highly complex and varied, the specific agent considered here—imipramine—will simply be treated as a mood-stabilising agent, useful clinically in the treatment of a variety of depressive illnesses. In general, the tricyclic compounds, which include imipramine, desipramine, etc. (iminodibenzyl derivatives) and amitriptyline, nortriptyline, protriptyline, etc. (dibenzocycloheptene derivatives), have been shown to be more effective when used clinically as antidepressant medication than MAO inhibitors (Wechsler et al., 1965), and among the tricyclic compounds themselves, amitriptyline, which is intermediate in action between imipramine and chlorpromazine, was shown to be slightly more effective in depressive disorders characterised by agitation, anxiety, and schizophrenic-like symptoms.

Imipramine, which is structurally similar to chlorpromazine, has been shown to induce or enhance the resting rhythm of the electroencephalogram: at low doses, in experimental animals, there is synchronisation of the cortical EEG and a decrement in fast and low amplitude activity; at intermediate doses, desynchronisation of EEG activity occurs, with a slowing in frequency; and at high doses, imipramine produces hypersynchronisation of EEG activity, with the possibility of EEG seizures.

Several studies have attributed the effect of imipramine to its action on brain monoamines, although this relationship remains to be explored considerably further before any descriptive statement can be made regarding a central mechanism of action for this compound or corollary of its behavioural effects.

An absence of any significant effect of imipramine on monoamine oxidase activity has been shown in several studies (Exer and Pulver, 1960; Kivalo et al., 1961; Pletscher and Gey, 1959, 1962), and a lack of effect on brain monoamines has also been indicated in rats (Sulser et al., 1962; Vernier, 1961). In contrast to these findings, however, there have been reports of elevated levels of brain serotonin resulting from imipramine treatment (Costa *et al.*, 1960; Kivalo *et al.*, 1961). In mice treated with imipramine hydrochloride (20 mg/kg), there was an elevation in whole brain serotonin, a slight elevation in its chief metabolite in brain, 5-hydroxyindoleacetic acid, an increase in brain serotonin turnover time, with no alteration in brain MAO activity (Essman, 1970). These findings have tentatively suggested that one central effect of this compound in mice may be to increase the synthesis and degradation of serotonin in brain. The brain level of imipramine, following injection (40 mg/kg, i.p.), reached a peak at 45 minutes after such treatment, with a brain level of 14 μg/g (Gilett *et al.*, 1961). A 30 per cent inhibition of brain cholinesterase activity has been reported with injection of 10 mg/kg of imipramine (Pulver, 1960), and inhibition of respiratory activity in rat brain cortex slices and a reduction in oxidative phosphorylation in rat brain mitochondria has also been reported (Abadon *et al.*, 1961).

The effect of imipramine on the central nervous system has been interpreted as non-specific and stimulatory for neurons, whereas for glia a proposed specific effect on RNA synthesis has been proposed (Hydén, 1963). These conclusions were based on experiments in which the RNA content of single cells was altered by imipramine treatment, such that there was an 18 per cent increase in neuronal RNA and a 45 per cent decrease in glial RNA. This finding bears some relationship to the suggestion that compounds that elevate neuronal RNA and deplete glial RNA may be effective in antagonism of the amnesic effect of electroconvulsive shock (Essman, 1966; Essman and Golod, 1968; Essman and Essman, 1969). Some support for this relationship may be found, in that imipramine-treated mice given electroconvulsive shock immediately following acquisition training for a single trial passive avoidance response showed a significantly reduced incidence of an electroshock-induced retrograde amnesia than did control-treated mice (Essman, 1970).

The behavioural effects of imipramine, in animals, may be broadly viewed as sedative, with only a very minimal effect on spontaneous locomotor activity. In behavioural studies, rats trained to acquire a maze response showed an increase in response latency in the acquisition of such behaviour independent of the nature of the motivated stimulus. In doses of 5 to 20 mg/kg, i.p., error performance in a water maze was decreased; however, response time was increased (Latz, 1964). Conditioned avoidance responses have been reduced at high doses of imipramine (100 mg/kg, p.o.), in rats (Theobald, 1959); however, at lower doses, conditioned avoidance responses were not negatively affected and

performance thereof appeared to be enhanced (Maxwell and Palmer, 1961; Maxwell, 1964). It appears as though discrete conditioned avoidance responses are negatively affected by imipramine in animals, at high doses, within a range in which induced synchronisation of the electrocorticogram is a corollary. At doses of 5 to 20 mg/kg, i.p., the response rate and incidence of shock avoidance was decreased by imipramine treatment (Theobald *et al.*, 1964; Carlton, 1961), although other studies have not consistently demonstrated a response decrement in animals treated with higher doses of imipramine (Scheckel and Boff, 1964; Heise and Boff, 1962). There has been some indication (Shchelkunov, 1962) that the effect of imipramine on performance becomes more apparent when the reinforcing stimulus employed was food rather than shock. The reduction of food reinforcement, produced by imipramine, did not affect the percentage of shocks taken by the animal (Goldberg and Johnson, 1964).

A variety of studies would appear to indicate that at low doses imipramine acts as a mild analeptic, whereas at high doses it serves as a depressant. Discriminatory behaviour is improved or facilitated, particularly in the case of classical secretory or motor responses when low doses of imipramine are given, and under such dose conditions, maze errors and non-discriminated avoidance behaviour has been observed to be facilitated.

Certain similarities between central effects of imipramine and those of lithium salts have been pointed out (Essman, 1970), which perhaps lends some support to the view (Schou, 1963) that these compounds fall within the common category designated as 'normothymoleptics', or mood stabilisers. The alteration of the EEG in the direction of a recruiting response, resulting in high amplitude slow waves, in cats and rabbits, and the reduction or suppression of arousal, produced by electrical stimulation of the reticular formation, or by auditory or painful stimulation, has been shown for imipramine (Sigg, 1959). The increase in the arousal threshold to reticular stimulation by imipramine has also been demonstrated in cats (Bradley and Key, 1959), and in doses of 0·1 to 2·0 mg/kg, imipramine was effective in blocking the activation of electrocortical responses induced by sensory stimulation. A critical parameter in the evaluation of the central effects of imipramine appear to reside in the dose at which this compound is administered; for example, low doses led to decreased arousal thresholds for sensory stimuli and direct electrical stimulation of the reticular formation, whereas higher doses (8 to 20 mg/kg) depressed the excitability of the arousal system (Rubio-Chevannier *et al.*, 1961). Alterations in threshold for the rage response also appears to be dose-dependent in that low doses (2 to 5 mg/kg) resulted in decreased threshold for rage responsiveness, whereas higher doses (8 to 10 mg/kg) decreased autonomic responsivity, caused rage to disappear, and increased threshold. These findings may possibly point toward the direct or indirect enhancement of hypothalamic excitability, which could possibly serve to account for the clinically antidepressant nature of imipramine action (Peñaloza-Rojas, 1961).

C. Miscellaneous Indirect Stimulants

There has been a variety of compounds that can be broadly classed within an area considered as indirect stimulants. However, the nature of such compounds and their interrelationship with one another is of such a diverse nature and their behavioural effects have sometimes been rather far removed from their intended clinical use.

Recent clinical interest in the use of lithium salts, in the treatment of the manic phase of manic-depressive illness, and the variety of metabolic effects and behavioural alterations induced by compounds within the lithium family, suggest that lithium salts, as possible indirect stimulants of central nervous system activity, may be useful to consider both experimentally, as well as clinically, within this general area.

Lithium

The initial studies, from which the clinical application of lithium salts to the treatment of the manic phase of manic-depressive illness emerged, were conducted in guinea-pigs (Cade, 1949). It was noted that the result of the administration of lithium salts to these animals was lethargy and protection from urea-induced convulsions. There has been little experimental work dealing with the effect of lithium salts on behaviour since most of these considerations have been explored in human subjects within the context of therapeutic application. The effect of lithium on the electrical activity of the nervous system has been considered (Mayfield, 1966), and the results of EEG studies indicate a widening of the frequency spectrum and diffuse slowing. Background rhythm in these recordings has been both potentiated as well as disorganised by lithium treatment, with sensitivity to hyperventilation also occurring. There is some indication that cerebral ADP and respiration is stimulated by lithium, as indicated from studies of its effects on isolated rat brain mitochondria (Kraal, 1967).

It was noted, in man, that there was a higher retention and tolerance to lithium during manic attack, as compared with healthy persons, and that this increase in retention is reduced following the attenuation of the manic attack (Trautner, 1955). Following the ingestion of lithium salts, it was noted that whereas animal subjects excreted 50 to 70 per cent, manic patients excreted less than 20 per cent. It should, however, be pointed out that different doses of lithium salts were given to the control and manic groups (Gershon and Yuwiler, 1960).

Another hypothesis concerned with the effect of lithium has suggested central nervous system catecholamines, which increased during mania and decreased during depression. Norepinephrine, available to central adrenergic receptors has, in animal studies, been shown to be decreased by lithium chloride (Schanberg and Schildkraut, 1967). A decrease in brain level of normetanephrine and an increase in the level of deanimated catecholes resulted from lithium chloride treatment (Schanberg et al., 1966), suggesting that it may decrease the availability of norepinephrine to adrenergic receptor sites in mania. There has been some suggestion that the relative rates of release and re-uptake of norepinephrine at central adrenergic nerve endings may be related to alterations in mood states (Benney and Davis, 1965; Susler et al., 1964). These data have indicated that the therapeutic efficacy of lithium treatment in manic states may partially result from an increased re-uptake of norepinephrine, with a resulting decrease in norepinephrine available for interaction with receptor sites.

There has been some degree of experimental work relating the effects of lithium to other electrolytes. Following lithium chloride treatment in rats there was an elevation of calcium and magnesium execretion after 12 days, whereas phosphate excretion rose after 20 days (Gotfredson et al., 1969). Lithium chloride injection in rats led to an elevation of brain glycogen level, and in its specific activity in brain blood, glucose levels were also affected during the first two hours of lithium chloride treatment, following which there was a decrease in level (Plenge, 1969). In rats given oral doses of lithium salts there was no recorded effect on brain amine levels; however, there was a reduced depletion of 5-hydroxytryptamine in the nerve terminals of lithium-treated animals that were given a tryptophan hydroxylase inhibitor (Corrodi et al., 1969); these authors have concluded that prolonged administration of low doses of lithium salts lead to a reduction in the activity of 5-hydroxytryptamine neurons or, possibly, the inhibition of 5-hydroxytryptamine release at nerve terminals following impulse stimulation. An earlier conclusion regarding the central effect of lithium on amines was that it did not alter brain amine levels (Schou, 1967). This same investigator suggested earlier (Schou, 1963) that there were parallels between the therapeutic effects of lithium salts and imipramine, which were classed as 'normothymoleptics', in that both of these compounds did not affect 'normal behaviour', led to no apathy or impairment of consciousness or intellectual functions, and had no euphoriant or mood-depressive properties. These suggested parallels have beeen studied in mice (Essman, 1970—in press), and several behavioural and biochemical correlates of acute lithium salt treatment have emerged.

The administration of doses of lithium carbonate, ranging from 1·18 to 4·70 mEq/kg, in mice, resulted in detectable amounts of brain lithium by 15 minutes following intraperitoneal injection and persisting for at least 45 minutes following injection. Brain magnesium concentration was significantly elevated for at least 60 minutes following treatment. Brain serotonin concentration was elevated at 15 minutes following lithium injection, and at this time, for the lowest dose, there was a significant reduction in brain serotonin turnover rate, and an elevation in turnover time, suggesting that brain serotonin synthesis and degradation at one specific time following lithium treatment was reduced. It was also found that a conditioned avoidance response, for which post-training electroshock resulted in a retrograde amnesia in animals tested 24 hours following the training ECS sequence, was reinstated in approximately 30 per cent of the animals by 48 or 72 hours later, where such animals had been pre-treated with 2·35 mEq/kg of lithium carbonate 30 minutes prior to training.

In a clinical study, patients suffering from affective psychoses, when treated with lithium carbonate, showed that during the course of therapy, clinical recovery was accompanied by a rise in total body water and a significant increase in intracellular water, suggesting that altered electrolyte levels in the central nervous system may be related to such pathology or the mechanism whereby lithium treatment effects clinical recovery (Mangoni et al., 1969).

The efficacy with which lithium salts have been used in the treatment of affective psychosis, particularly in the therapy of mania, has received some attention. Utilising the frequency of manic attack as a measure of therapeutic effectiveness, it was reported that 39 out of 48 patients, treated with lithium salts, showed a reduced frequency of attack (Schou, 1959). When patients were rated for the intensity of attack (i.e. activity level, mood, sleep, etc.), it was shown that such intensity was reduced in 18 out of 28 subjects, when compared to a placebo group (Maggs, 1963). In 19 patients clinically diagnosed as manic, and exhibiting hyperactivity, elation, and pressured speech, treatment with lithium carbonate and maintenance of serum levels below 2 mEq/litre, resulted in a reduced duration of attack in 17 out of 25 patients. Using a phenothiazine baseline as a control, wherein manic attack can last as long as six months, the attacks were reduced to approximately two weeks with lithium treatment; it was thereby concluded that lithium represents a treatment of choice for those patients who do not respond to phenothiazines (Wharton and Fieve, 1966). In a double-blind experiment, testing the effectiveness of lithium carbonate, as compared with imipramine in the treatment of acute depression, it was concluded that imipramine exerted a considerably greater antidepressant effect, as measured by clinical ratings, than did lithium, although the latter did show some degree of effectiveness as an antidepressant (Fieve et al., 1968).

It is apparent that the effects of lithium salts on behaviour is, in its present state, poorly understood and sparingly studied. It remains for a considerable amount of animal and human experimental work to clarify the nature of the mechanisms and effects that this potentially useful psychoactive agent may possess.

III. CENTRAL NERVOUS SYSTEM STIMULANTS

The central nervous system stimulants represent a class of compounds, the effects of which are sometimes outside the borders of traditional psychoactive compounds. They are, in most respects, older, and their therapeutic applicability has been rather limited and, to a large extent, as yet unexplored. Central nervous system stimulation implies that a portion or portions of that system increase their activity, as defined either by metabolic or electrophysiological alterations. The nature by which the initiation and/or spread of such excitation occurs may involve either direct stimulation or, possibly, the interference with inhibitory mechanisms. The relevance of such compounds in psychopharmacology becomes apparent when effects on behaviour, affective states, learning, or performance are apparent, whereas in other instances the behavioural effect of such agents may, through behavioural criteria, be defined as stimulatory, whereas the central nervous system effects may be less apparent. There appear to be rather narrow borders separating stimulant effects in the central nervous system, as characterised by increased activity and subsequent depression, from the type of massive stimulation which, for most of such compounds, eventuates in seizure discharges and overt convulsions. With this consideration taken into account, this central nervous stimulant considered on both a behavioural and physiological level will, for the most part, be limited to investigations wherein subconvulsive doses have been employed.

1. CAMPHOR

This compound, which is a mild irritant and antiseptic, produces consistent convulsions in large doses, and these irregular clonic events are probably medullary in nature. It does not selectively stimulate respiration, and when administered in small amounts it relaxes the gastro-intestinal tract. Camphor monobromate has been used in the treatment of headache and other neurological conditions and camphor spirit has historically been used in the treatment of hysteria and related excited states. In mammals, the convulsive action of camphor appears to be confined above the optic thalami and direct application of this compound to the cerebral cortex results in Jacksonian and generalised epileptoform seizures.

There has been little interest in using camphor in behavioural studies, although for comparative purposes, with other agents in this class, it might be of interest to ascertain its relative behavioural effects. Camphor (50 mg/kg), given to cats (p.o.) had less of a CNS stimulant effect than either caffeine or theophylline, and was 1·1 times less efficient as a CNS stimulant than the amphetamines. Within 24 hours after camphor treatment, the animals showed reduced alertness (Müller-Calgan and Hotovy, 1961).

2. NICOTINE

This compound, which in traditional pharmacological classification has not usually been included among the central nervous system stimulants, has been included here at this time for several reasons: it stimulates both sympathetic and parasympathetic ganglia; grossly stimulates skeletal muscle, carotid body receptors, and the supraoptic nucleus of the hypothalamus; leads to convulsions when introduced intravenously in sufficient concentrations; and acts directly on the walls of the blood vessels, liberating norepinephrine present in the vascular wall, leading to vaso-constriction. The direct central effects of this compound resemble, in many respects, those observed with other compounds within this general class. The effects of nicotine and nicotine derivatives, from tobacco smoking, on the central nervous system has recently been comprehensively summarised

(Murphree, 1967). The stimulant-like properties of nicotine have been known for many years and the name of this drug is actually derived from one of the early names given to tobacco; when first introduced in France, following its introduction of use in the Spanish peninsula, the raw derivative was named 'nicotina' in honour of the French Ambassador at Lisbon, Jean Nicot, who, in approximately 1560, made this introduction.

The central effects of nicotine have been ascribed preferentially to the cholinergic portion of the meso-diencephalic activating system, based on evidence of its activation of the EEG following i.p. treatment (1 to 2 mg/kg) in the rabbit. Doses of 2 to 6 mg/kg led to convulsions, the origin of which was in the hippocampus (Floris et al., 1962). The local effects of nicotine within the central nervous system have been studied in cats given 10 to 20 y per kg, in which EEG arousal was produced in animals with mid-pontine sections; this was also observed with rabbits with pre-pontine sections, in dogs with mid-pontine transsections and in deafferented dog brains prepared by pretrigeminal transsection, bilateral destruction of II and III nerves and application of lidocaine to olfactory mucosa (Knapp, 1961). Administration of 20 per cent of the convulsive dose of nicotine, i.v., was shown to reach peak levels in the cerebral cortex, cerebellum, and brain stem within 5 to 10 minutes after injection (Yamamoto et al., 1967).

Some evidence for the metabolic effects of nicotine may be found in studies in which administration of 1 mg/ml resulted in a release of 58 per cent of the total serotonin present in rabbit thrombocytes. The urinary excretion of 5-hydroxyindole acetic acid increased significantly after 5 to 10 cigarettes a day were smoked (Schuvelein and Werle, 1962). In the mouse, there is evidence to indicate that whole-brain serotonin levels in nicotine sulphate-treated (1 mg/kg) animals do not appreciably change by one hour after i.p. injections, whereas agents or events that modify the brain level of serotonin are less effective in causing its elevation if these animals have been treated with nicotine (Essman et al., 1968).

The behavioural effects of nicotine have been explored to some extent although the findings are by no means consistent. A graded increase in motor activity was observed with i.v. injections of from 0·18 to 0·43 mg/kg. Motor activity was increased as a function of dosage (Bonta et al., 1960). There have been studies in which the effects of nicotine appear generally to impair performance. In rats trained to discriminate between colours, doses of from 0·5 to 0·75 mg/kg depressed colour discrimination performance for the first day; in doses of 1·5 to 2 mg/kg, performance was depressed for the first four days with a return to normal performance levels by the fifth day; at a dose of 2·5 mg/kg, performance was depressed for five weeks before tolerance levels were reached and performance was again stabilised at normal levels. All injections were given for this study by the subcutaneous route (Mercier and Desaigne, 1960). The daily injections of nicotine in doses from 0·05 to 1 mg either s.c. or i.p. over several months led to a significant reduction of performance in maze behaviour as measured by running-time and the number of errors (Eisenberg, 1948, 1954). In rats, 0·1 mg/kg of nicotine was shown to affect the rate at which conditioned responses were elaborated, and such facilitation emerged as a function of age; 55-day-old rats elaborated conditioned responses by 8 days when treated with nicotine, as compared with 14 days required by controls; at 61 days of age, nicotine-treated rats required 4 days, as compared with 11 days for controls; and, at 131 and 158 days of age, nicotine treatment did not affect the rate of CR elaboration (Linuchev and Michelson, 1965).

Significant behavioural effects of nicotine have also been reported. The acquisition of a conditioned response was made easy by nicotine treatment in rats, and there was a greater per cent of conditioned responses apparent in young drug-treated rats than in the adult animals (Robustelli, 1966). Temporally-dependent effects of nicotine (0·05 to 0·4 mg/kg) were observed for rats on an operant task; the response rate on a variable-interval schedule decreased as a function of increased dose (Morrison, 1967). Enhanced performance in shock-avoidance conditioning has been demonstrated in mice (Oliverio, 1967), and the beneficial effect of nicotine (0·05 to 0·4 mg/kg) on bar-pressing rate in rats was abolished by prior treatment with physostigmine. A reduced rate was potentiated by physostigmine and an increased rate was reduced by physostigmine, suggesting a central interaction (Morrison, 1968). In rats trained to avoid electric shock by pushing a pattern on the door of a goal box, a two-pattern choice was improved (0·2 mg/kg s.c. of nicotine sulphate), whereas a five-pattern choice was unaffected by such drug treatment (Bovet-Nitti, 1966). The maze learning performance of nicotine-treated rats was superior to that of controls, when the drug was administered post-trial. The Maudsley 'reactive' strain achieved better scores under these conditions than rats from a 'non-reactive' strain (Garg and Holland, 1968). In a light-shock shuttle box, ease of avoidance acquired by nicotine treatment was shown to be strain dependent; strains of mice that were characterised by low performance scores acquired the greatest degree of ease of avoidance by nicotine whereas in two strains of mice with a high initial level of performance, avoidance was impaired

by nicotine treatment. Nicotine sulphate (0·5 mg/kg, i.p.) was given 15 minutes before the conditioning test (Bovet et al., 1966). It is of interest in this study to note that the 15 minute pretest injection of nicotine sulphate led to significant increase in avoidance responding in Swiss mice. It has been shown (Essman, 1969) that Swiss mice conditioned in a passive avoidance situation, 15 minutes following i.p. injection of 1 mg/kg, are much more highly susceptible to the memory-disruptive effects of post-conditioning treatments than are mice tested under such conditions 45 or 60 minutes following injection. The point in question, therefore, is whether increased avoidance responding is in fact a true indication of the stability of such avoidance behaviour and to what extent both these measures are influenced by the central effects of nicotine.

The mating behaviour of rats was shown to be completely unaffected at doses of 0·1 and 0·2 mg/kg of nicotine and even at doses (2 mg/kg) leading to overt depression mating behaviour was still unaffected (Bignami, 1966). The rearing activity of rats was affected by nicotine bitartrate (0·8 mg/kg), such that injection prior to each daily trial that measured rearing behaviour in males and females of a 'reactive' and 'non-reactive' strain resulted generally in better rearing behaviour; 'non-reactive' rats reared more than rats of the 'reactive' strain and males obtained higher 'rearing scores' than females (Garg, 1969).

The effects of nicotine in man are largely found in anecdotal and extremely subjective reports and it is, therefore, difficult to summarise such findings within an experimental context. Transient nocturnal motor aphasias, of 10 to 15 minute duration, have been observed in human subjects as a consequence of nicotine, with some indication of alterations in blood flow (Sörgel, 1961).

The amount of nicotine present in a single inhaled cigarette has been estimated as equivalent to an intravenous dose of 1 to 2 μg/kg. (The Editor, Brit. med. J., 1968). During a six-hour period within which subjects smoked an average of ten cigarettes (≃10 to 20 μg/kg, i.v.), concentration was decreased and fatigue increased, as measured on the Nowlis Mood Scale. Tracking and vigilance, measured on a simulated driving task did not differ between smokers and non-smokers (Heimstra et al., 1967). A decrease in performance on a tracking task has been reported in subjects after smoking four cigarettes (Wenzel and Davies, 1961).

The effect of nicotine on tapping was shown to cause the delay of inhibition for rate of tapping, the occurrence of rest pauses, and to produce changes in average gap length. The extent of the effect was not dependent on the initial tapping ability of the subject (Frith, 1967). In 20 male subjects nicotine was shown to promote the consolidation of pursuit rotor learning (Frith, 1968).

3. NIKETHAMIDE

Nikethamide, a derivative of nicotinic acid, in large doses, leads to convulsions. It has a variety of effects, including vascular changes, salivation, respiratory stimulation, etc. Comparatively little is known about the site and mechanism of action, although it has been indicated as a stimulant at all levels of the cerebral spinal axis (Esplin and Zablock, 1965). This compound stimulates the parasympathetic nervous system and inhibits cholinesterases, at least peripherally. The behavioural effects of this compound have been very sparingly treated, although the fact that it has been shown to interact with central nervous system depressants, particularly barbiturates, represents one area of interest for behavioural studies. Although nikethamide is only a weak antagonist of barbiturates, it may lead to convulsions in the absence of full arousal under even light barbiturate anaesthesia. The initial excitation is followed by prolonged anaesthesia. A lethal dose of nikethamide is increased in a similar regard by small amounts of barbiturates. There are, in view of these interactions, several areas of interest in behavioural studies where further exploration is indicated.

4. PENTYLENETETRAZOL

Pentylenetetrazol appears to act in the entire nervous system from the brain stem to the cortex, although some localisation of its convulsive action has been attempted. Because of the considerations involving interactions between the cerebral cortex and subcortical sites, the primary site of action of pentylenetetrazol cannot be solely attributed to the cortical changes it leads to. Cortical stimulation by this compound leads to subsequent spread of anterior horn cells by way of the pyramidal tract, and then to subcortical structures. Extrapyramidal motor nuclei and the thalamus are involved, with lesser involvement of the diffuse projection system. The suggestion has been made that the excitatory effect of this compound may be due to a decrease in neuronal recovery time (Eyzaguirre and Lilienthal, 1949). The relative refractory period of nerve was shortened by large doses of pentylenetetrazol, and repetitive discharge occurred. Stimulation of excitatory and inhibitory neurons by this compound has been suggested (Lewin and Esplin, 1961) on the ground that seizures result from excitation of cerebral structures relatively unopposed by inhibition.

Pentylenetetrazol has a history of use in neurological and psychiatric practice; it has been used as a substitute for electroconvulsive therapy, but in this respect appeared to be somewhat less effective, with additional unwanted side effects. It has been used as a diagnostic aid in epilepsy, where, as an EEG activator, it can sometimes stimulate latent epileptogenic foci. Subconvulsive doses of pentylenetetrazol have been recommended for use in cases presenting signs of senility (Goodhart and Helenore, 1963), as a means of increasing alertness, regularising sleep and eating habits, and improving sociability. Some studies have indicated that disorientation, confusion, and memory disorders in geriatric patients diagnosed as psychotic, with cerebral arteriosclerosis or associated chronic brain syndrome, may benefit by pentylenetetrazol treatment (Wolff, 1962). There is some question whether well-controlled studies demonstrate that the use of pentylenetetrazol in a geriatric population exerts positive effects in a significant direction.

There has been some indication in animal studies that subconvulsive doses of pentylenetetrazol may exert a beneficial effect for various learning conditions. Mice, given pentylenetetrazol (1 to 30 mg/kg, p.o.) showed ease of acquisition of one-trial learning and retention; this was observed when the drug was administered either 30 minutes before or after the training trial. The most striking results in this study were obtained when pentylenetetrazol was given before the trial (Irwin and Benuzzi, 1966). The effects of pretrial pentylenetetrazol treatment (8 to 20 mg/kg) on discrimination learning in rats has been studied (Hunt and Krivanek, 1966); it was found that it reduced responsiveness in both a maze situation or in a bar-pressing situation, but enhanced the ability to learning both successive and simultaneous discriminations. The effect of pentylenetetrazol appeared dose-dependent in that the effect increased as dosage increased, and it was suggested that the drug may act by expanding the range of stimulus situation cues to which the animal will respond at any given time. In rats trained to lever press for water reinforcement, treatment with pentylenetetrazol for 5 to 7 weeks (10 to 40 mg/kg) led to differential effects. At 10 mg/kg there was a slight reduction in initial response rates; at 20 mg/kg there was a significant reduction in initial response rates during the first two periods of fixed-ratio and fixed interval responding; there was no significant effect with 30 mg/kg; and, at 40 mg/kg there was complete disruption of fixed-ratio and fixed-interval responding in excess of one hour (Kahan, 1966). These findings indicate that the effects of chronic pentylenetetrazol treatment may affect different response systems in an adverse rather than a positive manner, and perhaps the nature of the motivational stimuli (positive versus negative reinforcement) or the situational cues (visual, somatosensory, etc.) constitute relevant determinants of the direction of the pentylenetetrazol effect. The effect of post-trial injections of pentylenetetrazol was investigated in rats given a brightness discrimination task. The drug was given after trials for a black-white discrimination in a Y-maze (20 mg/kg, i.p.). Pentylenetetrazol treatment resulted in better performance than controls, although, as demonstrated in the previous study, there was some reduction in maze running time (Krivanek and Hunt, 1967). The authors interpret their findings in terms of a direct drug effect on the central nervous system, and their finding of decreased running speed, induced by this agent, appears to be a good point in favour of the argument that the result cannot clearly be explained in terms of improvement in performance alone.

Mice, studied in an actophotometer and treated with pentylenetetrazol, were shown to maintain levels of motor activity (exploratory behaviour) which, in control animals, decreases following a brief exposure to such apparatus (Greenblatt and Osterberg, 1961). This finding may possibly argue in favour of an antifatigue effect of this compound in subconvulsive doses or, again, perhaps may indicate that enhanced responsiveness to available sensory cues may be stimulated by the action of this drug.

5. PICROTOXIN

In unanaesthetised animals and man it appears that this CNS stimulant exerts little overt effect until doses approximating convulsive levels are reached, although it has been indicated that respiration is stimulated with subconvulsive doses (Modell, 1966). The drug, generally, may be considered as a brainstem stimulant. However, generally, it seems to stimulate the central nervous system at all levels. It is capable of blocking presynaptic inhibition (Eccles et al., 1963) and it has been suggested that this effect may be related to the role of gamma amino butyric acid (Esplin and Zablocka, 1965).

Motor activity, as measured by the co-ordinated running and walking in mice, was shown to remain unaffected at several doses of picrotoxin (Dews, 1953). The post-trial injection of picrotoxin in rats treated to acquire a maze response has been shown to better responses (Breen and McGaugh, 1961). A 14 unit T-maze was used with rats that were descendants of Tryon 'maze dull' and 'maze bright' sublines. Injections at three dose levels (0·75, 1·0, and 1·25 mg/kg) were given 30 seconds following a food-reinforced trial. Initial errors in the maze

acquisition behaviour of these animals indicated that medium and high doses improved acquisition in the 'maze dull' animals but the 'bright' rats showed no improvement. The degree to which picrotoxin was helpful in maze running appeared dependent on dosage and strain, and the effect as seen with post-trial administration obviates motivational or performance variables with which this stimulant might possibly interact.

6. STRYCHNINE

This central nervous system stimulant appears to act principally on synapses of the spinal cord, possibly blocking inhibitory substance at that site which mediates such transmission; thereby afferent input becomes capable of discharging motor neurons. Voluntary muscles do not seem to be directly involved with the action of this drug whereas vasomotor centres of the medulla and spinal cord are stimulated. Strychnine depresses the activity of postsynaptic inhibitory synapses and has also been shown to inhibit cholinesterase in vitro (Nachmansohn, 1938).

Subconvulsive doses of strychnine administered to mice did not lead to any increase in locomotor activity at several doses (Dews, 1953). As early as 1917, Lashley indicated that strychnine sulphate was capable of improving maze acquisition in rats. Several more recent studies have indicated that central nervous system stimulation by such agents as strychnine becomes capable of enhancing perseverating neural activity which, in turn, allows for an increase in the degree of consolidation. The effects of low and high doses of strychnine sulphate were studied in rats trained on a food-reinforced multiple unit maze, and for a certain portion of the acquisition period rats were given strychnine injections at the two-dose level ten minutes before the trials began. It was generally concluded that low doses of strychnine (0·33 mg/cc) were capable of making maze acquisition by some animals easier, and high doses (1·00 mg/cc) could similarly disrupt maze learning by other animals (McGaugh, 1961). The effects of strychnine on rats given massed training trials for a simultaneous visual discrimination involving black-white and pattern discrimination for shock avoidance resulted in reduced errors and trials to standards involved in such maze learning (McGaugh and Thompson, 1962). The effects of variations in the training-drug injection interval on the degree of helpfulness brought about by strychnine in rats was considered in another study (McGaugh et al., 1962), where it was concluded that strychnine sulphate treatment improved aptitude for as long as 15 minutes after training. The degree of facilitation was an approximate equivalent for injection given both before as well as after training; however, sex and strain seemed to constitute relevant variables in this investigation. The visual successive discrimination problem was used with rats given strychnine sulphate (1 mg/kg) ten minutes prior to training trials. Such treatment in both 'maze bright' and 'maze dull' subline strains resulted in significantly more rapid learning as measured by number of trials to criterion. There was some indication that a number of 'poor learners' required more time to reach criterion than did controls, possibly because of repetitive errors (Petrinovich, 1963).

The view that more efficient consolidation of the memory trace occurs when strychnine injections are given a few seconds or a few minutes following a task rests basically on the assumption that this drug is rapidly destroyed by the body and does not remain to affect subsequent performance or training; should it remain, the effect might be expected to affect performance rather than an already consolidated memory trace. Hooded female rats were given strychnine sulphate (1·25 mg/kg, i.p.) either 24 hours or 72 hours before testing in a shock maze to which there was previous adaptation; as compared with two control groups, the strychnine-treated animals made fewer maze errors, and this could be attributable to its performance effects persisting for as long as three days (Cooper and Krass, 1963). Such experimental evidence as that indicating persistent performance effects of strychnine represent a major criticism of its possible facilitating effects. The post-trial administration of strychnine as employed in several studies, meets any possible objection to its sensory, sensorimotor, or motivational effects during actual training. In a study with female Sprague-Dawley rats in a Lashley III alley maze with water-reinforcement, strychnine sulphate (1 mg/kg, i.p.) was given either two days prior to training, immediately following training, or two days prior to five retention trials which followed two training trials (Greenough and McGaugh, 1965). It was predicted that drug treatment immediately following training would lead to the best results if the drug selectively aided the memory consolidation process, and not performance; the data indicated that there were no differences between treatment conditions as far as error incidence was concerned on the two training trials and the five criterion trials. This experiment, therefore, does not actually support the view that strychnine sulphate enhances the process by which memory consolidation takes place nor does it clearly support the view that the effects of strychnine may be attributable to the persistent performance change that such treatment may modulate.

Another view has been that the effects of strychnine on learning may be based on a reduction in activity. The effects of strychnine on home cage activity and oxygen consumption were measured and in some of the measures, including crossing, rearing, hanging, grooming, and digging, there was a linear reduction in such activity with increased dosage. Oxygen consumption did not decrease as a function of dosage but, in fact, increased in two of the three strains that were studied. It was concluded (Calhoun, 1965) that the reduction in activity resulting from strychnine treatment probably does not represent the necessary condition for determining the effects of this drug on learning.

Utilising negative reinforcement, male Wistar albino rats were studied in a situation in which lever-pressing behaviour was required to avoid shock, the onset of which was signalled by a buzzer. The acquisition of avoidance behaviour in this situation was measured by latency and the number of avoidance responses. Conditioned avoidance was significantly enhanced in rats given 1 mg/kg of strychnine sulphate whereas at a lower dose (0·5 mg/kg) avoidance behaviour did not differ from that of saline-treated controls (Gibby et al., 1965).

An alternation problem was used to study the effects of strychnine in rats genetically selected on the basis of low acetylcholinesterase activity in the cerebral cortex. Successive alternation of sides of a single unit T-maze were reinforced with water, and strychnine treatment (1 mg/kg, i.p.) was given each day after the first or second of four trials. Significantly better performance was observed in the drug-treated animals on these trials following injection (Petrinovich et al., 1965). The strain of animal used in this type of study and the dose of strychnine administered appear to be important considerations in the outcome of such studies. For example, no improvement of maze learning has been reported with hooded rats given doses of 0·75 or 1 mg/kg of strychnine (Prien et al., 1963). With Long-Evans hooded rats, strychnine sulphate (1 mg/kg) did not lead to any improvement of mass learning (Louttit, 1965). Although these strains differ from the descendants of the Tryon strains, in which other investigators have reported a positive enhancing effect of strychnine sulphate, the dose used was comparable to that in which improvements have been reported. Some evidence for improved performance in Long-Evans hooded rats has been provided (Petrinovich, 1967) although indications are that for benefit to occur, the dose must be considerably lower (0·125 mg/kg) than that employed with the Tryon strains. At a higher dose in the Long-Evans rats (1·75 mg/kg) significantly more efforts were made in a multiple unit Lashley III maze using food-reinforcement.

The effects of post-trial injections of strychnine have been studied in rats trained on a brightness discrimination task with food-reinforcement in a Y-maze. Strychnine sulphate (0·33 mg/kg, i.p.) was administered after trials and the drug-treated animals differed significantly from saline controls in terms of incidence of errors and trials required to reach criterion. These data have also been interpreted in support of a drug-induced improvement of central nervous system processes rather than to a performance effect (Krivanek and Hunt, 1967).

One of the problems raised by studies that have indicated that strychnine is capable of improving learning or enhancing the processes by which the neural memory trace is consolidated, is that no firm groundwork has been laid to provide the framework within which the central effects of strychnine can be reconciled with such behavioural improvements. One possible approach to this problem has been made in studies in which doses of strychnine sulphate comparable to those shown to improve learning ability and/or consolidation have also led to increases in brain levels of ribonucleic acid (RNA) (Carlini and Carlini, 1965). This study, in which still another strain of rat—the Wistar—was used, indicated that six daily i.p. injections led to a significantly higher level of whole brain RNA. This 27 per cent increase in whole-brain RNA has been offered in support of the hypothesis that strychnine may improve learning through some influence with RNA activity, possibly as a result of an increased neural activity resulting from strychnine. The problem in such an argument is that not all drugs that increase or decrease whole-brain RNA level necessarily correlate with increases or decreases in learning ability or efficiency.

The generalisation that informational capacity occurring on a molecular level becomes grossly applicable to the results of generalised central nervous system stimulation on which a measure encompassing the whole brain is based, must be approached with some degree of caution.

7. XANTHINES

The xanthines are a group of alkaloids possessing central nervous stimulant properties that have, except for a few members of this class of drug, been limited in their application in behavioural study. Although this class of compound has strong effects on cellular metabolism, such studies have not been extensively conducted in the central nervous system, but have been largely confined to muscle. Most of the compounds exert respiratory stimulant effects, which are probably central in origin.

(a) *Caffeine.* This compound appears to be the most active of the xanthine group, both in terms of its CNS effect and its respiratory stimulant properties. It has been shown to increase locomotor activity in mice (Dews, 1953), although in rats, initially high locomotor activity rates were not increased by the drug to a significant degree (Greenblatt and Osterberg, 1961). The behaviour of Siamese fighting fish (*Betta splendens* Regan) was stimulated with caffeine (Ketusinh *et al.*, 1962). The sensitivity to caffeine toxicity has been shown to increase with age, males being more susceptible than females. Increases in caffeine toxicity has resulted from starvation, pneumonia, diabetes, and elevated environmental temperature, and toxicity can be potentiated by iproniazid and meprobamate. In isolated rats, caffeine treatment resulted in self-aggressive behaviour, whereas in group-housed rats, aggressive behaviour was directed toward other animals within the group. The formation of gastric ulcers can also be aggravated by caffeine (Peters, 1967).

An inhibition of chains of alimentary reflexes in dogs was produced by caffeine administration (Voronin and Napalkov, 1963), and it was also shown to impair 'negative' conditional reflexes in dogs, while enhancing 'positive' conditional reflexes; this was interpreted as a decrease in 'internal inhibition' (Pavlov, 1927). Intramuscular administration of caffeine (16 mg/kg) in dogs resulted in a decreased latency of conditioned responses, an increase in the effect of reinforced stimuli, and a decrease in the effect of non-reinforced stimuli (Wolff and Gantt, 1935).

One obvious point regarding the behavioural effect of this stimulant is the extent to which it may be active in attenuating fatigue or in enhancing motor performance. Small doses of caffeine were shown to affect swimming endurance of mice only slightly (Von Nieschulz, 1963). The oral administration of caffeine (4 mg/kg) to mice resulted in a stimulant effect, with maximum stimulation in doses of from 8 to 32 mg/kg. Exploratory activity was decreased, as a function of dose, within this range; however, at a considerably higher dose (128 mg/kg) exploratory activity was increased (Boissier and Simon, 1967). The drug has been credited with learning enhancement properties in several studies in which its performance for antifatigue effects were not considered to play a major role. In rats, trained in a food approach-shock avoidance situation, the running speed of the animals was studied and, under shock-escape conditions, this running speed was increased (Barry and Miller, 1965). Isolated rats, which did not initially show an escape response from auditory stress, showed enhanced auditory escape behaviour following caffeine administration

(Pletnikoff, 1962). In rats, trained to suppress reinforcement, caffeine treatment increased the level of performance, and it was noted that these effects were more pronounced in animals with poorer learning results (Tonini, 1961). The post-training effects of caffeine were considered to improve avoidance behaviour, conditioned to a black-white and horizontal-vertical discrimination (Pare, 1961). Rats were trained with massed trials to criterion, and five seconds after reaching criterion, were given caffeine injections (30 mg/kg). Similar injections were given at two minutes or one hour after reaching criterion, and retention testing was carried out two days after injection. Those animals treated with caffeine five seconds after reaching criterion showed reduced errors on the retention trials and the magnitude of errors was positively related to the acquisition criterion-caffeine injection interval. In an approach avoidance conflict situation, caffeine (20 to 40 mg/kg) reduced approach performance, and it was assumed, on this basis, that the stimulant effects of this compound could be counteracted by reduced approach motivation (Barry and Miller, 1962).

The effects of caffeine on human performance have been studied in a variety of ways, and it has been generally concluded that the drug is capable of mobilising intellectual resources (Nash, 1962). In so far as performance is concerned, caffeine (500 mg), given intravenously during a rest period following cycling to exhaustion, significantly increased work output during a second cycling period (Foltz et al., 1942). Subjective signs of fatigue were attenuated by caffeine (450 mg) given to subjects required to participate in an all-day hiking excursion (Seashore and Ivy, 1953). Motor tests, involving co-ordination, also showed improvements under these conditions. Studies on the effects of caffeine on motor co-ordination and control were reviewed, with the conclusion that little or no effect results on tasks involving reaction time, and hand steadiness could be impaired. The decrement in performance, produced by alcohol can be counteracted by caffeine, and the rate of finger tapping can be increased (Weiss and Laties, 1962). The administration of caffeine (300 mg), one and a half hours prior to testing subjects on tasks of tracking, manual dexterity, Whipple steadiness, nonsense syllables, and arithmetic sums, in a double-blind design, was shown to result in an increase of muscle tension, and when caffeine was combined with meprobamate, to reduce the muscle tension, performance was improved (Wenzel and Davis, 1961).

In another study, a double-blind design was used to determine the effects of caffeine (500 mg) on test performance interrupted by delayed audio-feedback stress. In a colour discrimination test, performance was improved by caffeine (Forney and Hughs, 1965). In doses of 150 and 200 mg caffeine was shown to counteract a performance decrement caused by fatigue or sleep deprivation. This was evaluated on the basis of tests on alertness, psychomotor co-ordination, and mood, as assessed by a self-rating inventory. Whereas objectively measured performance was not demonstrably affected by caffeine, feelings of alertness and physical activity were enhanced in some subjects, with a further indication that the threshold for critical flicker fusion was increased (Goldstein et al., 1965). Doses of 100 to 300 mg of caffeine reduced the time-related decrement associated with tasks including tapping rate, visual reaction time, and tracking; fatigue was apparently mitigated by a revision of the initial performance level. The effect of caffeine was related to possible stimulation of the reticular system in a study in which human subjects were given caffeine 15 minutes prior to testing for judgements of brightness of a test circle surrounded by an annulus, the luminance of which was less than the test patch. In caffeine-treated subjects, there was an elimination of the enhancement of test circle brightness produced under these conditions (Kleman, 1961).

There has been some indication that there are wide individual differences in sensitivity to the central effects of caffeine. In a placebo-controlled, double-blind study, subjects were given de-caffeinated coffee, with and without caffeine added (150 mg) one hour prior to bed-time. For some individuals there was a significant delay in the onset of sleep. However, it was noted that heavy coffee drinkers reacted with appreciably less frequency to such delays. The plasma levels of caffeine were similar for all individuals, indicating that the absorption of the drug was comparable, regardless of whether sleep onset was delayed or not (Goldstein and Warren, 1961). Findings such as these suggest that the central effects of caffeine may be subject to individual variability, perhaps on the basis of previous adaptation to baseline levels of stimulation provided by continued use of this drug.

The use of caffeine, as an adjunct to pharmacotherapy, has been made in only a few studies. In one study the combined use of caffeine with amobarbital in the treatment of 2,905 psychiatric patients, over a 10-year period, resulted in remission in 96·9 per cent, with no improvement shown in 3·1 per cent (Yagodka et al., 1965). In combined treatment with 55·91 per cent acetyltryptophamate, 44·09 per cent of caffeine was given over a 3 to 9 month period to 80 psychiatric in-patients and out-patients with diverse diagnoses. Chronic schizophrenics showed an increased efficiency in performance on psychomotor tasks, and 19 out of 29 schizophrenic patients showed marked to very good improvement (Sivadon *et al.*, 1965). In combination with 0·25 to 1·5 g of glutamic acid, caffeine was shown to be effective in the treatment of aphasic and asthenic children. Vocabularies were increased under these conditions, and the incidence of reported headache was decreased (Chernonordik, 1964). Unfortunately, it is difficult to assess the independent contributions of caffeine as a psychotherapeutic agent, and it is, further, difficult to separate the therapeutic effects of the compound from the many other complex variables that apparently make a significant contribution in uncontrolled studies of psychiatric populations.

(b) *Theobromine and Theophylline.* These compounds are weaker central nervous system stimulants and respiratory stimulants than caffeine. To some extent, the compounds are capable of enhancing reflex excitability and acting directly on lower motor centres. There is some indication of a weak pressor effect, and theophylline is an effective bronchodilator and has sometimes been used extensively in the treatment of bronchial asthma. These compounds are only weakly effective in increasing basal metabolic rate. High doses are capable of producing insomnia, restlessness, and excitement, which may sometimes end in mild delirium. At high doses, sensory disturbances such as flashes of light and ringing in the ears may develop. There has been little indication of any behavioural application of these compounds either in animal studies or in man.

(c) *Uric Acid.* Uric acid, as the only member of the xanthene family that is endogenous to animals and man, has been considered as a central nervous system stimulant (Orowan, 1955; Ritchie, 1965). There has been some suggestion that uric acid serves to maintain a high level of cognitive and intellectual functions (Orowan, 1955), and that it may be related to intelligence test performance (Stetten and Heron, 1959). It appears to be well correlated with achievement (Brooks and Mueller, 1966). The endogenous effects of this compound may possibly implement performance variables rather than cognitive or intellectual ability in as much as senile and senescent patients did not show appreciably lower serum uric acid level (Kral *et al.*, 1967) and in several patients intellectual impairment attending Down's syndrome, serum uric acid levels were elevated (Coburn *et al.*, 1967).

The effects of uric acid administration studied in a behavioural context have already appeared in a few investigations; some of these (Essman, 1970a) have indicated that in mice, uric acid (0·75 mg/kg) led to significant positive saving scores when animals were trained and tested in a water maze; when endogenous uric acid was partially oxidised by uricase, impairment of maze acquisition, as measured by response latency and errors, was noted. Under the same conditions, mice treated with xanthine (2 or 5 mg/kg, i.p.) had no effect on maze acquisition or reversal of the maze habit. Under parallel conditions, it was shown that uric acid treatment led to an elevation of whole-brain RNA whereas uricase treatment led to a decreased brain RNA level. Whereas the acquisition of a conditioned passive avoidance response was not altered by uric acid treatment in doses ranging from 0·5 to 20 mg/kg, a significant degree of antagonism toward the amnesic effect of electroconvulsive shock was achieved throughout this dose range when mice were given such amnesia-producing treatment 10 seconds following training for acquisition of passive avoidance behaviour. In this same series of studies, it was shown that uric acid, by one hour after its systemic administration in mice, resulted in a reduced synthesis and degradation in brain serotonin and also attenuated the brain serotonin turn-over which is commonly produced by electroshock.

Anecdotal evidence concerning a possible relationship between the elevated serum uric acid levels characterising individuals afflicted with gout and the sometimes high level of intellectual professional achievement has found partial support in historical study. The specific role of endogenous uric acid in behaviour and the behavioural effects of exogenous uric acid remain as a relatively unexplored area of possible interest.

IV. HYPNOTICS, SEDATIVES, AND ANAESTHETICS

A. Barbiturates

The barbiturates represent a class of compounds that has been in clinical use for a considerable period of time. This survey of the experimental literature combines studies in animals and in man in the form of a general overview of the compounds in terms of their behavioural effects. The exhaustive literature on this subject has been reviewed on several prior occasions and will not be repeated here. The barbiturates, in terms of their effects on animals and man are treated in alphabetical sequence, which does not, therefore, imply that any hierarchy of importance should be assigned to one drug over another within this class.

Amobarbital. This compound, which was first

synthesised in 1923, has been shown to exert a blocking effect on acetylcholine in peripheral cholinergic junctions in the superior cervical ganglion of cats. This effect has been interpreted as a reduction in the responsiveness of the post-junctional effector cell (Matthews and Quilliam, 1962). Its neurophysiological effects have been generally studied and, in humans, intracarotid injection of 75 to 200 mg leads to the appearance of slow waves on the side ipsilateral to the injection site. An increase in the average frequency and reduction in rhythmicity occurred on the contralateral side, suggestive of a tendency toward desynchronisation (Barlow et al., 1964). Positive bilateral EEG effects have been observed in human patients with brain pathology when given amobarbital in doses of 0·2 to 0·3 g (Flodmark and Leissner, 1965). The administration of amobarbital sodium to humans with focal epilepsy indicated that blood flow and the effect of the drug were confined to the ipsilateral hemisphere with approximately 35 per cent of the injected dose absorbed into the brain (Iannone and Morrell, 1961). In patients with and without motor disturbances, the injection of amobarbital sodium was shown to impair the perfused hemisphere earlier and more completely (Gilman et al., 1963). An ipsilateral slowing in EEG was shown in patients with brain pathologies given intracarotid amobarbital sodium. However, at doses less than 20 mg no such changes were observed (Tengesdal, 1963). A secondary bilateral synchrony was shown in epileptic patients given intracarotid amobarbital sodium. When such injection was given on the side ipsilateral to the triggering focus, a suppression of discharges on both sides occurred. A slight reduction in amplitude occurred only on the ipsilateral side when the drug was injected on the side contralateral to the triggering focus (Perez-Borja and Rivers, 1963).

A 20 to 50 mg dose of amobarbital in humans is indicated for sedation, and a hypnotic effect achieved with doses from 100 to 300 mg. In humans experiencing anxiety states, side effects of amobarbital treatment have been noted; these have included headache, irritability, and discomfort (McDowell et al., 1966). In normal human subjects, sedation and some clouding of mental capacity has been observed; however, under these conditions it has been noted that the drug effect is sometimes difficult to distinguish from that of a placebo (Hawkins et al., 1961).

The behavioural effects of amobarbital generally are sometimes difficult to assess; for example, in the dog, an intra-arachnoid injection of 50 mg did not generally alter the behavioural status of the animal; however, the animals did manifest a variety of signs, including coughing, sneezing, hiccuping, licking,

vomiting, defecation, and motor ataxia within one hour after an intraventricular injection of the drug at the same dosage. Some effect, under these conditions of drug administration, could be observed for as long as seven hours later when the animals showed a marked reduction in appetite, random wandering, panting, and unusual barking (Kobayashi, 1962). Signs such as these, in the dog, perhaps point to a possible motivational role played by treatment with amobarbital. Male albino Sprague-Dawley rats, tested in a situation for escape, avoidance, and approach, had their running speed affected as a function of amobarbital dosage (Barry and Miller, 1965). A gross decrease in running speed was observed under avoidance conditions; secondarily, under escape conditions; and minimally, under approach conditions. This observation again points to the possible motivational role played by this compound, to the extent that the same response under different motivational stimulus conditions can be affected differentially. Motivational factors in a social situation has also been demonstrated in rats (Chance and Silverman, 1964) where a dose of 5 mg/kg reduced social exploration, mating responses, and submissive behaviour, and also led to reduced escape behaviour; under these same conditions, an increase in aggressive behaviour was noted following the drug administration. Hoarding behaviour has been measured in rats (Torres, 1964), and amobarbital sodium exerted a differential effect, depending on whether these animals were judged to be shy or non-shy. Hoarding behaviour in shy rats was increased by drug treatment, whereas in the more aggressive animal there was no effect upon hoarding. Improved performance was shown in rats given amobarbital sodium (20 mg/kg) in order to reduce fear; however, when this effect was assessed in a non-drug state, there was no transfer (Miller, 1961). This observation points to the possible state-dependent effect of this compound on motivational conditions. Where reinforcement incidence was varied, rats receiving 100 per cent reinforcement showed a greater increase in running time as a result of amobarbital sodium treatment (20 mg/kg) than animals having received 50 per cent reinforcement (Wagner, 1963).

The motivational component relating to amobarbital effects in man is difficult to assess; some investigators (Hawkins et al., 1961) have observed that in normal human subjects there was little change in mood, and a t.i.d. dose of 60 mg in out-patients was minimally effective in reduction of anxiety (McDowell et al., 1966). Similarly, amobarbital has been shown to be no more effective than a placebo in the reduction of anxiety of outpatients (Black, 1966). When amobarbital (1 g) was combined with trifluoperazine (1 g) a greater reduction in anxiety in human psychoneurotic outpatients was achieved than was noted with amobarbital alone (May, 1961). No significant improvement with a 65 mg (t.i.d.) dose of amobarbital was achieved in human patients characterised by anxiety and depression (Wing and Lader, 1965), whereas psychosomatic symptoms have been shown to disappear more rapidly, and an attenuation of depressive mood has been achieved in patients given an i.v. injection of amobarbital sodium (Kraines, 1965). An increase in the capacity to evoke emotional responses in schizophrenic patients, given amobarbital sodium, was observed, whereas under non-drug conditions these responses could not be elicited (Bazin, 1964).

The effects of amobarbital on learning and performance has been studied in animals, and noteworthy in this regard is a study in which pigeons, trained to peck a key on a positive reinforcement schedule, were given amobarbital in a dose range of 6 to 60 mg/kg, i.m. The rate of key-pecking response appeared to be dependent on key-pecking behaviour in the absence of the drug, and the effects of an inhibitory stimulus was not clearly affected by amobarbital treatment (Dews, 1964). With amobarbital sodium, chronic administration in varying doses to dogs in a conditioning situation led to an increase in internal inhibition with small doses, whereas larger doses weakened internal inhibition (Sofronod and Tsovkallo, 1964). In oral doses of 0·1 g and 0·3 g, positive conditioned reflexes were reduced and rather pronounced fluctuations in these conditioned reflexes were observed (Guseva, 1964). When male albino rats were trained in a conflict situation, either under amobarbital sodium or placebo, an increase in the approach performance was achieved when these animals were given 20 mg/kg, i.p.; this increase was independent of conflict training drug conditions (Barry et al., 1962). The decreases noted in running speeds, which characterise the extinction of a response, were further attenuated in female albino rats given 15 mg/kg of amobarbital sodium (Stretch et al., 1964). In albino Sprague-Dawley rats, the effects on the startle response were shown to be dose-dependent (Chi, 1965), while the intensity of a visual stimulus, used with male albino Wistar rats, differentially affected a performance increment resulting from amobarbital sodium treatment (20 mg/kg, i.p.) (Powell et al., 1966). A dose-dependent increment in learning was shown to result from amobarbital sodium treatment in Abrams Wistar albino rats; however, a learning decrement was noted at higher doses (Kamano et al., 1966). In another study, using the same strain of rats, amobarbital sodium (20 mg/kg, i.p.) did not affect the

acquisition of a conditioned emotional response; however, CAR acquisition rate was significantly increased (Kamano et al., 1966).

In human subjects, reaction time to visual stimuli, tapping speed, hand coordination, and standing steadiness, were all affected by amobarbital treatment. At a dose of 150 mg, impairment was apparent; however, at a dose of 300 mg, improved performance was noted. When the dose was increased to 450 mg, impairment again occurred (Idestron and Cadenius, 1963). In normal subjects given amobarbital, increase in reaction time to a light onset, by removal of the finger from a button, was increased.

Perceptual studies, involving amobarbital, have indicated that several diverse capacities can be impaired with a 150 mg dosage. This deficit was noted in critical flicker fusion, counting behaviour, and tone discrimination (Idestron and Cadenius, 1963). The impairment of critical flicker fusion thresholds was impaired with 100 mg of amobarbital; however, the degree of impairment was appreciably reduced when the amobarbital was combined with 15 mg of dexamphetamine sulphate (Turner, 1965). In pre-morbid neurasthenic subjects, an increase in imagery was observed following a 200 mg dose of amobarbital (Pervov, 1965). When thought disorder scores were compared in normal subjects receiving 200 mg of amobarbital and non-drug-treated controls, there was no significant emerging difference (Beach et al., 1961). No significant effect of amobarbital sodium was noted in either schizophrenic or normal subjects for Gorham's Proverbs Test and Serial Sevens Task (Cohen et al., 1962).

Barbital. This compound was first introduced for clinical use in 1903 and, primarily because of its sedative and hypnotic effects of long duration, it has not been extensively studied on a behavioural level in either animals or man. Since side effects are not infrequent with average doses (i.e. fever, dermatitis, prolonged depression, etc.), and prolonged ingestion of even average dosages can lead to severe behavioural and neurological conditions, and withdrawal, after prolonged use, can lead to an abstinence syndrome which includes convulsions, this compound does not represent an ideal choice for behavioural investigation. Sodium barbital induces narcosis in rats, which appears to be a direct function of the rate at which this compound accumulates in the brain (Markova, 1961), and the rate of such accumulation in rats appears to be age-dependent, in as much as younger rats showed a greater rate of sodium barbital accumulation. A suggested site of action of this compound has been the reticular area of the brain stem leading to consequent cortical involvement, and this possibly might account for the withdrawal seizures noted for this drug (Essig and

Flanary, 1961). In cats given 40 to 200 mg/kg s.c. or i.m. of sodium barbital, chronic changes, characterised by lower excitability, were more apparent than were such excitability alterations in the subcortical areas; a reduction in excitability was initially noted in the motor and visual cortex (Fan, 1965).

The increase in excitability of the central nervous system, following withdrawal of barbital sodium, appears to be linked to adrenocortical hyperactivity. In female Wistar albino rats, the levels of adrenal ascorbic acid during habituation showed marked rises after sodium barbital treatment (Leonard, 1966b). In female Wistar albino rats chronically treated with sodium barbital, an appreciable increase in brain ammonia and lactate was observed in some substrains during habituation, whereas in other strains the elevation of brain ammonia occurred in the absence of any lactate changes; in all substrains treated chronically with sodium barbital, a decrease in ATP and creatine phosphate was observed (Leonard, 1966a).

Cyclobarbital. This compound, which has a short duration of hypnotic and sedative action, has been shown to initiate alpha activation in EEG, and reduce both amplitude and frequency (150 mg), whereas at the same dosage, sleep is induced when given i.v. to human patients; the duration of such sleep was markedly potentiated when cyclobarbital was combined with 40 mg of prothitendyl (Itil, 1962). A side effect of such combined treatment also seemed to be abolished (Itil, 1963).

In psychotic patients with acute psychomotor agitation, the combination of cyclobarbital and prothitendyl resulted in relief of these symptoms and alleviation of symptomology in reactive depressive neurasthenic and psychotic patients without any evidence of side effects (Quandt, 1961).

In normal human subjects, arithmetic and memory tests showed impairment following administration of 360 mg of cyclobarbital (Smith and Sullivan, 1965). Impaired performance, as a function of dosage for a combination of cyclobarbital and amphetamines, was noted in normal human subjects performing a disc-dotting task and series of arithmetic tests (Dickens *et al.*, 1965). 300 mg of cyclobarbital served to impair arithmetic performance and motor co-ordination in normal human subjects. A combination of cyclobarbital with amphetamines appeared to increase the production of elation and haziness in normal subjects (Editorial, *Brit. med. J.*, 1962).

Heptabarbital. This barbiturate, which exerts a short duration sedative and hypnotic effect, has been shown to lead to approximately the same incidence of confusional states and sedative effect as does butobarbital, when given to human patients (Tweedy, 1962), in a dose of 400 mg. The same dosage given to a population of depressed patients and normal controls exerted a marked effect on the duration of periods of rapid eye movement during sleep and the frequency of eye movements during these intervals. The wakening time periods were also decreased (Oswald *et al.*, 1963).

Hexobarbital. This barbiturate, possessing a hypnotic and sedative effect of short duration, has been shown to result in a dose-dependent reduction on the frequency of discharge in neurons of visual cortex, particularly in intervals between 10 to 100 msec, when given to cats in doses of 2 to 10 mg/kg (Herz and Fuster, 1964). When doses of hexobarbital were given in two successive 50 mg/kg doses, rather than a single 100 mg/kg dose daily, to rats, a decrease was noted in the duration of narcosis. Under these conditions, tolerance was developed more rapidly in male mice and rats than in females (Remmer, 1964). Apparently, in rodents, hexobarbital is subject to rapid oxidation, so that the catabolising enzyme system is not stimulated, whereas with a slower rate of oxidation, activity of the enzyme system is called on; this latter situation is apparent in dogs. Female dogs, treated with phenobarbital, where oxidation rate is accelerated, leads to a more rapid elimination of hexobarbital (Remmer and Siegert, 1964). A temperature-dependent relationship has been demonstrated for the uptake of hexobarbital, and the sleeping time resulting in mice given 100 to 196 mg/kg (Winne, 1964). At 21 °C, brain concentration of hexobarbital was lower, and sleeping time was longer than when comparable doses of this barbiturate was administered at 37 °C. A drop in body temperature resulted when the drug was given to mice at room temperature, and under conditions where animals were pre-treated with chlorpromazine, hexobarbital sleeping time was increased and the brain concentration was lowered.

Pentobarbital. Pentobarbital has been more extensively studied than most of the barbiturates discussed above, and brain mechanisms affected probably include the reticular formation which regulates recovery with a depression of thalamic relay nuclei occurring at higher doses (Schwartz *et al.*, 1962). In cats, a reduction of the hypothalamic effects of spinal cord reflexes was observed with moderate pentobarbital anaesthesia and peripherally-evoked hypothalamic potentials disappeared. With deepened anaesthesia, the hypothalamic facilitation of monosynaptic reflexes was abolished, and there was little or no effect on persistent polysynaptic responses with hypothalamic stimulation (Feldman and Wagman, 1962). Intravenous administration of 1 to 35 mg/kg of pentobarbital sodium to cats exerted a dose-dependent reaction. In an awake preparation there was an increased amplitude of fast activity in the cortex, and a slight increase in slow wave amplitude in a sleeping preparation (Bradley and Nicholson, 1962).

Pentobarbital, given to rhesus monkeys (5 mg/kg) resulted in marked fluctuations in the intensity of painful stimulation that was tolerated (Weitzman and Rose, 1962). With very deep narcosis produced by a 60 mg/kg pentobarbital sodium dose, vestibular eye reflexes were suppressed (Jongkees, 1961).

Learning has been considered in several studies using pentobarbital; for example, under pentobarbital anaesthesia diffuse motor conditioned reflexes, involving various parts of the body, including the forelegs, were developed in dogs. The latency of such responses were long and somewhat variable (Teitelbaum et al., 1961). Lever pressing to reduce painful stimulation was abolished when sufficient doses of pentobarbital were administered to rhesus monkeys (Malis, 1962). When pentobarbital sodium (13 mg/kg) was given to male albino rats, the CAR established was the same as that resulting in control animals. With this continuance of the barbiturate treatment in animals that had acquired the response while under the influence of the drug, a sharp fall in the percentage of CARs resulted when the response was explored in the absence of reinforcement. Following re-learning, in the absence of pentobarbital sodium, the CAR became independent of the presence or absence of the drug (Holmgren and Condi, 1964). A response, relearned by rats given 25 mg/kg of pentobarbital sodium, was not transferred to the non-drugged state, whereas re-learning under the non-drug state was similarly not transferred to the drug state (Overton, 1964). In pigeons, trained to press a colour-illuminated response key, a considerable initial decrement in accuracy was observed following administration of pentobarbital sodium (5 or 10 mg/kg); however, relatively fast recovery of response accuracy to normal levels occurred thereafter (Berryman et al., 1962).

In human subjects it has been implied that pentobarbital probably interferes with the ability to attend maximally in a response task. Normal subjects, given 100 mg per 150 lb of body weight, i.v., of pentobarbital, showed a reduced span on the Running Memory Span Test, although no difference between drug- and control-treated subjects emerged on the Stropp Test (Quarton and Talland, 1962). Normal males, given pentobarbital (100 mg/68 kg, i.v.), showed impaired organisation, rehearsal, and other strategies by which information storage was accomplished and by which it was usually made subsequently available for recall (Talland and Quarton, 1965).

Phenobarbital. This barbiturate, which was the second of this series to be introduced in 1912, has sedative, hypnotic, and anticonvulsive effects of long duration. Its central effects have been explored in several respects. In cats, a 10 to 30 mg/kg, i.v., dose of phenobarbital resulted in high voltage, slow waves in the EEG, recorded in the sensory area and also in the thalamus; multiple spikes occurred in the amygdala, and low voltage fast activity was observed in the hippocampus (Kido and Yamamoto, 1961). Relatively high doses of phenobarbital (45 mg/kg) given to rats resulted in a slight tendency toward habituation to arousal in response to shock (Kelemen et al., 1961). In mice, phenobarbital has been shown to depress motor activity and the thermoregulatory centres (Heim and Estler, 1961).

Behavioural effects of phenobarbital have been observed where, for example, rats trained to press a disc or lever for food reinforcement showed increased response rates as a result of phenobarbital treatment (Kelleher et al., 1961). In a task requiring schizophrenic patients to become conditioned in a verbal situation of the Taffel-type, wherein the emission of words was verbally reinforced by the experimenter, a statistically significant degree of facilitation of such conditioning was achieved by phenobarbital over other drug conditions in which triflupromazine and fluphenazine were used (Vestre, 1965).

Secobarbital. This barbiturate, resulting in short duration hypnotic action, sometimes has associated side effects, including drowsiness, dizziness, or headache, but appears effective in inducing sleep.

In man, the subjective effects of secobarbital (50 mg/70 kg), although it is capable of impairing performance on objective tests, appears minimal as compared with amphetamines (Smith et al., 1963). In tasks where sustained attention is required by experimenter-paced tests, secobarbital (100 to 200 mg) in normal subjects resulted in little performance decrement, but caused a considerably greater decrement in tasks not dependent on sustained attention (Kornetsky and Orzack, 1964).

In male schizophrenic patients, tested for sustained attention, response latency, psychomotor output, and cognition, sustained attention was affected to a greater degree by chlorpromazine than by secobarbital, whereas on the other tasks, the barbiturate did exert effects (Latz, 1963).

Thiopental. This sedative of ultra-short duration of action has sometimes been used in psychiatric practice for narcosynthesis, and i.v. injections of thiopental sodium up to 300 mg in schizophrenic patients resulted in increase in EEG activity, particularly in the beta range (Sila *et al.*, 1962). Doses of 6 mg/kg of thiopental have been shown to exert a beneficial influence on central nystagmus (Jongkees, 1961). Average sleep threshold in depressed female patients was differentially affected with i.v. administration of 0·5 mg/kg of thiopental. In those patients with endogenous depression, the average sleep threshold was significantly lowered, as compared with patients with psychogenic depression (Bojanovsky, 1965).

The barbiturates, generally, because of differences in both the onset and duration of their central action, hold some potential as tools for the investigation of a number of varying behaviours in animals and man. The central effects of barbiturates would appear to warrant their use, particularly for comparative purposes, in behavioural studies in which psychoactive drugs, exerting similar central neurophysiological or metabolic effects, are employed.

B. Sedatives

Bromides. Bromide was first discovered in 1826, although its effect on the central nervous system was not observed until some time later. Its initial and still common use has been in the treatment of epilepsy and, generally, for use as a central nervous system depressant. The depression attending administration of bromine salts has been recognised as due to the bromide ion and the particular cation with which it is associated and does not appear to alter its depressant action. There have been a few experiments investigating the physiological correlates of bromide. It has been shown that during bromide intoxication fast activity in the EEG may occur when blood bromide levels are low, although diffuse slow activity has been linked to high blood level (Greenblatt *et al.*, 1945).

Behavioural studies with bromide are small in number, although some investigations have appeared. In dogs with excited forms of 'experimental neurosis', where there was an absence of the ability to differentiate between positive and negative conditional stimuli, such that these animals responded with salivary secretion to all stimuli, potassium bromide (2 g daily) was given (Pavlov, 1927, 1941), and it was observed under these conditions that there was a restoration of negative conditional reflexes without impairment of positive conditional reflexes. It was therefore concluded that 'bromides should not be regarded as sedatives diminishing the excitability of the CNS; they simply regulate the activity of the nervous system by strengthening the intensity of internal inhibition' (Pavlov, 1927). Similar results were also obtained in normal dogs (Wolff and Gantt, 1935). In 'neurotic sheep', a single dose of 2·5 g of sodium bromide diminished 'internal restlessness' without impairment of positive motor conditional reflexes (Anderson and Paramenter, 1941). Doses of 0·018 to 0·036 g of sodium bromide, s.c., given to rats, produced a slight and variable effect on lever pressing under a periodic food reinforcement schedule. It is possible that, because of a reduction in interest in bromides, few additional studies concerned with its behavioural effects have been reported.

Chloral Hydrate. This compound, in doses of 1 or 2 g, leads to sedation without any prior excitation within 10 to 15 minutes, and results in sleep, usually within one hour. The sleep state, interestingly, is often accompanied by frequent dreaming and vivid recall of such dreams, and the total period of sleep is usually from 5 to 8 hours. The sleep state is not an excessively deep one and has usually been referred to as physiological sleep, in that arousal from the sleep state can usually be accomplished quite easily. Behavioural studies with this compound have been virtually absent in the experimental literature.

C. General Anaesthetics

The general anaesthetics consist of volatile liquids and gases which, following administration via the pulmonary route, become capable of inducing various degrees of anaesthesia. Varying areas of the nervous system are differentially sensitive to the effects of anaesthesia. Anaesthetics have been shown initially to affect active pathways in the brain stem (French, 1953) and the neural basis of anaesthesia has been attributed to several factors, which include a reduction for blockage of corticopetally-conducted impulses through the multisynaptic medial brain-stem system, depression of local cortical events excited by afferent volleys over non-blocked lateral brain stem pathways, and elimination of the normal influences of the central cephalic brain-stem activating system on the cortex and diencephalon. There are, in addition to rather well-documented electrophysiological data, additional findings that suggest rather diverse metabolic effects in the brain. Exposure to ether has been shown to increase cerebral ATP, CoA, and hexokinase activity, and decrease ADP creatine, phosphate, and glycogen (Estler, 1962). During anaesthesia, cellular respiration, lactic acid accumulation, and inorganic phosphate level were shown to decrease (McIlwain, 1966). Brain level, after ether exposure in rats, almost doubled after 20 minutes of exposure (Anderson and Bonnycastle, 1960). General anaesthetics have also been indicated as activators of the supraoptic-hypophyseal mechanisms concerned with the secretion of antidiuretic hormones (Craig *et al.*,

1945) and an increase in the input of 17-hydroxy-corticosteroids has been recorded at ten minutes following ether administration (Suzuki *et al.*, 1959). Behavioural studies concerned with the effects of general anaesthetics have usually been in two general areas. One of these has concerned memory consolidation, and the other, more generally, has dealt with perceptual studies.

Those mechanisms involved in memory consolidation have been related in several respects to general anaesthetics. Diethyl ether has been shown to impair the retention of an avoidance response conditioned immediately prior to anaesthesia (Essman and Jarvik, 1961). In this instance a retrograde amnesia for the conditioned response was demonstrated when mice were tested at 24 hours following the conditioning trial. Similar results, with rats, were obtained in a study in which animals were trained to bar-press for water reinforcement, and an avoidance response was established by electrifying the bar and reinforcement nozzle. Animals were anaesthetised with ether either 10 seconds, 5 minutes, or 10 minutes following the training shock and were re-tested for retention of avoidance behaviour 24 hours later. Rats given ether 10 seconds and 5 minutes after shock, showed significantly less avoidance than unanaesthetised controls (Pearlman *et al.*, 1961). In another study, diethyl ether was administered to mice at varying intervals following a single trial shock-avoidance conditioning situation. Interference with retention was recorded for ether anaesthesia, induced as long as 24 minutes after training (Abt *et al.*, 1961). The amnesic effects of ether anaesthesia and electroconvulsive shock were compared in mice where presentation of these conditions, immediately following a single training trial (40 or 70 seconds) was comparable in amnesic efficiency to a single ECS. The interaction of temperature and duration of anaesthesia has also been indicated, in that, at higher ambient temperatures, a shorter anaesthetic duration was sufficient to produce retrograde amnesia in mice (Herz *et al.*, 1966).

Subsequent to the completion of memory consolidation, there has been some indication that retention may be improved. Anaesthesia, at lower concentrations, results in only a slight deviation from normal fast cortical activity and, under such conditions, patients are unable to form new memories, although other functions, as measured by response to spoken voice, problem solving, and ability to recall old memories, remain intact (Artusio, 1955). The suggestion that memory may be improved by means of a reduction in interference and retroactive inhibition due to new learning has been explored. Human subjects, given nitrous oxide, following learning of a list of nonsense syllables, after which a new list of stimuli (interference stimuli) were presented; memory for the original list was then tested. A significant reduction in memory loss for the original learning was shown in the group of subjects anaesthetised with nitrous oxide.

The extent to which anaesthetics affect participation during consciousness has been investigated. A nitrous oxide-oxygen mixture (80/20) was administered to five monkeys while they were working for liquid reinforcement (Jarvik, 1961). In one experiment, they were required to distinguish the figure 3 from the figure 4 and, in another experiment, they were required to delay their response for two seconds, or longer. The accuracy of visual discrimination in the anaesthetised animals was depressed, as compared to control levels, and total response rates were also depressed. Perseveration errors markedly increased and, based on these findings, it was concluded that impairment of discriminative behaviour results from nitrous oxide treatment. In a study in which normal adults were required to judge the length of randomly presented lines while inhaling a nitrous oxide-oxygen mixture, the length of the shorter line was consistently overestimated, and the magnitude of such overestimation was an increasing function of the percentage of nitrous oxide in the mixture. The same degree of overestimation also emerged for the longer line. Measures of visual acuity and pupillary size were not affected by drug treatment, and the findings were interpreted in terms of an effect on the process of sensory input rather than reduced sensory capacity (Steinberg *et al.*, 1961). Subjects, tested on four intellectual factors (verbal, numerical, inducted, and special areas) showed a deterioration of performance as a result of nitrous oxide treatment (Frankenhaeuser, 1961). Normal adults were tested, using a 'missing scan method' with the letters A through H presented at either a rapid or slow rate, with one missing letter. At both 15 or 25 per cent nitrous oxide no impairment was demonstrated at the fast speed, but at a slow presentation rate, with 15, 25, and 35 per cent nitrous oxide, recall of the missing letter was impaired (Berry, 1965). Cognitive tests, given during nitrous oxide inhalation, revealed a concentration difficulty and personality dissociation in some subjects (Steinberg, 1956). Subjective reports included feelings of distance, dreaminess, and loss of control of action. There were also some reports of hallucinations and illusions, mainly auditory, with euphoria and irrelevant or exaggerated thoughts or emotions.

Some performance studies have been conducted with trichloroethylene, in which it has been shown, for example, that at doses of 200 to 800 ppm there was no effect on spontaneous motility or learning; however, exploratory activity in rats was increased, speed was accelerated, physical capacity was reduced, and emotional reactions were attenuated (Grandjeau and Bättig, 1964). Rats, exposed to 125 ppm of trichloroethylene, showed an impaired ability to prevent shock in a discrete avoidance situation after 4-hour periods of inhalation, given daily (Goldberg et al., 1964). Rats, exposed for eight hours of trichloroethylene (400 to 800 ppm),

showed a reduced frequency spontaneous left-right alterations in a T-maze, and at 400 and 600 ppm, running speed was significantly increased. At 200 ppm, running speed was markedly reduced. The concentration of the gas appears to affect motor performance as a function of its concentration, and this may well be a function of its ability selectively to depress inhibitory neurons at lower doses and more generally depress mixed neurons at higher concentrations (Zahner, 1962).

V. PSYCHOTOMIMETIC AGENTS

Compounds, which in man exert a psychotomimetic effect (i.e. hallucinations, novelty of experience, hypersuggestibility, spontaneous insights and emotions, impairment of memory and difficulty in concentration, depersonalisation, etc.), have had a long history in folklore and observational literature. There is a variety of such compounds, the detailed treatment of which, in the present context, would be far in excess of the scope of this survey, so that in order to bring this class of compound into focus, and view it in the context of the present overview, three representative compounds have been selected for inclusion; these are: mescaline, cannabis, and lysergic acid diethylamide (LSD-25).

Mescaline. Mescaline is an active component of the cactus plant *Lophophora Williamsii*, as well as a number of other Central and South American varieties of cactus plant. It is a compound closely related in structure to the catecholamines, and exerts a number of rather profound physiological and metabolic effects in the central nervous system. In small quantities, mescaline induces a state of relaxation and, as a function of dosage, can induce hallucinations, followed by sleep and fatigue. The effects of the compound are similar to those of LSD, except that mescaline is considerably less potent as a hallucinogenic agent. The compound results in minimal changes in the resting EEG, which are generally in the direction of desynchronisation and alpha frequency acceleration. It has been reported that alpha rhythms in man were blocked when visual experiences followed mescaline administration (Chweitzer et al., 1937). Alpha frequencies, in a group of seven schizophrenic patients, showed acceleration of 20 to 30 per cent in three subjects following oral administration of 300 mg, whereas in the others, it was unchanged (Rubin et al., 1942). Following the injection of 300 to 350 mg of mescaline, alpha activity was suppressed during the occurrence of visual hallucinations, with the occasional appearance of spike and wave complexes similar to those observed in epilepsy (Endo, 1952). With the oral

administration of 5 mg/kg of mescaline to 21 former narcotics addicts, visual hallucinations, tremors, and other behavioural changes appeared in the absence of any observable change in EEG, whereas in those instances in which EEG changes were observed, these were always accompanied by behavioural changes; euphoria, relaxation, and/or drowsiness, generally were associated with EEG desynchronisation (Wikler, 1952). Alpha activity in the EEG was decreased or abolished in 80 per cent of 25 schizophrenic patients given 500 mg of mescaline, but this change did not appear to be associated with a wide variety of clinical signs and symptoms observed (Denber and Merlis, 1955). It has been concluded (Denber, 1955) that the drug acts on the diencephalon on the basis of evidence indicating spiking, and slow wave discharges were decreased in 12 epileptic patients following intravenous (250 to 500 mg) injection (Denber, 1955).

The effects of mescaline on the metabolism of the brain are not well understood; no significant alterations in cerebral blood flow, oxygen consumption, or glucose utilisation were observed in normal subjects experiencing the hallucinogenic effects of 80 to 100 mg of mescaline extract (Kety, 1955). It has been reported that mescaline inhibits cerebral oxidations *in vitro* (Quastel and Wheatly, 1933), and the effect of low concentrations of mescaline were not observed in glycolysis and respiration of unstimulated cerebral tissue maintained *in vitro;* however, with electrical stimulation, a clearly inhibitory effect was demonstrated (Lewis and McIlwain, 1954). It was concluded that this compound may prevent changes in activity level involving the tissue response to excitation.

In animal studies, it has been shown that mescaline (10 to 100 mg/kg, p.o.) failed to block conditioned avoidance behaviour and did not antagonise the blocking properties on such behaviour caused by chlorpromazine, reserpine, and morphine (Cook and Weidley, 1957). In rats trained to jump a barrier at the sound of a tone in order to avoid a subsequent foot shock, mescaline had no effect on the acquisition of the conditioned response; it was observed, however, that 80 minutes following drug administration the animals responded to a tone following the simultaneous presentation of tone and shock by responding to the post-shock tone in a manner that suggested painful experience (leaping, squealing, etc.). It was concluded that the rat was hallucinating the sensation of pain in response to the tone (Sivadjian, 1934). In rats conditioned to avoid electroshock, similar evidence has emerged in that the CS was apparently capable of replacing the shock stimulus in terms of the responses made by the rat (Courvoisier, 1956). Mescaline, given to dogs (Bridger and Gantt, 1955; Stephens and Gantt, 1956) in doses of 35 mg/kg abolished a cardiac conditioned response, while causing relatively little change on a motor conditioned response; the latter disappeared when the dose of mescaline was increased to 70 mg/kg, and the dogs responded to the CS alone in a manner similar to their response to electric shock in a control period.

A detailed treatment of the symptoms produced by mescaline in non-psychotic human subjects has been presented (Beringer, 1927), and it is concluded that the effects of this compound are highly dose-dependent, as well as dependent on individual differences and the nature of the circumstances under which the drug is administered. In attempts to ascertain certain constants of the hallucinatory experience produced by mescaline, these studies have been considered largely undecisive (Wikler, 1957).

Lysergic Acid Diethylamide (LSD-25). The discovery of the behavioural effects of 4-lysergic acid diethylamide (LSD-25), in 1943, by Hofmann has resulted in a vast literature dealing with the effects of the compound in animals and man. Perhaps one of the most effective descriptions of the hallucinogenic properties of this compound may be found in a translation of the original report of its discoverer (Hofmann, 1955):

'Last Friday, April 16, 1943, I was forced to stop my work in the laboratory in the middle of the afternoon and to go home, as I was seized by a peculiar restlessness associated with a sensation of mild dizziness. Having reached home, I lay down and sank in a kind of drunkenness which was not unpleasant and which was characterised by extreme activity of imagination. As I lay in a dazed condition with my eyes closed (I experienced daylight as disagreeably bright) there surged upon me an uninterrupted stream of fantastic images of extraordinary plasticity and vividness and accompanied by an intense, kaleidoscope-like play of colors. This condition gradually passed off after about two hours.'

A subsequent report dealt with an intentional experiment in which, following the accidental ingestion of LSD-25, the investigator took 0·25 mg of this compound. The laboratory notes, discontinued within 40 minutes following the oral ingestion of the compound, read—

'April 19, 1943: Preparation of an 0·5% aqueous solution of 4-lysergic acid diethylamide tartrate.
4:30 P.M.: 0·5 cc (0·25 mg LSD) ingested orally. The solution is tasteless.
4:50 P.M.: no trace of any effect.
5:00 P.M.: slight dizziness, unrest, difficulty in concentration, visual disturbances, marked desire to laugh . . .'

The reported effects are vividly related in a later description (Hofmann, 1968) of the subjective experiences that followed—

'The last words could only be written with great difficulty. I asked my laboratory assistant to accompany me home as I believed that my condition would be a repetition of the disturbance of the previous Friday. While we were still cycling home, however, it became clear that the symptoms were much stronger than the first time. I had great difficulty in speaking coherently, my field of vision swayed before me, and objects appeared distorted like images in curved mirrors. I had the impression of being unable to move from the spot, although my assistant told me afterwards that we had cycled at a good pace . . . .

'By the time the doctor arrived, the peak of the crisis had already passed. As far as I remember, the following were the most outstanding symptoms: vertigo, visual disturbances; the faces of those around me appeared as grotesque, colored masks; marked motor unrest, alternating with paresis; an intermittent heavy feeling in the head, limbs and the entire body, as if they were filled with metal cramps in the legs, coldness and loss of feeling in the hands, a metallic taste on the tongue, dry, constricted sensation in the throat; feeling of choking; confusion alternating between clear recognition of my condition, in which state I sometimes observed, in the manner of an independent, neutral observer, that I shouted half insanely or babbled incoherent words. Occasionally I felt as if I were out of my body.

'The doctor found a rather weak pulse but an otherwise normal circulation . . . . Six hours after ingestion of the LSD-25 my condition had already improved considerably. Only the visual disturbances were still pronounced. Everything seemed to sway and the proportions were distorted like the reflections in the surface of moving water.

Moreover, all objects appeared in unpleasant, constantly changing colors, the predominant shades being sickly green and blue. When I closed my eyes, an unending series of colorful, very realistic and fantastic images surged in upon me. A remarkable feature was the manner in which all acoustic perceptions (e.g., the noise of a passing car) were transformed into optical effects, every sound causing a corresponding colored hallucination constantly changing in shape and color like pictures in a kaleidoscope. At about 1 o'clock I fell asleep and awakened next morning somewhat tired but otherwise feeling perfectly well.'

The effects of LSD on the electrical activity of the brain are complex and difficult to compare with those of other psychoactive compounds. LSD does not result in EEG arousal (Bradley and Key, 1958), and these authors have further shown that, in cats, there is an apparent fall in threshold for arousal. Cats and monkeys showed initial excitement and fast low amplitude EEG (Bradley and Elkes, 1957), and the threshold for arousal to afferent stimulation, but not to direct stimulation of the reticular formation, was lowered (Bradley, 1957). In the conscious cat, LSD resulted in alerting of behaviour and electrical activity (Bradley and Hance, 1957) and the electrical after-discharge in motor cortex was increased in cats and monkeys, whereas it was decreased as a result of LSD treatment in the amygdala and thalamus (Delgado and Mihailovic, 1956).

Various alterations in brain metabolism have been demonstrated in both acute as well as chronic treatment of animals with LSD. *In vitro* inhibition of oxidative phosphorylation has been demonstrated (Abood and Romanchek, 1957) in rat brain, whereas the oxygen consumption in brain homogenates was shown to increase where guinea-pig tissue was used (Mayer-Gross *et al.*, 1953). Several studies in rabbits (Cahn *et al.*, 1957, 1958) have indicated that LSD reduces cerebral glucose consumption, results in a depletion of cerebral sodium and potassium, reduces blood sodium and potassium, reduces cerebral blood flow, and interferes with carbohydrate metabolism. In chronically treated rabbits, some of these effects were partially antagonised by ATP or Vitamin C.

The behavioural effects of LSD have been explored over a rather wide range of animal species. In spiders, for example, it has been shown that oral administration of LSD (0·03 to 0·05 μg) resulted in a pronounced reduction in the number of webs that were built with an increased degree of regularity and precision in the structure of the completed webs (Witt, 1956). Other species, such as snails, fish, salamanders, pigeons, mice, rats, cats, dogs, and monkeys, have been used in a wide variety of experiments in which the effects of LSD have been studied independently or in interaction with other pharmacological agents. In general, these studies have indicated that motor performance, specifically in motor tasks, or motor performance as a component of learned behaviour, is impaired and that a variety of perceptual tasks are also subject to alterations due to this psychoactive compound. There have been relatively few behavioural studies concerned with the biochemical mode of action in relation to the onset of behavioural effect. Since several systems in the brain are apparently affected by LSD, variations in time course may be an important factor in the consideration of any specific behavioural effect emerging. The question of LSD-induced inhibition in the central nervous system is also of interest in so far as considering the nature of the LSD-induced perceptual effects; the differential inhibition of dendritic over somatic synapses may be an important component of the hallucogenic effects of this and similar compounds (Marrazzi, 1960). The suppression by hallucogenic compounds such as LSD of sensory stimuli that compete may be considered as a possible requisite to the suppression of cognitive stimuli. LSD, for example, is capable of blocking the establishment of conditioned responses through inhibition of conditioned stimuli, and there is the suggestion (Marrazzi, 1960) of direct inhibition of cognitive stimuli, which may perhaps be analogous to memory traces. This realm is extremely difficult to evaluate in as much as there is little clear evidence of memory impairment due to LSD, and this factor would, in addition, be difficult to separate from the performance effects and possible dissociation effects produced by this compound. There is also evidence in animal studies (Brunaud and Siou, 1959) that rodents, following LSD administration, show increased activity and sensitivity to stimuli, and an excitatory phase has been reported in numerous studies to occur following LSD administration over a wide species range.

Sensory and perceptual studies concerned with the effects of LSD in man have been largely confined to the visual system, and in this regard it may be useful to consider that the LSD state is accompanied by an often-reported period of hyper-suggestibility. The increased level of attention and highly directed stimulus specificity would seem to present a variable relevant to task direction and subject orientation in any task requiring subjective judgements. An increase in the duration and intensity of visual after-images has been reported (Keeler, 1965). Target fixation is increased in duration under the effects of LSD (Kohn and Bryden, 1965). Other investigators have observed that hue discrimination was decreased and there was a corresponding increase in reported colour perception induced by flickering light; colour perception reported as a result of flickering white light was enhanced by concurrent administration of tones (Hartman and Hollister, 1963). The complexity of interactions between differing modes of sensory stimulation and the resulting synaesthetic results in man contrast somewhat with evidence of stimulus suppression by LSD and inhibition of competing sensory stimuli, particularly as have emerged in studies with animals. Whether LSD results in inhibition or potentiation through specific sensory systems seems to be dependent not only on the specific task in which that subject may be involved, but also perhaps on those sets, attitudes, and experimental dispositions that are created within the context of the experiment itself. It would appear that a more critical evaluation of stimulus interaction in human perceptual tasks, as affected by LSD, is warranted, and the available experimental evidence does not, at present, allow for any conclusive statement regarding a specific perceptual effect independent of all of the many other contributory factors.

Marihuana (Cannabis). Marihuana is probably the most widely used, or abused, of drugs generally classed as hallucinogens. This material, one species of hemp *Cannabis Sativa L*, has been known variously by several names, depending on its variety and preparation. Marihuana, the most commonly designated referent, is the name given to the leaves and flowering tops of the cannabis plant, and this designation is used extensively in the western hemisphere. Another very common referent is hashish; this term has been generally used to refer to Indian hemp and is, in fact, the preparation of resin or resinous leaves of this plant, derived from Egypt, Iran, and Turkey. There are several other names by which this plant and its derivatives are known; among these are, *charas*, which consists of the tops of the female plants of cannabis, from which a raw resin is extracted. *Chira* is the name given to charas, as used in the Balkans and North Africa. *Esrar*, which means secret, is the Turkish designation of the principal element of hemp, obtained by using pure water or alcoholised water as a medium. *Madjun* is a preparation obtained by soaking cannabis with butter and water and mixing this product with nuts, ground almond, sugar, or honey. *Ganja* is the Indian designation of the flowering tops of the cultivated female plants. *Takuri*, the Tunisian designation, consists of the tops of the female hemp plant which are dried and minced into small particles for smoking. *Kif* is the Moroccan version of Takuri. *Bhang* is an Indian variety obtained by roughly powdering the dried hemp weeds. *Ajamba* is the designation used to refer to central African cultivated hemp. It also refers to a variety of Indian hemp grown in Brazil.

The *Cannabis Sativa* plant, when used by man for smoking, swallowing, chewing, etc., leads to a variety of behavioural signs, including excitement, euphoria, or possibly depression and sleep. More pronounced effects include hallucinations and aggressiveness.

The psychoactive effect of marihuana, or marihuana derivatives, appear mainly accounted for by the content of tetrahydrocannabinols. The majority of the work in which the use of cannabis, crude extracts of the cannabis plant, or distillates of the hemp resin, sometimes referred to as 'red oil', has been studied, and it is largely on the basis of these studies that the consideration of marihuana was based.

Several behavioural effects of marihuana or cannabis derivatives have been reported in animal studies. A possible bioassay method for the activity of marihuana has been reported (Loewe, 1944) and the description of the effects of cannabis in dogs on motor functions has been extensively reviewed in this respect. In general, locomotor ataxia, without effects on righting reflexes or escape reactions, is apparent. Dogs, treated with cannabis, have been observed to show excessive startle reflexes on presentation of sensory stimuli. Muscle tremor has also been observed in some species. The effects of cannabis have also been seen in mice where there is a generalised decrease in their spontaneous locomotor activity (Valle, 1961). Corneal anaesthesia in rabbits has also been employed as a possible bioassay in the evaluation of cannabis activity (Gayer, 1928). The use of this bioassay method has been employed in the preparation of a *cannabis sativa* extract (Carlini and Kramer, 1965), in which it was determined that the extract prepared gave complete corneal areflexia within five minutes following the intravenous injection of 0·5 mg/kg to rats. In their study, these authors demonstrated that injection of 30 to 50 mg of the marihuana extract in rats resulted in excitation, with signs of increased spontaneous activity within three to five minutes following such injection. Excitation became more pronounced by 30 minutes and violent reactions developed to sensory stimuli, including air blasts or the presentation of a glass stick which resulted in active biting behaviour. Interanimal fighting occurred at this time, but with continued elapse of time there were indications of depression and abstinence from food-seeking behaviour. Excessive reactivity to touch was noted, with vocalisation occurring. By 100 to 150 minutes following the drug injection there was apparent cataonic stupor, and the signs of the drug effect had disappeared by approximately 12 to 15 hours following injection. An earlier onset of the depressive phase following marihuana, with the injection of the extract in doses of 100 to 150 mg/kg, occurred. A dose of 10 mg/kg was shown to be non-toxic in rats, and produced mild excitation with a slight increase in motor activity; this occurred withinapproximately five minutes following injection and did not end in signs of depression, by approximately two hours following treatment. These same authors investigated the effect of the marihuana extract given to Wistar rats by the i.p. route, three minutes before or 30 seconds after trials in a Lashley III alley maze. Rats, given the cannabis extract three minutes prior to the trials showed better performance than did controls. Animals receiving the same dose by post-trial injection showed an increase in the length of time in maze performance, although there was no increase in the number of maze errors, as compared with control animals. Of 32 rats receiving the cannabis extract, five were disrupted by this treatment. The results of this study were discussed in view of a perseveration-consolidation theory of memory, although, in the light of this interpretation, it is not clear as to the specific role played in this hypothesised memory model by cannabis extract; it has been previously shown that the RNA content in rat brain was not affected by cannabis (Carlini and Carlini, 1966) and in view of the fact that post-trial injections had no effect on the facilitative maze performance observed with pre-trial injections, this finding is difficult to resolve with others in which post-trial injection of central nervous system stimulants has, on occasion, been observed to promote maze acquisition. In another study with a *cannabis sativa* extract, in a dose of 2·5 mg/kg (Salustiano *et al.*, 1966) the fighting time, in mice, induced by isolation, was reduced and, in aggregated mice, there was an increased toxicity to amphetamine. The cannabis extract was less efficient than chlorpromazine in protecting against the toxic effects of amphetamines in these conditions and was generally viewed, within the context of this experiment, to have tranquilising properties. In a related study (Santos *et al.*, 1966) alcoholic extracts from two samples from *cannabis sativa* were tested for their effect on isolation-induced aggressive behaviour and spontaneous locomotor activity of mice. Aggressiveness was suppressed by a northeastern Brazilian extract, and this was found to be more potent by a factor of 15 than an extract prepared from western Brazilian marihuana. It is of interest to note that the bioassay procedure in which both extracts were assayed by the corneal areflexia method in rabbits showed the same degree of activity, even though the ability to suppress

aggressive behaviour was dramatically different. Fighting time in isolated mice was reduced from 21·9 to 11·8 seconds, with a dose of 2·5 mg of the more potent extract. Locomotor activity, however, was not altered by doses up to 10 mg/kg, and in order to reduce locomotor activity to 60 per cent of baseline levels, a dose of 80 mg/kg was necessary. An interesting contrast to this finding is seen in a more recent study (Carlini and Masur, 1969) in which the development of aggressive behaviour in rats was mediated by the chronic administration of a marihuana extract. In this study, chronic daily injection of a marihuana extract, given to rats ranging in age from two to six months, induced aggressive fighting behaviour. Where the aggressive behaviour was more carefully controlled through the means of shock-induced fighting, the effect of the marihuana extract on daily administration was to potentiate such aggressive behaviour. It was of interest to note that in the doses used, 10 to 20 mg/kg, there were no such differences observed in the rats, and similar aggressive behaviour was not obtained through the use of other drugs chronically administered, such as caffeine, amphetamine, or amobarbital sodium. These investigators further observed that deprivation of food markedly increased the aggressive behaviour induced by the chronic administration of the marihuana extract. This finding is of interest in light of the observation that there is increased appetite produced through the chronic consumption of cannabis, and this may well be reflected in the observation made in the present study. It was further noted in this investigation that with an increase in ambient temperature there was a decrease in the aggressive behaviour induced by chronic administration of the marihuana extract, whereas when the ambient temperature was reduced, this led to an increase in the aggressive behaviour it induced. This finding is of interest in the light of the observation (Garattini, 1965) that a 'hashish extract' lowered the body temperature of rats, and at a dose of 150 mg/kg the reduction in body temperature was approximately equivalent to that produced by 5 mg/kg of chlorpromazine. Admittedly, the doses of 10 to 20 mg/kg are considerably below the dose reported for body temperature reduction. However, it is quite possible that a thermolytic effect of marihuana may be indicated and, therefore, the degree to which aggressive behaviour is expressed may well be the function of the extent to which body temperature is brought into equilibrium with the ambient temperature.

In another respect, if, at the dose of the marihuana extract used in this study, a thermolytic is indicated, the increase in aggressive behaviour may likely be a form of thermoregulatory behaviour in the light of the possibility that body temperature is actually reduced at lower ambient temperature in rats chronically treated with a marihuana extract.

The effects of marihuana extracts or derivatives have been described in man. The results have been summarised for a reasonably large group of subjects (Allentuck and Bowman, 1942). These authors have detailed the effects following ingestion of marihuana and several synthetic derivatives, resulting in relaxation, sedation, with concommitant sensations of pleasure. Also noted was the appearance of a variety of autonomic signs within 30 minutes to one hour following drug administration, and by two to three hours, there were indications of increased psychomotor activity, euphoria, and alterations in temporal and spatial perception in these subjects. This was followed or accompanied by drowsiness and subsequently, by sleep, the duration of which was approximately from one to six hours. Among those subjects in the population (in this instance, nine) that were considered 'unstable', the ingestion of marihuana precipitated a schizophrenic-like psychosis, or affective disorders with paranoid signs and psychopathic indications.

There seems to be some degree of doubt regarding the extent to which personality changes occur as a result of marihuana use. There has been some indication that intellectual performance shows some slight impairment, the degree of which is increased as a function of dosage (Halpern, 1944). One of the problems in assessing the behavioural effects of marihuana in man objectively seems to be indicated by the exceedingly small number of objective experimental studies that have been conducted. In one study (Clark and Nakashima, 1968) volunteer subjects, ranging in age from 21 to 40, who had had no previous experience with marihuana, nor any history of any previous psychiatric disorder were employed. Doses of an alcohol extracted from reconstituted oily concentrate of raw marihuana was administered in doses ranging from 0·0125 to 0·03 g per lb of body weight. Tests, randomly presented from one-and-a-half to four hours following the administration of the drug, consisted of hand and foot reaction time to simple and complex visual signals, a digit code, depth perception, consisting of the positioning of vertical white rods at 16 feet, visual flicker fusion, auditory frequency discrimination, duration of after-image induced by the Archimedes spiral, mirror pattern tracing, and visual motor co-ordination, as measured by a pursuit motor apparatus. Both simple and complex reactions were affected by the marihuana extract and the magnitude of their effect appeared dose-related, although considerable variability occurred in subjects. Complex reaction time was severely

affected by marihuana in simple reaction time. Impairment of the learning of the digit code was apparent in most of the subjects tested on this task, although for some subjects the learning behaviour was unaltered. At higher dose levels, a greater impairment of acquisition of this material was apparent, although again, for this task, there was considerable variability from subject to subject in the extent to which increases in dosage increased the performance. It was, however, generally noted that performance became impaired as the function of dosage over the total of 250 trials given for the acquisition of the digit code. Depth perception measured showed no consistent trend in so far as their effects by the marihuana extract, and there was considerable variability. There is, unfortunately, no information given on the effects of marihuana on visual flicker fusion, even though this is reported as one of the tests in the battery employed. Auditory frequency discrimination appeared to be unchanged at all with the dose levels used, and the after-image induced by the Archimedes spiral again appeared extremely variable even in control subjects not treated with marihuana, so that in terms of obtaining a baseline, the only conclusion drawn was that the drugs affect a shortening of the duration of the after-image. There was some subjective report indicating a pleasurable sensation by looking at the whirling spiral by subjects treated with marihuana extracts. The mirror tracing was subject to practice effects and did not appear to be impaired by marihuana, although, again, subjective reports appeared to indicate that the task was made easier due to the relaxation produced by the drug. The pursuit rotor task did not appear to discriminate any differences emerging as a function of drug treatment; however, at the highest dose level there was some indication of a performance decrement in some subjects.

The above study points out very clearly the extent to which inter- and intra-subject variability can lead to difficulties in assessing the effects of marihuana or marihuana derivatives on behaviour in man. The choice of tasks, leading to limitations of this variability appears to be a desirable end point in the design of subsequent studies. An interesting evaluation of the clinical and psychological effect of marihuana in man has also appeared recently (Weil et al., 1968). Marihuana treatment in 'marihuana naive' subjects did not yield a strong subjective experience commonly accompanying marihuana intoxication, where either 4·5 or 18 mg of tetrahydrocannabinal were given. However, under these conditions, there was a dose-related performance impairment. Experienced marihuana users, when given a high dose of tetrahydrocannabinal, improved on two of the three behavioural tasks given to them. Marihuana users improved from baseline levels on digit simple substitutions and pursuit rotor performance. It may be observed that these are tasks that require sustained performance and, perhaps, this may be a factor that discriminates the differences in improved, compared with impaired, performance in marihuana users, as compared with marihuana naive subjects, respectively. Another study (Myers and Caldwell, 1969) showed that marihuana naive subjects showed no differences in either visual or sensory threshold after smoking one 300 mg marihuana cigarette. The content of such a cigarette is judged to be equivalent to approximately 3·966 mg of Δ^9-tetrahydrocannabinal.

The subjective effects of marihuana can generally be summarised as consisting of an elevation of mood, with increases in the extent to which euphoria is reported. There are accompanying distortions of visual perception and in body image. There have been reports of dream-like states, or dream images, and intermittent periods, consisting of sleeping illusory experiences. Distortions of space, time, have been indicated. There have been subjective indications of withdrawal with marihuana use from one extreme to aggressive behaviour and activation on the other. It appears that the wide variety and range of the subjective effects of marihuana and its derivatives in man are dependent on a large number of variables; these include the personality of the user, the dose used, the chronicity of use, the circumstances under which the drug is used, including the environment within which it is used, and many other social factors that determine the outcome or magnitude of a subjective experience associated with this hallucogenic agent.

EVALUATION OF THE PRESENT STATUS OF PSYCHOPHARMACOLOGY AND PERSPECTIVES FOR THE FUTURE

The present status of psychopharmacology presents a difficult evaluative task for which significant interrelationships between the behavioural effect of psychoactive agents and the inferences resulting from such data constitute a basis on which a set of rules for such interrelationships can emerge. It is apparent that a variety of studies can generate meaningful hypotheses that should and, in some cases, have been tested in animals and man; however, there are indeed many shortcomings that limit both generality and the validity of inference which, perhaps, should serve as guidelines for future research in this area. There are many considerations, which perhaps are more fundamentally pharmacological than behavioural, that appear to constitute limiting factors in both the interpretation and applicability of results; first among these, of course, is the character of any specific drug used in conjunction with behavioural studies and the nature of its onset and duration of action, site of action, and mode of action. In this respect, the vehicle in which the compound is administered and the route by which it is administered, probably constitute important initial considerations. In this connection the dose range over which any given compound is tested for behavioural conditions is often overlooked by investigators who are satisfied at accepting a given effective dosage based on previous findings. The sample on which a given compound is tested behaviourally can often create problems that have pronounced significance for the interpretation of any

emerging results, and the choice of an appropriate control both behaviourally and pharmacologically is an exceedingly important aspect of any experimental design. The behavioural method used to evaluate the psychoactive effect of a given compound, or to test a hypothesis regarding its effect on some specific behavioural component, often overlooks the obvious possibility that the behaviour measured may not necessarily be identical with those behavioural processes inferred from the results of such measurements. The time course over which drug activity is assumed and behavioural capacity for performance is evaluated, are often not coincident with one another, or may, in fact, generate a complex series of interactions that are especially dependent on the number of behavioural controls and/or the number of pharmacological treatments. The question of pharmacological equivalents can arise as a problem in the evaluation of behavioural effects where more than one psychoactive agent is employed under parallel or sequential behavioural conditions; equivalence of effective dosage is not necessarily a sufficient basis for evaluating behavioural differences and, similarly, equivalence assumptions do not necessarily apply for identical routes of drug administration, or assumptions regarding onset and time course of action in relation to a given behavioural task and, particularly, multiple tasks.

It would appear that the field of psychopharmacology is beset by as many methodological considerations as there are disciplines within which the behavioural effect of a drug can be of concern. It would also appear that one of the tasks in this field presented for the future to contend with is to interrelate multidisciplinary approaches as they bear on the effects of drugs on behaviour. It therefore seems apparent that the entire character of psychopharmacology, as presented in this chapter, will probably be completely changed when this subject is again dealt with in a future edition of this *Handbook*.

REFERENCES

ABADON, P. N., AHMED, K., and SCHOLEFIELD, P. G. (1961) Biochemical studies on Tofranil. *Canad. J. Biochem.*, **39**, 551–558.

ABOOD, L. G. (1955) Effect of chlorpromazine on phosphorylation of brain mitochondria. *Proc. soc. exp. biol. Med.*, **88**, 688–690.

ABOOD, L. G. and ROMANCHEK, R. L. (1957) The chemical constitution and biochemical effects of psychotherapeutic and structurally related agents. *Ann. N.Y. Acad. Sci.*, **66**, 812–825.

ABT, J. P., ESSMAN, W. B., and JARVIK, M. E. (1961) Ether-induced retrograde amnesia for one-trial conditioning in mice. *Science*, **133**, 1477–1478.

AGATHON, M. (1964) Intéret de la méthodes des images consécutives dans l'étude de l'action des drogues psychotropes. *Rev. Neuropsych. Infant. Hyg. Ment. Enfan.*, **12**, 209–216.

ALLENTUCK, S. and BOWMAN, K. M. (1942) The psychiatric aspects of marihuana intoxication. *Amer. J. Psychiat.*, **99**, 248–251.

ALLES, G. A. and FEIGEN, G. A. (1942) The influence of benzedrine on work decrement and patellar reflex. *Amer. J. Physiol.*, **136**, 392–400.

ANDERSON, E. G. and BONNYCASTLE, D. D. (1960) *J. Pharm. exp. Ther.*, **130**, 138–143.

ANDERSON, O. D. and PARAMENTER, R. (1941) A long term study of the experimental neuroses in the sheep and dog. *Psychosom. med. Monogr.*, **2**, 1–150.

APPEL, J. B. (1963) Drugs, shock intensity, and the CER. *Psychopharmacologia*, **4**, 148–153.

ARELLANO, Z. A. P. and JERI, V. R. (1956) Scalp and basal EEG during the effect of reserpine. *Amer. Med. Assoc. Arch. Neurol. Psychiat.*, **75**, 525–533.

ARTUSIO, J. F., JR. (1955) Ether analgesic during major surgery. *J. Amer. med. Assn.*, **157**, 33–36.

AZIMA, H. (1958) The possible dream-inducing capacity of the whole root of *rauwolfia serpentina*. *Canad. psychiat. Assn. J.*, **3**, 47–51.

BALZER, H., HOLTZ, P., and PALM, D. (1961a) Reserpin und Aminobuttersäueregehalt des Gehirns. *Experientia*, **17**, 38–40.

BALZER, H., HOLTZ, P., and PALM, D. (1961b) Reserpin und Glykogengehalt der Organe. *Experientia*, **17**, 304–305.

BARKOV, N. K. (1961a) The analgesic properties of certain phenothiazine derivatives. *Bull. exp. biol. Med.*, **50**, 950–952.

BARKOV, N. K. (1961b) The influence of phenothiazine derivatives on the action of analgesics. *Bull. exp. biol. Med.*, **51**, 185–188.

BARLOW, J. S., ROVIT, R. L., and GLOOR, P. (1964) Correlation analysis of EEG changes induced by unilateral carotid injection of amobarbital. *Electroenceph. clin. Neurophysiol.*, **16**, 213–220.

BARRY, H. and MILLER, N. E. (1962) Effects of drugs on approach-avoidance conflict tested repeatedly by means of a 'telescope alley'. *J. comp. physiol. Psychol.*, **55**, 201–210.

BARRY, H., MILLER, N. E., and TIDD, G. E. (1962) Control for stimulus change while testing effects of amobarbital on conflict. *J. comp. physiol. Psychol.*, **55**, 1071–1074.

BARRY, H. and MILLER, N. E. (1965) Comparison of drug effects on approach, avoidance and escape motivation. *J. comp. physiol. Psychol.*, **59**, 18–24.

BARTLET, A. L. (1960) The 5-hydroxytryptamine content of mouse brain and whole mice after treatment with some drugs affecting the central nervous system. *Brit. J. Pharmacol.*, **15**, 140–146.

BAZIN, YE F. (1964) Kvoprosu ob ispol'-zovanii amitalkofeinovogo rastormazhivaniya khronicheski bol'nykh shizofreniyey dlya izacheniya ikh psikhoptaologii i otsenki lechebnogo prognoza. *Voprosy Psikhiatrii Nevropatologii*, **10**, 312–326.

BEECH, H. R., DAVIES, B. II, and MORGENSTERN, F. S. (1961) Preliminary investigation of the effects of sernyl upon cognitive and sensory processes. *J. ment. Sci.*, **107**, 509–513.

BENTE, D. and ITIL, T. M. (1954) Zur Wirkung des Phenothiazinkörpers Megaphen auf das menschliche Hirnstrombild. *Arzneimittel-Forsch.*, **4**, 418.

BERGSTRÖM, L., HÄKKINEN, V., JAUHIAINEN, T., and KAHRI, A. (1964) The effects of chlorpromazine on the perceptual manifold of the sense of hearing. *Ann. Acad. Sci. Fenn.*, Series A: V. Medica, **106**, 1–12.

BERINGER, K. (1927) Der Meskalinrausch. *Monogr. neurol. Psychiat.*, 1–315.

BERRY, C. (1965) Effects of a drug and immediate memory. *Nature*, **207**, 1012.

BERRYMAN, R., JARVIK, M. E., and NEVIN, J. A. (1962) Effects of pentobarbital lysergic acid diethylamide and chlorpromazine on matching behavior in the pigeon. *Psychopharmacologia*, **3**, 60–65.

BESSER, G. M., DUNCAN, C., and QUILLIAM, J. P. (1966) Modification of the auditory flutter fusion threshold by centrally acting drugs in man. *Nature*, **211**, 751.

BHARGAVA, K. P. and BORISON, H. L. (1955) Comparative effects of some Rauwolfia alkaloids on central vasoregulatory mechanism. *Fed. Proc.*, **15**, 401.

BIEL, J. H. (1968) Chemopharmacologic approaches to the treatment of mental depression. In *Drugs Affecting the Central Nervous System*, Vol. 2 (Ed. Burger, A.). New York: Marcel Derker, Chapter 3.

BIGNAMI, G. (1966) Pharmacologic influence on mating

behavior in the male rat. *Psychopharmacologia*, **10**, 44–58.

BLACK, A. A. (1966) Factors predisposing to a placebo response in new outpatients with anxiety states. *Brit. J. Psychiat.*, **112**, 557–567.

BLOGOVSKI, M. (1959) Exploration of an elevated maze used as a neuropharmacological test (In French), *Compt. Rend.*, **249**, 2868–2870.

BOISSIER, J. R., DUMONT, C., RATOUIS, R., and PAGNY, J. (1961) Tentative de pharmacologie prévisionelle dans le domaine des neuroleptiques: actions sédative centrale et adrénolytique de la N(diméthoxy-s,4 Phénéthyl)N′ (chloro-2-phényl) pipérazine. *Arch. int. pharmacodyn. Thérap.*, **133**, 29–49.

BOISSIER, J. R. and SIMON, P. (1964) Dissociation of two components in the investigation of behavior of the mouse. *Arch. int. pharmacodyn. Thérap.*, **147**, 372–387.

BOISSIER, J. R., SIMON, P., and LWOFF, J. M. (1964) Use of a specific reaction of mice (method of the perforated board) for the study of psychotropic drugs (In French). *Thérapie*, **19**, 571–589.

BOISSIER, J. R. and SIMON, P. (1967) Influence de la cafeine surle comportement en situation libre de la souris. *Arch. int. pharmacodyn. Thérap.*, **166**, 362–368.

BOJANOVSKÝ, J. (1965) The use of thiopental in a differential diagnosis of endogenous and psychogenic depressions. *Activitas nervosa Superior*, **7**, 291–292.

BONTA, I. L., DELVER, A., SIMONS, L., and deVOS, C. J. (1960) A newly developed motility apparatus and its applicability in two pharmacological designs. *Arch. int. pharmacodyn. Thérap.*, **129**, 381–394.

BOVET, D., BOVET-NITTI, F., and OLIVERIO, A. (1966) Effects of nicotine on avoidance conditioning in inbred strains of mice. *Psychopharmacologia*, **10**, 1–5.

BOVET-NITTI, F. (1966) Facilitation of simultaneous visual discrimination by nicotine in the rat. *Psychopharmacologia*, **10**, 59–66.

BRADLEY, P. B. (1957) Recent observations on the action of some drugs in relation to the reticular formation of the brain. *Electroenceph. clin. Neurophysiol.*, **9**, 372.

BRADLEY, P. B. and ELKES, J. (1957) The effects of some drugs on the electrical activity of the brain. *Brain*, **80**, 77–117.

BRADLEY, P. B. and HANCE, A. J. (1957) The effect of chlorpromazine and methopromazine on the electrical activity of the brain in the cat. *Electroencephalog. clin. Neurophysiol.*, **9**, 2.

BRADLEY, P. B. and KEY, B. J. (1958) The effects of drugs on arousal responses produced by electrical stimulation of the reticular formation of the brain. *Electroencephalog. clin. Neurophysiol.*, **10**, 97–110.

BRADLEY, P. B. and KEY, B. J. (1959) A comparative study of the effects of drugs on the arousal system of the brain. *Brit. J. Pharmacol.*, **14**, 340.

BRADLEY, P. B. and NICHOLSON, A. N. (1962) The effect of some drugs on hippocampal arousal. *Electroenceph. clin. Neurophysiol.*, **14**, 824–834.

BRADY, J. V. (1956) Assessment of drug effects on emotional behavior. *Science*, **123**, 1033–1034.

BREEN, R. A. and McGAUGH, J. C. (1961) Facilitation of maze-learning with post-trial injection of picrotoxin. *J. comp. physiol. Psychol.*, **54**, 498–501.

BRIDGER, W. H. and GANTT, W. H. (1955) The effect of mescaline on higher nervous activity (differentiated conditional reflexes). *J. Pharmacol.*, **113**, 7–8.

BRIMBLECOMBE, R. W. (1963) Effects of psychotropic drugs on open-field behaviour in rats. *Psychopharmacologia*, **4**, 139–147.

BRIMER, A., SCHNIEDEN, H., and SIMON, A. (1964) The effect of chlorpromazine and chlordiazepoxide on cognitive functioning. *Brit. J. Psychiat.*, **110**, 723–725.

BROOKS, G. W. and MUELLER, E. (1966) Serum urate concentrations among university professors; relation to drive, achievement, and leadership. *J. Amer. med. Assn.*, **195**, 415–418.

BROWN, B. B. (1960) CNS drug actions and interactions in mice. *Arch. int. pharmacodyn. Thérap.*, **128**, 391–414.

BRUNAUD, M. and SIOU, G. (1959) Action des substances psychotropes chez le rat, sur un état d'agressivité provoque. In *Neuro-psychopharmacology*, Vol. I (Ed. Bradley, P. B., Deniker, P., and Radouco-Thomas, C.). Amsterdam: Elsevier, pp. 282–286.

BUCHEL, L., LEVY, J., and TANGUY, O. (1962) The importance of antagonism and synergism in the pharmacological study of neuroleptics (In French). *J. Physiol. (Paris)*, **54**, 771–786.

BUNNEY, W. E. Jr. and DAVIS, J. M. (1965) Norepinephrine in depressive reaction. *Arch gen. Psychiat.*, **13**, 483.

BURGE, E. (1961) Einfluss von Tranquillizer-Substanzen auf die Alkoholwirkung. *Monatschr. Unfallheilkunde Versicherungsmedizin.*, **24**, 99–102.

CADE, J. F. J. (1949) Lithium salts in the treatment of psychotic excitement. *Med. J. Australia*, **36**, 349.

CAHN, J., HEROLD, M., DUBRASQUET, M., ALANO, J., BARRÉ, N., and BURET, J. P. (1957) Contribution à un concept biochimique des psychoses expérimentales. I. Effets du diéthylamide de l'acide lysergique sur le bilan humoral et le métabolisme cérébral du lapin *in vivo*. *Compt. rend. soc. Biol.*, **151**, 1820.

CAHN, J., HEROLD, M., GEORGES, G., and PIERRE, R. (1958) Action de la sérotonine sur le système nerveux central. *Thérapie*, **13**, 464.

CALHOUN, W. H. (1965) The effect of strychnine sulfate on the home cage activity and oxygen consumption in 3 inbred strains of mice. *Psychopharmacologia*, **8**, 227–234.

CARLINI, G. R. S. and GARLINI, E. A. (1965) Effects of strychnine and *Cannabis Sativa* (Marihuana) on the nucleic acid content in brain of the rat. *Med. pharmacol. Exp.*, **12**, 21–26.

CARLINI, E. A. and KRAMER, C. (1965) Effects of *Cannabis sativa* (Marihuana) on maze performance of the rat. *Psychopharmacologia*, **7**, 175–181.

CARLINI, E. A. and MASUR, J. (1969) Development of aggressive behavior in rats by chronic administration of *Cannabis sativa* (Marihuana). *Life Sciences*, **8**, 607–620.

CARLTON, P. L. and DIDAMO, P. (1961) Augmentation of the behavioral effects of amphetamine by atropine. *J. pharmacol. exp. Therap.*, **132**, 91–96.

CASEY, J. F., LASKY, J. J., KLETT, C. J., and HOLLISTER, L. E. (1960) Treatment of schizophrenic reactions with phenothiazine derivatives. A comparative study of chlorpromazine, triflupromazine, mepazine, prochlorperazine, perphenazine and phenobarbital. *Amer. J. Psychiat.*, **117**, 97–105.

CHANCE, M. R. A. and SILVERMAN, A. P. (1964) The structure of social behavior and drug action. In *Animal Behavior and Drug Action* (Ed. H. Steinberg, A. V. S. de Reuck, and J. Knight). Boston: Little, Brown, Pp. 65–82.

CHEN, G. M. and WESTON, J. K. (1960) The analgesic and anesthetic effect of 1-(1-phenylcyclohexyl) piperidine HCl on the monkey. *Anesth. Analg.*, **39**, 132–137.

CHEN, G., BOHNER, B., and BRATTON, A. C. Jr. (1963) The influence of certain central depressants on fighting behavior of mice. *Arch. int. Pharmacodyn.*, **142**, 30–34.

CHERNOMORDIK, A. B. (1964) Novye aredstva spet sificheskoy terapii kolienteritov-pobimiksin Mi nitrofuranovye preparaty. *Pediatriia*, **43**, 72–73.

CHI, C. C. (1965) The effect of amobarbital sodium on conditioned fear as measured by the potentiated startle response in rats. *Psychopharmacologia*, **7**, 115–122.

CHWEITZER, A., GEBLEWICZ, W., and LIBERSIN, W. T. (1937) Action de la méscaline sur les ondes alpha (rhythme de Berger) chez l'homme. *C. R. Soc. Biol., Paris*, **124**, 1296–1299 (abstract).

CLARK, L. D. and NAKASHIMA, E. N. (1968) Experimental studies of marihuana. *Amer. J. Psychiat.*, **125**, 135–140.

COBURN, S. P., SEIDENBERG, M., and MERTZ, E. T. (1967) Clearance of uric acid, urea, and creatinine in Down's syndrome. *J. appl. Physiol.*, **23**, 579–580.

COHEN, B. D., ROSENBAUM, G., LUBY, E. D., and GOTTLIEB, J. S. (1962) Comparison of phencyclidine hydrochloride (Sernyl) with other drugs. Stimulation of schizophrenic performance with phencyclidine, hydrochloride (Sernyl), lysergic acid diethylamide (LSD-25), and amobarbital (Amytal) sodium: II. Symbolic and sequential thinking. *Arch. gen. Psychiat.*, **6**, 395–401.

COLE, J. (1966) The importance of individual studies in testing drugs. Observations on three rats given Niamid and reserpine. *Arzneimitt.-Forsch.*, **16**, 91–94.

COLE, S. O. (1966) Comments on the effect of amphetamine in avoidance conditioning. *Psychol. Rep.*, **19**, 41–42.

COOK, L., WEIDLEY, E., MORRIS, R. W., and MATTIS, P. A. (1953) Neuropharmacological effects of chlorpromazine (thorazine hydrochloride). *J. Pharmacol.*, **113**, 11–12.

COOK, L. and WEIDLEY, E. (1957) Behavioral effects of some psychopharmacological agents. *Ann. N. Y. Acad. Sci.*, **66**, 740–752.

COOPER, R. M. and KRASS, M. (1963) Strychnine: duration of the effects on maze learning. *Psychopharmacologia*, **4**, 472–475.

CORRODI, H., FUXE, K., and SCHOU, M. (1969) Effect of prolonged lithium administration on cerebral monoamines in the rat. *Proc. 2nd Int. Meeting of Int. Soc. for Neurochem.*, p. 136.

COSTA, E., GARATTINI, S., and VALZELLI, L. (1960) Interactions between reserpine, chlorpromazine, and imipramine. *Experientia*, **16**, 461.

COSTA, E., PSCHEIDT, G. R., VANMETER, W. G., and

HIMWICH, H. E. (1960) Brain concentrations of biogenic amines and EEG patterns of rabbits. *J. pharmacol. exp. Therap.*, **130**, 81–88.

COURVOISIER, S., FOURNEL, J., DUCROT, R., KOLSKY, M., and KOETSCHET, P. (1953) Propriétés pharmacodynamiques du chlorhydrate de chloro-3-(diméthylamino-3′-propyl)-10-phénothiazine (4560 R.P.); Etude expérimentale d'un nouveau corps utilisé dans l'anesthésie potentialisée et dans l'hibernation artificielle. *Arch. int. Pharmacodynam.*, **92**, 305–361.

COURVOISIER, S. (1956) Pharmaco-dynamic basis for the use of chlorpromazine in psychiatry. *J. clin. Psychopath.*, **17**, 25–37.

COURVOISIER, S., DUCROT, R., and JULOU, L. (1958) Nouveaux aspects expérimentaux de l'activité centrale des dérivés de la phénothiazine. In *Psychotropic Drugs* (Ed. Garattini, S. and Ghetti, V.). Amsterdam: Elsevier, p. 373.

CRAIG, F. N., VISSCHER, F. E., and HOUCK, C. R. (1945) Renal function in dogs under ether or cyclopropane anesthesia. *Amer. J. Physiol.*, **143**, 108–118.

DAS, N. N., DASGUPTA, S. R., and WERNER, G. (1954) Changes of behavior and EEG in rhesus monkeys caused by chlorpromazine. *Arch. int. Pharmacodyn.*, **99**, 451–457.

DASGUPTA, S. R. and WERNER, G. (1955) Inhibitory actions of chlorpromazine on motor activity. *Arch. int. pharmacodyn. Thérap.*, **100**, 409–417.

DAVIS, J. M. (1965) Efficacy of tranquilizing and antidepressant drugs. *Arch. Gen. Psychiat.*, **13**, 552–572.

DELAY, J., DENIKER, P., and HARL, J. M. (1952) Utilisation en thérapeutique d'une phénothiazine d'action centrale élective (4560RP). *Ann. méd. psychol.*, **110**, 112–117.

DELAY, J. and DENIKER, P. (1952) Trente-huit cas de psychoses traitées par la cure prolongée et continue de 4560RP. Le Congrès des Al. Neurol. Langue Fr. In *Compt. rend. Congr.* Paris: Masson et Cie.

DELGADO, J. M. R. and MIHAILOVIC, L. (1956) Use of intracerebral electrodes to evaluate drugs that act on the central nervous system. *Ann. N. Y. Acad. Sci.*, **64**, 644–666.

DE MAAR, E. W. J., MARTIN, W. R., and UNNA, K. R. (1958) Chlorpromazine. II. The effects of chlorpromazine on evoked potentials in the midbrain reticular formation. *J. Pharmacol.*, **124**, 77–85.

DENBER, N. C. B. (1955) Studies on mescaline. No. 3: Action in epileptics. *Psychiat. Quart.*, **29**, 432–437.

DENBER, H. C. B. and MERLIS, S. (1955) Studies on mescaline. No. 1: Action in schizophrenic patients. *Psychiat. Quart.*, **29**, 421–429.

DEWS, P. B. (1953) The measurement of the influence of drugs on voluntary activity in mice. *Brit. J. pharmac. Chemother.*, **8**, 46–48.

DEWS, P. B. (1956) Comparison of effects of phenobarbital and chlorpromazine on discriminatory performance in pigeons. *J. Pharmacol.*, **116**, 16.

DEWS, P. B. (1964) A behavioural effect of amobarbital. *Naunyn-Schimiedeberg's Archiv für experimentelle Pathologie und Pharmakologia*, **248**, 296–307.

DICKENS, D. W., LADER, M. H., and STEINBERG, H.

(1965) Differential effects of two amphetamine-barbiturate mixtures in man. *Brit. J. Pharmacol. Chemo.*, **24**, 14–23.

DiMascio, A., Havens, L. L., and Snell, J. E. (1961) A comparison of four phenothiazine derivatives: a preliminary report on the assessment of chlorpromazine, promethiazine, perphenazine, and trifluoperazine. In *Recent Advances in Biological Psychiatry*, Vol. 3 (Ed. Wortis, J.). New York: Grune Stratton, Pp. 68–76.

Dobkin, A. B., Gilbert, R. G., and Lamoureaux, L. (1954) Physiological effects of chlorpromazine. *Anaesth.*, **9**, 157–174.

Domer, F. R. and Schueler, F. W. (1960) Investigations of the amnesic properties of scopalamine and related compounds. *Arch. int. pharmacodyn. Thérap.*, **127**, 449–458.

Driever, C. W., Bousquet, W. F., and Miya, T. S. (1966) Stress stimulation of drug metabolism in the rat. *Inter. J. Neuropharm.*, **5**, 199–205.

Eccles, J. C., Schmidt, R. F., and Willis, W. D. (1963) Pharmacological studies on presynaptic inhibition. *J. Physiol.*, **168**, 500–530.

The Editor (1968) Effects of nicotine. (Editorial). *Brit. med. J.*, No. 5584, 73–74.

Editorial (1962) Amphetamine-barbiturate combinations. *Brit. med. J.*, No. 5317, 1456–1457.

Ehringer, H., Hornykiewicz, O., and Lechner, K. (1960) The effect of chlorpromazine on catecholamine and 5-hydroxytryptamine metabolism in the rat brain (In German). *Arch. Exp. Pathol. Pharmakol.*, **239**, 507–519.

Endo, K. (1952) Experimental study of mescaline intoxication on relation between clinical picture and EEG in man. *Folia. psychia. neur. Jap.*, **6**, 104–113.

Ernsting, M. J. E., Kafoe, W. F., Nauta, W. T., Oosterhuis, H. K., and DeWarrt, C. (1960) Biochemical studies on psychotropic drugs. 1. The effects of psychotropic drugs on γ-aminobutyric acid and glutamic acid in brain tissue. *J. Neurochem.*, **5**, 121–127.

Esplin, D. W. and Zablock, B. (1965) Central nervous system stimulants. In *The Pharmacological Basis of Therapeutics* (Ed. Goodman, L. S. and Gilman, A.). New York: Macmillan, Chapter 18.

Essenberg, J. M. (1948) The effect of nicotine on maze learning ability of albino rats. *Fed. Proc.*, **7**, 31–32.

Essenberg, J. M. (1954) The effect of nicotine on maze behavior of albino rats. *J. Psychol.*, **37**, 291–295.

Essig, C. F. and Flanary, H. G. (1961) Convulsive aspects of barbitalsodium withdrawal in the cat. *Exptl. Neurol.*, **3**, 149–159.

Essman, W. B. (1966) Effect of tricyanoaminopropene on the amnesic effect of electroconvulsive shock. *Psychopharmacologia*, **9**, 426.

Essman, W. B. (1967) Changes in memory consolidation with alterations in neural RNA. *Proc. Coll. Int. Neuropsychopharm.*, 108.

Essman, W. B. (1969) Alterations in brain serotonin metabolism mediating enhanced memory consolidation. In *The Present Status of Psychotropic Drugs* (Ed. Cerletti, A. & Bové, F. J.). Amsterdam: Excerpta Medica, Pp. 305–306.

Essman, W. B. (1970) Central nervous system metabolism, drug effects, and higher functions. In *Drugs and Cerebral Function* (Ed. Smith, W. L.). Springfield Ill.: Chas. Thomas, 151–175.

Essman, W. B. (1970a) The role of biogenic amines in memory consolidation. In *The Biology of Memory* (Ed. Adám, G.) Budapest: Hungarian Academy of Sciences (In Press).

Essman, W. B. and Essman, S. G. (1969) Enhanced memory consolidation with drug-induced regional changes in brain RNA and serotonin metabolism. *Pharmako-Psychiat. Neuropsychopharm.*, **12**, 28–34.

Essman, W. B. and Golod, M. I. (1968) Reduction of retrograde amnesia by TCAP: drug dosage and electroshock intensity. *Comm. Behav. Biol.*, **1**, 183–187.

Essman, W. B. and Jarvik, M. E. (1961) Impairment of retention for a conditioned response by ether anesthesia in mice. *Psychopharmacologia*, **2**, 172–176.

Essman, W. B., Steinberg, M. L., and Golod, M. I. (1968) Alterations in the behavioral and biochemical effects of electroconvulsive shock with nicotine. *Psychon. Sci.*, **12**, 107–108.

Essman, W. B. and Sudak, F. N. (1962) Effect of body temperature reduction on response acquisition in mice. *J. appl. Physiol.*, **17**, 113–116.

Estler, C. (1962) Changes in cerebral hexokinase activity in white mice under the influence of central stimulants. *Archiv für Experimentelle Pathologie und Pharmakologie*, 292–293.

Exer, B. and Pulver, R. (1960) Some metabolic effects of Tofranil and metabolites. *Chimia*, **14**, 30.

Eysenck, H. J. (1960) *Experiments in Personality*. London: Routledge & Kegan Paul.

Eyzaguirre, C. and Lilenthal, J. L. Jr. (1949) Veratrinic effects of pentamethylenetetrazol (metrazol) and 2,2-bis (p-chlorophenyl)1,1,1 trichloroethane (DDT) on mammalian neuromuscular function. *Proc. soc. exp. biol. Med.*, **70**, 272–275.

Fan, C. (1965) K mekhanizmu tsentral'-nogo deystrivya medinala i khloralgidrata. *Farmakol. Toksikol.*, **28**, 647–649.

Feldman, S. and Wagman, I. H. (1962) Hypothalamic effects on spinal reflexes and their alteration by pentobarbital. *Exper. Neurol.*, **5**, 250–268.

Fieve, R. R. and Platman, S. E. (1968) Prophylactic lithium? *Lancet*, **ii**, 830.

Flodmark, S. and Leissner, P. (1965) Clinical detection of blood-brain barrier alteration by means of EEG. Part II: A comparison between the barbitone-EEG method and isotope encephalometry with RISA. *Acta Neurologica Scand.*, **41**, 179–192.

Floris, V., Morocutti, G., and Ayala, G. F. (1962) Azione della nicotina sull' attivitá bioelettrica della corteccia del talamo e dell'ippocampo nel coniglio. Su' azione di 'arousal' a convulsivante primitiva sulle strutture ippicampotalamiche. *Boll. So. Ital. Biol. Speriment.*, **38**, 407–410.

Foltz, E. E., Ivy, A. C., and Barborka, C. J. (1942) The use of double work periods in the study of fatigue and the influence of caffeine on recovery. *Amer. J. Physiol.*, **136**, 79–86.

FORNEY, R. B. and HUGHS, F. W. (1965) Effect of caffeine and alcohol on performance under stress of audiofeedback. *Quart. J. Stud. Alcohol.*, **26**, 206–212.

FRANKENHAEUSER, M. and BECKMAN, M. (1961) The susceptibility of intellectual functions to a depressant drug. *Scand. J. Psychol.*, **2**, 93–99.

FRANKS, C. M. and TROUTON, D. (1958) Effects of amobarbital sodium and dexamphetamine sulfate on the conditioning of the eyeblink response. *J. comp. physiol. Psychol.*, **51**, 220–222.

FRENCH, J. D., VERZEANO, M., and MAGOUN, H. W. (1953) A neural basis of the anesthetic state. *Arch. Neurol. Psychiat.*, Chicago, **69**, 519–529.

FRITH, C. D. (1967) The effects of nicotine on tapping: III. *Life Sciences*, **6**, 1541–1548.

FRITH, C. D. (1968) The effects of nicotine on the consolidation of pursuit rotor learning. *Life Sciences*, **7**, 77–84.

GOLOYAN, A. A. (1961) Changes in neurosecretion during various effects on the central nervous system. *Pathol. Biol.* (Paris), **9**, 682–684.

GANGLOFF, H. and MONNIER, M. (1955) Topische Bestimmung des zerebralen Angriffs von Reserpin (Serpasil). *Experientia*, **11**, 404–407.

GARATTINI, S. (1965) Effects of a cannabis extract on gross behaviour. In *Hashish, its Chemistry and Pharmacology* (Ed. Wolstenholme, G. E. & Knight, J.). London: Churchill, pp. 70–78.

GARATTINI, S. and SIGG, E.B. (Ed.) *Aggressive Behaviour*. Amsterdam: Excerpta Medica.

GARDNER, M. J., HAWKINS, H. M., JUDAH, L. N., and MURPHREE, O. D. (1955) Objective measurement of psychiatric changes produced by chlorpromazine and reserpine in chronic schizophrenia. *Psychiat. Res. Rep.*, **1**, 77–82.

GARG, M. and HOLLAND, H. C. (1968) Consolidation and maze learning: a further study of post-trial injections of a stimulant drug (nicotine). *Int. J. Neuropharmacol.*, **7**, 55–59.

GARG, M. (1969) The effects of some central nervous system stimulant and depressant drugs on rearing activity in rats. *Psychopharmacologia*, **14**, 150–156.

GAYER, H. (1928) Pharmakologische Wertbestimmung von orientalischen Haschisch und Herba *cannabis indica*. *Naunyn-Schmiedebergs Arch. exp. Pathol. Pharmak.*, **129**, 312–318.

GELLER, I., BACHMAN, E., and SEIFTER, J. (1963) Effects of reserpine and morphine on behavior suppressed by punishment. *Life Sciences*, **4**, 226–231.

GERSHON, S. and YUWILER, A. (1960) Lithium ion: a specific psychopharmacological approach to the treatment of mania. *J. Neuropsychiat.*, **1**, 229–241.

GEY, K. F. and PLETSCHER, A. (1961) Einfluss von Chlorpromazin und Chlorprothixen auf den Monoaminstoffwechsel des Rattenhirns. *Helv. Physiol. Pharmacol. Acta*, **19**, C22–C24.

GIBBY, R. G., Sr., GIBBY, R. G., Jr., KISH, G. B., and THEOLOGUS, G. C. (1965) Enhancement of avoidance learning by strychnine sulfate. *Psychol. Rep.*, **17**, 123–126.

GILETTE, J. R., DINGELL, J. V., SULSER, F., KUNTZMAN, R., and BRODIE, B. B. (1961) Isolation from rat brain of a metabolic product, desmethylimipramine, that mediates the antidepressant activity of imipramine (Tofranil). *Experientia*, **17**, 417.

GILMAN, S., MACFADYEN, D. J., and DENNY-BROWN, D. (1963) Decerebrate phenomena after carotid amobarbital injection. *Arch. Neurol.*, **8**, 662–675.

GLASKY, A. J. and SIMON, L. N. (1966) Magnesium pemoline: enhancement of brain RNA polymerases. *Science*, **151**, 702–703.

GOLDBERG, M. E. and JOHNSON, H. E. (1964) Potentiation of chlorpromazine-induced behavioural changes by anticholinesterase agents. *J. Pharm. Pharmacol.*, **61**, 60–61.

GOLDBERG, M., JOHNSON, H., POSSANI, U., and SMYTH, H. (1964) Behavioral response of rats during inhalation of trichloroethylene and carbon disulfide fumes. *Acta Pharmacologica et Toxicologica*, **21**, 31–44.

GOLDBERG, S. C., KLERMAN, G. L., and COLE, J. O. (1965) Changes in schizophrenic psychopathology and ward behaviour as a function of phenothiazine treatment. *Brit. J. Psychiat.*, **111**, 120–133.

GOLDMAN-EISLER, F., SKARBEK, A., and HENDERSON, A. (1966) Breath rate and the selective action of chlorpromazine on speech behaviour. *Psychopharmacologia*, **8**, 415–427.

GOLDSTEIN, A. and WARREN, R. (1961) Individual differences in sensitivity of people to the central effects of caffeine. *Fed. Proc.*, **20**, 394.

GOLDSTEIN, A., KAISER, S., and WARREN, R. (1965) Psychotropic effects of caffeine in man. II. Alertness, psychomotor coordination, and mood. *J. Pharmacol. exp. Therap.*, **150**, 146–151.

GOLDSTEIN, S., BOARDMAN, W. K., and LHAMON, W. T. (1958) Effect of quinal barbitone, dextroamphetamine and placebo on apparent time. *Brit. J. Psychol.*, **49**, 324–328.

GOODHART, R. S. and HELENORE, J. C. (Eds.) (1963) *Modern Drug Encyclopedia and Therapeutic Index*. 9th ed. New York: Reuben H. Donnelley.

GOTFREDSEN, C. F., MELLERUP, E. T., and RAFAELSEN, O. J. (1969) Lithium and some other psychopharmaca. Effect on electrolyte distribution and excretion in rat. *Proc. 2nd Int. Meet. Int. Soc. Neurochem.*, p. 196.

GRANDJEAU, E. and BÄTTIG, K. (1964) Le spectre des éffets du trichlorethylene sur le comportement du rat. *Arch. int. pharmacodyn. Thérap.*, **147**, 333–350.

GREENBLATT, M., LEVIN, S., and SCHEGLOFF, B. (1945) EEG findings in cases of bromide intoxication. *Arch. neurol. Psychiat.*, Chicago, **53**, 431–436.

GREENBLATT, E. N. and OSTERBERG, A. C. (1961) Effect of drugs on the maintenance of exploratory behavior in mice. *Fed. Proc.*, **20**, 397.

GREENOUGH, W. T. and McGAUGH, J. L. (1965) The effect of strychnine sulfate on learning as a function of time of administration. *Psychopharmacologia*, **8**, 290–294.

GROH, G. and LEMIEUX, M. (1964) The effects of three psychotropic drugs on spider web formation. In *The Butyrophenones in Psychiatry* (Ed. Lehmann, H. E. and Ban, T. A.). Quebec: Quebec Psychopharmacological Assn., p. 53.

GROSS, C. G. and WEISKRANTZ, L. A. (1961) The effect of two "tranquilizers" on auditory discrimination and delayed response performance in monkeys. *Quart. J. exp. Psychol.*, **13**, 34–39.

GUSEVA, YE G. (1964) Izmeneniye predela different-serovochnogo tormozheniya pod vliyaniyem kofeina i amitalnatrya. *Zhurnal Vysshey Nervnoy Deyatel'nosti*, **14**, 480–488. (Abstract).

HALPERN, F. (1944) Intellectual functioning, emotional reactions and personality structure. In *The Marihuana Problem in the City of New York*. Lancaster: Caitell Press, pp. 81–132.

HARTELIUS, H. (1950) Further experiences of the use of malononitrile in the treatment of mental illness. *Amer. J. Psychiat.*, **107**, 95–101.

HARTMAN, A. M. and HOLLISTER, L. E. (1963) The effect of mescaline lysergic acid diethylamide and psilocybin on color perception. *Psychopharmacologia*, **4**, 441–451.

HARTMANN, E. (1966) Reserpine: its effect on the sleep-dream cycle in man. *Psychopharmacologia*, **9**, 242–247.

HAWKINS, D. R., PACE, R., PASTERNACK, B., and SANDIFER, M. G., Jr. (1961) A multivariate psycho-pharmacologic study in normals. *Psychosom. Med.*, **23**, 1–17.

HAYS, S. B. (1965) Some effects of reserpine, a tran quilizer on the house fly. *J. Econ. Entomol.*, **58**, 782–783.

HEARST, E. and WHALEN, R. E. (1963) Facilitatory effects of d-amphetamine in discriminated avoidance performance. *J. comp. physiol. Psychol.*, **56**, 124–128.

HECHT, K. (1963) Comparative investigations of some centrally acting drugs with a conditioned-reflex motoric food method and a conditioned-reflex escape method. In *Psychopharmacological Methods* (Ed. Votava, Z., Horváth, M. and Vinar, O.). New York: Macmillan, p. 58.

HEIM, F. and ESTLER, C. J. (1961) Der Einfluss von Phenobarbital (Luminal) auf einige Funktionen und Metaboliten des Gehirns normaler und zentralerregter weisser Mäuse. *Klinische Wochenschrift*, **39**, 798–801.

HEIMSTRA, N. W. and MCDONALD, A. (1962) Social influence on the response to drugs. III. Response to amphetamine sulfate as a function of age. *Psycho-pharmacologia*, **3**, 212–218.

HEISE, G. A. and BOFF, E. (1962) Continuous avoidance as a baseline for measuring behavioral effects of drugs. *Psychopharmacologia*, **3**, 264–282.

HERR, F., STEWART, J., and CHAREST, M-P. (1961) Tranquilizers and antidepressants: a pharmacological comparison. *Arch. int. pharmacodyn. Thérap.*, **134**, 328–342.

HERZ, A. and FUSTER, J. M. (1964) Über das Entladungs-muster von Neuronen des optischen Cortex und dessen Veränderung durch Barbiturate und Amphetamin. *Naunyn-Schmiedeberg's Archiv. für exp. pathol. Pharmakol.*, **246**, 25–26.

HERZ, M., PEEKE, H., WYERS, E. (1966) Amnesic effects of ether and electroconvulsive shock in mice. *Psychonom. Sci.*, **4**, 375–376.

HIEBEL, G., BONVALLET, M., and DELL, P. (1954) Sympathetic tonus, central electrical activity and waking state. Effects of chlorpromazine (Largactil)

and of a dextrorotary benzedrine. *EEG Clin. Neurophysiol.*, **6**, 160.

HOEHN-SARIC, R., BACON, E. F., and GROSS, M. (1964) Effects of chlorpromazine on flicker fusion. *J. nerv. ment. Dis.*, **138**, 287–292.

HOFMANN, A. (1955) Discovery of d-lysergic acid diethylamide—LSD. *Sandoz Excerpta*, **1**, 1.

HOFMANN, A. (1968) In *Drugs Affecting the Central Nervous System* (Ed. Berger, A.). New York: Marcel Dekker, pp. 169–235.

HOLLISTER, L. E., DEGAN, R. O., and SCHULTZ, S. D. (1962) An experimental approach to facilitation of psychotherapy by psychotomimetic drugs. *J. ment. Sci.*, **108**, 99–100.

HOLMGREN, B. and CONDI, C. (1964) Conditioned avoidance reflex under pentobarbital. *Boletin del instituto de estudios medicos y biologicos*, **22**, 21–38.

HOLZBAUER, M. and VOGT, M. (1956) Depression by reserpine of the noradrenaline concentration in the hypothalamus of the cat. *J. Neurochem.*, **1**, 8–11.

HUNT, E. and KRIVANEK, J. (1966) The effects of pentylenetetrazol and methylphenoxypropane on discrimination learning. *Psychopharmacologia*, **9**, 1–16.

HUNT, H. F. (1956) Some effects of drugs on classical (type S) conditioning. *Ann. N.Y. Acad. Sci.*, **65**, 258–267.

HYDÉN, H. (1963) Biochemical and functional interplay between neuron and glia. *Rec. adv. biol. Psychiat.*, **6**, 31.

HYDÉN, H. and HARTELIUS, H. (1948) Stimulation of the nucleoprotein production in the nerve cells by malononitrile and its effect on psychic functions in mental disorders. *Acta Psychiat.*, Suppl. 48.

IANNONE, A. M. and MORRELL, F. (1961) Experience with intracarotid amytal in man. *Electroenceph. clin. Neurophysiol.*, **13**, 306.

IDESTRÖM, C. M. and CADENIUS, B. (1963) Chlordiazepoxide, dipiperon, and amobarbital: dose effect studies on human beings. *Psychopharmacologia*, **4**, 235–246.

INNES, I. R. and NICKERSON, M. (1965) Drugs acting on postganglionic adrenergic nerve endings and structures innervated by them (sympathomimetic drugs). In *The Pharmacological Basis of Therapeutics* (Ed. Goodman, L. S. and Gilman, A.). New York: Macmillan, Chapter 24.

IRWIN, S. (1961) Correlation in rats between the loco-motor and avoidance suppressant potencies of eight phenothiazine tranquilizers. *Arch. int. Pharmacodyn.*, **132**, 279–286.

IRWIN, S. and BENUAZIZI, A. (1966) Pentylenetetrazol enhances memory function. *Science*, **152**, 100–102.

ISBELL, H. and LOGAN, C. R. (1957) Studies on the diethylamide of lysergic acid (LSD-25). II. Effects of chlorpromazine, azacyclonol, and reserpine on the intensity of the LSD-reaction. *Amer. med. assn. Arch. Neurol. Psychiat.*, **77**, 350–358.

ITIL, T. (1962) Die Problematik der Schlafstörungen und deren Beeinflussung. *Arzneimittel Forschung*, **12**, 399–407.

ITIL, T., STOERGER, R., and RAJOTTE, P. (1963) Clinical and electroencephalographic study of a new hypno-sedative combination and its constituents. *Dis. nerv. Syst.*, **24**, 476–483.

JANSSEN, P. A., JAGENEAU, A. H., and NEMEGEERS, C. J. (1960) Effects of various drugs on isolation-induced fighting behavior of male mice. *J. pharmacol. exp. Therap.*, **129**, 471–475.

JANSSEN, P. A., VAN DE WESTERINGH, C., JAGENEAU, A. H., DEMOEN, P. J., HERMANS, B. K., VAN DAELE, G. H., SCHELLEKENS, K. H., VANDER EYCKEN, C. A., and NIEMEGEERS, C. J. (1960) Chemistry and pharmacology of CNS depressants related to 4-(4-hydroxyphenyl-piperidino)butyrophenone. I. Synthesis and screening data in mice. *J. med. pharm. Chem.*, **1**, 281–297.

JARVIK, M. (1961) Nature of efficiency decrement produced by N₂O on monkeys in a visual discrimination and delayed response test. *J. pharmacol. exp. Therap.*, **131**, 108–114.

JONGKEES, L. B. W. (1961) The influence of some drugs upon the function of the labyrinth. *Acta otolaryngologica*, **53**, 281–286.

KAHAN, S. A. (1966) The effects of metrazol on operant response rates. *Physiol. Behav.*, **1**, 117–123.

KAMANO, D. K., MARTIN, L. K., OGLE, M. E., and POWELL, B. J. (1966) Effects of amobarbital on the conditioned emotional response and conditioned avoidance response. *Psychol. Rec.*, **16**, 13–16.

KAMANO, D. K., MARTIN, L. K., and POWELL, B. J. (1966) Avoidance response acquisition and amobarbital dosage levels. *Psychopharmacologia*, **8**, 319–323.

KEELER, M. H. (1965) The effects of psilocybin on a test of after image perception. *Psychopharmacologia*, **8**, 131–139.

KELEMAN, K. and DANIEL, B. (1961) [Effects of drugs on protective reflex activities in rats]. *Kiserl Orvustud*, **13**, 419–429.

KELLEHER, R. T., FRY, W., DEEGAN, J., and COOK, L. (1961) Effects of meprobamate on operant behavior in rats. *J. pharmacol. exp. Therap.*, **133**, 271–280.

KETUSINH, OU., NILVESES, N., and CHENPANICH, K. (1962) Der siamesische Kampffsch (*Betta splendens Regan*) als Versuchstier für Psychopharmaka: Wirkungen und Gegenwirkungen zentralstimulierender und hemmender Pharmaka auf die Kampfestellungs-reaktion. *Arch. exp. pathol. Pharmakol.*, **243**, 301–302.

KETY, S. S. (1955) Consideration of pharmacological agents on the over-all circulation and metabolism of the brain. In *Neuropharmacology* (Ed. H. A. Abrahmson). New York: Josiah Macy, Jr. Foundation, pp. 13–89.

KIDO, R. and YAMAMOTO, K. (1961) An analysis of tranquilizers in chronically electrodes-implanted cat. *Biochem. Pharmacol.*, **8**, 42.

KILLAM, E. K. and KILLAM, K. F. (1956) A comparison of the effects of reserpine and chlorpromazine to those of barbiturates on central afferent systems in the cat. *J. pharmacol. exp. Therap.*, **116**, 35.

KILLAM, E. K., KILLAM, K. F., and SHAW, T. (1957) The effects of psychotherapeutic compounds on central afferent and limbic pathways. *Ann. N. Y. Acad. Sci.*, **6**, 784–805.

KILLAM, E. K. and KILLAM, K. F. (1959) Phenothiazine-pharmacologic studies. In *The Effect of Pharmacologic Agents on the Nervous System* (Ed. Braceland, F. J.). Baltimore: Williams and Wilkins.

KIRPEKAR, S. M. and LEWIS, J. J. (1959) Some effects of reserpine and hydrallazine upon tissue respiration and the concentration of adenosine nucleotides in certain tissues. *Brit. J. Pharmacol.*, **14**, 40–45.

KIVALO, E., RINNE, U. K., and KARINKANTA, H. (1961) The effect of imipramine on the 5-hydroxy-tryptamine content and monoamine oxidase activity of the rat brain and on the excretion of 5-hydroxyindoleacetic acid. *J. Neurochem.*, **8**, 105.

KLEMAN, J. P., DIAMOND, A. L., and SMITH, E. (1961) Effects of caffeine on enhancement in foveal simultaneous contrast. *J. exp. Psychol.*, **61**, 18–22.

KLERMAN, G. L. and DIMASCIO, A. (1961) Psychological effects of piperazine phenothiazine. *Fed. Proc.*, **20**, 393.

KNAPP, D. E. (1961) Evidence for a nicotinic receptor in the central nervous system related to EEG arousal. *Fed. Proc.*, **20**, 307.

KNEIP, P. (1960) Climbing impulse and climbing test (In German). *Arch. int. pharmacodyn. Thérap.*, **126**, 238–245.

KOBAYASHI, T. (1962) Drug administration to cerebral cortex of freely moving dogs. *Science*, **135**, 1126–1127.

KOHN, B. and BRYDEN, M. P. (1965) The effect of lysergic acid diethylamide (LSD-25) on perception with stabilized images. *Psychopharmacologia*, **7**, 311–320.

KORNETSKY, C., VATES, T. S., and KESSLER, E. K. (1959) A comparison of hypnotic and residual psychological effects of single dose of chlorpromazine and secobarbital in man. *J. pharmacol. exp. Thérap.*, **127**, 51–54.

KORNETSKY, C. (1960) Alterations in psychomotor functions and individual differences in responses produced by psychoactive drugs. In *Drugs and Behavior* (Ed. Uhr, L. & Muller, J. G.). New York: John Wiley, pp. 297–312.

KORNETSKY, C. and ORZACK, M. H. (1964) A research note on some of the critical factors on the dissimilar effects of chlorpromazine and secobarbital on the digit symbol substitution and continuous performance tests. *Psychopharmacologia*, **6**, 79–86.

KOSTOWSKI, W. (1966) A note on the effects of some psychotropic drugs on the aggressive behavior in the ant. *Formica rufa. J. pharmac. Pharmacol.*, **18**, 747–749.

KRAINES, S. H. (1965) Sodium amytal hypnosis and psychotherapy. *Amer. J. Psychiat.*, **122**, 458–460.

KRAL, V. A., SOLYOM, L., and ENESCO, H. E. (1967) Effect of short-term oral RNA therapy on the serum uric acid level and memory function in senile versus senescent subjects. *J. Amer. Geriat. Soc.*, **15**, 364–372.

KRIECKHAUS, E. F., MILLER, N. E., and ZIMMERMAN, P. (1965) Reduction of freezing behaviour and improvement in shock avoidance by d-amphetamine. *J. comp. dhysiol. Psychol.*, **60**, 36–40.

KRIVANEK, J. and HUNT, E. (1967) The effects of post-trial injection of pentylenetetrazol, strychnine and mephenesin on discrimination learning. *Psychopharmacologia*, **10**, 189–195.

KULKARNI, A. S., THOMPSON, T., and SHIDEMAN, F. E. (1966) Effect of reserpine administered during infancy on brain catecholamines and adult behavior in the rat. *J. Neurochem.*, **13**, 1143–1148.

LATZ, A. (1963) The differential effects of chlorpromazine and secobarbital on sustained attention in chronic schizophrenics. *Fed. Proc.*, **22**, 509.

LATZ, A. (1964) Alterations in the performance of mice on a learned task after the administration of antidepressant drugs. *Fed. Proc.*, **23**, 103.

LEBLANC, J. (1958) Effect of chlorpromazine on swimming time of rats at different temperatures. *Proc. soc. exp. biol. Med.*, **98**, 648–650.

LEHMANN, H. E. and HANRAHAN, G. E. (1954) Chlorpromazine, a new inhibiting agent for psychomotor excitement and manic states. *Amer. med. assn. Arch. Neurol. Psychiat.*, **71**, 227–237.

LEONARD, B. E. (1966a) The effect of the chronic administration of barbitone sodium on labile compounds in the rat brain. *Biochem. Pharmacol.*, **15**, 255–262.

LEONARD, B. E. (1966b) The effect of the chronic administration of barbitone sodium on pituitary-adrenal function in the rat. *Biochem. Pharmacol.*, **15**, 263–268.

LEWIN, J. and ESPLIN, D. W. (1961) Analysis of the spinal excitatory action of pentylenetetrazol. *J. pharmacol. exp. Therap.*, **132**, 245–250.

LEWIS, J. L. and MCILWAIN, H. (1954) The action of some ergot derivatives, mescaline, and dibenamine on the metabolism of separated mammalian cerebral tissues. *Bio. Chem. J.*, **57**, 680–684.

LINDAN, O., QUASTEL, J. H., and SVED, S. (1957) Biochemical studies on chlorpromazine. 1. The effect of chlorpromazine on respiratory activity of isolated rat brain cortex. *Canad. J. Biochem. Physiol.*, **35**, 1135–1144.

LINUCHEV, M. N. and MICHELSON, M. J. (1965) Action of nicotine on the rate of elaboration of food motor conditioned reflexes in rats of different ages. *Activ. Nerv. Sup.*, **7**, 25–30.

LOEWE, S. (1944) Pharmacological study. In *The Marihuana Problem in the City of New York.* Lancaster: Cattell Press.

LONGO, V. G. and SILVESTRINI, B. (1957) Action of eserine and amphetamine on the electrical activity of the rabbit brain. *J. pharmacol. exp. Therap.*, **120**, 160–170.

LOUTTIT, R. T. (1965) Central nervous system stimulants and maze learning in rats. *Psychol. Rec.*, **15**, 97–102.

LUCO, J. V., MARTORELL, R., and REID, A. (1949) Effect of amphetamine on the synaptic transmission of sympathetic ganglion and spinal cord. *J. Pharmacol.*, **97**, 171–176.

LUDVIGSON, H. W. (1960) The effects of chlorpromazine and 4-amphetamine on eyelid conditioning. Ph.D. Thesis, State University of Iowa.

MCDOWALL, A., OWEN, S., and ROBIN, A. (1966) A controlled comparison of diazepam and amylobarbitone in anxiety states. *Brit. J. Psychiat.*, **112**, 629–631.

MCGAUGH, J. L. (1961) Facilitative and disruptive effects of strychnine sulfate on maze learning. *Psychol. Rep.*, **8**, 99–104.

MCGAUGH, J. L. and THOMSON, C. W. (1962) Facilitation of simultaneous discrimination learning with strychnine sulfate. *Psychopharmacologia*, **3**, 166–172.

MCGAUGH, J. L., THOMPSON, C. W., WESTBROOK, W. H., and HUDSPETH, W. J. (1962) A further study of learning facilitation with strychnine sulfate. *Psychopharmacologia*, **3**, 352–360.

MCILWAIN, H. (1966) *Biochemistry and the Central Nervous System.* Boston; Little, Brown & Co., pp. 338–345.

MAGGS, R. (1963) Treatment of manic illness with lithium carbonate. *Brit. J. Psychiat.*, **109**, 56–65.

MALHOTRA, C. L. and PUNDLIK, P. G. (1965) The effect of reserpine on the acetylcholine concentration in hypothalamus, ileum, and heart of the dog after bilateral vagotomy and ganglionic blockade. *Brit. J. Pharmacol. Chemotherap.*, **24**, 119–123.

MALIS, J. L. (1962) Effects of drugs on the regulation of an aversive stimulus in the monkey. *Fed. Proc.*, **2**, 327.

MANGONI, A., ANDREOLI, V., CABIBBE, F., and MANDELLI, V. (1969) Body fluids distribution in manic and depressed patients treated with lithium carbonate. *Proc. 2nd Int. Meet. Int. Soc. Neurochem.*, pp. 279–280.

MARAZZI, A. (1953) Some indications of cerebral humoral mechanisms. *Science*, **118**, 367–370.

MARAZZI, A. S. and HART, E. R. (1955) Amphetamine effect on midbrain synapses. *Science*, **121**, 365.

MARAZZI, A. S. (1960) The action of psychotogens and a neurophysiological theory of hallucination. *Amer. J. Psychiat.*, **116**, 911–914.

MARKOVA, I. O. (1960) Age sensitivity to barbiturate and its dependence on the development of the hypophyseal-adrenal system. *Biull. eksper. biol. i med.*, **50**, 87–90.

MATTHEWS, E. K. and QUILLIAM, J. P. (1962) Central depressant drugs and acetylcholine release. *Fed. Proc.*, **2**, 239 (Abstract).

MAXWELL, D. R., PALMER, H. T., and RYALL, R. W. (1961) A comparison of the analgesic and some other central properties of methotrimeprazine and morphine. *Arch. int. pharmacodyn. Thérap.*, **132**, 60–73.

MAXWELL, D. R. and PALMER, H. T. (1961) Demonstration of anti-depressant or stimulant properties of imipramine in experimental animals. *Nature*, **191**, 84–85.

MAXWELL, D. R. (1964) The relative potencies of various antidepressant drugs in some laboratory tests. In *Neuropsychopharmacology*, Vol. 3 (Ed. Bradley, P. B., Flügel, F. & Hoch, P.). Amsterdam: Elsevier, pp. 501–506.

MAY, A. R. (1961) Drug treatment of neurotic symptoms with a combination of trifluoperazine and amylobarbitone (amylozine). *Medical Press* (Lond.) **245**, 269–272.

MAY, P. and EBAUGH, F. (1953) Use of hypnotics in aging and senile patients. *J. Amer. med. Assn.*, **152**, 801.

MAYER-GROSS, W., MCADAM, W., and WALKER, J. W. (1953) Further observations on the effects of lysergic acid diethylamide. *J. ment. Sci.*, **99**, 804.

MAYFIELD, D. and BROWN, R. G. (1966) The Clinical Laboratory. Electroencephalographic effects of lithium. *J. Psychiat. Res.*, **4**, 207–219.

MERCIER, J. and DESSAIGNE, S. (1960) Détermination de l'accoutumance expérimentale par une méthode psychologique (IVᵉ Memoire). Etude de quelques drogues sympathicomimétiques, de la nicotine et de la cocaine. *Ann. pharm. Franc.*, **18**, 502–518.

MILLER, N. E. (1961) Some recent studies of conflict behavior and drugs. *Amer. Psychol.*, **16**, 12–24.

MITCHELL, J. C. and KING, F. A. (1960) The effects of chlorpromazine on water maze learning, retention, and stereotyped behavior in the rat. *Psychopharmacologia*, **1**, 463–468.

MODELL, W. (1966) Choice of stimulants to the medulla. In *Drugs of Choice*. New York: C. V. Mosby, Chapter 12.

MONROE, R. R., HEATH, R. G., MICKLE, W. A., and MILLER, W. (1955) A comparison of cortical and subcortical brain waves in normal barbiturate, reserpine, and chlorpromazine sleep. *Ann. N. Y. Acad. Sci.*, **61**, 56–71.

MORRISON, C. F. (1967) Effects of nicotine on operant behaviour of rats. *Int. J. Neuropharmacol.*, **6**, 229–240.

MORRISON, C. F. (1968) The modification by physo-stigmine of some effects of nicotine on bar-pressing behaviour of rats. *Brit. J. pharmacol. Chemotherap.*, **32**, 28–33.

MÜLLER-CALGAN, H. E. and HOTOVY, R. (1961) Verhaltensänderung der Katze durch verschiedene Zentralerregendwirkende Pharmaka. 2. Mitteilung. *Arzneimittel Forsch.*, **11**, 775–783.

MURPHREE, H. B. (1967) Methodology for the clinical evaluation of analgesics. *J. New Drugs*, **6**, 15–22.

MYERS, S. A. and CALDWELL, D. F. (1969) The effects of marihuana on auditory and visual sensation: a preliminary report. *New Physician*, **18**, 212–215.

NACHMANSOHN, D. (1938) Sur l'action de la strychnine. *Seanc. Soc. Biol.*, **129**, 941–943.

NASH, H. (1962) *Alcohol and caffeine. A study of their psychological effects.* Springfield, Ill.: Chas. C. Thomas.

NASH, H. (1962) Psychologic effects of amphetamines and barbiturates. *J. nerv. ment. Dis.*, **134**, 203–217.

NATHANSON, M. H. (1937) The central actions of beta-aminopropylbenzene (benzedrine)—clinical observations. *J. Amer. med. Assn.*, **108**, 528–531.

NICOLAOU, G. T. and KLINE, N. S. (1955) Reserpine in the treatment of disturbed adolescents. *Psychiat. Res. Rep.*, **1**, 122–132.

NORTON, S., DEBEER, E. J., and TAMBURRO, J. (1957) Comparison of the effects of chlorpromazine and pentobarbital on cat behaviour. *J. Pharmacol.*, **119**, 173.

OLIVERIO, A. (1967) Analysis of the 'anti-fatigue' activity of amphetamine. Role of central adrenergic mechanisms. *Il Farmaco (Milano)*, **22**, 441–449.

OROWAN, E. (1955) The origin of man. *Nature*, **175**, 683–684.

OSWALD, I., BERGER, R. J., JARAMILLO, R. A., KEDDIE, K. M. G., OLLEY, P. C., and PLUNKETT, G. B. (1963) Melancholia and barbiturates: A controlled EEG body and eye movement study of sleep. *Brit. J. Psychiat.*, **109**, 66–78.

OTIS, L. S. (1964) Dissociation and recovery of a response learned under the influence of chlorpromazine of saline. *Science*, **143**, 1347–1348.

OVERALL, J. E., HOLLISTER, L. E., HONGFIELD, G., KIMBELL, I. H. Jr., MEYER, F., BENNETT, J. L., and CAFFEY, E. Jr. (1963) Comparison of acetophenazine with perphenazine in schizophrenics: demonstration of differential effects based on computer-derived diagnostic models. *Clin. Pharmacol. Therap.*, **4**, 200–208.

OVERALL, J. E., HOLLISTER, L. E., MEYER, F. (1964) Imipramine and thioredazine in depressed and schizophrenic patients. Are there specific antidepressant drugs? *J. Amer. med. Assn.*, **189**, 805–806.

OVERTON, D. A. (1964) State-dependent or "dissociated" learning product by pentobarbital. *J. comp. physiol. Psychol.*, **57**, 3–12.

PAASONEN, M. K. and VOGT, M. (1956) The effect of drugs on the amount of Substance P and 5-hydroxy-tryptamine in mammalian brain. *J. Physiol. (Lond.)*, **131**, 617–626.

PARE, W. (1961) The effect of caffeine and seconal on a visual discrimination task. *J. comp. physiol. Psychol.*, **54**, 506–509.

PAVLOV, I. P. (1927) *Conditioned Reflexes.* London: Oxford Univ. Press.

PAVLOV, I. P. (1941) *Conditioned Reflexes and Psychiatry.* New York: International Publishers.

PEARLMAN, C. A., Jr., SHARPLESS, S. K., and JARVIK, M. E. (1961) Retrograde amnesia produced by anesthetic and convulsive agents. *J. comp. physiol. Psychol.*, **54**, 109–112.

PENALOZA-ROJAS (1961) see: Hernandez-Peon, R. (1960) Physiology of pain. *Acta Neurol. (Nap.)*, **6**, 174–182.

PEREZ-BORJA and RIVERS, M. H. (1963) Some scalp and depth electrographic observations on the action of intracarotid sodium amytal injection on epileptic discharges in man. *Electroenceph. clin. Neurophysiol.*, **15**, 588–598.

PERVOV, L. G. (1965) Izuchenie obraznogo myshlenila i vozmozhnost' medikamentoznogo vozdeistviia na nego u bol'nykh nevradenief. *Zh. Nevropat Psikhiat Korsakov*, **65**, 715–720.

PETERS, J. M. (1967) Factors affecting caffeine toxicity. A review of the literature. *J. clin. Pharmacol.*, **7**, 131–141.

PETRINOVICH, L. (1963) Facilitation of successive discrimination by strychnine sulfate. *Psychopharmacologia*, **4**, 103–113.

PETRINOVICH, L., BRADFORD, D., and McGAUGH, J. L. (1965) Drug facilitation of memory in rats. *Psychon. Sci.*, **2**, 191–192.

PETRINOVICH, L. (1967) Drug facilitation of learning: strain differences. *Psychopharmacologia*, **10**, 375–378.

PLAS, R. and NAQUET, R. (1961) Contribution to the neurophysiological study of imipramine. *CR Soc. Biol.*, **155**, 547–550 and 840–843.

PLENGE, P., MELLERUP, E. T., and RAFAELSEN, O. J. (1969) Lithium action on the carbohydrate metabolism in rat brain, muscle, and liver. *Proc. 2nd Int. Meet. Int. Soc. Neurochem.*, p. 321.

PLETSCHER, A., SHORE, P. A., and BRODIE, B. B. (1955) Serotonin release as a possible mechanism of reserpine action. *Science*, **122**, 374–375.

PLETSCHER, A. and GEY, K. F. (1959) Pharmacological influence of 5-hydroxytryptamine metabolism in the brain and monoamine oxidase inhibition in vitro. *Helvet. physiol. pharmacol. Acta*, **17**, C35.

PLETSCHER, A. and GEY, K. F. (1960) The effect of chlorpromazine on pharmacological changes in 5-hydroxytryptamine and noradrenaline content in the brain (In German). *Med. Exp.*, **2**, 259–265.

PLETSCHER, A. and GEY, K. F. (1962) Action of imipramine and amitriptyline on cerebral monoamines as compared with chlorpromazine. *Med. Exper.*, **6**, 165.

PLOTNIKOFF, N. (1962) Bioassay of psychoactive agents on escape from auditory stress. *Fed. Proc.*, **21**, 420.

PLOTNIKOFF, N. (1966) Magnesium pemoline: antagonism of retrograde amnesia in rats. *Fed. Proc.*, **25**, 262.

PLOTNIKOFF, N. (1966) Magnesium pemoline: Enhancement of learning and memory of conditioned avoidance response. *Science*, **151**, 703–704.

POWELL, B. J., MARTIN, L. K., and KAMANO, D. K. (1965) Failure to find improved shuttle box avoidance performance using d-amphetamine sulfate. *Psychol. Rep.*, **17**, 330.

POWELL, B. J., OGLE, M. E., MARTIN, L. K., and KAMANO, D. K. (1966) CS intensity, amobarbital sodium and the conditioned avoidance response. *Psychol. Rep.*, **18**, 645–656.

PREIBISCH-EFFENBERGER, R. and KNOTHE, J. (1965) Der Einfluss zentralwirkender Pharmaka auf die Wortverständlichkeit des Normalhörenden bei binauraler Testsprache. *Z. Laryng. Rhinol. Otol. u. Grenzgeb.*, **44**, 619–630.

PRESTON, J. B. (1956) Effects of chlorpromazine on the central nervous system of the cat: a possible neural basis for action. *J. Pharmacol.*, **118**, 100–115.

PRIEN, R. F., WAGNER, M. J. Jr., and KAHN, S. (1963) Lack of facilitation in maze learning by picrotoxin and strychnine sulfate. *Amer. J. Psychol.*, **204**, 488–492.

PULVER, R., EXER, B., and HERRMANN, B. (1960) Einige Wirkungen des (γ-Dimethylaminopropyl)iminobenzyl-HCl und seiner Maetabolite auf den Stoffwechsel von Neurohormonen. *Arzneimittel-Forsch.*, **10**, 530.

QUANDT, J. (1961) Erfahrungen mit Itridal unter besonderer Berücksichtigung der Behandlung akuter psychomotorischer Erregungszustände. *Medizinische Welt.*, **29/30**, 1523–1525.

QUARTON, G. C. and TALLAND, G. A. (1962) The effects of methamphetamine and pentobarbital on two measures of attention. *Psychopharmacologia*, **3**, 66–71.

QUASTEL, J. H. and WHEATLEY, H. J. N. (1933) Effects of amines on oxidation of the brain. *Biochem. J.*, **27**, 1609–1613.

RAHMANN, H. (1963) Einfluss von Koffein auf das Gedächtnis und das Verhalten von Goldhamstern. *Pflüg. Archiv.*, **276**, 384–397.

REMMER, H. (1964) Gewöhnung an Hexobarbital durch beschleunigten Abbau. *Arch. Int. Pharmacodyn.*, **152**, 346–359.

REMMER, H., SIEGERT, M., and NEUHAUS, G. (1964) Die Elimination von Glutethimid und von langwirkenden Barbituraten nach toxisch und therapeutisch wirksamen Dosen. *Naunyn Schmiedelberg Arch. Exp. Path.*, **245**, 471–483.

RINALDI, F. and HIMWICH, H. E. (1955a) Drugs affecting psychotic behavior and the function of the mesodiencephalic activating system. *Dis. nerv. Syst.*, **16**, 133–141.

RINALDI, F. and HIMWICH, H. E. (1955b) A comparison of effects of reserpine and some barbiturates on the electrical activity of cortical and subcortical structures of the brain of rabbits. *Ann. N.Y. Acad. Sci.*, **61**, 27–35.

RITCHIE, J. M. (1965) The Xanthines. In *The Pharmacological Basis of Therapeutics* (Ed. Goodman, L. S. and Gilman, A.). New York: The Macmillan Co., pp. 354–366.

ROBUSTELLI, F. (1966) Azione della nicotina sul condizionamento di salvaguardia di ratti di un mese. (Action of nicotine on avoidance conditioning in 1-month-old rats). *R.C. Accad. Napoli*, **40**, 490–497.

RONCO, P. and CACOPARDO, A. (1957) La percezione visiva in alcoolisti cronici sotto l'azione della reserpina e della clorpromazina. *Acta Neurol.*, **12**, 507–516.

ROSNER, H., LEVINE, S., HESS, H., and KAY, H. (1955) A comparative study of the effect on anxiety of chlorpromazine, reserpine, phenobarbital, and a placebo. *J. nerv. ment. Dis.*, **122**, 505–512.

RUBIN, A. A., MALAMUD, W., and HOPE, J. M. (1942) The EEG and psychopathological manifestations in schizophrenia as influenced by drugs. *Psychosom. Med.*, **4**, 355–361.

RUBIO-CHEVANNIER, H., BACH-E-RITA, G., PEÑALOZA-ROJAS, J., and HERNANDEZ-PÉON, R. (1961) Potentiating action of imipramine upon 'reticular arousal'. *Exp. Neurol.*, **4**, 214.

SALUSTIANO, J., HOSHINO, K., and CARLINI, E. A. (1966) Effects of cannabis sativa and chlorpromazine on mice as measured by two methods used for evaluation of tranquilizing agents. *Med. Pharmacol. Exp.*, **15**, 153–162.

SANDBERG, F. (1959) A comparative quantitative study of the central depressant effect of seven clinically used phenothiazine derivatives. *Arzneimitt. Forsch.*, **9**, 203–206.

SANTOS, M., SAMPAIO, M. R. P., FERNANDES, N. S., and CARLINI, E. A. (1966) Effects of *Cannabis sativa* (Marihuana) on the fighting behavior of mice. *Psychopharmacologia*, **8**, 437–444.

SCHALLEK, W., KUEHN, A., and SEPPELIN, D. K. (1956) Central depressant effects of methylprylon. *J. Pharmacol. exp. Therap.*, **118**, 139–147.

SCHANBERG, S., SCHILDKRAUT, J. J., and KOPIN, I. J. (1967) The effects of psychoactive drugs on norepinephrine-H³ metabolism in brain. *Biochem. Pharmacol.*, **16**, 393–399.

SCHECKEL, C. L. and BOFF, E. (1964) Behavioral effects of interacting imipramine and other drugs with d-amphetamine, cocaine, and tetrabenazine. *Psychopharmacologia*, **5**, 198–208.

SCHIEVELBEIN, H. and WERLE, E. (1962) Freisetzung von 5-Hydroxytryptamin durch Nicotin. *Psychopharmacologia*, **3**, 35–43.

SCHILDKRAUT, J. J., SCHANBERG, S. M., and KOPIN, I. J. (1966) The effects of lithium ion on H^3-norepinephrine metabolism in brain. *Life Sciences*, **5**, 1479.

SCHNEIDER, R. A. and COSTILOE, J. P. (1956) Inhibition and facilitation of the conditioned galvanic skin reflex by centrally acting drugs. (Chlorpromazine, amobarbital and methylphenidylacetate). *Clin. Res. Proc.*, **4**, 45.

SCHNEIDER, J. A. and EARL, A. E. (1954) Effects of Serpasie on behavior and autonomic regulating mechanisms. *Neurol.*, **4**, 657–667.

SCHNEIDER, J. A. (1955) Further characterization of central effects of reserpine (Serpasil). *Amer. J. Physiol.*, **181**, 64–68.

SCHOU, M. (1959) Lithium in psychiatric therapy. Stocktaking after 10 years. *Psychopharmacologia*, **1**, 65–78.

SCHOU, M. (1963) Normothymoleptics 'mood normalizers'. Are lithium and imipramine drugs specific for affective disorders? *Brit. J. Psychiat.*, **109**, 803.

SCHOU, M. (1967) Lithium, sodium and manic depressive psychosis. In *Molecular Basis of Some Aspects of Mental Activity*, Vol. 2 (Ed. Walaas, O.). New York: Academic Press, p. 457.

SCHWARTZ, M., SHAGALL, C., BITTLE, R., and FLAPAN, N. (1962) Dose related effects of pentobarbital on somatosensory evoked responses and recovery cycles. *Electroenceph. clin. Neurophysiol.*, **14**, 898–903.

SEASHORE, R. H. and IVY, A. C. (1953) Effects of analeptics in relieving fatigue. *Psychol. Monographs*, **67**, 1–16.

SEN, G. and BOSE, K. C. (1931) *Rauwolfia serpentina*, a new Indian drug for insanity and high blood pressure. *Ind. med. Wld.*, **2**, 194–201.

SHCHELKUNOV, YE. (1963) 1. Usiliniye tofranilom i khloratsizinom antirezerpinovogo deystviya fenamina v apytakh na krysakh s uslovnymi refleksami. *Activitas Nervosa Superior*, **5**, 4–12.

SHEPPARD, C., BHATTACHARYYA, A., DIGIACOMO, M., and MERLIS, S. (1964) Effects of acetophenazine dimaleate on paranoid symptomatology in female geriatric patients. Double-blind study. *J. Amer. geriat. Soc.*, **12**, 884–888.

SHUGAYEV, V. A. (1965) Vliyaniye reserpina, na uslovnoreflektomuya deyetel 'nost' belykh myshey. *Farmakol. Toksikol.*, **28**, 3–4.

SIGG, E. B. (1959) Pharmacological studies with Tofranil. *Canad. psychiat. Assoc. J.*, **4**, 75.

SILA, B., MOWRER, M., ULETT, G., and JOHNSON, M. (1962) The differentiation of psychiatric patients by EEG changes after sodium pentathol. *Proc. Neurol. Psychiat.*, **17**, 191–199.

SIVADJIAN, J. (1934) Etude pharmacologique d'un réflex conditioné. *C. R. Acad. Sci., Paris*, **199**, 884–886 (abstract).

SIVADON, P., FERNANDEZ, A., and ROSENBERGER-DEBIESSE, J. (1965) L'acétyltryptophanate de caféine en pratique psychiatrique. *Ann. Medicopsychol.*, **123**, 153–158.

SMITH, G. M. and BEECHER, H. K. (1959) Amphetamine sulfate and athletic performance. I. Objective effects. *J. Amer. med. Assn.*, **170**, 542.

SMITH, G. M., WEITZNER, M., and BEECHER, H. K. (1963) Increased sensitivity of measurement of drug effects in expert swimmers. *J. pharmacol. exp. Therap.*, **139**, 114–119.

SMITH, S. E. and SULLIVAN, T. J. (1965) The effect of cyclobarbitone on mental performance: A teaching experiment. *J. med. Educat.*, **40**, 294–297.

SOFRONOV, M. S. and TSOBKALLO, G. I. (1959) Changes in the higher nervous activity of dogs in chronic use of Barbamyl. *Physiol. patologii nerv. Sist., Moscow*: Acad. Sci., U.S.S.R., 717–730.

SÖRGEL, H.-J. (1961) Nicotinschäden am Zentralnervensystem. *Deutsche Gesundheitswesen*, **16**, 686–690.

STARK, P. and TOTTY, C. W. (1967) Effects of amphetamines on eating elicited by hypothalamic stimulation. *J. pharmacol. exp. Therap.*, **158**, 272–278.

STEIN, L. (1956) Reserpine and the learning of fear. *Science*, **124**, 1082–1083.

STEIN, L. (1964) Amphetamine and neural reward mechanisms. In *Animal Behaviour and Drug Action* (Ed. Steinberg, H., de Reuck, A. V. S., & Knight, J.) Ciba Foundation Symposium with the coordinating committee for symposia on drug action. Boston: Little, Brown., pp. 91–113.

STEIN, L. (1965) Facilitation of avoidance behavior by positive brain stimulation. *J. comp. physiol. Psychol.*, **60**, 9–19.

STEINBERG, H. (1956) 'Abnormal behavior' induced by nitrous oxide. *Brit. J. Psychol.*, **47**, 183–193.

STEINBERG, H., LEGGE, D., and SUMMERFIELD, A. (1961) Drug-induced changes in visual perception. In *Neuro-Psychopharmacology*, Vol. 2 (Ed. Rothlin, E.). Amsterdam: Elsevier, pp. 392–396.

STEINBERG, H. and WATSON, R. H. J. (1959) Chlorpromazine inhibition of reactions of rats to unfamiliar surroundings. *J. Physiol.* (Lond.), **147**, 20P.

STEPHENS, J. H. and GANTT, W. H. (1956) The differential effect of morphine on cardiac and motor conditional reflexes—schizokinesis. *Johns Hopkins Hosp. Bull.*, **98**, 245–254.

STETTEN, D. and HERON, S. Z. (1959) Intellectual level measured by Army classification Battery and uric acid concentration. *Science*, **129**, 1737.

STEWART, J. (1962) Differential response based on the physiological consequences of pharmacological agents. *Psychopharmacologia*, **3**, 132–138.

STONE, G. C., BERNSTEIN, B. M., HAMBOURGER, W. E., and DRILL, V. A. (1960) Behavioral and pharmacological studies of thiopropazate, a potent tranquilizing agent. *Arch. int. pharmacodyn. Thérap.*, **127**, 85–103.

STRETCH, R., HOUSTON, M., and JENKINS, A. (1964) Effects of amobarbital on extinction of an instrumental response in rats. *Nature*, **201**, 472–474.

STRICKLAND, K. P. and NOBLE, D. M. (1961) The *in vitro* incorporation of inorganic P^{32} into the phosphatides of different areas of brain. The effect of chlorpromazine administered *in vitro* and *in vivo*. In *Regional Neurochemistry* (Ed. Kety, S. S. and Elkes, J.). London: Pergamon, p. 489.

SULSER, F., WATTS, J., and BRODIE, B. B. (1962) On the mechanism of antidepressant action of imipraminelike drugs. *Ann. N. Y. Acad. Sci.*, **96**, 279–288.

SULSER, F., BICKEL, M. H., and BRODIE, B. B. (1964) The action of desmethylimipramine in counteracting sedation and cholinergic effects of reserpine-like drugs. *J. pharmacol. exp. Therap.*, **144**, 321–330.

SUZUKI, T., YANASHITA, K., and MITAMURA, J. (1959) Effect of ether anesthesia on 17-hydroxycorticosteroid secretion in dogs. *Amer. J. Physiol.*, **197**, 1261–1262.

SWADON, P., FERNANDEZ, A., and ROSENBERGER-DEBIESSE, J. (1965) L'acétyl-tryptophante de caféine en pratique psychiatrique. *Annal. Med-Psycholog.*, **123**, 153–158.

SWAIN, J. M. and LITTERAL, E. G. (1960) Prolonged effect of chlorpromazine: EEG findings in a senile group. *J. nerv. ment. Dis.*, **131**, 550–553.

SZATMARI, A. (1956) Clinical and electroencephalogram investigation on largactil in psychosis (preliminary study). *Amer. J. Psychiat.*, **112**, 788–794.

TAESCHLER, M. and CERLETTI, A. (1959) Differential analysis of the effects of phenothiazine-tranquilizers on emotional and motor behavior in experimental animals. *Nature*, **184**, 823.

TALLAND, G. A. and QUARTON, G. C. (1965) The effects of methamphetamine and pentobarbital on the running memory span. *Psychopharmacologia*, **7**, 379–382.

TEITELBAUM, H. A., NEWTON, J. E. O., GLIEDMAN, L. H., and GANTT, W. H. (1961) Conditioned reflex formation under pentobarbital. *Psychosom. Med.*, **23**, 446.

TEITELBAUM, P. and DERK, P. (1958) The effect of amphetamine on forced drinking in the rat. *J. comp. physiol. Psychol.*, **51**, 801–810.

TENGESDAL, M. (1963) Experiences with intracarotid injections of sodium amytal. A preliminary report. *Acta Neurol. Scand.*, **39**, 329–343.

TERZIAN, H. (1952) Electroencephalographic study of the central action of largactil (4560 R.P.). *Rass. neurol. vegetativa*, **9**, 211–215.

THEOBALD, W. (1959) The course of a conditioned avoidance response in rats after treatment with Tofranil and reserpine combined. *Med. Exp.*, **1**, 102–108.

THEOBALD, W., BUCH, O., KUNG, H. A., MORPURGO, C., WILHELMI, G., and STENGAR, E. G. (1964) Comparative pharmacological investigations with Tofranil, Pertofane, and Ensidon. *Arch. int. Pharmacodyn.*, **148**, 560.

TONINI, G. (1961) Individual variations of pharmacological central reactions. *Biochem. Pharmacol.*, **8**, 59.

TORRES, A. A. (1964) Effects of chlorpromazine and amytal on hoarding in "shy" and "nonshy" rats. *Psychol. Rep.*, **14**, 359–365.

TRAUTNER, E. M., MORRIS, R., NOACK, C. H., and GERSHON, S. (1955) The excretion and retention of ingested lithium and its effect on the ionic balance of man. *Med. J. Australia*, **2**, 280–291.

TURNER, M., BERARD, E., TURNER, N., and FRANCO, N. (1956) Modifications électro-encéphalographiques, électrodermographiques et électromyographiques provoqués par la chlorpromazine chez l'homme. *EEG Clin. Neurophysiol.*, **8**, 25–34.

TURNER, P. (1965) Effect of a mixture of dexamphetamine and amylobarbitone on critical flicker fusion frequency. *J. pharm. Pharmacol.*, **17**, 388–389.

TWEEDY, P. S. (1962) A clinical trial of heptabarbitone (Medomin). *Gerontologia Clinica*, **4**, 276–280.

VALLE, J. R. (1961) Studies on *Cannabis sativa* (Portugese). *Rev. Inst. A. Lutz (S. Paulo)*, **21**, 83–98.

VERNIER, V. G. (1961) The pharmacology of antidepressant agents. *Dis. nerv. Syst.*, **22**, 7–13.

VESTRE, N. D. (1965) Relative effects of phenothiazines and phenobarbital on verbal conditioning of schizophrenics. *Psychol. Rep.*, **17**, 289–290.

VIVIANO, M. (1956) Ricerche psicocronometriche in soggetti trattati con reserpina. *Nota preventiva Neuropsichiatria*, **12**, 67–72.

VON NIESCHULZ, O. (1963) Swimming tests with mice. *Medicum Experimentalis*, **8**, 135–140.

VORONIN, L. G., TOLMASSKAIA, E. S., GUSEL'NIKOVA, K. G., and GUSEL'NIKOV, V. I. (1961) Electrophysiological studies on the mechanism of action of aminazin. (In Russian). *Zhur. nervopat. psikhiat.*, **61**, 208–217.

VORONIN, L. G. and NAPALKOV, A. V. (1963) Complex systems of conditioned reflexes in the analysis of drug effects. In *Psychopharmacological Methods* (Ed. Votava, Z., Horvath, M., and Vinar, O.). New York: Macmillan, p. 182.

WAGNER, A. R. (1963) Sodium amytal and partially reinforced runway performance. *J. exp. Psychol.*, **65**, 474–477.

WALK, R. D., OWENS, J. W. M., and DAVIDSON, B. S. (1961) Influence of reserpine on avoidance conditioning, exploratory behavior, and discrimination learning in the rat. *Psychol. Rep.*, **8**, 251–258.

WECHSLER, H., GROSSER, G. H., and GREENBLATT, M. (1965) Research evaluating antidepressant medications on hospitalized mental patients: a survey of published reports during a five-year period. *J. nerv. ment. Dis.*, **151**, 231–239.

WECHSLER, M. B. and ROIZIN, L. (1960) Tissue levels of chlorpromazine in experimental animals. *J. ment. Sci.*, **106**, 1501.

WEIL, A. T., ZINBERG, N. E., and NELSON, J. M. (1968) Clinical and psychological effects of marihuana in man. *Science*, **162**, 1234–1242.

WEISKRANTZ, L. and WILSON, W. A. (1956) Effect of reserpine on learning and performance. *Science*, **123**, 1116–1118.

WEISS, B. and LATIES, V. G. (1962) Enhancement of human performance by caffeine and the amphetamines. *Pharmacol. Rev.*, **14**, 1–36, 62–85.

WEISS, B. and LATIES, V. G. (1963) Effects of amphetamine, chlorpromazine and pentobarbital on behavioral thermoregulation. *J. pharmacol. exp. Therap.*, **140**, 1–7.

WEITZMAN, E. D. and ROSS, G. S. (1962) A behavioral method for the study of pain perception in the monkey. *Neurology*, **12**, 264–272.

WENZEL, D. G. and DAVIS, P. W. (1961) The effect of caffeine and nicotine as tension-inducing agents and the ability of meprobamate to counteract such effects upon performance. *Tech. Rep. Off. Nav. Res. Armed Svc. Tech. Inf. Agency*, 1–11.

WENZEL, D. G. and RUTLEDGE, C. O. (1962) Effects of centrally-acting drugs on human motor and psychomotor performance. *J. pharmaceut. Sci.*, **51**, 631–644.

WHARTON, R. N. and FIEVE, R. R. (1966) The use of

lithium in the affective psychoses. *Amer. J. Psychiat.*, **123**, 706–712.

WIKLER, A. (1952) Clinical and EEG studies on the effects of mescaline, N-allylnormorphine and morphine in man. *Electroenceph. clin. Neurophysiol.*, **4**, 378–379.

WIKLER, A. (1957) *The Relation of Psychiatry to Pharmacology.* Baltimore: Williams and Wilkins.

WING, L. and LADER, M. H. (1965) Physiological and clinical effects of amylobarbitone sodium therapy in patients with anxiety states. *N. neurol. neurosur. Psychiat.*, **28**, 78–87.

WINNE, I. D. (1964) Experimentelle und biometrische Untersuchungen über den Zusammenhang von Gehirnkonzentration, Eliminationsgeschwindigkeit, Schlafzeit, und Korpertemperatur bei der Hexobarbitalnarkos. *Naunyn-Schmiedebergs. Arch. für exp. pathol. Pharmak.*, **247**, 278–294.

WITT, P. N. (1955) Die Wirkung einer einmaligen Gabe von Largachtil auf den Netzbau der Spinne Zilla-x-notata. *Monatsschr. Psychiat. Neurol.*, **129**, 123–128.

WITT, P. N. (1956) *The Effect of Substances on the Construction of Webs by Spiders as a Biological Test.* Berlin: Springer.

WOLFF, H. G. and GANTT, W. H. (1935) Sodium isoamylethyl-barbiturate, sodium bromide and chloral hydrate. Effect on the highest integrative functions. *Arch. neurol. Psychiat., Chicago*, **33**, 1030–1057.

WOLFF, K. (1962) Treatment of the confused geriatric patient. *Dis. nerv. Syst.*, **23**, 199–203.

WU, H.-J. (1961) Sravenie mekhanizma deistviia rezerpina i nekotorykh tranviliziruiushchikh veshchestv (aminzina, difatsila, antifeina, strofantidina i sigetina). *Bull. Biol. Med. exp. URSS*, **51**, 76–81.

YAGODKA, P. N., NARODITSKAYA, V. F., POTAPOVA, A. A., and SOMLINA, A. I. (1965) Kombirovannoye parenteral' noye primeneniye barbamila s kofeinom na sovremennom etape razvitiye psikhiatricheskoy terapil. *Zh. Nervopatol. Psiph. Korsakova*, **65**, 757–764.

YAMMOTO, I., INOKI, R., TAMARI, Y., and IWATSUBO, K. (1967) Effect of reserpine on brain levels of 14-C-nicotine in relation to nicotine-induced convulsions. *Arch. int. pharmacodyn. Thérap.*, **166**, 102–109.

ZAHNER, H. (1961) Die Wirkung von Trichloraethylen auf das spontane links-rechts Alternieren der Ratte. *Medicine Experimentalis*, **41**, 191–196.

22

The Effects of Psychological Treatment

S. J. RACHMAN

In the first edition of this *Handbook*, Eysenck carried out a detailed analysis of the effects of psychotherapy. The present chapter is a development of that work and not a replacement. In a few places it has been necessary to include parts of the previous chapter* in order to sustain the line of argument, but most of the material and discussion is new. The section on spontaneous remission begins with Eysenck's argument, adds new evidence and develops the discussion along two additional avenues. The section on psychoanalysis contains new material, and in particular an account of the report of the Fact-Gathering Committee of the American Psychoanalytic Association. The section on the effects of psychotherapy assumes the earlier material and deals with recent studies, the self-concept, and Rogerian therapy. The section on behavioural treatment is an addition.

In a somewhat unsuccessful attempt to contain this analysis within a reasonable space, certain types of data were excluded from consideration. Except in those few instances where it was impossible to do so, we have excluded material on counselling, therapy with children, and reports on uncontrolled studies. The primary emphasis is on *neurotic disorders of adulthood* with supplementary discussions included as necessary.

SPONTANEOUS REMISSION

In the earlier edition of this *Handbook* (Eysenck, 1960) it was argued that an accurate evaluation of psychotherapeutic effects is impeded by the methodological shortcomings found in most studies. It was felt that in examining the large body of studies without control groups we cannot, in the nature of the case, draw any definite conclusions. What we can do, however, is to try to provide a base-line with which to compare the results of treatment; a baseline derived from the best available estimate of remission in the absence of psychotherapy. Our efforts along these lines will, of course, suffer from certain obvious defects. The matching of cases is difficult enough when the same investigator selects the treatment and control groups; it becomes almost impossibly complex when all we have to go on is the usually very inadequate account given in a written report. The nature and severity of the illness and the standards of recovery are not discussed in sufficient detail to make exact comparisons possible. Data on duration of treatment and the length of follow-up are not given in sufficient detail to enable the reader to form an accurate judgement of the time intervals involved. When all these difficulties are added to those usually implied in any actuarial comparison, it will be realised that not too much faith should be placed in the *precision* of the comparisons given.

Three attempts are worth mentioning in this connection as giving us some help in finding the requisite base-line. The first study to be quoted is a rather indirect one by Shepherd and Gruenberg (1957) in which they attempt to estimate the duration of neurotic illnesses not treated by psychotherapy by reference to the general rule stating that

* The introductory section on Spontaneous Remission incorporates some of Eysenck's original chapter.

the prevalence of an illness in a population is equal to the product of its incidence and duration. They quote figures relating to both incidence and prevalence from the Health Insurance Plan of Greater New York (HIP)—

'From these data age-specific curves are plotted [in Fig. 22.1] for cases reported as receiving a service in any one year and for cases receiving a service for psychoneurotic illness *for the first time* from H.I.P. in 1951, having been H.I.P. enrolees for at least three previous years without having a service for a psychoneurotic illness. While it is recognized that these are not direct estimates of momentary prevalence nor direct measures of the date of onset, they are superior to most of the other data available in that they are from a large population and that both measures derive from the same data. Because the reports stem from many different physicians trained in many different schools and practicing in diverse groups, it is not possible to know just what criteria were being used to make and record these diagnoses. They undoubtedly varied widely. However, whether from accident or from consistency, both the "prevalence" curve and the "incidence" curve are similar to those obtained from other sources of data.'

It will be noticed in Fig. 22.1 that the incidence and prevalence curves are not only of the same shape, but are very close to one another, running almost parallel.

From this it may be concluded that the variations in prevalence are due, predominantly, to variations in incidence, since apparently the average duration of the neuroses reported in this population does not vary equally with age. Since the prevalence curve here is only slightly higher than the incidence curve, it follows that the average duration of these illnesses is of between one and two years. The authors sum up their study as follows—

'While it is well known that neurotic illnesses can occur at any age and exhibit extremely long courses as well as very brief courses, the available data are remarkably consistent in suggesting that neurotic illnesses are not characteristic of early adult life, that there is a rising incidence and prevalence during the twenties and thirties, a parallel rising prevalence continuing into the forties, and then a rapid decline in prevalence of recognized neuroses. From these data it is perfectly clear that, in the mass, neuroses must have a limited course even if untreated; in fact, the best available data would suggest an average duration between one and two years.'

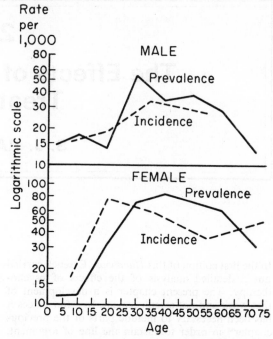

Fig. 22.1. Average annual prevalence of psychoneuroses in 1948–1951 and incidence of new cases in 1951, for enrolees in HIP

The prevalence curves reflect the average annual experience over the years 1948–1951 of all HIP enrolees with twelve months of coverage in any one of those calendar years. There was a total of 60,302 person-years of exposure over this period; 2,714 of these person-years were characterised by the existence of one or more services related to mental illness.

The new case curves show the experience in 1951 of 6,643 enrolees who had entered HIP by January 15, 1948, were still in the Plan on December 31, 1951, and had not received service related to psychoneurosis in 1948, 1949, or 1950 (*quoted by permission of* Shepherd and Gruenberg, 1957).

As a rough-and-ready estimate of our base-line, therefore, we appear to have a figure suggesting that neurotic disorders will tend to remit spontaneously over a period of two years or so. The calculations are rather indirect, and we must next turn to direct studies.

The first of these is an evaluation by Landis (1938) who begins his discussion by pointing out that—

'. . . before any sort of measurement can be made, it is necessary to establish a base-line and a common unit of measure. The only unit of measure available is the report made by the physician stating that the patient has recovered, is much improved, is improved or unimproved. This unit is probably as satisfactory as any type of human subjective judgement, partaking of both the good and bad points of such judgements.'

For a unit, Landis suggests 'that of expressing therapeutic results in terms of the number of patients recovered or improved per hundred cases admitted to the hospital'. As a alternative, he suggests 'the statement of therapeutic outcome for some given group of patients during some stated interval of time'.

Landis realised quite clearly that in order to evaluate the effectiveness of any form of therapy, data from a control group of non-treated patients would be required to compare the effects of therapy with the spontaneous remission rate. In the absence of anything better, he used the amelioration rate in state mental hospitals for patients diagnosed under the heading of 'neuroses'. As he points out—

'There are several objections to the use of the consolidated amelioration rate . . . of the . . . state hospitals . . . as a base rate for spontaneous recovery. The fact that psychoneurotic cases are not usually committed to state hospitals unless in a very bad condition; the relatively small number of voluntary patients in the group; the fact that such patients do get some degree of psychotherapy especially in the reception hospitals; and the probably quite different economic, educational, and social status of the State Hospital group compared to the patients reported from each of the other hospitals—all argue against the acceptance of (this) figure . . . as a truly satisfactory base line, but in the absence of any better figure this must serve.'

Actually, the various figures quoted by Landis agree very well. The percentage of neurotic patients discharged annually as recovered or improved from New York state hospitals is seventy (for the years 1925–1934); for the United States as a whole it is sixty-eight (for the years 1926–1933). The percentage of neurotics discharged as recovered or improved within one year of admission is sixty-six for the United States (1933) and sixty-eight for New York (1914). The consolidated amelioration rate of New York state hospitals, 1917–1934, is 72 per cent. As this figure is the one chosen by Landis, we may accept it in preference to the other very similar ones quoted. By and large, we may thus say that of severe neurotics receiving, in the main, custodial care, and very little, if any, psychotherapy, over two-thirds recovered or improved to a considerable extent. 'Although this is not, strictly speaking, a basic figure for "spontaneous" recovery, still any therapeutic method must show an appreciably greater size than this to be seriously considered.'

Another estimate of the required base-line is furnished by Denker (1946). Here is a description of his procedure—

Five hundred consecutive disability claims due to psychoneurosis, treated by general practitioners throughout the country, and not by accredited specialists of sanatoria, were reviewed. All types of neurosis were included, and no attempt was made to differentiate the neurasthenic, anxiety, compulsive, hysteric, or other states, but the greatest care was taken to eliminate the true psychotic or organic lesions which in the early stages of illness so often simulate neurosis. These cases were taken consecutively from the files of the Equitable Life Assurance Society of the United States, were from all parts of the country, and all had been ill of a neurosis for at least three months before claims were submitted. They, therefore, could be fairly called 'severe', since they had been totally disabled for at least a three months' period, and rendered unable to carry on with any 'occupation for remuneration or profit' for at least that time.

These patients were regularly seen and treated by their own physicians with sedatives, tonics, suggestion, and reassurance, but in no case was any attempt made at anything but this most superficial type of 'psychotherapy' which has always been the stock-in-trade of the general practitioner. Repeated statements, every three months or so by their physicians, as well as independent investigations by the insurance company, confirmed the fact that these people actually were not engaged in productive work during the period of their illness. During their disablement, these cases receive disability benefits. . . . It is appreciated that this fact of disability income may have actually prolonged the total period of disability and acted as a barrier to incentive for recovery. One would, therefore, not expect the therapeutic results in such a group of cases to be as favourable as in other groups where the economic factor might act as an important spur in helping the sick patient adjust to his neurotic conflict and illness.

The cases were all followed up for at least a five-year period, and often as long as ten years after the period of disability had begun. The criteria of 'recovery' used by Denker were as follows: (a) return to work, and ability to carry on well in economic adjustments for at least a five-year period; (b) complaint of no further or only very slight difficulties; (c) making of successful social adjustments. Using these criteria, which are very similar to those usually used by psychiatrists, Denker found that 45 per cent of the patients recovered after one year and another 27 per cent after two years, making 72 per cent in all. Another 10 per cent, 5 per cent, and 4 per cent recovered during the third, fourth, and fifth years, respectively, making a total of 90 per cent recoveries after five years.

The recovery of the patients in Denker's sample

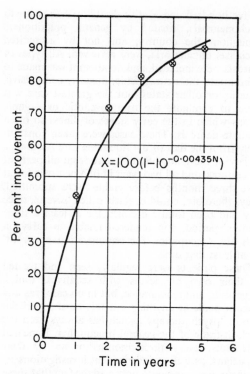

$$X = 100(1 - 10^{-0.00435N})$$

Fig. 22.2 Improvement shown by five hundred severe neurotics, not receiving psychotherapy, after between one and five years

In the formula, X denotes the proportional improvement while N denotes the number of weeks lapsing from the beginning of the experiment

as a function of time is plotted in Fig. 22.2. An exponential curve has been fitted to these data. The formula for this curve is—

$$X = 100(1 - 10^{-0.00435N})$$

where X stands for the amount of improvement achieved in percent and N for the number of weeks elapsed. While the exact values in this formula should not be taken too seriously, its general form is, of course, that of the typical learning curve with which psychologists are familiar. It will be seen later that many other data are in good agreement with the generalisation embodied in this formula.

The Landis and Denker studies supplement each other in a variety of ways. The patients Landis is discussing were largely working-class; those reported on by Denker almost entirely middle-class. The criterion of recovery in the Landis study was probably more lenient, that of the Denker study less lenient than the criteria usually applied by psychotherapists to their own cases. In spite of these differences the recovery figures for the two samples

are not too dissimilar. If we take a period of about two years for each base-line estimate, which appears to be a reasonable figure in view of the fact that psychotherapy does not usually last very much longer than two years and may sometimes last less, we may conclude with some confidence that about two-thirds of neurotics show recovery or considerable improvement, without the benefit of systematic psychotherapy, after a lapse of two years from the time that their disorder is notified, or they are hospitalised. These figures are less optimistic than those given by Shepherd and Gruenberg who seem to suggest 100 per cent remission after two years; this is probably because the severity of their cases appears to have been rather less than that of those studied by Landis and Denker. When we bear in mind the different methods used by these two investigators and the very divergent samples studied, we cannot but conclude that the estimates of the rate of spontaneous remission are sufficiently similar to enable us to form a crude estimate as to the facts of the case.*

Recognition that the majority of neurotic disorders can be expected to remit within two years in the absence of formal psychiatric treatment is the first step in what will undoubtedly prove to be a long and complex process of investigation. Many people have already recommended that we now focus attention on the remission rates that occur in different diagnostic categories and there can be little argument that this is a necessary and inevitable development. We already have many indications of the variation that occurs between diagnostic groupings but a systematic analysis has yet to be conducted. We may also draw attention to some other interesting problems that have emerged from a recognition of the occurrence of spontaneous remissions and that merit attention. Every investigation reported so far has found evidence of a group of patients who fail to remit spontaneously— the figures range from 20 per cent to as high as 50 per cent—and we need to identify and describe these persisting disorders with accuracy. We also need to investigate the reasons why these disorders persist and, indeed, show deterioration in numbers of cases. Another important problem that will require some explanation arises from the observation that *treated*

* It may be of interst in this connection to recall some historical comments by Bockover (1956), who points out that 'early American mental hospitals recognised the importance of psychologic and social influences in what was called "moral treatment" of the mentally ill'. He points out that Worcester State Hospital showed a recovery and improvement rate of 60 per cent between 1833 and 1846, and Bloomingdale Hospital one of 65 per cent between 1821 and 1844. For the Worcester State Hospital it is claimed that between 1833 and 1946, 50 per cent of patients had no relapse.

patients rarely show an improvement rate in excess of the spontaneous remission rate and quite frequently show an improvement rate that is considerably lower than that of the spontaneous improvements. Even if we allow for the likelihood that therapy may make some patients worse it seems most improbable that the large discrepancy between treated improvement rates and spontaneous improvement rates can be accounted for satisfactorily in this manner. We feel that the large discrepancies that have been recorded may be attributable to the selection of unrepresentative samples of patients for inclusion in certain treatment series. For example, if a treatment series includes a disproportionately large number of 'hard core' patients then the improvement rate may well fail to reach the spontaneous improvement rate of two-thirds. A second factor that may contribute to treated improvement rates that fall below the spontaneous figure is the duration of treatment and follow-up (where applicable). If the treatment period is relatively brief, then the outcome figures may again fall below those of the spontaneous improvement rate which is usually quoted in terms of a 2-year period.

Some interesting pointers that may facilitate the investigation of some of these problems are provided in a monograph by Greer and Cawley (1966). They carried out a 4 to 6-year follow-up investigation of 160 neurotic patients who were consecutive admissions to the Maudsley Hospital. The investigation was extensive and thorough and only certain findings

can be mentioned here. One of their conclusions was that 'two of the principal prognostic indicators in neurotic illness are pre-morbid personality and the nature of the illness' (p. 88). These indicators were not necessarily related to each other. In regard to diagnostic groupings they found that patients with depressive, hysterical or anxiety reactions had the most favourable outcomes while those with obsessive-compulsive or hypochondriacal symptoms had a poor prognosis. Patients with obsessive reactions were found to have the longest duration of symptoms and depressive patients to have the shortest duration. Patients with anxiety and hysterical reactions had illness durations of moderate length. These findings, illustrated in Fig. 22.3, lead to the suggestion that the obsessional and hypochondriacal patients may constitute a disproportionate number of the 'hard core' patients.

Other factors found to be related to prognosis included a number of variables related to pre-morbid personality and precipitating events. The variables found to be—

'significantly associated with a favourable prognosis include: (*a*) married civil status; (*b*) normal pre-morbid personality; (*c*) satisfactory pre-morbid social adjustment with respect to work record, inter-personal relations and marital relations; (*d*) evidence of precipitating factors preceding the onset of illness; (*e*) less than 5 years duration of symptoms; (*f*) presence of

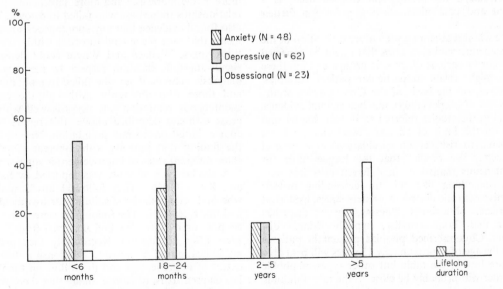

Fig. 22.3 The duration of different types of neurotic illness

(Based on the data reported by Greer and Cawley in 'Some observations on the natural history of neurotic illnesses', *Australian Med. Assn.*, 1966)

depressive symptoms and absence of disorders of thought content—in particular, hypochondriacal preoccupations; (*g*) a diagnosis of depressive or hysterical reactions; (*h*) ... patient lives in a domestic group the members of which show a sympathetic and tolerant attitude towards him ...'

Some of the main variables found to be associated with an unfavourable prognosis included disturbed pre-morbid personality, unsatisfactory interpersonal relations, unsatisfactory work record, absence of precipitating factors, duration of more than 5 years, disorders of thought content. Equally interesting are some of the variables that appeared, in this study at least, to have no significant relationship to outcome in neurotic disorders. They include: 'age, sex, social class, family history, childhood environment, neurotic traits in childhood, intelligence, pre-morbid sexual adjustment, a history of previous psychiatric illness, length of stay in hospital, presence or absence of associated organic disease, material circumstances after discharge from hospital, and occurrence of stressful events since discharge' (p. 88).

The findings reported in this study are of considerable potential value provided they are used with care. Firstly, it is likely that the sample is in certain respects atypical. It probably contained a disporportionately large number of severe cases and, in addition, the Maudsley Hospital is a major teaching institution and in this sense uncharacteristic. Nevertheless, the monograph can be used as a sound and convenient starting point for further studies.

We will not attempt a premature estimation of the spontaneous remission rates that might be expected to occur in various diagnostic groups or how these rates might relate to particular patient variables. However, on the basis of the Greer-Cawley study, the work of Marks (1969), much anecdotal evidence found in the studies referred to in this chapter and also on the basis of clinical observations, we are prepared to risk certain speculations of a general character. We predict that the league table for spontaneous remissions in different disorders may look something like this (in descending order): affective neurotic disorders, anxiety states, hysterical disorders, obsessional illnesses, sexual disorders other than homosexuality, hypochondriacal disorders. Circumscribed phobias present in patients over the age of approximately 15 years will probably feature low in the table but other types of phobic disorder will probably be close to the rate obtaining in anxiety states.

Variables other than diagnostic category must also be taken into account as the spontaneous remissions are neither complete nor wholly absent in any of the diagnostic groupings. The nature of these other contributing factors has been alluded to in the discussion on the Greer-Cawley study and no doubt will be elaborated in time. Even though they found a clear relationship between long-term duration of the disorder and poor prognosis, we can anticipate certain matters that will be dealt with later in this chapter by saying that the relationship between long-term duration and poor prognosis does not hold up with certain forms of treatment. This is demonstrated most clearly in the treatment of circumscribed phobias which, even though they probably have a low spontaneous remission rate, respond well and promptly to desensitisation.

Global estimates of remission can be supplemented by a number of reports and investigations carried out on smaller samples of patients. Wallace and Whyte (1959) reported on the progress made by '83 psychoneurotic patients who had been promised psychotherapy and who failed to receive it' because of an absence of adequate facilities. The patients were followed up three to seven years later and valid information was obtained on 49 of them. The overall spontaneous improvement rate was 65·3 per cent and the improvement rate for each diagnostic group was: anxiety states 68 per cent; hysteria 50 per cent; miscellaneous 75 per cent. Seven patients who had obtained treatment in the interim were excluded from the analysis. Wallace and Whyte found that those patients who had recovered tended to have more stable marriages and more satisfactory group relationships than those who failed to recover. They also found evidence that any spontaneous improvements that take place tend to occur within the first three years. Wallace and Whyte could detect no significant differences in respect to recovery and diagnosis between those who failed to reply initially and those who did reply. Although the overall spontaneous remission rate accords well with the gross estimate described above, this report is, of course, based on a small population. Nevertheless, the finding that patients with different diagnoses show different rates of improvement is suggestive.

A similar type of study was reported by Saslow and Peters (1956). They followed up 83 patients who had been considered suitable for treatment but had not received it. The follow-ups were conducted by post or by interview and occurred from 1 to 6 years after notification. Regrettably they provide no indication of a possible relationship between extent of improvement and the follow-up time that has elapsed. It is, of course, likely that there would be differences in the estimates provided at one year after notification and at 6 years after notification. Despite some flaws in their procedure, Saslow and

Peters's study did produce interesting data and their overall spontaneous remission rate figure is lower than usual. They state that '37 per cent were found significantly improved'. If we exclude from this overall rate the 16 per cent who were diagnosed as schizophrenic and the 4 per cent 'mental deficiency' then the remission figure would be increased—this is implied but not stated in their discussion. Even so, the figures are lower than usual. In addition to the reasons already suggested, it is possible that their findings can be accounted for by the inclusion of a surprisingly high proportion of patients with hysteria—30 per cent. Most of these patients had a poor outcome and while this observation is in keeping with that reported by Wallace and Whyte whose patients with hysteria showed a lower spontaneous remission rate than the rest of the sample, it is not consistent with Greer and Cawley's results.

Schorer et al. (1968) traced 138 patients who had been placed on a waiting-list for psychotherapy and of these, 55 (52%) were found to have received no treatment in the follow-up period which averaged 5 years. The spontaneous remission rate for these untreated patients, comprising neurotics and people with personality disorders, was 65 per cent ('proved to be definitely improved'). These improvements were widespread and included increased social effectiveness as well as significant changes in the presenting complaints. A group of 41 patients who obtained treatment elsewhere 'were found to be 78% improved—not significantly more than those who improved without treatment'. The authors comment on the similarity of their results to those reported by Wallace and Whyte (1959). They could detect 'little predictability about who would improve without treatment and who would not'.

Kedward (1969) found that the spontaneous remission rate showed little change in the period between a 1-year and 3-year follow-up among 346 patients diagnosed by their GP as having a psychiatric illness. The data are based on 82 per cent of the original sample of 422 patients some of whom had only mild illnesses. At the 3-year follow-up, '73% of all new cases were regarded as free from psychiatric symptoms' (p. 3)—a similar proportion as those said to be recovered within 1-year. The study indicates that maximum remission occurs within a year and also that there is a minority of patients whose illness runs 'a refractory course which continues longer than 3 years' (p. 3).

In their 5-year follow-up of 100 neurotic patients Giel, Knox, and Carstairs (1964) found that 71 per cent of the patients were recovered or much improved. In 90 per cent of these improved cases, the recovery had taken place within 2 years of their first attending an out-patient clinic. Although the rate of recovery observed in this group is consistent with the gross spontaneous remission rate, it cannot be quoted without reservation, as one half of the patients had received 'at least a modicum of out-patient care and 20 patients were temporarily admitted to hospital'. According to the authors, however, the untreated half of their sample did not show a different pattern of outcome to that of the treated group. 'No difference was found between the outcome of these patients (i.e. treated) and the remainder of the group. Evidence was not available to show that their treatment had shortened their period of disability or relieved their subjective distress. This study therefore confirms that any new treatment for the neuroses must show better than 70% improvement before it can claim to represent a significant therapeutic advance' (p. 162). They were unable to find evidence of a relationship between outcome and a variety of variables including diagnostic category, degree of disturbance, sudden onset and so on. However, 22 of the 24 cases with a history of less than three months illness had a good outcome. In those 58 instances where they were able to date the patient's improvement, it was found to have occurred within the first year after the initial contact in 79 per cent of the sample.

Although their attempts to obtain information about the prognostic variables involved in spontaneous remissions was not a notable success, the small study reported by Endicott and Endicott (1963) is still of some interest. They carried out a 6-month follow-up of 40 untreated psychiatric patients and although 'the groups are too small to allow statistical analysis' it was found that 52 per cent of the patients with neuroses or psychophysiological reactions improved, whereas only 9 per cent of the 'border line' and schizophrenic patients were so evaluated. The authors themselves draw attention to some of the main limitations of their study. 'From one point of view the most serious deficiency of the study was the brief duration of the waiting period' (p. 581). They add that 'a second limitation is the small size of the patient sample, especially when the sample is divided into improved and unimproved groups' (p. 581). After the second evaluation, those patients who still wanted treatment were taken into psychotherapy but 'it is of interest that after the passage of 6 months, only 12 out of the 33 remaining non-hospitalized patients still desired psychotherapy' (p. 537).

On similar lines, Cartwright and Vogel (1960) examined the characteristics of improvers and non-improvers—both before and during treatment. The study is difficult to evaluate as virtually no information about the patients is provided, other than that '30 subjects who applied to the University of Chicago

counselling centre for therapy were asked to participate in a research study' (p. 121). The patients 'pre-
therapy status' and their changes with and without
therapy were assessed on a Q adjustment scale and
on the TAT. Unfortunately, 8 of the 30 subjects
were lost before they had completed 6 interviews
and these 'attrition cases' were excluded from the
analysis. The remaining 22 subjects showed, on the
whole, improvements during the pretherapy period
and these improvements were apparently associated
with longer waiting periods. Despite their ill-chosen
outcome measures, the results obtained by the
authors are worth mentioning. Even in the very
short waiting period of 1 to 2 months, 5 out of 10
subjects reported positive changes on the Q sort and
3 out of 10 showed positive changes on the TAT.
Those subjects who waited from 2 to 6 months
before entering therapy showed evidence of greater
change, in that 6 out of 12 reported positive changes
on the Q sort and almost all (9 out of 12) showed
positive changes on the TAT. An evaluation of the
effects of therapy is virtually precluded by the fact
that the results on the two measures (the TAT and the
Q sort) tend to disagree. Incidentally, the claim by
Cartwright and Vogel that self-report on the Q sort
'reflected their deep improvement on the conscious
level in an improved self-description' is an odd
remark. Presumably, advocates of the TAT would
regard *their* findings as reflecting deep improvement
as well.

In a more recent study, Jurjevich (1968) preferred
to examine the spontaneous remission of particular
symptoms rather than work in diagnostic categories.
Two groups of 50 and of 62 psychiatric out-patients
were retested on a symptom check-list after about
10 days or after 6 months. 'Significant reduction of
symptoms occurs after longer intervals (i.e. 6
months) on the raw and weighted full scales, raw
scales of anxiety and psychosomatic complaints and
weighted scales of anxiety immaturity and com-
pulsiveness' (p. 199). Analysing the results in a slightly
different way, the author found that 60 per cent of
the patients were improved within 6 months.
Jurjevich draws attention to the fact that 'about
1/3rd of the subjects do not seem to possess self-
restorative mechanisms, tending to remain stable
in their maladjustment or even to become worse.
This finding gives support to the psychiatric rule
of thumb that about 2/3rds of patients recover with
or without treatment, and 1/3rd remain unchanged
in spite of treatment of various types if sufficient
time is given for the operation of (spontaneous)
homeostatic psychological processes' (p. 196). His
analysis shows that of the 40 per cent of patients who
were not improved within 6 months, 13 per cent
were unimproved and 27 per cent were worse.

Detailed analysis of the symptom changes showed
that the most changeable symptoms, over the 6
month period, included cardiac acceleration, twitch-
ing, bad dreams, irritation, and so on. Although the
overall findings are consistent with the gross
spontaneous remission rate estimate, the smallness
of the sample and the relatively short period of
observation place limitations on the generality of
the data.

Cremerius (1969) has argued that there is a very
small spontaneous remission rate in 'organneuro-
tischen Beschwerden'. He selected from a polyclinic
sample of 21,500 patients (seen between 1949 and
1951) those patients who had what can be described
as 'organ functional syndromes'. This initial screening process produced no fewer than 7,400 patients.
A staggeringly high figure of this order (implying
that every third patient attending the polyclinic had
important neurotic features in his illness) raises
serious questions about the nature of the diagnoses
employed. An examination of the 6 groups of syndromes described by Cremerius feeds these doubts.
The groups are: functional stomach syndromes;
functional cardiovascular syndromes; functional
syndrome of the lower digestive tract; functional
respiratory syndrome; functional headache syndrome; functional ailments of a heterogeneous and
changing nature. In the functional respiratory
group for example we find that patients with chronic
bronchitis are included. It is possible that we are
encountering linguistic problems because the terms
'Neurosen' and 'Psychoneurosen' are distinguished
in German but rarely distinguished in English usage.
For example, Psychrembel (1964) in his *Klinisches
Wörterbuch* contrasts the 'Psychoneurosen' which are
psychic disorders (and include behavioural disturbances and abnormal experiences) with 'Neurosen'
which are manifested in physical symptoms. It is
extremely unlikely that this large group of patients
would be diagnosed as 'neurotic' in a British or
American polyclinic or general hospital.

Of the 7,400 patients with organ neuroses,
Cremerius selected 2,330 (excluding those whose
illnesses has lasted for less than 2 years) and sent
them a letter requesting them to re-attend the clinic
11 to 30 years after initial admission. In other
words, two-thirds of the sample were excluded and
these exclusions ensured that patients with short-
lived illnesses were not assessed. The remaining one-
third of the sample who were contacted, showed a
very poor response. Only 15 per cent (371 cases)
reattended as requested. Stated in another way, only
1 out of every potential 200 patients was reassessed.
As noted above, patients with short-lived illnesses
were specifically excluded. In addition, as will be
shown presently, a comparable study carried out by

Friess and Nelson (1942) indicated that the patients who failed to respond to this type of request for reattendance show a disproportionately large number of recoveries. Moreover, it seems extremely unlikely that patients with distressing illnesses would fail to seek other treatment for 11 to 30 years after a diagnosis had been reached, and indeed, there is internal evidence in Cremerius's paper to show that at least some of them were treated in the interim.

In view of all these limitations the Cremerius study can add little to our understanding of the spontaneous remission rate of neurotic disorders. For the record it is worth mentioning that the spontaneous remission rate was extremely low (8%) and the majority of patients either showed a persistence of the original difficulty, or the original organ neurosis had changed to 'psychic symptoms' (approximately 24%) or to physical syndromes (approximately 26%).

The views on spontaneous remission presented here have not gone unchallenged. Broadly, two types of criticisms have been raised. It has been argued that neuroses do not remit spontaneously or, if they do, it is not a spontaneous process (e.g. Goldstein, 1960; Kiesler, 1966; Rosenzweig, 1954). Another point of view is illustrated by the work of Bergin (1970) who agrees that spontaneous remission of neuroses does occur but that a more accurate estimate of the rate of occurrence of these remissions is in the region of 30 per cent.

The claim that spontaneous remission of neuroses does not occur at all is a matter for demonstration rather than argument. The evidence described in this chapter, despite its shortcomings, seems to us to demonstrate its occurrence. The related but different question of whether or not 'spontaneous remission' is an apt or a misleading description of the phenomenon can, of course, be debated. Nevertheless, we feel that a satisfactory definition can be agreed on and that even if such agreement cannot be obtained, the varying opinions on the subject are all capable of being defined in such a way as to prevent confusion. We can begin by dismissing those simple-minded views that suggest that the term spontaneous means 'uncaused'. It has been pointed out in previous publications that it is not the mere passage of time that produces an improvement in neurotic disorders; it must be events in time that are responsible (Eysenck and Rachman, 1965, page 277). The attribution of causal influences is, of course, difficult but it is quite wrong to give the impression that no theory exists that can come to grips with these questions. Eysenck (1963) has in fact proposed a theory of how and why spontaneous remissions occur and also of the circumstances in which spontaneous remission should not be expected to

occur. It should be clear from earlier publications and the present work that the term 'spontaneous remission' is used to describe improvements in neurotic disorders that occur in the absence of any formal psychiatric treatment. Undergoing a psychiatric examination (even with a possible view to later treatment) does not constitute treatment. Discussing one's problems with a relative, lawyer, priest, neighbour or even a dark stranger does not constitute treatment. Events such as promotion, financial windfalls, successful love affairs may all be therapeutic but, regrettably perhaps, they cannot be considered as forms of psychological treatment. These acts and events are all potentially therapeutic and undoubtedly contribute to the process of spontaneous remission. Current research interest in those life events that precipitate psychiatric disorders encourages us in the hope that attention will also be turned to those life events that have a *therapeutic* value. Within the context of an examination of the effects of psychotherapy, however, improvements in neurotic disorders that occur in the absence of formal psychological treatment can justifiably be regarded as 'spontaneous'.

On the question of quantitative estimates of the rate of spontaneous remission of neuroses, Bergin's (1970) estimate of 30 per cent differs so widely from our own that it is imperative to examine his figures and arguments in some detail. Bergin begins by saying that 'there has actually been a substantial amount of evidence lying around for years on this question'. He concludes from this evidence that, 'generally, rates are lower than the Landis-Denker figures, thus justifying those critics who have emphasised the inadequacy or irrelevance of these baselines'. Bergin then presents a Table containing fourteen studies and he provides percentage improvement rates for each. As he remarks, the rates vary from 0 to 56 per cent and 'the median* rate appears to be in the vicinity of 30 per cent!' Admitting that his figures 'have their weaknesses' Bergin nevertheless feels that 'they are the best available to date' and that they rest 'upon a much more solid base than the Landis-Denker data'. Before making a detailed examination of what Bergin considers to be the best available data, two points should be borne in mind. In the first place it seems to us to be a curious procedure in which one unearths new data and then calculates a median rate of improvement while ignoring the 'old' data. The 'new' data (actually, some of them are chronologically older than those of Landis-Denker) should have been considered in conjunction with,

* In future studies, the inclusion of median rates *would* be helpful, particularly for prognostic use (Passingham, 1970).

or at least in the light of, the existing information. The second point is that although Bergin has considered some new evidence, he seems inexplicably to have missed a number of more satisfactory and indeed more recent studies that are pertinent to the question of spontaneous recovery rates. His estimate of a 30 per cent spontaneous recovery rate is in fact based on fourteen studies which are incorporated in Table 8 of his work. It will be noticed immediately that the list omits some of the studies discussed earlier in this chapter.

The fourteen studies are given with the percentage improvement rates quoted by Bergin. They are: Friess and Nelson (1942a and b)—29%, 35%; Shore and Massimo (1966)—30%; Orgel (1958)— 0%; Masterson (1967)—38%; Vorster (1966)— 34%; Hastings (1958)—46%; Graham (1960)— 37%; O'Connor (1964)—0%; Cappon (1964)—0%; Endicott and Endicott (1963)—52%; Koegler and Brill (1967)—0%; Paul (1967)—18%; Kringlen (1965)—25%.

Bergin gives a spontaneous remission rate of 0 per cent for Cappon (1964). The first surprise about Cappon's paper is its title—'Results of Psychotherapy'. He reports on a population consisting of 201 consecutive private patients 'who underwent therapy between 1955 and 1960'. Their diagnoses were as follows: psychoneuroses 56%, psychopathic personality 25%, psychosomatic reactions 8%, psychosis 8%, and other 3%. Only 10 per cent received medication and 3·5 per cent were hospitalised. As 163 had ended their therapy in 1960, 'this was the operative sample'. Cappon describes his treatment as being 'applied Jungian'. The results of the treatment were 'admittedly modest' and the follow-up was conducted by mail. Unfortunately, only 53 per cent of the patients returned their forms and the follow-up period varied from 4 to 68 months. In addition the follow-up sample 'was biased in that these patients did twice as well at the end of therapy as rated by the therapist, as those who did not return the forms'. It is also noted that 'the operative patient sample ($N = 158$) was still different (sicker) from a controlled normal sample, at the time of the follow-up. Patients showed more than 4 times the symptoms of normals. This ensured the fact that the sample was indeed composed of patients'. The measure on which this conclusion is based is the Cornell Medical Index.

Cappon states that, 'the intention of this work was not so much to prove that results were actually due to psychotherapy as to show some of the relationships results. Consequently, there was no obsessive preoccupation with "controls" as the sine qua non dictate of science.' We seem in the midst of all this to have strayed from the subject of spon-

taneous remissions. In fact, Cappon does make some brief comments on the subject. He argues that, 'if worsening rather than improvement were rated, 4 to 15 times as many patients changed (got worse) in the follow-up (control) period combined with the therapeutic (experimental) period, depending on the index used'. He then argues that as the follow-up period averaged some 20 months and the therapeutic period some 6½ months, 'this fact alone casts great doubt on Eysenck's data on spontaneous remission which led him to the false conclusion that patients did better without treatment than with treatment'. Leaving aside the fact that Cappon unfortunately lost approximately half of his sample between termination of treatment and follow-up, we can perhaps leave uncontested his conclusion that many of the patients got worse after treatment. At best (?), Cappon's report adds support to the belief that some patients get worse after psychotherapy. It tells us nothing at all about spontaneous remission rates and indeed, far from giving a spontaneous remission rate of 0 per cent, Cappon does not provide *any figures* on which to calculate a rate of spontaneous remission. Bergin's figure of a 0 per cent spontaneous remission rate would appear to be drawn from Cappon's introductory description of his patients in which he says that they 'had their presenting or main problem or dysfunction for an *average of 15 years* before treatment' (original italics). Clearly one cannot use this single sentence description in attempting to trace the course of neurotic disorders or to determine their spontaneous remission rate. Nearly half Cappon's patients apparently had disorders other than neurotic; we are not aware that they had been untreated prior to attending Cappon; we cannot assume that their diagnosis at the beginning of treatment would correspond with their condition in the years prior to treatment; we don't know whether the 201 patients constitute 90 per cent of the relevant population or even 0·00001 per cent of that population. Without labouring the point, we can firmly disregard this incidental sentence as evidence for or against the occurrence of spontaneous remission and conclude that Bergin's use of these data is unjustified.

Bergin also gives a 0 spontaneous remission rate for the paper by O'Connor *et al.* (1964). Once again, the title, 'The effects of psychotherapy on the course of ulcerative colitis', is surprising. At this point we have to remind ourselves that the subject under discussion is the spontaneous remission rate in neurotic disorders. Ulcerative colitis is defined by O'Connor and his co-authors as 'a chronic nonspecific disease characterised by inflammation and ulceration of the colon and accompanied by systemic manifestations' (p. 738). According to them, 'its course is marked by remissions and exacerbations, its aetiology is considered multifactorial and it has been variously attributed to infections, genetic, vascular, allergic and psychological phenomena' (p. 738). It will not pass unnoticed that 'psychological phenomena' are only one in a list of five types of attribution, nor indeed that the course of the disease is 'marked by remissions'. We have then some information of interest to gastroenterologists, namely that patients who have ulcerative colitis can show remissions. The study actually compares the progress made by 57 patients with colitis who received psychotherapy and 57 patients who received no such treatment. Apparently, patients in both groups continued to receive medical and even surgical treatment. Nevertheless, as a group, the ones who had psychotherapy did better overall. In the treated group, '19 patients were diagnosed as schizophrenic, 3 were psychoneurotic, 34 were diagnosed as having personality disorders and 1 received no diagnosis'. In the control group, however, '3 of the patients were diagnosed as schizophrenic, 3 as psychoneurotic and 14 as having personality disorders. The remaining 37 control patients were not diagnosed because of the lack of overt psychiatric symptoms'. As only 3 of the control group subjects were diagnosed as psychoneurotic, the spontaneous remission rate over the 15-year period would have to be expressed as the number of spontaneous remissions for a group with an N of 3. Bergin's use of the data in this report also raises a serious methodological point. He quotes the spontaneous remission rate for colitis patients as 0 per cent over 15 years. In fact, no such percentage rate can be obtained from the report as all the results are given as group means—in other words, it is perfectly possible and indeed likely, that numbers of patients experienced remissions even though the *group* mean shows little change. For the study as a whole, we are in no position to conclude what the spontaneous remission rate in 3 neurotic patients with ulcerative colitis was.

Orgel's (1958) report on 15 *treated* cases of peptic ulcer is quoted as showing a 0 per cent remission rate. Bergin appears to argue that because the patients had suffered from stomach ulcers from 4 to 15 years prior to entering treatment, this indicates a remission rate of 0. Factually, Bergin is incorrect in stating that the peptic ulcers 'had persisted from 4 to 15 years without change'. Several of the patients had experienced remissions prior to entering psychoanalytic treatment. Furthermore, some of them experienced remissions and recurrences *during* the treatment. Far more serious, however, is Bergin's assumption that these 15 ulcer cases are representative of the relevant population—it is possible that 1,500

cases not seen by the psychoanalyst experienced a different course in their illness. In addition, the introduction of material on the 'natural history' of patients with *peptic ulcer* into a discussion on spontaneous remissions in neurotic disorders is not justified.

In his table, Bergin quotes a 37 per cent spontaneous improvement rate for a study by Graham (1960). In the text he says, 'Hastings (1958) found a 46% (spontaneous remission) rate for neurotics and Graham (1960) observed a range from 34 to 40% for sexual problems'. What Graham actually reports in his brief paper is a comparison of the sexual behaviour of 65 married men and women (before beginning psychoanalytic treatment) with that of 142 married men and women who had been in treatment for from several weeks to 49 months. He found that for most (but not all) of the comparisons, the patients in treatment expressed greater satisfaction in and greater frequency of sexual activity than did the patients awaiting treatment. Of course, this tells us nothing about the spontaneous remission of neurotic disorders. It is simply a comparison of the sexual activity of two groups of people at a particular point in time. We are given no details about the patients in either group—not their diagnosis, nor even their ages. We are told that before treatment the men in this sample ($N = 25$) shared a mean level of satisfaction of 2·81 but this figure is nowhere explained. We do not know what the range is nor are we told how the figure is derived. At very best a study of this type might tell us what the spontaneous remission rate in sexual disorders is, but as we do not know what complaint these patients had nor how they progressed, the study tells us precisely nothing about the spontaneous remission rate in sexual (or neurotic) disorders.

From a study of the sexual life of potential patients, Bergin turns to a study that reports the fate of 10 juvenile delinquents (Shore and Massimo, 1966). As the patients comprising the untreated group of 10 were not suffering from neurotic disorders, their inclusion in an estimation of spontaneous remission in neuroses is difficult to justify. Although Bergin's discussion of this report adds nothing to our understanding of remission in neuroses, his handling of the data requires some comment. According to him, 3 of the 10 untreated delinquents remitted spontaneously (actually, on a basis of 'known offences' the figure should be 4 out of 10). A major point, however, is that Bergin uses this figure of 3 out of 10 remitting, to obtain a percentage remission rate of 30. This figure is then included in his table and added to other studies with much larger samples to yield a median rate of remission—surely a dubious way of proceeding. The point is emphasised by referring back to some of the studies which provided the material for a gross spontaneous remission rate. It will be recalled that the studies of Landis, Denker and Shepherd, and Gruenberg dealt with hundreds and even thousands of cases. In any event, readers interested in the 'natural history' of delinquency may prefer to study the thorough and extensive investigation carried out by Teuber and Powers (1953).

We next turn to the Masterson (1967) study for which Bergin quotes a spontaneous recovery rate of 'only 38%'. Masterson reports the clinical status of 72 patients (from an original group of 101) who received treatment in an out-patient clinic during their adolescence. It is immediately apparent, therefore, that we are dealing not with an investigation of spontaneous remission but with a follow-up study of the effects of treatment administered during adolescence. We then learn that 'during the 5-year follow-up period, 38 patients received out-patient treatment, 11 received in-patient treatment, and 31 received no treatment' (p. 1340). In other words, nearly 60 per cent of the sample received further treatment during the follow-up period—hardly then a measure of spontaneous recovery. The matter is further complicated by the fact that Masterson used two methods for evaluating the psychiatric status of the patients. In the first place he apparently used the psychiatrist's 'clinical judgement to rate the level of impairment of functioning'. Later we read that 'we re-defined impairment not in terms of functioning but in terms of underlying conflict with regards to dependency needs and sexual and aggressive impulses' (p. 1339). The level of impairment observed in 72 adolescents at follow-up is summarised by Masterson in a table on page 1340. A simple combination of the patients showing minimal or mild impairment at this stage yields a total of 27 out of 72—the source, apparently, of Bergin's conclusion that the sample showed a 38 per cent spontaneous remission rate. It turns out, however, that relatively few of the 72 patients had a diagnosis of neurosis. In Masterson's own words, 'breaking this down by diagnosis, we note that those with character neurosis did well, all having only minimal or mild impairment functioning, whereas those with schizophrenia and personality disorder did poorly, 75% having moderate or severe impairment of functioning. When the personality disorder group is further sub-divided by type we find that 100% of the sociopaths, 63% of those with a passive aggressive disorder, 75% of the miscellaneous, and 8% of epileptics continued to have severe or moderate impairment of functioning' (p. 1340). If we now exclude the patients with schizophrenia and the psychopaths from our consideration, an interesting sum emerges. The remission rate, with

schizophrenics and psychopaths omitted, is exactly 50 per cent but we hasten to add that this is *not* a spontaneous remission rate, as an unspecified number of this remaining group received treatment during the period under consideration and also because some of the diagnostic labels (e.g. 'passive-aggressive') are ambiguous. It can thus be seen that Bergin's statement that 'Masterson found only 38% spontaneous recovery of adolescent disorders' is misleading.

Kringlen's study is described by Bergin as follows: 'Kringlen (1965) followed the course of a sample of neurotics for 13 to 20 years and found that spontaneous changes varied with diagnosis. The overall spontaneous improvement rate was 25%.' In fact, the rate was neither spontaneous nor was it 25%. Kringlen carried out a carefully conducted long-term follow-up study of 91 obsessional patients who were seen for 13 to 20 years after admission to hospital. On admission, 'most of the patients got some form of somatic therapy, either ECT or drugs' (p. 714). Of these, 44 per cent were improved on discharge. During the follow-up period 'most of the patients received some form of treatment; 32 by drugs, 9 by ECT, 7 psychotherapy, 3 leucotomy and 7 a mixture of several forms of therapy' (p. 716). Thirty-three of the 91 patients had received in-patient psychiatric treatment.

The outcome figures for Kringlen's patients, irrespective of type of treatment, were not too encouraging. Combining the cured, much improved, and slightly improved groups we find that only 28 (30%) had changed favourably at the 3 *month* follow-up period, 46 (50%) at the 5 *year* follow-up and 44 (48%) at the 10 year follow-up period. We can only conclude from all of this that slightly under half the obsessional patients were improved during a course of in-patient treatment and that the figure for the group as a whole increases only slightly after 5 or even 10 years, despite further treatment.

Bergin quotes Paul's (1966) experiment as yielding a spontaneous remission rate of 18 per cent. He says, 'that after 2 years speech-anxious neurotic students spontaneously improved on speech anxiety at the rate of 22% and on more general anxiety at 18%'. Bergin is perhaps justified in praising the thoroughness of this study but, unfortunately, it tells us nothing whatever of the spontaneous remission rate in neuroses and nor indeed was it designed to do so. It was concerned with the treatment of fear of public-speaking. Contrary to Bergin's description, the students were *not* neurotic but were drawn from the normal undergraduate population of '710 students enrolled in public speaking' (Paul, 1966). Paul states that 'students who, prior to contact, had entered treatment elsewhere or dropped the speech course were also excluded' (p. 25). He also points out that in the final screening of the subjects 'those students who have received previous psychological treatment... were to have been dropped' (p. 25); in the event, however, 'no subject need to be excluded for these reasons.' In other words, any student who had received psychological treatment in the past, or was currently receiving such treatment, was automatically excluded. Moreover, each subject was subjected to extensive psychological investigation before and after treatment; no fewer than 5 types of psychological tests were administered. The means obtained by the students on these tests did not fall into a neurotic classification on any of the 5 tests. A comparison between the mean scores obtained by Paul's 'no-treatment control' subjects and those reported in an earlier study by Endler *et al.* (1962) on a group of subjects drawn from the same university (Illinois) shows quite clearly the essential 'normality' of the experimental subjects. The pre-treatment means for the control subjects are given first and are followed by the means recorded for the Illinois University undergraduates in 1962, which are given in parentheses. On the SR Inventory of Anxiousness sub-test entitled 'contest' the mean was 33·4 (32·9); the 'interview' item mean was 34·1 (31·62 with a standard deviation of 9·9); the 'examination' item mean was 38·9 (37·6, and standard deviation of 10·9). On a measure of general anxiety, Cattell's IPAT, the mean was 35·6 with a standard deviation of 11·7 (34·5 and standard deviation of 7·4). For the Pittsburgh scales of extraversion and of emotionality, the normative data were reported by Bendig in 1962 on a sample of 200 students. Paul's subjects obtained a pre-treatment mean of 16·3 and Bendig's group had a mean of 17·6. On the emotionality scale, Paul's subjects had a mean of 17·8 with a standard deviation of 6·1 and Bendig's a mean of 14·6 with a standard deviation of 7.

The students used by Paul as experimental subjects in an analogue study cannot justifiably be included in an attempt to determine the spontaneous remission rate of neurotic disorders, any more than the large number of subjects who have been used in the numerous similar analogue studies (see review; Rachman, 1967).

Although the report by Hastings (1958) is not strictly speaking a paper on spontaneous remission rates, Bergin's inclusion of it is at least defensible. The spontaneous remission rate of 46 per cent quoted by Bergin, while correct, needs some elaboration in order to be appreciated. Hastings followed up 1,638 patients who were consecutive admissions to a psychiatric ward between 1938 and 1944. As the treatment available was extremely limited, he regards the outcome of these patients

as a measure of spontaneous remission and he also argues that it is most unlikely that these patients received further treatment during the follow-up period as they resided in a rural community. The follow-ups, which ranged from 6 to 12 years, were almost all conducted by interview (two-thirds of the original sample were interviewed). Among the neurotics, Hastings concluded that 'taken as a group (371 cases) the outlook for satisfactory adjustment without specialized therapy appears fairly good' (p. 1065). Of this group, 46 per cent were classified into the 'excellent' or 'good' outcome groups. However, it is probable that the outcome figures are deflated by the exceedingly poor outcome (25%) observed in the surprisingly large group who were diagnosed as suffering from 'hypochondriasis'—no fewer than 95 out of the total of 371 cases. The 14 anxiety neurotics had a good outcome (65%), the 23 obsessionals moderate to poor (44%), and the 73 hysterics had a moderate outcome (56%). Although the figures obtained by Hastings do not reflect a true spontaneous remission rate—'minimal treatment rate' would be a better description—the findings are of some interest because of the personal assessments carried out and also because of the long follow-up period.

The study by Endicott and Endicott (1963) in which a 52 per cent spontaneous remission rate was obtained over a period of six months is justifiably included in Bergin's table and has, of course, already been discussed above.

Bergin's use of Vorster's (1966) paper is puzzling. He states that, 'Vorster (1966) reported that only 34% of his neurotic sample had improved after more than 3 years'. Apart from some asides in the introduction, Vorster makes no mention of spontaneous remissions in his data. In fact he reports an 80 per cent improvement rate in 65 treated neurotic patients, 55 of whom received private treatment. The age range of the sample was from 9 to 52 years and he provides meagre follow-up information. Twenty-four of the cases were followed up for either months or years. The results of the treatment were assessed by the therapist (i.e. Vorster himself). The treatment consisted of psychotherapy which varied from eclectic to 'psychoanalysis bordering on the orthodox', narcoanalysis (beneficial in 7 out of 8 cases), some drugs, 'temporary hospitalisation', 'behaviour therapy' principles. An evaluation of Vorster's therapeutic claims is not our present concern. We have, however, been unable to trace the origin of the 34 per cent spontaneous remission rate quoted by Bergin and we willingly admit defeat.

Bergin's use of the report by Friess and Nelson (1942) is extremely uncritical. He quotes two spontaneous remission figures: 'Twenty of the no-therapy group of 70 had improved, or 29%. 23 of the 66 subjects with 2 therapy sessions had improved, or 35%'. He then concludes that, 'thus, after 5 years and upon careful examination by skilled clinicians, these cases showed recovery rates less than half the rates reported among Landis and Denker's admittedly inadequate samples'. The report by Friess and Nelson is a 5-year follow-up of patients who attended a general medical clinic in the period September 1932 to December 1933. The authors selected from the clinic records 498 patients for whom a retrospective diagnosis of psychoneurosis was determined. These 498 patients constituted 14 per cent of the total clinic sample and 269 were traced in the follow up study, i.e. just over half the complete group. Of the 269 patients who were traced, 177 were interviewed, 69 were visited by a social worker and/or supplied the information by post. The remaining patients were traced but little information was available as they were either in state psychiatric institutions or had died during the 5-year period.

The diagnoses seem somewhat atypical and a substantial number of the patients can at most be regarded as suffering from psychosomatic disorders. For example, 111 (41%) had a diagnosis 'referred to the gastro-intestinal tract. In the order of their frequency the symptoms were abdominal pain, belching or flatulence, nausea, constipation, vomiting, halitosis, sore tongue, anorexia, difficulty in swallowing, and rectal pain' (p. 545). Fifty-seven of the patients had skeletal symptoms, mainly aches and pains in muscles or joints. Of the 269 patients, only 7 had 'phobias' (from the brief description supplied, they were probably obsessional) and 4 of them had tics. As can be seen, this was scarcely a representative sample of neurotic disorders. No matter. If we examine the data on the *entire* sample of 269 patients we find that 115 had no psychiatric care whatever. This figure excludes the 15 patients for whom an incorrect diagnosis had been made and the 11 patients who had died during the 5-year period. We find that 50 of these untreated patients (i.e. 44%) were found to be either cured or improved. Sixty-five were found to be unchanged or worse (i.e. 55%). Of this total, 14 were categorised as 'worse' and 1 was in a state psychiatric hospital. Bergin's figure of 29 per cent is at underestimation of the spontaneous remission rate but in this instance it can (and will) be explained. Before doing so, however, it is instructive to compare the spontaneous remission figures with the remissions found in the group who had received 'much psychiatric care'. Of the 36 treated patients, none was cured and 10 got worse (including 4 in state psychiatric hospitals). Only 12 out of 36 showed any improvement. These

figures can be compared with those reported for the patients who had received no psychiatric care. Of the 116 untreated patients in this group, 23 were cured, 27 were improved and and 15 were worse (including 1 in a state psychiatric hospital). Stated in a slightly different way, none of the *treated* patients was cured but one-fifth of the *untreated* patients were cured. If we combine the cured and improved categories, it is seen that 33 per cent of the treated patients show some recovery whereas slightly under half the untreated patients show some degree of recovery. Nearly one-third of the treated patients were worse at follow-up whereas only 8 per cent of the untreated patients were found to be worse. Friess and Nelson sum up: 'there was no noteworthy difference between the psychiatrically and non-psychiatrically treated groups' (p. 557).

Bergin's figure of a 29 per cent spontaneous remission rate is obtained by relying exclusively on the patients who were interviewed at the end of the 5-year period, despite the fact that Friess and Nelson specifically draw attention to the higher remission rate obtained from those patients who did not re-attend the clinic when invited. They even mention three of the most prominent reasons given by the patients who declined the invitation. They were: there was no need to return to the clinic as they had improved; it was difficult or inconvenient for them to re-attend; they were dissatisfied with the treatment they had received. The essential point is, however, that the people who accepted the clinic invitation to reattend were *demonstrably unrepresentative*. A significantly larger proportion of the refusers were well. Of the 48 untreated patients who refused the invitation to re-attend (but were visited by the social worker and/or supplied information by post), no fewer than 30 were cured or improved. This yields a spontaneous remission index of 62 per cent (10 patients were unchanged, 6 were worse and 2 had been incorrectly diagnosed). If this finding were repeated in the 229 patients who were neither traced nor contacted (and this is a reasonable expectation) then the spontaneous remission rate would approximate the usual figure, despite the fact that it is doubtful whether the sample from this clinic is a typically neurotic one. If, however, we were unwise and decided to ignore the demonstrated distortion of the sample and we were also to suppress our doubts about the nature of the disorders under consideration, we would settle on the spontaneous remission rate of 44 per cent described above. Fortunately, the shortage of adequate studies is not so desperate that it demands an unwise use of such doubtful information.

The study by Koegler and Brill (1967) does not provide figures on spontaneous remission rate and is discussed in the section on psychotherapy (p. 829). In all, Bergin's substitution of a 30 per cent spontaneous remission rate appears to be ill-founded.

In fact, the available evidence does not permit a revision of Eysenck's (1952) estimate of a gross spontaneous remission rate of approximately 65 per cent of neurotic disorders over a two-year period. However, the evidence that has been presented since that original estimate was attempted, emphasises the need for more refined studies and more accurate statistics. In particular, it is now possible to say with a high degree of certainty that the gross spontaneous remission rate is not constant across different *types* of neurotic disorder. It is, for example, probable that obsessional disorders show a lower rate of spontaneous remission than anxiety conditions. Future investigators would be well advised to analyse the spontaneous remission rates of the various neuroses within rather than across diagnostic groupings. If we proceed in this manner it should eventually be possible to make more accurate estimates of the likelihood of spontaneous remission occurring in a particular type of disorder and, indeed, for a particular group of patients.

Although the gross spontaneous remission rate has thus far been based on a two-year period of observation (and this serves well for many purposes), attempts to understand the nature of the process will, of course, be facilitated by an extension of the periods of observation. The collection of reliable observations on the course of spontaneous remission will, among other things, greatly assist in making prognoses.

Naturally, the determination of a reliable rate of spontaneous remission is only the first stage in a process of exploration. Both for its own sake and for practical reasons, we need to approach an understanding of the causes of spontaneous remission. Eysenck (1963) has adumbrated a theory to account for remissions and relapses which draws attention to the possible role of individual differences in personality. In addition, there are numerous bits of incidental information pertinent to the subject which are contained in clinical reports, follow-up studies and the like (e.g. Stevenson, 1961). Respond-ents who have recovered from neurotic disorders often attribute their improvements to the occurrence of fortunate *events*. Some of the more commonly mentioned are financial gains, improvements in occupation, successful marriages and personal relationships, and amelioration of pressing difficulties, and so on (Friess and Nelson, 1942; Imber *et al.*, 1968). The identification of these restorative events and study of the manner in which they affect the process of remission would be of considerable value.

Unfortunately, the encouragement that can be derived from the occurrence of spontaneous remissions in neuroses must be tempered by recognition of the fact that a sizeable minority of patients do not remit spontaneously. Approximately one-third of all neurotic patients do not improve spontaneously and it could be that, in the future, it is this group of people who will absorb the attentions of clinicians and research workers. Such a redirection of effort must, of course, depend on an accurate system of identification and prognosis. The size of the problem can be estimated from the current rates of rejection, defection, and failure reported by psychotherapists.

Recognition of the occurrence of spontaneous remissions in neurotic disorders leads us to consider the possibility (and utility) of establishing and determining an index of spontaneous deterioration. Although some neurotic behaviour (e.g. specific phobias) is relatively unchanging, much neurotic behaviour is not stable and it follows that the changes that occur can move in a positive or negative direction. Fortunately, the majority of the changes are towards improvement. It seems highly probable that a proportion of the remaining third who do not improve, get *worse* over time. At present it is not possible to say much that is useful on this topic but it is to be hoped that future studies of the course of neurotic behaviour patterns will also explore the occurrence of deteriorations and the factors that contribute to this process. In time, it should be possible to determine the spontaneous remission index *and* the spontaneous deterioration index for various types of neurotic disorder.

THE EFFECTS OF PSYCHOANALYTIC TREATMENT

Two of the major conclusions reached in the earlier edition of this *Handbook* were: 'when untreated neurotic control groups are compared with experimental groups of neurotic patients treated by means of psychotherapy, both groups recover to approximately the same extent' and, 'neurotic patients treated by psychoanalytic psychotherapy do not improve more quickly than patients treated by means of eclectic psychotherapy, and may improve less quickly when account is taken of the large proportion of patients breaking off treatment' (Eysenck, 1960, pp. 719–720). These conclusions gave rise to controversy and although many aspects of the dispute have not been satisfactorily resolved, there appears to be fairly wide (although by no means universal) agreement that the case for psychotherapy has not been proven. There is also general agreement on the need for controlled studies of the effect of psychotherapy and a recognition that reports of uncontrolled studies of psychotherapy are of very little value. With the exception of psycho-analytic treatment, this chapter will therefore deal primarily with studies in which controls have been employed.

It was felt that psychoanalysis requires further examination even in the absence of controlled studies. It can be argued that most forms of psycho-therapy owe their genesis, to a small or large extent, to psychoanalytic theory and technique. Secondly, the evaluation of psychoanalytic results presents serious difficulties that are particular to it. Furthermore, even when a measure of agreement has been reached on evaluating other forms of psychotherapy, disputes about *psychoanalysis* are still evident. For example, Bergin (1970) is critical of many of the arguments and conclusions proposed in the earlier edition of this *Handbook* but finds himself in agreement with the conclusions regarding the effect of psychotherapy, other than psychoanalysis. He says, 'while there are several modest differences between my and Eysenck's evaluation of the cases so reported, the overall conclusion is virtually identical. Eysenck finds a 64% improvement rate with a range from 41 to 77 and I find a 65% rate with a range from 42 to 87. I analysed 8 additional studies not reviewed by Eysenck and these yielded essentially the same mean and range of improvement'. As Bergin observes, 'it is striking that we should agree so closely on the results of eclectic psychotherapy and differ so sharply on our evaluations of psychoanalysis'. For these reasons we have decided to include a discussion of psychoanalytic treatment even though there is an absence of suitable controlled studies.

An evaluation of psychoanalysis presents numer-ous difficulties, and one of the most serious is how to deal with the gross biases that operate in the selection for treatment and the related problem of premature terminations of treatment. Recent in-formation on these topics confirms earlier obser-vations of an enormous selection bias and a staggeringly high rate of premature terminations, such that, even if one were to conclude that psycho-analysis is an extraordinarily effective treatment it would be necessary to add the qualification that it has an extremely narrow range of applicability. A second qualification would be that there is a strong risk that patients will not complete treatment. Again, even if one put the best possible face on the effects of psychoanalytic treatment, the premature termin-ation rate demonstrates a serious deficiency in the criteria and techniques used by psychoanalysts in selecting patients for treatment.

One of the implications to flow from estimates of the gross spontaneous remission rate in neurotic disorders is that any form of treatment for these disorders must attain a success rate as good as or, preferably, better than the gross rate. It is unlikely, however, that crude comparisons between treated and untreated groups of heterogeneous patients will advance our knowledge and understanding at any-thing more than a snail's pace. The more economic and sensible course is to attempt comparisons between treated and untreated groups of neurotic patients with similar disorders (and, hence, similar prognoses). On strictly scientific grounds the inclu-sion of untreated control groups is a prerequisite for the evaluation of treatment techniques. The undesira-bility of withholding treatment from large numbers of patients (particularly where long-term follow-ups are envisaged) is too obvious to require elaboration. Several alternatives, however, can be employed such as own-controls, brief waiting periods, placebo trials and the rest (*see* Strupp and Bergin's (1969) review).

In any therapeutic evaluation study there are numerous problems to be contended with: diagnostic problems, outcome criteria, duration of treatment, patient selection and matching, and so on. Each of these problems, and many others, become even more prominent in attempting to assess the effects of psychoanalysis than is the case with other forms of treatment. Strict psychoanalytic theory implies its own somewhat idiosyncratic diagnostic concepts, criteria of success, the nature of failure and, indeed, perhaps central to all of these, the *purpose* of treat-ment. Although we are frequently confronted with outcome criteria such as 'total functioning' which are as extravagant as they are nebulous, it is nevertheless possible to reach some agreed definitions (e.g. *see* Knight, 1941). In our opinion, however, evaluations of psychoanalysis (and comparative studies) cannot even be contemplated until agreement is reached on the purpose of the treatment; i.e. are we trying to help the patient overcome his difficulties and com-plaints or are we hoping to change his 'character structure' (*see* Hamburg *et al.*, 1967). It is not our present purpose, however, to embark on an extensive investigation of these problems. Nor do we wish to multiply or exaggerate the number and nature of these problems; they will speak for themselves.

Most of the information on the effectiveness of psychoanalysis consists of single case-reports (which we can largely discount) and series of patients treated by a single analyst or, more commonly, at a particular clinic. We have, in addition, access to a few studies that have compared psychoanalytic and other types of treatment. Although some seemingly extravagant claims are made on behalf of the therapeutic value of psychoanalysis (e.g. 'Psychoanalysis has emerged not only as the most effective method known for the study of the human psyche, but as the most effective method known for the treatment of emotional disorders' (Brody, 1962, p. 732)), it is significant that the *authors* of the reports to be dealt with rarely make specific claims for the therapeutic value of psychoanalytic treatment. Indeed in some instances specific disclaimers are recorded.

The most suitable starting point for an examination of the results of psychoanalytic therapy is the commendable survey attempted by Knight in 1941. He tried to remedy the fact that 'to the knowledge of the writer there is not a single report in the literature on the therapeutic results of an analyst in private practice or of any such group of analysts' (p. 434). After carefully listing the great difficulties involved in his task, Knight proposed five criteria on which to base the outcome of treatment and then analysed the 'brochure reports' of the Berlin Institute (1920–1930), London Clinic (1926–1936), Chicago Institute (1932–1937), Menninger Clinic (1932–1941) and the work of Hyman and Kessel. Each of these reports is analysed separately and jointly to provide a composite picture of the results. A total of 952 cases are listed by diagnosis and therapeutic result, with the appropriate words of caution on both scores. A specific point of importance is that the analysis of results from the Berlin, London, and Chicago Clinics includes only those patients who had completed *at least 6 months* of analysis. And, 'in order to promote uniformity this same selection was used in the study of the Menninger Clinic cases and of course in the composite table . . . however, the writer is well aware that the excluded cases, i.e. those treated less than 6 months, represent an important group of "failures" . . . it is emphasized here again that this group deserves special study, statistical analysis and evaluation of the failure factors' (p. 438).

By its very nature the information compiled by Knight cannot provide us with an answer to the question of whether or not psychoanalysis is effective. Nevertheless, the interclinic and inter-diagnostic comparisons are of some interest (especially for connoisseurs) and provide a general, if somewhat blurred picture of analytic practice. Knight's overall conclusion, given in his composite table, is that the percentage cured and much improved rate for psychoanalytic treatment is 55·9 per cent. Some additional information can be obtained by analysing subcategories separately or in different combinations. For example, one can exclude the psychotic cases (who tended to do worse than

neurotics) and the improvement rate increases. On the other hand, if we include the 292 patients who broke off treatment before completing 6 months of analysis, then the overall improvement rate drops drastically. If we adopt both of these procedures (i.e. exclude the psychotics and include the premature terminators) we arrive at an overall recovery rate of 30 per cent.

The interesting aspects of this information should not, however, cloud the main issue: these brochure reports do not demonstrate the effects, positive or negative, of psychoanalytic treatment.

Bergin (and others) have taken the view that premature terminations of psychoanalytic treatment should be excluded when one attempts to evaluate its efficacy. As the majority of patients who break off the treatment appear to do so after having received what would be regarded by any other psychotherapist as a great deal of treatment, we are of the opinion that the terminators should be included as failures, unless there is demonstrable evidence to the contrary. There is, however, a more serious methodological problem lying beneath the surface. As will be shown presently, some reports of psychoanalytical treatment claim astonishingly high rates of recovery (e.g. Bergin obtains a figure of 91 %). It seems likely to us that these figures may be an artefact of the psychoanalytic procedure in that the therapist does not regard the patient as having completed his analytic treatment unless and until he has recovered. To take an extreme case, if a patient has failed to recover after seven years of psychoanalytic treatment and consequently decides to discontinue attendance, then he would be regarded as a premature terminator rather than a failed case. If one adopts the view, as most analysts do, that psychoanalytic treatment *is a complete treatment* then it follows that failures can occur only as a result of an incomplete analysis. It is only by coming to grips with this point of view that enables one to understand why the premature temination rates are so high. Here we are forced to recall Galen's famous observation: 'All who drink this remedy recover in a short time, except those whom it does not help, who all die and have no relief from any other medicine. Therefore it is obvious that it fails only in incurable cases'.* We might also note, in passing, that the average duration

* See for example Brody's (1962) comments on the report of the American Psychoanalytic Association. He says that 'one might draw the conclusion that of the patients who undertook analysis for neurotic reactions and completed treatment, 97 per cent were cured or improved'. Then, later, on the same page (p. 732), he points out that 'the patients who undertook analysis for neurotic reactions but did not complete their treatment, 50 per cent discontinued because they were improved. The other half discontinued treatment because of external reasons'.

of psychoanalytic treatment is 3 to 4 years. As argued above, the spontaneous remission rate in neurotic disorders is approximately 66 per cent over a 2-year period—consequently one would expect a group of patients undergoing psychoanalysis to show an overall recovery rate in excess of 66 per cent.

Bieber *et al.* (1962) carried out a questionnaire investigation of patients receiving psychoanalytic treatment procedurally similar to that conducted by the American Psychoanalytic Association (*see* below) but more successful. Of the 100 members of the Society of Medical Psychoanalysts, 70 responded to a request that they complete questionnaires on homosexual male patients in their care. Each psychoanalyst was requested to complete three copies and in the event that they were treating fewer than three homosexuals, they were asked to complete the questionnaires on heterosexual male patients. These heterosexual patients formed the comparison sample. The analysts were given 'unrestricted choice' in the selection of comparison patients, and few of them had been in therapy for less than 100 hours. These initial questionnaires were supplemented and the sample of therapists was also extended at a later stage. Varying degrees of information were finally obtained on 106 male homosexual patients and 100 heterosexual male comparison cases. As the authors point out, the samples were by no means random. In addition to the selection carried out by the responding therapists, the patient sample was as unrepresentative of the general population as in all the psychoanalytic reports and surveys emerging from the United States. The patients were predominantly from higher than average socio-economic classes, significantly well-educated (two-thirds having completed university education), and two-thirds were in professional occupations. Obviously, the selection bias and unrepresentative character of the samples precludes any generalisations about homosexual patients or their similarities and differences with other types of patients. The authors draw attention to these factors and mention, among other studies, the composition and nature of a British sample reported by Westwood (1960). The generality of Bieber's findings is further limited by the psychoanalytic bias incorporated in the questionnaires and interpretations placed on the data. Despite all these shortcomings some interesting suggestions emerged from their fairly extensive survey.

Of course, their comparison group is in no sense a control group and is wholly irrelevant to a consideration of the effects of treatment. Their results cannot be used to prove or disprove the putative benefits of psychoanalytic treatment but they are not without interest. Of the 106 homosexuals treated, 27 per cent became exclusively heterosexual while 15 of the 30 patients who began treatment as bisexual eventually became heterosexual. Only 19 per cent (14 out of 72) of those who began treatment as exclusively homosexual eventually became heterosexual. Only 7 per cent of those patients who had fewer than 150 hours of treatment became heterosexual whereas 47 per cent of those who had 350 or more hours of analysis became heterosexual. The 'favourable prognostic indicators' included bisexuality, motivation to become heterosexual, heterosexual genital contact at some time, under 35 years of age. The relevance of these indicators is discussed in Chapter 5.

In 1952 the American Psychoanalytic Association commendably set up a Central Fact-gathering Committee (Hamburg *et al.*, 1967) to compile what is described as an 'experience survey'. All members of the Association were sent questionnaires to be completed on up to 25 patients per analyst. The Committee received approximately 10,000 completed questionnaires from about 800 participants (i.e. approximately 80 per cent of the analysts complied with this first request). The second questionnaire, entitled final, yielded a far less satisfactory response and they were able to obtain information on only 3,000 patients. The initial report requested information on the vital statistics of patients and their presenting symptoms while the final report requested information about the outcome of treatment. The loss of information on more than two-thirds of the patients is unfortunate, and the Committee was understandably puzzled by this sharp reduction in the number of participating analysts. They point out, quite correctly, that their sample is likely to be biased because of this lost material and 'any conclusions based on this set of data must be qualified by our doubts about the representativeness of the sample' (p. 847). One need not take too seriously Brody's suggestion that the participating analysts failed to return the majority of the questionnaires because of 'resistance' (Brody, 1962, p. 731). The important fact to bear in mind is that only 300 of the original 800 participants submitted final reports (i.e. outcomes) on neurotic patients who had been analysed. In addition it should be noted that the range of the number of patients reported by each therapist was from 1 to 24, the mode being one patient-report and the median about 6.

The Committee found that of the 595 cases of neurotic reactions who had undertaken analysis, only 306 were reported as having been completely analysed, that is, approximately 50 per cent and the average duration was 3 to 4 years. The Committee then sent follow-up questionnaires to the participants who had reported on the 306 completely analysed patients. They received only 210 replies, that is only 70 per cent. Of these 210 supplementary questionnaires, 80 patients were listed as cured. In 35 of these, all of the symptoms were reported as cured, and in 45 patients residual symptoms remained. In the 130 remaining questionnaires the improvement rates were high, and the Committee concluded that: 'one might draw the conclusion that about 97% of the patients who undertake analysis for neurotic reactions and complete it, are "cured" or "improved".' Of the 50 per cent who do not complete their analysis, about half discontinued apparently because they were improved. The other half discontinued because of 'external' reasons or, because they did not improve, or were considered untreatable, or they were transferred to other analysts, or required hospitalisation. The most frequent reason given for discontinuing, apart from being improved, was 'external reasons'.

In the light of this striking improvement rate, some of the other findings of the Committee are a little surprising. For example, 650 analysts were asked about their expectations of treatment outcome, given a young person whom one could analyse for four years or more, with all conditions favourable. The analysts were asked to estimate the expected results for patients with neuroses, character disorders, and so on. The opinions were candid. Forty-five percent of the analysts who replied, 'expected no cure in any of the conditions'.

Analysing the admittedly unrepresentative data, the Committee found that '96·6% of the patients reported that they felt benefited by their treatment'. Similarly, 97·3 per cent of the patients were 'judged by their therapist to be improved in total functioning'. Once more, 'virtually all patients reported to their therapists that they felt benefited by completed treatment'. Similarly impressive results were reported for the effect of treatment on the 'character structure' of the patients.

There is only one finding that jars. The 'overall incidence of symptom cure is only 27%'. Whatever the temptation, these findings do not permit the conclusion that psychoanalysis is capable of achieving anything except a removal of the patient's symptoms.

As already noted, the subgroup on which the analysis was carried out is 'significantly different from parent group of 10,000 in the distribution of patients between psychoanalysis and psychotherapy, and in this respect, at the very least, is *not* a random sample' (p. 854). To this we may add the unknown effects that might arise from the *literal* loss of a great deal of the data between the inception of the study in 1952 and the appearance of the report some 15 years later. Moreover, an astonishingly large number of patients did not complete treatment. 'Of the 2,983 reports examined, 43% were in psychoanalysis, 47% in psychotherapy, and 10% in both at different times. Of those in psychoanalysis, 57% completed treatment and 43% did not. In psychotherapy these figures were 37% (completed) and 63% (did not); in both, 47% completed and 53% did not complete.' The Committee adds that 'there is no information in the study as to whether termination was initiated by therapist or patient' (p. 854). The salient feature to emerge from all this is that *more patients terminated therapy prematurely than completed it.* The raw figures are as follows: 1,589 did not complete treatment and 1,393 did complete it. The Committee report does throw a small ray of light on the fate of patients who terminate their analysis before completion. It would appear from their inadequate figures that slightly under half of the premature terminators were 'improved'. Regrettably there are no data provided on the effects of an incomplete analysis on character structure, total functioning or symptoms.

One of the more interesting aspects of this report and one for which the Committee can be commended, is the information provided on the vital statistics of the patient sample. The Committee points out that the patient sample is highly selected and that they are grossly unrepresentative of the US population. For example 60 per cent of all the patients were *at least* college graduates—compared with 6 per cent in the general population. The income and professional status of the group are both well above the US average. In 94 per cent of cases, the treatment was carried out privately. The frequency of the treatment (in analysis) revealed that 61 per cent of the patients attended their analyst 4 or 5 times a week. Approximately one-sixth of all the patients in this sample had undergone previous analysis. Nearly 7 per cent of the sample were themselves psychiatrists (undergoing a training analysis?).

The Committee expressed the view that the figures cannot 'be used to prove analytic therapy to be effective or ineffective' and, apart from providing some interesting peripheral information, we hope that this survey might prompt others to carry out scientific enquiries into the effectiveness of psychoanalytic therapy.

In 1961, Professor Barendregt of Amsterdam University published an interesting follow-up study of three groups of patients. These were derived from a number of patients who were tested psychologically when they applied for psychotherapy at the Institute for Psychoanalysis in Amsterdam. After about 2½ years the patients were re-tested. Of these patients, 47 (Group A) had been given psychoanalysis; 79 patients (Group B) had been given psychotherapy other than psychoanalysis, and not at the Institute; 74 patients (Group C) did not have any form of psychotherapy or any therapeutic contact during the period. The follow-up study is concerned with a comparison of the changes that occurred and it is obviously of central importance to know why patients were assigned to the various groups. It will be seen that this was not a control study in the ordinary sense but rather a comparison study which in its important respects should be thought of as retrospective. The 'patients were classified into group B for various reasons. The decision in favour of psychotherapy for a number of patients was made for practical reasons (mainly financial), when psychoanalysis would actually have been more desirable . . . for some of the patients in Group C psychoanalysis or psychotherapy was advised but impractical. Moreover, patients for whom psychoanalysis had been indicated and were put on a waiting list, were included in the control group if by the time of the second psychological examination they were still awaiting treatment.' Barendregt considers the possibility that selection may have vitiated the effects of any comparison between the groups but concludes that it is not too likely. The criteria of change were, unfortunately, not chosen with the care that might have been given and included two projective tests of doubtful validity. A third reservation attaching to the study is the fact that the psychoanalytic treatment was carried out predominantly by inexperienced psychoanalysts.

The results of the study did not yield evidence in favour of the therapeutic usefulness of either psychoanalysis or psychotherapy. The positive outcome on one or two predictions relates to incidental effects; thus, it is not the patient's sense of well-being or his neuroticism that is affected, but rather his score on the Lie Scale, i.e. a score, the meaning of which is difficult to ascertain. The author concludes that, 'all the same this study is felt to have been useful. For one thing the patients' opinion of feeling better after some time of psychotherapy has proved to be of little meaning in favour of psychotherapy.* For another, the present study has shown two ways which may possibly lead to compelling evidence of the usefulness of psychotherapy. However, such evidence has not been arrived at by this investigation.'

In their statistical appraisal of the putative effects of psychoanalytic psychotherapy Duhrssen and Jorswieck (1969) compared the number of occasions on which three types of patients were admitted to hospital for any complaint in a five-year pre-treatment period and a five-year post treatment period. The sheer number of hospital admissions was

* See also Koegler and Brill (1967, p. 55) for example.

obtained from insurance cards, and the nature and cause of the admission was not specified in their study. Nonetheless, they compared 125 patients who completed psychoanalysis during 1958 with another 100 patients who were on a psychiatric waiting list and yet another 100 normal subjects. They found that there was no significant difference between the treated and untreated groups before psychoanalysis but that both groups of patients had more admissions to hospital prior to treatment than did the normals. After psychoanalysis, however, the treated group had fewer hospital admissions than the untreated group, which showed no change in the number of days spent in hospital.

The authors' idea of using number of hospital admissions as an index of response to treatment is interesting but peripheral and in the absence of direct evidence on the psychological state of the treated and untreated patients, can tell us very little about the effects of psychoanalytic treatment. Their study also suffers from other defects such as a failure to explain why the treated patients *were* treated whereas the waiting list controls were not treated. One wonders why the untreated subjects were expected to or required to wait 5 years before receiving treatment, unless they did in fact receive treatment during the 5-year follow-up period. This point is not made clear in the paper. Certainly one needs to know what type of patients they were and what sort of disorders they had that enabled them to wait patiently over a 5-year period while expecting to be given treatment. Another serious limitation of this study is the absence of *psychological* information about the patients and the curious but striking absence of any psychological assessment either before or after the treatment period.

Although Klein's (1960) paper is mainly concerned with the putative changes that occur during psychoanalytic treatment, some of the information is relevant to the present discussion. She carried out a retrospective analysis of 30 patients who had completed a minimum of 200 analytic sessions (4 to 5 times weekly, who had been out of treatment for more than one year, and who had an original diagnosis of neurosis). The 'arbitrary length of treatment' chosen in this study 'automatically rules out those patients whose psychoanalytic treatment at the clinic is discontinued early' (p. 156). Klein admits that 'this procedure may appear to favour a trend of excluding treatment failures . . . but we were interested primarily in finding a method for studying therapeutic changes' (p. 156). The degree of selection involved in assembling these 30 patients is indicated by the fact that they were chosen from an original group of 288. The demographic characteristics of the 30 patients are comparable to those reported by the Fact-Finding Committee of the American Psychoanalytic Association described above. Klein's description of the criteria for selecting patients for psychoanalytic treatment at the clinic (Columbia University Psychoanalytic Clinic) are of interest. The patient 'must possess sufficient motivation to improve his current functioning'. The assessing psychoanalyst then attempts to assess the patient's degree of rigidity and his ego strength. In both instances they have to be favourable before the patient is considered suitable for treatment. In addition the patients whose 'prognosis is most favourable and who are, therefore, regarded as most suitable for psychoanalytic treatment are those who present structured symptomotology of a relatively short duration' (p. 155). Furthermore, the selected patients 'are expected to be capable of a degree of effective functioning, either currently or in the recent past'. Again, 'these patients must be capable of significant pleasure response'. To complete the list, the patients must 'have the ability to form affective relationships with others and a history of having been capable of such relationships in the past'. It is reassuring that 'these basic criteria of psychoanalyzability are used flexibly' (p. 155).

The selection of patients for this retrospective study was based on the diagnosis made at the end of the third month of treatment and patients with 'schizotypal disorders' were excluded as it is the policy of the clinic not to undertake treatment of these patients by standard psychoanalytic technique. In view of the formidable list of excluding criteria and the apparent intensiveness of the screening procedures, it therefore comes as something of a surprise when we are told that at the time of the follow-up study '7 of the 30 cases, originally diagnosed as psychoneurosis, were diagnosed schizotypal disorder by the 5 interviewers' (p. 170).

It was found that 76 per cent of this group of 30 patients rated themselves as having shown considerable improvement at the follow-up period.

This favourable outcome was consistent with the conclusion reached by the psychoanalytic raters who examined the case notes of each patient. It is, however, unfortunately necessary to qualify the impression given by these overall results. The ratings made by the psychoanalytic judges were not blind. The raters were aware that the patients had completed analytic treatment and, also, 'had the knowledge of the patients functioning at all three periods when rating any one period'. Secondly, 'about one half of the patients in our sample' had had previous therapy. There would appear to be a strong likelihood that the sample under consideration is far from being representative and the absence of any control group is, of course, an obvious shortcoming.

Finally, it is noted that after the follow-up 'more than one fourth of the group had returned to treatment with an analyst, usually on a one to two times per week basis' (p. 165).

The serious question of selection bias in any attempts to assess the effects of psychoanalysis is underscored by some incidental information that emerges from the work by Knapp and others (1960) who attempted to determine criteria for successful analytic treatment. Like Klein and the Fact-gathering Committee, these workers found that analytic patients had a disproportionate number of highly educated and sophisticated patients. For example, in their sample of 100 cases no fewer than 64 had received post-graduate education. Seventy-two per cent were in professional and academic work and approximately half of all the cases were 'engaged in work related to psychiatry and psychoanalysis' (p. 463). They also found that 'interviewers accepted approximately one third of all applicants'. The wholly unrepresentative nature of the patients who receive psychoanalysis (at least in the USA) is confirmed by the work of Hollingshead and Redlich (1958).

The extreme bias operating in the selection of patients who are chosen for psychoanalytic treatment would, of itself, make any attempts at generalisation about the effects of the treatment risky. As noted above, the extremely high rejection rate is further compounded by the unacceptably large number of patients (roughly one half) who terminate prematurely. Rightly or wrongly, psychoanalysts appear to believe that their method of treatment is suitable only for a tiny fraction of the population of psychiatric cases in the community. Moreover, in considerations of social utility, one has to bear in mind that psychoanalysis is extremely time-consuming. Given that the average course of analytic treatment takes 3 to 4 years (see above), and that an analyst using classical analysis is unlikely to carry more than 8 patients at any one time, we estimate that a practising psychoanalyst will complete treatment on roughly two or three patients per year. Carrying these calculations a little further, we find that a psychiatric clinic or hospital that aims to complete treatment on a thousand cases a year would require in the region of 300 to 500 full-time psychoanalysts. Viewed in this perspective it seems reasonable to us that if psychoanalytic treatment is to be practised, then we have grounds for expecting it to do more than provide relief for a highly selected and tiny group of people (e.g. it could be argued that the treatment process might increase our understanding of psychological processes or mechanisms). The point is that, judged on grounds of social utility, psychoanalytic treatment has little justification. Naturally, its scientific value needs to be judged by other criteria (Rachman, 1963).

The comparative study reported by Cremerius (1962) is, unfortunately, defective in the same respect as the Barendregt study in that the selection of patients for psychoanalytic treatment was not random. In both studies, patients were very carefully selected and those thought most likely to benefit from psychoanalytic treatment were given prime choice, and constituted a small minority of the total patient pool. As we have already seen in earlier reports, those patients who are selected for psychoanalysis are a highly unrepresentative sample of the population and include a grossly disproportionate number of highly-educated, persistent patients from the middle classes. The Cremerius report deals with the fate of 605 neurotic out-patients who were treated by some form of psychotherapy during the period from 1948 to 1951. A further 175 patients were excluded because they were not considered suitable for psychotherapy either because they refused treatment, were of an inappropriate age, suspected of having a psychotic disorder etc. The majority of patients were between 30 and 50 years of age and the sexes were equally distributed. About one-third of the patients expressed a wish for psychotherapy and about one-half had no idea what psychotherapy was and, hence, had no desire for such treatment. These ideas and views played a considerable part in the selection of therapy. Nine per cent (56 cases) were treated by analytic therapy, 160 cases (27%) by verbal discussion and psychotherapy, 194 (32%) received hypnotic treatment, 40 cases (7%) had narcohypnotic treatment, 105 (17%) received autogenic training and 50 cases (8%) received a combination of treatments. A majority of patients who were psychoanalysed had psychosomatic symptoms whereas very few of those who received hypnosis or narcohypnosis had such a

diagnosis. This treatment allocation correlated highly with social class in the expected direction.

The figures for the outcome of therapy in 573 cases are shown in Table 22.1. The criteria for outcome of treatment were the same for all groups but it will be noticed that the outcome categories given at the end of treatment do not include patients who were unchanged or worse at the end of treatment. For the total sample the overall improvement rate is 78 per cent. The figures at termination of treatment are most favourable for hypnosis and least favourable for combined treatment methods. Psychoanalysis is inferior to hypnosis and superior to the combined method and seems roughly comparable to autogenic training, as far as success rate at termination is concerned. The proportion of patients who abandoned therapy (presumably this figure includes unchanged or deteriorated cases as well) was largest for psychoanalysis and autogenic training. This failure (?) rate occurs in spite of the rigorous selection which isolated those patients deemed most likely to succeed with psychoanalytic treatment. Within diagnostic categories, hysteria and anxiety neuroses showed the best results with the remarkable figures of 97 per cent and 94 per cent of 'cures and improvements'. Depression, hypochondria, and obsessional disorders did rather less well and showed fewer instances in which the symptoms disappeared. However, 92 per cent of all patients were at work at the end of treatment compared with only 63 per cent prior to treatment.

The follow-ups were carried out between 8 and 10 years after termination and the excellent figure of 86 per cent were traced. The figures shown in Table 22.1 exclude those cases in which the symptom remained unchanged (38%). One of the most notable features of the follow-up figures is the sharp reduction in the overall percentage of improvements—a fall from 78 to 25 per cent. The most striking change

Table 22.1. The Effects of Different Types of Therapy—Cremerius's Study (1962)

Therapy	Position at end of treatment			Position at follow-up		
	Abolition of symptom (per cent)	Symptom improvement (per cent)	Treatment terminated (per cent)	Abolition of symptom (per cent)	Symptom improvement (per cent)	Symptom substitution or worsening (per cent)
Analytic psycho-therapy	41	29	30	21	31	18
Verbal discussion	48	33	19	12	13	37
Hypnosis	54	31	15	7	10	47
Autogenic training	38	32	30	12	17	28
Combined methods	32	26	42	7	14	39
Total (per cent)	47	31	22	11	14	37

is the large deterioration in the group of patients treated by hypnosis. The patients who received psychoanalytic treatment show a much smaller deterioration, and the difference between these two types of treatment at follow-up is statistically significant. In addition to this difference between treatment types, the figures also suggest some differences in outcome for diagnostic categories. These figures are shown in Table 22.2 below. They indicate a marked degree of so-called symptom substitution; this is particularly noticeable in hysterics, but also in anxiety conditions, and depressions. The hypochondrical group shows a large number of patients who got worse and the obsessionals an extremely high percentage of patients with unchanged symptomatology. Two-thirds of the patients with this disorder show little variation in their condition over an 8- to 10-year period. As mentioned earlier, the most striking feature of these figures is the exceedingly poor recovery rate over the long term—averaging only 25 per cent compared with the figure of 73 per cent improved at termination of therapy. The suggestion that patients who received psychoanalytic therapy do slightly better over the long-term despite the absence of any such superiority at the time of treatment termination, is interesting and might be worth investigating in a more appropriate control study where the selection of patients is correctly randomised. We might also draw attention to the fact that those patients who received psychoanalytic treatment had, of course, a great deal more treatment than did the patients in other groups. They received in the region of approximately 300 hours of treatment as opposed to a dozen hours or less for some of the other groups. Another important comparison would, of course, involve types of treatment more frequently used in Britain and the US. In terms of Anglo-Saxon practice, the German methods are unusual.

The study reported by Lakin Phillips (1957) also compares an unorthodox method with psychoanalytic treatment. The comparison treatment was de-veloped by Phillips and is based on 'interference' theory.

Very briefly, interference theory constitutes the viewpoint that behaviour—psychological or other-wise—is a result of various assertions made by the individual about himself or about his relationship with others. The person chooses now one kind of behaviour, now another, depending on what kind of behaviour seems likely to bring (from the environ-ment) confirmation of his assertions. Certain behaviour possibilities 'interfere' with each other; i.e. the person cannot do both at the same time. However, since possible behaviour is always selected by a person on the basis of its appropriateness to the environment, the whole process with which we are concerned goes on 'in the open'. 'Depth views which regard the mental life of people as having a kind of reservoir from which diabolical forces spring are entirely anathema to the present viewpoint' (Phillips, 1957).

The treatment used by Phillips is directive and involves an analysis of the patients prevailing diffi-culties and choices. The problems are examined with the guidance of the therapist and the most desirable practical possibilities are then encouraged in a form of behavioural prescriptions.

Before comparing the effects of this treatment with that of analysis, it should be noted that the samples of the two groups were selected on quite different principles and, for this reason (among others), the study cannot be regarded as a satisfactory test of either treatment technique. The results of the com-parison are shown in Table 22.3 (p. 828). Before turning to the table, however, it should be noted that the number of interviews required by the inter-ference method was less than half that required by psychoanalytic methods, a difference that was statistically significant. On the basis of his research, Phillips argues that the results 'suggest strongly that there are real differences in the effectiveness and efficiency of outpatient, parent-child psychotherapy when assertion therapy and psychoanalytic-derived depth methods are compared'. Particularly striking,

Table 22.2. The Effects of Therapy on Different Diagnostic Groups—Cremerius's Study (1962)

	Condition at follow-up				
	Symptom abolition (per cent)	Symptom improvement (per cent)	Symptom unchanged (per cent)	Symptom worse (per cent)	Symptom substitution (per cent)
Hysteria	9	11	24	3	53
Anxiety state	9	12	31	3	45
Obsessive-compulsive	5	10	67	9	9
Hypochondria	6	13	52	21	8
Neurasthenia	8	16	29	5	42
Neurotic depression	12	15	19	14	40

Table 22.3. Comparing the efficiency and effectiveness of hypothetical (ideal) therapy, assertion-structured therapy, and depth-oriented therapy
(*quoted by permission from* Phillips, 1957)

	Number applying for therapy	Number treated from among applicants	Number refused treatment by clinicians	Number who them-selves refuse treatment	Number completing 3 or more interviews	Number benefited by 3 or more interviews	Percentage of original applicants benefited
Hypothetical group	100	90	5	5	90	90	81
Assertion-structured therapy	59	53	—	6	53	51	86·4
Psychoanalytic depth-oriented therapy	190	45	103	42	45	21[1] (patients' rating) 33[1] (therapists' rating)	11·05[1] (patients' rating) 17·3[1] (therapists' rating)

[1] Therapists' ratings were available for all forty-five patients who completed three or more interviews. Only twenty-seven of these forty-five patients returned questionnaires rating their therapy experience; the twenty-one who rated themselves as having improved somewhat supplied the figure used here.

in looking at the figures for psychoanalytic therapy, is the fact that of all those applying for therapy only 25 per cent (45 out of 190!) were actually accepted for therapy. Apart from the wider import of these high rejection figures, their occurrence creates enormous difficulties for anyone attempting to assess the affectiveness of psychoanalytic treatment. The outcome figures show that 51 of the 53 children were benefited by Phillips's therapy but only 21 out of 45 were so benefited by psychoanalytic therapy—a significant difference.

Phillips concludes very firmly that

'one may produce certain arguments against interpreting these results as being in any way adverse as far as psychoanalytic depth-derived, parent-child, outpatient treatment cases are concerned. One might say that the methods used are not "true psychoanalysis" of children. However, the record of 'true' psychoanalysis of children is hardly better, if as good: witness the work of Klein and Anna Freud. The argument for depth-derived practices cannot be bolstered on the basis of probable value latent upon unstudied and unreported upon therapeutic results . . . the hard reality here is that there are no convincing results of a follow-up nature that can be used to support psychoanalytically derived treatment of children.'

A fourth study comparing psychoanalytic and other types of psychotherapy was reported by Ellis (1957). Ellis has himself used psychoanalytic

psychotherapy of the orthodox type in addition to psychoanalytic type psychotherapy and also what he calls 'rational psychotherapy'. Briefly, 'the main emphasis of the therapist . . . is on analysing the client's current problems . . . and concretely showing him that these emotions arise, not from past events or external situations, but from his present irrational attitudes toward, or illogical fears about, these events and situations.' Two groups, closely matched as to diagnosis, age, sex, and education were constituted. Each consisted of 78 cases and the first group consisted of patients treated with rational techniques over an average period of 26 sessions. The second group of 78 patients was treated with psychoanalytic-orientated techniques over an average of 35 sessions. In addition, there was a group of 16 patients who were treated by orthodox psychoanalysis over an average of 93 sessions. They were all treated by Ellis himself and he rated them at the termination of treatment in terms of whether the patient had made, (*a*) little or no progress while being seen, (*b*) some distinct improvement, or (*c*) considerable improvement.

Ellis found that, 'therapeutic results appear to be best for patients treated with rational analysis and poorest for those treated with orthodox analysis . . . significantly more clients treated with rational analysis showed considerable improvement and significantly fewer showed little or no improvement than clients treated with the other two techniques.' The actual proportions of cases showing distinct or considerable improvement were 90 per cent for rational psychotherapy, 63 per cent for psychotherapy and 50 per cent for orthodox psychoanalysis. These figures should be seen in the light of the fact that orthodox analysis was carried on for three times as many sessions as rational psychotherapy. Ellis concludes that, 'while the obtained data of the study do not offer incontrovertible proof of the superiority technique of rational psychotherapy, they strongly indicate that neither orthodox nor liberally psychoanalytical procedures may be the very last word in effective technique'.

Of course, without the use of a non-treated control group it is impossible to say whether the patients treated by rational psychotherapy did better than those treated analytically because analytic therapy had a positive effect, or because analytic therapy had a negative effect. The former appears to be the more likely hypothesis but cannot be confirmed or disconfirmed in this study (rater contamination, poor outcome criteria, etc.).

With the exception of the study by Barendregt all these comparison studies involve psychoanalysis matched against some form of treatment about which little is known with certainty. This fact, coupled with the other limitations involved in all the studies (including Barendregt's), do not allow of a reasonable conclusion. In none of the studies was psychoanalysis shown to be superior at the termination of treatment, in two studies it was found to be worse, and in one study it was found to be equally effective at termination and superior over the long term. Clearly, what is needed is a sound comparative study and, if possible, the inclusion of an untreated control group. Because of the obvious difficulties involved in any long-term study of untreated patients, perhaps the best we can hope for at the moment is a carefully controlled comparison study between psychoanalysis and one of the more widely used treatment techniques; e.g. conventional supportive psychiatric care and/or drug treatments, and, most interesting of all perhaps, behaviour therapy.

We can find no acceptable evidence to support the view that psychoanalytic treatment is effective.

THE EFFECTS OF PSYCHOTHERAPY

In 1952, Eysenck carried out an examination of the evidence relating to the effects of psychotherapy and came to the conclusion that the emperor had no clothes. The initial reactions of disbelief and shock have passed and now, 18 years later, the time is ripe for a re-examination of the emperor's sartorial progress. With a few notable exceptions, most writers appear to have accepted the need for satisfactory evidence to support the claim that psychotherapy is beneficial. Most writers also appear to accept the view that in the absence of suitable control groups, investigations cannot provide a conclusive result.

Working within these terms of reference, several writers (Cross, 1964; Dittmann, 1966; Kellner, 1967; Bergin, 1970) have concerned themselves primarily with the evidence emerging from studies incorporating control groups. In most instances the writers concluded that there is now modest evidence to support the claim that psychotherapy produces satisfactory results. It is, however, a little discouraging to find that with successive reports the claims appear to become increasingly modest.

Although there is a continuing theme in these discussions on the outcome of psychotherapy, the writers concerned are by no means in agreement. Discussing the earlier reviews, Bergin says—

'Cross (1964) for example, reviewed nine control studies and determined that six were favourable to therapy, whereas our own review of the same reports yielded only one that approximated adequacy and even that one is subject to criticism (Rogers and Dymond, 1954). Dittmann (1966) added five more studies to Cross's group, considered four of them to be positive evidence, and concluded that ten out of fourteen controlled outcome studies were favourable to psychotherapy. Actually, only two of the studies indicate that psychotherapy had any effect and neither of them would be generally acceptable as evidence. Thus, these authors claim *strong* support for the average cross-section of therapy, whereas I would argue for a more modest conclusion.'

While we agree with Bergin's assessment of these reviews, it should in fairness be pointed out that both Cross and Dittmann were more tentative and cautious than Bergin allows. For example, Cross mentions that some important 'cautions must be kept in mind'. The work referred to in his review consisted of 'quite brief or superficial' treatment, the measurement techniques were 'of questionable or unproven validity', and for some of the studies 'the method of control itself is questionable'. For these reasons he specifically urges caution, 'even though the reviewed studies are the most careful which have been done, various limitations proscribe any strong conclusions' (p. 416). It should also be remembered that four of the largest and best designed studies produced *negative* results—Teuber and Powers (1951); Barron and Leary (1955); Fairweather and Simon (1963); Imber *et al.* (1957). In regard to the last-mentioned study, Cross placed a more optimistic interpretation on the data than the authors themselves. As will be shown below, the authors made no claims for psychotherapy, and their findings were sometimes contradictory, often fluctuating and finally, inconclusive. Cross himself points out that the Rogers and Dymond study uses a questionable method of control, and this investigation is also discussed below.

Bergin's rejection of the conclusion reached by Dittmann is understandable. Even Dittman, however, has his reservations: 'My impression is that studies of the outcome of psychotherapy have finally allowed us to draw conclusions on other bases than intuition, but the conclusions, themselves, are modest, and are moreover, diluted by confusion'. All the same, he felt that 1966 was 'a year of bumper crop in outcome studies'. Dittmann claims that 4 out of the 5 control studies described by him were favourable to the position that psychotherapy is effective. Two of these studies can be dismissed immediately. The first is the study by O'Connor *et al.* (1964), referred to in an earlier section. It deals with 57 patients with colitis who also received psychiatric treatment. Their 57 so-called control subjects, like the treated ones, received medical and even surgical treatment during the course of the study. Moreover, whereas the treated patients were said to have psychiatric problems, only a minority of the so-called controls were so described. A second study quoted by Dittmann used as the criterion for improvement after psychotherapy a measurement of 'time perspective' as interpreted on the basis of TAT stories (Ricks *et al.*, 1964). The study by Seeman *et al.* involved very small numbers of children, and in any event on one of the major outcome criteria (teacher ratings) no differences emerged. The report by May and Tuma (1965) showed that patients given drugs improved more than those who did not receive drugs; it produced no evidence that psychotherapy was effective. The study by Ashcroft and Fitts (1964) cannot be assessed satisfactorily because they used an unpublished test as their criterion of outcome. As Dittmann allows, 'the results are complicated because of the many subscores of the test and the methods of analysis, but clearly favour the treatment group.'

At this point, it is necessary to digress. In view of the significance attached to Q-sorts and self-acceptance tests by research therapists and theorists, a consideration of this approach is required before progressing deeper in the outcome literature.

Self-concepts

Measurements of the self-concept feature prominently in outcome studies, and the notion of changes in self-concept is also a central feature of non-directive therapy. It seems desirable therefore to examine the idea and its measurement in detail. Such an examination may also be thought of as being instructive in so far as the assessment of assessment is concerned.

Wylie (1961) has neatly summarised the predictions that flow from theories of self-concept psychotherapy. It is to be expected that successful therapy will produce various changes in self-concept, such as the following: 'increased agreement between self-estimates and objective estimates of the self . . . increased congruence between self and ideal-self, if this congruence is very low at the outset of therapy . . . slightly decreased self-ideal congruence if this congruence is unwarrantedly high at the outset of therapy . . . increased consistency among various aspects of the self-concept' (p. 161).

Wylie mentions, among other difficulties, many of the problems involved in attempts to relate changes in self-concept to psychotherapy. Two of the major problems are the possibility of mutual contamination between measures of improvement and measures of self-concept (p. 165) and the serious problems of scaling (for example, 'neither can one say that equal numerical changes involving different scale ranges are psychologically comparable' (p. 166)). Like Wylie, Crowne and Stephens (1961) draw attention to the large variety of tests that have been evolved to measure self-regard, self-acceptance and the like. They comment unfavourably on the assumption that these tests are equivalent 'despite their independent derivation and despite the relative lack of empirical demonstration that there is a high degree of common variance among them' (p. 107). They point out that there is a serious absence of information on both the reliability and validity of these tests. For example:

'Criterion validation of self-acceptance tests is of course logically impossible . . . face validity however, has apparently been assumed without question (and this) implies adherence to a further assumption . . . that of the validity of self-reports. In terms of these assumptions, a self-acceptance test is valid if it looks like a self-acceptance test and is similar to other tests and what a person says about himself self-evaluatively is accepted as a valid indication of how he "really" feels about himself' (p. 106).

Another major difficulty with these tests is the often

dubious assumption that the items chosen represent a fair sample of the possible parameters. They argue that it is 'of importance to draw one's sample of test items in such a way as represent their occurrence in the population'. Although they are not entirely consistent on this subject, writers generally assume that the self-reports given by subjects are valid. Crowne and Stephens draw attention to reports of extremely high correlations between self-concept rating scales and social desirability scales. In one study, for example, the correlations between Q sort and a social desirability score were found to be 0·82, 0·81, and 0·66. Social desirability correlated 0·82 with the ideal-self rating scale score and 0·59 with the ideal-self Q sort. In a study conducted on students, correlations of 0·84 and 0·87 were found between items on a Q sort and a social desirability scale. In a psychiatric sample the correlation was found to be 0·67. Another study quoted by them produced what is probably a record correlation of 0·96 (between social desirability and an ideal-self score). They conclude quite firmly that 'failure to control for social desirability in the self-acceptance assessment operations would make the results, no matter what the outcome, uninterpretable in terms of self-acceptance' (p. 116). They even go so far as to suggest that in the absence of suitable controls, the tests in question 'may better be interpreted as a measure of social desirability than of self-acceptance'.

In all, Crowne and Stephens were unimpressed.

'The failures of self-acceptance research can be traced, at least in a large part, to neglect of several crucial psychometric and methodological principles: the unsupported assumption of equivalence of assessment procedures, the absence of any clear construct level definition of the variable, failure to construct tests in accord with principles of representative sampling, and questions concerning the social desirability factor in self-report tests' (p. 119).

Although not as harsh in their judgements, Lowe (1961) and Wittenborn (1961) are also critical of self-concept procedures.

Moving from a consideration of the general status of self-concept research, we may now examine its specific application in the assessment of abnormal behaviour and the effects of psychotherapy. We strike an immediate difficulty in attempting to define the relationship between the self-concept and adjustment. Although there is fairly good agreement that low self-regard is related to maladjustment, high self-regard may indicate one of *three* things. It may be a sign of good adjustment or of denial of problems or yet again, of 'unsophisticated conventionality'

(Wylie, 1961). For example, Crowne and Stephens mention a study by Bills in which subjects with high self-acceptance scores were found to be more maladjusted than low scorers. Summarising a good deal of the literature, Wylie concluded that 'there is much overlap between groups' (i.e. neurotics, non-psychiatric patients, normals). Comparisons between psychotics and normals have been contradictory with at least 'three investigators reporting no significant difference between psychotic and normal controls' (p. 216). Considering the range from normal through various types of abnormality she concludes that 'a clear linear downward trend in self-regard is *not* found' (p. 216). In four studies, in fact, a curvilinear relationship between self-regard and severity of maladjustment was observed. An important aspect of this research was the finding that subjects who were judged to be the best adjusted in various studies had high self-regard, 'but their self-regard was not necessarily significantly better than that of the most poorly adjusted subjects'. Wylie concluded that, 'we can see that the level of self-regard is far from being a valid indicator degree of pathology' (p. 217).

Although therapeutic claims on behalf of psychotherapy have sometimes been made on the basis of changes in self-concept scores, the omission of control groups is a crucial deficit. In addition to the general inadequacies of the self-concept notion and its measurement (some of which have been enumerated above), it is necessary to draw attention to one further limitation. Dymond (1955) observed that a small group of 6 subjects who showed spontaneous remission and decided not to take therapy after being on a waiting-list, 'appeared to have improved in adjustment, as measured from their self-description, about as much as those who went through therapy successfully' (p. 106). Their Q scores increased from 33 to 47·3 (significant at the 2 per cent level). A comparison group of six apparently successfully treated patients (although there are some confounding variables here) showed changes from 34·8 to 48·3. The two groups were 'not initially differentiable in terms of adjustment status at the beginning of the study'. Instead of drawing what would appear to be the obvious conclusion, however, Dymond states that 'no deep reorganisation appears to take place' (in the untreated patients). 'The "improvement" appears to be characterised by a strengthening of neurotic defences and a denial of the need for help' (p. 106). If Dymond's attempted explanation is correct, then presumably one would be entitled to conclude that a similar process occurs when self-concept changes occur after psychotherapy. That is, can psychotherapy also be 'characterised by a strengthening of neurotic defences?'

Further evidence that significant changes in self-concept occur without psychotherapy was provided by Taylor (1955). He found that subjects who were required to do self and self-ideal reports repeatedly, showed the changes usually attributed to psychotherapy. The subjects showed an increase in the correlation between the descriptions of self and self-ideal, increased consistency of self-concept, and an increase in positive attitudes towards the self. Although these improvements are said by Taylor to be smaller in magnitude than those reported for cases of psychotherapy, this is doubtful. The comparisons he made are between his experimental group of 15 subjects and 3 single case reports of disturbed patients. Either way his conclusion is consistent with Dymond's and interesting in itself: 'significant increases in positiveness of self-concept, and in positive relationship between the self and self-ideal, may be valid indexes of improvement wrought by therapy, but increased consistency of self-concept is achieved so readily by self-description without counselling that it would seem a dubious criterion, especially when self-inventories or Q sorts are used in conjunction with therapy.'

Writers on the subject have expressed the following views. 'When such tests are used in further research as if they had been carefully and adequately constructed, little can ensue but error and confusion. And such seems to be the case in self-acceptance research. Perhaps it is true that these tests are not yet used commonly in clinical settings where their inadequacies could lead to disservice to the client...' (Crowne and Stephens, 1961). Lowe (1961) cautiously concluded that 'there is in short no complete assurance that the cognitive self-acceptance as measured by the Q sort is related to the deeper level of self-integration that client centred therapy seeks to achieve' (p. 331). Concluding her analysis of 29 research studies Wylie (1961) said, 'of course nothing can be concluded from these studies concerning the role of therapy in causing the reported changes' (p. 182).

Kellner's Assessment

Kellner (1967) has argued that the case for the effectiveness of psychotherapy is a sound one, and supports his conclusion by a reasonably detailed consideration of several studies. Many other studies are mentioned in passing and will not be taken up here, particularly as numbers of them are discussed elsewhere in this chapter. Here we will confine ourselves to those studies (other than with children or by counselling) on which Kellner bases the main force of his argument. We will not take up his discussion of those studies in which psychotherapy failed to produce results more satisfactory than the improvements observed in controls. We might mention, however, that Kellner's attempts to explain the negative results frequently reported are less than satisfactory. In his discussion of the Barron-Leary study, for example, he suggests that the untreated patients were probably less disturbed than their treated counterparts—despite evidence to the contrary contained in the study itself. On the other hand, his reservations about the use of various outcome criteria appear to be well-grounded. He notes, for example, that MMPI scores are generally inappropriate and that 'self-acceptance, if used as the only measure, is at present an inadequate criterion of improvement' (p. 345). He also notes a number of studies in which this type of assessment has failed to pick up therapeutic changes.

Kellner attaches significance to the two studies reported by Ends and Page (1957, 1959) in which they assessed the effects of various types of psychotherapy on hospitalised male alcoholics. As we feel these studies do not support the notion that psychotherapy is effective, it is necessary to consider them with care. Kellner describes the first of these studies in some detail and points out that 63 (out of an original group of 96!) completed the programme: each of four therapists had 15 sessions with four different groups of patients. The methods of therapy were client-centred, psychoanalytic derivation, learning theory (an inappropriate designation) and lastly, a social discussion group which served as control. In addition to the specific therapy, all patients participated in other presumably therapeutic activities during their stay in hospital. These included A.A. meetings, lectures, physical treatments and so on. The outcome of therapy was evaluated by changes occurring in the self-ideal correlation. As Kellner points out, the MMPI used initially was discontinued, and the evaluation of therapy depended almost entirely on Q-sort analysis. He states that 'one and a half years after discharge from hospital the degree of improvement was judged by independent raters' (p. 345). He goes on to say that the 'ratings one and a half years after discharge showed a significant improvement in the two groups which had shown changes in the Q sort'. On the Q-sort analysis itself there were greater 'reductions in the discrepancy between self and ideal in the client-centred group and in the psychoanalytic group'. The second study (Ends and Page, 1959) is referred to briefly and Kellner points out that although the self-ideal correlation again 'discriminated significantly between treated patients and untreated controls' only the paranoia scale of the MMPI discriminated significantly. As Kellner regards MMPI scores as an unsatisfactory measure of outcome (and in any event these scores failed to show therapeutic changes) we will confine ourselves largely to a consideration of the other two measures, i.e. Q-sort analyses and follow-up ratings.

The Q-sort analyses are fairly complex and will be discussed at some length below. The follow-up data that appeared to have influenced Kellner's judgement of these studies are scanty and can be discussed fairly briefly. Ends and Page claim that the follow-up data show significant success for the psychotherapy groups but point out that the 'results are by no means unequivocal' (p. 275). We might add that they are by no means clearly described. Although it is implied that follow-ups were carried out on three occasions, the results are all presented in a single table so that it is impossible to sort out the patients' progress at various stages. To make matters worse it is not at all clear how the follow-ups were conducted or the data analysed. They say: 'follow-up data from county welfare officers, from the hospitals own follow-up clinic, and from hospital admission records were analysed. The initial follow-up was made six months after discharge by county welfare officers using a standard interview form. The one-year and one-and-a-half year follow-ups were made through the hospital follow-up clinic and hospital admission records' (p. 275). The results are presented in five categories but, unfortunately, the categories deal with different types of data and different time periods. For example a rating of 'greatly improved' was given when there was no evidence of further alcoholic episodes during the one-and-a-half-year period. The rating of 'possibly improved' was given when there was evidence of one or two brief episodes within the *first three months* following discharge and, 'as far as could be determined no evidence of a reversion to the former pattern during the follow-up period'. They define recidivism as 'readmission to *the same* hospital for alcoholism' (our emphasis). It is in no way made clear that the patients were actually interviewed—in the context of the discussion it seems unlikely, but one cannot be sure. Secondly, it would appear that the follow-ups at the one-year and one-and-a-half-year periods were carried out by examining the information that happened to be present in the hospital's clinic and records. On the basis of their criterion for recidivism, it seems quite possible that their one-year and one-and-a-half-year follow-ups did not include the full sample, but only those patients who made contact with the hospital after discharge. If this is the case then the most that one can conclude is that patients who had undergone psychotherapy did not return to the same hospital

and *not* that they were necessarily improved or abstinent. In view of their description of the composition of the category 'possibly improved' there appears to be no certainty that the patients did not resume drinking after three months. As Kellner puts it 'fewer patients from the client-centred group had been readmitted to the hospital'. His description of the follow-up procedure may, however, be slightly misleading. We cannot be sure that 'the degree of improvement was judged by independent raters' one and a half years 'after discharge from hospital'.

In dealing with the first study, we feel that Kellner might have drawn attention to the extremely high defection rate—no fewer than 33 of the original 96 patients failed to complete the programme, i.e. a 30 per cent loss rate. It is not stated whether the defections were more common in one or other of the groups nor whether the defectors were comparable in initial status to the patients who completed the programme. Kellner might also have noticed that although Ends and Page excluded the MMPI data from their first study because 'preliminary analysis revealed that physical and psychological treatment effects were confounded in the MMPI profiles', scores from the same test *were included* in the second study. The authors' inclusion of the MMPI data in the later study is doubly puzzling in view of their stated reason for excluding it from their first study, i.e. physical and psychological treatment effects were confounded. It is nowhere explained how they reached this conclusion or how they were able to decide that the Q-sort analysis 'held such confounding to a minimum'. In any event, they appear to have changed their minds in the second study.

Their Q-sort analyses are atypical and sometimes difficult to follow. Certainly their justification for using some of the analyses is highly doubtful. They carry out a large number of comparisons between different variations of the self and ideal-self correlations and find a number of significant 'movement indexes'. The client-centred group show two significant changes, the analytic group three significant changes, the learning theory group two significant changes and two negatives, and the controls one negative. A conclusion drawn from the comparisons is that the patients who received psychotherapy showed significant improvements, the control subjects showed little change, and the 'learning therapy' patients deteriorated slightly.

This conclusion appeared to be supported in their second study when they compared 28 patients who received twice as much client-centred therapy (i.e. 30 sessions) and 28 control patients who were simply assessed at the termination of the 6-week therapy period. In this comparison, however, the control patients were found to show some degree of improvement although not as large as the treated patients. One curious factor to notice here is that this second control group showed statistically significant improvements on 5 of the 8 comparisons whereas the control group in the earlier study showed only one positive change and one negative change. The improvements observed in this second control group are, however, explained by Ends and Page as having 'gained minimally in self-acceptance only by a defensive manoeuvre that appears to be unstable at the outset' (p. 12). The matter is made even more intriguing by comparing the control patients in the second study with the treated patients of the first study. The treated patients showed significant improvement on only *four* of the indexes. The major surprises, however, occur when the authors compare the patients who had 30 sessions of therapy with an additional control group of 28 patients who were simply re-tested after a two-week wait period. 'In general, (Figure 6) reveals that the control group made greater gains on 5 of the indexes than did the therapy group' (p. 23). Apparently these improvements represent 'a defensive reaction' otherwise known as a 'flight into health'. This interpretation we are told is 'supported by a wealth of clinical observation' and a 'flight into health' is distinguished from 'truly integrated therapeutic change'. The difference in improvement scores between the treated and untreated groups is explained by the claim that group therapy 'retards the flight into health' (p. 27). This flight into health apparently occurs 'as a defense against self-examination and criticism' and, on average, occurs between the tenth and fifteenth therapy session. However, 'this phenomenon seems to occur with or without therapy' (p. 24). We might note, incidentally, that if it occurs between the tenth and fifteenth therapy session, the successful results obtained in the first study (in which 15 treatment sessions were given) appear to be fortunate.

On the MMPI results (considered in the first study to be confounding) the treated and untreated patients were found to produce significantly different results on only two of the thirteen comparisons. The treated group showed significantly greater decreases in the paranoia scale and the untreated patients showed significantly greater decreases in the Hy scale. We are also informed in the *second* study that the patients who received 15 treatment sessions, i.e. those in the first study, 'demonstrated no significant change from pre to post on any of the MMPI scales' (p. 14). Moreover, only one significant difference on the MMPI scales was observed between those patients who received 15 and those who received 30 treatment sessions. This is explained by Ends and Page on the grounds that the pretreatment scores 'suggest that the (first treated) group were

somewhat healthier to start with as far as scale elevation is concerned. One would, therefore, expect less change on the MMPI scales simply because (this) group needed to move less, and, indeed, had less room in which to move since they began closer to the normal means for the scale' (p. 14). However, the same comment could be made about the untreated patients as they also show consistently lower MMPI scores than the patients who received 30 treatment sessions. We may even extend the argument to the analysis of the Q-sort data, as the control group has a z score of 0·406 prior to treatment while the treated group had a score of 0·303.

Almost all of the conclusions reached by Ends and Page are doubtful. Conclusion number 6 is particularly misleading. They state that, 'the flight into health phenomenon occurs in those not participating in group psychotherapy. Following the inevitable collapse, those not receiving group therapy show no indications of reintegration in a therapeutic sense but instead recover by re-erecting a structure only superficially different from the initial one' (p. 29). As the so-called flight into health phenomenon (i.e. improved self-acceptance) was most clearly observed in the group re-tested after two weeks, it is hard to see how they can speak of an 'inevitable collapse'. This control group was *not* retested after the second week. It is not possible to say whether or not they 'collapsed', or whether they 're-erected superficial structures' or showed no indication of 're-integration'. On the contrary, when last tested, they were showing considerable improvement.

It can be seen then that the studies by Ends and Page have serious shortcomings. The defection rate is extremely high and contains possible biasing factors. The selection of outcome measures, Q-sorts and MMPI scores, is unfortunate. The follow-up data are scanty and confounded. The Q sort and MMPI scores suggest quite different conclusions. One of the untreated control groups shows considerable improvement after a two-week wait period—greater than that seen in treated patients. Their exclusion of MMPI data from the first study is inconsistent. Their explanation of improvement in the untreated controls is unconvincing and, even if accepted, could be applied with equal significance to the improvements observed in some of the treated patients. As a great deal of time and effort was put into these studies it is a pity that the authors did not pay more attention to the accumulation of 'hard' information such as status at follow-up determined by direct interview. The total absence of follow-up data in the second study is particularly unfortunate.

The study by Shlien, Mosak, and Dreikurs (1962) is frequently quoted as evidence in support of the effectiveness of psychotherapy. They compared the effects of unlimited client-centred therapy with time-limited client-centred therapy and time-limited Adlerian therapy. They included in addition, two control groups. One control group consisted of normal people, and can be dismissed as irrelevant. The other control group consisted of patients who requested therapy but did not receive it. These untreated controls were retested after *three months*. The sole criterion of therapeutic effectiveness was a self-ideal Q sort.

The authors claimed to have demonstrated the effectiveness of psychotherapy and drew attention to the effectiveness of time-limited therapy. Apart from serious weaknesses in the experimental design, the authors reported their results in brief form and, regrettably, omitted some vital details. For example, *all* their results are presented as averages (mean or median?) and these are shown in the form of a graph. No actual figures are provided. It is nowhere stated what sort of patients they were dealing with. They do not indicate why the untreated group remained untreated. Nor do they state whether the allocation of patients to the treatment or no-treatment conditions was random—in the context of the report it seems highly unlikely.

In regard to the experimental design used, one of the control groups is irrelevant. The other control group comprised untreated patients who may or may not have been retested at the follow-up period twelve months later. In any event they appear to have carried out the Q sort on only two occasions as compared with four occasions for each of the treated groups. The sole criterion on which the effects of therapy are based is the Q sort—generally agreed to be inadequate (e.g. Kellner, 1967). We are provided with no information about the psychiatric status of the patients either before or after treatment, nor are we told anything about their actual behaviour. In regard to the results themselves, the treatment groups appear to have shown substantial increases in self-ideal correlations. The untreated control group, on the other hand, showed a surprisingly unchanging course. Prior to treatment the self-ideal correlation for this group is precisely zero and at the end of the three-month waiting period it is still precisely zero. In the graph containing the results of the study they appear to be precisely zero at the 12 month follow-up period as well, but this may be misleading because it is by no means certain that they were retested at the follow-up occasion. In any event this remarkable stability is somewhat unusual. Ends and Page, for example, found that their two-week waiting control patients showed an increase in self-ideal correlation of 0·25, i.e. they improved from 0·35 to 0·60 on re-test after two weeks. As

mentioned earlier, other workers have found similar 'spontaneous' changes in this type of correlation. In sum, the Shlien study will do as an exploratory investigation but as evidence in support of the effectiveness of psychotherpy it is unconvincing.

Although Kellner's appraisal of the evidence appears to be over-optimistic, some of his comments on the problems of research into psychotherapy are well taken. In particular, he argues the case for increased specificity in a persuasive manner. Certainly, the treatment of a mixed bag of patients with a mixed bag of techniques is unlikely to further our understanding of the nature and possible effects of psychotherapy.

Phipps Clinic Study

The by now well-known study of the effects of psychotherapy on psychiatric outpatients carried out at the Phipps Clinic has celebrated its 10th birthday and the status of 34 of the original group of patients at the 10-year follow-up period has now been described by Imber *et al.* (1968). The patients were originally assigned at random to one of three forms of treatment: 'individual psychotherapy, in which a patient was seen privately for one hour for once a week: group therapy, in which groups of 5 to 7 patients were seen for $1\frac{1}{2}$ hours once a week: and minimal contact therapy, in which the patient was seen individually for not more than one half hour once every two weeks' (p. 71). The treatment was carried out by second-year psychiatric residents who took no part in the evaluations of their patients. These evaluations took place at the end of 6-months of treatment and again 1, 2, 3, 5, and 10 years from the time of the initial treatment contact. A variety of assessments was carried out and the two main criteria were personal discomfort and social effectiveness. Significant improvements were observed in all three groups but some fluctuations occurred during the 10-year period, particularly among those patients who had minimal treatment. The main changes occurred within the first 2 years after treatment outset and, with some exceptions, tended to hold up at the 10 year follow-up period. As the authors remark, 'it does seem somewhat improbable that differences consequent to a brief therapeutic experience a decade earlier should persist in such a striking fashion'. Their argument is supported by a number of points the most prominent of which is that some of the differences between treatments were absent at the 5-year follow-up period but present at the 10-year follow-up period. An overall evaluation of this admirably persistent investigation is complicated by fluctuations in the results and by an unfortunate lack of correspondence between the two major criteria. The omission of an untreated control group is understandable, but unfortunate as it precludes any conclusions about the effect of psychotherapy *per se*. In view of the earlier discussion of possible events contributing to the spontaneous remission of neurotic disorders, the authors' findings on their patients' explanation of their improvements are interesting.

'Although improved patients tended to associate their better current condition to a change in their socio-economic situation or to their adaptation to general life circumstances, including symptoms, it cannot be determined whether psychotherapy fostered these changes or whether they occurred quite independently of the treatment experienced. In any event, it is clear that, in retrospect, patients conceive of improvement as a function of adjustment to their lot in life or to a change in external socio-economic circumstances' (p. 80).

It is tempting to conclude from this study that psychotherapy was effective and that more psychotherapy was more effective (even when administered by inexperienced therapists). However, in view of the limitations of the study and the unclear outcome, we share the authors' caution. Although the results are inconclusive, they do encourage the possibility that psychotherapy may be beneficial, even if it is provided in a brief and limited form by inexperienced therapists.

UCLA Study

Despite some unfortunate inadequacies in the analysis and reporting of their data, the study by Brill and co-workers (1964) contains interesting information. They carried out a long-term, double-blind study of the use of placebos, prochlorperazine, meprobamate, and phenobarbital 'in conjunction with brief visits' in the treatment of 299 predominantly neurotic outpatients. The selection of patients was carried out in a systematic fashion and, on acceptance for the trial, they were randomly allocated to one of the three drug treatments or to psychotherapy (given weekly for one hour's duration), or to a placebo control, or to a no-treatment waiting-list control. The authors conclude that the 'patients in all 5 groups showed a tendency to improve, in contrast to a lack of improvement in the patients who were kept on a waiting-list and received no treatment' (p. 594). They add that 'the lack of any marked differences would suggest that neither a specific drug nor the length of the psychotherapeutic sessions was the crucial factor in producing improvement in this sample of patients' (p. 594). We may add that the patients receiving placebos did as well as the treated groups.

One of the most interesting findings was the resistance encountered by the investigators when the study was introduced and carried out. They comment on the 'prejudice in favour of psychotherapy among patients and therapists' and point out that the 'extent of the bias in favour of psychotherapy, even in beginning residents who had had very little experience with it, was quite startling' (p. 591). This was particularly surprising as 'all of this took place at a time when, in fact, no one knew how effective or ineffective drug treatment was.'

The effects of the treatment were assessed by a variety of procedures. The therapists rated the improvements on a symptom check-list and a 16-item evaluation form. The patient was required to complete a similar item-evaluation and one relative or close friend did likewise. In addition, a social worker carried out an evaluation of each patient—unfortunately, the value of this information is limited by the fact that the valuation was carried out after the social workers had read the reports on each patient. Lastly, the patients were required to complete MMPI tests. The before and after profiles for each patient were drawn on the same profile sheet and two independent psychologists sorted the profiles into degrees of improvement or lack of improvement. Although their evaluations agreed rather well ($r = 0.85$), their conclusions differed on one of the most crucial comparisons, i.e. whether the treated groups were improved to a significantly greater extent than the untreated controls.

It will be realised that this study required a great deal of effort and careful planning. It is particularly unfortunate, therefore, that their handling of the resulting information was so inadequate. In fact, it is extremely difficult to evaluate the information provided because they rarely give the actual figures obtained and rely almost exclusively on graphic presentations. The absence of basic information such as the means and standard deviations on the various measures before and after treatment is particularly serious. Matters are further confounded by their failure to give adequate descriptions of many of the assessment procedures employed. For these reasons and because they were almost exclusively concerned with intergroup comparisons, we are not able to say with certainty whether any of the groups was in fact significantly improved. In order to reach a conclusion on this point one would need to have the means and standard deviations of the pre- and post-treatment assessment (subject, of course, to the usual tests of significance). The study is also limited by the unfortunately high rate of drop-outs—43·5 per cent of the selected subjects either dropped out of treatment or were not reassessed, or both. Despite the remarks made by the authors, there are indications that the drop-outs were somewhat different from the treated subjects. In their own words 'the drop-out group may be characterised as less intelligent, less passive and more inclined to act out their problems' (p. 584). As the data for the groups are not provided, the matter remains in a degree of doubt except for the IQ scores which are presented graphically. This shows the completed subjects to have a mean IQ of approximately 125. They were a group of superior intelligence and the drop-outs were of high average intelligence (approximately 115).

One of the major drawbacks to this study is the doubt that surrounds the degree of improvement, if any, shown by the treated and placebo groups. In some of the graphical presentations (e.g. Fig. 5) they appear to have made 'doubtful' to 'slight' improvement. In other representations the changes seem to be slightly larger. Bearing in mind all these shortcomings, one can probably agree with the general conclusion reached by Brill and his colleagues to the effect that the treated (and placebo) groups showed slight improvement over a period of one year. They could detect no differences between the improvements registered by the three drug-treated groups, the placebo group, and the psychotherapy group. All these groups, however, appeared to do better than the untreated, waiting-list controls. Taken at face value the main conclusion regarding the effects of psychotherapy would appear to be that it may have produced a slight improvement overall and this degree of improvement was neither smaller nor greater than that observed in patients who received placebos. The conclusion that psychotherapy is no more effective than an inert tablet can be avoided, however, by drawing attention to the shortcomings enumerated above. And one may also add that the psychotherapy was given for only 5 months and that much of it was conducted by trainee psychotherapists. As an attempt to evaluate psychotherapy the study must be regarded as inconclusive.

The information discussed so far is based on the condition of the patients at termination of treatment (mean duration 5·5 months). Koegler and Brill (1967) later reported their condition after a 2-year follow-up period. Their findings are striking: 'The most marked improvement is in the rated status of the waiting-list (i.e. untreated) patients' (p. 77). At follow-up there were no significant differences between any of the groups. This suggests that at very best, treatment (by drugs, psychotherapy, or placebo) achieves improvement more quickly. The authors quote Jerome Frank's notion that '. . . the function of psychotherapy may be to accelerate a process that would occur in any case.'

In regard to the question of spontaneous remissions, it will be recalled that Bergin was quoted as giving a zero rate for this study. In fact, it is impossible to work out a percentage remission *rate* from the information given. The results are reported for the no-treatment waiting-list control group *as a group* and while it is true that at termination they had shown relatively little change as a group, there is no way of determining whether any of the 20 remaining patients concerned (14 of the original 34 were lost) remitted spontaneously. Nevertheless, they caught up *within 2 years* and were then no different from the other groups of patients.

In the study by Greer and Cawley (1966), mentioned earlier, the relationship between treatment and outcome was also examined. It will be recalled that all the patients were sufficiently ill to require in-patient care and they received the following types of treatment. Sixty-three received supportive treatment, forty-two had physical treatment, ten underwent leucotomy, twenty-eight had psychotherapy and nineteen had psychotherapy combined with physical treatment. Thirteen patients received no treatment 'as they remained in hospital less than 2 weeks and in most cases discharged themselves against medical advice'. At discharge, the group of patients who had received psychotherapy 'had a significantly more favourable outcome than the remainder'. The mean outcome score for the twenty patients concerned was 1·96; the mean score for the nineteen patients who had psychotherapy and physical treatment was 2·11, and the mean outcome for those thirteen patients who received no treatment was 2·15. The worst outcome was recorded by the patients who underwent leucotomy and they had a mean score of 2·60. Although this trend was seen to continue at 'final outcome' (i.e. the follow-up), the difference between the patients who had psychotherapy and those who had no treatment was no longer significant. The significant advantage for the psychotherapy patients in relation to those who had received supportive treatment or physical treatment was maintained. The patients who had undergone leucotomy had the worst outcome of all but their numbers were small. The more favourable outcome for psychotherapy patients when discharged from hospital may be misleading. Although no direct information is provided on the selection procedures in operation at the time of the patients stay in hospital, there are significant indications that the patients who received psychotherapy were unrepresentative of the total patient sample. Greer and Cawley were aware of the significance of the factor of patient selection and carried out some comparisons between the patients who received psychotherapy and the remainder. It was found that the psychotherapy patients 'differed from the other group in several important respects'. All the patients receiving psychotherapy had a history of precipitating factors and none of the 16 patients whose symptoms were regarded as being of life-long duration had received psychotherapy. In addition a significantly higher proportion of psychotherapy patients were married and significantly fewer of them had an unfavourable pre-morbid personality. All these features had previously been demonstrated by the authors to relate significantly to outcome, 'so patients who had received psychotherapy would be expected to have had a more favourable prognosis, irrespective of treatment.' They concluded that it would not be justifiable to ascribe the difference in outcome between the psychotherapy group and the rest of the sample to the effect of the particular treatment. Having pointed out that the patients selected for psychotherapy had a favourable prognosis irrespec-

tive of the particular treatment given, they go on to point out that 'this argument does not necessarily demonstrate that psychotherapy was *ineffective* in these patients. From the findings of the present study we are not entitled to draw any conclusions regarding the efficacy of psychotherapy' (p. 83). As we have already seen, however, the Greer-Cawley study contains a considerable amount of useful information on the course of neurotic illnesses. In regard to improvement rates and eventual outcome they unearthed a disconcerting finding. The correlation between immediate outcome (i.e. condition at discharge) and final outcome is very low $-r = 0 \cdot 19$.

To sum up, it is disappointing to find that the best studies of psychotherapy yield such dispiriting results and that the poor studies are so over-optimistic.

THE NEGATIVE EFFECTS OF PSYCHOTHERAPY

It is sometimes observed that patients get worse during or after a course of psychotherapy. This statement cannot be taken to imply that the psychotherapy *causes* the deterioration, any more than one can presume that positive changes observed after psychotherapy are the result of that treatment. As a minimum, it is necessary in both cases to demonstrate that the positive or negative changes are greater than those that might be expected to occur in the absence of psychotherapy. Bergin (1970) has accumulated some reports on the presumed deterioration effect but the quality of the evidence is not high and certainly cannot be taken as proof of the claim that psychotherapy causes some patients to deteriorate. If, as seems to be the case, some patients do deteriorate spontaneously (i.e. in the absence of formal treatment), the occurrence of deterioration during or after psychotherapy is not adequate evidence that the therapy produced the negative changes. Before reaching a firm conclusion on such a serious matter it is desirable that we should accumulate unequivocal evidence.

Over and above the clinical necessity of obtaining information about possible deteriorative effects of psychotherapy, this possibility is a central feature of the important argument about the so-called 'average therapeutic effect'. As noted earlier, there is fairly good agreement on the insufficiency of the available evidence concerning the positive effects of psychotherapy. Most writers also agree that the therapeutic claims made for psychotherapy range from the abysmally low to the astonishingly high and, furthermore, they would tend to agree that, on average, psychotherapy appears to produce approximately the same

amount of improvement as can be observed in patients who have not received this type of treatment. The 'average effect' argument is well stated by Bergin (1967):

'while some research studies reveal little difference in the *average amount* of change occurring in experimental and control groups, a significant increase in the variability of criterion scores appears at post-testing in the treatment groups. This conclusion was drawn from seven (well designed) psychotherapy outcome studies and was startling in that it directly implied that some treatment cases were improving while others were deteriorating, thus causing a spreading of criterion scores at the conclusion of the therapy period which did not occur among the control subjects. Evidently there is something unique about psychotherapy which has the power to cause improvement beyond that occurring among controls, but equally evident is a contrary deteriorating impact that makes some cases worse than they were to begin with: when these contrary phenomena are lumped together in an experimental group, they cancel each other out to some extent and the overall yield in terms of improvement (in these particular studies) is no greater than the change occurring in a control group via "spontaneous remission factors"' (Bergin, 1967, p. 184).

Before examining some of these findings in more detail, Bergin's qualification should be borne in mind. He states that the finding of increased variability at the end of treatment occurs 'in these particular studies'. It certainly cannot be said to be a universal observation.

Bergin's intriguing argument has numerous implications. Here we will draw attention to what seems to us to be one of the most important. If he is correct, then one of the two conclusions given here must follow: either, psychotherapy is capable of helping a lot of people and also making an approximately equal number of people worse; or, very few patients are made worse by psychotherapy and an equally small number are improved by psychotherapy. As possible corollaries to these alternatives, we would have to add that either there are a large number of effective therapists and an equally large number of deplorable therapists or, most therapists are relatively ineffective and also relatively harmless.

Turning now to the evidence presented by Bergin in support of his case, we must preface it by saying that he is perhaps a little uncritical in his use of the data. In particular, he seems satisfied with the results obtained from a variety of tests and other measures that are either inappropriate or not known to be reliable or valid. One of the studies Bergin quotes in support is that by Cartwright and Vogel (1960). He quotes from their paper as follows: 'thus, as measured by the Q score, adjustment changes, regardless of direction, were significantly greater during a therapy period than during the no-therapy period' (p. 122). Unfortunately, Bergin does not quote the very next sentence in the Cartwright paper. It reads as follows: 'this was not true for the adjustment changes as measured by the TAT.' Moreover, inspection of Table 1 in the paper by Cartwright and Vogel shows that on both measures used in this study (Q scores and TAT scores) the 22 experimental subjects showed greater variance in the *pre*-therapy period than during the therapy period itself. Although no figures are given it is not likely that these differences are statistically significant. In any event, the study referred to by Bergin cannot be said to support the general case that therapy increases variance.

The next study to be considered is that of Barron and Leary (1955). It will be recalled that they carried out a reasonably well-controlled study of psychotherapy and found that it produced changes no greater than those observed in a non-treated group. In 1956, Cartwright re-analysed some of their data and concluded that although there was no difference between the two groups on average, 'it seems that some therapy patients deteriorated to a greater extent than did the waiting list controls, while some therapy patients did improve significantly more than the controls'. Unfortunately, as noted by Bergin, this effect 'occurred only for individual and not for group therapy' (Bergin, 1966, p. 236). Even if this

evidence were acceptable it still leaves unresolved the mystery of why the patients treated by group therapy, although showing the average effect, did *not* show an increased variance. On the face of it, the 'average effect' observed in patients treated by group therapy *cannot* be accounted for by Bergin's hypothesis. This exception (and there are others) means that even if Bergin's attempted explanation has merit, it cannot be a complete explanation of the so-called average effect of psychotherapy. There is a further complication. Barron and Leary in their first Table (p. 242) provide the *pretreatment* means and standard deviations for the three groups on the MMPI. On three of the subscales quoted by Bergin in support of his argument (F, K, Sc) the standard deviations in the group of patients who eventually received individual psychotherapy are greater than those observed in the no-treatment control group. Lastly, one may point out that the MMPI is far from being a satisfactory measure of putative psychotherapeutic changes.

A third piece of evidence offered by Bergin is taken from the study by Rogers and Dymond (1954). He says, 'it is even more fascinating that Cartwright himself participated in a study in which a similar phenomenon occurred . . . but it was never emphasized in proportion to its true import' (p. 236) Bergin calls this phenomenon 'client-deterioration' and says that 'a careful reading of the report indicates that of 25 therapy subjects, 6 or 24%, declined in self-ideal correlation between pretherapy and follow-up testing' (p. 236). Unfortunately, 7 of the *control* group subjects also showed a decline in self-ideal correlations (*see* Rogers and Dymond, Table 2, p. 66). Moreover if we examine the self-ideal correlations in the treated group we find that *at the end of treatment* only two of them have 'deteriorated' and of these, one subject moved from −0·12 to −0·17. The figures quoted by Bergin refer to the differences between pre-therapy correlations and *follow-up* testing. This is, of course, entirely permissible but it is not consistent with Bergin's statement of the position—*see* above where he states 'a significant increase in the variability of criterion scores appears at *post-testing* in the treatment groups' (our italics). If we are to place any reliance on these scores obtained from a self-acceptance type of Q sort, we would have to conclude that the increased variance occurs *after* the termination of treatment, i.e. in the follow-up period. The number of patients who show such 'deterioration' in the follow-up period is similar to that obtained in the untreated control group.

Bergin also makes use of the study reported by Fairweather *et al.* (1960) which he says 'yielded similar results'. Bergin then quotes two sections from the report by Fairweather *et al.* and these are indeed representative of their views but, nevertheless, somewhat misleading. As Fairweather says 'the control group *usually* had the smallest variance and the three psychotherapy groups the largest' (our italics). However, the detailed results provided in this report are considerably more complex than this quotation indicates. One of the major determinants of the variance observed was the diagnostic category of the patients concerned and, furthermore, the mean variances for the control group subjects were often *larger* than those obtaining in the treated group. Regarding the question of diagnostic category, on all five of the major comparisons, the non-psychotic patients had smaller mean variances than the two other groups of patients (short-term psychotics and long-term psychotics). In regard to treatment groups, in every one of the numerous comparisons made, the control group (i.e. untreated) patients showed a larger mean variance than at least one of the treated groups. In some of the comparisons the non-psychotic control patients showed larger mean variances than *all* the treated groups (e.g. self-report change scores shown in Table 17, change scores for five ideal-sort scales on Table 20). The results of this study are detailed and complex and repay inspection. They cannot be discussed at length here but it should be remembered that in any event, the post-treatment ratings and psychometric scores were shown to have practically no relation to the clinical condition of the patient at the six month follow-up period.

Of the other studies discussed by Bergin, one deals with a brief (three session) counselling study, another is the report by Powers and Witmer (1951), and the last is the Wisconsin project by Rogers and his colleagues, which will be discussed below. The Powers and Witmer report does, in fact, provide some support for Bergin's position.

In sum then, the evidence in support of Bergin's contention is scanty. Although it seems likely that the 'deterioration phenomenon' may provide a partial explanation for some of the so called average psychotherapeutic outcome figures, it is most unlikely that this will provide a complete explanation. It has already been shown that even untreated patients show deterioration and, furthermore, such deterioration varies between different diagnostic groupings. The possibility that improvements and deteriorations in psychotherapy are determined, at least to some extent, by the effectiveness of the therapist is discussed by Bergin and has, of course, been the subject of extensive research by Truax and his colleagues. Lastly, we should add that another determinant of therapeutic outcome (and probably the most important) is the selection of the appropriate and effective method of treatment for the particular disorder concerned.

We feel that, at best, Bergin's explanation is incomplete. In a sense, this is a reassuring evaluation. Acceptance of his point of view as a complete explanation would imply one of the two following combinations mentioned above; psychotherapy is harmful as often as it is helpful and/or psychotherapy is conducted by therapists who are harmful about as often as they are helpful. Although this 'helpful-harmful' hypothesis has been given a prominent place in the arguments of the Rogerian school of psychotherapy, it is, fortunately, not an essential feature. The major tenets of the Rogerian position were elaborated some years prior to the appearance of this argument.

ROGERIAN PSYCHOTHERAPY

The intensive and extensive growth of Rogerian psychotherapy has undoubtedly been one of the most important developments to have occurred in the field of psychotherapy during the past decade. The necessary and sufficient conditions of therapeutic change were stated by Rogers (1957) with admirable clarity and lack of equivocation. He boldly attempted to specify 'a single set of preconditions' which, he felt, were necessary to produce therapeutic change. These pre-conditions were, he argued, operative in *all* effective types of psychotherapy. The necessary and sufficient conditions that have received the greatest amount of attention all relate to the therapist's attitude, set and/or behaviour. It is argued that constructive personality change is facilitated when the therapist is warm, empathic, and genuine.

Rogers claimed that 'if one or more of these conditions is not present, constructive personality change will not occur'.* He added that, when these conditions are present in large measure, then the

* The 'necessary and sufficient conditions' of effective therapy postulated by Rogers in 1957 are neither necessary nor sufficient. Their insufficiency is indicated by the recent addition of a fourth ingredient of self-exploration and by the therapeutic failure of the Wisconsin project. The evidence presented by Truax and Carkhuff also shows that in numerous studies therapeutic changes were observed even though one of the 3 therapist conditions was low. For example, 'The Hopkins data, then, suggests that *when one of the 3 conditions is negatively related to the other two* (original italics) in any sample of therapists, then patient outcome is best predicted by whichever 2 conditions are most closely related to each other' (Truax and Carkhuff, p. 91). The three conditions may be facilitative but they are not necessary.

resulting personality change is more marked. One of the most radical aspects of Rogers's position was the argument that the treatment *technique* is not 'an essential condition of the therapy'. He states that 'the techniques of the various therapies are relatively unimportant except to the extent that they serve as channels for fulfilling one of the conditions.' Rogers's theory is consistent, even to the extent of conceding that his own form of therapy is convenient but not essential. He says, 'in terms of the theory here being presented, this technique (client-centred) is by no means an essential condition of therapy.'

He also adopts a radical view on the question of training. A successful therapist is a person who can provide high levels of the three therapist conditions and 'intellectual training and the acquiring of information' does not produce a successful therapist.

In the first major outcome study reported by Rogers and his colleagues, a successful result was claimed (Rogers and Dymond, 1954). In the earlier edition of this *Handbook*, it was argued that this claim could not be sustained. In view of the fact that no proper control group was provided and the 'waiting control group' was not matched on the most crucial variable, the outcome of this study was inconclusive.

In 1967, Rogers and his colleagues produced a massive report on a treatment trial carried out on 28 schizophrenic patients, 16 of whom were treated. Although this study served the useful function of clarifying and refining the methodological procedures involved in a task of this magnitude, the *therapeutic* results were disappointing. Despite the intensive measurement and data analysis undertaken by the group, they were not able to confirm either of the two crucial predictions. The treated patients did not do better than the untreated controls. The patients who experienced high levels of the three crucial therapist conditions did not necessarily do better than those patients who experienced low levels of these conditions. Although considerable progress was made in the development of the assessment techniques, some disconcerting findings also emerged. It was found, for example, that the scales for measuring one of the three conditions had a reliability so low that it precluded any useful result. It was also found that the therapist's assessment of their own behaviour differed significantly from that perceived by the patient or by an independent assessor. It was found also that the therapist variables thought to be important for neurotic patients did not apply to the schizophrenic group.

Obviously, it is not possible to discuss the wealth of complex data in detail. It can be said with certainty, however, that this work by Rogers and his colleagues makes an important methodological contribution and is pertinent not only to Rogerian therapy but to all evaluations of psychotherapy. Nonetheless, the failure to obtain evidence of positive therapeutic effects in this intensive and carefully planned and executed study is a major setback for Rogerian theory and therapy. Rogers's initial theory notwithstanding, the disappointing outcome of this study may well be attributable to what seems to have been an unwise selection of patients. For implicit and explicit reasons schizophrenic patients seem to be less promising material for this type of treatment than other types of patients (e.g. personality problems).

Apropros the earlier discussion on the putative increases in variance observed after average therapy, the Wisconsin study provided scant support for this position. It is also worth noticing that in other studies reported by this group, treated patients do not always show increased variance. For example, Carkhuff and Truax (1965) in a study on the effectiveness of lay therapists showed that after treatment only one out of the 74 patients showed a deterioration. In this instance the effect of treatment was to *reduce* the variance.

Truax and Carkhuff (1967) have provided a coherent and important contribution to this subject. They describe and discuss in considerable detail the methodology involved in measuring the therapist conditions and they also assess the relations between the measures and across measures and therapeutic effect. In addition, they propose a 'fourth major ingredient of effective therapeutic encounters', namely, the patient's depth of self-exploration. As the present chapter is concerned with the outcome of therapy, we will not examine their interesting accounts of how the therapeutic encounter can be assessed and quantified, nor their analysis and recommendations for the training of therapists.

They discuss and describe a substantial number of experiments concerned with the reliability of therapist condition ratings and the relationship between these measures and therapeutic outcome. Unfortunately, however, most of these studies lack adequate control groups. The control studies are few in number but they do, in general, encourage the view that satisfactory therapeutic conditions do facilitate therapeutic improvement. In view of the serious setback in the Wisconsin study mentioned above and for other reasons that will be gone into presently, we feel that a definitive conclusion on the effectiveness of this type of therapy must await confirmation.

Some of the reasons that account for this cautious

attitude include the following. In the control studies, differences in the therapeutic conditions obtaining in various groups are sometimes extremely small. In the Dickenson and Truax (1966) study with college under-achievers, although they found significant differences between the groups receiving high and low conditions, an inspection of the ratings for the three groups shows that the *actual* differences are very slight. The mean ratings for the three groups were 13·2, 13·4, and 12·6 (presumably out of a possible total of 19). It will be seen that the differences are very slight despite the fact that group 3 received conditions that were (statistically) significantly lower than the other two groups. In spite of this very small difference in therapist conditions the outcome measures between the groups were quite substantial. The study by Truax, Wargo, and Silber (1966) on delinquent girls, although successful in the main, produced real differences that were comparatively slight (i.e. time out of institutions). Teasdale (1969) among others, has drawn attention to the need for independent confirmation of their findings by research workers outside the Truax, Rogers group. Many of the detailed difficulties that arise in evaluating the Rogerian approach are admirably discussed by Shapiro (1969) whose review is, in general, favourable. Among the many important points discussed in this paper, we will draw attention to only a few. Shapiro points out that the three scales contain ambiguities in terminology; the reliabilities of the scales are occasionally dangerously low; there is little evidence on the validity of the scales; the functional independence of the three therapeutic conditions is doubtful (*see also* the recent work by Muehlberg *et al.*, 1969 and Collingwood *et al.*, 1969). Discussing the outcome studies, Shapiro notes the presence of some contradictory and inconclusive results and suggests 'that that simple hypothesis of positive association between conditions and outcome leaves much to be accounted for.' He also draws attention to the inadequacies of the measures of change used in many of these studies —the shortcomings of some of the more popularly used ones, such as the MMPI and the Q sort, have already been discussed earlier.

There are other difficulties. Even though Truax and Carkhuff present some evidence on the connection between the therapist conditions and degree of self-exploration, it has not been shown that there is a necessary connection between self-exploration and therapeutic outcome. Perhaps the most important limitation in all this work is their tendency to over-emphasise the importance of therapist conditions, and the consequent lack of importance attached to treatment *technique* variables, the *nature* of the

patient's psychological difficulties, and, of course, the combination and interaction of these two determinants. The evidence on varying rates of spontaneous remission in different diagnostic categories and the differences in the natural history of various neurotic and other disorders have been discussed above. Neglect of this information certainly limits the value of the Rogerian approach. The importance of selecting an effective technique is adequately demonstrated in the research on behaviour therapy (*see* below). And in this connection it is worth noticing that the successful results obtained with automated desensitisation are a source of embarrassment to the Rogerian position (also, effective physical treatments, drugs etc.). Leaving aside the therapist conditions, it seems entirely reasonable to suggest that the chances of a course of therapy proving effective are determined to a very considerable extent by selecting the appropriate treatment technique for the particular disorder. Starting from this position it is far easier then to include the contribution made by the therapist or more accurately, the therapist conditions. It seems entirely reasonable to expect (even in the absence of the work by Truax and Carkhuff) that therapists will differ in skill and effectiveness. The Rogerian work has served the important function of preparing the ground for an improved understanding of the way in which a therapist can facilitate the treatment process. Neglecting to consider the treatment technique and the psychological problem presented, is likely to retard rather than facilitate our understanding of the contribution made by the conditions the therapist offers. If, on the other hand, attempts were made to investigate these conditions in the context of the correct technique for the appropriate problem, we might look forward to some valuable findings.

It is suggested that this type of approach could be facilitated by recasting the Rogerian approach in terms of learning theory. Truax and Carkhuff have, in fact, made the initial steps in this direction by proposing that therapists who are high on the three conditions are potent positive reinforcers. Similarly, those therapists who are low on these qualities are ineffective or even negative reinforcers. They suggest that the potent therapist provides positive reinforcement of 'approach response to human relating', reinforcement of self-exploratory behaviour, the elimination of specific fears, the 'reinforcement of positive self-concepts and self-valuations' (p. 151–152). Parts of this model bear some resemblance to Wolpe's (1958) view of non-systematic desensitisation which, he argues, can be used to explain the fact that most forms of therapy are capable of producing at least some therapeutic successes. Similarly, the Truax and Carkhuff model is congruent with some of the views put forward by Krasner (1962) on the reinforcing powers of a therapist.

We would suggest that if the Rogerian research proceeds from this model, it should be possible to bring about a fruitful integration with behavioural techniques, and the ensuing combination might be valuable.

BEHAVIOURAL TREATMENT

Behaviour therapy may prove to be the most significant advance in psychological treatment to be recorded by modern psychology. Substantial progress has been achieved in the past decade in establishing a firm experimental foundation on which to base the treatment of psychiatric patients, particularly those suffering from neurotic complaints (Wolpe, 1958; Eysenck and Rachman, 1965; Franks, 1969; Marks, 1969).

This Chapter is restricted to a discussion of techniques for treating neurotic conditions in which anxiety is a central feature. On the whole, deficit disorders are managed by operant procedures (*see* Ullman and Krasner, 1965; Ayllon and Azrin, 1968) and sexual disorders by aversion therapy (*see* Chapter 5).

Desensitisation

Systematic desensitisation is a technique for treating neurotic disorders in which anxiety is a central element. Since its development by Professor Wolpe in 1950, it has been used extensively in the treatment of neurotic patients (Marks, 1969; Rachman, 1968). The procedure and its rationale have also been the subject of numerous experimental investigations (Rachman, 1967).

Desensitisation involves the gradual and graduated imaginal presentation of anxiety-evoking stimuli while the patient is deeply relaxed. After the completion of the usual psychiatric investigations, the therapist and the patient construct a graded list of situations that provoke anxiety in the patient (this list is referred to as a 'hierarchy'). The patient is also given instruction in deep relaxation. When these preliminaries are completed the therapist relaxes the patient and then presents the least provocative items in the hierarchy. After relatively few presentations the patient generally finds that he can tolerate the previously disturbing image with tranquillity. The therapist then deals with successive items in the hierarchy and, proceeding in a gradual manner, eventually desensitises the patient to the entire hierarchy. The patient's newly acquired ability to tolerate the anxiety-evoking stimuli in imagination

usually transfers to the real life situation. The treatment sequence is 'relax—imagine the scene—relax and can be illustrated by the simple example of acrophobia. Here the patient might first be relaxed while imagining that he is standing on a well-protected first-floor balcony. When he can tolerate that image he is asked to imagine being on a second-storey balcony, and so on, until he is able to tolerate reasonable and realistic heights.

Much of our recently acquired knowledge about phobias has been obtained from the study of normal subjects who are frightened of spiders, snakes, worms, and so on. In 1963, Lang and Lazowik reported an experiment carried out on non-psychiatric subjects who suffered from an excessive fear of snakes. This pioneer experiment was carefully and elaborately prepared and the experimental design and execution were of high quality. The aims of the experiment are described by Lazovik and Lang as follows—

1. To evaluate the changes in snake phobic behaviour that occur over time, particularly the effect of repeated exposure to the phobic object.
2. Compare these changes with those that follow systematic desensitisation therapy.
3. Determine the changes in behaviour that are a direct function of the desensitisation process.

They chose to study snake phobias because of their fairly common occurrence and also because of the assumed symbolic sexual significance attributed to snakes. The twenty-four subjects who participated in the research were selected by a combination of interview, questionnaire, and direct exposure to non-poisonous snakes. Only those subjects who rated their fears as intense and whose behaviour in the presence of the snake confirmed this subjective report, were used in the experiment. The subjects were divided into two matched groups, an experimental group consisting of 13 subjects and a control group comprising 11 subjects. The experimental treatment comprised two essential parts, training and desensitisation proper. The training procedure consisted of five sessions of 45 minutes duration, during which an anxiety hierarchy consisting of 20 situations involving snakes was constructed. The subjects were then trained in deep relaxation and taught how to visualise the feared scenes vividly while under hypnosis.

Following this training period, the experimental subjects were given 11 sessions of systematic desensitisation during which they were hypnotised and instructed to relax deeply. The anxiety items from the hierarchy were then presented, starting with the least frightening scenes and working up the scale to the most frightening scenes. As the experimental design demanded that each treated subject receive only 11 treatment sessions, some of the subjects were not desensitised to all of the items in the hierarchy. In order to assess the effectiveness of reality training, half the experimental subjects were exposed to the snake before treatment on a number of occasions. The control subjects did not participate in desensitisation but they were evaluated at the same time as their opposite numbers in the experimental series and their behaviour in the presence of the snake was ascertained at the beginning and the end of the experiment. All the available subjects were seen and evaluated six months after this completion of therapy.

The authors summarised their results in the following way—

'The results of this present experiment demonstrate that the experimental analogue of desensitisation therapy effectively reduces phobic behaviour. Both subjective rating of fear and overt avoidance behaviour were modified and these gains were maintained or increased at the six-month follow-up. The results of objective measures were, in turn, supported by extensive interview material. Close questioning could not persuade any of the experimental subjects that their desire to please the therapist had been a significant factor in their change. Furthermore, in none of these interviews was there any evidence that other symptoms appeared to replace the phobic behaviour. The fact that no significant change was associated with the pre-therapy training argues that hypnosis and general muscle relaxation were not in themselves vehicles of change. Similarly, the basic suggestibility of the subject must be excluded . . . clearly the responsibility for the reduction in the phobic behaviour must be assigned to the desensitisation process itself.'

Lang and Lazovik also found a connection between the degree of improvement and the amount of progress made in the desensitisation of hierarchy items within the 11 sessions provided by the experiment. They also make three general points on the basis of their results. Firstly, as has been argued on previous occasions (*see* Eysenck and Rachman,

1965), it is not necessary to 'explore with the subject, the factors contributing to the learning of a phobia or its unconscious meaning in order to eliminate the fear behaviour'. Secondly, they were not able to find any evidence to support the presumed claim that symptom substitution will arise if the symptoms are treated directly.

Lang, Lazovik, and Reynolds (1966) later completed a study that included the experimental treatment of 23 subjects by systematic desensitisation, 11 untreated controls and a further 10 subjects (a particularly important addition) who received the same preliminary training as the desensitisation group and participated in the same number of interview sessions. The major difference was that the pseudo-therapy group subjects were relaxed in the interview sessions but not desensitised—instead, the therapist carefully avoided presenting any anxiety-provoking stimuli. The subjects were under the impression that they were being given a form of dynamic or interpretive therapy. The essential difference in the treated and pseudo-therapy groups lay then in the use of systematic desensitisation. Consequently any difference in the treatment outcome must be attributed to the use of this behaviour therapy technique. The results were clearcut and indicated that the subjects treated by systematic desensitisation showed significant reductions in phobic behaviour. The untreated subjects and the subjects who participated in pseudotherapy showed no improvement whatever. Among the subsidiary observations made by those research workers, the following are of particular interest. None of the successfully treated subjects showed signs of developing substitute symptoms. Again, it was found to be unnecessary to delve into the presumed basic causes of their fear of snakes. Simply being in a therapeutic relationship with the therapist is not sufficient to effect changes in the phobia. Successful therapy is independent of the subject's basic suggestibility (as assessed on the Stanford scale). The systematic desensitisation of the specific fear generalises positively to other fears, and an all-round improvement is observed.

Virtually all the conclusions reached by Lang and his colleagues have been confirmed by other experimenters. The extent of these investigations can be gauged from the summary tables (Table 22.4). It is fair to say that such widespread agreement has rarely been achieved in any other psychotherapeutic undertaking.

These studies, in addition to the support they provide for Wolpe's work and Lang's experiments, have also explored the nature of desensitisation in closer detail. For example, attempts have been made to isolate the effective elements in the treatment.

Table 22.4. Experimental Studies of Desensitisation

Author	Type of anxiety	Desensitisation Indiv.	Group	Other	Type of control	Sample	Assessment Subj.	Behav.	Psycho-metric	Outcome: Desens. more effective?
Lang and Lazowik (1963)	Snake phobia	Yes	—	—	No-treatment after prelim. training	E = 13 C = 11	Yes	Yes	Yes	On all 3 measures
Lang et al. (1966)	Snake phobia	Yes	—	—	Pseudo-therapy	E = 10 C = 10	Yes	Yes	Yes	On all 3 measures
Rachman (1965)	Spider phobia	—	Yes	—	Relax. only or desens. only or no-treat-ment	N = 12	Yes	Yes	Yes	On subjective and behav. measures
Davison (1965)	Snake phobia	Yes	—	—	Relax. only or desens. only or no-treat-ment	N = 28	Yes	Yes	Yes	On all measures
Paul (1966)	Public speaking	Yes	—	—	Insight, attention, no-treatment	N = 60	Yes	Yes	Yes	On all measures
Paul and Shannon (1966)	Public speaking	—	Yes	—	No-treatment	N = 20	Yes	Yes	Yes	On all measures
Kondas (1967)	Examinations	—	Yes	—	Relaxation, no-treatment, hierarchy only	N = 36	Yes	—	Yes	On all measures
Lazarus (1961)	Acrophobia etc.	—	Yes	—	Relaxation and insight	N = 35	Yes	—	Yes	Both measures
Cooke (1966)	Rats	Yes	—	in vivo	No-treatment	N = 12	Yes	Yes	—	Both measures
Lomont and Edwards (1966)	Snake phobia	Yes	—	—	Without relaxation	N = 22	Yes	Yes	Yes	On 3 of 5 measures
Johnson and Sechrest (1968)	Test anxiety	—	Yes	—	Relaxation, no-treatment	N = 33	Yes	Yes	Yes	Only on achievement tests
Ramsay et al. (1966)	Animals	Yes	—	—	Massed practice	N = 20	Yes	Yes	—	Yes, when spaced
Moore (1965)	Asthma attacks	Yes	—	—	Within subject, relaxation only	N = 12	Yes	Yes	—	On peak flow measure

continued overleaf

Table 22.4. (Continued)

Author	Type of anxiety	Desensitisation			Type of control	Sample	Assessment			Outcome: Desens. more effective?
		Indiv.	Group	Other			Subj.	Behav.	Psychometric	
Garfield et al. (1967)	Snake phobia	—	Yes	in vivo	Vs. in vivo but inadequate	N = 7	Yes	Yes	—	in vivo adds something?
Katahn et al. (1966)	Examinations	—	Yes	+ Counselling	No-treatment	N = 28	Yes	—	Yes	Yes?
Emery and Krumbolz (1967)	Examinations	Yes	—	+ Standard hierarchy	No-treatment	N = 36	Yes	Yes	Yes	On subjective and psychometric
Garlington and Cotler (1968)	Examinations	—	Yes	—	No-treatment	N = 32	Yes	Yes	Yes	On subjective and psychometric
Suinn (1968)	Examinations	Yes	Yes	—	No-treatment	N = 32	Yes	—	Yes	On subjective and psychometric
Zeisset (1968)	Interviews	Yes	—	—	No-treatment, relax, attention	N = 48 psychotics	Yes	Yes	—	On both measures
Donner and Guerney (1968)	Examinations	—	Yes	Automated	No-treatment, therapist absent	N = 42	Yes	Yes	Yes	On all measures
Lanyon et al. (1968)	Spider phobia	Yes	—	Massed	Massed, pseudo-treatment	N = 17	Yes	Yes	Yes	Trend on all measures
Melamed and Lang (1967)	Snake phobia	Yes	—	Automated	Automation, no-treatment	N = 21	Yes	Yes	Yes	On all measures
Kahn and Baker (1968)	Mixed phobias	Yes	—	Self-treatment	Self-treatment	N = 16	Yes	—	Yes	Self-treatment equally effective?
Donner and Guerney (1969)	Test anxiety	—	Yes	Automated	No-treatment	E = 11, E² = 12, C = 10	Yes	Yes	Yes	On all measures
Cohen (1969)	Test anxiety	—	Yes	—	No-treatment	E = 13, C = 8	Yes	Yes	Yes	On all measures
Oliveau et al. (1969)	Snake phobia	—	Yes	—	Praise/instructions (?)	N = 32	Yes	Yes	—	Yes; importance of instructions
Cotler and Garlington (1969)	Snake phobia	Yes	—	—	No-treatment	E = 12, C = 7	Yes	Yes	Yes	Yes, all measures

Study	Phobia			Treatment	Control	N				Results
Crighton and Jehu (1969)	Test anxiety	—	Yes	—	Psychotherapy	E = 10 C = 7	Yes	Yes	Yes	No
O'Neill and Howell (1969)	Snake phobia	—	Yes	—	(a) *in vivo* (b) slides	E = 10 C¹ = 10 C² = 10	Yes	Yes	Yes	All groups improved
Robinson and Suinn (1969)	Spiders	Yes	Yes	—	Group vs. individual	E = 10 C = 10	—	Yes	Yes	All measures; massing effective
Mann and Rosenthal (1969)	Test anxiety	—	Yes	Vicarious	No-treatment	E¹ = 25 E² = 25 C = 21	Yes	Yes	Yes	On all 6 measures
Willis and Edwards (1969)	Mice phobia	—	Yes	Implosion	No-treatment	E¹ = 16 E² = 16 C = 16	Yes	Yes	Yes	On all 6 measures
Crowder and Thornton (1970)	Snake phobia	Yes	—	—	No-treatment	E¹ = 10 E² = 10 C = 9	—	Yes	Yes	Yes, but muscle relaxation redundant
Nawas, Fishman, and Pucel (1970)	Snake phobia	—	Yes	—	Pseudo-treatment No-treatment	E¹ = 10 E² = 10 C¹ = 10 C² = 10	—	Yes	—	Yes
Miller and Nawas (1970)	Snake phobia	—	Yes	—	Pseudo-treatment No-treatment	E¹ = 10 E² = 10 C¹ = 10 C² = 10	Yes	Yes	—	Yes
Nawas, Welsch, and Fishman (1970)	Snake phobia	—	Yes	—	Pseudo-treatment No-treatment	E¹ = 10 E² = 10 E³ = 10 C¹ = 10 C² = 10	—	Yes	—	Yes, but muscle relaxation redundant
Mitchell and Ingham (1970)	Test anxiety	—	Yes	—	No-treatment No-contact	E = 31 C¹ = 6 C² = 22	Yes	Yes	Yes	Yes
McGlynn and Mapp (1970)	Snake phobia	—	Yes	—	No-treatment	E¹ = 8 E² = 8 E³ = 8 C = 7	—	Yes	—	Yes
Proctor (1969)	Snake phobia	—	Yes (?)	—	No-treatment	E = 54 C = 9	Yes	3	—	Yes on 3 out of 4 measures
Cotler (1970)	Snake phobia	—	Yes	Automated	No-treatment	E = 16 C = 12	Yes	Yes	Yes	Yes, all measures
Barrett (1969)	Snake phobia	Yes	—	—	(i) No-treatment (ii) Implosion	N = 36	Yes	Yes	Yes	Both more effective than control; implosion quicker but less stable

Thus far the evidence indicates that desensitisation effects are probably the result of the combined action of relaxation instructions and graduated image presentations (Rachman, 1965; Davison, 1967; Kondas, 1967; Lomont and Edwards, 1968). However, the role and action of muscle relaxation training has now been re-examined (Rachman, 1968a; Nawas *et al.*, 1970).

The present state of the experimental evidence on desensitisation permits the following conclusions. Desensitisation therapy effectively reduces phobic behaviour. The elimination of phobic behaviour is analogous to the elimination of other responses from the subject's repertoire. It is not necessary to ascertain the origin of the phobia in order to eliminate it. Neither is it necessary to change the subject's basic attitudes or to modify his personality. The elimination of a phobia is not followed by symptom substitution. The response to treatment is not related to suggestibility. Relaxation or hypnosis alone do not reduce the phobia. Relaxation and hypnosis accompanied by pesudotherapeutic interviews do not reduce the phobia. The establishment of a therapeutic relationship with the patient does not of itself reduce the phobia. Desensitisation administered in the absence of relaxation appears to be less effective than systematic desensitisation treatment. Interpretive therapy combined with relaxation does not reduce phobic behaviour. A limited number of observations raise the possibility that reductions in fears produced by desensitisation occur almost immediately; in a large minority of instances, a proportion of the fear-reduction accomplished in experimental treatment sessions reappears within 24 hours.

Although some of these conclusions are tentative (the last two in particular), as a body they constitute a very important advance in our ability to reduce phobias. It is clear, nevertheless, that a great deal still needs to be investigated and understood. Perhaps the most immediate need is for further experimental studies that attempt to apply these findings to psychiatric patients. While it is true that the clinical reports that have been published to date are, with some exceptions, consistent with the experimental evidence discussed in this paper, there remains a need for careful experimental investigation of the clinical application of desensitisation. The bulk of the work reported so far has, of course, been carried out on phobic subjects. There is, therefore, a need for further investigation of both psychiatric and non-psychiatric subjects who suffer from complaints other than excessive fears or phobias. Clearly, it is necessary to find other psychiatric and non-psychiatric analogues on which to carry out similar experiments to those already described.

One such example is the study carried out by Moore (1965) on asthmatic patients. From an experimental point of view the full range of applicability of desensitisation needs to be explored.

On the technical side it is becoming increasingly important to refine and extend the present methods of assessing therapeutic changes. The inclusion of physiological measures is an obvious step and work on the subject is gathering momentum (e.g. Lang, 1969; Matthews, 1970) but is still replete with technical difficulties.

Finally, two theoretical advances are worth noting. When behaviour therapy was first introduced, numerous objections were raised, particularly in psychoanalytic circles. Two of the most serious and widely expressed criticisms were these. Firstly, it was argued that the tendency of behaviour therapists to treat manifest neurotic behaviour would, if successful, lead to symptom substitution. That is to say, the patient would develop new and possibly even worse symptoms if the so-called defensive reactions were removed by the behaviour therapist. This phenomenon of symptom substitution has, in the event, proved to be of minimal importance and occurs very rarely. In none of the experiments described above was symptom substitution observed even though it was in almost all cases carefully sought. In the clinical reports also, the occurrence of symptom substitution is rare (Rachman, 1968).

A second objection raised was that it is impossible to bring about the reduction or elimination of neurotic symptoms and behaviour unless one first eliminates the presumed basic cause of the illness. It was said that behaviour therapy could not succeed because it was directing its attention to the wrong area. This objection, too, has now been firmly eliminated. In the experimental investigations and the clinical reports there is overwhelming evidence that substantial improvements in abnormal behaviour can be obtained by systematic desensitisation (and other methods of behaviour therapy) even when little or no attention is paid to the possible or presumed underlying causes of the illness.

Flooding

The possibility that patients suffering from phobic conditions (and possibly, other disorders) might derive benefit from being exposed to overwhelmingly provocative stimulation under controlled conditions, has been considered by clinicians and experimenters over the years. Experimental investigations have been reported by, among others, Masserman (1943) and Polin (1953); it was raised as a theoretical possibility by Wolpe (1958), and applied in the treatment of patients with excessive fear of examinations by Malleson (1961). The revival of interest in this topic is attributable to the work of Stampfl and his colleagues on the method they describe as 'implosion'. This work has aroused a good deal of interest because of the claims made for the speed and wide applicability of the method. Some dramatic changes have been described and these, not surprisingly, attract attention. The choice of the term 'implosion' is perhaps unfortunate—it suggests a great deal but is almost certainly misleading. For most people it will probably have an association with the word explosion and it seems that the term was borrowed from physics. In any event, the suggestion, however faint, that something *inside* the patient undergoes a bursting release or disintegration, is not borne out by the available facts. 'The noun implies a bursting from within. It was chosen to depict the onslaught of the cues and the subsequent intense anxiety reaction which is followed by the collapse of the symptoms because of the extinction of the anxiety which supports them' (Hogan and Kirchner, 1967). As this quotation indicates, the term implosion was introduced partly because of its overtones and partly because it is linked with a hypothesised sequence of events and a theoretical mechanism postulated to account for this sequence. Both the hypothesised events and the explanation for them can be challenged. In all, it seems preferable at this early stage to use a term that is descriptive rather than explanatory. An accurate title would be 'prolonged exposure to high intensity stimulation' but this is too cumbersome for ordinary use and the alternative term 'flooding' is suggested as a substitute.

It is assumed by implosive therapists that neurotic symptoms can be viewed as avoidance behaviour that is 'reinforced because it successfully helps the organism to evade repressed cues associated with the original situation which elicits greater anxiety' (Hogan and Kirchner, 1967). This avoidance behaviour is an attempt to protect the organism from an original fear of an object or event, acquired in its life history, that continues to evoke intense anxiety. Implosive therapy attempts to extinguish both the avoidance response patterns and the anxiety reactions themselves. Stampfl and Levis (1968) explain the treatment in this way: 'Exposure to cues representing or approximating these events is likely to elicit relatively high levels of anxiety. Their repetition in the absence of a primary reinforcer, however, should lead to a decrement in their aversiveness through the principle of generalization of extinction and thereby to a reduction in the avoidance reactions which constitute symptomatic behaviour' (page 33). Thus far, implosive therapy bears some resemblance to formulations proposed by behaviour therapists such as Wolpe (1958),

Eysenck and Rachman (1967), and so on. It will also be noticed that the implosive therapists similarly place considerable emphasis on Mowrer's theorising. The important theoretical divergence between implosive therapy and other forms of behaviour therapy begins when Stampfl and his colleagues attempt to 'synthesise behaviouristic and Freudian concepts' (Hogan and Kirchner, 1967). A similar view is expressed by Stampfl and Levis (1967): 'a strong emphasis is also placed upon stimuli which might be described as "hidden", "inner", or unreportable by the patient'. Hogan and Kirchner explain that a large number of stimuli can be associated with the original trauma and that the 'most threatening of these cues becomes repressed— an idea analogous to Freud's primal repression. Stimulus generalization, or what Freud called repression proper, also occurs . . . .' This Freudian influence naturally determines the flavour of the treatment technique and it can be described quite fairly as an attempt to extinguish the anxiety associated with repressed memories. The implosive therapists therefore attempt to 'recreate the original trauma' (Hogan, 1968), or at least the presumed trauma. According to Hogan, the 'usual areas of conflict are related to fears, rejections, prior humiliations or deprivations, or conflicts related to expression of, or fear of aggression, sexual problems of various types, and guilt-related behaviour.' In practice, this means that the therapists devote a good deal of attention to castration, Oedipal and related themes. As one might expect, the therapists encounter difficulty in determining the accuracy of their selection of cues. Stampfl and Levis (1967) imply that if the cues elicit anxiety, then this confirms their selection.

In an informative introduction to a report on short-term implosive therapy, Hogan and Kirchner (1967) mention several important hypotheses associated with, or implied, by implosive therapists. They include the following. The subject's fear was learned while he was experiencing intense anxiety. Such fear reactions can only be 'unlearned under similar conditions'. In order to be successful the treatment must ensure that the patient experiences 'the extreme anxiety associated with those cues' (i.e. those involved in the traumatic experience). Experiencing intense anxiety in the absence of the real occurrence of the feared stimulus, will be followed by a reduction in anxiety. The amount of anxiety 'manifested by the organism is proportionate to the number of significant cues presented.' The amount of extinction of the fear response is directly related to the degree of unreinforced anxiety the subject experiences. As the stimuli assumed to be related to the traumatic origin of the fear are, of course, presented in imagination only, it is assumed that the reduction of anxiety the patient undergoes while imagining stimuli will transfer to the actual stimuli themselves, and the patient will experience an improvement.

Only the last-mentioned of these assumptions has received experimental support to date, and that support is of an indirect nature.

The early evidence on the effects of flooding was reviewed by Rachman (1969) who found it to be inadequate but promising. Later studies have produced conflicting results which seem to emphasise our vague understanding of the process involved. Boulougouris, Marks, and Marset (1970) obtained particularly encouraging results with 16 phobic patients, and Barrett (1969) was successful with snake-phobic volunteers. On the other hand, Hodgson and Rachman (1970), Willis and Edwards (1969), Mealia (1968), and Fazio (1970) have all been unsuccessful.

At least one of Stampfl's major assumptions has already been undermined. The psychodynamic aspects of the theory seem to be redundant as Hogan and Kirchner (1967) have reported reductions in fear among rat-phobic subjects after a remarkably brief amount of implosion therapy. In another study, Kirchner and Hogan (1966) observed reductions in fear after a single, group-administered session of implosion. In neither of these experiments were attempts made to relate the implosive material to the presumed or actual trauma that generated the fears. More recently Hogan and Kirchner (1968) reported successful results with ten snake-phobic subjects after one implosion session and, again, no attempt was made to ascertain the dynamic origin or significance of the subjects' phobias. A defence of Stampfl's position would demand the assumption that all of the subjects had undergone similar, if not identical, experiences with snakes and/or that they all attributed the same psychodynamic significance to snakes. This is most unlikely. These experiments do, however, share one obvious feature: the subjects in each study (and the patients described in case-studies) are exposed to material that arouses intense emotional reactions in a defined and controlled situation ('in the absence of primary reinforcement').

Despite its theoretical weaknesses, the *technique* has an appeal and would seem to be worth investigating. The idea of extinguishing surplus and deviant reactions by prolonged exposure to high intensity stimulation is one that has some support from animal experiments and is a reasonably sound basis in experimental psychology. Moreover, some of the case-reports described by the workers employing implosion have a dramatic quality that cannot but evoke interest (Stampfl, 1967; Stampfl and Levis, 1969). It might, however, be of some value if we

could, at this early stage, focus on what appear to be some of the central issues involved.

From the clinical point of view it is, of course, necessary to demonstrate first and foremost that the technique is capable of producing significant and enduring improvements. The accumulation of such evidence can (and probably should be) approached from two points. In the first place, it is easy to carry out analogue studies of the type employed in research work on desensitisation (Rachman, 1967). A second line of approach would be to examine the effects of technique on psychiatric patients. As there is a possibility, however, that the technique may, if incorrectly used, produce an increase rather than a decrease in anxiety and related disturbances, this development should probably be postponed until the analogue studies have provided more detailed and reliable guides.

Even if it is demonstrated that the technique is capable of producing lasting reductions in anxiety and other unadaptive behaviour, it will still be necessary to examine the assumptions proposed by Stampfl and his colleagues, and, in particular, a great deal of doubt must attach to their insistence on the importance of psychodynamic material. As yet, we are not even in a position to state that the content of the fear-evoking instructions need be related to the abnormal behaviour the therapist is attempting to reduce or eliminate. It is, for example, perfectly possible that the arousal of high levels of anxiety may be the key factor involved,* even if the material used to provoke such anxiety is entirely irrelevant to the target behaviour. This point is discussed in a little more detail below.

In detailing the assumptions underlying the use of implosion therapy, it was pointed out that the workers concerned have assumed that a reduction in the anxiety evoked by imaginal representations of the relevant images and memories will be followed by a reduction in anxiety in the face of the real object or event. It was said that the evidence on this point is as yet, indirect. While it is true that there is some evidence that imaginal evocations of images relating to a fear of rats or snakes can be followed by a reduction in avoidance behaviour in the presence of the real object, no attempt has yet been made to ascertain the degree of fear reduction obtained when the imaginal stimulus is presented and *then* to determine the amount of fear evoked in the presence of the real object. If the experience gained with the desensitisation method is any guide, then we can

---

* Recent clinical findings have made it clear that the evocation of high levels of anxiety (or arousal) is *not* necessary for therapeutic results. Whether such evocation is facilitative remains to be proved.

happily expect that a reduction in imaginally induced fear will be followed by similar reductions in real life. There is, however, some evidence from this source (e.g. Cooke, 1965; Barlow *et al.*, 1969) that desensitisation in face of the real object is marginally more efficient than desensitisation to the imaginal object. Therapists have for some time past considered the possible effects of exposing neurotic patients to their most feared situation, but have rarely tried it in practice. Meyer (1967) has, however, attempted a technique of this type in the treatment of obsessional patients and reported extremely interesting results.

An aspect of the implosive method that is of considerable theoretical and practical importance is the duration of the treatment session and, closely related to this, the point at which the treatment session can be terminated with safety. On theoretical grounds, we may expect that the premature termination of a treatment session (i.e. when the patient is still at an exceedingly high level of arousal) may result in an increase rather than a reduction in anxiety.

It is worth mentioning in passing, that similar deductions are implicit in Bandura's (1968) theorising about the effects of modelling treatment. Similarly, Hinde (1968) has shown that the length of time for which 'an animal is exposed to a frightening stimulus is a really crucial variable in establishing habituation' of the fear response. He continues, 'if the periods of exposure are too short the intensity of the animal's response may be increased rather than decreased' (page 83). There is, in fact, one small piece of experimental evidence on fearful non-psychiatric subjects indicating that this may occur (Rachman, 1966).

The flooding (or implosive) techniques raise many fascinating problems and not the least of these, is the manner in which they operate. There seems to be universal and quite reasonable agreement, that some form of extinction process is involved. If this can be confirmed, then it will provide an extremely useful link with some of the other methods of behaviour therapy (e.g. desensitisation, modelling techniques, and so forth). In this connection it will be interesting to discover whether or not the patient or subject has to be saturated with images that are relevant to the target behaviour, or, whether one can achieve much the same result by evoking high levels of anxiety using standard (even tape-recorded) instructions. It is implied in much of the thinking on this subject that strong emotional reactions are in some way self-limiting. It is, for example, conceivable that implosion and related techniques operate by bringing about a type of 'exhaustion' of the patient's ability to respond emotionally and, during this refractory phase, he is able rapidly to habituate to the formerly fear-evoking stimuli. This hypothesis can be tested by comparing the effects of anxiety-evoking material that is related to the feared object with anxiety-evoking material that is unrelated to the feared object.

Finally, some recent observations taken during the exploratory stages of a research project may be of interest. These preliminary observations (Hodgson and Rachman, 1970) indicate that in some patients at least, there is a very rapid recovery from an imaginal flooding session—of the order of minutes. Secondly, post-flooding session avoidance tests seem to suggest that mildly fearful items are weakened much more rapidly than anxiety hierarchy items that are high on the list. These high anxiety items appear to be fairly resistant to change, an observation concordant with the evidence from desensitisation.

Among others, the following problems seem worthy of early investigation. The therapeutic effects reported by Stampfl and his colleagues need to be replicated. The stability of observed improvements needs to be ascertained. The nature and means of presenting the 'implosive' material need to be investigated (e.g. Should the images be related to the target behaviour? Should the therapist draw attention to and increase the subjects' bodily reactions? Should the images be mainly realistic or mainly fantastic? Are tape-recordings effective?) The optimal duration and frequency of treatment sessions need to be determined. The conditions that may produce undesirable changes need to be discovered. The nature and significance of the physiological changes associated with 'implosive' sessions need to be investigated. For experimental purposes it seems wise to control the time that elapses between the termination of the treatment session(s) and the conduct of the behavioural avoidance tests. On the theoretical side, the extinction hypothesis needs to be tested and, closely related, it is necessary to discover whether the evoked emotional reactions are self-limiting. Do the therapeutic effects result from the prevention of avoidance responses (hence, extinction) as suggested by Stampfl and co-workers? Or are the effects produced by a rapid extinction process which is facilitated by subjecting the subject to preparatory (non-specific?) emotional arousal?

These suggestions are, of course, offered on the assumption that the recently made claims for the therapeutic value of 'implosion' are confirmed. Increased understanding of an ineffective procedure, however elaborate and elegant the contributory experimentation, would not constitute an unique achievement in clinical psychology.

Modelling

Another development of great potential value is the research on modelling techniques so ably presented by Bandura (1969). The steadily accumulating experimental evidence uniformly shows that these techniques can produce substantial reductions in fear. If modelling procedures stand up to the transfer from laboratory to clinic, modelling will have a central place in the next edition of this *Handbook*.

Clinical Results

The clinical effectiveness of behaviour therapy (and desensitisation in particular) is attested to by two types of evidence: individual case histories and field trials. A large number of illustrative case histories are now available, and many of them have been conveniently assembled and reproduced in three or four texts. Descriptions of the clinical method are contained in *Behaviour Therapy and the Neuroses*, edited by H. J. Eysenck; *Causes and Cures of Neurosis*, by Eysenck and Rachman; *Psychotherapy by Reciprocal Inhibition*, by Wolpe; *Case Studies in Behaviour Modification*, by Ullmann and Krasner; *Fears and Phobias*, by Marks; *The Practice of Behavior Therapy*, by Wolpe.

The first major report on the clinical effectiveness of desensitisation and other methods of behaviour therapy was provided by Wolpe in 1958. He described the results obtained in the treatment of 210 neurotic patients. Wolpe accepted every patient referred provided that the diagnosis of neurosis had been confirmed. The composition of the sample is adequately described, and it is clear that the majority of his patients were suffering from anxiety states of one type or another. The patients suffering from anxiety were not, however, subdivided into phobics and related conditions, so that it is not possible to provide an accurate estimate of the degree of success obtained with specifically phobic disorders. However, 135 of the 210 patients reported in this publication were described as being anxiety neurotics; an examination of the cases in detail makes it fairly clear that many of them were, in fact, complaining of phobic symptoms of one variety or another.

Wolpe assessed the effectiveness of therapy in terms of five criteria: symptomatic improvement, increased productiveness, improved adjustment and pleasure in sex, improved interpersonal relationships, and the ability to deal with reasonable reality stresses. Each patient was classified in terms of these criteria into one of five categories: apparently cured, much improved, moderately improved, slightly improved and unimproved. Of the 210 patients treated, approximately 90 per cent were apparently cured or much improved after treatment.

This exceptionally successful result must be regarded with a measure of reserve because of the incomplete nature of the follow-up investigations. It was impossible, for practical reasons, to arrange long-term follow-ups for the majority of these patients, and it seems probable in view of more recent evidence that a proportion of them did not maintain their initial improvements. Another possible source of inflation in this figure can be traced to Wolpe's exclusion from the final assessment of those patients who had not completed a minimum of fifteen treatment sessions. This is an unusually stringent criterion, and one that most of the later clinicians have not used.

This report by Wolpe was the first major account of the systematic attempt to apply principles of learning theory to the treatment of neurotic disturbances. As a pioneering effort, it cannot, of course, be expected to provide a full answer to the problem of psychotherapy. It is true, nevertheless (and this can be said with increasing confidence, in view of more recent evidence), that the therapy and general approach developed by Wolpe constitutes an advance in our ability to treat neurotic disturbances and phobias in particular.

Wolpe's work is attractive for a number of reasons, in addition to the encouraging therapeutic outcome he obtained. In the first place, it is based on sound psychological principles and was developed in a systematic and logical manner from existing theoretical notions and specially devised experiments. It has the further advantage of being stated and described in such a manner as to permit careful experimental investigation of both the assumptions and actual procedures involved.

In 1963, Lazarus reported on the treatment of 408 patients. These neurotic patients were treated on the lines proposed by Wolpe and were assessed in similar manner. Lazarus was able to obtain significant improvement in 321 of his patients, that is, 78 per cent. He then went on to carry out a detailed analysis of the results obtained with 126 patients who were suffering from what he describes as 'severe neurosis'. This sub-analysis was carried out in an attempt to clarify the position in regard to the effectiveness of behaviour therapy with more complex and severe disorders.

Lazarus discovered that the recovery rate of severe cases was only 62 per cent. This figure is, of course, lower than that obtained in the total series and also lower than that obtained by Wolpe in his major report. The suggestion arising from this subanalysis is that while behaviour therapy is probably effective in treating complex neurotic disorders, it may well prove to be more effective in treating simple disorders. Another difference that might account for the reduced improvement rate in Lazarus's group is the fact that each of the 126 severely neurotic patients was followed up for a mean duration of two years.

Other clinical reports have been provided by Hussein (1962), Burnett and Ryan (1965), and by Schmidt *et al.* (1965). As these three clinical reports all described variations on conventional behaviour therapy, and because they dealt with a conglomeration of different types of patient, they will not be discussed in any detail here. It is sufficient to say that the success rates varied between 60 per cent and 95 per cent and that the suggestion emerged from the paper by Schmidt *et al.* that patients who had chronic and complicated disorders tended on the whole to do less well than those patients who were less severely ill.

Humphrey (1966) reported a comparison trial between behaviour therapy and psychotherapy in treating neurotic disorders in children. Both methods produced successful results, but behaviour therapy was slightly more effective and was significantly quicker than psychotherapy. The long-term results from behaviour therapy were found to be superior. The value of this trial is limited by inadequate agreement between the independent assessors and by a slight overlap in methods of therapy, both of which were carried out by the same therapist.

Cooper (1963) reported a retrospective study on the effects of behaviour therapy. He carried out a follow-up study of thirty patients who had received various types of behaviour therapy at the Maudsley Hospital between 1954 and 1960. Cooper attempted to construct a retrospective control group by matching them with another thirty patients who had been treated at approximately the same time. In fact, he was able to extract only sixteen matched controls from hospital records.

The progress of these matched pairs of patients (ten phobics, four obsessionals, one stammerer, and one case of writer's cramp) was then estimated by two independent assessors. Retrospective assessments were made of their progress at the end of treatment, one month, and one year after treatment. Cooper stated that the 'only striking finding is at the end of treatment for the 10 phobic patients, 9 of whom showed definite improvement in the symptom treatment compared to only 5 of the control cases'. The superior improvement observed in the phobic patients was not apparent at the follow-up assessment, however. Cooper also pointed out that none of the patients had developed substitute symptoms.

Unfortunately, the value of Cooper's study is undermined by several factors. The selection of patients was not properly randomised, as the match-

ing was carried out retrospectively, and as Cooper himself points out, 'in some of these cases, behaviour therapy suffered the fate of all new forms of treatment and was tried as a last resort, and some cases were taken on as much experimentally as therapeutically. This was particularly so in obsessional patients . . .'.

Some of the treatment was carried out by students, or by psychologists who had no previous experience of behaviour therapy (many of the control patients were treated by trainee psychiatrists.) Thirdly, Cooper provides few details about the nature of the behaviour therapy used. His statement that the phobic patients were treated by Wolpe's methods of reciprocal inhibition and desensitisation is misleading. In fact, fewer than twenty of the patients in the matched group of therapy cases were treated by the method Wolpe used in practically all his phobic cases, namely desensitisation based on relaxation. Consequently, Cooper's comparison of the results with those reported by Wolpe appears to be unjustified.

Cooper failed to indicate in a clear manner that he was, in fact, comparing different types of behaviour therapy. Moreover, he was comparing different types of patients—many of the Maudsley group were people who required in-patient hospital care. The great majority of Wolpe's patients were treated on an out-patient basis. A further drawback to Cooper's study was the fact that the assessors worked solely from the case notes and did not interview any of the patients in either the treatment or the control groups. Cooper himself interviewed fourteen of the thirty behaviour-therapy patients and none of the controls. For these reasons Cooper's conclusions cannot be accepted at face value.

In an extension of Cooper's study, Marks, Gelder, and Cooper (1965) arrived at a similar conclusion when they examined an additional thirty-seven patients treated at the Maudsley Hospital. They claimed that in none of the treatment groups was behaviour therapy less effective than other methods of treatment, and that *in the phobias* it was more effective. The development of fresh symptoms after successful behavioural treatment was not a hazard.

Behaviour therapy can be effective in severe chronic cases where other methods have been tried and failed, and in some conditions (i.e. monosymptomatic phobias) it may even be the first consideration for treatment. The finding that severe chronic patients do not respond as successfully to behaviour therapy as do other types of neurotic patients has in fact received further support in a prospective study recently completed.

Gelder and Marks (1966) described a control trial of behaviour therapy with twenty severe agoraphobic patients. These patients were carefully matched and placed into either the treatment or control group. The therapy consisted of graded retraining in real-life situations together with Wolpe's technique of desensitisation in imagination. The control treatment was based on brief 're-educative psychotherapy,' and both types of treatment were given three times weekly.

In each group seven out of the ten patients improved symptomatically. In both instances, however, the patients were left with much residual disability. This disappointing result appears to have resulted from the fact that the patients concerned were severely ill. The mean duration of the agoraphobic illness was more than seven years, and all the patients were deemed to require in-patient care. As has already been shown in other studies, severely ill patients do not respond as well to behaviour therapy as those with less incapacitating disorders.

Closer inspection of the results indicate, however, that the patients who were treated by behaviour therapy had improved slightly more (but not statistically so) than the other group. Moreover, the behaviour-therapy group showed 'greater improvement in work capacity . . . at the end of treatment'. A similar finding was reported by Hain and others (1966).

That the relatively poor results obtained in this control trial can best be attributed to the severity of the illness affecting these patients gained some support from another study reported by Gelder, Marks, and Wolff (1967). They reported that a less-satisfactory response to treatment was found in severe agoraphobics than among moderately disturbed (out-patient) phobics.

Although Gelder and Marks did not provide the mean number of sessions of treatment given to the severe agoraphobics, it is apparent from the duration of the treatment (given approximately three times a week) that these patients required considerably more treatment than those described either by Lazarus (1965) or by Meyer and Crisp (1966) or by Hain, Butcher, and Stevenson (1966). The suggestion made by Gelder and Marks that the slightly better outcome for patients who received behaviour therapy can be accounted for by the longer duration of treatment is not entirely consistent with the observations reported by Hain and others, who found that there was no correlation in their group of patients, between duration of treatment and therapeutic outcome. Wolpe (1964) himself, however, reported that sixty-five patients with complex neuroses needed an average of 54·8 treatment sessions, whereas twenty-one patients with simple neuroses only required an average of 14·9 sessions.

As in every study on the subject, both clinical and

experimental, Gelder and Marks could find no evidence that symptom substitution constitutes a problem. They also emphasise, however, the difficulty encountered in selecting patients for behaviour therapy.

These psychiatrists recently added another field trial to their valuable investigations. Gelder, Marks, and Wolff (1967) carried out a controlled enquiry into the comparative effectiveness of desensitisation, individual psychotherapy or group psychotherapy in the treatment of phobic states. Forty-two moderately disturbed phobic patients were treated on an out-patient basis by one of these three methods. The patient groups were extremely carefully matched and consisted of the following cases: desensitisation group—eight agoraphobics, four social phobics, four with specific phobias; group therapy—seven agoraphobics, three social phobias, six specific phobias; individual psychotherapy—seven agoraphobics, three social phobias. They summed up their major findings in this way—

'All raters agreed that, of the three treatments, desensitization produced more patients whose symptoms improved at the end of treatment and follow-up.

'Symptoms, especially the presenting phobias, improved faster with desensitization than with psychotherapy. After 6 months, desensitization patients had changed more significantly than others, but this difference diminished later, as the patients in psychotherapy went on improving slowly. Only two patients lost their symptoms completely, both with desensitization. At follow-up the degree of improvement still tended to be greater in those who had been treated with desensitization, but the difference was no longer statistically significant.

'Ratings of social adjustment were less sensitive and reliable than symptom ratings; however, greater and more rapid improvement occurred in work and leisure adjustment with desensitization . . . (pp. 71–72). The number of patients whose phobias were rated much improved by two of three raters at the final rating were: desensitization 9/16; group therapy 2/16; individual therapy 3/10 (p. 60).'

In assessing these results, it is important to note that the desensitisation group was treated weekly for about nine months and then re-assessed nine months later. The patients in group therapy received eighteen months of treatment, and their results do not include a follow-up. The patients who received individual therapy were treated for a year and re-assessed six months later. Gelder *et al.* (1967), commenting on their results, occasionally fail to take these differences fully into account.

Although the groups were extremely well matched in particulars, it is a pity that only ten patients were included in the individual therapy group. Perhaps the main weakness in this study is the crudity of the assessment measures (mostly five-point rating scales), but this is a difficulty with which all research workers can sympathise.

In examining the outcome of this trial, it is also worth remembering that many of the subsidiary measures (e.g. of obsessions and also of the therapist's rating of depression) deal with minor problems, and it is no surprise therefore that the three treatment groups rarely differ in these respects. Neither desensitisation nor psychotherapy can produce superior results with subsidiary problems that are slight to begin with—simply, there is little room for change.

Finally, some of the authors' concluding comments are arguable. Nevertheless, Marks and Gelder's investigations are the best field trials available and need to be studied carefully.

Gillan (1970) recently completed an investigation into the comparative effectiveness of desensitisation, psychotherapy, and pseudotherapy in the management of phobic patients. There were eight patients in each group and the effects of treatment were assessed by clinical ratings (independent, self, and therapists), psychometrics, and physiological indices. On all the main clinical measures the desensitised patients were found to be significantly better; the patients treated by psychotherapy or pseudotherapy showed little change. These results persisted at the three-month follow-up.

The report made by Meyer and Crisp (1966) is particularly interesting, because they describe their experiences with the use of behaviour therapy in a general psychiatric department which offers a wide range of diagnostic and treatment services, and which caters for a heterogeneous group of patients. They quote the results obtained with fifty-four cases of mixed neurotic and behaviour disorders ranging from agoraphobia to encopresis. A variety of behavioural methods was used, and desensitisation was the most common. The overall improvement rate was 70 per cent in a mean of twenty-five sessions. Only two relapses were noted and both of these were successfully re-treated.

Hain, Butcher, and Stevenson (1966) presented a similar report of their clinical experiences except that they used only desensitisation therapy. The work was, however, done in a general psychiatric department which resembles that in which the Meyer and Crisp study was conducted. All of the twenty-seven patients treated by Hain and his colleagues were diagnosed as suffering from psychoneuroses, and the duration of their symptoms ranged from four months to fifty years, with a mean of 8·6 years. The major symptoms encountered in these patients were fears and anxiety, and phobias. Seventy-eight per cent of the patients showed symptomatic improvement. These figures are, of course, strikingly similar to those reported by Meyer and Crisp.

The mean number of sessions required to treat patients was nineteen; this figure is also similar to Meyer and Crisp's experience. Hain et al. found there was no correlation between the degree of improvement obtained and the duration of treatment. The greatest improvement (in addition to the removal of the presenting symptom) was found in occupational functioning. Once again, although it was sought, no evidence of symptom substitution was elicited. Like Meyer and Crisp, these authors make some interesting comments about the practical difficulties encountered in the routine use of behaviour therapy (e.g. the selection of patients, the assessment of improvement, and so on).

Naturally, it is not sufficient merely to state that behaviour therapy can successfully induce improvement in neurotic conditions, particularly anxiety states. Ideally, one would like to know what the effective act in these types of treatment is. It has already been argued that a number of the variables involved in desensitisation therapy are not capable of inducing these improvements in isolation. For example, there is clear evidence that sheer muscle relaxation cannot by itself produce therapeutic improvements. Similarly, the improvements cannot be attributed to suggestibility, nor to hypnosis.

A more serious possibility is the one raised by Cooper (1963), Meyer and Gelder (1963), and by Murray (1962), among others. Pointing to the measure of success that can be obtained by other forms of treatment, it has been argued that the primary cause of the therapeutic improvements must be attributed to the patient-therapist relationship that develops during the course of treatment. However, if this were the main vehicle of change, then it would be difficult to account for the fact that in most studies behaviour therapy appears to be more effective than other types of treatment—or, indeed, for the success of automated desensitisation (see Table 22.4). Fortunately, we have some direct and indirect evidence that puts us in a position to estimate the contribution made to the progress of the therapy by the relationship between the patient and the therapist.

It should be pointed out initially that the contribution made by the relationship almost certainly varies with the type of disorder under consideration. In some types of disorder, particularly those that are complex and long lasting, the relationship seems to be of some significance. Examples of this type are provided by Meyer and Gelder (1963). In other disorders, however, such as enuresis, the relationship is of virtually no significance in determining the outcome of behavioural treatment.

Costello (1965) has drawn attention to an important difference between conventional types of psychotherapy and behaviour therapy. He points out that many psychotherapists actively encourage the patient to form a close and even dependent emotional relationship with the therapist. In behaviour therapy, this type of emotional bond is discouraged as it is considered to be a possible source of interference with the relearning process.

Obviously, the behaviour therapist requires the co-operation of his patients and at all times avoids giving them cause for distrust or distress. It must also be recognised that the therapist is a potential and powerful source of social reinforcement (see Ferster, 1958). The therapist can also facilitate the reduction of anxiety in a formal manner (by relaxation, etc.), or in a informal manner by verbal conditioning and reassurance. In the treatment of children he can reduce anxiety by directly comforting the patient (Bentler, 1963).

Commenting on this problem, Eysenck and Rachman (1965) say that

'it is preferable, and indeed necessary, to analyse the effect of the relationship in learning-theory terms rather than in psychoanalytic or psychodynamic manner. Explanations that rely on the concepts of psychosexuality and/or unconscious motives and ideas cannot accommodate some of the available evidence. In particular, the results obtained in the treatment of enuresis defy explanation in dynamic terms. Similarly, it is impossible to speak of a transference or countertransference effect in attempting to account for the successful reduction of neurotic disturbances in animals by means of direct comforting and soothing (see the work of Anderson and Paramenter, 1941; Masserman, 1943; Haslerud et al., 1954; for examples).'

One might also add the recently accumulated evidence on the experimental use of systematic desensitisation treatment for excessive fears in normal subjects. In many of these studies the extent and degree of the interaction between the therapist and the subject was minimal. Nevertheless, significant reductions in fear were regularly obtained. Moreover, in some studies, such as that reported by Lang, Lazovik, and Reynolds (1965), even though a positive relationship was formed between the therapist and the subject, very little therapeutic change was produced except when systematic desensitisation was conducted.

In the pseudo-therapy group used by these workers, the subjects reported that they had in fact developed a positive relationship. However, their fear of snakes was not significantly reduced despite the growth of such a relationship. It should be mentioned, however, that Paul (1966) obtained some evidence of beneficial effects emerging from the development of a relationship between the therapist and the subject. He noted that some subjects showed a measure of improvement that can apparently be attributed to their positive feelings regarding the pseudotherapists.

It seems reasonable to conclude that 'the chief therapeutic contribution is made by the *deliberate and systematic* inhibition or extinction of the neurotic habit patterns—by deliberately facilitating the learning process' (Eysenck and Rachman, 1965).

Direct evidence in support of this conclusion can be found in the number of case reports. Wolpe (1962) described in great detail the treatment of a patient suffering from travel phobias, and demonstrated very clearly the close correspondence between the stages completed in the desensitisation of the travel hierarchy and the actual changes in the behaviour of the patient outside the consulting room (see also Clark, 1963 and the excellent example provided by Marks and Gelder and referred to by Feldman on page 161 above).

If the effective mechanism in behaviour therapy is conceived of as being a relearning process, then it should be possible to manipulate and measure the techniques in a similar manner to the familiar learning processes. In 1963, Wolpe attempted the exercise by quantifying the relationships between the amount of training (learning trials) and the development of the learned reaction; he was able to demonstrate some interesting differences between what he called *proximation phobias* and other phobias.

He found, for example, that 'in claustrophobias and phobias in which anxiety arises with increasing proximity to a feared object', only a small number of practice trials (i.e. desensitisation presentations of the scene) were required to reduce the anxiety experienced at a far distance from the feared object. As the feared object is approached, however, an increasing number of practise trials is required. This positively accelerating curve is a familiar feature of many learning processes.

In the case of agoraphobias and other phobias that increase in intensity with the number of objects involved, the initial items on the hierarchy may be difficult to overcome (i.e. may require many practice trials). In this case the learning curve corresponds to a negatively accelerating function. Here it can be seen that the three cases treated by Wolpe required a large number of scene presentations in order to cope with the initial items in the hierarchial list.

Translated into actual clinical practice this means that agoraphobics, for example, require a great deal of desensitisation treatment before they can be helped to make the initial break out of their encapsulated circles. Once they have succeeded in moving beyond the restriction imposed by their phobic reactions, their progress tends to be fairly rapid and can ordinarily be achieved with considerably less effort than that which has gone into the initial attempts to get the person moving again.

Apart from their relevance to the consideration of isolating the effective mechanisms in behaviour therapy, these quantitative findings of Wolpe's show how therapeutic actions and reactions can be measured. Furthermore, they indicate how the lawful progression of the therapeutic learning process can be brought under close examination. The accumulation of further quantified observations of this type is highly desirable, and it is to be hoped that eventually one may be in the position to make reasonably accurate prognoses for the various types of phobias. It should also be possible to make reasonably accurate predictions about the expected speed of progression from session to session with different types of disorders and different types of patients.

The evidence to date on the effectiveness of behaviour therapy has been summarised by Rachman (1968) in this way: 'It is a promising technique which is virtually certain to be effective in a large number of phobic and anxiety states, but the treatment of severe chronic patients needs to be improved. There is, of course, a need for further prospective controlled trials of the methods of behaviour therapy.'

CONCLUDING COMMENTS

The available evidence does not permit a revision of Eysenck's original estimate of the gross spontaneous remission rate in neurotic disorders—roughly two-thirds of such patients will recover within two years. It is clear, however, that remission rates are not constant across different types of neurosis and future research should be directed at a refinement of the gross rate. Attention has also been centred on the sizable minority of neurotic patients who fail to remit spontaneously. This group and those patients who deteriorate spontaneously, require investigation. On the theoretical side, the Eysenckian hypothesis needs to be explored and perhaps related to a study of the events, actions, and processes that have a restorative effect.

Outcome studies of psychoanalysis are rare, and the available studies are generally of poor quality. There is still no acceptable evidence to support the claim that psychoanalysis is therapeutically effective. Samples of patients undergoing this form of therapy in the US are wholly unrepresentative of the population; the majority of them come from an otherwise privileged group.

A number of investigations into the effectiveness of psychotherapy have been reported. The assessment and interpretation of these results vary. Some writers feel that they provide modest evidence in support of therapeutic claims but the present evaluation is less optimistic: the results rarely show that treated patients do better than untreated controls or patients receiving placebos. The Rogerian approach offers the advantage of clear exposition and has been the subject of concentrated research. Methodological advances have been achieved slowly but systematically and one can expect further progress in this direction. This approach will benefit from an explicit recognition of the variations between disorders and a more rigorous selection of suitable cases. The use of these research methods in studies of the therapist's behaviour in the behavioural techniques would be of interest.

Behavioural therapy has made rapid progress and most notably in the establishment of a firm experimental basis for therapy. The most prominent technique for treating neurotic disorders, desensitisation, has been shown to be effective in a large number of experiments. The uniformity of these results is as reassuring as it is unusual. Some of the new methods, such as flooding and modelling, appear to be of considerable promise.

On the clinical side, the results are encouraging but still limited. Rigorous testing in the field is a prerequisite for further advances and the range of applicability of the techniques is still to be determined. On the theoretical side, some interesting developments have occurred and there are fascinating problems that remain to be investigated.

REFERENCES

ASHCRAFT, C. and FITTS, W. (1964) Self-concept change in psychotherapy. *Psychother. Theor. Res. Pract.*, **1**, 115–118.

AYLLON, T. and AZRIN, N. (1968) *The Token Economy*. New York: Appleton.

BANDURA, A. (1969) *Principles of Behavior Modification*. New York: Holt.

BARENDREGT, J. T. (1961) *Research in Psychodiagnostics*. Paris: Mouton.

BARLOW, D., LEITENBERG, H., AGRAS, S., and WINCZE, J. (1969) The transfer gap in systematic desensitization. *Behav. Res. Ther.* **7**, 191–196.

BARRON, F. and LEARY, T. (1955) Changes in psychoneurotic patients with and without psychotherapy. *J. consult. Psychol.*, **19**, 239–245.

BARRETT, C. (1969) Systematic desensitization versus implosive therapy. *J. abnorm. Psychol.*, **74**, 587–592.

BENDIG, A. (1962) Pittsburgh scale of social introversion—extroversion and emotionality. *J. Psychol.*, **53**, 199–210.

BENTLER, P. M. (1962) An infant's phobia treated with reciprocal inhibition therapy. *J. child Psychol. Psychiat.*, **3**, 185–189.

BERGIN, A. E. (1963) The effects of psychotherapy: negative results re-visited. *J. counsel. Psychol.*, **10**, 244–250.

BERGIN, A. E. (1966) Some implications of psychotherapy research for therapeutic practice. *J. abnorm. Psychol.*, **71**, 235–246.

BERGIN, A. E. (1967) Further comments on psychotherapy research. *Int. J. Psychiatry*, **3**, 317–323.

BERGIN, A. E. (1971) The evaluation of therapeutic outcome. In *Handbook of Psychotherapy and Behavior Change* (Ed. Bergin, A. and Garfield, S.). New York: Wiley.

BIEBER, I. (Ed.) (1962) *Homosexuality: A psychoanalytic study*. New York: Basic Books.

BOCKOVER, J. (1956) Moral treatment in American psychiatry. *J. nerv. ment. Dis.*, **124**, 167–194.

BOULOUGOURIS, J., MARKS, I., and MARSET, P. (1970) Superiority of flooding (implosion) to desensitization for reducing pathological fear. *Behav. Res. Ther.*, **9**, 7–16.

BRILL, N., KOEGLER, R., EPSTEIN, L., and FORGY, E. (1964) Controlled study of psychiatric out-patient treatment. *Arch. gen. Psychiatry*, **10**, 581–595.

BRODY, M. (1962) Prognosis and results of psychotherapy. In *Psychosomatic Medicine* (Ed. Nodine, J. and Moyer, J.). Philadelphia: Lea & Febiger.

BURNETT, A. and RYAN, E. (1963) The applications of conditioning techniques in psychotherapy in a day-care treatment hospital. Unpublished Report.

CAPPON, D. (1964) Results of psychotherapy. *Brit. J. Psychiatry*, **110**, 34–75.

CARTWRIGHT, D. S. (1956) Note on 'changes in psychoneurotic patients with and without psychotherapy'. *J. consult. Psychol.*, **20**, 403–404.

CARTWRIGHT, D. S. and VOGEL, J. (1960) A comparison of changes in psychoneurotic patients during matched periods of therapy and no-therapy. *J. consult. Psychol.*, **24**, 121–127.

CLARK, D. F. (1963) Treatment of a monosymptomatic phobia by systematic desensitization. *Behav. res. Ther.*, **1**, 89–104.

COHEN, R. (1969) The effects of group interaction and progressive hierarchies. *Behav. Res. Ther.*, **7**, 15–26.

COLLINGWOOD, T., HEFELE, T., MUEHLBERG, N., and DRASGOW, J. (1970) Toward identification of the therapeutically facilitative factor, *J. clin. Psychology*, **26**, 119–120.

COOKE, G. (1966) The efficacy of two desensitization procedures: an analogue study. *Behav. Res. Ther.*, **4**, 17–24.

COOPER, J. E. (1963) A study of behaviour therapy in thirty psychiatric patients. *The Lancet*, **i**, 411–415.

COOPER, J. E., GELDER, M. G., and MARKS, I. M. (1965) Results of behaviour therapy in 77 psychiatric patients. *Brit. med. J.*, **1**, 1222–1225.

COSTELLO, C. G. (1963) Behaviour therapy: Criticisms and confusions. *Behav. Res. Ther.*, **1**, 159–162.

COTLER, S. (1970) Sex differences and generalization of anxiety reduction with automated desensitization. *Behav. Res. Ther.*, **8**, 273–286.

COTLER, S. and GARLINGTON, W. (1969) The generalization of anxiety reduction following desensitization. *Behav. Res. Ther.*, **7**, 35–40.

CREMERIUS, J. (1962) *Die Beurteilung des Behandlungserfolges in der Psychotherapie*. New York: Springer Verlag.

CREMERIUS, J. (1969) Spätschicksale unbehandelter Neurosen. *Die Berliner Arztekammer*, **12**, 389–392.

CRIGHTON, J. and JEHU, D. (1969) Treatment of exam anxiety. *Behav. Res. Ther.*, **7**, 245–248.

CROSS, H. J. (1964) The outcome of psychotherapy. *J. consult. Psychol.*, **28**, 413–417.

CROWDER, D. and THORNTON, D. (1970) Effects of systematic desensitization, programmed fantasy and bibliotherapy on a specific fear. *Behav. Res. Ther.*, **8**, 35–42.

CROWNE, D. and STEPHENS, M. (1961) Self-acceptance and self-evaluative behavior: A critique of methodology. *Psychol. Bull.*, **58**, 104–121.

DAVISON, G. (1968) Systematic desensitization as a counterconditioning process. *J. abnorm. Psychol.*, **73**, 91–99.

DENKER, P. (1946) Results of treatment of psychoneuroses by the G.P. *N. Y. State J. Med.*, **46**, 2164–2166.

DICKENSON, W. and TRUAX, C. (1966) Group counselling with college under-achievers. *Personn. Guidance J.*, **45**, 243–247.

DITTMANN, A. (1966) Psychotheraeutpic processes. In *Annual Review of Psychology* (Ed. Farnsworth, P., McNemar, Q., and McNemar, L.,). Palo Alto: Ann. Reviews.

DONNER, L. and GUERNEY, B. (1969) Automated group desensitization. *Behav. Res. Ther.*, **7**, 1–15.

DUHRSSEN, A. and JORSWIECK, E. (1969) Eine empirisch-statische Untersuchung zur Leistungsfahigkeit psychoanalytischer Behandlung. *Die Berliner Arztekammer*, **12**, 385–389.

DYMOND, R. (1955) Adjustment changes in the absence of psychotherapy. *J. consult. Psychol.*, **19**, 103–107.

ELLIS, A. (1957) Outcome of employing 3 techniques of psychotherapy. *J. clin. Psychol.*, **13**, 344–350.

EMERY, J. and KRUMBOLZ, J. (1967) Standard vs. individual hierarchies in desensitization to reduce test anxiety. *J. counsel. Psychol.*, **14**, 204–209.

ENDICOTT, N. and ENDICOTT, J. (1963) 'Improvement' in untreated psychiatric patients. *Arch. gen. Psychiatry*, **9**, 575–585.

ENDLER, N. S. (1962) An S-R inventory of anxiousness. *Psychol. Monogr.*, **76**, No. 536.

EISENBERG, L., CONNERS, K., and LAWRENCE, S. (1965) A controlled study of the differential application of out-patient psychiatric treatment for children. *Jap. J. child Psychiatry*, **6**, 125–132.

ENDS, E. and PAGE, C. (1957) A study of 3 types of group psychotherapy with hospitalised male inebriates. *Quart. J. Stud. Alcohol*, **18**, 263–277.

ENDS, E. and PAGE, C. (1959) Group psychotherapy and concomitant psychological change. *Psychol. Monogr.*, **73**.

EYSENCK, H. J. (1960) The effects of psychotherapy. In *Handbook of Abnormal Psychology* (Ed. Eysenck, H.J.). London: Pitman Medical.

EYSENCK, H. J. (Ed.) (1960) *Behaviour Therapy and the Neuroses*. Oxford: Pergamon Press.

EYSENCK, H. J. (1963) Behaviour therapy, spontaneous remission and transference in neurotics. *Amer. J. Psychiat.*, **119**, 867–871.

EYSENCK, H. J. (Ed.) (1964) *Experiments in Behaviour Therapy*. Oxford: Pergamon Press.

EYSENCK, H. J. (1968) A theory of the incubation of anxiety/fear responses. *Behav. Res. Ther.*, **6**, 309–322.

EYSENCK, H. J. (1969) Relapse and symptom substitution after different types of psychotherapy. *Behav. Res. Ther.*, **7**, 283–287.

EYSENCK, H. J. and RACHMAN, S. (1965) *The Causes and Cures of Neurosis*. London: Routledge & Kegan Paul.

FAIRWEATHER, G., SIMON, R., GEBHARD, M., WEINGARTEN, E., HOLLAND, J., SANDERS, R., STONE, G., and REAHL, J. (1960) Relative effectiveness of pscyhotherapeutic programs. *Psychol. Monogr.*, **74**.

FAZIO, A. (1970) Treatment components in implosive therapy. *J. abnorm. Psychol.*, **76**, 106–109.

FRANKS, C. (Ed.) (1969) *Behavior Therapy: Appraisal and Status*. New York: McGraw-Hill.

FRIESS, C. and NELSON, M. J. (1942) Psychoneurotics five years later. *Amer. J. med. Sci.*, **203**, 539–558.

GARFIELD, Z., DARWIN, P., SINGER, B., and McBREHSTY, J. (1967) Effect of 'in vivo' training on experimental desensitization of a phobia. *Psychol. Reports.* **20**, 515–519.

GARLINGTON, W. and COTLER, S. (1968) Systematic desensitization of test anxiety. *Behav. Res. Ther.*, **6**, 247–256.

GELDER, M., MARKS, I., and WOLFF, H. (1967) Desensitization and psychotherapy in the treatment of phobic states. *Brit. J. Psychiatry*, **113**, 53–73.

GIEL, R., KNOX, R. and CARSTAIRS, G. (1964) A 5-year follow-up of 100 neurotic out-patients. *Brit. med. J.*, **2**, 160–163.

GILLAN, P. (1970) Behaviour therapy and psychotherapy: a comparative investigation, Ph.D. Thesis, London University.

GOLDSTEIN, A. (1960) Patient's expectancies and non-specific therapy as a basis for (un-) spontaneous remission. *J. clin. Psychol.*, **18**, 399–403.

GRAHAM, S. R. (1960) The effects of psychoanalytically oriented psychotherapy on levels of frequency and satisfaction in sexual activity. *J. clinical Psychol.*, **16**, 94–95.

GREER, H. and CAWLEY, R. (1966) *Some observations on the natural history of neurotic illness.* Australian Medical Association.

HAIN, J., BUTCHER, R., and STEVENSON, I. (1966) Systematic Desensitization Therapy: An analysis of results in twenty-seven patients. *Brit. J. Psychiatry*, **112**, 295–308.

HAMBURG, D. A. (Ed.) (1967) *Report on an ad hoc committee on central fact-gathering data (plus appendices).* New York: American Psychoanalytic Association.

HASTINGS, D. W. (1958) Follow-up results in psychiatric illness. *Amer. J. Psychiatry*, **114**, 1057–1066.

HENRY, W. and SHLIEN, J. (1958) Affective complexity and psychotherapy. *J. proj. Techniques*, **22**, 153–162.

HINDE, R. (1968) *The Role of Learning in Psychotherapy* (Ed. R. Porter). London: Churchill.

HOGAN, R. (1968) The implosive technique. *Behav. Res. Ther.*, **6**, 423–432.

HOGAN, R. and KIRCHNER, J. (1967) A preliminary report of the extinction of learned fears via short term implosive therapy. *J. abnorm. Psychol.*, **72**, 106–109.

HOGAN, R. and KIRCHNER, J. (1968) Implosive, eclectic verbal and bibliotherapy in the treatment of fears of snakes. *Behav. Res. Ther.*, **6**, 167–172.

HOLLINGSHEAD, A. and REDLICH, F. (1958) *Social Class and Mental Illness.* New York: Wiley.

HUMPHREY, J. (1966) Behaviour therapy with children: an experimental evaluation. Ph.D. Thesis. Univ. of London.

HUSSAIN, A. (1964) Behavior therapy using hypnosis. In *The Conditioning Therapies* (Ed. Wolpe, J., Salter, A., and Reyna, L). New York: Holt, Rinehart & Winston.

IMBER, S., NASH, E., HOEHN-SARIC, R., STONE, A., and FRANK, J. (1957) Improvement and amount of therapeutic contact. *J. consult. Psychol.*, **77**, 283–293.

IMBER, S. (1968) A ten-year follow-up of treated psychiatric out-patients. In *An Evaluation of the Results of the Psychotherapies* (Ed. Lesse, E.). Springfield: C. C. Thomas.

JOHNSON, S. and SECHREST, L. (1968) Comparison of desensitization and progressive relaxation in treating test anxiety. *J. consult. clinical Psychol.*, **32**, 280–286.

JURJEVICH, R. M. (1968) Changes in psychiatric symptoms without psychotherapy. In *An Evaluation of the Results of the Psychotherapies* (Ed. Lesse, E.) Springfield: C. C. Thomas.

KAHN, M. and BAKER, B. (1968) Desensitization with minimal therapist contact. *J. abnorm. Psychol.*, **73**, 198–200.

KATAHN, M. *et al.* (1966) Group counseling and behavior therapy with test anxious college students. *J. consult. Psychol.*, **30**, 544–549.

KEDWARD, H. (1969) The outcome of neurotic illness in the community. *Soc. Psychiat.*, **4**, 1–4.

KELLNER, R. (1967) The evidence in favour of psychotherapy. *Brit. J. med. Psychol.*, **40**, 341–358.

KIESLER, D. (1966) Some myths of psychotherapy. *Psychol. Bull.*, **65**, 110–136.

KLEIN. H. (1960) A study of changes occurring in patients during and after psychoanalytic treatment. In *Current Approaches to Psychoanalysis* (Ed. Hoch, P. and Zubin, J.). New York: Grune and Stratton.

KNAPP, P., LEVIN, S., MCCARTER, R., WERNER, H., and ZETZEL, E. (1960) Suitability for psychoanalysis: A review of 100 supervised analytic cases. *Psychoanal. Quart.*, **29**, 459–477.

KNIGHT, R. P. (1941) Evaluation of the results of psychoanalytic therapy. *Amer. J. Psychiat.*, **98**, 34–446.

KONDAS, O. (1967) Reduction of examination anxiety and 'stage-fright' by group desensitization and relaxation. *Behav. Res. Ther.*, **5**, 275–282.

KOEGLER, R. and BRILL, N. (1967) *Treatment of Psychiatric Out-patients*. New York: Appleton Century Crofts.

KRASNER, L. (1962) The therapist as a social reinforcement machine. In *Research in Psychotherapy*. Washington, D.C.: American Psychological Association.

KRINGLEN, E. (1965) Obsessional neurosis: a long term follow-up. *Brit. J. Psychiat.*, **111**, 709–714.

LADER, M. and MATTHEWS, A. (1968) A physiological model of phobic anxiety and desensitization. *Behav. Res. Ther.*, **6**, 411–421.

LADER, M. and WING, L. (1966) *Physiological Measures, Sedative Drugs and Morbid Anxiety*. Maudsley Monographs, No. 14.

LANDIS, C. (1937) A statistical evaluation of psychotherapeutic methods. In *Concepts and Problems of Psychotherapy* (Ed. L. E. Hinsie). New York: Columbia N.P.

LANG, P. (1969) *Behavior Therapy: Appraisal and Status* (Ed. C. Franks). New York: McGraw-Hill.

LANG, P. and LAZOVIK, A. (1963) The experimental desensitization of a phobia. *J. abnorm. soc. Psychol.*, **66**, 519–525.

LANG, P., LAZOVIK, A., and REYNOLDS, D. (1966) Desensitization, suggestibility and pseudotherapy. *J. abnorm. Psychol.*, **70**, 395–402.

LANYON, R., MANOSOVITZ, M., and IMBER, R. (1968) Systematic desensitization: Distribution of practice. *Behav. Res. Ther.*, **6**, 323–330.

LAZARUS, A. A. (1961) Group therapy of phobic disorders. *J. abnorm. soc. Psychol.*, **63**, 504–512.

LAZARUS, A. A. (1963) The results of behaviour therapy in 126 cases of severe neurosis. *Behav. Res. Ther.*, **1**, 65–786.

LESSE, S. (1968) (Ed.) *An Evaluation of the Results of the Psychotherapies*. Springfield: C. C. Thomas.

LEVIS, D. and CARRERA, R. (1967) The effects of 10 hours of implosive therapy in the treatment of out-patients. *J. abnorm. Psychol.*, **72**, 504–508.

LEVITT, E. (1963) Psychotherapy with children: a further evaluation. *Behav. Res. Ther.*, **1**, 45–51.

LOMONT, J. F. (1965) Reciprocal inhibition or extinction? *Behav. Res. Ther.*, **3**, 209–220.

LOMONT, J. F. and EDWARDS, J. E. (1967) The role of relaxation in systematic desensitization. *Behav. Res. Ther.*, **5**, 11–26.

LOWE, C. (1961) The self-concept: Fact or artifact? *Psychol. Bull.*, **58**, 325–336.

McGLYNN, F. and MAPP, R. (1970) Systematic desensitization of snake-avoidance following 3 types of suggestion. *Behav. Res. Ther.*, **8**, 197–201.

MALLESON, N. (1959) Panic and phobia. *Lancet*, i, 225–227.

MARKS, I. (1969) *Fears and Phobias*. London: Heinemann.

MARKS, I. and GELDER, M. (1965) A controlled retrospective study of behaviour therapy in phobic patients. *Brit. J. Psychiat.*, **111**, 561–573.

MARKS, I. and GELDER, M. (1966) Severe Agoraphobia. A controlled prospective trial of behaviour therapy. *Brit. J. Psychiat.*, **112**, 309–320.

MARKS, I. M. and GELDER, M. G. (1966) Different ages of onset in varieties of phobia. *Amer. J. Psychiat.*, **123**, 218–221.

MASSERMAN, J. H. (1955) *The Practice of Dynamic Psychiatry*. New York: Saunders.

MASSIMO, J. and SHORE, M. (1963) The effectiveness of a comprehensive vocationally oriented psychotherapeutic program for delinquent boys. *Amer. J. Orthopsychiat.*, **33**, 634–642.

MASTERSON, J. (1967) The symptomatic adolescent five years later. *Amer. J. Psychiat.*, **123**, 1338–1345.

MATHEWS, A. (1970) Psychophysiology and behaviour therapy. (In preparation.)

MAY, P. and TUMA, A. (1965) Treatment of schizophrenia. *Brit. J. Psychiat.*, **111**, 503–510).

MEALIA, W. (1968) The comparative effectiveness of systematic desensitization and implosive therapy. Ph.D. Dissert., Univ. Missouri.

MELAMED, B. and LANG, P. (1967) *Study of the Automated Desensitization of Fear*. Conf. Midwestern Psychol. Assn., Chicago.

MEYER, V. and CRISP, A. H. (1966) Some problems of behaviour therapy. *Brit. J. Psychiat.*, **112**, 367–382.

MEYER, V. (1967) Modification of expectations in cases with obsessional rituals. *Behav. Res. Ther.*, **4**, 273–280.

MILLER, H. and NAWAS, M. (1970) The comparative effectiveness of pairing aversive imagery with relaxation, neutral tasks and muscular tension in reducing snake phobias. *Behav. Res. Ther.*, **8**, 63–68.

MITCHELL, K. and INGHAM, R. (1970) The effects of general anxiety on group desensitization of test anxiety. *Behav. Res. Ther.*, **8**, 69–78.

MOORE, N. (1965) Behaviour therapy in bronchial asthma: a controlled study. *J. psychosom. Res.*, **9**, 257–274.

MUEHLBERG, N., PIERCE, R., and DRASGOW, J. (1969) A factor analysis of therapeutically facilitative conditions. *J. clin. Psychol.*, **25**, 93–95.

MURRAY, E. J. (1962) Paper read at A.P.A. Conv. St. Louis. Quoted by Costello, C. G. (1963).

NAWAS, M., FISHMAN, S., and PUCEL, J. (1970) A standardized desensitization program. *Behav. Res. Ther.*, **8**, 49–56.

O'CONNOR, J., DANIELS, G., KARSH, A., MOSES, L., FLOOD, C., and STERN, L. (1964) The effects of psychotherapy on the course of ulcerative colitis. *Amer. J. Psychiat.*, **120**, 738–742.

OLIVEAU, D., AGRAS, S., LEIBENBERG, H., MOORE, R., and WRIGHT, D. (1969) Systematic desensitization, instructions and positive reinforcement. *Behav. Res. Ther.*, **7**, 27–35.

O'NEIL, D. and HOWELL, J. (1969) Three modes of hierarchy presentation in desensitization. *Behav. Res. Ther.*, **7**, 289–294.

ORGEL, S. (1958) Effect of psychoanalysis on the course of peptic ulcer. *Psychosom. Med.*, **20**, 117–125.

PASSINGHAM, R. (1970) Personal communication.

PAUL, G. (1966) *Insight versus Desensitization in Psychotherapy*. Stanford: Stanford University Press.

PAUL, G. and SHANNON, D. (1966) Treatment of anxiety through systematic desensitization in therapy groups. *J. abnorm. Psychol.*, **71**, 124–135.

PHILIPS, E., RAIFORD, A., and EL-BATRAWI, S. (1965) The Q-sort Re-evaluated. *J. consult. Psychol.*, **29**, 422–425.

PHILLIPS, E. L. (1957) *Psychotherapy*. London: Staples.

POLIN, A. (1959) The effect of flooding and physical suppression as extinction techniques on an anxiety-motivated avoidance response. *J. Psychol.*, **47** 253–255.

PROCTOR, S. (1969) Duration of exposure of items and pretreatment training as factors in systematic desensitization therapy. In *Advances in Behaviour Therapy, 1968* (Ed. R. Rubin and C. Franks). New York: Academic Press.

PSYCHREMBEL, W. (1964) *Klinisches Wörterbuch*. Gruyter: Berlin.

POWERS, E. and WITMER, H. (1951) *An Experiment on the Prevention of Delinquency*. New York: Columbia Univ. Press.

RACHMAN, S. (1965) Studies in desensitization: I. The separate effects of relaxation and desensitization. *Behav. Res. Therapy*, **3**, 245–252.

RACHMAN, S. (1966) Studies in desensitization: III. Flooding. *Behav. Res. Ther.*, **4**, 1–6.

RACHMAN, S. (1967) Systematic desensitization. *Psychol. Bull.*, **67**, 93–103.

RACHMAN, S. (1968) *Phobias: Their Nature and Control*. Springfield: Thomas.

RAMSAY, R. W., BARENDS, J., BREUKER, J., and KRUSEMAN, A. (1966) Massed versus spaced desensitization of fear. *Behav. Res. Ther.*, **4**, 205–208.

ROGERS, C. R. (1957) The necessary and sufficient conditions of therapeutic personality change. *J. consult. Psychol.*, **21**, 95–103.

ROGERS, C. R. and DYMOND, R. (1954) *Psychotherapy and Personality Change*. Chicago: Chicago Univ. Press.

ROGERS, C. R., GENDLIN, E., KIESLER, D., and TRUAX, C. (1967) *The Therapeutic Relationship and its Impact: A study of psychotherapy with schizophrenics*. Madison: U. Wisconsin Press.

ROSENWEIG, S. (1954) A transvaluation of psychotherapy: a reply to Eysenck. *J. abnorm. soc. Psychol.*, **49**, 298–304.

SASLOW, G. and PETERS, A. (1956) Follow-up of 'untreated' patients with behaviour disorders. *Psychiat. Quart.*, **30**, 283–302.

SCHORER, C., LOWINGER, P., SULLIVAN, T., and HARTLAUB, G. (1968) Improvement without treatment. *Dis. nerv. System*, **29**, 100–104.

SHAPIRO, D. (1969) Empathy, warmth and genuineness in psychotherapy. *Brit. J. soc. clin. Psychol.*, **8**, 350–361.

SHEPHERD, M. and GRUENBERG, E. (1957) The age for neuroses. *Millbank Memor. Quart. Bull.*, **35**, 258–265.

SHLIEN, H., MOSAK, H., and DREIKURS, R. (1962) Effect of time limits: a comparison of two psychotherapies. *J. counsel Psychol.*, **9**, 31–34.

SHORE, M. and MASSIMO, J. (1966) Comprehensive vocationally oriented psychotherapy for adolescent boys: a follow-up study. *Amer. J. Orthopsychiat.*, **36**, 609–615.

STAMPFL, T. (1967) Implosive therapy. In *Behavior Modification Techniques in the treatment of Emotional Disorders* (Ed. S. Armitage). Michigan: V. A. Publ.

STAMPFL, T. and LEVIS, D. (1967) Essentials of implosive therapy. *J. abnorm. Psychol.*, **72**, 496–503.

STAMPFL, T. and LEVIS, D. (1968) Implosive therapy—a behavioral therapy? *Behav. Res. Ther.*, **6**, 31–36.

STEVENSON, I. (1961) Processes of 'spontaneous' recovery from the psychoneuroses. *Amer. J. Psychiat.*, **117**, 1057–1064.

STRUPP, H. and BERGIN, A. (1969) Some empirical and conceptual bases for coordinated research in psychotherapy. *Int. J. Psychiatry*, **7**, 18–90.

SUINN, R. (1968) The desensitization of test anxiety by group and individual therapy. *Behav. Res. Ther.*, **6**, 385–388.

TAYLOR, D. (1955) Changes in the self-concept without psychotherapy. *J. consult. Psychol.*, **19**, 205–209.

TEASDALE, J. (1969) Research in psychotherapy. Unpublished M.S.

TRUAX, C. and CARKHUFF, R. (1967) *Toward Effective Counseling and Psychotherapy*. Chicago: Aldine Press.

TRUAX, C., FRANK, I., and IMBER, S. (1966) Therapist empathy, genuineness, and warmth and patient outcome. *J. consult. Psychol.*, **30**, 395–401.

TRUAX, C., WARGO, D., and SILBER, L. (1966) Effects of high accurate empathy and non-possessive warmth during group therapy with female delinquents. *J. abnorm. Psychol.*, **71**, 267–274.

ULLMANN, L. and KRASNER, L. (1965) *Case Studies in Behavior Modification*. New York: Holt, Rinehart and Winston.

VORSTER, D. (1966) Psychotherapy and the results of psychotherapy. *S. African med. J.*, **40**, 934–936.

WALLACE, H. and WHYTE, M. (1959) Natural history of the psychoneuroses. *Brit. med. J.*, **1**, 144–148.

WITTENBORN, J. (1961) Contributions and current status of Q methodology. *Psychol. Bull.*, **58**, 132–142.

WOLPE, J. (1958) *Psychotherapy by Reciprocal Inhibition*. Stanford: Stanford Univ. Press.

WOLPE, J. (1963) Behaviour therapy in complex neurotic states. Paper read at Reading Conference of Br. Psychol. Soc.

WOLPE, J. (1968) *The Practice of Behavior Therapy*. Oxford: Pergamon Press.

WYLIE, RUTH (1961) *The Self Concept*. University of Nebraska Press.

ZEISSET, R. (1968) Desensitization and relaxation in the modification of psychiatric patients interview behaviour. *J. abnorm. Psychol.*, **73**, 18–24.

Index of Authors

Index of Subjects